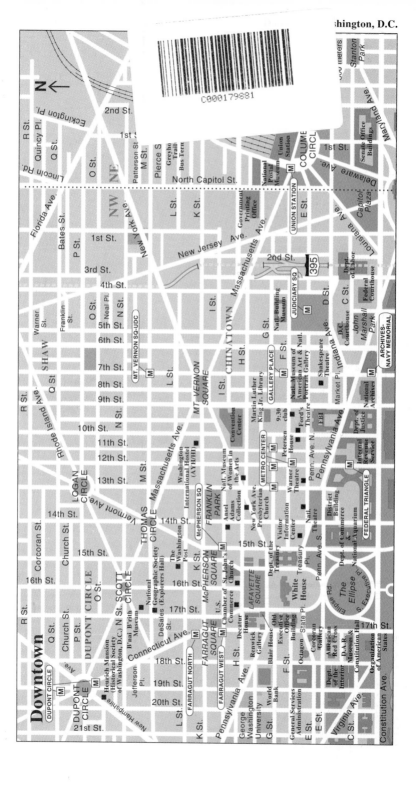

Central Washington, D.C.

MT. PLEASANT

CLEVELAND PARK

Klingle St.

Washington National Cathedral

Klingle St.

Cathedral Ave.

National Zoo

Adams Mill Rd.

Irving St.

16th St.

14th St.

13th St.

Columbia Rd.

Harvard St.

Woodley Rd.

GLOVER PARK

Massachusetts

WOODLEY PARK-ZOO

M

Calvert St.

Euclid St.

15th St.

Calvert St.

Vice Presidential Mansion

ADAMS-MORGAN

Calvert St.

Observatory

La. U.S. Naval Observatory

Ave.

EMBASSY ROW

Rock Creek Park

Rock Creek Pkwy.

KALORAMA CIRCLE

Columbia Rd.

Florida Ave.

12th St.

Whitehaven Park

Dumbarton Oaks Park

Waterside Dr.

U St.

U ST/CARDOZO

M

37th St.

Montrose Park

Rock Creek

Florida

Ave.

DUPONT CIRCLE

New Hampshire Ave.

16th St.

15th St.

Vermont Ave.

R St.

R St.

SHERIDAN CIRCLE

20th St.

Q St.

DUPONT CIRCLE

LOGAN CIRCLE

Georgetown University

Wisconsin Ave.

28th St.

Q St.

Q St.

DUPONT CIRCLE

M

P St.

M

14th St.

13th St.

12th St.

34th St.

P St.

SCOTT CIRCLE

THOMAS CIRCLE

GEORGETOWN

30th St.

NEW DOWNTOWN

Connecticut Ave.

FARRAGUT SQUARE

MCPHERSON SQUARE

C&O Canal

M St.

26th St.

23rd St.

FARRAGUT NORTH

K St.

M

McPHERSON SQ

M

White hurst Fwy.

Key Br.

WASHINGTON CIRCLE

FARRAGUT WEST

M

Pennsylvania Ave.

New York Ave.

66

M

H St.

FOGGY BOTTOM-GWU

GWU

LAFAYETTE SQUARE

M

METRO CENTER

ROSSLYN

Theodore Roosevelt Memorial

George Washington Pkwy.

Rock Creek Pkwy.

JAUREZ CIRCLE

G St.

F St.

FOGGY BOTTOM

18th St.

White House

17th St.

15th St.

E St.

OLD DOWNTOWN

M

ROSSLYN

M

Theodore Roosevelt Island

Virginia Ave.

E St.

The Ellipse

E St.

FEDERAL TRIANGLE

66

Roosevelt Bridge

50

Constitution Ave.

14th St.

SMITHSONIAN

50

66

50

ARLINGTON CEMETERY

George Washington Pkwy.

Ladybird Johnson Park

Memorial Bridge

Lincoln Memorial

Independence Ave.

West Potomac Park

Washington Monument

U.S. Holocaust Memorial Museum

Kutz Br.

Raoul Wallenberg Pl.

Tidal Basin

East Basin Dr.

C St.

M

14th St.

12th St.

Maine Ave.

ARLINGTON CEMETERY

M

Memorial Dr.

Columbia Island

Potomac River

Outlet Br.

Jefferson Memorial

Francis Ca Memorial I

395

VIRGINIA

Jefferson Davis Hwy.

Visitors Center

East Potomac Par

395

1

Pentagon

PENTAGON

M

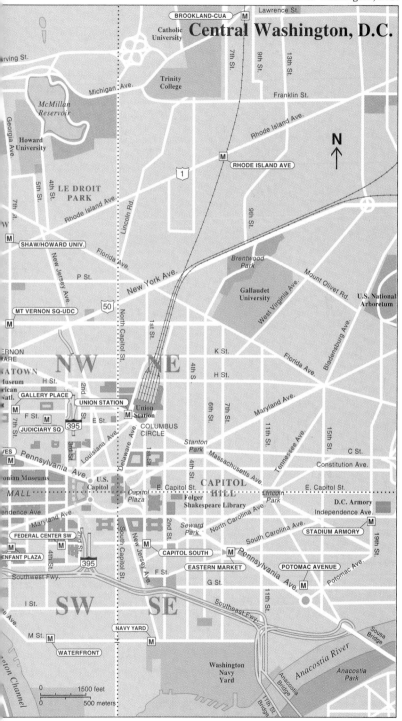

Central Washington, D.C.

The Mall Area, Washington, D.C.

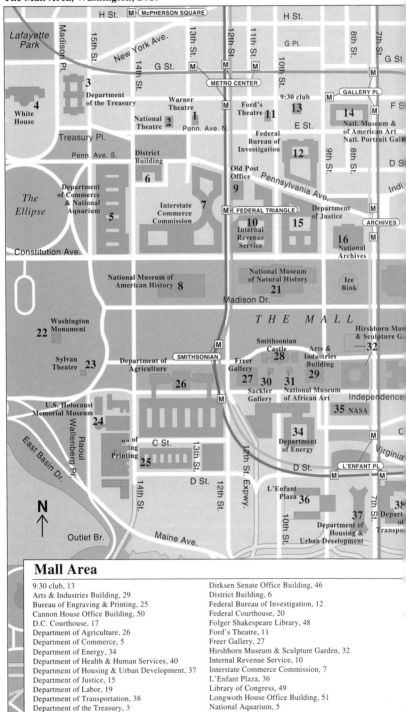

Mall Area

9:30 club, 13
Arts & Industries Building, 29
Bureau of Engraving & Printing, 25
Cannon House Office Building, 50
D.C. Courthouse, 17
Department of Agriculture, 26
Department of Commerce, 5
Department of Energy, 34
Department of Health & Human Services, 40
Department of Housing & Urban Development, 37
Department of Justice, 15
Department of Labor, 19
Department of Transportation, 38
Department of the Treasury, 3

Dirksen Senate Office Building, 46
District Building, 6
Federal Bureau of Investigation, 12
Federal Courthouse, 20
Folger Shakespeare Library, 48
Ford's Theatre, 11
Freer Gallery, 27
Hirshhorn Museum & Sculpture Garden, 32
Internal Revenue Service, 10
Interstate Commerce Commission, 7
L'Enfant Plaza, 36
Library of Congress, 49
Longworth House Office Building, 51
National Aquarium, 5

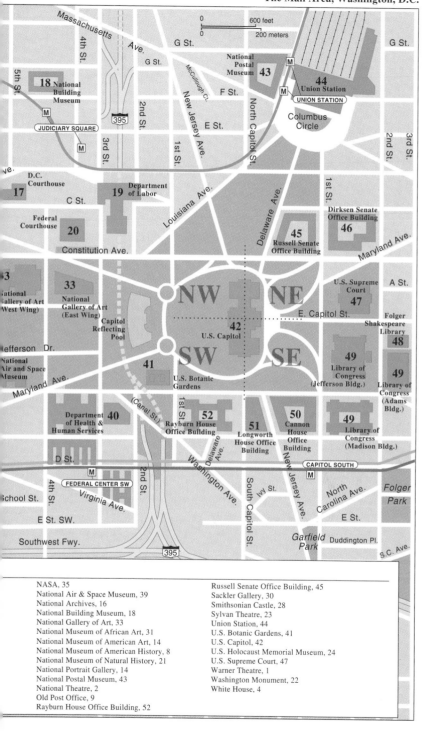

NASA, 35
National Air & Space Museum, 39
National Archives, 16
National Building Museum, 18
National Gallery of Art, 33
National Museum of African Art, 31
National Museum of American Art, 14
National Museum of American History, 8
National Museum of Natural History, 21
National Portrait Gallery, 14
National Postal Museum, 43
National Theatre, 2
Old Post Office, 9
Rayburn House Office Building, 52

Russell Senate Office Building, 45
Sackler Gallery, 30
Smithsonian Castle, 28
Sylvan Theatre, 23
Union Station, 44
U.S. Botanic Gardens, 41
U.S. Capitol, 42
U.S. Holocaust Memorial Museum, 24
U.S. Supreme Court, 47
Warner Theatre, 1
Washington Monument, 22
White House, 4

White House Area, Foggy Bottom, and Nearby Arlington

N

Prospect St.

GEORGETOWN

33rd St.

N St.

Old Stone House

Olive St.

M St.

31st St.

Rock Creek

24th St.

New Hampshire Ave.

C&O Creek

South St.

Whitehurst Fwy.

K St. (under expressway)

29

26th St.

25th St.

L St.

WASHINGTON CIRCLE

G.W. Hosp.

FOGGY BOTTOM-GWU

66

M

George Washington University

Francis Scott Key Br.

Potomac River

Thompson Boat Center

Watergate Hotel

Watergate Hotel Complex

JUAREZ CIRCLE

24th St.

23rd St.

22nd St.

FOGGY BOTTOM

Fort Myer Dr.

N. Moore St.

N. Lynn St.

N. Kent St.

19th St.

George Washington Pkwy.

Theodore Roosevelt Memorial

Theodore Roosevelt Island

Rock Creek Pkwy.

Kennedy Center for the Performing Arts

Virginia

ROSSLYN

M

Wilson Blvd.

State Department

ROSSLYN

Fairfax Dr.

Arlington Ridge Rd.

66

Theodore Roosevelt Br.

66

50

National Academy of Science

50

N. Nash St.

50

NW

SW

Henry Bacon

Lincoln Memorial

Marine Corps War Memorial (Iwo Jima Statue)

Mead Dr.

12th St.

Netherlands Carillon

George Washington Memorial Pkwy.

Arlington Memorial Br.

Ericsson Memorial

ARLINGTON

Ladybird Johnson Park

M

ARLINGTON CEMETERY

Memorial Dr.

Columbia Island

Grave of President John F. Kennedy

Jefferson Davis Hwy.

Arlington House

Robert E. Lee Memorial

Visitor Center

ARLINGTON NATIONAL CEMETERY

Tomb of the Unknown Soldier

Lyndon B. Johnson Memorial

VIRGINIA

0   1500 feet

0   500 meters

Pentagon, National Airport

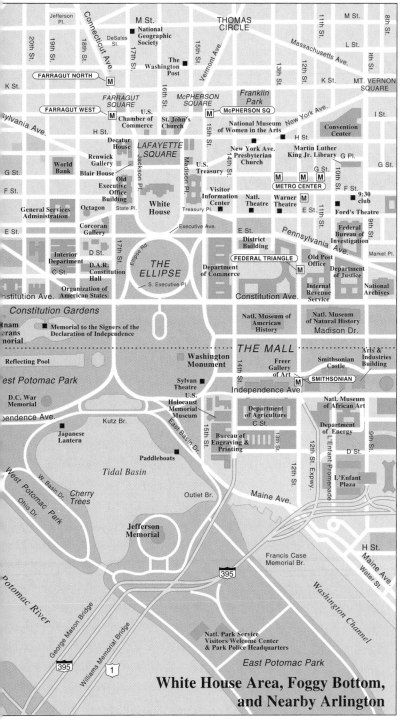

White House Area, Foggy Bottom, and Nearby Arlington

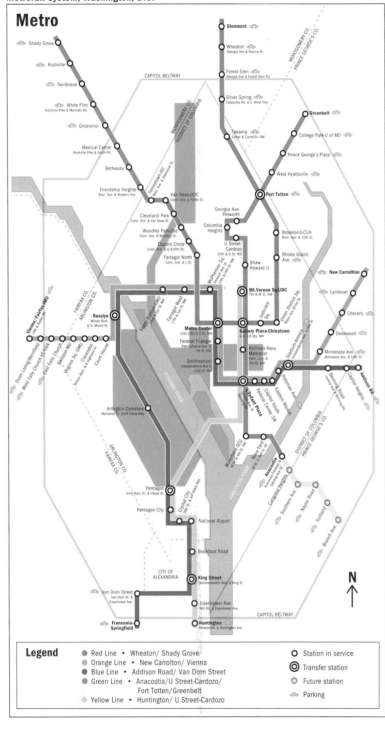

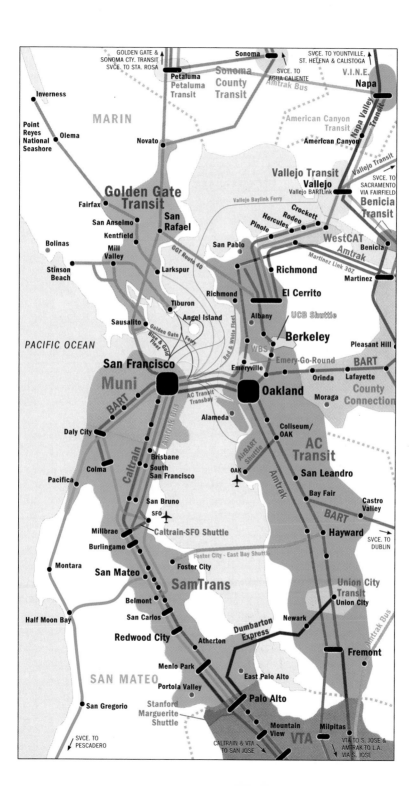

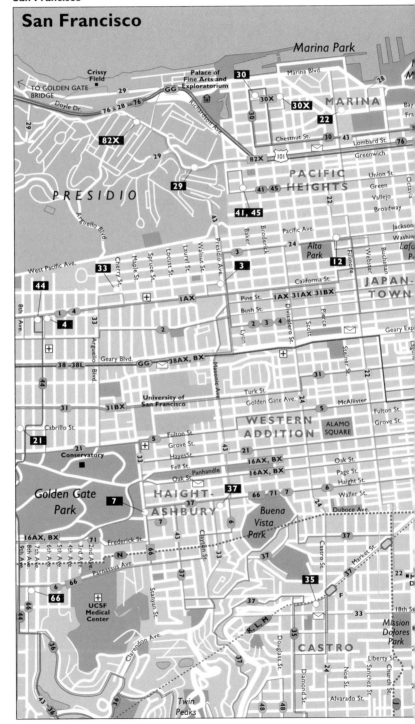

San Francisco

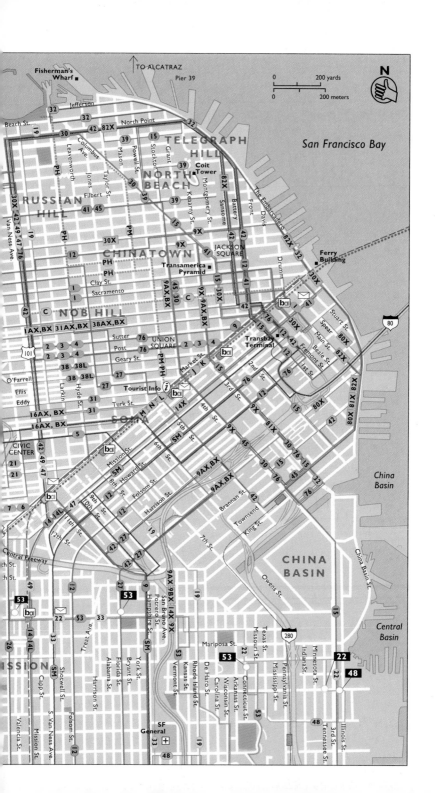

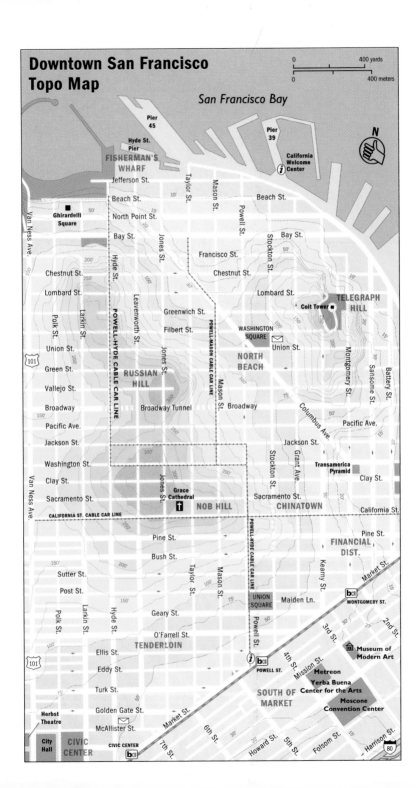

Downtown San Francisco
Topo Map

San Francisco Bay

N

FISHERMAN'S WHARF

Pier 45
Hyde St. Pier
Pier 39
California Welcome Center

Jefferson St.
Beach St.
Beach St.
Ghirardelli Square
North Point St.
Bay St.
Bay St.
Francisco St.
Chestnut St.
Chestnut St.
Lombard St.
Lombard St.

Taylor St.
Mason St.
Powell St.
Stockton St.

Coit Tower
TELEGRAPH HILL

Greenwich St.
Filbert St.
WASHINGTON SQUARE
Union St.

POWELL-HYDE CABLE CAR LINE
POWELL-MASON CABLE CAR LINE

RUSSIAN HILL
NORTH BEACH

Polk St.
Larkin St.
Leavenworth St.
Jones St.
Hyde St.

Union St.
Green St.
Vallejo St.
Broadway
Broadway Tunnel
Broadway
Pacific Ave.
Jackson St.
Washington St.
Clay St.
Sacramento St.

Montgomery St.
Sansome St.
Battery St.
Columbus Ave.
Pacific Ave.
Jackson St.

Transamerica Pyramid
Clay St.

Grace Cathedral
NOB HILL
Stockton St.
Grant Ave.
Sacramento St.
CHINATOWN
California St.

CALIFORNIA ST. CABLE CAR LINE

Van Ness Ave.

Pine St.
Bush St.
Pine St.
FINANCIAL DIST.
Market St.

Sutter St.
Post St.
Taylor St.
Mason St.
POWELL-HYDE CABLE CAR LINE
Kearny St.
MONTGOMERY ST.

Geary St.
O'Farrell St.
UNION SQUARE
Maiden Ln.
Powell St.

TENDERLOIN
Ellis St.
Eddy St.
POWELL ST.

Polk St.
Larkin St.
Hyde St.

3rd St.
2nd St.
Museum of Modern Art

Turk St.
Golden Gate St.
McAllister St.
Market St.
4th St.
Mission St.

Metreon
Yerba Buena Center for the Arts
SOUTH OF MARKET
Moscone Convention Center

Herbst Theatre
City Hall
CIVIC CENTER
CIVIC CENTER

6th St.
7th St.
5th St.
Howard St.
Folsom St.
Harrison St.

Van Ness Ave.
101

0   400 yards
0   400 meters

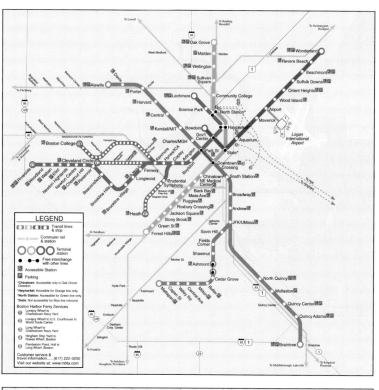

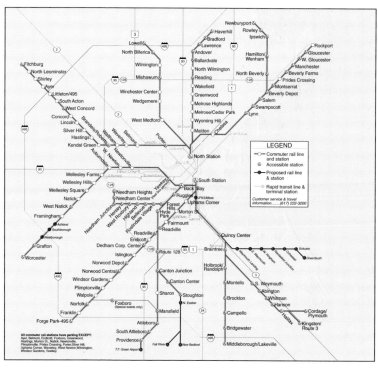

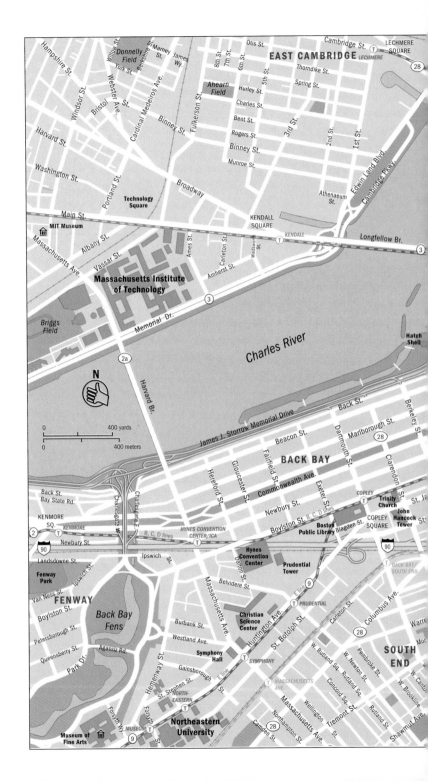

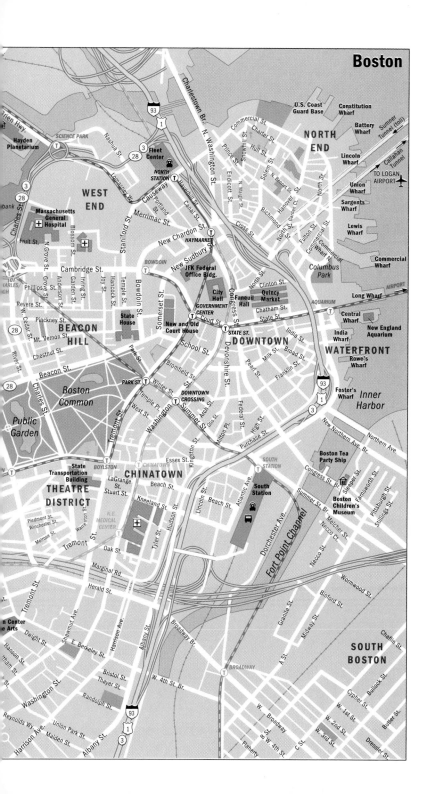

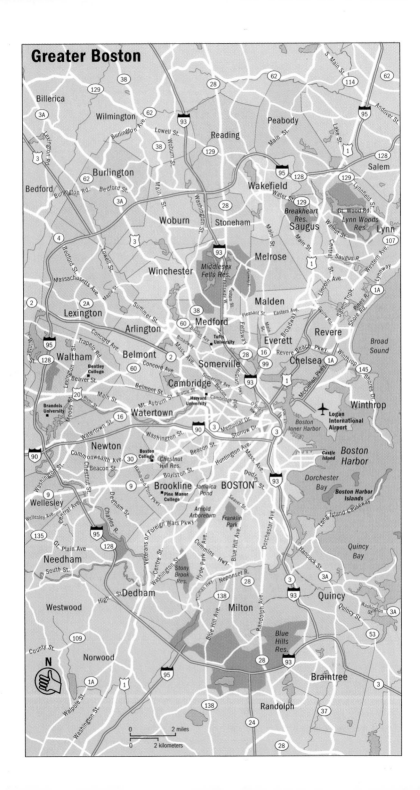
Greater Boston

▨ Let's Go writers travel on your budget.

"Guides that penetrate the veneer of the holiday brochures and mine the grit of real life."

—*The Economist*

"The writers seem to have experienced every rooster-packed bus and lunar-surfaced mattress about which they write."

—*The New York Times*

"All the dirt, dirt cheap."

—*People*

▨ Great for independent travelers.

"The guides are aimed not only at young budget travelers but at the independent traveler; a sort of streetwise cookbook for traveling alone."

—*The New York Times*

"Flush with candor and irreverence, chock full of budget travel advice."

—*The Des Moines Register*

"An indispensible resource, *Let's Go*'s practical information can be used by every traveler."

—*The Chattanooga Free Press*

▨ Let's Go is completely revised each year.

"Only *Let's Go* has the zeal to annually update every title on its list."

—*The Boston Globe*

"Unbeatable: good sightseeing advice; up-to-date info on restaurants, hotels, and inns; a commitment to money-saving travel; and a wry style that brightens nearly every page."

—*The Washington Post*

▨ All the important information you need.

"*Let's Go* authors provide a comedic element while still providing concise information and thorough coverage of the country. Anything you need to know about budget traveling is detailed in this book."

—*The Chicago Sun-Times*

"Value-packed, unbeatable, accurate, and comprehensive."

—*Los Angeles Times*

Let's Go

USA

INCLUDING COVERAGE OF CANADA
2001

Kevin Hoffman Yip editor
Stephanie L. Coon associate editor
Jonathan Hall associate editor
Daisy Stanton map editor

researcher-writers

Blair Baldwin	Kate Kraft
Edward B. Colby	Andy Lynn
Sarah J. Hines	John Mazza
Joanie Hubble	Maureen Shannon
Amy Kirkcaldy	Jessica Tanner

Macmillan

HELPING LET'S GO If you want to share your discoveries, suggestions, or corrections, please drop us a line. We read every piece of correspondence, whether a postcard, a 10-page email, or a coconut. Please note that mail received after May 2001 may be too late for the 2002 book, but will be kept for future editions. **Address mail to:**

> Let's Go: USA
> 67 Mount Auburn Street
> Cambridge, MA 02138
> USA

Visit Let's Go at **http://www.letsgo.com,** or send email to:

> feedback@letsgo.com
> Subject: "Let's Go: USA"

In addition to the invaluable travel advice our readers share with us, many are kind enough to offer their services as researchers or editors. Unfortunately, our charter enables us to employ only currently enrolled Harvard students.

Published in Great Britain 2001 by Macmillan, an imprint of Macmillan Publishers Ltd, 25 Eccleston Place, London, SW1W 9NF, Basingstoke and Oxford.
Associated companies throughout the world
www.macmillan.com

Maps by David Lindroth copyright © 2001, 2000, 1999, 1998, 1997, 1996, 1995, 1994, 1993, 1992, 1991, 1990, 1989, 1988 by St. Martin's Press.

Published in the United States of America by St. Martin's Press.

ISBN: 0-333-90144-4
First edition
10 9 8 7 6 5 4 3 2 1

Let's Go: USA is written by Let's Go Publications, 67 Mount Auburn Street, Cambridge, MA 02138, USA.

Let's Go® and the thumb logo are trademarks of Let's Go, Inc.
Printed in the USA on recycled paper with biodegradable soy ink.

CONTENTS

DISCOVER THE UNITED STATES 1
When to Go 1
Things to Do 2
Suggested Itineraries 4

LIFE AND TIMES 7
THE UNITED STATES 7
History 7
2000's News 15
A Civics Primer 16
The Arts 16
The Media 25
Sports 26
Food 27
CANADA 28
A Brief History 28
Culture 30

ESSENTIALS 31
Facts for the Traveler 31
Getting There 65
Getting Around 73
Additional Information 80

NEW ENGLAND 86
☆ MAINE 86
MAINE COAST 87
Portland 88
South of Portland 90
Mt. Desert Island 91
Northern Maine Coast 94
☆ NEW HAMPSHIRE 95
Portsmouth 95
White Mountains 97
☆ VERMONT 102
Vermont Ski Resorts 102
Burlington 103
☆ MASSACHUSETTS 110
BOSTON 111
Getting There and Away 111
Getting Around 111
Orientation 112
Practical Information 112
Accommodations 112
Food 114
Sights 117
Museums 121
Entertainment 122
Nightlife 124
CAPE COD 130
Upper Cape 132
Lower Cape 132
Martha's Vineyard 136
WESTERN MASSACHUSETTS 139
The Berkshires 139
The Pioneer Valley 142
☆ RHODE ISLAND 143
Providence 143
Newport 145
☆ CONNECTICUT 148
Hartford 148
New Haven 149

EASTERN CANADA 152
NOVA SCOTIA 152
Atlantic Coast 152
Halifax 155
NEW BRUNSWICK 157
Saint John 158
PRINCE EDWARD ISLAND 160
QUÉBEC 162
MONTRÉAL 163
Getting There and Away 163
Getting Around 163
Orientation 166
Practical Information 166
Accommodations 167
Bon Appetít 168
Sights 169
Museums 171
Nightlife 172
Entertainment 173
Québec City 173
ONTARIO 179
TORONTO 181
Getting There and Away 181
Getting Around 181
Orientation 182
Practical Information 184
Accommodations 184
Food 185
Sights 186
Entertainment 187
Festivals 188
Nightlife 188
Daytrips From Toronto 190
Ottawa 190

MID-ATLANTIC 196
☆ NEW YORK 196
NEW YORK CITY 198
Orientation 198
Getting There and Away 200
Getting Around 201
Practical Information 202
Accommodations 203
Food 206
Sights 213
Museums 224
Galleries 226
Shopping 227
Entertainment 228
Nightlife 230
The Catskills 236
Albany 237
Niagara Falls 243
NORTHERN NEW YORK 245
☆ NEW JERSEY 250
Atlantic City 250
☆ PENNSYLVANIA 254
PHILADELPHIA 255
Getting There and Away 255
Getting Around 255
Orientation 256
Practical Information 256
Accommodations 258

Food 258
Sights 260
Entertainment 264
Nightlife 264
Daytrip From Philadelphia 265
Lancaster County 266
Pittsburgh 270
★ DELAWARE 274
Delaware Seashore 275
★ MARYLAND 277
Baltimore 277
WASHINGTON, D.C. 287
Getting There and Away 288
Orientation 288
Practical Information 290
Accommodations 290
Food 291
Sights 294
Museums on the Mall 298
Entertainment 299
Nightlife 299
Daytrips From D.C. 301
★ VIRGINIA 302
Richmond 302
Williamsburg 309
Virginia Beach 312
Charlottesville 315
Shenandoah National Park 318
★ WEST VIRGINIA 322

THE SOUTH 328
★ KENTUCKY 330
Louisville 331
Lexington 334
★ TENNESSEE 339
Nashville 339
Memphis 349
★ NORTH CAROLINA 355
The Research Triangle 356
CAROLINA MOUNTAINS 360
Asheville 362
NORTH CAROLINA COAST 364
Outer Banks 364
★ SOUTH CAROLINA 368
Charleston 368
Myrtle Beach and the Grand Strand 373
★ GEORGIA 375
Atlanta 376
Savannah 387
★ ALABAMA 390
Montgomery 390
Birmingham 393
Mobile 396
★ MISSISSIPPI 397
Jackson 398
★ LOUISIANA 402
NEW ORLEANS 403
Getting There and Away 404
Getting Around 404
Orientation 404
Practical Information 406
Accommodations 406
Food 407
Sights 409
Museums 412
Entertainment 412
Nightlife 413
ACADIANA 418

★ ARKANSAS 420
Little Rock 420

★ FLORIDA 426
St. Augustine 426
Orlando 432
Disney World 435
Life Beyond Disney 438
Fort Lauderdale 441
Miami and Miami Beach 444
FLORIDA KEYS 452
Practical Information 452
Key West 453
GULF COAST 456
Tampa 456
St. Petersburg and Clearwater 459

GREAT LAKES 466
★ OHIO 466
Cleveland 467
Cincinnati 473
★ MICHIGAN 477
Detroit 477
Ann Arbor 482
★ LAKE MICHIGAN SHORE 485
Southern Michigan Shore 486
Central Michigan Shore 487
Northern Michigan Shore 489
UPPER PENINSULA 491
Isle Royale National Park 494
★ INDIANA 495
Indianapolis 495
Bloomington 497
★ ILLINOIS 499
CHICAGO 499
Getting There and Away 499
Getting Around 500
Orientation 500
Practical Information 502
Accommodations 503
Food 504
Sights 506
Museums 510
Outdoors 511
Entertainment 512
Nightlife 513
Daytrips From Chicago 514
★ WISCONSIN 516
Milwaukee 516
Madison 521
Door County 524
Apostle Islands 526
★ MINNESOTA 528
Minneapolis and St. Paul 529
Duluth 536
Chippewa National Forest 538
Iron Range 539
Voyageurs 540

GREAT PLAINS 542
★ NORTH DAKOTA 542
Fargo 544
★ SOUTH DAKOTA 549
The Badlands 550
BLACK HILLS REGION 553
★ IOWA 559
Des Moines 560
★ NEBRASKA 566

Omaha 566
Lincoln 568
☆ KANSAS 571
Wichita 572
☆ MISSOURI 574
St. Louis 574
Kansas City 581
☆ OKLAHOMA 586
Tulsa 587
Oklahoma City 589

☆ TEXAS 591
San Antonio 592
Austin 598
Dallas 603
Houston 609
WESTERN TEXAS 617

ROCKY MOUNTAINS 623
☆ IDAHO 623
Boise 624
Ketchum and Sun Valley 626
☆ MONTANA 631
Missoula 636
Waterton-Glacier Peace Park 638
☆ WYOMING 644
Yellowstone 645
Grand Teton 654
Buffalo and Sheridan 661
☆ COLORADO 668
Denver 669
Boulder 676
Rocky Mountain National Park 680
Vail 683
Aspen 684
SAN JUAN MOUNTAINS 691
Durango 695

THE SOUTHWEST 700
☆ NEVADA 700
Las Vegas 702
☆ UTAH 707
Salt Lake City 708
☆ ARIZONA 727
Practical Information 727
GRAND CANYON 727
South Rim 728
North Rim 732
Flagstaff 734
Navajo Reservation 741
Phoenix 747
Tucson 752
☆ NEW MEXICO 759
Santa Fe 760
Albuquerque 766

☆ CALIFORNIA 779
LOS ANGELES 779
Getting There and Getting Away 781
Getting Around 781
Orientation 782
Practical Information 782
Accommodations 783
Food 787
Sights 790
Entertainment 797
Nightlife 799
Seasonal Events 801

South Bay Beaches 801
Orange County 802
San Diego 805
Tijuana 811
THE CALIFORNIA DESERT 812
Joshua Tree National Park 813
Death Valley 815
THE CENTRAL COAST 816
Santa Barbara 816
Santa Cruz 823
SAN FRANCISCO 825
Getting There and Away 826
Getting Around 826
Orientation 827
Practical Information 828
Accommodations 828
Food 831
Sights 833
Museums 841
Entertainment 842
Nightlife 843
THE BAY AREA 845
Berkeley 845
Marin County 850
WINE COUNTRY 853
Napa Valley 853
Sonoma Valley 856
NORTHERN CALIFORNIA 858
Redwood National Park 859
GOLD COUNTRY 861
THE SIERRA NEVADA 863
Lake Tahoe 863
Yosemite National Park 868

THE PACIFIC NORTHWEST 876
☆ WASHINGTON 876
Seattle 877
San Juan Islands 891
OLYMPIC PENINSULA 893
Olympic National Park 894
CASCADE RANGE 897
EASTERN WASHINGTON 901
☆ OREGON 902
Portland 903
OREGON COAST 910
INLAND OREGON 913
Eugene 913

WESTERN CANADA 920
BRITISH COLUMBIA 920
Vancouver 920
Vancouver Island 928
THE YUKON TERRITORY 932
ALBERTA 936
The Rockies 936
Calgary 940

☆ ALASKA...................... 943
Getting There and Away 944
Anchorage 944
Fairbanks 950
SOUTHEAST ALASKA 952
Ketchikan 952
Juneau 953

DISTANCE CHART 956

INDEX 959

MAPS

USA & Canada xii
USA Transport xiii
The United States xiv–xv
USA National Park System xvi–xvii

New England 87
Boston 113
Cape Cod 131

Eastern Canada 153
Montréal 164–165
Vieux-Québec 175
Ontario and Upstate New York 180
Toronto 183
Ottawa 191

Mid-Atlantic 197
South Manhattan 199
Downtown Philadelphia 257
Pittsburgh 271
Central Baltimore 279
Washington, D.C. 289
Downtown Richmond 303

The South 328–329
Nashville 341
Downtown Memphis 351
Downtown Atlanta 377
New Orleans 403
Downtown New Orleans 405

Florida Peninsula 427
Orlando Theme Parks 433
Miami 445
South Beach 447

Great Lakes 467
Downtown Cleveland 469
Downtown Cincinnati 475
Downtown Detroit 479
Downtown Chicago 501
Downtown Minneapolis/St. Paul 531

Great Plains 543
Downtown St. Louis 575
Kansas City 583

Texas 591
Downtown San Antonio 593
Downtown Austin 599
Downtown Dallas and City Overview 605
Houston 611
El Paso and Ciudad Juarez 621

The Rocky Mountains 625
Yellowstone and Grand Teton National Parks 647
Denver 671

The Southwest 701
Las Vegas: The Strip 703
Salt Lake City 709
National Parks of Utah 715
Grand Canyon National Park 729
Downtown Phoenix 749
Downtown Tucson 753
Santa Fe 761
Albuquerque 767

California 780
Los Angeles Overview 783
L.A. Westside 785
Downtown San Diego 807
San Francisco Bay Area 827
Downtown San Francisco 829
Yosemite 869

The Pacific Northwest 877
Seattle 878–879
Downtown Portland 905

British Columbia and the Yukon Territory 921
Downtown Vancouver 923
Alberta 937

Alaska 943

⊞ Hospital	✈ Airport	🏛 Museum	▲ Mountain
🚓 Police	🚌 Bus Station	♠ Hotel/Hostel	Park
✉ Post Office	🚂 Train Station	⛺ Camping	
ⓘ Tourist Office	M METRO STATION	🍴 Food & Drink	Beach
🏦 Bank	⚓ Ferry Landing	🛍 Shopping	
🏴 Embassy/Consulate	✝ Church	♪ Arts & Entertainment	Water
▪ Site or Point of Interest	✡ Synagogue	🌙 Nightlife	
☎ Telephone Office	☪ Mosque	💻 Internet Café	The Let's Go thumb always points NORTH.
🎭 Theater	♜ Castle	▬▬▬ Pedestrian Zone	

RESEARCHER-WRITERS

Blair Baldwin *Texas, Louisiana, Mississippi, Oklahoma*

Reading through episode after episode of Blair's outrageous travelogue, we office-types couldn't believe what this seasoned backpacker would do for research. A Yankee in Texas and the Deep South, Blair set out to give *Let's Go: USA* deeper coverage of what makes this region unique. It was for the readers of this book that he braved so many saloons, nightclubs, and beaches.

Edward B. Colby *Southern New England, New York, Toronto, east of the Mississippi*

A budding journalist and heir to this traditionally tough itinerary, Ned endured the long haul, sending back crafted copy sprinkled with the creative quips and lucid observations that have come to be affectionately called "Nedisms." Ever a wit, Ned injected life into every syllable, and even attracted the attention of local media as he blazed his western trail.

Sarah J. Hines *Northern New England, Québec, Ontario, the Maritimes*

With an undying drive, Sarah tackled the rugged mountains and sea-swept coast-line of New England, as well as the raging nightlife of Canada's eastern cities, delivering top-notch research and creative copy. Back at headquarters, we boasted of our hard-core RW who battled sickness and faulty laptops without so much as a wince.

Joanie Hubble *Montana, Idaho, Wyoming, Utah, Colorado*

Fresh from the woods of Montana, Joanie burst onto the *Let's Go* scene, wrestled bears in Yellowstone, climbed jagged cliffs in the Rockies, and got muddy in her mean pickup. Faced with scorched earth and mountain roads without guardrails, this true outdoorswoman pushed onward, harnessing the wild moose that was her copy. No sooner had she finished than she was back in the hills, teaching some tenderfoots how to rough it.

Amy Kirkcaldy *Iowa, Nebraska, the Dakotas, Wyoming, Colorado*

We sent all the way to Spain for this senorita, who returned to her homeland to come see those big skies. With the skill of Picasso and the grace of a matador, Amy mastered the art of researching. Tireless through car troubles, lonely roads, and dirty dorms, this researcher made what a traveler once told her— "you must have the best job in the world" —into a reality.

Kate Kraft *Georgia, Florida*

No one has ever worked so hard in the Sunshine State as Kate. Her meticulous research, thoughtful writing, and spot-on timing drew gasps from editors back in the office. Hailing from Atlanta, GA, Kate was no stranger to this territory—her experience and excellent judgment helped her to give this jam-packed region the tender, loving care its due.

Andy Lynn *North Carolina, Kentucky, Tennessee, Alabama, Arkansas, Kansas*

There is little left south of the Mason-Dixon that Andy has not seen, explored, evaluated, mocked, or eaten. Even beyond his finely-tuned editing work and careful investigation of all things barbecue, Andy was a constant source of surprise. Held by no man's itinerary, he skipped from state to state at his own pace, ever willing to take his region head-on, chew it up, and spit it out. Who needs rest days? Hail Andy—the Southern conqueror.

John Mazza *Virginia, West Virginia, Delaware, Maryland, Pennsylvania, New Jersey*

In between revamping a *Let's Go* city guide, John moonlighted as USA researcher-writer, changing between Capitol Hill casual, D.C. punk, and Lancaster straw hats almost daily. Out of place in neither a Appalachian hoe-down nor an Atlantic City craps hall, John's in-depth researching techniques had him often confused for a local. John charmed and impressed us to the very end, and even led one of our editors to come to terms with the truth about his home state.

Maureen Shannon *Arizona, Utah, Colorado, New Mexico, Western Texas*

Moe turned a good copy into something better than anyone had ever imagined. If there was something great in the Southwest that we didn't cover, this researcher found it and turned it into sparking prose. Despite having the longest and hottest itinerary, Moe remained a true trailblazer; she let no travel brochure tell her what *real* traveling is about.

Jessica Tanner *Minnesota, Wisconsin, Iowa, Illinois, Michigan*

Jessica donned a cheese hat and painstakingly worked and reworked our coverage of the Great Lakes region, making us drool as we awaited her polished copy by post. At home on her old stompin' ground, Jessica went unfazed by computer glitches and a car that wouldn't go. Her skill and devotion served her as she ruthlessly improved coverage of the land that she loves so dearly.

REGIONAL RESEARCHER-WRITERS

Kaya Stone	*South Carolina*
Laela Sturdy	*Oregon and Washington*
Carletta Bruno	*Oregon*
Adam Scheuer	*British Columbia and Alberta*
Anne Browning	*Northern British Columbia, the Yukon, and Alaska*
Tom Mercer	*Alaska Panhandle*
Elizabeth Aranow	*Central Alaska*
Christopher A. Amar	*Gold Country, Sierra Nevadas*
Efrat Kussell	*Bay Area, North Coast, Central Coast*
Anna Portnoy	*L.A., Orange County*
Jeffrey T. Rowes	*Big Bear, San Diego, Desert, Las Vegas*
Yayoi Shionoiri, Thandi O. Parris, Christian Lorentzen, Matthew Murray, Daniel Levi, Bart St. Claire, Joseph Turian, Ian Pervil, the inimitable T.J. Kelleher, and Matt Daniels	*Noo Yauk City!*
Randy Gomes	*Washington, D.C., and environs*
Morgan Rodman	*Washington, D.C., and environs*
Julie K. Allen	*Boston and environs*
Jeff Sheng	*Boston and environs*
Alex Olson	*San Francisco and environs*
Jesse Green	*San Francisco and environs*
Dimple Chaudhary	*San Francisco and environs*

REGIONAL EDITORS

Marly Ohlsson	*Editor, Alaska & The Pacific Northwest (not neglecting Western Canada)*
Matt Brischetto	*Associate Editor, Alaska & The Pacific Northwest*
Nathan Foley-Mendelssohn	*Editor, California*
Michael Murakami	*Associate Editor, California*
Valerie De Charette	*Editor, New York City*
Terry Chang	*Editor, Washington, D.C.*
Keja Valens	*Editor, San Francisco*
Sarah Rotman	*Editor, Boston*
Chris Blazejewski	*Associate Editor, Boston and San Francisco*

ACKNOWLEDGMENTS

TEAM USA THANKS. Nick, an inspiration. Our outstanding RWs: Blair, Ned, Sarah, Joanie, Amy, Kate, Andy, John, Moe, and Jessica. Daisy, a great gal and a mean mapper. Singing Beach. Aarup, when you were there, you were there. Team North America. Kaya, an ol' vet, for helping us out in a pinch. All the RWs whose work went into the guide. Our inspirationally energetic hamsters. The nameless proofers. All those who came before us. Boom.

KEVIN THANKS. Stephanie and Jon: awesome editors, awesome folk. Nick, you steered this book in the right direction and always livened our spirits. To the researchers: this is your book. To T.J., for hiring me in the first place. To family. To Mom, you brought me life and keep on giving it. To Dad, you're an inspiration is so many ways. To my bros, Jeff and Greg. To friends: Geoff, Lindsay, Nick, Carlos, Oorlagh, Bartek, Stella, Cliona, Alex S., Alex P., Sahir, Dan, Brian, Anthony. You all enrich my life more than anything.

STEPHANIE THANKS. Kevin for the wildlife, Jon for "lunch breaks." Nick and his life-saving Wrap runs. My Southern researchers. Love to my family, for visiting me and taking me to exciting places. My summer roommates—Paul, John, Kate—you rock. Real roommates—Ellen, Viv, Amy, Emily—you rock too. Thanks to Scott and Rebecca for keeping me company. Love to Summer and Chris, for giving me a reason to stay in Boston this summer.

JONATHAN THANKS... Goodness. Kevin and Stephanie for their brilliance as editors, as people, and on the beach. Nick for his vision and his infectious laidback-ness. My unparalleled researchers. My family who I love more than life. Kate, my best friend and companion. Dan Fisher, Ricat, Stephen and his troublesome colon, Debiak, Philip V., Alex K., the elusive Tony-ball and Joe Fox, Prem Das, Oatnut, Sting, Stewart, Mo, Alberto, and Beer. Special thanks to Andy for making the mark.

Editor
Kevin Hoffman Yip
Associate Editors
Stephanie L. Coon, Jonathan Hall
Managing Editor
Nicholas Grossman
Map Editor
Daisy Stanton

Publishing Director
Kaya Stone
Editor-in-Chief
Kate McCarthy
Production Manager
Melissa Rudolph
Cartography Manager
John Fiore
Editorial Managers
Alice Farmer, Ankur Ghosh, Aarup Kubal, Anup Kubal
Financial Manager
Bede Sheppard
Low-Season Manager
Melissa Gibson
Marketing & Publicity Managers
Olivia L. Cowley, Esti Iturralde
New Media Manager
Daryush Jonathan Dawid
Personnel Manager
Nicholas Grossman
Photo Editor
Dara Cho
Production Associates
Sanjay Mavinkurve, Nicholas Murphy, Rosalinda Rosalez, Matthew Daniels, Rachel Mason, Daniel Visel
Some Design
Matthew Daniels
Office Coordinators
Sarah Jacoby, Chris Russell

Director of Advertising Sales
Cindy Rodriguez
Senior Advertising Associates
Adam Grant, Rebecca Rendell
Advertising Artwork Editor
Palmer Truelson

President
Andrew M. Murphy
General Manager
Robert B. Rombauer
Assistant General Manager
Anne E. Chisholm

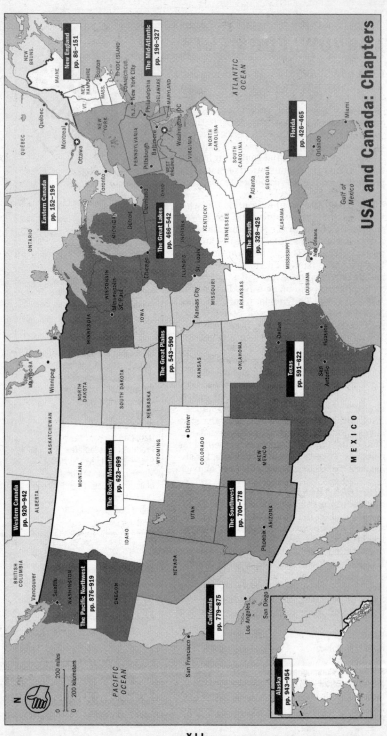

USA and Canada: Chapters

New England pp. 86–151

The Mid-Atlantic pp. 196–327

Eastern Canada pp. 152–195

The Great Lakes pp. 466–542

Florida pp. 426–465

The South pp. 328–425

The Great Plains pp. 543–590

Texas pp. 591–622

The Rocky Mountains pp. 623–699

The Southwest pp. 700–778

Western Canada pp. 920–942

The Pacific Northwest pp. 876–919

California pp. 779–875

Alaska pp. 943–954

PACIFIC OCEAN

ATLANTIC OCEAN

Gulf of Mexico

MEXICO

N

0   200 miles
0   200 kilometers

BRITISH COLUMBIA
Vancouver
Seattle
WASHINGTON
OREGON
San Francisco
Los Angeles
San Diego
CALIFORNIA
NEVADA
IDAHO
MONTANA
ALBERTA
Winnipeg
MANITOBA
SASKATCHEWAN
NORTH DAKOTA
SOUTH DAKOTA
WYOMING
Denver
COLORADO
UTAH
Phoenix
ARIZONA
NEW MEXICO
NEBRASKA
KANSAS
OKLAHOMA
San Antonio
Houston
Dallas
MINNESOTA
Minneapolis-St. Paul
IOWA
MISSOURI
Kansas City
ARKANSAS
LOUISIANA
New Orleans
MISSISSIPPI
ALABAMA
TENNESSEE
KENTUCKY
WISCONSIN
MICHIGAN
Chicago
ILLINOIS
INDIANA
St. Louis
Detroit
Cleveland
OHIO
Toronto
ONTARIO
QUÉBEC
Ottawa
Montréal
Québec
NEW BRUNS.
MAINE
NEW HAMPSHIRE
Boston
MASS.
RHODE ISLAND
CONNECTICUT
VT.
NEW YORK
New York City
N.J.
Philadelphia
DELAWARE
MARYLAND
Washington, D.C.
Baltimore
Pittsburgh
PENNSYLVANIA
WEST VIRGINIA
VIRGINIA
NORTH CAROLINA
SOUTH CAROLINA
GEORGIA
Atlanta
Orlando
Miami
FLORIDA

XII

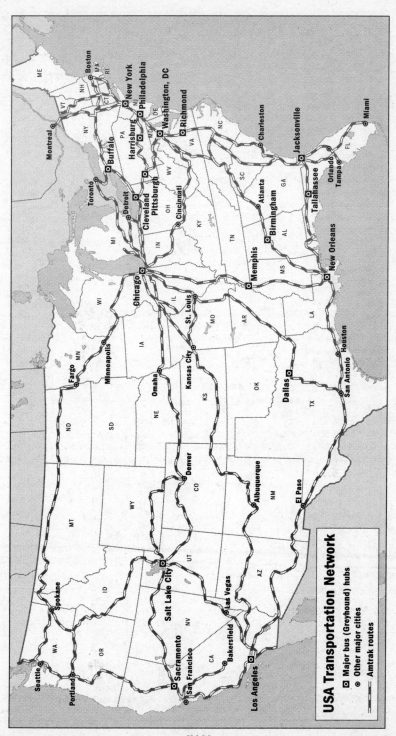

USA Transportation Network

◎ Major bus (Greyhound) hubs
◉ Other major cities
≈≈≈ Amtrak routes

The United States

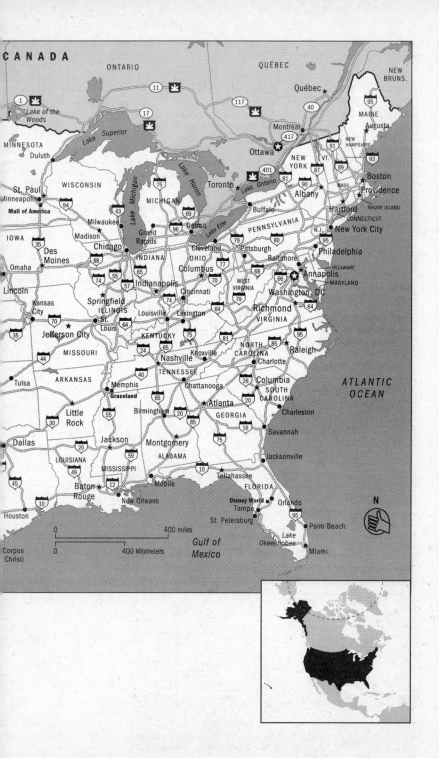

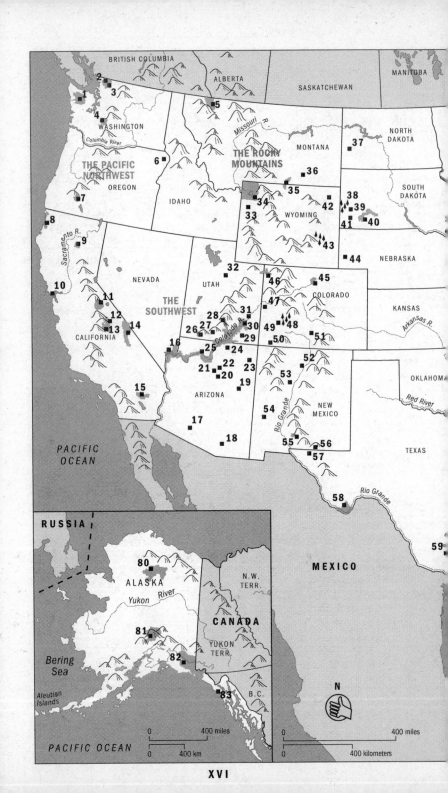

BRITISH COLUMBIA

ALBERTA

SASKATCHEWAN

MANITOBA

THE PACIFIC NORTHWEST

WASHINGTON

Columbia River

OREGON

IDAHO

Missouri R.

MONTANA

THE ROCKY MOUNTAINS

NORTH DAKOTA

SOUTH DAKOTA

WYOMING

NEBRASKA

Sacramento R.

NEVADA

UTAH

THE SOUTHWEST

CALIFORNIA

COLORADO

KANSAS

Arkansas R.

Colorado R.

ARIZONA

NEW MEXICO

OKLAHOMA

Red River

Rio Grande

TEXAS

PACIFIC OCEAN

Rio Grande

RUSSIA

ALASKA

Yukon River

N.W. TERR.

CANADA

YUKON TERR.

MEXICO

Bering Sea

B.C.

Aleutian Islands

PACIFIC OCEAN

N

| 0 | 400 miles |

| 0 | 400 km |

| 0 | 400 miles |

| 0 | 400 kilometers |

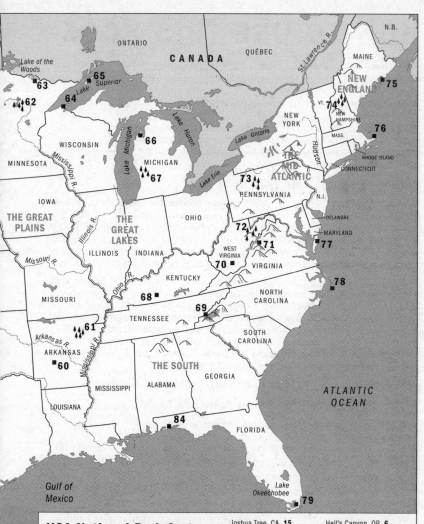

USA National Park System

National Monuments
Bandelier, NM, **52**
Black Canyon, CO, **49**
Canyon de Chelly, AZ, **23**
Colorado, CO, **47**
Devils Tower, WY, **42**
Dinosaur, CO, **46**
Gila Cliff Dwellings, NM, **54**
Great Sand Dunes, CO, **51**
Lassen Volcanic, CA, **9**
Little Bighorn, MT, **36**
Mt. Rushmore, SD, **39**
Natural Bridges, UT, **29**
Navajo, AZ, **24**
Organ Pipe, AZ, **17**
Petroglyph, NM, **53**
Scotts Bluff, NE, **44**
Sunset Crater, AZ, **21**
Timpanogos Cave, UT, **32**
Walnut Canyon, AZ, **20**
White Sands, NM, **55**
Wupatki, AZ, **22**

National Parks
Acadia, ME, **75**
Arches, UT, **31**
Badlands, SD, **40**
Big Bend, TX, **58**
Bryce Canyon, UT, **27**
Canyonlands, UT, **30**
Capitol Reef, UT, **28**
Carlsbad Caverns, NM, **56**
Crater Lake, OR, **7**
Death Valley, CA, **14**
Denali, AK, **81**
Everglades, FL, **79**
Gates of the Arctic, AK, **80**
Glacier, MT, **5**
Glacier Bay, AK, **83**
Grand Canyon, AZ, **25**
Grand Teton, WY, **33**
Great Smoky Mts., TN, **69**
Guadalupe Mts., TX, **57**
Hot Springs, AR, **60**
Isle Royale, MI, **65**

Joshua Tree, CA, **15**
Kings Canyon, CA, **12**
Mammoth Cave, KY, **68**
Mesa Verde, CO, **50**
Mt. Rainier, WA, **4**
New River Gorge, WV, **70**
North Cascades, WA, **2**
Olympic, WA, **1**
Petrified Forest, AZ, **19**
Redwood, CA, **8**
Rocky Mt., CO, **45**
Saguaro, AZ, **18**
Sequoia, CA, **13**
Shenandoah, VA, **71**
Theodore Roosevelt, ND, **37**
Voyageurs, MN, **63**
Wind Cave, SD, **41**
Wrangell-St. Elias, AK, **82**
Yellowstone, WY, **34**
Yosemite, CA, **11**
Zion, UT, **26**

National Recreation Areas
Bighorn Canyon, MT, **35**
Golden Gate, CA, **10**

Hell's Canyon, OR, **6**
Lake Mead, NV, **16**
Ross Lake, WA, **3**

National Forests
Allegheny, PA, **73**
Black Hills, SD, **48**
Chippewa, MN, **62**
Grand Mesa, CO, **48**
Manistee, MI, **67**
Medicine Bow, WY, **43**
Monongahela, WV, **72**
Ozark, AR, **61**
White Mts., NH, **74**

National Lakeshores
Apostle Islands, WI, **64**
Sleeping Bear Dunes, MI, **66**

National Seashores
Assateague, MD, **77**
Cape Cod, MA, **76**
Cape Hatteras, NC, **78**
Padre Island, TX, **59**
Gulf Islands, FL, **84**

HOW TO USE THIS BOOK

WELCOME TO LET'S GO: USA 2001!
About seven months ago, three editors, ten researcher-writers, and nearly forty regional editors and writers came upon a task of unspeakable proportions: revisit every single city in these thousand pages, drive down every road, and check every price and every fact, from the price of a bottomless cup of coffee in the Florida Keys to instructions on chartering a plane in the Arctic circle. An incredible task it was, but **The United States of America** deserves nothing less. This is a nation of anything and everything, a world unto itself, a phenomenon, and a land so immense that it nearly busted the seams of this book.

THE ORGANIZATION OF THIS BOOK

INTRODUCTORY MATERIAL. The first chapter, **Discover The United States of America,** of this book provides you with an overview of travel in the US, including **Suggested Itineraries** that give you an idea of what you shouldn't miss and how long it will take to see it. The **Life & Times** chapter provides you with a general introduction to the history and culture of the USA. Meanwhile, the **Essentials** section outlines the practical information you will need to prepare for and execute your trip.

THE MEAT. We start our coverage on the East Coast with our home, **New England,** ramble onward to that foreign land of **Eastern Canada,** gleefully hopscotch to the megalopolis that is the **Mid-Atlantic,** ride our ponies south to the **South,** enjoy a few surreal weeks in **Florida,** space-warp north to the land of cheese-heads, the **Great Lakes,** drive (and drive and drive) to the **Great Plains,** *do* **Texas,** get high in the **Rockies,** cartwheel to the **Southwest,** cruise through **California,** and finally, well...go to the **Pacific Northwest, Western Canada, and Alaska.** The **black tabs** in the margins will help you to navigate between chapters quickly and easily!

APPENDIX. Check out the appendix for a nifty and ever-useful mileage chart!

A FEW NOTES ABOUT LET'S GO FORMAT

RANKING ESTABLISHMENTS. In each section (accommodations, food, etc.), we list establishments in order from best to worst. Our absolute favorites are so denoted by the highest honor given out by Let's Go, the Let's Go thumbs-up (🖐). For sights, we usually group attractions in whatever order we feel is most logical.

PHONE CODES AND TELEPHONE NUMBERS. The **phone code** for each region, city, or town appears opposite the name of that region, city, or town, and is denoted by the ☎ icon. **Phone numbers** in text are also preceded by the ☎ icon.

GRAYBOXES AND WHITEBOXES. Grayboxes at times provide wonderful cultural insight, at times simply crude humor. In any case, they're usually amusing, so enjoy. **Whiteboxes,** on the other hand, provide important practical information, such as warnings (🖐), helpful hints and further resources (🖐).

UNIQUE AND USEFUL SECTIONS. Check out our expanded coverage of scenic drives and roadtrips, noted in text like this: *Scenic Drive: Apache Trail.*

A NOTE TO OUR READERS The information for this book was gathered by *Let's Go* researchers from May through August of 2000. Each listing is based on one researcher's opinion, formed during his or her visit at a particular time. Those traveling at other times may have different experiences since prices, dates, hours, and conditions are always subject to change. You are urged to check the facts presented in this book beforehand to avoid inconvenience and surprises.

DISCOVER THE UNITED STATES

Stretching from below the Tropic of Cancer to above the Arctic Circle and spanning the North American continent, the United States is big. It is a country defined by open spaces and an amazing breadth of terrain. From sparse deserts to lush forests to snow-capped peaks to rolling fields of grain, the American landscape sprouts new views from state to state—even from neighborhood to neighborhood.

America's accumulation of wealth and prestige since WWII has heightened both its patriotism and its interior divisions. Americans have reason to be proud: in this fair country, world-class creature comforts exist minutes away from acres of country quiet—and most of it is accessible, at least in theory, to everyone. However, the contrast between the overall abundance of wealth and the many who struggle to make ends meet is a constant confrontation. Though class lines aren't openly acknowledged, they drive people's daily lives, aspirations, and politics. Wealthy people may run the big show, but the middle-class masses inspire America's ideological orientation towards unpretentious family values. Through centuries of immigration, the US has absorbed and integrated millions of immigrants to create the cultural amalgamation that now defines the population, contributing to the proud spirit of diversity which pervades the country, and also clashing in situations of discrimination and misunderstanding.

America does indeed live up to its reputation as the land of plenty, but plentifulness leads often to too-muchness, as the proliferation of chain motels, superficial cafes, and growing acres of cookie-cutter suburbs attests to. As this child of many continents has risen from a colonial experiment to a position of supreme economic and political power, its largesse continues to both impress and overwhelm.

FACTS AND FIGURES

POPULATION: 270,262,000

FOUR LARGEST CITIES: New York City, Los Angeles, Houston, Philadelphia

RELIGIOUS AFFILIATION: Protestant 58%, Roman Catholic 21%, other Christian 6%; Jewish 2%; Muslim 2%; other 2%; nonreligious 9%

MILES DRIVEN EACH YEAR: 1½ trillion (to the sun and back 7,500 times)

URBAN/RURAL POPULATION: urban 77%; rural 23%

ETHNICITY: White 73%; Black 12%; Hispanic 11%; Asian and Pacific Islander 3½%; Native American 1%

WHEN TO GO

In general, the US tourist season runs during the summer months between Memorial Day to Labor Day, (May 28-Sept. 3, 2001); in Canada, the tourist season starts around mid-July. National parks become inundated with visitors during the high season, though cities are less affected. For regions where winter sports are big or that have mild winters, the tourist season is generally inverted (Dec.-Mar.). For a chart detailing many of the festivals in the USA and Canada, see **Festivals**, p. 31.

THINGS TO DO

Neither these two nor this book's one thousand pages can begin to do justice to the vibrant, unparalleled, and above all, diverse offerings of the North American continent. No two trips to the New World are ever the same, and visitors to two different regions may feel like they've visited different countries. There are, however, a few common themes in the States and Canada that deserve mention and that should be a part of any thorough exploration.

SCENIC DRIVES

News commentator and stalwart American patriot Charles Kuralt once said, "thanks to the interstate highway system, it is now possible to travel from coast to coast without seeing anything." The interstate system is the fastest, most efficient, most sensible, worst way of driving through America. The incredible network of backroads in the US afford a view of the real country, unobstructed by vision-blocking soundproofers and gas-spewing trailers and with rest-stops with more character than the next Burger King. **Blue Ridge Parkway,** VA (p. 320), connects two national parks—Shenandoah and Great Smoky Mountains—passing tremendous green mountains and rustic Appalachian wilderness. In the North, the **Lake Superior North Shore Drive,** MN (p. 540), traces the dramatic, cliff-lined shore of the greatest Great Lake, passing waterfalls, lighthouses, and looming forests. Connecting San Antonio with Austin, TX, the **Texas Hill Country Drive** (p. 596) goes deep into the heart of Texas—broad-rim hats and dusty jeans country—where the Western landscape is dotted with ethnic enclaves and pristine vineyards. Just outside Phoenix, AZ, the **Apache Trail** (p. 752) curves around stark cactus-laden desert mountains, looming over, and contrasting surreally with, smurf-blue reservoirs. The **San Juan Skyway** (p. 695), in southern CO, ascends to breathtaking heights under snow-capped mountains and past bottomless gorges. **Going-to-the-Sun Road** (p. 642), in the Waterton-Glacier Peace Park, MO, skirts mountainous landscape too beautiful for words and then descends into rainforest.

DIAMONDS IN THE ROUGH

Sure, everyone knows the big'uns. New York has...well, everything. And for vivacity, glamour, great weather, and unbeatable smog, nothing tops Los Angeles. But the real reason to buckle up for the great American journey, besides the great American wilderness, is to enjoy the smaller, less obvious cities and towns on the way. Lost between the twin metropoli of New York and Boston, the smaller college town of **Providence, RI** (p. 143), beckons with fast-paced energy on a slower, more inviting pace. The "staid" Midwest boasts **Minneapolis-St. Paul, MN** (p. 524), a sprawling and unsung urban center with the sights and diversity to rival even the most famous of American cities. In **Asheville, NC** (p. 362), relics of conspicuous consumption from days passed provide a gilded backdrop for its current funky population. The legendary nightlife of **Austin, TX** (p. 598), thrives on the city's mix of Southwestern grit, collegiate energy, and dot-com optimism. The gentility of the Old South lives on in cities like **Vicksburg** and **Natchez, MI** (p. 399 and p. 400), where time passes just a little slower than anywhere else in the country. Only the most liberal-minded and fun-loving traveler need stop in the eclectic town of **Boulder, CO** (p. 676), a place of many Rocky Mountain highs. Countless adventurers find a warm welcome in **Flagstaff, AZ** (p. 734), perhaps the greatest crossroads in the US.

AMERICANA

America enshrines the biggest, smallest and zaniest of everything. Kitschy roadside attractions dot the country's dusty roads, putting on public display a vast and truly baffling material culture, most often for a modest fee. The **Museum of Early American Farm Machinery and Very Old Horse Saddles with a History** houses rusted relics of happier days in Chalk Hill, PA (p. 274). Out west in Polson, MT, the **Miracle of America Museum** makes it clear that reg'lar old American living is downright miraculous (p. 638). **Wall Drug's** notorious billboards lure tourists to the Badlands of

▧ LET'S GO PICKS

BEST OPPORTUNITIES FOR PUBLIC BATHING: Hot springs are a therapeutic diversion from the hard work of travel; the best are at Hot Springs, AR (p. 422); Saratoga, WY (p. 667); Truth or Consequences, NM (p. 773); and Hot Springs, SD (p. 556). For just plain skinny dippin', try Hippie Hollow in Austin, TX (p. 601).

BEST SUNSPOTS: To watch the sun rise first, head to Cadillac Mt. in Acadia National Park, ME (p. 87). To see the best sunset on earth, go to the pier in Clearwater, FL (p. 459).

BEST FOR SPELUNKERS: Don't forget to explore the underground. Highest marks go to Mammoth Cave, KY (p. 333), and Carlsbad Caverns, NM (p. 778).

BEST GATORS: America's most impressive creatures. Get up-close and scarily personal in Nachitoches, LA (p. 416); the Everglades, FL (p. 450); and St. Augustine, FL (p. 426).

BEST BIG ART: Everything's big in America. Twenty-seven factory buildings are needed to hold the exhibits at the Museum of Contemporary Art in North Adams, MA (p. 140). The yet-unfinished sculpture of Crazy Horse (p. 555) will be 563 ft. when it is completed, making the 60 ft. presidential heads on nearby Mt. Rushmore (p. 554) seem like child's play.

BEST WAY TO ESCAPE AMERICA: Tibetan cuisine, rare in the US, is authentically served at the Snow Lion restaurant in Bloomington, IN (p. 497), owned by the Dalai Lama's nephew. Made in Tajikstan and shipped to Boulder, CO (p. 676), the building of the Dushanbe teahouse is a gift between sister cities—a tasty tribute to international relations.

BEST EXTRA-TERRESTRIALS: Many claim Roswell, NM (p. 776) and Sedona, AZ (p. 739) have hosted a few *really* long-distance travelers.

South Dakota from as far away as Amsterdam—that's right, in Holland—and have turned a marketing ploy into a cultural phenomenon (p. 552). At the **Tinkertown Museum** in Albuquerque, NM, the pants of the world's tallest man, among other thingamabobs, are walled-in by countless glass bottles (p. 770). That's no match for the **beer can house** in Houston, TX, however, which needs no explanation (p. 613). America also claims the world's largest **kaleidoscope** (Kaleidoworld in Mt. Tremper, NY, p. 236) and **wooden cross** (Cross in the Woods in Petoskey, MI, p. 490), neither of which can quite compete with the magnitude of **Car Henge,** a scale model of Stonehenge built from 36 old cars just north of Alliance, NE (p. 571). Bigger and brighter still are the casinos of **the Strip** in Las Vegas, NV (p. 702) and **the Boardwalk** in Atlantic City, NJ (p. 252). No tribute to the American value of individual rights stands so proud as **"The Tree That Owns Itself"** (and its shade) in Athens, GA (p. 385). And no tour of American kitsch would be complete without a trip to the heart and soul of all Americana, Elvis's **Graceland** (p. 352).

NATIONAL PARKS

From ancient glaciers to an endless sea of blinding white gypsum to haunting red buttes to endless pitch-black caves, the national parks of the US and Canada protect some of the most phenomenal natural beauty in the world. While much of the land's beauty can be seen along the byways, the truly miraculous works of nature are cared for by the national parks services. In the East, parks like **Acadia N.P.**, ME (p. 93), **Adirondacks State Park**, NY (p. 245), **Shenandoah N.P.**, VA (p. 318), and **Great Smokey Mountains N.P.**, TN (p. 345) preserve pristine green mountains, lush valleys, and vivid foliage in the fall. By far the most popular parks, however, lie out west. **Yellowstone N.P.**, WY (p. 645), **Grand Canyon N.P.**, AZ (p. 727), and **Yosemite N.P.**, CA (p. 868), draw hordes of trekkers, trailers, and tourists in the warmer months. Every local will tell you that you have to see their park "at least once in your life;" they speak the truth at these, the big three. Smaller, but not less breathtaking wonders can be found in the otherworldly hoodoos of **Bryce Canyon N.P.**, UT (p. 721), the varied and dramatic terrain of **Waterton-Glacier Peace Park,** MO (p. 638), and the awesome mountains of **Grand Teton N.P.**, WY (p. 654).

SUGGESTED ITINERARIES

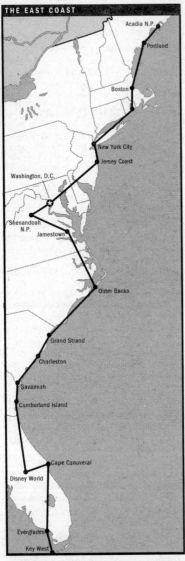

THE EAST COAST

Acadia N.P.

Portland

Boston

New York City

Jersey Coast

Washington, D.C.

Shenandoah N.P.

Jamestown

Outer Banks

Grand Strand

Charleston

Savannah

Cumberland Island

Cape Canaveral

Disney World

Everglades

Key West

tacular results, and then head down the coast. The youthful Portland, ME (p. 88) will whet your appetite for city life, and the thriving culture of Boston, MA (p. 111) will satisfy it. Cape Cod (p. 130) awaits with pristine beaches, while Newport, RI (p. 145) preserves the must-see summer estates of America's wealthiest Industrialists. Then on to New York City (p. 236), to which so many superlatives cannot do justice—give yourself some time to take it all in. The Jersey Shore (p. 253) offers R&R on what are arguably the best beaches in the Northeast. Washington, D.C. (p. 287) deserves a few days, as does the placid Shenandoah National Park (p. 318). They'll act out colonial history for you in Williamsburg, VA (p. 309), but you can find solitude on the long stretches of sand of the Outer Banks (p. 364). The more built-up Grand Strand (p. 373) and the city of Charleston, SC (p. 368) beckon partyers back to the mainland. Savannah (p. 387) and stunning Cumberland Island (p. 387) will leave Georgia on your mind, but Disney World (p. 435) will leave you blissfully mind-numb. Give the Space Coast of Florida (p. 440) a fly-by, and definitely explore the vast, mysterious Everglades (p. 450). Celebrate the end of your journey with umbrella drinks on sugar-white beaches in Key West (p. 453).

THE NORTH: TRACING THE US-CANADIAN BORDER (6 WEEKS)

Crossing the continent at higher latitudes affords travelers time in the unique cities and less touristed parks of the North. Begin on the Canadian side of the border and take a whirlwind tour of the country's cosmopolitan eastern cities. Québec City (p. 173) and Montréal (p. 163) are predominantly French-speaking and overflow with culture. The pleasant city of Ottawa (p. 190) offers history and intriguing architecture, while Toronto (p. 181) boasts huge ethnic quarters and refreshing tidiness for a big city. Cross the border at the spectacular Niagara Falls (p. 243) and head west for the oft-stigmatized and underestimated city of Detroit (p. 477). Move quickly on to the main course, though: Chicago (p. 499). Wind down in the friendly and scenic lakeside communities of Wisconsin at Door County (p. 524) and the Apostle Islands (p. 526). Next, head to the surprisingly hip twin cities of St. Paul and Minneapolis (p. 529). The cute city of Duluth, MN (p. 536) combines a thriving shipping industry with endless waterfront recreation. Before leaving Minnesota, park the car and boat into the

EAST COAST: MAINE TO THE FLORIDA KEYS (6 WEEKS) I-95 and the sometimes commercial, sometimes scenic U.S. 1 parallel each other from the northern wilds of Maine down to the gorgeous Florida Keys. In spite of the many state-levied tolls, this strip gives a true cross-section of American life and culture, and encourages on-a-whim diversions. Begin on Mt. Desert Island, ME (p. 87) where mountain and ocean meet with spec-

TRACING THE US-CANADA BORDER

unspoiled expanse of Voyageurs National Park (p. 540). Stop in Fargo (p. 544), then speed out to the breathtaking Theodore Roosevelt (p. 547) and Yellowstone (p. 645) National Parks. Missoula, MT (p. 636) is surprisingly hip, and provides a much-needed stop before heading north to Waterton-Glacier Peace Park (p. 638) and the popular Banff National Park (p. 936) in Canada. Out on the Pacific coast, choose among the lively city scenes of Vancouver (p. 920) and Seattle (p. 877) or one of the world's last remaining old-growth temperate rainforests at Olympic National Park (p. 894). Or take your time and do all three.

SOUTH BY SOUTHWEST (8 WEEKS)
Striking straight across the American South from sea to shining sea—and even dipping into Mexico—this route highlights down-home Southern culture, Mexican-infused Southwestern culture, and canyon country. It can be driven all year. Warm up with big cities tempered by Southern hospitality in the triangle of Charleston, SC (p. 368), Savannah, GA (p. 387) and Atlanta (p. 376). Chug through Chattanooga, TN (p. 347), then follow virtually all American musics to their roots through Nashville (p. 339), Memphis (p. 349) and New Orleans (p. 403). Experience the unadulterated cajun culture of the Deep South in Acadiana, LA (p. 418) before heading out to the fun Texas cities of Houston (p. 609), San Antonio (p. 592), and Austin (p. 598). White Sands National Monument (p. 775) is truly other-worldly, while Truth or Conse-

quences, NM (p. 773) has mineral baths that can also take you to another place. The cities of Santa Fe (p. 760) and Albuquerque (p. 766) are worth a couple of days each. Then onto the astonishing Petrified Forest and Painted Desert (p. 745) via stopover in Gallup, NM (p. 772). Flagstaff, AZ (p. 734) is an inviting Southwestern city in its own right, and makes a convenient base for exploring the region near the indescribable Grand Canyon (p. 727). Page, AZ and the enormous man-made Lake Powell (p. 746) offer a great hostel and plenty to do outside and on the water. To the north, the idyllic wilderness of Zion National Park (p. 723) and startling hoodoos of Bryce Canyon (p. 721) in Utah provide travelers with a last gasp of clean air and natural beauty before plunging into the glitz of Las Vegas (p. 702). In California, Joshua Tree National Park (p. 813) is a worthy stop in the desert on the way to the Pacific coast. Savor sunny San Diego (p. 805), but bear witness to run-down Tijuana, Mexico (p. 811) where classes and cultures clash. Finish up in Los Angeles (p. 779) with a night on the town.

THE AMERICAN WEST (3-6 WEEKS)
This is the West that has blown the minds of generations of westward wanderers. Acculturate yourself to the region with tours of Tucson (p. 752), Phoenix (p. 747), and Flagstaff, AZ (p. 734). Hit the must-see Grand Canyon (p. 727) from the South Rim, and then mosey through the more tranquil Bryce Canyon (p. 721) and Zion (p. 723) National Parks in Utah. On to Albuquerque (p. 766) and Santa

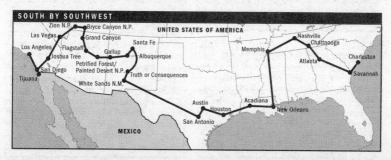

SOUTH BY SOUTHWEST

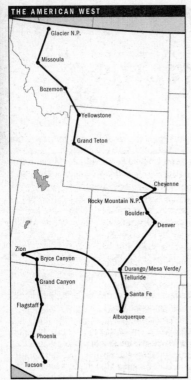

THE AMERICAN WEST

and quintessential beach culture. Las Vegas (p. 702), Tijuana (p. 811), and Joshua Tree (p. 813) are viable side trips. The 400 mi. stretch of shore-hugging Rte. 1 between LA and San Francisco—through Big Sur (p. 821) and Santa Cruz (p. 823)—is pure California: rolling surf, secluded beaches, dramatic cliffs, and quirky folks. San Francisco (p. 825), a groovin' city in itself, is only 3-4hr. from Yosemite National Park (p. 868). From San Fran, the slightly inland Rte. 101 hits Napa Valley wine country (p. 853) before reuniting with Rte. 1 (and the coast) and passing through primordial Redwood National Park (p. 859). Once past the trees, rejoin I-5 for a trip through Oregon to Portland (p. 903). Side trips to Crater Lake (p. 915) and Mt. Hood (p. 908) are well worth it. Before resettling with a cappucino in Seattle, the moonscape of Mt. St. Helens (p. 897) and the rainforests of Olympic National Park (p. 894) lie in wait. Vancouver, BC (p. 920) offers access to the outdoor havens of Vancouver Island (p. 928).

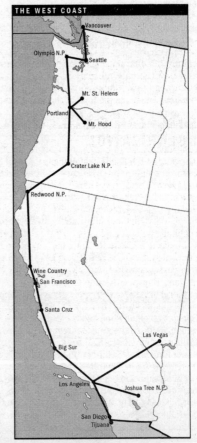

THE WEST COAST

Fe, NM (p. 760) as you approach more mountainous terrain. Spend some time in the hip and cattle-friendly area of Durango (p. 695) and Telluride, CO (p. 693), and take on the mile-high city of Denver (p. 669) and healthful Boulder (p. 676) before getting lost amongst the peaks of Rocky Mountain National Park (p. 680). Stopover in Cheyenne, WY (p. 664) for a boot-stompin' good time on your way to the magnificent Tetons (p. 654). The vastly popular Yellowstone National Park (p. 645) warrants an extra couple of days. Then, the towns of Bozeman (p. 633) and Missoula, MT (p. 636), culturally straddling East and West, make pleasant and unique stops for the weary. Cap off your trip, though, with more raw beauty in the rugged Glacier National Park (p. 639).

THE WEST COAST: FROM LA TO VANCOUVER, B.C. (2-6 WEEKS).

A tour of the West Coast offers the most cosmopolitan diversity, mountainscapes, and oceanfront property for your buck. Between sunny, boisterous Los Angeles and lush, mellow Vancouver, BC lies much natural (and artificial) diversion. L.A. (p. 779), America's western outpost of high culture, provides access to Hollywood (p. 784), famous art,

LIFE AND TIMES

THE UNITED STATES

HISTORY

IN THE BEGINNING

Archaeologists estimate that the **first Americans** crossed the Bering Sea from Siberia by land bridge during the last Ice Age, anywhere from 10,000 to 60,000 years ago. While these aboriginal Americans all shared an Asiatic ancestry, they developed several different cultures based largely on the area where they settled. Fishing provided the primary source of sustenance for the Subarctic, Northwest Pacific Coast, and Plateau societies. In California, Native Americans discovered a plentiful supply of flour in the process of leaching acorn pulp. Nomadic families in the relatively impoverished Great Basin survived on wild seeds, insects, and small animals. The Native Americans of the Plains Regions were greatly influenced by European colonization, as the introduction of the horse by 16th-century Spanish explorers made bison-hunting (and raiding) more profitable activities. For the Southwest, Eastern Woodlands, and Southeast civilizations, agriculture of common staples such as corn (maize), beans, squash, and tubers made more stable villages possible. These nine cultural groups composed the diverse Native American population that existed at the time of the first European exploration.

EUROPEAN EXPLORATION AND COLONIZATION

The date of the first European exploration of North America is difficult to pinpoint. The earliest Europeans to stumble upon the "New World" were likely sea voyagers blown off-course by storms. The traditional "discovery" of the Americas was in 1492, when **Christopher Columbus** found his voyage to the East blocked by Hispaniola in the Caribbean Sea. Believing he had reached the spice islands of the East Indies, he erroneously dubbed the inhabitants "Indians." In return for an efficient agricultural system, the Europeans gave the Native Americans pestilence, persecution, and slavery.

Many Europeans came to the Americas (named after Italian explorer Amerigo Vespucci) in search of gold and silver; most were unsuccessful, but European colonization persisted. The Spanish originally boasted the most extensive American colony, which included the areas known today as New Mexico, Arizona, California, and Florida. At the same time that Spain was building her colony in the Southern territories, the French and Dutch created more modest empires to the north. It was the English, however, who most successfully settled the vast New World. After a few unsuccessful attempts, the English finally managed to establish a colony at **Jamestown** in 1607. Their success hinged on a strain of indigenous weed called tobacco, which achieved wild

1000
Leif Eriksson establishes a colony in Newfoundland

1513
Ponce de León discovers Florida

1590
English settlers at Roanoke disappear

1619
The legislative body of the House of Burgesses created in Jamestown

1671
France lays claim to all of western North America

1732
The last of the 13 original colonies is founded (Georgia)

popularity in England. While the Virginia settlements were commercially focused and organized by the Virginia Company of London, other English colonists saw the New World as an escape from the religious persecution of England's king, Charles I. These **Puritans** settled in present-day Massachusetts, where Native Americans taught them how to live in a harsh land. Grateful for their hard-won survival, the Puritans celebrated with a huge feast. **Thanksgiving,** one of the most treasured holidays in American culture, continues to stuff families with turkey, gravy, and cranberry sauce every fourth Thursday in November.

REBELLION AND REVOLUTION

1765
Stamp Act levies tax on colonies

1773
Tea Act passed; Boston responds with the Boston Tea Party (see The Freedom Trail, p. 117)

1774
First Continental Congress meets

1775
Second Continental Congress meets

1783
Last British troops in America leave New York

In order to protect her holdings in the Americas, Great Britain entered into the French and Indian War against France in 1754. Although ultimately successful, the struggle more than doubled Great Britain's government expenditures and raised awareness of the high price of colonialism. In order to offset the burden of this price on British taxpayers, the powers that be decided to shift more responsibility onto the 13 original colonies, who had previously been taxed lightly. The authorization of new taxes for the American colonies angered colonists, who responded with the call for "no taxation without representation." In the first meeting of the Continental Congress, independence from Britain was not necessarily the consensus, although fighting between colonists and British troops convinced the Second Continental Congress to prepare the 13 colonies for war. In 1776, a **Declaration of Independence** was drafted and then adopted on July 4th. This date remains the marker of independence for the US; barbecues and fireworks serve as traditional celebration for the success of the American Revolution against the British.

LIFE, LIBERTY, & THE CONSTITUTION

1787
Constitutional Convention meets in Philadelphia

1787-88
Constitution ratified by state conventions

1791
Bill of Rights ratified as first ten amendments to the Constitution

After achieving its independence, the country experimented with a loose confederated government until 1787, when the several state legislatures sent a distinguished group of 55 men to draft what is now the world's oldest written **Constitution.** While the **Federalists** supported a strong central government free from popular influence, **Jeffersonians** (Anti-Federalists) favored states' rights and feared the cutthroat individualism and domineering government that a central government would bring.

The Constitution's **Bill of Rights,** which included the rights to free speech, freedom of the press, and freedom of religion along with the controversial right to bear arms, remains a cornerstone of the American political system. In spite of the supposed inalienability of these rights, the original words of the document's authors are still interpreted differently according to the political climate of each era. In 1896, Justice Henry Billings Brown used the Constitution to support segregation in *Plessy v. Ferguson,* whereas Chief Justice Earl Warren cited the same document to destroy the practice in the 1950s. The Constitution, with its malleability and responsiveness to changing mores, reflects the country's longing for just governance.

MANIFEST DESTINY

1819
Florida is acquired from Spain

Looking toward the land beyond the Mississippi, President Thomas Jefferson purchased the **Louisiana Territory** (one-fourth of the present-day United States) from Napoleon in 1803 for less than 3¢ an acre. The next year, Jefferson sent the Lewis and Clark expedition to explore the territory and to find an aqueous trade route to the Pacific Ocean. Lewis and Clark never found a trade route, but they did chart the vast extent of land which lay west of the Mississippi. After the War of 1812 with Britain, the westward movement gained momentum. **Manifest Destiny,** a belief that the United States was destined by God to rule the continent, captured the ideological imagination of the era. The acquisition of the Southwest, California, and Oregon territory gave the US access to the West Coast, and droves of people migrated west in covered wagons along the grueling Oregon Trail in search of land, fortune, and a new life.

The **Homestead Act** of 1862, which distributed government land to those who would farm and live on it, prompted the cultivation of the Great Plains. This large-scale settlement led to bloody battles with the Sioux, Hunkpapas, and Cheyenne tribes who had long inhabited the plains. From 1866-1891 the US fought a continuous war against the remaining 300,000 "Indians." At **Custer's Last Stand** in 1876, a group of Native Americans led by Crazy Horse and Sitting Bull massacred General Custer's army, which prompted a furious reaction. The Native Americans were routed out, their land taken away, and their communities relegated to reservations. Much of the legend of the **Wild West** revolves around tall tales of brave white settlers and stoic cowboys fending off attacks by the "Indians."

AMERICA'S PECULIAR INSTITUTION

The first **Africans** were brought to America in 1619, prisoners aboard a Dutch slave ship headed for Jamestown, Virginia. The infusion of African slave labor led to the decline of indentured servitude, a system by which poor Europeans would provide seven years of labor in exchange for their Atlantic crossing. From the late-16th century and into the 17th century, as the demand for cheap labor increased, white settlers systematically invaded and terrorized Native American communities in search of slaves. As white indentured servitude tapered off and Native Americans suffered fatally from European diseases, white America relied heavily on the African slave trade to fill the gap. Thousands of Africans were taken from their homes and forced across the Atlantic in the dark holds of slave ships, a harrowing journey known as the **Middle Passage.** Once in the US, they were auctioned. This practice would last until 1807, when the slave trade was abolished. Slave ownership, however, would continue until the late 19th century, forming one of the most brutal chapters in the country's short history.

Slavery exacerbated existing ideological differences between the North and the South. Because the federal government was created relatively weak in order to prevent the "tyranny" of pre-Revolution days from reappearing, each state could decide to allow or prohibit slavery independently. As the Northern states became more insistent that territories and new states should be kept free of slavery, the Southern states counteracted by citing the Revolutionary ideal of states' rights to self-determination. Northern abolitionists also joined with free African-Americans to form the elusive **Underground Railroad,** an escape route for slaves into the free northern states. Southerners who invaded

THE USA

1820
Missouri Compromise establishes that slavery is to be limited to territories or states south of the 36º30' line

1846
Texas annexed

1848
Victory in Mexican War adds California and most of the Southwest to US territory

1850
Fugitive Slave Act requires runaway slaves in free states to be returned to their owners

1854-9
"Bleeding Kansas" serves as a prelude to the Civil War, as pro-slavery and anti-slavery camps war over Kansas's admission into the Union as a free or slave state

1857
Slave Dred Scott sues for his freedom in a Missouri court; Supreme Court Chief Justice Roger Taney declares that African-Americans are not citizens and therefore do not possess the right to sue in federal courts

the north to retrieve their "property" fueled existing tensions between these two separate halves of a nation, split by economic and societal differences. It would take a fierce and bloody call to arms to decide which identity would prevail.

"A HOUSE DIVIDED"—THE CIVIL WAR

1863
Lincoln issues the Emancipation Proclamation, which freed all slaves in rebel territory (but not in the four Union slave states); Battle of Gettysburg in southern Pennsylvania causes heavy casualties for both sides and turns the tide of the war in the North's favor

Tensions between the North and South came to a head when an anti-slavery President, **Abraham Lincoln,** was elected in 1860. South Carolina seceded from the Union, but Lincoln refused to officially recognize the secession. Twelve states followed in 1861, and 1862 witnessed the birth of a united **southern Confederacy** under the lead of Jefferson Davis. Most federal forts in the South were converted to Confederate control, although Fort Sumter in Charleston, South Carolina, remained staffed by Union troops. On April 12, 1861, Southern troops fired shots at the fort, and the Civil War began. For four years the country endured a savage and bloody war, fought by the North to restore the Union and by the South to break it.

1864
Union general William Tecumseh Sherman forces Confederate evacuation of Atlanta; Lincoln is re-elected

Lincoln led the North to victory, but the price was high. The war claimed more American lives than any other in history, and many families were divided against each other as brothers took up different uniforms and loyalties. Lincoln was assassinated on April 14, 1865, by a Southern sympathizer named John Wilkes Booth, too late to prevent his mark on American history. Despite his untimely death, Lincoln would be forever memorialized in public memory as the President who saved the Union and abolished slavery.

1865
13th Amendment abolishing slavery is ratified after the end of the war

RECONSTRUCTION AND INDUSTRIALIZATION

1868
Despite being rejected by all Southern states except Tennessee, the 14th Amendment is ratified and provides African-Americans with the rights of citizenship

The period after the war brought Reconstruction to the South and Industrial Revolution to the North. The North's rapid industrialization rendered it a formidable contender in the world economy, while the South's agricultural economy began a slow decline. Injured and embittered by the war and dependent on an outdated agricultural tradition, Southerners struggled to readjust to the new economic and social situations forced upon them. The newly freed blacks faced a difficult transition from plantation to free life. **Jim Crow** laws continued to restrict blacks' freedom, while white politicians espousing the "separate but equal" doctrine prohibited blacks from frequenting the same establishments, schools, and even drinking fountains as whites. Though black colleges were established and prominent blacks were able to gain some degree of political power, others were relegated to a life of share-cropping for white landowners.

1876
Alexander Graham Bell receives a US patent for his invention, the telephone

During the North's **"Gilded Age"** of the 1870s, captains of industry such as George Vanderbilt, Andrew Carnegie, and John D. Rockefeller built commercial empires and enormous personal fortunes amidst an atmosphere of widespread political and economic corruption. The burden of the concentration of massive wealth in a few hands landed most heavily on the powerless masses—on hapless farmers toiling in a dying agricultural economy and on workers facing low wages, violent strike break-ups, and unsafe working conditions. Yet the fruits of the industrial age, including railroads, telegraphs, and telephones, made transportation and communication across the vast nation easier.

1881
Rockefeller's Standard Oil becomes the US's first trust company

GLOBAL IMPERIALISM AND WWI

The racism expressed in Jim Crow laws and Native American genocide didn't end at domestic borders. The United States' victory in the **Spanish-American War** in 1898 validated the American sense of Anglo-Saxon superiority, and the belief that its influence could be extended worldwide. The United States caught imperial fever, acquiring colonies in the Philippines, Puerto Rico, and Cuba. Meanwhile, large industrial monopolies came under attack from the Progressive Party. A new breed of journalists, nicknamed "muckrakers," began exposing the corruption rampant in big business.

In 1901, at age 42, **Teddy Roosevelt** became the youngest president in history. In response to the corrupt, monopolistic practices of big business, Roosevelt promoted anti-trust reforms to regulate large companies. In foreign affairs Roosevelt established the US as an international police power, recommending that the nation "speak softly and carry a big stick."

After vowing to keep the US out of "Europe's War," President **Woodrow Wilson** reluctantly entered **World War I** in its closing stages. US troops landed in Europe in 1917 and fought until Germany's defeat the next year. Though the metal-consuming war jump-started America's industrial economy and established the United States as a major international power, the frightful toll of the Great War—10 million people dead, including 130,174 Americans—disillusioned and shocked Americans.

ROARING 20S, GREAT DEPRESSION, AND WWII

Americans returned their attentions to their own continent, busting with money but ruffled by the winds of change. Labor unrest and racial tension were blamed on communist influences, and the US would experience increased paranoia of communism (a **"Red Scare"**) over the course of 1919. During the same year, the perceived moral decline of America was addressed by establishing the immensely unpopular **Prohibition,** which outlawed all alcohol. Among the younger generations, however, restrictive conventions were exuberantly tossed aside. In celebration of the free-wheelin', booze-smugglin' **"Jazz Age,"** women shucked their undergarments aside and bared their shoulders to dance the Charleston. Women **suffragists** also mobilized for the right to vote, which the 19th Amendment to the Constitution granted in 1920.

The **"Roaring 20s"** were largely supported by overextended credit. The facade crumbled on "Black Thursday," October 24, 1929, when the New York Stock Exchange crashed, launching the **Great Depression.** In an urbanized, mechanized age, millions of workers (25-50% of the work force) were left unemployed and struggled to provide food and housing for their families. The United States was unable to rebound from the Great Depression as it had from previous depressions. The experience of the Depression imprinted a generation of Americans with a compulsion to hoard, an appreciation of money, and a skepticism of the economy. Under the firm rule of President **Franklin D. Roosevelt,** the US began a decade-long recovery.

1898
USS Maine sinks in Havana Harbor; US demands that Spain evacuate from Cuba; Spanish-American War begins

1914
In response to outbreak of war in Europe, Wilson releases an official proclamation of neutrality

1919
Versailles Treaty ends World War I

1920
Warren Harding wins the Presidency by pledging a "return to normalcy"

1923
Harding's death in office reveals a series of scandals that show his administration to be one of the most corrupt in American history

1933
During his first 100 days in office, as part of his New Deal, Roosevelt passes bills and establishes programs to address the failure of banks, growing unemployment, and agricultural depression

THE USA

THE USA

1942
Paranoia over the war causes the entire Japanese-American population of the West Coast to be placed in "relocation centers"

As the German Nazi regime plowed through Europe, anxious Americans largely stood aside and watched, unaware of the Holocaust. The Japanese attack on Pearl Harbor, Hawaii, on December 7, 1941, brought America reluctantly into **World War II**. The war existed on two fronts, as the Allied powers fought both the Germans in Europe and the Japanese in the Pacific. The European front was resolved first, with the formal German surrender on May 8, 1945. The war in the Pacific continued until August, when the US dropped two newly developed **nuclear bombs** on Japan, at Hiroshima on August 6, 1945, and at Nagasaki three days later, killing 80,000 civilians.

THE COLD WAR

1949
Soviet Union detonates its first nuclear bomb, making it and the US the only nuclear powers in the world

1950
State Department official Alger Hiss convicted of perjury concerning his involvement with an alleged Communist espionage ring

1951
Julius and Ethel Rosenburg convicted of providing atomic secrets to the Soviet Union

1952
World War II general Dwight D. Eisenhower elected President after promising to end Korean War

1955
Eisenhower meets with Soviet leader Nikita Krushchev

1963
Oswald is killed by Jack Ruby at Dallas County Jail two days after Kennedy's assassination

Spared the wartime devastation of Europe and East Asia, the US economy boomed in the post-war era, solidifying the nation's status as the world's foremost economic and military power. The 50s are nostalgically recalled as a time of prosperity and social normalcy; TV sitcoms and suburban houses with glowing green lawns and dishwashers typified the American dream.

The ideological gulf between the two nuclear powers—the democratic, capitalist America and the totalitarian, communist Soviet Union—initiated a half-century of **Cold War** between the two nations. Tension with the Soviet Union heightened as President Harry Truman exaggerated the Soviet threat in order to gain support for his foreign policy of **Communist containment.** Amidst a cloud of anti-Communist hysteria, **McCarthyism** took root. A powerful congressional committee, the House Un-American Activities Committee led by Senator Joseph McCarthy, saw communists everywhere: thousands of Americans were blacklisted. "McCarthyism" was meant to be a patriotic stand against Communism, but in retrospect the era is seen as a smear campaign of groundless accusations.

Fear of communism had grown in the US since the Russian Revolution in 1917, but the feverish intensity it gained during the McCarthy era ultimately led to American military involvement in Asia, where communism was beginning to take hold. From 1950 to 1953, the United States fought the **Korean War** on behalf of the South Koreans who were attacked by the Communist North Korean government. The premises established in Korea were carried over to the Vietnam conflict. The Soviet launch of Sputnik, the first artificial satellite, in 1957, renewed fears that communism was getting ahead. The **Cuban Missile Crisis** in 1962, when President John F. Kennedy narrowly negotiated the removal of Soviet missiles from a Cuban base, reinforced the notion that the United States must protect the world from Soviet invasion and nuclear assault.

In 1963, **President Kennedy** was assassinated during a campaign parade in Dallas, Texas, by Lee Harvey Oswald, aiming out the window of the nearby Texas Book Depository (p. 606). Though numerous conspiracy theories have been suggested, it appears that Oswald acted alone. The assassination of the young, charismatic President mirrored the loss of innocence America was confronting. Playing into a larger cultural revolution unfolding in America, the 60s witnessed mounting social unrest linked to entrenched racism and the escalation of the Vietnam conflict.

VIETNAM AND CIVIL RIGHTS

High on their role as global policemen staying the tide of communism, the United States became embroiled in Vietnamese politics, culminating in a large-scale deployment of combat troops in 1965 to protect the south Vietnamese government from Ho Chi Minh's socialist government to the north. The **Vietnam War** became a symbol for America's credibility as a protector of nations struggling with communism, making retreat difficult even when it became apparent that the situation in Vietnam was not clear-cut and that victory was unlikely. Though Americans had at first supported the war, opposition grew as it dragged on and its moral premises were questioned. The use of TV and photographic media to cover the war contributed to the harsh and hopeless vision of the situation in Vietnam. The mounting human costs of Vietnam—and growing suspicion of America's motives—catalyzed wrenching generational clashes reflected vividly in the stacks of burning draft cards and anti-war demonstrations on college campuses. The mantra "Make Love, Not War," shouted among long-haired, scantily-clad bodies rolling in the mud at the 1969 **Woodstock** music festival, came to symbolize the hippie generation.

The Vietnam War was not the only cause that captured the hearts and lungs of idealistic young Americans. Rosa Parks' refusal to give up a bus seat in Montgomery, Alabama, in 1955 sparked the **civil rights movement**, a time of intense protests by African Americans, who organized countless demonstrations, marches, and sit-ins in the heart of a defiant and often violent South. Activists were drenched with fire hoses, arrested, and even killed by local whites and policemen. The movement peaked with the March on Washington in 1963, where **Dr. Martin Luther King, Jr.** delivered his famous "I Have A Dream" speech calling for non-violent racial integration. The tone of the civil rights movement changed as blacks became fed up with peaceful moderation, and gathered around the more aggressive rhetoric of **Malcolm X,** a converted Black Muslim who espoused separatist "Black Power." The militant Black Panthers resorted to terrorist tactics to assert the rights of African Americans.

The second wave of the **women's movement** accompanied the civil rights movement. Sparked by Betty Friedan's landmark book, *The Feminine Mystique,* American women sought to change the delineation between men's and women's roles in society, demanding access to male-dominated professions and equal pay. The sexual revolution, fueled by the birth control pill, heightened debate over a woman's right to choose abortion. The 1973 Supreme Court decision *Roe v. Wade* legalized abortion, but the battle between abortion opponents and pro-choice advocates still divides the nation today.

Despite a spate of civil rights legislation and anti-poverty measures passed under President Lyndon B. Johnson's **Great Society** agenda, the specter of the war overshadowed his presidency. By the end of these tumultuous years, the nation had dropped 7 million tons of bombs on Indochina—twice the amount used against America's World War II enemies—and victory was still unattainable. In 1972, as President Richard Nixon was attempting to "honorably" extricate the United States from Vietnam, five burglars were caught breaking into the Democratic National Convention Headquarters in the **Watergate**

THE USA

1964
President Lyndon B. Johnson pushes the Civil Rights Act through Congress despite a 57-day filibuster by Southern senators

1965
Six days of riots are sparked in the Watts neighborhood of L.A. when a white police officer pulls over a young African American for drunk driving

1968
An army photographer's secret camera captures the slaughter of 560 civilians, mostly women and children, in the Vietnamese village of My Lai by a platoon of American G.I.s; Martin Luther King, Jr. is assassinated in Memphis, TN

1970
Four student anti-war protesters are killed by National Guardsmen at Ohio's Kent State University

1972
The Equal Rights Amendment, which would outlaw discrimination against women, is approved by Congress but fails to gain ratification in a sufficient number of states by 1982

1972
Nixon and Soviet leader Leonid Brezhnev meet in Moscow for the first of two Strategic Arms Limitation Talks

THE USA

1974
President Gerald Ford issues an unconditional pardon for Nixon

1976
Democrat Jimmy Carter wins the Presidency from incumbent Ford by the smallest electoral margin since 1916

apartment complex. Their botched attempt to bug the Democratic offices ultimately led to a broader scandal involving the President himself. Caught by his own audiotape, Nixon fought Congress but ultimately resigned from the Presidency.

By the mid-70s, America was firmly disillusioned with the idealistic counter-culture of the previous decade. More frivolous forms of fun, such as dancing in platform shoes and powder blue suits under flashing colored lights—a phenomenon known as **"disco"**—became the mark of a generation that just wanted to have fun. Unfortunately, the international situation continued to be tenuous. The oil-rich Arab nations boycotted the US, causing an **energy crisis** which drove up gas prices, frustrated autophilic Americans, and precipitated an economic recession. The oil crisis also forced the US to develop more energy-efficient technology, lending economic credibility to the environmentalist movement.

BIG 80S

1983
Reagan authorizes an invasion of the Caribbean island of Grenada in order to combat Cuban influence

1987
Reagan negotiates the Intermediate-range Nuclear Forces treaty with Soviet Leader Mikhail Gorbachev, the first arms-limitation pact to result in the destruction of existing weapons

In 1980 **Ronald Reagan,** a politically conservative actor and former California governor was elected to the White House. Reagan knew how to give the people what they wanted: money. He cut government spending on public programs and lowered taxes. Though the decade's conservatives did embrace certain right-wing social goals like school prayer and the campaign against abortion, the Reagan revolution was essentially economic. **Reaganomics** handed tax breaks to big business, spurred short-term consumption, and deregulated savings and loans. Although these measures were successful in the short-run by suppressing inflation and unemployment, long-term repercussions included a massive increase in the budget deficit. Whereas the US had been a creditor nation in 1980, the end of the decade saw the nation as the world's largest debtor.

On the foreign policy front, Reagan aggressively swelled the military budget and sent weapons and aid to right-wing "freedom fighters" in Guatemala, Nicaragua, and Afghanistan. The Iran-Contra affair at the end of his second term revealed that profit from arms sold to Iran had been used to fund the **Contras** of Nicaragua in their attempt to overthrow the leftist Sandinista regime. But even as the affair was received negatively by the American public, Reagan remained a popular president. For middle America, his administration represented a return to traditional values after the radicalism and revolution of the 60s and 70s, a legacy that helped his vice-president George Bush to victory in the 1988 Presidential election.

90S—WE ARE THE WORLD

1993
First lady Hillary Clinton is appointed by her husband as the head of the Task Force on National Health Care Reform, whose policy will be defeated in Congress

The US remained an active police force in the world through the early 90s, as President Bush instigated **"Operation Desert Storm"** in 1990 as a response to Iraq's invasion of its neighboring country, Kuwait. The war freed Kuwait, but its popularity in the US was compromised by the recession that followed. The large deficit created by Reagan's administration prevented the typical cure of increased government spending, and the public replaced Bush in the 1992 Presidential election with the young, saxophone-tooting Democrat **Bill Clinton,** who promised a new era of governmental activism after years of laissez-faire rule.

Also in 1992, fire and riots swept Los Angeles in the wake of the **Rodney King** controversy. Although a videotape captured the scene of four white policemen brutally beating King, an African American, during a traffic stop, a jury had acquitted the policemen of any wrong-doing. Angry mobs attributed the "not guilty" verdict to the color of King's skin. The day after the trial ended 25 murders had taken place, 1000 fires had swept the city, and 2400 National Guardsmen had moved in. These numbers only increased on the second day.

Clinton's young administration soon found itself plagued with its own problems, including an Arkansas real estate development called **Whitewater,** an alleged extramarital affair with Gennifer Flowers, and accusations of sexual harassment from Paula Jones. Clinton's public approval remained high, however, especially after the nation supported him in a struggle against the Congressional Republicans whose attempts to balance the budget led to two government shutdowns between 1995 and 1996. Clinton was elected to his second term in 1996.

New scandal erupted in 1998, as reports of an inappropriate relationship between Clinton and a 24-year-old White House intern, **Monica Lewinsky,** were plastered across American newspapers, magazines, and television. At first Clinton denied the allegations, although he would later admit that he lied. He was eventually **impeached** for perjury and obstruction of justice on the recommendation of Independent Counsel Kenneth Starr. The resulting trial in the Senate ended with a vote for informal censure over conviction, and Clinton remained in office.

2000'S NEWS

The US rang in the millennial new year without a hitch, defying all expectations that the **Y2K computer bug** would cause havoc. Although paranoia over Y2K complications did mean lower attendance at city-wide celebrations across the country than in previous years, New York's Times Square remained the happening place to be, as two million people crowded the area to watch the millennial ball drop.

The New Year also witnessed heightened controversy over the fate of **Elián Gonzales**, a 6-year-old Cuban boy found floating in an inner tube off the coast of Florida in November, 1999. His mother had died while attempting to relocate to the US, and his father still lived in Cuba, leaving the boy as the prize in a tug-of-war that pitted US-Cuban political tension against parental rights. While some wished to see him returned to his father, others (including his Miami relatives) preferred to consider him a political refugee. The late-night raid in April of the home where the boy had been staying successfully reunited him with his father in the US, In reponse, hordes of Miami Cuban Americans protested the government's strong-arm tactics on the streets of Little Havana. On June 29, Elián returned to Cuba; the mood in Miami was more of disappointment than violence.

Although the Presidential primaries essentially ended with the March 7 "Super Tuesday" wins of the two party frontrunners—Democratic Vice President **Al Gore** and Republican Texas Governor **George W. Bush** (the former president's son)—the long road leading up to the final battle was vitalized by Republican maverick **John McCain,** a moderate who appealed to political independents by speaking out against conservative dogma.

THE USA

1994
Republicans are voted into the majority of both houses of Congress

1995
Ex-football player O.J. Simpson, is acquitted of the alleged murder of his wife and lover in a nationally televised trial

1997
Timothy McVeigh is sentenced to death for the bombing of the Alfred P. Murrah Federal Building in Oklahoma City in 1995, the largest terrorist attack on US soil

March
Vermont legislature begins to consider legalizing gay marriage

March 1
In Michigan, a 6-year-old boy shoots and kills a classmate

March 3
Four white NYC police officers are acquitted of the 1999 shooting of African-American street vendor Amadou Diallo, who was shot 41 times

May 4
A 1000-acre "controlled fire" set by the National Park Service in New Mexico becomes a raging wildfire that consumes nearly 50,000 acres

May 19
The two houses of
the South Carolina
General Assembly
vote to remove the
Confederate battle
flag flying on the
State Capitol dome

But his renegade politics failed to win over the conservative old guard. The campaign only began to heat up with the selection of running mates. In an effort to balance his light political résumé, Bush chose the Secretary of Defense under his father, fellow oil businessman and hard-line conservative **Dick Cheney** as his Vice Presidential partner. Gore made history in selecting Connecticut Senator **Joseph Lieberman,** the first Jewish candidate on a major Presidential ticket.

Microsoft, the child company of Bill Gates, the world's richest Man, underwent a legal battle against the US Justice Department in early 2000, as executives attempted to deny allegations that their company violated antitrust statutes. A federal court has required Microsoft to split up into separate operating system and applications companies, a decision immediately appealed in federal court.

America's Two-Party System
Elected representatives in the US are usually members of the Republican or Democratic Parties, which span a narrow (and right-leaning) political spectrum. The Republican Party is more conservative and is divided into two warring camps: social traditionalists grudgingly share a tent with their libertarian, pro-business colleagues. The Democrats are also plagued by internal conflict, as the centrist, "New Democrats" lock horns with the party's dwindling liberal contingent.

A CIVICS PRIMER

The US government functions on two separate levels. Certain laws are established on a national level by the **federal government,** while **states** and **localities** determine their own laws and regulations on matters that fall outside the federal government's scope. The federal government is further divided by focus into a system of three branches—the **executive, legislative,** and **judicial**—each of which can regulate the actions of the others. The **president** and **vice-president** head the executive branch and are elected every four years. Most federal agencies fall under the authority of the executive branch, which consists of thirteen departments. The heads of the departments, known as the Secretaries, comprise the Cabinet, used by the president as a source of advice and guidance for policy decisions. The legislative branch contains two representative bodies, the **House of Representatives** and the **Senate,** where laws and budgets are debated and passed before being submitted for presidential approval. The population of each state directly elects the members of these two bodies, jointly referred to as Congress. The **Supreme Court** of the United States, 13 circuit courts of appeal, and 90 district courts comprise the last branch of the federal government, the judicial. The Supreme Court's nine justices, appointed for life by the President upon approval of the Senate, hold the power to strike down laws that violate constitutional principles.

THE ARTS

While the US's early artistic endeavors owed much to age-old European tradition, it did not take long for hearty American individualism to make its mark on the global canon. From the blockbuster movies of Hollywood to the 19th century Transcendental literature of New England to the musical amalgam that came to be known as jazz, America has established herself time and again as an innovator in the theater of world arts.

LITERATURE

THE FIRST FEW PAGES
The first bestseller printed in America, the *Bay Psalm Book,* was published in Cambridge in 1640. Like much of the literature

read and published in 17th- and 18th-century America, this chart-buster was religious in nature. Most of these early works gather dust on academic bookshelves; America did not create any enduring classics until the early 1800s, when her artists began to cultivate a substantial literary tradition expressing the unique American experience. James Fenimore Cooper's *Last of the Mohicans* (1826), Nathaniel Hawthorne's *Scarlet Letter* (1850), and Herman Melville's *Moby Dick* (1851)—among the first great American novels—all feature strong yet innocent individualists negotiating the raw American landscape. By the mid-nineteenth century, the **New England Transcendentalists** began writing sparse, less romantic works in a firm attempt to portray a down-to-earth culture distinct from that of their European forebearers. The work of Henry David Thoreau (*Walden Pond*), Ralph Waldo Emerson, and Walt Whitman (*Leaves of Grass*) embodied a spirit of anti-materialism by focusing on self-reflection and a retreat into nature.

Literature provided 19th-century American women the opportunity both to express themselves and to comment critically on their society. In 1852, Harriet Beecher Stowe published *Uncle Tom's Cabin*, an exposé of slavery that became internationally popular and was a major factor in starting the Civil War. The poet Emily Dickinson secretly scribbled away in her native Amherst, Massachusetts, home; her untitled, unpunctuated, and uncapitalized verses weren't discovered until after her death in 1886.

By the end of the nineteenth century, the older generation of academic New England writers had been displaced by more middle-class, journalistic **realists** who sought to portray life as it really was, focusing on the ordinary and the local rather than the magnificent and the remote.

EARLY TWENTIETH CENTURY EXPLORATIONS

The 20s marked a time of increasing angst, and a reflective, self-centered movement fermented in American literature. F. Scott Fitzgerald's works (*The Great Gatsby*) portray restless individuals, financially secure but unfulfilled by their conspicuous consumption. Many writers moved abroad in search of refuge during this tumultuous time. This **lost generation** included Fitzgerald, Ernest Hemingway (*The Sun Also Rises*), T.S. Eliot ("The Waste Land"), Ezra Pound, and e.e. cummings, poets and writers whose sophisticated works used foreign settings but focused on American issues. On the home front, the Harlem Renaissance, a timely gathering of African-American artistic energy in New York City, fed off the excitement of the Jazz Age. Langston Hughes, Nella Larsen, and Zora Neale Hurston (*Their Eyes Were Watching God*) exposed the black American experience to a broad scope of readers.

As America struggled to recover from the Great Depression, the plight of decaying agricultural life and faltering industry of the **Deep South** and **West** began to infiltrate literature. William Faulkner (*The Sound and the Fury*) juxtaposed avant-garde stream-of-consciousness techniques with subjects rooted in the rural South. The plays of Tennessee Williams (*A Streetcar Named Desire*) portray the family dynamics within lower-class, uprooted Southern families. In his remarkable autobiography, *Black Boy* (1945), Richard Wright recounts the harsher side of the African-American experience in the South.

THE USA

NATHANIEL HAWTHORNE (1804-1864) Employed probing character studies and sharp allegory in an honest attempt at understanding the roots of America.

HERMAN MELVILLE (1819-1891) His characters from *Moby Dick*, Ahab and Ishmael, represented the two poles of the American psyche: the conqueror and the wanderer.

MARK TWAIN (1835-1910) A true original, he infused his unique creativity and acid wit into colorful yarns whose humor conveyed significant social critiques.

EDITH WHARTON (1862-1937) Detailed the genteel yet vicious life of upper-class New York society from a woman's point of view.

HENRY JAMES (1843-1916) A dense, ornate stylist of psychological fiction, he brought a sensitive eye to the portrayal of his very human characters.

T.S. ELIOT (1888-1965) Revitalized American poetry with his experiments in style and diction. Offered social critique by blending obscure and multicultural allusions with traditional literary forms.

ERNEST HEMINGWAY
(1899-1961)
Using simple, straightforward language, he sought to strip fiction to its essentials.

VLADIMIR NABOKOV
(1899-1977)
A taboo-shattering Russian émigré who ironically brought more to the art of English prose styling than any other 20th-century writer.

FLANNERY O'CONNOR
(1925-1964)
Amidst calm Southern society, her characters confront a world of eerie violence and hidden evil.

KURT VONNEGUT, JR.
(1922-)
A fierce, wholly irreverent satirist of the absurdity of 20th-century American civilization.

TIM O'BRIEN
(1946-)
By blending fiction and memoir, his collection of short stories titled *The Things They Carried* gently probes the problems faced by Vietnam veterans in re-entering society.

MODERN DESPAIR

In the conformist 50s, literature provided alternative commentary on America's underlying social problems. Ralph Ellison's *Invisible Man*, published in 1952, confronted a broad audience with the division between white and black identities in America. Gwendolyn Brooks, the first black writer to win a Pulitzer Prize, published intense poetry which highlighted social problems such as abortion, gangs, and drop-outs. The **Beats**, spearheaded by cult heroes Jack Kerouac (*On the Road*) and Allen Ginsberg ("Howl"), lived wildly and proposed a more free-wheeling attitude. The playwright Arthur Miller delved into the American psyche with *The Crucible* (1953), an allegory of McCarthyism (p. 12).

As the rules of established society began to crumble in the **60s**, writers began to explore more outrageous material. Anne Sexton and Sylvia Plath led the movement towards "confessional poetry;" Sexton delves into the depths of her own mental breakdown, while Plath exposes her psychological deterioration and hints at her eventual suicide in *The Bell Jar* (1963). James Baldwin's essays and stories warn white America of the explosions to come and caution black America against the self-destructive excesses of racial hatred. John Cheever (*Bullet Park*) and John Updike (*Rabbit, Run*) explore the terrifying ennui of **suburban America**.

CONTEMPORARY LITERATURE

In more recent fiction, the search for identity and the attempt to reconcile **artistic and social agendas** has continued. Toni Morrison (*Beloved*) won the Nobel Prize, viscerally interpreting the tension between gender, ethnic, and cultural identities. Raymond Carver, in his numerous short stories, charts the hopelessly misdirected, yet strangely hopeful lives of people stuck amidst the fog of modern society. The fast pace and commercialism of modern society has been the subject of many a novel. In *Bright Lights Big City* (1987), Jay McIntire exposes the fast-living Wall Street of the 80s. Don Delillo's *White Noise* (1991) heats up to the tune of a chemical holocaust. Most of Richard Ford's books (*Independence Day*) are about guys in mid-life crises—which everyone seems to be going through these days.

> # ON THE ROAD
> The roadtrip that you, traveler, are about to embark on is the stuff of poetry. To take to the open road in search of a new life, new experiences, and a new understanding of America has fueled the creativity of authors before the first Ford Model T rolled off the assembly line. As American poet Walt Whitman exclaimed in 1856, "Afoot and light-hearted, I take to the open road...From this hour, freedom!" Some recommended reads:
> *Adventures of Huckleberry Finn* (1884) by Mark Twain. A carefree lad's misadventures typify the American roadtrip spirit.
> *On the Road* (1957) by Jack Kerouac. A beat's odyssey.
> *Travels with Charley: In Search of America* (1962) by John Steinbeck. A veteran writer takes to the road to rediscover his homeland.
> *Zen and the Art of Motorcycle Maintenance* (1974) by Robert Pirsig. A critique of modern values set in a cross-country roadtrip.
> *Blue Highways: A Journey into America* (1982) by William Least Heat-Moon. A trip through the back-roads of small-town America.

MUSIC

Weened on the fertile, if not easy, intermingling of cultures, America has plenty of homegrown music. While American-born jazz, rock, and rap styles have imitators and innovators outside the States, American artists continue to dominate and define the musical genres that are rightfully their own.

ROOTS IN THE BLACK SOUTH

The unnerved climate of the South during and after slavery flooded the New World with renegade artists and musical styles. In the days of slave driving and plantation farming, slaves sung work songs that fused African rhythm and call-and-response form with Christian hymns and a consciousness shaped by hardship and hope. After emancipation, music for still-oppressed blacks became a primary vehicle of African American religiosity, solidarity, and grievance. From ragtime, the upbeat, piano-banging dance music of the 19th century, to the deep South's tradition of low-down, moanful blues, early African-American musics defined what would come to be called **soul**. Still a vital category in African-American music, soul encompasses a range of musical styles and expressions. The ecstatic joy of a rousing gospel chorus, the deep melancholy of timeless spirituals like "Swing Low, Sweet Chariot" and "Nobody Knows the Trouble I've Seen," or the reflective lyricism of current hip-hop all evince soul. Recent artists in rhythm & blues (R&B), jazz, pop, funk, and rap genres continue to be described as "soulful" in that they embody the legacy of a resilient and expressive African-American voice. In some ways, some say, even Michael Jackson is a soul artist.

BLUES

The blues epitomizes soul music. Thought to have originated from a blend of Northwest African calls and Native American song and verse forms, the blues allowed Southern black singers to vent the woes of hard love and a harder life. Today, the blues attracts the "down and out" listener and artist, and has heavily influenced the development of other popular music styles, notably jazz and rock and roll. To most Americans, nothing seems as appropriate as singin' the blues when your baby done left you or you're down in the dumps. That's what we do.

JAZZ

In the early 20th century, black musicians in New Orleans took Southern blues and ragtime, and the instruments of the brass band, into new territory with an intellectual music called jazz. Jazz's emphasis on **improvisation** and unique tonal and harmonic rules distinguished it from all other genres fearing performance spontaneity and occasional dissonance. Some music historians say that jazz is the one truly American art form. Despite its roots in popular music, jazz certainly befits its label as "art music." It has long thrived on the tension between the popular and the elitist; it embraces both the catchy and the esoteric. As a medium of African-American artistic expression, jazz artists have used their music to convey social and political attitudes.

Out of the black South still other musical styles were born: a bluesy, accordion-based music of the Creole-speaking population called **zydeco**, the uplifting **gospel** music of the church choir, and the foot-stomping, banjo-twanging Southern mainstay, **bluegrass.** But distinctively American musics also developed elsewhere.

THE USA

W.C. HANDY
(1873-1958)
As a student of Southern music, Handy introduced "blue (flatted) notes" into popular songs, giving birth to a distinctive, sorrowful sound. "Memphis Blues" (1913)

DUKE ELLINGTON
(1899-1974)
Groomed to be a professional pianist, the Duke renounced tradition to pioneer jazz as an instrumentalist, a composer and a bandleader. "It Don't Mean a Thing If It Ain't Got That Swing" (1932)

THE USA

JOHNNY CASH
(1932-)
An occasionally disaffected singer/songwriter, Cash's popularity brought country music into the limelight around mid-century. "I Walk the Line" (1958)

WOODY GUTHRIE
(1912-1967)
While still a teen, Woody hopped a freight train west. A roaming romantic in the midst of the Depression, he wrote quite a few sentimental classics. "Hard Travelin'"

BRUCE SPRINGSTEEN
(1949-)
Elvis may have been King, but Bruce—a.k.a. the Boss—wears the pants. A simple songwriter/rocker hailing from Freehold, New Jersey, Springsteen's denim look and energetic performances defined rock and roll as an ever-wild American institution. "Born to Run" (1975)

SUGAR HILL GANG
The first true rap artists, the Gang inflected playful rhymes over simple electronic dance beats, getting, as they say, the party started. "Rapper's Delight" (1979)

COUNTRY

Country music began in the Appalachian Mountains among poor, rural whites putting a new spin on their ancestral European folk traditions. Simple melodies and sentimental lyrics served numerous ends: as work songs, as love songs and "cowboy ballads," and when occasion called, as the rallying cry of an old-fashioned hoedown. Commercially, country music didn't become popular until it was given a boost by radio and the Nashville's famous 30s program, the *Grand Ole Opry.* Roadtrippers be warned: country music today monopolizes the radio waves over much of the continent.

FOLK

So-called American folk music is not a collective repository of ageless songs from nameless authors, but rather popular music by artists who maintain the spirit of such songs. From **Woody Guthrie**'s celebratory "This Land is Your Land" sung in the midst of the Great Depression, to the political and personal musical monologues of **Bob Dylan** or today's **Ani DiFranco**, American folk music keeps the tradition of simple song-style and direct lyrics alive. Folk musicians are still some of our most lucid social commentators, whether preaching love of country or satirizing American life.

ROCK AND ROLL

No one can say just who started rock and roll, though **Elvis Presley** was the first to be crowned "King." What followed Elvis's success in the 50s and 60s was a contest of one-upmanship among rock and roll musicians: when one band cranked up their amps, the next band cranked 'em up higher, and the next cranked 'em up with strategically-torn speakers, generating a wonderfully grating sound. **Chuck Berry**'s "Rock and Roll Music" (1957) inaugurated a new musical era not only in America, but in Europe (especially Britain) as well. In the decades after, rock-and-roll's driving, danceable rhythms, rebellious attitude, and fascination with electric instruments would dominate the popular music charts. Today, rock music is unfamiliar to none but the oldest generation of Americans. The general category of "rock" is divided chronologically into **oldies** (the Beach Boys, Jerry Lee Lewis), **classic rock** (Led Zeppelin, Bruce Springsteen), and **modern rock** (Pearl Jam, Dave Matthews); **pop, heavy metal,** and **alternative** also fall under its heading.

RAP

Largely an urban phenomenon, rap music owes its beginnings to **reggae** DJs who improvised rhymes over pre-recorded music in a style called **dub.** The practice took off in New York City among dance DJs of all kinds in the late 70s. Soon, rap artists were keeping it real with syncopated rhymes over drum-heavy tape loops, record scratching, and digital samples. Lyrically, the subject-matter of rap music runs the gamut from hardcore sex and violence to class and race consciousness, from egoistic self-aggrandizement to lofty spiritual concerns.

FILM

Of all artistic media, American film has had, for better or worse, the greatest cultural impact domestically and abroad in the 20th century. Popularly celebrated movie stars began setting fashions and influencing common perceptions of beauty and glamour well before World War II. Throughout the United States, movie catch-phrases are part of the vernacular, movie stars are more recognizable (and occasionally have more political power) than politicians, and the archetypal Hollywood movie studio plotline is the foundation of the average American's grandest aspirations, or the American Dream.

SCENE ONE, TAKE ONE!

The most common aspects of American cinema can be traced back to their roots in the 1910s. Pioneering director D.W. Griffith (*The Birth of a Nation, Intolerance*) defined the medium, introducing both the stylistic plot conventions and the techniques like cuts, pans, and tracking that became the bread-and-butter of the Hollywood film studios.

Hollywood, California, owing to its sunny, film-friendly climate, proximity to a variety of photogenic terrain, and previous prominence as a theater center, quickly became the center of the movie business. As industry churned and began to give rise to a consumer market, America's thirst for quick, wrapped-and-packaged entertainment ballooned. By the period just after World War I, actors like Charlie Chaplin, Buster Keaton, and Mary Pickford were household names. Free from the control of domineering studios, these film artists brought a playful, exuberant, and innovative attitude to their work.

It was not long, however, before the wild success of the movies gave rise to expansion of the **studio system.** Giant production houses like Paramount, MGM, and Warner took up root on the West Coast, and turned movies into big business. Film became a commodity, and studio executives' wages were earned by the rapid production and dissemination of their celluloid product: some studios would push out up to a film a week. The entrance of money into the filmmaking equation, along with the enactment of the "production code," a series of conservative guidelines that effectively banned the depiction of even the slightest sexual innuendo or unpunished immorality, resulted in a legacy of formulaic, happy-go-lucky, rather superficial films.

In truth, however, American film's **golden age** still took place during the height of the studio era, fueled by those who transcended the studio system's confines. Victor Fleming's *Gone with the Wind* (1939), a Civil War epic, was the first large-scale movie extravaganza, redefining the bounds of cinematic scale. Frank Capra, in his surprisingly probing morality plays like *It's a Wonderful Life* (1946) and *Mr. Smith Goes to Washington* (1939), brought a conscience to entertainment. Michael Curtiz's *Casablanca* (1942), starring the moody Humphrey Bogart, fine-tuned the art of creating cinematic romance. In 1941, Orsen Welles unveiled his intricate masterpiece, *Citizen Kane*, a landmark work whose innovations expanded contemporary ideas about the potential of film. Fantasy and mindless fun, however, still sold tickets and appeased the censors; Walt Disney's animated *Snow White* (1937) and Fleming's *The Wizard of Oz* (1939) kept producers well-fed.

ALL GLITTER, SOME GOLD

The film industry met lean times following WWII. The spread of television into nearly every home and rising production costs deeply affected the industry. While the production code's influ-

AMERICAN FILM GENRES

WESTERNS
Stagecoach (1939). A band of motley pioneers starts a good ol' Western ruckus.
True Grit (1969). A young tomboy girl goes off into the raw Western wild to avenge her father's death.
Unforgiven (1992). A retired killer gets drawn back into the world of self-defeating violence.

THRILLERS
Psycho (1960). Alfred Hitchcock defined the genre with this classic tale of deceit and insanity.
Silence of the Lambs (1991). A FBI agent tracks one madman with the help of another.

DRAMA
Casablanca (1942). Amid the chaos of WWII, some lonely souls unite.
The Godfather (1972). Stylistically innovative with a downright captivating storyline, this film launched the Italian mafia genre.
One Flew Over the Cuckoo's Nest (1975). A gripping allegory and a beautiful portrait of the insane asylum that is modern life.

THE USA

COMEDY

Dr. Strangelove
(1964). Dry, black
humor mixes with
occasional hilarity
to lampoon the
Cold War better
than any other film.
*National Lam-
poon's Vacation*
(1983). Your aver-
age American fam-
ily's misadventure
on the road. May
your trip be no less
hilarious.
Austin Powers
(1997). A Cana-
dian-American's
take on 60s Brit-
ain. Most Ameri-
cans, at least, find
it very funny.

YOUTH

Easy Rider (1969).
Two bikers head
out on the road to
"find America."
They should have
taken *Let's Go*.
The Outsiders
(1983). Featuring
young versions of
future stars in a
simple plot of
down-and-out boys
versus the rest.
*Ferris Bueller's Day
Off* (1986). A high
schooler plays sick
one day and
embarks on an
adventure in the
city. Inspiration for
countless school
absences.

ACTION

Terminator II
(1991). Arnold's
return launched
the special-effects-
heavy blockbuster.
This one has a
decent plot to
boot.
The Fugitive
(1993). A wrong-
fully-convicted Har-
rison Ford escapes
from prison and
tracks the one-
armed man who
killed his wife.

ence dwindled, new constraints began to arise. Heightened tensions with the Soviet Union and conflicts against Communism abroad led to widespread communist witch-hunts. The film industry, under government pressure, took up the policy of **blacklisting** any artists with suspected ties to Communism (or even leftism). The result of these two influences—dwindling box office returns and constant paranoia—resulted in a slew of films that were sensational enough to draw crowds away from their television sets and yet highly conservative and uninnovative. There were, of course, those who broke the mold, like master of intrigue and suspense Alfred Hitchcock and the ever-free-thinking Orsen Welles.

The 50s also saw the emergence of a cult of **glamour** surrounding the most luminous stars. Cloaked in glitz and scandal, sex symbols Marilyn Monroe, James Dean, and Elizabeth Taylor drew audiences to movies by name recognition alone. Along with actors Marlon Brandon (*A Streetcar Named Desire*) and Audrey Hepburn (*Breakfast at Tiffany's*), these stars brought their own, personal mystique to the screen, while adding much to the art of cinematic performance.

REBELS WITH A CAUSE

The 60s and early 70s saw the widespread **social upheaval** and tension between generations. The studio system proved entirely incapable of responding to the demands of the young, more liberal-thinking audiences. *Cleopatra* (1963), starring Elizabeth Taylor, a last-ditch effort to attract crowds in the style of the 50s, proved to be a financial disaster. Rethinking their battle plans, many studios enlisted directors influenced by the French New Wave, and artists from other media to direct features, including Sidney Lumet, John Frankenheimer, and Robert Altman.

With the studios more willing to take a gamble and the introduction of a movie ratings board (MPAA) to replace censorship, the work of a number of **innovative filmmakers** began to enter the mainstream. Stanley Kubrick, in *Dr. Strangelove* (1964), *2001: A Space Odyssey* (1968), and *A Clockwork Orange* (1971), brought a literary importance to filmmaking. Dennis Hopper's *Easy Rider* (1969), a film about counter-cultural youth rebellion, and the acclaimed documentary *Woodstock* (1970) opened the door to social critique. John Schlesinger's *Midnight Cowboy* (1969) demonstrated mature treatment of adult subjects.

By the 70s, experimentalism largely gave way to more polished treatment of equally serious issues. Film-schooled directors like Martin Scorsese (*Taxi Driver*), Francis Ford Coppola (*The Godfather*), and Michael Cimino (*The Deer Hunter*), brought technical skill to their exploration of the darker side of humanity. An influx of foreign filmmakers, like Milos Forman (*One Flew Over the Cuckoo's Nest*) and Roman Polansky (*Chinatown*), introduced a new perspective to the American film scene.

BACK TO BUSINESS

Driven by the global mass distribution of American cinema and the development of high-tech special effects, the late 70s and 80s witnessed the revitalization of the **blockbuster**. Directors like George Lucas with his *Star Wars* trilogy, and Steven Spielberg with *E.T.* (1982) and *Raiders of the Lost Ark* (1981), created enormously successful movies whose success spanned the globe. Though such films were often criticized for overreliance on special effects and lack of a substantive storyline, they almost single-handedly returned Hollywood to its former status as king.

Despite the profit-orientation of Hollywood, quite a bit of highly imaginative work came out of the period, including the thoughtful critique of 80s materialism and self-absorption, *Rain Man* (1988), and the disturbing exploration of the primal terror beneath the tranquil surface of suburbia, David Lynch's *Blue Velvet* (1986).

INDEPENDENTS, INDEPENDENCE DAY

The revival of the blockbuster continued strong into the 90s, with such high-budget money-makers as the alien invasion flick *Independence Day* (1996) to the extravagant marine love-story *Titanic* (1997) still drawing the largest crowds. The emergence of independent, or **indie,** films—films that are either produced independent from any major studio or at least do not follow the standard studio conventions—marks the most interesting turn for cinema in the last several years. Brothers Joel and Ethan Coen have created some of the most creative and original work of late, including the gruesome comedy *Fargo* (1996) and the hilarious, off-beat *The Big Lebowski* (1998). Quentin Tarantino's (*Reservoir Dogs*, *Pulp Fiction*) cool yet hypercharged action, Mike Figgis' (*Leaving Las Vegas*) unpretentious drama, and Curtis Hanson's (*L.A. Confidential*) tight plot-weaving, have all injected new life into American cinema. The 21-year-old John Singleton directed *Boyz N the Hood* (1991), a hard-hitting portrayal of life in poverty-stricken South Central Los Angeles. Hollywood has picked up on the indie trend and recently released a number of films with a distinctly un-Hollywood slant, like newcomer Sam Mendes' acclaimed exploration of suburban angst, *American Beauty* (1999).

VISUAL ART

Snobbish and Eurocentric art historians have often glossed over American art as a pale reflection of European trends. Notable modern art historians like Robert Rosenblum, however, reject that view, finding uniquely American themes in American art. Raw and uncontrolled nature, for one, is reflected not only in the grandiose 19th-century landscape paintings that sought to capture the beauty of the untamed West, but also in the unwieldy lines and shapes of a 20th-century American brand of abstract expressionism.

ART IN THE NEW WORLD

Colonial America produced art of a limited scope. Subject-matter for New World artists was not an issue of prerogative: the only livelihood in art was in painting portraits for wealthy patrons. Some gifted (and willing) painters accompanied expeditions into unexplored territory in order to record the places and people they found. These two genres—portraiture and landscape painting—grew increasingly stylized into the mid-19th century. George Fuller made intimate portraits contrasting murky background with a glowing illumination of his subjects. Winslow Homer created memorable seaside scenes and sweeping Civil War era farmscapes.

THE USA

Speed (1994). There's a bomb on the bus! And if the speed drops below 50mph, it will explode. A high-octane adventure decorated with Keanu Reeves and Sandra Bullock.

INDEPENDENT
My Own Private Idaho (1991). A narcoleptic male prostitute faces unending tragedy in this adaption of Shakespeare's *Henry IV, Part II*.
Pulp Fiction (1994). This film launched Quentin Tarantino as a director, revived the John Travolta's ailing career, and did much to bring indie films into the mainstream.
Clerks (1994). An unpolished, goofy comedy about youth and convenience stores.

WINSLOW HOMER (1836-1910) Homer combined loose watercolor technique and a shrewd observer's eye to reproduce the many moods of Nature on canvas. His style marked the growing creative freedom of American painters.

ALFRED STIEGLITZ
(1864-1946)
A zealous and influential advocate of art photography in the face of elitist scepticism, Stieglitz exhibited his work and that of new crop of art photographers both in his publications and the venues he oversaw.

WILLEM DE KOONING
(1904-1997)
Blending figurative images with vigorous strokes and splatters on a single canvas, de Kooning not only straddled old and new styles, but allowed them to comment on each other in his work.

ANDY WARHOL
(1928-1987)
The name associated with pop art, Warhol mass-produced loud, colorful images of cultural icons like Marilyn Monroe.

NAN GOLDIN
(1953-)
Since the 70s, Goldin has opened up the seedy underbelly of urban life to photographic exploration. A master at exposing moments of pure, emotive expression, Goldin frames all her subjects—from prostitutes to couples smoking in bed—with thought and poignancy.

NEW ATTITUDES FOR THE NEW CENTURY

In the early 20th century, Alfred Stieglitz championed photography as a legitimate art form with his meticulously composed stills. His wife, Georgia O'Keefe, preferred to paint surreal, pastel visions of desert bones and suggestive flowers. But other artists took a more socially-engaged stance toward their vocation. In colorful, narrative paintings of distinctly American scenes, Edward Hopper and Thomas Hart Benton explored the innocence and mythic values of the country during its emergence as a superpower. **Photography,** though, became the medium of choice for artists with a social conscience. Lewis Hine photographed the urban poor while Dorthea Lange and Walker Evans captured the plight of destitute farmers during the Great Depression. Ansel Adams's crisp photographs of pristine landscapes, while not politically motivated, helped to establish the National Park system.

DRIVEN TO ABSTRACTION

By the 40s, the **abstract expressionist** movement in Europe had been reborn in the States, where anxiety over international tension and the threat of war was rampant. In this climate, many artists thought realism's tight control over images insincere. Willem de Kooning's masterful work documents the movement from realistic to abstracted images. The found-object compositions of Robert Rauchenburg, along with Jackson Pollock's energetic drip paintings, reflect the ironic mix of swaggering confidence and frenetic insecurity that characterized Cold War America.

The new art earned the appreciation of art purists through figures like Mark Rothko, who perfected the subtle aesthetics and emotional impact of abstract art in his color field paintings. Other artists strove for a more global impact. Jasper Johns incorporated iconic images like the American flag into his folksy paintings, ushering in the age of **pop** art. Practiced most memorably by Roy Lichtenstein and Andy Warhol, pop art used graphic, cartoonish images to satirize the icons of American life and popular culture, blurring the line between art and everything else.

NEW IN THE ART WORLD

In the 70s, photography finally came into its own as the back-to-basics 35mm photographs of Gary Winnogrand and Lee Friedlander, as well as the freakish work of Diane Arbus, stretched the bounds of art photography. The 80s art boom, stationed around private galleries in New York City and Los Angeles, began a retreat from the realism of photography, and ushered in a decade of slick, idyllic paintings. Julian Schnabel and David Hockney, in particular, garnered the accolades of art critics and investors with a taste for pretty things. But as part of an eventual backlash to 80s materialism, artists began to produce **ultrarealistic** depictions of the harshness in human life. The bare-all photographs of Nan Goldin, as well as the manipulated images of Cindy Sherman (a photographer who places herself in scenes taken out of anything from popular movie stills to gruesome pornography) and Kiki Smith (who makes body part sculptures), are typical of recent artists who try to deconstruct the meaning of identity and the human body. Abstract art, though, hasn't died on the gallery floor; Brice Marden's squiggly lines still sell big.

ARCHITECTURE AND PUBLIC ART
American architecture of earlier days may have scraped together the leftovers of passé European styles, but the 20th-century architect **Frank Lloyd Wright** gave America its own architectural mode. Wright's opuses—the Fallingwater house in Pennsylvania (see p. 274) and the Guggenheim Museum in NYC (see p. 224)—demonstrate an angular aesthetic and attention to environmental cohesiveness. More recently, Frank Gehry has moved the craft of architecture into the 21st century with his feats of impossible engineering and optical effects.

Public art has had an established role in most American cities; some devote a full 1% of their funds to it. Not only do sculptures and installations adorn city parks and the lobbies of public buildings, but experiential walk-through environments like Maya Lin's Vietnam Veterans Memorial in Washington, D.C. (see p. 295) are often commissioned in larger cities.

THE MEDIA
America is wired. Images, sounds, and stories from the boob tube, radio, internet, and advertisements infiltrate every aspect of the American lifestyle. Because of the media's power, constant debate centers on censorship and freedom. Censored or not, new media spread like (poison) ivy every second.

TELEVISION
There are television sets in 98% of US homes. Competition between the six national **networks** (ABC, CBS, NBC, Fox, and two newcomers: UPN and WB), cable television, and satellite TV has triggered exponential growth in TV culture over the past few years. The premium hours of prime time (8-11pm EST) are filled with half-hour situational comedy shows, one-hour drama programs, and special programming such as made-for-TV movies and national sporting events. Daytime programming concerns itself with less high-brow fodder, offering a pastiche of trashy soap operas and trashier talk shows, with the occasional game show to lighten the melodrama.

One need not be bound to the networks, however, as **cable** provides special-interest channels that cover every subject from cooking to sports to science fiction. Some hotel rooms come equipped with basic cable, while others will even offer premium stations like HBO that air recently-released movies along with stand-by favorites. Pay-per-view channels are also available in some hotel rooms, although (as the name suggests) the privilege comes at a cost.

Television is the point of entry to **world-wide news** for most Americans. Twenty-four hour news coverage is available on CNN, a cable station. Each network presents local and national nightly news, usually at 5 and/or 11 p.m. EST, while prime time "newsmagazines" like *60 Minutes*, *Dateline*, and *20/20* specialize in investigative reports and exposés.

The **Public Broadcasting Station** (PBS) is commercial-free, funded by viewer contributions, the federal government, and corporate grants. Its repertoire includes educational children's shows like *Sesame Street* and *Mister Roger's Neighborhood*, nature programs, mystery shows, and British comedy shows.

FRANK LLOYD WRIGHT
(1867-1959) As a budding architectural genius, Wright left school at 18 for Chicago, where a boom in innovative construction was going on. Wright signed on, embarking on a long and prolific career designing unique dwellings.

THE USA

TEEN SHOWS
Dawson's Creek (WB) offers high school melodrama on the water, while *Buffy the Vampire Slayer* (WB) fights the forces of evil on a California college campus.
DRAMAS
ER (NBC) rips through fast-paced scenes in a Chicago hospital. On *Law & Order* (NBC), police and district attorneys tackle a new homicide case each week.
SITCOMS
That 70s Show (FOX) features Wisconsin teenagers in the 70s. *Will & Grace* (NBC) boasts the first gay male lead character in prime time.
OTHER
The Simpsons (FOX), a classically irreverent cartoon.

MAJOR DAILIES
The New York Times
The Wall Street Journal
The Chicago Sun-Times

NEWSMAGAZINES
Time
Newsweek

FASHION
Cosmopolitan
Vogue

CULTURE
The New Yorker

ENTERTAINMENT
People
Rolling Stone

PRINT

Despite the onset of more sophisticated technologies like TV and the Internet, Americans still cherish the feel of glossy pages and the smell of newsprint. Newsstands crowd city corners and transportation terminals, while suburban and rural America keeps contact with the larger culture via mail subscriptions and paperboys. Major daily **newspapers** like the *New York Times* wire their stories across the country so that editions can be printed for each major city or region. Sunday editions are always stuffed, feeding the time-honored American tradition of spending lazy Sundays loafing around the house, catching up on goings-on in the world. Print media also dominate the market for beach-, bathroom-, and waiting-room reading. From glitzy **tabloids** like the *National Enquirer* to the most influential and respected news organs, almost all American media suffers the banal criticism of being sensational and exploitative. But isn't that why we like it so much?

SPORTS

Nowhere do Americans express their team spirit so much as in and around the sports arena. Unfortunately, a growing phenomenon of sports-related riots plagues both professional and college events—and soccer hasn't even caught on yet.

AUTO RACING

Start your engines! Although baseball is officially America's favorite pastime, it is **NASCAR auto racing** that draws the most fans of any sport on Memorial Day weekend (in late May) with the Indianapolis 500. Here, average family vehicles are transformed into 185+ m.p.h. powerhouses through the sponsorship of automobile manufacturers and brand-name companies like Spam, Cheerios, and Tide. The cars tear around a banked track hundreds of times, while wide-eyed and open-mouthed fans throw down countless beers and hot dogs. Now that's a sport!

BASEBALL

For those who don't like fast-paced sports, pollution, or noisy fans, most large cities host **Major League Baseball** (MLB) teams. The slow, methodical game of baseball—stopping play and changing sides so often that both the fans and the players need to partake of a seventh-inning stretch—captures the hearts of dreaming boys and grown men alike. Major-league games are often cheap and easy to get tickets to, and they are worth the price. Minor-league games are even cheaper, and are slowly gaining popularity among fans fed up with the whining (and striking) of the discontent big shots.

(AMERICAN) FOOTBALL

Like auto-racing and beer-swilling, football and basketball rival baseball for the title of the country's favorite pastime. The **National Football League** (NFL) is full of beefy men made beefier by shoulder pads; this ain't no European "football." The American-rules game is especially dear to middle America, where the end of the maniacal football season segues nicely into the equally maniacal basketball season.

BASEBALL is played in nine innings. Each team takes a turn at bat per inning. A pitcher throws the ball over home plate. The batter either walks (due to poor pitching), hits, or strikes out (missing 3 good pitches). If he hits, he runs around as many bases as he can without being thrown out (tagged with the ball). When a player makes it around the whole diamond (4 bases), a run is scored.

Each team in **FOOTBALL** tries to run, pass, or kick the ball into a given endzone (at the end of a 100-yard field) or between the uprights (vertical bars marking a goal for kicked balls). The defense does whatever it can to stop this. Play stops when the ball-holder is tackled.

BASKETBALL

Professional basketball teams hail from almost every major city, making up the **National Basketball Association** (NBA). NBA players have come a long way since the first teams were playing with peach baskets and Converse All-Star sneakers. Today, professional basketball players can jump so high and pass so fast that the Association had to move the three-point shooting line back in order to compensate. But football and basketball are not only for professionals: enthusiasm for college and playground traditions often surpasses that for the pros. With spite for overpaid athletes, or maybe just to relive their college days, many Americans are known to live and die by, and bet large amounts of money on their college's football team in the bowl games or its basketball team in the NCAA tournament, fondly called March Madness.

OTHER SPORTS

Other sports claim smaller niches of the American spectatorship. The internationally publicized **US Open** (tennis) and **US Open** (golf) never seem to confuse fans on the home turf. The **Kentucky Derby** (horse racing), a peculiarly American sporting event, hones the betting strategies of seasoned gamblers and tries the tolerance of seasoned boozers. Ice hockey is most popular in the northeast; the **National Hockey League** (NHL) endures the competition with neighbors to the north, in Canada. **Major League Soccer** (MLS) and **women's basketball** (WNBA) are both budding, but not yet out of control, sports.

PHYSICAL ALTERNATIVES

In the past decade, physical fitness has caught on among Americans generally. Work-out enthusiasts have gone from Jane Fonda-type classic **aerobic workouts** to Billy Blanks's hardcore martial arts-inspired Tae Bo, from Cindy Crawford-style light exercise (helped along by a personal trainer) to "spinning" (group bike workouts set to pumping music) and kick-boxing. There is always a new way to burn fat, it seems. Along the beaches of California, you'll find hardbodies equipped with surf boards and in-line skates. In the Northeast, a new crop of suburban yuppies can be spotted powerwalking and cycling on expensive custom-made bikes. Of course, Americans like to do it all in as little time and as much style as possible; thus, the eight minute work-out and matching Spandex gear. In the winter, skiing, snowboarding, and ice skating are popular **recreational sports**, while during the rest of the year, families and bored teenagers nationwide resort to bowling and miniature golf for good, and usually clean, fun.

FOOD

There is more to American food than McDonald's, despite the common perception overseas. Due to the size, geographic, and ethnic diversity of the States, however, it is not easy to nail down exactly what American food is. Ask the average American what he thinks is his native cuisine, and you'll probably hear about hamburgers, fried chicken, and hot dogs—basic **fast food** fare. Simply put, these offerings are what can be found anywhere in the country (and increasingly, the world), and therefore are easily associated with "American food." The truth is that real American food is best found at the regional level, where agricultural produc-

---

The obvious goal of **BASKETBALL** is to put the ball through the hoop. Five-person teams dribble (bounce on the floor) and pass the ball down the court. A shot from inside the 3-point arc is worth 2 points; from outside, it's worth 3. When one team scores, the other gets the ball.

THE USA

NORTHEAST
Roast turkey, clam chowder, seafood (lobster, soft-shell crabs), cornbread.

SOUTHEAST
Fried chicken, breaded and fried steak ("chicken-fried steak"), collard greens.

LOUISIANA
Crawfish, catfish, jambalaya (rice cooked with ham, sausage, shrimp and herbs), gumbo (a soup with okra, meat, and misc. vegetables).

TEXAS
Beef, BBQ, and Tex-Mex are the only three words you need to know

SOUTHWEST
Green chiles, Mexican-influenced.

CALIFORNIA
Salads, wrapped sandwiches, smoothies, Asian-influenced food.

tion, immigration patterns, and local culture have resulted in food that goes beyond the hot dog (which is German, anyway).

Travelers through the states will probably come across some commonalities. Most Americans in between diets cherish a big breakfast, often referred to as a **lumberjack breakfast**. The full deal includes fried eggs, several strips of salty bacon, small links of breakfast sausage, hash browns (fried potatoes), buttered toast, pancakes (a.k.a. flapjacks) with maple syrup, coffee, and orange juice. In the South, grits, a tasteless, mushy gruel is added to the mix, often topped with a gravy made from pork fat. For the non-lumberjack, a bowl of cereal and milk or oatmeal is an acceptable alternative.

Lunch and dinner (supper, in the middle of the country) are far less standardized than breakfast. Urbanites are often drawn to the exotic allure of **international cuisine**, which is fairly abundant in most cities. For everyone, Chinese takeout and pizza have become so Americanized that someone accustomed to the real thing may scarcely recognize the American versions. Many will still flock to the **staples** of their youth occasionally: a simple white bread sandwich for lunch and a dinner of neatly arranged meat, potatoes, and vegetables. The next day, of course, it's back to sushi.

CANADA

O Canada! The second largest country in the world, Canada covers almost 10 million square kilometers (3.85 million square miles). Still, just over 30 million people inhabit Canada's 10 provinces and three territories, which is roughly the population of California. Well over half the population crowds into either Ontario or Québec, while the newly declared territory, Nunavut, has under 30,000. Framed by the Atlantic coastline in the east and the Pacific Ocean in the west, Canada extends from fertile southern farmlands to frozen northern tundra.

The name Canada is thought to derive from the Huron-Iroquois word "kanata," meaning "village" or "community." This etymology betrays the early settlers' dependence on indigenous peoples as well as the country's origins as a system of important trading posts. The early French and English colonists were distant and culturally distinct from each other. To this day the two linguistic groups fight to retain political dominance in the Canadian governing body, though it was only in the 70s that tension between **anglophones** and **francophones** flared briefly into terrorist acts of violence. The concerns of the First Nation people and a rapidly increasing allophone population—people whose first language is neither English nor French—have also become intertwined in the struggle. For crucial info on travel in Canada, see **Essentials,** in the front of this book (p. 31).

A BRIEF HISTORY

circa 8000 B.C.E.
First human inhabitants populate Canadian lands

Although archaeologists are uncertain about the exact timing, recent data indicates that the **first Canadians** arrived at least 10,000 years ago by crossing Beringia, the Asian-Alaskan land bridge. Their descendants flooded the continent, fragmenting into disparate tribes. The first **Europeans** known to explore the area were the Norse, who settled in northern Newfoundland around the year 1000. England came next; John Cabot sighted Newfoundland in 1497. When Jacques Cartier, landing on the gulf of the St. Lawrence River, claimed the mainland for the French crown in 1534, he touched off a rivalry that persisted until Britain's 1759 capture of Québec in the Seven Years' War and France's total capitulation four years later.

The movement to unify the British North American colonies gathered speed after the American Civil War, when US military might and economic isolationism threatened the independent and continued existence of the British colonies. On March 29, 1867, Queen Victoria signed the **British North America Act** (BNA), uniting Nova Scotia, New Brunswick, Upper Canada, and Lower Canada (now Ontario and Québec). Though still a dominion of the British throne, Canada at last had its country—and its day: the BNA was proclaimed on July 1, now known as Canada Day.

Since that time, Canada has expanded territorially and economically. The years following consolidation witnessed sustained economic growth and settlement in the west with the completion of the trans-continental railway. The country quickly grew to encompass most of the land it covers today. Participation in World War I earned the Dominion international respect and a charter membership in the League of Nations. It joined the United Nations in 1945 and was a founding member of the **North Atlantic Treaty Organization** in 1949. The Liberal government of the following decade created a national social security system and a national health insurance program. Pierre Trudeau's government repatriated Canada's constitution in 1981, freeing the nation from Britain in constitutional legality (though Elizabeth II remains nominal head of state). Free to forge its own alliances, the country signed the controversial **North American Free Trade Agreement** (NAFTA) in 1992 under the leadership of Conservative Brian Mulroney.

In recent years, Canada has faced both internal political tensions and ever-increasing Americanization pressure. **Mulroney** strove hard to mold a strong, unified Canada, but will probably go down in Canadian history as the leader who nearly tore the nation apart in an effort to bring it together. (Canadians today also know and despise Mulroney as the wicked PM who introduced the universally bemoaned 7% Goods and Services Tax.) His numerous attempts to negotiate a constitution that all 10 provinces would ratify (Canada's present constitution lacks Québec's support) consistently failed, flaring century-old regional tensions and spelling the end of his government.

The ever-present question of **Québec's separation** remains unsettled; an October 1996 referendum rejected separation by a mere 1.2% margin. Still, the Canadian government has made strides in appeasing other underrepresented groups. With the 1999 establishment of Nunavut, a huge new territory carved out of the Northwest Territories, Canada gave political control of much of the frozen North to the 85% Inuit population there.

In addition to fretting over the independence wishes of their numerous constituents, Canadian policy-makers continue to struggle for Canada's **cultural independence** from the US. Media domination by their southern neighbor has put a bit of a strain on Canadian pride, so much so that Canada's radio stations are required by law to play at least 30% Canadian music. But increasing "brain drain," the southward emigration of Canada's top intellectuals, has dashed many a hope for cultural renewal.

1000 C.E.
Leif Eriksson and friends are the first Europeans to reach the Canadian coast

1763
The French cede disputed Canadian territories to the British

1867
Queen Victoria unites Eastern Canada as a dominion of the British crown

1917-19, 1939-45
Important contributions to both World Wars win Canada status and respect among world powers.

1970
After a decade of terrorist bombings and robberies, the Front de Liberation du Québec kidnaps two officials, killing one. Trudeau declares a brief period of martial law until the crisis is abated.

1990
Elijah Harper, Manitoba legislator and hero of Canada's First Nation, rejects a constitution accord made palatable to Québec at the expense of native peoples.

1999
A new Inuit-dominated territory, Nunavut, is declared.

ROBERT SERVICE
(1874-1958)
Called the "Canadian Kipling," Service mostly wrote descriptive verse about the still-frontier of Canada's northwest at the turn of the century.

MARGARET ATWOOD
(1939-)
Resisting the label of "feminist," Atwood explores the dimensions of human relationships in contemporary society through the eyes of female characters.

NEIL YOUNG
(1945-)
Teaming up first with Crosby, Stills and Nash, and then with aggressive artists like Sonic Youth and Pearl Jam, Young just keeps on rockin' (in the free world). *Harvest* (1972)

DENYS ARCAND
(1941-)
Arcand directed a number of award-winning films weaving together intelligent dialogue and provocative imagery to address disillusionment and despair in the modern world. Yes, it happens even in Canada.

CULTURE

Canada has two official languages, English and French. *Québécois* pronunciation of French can be perplexing to European French-speakers, and the protocol is less formal. There are also numerous native languages. Inuktitut, the Inuit language, is widely spoken in Nunavut and the Northwest Territories.

Most noted **Canadian literature** is post-1867. The opening of the Northwest and the Klondike Gold Rush (1898) provided fodder for the adventure tale—Jack London (*The Call of the Wild, White Fang*) and Robert Service (*Songs of a Sourdough, The Trail of '98*) both penned stories of prospectors and wolves based on their mining experience in the north. In the Maritimes, L.M. Montgomery authored one of the greatest coming of age/romance novels of all times, *Anne of Green Gables*. Prominent contemporary English-language authors include Margaret Atwood, best known for the futuristic bestseller *The Handmaid's Tale*, and Sri Lankan-born poet and novelist Michael Ondaatje, whose *The English Patient* received the prestigious Booker Prize. Canada also boasts three of the world's most authoritative cultural and literary critics: Northrop Frye, Hugh Kenner, and pop phenom Marshall McLuhan. The *Québecois* literary tradition is becoming more recognized, and has been important in defining an emerging cultural and political identity.

Canada's contribution to the world of **popular music** includes a range of artists with varying levels of musical ability. Neil Young, Joni Mitchell, Bruce Cockburn, Rush, Cowboy Junkies, Bare Naked Ladies, k.d. lang, Bryan Adams, Crash Test Dummies, Sarah McLachlan, and the Tragically Hip are all Canucks. Recent chart-toppers include Alanis Morissette, country goddess Shania Twain, and Céline Dion, who's everything she is because we loved her. Canada is also home to *Québecois* folk music and several world-class orchestras, including the Montréal, Toronto, and Vancouver Symphonies.

On the **silver screen**, Canada's National Film Board (NFB), which finances many documentaries, has gained worldwide acclaim. The first Oscar given to a documentary went to the NFB's 1941 *Churchill Island*. Since then, *Québecois* filmmakers have caught the world's eye with Oscar-nominated movies like *Le declin de l'empire americain*, directed by Denys Arcand. He also directed the striking *Jesus de Montréal*, and art flick *Léolo* which was deemed a classic by critics. François Girard provoked gasps with *Thirty-two Short Films about Glenn Gould*, and actress Sheila McCarthy shone in *I Have Heard the Mermaids Singing*.

Many famous **television** actors and comedians are from Canada, including Dan Aykroyd (*Blues Brothers, Ghostbusters*), Mike Meyers (*Saturday Night Live, Wayne's World, and Austin Powers*), Michael J. Fox (*Back to the Future, Spin City*), newscaster Peter Jennings, *Jeopardy* host Alex Trebek, and Captain James T. Kirk himself, William Shatner (*Star Trek*). The Canadian comedy troupe SCTV spawned the careers of big-time laughmasters Martin Short, the late John Candy, and Rick Moranis.

ESSENTIALS

FACTS FOR THE TRAVELER

WHEN TO GO

Climate and goings-on vary greatly across the continent, so when to go depends on where you plan to go and what you plan to do there. For most of the country, the period between Memorial Day and Labor Day (May 28 to Sept. 3, 2001) is the tourist high-season; Florida, the Southwest, and southern California perhaps see as many visitors in the winter, while colder climes in the north draw the masses with winter attractions like skiing and snowshoeing. Avoid travel on major holidays, especially American Thanksgiving and the Christmas-New Year's period.

NATIONAL HOLIDAYS

USA

Date in 2001	Holiday
January 1	New Year's Day
January 15	Martin Luther King, Jr. Day
February 19	Presidents Day
May 28	Memorial Day
July 4	Independence Day
September 3	Labor Day
October 8	Columbus Day
November 11	Veterans Day
November 22	Thanksgiving
December 25	Christmas Day

CANADA

Date in 2001	Holiday
January 1	New Year's Day
April 15	Easter Sunday
April 16	Easter Monday
May 21	Victoria Day
July 1	Canada Day
September 3	Labour Day
October 8	Thanksgiving
November 11	Remembrance Day
December 25	Christmas Day
December 26	Boxing Day

FESTIVALS

Some of the most popular festivals are listed below, along with the page numbers of their respective descriptions in the guide. This list is not exhaustive; refer to Sights and Entertainment sections of specific cities for more festivals.

USA

Month	Festival and Location
January	Elvis Presley's Birthday Tribute, Memphis, TN (p. 349)
	Western Stock Show, Rodeo, and Horse Show, Denver, CO (p. 669)
	Winter Carnival, St. Paul, MN (p. 524)
February	Mardi Gras, New Orleans, LA (p. 403)
	Ashland Shakespeare Festival, Ashland, OR (p. 916)
	Gasparilla Pirate Festival, Tampa, FL (p. 456)
March	South by Southwest, Austin, TX (p. 598)
April	New Orleans Jazz and Heritage Festival, New Orleans, LA (p. 403)
	Fiesta San Antonio, San Antonio, TX (p. 615)
May	Memphis in May International Festival, Memphis, TN (p. 349)
	Spoleto Festival USA (theater, dance, opera), Charleston, SC (p. 368)
June	Portland Rose Festival, Portland, OR (p. 903)
	Chicago Blues Festival, Chicago, IL (p. 499)
	Summerfest, Milwaukee, WI (p. 524)
	Aspen Music Festival, Aspen, CO (p. 684)

July	**Tanglewood,** Lenox, MA (p. 143)
	Frontier Days, Cheyenne, WY (p. 664)
	Aquatennial, Minneapolis, MN (p. 524)
August	**Newport Folk Festival and JVC Jazz Festival,** Newport, RI (p. 145)
September	**Bumbershoot,** Seattle, WA (p. 877)
	La Fiesta de Santa Fe, Santa Fe, NM (p. 760)
November	**Hot Air Balloon Rally,** Albuquerque, NM (p. 766)
	Macy's Thanksgiving Day Parade, New York, NY (p. 196)

CANADA

Month	Festival and Location
January	**Annual Polar Bear Swim,** Vancouver, B.C. (p. 920)
February	**Winterlude,** Ottawa, ON (p. 190)
	Winter Carnival, Québec City, QC (p. 173)
May	**Stratford Shakespeare Festival** (through Nov.), Stratford, ON (p. 190)
	Canadian Tulip Festival, Ottawa, ON (p. 190)
June	**International Jazz Festival,** Montréal, QC (p. 163)
July	**Nova Scotia International Tattoo Festival,** Halifax, NS (p. 152)
August	**Canadian National Exhibition,** Toronto, ON (p. 188)

CLIMATE

This chart gives the average high/low temperatures in degrees Fahrenheit and the average rainfall in inches during four months of the year. To convert from Fahrenheit to Celsius, subtract 32 and divide by 2.

SEASONAL	JANUARY		APRIL		JULY		OCTOBER	
TEMP. (HI/LO), precipitation	°F	in.	°F	in.	°F	in.	°F	in.
Atlanta	51/33	4.9	73/51	4.4	89/70	4.7	74/53	2.5
Chicago	29/19	1.6	59/40	3.7	83/67	3.6	64/49	2.3
Dallas	54/35	1.7	84/56	3.6	98/76	2.0	80/57	2.5
Las Vegas	56/33	0.5	77/51	0.2	105/76	0.5	82/54	0.3
Los Angeles	67/47	3.7	71/56	1.2	84/64	0.0	79/59	0.2
New Orleans	62/43	5.0	79/59	4.5	91/73	6.7	79/59	2.7
New York	38/26	3.2	61/43	3.8	85/68	3.8	66/49	3.4
Seattle	45/34	5.9	58/41	2.5	74/54	0.9	60/45	3.4

DOCUMENTS AND FORMALITIES

EMBASSIES AND CONSULATES

Contact your nearest embassy or consulate to obtain info regarding visas and passports to the United States and Canada. The **US State Department** provides contact info for US overseas stations which can be found on the Internet at www.state.gov/www/about_state/contacts/keyofficer_index.html. A similar listing for the Canadian Ministries of Foreign Affairs can be found at www.dfait-maeci.gc.ca/dfait/missions/menu-e.asp.

US EMBASSIES

Australia, Moonah Pl., Canberra, ACT 2600 (☎02 6214 5600; fax 6214 5970; www.usis-australia.gov/embassy/).

Canada, 100 Wellington St., Ottawa, ON K1P 5T1 (☎613-238-5335 or 238-4470; fax 238-5720; www.usembassycanada.gov).

Ireland, 42 Elgin Rd., Ballsbridge, Dublin 4 (☎01 668 8777; fax 668 9946; www.usembassy.ie).

New Zealand, 29 Fitzherbert Terr., Thorndon, Wellington (☎04 472 2068; fax 472 3537; http://usembassy.state.gov/wellington).

South Africa, 877 Pretorius St., Arcadia 0083, P.O. Box 9536 Pretoria 0001 (☎012 342 1048; fax 342 2244; http://usembassy.state.gov/pretoria).

UK, 24/31 Grosvenor Sq., London W1A 1AE (☎0171 499 9000; fax 495 5012; www.usembassy.org.uk).

US CONSULATES

Australia, MLC Centre, 19-29 Martin Pl., 59th fl., Sydney NSW 2000 (☎02 9373 9200; fax 9373 9125); 553 St. Kilda Rd., P.O. Box 6722, Melbourne, VIC 3004 (☎03 9625 1583; fax 9510 4646); 16 St. George's Terr., 13th fl., Perth, WA 6000 (☎08 9231 9400; fax 9231 9444).

Canada, 615 Macleod Trail #1050, S.E., Calgary, AB T2G 4T8, (☎403-266-8962; fax 264-6630); Cogswell Tower #910, Scotia Sq., Halifax, NS, B3J 3K1, (☎902-429-2480; fax 423-6861); P.O. Box 65, Postal Station Desjardins, Montréal, QC H5B 1G1 (☎514-398-9695; fax 398-0973); 2 Place Terrasse Dufferin, C.P. 939, Québec, QC, G1R 4T9 (☎418-692-2095; fax 692-4640); 360 University Ave., Toronto, ON, M5G 1S4 (☎416-595-1700; fax 595-0051); 1095 West Pender St., Vancouver, BC V6E 2M6 (☎604-685-4311; fax 685-5285).

New Zealand, Yorkshire General Bldg., 4th fl., 29 Shortland St., Auckland (☎09 303 2724; fax 366 0870); Price Waterhouse Ctr., 109 Armagh St., 11th fl., Christchurch (☎03 379 0040; fax 379 5677).

South Africa, Broadway Industries Centre, P.O. Box 6773, Heerengracht, Foreshore, Cape Town (☎021 214 280; fax 211 130); Durban Bay House, 333 Smith St., 29th fl., Durban (☎031 304 4737; fax 301 8206); 1 River St. c/o Riviera, Killarney, Johannesburg (☎011 646 6900; fax 646 6913).

UK, Queen's House, 14 Queen St., Belfast, N. Ireland BT1 6EQ, PSC 801, Box 40, APO AE 09498-4040 (☎0123 232 8239; fax 224 8482); 3 Regent Terr., Edinburgh, Scotland EH7 5BW, PSC 801 Box 40, FPO AE 90498-4040 (☎0131 556 8315; fax 557 6023).

CANADIAN EMBASSIES

Australia, Commonwealth Ave., Canberra, ACT 2600 (☎02 6273 3844; fax 6273 3285).

Ireland, 65 St. Stephen's Green, Dublin 2 (☎01 478 1988; fax 478 1285).

New Zealand, 61 Molesworth St., 3rd fl., Thorndon, Wellington (☎04 473 9577; fax 471 2082).

South Africa, 1103 Arcadia St. Hatfield, Pretoria 0083 (☎012 422 3000; fax 422 3052).

UK, Canada House, Trafalgar Square, London, SW1Y 5BJ (☎0171 258 6600; fax 258 6533).

US, 501 Pennsylvania Ave. NW, Washington, D.C. 20001 (☎202-682-1740; fax 682-7726).

CANADIAN CONSULATES

Australia, Quay West Bldg., 111 Harrington St., Level 5, Sydney NSW, 2000 (☎02 9364 3000; fax 9364 3098); 123 Camberwell Rd., Hawthorn East, Melbourne, VIC 3123 (☎03 9811 9999; fax 9811 9969); 267 St. George's Terr., 3rd fl., Perth WA 6000 (☎08 9322 7930; fax 9261 7706).

New Zealand, Jetset Centre, Level 9, 48 Emily Pl., Auckland (☎09 309 3680; fax 307 3111).

South Africa, Reserve Bank Bldg., 360 St. George's Mall St., 19th fl., Cape Town 8001 (☎021 423 5240; fax 423 4893); 25/27 Marriott Rd., Durban 4000 (☎031 309 8434; fax 309 8432).

UK, 30 Lothian Rd., Edinburgh, Scotland EH1 2DH (☎0131 220 4333; fax 245 6010).

US, 1251 Ave. of the Americas, New York, NY 10020-1175 (☎212-596-1600; fax 596-1666); 550 S. Hope St. 9th fl., Los Angeles, CA 90071-2627 (☎213-346-2700; fax 620-8827); 2 Prudential Plaza, 180 N. Stetson, Ave., Ste. 2400, Chicago, IL 60601 (☎312-616-1860; fax 616-1877).

EMBASSIES IN THE USA AND CANADA

IN WASHINGTON, DC (USA)

Australia, 1601 Massachusetts Ave., 20036 (☎202-797-3000; fax 797-3168). **Canada,** 501 Pennsylvania Ave., 20001 (☎202-682-1740; fax 682-7726). **Ireland,** 2234 Mass. Ave., 20008 (☎202-462-3939; fax 232-5993). **New Zealand,** 37 Observatory Circle, 20008 (☎202-328-4800; fax 667-5227). **UK,** 3100 Mass. Ave., 20008 (☎202-588-6500; fax 588-7870). **South Africa,** 3051 Mass. Ave., 20008 (☎202-232-4400; fax 265-1607).

> **ENTRANCE REQUIREMENTS**
>
> **Passport** (below). Required for all visitors to the US and Canada.
>
> **Visa** (p. 35). A visa is usually required to visit the US and Canada, but can be waived.
>
> **Work Permit** (p. 84). Required for all foreigners planning to work in Canada or the US.
>
> **Driving Permit** (p. 76). Required for all those planning to drive.

IN OTTAWA, ONTARIO (CANADA)

Australia, 50 O' Connor St. #710, K1P 6L2; (☎613-236-0841; fax 236-4376). **Ireland,** 130 Albert St. #700, K2P 5G4; (☎613-233-6281; fax 233-5835). **New Zealand,** 99 Bank St. #727, K1P 6G3; (☎613-238-6097; fax 238-5707). **UK,** 310 Summerset St., K2P 0J9; (☎613-230-2961; fax 230-2400). **US,** 100 Wellington St., K1P 5T1; (☎613-238-5335). **South Africa,** 15 Sussex Dr., K1M 1M8; (☎613-744-0330; fax 741-1639).

PASSPORTS

REQUIREMENTS. All foreign visitors except Canadians need valid passports to enter the United States and to re-enter their own country. Returning home with an expired passport is illegal and may result in a fine. Canadians need to demonstrate proof of Canadian citizenship, such as a citizenship card with photo ID. The US does not allow entrance if the holder's passport expires in under six months.

PHOTOCOPIES. Be sure to photocopy the page of your passport with your photo, passport number, and other identifying info, as well as any visas, travel insurance policies, plane tickets, or traveler's check serial numbers. Carry one set of copies in a safe place, apart from the originals, and leave another set at home. Consulates also recommend that you carry an expired passport or an official copy of your birth certificate in a part of your baggage separate from other documents.

LOST PASSPORTS. If you lose your passport, immediately notify the local police and the nearest embassy or consulate of your home government. To expedite its replacement, you will need to know all info previously recorded and show ID and proof of citizenship. In some cases, a replacement may take weeks to process, and it may be valid only for a limited time. Any visas stamped in your old passport will be irretrievably lost. In an emergency, ask for immediate temporary traveling papers that will permit you to re-enter your home country. Your passport is a public document belonging to your nation's government. You may have to surrender it to a US government official, but if you don't get it back in a reasonable amount of time, inform the nearest mission of your home country.

NEW PASSPORTS. File any new passport or renewal applications well in advance of your departure date. Most passport offices offer rush services for a steep fee. Citizens living abroad who need a passport or renewal should contact the nearest consular service of their home country.

Australia: Citizens must apply for a passport in person at a post office, a passport office, or an Australian diplomatic mission overseas. Passport offices are located in Adelaide, Brisbane, Canberra, Darwin, Hobart, Melbourne, Newcastle, Perth, and Sydney. New adult passports cost AUS$128 (for a 32-page passport) or AUS$192 (64-page), and a child's is AUS$64/AUS$96. Adult passports are valid for 10 years and child passports for 5 years. For more info, call toll-free (in Australia) ☎ 13 12 32, or visit www.dfat.gov.au/passports.

Canada: Citizens may cross the US-Canada border with any proof of citizenship.

Ireland: Citizens can apply for a passport by mail to either the Department of Foreign Affairs, Passport Office, Setanta Centre, Molesworth St., Dublin 2 (☎01 671 16 33; fax 671 1092; www.irlgov.ie/iveagh), or the Passport Office, Irish Life Building, 1A South Mall, Cork (☎021 27 25 25). Obtain an application at a local Garda station or post office, or request one from a passport office. 32-page passports cost IR£45 and are valid for 10 years. 48-page passports cost IR£55. Citizens under 18 or over 65 can request a 3-year passport (IR£10).

New Zealand: Application forms for passports are available in New Zealand from most travel agents. Applications may be forwarded to the Passport Office, P.O. Box 10526, Wellington, New Zealand (☎0800 22 50 50 or 4 474 8100; fax 4 474 8010; www.passport.govt.nz). Standard processing time in New Zealand is 10 working days for correct applications. The fees are adult NZ$80 and child NZ$40. Children's names can no longer be endorsed on a parent's passport—they must apply for their own, which are valid for up to 5 years. An adult's passport is valid for up to 10 years.

South Africa: South African passports are issued only in Pretoria. However, all applications must still be submitted or forwarded to the applicable office of a South African consulate. Tourist passports, valid for 10 years, cost around ZAR165. Children under 16 must be issued their own passports, valid for 5 years, which cost around ZAR120. Time for the completion of an application is normally 3 months or more from the time of submission. For further info, contact the nearest Department of Home Affairs Office (http://usaembassy.southafrica.net/VisaForms/Passport/Passport2000.html).

United Kingdom: Full passports are valid for 10 years (5 years if under 16). Application forms are available at passport offices, main post offices, travel agents, and online (www.ukpa.gov.uk/forms/f_app_pack.htm). Apply by mail or in person to one of the passport offices, located in London, Liverpool, Newport, Peterborough, Glasgow, or Belfast. The fee is UK£28, UK£14.80 for children under 16. The process takes about four weeks, but the London office offers a five-day, walk-in rush service; arrive early. The UK Passport Agency can be reached by phone at ☎0870 521 04 10. More info is available at www.open.gov.uk/ukpass/ukpass.htm.

United States: Citizens may cross the US-Canada border with any proof of citizenship.

VISAS

US. As of August 2000, citizens of most other countries need a visa—a stamp, sticker, or insert in your passport specifying the purpose of your travel and the permitted duration of your stay—in addition to a valid passport for entrance to the US. To obtain a visa, contact a US embassy or consulate (see p. 32).

Citizens of Australia, Austria, Belgium, Denmark, Finland, France, Germany, Iceland, Ireland, Italy, Japan, Luxembourg, the Netherlands, New Zealand, Norway, Portugal, San Marino, Singapore, Slovenia, Spain, Sweden, Switzerland, the United Kingdom and Uruguay can waive US visas through the **Visa Waiver Pilot Program.** Visitors qualify if they are traveling only for business or pleasure (*not* work or study), are staying for fewer than 90 days, have proof of intent to leave (e.g., a return plane ticket), an I-94W form (arrival/departure certificate attached to your visa upon arrival), and are traveling on particular air or sea carriers.

All travelers planning a stay of more than 90 days (180 days for Canadians) must obtain a visa. The **Center for International Business and Travel (CIBT),** 23201 New Mexico Ave. NW #210, Washington, D.C. 20016 (☎202-244-9500 or 800-925-2428), secures travel "pleasure tourist," or **B-2** visas to and from all possible countries for a variable service charge (6-month visa around $45). If you lose your I-94 form, you can replace it at the nearest **Immigration and Naturalization Service (INS)** office (☎800-375-5283; www.ins.usdoj.gov), although it's unlikely that the form will be replaced within the time of your stay. **Visa extensions** are sometimes attainable with a completed I-539 form; call the forms request line (☎800-870-3676).

Be sure to double-check on entrance requirements at the nearest US embassy or consulate, or consult the **Bureau of Consular Affairs** web page at http://travel.state.gov/visa;visitors.html.

CANADA. Citizens of Australia, France, Germany, Ireland, Italy, Japan, Mexico, New Zealand, the UK, and the US may enter Canada without visas for stays of 90 days or less if they carry proof of intent to leave; South Africans need a visa to enter Canada ($75 for a single person, $400 for a family). Citizens of other countries should contact their Canadian consulate for more info. Write to Citizenship and Immigration Canada for the useful booklet *Applying for a Visitor Visa* at Information Centre, Public Affairs Branch, Jean Edmonds Tower South, 365 Laurier

Ave. W., Ottawa, ON K1A 1L1 (☎888-242-2100 or 613-954-9019; fax 954-2221), or consult the electronic version at http://cicnet.ci.gc.ca. Extensions are sometimes granted; call the nearest Canada Immigration Centre listed in the phone directory.

IDENTIFICATION

When you travel, always carry two or more forms of identification on your person, including at least one photo ID. A passport combined with a driver's license or birth certificate usually serves as adequate proof of your identity and citizenship. Many establishments, especially banks, require several IDs before cashing traveler's checks. Never carry all your forms of ID together. It is useful to carry extra passport-size photos to affix to the various IDs or railpasses you may acquire.

DRIVER'S LICENSE. A foreign driver's license is usually acceptable for driving in the United States and Canada for a temporary period. To rent a car and to avoid the incredulousness of a disgruntled Southern sheriff, purchase an **International Driving Permit** (see p. 76) from a certified agent. A driver's license without an attached photo will seldom be accepted.

STUDENT AND TEACHER IDENTIFICATION. While less widely recognized in the US and Canada than in Europe, the **International Student Identity Card (ISIC)** is still the most widely accepted form of student identification. Flashing this card can often procure you discounts for sights, theaters, museums, transportation, and other services. You must present an ISIC card to purchase reduced-rate student fare airplane tickets. Cardholders have access to a toll-free 24hr. ISIC helpline whose multilingual staff can provide assistance in medical, legal, and financial emergencies overseas (☎877-370-4742 in the US and Canada; elsewhere call collect 715-345-0505).

Many student travel agencies around the world issue ISICs, including STA Travel in Australia and New Zealand; Travel CUTS in Canada; USIT in Ireland and Northern Ireland; SASTS in South Africa; Campus Travel and STA Travel in the UK; Council Travel, STA Travel, and via the web (www.counciltravel.com/idcards/default.asp) in the US (see **Budget and Student Travel Agencies,** p. 65). When you apply for the card, request a copy of the *International Student Identity Card Handbook*, which lists some of the available discounts in the US and Canada. You can also write to Council for a copy. The card is valid from September of one year to Dec. of the following year and costs AUS$15, CDN$15, or $22. Applicants must be at least 12 years old and degree-seeking students of a secondary or post-secondary school. Because of the proliferation of phony ISICs, many airlines and some other services require additional proof of student identity, such as a signed letter from the registrar attesting to your student status that is stamped with the school seal or your school ID card. The **International Teacher Identity Card (ITIC)** offers similar but limited discounts. The fee is AUS$13, UK£5, or $22. For more info on these cards, contact the **International Student Travel Confederation (ISTC)**, Herengracht 479, 1017 BS Amsterdam, Netherlands (☎31 20 421 28 00; fax 421 28 10; email istcinfo@istc.org; www.istc.org).

YOUTH IDENTIFICATION. The International Student Travel Confederation also issues a discount card to travelers who are 25 years old or younger, but not students. This one-year card, known as the International Youth Travel Card (IYTC) and formerly as the GO25, offers many of the same benefits as the ISIC, and most organizations that sell the ISIC also sell the IYTC. To apply, you will need either a passport, valid driver's license, or copy of a birth certificate and a passport-sized photo with your name printed on the back. The fee is $22.

CUSTOMS

Upon entering the United States or Canada, you must declare certain items from abroad and pay a duty on the value of those articles that exceed the allowance established by the US or Canada's customs service. Keeping receipts for purchases made abroad will help establish values when you return. It is wise to make a list, including serial numbers, of any valuables that you carry with you from home; if you register this list with customs before your departure and have an official stamp it, you will avoid import duty charges and ensure an easy passage upon your return. Be especially careful to document items manufactured abroad, and don't try to bring perishable food over the border.

Upon returning home, you must declare all articles acquired abroad and pay a **duty** on the value of articles that exceed the allowance established by your country's customs service. Goods and gifts purchased at **duty-free** shops abroad are not exempt from duty or sales tax at your point of return; you must declare these items as well. "Duty-free" merely means that you need not pay a tax in the country of purchase. For more specific info on customs requirements, contact the following info centers:

FURTHER RESOURCES

Australia: Australian Customs National Information Line (in Australia call ☎01 30 03 63, from elsewhere call ☎61 2 6275 6666; www.customs.gov.au).

Canada: Canadian Customs, 2265 St. Laurent Blvd., Ottawa, ON K1G 4K3 (☎613-993-0534 or 800-461-9999; www.revcan.ca).

Ireland: Customs Information Office, Irish Life Centre, Lower Abbey St., Dublin 1 (☎01 878 8811; fax 878 0836; taxes@revenue.iol.ie; www.revenue.ie/customs.htm).

New Zealand: New Zealand Customhouse, 17-21 Whitmore St., Box 2218, Wellington (☎04 473 6099; fax 473 7370; www.customs.govt.nz).

South Africa: Commissioner for Customs and Excise, Privat Bag X47, Pretoria 0001 (☎012 314 9911; fax 328 6478; www.gov.za).

United Kingdom: Her Majesty's Customs and Excise, Passenger Enquiry Team, Wayfarer House, Great South West Road, Feltham, Middlesex TW14 8NP (☎020 8910 3744; fax 8910 3933; www.hmce.gov.uk).

MONEY

No matter how low your budget, if you plan to travel for more than a couple of days, you will need to keep handy a larger amount of cash than usual. Carrying it around with you, even in a money belt, is risky, and personal checks from another country, or even another state, will probably not be accepted no matter how many forms of identification you have (some banks even shy away from accepting checks).

Many Canadian shops, as well as vending machines and parking meters, accept US coins at face value. Stores often convert the price of your purchase for you, but they are not legally obligated to offer a fair exchange. During the past several years, the Canadian dollar has been worth roughly 30% less than the US dollar.

CURRENCY AND EXCHANGE

The main unit of currency in the US and Canada is the **dollar,** which is divided into 100 **cents.** Paper money is green in the US; bills come in denominations of $1, $5, $10, $20, $50, and $100. Coins are 1¢ (penny), 5¢ (nickel), 10¢ (dime), and 25¢ (quarter). Paper money in Canada comes in denominations of $5, $10, $20, $50, and $100, which are all the same size but color coded by denomination. Coins are 1¢, 5¢, 10¢, 25¢, $1, and $2. The $1 coin is known as the **Loonie,** the $2 the **Toonie.**

The following currency chart is based on August 2000 exchange rates between US dollars (US$), Canadian dollars (CDN$), British pounds (UK£), Irish pounds (IR£), Australian dollars (AUS$), New Zealand dollars (NZ$), South African Rand (ZAR), and European Union euros (EUR€). Check a large newspaper or the web (letsgo.com) for the latest exchange rates.

CURRENCY EXCHANGE

THE GREENBACK (THE US DOLLAR)	
CDN$1 = $0.68	US$1 = CDN$ 1.48
UK£1 = $1.45	US$1 = UK£ 0.69
IR£1 = $1.13	US$1= IR£ 0.88
AUS$1 = $0.57	US$1= AUS$ 1.76
NZ$1 = $0.43	US$1 = NZ$ 2.40
ZAR1 = $0.14	US$1 = ZAR 7.03
EUR€1 = $0.89	US$1= EUR€ 1.12
THE LOONIE (THE CANADIAN DOLLAR)	
US$1 = $1.48	CDN$1 = US$ 0.68
UK£1 = $2.15	CDN$1 = UK£ 0.47
IR£1 = $1.67	CDN$1= IR£ 0.60
AUS$1 = $0.84	CDN$1= AUS$ 1.19
NZ$1 = $0.63	CDN$1 = NZ$ 1.59
ZAR1 = $0.21	CDN$1 = ZAR 4.76
EUR€1 = $1.31	CDN$1= EUR€ 0.76

TRAVELER'S CHECKS

Traveler's checks are one of the safest and least troublesome means of carrying funds, since they can be refunded if stolen. In both the US and Canada, traveler's checks are widely accepted in both rural and urban areas. Several agencies and banks sell them, usually for face value plus a small percentage commission. **American Express** and **Visa** are the most widely recognized. If you're ordering checks, do so well in advance, especially if you are requesting large sums.

Each agency provides refunds if your checks are lost or stolen, and many provide additional services, such as toll-free refund hotlines in the countries you're visiting, emergency message services, and stolen credit card assistance.

In order to collect a **refund for lost or stolen checks,** keep your check receipts separate from your checks and store them in a safe place or with a traveling companion. Record check numbers when you cash them, leave a list of check numbers with someone at home, and ask for a list of refund centers when you buy your checks. Never countersign your checks until you are ready to cash them, and always bring your passport with you when you plan to use the checks.

American Express: Call ☎ 800-251-902 in Australia; in New Zealand ☎ 0800 441 068; in the UK ☎ 0800 52 13 13; in the US and Canada ☎ 800-221-7282. Elsewhere, call US collect ☎ 801-964-6665; www.aexp.com. American Express traveler's checks are available in US (but not Canadian) dollars. Checks can be purchased for a small fee (1-4%) at American Express Travel Service Offices, banks, and American Automobile Association offices. AAA members (see p. 77) can buy the checks commission-free. American Express offices cash their checks commission-free (except where prohibited by national governments), but often at slightly worse rates than banks. *Cheques for Two* can be signed by either of two people traveling together.

Citicorp: Call ☎ 800-645-6556 in the US and Canada; in Europe, the Middle East, or Africa, call the UK office at ☎ 44 020 7508 7007; from elsewhere, call US collect ☎ 1-813-623-1709. Traveler's checks in 7 currencies. Commission 1-2%. Guaranteed hand-delivery of traveler's checks when a refund location is not convenient. Call 24hr.

Thomas Cook MasterCard: From the US, Canada, or Caribbean call ☎ 800-223-7373; from the UK call ☎ 0800 622 101; from elsewhere, call ☎ 44 1733 318 950 collect. Available in 13 currencies. Commission 2%. Offices cash checks commission-free.

Visa: Call ☎ 800-227-6811 in the US; in the UK ☎ 0800 895 078; from elsewhere, call ☎ 44 1733 318 949 and reverse the charges. Any of the above numbers can tell you the location of their nearest office.

ESSENTIALS

CREDIT CARDS

Credit cards are generally accepted in all but the smallest businesses in both the United States and Canada. Major credit cards—**MasterCard** and **Visa** are welcomed most often—can be used to extract cash advances in dollars (both US and Canadian) from associated banks and teller machines throughout both countries. Credit card companies get the wholesale exchange rate, which is generally 5% better than the retail rate used by banks and other currency exchange establishments. **American Express** cards also work in some ATMs, as well as at AmEx offices and major airports. All such machines require a **Personal Identification Number (PIN)**. You must ask your credit card company for a PIN before you leave; without it, you will be unable to withdraw cash with your credit card outside your home country. If you already have a PIN, check with the company to make sure it will work in Canada and the US. Credit cards often offer an array of other services, from insurance to emergency assistance; check with your company.

CREDIT CARD COMPANIES. Visa (US ☎ 800-336-8472) and **MasterCard** (US ☎ 800-307-7309) are issued in cooperation with individual banks and some other organizations. **American Express** (US ☎ 800-843-2273) has an annual fee of up to $55, depending on the card. Cardholder services include the option of cashing personal checks at AmEx offices, a 24-hour hotline with medical and legal assistance in emergencies (☎ 800-554-2639 in US and Canada; from abroad call US collect ☎ 202-554-2639), and the American Express Travel Service. Benefits include assistance in changing airline, hotel, and car rental reservations, baggage loss and flight insurance, sending mailgrams and international cables, and holding your mail at one of the more than 1700 AmEx offices around the world. The **Discover Card** (US ☎ 800-347-2683; outside US, call ☎ 801-902-3100) offers small cashback bonuses on most purchases, but it may not be readily accepted in Canada or the US.

CASH (ATM) CARDS

Cash cards—popularly called **ATM** (Automated Teller Machine) cards—are widespread in both rural and urban parts of the US and Canada. You can access any US and most foreign banks through this system. Check your card to see which international money networks it uses, then look for ATM machines using the same (most machines will use all). The two major international money networks are **Cirrus** (US ☎ 800-424-7787) and **PLUS** (US ☎ 800-843-7587). **NYCE** is a major US network. ATMs often offer superior exchange rates—up to 5% better than the retail rate used by banks and other currency exchange establishments. Typically the ATM you use will add a $1-1.50 surcharge and your home bank may charge $1-5 charge per withdrawal. A $200-500 daily cash withdrawal limit is generally imposed by your home bank (check before you leave). Be sure to memorize your PIN code in numeric form since machines often don't have letters on their keys. Also, if your PIN is longer than four digits, ask your bank whether you need a new number.

Visa TravelMoney (☎ 800-847-2911) is a system allowing you to access money from Visa ATMs (check www.visa.com/pd/atm, www.mastercard.com/atm for locations). You deposit an amount before you travel (plus a small administration fee), and you can withdraw up to that sum. The cards, which give you the same favorable exchange rate for withdrawals as a regular Visa, are especially useful if you plan to travel through many countries. Check with your local bank to see if it issues TravelMoney cards. **Road Cash** (US ☎ 877-762-3227; www.roadcash.com) issues cards in the US with a minimum $300 deposit.

GETTING MONEY FROM HOME

AMERICAN EXPRESS. Cardholders can withdraw cash from their checking accounts at any of AmEx's major offices and many representative offices (up to $1000 every 21 days; no service charge, no interest). AmEx "Express Cash" withdrawals from any AmEx ATMs in the USA or Canada are automatically debited from the cardholder's checking account or line of credit. Green card holders may withdraw up to $1000 in any seven-day period (2% transaction fee; minimum $2.50, maximum $20). To enroll in Express Cash, cardmembers should call ☎ 800-227-4669 in the US; outside the US call collect ☎ 336-668-5041.

WESTERN UNION. Travelers from most of the world can wire money to and from their home country or state through Western Union's money transfer services. In the US, call ☎ 800-325-6000; in Canada ☎ 800-235-0000; in the UK ☎ 0800 833 833. To wire money within the US using a credit card, call ☎ 800-225-5227. The rates for sending cash are generally $10-11 cheaper than with a credit card, and the money is usually available at the place you're sending it to within an hour. To find the nearest Western Union location online, consult www.westernunion.com.

FEDERAL EXPRESS. Some people choose to send money internationally or nationally in cash via FedEx to avoid transmission fees and taxes. In the US and Canada, call ☎ 800-463-3339; in the UK ☎ 0800 123 800; in Ireland ☎ 800 535 800; in Australia ☎ 13 26 10; in New Zealand ☎ 0800 733 339; and in South Africa ☎ 021 551 7610. While FedEx is reasonably reliable, note that this method is illegal and somewhat risky.

COSTS

The cost of your trip will vary considerably, depending on where you go, how you travel, and where you stay. The single biggest cost of your trip will probably be your round-trip **airfare** to the USA (see p. 65). On land, **accommodations** start at about $12 per night in a hostel bed, while a basic sit-down meal costs about $10 depending on the region. If you stay in hostels and prepare your own food, you'll probably spend from $30-40 per person per day. A slightly more comfortable day (sleeping in hostels/guesthouses and the occasional budget hotel, eating one meal a day at a restaurant, going out at night) would run US$50-65; for a luxurious day, the sky's the limit. Transportation costs will increase these figures. **Gas** prices have risen significantly in the US over the past year. A gallon of gas now costs about $1.60 per gallon (40¢ per L), but prices vary widely according to state gasoline taxes. In Canada, gas costs CDN60-70¢ per L (CDN$2-2.65 per gallon). Before you go, spend some time calculating a reasonable per-day **budget** to meet your needs. Don't forget to factor in emergency reserve funds (at least $200) when planning how much money you'll need.

TIPS FOR STAYING ON A BUDGET

Considering that saving just a few dollars a day over the course of your trip might pay for days or weeks of additional travel, the art of penny-pinching is well worth learning. Learn to take advantage of freebies: for example, museums will typically be free once a week or once a month, and cities often host free open-air concerts and/or cultural events (especially in the summer). Bring a sleepsack (see p. 49) to save on sheet charges in hostels, and do your **laundry** in the sink (unless you're explicitly prohibited from doing so). You can split **accommodations** costs (in hotels and some hostels) with trustworthy fellow travelers; multi-bed rooms almost always work out cheaper per person than singles. The same principle will also work for cutting down on the cost of **restaurant** meals. You can also buy food in supermarkets instead of eating out; you'd be surprised how tasty (and cheap) simple bread with cheese or spread can be.

 TIPPING AND BARGAINING. In the US, it is customary to tip waitstaff and cab drivers 15-20%, at your discretion. Tips are usually not included in restaurant bills, unless you are in a party of 6 or more. At the airport and in hotels, porters expect at least a $1 per bag tip to carry your bags. Tipping is less compulsory in Canada; a good tip signifies remarkable service. Bargaining is generally frowned upon and fruitless in both countries.

TAXES

In the US, sales tax is similar to the European Value-Added Tax and ranges from 4-10% depending on the item and the place; in many states, groceries are not taxed. *Let's Go* lists sales tax rates in the introduction to each state; usually these taxes are not included in the prices of items.

In Canada, you'll quickly notice the 7% goods and services tax (GST) and an additional sales tax in some provinces. See the provinces' introductions for info on local taxes. Visitors can claim a rebate of the GST they pay on accommodations of less than one month and on most goods they buy and take home, so be sure to save your receipts and pick up a GST rebate form while in Canada. The total claim must be at least CDN$7 of GST (equal to CDN$100 in purchases) and made within one year of the date of the purchase; further goods must be exported from Canada within 60 days of purchase. A brochure detailing restrictions is available from local tourist offices or through Revenue Canada, Visitor's Rebate Program, 275 Pope Rd., Summerside, PEI C1N 6C6 (☎ 902-432-5608 or 800-668-4748).

SAFETY AND SECURITY

Crime is mostly concentrated in the cities, but being safe is a good idea no matter where you are. Washington, D.C.; Newark, NJ; New Orleans, LA; Miami, FL; Atlanta, GA; Los Angeles, CA; Detroit, MI; and St. Louis, MO, are the most dangerous cities in the United States, but that does not mean you should not visit them. Common sense and a little bit of thought will go a long way in helping you to avoid dangerous situations.

EMERGENCY = 911. For emergencies in the US and Canada, dial **911**. This number is toll-free from all phones, including coin phones. In a very few remote communities, 911 may not work. If it does not, dial 0 for the operator and request to be connected with the appropriate emergency service. In national parks, it is usually best to call the **park warden** in case of emergency. *Let's Go* always lists emergency contact numbers.

BLENDING IN. Tourists are particularly vulnerable to crime because they often carry large amounts of cash and are not as street savvy as locals. To avoid unwanted attention, try to blend in as much as possible: leave the fanny pack, pulled-up socks, and weird shoes at home. The gawking camera-toter is a more obvious target than the low-profile traveler. Familiarize yourself with your surroundings before setting out; if you must check a map on the street, duck into a cafe or shop. Also, carry yourself with confidence. If you are traveling alone, remember Little Red Riding Hood: be sure that someone at home knows your itinerary and *never admit that you're traveling alone.*

EXPLORING. Extra vigilance is always wise, but there is no need to panic when exploring a new city or region. Find out about **unsafe areas** from tourist offices, from the manager of your hotel or hostel, or from a local whom you trust. You may want to carry a **whistle** to attract attention, and you must memorize the emergency number of the city or area. Whenever possible, *Let's Go* warns of unsafe neighborhoods and areas, but there are some good general tips to follow.

When walking at night, stick to busy, well-lit streets and avoid dark alleyways. Do not attempt to cross through parks, parking lots, or other large, deserted areas. Buildings in disrepair, vacant lots, and unpopulated areas are all bad signs. The distribution of people can reveal a great deal about the relative safety of the area; look for children playing, women walking in the open, and other signs of an active community. Keep in mind that a district can change character drastically between blocks. If you feel uncomfortable, leave as quickly and directly as you can, but don't allow fear to turn you into a hermit. Careful, persistent exploration will build confidence and make your stay in an area that much more rewarding.

GETTING AROUND. Driving in the US and Canada is generally safe. It is a good idea to drive during the day, because you can get help faster if you run into trouble on the highways, and you can avoid trouble in the city streets at night. Learn local driving signals and wear a seatbelt. Most states require seatbelts by law, and they are proven to save lives in the case of auto accidents. Children under 40 lbs. should only ride in a specially-designed carseat, available for a small fee from most car rental agencies. Study route maps before you hit the road, and, if possible, figure out gas station availability before you set out. (You should have no problem finding stations if you are driving on major roads.) If you plan on spending a lot of time on the road, you may want to bring spare parts. Also, if traveling in the winter, it is a good idea to have a blanket, a shovel, emergency flares, a needle and thread, and some chocolate, in case of getting stuck in a snowstorm. For long drives in desolate areas, invest in a cellular phone and a roadside assistance program (see p. 77). If your car breaks down, wait for the police to assist you. Be sure to park your vehicle in a garage or well-traveled area, and use a steering wheel locking device in larger cities. **Sleeping in your car** is one of the most dangerous (and often illegal) ways to get your rest.

Public transportation across states (buses and trains) is generally safe. Occasionally, the stations that the buses or trains leave you at are dangerous; *Let's Go* warns of these stations where applicable. If possible, avoid using public transportation late at night unless you are in a large group. **Taxis** are oftentimes driven by people who don't speak English, but they are safe.

Let's Go does not recommend **hitchhiking** under any circumstances, particularly for women—see **Getting Around,** p. 80 for more info.

SELF DEFENSE. There is no sure-fire set of precautions that will protect you from all of the situations you might encounter when you travel. A good self-defense course will give you more concrete ways to react to different types of aggression. **Impact, Prepare, and Model Mugging** can refer you to local self-defense courses in the United States (☎ 800-345-5425) and Vancouver, Canada (☎ 604-878-3838). Workshops (2-3hrs.) start at $50 and full courses run $350-500. Both women and men are welcome.

FINANCIAL SECURITY

PROTECTING YOUR VALUABLES. Theft in the US is more rampant in big cities and at night. To prevent easy theft, don't keep all your valuables (money, important documents) in one place. **Photocopies** of important documents allow you to recover them in case they are lost or filched. Carry one copy separate from the documents and leave another copy at home. Label every piece of luggage both inside and out. *Don't put a wallet with money in your back pocket.* Never count your money in public and carry as little as possible—keep some aside in case of an emergency. If you carry a purse, buy a sturdy one with a secure clasp, and carry it crosswise on the side, away from the street with the clasp against you. Secure packs with small combination padlocks which slip through the two zippers. A **money belt** is the best way to carry cash; you can buy one at most camping supply stores. A nylon, zippered pouch with a belt that sits inside the waist of your pants or skirt combines convenience and security. A **neck pouch** is equally safe, although far less accessible and discreet. Valuables in a fanny pack will be stolen.

CON ARTISTS AND PICKPOCKETS. Among the more colorful aspects of large cities are **con artists.** Con artists and hustlers often work in groups, and children are among the most effective. Con artists possess an innumerable range of ruses. Be aware of certain classics: sob stories that require money, rolls of bills "found" on the street, mustard spilled (or saliva spit) onto your shoulder, directions asked—all distracting you for enough time to snatch your bag. Try to rent a car with a phone so you can call the police; be careful when driving, and if you get bumped, be wary. In general, if you are harassed, do not respond or make eye contact, walk away quickly, and keep a solid grip on your belongings. Contact the police if a hustler is particularly insistent or aggressive.

In city crowds and especially on public transportation, **pickpockets** are amazingly deft at their craft. Rush hour is no excuse for strangers to press up against you on the metro. If someone stands uncomfortably close, move to another car and hold your bags tightly. Also, be alert in public telephone booths. If you must say your calling card number, do so very quietly; if you punch it in, make sure no one can look over your shoulder.

ACCOMMODATIONS AND TRANSPORTATION. Never leave your belongings unattended; crime occurs in even the most demure-looking hostel or hotel. If you feel unsafe, look for places with either a curfew or a night attendant. *Let's Go* lists locker availability in hostels and train stations, but you'll need your own **padlock.** Lockers are useful if you plan on sleeping outdoors or don't want to lug everything with you, but don't store valuables in them. Most hotels also provide lock boxes free or for a minimal fee.

Be particularly careful on **buses;** carry your backpack in front of you, avoid checking baggage on trains, and don't trust anyone to "watch your bag for a second." Thieves thrive on **trains;** professionals wait for tourists to fall asleep and then carry off everything they can. When traveling in pairs, sleep in alternating shifts; when alone, use good judgement in selecting a train compartment: never stay in an empty one, and use a lock to secure your pack to the luggage rack. Keep important documents and other valuables on your person.

If you travel by **car,** try not to leave valuable possessions—such as radios or luggage—in it while you are away. If your tape deck or radio is removable, hide it in the trunk or take it with you. If it isn't, at least conceal it under something else. Similarly, hide baggage in the trunk—although savvy thieves can tell if a car is heavily loaded by the way it sits on its tires.

Drivers should take necessary precautions against **carjacking,** which has become one of the most frequent crimes committed in the US. Carjackers, who are usually armed, approach their victims in their vehicles and force them to turn over the automobile. Carjackers prey on cars parked on the side of the road and cars stopped at red lights. If you are going to pull over on the side of the road, keep your doors locked and windows up at all times and do not pull over to help a car in the breakdown lane; call the police instead.

For info on the perils of **hitchhiking,** see p. 80.

DRUGS AND ALCOHOL

In the US, the drinking age is 21; in Canada it is 19, except in Alberta, Manitoba, and Québec, where it is 18. Drinking restrictions are particularly strict in the US; the youthful should expect to be asked to show government-issued identification when purchasing any alcoholic beverage. Drinking and driving is prohibited everywhere, not to mention dangerous and idiotic. Open beverage containers in your car will incur heavy fines; a failed breathalyzer test will mean fines, a suspended license, imprisonment, or all three. Most localities restrict where and when alcohol can be sold under restrictions known as "blue laws." Sales usually stop at a certain time at night and are often prohibited entirely on Sundays.

Narcotics like marijuana, heroin, and cocaine are highly illegal in the US and Canada. If you carry prescription drugs while you travel, it is important that you keep a copy of the prescription with you, especially at border crossings.

HEALTH

Common sense is the simplest prescription for good health. Travelers complain most often about their feet and their gut, so take precautionary measures: drink lots of fluids to prevent dehydration and constipation, wear sturdy, broken-in shoes and clean socks, and use talcum powder to keep your feet dry. To minimize the effects of jet lag, "reset" your body's clock by adopting the time of your destination as soon as you board the plane.

BEFORE YOU GO

Preparation can help minimize the likelihood of contracting a disease and maximize the chances of receiving effective health care in the event of an emergency. For minor health problems, bring a compact **first-aid kit** (see p. 49). In your **passport,** write the names of any people you wish to be contacted in case of a medical emergency and list any **allergies** or medical conditions you would want doctors to be aware of. Allergy sufferers might want to obtain a full supply of any necessary medication before the trip. Matching a prescription to a foreign equivalent is not always easy, safe, or possible. Carry up-to-date, legible prescriptions or a statement from your doctor stating the medication's trade name, manufacturer, chemical name, and dosage. While traveling, be sure to keep all medication with you in your carry-on luggage.

IMMUNIZATIONS AND PRECAUTIONS. Travelers over two years old should be sure that the following vaccines are up to date: MMR (for measles, mumps, and rubella); DTaP or Td (for diptheria, tetanus, and pertussis), OPV (for polio), HbCV (for haemophilus influenza B), and HBV (for hepatitus B).

USEFUL ORGANIZATIONS. The **US Centers for Disease Control and Prevention (CDC)** (877-394-8747; www.cdc.gov/travel), is an excellent source of info for travelers, and maintains an international fax info service. The CDC's comprehensive booklet *Health Information for International Travelers*, an annual rundown of disease, immunization, and general health advice, is free on the website or US$22 via the Government Printing Office (☎202-512-1800). The **US State Department** (http://travel.state.gov) compiles Consular Information Sheets on health, entry requirements, and other issues for various countries. The **British Foreign and Commonwealth Office** also gives health warnings for individual countries (www.fco.gov.uk).

MEDICAL ASSISTANCE ON THE ROAD. Health care in the US and Canada is good. One thing to do before you leave: make sure you have some sort of travel insurance. Medicare (for US citizens in Canada) and most health insurance plans cover members' medical emergencies during trips abroad, but you should check with your insurance carrier to be sure, because you may have to purchase additional coverage (see **Insurance,** p. 47).

ENVIRONMENTAL HAZARDS

HEAT EXHAUSTION AND DEHYDRATION. Heat exhaustion, characterized by dehydration and salt deficiency, can lead to fatigue, headaches, and wooziness. Avoid it by drinking plenty of fluids (enough to keep your urine clear) and eating salty foods. Wear a hat, sunglasses, and a lightweight longsleeve shirt in hot sun, and take time to acclimate to a hot destination before seriously exerting yourself. Continuous heat stress can eventually lead to **heatstroke,** characterized by rising body temperature, severe headache, and cessation of sweating. Heatstroke victims must be cooled off with wet towels and taken to a doctor as soon as possible. The risks of heat exhaustion and dehydration are high in the Southwest and in the desert, because the heat is dry and sweat evaporates very quickly.

HYPOTHERMIA AND FROSTBITE. A rapid drop in body temperature is the clearest warning sign of overexposure to cold. Victims may shiver, feel exhausted, have poor coordination or slurred speech, hallucinate, or suffer amnesia. Seek medical help, and *do not let hypothermia victims fall asleep*—their body temperature will continue to drop and they may die. To avoid hypothermia, keep dry, wear layers, and stay out of the wind. In wet weather, wool and synthetics such as pile retain heat. Most other fabric, especially cotton, will make you colder. When the temperature is below freezing, watch for **frostbite.** If a region of skin turns white, waxy, and cold, do not rub the area. Drink warm beverages, get dry, and slowly warm the area with dry fabric or steady body contact, until a doctor can be found.

HIGH ALTITUDE. Travelers to high altitudes (e.g. the Rocky Mountains) must allow their bodies a couple of days to adjust to lower oxygen levels in the air before exerting themselves. Alcohol is more potent at high elevations.

PREVENTING DISEASE

INSECT-BORNE DISEASES

Many diseases are transmitted by insects—mainly mosquitoes, fleas, ticks, and lice. Be aware of insects in wet or forested areas, while hiking, and especially while camping. Mosquitoes are most active from dusk to dawn. Use insect repellents, such as DEET. Wear long pants and long sleeves (fabric need not be thick or warm; tropic-weight cottons can keep you comfortable in the heat) and buy a mosquito net. Wear shoes and socks, and, if no one can see you, tuck long pants into socks. Wear a hat. Soak or spray your gear with permethrin, which is licensed in the US for use on clothing. Natural repellents can be useful supplements: taking vitamin B-12 pills regularly can repel insects, as can garlic pills. Calamine lotion or topical cortisones (like Cortaid) may stop insect bites from itching, as can a bath with a half-cup of baking soda or oatmeal.

Lyme disease: A bacterial infection carried by ticks, causing a circular bull's-eye rash around the bite, fever, headache, tiredness, and aches and pains. Antibiotics are effective if administered early. Untreated, Lyme can cause problems in joints, the heart, and the nervous system. Take extra care in rural and forested regions to periodically pause while walking to brush off ticks using a fine-toothed comb on your neck and scalp. Do not try to remove ticks by burning them or coating them with nail polish remover or petroleum jelly. If you find a tick attached to your skin, grasp the tick's head parts with tweezers as close to your skin as possible and apply slow, steady traction. Removing a tick within 24 hours greatly reduces risk of infection.

FOOD- AND WATER-BORNE DISEASES

Travelers in the US and Canada experience food- and water-related illness much less often than in most parts of the world, thanks to good water-treatment facilities and fairly well-maintained restaurant standards. The tap water in the US and Canada is treated to be safe for drinking.

Traveler's diarrhea: A temporary (and fairly common) reaction to the bacteria in unfamiliar water and food ingredients. Symptoms include nausea, bloating, urgency, and malaise. Try quick-energy, non-sugary foods with protein and carbohydrates to keep your strength up and plenty of water and electrolytes to avoid dehydration.

Parasites: Giardiasis is present in the untreated water from streams or lakes and causes a very uncomfortable and difficult to treat intestinal disease. Drink only tap water, including public water fountains and campground pumps. If you are backpacking, carry water with you or use a water filter.

AIDS, HIV, STDS

Acquired Immune Deficiency Syndrome (AIDS) is a growing problem around the world. The World Health Organization estimates that there are 30 million people infected with HIV, and women now comprise 40% of all new infections. In recent years, however, the spread of the disease has been markedly curbed in the US. The easiest mode of HIV transmission is through direct blood-to-blood contact with an HIV positive person; *never* share intravenous drug, tattooing, or other needles. A more common mode of transmission is sexual intercourse: wear a rubber.

For more info on AIDS, call the **US Center for Disease Control's** 24-hour hotline at ☎ 800-342-2437, or contact the **Joint United Nations Programme on HIV/AIDS (UNAIDS),** 20 av. Appia 20, CH-1211 Geneva 27, Switzerland (☎ 41 22 791 36 66, fax 791 41 87). Council's brochure, *Travel Safe: AIDS and International Travel*, is available at all Council Travel offices and on their website (www.ciee.org/Isp/safety/travelsafe.htm). If you are **HIV positive,** contact the Bureau of Consular Affairs, #4811, Department of State, Washington, D.C. 20520 (☎ 202-647-1488; auto-fax 647-3000; http://travel.state.gov). According to US law, HIV positive persons are not permitted to enter the US. However, HIV testing is conducted only for those who are planning to immigrate permanently. Travelers from areas with particularly high concentrations of HIV positive persons or persons with AIDS may be required to provide more info when applying. Travelers to Canada who are suspected of being HIV positive will be required to submit to HIV testing.

Sexually transmitted diseases (STDs) such as gonorrhea, chlamydia, genital warts, syphilis, and herpes are easier to catch than HIV, and some can be just as deadly. **Hepatitis B** and **C** are also serious sexually-transmitted diseases. Warning signs for STDs include: swelling, sores, bumps, or blisters on sex organs, rectum, or mouth; burning and pain during urination and bowel movements; itching around sex organs; swelling or redness in the throat; flu-like symptoms with fever, chills, and aches. If these symptoms develop, see a doctor immediately. When having sex, condoms may protect you from certain STDs, but oral or even tactile contact can lead to transmission.

INSURANCE

Travel insurance generally covers four basic areas: medical/health problems, property loss, trip cancellation/interruption, and emergency evacuation. Although your regular insurance policies may well extend to travel-related accidents, you may consider purchasing travel insurance if the cost of potential trip cancellation/interruption is greater than you can absorb.

Medical insurance (especially university policies) often covers costs incurred abroad; check with your provider. Medicare covers travel to Canada. Canadians are protected by their home province's health insurance plan for up to 90 days after leaving the country; check with the provincial Ministry of Health or Health Plan Headquarters for details. **Homeowners' insurance** (or your family's coverage) often covers theft during travel and loss of travel documents (passport, plane ticket, railpass, etc.) up to $500.

ISIC and **ITIC** provide basic insurance benefits, including $100 per day of in-hospital sickness for a maximum of 60 days, $3000 of accident-related medical reimbursement, and $25,000 for emergency medical transport (see **Identification,** p. 36). Cardholders have access to a toll-free 24-hour helpline whose multilingual staff can provide assistance in medical, legal, and financial emergencies overseas (US and Canada ☎877-370-4742, elsewhere call the US collect 713-342-4104.) **American Express** (☎800-528-4800) grants most cardholders automatic car rental insurance (collision and theft, but not liability) and ground travel accident coverage of $100,000 on flight purchases made with the card.

Prices for travel insurance purchased separately generally run about $50 per week for full coverage, while trip cancellation/interruption may be purchased separately at a rate of about $5.50 per $100 of coverage.

INSURANCE PROVIDERS. Council and **STA** (see p. 65) offer a range of plans to supplement insurance coverage. Other private insurance providers in the **US** and **Canada** include: **Access America** (☎800-284-8300; fax 804-673-1491); **Berkely Group/Carefree Travel Insurance** (☎800-323-3149 or 516-294-0220; fax 516-294-1095; email info@berkely.com; www.berkely.com); **Globalcare Travel Insurance** (☎800-821-2488; fax 781-592-7720; www.globalcare-cocco.com); and **Travel Assistance International** (☎800-821-2828 or 202-828-5894; fax 202-828-5896; email wassist@aol.com; www.worldwide-assistance.com). Providers in the **UK** include **Campus Travel** (☎01865 258 000; fax 792 378) and **Columbus Travel Insurance** (☎020 7375 0011; fax 375 0022). In **Australia,** try **CIC Insurance** (☎02 9202 8000; fax 9202 8220).

PACKING

Pack according to the extremes of climate you may experience and the type of travel you'll be doing. **Pack light:** a good rule is to lay out only what you absolutely need, then take half the clothes and twice the money. The less you have, the less you have to lose (or store, or carry on your back). Don't forget the obvious things: no matter when you're traveling, it's always a good idea to bring a rain jacket (Gore-Tex is a miracle fabric that's both waterproof and breathable), a warm jacket or wool sweater, and sturdy shoes and thick socks. You may also want to add one outfit beyond the jeans and t-shirt uniform, a collared shirt and a nicer pair of shoes if you have the room. Remember that wool will keep you warm even when soaked through, whereas wet cotton is colder than wearing nothing at all.

NEW CENTRAL HOSTEL

250-bed hostel open all year
bunks and large doubles with regular mattresses • 4 beds per room, private
rooms smoking and nonsmoking rooms

$17*

*per night (depending on bed and season)
travelers' check, VISA, MasterCard accepted
passport and travel documents requested • no membership required

pillows with cases, sheets and blankets provided
laundry • full kitchen
fax service • locker and safety deposit boxes

Check in: 24 hours a day • Check out: by 11 a.m.
No curfew • Parties / social activities

NEW CENTRAL HOSTEL
1412 Market Street
San Francisco, CA 94102
(415) 703-9988
Fax: (415) 703-9986

ï **Shared Accommodations**
ï **Double Rooms**
ï **Private Rooms**
ï **Free linen, kitchen**
ï **Weekly Rates**

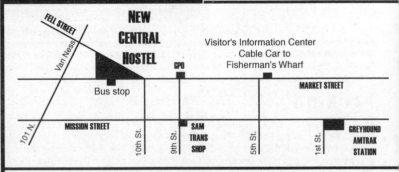

Transportation: city bus stops at front door
Attractions: Fisherman's Wharf, Haight-Ashbury, Union Square, Civic Center,
Golden Gate Bridge and Park, Alcatraz, Cable Cars, restaurants, shopping,
major museums and art galleries, bars, pubs and clubs

Visitor's Information Center, Post Office, hospital and downtown areas are all
within walking distance

SLEEPSACKS. Some youth hostels require that you have your own sleepsack or rent one of theirs. If you plan to stay in hostels you can avoid linen charges by making the requisite sleepsack yourself: fold a full size sheet in half the long way, then sew it closed along the open long side and one of the short sides. Sleepsacks can also be bought at any Hostelling International store.

WASHING CLOTHES. Laundromats are common in North America, but it may be cheaper and easier to use a sink. Bring a small bar or tube of detergent soap, a small rubber ball to stop up the sink, and a travel clothes-line.

CONVERTERS AND ADAPTERS. In the USA and Canada, electricity is 110V. 220V electrical appliances don't like 110V current. Visit a hardware store for an adapter (which changes the shape of the plug) and a converter (which changes the voltage). Don't make the mistake of using only an adapter (unless appliance instructions explicitly state otherwise).

TOILETRIES. Toothbrushes, towels, cold-water soap, talcum powder (to keep feet dry), deodorant, razors, tampons, and condoms are readily available. **Contact lenses,** on the other hand, can be expensive, so bring enough extra pairs and solution for your entire trip. Machines which heat-disinfect contact lenses will require a small converter (about $20) to 110V; consider switching temporarily to a chemical disinfection system. Also bring your glasses and a copy of your prescription in case you need emergency replacements.

FILM. If you're not a serious photographer, you might want to consider bringing a **disposable camera** or two rather than an expensive permanent one. Despite disclaimers, airport security X-rays *can* fog film, so either buy a lead-lined pouch, sold at camera stores, or ask the security to hand inspect it. Always pack it in your carry-on luggage, since higher-intensity X-rays are used on checked luggage.

FIRST-AID KIT. No matter how you're traveling, it's always a good idea to carry a first-aid kit including bandages, aspirin or another pain killer, antibiotic cream, a thermometer, a Swiss army knife with tweezers, moleskin, decongestant for colds, motion sickness remedy, medicine for diarrhea or stomach problems (antacid and Immodium), sunscreen, insect repellent (you might want to get an extra-strength repellent if you plan on camping), burn ointment, and a syringe for emergency medical purposes (get a letter of explanation from your doctor).

OTHER USEFUL ITEMS. Other useful items include: an umbrella; sealable plastic bags (for damp clothes, soap, food, shampoo, and other spillables); alarm clock; waterproof matches; sun hat; needle and thread; safety pins; sunglasses; pocketknife; plastic water bottle; compass; rope (makeshift clothesline and lashing material); towel; padlock; rubber bands; flashlight; cold-water soap; earplugs; electrical tape (for patching tears); tweezers; garbage bags; a small calculator for currency conversion; a pair of flip-flops for the shower; a money-belt for carrying valuables.

IMPORTANT DOCUMENTS. Don't forget your passport, traveler's checks, ATM and/or credit cards, and adequate ID (see p. 36). Also check that you have a hostelling membership card (see p. 51) and a driver's license (see p. 76), if you need them.

ACCOMMODATIONS

HOTELS

Hotel rooms in the US vary widely in cost depending on the region in which the hotel is located. The cheapest hotel single in the Northeast would run about $60 per night, while it is possible to stay for $30 a night in a comparable hotel in the South, West, or Midwest regions. The most reliable national budget chains include Motel 6, Super 8, and Econolodge.

Hotels tend to be more expensive with proximity to tourist attractions or cities. The best bargains are usually located on the outskirts of a city, typically on a busy road such as an interstate. Almost all hotels in the US take reservations, and for busy seasons they are highly recommended. Note that busy seasons can also mean an increase in the average price for any available hotel room.

HOTEL CHAIN	TELEPHONE	La Quinta Inn	☎800-531-5900
Best Western	☎800-528-1234	Motel 6	☎800-891-6161
Comfort Inn	☎800-221-2222	Ramada Inn	☎800-272-6232
Days Inn	☎800-325-2525	Red Carpet Inn	☎800-251-1962
Econo Lodge	☎800-446-6900	Select Inn	☎800-641-1000
Embassy Suites Hotel	☎800-362-2779	Sleep Inn	☎800-221-2222
Hampton Inn	☎800-426-7866	Super 8 Motel	☎800-800-8000
Hilton Hotel	☎800-445-8667	Travelodge	☎800-255-3050
Holiday Inn	☎800-465-4329	YMCA	☎800-922-9622
Howard Johnson	☎800-654-2000		

ESSENTIALS

HOSTELS

Hostels are generally dorm-style accommodations, often in single-sex large rooms with bunk beds, although some hostels do offer private rooms for families and couples. They sometimes have kitchens and utensils for your use, bike or moped rentals, storage areas, and laundry facilities. There can be drawbacks: some hostels close during certain daytime "lock-out" hours, have a curfew, don't accept reservations, impose a maximum stay, or, less frequently, require that you do chores. In the USA and Canada, a bed in a hostel will average around $15.

For their various services and lower rates at member hostels, hostelling associations, especially **Hostelling International (HI),** can definitely be worth joining. HI hostels are scattered throughout both countries, and many accept reservations via the International Booking Network (☎02 9261 1111 from Australia, ☎800-663-5777 from Canada, ☎1629 58 14 18 from England and Wales, ☎1232 32 47 33 from Northern Ireland, ☎01 830 1766 from the Republic of Ireland, ☎09 379 4224 from New Zealand, ☎541 55 32 55 from Scotland, and ☎800-909-4776 from the US; www.hiayh.org/ushostel/reserva/ibn3.htm) for a nominal fee. HI's umbrella organization's web page lists the web addresses and phone numbers of all national associations and can be a great place to begin researching hostelling in a specific region (www.iyhf.org). Other comprehensive hostelling websites include www.hostels.com. To join HI, contact one of the following organizations:

Australian Youth Hostels Association (AYHA), 422 Kent St., Sydney NSW 2000 (☎02 9261 1111; fax 9261 1969; www.yha.org.au). One-year membership AUS$49, under 18 AUS$14.50.

Hostelling International-Canada (HI-C), 400-205 Catherine St., Ottawa, ON K2P 1C3 (☎613-237-7884 or 800-663-5777; fax 237-7868; email info@hostellingintl.ca; www.hostellingintl.ca). CDN$25, under 18 CDN$12.

An Óige (Irish Youth Hostel Association), 61 Mountjoy St., Dublin 7 (☎1 830 4555; fax 830 5808; email anoige@iol.ie; www.irelandyha.org). IR£10, under 18 IR£4, families IR£20.

Youth Hostels Association of New Zealand (YHANZ), P.O. Box 436, 173 Cashel St., Christchurch 1 (☎03 379 9970; fax 365 4476; email info@yha.org.nz; www.yha.org.nz). NZ$40, ages 15-17 NZ$12, under 15 free.

Hostels Association of South Africa, 3rd fl. 73 St. George's St. Mall, P.O. Box 4402, Cape Town 8000 (☎021 424 2511; fax 424 4119; email info@hisa.org.za; www.hisa.org.za). ZAR55, under 18 ZAR30, lifetime ZAR250.

Scottish Youth Hostels Association (SYHA), 7 Glebe Crescent, Stirling FK8 2JA (☎01786 89 14 00; fax 89 13 33; www.syha.org.uk). UK£6, under 18 UK£2.50.

Youth Hostels Association (England and Wales) Ltd., Trevelyan House, 8 St. Stephen's Hill, St. Albans, Hertfordshire AL1 2DY, UK (☎01727 85 52 15; fax 84 41 26; www.yha.org.uk). UK£12, under 18 UK£6, families UK£24.

Hostelling International Northern Ireland (HINI), 22-32 Donegall Rd., Belfast BT12 5JN, Northern Ireland (☎01232 32 47 33; fax 43 96 99; email info@hini.org.uk; www.hini.org.uk). UK£7, under 18 UK£3, families UK£14.

Hostelling International-American Youth Hostels (HI-AYH), 733 15th St. NW, #840, Washington, D.C. 20005 (☎202-783-6161 ext. 136; fax 783-6171; email hiayh-serv@hiayh.org; www.hiayh.org). $25, under 18 free, over 55 $15.

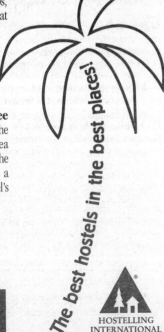
ESSENTIALS

BED AND BREAKFASTS

For a cozy alternative to hotel rooms, B&Bs (private homes with rooms available to travelers) range from the acceptable to the sublime. Hosts will sometimes go out of their way to be accommodating by accepting travelers with pets, giving personalized tours, or offering home-cooked meals. On the other hand, many B&Bs do not provide phones, TVs, or private bathrooms. Rooms in B&Bs generally cost $50-70 for a single and $70-90 for a double. For more info see Nerd World's Bed and Breakfasts by Region (www.nerdworld.com/users/dstein/nw854) or try **Bed & Breakfast Central Information (BBCI)**, P.O. Box 38279, Colorado Springs, CO 80937 (fax 719-471-4740; email bbci@bbonline.com; www.bbonline.com/bbci). The National Network of Bed and Breakfast Reservations Services (TNN) provides links to booking agencies for each US state and certain regions of Canada (www.go-lodging.com).

YMCA AND YWCAS

Not all **Young Men's Christian Association (YMCA)** locations offer lodging; those that do are often located in urban downtowns, which can be convenient but a little gritty. YMCA rates are usually lower than a hotel's but higher than a hostel's and may include TV, air conditioning, pools, gyms, access to public transportation, tourist info, safe deposit boxes, luggage storage, daily housekeeping, multilingual staff, and 24-hour security. Many YMCAs accept women and families (group rates often available), and some will not lodge people under 18 without parental permission. There are several ways to make a reservation, all of which must be made at least two weeks in advance and paid for in advance with a traveler's check, US money order, certified check, Visa, or Mastercard in US dollars.

YMCA of the USA, 101 North Wacker Drive, Chicago, IL 60606 (☎800-872-9622; fax 312-977-9063; www.ymca.net). A listing of the nearly 2400 Y's across the US and info on prices, phone numbers and addresses, but no reservation service.

YMCA Canada, 42 Charles St. 6th flr., Toronto ON M4Y 1T4 (☎416-967-9622; fax 967-9618; email sevices@ymca.ca; www.ymca.ca), offers info on Ys throughout Canada.

YWCA of the USA, Empire State Building, 350 Fifth Avenue #301, New York, NY 10118 (☎212-273-7800; fax 465-2281; www.ywca.org). Publishes a directory ($8) on YWCAs across the USA.

DORMS

Many **colleges and universities** open their residence halls to travelers when school is not in session (May-Sept.)—some do so even during term-time. These dorms are often close to student areas—good sources for info on things to do—and are usually very clean. Getting a room may take a couple of phone calls and require advanced planning, but rates tend to be low, and many offer free local calls. *Let's Go* lists colleges which rent dorm rooms among accommodations listings.

HOME EXCHANGES AND HOME RENTALS

Home exchange offers the traveler various types of homes (houses, apartments, condominiums), plus the opportunity to live like a native and to cut down on accommodation fees. For more info, contact **HomeExchange.Com** (☎805-898-9660; www.homeexchange.com), **Intervac International Home Exchange** (☎800-756-4663, www.intervac.com), or **The Invented City: International Home Exchange** (US ☎800-788-2489, elsewhere call ☎415-252-1141; www.aitec.edu.au/~bwechner/Documents/Travel/Lists/HomeExchangeClubs.html). Home rentals are more expensive than exchanges, but they can be cheaper than comparable hotels. Both home exchanges and rentals are ideal for families with children, or travelers with special dietary needs; you often get your own kitchen, maid service, TV, and telephones.

FURTHER READING: ACCOMMODATIONS

Campus Lodging Guide (18th Ed.). B&J Publications ($15).

The Complete Guide to Bed and Breakfasts, Inns and Guesthouses in the US, Canada, and Worldwide, Pamela Lanier. Ten Speed Press ($17).

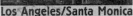

CAMPING AND THE OUTDOORS

Camping is probably the most rewarding way to slash travel costs. Considering the sheer number of public lands available for camping in both the United States and Canada, it may also be the most convenient option. Well-equipped campsites (usually including prepared tent sites, toilets, and water) go for $5-20 per night in the US and CDN$10-30 in Canada. **Backcountry camping,** which lacks all of the above amenities, is often free, but can cost up to $20 at some national parks. In general, the more popular the wilderness region, the better-equipped and the more expensive the campsites. Most campsites are first come first served, though a few accept reservations, usually for a small fee. Outside of national parks, the ubiquitous **Kampgrounds of America (KOA)** offer a ritzy kamping experience at a premium. All of the comforts of home go for about $20-30 a night for a tent site. It is not legal or safe to camp on the side of the road, even on public lands; *Let's Go* lists areas where dispersed roadside camping is permitted.

NATIONAL PARKS

National Parks protect some of the most spectacular scenery in North America (see p. 3). Though their primary purpose is preservation, the parks also host recreational activities such as ranger talks, guided hikes, marked trails, skiing, and snowshoe expeditions. For info, contact the **National Park Service,** Office of Public Inquiries, 1849 C St. NW, #1013, Washington, D.C. 20240 (☎202-208-4747). The slick and informative webpage (www.nps.gov) lists info on all the parks, detailed maps, and fee and reservation data. The **National Park Foundation,** 1101 17th St. NW, #1102, Washington, D.C. 20066 (☎202-785-4500) distributes *The Complete Guide to America's National Parks* by mail-order ($16, plus $3 shipping); a guide to national parks is available online at www.nationalparks.org.

Entrance fees vary. The larger and more popular parks charge a $4-20 entry fee for cars and sometimes a $2-7 fee for pedestrians and cyclists. The **National Parks Pass** ($50), available at park entrances, allows the passport-holder's party entry into all national parks for one year. National Parks Passes can also be bought by writing to National Parks Pass, 27540 Ave. Mentry Valencia, CA 91355 (send $50 plus $3.95 shipping and handling) or on the National Parks Service website. For an additional $15, the Parks Service will affix a **Golden Eagle Passport** hologram to your card, which will allow you access to sites managed by the US Fish and Wildlife Service, the US Forest Service, and the Bureau of Land Management. US citizens or residents 62 and over qualify for the lifetime **Golden Age Passport** ($10 one-time fee), which entitles the holder's party to free park entry, a 50% discount on camping, and 50% reductions on various recreational fees for the passport holder. Persons eligible for federal benefits on account of disabilities can enjoy the same privileges with the **Golden Access Passport** (free). Golden Age and Golden Access Passports must be purchased at a park entrance with proof of age or federal eligibility, respectively. All passports (not the Parks Pass) are also valid at National Monuments, Forests, Wildlife Preserves, and other national recreation sites.

Most national parks have both backcountry and developed **camping;** some welcome RVs, and a few offer grand lodges. At the more popular parks in the US and Canada, reservations are essential, available through MISTIX (☎619-452-8787 or 800-365-2267; reservations.nps.gov) no more than five months in advance. Indoor accommodations should be reserved months in advance. Campgrounds often observe first come, first served policies, and many fill up by late morning. Some limit your stay and/or the number of people in a group.

NATIONAL FORESTS

Often less accessible and less crowded, **US National Forests** (www.fs.fed.us) are a purist's alternative to parks. While some have recreation facilities, most are equipped only for primitive camping—pit toilets and no water are the norm. Entrance fees, when charged, are $10-20, but camping is generally free or $3-4. Some specially designated wilderness areas have regulations barring all vehicles. Neces-

FACTS FOR THE TRAVELER

ESSENTIALS

HOSTELLING INTERNATIONAL
choose the EAST COAST

Hostelling International-Boston
is located downtown in the Fenway. This hostel is close to Boston's best museums, restaurants, and night spots, and only two blocks from the subway. At the hostel, you'll find special activities offered every day, including walking tours, trips to baseball games and more.

Open 24 hours
12 Hemenway Street
Boston, Massachusetts 02115
For toll-free reservations
within the U.S. call
800-909-4776, code 07
Telephone: 617-536-9455

From $24-26 a night!

Hostelling International-New York is located on Manhattan's Upper West Side. This hostel is just a block from the subway, and close to Central Park and Columbia University. The hostel also offers special tours and activities, a coffee bar, a cafeteria and more.

Open 24 hours
891 Amsterdam Avenue
New York, NY 10025
For toll-free reservations
within the U.S. call
800-909-4776, code 01
Telephone: 212-932-2300

From $27-29 a night!

Hostelling International-Washington, D.C.,
is near the White House, Smithsonian Museums and the Metro rail system - a capital location! The hostel offers tours, movies, concert trips, and other special programs year-round.

Open 24 hours.
1009 11th Street, N.W.
Washington, D.C. 20001
For toll-free reservations
within the U.S. call
800-909-4776, code 04
Telephone: 202-737-2333

From $22-25 a night!

The best hostels in the best places – see it all!

Quality downtown accommodations!
www.hiayh.org

HOSTELLING INTERNATIONAL

sary wilderness permits for backpackers can be obtained at the US Forest Service field office in the area. If you are interested in exploring a National Forest, *The Guide to Your National Forests* is available at all Forest Service branches, or call or write the main office (USDA, Forest Service, Office of Communications, Sydney R. Yates Building, 201 14th St. SW, Washington, D.C. 20090; ☎202-205-0957; fax 205-0885). This booklet includes a list of all national forest addresses; request maps and other info directly from the forest(s) you plan to visit. Reservations, with a one-time $16.50 service fee, are available for most forests, but are usually unnecessary except during high season at the more popular sites. Write or call up to one year in advance to National Recreation Reservation Center, P.O. Box 900, Cumberland, MD 21501-0900 (☎518-885-3639 or 800-280-2267; fax 301-722-9802; www.reserveusa.com).

CANADA'S NATIONAL PARKS

Less trammeled than their southern counterparts, these parks boast at least as much natural splendor. Park entrance fees range from CDN$3-7 per person, with family and multi-day passes available. Reservations are offered for a limited number of campgrounds with a CDN$7 fee. For these reservations, or for info on the over 40 parks and countless historical sites in the network, call **Parks Canada**, 25 Edy St., Hull, QC, Canada KIA OM5 (☎888-773-8888 for trip planning info), or consult the useful webpage (http://parkscanada.pch.gc.ca). A patchwork of regional passes are available at relevant parks; the best is the Western Canada Pass, which covers admission to all the parks in the Western provinces for a year (CDN$35 per adult, CDN$70 per group— up to seven people).

WILDERNESS SAFETY

Stay warm, stay dry, and stay hydrated. The vast majority of life-threatening wilderness situations result from a breach of this simple dictum. On any hike, however brief, you should pack enough equipment to keep you alive should disaster befall. This includes **raingear, hat** and **mittens, a first-aid kit, a reflector, a whistle, high energy food,** and extra **water.** Dress in warm layers of **synthetic materials** designed for the outdoors, or **wool.** Fleece jackets and Gore-Tex raingear are excellent choices. Never rely on **cotton** for warmth, unless you're after that inner warmth that comes from wearing "the fabric of our lives." In the wild, this "death cloth" will be absolutely useless should it get wet. Weather can change suddenly anywhere on that continent. Check **weather forecasts** and pay attention to the skies when hiking.

Whenever possible, let someone know when and where you are hiking, either a friend, your hostel, a park ranger, or a local hiking organization. If you are hiking in an area which might be frequented by bears, ask local rangers for info on bear behavior before entering any park or wilderness area, and obey posted warnings.

CAMPERS AND RVS

Much to the chagrin of more purist outdoorspeople, the US and Canada are havens for the corpulent, home-and-stove on wheels known as "**recreational vehicles**" **(RVs).** Most national parks and small towns cater to RV travelers, providing campgrounds with large parking areas and electric outlets ("full hook-up"). Especially for older travelers or families, RVs can be a convenient way to view the continent without sacrificing independence, mobility, and creature comforts.

Renting an RV will always be more expensive than tenting or hostelling, but the costs compare favorably with the price of staying in hotels and renting a car (see **Rental Cars,** p. 80), and the convenience of bringing along your own bedroom, bathroom, and kitchen makes it an attractive option.

ORGANIZED ADVENTURE TRIPS

Organized adventure tours offer another way of exploring the wild. Activities include hiking, biking, skiing, canoeing, kayaking, rafting, climbing, photo safaris, and archaeological digs. Consult tourism bureaus, which can suggest parks, trails, and outfitters. Other good sources for organized adventure options are the stores

ENVIRONMENTALLY RESPONSIBLE TOURISM. The idea behind responsible tourism is to leave no trace of human presence behind. A campstove is the safer (and more efficient) way to cook than using vegetation, but if you must make a fire, keep it small and use only dead branches or brush rather than cutting vegetation. Make sure your campsite is at least 150 ft. (50m) from water supplies or bodies of water. If there are no toilet facilities, bury human waste (but not paper) at least four inches (10cm) deep and above the high-water line, and 150 ft. or more from any water supplies and campsites. Always pack your trash in a plastic bag and carry it with you until you reach the next trash receptacle. For more info on these issues, contact one of the organizations listed below.

Earthwatch, 680 Mt. Auburn St., Box 403, Watertown, MA 02272, USA (☎617-776-0188; email info@earthwatch.org; www.earthwatch.org).

Ecotourism Society, P.O. Box 755, North Bennington, VT 05257, USA (☎802-447-2121; email ecomail@ecotourism.org; www.ecotourism.org/tesinfo.html).

EcoTravel Center: www.ecotour.com.

National Audobon Society, Nature Odysseys, 700 Broadway, New York, NY 10003 (☎212-979-3066; email travel@audobon.org; www.audobon.org).

Tourism Concern, Stapleton House, 277-281 Holloway Rd., London N7 8HN, UK (☎020 7753 3330; www.gn.apc.org/tourismconcern).

and organizations specializing in camping and outdoor equipment listed above. Sales reps at REI, EMS, or Sierra often know of a range of cheap, convenient trips. They may give training programs for people who want to have an independent trip.

Specialty Travel Index, 305 San Anselmo Ave., #313, San Anselmo, CA 94960 (☎800-442-4922; www.specialtytravel.com) is a directory listing hundreds of tour operators worldwide.

The Sierra Club, 85 Second St., Second Floor, San Franciso, CA 94105 (email national.outings@sierraclub.org; www.sierraclub.org/outings) plans many adventure outings at all of its branches throughout Canada and the US.

TrekAmerica, P.O. Box 189, Rockaway, NJ 07866 (☎973-983-1144 or 800-221-0596; www.trekamerica.com) operates small group adventure tours throughout the US, including Alaska, Hawaii, and Canada. Tours are for 18- to 38-year olds and run 1-9 weeks.

Roadrunner Hostelling Treks, 9741 Canoga Ave., Chatsworth, CA 91311 (☎800-873-5872 or ☎44 1892 51 27 00 in Europe and the UK; www.americanadventures.com) offers inexpensive guided trips (maximum 13 travelers) in the US and Canada which include hostel stays.

USEFUL PUBLICATIONS AND WEB RESOURCES

A variety of publishing companies offer hiking guidebooks to meet the educational needs of novice or expert. For info about camping, hiking, and biking, write or call the publishers listed below to receive a free catalogue.

Sierra Club Books, 85 Second St. 2nd fl., San Francisco, CA 94105-3441 (☎415-977-5500; www.sierraclub.org/books). Books on many national parks and several series on different regions of the US, all with an adventurous bent.

The Mountaineers Books, 1001 SW Klickitat Way, #201, Seattle, WA 98134 (☎206-223-6303 or 800-553-4453; www.mountaineers.org). Over 400 titles on hiking (the *100 Hikes* series), biking, mountaineering, natural history, and conservation.

Wilderness Press, 1200 Fifth St., Berkeley, CA 94704 (☎510-558-1666; www.wildernesspress.com). Over 100 hiking guides and maps for the western US including *Backpacking Basics* ($10), as well as guides to New England and Minnesota.

Woodall Publications Corporation, 13975 W. Polo Trail Dr., Lake Forest, IL 60045 (☎847-362-6700 or 800-323-9076; www.woodalls.com). Covering the US and Canada, Woodall publishes the annually updated *Woodall's Campground Directory* ($22) and *Woodall's Plan-it, Pack-it, Go!: Great Places to Tent, Fun Things To Do* ($13).

For topographical maps of Canada, write the **Center for Topographic Information,** Canada Map Office, 130 Bentley Ave., Nepean, ON K1A 0E9 (☎613-952-7000 or 800-465-6277; http://maps.NRCan.gc.ca). In the US, contact the **US Geological Survey Information Services,** Box 25286, Denver CO 80225 (☎800-435-7627; http://mapping.usgs.gov/mac/findmaps.html).

KEEPING IN TOUCH

MAIL

SENDING MAIL TO THE US AND CANADA

Envelopes should be marked "air mail" or "par avion" to avoid having letters sent by sea.

Australia: Allow 4-6 work days for regular **airmail** to the US; 5-7 work days to Canada. Postcards cost AUS$1; letters up to 50g cost AUS$1.50; packages up to ½kg AUS$11.50, up to 2kg AUS$40. **EMS** can get a letter to the US or Canada in 2-5 work days for AUS$30. www.auspost.com.au/pac.

Ireland: Allow 4-6 work days for regular airmail to the US and Canada. Postcards and letters up to 25g cost IR£0.45. Add IR£2.30 for Swiftpost International. www.anpost.ie.

New Zealand: Allow 4-10 work days for regular airmail to the US and Canada. Postcards NZ$1.10. Letters up to 200g cost NZ$1.50-5; small parcels up to 0.5kg NZ$11.80, up to 2kg NZ$35.80. www.nzpost.co.nz/nzpost/inrates.

UK: Allow 4-6 work days for airmail to the US and Canada. Letters up to 20g cost UK£0.65; packages up to 0.5kg UK£4.55, up to 2kg UK£17.30. UK Swiftair delivers letters a day faster for UK£2.85 more. www.royalmail.co.uk/calculator.

Additionally, **Federal Express** (Australia ☎13 26 10; US and Canada ☎800-247-4747; New Zealand ☎0800 73 33 39; UK tel. ☎0800 12 38 00; www.fedex.com) handles express mail services from most of the above countries to the US and Canada.

RECEIVING MAIL

General Delivery: Mail can be sent to the USA through **General Delivery** to almost any city or town with a post office. Address letters to:

Elvis PRESLEY
General Delivery
Post Office Street Address
Memphis, TN 38101 or VICTORIA, BC V8W 1L0
USA or Canada.

The mail will go to a special desk in the central post office, unless you specify a post office by street address or postal code. As a rule, it is best to use the largest post office in the area, and mail may be sent there regardless of what is written on the envelope. It is usually safer and quicker to send mail express or registered. When picking up your mail, bring a form of photo ID, preferably a passport. There is generally no surcharge; if there is a charge, it generally does not exceed the cost of domestic postage. If the clerks insist that there is nothing for you, have them check under your first name as well. *Let's Go* lists post offices in the **Practical Information** section for each city and most towns.

American Express: AmEx's travel offices throughout the world will act as a mail service for cardholders if you contact them in advance. Under this free **Client Letter Service,** they will hold mail for up to 30 days and forward upon request. Address the letter in the same way shown above. Some offices will offer these services to non-cardholders (especially those who have purchased AmEx Travelers Cheques), but you must call ahead to make sure. A complete list is available free from AmEx (☎800-528-4800).

SENDING MAIL HOME FROM THE USA AND CANADA

Aerogrammes, printed sheets that fold into envelopes and travel via airmail, are available at post offices. It helps to mark "airmail," though "par avion" is universally understood. Most post offices will charge exorbitant fees or simply refuse to

send aerogrammes with enclosures. Airmail from the USA averages 4 to 7 work days, although times are more unpredictable from smaller towns. The cost is 60¢; a simple postcard is 55¢. A **standard letter** can be sent to abroad in about 4-7 work days for $1. For packages up to 4lbs., use **Global Priority Mail,** for delivery to major locations in 3-5 work days for a flat-rate ($5).

If regular airmail is too slow, **Federal Express** (US ☎800-247-4747) can get a letter from New York to Sydney in 2 work days for a whopping $30. By **US Express Mail,** a letter would arrive within 4 work days and would cost $15.

Surface mail is by far the cheapest and slowest way to send mail. It takes one to three months to cross the Atlantic and two to four to cross the Pacific—appropriate for sending large quantities of items you won't need to see for a while. When ordering books and materials from abroad, always include one or two **International Reply Coupons (IRCs)**—a way of providing the postage to cover delivery. IRCs should be available from your local post office and those abroad ($1.05).

TELEPHONES

PLACING INTERNATIONAL CALLS. To call the US or Canada from home or to place an international call from the US or Canada, dial:
1. The **international dialing prefix.** To dial out of **Australia,** dial 0011; the **Republic of Ireland, New Zealand,** or the **UK,** 00; **South Africa,** 09; **Canada** or the **US,** 011.
2. The **country code** of the country you want to call. To call **Australia,** dial 61; the **Republic of Ireland,** 353; **New Zealand,** 64; **South Africa,** 27; the **UK,** 44; **Canada** or the **US,** 1.
3. The **city** or **area code.** *Let's Go* lists the area codes for cities and towns next to the city or town name.
4. The **local number.**

CALLING HOME FROM CANADA AND THE USA

A **calling card** is probably your best and cheapest bet. Calls are billed either collect or to your account. **MCI WorldPhone** also provides access to MCI's Traveler's Assist, which gives legal and medical advice, exchange rate info, and translation services. Other phone companies provide similar services to travelers. **To obtain a calling card** from your national telecommunications service before you leave home, contact the appropriate company below.

US: AT&T (☎888-288-4685); **Sprint** (☎800-877-4646); or **MCI** (☎800-444-4141; from abroad dial the country's MCI access number).

Canada: Bell Canada **Canada Direct** (☎800-565-4708).

UK: British Telecom **BT Direct** (☎0800 34 51 44).

Ireland: Telecom Éireann **Ireland Direct** (☎800 250 250).

Australia: Telstra **Australia Direct** (☎13 22 00).

New Zealand: Telecom New Zealand (☎0800 000 000).

South Africa: Telkom South Africa (☎09 03).

To call home with a calling card, contact the North American operator for your service provider. Wherever possible, use a calling card for international phone calls; long-distance rates for national phone services are often exorbitant. You can usually make direct international calls from pay phones, but if you aren't using a calling card you may need to drop your coins as quickly as your words. Prepaid phone cards and occasionally credit cards can be used for direct international calls, but they are still less cost-efficient. In-room hotel calls invariably include an arbitrary surcharge.

The expensive alternative to dialing direct or using a calling card is using an international operator to place a **collect call.** An English-speaking operator from your home nation can be reached by dialing the appropriate service provider listed above, and they will typically place a collect call even if you don't possess one of their phone cards.

ESSENTIALS

CALLING WITHIN USA AND CANADA

The simplest way to call within the country is to use a coin-operated phone. You can also buy **prepaid phone cards,** which carry a certain amount of phone time depending on the card's denomination. The time is measured in minutes or talk units (e.g. one unit/one min.), and the card usually has a toll-free access telephone number and a personal identification number (PIN). To make a phone call, you dial the access number, enter your PIN, and, at the voice prompt, enter the phone number of the party you're trying to reach. Phone rates tend to be highest in the morning, lower in the evening, and lowest on Sunday and late at night.

GETTING THERE

BY PLANE

When it comes to airfare, a little effort can save you a bundle. If your plans are flexible enough to deal with the restrictions, courier fares are the cheapest. Tickets bought from consolidators and standby seating are also good deals, but last-minute specials, airfare wars, and charter flights often beat these fares. The key is to hunt around, to be flexible, and to persistently ask about discounts. Students, seniors, and those under 26 should never pay full price for a ticket.

DETAILS AND TIPS

Timing: Airfares to the US and Canada peak in the summer, and holidays are also expensive periods in which to travel. Midweek (M-Th morning) round-trip flights run $40-50 cheaper than weekend flights, but the latter are generally less crowded and more likely to permit frequent-flier upgrades. Return-date flexibility is usually not an option for the budget traveler; traveling with an "open return" ticket can be pricier than fixing a return date when buying the ticket and paying later to change it.

Route: Round-trip flights are by far the cheapest; "open-jaw" (arriving in and departing from different cities) and round-the-world, or RTW, flights are pricier but reasonable alternatives. Patching one-way flights together is the least economical way to travel. Flights between capital cities or regional hubs will offer the most competitive fares.

Gateway Cities: Flights between capitals or regional hubs will offer the cheapest fares. The cheapest gateway cities in North America are typically New York, Chicago, Atlanta, Houston, and Los Angeles.

Boarding: Whenever flying internationally, pick up tickets for international flights well in advance of the departure date, and confirm by phone within 72hrs. of departure. Most airlines require that passengers arrive at the airport at least two hours before departure. One carry-on item and two pieces of checked baggage are the norm for non-courier flights. Consult the airline for weight allowances.

Fares: Round-trip fares from Western Europe to the US range from $100-400 (during the off-season) to $200-550 (during the summer).

BUDGET AND STUDENT TRAVEL AGENCIES

A knowledgeable agent specializing in flights to the US and Canada can make your life easy and help you save, too, but agents may not spend the time to find you the lowest possible fare—they get paid on commission. Those holding **ISIC and IYTC cards** (see **Identification,** p. 36) qualify for big discounts from student travel agencies. Most flights from budget agencies are on major airlines, but in peak season some may sell seats on less reliable chartered aircraft.

usit world (www.usitworld.com). Over 50 **usit campus** branches in the UK (www.usitcampus.co.uk), including 52 Grosvenor Gardens, London SW1W 0AG (☎0870 240 1010); Manchester (☎0161 273 1721); and Edinburgh (☎0131 668 3303). Nearly 20 usit now offices in Ireland, including 19-21 Aston Quay, O'Connell Bridge, Dublin 2 (☎01

ESSENTIALS

602 1600; www.usitnow.ie), and Belfast (☎02890 327 111; www.usitnow.com).
Offices also in Athens, Auckland, Brussels, Frankfurt, Johannesburg, Lisbon, Luxembourg, Madrid, Paris, Sofia, and Warsaw.

Council Travel (www.counciltravel.com). US offices include: Emory Village, 1561 N. Decatur Rd., Atlanta, GA 30307 (☎404-377-9997); 273 Newbury St., Boston, MA 02116 (☎617-266-1926); 1160 N. State St., Chicago, IL 60610 (☎312-951-0585); 931 Westwood Blvd., Westwood, Los Angeles, CA 90024 (☎310-208-3551); 254 Greene St., New York, NY 10003 (☎212-254-2525); 530 Bush St., San Francisco, CA 94108 (☎415-566-6222); 424 Broadway Ave E., Seattle, WA 98102 (☎206-329-4567); 3301 M St. NW, Washington, D.C. 20007 (☎202-337-6464). For US cities not listed, call ☎800-226-8624. In the UK, 28A Poland St. (Oxford Circus), London, W1V 3DB (☎020 7437 7767).

STA Travel, 6560 Scottsdale Rd. #F100, Scottsdale, AZ 85253 (☎800-777-0112; fax ☎602-922-0793; www.sta-travel.com). A student travel organization with over 150 offices worldwide. Ticket booking, travel insurance, railpasses, and more. US offices include: 297 Newbury St., Boston, MA 02115 (☎617-266-6014); 429 S. Dearborn St., Chicago, IL 60605 (☎312-786-9050); 7202 Melrose Ave., Los Angeles, CA 90046 (☎323-934-8722); 10 Downing St., New York, NY 10014 (☎212-627-3111); 4341 University Way NE, Seattle, WA 98105 (☎206-633-5000); 2401 Pennsylvania Ave., Ste. G, Washington, D.C. 20037 (☎202-887-0912); 51 Grant Ave., San Francisco, CA 94108 (☎415-391-8407). In the UK, 11 Goodge St., London WIP 1FE (☎020 7436 7779 for North American travel). In New Zealand, 10 High St., Auckland (☎09 309 0458). In Australia, 366 Lygon St., Melbourne Vic 3053 (☎03 9349 4344).

Travel CUTS (Canadian Universities Travel Services Limited), 187 College St., Toronto, ON M5T 1P7 (☎416-979-2406; fax 979-8167; www.travelcuts.com). 40 offices across Canada. Also in the UK, 295-A Regent St., London W1R 7YA (☎020 7255 1944).

Other organizations that specialize in finding cheap fares include:

Cheap Tickets (☎800-377-1000; www.cheaptickets.com) offers cheap domestic flights.

Travel Avenue (☎800-333-3335; www.travelavenue.com) searches for best available published fares and then uses several different consolidators to attempt to beat that fare. They also offer package deals, which include car rental and hotel reservations, to many destinations.

 FLIGHT PLANNING ON THE INTERNET. The Web is a great place to look for travel bargains—it's fast, it's convenient, and you can spend as long as you like exploring options without driving your travel agent insane.

Many airline sites offer special last-minute deals on the Web. Other sites do the legwork and compile the deals for you—try www.bestfares.com, www.one-travel.com, www.lowestfare.com, and www.travelzoo.com.

STA (www.sta-travel.com) and **Council** (www.counciltravel.com) provide quotes on student tickets, while **Expedia** (msn.expedia.com) and **Travelocity** (www.travelocity.com) offer full travel services. **Priceline** (www.priceline.com) allows you to specify a price, and obligates you to buy any ticket that meets or beats it; be prepared for antisocial hours and odd routes. **Skyauction** (www.skyauction.com) allows you to bid on both last-minute and advance-purchase tickets.

Just one last note—to protect yourself, make sure that the site uses a secure server before handing over any credit card details. Happy hunting!

COMMERCIAL AIRLINES

The commercial airlines' lowest regular offer is the **APEX** (Advance Purchase Excursion) fare, which provides confirmed reservations and allows "open-jaw" tickets. Generally, reservations must be made 7 to 21 days in advance, with 7- to 14-day minimum up to 90-day maximum stay limits, and hefty cancellation and change penalties (fees rise in summer). Book peak-season APEX fares early, since by May you will have a hard time getting the departure date you want.

ESSENTIALS

Although APEX fares are probably not the cheapest possible fares, they provide a sense of the average commercial price, from which to measure other bargains. Many airlines offer **"e-fares,"** special, last-minute fares available over the internet; check airline webpages for details. www.sta-travel.com is a pretty reliable website offering deals for student travelers. Specials in newspapers may be cheaper but have more restrictions and fewer available seats.

NORTH AMERICAN CARRIERS

Air Tran (☎800-247-8726; www.airtran.com). Consumer Relations, Dept. INT, 9955 Air-Tran Blvd., Orlando, FL 32827. A budget carrier which also offers the "X-Fares Standby Program" for 18- to 22-year-olds (☎888-493-2737).

Air Canada (☎800-776-3000 from the US, 888-247-2262 from Canada; www.aircanada.ca). Ask about "Websaver" fares (☎800-776-3030 in US, 888-776-3030 in Canada, W-F).

America West (☎800-235-9292; www.americawest.com). 4000 Sky Harbor Blvd., Phoenix, AZ 85034. Services primarily the Western US.

American (☎800-433-7300; www.americanair.com). P.O. Box 619612, Dallas-Ft. Worth International Airport, TX 75261. Offers "College SAAvers" fares for full-time college students.

Continental (☎800-525-0280; www.flycontinental.com). Great deals for senior citizens in the "Freedom Club;" call ☎800-441-1135.

Northwest (☎800-225-2525; www.nwa.com). 5101 Northwest Dr., St. Paul, MN 55111-3034.

Southwest (☎800-435-9792; www.iflyswa.com). P.O.Box 36611, Dallas, TX 75235.-1611 A budget carrier with an ultra-friendly, laissez-faire attitude.

TWA (☎800-221-2000; www.twa.com). Customer Relations, 1415 Olive St., St. Louis, MO 63103. Offers last minute "TransWorld specials" via email.

United (☎800-241-6522; www.ual.com). P.O. Box 66100, Chicago, IL 60666.

TRAVELING FROM WITHIN NORTH AMERICA

Basic round-trip fares across the US (New York to Los Angeles) go for about $300-600. Flights that cover just a portion of the United States may actually be more expensive, depending on how frequented the route is (the more the cheaper). Standard commercial carriers like American and United will probably offer the most convenient flights, but they may not be the cheapest, unless you manage to grab a special promotion or airfare war ticket. You will probably find flying one of the "discount" options listed below a better deal, if any of their limited departure points is convenient for you.

TRAVELING FROM THE UK AND IRELAND

Airfares from Britain and Ireland peak between June and Sept. and near holidays. Expect round-trip fares from either London or Dublin to both New York or Boston to range from about $300 to $1000, to Los Angeles $500-1500.

European travelers will experience the least competition for inexpensive seats during the off season, but "off season" need not mean the dead of winter. Peak-season rates generally take effect from mid-May until mid-September. If you can, take advantage of cheap off-season flights within Europe to reach an advantageous point of departure for North America. (London is a major connecting point for budget flights to the US; New York City is often the destination.)

TRAVELING FROM AUSTRALIA AND NEW ZEALAND

Flights from Sydney to Los Angeles will cost between $900-1200. Traveling from Auckland to Los Angeles is a tad cheaper at around $700-1100. **Qantas** (☎13 13 13 or US ☎800-227-4500; www.qantas.com.au), **United** (see above), and **Air New Zealand** (☎0800 737 000 in New Zealand; ☎13 24 76 in Australia; www.airnewzealand.co.nz) fly between Australia or New Zealand and the US. Advance purchase fares from Australia have extremely tough restrictions. If you are uncertain about your plans, pay extra for an advance purchase ticket that has only a 50%

ESSENTIALS

penalty for cancellation. Many travelers from Australia and New Zealand take **Singapore Air** (☎02 93 500 100 in Australia; ☎0800 808 909 in New Zealand; www.singaporeair.com) or other East Asian carriers for the initial leg of their trip.

TRAVELING FROM SOUTH AFRICA
Traveling from either Cape Town or Johannesburg to New York will cost from $900 to $1400. Most flights into the US will go through either Boston, New York, or Washington DC. Standard commercial carriers like Virgin Atlantic will probably offer the most convenient flights. **South African Airways** (www.saa.co.za), **American**, and **Northwest** (see above) connect South Africa with North America.

COURIER FLIGHTS
Those who travel light should consider courier flights. Couriers help transport cargo on international flights by using their checked luggage space for freight. Generally, couriers must travel with carry-ons only and must deal with complex flight restrictions. Most flights are round-trip only, with short fixed-length stays (usually one week) and a limit of one ticket per issue. Schedules and itineraries may also change or be cancelled at the last moment (as late as 48 hours before the trip, and without a full refund), and check-in, boarding, and baggage claim are often much slower. As always, pay with a credit card if you can, and consider traveler's insurance against trip interruption. Generally, you must be over 21 (in some cases 18). In summer, the most popular destinations usually require an advance reservation of about two weeks (you can usually book up to two months ahead). Super-discounted fares are common for "last-minute" flights (three to 14 days ahead). Info on courier flights is available at www.courier.org.

STANDBY FLIGHTS
Traveling standby requires considerable flexibility in arrival and departure dates and cities. Companies dealing in standby flights sell vouchers rather than tickets, along with the promise to get to your destination (or near your destination) within a certain window of time (typically one to five days). You call in before your specific window of time to hear your flight options and the probability that you will be able to board each flight. You can then decide which flights you want to try to make, show up at the appropriate airport at the appropriate time, present your voucher, and board if space is available. Vouchers can usually be bought for both one-way and round-trip travel. You may receive a monetary refund only if every available flight within your date range is full; if you opt not to take an available (but perhaps less convenient) flight, you can only get credit toward future travel. Carefully read agreements with any company offering standby flights as tricky fine print can leave you in a lurch. To check on a company's service record in the US, call the Better Business Bureau (☎212-533-6200). It is difficult to receive refunds, and clients' vouchers will not be honored when an airline fails to receive payment in time. One established standby company in the US is **Airhitch**, 2641 Broadway, 3rd fl., New York, NY 10025 (☎800-326-2009; fax 864-5489; www.airhitch.org) and Los Angeles, CA (☎888-247-4482), which offers one-way flights to and from Europe from the Northeast ($159), West Coast and Northwest ($239), Midwest ($209), and Southeast ($189). Intracontinental connecting flights within the US cost $79-139. Airhitch's head European office is in Paris (☎33 01 47 00 16 30); there's also one in Amsterdam (☎31 20 626 32 20).

TICKET CONSOLIDATORS
Ticket consolidators, or **"bucket shops,"** buy unsold tickets in bulk from commercial airlines and sell them at discounted rates. The best place to look is in the Sunday travel section of any major newspaper, where many bucket shops place tiny ads. Call quickly, as availability is typically extremely limited. Not all bucket shops are reliable establishments, so insist on a receipt that gives full details of restrictions, refunds, and tickets, and pay by credit card. For more info, check the website **Consolidators FAQ** (www.travel-library.com/air-travel/consolidators.html).

ESSENTIALS

TRAVELING WITHIN THE US AND CANADA

Travel Avenue (☎800-333-3335; www.travelavenue.com) searches for best available published fares and then uses several different consolidators to attempt to beat that fare. **NOW Voyager,** 74 Varick St., #307, New York, NY 10013 (☎212-431-1616; fax 219-1793; www.nowvoyagertravel.com) arranges discounted flights, within the US and to the world. Other consolidators worth trying are **Interworld** (☎305-443-4929; fax 443-0351); **Pennsylvania Travel** (☎800-331-0947); **Rebel** (☎800-227-3235; email travel@rebel-tours.com; www.rebeltours.com); **Cheap Tickets** (☎800-377-1000; www.cheaptick-ets.com); and **Travac** (☎800-872-8800; fax 212-714-9063; www.travac.com). Yet more consolidators on the web include the **Internet Travel Network** (www.itn.com); **Surplus-Travel.com** (www.surplustravel.com); **Travel Information Services** (www.tiss.com); **TravelHUB** (www.travelhub.com); and **The Travel Site** (www.thetravelsite.com). Keep in mind that these are just suggestions to get you started in your research; *Let's Go* does not endorse any of these agencies. As always, be cautious, and research companies before you hand over your credit card number.

TRAVELING FROM THE UK, AUSTRALIA, AND NEW ZEALAND

In London, the **Air Travel Advisory Bureau** (☎020 7636 5000; www.atab.co.uk) can provide names of reliable consolidators and discount flight specialists. From Australia and New Zealand, look for consolidator ads in the travel section of the *Sydney Morning Herald* and other papers.

CHARTER FLIGHTS

Charters are flights a tour operator contracts with an airline to fly extra loads of passengers during peak season. Charter flights fly less frequently than major airlines, make refunds particularly difficult, and are almost always fully booked. Schedules and itineraries may also change or be cancelled at the last moment (as late as 48 hours before the trip, and without a full refund), and check-in, boarding, and baggage claim are often much slower. However, they can also be cheaper.

Discount clubs and **fare brokers** offer members savings on last-minute charter and tour deals. Study contracts closely; you don't want to end up with an unwanted overnight layover. **Travelers Advantage,** Stamford, CT, USA (☎800-548-1116; www.travelersadvantage.com; $60 annual fee includes discounts, newsletters, and cheap flight directories) specializes in travel and tour packages.

GETTING AROUND

BY TRAIN

Locomotion is still one of the cheapest (and most pleasant) ways to tour the US and Canada, but keep in mind that discounted air travel may be cheaper, and much faster, than train travel. As with airlines, you can save money by purchasing your tickets as far in advance as possible, so plan ahead and make reservations early. It is essential to travel light on trains; not all stations will check your baggage.

AMTRAK

Amtrak is the only provider of intercity passenger train service in the US. (☎800-872-7245; www.amtrak.com. New York to Boston $50; New York to Chicago $150.) Most cities have Amtrak offices which directly sell tickets, but tickets must be bought through an agent in some small towns. The informative web page lists up-to-date schedules, fares, arrival and departure info, and makes reservations. **Discounts** on full rail fares are given to: senior citizens (10% off), students with a Student Advantage card (15% off; call 800-96-AMTRAK to purchase the $20 card), travelers with disabilities (15% off), children 2-15 accompanied by an adult (50% off), children under 2 (free), and current members of the US armed forces, active-duty veterans, and their dependents (25% off). "Rail SALE" offers online discounts of up to 90%; visit the Amtrak web site for details and reservations. Amtrak also offers some **special packages:**

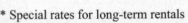

All-aboard America: This fare divides the Continental US into 3 regions: Eastern, Central, and Western.

Air-Rail Vacations: Amtrak and United Airlines allow you to travel in 1 direction by train and return by plane, or to fly to a distant point and return home by train. The train portion of the journey can last up to 30 days and include up to 3 stopovers. A multitude of variations are available; call ☎ 800-437-3441.

North America Rail Pass: A 30-day pass offered in conjunction with Canada's VIA Rail which allows unlimited travel and unlimited stops throughout the US and Canada for 30 consecutive days; $656 during peak season (June 1-Oct. 15) and $459 during off-season. A 15-day Northeastern North America Pass is available to international residents only; $400 during peak season, $300 off-season.

VIA RAIL

Via Rail, P.O. Box 8116, Station A, Montreal, QC H3C 3N3 (☎ 800-842-7733; www.viarail.ca), is Amtrak's Canadian analogue. **Discounts** on full fares are given to: students with ISIC card and youths under 24 (40% off full fare); seniors 60 and over (10% off); ages 2-15, accompanied by an adult (50% off); children under 2 (free on the lap of an adult). Reservations are required for first-class seats and sleep car accommodations. "Supersaver" fares offer discounts of 35% and more. Call for details. The **Canrail Pass** allows unlimited travel on 12 days within a 30-day period. Between early June and early October, a 12-day pass costs CDN$616 (seniors and youths and students with an ISIC, CDN$545). Off-season passes cost CDN$390 (seniors, youths, and students, CDN$355). Add CDN$30-52 for each additional day of travel. Call for info on seasonal promotions such as discounts on Grayline Sightseeing Tours.

BY BUS

Buses generally offer the most frequent and complete service between the cities and towns of the US and Canada. Often a bus is the only way to reach smaller locales without a car. In rural areas and across open spaces, however, bus lines tend to be sparse. *Russell's Official National Motor Coach Guide* ($15.70 including postage) is an invaluable tool for constructing an itinerary. Updated each month, *Russell's Guide* has schedules of every bus route (including Greyhound) between any two towns in the United States and Canada. Russell's also publishes two semiannual *Supplements* which are free when ordered with the main issue; a Directory of Bus Lines and Bus Stations, and a series of Route Maps (both $8.40 if ordered separately). To order any of the above, write **Russell's Guides, Inc.,** P.O. Box 278, Cedar Rapids, IA 52406 (☎ 319-364-6138; fax 364-4853).

GREYHOUND

Greyhound (☎ 800-231-2222; www.greyhound.com) operates the largest number of routes in the US, though local bus companies may provide more extensive services within specific regions. Schedule info is available at any Greyhound terminal, on the web page, or by calling the 800 number. Reserve with a credit card over the phone at least 10 days in advance, and the ticket can be mailed anywhere in the US. Otherwise, reservations are available only up to 24 hours in advance. You can buy your ticket at the terminal, but arrive early.

If **boarding at a remote "flag stop,"** be sure you know exactly where the bus stops. You must call the nearest agency and let them know you'll be waiting and at what time. Catch the driver's attention by standing on the side of the road and flailing your arms wildly—better to be embarrassed than stranded. If a bus passes (usually because of overcrowding), a later, less-crowded bus should stop. Whatever you stow in compartments underneath the bus should be clearly marked; be sure to get a claim check for it and make sure your luggage is on the same bus as you.

Advance purchase fares: Reserving space far ahead of time ensures a lower fare, although expect a smaller discount during the busy summer months (June 5-Sept. 15). For tickets purchased more than 7 days in advance, the one-way fare anywhere in the

US will not exceed $80, while the round-trip price is capped at $158 (from June-Sept., the one-way cap is $89 and the round-trip $178). Fares are often reduced even more for 14-day or 21-day advance purchases on many popular routes; call the 800 number for up to the date pricing, or consult the user-friendly web page.

Ameripass: Call ☎888-454-7277. Allows adults unlimited travel for 7 days ($209), 15 days ($319), 30 days ($429), or 60 days ($599). Prices for students with a valid college ID and for senior citizens are slightly less: 7 days $189/$279/$379/$509). Children's passes are half the price of adults. The pass takes effect the first day used. Before purchasing an Ameripass, total up the separate bus fares between towns to make sure that the pass is really more economical, or at least worth the unlimited flexibility it provides. **TNM&O Coaches, Vermont Transit, Carolina Trailways,** and **Valley Transit** are Greyhound subsidiaries, and as such will honor Ameripasses; actually, most bus companies in the US will do so, but check for specifics.

International Ameripass: For foreign visitors only. A 7-day pass is $179, 15-day pass $269, 30-day pass $369, 60-day pass $499. Call ☎888-454-7277 for info. International Ameripasses are not available at the terminal; they can be purchased in foreign countries at Greyhound-affiliated agencies; telephone numbers vary by country and are listed on the web page. Passes can also be ordered at the web page, or purchased in Greyhound's International Office, in Port Authority Bus Station, 625 Eighth Ave., New York, NY 10018 (☎212-971-0492 or 800-246-8572; fax 402-330-0919; email intlameripass@greyhound.com). **Australia:** ☎049 342 088. **New Zealand:** ☎64 9 479 65555. **South Africa:** ☎27 11 331 2911. **UK:** ☎44 01342 317 317.

GREYHOUND CANADA TRANSPORTATION

Unrelated to Greyhound Lines, Greyhound Canada Transportation, 877 Greyhound Way, Calgary, AB T3C 3V8 (☎800-661-8747; www.greyhound.ca) is Canada's main intercity bus company. The web page has full schedule info.

Discounts: Seniors (10% off); students (25% off with an ISIC; 10% off with other student cards); a companion of a disabled person free; ages 3-7 50%; under 3 free. If reservations are made 7 days or more in advance, a friend travels half-price. A child under 16 rides free with an adult if reserved 7 days in advance.

Canada Pass: Offers 7-, 15-, 30-, and 60-day unlimited travel on all routes for North American residents, including limited links to northern US cities. 7 day advance purchase required. (7-day pass CDN$230; 15-day pass CDN$360; 30-day pass CDN$420; 60-day pass CDN$535).

International Canada Pass: For foreign visitors. Same prices as the Canada Pass. The "Plus" pass adds travel to Québec and the Maritime provinces for a few dollars more; this pass can be purchased only overseas at select travel agencies, including those listed above for Greyhound Lines. Goods and services tax (GST) at 7% is added to fares.

BY CAR

"I" (as in "I-90") refers to Interstate highways, "U.S." (as in "U.S. 1") to United States highways, and "Rte." (as in "Rte. 7") to state and local highways. For Canadian highways, "TCH" refers to the Trans-Canada Hwy., while "Hwy." or "autoroute" refers to standard automobile routes.

INTERNATIONAL DRIVING PERMIT

If you do not have a license issued by a US state or Canadian province or territory, you might want an **International Driving Permit (IDP).** While the USA allows you to drive with a foreign license for up to a year, and in Canada for six months, it may help with police if your license is written in English. You must carry your home license with your IDP at all times. You must be 18 to obtain an IDP, it is valid for a year, and must be issued in the country in which your license originates. Contact these offices to apply:

Australia: Contact your local Royal Automobile Club (RAC) or the National Royal Motorist Association (NRMA) if in NSW or the ACT (☎08 9421 4444; www.rac.com.au/travel). Permits AUS$15.

Canada: Contact any Canadian Automobile Association (CAA) branch office or write to CAA, 1145 Hunt Club Rd., #200, K1V 0Y3. (☎613-247-0117; www.caa.ca/CAAInternet/travelservices/internationaldocumentation/idptravel.htm). Permits CDN$10.

Ireland: Contact the nearest Automobile Association (AA) office or write to the UK address below. Permits IR£4. The Irish Automobile Association, 23 Suffolk St., Rockhill, Blackrock, Co. Dublin (☎01 677 9481), honors most foreign automobile memberships (24hr. breakdown and road service ☎800 667 788; toll-free in Ireland).

New Zealand: Contact your local Automobile Association (AA) or their main office at Auckland Central, 99 Albert St. (☎9 377 4660; www.nzaa.co.nz). Permits NZ$8.

South Africa: Contact the Travel Services Department of the Automobile Association of South Africa at P.O. Box 596, 2000 Johannesburg (☎11 799 1400; fax 799 1410; http://aasa.co.za). Permits ZAR28.50.

UK: To visit your local AA Shop, contact the **AA Headquarters** (☎0990 44 88 66), or write to: The Automobile Association, International Documents, Fanum House, Erskine, Renfrewshire PA8 6BW. To find the location nearest you that issues the IDP, call ☎0990 50 06 00 or 0990 44 88 66. For more info, see www.theaa.co.uk/motoringandtravel/idp/index.asp. Permits UK£4.

US: Visit any American Automobile Association (AAA) office or write to AAA Florida, Travel Related Services, 1000 AAA Drive (mail stop 100), Heathrow, FL 32746 (☎407-444-7000; fax 444-7380). You don't have to be a member to buy an IDP/IADP. Permits $10. AAA Travel Related Services (☎800-222-4357) provides road maps, travel guides, emergency road services, travel services, and auto insurance.

AUTOMOBILE CLUBS

Most automobile clubs offer free towing, emergency roadside assistance, travel-related discounts, and random goodies in exchange for a modest membership fee. Travelers should strongly consider membership if planning an extended roadtrip.

▨ **American Automobile Association (AAA),** (for emergency road service call ☎800-AAA-HELP/800-222-4357; www.aaa.com). Offers free trip-planning services, roadmaps and guidebooks, 24-hour emergency road service anywhere in the US, free towing, and commission-free traveler's checks from American Express with over 1,000 offices scattered across the country. Discounts on Hertz car rental (5-20%), Amtrak tickets (10%), and various motel chains and theme parks. AAA has reciprocal agreements with auto associations in other countries which often provide you full benefits while in the US. Memberships vary depending on which AAA branch you join, but hover between $50-60 for the first year and less for renewals and additional family members; call ☎800-564-6222 to sign up.

▨ **Canadian Automobile Association (CAA),** 1145 Hunt Club Rd., #200, Ottawa, ON K1V 0Y3 (☎800-CAA-HELP/800-222-4357; www.caa.ca). Affiliated with AAA (see above), the CAA provides the same membership benefits, including 24hr. emergency roadside assistance, free maps and tourbooks, route planning, and various discounts. Basic membership is CDN$66 and CDN$24 for associates; call ☎800-564-6222 to sign up.

Mobil Auto Club, 200 N. Martingale Rd., Schaumbourg, IL 60174 (☎800-621-5581 for info; 800-323-5880 for emergency service). Benefits include locksmith reimbursement, towing (free up to 10 mi.), roadside service, and car-rental discounts. $7 per month covers you and another driver.

ON THE ROAD

Tune up the car before you leave, make sure the tires are in good repair and have enough air, and get good maps. *Rand McNally's Road Atlas*, covering all of the US and Canada, is one of the best (available at bookstores and gas stations, $11). A **compass** and a **car manual** can also be very useful. You should always carry a **spare tire** and **jack, jumper cables, extra oil, flares,** a **flashlight,** and **blankets** (in case you break down at night or in the winter). Those traveling long undeveloped stretches of road may want to consider renting a **car phone** or purchasing a **cell phone** in case of a breakdown. When traveling in the summer or in the desert bring five gallons of **water** for drinking and for the radiator. In extremely hot weather, use the air conditioner with restraint; if you see the car's temperature gauge climbing, turn it off. Turning the heater on full blast will help cool the engine. If radiator fluid is steaming, turn off the car for half an hour. *Never pour water over the engine to cool it.* Never lift a searing hot hood. In remote areas, remember to bring emergency food and water.

Sleeping in a car or van parked in the city is extremely dangerous—even the most dedicated budget traveler should not consider it an option. While driving, be sure to buckle up—seat belts are **required by law in many regions of the US and Canada. The speed limit** in the US varies considerably from region to region. Most urban highways have a limit of 55mph (63km per hr.), while rural routes range from 65mph (104kph) to 80mph (128kph). Heed the limit; not only does it save gas, but most local police forces and state troopers make frequent use of radar to catch speed demons. The **speed limit in Canada** is 100kph (63mph).

HOW TO NAVIGATE THE INTERSTATES

In the 50s, President Dwight "Ike" Eisenhower envisioned a well-organized **interstate highway system.** His dream has been realized: there is now a comprehensive, well-maintained, efficient means of traveling between major cities and between states. Luckily for the traveler, the highways are named with an intuitive numbering system. Even-numbered interstates run east-west and odd ones run north-south, decreasing in number toward the south and the west. North-south routes begin on the West Coast with I-5 and end with I-95 on the East Coast. The southernmost east-west route is I-4 in Florida. The northernmost east-west route is I-94, stretching from Montana to Wisconsin. Three-digit numbers signify branches of other interstates (e.g., I-285 is a branch of I-85), which are often bypasses skirting around large cities.

RENTING

The cost of car rental is often prohibitive for one-way trips between two cities, but local trips may be reasonable. **Rental agencies** fall into two categories: national companies with hundreds of branches, and local agencies serving a city or region.

National chains usually allow cars to be picked up in one city and dropped off in another (for a hefty charge, sometimes in excess of $1000); occasional promotions linked to coastal inventory imbalances may cut the fee dramatically. By calling a toll-free number, you can reserve a reliable car anywhere in the country. Generally, airport branches carry the cheapest rates. However, like airfares, car rental prices change constantly and often require scouting around for the best rate. Drawbacks include steep prices (a compact rents for about $35-45 per day) and high minimum ages for rentals (usually 25). Most branches rent to ages 21-24 with an additional fee, but policies and prices vary from agency to agency. If you're 21 or older and have a major credit card in your name, you may be able to rent where the minimum age would otherwise rule you out. **Alamo** (☎800-327-9633; www.alamo.com) rents to ages 21-24 with a major credit card for an additional $20 per day, **Enterprise** (☎800-736-8222) rents to customers aged 21-24 with a variable surcharge, and many **Dollar** (☎800-800-4000; www.dollar.com) and **Thrifty** (☎800-367-2277; www.thrifty.com) locations do likewise for varying surcharges. **Rent-A-Wreck** (☎800-944-7501; www.rent-a-wreck.com) specializes in supplying vehicles that are past their prime for lower-than-average prices; a bare-bones compact less than 8 years old rents for around $20-25; cars 3-5 years old average under $30.

Most rental packages offer unlimited mileage, although some allow you a certain number of miles free before the usual charge of 25-40¢ per mile takes effect. Most quoted rates do not include gas or tax, so ask for the total cost before handing over the credit card; many large firms have added airport surcharges not covered by the designated fare. Return the car with a full tank unless you sign up for a fuel option plan that stipulates otherwise. When dealing with any car rental company, ask whether the price includes insurance against theft and collision. There may be an additional charge for a collision and damage waiver (CDW), which usually comes to about $12-15 per day. Some major credit cards (including Master-Card and American Express) will cover the CDW if you use their card to rent a car; call your credit card company or inquire at the rental agency for specifics.

BUYING

Adventures on Wheels, 42 Rte. 36, Middletown, NJ 07748 (☎ 732-583-8714 or 800-943-3579; email info@wheels9.com; www.wheels9.com), sells travelers a motorhome, camper, minivan, station wagon, or compact car, organizes its registration and provides insurance, and guarantees they will buy it back after you have finished your travels. Cars with a buy-back guarantee start at $2500. Buy a camper for $6500, use it for six months, and sell it back for $3000-4000. The main office is in New York/New Jersey; there are other offices in Los Angeles, San Francisco, and Miami. Vehicles can be picked up at one office and dropped off at another

AUTO TRANSPORT COMPANIES

These services match drivers with car owners who need cars moved from one city to another. Would-be travelers give the company their desired destination and the company finds a car which needs to go there. The only expenses are gas, tolls, and your own living expenses. Some companies insure their cars; with others, your security deposit covers any breakdowns or damage. You must be at least 21, have a valid license, and agree to drive about 400 mi. per day on a fairly direct route. Companies regularly inspect current and past job references, take your fingerprints, and require a cash bond. Cars are available between most points, although it's easiest to find cars for traveling from coast to coast; New York and Los Angeles are popular transfer points. If offered a car, look it over first. Think twice about accepting a gas guzzler, since you'll be paying for the gas. With the company's approval, you may be able to share the cost with several companions.

Auto Driveaway Co., 310 S. Michigan Ave., Chicago, IL 60604-4298 (☎312-341-1900 or 800-346-2277; email nationalhq@autodriveaway.com; www.autodriveaway.com).

Across America Driveaway, 9905 Express Dr., Highland, IN 46322 (☎219-934-2000 or 800-619-7707; email Schultz!@gte.net; www.schultz-international.com). Offices in L.A. (☎800-964-7874 or 310-798-3377) and Dallas (☎214-745-8892).

BY BICYCLE

Before you pedal furiously onto the byways of America astride your banana-seat Huffy, remember that safe and secure cycling requires a quality helmet and lock. A good helmet costs about $40—much cheaper than critical head surgery. U-shaped **Kryptonite** or **Citadel** locks ($30-60) carry insurance against theft for 1 or 2 years if your bike is registered with the police. **Bike Nashbar,** 4111 Simon Rd., Youngstown, OH 44512 (☎800-627-4227; fax 456-1223), will beat any nationally advertised in-stock price by 5¢, and ships anywhere in the US and Canada. They also field questions about repairs and maintenance (☎330-788-6464; open M-F 8am-6pm).

Adventure Cycling Association, P.O. Box 8308, Missoula, MT 59807 (☎406-721-1776 or 800-755-2453; fax 721-8754; email acabike@aol.com; www.adv-cycling.org). A national, non-profit organization that researches and maps long-distance routes and organizes bike tours long and short for members (75-day Great Divide Expedition, $2800, 9-day trip $650). Annual membership $30; includes access to maps and routes and a subscription to *Adventure Cyclist* magazine.

The Canadian Cycling Association, 1600 James Naismith Dr., #212A, Gloucester, ON K1B 5N4 (☎613-748-5629; fax 748-5692; email general@canadian-cycling.com; www.canadian-cycling.com). Provides info for cyclists of all abilities, from recreational to racing. Distributes *The Canadian Cycling Association's Complete Guide to Bicycle Touring in Canada* (CDN$24), plus guides to specific regions of Canada, Alaska, and the Pacific Coast.

BY MOTORCYCLE

Those considering a long journey on a bike should contact the **American Motorcyclist Association,** 13515 Yarmouth Dr. in Pickering, OH 43147 (☎614-856-1900 or 800-262-5646; fax 856-1920; email ama@ama-cycle.org; ama-cycle.org), the linchpin of US biker culture. A full membership ($29 per year) includes a subscription to the extremely informative *American Motorcyclist* magazine, discounts on insurance, rentals, and hotels, and a kick-ass patch for your riding jacket. For an additional $25, members benefit from emergency roadside assistance, including pick-up and delivery to a service shop. And of course, take a copy of Robert Pirsig's *Zen and the Art of Motorcycle Maintainance* (1974) with you.

BY THUMB

Let's Go urges you to consider the great risks and disadvantages of **hitchhiking** before thumbing it. Hitching means entrusting your life to a randomly selected person who happens to stop beside you on the road. While this may be comparatively safe in some areas of Europe and Australia, it is generally *not* so in the US or Canada. We do not recommend it. We strongly urge you to find other means of transportation and to avoid situations where hitching is the only option.

ADDITIONAL INFORMATION

SPECIFIC CONCERNS

WOMEN TRAVELERS

In the US, a woman should expect to be treated just as a man would be; though sexism still exists, it is considered unacceptable behavior. If you are treated unfairly because you are a woman, this is grounds for complaint.

Women exploring on their own inevitably face some additional safety concerns, but it's easy to be adventurous without taking undue risks. Generally, it is safe to travel in the US as a woman, but common sense still applies; women are targeted for muggings and swindlings, as well as general harassment. Watch out for vendors who may try to take advantage of you. Avoid downtrodden neighborhoods, especially at night, and avoid solitary, late-night treks or subway rides. If you are camping in isolated areas or traveling in big cities you are unfamiliar with, try to travel with partners. In more rural areas, rowdy bars can also be risky. Wherever you go, walk purposefully and self-confidently; women who look like they know what they are doing and where they are going are less likely to be harassed. When traveling, always carry extra money for a phone call, bus, or taxi. **Hitching** is never safe for lone women, or even for two women traveling together. Consider approaching older women or couples if you're lost or feel uncomfortable.

Don't hesitate to seek out a police officer or a passerby if you are being harassed. *Let's Go: USA* lists emergency numbers (including rape crisis lines) in the **Practical Information** listings of most cities, and you can always dial **911**. An **IMPACT Model Mugging** self-defense course will not only prepare you for a potential attack, but will also raise your level of awareness of your surroundings as well as your confidence (see **Self Defense**, p. 43).

The **National Organization for Women (NOW)** (email now@now.org; now.org) can refer women travelers to rape crisis centers and counseling services. Main offices include 150 W. 28th St., # 304, New York, NY 10001 (☎212-627-9895) and 1000 16th St. NW, # 700, Washington, D.C. 20036 (☎202-331-0066).

FURTHER READING

A Journey of One's Own: Uncommon Advice for the Independent Woman Traveler, Thalia Zepatos. Eighth Mountain Press ($17).

Adventures in Good Company: The Complete Guide to Women's Tours and Outdoor Trips, Thalia Zepatos. Eighth Mountain Press ($7).

Active Women Vacation Guide, Evelyn Kaye. Blue Panda Publications (US$18).

Travelers' Tales: Gutsy Women, Travel Tips and Wisdom for the Road, Marybeth Bond. Traveler's Tales ($8).

TRAVELING ALONE

There are many benefits to traveling alone, among them greater independence and challenge. As a lone traveler, you have greater opportunity to interact with the region you're visiting. Without distraction, you can write a great travel log in the grand tradition of Mark Twain, John Steinbeck, and Charles Kuralt.

Connecting: Solo Traveler Network, P.O. Box 29088, 1996 W. Broadway, Vancouver, BC V6J 5C2, Canada (☎604-737-7791; email info@cstn.org; www.cstn.org). Bi-monthly newsletter features going solo tips, single-friendly tips, and travel companion ads. Annual directory lists holiday suppliers that avoid single supplement charges. Advice and lodging exchanges facilitated between members. Membership $25-35.

Travel Companion Exchange, P.O. Box 833, Amityville, NY 11701 (☎800-392-1256 or 516-454-0880; www.travelalone.com). Publishes the pamphlet *Foiling Pickpockets & Bag Snatchers* ($4) and *Travel Companions*, a bi-monthly newsletter for single travelers seeking a travel partner (subscription $48).

FURTHER READING: TRAVELING ALONE

Traveling Solo, Eleanor Berman. Globe Pequot ($17).
The Single Traveler Newsletter, P.O. Box 682, Ross, CA 94957 (☎415-389-0227). 6 issues $29.

OLDER TRAVELERS

Senior citizens are eligible for a wide range of discounts on transportation, museums, movies, theaters, concerts, restaurants, and accommodations. If you don't see a senior citizen price listed, ask, and you may be delightfully surprised.

Agencies for senior group travel are growing in enrollment and popularity. These are only a few:

ElderTreks, 597 Markham St., Toronto, ON, Canada, M6G 2L7 (☎416-588-5000 or 800-741-7956; fax 588-9839; email passages@inforamp.net; www.eldertreks.com).

Elderhostel, 75 Federal St., Boston, MA 02110-1941 (☎877-426-8056 or 617-426-7788; email registration@elderhostel.org; www.elderhostel.org). Programs at colleges, universities, and other learning centers in the US on varied subjects lasting 1-4 weeks. Must be 55 or over (spouse can be of any age).

The Mature Traveler, P.O. Box 50400, Reno, NV 89513 (☎800-460-6676 or 775-786-7419). Soft-adventure tours for seniors. Subscription $30.

FURTHER READING: OLDER TRAVELERS

No Problem! Worldwise Tips for Mature Adventurers, Janice Kenyon. Orca Book Publishers ($16).
A Senior's Guide to Healthy Travel, Donald L. Sullivan. Career Press ($15).
Unbelievably Good Deals and Great Adventures That You Absolutely Can't Get Unless You're Over 50, Joan Rattner Heilman. Contemporary Books ($13).

BISEXUAL, GAY, AND LESBIAN TRAVELERS

American cities are generally accepting of all sexualities, and thriving gay and lesbian communities can be found in most cosmopolitan areas. Most college towns are gay-friendly as well. In rural areas, however, homophobia can be rampant. In light of the anti-gay legislative measures narrowly defeated in various states, and not-so-isolated gay-bashing incidents, homophobia is still all too common.

BOOKSTORES AND INFORMATION SERVICES

Gay's the Word, 66 Marchmont St., London WC1N 1AB (☎0171 278 7654; email gays.theword@virgin.net; www.gaystheword.co.uk). The largest gay and lesbian bookshop in the UK. Mail-order service available. No catalogue of listings, but they will provide a list of titles on a given subject.

Giovanni's Room, 345 S. 12th St., Philadelphia, PA 19107 (☎215-923-2960; fax 923-0813; email giophilp@netaxs.com). An international feminist, lesbian, and gay bookstore with mail-order service which carries the publications listed below.

International Gay and Lesbian Travel Association, 4331 N. Federal Hwy., #304, Fort Lauderdale, FL 33308 (☎954-776-2626 or 800-448-8550; fax 954-776-3303; email

IGLTA@aol.com; www.iglta.com). An organization of 1350+ companies serving gay and lesbian travelers worldwide. Call for lists of travel agents, accommodations, and events.

International Lesbian and Gay Association (ILGA), 81 rue Marché-au-Charbon, B-1000 Brussels, Belgium (☎32 2 502 24 71; email ilga@ilga.org; www.ilga.org). Not a travel service. Provides info such as homosexuality laws of individual countries.

FURTHER READING: BISEXUAL, GAY, AND LESBIAN TRAVELERS

Spartacus International Gay Guide. Bruno Gmunder Verlag ($33).

Damron Men's Guide, Damron Road Atlas, Damron's Accommodations, and *The Women's Traveller.* Damron Travel Guides ($14-19). For more info, call 415-255-0404 or 800-462-6654 or check their website (www.damron.com).

Ferrari Guides' Gay Travel A to Z, Ferrari Guides' Men's Travel in Your Pocket, Ferrari Guides' Women's Travel in Your Pocket, and *Ferrari Guides' Inn Places.* Ferrari Guides ($14-16). For more info, call 602-863-2408 or 800-962-2912 or check their web site (www.q-net.com).

Gayellow Pages ($16). (212-674-0120; gayellowpages.com; email gayellow@banet.net).

TRAVELERS WITH DISABILITIES

Federal law dictates that all public buildings should be handicap accessible, and recent laws governing building codes have made disabled access more the norm than the exception. Businesses, transportation companies, national parks, and public services are compelled to assist the disabled in using their facilities.

Those with disabilities should inform airlines, buses, trains, and hotels of their disabilities when making arrangements for travel; some time may be needed to prepare special accommodations. Call ahead to restaurants, hotels, parks, and other facilities to find out about the existence of ramps, the widths of doors, the dimensions of elevators, etc. Major airlines and **Amtrak** (☎800-872-7245; see p. 73) will accommodate disabled passengers if notified at least 72hr. in advance. Amtrak offers 15% discounts to disabled passengers, and hearing impaired travelers may contact Amtrak using teletype printers (☎800-872-7245). **Greyhound** (see p. 75) will provide free travel for a companion; if you are without a fellow traveler, call Greyhound (☎800-752-4841) at least 48 hours, but no more than one week, before you leave and they'll arrange assistance where needed. Hertz, National, and Avis **car rental** agencies have hand-controlled vehicles at some locations (see **Renting,** p. 78). To visit a national park or any other sight managed by the US National Park Service, you can obtain a free **Golden Access Passport** (see **National Parks,** p. 55).

FOR MORE INFORMATION

Access-Able Travel Source, LLC, P.O. Box 1796, Wheat Ridge, CO 80034 (☎303-232-2979, fax 239-8486; www.access-able.com, e-mail bill@access-able.com). A database on traveling the US for disabled travelers, started by two avid disabled travelers. Provides info on access, transportation, accommodations, and various other resources.

Mobility International USA (MIUSA), P.O. Box 10767, Eugene, OR 97440 (☎541-343-1284 voice and TDD; fax 343-6812; email info@miusa.org; www.miusa.org). Sells *A World of Options: A Guide to International Educational Exchange, Community Service, and Travel for Persons with Disabilities* ($35).

Moss Rehab Hospital Travel Information Service (☎215-456-9600; www.mossresourcenet.org). A telephone and internet info resource center on travel accessibility and other travel-related concerns for those with disabilities.

Society for the Advancement of Travel for the Handicapped (SATH), 347 Fifth Ave., #610, New York, NY 10016 (☎212-447-1928; fax 725-8253; email sathtravel@aol.com; www.sath.org). Advocacy group which publishes quarterly color travel magazine *OPEN WORLD* (free for members or $13 for nonmembers) and a wide range of info sheets on disability travel facilitation and accessible destinations. Annual membership $45, students and seniors $30.

The following organizations arrange tours or trips for disabled travelers:

Directions Unlimited, 720 N. Bedford Rd., Bedford Hills, NY 10507 (☎914-241-1700 or 800-533-5343; fax 241-0243; email cruisesusa@aol.com). Specializes in arranging individual and group vacations, tours, and cruises for the physically disabled. Group tours for blind travelers.

The Guided Tour Inc., 7900 Old York Rd.,#114B, Elkins Park, PA 19027-2339 (☎215-782-1370 or 800-783-5841; email gtour400@aol.com; www.guidedtour.com). Runs travel programs for persons with developmental and physical challenges around the US.

FURTHER READING: DISABLED TRAVELERS
Resource Directory for the Disabled, Richard Neil Shrout. Facts on file ($45).

MINORITY TRAVELERS

Racial and ethnic minorities sometimes face blatant and, more often, subtle discrimination and/or harassment, though regions in the US and Canada differ drastically in their general attitudes towards race relations. Verbal harassment is now less common than unfair pricing, false info on accommodations, or inexcusably slow or unfriendly service at restaurants. The best way to deal with such encounters is to remain calm and report individuals to a supervisor and establishments to the Better Business Bureau for the region (the operator will provide local listings); contact the police in extreme situations. *Let's Go* always welcomes reader input regarding discriminating establishments.

In larger cities, African-Americans can usually consult chapters of the Urban League and the **National Association for the Advancement of Colored People (NAACP)** (www.naacp.org) for info on events of interest to African-Americans.

FURTHER READING: MINORITY TRAVELERS
Go Girl! The Black Woman's Book of Travel and Adventure, Elaine Lee. Eighth Mountain Press ($18).
The African-American Travel Guide, Wayne Robinson. Hunter Publishing ($16).
Traveling Jewish in America, Jane Moskowitz. Wandering You Press ($14.50).

TRAVELERS WITH CHILDREN

Family vacations often require that you slow your pace, and always require that you plan ahead. When deciding where to stay, remember the special needs of young children; if you pick a B&B or a small hotel, call ahead and make sure it's child-friendly. If you rent a car, make sure the rental company provides a car seat for younger children. Be sure that your child carries some sort of ID in case of an emergency or he or she gets lost, and arrange a reunion spot in case of separation when sight-seeing.

Restaurants often have children's menus and discounts. Virtually all museums and tourist attractions also have a children's rate. Children under two generally fly for free or 10% of the adult airfare on domestic flights (this does not necessarily include a seat). Fares are usually discounted 25% for children from 2 to 11.

FURTHER READING: TRAVELERS WITH CHILDREN
Backpacking with Babies and Small Children, Goldie Silverman. Wilderness Press ($10).

Have Kid, Will Travel: 101 Survival Strategies for Vacationing With Babies and Young Children, Claire and Lucille Tristram. Andrews and McMeel ($9).

Kidding Around Boston, San Francisco, Washington D.C., Atlanta, Austin, Chicago, Miami, Nashville OR *Portland.* John Muir ($8).

Adventuring with Children: An Inspirational Guide to World Travel and the Outdoors, Nan Jeffrey. Avalon House Publishing ($15).

DIETARY CONCERNS

Vegetarians should have no problem finding suitable cuisine on either coast (the West Coast, especially, is extremely vegetarian friendly) and in most major cities, although small-town America may meet veggie requests with a long, blank stare and a pile of mashed potatoes. For more info, contact:

North American Vegetarian Society, P.O. Box 72, Dolgeville, NY 13329 (☎518-568-7970; email navs@telenet.com; www.cyberveg.org/navs/). Publishes *Transformative Adventures,* a guide to vacations and retreats ($15), and the *Vegetarian Journal's Guide to Natural Food Restaurants in the US and Canada* ($12).

Travelers who keep **kosher** should contact synagogues in larger cities for info on kosher restaurants; your own synagogue or college Hillel should have access to lists of Jewish institutions across the nation.

The Jewish Travel Guide lists synagogues, kosher restaurants, and Jewish institutions in the US and Canada. Available from Vallentine-Mitchell Publishers, Newbury House 890-900, Eastern Ave., Newbury Park, Ilford, Essex, UK IG2 7HH (☎0181 599 88 66; fax 599 09 84). It is available in the US ($16) from ISBS, 5804 NE Hassalo St., Portland, OR 97213-3644 (☎800-944-6190).

ALTERNATIVES TO TOURISM

For an extensive listing of "off-the-beaten-track" and specialty travel opportunities, try the **Specialty Travel Index,** 305 San Anselmo Ave., #313, San Anselmo, CA 94960, USA (☎415-455-1643 or 888-624-4030; www.spectrav.com; US$6). Transitions Abroad (www.transabroad.com) publishes a bimonthly on-line newsletter for work, study, and specialized travel abroad.

STUDYING ABROAD

US. Foreign students can take advantage of most educational opportunities in the US, including secondary schools, colleges, English language programs for all levels, and even vocational training. Although revised immigration laws from 1996 prohibit foreign students from attending public elementary or middle school, public high schools (with a maximum stay of one year) and secondary institutions remain accessible with the **F-1 student visa.** Vocational students would need to secure a **M-1 visa,** which is more difficult to obtain than the F-1.

Those interested in studying in the US should first consider which program or institution they would like to join. The Web offers an exhaustive index of **study abroad** opportunities for foreign students, including www.petersons.com and www.studyabroad.com for academic programs and www.aipt.org for vocational and professional exchanges. Study abroad can also be arranged through particular institutions, such as universities and English language schools. Participation in a program needs to be secured before arranging for a visa, which should be done at the US Embassy or Consulate located in the country of permanent residence.

Most study abroad programs in the US require a base level of proficiency in English before admission can be granted. Applicants usually prove their skills by taking the **TOEFL,** a standardized test offered in most countries. Test times and locations can be obtained at www.toefl.org (email toefl@ets.org) or by calling or writing TOEFL services: P.O Box 6151, Princeton, NJ 08541 (☎609-771-7100).

CANADA. Just as in the US, prospective students should choose and be accepted to a program of study before applying to live in Canada as a foreign student. Authorization for study in Canada occurs on a provincial level and requires proof of admission to an institution, financial solvency to pay all expenses incurred, and ability to meet other visitation requirements, such as visas.

WORKING ABROAD

US. Foreign students living in the US are prohibited from taking an off-campus job during the first year of their study and can only accept such a job after the first year upon permission from the INS. Technical students are allowed to work only as a function of their training. Visitors to the US under the regular visitation visa (the B-2 visa) are prohibited from taking any type of employment.

To work in the US without immigrating, one must obtain a work visa or participate in a cultural exchange program. **Work visas** are extremely difficult to procure and require the presence of extraordinary circumstances, such as extensive education or prominence in a particular academic or professional field. Cultural exchanges are easier to arrange and are intended to facilitate multi-culturalism in education, arts, and sciences. The US Information Agency organizes a variety of cultural exchanges (www.usinfo.state.gov).

CANADA. Foreign students living in Canada are allowed to work only under exceptional circumstances, such as unforeseen loss of expected funding. In order to work in Canada without immigrating, one must be sponsored by a Canadian employer who can prove that foreign assistance is needed to fill a Canadian employee market shortage. An Employment Authorization (EA) can be issued to a foreign worker only if he or she is sponsored by a Canadian employer and if a Human Resources Development Canada officer agrees that the foreign worker will produce a net benefit for Canada and Canadians.

OTHER RESOURCES

USEFUL PUBLICATIONS

MISCELLANEOUS

Specialty Travel Index, 305 San Anselmo Ave., #313, San Anselmo, CA 94960 (☎888-624-4030 or 415-455-1643; fax 459-4974; email spectrav@ix.netcom.com; www.spectrav.com). Published twice yearly, this is an extensive listing of "off the beaten track" travel opportunities. One copy $6, one-year subscription (2 issues) $10.

TRAVEL BOOK PUBLISHERS

Hippocrene Books, Inc., 171 Madison Ave., New York, NY 10016 (☎212-685-4371; orders 718-454-2366; fax 454-1391; email contact@hippocrenebooks.com; www.netcom.com/~hippocre). Free catalogue. Publishes travel reference books and guides.

Hunter Publishing, 130 Campus Drive, Edison, NJ 08818-7816 (☎800-255-0343; fax 417-0482; email kimba@mediasoft.net; www.hunterpublishing.com). Has an extensive catalogue of travel books, guides, language learning tapes, and quality maps, and the *Charming Small Hotel Guide to New England* or *Florida* ($15).

Rand McNally, 150 S. Wacker Dr., Chicago, IL 60606 (☎312-332-2009 or 800-234-0679; fax 443-9540; email storekeeper@randmcnally.com; www.randmcnally.com). Publishes a number of comprehensive road atlases (each $8).

THE WORLD WIDE WEB

The Internet can provide factual info without the hassle of calling, and can facilitate hotel, hostel, and car rental reservations. Listed below are sights that would be useful to a budget traveler.

Microsoft Expedia (expedia.msn.com) has everything you'd ever need to make travel plans on the web: compare flight fares, look at maps, make reservations. FareTracker, a free service, sends you monthly mailings about the cheapest fares to any destination.

The CIA World Factbook (www.odci.gov/cia/publications/factbook/index.html) has tons of vital statistics on the United States and Canada. Check it out for an overview of either country's economy, and an explanation of its system of government.

Shoestring Travel (www.stratpub.com), an alternative to Microsoft's monolithic site, is budget travel e-zine that features listings of home exchanges, links, and accommodations info.

Tourism Offices Worldwide Directory (http://mbnet.mb.ca/lucas/travel/tourism-offices.html) will give you tourism offices for all fifty states and Canada, as well as consulate and embassy addresses.

City Net (www.city.net) dispenses info on renting a car, restaurants, hotel rates, and weather for a wide array of cities and regions across the US and Canada.

Let's Go (www.letsgo.com). A shameless plug. Stories from the road, currency conversion, travel link database, weather, a hoppin' message board, and *love*.

FURTHER READING: THE WORLD WIDE WEB

How to Plan Your Dream Vacation Using the Web, Elizabeth Dempsey. Coriolis Group ($25).
Nettravel: How Travelers Use the Internet, Michael Shapiro. O'Reilly & Associates ($25).
Travel Planning Online for Dummies, Noah Vadnai. IDG Books ($25).

NEW ENGLAND

New England has fancied itself an intellectual and political center since before the States were United. Students and scholars funnel into New England's colleges each fall, and town meetings still evoke the spirit of popular government which once inspired American colonists to create a nation. Numerous historic landmarks recount every step of the young country's break from "Old" England.

The region's unpredictable climate can be particularly dismal during the harsh, wet winter from November to March, when rivers, campgrounds, and tourist attractions freeze up. Nevertheless, today's visitors find adventure in the rough edges that irked early settlers, flocking to New England's dramatic, salty coastline to sun on the sand or heading to the slopes and valleys of the Green and White Mountains to ski, hike, bike, and canoe. In the fall, the nation's most brilliant foliage bleeds and burns, transforming the entire region into an earth-sized kaleidoscope.

HIGHLIGHTS OF NEW ENGLAND

SEAFOOD. Head to Maine (see below) for the best lobster around, and don't forget to try New England clam "chowda" before you leave.

SKIING. Enthusiasts flock to the mountains of New Hampshire and Vermont; the most famous resorts include Stowe (p. 107) and Killington (p. 103).

BEACHES. Cape Cod (p. 130) and Nantucket, MA (p. 138) have the region's best.

COLONIAL LANDMARKS. They're everywhere, but a walk along the Freedom Trail in Boston, MA (p. 111) is a great place to start.

SCENIC NEW ENGLAND. Take a drive along Rte. 100 in the fall, when the foliage is at its most striking, or hike the Appalachian Trail (p. 94) for a view on foot.

MAINE

Nearly a thousand years ago, Leif Eriksson and his band of Viking explorers set foot on the coasts of Maine. Moose roamed the sprawling evergreen wilderness, the cry of the Maine coon cat echoed through towering mountains, and countless lobsters crawled in the ocean deep. A millennium has not changed much. Forests still cover nearly 90% of Maine's land, an area larger than the entire stack of New England states to the south, and the inner reaches of the state stretch on for mile after uninhabited mile, while some more populated locales dot a harsh and jagged coastline.

🛈 PRACTICAL INFORMATION

Capital: Augusta.
Visitor Info: Maine Tourism Information, 325B Water St., Hallowell (☎207-623-0363 or 888-624-6345; www.visitmaine.com). Send mail to P.O. Box 2300, Hallowell 04347. **Bureau of Parks and Lands,** State House Station #22 (AMHI, Harlow Bldg.), Augusta 04333 (☎207-287-3821). **Maine Forest Service,** Bureau of Forestry, State House Station #22, Harlow Bldg., 2nd fl., Augusta 04333 (☎207-287-2791).
Postal Abbreviation: ME. **Sales Tax:** 6%. **Area code:** 207.

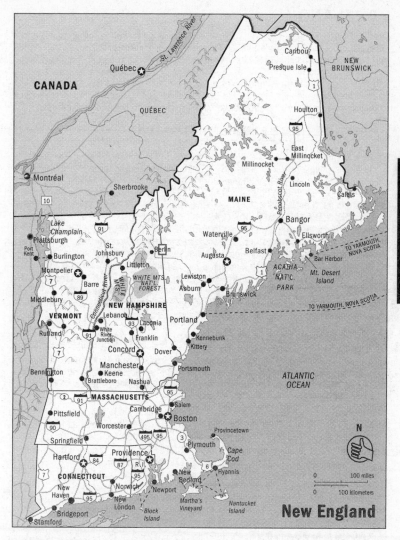

New England

MAINE COAST

As the puffin flies, the Maine coast from Kittery to Lubec measures 228 mi., but if untangled, all of the inlets and rocky promontories would stretch out 3478 mi. The meandering, two-lane **U.S. 1** hugs the coastline, stringing the port towns together, and is the only option for most points north of Portland. In summer, the traffic pace is often slow; be prepared to take your time and stop at one of the innumerable makeshift red wooden lobster signs that speckle the roadsides for a freshly boiled one. Lesser roads and small ferry lines connect the remote villages and offshore islands. **Visitor Info: Maine Information Center,** in Kittery, 3 mi. north of the Maine-New Hampshire bridge. (☎207-439-1319. Open daily 8am-6pm; mid-Oct. to June 9am-5pm.) **Greyhound** serves points between Portland and Bangor along I-95, as well as the town of Brunswick, but to explore most coastal points you need a car.

PORTLAND ☎207

During the 4th of July fireworks of 1866, a young boy playing on a Portland wharf inadvertently started a fire which destroyed over three-fourths of the city. The formal Victorian reconstruction that survives in the Old Port Exchange stands in stark contrast to Portland's spirited youth culture. Here, teenagers and 20-somethings gather in bars, restaurants, and cafes near the wharf and flood the streets in talkative groups or couples, even after stores close down. Outside the city, ferries run to the Casco Bay Islands while Sebago Lake provides sunning and water skiing.

GETTING THERE AND GETTING AROUND

Buses: Concord Trailways, 100 Sewall St. (☎828-1151). To: Boston (2hr., 11 per day, $17) and Bangor (2hr., 4 per day, $21). Metro buses #5 and 3 run to and from the station. Office open daily 5:30am-8:30pm. **Greyhound/Vermont Transit,** 950 Congress St. (☎772-6587), on the western outskirts of town. *Be cautious here at night.* Take bus #1 "Congress St." downtown. Office open daily 6:30am-7:15pm. To: Boston (2hr., 9 per day, $15) and Bangor (2½-3½hr., 6 per day, $19).

Ferries: Prince of Fundy Cruises, P.O. Box 4216, 468 Commercial St. (☎775-5616, 800-341-7540 or 800-482-0955). Ferries to Yarmouth, NS, leave from the Portland International Ferry Terminal, on Commercial St. near the Million Dollar Bridge. Runs May to mid-June and mid-Sept. to late Oct. Boats depart Portland at 9pm; the 11hr. trip takes the whole night. Cabins available. $60, ages 5-14 $30, car $80, bike $7; late June to mid-Sept. $80/$40/$98/$10. Reservations strongly recommended.

Public Transit: Metro Bus (☎774-0351) offers service in and around downtown. Most routes run 6am-7pm. $1, seniors with Medicaid card 50¢, under 5 free, transfers free.

ORIENTATION AND PRACTICAL INFORMATION

Downtown sits near the bay, along **Congress St.** between State and Pearl St. A few blocks south lies the **Old Port** on Commercial and Fore St. These two districts contain most of the city's sights and attractions. **I-295** (off I-95) forms the western boundary of downtown.

Visitor Info: Visitors Information Bureau, 305 Commercial St. (☎772-5800), at Center St. Open M-F 8am-6pm, Sa-Su 10am-6pm; mid-Oct. to mid-May M-F 9am-5pm, Sa-Su 10am-5pm.

Hotlines: Rape Crisis, ☎774-3613. **Crisis Hotline,** ☎800-660-8500. Both 24hr.

Hospitals: Maine Medical Center, 22 Bramhall St. (☎871-0111). **Women's Community Health Services,** ☎773-7247 or 800-666-7247. Open daily 9am-5pm.

Internet Access: JavaNet Cafe, 37 Exchange St. (☎773-2469). Open M-Th 7:30am-11pm, F 7:30am-midnight, Sa 8am-midnight, Su 8am-10pm. $6 per hr.

Post Office: 400 Congress St. (☎871-8426). Open M-F 8am-7pm, Sa 9am-1pm. **ZIP code:** 04112. **Area code:** 207.

ACCOMMODATIONS

Portland has some inexpensive accommodations, but prices jump during the summer. At Exit 8 off I-95, **Super 8** and budget rates congregate. (☎854-1881. A few singles at $35; most start around $60.)

Oak Leaf Inn, 51A Oak St. (☎773-7882). This casual, elegant inn has quickly converted several of its guest suites into welcoming 4-6 bed dorms for stranded hostelers seeking the now non-existent Portland Youth Hostel. Modest common room with TV and fridge. 20 beds total. Dorms $22, $27 non-members. Reservations strongly recommended.

YMCA, 70 Forest Ave. (☎874-1111), on the north side of Congress St., 1 block from post office. Men only. Unspectacular but tidy singles with access to kitchen, pool, and exercise facilities. 85 rooms. Singles $31.50 per night, $104 per week. Key deposit $10. Check-in 11am-8:30pm.

The Inn at St. John, 939 Congress St. (☎773-6481 or 800-636-9127), across from the bus station. An upscale environment makes for a pricier alternative. Free local calls and parking. Continental breakfast included. Kitchen, laundry facilities, and bike storage available. Tidy, tasteful singles and doubles start at $55 weekday, $65 weekend; $50 in winter. Rooms with private bath are available.

Wassamki Springs, 56 Saco St. (☎839-4276), in Scarborough. Closest campground (10min.) to Portland. Drive 6 mi. west on Congress St. (becomes Rte. 22, then County Rd.), then turn right on Saco St. Flocks of migrant Winnebagos nest among cozy, fairly private sites bordering a lake encircled by sandy beaches. Free showers and flush toilets. Sites $21 for 2 people, with hook-up $23-25; $4 per additional person; add $2 for lakefront sites. Reserve 2 weeks in advance, especially July-Aug. Open May to mid-Oct.

◯ FOOD

Portland's harbor overflows with the ocean's fruits, but non-aquatic and vegetarian fare aren't too hard to find either.

Federal Spice, 225 Federal St. (☎774-6404), just off Congress St. A favorite among Portland's youth, the Fed spices all its entrees (all under $6) with fiery Caribbean, South American, and Asian ingredients. Open M-Sa 11am-9pm.

Gilbert's Chowder House, 92 Commercial St. (☎871-5636). The local choice for seafood. A large bowl of chowder in a bread bowl is a meal in itself ($6). On summer nights Gilbert's patio on the water is one of the nicest spots in town. Open Su-Th 11am-9pm, F-Sa 11am-10pm; Oct.-May call for hrs.

Old Chicago Pasta and Pizza, 375 Fore St. (☎773-3333). Calzones ($8) and brick oven pizzas are tasty, especially with one of 110 brews. 3 upstairs dining rooms overlooking the harbor and Th pint nights ensure this joint's popularity. Open daily 11am-1am.

👁 SIGHTS

Primordial offshore islands with secluded beaches and relatively undeveloped interiors lie just a ferry ride from the city proper. America's oldest ferry service, **Casco Bay Lines,** on State Pier near the corner of Commercial and Franklin, runs year-round to these nearby islands. Daily **ferries** depart approximately every hour for **Peaks Island.** (☎774-7871. Operates M-Sa 5:45am-10:30pm. Round-trip $5.25.) On the island, you can rent a bike at **Brad's Recycled Bike Shop.** (115 Island Ave. ☎766-5631; $5 per hr., $8.50 for up to 3hr., $12 per day.) Waves crash on **Long Island's** quiet, unpopulated beach; Casco Bay Lines runs ten ferries there daily. Starting at Long Island, you can island-hop by catching later ferries to other islands. (Same price as Peaks ferry.) Getting to more than two islands will take all day. **Two Lights State Park,** across the Million Dollar Bridge on State St. and south along Rte. 77 to Cape Elizabeth, is a wonderful place to picnic and relax and is not usually crowded. (☎799-5871. $2, ages 3-11 50¢.)

The sea calls, but Portland does have landlubber activities. The **Portland Museum of Art,** at the intersection of Congress, High, and Free St., collects American art by John Singer Sargent, Wyeth, and Winslow Homer. (7 Congress Sq. ☎775-6148 or 800-639-4067. Open May 31 to Oct. 11 M-W and Sa-Su 10am-5pm, Th-F 10am-9pm. $6, students and seniors $5, ages 6-12 $1; free F 5-9pm.) The **Wadsworth-Longfellow House** was the home of 19th-century poet Henry Wadsworth Longfellow and is now a museum of social history and US literature focusing on late 18th- and 19th-century antiques as well as on the life of the poet. (489 Congress St. ☎879-0427. Purchase tickets at 489 Congress St. House open daily June-Oct. 10am-5:30pm. Gallery and museum store also open Nov.-May W-Sa noon-4pm. $6, students and seniors $5, ages 6-18 $2. Price includes admission to a neighboring history museum with rotating exhibits. Tours every 30-40min.)

🎵🎭 ENTERTAINMENT AND NIGHTLIFE

Portland's spirited youth culture shows in its many summer theater and orchestra performances; signs for these productions decorate the city, and schedules are available at the visitors center (see **Practical Information,** opposite). The **Portland Symphony** presents concerts renowned throughout the northeast (☎842-0800; 50% student discount). Info on Portland's jazz, blues, and club scene packs the *Casco Bay Weekly* and *FACE*, both of which are free in many restaurants and stores.

Traditionally on the first Su in June, the **Old Port Festival** (☎772-6828) fills several blocks from Federal to Commercial St. with as many as 50,000 people. On summer afternoons during the **Noontime Performance Series,** a variety of bands perform in Portland's Monument Sq. and Congress Sq. (☎772-6828; mid-June to Aug.)

For a taste of the hometown spirit, the **Portland Sea Dogs,** an AA minor-league baseball team, take the field from Apr. to mid-Sept. at **Hadlock Field** on Park Ave. (☎879-9500; $4-6, under 17 $2-5).

After dark, the Old Port area, known as "the strip," especially **Fore St.** between Union and Exchange St., livens up with pleasant-if-touristy shops and a few good pubs. **Brian Boru,** 57 Center St., provides a mellow pub scene. The brew nachos ($5) are good, as are $2 pints all day Su. (☎780-1506. Open daily 11:30am-1am.) **Gritty MacDuff's,** 396 Fore St., brews its own sweet beer ($3 pints) for adoring locals and entertains with live bluegrass and jazz two to three times a week. (☎772-2739. Open daily 11:30am-1am. No cover.) The English pub around the corner, **Three Dollar Dewey's,** 241 Commercial St., serves over 100 different beers (36 on tap at $3-3.50), along with great chili (cup $3.50) and free popcorn. (☎772-3310. Open Su-Th 11:30am-midnight, F-Sa 11:30am-1am.) The **Dry Dock Restaurant & Tavern,** 84 Commercial St., is a great place to relax with a few drinks and friends. The bar is outside with a great waterfront view. (☎774-3550. Open daily 11am-1am.)

SOUTH OF PORTLAND ☎207

OLD ORCHARD BEACH. A kingdom of delightful tackiness, Old Orchard Beach reigns 10 mi. south of Portland on U.S. 1 (or take Exit 5 off I-95 south and follow signs). The plastic jewel in the beach's crown is the **Wonderland Arcade.** The rides aren't spectacular for those with high hopes, but the simple, happy carnival atmosphere is blissfully anachronistic. Parking costs $3, and East Grand Ave. is packed with seaside hotels and motels, the cheapest of which cost around $40 for a double.

KENNEBUNK. Kennebunk and its coastal counterpart 8 mi. east, **Kennebunkport,** are more tasteful (and expensive) than Old Orchard. Both of these towns are popular hideaways for wealthy authors and artists—Kennebunkport reluctantly grew famous as the summer home of former President Bush. Rare and used bookstores line U.S. 1 just south of Kennebunk, while art galleries fill the town itself. You could spend a day (and a fortune) exploring all the little shops in town. Even more terrifying than its monied homogeneity, though, is the **Maritime Productions' Chilling and Unusual Theatre Cruise,** a 2hr. cruise and performance narrating true tales of haunted lighthouses, ghost ships, shipwrecks, and cannibalism in New England's maritime past and present. (☎967-4938 or 967-5595. Departs twice daily from Kennebunkport Marina on Ocean Ave. 3:30pm matinee cruise $26, seniors $24, children $22; 6:30pm sunset cruise $30 all ages.) The 55 ft. gaff rigged **Schooner Eleanor** provides a more sedate 2hr. ocean experience. (☎967-8809. Leaves from Arundel Wharf, Ocean Ave. $38. Call for reservations and departure times.) The **Kennebunk-Kennebunkport Chamber of Commerce,** 17 U.S. 100/Western Ave., in Kennebunkport, has a free guide. (☎967-0857. Open daily 9am-6pm; off-season 9am-5pm.)

OGUNQUIT. South of Kennebunk on U.S. 1 lies Ogunquit, which means "beautiful place by the sea." The long, sandy shoreline is probably the best beach north of Cape Cod. Ogunquit also has one of New England's largest (although seasonal) gay communities. The **Ogunquit Information Bureau,** on U.S. 1, has info. (☎646-2939. Open M-Th noon-5pm, F and Su noon-6pm, Sa 10am-6pm; early Sept. to late May daily 9am-5pm.) The **Rachel Carson National Wildlife Refuge,** ½ mi. off U.S. 1 on Rte. 9, provides a secluded escape from the tourist throngs. A trail winds through the salt marsh, home to over 200 species of shorebirds and waterfowl. (☎646-9226. Open M-F 8am-4:30pm, Sa-Su 10am-2pm; off-season M-F 8am-4:30pm. Trail open daily sunrise-sunset. Free.) In nearby Wells, the **National Estuarine Research Reserve,** at the junction of U.S. 1 and Rte. 9, sprawls over meadows and beaches and offers tours of the estuary, bird life, and wildflowers (open daily 8am-5pm). Nearby **Perkins Cove,** which is accessible only by a very windy and narrow road, charms the argyle socks off the polo shirt crowd with boutiques hawking seashell sculptures. The two **Barnacle Billy's** restaurants, 20 yd. apart on Oar Weed Rd., practice an interesting division of labor. The original (a lobster pound) broils, bakes, and sautés lobsters, while their newer full-service location has a bigger menu. (☎646-5575. Both open daily noon-9:30pm with free parking for patrons.) Weather-permitting, biking is the best way to travel Maine's rocky shores and spare yourself the thick summer traffic. **Wheels and Wares,** U.S. 1 on the Wells/Ogunquit border, rents mountain bikes. (☎646-5774. Open daily 10am-5pm. $20 per day, $25 per 24hr.) **Moody,** just south of Ogunquit, has budget motels.

MT. DESERT ISLAND ☎207

Mt. Desert Island is anything but deserted. During the summer, the island swarms with tourists lured by the thick forests and mountainous landscape. Roughly half of the island is covered by Acadia National Park, which harbors some of the last protected marine, mountain, and forest environments on the New England coast. Bar Harbor, on the eastern side, is by far the most crowded and glitzy part of the island. Once a summer hamlet for the very wealthy, the town now welcomes a motley mélange of R&R-seekers; though the monied have fled to the more secluded Northeast and Seal Harbor, the town still maintains its overpriced traditions.

▐ GETTING THERE AND GETTING AROUND

Buses: Greyhound/Vermont Transit (☎800-451-3292) leaves for Bangor ($9.50) and Boston ($40) daily May-June and Sept.-Oct. 6:45am; July-Aug. 8am; in front of Fox Run Travel, 4 Kennebec St. (☎288-3366). Tickets are sold at Fox Run (open M-F 9am-5pm). 15% discount for Student Advantage cardholders, 10% for seniors. Fox Run is open for last-minute ticket purchases for buses departing after normal business hours.

Ferries: Beal & Bunker (☎244-3575), from Northeast Harbor on the town dock. To: Great Cranberry Island (20min., 6 per day; $10, under 12 $5). Open daily late June to Sept. 8am-4:30pm; call for winter hrs. **Bay Ferries** (☎888-249-7245), Bar Harbor. To: Yarmouth, NS (2¾hr., 2 per day; $55, ages 5-12 $25, seniors $50, car $80, bike $25). Reservations recommended, $5 fee. Car price does not include driver/passengers.

Bike Rental: Bar Harbor Bicycle Shop, 141 Cottage St. (☎288-3886). Mountain bikes $10 for 4hr., $15 per day. Helmet, lock, and map. 20% discount for rentals of 5 days or longer. Driver's license, cash deposit, or credit card required. Open daily 8am-8pm; Sept.-June 9am-6pm.

National Park Canoe Rentals, at the north end of Long Pond off Rte. 102, in Pond's End (☎244-5854); or on the pier at the end of West St., Bar Harbor (☎288-0007). Canoe rental $22 for 4hr., $32 per day; kayak rental $25 per half-day, $45 per day. Open mid-May to mid-Oct. daily 8am-5pm. Reservations are strongly recommended.

Free Shuttles: service the island Jun.-Aug., linking hotels, campgrounds, village centers, and the airport with destinations in Acadia. Seven shuttle routes cover the island (transporting bikes as well as people), allowing riders to bypass Acadia's vehicle permit fees while maintaining a cleaner environment. Shuttles leave from the village green in Bar Harbor every 30min., running daily 9am-11pm; pick up a schedule at any info center or the village green for specific routes and operating times.

✳❓ ORIENTATION AND PRACTICAL INFORMATION

Mt. Desert Island is shaped roughly like a really big lobster claw, 14 mi. long and 12 mi. wide. To the east on Rte. 3 lie **Bar Harbor** and **Seal Harbor.** South on Rte. 198 near the cleft is **Northeast Harbor.** Across Somes Sound on Rte. 102 is **Southwest Harbor,** where fishing and shipbuilding thrive without the taint of tacky tourism. **Rte. 3** runs through Bar Harbor, becoming **Mt. Desert St.;** it and **Cottage St.** are the major east-west arteries. **Rte. 102** circuits the western half of the island.

Visitor Info: Acadia National Park Visitors Center (☎288-4932 or 288-5262), 3 mi. north of Bar Harbor on Rte. 3. Open daily mid-June to mid-Sept. 8am-6pm; mid-Apr. to mid-June and mid-Sept. to Oct. 8am-4:30pm. **Park Headquarters** (☎288-3338), 3 mi. west of Bar Harbor on Rte. 233, provides visitor info during the off-season (Nov.-Mar.).

Open year-round M-F 8am-4:30pm. **Bar Harbor Chamber of Commerce** (☎288-5103), in the Marine Atlantic Ferry Terminal, Rte. 3. Open M-F 8am-5pm, Sa-Su noon-5pm; in winter M-F 8am-4pm. **Mt. Desert Island Regional Chamber of Commerce** (☎288-3411), on Rte. 3 at the entrance to Thompson Island. In the same building is a state-owned **Acadia National Park Information Center** (☎288-9702). Both open daily July-Aug. 9am-8pm; mid-May to June 10am-6pm and Sept. to mid-Oct. 9am-6pm.

Hotlines: Downeast Sexual Assault Helpline, ☎800-228-2470. **Mental Health Crisis Line,** ☎800-245-8889. Both 24hr.

Emergency: Acadia National Park Law Enforcement, ☎288-3369.

Post Office: 55 Cottage St. (☎288-3122). Open M-F 8am-4:45pm, Sa 9am-noon. **ZIP code:** 04609. **Area code:** 207.

⌐ ACCOMMODATIONS

Grand hotels and prices linger from the island's exclusive resort days. Still, a few reasonable establishments do exist, particularly on **Rte. 3** north of Bar Harbor. Camping spots cover the island, especially **Rte. 198** and **102**, well west of town.

Bar Harbor Youth Hostel (HI-AYH), 27 Kennebec St. (☎288-5587), Bar Harbor. In the parish house of St. Saviour's Episcopal Church, down the road from the bus stop. 2 large dorm rooms accommodate 20 guests in cheery red-and-white bunks. A perfect location, common room with TV and piano, full kitchen, weekly movie nights, and occasional pancake breakfasts ($4) compensate for only 2 showers and an 11pm curfew. Lockout 9am-5pm. Open mid-June to Sept. Dorms $12, non-members $15. Linen $2.

Mt. Desert Island YWCA, 36 Mt. Desert St. (☎288-5008), Bar Harbor, near downtown. Women only. Common room, kitchen, laundry. Simple singles with shared bath $30 per night; doubles $25 per person; solarium with 7 beds $20 per bed; weekly rates $90/$75/$65. $25 deposit. Open daily 9am-9pm; off-season M-F 9am-4pm. Reserve early.

White Birches Campground (☎244-3797), Southwest Harbor, on Seal Cove Rd. 1 mi. west of Rte. 102. 60 widely spaced, wooded sites offer an escape from the touristy areas. $20 for up to 4 people, with hook-up $24; weekly $120/$144; $2 per additional person. Free hot showers, fireplace, bathrooms. Open daily mid-May to mid-Oct. 8am-8pm for check-in. Reservations recommended, especially in July and Aug.

Acadia National Park Campgrounds: Blackwoods (☎288-3274, reservations 800-365-2267), 5 mi. south of Bar Harbor on Rte. 3. Over 300 wooded sites seem tightly packed when campgrounds reach full occupancy in summer. When the throngs depart, the charm of the campground's thick, deep, dark woods returns, as does the larger wildlife. Mid-Mar. to mid-Dec. $18; mid-Dec. to mid-Mar. free. Group sites also available. Reserve in summer. **Seawall** (☎244-3600), off Rte. 102A on the western side of the island, 4 mi. south of Southwest Harbor and a 10min. walk from the ocean. Seawall is slightly more rustic with toilets but no hook-ups. Showers available ($1 per 6min.). A total of 213 sites; first come, first served walk-in sites are $12; drive-in and RV sites $18. Open daily late May to Sept. 7:15am-9pm. See **Acadia National Park,** p. 93.

◖ FOOD

■ **Beal's** (☎244-7178 or 800-245-7178), off Main St. at the end of Clark Point Rd., Southwest Harbor, goes easy on the frills, offering lobster at superb prices on an outdoor, picnic-tabled patio overlooking the pier. Pick a live crustacean from a tank ($10-13), and (s)he'll be buttered and steaming red in minutes. Kitchen closed off-season, but fresh seafood is sold. Open daily mid-May to early Sept. 9am-8pm; off-season 9am-5pm. Hrs. vary with weather.

■ **Freddie's Route 66 Restaurant,** 21 Cottage St., (☎288-3708), Bar Harbor. Freddie's walls, ceilings, and airwaves are absolutely crammed with neon signs, wind-up metal cars, boob tubes showing Casper in black and white, and the gloriously upbeat tunes of the 50s. $9 is well spent on a Cadillac burger, $15 for a seafood pie. Open daily mid-May to mid-Oct. 11am-2:30pm and 4:30-10pm.

Jordan's, 80 Cottage St. (☎288-3586), Bar Harbor. A breakfast joint specializing in blueberry-packed muffins and pancakes. Open daily 5am-2pm except for 3 weeks in Nov.

The Colonel's Deli Bakery and Restaurant (☎276-5147), on Main St. in Northeast Harbor. Sandwiches so big it's hard to get one into your mouth ($6-10). Take one with you for a cheap dinner in the national park. Open mid-Apr. to Oct. daily 6:30am-9pm.

👁 SIGHTS

The staff at the **Mt. Desert Oceanarium,** at the end of Clark Pt. Rd. near Beal's in Southwest Harbor, knows its sea stuff. The main museum, reminiscent of a grammar school science fair, fascinates children and some adults. (☎244-7330. Open mid-May to late Oct. M-Sa 9am-5pm. Ticket for all 3 facilities $13, ages 4-12 $10.) Cruises head out to sea from a number of points. **Bar Harbor Whale Watch Co.,** 1 West St. at the waterfront, offers both whalewatching (2-3 per day; $39, ages 5-15 $20, under 5 $8) and lobster, fishing, and seal-watching trips (2-5 per day; $18/$15/$5). (☎288-2386. Open May-Oct; call for exact schedule. Reservations recommended.) The **Acadian Whale Watcher,** Golden Anchor Pier, West St., has occasional sunset cruises. (☎288-9794 or 800-247-3794. Operates May-Nov. Buy tickets at corner of Cottage and Main St. 2-3 trips per day, whale watch/puffin tour combo $36, $20 for kids ages 6-14.) **Wildwood Stables,** along Park Loop Rd. in Seal Harbor, takes tourists on explorations of the island via horse and carriage. (☎276-3622. 1hr. tour $13.50, seniors $12.50, ages 6-12 $7, ages 2-5 $4. 2hr. tour $17.50/$16.50/$8/$5. Reservations recommended.)

🎵🎭 ENTERTAINMENT AND NIGHTLIFE

Most after-dinner pleasures on the island are simple and cluster in Bar Harbor. **Ben and Bill's Chocolate Emporium,** 66 Main St., near Cottage St., boasts 50 flavors of homemade ice cream, including—no kidding—lobster. (☎288-3281. Open daily mid-Feb. to Jan. 9am-midnight. Cones $3-4.) **Geddy's Pub,** 19 Main St., gives a backwoods backdrop of weathered wooden signs, beat-up license plates, and moose head trophies to the dancing frenzy that breaks out nightly. Live music until 10:30pm, when tables are moved aside for a DJ and dance floor. Pub-style dinner served until 9:30pm, pizzas ($10) until 10pm. (☎288-5077. Open daily Apr.-Oct. 11:30-12:30am; winter hrs. vary. No cover.) Locals prefer the **Lompoc Cafe & Brew Pub,** 36 Rodick St., off Cottage St., which features Bar Harbor Real Ale and live jazz, blues, Celtic, rock, and folk. (☎288-9392. Open daily May-Oct. 11:30am-1am. Shows F-Sa nights. No cover.) The Art Deco **Criterion Theater,** on Cottage St., shows flicks in the summer. (☎288-3441. 2 evening movies daily. Box office opens 30min. before show. $7, seniors $6, under 12 $4.50; balcony seats $7.75.)

ACADIA NATIONAL PARK   ☎207

The jagged, rocky oceanside perimeter of Acadia National Park's 38,500 acres is gradually obscured, then enveloped by thick pine forests as you move inland. Fern-shrouded streams and 120 mi. of hiking trails and carriage roads criss-cross the rugged, coastal terrain. Fearing the island would one day be overrun by cars, millionaire and expert horseman John D. Rockefeller funded the creation of these carriage roads, now accessible to mountain bikes.

Precipice Trail (1½ mi.), one of the most popular and strenuous hikes, is closed June to late Aug. to accommodate nesting peregrine falcons; venture down the meandering cliff and ledge trail prepared to use the iron rungs and ladders that are necessary to complete the hike intact. The **Cadillac Summit Trail** (¼ mi.), atop its mountain namesake, is paved and wheelchair accessible. Hike either the **Cadillac Mountain North** (4½ mi.) or **South Ridge** (7½ mi.) trails, or cruise along the paved **auto road** to the top. At 1530 ft., Cadillac Mountain is the highest point on the Atlantic seaboard north of Brazil; from its peak, be the first person in the US to witness 🌄**sunrise** on any summer morning (4-4:30am in summer).

About 4 mi. south of Bar Harbor on Rte. 3, **Park Loop Rd.** runs along the shore of the island, where great waves crash against steep granite cliffs. The sea comes into **Thunder Hole** with a bang at half-tide. Practice your backfloat in the relatively warm **Echo Lake** or at **Sand Beach,** both of which have lifeguards in the summer.

Touring the park by auto costs $10 for seven days, $5 per pedestrian or cyclist. Seniors can purchase a lifetime pass for $10. The *Biking and Hiking Guide to the Carriage Roads* ($6), available at the visitors center and in bookstores, offers invaluable directions for the more labyrinthine trails. To spend the night in or near the park (and you should!), see Mt. Desert Island's **Accommodations,** p. 92.

NORTHERN MAINE COAST

Much like the coastal region south of Portland, the north offers the traveler unforgettable beaches, windswept ocean vistas, and verdant forests—for a price. Lodging in L.L. Bean country isn't cheap, but just passing through can give all the flavor, without the guilt. U.S. 1 is northern Maine's only thoroughfare; public transportation is non-existent, and traffic barely creeps along on rainy weekends in Freeport.

FREEPORT. About 20 mi. north of Portland on I-95, Freeport once garnered glory as the "birthplace of Maine." The 1820 signing of documents declaring the state's independence from Massachusetts took place at the historic **Jameson Tavern,** 115 Main St., right next to L. L. Bean. Freeport is now known as the factory outlet capital of the world, with over 100 downtown stores attracting urbanites sick of the woods. The granddaddy of them all, **L.L. Bean,** began making Maine Hunting Shoes here in 1912. The megamogul now sells everything in outdoor gear and outfits America's youth with backpacks guaranteed for life. The **factory outlet,** 11 Depot St., behind Bannister Shoes, is the place for bargains. (☎865-4057 or 800-341-4341. Open daily 9am-10pm; Jan. to late May 9am-9pm.) The multi-storied **retail store,** 95 Main St. (☎865-4761), is open 24 hours day, 365 days a year, and generates a madness that could transform even the most indoorsy herb into a backwoods renegade.

CAMDEN. In the summer, khaki-clad crowds flock to Camden, 100 mi. north of Portland, to dock their yachts alongside the tall-masted schooners in Penobscot Bay. Cruises are generally out of the budgeteer's price range, but the **Camden-Rockport Lincolnville Chamber of Commerce,** on the public landing in Camden behind Cappy's Chowder House, can tell you which are most affordable. They also have info on the sparse budget accommodations. (☎236-4404 or 800-223-5459. Open M-F 9am-5pm, Sa 10am-5pm, Su 10am-4pm; mid-Oct. to mid-May closed Su.) The **Camden Hills State Park,** 1¼ mi. north of town on U.S. 1, is almost always full in July and Aug. but you are fairly certain to get a site if you arrive before 2pm. This beautiful coastal retreat offers more than 25 mi. of trails, including one which leads up to **Mt. Battie** and has a harbor view. (☎236-3109; reservations 287-3824 or 800-332-1501. Sites $17, ME resident $13, day use $2. Free showers. Open mid-May to mid-Oct.). The folks at **Maine Sports,** on U.S. 1, in Rockport just south of Camden, teach/lead/rent/sell a wide array of sea-worthy vehicles. **Kayaks** will only be rented to those with paddling experience,

---

THE APPALACHIAN TRAIL
Stretching 2160 mi. from Mt. Katahdin, ME, to Springer Mountain, GA, the Appalachian Trail, or "AT," follows the path of the Appalachian Mountains along the eastern United States. Use of the AT is free, although only foot travelers may access it. The Trail cuts through 14 states, 8 national forests, and 6 national parks; 98% of it is on public land. Generally, the AT is very accessible, crossed by roads along its entire length except for the northernmost 100 mi. Although many sections make excellent day hikes or overnights, about 2500 "through-hikers" attempt a continuous hike of the AT annually. 3-sided first come, first served shelters dot the trail, spaced about a day's journey apart. Hikers take advantage of the many streams and nearby towns to stock up on water and supplies. White blazes on rocks and trees mark the entire length of the main trail, while blue blazes mark side trails. Numerous publications are available to facilitate your journey; contact the Center for AT Studies, P.O. Box 525, Hot Springs, NC 28743 (☎704-622-7601, M-Sa 10am-10pm; fax 704-622-7601; email atcenter@trailplace.com; www.trailplace.com) for more info, including a list of publications.

but anyone can join a tour. (☎236-8797. Open daily 8am-9pm; Sept.-May Su-Th 9am-6pm, F 9am-8pm. 2hr. harbor tour $35. Full-day singles rental $25-40, doubles $35-55, depending on whether it's a sea or lake kayak; ask about overnights to nearby islands.) The **Maine State Ferry Service** (☎789-5611), 5 mi. north of Camden in Lincolnville, floats over to Islesboro Island. (20min., 7-9 per day; last return trip 4:30pm. Round-trip $4.50, with bike $8.50, car and driver $13. Parking $4.) The ferry also has an agency on U.S. 1 in **Rockland**, 517A Main St. (☎596-2202), that shuttles to North Haven, Vinalhaven, and Matinicus. Rates and schedules change with the weather.

SEARSPORT. Forty-five mi. south of Bar Harbor on U.S. 1 lies Searsport, a respite from the commercialization of Camden and Freeport, but well known as the antique capital of Maine. Here, first-time buyers and lifelong collectors scour multi-tudinous shops for ancient and colonial treasures. A stay at the **Searsport Penobscot Bay Hostel (HI)**, 132 W. Main St./U.S. 1, merits a trip to this oceanside town. Once a sea captain's getaway, and later a bed and breakfast, the colonial homestead is now a spacious, relaxing, home-decorated hostel. (☎548-2506 or 877-334-6783. Open mid-Apr. through Oct. Office hours 8am-10am, 5pm-10pm, 10pm curfew. 10 beds $15, non-members $18. Doubles $40/$50 per person.) Each of the 19th-century village buildings composing the **Penobscot Marine Museum** features a different aspect of colonial New England maritime livelihood. The buildings, including Old Town Hall, the Congregational Church, and Captain Jeremiah Merithew's House, are concentrated along **Church St.**, off U.S. 1. (☎548-2529. Open late May to mid-Oct. M-Sa 10am-5pm, Su noon-5pm. $6; ages 6-15, $2; seniors $5; family $14.)

NEW HAMPSHIRE

There are two sides to New Hampshire: the rugged landscape and natural beauty of the White Mountains, and the tax-free outlets, tourist traps, and state liquor stores that line most of the highways. The first colony to declare its independence from Great Britain, New Hampshire has retained its backwoods libertarian charm and its motto, "Live Free or Die!"

⚡ PRACTICAL INFORMATION

Capital: Concord.
Visitor Info: Office of Travel and Tourism, P.O. Box 856, Concord 03302 (☎603-271-2666 or 800-386-4664; www.visitnh.gov). **Outdoor report:** ☎800-258-3608, 24hr. **Fish and Game Dept.,** 2 Hazen Dr., Concord 03301 (☎603-271-3421), furnishes info on hunting and fishing regulations and license fees. **U.S. Forest Service,** 719 North Main St., Laconia 03246 (☎603-528-8721). Open M-F 8am-4:30pm.
Postal Abbreviation: NH. **Sales Tax:** 8% on meals and lodgings. **Area Code:** 603.

PORTSMOUTH   ☎603

Although New Hampshire's seacoast is the smallest in the nation, with only 13 miles fronting the Atlantic Ocean, the state makes the most of its toehold on the water. Portsmouth, once the colonial capital, is one of the nicest seaside towns north of Boston. Most buildings date to the 18th century, while a handful were built in the mid-17th century. Although not large by any standards, Portsmouth is exceptionally cultured—and expensive. History is the main attraction, seafood reigns supreme, and a pint of local ale is the mainstay after dinner.

⚡ **PRACTICAL INFORMATION.** Just 57 mi. north of Boston, Portsmouth is situated at the junction of U.S. 1, 1A, and I-95. The town is best navigated by foot; leave your car in one of the inexpensive lots ($2-4 per day) downtown. State St. runs north-south through downtown and is bisected by Pleasant and Fleet St. **Buses: Vermont Transit/Greyhound,** 1 Market Sq. (☎436-0163), heads to Portsmouth from

Boston (7 per day, 1hr., $13). **Public Transit: Seacoast Trolley** (☎431-6975) runs hourly in summer from 10am-5pm, with 17 stops in and around Portsmouth ($2). **Wade's Taxi:** ☎436-0044. **Visitor Info: Greater Portsmouth Chamber of Commerce,** 500 Market St., outside downtown. (☎436-1118. In summer, open M-W 8:30am-5pm, Th-F 8:30am-7pm, Sa-Su 10am-5pm; rest of year, open M-F 8:30am-5pm.) **Hospital: Portsmouth General** (☎436-5110), a few miles from town at 333 Borthwick Ave. **Post Office:** 80 Daniel St. (☎431-1300). Open M-F 8am-5pm, Sa 9am-noon. **Zip code:** 03801. **Area code:** 603.

⌐⌐ ACCOMMODATIONS AND FOOD. Portsmouth is not the best place to spend the night unless you can afford to part with your Ben Franklins. Accommodations in town are pricey; try U.S. 1A south of Portsmouth for typically drab motels. A nice alternative is **Camp Eaton** in York Harbor, ME, about 15 mi. north of Portsmouth off Rte. 1. Although the wooded sites are still pricey, oceanside vistas and immaculate bathrooms ease the pain. (☎207-363-3424. Sites $29 for 2.) The best bet may be to splurge and stay right in Portsmouth to take advantage of the great nightlife without having to drive out of town late at night.

Portsmouth offers plenty of other dining options, with many fine establishments dotting Market St. Unfortunately, prices are not the budget traveler's friend here. ◼**The Friendly Toast,** 121 Congress St., a block and a half from Market Sq., is a local landmark, cluttered with the most ghastly artifacts the 50s could produce: mannequin limbs, pulp novels, formica furniture, and stroke-inducingly bad art. Most menu items ($6-7) are too large to finish, and come with ungodly portions of pan-hot homefries. Breakfast is served all day, and the Toast is very vegetarian-friendly. (☎430-2154. Open M-Th 7am-11pm, F 7am through Su 9am.) At **Gilly's Lunchcart,** 175 Fleet St., semi-inebriated folk trail out the door and into the street awaiting heavenly hotdogs with the works for $1.25 in the wee hours of any given night. Top it off with fries for $1-3. (Open M-Sa 11:30am-2:30am, Su 4pm-2:30am.)

◼◼ SIGHTS AND ENTERTAINMENT. Modern Portsmouth sells itself with its colonial past. The most prestigious and well-known example is **Strawberry Banke,** on the corner of Marcy and Hancock streets. The community was first settled as Strawberry Banke in 1630 and did not assume the name of Portsmouth until 1653. The **museum** is a collection of several dozen original buildings from that period. Costumed interpreters and craftsmen give visitors a feel for what life was like before the Revolution. (☎433-1100. Open daily mid-Apr. to late Oct. 10am-5pm. $12, seniors $11, ages 7-17 $8; Th half-price. Tickets are good for 2 days.) For something more modern, try the **USS Albacore,** a research submarine built locally at the Portsmouth Naval Shipyard. The sub was retired in 1972, returned to Portsmouth in 1984, and has since served as a museum of both marine exploration and naval life. (☎436-3680. Open daily 9:30am-5:30pm, May-Oct. Hours vary in winter. $4, seniors $3, under 18 $2.) Deprive yourself of sleep and peace of mind with **Ghostly Tours of Portsmouth, NH.,** as hooded guides lead visitors on a candlelit tour through Old Portsmouth, recounting ghost stories and witch tales along the way. (☎433-8888. Open June-Oct. Tours run Tu-Sa at 7pm, depart from the **Rusty Hammer Restaurant,** 49 Pleasant St, and cost $7 per person. Tour times vary; call for reservations.)

NEW HAMPSHIRE SKI RESORTS ☎ 603

The various ranges within the White Mountains offer numerous opportunities for skiing. **Ski-93** is a service which provides information and reservations for five ski resorts in the White Mountains. (☎745-8101 or 800-937-5493. *P.O. Box 517, Lincoln 03251.*) Winters in New England are long, so skiing is generally available from Nov. through Apr., but can vary drastically seasonally or with weather changes.

CRANMORE. In North Conway close to the outlets, Cranmore offers 39 trails and ski vacations complemented by great shopping. The 350 ft. half-pipe is a huge summer draw. *(☎800-786-6754. Lift tickets $29, ages 6-12 $15; lift operates from 8:30am-4pm.)*

ATTITASH. Located along U.S. 302 near North Conway, Attitash is expensive, but offers two mountains, 68 trails (20% beginner, 47% intermediate, 33% expert), and 25 acres of glades. Mountain biking, horseback riding, waterslides, and a $9 alpine slide keep the resort busy in summer. (☎374-2368. *Lift tickets for weekends/weekdays/ holidays $48/$42/$50, children $30/$27/$30. Alpine slide open 10am-6pm. Single ride $9, double $15, unlimited $21.)*

WILDCAT MOUNTAIN. Just outside Pinkham Notch on Rte. 16, Wildcat offers a superb view of the Whites from its 4062 ft. peak, as well as 44 trails (25%, 40%, 35%). Gondola rides are $9 in the summer. (☎888-754-9453. *Lift tickets for weekends/weekdays $49/$39, ages 5-15 and 65+ $39/$25; two-day weekend $89/$75.)*

LOON MOUNTAIN. Three mi. east of Lincoln on Rte. 112., Loon guarantees less-crowded conditions on their 43 trails by limiting ticket sales. They have biking and horseback riding when the weather warms and the annual **Highland Games** during the third week in Sept. (☎745-8111. *Lift tickets for weekends/weekdays $47/$40, teens $41/$33, children $29/$25.)*

CANNON MOUNTAIN. Just off I-93 in Franconia Notch State Park, Cannon has 42 trails (30%, 30%, 40%) at slightly lower prices than other local resorts. Summer hiking, biking, and swimming keep athletes in shape, while the Aerial Tramway (see p. 100) schleps the rest of us up the mountain. (☎823-5563. *Lift tickets for weekends/weekdays $42/$30, teens $35/$30, children and seniors $27/$20.)*

WHITE MOUNTAINS   ☎603

780,000 acres of mountainous national forest, maintained by the US Forest Service, provide a playground for outdoor enthusiasts. Year-round hiking and camping, as well as warmer weather alternatives like canoeing, kayaking, and fishing, supplement the White Mountains' intense winter skiing options. Campsites and cabins can be found throughout the mountains, by lakes and rivers, and deep within the wilderness. The White Mountain National Forest also harbors dozens of geological wonders and provides a relatively undisturbed refuge for some awe-inspiring animals, like the moose and black bears that occasionally surprise hikers.

▐ GETTING THERE AND GETTING AROUND

Finding the White Mountains by bus is considerably easier than getting around once there. **Concord Trailways** (☎228-3300 or 800-639-3317) runs from Boston to Concord (18 per day, $12); Conway (1 per day, $26); and Franconia (1 per day, $26). **Vermont Transit** (☎800-451-3292) stops its Boston-to-Vermont buses in Concord (3 per day, $11) at the Trailways terminal, 30 Stickney Ave. The **Appalachian Mountain Club (AMC)** runs a **shuttle** between locations on the Appalacian Trail in the White Mountains. Consult AMC's *The Guide* for a complete map of routes and times; reservations are recommended for all stops and required for some. (☎466-2727. Service operates early June to early Oct. daily 8:45am-3:30pm. $7, non-members $8.)

▐ ORIENTATION AND PRACTICAL INFORMATION

The White Mountains can be daunting to an unfamiliar traveler. The immense forest is bordered by a dozen or so distinctive towns and contains several commercial ski resorts. Many of this region's highlights can be found within three areas: **Pinkham Notch,** the popular center of the region; **Franconia Notch Area,** northwest of the National Forest; and **North Conway,** a happening gateway town. **Visitor Info:** A map of the White Mountains area is super-helpful and can be obtained for free from local town info booths and the **White Mountain Attraction Center,** P.O. Box 10, N. Woodstock 03262, at Exit 32 from I-93. (☎745-8720. Open daily 8:30am-5:30pm.) **US Forest Service Ranger Stations** dot the main highways throughout the forest, also providing maps and info on trail locations and conditions and a handy free guide to the local **backcountry facilities.** Stations include: **Androscoggin** (☎466-2713), on Rte. 16, 5 mi. south of the U.S. 2 junction in Gorham; **Ammonoosuc** (☎869-2626), on Trudeau Rd. in Bethlehem, west of U.S. 3 on U.S. 302; and **Saco** (☎447-5448), on the Kancamangus Hwy. in Conway, 100 yd. off Rte. 16. (Ranger stations open daily 8am-4:30pm; Ammonoosuc only open M-F.) **Pinkham Notch Visitors Center** (☎466-2721 or 466-

2727 for reservations), 10 mi. north of Jackson on Rte. 16 in Gorham, is the area's best source of info on weather and trail conditions. The center, run by the AMC, also handles reservations at any of the AMC lodgings and sells the complete line of AMC books, trail maps, and outdoor accessories. (Open daily 6:30am-10pm.)

CAMPING

The US Forest Service maintains over 20 **designated campgrounds:** six are directly accessible by car off the Kancamagus Hwy., the others are sprinkled along hiking trails. (☎800-280-2267 or 877-444-6777 for info. Sites $12-16. Cars parked at campsite do not require a parking pass. Bathrooms and firewood usually available. Reservation fee $10. Reserve 2 weeks in advance, especially July-Aug.) Camping is less expensive or free of charge at the many backcountry **campsites,** only accessible via hiking trails. The **US Forest Service** (☎528-8721) and the AMC's free two-page handout, *Backpacker Shelters, Tentsites, Campsites, and Cabins in the White Mountains* are both good sources of info. Neither camping nor fires are allowed above the tree line (approximately 4000 ft.), within 200 ft. of a trail, or within ¼ mi. of roads, huts, shelters, tent platforms, lakes, or streams. Rules vary depending on forest conditions; backpackers should call the Forest Service before settling into a campsite. Campers should note that a $5 **parking pass,** valid for one week, is required for any car parked at a trailhead in the forest.

ACCOMMODATIONS

The White Mountain Forest also rents land to the **AMC,** which has its main base in the mountains at the Pinkham Notch Visitors Center and maintains eight backcountry huts, spaced about a day's hike apart, along the Appalachian Trail. Guests must provide their own sleeping bags or sheets; dinner and breakfast are included with each night's stay. (Bunk with 2 meals $56, children $35; non-members $62/$39.) All huts open for full service June to mid-Oct.; self-service rates with no meals are available at other times ($16, non-members $18; call the AMC for reservations). The club runs two car-accessible **lodgings** in the White Mountains: **Joe Dodge Lodge** (see **Pinkham Notch,** p. 99) and the **Crawford Hostel**—actually an isolated set of several spartan cabins situated against a mountainous backdrop east of Bretton Woods on U.S. 302. The hostel's main lodge includes a modest kitchen and library, while the front desk sells limited supplies, including trailguides, candy, and first-aid kit material. The cabins' 24 bunks fill up quickly, so make reservations. (☎846-7773, reservations 466-2727. Clean toilets, showers. Bring a sleeping bag/linens and food. Curfew 9:30pm. $18, non-members $20.)

HIKING, BIKING, AND DRIVING

If you intend to spend a lot of time in the area and are planning to do a significant amount of hiking, the *AMC White Mountain Guide* is invaluable ($22; available in most bookstores and huts). The guide includes full maps and descriptions of all the mountain trails. Hikers should bring three layers of clothing in all seasons: one for wind, one for rain, and at least one for warmth, as weather conditions change at a moment's notice. Black flies and swarms of mosquitoes can ruin a trip, particularly in June, so carry insect repellent. After hiking, cycling is the next most popular way to tour the White Mountains. Many areas are accessible by bike, and paths are specifically provided for bikers in some locations. The *New Hampshire Bicycle* guide and map or the US Forest Service's bike trail guides, available at info centers, or *30 Bicycle Tours in New Hampshire* ($13), available at local bookstores and outdoor equipment stores, can help with planning.

To see the National Forest without much exertion, drive the ⬛**Kancamagus Scenic Highway** that connects the towns of Lincoln and Conway. The 35 mi. drive requires at least an hour, though the vistas typically lure drivers to the side of the road for a picnic. Remember to purchase a **National Forest parking pass** ($5; valid for one week) if you plan to leave your car at a trailhead or picnic ground parking lot. Check your gas at Lincoln or North Woodstock (no gas is available for 35 mi.), then head east on **the Kanc** (officially Rte. 112; clearly marked) to enjoy the scenic splendor stretching all the way to Conway.

PINKHAM NOTCH   ☎ 603

New Hampshire's easternmost Notch lies in the shadow of the tallest mountain in the Northeast, Mt. Washington. Its proximity to the peak makes Pinkham more crowded and less peaceful area than others in the area. The **Pinkham Notch Visitors Center,** the AMC's main info center in the White Mountains and the starting point for most trips up Mt. Washington, lies between Gorham and Jackson on Rte. 16. To get to Pinkham Notch from I-93 S, take Exit 35 from I-93 and travel north on U.S. 3 until it meets U.S. 302; take U.S. 302 until it meets Rte. 16, then take it north.

From just behind the Pinkham Notch Visitors Center all the way up to the summit of Mt. Washington, **Tuckerman's Ravine Trail** takes 4-5hr. of steep hiking each way. Authorities urge caution when climbing—Mt. Washington claims at least one life every year. A gorgeous day here can suddenly turn into a chilling storm, with whipping winds and rumbling thunderclouds. It has never been warmer than 72°F atop Mt. Washington, and the average temperature on the peak is a bone-chilling 26.7°F. With an *average* wind speed of 35 mph and gusts that have been measured up to an astounding 231 mph, Mt. Washington is the windiest place in the world. As long as you take proper measures, the climb is stellar and the view on the way up well worth it. Motorists can take the **Mt. Washington Auto Rd.,** a paved and dirt road that winds 8 mi. to the summit. Motorists scaling the mountain by car receive bragging rights in the form of a free "This Car Climbed Mt. Washington" bumper sticker; delay affixing it to said bumper until your car has proven its engine and brakes can handle the challenge. The road begins at **Glen House,** 3 mi. north of the visitors center on Rte. 16. (☎466-3988. Road open daily mid-June to mid-Sept. 7:30am-6pm; mid-May to mid-June and mid-Sept. to mid-Oct. 8:30am-5pm. $15 per car and driver, $6 per passenger, ages 5-12 $4.) **Guided van tours** to the summit include a 30min. presentation on the mountain's natural history ($20, ages 5-12 $10). On even the most beautiful summer days, the summit is likely to be covered with clouds, giving you a slim chance of getting a good view. So enjoy the **snack bar,** offering sandwiches ($2-4) and drinks ($1-2) at reasonable rates. (☎466-3347. Open late May to mid-Oct. daily 8am-6pm.) A **museum** is run by the **Mt. Washington Observatory.** (☎466-3388. Open daily late May to mid-Oct. 9am-7pm.)

AMC's huts offer the best lodging near the mountain. At **Joe Dodge Lodge,** immediately behind the Pinkham Notch Visitors Center, a stay includes a comfortable bunk with two delicious and sizeable meals. The lodge offers over 100 bunks, but has no self-service kitchen—all meals are prepared and served by staff. ($45, children $30; non-members $49/$33. Off-season $42, children $28; non-members $46/$30. Without meals $29, children $19; non-members $31/$21.) **Hermit Lake Shelter,** situated about 2hr. up the Tuckerman Ravine Trail, has bathrooms but no shower, and sleeps 72 people in eight lean-tos and three tent platforms ($7 per night; buy nightly passes at the visitors center). **Carter Notch Hut** lies to the east of the visitors center, a 4 mi. hike up the 19 mi. **Brook Trail;** it has 40 bunks and a functioning kitchen with gas stove. Just 1½ mi. from Mt. Washington's summit sits **Lakes of the Clouds,** the largest, highest, and most popular of the AMC's huts (room for 90); additional sleeping space for six backpackers in its basement refuge room can be reserved from any other hut. (☎466-2727. $16, non-members $18. Reservations recommended for stays at any of the AMC's huts.)

FRANCONIA NOTCH AREA   ☎ 603

Located in the northwestern expanse of the forest, Franconia Notch is not actually part of the White Mountains National Forest but a state park owned and maintained by the state of New Hampshire. Formed by glacial movements that began during an ice age 400 million years ago, the Notch comprises imposing granite cliffs, waterfalls, endless woodlands, and the famous rocky profile known as the "Old Man of the Mountain" which has come to adorn New Hampshire state highway signs.

NEW ENGLAND

☷ PRACTICAL INFORMATION. All but one of the area highlights are directly accessible from I-93. Beginning from Lincoln, traveling north on I-93, ☷The Flume, a 2 mi. walk through a spectacular granite gorge, is the first essential stop within Franconia Notch (parkway Exit 1). The moss-covered canyon walls are 90 ft. high, and the walk takes visitors over centuries-old covered bridges and past the 45 ft. Avalanche Falls. Tickets can be purchased from the **The Flume Visitors Center,** which also shows an excellent 15min. film that acquaints visitors with the landscape and geological history of the area. (☎745-8391. Open daily May-Oct., 9am-5pm; 9am-5:30pm in July-Aug. Tickets $7, ages 6-12 $4.) A 9 mi. recreational **bike path** also begins at the visitors center and parallels I-93 north through the park.

☷☷ ACCOMMODATIONS AND FOOD. The beauty of Franconia Notch makes it an ideal place for camping. **Lafayette Place Campground,** with nearly 100 sites, is nestled smack in the middle of the Franconia Notch State Park. (☎388-4373. Open mid-May to mid-Oct., weather permitting. Lafayette's location makes it extremely popular; reservations are recommended at least one week in advance. Coin-operated showers. Sites for 2 $15, $8 per additional person.) **Fransted Campground,** 3 mi. north of the Notch on Rte. 18, is one option if Lafayette is already full. (☎823-5675. Open May to mid-Oct. Showers and bathroom. Family sites $18, $2 extra for a site either along the brook or with water and electricity.) **Woodstock Inn & Station** offers a nice but not cheap—from $79—alternative to camping (☎745-3951). **Polly's Pancake Parlor,** on Rte. 117 in Sugar Hill, just 2 mi. from Exit 38 off I-93, is a homey cabin restaurant with a maple-leaf theme, Civil War-era photographs on one wall, and a dining room overlooking Mt. Washington. The parlor offers a stack of six superb pancakes for $6, unlimited superb pancakes for $11. (☎823-5575. Open weekends Apr. and Nov. 7am-2pm, then daily May-Oct. 7am-3pm.)

☷ SIGHTS. Franconia is best known for the **Old Man of the Mountain,** a 40 ft. human profile formed by five ledges of stone atop a 1200 ft. cliff on Cannon Mountain. Nathaniel Hawthorne addressed this geological visage in his 1850 story "The Great Stone Face," and the landmark has since graced state license plates as the symbol of the Granite State. The exit for "Old Man" parking is clearly marked, and a 10min. walk down the designated path brings viewers to the bank of **Profile Lake,** which affords the best available view. The 80-passenger **Cannon Mountain Aerial Tramway** climbs over 2,000 ft. in 7min. and carries visitors to the summit of The Great Cannon Cliff, a 1000 ft. sheer drop into the cleft between Mt. Lafayette and Cannon Mountain. The tram offers unparalleled vistas of Franconia Notch along its ascent, and even better views can be had from the summit. (☎823-8800. Open daily May-Oct. 9am-4:30pm; July-Aug. 9am-5:30pm. One-way $7, round-trip $9, ages 6-12 $5). Skilled mountaineers will enjoy climbing instead, via the aptly named "Sticky Fingers" or "Meat Grinder" routes. Between Exits 1 and 2 on I-93, visitors can find a well-marked turnoff for **The Basin,** a whirlpool along the Pemigewasset River that has been carved out as a 15 ft. waterfall erodes a massive base of granite. It's fully wheelchair-accessible—the path is paved—but swarms of gnats may discourage picnickers in the summer. On steamy **summer** days, the lifeguard-protected beach at **Echo Lake** just off parkway Exit 3 offers cool waters, often with crowds. The lake is accessible even when the lifeguard is not on duty. (☎823-5563. Lifeguard on duty mid-June to Sept. daily 10am-5pm. Park admission $2.50, under 12 and over 65 free.)

☷ HIKING. Myriad trails lead up into the mountains on both sides of Franconia Notch, providing excellent day hikes and views. Be prepared for severe weather, especially above 4000 ft. The **Lonesome Lake Trail,** a relatively easy hike, winds its way 1½ mi. from Lafayette Place Campground to **Lonesome Lake,** where the AMC operates its westernmost summer hut (see **Practical Information,** p. 100). The **Greenleaf Trail** (2½ mi.), which starts at the Aerial Tramway parking lot, and the **Old Bridle Path** (3 mi.), from Lafayette Place, are much more ambitious. Both lead up to the AMC's Greenleaf Hut near the summit of Mt. Lafayette and overlooking Echo Lake. This is a favorite destination for sunset photographers. From Greenleaf, a 7½ mi. trek east along **Garfield Ridge** leads to the AMC's most remote hut, the **Galehead.**

This area can keep you occupied for days; adequate supplies and equipment are needed before starting out. A campsite on Garfield ridge costs $5.

NEAR FRANCONIA: LOST RIVER
Outside of Franconia Notch State Park, **⊠Lost River,** located 6 mi. west of North Woodstock on Rte. 112, is a glacial gorge with numerous caves and rock formations. The reservation also maintains an elaborate nature garden and a forestry museum. The walk through the gorge is less than 1 mi, in length, but can take a while; each creatively-named cavern (such as the Lemon Squeeze) is open for exploration to those agile (and willing) enough to wrench through. (☎745-8031. *Open daily May-Oct. 9am-5pm. Last ticket sold 1 hr. before close. $8.50, children 6-12 $5.)*

NORTH CONWAY AND CONWAY ☎603
The town of North Conway serves as one of New Hampshire's most popular vacation destinations because of its proximity to ski resorts in winter, foliage in the fall, and hiking and shopping year-round. Rte. 16, the traffic-infested main road, houses **outlet stores** from big-buck labels like Banana Republic, J. Crew, Liz Claiborne, and Brooks Brothers. The town of Conway, several miles south, has fewer touristy shops, but several excellent mealtime and lodging options.

◪ PRACTICAL INFORMATION. A number of stores in the North Conway area rent outdoor equipment. For ski goods in winter or biking gear during other seasons, **Joe Jones,** in North Conway on Main St. at Mechanic, is suitable. A second branch lies a few miles north of town on Rte. 302. (☎356-9411. Open daily July-Aug. 9am-9pm; Sept.-Nov. and Apr.-June Su-Th 10am-6pm, F-Sa 9am-6pm. Alpine skis, boots, and poles $12 for 1 day, $22 for 2 days. Cross-country equipment $10/$16; snowboards $20/$35.) **Eastern Mountain Sports (EMS),** on Main St. in the Eastern Slope Inn, distributes free info on the area, sells camping equipment, and rents tents (2-person $15 for 1 day, $20 for 3; 4-person $20 for 1 day, $25 for 3), sleeping bags ($10 for 1 day, $15 for 3), and other equipment. The knowledgeable staff can provide first-hand info on climbing and hiking in North Conway. (☎356-5433. Open June-Sept. M-Sa 9am-9pm, Su 9am-6pm; Oct.-May daily 9am-6pm.)

▛ ACCOMMODATIONS. The **⊠White Mountains Hostel (HI-AYH),** 36 Washington St. off Rte. 16 at the intersection of Rte. 153 in the heart of Conway, is maintained by incredibly friendly folk and kept meticulously clean. The hostel has 43 comfy bunks on several floors, and each bed comes with clean linen and a pillow. (☎447-1001 or 800-909-4776, ext. 51. Kitchen and Internet use. Reception 7-10am and 5-10pm. Check-out 10am. Reservations recommended during the summer and peak foliage season. Open Dec.-Oct. $16, non-members $19, includes light breakfast; private rooms $45/$48.) The hostel at the beautiful **Cranmore Mt. Lodge,** 859 Kearsarge Rd., North Conway, has 40 bunks. The lodge is a few miles from downtown, but its recreation room, pool, jacuzzi, trails, cable TV, refrigerator, microwave, and duck pond are all at the disposal of guests. A delicious full country breakfast, included with each overnight stay, may compensate for the tight bunkrooms and thin mattresses. (☎356-2044 or ☎800-356-3596. Check-in 3pm, check-out 11am. $17, linen and towel included.)

◖ FOOD. As for eateries, **Horsefeathers** on Main St. in North Conway promises that "if you don't like it, we'll make it right;" they offer burgers for $7-7.50 and other entrees for a few bucks more. (☎356-2687. Kitchen open daily 11:30am-11:45pm; bar open until 1am.) Across the way, adjacent to Olympia Sports, **Morning Dew** caffeinates a great percentage of the local populus. This hole-in-the-wall coffee shack offers bagels, juice, and the daily paper in addition to every variety of coffee. (Open daily 7am-9pm.) Stay wired with a bagful of penny candy from **Zeb's General Store,** which also sells everything New England, from pure maple syrup to wooden signs and moose memorabilia. (☎356-9294. Open mid-June to Dec. 9am-10pm, with hrs. varying during other months.) Several miles south in **Conway,** pink, green, and purple pastels mark **Cafe Noche,** 147 Main St., which offers authentic Mexican food with many vegetarian choices. Mexican tunes filter through the restaurant and onto the outdoor patio, shaded by a giant maple and colorful umbrellas. Local patrons recommend the Montezuma Pie, a sort of Mexican lasagna ($7), or the garden burger ($4). (☎447-5050. Open M-Th, Su 11:30am-9pm, F-Sa 11:30am-9:30pm.)

VERMONT

No other state is as aptly named as Vermont. The lineage of the name extends back to Samuel de Champlain, who in 1609 dubbed the area "green mountain" in his native French. The Green Mountain range defines Vermont, spanning the length of the state from north to south and filling most of its width as well. Over the past few decades, ex-urbanite yuppies have invaded, creating some tension between the original, pristine Vermont and the packaged Vermont of trendy businesses. Happily, the former still seems to prevail; visitors can frolic in any of the 30 state forests, 80 state parks, or the mammoth 186,000-acre Green Mountain National Forest.

⁊ PRACTICAL INFORMATION

Capital: Montpelier.
Visitor Info: Vermont Information Center, 134 State St., Montpelier 05602 (☎802-828-3237; www.travel-vermont.com). Open M-F 8am-8pm. **Dept. of Forests, Parks and Recreation,** 103 S. Main St., Waterbury 05676 (☎802-241-3670). Open M-F 7:45am-4:30pm. **Vermont Snowline** (☎802-229-0531) gives snow conditions. Nov.-May 24hr.
Postal Abbreviation: VT. **Sales Tax:** 5%; 9% on meals and lodgings. **Area code:** 802.

VERMONT SKI RESORTS   ☎802

Come winter, skiers pour into Vermont and onto the Northeast's finest slopes, which become havens for hikers and cyclists in the summer and fall. Towns surrounding each of the mountains make their livelihood on this annual flood, thus offering a range of accommodations options. For more info, contact **Ski Vermont,** 26 State St., P.O. Box 368, Montpelier 05601 (☎223-2439; fax 229-6917. Open M-F 7:45am-4:45pm), or visit the comprehensive website at www.skivermont.com, which also provides links to the websites of major resorts. Helpful info can also be obtained from the Vermont Information Center (see **Practical Information** above). Cheaper lift tickets can be found off-season before mid-Dec. and after mid-Mar.

SMUGGLER'S NOTCH. Just north of Stowe on Rte. 108 W lies Smuggler's Notch, recently voted the #1 ski resort in the US by *SKI Magazine.* Smuggler's three mountains, 67 trails, and the only triple blackdiamond run in the East make it a hotspot in winter, while the resort's package deals and warm weather canoeing and hiking options attract visitors throughout the year. *(☎644-8851 or ☎800-451-8752. Lift tickets $44 weekday/$48 weekend, youth $32/$34; 5 night/5 day lodging lift packages start at $95 per adult per day in winter.)*

STOWE MOUNTAIN RESORT. 59% of Stowe's 48 trails are ranked at the intermediate level (16% beginner, 25% expert), with one-day lift tickets for $54, making it a popular resort for families. Stowe's summer facilities may be more impressive: a golf course and country club, mountain biking and alpine slides (single ride $8, ages 6-12 and seniors $7), and a skate park with half-pipe called the "launch zone." *(☎253-3000 or ☎800-253-4754. All-day pass $15, junior/senior $12; half-day $8/$6.50.)*

MT. SNOW. West of Brattleboro on Rte. 100 in the town of West Dover, this popular resort boasts 134 trails (20% beginner, 60% intermediate, 20% expert), 26 lifts, excellent snowmaking capabilities, as well as the first snowboard park in the Northeast. In the summer, mountain bikers can take advantage of 45 mi. of trails. *(☎800-245-7669. Open mid-Nov. to late Apr. M-F 9am-4pm, Sa-Su 8am-4pm. Lift tickets $52 weekends/$49 weekdays, ages 13-19 $46/$44, seniors and 12 and under $33/$31.)*

KILLINGTON. At the junction of U.S. 4 and Rte. 100 N in Sherburne, Killington's seven mountains and 205 trails cover the most terrain and entertain the East's longest ski season (mid-Oct. to early June). Snowboarding and ice-skating are also popular there in winter, hiking and biking in the summer. (☎422-3333 or ☎800-621-6867. Lift tickets $56, ages 13-18 $49, 6-12 $26.)

BURKE. For some of the most reasonable lift ticket prices in Vermont, head to Burke, off I-91 in northern Vermont. 30% of the trails are beginner, 40% intermediate, and 30% expert. In summer, visitors can find almost any recreation, from rock climbing to fishing, as well as hike and bike 200 mi. of trails. (☎626-3305. Lift tickets Sa-Su $42, ages 13-18 $37, 12 and under $28; M-F $25; off-season $20).

JAY PEAK. In Jay on Rte. 242, Jay Peak sits just inside the US-Canadian border in Vermont's Northeast Kingdom, catching more snowfall each year than any other New England resort. With some of the East's best Glades and ample opportunities for woods-skiing, Jay Peak is an appealing option for thrill-seekers. 63 trails, 40% of which are expert. Excellent fishing and mountain biking abound in summer. (☎988-2611 or ☎800-451-4449. Lift tickets $49, ages under 15 $37; after 2:45pm $12.)

OTHER RESORTS. Stratton (☎297-2200 or ☎800-787-2886; 90 trails, 12 lifts), on Rte. 30 N in Bondville; **Sugarbush** (☎583-2381 or ☎800-537-8427; 112 trails, 18 lifts, 4 mountains). **Cross-country resorts** include the **Trapp Family Lodge, Stowe** (see p. 107); **Mountain Meadows, Killington** (☎775-7077; 90 mi. of trails); and **Woodstock** (☎457-1100; 40 mi. of trails).

BURLINGTON ☎802

Tucked between Lake Champlain and the Green Mountains, the largest city in Vermont successfully bridges the gap between the urban and the rustic. Five colleges, including the University of Vermont (UVM), give the area a youthful, progressive flair; bead shops pop up next door to mainstream clothing stores without disrupting local harmony. Along Church St.—downtown's bustling marketplace—numerous sidewalk cafes offer both a taste of the middle-class hippie atmosphere and a great venue for people-watching.

▐ GETTING THERE AND GETTING AROUND

Trains: Amtrak, 29 Railroad Ave., Essex Jct. (☎879-7298), 5 mi. east of Burlington on Rte. 15. To New York (9¾hr., 1 per day, $59) and White River Junction (2hr., 1 per day, $16). Station open daily 8:30am-noon and 8-9pm. CCTA bus to downtown runs every 30min. M-F 5:55am-6:05pm, Sa 6:45am-7:40pm.

Buses: Vermont Transit, 345 Pine St. (☎864-6811 or 800-451-3292), at Main St. To: Boston (4¾hr., 5 per day, $46.50); Montréal (2½hr., 4 per day, $19); White River Junction (2hr., 5 per day, $15); Middlebury (1hr., 3 per day, $7.50); and Albany (4¾hr., 3 per day, $35). Open daily 5:30am-7:30pm.

Public Transit: Chittenden County Transit Authority (CCTA) (☎864-0211). Downtown Burlington is definitely walkable, but if visitors are planning to venture out of the city center, CCTA provides unbeatable access and frequent, reliable service. Pick up connections with Shelburne and other outlying areas downtown at the intersection of Cherry and Church St. Buses operate every 30min. M-Sa roughly 6:15am-9:20pm, depending on routes. Fare $1; seniors, disabled, and under 18 50¢; under 5 free.

Bike Rental: Ski Rack, 85 Main St. (☎658-3313 or 800-882-4530). Mountain bikes $8 for 1hr., $14 for 4hr., and $22 for 24hr. Helmet and lock included. In-line skates $8 for 4hr., $12 per day. Credit card required for rental. Open M-Th 10am-7pm, F 10am-8pm, Sa 9am-6pm, Su 11am-5pm.

▐ PRACTICAL INFORMATION

Visitor Info: Lake Champlain Regional Chamber of Commerce, 60 Main St., Rte. 100 (☎863-3489). Open M-F 8:30am-5pm, Sa-Su 9am-5pm; Oct.-May M-F 8:30am-5pm.

NEW ENGLAND

Hotlines: Women's Rape Crisis Center, ☎863-1236. **Crises Services of Chittenden County,** ☎863-2400. Both 24hr.

Internet Access: Kinko's, 199 Main St. (☎658-2561). 20¢ per min. Open 24hr.

Post Office: 11 Elmwood Ave. (☎863-6033), at Pearl St. Open M-F 8am-5pm, Sa 8am-1pm. **ZIP code:** 05401. **Area code:** 802.

▌ A PLACE TO LAY YOUR HEAD

The chamber of commerce has the complete rundown on area accommodations. B&Bs are generally found in the outlying suburbs. Reasonably priced hotels and guest houses line **Shelburne Rd.** south of downtown. **Mrs. Farrell's Home Hostel (HI-AYH)** is a welcoming abode for the homesick traveler. Six beds are split between a clean, comfortable basement and a lovely garden porch. Even if Mrs. Farrell has no available beds, she can refer you to an overflow location. The hostel is 3 mi. north of downtown via North Ave. and is accessible by public transportation; get directions when you call for reservations. (☎865-3730. Free coffee and bagels. Linen $1. Partial wheelchair access; full access expected soon. Dorms $15, non-members $17.) The **North Beach Campsites,** on Institute Rd. beside the high school 1½ mi. north of town by North Ave., have a spectacular view and access to a pristine beach on Lake Champlain. Take Rte. 127 to North Ave., or the "North Ave." bus from the main terminal on Pine St. (☎862-0942. 137 sites. Open May to mid-Oct. Sites $18, with electricity $22, full hook-up $25. Showers 25¢ per 5min. Beach closes at 9pm; free to registered campers, $5 non-campers.) The **Shelburne Campground,** on Shelburne Rd., lies 1 mi. north of Shelburne and 5 mi. south of Burlington by Rte. 7; buses to Shelburne South stop right next to the campground. (☎985-2540. Pool, laundry facilities. Open May-Oct. Sites for 2 $19, with water and electricity $21, full hook-up $27; $2 per additional person. Showers 25¢ per 5min.) See **Champlain Valley,** p. 105, for more camping.

◐ FOOD

Church Street Marketplace, and its adjacent sidestreets, has approximately 85 restaurants, making Burlington a food-lover's paradise. Visitors could eat downtown for weeks without hitting the same place twice; not bad for a city of only 40,000.

■ **Sweetwater's,** 120 Church St. (☎864-9800). Incredibly high ceilings and vast wall paintings dwarf those who come for delicious $3-3.50 soups and $6-7 sandwiches. Try the Duck Quesadillas for $9, served with cranberry mayo. In the summer, ask to be seated outdoors to observe the goings-on of Church St. Marketplace. Open M-Sa 11:30am-2am, Su 10:30am-midnight; food served M-Sa until 1am, Su until 11pm.

Liquid Energy Cafe, 57 Church St. (☎860-7666). Fills California's shoes in the East with its attitude and bright, airy interior. Nonchalant staff and patrons define "chill" while blending funky ingredients into delicious smoothies. Free Internet access. Open M-Th 7am-8pm, F 7am-9pm, Sa 9am-9pm, Su 9am-6pm.

Ben & Jerry's, 36 Church St. (☎862-9620), is considered the company's birthplace (see p. 108) after its original shop, a converted gas station at 169 Cherry St., was burned down and abandoned. Cones $2-3. Open Apr.-Nov. Su-Th 11am-11pm, F-Sa 11am-midnight; Dec.-Mar. Su-Th 11am-10pm, F-Sa 11am-11pm.

◉ SIGHTS

The **Shelburne Museum,** 7 mi. south of Burlington in Shelburne, houses one of the best collections of Americana in the country. A 19th-century General Store and adjacent apothecary are among the 37 buildings composing the splendid 45-acre museum. A covered bridge, lighthouse, and 1950s house are displayed beside Degas, Cassat, Manet, Monet, Rembrandt, and Whistler paintings. (☎985-3346. Open daily mid-May to Oct. 10am-5pm. Hours vary from Oct.-May; several buildings only open in summer. Tickets are valid for 2 days; $17.50, 14 and under $7.) Five mi. farther south on U.S. 7, the **Vermont Wildflower Farm** has a seed shop and 6½ acres of wildflower gardens. (☎425-3641. Open Apr.-Oct. daily 10am-5pm. $3; off-season admission only $1.50.)

NEW ENGLAND

Amateur historians delight in Victorian **South Willard St.**, where you'll find **Champlain College** and the **University of Vermont,** founded in 1797. **City Hall Park,** in the heart of downtown, and **Battery St. Park,** on Lake Champlain near the edge of downtown, are bucolic. For insomniac boaters, the **Burlington Community Boathouse,** at the base of College St. at Lake Champlain, is open late to rent light craft for a cruise on the lake. *(☎865-3377. Open June-Aug. 24hr.; daily mid-May to June and Sept. to mid-Oct. 6am-10pm. Sailboats $20-35 per hr.)* The **Spirit of Ethan Allen** scenic cruise departs from the boathouse at the bottom of College St. Live commentary complements mountain scenery and a close-up view of the famous **Thrust Fault,** which is not visible from land. *(☎862-9685. Cruises late May to mid-Oct. daily 10am, noon, 2, and 4pm. $9.40, ages 3-11 $4.15. Sunset cruise lasts 1hr. longer and sails at 6:30pm Su-Th; adults $10, ages 3-11 $5.20.)* The **Ethan Allen Homestead** rests northeast of Burlington on Rte. 127. In the 1780s, Allen forced the surrender of Fort Ticonderoga and helped establish the state of Vermont. He built his cabin in what is now the Winooski Valley Park. *(☎865-4556. Open mid-May to mid-June daily 1-5pm; June to mid-Oct. M-Sa 10am-5pm, Su 1-5pm. Last tour 4:15pm. $4, seniors $3.50, ages 5-17 $2, families $12.)*

🎵🎹 ENTERTAINMENT AND NIGHTLIFE

UVM and several other nearby college fuel Burlington's youthful, kickin' atmosphere. The town's locus is Church St. Marketplace, a pedestrian haven for tie-dye seekers and ice cream lovers, where all are entertained by off-beat puppeteers and musicians. In the summer, the **Vermont Mozart Festival** (☎862-7352 or 800-639-9097) brings Bach, Beethoven, and Mozart to barns, farms, and meadows throughout the area. The **Discover Jazz Festival** (☎863-7992) features over 1000 musicians in both free and ticketed performances. The **Flynn Theater Box Office,** 153 Main St., handles sales for the Mozart and jazz performances (☎863-5966; open M-F 10am-5pm, Sa 11am-4pm). The **Champlain Valley Folk Festival** (☎800-769-9176) croons in early Aug.

Immortalized by ex-regulars Phish on their album *A Picture of Nectar,* **Nectar's,** 188 Main St., rocks with inexpensive food, such as the locally acclaimed gravy fries ($3-5), and nightly live tunes. (☎658-4771. Open M-F 5:45am-2am, Sa 7:30am-1am, Su 7:30am-2am. No cover.) The **Red Square,** 136 Church St., is one of Burlington's most popular night spots with live music nightly. Bands play in the alley if the crowd gets large. (☎859-8909. No cover.)

🚗 DAYTRIP FROM BURLINGTON

CHAMPLAIN VALLEY. Lake Champlain, a 100 mi. long lake between Vermont's Green Mountains and New York's Adirondacks, is often referred to as "Vermont's West Coast." You can take a bridge or a ferry across the lake; the ferry offers fantastic views. The **Lake Champlain Ferry,** located on the dock at the bottom of King St., sails daily from Burlington to Port Kent, NY, and back. (☎864-9804. 1hr. Late June to Aug. 12-14 per day, 8am-7:30pm; mid-May to late June and Sept. to mid-Oct. 9 per day, 8am-6:35pm. $3.25, ages 6-12 $1.25, car $12.75). The same company also travels from Grand Isle to Plattsburg, NY, and 14 mi. south of Burlington from Charlotte, VT, to Essex, NY (either fare $2.25, ages 6-12 50¢, with car $7).

Mt. Philo State Park, 15 mi. south of Burlington off Rte. 7, offers pleasant camping and gorgeous views of the Champlain Valley; take the Vermont Transit bus from Burlington south along U.S. 7 toward Vergennes. (☎425-2390. Open mid-May to mid-Oct. daily 10am-sunset. 8 tent sites without hook-ups $11, 2 lean-tos $15. Entrance fee $2, ages 4-14 $1.50.) The marsh of the **Missisquoi National Wildlife Refuge** sits at the northern end of the lake west of Swanton, VT along Rte. 78. Also north of the lake, **Burton Island State Park** is accessible only by ferry from Kill Kare State Park, 35 mi. north of Burlington and 3½ mi. southwest off U.S. 7 near St. Albans Bay. (☎524-6353. Open late May to early Sept. daily 8am-8pm; call for schedule. $4.) The campground has 19 tent sites ($13) and 26 lean-tos ($19; $4 per additional person). The state park on **Grand Isle,** just off U.S. 2 north of Keeler Bay, also offers camping. (☎372-4300. Open mid-May to mid-Oct. 123 sites for 4 $13, $3 per additional person; 34 lean-tos $17/$4; 1 cabin $34. Reservations are highly recommended, especially for summer weekends.)

MIDDLEBURY   ☎802

Unlike the many Vermont towns that seem to shy away from association with local colleges, Middlebury, "Vermont's Landmark College Town," welcomes the energy and culture stimulated by Middlebury College. The result is a traditional Vermont atmosphere tinged both with vitality and history.

▨ PRACTICAL INFORMATION. Middlebury stretches along U.S. 7, 42 mi. south of Burlington. **Vermont Transit** stops at the Exxon station, 16 Court St., west of Main St. (☎388-4373; station open M-Sa 6am-9pm, Su 7am-9pm). Buses run to Burlington (1hr., 3 per day, $7.50); Rutland (1½hr., 3 per day, $7.50); Albany (3hr., 3 per day, $28); and Boston (6hr., 3 per day, $43). There is no public transportation in Middlebury, but the **Bike Center,** 74 Main St., rents bikes starting at $15 per day (☎388-6666; open M-Sa 9:30am-5:30pm). The staff at the **Addison County Chamber of Commerce, 2** Court St., in the historic Gamaliel Painter House, has area info (☎388-7951; open M-F 9am-5pm; limited weekend hrs. in summer; maps of Middlebury are outside if you arrive after hours). **Post Office:** 10 Main St. (☎388-2681; open M-F 8am-5pm, Sa 8am-12:30pm). **ZIP code:** 05753. **Area code:** 802.

▟ ACCOMMODATIONS. Lodging with four walls and no mosquitoes does not come cheaply in Middlebury; be prepared to trade an arm and a leg for an extended stay. The **Sugar House Motor Inn,** just north of Middlebury on Rte. 7, offers basic motel rooms with free local calls, refrigerators, and microwaves. (☎388-2770. Rooms start at $60 but the owner may be willing to make a deal off-season.) On the southern edge of Middlebury, the **Greystone Motel,** 2 mi. south of the town center on Rte. 7, has ten basic rooms (☎388-4935; singles $65; doubles $75). The best budget accommodations are to be found in the great outdoors. **Branbury State Park,** 7 mi. south on U.S. 7, then 4 mi. south on Rte. 53, stretches along Lake Dunmore, offering idyllic frisbee fields and camping grounds. (☎247-5925. Open late May to mid-Oct. 40 sites $13; lean-tos $19. Canoe rentals $5 per hr., $30 per day; paddle boats $5 per 30min. Showers 25¢ per 5min.) **River's Bend Campground,** 3 mi. north of Middlebury off Rte. 7 on the Dog Team Rd. in New Haven, is clean and appropriately named, but can be difficult to find. (☎388-9092 or 888-505-5159. 65 sites for 2 with water and electricity $20, river sites $24; $6 per additional adult. Fishing, swimming, picnicking facilities $3. Canoe rental $6 per hr. Showers 25¢ per 5min.)

◖▤ FOOD AND NIGHTLIFE. Middlebury's many fine restaurants cater chiefly to plump wallets, but the year-round presence of students ensures the survival of cheaper places. **Noonie's Deli,** in the Marbleworks building just behind Main St., is a student favorite and makes terrific $4-5 sandwiches on homemade bread. (☎388-0014. Open daily 8am-8pm.) Students also flock to **Mister Up's,** a popular nighttime hangout on Bakery Ln. just off Main St., for an impressively eclectic menu including sandwiches ($6-7), hamburgers ($5-7), and an extensive salad bar. (☎388-6724. Open M-Sa 11:30am-midnight, Su 11am-midnight.) Decked with cacti and porcelain flamingoes, **Amigos,** 4 Merchants Row, offers fajitas, burritos, and other Mexican favorites. (☎388-3624. Open M-Th 11:30am-9pm, F-Sa 11:30am-10:00pm, Su 4-9pm; bar open daily until midnight, depending on the crowd. Live music F-Sa.)

◪ SIGHTS. The **Vermont State Craft Center** at Frog Hollow exhibits and sells the artistic productions of Vermonters. (☎388-3177. Open M-Th 9:30am-5:30pm, F-Sa 9am-6pm, Su 11am-5pm.) **Middlebury College** hosts cultural events; the architecturally striking concert hall in the college **Arts Center,** just outside of town, resonates with a terrific concert series. The campus **box office** has details on events sponsored by the college. (☎443-6433. Open Sept.-May Tu-Sa noon-4pm and 1hr. before start of show.) Tours from the **Admissions Office,** in Emma Willard Hall on S. Main St., showcase the campus. (☎443-3000. Tours Sept. to late May daily 9am and 1pm. In July and Aug. Self-guided tour brochures available.) Too poor for a pint? Trek ¾ mi. north of town to the **Otter Creek Brewery** for free samples. (793 Exchange St. ☎800-473-0727. Tours daily at 1, 3, and 5pm.) Fifteen mi. east of the Middlebury College campus, the **Middlebury College Snow Bowl** entertains skiers in winter with 15 trails and lifts. (☎802-388-4356.)

STOWE ☎802

Stowe winds gracefully up the side of Mt. Mansfield (Vermont's highest peak, at 4393 ft.). The village self-consciously fancies itself an American skiing hotspot on par with its ritzier European counterparts. In fact, Stowe has something of an obsession with all things Austrian, which may account for the proliferation of Austrian-type chalets and restaurants dotting the mountain's ascending road.

🏠 PRACTICAL INFORMATION. Stowe is 12 mi. north of I-89's Exit 10, which is 27 mi. southwest of Burlington. The ski slopes lie along **Rte. 108** (Mountain Rd.), northwest of Stowe. **Vermont Transit** (☎244-6943 or 800-451-3292; open daily 8am-8pm) comes only as close as **Depot Beverage**, 1 River Rd., in Waterbury, 10 mi. from Stowe. **Peg's Pick-up DBA Stowe Taxi** will take you into Stowe for about $20, but you should call ahead (☎253-9433). In winter, the **Stowe Trolley** (☎253-7585) runs irregularly between the important locations in the village. (In summer, 1¼hr. tours M, W, F 11am, $5. In winter, every 20min. 8-10am and 2-4:20pm; every hr. 11am-1pm and 5-10pm, $1; weekly pass $10.) **Visitors Info: Stowe Area Association** on Main St. (☎253-7321 or 800-247-8693. Open M-F 9am-8pm, Sa 10am-5pm, Su 10am-5pm; late Apr. to early May closed Sa-Su.) **Post Office:** 105 Depot St., off Main St. (☎253-7521. Open M-F 7:15am-5pm, Sa 9am-noon.) **ZIP code:** 05672. **Area code:** 802.

🛏 ACCOMMODATIONS. At the base of Mt. Mansfield, **Mt. Mansfield Hostel**, 6992 Mountain Rd., 7 mi. from town (shuttles run to town during ski season), is Stowe's best lodging bargain by far. Also, meals are cheap and gigantic: the excellent breakfast will run you $5, dinner $7. (☎253-4010. 48 beds; $12 in the summer, $15 in the spring and fall; in ski season Su-Th $19, F-Sa $24. Reserve by phone far in advance for ski and foliage seasons.) **Foster's Place,** on Mountain Rd., offers dorm rooms with a lounge, game room, and hot tub/sauna in a recently renovated school building. (☎253-9404. Singles with shared bath $39; private bath $49; quad $75. Reservations recommended.) **Gold Brook Campground,** 1½ mi. south of the town center on Rte. 100, is the only camping area open year-round in Stowe. (☎253-7683. Showers, laundry, horseshoes, skateboard ramp. Tent sites for 2 $18, with hook-up $20-27, $5 per additional person.) **Smuggler's Notch State Park,** 7248 Mountain Rd./Rte. 108, 8 mi. west of Stowe, just past the hostel, keeps it simple with hot showers, tent sites, and lean-tos. (☎253-4014. Open late May to mid-Oct. Sites for 4 $12, $3 per additional person up to 8; lean-tos $16/$4. Reservations recommended.)

🍴 FOOD. Mac's Deli is a convenient stop for a sandwich ($3) or sub ($4) to go. Located in Mac's Stowe Grocery Store, S. Main St. by the intersection of Rte. 100 and Rte. 108, the deli has awful good sandwiches but no seating. In winter, they serve piping hot soups at $2.25 per pint. (☎253-4576. Open daily 7am-9pm.) The **Depot Street Malt Shoppe,** 57 Depot St., is reminiscent of decades past; felt sports pennants and plastic 45s bedeck the walls. While the cost of a 50s-style cherry or vanilla coke has been adjusted for inflation, prices remain reasonable, with meals ranging from $3-8. (☎253-4269. Open daily 11am-9pm.) The **Sunset Grille and Tap Room,** 140 Cottage Club Rd. off Mountain Rd., is a favorite among sportsfans with its 20 TVs (including three big screens) and pool and airhockey tables. The restaurant adjacent to the bar offers barbecue fare. (☎253-9281. Open daily for dining 11:30am-midnight; bar open until 2am, 1am on Sa.) The pub-like atmosphere of **The Shed,** on Mountain Rd., along with six potent homemade microbrews and unbeatable M-F specials, make it another nighttime hotspot. (☎253-4364.)

⛷ OUT OF DOORS. Stowe's ski offerings include the **Stowe Mountain Resort** (☎253-3000 or ☎800-253-4754) and **Smuggler's Notch** (☎664-1118 or ☎800-451-8752. See **Vermont Ski Resorts,** p. 102 for more info.) Nearby, the hills are alive with the sound of the area's best cross-country skiing at the **Von Trapp Family Lodge,** Luce Hill Rd., 2 mi. off Mountain Rd. Yes, it *is* the family from *The Sound of Music*, and it is divine. Don't stay here unless you have a rich uncle in Stowe—prices for lodging climb to $345 in the high season. There's no charge to visit, however, and the lodge does offer fairly inexpensive rentals and lessons for their cross-country ski

NEW ENGLAND

trails. (☎253-8511. Trail fee $14; ski rentals $16; lessons $14-40 per hr.; ski school package includes all three for $35; discounts for kids.) **A.J.'s Ski and Sports,** at the base of Mountain Rd., rents snow equipment in winter, bikes and in-line skates during other seasons. (☎253-4593. Skis, boots, and poles: downhill $24 per day, 2 days $46; cross-country $12/$22. Snowboard and boots $24 per day. 20% discount with advance reservations. Mountain bike or in-line skates, $7 1hr., $16 half-day, $24 full-day, necessary padding/helmet included. Open in summer daily 9am-6pm; in winter Su-Th 8am-8pm, F-Sa 8am-9pm.)

In summer, Stowe's frenetic pace drops off—as do its prices. **Action Outfitters,** 2160 Mountain Rd. (☎253-7975; open daily 9am-5:30pm), rents mountain bikes ($6 per hr., $14 per half-day, $30 full-day), in-line skates ($6/$12/$18), and canoes ($30 per day; life jackets, paddles, and a car rack are included in the rental price.) Stowe's 5½ mi. **asphalt recreation path,** perfect for cross-country skiing in the winter and biking, skating, or strolling in the summer, runs parallel to the Mountain Rd.'s ascent and begins behind the church on Main St. in Stowe. Before you set out on the path check out **Shaw's General Store,** 54 Main St. (☎253-4040), for pretty much anything, including Vermont-made shoes.

Fly fisherfolk should head to the **Fly Rod Shop,** 3 mi. south of Stowe on Rte. 100, to pick up the necessary fishing licenses ($38 per year, $25 per week, $11 per day; $20 per year for VT residents) and rent fly rods and reels for $10 per day. The owner can show you how to tie a fly, or you can stick around for free fly-fishing classes on the shop's own pond. (☎253-7346 or ☎800-535-9763. Open Apr.-Oct. M-F 9am-6pm, Sa 9am-5pm, Su 10am-4pm; after fishing season, M-F 9am-5pm, Sa 9am-4pm, Su 10am-4pm.) To canoe on the nearby Lamoille River, **Umiak,** Rte. 100, 1 mi. south of Stowe Center, can help. The store (named after a unique type of kayak used by the Inuit) rents regular ol' kayaks and canoes in the summer and offers a full-day river trip for $30 per person. (☎253-2317. Rental and transportation to the river included. Open daily Apr.-Oct. 9am-6pm; winter hrs. vary. Sport kayaks $10 per hr., $20 per 4hr.; canoes $10/$25.) Located in a rustic red barn, **Topnotch Stowe,** 4000 Mountain Rd., offers 1hr. horseback-riding tours through woods and streams. (☎253-6244. Tours daily late May through Nov. 11am, 1, and 3pm; $25. Reservations required.)

NEAR STOWE: ROUTE 100 GLUTTONY

If you haven't already made yourself sick on **Ben & Jerry's** ice cream, Rte. 100 features a bona fide food fiesta south of Stowe. Begin at Ben & Jerry's and drive north on Rte. 100 towards Stowe. The first stop is the **Green Mountain Chocolate Company** (☎244-1139) and **Cabot Annex Store** (☎244-6334), home to rich chocolate truffles and Vermont's best cheddar (open daily 9am-6pm). Cheddar samples are free, but fork over some cash for the chocolate. Leave room in your stomach for the **Cold Hollow Cider Mill.** In addition to the potent beverage, cider spin-offs include the 35¢ jelly and doughnuts. (☎244-8771. Call for a cider-making schedule. Open daily 8am-6pm.) Finally, maple is everywhere at the **Stowe Maple Products** maple museum and candy kitchen. Mar. and Apr. is syrup season, but they sell the goods all year. (☎253-2508. Open daily 8am-6pm.)

BEN & JERRY: TWO MEN, ONE DREAM, AND LOTS OF CHUNKS

In 1978, Ben Cohen and Jerry Greenfield enrolled in a Penn State correspondence course in ice cream making, converted a gas station into their first shop, and launched themselves on the road to a double scoop success story. Today, **Ben and Jerry's Ice Cream Factory,** north of Waterbury on Rte. 100, is a mecca for ice cream lovers. On a 30min. tour of the facilities, you can taste the sweet success of the men who brought "Lemongrad" to Moscow and "Cherry Garcia" to San Francisco. The tour tells Ben & Jerry's history, showcases the company's social consciousness, and awards a free sample at the end. *(☎882-1260. Tours Nov.-May daily every 30min. 10am-5pm; June every 20min. 9am-5pm; July-Aug. every 10min. 9am-8pm; Sept.-Oct. every 15min. 9am-6pm. $2, seniors $1.75, under 13 free.)*

WHITE RIVER JUNCTION ☎ **802**

The intersection of I-89 and I-91 marks White River Junction, which serves as the bus center for most of Vermont. **Vermont Transit** (☎ 295-3011 or ☎ 800-552-8737; office open daily 7am-9pm), on U.S. 5, behind the Mobil station 1 mi. south of downtown White River Junction, makes connections to New York (7½hr., 3 per day, $60); Burlington (2hr., 4 per day, $18); Montréal (5hr., 5 per day, $45); and smaller centers on a less regular basis. **Amtrak** (☎ 295-7160; office open daily 9am-noon and 5-7pm), on Railroad Rd. off N. Main St., rockets once per day to New York (7½hr.; M-Th and Sa $58, F and Su $64); Essex Jct. (near Burlington, 2hr.; $16/$24); Montréal (4½hr.; $30/$30); and Philadelphia (9hr.; $75/$68).

There's not much in White River Junction to attract tourists, but if you must stay in town, virtually the only choice for lodging is the old-style **Hotel Coolidge (HI-AYH),** 17 S. Main St., across the road from the retired Boston and Maine steam engine. From the bus station, walk to the right on U.S. 5 and down the hill past two stop lights (1 mi.) into town. The 26-bed dorm-style hostel-ette is tidy and relatively private. (☎ 295-3118 or ☎ 800-622-1124. Dorm beds $19, non-members $22; couple rooms are $29/$32.) The **Polkadot Restaurant,** 1 N. Main St., doles out cheap sandwiches ($2-5) and sit-down meals. (☎ 295-9722. Open M 5am-2pm, Tu-Su 5am-7pm.)

An **info booth** next to the Texaco station at the intersection of U.S. 5 and I-91 will let you in on what little there is to do in White River Junction. The **Upper Valley Chamber of Commerce,** 61 Old River Rd., about 1 mi. south of town off U.S. 4, also has area info (☎ 295-6200: generally open Tu and Th mornings). **Post Office:** 27 South St. (☎ 296-3246; open M-F 8am-noon, 1-4:30pm, Sa 8-11am). **ZIP code:** 05001.

BRATTLEBORO ☎ **802**

The colonial brick facade of Brattleboro's Main St. contains more than its fair share of sporting goods stores, but their presence is warranted by the town's popularity as a starting point for adventures in the southern Green Mountains and along the Connecticut River. Foliage season in Oct. is the most beautiful, and thus the most expensive time for a visit to this region of Vermont.

⚑ PRACTICAL INFORMATION. The **Amtrak** (☎ 254-2301) Montréaler train from New York and Springfield, MA, stops in Brattleboro behind the museum on Vernon St. Trains depart once per day for Montréal (6hr., $39); New York (6hr., $46-51); and Washington, D.C. (9¾hr., $79). **Greyhound** and **Vermont Transit** roll into town at the parking lot behind the Citgo station off Exit 3 on I-91, on Putney Rd. (☎ 254-6066. Open M-F 8am-4pm, Sa-Su 8am-3:20pm.) Buses run to New York (5hr., 4 per day, $37-39); Burlington (3½hr., 3 per day, $26.50); Montréal (6½hr., 2 per day, $47-$50); and Boston (3hr., 2 per day, $22). To get downtown from the bus station, take the infrequent **Brattleboro Town Bus,** which runs on Putney Rd. to Main St. (☎ 257-1761; runs M-F 6:30am-6pm; fare 75¢, children 25¢). The **Chamber of Commerce,** 180 Main St., provides the *Brattleboro Main Street Walking Tour,* detailed town maps, and brochures galore for local outdoor activities (☎ 254-4565; open M-F 8:30am-5pm). In the summer and foliage seasons, an **info booth** (☎ 257-1112), on the Town Common off Putney Rd., operates from 9am-5pm. **Post Office:** 204 Main St. (☎ 254-4110; open M-F 7:30am-5:30pm, Sa 8am-1pm). **ZIP code:** 05301. **Area code:** 802.

⚑ ACCOMMODATIONS. Economy lodgings such as **Super 8** and **Motel 6** proliferate on Rte. 9 (singles generally $49-$69), although privately owned establishments can offer slightly better deals. The simple **Molly Stark Motel** sits 4 mi. west on Rte. 9. (☎ 254-2440. Singles start at $35 in winter, $41 in summer.) Renovated to mimic 1930s style, the Art Deco **Latchis Hotel,** 50 Main St. at Flat St., rents 30 decent rooms in an unbeatable location. (☎ 254-6300. Singles start at $55, doubles at $75; rates slightly higher during foliage season and holidays. Reservations recommended.) For those short on cash, the **Vagabond Hostel (HI-AYH),** 25 mi. north on Rte. 30, offers decent bunks and extensive facilities for a reasonable price. The hostel operates as a ski lodge and offers meals in the winter. (☎ 874-4096. 84 bunks, game room, kitchen. Group rates and meal plans available. Mid-June to Oct. $15, non-members $17; Thanksgiving-Mar. $20.) **Fort Dummer State Park** is 2 mi. south of town on U.S. 5; turn left on Fairground Ave. just before the I-91 interchange, then right on S. Main St. which becomes Old Guilford Rd. until you hit the park. Named for the first white settlement in Vermont, the park offers campsites with fireplaces, picnic tables, bathroom facilities, hiking trails, a playground, and a lean-to with wheelchair access. (☎254-2610. 51 sites. $11; $3 per additional person; ten lean-tos $17/$4. Day use of park $2, children $1.50. Firewood $2 per armload. Hot showers 25¢ per 5min. Reservations accepted.) **Molly Stark State Park,** 15 mi. west of town on Rte. 9 in a secluded location, provides basically the same facilities as Fort Dummer for the same prices. This park also has RV sites without hook-ups for $11. (☎464-5460. Open late May to mid-Oct.)

☐☐☐ **FOOD AND NIGHTLIFE.** One mi. north of town on Rte. 5, across Putney Rd. from the Vermont Canoe Touring Center, the casual **Marina Restaurant** is perched atop the bank of the West River, offering an unsurpassed view from the porch or outdoor terrace. Favorites include the $5.75 shrimp and chip basket and the $6 rajun cajun chicken. (☎257-7563. Open in summer M-Sa 11:30am-10pm, Su 11am-9pm. Closed M, Tu from late Oct. to mid-March. Live music Su 3-7pm. Blues Jam, 9pm-midnight on the 2nd and last W of every month.) The **Backside Cafe,** 24 High St., inside the Mid-town Mall, features a breakfast of farm-fresh eggs cooked to perfection, while locals rave about the sandwiches ($5); try either on their upstairs covered patio. (☎257-5056. Open M-Th 7:30am-3:30pm, F 7:30am-4pm and 5-9pm, Sa 8am-3pm, Su 9am-3pm.) At the **Latchis Grille,** 68 Flat St., next to the Latchis Hotel, patrons dine in inexpensive elegance and sample beer brewed on the premises by **Windham Brewery.** (☎254-4747. Lunch and dinner $6-19. 7 oz. beer sampler $2. Open W-Th 5:30-9pm, F-Su noon-3pm, 5:30-9:30pm, closes 8:45pm on Su.) With locally grown fruits, vegetables, and cider to boot, the **farmers markets** have what you need. (☎254-9567. W 11am-2pm on Main St.; Sa 9am-2pm on Rte. 9 just 2 mi. west of town.) At night, rock, blues, R&B, and reggae tunnel through the **Mole's Eye Cafe,** located downstairs at 4 High St., off Main St. Offering traditional pub fare for under $7 and live music F-Sa 9pm (cover $3-4), the Mole's Eye is more akin to a bar than a cafe. (☎257-0771. Open M-Sa 11:30am-1am.)

☐ **SIGHTS.** Brattleboro's natural beauty, especially along its rivers, is its main attraction. The region can be explored by canoe from the **Vermont Canoe Touring Center,** 1 mi. north of town on Putney Rd. (☎257-5008. Open late May to early Sept. daily 9am-dusk; otherwise call for reservations. Rentals $10 for 1hr., $15 2hr., $20 half-day, and $30 full-day.) The **Brattleboro Museum and Art Center** resides in the old Union Railroad Station at the lower end of Main St. and houses a changing and eclectic collection of very modern art. (☎257-0124. Open mid-May to Nov. Tu-Su noon-6pm. $3, students and seniors $2, under 19 free.) The **Gallery Walk** is a free walking tour of Brattleboro's plentiful art galleries on the first Friday of every month.

MASSACHUSETTS

Massachusetts regards itself, with some justification, as the intellectual center of the nation. From the 1636 establishment of Harvard, the oldest university in America, Massachusetts has attracted countless intellectuals and *literati*. This little state also offers a large variety of cultural and scenic attractions. Boston, the revolutionary "cradle of liberty," has become an ethnically diverse urban center. Resplendent during the fall foliage season, the Berkshire Mountains fill western Massachusetts with a charm that attracts thousands of visitors. The seaside areas from Nantucket to Northern Bristol feature the stark oceanic beauty that first attracted settlers to the North American shore.

7 PRACTICAL INFORMATION

Capital: Boston.

Visitor Info: Office of Travel and Tourism, 10 Park Plaza (Transportation Building), Boston 02202 (617-727-3201 or 800-447-6277 for guides; www.mass-vacation.com). Offers a complimentary, comprehensive *Getaway Guide.* Open M-F 8:45am-5pm.

Postal Abbreviation: MA. **Sales Tax:** 5%; 0% on clothing and pre-packaged food.

BOSTON ☎617

Like most sizeable American cities, Boston betrays the limits of the "melting pot" metaphor. The city is, and has been for much of its history, an uneasy stew of different racial, ethnic, religious, economic, and political groups. Its small geographical size and dramatically differentiated neighborhoods make these contrasts easy to see: the towering corporate sanctuaries of the Financial District are visible from the tortuous streets of the North End; phenomenally expensive Beacon Hill is just across the Boston Common from the nation's first Chinatown. Walking the Freedom Trail may show you early America's textbook history, but wandering the streets of Boston's neighborhoods will give you a glimpse of a people's history that is constantly changing and very much alive.

■ GETTING THERE AND AWAY

Airport: Logan International (☎561-1800), in East Boston. T: Blue Line-Airport. A free **Massport Shuttle** connects all terminals with the T-stop (bus #22 serves terminals A and B; bus #33 serves terminals C, D, and E). **US Shuttle** (☎877-748-8853) departs every 30min. to many areas in downtown Boston (24hr. service; 24hr. advanced reservation required). The **Airport Water Shuttle** runs between Rowes Wharf and Logan Airport (every 15min. M-F 6am-8pm; every 30min. F 8-11pm, Sa 10am-11pm, Su 10am-8pm; $10) while the **City Water Taxis** connect the airport with other landings (every 10min. daily Apr. to Oct. 15 7am-7pm). A **taxi** to downtown costs $15-20.

Trains: Amtrak. T: Red Line-South Station. Frequent daily service to New York City (5hr., $44-65); Washington, D.C. (9hr., $62-87); Philadelphia (7hr., $53-80); and Baltimore (8½hr., $62-87).

Buses: T: Red Line-South Station and T: Orange Line-Back Bay are the two main bus terminals. **Greyhound** provides daily service to New York City (4½hr., every 30min., $34); Washington, D.C. (10hr., every hr., $52); Philadelphia (7hr., every hr., $46); and Baltimore (10hr., every hr., $52). **Vermont Transit** (☎800-862-9671), administered by Greyhound, goes north to Burlington, VT (5hr., 6 per day, $45); Portland, ME (2½hr., 8 per day, $24); and Montréal (8hr., 6 per day, $52). **Bonanza** (☎720-4110) has frequent daily service to Providence, RI (16 per day, $8.75); Newport, RI (5 per day, $15); and Woods Hole, MA (1¾hr., 11-15 per day 8am-10pm, $15). **Plymouth & Brockton** (☎508-746-0378) travels between South Station and Cape Cod. Ride to Provincetown (3¼hr., 5 per day, $21). **Peter Pan Trailways** (☎800-343-9999) runs to Springfield (13 per day, $18); Albany (3 per day, $25); and New York City (21 per day, $34).

⊏ GETTING AROUND

Public Transit: Massachusetts Bay Transportation Authority (MBTA) (☎722-3200 or 222-5000). The **subway** system, known as the **T,** consists of the Red (2 lines split at JFK/UMass); Green (splits into 4 lines B, C, D, and E); Blue; and Orange Lines. Maps available at info centers and T-stops. Lines run daily 5:30am-12:30am. Fare $1, seniors 25¢, under 12 40¢. **MBTA Bus** service covers the city and suburbs more extensively than the subway. Fare 75¢, seniors 15¢. Bus and T schedules available at various subway stations, including Park St. and Harvard Sq. The **MBTA Commuter Rail** reaches suburbs and the North Shore, leaving from North Station, Porter Sq., Back Bay, and South Station T stops. Fares are determined by zone $1-5.75. **Vistors passes** 1-day $6, 3-day $11, 7-day $22.

Taxis: Checker Taxi, ☎536-7008. **Boston Cab,** ☎536-5010.
Car Rental: Dollar Rent-a-Car (☎634-0006 or 800-800-4000), at various locations including **Logan Airport.** Open 24hr. Under 25 $20 surcharge per day. 10% AAA discount. Must be 21 with major credit card.
Bike Rental: Community Bicycle Supply, 496 Tremont St. (☎542-8623), in Back Bay. T: Green Line-Arlington. Open Mar.-Sept. M-F 10am-8pm, Sa 10am-6pm, Su noon-5pm; Oct.-Feb. M-Sa 10am-6pm. $5 per hr., $20 per 24hr., $90 per week. Major credit card required.

✷ ORIENTATION

Boston sits on a peninsula that juts into the protective waters of Boston Harbor. **Downtown** is still the same compact 3 sq. mi. settled in 1630, but important urban and residential neighborhoods inflate its metropolitan area. Aristocratic **Beacon Hill** marks the territory west of Downtown. The **Fitzgerald Expressway I-93** divides Downtown from the Italian **North End,** which in turn lies across the Charles River from up-and-coming **Charlestown** and is separated from ethnic **East Boston** by the Inner Harbor. **Chinatown** and the **Theater District** lie to the south. At the center of all these neighborhoods is the green **Boston Common.** West of the Common, the brownstones of **Back Bay** stand upon a landfill (don't worry, the smell subsided 100 years ago). The **Mass Pike I-90,** which continues west across the state, separates the Back Bay from the artsy **South End.** Home of the Red Sox, the **Fenway** spreads out along the Charles River to the east of Back Bay. Across the river, you'll find Boston's Left Bank, the Kremlin on the Charles, otherwise known as **Cambridge** (see p. 125).

◪ PRACTICAL INFORMATION

Visitor Info: Greater Boston Convention & Visitors Bureau, 2 Copley Pl., # 105 (☎536-4100), in Back Bay. T: Green Line-Copley. Open M-F 8:30am-5pm. Kiosk at Center Court of **Prudential Center** open M-F 9am-6pm, Sa-Su 10am-6pm. **Boston National Historic Park Visitors Center,** 15 State St. (☎242-5642), near the Old State House Downtown. T: Orange Line/Blue Line-State. Open daily 9am-5pm.
Hotlines: Rape Hotline, ☎492-7273. **Gay and Lesbian Helpline,** ☎267-9001.
Post Office: 25 Dorchester Ave. (☎267-8162), behind South Station. Open 24hr. **ZIP code:** 02205. **Area code:** 617.

◤ ACCOMMODATIONS

Finding cheap lodging in Boston is almost always difficult (if not impossible). Planning ahead is essential in order to get a room during the college-rush times in Sept., May, and June. Reservation services like the **Central Reservation Service** (☎800-332-3026 or 617-569-3800; www.bostonhotels.net; free), **Boston Reservations** (☎332-4199; $5 fee), and the **Hotel Reservations Network** (☎800-964-6835; www.hoteldiscount.com; free) promise to find discounted rooms, even during sold-out periods like Boston's **fall foliage** leaf-watching craze, which peaks in early Oct. **Room tax** in Boston is 12.45%.

▨ **Hostelling International-Boston (HI-AYH),** 12 Hemenway St. (☎536-9455), in Back Bay. From T: Green B, C, or D Line-Hynes/ICA, turn left on Mass. Ave., then right on Boylston St., and walk 1 block to Hemenway St. Laundry, kitchen, storage, in-room lockers, email kiosks in the lobby ($1 per 8min.). Shared bathrooms. Open 24hr. Check-in noon-10pm. Check-out by 11am. 6-bed dorm rooms (co-ed or single-sex) $24, non-members $27; double rooms $72, $78. 200 beds. $10 deposit for linen refunded at check-out. $5 refundable deposit for padlock. Photo ID required for check-in. Reservations recommended (credit card required). Wheelchair accessible.

Back Bay Summer Hostel (HI-AYH), 512 Beacon St. (☎353-3294), in Back Bay. From T: Green B, C, or D Line-Hynes/ICA, turn right on Mass. Ave., then left on Beacon St. BU dorms-turn-hostel in the summer. Kitchen, laundry. No sleeping bags; linen included. 200 beds. Open early June to Aug. 15. Check-in after noon. Check-out by 11am. Singles $53, non-members $56; doubles and triples $53/$56. $10 key deposit.

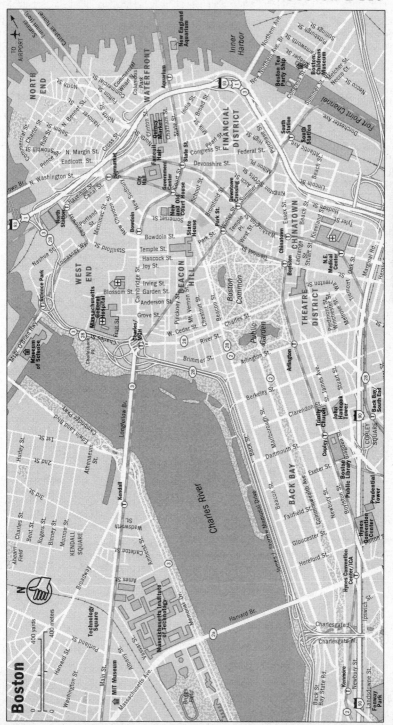

Boston

N

400 yards
400 meters

MIT Museum

KENDALL SQUARE

Massachusetts Institute of Technology

Technology Square

Charles River

WEST END

Museum of Science

Science Park

NORTH END

WATERFRONT

Inner Harbor

New England Aquarium

Boston Tea Party Ship

Boston Childrens Museum

Fort Point Channel

TO AIRPORT

FINANCIAL DISTRICT

South Station

Faneuil Hall

Quincy Market

City Hall

Government Center

New and Old Court House

State St

Downtown Crossing

North Station

Bowdoin

State House

BEACON HILL

Boston Common

CHINATOWN

N.E. Medical Center

THEATRE DISTRICT

BACK BAY

Public Garden

Arlington

Copley

Trinity Church

John Hancock Tower

Boston Public Library

Prudential Tower

Hynes Convention Center

Hynes Convention Center / ICA

COPLEY SQUARE

Back Bay South End

Charlesgate E.
Charlesgate W.

Kenmore

Fenway Park

Public Garden

Charles/MGH

Massachusetts General Hospital

Beantown Hostel, 222 Friend St., 3rd fl. (☎723-0800), and **Irish Embassy Hostel,** 232 Friend St. (☎723-0800), above the Irish Embassy Pub. From T: Orange Line/Green Line-North Station, with the Fleet Center on your right, head down Causeway and turn left down Friend St. (between Canal and Portland St.). Check-in for both hostels at Beantown. 110 beds in 6-10 bed-rooms, both single-sex and mixed. Free buffet dinner Tu-W, F-Sa 8pm in the **Irish Embassy Pub.** Linen deposit $10 (no sleeping bags or sleep-sheets). Lockers 50¢. Kitchen in Irish Embassy. Laundry in Beantown. Curfew 1:45am. Check-out 10am. $22. Reservations recommended. Wheelchair access on Portland St.

YMCA of Greater Boston, 316 Huntington Ave. (☎536-7800), in the Fenway. T: Green E Line-Northeastern. Just down the street from Symphony Hall and the MFA. Basic dorm rooms (no A/C, but most have TV). Hallway bathrooms. Cafeteria, pool, and gym. Reception 24hr. Check out before 11am. Key deposit $5. Singles $42; doubles $62; triples $81. With HI card $38/$56/$81. Breakfast included. Reservations recommended 2 weeks in advance. No children under 16. 10-day maximum stay. Men only except mid June to early Sept. Wheelchair accessible.

YWCA Berkeley Residence, 40 Berkeley St. (☎482-8850), a 3min. walk from T: Orange Line-Back Bay. Hostel-style accommodations for *women only.* Although the Residence is on the outskirts of downtown, the train is nearby and intrepid strollers can hoof it to many of Boston's signature attractions. Shared bathrooms. Breakfast included. On-site laundry. 13-night max. stay. Singles $51; doubles $86; triples $99.

The Buckminster, 645 Beacon St. (☎236-7050 or 800-727-2825; fax 617-262-6068), adjacent to Fenway Park. T: Green B, C, or D Line-Kenmore. Built in 1903, the Buckminster offers fancy lodging for the tourist willing to put up a little cash. Private bath, TV, and phone. Parking next door $20 per night. Check-in 3pm. Check-out 5pm. Singles $69-99; doubles $75-129; suites $105-159. Wheelchair accessible.

The Farrington Inn, 23 Farrington Ave. (☎787-1860 or 800-767-5337), in Allston. From T: Green B Line-Harvard Ave., turn right onto Harvard Ave., pass the Brighton Ave. intersection; Farrington Ave. is a small side-street on the right. This functional hotel/hostel has singles, doubles, and apartments. Porches on every floor encourage guest intermingling. Rooms are tidy, and common areas feature antiques, worn Oriental rugs, and classical music. Showers, kitchens, and TV available in most rooms. Most rooms have A/C. Free parking and local calls. Breakfast included. Reception 24hr. Check-out 11am, but flexible. Book ahead in summer. Apartment shares in summer $60-80; in winter $45-55. Singles, doubles, apartments $40-175.

Anthony's Town House, 1085 Beacon St. (☎566-3972), in Brookline. T: Green C Line-Hawes St. Anthony's Town House is a decent value for the price, featuring a variety of comfortable if quirky rooms. All rooms have semi-private baths, A/C, and cable TV. Long singles and large doubles in this handsome brownstone $80-95 in summer. Two suites with double beds and kitchen are suitable for families.

◘ FOOD

Boston is no longer known as the land of beans and cod—trendy bistros, pan-Asian, and ethnic restaurants of all stripes have hit Boston. On the other side of the Boston food scene are the places that have been here forever—greasy-spoon diners, soul-food and barbecue joints, and welcoming pubs. You can find anything here you want, from Ethiopian to Malaysian to a good old-fashioned burger and fries.

DOWNTOWN

Blossoms Cafe, 99 High St. (☎423-1911), at Federal St. From T: Red/Orange Line-Downtown Crossing, walk 5 blocks down Summer St., turn left on High St. and walk 2 blocks. This California-style cafe emphasizes freshness, serving salads with homemade dressings, soups, sandwiches, pizza and hot entrees. Prices are surprisingly low for the money-manic Financial District: under $5 for sandwiches, and nothing on the menu above $7. Wheelchair accessible. Cash only. Open M-F 7am-4pm.

Durgin Park, 30 North Market St. (☎227-2038), in Faneuil Hall. T: Green/Blue Line-Government Center. Serving New England classics since 1827, their menu hasn't changed a bit: prime rib (2 cuts, $13 or $17), Yankee Pot Roast, cornbread, baked beans, and Indian Pudding to name a few. Seating is family-style so be prepared to meet new people. Entrees $8-18. Open M-Sa 11:30am-10pm, Su 11:30am-9pm; lunch 11:30am-2:30pm. Wheelchair accessible.

Sultan's Kitchen, 72 Broad St. (☎728-2828 or 338-7819). From T: Orange/Blue Line-State, head toward the water on State St., then turn right on Broad St. Don't let the demure blue facade fool you into passing by; behind it, you'll find delicious Turkish food, from hearty curried lentil soup ($3.50) to tandoori chicken kebab sandwiches ($6.25). Open M-F 11am-5pm, Sa 11am-3pm.

Country Life Vegetarian, 200 High St. (☎951-2685), at Broad St. T: Blue Line-Aquarium. Yellow signs lead you under the I-93 overpass to this self-serve, all-you-can-eat buffet restaurant serving tasty vegan foods. The menu changes daily, but specialties include BBQ chickettes and Thai stir-fry. Lunch buffet $7, dinner $8. Open daily 11:30am-3pm; Su, Tu-Th 5-8pm, Su brunch 9:30am-3pm.

NORTH END

Boston's "Little Italy" is the place to come for authentic Italian fare. If just want to sip espresso and people-watch, head to **Caffé Paradiso,** 255 Hanover St. (☎742-1768; open daily 6:30-2am) or **Caffé Vittoria,** 296 Hanover St. (☎227-7606; open M-F 8am-midnight, Sa-Su 1pm-12:30am). For cannoli to go, try **Mike's Pastry,** 300 Hanover St. (☎742-3050; open daily 9am-9pm) or **Modern Pastry,** 257 Hanover St. (☎523-3783; open in summer Su-Th 8am-10pm, F-Sa 8am-11pm; in winter Su-Th 8am-9pm, F-Sa 8am-10pm). **Bova's Bakery,** 134 Salem St. (☎523-5601), is open daily 24 hours.

🏠 **La Famiglia Giorgio's,** 112 Salem St. (☎367-6711). T: Green/Orange Line-Haymarket. Giorgio's is one of the most popular and most affordable restaurants in the North End, though the crowd is often more tourists than locals. The decor is minimal, portions are enormous, and the cooks don't skimp on the cream. Lunch specials ($5.50) are a bargain that can't be beat. Open M-Sa 11am-10:30pm, Su noon-10:30pm.

Artú, 6 Prince St. (☎742-4336). T: Green/Orange Line-Haymarket. Just off Hanover St., this simple but tastefully appointed *rosticceria-trattoria* serves up a variety of traditional, hearty Italian specialties. Locals rave about the grilled vegetable antipasti ($5.25) and the Roast Lamb Panini ($5; lunch only). Dinner entrees, including a variety of fresh seafood options, start at $8.75. Open daily 11am-11pm.

CHINATOWN

Chinatown is the place to go for great Asian food anytime, but it also happens to be the one place in Boston where you can get a full meal until 3 or 4am. Weekend morning dim sum is popular at **Chau Chow City,** 83 Essex St. (☎338-8158) and **China Pearl,** 9 Tyler St. (☎426-4338).

🏠 **Penang,** 685-691 Washington St. (☎451-6373). T: Orange Line-Chinatown. Though self-billed as Malaysian, the poly-ethnic menu is an amalgam of Indian, Cantonese, Szechuan, Thai, and Siamese cuisine. The *roti canai* bread with curry dipping sauce ($3) is divine, and the hearty noodle-in-soup dishes ($4-6) are perfect for those with large appetites and small wallets. Most entrees $6-14. Open Su-Th 11:30am-11:30pm, F-Sa 11:30am-midnight.

East Ocean City, 25-29 Beach St. (☎542-2504). T: Orange Line-Chinatown. Patrons can greet their meal at the door, where fish and crabs swim about in bubbling tanks. Tuxedo-clad waiters hurry patrons into a nondescript interior peopled with Hong Kong emigres, who down fried rice dishes with beef, chicken, seafood, or vegetable toppings ($7-9). Open Su-Th 11am-3am, F-Sa 11am-4am.

Dong Khanh, 83 Harrison Ave. (☎426-9410). T: Orange Line-Chinatown. This simple restaurant serves up fantastic traditional Vietnamese cuisine such as *Pho Dac Biet* (beef noodle soup) and rice plates with meats and vegetables ($4-5). Fresh strawberry, coconut, or lychee fruit juices ($2-2.50) are a great complement to any meal. Cash only. Open daily 9:30am-10:30pm.

BACK BAY

▓ **Pour House Bar and Grill,** 907 Boylston St. (☎236-1767), at Hereford St. T: Green B, C, or D Line-Hynes/ICA. Eating here won't put you in the poor house. A "Stately" burger menu features the Massachusetts (plain and proper), the Wisconsin (chunks of blue cheese), and the Hawaiian (teriyaki style with pineapple), all $3.25-3.55. Take advantage of half-price Burger Mania every Sa 6-10pm. Mexican Madness every Th 6-10pm features half-price border bargains (burritos and tacos regularly $5-6). W 6-10pm are "buck, buck and a half" chicken nights (grilled chicken sandwiches $2.50). Open daily 8am-2am. Dinner served until 10pm. Wheelchair accessible. 21+ after 8pm.

▓ **Trident Booksellers and Cafe,** 338 Newbury St. (☎267-8688). T: Green B, C, or D Line-Hynes/ICA. A haven for the health food-seeking, liberal literati; customers lunch on veggie burgers and salads ($7-8) or sip fresh juice smoothies ($3-4) before or after perusing the wide selection of special interest books and periodicals. Come at night for luscious desserts ($3) and caffeine concoctions. Open daily 9am-midnight. For the same menu to go, visit the Trident's take-out only branch **Bodhi Cafe** across the street.

Cafe Jaffa, 48 Gloucester St. (☎536-0230). T: Green B, C, or D Line-Hynes/ICA. In this casual Israeli eatery, enormous sandwiches are stuffed with your choice of grape leaves, baba ghanoush, kabobs, chicken or beef schwarma, falafel, or hummus. Turkish coffee $2.25. Lunch specials M-F 11am-2:30pm. Open M-Th 11am-10:30pm, F-Sa 11am-11pm, Su noon-10pm.

SOUTH END

The South End is quickly becoming the hottest neighborhood in the Boston culinary scene, especially in the area around Tremont St. Unfortunately, it's not right on the T, so you'll have to hoof it from Back Bay Green and Orange Line stops.

▓ **Addis Red Sea,** 544 Tremont St. (☎426-8727). From T: Green Line-Arlington, walk 1 block away from the Public Gardens, turn left on Berkeley St., and walk 7 blocks to Tremont St., then turn right; it's on the left after Hanson St. The best Ethiopian restaurant in Boston. Start off with the delightful *Ye-Miser Selatta* ($6), lentils laced with tomatoes, onions, and peppers in a tangy lemon dressing (eaten with your hands, of course, on the spongy *injera* bread). For entrees, choose from fish, chicken, beef, lamb or vegetarian dishes, all seasoned to perfection. Open M-F 5-11pm, Sa-Su noon-11pm.

▓ **Bob the Chef's,** 604 Columbus Ave. (☎536-6204), at Northampton St. From T: Orange Line-Mass. Ave., turn right on Mass. Ave., walk 1 block, turn right on Columbus Ave., then walk another block. Across the street from the old NAACP building, Bob the Chef's was once a hangout for Civil Rights revolutionaries. Now under new management, Bob's has a sleek interior but the same funky soul. Tender ribs, collard greens, and "glori-fried" chicken melt in your mouth, but save room for the divine peach cobbler or sweet potato pie. Entrees $7-14. Live jazz Th-Sa 7:30pm-midnight (cover $5). Su all-you-can-eat jazz brunch. Open Tu-W 11:30am-10pm, Th-Sa 11:30am-midnight, Su 11am-9pm.

▓ **Le Gamin Cafe,** 550 Tremont St. (☎654-8969), at Waltham St. From T: Green Line-Arlington, walk 1 block down Boylston away from the Public Gardens, turn left on Berkeley St., walk 7 blocks, turn right on Tremont St.; it's a few blocks down on the left. This romantic underground grotto on trendy Tremont St. serves expertly prepared crepes (goat cheese and leek $7.25, smoked salmon salad $11). Breakfast served daily, including croissants, french toast, espresso drinks and coffee. Open M-F 10am-midnight, Sa-Su 8am-midnight.

THE FENWAY

Near Boston University and Kenmore Sq., you'll find cheap student dives and a few late-night spots. Near the Symphony, there are a few good restaurants and bars.

▓ **Betty's Wok & Noodle Diner,** 250 Huntington Ave. (☎424-1950), opposite Symphony Hall. T: Green E Line-Symphony. This brand-spanking new diner looks like a (stylish) throwback to the 50s, but there is nothing old about the incredibly fresh, made-to-order Asian-Latino cuisine. Lounge on dark red vinyl-covered wall benches while waiting for your own creation of noodles or rice, veggies and/or meat, and one of Betty's Lucky Seven sauces to be prepared before your eyes. Entrees start at $8. Open Tu-Th noon-10pm, F-Sa noon-11pm.

Delihaus, 476 Commonwealth Ave. (☎247-9712). T: Green B, C, or D Line-Kenmore. The combination of diner food (cheap, greasy, and delicious), punk music, and late hours packs students into Delihaus when the clubs close. Painfully hip waitstaff serves breakfast all day (pancakes $3.50), beer ($3.50, more for specialty Belgian brews), and perfect sweet potato fries with horseradish sauce ($3.95). Coffee (95¢) includes 2 free refills. Open daily 9am-3am.

◼ SIGHTS

THE FREEDOM TRAIL

A great introduction to Boston's history lies along the red-painted line of the Freedom Trail (FT), a 2½ mi. path through the historic landmarks of downtown Boston. Even on a trail dedicated to freedom, however, some sights charge admission. Starting at their **visitors center,** the National Park Service offers free tours of the trail's free attractions. *(Visitors center: ☎536-4100. Red/Green Line-Park Street. Open M-Sa 8:30am-5pm, Su 9am-5pm. Tours depart from the National Park Service office at 15 State St., opposite the entrance to the Old State House. In spring and fall M-F 2pm, Sa-Su 10, 11am, and 2, 3pm; in summer daily 10, 11am, and 1, 2, 3pm. Arrive 30min. early to sign up.)*

The Freedom Trail begins at another **visitors center,** in **Boston Common** where you can pick up decent free maps or buy more detailed ones. *(T: Red/Green Line-Park St. Open M-Sa 8:30am-5pm, Su 9am-5pm.)* The FT runs uphill to the **Robert Gould Shaw and 54th Regiment Memorial,** on Beacon St. The memorial honors the first black regiment of the Union Army in the American Civil War and their Bostonian leader, all made famous by the movie *Glory.* The trail then crosses the street to the magnificent and ornate **State House.** *(☎727-3676. Open M-F 9am-5pm, Sa and holidays 10am-4pm. Free guided tours M-F 10am-3:30pm. Tours begin in Doric Hall on the 2nd floor.)* Passing the **Park St. Church,** the trail reaches the **Old Granary Burial Ground** in which John Hancock, Samuel Adams, and Paul Revere rest. **King's Chapel and Burial Ground,** New England's oldest Anglican church, stands on Tremont St.; the latest inhabitants are Unitarian. Colonists founded the Chapel in 1686; more recently, the cemetery has come to inter the earthly remains of John Winthrop. *(Chapel: ☎227-2155. Open in summer daily 9:30am-4pm; in spring and fall M, F-Sa 10am-4pm; in winter Sa 10am-2pm or by appointment. Unitarian services held W 12:15pm, Su 11am. Burial Grounds: open daily 8am-5:30pm; in winter 8am-3pm.)*

The **Old South Meeting House** was the site of the preliminary get-together that set the mood for the **Boston Tea Party.** *(☎482-6439. Open daily in summer 9:30am-5pm, in winter 10am-4pm. $3, students and seniors $2.50, under 6 free.)* Formerly the seat of British government in Boston, the **Old State House** now serves as a museum and the next stop on the trail. *(20 Washington St. ☎720-1713. Open daily 9am-5pm. $3, students and seniors $2, ages 6-18 $1.)* The Trail continues past the site of the **Boston Massacre** and through **Faneuil Hall,** a former meeting hall and current mega-food court. Lectures are given every 30min. in the upstairs Great Hall when the city is not holding a function. *(Hall open daily 9am-5pm; enter through rear center doors.)* Heading into the North End, the path passes the **Paul Revere House.** *(19 North Sq. ☎523-2338. Open daily Apr. 15 to Oct. 9:30am-5:15pm, Nov. to Apr. 14 9:30am-4:15pm. $2.50, students and seniors $2, ages 5-17 $1.)* Next, the **Old North Church** is where Revere's friend Robert Newman hung lanterns to warn the Charlestown rebels of the British approach. *(193 Salem St. ☎523-6676. Open daily in summer 9am-6pm; in winter 9am-5pm. Services on Su 9am, 11am, and 4pm.)* **Copp's Hill Burying Ground** provides a resting place for numerous colonial Bostonians, including Prince Hall, a freed slave, soldier, and founder of Boston's first school for black children, as well as a nice view of the Old North Church. Nearing its end, the FT heads over the Charlestown Bridge to the newly renovated **USS Constitution** and its companion museum. *(☎426-1812. Open daily 9:30am until 10min. prior to sunset. Free tours every 30min. until 3:50pm.)* The final stop on the trail, the **Bunker Hill Monument,** isn't on loan from Washington. The fraudulent obelisk is actually on Breed's Hill, the site of colonial fortification during the battle; Bunker Hill is about ½ mi. away. A grand view awaits those willing to climb the 294 steps to the top. *(Open daily 9am-4:30pm.)* To return to Boston, follow the FT back over the bridge, take the T from the Orange Line-Community College stop near Bunker Hill, or hop on a **Harbor Ferry** from one of the piers near the Constitution. *(Ferries run between Lovejoy Wharf, adjacent to the Fleet Center, Boston Long Wharf, near the New England Aquarium, and the Charlestown Navy Yard/USS Constitution M-F every 20min. 6:30-11:10am and 3:10-6:30pm, every hr. 11:10am-3:10pm; Sa-Su every 30min. 10am-6pm. Fares collected aboard vessels. $1, ages 5-11 50¢.)*

DOWNTOWN

Downtown Boston is the historical and financial heart of the city, and it is usually the first and often the only place that many visitors to Boston see. Old and new rub shoulders in this mini-metropolis, where skyscrapers overshadow stately colonial buildings and subways rumble beneath the cobblestones. In the center of downtown Boston's three main districts—**Government Center, Downtown Crossing,** and the **Financial District**—is the sprawling **Boston Common,** where yuppies, hippies, and everyone in between come to sit in the sunshine.

GOVERNMENT CENTER. At the mouth of the Green/Blue Line-Government Center T stop lies a large brick plaza, home to the **J.F.K. Building** and Big Brother-esque **City Hall.** City Hall's architecture was designed to express symbolically the structure of government—rising up from the plaza, the bricks of the lower level enclose the offices that the public use, while the highest reaches of the building hold the offices of bureaucracy with which the public has little contact. The plaza was originally intended to be a gathering place, but aside from the occasional concert, it serves mainly as a walkway from the T station to the bustling **Quincy Market** area, a commercialized outdoor market. It's worth the short walk to the **Holocaust Memorial,** six luminous 54 ft. high glass towers that pay tribute to all victims of the Holocaust, both Jews and Gentiles. Resembling smokestacks, the towers recall the six main concentration camps. The 6 million numbers etched into the glass towers, quotations from survivors, and facts about the Holocaust create a powerful, beautiful, and extremely educational memorial—it's especially sobering at night. To get there, walk past City Hall, and turn left on Congress St. before Quincy Market.

DOWNTOWN CROSSING. Centered around **Washington St.,** Downtown Crossing is a great place to buy something quickly and cheaply. At the heart of the Washington St. shopping district lies the symbol of bargain hunting, **Filene's Basement,** where there are generous discounts on many top of the line labels. Independent shops and fancy department stores that in pre-mall years drew suburban folks to Boston's best shopping have long since given way to chain retail stores, but it's still a convenient place to shop in the open air.

FINANCIAL DISTRICT. Boston's first skyscraper, the stylish 495 ft. **Custom House Tower,** and its signature clock stand out in the city skyline against their drab Financial District neighbors. Worth a visit is the small **observation balcony** at the top of the tower where you can take in breathtaking views of the harbor and downtown area, as well as meet the **Peregrine falcons** who nest there. *(3 McKinley Sq. ☎ 310-6300. From T: Orange/Blue Line-State, walk down State St. towards the harbor to India St. Free tours to observation balcony daily 10am and 4pm.)* The **Batterymarch Building** was the first **Art Deco** building in the city of Boston. One of the characteristics of the Art Deco style is the shifting of the exterior color from dark at the base to light at the top, giving the impression of greater height. *(60 Batterymarch St., at Broad St.)*

BOSTON COMMON. Bordered by Beacon, Boylston, and Tremont St., the **Boston Common** has been used over the centuries as the scene of public rallies and celebrations, recreation, military training, public punishment and burial, as well as a pasture for cows and sheep. In 1728, the first tree-lined pedestrian mall was laid out in the Common, and in the 19th century, enthusiasm for the American parks movement led to new walkways, statues, plaques, fountains, and gates. Today, you can picnic with squirrels and pigeons, wade in the **Frog Pond** in summer (the frogs have

FORNICATING FALCONS Since 1987, the **Custom House Tower** has been the site of a nest for a pair of Peregrine falcons as part of an effort to restore the bird to Massachusetts. The Peregrine falcon is considered the fastest bird on earth, capable of diving from great heights at speeds of up to 200 mph to capture its prey. Once prominent in the New England area, they suffered almost total extinction in the 50s because of the pesticide DDT. Recovery efforts from state and federal wildlife agencies have included setting up breeding nests in selected locations, such as the one at the Custom House. These falcons, one of the most productive pairs of falcons in New England, have laid 64 eggs and raised 36 chicks. The falcons are the two oldest Peregrines known to exist in the area and can often be seen hovering above downtown. Thanks to such recovery efforts, the Peregrine falcon was removed from the federal list of endangered species in 1999.

been evicted) or **ice-skate** on it in the winter, watch old movies on a big screen for free during the **Classic Film Festival,** or refine your cultural polish during the free **Shakespeare** performances in the Bandstand in late June. Upcoming events are posted at the **Visitor Information Center.** (☎ 635-2147 for ice skating info. T: Green/Red Line-Park Street. Classic films shown on the Parade Grounds June-Aug. Tu at dusk.)

THE WATERFRONT

The waterfront area, bounded by Atlantic and Commercial St., runs along Boston Harbor from South Station to the North End. Stroll down Commercial, Lewis, or Museum Wharf for a view of the harbor and a breath of sea air. Catering to all ages, **New England Aquarium,** on Central Wharf, presents cavorting penguins, giant sea turtles, and a bevy of briny beasts in a 200,000 gallon tank and over 70 galleries. Aboard *Discovery*, a floating platform moored next to the Aquarium, you can watch sea lions perform or visit the harbor seals and sea otters. A new IMAX theater is scheduled for completion in 2001. (☎ 973-5200 or 973-0223. From T: Blue Line-Aquarium turn left and walk down Central Wharf. Open Sept.-June M-F 9am-5pm, Sa-Su 9am-6pm; July-Aug. M-Tu, F 9am-6pm, W-Th 9am-8pm, Sa-Su 9am-7pm. $12.50, ages 3-11 $6.50, seniors $10.50. W 4-8pm $1 off.) If you're having trouble getting your blood boiling about Revolutionary Boston, the **Boston Tea Party Ship and Museum,** on the Congress St. Bridge, is the place to come, particularly for visitors with children. Costumed actors draw the audience into an irreverent re-enactment of the inflammatory town meeting in Old South and the treasonous Tea Party itself. (☎ 338-1773. From T: Red Line-South Station walk down Atlantic Ave. to Congress St. and turn onto the bridge. Open spring and fall 9am-5pm, in summer 9am-6pm. $8, students $7, children $4.)

BEACON HILL

As the economy booms and *nouveau-riche* neighborhoods spring up overnight, none will ever match the old money class of Beacon Hill. Amid elm trees and gas lanterns, in the cramped brick townhouses overlooking the Common, live the wealthiest families in Boston. The neighborhood's elite destiny was established in 1797 when the **State House** was built at the base of the hill by Charles Bullfinch. The most opulent homes line Mt. Vernon and Chestnut St., as well as **Louisberg Square.**

The neighborhood has traditionally been divided into three districts, the South Slope, the Flat of the Hill, and the North Slope. The **South Slope** was the original Beacon Hill, consisting of everything between Beacon St. and Pinckney St., bordered by Charles St. and the State House. The **Charles Street** area, called the **Flat of the Hill,** provides a nice place to stroll past antique stores and other shops and restaurants, as well as the pedestrian-friendly **Esplanade** park. The **North Slope,** starting above Pinckney St., was originally denied "Beacon Hill" status by the Brahmins—instead, it was considered part of the low-income **West End** (see **The Old West End,** below). The North Slope housed 19th-century African Americans and European immigrants, as well as sailors, artists, poets, and other "morally emancipated" folk.

NEW ENGLAND

THE SOUTH SLOPE. The cornerstone of posh Beacon Hill is the **Massachusetts State House,** at Beacon St. and Park St., which has an interior just as splendid as the exterior. (☎727-3676. T: Red/Green Line-Park St. Open M-F 9am-5pm. 30min. tours 10am-3:30pm, or pick up a yellow brochure at the door and guide yourself.) Author **Oliver Wendell Holmes** first dubbed the elite 19th-century Beacon Hill families the "Boston Brahmins." The only Brahmin house open to the public is the four-story **Nichols House,** 55 Mt. Vernon St. (☎227-6993. T: Red/Green Line-Park St. Open May-Nov. Tu-Sa noon-4:15pm; Feb.-May, Nov.-Dec. M, W, and Sa only; closed Jan. $5.)

NORTH SLOPE (THE OLD WEST END). In the early 1900s, the West End was home to many Italian, Jewish, and Irish immigrants, as well as African-Americans. Though rich in character, the area was financially poor and considered by the city to be an eyesore. In the 60s, the city of Boston decided that it needed better infrastructure—hospitals, roadways, research centers, apartment housing—and completely demolished the West End to accommodate new construction. The only building left intact was the first **Harrison Gray Otis House,** built in 1796 by premier Boston architect Charles Bulfinch. The tours of his house are excellent, providing insight into the origins of Beacon Hill culture and its changes over time. (141 Cambridge St. ☎227-3956. T: Red Line-Charles/MGH. Open W-Su 11am-5pm. Last tour at 4pm. $4, seniors $3.50, students and children $2.) Also on the North Slope is the **Black Heritage Trail,** which highlights some of the most controversial and historic hotspots in the fight against slavery. Many of these sights are now homes to Beacon Hill residents and lack much description and identification, so the free 2hr. walking tour given by the National Park Service is highly suggested. It covers 1½ mi. and 14 sites, including the **African Meeting House,** the oldest black church in America. (Trail begins at the Robert Gould Shaw Memorial on the corner of Park St. and Beacon St., across from the State House. ☎742-5415. Tours meet at the Robert Gould Shaw Memorial in summer T-Sa 10am, noon, and 2pm; to arrange other times, call 24hr. in advance.)

FLAT OF THE HILL. Through the great art of window-shopping, even budget-savvy travelers can appreciate the offerings of **Charles St.,** Beacon Hill's main commercial street. More than 40 antique stores, independent retail stores selling artsy doo-dads, neighborhood service shops, markets, and several good restaurants line every block. The **Esplanade Park** bordering the Charles River is often crowded with runners, dog-walkers, and in-line skaters. On the southern edge of the park lies the **Hatch Shell,** a free outdoor concert venue that also plays movies F at sunset.

NORTH END

The east tip of Boston contains the historic **North End.** (T: Green/Orange Line-Haymarket.) Now an Italian neighborhood, the city's oldest residential district overflows with window boxes, Italian flags, fragrant pastry shops, *crèches*, Sicilian restaurants, and Catholic churches. The most famous of the last, **Old St. Stephen's Church,** is the classic colonial brainchild of Charles Bulfinch. (24 Clark St. at Hanover St. ☎523-1230. Open daily 7am-dusk and during services.) Down the street, the sweet-smelling **Peace Gardens** provide a respite from the clamor of the North End.

CHINATOWN

Two blocks from South Station and southwest of the Common, Boston's **Chinatown** demarcates itself with an arch and huge Fu dogs at its Beach St. entrance, bilingual signs, and pagoda-topped telephone booths throughout. This is the place for good Asian food, Chinese slippers, and "1000-year-old eggs." Many restaurants stay open until 3 or 4am. *Do not walk alone here at night.* Chinatown holds two big festivals each year. The first, **New Year,** usually celebrated on a Su in Feb., includes lion dances, fireworks, and kung fu exhibitions. The **August Moon Festival** honors a mythological pair of lovers at the time of the full moon, usually on the 2nd or 3rd Su in Aug. (T: Orange Line-Chinatown.)

BACK BAY

The elegant Back Bay district of Boston did not exist until 1857, when developers filled in the foul-smelling tidal flats between Beacon Hill and Brookline. The **Public**

Gardens mark the eastern boundary of Back Bay where the landfill project began. The heart of Back Bay is **Copley Square,** framed by H. H. Richardson's **Trinity Church** and the majestic **Boston Public Library.** Nearby, the **John Hancock Tower** soars above the neo-Gothic **New Old South Church.** The **Prudential Tower** on Huntington Ave. is alternately beloved and despised by locals, but is a landmark nonetheless. Radiating out from Copley Sq. are **Huntington Ave.,** the sculpture-studded **Commonwealth Ave.,** and **Boylston St.,** which parallels the upscale, commercial **Newbury St.**

PUBLIC GARDENS. Across from the Common on Charles St., the title characters from the children's book *Make Way for Ducklings* (hallowed in bronze) point the way to the **Public Gardens,** where peddle-powered **Swan Boats** glide around a quiet pond lined with shady willows. *(T: Green Line-Arlington. Swan rides $3 for a 15min. ride.)*

COPLEY SQUARE. The lush lawn and elegant fountains of Copley Sq. are hemmed by Boston landmarks on all sides. *(T: Green Line-Copley.)* The John Hancock Observatory is on the 60th floor of the 790 ft., 62-story **John Hancock Tower,** which is the tallest building in the US north of New York City. As is to be expected, the view of Boston and its environs (all the way up to New Hampshire on clear days) is stunning, though not a 360° panorama. *(☎572-6429. Open M-Sa 9am-10pm, Apr.-Oct. Su 9am-10pm, Nov.-Mar. Su 9am-5pm. $6, seniors and ages 5-17 $4, military and children under 5 free.)* Dominating Copley Sq. is the imposing Romanesque Revival **Trinity Church,** erected between 1872 and 1877, and widely regarded as the pinnacle of architect Henry Hobson Richardson's career. The church's cloister and hidden garden are enchanting, perhaps because they are rather difficult to find—go around to Clarendon St. Be sure to look up at the reflection of the church in the windows of the Hancock Tower. Founded on April 3, 1848, the **Boston Public Library** was the first major free municipal library in the US. When you first see it, however, it may feel more like an art museum than a large public research library. The greatest artistic treasures are hidden on the 3rd floor in the Sargent gallery, named for John Singer Sargent, who created the grand mural that adorns the walls. *(☎536-5400. Open M-Th 9am-9pm, F-Sa 9am-5pm. Free guided Art and Architecture Tours of the Library year-round M 2:30pm, Tu and Th 6pm, F-Sa 11am; Oct.-May Su 2pm.)*

NEWBURY AND BOYLSTON STREETS. The ritziest promenade in all of Boston is **Newbury St.,** where the city's rich and trendy go to be seen. In the eight-block stretch between Arlington St. and Mass. Ave., there are over 40 restaurants, more than 100 stores, 40 art galleries, and almost 100 hair salons. The most upscale stores are clustered on the side of Newbury closest to the Public Gardens. **Boylston St.** runs parallel to Newbury St. and is considered the more modest of the two commercial strips. Fairly inexpensive bars can be found here, as well as common retail stores. *(T: Green Line-Arlington, Copley, or Hynes/ICA.)*

COMMONWEALTH AVENUE MALL. The name "mall" can be misleading, as there are no stores here. Rather, the 220 ft. wide Parisian boulevard is the address for some of Back Bay's most impressive townhomes, with a tree-lined 100 ft. wide pathway cutting through the center. **Frederick Law Olmsted** designated the area as part of his **Emerald Necklace** park system that encircles Boston and lends the Green line its color. The park is perhaps best known for its **public sculpture**—every block or so there is a sculpture or monument, ranging from former presidents to social activists to the Viking **Leif Eriksson,** who, some 19th-century historians theorized, may have explored as far south as Boston and Cambridge. *(T: Green Line-Arlington.)*

🏛 MUSEUMS

▨ **Isabella Stewart Gardner Museum,** 280 the Fenway (☎566-1401), a few hundred yards from the MFA. T: Green E Line-Museum. This astounding private collection remains exactly as Mrs. Gardner arranged it a century ago. The Venetian-style *palazzo* garners as much attention as the Old Masters, and the smell of the courtyard garden alone is worth the price of admission. Open Tu-Su 11am-5pm. $10, Sa-Su $11; students Tu, Th $5, W $3; seniors $7; under 18 free.

Museum of Fine Arts (MFA), 465 Huntington Ave. (☎267-9300), in the Fenway. T: Green E Line-Museum. Boston's most famous museum contains one of the world's finest collections of Asian ceramics, outstanding Egyptian Nubian art, a showing of Impressionists, and superb American art. Two unfinished portraits of George and Martha Washington, begun by Gilbert Stuart in 1796, merit a gander. Open M-Tu 10am-4:45pm, W-F 10am-9:45pm, Sa-Su 10am-5:45pm. $12; students and seniors $10; ages 7-17 M-F until 3pm $5, otherwise free; $2 off Th-F after 5pm; free W after 4pm. Special entrance fees apply for exhibits in the Gund Gallery.

Museum of Science, Science Park (☎723-2500), on the Charles River. T: Green Line-Science Park. Contains the largest "lightning machine" in the world, a hands-on activity center, and live-animal demonstrations. Within the museum, the **Hayden Planetarium** features models, lectures, films, and laser and star shows. Travel the world in the **Mugar Omni Theater**; films on scientific subjects show on a 4-story, domed OmniMax screen. Exhibit hall open daily 9am-5pm; July 5 to Labor Day Sa-Th 9am-7pm, F 9am-9pm. Exhibit Hall admission $10, children and seniors $7. Omni Theater, Planetarium, and Laser Show admission $7.50/$5.50. Omni shows $2.50 off T and W after 7pm.

Children's Museum, 300 Congress St. (☎426-8850), on the waterfront. T: Red Line-South Station. Kids of all ages wind through hundreds of hands-on exhibits and learn a little something to boot. Open M-Th, Sa-Su 10am-5pm, F 10am-9pm. $7, ages 2-15 and seniors $6, under 2 $2. F 5-9pm $1.

John F. Kennedy Presidential Library (☎929-4500), Columbia Point just off I-93 in Dorchester. T: Red Line-JFK/UMass, then take the free shuttle bus marked JFK to the library (every 20min. 8am-5pm). Dedicated "to all those who through the art of politics seek a new and better world." The looming white structure, designed by I.M. Pei, overlooks Dorchester Bay. No conspiracy theories here; the museum contains exhibits tracing Kennedy's career from the campaign trail to his tragic death. Open daily 9am-5pm. $8, seniors and students $6, children 13-17 $4, children under 12 free.

Institute of Contemporary Art (ICA), 955 Boylston St. (☎266-5152), in Back Bay. T: Green Line B, C, or D-Hynes/ICA. Boston's lone outpost of the avant-garde attracts major modern artists while aggressively promoting lesser-known work. Innovative, thought-provoking exhibits change every 8 weeks. The museum also presents experimental theater, music, dance, and film. Open W noon-5pm, Th noon-9pm, F noon-7pm, Sa-Su noon-5pm. $6, students and seniors $4, children under 12 free. Free Th 5-9pm. 2 for 1 with AAA card.

🎵 ENTERTAINMENT

Publications like *The Boston Phoenix*, *Stuff@Night*, the *Boston Globe* Calendar section, and websites like ae.boston.com and boston.citysearch.com offer complete lists of what's happening in the Hub. For tickets to most events throughout the area, contact **Bostix** (☎723-5181 or 482-2849), **Ticketmaster** (www.ticketmaster.com), **NEXT** (☎423-6000). Although ticket prices can be steep, there are ways to cut costs. **Student rush** tickets go on sale for many shows an hour before the performance. Bostix sells **remainder half-price tickets** the day of the show. Many of the area's universities (especially Emerson College, Boston University, and Harvard) put on quality **student productions,** which are generally inexpensive or even free. Some venues accept **volunteer ushers,** where you can see the show at a reduced price or even free in exchange for less than an hour of stuffing programs or seating patrons. Contact individual venues for information on special pricing events.

THEATER. Boston is known as a try-out town; many shows test the waters here before heading for Broadway. The major theater venues are clustered around the **Theatre District** (T: Green Line-Boylston), including the **Wang Center,** a tour stop for blockbuster musicals *Phantom of the Opera* and *Miss Saigon*, as well as the home of the annual holiday production of *The Nutcracker.* Two of Boston's long-running shows are thoroughly entertaining and worth the splurge to see them at the **Charles Playhouse: Blue Man Group** dazzles audiences of all ages with drums, music, paint, lights, twinkies, marshmallows, and rolls of toilet paper. (☎800-BLUEMAN/

258-3626. $39-49, student rush $25.) **Shear Madness** is a wacky murder-mystery. (☎426-5225. $34, student rush $29.) The **Huntington Theater Company,** 264 Huntington Ave. (☎266-0800), in the Fenway, is a well-respected theater that produces quality contemporary and classic plays. For more avant-garde productions, check out what's playing at the **Boston Center for the Arts,** 539 Tremont St. (☎426-2748), in the South End, which hosts several performance groups in its three theaters.

CLASSICAL MUSIC AND DANCE. Symphony Hall, 301 Mass. Ave., is home to both the world-renowned **Boston Symphony Orchestra (BSO),** under the direction of Seiji Ozawa, and her lighter-hearted little sister, the **Boston Pops.** (☎266-1492. Orchestra season Oct.-Apr., with concerts on Tu, Th, Sa night, F afternoon, and some F nights. $22-67; rush tickets available Tu and Th 5pm, F 9am $10; rehearsal tickets W night, Th morning $12. Pops season May-July Tu-Su nights. Balcony tickets $14-34, table tickets $36-53. Free concerts at the Hatch Shell on the Esplanade in early July, including the July 4th concert.) The **Boston Ballet** (☎695-6950) performs at the Wang Center and is best known for its holiday performance of *The Nutcracker*, a six-week run that draws over 140,000 people.

COMEDY CLUBS. Situated in crowded Quincy Market, the **Comedy Connection** features local and national comedians, many of whom have shows on HBO, Showtime and BET. Th nights feature Frank Santos, the "R-Rated Hypnotist." (☎248-9700. Local acts Su-W $10 and national acts F-Sa $13-37. Call ahead for tickets as all shows frequently sell out. 18+.) The **Improv Asylum Theater,** 216 Hanover St., in the North End, puts on 1½hr. shows comprised of sketches generated by audience suggestions. (☎263-6887. Mainstage shows Th 8pm $12, F-Sa 8, and 10pm $15. $2 discount with student ID. Th night 2-for-1 with student ID. Advance purchase recommended.) **Nick's Comedy Stop,** 100 Warrenton St., in the Theater District, features local comedians as well as national acts. Past performers have included Dennis Leary, Jay Leno, and Jerry Seinfeld. (☎482-0930. Th 8pm. F-Sa 8:30pm. Th $10, F $14, Sa $15. 16+.)

BILLIARDS. If ever a public pool parlor could be described as swank, it's **Boston Billiard Club,** 126 Brookline Ave. (☎536-7665), in the Fenway. **Jillian's,** 145 Ipswich St., at the end of Lansdowne St., has 55 billiard tables as well as arcade games on the 2nd floor. (☎437-0300. 2 people $10 per hr., 4 people $14 per hr.) **The Rack,** 24 Clinton St., downtown, is the home of affluent, young urban professionals who double as pool sharks after hours. (☎725-1051. Open daily 11:30-2am. Proper dress required. 21+.)

SPECTATOR SPORTS. Catch a **Red Sox** game at **Fenway Park,** the oldest and the smallest baseball park in the major leagues. (☎482-4769 or 267-1700 for tickets. Tickets: Bleachers $14, grandstand $28, field boxes $45.) If you are a basketball or hockey fan, head to the **Fleet Center,** 50 Causeway St. Replacing the Boston Garden in 1995, this corporate-named entertainment complex seats up to 20,000 for concerts, pro-wrestling, figure skating, and the circus. It is also the home of the **Celtics** and the **Bruins.** (☎624-1750. Box office summer hours M-F 10am-5pm; in season daily 10am-7pm. Celtics tickets $10-140, Bruins $20-140. Tours available in summer Th-Sa 12pm and 2pm; adults $5, seniors, students, and children $4.)

SPECIAL SPORTS EVENTS. The 105th **Boston Marathon** will occur on April 16, 2001. The whopping 26 mi. run snakes from Hopkinton to Copley through the city and over "Heartbreak Hill." Part of local tradition on Patriot's Day for over 100 years, the Boston Marathon attracts thousands of runners from all over the world who are cheered on by thousands of spectators lining the route. You don't need any tickets—just come. For the serious race watchers, getting there before noon is a must to secure a spot in the front row. Since 1965, the **Head of the Charles Regatta,** the world's largest single-day race, has been a mecca for thousands of rowers and revelers who descend on the Charles River to participate in the pageantry. The 36th Head of the Charles occurs the 3rd weekend of Oct. (Oct. 19-21, 2001).

NEW ENGLAND

◪ NIGHTLIFE

Before you set out to paint the town red, there are a few things to know about night-life in Boston. First, nearly every place requires *21+ ID* to get in. Boston bars and clubs are notoriously strict about the minimum age. Second, *closing time is 2am*—after hours does not exist in Puritan Boston (though some restaurants in Chinatown stay open until 3 or 4am if you have the munchies). Do the math and you'll realize that the T stops running two hours before last call, so bring some extra cash for the taxi ride home. If **clubbing** is your thing, head to Lansdowne St. in Kenmore Sq. or Boylston St. in the Theater District. However, if you expect the hipster scene of NYC or London, you may be in for a disappointment—Boston is better suited to the pubbers than the clubbers. Irish and faux-Irish pubs, student dives, swanky lounges—Boston has it all. The **live music** scene in Boston is also fabulous, from Irish folk to jazz to rhythm and blues. (You can't expect anything less than rocking from the city that gave the world Aerosmith, the Pixies, the Mighty Mighty Bosstones, and New Kids on the Block.)

DANCE CLUBS

Avalon, 15 Lansdowne St. (☎262-2424). T: Green B, C, or D Line-Kenmore. Across the street from Fenway Park in a line of other clubs, the Avalon stands out with its trippy interior. The roomy dance floor, surrounded by 3 bars, offers house and techno dance music. Su is gay night. Open daily 10pm-2am. Cover $10-15. 19+ except on Sa 21+.

Axis, 13 Lansdowne St. (☎262-2424). T: Green B, C, or D Line-Kenmore. Th nights have international guest DJs downstairs and local DJs upstairs. F night Spin Cycle is mainly techno and house. Open daily 10pm-2am. Cover ages 19-21 $15, 21+ $12. Sa "X-nights;" cover $10, 21+.

Bill's Bar, 5½ Lansdowne St. (☎421-9678). T: Green B, C, or D Line-Kenmore. Hip-hop night draws an enthusiastic crowd. Other theme nights include Reggae Su, Funk and Groove W, Underground Th, and Nocturnal F. Beer $4, cocktails $5. Dress code on dance and hip-hop nights. Open W-M 9pm-2am. Cover $5-7, F-Sa $12-15. 19+.

Envy, 25 Boylston Pl. (☎542-3689). From T: Green Line-Boylston, cross the street and turn right, then make the first left. Envy is on the left. "The Alley," as Boylston Pl. is known, is home to numerous clubs that differ little from each other. Envy is a huge club decked out in murals by a Hollywood film artist. DJ plays techno-ized 70s and 80s standards—nothing new, but still fun. Proper dress required. Beer $3.50-4, cocktails $5-6. Open F-Sa and every other W 9pm-2am. W $15 cover; F-Sa $5 cover.

BARS AND PUBS

▨ **The Littlest Bar,** 47 Province St. (☎523-9766), Downtown. From T: Red Line/Green Line-Park St., walk down Tremont St. away from the Common, turn right on Bromfield St., then left on Province St. Somehow they find a way to cram person after person into this closet-like bar—it's inevitable that everyone's chummy by the end of the evening. While the rest of the city awaits the weekend, live Irish music during the week makes this one of the most happening places around. Bud $2.50. Open daily until 2am.

Cactus Club, 939 Boylston St. (☎236-0200), in Back Bay. From T: Green Line-Hynes/ICA, walk across the overpass towards the Convention Center; it's in the 2nd block on the left side of the street. A slightly timid crowd scopes, but doesn't scam, their yuppie neighbors; perhaps the margaritas ($5) are to blame for the slightly frosty pick-up scene. The truly bold purchase their drinks in a "Big Bowl" ($11) with extra straws in the hopes of finding a friend or three with whom to share. Open daily 11:30am-2am.

Delux Cafe, 100 Chandler St. (☎338-5258), in the South End. From T: Orange Line-Back Bay, turn left on Dartmouth St., walk 1 block, turn left on Chandler St. and walk another block; it's on the right after Clarendon St. Quirkiness is the keyword at Delux Cafe, where a shrine to Elvis sits beside a fake Christmas tree and golden oldies music competes for distraction with screenings of Scooby Doo episodes. Drinks $2.50-3.75. Open M-Sa 5pm-1am; dinner served until 11:30pm. Cash only.

Sunset Grill & Tap, 130 Brighton Ave. (☎254-1331), in Allston. From T: Green B Line-Harvard Ave., walk right down Brighton Ave.; it's across the street from Pho Pasteur. Come to Sunset for the beer: with 112 varieties on tap, over 400 in bottles, and a selection that changes every 2 weeks, Sunset is a malt-lover's heaven. Beer starts at $3.50 a pint. "Midnight Madness" Su-Tu 11:30pm-1am: free appetizer buffet with a 2-drink minimum purchase. Open daily 11:30am-1am.

Wonder Bar, 186 Harvard Ave. (☎351-2665), at Comm. Ave. in Allston. The Wonder Bar is *swank:* live jazz nightly, a downstairs lounge (velvet included), and a dress code to boot (no sneakers, no hats, no ripped jeans). The scene is at its most happening late into the night, but there is also a swinging after-work crowd until around 7:30pm on weekdays. Beer $3.75-4; wine $5-7. Live jazz nightly at 9:30pm. Bar open daily 5pm-2am; lounge Th-Sa 10:30pm-2am.

LIVE MUSIC

Wally's Cafe, 427 Mass. Ave. (☎424-1408), at Columbus Ave. in the South End, accessible via the #1 bus or T: Orange Line-Mass. Ave. Established in 1947, Wally's is Boston's longest-running jazz joint, and the place has only improved with age. The beer ($2.75, $3.75 during music) flows freely. Blues M 9pm-2am, jazz Tu-W and F-Sa 9pm-2am, Latin jazz Th 9pm-2am. Open M-Sa 9am-2am, Su noon-2am. 21+.

Harper's Ferry, 158 Brighton Ave. (☎254-9743), in Allston. From T: Green B Line-Harvard Ave., walk left down Brighton Ave. A must-stop for blues aficionados, this is Bo Diddley's favorite joint in town. Featured bands usually play Chicago-style blues. In addition to live nightly rhythm and blues acts, Harper's promises a relaxed atmosphere, plenty of pool tables, and a casual down-home scene. Beer $3-4. Live music nightly at 9:30pm. Open daily 1pm-2am. Cover $2-10.

GAY AND LESBIAN NIGHTLIFE

For updated listings for gay and lesbian nightlife, pick up a copy of *Bay Windows*, available in many businesses in the South End. All bars and restaurants in the **South End** are gay-friendly, but some cater exclusively to a gay crowd (sorry, ladies, these are mostly boys' night out places). **The Eagle,** 520 Tremont St. (☎542-4494), draws an older crowd of men. **The Fritz,** 26 Chandler St. (☎482-4428), is a popular gay sports bar. **Moonshine** and **Satellite Lounge** at Club Cafe, 209 Columbus Ave. (☎536-0966), are video bars that attract a mixed crowd of young gay professionals. **Jacque's,** 71 Broadway (☎426-8902), is the oldest gay bar in Boston, catering mostly to a transgendered crowd, with drag shows and live music. In the Fenway, strictly leather-and-Levis **Ramrod** has recently spawned another floor of non-leather earthly delights—**The Machine** (☎266-2986) dance club. Other Fenway fun can be had at the **Lava Bar,** 575 Commonwealth Ave. (☎267-7707), where DJs spin hip-hop, house, and world beat for a mixed crowd; Sa nights are hailed as the best lesbian nights in Boston. If you wanna boogie, check out **Avalon Sundays** (see p. 124) for cruisy, crazy fun. On F-Sa nights, the low-key gay bar **Chaps** transforms into **Vapor,** 100 Warrenton St. (☎695-9500), when a gay and lesbian crowd grooves to house and dance mixes under the lights. The most popular scene, however, is **Axis Mondays** (p. 124), when a mixed straight and gay crowd pack the dance floor as one of area's best DJs spins the latest dance hits; at 12:30am, the real fun begins with a raunchy drag show—be prepared for foul language, fabulous costumes, and real attitude.

CAMBRIDGE ☎617

Cambridge began its career as an intellectual and publishing center in the colonial era. Harvard, the nation's first university, was founded as a college of divinity here in 1636. The Massachusetts Institute of Technology (MIT), founded in Boston in 1861, moved to Cambridge in 1916, giving the small city a second academic heavyweight. Today, the city takes on the character of both the universities and the taxpaying Cantabrigians. Town and gown mingle and contrast, creating a patchwork of diverse flavors that change as you move from square to square. Bio-tech labs and computer science buildings radiate out from MIT through Kendall Sq., and their

NEW ENGLAND

gentrifying influence is slowly overtaking Central Sq. Harvard Sq., on the other side of the city, offers Georgian buildings, stellar bookstores, coffeehouses, street musicians, and prime people-watching opportunities.

🛈 PRACTICAL INFORMATION. Cambridge is best reached by a 10min. T-ride outbound from downtown Boston. The city's main artery, **Massachusetts Ave.** ("Mass. Ave."), parallels the Red Line, which makes stops at a series of squares along the road. The **Kendall Sq./MIT** stop is just across the Longfellow Bridge from Boston. The subway continues outbound through **Central Sq., Harvard Sq.,** and **Porter Sq.** The *Old Cambridge Walking Guide* provides an excellent self-guided tour ($2). **Post Office:** 125 Mt. Auburn St. (☎876-9280. Open M-F 7:30am-6pm, Sa 7:30am-3pm; self-service available M-F 7am-6:30pm, Sa 7am-3:30pm.) **ZIP code:** 02138. **Area code:** 617. For budget **accommodations,** head back to Boston (see p. 111).

🍴 FOOD. Cambridge culinary culture is a microcosm of the United Nations, from Portugal to Pamplona, Afghanistan to Algiers. The best part about Cambridge, however, is dessert—whether you crave decadent hot chocolate, an ice cream sundae, or just a cup of coffee. At **🖾Charlie's Kitchen Bar and Grill,** 10 Eliot St., fickle tastes and changing trends don't bother anyone. Although occasionally frequented by ironic hipsters in search of kitsch, this joint is the official dinner spot of the *Let's Go* staff, and the $5 double cheeseburger special is the staple of our diets. Frozen in 1983 America, Charlie's tiled walls, booths, and jukeboxes offer a timelessness lost elsewhere in Harvard Sq. (☎492-9646. Open Su-W noon-12:30am, Th-Sa noon-1:30am.) **🖾Campo de Fiori,** 1350 Mass. Ave., in the Holyoke Center, hits the spot with rave reviews, a prime location in the Holyoke Arcade, and a scrumptious signature *pane romano.* The counter service is quick despite the crowds, making this an unusual option on the fast food roster. (☎354-3805. Open M-F 8am-8pm, Sa 11-6pm. *Pane Romano* $3-4.50, sandwiches $4-5.50.) With its signature "smoosh-ins," **🖾Herrell's Ice Cream,** 15 Dunster St., delivers ice cream lovers more than 2500 different possibilities, including frozen yogurt and "no-moo" vegan options. All flavors, fudges, and whipped creams are prepared on site. Lick your heart out in the a converted bank vault in the back decorated with aquatic murals. (Open daily noon-midnight.) **Pinocchio's,** 74 Winthrop St., or "Noke's," as patrons lovingly dub it, serves Sicilian-style deep dish pizza with a variety of toppings, including tomato and basil, spinach, and good ol' pepperoni. (☎876-4897. Open M-Sa 11am-1am, Su 2pm-midnight. Steak and cheese $5, slices $2.)

🖾 SIGHTS. The **Massachusetts Institute of Technology (MIT)** supports cutting-edge work in the sciences. Free campus tours highlight the Chapel, designed by Eero Saarinen, and an impressive collection of modern outdoor sculpture. Contact **MIT Information** for more details. *(77 Mass. Ave. ☎253-1875. T: Red Line-Kendall/MIT. Open M-F 9am-5pm; tours, M-F 10am and 2pm, meet in the lobby.)* The **MIT Museum** contains a slide rule collection and wonderful photography exhibits, including the famous stop-action photos of Harold Edgerton. *(265 Mass. Ave. ☎253-4444. Open Tu-F 10am-5pm, Sa-Su noon-5pm. $3, students and seniors $1, under 5 free.)*

In all its red-brick-and-ivy dignity, **Harvard University,** farther down Mass. Ave. from Boston, finds space for Nobel laureates, students from around the world, and the occasional party. The **Harvard Events and Information Center,** at the Holyoke Center in Harvard Sq., distributes free guides to the university, its museums, and all upcoming events, as well as offering 1hr. tours of Harvard Yard. Pick up a comprehensive map of Harvard for $1. *(1350 Mass. Ave. ☎495-1573. Tours in summer M-Sa 10, 11:15am, 2 and 3:15pm, Su 1:30 and 3pm; Sept.-May M-F 10am and 2pm, Sa 2pm.)* The university revolves around **Harvard Yard,** a grassy oasis amid the Cantabrigian bustle. The **Harry Elkins Widener Memorial Library** stands as the largest academic library in the world, containing 4½ million of the university's 13½ million books. Visitors are not allowed inside. The extravagantly ornate **Memorial Hall,** just outside the Yard's northern gate, is a secular cathedral dedicated to the Union dead.

The most notable of Harvard's museums, the **Fogg Art Museum** gathers a considerable collection of works ranging from ancient Chinese jade to contemporary photography, as well as the largest Ingres collection outside of France. Across the street, the modern exterior of the **Arthur M. Sackler Museum** holds a rich collection of ancient Asian and Islamic art. Another of Harvard's art museums, the **Busch-Reisinger Museum,** on the 2nd fl. of the Fogg, displays Northern and Central European sculpture, painting, and decorative arts, especially German Expressionism. *(32 Quincy St. and 485 Broadway. ☎495-9400 for all 3. All open M-Sa 10am-5pm, Su 1-5pm. $5, students $3, seniors $4; free on W, Sa before noon, and for guests under 18. Wheelchair access on Prescott St.)* Peering down at the Fogg, Le Corbusier's piano-shaped **Carpenter Center** displays student and professional work with especially strong photo exhibits and a great, largely foreign, film series at the **Harvard Film Archive,** located inside the Center. Pick up schedules outside the door. *(24 Quincy St. ☎495-3251. Center open M-Sa 9am-11pm, Su noon-11pm; during term-time, daily 9am-11pm. Most shows $6, students and seniors $5, under 8 free.)* The **Botanical Museum,** one of Harvard's several **Museums of Natural and Cultural History,** draws huge crowds to view the Ware collection of glass flowers. *(24 Oxford St. ☎495-3045. Open M-Sa 9am-5pm, Su 1-5pm. $5, students and seniors $4, ages 3-13 $3. Admission includes all the museums.)*

The **Longfellow House,** now a National Historic Site, headquartered the Continental Army during the early stages of the Revolution. The poet Henry Wadsworth Longfellow, for whom the house is named, lived here later. *(105 Brattle St. ☎876-4491.)* The **Mt. Auburn Cemetery** lies about 1 mi. up the road at the end of Brattle St. The nation's first botanical garden/cemetery has 174 acres of beautifully landscaped grounds worked by Louis Agassiz, Charles Bullfinch, Dorothea Dix, Mary Baker Eddy, and Longfellow. Locals say it's the best birdwatching site in Cambridge. The central tower offers a stellar view of Boston and Cambridge. *(580 Mt. Auburn St. ☎547-7105. Open Su-Sa 8am-7pm; tower closes 1hr. earlier. Greenhouse: M- Sa 8am-4pm. Free. Wheelchair accessible.)*

📷📺 **ENTERTAINMENT AND NIGHTLIFE.** In warm weather, street performers ranging from Andean folk singers to magicians crowd every brick sidewalk of Harvard Sq. and nearby **Brattle Sq.** The **American Repertory Theater (ART),** 64 Brattle St., in the Loeb Drama Center, produces shows from late Nov. to early June. *(☎547-8300. Box office open M 11am-5pm, Tu-Su 10am-5pm, or until showtime. Tickets $25-55. Student rush tickets available 30min. before shows, $12 cash only; seniors $5 off ticket price.)*

Harvard Sq. is a lively scene weekend nights in the summertime, while other times of the year Harvard grads and undergrads crowd the bars, blowing off steam and throwing back shots. **Central Sq.** is a bar-hopper's heaven—a true neighborhood not yet overtaken by tourist capital. Here you'll find blues lounges, communist republics, and some of the best live music anywhere.

📷**The Cellar,** 991 Mass. Ave., in Central Sq., is frequented by Hemingway aspirants, *Let's Go* lushes, and students who think they are expatriates just because they've taken a 5min. walk out of Harvard Sq. But, hey, with pint-sized whiskey sours and gin and tonics ($3 Su-Th, $4 F-Sa) such delusion comes cheap. (☎876-2580. Open daily until 1am. Pilsner $3.) The homespun acts of the 📷**The Cantab Lounge,** 738 Mass. Ave., are its primary claim to fame: Little Joe Cook and the Thrillers, a Cambridge institution who blend blues and 50s rock, takes the stage Th-Sa. (☎354-2685. Open Su-W 8pm-1am, Th-Sa 8pm-2am. Each Tu a local bluegrass band plays at 9pm. Folk or blues bands 9pm Su and W. Poetry Slams W. Domestic beers $3, imports $4. Bar food and sandwiches $4.50-7. Cover W-Su $3-8.)

📷**The Middle East,** 472 Mass. Ave., in Central Sq., features live bands every night. The Middle East is a well-known hot-spot for a young, underground-type crowd. (☎864-3278 or 492-5162. Open Su-W 9pm-1am, Th-Sa 9pm-2am. Advance tickets for all shows are available at the Middle East Box Office and Ticketmaster locations. Bottled beers $3.50. Cover for upstairs and downstairs average $5-8. Shows 18+.) For live music, head to **Club Passim,** 47 Palmer St. This brick-floored, subterranean locale is a premier national venue presenting new and established folk and acoustic musical performers. Sitting in the intimate 125-seat audience, you can relive the days when Joan Baez graced the stage (and Bob Dylan played in between her sets). (☎492-5300. Open daily 11am-11pm. Shows nightly 8pm. Open mike night Tu $5. Cover $5-12. No alcohol.)

SALEM
☎ 978

Salem ain't trying that hard to free itself from certain stereotypes. The **Salem Witch Museum,** 19½ Washington Sq., gives a melodramatic but informative multi-media presentation that details the history of the infamous 17th-century witch trials. (☎ 745-1692. Open daily 10am-7pm; Sept.-June 10am-5pm. $6, seniors $5.50, ages 6-14 $4.) Escape the sea of witch kitsch at the **Witch Trials Memorial,** off Charter St., where engraved stones commemorate the trials' victims.

Salem's **Peabody Essex Museum,** on the corner of Essex and Liberty St., recalls the port's former leading role in Atlantic whaling and merchant shipping. Admission includes four historic Salem houses. (☎ 800-745-4054, recorded info 745-9500. Open M-Sa 10am-5pm, Su noon-5pm; Nov.-May closed M. $10, students and seniors $8, ages under 17 free.) The **Salem Maritime National Historic Site,** consisting of three wharves and 12 historic buildings jutting out into Salem Harbor on Derby St., is a respite from the barrage of commercial attractions. (☎ 740-1650. Open daily July-Aug. 9am-6pm, Sept.-May 9am-5pm.) Built in 1668 and officially named the Turner-Ingersoll Mansion, Salem's **House of Seven Gables,** 54 Turner St., became the "second most famous house in America" after the release of Nathaniel Hawthorne's Gothic romance of the same name. (☎ 744-0991. Open M-Sa 10am-5pm, Su noon-5pm. $8, ages 6-17 $5. Guided tour only.)

The **Salem Visitors Center,** 2 New Liberty St., has free maps, public restrooms, historical displays, and a gift shop. (☎ 740-1650. Open in summer daily 9am-6pm; in winter 9am-5pm.) The town is packed during Oct. with the **Haunted Happenings** festival (☎ 744-0013). Salem, 20 mi. northeast of Boston, is accessible by the Rockport/Ipswich commuter train from Boston's North Station (☎ 617-722-3200; $3.50), by bus #450 or 455 from Haymarket ($2.25), or driving by taking I-95 or U.S. 1 N to Rte. 128, then following Rte. 114 into the center of Salem. **Area code:** 978.

LEXINGTON
☎ 781

"Stand your ground. Don't fire unless fired upon, but if they mean to have a war, let it begin here," said Captain John Parker to the colonial Minutemen on April 19, 1775. Although no one is certain who fired the first shot, the American Revolution did indeed erupt in downtown Lexington. The site of the fracas lies in the center of town (Mass Ave.) at the Battle Green, where a Minuteman Statue still watches over Lexington. The fateful command itself was issued from across the street at the **Buckman Tavern,** 1 Bedford St., which housed the minutemen on the eve of their decisive battle. The nearby **Hancock-Clarke House,** 36 Hancock St., and the **Munroe Tavern,** 1332 Mass. Ave., also played significant roles in the birth of the Revolution. (Buckman: ☎ 862-5598. Hancock-Clarke: ☎ 861-0928. Munroe: ☎ 674-9238. All open Apr.-Oct. M-Sa 10am-5pm, Su 1-5pm. $4 per site, ages 6-16 $2. Combination ticket for all 3 houses, $10.) All three can be seen on a 30min. tour that runs continuously. You can also survey exhibits on the Revolution at the **Museum of Our National Heritage,** 33 Marrett Rd./Rte. 2A, which emphasizes a historical approach to understanding popular American life. (☎ 861-6559. Open M-Sa 10am-5pm, Su noon-5pm. Free. Wheelchair accessible.) An excellent model and description of the Battle of Lexington decorates the **visitors center,** 1875 Mass. Ave., behind the Buckman Tavern. (☎ 862-2480. Open daily Apr.-Oct 9am-5pm, 10am-4pm off-season.)

Picky eaters flock to the 33-acre **Wilson Farm,** 10 Pleasant St., for freshly picked fruits and veggies and over 30 varieties of freshly baked bread and pastry. (☎ 862-3900. Open M and W-F 9am-8pm, Sa 9am-7pm, Su 9am-6:30pm; call for winter hrs.) The road from Boston to Lexington is easy. Drive straight up Mass. Ave. from Boston or Cambridge, or bike up the **Minuteman Commuter Bike Trail,** which runs into downtown Lexington (access off Mass. Ave. in Arlington, or Alewife in Cambridge). MBTA bus #62 from Alewife in Cambridge runs to Lexington (60¢). **Area code:** 781.

CONCORD
☎ 978

Concord, the site of the second conflict of the American Revolution, is famous for both its military history and its status as a 19th-century intellectual center. The **Concord Museum,** 200 Lexington St. on the Cambridge Turnpike, lies across the street from Ralph Waldo Emerson's 19th-century home. This recently refurbished museum houses a reconstruction of Emerson's study alongside Paul Revere's lantern. Period rooms, with an exhaustive collection of decorative arts, walk you through three centuries of Concord's history. (☎369-9763. Open M-Sa 9am-5pm, Su noon-5pm; Jan.-Mar. M-Sa 11am-4pm, Su 1-4pm. $7, students and seniors $6, ages 6-18 $3, families $16.) Down the road from the Concord Museum, you'll find the **Orchard House,** 399 Lexington Rd., home of the illustrious and multi-talented Alcotts, where Louisa May wrote *Little Women.* (☎369-4118. Open M-Sa 10am-4:30pm, Su 1-4:30pm; Nov.-Mar. M-F 11am-3pm, Sa 10am-4:30pm, Su 1-4:30pm. $7, students and seniors $6, ages 6-17 $4, families $16. Guided tour only.) Further down the road lies **Wayside,** 455 Lexington Rd., the former residence of the Alcotts and Hawthornes. (☎369-6975. Open May to Oct. M-Th 10am-5pm. $4, under 17 free. Guided tour only.) Today, Emerson, Hawthorne, Alcott, and Thoreau reside on "Author's Ridge" in the peaceful **Sleepy Hollow Cemetery** on Rte. 62, three blocks from the center of town.

Over the **Old North Bridge,** you'll find the spot from which "the shot heard 'round the world" was fired. From the parking lot, a 5min. walk brings you to the **North Bridge Visitors Center,** 174 Liberty St., where you can learn about the town's history, especially its involvement in the Revolutionary War. (☎369-6993. Open daily Apr.-Oct 9am-5pm; in winter 9am-4pm.) The **Minuteman National Historical Park,** best explored along the adjacent 5½ mi. **Battle Rd. Trail,** includes an impressive **visitors center** that hosts battle reenactments and a multimedia presentation on the "Road to Revolution." (☎781-862-7753. Off Rte. 2A between Concord and Lexington. Open Apr.-Nov. daily 9am-5pm; in winter 9am-4pm.)

A night's stay in Concord will suck your wallet dry; consider making the trek 13 mi. northwest to the secluded, family-run **Friendly Crossways Hostel and Conference Center,** 247 Littleton County Rd. in Littleton. Set in rural Massachusetts on 40 acres of gardens, forest and cornfields, this big, beautiful hostel offers an escape from a busier (and costlier) New England. Buffet-style meals (breakfast $5, lunch $10, dinner $15) are served in the dining hall, or guests may use the kitchen. Common area with TV and conference room. (☎456-9386 or 456-3649. Check-in 8-10am and 5-11pm; after 10pm ring the owner's private residence. Check-out before 10am. 50 beds, $12-17, non-members add $3. Linen $5.) Both Littleton and Concord, north of Boston, are served by commuter rail trains from **North Station** (☎722-3200; fare $2.50, seniors and ages 5-11 $1.25). **Area Code:** 978.

NEAR CONCORD: WALDEN POND.

In 1845, Thoreau retreated 1½ mi. south of Concord "to live deliberately, to front only the essential facts of life" (though the harsh essence of *his* life was eased from time to time by his mother's home cooking; she lived within walking distance of his cabin). Here he wrote his famous book *Walden.* The **Walden Pond State Reservation,** on Rte. 126, draws picnickers, swimmers, and boaters, and is mobbed in summer (though still mighty pleasant). No camping, pets, or novelty flotation devices are allowed. (☎369-3254. Open daily 7am-8pm. Parking $2.) When Walden Pond swarms with crowds, head east from Concord center on Rte. 62 to another of Thoreau's haunts, **Great Meadows National Wildlife Refuge,** on Monsen Rd. (☎443-4661. Open daily dawn-dusk. Free.)

PLYMOUTH   ☎508

Despite what American high school textbooks say, the Pilgrims' first step onto the New World was *not* at Plymouth. They stopped first at Provincetown, but promptly left because the soil was so inadequate. **Plymouth Rock** itself is a rather small stone that has dubiously been identified as the actual rock on which the Pilgrims disembarked. A stepping stone to the nation, it served as a symbol of liberty during the American Revolution, then was moved three times, and was chipped away by tourists before landing at its current home beneath an extravagant portico on Water St., at the foot of North St. After several vandalization episodes, it's under high security.

Three mi. south of town off Rte. 3A, the historical theme-park of **Plymouth Plantation** recreates the Pilgrims' early settlement. In the **Pilgrim Village,** costumed actors play the roles of actual villagers carrying out their daily tasks, based upon William

Bradford's record of the year 1627, while the **Wampanoag Summer Encampment** represents a Native American village of the same period. The plantation sends a historian to England each summer to gather more info about each villager. (☎746-1622. Open daily Apr.-Nov. 9am-5pm. $17, ages 6-12 $9.50. Pass good for 2 consecutive days.) The **Mayflower II**, built in the 50s to recapture the atmosphere of the original ship, is docked off Water St. (Open Apr.-Nov. daily 9am-5pm. $7, ages 6-12 $4.50. Admission to both sights $19, students and seniors $17, ages 6-12 $11.) The nation's oldest museum in continuous existence, the **Pilgrim Hall Museum,** 75 Court St., houses Puritan crafts, furniture, books, paintings, and weapons. (☎746-1620. Open daily Feb.-Dec. 9:30am-4:30pm. $5, seniors $4.50, ages 5-17 $3, families $14.)

Bogged down in history? A trip down Federal Furnace Rd. or Rte. 44 in early fall leads you to the heart of **Cranberry Country. Cranberry World,** 225 Water St., celebrates one of the three indigenous American fruits (the others are the blueberry and the Concord grape). Exhibits, including a small cranberry bog in front of the museum, show how cranberries are grown, harvested, and sold. (☎747-2350. Open May-Nov. daily 9:30am-5pm. Free, and free samples!) **The Plymouth Bay Winery,** 114 Water St. has free wine tasting. Try peach, raspberry, blueberry, and the local favorite: cranberry! (☎746-2100. Open daily 10am-5pm. 21+.)

A few blocks from the center of town, the **Bunk and Bagel,** 51 Pleasant St., has a cheerful, homey atmosphere and the cheapest beds in Plymouth. Bunks come with a bagel. (☎830-0914. Reception daily 7am-9pm. 5-8 hostel beds with common bath. Linen provided. Dorms $20-25.) Majestic **Myles Standish Forest,** 7 mi. south of Plymouth via Exit 3 off Rte. 3, offers 450 wooded sites. (☎866-2526. Office open daily Apr.-June 8am-10pm; July-Aug. 24hr.; Sept.-Oct. 8am-midnight. Sites $6-7.) The natives bite at **Wood's Seafood Restaurant,** Town Pier. A fish sandwich with fries is $4; prices vary with fresh market prices. (☎746-0261. Open daily June-Aug. 11am-9pm; Sept.-May 11am-8:30pm.) Zip back to modern times at **Sean O'Toole's Public House,** 22 Main St., with live music and a traditional Irish pub atmosphere (☎746-3388. Open daily 4:30pm-12:30am.) **Plymouth Visitor's Information Center** is located at 130 Water St. (☎747-7525 or 800-872-1620. Open daily Apr.-May 9am-5pm; June 9am-6pm; July-Aug. 9am-9pm; Sept.-Nov. 9am-5pm.) **Area code:** 508.

CAPE COD   ☎508

Henry David Thoreau once said: "At present [this coast] is wholly unknown to the fashionable world, and probably it will never be agreeable to them." Think again, Hank. In 1602, when English navigator and Jamestown colonist Bartholomew Gosnold landed on this peninsula in southeastern Massachusetts, he named it in honor of all the codfish he caught in the surrounding waters. In recent decades, tourists have replaced the plentiful cod, and the area has as many taffy shops as fishermen. This small strip of land supports a diverse set of landscapes—long, unbroken stretches of beach, salt marshes, hardwood forests, deep freshwater ponds carved by glaciers, and desert-like dunes sculpted by the wind. Thankfully, the Cape's natural landscape has been protected from the tide of commercialism by the **Cape Cod National Seashore.** Blessed with an excellent hostel system, Cape Cod is an option for budget travelers, though in general it attracts services more affluent tourists. The Cape also serves as the gateway to **Martha's Vineyard** and **Nantucket,** two islands with unsurpassed natural beauty. Ferries shuttle from Falmouth, Woods Hole, and Hyannis to Martha's Vineyard, and from Hyannis to Nantucket; see **Martha's Vineyard** (p. 136) and **Nantucket** (p. 138) for info.

✦ 🔃 ORIENTATION AND PRACTICAL INFORMATION

Terminology for locations on the Cape can be confusing. **Upper Cape** refers to the more suburbanized and developed part of Cape Cod, closer to the mainland. Proceeding eastward away from the mainland, you travel "down Cape" until hitting the **Lower Cape;** the National Seashore encompasses much of this area. Cape Cod resembles a bent arm, with **Woods Hole** at its armpit, **Chatham** at the elbow, and

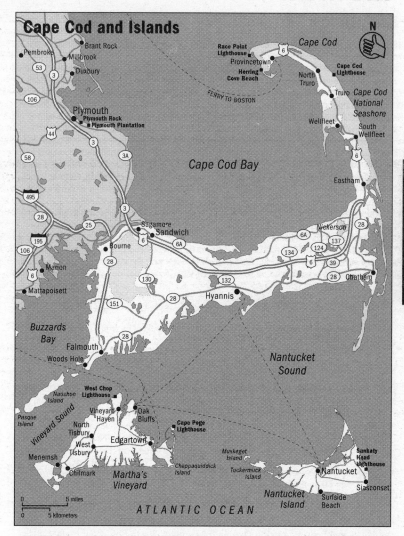

Cape Cod and Islands

N

Race Point Lighthouse
Cape Cod
Provincetown
Herring Cove Beach
Cape Cod Lighthouse
North Truro
Truro
Cape Cod National Seashore
Wellfleet
South Wellfleet

FERRY TO BOSTON

Pembroke
Millbrook
Brant Rock
53
3
Duxbury
106
Plymouth
Plymouth Rock
Plymouth Plantation
44
3
58
3A
495
28
25
Sagamore
Sandwich
6
6A
Bourne
28
106
195
6
Marion
130
6
Mattapoisett
151
28
Hyannis

Cape Cod Bay

Eastham

Nickerson
6A
124
134
6
39
28
Chatham
137
28
132

Buzzards Bay
Falmouth
28
Woods Hole

Nantucket Sound

West Chop Lighthouse
Nashon Island
Vineyard Haven
Oak Bluffs
Cape Poge Lighthouse
Pasque Island
North Tisbury
Edgartown
West Tisbury
Menemsha
Chilmark
Martha's Vineyard
Chappaquiddick Island
Muskeget Island
Tuckernuck Island
Sankaty Head Lighthouse
Nantucket
Siasconset
Nantucket Island
Surfside Beach

ATLANTIC OCEAN

0   5 miles
0   5 kilometers

NEW ENGLAND

Provincetown at its clenched fist. Travel times on the peninsula are often inconsistent; a drive from the Sagamore bridge to Provincetown can take anywhere from 2 to 4hrs. Leaving the Cape can be equally annoying; the area's weekend warriors can turn a Su departure into a hellacious 6hr. odyssey.

If you're up for some exercise, cycling is the best way to travel the Cape's gentle slopes. The park service can give you a free map of trails or sell you the detailed *Cape Cod Bike Book* ($3; available at most Cape bookstores). The 135 mi. **Boston-Cape Cod Bikeway** connects Boston to Provincetown at land's end. If you want to bike this route, pick up a bicycle trail map of the area. These are available at some bookstores and most bike shops. The trails that line either side of the **Cape Cod Canal** in the National Seashore rank among the country's most scenic, as does the 25 mi. **Cape Cod Rail Trail** from Dennis to Wellfleet. For discount coupons good for bargains at restaurants, sights, and entertainment venues throughout the Cape, pick up a free copy of *The Official 2001 Guide to Cape Cod* or the *Cape Cod Best Read Guide*, available at most Cape info centers. **Area code:** 508.

UPPER CAPE

HYANNIS. Hyannis is not the Cape Cod idyll most people expect. John F. Kennedy spent his summers on the beach in nearby Hyannisport, but the town itself sees more action as a transportation hub than as a tourist destination. Island ferries and buses to destinations throughout the Cape leave from Hyannis; hop on one and get out of town—the Kennedys *aren't* going to meet you at the bus station.

About 3 mi. up the road from the bus station, the **Hyannis Area Chamber of Commerce,** 1481 Rte. 132, distributes the free *Hyannis Guidebook* and has a campground guide for the whole Cape. (☎362-5230 or 800-449-6647. Open June-Sept. M-Sa 9am-5pm, Su 10am-2pm; Oct.-May M-Sa 9am-5pm.) If you must stay in Hyannis, there are a bunch of your run-of-the-mill cheap motels. Hyannis does have a few good beaches, however. **Kalmus Park,** on Ocean St. in Hyannisport, is popular with windsurfers. **Orrin Keyes,** on Sea St., attracts more of a local crowd. **Veteran's Park Beach,** off Ocean St., is a favorite of families. All three beaches have parking (M-F $8, Sa-Su $10), lifeguards, bathhouses, snack bars, and picnic areas.

Hyannis is tattooed midway across the Cape's upper arm, 3 mi. south of Rte. 6 on Nantucket Sound. **Plymouth & Brockton** (☎771-6191) runs five Boston-to-Provincetown buses per day with 30min. layovers at the **Hyannis Bus Station,** 17 Elm St. Other stops besides Boston (1¾hr., $12) and Provincetown (1½hr., $9) include Plymouth, Barnstable, Yarmouth, Eastham, Wellfleet, and Truro. **Bonanza Bus Lines** (☎800-556-3815) operates a line to New York City (6hr., 7 per day, $29).

SANDWICH. The oldest town on the Cape, Sandwich cultivates an old-fashioned charm, more old New England-esque than touristy. The beauty and workmanship of Sandwich glass was made famous by the Boston & Sandwich Glass Company, founded in 1825. Master glassblowers shape works of art from blobs of molten sand at **Pairpoint Crystal,** on Rte. 6A just across the town border in Sagamore. (☎888-2344. Open M-F 9am-noon and 1-4:30pm. Free.) To enjoy the town's considerable collection of older pieces, tiptoe through the light-bending exhibits at **The Sandwich Glass Museum,** 129 Main St., in Sandwich center. (☎888-0251. Open daily Apr.-Oct. 9:30am-5pm; Nov.-Mar. W-Su 9:30am-4pm; closed in Jan. $3.50.) The gorgeously floral **Heritage Plantation of Sandwich,** Grove St., features a working 1912 carousel, antique automobiles, military and art museums, and 76 acres of landscaped gardens. (☎888-3300. Open daily mid-May to mid-Oct. 10am-5pm. $9, seniors $8, ages 6-18 $4.50. Wheelchair accessible.)

The best beach on the Upper Cape, the **Sandy Neck Beach,** on Sandy Neck Rd. 3 mi. east of Sandwich off Rte. 6A, extends 6 mi. along Cape Cod Bay with beautifully polished, egg-sized granite cobbles and verdant dunes. Hike only on marked trails; the plants are very fragile. The **Shawme-Crowell State Forest,** at Rte. 130 and Rte. 6, provides 285 wooded campsites with showers and campfires, but no hook-ups (☎888-0351; $6). Parking is at **Scusset Beach,** on the canal near the junction of Rte. 6 and Rte. 3. Scusset Beach also offers swimming and a fishing jetty. (☎888-0859. $2 per car.) The family-oriented **Peters Pond Park Campground,** on Cotuit Rd. in south Sandwich, combines waterside sites with swimming, fishing, rowboat rentals ($15 per day), showers, and a grocery store. (☎477-1775. Open mid-Apr. to mid-Oct. Sites $24-28, with hook-up $30-50. No pets are allowed.)

Sandwich lies at the intersection of Rte. 6A and Rte. 130, about 13 mi. from Hyannis. The **Plymouth & Brockton** bus makes its closest stop in Sagamore, 3 mi. northwest along Rte. 130.

LOWER CAPE

CAPE COD NATIONAL SEASHORE. As early as 1825, the Cape had suffered so much man-made damage that the town of Truro required local residents to plant beach grass and keep their cows off the dunes. Further conservation efforts culminated in 1961 with the creation of the **Cape Cod National Seashore,** which includes much of the Lower Cape from Provincetown to Chatham and has largely escaped the commercialism that afflicts most American seacoasts. Over 30 mi. of wide, soft, uninterrupted beaches lie under the tall clay cliffs and towering 19th-century lighthouses of this protected area. Just a short walk away from the lifeguards, the sea of umbrellas and coolers fades into the distance.

Beachgoers at the Cape face a difficult question: ocean or bay? While the ocean beaches entice with whistling winds and surging waves, the water on the bay side rests calmer and gets a bit warmer. The National Seashore oversees six beaches: **Coast Guard** and **Nauset Light** in Eastham; **Marconi** in Wellfleet; **Head of the Meadow** in Truro, and **Race Point** and **Herring Cove** in Provincetown. Herring Cove has special facilities which allow disabled travelers access to the water. (Parking at all beaches $7 per day, $20 per season; mid-Sept. to late June free.)

To park at any other beach, a town permit is required. While each town has a different beach-parking policy, all require proof of lodging in their town. Permits generally cost $5-10 per day, $20-25 per week, or $50-100 per season and can be bought at town halls. Call the appropriate town hall before trying to get around the parking permit; beaches are sometimes miles from any other legal parking and police with tow-trucks hover like vultures. Parking lots fill up by 11am or earlier; it is often easier to rent a bike and ride in. Most town beaches do not require bikers and walkers to pay an entrance fee. Wellfleet and Truro stand out among the ocean beaches as great examples of the Cape's famous endangered sand dunes. **Cahoon Hollow Beach,** with spectacular, cliff-like dunes, and **Duck Harbor Beach,** overlooking the bay in Wellfleet, provide two particularly beautiful vistas.

Among the best of the seashore's 11 self-guiding **nature trails,** the **Great Island Trail,** in Wellfleet, traces an 8 mi. loop through pine forests and grassy marshes and along a ridge with a view of the bay and Provincetown. The **Atlantic White Cedar Swamp Trail,** a 1¼ mi. walk, leads to dark, swampy waters under towering trees, beginning at Marconi Station site in south Wellfleet. The **Buttonbush Trail,** a ¼ mi. walk with Braille guides and a guide rope for the blind, leaves the Salt Pond Visitors Center (see below). There are also three park **bike trails:** Nauset Trail (1½ mi.), Head of the Meadow Trail (2 mi.), and Province Lands Trail (5 mi.). The accessible **National Seashore's Salt Pond Visitors Center,** at Salt Pond, off Rte. 6 in Eastham, offers a free 10min. film every 30min. and a museum with exhibits on the Cape's natural and contemporary history. (☎255-3421. Open daily 9am-5pm; Sept.-June 9am-4:30pm.) **Camping** on the national seashore is illegal. Permits for fishing and campfires can be purchased at the visitors center.

EASTHAM. Popular with Cape bikers, the **Mid-Cape Hostel (HI-AYH),** 75 Goody Hallet Dr., occupies a quiet, wooded spot in Eastham, convenient to the lower part of the Cape. On the Plymouth-Brockton bus to Provincetown, ask to be let off at the traffic circle in Orleans (not the Eastham stop). Walk out on the exit to Rock Harbor, turn right on Bridge Rd., and take a right onto Goody Hallet Rd. ½ mi. from Rte. 6. The hostel has eight cabins with a total of 78 beds, a kitchen, and a relaxed atmosphere that attracts groups. (☎255-2785. Open mid-May to mid-Sept. Checkout 7:30-10am, check-in 5-10pm. 5-day maximum stay. Members $15, non-members $18. Reservations essential July-Aug.)

WELLFLEET. Thoreau modeled the character of John Newcomb in *Cape Cod* (1864) after a Wellfleet oysterman. Today, Wellfleet is less known as a port than as a cute town that attracts quite a few artists to its shores. Hundreds species of birds inhabit the **Wellfleet Wildlife Sanctuary,** on Rte. 6; follow signs for the Audobon Society. Seven walking trails wind through salt marshes, tidal flats, and fields. (☎349-2615. Open daily 8:30am-5pm; mid-Oct. to May Tu-Su 8:30am-5pm. $3, seniors and ages 6-12 $2.) **Gull Pond,** off Gull Pond Rd., which is off Rte. 6 past the town center in Wellfleet, provides for some of the Cape's best paddling; heading north on Rte. 6, take the first right after the police/fire department. **Maurice's Campground,** 80 Rte. 6 offers 200 sites as well as a playground, basketball court, and direct access to the Cape Cod Rail Trail. (☎349-2029. Office open daily mid-May to mid-Oct. 9am-9pm. Sites $22, with hook-up $25.) **Paine's Campground,** 180 Old County Rd., is harder to find, but has special sections for families. To get there on Rte. 6 E, turn right just before the Citgo station and follow the signs to Paine's. (☎349-3007 or 800-479-3017. Office open May to mid-Oct. 9am-9pm. Tent sites for 2 $18-24.) Family-owned **Moby Dick's Restaurant,** on Rte. 6, offers Cape Cod favorites. (☎349-9795. Open daily mid-May to late Sept. 11:30am-10pm. Clam chowder $3.75, lobster rolls $12.)

TRURO. Head down Highland Rd., off Rte. 6, to visit one of Thoreau's favorite places and to catch a panoramic view of the Lower Cape from the Cape Cod Lighthouse. Recently moved over 400 ft. inland, the lighthouse lies adjacent to the **Truro Historical Museum,** a former hotel that transports visitors back in history with shipwreck mementos, early whaling gear, and Victorian-style furnished rooms. (☎487-3397. Open daily June-Oct. 10am-4:30pm. $3, $5 for a lighthouse/museum combo ticket, under 12 free.) The picturesque ½ mi. **Cranberry Bog Trail,** North Pamet Rd., provides a secluded setting for a walk; get a map at the Salt Pond Visitors Center (see above). Directly across the road from the trail lies the noteworthy **Truro Hostel (HI-AYH),** N. Pamet Rd. Take the N. Pamet Rd. Exit off Rte. 6; follow it 1½ mi. to the east. The hostel offers an escape from the crowds with plenty of space, 42 beds, a large kitchen, great ocean views, and access to Ballston Beach. (☎349-3889 or 800-909-4776, ext. 15. Open late June to early Sept. Reception daily 8-10am and 5-10pm. $14, non-members $17. Reservations essential in July and Aug.) Several popular campgrounds nestle among the dwarf pines of North Truro. Just 7 mi. southeast of Provincetown on Rte. 6, **North Truro Camping Area,** on Highland Rd. ½ mi. east of Rte. 6, has small sandy sites, heated restrooms, hot showers, and cable TV with hook-up. (☎487-1847. Sites for 2 $16, full hook-up $24; $8 per additional person.) **Horton's Camping Resort,** 71 South Highland Rd., offers 200 wooded and open sites with views of the ocean, as well as restrooms and hot showers. (☎487-1220. Sites for 2 $19-23, with hook-up $26-28; $8 per additional person.)

PROVINCETOWN ☎508

At Provincetown, Cape Cod ends and the wide Atlantic begins. The National Seashore protects two-thirds of "P-Town" as conservation land; the inhabited third touches the harbor on the south side of town. This former whaling village has diversified and now includes a prominent gay and lesbian contingent. P-Town is far from inexpensive, but there are many options for the budget travelers. Commercial St., the town's main drag, is home to countless art galleries, novelty shops, and trendy eateries, as well as parades and drag shows.

⚐ PRACTICAL INFORMATION. The Plymouth & Brockton Street Railway (☎771-6191) has buses connecting to a local in Hyannis which will take you all the way to Provincetown (3¼hr.; $21). **Bay State Cruises** sends regular and high speed ferries between Boston and P-town. (☎487-9284 or 617-748-1428. 3hr.; $18 one-way, seniors $15, ages 5-14 $14. High-speed ferries run May 20 to Oct. 9; 2hr., $25 one-way, $40 round-trip.) **Boston Harbor Cruises** uses high-speed catamarans to make the trip in 90min. (☎617-227-4321. $20 one-way, $39 round-trip; seniors $18/30; ages 4-12 $16/25.) To get around in Provincetown, Herring Cove Beach, and North Truro, take **The Shuttle.** Tickets are available on the bus or at the Chamber of Commerce. (☎385-8326 or 800-352-7155; TDD 385-4163. Daily June 24 to Sept. 17 every 20min, 7:15am-12:15am; Sept. 18 to Oct. 15 in Provincetown only. $1, seniors, disabled, and under 17 50¢, under 6 free. One-day pass $3, bulk tokens 25% discount.) **Ptown Bikes,** 42 Bradford St., hands out free locks and maps with their beach cruisers and mountain bikes. (☎487-8735. Open daily 9am-7pm. $3 per hr., minimum 2hr. $10-16 per day, $40-65 per week. Helmet $1 per day, $5 per week.) You'll find the helpful **Provincetown Chamber of Commerce** on MacMillian Wharf. (307 Commercial St. ☎487-3424. Open daily June-Sept. 9am-4pm; reduced off-season hours.) National Seashore information can be found at the **Province Lands Visitors Center,** Race Point Rd. off Rte. 6. (☎487-1256. Open daily May 15 to Labor Day 9am-5pm.) **Area Code:** 508.

⚐ ACCOMMODATIONS. Provincetown teems with expensive places to lay your head—the most comfortable budget options are the hostels 10 mi. away in Truro or a bit farther in Eastham. But if the temptation of P-town nightlife is too much, a few decent quasi-cheap accommodations exist. Prices here drop drastically off-season.

   Outermost Hostel, 28 Winslow St. (☎487-4378), a short walk from the center of town to a quiet location 300 ft. past the Pilgrim Monument. 30 beds in 5 cramped cottages go for $15 each, including kitchen access and parking. Open mid-May to mid-Oct. Reception daily 8-9:30am and 6-9:30pm. Check-out 9:30am. Linen rental $3. Key deposit $10. Reservations recommended for weekends and July-Aug.

The Cape Codder, 570 Commercial St. (☎487-9815), in the quiet East End, welcomes you in crisp, classic Cape Cod style, right down to the wicker furniture and private beach access. Room 16 has a view of the beach. Shared bathrooms feature impeccable cleanliness and an antique tub. Parking and continental breakfast included in season. Open May-Oct. Singles $33-45; doubles $45-65, $5 each additional person.

Dunham House Bed and Brew, 3 Dyer St. (☎487-3330). Catering to artists and return-ing guests, Dunham House has 5 rooms (named according to Monopoly board squares) available in the homestead. Open May-Oct. Rooms $40-60 depending on size, length of stay, and your bargaining capacity.

Sunset Inn, 142 Bradford St. (☎487-9810 or 800-965-1801). This inn inspired great American Realist Edward Hopper's *Rooms for Tourists*. Parking and continental break-fast included. Closed in winter. Rooms with shared bath $69-79, with private bath and A/C $99-135. Reduced rates spring and fall.

Dune's Edge Campground, 386 Rte. 6 (☎487-9815), on the right side at the East End. 100 shaded sites packed together in an idyllic setting. Office open July-Aug. 8am-10pm, May-June and Sept. 9am-8pm. Sites $26, with partial hook-up $32.

◘ FOOD. Sit-down meals in Provincetown cost a bundle. The Commercial St. extension next to MacMillian Wharf and the Aquarium Mall farther west on Com-mercial St. offer a selection of fast food to go with nearby benches and picnic tables. For a gourmet picnic, head to the East End's **Angel Foods,** 467 Commercial St. (☎487-6666. Open 8am-10pm in season; reduced off-season hrs.)

Mayflower Family Dining, 300 Commercial St. (☎487-0121), has given visitors walls lined with ancient caricatures and stomachs lined with solid food since 1921. Try the fish and chips ($8.50) or crab cakes ($10) or splurge on the cheapest lobster in town ($12 for 1¼ lb.). Open daily Apr.-Nov. 11:30am-10pm. Cash only.

Spiritus, 190 Commercial St. (☎487-2808), dishes out whole wheat pizza and doubles as an art gallery and coffee shop. Slices $2. Open daily Apr.-Oct. noon-2am.

Cafe Crudite, 338 Commercial St. (☎487-6237). A casual restaurant with deliciously fresh veg-etarian, vegan and macrobiotic options. Tasty Greek salad and daily specials such as roasted chipotle BLT with tempeh bacon. Lunch served daily 11:30am-4pm, dinner from 5:30pm.

▣◪ SIGHTS AND ENTERTAINMENT. Provincetown is acknowledged as the original site of the Pilgrims' 1620 arrival in Massachusetts, which is marked by the **Pilgrim Monument** and **Provincetown Museum** on High Pole Hill. (☎487-1310. Open daily Apr.-Nov. 9am-5pm; July-Aug. until 7pm. $6, ages 4-12 $3.) The Provincetown **Art Associa-tion and Museum** lies near the artsy East End and was founded in 1914 during Prov-incetown's heyday as a seasonal colony for painters and other artists. (460 Commercial St. ☎487-1750. Open daily July 4 to Labor Day noon-5pm and 8-10pm, Apr.-Sept. reduced hours. $3, seniors and children $1.) Provincetown's natural waterfront provides spectacular walks. Directly across from Snail Rd. on Rte. 6, an unlikely path will lead you to a world of rolling **sand dunes;** look for the shacks where writers like Tennessee Williams, Norman Mailer, and John Dos Passos penned their days away. From Race Point Rd., you can reach the **National Seashore beaches** and **walking and biking trails.** The **visitors center** offers free daily guided tours and activities during the summer, as well as an unbeatable 360° view from their observation deck. The 1¼ mi. **Breakwater Jetty,** at the west end of Commercial St., whisks you away from the crowds and down to a secluded peninsula of endless beach, bearing two working lighthouses and the remains of a Civil War fort. Today, Provincetown seafarers carry telephoto lenses, not harpoons, when they go whale hunting. **Whale-watching cruises** are some of P-town's most popular attractions. Cruise companies claim that whales are sighted on 99% of the journeys, and most promise free trips to the unlucky 1%. (Tickets cost about $19 for a 3hr. cruise. Cape Cod Whale Watch ☎487-4079, Dol-phin Fleet ☎349-1900, and Portuguese Princess ☎487-2651 all leave from MacMillian Wharf.)

◪ NIGHTLIFE. Provincetown's nightlife is almost totally gay- and lesbian-ori-ented, but all are welcome. Most of the clubs and bars on Commercial St. charge around $5, and shut down at 1am. Live music drives **Antro,** 258 Commercial St., with nightly shows and techno music after 10pm. (☎487-8800. Open daily May-Oct. $15 shows at 8 and 9:30pm; $5 after the shows.) **Governor Bradford,** 312 Commercial St., has drag karaoke nightly, never charges cover, and offers $3 beer. (☎487-2781. Open daily 11:30am-1am; kitchen closes at 11pm.) **Vixen,** 333 Commercial St., caters mostly to women with big-name shows and a steamy dance floor. (☎487-6424. Open daily 5pm-1am.) **Steve's Alibi,** 293 Commercial St., is a local hangout with a laid-back atmosphere and tiny tables crunched together to promote socializing. (☎487-2890. Open daily 10am-1am. $5 cover for shows nightly at 6, 9, and 11pm.)

MARTHA'S VINEYARD   ☎508

From remote whaler's outpost to choice destination of the rich and famous, the Vineyard has experienced numerous identity shifts in its history. Native American Wampanoags have long called the island home, and they still retain part of their original lands in the rural southwestern part of the island. In the 1960s the Vineyard was a liberal hippie haven; aging hippies who still live here appreciate the "clothing optional" beaches. In the past decade, the Vineyard has seen an unbelievable boom in wealth and population. The Vineyard economy depends on summer tourism, and locals have mixed feelings about the new construction, inflated price of land, and damage to the fragile ecosystem that comes along with the thousands of seasonal visitors. Still, there's a reason why families, honeymooners, celebrities—even presidents and royalty—flock here: the island's verdant meadows, dramatic cliffs, and unbeatable beaches.

⌷ GETTING THERE AND GETTING AROUND

Buses: Bonanza (☎800-556-3815) stops at the Ferry Terminal in Woods Hole and departs, via Bourne, for Boston (1¾hr.; 11-15 per day 8am-10pm; $15) and New York City (6hr.; 6 per day, early Sept. to late June 5 per day; $45).

Ferries: The **Steamship Authority** sends 24 boats per day on the 45min. ride from Woods Hole to Vineyard Haven and Oak Bluffs. Boats to Oak Bluffs run from 10:45am to 6:15pm mid-May to mid-Oct., while Vineyard Haven operates the approximate hours of 7am to 9:30pm year-round. (☎477-8600 or 693-9130. One-way: $5, ages 5-12 $2.50, cars $52, bikes $3. Oct. 15 to May 14 car reservations drop to $21-31.) Reserve cars months in advance in summer.

Taxis: AdamCab, ☎693-3332 or 281-4462, **Atlantic Cab,** ☎693-7110, and **All Island,** ☎693-2929 or 800-693-8294. To go from Vineyard Haven to Oak Bluffs costs $8-9; Vineyard Haven to Edgartown $15.

Public Transit: Martha's Vineyard Regional Transit Authority runs summer shuttles between and within the various towns on the island. Buses run between **Vineyard Haven** (Ferry Terminal) and **Edgartown** (Church St.) late June through Labor Day every 30min daily 5:30am to 12:45am; late May to late June and early Sept. to early Oct. every 30min. 7am-8pm. Pick up a complete schedule and map (available at the ferry terminals) detailing all 11 routes, including the popular route between **South Beach** and Edgartown. (Fare $1.50. Recorded info ☎508-627-7448, additional info 508-693-4633. 50¢ per town. Most buses have bike racks.) **Island Transport** supplements the coverage with trips in and out of **Oak Bluffs** to Vineyard Haven and Edgartown (☎508-693-1589. Late May to late June and early Sept. to early Oct. every 30min. Su-Th 8am-6:30pm, F-Sa 8am-11:30pm; late June to Labor Day every 15-30min. 6am-12:30am. Oak Bluffs to Vineyard Haven or Edgartown $1.75.)

Bike Rental: Martha's Bike Rental (☎693-6593), at the corner of Beach St. and Beach Rd. in Vineyard Haven. $8 per day for a 3-speed, $20 per day for a mountain or hybrid. Open daily June-Aug. 8am-6pm; mid-Mar. to Nov. 9am-5pm.

ⓘ PRACTICAL INFORMATION

Visitor Info: Martha's Vineyard Chamber of Commerce (☎693-0085), Beach Rd., Vineyard Haven. Open M-F 9am-5pm.

Medical Services: Vineyard Walk-In Medical Center, 108 State Rd. (☎693-6399). Open daily June-Oct. 9am-1pm; Nov.-May 9am-noon. Call for afternoon appointments.

Post Office: Beach Rd., Vineyard Haven (☎693-2815). Open M-F 8:30am-5pm, Sa 9:30am-1pm. **ZIP code:** 02568. **Area code:** 508.

ACCOMMODATIONS

Truly budget accommodations in Martha's Vineyard are almost nonexistent. The Chamber of Commerce provides a list of inns and guest houses; all recommend reservations for July and Aug., especially on weekends.

Martha's Vineyard Hostel (HI-AYH), Edgartown-West Tisbury Rd. (☎693-2665), West Tisbury. The fantastic hostel provides the 78 cheapest beds on the island. Right next to the bike path with a great kitchen and a volleyball court. Reception daily Apr.-Nov. 7:30-10am and 5-10pm. Light chores required. $15, non-members $18. Linen $2. Internet $1 per 8min. Lockers 75¢. Bike rental $15 per day. Reservations essential.

Nashua House, 30 Kennebec Ave. (☎693-0043). Cute, clean, cozy, and with a Van Gogh in all 15 rooms, this old Victorian house in the heart of Oak Bluffs is the best deal on the island for those needing more privacy than the hostel can provide. Shared bath. Open Apr.-Oct. Singles and doubles $70-100.

Attleboro House, 42 Lake Ave. (☎693-4346), overlooking the harbor in Oak Bluffs. No frills but homey atmosphere in one of Oak Bluffs' famous gingerbread houses. Eleven tiny rooms. Some have sink, all have porches. Check-in 1pm. Check-out 11am. Continental breakfast. Shared bath. No maid service. Open May to mid-Sept. Doubles $75-115; suites $115-200; extra person $15-25.

Martha's Vineyard Family Campground (☎693-3772), 1½ mi. from Vineyard Haven on Edgartown Rd. 185 shaded sites in an oak forest. Groceries and metered showers nearby. Open mid-May to mid-Oct. Office open daily 8am-9pm; in spring and fall 8:30-10:30am and 5-8pm. Sites for 2 $32; ages 2-18 $2, $10 per additional person. Single campers receive $10 off before June 20 and after Labor Day. Cabins with 4-6 beds $90-100. No pets or motorcycles.

FOOD

Cheap sandwich and lunch places dot the Vineyard, especially in Vineyard Haven and Oak Bluffs. Fried-food shacks across the island sell clams, shrimp, and potatoes, which generally cost at least $15. Several **farm stands** sell inexpensive produce; the Chamber of Commerce map shows their locations.

The Newes From America, 23 Kelley St. (☎627-4397), in Edgartown. Voted best bar/pub on the island. Traditional pub fare served in an old-time colonial setting. Sandwiches $6-8; fish 'n' chips $9.50. Home-brewed beer $3. Open daily 11am-midnight; kitchen open 11:30am-11pm.

Louis', 350 State Rd. (☎693-3255), in Vineyard Haven. Take-out Italian food that won't break the bank. Try the fresh pasta with meat sauce ($5.25) or the vegetable calzone ($5.50). Cheese pizzas $8.50-10.75. Open M-Sa 11am-9pm, Su 4-9pm.

Black Dog Bakery, on Water St. (☎693-4786), in Vineyard Haven. A range of creative and delicious pastries and breads (40¢-$3.25) tempt patrons, but for the love of God, please don't buy another sweatshirt. Open daily in summer 5:30am-7pm.

Mad Martha's, 10 Circuit Ave. (☎693-9151), in Oak Bluffs. This island institution scoops out outstanding homemade ice cream and frozen yogurt. Two scoops $3. Open daily in season 11am-midnight. Also at 7 N. Water St. (☎627-8761) in Edgartown and 8 Union St. (☎693-5883) in Vineyard Haven.

SIGHTS

Exploring the Vineyard can involve much more than zipping around on a moped. Head out to the countryside, hit the beach, or trek down one of the great trails. **Felix Neck Wildlife Sanctuary,** on the Edgartown-Vineyard Haven Rd., offers five trails which meander through 350 acres. *(☎627-4850. Office open M-Sa 8:30am-4pm, Su 10am-3pm; $3, seniors and under 12 $2.)* **Menemsha Hills Reservation,** off North Rd. in Menemsha, has 4 mi. of trails along the rocky Vineyard Sound beach leading to the island's 2nd-highest point. **Cedar Tree Neck** on the western shore harbors 250 acres of headland off Indian Hill Rd. with trails throughout, while the **Long Point** park in West Tisbury preserves 550 acres and a shore on the Tisbury Great Pond. The largest conservation area on the island, **Cape Pogue Wildlife Refuge and Wasque Reservation,** floats on Chappaquiddick Island. *(☎627-3599.)*

NEW ENGLAND

Two of the best beaches on the island, **South Beach,** at the end of Katama Rd., 3 mi. south of Edgartown; and **State Beach,** on Beach Rd. between Edgartown and Oak Bluffs, are free and open to the public. South Beach boasts sizeable surf and an occasionally nasty undertow. State Beach's warmer waters once set the stage for parts of *Jaws,* the granddaddy of classic beach-horror films. For the best sunsets on the island, stake out a spot at **Gay Head** or the **Menemsha Town Beach.**

Chicama Vineyards, off State Rd. in West Tisbury, offers free tours and wine tasting. *(☎888-244-2262. Open June-Sept. M-Sa 11am-5pm, Su 1-5pm.)* **Oak Bluffs,** 3 mi. west of Vineyard Haven on Beach Rd., is the most youth-oriented of the Vineyard villages. Highlights of a tour of **Trinity Park** near the harbor include the famous "Gingerbread Houses" (minutely detailed, elaborate pastel Victorian cottages) and the Oak Bluffs's **Flying Horses Carousel,** at the end of Circuit Ave. It's the oldest in the nation (built in 1876), and is composed of 20 handcrafted horses with real horsehair. *(☎693-9481. Open daily mid-June to Aug. 10am-10pm; Aug. to mid-June hrs. vary. Fare $1.)* **Gay Head,** 22 mi. southwest of Oak Bluffs on State Rd., offers just about the best view of the sea in all of New England. The native Wampanoag frequently saved sailors whose ships wrecked on the breathtaking **Gay Head Cliffs.** The 100,000-year-old precipice shines in brilliant colors and supports one of five lighthouses on the island. **Menemsha** and **Chilmark,** a little northeast of Gay Head, share a scenic coastline; Chilmark claims to be the only working fishing town on the island. Tourists can fish off the pier. **Vineyard Haven** has more artsy boutiques and fewer tacky t-shirt shops than other towns on the island.

NANTUCKET   ☎508

Nantucket is far enough away to ward off tourists, but not so secluded that it ain't worth the two-hour ferry ride to get there. Once the home of the biggest whaling port in the world—Herman Melville's *Moby Dick* is based on a Nantucket whaling incident—Nantucket has a lot of history to be proud of. Beyond its rich past, Nantucket offers dune-covered beaches, wild flowers, cobblestone streets, and spectacular bike paths. Although a famed preppy mecca, it is possible to enjoy a stay on the island without holding up a convenience store to do so. During the first and last weeks of the tourist season, prices tend to drop. There is only one town on the island, where the ferries unload their passengers. The hostel is a few miles south.

⑦ PRACTICAL INFORMATION. From Hyannis there are two ferry companies two blocks from the bus station that leave for Nantucket; both companies have slow boats (2hr. one-way) and fast boats (1hr.). **Hyline** runs slightly faster boats to Straight Wharf on Nantucket. (☎778-2600. Slow boat: 5 per day in summer, 3 per day in winter; one-way $12.50, ages 5-12 $6.25. Fast boat: 6 per day year-round; $31/$25; $2 discount for HI-AYH members on all trips.) The **Steamship Authority** floats into Steamboat Wharf on Nantucket, and ships cars. (☎477-8600. Slow boat: 4-6 per day 7:30am-8:30pm; one-way $12.50, ages 5-12 $6.25. Fast boat: 6 per day; $23/7.25; in summer car passage $158. Both ferries charge $5 for bicycles.) **Nantucket Regional Transit Authority** (☎228-7025) runs five shuttle bus routes throughout the island. Buses to **Sconset** and **Surfside** leave from Washington and Main St., near the lamp post. Buses to **Miacomet** leave from Washington and Salem St., one block up from Straight Wharf. Buses to **Madaket** leave from Broad St. in front of the Peter Foulger Museum. (Buses depart every 30min. 7am-11:30pm, Surfside/Hostel bus runs every 40min. 10am-5:20pm. Fare is 50¢-$1, seniors and under 6 free.) **Young's Bicycle Shop** rents bikes from Steamboat Wharf. All-terrain or hybrid bikes (with baskets for picnic supplies) are $25 per day and $90 per week, though if you bring the bike back by 5pm the same day you save $5. Childrens' bikes are $15 per day and $65 per week. (☎228-1151. Open daily 8am-6pm; in winter 9am-5pm.) Bus map, schedules, and multi-day passes are available at the **visitors center,** 25 Federal St. (☎228-0925. Open daily 9am-5:30pm.) Renting bikes is a great option: there are three beautiful **bike paths** that wind from town through wildflower paths and along dune-covered beaches (to Madaket Beach 5 mi., Surfside Beach 2½ mi., and Siasconset 6 mi). **Area code:** 508.

▐▐ ACCOMMODATIONS AND FOOD. Occupying an old lifesaving station, the **Nantucket Hostel (HI-AYH),** 51 Western Ave., sits pretty at Surfside Beach, 3½ mi.

from town at the end of the Surfside Bike Path. Take the Miacomet Loop Shuttle to Surfside Rd. and walk 1 mi. south on Surfside. (☎228-0433. Open late Apr. to mid-Oct. 49 beds, full kitchen. Check-in 5-10pm. Lockout 10am-5pm. Curfew 11pm. $15, non-members $18. Linen $2. Reservations essential.) In the heart of Nantucket Town, **Nesbitt Inn,** 21 Broad St., offers 13 rooms in the oldest Victorian guest house on the island. The friendly owners make sure guests are comfortable with a fire-place, deck, and free continental breakfast. (☎228-0156. Open Mar.-Dec. Reception 7am-10pm. Singles $65; doubles $75; Oct.-Apr. $10 less. Reservations and deposit required.) Meals on Nantucket are pricey. The standard entree runs about $15-20, but the frugal gourmet can still dine well. **Something Natural,** 50 Cliff Rd., has gained somewhat of a cult following by churning out enormous sandwiches with heart and pizzazz (whole sandwich $7), though their half sandwiches ($4-5) are enough to fill most mortals. (☎228-0504. Open daily May-Oct. 15 7:30am-5:30pm.) **Henry's Sand-wiches,** Steamboat Wharf, piles 'em high with cold cuts and tons of toppings. (☎228-0123. Open daily May to Oct. 15 7:30am-5:30pm.)

🔷 **SIGHTS.** The remarkable natural beauty of Nantucket is well protected; over 36% of the island's land can never be built upon. For a great bike trip, head east from Nantucket Town on Milestone Rd. and turn left onto any path that looks promising. For a day on the sand, **Dionis** and **Jetties** both have rolling dunes and calm water (Jetties is also the closest beach to town, and predictably more busy). For isolated expanses made for walking, head east to the beaches of **Siasconset** and **Wauwinet. Nobadeer** and **Cisco** are good areas for surfing. For another sort of aquatic adventure, **Nantucket Island Community Sailing** rents **kayaks.** *(Near Jetties Beach. ☎228-6600. 1 person kayaks $15 per hr., $25 per half-day; 2 person kayaks $20/$30.)* You can only kayak in the protected waters of Nantucket Sound, but if you take one out to a nearby salt marsh, or head across the harbor to an isolated beach on the Coatue peninsula, you'll be able to enjoy a picnic undisturbed by other beach-goers. *(☎228-6600. Open daily late June to Labor Day 9am-5pm.)* **Barry Thurstons** rents out rods and reels and gives beginners enough advice to get started fishing. *(At Candle St. and Washington St. ☎508-228-9595. Coming from Straight Wharf turn left on the 3rd street up from the dock and walk 1 block. Open daily Apr.-Dec. 8am-6pm. $20 per 24hr.)* The fasci-nating **Nantucket Whaling Museum** explains the glories and hardships of the old whaling community through exhibits and talks on whales and whaling methods. The **Peter Foulger Museum** gives an overview of Nantucket's history. A visitor's pass allows access to both museums and seven other historical sights run by the historical association. *(Whaling: ☎228-1736, Broad St. in Nantucket Town. Foulger: ☎228-1894, Broad St. Both museums open daily early June to mid-Oct. 10am-5pm; May to early June and mid-Oct. to early Dec. 11am-3pm. $5, children $3. Visitor's Pass $10/$5.)*

WESTERN MASSACHUSETTS

THE BERKSHIRES ☎413

Famous for great cultural events in the summer, rich foliage in the fall, and skiing in the winter, the Berkshire Mountains have long been a vacation destination for Bos-ton and New York urbanites seeking a country escape. Sprinkled with small New England towns, the Berkshires offer a plethora of churches, fudge shops, country stores, and scenic rural drives. To see sights located far from the town centers, you'll have to travel along the region's winding and occasionally bumpy roads.

✦🔢 ORIENTATION AND PRACTICAL INFORMATION

Filling the western third of Massachusetts, the Berkshire region is bordered to the north by Rte. 2 (the Mohawk Trail) and Vermont, to the west by Rte. 7 and New York, to the south by the Mass. Pike and Connecticut, and to the east by I-91. **Visitor Info: Berkshire Visitors Bureau,** 2 Berkshire Common (☎443-9186 or 800-237-5747), Plaza Level, in Pittsfield (open M-F 8:30am-5pm) and an **information booth** (open M-

NEW ENGLAND

F 9am-5pm) on the east side of Pittsfield's rotary circle. Berkshire County's 12 state parks and forests cover 100,000 acres and offer numerous camping and hiking options. For info, stop by the **Region 5 Headquarters,** 740 South St., in Pittsfield. (☎442-8928. Open M-F 8am-5pm.) **Area code:** 413.

THE MOHAWK TRAIL

Perhaps the most famous highway in the state, the **Mohawk Trail (Rte. 2)** provides a meandering drive that showcases the beauty of the Berkshires, as well as numerous roadside Indian trading posts. During fall foliage weekends, the awe-inspiring reds and golds of the surrounding mountains draw crowds of leaf-peepers. Several spectacular overlooks highlight the western half of the trail, while the town of Millers Falls marks its eastern terminus.

SHELBURNE FALLS. Several miles west from I-91, the village of Shelburne Falls is home to a few unusual attractions. **The Bridge of Flowers,** originally a trolley crossing, runs across the Deerfield River between Shelburne and neighboring Buckland. Each year over 500 different flowers and plants bloom on the bridge, which claims to be a one-of-a-kind. A few hundred ft. south of the main drag, over 50 **Glacial Potholes,** including the "world's largest pothole of record," can be viewed from a calming scenic overlook above the river. **Springbrook Family Camping** has 100 campsites, an outdoor swimming pool, and an unbeatable hillside view. (Patten Rd.; follow the signs from Rte. 2. ☎625-6618. Open mid-May to mid-Oct. 9am-9pm. Sites $20.)

CHARLEMONT. Five mi. west of tiny Charlemont, off Rte. 2, the **Mohawk Trail State Forest** offers campsites along a river ($12, Mass. residents $10) and rents cabins. (☎339-5504. Reservations required at least two weeks in advance.) Whitewater raft on the Deerfield River (Apr.-Oct.) with **Crabapple Whitewater** (☎800-553-7238; differing skill levels available), or with **Zoar Outdoor** (☎800-532-7483; kayaking and canoeing also available), both in Charlemont.

NORTH ADAMS. Once a large industrial center—100 trains per day passed through its state-of-the-art Hoosac Tunnel at one time—North Adams went into decline for many years. Bolstered by a popular new art museum, however, the city is on the upswing again, as it finds new uses for its many factory buildings. The two-year-old ▓**Museum of Contemporary Art** comprises 27 old factories and is the largest center for contemporary visual and performing arts in the country. The museum exhibits art that, because of its size and complexity, can't be exhibited anywhere else. (87 Marshall St. ☎662-2111. Open June-Oct. daily 10am-6pm, Nov.-May Tu-Su 10am-4pm. $8, ages 6-16 $3, Nov.-May $6, seniors $4, ages 6-16 $2.) North Adams is also home to the **Western Gateway,** on the Furnace St. bypass off Rte. 8, a railroad museum, gallery, and noted state historic site. (☎663-6312. Open daily 10am-5pm. Free, donations encouraged. Live music in summer Th 7pm.) On Rte. 8, ½ mi. north of downtown North Adams, lies **Natural Bridge State Park,** a white marble bridge formed during the last Ice Age and the only natural, water-eroded bridge on the continent. (☎663-6392. Open late May to mid-Oct. daily 9am-5pm. $2 per vehicle.)

MT. GREYLOCK. The highest peak in Massachusetts (3491 ft.) is south of the Mohawk Trail and only accessible by Rte. 2 to the north and U.S. 7 to the west. By car, take Notch Rd. from Rte. 2 between North Adams and Williamstown, or take Rockwell Rd. from Lanesboro on U.S. 7. The roads up are rough but the views of the surrounding area are breathtaking in all seasons. Hiking trails begin from nearly all the towns around the mountain; grab free maps at the **Mt. Greylock Visitors Information Center,** 50 Rockwell Rd. (☎443-0011. Open daily 9am-5pm.) Climb the tricky winding staircase of the massive, 92 ft. tall **War Memorial** at the summit for a breathtaking view. The nearby **Bascom Lodge** is built from the rock excavated for the monument, and serves breakfast, lunch, and dinner. (☎743-1591. Open mid-May to mid-Oct. 6am-10pm; snack bar open daily 10am-4pm. Meals $6-14. Rooms $27, under 12 $13; private doubles $65.) Two mi. shy of the summit off Rockwell Rd., there are 35 **primitive camping** sites. (☎443-0011, 877-422-6762 for reservations. $6, Mass. residents $5. Water available at Bascom Lodge.)

WILLIAMSTOWN. Small and quiet, Williamstown is home to the prestigious Williams College and several artistic attractions, including the renowned 47-year-old Williamstown Theater Festival. The Mohawk Trail ends in Williamstown at its junction with U.S. 7. Here, an **info booth** provides an abundance of free local maps and seasonal brochures, and can help you find a place to stay in one of Williamstown's many reasonably priced B&Bs. (☎458-4922. Staffed July-Oct. daily 10am-6pm, May-June F-Su 10am-6pm.) The **Hopkins Memorial Forest** (☎597-2346) offers over 2250 acres that are free for hiking and cross-country skiing. Take U.S. 7 N, turn left on Bulkley St., follow Bulkley to the end, and turn right onto Northwest Hill Rd. At **Williams College,** the 2nd-oldest in Massachusetts (est. 1793), lecturers compete with the beautiful scenery of surrounding mountains for the students' attention. Maps of the brick-laden campus are available from the **Admissions Office,** 988 Main St., in Mather House. (☎597-2211. Open M-F 8:30am-4:30pm. 2-6 tours M-F year-round, 1-2 tours Sa June-Nov.) In the summer, be sure to check out the star-studded ▧**Williamstown Theater Festival.** (☎597-3400. June-Aug.) Past performers include Gwyneth Paltrow, along with her mother, Blythe Danner, and other acting luminaries.

Williamstown has many affordable motels east of town on Rte. 2. The welcoming **Maple Terrace Motel,** 555 Main St. (Rte. 2) has bright rooms with cable TV and a refrigerator, a heated outdoor pool and free continental breakfast. (☎458-9677. Office open daily 8am-10:30pm. Singles $46-88; doubles $56-93.) Popular **Pappa Charlie's Deli,** 28 Spring St., offers sandwiches such as the "Dr. Johnny Fever" and the $4.65 "Maria Tucci." (☎458-5969. Open M-Th 8am-9pm, F-Sa 8am-10pm, Su 9am-9pm; Sept.-June M-Th 8am-9pm, F-Sa 8am-10pm, Su 9am-9pm.)

PITTSFIELD. South of Williamstown, the first major town along Rte. 7 is Pittsfield, the county seat of Berkshire County. Though not as scenic as neighboring towns, Pittsfield bustles with activity. Recreational possibilities abound at the **Pittsfield State Forest,** 4 mi. northwest of town, off Rte. 20., with camping and scheduled outdoor activities. (☎442-8992. Sites $6.) **Herman Melville's** home, **Arrowhead,** 3½ mi. south of Pittsfield, off Rte. 7, inspired the author during his most productive period and somehow reminded him of his days in the Atlantic. Inside, the **Berkshire County Historical Society** has exhibits on 19th-century country life and the role of women on the farm. (780 Holmes Rd. ☎442-1793. Open late May to late Oct. 9:30am-5pm, Nov. to late May by appointment only. $5, seniors $4.50, students with ID $3, ages 6-15 $1. 40min. tours on the hr.) The **Berkshire Museum** has a large collection of Winslow Homer and Hudson River School paintings, natural history exhibits, an aquarium, and an art-house cinema. (39 South St. ☎443-7171. Open Aug. M-Sa 10am-5pm, Su noon-5pm; Sept.-July Tu-Sa 10am-5pm, Su 1-5pm. $6, seniors $5, 3-18 $4.)

LENOX. Tanglewood is the famed summer home of the **Boston Symphony Orchestra,** one of the Berkshires' greatest treasures. South on Rte. 7, a short distance west of Lenox Center on Rte. 183 (West St.), Tanglewood concerts include a variety of music styles, from Ray Charles to James Taylor, but its bread-and-butter is top-notch classical music. Lawn tickets and picnics make for a great evening or Su afternoon. There are chamber concerts on Th evenings, the Boston Pops give three summer concerts, and the young musicians of the Tanglewood Music Center, a premier training institute, perform throughout the summer. The summer ends with a jazz festival over Labor Day weekend. (☎637-5165. Orchestral concerts held July-Aug. F 8:30pm with 6pm prelude, Sa 8:30pm, Su 2:30pm. Tickets $16-82, lawn seats $14-17. Open rehearsals held Sa 10:30am. Call for schedule of special events and prices.) The **Edith Wharton Restoration at the Mount,** at the junction of Rte. 7 and 7A, showcases the home of the turn-of-the-century Pulitzer Prize-winning author. (2 Plunkett St. ☎637-1899. Open late May to Oct. daily 9am-2:30pm. $6, seniors $5.50, ages 13-18 $4.50. Tours on the hr.) On the same grounds, **Shakespeare & Company** produces top-notch Elizabethan and experimental theatre in five different performance spaces. (☎637-3353. Ticket prices and show times vary; call ahead for info.)

STOCKBRIDGE. The must-see ▧**Norman Rockwell Museum,** on Rte. 183, ½ mi. south from the junction of Rte. 7 and 102, contains over 1000 works, including many of Rockwell's *Saturday Evening Post* covers. (☎298-4100. Open daily 10am-

NEW ENGLAND

5pm. $9, children 18 and under free.) **Chesterwood,** ¾ mi. away, reveals the studio
and estate of artist Daniel Chester French, the creator of several famous public
monuments, including the Abraham Lincoln memorial in Washington, D.C. (☎298-
3579. Open daily May-Oct. 10am-5pm. $8.50, ages 13-18 $5, ages 6-12 $3. Follow the
signs from the Rockwell Museum.) Rte. 7 S passes the **Wagon Wheel Motel,** at the
junction with Rte. 20. (☎445-4532. In summer Su-Th $40, F-Sa $100; off-season $35.)
Summer weekend rates are high throughout the Berkshires, starting at $100. A
cheaper option is **October Mountain State Forest,** north on U.S. 20 for about 3 mi. to
Walker Rd., which has toilets and showers. (☎243-1778. Sites $6.) About 10 mi. east
on Rte. 20, in Becket, the **Jacob's Pillow Dance Festival** showcases extraordinary performances from June-Aug. (☎243-0745. Call for ticket prices and showtimes.)

ROUTE 7. Paralleling the Appalachian Trail as it meanders through western Massachusetts, Route 7 offers the road-bound some of the same natural beauty that
brave through-hikers are treated to on the way from Georgia to Maine—but those
traveling by car get to sample numerous high-quality artistic venues along the way.

THE PIONEER VALLEY ☎413

Northampton and Amherst in the Pioneer Valley offer classic small-town New
England charm. Springfield, the state's 3rd-largest city, is the major industry and
transportation hub of the region. The MassPike (I-90) and I-91 are the area's speedy
interstates, but there are better routes for aesthetes with time on their hands. Rte.
20 meanders above, below, and around the Pike, and in the north-south direction. I-
91 can be substituted by Rte. 47 and 63, which snake along the Connecticut River.

AMHERST. On I-91, about 15min. north of Springfield, lie academic hubs **Northampton** and **Amherst,** home to numerous colleges. The largest is the gargantuan and
unsightly **University of Massachusetts-Amherst** in Amherst. (☎545-0222. Tours daily
11am and 1:15pm; June-July M-F 11am and 1:15pm.) Prestigious **Amherst College**
shares the town with the main UMass campus. (☎542-2328. Open M-F 8:30am-
4:30pm. Tours mid-Sept.-mid-Dec. and Feb.-early May at 9 and 11am and 1 and 3pm,
Sa in the fall at 11am.) Nearby, the all-female **Smith** and **Mount Holyoke** colleges, and
the small, alternative **Hampshire College** round-out the **Five-College Consortium.** The
⬛**Black Sheep Deli and Bakery,** 79 Main St., is a mainstay, offering huge, ultra-fresh
gourmet sandwiches, along with pastas and salads. Mouth-watering vegetarian
choices are plentiful. (☎253-3442. Open Su-Th 7am-8pm, F-Sa 7am-10pm.) Dubbed
"the mecca of the Northeast" by Amherst students, **Antonio's,** 31 N. Pleasant St.,
makes deliciously creative pizza with toppings like chicken-blue-cheese or black-
bean-avocado. (☎253-0808. Open daily 10:30am-1:15am. Slices $1.25-2.75.)

NORTHAMPTON. Northampton is a beautiful town that boasts a number of restaurants and shops, on Main and Pleasant St. The nonprofit **Ten Thousand Villages,** 82
Main St., sells handicrafts from around the world, many under $10. (☎582-9338.
Open M-W 10am-6pm, Th-Sa 10am-8pm.) On the Smith campus, the professional
New Century Theatre recently celebrated its 10th anniversary with four summertime
productions. (Green St. ☎585-3220. Box office open Tu-Sa noon-6pm, Su 11am-
3pm. $18, seniors $16, same-day student rush tickets $9.) The **Academy of Music,** a
former opera house and the 6th-oldest theater in the US, shows quality domestic
and international films. (274 Main St. Call ☎584-8435 for schedule.) The 200 riverside acres of **Look Memorial Park,** on the Berkshire Trail (Rte. 9) not far from
Northampton, make for pleasant picnicking. (☎584-5457. Open daily dawn-dusk.
Facilities open April to mid-Oct. daily 11am-7pm. $3 per vehicle Sa-Su, $2 M-F.)
Award-winning **La Veracruzana,** 31 Main St. in Northampton, is the hotspot for Mexican food. Try the excellent enchiladas ($6-7) with one of nine salsas at their salsa
bar. (☎586-7181. Open Su-M 11am-10pm, Tu-Sa 11am-midnight.) For more info,
visit or call the **Greater Northampton Chamber of Commerce,** 99 Pleasant St. (☎584-
1900; open M-F 9am-5pm; additional hrs. June to early Oct. Sa-Su 10am-2pm). **Peter
Pan Trailways,** 1 Roundhouse Plaza (☎586-1030; station open daily 7am-6pm), runs
buses to Boston (10 per day, 3hr., $23) and New York (9 per day, 4¼hr., $34).

SPRINGFIELD. For the budget traveler, Springfield is no more than a transportation hub, so get in and get out. **Visitor Info: Greater Springfield Convention and Visitors Bureau,** in the Tower Sq. building at 1500 Main St. (☎787-1548; open M-F 9am-5pm). Most budget motels are in West Springfield, at Exits 13A and 13B off I-91. **Peter Pan Bus Line** provides service to Boston (16 per day, 2hr., $19) and New York (16 per day, 3½hr., $29). (1776 Main St. ☎781-3320. Station open 5:30am-9:45pm.) **Amtrak,** at 66 Lyman St., runs trains to New York (3½hr., 7 per day, $36) and Boston (2½hr., 2 per day, $21). Station open 5am-12:45am. But it's not only Peter Pan bus lines that call Springfield home: in 1891, Dr. James Naismith invented the game of basketball here, and the city has been identified with it ever since. Today, visitors to the **Basketball Hall of Fame,** 1150 W. Columbus Ave., adjacent to I-91, can see Bob Lanier's size 22 sneakers and play a virtual one-on-one with Bill Walton. (☎781-6500. Open July to early Sept. M-Sa 9am-7pm, Su 9:30am-5:30pm, mid-Sept.-June daily 9:30am-5:30pm. $8, seniors and ages 7-15 $5.)

RHODE ISLAND

Despite its diminutive stature (it is the smallest state in the Union), Rhode Island has never felt pressure to conform. Founded by religious outcast Roger Williams during colonial days, it was the first state to pass laws against slavery. Though you can drive through the whole of Rhode Island in 45min., the Ocean State's 400 mi. coastline deserves a longer look. Small, elegant hamlets speckle the shores winding to Connecticut, while the inland roads remain quiet, exuding New England charm.

▇ PRACTICAL INFORMATION

Capital: Providence.
Visitor Info: Dept. of Tourism, 1 West Exchange St., Providence 02903 (☎401-222-2601 or 800-556-2484; www.visitrhodeisland.com). Open M-F 8:30am-5pm. **Division of Parks and Recreation,** 2321 Hartford Ave., Johnston 02919 (☎401-222-2632). Open M-F 8:30am-4pm.
Postal Abbreviation: RI. **Sales Tax:** 7%.

PROVIDENCE   ☎401

Seven colleges inhabit the seven hills of Providence, luring a community of students, artists, and academics to join the native working class and state representatives. Providence has cobbled sidewalks and colonial buildings, a college town atmosphere, and more than its share of bookstores and cafes. In the area around the colleges, students on tight budgets support a plethora of inexpensive restaurants and shops. Affordable accommodations are hard to find, but Providence's compact size makes it a pleasurably walkable city. Its local color stems in part from constant allegations of corrupt city government: longtime mayor, Buddy Cianci, served a jail term and a term of office while on probation for attacking his estranged wife's suspected lover.

▐ GETTING THERE AND GETTING AROUND

Amtrak, 100 Gaspee St. (☎727-7379 or 800-872-7245; station open daily 5am-11pm; ticket booth open 5am-9:45pm), operates from a gleaming white structure near the state capitol, a 10min. walk from Brown University or downtown. Trains set out for Boston (1hr., 11 per day, $17-19; 2 high-speed Acela trains per day take only 30min.) and New York (4hr., 12 per day, $44-63; 2 Acela trains, 3¼hr.). **Greyhound,** 102 Fountain St. in downtown Providence (☎454-0790; station open daily 6:30am-8:45pm), runs buses to Boston (1 hr., 12 per day, $7.50) and New York (4hr., 13 per day, $13.50). **Bonanza,** 1 Bonanza Way at Exit 25 off I-95 (☎751-8800; station open daily 4:30am-11pm), also has frequent service to Boston (1hr., 18 per day, $9) and New

York (4hr., 6 per day, $37). **Rhode Island Public Transit Authority (RIPTA),** 265 Melrose St. (☎781-9400; M-F 7am-6pm, Sa 8am-6pm), runs an **info booth** at Kennedy Plaza, which provides route and schedule assistance and free bus maps. RIPTA's service includes Newport ($1.25) and other points. (Buses run daily 5am-midnight; hrs. vary by route. Fare 25¢-$5; base fare $1.25; within Providence, 50¢.)

✴🛈 ORIENTATION AND PRACTICAL INFORMATION

The downtown business district clusters in the area bounded by **I-95** on the west, **I-195** to the south, the Providence River to the east, and the state capitol to the north. **Brown University** and the **Rhode Island School of Design (RISD),** pronounced *RIZ-dee*, sit atop a steep hill, a 10min. walk east of downtown. **Visitor Info: Providence/Warwick Convention and Visitors Bureau,** 38 Exchange Terr. in downtown (☎274-1636 or 800-233-1636; open M-Sa 9am-5pm). The **Providence Preservation Society,** 21 Meeting St. at the foot of College Hill (☎831-7440; open M-F 9am-5pm), provides detailed info on historic Providence. **Post Office:** 2 Exchange Terr. (☎421-4361; open M-F 7:30am-5:30pm, Sa 8am-2pm.) **ZIP code:** 02903. **Area code:** 401.

▟ ACCOMMODATIONS

Downtown motel rates make Providence an expensive overnight stay. Rooms fill up far in advance for the graduation season in May and early June. Head 10 mi. south on I-95 to Warwick/Cranston for cheaper motels.

Catering largely to the international visitors of the universities, the stained-glass-windowed **International House of Rhode Island,** 8 Stimson Ave., off Hope St. near the Brown campus, has three comfortable, welcoming rooms, but they are often full. Amenities include kitchen, private bath, TV, and a fridge. (☎421-7181. Reception M-F 9:30am-5pm. Singles $50, students $35; doubles $60/$45; $5 per night off for stays of 5 nights or more. Reservations required; many international visitors stay for weeks at a time.) Three mi. outside of Providence on Rte. 6 in Seekonk, MA, the **Town 'n' Country Motel** has reasonable rooms (☎508-336-8300. Singles $44; doubles $50). The nearest **campgrounds** lie a 30min. drive from downtown. One of the closest, in Coventry, RI, **Colwell's Campground,** provides showers and hook-ups for 75 sites on the shore of the Flat River Reservoir. From Providence, take I-95 S to exit 10, then head west 9½ mi. on Rte. 117 to Peckham Ln. (☎397-4614. Check-in 9am-7pm. Sites $14, with electricity $16.)

◖ FOOD

A variety of impressive food is found in three areas in Providence: **Atwells Ave.** in the Italian district, on Federal Hill just west of downtown; **Thayer St.,** on College Hill to the east, home to off-beat student hangouts and ethnic restaurants; and **Broad St.,** in the southwest part of town, with many inexpensive international eateries. **Geoff's Superlative Sandwiches,** 163 Benefit St., attracts a diverse clientele with 102 creatively-named sandwiches, such as the "Buddy Cianci," the "Marlene Dietrich," and the "Embryonic Journey." Grab a green dessert from the huge pickle barrel on your way out (☎751-2248; sandwiches $4-6; open M-F 8am-9pm, Sa-Su 10am-9pm). Shoot the breeze with Providence locals at the **Seaplane Diner,** 307 Allen's Ave., near I-195 downtown. A classic diner, Seaplane has quick service and cheap homestyle breakfast and lunches (☎941-9547; open M-F 5am-3pm, Sa 5am-1pm, F-Sa midnight-4am). **Louis' Family Restaurant,** 286 Brook St., has made the entire community its family because of its friendly service. In recent years, students have rallied to save the diner from Brown's expansion. Try the "Henry Hample" ($3), a vegan eggplant Florentine sub, or any number of specials drawn on placards above the counter (☎861-5225; open daily 6am-3pm). For a gastronomic challenge, head to **The Original Riccotti's** on Federal Hill at 133 Atwells Ave. As "home of the 29 in. sub" ($13.50), Ricotti's is a bargain for two or more (☎621-8100; open M-F 8am-8pm, Sa 10am-8pm).

SIGHTS

Exhibiting just a smattering of the world-renowned art school's hoard, the **RISD Museum of Art** gathers Egyptian, Indian, Impressionist, medieval, and Roman art, as well as a gigantic 12th-century Japanese Buddha, into a small but pleasant space. *(224 Benefit St. ☎454-6500. Open Tu-Su 10am-5pm. $5, students $2, seniors $4, ages 5-18 $1. Free every 3rd Th 5-9pm and last Sa of month.)* Notable historic sights in Providence cluster around the 350-year-old neighborhood of **College Hill. Brown University,** established in 1764, includes several 18th-century buildings and provides a fitting starting point for a historic walking tour of Providence. The Office of Admissions, housed in the historic **Carliss-Brackett House,** gives free 1hr. walking tours of the campus *(45 Prospect St. ☎863-2378. Open M-F 8am-4pm. Tours M-F 10, 11am, 1, 3, and 4pm.)* In addition to founding Rhode Island, in 1638 Roger Williams founded the *first* **First Baptist Church of America.** Its 1775 incarnation stands today at 75 N. Main St. *(☎454-3418. Open M-F 10am-noon and 1-3pm, Sa 10am-noon. Free.)* Down the hill, the **Rhode Island State Capitol** supports the 4th-largest free-standing marble dome in the world. *(☎222-2357. Open M-F 8:30am-4:30pm. Free tours M-F 10 and 11am; reservations appreciated for individual groups. Free self-guide booklets available in room 220.)* John Quincy Adams called the **John Brown House Museum,** the 18th-century home of the Rhode Island entrepreneur and revolutionary, "the most magnificent and elegant private mansion" on the continent. *(52 Power St. ☎331-8575. Open Tu-Sa 10am-5pm, Su noon-4pm. $6, students and seniors $4.50, ages 7-17 $3.)* The New England textile industry was born in 1793 when Samuel Slater used plans smuggled out of Britain to build the first water-powered factory in America. In Pawtucket, the **Slater Mill Historic Site** preserves fabric heritage with working machinery in three historic buildings. *(67 Roosevelt Ave. ☎725-8638. Open June-Oct. M-Sa 10am-5pm, Su 1-5pm; Mar.-June and Nov.-Dec. Sa-Su 1-5pm. Tours leave roughly every 2hr. $7, seniors $6, 6-12 $5.50.)* If you're ready for some hardball, the **Pawtucket Red Sox** (AAA) take the field Apr. through early Sept. in the resplendent **McCoy Stadium,** 1 Columbus Ave. in Pawtucket. *(☎724-7300. Box seats $7; general admission $5, seniors and under 13 $4.)*

ENTERTAINMENT AND NIGHTLIFE

For film, theater, and nightlife listings, read the "Weekend" section of the F *Providence Journal* or the *Providence Phoenix.* The nationally acclaimed **Trinity Repertory Company,** 201 Washington St., offers $10 student rush tickets 2hr. before performances when available. *(☎351-4242. Tickets $26-42.)* For splashier productions, contact the **Providence Performing Arts Center,** 220 Weybosset St., which hosts a variety of concerts and Broadway musicals. *(☎421-2787. Box office open M-F 10am-6pm, Sa noon-5pm.)* The **Cable Car Cinema and Cafe,** 204 S. Main St., shows artsy and foreign films in a kinder, gentler setting—on couches instead of chairs. *(☎272-3970. Tickets $7.)*

Brownies, townies, and RISDs rock the night away at several hot spots throughout town. Mingle with the local artist community at **AS220,** 115 Empire St. between Washington and Westminster St., a cafe/bar/gallery/music and improv performance space. *(☎831-9327. Open M-F 10am-1am, Sa noon-5pm and 7pm-1am, Su 7pm-1am. Cover $3-5.)* Gay and straight alike favor **Gerardo's,** 1 Franklin Sq. on Allen's Ave., where DJ beats and karaoke fill a neon pink and blue disco dance hall. *(☎274-5560. Th-Su cover varies; open Su-Th 4pm-1am, F-Sa 4pm-2am.)*

NEWPORT   ☎401

Money has always found its way into Newport. Once supported by slave trade profits, the coastal town later became the summer home of America's elite and thus the site of some of the nation's most opulent mansions. Today, Newport is a high-priced tourist town, but its numerous arts festivals—and the awe-inspiring extravagance of its mansions—are reason enough for those on a tight budget to visit.

PRACTICAL INFORMATION. The place to start any visit to Newport is the **Newport County Convention and Visitors Bureau,** 23 America's Cup Ave. in the New-

port Gateway Center (☎845-9123 or 800-976-5122; www.gonewport.com; open Su-Th 9am-5pm, F-Sa 9am-6pm). **Bonanza Buses** (☎846-1820) depart from the Center, as do the buses of **Rhode Island Public Transit Authority (RIPTA)** (see p. 143). **Ten Speed Spokes,** 18 Elm St., rents bikes. (☎847-5609. Open M-Th 10am-6pm, F-Sa 9am-6pm, Su 11am-5pm. Mountain bikes $5 per hr., $25 per day. Must have credit card and photo ID.) **Post Office:** 320 Thames St. (☎847-2329; open M-F 8:30am-5pm, Sa 9am-1pm). **ZIP code:** 02840. **Area code:** 401.

⌐ ACCOMMODATIONS. Guest houses account for the bulk of Newport's accommodations. Most offer a bed and continental breakfast with colonial intimacy. Those willing to share a bathroom or forego a sea view might find a double for $65; singles are almost nonexistent. Many hotels and guest houses book solid two months in advance for summer weekends. The best weekday deal in the area is the **Newport Gateway Hotel,** 31 W. Main Rd., just across the town line in Middletown. The Gateway has clean, comfortable doubles with A/C and cable TV, a few minutes from Newport's harborfront. (☎847-2735. Su-Th $45-95; F-Sa $125-195 with 2-night minimum. $15 each additional person.) Just up the road, **Motel 6,** 249 J.T. Connel Hwy, provides a second affordable option for budget travelers. Follow Broadway out of Newport into Middletown, turn left on W. Main St., and follow Connelton Hwy. for 1½ mi. (☎848-0600 or 800-466-8356. Singles $59-69; doubles $65-75, $3 per additional person.) Campsites await at **Fort Getty Recreation Area,** on Fort Getty Rd. on Conanicut Island. The nearby Fox Hill Salt Marsh has great birdwatching. (☎423-7264, reservations ☎423-7211. RV sites $25; tent sites $20. Showers and beach access. Reservations recommended 1-2 months in advance. Tent sites available late May-Oct.)

☐ FOOD. While many restaurants are pricey, cheap food can be found in Newport. Most of Newport's restaurants line up on **Thames St.,** where ice cream parlors abound. Good, hearty breakfasts ("Portuguese Sailor," $5) are prepared before your eyes at the **Franklin Spa,** 229 Spring St. (☎847-3540; open M-F 6am-3pm, Sa-Su 7am-3pm.) Shack up with some choice mollusks alongside a severely incapacitated lobster boat at **Flo's Clam Shack,** Rte. 138A/Aquidneck Ave., across from Easton Beach (☎847-8141. Open Su-Th 11am-9pm, F-Sa 11am-10pm. Fried clams $11.) **Dry Dock Seafood,** 448 Thames St., serves fresh fish quickly. (☎847-3974. Open daily 11am-9pm; in off-season Tu-Su 11am-9pm. Entrees $7-15, baked fish of the day $8.)

☐ SIGHTS. George Noble Jones built the first "summer cottage" in Newport in 1839, thereby kicking off an extravagant string of palatial summer estates. Five of the mansions lie south of downtown on Bellevue Ave. A self-guided walking tour or a guided tour by the **Preservation Society of Newport** will allow you to ogle at the extravagance; purchase tickets at any mansion. *(424 Bellevue Ave. ☎847-1000. Open M-F 9am-5pm; mansions open M-F 10am-5pm. $9-12, ages 6-17 $4. Combination tickets available.)* **The Marble House** is the must-see of the mansions. Built for $11 million in 1892 as a 39th birthday present for William K. Vanderbilt's wife Alva, it contains over 500,000 cubic ft. of marble, silk walls, and rooms covered entirely in gold. *(☎847-1000. Open Apr.-Oct. M-F 10am-5pm; Jan.-Mar. Sa-Su 10am-4pm. $9, ages 6-17 $4.)* The father of William Mayes, a notorious Red Sea pirate, opened the **White Horse Tavern** at Marlborough St. and Farewell St. in 1687, making it the oldest continuously operated drinking establishment in the country. *(☎849-3600. Open W-M 11:30am-2:30pm for lunch and 6-10pm each day for dinner. Beer $3-4.)* The oldest synagogue in the US, the beautifully restored Georgian **Touro Synagogue,** dates back to 1763. *(85 Touro St. ☎847-4794. Visits by free tour only. Tours every 30min. late May to late June M-F 1-2:30pm, Su 11am-2:30pm; early July to early Sept. Su-F 10am-4:30pm. Call for off-season tour schedule.)* Die-hard tennis fans will feel right at home in Newport, where the stately **Tennis Hall of Fame** hosts the last two professional grass court tournaments in the U.S. each summer and has the largest tennis museum in the world. *(194 Bellevue Ave. ☎849-3990. Open daily 9:30am-5pm. $8, students and seniors $6, under 17 $4, families $20.)* Eight miles north of Newport in Portsmouth, the **Green Animals Topiary**

Gardens, Cory's Lane, holds 21 shrubs amazingly sculpted into the likes of giraffes and lions. (☎683-1267. May-Oct. open daily 10am-5pm. $9, ages 6-17 $4.)

Newport's gorgeous beaches are frequently as crowded as the streets. The most popular is **Easton's Beach,** or First Beach, on Memorial Blvd. (☎848-6491. Open late May to early Sept. M-F 9am-9pm, Sa-Su 8am-9pm. Parking M-F $8, Sa-Su $10; before 10am in the summer $6.) For a nice walk by the sea, traverse the **Cliff Walk,** a 3½ mi. dirt trail on Newport's eastern shore. Start at Easton Beach or halfway through the trail at Narragansett Ave. **Fort Adams State Park,** south of town on Ocean Dr. 2½ mi. from the visitors center, offers showers, picnic areas, and two fishing piers. (☎847-2400. Park open sunrise to sunset.) Good beaches also line Little Compton, Narragansett, and the shore between Watch Hill and Point Judith; for more details the free *Ocean State Beach Guide*, available at the **Visitors Center,** ought not be missed.

■ **ENTERTAINMENT.** In June, July and Aug., Newport gives lovers of classical, folk, blues, jazz, and film each a festival to call their own. The oldest and best-known jazz festival in the world, the **Newport Jazz Festival** has seen the likes of Duke Ellington and Count Basie; bring your beach chairs and coolers to Fort Adams State Park to join the fun Aug. 10-12, 2001 (☎847-3709; tickets $40 per day, under 12 $15). Also at Fort Adams State Park, on Aug. 3-5, 2001, folk singers (former acts include Bob Dylan, Joan Baez, and the Indigo Girls) entertain at the **Newport Folk Festival** (☎847-3709; tickets $40, under 12 $15). **Newport Music Festival,** July 6-22, 2001, will bring pianists, violinists, and other classical musicians from around the world for two weeks of concerts in the ballrooms and lawns of the mansions. (☎846-1133; box office ☎849-0700. Box office open daily 10am-5pm. Tickets $30-35.)

For crawling types, a number of pubs and clubs line Thames St. **One Pelham East,** 274 Thames St., packs 'em in for alternative cover bands. (☎847-9460. Live music nightly; cover varies. Open M-F 3:30pm-1am, Sa-Su 1pm-1am.) **The Newport Blues Cafe,** 286 Thames St., has rocking blues music seven nights per week. (☎841-5510. Open 6pm-1am. Dinner 6-10pm; live music after 9:30pm. Cover varies; non-passport foreign IDs not accepted.) For art-house films, go to the **Jane Dickens Theatre,** 49 Truro St. (☎846-5252. $6.50, senior $4.) For more mainstream movies, head to the **Opera House Cinema,** 19 Truro St. (☎847-3456. $7, children $4.)

NEAR NEWPORT: BLOCK ISLAND

A popular daytrip 10 mi. southeast of Newport in the Atlantic, sand-blown **Block Island** possesses an untamed natural beauty. Block Island was originally called by its Mohegan name *Manisses*, or "Isle of Little God." One-quarter of the island is protected open space; local conservationists hope to increase that to 50%. The 11 square mi. island is not as well-known as its larger Massachusetts counterparts Martha's Vineyard and Nantucket, but countless visitors still swell its population during the summer months. The **Interstate Navigation Co.** (☎783-4613) provides **ferry service** to Block Island from Galilee Pier in Point Judith, RI. (1¼hr. 8-9 per day, Sept.-June schedule varies. $8.40, ages 5-11 $4.10. Cars by reservation $26.30, driver and passengers extra; bikes $2.30) Additional summer service runs from New London, CT. (2hr., mid-June to mid-Sept. Sa-Th 1 per day, F 2 per day, $15, ages 5-11 $9.) **Viking Lines** (☎631-668-5709) also runs a daily ferry from Montauk, Long Island, to Block Island during the summer (1¾hr. 1 per day, 9am. $23, ages 5-12 $10).

The island does not permit camping; it's best to take a daytrip unless you're willing to shell out $60 or more for a room in a guest house. Moderately priced restaurants hover near the ferry dock in Old Harbor; several dot New Harbor 1 mi. inland. Cycling is the ideal way to explore the tiny (7 mi. by 3 mi.) island; the **Old Harbor Bike Shop,** directly to the left of the ferry exit, rents just about anything on wheels. (☎466-2029. Mountain bikes $5-8 per hr., $20-30 per day; mopeds $27/$75. Jeeps $80 half-day, $110 full-day. Must be 21+ with credit card. Open mid-May to mid-Oct. daily 8:30am-7pm.) The **Block Island Chamber of Commerce** (☎466-2982) is located at the ferry dock in Old Harbor Drawer D and in an office behind Finn's Fish Market (open daily in summer 9am-5pm; hours vary off-season). **Area Code:** 401.

NEW ENGLAND

CONNECTICUT

Connecticut, the third-smallest state in the Union, resembles a patchwork quilt with industrialized centers (like Hartford and New Haven), serene New England villages, and lush woodland beauty. Perhaps it is this diversity that attracted such famous residents as Mark Twain, Harriet Beecher Stowe, Noah Webster, and Eugene O'Neill, and inspired the birth of the American Impressionist movement and the American musical—both Connecticut originals. Home to Yale University and the nation's first law school, Connecticut has an equally rich intellectual history. This doesn't mean that the people of Connecticut don't know how to let their hair down—this is the state that also brought us the lollipop, the three-ring circus, and the largest casino in the United States.

◪ PRACTICAL INFORMATION

Capital: Hartford.
Visitor Info: Connecticut Vacation Center, 865 Brook St., Rocky Hill 06067 (☎800-282-6863; www.state.ct.us/tourism). Open M-F 9am-4:30pm.
Postal Abbreviation: CT. **Sales Tax:** 6%.

HARTFORD   ☎860

Hartford may be the world's insurance capital, but it has more to offer travelers than financial protection: several high-quality museums, a lively theater scene, and the only hostel in all of Connecticut and Rhode Island.

◪ **PRACTICAL INFORMATION.** Hartford marks the intersection of I-91 and I-84. Union Place, in the northeast part of the city between Church and Asylum St., houses **Amtrak,** which runs trains north and south (☎727-1778; office open daily 5:30am-9pm), and **Greyhound** (station open daily 6am-9pm), which runs buses to New York (2½hr., 19 per day, $20) and Boston (2½hr., 10 per day, $20). **Visitor Info: Greater Hartford Convention and Visitors Bureau,** 1 Civic Center Plaza, 3rd fl. (☎728-6789 or ☎800-446-7811; open M-F 9am-4:30pm); the **Old State House,** 800 Main St. (☎522-6766; open M-F 10am-4pm, Sa 11am-4pm); and **Connecticut Transit's Information Center**, at State and Market St., which doles out helpful maps and public transportation info (☎525-9181; open M-F 7am-6pm). **Post Office:** 141 Weston St. (☎524-6074; open M-F 7am-6pm, Sa 7am-3pm). **ZIP code:** 06101. **Area code:** 860.

◪◪ **ACCOMMODATIONS AND FOOD.** The excellent **Mark Twain Hostel (HI-AYH),** 131 Tremont St., offers welcoming accommodations, not far from the center of town. Tremont St. is past the Mark Twain House on Farmington Ave. and is accessible by the "Farmington Ave." bus west. (☎523-7255. Check-in 9am-10pm. Dorms $15, non-members $18.) In the heart of downtown, the **YMCA,** 160 Jewell St., by Bushnell Park, offers dorm-like rooms at reasonable rates and use of a gym, pool, and racquetball courts. (☎246-9622. Singles $19, with private bath $24. $5 key deposit. Must be 18+ with ID. Check-in 7:30am-10pm. Check-out noon. No reservations accepted.) Many restaurants hover within a few blocks of downtown. Hartford's oldest eatery, the **Municipal Cafe,** 485 Main St., is a popular and friendly place to catch breakfast or lunch. The breakfast special means bacon, ham, or sausage with two eggs, toast, and coffee or tea for $4.25. Hot lunches and dinner plates go for $4-6. (☎278-4844. Open daily 7am-2:30pm.) **Black-Eyed Sally's BBQ & Blues,** 350 Asylum St., serves nicely priced, down-home cooking. Sally's image warns patrons that the only thing worse than a barbecue sandwich without sauce is "skinny dippin' with yer mother." (☎278-7427. Open M-W 11:30am-10pm, Th 11:30am-11pm, F 11:30am-midnight, Sa 5pm-midnight, Su 5-9pm. Live blues Th-Sa nights.)

◪ **SIGHTS.** The ▨Wadsworth Athenaeum, 600 Main St., has absorbing collections of contemporary and Baroque art, including one of three Caravaggios in the US.

(☎278-2670. Open Tu-Su 11am-5pm. $7, seniors and students $5, ages 6-17 $3. Free all day Th and Sa before noon. Call ahead for tour and lecture info.) Designed by Charles Bulfinch in 1796, the gold-domed **Old State House,** 800 Main St., housed the state government until 1878. Now, well-dressed historic actors welcome tourists to the chambers, a rotating art exhibit hall, and a museum of oddities including a mounted two-headed calf. *(☎522-6766. Open M-F 10am-4pm, Sa 11am-4pm.)* The **Mark Twain House,** 351 Farmington Ave., and **Harriet Beecher Stowe House,** 71 Forest St., both just west of the city center on Farmington Ave., colorfully reflect their authors' life and times. From the Old State House, take any "Farmington Ave." bus west. An entertaining tour of the intricately textured Twain homestead, where the author penned *The Adventures of Huckleberry Finn*, poignantly recalls Twain's energetic life and family tragedies. After the publication of *Uncle Tom's Cabin*, Stowe, whom Abraham Lincoln called "the little lady that started the big war," lived in her homey, modest cottage next door. *(Twain House: ☎493-6411. Open M-Sa 9:30am-5pm, Su noon-5pm; Jan.-Apr. and Nov. closed Tu. $9, seniors $8, ages 13-18 $7, ages 6-12 $5. Stowe House: ☎525-9317. Open June to early Oct. M-Sa 9:30am-4:30pm, Su noon-4:30pm; off-season Tu-Sa 9:30am-4pm, Su noon-4pm. $6.50/$6/ages 6-16 $2.75.)*

🎭 **ENTERTAINMENT.** In addition to its undisputed status as the insurance capital of the world, Hartford is also home to a burgeoning 20-block **Arts & Entertainment District** downtown. The **Hartford Stage Company,** a Tony Award-winning regional troupe, mounts six productions of classics and contemporary works each year. (50 Church St. ☎527-5151. Tickets $26-40; call for showtimes.) **TheaterWorks** is an up-and-coming off-Broadway-type theater which produces recent American plays. (233 Pearl St. ☎527-7838. Tickets $18-25; performances Tu-Sa 8pm, Su 2:30pm.) For a variety of performance options, head to **The Bushnell,** home of Hartford's symphony, ballet, and opera companies. (166 Capitol Ave. ☎246-6807. Box office open M-Sa 10am-5pm, Su 12-4pm.)

NEW HAVEN   ☎203

Simultaneously university town and depressed city, New Haven has gained a reputation as something of a battleground—academic types and a working-class population live uneasily side by side. While most of New Haven continues to decay, Yale has begun to renovate its neo-Gothic buildings, convert its concrete sidewalks to brick, and generate a thriving collegiate coffeehouse, bar, and bookstore scene.

🔷 **PRACTICAL INFORMATION.** New Haven lies at the intersection of I-95 and I-91, 40 mi. south of Hartford, and is laid out in nine squares. Between Yale University and City Hall, the central square, called **the Green,** provides a pleasant escape from the hassles of city life. *At night, don't wander too far from the immediate downtown and campus areas; surrounding sections are notably less safe.* **Amtrak,** Union Station on Union Ave. Exit 1 off I-91 (☎773-6178; ticket office open daily 6:30am-10:30pm), runs out of a newly renovated station in tough area to New York (1½hr., 12 per day, $22); Boston (2½hr., 8 per day, $33); Washington, D.C. (6hr., 12 per day, $61); and Mystic (1¼hr., 2 per day, $15). Also at Union Station, **Greyhound** (☎772-2470; ticket office open daily 6:15am-9:45pm) runs frequently to: New York (1½hr., 11 per day, $19); Boston (4hr., 13 per day, $27); and Providence (2½hr., 7 per day, $19.50). **Visitor Info: Greater New Haven Convention and Visitors Bureau,** 59 Elm St. (☎777-8550; open M-F 8:30am-5pm) and another location at 350 Long Wharf Dr. **Internet access: New Haven Public Library,** 13 Elm St. ½hr. access per day with photo ID. (☎946-8130. Open M-Th 9am-9pm, F-Sa 9am-5pm, Su 1-5pm. Closed Sa-Su in July and Aug.) **Area code:** 203.

🛏 **ACCOMMODATIONS.** Inexpensive lodgings are sparse in New Haven; the hunt quickens around Yale Parents Weekend (mid-Oct.) and commencement (early June). Head 10 mi. south on I-95 to **Milford** for affordable motels. **Hotel Duncan,** 1151 Chapel St., located in downtown New Haven, has old-fashioned charm, inexpensive rooms with cable TV, and the oldest manually operated elevator in the state. John

Hinckley stayed here when he was stalking Jodie Foster in the fall of 1980, a few months before he shot President Reagan. (☎787-1273. Singles $44; doubles $60; suite with fridge $70. Reservations recommended for F-Su.) **Motel 6,** 270 Foxon Blvd., Exit 8 off I-91, keeps 58 rooms at good prices. (☎469-0343 or 800-466-8356. Su-Th singles $52, doubles $60; F-Sa $58/$66.) **Hammonasset Beach State Park,** 20min. east on I-95 N from New Haven, Exit 62 in Madison, offers 558 sites in a beautiful setting. (☎245-1817. Office open mid-May to Oct. 8am-11pm. Sites $12.)

⌸ FOOD. For great authentic Italian cuisine, work your way along Wooster St., in Little Italy 10min. east of downtown. The finest brick oven pizza can be found at **Pepe's,** 157 Wooster St. Try a small red or white sauce clam pie for $9. (☎865-5762. Open M, W-Th 4-10pm, F-Sa 11:30am-11pm, Su 2:30-10:30pm.) No condiments are allowed at **Louis' Lunch,** 263 Crown St. Cooked vertically in original cast iron grills, these $3.25 burgers are too fine for ketchup or mustard. (☎562-5507. Open Tu-W 11am-4pm, Th-Sa 11am-2am.) Indian restaurants dominate the neighborhood southwest of downtown, by Howe St. The $6 all-you-can-eat lunch buffet at **India Palace,** 65 Howe St., is one of the best deals in town. (☎776-9010. Open until 10:30pm; lunch served M-F 11:30am-3pm.)

◈ SIGHTS. The Yale University Campus provides the bulk of the city's sights and museums. Each campus building was designed in the English Gothic and Georgian Colonial styles, many of them with intricate moldings and a few with gargoyles. The **Yale Visitors Center** faces the Green at 149 Elm St. (☎432-2300. Open M-F 9am-4:45pm, Sa-Su 10am-4pm. Free tours M-F 10:30am and 2pm, Sa-Su 1:30pm. Tours last 1¼hr.) Wander into the charming Old Campus, bordered by Chapel, College, Elm, and High St., and view Connecticut Hall, the university's oldest building. One block north, on the other side of Elm St., **Sterling Memorial Library,** 120 High St., is designed to resemble a monastery—even the telephone booths are shaped like confessionals. Apparently the creator of the massive **Beinecke Rare Book and Manuscript Library** wasn't fond of windows: this massive modern white structure has none. Instead, it's paneled with Vermont marble cut thin enough to be translucent. The building protects one of five Gutenberg Bibles in the US and an extensive collection of William Carlos Williams's writings. (121 Wall St. ☎432-2977. Open M-F 8:30am-5pm, Sa 10am-5pm. Closed Sa in Aug.)

Open since 1832, the **Yale University Art Gallery,** on the corner of York, claims to be the oldest university art museum in the Western Hemisphere. The museum holds over 100,000 pieces from around the world, including works by Monet, Picasso, and 13th-century Italian artists. (1111 Chapel St. ☎432-0600. Open Sept.-July Tu-Sa 10am-5pm, Su 1-6pm. Free.) The **Peabody Museum of Natural History,** off I-91 at Exit 3, houses Rudolph F. Zallinger's Pulitzer Prize-winning mural, which portrays the North American continent before European settlement. Other exhibits include a 100-million-year-old, three-ton turtle, an Egyptian mummy residing in an "house of eternity," and a strange talking head, Dr. Dolittle. (170 Whitney Ave. ☎432-5050. Open M-Sa 10am-5pm, Su noon-5pm. $5, seniors and ages 3-15 $3.)

▣ ◪ ENTERTAINMENT AND NIGHTLIFE. Pick up a free copy of *The Advocate* to find out what's up. **The Shubert Theater,** 247 College St., brings in top Broadway productions. (☎562-5666 or 800-228-6622. Box office open M-Sa 10am-5pm, Su 11am-3pm.) **The Yale Repertory Theater,** 1120 Chapel St., boasts illustrious alums like Meryl Streep, Glenn Close, and James Earl Jones. (☎432-1234. Open Oct.-May M-Sa 11am-5pm, June-Sept. M-F 10am-5pm. Tickets $10-30. Half-price student rush tickets on the day of a show.) In summer, the city hosts **concerts** on the Green (☎946-7821), including the **New Haven Symphony** (☎865-0831, box office ☎776-1444; open M-F 10am-5pm). During the last two weeks of June, New Haven hosts the **International Festival of Arts & Ideas,** an extravaganza of theater, music, visual arts, dance, and "ideas." (Many events are free. Call ☎888-278-4332 for more info.)

Toad's Place, a club at 300 York St., has hosted gigs by Bob Dylan and the Stones. (☎562-5694, recorded info ☎624-8623. Box office open daily 11am-6pm; buy tickets at the bar after 8pm. Bar open Su-Th 8pm-1am, F-Sa 8pm-2am; closed when there is not a show.) **Bar,** 254 Crown St., is a hip hangout, replete with a pool table, jazzy lounge room, dance floor/theater, homemade beers and brick-oven pizzas. The popular party every Tu night attracts a large gay crowd. (☎495-8924. Open Su-Tu 4pm-1am, W 11:30am-2:30am, Th 5pm-1am, F 11:30am-2am, Sa 5am-2am.)

MYSTIC AND THE CONNECTICUT COAST   ☎860

Connecticut's coastal towns were busy seaports in the days of Herman Melville and Richard Henry Dana, but the dark, musty inns filled with tattooed sailors swapping sea stories are history. Today, the coast is mainly a resort and sailing base.

🛈 PRACTICAL INFORMATION. The **Mystic Tourist and Information Center,** Bldg. 1d in Old Mystick Village, off Rte. 27, provides info on attractions and accommodations. (☎536-1641. Open M-Sa 9am-6pm, Su 10am-5pm.)

📍 ACCOMMODATIONS. It is almost impossible to find budget-friendly lodgings in Mystic, and pricier offerings need to be reserved well in advance. Close to Mystic is **Seaport Campgrounds,** on Rte. 184, 3 mi. north on Rte. 27 from Mystic. (☎536-4044. Open daily mid-Apr. to late Oct. Sites $28, with water and electricity $32; $5 per additional person; seniors 10% discount.) **Stonington** makes a more affordable base from which to explore the shore and also boasts a beautiful downtown area on the water. The **Sea Breeze Motel,** 5 mi. north of Mystic at 812 Stonington Rd./Rte. 1, rents big, clean rooms with A/C and cable TV, though the walls are thin. (☎535-2843. Singles $55, F-Sa $85; doubles $69-75, F-Sa $99. Rates much lower in winter.)

🍴 FOOD AND NIGHTLIFE. Mystic Pizza, 56 W. Main St., the town's most renowned eatery, has been serving its tasty "secret recipe" pizzas since 1973. The 1988 Julia Roberts film by the same name further contributed to the popularity of the bright and lively restaurant/take-out joint. (☎536-3737 or 536-3700. Open 10am-11pm. Slices $2; small pizza $5.25; large $9.75.) **Christine's Cafe,** 4 Pearl St. off W. Main St., serves enormous and satisfying sandwiches with titles taken from the owner's album, such as the "Good Rockin' Daddy" or the "Trickle Down." (☎536-1244. Open M 10am-6pm, Tu-F 10am-12:30am, Sa 8:30am-12:30am, Su 10am-10pm. Hours vary off-season. Live acoustic music Tu-Su nights. Sandwiches $3-7.) For consistently good seafood, head to **Cove Fish Market,** a classic New England take-out stand 1 mi. east of downtown on Old Stonington Rd. (☎536-0061. Open mid-May through early Sept. 11am-8pm; Feb. through mid-May and early Sept. to mid-Oct. F-Sa 11am-8pm, Su 11am-7pm. Fish market open year-round 9am-6pm.) **Trader Jack's,** 14 Holmes St., near downtown, pours $2.75 domestic beers. Happy hour (M-F 5-6:30pm) will make you smile with half-price appetizers and 50¢ off all drinks except wine. (☎572-8550. No cover. Food 5pm-midnight; last call Su-Th 1am, F-Sa 2am.)

🔲 SIGHTS. Mystic Seaport, 1 mi. south on Rte. 27 from I-95 at Exit 90, offers a look back at Melville's Connecticut, with 17 acres of recreated village, scrimshaw carvings, and a working wood-only shipyard where a reproduction of the *Amistad* was completed last year. (☎572-5315. Open daily Apr.-Oct. 9am-5pm; Nov.-Mar. 10am-4pm. $16, seniors $15, ages 6-12 $8. Audio tours $3.50.) Seaport admission entitles visitors to **Sabino Charters'** steamboat cruise on the **Mystic River** for a few dollars more. (☎572-5351. 30min. trips mid-May to early Oct. daily on the hr. 11am-4pm. $4.50, ages 6-12 $3.50 after Seaport admission.) If walking through a fishing village puts you in the mood for aquatic life, seals, penguins, sharks, and dolphins await at one of the Northeast's finest aquariums, the **Mystic Marinelife Aquarium,** at Exit 90 off I-95. (55 Coogan Blvd. ☎572-5955. Open daily 9am-5pm; July to early Sept. 9am-6pm. $15, seniors $14, ages 3-12 $10.) The **Denison Pequotsepos Nature Center,** 1½ mi. east of downtown at 109 Pequotsepos Rd., offers a relaxing refuge from the droves of tourists with great bird watching and 7½ mi. of scenic trails through meadows, fields, brooks, ponds, and woodland. Indoors, be sure to take in "Night in the Meadow," and learn how little American toads work their mojo. (☎536-1216. Park center open M-Sa 9am-5pm, Su 10am-4pm; park open dawn-dusk. $4, seniors $3, ages 6-12 $2.)

EASTERN CANADA

HIGHLIGHTS OF EASTERN CANADA

FOOD. Fresh seafood abounds, particularly on Prince Edward Island (p. 160). Delicious *Québecois* cuisine fills the restaurants of Québec City, QC (p. 176).

COASTAL TOWNS. Say "cheese" in the photo-opportune, picturesque towns of Yarmouth, NS (p. 154) and Fundy, NB (p. 159).

NIGHTLIFE. Québec offers up terrific nightlife opportunities in Montréal (p. 163). What's more, the drinking age is a mere 18.

TORONTO. Ethnic neighborhoods and fabulous museums provide fodder for long days of exploration (p. 181).

NOVA SCOTIA

Around 1605, French colonists joined the indigenous Micmac Indians in the Annapolis Valley and on the shores of Cape Breton Island. During the American Revolution, Nova Scotia declined the opportunity to become the 14th American state, establishing itself as a refuge for fleeing British loyalists. Subsequent immigration waves infused Pictou and Antigonish Counties with a Scottish flavor. As a result of these multinational immigrants, Nova Scotia's population is a cultural "mixed salad." This diversity is complemented by the province's four breathtaking geographies: the rugged Atlantic coast, the lush Annapolis Valley, the calm of the Northumberland Strait, and the magnificent highlands of Cape Breton Island.

◪ PRACTICAL INFORMATION

Capital: Halifax.
Visitor Info: Tourism Nova Scotia, P.O. Box 519, Halifax, NS B3J 2R7 (☎800-565-0000 in the US and Canada, ☎902-425-5781 elsewhere; www.explore.gov.ns.ca).
Drinking Age: 19.
Postal Abbreviation: NS. **Provincial Sales Tax:** 15% GST.

ATLANTIC COAST   ☎902

LIGHTHOUSE ROUTE. Nova Scotia's **Lighthouse Route** (Hwy. 333) extends south of Halifax and continues along the Atlantic Coast the entire way to Yarmouth, linking tiny coastal villages. Here, dilapidated fishing boats and lobster traps are tools of a trade, not just props for tourists. Blue signs with lighthouse symbols clearly mark the route's twists and turns. A lighthouse-turned-post office sits atop a peninsula of enormous, slippery rocks, luring a healthy number of tourists to **Peggy's Cove,** off Hwy. 333, 43km southwest of Halifax. Picturesque, weather-worn houses speckle a rocky highland landscape as sea-battered fishing vessels bob gently in the cove. The town recently stepped into the limelight when local fishermen bravely weathered the sea and fog in their own vessels to search for survivors of the 1998 Swissair plane crash. Early arrivals avoid the crowds, and early birds wake up with $2 espresso and $1 just-baked cookies from **Beales Bailiwick.** (☎823-2099. Open daily Apr.-Nov. 9am-8pm.)

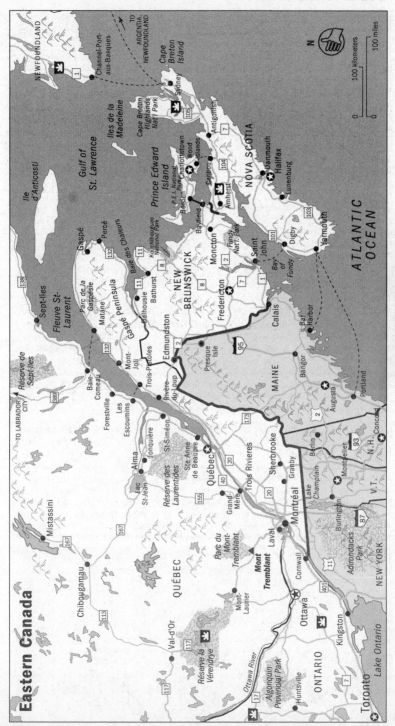

EASTERN CANADA

MAHONE BAY. Offering a few more tourist amenities is the slightly larger coastal town of Mahone Bay; take Hwy. 333 W to Hwy. 3 and head west for about 90km. The **tourist office** is at 165 Edgewater St. (☎624-6151. Open daily July-Aug. 9am-7pm; May and Oct. 10am-5pm; June and Sept. 10am-6pm.) The **Wooden Boat Festival,** a celebration of the region's heritage, includes a boat-building contest and race, and a parade of old-style schooners (☎624-8443; Aug. 1-5, 2001). Avast, ye scurvy dog! **Mug & Anchor Pub,** 634 Main St., tames a mate's appetite for seafood (fish and chips $8) and draft beer beneath wooden beams laden with an impressive collection of coasters. (☎624-6378. Open daily 11am-9:30pm; bar open Su-Th 11am-midnight, F-Sa 11am-1am.)

LUNENBERG. Dark-trimmed Victorian houses and occasional German flags hint at Lunenburg's status as Canada's oldest German settlement and an UNESCO World Heritage Site. The town may be better known for producing the undefeated racing schooner **Bluenose,** which now adorns the Canadian dime and Nova Scotia's license plate. Explore the schooner and ocean-going history at the **Fisheries Museum of the Atlantic,** on Bluenose Dr. by the harbor front. (☎634-4794. Open daily mid-May to mid-Oct. 9:30am-5:30pm; call for winter hrs. $7, seniors $5.50, ages 6-17 $2.) Several B&Bs dot the roadsides in this area, but don't expect bargains. **Brook House B&B,** 3 Old Blue Rocks Rd., is as good as it gets. (☎634-3826. Singles $55; doubles $65. 10% discount for students and seniors. Reservations recommended.) The **tourist office,** in the new blockhouse on Blockhouse Hill Rd., has info. (☎634-8100 or 634-3656. Open daily July-Sept. 9am-8pm; May-June and Oct. 8am-6pm.)

OVENS NATURAL PARK. Steeped in lore that extends from Native Canadian legends to tales of the Nova Scotia Gold Rush, ■Ovens Natural Park has an almost spiritual quality, marred only by efforts to package it for tourists. The park features a spectacular trail along a cliff to a set of natural sea caves (the "ovens" from which the area takes its name) and the region's best **campground.** Overlooking the ocean, amenities include access to the caves, free hot showers, a heated swimming pool, flush toilets, a restaurant, and a store. (☎766-4621. Open May-Oct. Check-in before dusk. 65 sites $20, with water and electricity $23, full hook-up $25-30. Private cottages from $50. Park admission $5; seniors and ages 5-12, $3.)

LAHAVE. Hwy. 332 continues along the shore and into the town of **East LaHave,** where a **cable ferry** runs across the LaHave River to LaHave. (Every 30min. 7am-11pm, by demand 11pm-7am. $3 per car or person). There is no actual ferry terminal, just a small turnoff from the road with a sign, so be on the lookout. The **Lahave Marine Hostel (HI-C),** located above the **Lahave Bakery,** is run by the bakery proprietor. A homey apartment with a wood-burning stove, the hostel overlooks the river, has eight beds, and offers kitchen and laundry facilities. Forego cooking yourself and try some delicious cheese and herb bread ($2.75) downstairs. Call ahead or arrive during bakery hours. (☎688-2908. Bakery open daily 9am-7pm; mid-Sept. to June 10am-5pm. Hostel open June-Oct. Dorms $12, non-members $14.)

YARMOUTH. The port of Yarmouth, 339km from Halifax on the southwestern tip of Nova Scotia, has a major **ferry terminal,** 58 Water St., where boats set out across the **Bay of Fundy** to Maine (open daily 8am-5pm). Life here seems to revolve around the ferries. **Bay Ferries** (☎742-6800 or 888-249-7245) provides service to Bar Harbor, ME. (2½hr.; 2 per day; US$56, seniors US$50, ages 5-12 US$25, car US$80, bike US$25. Reservations recommended, US$5 fee. US$3 departure fee for all passengers. Car prices do not include driver/passenger.) **Prince of Fundy Cruises** sails 11hr. from Yarmouth to Portland, ME. (☎800-341-7540. Cruise departs daily early May to mid-Oct. 10am. Prices: early May to mid-June and mid-Sept. to mid-Oct. US$60, ages 5-14 US$30, car US$80, bike US$7; mid-June to mid-Oct. US$80/ $40/$98/$10. Add US$3 passenger tax.) **Avis** can rent you a car at 42 Starr's Rd., and at a desk in the ferry terminal. (☎742-3323. $30-60 per day with 200 free km, 15¢ per additional km. Reserve ahead; must be 21+.) The **info center,** 228 Main St., uphill and visible from the ferry terminal, houses both **Nova Scotia Information** (☎742-5033) and **Yarmouth Town and County Information.** (☎742-6639. Both open mid-June to mid-Oct.; hrs. vary.) The **Ice House Hostel** and adjacent **Churchill Mansion Inn** overlook Darling Lake, 15km from Yarmouth on Rte. 1. Take Old Post Rd. on the left; the hostel and inn are on your right. Seven beds are split between the hostel and a cabin outside the inn. Guests have access to all inn facilities, and when the hostel is full, guests can stay at the inn for hostel rates. (☎649-2818. Open May-Nov. Shared bath. Pick-up from ferry. Dorms $10 or US$7. Reservations recommended.) **Area code:** 902.

HALIFAX   ☎902

Once considered by the British to be a strategic naval point in their ongoing skirmishes with the French, Halifax was established with the completion of the Halifax Citadel in 1749. The fortress was never attacked, and today, summertime cruise ships spill droves of linen-clad wayfarers into the port in search of maritime souvenirs. Why else are they coming? Despite being Eastern Canada's largest city, Halifax is manageable, tree-filled, and laid-back, and maintains a first-rate nightlife and cultural scene.

⌐ GETTING THERE AND GETTING AROUND

Airport: Halifax International, 40km from the city on Hwy. 102 into town. **The Airbus** (☎873-2091; 21 per day, 7:15am-11:15pm; $12, under 10 free with adult) and **Ace Y Share-A-Cab** (☎429-4444; 5am-9pm; phone 1 day ahead; $25, $39 for 2) run between the airport and town.

Trains: VIA Rail, 1161 Hollis St. (☎494-7920 or 800-561-3952), at South St. in the South End near the harbor. To: Montréal ($190) and Québec City ($100). Open daily 9am-5:30pm.

Buses: DRL Bus Lines and **Acadian Lines** share a terminal at 6040 Almon St. (☎454-9321), near Robie St.; take bus #7 or 80 on Robie St. DRL travels down the coast to Yarmouth (6hr., M-F 1 per day, $38). Acadian covers most of the remainder of Nova Scotia and Canada: Annapolis Royal (3-5hr., 1 per day, $31); Charlottetown, P.E.I. (8½hr., 1-2 per day, $60); and North Sydney (6-8hr., 2 per day, $56). Seniors 25% discount, ages 5-11 50%. Station open daily 6:30am-11:30pm.

Public Transit: Metro Transit, (☎490-6600). Efficient and thorough; maps and schedules at any info center. Fare $1.65, seniors and ages 5-15 $1.15, under 5 free. Buses run daily roughly 6am-11pm. Bus info M-F 7:30am-10pm.

Ferries: Dartmouth-Halifax Ferry (☎490-6600), on the harbor front. 15min. crossings depart from both terminals every 15-30min. June-Sept. M-F 7am-11:30pm, Sa 6:30am-11:30pm, Su noon-5:30pm; no Su service Oct.-May. Same fares as Metro Transit.

Taxi: Ace Y Cab, ☎429-4444.

▣🛈 ORIENTATION AND PRACTICAL INFORMATION

Barrington St., the major north-south thoroughfare, runs straight through downtown. Approaching the Citadel and the Public Garden, **Sackville St.** cuts east-west parallel to **Spring Garden Rd.,** Halifax's shopping thoroughfare. Downtown is flanked by the less affluent **North End** and the mostly quiet and arboreal **South End,** on the ocean. Traffic is light, and parking is available by the waterfront for $3-7.

Visitor Info: Halifax International Visitors Center, 1595 Barrington St. (☎490-5946). Open daily 8:30am-8pm; off-season closes between 5-7pm. Free **Internet access** (15min.).

Hotlines: Sexual Assault, ☎425-0122. **Crisis Centre,** ☎421-1188. Both 24hr.

Royal Canadian Mounted Police (the Mounties), ☎426-1323.

Post Office: Main Station, 1680 Bedford Row (☎494-4000). Open M-F 7:30am -5:15pm. **Postal code:** B3K 5M9. **Area code:** 902.

ACCOMMODATIONS

Affordable summer accommodations come easy, but popular ones, like the universities and the hostel, are usually booked. Expect difficulty during major events, such as the Tattoo Festival (see **Entertainment,** below).

Halifax Heritage House Hostel (HI-C), 1253 Barrington St. (☎422-3863). A 3min. walk from the heart of downtown. Behind the brick facade is a newly renovated hostel with a high-ceilinged TV room, kitchen, laundry facilities, and 4- to 8-bed dorms. Office closed noon-4pm. Check-in 4-11pm. Dorms $18, non-members $23. Linen $1.55. Parking $5.

St. Mary's University, 923 Robie St. (☎420-5049 or 420-5485). Just a short distance from pubs and clubs, St. Mary's has hundreds of rooms in the summer. Open May-Aug., call for reservations. Singles $23; doubles $33.

Dalhousie University, 6136 University Ave. (☎494-8840). Now merged with the Technical University, "Dal" has a large selection of summer housing options. Open May-Aug. Singles $37, students $25; doubles $56/$43. Prices include tax. Call ahead for reservations and directions.

Laurie Provincial Park, 25km north of Halifax on Hwy. 2 (☎861-1623). Rustic campsites on Grand Lake. Open June-Sept. Check-in before dusk. No showers. Sites $10.

FOOD

Dozens of downtown restaurants double as nightspots come dusk. Grab a bite before 9 or 10pm, as most places close their doors or kitchens by this time; then, let the drinking begin. **Granite Brewery,** at 1222 Barrington St., produces three of their own microbrewed beer labels and tasty pub food. The $5 "Peculiar" brew is strangely appealing and goes well with the hearty $5.25 beef-and-beer stew. (☎423-5660. Open M-Sa 11:30am-1am, Su noon-11:30pm.) At **Mediterraneo Restaurant,** 1571 Barrington St., students and civilians gather over Middle Eastern dishes. (☎423-4403. Open M-Sa 7am-10pm, Su 7am-9pm. Falafel sandwich $4-5, full breakfast served until 11am for $2.50-5.) For killer food in a casual, fun atmosphere, try **The Atrium,** 1740 Argyle St., which is also a popular nightspot. (☎422-5453. Open M-Tu 11am-2am, W-Su 11am-3:30am. Kitchen closes at 9pm. Seafood dishes around $6-8, daily specials $6-7. Famous 15¢ wings daily 4-9pm.)

SIGHTS

Stroll up to the star-shaped **Halifax Citadel National Historic Park,** in the heart of Halifax on Sackville St., and the old **Town Clock,** at the foot of **Citadel Hill,** for a fine view of the city and harbor. Small exhibits and a 1hr. film relay the relevant history of the British fortress. Come any day at noon to see the pageantry of preparation for the **noonday cannon firing.** (☎426-5080. Open daily mid-June to early Sept. 9am-6pm; early Sept. to mid-Oct. and mid-May to mid-June 9am-5pm. In summer $6, seniors $4.50, ages 6-16 $3, family $14.75. Parking $2.75. Nov.-Apr. free.)

The **Halifax Public Gardens,** across from the Citadel near the intersection of South Park and Sackville St., are ideal for strolling, snoozing, or picnicking. The Roman statues, Victorian bandstand, gas lamps, exquisite horticulture, and overfed loons on the pond are all properly British. From July through Sept., watch for concerts on Su afternoons at 2pm. (☎424-4248. Open daily 8am-sunset.)

Point Pleasant Park, 186 car-free wooded acres at the southern tip of Halifax (take bus #9 from Barrington St. downtown), remains one of England's last imperial holdings, leased to the city of Halifax for 999 years at the bargain rate of one shilling per year. Inside the park, the **Prince of Wales Martello Tow**er, an odd fort built by the British in 1797, honors Prince Edward's obsession with round buildings—with no corners, there's no place for ghosts to hide. (Tower open daily July-Sept. 10am-6pm.) A little farther from downtown, **The Dingle** or **Sir Sandford Fleming Park** on Dingle Rd. provides ocean access for escaping the occasionally scorching summer heat. But if you're really *hot* (wink wink), go to **Crystal Crescent Beach,** off Rte. 349, Halifax's clothing-optional locale.

BOOM. What do you get when you cross 225 tons of TNT, a few barrels of butane, a hell of a lot of picric acid, and a lone spark? On Dec. 6, 1917, the citizens of Halifax discovered the answer—the biggest boom before the Atomic Age. Tragically, over 2000 people lost their lives when *Mont Blanc*, a French ship heavy with acid and TNT, collided with *Imo*, a Belgian relief ship. Both vessels began to burn, luring hapless spectators to the docks. Frantic soldiers evacuated the *Mont Blanc* by paddling lifeboats to the opposite shore. An hour later, the explosion leveled 325 acres of the city, throwing a half-ton anchor 4½km and a cannon barrel 7½km in opposite directions. Windows shattered 100km away, and shock waves were felt for 650km. The **Maritime Museum of the Atlantic** has an exhibit and short film on the explosion. *(1675 Lower Water St. ☎424-7490. Open M-Sa 9:30am-5:30pm, Su 1-5:30pm. In winter, open Tu-Sa 8:30am-5pm, Su 1-5pm. June to late Oct. $6, seniors $5, ages 6-17 $2; family $15. Late Oct. to May 31 free.)*

🎵🎶 ENTERTAINMENT AND NIGHTLIFE

The **Neptune Theater,** 1593 Argyle St., presents the area's most noteworthy professional stage productions. (☎429-7070. Box office open M-Sa 9am-5pm. Tickets $18-33, student and senior discounts). **The Nova Scotia International Tattoo Festival** is Halifax's biggest summer event. The festival runs through the first week of July, featuring military groups and international performers; at noon, the Metro area overflows with free entertainment. Later, a 3hr. show takes place in the Metro Centre. (☎420-1114, ticket info 451-1221. Tickets $12-24, seniors and under 13 $10-22.) The **Atlantic Jazz Festival** (☎492-2225 or 800-567-5277) jams for a week in mid-July with ticketed and free concerts. In Aug., street performers from around the world display random talents at **Buskerfest** (☎429-3910). At the end of Sept., the **Atlantic Film Festival** (☎422-3456) wraps up the season with Canadian and international films. The **Halifax Event Line** (☎451-1202) knows what's going on.

Halifax boasts an intoxicating nighttime scene—the pub per capita ratio is "the highest in Canada," which makes bar-hopping common and easy. The free *Coast* lists special goings-on. **The Dome** (that's "the Liquordome" to locals), 1740 Argyle St., is a four-club establishment that offers dining by day, and attracts a 20- and 30-something crowd to party at nightfall. The **Seahorse Tavern,** 1665 Argyle St., is the oldest tavern in Nova Scotia. Purple-haired students chat with paralegals in a dark basement room with carved woodwork and benches aplenty. (☎423-7200. Open M-W noon-1am, Th-Sa noon-2am.) Amidst nautical decor, the **Lower Deck** in the Historic Properties region on Upper Water St., offers excellent Irish folk music. (☎425-1501. Open daily 11am-12:30am. Cover $2-5.) Huge and always packed, **Peddler's Pub,** in Barrington Place Mall on Granville St., is favored for good pub food. (☎423-5033. Open M-Sa 11am-10:30pm, Su 11am-8pm. Wings $5; steamed mussels $4.50.) The city's hottest gay spot and best sound system are both inside **Reflections Cabaret,** 5184 Sackville St. (☎422-2957), where pounding bass overtakes dancers' heartbeats nightly until 4am.

NEW BRUNSWICK

Powerful South Indian Ocean currents sweep around the tip of Africa and ripple thousands of miles through the Atlantic before coming to a spectacular finish at New Brunswick. The Bay of Fundy witnesses the world's highest tides, which can ebb and flow through a staggering 48-foot cycle. Away from the ocean's violent influence, vast unpopulated stretches of forest swathe the land in timeless wilderness. In the 17th century, French pioneers established the farming and fishing nation of *l'Acadie* on the northern and eastern coasts. Later, British Loyalists, fleeing in the wake of the American Revolution, settled on the shores of the bay. After complaining about the distant government in Halifax, the colonists were granted self-government by the Crown, and New Brunswick was born. Over a third of the province's population is French-speaking, but English is more widely used.

▨ PRACTICAL INFORMATION

Capital: Fredericton.
Visitor Info: Dept. of Economic Development and Tourism, P.O. Box 6000, Fredericton E3B
  5C3. Call **Tourism New Brunswick** (☎ 800-561-0123) from anywhere in Canada.
Postal Abbreviation: NB. **Drinking Age:** 19. **Sales Tax:** 15%. **Area Code:** 506.

SAINT JOHN   ☎ 506

The city of Saint John (never abbreviated to distinguish it from St. John's, Newfoundland) was founded literally overnight on May 18, 1783, by the United Empire
Loyalists, a band of about 10,000 American colonists holding allegiance to the British crown. But the town's remarkable history is a mere detail to the thousands who
flock here just to witness the Bay of Fundy's tides and the "Reversing Falls."

■▨ **ORIENTATION AND PRACTICAL INFORMATION.** Saint John's downtown
is bounded by **Union St.** to the north, **Princess St.** to the south, **King Sq.** to the east,
and **Market Sq.** and the harbor to the west. Find free parking on many sidestreets
outside of the immediate downtown area; parking garages downtown are fair-
priced, though. Fort Latour Harbor Bridge (toll 25¢) on Hwy. 1 links Saint John to
West Saint John, as does a free bridge on Hwy. 100. **Via Rail** (☎ 857-9830) has a station in Moncton; take an SMT bus from Saint John. **SMT,** 300 Union St. (☎ 648-3555)
buses to Moncton (2hr., 2 or 4 per day, $23); Montréal (14hr., 2 per day, $94); and
Halifax (6-6½hr., 5 per week, $65). Station open daily 7:30am-9pm. **Saint John Transit**
runs until roughly 12:30am. (☎ 658-4700. Fare $1.55, under 14 $1.30.) Late June to
early Oct., 2hr. tour of historic Saint John leaves from Barbara General Store at Loy-
alist Plaza and Reversing Falls ($15, ages 6-14 $5). **NFL Bay Ferries** (☎ 888-249-7245)
on Lancaster St. (follow ferry signs after Exit 109 from Hwy. 1), crosses to Digby,
NS (3hr., 2-3 per day; $30, seniors $25, ages 5-12 $15, cars $60). The **City Center Information Center,** at Market Sq., has info. (☎ 658-2855. Open daily 9am-8pm, Sept.-May
9am-6pm.) **Post Office:** Station B, 41 Church Ave. W, in W. Saint John. (☎ 672-6704.
Open M-F 8am-5pm.) **Postal code:** E2L 3W9. **Area Code:** 506.

▌ **ACCOMMODATIONS.** There are number of nearly identical motels on the 1100
to 1300 blocks and then farther along on the 1700 block of **Manawagonish Rd.** in the
western part of town (singles $35-50). Saint John Transit has bus directions (see
Practical Information, above); by car, avoid the 25¢ bridge toll by taking Hwy. 100 into
West Saint John, turn right on Main St., and head west until it turns into Manawagonish Rd. The rooms at the **Saint John YMCA/YWCA (HI-C),** 19-25 Hazen Ave., are clean
and unremarkable. Access to recreational facilities, pool, workout room is
included. From Market Sq., head two blocks up Union St.; the hostel is on the left.
(☎ 634-7720. Open daily 5am-11pm; guests arriving on evening ferry can check-in
later. Singles $20, non-members $30. Summer reservations recommended.) The **University of New Brunswick at Saint John** on Tucker Park Rd. offers neat, furnished rooms
a 10min. drive from downtown. Take Somerset St. onto Churchill Blvd. and turn left
onto Tucker Park Rd. (☎ 648-5768. Open May-Aug. Reception M-F 8am-4pm. Singles
$29, students $18; doubles $42/$30.) Partially wooded tent sites at the **Rockwood Park
Campground** are just off Lake Drive S. in Rockwood Park. Take the "University" bus
to the Mt. Pleasant stop and follow the signs. (☎ 652-4050. Showers. Open May-Sept.
Sites $15, with hook-up $18; weekly $65/$95.)

▍ **FOOD.** The butcher, baker, fishmonger, produce dealer, and cheese merchant
sell fresh goodies at **City Market,** 47 Charlotte St., between King and Brunswick Sq.
The market may be the best place to look for **dulse,** sun-dried seaweed from the
Bay of Fundy; it is best described as "ocean jerky." A $1.50 bag is more than a sam-
ple. (☎ 658-2820. Open M-Th 7:30am-6pm, F 7:30am-7pm, Sa 7:30am-5pm.) **Billy's
Seafood Company,** 49-51 Charlotte St. is scrumptious, though pricey. Fresh oysters
(6 for $10) and fish and chips ($11) are superb, or splurge for their seasonally
priced specialty: lobster. (☎ 672-3474. Open M-Th 11am-10pm, F-Sa 11am-11pm, Su

4-10pm.) **Reggie's Restaurant,** 26 Germain St., is the local hub, providing homestyle North American fare. The breakfast special will fill you up: two eggs, sausage, homefries, and toast for $3.50, served daily 6 to 11am. (☎ 657-6270. Open M-Tu 6am-7pm, W-F 6am-8pm, Sa-Su 6am-6pm.)

🖸 **SIGHTS.** Saint John's main attraction is the **Reversing Falls,** a natural phenomenon caused by the powerful Bay of Fundy tides (for more on the tides see **Fundy,** below). Though the name may suggest 100 ft. walls of gravity-defying water, the "falls" are actually beneath the surface of the water. Two hr. before high tide, and again 2hr. after, patient spectators see the flow of water at the nexus of the Saint John River and Saint John Harbor slowly halt and change direction. More amazing than the event itself is the number of people captivated by it. The **Reversing Falls Tourist Centre,** at the west end of the Hwy. 100 bridge (take the west-bound "East-West" bus), distributes tide schedules and shows a 12min. film on the phenomenon. *(☎ 658-2937. Center open daily May-Oct. 8am-8pm. Screenings every 15min.; $1.75.)* **Moosehead Breweries,** in West Saint John, is the oldest independent brewery in Canada. *(89 Main St. ☎ 635-7000. 1hr. tours with samples mid-June to Aug. 9:30am and 2pm. Call for times. Tours limited to 20 people; make reservations 2-3 days in advance. Free.)*

FUNDY NATIONAL PARK   ☎ 506

Twice each day, the world's largest tides withdraw over one kilometer into the Bay of Fundy, exposing a vast stretch of seashore teeming with hardy aquatic lifeforms. The dramatic contrast between the two tidescapes, and the rapidity with which the waters rise and fall (1m per 3min.), is enough to draw thousands of tourists each year to Fundy National Park. Located an hour's drive southeast of Moncton on Hwy. 114, the park occupies 260 square kilometers of New Brunswick's coast and offers exquisite campgrounds and recreation facilities, as well as a variety (wooded, oceanside, swampy, etc.) of hiking trails. Visits to the park in chillier September and October catch the fall foliage and avoid the crush of vacationers.

🛈 **PRACTICAL INFORMATION. Park Headquarters,** P.O. Box 1001, Alma, New Brunswick, E4H 1B4, in the southeastern corner of the Park facing the Bay, across the Upper Salmon River from the town of Alma, includes the administration building and the **visitors center.** (☎ 887-6000. Open daily mid-Jun. to early Sept. 8am-10pm; mid-May to mid-June and early Sept. to early Oct. daily 8am-4:30pm, weekends until 5pm; in winter 8am-4:30pm, weekends 9am-4pm.) The other visitors center, **Wolfe Lake Information,** is at the northwest entrance off Hwy. 114. (☎ 432-6026. Open daily late June to early Sept. 10am-6pm.) No public transportation serves Fundy; the nearest bus depots are in Moncton and Sussex. (Entrance fee $3.50 per day, senior $2.75, ages 6-16 $1.75; family $7.) The free and invaluable park newspaper *Salt and Fir,* available at the entrance stations and info centers, includes a map of hiking trails and campgrounds, as well as a schedule of activities. **Weather info:** ☎ 887-6000.

🏕️ **CAMPING AND ACCOMMODATIONS.** The park operates four **campgrounds** totaling over 600 sites. Getting a site is seldom a problem, but landing one at your campground of choice may be a little more difficult. The park accepts no reservations; all sites are first come, first served. **Headquarters Campground,** closest to civilization, is usually in highest demand. If a site is full, put your name on the waiting list; at noon, the names of those admitted for the night are read. (Open year-round. Sites $13, with hook-up $19.) **Chignecto North Campground,** off Hwy. 114, 5km inland from the headquarters, provides more private wooded sites. (Open mid-May to mid-Oct. Sites $13, with hook-up $17-19.) **Point Wolfe Campground,** scenically located along the coast 7km west of headquarters, stays cooler and more insect-free than the inland campgrounds and has direct access to several beautiful oceanside hikes. (Open late June to early Sept. Sites $13). Year-round wilderness camping is also available in some of the most scenic areas of the park, especially **Goose River** along the coast. The campsites, all with fireplaces, wood, and an outhouse, take a $3 per person per night permit fee. Or opt for a degree of domestication while remaining burrowed within the park's splendor at the **Fundy National Park Hos-**

tel **(HI-C)**, near Devil's Half Acre about 1km south of the park headquarters. The 16-bed hostel has a full kitchen, showers, laundry facilities and a common room. (☎ 887-2216. Open mid-May to mid-Oct. Check-in 8-10am and 5-10pm. Dorms $12, non-members $15. Wheelchair accessible.)

⬤ FOOD. Refuel with basic groceries or a home-cooked meal at **Harbor View Market and Coffee Shop** on Main St. in Alma. The breakfast special of two eggs, toast, bacon, and coffee runs $4.50. (☎ 887-2450. Open daily July-Aug. 7:30am-8:30pm; Sept.-June M-F 8am-6pm, Sa-Su 8am-7pm.) A trip into Alma is more than worthwhile if only for a sticky bun ($1) from ■**Kelly's Bake Shop.** Replenish lost hiking calories (plus some!) with fresh baked bread, cookies, pies, and peanut butter balls. Baked goods start at 60¢. (☎ 887-2460. Open May-Sept. 7am-8pm.)

▨ OUTDOORS. The park maintains 104km of trails year-round, about 35km of which are open to mountain bikes. Be sure to bring your own though—no rental outfits serve the island. *Salt and Fir* contains detailed descriptions of all trails, including where to find waterfalls and ocean views. Moose are most common along Hwy. 114, between Wolfe Lake and Caribou Plain. Hike the ■**Caribou Plain Trail** (3½km loop) at dusk and you'll likely spot several dining in the swamps. Deer live throughout the park; thieving raccoons run thick. Peregrine falcons are hard to spot. Most recreational facilities operate only during the summer season (mid-May to early Oct.), and include free daily interpretive programs designed to help visitors get to know the park. The park staff leads beach walks and evening theater and campfire gatherings, usually involving storytelling, forest education, and singing. For a fee, visitors can take a spooky nocturnal 3hr. guided tour through the woods. (Tours held twice per week $12, children $8, family $33.)

NEAR FUNDY: KOUCHIBOUGUAC

Unlike Fundy's rugged forests and high tides, **Kouchibouguac National Park** (the name meaning "river of the long tides") features warm lagoon waters, salt marshes, peat bogs, and white sandy beaches. Bask in the sun along the 25km stretch of barrier islands and sand dunes, or float down canoe waterways. Rent canoes ($6 per hr., $30 per day), kayaks ($6 per hr., $30 per day), and bikes ($4 per hr., $26 per day) at **Ryans Rental Center** in the park between the South Kouchibouguac Campground and Kelly's Beach. (☎ 876-3733. Open daily June-Aug. 8am-9pm; May Sa-Su 8am-5pm.) The park operates two campgrounds in the summer. **South Kouchibouguac** has 311 sites with showers. (Late June to early Sept. $16.25, with hook-up $22. Mid-May to late June and early Sept. to mid-Oct. $13/$18. Reservations recommended July-Aug.) **Côte-à-Fabien** has 32 sites ($14), but no showers. Off-season campers take advantage of primitive sites within the park and several commercial campgrounds just outside of the park (park entrance fee $3.50, ages 6-16 $1.75). The **park info center** is at the park entrance on Hwy. 117 just off Hwy. 11, 90km north of Moncton. (☎ 876-2443. Open daily 8am-8pm; mid-Sept. to mid-June 9am-5pm. Park administration open year-round M-F 8am-4:30pm.)

PRINCE EDWARD ISLAND

Prince Edward Island, now more commonly called "P.E.I." or "the Island," began as St. John's Island. The name switch came in 1799, when residents renamed their home to honor Prince Edward, son of King George III, in response to his interest in the territory's welfare. The smallest province in Canada attracts most of its visitors thanks to the beauty made famous by Lucy Maud Montgomery's novel *Anne of Green Gables*. The fictional work did not exaggerate the wonders of natural life on the island; the soil, made red by its high iron-oxide content, contrasts the green crops and shrubbery, turquoise waters, and purple roadside lupin. On the north and south shores are some of Canada's finest beaches. Relentlessly quaint (and fun) island towns all over P.E.I. seem to exist more for visitors than for residents.

PRACTICAL INFORMATION

Charlottetown is the capital of P.E.I; **Queen St.** and **University Ave.** are its main thoroughfares, straddling **Confederation Centre** on the west and east, respectively. The most popular beaches—**Cavendish, Brackley,** and **Rustico Island**—lie on the north shore in the middle of the province, opposite Charlottetown. **Confederation Bridge** meets P.E.I. at Borden-Carleton, 56km west of Charlottetown on Hwy. 1.

Ferries: Northumberland Ferry (☎566-3838 or 800-565-0201 from P.E.I. and Nova Scotia), in Wood Islands 61km east of Charlottetown on Trans-Canada Hwy. To: Caribou, NS (1¼hr.; 6-10 per day; pedestrians $11, vehicles $49).

Driving: Confederation Bridge, the longest continuous marine span bridge in the world, extends over the 15km from P.E.I. to the mainland. Toll $36.25 to exit the island.

Taxis: City Cab, ☎892-6567. Runs 24hr.

Bike Rental: MacQueens, 430 Queen St. (☎368-2453). Road and mountain bikes $25 per day, $100 per week; children half-price. Must have credit card or $75 deposit. Open M-Sa 8:30am-5:30pm.

Beach Shuttles: ☎566-3243. Picks up at the **P.E.I. Visitor Information Centre** at 178 Water St. and the hostel (call for additional points), and drops off in Cavendish (45min.; 2 per day June and Sept., 4 per day July-Aug.; $10, same-day round-trip $16).

Visitor Info: P.E.I. Visitor Information Centre, P.O. Box 940, C1A 7M5 (☎368-4444 or 888-734-7529), by the waterfront in Charlottetown. Open daily June 8am-8pm; July-Aug. 8am-10pm; Sept. to mid-Oct. 9am-6pm; mid-Oct. to May M-F 9am-4:30pm.

Crisis Line: Crisis Centre, ☎566-8999. 24hr.

Drinking Age: 19.

Post Office: 135 Kent St., Charlottetown C1A 7N7. (☎628-4400. Open M-F 8am-5:15pm. **Postal abbreviation:** PEI. **Area code:** 902.

ACCOMMODATIONS

B&Bs and **country inns** crowd every nook and cranny of the province; some are open year-round, but the most inexpensive are closed off-season. Rates hover around $35-40 for singles and $50 for doubles, but you won't land those prices unless you call in advance. Many of the island's visitors centers, including Charlottetown's, display daily vacancy listings for the island's inns, B&Bs, campgrounds, and other accommodations. Fifteen farms participate in a provincial **Farm Vacation** program, in which tourists spend time with a farming family. (☎651-2620. From $35 per night for a double).

The **Charlottetown International Hostel (HI-C),** 153 Mt. Edward Rd., across the yard from the University of P.E.I. (UPEI), is housed in a large green barn. Take Belvedere one long block east of University Ave., then turn left onto Mt. Edward Rd. Join the outgoing hostel staff for movie night or an occasional campfire. (☎894-9696. Kitchen facilities, showers, TV lounge. Open June to early Sept. Check-in 7-10am and 4pm-midnight. Curfew midnight. Lockout 10am-4pm. Dorms $15.50, non-members $19.50. Linen $1. Bike rental $15.) Located off of Belvedere Rd., the **UPEI** runs a dorm-style B&B in Marian and Bernardine Halls, but lacks the Victorian frills. (☎566-0362 Sept.-May; ☎566-0442 June-Aug. Marian: July-Aug. singles $36, doubles $46; May-June $32/$39. Bernardine: $47/$53/$46/$48. Check-in for all locations at Blanchard Hall.) **Le Goéland,** in Cape Egmont, is a hostel by the sea with some campsites and direct access to the beach and hiking trails. The staff hosts musical and bonfire evenings. From Summersire, follow Rte. 2 W to the Rte. 124 intersection. Follow 124 into the town of Mont Carmel. Turn right onto Rte. 11, and follow for 6km. (☎854-2546. Dorms $14; sites $8; $3 extra per person.)

Prince Edward Island National Park operates three campgrounds during the summer and one off-season. Campgrounds often reach full capacity in summer; reservations are strongly recommended, and must be made at least three days in advance. (☎800-414-6765 for reservations; info 672-6350 or 963-2391. In summer, 462 primitive sites with showers, toilets, kitchen access, laundry facilities $15-19;

110 sites with hook-up $20-21. In winter, primitive sites $8.) **Cavendish Campground** has a beach-side location—reservations are particularly handy. (Seasons vary, but expect to find a campground open mid-June to mid-Sept.) Privately-owned campgrounds saturate the island and provide a convenient alternative when campsites are unavailable at the national park (brochures available at info centers).

FOOD

The quest for food often boils down to the search for **lobster.** The coveted crustaceans start around $9 per lb. Fresh seafood, including world-famous **Malpeque oysters,** is sold along the shores of the island, especially in North Rustico on the north shore. The back of the *P.E.I. Visitor's Guide* lists fresh seafood outlets. The **Charlottetown Farmers' Market,** on Belvedere Ave. opposite UPEI, sells the freshest fruits and veggies around in summer. (☎368-4444. Open July-Aug. W and Sa 9am-2pm; in winter Sa 9am-2pm.)

The cosmopolitan young clientele at **Beanz,** 52 University Ave., bask on a sunny outdoor terrace and wash down homemade sandwiches ($3-4) with great espresso. (☎892-8797. Open M-F 6:30am-6pm, Sa 8am-6pm, Su 9am-5pm.) **Shaddy's,** 44 University Ave., has a bit of it all, including lobsters (seasonal $15-$20) and non-aquatic Lebanese and Canadian fare. (☎368-8886. Open daily 10am-9:30pm, sometimes later in summer. Sandwiches $4-7.)

SIGHTS

Green Gables House, off Rte. 6 in Cavendish just west of Rte. 13, is a shrine for adoring Lucy Maud Montgomery readers—a surprising number of which are from Japan. The traditionally furnished house and its surroundings served as inspiration for this P.E.I. native's first novel; add a few sappy L.M. Montgomery films and memorabilia, and most visitors can't escape without purchasing a special edition copy of *Anne,* if not a commemorative thimble. Arrive in early morning or the evening to escape crowds. *(☎963-3370. Open daily July-Aug. 9am-8pm; May-June and Sept.-Oct. 9am-5pm. $5, seniors $4, ages 6-16 $2.50, families $12. Off-season discounts.)*

Prince Edward Island National Park consists of a 32km coastal strip embracing some of Canada's finest beaches. Wind-sculpted sand dunes and salt marshes undulate along the park's terrain. The park is home to many of the Island's 300-odd species of birds, including the endangered piping plover. *(☎963-7830 or 963-7831. Campgrounds, programs, and services from early July to mid-Aug.)* The stretches of beach on the **eastern coast** of P.E.I. are considerably less touristed than those in the west, perhaps due to the rougher surf. **Lakeside,** a beach 35km east of Charlottetown on Rte. 2, is unsupervised and often nearly deserted on July and Aug. weekdays. Trot along the surf atop a sturdy steed from **Gun Trail Ride,** located right beside the golf course. *(☎961-2076. Open daily June to early Sept. 9am-9pm. $10.)* **Basin Head Beach,** 95km east of Charlottetown, makes a relaxing daytrip, with over 11km of unsupervised white sand. Celtic concerts are held throughout the summer at the ◨**College of Piping,** 619 Water St. E, in Summerside. Scottish *Ceilidhs*, with bagpipes and traditional dance, happen Tu and Th at 7pm. Call for full schedule. *(☎877-224-7473. $10, seniors $9, students and children $7.)*

QUÉBEC

Home to 90% of Canada's French-speaking population, Québec continues to fight for political and legal recognition of its separate cultural identity. Originally populated by French fur trading settlements along the St. Lawrence River, Québec was ceded to the British in 1759. Ever since, anti-federalist elements within *Québecois* society have rankled under control of the largely Anglicized national government. Visitors will likely never notice these underlying tensions though, as the majority of the struggle goes on behind closed doors in Ottawa. Instead, Montreal's renowned nightlife and Québec City's centuries-old European flair distinguish Québec among Canada's provinces.

7 PRACTICAL INFORMATION

Capital: Québec City.
Visitor Info: Tourisme Québec, C.P. 979, Montréal, PQ H3C 2W3 (☎800-363-7777, 514-873-2015 in Montréal; www.tourisme.gouv.qc.ca). Open daily 9am-5pm. **Canadian Parks Service,** Québec Region, 3 Passage du D'or, C.P. Box 6060, Haute-Ville, PQ GIR 4V7 (☎800-463-6769, 418-648-4177 in Québec City).
Postal Abbreviation: PQ. **Drinking Age:** 18.
Provincial Sales Tax: 7.5%, plus 7% GST.

MONTRÉAL   ☎514

This island city, named for the royal mountain in its midst, has been coveted territory for over 300 years. Wars and sieges have brought governments in and out like the tide, including a brief takeover by American revolutionaries in late 1775. Despite, or perhaps due to, these conflicts, Montréal has grown into a diverse city with a cosmopolitan air. Although less than an hour from the US-Canada border, Montréal's European legacy is immediately evident. Fashion that rivals Paris, a nightlife comparable to London, and cuisine from around the globe all attest to this international influence. Whether you credit the international flavor or the large student population of the city, it is hard not to be swept up by the vibrancy that courses through Montréal's *centre-ville*.

✈ GETTING THERE AND AWAY

Airports: Dorval (info ☎394-7377), 25min. from downtown by car. From the Lionel Groulx Métro stop, take bus #211 to Dorval Train Station, then transfer to bus #204. Handles international and domestic flights. **Autocar Connaisseur-Grayline** (☎394-7369) runs a minivan to Dorval from 777 rue de la Gauchetière, at University St., stopping at any downtown hotel if you call in advance. Vans run M-F 5:20am-11:00pm every 20min., Sa-Su every 30min. $9.25, under 5 free. Taxi to downtown $30-35. **Mirabel International** (☎450-476-3010, for info ☎800-465-1213), 45min. from downtown by car, handles all flights from outside the US or Canada. Taxi to downtown $60.
Trains: Central Station, 895 rue de la Gauchetière Ouest, under Queen Elizabeth Hotel. Métro: Bonaventure. Served by **VIA Rail** (☎989-2626 or 800-561-9181, in the US 800-842-7245). To: Québec City (3hr., 3-4 per day, $51, seniors $46, students $33, ages 2-11 $26); Ottawa (2hr., 4 per day, $40/$36/$26/$20); and Toronto (4-5½hr., 6 per day, $97/$87/$63/$49). Discount tickets must be bought 5 or more days in advance. Ticket counter open daily 6am-9pm. **Amtrak** goes to New York (10hr., 1 per day, US$65) and Boston (13hr., 1 per day, US$115). Ticket counter open daily 8am-5pm.
Buses: Voyageur, 505 bd. de Maisonneuve Est (☎842-2281). Métro: Berri-UQAM. To: Toronto (6¾hr., 7 per day, $90, students $62); Ottawa (2½hr., 17-18 per day, $29); and Québec City (3hr., 18 per day, $40/$30). **Greyhound** (☎287-1580). To New York City (7½-8¾hr., 7 per day, $103.50) and Boston (7hr., 7 per day, $84).

▐ GETTING AROUND

Public Transit: STCUM Métro and Bus (☎288-6287). Safe and extremely efficient. The 4 Métro lines and most buses operate daily 5:30am-12:30am; some have early morning schedules as well. Get maps at the tourist office or any Métro station booth. Buses are well-integrated; transfer tickets from bus drivers are valid as subway tickets, and vice versa. Fare for train or bus $2, 6 tickets $8.25. 1-day unlimited tourist pass $5, 3-day $12; weekly $12.50. Passes sold at any downtown Métro station.
Taxis: Taxi Pontiac, ☎761-5522. **Champlain Taxi Inc.,** ☎273-2435.
Car Rental: Via Route, 1255 rue MacKay (☎871-1166), at Ste-Catherine. Rates from $40 per day; special 4hr. rental $25. Must be 21+ with credit card. Open M-F 7am-7pm, Sa 7:30am-5pm, Su 9am-9pm.

EASTERN CANADA

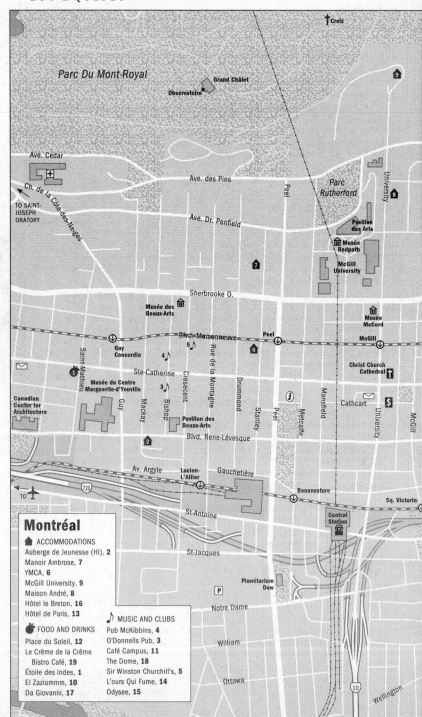

Montréal

🏠 **ACCOMMODATIONS**
Auberge de Jeunesse (HI), **2**
Manoir Ambrose, **7**
YMCA, **6**
McGill University, **9**
Maison André, **8**
Hôtel le Breton, **16**
Hôtel de Paris, **13**

🍴 **FOOD AND DRINKS**
Place du Soleil, **12**
Le Crême de la Crême
   Bistro Café, **19**
Étoile des Indes, **1**
El Zaziummm, **10**
Da Giovanni, **17**

♪ **MUSIC AND CLUBS**
Pub McKibbins, **4**
O'Donnells Pub, **3**
Café Campus, **11**
The Dome, **18**
Sir Winston Churchill's, **5**
L'ours Qui Fume, **14**
Odysee, **15**

Parc
Jeanne-Mance

Ave. du Parc

Duluth

400 yards

400 meters

10 Roy

Ave. des Pins

Parc
Lafontaine

Sherbrooke 🔽

Prince Arthur

11 🎵

12 SQUARE
SAINT-LOUIS

LATIN
QUARTER

13

TO
OLYMPIC PARK

Ilton

St-Denis

St-Hubert

Berri

Sherbrooke E.

14 🎵

Sherbrooke O.

15 🎵

Blvd. St-Laurent

Musée de
l'humor

Ontario

National
Library

16

Pl.-des-Arts 🔽

St-Laurent

Blvd. Maisonneuve

Berri-UQAM

Beaudry

M

PLACE DES
ARTS
Musée d'Arts
de Montréal

Ste-Catherine

18 🎵

CHINESE
QUARTER

17

Université de
Québec
à Montréal

Rue de Bleury

Jeanne-Mance

St-Urbain

Blvd. Rene-Lévesque

Gauchetière

Ave. Viger

P

SQ.
VIGER

Pl. d'Armes 🔽

Champ de Mars 🔽

Palais de Congrès

Berri

TO
ÎLE SAINTE-HÉLÈNE,
AQUARIUM & AMUSEMENT PARK

Musée
Artur Pascal

St-Antoine

Parc
Champs-de-Mars

St-Jacques

PL.
D'ARMES

Palais
de Justice

Vieux Palais
de Justice

St-Paul

Notre-Dame

St-François-Xavier

St-Sulpice

VIEUX-
MONTRÉAL

St-Vincent

Jacques-Cartier

ℹ️

Musée de
Château
Ramezay

Centaur
Theatre

Notre-Dame
Basilica

St-Paul

19

St-Jean

Pl.
Royale

de la Commune

VIEUX-PORT

Tour de
l'Horloge

Centre
Histoire
ontréal

St-Pierre

Quai Jacques Cartier

Quai de l'Horloge

Musée
rc-Aurèle

IMAX

Quai King Edward

Quai Alexandra

Le Pélican

Fleuve St-Laurent

Driver/Rider Service: Allo Stop, 4317 rue St-Denis (☎985-3032). Matches passengers with member drivers; part of the rider fee goes to the driver. To: Québec City ($15), Toronto ($26), Sherbrooke ($9), New York City ($50), and Boston ($42). Riders and drivers fix their own fees for rides over 1000 mi. Annual membership fee required ($6, drivers $7). Open daily 9am-6pm.

Bike Rental: Cycle Pop, 1000 Rachel Est (☎526-2525). Métro: Mont-Royal. 21-speeds $20 per day, $40 per weekend. Open M-W 10am-6pm, Th-F 10am-9pm, Sa-Su 9am-5pm. Credit card or $250 deposit required.

⚑ ORIENTATION

Two major streets divide the city, making orientation convenient. The one-way **bd. St-Laurent** (also called **"The Main"**) runs north through the city, splitting Montréal and its streets east-west. The Main also serves as the unofficial French/English divider; English **McGill University** lies to the west, while slightly east is **St-Denis,** a parallel two-way thoroughfare which defines the French student quarter (also called the *quartier latin* or the "student ghetto"). Montréal's population is 85% Francophone, but most are bilingual. **Rue Sherbrooke,** which is paralleled by **de Maisonneuve** and **Ste-Catherine** downtown, runs east-west almost the entire length of Montréal. The **Underground City** runs north-south, stretching from **rue Sherbrooke** to **rue de la Gauchetière** and **rue St. Antoine.** For easy navigation, a free map from the tourist office will help. Parking is expensive and often difficult to find along the streets (meters are 25¢ for 10min.; $30 tickets are common); try the lots—especially those on the outskirts—for more reasonable parking prices. The **Métro** avoids the traffic and parking hassles by whisking riders throughout the city.

NEIGHBORHOODS

Montréal has matured from a riverside settlement of French colonists into a hip metropolis. A stroll along **Rue Ste-Catherine,** the flashy commercial avenue, is a must; it is here where European fashion tussles Canada, fragments of overheard conversation morph between English and French, and upscale retail intermingles with tacky souvenir stores and debaucherous nightclubs. Global flavor is as pervasive as Canadian beer in Montréal.

A small **Chinatown** orients itself along **rue de la Gauchetière,** near Vieux Montréal's **Place d'Armes. Little Greece,** a bit farther than you might care to walk from downtown, is just southeast of the **Outremont** Métro; stroll by **rue Hutchison** between **ave. Van Horne** and **ave. Edouard-Charles.** At the northern edge of the town's center, **Little Italy** occupies the area north of **rue Beaubien** between **rue St-Hubert** and **Louis-Hémon.** Walk east from Métro: Beaubien. **Rue St-Denis,** home to the city elite at the turn of the century, still serves as the **Latin Quarter's** main street, although restaurants of all flavors are also clustered along **rue Prince Arthur** (Métro: Berri-UQAM or Sherbrooke). **Bd. St-Laurent,** north of Sherbrooke, is perfect for walking or biking. Originally settled by Jewish immigrants, this area now functions as a sort of multicultural welcome wagon, home to Greek, Slavic, Latin American, and Portuguese immigrants. Many attractions between **Mont Royal** and the **Fleuve St-Laurent** are free, from parks (Mont Royal and Lafontaine) and universities (McGill, Montréal, Concordia, Québec at Montréal) to architectural spectacles. **Carré St-Louis** (Métro: Sherbrooke) hosts a beautiful fountain and sculptures. **Le Village** is a gay village in Montréal from rue St-Denis Est to Papineau along rue Ste-Catherine Est. Both the Latin Quarter (above) and the area along rue St-Denis foster a very liberal, gay-friendly atmosphere (Metro: Sherbrooke or Mont-Royal).

ⓘ PRACTICAL INFORMATION

Visitor Info: Infotouriste, 1001 rue de Square-Dorchester (☎873-2015 or 800-363-7777; www.tourisme.montreal.org), at Peel and Ste-Catherine between rue Peel and rue Metcalfe. Métro: Peel. Open daily 8am-7:50pm; Sept.-June 9am-6pm. In **Old Montréal,** 174 rue Notre-Dame Est at Place Jacques Cartier. Open daily 9am-7pm; daily Sept.-Oct. 9am-5pm; Nov. to early Mar. Th-Su 9am-5pm; daily late Mar. to early June 9am-5pm.

Youth Travel Office: Tourisme Jeunesse, 4008 rue St-Denis (☎252-3117 or 844-0287). Métro: Sherbrooke. A non-profit organization that inspects and ranks all officially recognized youth hostels in Québec. Open M-W 10am-6pm, Th-F 10am-9pm, Sa 10am-6pm, Su 10am-5pm. **Travel CUTS,** McGill Student Union, 3480 rue McTavish (☎398-0647). Métro: McGill. Specializes in budget travel for college students. Open M-F 9am-5pm.

Currency Exchange: Currencies International, 1250 rue Peel (☎392-9100). Métro: Peel. Open in summer M-W 8:30am-8pm, Th-F 8:30am-9pm, Sa 8:30am-7pm, Su 9am-6pm; call for winter hours. **Thomas Cook,** 777 rue de la Gauchetière Ouest (☎397-4029). Métro: Bonaventure. Open M-F 8:30am-7pm, Sa 9am-4pm, Su 10am-3pm. Rue Ste-Catherine is lined with other small bureaus de change—watch out for high commissions. Most ATMs are on the PLUS system and charge only the normal transaction fee for withdrawals abroad; ask your bank about fees.

American Express, 1141 rue de Maisonneuve (☎284-3300), at Peel. Métro: Peel. Travel agency; traveler's checks and currency exchange. Open M-F 9am-5pm.

Hotlines: Tel-aide, ☎935-1101. **Sexual Assault,** ☎934-4504. **Suicide-Action,** ☎723-4000. All 3 operate 24hr. **Rape Crisis,** ☎278-9383. Operates M-F 9:30am-4:30pm; call Tel-aide after hours.

Post Office: Succursale (Postal Station) "B," 1250 rue Université (☎395-4539), at Cathcourt. Open M-F 8am-5pm. **Postal code:** H3B 3B0. **Area code:** 514.

ᚱ ACCOMMODATIONS

The **Québec Tourist Office** (☎800-363-7777) is the best resource for info about hostels, hotels, and *chambres touristiques* (rooms in private homes or small guest houses). B&B singles cost $25-40, and doubles run $35-75. Or, take your B&B inquiries directly to the **Downtown Bed and Breakfast Network,** 3458 ave. Laval, H2X 3C8, near Sherbrooke; the managers run their own modest hideaway and maintain a list of 80 other homes downtown. (☎289-9749 or 800-267-5180; www.bbmontreal.qc.ca. Open daily 9am-9pm. Singles $40-65; doubles $45-75.)

Ranging from quaint to seedy, any of the least expensive *maisons touristiques* and hotels cluster around **rue St-Denis.** The area, which abuts Vieux Montréal, flaunts lively nightclubs and a number of funky cafes and bistros.

▧ Auberge de Jeunesse, Montréal Youth Hostel (HI-C), 1030 rue MacKay (☎843-3317). Métro: Lucien-L'Allier. Airport shuttle drivers will stop here if asked. If only the life of a hosteler were always this cushy; with a full bathroom in every room, A/C, a complete kitchen, laundry facilities, pool tables, and a petit cafe whipping up gourmet creations, the Montréal Youth Hostel is synonymous with heaven. The 250 beds (3-10 per room) fill quickly in summer, attesting to Montréal's popularity, but if you're hesitant to check out nightlife alone, join staff and guests for a bi-weekly pub crawl (F and Tu 8:30pm). Some parking. 1-week maximum stay; in winter 10 days. Reception 24hr. Dorms $19, non-members $24. Private doubles $26/$32 per person. Linen $2.10.

McGill University, Bishop Mountain Hall, 3935 rue de l'Université, H3A 2B4 (☎398-6367). Métro: McGill. Follow Université through campus, then catch your breath and bear right when the road seems to terminate in a parking lot atop the steep hill. Kitchenettes on each floor. 1000 beds. Fast, free Internet access. Common room with TV and laundry facilities. Reception daily 7am-10pm; a guard will check you in late. Open May 15 to Aug. 15. Singles $40, students and seniors $33; weekly $230/$200; prices include tax. Full breakfast M-Th 7:30-9:30am $6.

Hotel Le Breton, 1609 rue St-Hubert (☎524-7273), around the corner from the bus station and 2 blocks east of St-Denis. Métro: Berri-UQAM. Although the neighborhood is neither particularly wholesome nor attractive, the 13 rooms are clean and comfortable with a TV, some with A/C. Reception 8am-midnight. Make reservations 2 weeks in advance. Non-smoking rooms available. Front door remains locked. Rooms $40-55.

Université de Montréal, Residences, 2350 rue Edouard-Montpetit, H2X 2B9, (☎343-6531), off Côte-des-Neiges. Métro: Edouard-Montpetit. Located on the edge of a beau-

EASTERN CANADA

tiful campus; try the East Tower for great views. Laundry facilities. Free local calls, sink in each room. The noon check-out is strictly enforced. Reception 24hr. Cafe with basic foods open M-F 7:30am-2:30pm. Open early May to mid-Aug. Singles $26. Parking $7.

Hôtel de Paris, 901 Sherbrook E. (☎522-6861). Métro: Sherbrook. Misleading in appearance, the facade of this seemingly modest-sized 19th-century flat conceals a brand new 100-bed hostel with kitchen and a score of hotel rooms. Single-sex dorm rooms $19. Linen $2. Hotel rooms start at $55.

Maison André Tourist Rooms, 3511 rue Université (☎849-4092). Métro: McGill. Mme Zanko spins great yarns in her antique, well located house. Guests have been returning to this bastion of European cleanliness and decor for over 30 years. No smoking. Singles $26-35; doubles $38-45; $10 per additional person. Reservations recommended.

YMCA, 1450 rue Stanley at Ste-Catherine's (☎849-8393), downtown. Métro: Peel (right across the street from the station). A far cry from luxury, the Y compensates with impeccable, ideally located rooms (they're tiny, but equipped with TV and phone) and allow guests access to newly renovated facilities. Singles $40 for men, $46 for women; doubles $56; triples $66; quads $76. Reserve 2 weeks in advance.

Manoir Ambrose, 3422 rue Stanley (☎288-6922), just off Sherbrooke. Métro: Peel. Somewhat upscale both in price and appearance, the 22 Victorian-furnished rooms have TVs, phones, and an excellent location. Doubles $55, with private bath $65; $10 per additional adult. Continental breakfast included. Reservations recommended 1 month in advance.

Camping Alouette, 3449 de l'Industrie (☎450-464-1661), 30km from the city. Follow Autoroute 20, take Exit 105, and follow the signs to the campground. Find the privacy that is lacking in Montreal's bustling hostels. Pool, laundry facilities, a small store, and a daily shuttle to and from Montréal. Sites for 2 $19, with hook-up $27; $2 per additional person. Showers 25¢. Shuttle $10 per person round-trip.

☼ BON APPETÍT

Affordably- to astonomically-priced restaurants pack in along **bd. St-Laurent** and on the western half of **Ste-Catherine.** In the Latin Quarter, energetic **rue Prince Arthur** jams Greek, Polish, and Italian restaurants into a tiny area, and maître-d's stand in front of their restaurants to court you. The accent changes slightly at **ave. Duluth,** where Portuguese and Vietnamese establishments prevail. Extending north of Maisonneuve on **Rue St-Denis,** you'll find the French Student Quarter, which has many small cafes and eateries, most catering to student budgets. If you'd like wine at an unlicensed restaurant, buy your own at a *dépanneur* or the **SAQ (Sociéte des alcohols du Québec);** the eateries are concentrated on the **bd. St-Laurent,** north of Sherbrooke, and on the pedestrian precincts of rue Prince Arthur and rue Duluth.

All restaurants are required by law to post their menus outside (although many white out the prices), so shop around. Consult the free *Restaurant Guide,* published by the **Greater Montréal Convention and Tourism Bureau** (☎844-5400), which lists over 130 restaurants by type of cuisine. For preparing your own meals, head to the markets: the **Atwater Market** (Métro: Lionel-Groulx); the **Marché Maisonneuve,** 4375 rue Ontario Est (Métro: Pie-IX); the **Marché St-Jacques** (Métro: Berri-UQAM, at Ontario and Amherst); or the **Marché Jean-Talon** (Métro: Jean Talon). Call ☎937-7754 9am to 4pm daily. All markets open M-W 8am-6pm, Th 8am-8pm, F 8am-9pm, Sa 8am-5pm, Su 8am-5pm. Closest to the Montréal hostel is Provigo **SuperMarché,** on the corner of Maisonneuve and Rue du Fort (☎932-3756; open daily 8am-9pm).

■ **La Creme de la Creme Bistro Cafe,** 21 rue De La Communne est (☎874-0723), down by the water in Old Montreal. Provincial French decor and refreshingly reasonable prices distinguish this brick basement cafe from the other eateries lining Old Montréal's streets. Baguette sandwiches served with salad are $6-8, but even more impressive are their scandalously large wedges of chocolate cake ($3-4). If you can handle all that, move onto the bar to get an early start on Montréal's hoppin' nightlife. Open Jun.-Sept. daily 11am-midnight. Hours vary during other seasons.

SMOKED MEAT ON RYE Any true Montréalian (not those artsy downtown types) will agree that Smoked Meat—a spicy, salty, greasy cured beef brisket—is a delicacy not to be compared with anything else in the world. The great landmark ■ **Ben's Delicatessen,** 990 bd. de Maisonneuve, at Metcalfe, in the heart of downtown, is often said to be the originator of this artery-clogging delicacy, which resembles pastrami or even corned beef (☎ 844-1000). The story has it that Ben Kravitz, a native Lithuanian, longed for the briskets of his native land and, in an effort to recreate them, invented Smoked Meat. Famous in Montréal, cafes as far away as Halifax fly in meat from Ben's to serve to their adoring customers. A proper Smoked Meat sandwich is served hot with mustard on seedless rye, with fries, vinegar, a half-sour pickle, and black cherry soda. (At Ben's, that'll be about $6.)

■ **Au Pain Doré,** 5214 Côte des Neiges (☎ 342-8995), near rue Jean Brillant. Such delicious pastries are rarely found within France, nevermind on this side of the prime meridian. Why not treat yourself to a purely butter/carbohydrate diet and drop some extra cash here to buy food for your entire stay? Chocolatines are excellent, as are the croissants, breads, muffins, and pretty much everything else. Also offers a selection of cheeses. Baguettes $1.50-4. Open M-W 8:30am-7pm, Th-F 8:30am-7:30pm, Sa-Su 8:30am-5:30pm.

Etoile des Indes, 1806 Ste-Catherine Ouest (☎ 932-8330), near St-Mathieu. Métro: Guy-Concordia. The best Indian fare in town, according to locals. The brave should try their bang-up Bangalore *phal* dishes. Dinner entrees $5-15; lunch specials $5-8 are your best bet for value. Open M-Sa noon-2:30pm and 5-11pm, Su 5-11pm.

El Zaziummm, 51 Roy Est (☎ 844-0893), a St-Laurent side street. Primary-colored patio floorboards introduce patrons to the intoxicating atmosphere of this wee Mexican eatery. Entrees $8-15. Open M-Tu 4-11pm, W-Su noon-11:30pm; in winter daily 4-11pm.

Place du Soleil Cafe, 3603 Ave. Laval (☎ 499-3658), in Square St. Louis. This little ice cream parlor vends great licks to the kids, lovers, punks, and others who meander through the park or sit by the fountain. Cones $1.75-2.50, wraps and sandwiches $2.50-7. Open daily May-Nov. 11am-11pm.

🔘 SIGHTS

MONT-ROYAL, LE PLATEAU, AND THE EAST

Package tickets for the Funiculaire, Biodôme, Gardens, and Insectarium are a decent deal. *($22.50, students and seniors $15.75, ages 6-17 $12.00.)*

FUNICULAIRE. Home to the 1976 summer Olympic games, **Olympic Park** still provides entertainment enough for a day away from the city's center. The park's daring architecture is most poignantly represented by the inclined tower (the world's tallest) adjoined to what now serves as the Expos' baseball stadium—together, the two form a structure uncannily reminiscent of the starship *Enterprise* from TV's "Star Trek." Riding the Funiculaire to the top of the tower grants a panoramic view of Montréal. *(3200 rue Viau. ☎ 252-8687. Métro: Viau, Pie IX. Tours offered daily in both French and English. Call for times. $5.25, ages 5-17 $4.25. Funiculaire open June-Sept. M noon-9pm, Tu-Th 10am-9pm, F-Su 10am-11pm; early Sept. to mid-June M noon-6pm, Tu-Su 10am-6pm. $9, seniors and ages 5-17 $5.50.)*

BIODÔME. The fascinating ■Biodôme is the most recent addition to Olympic park. Housed in the former Olympic Vélodrome, the Biodôme is a "living museum" in which four complete ecosystems have been reconstructed: the Tropical Forest, Laurentian Forest, the St-Laurent marine ecosystem, and the Polar World. Stay alert and you might spot the more elusive of the 6200 vertebrates subsisting here. *(4777 ave. Pierre-de-Coubertin. ☎ 868-3000. Métro: Viau. Open daily in summer 9am-7pm; off-season 9am-5pm. $9.50, students and seniors $7, ages 6-17 $4.75.)*

THE GARDENS. In the summer, a free shuttle will take you across the park to the **Jardin Botanique (Botanical Gardens).** The Japanese and Chinese landscapes showcase the largest *bonsai* and *penjing* collections outside of Asia. Beware: the gardens also harbor an **insectarium** with astounding collections of mounted and live exotic bugs, including at least a dozen breathing fist-sized spiders. *(4101 rue Sherbrooke Est. ☎872-1400; Métro: Pie-IX. Gardens open daily 9am-7pm; Sept.-June 9am-5pm. $9.50, students and seniors $7, ages 6-17 $4.75; Sept.-June $6.75/$5.25/$3.50.)*

PARC DU MONT-ROYAL. The Parc du Mont-Royal was inaugurated in 1876 and climbs up to the mountain from which the city took its name. From rue Peel, hardy hikers can take a foot path and stairs to the top or to the lookouts on Camillien-Houde Pkwy. and the Mountain Chalet. Like New York's Central Park, this one too is a Frederick Law Olmsted original. The **30m cross** at the top of the mountain commemorates the 1643 climb by de Maisonneuve, founder of Montréal. In winter, his proverbial progeny congregate here to ice-skate, toboggan, and cross-country ski. In summer, Mont-Royal welcomes joggers, cyclists, picnickers, and amblers. *(Camilien-Houde Pkwy. ☎844-4928. Métro: Mont-Royal or Bus #11. Officially open 6am-midnight.)*

ST. JOSEPH'S. An acclaimed religious site that attracts pilgrims from all over the globe, ▧**St. Joseph's Oratory** is credited with a long list of miracles and unexplained healings. The **Votive Chapel,** in which hangs the crutches and canes of thousands of healed devotees, pulses with the heat of 10,000 candles. *(3800 ch. Queen Mary, ☎733-8211. Open daily 6am-9:30pm. Metro: Cote-des-Nieges.)*

THE UNDERGROUND CITY

To those attracted to the chic, cosmopolitan Montréal but could do without its sub-zero winters, hibernation is an option. Twenty-nine km of tunnels link Métro stops and form the ever-expanding "prototype city of the future," connecting railway stations, two bus terminals, restaurants, banks, cinemas, theaters, hotels, two universities, two department stores, 1700 businesses, 1615 housing units, and 1600 boutiques. And there aren't any streets to speak of; rather, residents bustle through the hallways and tunnels of this sprawling mall-like, "sub-urban" city. The city can be entered from most downtown Métro stops, though a good start to an adventure is the **Place Bonaventure.** Canada's largest commercial building sports a melange of shops, each selling products imported from a different country. The tourist office supplies treasure maps of the tunnels and underground attractions. *(900 rue de la Gauchetière Ouest. ☎397-2325. Métro: Bonaventure. Shops open daily 9am-9pm.)*

At the McGill stop lies some of the Underground City's finest offerings. Here, beneath the **Christ Church Cathedral** waits **Promenades de la Cathédrale,** one of the Underground's primary shopping complexes. *(635 Ste-Catherine Ouest. Church ☎843-6577. Open daily 8am-6pm. Promenades ☎849-9925.)* Three blocks east, passing through Centre Eaton, of grand department store fame, the **Place Montréal Trust** is famous for its modern architecture and decadent shopping area. Still, there's no charge for an innocent peek around.

VIEUX MONTRÉAL (OLD MONTRÉAL)

In the 17th century, the city of Montréal struggled with Iroquois tribes for control of the area's lucrative fur trade and erected walls encircling the settlement for defense. Today the remnants of those ramparts delineate the boundaries of Vieux Montréal, the city's first settlement, on the stretch of river bank between **rues McGill, Notre-Dame,** and **Berri.** The fortified walls that once protected the quarter have crumbled, but the beautiful 17th- and 18th-century mansions of politicos and merchants retain their splendor. Take the Métro to **Place d'Armes** or **Champ-de-Mars.**

NOTRE-DAME-DE-MONTRÉAL. A couple blocks south of the Place d'Armes, Notre-Dame-de-Montréal towers above the memorial to de Maisonneuve in the bordering square. One of North America's largest churches and an historic center for the city's Catholic population, the neo-Gothic basilica once hosted Québec separatist rallies. Most impressive are the extremely ornate and detailed hand-painted designs covering the pillars and ceiling. *(116 rue Notre-Dame Ouest. ☎ 842-2925. Open daily 7am-8pm; early Sept. to late June M-Sa 8:30am-6pm, Su 1:30-6pm. $2 entrance fee, free to those entering to pray.)*

CATHÉDRALE MARIE REINE DU MONDE. On the block bordered by René-Lévesque, Cathédrale, and Metcalf, Cathédrale Marie Reine du Monde is a scaled-down replica of St. Peter's in Rome and a rival of Notre-Dame-de-Montréal for grandeur. A Roman Catholic basilica, it was built in the heart of Montréal's Anglo-Protestant area. *(☎ 866-1661. Open M-F 7am-7:30pm, Sa 7:30am-8:30pm, Su 8:30am-7:30pm. At least 3-4 masses offered daily. Free.)*

CHÂTEAU RAMEZAY. The grand Château Ramezay, built in 1705 for the French viceroy, houses a museum of Québecois, British, and American 18th-century artifacts. *(280 rue Notre-Dame Est. 861-3708. Métro: Champ-de-Mars. Open daily 10am-6pm; Oct.-May Tu-Su 10am-4:30pm. $6, students and seniors $3, under 6 free. Tours available by reservation. Partially wheelchair accessible; assistance may be required.)*

OTHER ATTRACTIONS. The **Sulpician Seminary,** built in 1685, is still a functioning seminary. The clock over the facade, built in 1701, is the oldest public timepiece in North America. *(130 rue Notre-Dame Ouest. Métro: Place D'Armes.)* At rue Bonsecours and rue St-Paul stands the 18th-century **Notre-Dame-de-Bonsecours,** founded as a sailors' refuge by Marguerite Bourgeoys, leader of the first order of non-cloistered nuns. The church displays archaeological finds from beneath its floors. *(400 rue St-Paul Est. Métro: Champ-de-Mars.)* **Place Jacques Cartier** is the site of Montréal's oldest market. Here the modern European character of Montréal is most evident; cafes line the square, and street artists strut their stuff during the summer. *(Rue St. Paul. Metro: Champ-de-Mars.)* The **Vieux Palais de Justice,** built in 1856 in Place Vaugeulin, stands across from City Hall. **Rue St-Jacques** in the Old City, established in 1687, is Montréal's Wall St.

ST-LAURENT AND ILE. STE-HELENE

Saute-Moutons Jet-Boating tours are a unique but expensive way of experiencing the rapids of the St. Lawrence without getting soaked. *(Clock Tower Pier. ☎ 284-9607. Metro: Champ-de-Mars. 10am-6pm in summer, with prices starting at $60. Call ahead.)* **Les Descentes sur le Saint-Laurent** in LaSalle provides **rafting adventures.** *(Free shuttle from the Info Centre at 1001 rue du Square-Dorchester. ☎ 767-2230 or 800-324-7238. Metro: Peel. 1½hr. tours. Prices and departure times vary, but begin around $30.)*

LA RONDE. La Ronde is the best among many good reasons to visit **Ile Ste-Helene,** an island in the St. Lawrence just off shore from Vieux Montréal. This amusement park, with its free-fall drop and one of the largest wooden rollercoasters in North America, is popular with locals and visitors alike. *(☎ 872-4537 or 800-797-4537. Metro: Ile-Sainte-Helene. Rides open daily in summer 11am-11pm, grounds open until midnight; hours vary off-season. Unlimited passes $29.)* The **International Fireworks Competition** takes place every June and July at La Ronde, but you can avoid the park's steep prices by watching from Mont-Royal or the very crowded Pont Jacques-Cartier. *(☎ 872-4537.)*

LE VIEUX FORT. Originally built in 1820 to defend Canada's inland waterways from the imperialistic Americans to the south, Le Vieux Fort now contains the **Stewart Museum**, which houses a large collection of weapons, war instruments, and strategic maps. Sit tight for musket firing by costumed colonials daily in summer at 3pm. *(☎ 861-6701. Metro: Ile-Sainte-Helene. Open daily 10am-6pm; Sept-May W-M 10am-5pm. $6, students and seniors $4, families $12.)*

🏛 MUSEUMS

The **McGill University** campus extends up Mont Royal. Composed predominantly of Victorian-style buildings set on pleasant greens, the university bears the impact of the British on the city. The campus also contains the site of the 16th-century Native American village of **Hochelaga** and the **Redpath Museum of Natural History,** with rare fossils and two genuine Egyptian mummies. *(☎ 398-4086. Main gate at rue McGill and Sherbrooke; Métro: McGill. Open M-Th 9am-5pm, Su 1-5pm; Sept. to late June M-F 9am-5pm, Su 1-5pm. Free.)*

Musée des Beaux-Arts, 1380 rue Sherbrooke Ouest (☎285-2000; Métro: Guy-Concordia), about five blocks west of the McGill entrance. Impressive visiting exhibits; its small permanent collection touches upon all major artistic periods and includes Canadian and Inuit work. Open Tu-Su 11am-6pm. Permanent collection free. Temporary exhibits $12, students and seniors $6, under 12 $3; half-price W 5:30-9pm.

McCord Museum, 690 rue Sherbrooke Ouest (☎398-7100; Métro: McGill). Textiles and ornate costumes, paintings and prints, and a photographic archive with 700,000 works trace Canadian history from Confederation onward. Open daily June to Sept. 10am-5pm, Sept.-June Tu-F 10am-6pm, Sa-Su 10am-5pm. $8.50, students $5, seniors $6, ages 7-12 $2, families $17. Free Sa 10am-noon.

Canadian Centre for Architecture, 1920 ave. Baile. (☎939-7026; Métro: Guy-Concordia or Atwater). One of the world's most important collections of architectural prints, drawings, photographs, and books. Open in summer Tu-Su 11am-6pm; hrs. vary in other seasons. $6, students $3, seniors $4, under 12 free.

Musée d'Art Contemporain, 185 rue Ste-Catherine Ouest at Jeanne-Mance (☎847-6226; Métro: Place-des-Arts). Works by *Québecois* artists, as well as textile, photography, and avant-garde exhibits. Open Tu and Th-Su 11am-6pm, W 11am-9pm. $6, seniors $4, students $3, under 12 free.

Montréal Museum of Decorative Arts, 2200 rue Crescent (☎284-1252; Métro: Guy-Concordia, then transfer to bus #24 Pie-IX). A slew of innovative and absurd decorative pieces. Open Tu-Su 11am-6pm, W 11am-9pm. $4, students $3, under 12 free.

◪ NIGHTLIFE

Combine a loosely-enforced drinking age of 18 with thousands of taps flowing unchecked till 3am and what results is the unofficially titled "nightlife capital of North America." Most pubs and bars offer the ever-popular weekday "happy hour," usually from 5 to 8pm, where bottled drinks may be two-for-one, and mixed drinks may be double their usual potency. Although it has its share of skanky peepshows and *chateaus de sexe,* Montréal is less a depot of debauchery and more a youthful city surging with energy at twilight and after. In summer, restaurants spill onto outdoor patios and streets clog with strollers, thespians, and couples holding hands. **Rue Prince Arthur** at St-Laurant is devoted solely to pedestrians who mix and mingle at cafes by day and clubs by night. (Métro: Sherbrooke). **Rue St-Denis,** north of Ste-Catherine, is rising as a nighttime hotspot. Montréal's **gay village,** stretching from Rue St-Hubert to Rue Papineau along Ste-Catherine Est, caters mostly to men, but interspersed are a few lesbian clubs (Métro: Papineau or Beaudry).

▨ Pub McKibbins, 1426 Bishop (☎288-1580). Fine fermented drinks within the dark mahogany confines of an enchanting Irish pub. Trophies and brass tokens ornament the walls, and dartboards animate the crowds; a fieldstone fireplace warms the quarters in winter. Ground yourself with the Shepard's Pie ($9) before your next Guinness. Open daily 11am-3am; kitchen closes at 10pm.

O'Donnells Pub, just down the street at 1224 Bishop (☎877-3128), south of Ste-Catherine. Enticing weekday dinner specials (fish and chips on F, $7). The tartan stools and cozy booths are quickly claimed W-Sa, when live traditional Irish music filters into the street, indiscriminately luring in students, tourists, and locals. Open daily noon-3am, kitchen closes at 10pm.

Sir Winston Churchill's, 1459 Crescent (☎288-0616). Perhaps the most impressive ratio of counter length to total area of any bar in all of Montréal. As if covering every inch of wall with bar counter weren't enough, 2 island watering holes take up the remaining floorspace. Every M is "dare to bare all"—we're talking heavy drinking here, folks. Open daily 10:30am-3am.

Cafe Campus, 57 Prince Arthur (☎844-1010). Unlike the more touristy meat-market discothèques, this hip club gathers a friendly student and 20-something crowd. Tu night is retro night, when sloshing pitchers of beer go for a measly $6. Cover: dancing $3, live music $5-$15. Open M-Sa 7pm-3am, Su 8:30pm-3am.

EASTERN CANADA

The Dome, 32 rue Ste-Catherine Est (☎875-5757), at the corner of St-Laurant. Attracts a more outrageous, eclectic, and international crowd to bump and grind. Cover $5. Open F-Sa, 10pm-3am.

L'ours Qui Fume, 2119 rue St-Denis (☎845-6998). A low-key, intimate venue for nightly live blues. Open daily 8pm-3am.

🎭 ENTERTAINMENT

THEATER

Productions in both French and English sustain another genre of nighttime entertainment in Montréal: theater. The **Théâtre du Nouveau Monde,** 84, Ste-Catherine Ouest, hosts French productions (☎866-8667; Métro: Place-des-Arts). The **Théâtre du Rideau Vert,** 4664 rue St-Denis (☎844-1793), stages *Québecois* works. **Centaur Theater,** 453 rue St-François-Xavier, has English-language plays, performed mainly Sept.-May (☎288-1229, ticket info 288-3161; Métro: Place-d'Armes). The city's exciting **Place des Arts,** 260 bd. de Maisonneuve Ouest, at rue Ste. Catherine Ouest and rue Jeanne Mance (☎842-2112 for tickets), houses the **Opéra de Montréal** (☎985-2258), the **Montréal Symphony Orchestra** (☎842-9951), and **Les Grands Ballets Canadiens** (☎849-8681). The **National Theater School of Canada,** 5030 rue St-Denis (☎842-7954), stages excellent student productions during the academic year. **Théâtre Saint-Denis,** 1594 rue St-Denis (☎849-4211), hosts traveling productions like *Cats*. Theater-goers should peruse the **Calendar of Events** (available at the tourist office and reprinted in daily newspapers), or call **Telspec** for ticket info (☎790-2222; open M-Sa 9am-9pm, Su noon-6pm). **Admission Ticket Network** also has tickets for various events (☎790-1245 or 800-361-4595; open daily 8am-midnight; credit card required).

SEASONAL AND OTHER ENTERTAINMENT

Like much of the city, Vieux Montréal is best seen at night. Street performers, artists, and *chansonniers* in various *brasseries* set the tone for lively **summer evenings** of clapping, stomping, and singing along. Real fun goes down on St-Paul, near the corner of St-Vincent. For a sweet Su afternoon, **Parc Jeanne-Mance** reels with bongos, dancing, and handicrafts (May-Sept. noon-7pm).

Québec is no different from the rest of Canada in its obsession with hockey. Between Oct. and Apr., be sure to attend a **Montréal Canadiens** hockey game at the new **Molson Centre,** 1250, de la Gauchetière Ouest, where Les Habitants (a nickname for the Canadiens) play. Dress and behavior at games can be quite formal; jackets and ties are not uncommon (☎932-2582; Métro: Bonaventure; call well in advance to reserve tickets). Baseball is also popular here, and the local MLB team, the **Montréal Expos,** plays at Olympic Park (☎790-1245; Métro: Pie IX).

But *Montréalais* don't just like to watch; in early June, the one-day **Tour de l'île,** a 64km circuit of the island, is the largest cycling event in the world, with 45,000 mostly amateur cyclists pedaling their wares. (Call ☎521-8356 by Apr. if you want to participate. Separate days for adults and children.)

Jazz fiends will command the street June 27 to July 8, 2001, during the annual **Montréal International Jazz Festival** (☎871-1881), with over 300 free outdoor shows scattered on a dozen stages near Métro Place-des-Arts.

QUÉBEC CITY   ☎418

Dubbed the "Gibraltar of America" because of the stone escarpments and military fortifications protecting the port, Québec City (generally shortened to just "Québec") sits high on the rocky heights of Cap Diamant where the Fleuve St-Laurent narrows and is joined by the St-Charles river. The name Québec is derived from the Algonquin word *kebek*, which means "place where the river narrows." Passing through the portals of North America's only walled city is like stepping into a European past; narrow streets and horse-drawn carriages greet visitors to the Old City (Vieux-Québec), and there are enough sights and museums to satisfy even the most voracious history buff for weeks. Along with the historical attachment, Canada's oldest city boasts a thriving French culture, standing apart from Montréal as the center of true *Québecois* culture. Never assume that the locals speak English—it has yet to make solid inroads here.

⌐ GETTING THERE AND AROUND

Airport: Québec's airport (☎692-0770) is far out of town and inaccessible by public transit. Taxi to downtown $30. By car, turn right onto Rt. de l'aéroport and then take either bd. Wilfred-Hamel or, beyond it, Autoroute 440 to get into the city. **Autobus La Québecois** runs a shuttle service between the airport and the major hotels of the city. (☎872-5525. Runs M-F 6 per day to and from the airport, 8:45am-9:45pm; Sa 7 per day 9am-8:45pm; Su 7 per day 9am-11:35pm. $46, under 12 free.)

Trains: VIA Rail, 450 rue de la Gare du Palais (☎692-3940), in Québec City. To: Montréal (3hr., M-F 4 per day, Sa-Su 3 per day); $51, seniors $46, students $33, ages 2-11 $26), Toronto (8hr., 3 per day, $129/$116/$84/$65), and Ottawa (3hr., 3 per day, $77/$69/$50/$39). Open daily 6am-8:30pm. Nearby stations at 3255, ch. de la Gare in Ste-Foy (open M-F 6am-9pm, Sa-Su 7:30am-9pm) and 5995, St-Laurent, Autoroute 20 Lévis. Open Th-M 4-5am and 8-10:30pm, Tu 4-5am, W 8-10:30pm.

Buses: Orlean Express, 320 Abraham Martin (☎525-3000). Open daily 5:30am-1am. Outlying stations at 2700 ave. Laurier, in Ste-Foy (☎650-0087; open M-Sa 6am-1am, Su 7am-1am), and 63, Hwy. Trans-Canada Ouest (Hwy. 132), in Lévis (☎837-5805; open daily 6am-2am). To: Montréal (3hr., every hr. 6am-8pm and 9:30pm and 11pm; $35, seniors $26, ages 5-11 $17); Ste-Anne-de-Beaupré (25min., 3 per day, $5); and the US via Montréal or Sherbrooke.

Public Transit: Commission de transport de la Communauté Urbaine de Québec (CTCUQ), 270 rue des Rocailles (☎627-2511 for route and schedule info). Open M-F 6:30am-10pm, Sa-Su 8am-10pm. Buses operate daily 6am-1am, although individual routes and hours of operation vary significantly. $2.25, students $1.50, seniors and children $1.30; advance-purchase tickets $1.60/$1/$1; under 5 free.

Taxis: Coop Taxis Québec, ☎525-5191.

Driver/Rider Service: Allo-Stop, 467 rue St-Jean (☎522-0056), will match you with a driver heading for Montréal ($15). Must be a member ($6 per year, drivers $7). Open daily 9am-6pm, Tu and F until 7pm.

Car Rental: Pelletier, 900 bd. Pierre Bertrand (☎681-0678). $35 per day, $50 with insurance; 250km free, 11¢ per additional km. Must be 25+ with credit card deposit of 20%. Open M-F 7am-8pm, Sa-Su 8am-4pm.

Bike Rental: Vélo Passe-Sport, 22 Cote du Palais (☎692-3643). 1hr. $6, 4hr. $15, 1 day $25. Credit card deposit of $40 required. Open daily May-Oct. 8am-6pm.

✴⃟ 7 ORIENTATION AND PRACTICAL INFORMATION

Québec's main thoroughfares run through both the Old City *(Vieux Québec)* and the more modern city outside it, generally parallel in an east-west direction. Within **Vieux Québec,** the main streets are **St-Louis, Ste-Anne,** and **St-Jean.** Most streets in Vieux Québec are one-way, the major exception being rue d'Auteuil, which borders the walls inside Vieux Québec—it's the best bet for parking. Outside the walls of Vieux Québec, both St-Jean and St-Louis continue (St-Jean eventually joins Chemin Ste-Foy and St-Louis becomes **Grande Allée**). **Bd. René-Lévesque,** the other major street outside the walls, runs between St-Jean and St-Louis. The Basse-ville (lower town) is separated from the Haute-ville (upper town, Old Québec) by an abrupt cliff roughly paralleled by rue St-Vallier Est.

Visitor Info: Centre d'information de l'office du tourisme et des congrès de la Communauté urbaine de Québec, 835 rue Wilfred Laurier (☎649-2608), in the Old City just outside the walls. Open daily 8:30am-7pm; Thanksgiving (mid-Oct.) to May 9am-5:30pm. Dealing primarily with provincial tourism, Maison du tourisme de Québec, 12 rue Ste-Anne (☎800-363-7777). Open daily 8:30am-7:30pm; early Sept. to mid-June 9am-5pm.

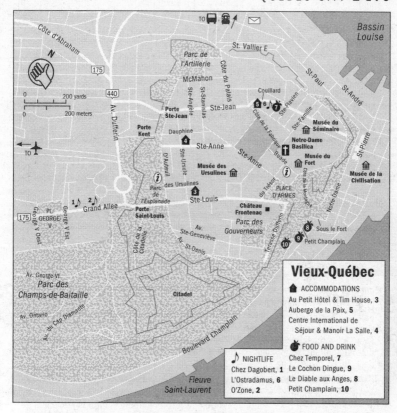

Vieux-Québec

⚓ ACCOMMODATIONS

Au Petit Hôtel & Tim House, 3
Auberge de la Paix, 5
Centre International de
  Séjour & Manoir La Salle, 4

🍴 FOOD AND DRINK

♪ NIGHTLIFE
Chez Dagobert, 1
L'Ostradamus, 6
O'Zone, 2

Chez Temporel, 7
Le Cochon Dingue, 9
Le Diable aux Anges, 8
Petit Champlain, 10

Hotlines: Tél-Aide distress center, ☎686-2433. Operates daily noon-midnight. **Viol-Secours (sexual assault line),** ☎522-2120. Counselors on duty M-F 9am-4pm and on-call 24hr. **Center for Suicide Prevention,** ☎529-0015. Operates daily 8am-midnight. **Info-Santé,** ☎648-2626, handles bi-gay-lesbian concerns. **Poison Control,** ☎656-8090.

Emergency: Police, ☎911 (city); 800-461-2131 (province). **Info-santé (medical info),** ☎648-2626. Both 24hr.

Post Office: 300 rue St-Paul (☎694-6176). Open M-F 8am-5:45pm. **Postal code:** G1K 3W0. **Area code:** 418.

📷 ACCOMMODATIONS

For Bed & Breakfast referrals, **Le Transit,** 1050 ave. Turnbull, Québec City G1R 2X8 (☎647-6802; call 8am-noon or 4-9pm) will help. Rooms start at $50 for one or two people, and hosts are usually bilingual. If parking is a problem (usually the case in Old Québec) and you must make use of the underground parking areas, ask your host about discount parking passes. Most places offer them, which means paying $8.50 rather than $12.50 for a 24hr. pass.

Centre international de séjour (HI-C), 19 rue Ste-Ursule (☎694-0755), 1 block north of rue St-Jean at Dauphine. Follow Côte d'Abraham uphill from the bus station until it joins ave. Dufferin. Turn left on St-Jean, pass through the walls, and walk uphill, to your right, on Ste-Ursule. If driving, follow St-Louis into the Old City and take the 2nd left past the walls onto Ste-Ursule. Diverse, young clientele, fabulous location, and an array of extras (laundry, microwave, TV, pool table, ping-pong tables, living room, kitchen, cafeteria, Internet access) make this place prime pickin's. Reduced rate parking at a city garage.

Check-out 10am. Lockout 11pm, but the front desk will let you in if you flash your key. 250 beds $17, non-members $21; private rooms $46/$50. Breakfast 8-10am (continental $3.75, full $4.50). Usually full July-Aug.; make reservations or arrive early.

Auberge de la Paix, 31 rue Couillard (☎694-0735). Take St-Jean into Vieux Québec, and take Couillard when it branches left. If you can manage without TV or Internet access for a few days, check yourself into this friendly, ideally located "peace hostel" (look for the peace sign suspended above the door). The atmosphere is laid-back (there are no locks on the doors, but this doesn't seem to be a problem). Continental breakfast included (8-10am). Curfew 2am with all-day access. Kitchen open all day. 60 beds in 14 co-ed rooms, $19. Linen $2.50. Reservations necessary July-Aug.

Au Petit Hôtel, 3 ruelle des Ursulines (☎694-0965), just off of rue Ste-Ursule. This tidy little hotel is a great deal for 2 people. TV, free local phone, private bath, and refrigerator in each room. May-Oct. rooms from $60 for 1 or 2 occupants, continental breakfast included; Nov.-May rooms from $45. Audaciously combines a downtown location with free parking in winter ($5 May-Oct.).

Montmartre Canadien, 1675, ch. St-Louis (☎686-0867). Located on the outskirts of the city in Sillery, this small white house behind the main building at 1669 is ideal for those willing to trade proximity for privacy; located in a religious sanctuary run by Assumptionist monks, the grounds have a relaxed, almost ascetic setting. Take bus #25 or 11. Dirt cheap, immaculate singles $17; doubles $30; triples $42. Common showers. Reserve 2-3 weeks in advance.

Universite Laval, Pavillon Alphonse-Marie-Parent (☎656-2921), rents beds from May-Aug. Linen, towels and phones. Singles $25, students $21; doubles $35/$30.

Manoir La Salle, 18 rue Ste-Ursule (☎692-9953), opposite the youth hostel. The clean private rooms in this ornate Victorian mansion fill quickly, especially in summer. Shared bathrooms. Singles $35; doubles $55, with private bath $70. Reservations necessary.

Tim House, 84 rue Ste-Louis (☎694-0776). Adjacent to Au Petit Hotel and run by the same folks (check-in at Au Petit). A lovely B&B. 3rd fl. rooms have shared baths; a delectable breakfast is included. Rooms $40-70, depending on the season. Reservations necessary. Parking $5.

You can obtain a list of nearby **campgrounds** from the **Maison du Tourisme de Québec** (see **Practical Information,** p. 174), or write to **Tourisme Québec,** Montréal, PQ H3C 2W3 (☎800-363-7777; open daily 9am-5pm). A good camping option is **Municipal de Beauport,** Beauport. Take Autoroute 40E, get off at Exit 321 at rue Labelle onto Hwy. 369, turn left, and follow the signs marked "camping." Bus #55 to 800 will also take you to this 135-site campground on a hill over the Montmorency River. A swimming pool, canoes ($8 per hr.), showers ($1 per 5min.), and laundry facilities ($1 per load) are available. (☎666-2228. Open June to early Sept. Sites $19, with hook-up $24; $114/$144 per week.)

◐ L'HAUTE CUISINE

In general, rue Buade, St-Jean, and Cartier, as well as the **Place Royale** and **Petit Champlain** areas offer the widest selection of food and drink. The **Grande Allée** may seem like heaven to the hungry, but its prices may encourage you to keep strolling.

The best bet for a simple and affordable meal doesn't have to be a fast-food joint. Traditional *Québecois* food is not only appetizing, but often economical. One of the most filling yet inexpensive meals is a *croque-monsieur*, a large, open-faced sandwich with ham and melted cheese (about $6), usually served with salad. *Québecois* French onion soup, slathered with melted cheese, is not to be missed and can be found in virtually every restaurant and cafe. It is usually served with either bats of French bread or *tourtière*, a thick meat pie. Other specialties include the ever-versatile *crêpe*, stuffed accordingly to serve as either an entree or a dessert. The **Casse-Crêpe Breton,** 1136 St-Jean, offers many choices of fillings in their "make your own combination" crêpes for dinner ($3.50-6), as well as scrumptious dessert options. (Open daily 7:30am-midnight). **Pâtisserie au Palet d'Or,** 60 rue Garneau, bursts with culinary excellence—$3.50 will win you a salmon sandwich and $1.60 a golden baguette. (☎692-2488. Open daily 7am-9pm.)

▓ **Le Diable aux Anges,** 28 Boul. Champlain and 39 Petit Champlain (☎692-4674). Enhances the European aura of rue Petit Champlain with its dimly lit, colonial interior. A number of traditional *Québecois* dishes offer seldom-found variety to the usual cafe/bistro fare. Breakfast is the best value, with many items offered a la carte. Try the *Oeuf Gaspesiene* ($10), an English muffin topped with smoked salmon, poached egg, and hollandaise sauce, with herbed potatoes, fruit, and beans. Open 9am-11pm.

Le Café Buade, 31 rue Buade (☎692-3909), is renowned for its succulent prime rib, but it'll cost you $15-20. For those short on money, breakfast ($4) and lunch specials ($11) are large and delicious. Open daily 7am-midnight.

Le Cochon Dingue, 46 bd. Champlain (☎692-2013), meaning "crazy pig," is quickly becoming a culinary landmark in Québec. Entrees are great; desserts heavenly. Consider spending your money on a few extra chocolate pear pies ($4) instead of the hog-themed t-shirt. Open June-Aug. M-Th 7am-midnight, F 7am-1am, Sa-Su 8am-1am; Sept.-May M-F 7am-11pm, Sa-Su 8am-11pm.

Chez Temporel, 25 rue Couillard (☎694-1813). Stay off the tourist path but remain within your budget at this genuine *café Québecois*, discreetly tucked in a side alley off rue St-Jean, near the Auberge de la Paix. Besides the usual cafe staples (sandwiches $4-7), it offers exotic spirits ($4.50). Open daily 7am-2am.

Restaurant Liban, 23 rue d'Auteuil (☎694-1888), off rue St-Jean. Grab a great lunch or a late-night bite to go, or enjoy it on their outdoor patio. Tabouleh and hummus plates $3.50, both with pita bread. Excellent falafel ($4.50) and baklava ($2). Open daily 9am-4:30pm.

◉ SIGHTS

The **Fortifications of Québec** compose a 6½km stretch of wall surrounding *Vieux Québec* (the Old City), inside of which are most of the city's historic attractions. Monuments are clearly marked and explained; still, you'll get more out of the town if you consult the *Greater Québec Area Tourist Guide*, which contains a walking tour of the Old City. Don't be tempted by bus tours; although it takes one to two days to explore all of Vieux Québec's narrow, hilly streets and historic sites on foot, this is by far the best way to absorb its charm. The **Funiculaire** will carry passengers between Upper-Town and Place Royal and the Quartier Petit-Champlain for $1.25. (☎692-1132. Open 7:30am-midnight.)

CAP DIAMANT. Climbing to the top of Cap Diamant for a view of the city is a good way to orient oneself. Take Terrasse Dufferin to the Promenade des Gouverneurs. Just north is the **Citadel,** the largest North American fortification still guarded by troops—who knows why? Resist the impulse to attack it. Visitors can witness the **changing of the guard** daily at 10am and the **beating of the retreat** W-Sa at 6pm. Tours also available. (☎694-2815. Open daily Apr. to mid-May 10am-4pm; mid-May to mid-June 9am-5pm; mid-June to Aug. 9am-6pm; Sept. 9am-4pm; Oct. 10am-3pm. $5.50, seniors $4, under 18 $2.75, family $13.75)

PLACE-ROYALE AND QUARTIER PETIT-CHAMPLAIN. One of Old Québec's highlights is the crowded thoroughfare of **Rue du Petit-Champlain,** the oldest street in North America. Along either side of this narrow passageway, modern visitors will find a host of cafes, craft shops, trendy boutiques, and restaurants. Each evening, the **Cafe-Theater Le Petit Champlain** presents *Québecois* music, singing, and dancing. (68 rue du Petit-Champlain. ☎692-2631. Call for schedules. Tickets for most shows $25-$30.) **Place-Royale,** home to the oldest permanent European settlement in Canada (dating from 1608), can be reached quickly by taking rue Sous-le-Fort from the bottom of the Funiculaire. The **Place-Royale Information Center** provides free 45min. tours of this historic district. (☎643-6631. Open 10am-5pm.) Dating back to 1688, **L'Eglise Notre-Dame-des-Victoires** is the oldest church in Canada. (32 rue Sous-le-Fort. ☎692-1650. Open May to mid-Oct. M-F 9:30am-5pm, Sa-Su 9:30am-4:30pm, rest of the year 10am-4:30pm. Free admission and tours.) The **Musee de la Civilisation** celebrates Québec's past, present, and future, with tours in English and French. It can be reached easily by walking down rue Sous-le-Fort at the bottom of the Funiculaire and following the series of signs. (85 rue Dalhousie. ☎643-2158. Open late June to early Sept. 10am-7pm; off-season Tu-Su 10am-5pm. $7, students $4, seniors $6.)

PARLIAMENT HILL. The **Assemblee Nationale,** at Grande Allee and Ave. Honore-Mercier, is located just outside the wall of the city. Finished in 1886, the building was designed in the style of Loius XIII. Lively debates can be observed from the visitors' gallery, and both English and French-speakers have recourse to simultaneous translation earphones. *(☎ 643-7239. Open late June to early Sept. M-F 9am-4:30pm, Sa-Su 10am-4:30pm; hours vary during rest of year. 30min. tours are free, but advance reservations are recommended.)* The **Capital Observatory,** just off Grande Allee, offers breathtaking views of the city from the highest observing place in town. *(1037 rue de la Chevrotiere. ☎ 644-9841. Open daily 10am-5pm. $4, students and senior $3.)*

BATTLEFIELDS. The **Parc des Champs-de-Bataille** or **Plains of Abraham,** located adjacent to the Citadel along Ave. George-VI, can be reached from Grande Allee. The interpretation center has exhibits on the history of the battlefields, where French forces under Montcalm fell to the British under General Wolfe in 1759. *(☎ 648-4071. Open daily mid-May to early Sept. 10am-5:30pm; call for times during the rest of the year.)* Located on the premises of the Battlefields Park, the **Musée du Québec** houses eclectic modern and *Québecois* art while playing host to visiting exhibitions. *(☎ 646-3330. Open daily June-Sept. 10am-6pm, W 10am-9pm; Sept.-June Tu-Su 10am-5pm, W 10am-9pm. $7, students $2.75, seniors $6.)*

CHÂTEAU FRONTENAC. The Château Frontenac, with its grand architecture and green copper roofs, is perhaps the most recognizable structure in the city and is thought to be the most photographed hotel in the world. Should you be windswept by the hype, the hotel provides tours of its opulence, highlighting its place in history with photographs of famous visitors, including the Allied leaders that conferenced here during World War II. *(1 rue des Carrieres. ☎ 692-3861 or 691-2166. Daily tours leave hourly 10am-6pm from mid-May to mid-Oct.; during the rest of the year, tours are Sa-Su only from 12:30pm-5pm; reservations highly recommended. $6.50, seniors $5.50, under 16 $3.75.)*

OTHER ATTRACTIONS. With its shimmering golden altar and ornate stained-glass windows, the **Notre-Dame de Québec Basilica** is one of the oldest cathedrals in North America. Located at rue de Buade and rue Ste-Famille, the Basilica shows a fantastic 45min. light show, the **"Act of Faith,"** which relays the history of the church. *(☎ 694-0665. Open daily 9:30am-4:30pm. Free. Shows daily May-Oct.; times vary. $7.50.)* The **Musée de l'Amerique Francaise,** located on the grounds of the **Québec Seminary** just down the street from the Basilica, is an excellent museum whose informative exhibits recount the details of Francophone settlement in North America. *(9 rue de l'Universite. ☎ 692-2843. Open Tu-Su 10am-5pm. $3, students and seniors $2.)*

🎵🎭 ENTERTAINMENT AND NIGHTLIFE

Images of "Le Bonhomme de Neige" will plaster the snow-covered city in anticipation of the raucous annual **Winter Carnival,** which breaks the tedium of northern winters and lifts spirits from Jan 26 to Feb. 11, 2001 *(☎ 626-3716).* The annual **Summer Festival,** with free outdoor concerts and lavish merrymaking, will mean packed hostels from July 5 to July 15, 2001 *(☎ 692-4540).* Throughout the summer, the **Plein Art** exhibition floods the Pigeonnier on Grande-Allée with arts and crafts *(☎ 694-0260).* **Les nuits Black,** Québec's burgeoning jazz festival, bebops the city for two weeks in late June. But Québec's most festive day of the year—eclipsing even Canada Day—is June 24, **la Fête nationale du Québec** (St-Jean-Baptiste Day). This celebration of *Québecois* culture features free concerts, a bonfire, fireworks, and 5 million roaring drunk acolytes of John the Baptist *(☎ 640-0799).*

OUTSIDE THE WALLS. The Grande Allée's many restaurants are interspersed with *Bar Discothèques,* where 20-something crowds dance till dawn. **Chez Dagobert,** 600 Grande Allée, saturates the air with pop and dance sounds. Two dance floors and an adjoining bar give plenty of room to mingle. *(☎ 522-0393. Outside bar open daily 3pm-3am, inside club 10pm-3am. No cover.)* A bit less hectic is **O'Zone,** 570 Grande Allée, where the folks linger at the bar before ascending to the 2nd-story dance floor for a latenight medley of rock, alternative, dance, and hip-hop. *(☎ 529-7932. Open M-Sa*

11am-3am, Su 1pm-3am. No cover.) The gay scene in Québec City is limited, but alive. **Le Ballon Rouge,** 811 St-Jean, several blocks beyond the walls of the Old City, is a favorite dance club where dimly lit pool tables coexist with neon rainbows, and tight clothing is essential. (☎647-9227. Open daily 5pm-3am. No cover.)

INSIDE THE WALLS. Québec City's young, visible punk contingent clusters around rue St-Jean and several nearby sidestreets, but more laid-back nightclubs find a niche here too. A more traditional Québec evening awaits at **Les Yeux Bleux,** 1117½ rue St-Jean, a local hangout where *chansonniers* perform nightly. (☎694-9118. Open daily 8pm-3am. No cover.) **La Fourmi Atomik,** 33 rue d'Auteuil, features underground rock and themed music nights. (☎694-1473. Open daily 1pm-3am; Oct.-May 4pm-3am. No cover. 18+.) **L'Ostradamus,** 29 rue Couillard, throws live jazz/techno over its smoke-drenched, "spiritual" ambience with artsy Thai decor. (☎694-9560. Open daily 8pm-3am. Cover some nights $4.)

DAYTRIP FROM QUÉBEC CITY

ILE-D'ORLÉANS. Originally called *Ile de Bacchus* because of the multitudinous wild grapes fermenting here, the **Ile-d'Orléans** remains a sparsely populated retreat of small villages and endless strawberry fields. The island is located about 10km downstream from Québec on the St-Laurent, making it an ideal excursion by car (public transportation doesn't access the island, and the highway stretch to the island makes biking impossible). Take Rte. 75 to Autoroute 440 Est, on to Rte. 368, and cross over the only bridge leading to the island (Pont de l'Ile). A tour of the island covers 64km. **The Manoir Mauvide-Genest,** in St-Jean, is a private museum flaunting crafts and traditional colonial furniture. (*1451, ch. Royal.* ☎*829-2630. Open daily June to mid-Oct. 10am-5pm. $4, students and seniors $2.50, under 14 $2.*)

Exiting Ile-d'Orléans, turn right (east) onto Hwy. 138 (bd. Ste-Anne) to view the splendid **Chute Montmorency** (Montmorency Falls). In winter, vapors from the falls form a frozen mist that screens the running water. About 20km along Hwy. 138 lies **Ste-Anne-de-Beaupré** (Orlean Express buses link it to Québec City for $5, see **Practical Information**). This small town's entire *raison d'être* is the famous double-spired **Basilique Ste-Anne-de-Beaupré,** which houses the alleged forearm bone of Ste. Anne, mother to the Virgin Mary. How did it get to Canada? The pilgrims who visit by the hundreds of thousands each year don't question the logistics, and the church's miraculous power is evidenced by the racks of discarded crutches inside. (*10018 ave. Royale.* ☎*827-3781. Open daily early May to mid-Sept. 6am-9:30pm.*)

ONTARIO

Now an Anglo political counterbalance to French Québec, this populous central province raises the ire of peripheral regions of Canada due to its high concentration of power and wealth. In the south, world-class Toronto shines—multicultural, enormous, vibrant, clean, and generally safe. Yuppified suburbs, an occasional college town, and farms surround this sprawling metropolis. In the east, the national capital Ottawa sits on Ontario's border with Québec. To the north, layers of cottage country and ski resorts give way to a pristine wilderness that is as much French and Native Canadian as it is British.

PRACTICAL INFORMATION

Capital: Toronto.

Visitor Info: Customer Service Branch of the **Ontario Ministry of Culture, Tourism, and Recreation** (☎800-668-2746, 24hr. automated info). Send written requests to **Tourism Ontario,** 1 Concord Gate, 9th fl., Dawn Mills, ON M3C 3NC.

Drinking Age: 19. **Postal Abbreviation:** ON. **Sales Tax:** 8%; 5% on rooms; 7% GST.

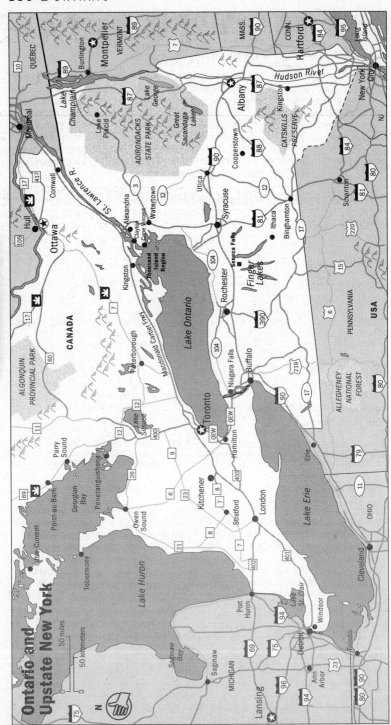

Ontario and Upstate New York

TORONTO ☎ 416

Once a prim and proper Victorian city where even window-shopping was prohibited on the Sabbath, Toronto is now dubbed the world's most multicultural by the United Nations. The city has spent millions in recent decades on spectacular public works projects: the world's tallest "free-standing" structure (the CN tower), the biggest retractable roof (the Sky Dome), outstanding lakefront development, and sponsorship of arts and museums. Cosmetically, Toronto's skyscrapers and neatly gridded streets aspire to the urban grandeur of New York, drawing Hollywood producers seeking to make a New York movie at Toronto prices. But New York it is not; one film crew, after dirtying a street to make it look more like a gritty "American" avenue, went on coffee break and returned to find their set spotless again, swept by the vigilant city maintenance department.

✈ GETTING THERE AND AWAY

Airport: Pearson International (☎247-7678), about 20km west of Toronto via Hwy. 401. Take bus #58A west from Lawrence W. subway. **Pacific Western Transportation** (☎905-564-6333) runs buses every 20min. to downtown hotels ($13.75, round-trip $23.65) and every 40min. to Yorkdale ($7.60), York Mills ($8.70), and Islington ($7.10) subway stations. Buses run 5:30am-12:15am.

Trains: All trains leave from **Union Station,** 65 Front St. (☎366-8411), at Bay and York. Subway: Union. **VIA Rail** (☎366-8411) cannonballs to Montréal (5½hr., 7 per day, $97); Windsor (4hr., 4-5 per day, $72); New York City (12hr., 2 per day, $95); and Chicago (11hr., 2 per day, $146). Ticket office open M-F 8am-11:30pm, Sa 8am-6:30pm, Su 7am-11:30pm; station open M-Sa 5:30am-12:45am, Su 6:30am-12:45am.

Buses: Trentway-Wagar (☎393-7911) and **Greyhound** (☎367-8747) operate from 610 Bay St., just north of Dundas St. Subway: St. Patrick or Dundas. Trentway-Wagar has service to Montréal (7hr., 7 per day, $79). Greyhound goes to Ottawa (5½-7hr., 9 per day, $56); Calgary (49hr., 5 per day, $269); Vancouver (2½ days, 3 per day, $312); and New York City (11hr., 8 per day, $104). Ticket office open daily 5am-1am.

▣ GETTING AROUND

The TTC's subway and streetcars are the easiest way to get around the city, but if you must drive, avoid rush hour (4-7pm). A flashing green light means that you can go straight or turn left freely, as the opposing traffic has a red light. **Parking** on the street is hard to find and usually carries a 1hr. limit, except on Su and at night (until 7am), when spaces are free and abundant. Day parking generally costs inbound daytrippers $3-4 at outlying subway stations; parking overnight at the subway stations is prohibited. Parking lots within the city run at least $12 for 24 hours. (7am-7am), although some all-day lots downtown on King St. sell unguarded spots for $4-6. Free, unmetered parking is available in **Rosedale,** a residential neighborhood northeast of Bloor and Sherbourne St., about 3km from downtown. To combat transportation problems, city officials enforce traffic and parking regulations zealously, so don't tempt them. Towing is a common occurrence, even for locals; the **non-emergency police number** (☎416-808-2222) has an answering system to help you find your car's temporary new home.

Ferries: Toronto Island Ferry Service (☎392-8194, recording 392-8193). Ferries to Centre Island, Wards Island, and Hanlans Point leave from the foot of Bay St. Service daily every 30min. 8am-11:45pm; less often in winter. Round-trip $5; seniors, students, and ages 15-19 $3; ages 2-14 $2.

Public Transit: Toronto Transit Commission (TTC) (☎393-4000). A network of 2 long subway lines and many bus and streetcar routes. After dark, buses are required to stop anywhere along a route at a female passenger's request. Subway service begins M-Sa 6am and Su 9am, with the last trains leaving downtown at 1:30am; buses cover subway routes after that. Fare $2 (5 tokens $8), seniors and students with ID $1.40, under 13

50¢ (10 for $4). M-Sa 1-day travel pass $7. Su and holidays, families receive unlimited travel for $7. Free transfers among subway, buses, and streetcars, but only at stations.

Taxis: Co-op Cabs, ☎ 504-2667.

Jump-On/Jump-Off Service: Moose Travel Co. Ltd. (☎ 905-853-4762 or 888-816-6673). A series of expeditions founded by former backpackers, in which you can hop on and off a bus full of hostelers at dozens of destinations throughout Eastern Canada at your own convenience. 3-6 days of travel time can spread over 5 months. Offers 3 routes through Ontario and Québec ($219-379).

Bike Rental: Brown's Sports and Bike Rental, 2447 Bloor St. W. (763-4176). $22 per day, $48 per weekend, $55 per week. $300 deposit or credit card required. Open M-W 9:30am-6pm, Th-F 9:30am-8pm, Sa 9:30am-5:30pm.

▦ ORIENTATION

Toronto's streets form a grid pattern. Addresses on north-south streets increase toward the north, away from Lake Ontario. **Yonge St.** is the main north-south route, dividing the city and the streets perpendicular to it into east and west. Numbering for both sides starts at Yonge St. and increases as you move away in either direction. West of Yonge St., the main arteries are **Bay St., University Ave., Spadina Ave.,** and **Bathurst St.** The major east-west routes include, from the water north, **Front St., Queen St., Dundas St., College St., Bloor St.,** and **Eglington St.**

Downtown Toronto splits into many distinctive neighborhoods. Thanks to zoning regulations that require developers to include housing and retail space in commercial construction, many people live downtown. **Chinatown** centers on Dundas St. W. between Bay St. and Spadina Ave. Formerly the Jewish market of the 1920s, **Kensington Market,** on Kensington Ave., Augusta Ave., and the western half of Baldwin St., is now a largely Portuguese neighborhood with many good restaurants, vintage clothing shops, and an outdoor bazaar. A strip of old factories, stores, and warehouses on **Queen St. W.,** from University Ave. to Bathurst St., is a good place to shop during the day and go club-hopping at night. The ivy-covered Gothic buildings and magnificent quadrangles of the **University of Toronto** occupy about 200 acres in the center of the city. **The Annex,** Bloor St. W. at the Spadina subway, has an artistic ambiance and an excellent range of budget restaurants (see **Food,** below). Afterwards, hit the numerous bars and nightclubs along Bloor St. heading west. **Yorkville,** just north of Bloor between Yonge St. and Avenue Rd., was once the communal home of flower children and folk guitarists. **Cabbagetown,** just east of Yonge St., bounded by Gerrard St. E., Wellesley, and Sumach St., takes its name from the Irish immigrants who used to plant the vegetable in their yards. Today, professionals and the only crowing rooster in the city inhabit the renowned Victorian houses. The **Gay and Lesbian Village,** around Church and Wellesley St., offers fine outdoor cafes.

On Front St. between Sherbourne and Yonge St., the **Theater District** supports enough venues to whet any cultural appetite. Music, food, ferry rides, dance companies, and art all dock at the **Harbourfront** (☎ 973-3000), on Queen's Quay W. from York to Bathurst St., on the lake. The three main **Toronto Islands,** accessible by ferry (see **Practical Information,** above), offer beaches, bike rentals, and an amusement park. East from the harbor, the beaches along and south of Queen's St. E., between Woodbine and Victoria, boast a popular boardwalk. Five km east of the city center, the rugged 16m stretch of **Scarborough Bluffs** rises over the lakeshore.

Three more ethnic enclaves lie 15 to 30min. from downtown by public transit. **Corso Italia** surrounds St. Clair W. at Dufferin St.; take the subway to St. Clair W. and bus #512 west. **Little India** is at Gerrard St. E. and Coxwell; ride the subway to Coxwell, then take bus #22 south to the second Gerard St. stop. Better known as **"the Danforth," Greektown** (subway: Pape) is on Danforth Ave. at Pape Ave.

For an extended stay or travel outside the city center, it is best to buy the orange *Downtown and Metro Toronto Visitor's Map Guide* from a drug store or tourist shop ($2.50). The *Ride Guide*, free at all TTC stations and tourism info booths, explains metro area subway and bus routes.

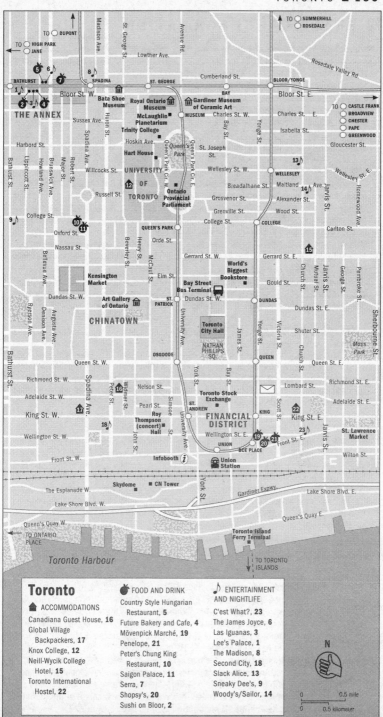

TO DUPONT

TO HIGH PARK
JANE

TO SUMMERHILL
ROSEDALE

Madison Ave.
St. George St.
Avenue Rd.
Lowther Ave.

Rosedale Valley Rd.

BATHURST
SPADINA
ST. GEORGE
BLOOR/YONGE
Cumberland St.

Bloor St. W.
Bloor St. E.

Bata Shoe Museum
Royal Ontario Museum
Gardiner Museum of Ceramic Art

THE ANNEX
Sussex Ave.
MUSEUM
Charles St. W.
BAY

TO CASTLE FRANK
BROADVIEW
CHESTER
PAPE
GREENWOOD

McLaughlin Planetarium
Trinity College
Charles St. E.
Isabella St.
Gloucester St.

Harbord St.
Spadina Ave.
Hoskin Ave.
Hart House

Queen's Park Cir. W.
Queen's Park Cir. E.
St. Joseph St.
Wellesley St. W.

WELLESLEY

Willcocks St.
UNIVERSITY
Breadalbane St.
Maitland

Robert St.
Major St.
Brunswick Ave.
Russell St.
OF
TORONTO
Ontario Provincial Parliament
Grosvenor St.
Alexander St.
Jarvis St.
Homewood Ave.

Wellesley St. E.

Grenville St.
Wood St.

College St.
Oxford St.
Nassau St.
QUEEN'S PARK
Orde St.
College St.
COLLEGE
Carlton St.

Bellevue Ave.
Lippincott St.
Howland Ave.

Gerrard St. W.
Gerrard St. E.

World's Biggest Bookstore
Gould St.

Kensington Market
Dundas St. W.
Bay Street Bus Terminal
ST. PATRICK
Dundas St. E.
DUNDAS

Denison Ave.
Augusta Ave.
Ryerson Ave.
Beverley St.
Henry St.
McCaul St.
Elm St.

Art Gallery of Ontario
CHINATOWN

Church St.
Mutual St.
George St.
Pembroke St.
Sherbourne St.

Moss Park

Toronto City Hall
Shuter St.

OSGOODE
NATHAN PHILLIPS SQ.
Queen St. W.
James St.
Yonge St.
Victoria St.
QUEEN
Queen St. E.
Church St.

Richmond St. W.
Nelson St.
Richmond St. E.
Lombard St.

Adelaide St. W.
Adelaide St. E.

King St. W.
Toronto Stock Exchange
ST. ANDREW
Pearl St.
Roy Thompson (concert) Hall
FINANCIAL DISTRICT
KING
King St. E.

St. Lawrence Market

Spadina Ave.
Peter St.
Widmer St.
Simcoe St.
John St.
University Ave.
York St.
Bay St.
Scott St.
Jarvis St.

Wellington St. W.
Wellington St. E.
UNION
BCE PLACE
Front St. E.
Wilton St.

Infobooth
Union Station

Front St. W.

The Esplanade W.
Skydome
CN Tower
Gardiner Expwy
Lake Shore Blvd. E.
Lake Shore Blvd. W.
York St.

Queen's Quay W.
Queen's Quay E.

TO ONTARIO PLACE

Toronto Island Ferry Terminal

Toronto Harbour
TO TORONTO ISLANDS

Toronto

🏠 ACCOMMODATIONS

Canadiana Guest House, 16
Global Village Backpackers, 17
Knox College, 12
Neill-Wycik College Hotel, 15
Toronto International Hostel, 22

🍴 FOOD AND DRINK

Country Style Hungarian Restaurant, 5
Future Bakery and Cafe, 4
Mövenpick Marché, 19
Penelope, 21
Peter's Chung King Restaurant, 10
Saigon Palace, 11
Serra, 7
Shopsy's, 20
Sushi on Bloor, 2

🎵 ENTERTAINMENT AND NIGHTLIFE

C'est What?, 23
The James Joyce, 6
Las Iguanas, 3
Lee's Palace, 1
The Madison, 8
Second City, 18
Slack Alice, 13
Sneaky Dee's, 9
Woody's/Sailor, 14

N

0   0.5 mile
0   0.5 kilometer

🛂 PRACTICAL INFORMATION

Visitor Info: The **Metropolitan Toronto Convention and Visitors Association (MTCVA),** 207 Queens Quay W. (☎203-2500 or 800-363-1990), mails out info and answers questions by phone. For in-person assistance, head to the **Info T.O.,** 255 Front St. W., at the Metro Toronto Convention Centre. Open M-F 8am-5pm.

Student Travel Office: Travel CUTS, 187 College St. (☎979-2406), just west of University Ave. Subway: Queen's Park. Open M and Th-F 9am-5pm, Tu 9:30am-5pm, W 9am-7pm, Sa 10am-3pm. Second office at 74 Gerrard St. E. (☎977-0441). Subway: College. Open M-F 10am-6pm.

Currency Exchange: Toronto Currency Exchange, 363 Yonge St. (☎598-5096), at Dundas St., offers the best rates around. Open daily 10am-8pm. Also at 2 Walton St. (☎599-5821). Open daily 8:30am-5:30pm. **Royal Bank of Canada,** 200 Bay St. Plaza (☎800-769-2511, foreign exchange 974-5535), exchanges around the city. Branches generally open M-F 10am-4pm; call for each branch's specific hrs. **Money Mart,** 617 Yonge St. (☎920-4146), has 24hr. service and some fees. Subway: Bloor/Yonge. French- and English-speaking **ATMs** across the city are perhaps the easiest way to get Canadian currency. Fees, however, are $1-2.

Hotlines: Rape Crisis, ☎597-8808. **Services for the Disabled, Info Ability** ☎800-665-9092. **Toronto Gay and Lesbian Phone Line,** ☎964-6600. Open M-F 7-10pm. **Events Hotline,** ☎392-0458.

Post Office: Adelaide Station, 31 Adelaide St. E. (☎214-2353 or 214-2352). Subway: King. Open M-F 8am-5:45pm. **Postal code:** M5C 1J0. **Area code:** 416 (city), 905 (outskirts). In text, 416 unless noted otherwise.

🛏 ACCOMMODATIONS

Cut-rate hotels concentrate around Jarvis and Gerrard St. The University of Toronto provides cheap sleep for budget travelers; contact the **U of T Housing Service,** 214 College St., at St. George St., for $20-45 rooms (☎978-8045; open M-F 8:45am-4:30pm; reservations recommended). The **Downtown Association of Bed and Breakfast Guest Houses** places guests in renovated Victorian homes (☎483-8032; singles $50-85, doubles $75-130). Because it is difficult to regulate these registries, visit a B&B before you commit.

Global Village Backpackers, 460 King St. W. (☎703-8540 or 888-844-7875). Subway: St. Andrew. An efficient, highly social backpacker support system, with staff that make you feel at home. 195 beds in the centrally located, brightly colored former Spadina Hotel. Travelers convene at the cool bar and by the pool table inside and on the outdoor patio, where BBQs are held nightly 7-9:30pm. Lockers and Internet access available. Kitchen, laundry, in-house Travel CUTS branch. Reception 24hr. Dorms $25; doubles $56 during summer, slightly less off-season. $2-4 off for ISIC or HI members.

Canadiana Guest House & Backpackers, 42 Widmer St., off Adelaide St. W. (☎598-9090 or 877-215-1225). Subway: Osgoode. 70 extra-long homemade beds in attractive, newly renovated Victorian townhouses. Small, comfortable living room, A/C, free continental breakfast, and Internet access for a slightly older and quieter hostel crowd. Kitchen and locker facilities available. Check-in 8am-midnight during summer; 8am-11pm in winter. Dorms $25; private doubles $60.

Neill-Wycik College Hotel, 96 Gerrard St. E. (☎977-2320 or 800-268-4358). Subway: College. Small, clean rooms, some with beautiful views of the city. Kitchen on every floor. Laundry, roof deck, sauna. Family rooms and lockers available. Open early May to late Aug. Check-in after 4pm. Check-out 10am. Dorms $20; singles $35; doubles $52. Students, seniors, and HI members get a 20% discount.

Toronto International Hostel (HI-C), 76 Church St. (☎971-4440 or 877-848-8737), at King. Subway: Dundas. Recently relocated hostel in a great downtown location. Kitchen, laundry facilities, and a lounge. Reception 24hr. Check-in after noon. Check-out 11am. Dorms $19, non-members $23. Linen $2. Reservations recommended in the summer. Additional location June-Aug. at 76 Mutual St. (☎971-7073; $22.50/27).

Knox College, 59 St. George St. (978-0168; call M-F 10am-5pm). Subway: Queen's Park or St. George. In the heart of campus, Canada's picturesque Presbyterian Seminary offers huge rooms with wooden floors around an idyllic courtyard. The movie *Good Will Hunting* used Knox rooms to simulate the interiors of Harvard and MIT. Open mid-May to late Aug. Singles $35, students $33; doubles $45. Reserve rooms at least 3 weeks ahead of time; 1 night's deposit required in advance.

YWCA-Woodlawn Residence, 80 Woodlawn Ave. E. (☎923-8454), off Yonge St. Subway: Summerhill. 144 rooms for women only, in a nice neighborhood uptown. Breakfast, kitchen, TV lounges, and laundry facilities. Reception M-F 7:30am-11:30pm, Sa-Su 7:30am-7:30pm. Small, neat singles $48-54; doubles $62; private bath available. Beds in basement dormitory $22. 10% senior discount. Linen $3 deposit.

◐ FOOD

An immigration surge has made Toronto a haven for international food, with over 5000 restaurants squeezed into the metropolitan area. **Village by the Grange,** at McCaul and Dundas near the Art Gallery of Ontario, is a vast collection of super-cheap restaurants and vendors—Chinese, Thai, Middle Eastern, you name it (generally open 11am-7pm). "L.L.B.O." posted on the window of a restaurant means that it has a liquor license. The cheapest options are hot-dog stands (offerings range from basic to vegetarian to venison $2-3) that line most main streets in Toronto. Some of the standouts can be found on **Bloor St. W.** and in **Chinatown.** For fresh produce, go to **Kensington Market** or the **St. Lawrence Market** at King St. E. and Sherbourne, six blocks east of the King subway stop.

THE ANNEX

Serra, 378 Bloor St. W. (☎922-6999). Subway: Spadina. A quiet, tastefully decorated oasis amid the bustle of the Annex. Delicately prepared angel hair and grilled chicken ($9.45). Open daily noon-midnight.

Sushi on Bloor, 515 Bloor St. W (☎516-3456). Subway: Bathurst. This friendly, well-lit joint is filled with hipsters scarfing down fresh, reasonably priced sushi (6 pieces $4-5), including lunch ($6) and dinner (starting from $5.50) specials. Open daily noon-11pm.

Future Bakery & Cafe, 483 Bloor St. W. (☎922-5875). Subway: Spadina. Fresh baked cakes ($4.25) and pastries charge up the young student crowd by day, and beer ($4-5) on the street corner patio winds them down after dark. Open daily 7:30am-2am.

Country Style Hungarian Restaurant, 450 Bloor St. W. (☎537-1745). Subway: Spadina. Hearty stews, soups, and casseroles, just like in Hungary. Meals come in small (plenty) and large (huge) portions. Schnitzel $9.75. Entrees $4-11. Open daily 11am-10pm.

CHINATOWN

Saigon Palace, 454 Spadina Ave. (☎968-1623), at College St. Subway: Spadina. An unassuming Vietnamese restaurant with great spring rolls and natural juice drinks ($3). Popular with locals. Beef, chicken, or vegetable dishes over rice or noodles $4-8. Open M-Th 9am-10pm, F-Sa 9am-11pm.

Peter's Chung King Restaurant, 281 College St. W. (☎928-2936). Subway: Spadina. A picture of Chris de Burgh (of "Lady in Red" fame) adorns the window, with Chris's note proclaiming "Wonderful Food!" He's not the only one who thinks so: Peter's is consistently named one of Toronto's best Chinese restaurants. Garlic shrimp $9; soy sauteed green beans $7. Open M-Th noon-10pm, F noon-11pm, Sa 1-11pm, Su 1-10pm.

THEATER/ST. LAWRENCE DISTRICT

▨ **Mövenpick Marché** (☎366-8986), in BCE Place at Yonge and Front St. Probably the only restaurant that requires a map. Browse through and pick a meal from the 14 culinary stations, including bakery, bar, pasta, seafood, salad, and grill. Haute cuisine at its finest and cheapest. Entrees run $8-10. Open Su-Th 7:30am-2am, F-Sa 7:30am-4am.

EASTERN CANADA

Shopsy's, 33 Yonge St. (☎365-3333), at Front St. 1 block from Union Station. Other locations at 284A King St. W. (☎599-5464) and 1535 Yonge St. (☎967-5252). The definitive Toronto deli. 300 seats. Snappy service. Hot dog $3.79. Open M 6:30am-10pm, Tu-W 6:30am-11pm, Th-F 6:30am-midnight, Sa 8am-midnight, Su 8am-9pm.

Penelope, 6 Front St. E. (☎351-9393). Subway: St. Andrew. Generous portions of Greek fare in the middle of the financial district. Pre-theater dinner special $11; mouth-watering roast lamb $13. Open daily 10:30am-11pm.

THE DANFORTH

Mr. Greek, 568 Danforth Ave. (☎461-5470), at Carlaw. Subway: Pape. A friendly, bustling cafe serving shish kebabs, salads, and wine amidst Greek music. Family atmosphere; speedy service. Classic gyros or souvlaki dinner $10.50. Open Su-Th 10am-1am, F-Sa 10am-4am.

◉ SIGHTS

A walk through the city's neighborhoods can be one of the most rewarding (and cheapest) activities in Toronto. Signs and streetside conversations change languages frequently, and the main thoroughfares are usually full of frenetic activity. For an organized expedition, the **Royal Ontario Museum** leads seven free **walking tours.** (☎586-5797. Tours June-Sept. W 6pm and Su 2pm. Destinations and meeting places vary; call for specific info.) The green and tidy **University of Toronto** conducts free 1hr. walking tours of Canada's largest university. Tours meet at the Nona MacDonald visitors center at King's College Circle. (☎978-5000. Tours June-Aug. M-F 11am and 2pm, Sa 11am.) Other free trips within the city revolve around architectural themes, sculptures, or ghost haunts.

ARCHITECTURE

Toronto's **CN Tower** stands as the world's tallest free-standing structure, a mammoth concrete symbol of human ingenuity that is visible from nearly every corner of the city. The tower offers a heavenly view (especially on a cloudy day), and trusting souls lie down on the sturdy glass floor despite the frightening void below them. (☎360-8500. Subway: Union. Open daily 9am-11pm. $16, seniors $14, ages 4-12 $11. $5.50 more for the Sky Pod.) The curving twin towers and two-story rotunda of the innovative **City Hall** is at Queen and Bay St.; brochures for self-guided tours of this 60s creation are available (☎338-0338. Subway: Osgoode. Open M-F 8:30am-4:30pm). In front of City Hall, **Nathan Phillips Sq.** is home to a reflecting pool (which becomes a skating rink in winter) and numerous events, including live music every W. (June to early Oct. noon-2pm.) The Ontario government legislates in the stately **Provincial Parliament Buildings,** at Queen's Park in the heart of the city. (☎325-7500. Subway: Queen's Park. 30min. tours M-F 10am-3pm, Sa-Su 10am-3pm late May-early Sept. Call ahead for Parliamentary schedule. Free gallery passes available at south basement door when the house is in session.) Straight out of a fairy tale, the 98-room **Casa Loma,** atop a hill near Spadina a few blocks north of the Dupont subway stop, is a classic tourist attraction. An eerie underground tunnel and two formidable towers add to the magic of the only turreted castle in North America. (☎923-1171 or 923-1172. Open daily 9:30am-4pm. $10, seniors and ages 14-17 $6.50, ages 4-13 $6.) Visitors are treated to an engaging tour of old-school 19th-century Toronto next door at the **Spadina House,** a six-acre estate relic from 1866. (285 Spadina Rd. ☎392-6910. Open Apr.-Sept. Tu-Su noon-5pm. $5, seniors and ages 12-17 $3.25, ages 6-11 $3.)

MUSEUMS

Toronto is home to a variety of intriguing museums. The **Art Gallery of Ontario (AGO),** on three blocks of University Ave. downtown, showcases an enormous collection of Western art from the Renaissance to the 90s, concentrating on Canadian artists. Exhibits in the past year have featured Charlotte Solomon and Man Ray. (317 Dundas St. W. ☎979-6648. Subway: St. Patrick. Open Tu and Th-F 11am-6pm, W 11am-

8:30pm, Sa-Su 10am-5:30pm. $6 donation suggested.) A shoe-shaped glass-and-stone edifice houses the **Bata Shoe Museum,** which examines what it would be like to walk a mile in the Inuits' *and* Princess Diana's shoes. The diverse collection focuses on the role of footwear in culture, religion, and gender issues. *(327 Bloor St. W. ☎ 979-7799. Subway: St. George. Open Tu-W and F-Sa 10am-5pm, Th 10am-8pm, Su noon-5pm. $6, seniors and students $4, ages 5-14 $2, families $12. Free first Tu of every month.)* The **George R. Gardiner Museum of Ceramic Art** traces the history of ceramics with a collection dating back to the Renaissance. *(111 Queen's Park. ☎ 586-8080. Subway: Museum. Open M, W, and F 10am-6pm, Tu and Th 10am-8pm, Sa-Su 10am-5pm. $5, students and seniors $3. Free first Tu of every month.)* Across the street, the **Royal Ontario Museum (ROM)** houses artifacts from ancient civilizations (Greek, Chinese, and Egyptian), a bat cave, and a giant T-rex. *(100 Queen's Park. ☎ 586-5549. Open M-Th and Sa 10am-6pm, F 10am-9:30pm, Su 11am-6pm. $15, seniors and students $10, ages 5-14 $8. F after 4:30pm free.)* A visit to the city's museums would not be complete, however, without an excursion to **The Hockey Hall of Fame,** the glorified home of Canada's national pastime. Get in on the action in several interactive exhibits, or call your own bilingual play-by-play of some of hockey's greatest goals. *(In BCE Place. Subway: BCE Place. Open mid-June to early Sept. M-Sa 9:30am-6pm, Su 10am-6pm; off-season M-F 10am-5pm, Sa 9:30am-6pm, Su 10:30am-5pm. $12, seniors and under 18 $7.)*

ACTIVITIES

Toronto crawls with **biking** and **hiking** trails. For a map of the trails, call **MetroParks** *(☎392-8186),* which has info on local facilities and activities. It might not be the Caribbean, but the **beaches** on the southeast end of Toronto now support a permanent community. A popular "vacationland," the **Toronto Islands Park,** on Centre Island, has a boardwalk, bathing beaches, canoe and bike rentals, and an amusement park. The park is on a 9km strip of connected islands opposite downtown. *(Open mid-May to early Sept.)*

The **Ontario Science Center,** at Eglington Ave. E., presents more than 650 interactive exhibits, showcasing humanity's greatest innovations. *(770 Don Mills Rd. ☎696-3127. Museum open daily 10am-6pm; early Sept.-June 10am-5pm. Omnimax shows every hr. on the hr. 11am-6pm; Sept.-June 11am-5pm. Museum $12, ages 13-17 and seniors $7, ages 5-12 $6; with Omnimax film $17/$11.)* The **Metro Toronto Zoo,** Meadowvale Rd. off Exit 389 on Hwy. 401, keeps over 6600 animals in a 710-acre park that features sections re-creating the world's seven geographic regions and rare wildlife including a Komodo dragon and a Tasmanian devil. *(☎392-5900. Take bus #86A from Kennedy Station. Open daily mid-Oct. to mid-Mar. 9:30am-4:30pm; mid-Mar. to mid-May and early Sept. to mid-Oct. 9am-6pm; late May to early Sept. 9am-7pm. Last entry 1hr. before closing. $13, seniors $10, ages 4-14 $8. Parking $6.)*

♫ ENTERTAINMENT

The monthly *Where Toronto,* available free at tourism booths, gives the lowdown on arts and entertainment. **T.O. Tix** sells half-price tickets on performance day at 208 Yonge St., north of Queen St. at Eaton's Centre. (Subway: Queen. ☎536-6468. Open Tu-Sa noon-7:30pm; arrive before 11:45am for first dibs.) **Ticketmaster** (☎870-8000) supplies tickets for many Toronto venues, but with a hefty service charge.

MUSIC. Ontario Place, 955 Lakeshore Blvd. W (☎314-9811, recording 314-9900), features cheap summer entertainment. Top pop artists perform in the **Molson Amphitheater.** (☎260-5600. Park open mid-May to early Sept. daily 10:30am-midnight. Ticketmaster handles tickets; $20-125.) **Roy Thomson Hall,** 60 Simcoe St., at King St. W, is both Toronto's premier concert hall and the home of the **Toronto Symphony Orchestra** from Sept. to June. (☎593-4828; box office 872-4255. Subway: St. Andrews. Open M-F 10am-6pm, Sa noon-5pm, Su 2hr. before performances. Tickets $24-77, $22-48 for matinees. $15 rush tickets available on concert days M-F 11am and Sa 1pm.) The same ticket office serves **Massey Hall,** Shuter St. (☎593-4828; subway: Queen), a great hall for rock and folk concerts and musicals.

THEATER. The **St. Lawrence Centre,** 27 Front St. E., stages excellent drama and chamber music recitals in two different theaters. (☎366-7723. Box office open M-Sa 10am-6pm; in winter performance days 10am-8pm, non-performance days 10am-6pm. Ask for possible student and senior discounts.) **Canadian Stage** performs free summer Shakespeare ($5 donation suggested) amid the greenery of **High Park,** on Bloor St. W. at Parkside Dr. Year-round performances at the St. Lawrence Centre include new Canadian works and time-honored classics. (Box office ☎368-3110. Subway: High Park. Open M-Sa 10am-6pm. Call for schedule.) Several blocks west in the Harbourfront Centre, the **Soulpepper Theatre Company,** 231 Queen's Quay W, presents enthralling performances of masterpieces ranging from Shakespeare to Pinter. (☎973-4000. $41-46, students $25, rush tickets $18.)

AMUSEMENTS. Canada's answer to Disney is **Canada's Wonderland,** 9580 Jane St., 1hr. from downtown but accessible by public transit; take **Vaughn Transit** (☎905-832-8527) from the Richmond Hill area or the **Go Bus** (☎869-3200) from the Yorkdale or York Mills subway stations ($3.75 each way). Splash down water rides or try your stomach on the backwards, looping roller-coasters. (☎905-832-7000. Open daily late June to early Sept. 10am-10pm; open in fall Sa-Su, closing times vary. Waterpark open daily in summer 11am-8pm. $43, seniors and ages 3-6 $21.50.)

SPORTS. From Apr. to early Oct., the **Toronto Blue Jays** play hardball at the enormous modern monstrosity, **Sky Dome.** (Front and Peter St. ☎341-1111, tickets 341-1234. Subway: Union, follow the signs. Tickets $7-42.) To get a behind-the-scenes look at the Sky Dome, take the **tour.** (☎341-2770. Times vary. $9.50, seniors and under 16 $7.) The Sky Dome is also the home of the **Toronto Argonauts** of the Canadian Football League, as well as concerts and other events throughout the year. (Argonauts: ☎341-5151; concerts: ☎341-3663.) Hockey fans head for **The Air Canada Centre,** 40 Bay St., to see the knuckle-crackin' **Maple Leafs.** (☎815-5700. Subway: Union. Tickets $26-100.)

❋ FESTIVALS

Film fans choose the **Bloor Cinema,** 506 Bloor St. W. (☎532-6677), at Bathurst, or the **Cinématheque Ontario,** 317 Dundas St. W. (☎923-3456), at McCaul St. The ten-day **Toronto International Film Festival** (☎967-7371), held in mid-Sept., is one of the most prestigious festivals on the art-house circuit. Toronto hosts numerous other festivals as well. Groove to the rhythms of old and new talents—more than 1500 artists from 17 countries—at the ten-day **Du Maurier Ltd. Downtown Jazz Festival** (☎363-5200), at Ontario Place in late June. Also in June, the **Toronto International Dragon Boat Race Festival** (☎598-8945) continues a 2000-year-old Chinese tradition. The celebration includes traditional performances, foods, and free outdoor lunchtime concerts. From mid-Aug. through early Sept., the **Canadian National Exhibition (CNE),** the world's largest annual fair, brings an international carnival to Exhibition Place (☎393-6000. Open daily 10am-midnight. $8, seniors and children $5, under 6 free.) The city also rocks with the second-largest **gay pride celebration** in the world, also in late June, and a growing **street festival** and **fringe theatre festival** in mid-July.

◪ NIGHTLIFE

Toronto offers a seemingly limitless selection of bars, pubs, dance clubs, and late-night cafes, including the **Second Cup Coffee Co.,** a T.O. institution which has branches all over town. The city shuts down alcohol distribution daily at 2am, so most clubs close down then. The most interesting new clubs are on trendy **Queen St. W.** in the **Entertainment District,** and on **College St. W.** and **Bloor St. W.** Two comprehensive free entertainment magazines, *Now* and *Eye*, come out every Th. The gay scene centers around **Wellesley and Church St.** For the scoop on Toronto's gay scene, pick up the free, bi-weekly *fab*.

THE ANNEX

▨ **The James Joyce,** 386 Bloor St. (☎324-9400). Subway: Spadina. Live Celtic music every night and 2 happening pool tables are the highlight of this dark, traditional Irish pub. No cover. Open daily 11:30am-2am.

Lee's Palace, 529 Bloor St. W. (☎532-1598), just east of the Bathurst subway stop. Crazy creature art depicts a rock 'n' roll frenzy. Live alternative music nightly downstairs; batlike DJ dance club, the **Dance Cave,** swings upstairs. Pick up a calendar of bands. Box office opens 8pm, shows begin 10pm. Cover $3-20 downstairs; open M-Sa noon-2am. Cover after 10pm $4 upstairs F-Sa; open daily 8pm-3am.

The Madison, 14 Madison Ave. (☎927-1722), at Bloor St. Subway: Spadina. 2 pool rooms, 3 patios, and a kick-back but crowded atmosphere attract students and yuppies. 21 beers on tap. Pints $5. Wings $9. Open daily 11am-2am.

Las Iguanas, 513 Bloor St. W (☎532-3360). Subway: Spadina. Irreverent faux-calfskin booths and kitschy margaritas ($4.70) with plastic lizards on the glass. Su is wing night; fajitas are half-price on M. Open M-F noon-2am, Sa-Su 11am-2am.

DOWNTOWN

▨ **The Second City,** 56 Blue Jays Way (☎343-0011 or 888-263-4485), at Wellington St., just north of the Sky Dome. Subway: Union. One of North America's wackiest, most creative comedy clubs. Spawned comics Dan Akroyd, John Candy, Martin Short, Mike Myers, and a hit TV show (SCTV). Free improv sessions M-Th 10pm and Sa midnight. Free F midnight howl with guest improv troupe. M-Th show 8pm ($19), F-Sa 8pm and 10:30pm ($23-25), Su touring company's production $10. Reservations required.

C'est What?, 67 Front St. E. (☎867-9499). Subway: Union. A mellow manifestation of Canada's multiculturalism. A great bar, with live music most nights of the week, homemade microbrews and wines, and exceedingly friendly and talkative bartenders. Open M-F noon-2am, Sa 11am-2am, Su 11am-1am.

Top o' the Senator, 249-253 Victoria St. (☎364-7517). Attracts local and national jazz acts. Cover $5-30. Open Tu-Sa 8:30pm-1am, Su 8pm-midnight.

COLLEGE ST.

Sneaky Dee's, 431 College St. W. (☎603-3090), at Bathurst. A popular (if generic) bar replete with cheap beer ($2.50-4) and pool tables in back. DJ and dancing upstairs W-Sa 9:30pm. Open M-Th 11am-4am, F 11am-5am, Sa 9am-5am, Su 9am-4am.

THE DANFORTH

Iliada Cafe, 550 Danforth Ave. (☎462-0334). Subway: Pape. Sip frappes and nibble at fresh baklava ($2.75) in this softly lit hangout spot, which serves a young, diverse clientele. Open Su-Th 9am-2am, F-Sa 9am-3am.

THE GAY AND LESBIAN VILLAGE

Woody's/Sailor, 465-467 Church St. (☎972-0887), by Maitland. Subway: Wellesley. *The* established gay bar in the Church and Wellesley area. Neighborhood atmosphere; walls are lined with art nudes. Come to relax before heading to the clubs, but don't miss "Bad Boys Night Out" Tu, "Best Legs" Su 11pm, and "Best Chest" Th at midnight. Bottled beer $4.50. Open daily 11am-2am.

Slack Alice, 562 Church St. (☎969-8742). Subway: Wellesley. This cafe and bar offers international food (entrees $7-14), an outdoor patio, and a happy hour from 4-7pm, all of which draw in a mostly lesbian and gay crowd. A DJ and dancing spice things up on weekends. Open daily 11am-2am.

YOUR CHARIOT AWAITS... If you find the subway crowded but don't want to hail a cab, rickshaws will sweep you off your feet. Originally from Hong Kong, these human-drawn carriages have caught on all over Canada. In Toronto, companies like **Rickshaw Services of Toronto** (☎410-4593) will cart you through the city streets courtesy of other people's backs. Rates are about $3 per block per person.

⚑ DAYTRIPS FROM TORONTO

ONATION'S NIAGARA ESCARPMENT. As beautiful as its name is strange, Onation's Niagara Escarpment passes west of Toronto as it winds its way from Niagara Falls to Tobermory at the tip of the Bruce Peninsula. Along this rocky 724km ridge, the **Bruce Trail** snakes through parks and private land. Hikers are treated to spectacular waterfalls, the breathtaking cliffs along **Georgian Bay,** and unique flora and fauna, including an old growth forest. Because the Escarpment is registered as a UN world biosphere reserve, future land development is limited to that which can exist symbiotically with the natural environment. For maps and Escarpment info, write or call the **Niagara Escarpment Commission,** 232 Guelph St., Georgetown L7G 4B1 (☎905-877-5191). Specifics on the Bruce Trail can be obtained from the **Bruce Trail Association,** P.O. Box 857, Hamilton L8N 3N9 (☎905-529-6821).

STRATFORD. The **Stratford Shakespeare Festival,** held in nearby Stratford since 1953, has proven to be the lifeblood of this picturesque town named for the Bard's own village. The prestigious festival runs from early May to early Nov., with about 15 Shakespearean and non-Shakespearean plays performed in three theaters. During midsummer (July-Aug.), up to six different shows play per day (none on M), with matinees beginning at 2pm and evening performances at 8pm. For complete info about casts and performances, call ☎800-567-1600. Tickets are expensive ($49-75), but a few good deals lower the stakes, including **rush tickets,** sold at 9am on the morning of the show at the box office, theater, or at 9:30am by phone ($38-48); matinees for seniors and students from Sept.-Nov. (from $22); general student discounts ($26-27); and half-price for some performances in the fall. The box office is open M-Sa 9am-8pm, Su 9am-2pm.

OTTAWA ☎613

Legend has it that in the mid-19th century, Queen Victoria chose Ottawa as Canada's capital by closing her eyes and pointing a finger at a map, but perhaps political savvy rather than blind chance guided her to this once remote logging town. As a stronghold for neither French nor English interests, Ottawa became a perfect compromise. Today, faced with the increasingly tricky task of forging national unity while preserving local identities, Ottawa continues to play cultural diplomat to larger Canada. Despite the city's reputation for being boring—owing to its historic, polished feel and the careful grooming that makes it easy to navigate—an evening stroll through Byward Market reveals Ottawa's lively other side.

⬛ GETTING THERE AND GETTING AROUND

Airport: Ottawa International (☎248-2125), 20min. south of the city off Bronson Ave. Take bus #96 from MacKenzie King Bridge. Info desk in arrival area open 9am-9pm. **Kasbary Transport, Inc.** runs shuttles (☎736-9993) between the airport and all downtown hotels (every 30min. 4:40am-2am; call for later pick-up. $9, seniors and ages 11-18 $6). Call for pick-up from smaller hotels.

Trains: VIA Rail, 200 Tremblay Rd. (☎244-8289), east of downtown, off the Queensway at Alta Vista Rd. To: Montréal (2hr., 4 per day, $40); Toronto (4hr., 5 per day, $85); and Québec City via Montréal (7hr., 2 per day, $75). Ticket office open M-F 5am-9pm, Sa 6:30am-7pm, Su 8:20am-9pm.

Buses: Voyageur, 265 Catherine St. (☎238-5900), between Kent and Lyon. Serves primarily eastern Canada. To: Montréal (2½hr., on the hr. 7am-11pm, $27.50). **Greyhound** (☎237-7038) leaves from the same station, bound for western Canada and southern Ontario. To: Toronto (5hr., 7 per day, $56.50). For service to the US you must first go to Montréal or Toronto; the Québec City-bound passes through Montréal (6hr., every hr., $64.20). Station open daily 6:30am-12:30am. The blue **Hull City** buses (☎819-770-3242) connect Ottawa to Hull, across the river.

Public Transit: OC Transpo, 1500 St. Laurent (☎741-4390). Buses congregate on Rideau Centre. Fare $2.25, express (green buses) $3.50, ages 6-11 $1.25.

Taxis: Blue Line Taxi, ☎238-1111. **Capital,** ☎744-3333.

EASTERN CANADA

Ottawa

🏠 ACCOMMODATIONS

Gatineau Park Campgrounds, **1**
Gatineau Park International Hostel, **2**
Ottawa International Hostel (HI), **10**
University of Ottawa Residences. **12**
YMCA/YWCA, **11**

🍅 FOOD AND DRINKS

Coffee Revolution, **9**
Las Palmas, **3**
Mamma Grazzi's Kitchen, **7**
Rideau Deli, **8**

♪ MUSIC AND CLUBS

The Lookout, **4**
Minglewoods, **6**
Zaphod, **5**

Bike Rental: Rent-A-Bike-Vélocationo, 1 Rideau St. (☎ 241-4140), behind the Château Laurier Hotel. Open daily Apr.-Oct. 9am-8pm. $7 per hr., $16 per 4hr., $20 per day; tandems $15/$38/$50. Maps, locks, helmets free. Family deals. Credit card required.

✴ ORIENTATION

The **Rideau Canal** divides Ottawa into the eastern lower town and the western upper town. West of the canal, Parliament buildings and government offices line **Wellington St.,** one of the city's main east-west arteries, which runs directly into the heart of downtown and crosses the canal. **Laurier** is the only other east-west street which permits traffic from one side of the canal to the other. East of the canal, Wellington St. becomes **Rideau St.,** surrounded by a fashionable shopping district. North of Rideau St. lies the **Byward Market,** a shopping area which hosts a summertime open-air market and much of Ottawa's nightlife. **Elgin St.,** a primary north-south artery stretching from the Queensway (Hwy. 417) to the War Memorial just south of Wellington in front of Parliament Hill, is also home to a number of pubs and nightlife spots. **Bank St.,** which runs parallel to Elgin three blocks to the west, services the town's older shopping area. The canal itself is a major access route. In winter, thousands of Ottawans skate to work on this, the world's longest skating rink; in summer, power boats breeze by regularly. Bike paths and pedestrian walkways also line the canals. Parking downtown is painful (to find as well as to pay for); meters often cost 25¢ for 10min. Stash your car near the hostels and hop on the OC Transpo buses or walk. All the best attractions, restaurants, lodgings, clubs, and parks are within easy walking distance of one another.

🛈 PRACTICAL INFORMATION

Visitor Info: National Capital Commission Information Center, 90 Wellington St. (☎ 239-5000 or 800-465-1867 in Canada), opposite the Parliament Buildings. Open daily early May-early Sept. 8:30am-9pm; early Sept.-early May 9am-5pm. For info on Hull and Québec province, contact the **Association Touristique de l'Outaouais,** 103 rue Laurier, Hull (☎ 819-778-2222 or 800-265-7822). Open mid-June to Sept. M-F 8:30am-8pm, Sa-Su 9am-6pm; off-season M-F 8:30am-5pm, Sa-Su 9am-4pm.

Hotlines: Ottawa Distress Centre, ☎ 238-3311, English-speaking. **Tel-Aide,** ☎ 741-6433, French-speaking. **Rape Crisis Centre,** ☎ 562-2333. All 24hr.

Bi-Gay-Lesbian Organization: Gayline-Telegai (☎ 238-1717) has info on local bars and special events. Open daily 7-10pm.

Post Office: Postal Station B, 59 Sparks St. (☎ 844-1545), at Elgin St. Open M-F 8am-6pm. **Postal code:** K1P 5A0. **Area code:** 613 in Ottawa; 819 in Hull.

🏠 ACCOMMODATIONS

Finding inexpensive lodging in downtown Ottawa can be difficult, especially in the summer. However, fantastic budget options exist if you avoid hotels. Advance reservations are strongly recommended, especially if you stay through Canada Day (July 1). A complete list of B&Bs can be found in the *Ottawa Visitors Guide;* **Ottawa Bed and Breakfast** represents ten B&Bs in the Ottawa area (☎ 563-0161; singles $49-54; doubles $59-64).

Ottawa International Hostel (HI-C), 75 Nicholas St., K1N 7B9 (☎ 235-2595), in downtown Ottawa. The site of Canada's last public hanging, the former Carleton County Jail now incarcerates travelers. Cells contain 4-8 bunks and minimal personal space. Communal showers, kitchen, laundry facilities, lounges, and a cast of friendly regulars. Many organized activities (biking, canoeing, tours, and pub crawls) keep visitors happy. In winter, doors locked 2-7am. Dorms $16, non-members $21; private rooms from $46/$50. Linen $2. Parking $4.28 per day.

Gatineau Park International Hostel (HI-C), 66 Carman Rd. (☎ 819-459-3180), 20min. from downtown Ottawa. Take Hwy. 5 north to its end, turn left at the intersection, and the hostel is 5km down the road, on the left. By bus, take the #1 Maniwaki and ask the driver to stop at the intersection of Hwy. 105 and Chemin Carman. Call the hostel in advance for shuttle service from here. For an idyllic retreat from the city, take advantage of this smaller hostel's proximity to Gatineau Park. Dorms $17, non-members $20.

University of Ottawa Residences, 100 University St. (☎564-5400), in the center of campus, an easy walk from downtown. From the bus and train stations, take bus #95. Clean dorms in a concrete landscape. Free linen, towels. Open early May to late Aug. Check-in 4:30pm. Parking $8 per day, $5 after 4pm and Sa-Su. Singles $35; doubles $44. Students with ID $25/$37.

YMCA/YWCA, 180 Argyle Ave. (☎237-1320), at O'Connor St., close to the bus station and only a 10min. walk from Ottawa's main sights; walk left on Bank St. and right on Argyle. Good-sized rooms in a high-rise. Free local calls from most rooms. Kitchen and gym facilities. Reception Su-Th 7am-11pm, F-Sa 24hr. Singles with shared bath $42, with private bath $49; doubles $49. Parking $9.25. Weekly and group rates available.

Gatineau Park (☎819-827-2020; reservations 456-3016), northwest of Hull. Three rustic campgrounds within 45min. of Ottawa: **Lac Philippe Campground,** 248 sites with facilities for family camping, trailers, and campers; **Lac Taylor Campground,** with 33 semi-rustic sites; and **Lac la Pêche,** with 36 campsites accessible only by canoe. Lac Philippe and Lac Taylor are open year-round; daily 9am-6pm, in winter 9:30am-6pm. La Pêche is available mid-May to mid-Oct. Camping permits required for Taylor and Philippe ($16; mid-June to mid-Oct. $19) available at the campground entrance. Pay for a site at La Pêche ($15; off-season $12) on Eardley Rd.

FOOD

Ottawa's **Byward Market,** on Byward St. between York and Rideau St., is rather European in style; tables of fresh fruits, vegetables, plants and flowers are occasionally punctuated with maple syrup stands that remind passers-by that they're in Canada. (☎562-3325. Open daily in warmer weather 8am-5pm. Boutiques open later.) Outdoor and patio dining options are plentiful in the warmer weather, while the area surrounding Byward Market is concentrated with dozens of pubs and restaurants.

Father and Sons, 112 Osgoode St. (☎233-6066), at the eastern edge of the U of O campus, is a student favorite, and for good reason. The menu presents quality, tavern-style food with some Lebanese dishes thrown in. Falafel platter ($7) or a triple-decker sandwich ($7.25) are delicious. 15¢ wings all day M and Sa, 30¢ otherwise. Open daily 7am-2am. Kitchen open until midnight in winter.

Mamma Grazzi's Kitchen, 25 George St. (☎241-8656). This little Italian hideaway is located in a stone building in one of the oldest parts of Ottawa. Regulars rave about the thin-crust pizza ($8-13). Be patient; it's worth the wait. Open Su-Th 11:30am-10pm, F-Sa 11:30am-11pm.

Coffee Revolution, 115 Rideau St. (☎562-5678). Brick walls and exposed ceiling pipes give a dark ambiance to this coffee joint by day, bistro by night. Try the weekday breakfast special: 2 eggs, 2 pieces of toast, homefries, and coffee for $2. Lunch and dinner options include burgers ($6-7), pasta ($8-9), and wraps ($6-9). Open M-F 7am-midnight, Sa-Su 8am-1am, depending on the crowd.

Rideau Deli, 113 Rideau St. (☎562-8147). Quick-stop sandwiches are rarely so cheap and appetizing ($2). Open M-W 9:30am-6pm, Th 9:30am-7pm, F 9:30am-8pm, Sa 9:30am-5pm, Su 11:30am-5pm.

SIGHTS

THE HUB. Parliament Hill, on Wellington at Metcalfe St., distinguished by Gothic architecture, towers over downtown. Warm your hands or raise a skeptical Québecois eyebrow over the **Centennial Flame** at the south gate, lit in 1967 to mark the 100th anniversary of the Dominion of Canada's inaugural session of Parliament. The Prime Minister can occasionally be spotted at the central parliament structure, **Centre Block,** which contains the House of Commons, Senate, and Library of Parliament. Free tours of Centre Block (in English or French) depart every 30min. from the white **Infotent** by the visitors center. (☎992-4793. *Tours mid-May to Sept. M-F 9am-8:30pm, Sa-Su 9am-5:30pm; Sept. to mid-May daily 9am-4:30pm. Info-tent open mid-May to mid-June daily 9am-5pm; mid-June to Aug. 9am-8pm.)* On display behind the library, the bell from Centre Block is the only part of the original 1859-66 structure to survive a 1916 fire; according to legend, the bell crashed to the ground after chiming at midnight on the night of the flames. A carillon of 53 bells now hangs in the Peace Tower. When Parliament is in session, you can watch Canada's government officials squirm on the hot seat during the official **Question Period** in the House of Commons chamber. *(Mid-Sept. to Dec. and Feb. to mid-June M-Th 2:15-3pm, F 11:15am-noon.)*

Those interested in trying to make a statuesque soldier smile should attend the **Changing of the Guard,** on the broad lawns in front of Centre Block. *(☎ 993-1811. Late June to late Aug. daily 10am, weather permitting.)* At dusk, Centre Block and its lawns transform into the set for **A Symphony of Sound and Light,** which relates the history of the Parliament Buildings and the nation. *(Shows mid-May to early Aug. W-Su 9:30 and 10:30pm; early Aug. to early Sept. W-Su 9 and 10pm. Performances alternate between French and English; for specifics, call ☎ 239-5000)* A 5min. walk west along Wellington St., the **Supreme Court of Canada** *(☎ 995-5361)* cohabits with the **Federal Court.** *(Open daily 9am-5pm; Sept.-May hrs. vary. Alternating French and English 30min. tours every 30min.; no tours Sa-Su noon-1pm. Free.)*

PARKS AND OTHER ATTRACTIONS. East of the Parliament Buildings at the junction of Sparks, Wellington, and Elgin St. stands **Confederation Sq.** with its enormous **National War Memorial,** dedicated by King George VI in 1939. The structure symbolizes the triumph of peace over war, an ironic message on the eve of World War II. **Nepean Point,** several blocks northwest of Rideau Centre and the Byward Market, behind the National Gallery of Canada, provides a panoramic view of the capital. The **Governor-General,** the Queen's representative in Canada, resides at **Rideau Hall** *(☎ 998-7113).* Dress up for the open house on New Year's Day or Canada Day and they'll let you view the interior. Otherwise, gawk from 24 Sussex Drive, the **Prime Minister's residence.** Free tours leave from the main gate at 1 Sussex Dr. *(☎ 800-465-6890 for tour info).* Witness the production of "Toonies" ($2 coins) and other currency at the **Royal Canadian Mint,** 320 Sussex Drive. The tour schedule varies, call ☎ 800-276-7714 or 993-8990.

Ottawa has managed to skirt the traditional urban vices of pollution and violent crime; the multitude of parks and recreation areas may make you forget you're in a city at all. A favorite destination for Ottawans who want to cycle, hike, or fish, **Gatineau Park** (see **Accommodations,** above) occupies 356 sq. km in the northwest. Artificial **Dow's Lake,** accessible by the Queen Elizabeth Dwy., extends off the Rideau Canal 15min. south of Ottawa. **Dow's Lake Pavilion,** near Preston St., rents pedal boats, canoes, and bikes. *(101 Queen Elizabeth Driveway. ☎ 232-1001. Open daily mid-May to Sept. 8am-8pm. Rentals by the hr. and half-hour. Prices vary.)*

🏛 MUSEUMS

Geographically concentrated and manageable, many of Ottawa's notable museums (most of which are wheelchair accessible) double as architectural marvels.

The National Gallery, 380 Sussex Dr. *(☎ 990-1985 or 800-319-2787).* A spectacular glass-towered building adjacent to Nepean Pt. holds the world's most comprehensive collection of Canadian art complemented by outstanding European, American, and Asian works. The building's exterior, a work of art in itself, parodies the neo-Gothic buttresses of the opposing Library of Parliament. Open daily May-Oct. 10am-6pm, Th 10am-8pm; hrs. vary off-season. Free; special events $10-12, students and seniors $6-8, under 18 free.

The Canadian Museum of Civilization, 100 Laurier St. *(☎ 776-7000).* Housed in a striking, sand-dune-like structure across the river in Hull. Journey amidst life-sized dioramas that attempt to put 1000 years of Canadian history into perspective. Open daily Apr.-Oct. 9am-6pm, Th. 9am-9pm; hrs. vary off-season. $8, seniors $7, under 18 $6, children $3.

The Canadian War Museum, 330 Sussex Dr. *(☎ 776-8600),* next to the National Gallery. A poignant exhibit of Canadian citizens at war from colonial times to UN Peacekeeping Missions. Open daily 9am-5pm, Th 9am-8pm. $4, students and seniors $3, children $2. Half-price Su, free after 4pm on Th.

The Canadian Museum of Contemporary Photography, 1 Rideau Canal *(☎ 990-8257),* on the steps between the Château Laurier and the Ottawa Locks. Modern Canadian life is freeze-framed, making for endless contemplation. Open F-Tu 11am-5pm, W 4-8pm, Th 11am-8pm. Free.

EASTERN CANADA

The Canadian Museum of Nature, 240 McLeod St. (☎566-4700), at Metcalf. An exploration of the natural world from dinosaur to mineral through multimedia displays. Open daily May-early Sept. 9:30am-5pm, Th 9:30am-8pm; hrs. vary during off-season. $5, students $4, seniors and ages 3-12 $2, families $12; Th half-price 9:30am-5pm, free after 5pm.

National Library Archives, 395 Wellington St. (☎995-5138), at Bay St. History buffs easily lose themselves in the oodles of Canadian publications, old maps, photographs, letters, and often random and eclectic historical exhibits. Reading room open M-F 8:30am-10pm, Sa-Su 8am-6pm. Call ahead.

Laurier House, 335 Laurier Ave. E. (☎992-8142). Liberal Prime Minister William Lyon Mackenzie King governed from the elegant house for most of his lengthy tenure. Admire all that he accumulated, including the crystal ball he used to consult his long-dead mother on matters of national importance. Open Apr.-Sept. Tu-Sa 9am-5pm, Su 2-5pm; Oct.-Mar. Tu-Sa 10am-5pm, Su 2-5pm. $2.25, seniors $1.75, students $1.25, under 5 free.

National Museum of Science and Technology, 1867 St. Laurent Blvd. (☎991-3044), at Smyth. Explore the wonderful world of modern tech with touchy-feely exhibits. The museum entrance is on Lancaster Rd., 200m east of St. Laurent. Open daily May-Sept. 9am-6pm, F until 9pm; hrs. vary off-season. $6, students and seniors $5, ages 6-14 $2, family rate including 2 adults, 2 children $12.

National Aviation Museum (☎993-2010), in front of the Rockcliffe Flying Club on Prom. de l'Aviation and Rockcliffe Pkwy. north of Montréal St. The history of human flight and over 120 aircraft. Take bus #95 and transfer to #198. Open daily May-Sept. 9am-5pm, Th 9am-9pm; hrs vary during off season. $6, students and seniors $5, ages 6-15 $2.

 NIGHTLIFE

Those pubcrawlers who recall nightlife being centered across the Ottawa River may want to reconsider before heading over to **Hull, Québec.** At one time grinding and gnashing until 3am, many nightclubs have since been bought out due to increasing crime. Coupled with Ottawa's decision to allow nightspots to serve alcohol until 2am, the capital city is once again where it's at. For a taste of it all, wander about **Byward Market** and the surrounding area, where streets typically overflow with pedestrians in the evening. **The Atomic,** 137 Besserer Street, lures clubbers through its silver doors with the most up-to-date music scene in Canada, spinning techno and rave still virgin to the airwaves. Since good health is a priority, Cybertonic juice and vitamin drinks are served along with the booze. (☎241-2411. Open Th 10pm-3am, cover $5; F 10pm-5am, cover $7 before 1am, $10 after; Sa 10pm-8am, cover $10 before 1am, $12 after). Experience life, the universe, and a bit of everything else at **Zaphod,** 27 York St., in Byward Market, a popular alternative club famous for their $6.50 Pangalactic Gargle Blasters. (☎562-1010. Live bands on weekends, music on weekdays. Cover $2-10 depending on the band playing. Open daily 3pm-2am.) **The Lookout,** 41 York St. next to Zaphod's, is a hoppin' gay club that attracts anyone in the mood for intense dancing. (☎789-1624. Open daily 3pm-2am.) **Minglewoods,** 101 York St. on the corner of Dalhousie, is pure Canadian with its slew of domestic beers on tap. The three levels include a bar, pool room, and dance floor to accommodate the teeming crowd that gathers here regardless of day or time. (☎562-2611. Open daily from 11:30am-2am.)

FESTIVALS

Ottawans seem to celebrate everything, even the bitter Canadian cold. All-important is **Canada Day,** July 1, which involves fireworks, partying in Major's Hill Park, concerts, and all-around merrymaking. During the first three weekends of Feb., **Winterlude** (☎239-5000) lines the Rideau Canal with ice sculptures illustrating how it feels to be an Ottawan in the winter (frozen). For a week in mid-May, the **Tulip Festival** (☎567-5757) explodes with a kaleidoscope of more than a million buds around Dow's Lake. Music fills the air during the **Dance Festival** (☎237-5158), in mid-June, and the **Jazz Festival** (☎594-3580), in mid-July; both hold free recitals and concerts as well as pricier events. During Labor Day weekend, hundreds of international balloons take to the sky at the **Hot Air Balloon Festival** (☎819-243-2330).

MID-ATLANTIC

From the Eastern seaboard of New York south through Virginia, the mid-Atlantic states claim not only a large slice of the nation's population, but several of its major historical, political, and economic centers. This region has witnessed the rotation of US capitals; first Philadelphia, PA, then Princeton, NJ, Annapolis, MD, Trenton, NJ, New York City, and finally Washington, D.C. During the Civil War, the mid-Atlantic even housed the Confederacy's capital, Richmond, VA. Urban centers (and suburban sprawl) cover much of the land, but the great outdoors have survived. The Appalachian Trail meanders through the region and New York's Adirondacks compose the largest US park outside of Alaska.

HIGHLIGHTS OF THE MID-ATLANTIC

NEW YORK, NY. The Big Apple combines world-class museums (p. 224) with top-notch arts and entertainment venues (p. 228).

WASHINGTON, D.C. The impressive Smithsonian Museum (p. 298), the White House (p. 296), the Capitol (p. 294), and a slew of monuments (p. 295) comprise some of the coveted attractions of the nation's capitol.

SCENIC DRIVES. The Blue Ridge Pkwy. (p. 320) is justifiably famous. A more hidden drive is the gorgeous backcountry road from Carter's Grove Plantation to Colonial Williamsburg, VA (p. 309).

HISTORIC SITES. Four-time battlefield Fredericksburg, VA (p. 306); Harper's Ferry, WV (p. 322); and Gettysburg, PA (p. 268) are the best places to relive the Civil War. Philadelphia, PA (p. 255) abounds with colonial landmarks.

NEW YORK

This state offers a little bit of everything: the excitement of New York City, the grandeur of Niagara Falls, and the fresh natural beauty of the Catskills and the Adirondacks. While "The City" attracts cosmopolitan types looking for adventure year-round, those seeking a more mellow New York experience head upstate. Here, surrounded by the beauty of some of the state's landscape, you may find it difficult to remember that smog and traffic exist. The cities that dot upstate New York have a sweet natural flavor that hold their own against the tang of the Big Apple.

PRACTICAL INFORMATION

Capital: Albany.

Visitor Info: Division of Tourism, 1 Commerce Plaza, Albany 12245 (☎518-474-4116 or 800-225-5697; www.iloveny.state.ny.us). Operators available M-F 8:30am-5pm; voice mail otherwise. **New York State Office of Parks and Recreation and Historic Preservation,** Empire State Plaza, Agency Bldg. 1, Albany 12238-0001 (☎518-474-0456). Open M-F 9am-5pm. **Bureau of Public Lands** of the **Division of Lands and Forests,** DEC, 50 Wolf Rd., Room 438, Albany 12233-4255 (☎518-457-7433). A full pamphlet of the locations and facilities of all **state campgrounds** is available from any park ranger's office or by calling ☎457-2500; reservations for campgrounds ☎800-456-2267 or www.park-net.com.

Postal Abbreviation: NY. **Sales Tax:** 8.25%.

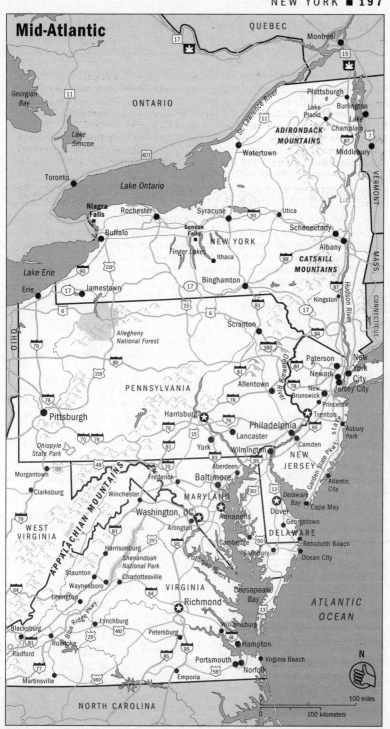

Mid-Atlantic

NEW YORK CITY ☎212

Immensity, diversity, and a tradition of defying tradition characterize the city known as "the Crossroads of the World." Since its earliest days, New York has scoffed at the timid offerings of other American cities. It boasts the most immigrants, the tallest skyscrapers, the biggest museum in the Western Hemisphere, and the largest landfill ever (otherwise referred to as Staten Island). Even the vast blocks of concrete have their own gritty charm. Returning from a dull vacation in rural Westchester, talespinner O. Henry noted, "there was too much fresh scenery and fresh air. What I need is a steam-heated flat and no vacation or exercise."

New York City is full of folks. The stars are shielded by a blanket of pollution. The buildings are tall, the subway smelly, the people rushed, the beggars everywhere. But for every inch of grime, there's a yard of silver lining. Countless people mean countless pockets of culture—you can find every kind of ethnicity, food, art, language, attitude. It's possible to be alone, but that's not the point—plunge into the fray and you'll find 8 million stories, curmudgeonly humor, innovative ideas, and a fair share of madness. The architecture, from colonial to Art Deco, reveals the stratae of history that NYC embodies. Meanwhile, there's flamenco at an outdoor cafe, jazz in historic speakeasies, jungle/illbient under a bridge, Eurotechno at a flashy club—whatever the question, New York has the answer.

For the coverage this city deserves, see our city guide, *Let's Go: New York City*, and the *Let's Go Map Guide: New York City*.

✤ ORIENTATION

Five **boroughs** comprise New York City: Brooklyn, the Bronx, Queens, Staten Island, and Manhattan. **Manhattan** Island is 13 mi. long and 2½ mi. wide, and houses the 3rd-largest population of the boroughs, after Brooklyn and Queens. **Queens,** the largest of the boroughs, faces Manhattan's east midtown from across the East River. **Brooklyn,** due south of Queens, would be America's 4th-largest city if it weren't a part of New York. Residential **Staten Island,** southwest of Manhattan, has repeatedly sought secession from the city. North of Manhattan, the **Bronx** is the only borough connected by land to the rest of the US; the two main regions are upscale Riverdale and the economically depressed South Bronx.

MANHATTAN. From the window of an approaching plane, it can seem a monolithic concrete jungle. Up close, Manhattan breaks down into manageable neighborhoods that change abruptly from street to street. Subway directions are in parentheses. Manhattan's east/west division refers to an establishment's location in relation to the two borders of Central Park—**Fifth Ave.** on the east side and **Central Park West** on the west. Below 59th St. where the park ends, the West Side begins at the western half of 5th Ave. **Uptown** (59th St. and up) refers to the area north of Midtown. **Downtown** (34th St. and down) means the area south of Midtown. (Keep in mind, though, that "uptown" and "downtown" are also simply relative terms, and you can be downtown of Uptown if you're just in Midtown. Get it?) Streets run east-west. Avenues run north-south. Numbers increase from south to north along the avenues, but you should always ask for a cross street when getting an avenue address. This plan becomes very chaotic below 14th St.; get a good map and ask for directions.

New York began at the southern tip of Manhattan, in the area around **Battery Park** where the first Dutch settled (1, 9 to South Ferry; 4, 5 to Bowling Green). The nearby harbor, with the **South St. Seaport** tourist magnet, provided the commercial opportunities that helped NYC to succeed (2, 3, 4, 5, J, M, Z to Fulton St.). Historic Manhattan, however, lies in the shadows of the imposing financial buildings around **Wall St.** (4, 5 to Bowling Green) and the civic offices around **City Hall** (2, 3 to Park Pl.; 4, 5, 6, J, M, Z to Chambers St./Brooklyn Bridge/City Hall). A little farther north, neighborhoods rich in the cultures brought by late 19th-century immigrants sit below Houston St. (pronounced *HOW-ston*, unlike the Texas city)— **Little Italy, Chinatown** (J, N, R, 6, A, C, E, 1, 9 to Canal St.), and the southern blocks

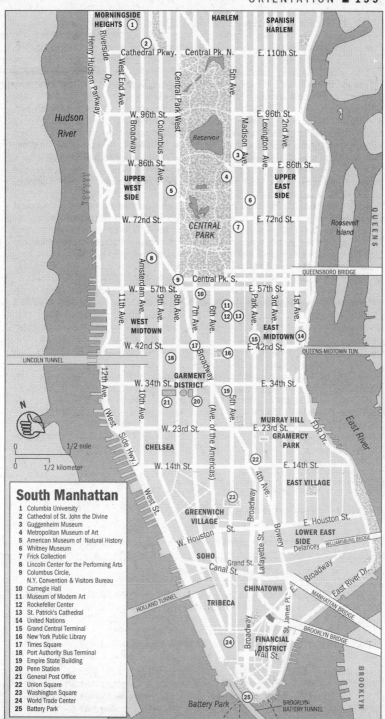

MID-ATLANTIC

South Manhattan

1 Columbia University
2 Cathedral of St. John the Divine
3 Guggenheim Museum
4 Metropolitan Museum of Art
5 American Museum of Natural History
6 Whitney Museum
7 Frick Collection
8 Lincoln Center for the Performing Arts
9 Columbus Circle,
   N.Y. Convention & Visitors Bureau
10 Carnegie Hall
11 Museum of Modern Art
12 Rockefeller Center
13 St. Patrick's Cathedral
14 United Nations
15 Grand Central Terminal
16 New York Public Library
17 Times Square
18 Port Authority Bus Terminal
19 Empire State Building
20 Penn Station
21 General Post Office
22 Union Square
23 Washington Square
24 World Trade Center
25 Battery Park

of the historically Jewish **Lower East Side** (G, M, E, J, Z to Essex/Delancey St.). Once home to Eastern European and Russian Jews, Delancey and Elizabeth St. now offer pasta and Morroccan silks. The up-and-coming nook of high fashion (some call it **NoLIta** for "North of **Little Italy**"), extends roughly down from Houston to Spring St. and over from Lafayette to the Bowery. To the west lies **TriBeCa** ("Triangle Below Canal St.;" 1, 9 to Franklin St.; A, C, E to Canal St.), the industrial-chic home of the late John F. Kennedy, Jr. and his wife Carolyn. **SoHo** (for "South of Houston;" C, E to Spring St.; N, R to Prince St.), a former warehouse district just north of TriBeCa, shelters art galleries, chic boutiques, and pouting waifs. Above SoHo thrives **Greenwich Village,** whose jumbled streets, trendy shops, and cafes have long housed intense political and artistic activity (1, 9 to Christopher St. or Houston St.; A, B, C, D, E, F, to W 4th St.; N, R to 8th St.). **The Village** primarily indicates the western part (from Broadway west to the Hudson River); the (cheaper, younger, and trendier) area east of Broadway is called the **East Village** (6 to Astor Pl.).

A few blocks north of Greenwich Village, stretching across the west teens and 20s, lies **Chelsea** (C, E to 23rd St.; 1, 9 to 28th St. or 23rd St.). East of Chelsea, **Gramercy Park's** pastoral collection of elegant brownstones seem straight out of Edith Wharton's *Age of Innocence* (N, R, 6 to 23rd St.). **Midtown Manhattan,** 34th to 59th St., boasts skyscrapers that support over a million elevated offices. East Midtown's department stores outfit New York (S, 4, 5, 6, 7, to Grand Central; N, R to Fifth Ave.; B, Q to 57th St.); West Midtown's **Theater District** and **Times Square** entertain (N, R, S, 1, 2, 3, 7, 9 to Times Sq.; C, E to 50th St.; B, D, E to Seventh Ave.). North of Midtown, **Central Park** slices Manhattan into East and West. The **Upper West Side's** cultural venues and Central Park West's residences neighbor Columbus Ave.'s chic boutiques and sidewalk cafes (1, 9, 2, 3 anywhere between 59th St./Columbus Circle and 96th St.). The **Upper East Side's** galleries and museums create an even more rarefied atmosphere amidst the elegant apartments of Fifth and Park Ave. (4, 5, 6 anywhere between 59th St. and 96th St.).

Above E. 97th St., commuter trains emerge from the tunnel, marking where the Upper East Side's opulence ends and the *barrio* begins (6 to 110th St.). Above W. 110th St., in **Morningside Heights,** sits the Ivy League's **Columbia University. Harlem** produced the Harlem Renaissance of black artists and writers in the 20s and the revolutionary Black Power movement of the 60s (1, 9 anywhere between 125th and 145th St.; A, B, C, D anywhere between 125th St. and 145th St.). **Washington Heights,** north of Harlem, is home to Fort Tryon Park and various immigrant communities (A, C, 1, 9 to Washington Heights).

◹ GETTING THERE AND AWAY

From New Jersey, there are three ways to reach the city by car. The **George Washington Bridge** crosses the Hudson River into northern Manhattan and gives easy access to either Harlem River Dr. or the West Side Hwy. From the NJ Turnpike you'll probably end up going through Weehawken, NJ, to the **Lincoln Tunnel,** which exits in Midtown in the west 40s. The **Holland Tunnel** connects to lower Manhattan, exiting into the SoHo and TriBeCa area. Coming from New England or Connecticut on I-95, follow signs for the **Triboro Bridge.** From there get onto **FDR Dr.,** which runs along the east side of Manhattan and exits onto city streets every 10 blocks or so. Another option is to look for the **Willis Ave. Bridge exit** on I-95 to avoid the toll, and enter Manhattan north on the FDR Drive. From Upstate, take the Saw Mill Pkwy. south; it becomes the West Side Hwy. in Manhattan. Expect $4-7 **tolls.**

Hitchhiking is illegal in New York State, and cops strictly enforce the law within NYC. *Hitching in and around New York City is suicidal; don't do it.*

John F. Kennedy Airport (JFK) (☎ 718-244-4444), 12 mi. from Midtown in southern Queens, handles most international flights. The yellow, white, and blue "long-term parking lot" bus runs every 15min. from any airport terminal to the **Howard Beach-JFK subway station.** From there, take the **A train** to the city (1hr.). **New York Airport Service**

Bus (☎ 718-875-8200) runs every 15-30min. between JFK or LaGuardia and Grand Central Terminal, Penn Station, Port Authority, and midtown hotels (1hr.), 6am-midnight; $13-15. The **SuperShuttle** (☎ 258-3826) will drop you off anywhere in Manhattan between Battery Park and 227th St. On call 24hr.; $13-15. Inquire at JFK Ground Transportation Centers. A **taxi** from JFK to Manhattan costs $30 (plus tolls and tip).

LaGuardia Airport (☎ 718-533-3400), 6 mi. from midtown in NW Queens; domestic flights and air shuttles. **New York Airport Service** and **SuperShuttle** (see **JFK** above). With extra time and light luggage, one can take the **M60 bus** (daily 4:50am-1am; $1.50), which connects in Manhattan to the 1 and 9 trains at 116th St. and Broadway, the 2 and 3 at 125th St. and Lenox Ave., and the 4, 5, and 6 at 125th St. and Lexington Ave; in Queens to the N train at Astoria Blvd. and 31st St. Alternatively, the MTA **Q33** and **Q47** buses ($1.50) transfer at the 74th St./Broadway-Roosevelt Ave./Jackson Hts. subway stop in Queens to the 7, E, F, G, or R trains into Manhattan ($1.50). Travel time: at least 1½hr. **Taxis** to Manhattan are $16-26 (plus tolls and tip). A **water shuttle** is cheaper than a cab and takes less time ($15, round-trip $25).

Newark International Airport (☎ 973-961-6000), 12 mi. west of midtown in Newark, NJ; domestic and international flights. Often cheaper than JFK or LaGuardia. **Olympia Airport Express** (☎ 964-6233) travels between Newark and Grand Central, Penn Station, and Port Authority every 20-30min. 6am-midnight (25min.-1hr., $10; tickets may be purchased on the bus). The **SuperShuttle** also goes to Manhattan ($17.50-22.50, see **JFK,** above). **New Jersey Transit Authority (NJTA)** (☎ 973-762-5100) runs an **Air Link bus #302** ($4) between the airport and Newark's Penn Station (not Manhattan's). From there bus #108 ($3.25, exact change) goes to Port Authority. **PATH trains** (☎ 800-234-7284; $1) run from Newark Penn Station into Manhattan, stopping at the World Trade Center, Christopher St., 6th Ave., 9th St., 14th St., 23rd St. and 33rd St. (20-30min.) $34-51 **taxi** fare negotiable.

Trains: On the East side, **Grand Central Terminal,** 42nd St. and Park Ave. (subway: #4, 5, 6, 7 or S to 42nd St./Grand Central), handles **Metro-North** (☎ 800-638-7646) commuter lines to Connecticut and NY suburbs. **Amtrak** (☎ 800-872-7245) runs out of **Penn Station,** 33rd St. and 8th Ave. (subway: 1, 2, 3, 9, or A, C, E to 34th St./Penn Station). To: Washington, D.C. (3-4hr., $67-118); Boston, MA (4-6hr., $50-71); and Philadelphia (1½hr., $43-77). The **Long Island Railroad (LIRR)** (☎ 718-217-5477) and **NJ Transit** (☎ 973-762-5100) commuter rails also chug from Penn Station. Nearby at 33rd St. and 6th Ave., you can catch a **PATH** train to New Jersey (☎ 800-234-7284).

Buses: Greyhound and Peter Pan buslines leave the Port Authority Terminal, 41st-42nd St. and 8th Ave. (☎ 435-7000; subway: A, C, E to 42nd St.-Port Authority). Watch for con-artists and pickpockets, especially at night. To: Boston, MA (4½hr., $39); Philadelphia, PA (2hr., $20); and Washington, D.C. (4½hr., $39).

▄ GETTING AROUND

PUBLIC TRANSIT

Information: NYC Transit Information Bureau (☎ 718-330-1234, 718-330-4847 for non-English-speakers; open daily 6am-9pm) has **subway maps,** as do token booths and the visitors bureau. The *Manhattan Yellow Pages* contains detailed subway, PATH, and bus maps. Subways and buses are run by the **Metropolitan Transit Authority (MTA).**

MetroCards and Transfers: The main form of currency for the subway and buses. With the purchase of a $15 card, you get one free ride. MetroCards can make free subway-bus, bus-subway, and bus-bus transfers. When the card is swiped on the initial ride, a free transfer (good for 2hr.) is electronically stored on your MetroCard. Without the MetroCard (using tokens), bus-subway or subway-bus transfers are not free. 1 MetroCard can store up to 4 transfers for people traveling in a group. Passengers on a north-south bus can generally only transfer to a bus going east-west. The 1-day ($4), 7-day ($17), and 30-day ($63) **"Unlimited Rides" MetroCards** (as opposed to "Pay-Per-Ride" cards) allow unlimited use, and are good for tourists visiting many sights.

MID-ATLANTIC

Buses: $1.50. Buses take tokens, MetroCards, and exact change—not bills. Buses are often slower than subways, but are relatively safer and cleaner. Buses stop roughly every 2 blocks and run crosstown (east-west), as well as uptown and downtown (north-south). For subway-bus transfers, see MetroCard and Transfers, above. Ring to get off. Look for blue signposts announcing bus numbers or glass-walled shelters displaying a map of the route and a schedule of arrival times.

Subway: Operates 24hr. a day, 365 days a year. $1.50. Groups of 4 may find a cab to be cheaper and more expedient for short distances. Long distances are best traveled by subway; once inside, a passenger may transfer onto any other train without restrictions. "Express" trains run at all hours and stop only at certain major stations; "locals" stop everywhere. Be sure to check the letter or number and the destination of each train, since trains with different destinations often use the same track. When in doubt, ask the conductor, who usually sits near the middle of the train. On the train, pay attention to the often garbled announcements—trains occasionally change mid-route from local to express or vice-versa. Rush-hour crowds make air and seating scarce. You'll see **glass globes** outside of most **subway entrances.** If the globe is green, the entrance is open 24hr. A red globe indicates that the entrance is somehow restricted.

SUBWAY SAFETY In crowded stations (most notably those around 42nd St.), pickpockets find work; violent crimes occasionally occur in stations that are deserted. Stay alert and stick to well-lit areas; most stations have clearly marked "off-hours" waiting areas that are under observation and significantly safer. When boarding, pick a car with a number of other passengers in it, or sit near the middle of the train, in the conductor's car. *For safety reasons, try to avoid riding the subways between midnight and 7am, especially above E. 96th St. and W. 120th St. and outside Manhattan.*

OTHER TRANSPORTATION

Taxis: Most people in Manhattan hail yellow (licensed) cabs on the street. Call 411 to ask for a cab dispatcher.

Car Rental: AAMCAR Rent-a-Car, 315 W. 96th St., between West End Ave. and Riverside Dr. (☎222-8500). **Dollar,** at JFK ☎718-656-2400; at LaGuardia ☎718-244-1235. **Enterprise,** ☎800-566-9249. **Nationwide,** 241 W. 40th St., between 7th and 8th Ave. (☎867-1234).

Bike Rental: Pedal Pushers, 1306 2nd Ave. between 68th and 69th St. (☎288-5592). 3-speeds $4 per hr., $10 per day, $12 overnight; 10-speeds $5/$14/$14; mountain bikes $6/$17/$25. Overnight rentals require $150 deposit on a major credit card, regular rentals only require major credit card, passport, or a NY state driver's license deposit. Open F-M 10am-6pm, W 10am-7pm, Th 10am-8pm. Helmet $2 per day.

■ PRACTICAL INFORMATION

Visitor Info: Times Square Visitors Center, 1560 Broadway, between 46th and 47th St. (☎869-5453). Open daily 9am-6pm. Other locations: Grand Central terminal, south side of main concourse; Penn Station terminal, south side of Amtrak rotunda.

Help Lines: AIDS Hotline, ☎447-8200. Open daily 9am-9pm; 24hr. recording. **Crime Victims' Hotline,** ☎577-7777. **Sex Crimes Report Line,** ☎267-7273. Both 24hr.

Medical Services: Walk-in Clinic, 55 E. 34th St. (☎252-6001, ext. 2), between Park and Madison Ave. Open M-Th 8am-8pm, Sa 9am-3pm, Su 9am-2pm.

Post Office: 421 8th Ave. (☎330-2902), across from Madison Sq. Garden. Open 24hr. For General Delivery, mail to and use the entrance at 390 9th Ave. **ZIP code:** 10001.

Area code: 212 or 646 (Manhattan); 718 (other 4 boroughs); 917 (cell phones). In text 212, unless noted.

ACCOMMODATIONS

The cost of living in New York is *very high*. A night at a full-service establishment runs $125 (plus 13.4% hotel tax), but you can get a bed for under $60 a night.

HOSTELS: BELOW 72ND ST.

Chelsea International Hostel, 251 W. 20th St. between 7th and 8th Ave., in Chelsea (☎ 647-0010; fax 727-7289). Subway: 1, 9, C, or E to 23rd St. On a block with a police precinct. Overflowing with funky youth travelers. Congenial staff offers pizza W night. All rooms have sink, and guests have access to a backyard garden. Kitchens and laundry available. Internet access. Check-in 8am-6pm. Key deposit $10. Smallish but adequate 4- and 6-person dorms $25; private rooms $60. Reservations recommended.

Chelsea Center Hostel, 313 W. 29th St. between 8th and 9th Ave., in Chelsea (☎ 643-0214; fax 473-3945). Subway: 1, 2, 3, 9, A, C, or E to 34th St. To enter, ring the labeled buzzer at the door. Knowledgeable, multi-lingual staff. Room for 22 guests in this home-turned-hostel, 16 of whom stay in a spacious basement room with a summer camp feel. 5 others stay in a bedroom on the main floor. 2 showers. Light breakfast included. Linen provided. 2-week max. stay. Check-in 8:30am-10:30pm. Flexible lockout 11am-5pm. Dorm beds $28. Cash and traveler's checks only. Call ahead.

YMCA—McBurney, 206 W. 24th St., between 7th and 8th Ave., in Chelsea (☎ 741-9226; fax 741-8724). Subway: 1, 9, C, or E to 23rd St. No-frills, clean rooms. All rooms have TV. Free access to pool and athletic facilities. 25-day max. stay. 24hr. door security. Reception 8am-11pm. Check-out noon. Singles $59-71; doubles $72-82; triples $94-104; quads $105-115; with A/C add $5. Key deposit $5. Usually has vacancies, but reservations are advisable. Wheelchair accessible.

International Student Hospice, 154 E. 33rd St., between Lexington and 3rd Ave., in Gramercy (☎ 228-7470). Subway: 6 to 33rd St. Up a flight of stairs in a brownstone with a brass plaque saying "I.S.H." Resembles a house full of bric-a-brac. Rooms for 1-4 people and tiny hall bathroom. $28 per night including tax. Call ahead.

Aladdin Hotel, 317 W. 45th St., between 8th and 9th Ave. (☎ 246-8580; fax 246-6036). Subway: 1, 2, 3, 9, A, C, E, N, or R to 42nd St.-Times Sq. Its lobby and common room/smoking lounge look like a club or a circus. International travelers fill rooftop garden. Internet access $1 per 3min. Lockers of various size $3-5. Laundry facilities. 4-bed dorms $35 per bed; singles and doubles with shared bath $87-99. Reserve at least one week in advance.

Big Apple Hostel, 119th W. 45th St., between 6th and 7th Ave. (☎ 302-2603; fax 302-2605). Subway: 1, 2, 3, 9, A, B, C, D, E, F, N, Q, or R to 42nd St.-Times Sq. Centrally located, this hostel has clean, carpeted rooms, kitchen with refrigerator, luggage room, big back deck with grill, and laundry facilities. Americans accepted with out-of-state photo ID or other proof that they're tourists. Reception 24hr. Safe deposit 25¢. Internet access $1 per 5min. Bunk in dorm-style room with shared bath $30; singles and doubles $80. No reservations Aug.-Sept., but they'll hold a bed if you call after 11:30am day-of; advance reservations accepted Oct.-June through website or by fax—send your credit card number. No wheelchair access.

YMCA—Vanderbilt, 224 E. 47th St. (☎ 756-9600; fax 752-0210), between 2nd and 3rd Ave. Subway: 6 to 51st St.; or E or F to Lexington/3rd Ave. Convenient and well-run, with reasonable security. Clean, bright lobby bustles with international visitors. Each small room has A/C and cable TV; usually enough bathrooms to go around. Free use of well-equipped gym and safe boxes. Wheelchair accessible. Five shuttles per day to the airports. 25-night maximum stay. Check-in 3pm. Check-out 11am; luggage storage until departure $1 per bag. Key deposit $10. Singles $68; doubles $81, with sink $83. Make reservations 2-3 weeks in advance and guarantee with a deposit.

West Side YMCA, 5 W. 63rd St., near Central Park W. (☎ 875-4273 or 875-4173; fax 875-1334). Subway: 1, 9, A, B, C, or D to 59th St. Institutionalized atmosphere behind Moorish facade. Access to pool and gym, with cafe and central location. All rooms have A/C and cable TV. Shuttle buses to airports available ($14 to LaGuardia, $16 to JFK). Luggage storage. 25-day max. stay. Check-in 2:30pm. Check-out noon. Singles $72, with bath $105; doubles (bunk beds) $84, with bath (double bed) $120. Membership fees included. Deposit required to reserve. Wheelchair accessible.

HOSTELS: ABOVE 72ND ST. AND OUTER BURROUGHS

International Student Center, 38 W. 88th St., between Central Park W. and Columbus Ave. (☎ 787-7706; fax 580-9283). Subway: B or C to 86th St. Open only to foreigners aged 18-30; foreign passport or valid visa required. No-frills, livable dorms include showers and linens. Single and co-ed rooms available. Large TV lounge with kitchen and fridge. 1-week maximum stay (flexible in winter). Reception 8am-11pm. Key deposit $10. 8- to 10-bed dorms $15. No reservations and generally full in summer—call after 10:30am day-of to check vacancies. No wheelchair access; lots of stairs.

De Hirsch Residence, 1395 Lexington Ave., at 92nd St. (☎ 415-5650 or 800-858-4692; fax 415-5578). Subway: 6 to 96th St. Affiliated with the 92nd St. YMHA/YWHA. Some of the larger, cleaner, and more convenient hosteling in the city. Rooms near huge hall bathrooms, kitchens, and laundry on every other floor. Single-sex floors, strictly enforced. 24hr. access and security. Access to facilities of 92nd St. Y, including gym, pool, and reduced rates for concerts. Activities like video nights and walking tours of NYC. All have A/C. Rents by the month. Single $945 per month; shared room $655-765 per person per month. Wheelchair accessible.

New York International HI-AYH Hostel, 891 Amsterdam Ave., at 103rd St. (☎ 932-2300; fax 932-2574). Subway: 1, 9, B, or C to 103rd St. In a block-long, landmark building—the largest in the US, with 624 beds. Shares site with several eateries, the **CIEE Student Center** (☎ 666-3619), a depot for travelers, and a **Council Travel** office. Soft carpets and spotless bathrooms. Members' kitchens and dining rooms, laundry machines, TV lounges, and large garden. Walking tours and outings. Internet access. Key-card entry to rooms. Linen and towels included. Secure storage area and lockers. 29-night max. stay, 7-nights in summer. Open 24hr. Check-in any time. Check-out 11am (late check-out fee $5). Nov.-Apr. 10- to 12-bed dorms $27; 6- to 8-bed dorms $30; 4-bed dorms $33. May-Oct. dorms $2 more. Non-members $3 more. Groups of 4-9 may get private rooms with bath ($120); groups of 10 or more definitely will. Credit card reservations a must; 1-night deposit to confirm reservations. Wheelchair accessible.

Manhattan Youth Castle, 1596 Lexington Ave. between 101st and 102nd St. (☎ 831-4440; fax 722-55746). Subway: 6 to 103rd St. Small and affordable, in the friendly area bordering Spanish Harlem and the Upper East Side. Helpful staff offers themed tours of the city. 3-week maximum stay. Passport ID required. Key deposit $5. $20-30 per person per day; $120-180 per person per week. Reservations recommended. Call 2 months in advance for summer, otherwise 2 weeks is sufficient.

Central Park Hostel, 19 W. 103rd St., near Manhattan Ave. (☎ 678-0491). Subway: B, C to 103rd St. Slightly away from the heart of Manhattan, this hostel makes up for it with its renovated cleanliness. Shared bathrooms. Linen/towels provided. Lockers available. A/C. 2-week max. stay. Dorm $25; private double $75.

Jazz on the Park, 36 W. 106th St., at Central Park W. (☎ 932-1600). Subway: B or C to 103rd St. Clean, newly renovated hostel-dom. Chic, modern decor. Lockers and A/C to make you a real cool cat. Internet access. Java bar hosts live bands and other assorted hepcats. Taxes, linens, towels, and breakfast included. Check-out 11am. 12- to 14-bed dorms $30; 4-bed dorms $34. No wheelchair access.

Uptown Hostel, 239 Lenox/Malcolm X Ave., at 122nd St. (☎ 666-0559; fax 663-5000). Subway: 2 or 3 to 125th St. Gisèle helps long-term travelers find uptown apartments and temporary jobs. Bunk beds in clean, comfy rooms. Big hall bathrooms. Wonderful common room and kitchen. Key deposit $10. Check-in 11am-8pm. Lockout June-Aug. 11am-4pm. Sept.-May singles $17, doubles $23; June-Aug. singles $20, doubles $25. Call as far in advance as possible in summer, 2 days in advance the rest of the year.

Sugar Hill International House, 722 St. Nicholas Ave., at 146th St. (☎ 926-7030). Subway: A, B, C or D to 145th St. Reassuring, lively neighborhood, across from subway. Brownstone with enormous rooms (25-30 beds total). Staff is a wealth of Harlem history and entertainment. Rooms for 2-10 people. All-female room available. Internet access $1 per 10min. Facilities include kitchens, stereo, and library. 2-week maximum stay. Check-in 9am-10pm. Check-out 11am. Key deposit $10. Rooms $25-30. Call 1 month in advance during off-season. No reservations accepted July-Sept. Passport ID required. Owners also run the 4-floor **Blue Rabbit Hostel,** 730 St. Nicholas Ave. (☎491-3892). Has more doubles and privacy. Cats, common room, and kitchen.

YMCA—Flushing, 138-46 Northern Blvd. between Union and Bowne Sts., in Flushing, Queens (☎718-961-6880; fax 718-461-4691). Subway: 7 to Main St.; from there walk 10min. north on Main St. (the avenue numbers should get smaller), and turn right onto Northern Blvd. Popular with neighborhood families for activities, as well as for offering co-ed accommodations. The area between Y and Flushing's shopping district is well populated, but neighborhood deteriorates north of Northern Blvd. Carpeted, small, clean rooms with TV and A/C. Hall bathrooms and public telephones. Daily maid service. Gym, squash, and swimming facilities included. Free breakfast vouchers at local diner. 25-night maximum stay (longer stays possible with advance arrangements). Singles $50; doubles $70; triples $80. Key deposit $10. Photo ID required. Reserve at least a month in advance for summer, 1 week otherwise.

HOTELS: BELOW MIDTOWN

Pioneer Hotel, 341 Broome St. between Elizabeth St. and the Bowery. (☎226-1482; fax 266-3525). Subway: N or R to Canal and walk north several blocks to Broome. The Pioneer is a good, no-frills place to stay if you want to be close to nightlife of SoHo and East Village. All rooms have TV, sinks, and ceiling fans. Rooms with private bath have A/C. Generally tight security at night. Check-out 11am. Singles $62; doubles $70, with bath $82; triples with bath $138. Reservations recommended, at least 6 weeks in advance during peak season.

St. Mark's Hotel, corner of St. Mark's Pl. and 3rd Ave. (☎674-2192). Renovated, and perhaps the most exciting location in the city. Call ahead for reservations. Doubles with private bath and cable TV $100, tax included. Cash or travelers checks only.

Larchmont Hotel, 27 W. 11th St., between 5th and 6th Ave., in Greenwich (☎989-9333; fax 989-9496). Subway: 4, 5, 6, N, R, or L to 14th St./Union Sq. Spacious, clean rooms in a whitewashed brownstone on a quiet block. Clientele ranges from Californian 20-somethings to European retirees. A/C, TV, desks, closets, and wash basins in all rooms. Shared bath. Continental breakfast included. Singles $70-95; doubles $90-115; queen-size bed $109-125. Reserve 5-6 weeks in advance.

Hotel 17, 225 E. 17th St., between 2nd and 3rd Ave., near Gramercy Park (☎475-2845; fax 677-8178). This historic site served as the setting for Woody Allen's *Manhattan Murder Mystery;* Madonna had her portrait done here. Mostly foreign crowd. Beautiful, high-ceilinged rooms with sink and A/C. Check-out noon. Singles $81; doubles $110; triples $171 (tax included). If staying for 5 days in a triple, $160 per night.

Carlton Arms Hotel, 160 E. 25th St., between Lexington and 3rd Ave., in Gramercy (☎679-0680). Subway: 6 to 23rd St. Each room is decorated by a different artist; one indulges childhood fantasies with stuffed animals and blackboard walls. All 54 rooms have sinks. $6-8 discounts for students and foreign travelers. Pay for 7 or more nights up front and get a 10% discount. Check-out 11:30am. Singles $63, with bath $75; doubles $80/$92; triples $99/$111; quads $105/$117. Reserve for summer 2 months in advance; confirm 10 days in advance.

Gershwin Hotel, 7 E. 27th St., between 5th and Madison Ave., in Gramercy (☎545-8000; fax 684-5546). Subway: 6, N, or R to 28th St. Pristine yet funky hotel full of pop art, random furniture, and artsy 20-somethings. Has spaces for poetry, comedy, concerts, and open-mic nights. Internet $1 per 4min. 21-night max. stay. Check-out 11am. Reception 24hr. 8-12 bed dorms $30 per bed, with TV and phone $50; 4-bed dorms $40; 2-bed dorms $60. Private rooms (single or double occupancy) $99-169; triples and quads add $10 per person.

Senton Hotel, 39-41 W. 27th St., between 6th Ave. and Broadway, in Gramercy (☎684-5800; fax 545-1690). Subway: R to 28th St. Comfortable beds in spacious quarters. A/C, cable TV, VCR, and refrigerators in every room. The hotel is renovating; some rooms have been completed. Security 24hr. Singles $57; with private bath $68; doubles $78; 2-room suites with 4 double beds $83.

Murray Hill Inn, 143 E. 30th St., between Lexington and 3rd Ave., in Murray Hill (☎683-6900 or 888-996-6376). Subway: 6 to 28th St. Clean, floral-print rooms exude a Holiday Inn feel at reasonable prices. 5 floors—no elevator. All rooms have sink, A/C, cable TV, and phone. 21-day max. stay. Check-in 2pm. Check-out noon. Singles $75, private bath $115; doubles $95/$125. Extra bed $10.

Herald Square Hotel, 19 W. 31st St., at 5th Ave., near Herald Sq. (☎279-4017 or 800-727-1888; fax 643-9208). Subway: B, D, F, N, or R to 34th St. In the Beaux-Arts home of the original *Life* magazine. Small, pleasant rooms have undergone recent renovations; all include cable TV, safe, phone, voicemail messaging, and A/C. Singles $60, with bath $85; doubles $115; twins $130; triples $140; quads $150. 10% discount for international students. Reserve 2-3 weeks in advance.

Hotel Stanford, 43 W. 32nd St., between 5th Ave. and Broadway, near Herald Sq. (☎563-1500 or 800-365-1114; fax 629-0043). Subway: B, D, F, N, or R to 34th St. In NY's Korean district, this glitzy hotel's lobby sparkles with a marble floor. Adjoins the **Maxim Bar** and the **Pari Pari Ko Bakery,** which serves up Korean pastries. Impeccably clean rooms, with firm mattresses, plush carpeting, cable TV, A/C, small refrigerators. Continental breakfast included. Check-out noon; fee for late check-out. Singles $90-110; doubles and triples $120-150. Reservations recommended.

HOTELS: ABOVE MIDTOWN AND OUTER BOROUGHS

Broadway Inn, 264 W. 46th St., at 8th Ave., in Times Square (☎997-9200 or 800-826-6300; fax 768-2807). Subway: 1, 2, 3, 9, 7, N, R, or S to 42nd St.-Times Square. These quiet, clean rooms have the dignity of a European B&B. TV, dataport jack, private bath, and A/C in all rooms. Continental breakfast included. Singles $95-115; doubles $135-195 (high-end includes jacuzzi); suites (for 2 adults and 2 children 6-12 or 3 adults) $195-225. No wheelchair access.

Amsterdam Inn, 340 Amsterdam Ave., at 76th St. (☎579-7500; fax 579-6127). Subway: 1 or 9 to 79th St. Safe and well-located, the 25 rooms are small but renovated and clean. 2-flight walk up to the "first" floor. All rooms have A/C and color TV. Check-in 3pm. Check-out 11am. Singles $75; doubles $95; with private bath $115-125.

Hotel Belleclaire, 250 W. 77th St., corner of Broadway. (☎362-7700). Check-in 3pm. Check-out noon. Economy (shared bath) room $99; queen bed $169; two double beds $189. Reservations recommended.

Hayden Hall, 117 W. 79th St., off Columbus Ave. (☎787-4900; fax 496-3975). Subway: B or C to 81st St. Great location, but dingy. Good weekly rates. Singles and doubles with shared bath $50; 2- to 3-person room with private bath $90; 4-person room $100; 2-room suite for up to 4 $125. Reservations recommended.

DORMITORIES

Columbia University, 1230 Amsterdam Ave., at 120th St. (☎678-3235; fax 678-3222). Subway: 1, 9 to 116th St. Whittier Hall sets aside 10 rooms year-round, all clean and equipped with full beds. Max. 4 people per room. Generally tight 24hr. security. Not the safest neighborhood, but well-populated until fairly late. 1-week max. stay. Singles $55; doubles with A/C and bath (some with kitchen) $75. Reserve in Mar. for May-Aug., in July for Sept.-Dec. Credit card deposit required.

New York University, 14a Washington Pl. (☎998-4621). NYU summer school students get priority and lower rates, and housing is only available for individuals. Options in the East and West Villages as well as near South St. Seaport. Minimum age 17, unless an approved summer school student. 11-12 week max. stay. 3 week minimum stay. Reception M-Tu 9am-5pm, W-Th 9am-7pm, Su 9am-2pm. Call for prices.

◘ FOOD

New York will dazzle you with its culinary bounty. City dining, like the population, spans the globe, ranging from sushi bars to wild combinations like Afghani/Italian and Mexican/Lebanese.

LOWER MANHATTAN

Lower Manhattan eateries cater to sharply clad Wall St. brokers and bankers on lunch break; they offer cheap food prepared grease-lightning-fast, always available as takeout. Fast-food joints pepper Broadway near Dey and John St., steps away from the overpriced offerings of the Main Concourse of the World Trade Center. In the summer, food **pushcarts** form a solid wall along Broadway between Cedar and Liberty St. If you prefer that comforting suburban fare, **Pier 17** at South St. Seaport has a food court worthy of its mini-mall.

Zigolini's, 66 Pearl St., at Coenties Alley (☎425-7171). One of the few places in the area where you can get an indoor, air-conditioned seat most of the time, although there is more seating outside. Serves filling sandwiches ($5-7) and great pasta ($7-11), Zigolini's also offers the option of creating your own sandwich. Open M-F 7am-7pm.

LITTLE ITALY

A chunk of Naples has migrated (and unfortunately sold out) to this lively, compact quarter roughly bounded by Canal, Lafayette, Houston St., and the Bowery. **Mulberry St.** is the main drag and the appetite avenue of Little Italy. Stroll here after 7pm to catch street life, but arrive earlier to get a good table.

Da Nico, 164 Mulberry St. between Broome and Grand St. (☎343-1212). Cheap, tasty food in a lovely environment or tree-shaded garden in back—frequented by Al Pacino and Johnny Depp. Lunch: pasta $6-10, entrees $6.50-12.50. Dinner: pasta $10-15, entrees $11-25. Open Su-Th 11am-11pm, F-Sa 11am-midnight.

Caffè Palermo, 148 Mulberry St. between Grand and Hester St. (☎431-4205). The best of the *caffè* offerings along Mulberry. In summers, Palermo opens onto the street. Most pastries $3-5. The staff takes much pride in its tasty *tiramisù* ($5); the cannoli ($2.75) and cappuccino ($3.25) are also quite good. Open daily 10am-midnight.

CHINATOWN

Join the crowds that push through the narrow, chaotic streets of one of the oldest Chinatowns in the US. More than 300 restaurants squished into this tiny area serve some of the best Chinese, Thai, and Vietnamese eats around.

🍴 **Hop Kee,** 21 Mott St., at the corner of Mosco St. (☎964-8365). Bare bones in the ambiance department, but this is *real* Chinese food. Their specialties are expensive—snails Cantonese-style ($10.25) and pineapple with roasted duck ($14.75)—but dishes like beef chow fun are only $4.10. Open daily 11am-4am.

🍴 **H.S.F. Restaurant,** 46 Bowery (☎374-1319). Order their buffet special, where they bring you a pot of boiling broth and you pick vegetables, dumplings, etc. from their huge buffet and cook it at your table ($19.95 per person, all-you-can-eat; served after 5). Also known for their dim sum. Open daily 8am-4:30pm.

🍴 **Hong Kong Egg Cake Co.,** on the corner of Mott and Mosco St., in a small red shack—just follow the line wrapped around the corner. Cecelia Tam will make you a dozen soft, sweet egg cakes ($1) fresh from the skillet that she's been at for 19 years. Open W-Th and Sa-Su 10:30am-5pm.

Chinatown Ice Cream Factory, 65 Bayard St., at Mott St. (☎608-4170). Homemade lychee, taro, ginger, red bean, or green tea ice cream. 1 scoop $2, 2 $3.60, 3 $4.60. Open Su-Th noon-11:30pm, F-Sa 11:30am-11:30pm.

SOHO AND TRIBECA

In SoHo, food is all about image, so don't be surprised if you find it hard to get a cheap meal. Often the best deal in SoHo is brunch, when the neighborhood shows its most good-natured front. Dining in TriBeCa is generally a much funkier (and blessedly cheaper) experience than in SoHo. TriBeCa's restaurants are often hidden among the hulking warehouses.

🍴 **Space Untitled,** 133 Greene St., near Houston St. (☎260-8962). The best of SoHo—huge, warehouse-like space with plenty of bar stools and chairs to make yourself comfortable. Sandwiches $3-7; fabulous desserts $1.75-4.50. Coffee $1.50-2; wine and beer $4.50. Open M-Th 8am-10pm, F-Sa 8am-11pm, Su 8am-9pm.

MID-ATLANTIC

■ **Penang,** 109 Spring St. between Mercer and Greene St., in SoHo (☎274-8883). Excellent Malaysian cuisine served in an exotic setting. Savor the award-winning *roti canai* $4.25 or the tasty *poh-piah* (steamed spring rolls) $6. Entrees ($8-20) are generally pricey, but worth it. At $9, cocktails may bruise your funds, especially since you'll want a few while waiting for a table on weekends. Open M-Th noon-midnight, F-Sa noon-1am.

■ **Le Gamin Cafe,** 50 MacDougal St. between Prince and Houston St., in SoHo (☎254-4678). Always packed with locals, this very European cafe offers simple French-inspired fare. The *salade de chevre chaudaux noix* (goat cheese croutons, tomato, mesclun, and walnuts, $9) is sumptuous. Crepes $3.50-8. Open daily 8am-midnight.

Bar Odeon, 138 W. Broadway between Thomas and Duane St., in TriBeCa (☎233-6436). Tasty French-American served in a casual setting. Entrees $11-20. Open M-Th 11:30am-midnight, F-Su 11-12:30am.

Bubby's, 120 Hudson St., at N. Moore St., in TriBeCa (☎219-0666). Rough brick walls, window seats, and walls of windows add to this cafe's stylish simplicity. Scones, muffins, and pies keep this place packed with locals; entrees ($9-15) are a bit expensive, but great soups and salads ($5-10) will fill you up. Brunch Sa-Su 9am-4:45pm; expect a wait. Open M-Tu 8am-11pm, W-F 8am-3am, Sa 9am-3am, Su 9am-10pm.

LOWER EAST SIDE

Cultures clash here, where pasty-faced punks and trustafarians dine alongside an older generation conversing in Polish, Hungarian, and Yiddish. The neighborhood took in the huddled masses, and in return got lots of cool places to eat, including the city's finest **kosher Jewish eateries.** Nearby **NoLIta** has sleek, hip restaurants if corned beef and potato *latkas* are too heavy for you.

■ **Katz's Delicatessen,** 205 E. Houston St., near Orchard St. (☎254-2246). Since 1888, Katz's has remained an authentic Jewish deli. Katz's widened its appeal with its "Send a salami to your boy in the army" campaign during WWII. Every president in the last 2 decades has proudly received a Katz salami. The food is orgasmic (as Meg Ryan confirmed, when she made a loud scene here in *When Harry Met Sally*), but you pay extra for the atmosphere. Heroes $5.10, knishes $2.25, franks $2.15, sandwiches around $9. Open Su-Tu 8am-10pm, W-Th 8am-11pm, F-Sa 8am-3am.

■ **Economy Candy,** 108 Rivington St. (☎254-1531). Imported chocolates, jams, and confections fill this store, all at rock-bottom prices. Step into this sweet-tooth's heaven and treat yourself to a huge bag of gummi bears ($2) or a pound of chocolate-covered apricots ($5). They also have cotton candy ($2), and Turkish desserts, as well as a selection of spices. Open M-F 8:30am-6pm, Sa 10am-5pm, Su 8:30am-5pm.

■ **Guss Lower East Side Pickle Corp.,** 35 Essex St., at Hester St. (☎254-4477 or 800-252-4877). Pickles and poultry used to be sold in pushcarts until 1938, when they were abolished for hygiene and health reasons. Guss still sells glorious gherkins straight out of vats, from super-sour to sweet (individual 50¢-$2; quart $4). Cole slaw, pickled tomatoes, and t-shirts ($10) are also available. Open Su-Th 9am-6pm, F 9am-4pm.

■ **Rice,** 227 Mott St. between Prince and Spring St., in NoLIta (☎226-5775). Fantastic food—and darn cheap. Standard favorites here—basmati, jasmine, sticky, and Japanese, with sauces ranging from mango chutney to Aleppo yogurt ($1). Add ratatouille, shrimp coconut curry, or chicken satay, among other enticing toppings ($3.50-8). Crowds spill out into the street waiting for tables. Beer only. Open daily noon-midnight. Cash only.

Cafe Gitane, 242 Mott St., at Prince St. (☎334-9552). A focal point of NoLIta life, this cafe specializes in seeing and being seen. Always crowded, a rack of glossy fashion mags invites all to linger. Salads $5-7, glass of wine $5-7, tasty grilled eggplant with goat cheese and pesto on watercress $8. Open daily 9am-midnight. Cash only.

EAST VILLAGE AND ALPHABET CITY

First and **2nd Ave.** are the best for restaurant-exploring. **St. Mark's Place** hosts a slew of inexpensive and popular village institutions, and at night, **Avenue A** throbs with bars and sidewalk cafes. Twenty-six cheap Indian restaurants line **6th St.** between 1st and 2nd Ave. If you look indecisive, anxious managers may offer free wine or discounts on already cheap food.

■ **Frank's,** 88 2nd Ave., at E. 5th St. (☎420-0202). An adorable sliver of a place with a friendly bistro feeling. Breakfasts served in sets ($6 or $9); lunch menu centers around sandwiches ($6-8) and pasta ($9-10). M-F 5:30-7pm is Aperitivo Hour—free antipasti until 6:30pm. Expect a wait for seats. Open for lunch daily 10:30am-4pm; dinner M-Th 5pm-1am, F-Sa 5pm-2am, Su 5pm-midnight.

■ **Dojo Restaurant,** 24 St. Mark's Pl. between 2nd and 3rd Ave. (☎674-9821). One of the most popular restaurants and hangouts in the East Village, it offers vegetarian and Japanese foods that combine the healthy with the inexplicably tasty. You can even take home a container of Dojo's renowned carrot dressing. Soyburgers with brown rice and salad $3.50. Dojo salad $5. Beer $2.75-4; pitchers $12-15. Outdoor tables imbued with noisy St. Mark's ambience. Open Su-Th 11am-1am, F-Sa 11am-2am.

Flor's Kitchen, 149 1st Ave., at 9th St. (☎387-8949). Small Venezuelan restaurant serving up *arepas* (filled corn cakes, $2.75-3.25) and *empanadas* ($2.75). Open M-Th 11am-11pm, F-Sa 11am-midnight, Su 10am-10pm.

Mama's Food Shop, 200 E. 3rd St. between Ave. A and B (☎777-4425). See laid-back Villagers obeying Mama's order to "Shut up and Eat." Fried chicken or salmon (each $7) with sides like honey-glazed sweet potatoes and broccoli or couscous ($1 each). Vegetarian dinner includes any 3 sides ($7). Bread pudding and cobbler come by the ½ pint ($3), if you have room left for dessert. Open M-Sa 11am-11pm. Mama has recently created a doppelganger for herself with **Step Mama's,** across the street at 199 E. 3rd St. (☎228-2663), which sells sandwiches, soups, and sides. The nourishment continues next door at **Mama's Milk,** a new, creative smoothie shop.

GREENWICH VILLAGE

The West Village's artistic angst has been channeled into many creative (and cheap) food venues, which line the major avenues. Aggressive and entertaining street life makes stumbling around and deciding where to go almost as much fun as eating. The European-style bistros of **Bleecker St.** and **MacDougal St.,** south of Washington Sq. Park, have perfected the homey "antique" look.

Chez Brigitte, 77 Greenwich Ave. between 7th Ave. and Bank St. (☎929-6736). This hole-in-the-wall French diner-cum-bistro is the darling of the *New Yorker* for its $7.50-9 French entrees. Cash only. Open daily 11am-10pm.

John's Pizzeria, 278 Bleecker St. between 7th Ave. S and Morton St. (☎243-1680). They don't serve slices, and only have standard toppings like pepperoni, anchovies, mushrooms, and the like, but John's is widely regarded as Manhattan's best pizzeria. Two sizes, small and large, $9-19.50. Cash only. Open M-Th 11:30am-11:30pm, F-Sa 11:30am-12:30pm, Su noon-11:30pm.

Eva's, 11 W. 8th St. between MacDougal St. and 5th Ave. (☎677-3496). Refreshing health food. Massive veggie plate with falafel, grape leaves, and eggplant salad $5.55. Open M-Sa 11am-11pm, Su 11am-10pm.

MIDTOWN

East of 5th Ave. on **Lexington Ave.,** Indian restaurants battle for customers. Liberally sprinkled throughout, Korean corner shops are equal parts grocery and buffet. **Hell's Kitchen,** slowly gentrifying, offers cool new eateries. The best food offerings in **Chelsea** come from the large Mexican and Central American community in the southern section of the neighborhood, although the gay community has engendered a huge resurgence of hip cafes. From 14th to 22nd St., eateries offer combinations of Central American and Chinese cuisine, as well as Cajun and Creole specialties. **West Midtown** is mostly expensive and late-night restaurants geared to theater-goers, while **East Midtown** has more variety.

■ **Pete's Tavern,** 129 E. 18th St., at the corner of Irving Pl., near Union Sq. (☎473-7676). "NY's oldest original bar," legend has it that O. Henry wrote "The Gift of the Magi" in one of its booths. Since 1864, this tavern continues to serve sandwiches ($7) and entrees (veal cutlet parmigiana $10) at modest prices, retaining its old pub atmosphere. Kitchen open daily 11am-1am.

Soups on Seventeen, 307 W. 17th St., off 8th Ave., in Chelsea (☎255-1505). Daily rotations of soup, sandwich, or salad with bread, fruit, and cookie. $5-7 for 16 oz., $9-13 for 32 oz. Open M-Sa 11am-7pm.

Hourglass Tavern, 373 W. 46th St. between 8th and 9th Ave., in West Midtown (☎265-2060). A dark, crowded joint on Restaurant Row with a changing menu featuring fresh fish, filet mignon, New York select steak, and various pasta dishes. Servers flip an hourglass at your table when you sit down; the 59-min. time limit is strictly enforced when crowds are waiting. *Prix fixe* entrees ($12-16) include soup and salad. Open M-W 5-11:15pm, Th-F 5-11:30pm.

Food Bar, 149 8th Ave., in Chelsea (☎243-2020). A truly fabulous eatery that features relatively cheap sandwiches ($7) and large-portioned entrees ($11). Sit at a window seat to people-watch. Take-out available. Open M-Th 11am-4pm and 5-11:30pm, F 11am-4pm and 5pm-midnight, Sa 5pm-midnight, Su 5-11:30pm.

Mary Ann's, 116 8th Ave., at 16th St., in Chelsea (☎633-0877). Benevolent waiters serve huge portions of inventive Mexican cuisine in this white-walled restaurant slung with lights. Entrees $8-12. Corona with entree on Th $1. Open M-Tu noon-10:30pm, W-Th 11:30am-11pm, F-Sa 11:30am-11pm, Su noon-10pm. Cash only.

Coffee Shop Bar, 29 Union Sq. West facing Union Sq. Park (☎243-7969). Open 23hr. a day, this hangout serves classic American diner fare with a Brazilian twist. Good for dessert ($5-6), a very late dinner ($8-17), or watching others have dinner. Beers $4-6. Open daily 7am-6am.

Manganaro's, 488 9th Ave. between 37th and 38th St., in West Midtown (☎563-5331 or 800-4-SALAMI). This classy Italian grocery and restaurant retains all the authentic flavor of pre-gentrified Hell's Kitchen. The staff will construct the sandwich of your dreams; or select one from their vast menu ($3-12). Open M-F 8am-7pm, Sa 9am-7pm; Dec.-May also Su 11am-5pm.

Coldwaters, 988 2nd Ave. between 52nd and 53rd St., in East Midtown (☎888-2122). Brunch (11am-3pm; $9) tempts daily with 2 drinks (alcoholic or non) and choice of entree, salad, and fries. Dinner entrees come with all-you-can-eat salad, fries or baked potato, and a basket of fresh garlic bread. Idaho Rainbow Trout $10. Cajun Catfish $12. Open daily 11am-3am.

UPPER EAST SIDE

Meals descend in price as you move east from **5th Ave.'s** overpriced museum cafes toward **Lexington, 3rd,** and **2nd Ave.**

Jackson Hole Wyoming, 232 E. 64th St. between 2nd and 3rd Ave. (☎371-7187). Home of the famed 7 oz. burger and offering over 25 different kinds of burgers and 25 chicken sandwiches, Jackson Hole is synonymous with grease, which is synonymous with TASTE! Burgers, chicken sandwiches, and platters $6-11. Open 10am-1am.

EJ's Luncheonette, 1271 3rd Ave., at 73rd St. (☎472-0600). Scrumptious fare, like the buttermilk pancakes ($6), served in hip 50s diner-style decor, has gained the loyalty and devotion of many Upper Eastsiders. After all, what could be better than breakfast served all day? Open M-Sa 8am-11pm, Su 8am-10:30pm.

UPPER WEST SIDE

Large and trendy restaurants spill onto the sidewalk, providing the perfect people-watching post. Intermingled among these are cheap pizza joints and hotdog hole-in-the-walls. The budget traveler should have no trouble finding affordable, satisfying meals along **Broadway, Amsterdam,** or **Columbus.**

Ollie's, 1991 Broadway between 67th and 68th St. (☎595-8181). Inside this big, seemingly un-Asian joint is one of NY's best noodle shops. Just looking at the extensive menu of noodle soups ($6), fried rice (around $7), seafood ($10-14), and meat dishes ($8-10) will make you full. Lunch special M-F 11:30am-3pm (entree, soup, and rice) $6. Open M-Th and Su 11:30am-midnight, F-Sa 11:30am-1am.

Big Nick's Pizza and Burger Joint, 2173 Broadway, at 77th St. (☎362-9238). Serving West Side's "compulsive noshers, weekend partyfolk, mellow-groovy happyfolk, dedicated loners, lovers after the afterglow." Great pizza and burgers since 1962. They also have "diet delights," but why turn away a plate-sized burger? Open 24hr.

▨ **Cafe Lalo,** 201 W. 83rd St. between Broadway and Amsterdam Ave. (☎496-6031). A wall of French windows allows live jazz to escape onto the street. Perfect cakes $5 per slice; full bar available. Wonderful ambiance, *sans blague!* Open M-Th 8am-2am, F 8am-4am, Sa 9am-4am, Su 9am-2am.

▨ **Zabar's,** 2245 Broadway between 80th and 81st St. (☎787-2000). This Upper West Side institution often featured on TV's "Mad About You" sells everything you need for a 4-star meal at home. The adjoining cafe serves pastries, food (soup and sandwich combo $5.49, entree with 2 sides lunch special $6), and great coffee. Cafe open M-Sa 7:30am-7pm, Su 8am-6pm; store open M-F 8am-7:30pm, Sa 8am-8pm, Su 9am-6pm.

HARLEM AND MORNINGSIDE HEIGHTS

In Harlem, ethnic food is everywhere: Jewish food in Washington Heights; various Latino and Cuban foods in the Hispanic communities; and, of course, East and West African, Caribbean, Creole, and some of the best soul food. **Lenox Ave., 125th St.,** and **116th St.** are the places to go. The cafes and restaurants in Morningside Heights cater to **Columbia University.** This usually means late hours and a starving student's price range.

▨ **Copeland's,** 547 W. 145th St. between Broadway and Amsterdam Ave. (☎234-2357). Excellent soul food accompanied by live music. Entrees pricey ($11-26), so you may want to check out Copeland's "cafeteria" next door—same food, more options, entrees $4-11. Popular mid-week jazz buffet (all-you-can-eat $15) Tu-Th 4:30-10:30pm. Gospel brunch Su with live jazz, all-you-can-eat buffet, and complimentary champagne $17. Open Tu-Th 4:30-11pm, F-Sa 4:30pm-midnight, Su noon-9pm; cafeteria M-F 8am-11:30pm, Sa 8am-12:30am, Su 8am-1am.

▨ **Sylvia's,** 328 Lenox Ave., at 126th St. (☎996-0660). This soul food has enticed New Yorkers for close to 40 years; now European tour groups arrive in buses. Sylvia, the proclaimed "Queen of soul food," accents her "World-Famous Talked-about BBQ Ribs Special" with "sweet spicy sauce" and a side of collard greens and macaroni and cheese ($11). Lunch special $7. Free live jazz and R&B F 6-9pm. Gospel Brunch Su. Open M-Sa 7:30am-10:30pm, Su 11am-8pm.

▨ **Manna's Too!!,** 486 Lenox Ave. between 134th and 135th St. (☎234-4488). This recently opened restaurant and deli might just be the best thing in Harlem. The variety of soul food options are unbelievable and the salad bar is as fresh as they come. Simply put, the food speaks for itself. And the sweet aroma coming from the bakery in back is quite hard to ignore. Homemade cakes $2.50; peach cobbler $3. Cash only. Open M-Sa 7am-8pm, Su 10am-7pm.

Tom's Restaurant, 2880 Broadway, at 112th St. (☎864-6137). Immortalized as the storefront featured in *Seinfeld,* this diner is about as cheap and average as it gets. Offers luxurious milkshakes. Greasy, but tasty, burgers ($3-8), excellent fries ($2), and entrees ($6-8). Cash only. Open Th-Su 6am-1:30am, F-Sa 24hr.

BROOKLYN

Brooklyn's restaurants, delis, and cafes offer all the flavors and varieties of cuisine that can be found in Manhattan, and often at lower prices. Brooklyn Heights and Park Slope offer nouvelle cuisine but specialize in pita bread and *baba ghanoush.* **Williamsburg** has cheap eats in a funky, lo-fi atmosphere, **Greenpoint** is a borscht-lover's paradise, and **Flatbush** serves up Jamaican and other West Indian cuisine. For those who didn't get their international fill in Manhattan, Brooklyn has a Chinatown in Sunset Park and a Little Italy in Carroll Gardens.

▨ **Junior's,** 386 Flatbush Ave. extension, at De Kalb St. (☎718-852-5257). Subway: 2, 3, 4, 5, B, D, Q, M, N, or R to Atlantic Ave. Touted by *New York Magazine* as the home of "the world's finest cheescake" ($4.25), this is diner-land Brooklyn-style. Eat roast beef and brisket to your heart's delight. 10 oz. steakburgers start at $6. Open Su-Th 6:30am-12:30am, F-Sa 6:30am-2am.

▨ **Brooklyn Moon,** 745 Fulton St., at Lafayette St., in Fort Greene (☎718-243-0424). Subway: G to Fulton St.; C to Lafayette Ave. Comfy couches and local art on ochre sponge-painted walls. Salmon burger $6.50; apple salad $4.25. Readings held on F open mic night at 10:30pm, when aspiring bards from all over NYC hold forth. Occasional performances and readings by authors like Jamaica Kincaid and Amiri Baraka. Open Tu-Th 11am-10pm, F 11am-1am, Sa-Su 11am-10pm.

■ **Philip's Confections,** 1237 Surf Ave., at the entrance to the B, D, F, and N train, in Coney Island. (☎718-372-8783). Famous salt-water taffy 95¢ per ¼ lb.; candy or caramel apple 95¢; lime rickeys 65¢. Open Su-Th 11am-3am, F-Sa 11am-4am.

Roy's Jerk Chicken, 3125 Church Ave. between 31st and 32nd St., in Flatbush (☎718-826-0987). Subway: 2 or 5 to Church Ave. and 2 blocks east. Jerk chicken is a delicious Jamaican specialty. You can also sample one of the many other enticing entrees ($6-7). Open M-Th 9am-2am, F-Su 24hr. Cash only.

Hammond's Finger Lickin' Bakery, 5014 Church Ave., at Utica Ave. in Flatbush (☎718-342-5770). Subway: 3 or 4 to Utica Ave.; 2 blocks east. West Indian pastries. Carrot cake $1.25. Open M-F 8:30am-8pm, Sa-Su 8:30am-9pm. Cash only.

Sea Lane Bakery, 615 Brighton Beach Ave. between 6th and 7th St. (☎718-934-8877). Subway: D and Q to Brighton Beach. The best Jewish bakery in Brighton. You can't go wrong with 99¢ danishes or strudel with mixed fruit ($4). Open daily 6am-9pm.

QUEENS

Nearly every ethnic group is represented in Queens. **Astoria** specializes in cheap eats. Take the G or R train to Steinway St. and Broadway and start browsing—the pickings are good in every direction. In **Flushing,** excellent Chinese, Japanese, and Korean restaurants flourish, often making use of authentic ingredients such as skatefish, squid, and tripe. **Bell Blvd.** in Bayside, out east near the Nassau border, is the center of Queens nightlife for the young, white, and semi-affluent. **Jamaica Ave.** in downtown Jamaica and **Linden Blvd.** in neighboring St. Albans are lined with restaurants specializing in African-American and West Indian food.

■ **Jackson Diner,** 37-47 74th St., Jackson Heights, at 37th Ave. (☎718-672-1232). Subway: E, F, G, or R to Jackson Heights/Roosevelt Ave.; 7 to 74th St./Broadway, then walk north toward 37th Ave. Possibly the best Indian food in New York. Savor the *saag ghost* (lamb with spinach, tomato, ginger, and cumin; $10). Lunch specials $6-7.50. Open M-F 11:30am-10pm, Sa-Su 11:30am-10:30pm.

■ **The Lemon Ice King of Corona,** 52-02 108th St., at Corona Ave. (☎718-699-5133). Subway: 7 to 111th St.; a healthy walk back 1 block to 108th and south 10 blocks. Keep walking—it's worth it. The Emperor of Cool scrapes up juicy frozen treats outdoors. Every flavor you could want, including bubblegum, blueberry, cantaloupe, cherry, and, of course, lemon ($1-1.50). Open daily 10am-midnight.

Kum Gang San, 138-28 Northern Blvd. (☎718-461-0909). Subway: 7 to Main St.; walk north on Main St. and take a right on Northern Blvd. (about 10min.). Good Korean food in an elegant setting. A complete lunch special can get you chicken teriyaki with salad, noodles, a California roll, and a dumpling all for $6-9. Open 24hr.

THE BRONX

The Italian neighborhood of **Belmont,** which centers around the intersection of Arthur Ave. and 187th St., brims with streetside *caffè*, pizzerias, restaurants, and mom-and-pop emporiums vending Madonna 45s and imported espresso machines, all without the touristy frills of Little Italy. To get to **Arthur Ave.,** take the C or D train to Fordham Rd. and walk five blocks east.

■ **Dominick's,** 2335 Arthur Ave., near 186th St. (☎718-733-2807). Always packed, this small family-style Italian eatery sports an extra bar upstairs. Waiters seat you at a long table and simply ask what you want. No menu here and no set prices—locals are happy to give advice. Linguine with mussels and marinara ($7), marinated artichoke ($7), and veal *francese* ($12) are all house specials. Arrive before 6pm or after 9pm, or expect a 20min. wait. Open M and W-Sa noon-10pm, F noon-11pm, Su 1-9pm.

De Lillo Pastry Shop, 606 E. 187 St. between Hughes and Arthur Ave. (☎718-367-8198). Crowded, but it's worth your while for the excellent baked goods ($1-2). Cappuccino $2.25; espresso $2. Open daily 8am-7pm; closed M July-Aug.

🔎 SIGHTS

Yikes! Where to begin? You'll get a crick in your neck if you keep looking up at the skyscrapers without the proper guidance. Just pull out that friend of friends, *Let's Go!* Walk around the city like a native—follow our sights write-ups, listed by neighborhood, perfect for a relaxed but informed stroll through the Big City. Shed your insecurities, get into your walking shoes (the strappy python ones, please, this is New York, after all), and get to know everything, from the famous to the hidden.

THE STATUE OF LIBERTY AND ELLIS ISLAND

The **Statue of Liberty** stands at the entrance to New York Harbor and has welcomed millions of immigrants to America. The statue was given by the French in 1886 as a sign of goodwill. Today, she lifts her lamp to tourists galore, who make the ferry voyage to Liberty Island. While the Statue embodies the American Dream, **Ellis Island** chronicles the harsh realities of starting over in the New World. Once a processing center, it now houses an enlightening **museum.** *(☎363-3200. Ferry info 269-5755. Ferries leave for Liberty and Ellis Island from Battery Park daily 9am-3:45pm every 30min., 20min. on weekends; call for winter and updated hours. $7, seniors $6, ages 3-17 $3.)*

LOWER MANHATTAN

The southern tip of Manhattan is a motley assortment of cobblestones and financial powerhouses. The Wall St. area, less than a ½ mi. long, is the most densely built in all New York, creating one of the highest concentrations of skyscrapers in the world. Crooked streets retain NY's original Dutch layout; lower Manhattan was the first part of the island to be settled.

BATTERY PARK. Battery Park, named for a battery of guns that the British stored there from 1683 to 1687 and built on landfill, is now a peaceful residential area forming the southernmost toenail of Manhattan Island. On weekends the park is mobbed with people on their way to the Liberty and Ellis Island ferries, which depart from here, and in-line skaters pushing aerodynamic baby buggies. *(The 1 and 9 trains to South Ferry terminate at the southeastern tip of the park; the 4 and 5 stop at Bowling Green, just off the northern tip.)*

WALL STREET. Once the northern border of the New Amsterdam settlement, Wall St. takes its name from the wall built in 1653 to shield the Dutch colony from a British invasion from the north. By the early 19th century, the area was the financial capital of the US. In **Federal Hall,** the original City Hall, the trial of John Peter Zenger in 1735 helped to establish freedom of the press. *(26 Wall St. ☎825-6888.)* On the southwest corner of Wall and Broad St. stands the **New York Stock Exchange,** where over 3000 companies exchange 228 billion shares of stock valued at $13 trillion. Arrive early; tickets usually run out by 1pm. The observation gallery overlooks the exchange's zoo-like main trading floor. *(☎656-5165. Open to the public M-F 9am-4:30pm. Free.)* Around the corner, at the end of Wall St., rises the seemingly ancient **Trinity Church.** Its Gothic spire was the tallest structure in the city when first erected in 1846. The vaulted interior feels positively medieval. As recently as 1991, archaeologists found the remains of over 20,000 slaves buried only 20 ft. underground at the corner of Duane and Elk St. Congress declared the **African Burial Ground** a national landmark. Nearby is the neo-Renaissance Federal Reserve Bank of NY, modeled after the 15th-century Palazzo Strozzi. *(33 Liberty St.)*

WORLD TRADE CENTER. Walk up Broadway to Liberty Park, and in the distance you'll see the twin towers of the World Trade Center, the city's tallest buildings. Two World Trade Center has an **observation deck** on the 107th fl. *(☎323-2340. Ticket booth on the mezzanine. Open daily June-Aug. 9:30am-11:30pm; Sept.-May 9:30am-9:30pm. $12.50, students $10.75, seniors $9.50, ages 6-12 $6.25, under 6 free.)* Farther north on Broadway, City Hall Park and **City Hall** serve as the focus of the city's administration. The Colonial château-style structure, completed in 1811, may be the finest piece of architecture in the city.

SOUTH STREET SEAPORT. Turn left off Broadway onto Fulton St. and head for the South St. Seaport. New York's shipping industry thrived here for most of the 19th century. The city's revitalization has transformed the historic district, in all its fishy and foul-smelling glory, into the ritzy South St. Seaport complex, which includes a shopping mall known as **Pier 17.** The commercialism is made palatable by a restored 18th-century market, graceful galleries, and seafaring schooners. *(Visit the Seaport Museum Visitors Center, 12-14 Fulton St., for info on the myriad sights of the area. ☎ 748-8600.)* The pervading stench comes from the **Fulton Fish Market,** the largest fresh-fish mart in the country (and a notorious former mafia stronghold), on South St., on the other side of the overpass. *(☎ 748-8786. Market opens at 4am. Crack-of-dawn tours available June-Oct.)*

FAMOUS BUILDINGS. The neo-Gothic **Woolworth Building** towers south of City Hall. F. W. Woolworth erected it in 1913 to house the offices of his five-and-dime empire. The Chrysler Building robbed "the cathedral of commerce" of its tallest building status in 1930. Arches and mosaics adorn the lobby of Cass Gilbert's Versailles. *(233 Broadway.)* A block and a half south on Broadway, **St. Paul's Chapel** is Manhattan's oldest public building in continuous use; it hasn't missed a day since George Washington prayed here in his personal pew on Inauguration Day. *(Open M-F 9am-3pm, Su 7am-3pm.)*

LOWER EAST SIDE

Down below Houston St. lurks the trendily seedy Lower East Side, where old-timers rub shoulders with heroin dealers and hip 20-somethings. Two million Jews swelled the population of the Lower East Side in the 20 years before World War I; immigrants still come here, although now they are mostly Asian and Hispanic. A lot of East Village artists and musicians have recently moved in as well, especially near Houston St., but the down-trodden element remains.

EAST BROADWAY. Remnants of the Jewish ghetto that inspired Jacob Riis's compelling work *How the Other Half Lives* still exist. From Grand St., follow Essex St. three blocks south to East Broadway. This street epitomizes the Lower East Side's fusion of cultures. Buddhist temples sit next to Jewish religious supply stores.

TENEMENT MUSEUM. The area around Orchard and Delancey St. is one of Manhattan's bargain shopping centers. Between Broome and Delancey St., the **Lower East Side Tenement Museum** is a preserved tenement house of the type that proliferated in this neighborhood in the early part of the century. The **gallery** offers free exhibits and photographs documenting Jewish life on the Lower East Side. *(90 Orchard St. ☎ 431-0233. Call for info on tours of tenement and neighborhood. Around $9.)*

SOHO AND TRIBECA

SOHO. The architecture in SoHo is American Industrial (1860-1890), notable for its cast-iron facades. Its inhabitants are New York's prospering artistic. Here, **galleries** reign supreme (see **Galleries,** p. 226) and chic boutiques fill the gaps. While the shopping in SoHo is probably well beyond a budget traveler's means, those seeking that hidden gem should check out the **Antiques Fair and Collectibles Market** on the corner of Broadway and Grand St. *(Open Sa-Su 9am-5pm.)*

TRIBECA. TriBeCa has been anointed (by resident Robert DeNiro and others) as one of the hottest neighborhoods in the city—though you wouldn't guess it. Hidden inside the industrial warehouses are lofts, restaurants, bars, and galleries, maintaining SoHo's trendiness without the upscale airs. Admire the cast-iron edifices lining White St., Thomas St., and Broadway, the 19th-century Federal-style buildings on Harrison St., and the shops, galleries, and bars on Church and Reade St.

GREENWICH VILLAGE AND WASHINGTON SQUARE

The Village and its residents have defied convention for almost two centuries. Greenwich Village was once the nexus of New York bohemia and retains a reputation as the counter-culture capital of the East Coast. Narrow brownstone-lined streets meander haphazardly through the Village without regard to grids; most famously, W. 4th St. intersects W. 10th St. at Sheridan Sq.

GREENWICH VILLAGE. The **West Village** (west of 6th Ave.) boasts eclectic summer street life and excellent nightlife. The area has a large, visible gay community around **Sheridan Sq.** These are the home waters of the 1969 Stonewall Riot that helped galvanize the gay community. **Christopher St.** swims in restaurants and shops. *(Subway: 1 or 9 to Christopher St./Sheridan Sq.)* Once a literary hotbed of activity, off 10th St. and 6th Ave. you'll see an iron gate and street sign that reads **"Patchin' Place."** The 145-year-old buildings lining this path once housed e.e. cummings, Theodore Dreiser, and Djuna Barnes. **75½ Bedford St.** is the narrowest building in the Village, only 9½ ft. in width. Writer Edna St. Vincent Millay lived here in the 20s, when she founded the nearby **Cherry Lane Theater.** *(38 Commerce St.)* Actors Lionel Barrymore and Cary Grant both lived here after her departure.

WASHINGTON SQUARE PARK. Washington Sq. Park beats at the heart of the Village, as it has since the district's days as a suburb. *(Subway: A, B, C, D, E, F, or Q to W. 4th St./Washington Sq.)* The marshland here was once home to Native Americans and freed slaves, then a colonial cemetery, and by the 1820s a park and parade ground. Posh residences (described in Henry James' *Washington Square*) made the area center of the social scene. Society has long since gone north, the drug dealers came and went (most of them), and **New York University** moved in. The country's largest private university and one of the city's biggest landowners (along with the city government, the Catholic Church, and Columbia University), NYU's buildings and students blanket the area. *(For info and free maps of campus at 50 W. 4th St. ☎ 998-4636.)* But the Village has another center of higher education (yes, really): **The New School.** During WWII the college became known for offering positions to European intellectuals fleeing the Nazis; its faculty have included John Dewey and W.E.B. DuBois.

The north side of the park, called **The Row,** showcases a stretch of elegant Federal-style brick residences largely built in the 1830s. Also NYU owned, **Washington Mews** is a row of ivy-covered colonial houses. South of the park on MacDougal St. are the Village's finest coffeehouses, which saw their glory days in the 50s when beatnik heroes Jack Kerouac and Allen Ginsberg attended jazz-accompanied poetry readings at **Le Figaro** and **Cafe Borgia.** These sidewalk cafes still provide some of the best coffee and people-watching in the city. Nearby is what the *New York Times* proclaimed the ugliest piece of public art in the city, a work by Picasso. *(Corner of Bleecker St. and LaGuardia Pl.)*

EAST VILLAGE AND ALPHABET CITY

The East Village, a comparatively new creation, was carved out of the Bowery and the Lower East Side as rents in the West Village soared and its residents sought accommodations elsewhere. East Villagers embody the alternative spectrum, with punks, hippies, ravers, rastas, guppies, goths, beatniks, and seemingly everyone else coexisting amid an anarchic tangle of cafes, bars, and theaters. Allen Ginsberg, Jack Kerouac, and William S. Burroughs all eventually eschewed the Village establishment to develop a junked-up "beat" sensibility east of Washington Sq. Park in the 50s, as did the pioneers of Punk in the 80s.

ASTOR PLACE. The **Joseph Papp Public Theater** resides at Lafayette St., just below Astor Place, in John Jacob Astor's civic donation, the city's first free library. *(☎ 598-7150.)* Astor's 1867 **New York Shakespeare Festival** converted it into a theater. The intersection of **Astor Pl.** (at the juncture of Lafayette, 4th Ave., and E. 8th St.) is distinguished by a large black cube balanced on its corner. (If you push it, it will turn.)

COOPER UNION. Astor Pl. prominently features the rear of the Cooper Union Foundation Building, built in 1859 to house the **Cooper Union for the Advancement of Science and Art,** a tuition-free technical and design school founded by self-educated industrialist Peter Cooper. The school's free lecture series has hosted notable Americans since the mid-19th century. Cooper Union was the first college intended for the underprivileged; and the American Red Cross and NAACP began here as well. *(7 E. 7th Ave. ☎ 353-4199.)* Across Cooper Sq. south are the offices of America's largest free newspaper, the **Village Voice.** At 156 2nd Ave. stands a Jewish landmark, the **Second Avenue Deli.** *(☎677-0606.)* The "Yiddish Rialto," the stretch of 2nd Ave. between Houston and 14th St., comprised the Yiddish theater district in the early part of this century.

ST. MARK'S PLACE. St. Mark's Place (where E. 8th St. would be) has long been the geographical and spiritual center of the East Village. In the 1960s, the street was the Haight-Ashbury of the East Coast, giving San Francisco a run for its hashish. In the late 70s it taught King's Rd. how to be punk as mohawked youths hassled passers-by from the brownstone steps of Astor Pl.; the Ramones, Blondie, the Talking Heads and the New York Dolls all played at the legendary dive **CBGB's.** St. Mark's walks the line between unabashed sleaze (count the tattoo parlors) and homogenized cheeze, although alternateens dissipate as you move eastward.

ALPHABET CITY. In Alphabet City, east of 1st Ave. and south of 14th St., the avenues run out of numbers and adopt letters. During the area's heyday in the 60s, Jimi Hendrix played open-air shows here to bright-eyed love children. There has been a great deal of drug-related crime in the recent past, although locals have done an admirable job of making the area livable and have started a number of pretty community gardens. Alphabet City is generally safe during the day, and the nightlife on Ave. A ensures some protection there, but avoid straying east of Ave. B at night. Alphabet City's extremist Boho activism has made the neighborhood chronically ungovernable; police officers once set off a riot when they attempted to evict a band of the homeless and their supporters in **Tompkins Sq. Park.** *(E. 7th St. and Ave. A.)* The park still serves as an epicenter for many a churlish misfit, and, if you're looking, a few free-growing marijuana plants were found here by the police in 1997. East of the park, countless **memorial murals** attest to the scars left by the drug war. Many other murals colorfully celebrate the neighborhood.

LOWER MIDTOWN AND CHELSEA

BUILDINGS. Unfortunately, there's nothing to see where **Andy Warhol's Factory** once churned out Pop Art. *(19 E. 32nd St., between 5th and Madison Ave.)* The hulking **armory** is notable only for having hosted the infamous art exhibition in 1913 that brought Picasso, Matisse, and Duchamp—who Teddy Roosevelt called "a bunch of lunatics"—to the shores of America. *(68 Lexington Ave., at 26th St.)* Another member of the "once-world's-tallest-building" club is the eminently photogenic **Flatiron Building.** Considered the world's first skyscraper, it was originally named the Fuller Building, but its dramatic wedge shape, imposed by the intersection of Broadway, 5th Ave., 22nd St., and 23rd St., quickly earned it its current name.

UNION SQUARE. A few blocks away, Union Sq. sizzled with High Society intrigue before the Civil War. Early in this century, the name gained dual significance when the neighborhood became a focal point of New York's Socialist movement, which held its May Day celebrations in **Union Sq. Park.** Later, the workers and everyone else abandoned the park to drug dealers and derelicts. In 1989 the city began reclaiming it. The park is now pleasant and safe, though not necessarily pristine. *(Between Broadway and Park Ave., and 17th and 14th St.)*

CHELSEA. Home to some of the most fashionable clubs, bars, and restaurants in the city, Chelsea has lately undergone something of a rebirth. A large gay and lesbian community and an increasing artsy-yuppie population have given the area, west of 5th Ave. between 14th and 30th St., the flavor of a lower-rent West Village. Chelsea has become home to innovative **art galleries** that escape SoHo's exorbitant rent (see **Museums and Galleries,** p. 224). The historic **Hotel Chelsea,** between 7th and 8th Ave., has sheltered many an artist, most famously Sid Vicious of the Sex Pistols. Edie Sedgwick torched the place with a cigarette between Warhol films. Countless writers spent their days searching for inspiration and mail in the lobby, including Arthur Miller, Vladimir Nabokov, Arthur C. Clarke, and Dylan Thomas. *(222 W. 23rd St. ☎243-3700.)* Chelsea's **flower district,** a sprawling market on 28th St. between 6th and 7th Ave., blooms during the wee hours.

WEST MIDTOWN

UGLY BUILDINGS. Penn Station is one of the least engrossing pieces of architecture in West Midtown, but serves its function as a major subway stop and train terminal. *(33rd St. and 7th Ave. Subway: 1, 2, 3, 9, A, C, or E to 34th St./Penn Station.)* The original Penn Station, a classical marble building modeled on the Roman Baths of Caracalla, was demolished in the 60s. The railway tracks were then covered with the uninspiring **Madison Sq. Garden.** Facing the Garden at 421 8th Ave. is New York's immense main post office, the **James A. Farley Building.**

SHOPPING. East on 34th St., between 7th Ave. and Broadway, in Herald Sq., stands **Macy's,** the Goliath of department stores. It sponsors the **Macy's Thanksgiving Day Parade,** a NYC tradition buoyed by ten-story Snoopys, marching bands, floats, and hoopla. For cheaper clothing, the area surrounding Macy's, between Broadway and 8th Ave. in the 30s, is the **Garment District,** once a redlight district, and, in the 1930s, purportedly the largest concentration of apparel workers in the world.

HELL'S KITCHEN. The area in the 30s and 40s, around 10th, 11th, and 12th Ave., is known as Hell's Kitchen, and, although it is quickly becoming swallowed by the gentrifying monsters of Chelsea and the Upper West Side, it was once the inspiration for Leonard Bernstein's gangs in *West Side Story.* It is home to the **Jacob Javits Center,** host to some of the grandest-scale events in the world, like its famous motorcycle and car shows. *(Along 12th Ave. between 34th and 38th St.)* Nearby is the **John Jay College of Criminal Justice.** In 1990, students of the College took it over for two weeks in protest of tuition hikes, until the administration was violently reinstated. *(899 10th Ave., at 58th St.)*

TIMES SQUARE. The billboards of Times Square flicker at the intersection of 42nd St. and Broadway. Once considered the dark and seedy core of the Big Apple by most New Yorkers, the Square is working hard to improve its image. Mayor Giuliani promised to excise the pornography industry from the area, although many locals complain of the consequential "Disney-fication" of the area. Disney is planning an entertainment complex and 47-story hotel to replace the closed-down porn shops along 42nd St. between 7th and 8th Ave. Still, Times Square is Times Square. *(Subway: 1, 2, 3, 7, 9, A, C, E, N, R, or S.)* On 42nd St. between 9th and 10th Ave. lies **Theater Row,** which *is* American theater. The fabled **Theater District** stretches from 41st to 57th St. along Broadway, 8th Ave., and the connecting streets. Approximately 37 theaters remain active, most of them around 45th St.

CARNEGIE HALL. How do you get to Carnegie Hall? Practice, my dear, practice. Or, walk to 57th St. and 7th Ave. Founded in 1891, Carnegie Hall is New York's foremost soundstage. Tchaikovsky, Caruso, Toscanini, Bernstein, the Beatles, and the Rolling Stones have played Carnegie. Other notable events include a 1934 lecture by Albert Einstein and Martin Luther King Jr.'s last public speech on Feb. 28, 1968. Carnegie Hall's **museum** displays artifacts and memorabilia from its illustrious century of existence *(☎ 903-9790. 1hr. tours are given M-Tu and Th-F at 11:30am, 2, and 3pm. $6, students and seniors $5, under 12 $3. Museum open M-Tu and Th-F 11am-4:30pm. Free.)*

EAST MIDTOWN AND FIFTH AVENUE

THE EMPIRE STATE. The Empire State Building retains its place in the hearts and minds of New Yorkers even though it is no longer the tallest building in the US, or even the tallest in New York (stood up by the World Trade Center). But the Empire State remains New York's classic landmark, continuing to dominate postcards, movies, and the city's skyline. The limestone and granite structure, with glistening ribbons of stainless steel, stretches 1454 ft. into the sky, and its 73 elevators run through 2 mi. of shafts. The nighttime view from the top is spectacular. The Empire State was one of the first true skyscrapers, and was finished only 20 months after the contract was signed; it is a monolithic example of industrialization during the 30s. *(5th Ave. between 33rd and 34th St. ☎ 736-3100. Observatory open daily 9:30am-midnight; tickets sold until 11:30pm. $9, children under 12 $4, seniors $7.)*

ALL LIT UP One foggy night in 1945, a US Army B-25 bomber crashed into the 78th and 79th floors of the Empire State Building, shooting flames hundreds of feet in the air. Burning debris hurled for blocks, although the steel frame swayed less than 2 in. Fourteen people lost their lives in the bizarre accident. Mind you, this was not the skyscraper's first brush with aeronautical mayhem. Its tower, originally intended as a mooring mast for airships, docked two blimps there in 1931 and, in the same year, King Kong, the giant ape, fought planes from atop the famous tower.

NEW YORK PUBLIC LIBRARY. The New York Public Library opens its musty yet beautiful arms on the west side of 5th Ave. between 40th and 42nd St. On sunny afternoons, throngs of people perch on the marble steps. This is the world's 7th-largest research library; see the immense 3rd fl. reading room. (☎869-8089. Open M-Sa 10am-6pm, Tu-W 11am-7:30pm. Free tours Tu-Sa 11am and 2pm.) **Bryant Park** spreads out behind the library. The stage at the head of the park hosts free cultural events throughout the summer, including screenings of classic films, jazz concerts, and live comedy. (☎484-1222 for a schedule of events. Open 7am-9pm.)

GRAND CENTRAL TERMINAL. To the east along 42nd St., Grand Central Terminal sits where Park Ave. would be. The former main transportation hub of the city, where dazed tourists first got a glimpse of the glorious city, Grand Central has been renovated, and now the galaxy above the lobby glitters anew. The massive Beaux Arts front, with the famed 13 ft. clock, gives way to the dignified and echoey Main Concourse, a huge lobby area setting the backdrop for civilized commuting.

THE CHRYSLER BUILDING. The Chrysler Building, at 42nd St. and Lexington Ave., gives New York a touch of Gotham. Built by William Van Allen as an ode to the automobile, the building is topped by an Art Deco headdress and a spire modeled on a radiator grille.

THE UNITED NATIONS. To get out of the city for a while, head for the **United Nations Building,** located on 1st Ave. between 42nd and 48th St. A multicultural rose garden and a statuary park provide a lovely view of the East River. Inside, work your way through security check for informative tours of the **General Assembly**. Sometimes free tickets to sessions can be obtained when the U.N. is in session Oct. to May (☎963-4475. Visitor's entrance at 1st Ave. and 46th St. Daily tours 45min., every 15min. 9:15am-4:45pm, available in 20 languages. $7.50, students $4.50, over 60 $5.50, ages 6-14 $3.50.)

ROCKEFELLER CENTER. Between 48th and 51st St. and 5th and 6th Ave. stretches Rockefeller Center, a conjunction of business and art. On 5th Ave., between 49th and 50th St., the famous gold-leaf statue of Prometheus sprawls on a ledge of the sunken **Tower Plaza.** The Plaza serves as an open-air cafe in the spring and summer and as a world-famous ice-skating rink in the winter. The 70-story former RCA building, now the **GE Building,** seated at 6th Ave., is the center's most accomplished artistic creation. Every chair in the building sits less than 28 ft. from natural light. The **NBC Television Network** makes its headquarters here. The network offers an hour-long, behind-the-scenes tour tracing the history of NBC. The tour visits the studios of *Conan O'Brien* and *Saturday Night Live.* (Tours every 30min. M-Sa 9:30am-4:30pm. $17.50.)

RADIO CITY. Despite an illustrious history and a wealth of Art Deco treasures, **Radio City Music Hall** was almost demolished in 1979 to make way for new office high-rises. However, the public rallied and the place was declared a national landmark. First opened in 1932 the 5874-seat theater is still the largest in the world. The Rockettes, Radio City's vertically endowed chorus line, still dance on, and live performances by acts ranging from Tony Bennett to Phish fill the rest of the year. (At the corner of 6th Ave. and 51st St. ☎632-4041. Tours leaving every 30-45min. M-Sa 10am-5pm, Su 11am-5pm. $13.75, under 12 $9.)

SHOPPING. The stores on **5th Ave.** from Rockefeller Center to Central Park are the ritziest in the city. At **Tiffany & Co.,** on 57th St., everything from jewelry to housewares shines; the window displays are works of art in themselves, especially around Christmas. **F.A.O. Schwarz**, at 58th St., is one of the world's largest toy stores, including a Lego complex and a Barbie doll annex. Several notable **galleries** also live around 57th St. (see p. 226).

PLAZA HOTEL. On 5th Ave. and 59th St., at the southeast corner of Central Park, sits the legendary Plaza Hotel, built in 1907 at astronomical cost. Its 18-story, 800-room French Renaissance interior flaunts five marble staircases, countless ludicrously named suites, and a two-story Grand Ballroom. Past guests and residents include Frank Lloyd Wright and the Beatles. *Let's Go* recommends the $15,000-per-night suite.

OTHER SIGHTS. St. Patrick's Cathedral, New York's most famous church and the largest Catholic cathedral in America, stands at 51st St. and 5th Ave. Designed by James Renwick, its twin spires stretch 330 ft. into the air. (☎753-2261.) One of the monuments to modern architecture, Ludwig Mies Van der Rohe's dark and gracious **Seagram Building** looms over. Pure skyscraper, fronted by a plaza and two fountains, the Seagram stands as a paragon of the austere International Style. *(375 Park Ave., between 52nd and 53rd St.)*

CENTRAL PARK

General Information: ☎360-3444; for parks and recreation info call ☎360-8111 (M-F 9am-5pm). Main entrance: **subway** 1, 9 to 59th St./Columbus Circle; N to 59th St./5th Ave. The Central Park Conservancy, which runs the park and offers public programs, has four visitors centers that offer brochures, calendars of events, and **free park maps**, at **Belvedere Castle** (☎772-0210), located mid-park at 79th St.; the **Charles A. Dana Discovery Center** (☎860-1370), at 110th St. near 5th Ave.; the **North Meadow Recreation Center** (☎348-4867), mid-park at 97th St.; and the **Dairy**, mid-park near 65th St. The Dairy also showcases exhibits, books, and other collectibles reflecting the history of the park. Open Apr.-Oct. Tu-Su 10am-5pm, Nov.-Mar. Tu-Su 10am-4pm.

 Central Park is fairly safe during the day, but less so at night. Don't be afraid to go to events in the Park at night, but take large paths and go with someone. Do not wander the darker paths at night, especially if you are a woman. In an **emergency,** use one of the call-boxes located throughout the park. **24hr. Park Line** (☎570-4820).

This enormous park offers a pastoral refuge from the urban jungle of New York City. The landscaped gardens were carved out of the city's grid between 59th and 110th St. by designers Olmsted and Vaux in the mid-1840s. Once a geographical and social wasteland, their final product contains lakes, ponds, fountains, skating rinks, ball fields, tennis courts, a castle, an outdoor theater, a bandshell, and two zoos.

The southern half of the park affords more serene lakes and graceful promenades, while the northern half has more ragged edges (although the Conservatory Gardens on 5th Ave. at 105th St. are gorgeous). Nearly 1400 species of trees, shrubs, and flowers grow here, the work of distinguished horticulturist Ignaz Anton Pilat. Small metal four-digit plaques on lampposts are your map. The first two digits tell you the nearest street, and the second two whether you're on the east or west side of the Park (even numbers mean east, odds west).

The spectacular, free **Central Park Summerstage** concert program has indie acts and established artists each summer (at 72nd St.). The **Wollman Skating Rink,** near 64th St., sees wheels turn to blades in the cold. (☎396-1010. Ice- or roller-skating $15 for 2hr., $25 full-day, includes helmet and pads; $100 deposit.)

The **Friedsam Memorial Carousel** turns at 65th St. west of Center Dr. Brought from Coney Island and restored in 1983, it has 58 hand-carved horses. (Open M-Sa 10am-6pm, Su 10am-6:30pm, weather permitting; Thanksgiving to mid-Mar. Sa-Su 10am-4:30pm. $1.) The **Lake** provides a beautiful patch of blue, and the 1954 **Loeb Boathouse** supplies the necessary romantic nautical equipment. (Mid-park at 75th St. ☎517-2233. Open daily Apr.-Sept. 10am-6pm, weather permitting. Rowboats $10 per hr., $30 deposit.)

Strawberry Fields, a memorial to John Lennon, are located at 72nd St. and West Dr., directly across from the **Dakota Apartments** where Lennon was assassinated and where Yoko Ono still lives. On spring days, picnickers enjoy the 161 varieties of plants that bloom over the rolling hills around the star-shaped "Imagine" mosaic.

Alice in Wonderland, her friends, and **Hans Christian Andersen** live at 74th St. off 5th Ave. The NY Public Library sponsors free storytelling at the Andersen statue in the summer (usually Sa 11am). The **Swedish Cottage Marionette Theater,** at the base of Vista Rock near the 79th St. transverse, puts on regular puppet shows. (☎ 988-9093. *Shows usually Tu-F 10:30am and noon, Sa 1pm. Adults $5, children $4. Reservations required.*) Up the hill the **Delacorte Theater** hosts the wildly popular **Shakespeare in the Park** series each midsummer, which features celebrities every year for free. Come early—the theater seats only 1936 lucky souls. Large concerts often take place north of the theater, on the **Great Lawn.** Here, Paul Simon sang, the Stonewall 25 marchers rallied, and the New York Philharmonic and the Metropolitan Opera Company give free summer performances annually.

UPPER EAST SIDE

The Golden Age of East Side society began in the 1860s and progressed until WWI, as scores of wealthy people moved into the area. These days, the pristine sidewalks, gourmet bread stores, and fancy private schools of the Upper East prove they're still there.

MUSEUM MILE. Upper 5th Ave. is home to Museum Mile, which includes the **Metropolitan Museum of Art,** the **Guggenheim,** and the **Cooper-Hewitt,** among many others, while high-brow **galleries** and **auction houses** also strut their stuff here (see p. 224).

OTHER SIGHTS. At 59th St. and 3rd Ave., **Bloomingdale's** sits in regal splendor. **Park Ave.,** the street that time forgot, maintains a regal austerity with gracious buildings and landscaped medians. **Gracie Mansion,** at the north end of Carl Schurz Park, between 84th and 90th St. along East End Ave., has been the residence of New York mayors since Fiorello LaGuardia. (☎ 570-4751. *50min. tours by reservation only.*)

UPPER WEST SIDE

Broadway leads uptown to **Columbus Circle,** at 59th St. and Broadway, the symbolic entrance to the Upper West Side, the equally comfortable but much more liberal neighbor to the Upper East.

LINCOLN CENTER. Broadway intersects Columbus Ave. at Lincoln Center, the cultural hub of the city, between 62nd and 66th St. The seven facilities that constitute Lincoln Center—Avery Fisher Hall, the New York State Theater, the Metropolitan Opera House, the Library and Museum of Performing Arts, the Vivian Beaumont Theater, the Walter Reade Theater, and the Juilliard School of Music—accommodate over 13,000 spectators at a time (see **Classical Music,** p. 229).

SCENERY. Broadway and **Columbus Ave.** pulse with energy all day (and night) with stores, outdoor restaurants, millions of bars, and street vendors selling anything from back issues of *Maxim* to a rusty fan. The Upper West Side is covered with residential brownstones and beautiful buildings, especially along **Broadway, Central Park West,** and **West End Ave.**—take a scenic stroll.

HARLEM

The influx of rural black Southerners around WWI created the Harlem known today as one of the capitals of the black Western world. The 20s were Harlem's Renaissance; a thriving scene of artists, writers, and scholars lived fast and loose, producing cultural masterworks in the process. **The Cotton Club** and the **Apollo Theater,** along with numerous other jazz clubs, were on the musical vanguard, while Langston Hughes and Zora Neale Hurston changed the face of literature. Nevertheless, conditions for blacks were tough—they paid more than their white counterparts for unhealthy tenement rooms, and the murderous Klan paid occasional visits. In the 60s, riding the tidal wave of the civil rights movement, the revolutionary Black

Power movement flourished here. Recognizing the need for economic revitalization as a route to empowerment, members of the community began an attempt at redevelopment in the 70s. This attempt continues today as the city pumps money into the area and communities bond together to beautify the area and actively resist crime. Though poorer than many neighborhoods, it is culturally rich.

On the East Side above 96th St. lies **Spanish Harlem,** known as El Barrio ("the neighborhood"), and on the West Side lies Harlem proper, stretching from 110th to 155th St. **Columbia University** controls the area west of Morningside Dr. and south of 125th St., commonly known as **Morningside Heights.** On the West Side, from 125th to 160th St., most cultural and social life takes place in **Central Harlem.** To the far north, from 160th St. to 220th St., **Washington Heights** and **Inwood** are populated by Dominican and Jewish communities.

ST. JOHN THE DIVINE. The **Cathedral of St. John the Divine,** along Amsterdam Ave. between 110th and 113th St., is already the largest cathedral in the world, and it breaks its record with every stone added. Begun in 1812, construction isn't predicted to be over for another century or two. A trip down the overwhelming central nave leads to an altar dedicated to AIDS victims and a 2000 lb. natural quartz crystal. *(Open M-Sa 7am-6pm, Su 7am-8pm. Suggested donation $2, students and seniors $1. Vertical tours—you go up—given on the first and 3rd Sa of the month at noon and 2pm. $10. Reservations necessary. Regular horizontal tours Tu-Sa 11am, Su 1pm. $3.)*

RIVERSIDE DRIVE. Near Columbia, at 120th St. and Riverside Dr., is the **Riverside Church.** The observation deck in the tower commands an amazing view. Concerts make use of the world's largest carillon (74 bells), a gift of John D. Rockefeller, Jr. *(Bell tower open Tu-Sa 10:30am-5pm, Su 9:45-10:45am. Admission to observation deck Tu-Sa $2, students and seniors $1. Free tours Su 12:30pm.)* Diagonally across Riverside Dr. lies **Grant's Tomb,** the resting place of you-know-who. Mosaic tile benches around the monument were added in the mid-70s in the style of Dalí.

SUGAR HILL. African-Americans with "sugar," or money, moved to Sugar Hill in the 20s and 30s. W.E.B. DuBois, Thurgood Marshall, and Duke Ellington lived here alongside some of the city's most notable leaders and gangsters. It is also the birthplace of the Sugarhill Gang, whose "Rapper's Delight" was the first rap song to reach the Top 40. *(143rd to 155th St. between St. Nicholas and Edgecombe Ave.)*

WASHINGTON HEIGHTS. Washington Hts., the area north of 155th St., affords a taste of urban life with a thick ethnic flavor. On the same block, you can eat a Greek dinner, buy Armenian pastries and vegetables from a South African, and discuss the Talmud with a student at nearby **Yeshiva University.**

THE CLOISTERS. Get medieval at the Cloisters, a lovely monastery with airy archways, manicured gardens, the famed Unicorn Tapestries, and other pieces of the Met's collection of medieval art. *(Fort Tryon Park. ☎923-3700. Open Mar.-Oct. Tu-Su 9:30am-5:15pm, Nov.-Feb. 9:30am-4:45pm. Suggested donation $10, students and seniors $5; includes same-day admission to the Met on 5th Ave.)*

OTHER SIGHTS. 125th St., also known as Martin Luther King Jr. Blvd., spans the heart of traditional Harlem. Millions of people, fast-food joints, jazz bars, and the **Apollo Theater** keep the street humming day and night. *(☎749-5838, box office 864-0372.)* The silver dome of the **Masjid Malcolm Shabazz,** where Malcolm X was once a minister, glitters on 116th St. and Lenox Ave. *(☎662-2200. Services F at 1pm.)*

BROOKLYN

The gregarious streets of Brooklyn are an escape from tourist-infested Manhattan. Brooklyn is Dutch for "Broken Land," and the name fits—Brooklyn is a marvelously diverse terrain, where ultra-orthodox *Hasidim* rub elbows with black teenagers on a street covered with signs *en español.* Ethnic and religious groups don't always get along, but an indomitable pride in their home unites them. And they have reason to be proud—one out of every seven famous Americans is from here. What goes on here tends to go on outdoors, be it neighborhood banter, baseball games in the park, ethnic festivals, or pride marches.

MID-ATLANTIC

THE BROOKLYN BRIDGE. The Brooklyn Bridge gracefully spans the gap between Lower Manhattan and Brooklyn. Its arched towers were the greatest engineering feat of the 19th century. The 1 mi. walk along the pedestrian path reveals why every New York poet feels compelled to write about it, why photographers continually snap the bridge's airy spider-web cables, and why Frank Stella so well-represented it. A ramp across from Manhattan's City Hall begins the journey. *(Subway: 4, 5, or 6 to Brooklyn Bridge.)*

NEIGHBORHOODS. Head south on Henry St. after the Brooklyn Bridge, then turn right on Clark St. toward the river for a jaw-dropping view of Manhattan from the **Brooklyn Promenade.** Now-posh **Brooklyn Heights,** with beautiful old brownstones, tree-lined streets, and proximity to Manhattan, has hosted many authors, from Walt Whitman to Norman Mailer. *(Subway: 2, 3, 4, 5, N, or R to the Court St.-Borough Hall and follow Court St.)* Nestled at the northern border with Queens, **Greenpoint** is the seat of an active Polish community. *(Subway: E, F to Queens Plaza, then G to Greenpoint Ave.)* South of Greenpoint is **Williamsburg,** home to a new community of young artists following cheap rents out of Manhattan. *(Subway: J, M, Z to Marcy Ave.)* A small but growing number of hip restaurants, cafes, and bars has sprung up. In **Crown Heights** is the world headquarters of **ChaBad,** a Hasidic Jewish sect. *(770 Eastern Pkwy.)* **Bedford-Stuyvesant** boasts a wealthy African-American community and beautiful brownstones. Farther east into Brooklyn, if you walk along **Atlantic Ave.** or **Eastern Pkwy.,** is a bustling West Indian community.

OTHER SIGHTS. Prospect Park, designed by Frederick Law Olmsted and Calvin Vaux, is a 526-acre urban oasis; it pleased them more than their Central Park project. *(Subway: 2, 3 to Grand Army Pl.)* The striking Art Deco **Public Library** stands on **Grand Army Plaza,** at the northern corner of the Park. *(Open M 10am-6pm, Tu-Th 9am-8pm, F-Sa 10am-6pm, Su 1-5pm; closed Su June-Sept.)* **Greenwood Cemetery** is the permanent home of figures such as Samuel Morse and Horace Greeley and features tombstones shaped to tell the story of their owners deaths. *(5th Ave. and 25th St. ☎718-469-5277. Open daily 8am-4pm.)* The mammoth **Brooklyn Museum** rests at 200 Eastern Pkwy. *(☎718-638-5000. Open W-F 10am-5pm, Sa 10am-9pm, Su 11am-6pm. Suggested donation $4, students $2, seniors $1.50, under 12 free.)* Both a body of water and a mass of land, **Sheepshead Bay** lies on the southern edge of Brooklyn. Diners can catch daily seafood specials along Emmons Ave. Nearby **Brighton Beach,** nicknamed "Little Odessa by the Sea," has been homeland to Russian emigres since the turn of the century. *(Subway: D, Q.)*

CONEY ISLAND. At one time a resort for the City's elite, until the subway made it accessible to the masses, legendary Coney Island is now fading. The **Boardwalk** squeaks nostalgically as tourists are jostled by roughnecks. Enjoy a hot dog at the original **Nathan's,** at Surf and Sitwell Ave. The **Cyclone,** built in 1927, was once the most terrifying roller-coaster ride in the world. *(834 Surf Ave. Open mid-June to Sept. daily noon-midnight; Easter weekend to mid-June F-Su noon-midnight. $5.)* Meet a walrus, shark, or other ocean beast at the **New York Aquarium** *(Surf Ave. and W. 8th St. ☎718-265-3474. Open M-F 10am-5pm., Sa-Su 10am-6pm. $7.75, seniors and children $3.50.)*

QUEENS

Queens is NYC's largest borough, covering over a third of the city's total area. In this urban suburbia, the American melting pot bubbles away with a more than 30% foreign-born population. Immigrants from Korea, China, India, and the West Indies sort into neighborhoods where they try to maintain the memory of their homeland while striving for "the American Dream."

NEIGHBORHOODS. Flushing boasts colonial neighborhood landmarks, a bustling downtown, and a huge Asian immigrant population. *(Subway: 7 to Main St., Flushing.)* Nearby **Flushing Meadows-Corona Park** was the site of the 1939 and 1964 World's Fair, and now holds **Shea Stadium** (home of the Mets) and the simple yet interesting **New York Hall of Science,** on the corner of 111th St. and 48th Ave. *(☎718-699-0005, ext. 365.)* The **Unisphere,** a 380-ton steel globe in front of the nearby New York City Building, hovers over a fountain in retro-futuristic glory. This is the thing that nasty alien crashed into in the 1997 *Men In Black.* **Central Queens** is the borough's Jamaican and West Indian center. Buy succulent beef patties on Jamaica Ave. between 150th and 168th St., and spices on Linden Blvd. (birthplace of A Tribe Called Quest).

In the upper west corner lies **Astoria,** where Greek-, Italian-, and Spanish-speaking communities mingle amid lively shopping districts and cultural attractions. **Long Island City** is just south, across the river from the Upper East Side. Two sculpture gardens make for a worthwhile daytrip from Manhattan. From the Broadway subway station at 31st St., walk west along Broadway eight blocks toward the Manhattan skyline, leaving the commercial district for a more industrial area. At the end of Broadway, cross the intersection with Vernon Blvd. **Jackson Heights,** particularly around 73rd and 74th St., is home to many of the city's Indians, Pakistanis, Nepalese, and Iranians. Neighboring **Corona** is predominantly hispanic.

SCULPTURE. The **Socrates Sculpture Park,** started by sculptor Mark di Suvero, is stunning, if somewhat unnerving: 35 modern day-glo and rusted metal abstractions sit en masse in the middle of nowhere, on the site of what was once an illegal dump. *(☎718-956-1819. Park open daily 10am-sunset. Free.)* Two blocks south stands the **Isamu Noguchi Garden Museum,** established in 1985 next door to the world-renowned sculptor's studio. Twelve galleries display Noguchi's breadth of vision. *(32-37 Vernon Blvd. ☎718-721-1932. Open Apr.-Oct. W-F 10am-5pm and Sa-Su 11am-6pm. Suggested donation $4, students and seniors $2.)*

THE BRONX

While the media present "Da Bronx" as a crime-ravaged husk, the borough offers over 2000 acres of port land, a great zoo, turn-of-the-century riverfront mansions, grand boulevards, and thriving ethnic neighborhoods, including a Little Italy which shames Manhattan's. *Be careful in the South Bronx; do not venture there without someone who knows the area.*

THE BRONX ZOO. The most popular reason to come to the Bronx is the **Bronx Zoo/ Wildlife Conservation Park,** also known as the New York Zoological Society. The largest urban zoo in the US, it houses over 4000 animals. Soar into the air for a funky view of the zoo from the **Skyfari** aerial tramway ($2) that runs between Wild Asia and the **Children's Zoo.** *(☎718-330-1234. Subway: 2 to Pelham Pkwy. Open Apr.-Oct. M-F 10am-5pm, Sa-Su 10am-5:30pm; parts of the zoo close Nov.-Apr. $9, seniors and children 2-12 $5; W free. For disabled-access info, call ☎718-220-5188.)*

OTHER SIGHTS. North across East Fordham Rd. from the zoo, the **New York Botanical Garden** sprawls over forest and lake alike. *(☎718-817-8700. Subway: 4 or D to Bedford Park Blvd.; walk 8 blocks east. Open Apr.-Oct. Tu-Su 10am-6pm; July-Aug. Th and Sa grounds open until 8pm; Nov.-Mar. Tu-Su 10am-4pm.)* The **Museum of Bronx History,** at Bainbridge Ave. and 208th St., is on the premises of the landmark Valentine-Varian House. *(☎718-881-8900. Subway: D to 205th St. Open Sa 10am-4pm, Su 1-5pm, or by appt. $2.)*

Up in northern Bronx, to the east of **Van Cortlandt Park's** 1146 acres, lies the immense **Woodlawn Cemetery,** where music lovers can pay tribute at the resting places of jazz legends Miles Davis, Duke Ellington, and Lionel Hampton. Impressive Victorian mausoleums abound, as do other famous dead: Herman Melville, Roland H. Macy, and more. *(Subway: 4 to Woodlawn. Open daily 9am-4:30pm.)* Nearby, all the way up 242nd St. from Broadway, is Manhattan College, whose red-brick buildings cover stairs, squares, and plateaus like a life-sized game of chutes and ladders.

Belmont, the Bronx's Little Italy, is centered around Arthur Ave. and Tremont St. The much-maligned **South Bronx** still hosts millions of visitors, thanks to **Yankee Stadium,** which pumps millions of needed dollars into the poverty-stricken area. *(E. 161st St. at River Ave. Subway 4, C, or D to 161st St.)*

HIP-HOP (R)EVOLUTION In 1973, Bronx DJ Kool Herc began prolonging songs' funky drum "break" sections by using two turntables and two copies of the same record, switching to the start of the second copy when the first one ended and then doubling back. Dancers took up the rhythm's challenge, and by 1975 breakdancing had evolved in response to similar turntable manipulations by Afrika Bambaataa, Grandmaster Flash, Kool, and other denizens of the 174th St. area near the Bronx River. All in one break, the Bronx birthed the art of DJing, an acrobatic dance style, and the musical genre known as hip-hop/rap.

STATEN ISLAND

Unless you have a vested interest in Fresh Kills, the world's largest landfill and the highest hill on the Eastern Seaboard, or the following sights, it is more trouble to get to Staten Island than it is worth. However, the 30min. ferry ride from Manhattan's Battery Park to Staten Island is a perfect opportunity to cruise by the Statue of Liberty for free. The island is also connected to Brooklyn by the **Verrazano-Narrows Bridge,** the world's 2nd-longest (4260 ft.) suspension span. Because of the distances (and some dangerous neighborhoods in between), it's a bad idea to walk from one site to the next. Plan excursions with the bus schedule in mind.

SIGHTS. Sights on the island cluster around the beautiful 19th-century **Snug Harbor Cultural Center,** housing the **Newhouse Center for Contemporary Art,** a small American art gallery with a sculpture show in summer, and the **Staten Island Botanical Gardens.** *(1000 Richmond Terr. ☎ 718-448-2500. Call for hrs. Suggested donation $2. Gardens 718-273-8200.)* The **Jacques Marchais Museum of Tibetan Art** meditates in central Staten Island. *(388 Lighthouse Ave. ☎ 718-987-3500. Bus S74 to Richmond Rd. and Lighthouse Ave.; turn right and walk up the hill. Open Apr.-Nov. W-Su 1-5pm; Dec.-Mar. W-F 1-5pm. $3, seniors and students $2.50, under 12 $1.)*

🏛 MUSEUMS

For **museum** listings consult the following publications: *Time Out: New York, The New Yorker, New York* magazine and the Friday *New York Times* (Weekend section). Most museums close on Monday and are jam-packed on weekends. Many museums request a "donation" in place of an admission fee—don't be embarrassed to give as little as a quarter. Most museums are free one weeknight. In mid-June the **Museum Mile Festival** keeps the 5th Ave. museums' doors open late into the night and fills the streets with music and activities.

MAJOR COLLECTIONS

Metropolitan Museum of Art (The Met) (☎535-7710, 570-3949 for concerts and lectures), 1000 5th Ave. at 82nd St. Subway: 4, 5, or 6 to 86th St. The largest in the Western Hemisphere, the Met's art collection includes 3.3 million works from almost every period; particularly strong in Egyptian and non-Western sculpture and European painting. Open Su and Tu-Th 9:30am-5:15pm, F-Sa 9:30am-8:45pm. Suggested donation $10, students and seniors $5. (See also the **Cloisters,** p. 221.)

Museum of Modern Art (MoMA), 11 W. 53rd St. (☎708-9400), off 5th Ave. in Midtown. Subway: E or F to 5th Ave./53rd St. or B, D, Q to 50th St. One of the most extensive post-Impressionist collections in the world, founded in 1929 in response to the Met's reluctance to embrace modern art. Monet's sublime *Water Lily* room, numerous Picassos, and a great design collection are among the highlights. Open Sa-Tu and Th 10:30am-5:45pm, F 10:30am-8:15pm. $10, students and seniors $6.50, under 16 free. Pay-what-you-wish F 4:30-8:30pm. Films (free) require tickets in advance.

American Museum of Natural History (☎769-5100), Central Park West, 79th-81st St. Subway: B or C to 81st St. The largest science museum in the world, in an imposing Romanesque structure. The dinosaur exhibit is worth the lines. Brand-new Rose Planetarium. Open Su-Th 10am-5:45pm, F-Sa 10am-8:45pm. Suggested donation $10, students and seniors $7.50, children under 12 $6. **Imax** screen ☎ 769-5034.

Guggenheim Museum, 1071 5th Ave. (☎423-3500), at 89th St. Subway: 4, 5, or 6 to 86th St. The coiling building designed by Frank Lloyd Wright is as famous as the collection inside. The spiral gallery houses temporary exhibits, while the newly constructed **Tower Galleries** has a permanent collection of 19th- and 20th-century works, including several by Picasso, Matisse, Van Gogh, and Cézanne. Open Su-W 9am-6pm, F-Sa 9am-8pm. $12, students and seniors $7, under 12 free; F 6-8pm "pay-what-you-wish." Also: **Guggenheim Museum SoHo,** 575 Broadway (☎423-3500), at Prince St. Currently shows Andy Warhol's "Last Supper" for free. Open Th-M 11am-6pm.

Whitney Museum of American Art, 945 Madison Ave. (☎570-3676), at 75th St. Subway: 6 to 77th St. Futuristic fortress featuring the largest collection of 20th-century American art in the world, with works by Hopper, O'Keeffe, de Kooning, Warhol, and Calder. Open Tu-W and F-Su 11am-6pm, Th 1-9pm. $10, students and seniors $8, under 12 free. Free Th 6-9pm.

Cooper-Hewitt Museum, 2 E. 91st St. (☎849-8400), at 5th Ave. Subway: 4, 5, or 6 to 86th St. Andrew Carnegie's majestic Georgian mansion now houses the Smithsonian Institute's National Museum of Design. Playful exhibits focus on such topics as doghouses and the history of the pop-up book. Open Tu 10am-9pm, W-Sa 10am-5pm, Su noon-5pm. $8, students and seniors $5, under 12 free; free Tu 5-9pm.

The Frick Collection, 1 E. 70th St. (☎288-0700), at 5th Ave. Subway: 6 to 68th St. Henry Clay Frick left his house and art collection to the city, and the museum retains the elegance of his château. The Living Hall displays 17th-century furniture, Persian rugs, Holbein portraits, and paintings by El Greco, Rembrandt, Velázquez, and Titian. The courtyard is inhabited by elegant statues surrounding the garden pool and fountain. Open Tu-Sa 10am-6pm, Su 1-6pm. $7, students and seniors $5. Under 10 not allowed, under 16 must be accompanied by an adult. Group visits by appointment only.

Pierpont Morgan Library, 29 E. 36th St., at Madison Ave. (☎985-0610). J.P. Morgan and son left a stunning collection of rare books, sculptures, and paintings, including hand-written sheet music by Beethoven and Mozart, Thoreau's journal, a Guttenberg Bible (the first printed book), and a 12th-century, jewel-encrusted triptych believed to contain fragments of the Holy Cross. Open Tu-F 10:30am-5pm, Sa 10:30am-6pm, Su noon-6pm. $8, students and seniors $6, under 12 free.

SMALLER AND SPECIALIZED COLLECTIONS

Museum of the City of New York, 1220 5th Ave. (☎534-1672), at 103rd St. Subway: 6 to 103rd St. Details the history of the Big Apple. Open W-Sa 10am-5pm, Su noon-5pm. Suggested donation $7; students, seniors, and children $4.

Museum of American Illustration, 128 E. 63rd St. between Park and Lexington Ave. (☎838-2560). This museum has over 1500 works by legendary artists like Rockwell, Pyle, and Wyeth, and well-curated exhibits. Open Tu 10am-8pm, W-F 10am-5pm, Sa noon-4pm. Free.

Museum of Television and Radio, 25 W. 52nd St. (☎621-6600, 621-6800 for daily schedule), between 5th and 6th Ave. Subway: B, D, F, or Q to Rockefeller Center; or E or F to 53rd St. This museum is more an archive. With a collection of more than 95,000 TV and radio programs, the museum's library has a specially designed computerized cataloging system and private viewing consoles. Tours are free with admission; inquire at the desk. Open Tu-W and F-Su noon-6pm, Th noon-8pm; F until 9pm for theaters only. Suggested donation $6, students and seniors $4, under 13 $3.

The Children's Museum of New York, 212 W. 83rd St., off Amsterdam Ave. (☎721-1223). Subway: 1 or 9 to 86th St. Characters like Dr. Seuss' cat and Snoopy act as guides through the museum. Check out the "Body Odyssey" exhibit. Open Tu-Su 10am-5pm; winter W-Su 10am-5pm. Adults and children $6, seniors $3, under 1 free.

The Asia Society, 725 Park Ave. (☎517-2742), at 70th St. Subway: 6 to 68th St. Asian art exhibits accompanied by musical performances, films, and an acclaimed "Meet the Author" series. Open M-Sa 10am-6pm. $4, seniors and students $2; free daily noon-2pm. At 502 Park Ave., at 59th St., until uptown location is renovated.

International Center of Photography, 1133 Avenue of the Americas (6th Ave.), at 43rd St. (☎860-1777). Subway: B, D, F, or Q to 42nd St. The foremost exhibitor of photography in the city and a gathering place for its practitioners. Historical, thematic, and contemporary works, from fine art to photojournalism to celebrity portraits. Open Tu-Th 10am-5pm, F 10am-8pm, Sa-Su 10am-6pm. $6, students and seniors $4, under 12 $1.

Intrepid Sea-Air-Space Museum, Pier 86 (☎245-0072), at 46th St. and 12th Ave. Subway: A, C, or E to 42nd St. One ticket admits you to a veteran aircraft carrier, a Vietnam War destroyer, the only publicly displayed guided-missile submarine, and a lightship. Pioneer's Hall shows models, antiques, and film shorts. Open May-Sept. M-F 10am-5pm, Sa-Su 10am-6pm; Oct.-Apr. W-Su 10am-5pm. Last admission 1hr. before closing.

$12; students, seniors, ages 12-17, and veterans $9; ages 6-11 $6, 2-5 $2; active servicemen and under 2 free.

The Jewish Museum, 1109 5th Ave. (☎423-3200), at 92nd St. Subway: 6 to 96th St. The permanent collection of over 14,000 works, ranging from ancient Biblical artifacts to contemporary masterpieces, details the Jewish story. Open Su-M and W-Th 11am-5:45pm, Tu 11am-8pm. $8, students and seniors $5.50; Tu 5-8pm free.

El Museo del Barrio, 1230 5th Ave. (☎831-7272), at 104th St. Subway: 6 to 103rd St. El Museo del Barrio is the only museum in the U.S. devoted exclusively to the art and culture of Puerto Rico and Latin America. Begun in a classroom, the project has turned into a permanent museum. Open W-Su 11am-5pm. Suggested donation $4, students and seniors $2.

The Museum for African Art, 593 Broadway (☎966-1313), between Houston and Prince St. in SoHo. Subway: N or R to Prince St.; 6 to Spring St. African and African-American art that spans centuries and continents. Hands-on sculpture workshops available. Open Tu-F 10:30am-5:30pm, Sa-Su noon-6pm. $5, students and seniors $2.50.

National Museum of the American Indian, 1 Bowling Green (668-6624). Subway: 4 or 5 to Bowling Green. In the Beaux-Arts Customs House. The cream of the Smithsonian's collection of Native American artifacts. Open F-W 10am-5pm, Th 10am-8pm. Free.

New Museum of Contemporary Art, 583 Broadway (☎219-1222), between Prince and Houston St. Subway: N or R to Prince; B, D, F, or Q to Broadway-Lafayette. Dedicated to art's role in society; flaunts the hottest and most controversial. Open Su-W noon-6pm, Th-Sa noon-8pm. $6; artists, students, and seniors $3, under 18 free, Th 6-8pm free.

GALLERIES

Galleries are not only completely free, but they are where the avant-garde *goes down.* All are closed Monday. Check the free *Gallery Guide,* available at all museums and large galleries, for the most comprehensive list. **SoHo** is a wonderland of galleries; a particularly dense concentration lines Broadway between Houston and Spring St. Cutting-edge outposts have recently emerged in **Chelsea,** in reclaimed industrial spaces around W. 22nd St. between 10th and 11th Ave. **Madison Ave.** between 70th and 84th St. has a sampling of ritzy showplaces, and more galleries festoon **57th St.** between 5th and 6th Ave. This is just a browsing list.

SOHO

▨ **Artists Space.** Slide file of unaffiliated artists. 38 Greene St., at Grand St., 3rd fl. (☎226-3970). Open Tu-Sa 10am-6pm; summer W-Sa noon-6pm. Slide file open by appointment, usually F-Sa. Frequent free evening performances.

POP. Works by pop masters such as Warhol, Lichtenstein, and Haring. 473 W. Broadway, below Houston St. Open Tu-Sa 11am-6pm.

Drawing Center. Specializing exclusively in original works on paper—everything from Picasso to Kara Walker. 35 Wooster St. (☎219-2166). Open Tu and Th-F 10am-6pm, W 10am-8pm, Sa 11am-6pm; closed Aug.

Shakespeare's Fulcrum. Shows Actual Art—it requires the forces of nature for completion. 480 Broome St., at Wooster St. (☎966-6848). Open Tu-Sa 11am-6pm, Su 1-6pm.

Exit Art/The First World. A fun and happening "transcultural" and "transmedia" nonprofit space. 548 Broadway, between Prince and Spring St., 2nd fl. (☎966-7745). Open Tu-Th 11am-6pm; summer M-F 11am-6pm; closed Aug.

Printed Matter, Inc. Bookshop/gallery that lets you peruse books on art as well as books that are art. 77 Wooster St. (☎925-0325). Open Tu-F 10am-6pm, Sa 11am-7pm.

Thread Waxing Space. Mostly group shows with thematically curated exhibits, sometimes solo shows. 476 Broadway between Broome and Grand St., 2nd fl. (☎966-9520). Open Tu-Sa 10am-6pm.

Tony Shafrazi. Boasts being one of the first to display art by Haring and Basquiat. 119 Wooster St. between Prince and Spring St. (☎274-9300). Open Tu-Sa 10am-6pm.

Staley-Wise. Focuses on fashion photography. 560 Broadway, just south of Prince St., 3rd fl. (☎966-6223). Open Tu-Sa 11am-5pm.

CHELSEA

Sonnabend. Well-known American and European contemporary masters. 536 W. 22nd St. between 10th and 11th Ave. ☎627-1018. Open Tu-Sa 10am-6pm.

Dia Center for the Arts. Museum-sized, but with a sensibility for catching the current pulse. 548 W. 22nd St. between 10th and 11th Ave. ☎989-5566. Open W-Su noon-6pm; closed July-Aug. $6; students and seniors $3.

The Museum at Fashion Institute of Technology. Changing exhibits from photography and textiles to mannequin displays. 7th Ave. and 27th St. ☎217-5800. Open Tu-F noon-8pm, Sa 10am-5pm.

Taranto Gallery. Group and solo photo shows. 245 W. 19th St. between 7th and 8th Ave. ☎691-9040. Open M-F 9am-7pm, Sa 11am-5pm.

I-20. High quality contemporary art and an exhilarating view of the river and piers below. 529 W. 20th St., 11th fl. ☎645-1100. Open Tu-Sa 10:30am-6pm.

Gavin Brown's Enterprise Corp. Both a gallery and a social area, with a bar. 436 W. 15th St. between 9th and 10th Ave. ☎627-5258. Open Tu-Sa 10am-6pm.

57TH ST.

Fuller Building. 12 floors of galleries. 41 E. 57th St. between Madison and Park Ave. Most open M-Sa 10am-5:30pm, but call ahead to make sure; Oct.-May most closed M.

UPPER EAST SIDE

Gagosian. Represents an impressive group including Warhol, Yves Klein, and Richard Serra. 980 Madison Ave., near 77th St. ☎744-2313. Open M-Sa 10am-6pm.

M. Knoedler & Co., Inc. One of the oldest and most respected galleries in the city. 19 E. 70th St. between Madison and 5th Ave. ☎794-0550. Open M-Th 9:30am-5pm; summer M-F 9:30am-5pm.

Acquavella. Picasso, Degas, Cézanne, and Giacometti. 18 E. 79th St. between 5th and Madison Ave. ☎734-6300. Open M-F 10am-5pm; open Sa-Su for larger shows.

Auction Houses: Open to anyone, some auctions require tickets (first come, first served). **Sotheby's,** 1334 York Ave. ☎606-7000; ticket office 606-7171. Open M-Sa 10am-5pm, Su 1-5pm; closed Sa-Su in summer. **Christie's,** 20 Rockefeller Plaza. ☎636-2000. Open M-Sa 10am-5pm, Su 1-5pm.

SHOPPING

There is no easier place to blow your dough than NYC—everything from the world's (2nd) largest department store to sidewalk tables displaying bootleg Top 40 selections can be bought. Here's a quick walking tour of the city, style-wise.

The best place to start is downtown on the **Lower East Side,** where the really hip new designers sell their uneven hemlines and poly-nylon-shiny-rubber-weird-fabric shirts. (Orchard, Stanton, and Ludlow St.) Don't expect prices to reflect the relative namelessness of these designers—they are *artistes!* Next stop is **Chinatown,** where you can pick up a (fake) Kate Spade from any of the million vendors along Canal St. and they'll stick the label on for you. Pick up other bootleg items right off the sidewalk, from CDs to Polo shirts. Walk up to **SoHo** to spend some major cash, this time on hip but established designers. Wooster, Prince, and West Broadway are home to the likes of Rowley and Sui, but Broadway is cheaper, with the NYC staple Canal Jeans Co. (between Spring and Prince St.) and many $10 hoochie stores. **Greenwich Village** has a mish-mash of offerings, from the largest comic book store (Forbidden Planet) to Cheap Jack's Vintage Clothing. Just east of Broadway is the more risqué **East Village,** a den of tattoo parlors, silver trinkets, sex shops, and cheap CD stores (centered on St. Mark's Pl.) Find some fashionable enclaves on 9th St. farther east and a number of good vintage stores all over. **Midtown** is mostly Macy's at Herald Sq. and bookstores, although you can find one of everything (usually expensive). Right between Midtown and the Upper East Side is **Fifth Ave.** and **57th St.** Peruse these for a look at the really unattainable—flagships from Chanel, Armani, Prada, Klein, Vuitton, Tiffany's & Co., etc. plus elite department stores like Bergdorf, Saks, and Bloomingdale's. To keep the kids quiet while you shop at Versace, stop at F.A.O. Schwartz on 5th Ave. and 58th St. **Uptown** has everything, from cute boutiques along **Columbus Ave.** on the West Side to the cheapest kicks and FuBu gear on 125th St. in **Harlem.** The outer boroughs are a mixed bag, too far for most short-term visitors, although **Brooklyn** has the hippest vintage warehouse: Domsey's in Williamsburg.

🎵 ENTERTAINMENT

Although always an exhilarating, incomparable city, New York only becomes "New York" when the sun goes down. From the bright lights of Times Square to the smoky atmosphere of a Greenwich Village pub and stiletto-ed martinis sippers of a SoHo bar, the Big Apple pulls in a million directions at once. Find some performance art, hear some jazz, go to an all-night diner, twist the night away—heck, even get a tattoo. A cab home at 4:30am through empty streets is always sure to make your spirits soar. The city never sleeps and, for a few nights, neither should you.

Publications with noteworthy entertainment and nightlife sections are the *Village Voice, Time Out: New York, New York* magazine, and the Su edition of the *New York Times. The New Yorker* has the most comprehensive theater survey.

THEATER

Broadway is currently undergoing a revival and ticket sales are booming. Mainstream musicals receive more than their fair share of attention. Tickets cost about $50 each when purchased through regular channels. **TKTS** sells 25-50% discounted tickets to many shows on the day of the performance from a booth in the middle of Duffy Sq.—the northern part of Times Sq., at 47th and Broadway. (☎768-1818 for recorded info. Tickets sold M-Sa 3-8pm for evening performances, W and Sa 10am-2pm for matinees, Su 11am-7pm for matinees and evening performances. $2.50 service charge per ticket.) Less competitive lines form at the TKTS branch in the mezzanine of 2 World Trade Center. (Open M-F 11am-5:30pm, Sa 11am-3:30pm; Su matinee tickets sold on Sa.) For info on shows and tickets, call the **NYC/ON STAGE hotline** at ☎768-1818. **Ticketmaster** (☎307-4100, 800-755-4000) takes credit cards, but charges at least $2 more than other outlets.

Off-Broadway theaters have between 100 and 499 seats; only Broadway houses have over 500. Off-Broadway houses frequently offer more off-beat, quirky shows, with shorter runs. Occasionally these shows have long runs or make the jump to Broadway houses. Tickets cost $15-45. Many of the best Off-Broadway houses huddle in the Sheridan Sq. area of the West Village. TKTS also sells tickets for the larger Off-Broadway houses. **Off-Off-Broadway** means cheaper, younger theaters.

Shakespeare in the Park (☎539-8750) is a New York summer tradition. From June through Aug., two Shakespeare plays are presented at the **Delacorte Theater** in Central Park, near the 81st St. entrance on the Upper West Side, just north of the main road. Tickets are free, but lines form early.

FILMS

Many films open in New York weeks before they're distributed elsewhere, and the response of Manhattan audiences and critics can shape a film's success or failure. Check newspapers for times and locations. Big-screen fanatics should check out the cavernous **Ziegfeld,** 141 W. 54th St., one of the largest screens left in America, which shows first-run films. (☎765-7600. Subway: 1 or 9 to 51st St.) **The Kitchen,** 512 W. 19th St., between 10th and 11th Ave., is a world-renowned showcase for the off-beat and New York-based struggling artists. (☎255-5793, ext. 11. Subway: C or E to 23rd St.). Eight screens project art-house cinema at the **Angelika Film Center,** 18 W. Houston St., at Mercer St. (☎995-2000. Subway: 6 to Bleecker St., B, D, F, or Q to Broadway-Lafayette.) **Anthology Film Archives,** 32 2nd Ave., at E. 2nd St., is a forum for independent filmmaking. (☎505-5181. Subway: F to 2nd Ave.) The **New York International Film Festival** is here every Oct.; check the *Village Voice* or *Time Out.*

CHEAP SEATS To the budget traveler, the Great White Way's major theatrical draws may seem locked away in gilded Broadway cages. Never fear, however, *Let's Go*'s here! Er, that is to say, you can find cheap tickets, compadre. Should **Ticketmaster** and **TKTS** (see above) fail, other avenues remain open to you.

Rush Tickets: Some theaters distribute them on the morning of the performance; others make student rush tickets available 30min. before showtime. Lines can be extremely long, so get there *early*. Call the theater before to find out their policy.

Cancellation Line: No rush luck? Some theaters redistribute returned or unclaimed tickets several hours before showtime. You might have to sacrifice your afternoon—but, come on, Dame Edna is worth it! Once again, call before.

Hit Show Club: 630 9th Ave. (☎581-4211), between 44th and 45th St. This free service distributes coupons redeemable at the box office for 30% or more off regular ticket prices. Call for coupons via mail or pick them up them up at the club office.

Sold-out Shows: Even if a show is sold out to the general public, theaters reserve prime house seats, usually in the first few rows, for VIPs. However, house seats frequently remain unclaimed, in which case they are sold to the general public—for full price—on the day of the show. House seats can go on sale as early as the box office opens or as late as one hour before curtain, so call the theater for details.

Standing-room Only: Sold on the day of show, tend to be around $15 or $20. Call first, as some theaters can't accommodate standing room.

OPERA AND DANCE

You can do it all at **Lincoln Center**; there's usually opera or dance at one of its many venues. (☎546-2656. Subway: 1 or 9 to 66th St.) Check the New York Times listings. The **Metropolitan Opera Company's** premier outfit plays on a Lincoln Center stage as big as a football field. You can stand in the orchestra, $16; or all the way back in the Family Circle, $12. (☎362-6000. Season runs Sept.-Apr. M-Sa. Box office open M-Sa 10am-8pm, Su noon-6pm. Regular tickets run over $250; upper balcony around $50. The cheapest seats have an obstructed view.)

Next to the Met, the **New York City Opera** has come into its own. "City" has a split season (Sept.-Nov. and Mar.-Apr.) and keeps its ticket prices low. (☎870-5570. $25-92; $10 rush tickets, call the night before and wait in line morning of.) In July, the **New York Grand Opera** (☎360-2777) puts on free performances at the Central Park Summerstage every W night. A small company that garners standing ovations after *every* performance is the **Dicapo Opera Theatre**, 184 E. 76th St. between 3rd and Lexington Ave. (☎288-9438. Subway: 6 to 77th St. Tickets around $40.)

The **New York State Theater** in Lincoln Center is home to the late George Balanchine's **New York City Ballet.** Good tickets for the *Nutcracker* in Dec. sell out almost immediately. (☎870-5570. Season Nov.-Feb. and May-June; tickets $12-65.) The **American Ballet Theater** dances at the Metropolitan Opera House. (☎477-3030, box office 362-6000. Tickets $17-75.) **City Center** has some of the best dance in the city, from modern to ballet, including the **Alvin Ailey American Dance Theater** in Dec. 131 W. 55th St. (☎581-7907. Subway: 1 or 9 to 51st St.) **De La Guarda** (described as a trip to the rainforest, a disco, and an air show) dances at 20 Union Sq. East (☎239-6200), subway: L, N, R, 4, or 6 to Union Sq. Standing-room only $40-45, some $20 tickets sold 2hr. before.

CLASSICAL MUSIC

Start with listings in *Time Out*, the *New York Times*, *The New Yorker*, or *New York* magazine. Remember that many events are seasonal.

Lincoln Center has the most selection in its halls. The **Great Performers Series,** featuring famous and foreign musicians, packs the Avery Fisher and Alice Tully Halls and the Walter Reade Theater from Oct. until May (see above for contact info; tickets from $10). **Avery Fisher Hall** presents the annual **Mostly Mozart Festival.** Show up early; there are usually recitals 1hr. before the main concert that are free to ticketholders. (☎875-5766. July-Aug. Tickets $15-50.) The **New York Philharmonic** begins its regular season in mid-Sept. Students and seniors can sometimes get $10 tickets day-of; call ahead. Check about seeing morning rehearsals. (☎875-5709. Tickets $10-60.) For a few weeks in late June, Kurt Masur and friends lead the posse at **free concerts** on the Great Lawn in Central Park, at Prospect Park in Brooklyn, at Van Cortlandt Park in the Bronx, and elsewhere (☎875-5709). Free outdoor events at Lincoln Center occur all summer (☎875-4000).

Carnegie Hall, 7th Ave. at 57th St., is still the favorite coming-out locale of musical debutantes. (☎247-7800. Subway: N or R to 57th St.; D or E to 7th Ave. Box office M-Sa 11am-6pm, Su noon-6pm. Tickets $10-60.) A good, cheap way to absorb New York musical culture is to visit a **music school.** Except for opera and ballet productions ($5-12), concerts at these schools are free and frequent: the **Juilliard School of Music,** Lincoln Center (☎769-7406), the **Mannes School of Music** (☎580-0210), and the **Manhattan School of Music** (☎749-2802).

SPORTS

Most cities are content to field a major-league team in each big-time sport. New York opts for the Noah's Ark approach: two baseball teams, two hockey teams, NBA and WNBA basketball teams, two football teams, and a lonely MLS soccer squad. New York hosts a number of world-class events. Get tickets three months in advance for the prestigious **U.S. Open,** held in late Aug. and early Sept. at the USTA Tennis Center in Flushing Meadows, Queens. (☎888-673-6849; $33-69.) On the 3rd Su in Oct., 2 million spectators witness the 22,000 runners of the **New York City Marathon** (only 16,000 finish). The race begins on the Verrazano Bridge and ends at Central Park's Tavern on the Green.

The **New York Mets** bat at **Shea Stadium** in Queens (☎718-507-6387; $13-30). The legendary **New York Yankees** play ball at Yankee Stadium in the Bronx (☎718-293-4300; $8-30). Both the **New York Giants** and the **Jets** play football across the river at **Giants Stadium** (☎516-560-8200; from $25) in East Rutherford, NJ. The **New York/New Jersey Metrostars** play soccer in the same venue. The **New York Knickerbockers** (that's the Knicks to you), as well as the WNBA's **Liberty,** play basketball at **Madison Sq. Garden** (☎465-5867; from $22 and $8, respectively) and the **New York Rangers** play hockey there (from $25).

🎵 NIGHTLIFE

BARS

🍸 **Naked Lunch Bar and Lounge,** 17 Thompson St., at Grand St. (☎343-0828). Adorned with the roach-and-typewriter motif found in the novel and movie of the same name. The after-work crowd has no qualms about dancing in the aisle alongside the bar. Free BBQ hamburgers and hot dogs W. Beer $6. Occasional $7 cover F and Sa after 10pm. Take $2 off all drinks during Happy Hour Tu-F 5-9pm. Open Tu-F 5pm-4am, Sa 9pm-4am.

🍸 **NV and 289 Lounge,** 289 Spring St., near Varick St. (☎929-6868). Gothic playground meets post-industrialism. Two bars and dance floors. Mixed drinks are club priced ($8-10) and the cover ($10-20) could be much more for a night of pure fun. W and Su feature R&B, hip-hop, and reggae. Happy Hour W-Th 6-10pm. Open W-Su 10pm-4am.

🍸 **The Whitehorse Tavern,** 567 Hudson St. at W. 11th St. (☎243-9260). Dylan Thomas drank himself to death here, pouring 18 straight whiskies through an already tattered liver. Boisterous students and locals pay homage to the poet. Great jukebox. Outdoor patio. Beer $3-5. Open Su-Th 11am-2am, F-Sa 11am-4am.

🍸 **Tribe,** 132 1st Ave., at St. Mark's Pl. (☎979-8965). Behind the frosted glass windows lies a chic, friendly bar with colorful but subtle back lighting, complete with comfortable lounging areas. DJ nightly: M live music and DJ, Tu Salsa/Latin. Beer $5; cocktails $5-10. Open daily 5pm-4am.

bOb Bar, 235 Eldridge St. between Houston and Stanton St. (☎777-0588). Comfy and laid-back, with a hip-hop-inclined crowd. Happy Hour F 7-10pm $2 beers. While Tu alternates between Latin, reggae, and hip-hop (free), Th is strictly hip-hop ($5 cover after 10pm) in this small but happening bar. Open daily 7pm-4am.

MID-ATLANTIC

Orchard Bar, 200 Orchard St., between Houston and Stanton St. (☎673-5350). A long, narrow haunt frequented by hip Lower East Side scene-sters. Don't expect a sign outside. DJ after 10pm some weekend nights. F is proper house with one of NY's best DJs, Rob Salmon (free). Beer $4-5. Other drinks $5-6. Open daily 6pm-4am.

Potion Lounge, 370 Columbus Ave. between 77th and 78th St. (☎721-4386). Step into this silvery-blue lounge complete with local art on the walls, bubbles rising through pipes in the windows, and velvety sofas. Order a colorful layered drink ("potions" around $10) and watch a chemical miracle take place before your eyes. DJs on weekends. Open M-Th 6pm-midnight, F-Sa 6pm-4am.

Ozone, 1720 2nd Ave. between 89th and 90th Sts. (☎860-8950). Dim and elegant, Ozone's front room holds a classy bar, while the back has a mellow and comfortable lounge. Imported ($4) and domestic ($3) beers. Happy Hour daily 4-7pm. Live DJ spinning the latest in funk, jazz, and hip-hop F-Sa. Open Su-W 4pm-2am, Th-Sa 4pm-4am.

Moomba, 133 7th Ave. S., betweeen W. 10th and Charles St. (☎989-1414). Hip, candle-lit lounge with a mellow mood. Come for cocktails ($8-15) or Karoake (M; cover $5). Supposedly Madonna and Prince come here—but that's such a cliché NYC bar claim. Open daily 6pm-3am; Su brunch 11:30am-4pm.

Bbar (Bowery Bar), 40 E. 4th St., at the Bowery (☎475-2220). Bbar has long held court as a flagship of cooler-than-thou-ness. $5 beers. Tu night is "Beige," Erich Conrad's wonderfully flamboyant gay party. Open Su-Th 11:30am-3am, F-Sa 11:30am-4am.

Fun, 130 Madison St., at Pike St. (☎964-0303). In-the-know hipsters hang at this "never a cover, never a guest list" hangout, and so can you. Its whimsical decor is complete with hydraulic lifts for the bartenders. VJs and DJs rotate nightly. Tu playstation nights. Drinks start at $9 but are worth the phun. Open daily 8pm-4am.

MUSIC CLUBS

New York City has a long history of producing bands on the vanguard of popular music and performance, from the Velvet Underground to Sonic Youth to the Wu-Tang Clan. **Music festivals** provide the opportunity to see tons of bands at a (relatively) low price. The **CMJ Music Marathon** runs for four nights in the fall, including over 400 bands and workshops on the alternative music scene (☎877-633-7848). **The Digital Club Festival** (☎677-3530), a newly reconfigured indie-fest, visits New York in late July. The **Macintosh New York Music Festival** presents over 350 bands over a week-long period. For more experimental sounds, check out Creative Time's **Music in the Anchorage,** a June concert series happening in the massive stone chambers in the base of the Brooklyn Bridge. (☎206-6674, ext. 252 for info, or stop by **Other Music,** 4th St. between Broadway and Lafayette, for tickets and a brochure.) For the best listings, see *The Village Voice* and *Time Out: New York*.

Knitting Factory, 74 Leonard St. between Broadway and Church St. (☎219-3055). Walk up Broadway to Leonard St. Free-thinking musicians anticipate the apocalypse with a wide range of edge-pushing performances complemented by great acoustics. Several shows nightly. Summertime's **What is Jazz festival** is an open-ended exploration of the musical form that crosses genre boundaries. Shows $20-30 for entrance to the back room/performance space only; entry to the cozy bar up front is always free, as is the downstairs jazz space some nights. Box office open M-F 10am-11pm, Sa-Su 2-11pm; bar open M-F 4:30pm-2am, Sa-Su 6pm-2am.

Tramps, 51 W. 21st St. between 5th and 6th Ave. (☎727-7788). One of the best places to hear your favorite band if they've got a gig here. Small and well-designed so you can always see. Usually good hip hop and indie rock. Box office open M-F 11am-7pm, Sa noon-7pm, extended on night of show. Sets usually M-Th 8pm, Sa-Su 9pm. Doors open 1hr. before shows. Cover $5-20.

CBGB/OMFUG (CBGB's), 315 Bowery, at Bleecker St. (☎982-4052). The initials have stood for "country, bluegrass, blues, and other music for uplifting gourmandizers," since 1973, but the New York Dolls, Television, the Ramones, Patti Smith, and Talking Heads rendered the initials synonymous with punk. The music remains loud, raw, and hungry. Shows daily around 8pm. Cover $3-10. Next door, **CB's Gallery** (☎677-0455) presents softer live music.

Continental, 25 3rd Ave. between St. Mark's Pl. and Stuyvesant (☎529-6924). A dark club that hosts the loud set nightly. Come for noise, rock, and local punk. Iggy Pop, Debbie Harry, and Patti Smith have all played here—recently. Check lamp-posts and flyers for shows and times. Happy Hour daily half-price drinks. Shot of anything $2 with a beer. Cover free-$7.

Tonic, 107 Norfolk St. between Delancey and Rivington St. (☎358-7501). Artists like Cibo Matto, MC Paul Barman, and the members of Sonic Youth have used this space to put on conceptual, experimental music programs. Unexpected combination, collaboration, and juxtaposition are its functional principles. Films every M. Cover free-$10.

DANCE CLUBS

The New York club scene is an unrivaled institution. Honing in on the hippest club in New York isn't easy without connections. Clubs rise, war, and fall, and even those "in the know" can't always locate the hot spot, since many parties stay carefully underground, advertised only by word of mouth and carefully-distributed flyers. The right club on the wrong night can be a big mistake, particularly if you've already paid the $3-25 cover charge. Check out the cooler record stores for flyers. Flyers and staff at **8th St. Lab,** 69 E. 8th St., **Other Music,** 4th St. between Broadway and Lafayette, **Throb,** 211 E. 14th St., and **Phat Beats,** 2nd floor above Grey's Papaya on Avenue of the Americas at 8th St., will help guide you.

The rules are relatively simple. You have to have "the look" to be let in. Bouncers are the clubs' fashion police, and nothing drab or conventional will squeeze by. Most clubgoers wear black clothes or rave gear and their most attractive friends. These suggestions could change, though; hip is an elusive commodity. Call ahead to make sure you know what (and whom) you'll find when you arrive.

▓ **Centrofly,** 45 W. 21st. St. between 5th and 6th Ave. (☎627-7770). This is where the beautiful come to dance to the latest House and Techno. Although the patrons rave about the martinis ($11), it's the lights and decor that put the "fly" in Centrofly. Cover $20. Mixed drinks $8-10. Open M-Sa 10pm-5am. Call for weekly schedule.

▓ **Ohm,** 16 W. 22nd St. between 5th and 6th Ave. (☎229-2000). This warehouse-style space is one of the hottest clubs in the city. F is House and Trance, Sa hears latest Latin and International on the main floor, with hip-hop DJ Louie Passion keeping you on your feet downstairs. Mixed drinks $8-16. Open W-Sa 10pm-4am. Cover $20.

▓ **Spa,** 76 E. 13th St. between Broadway and 4th St. (☎388-1062). Don't be intimidated by the elegance of the crowd or the Herculean-sized bouncers. Just walk in with attitude. "Rock and Roll W;" other nights have hip-hop, house, and R&B. Th is a very popular gay night. Open Tu-Sa 10pm-4am. Cover F-Sa $20-25.

Cheetah, 12 W. 21st. St. between 5th and 6th Ave. (☎206-7770). Cheetah-print sofas and greenery create the setting for this club. A self-consciously trendy crowd struts it. Th is Clique, female DJ rotation with open bar 10-11pm. F is Great British House with open bar 10-11pm. Sa is Cherchez La Femme, hip hop and R'n'B with open bar 10-11pm. Beers $6. Open 10pm-4am. Cover charge usually $20-25.

Kilimanjaro, 95 Leonard St., at Broadway. (☎343-0957). Featuring the latest in hip-hop, reggae, and R&B, this club will take you to new heights of dancing enjoyment. Themed F always crowded, sweaty, and worth every minute. Drinks $7. Open F-Sa 11pm-4:30am. Cover: women $5 before midnight, $10 after; men $10-15.

Twilo, 503 W. 27th St. between 10th and 11th Ave. (☎268-1600). Perhaps the best of the widely-known NYC clubs, this warehouse-like complex features cavorting glam boys and their mixed friends. **Junior Vasquez** heats it up on Sa. Parties often run well past noon. Doors open around 11pm. Cover $20-25.

A2i's, 248 W. 14th St., between 7th and 8th Ave. (☎807-1775). Two metallic floors throbbing to urban beats laid down by a rotating crew of DJs. Booming BTUs and mid-riffs are the rule. Reggae M-Su; Hip Hop and House W-Sa. Cover $5-15. Drinks $6-12. Open W-M 11pm-4am.

101 on Seventh, 101 7th Ave., 1 block south of Christopher St. (☎620-4000). Featuring live R&B, funk, soul, and old-school hip-hop seven nights a week, this jumping spot is hard to walk past. Happy Hour 6-9pm, all drinks half-price. 1 drink minimum. Beer $6. Mixed drinks $6-8. Open Su-Th 6pm-3am, F-Sa 6pm-4am. No cover.

JAZZ JOINTS

The **JVC Jazz Festival** blows into the city with all-star performances from June to July. Tickets go on sale in early May, but many events are outdoors and free. Check the newspaper or call ☎501-1390. Annual festivals sponsored by major corporations bring in local talent and industry giants. The concerts take place throughout the city (some free) but center at TriBeCa's **Knitting Factory** (☎219-3055 in spring).

Apollo Theatre, 253 W. 125th St. between Frederick Douglass and Adam Clayton Powell Blvd. (☎749-5838; box office ☎531-5305). This Harlem landmark has heard Duke Ellington, Count Basie, Ella Fitzgerald, and Billie Holliday. A young Malcolm X shone shoes here. W is legendary Amateur Night ($13-30), where the audience plays judge, jury, and, many times, executioner. Order through Ticketmaster (☎307-7171) or at the box office. Open M-Tu and Th-F 10am-6pm, W 10am-8:30pm, Sa noon-6pm.

Detour, 349 E. 13th St. between 1st and 2nd Ave. (☎533-6212). Great nightly jazz and no cover—a perfect mix. One-drink minimum. Happy Hour M-F 4-7pm. Mixed drinks ($6), bottled beer ($4). Open M-Th 3pm-2am, F-Su 3pm-4am. Shows M-Th 9pm-midnight; F-Su 9:30pm-1:30am. Wheelchair accessible.

Fez, 380 Lafayette St. between 3rd and 4th St., under Time Cafe (☎533-2680). This lush club draws a photogenic crowd, especially on Th when the Mingus Big Band holds court. Sets at 9:30 and 11:30pm. $18, students pay $10 for 2nd set; reservations suggested. Other nights vary in musical genre. Cover $5-30; 2-drink minimum. Open Su-Th 6pm-2am, F-Sa 6pm-4am.

Lenox Lounge, 288 Lenox Ave. between 124th and 125th St. (☎427-0253). Glorious when Ella Fitzgerald, Billie Holiday, and Alvin Reed graced it, Lenox Lounge remains "one of the hidden treasures of Harlem." Intimate, with original 1939 decor. Jazz F, Sa. $10; M night jam session free. 2-drink minimum. First set 10pm; last set 1am. Open daily noon-4am.

Small's, 183 W. 10th St., at 7th Ave. (☎929-7565). Some of the best up-and-comers night after night, with the occasional luminary. The fact that it doesn't serve alcohol allows it to stay open all night, often providing over 10hr. of great music, and a late, late night showcase for musicians who still have chops left over from performances at other clubs. Cover $10. Free show Sa 6:30-9pm. Free non-alcoholic beverages. Open Su-Th 10pm-8am, F-Sa 6:30pm-8am. Call ahead for early bird specials (no cover).

Village Vanguard, 178 7th Ave. between W. 11th and Greenwich St. (☎255-4037). 65-years of memories of Leadbelly, Miles Davis, and Sonny Rollins. Every M the Vanguard Orchestra unleashes its Big Band sound at 9:30 and 11:30pm. Cover M-Sa $15, plus $10 drink minimum. Sets Su-Th 9:30 and 11:30pm, F-Sa 9:30, 11:30pm, and 1am. Doors open at 8:30pm. Reservations recommended. Cash and checks only.

GAY AND LESBIAN CLUBS

▓ **Splash,** 50 W. 17th St. between 5th and 6th Ave., in Chelsea (☎691-0073). Subway: 1 or 9 to 18th St.; F to 23rd St. One of the most popular gay mega-bars. Packed on weekends with muscular boys who love to flirt. Drinks $4-7. Open Su-Th 4pm-4am, F-Sa 4pm-5am. Cover varies, peaking at $7.

▓ **g,** 223 W. 19th St. between 7th and 8th Ave., in Chelsea (☎929-1085). Subway: 1 or 9 to 18th St. Glitzy, popular bar where well-exercised, pumped-up Chelsea boys try to win glances. Try a famous frozen Cosmo. Open daily 4pm-4am. No cover.

▓ **La Nueva Escuelita,** 301 W. 39th St., at 8th Ave., in Chelsea (☎631-0588). Subway: A, C or E to 42nd St. Latin dance club throbs with merengue, salsa, soul, hip-hop, and the best drag shows in NY. F, starting at 10pm, is Her/She Bar, with go-go gals, performances, and special events. (Her/She: ☎631-1093; $8 before midnight, $10 after.) Open Th-Sa 10pm-5am, Su 7pm-5am. Cover Th $5; F $10; Sa $15; Su 7-10pm $5, after 10pm $8.

Body & Soul, at Vinyl, 6 Hubert St., at Hudson St., in Greenwich Village (☎330-9169). Su evening throngs pack this place to wiggle-n-jiggle amid the lights and house music. A NYC must. Doors open at 4pm. $14 for non-members, $10 for members.

The Cock, 188 Avenue A, at 12th St., in Alphabet City (☎946-1871). Subway: 4, 5, 6, N, or R to Union Square/14th St. Busy rock-n-sleaze boy bar with a full offering of nightly diversions. Foxy Sa asks patrons to multiply their "Foxy dollars" through a gamut of ris-qué challenges. Call for the nightly entertainment fare. Open daily 9:30pm-4am.

Aspara, at the Gemini Lounge, 221 2nd Ave. between 13th and 14th St., in the East Village (☎254-5260). A seriously sexy party with gorgeous ladies trying to outdo each other on the wild tip. Come to dance hard, play hard, and strut your stuff. Every other Su 10pm-4am. Cover $8, with flyer $6.

MISCELLANEOUS HIPSTER HANGOUTS

BC No Rio, 156 Rivington St., near Clinton St. (☎254-3697; schedule info ☎539-6089). Subway: B, D, or Q to Essex St. Walk a block north and then 3 blocks east. A non-profit, community-run space featuring lots of hard-core and punk-related genres, as well as occasional poetry readings, art exhibitions, etc. No alcohol served. Cover $2-5. All ages.

Collective Unconscious, 145 Ludlow St., south of Houston St. (☎254-5277). A performance space collectively (and unconsciously) run by 21 local artists who put up their own shows and provide a venue/studio/rehearsal/you-name-it space for the downtown artistic community. Frequent open-mic events. Call for events schedule. No alcohol or other refreshments served, but BYOB is A-OK. Cover $3-9.

Galapagos, 70 N. 6th St., between Kent and Wythe St., in Williamsburg, Brooklyn (☎718-782-5188). Subway: L to Bedford St.; go south along Bedford and then west along N. 6th St. A bit deserted at night. One of the hipper cultural spots in the city. Puts up parties and a weekly film series. The people here *are* the Williamsburg arts scene. Great bar in an interesting futuro-sleek decor. DJ's every Tu-Sa. Events sometimes charge $5. Happy hour M-Sa 6pm-8pm. Open Su-Th 6pm-2am, F-Sa 6pm-4am.

Hell, 59 Gansevoort St., south of Hudson St. between Greenwich and Washington (☎727-1666). Hard-to-find but worth the trip. Open Sa-Th 7pm-4am, F 5pm-4am.

Nuyorican Poets Cafe, 236 E. 3rd St., between Ave. B and Ave. C (☎505-8183). Subway: F to 2nd Ave. Walk 3 blocks north and 3 blocks east. New York's leading joint for "poetry slams" and spoken-word performances. A mixed bag of doggerel and occasional gems. Workshops for your inner poet, DJ-enhanced parties, and occasional risque acts like "Erotic words en Español." Cover $10-12.

Soundlab (☎726-1724). Locations vary. Cultural alchemy in the form of an illbient happening, nomadic style. Call to find where the next Lab goes down; past locales include the base of the Brooklyn Bridge, a Financial District skyscraper, and a Chinatown park.

Sugar Shack, 2611 Frederick Douglass Blvd/8th Ave., at 139th St. (☎491-4422). Sexy lounge and soul food restaurant (entrees $10-12), with phenomenal daiquiris and smoothies ($6-12). M comedy night, W poetry series, Th 70s, F smooth jazz, and Sa R&B, hip-hop, and reggae. Ladies' Night Tu with $3 drinks. Reservations recommended. Open M-Th 5pm-midnight, F-Sa 5pm-3am, Su brunch all you can eat buffet ($14) 11am-5pm. Cover: M $5 ladies, $7 gents; W $5. 2-drink minimum.

LONG ISLAND ☎631

Long Island, a sprawling suburbia to the northeast of Manhattan, serves as a sleepy summertime resort for droves of wealthy Manhattanites reclaiming their sanity. As such, it is both expensive and difficult to navigate without a car. However, **Jones Beach** offers 6½ miles of beach only 40 minutes from the city, and **Fire Island** is an incredibly popular gay summertime getaway.

🛈 **PRACTICAL INFORMATION. Long Island Convention and Visitors Bureau:** ☎631-951-2423. **Long Island Railroad (LIRR)** services the island from Penn Station in Manhattan (☎718-217-5477; 34th St. at 7th Ave.; subway: 1, 2, 3, 9, A, C, or E) and stops in Jamaica, Queens (subway: E, J, or Z) before proceeding to "points east" ($4.75-15.25; lower in off-peak hrs.). To reach **Fire Island,** take the LIRR to Sayville, Bayshore, or Patchogue. The **Sayville ferry** (☎589-8980) serves Cherry Grove, the Pines, and Sailor's Haven (round-trip $9-11, under 12 $5). The **Bay Shore ferry** (☎516-665-

3600) sails to Fair Harbor, Ocean Beach, Ocean Bay Park, Saltaire, and Kismet (round-trip $11.50, under 12 $5.50). The **Patchogue ferry** (☎516-475-1665) shuttles to Davis Park and Watch Hill (round-trip $10, under 12 $5.50). Jam-packed **Jones Beach** is easily accessible by train: take the LIRR to Freeport, where a shuttle bus stops every 30min. and whisks to the ocean. The LIRR runs a package deal in summer ($11 from Manhattan). **Area Code:** 631 and 516; 631 unless noted.

JONES BEACH. When New York State Parks Commissioner Robert "God" Moses discovered Jones Beach in 1921, it was a barren spit of land off the Atlantic shore of Nassau County. Within ten years, he had created one of the finest public beaches in the world from almost nothing. There are nearly 2500 acres of beachfront, and the parking area accommodates 23,000 cars. In summertime, Jones Beach (☎516-785-1600) becomes a sea of umbrellas and blankets with barely a patch of sand showing. Along the 1½ mi. boardwalk, you can find deck games, rollerskating, mini-golf, basketball, and nightly dancing. The **Marine Theater** inside the park often hosts rock concerts. There are eight different public beaches on the rough Atlantic Ocean and the calmer Zachs Bay. The park closes at midnight, except to those with special fishing permits.

FIRE ISLAND. A gay hotspot and extraordinary naturistic site off Long Island's shores, Fire Island is a 32 mi. long barrier island buffering the South Shore from the roaring waters of the Atlantic. Cars are allowed only on the easternmost and westernmost tips of the island; there are no streets, only "walks," and deer roam boldly. A hip countercultural enclave during the 60s and home to the disco scene of the 70s, the island still parties loud.

Two of Fire Island's many resorts, **Cherry Grove** and **The Pines,** host predominantly gay communities. The Atlantic Ocean beaches are spectacular, and the scene rages late into the night. Cherry Grove is the more commercial of the two towns, with cheesy restaurants and souvenir shops lining the area around the ferry slip. The houses are uniformly shingled, small, crowded together, and generally overflowing with men, though lesbian couples come here, too. The Pines, a 10min. walk up the beach, is decidedly more male, upscale, and exclusive feeling. Both towns contain establishments advertising themselves as "guest houses." However, some of these may not be legally accredited and some may not be women-friendly. Be careful where you choose to stay; atmosphere varies. **Cherry Grove Beach Hotel** is a good bet, located on the Main Walk of Cherry Grove and close to the beach. (☎597-6600. Open May-Oct. Double beds, kitchenettes. From $70. Reservations required.) Fire Island's food generally entails unspectacular eats at astounding prices. You can make your own lunch from **Ocean Beach Trader,** one of the grocery stores on the strip. (Open M-Th 7am-8pm, F 7am-10:30pm, Sa 7am-9:30pm.)

Nightlife on Fire Island is everywhere, all the time. Most restaurants are open very late. The Pines' nightlife is active but feels as if you need to be a member of a secret club to get in. Start the night at 5pm at the bar next to the Botel (big hotel) for **Low Tea. High Tea** is at 8pm at the Pavilion, but disappear by 10pm for a "disco nap," because the **Island Club and Bistro** (more commonly known as the Sip and Twirl) starts grinding at 1:30am. From there you can move back to the **Pavilion** or you can make it a real Fire Island night, ending up at the **Meat Rack** (an area of the woods—follow the boardwalks) or on the **Dick Dock** (the Harbor, between FI Blvd. and Ocean Walk). Don't worry, though, the Gay Men's Health Crisis put condoms in the trees. How else are you going to occupy yourself until bedtime (dawn)?

The **Fire Island National Seashore** (☎516-289-4810 for the headquarters in Patchogue) is a daytime hotspot, offering summertime fishing, clamming, and guided nature walks. The facilities at **Sailor's Haven** (just west of the Cherry Grove community) include a marina, a nature trail, and a famous beach. Similar facilities at **Watch Hill** include a campground (☎597-6455; reservations required). The **Sunken Forest,** so called because of its location behind the dunes, is another natural wonder. Directly west of Sailor's Haven, its soil supports an unusual combination of holly, sassafras, and poison ivy laced together in a hulky mesh.

THE CATSKILLS   ☎ 845

The Catskills, home of Rip Van Winkle's century-long repose, remained in a happy
state of somnambulant obscurity for centuries. After the purple haze of Woodstock jolted the region to life in 1969, the Catskills had to undergo an extensive
detox period. Barring the occasional flashback, such as the 1994 and 1999 repeti-
tions of the rock festival, the state-managed Catskill Forest Preserve is today the
region's best attraction, offering travelers pristine miles of hiking and skiing trails,
adorably dinky villages, and crystal-clear fishing streams.

⑦ PRACTICAL INFORMATION. Traveling from I-87, the region is most easily
explored by following Rte. 28 W. **Adirondack/Pine Hill Trailways** provides excellent
service through the Catskills. The main stop is in **Kingston,** 400 Washington Ave., on
the corner of Front St. (☎ 331-0744 or 800-858-8555; ticket office open M-F 5:45am-
11pm, Sa-Su 6:45am-11pm). Buses run to New York City (2hr., 11 per day, $19; Tu-
Th same day round-trip $26). Other stops in the area include Woodstock, Pine Hill,
Saugerties, and Hunter; each connects with New York City, Albany, and Utica. Four
stationary **tourist cabooses** dispense info, including the extremely useful *Ulster
County: Catskills Region Travel Guide.* Located at the traffic circle in Kingston,
on Rte. 28 in Shandaken, on Rte. 209 in Ellenville, and on Rte. 9 W in Milton; open
May-Oct. 9am-5pm; hrs. vary depending on volunteer availability. Rest stop **visitors
centers** along I-87 can advise you on area sights and distribute excellent, free maps
of New York State. **Area code:** 845, unless otherwise noted.

CATSKILL FOREST PRESERVE. The 250,000-acre **Catskill Forest Preserve** contains
many small towns and outdoor adventure opportunities. Ranger stations distribute
free permits for backcountry camping, necessary for stays over three days. Still,
most of the **campgrounds** listed below sit at gorgeous trailheads that mark great day-
long jaunts. Reservations are vital in summer, especially weekends. (☎ 800-456-
2267. Sites $9-16; phone reservation fee $8; $2-3 more for partial hook-up at some
sites. Open May-Sept.) The **Office of Parks** (☎ 518-474-0456) distributes brochures on
the campgrounds. Required permits for **fishing** (non-NY residents $20 for five days)
are available in sporting goods stores and at many campgrounds. **Ski season** runs
from Nov. to mid-Mar., with popular slopes down numerous mountainsides along
Rte. 28 and Rte. 23A. Although hiking trails are maintained, some lean-to's are dilapidated and crowded. For more info, call the **Dept. of Environmental Conservation**
(☎ 256-3000). **Adirondack Trailways** buses from Kingston pass most trailheads.

WOODSTOCK. Signs advertising "Tie-Dyed T-shirts" and "Last incense for 20 mi.
sold here" might suggest to you that Woodstock, between Phoenicia and Kingston,
is *the* place to be for aging hippies. Although the famed 1969 concert was actually
held in nearby Saugerties, Woodstock has been a haven for artists since the turn of
the century. But the tie-dyed legacy has faded, and Woodstock has become expensive and touristy. Still, neo-hippie hipsters operate out of the **Woodstock School of Art**
on Rte. 212, accessible from Rte. 28 via Rte. 375. In addition to housing art classes,
a small gallery pays homage to Woodstock's artistic tradition. (☎ 679-2388. Open M-
Sa 9am-3pm.)

MT. TREMPER. ◙**Kaleidoworld,** on Rte. 28, fiercely competes with nature for the
title of most spectacular attraction in the Catskills. The two largest kaleidoscopes
in the world are displayed here, with the largest (56 ft.) leaving Woodstock-era veterans muttering, "I can see the music!" The adjacent Crystal Palace (included in
admission) features hands-on kaleidoscopes. (☎ 688-5328. Open daily 10am-7pm;
mid-Oct. to July closed Tu. $10, seniors $8, kids under 4 ft. 6 in. $8.) **Kenneth L. Wil-
son,** on Wittenburg Rd. 3¾ mi. from Rte. 212 (make a hard right onto Wittenburg
Rd., then turn right at the next intersection), has wooded **campsites,** showers, and a
quiet, wholesome atmosphere. The beach features a gorgeous panorama of mountains surrounding the looking-glass lake. Canoe rentals, fishing, and hiking round

out the options. (☎679-7020. Sites $12, plus a $2.50 service charge. Registration 8am-9pm. Day use $5, seniors free M-F. Canoes ½-day $10, full-day $15.)

PHOENICIA. Phoenicia is another beautiful spot in the Catskills. The **Esopus Creek,** to the west, has great trout **fishing,** and **The Town Tinker,** 10 Bridge St., rents inner-tubes for river-riding. (☎688-5553. Inner-tubes $7 per day, with seat $10. Driver's license or $50 deposit required. Tube taxi transportation $3. Life jackets $2. Open mid-May to Sept. daily 9am-6pm; last rental 4:30pm.) If tubes don't float your boat, the wheezing, 100-year-old **Catskill Mountain Railroad** can shuttle you for six scenic miles from Bridge St. to Mt. Pleasant. (40min., runs late May to early Sept. Sa-Su, 1 per hr. 11am-5pm. $4, round-trip $6, under 12 $2.) At the 65 ft. high **Sundance Rappel Tower,** off Rte. 214, visitors return to earth the hard way. (☎688-5640. 4 levels of lessons; beginner 3-4hr., $22. Lessons only held when a group of 8 is present. Reservations 1 week in advance required.) For a trip to the peak, head to Woodland Valley campground (below), where a 9¾ mi. hike to the 4204 ft. summit of **Slide Mt.** lends a view of New Jersey, Pennsylvania, and the Hudson Highlands.

The somewhat primitive **Woodland Valley** campground, off High St., 7 mi. southeast of Phoenicia, has flush toilets and showers, and provides access to many hiking trails. (☎688-7647. Sites $12, plus a $2.50 service charge; register between 8am-9pm. Open late May-early Oct.). The **Cobblestone Motel,** surrounded by mountains on Rte. 214, has friendly managers, an outdoor pool, and clean, newly renovated rooms, most with a kitchen and fridge. (☎688-7871. Doubles $49, large doubles $60, with kitchenette $69; 1-bedroom cottages $80, 3-room cottages with kitchen $99.)

PINE HILL. Pine Hill is nestled near **Belleayre Mt.,** which offers hiking trails and ski slopes. (☎254-5600 or 800-942-6904. Ski lift, lesson, and rental package M-F $52, Sa-Su $62; children $42/$52.) **Belleayre Hostel** is a lodging bargain; follow Rte. 28 past Big Indian, making a left on Main St. at the big white "Pine Hill" sign, then another left into the second parking lot. Bunks and private rooms in a rustic setting near Phoenicia. Amenities include a recreational room, kitchen access, **laundry** ($2), a picnic area, and sporting equipment. (☎254-4200. Bunks in summer $10, in winter $15; private rooms $30/$40; cabins for up to 4 $50/$60.)

HUNTER MT. AND HAINES FALLS. From Rte. 28, moving north on Rte. 42 and then east onto Rte. 23A leads through a gorgeous stretch along **Hunter Mt.,** one of the most popular **skiing** areas on the east coast (ski info ☎518-263-4223, accommodations ☎800-775-4641). During festivals held throughout the summer and fall, Hunter Mt. offers **Skyride,** the longest, highest chairlift in the Catskills. ($7, ages 3-12 $3.50, under 6 $1; $1 off with festival admission). Motels and outdoor stores dot the highway. Past Hunter Mt., **North Lake/South Lake campground** in Haines Falls has 219 campsites near two lakes, a waterfall, and hiking. (☎518-589-5058. $16, plus a $2.50 service charge; reserve 2 days in advance. Day use $5. Canoe rental $15.)

ALBANY
☎**518**

Although Albany proclaims itself "the most livable city in America," it suffers from an unhappy reversal of clichés. The city once known as Fort Orange comes up short in comparison with its southern sibling, the Big Apple. Established six years before the Pilgrims landed on the New England shore, it is the oldest continuous European settlement in the original 13 colonies and the capital of New York State.

🖪 PRACTICAL INFORMATION. Amtrak, at the intersection of East St. and Rensselaer, across the Hudson from downtown Albany (☎462-5710; station open daily 3:30am-midnight), has service to: New York City (2½hr., 11 per day, $40-47) and Buffalo (5hr., 4 per day, $46-56). **Greyhound,** 34 Hamilton St. (☎434-8095; station open 24hr.), runs buses to: Utica (1½-2hr., $20-22); Syracuse (3hr., $30-33); Rochester (4½hr., $34-37); and Buffalo (5-6hr., $44-48). *Be careful in this neighborhood at night.* From the same station, **Adirondack Trailways** (☎436-9651) connects to other upstate locales: Catskills (45min., 2 per day, $6); Lake George (1¾hr., 3 per day, $11); Lake Placid (3½hr., 3 per day, $25); and Kingston (4hr., 6 per day, $9). For local travel, the **Capital District Transportation Authority (CDTA),** 110 Watervliet Ave. (☎482-8822), serves Albany ($1), Troy ($1.25), and Schenectady ($1.35). Schedules are available at the Amtrak and Trailways stations. The **Albany Visitors Center,** 25 Quackenbush Sq. at Clinton Ave. and Broadway, runs trolley tours of downtown (☎434-0405; late June to late Sept. F 1pm and Sa 10:30am; $10, seniors $8.50, under 15 $4) and Albany's historic homes (open M-F 9am-4pm, Sa-Su 10am-4pm; trolley tour W 10am). **Post Office:** 45 Hudson Ave. (☎462-1359; open M-F 8am-5:30pm). **ZIP code:** 12207. **Area code:** 518.

▐▝▐ ACCOMMODATIONS AND FOOD. Pine Haven Bed & Breakfast, 531 Western Ave., offers gorgeous rooms with phone, TV, and A/C in an inviting setting. The big Victorian house stands at the convergence of Madison and Western Ave.; parking is in the rear (☎482-1574; single with shared bath $49, double $64; private bath $64/$79; breakfast included; reservations needed). **Thompson's Lake State Park,** on Rte. 157 north of East Berne, 18 mi. southwest of Albany, offers the closest camping, with 140 primitive sites, fishing, hiking, and a swimming beach. Follow Rte. 443 out of Albany and look for the signs for Thompson's Lake (☎872-1674; sites $13).

In "downtown" Albany, the best eating option entails getting "locked away" at the **Big House Brewing Company,** 90 N. Pearl St., at Sheridan St. The Big House serves pizzas, sandwiches, and burgers at prices that don't cry larceny ($6-7), alongside Al Capone Amber ale. (☎445-2739. Open Tu-Sa 4pm-late. Happy hour 4-7pm. Live bands Th-F. Dancing F-Sa.) At the vegetarian **Mother Earth's Cafe,** 217 Western Ave. at Quail St., students and locals kindle pacifist revolutions while munching Jamaican stir-frys ($5) and nature burgers ($4). Free live music nightly at 8pm. (☎434-0944. Open daily 11am-11pm.)

▣ SIGHTS. Albany's sights cluster downtown. The **Rockefeller Empire State Plaza,** between State and Madison St., is a $1.9 billion, towering, modernist Stonehenge. The plaza houses state offices, stores, a bus terminal, a post office, and a food court. *(Free parking M-F after 2pm.)* The huge flying saucer at one end of the Plaza is the **Empire Center for the Performing Arts,** also known as "The Egg," a venue for theater, dance, and concerts. *(☎473-1845. Box office open M-F 10am-5pm, Sa noon-3pm; in summer M-F noon-3pm; tickets $8-25.)* Across the street, the **New York State Museum** has in-depth exhibits on the state's history, people, and animals. *(☎474-5877. Open daily 10am-5pm. Free.)* The magnificent **New York State Capitol,** adjacent to the Plaza, has provided New York politicians with luxury quarters since 1899. *(☎474-2418. Call ahead for daily tour times. Tours begin M-F at 10am, noon, 2, and 3pm, at the senate staircase on the 1st fl. Free.)*

Bounded by State St. and Madison Ave. north of downtown, **Washington Park** has tennis courts, paddle boats, and plenty of room for celebrations and performances. The **Park Playhouse** stages free musical theater from July to mid-Aug. *(☎434-2035. Open Tu-Su 8pm.)* On Th during June and July, folks come **Alive at Five** to free concerts at the **Tricentennial Plaza,** across from Fleet Bank on Broadway. *(☎434-2032.)* For events, call the **Albany Alive Line.** *(☎434-1217, ext. 409.)*

Biking aficionados traverse the **Mohawk-Hudson Bikeway,** which passes along old railroad grades and canal towpaths as it weaves through the capital area. *(☎386-2225. Maps available at the visitors center.)* Rentals can be had at the **Down Tube Cycle Shop,** 466 Madison Ave. *(☎434-1711. Open M-F 11am-7pm, Sa 10am-5pm. Full-day $20.)*

COOPERSTOWN   ☎607

To earlier generations, Cooperstown evoked images of novelist James Fenimore Cooper's frontiersman hero, Leatherstocking, who roamed the woods around Lake Otsego. Tiny Cooperstown now recalls a different source of American legend and myth—baseball. Tourists file through the Baseball Hall of Fame, eat in baseball-themed restaurants, and sleep in baseball-themed motels. Fortunately for the tepid fan, baseball's mecca is surrounded by some non-baseball rural attractions.

⚡ PRACTICAL INFORMATION. Cooperstown is accessible from I-90 and I-88 via Rte. 28. Street parking is rare in Cooperstown; park in the free lots just outside of town on Rte. 28 south of Cooperstown, on Glen Ave. at Maple St.; or near the Fenimore House. From these lots, it's an easy 5-15min. walk to Main St. (Rte. 31). **Trolleys** also leave from the lots, dropping off riders at the Hall of Fame, the Farmer and Fenimore museums, Doubleday Field, the Chamber of Commerce, and downtown. (Trolleys run late June to mid-Sept. daily 8:30am-9pm; early June and late Sept. to Oct. Sa-Su 8:30am-6pm; all-day pass $2, children $1.) **Pine Hall Trailways** (☎800-858-8555) picks up visitors at Clancy's Deli on Rte. 28 and Elm St. for New York City (5½hr., 2 per day, $42) and Kingston (3¼hr., 2 per day, $20). **Cooperstown Area Chamber of Commerce:** 31 Chestnut St., on Rte. 28 near Main St. (☎547-9983; generally open daily 9am-5pm, but hrs. vary; call ahead). **Post Office:** 40 Main St. (☎547-2311; open M-F 8:30am-5pm, Sa 8:30am-noon). **ZIP code:** 13326. **Area code:** 607.

▐▐ ACCOMMODATIONS AND FOOD. Summertime lodging in Cooperstown seems to require a Major Leaguer's salary, and during peak tourist season (late June to mid-Sept.), many accommodation-seekers strike out. Fortunately, there are alternatives. The **Mohican Motel,** 90 Chestnut St., offers large beds, cable TV, and A/C at relatively affordable Cooperstown-area prices. (☎547-5101. Late June to early Sept. 2- to 6-people rooms range from $74-146; rates are about 50% lower in off-season.) **Glimmerglass State Park,** 7 mi. north of Cooperstown on Rte. 31 on the east side of Lake Otsego, has 37 pristine campsites in a gorgeous lakeside park. Daytime visitors can swim, fish, and boat ($6 per vehicle) from 11am-7pm. (☎547-8662, ☎800-456-2267 for reservations and a heinous $8 service charge. Sites $13; $2.50 registration fee; showers, dumping station; no hook-ups. Register daily 11am-9pm.) Closest to the Hall of Fame, **Cooperstown Beaver Valley Campground,** off Rte. 28 10min. south of Cooperstown, has spacious wooded sites, pool, recreation area, and boat rentals. (☎293-8131 or 800-726-7314; sites $28, with hook-up $31).

The **Doubleday Cafe,** 93 Main St., scores twice with a $6-8 Mexican dinner menu and eye-catching memorabilia of the Babe and others on the walls (☎547-5468; open daily 7am-10 or 11pm, depending on crowd; bar closes after kitchen). For elegant but affordable dining, the **Hoffman Lane Bistro,** on Hoffman Ln., off Main St. across from the Hall of Fame has light, airy rooms with checkered black-and-white tablecloths (☎547-7055; open M-Sa 11:30am-3:30pm and 5-9:30pm, with late-night menu served until midnight; clams over linguine $6). A Cooperstown institution, **Schneider's Bakery,** 157 Main St., has been feeding the locals delicious 45¢ "old-fashioneds" (doughnuts less sweet and greasy than their commercial cousins) since 1887 (☎547-9631; open M-Sa 6:30am-5:30pm, Su 7am-1pm in summer).

⬛ DIAMOND FIELDS OF DREAMS. The **▨National Baseball Hall of Fame and Museum** on Main St. is an enormous, glowing monument to America's national pastime. In addition to memorabilia from the immortals—everything from the bat with which Babe Ruth hit his famous "called shot" homerun in the 1932 World Series to the infamous jersey worn by 65 lb. White Sox midget Eddie Gaedel—the museum features a multimedia tribute to the sport, a candid display on African-American ballplayers' experiences in the Negro Leagues, art and movies about baseball, and history tracing the myth-making game to ancient Egyptian rituals. One exhibit reads, "In the beginning, shortly after God created Heaven and Earth, there were stones to throw and sticks to swing." You'll have to fight the crowds to get in: the daily turnstile count at the museum in the summer exceeds the town population. (☎547-7200. Open daily 9am-9pm; Oct.-Apr. 9am-5pm. $9.50, seniors $8, ages 7-12 $4.)

The free **annual ceremonies** for new inductees takes place on either the last weekend of July or the first weekend of Aug., on the field adjacent to the **Clark Sports Center** on Susquehanna Ave., a 10min. walk from the Hall. During the festivities, fans scramble for contact with the many Hall of Famers who sign autographs (at steep prices) along Main St. The annual **Hall of Fame Game** between two rotating major league teams concludes the festival on M at 2pm in the delightfully intimate

Doubleday Field. Plan accordingly—over 40,000 visitors are expected. Rooms must be reserved months in advance.

Nearby, the **Fenimore Art Museum,** Lake Rd./Rte. 80, features American folk art, Hudson River School paintings, James Fenimore Cooper memorabilia, and an impressive collection of Native American art. *(☎547-1400 or 888-547-1450. Open daily 10am-5pm; Oct.-Dec. and Apr.-May Tu-Su 10am-4pm. $9, ages 7-12 $4.)* Across the street, the **Farmer's Museum** offers exhibits on 19th-century rural life, with an operating farmstead and a recreated village. *(☎547-1450 or 547-1500. Open Apr.-May Tu-Su 10am-4pm, June-Sept. daily 10am-5pm, Oct.-Nov. 10am-4pm. $9, ages 7-12 $4. Combination tickets with Hall of Fame and Fenimore Art Museum $22/$9.50.)*

The **Glimmerglass Opera Company** is a world-renowned but tiny outfit. Shows are held at the historic Alice Busch Opera Theater; call for times and shows. *(18 Chestnut St. ☎547-2255. Opera Festival yearly July-Aug. Tickets M-Tu and Th $22-80, F-Su $45-90.)*

ITHACA AND THE FINGER LAKES   ☎607

According to Iroquois legend, the Great Spirit laid his hand upon the earth, and the impression of his fingers made the Finger Lakes: Canandaigua, Cayuga, Seneca, and others. Whether it was the Great Spirit or mere Ice Age glaciers, the results are spectacular. Vladimir Nabokov, Kurt Vonnegut, and Thomas Pynchon all brooded on the cliff at Cornell University. Trekkers stand beneath waterfalls in Ithaca's ruggedly carved gorges or sip another divine liquid that flows here—the rich wine of the Finger Lakes area's acclaimed vineyards.

◪ PRACTICAL INFORMATION. Ithaca Bus Terminal (☎272-7930; open M-Sa 7am-6pm, Su noon-5pm), 1710 W. State St. at Rte. 13 houses **Short Line** (☎277-8800) and **Greyhound** (☎272-7930), with service to New York City (5hr., 12 per day, $35); Philadelphia (7hr., 2per day, $53); and Buffalo (4hr., 5 per day, $25). **Tompkins Consolidated Area Transit (T-CAT)** (☎277-7433) is your only choice for getting out to Cayuga Lake without a car. Buses stop at Ithaca Commons, westbound on Seneca St. and eastbound on Green. (Fare 75¢-$1.50, less for seniors and students. Buses run daily.) The **Ithaca/Tompkins County Convention and Visitors Bureau,** 904 E. Shore Dr., Ithaca 14850, has the best map of the area ($3.50), hotel and B&B listings, and brochures. (☎272-1313 or 800-284-8422. Open late May to early Sept. M-F 8am-6pm, Sa 10am-5pm, Su 10am-4pm; mid-Sept. to Oct. M-F 8am-5pm; Nov. to late May M-F 8am-5pm.) **Post Office:** 213 N. Tioga St., at E. Buffalo (☎272-5455; open M-F 8:30am-5pm, Sa 8:30am-1pm). **ZIP code:** 14850. **Area code:** 607.

↥ ACCOMMODATIONS. As befits the town where Vladimir Nabokov penned *Lolita*, Ithaca is filled with typically cheap roadside motels, no questions asked. In summer, however, rooms are scarce and rates rise from about $40 to $100 per night. **Elmshade Guest House,** 402 S. Albany St., at Center St. three blocks from the Ithaca Commons, offers large, impeccably clean, well-decorated rooms with shared bath, cable TV, and a generous continental breakfast. This B&B is by far the best budget option in Ithaca. From the bus station, walk up State St. and turn right onto Albany St. (☎273-1707. Singles $40; doubles $55. Reservations recommended.) **The Economy Inn,** 658 Elmira Rd./Rte. 13, has just the basics, but is close to Buttermilk Falls and 2 mi. from downtown Ithaca. Rooms have A/C, cable TV, refrigerator, and free local calls. (☎277-0370. Singles from $30, Sa-Su $48; doubles $38/$65.) **The Wonderland Motel,** 654 Elmira Rd., has a pool, A/C, and free continental breakfast and local calls. (☎272-5252. Singles from $45; doubles from $55; Nov.-Mar. $35/$45. Rates significantly higher on weekends.) Three of the nearby state parks with camping are **Robert H. Treman** (☎273-3440), on Rte. 327 off Rte. 13; **Buttermilk Falls** (☎273-5761), Rte. 13 south of Ithaca; and **Taughannock Falls** (☎387-6739), north on Rte. 89. (Sites $15; $2 walk-on fee or $7.50 reservation fee by calling ☎800-456-2267. Cabins $122-239 per week plus $11 reservation fee.) The *Finger Lakes State Parks* has info on all area state parks and is available at any tourist office or park.

🍴 **FOOD.** Restaurants in Ithaca cluster in **Ithaca Commons** and **Collegetown.** For a night on the town, the free *Ithaca Times*, available at most stores and restaurants, has complete listings of entertainment options. The ⬛**Moosewood Restaurant,** 215 N. Cayuga, at Seneca St. in the Dewitt Mall, features an amazing selection of wonderfully fresh and creative vegetarian options. (☎273-9610. Open M-Th 11:30am-2pm and 5:30-9pm, F-Sa 11:30am-2pm, and Su 5:30-9pm; cafe M-Sa 2-4pm. Lunch $5.50; dinner $10-13. No reservations.) **Just a Taste,** 116 N. Aurora, near Ithaca Commons, has an extensive selection of fine wines ($2-5 glass), 25 beers, and tempting *tapas*. (☎277-9463. Open Su-Th 11am-3:30pm and 5:30-10pm, F-Sa 11am-3:30pm and 5:30-11pm.) **Joe's Restaurant,** 602 W. Buffalo St., at Rte. 13 (Meadow St.), serves Italian and American entrees ($8-20) with Joe's beloved bottomless salad. (☎273-2693. Open Su-Th 4-10pm, F-Sa 4-11pm.) **Rongovian Embassy to the USA ("The Rongo"),** Rte. 96 on the main strip in Trumansburg about 10 mi. from Ithaca, is worth the drive. Seek asylum in amazing Mexican entrees at this classic restaurant/bar, and plot a trip to "Nearvarna" on the huge wall map. (☎387-3334. Restaurant open Tu-Su 5-10pm; bar Tu-Su 4pm-1am. Bands W-Sa; cover $5. Enchiladas $12; beer $2.)

🎭 **NIGHTLIFE.** The area near Cornell called **Collegetown,** centering on College Ave., harbors student hangouts and access to a romantic path along the gorge. A smoky, red-walled cafe, **Stella's,** 403 College Ave., wears its pretension well. The dazzling $2.35 Italian soda with heavy cream and a few martinis might encourage you to strut your stuff at Stella's adjoining blue-walled jazz bar. (☎277-8731. Restaurant open daily 7am-1:30am; in summer M-F 8am-1am, Sa-Su 10am-1am. Jazz bar open daily 11am-1am.) Downtown, live bands and hip-hop acts perform at **The Haunt,** 114 W. Green St. (☎275-3447; small cover charge; 18+). High-minded moviegoers head to the **Cornell Cinema,** 104 Willard Straight Hall on the Cornell campus, a classic art-house theater with thrilling programming and prices. (☎255-3522. Tickets $4.50; students, seniors, and under 12 $4.)

📷 **SIGHTS. Cornell University,** youngest of the Ivy League schools, sits on a *steep* hill in Ithaca between two tremendous gorges. The **Suspension Bridge** above Fall Creek provides a heart-pounding walk above one gorge, while the **Central Avenue Stone Arch Bridge** above Cascadilla Creek has a brilliant sunset view. The **Information and Referral Center** in the Day Hall Lobby has info on campus sights and activities. (☎ 254-4636. Open M-F 8am-5pm; telephone staffed Sa 8am-5pm and Su noon-1pm. Tours Apr.-Nov. M-F 9, 11am, 1, and 3pm, Sa 9am and 1pm, Su 1pm; Dec.-Mar. daily 1pm.) The strangely pleasing cement edifice rising from the top of the hill—designed by I.M. Pei—houses Cornell's **Herbert F. Johnson Museum of Art,** at the corner of University and Central. The small collection of European and American painting and sculpture includes works by Giacometti, Matisse, O'Keeffe, de Kooning, and Hopper; the rooftop sculpture garden has an amazing view. (☎ 255-6464. Open Tu-Su 10am-5pm. Free.) At **Cornell Plantations,** a series of botanical gardens surround Cornell's great geological wonders. (☎255-3020. Open daily sunrise to sunset. Free.) Adventurous hikes into the Cornell gorge include the 1½ mi. **Founder's Loop,** which is well worth the time. The free *Passport to the Trails of Tompkins County*, available from the Visitor's Bureau, is a comprehensive trekking guide.

The fertile soil of the Finger Lakes area has made it the heart of New York's wine industry. Three designated **wine trails** provide opportunities for wine tasting and vineyard touring; locals say that the fall harvest is the best time to visit. The ten vineyards closest to Ithaca lie on the **Cayuga Trail,** with most located along Rte. 89 between Seneca Falls and Ithaca; call ☎800-684-5217 for info. The Finger Lakes Association (see **Practical Information,** above) has info on the **Seneca Lake Trail,** 21 wineries on the east side (Rte. 414) and west side (Rte. 14) of the lake, and the **Keuka Trail,** seven wineries along Rte. 54 and Rte. 76. Some wineries offer free picnic facilities and tours. All give free tastings; some require purchase of a glass ($2).

BUFFALO   ☎716

Girded by steel and concrete highways, Buffalo is a big, furry, overgrown town in a high-rise disguise. Fiery chicken wings and electric blues bands burn off the pain of the Bills' four recent Super Bowl defeats and the eternal minor league status of Bison baseball. From the downtown skyline to the small-scale pastel charm of historic Allentown, Buffalo trades the cosmopolitan for honest, modern Americana.

⚐ PRACTICAL INFORMATION. Greyhound (☎855-7533; station open 24hr.) buses from 181 Ellicott St. at N. Division St. To: New York (8½hr., 12 per day, $68); Boston (11½hr., 5 per day, $65); Niagara Falls, ON (1hr., 11 per day, $4); and Toronto (2½hr., 12 per day, $20). **Amtrak** (☎856-2075; office open M-F 7am-3:30pm) leaves from 75 Exchange St. at Washington St. for New York (8hr., 3 per day, $59) and Toronto (4hr., 1 per day, $16). The **Niagara Frontier Transit Authority (NFTA)** (☎855-7211 or 283-9319) offers bus and rail service throughout the city (fare $1.25), as well as free rides on the Main St. Metrorail and service to Niagara Falls (bus #40 "Grand Island" leaves from 181 Ellicott St., 13 per day, fare $1.85, seniors and ages 5-11 85¢). **Visitors center:** 617 Main St., in the Theater District. (☎852-2356 or 800-283-3256. Open M-F 9am-5pm, Sa-Su 10am-4pm. Tour $5.) **Post Office:** 701 Washington St. (☎856-4604; open M-F 8:30am-5:30pm, Sa 8:30am-1pm). **ZIP code:** 14203. **Area code:** 716.

⚑ ACCOMMODATIONS. The **Buffalo Hostel (HI-AYH),** 667 Main St., houses 48 beds and spotless floors in a safe neighborhood downtown. Friendly staff lead frequent group outings and make travelers feel at home. (☎852-5222. Reception daily 8-11am and 3pm-2am. Free linen, access to microwave, pool table, laundry facilities. Dorms $19, non-members $22.) Otherwise, budget lodgings are a rarity in Buffalo; **chain motels** cluster around the airport and I-90 8 to 10 mi. northeast of downtown. See **Niagara Falls** (p. 243) for campsites in the area.

◖▧ FOOD AND NIGHTLIFE. Frank and Teressa's Anchor Bar, 1047 Main St., serves up the original Buffalo Wing, invented here in 1964. (☎886-8920. 10 wings $6, 20 wings $9. Open Su noon-11pm, M-Th 11am-11pm, F-Sa 11am-1am.) Among the cute, boxy buildings of Allentown, the gothic facade of **Gabriel's Gate,** 145 Allen St., doesn't frighten its lunch crowd, who feast on taco salads ($5.25) or garden souvlaki ($5.25) under stuffed mooseheads or on the shaded patio. (☎886-0602. Open Su-Th 11:30am-1am, F-Sa 11:30am-2am.)

The city's surprisingly lively nightlife centers around **Chippewa St.** and **Franklin St.,** and on **Elmwood Ave.** The *Buffalo Beat* has event listings. **The Calumet Arts Cafe,** 56 W. Chippewa St., plays live jazz and blues on the weekends (☎855-2220; open Tu-W 5:30-10pm, Th-Sa 5:30pm-4am). **City SPoT,** on the corner of Delaware and Chippewa St., is the hip place to go for a wide array of cheap coffee and tea concoctions (☎854-7768; open 24hr.).

▨▧ SIGHTS AND ENTERTAINMENT. The **Albright Knox Art Gallery,** 1285 Elmwood Ave., houses over 6000 modern pieces, including a wonderful collection of Abstract Expressionist works. (☎882-8700. Bus #32 "Niagara." Open Su noon-5pm, Tu-Sa 11am-5pm. $4, seniors and students $3, families $8; free Sa 11am-1pm.) At the **Naval and Military Park,** on Lake Erie at the foot of Pearl and Main St., visitors can climb aboard a guided missile cruiser, a destroyer, and a WWII submarine. (☎847-1773. Open Apr.-Oct. daily 10am-5pm; Nov. Sa-Su 10am-4pm. $6, seniors and ages 6-16 $3.50.) An 1881 floating marine bicycle swims among the 300-piece collection at the **Pedaling History Bicycle Museum,** 3943 N. Buffalo Rd., Rte. 240/277 in Orchard Park, 12 mi. southeast of Buffalo. (☎662-3853. Open M-Sa 11am-5pm, Su 1:30-5pm; mid-Jan. to early Apr. M and F-Sa 11am-5pm, Su 1:30-5pm. $4.50, seniors $4, ages 7-15 $2.50, families $12.50.)

In winter, **Rich Stadium** (☎649-0015), in Orchard Park, hosts the four-time Super Bowl loser **Buffalo Bills.** The **HSBC Arena,** 1 Seymour H. Knox III Plaza (☎855-4000), is where hockey's **Buffalo Sabres,** who lost in the Stanley Cup Finals in 1999, slap the puck. The summer brings family fun with **Buffalo Bison** baseball (☎846-2000) at **Dunn Tire Park,** on Swan St. From I-90, take the Elm St. exit.

NIAGARA FALLS   ☎716

One of the seven natural wonders of the world, Niagara Falls also claims the title of one of the world's largest sources of hydro-electric power and daredevil risk-takers. Since 1901, when a 63-year-old schoolteacher, Annie Taylor, was the first to survive the beer-barrel plunge, the Falls have attracted many thrill-seekers. Modern day Taylors beware—heavy fines and possible death await the daring. For those of a sounder mind, outlet shopping, cheap motels, neon lights, and wacky funhouses cram the streets.

▐▘ GETTING THERE AND GETTING AROUND

Trains: Amtrak (☎285-4224), at 27th and Lockport St. 1 block east of Hyde Park Blvd. Take bus #52 to Falls/Downtown. To: New York City ($59) and Toronto ($16). Open Th-M 7am-11pm, Tu-W 7am-3pm.

Buses: Niagara Falls Bus Terminal (☎282-1331), 4th and Niagara St., sells **Greyhound** tickets for use in Buffalo. Open M-F 8am-4pm. To get a bus in Buffalo, take a 1hr. trip on bus #40 from the Niagara Falls bus terminal to the **Buffalo Transportation Center,** 181 Ellicott St. (see Buffalo **Practical Information,** p. 242).

Public Transit: Niagara Frontier Metro Transit System, 343 4th St. (☎285-9319), provides local city transit. Fare $1.25. **ITA Buffalo Shuttle** (☎800-551-9369) has service from Niagara Falls info center and major hotels to Buffalo Airport ($18).

Taxis: Blue United Cab, ☎285-9331. **Niagara Falls Taxi** in Canada, ☎905-357-4000.

✴▐ ORIENTATION AND PRACTICAL INFORMATION

Niagara Falls spans the US-Canadian border; addresses given here are in NY, unless noted. Take **U.S. 190** to the Robert Moses Pkwy., or else skirt the tolls (but suffer traffic) by taking Exit 3 to Rte. 62. In town, Niagara St. is the main east-west artery, ending in the west at **Rainbow Bridge,** which crosses to Canada (pedestrian crossings 25¢, cars $2.50). Numbered north-south streets increase toward the east. Outside of town, stores, restaurants, and motels line **Rte. 62 (Niagara Falls Blvd.).** Customs procedures, though relatively relaxed, are inevitable when crossing between the US and Canada. Many places in the Niagara area accept both American and Canadian currency.

Visitor Info: Orin Lehman Visitors Center (☎278-1796), in front of the Falls' observation deck; the entrance is marked by a garden. Open daily May-Sept. 8am-10:15pm; Oct. to mid-Nov. 8am-8pm; mid-Nov. to Dec. 8am-10pm; Jan.-Apr. 8am-6:15pm. An **info center** (☎284-2000) adjoins the bus station on 4th and Niagara St., a 10min. walk from the Falls. Open daily 8:30am-7:30pm; mid-Sept. to mid-May 9am-5pm. **Niagara Falls Canada Visitor and Convention Bureau,** 5515 Stanley Ave., ON L2G 3X4 (☎905-356-6061), has info on the Canadian side. Open daily 8am-8pm; off-season 8am-6pm. On the Canadian side, tune in to 91.9FM CFL2 for tourist info on the air.

Post Office: 615 Main St. (☎285-7561). Open M-F 7:30am-5pm, Sa 8:30am-2pm. **ZIP code:** 14302. **Area code:** 716 (NY), 905 (ON). In text, 716 unless otherwise noted.

▐▘ ACCOMMODATIONS

Many newlyweds spend part of their honeymoon by the awesome beauty of the falls, which are especially romantic at night. Cheap motels (from $25) advertising free wedding certificates line **Lundy's Lane** on the Canadian side and **Rte. 62** on the American side, while many moderately priced B&Bs overlook the gorge on **River Rd.** between the Rainbow Bridge and the Whirpool Bridge on the Canadian side. Reservations are always recommended.

Niagara Falls International Hostel (HI-C), 4549 Cataract Ave. (☎905-357-0770 or 888-749-0058), Niagara Falls, ON, just off Bridge St. An excellent hostel in a former brothel near the falls, about 2 blocks from the bus station and VIA Rail. 88 beds; can be cramped when full, but the staff is friendly, funky, and casual. Family rooms, laundry facilities, Internet access, pub crawls, nature hikes, barbecues, and parking. Check-out 10am. Reception 24hr. CDN$17.50, non-members CDN$22. Linen CDN$1.

Niagara Falls International Hostel (HI-AYH), 1101 Ferry Ave. (☎282-3700). From bus station, walk east on Niagara St., turn left onto Memorial Pkwy.; the hostel is at the corner of Ferry Ave. *From the falls, avoid walking alone on Ferry Ave. at night.* 46 beds in a friendly old house. Kitchen, TV lounge, limited parking. Family rooms available. Open Feb. to mid-Dec. Check-in 7:30-9:30am and 4-11pm. Lockout 9:30am-4pm. Curfew 11:30pm; lights out midnight. Dorms $14, non-members $17. Linen $1.50.

Olde Niagara House, 610 4th St. (☎285-9408). A country B&B just 4 blocks from the falls. Free pick-up at the Amtrak or bus station. Dorms $18-20 per person. Rooms with breakfast $45-55; in winter $35-45; student singles $25-45/$25-35.

All Tucked Inn, 574 3rd St. (☎282-0919 or 800-797-0919). Clean, nicely colored rooms with shared baths close to the attractions. Common TV room. Singles from $39; doubles from $59. Off-season $27/49. Continental breakfast included; discounts for *Let's Go* toters.

YMCA, 1317 Portage Rd. (☎285-8491), a 20min. walk from the Falls; at night take bus #54 from Main St. 58 beds. Fee includes full use of YMCA facilities; no laundry. Check-in 24hr. Dorm rooms for men only; singles $25, $96 weekly. Key deposit $10. Men and women can sleep on mats in the gym for $15.

Niagara Glen-View Tent & Trailer Park, 3950 Victoria Ave. (☎800-263-2570), Niagara Falls, ON. Close-by to the Falls, but bare and unwooded. Hiking trail across the street. Ice, showers, laundry facilities, pool. Shuttle from driveway to the foot of Clifton Hill in summer every 30min. 8:45am-2am. Sites CDN$35, with hook-up CDN$42 from June-Sept.; $28/$35 May and Oct. Office open daily 8am-11pm. Park open May to mid-Oct.

◉ FOOD

Corsaro's Sunrise Diner, 829 Main St. is a classic red-boothed hangout. (☎284-0959. Open M-Sa 7am-11pm, Su 7am-8pm. Two eggs and toast $1.50, sandwiches $2-4.) **Sardar Sahib,** 626 Niagara St., serves authentic and filling Indian food, emphasizing vegetarian specialities. (☎282-0444. Open daily 11:30am-midnight. Entrees $10 or less.) On the Canadian side, the restaurants on **Victoria Ave.** by Clifton Hill are touristy but inexpensive. **Simon's Restaurant,** 4116 Bridge St., ON, serves big breakfasts with giant homemade muffins (CDN69¢) and hearty diner dinners. (☎905-356-5310. Open M-Sa 5:30am-8:30pm, Su 5:30am-2pm.) **The Peninsula Bakery and Restaurant,** 4568 Erie Ave., ON, off Bridge St., has authentic Pan-Asian food. (☎905-374-8176. Open M 10am-7pm, W-Su 10am-10:30pm. Malaysian stir-fried noodles CDN$7.)

◉ SIGHTS

Although tourist snares abound on both sides, they're less rampant on the American shore. Official sights give more bang for your buck. From late Nov. to mid-Jan., Niagara Falls holds the **Festival of Lights** (☎905-374-1616), combining snow, ice, and spray from the Falls with concerts, fireworks, and night parades for a wondrous wintertime spectacle.

AMERICAN SIDE. The **Maid of the Mist Tour** is an exhilarating, drenching 30min. boat ride to the foot of both falls that has been thrilling tourists for over 150 years. (☎284-4233. *Tours in summer every 15min. M-Th 9:15am-5pm, F-Su 9:15am-6pm. $8.50 plus 50¢ elevator fee, ages 6-12 $4.80.)* The **Caves of the Wind Tour** lends out yellow raincoats for an exciting body-soaking trek to the base of the Bridal Veil Falls, including an optional walk to Hurricane Deck, where gale-force waves slam down on you from above. (☎278-1730. *Open May to mid-Oct.; hrs. vary depending on season and weather conditions. Trips leave every 15min. $6, ages 6-12 $5.50.)* For the less adventurous, **Niagara Wonders,** a 20min. movie on the Falls, plays in the info center. (☎278-1783. *Shows daily on the hr. 10am-8pm; in fall M-Su 10am-6pm. $2, ages 6-12 $1.)*

The **Master Pass,** available at the park's visitors center, covers admission to the theater, Maid of the Mist, **Schoellkopf's Geological Museum** in Prospect Park (home of the "greatest rock and flow story ever told"), a modest **Aquarium,** and the **Viewmobile,** a tram-guided tour of the park. (*Master Pass $21, ages 6-12 $16. Museum:* ☎278-1780. *Open daily Apr.-Oct. 9am-7pm; Nov.-Mar. 10am-5pm; $1. Dramatic film every 30min.*

Aquarium: 701 Whirlpool St. ☎285-3575. Open daily late May to early Sept. 9am-7pm; early Sept. to late May 9am-5pm. $6.75, ages 4-12 $4.75. Viewmobile: ☎278-1730. Runs daily every 15min. 8:30am-10:30pm; in winter 10am-5:30pm. $4.50, children $3.50.)

Continuing north, the **Niagara Power Project** features interactive demonstrations, videos, and displays on energy, hydropower, and local history. While there, you can cast off the fishing platform to reel in salmon, trout, or bass. *(5777 Lewiston Rd. ☎286-6661. Open daily 9am-5pm. Free.)* Further north in Lewiston, NY, the 200-acre state **Artpark,** at the foot of 4th St., focuses on visual and performing arts, with a variety of demonstrations. The theater presents opera, pops concerts, and jazz festivals. *(☎800-659-7275. Shows May-Dec.; call for schedule. Box office open M-Sa 10am-6pm, Su noon-4pm. Tickets $15-33.)* **Old Fort Niagara,** a French castle built in 1726, guards the entrance to the Niagara River and is now a prime picnic spot. A series of special reenactments throughout the summer brings the fort, once held by three different nations, back to 18th-century life. *(☎745-7611. Follow Robert Moses Pkwy. north from Niagara Falls. Open daily June 9am-6:30pm; July-Aug. 9am-7:30pm; hrs. vary off season. $6.75, seniors $5.50, ages 6-12 $4.50. Day use $5 per car.)*

CANADIAN SIDE. On the Canadian side of Niagara Falls (across Rainbow Bridge), **Queen Victoria Park** provides the best view of Horseshoe Falls. The falls are illuminated for 3hr. every night, starting 1hr. after sunset. Parking in Queen Victoria is expensive (CDN$9.75). **Park 'N' Ride** is a better deal, offering parking at Rapids View, across from Marineland at the south end of Niagara Pkwy. **People Movers** buses efficiently and comfortably take you through the 30km area on the Canadian side of the Falls, stopping at attractions along the way. *(☎357-9340. Mid-June to early Sept. daily 9am-11pm; hrs. vary off season. CDN$5, children CDN$2.50.)* Bikers, in-line skaters, and walkers enjoy the 32km **Niagara River Recreation Trail,** which runs from Fort Erie to Fort George and passes many interesting historical sights.

High above the crowds and excitement, **Skylon Tower** has the highest view of the falls at 775 ft.; on a clear day, you can see as far as Toronto. Its 520 ft. **Observation Deck** offers a calming, unhindered view of the falls. *(5200 Robinson St. ☎356-2651. Open daily 8am-11:30pm; in winter hrs. change monthly. CDN$8.50, seniors CDN$7.50, children CDN$4.50.)* The **Explorer's Passport** includes passage to **Journey Behind the Falls,** a tour behind Horseshoe Falls; **Great Gorge Adventure,** a long boardwalk next to the famous Niagara River Rapids, home to many lucky and not-so-lucky daredevils over the years; and the **Spanish Aero Car,** an aerial cable ride over the whirlpool waters. *(Passport: CDN$20, children CDN$10. Journey: ☎354-1551. CDN$6.50, children CDN$3.25. Adventure: ☎374-1221. Open daily mid-June to early Sept. 9am-9pm; hours fluctuate off-season. CDN$5, children CDN$2.50. Aero Car: ☎354-5711. Open year-round but hrs. vary; in winter, operation often closed due to inclement weather. CDN$5.50, children CDN$2.75.)*

Commercialism can be as much of a wonder as any natural one. The Canadian side of the falls offers the delightfully tasteless **Clifton Hill,** a collection of wax museums, funhouses, and overpriced shows. **Ripley's Believe It or Not Museum** displays wonders like wax models of unicorn men and a scary selection of medieval torture devices. Unfortunately, the authentic New Guinea Penis Guard, used for protection from hungry mosquitoes, is not for sale. *(4960 Clifton Hill. ☎356-2238. Open during summer daily 9am-2am; hrs. change off season. CDN$7.50, seniors CDN$5, ages 6-12 CDN$4.)*

NORTHERN NEW YORK

THE ADIRONDACKS   ☎518

In 1892, the New York State legislature demonstrated uncommon foresight, establishing the **Adirondacks State Park,** the largest US park outside Alaska and one of the few places left in the Northeast where hikers can spend days without seeing another soul. Unfortunately, increased pollution and development in recent years has damaged fish and tree populations, alerting locals and naturalists to the fragility of a seemingly immortal ecosystem. Despite this human intrusion, much of the area retains the splendor that has awed visitors for over a century.

MID-ATLANTIC

⚎ ORIENTATION. Of the six million acres in the Adirondacks Park, 40% are open to the public, offering a slew of outdoor activities. The 2000 mi. of winding trails that traverse the forest provide spectacular mountain scenery for hikers, snowshoers, and cross-country skiers; the rivers and streams that transect the mountain offer canoers and white water rafters the same, as well as the adventure of seasonal rapids. The hard-core might consider conquering Mt. Marcy, the state's highest peak (5344 ft.), or taking advantage of a dozen well known alpine centers. For those who prefer spectator sports, the town of Lake Placid, venue of the 1932 and 1980 winter Olympic Games, frequently welcomes national and international competitions. **Tupper Lake** and **Lake George** have carnivals every Jan. and Feb.; Tupper also hosts the **Tin Man Triathlon** in mid-July. In Sept., the hot air balloons of the **Adirondack Balloon Festival** paint the sky over Glens Falls.

⚎ PRACTICAL INFORMATION. The **Adirondack Mountain Club (ADK)** is the best source of info on outdoor activities in the region. Its offices are located at 814 Goggins Rd., Lake George 12845 (☎668-4447; open M-Sa 8:30am-5pm; Jan.-Apr. M-F 8:30am-4:30pm), and at Adirondack Loj Rd., P.O. Box 867, Lake Placid 12946 (☎523-3441; open Sa-Th 8am-8pm, F 8am-10pm), adjoining the Adirondack Loj. Call the Lake Placid number for the scoop on outdoor skills classes such as canoeing, rock climbing, whitewater kayaking, and wilderness medicine. For the latest backcountry info, visit ADK's **High Peaks Information Center,** 3 mi. east of Lake Placid on Rte. 73, then 5 mi. down Adirondack Loj Rd. The center also has washrooms and sells basic outdoor equipment, trail snacks, and a variety of extremely helpful guides to the mountains for $11-25 (open M-Th 8am-5pm, F 8am-10pm, Sa-Su 8am-8pm). Rock climbers should consult the experienced staff at the **Mountaineer** in Keene Valley, between I-87 and Lake Placid on Rte. 73. Snowshoes rent for $16 per day; ice-climbing boots and crampons $20 per day; rock shoes $12 per day. (☎576-2281. Open Su-Th 9am-5:30pm, F 9am-7pm, Sa 8am-7pm; off-season M-F 9am-5:30pm, Sa 8am-5:30pm, Su 10am-5:30pm.) The ADK and the Mountaineer can provide basic info on the conditions and concerns of backwoods travel.

Adirondacks Trailways (☎800-858-8555) services the region. From Albany, buses set out for Lake Placid, Tupper Lake, and Lake George. From the Lake George bus stop at Lake George Hardware, 35 Montcalm St., buses go to Lake Placid (2 per day, $14.40); Albany (4 per day, $11); and New York City (5 per day, $42). **Area code:** 518.

⚎ ACCOMMODATIONS. Two lodges near Lake Placid are also run by the ADK. The **Adirondack Loj** lures hikers off the trails with its cozy atmosphere. Situated on Heart Lake, the log cabin has 30 bunks and a den decorated with deer and moose trophies and warmed by an imposing fieldstone fireplace. In summer, guests swim, fish, and canoe on the premises (canoe or boat rental $5 per hr., guests $3); in winter, they explore the wilderness trails by renting snowshoes for $10 per day or cross-country skis for $20. (☎523-3441. Bunks $32; private room $52. Breakfast included, lunch $4.50, dinner $11.50. Lean-tos, campsites, and cabins also available; reservations highly recommended.) For a more rustic experience, hike 3½ mi. from the closest trailhead to the **John's Brook Lodge** in Keene Valley (call the Adirondack Loj for reservations); from Lake Placid, follow Rte. 73 15 mi. through Keene to Keene Valley and turn right at the Ausable Inn. The hike runs slightly uphill, but the meal that awaits you will reward the effort. A great place to meet friendly New Yorkers, John's Brook is no secret; beds fill completely on weekends. Make reservations one day in advance for dinner, earlier for a weekend. Bring sheets or a sleeping bag. (Rates start at $28 for a bunk July to early Sept.; dinner $11.50.)

Free camping is easy to come by. Inquire about the location of free trailside shelters before you plan a hike in the forest, or camp for free anywhere on public land in the **backcountry** as long as you are at least 150 ft. away from a trail, road, water source, or campground and below 4000 ft. in altitude. The State Office of Parks and Recreation (see New York **Practical Information,** p. 196) has more details.

LAKE PLACID ☎ 518

Melville Dewey, inventor of the Dewey Decimal Library Cataloging system, was the first person to promote Lake Placid as a summer resort, in 1850. Now the village is a winter sports mecca. Host to the Olympic Winter Games in both 1932 and 1980, this modest town has seen thousands of pilgrims and, aside from the manifold motels, has remained charmingly untainted by its popularity. World-class athletes train year-round in the town's extensive facilities, lending an international flavor which distinguishes Lake Placid from its Adirondack neighbors. The setting of the Adirondack High Peaks Region attracts droves of hikers and backpackers each year, although many would-be campers end up pitching their tents in a motel room—in the winter, temperatures can dip down to -40° F.

⚑ PRACTICAL INFORMATION. Lake Placid sits at the intersection of Rte. 86 and Rte. 73. The town's Olympic past defines the Lake Placid of today; the **Olympic Regional Development Authority,** 216 Main St., Olympic Center, operates the sporting facilities (☎ 523-1655 or 800-462-6236; open M-F 8:30am-4pm). Find info on food, lodging, and area attractions at the **Lake Placid-Essex County Visitors Bureau,** also in the Olympic Center (☎ 523-2445; open daily 9am-5pm; closed Su in winter). **Adirondack Trailways** (☎ 800-225-6815 for bus info) stops at Lake Placid Video, 324 Main St., and has extensive service in the area. Destinations include New York City ($51) and Lake George ($14.40). **Weather info:** ☎ 523-1363. **Post office:** 201 Main St. (☎ 523-3071; open M-F 8:30am-5pm, Sa 8:30am-2pm). **ZIP code:** 12946. **Area code:** 518.

☗ ACCOMMODATIONS. If you avoid the resorts on the west end of town, both lodgings and food can be had cheaply in Lake Placid. The **White Sled,** 3½ mi. east of town on Rte. 73, has a neat bunkhouse with 38 beds, three bathrooms, kitchen and barbecue facilities, and cable TV. For a little more, sleep in one of 15 motel rooms or rent the ten-bed cottage. The owner can provide visitors with information on Lake Placid and the Adirondacks and, if you're lucky, she will prepare her specialty, blueberry buckle. (☎ 523-9314. Bunks $18; motel rooms from $45.) If you prefer to stay right in town, the **High Peaks Hostel** offers slightly more crowded living quarters with Olympic proximity and a higher price. Located at 337½ Main St., across from the bowling alley and just a few blocks from Olympic Center, the hostel has kitchen facilities, a TV, and 14 bunks in two rooms. (☎ 523-3764; $22.) **Meadowbrook State Park,** 5 mi. west of town on Rte. 86 in Ray Brook, and **Wilmington Notch State Campground,** about 8 mi. east of Lake Placid on Rte. 86, are the region's best camping areas, although they may disappoint those who anticipate pristine Adirondack splendor. Both offer shady, wooded sites which accommodate two tents without hook-ups. (Meadowbrook ☎ 891-4351; Wilmington Notch ☎ 946-7172. Sites $10 per night, $2.50 surcharge for a first time registration). Unquestionably one of the state's most beautiful campgrounds, **Ausable Point** is located an hour from Lake Placid, 12 mi. south of Plattsburgh on Rte. 9, situated right on Lake Champlain (☎ 561-7080. $16 per night, $2.50 surcharge for first time registration.) For reservations at any New York State campground, call ☎ 800-456-2267.

◪ FOOD. Lake Placid Village, concentrated primarily along Main St., has a number of reasonably priced dining establishments. Glut at **Hilton Hotel's lunch buffet,** 1 Mirror Lake Drive, which includes sandwiches, soups, salads, and a hot entree for only $7. (☎ 523-4411. Buffet from noon-2pm.) The **Black Bear Restaurant,** 157 Main St., across from the municipal parking lot, features daily specials ($6-8) and a hearty breakfast ($3-6) or lunch ($6). Be sure to throw back a $3 bottle of the area's own brew, Saranac lager. (☎ 523-9886. Open 6am-10pm, depending on the crowd.) **The Cottage,** 5 Mirror Lake Drive, is worth a whirl if only for its spectacular view of Mirror Lake, where you can sometimes catch the US National canoeing or kayaking teams at practice. The salads and sandwiches, all priced under $8, are spectacular. (☎ 523-9845. Food served 11:30am-10pm; bar open 11:30am-midnight or 1am, depending on crowd.) **Mud Puddles**, 3 School St., is one of Lake Placid's few late night hotspots. (☎ 523-4446. Open 8am-3am. No cover M-F; Sa-Su $3.)

MID-ATLANTIC

■ **SIGHTS.** If you're planning to visit most of Lake Placid's Olympic attractions, the **Olympic Sites Passport** is your best bargain. For $16 per person, the pass includes entrance to the **Olympic Jumping Complex** (including chairlift and elevator ride), the **Mt. Van Hoevenberg Sports Complex,** the **Winter Olympic Museum,** and choice of either the **Scenic Gondola Ride** to the top of Little Whiteface or access to the **Veterans Memorial Highway** that climbs Whiteface Mountain. Purchase at any Olympic venue or at the Olympic Center Box Office (☎523-1655 or 800-462-6236).

The **Olympic Center** in downtown Lake Placid houses the 1932 and 1980 hockey arenas, as well as the petite, memorabilia-stuffed **Winter Sports Museum.** The museum features an 8min. intro video to Lake Placid and its Olympic history. *(☎523-1655 ext. 226. Open daily 10am-5pm. $4, seniors $3, children under 6 $2.)* Purchase tickets for a guided tour of the **Olympic Ski Jumps,** which, along with the **Kodak Sports Park,** make up the **Olympic Jumping Complex,** just east of town on Rte. 73. Admission gets you a chairlift and elevator ride to the top where you can watch summertime jumpers soaring off the astroturf-covered Olympic ramp into a swimming pool. *(Open 9am-4pm. $8, seniors and children $5.)* About 5 mi. east of town on Rte. 73, the **Olympic Sports Complex** *(☎523-4436)* at Mt. Van Hoevenberg offers bobsled rides down the actual Olympic track, no matter the season. In colder weather, the bobsleds run on ice and will set you back a chilly $30 per ride; in warmer weather, the sleds grow wheels and, oddly, cost only $25 per ride. While at the complex, consider whipping yourself into shape Olympian-style by taking a **mountain bike** run down one of the several cross-country ski paths. Bike rentals are available inside the complex. *(☎523-1402 or 523-3764. Open daily mid-June to early Sept.; on weekends early Sept. to early Oct. Bikes $10-40 per day; required helmet $3 per day).* Popular **Tour Boat Cruises** travel 16 narrated miles across Lake Placid. *(☎523-9704. Cruises depart daily at 10:30am and 2:30pm, 4pm cruise on weekends. $6.75 adults, $5.75 seniors, $4.75 children.)* For a bird's eye view, drive up Whiteface Mountain on the **Veterans Memorial Highway** just 11 mi. east of Lake Placid on Rte. 86. The alpine-style tollbooth at the bottom of the hill has info about the highway and is the starting point for a self-guided nature walk. Stop at one or two of the many parking areas on your way up for spectacular mountain vistas before reaching the observatory at the summit. *(☎946-7175. Open daily mid-May through early Oct., longer if weather permits. 8:30am-5pm. $8 car and driver; $5 motorcycle and driver; $4 each passenger.)*

THOUSAND ISLAND SEAWAY   ☎315

The Thousand Island region of the St. Lawrence Seaway spans 100 mi. from the mouth of Lake Ontario to the first of the many locks on the St. Lawrence River, forming a natural US-Canadian border. Although lucky Canada scored two-thirds of the islands when the two nations first parcelled them out, the US took the larger islands, thus laying claim to 50% of the total area. Surveys conducted by the US and Canadian governments determined that there are over 1700 islands in the seaway. The requirements for being an island stipulated that at least one square ft. of land should sit above water year-round and at least one tree should grow on it. These islands and countless rocky shoals make navigation tricky in the area. Locals divide people into two groups: those who *have* hit a shoal and those who *will* hit a shoal. But don't let this dire prediction deter you; not only is the Thousand Island region a fisherman's paradise with some of the world's best bass and muskie catch, it's the only area in the nation with a salad dressing named after it.

■ **PRACTICAL INFORMATION.** The Thousand Island region hugs the St. Lawrence just 2hr. from Syracuse by way of I-81 N. From south to north, **Cape Vincent, Clayton,** and **Alexandria Bay** ("Alex Bay" to locals) are the main towns in the area, although Alex Bay is by far the most cosmopolitan of the three. For Wellesley Island, Alexandria Bay, and the eastern 500 islands, stay on I-81 until you reach Rte. 12 E. For Clayton and points west, take Exit 47 and follow Rte. 12 until you reach Rte. 12 E. The **Clayton Chamber of Commerce,** 510 Riverside Dr., Clayton 13624, has the free *Clayton Vacation Guide* and *Thousand Islands Seaway Region Travel Guide* (☎686-3771; open daily mid-June to mid-Sept. 9am-4pm; mid-Sept. to mid-

June M-F 9am-4pm). The **Alexandria Bay Chamber of Commerce,** 24 Market St., Alexandria Bay 13607, is just off James St. (☎482-9531; open M-F 8:30am-4:30pm). The **Cape Vincent Chamber of Commerce** welcomes visitors at 175 James St., by the ferry landing (☎654-2481; open May-Oct. Tu-Sa 9am-5pm; also late May to early Sept. Su-M 10am-4pm). Access the region by bus with **Greyhound,** 540 State St., Watertown. Two buses run daily to New York City (7½hr., $47.50); Syracuse (1¾hr., $8.50); and Albany (5hr., $36). Station open M-F 8:30am-1pm and 3-5pm; Sa-Su only at departure times. **Thousand Islands Bus Lines** leaves for Alexandria Bay and Clayton from the same station, M-F at 1pm (☎287-2782; $5.60 to Alexandria, $3.55 to Clayton); return trips leave Clayton from the **Nutshell Florist,** 234 James St. (☎686-5791), at 8:45am, and Alexandria from the **Dockside Cafe,** 17 Market St. (☎482-9849), at 8:30am. Clayton's **post office:** 236 John St. (☎686-3311; open M-F 9am-5pm, Sa 9am-noon). **ZIP code:** 13624. Alexandria Bay's **post office:** 13 Bethune St. (☎482-9521; open M-F 8:30am-5:30pm, Sa 8:30am-1pm). **ZIP code:** 13607. Cape Vincent's **post office:** 362 Broadway St., across from village green (☎654-2424; open M-F 8:30am-1pm and 2-5:30pm, Sa 8:30-11:30am). **ZIP code:** 13618. **Area code:** 315.

▐ ACCOMMODATIONS AND CAMPGROUNDS. The idyllic **Tibbetts Point Lighthouse Hostel (HI-AYH),** 33439 County Rte. 6, along the western edge of the seaway on Cape Vincent, is situated where Lake Ontario meets the St. Lawrence River. Take Rte. 12 E into town, drive straight onto Broadway, and follow the river until the road ends. The lighthouse is still active, and the peaceful rhythm of the waves lulls you to sleep at night. Pick-up in Clayton is possible with one-day notice. (☎654-3450. Open mid-May to Oct. Check-in 5-10pm. Curfew 11pm. Two houses with 26 beds. Full kitchen with microwave. Dorms $12, non-members $15. Linen $1.) **Burnham Point State Park,** on Rte. 12 E 4 mi. east of Cape Vincent and 11 mi. west of Clayton, sports 52 campsites and three picnic areas. (☎654-2324. Open daily late May to early Sept. 8am-10pm. Showers. Tent sites $13, prime sites on the water $15. Boat Dockage $6 for the day, $13 overnight. $2.50 surcharge for each registration. Wheelchair accessible.) **Keewaydin State Park,** just south of Alex Bay, maintains 41 sites along the St. Lawrence River. Campers have free access to an Olympic-size swimming pool, which may explain why the park teems with tents in the thick of summer. (☎482-3331. Open daily late May to early Sept. 8am-11pm. Pool open 10am-7pm. Showers. Sites $13; $2.50 surcharge.) **Grass Point State Park,** halfway between Clayton and Alex Bay, is another appealing option to those with boats; there's a launch and 32 slips available, as well as 58 campsites and two picnic areas. (Open daily late May to mid-Sept. 8am-10pm. Rates equal to other state parks.) For reservations at any New York State campground, call ☎800-456-2267.

▣ EXPLORING THE SEAWAY. Any of the small towns that dot Rte. 12 will serve as a fine base for exploring the region, although Clayton and Cape Vincent tend to be less expensive than Alexandria Bay. **Uncle Sam Boat Tours,** 604 Riverside Dr. (☎686-3511), in Clayton, and on James St. in Alexandria Bay (☎482-2611), delivers the best view of the islands and the plush estates situated atop them, along with a fact-packed live narration and some sage wisdom on shoal-avoidance. Tours highlight **Heart Island** and its famous **Boldt Castle;** they do not cover the price of admission to the castle. George Boldt, former owner of New York City's elegant Waldorf-Astoria Hotel, financed Boldt Castle, a six-story replica of a Rhineland castle as a gift for his wife, who died before its completion. In his grief, Boldt stopped construction on the 120-room behemoth, which remains unfinished today. After extensive renovations necessitated by six decades of abandonment, this romantic monument is now open to the public. The castle grounds include magnificently sculptured gardens and several smaller stone buildings worth a glimpse. *(Tourism council: ☎800-847-5263. Uncle Sam: 2¼hr. tours leave daily from Alexandria Bay late Apr. to Oct. $13.50, children 12 and under $6.75. Daily lunch and dinner cruises $20.50-27.50 must be reserved in advance. Castle ☎482-9724; open daily mid-May to mid-Oct. 10am-6:30pm. $4.25, ages 6-12 $2.50.)* Endorsed by maniacal boaters, the **Antique Boat Museum,** 750 Mary St. in Clayton, houses practically every make and model of hardwood, freshwater boat ever conceived. (☎686-4104. Open daily mid-May to mid-Oct. 9am-5pm. $6, seniors $5, students $2, children under 5 free.) **French Creek Marina,** 250 Wahl St. (☎686-3621), off Strawberry Lane, 100m south of the 12/12E junction, rents 14 ft. fishing boats for $50 per day, launches boats for $5, and provides overnight docking for $20. **O'Brien's U-Drive Boat Rentals,** 51 Walton St., handles boat and jetski rentals in Alexandria Bay with 16 ft. fishing boats. (☎482-9548. Open daily May to early Oct. 8am-4:30pm. $70 per day; $300 deposit.) **Fishing licenses** are available at sporting goods stores or at the **Town Clerk's Office,** 405 Riverside Dr. in Clayton. (☎686-3512. Open M-F 9am-noon and 1-4pm. $11 per day, 5-day $20, season $35.) No local store rents equipment; bring rods or plan to buy.

NEW JERSEY

Travelers who refuse to get off the interstates envision New Jersey as a conglomeration of belching chemical plants and ocean beaches strewn with garbage and gamblers. This false impression belies the quieter delights hidden beyond the highway exit ramps. A closer look reveals that there is more to New Jersey than commuters, chemicals, and craps; the interior blooms with fields of corn, tomatoes, and peaches, and placid sandy beaches outline the southern tip of the state. The state shelters quiet hamlets, the Pine Barrens forest, and two world-class universities that clashed in the first ever intercollegiate football game: Rutgers and Princeton. Certainly, Atlantic City is gaudy and glitzy, and the Turnpike remains the zone of the road warrior, but those straying from the path will be pleasantly surprised. Hey, Bruce Springsteen calls it home.

🛈 PRACTICAL INFORMATION

Capital: Trenton.

Visitor Info: State Division of Tourism, 20 W. State St., P.O. Box 826, Trenton 08625 (☎609-292-2470; www.nj-tourism.com). **New Jersey Dept. of Environmental Protection and Energy, State Park Service,** 401 East State St., Trenton 08625 (☎609-292-2797).

Postal Abbreviation: NJ. **Sales Tax:** 6%; no tax on clothing.

ATLANTIC CITY   ☎609

More than any other American city, the geography of Atlantic City is subconsciously implanted into the minds of generations of Americans. For over 50 years, board-gaming strategists have been passing "Go" to collect their $200 and buying "Boardwalk" in efforts to control this coastal city as reincarnated on the *Monopoly* board. While *Monopoly* was created as a game for rainy days, it was the hot summer days of southern Jersey that catapulted Atlantic City to beachside hotspot status. The opulence, however, faded into neglect, still visible in decrepit streets and alleys, and then into a megadollar tackiness. With the legalization of gambling in 1976, casinos rose from the rubble of the boardwalk. Today, velvet-lined temples of glitter (each with a dozen restaurants and big-name entertainment) overlook the beach and draw all kinds, from international princes to local paupers.

📭 GETTING THERE AND GETTING AROUND

Atlantic City lies halfway down New Jersey's eastern seashore, accessible via the **Garden State Pkwy.** and the **Atlantic City Expwy.** and easily reached by train from Philadelphia or New York.

Airport: Atlantic City International (☎645-7895 or 800-892-0354). Located just west of Atlantic City in Pamona. Served by Spirit, USAirways, and Continental.

Trains: Amtrak, at Kirkman Blvd, near Michigan Ave. Follow Kirkman to its end, bear right, and follow the signs. To New York (2½hr., $40). Open daily 6am-10:15pm.

Buses: Greyhound (☎609-340-2000). Buses travel every 30min. between Port Authority (NYC) and most major casinos (2½hr., casino drop-off rates $30 round-trip). Many casinos, in addition to the round-trip discounts, will give gamblers between $15 and $20 in coins upon arrival. (Trump Plaza offers $20 for starting your gambling spree at their casino.) **New Jersey Transit** (☎215-569-3752 or 800-582-5946) offers hourly service between NYC and the transit station on Atlantic Ave. between Michigan and Ohio St. ($25, seniors $11 each way). **Gray Line Tours** (☎800-669-0051) offers several day-trips to Atlantic City (3hr.; $22 on weekdays, $24 on weekends). Don't pitch your ticket receipt, which is redeemable for cash, chips, or food from casinos when you arrive. Tropicana and the Sands offer $20 per person. The bus drops riders at the casino and picks you up later the same day. Call for nearest NYC bus pick-up locations. Call ☎800-995-8898 for info about economical overnight packages. Terminal open 24hr.

✦ 🕭 ORIENTATION AND PRACTICAL INFORMATION

Attractions cluster on and around the Boardwalk, which runs east-west along the Atlantic Ocean. Running parallel to the Boardwalk, Pacific and Atlantic Ave. offer cheap restaurants, hotels, and convenience stores. *Atlantic Ave. can be dangerous after dark, and any street farther out can be dangerous even by day.* Getting around is easy on foot and more pleasant on the boardwalk than in the neighborhoods. **Parking** at the Sands Hotel is free, but "for patrons only," so spend a dollar at the slots. Lots near the boards run $3-7.

Visitor Information: Atlantic City Convention Center and Visitors Bureau, 2314 Pacific Ave. (☎888-228-4748). A new visitors center has also been built on the Atlantic Expressway approximately 1 mi. after the Pleasantville Toll Plaza. Open Su-Tu 9am-5pm, W-Sa 9am-8pm.

Hospital: Atlantic City Medical Center (☎344-4081), at Michigan and Pacific Ave.

Hotlines: Rape and Abuse Hotline, ☎646-6767. 24hr. **Gambling Abuse,** ☎800-426-2537. 24hr. **AIDS Hotline,** ☎800-281-2437. Operates M-F 9am-5pm.

Post Office: Illinois and Pacific Ave. (☎345-4212). **ZIP code:** 08401. **Area code:** 609.

▐ ACCOMMODATIONS

Large, red-carpeted, and overpriced beachfront hotels have bumped smaller operators a few streets back. Smaller, privately owned hotels along **Pacific Ave.**, 1 block from the Boardwalk, charge about $60-95 in the summer. Reserve ahead, especially Sa-Su or face the plight of forking over all your blackjack earnings and then some for mediocre lodging. Many hotels lower their rates mid-week and in winter, when water temperature and gambling fervor drop significantly. Rooms in guest houses are reasonably priced, though facilities can be dismal. If you have a car, it pays to stay in **Absecon**, about 8 mi. from Atlantic City; Exit 40 from the Garden State Pkwy. leads to Rte. 30 and cheap rooms.

Inn of the Irish Pub, 164 St. James Pl. (☎344-9963), near the Ramada Tower just off the Boardwalk, has spacious, clean rooms with floral wall designs: the best budget accommodations in town. Porch is equipped with relaxing rocking chairs and refreshing Atlantic breeze. There's never a dull night in the house as the downstairs bar offers lively entertainment. Coin-op laundry in hotel next door. Restaurant offers a $2 lunch special and a $6 dinner special. Singles with shared bath $29, with private bath $40-52; doubles $60/$75; quad with shared bath $60. Key deposit $5. Room service charge $2.

Comfort Inn, 154 South Kentucky Ave. (☎348-4000 or 888-247-5337), near the Sands. Rooms with king size or 2 queen size beds and, true to Atlantic City swank, a jacuzzi. Includes continental breakfast, free parking, and an heated pool. Jan.-May $59, June $69-79, July $89, Aug. $99, early Sept. $69, late Sept. to Dec. $59. Rooms with ocean views $20 extra, but come with fridge, microwave, and a bigger jacuzzi. Call well in advance for Sa-Su and holidays.

Birch Grove Park Campground (☎641-3778), Mill Rd. in Northfield. About 6 mi. from Atlantic City, off Rte. 9. 50 sites. Attractive and secluded. Open Apr.-Oct. Sites $22 for 2, with 2-way hook-up $24, 4-way hook-up $27.

FOOD

The food in Atlantic City is, for the most part, reasonable. Although not recommended by nutritionists, 75¢ hot dogs and $1.50 pizza slices crowd the Boardwalk. After cashing in your chips, you can visit a casino buffet (lunch about $6-7; dinner $10). Less tacky and more tasty food can be found a little further from the seashore. For a complete rundown of local dining, pick up a copy of *Shorecast Insider's Guide At the Shore* or *Whoot* (both free) from a hotel lobby, restaurant, or local store. For real deal-seekers, loiter in gambling dens and score free pretzels, coffee, cookies, juice, and even yogurt provided to high rollers.

Atlantic City's most affordable eats are a mere flight of stairs away from the otherwise pricey town's cheapest beds. At one of the few AC spots where locals rule, the **Inn of the Irish Pub**, 164 St. James Pl., Erin Go Bragh is the theme and no item on the menu exceeds $6. The lunch special (M-F 11:30am-2pm) includes a pre-selected sandwich and a cup of soup for $2. Domestic drafts are $1. (☎345-9613. Open 24hr.) **Pacific Ave.** is cramped with steak, sub, and pizza shops. There's never a dull moment at the vibrant **White House Sub Shop**, 2301 Arctic Ave., which plays host to more celebrities than its national capital namesake, such as the late Frank Sinatra. Ol' Blue Eyes was rumored to have had these immense subs ($4-9) flown to him while he was on tour. (☎345-1564 or 345-8599. Open M-Th 10am-11pm, F-Sa 10am-midnight, Su 11am-11pm.) For the best pizza in town, hit **Tony's Baltimore Grille**, 2800 Atlantic Ave., at Iowa Ave. You'll always be in command of your musical destiny as large booths have personal jukeboxs. For a fishier twist, the $9 seafood special combines shrimp, crab cake, and scallops. (☎345-5766. Open daily 11am-3am. Bar open 24hr. Pasta $4-6; pizza $6-7.) One of the more palatable boardwalk options, **Custard and Snack House**, between South Carolina and Ocean Ave., makes 37 flavors of ice cream and yogurt, ranging from peach to tutti-frutti. If it's too chilly for dessert, coffee, tea, and hot cocoa (all $1) are warmer choices. (☎345-5151. Open Su-Th 10am-midnight, F-Sa 10am-3am. Cones $2.25.)

 CASINO$, THE BOARDWALK, AND BEACHES

All casinos on the Boardwalk fall within a dice toss of one another. The farthest south is **The Hilton** (☎347-7111), between Providence and Voston Ave., and the farthest north is **Showboat** (☎343-4000), at Delaware Ave. and Boardwalk. If you liked *Aladdin*, you'll love the **Taj Mahal**, 1000 Boardwalk (☎449-1000). Donald Trump's cartoonesque glittering castle is too ostentatious to be missed—it was neglected payments on this tasteless tallboy that cast the financier into his billion dollar tailspin. You, too, can board a magic carpet ride to bankruptcy with the perfect blend of splurging and misfortune. Speaking of *Monopoly*, Trump owns three other hotel casinos in the city: **Trump Plaza** (☎441-6000) and **Trump World's Fair** (☎344-6000) on the Boardwalk and **Trump Castle** (☎441-2000) at the Marina. Many a die is cast at **Caesar's Boardwalk Resort and Casino** (☎348-4411), at Arkansas Ave., which pales in comparison to the Las Vegas palace. The **Sands** (☎441-4000), at Indiana Ave., stands tall and flashy with its pink-and-green seashell motif.

> **BEFORE YOU LOSE YOUR SHIRT...** Contrary to popular belief, you don't *have* to spend a penny to enjoy yourself in Atlantic City's casinos; their vast, plush interiors and spotless marble bathrooms can entertain a resourceful, imaginative, and voyeuristic budget traveler for hours. The maze-like lobby of the **Trump Plaza** is especially conducive to games of hide-and-go-seek for the mature casino visitors. Open nearly all the time, casinos lack windows and clocks, denying you the time cues that signal the hours slipping away; keep your eyes on your watch, or you'll have spent five hours and five digits before you know what hit you. To curb inevitable losses, stick to the cheaper games—blackjack and slot machines. **TropWorld, Bally's Grand,** and **Taj Mahal** will allow you to gamble for hours on less than $10. Leave your fakes at home; the minimum gambling age of 21 is strictly enforced.

There's something for everyone in Atlantic City, thanks to the Boardwalk. Those under 21 (or those tired of the endless cycle of winning and losing) **gamble for prizes** at one of the many arcades that line the Boardwalk. It feels like real gambling, but the teddy bear in the window is easier to win than the convertible on display at Caesar's. The **Steel Pier,** an extension in front of the Taj Mahal, juts into the coastal waters with a ferris wheel that spins riders over the Atlantic. It also offers the rest of the usual amusement park suspects: roller coaster, tilt-a-whirl, carousel, kiddie rides, and many a game of "skill." Rides cost $2-3 each. (Open daily noon-midnight; call the Taj Mahal for winter hrs.) When you tire of spending money, check out the **beach,** although **Ventnor City,** just west of Atlantic City, offers more tranquil shores.

CAPE MAY ☎ 609

Lying at the southern extreme of New Jersey's coastline, Cape May is the oldest seashore resort in the US, and the money here is no younger. Once the summer playground of Upper Eastside New Yorkers, the town still carries the signs of affluent infiltration in the elegant restaurants of Beach Ave. but is no longer characterized by it. An afternoon ride through Cape May's residential side streets can be an aesthetic delight. Overgrown with roses and wrapped in starry white lights, gorgeous Victorian mansions and pastel porches are architectural candy. The resort's main attraction, however, continues to be the sparkling white beaches—perfect for play or a nap under the rays—which shun the commercialism of more modern beach towns. At night, candles flicker in the windows of 19th-century B&Bs by the shore, infusing an aura of Victorian romance into the passersby strolling the bricks.

■ **⁊ ORIENTATION AND PRACTICAL INFORMATION.** Despite its geographic isolation, Cape May is easily accessed. By car from the north, it is literally at the end of the road. Start digging for loose change as you follow the tollbooth-laden Garden State Pkwy. south as far as it goes, watch for signs to Center City, and you'll end up on Lafayette St. Alternately, take the slower, scenic Ocean Dr. 40 mi. south along the shore from Atlantic City. Rte. 55 brings beachgoers from Philadelphia. **NJ Transit** (☎215-569-3752 or 800-582-5946) makes a local stop at the bus depot on the corner of Lafayette and Ocean St. To: Atlantic City (2hr., 18 per day, $3.45); Philadelphia (3hr., 18 per day, $13.60); and New York City (4½hr., 3 per day, $27). **Cape Area Transit (CAT)** run buses on Pittsburgh Ave., Beach Dr., Lafayette St., and Ocean Ave. (☎889-0925 or 800-966-3758. Operates daily late June to Sept. 6 10am-10pm; late May to late June and Sept. 6 to mid-Oct. F 4-10pm, Sa 10am-10pm, Su 10am-4pm. $1 exact change.) **Cape May Seashore Lines** runs old-fashioned trains to further attractions along the 26 mi. to Tuckahoe four times per day (☎884-2675. $8, children $5). Bike the beach with the help of **Shields' Bike Rentals,** 11 Gurney St. (☎884-2453. Open 7am-7pm. $4 per hr., $9 per day; tandems $12 per hr.; surreys $24 per hr.) **Faria's,** 311 Beach Ave., rents beach necessities. (☎898-0988. Surfboard $16-20; umbrella or chair $6; bodyboard $8-16; wetsuit $15.) **Welcome center:** 405 Lafayette St. (☎884-9562; open daily 8:30am-4:30pm). **Chamber of Commerce:** 513 Washington St. Mall (☎884-5508; open M-F 9am-5pm, Sa-Su 10am-6pm) and in the **historic kiosk** at the south end of the mall. **Post Office:** 700 Washington St. (☎884-3578; open M-F 9am-5pm, Sa 8:30am-12:30pm). **ZIP code:** 08204. **Area code:** 609.

⌐ ACCOMMODATIONS. Sleeping does not come cheaply in Cape May. Luxurious hotels and Victorian B&Bs along the beach run $85-250 per night. Further from the shore, prices drop. Although the ▨**Hotel Clinton,** 202 Perry St., may lack presidential suites and A/C, the Italian family-owned establishment offers 16 breezy rooms, the most affordable rates in town, and priceless warmth and welcome from the colorful and charismatic proprietors. (☎884-3993. Open mid-June to Sept. Singles $30-35; doubles $40-45. Reservations recommended.) Next door, the **Parris Inn,** 204 Perry St., has one too many "r"s to be confused with that French capital, but it does rent spacious, comfortable rooms, most with private baths, TV, and A/C. (☎884-8015. Open mid-Apr. to Dec. Singles $55-65; doubles $85-95. Lower rates off-season.) Campgrounds line U.S. 9 just north of Cape May. In a prime seashore location, **Camp Island,** 709 Rte. 9, is only 2 mi. away from Victorian househunting. (☎800-437-7443. Sites $18-24, full hook-up $27.) More primitive, but only ten blocks from Cape May, **Depot Travel Park,** 800 Broadway, 2 mi. north on Rte. 626 (Seashore Rd.) off Rte. 9, is convenient for beach seekers. (☎884-2533. Open May-late Sept. Sites with water and electricity $21.75, full hook-up $26.)

🍴🎵 **FOOD AND NIGHTLIFE.** Cape May's cheapest food is the generic pizza and burger fare along **Beach Ave.** You'll have to shell out a few more clams for a more substantial meal at one of the pricey and plush beachside restaurants. Crawling with pedestrians hunting for the most heavenly fudge and saltwater taffy, the **Washington St. Mall** supports several popular food stores and eateries. A meal at the pub-like **Ugly Mug,** 426 Washington St. Mall, is worth battling through the initially suffo-cating smokescreen. Fresh air can be had on the patio as you inhale a New England cup o' chowder ($2) or the ever-popular "oceanburger" ($5.75). Summer means cover-free fun. (☎884-3459. Open M-Sa 11am-2am, Su noon-2am; hot food served until 11pm. Free pizza M 10pm-2am.) At the newly launched **Gecko's,** in the Carpen-ter St. Mall, Mexican chefs help hungry patrons triple their southwestern delight for $5.50 with the three-sister quesadilla. (☎898-7750. Open daily 10am-10pm.)

The rock scene collects around the barnacle and crustacean encrusted bar of **Car-ney's** on Beach Ave., with nightly entertainment in the summer. Unwind on the weekend with Su jams 3-7pm. (☎884-442. Open daily 11:30am-2am.) For a more cosmopolitan night scene, a borderline sophisticated crowd tends to congregate at **Cabana's,** across from the beach at the corner of Decatur St. and Beach Ave. You'll have to find a lot of sand dollars if you want a pricey entree, but there is no cover for the nightly blues or jazz. (☎884-8400. Open daily noon-2am.)

🏖 **HITTING THE BEACH.** The entire Jersey shore is blessed with foaming white-caps and glimmering beaches. Cape May's sands actually sparkle, dotted with the famous Cape May "diamonds" (quartz pebbles to the geology buffs). You can get horizontal and soak up some sun on a city-protected beach (off Beach Ave.), but don't while away the glorious days without a **beach tag,** required for beachgoers over 11. Tags are available from the vendors roaming the shore or from the **Beach Tag Office,** located at Grant and Beach Dr. (☎884-9522. Open daily 9:30am-5:30pm. Tags required daily June-Sept. 10am-5:30pm. Daily $4, 3-day $8, weekly $11, seasonal $17.)

Those in search of exercise and a spectacular view of the Delaware and New Jer-sey Shore can ascend the 199 steps to the beacon of the 1859 **Cape May Lighthouse** in **Cape May Point State Park,** west of town at the end of the point. (☎884-8626. Park open 8am-dusk. Lighthouse open daily Apr.-Nov. 8am-dusk; Dec.-Mar. Sa-Su 8am-dusk. $4, ages 3-12 $1.) In summer, several shuttles run the 5 mi. from the bus depot on Lafayette St. to the lighthouse. ($5, ages 3-12 $4.)

Even migratory birds flock to Cape May for a break from the long, southbound flight. Sneak a peak at these feathered vacationers from the **Cape May Bird Observa-tory,** on Cape May Point, a bird watcher's paradise. Bird maps, field trips, and workshops are all available here. (701 E. Lake Dr. ☎884-2736. Open Tu-Su 10am-5pm.)

PENNSYLVANIA

In 1681, Englishman William Penn, Jr. established the colony of Pennsylvania (Latin scholars can trace the etymology to "Penn's woods") in order to protect his fellow Quakers from persecution. A bastion of religious tolerance, the state grew quickly in population after attracting settlers of all ethnicities and beliefs. Since then, Pennsylva-nia has clung to the ideals of freedom from the drafting of the Declaration of Indepen-dence in Philadelphia to the present. In 1976, Philadelphia groomed its historic shrines for the nation's bicentennial celebration, and a quarter of a century later the long-standing colonial monuments serve as the centerpiece of the city's ambitious renewal program. Pittsburgh, the steel city with a raw image, was once dirty enough to fool streetlights into burning during the day but has recently initiated a cultural renaissance. Removed from the noise of its urban areas, Pennsylvania's landscape has retained much of the rustic beauty first discovered by colonists centuries ago, from the simple farms of Lancaster County to the deep gorges of the Allegheny Plateau.

🔋 PRACTICAL INFORMATION

Capital: Harrisburg.
Visitor Info: Pennsylvania Travel & Tourism, 453 Forum Bldg., Harrisburg 17120 (☎800-847-4852; www.state.pa.us). **Bureau of State Parks,** Rachel Carson State Office Bldg., 400 Market St., Harrisburg 17108 (☎800-637-2757). Open M-F 8am-4:30pm.
Postal Abbreviation: PA. **Sales Tax:** 6%.

PHILADELPHIA ☎215

With his band of Quakers, William Penn founded the City of Brotherly Love in 1682, after it had served as a colonial hub for 100 years. But it was Ben, not Penn, that transformed the town into the urban metropolis it is today. Benjamin Franklin, ingenious American ambassador, inventor, womanizer, and wit, almost singlehandedly built Philadelphia into an American colonial capital. Anything founded by Ben seems to bear his name, and in summer, at the peak of tourist season, his cocked-hatted and ruffled faux-colonial imitators roam the city making 1770s chitchat. Sightseers will have a field day in Philly, which abounds with historic attractions, world-class museums, and architectural accomplishments. The city's thriving ethnic neighborhoods deliver a range of culinary choices, while the native cheesesteak is a staple.

✈ GETTING THERE AND AWAY

Airport: Philadelphia International (☎937-6800 for info, 24hr.), 8 mi. southwest of Center City on I-76. The 20min. **SEPTA Airport Rail Line** runs from Center City to the airport. Trains leave 30th St., Suburban, and Market East Stations daily every 30min. 5:25am-11:25pm; $5 at window, $7 on train. Last train from airport 12:10am. **Airport Limelight Limousine** (☎782-8818) will deliver you to a hotel or a specific address downtown; $8 per person. Taxi to downtown $25.
Trains: Amtrak, 30th St. Station (☎824-1600), at Market St., in University City. To: New York (2hr.; 30-40 per day; $45, express trains $71); Boston (7hr., 10 per day, $59-69); Washington, D.C. (2hr., 33 per day, $40); Baltimore (2hr., 10 per day, $38); and Pittsburgh (8hr., 2 per day, $54-82). Office open M-F 5:10am-10:45pm, Sa-Su 6:10am-10:45pm. Station open 24hr.
Buses: Greyhound, 1001 Filbert St. (☎931-4075 or 800-231-2222), at 10th and Filbert in downtown Philadelphia 1 block north of Market near the 10th and Market St. subway/commuter rail stop. A populated, safe area. To: New York (2hr., 32 per day, $20); Boston (7hr., 19 per day, $29); Baltimore (2hr., 10 per day, $17); Washington, D.C. (3hr., 10 per day, $26); Pittsburgh (7hr., 8 per day, $39); and Atlantic City (2hr., 12 per day, $8.50). Station open daily 24hr. **New Jersey Transit** (☎569-3752), in the same station. To: Atlantic City (1hr., $10); Ocean City (2hr., $11); and other points on the New Jersey shore. Operates daily with buses to Atlantic City nearly every 30min.

🚉 GETTING AROUND

Public Transit: Southeastern Pennsylvania Transportation Authority (SEPTA), 1234 Market St. (☎580-7800; www.septa.org). Extensive bus and rail service to the suburbs. Buses serve the 5-county area; most operate 5am-2am, some 24hr. 2 major subway routes: the blue east-west **Market St. line** (including 30th St. Station and the historic area) and the orange north-south **Broad St. line** (including the stadium complex in south Philadelphia). *The subway is unsafe after dark;* buses are usually safer. Subway connects with commuter rails—the **R5** main line local runs through the western suburb of Paoli ($3.75-4.25). The SEPTA **R7** runs north to Trenton, NJ ($5). Pick up a free SEPTA system map, Philly's best street map, at any subway stop. Fare $1.60, 2 tokens $2.30, transfers 40¢. Unlimited all-day pass for both $5. In the tourist area, purple **Phlash** buses come by every 10min. and hit all major sights. Fare $1.50, day-pass $3.

Taxis: Yellow Cab, ☎922-8400. **Liberty Cab,** ☎389-2000.

Car Rental: Budget (☎492-9400), downtown at 21st and Market St., or in the 30th St. Station. Reliable and easy to find but relatively expensive. $50-60 per day with unlimited mi. Drivers must be 25+ with a major credit card.

Bike Rental: Frankenstein Bike Work, 1529 Spruce St. (☎893-4467). Open May-Sept. only Tu-Sa 10am-6pm, Su noon-4pm. Call ahead for M service. Cruisers $12 for 4hr., $15 per day.

◢ ORIENTATION

Penn planned his city as a logical and easily accessible grid, though the prevalence of one-way streets can cause many a migraine behind the wheel. The north-south streets ascend numerically from the **Delaware River,** flowing from **Penn's Landing** and **Independence Hall** on the east side to the **Schuylkill River** (SKOO-kill) on the west. The first street is **Front;** the others follow consecutively from 2 to 69. **Center City** runs from 8th St. to the Schuylkill River. From north to south, the primary streets are Race, Arch, JFK, Market, Chestnut, and South. The intersection of **Broad (14th) St.** and **Market** is the focal point of Center City, marked by the ornate City Hall. The **Historic District** stretches from Front to 8th St. and from Vine to South St. About 1 mi. west of Center City, the **University of Pennsylvania (UPenn)** sprawls on the far side of the Schuylkill River. **University City** includes the UPenn/Drexel area west of the Schuylkill River. This framework sounds simple, but Penn omitted the alleys in his system. Some can accommodate cars while others are too narrow, but street addresses often refer to alleys not pictured on standard AAA-type maps of the city. The **SEPTA transportation map,** available free from the tourist office, is probably the most complete map of the city.

Due to the proliferation of one-way streets, horrendous traffic, and outrageous parking fees, **driving** is not a good way to get around town. Parking near the historic sights will break the bank ($10 per day), but lower priced options scatter at a farther but walkable distance. If fortune is smiling upon you, meterless 2hr. parking spaces can sometimes be found on the cobblestones of Dock St. Day-long deals require vehicles to be in by 10am and out by 6pm. A well-secured lot on the corner of Race and 8th adheres to this policy ($5 all day). At 10th between Race and Vine St., a larger lot discounts on weekends and evenings ($4 Sa-Su and after 3pm.) Park outside the city and ride Philly's system of **buses** and its **subway** to most major downtown destinations. *Public transportation can be unsafe after dark.*

◪ PRACTICAL INFORMATION

Visitor Info: 1525 John F. Kennedy Blvd. (☎636-1666), the circular building by the fountain at 16th St. Free city guide with great map. Open daily 9am-6pm; in winter 9am-5pm. The **National Park Service Visitors Center** (☎597-8974, 627-1776 for a recording), at 3rd and Chestnut St., has info on **Independence Park,** including maps, schedules, and a branch of the tourist office. Open daily 9am-6pm; in winter 9am-5pm.

Hotlines: Suicide and Crisis Intervention, ☎686-4420. **Youth Crisis Line,** ☎787-0633. **Women Against Abuse,** ☎386-7777. All 3 24hr.

Gay, Lesbian, and Bisexual Info: Gay and Lesbian Counseling Services, ☎732-8255. Operates M-F 6-9pm, Su 5-8pm. **William Way Lesbian, Gay, and Bisexual Community Center** (☎732-2220). Info about gay events and activities. Open M-F noon-10pm, Sa 10am-5pm, Su 10:30am-8:30pm.

Post Office: 2970 Market St. (☎895-8000), at 30th St. across from the Amtrak station. Open 24hr. **ZIP code:** 19104. **Area code:** 215.

MID-ATLANTIC

Downtown Philadelphia

▲ ACCOMMODATIONS
Antique Row B&B, **3**
Bank St. Hostel (HI), **5**
Chamounix Hostel (HI), **1**
La Reserve, **2**

◤ ACCOMMODATIONS

Aside from its two hostels, inexpensive lodging in Philadelphia is uncommon, but if you make arrangements a few days in advance, comfortable rooms close to Center City can be had for around $60. The motels near the airport at Exit 9A on I-95 sacrifice location to be the most affordable motels in the area. The personable proprietors at **Antique Row Bed and Breakfast** and **La Reserve** (see below) will recommend rooms if they lack vacancy. **Bed & Breakfast Connections/Bed & Breakfast of Philadelphia**, in Devon, PA, books in Philadelphia and southeastern Pennsylvania but requires 20% payment. (☎610-687-3565. Call 9am-7pm. Singles $50-85; doubles $60-250. Reserve at least a week in advance.) The closest camping is across the Delaware River in New Jersey at **Timberline Campground**, 117 Timber Ln., 15 mi. from Center City. Take U.S. 295 S to Exit 18B (Clarksboro), follow straight through the traffic light ½ mi. and turn right on Friendship Rd. Timber Ln. is one block on the right. (☎609-423-6677. Sites $18, full hook-up $23.)

▨ **Chamounix Mansion International Youth Hostel (HI-AYH)** (☎878-3676 or 800-379-0017), in West Fairmount Park. Take bus #38 from lower Market St. to Ford and Cranston Rd., follow Ford Rd. to Chamounix Dr., turn left, and follow road to hostel. Aside from the standard bunk beds, you'll feel like royalty in suburban Philadelphia where a young, energetic staff maintains uncommonly lavish hosteling in a converted mansion. An ornate chandelier dangles in a designated quiet area fit for book reading or chess playing (table provided). Showers, kitchen, laundry, TV/VCR, piano, bikes, and Internet access ($1 per 5 min.). Free parking and discounted bus tokens. 80 beds. Private rooms are available for families and couples. Check-in 8-11am and 4:30pm-midnight. Lockout 11am-4:30pm. Curfew midnight. Dorms $11, non-members $14. Linen $2.

▨ **Bank Street Hostel (HI-AYH)**, 32 S. Bank St. (☎922-0222 or 800-392-4678). From the bus station, walk down Market St.; it's between 2nd and 3rd St. Subway: 2nd St. Very social hostel rests in a prime location within 2 blocks of both the historic district and the waterfront; super-convenient to South St. Travelers convene nightly to watch movies on the lounge's big screen TV. A/C, free coffee and tea, laundry facilities, kitchen, pool table, Internet access ($5 per 30min.). Lockout 10am-4:30pm, but they'll hold baggage. Curfew nightly 12:30am. 70 beds. Dorms $16, non-members $19. Linen $2. Cannot reserve rooms via phone; must mail payment in advance—call for details.

Antique Row Bed and Breakfast, 341 S. 12th St. (☎592-7802). Enchanting traditional B&B at the heart of colonial rowhouses. The engaging owner offers her guests expert restaurant referrals and an eclectic selection of good reads; she also serves a hearty morning meal. Free local calls. $60-100, depending on size of suite; reduced rate for longer stays.

La Reserve (a.k.a. **Bed and Breakfast Center City**), 1804 Pine St. (☎735-1137 or 735-0582). Entertains guests with an extravagant dining room that is often the site of lively dinner parties. Personable owner is a reliable source of Philadelphia advice and side-splitting humor. Full breakfast. $60-100.

Motel 6, 43 Industrial Hwy. (☎610-521-6650 or 800-466-8356), in Essington, Exit 9A off I-95. A generic option: large standard rooms with A/C and cable. Singles $50-60; doubles $56-65.

◖ FOOD

Street vendors are at the forefront of Philly specialties, hawking **cheesesteaks, hoagies, soft pretzels**, and **fruit salad**. Ethnic eateries gather in several specific areas: hip **South St.**, between Front and 7th; **18th St.** around Sansom; and **2nd St.**, between Chestnut and Market. **Chinatown**, bounded by 11th, 8th, Arch, and Vine St., offers well-priced vegetarian restaurants. The quintessential Philly cheesesteak rivalry squares off at 9th and Passyunk Ave., in South Philadelphia; **Pat's King of Steaks** (☎468-1546), the legendary founder of the cheesesteak, faces off against larger, more neon **Geno's Steaks**. Both offer cheesesteaks for $5 and stay open 24 hours. Whichever establishment you choose to visit, ordering a cheesesteak and the subsequent consumption of one will be an adventure. Prepare to order quickly and convincingly or risk being ejected to the back of the line. Be sure to grab a fistful of napkins to combat the deluge of grease that will pour from the sandwich. You may need a shower afterwards, but no Philly visit is complete without a cheesesteak.

Fresh fruit and other foodstuffs pack the mobbed streets of the immense **Italian Market,** which spans the area around 9th St. below Christian St. The **Reading Terminal Market,** 12th and Arch St., stocks globally diverse food under one roof—fabulous for lunch. Since 1893, food stands have clustered in the indoor market selling fresh produce and meats. Check the pamphlet available at vendors for events. (☎922-2317. Open M-Sa 8am-6pm.)

HISTORIC DISTRICT

Famous 4th St. Delicatessen (☎922-3274), 4th and Bainbridge St. A Philadelphia landmark since 1923, the Delicatessen has earned its stellar reputation by faithfully serving Jewish deli favorites like corned beef sandwiches ($6.75). Open M-Sa 7:30am-6pm, Su 7:30am-4pm.

Jim's Steaks, 400 South St. (☎928-1911). South St. bustles with activity, and at the heart of it rests this time warp back to 50s Philadelphia. People come in droves for the authentic Philly hoagie ($3.50-5); pass the time in line by inspecting the impressive wall of fame. Open M-Th 10am-1am, F-Sa 10am-3am, Su noon-10pm.

CHINATOWN

Singapore, 1006 Race St. (☎923-0303). Health-conscious Chinese food cravers flock to this therapeutic restaurant for options like the vegetarian roast duck ($8). The chef frequently hosts heart disease patients to share his wholesome cooking techniques. Open M-Th 11:30am-10pm, F 11:30am-11pm, Sa-Su noon-11pm.

Rangoon, 112 9th St. (☎829-8939). Spicy scents of Burmese cuisine float through the pretty pink interior. The crisp lentil fritters ($9) will whet your appetite for the tasty mint kabob ($9). Open daily 11:30am-10pm.

Harmony, 135 N. 9th St. (☎627-4520). The chef fled China in 1976 by swimming and now caters to Philadelphia's vegetarians. Space is limited but the dim lighting creates an intimate ambiance. Lovebirds warm up to each other by sharing a "Lovely Couple in Phoenix Nest" ($13). Open Su-Th 11:30am-10:30pm, F-Sa 11:30am-midnight.

CENTER CITY

Jamaican Jerk Hut, 1436 South St. (☎545-8644). Tropical paradise brightens an otherwise bleak urban area. While chefs jerk your Negril garlic shrimp ($10) to perfection, Bob Marley tunes jam in the backyard veranda. Open M-Th 10am-1am, F-Sa 10am-3am, Su 5-10pm. Live music F-Sa 7pm.

Taco House, 1218 Pine St. (☎735-1880). Loads of good, cheap Mexican food in a coffeehouse atmosphere. The tasty and affordable cheese crisps ($2) satisfy Mexican munchy cravings amid walls lined with local photography. Open Su-Th 11am-10pm, F-Sa 11am-11pm.

Samson St. Oyster House, 1516 Sansom St. (☎567-7683). Businesspeople and professionals seek seafood delight in the nautically decked dining room. As the name would indicate, oysters top the menu ($7.25 for half-dozen) but broiled bluefish ($7.50) and the popcorn shrimp po' boy ($6.25) also are great catches. Open daily 11am-11pm.

Alaska, 123 S. 18th St. (☎563-4424). Cafe-style relaxation with creamy creations. Features 3 diverse ice cream brands including Philly's famed Bassett's (regular $3). Open M-Th 11:30am-10pm, F-Su 11:30am-11pm.

UNIVERSITY CITY

Tandoor India Restaurant, 106 S. 40th St. (☎222-7122). Northern Indian cuisine with bread fresh from the clay oven (ask to see it). Lunch buffet $6; dinner buffet $9; entrees $7-11. 20% student discount with valid ID. Open M-F 11:30am-3pm and 4:30-10pm, Sa-Su 11:30am-3:30pm and 4:30-10pm.

Smokey Joe's, 210 S. 40th St. (☎222-0770), between Locust and Walnut St. The most popular UPenn bar and restaurant features hearty meals at student-friendly prices. All-you-can-eat pasta, broiled salmon, or BBQ baby ribs ($8). Lighter eaters can opt for the Palestra deal (salad, healthy sub, and drink for $7). Open daily 11am-2am; July-Aug. closed Su. In summer, no lunch Sa-Su. Local groups occasionally perform Su-Tu 10pm.

Abner's Cheesesteaks, 3813 Chestnut St. (☎662-0100), at 38th and Chestnut St. Local fast food attracts tipsy UPenn students deep into the night and better balanced businesspeople for lunch. Cheesesteak, large soda, and fries for $6. Open Su-Th 11am-midnight, F-Sa 11am-3am.

◉ SIGHTS

INDEPENDENCE MALL

The **Independence National Historical Park,** a small green bounded by Market, Walnut, 2nd, and 6th St., is comprised of a hash of historical buildings. (☎597-8974. *Open daily June-Aug. 9am-6pm; Sept.-May 9am-5pm. Free.)* Begin your trip down American history memory lane at the **visitors center,** 3rd and Chestnut, which dispenses detailed maps and brochures pertinent to the area (see **Practical Information,** above). One of the most popular of Philadelphia's historic landmarks, **Independence Hall** abounds with revolutionism and tourism. After Jefferson elegantly drafted the Declaration of Independence, the delegates signed the document here in 1776 and reconvened in 1787 to ink their names onto the US Constitution. *(Between 5th and 6th St. on Chestnut St. Open daily 9am-8pm; arrive early in summer to avoid a long line. Free guided tours daily every 15-20min. In summer, tours usually conclude around 6pm in favor of an open house format.)* The US Congress first assembled in nearby **Congress Hall,** at Chestnut and 6th. While soaking up the history, guests can take a reclining rest in one of the plush Senate chairs. *(Self-guided tour with rangers available to answer questions.)* Its predecessor, the First Continental Congress, united against the British in **Carpenters' Hall,** in the middle of the block bounded by 3rd, 4th, Walnut, and Chestnut St., now a mini-museum heralding the carpenters responsible for such architectural achievements as Old City Hall and the Pennsylvania State House. *(Open Tu-Su 10am-4pm.)* North of Independence Hall sits a 2080 lb. chunk of metal, originally built as a fully operative communication device. Nowadays at the **Liberty Bell Pavilion,** freedom may ring but the (cracked) **Liberty Bell** does not. *(Open 9am-8pm. Free.)*

The rest of the park preserves residential and commercial buildings of the Revolutionary era. On the northern edge of the Mall, a replica of Ben Franklin's home presides over **Franklin Court,** between 3rd and 4th St. The original abode was unsentimentally razed by the statesman's heirs in 1812 in order to erect an apartment complex. That project didn't endure, and today the imitation historical home exudes the same quirkiness that defined Franklin's character. The home contains an underground museum, a 20min. movie, a replica of his printing office, and phones that allow guests to lend an ear to the quips of long-dead political and literary luminaries. *(318 Market St. Open daily 10am-6pm. Free.)* On a more somber note, in Washington Sq., a statue of the army general and first American president namesake nobly presides over the **Tomb of the Unknown Soldier,** where an eternal flame commemorates the fallen heroes of the Revolutionary War.

Adjacent to the house where Jefferson drafted the Declaration of Independence, the **Balch Institute for Ethnic Studies** is a more academic glimpse into events in America's social history, such as the plight of Japanese Americans during World War II. *(18 S. 7th St. ☎925-8090. Open M-Sa 10am-4pm. $3; students, seniors, and under 12 $1.50; Sa 10am-noon free.)* Across the street, the **Atwater-Kent Museum** traces Philadelphia's History. Ben Franklin will probably feel like an old friend by the time you digest all of these Independent offerings. *(15 S. 17th. ☎922-3031. Open M-Th 10am-5pm, F 10am-3pm, Su noon-5pm.)*

OLD CITY CULTURAL DISTRICT

Religion and money are often at odds, but the two convene in the area above Market St. by the Delaware River to form the city's most unsung tourist region. A coin collector's delight, Philadelphia's branch of the **US Mint,** at 5th and Arch St., displays every US commemorative coin ever patented. Money does not grow on trees according to the self-guided tour that explains how it *is* made. (☎408-0230. Open July-Aug. daily 9am-4pm; Sept.-Apr. M-F 9am-4:30pm; May-June M-Sa 9am-4:30pm. Free.)

Long before the US Mint, a penniless Ben Franklin arrived in Philadelphia in 1723 and strolled by the colorful and clustered rowhouses that line the narrow **Elfreth's Alley,** near 2nd and Arch St. The vigorous neighborhood—the oldest continuously inhabited street in America—provides a shaded retreat from 21st century blaring horns and a window into the daily lives of Philadelphia patriots. A museum gives a peak inside and some alley history. (126 Elfreth's Alley. Open Tu-Sa 10am-4pm, Su noon-4pm; Jan.-Feb. Sa 10am-4pm, Su noon-4pm.) At the **Betsy Ross House,** arguably the most celebrated female patriot speaks through child-oriented placards to convey the seamstress skills that led her to sew the first Stars and Stripes in 1777. (239 Arch St. ☎627-5343. Open daily 10am-5pm. Suggested donation $2, children $1.)

On a quirkier foot, the Temple University School of Podiatric Medicine houses the **Shoe Museum,** on the corner of 8th and Race St. This 6th fl. collection features footwear from the famous feet of Reggie Jackson, Lady Bird Johnson, Dr. J, Nancy Reagan, and others. (☎625-5243. Tours W and F 9am-noon; tours are limited, call for appointment.) The powder-blue "marvel near the mint," **Benjamin Franklin Bridge,** off Race and 5th St., in addition to connecting Philadelphia to New Jersey, provides an expansive view of the city for un-vertigoed folks.

SOCIETY HILL AND THE WATERFRONT

Society Hill proper begins to the east of where Independence Mall ends, on Walnut St. between Front and 7th St. Independence Mall may halt at Walnut St. but the history continues to preside in 200-year-old townhouses over cobblestone walks illuminated by electric "gaslights." Flames don't have a chance in **Head House Sq.,** at 2nd and Pine St., which holds the distinction of being America's oldest firehouse and marketplace and now houses restaurants and boutiques. Bargain hunters can test their haggling skills at an outdoor **flea market** on summer weekends. (☎790-0782. Open June-Aug. Sa noon-11pm, Su noon-6pm.)

South of Head House Sq., the **Mummer's Museum** at Washington Ave. swells with the glitz and glamour of old costumes. Although it may look more like a Village People reunion, each Jan., Philadelphia laborers do their best Mardis Gras impression when construction workers, policemen, and other participants adorn themselves with sequins and feathers for a rowdy New Year's Day parade. (1100 S. 2nd St. ☎336-3050. Open Tu-Sa 9:30am-5pm, Su noon-5pm; closed Su July-Aug. Free string band concerts Tu evenings. $2.50, seniors and children $2.)

A looming, neon sign at the easternmost end of Market St. welcomes visitors to **Penn's Landing,** the largest freshwater port in the world. The USS Olympia, the oldest steel warship still afloat, served as Commodore Dewey's flagship during the Spanish-American War. The USS Becuna, a WWII submarine, also bobs at the dock. (☎923-8181. Tours daily 10am-5pm.) Philadelphian shipbuilding, cargo, and immigration unfold at the **Independence Seaport Museum.** Kids can get their sea legs under them at the "Boats Float" exhibit, which welcomes junior sailors aboard ships. (☎925-5439. Open 10am-5pm. Museum $5, seniors $4, children $2.50; museum and ships $7.50/$6/$3.50.) Finish the waterfront day in relaxing fashion at a free **waterfront concert** Apr. to Oct. (☎629-3257. Big bands Th nights, children's theater Su.)

CENTER CITY

As the financial and commercial hub of Philly, there's barely enough room to accommodate the professionals who cram into **Center City,** the area bounded by 12th, 23rd, Vine, and Pine St. Although rife with business activity during the daytime, the region retires early at night. Presiding over it all, the ornate wedding cake of thick granite and marble, **City Hall,** Broad and Market St., remains the nation's largest working municipal building. Until 1908, it reigned as the tallest building in the US, aided by the 37 ft. statue of William Penn stretching toward the heavens. A sentimentally historic municipal statute prohibited building higher than the apex of Penn's hat until Reagan-era entrepreneurs overturned the law in the mid-80s, launching independent and historical Philadelphia into the modernism of the skyscraper era. Unless you're afraid of heights, a commanding view of the city awaits in the building's tower. *(☎686-2840. Open M-F 10am-4pm; last elevator 4pm. Suggested donation $1. Tour daily 12:30pm.)* The country's first art museum and school, the **Pennsylvania Academy of Fine Art** dwells in the shadows of City Hall at Broad and Cherry St. Permanent displays include artwork by Winslow Homer and Mary Cassatt, while a June 2001 exhibit will celebrate notable creations of the Academy's own alumni. *(118 N. Broad St. ☎972-2060. Open M-Tu and Th-Sa 10am-5pm, W 10am-8pm, Su 11am-5pm. Tours M-F 11:30am and 1:30pm, Sa-Su noon and 2pm. $5, students with ID and seniors $4, ages 5-11 $3; additional charge for special exhibits.)* Across from City Hall, behind an alluring gate, lurks the mysterious **Masonic Temple.** The heavy wooden doors vault collections of books and other artifacts dating back to 1873 that can be viewed on a 45min. tour. *(1 N. Broad St., at JFK Blvd. ☎988-1917. Tours M-F hourly 10am-3pm except noon; Sept.-June Sa 10 and 11am. Free.)*

RITTENHOUSE SQUARE

The masons apparently left their mark in the brick-laden **Rittenhouse Sq. District,** a subset of Center City bounded by Broad, Market, South, and the Schuylkill River. This shaded region of town cradles the musical and dramatic pulse of the city, housing multiple performing arts centers. Not short on other means of tourist entertainment, Rittenhouse Sq. offers visitors two distinctly dissimilar museum options. For best results, digest your lunch before digesting the bizarre and often gory medical abnormalities displayed at the highly intriguing **Mütter Museum.** Among the potentially unsettling fascinations are a wall of skulls and human horns. *(19 S. 22nd St. ☎563-3737. Open Tu-Sa 10am-4pm. $8, students with ID, seniors, and ages 6-18 $5.)* Just south of the square, the more benign **Rosenbach Museum and Library** permanently displays the original manuscript of James Joyce's *Ulysses* and the collected illustrations of Maurice Sendak, among rotating exhibits. *(2010 Delancey St. ☎732-1600. Open Sept.-July Tu-Su 11am-4pm. Guided 1¼hr. tours $5, students, seniors, and children $3. Last tour 2:45pm.)*

PARKWAY/MUSEUM DISTRICT

Fittingly nicknamed "America's Champs-Elysées," the **Benjamin Franklin Pkwy.,** replete with a United Nations-esque international flag row, cuts a wide swath through William Penn's original grid of city streets. Built in the 20s, this tree-lined boulevard connects Center City with Fairmount Park and the Schuylkill River.

A modern assemblage of everything scientific, the **Franklin Institute** at 20th and Ben Franklin Pkwy., would make the old inventor proud and is even more interactive than standard science museums. The newly installed skybike allows guests to explore scientific theories while pedaling through the air. *(☎448-1200. Open daily 9:30am-5pm. $9.75, over 62 and ages 4-11 $8.50.)* Within the scientific depths of the Institute, the **Imax Theater** thrills audiences with 180° and 4½ stories of optical oohs and aahs. *(☎448-1111. Shows on the hr. Su-Th 10am-4pm, F-Sa 10am-9pm except for 6pm. $7.50. Advance tickets recommended.)* Not to be outdone, **Fels Planetarium** boasts an advanced computer-driven system that projects a simulation of life billions of years beyond ours. Lively laser shows flash and blind on F and Sa nights. *(☎448-1388. Shows M-F 12:15 and 2:15pm, Sa 10:15am, 12:15, and 2:15pm. $6, seniors and children $5. Exhibits and a show $12.75/$10.50. Exhibits and both shows $14.75/$12.50.)* Opposite Fels, at the **Academy of Natural Sciences,** 19th and Ben Franklin Pkwy., budding archaeologists can try their hand at dinosaur fossil digging. Through May 2001, guests will be able to putt their way through the museum full of live animals with the interactive Planet of Golf exhibit. *(☎299-1000. Open M-F 10am-4:30pm, Sa-Su and holidays 10am-5pm. $8.50, seniors and military $7.75, ages 3-12 $7. Wheelchair accessible.)*

Sylvester Stallone may have etched the sight of the **Philadelphia Museum of Art** into the minds of movie buffs everywhere when he bolted up the stately front stairs in *Rocky*, but it is the artwork that has solidified the museum's fine reputation. A world-class collection includes Picasso's *Three Musicians* and Toulouse-Lautrec's *At the Moulin Rouge*, as well as extensive Asian, Egyptian, and decorative art collections. Lighten up on W evenings with free films, talks, music, and food. The artistic adventure continues in 2001 when the work of Alice Neel will be on display. *(☎ 763-8100. Open Tu and Th-Su 10am-5pm, W 10am-8:45pm. Tours daily 10am-3pm. $8, students, seniors, and ages 5-18 $5; free Su before 1pm.)* A casting of the Gates of Hell outside the **Rodin Museum,** 22nd St., guards the portal of human passion, anguish, and anger in the most extensive collection of the prolific sculptor's works this side of the Seine. *(☎ 563-1948. Open Tu-Su 10am-5pm. $3 suggested donation.)*

In a reversal of convention, not to mention *Monopoly* rules, guests pay to get into prison, not out of it, at the castle-like **Eastern State Penitentiary,** on Fairmount Ave. at 22nd St. Once a ground-breaking institution of criminal rehabilitation, self- and and other-guided tours twist through the moldering dimness Al Capone once called home. *(☎ 236-3300. Open May to early Nov. Th-Su 10am-5pm. Tours hourly. $7, students and seniors $5, children $3, under 5 not permitted.)* **The Free Library of Philadelphia,** 20th and Vine St., scores with a library of orchestral music and one of the nation's largest rare book collections. Philadelphia art students frequently seek sketching subjects and inspiration amid the classical architectural appearance of the building. *(☎ 686-5322. Open M-W 9am-9pm, Th-F 9am-6pm, Sa 9am-5pm; Oct.-May also Su 1-5pm.)*

FAIRMOUNT PARK

Larger than any other city park and covered with bike trails and picnic areas, Fairmount Park offers city-weary vacationers the adventure of the great outdoors, not to mention stirring vistas of the Schuylkill River, within a stone's throw of urban museums. The Grecian ruins by the waterfall immediately behind the museum are the abandoned **Waterworks.** Free tours featuring Waterworks architecture, technology, and social history meet on Aquarium Dr. behind the Art Museum. *(☎ 685-4935. Open Sa-Su 1-3:30pm.)* Further down the river, the prevalent college influence on Philly is apparent in the spectacular line of crew clubs forming the historic **Boathouse Row.** *(Admission to most mansions $2.50.)* The Museum of Art hosts $3 guided tours of Boathouse Row on W and Su and trolley tours to some of the mansions in Fairmount Park. The area is Philly's most popular **in-line skating** spot. Rental blades are available from **Wilburger's** kiosk, on Kelly Dr. south of Boathouse Row, but you'll have to share the paths with the countless joggers who also seek recreation and the refreshment of a river breeze. *(☎ 765-7470. Open May to Sept. 6 W-F 4-8pm, Sa-Su 9am-6pm. $5 per hr., $25 per day.)* In the northern arm of Fairmount Park, trails follow the secluded Wissahickon Creek for 5 mi., as the concrete city fades to a distant memory. The **Japanese House and Garden,** off Montgomery Dr. near Belmont Ave. is designed in the style of a 17th-century *shoin;* the authentic garden offers the utmost in tranquility, leaving guests with all the peace of mind of a yoga class. *(☎ 878-5097. Open May to early Sept. Tu-Su 10am-4pm; mid-Sept. to Oct. Sa-Su 10am-4pm. $2.50, seniors and students $2.) Some neighborhoods surrounding the park are not safe. The park is not safe at night.*

UNIVERSITY CITY

The **University of Pennsylvania (UPenn)** and **Drexel University,** located across the Schuylkill from Center City, are in west Philly within easy walking distance of the 30th St. station. The Penn campus, a thriving assemblage of luscious green lawns, red brick quadrangles, and young Ivy League minds, contrasts sharply with the dilapidated buildings and deteriorating community surrounding it. Ritzy shops and hip cafes spice up 36th St. A statue of the omnipresent Benjamin Franklin, who founded the university in 1740, greets visitors at the entrance to the Penn campus on 34th and Walnut St. *Much of the area surrounding University City is unsafe at night—try not to travel alone.*

MID-ATLANTIC

The **University Museum of Archeology and Anthropology,** 33rd and Spruce St., journeys through three floors of the world's major cultures under a beautiful stone-and-glass rotunda. (☎898-4001. Open June-Aug. Tu-Sa 10am-4:30pm; Sept.-May Tu-Sa 10am-4:30pm, Su 1-5pm. Suggested donation $5, students and over 62 $2.50.) In 1965, Andy Warhol had his first one-man show at the **Institute of Contemporary Art,** 36th and Sansom St., which has stayed on the cutting edge to this day with changing exhibitions in all media. (☎898-7108. Open during academic terms W-F noon-8pm, Sa-Su 11am-5pm. $3, students, artists, and seniors $2; Su 11am-1pm free.) North of the University area, the **Philadelphia Zoo,** 34th and Girard St., the oldest zoo in the country, houses more than 1700 animals, wild exhibits, and kid-friendly programs. (☎243-1100. Open M-F 9:30am-4:45pm, Sa-Su 9:30am-5:45pm. $10, seniors and ages 2-11 $8. Parking $5.)

🎵 ENTERTAINMENT

The **Academy of Music,** Broad and Locust St., modeled after Milan's La Scala, houses the **Philadelphia Orchestra.** Under Wolfgang Sawallisch's expert baton-waving direction, the orchestra performs Sept. to May. (☎893-1930. Tickets $15-90. $5 general admission tickets go on sale at the Locust St. entrance 45min. before F-Sa concerts. Tu and Th student rush tickets 30min. before show $8.) The theater is also home to the **Pennsylvania Ballet,** tippy-toeing six runs yearly (☎551-7000; tickets $23-85).

The **Mann Music Center,** on George's Hill near 52nd and Parkside Ave. in Fairmount Park, hosts the Philadelphia Orchestra, jazz, and rock concerts with 5000 seats under cover and 10,000 on outdoor benches and lawns. Tickets are also available from the Academy of Music box office on Broad and Locust St. From June through Aug., free lawn tickets for the orchestra are available from the visitors center at 16th and JFK Blvd. on the day of a performance. (☎567-0707. Real seats $10-32.) The **Robin Hood Dell East** (☎685-9560), Strawberry Mansion Dr. in Fairmount Park, brings in top names in pop, jazz, gospel, and ethnic dance in July and Aug. The Philadelphia Orchestra holds several free performances here in summer, and as many as 30,000 people gather on the lawn.

Many of Philadelphia's most appealing cultural events take a leave of absence with the city's students come summertime. During the school year, however, theatrical entertainment bustles like a library during final exams. The students of the world-renowned **Curtis Institute of Music,** 1726 Locust St., give free concerts (mid-Oct. to Apr. M, W, F at 8pm). **Merriam Theater,** 250 S. Broad St., Center City, stages performances ranging from student works to Broadway hits (☎732-5446; box office open M-Sa 10am-5:30pm). The **Old City,** from Chestnut to Vine and Front to 4th St., comes alive the first F of every month (Oct.-June) for the **First Friday** celebration. The streets fill with live music, and many art galleries open their doors, enticing visitors with free food.

Philly gets physical with plenty of sports venues. Philly's four professional teams play a short ride away on the Broad St. subway line. Philadelphia's boys of summer, the baseball **Phillies** (☎463-1000), and football's **Eagles** (☎463-5500) play games at **Veterans Stadium,** Broad St. and Pattison Ave.; the **First Union Center,** across the street, fills to capacity on winter nights to support the NBA's **76ers** (☎339-7676) and the NHL's **Flyers** (☎755-9700). Call ☎336-3600 for general First Union Center information. General admission tickets for baseball and hockey start at $10; football and basketball tickets go for $15-50.

🎦 NIGHTLIFE

Check the Friday *Philadelphia Inquirer* for entertainment listings. *City Paper*, distributed Th, and the *Philadelphia Weekly,* distributed on W, have weekly listings of city events (free at newsstands and markets). Gay and lesbian weeklies *Au Courant* (free) and *PGN* (75¢) list events taking place throughout the Delaware Valley region. Along **South St.** toward the river, clubbers jam to the sounds of live music on weekends. Many pubs line **2nd St.** near Chestnut St., close to the Bank St. hostel. **Delaware Ave.** (a.k.a. **Columbus Blvd.**), running along Penn's Landing, has recently become a trendy local hotspot, full of nightclubs and restaurants attracting droves of young urban professionals and the college crowd. Most bars and clubs that cater to a gay clientele congregate along **Camac St., S. 12th St.,** and **S. 13th St.**

Kat Man Du, Pier 25 (☎629-1724), at N. Columbus Blvd. Who would've thunk tropical paradise could be found in the shadows of the Ben Franklin Bridge and on the banks of the Delaware River. Sport your favorite Hawaiian shirt as you escape to palm tree planet and an open-air deck at Philly's hottest summer venue. Open daily noon-2am. Happy hour M-F 5-7pm, $2 calls and domestic beers. 50¢ drafts Tu and Th 10pm-midnight. Cover M-Th after 8:30pm $5; F-Sa $8; Su $2, after 5pm $5.

The Khyber, 56 S. 2nd St. (☎238-5888). A speakeasy during the days of prohibition. A young crowd now gathers legally to listen to a range of punk, metal, and hip-hop music. The ornate wooden bar was shipped over from England in 1876. Belly-pleasing vegetarian sandwiches are $3. Open daily 11am-2am. Happy Hour M-F 5-7pm. Live music daily from 10pm. Cover $5-15.

The Trocadero (☎922-5483), 10th and Arch St. Aged 120 years, "the Troc," the oldest operative Victorian theater in the US, hosts big name bands. Upstairs, the Balcony bar may be open jointly or separately. Cover $6-16. Advance tickets through Ticketmaster.

Warmdaddy's (☎627-8400), on Front St. on the corner of Market St. Bayou dreamers will eat up this Cajun club renowned for its blues, diversity, and W night seafood bashes ($22 per person for lobster, shrimp, and crab). Open Tu-Sa 5pm-2am, Su noon-2am. Sets start at 7pm in summer, 8:30pm in winter. Tu free jam night. Cover W-Th and Su $5, F-Sa $10.

Woody's, 202 S. 13th St. (☎545-1893). An outgoing gay crowd frequents this lively, aptly named club. Lunch daily noon-3:30pm. Bar open M-Sa 11am-2am, Su noon-2am. Happy hour 5-7pm daily with 25¢ off all drinks. Voices and hearts sing M karaoke nights while minds stay sharp Tu trivia nights. Dance to country tunes Tu and Su, or grind to house music F-Sa. W is all ages night.

DAYTRIP FROM PHILADELPHIA

VALLEY FORGE. It was the winter of 1777-78, not the British, that almost crushed the Continental Army. When George Washington selected Valley Forge as the winter camp for his 12,000 troops following defeat at Germantown in Oct., the General could not have predicted the wretched fate that would befall his troops. Three arduous months of starvation, bitter cold, and disease nearly halved his forces. At times without blankets or even shoes, only crude meals of flour-and-water "firecake," women who volunteered nursing services, and hope sustained the men's spirits. But it was not until Baron Friedrich von Steuben arrived with fresh troops and supplies that recovery (and spring) seemed possible. Renewed, the Continental Army left Valley Forge and its harrowing memory on June 19, 1778, to win the Battle of Monmouth and help forge a nation.

The hills that once tried the frost-bitten soldiers roll through **Valley Forge National Historic Park.** Slightly more comfortable than frostbite is the 10 mi. self-guided auto tour which begins at the **visitors center.** The center also features a small museum and 18min. film. The tour passes **Washington's headquarters,** reconstructed soldier huts and fortifications, and the Grand Parade Ground where the Continental Army drilled. Visitors can also hop aboard a **bus tour.** The park has three picnic areas but no camping; those seeking to pitch a tent can obtain information at the visitors center which distributes a list of nearby campgrounds. Joggers can take a revolutionary trip down memory lane on a paved 6 mi. trail through deer-populated forests. (☎610-783-1077. Park open daily sunrise-sunset. Grounds free. Center open daily 9am-5pm. Film shown every 30min. 9am-4:30pm. Washington's headquarters $2, under 17 free. Audio tapes $9; tape player $15; no audio players rented after 2pm. Bus tours run hourly 9:30am-4pm. $5.50, children $4.50.)

Valley Forge lies 35min. from Philadelphia by car. To get there, take I-76 west from Philly for about 12 mi. Get off at the Valley Forge exit (Exit 24), then take Rte. 202 S for 1 mi. and Rte. 422 W for 1½ mi. to another Valley Forge exit. **SEPTA** runs buses to the visitors center M-F only; catch #125 at 16th and JFK (fare $3.10).

LANCASTER COUNTY ☎ 717

The Amish, the Mennonites, and the Brethren, three groups of German Anabaptists who fled persecution in Deutschland (thus the misnomer "Pennsylvania Dutch"), sought freedom to pursue their own religion in the rolling countryside of Lancaster County. They successfully escaped censorship, but they have not escaped attention. Ironically, the simplicity of the undeveloped, unassuming Amish lifestyle continues to fascinate a technologically dependent society. As a result, the "Plain Peoples's" chief industry is now tourism. Thousands of visitors flock to this pastoral area every year to glimpse a modest way of life that eschews modern conveniences like motorized vehicles, television, and cellular phones. Point but don't shoot; many Amish have religious objections to being photographed.

✈🛈 ORIENTATION AND PRACTICAL INFORMATION

Lancaster County covers an area almost the size of Rhode Island. County seat Lancaster City, in the heart of Dutch country, has red brick row houses huddled around historic **Penn Sq.** The rural areas are mostly accessible by car (unless you've got a horse and buggy), but it is easy to see the tourist sites with a bike or the willingness to walk the mile or two between public transportation drop-offs. You won't need to be married to travel the country roads of Lancaster where **Intercourse** suspiciously leads to **Paradise**. From Paradise, **U.S. 30 W** plots a straight course into **Fertility**. And you thought these were wholesome people. In all seriousness, visitors should be aware that the area is heavily Mennonite, so most businesses and all major attractions close on Su.

Trains: Amtrak, 53 McGovern Ave. (☎291-5080), in Lancaster City. To Philadelphia (1hr., 4-8 per day, $13) and Pittsburgh (6½hr., 3-5 per day, $52-78).

Buses: Capital Trailways (☎397-4861), on the ground fl. of the train station. To Philadelphia (2hr., 5 per day, $15) and Pittsburgh (6hr., 2 per day, $38). Open daily 7am-4:30pm.

Public Transit: Red Rose Transit, 45 Erick Rd. (☎397-4246). Service around Lancaster and the surrounding countryside. Buses run M-F 9am-3:30pm and after 6:30pm, Sa-Su all day. Base fare $1, over 65 free.

Visitor Info: Pennsylvania Dutch Visitors Bureau Information Center, 501 Greenfield Rd. (☎299-8901 or 800-735-2629), on the east side of Lancaster City off Rte. 30, dispenses info on the region, including excellent maps and walking tours. Open M-Sa 8am-6pm, Su 8am-5pm; daily Sept.-May 8:30am-5pm. **Downtown Lancaster Visitors Center,** at the corner of Queen and Vine St. Open M-F 8:30am-4:50pm, Sa 9am-3pm, Su 10am-2pm.

Post Office: 1400 Harrisburg Pike (☎396-6900). Open M-F 7:30am-7pm, Sa 9am-2pm. **ZIP code:** 17604. **Area code:** 717.

⌂ ACCOMMODATIONS

Hundreds of hotels and B&Bs cluster in this area, as do several working farms with guesthouses. Visitors centers can provide room information or, as part of a religious outreach mission, the amicable staff at the **Mennonite Information Center** (see **Sights,** below) will try to find you a Mennonite-run guest house for about the same price. About the only things that outnumber cows here are the campgrounds.

Smoketown Village Guest House, 2495 Old Philadelphia Pike (☎393-5975), 4 mi. east of Lancaster. Guests snuggle under Amish quilts in impeccably maintained floral rooms. Mennonite proprietors bubble with sightseeing suggestions. Continental breakfast awaits sleepy-eyed guests. Rooms with shared or private bath, TV, and A/C $32-38.

Kendig Tourist Home, 105 N. Ronks Rd. (☎393-5358 or 687-6294), left off Rte. 30 E just past Flory's Campgrounds. Spotless and homey rooms (all with TV, some with A/C and private bath) offer maximum comfort at minimal cost as the cornstalks grow outside your window. Hear the horses hooves and neighs of the Amish neighbors from dawn until the wee hours. Singles $26; doubles $36.

Pennsylvania Dutch Motel, 2275 N. Reading Rd. (☎336-5559), at Exit 21 off Pennsylvania Turnpike. Spacious, clean rooms with cable TV and A/C. The helpful hostess eagerly distributes written directions to major sights. Singles $50; doubles $54. Discounts Nov.-Mar.

Old Mill Stream Camping Manor, 2249 Rte. 30 E (☎299-2314). Shaded campground cramped between the family-oriented Dutch Wonderland amusement park and the Continental Inn, 4 mi. east of Lancaster City. The campground buzzes with a game room, playground, basketball court, volleyball court, and horseshoes. Laundry facilities and general store. Tenters are given stream-side sites. Office open daily 8am-9pm; off-season 8am-8pm. Sites $18, with hook-up $22. Reservations recommended.

◖ FOOD

Amish food, wholesome and generous in portion, is characterized by a heavy potato and vegetable emphasis. A palatable alternative to high-priced "family-style" restaurants endures at the **farmers markets** and produce stands which dot the roadway. At the ▧**Central Market,** in downtown Lancaster City at the northwest corner of Penn Sq., simply dressed Pennsylvania Dutch invade the city to sell affordable fresh fruit, meats, cheeses, vegetables, sandwiches, and desserts alongside more conventionally dressed vendors (open Tu and F 6am-4pm, Sa 6am-2pm). The Lancaster restaurant scene surrounds the market. One of the finest culinary options lurks in the depths of the Central Mall: **Isaac's Deli,** 44 N. Queen St., with the $5.25 Phoenix sandwich (ham, sliced pineapple, provolone) and classic $3 ice cream float. (☎394-5544. Open M-Th 10am-9pm, F-Sa 10am-10pm, Su 11am-9pm.) Nearby, **My Place,** 12 N. Queen St., can provide a slice of Italy or scrumptious pizza ($1.30) in Amish country. The filling cheesesteak hoagie ($4) will satisfy the ravenous while light eaters can pick at generous salads for $2-3. (☎393-6405. Open M-Th 10:30am-10pm, F-Sa 10:30am-11pm.) The huge **Bird-in-Hand Market** complex on Rte. 340 at the corner of Maple Ave. is more pricey than the Amish road stands but offers an array of non-perishable goods as well as ready-to-eat options. (☎393-9674. Open July-Aug. W-Sa 8:30am-5:30pm; Apr.-June and Nov. W and F-Sa 8:30am-5:30pm; Jan.-Mar. and Dec. F-Sa 8:30am-5:30pm.) At the **Amish Barn,** 3029 Old Philadelphia Pike, quilts surround the tables where patrons feed on Amish specialties such as $2 homemade chicken corn soup and $3.50 Amish barn apple dumpling. (☎768-8886. Open daily late May to Sept. 5 8am-9pm; Sept. 6 to Oct. and Apr. to Memorial Day 8am-8pm; Nov. 8am-7pm; closed Jan.-Mar.) Except for the chains, most restaurants close on Su.

◉ SIGHTS

To develop an understanding and appreciation of Amish culture, visit the informative **People's Place.** The complex covers most of a block with bookstores and craft shops. An exhibit called **20Q,** referring to the 20 most-asked questions about the Amish, details the nuances of the unique lifestyle from barn raising to hat styles. A film, *Who Are the Amish?*, takes care of any lingering curiosity. *(3513 Old Philadelphia Pike, on Main St./Rte. 340, in Intercourse, 11 mi. east of Lancaster City. ☎768-7171. Open M-Sa 9:30am-8pm; early Sept. to late May M-Sa 9:30am-5pm. Film shown every 30min. 9:30am-5pm; $5, seniors $4, under 12 $2.50. Film and 20Q $8/$7/$4.)* To get the story from the

---

PIE IN YOUR EYE The most distinctive culinary specialty of Lancaster County is the traditional Amish dessert, **shoofly pie,** popularized in the days before the refrigerator (or in contemporary Amish houses without refrigerators) because of its resistance to spoiling. Once removed from the oven, its treacly sweetness attracted droves of flies and thus gained its name from the constant "shoo fly" calls of its baker. Of equal authenticity if less publicity is the **whoopie pie,** a cookie-sized object with buttercream frosting sandwiched between two rounds of chocolate, pumpkin, or red velvet cake. These can be found at most bake shops for about 50¢ per pie.

people who live it, stop in the **Mennonite Information Center.** The Mennonites, unlike the Amish, believe that outreach is laudable and established this center to help tourists distinguish between the two faiths. Exceptionally cordial hostesses also offer to guide guests through a Mennonite Tabernacle reproduction. *(☎299-0964. Millstream Rd. off Rte. 30 east of Lancaster. Open M-Sa 8am-5pm.)* For the most authentic exploration of Amish country by car, wind through the verdant fields off U.S. 340 near Bird-in-the-Hand. Cyclists can capture the anti-electricity spirit on the tourism office's **Lancaster County Heritage Bike Tour,** a 46 mi., reasonably flat route past covered bridges and historic sites. A visit to Lancaster is not complete without using the locals' preferred mode of transportation; **Ed's 3 mi. buggy ride** bumps along an hour of scenic backwoods and countryside. *(On Rte. 896, 1½ mi. south of U.S. 30 W in Strasburg. M-Sa 9am-dusk. $7, under 10 $3.50.)* **Amish Country Tours** offers 2½hr. trips that include visits to one-room schools, Amish cottage industries, authentic farms, and a vineyard. *(☎786-3600. Tours given Apr.-Oct. M-Sa 10:30am and 2pm, Su 11:30am. $18, ages 4-11 $11.)* Tourist offices have info on the pseudo-Amish experiences available, from staying in an Amish-style house to watching a blacksmith. Old country crafts and food can be found at the **Pennsylvania Dutch Folk Festival,** but plan to visit early summer to catch it. *(☎610-683-8707. North of Lancaster off I-81 S, Exit 31. End of June and beginning of July. $10, ages 5-12 $5.)*

GETTYSBURG   ☎717

July 1-3, 1863, remain as perhaps the most memorable dates of the US Civil War. On those three sweltering summer days, Union and Confederate forces clashed at Gettysburg in bloody warfare, leaving lifeless men littered across the southern Pennsylvania countryside. The Union forces would ultimately prevail, derailing Southern hopes of advancement, but at a high price: over 50,000 casualties between North and South. Four months later, President Lincoln arrived in Gettysburg to dedicate the Gettysburg National Cemetery, where 979 unidentified Union soldiers rest. Today, the National Soldier's Monument towers where Lincoln commemorated the sacrifices of the Civil War soldier in his legendary Gettysburg Address. Each year, thousands of visitors visit these fields and are reminded of the President's call to "resolve that these dead shall not have died in vain."

🔢 PRACTICAL INFORMATION. Inaccessible by Greyhound or Amtrak, Gettysburg is in south-central Pennsylvania, off U.S. 15, about 30 mi. south of Harrisburg. In town, **Towne Trolley** will shuttle you to some locations, but not around the battlefield. (Runs Apr.-Oct. $1.) The **Gettysburg Travel Council,** 35 Carlisle St., is in the old train depot where Lincoln disembarked. (☎334-6274. Open daily 9am-5pm.) **Post Office:** 115 Buford Ave. **ZIP code:** 17325. **Area code:** 717.

📍 ACCOMMODATIONS. Follow Rte. 34 N to Rte. 233 to reach the closest hostel, **Ironmasters Mansion Hostel (HI-AYH),** 20 mi. away from Gettysburg, within the entrance of Pine Grove Furnace State Park and left at the Twirly Tap ice cream sign. Unusually large and luxurious, the 1820s building holds 46 beds in a tranquil and gorgeous area. Spacious porches, an ornate dining room, and the decadent jacuzzi make this hostel seem more like a Club Med resort. (☎486-7575. Reception 7:30-9:30am and 5-10pm. Laundry facilities available. Dorms $12, non-members $15. Linen $2. Internet access $3. By reservation only Dec.-Feb.) **Artillery Ridge,** 610 Taneytown Rd., 1 mi. south of the Military Park Visitors Center on Rte. 134, maintains over 200 campsites with access to showers, a riding stable, laundry facilities, a pool, nightly movies, a fishing pond, and bike rentals. Don't rely on catching a meal out of the pond; angling ethics insist that fish be caught and then thrown back. (☎334-1288. Open Apr.-Nov. Sites $15.50, with hook-up $21; $4 each additional person.) Surrounding the battlefield, multiple motels line Steinwehr Rd., but finding summer rates below $50 is difficult. Slightly less expensive options such as **The Red Carpet Inn,** 2450 Emmitsburg Rd. (☎334-5026 or 800-336-1345), are 4 mi. west of town down Steinwehr Rd., which becomes Emmitsburg.

HERSHEY'S CANDYLAND Around the turn of the century, Milton S. Hershey, a Mennonite resident of eastern Pennsylvania, discovered how to mass market a rare and expensive luxury—chocolate. Today, the company that bears his name operates the world's largest chocolate factory, in Hershey, about 45min. from Lancaster. East of town at **Hersheypark,** the **Chocolate World Visitors Center** presents a free, automated tour through a simulated chocolate factory. After the tour, visitors emerge into a pavilion full of chocolate cookies, discounted chocolate candy, and fashionable Hershey sportswear. Near the visitors center, the **Hershey Museum** probes more deeply into Milton Hershey's life and showcases his 19th-century Apostolic Clock with an hourly procession of clockwork apostles past a clockwork Jesus, while Satan periodically appears and a rooster crows to announce Judas's betrayal. *(Park: ☎534-3900. Open June M-F 10am-10pm; July-Aug. M-F 10am-10pm, Sa-Su 10am-11pm; call for hrs. May to early June and Sept. $30, over 54 and ages 3-8 $17; after 5pm $16. Visitors center: ☎800-437-7439. Opens with park and closes 2hr. earlier. "Free" tour: parking $5. Museum: ☎534-3439. Open daily 10am-6pm; Labor Day to Memorial Day 10am-5pm. $5, seniors $4.50, ages 3-15 $2.50. Theme park: ☎534-3860. Open daily mid-June to Aug. 10am-8pm; Sept. to mid-June 10am-5pm. $5.25, seniors $4.75, ages 3-12 $4.)*

⬛ **FOOD.** Hefty rations persist in the town's square and just beyond the entrance to the battlefield. Keep the historical juices flowing at the **Dobbin House,** 89 Steinwehr Rd., Gettysburg's first building (ca. 1776), where guests can create their own grilled burger ($6) and view an Underground Railroad shelter used as a "way station" for the protection of runaway slaves during the Civil War. (☎334-2100. Open Su-Th 9am-10pm, F-Sa 10am-11:30pm. Jazz on the 1st W of each month from 7:30pm.) Near the battlefield, **General Pickett's Restaurant,** 571 Steinwehr Rd., charges $6-12 for a southern-style all-you-can-eat buffet. (☎334-7580. Open M-Sa 11:30am-3:15pm and 4:30-8pm, Su 11:30am-8pm.)

⬛ **SIGHTS.** Visitors can explore Gettysburg in many ways. A sensible start is the **National Military Park Visitors Information Center,** which distributes free maps for an 18 mi. self-guided tour. *(97 Taneytown Rd. ☎334-1124, ext. 431. Visitors center open daily 8am-6pm; early Sept. to late May 8am-5pm. $3, seniors $2, under 15 $2. Park open daily 6am-10pm.)* General admission to the battlefield is free, but prepare to spare a penny or two for a more in-depth look at the historic grounds. Enlightening **park rangers** squeeze into the family wagon to personally guide you through the monuments and landmarks. *(2hr. tour $30 for up to 5 people. Personal tours are popular so arrive by 9am to ensure a time slot.)* If you're not comfortable with inviting a stranger ranger into your car or simply can't fit one, just follow the less comprehensive free walking tour.

Surround yourself with chilling sights and sounds of battle at the **Cyclorama Center,** next to the visitors center. The center shows a 20min. film on the battle every hour, and a 30min. light show revolves around a 9500 sq. ft. mural of the battle. *(☎334-1124, ext. 499. Open daily 9am-5pm. $3, seniors $2.50, ages 6-16 $2.)* Artillery Ridge Campgrounds (see above) rents **bikes** and conducts a 2hr. **horseback tour** by advanced reservation. *(Bikes $15 per half-day, $25 per full-day. Horseback tours $44.)* Adjacent to the campground's office is a meticulously detailed diorama of the Gettysburg battle, along with other exhibits. *($4.50, seniors and children $3.50.)* **Historic Tours** trundles visitors around the battlefield in buses that are nearly as old as the Battle of Gettysburg itself. *(☎334-8000. $12, children $9.)* Straight out of a Stephen King novel, candlelit **ghost walks and ghost stories** in a haunted cellar reawaken the dead. *(55 Steinwehr Ave. ☎337-0445 or 334-8838. Times vary. $6, under 8 free.)*

The grim **Jennie Wade House** preserves the kitchen where Miss Wade, the only civilian killed in the battle of Gettysburg, was mortally wounded by a stray bullet. The hole in the wall, through which the fatal bullet traveled, is still visible today. Legend has it that unmarried women who pass their finger through the fatal bullet hole will be engaged within a year. *(528 Baltimore St. ☎334-4100. Open daily May-Aug. 9am-9pm; Sept.-Apr. 9am-5pm. $5.75, ages 6-11 $3.50.)*

MID-ATLANTIC

PITTSBURGH   ☎412

Those who come to the City of Steel expecting sprawling industry and hordes of
soot-encrusted American Joes are bound to be disappointed. The decline of the
steel industry has meant cleaner air and rivers, and a recent economical renaissance has produced a brighter urban landscape. City officials are desperate to
provide Pittsburgh with a new image, going so far as to propose a theme park
filled with robotic dinosaurs. Throughout renewals, Pittsburgh's neighborhoods
have maintained strong and diverse identities. Admittedly, some of old, sooty
Pittsburgh survives in the suburbs, but one need only ride up the Duquesne
Incline and view downtown from atop Mt. Washington to see how thoroughly
Pittsburgh has entered a new age—and to understand why locals are so proud of
"The 'Burgh."

▐ GETTING THERE AND GETTING AROUND

Airport: Pittsburgh International (☎472-5526), 18 mi. west of downtown by I-279
and Rte. 60 N in Findlay Township. The Port Authority's **28x Airport Flyer** bus serves
downtown and Oakland from the airport (daily every 30min. 6am-11:58pm; $2).
Airline Transportation Company (☎471-2250 or 471-8900) runs to downtown (M-F
every 30min. 6am-11:30pm, Sa-Su every hr. 6am-11pm; $12). Cab to downtown
$30.

Trains: Amtrak, 1100 Liberty Ave. (☎471-6170), at Grant on the northern edge of downtown next to Greyhound and the post office. Generally safe inside, *but be careful walking from here to the city center at night.* To: Philadelphia (8½-11½hr., 2 per day, $44-
82); New York (10-13hr., 1 per day, $59-110); and Chicago (9½-10hr., 3 per day, $54-
100). Station open 24hr.

Buses: Greyhound (☎392-6526), on 11th St. at Liberty Ave. near Amtrak. To: Philadelphia (7hr., 9 per day, $39) and Chicago (8-12hr., 9 per day, $59.50). Open 24hr.

Public Transit: Port Authority of Allegheny County (PAT) (☎442-2000). Downtown: bus
fare free until 7pm; subway (between the 3 downtown stops) free. Beyond downtown:
bus fare $1.25, transfers 25¢, all-day weekend pass $3; subway $1.25, ages 6-11
half-price for bus and subway. Schedules, maps at most subway stations.

Taxi: Peoples Cab, ☎681-3131.

Car Rental: Rent-A-Wreck (☎367-3131 or 800-472-8353), on McKnight St. 7 mi. north
of downtown. $20-25 per day with 100 free mi.; 18¢ per additional mi. Must be 21+
with credit card; limited pre-approved cash rentals. Under 25 $3 per day surcharge.
Open M-F 8am-6pm, Sa 8am-4pm.

✦ ℹ ORIENTATION AND PRACTICAL INFORMATION

Pittsburgh's downtown, the **Golden Triangle,** is shaped by two rivers—the **Allegheny**
to the north and the **Monongahela** to the south—which flow together to form a third,
the **Ohio.** Streets in the Triangle that run parallel to the Monongahela are numbered
one through seven. The **University of Pittsburgh** and **Carnegie-Mellon University** lie east
of the Triangle in Oakland. Don't venture to one of Pittsburgh's many tight-knit
neighborhoods without getting directions first—the city's streets and 40-odd
bridges are notoriously difficult to navigate.

Visitor Info: Pittsburgh Convention and Visitors Bureau, 4 Gateway Center, 18th fl.
(☎281-7711 or 800-359-0758; www.pittsburgh-cvb.org), downtown on Liberty Ave.
Open M-F 9am-5pm, Sa-Su 9am-3pm. There are 4 visitors centers: downtown, Station
Sq. at the foot of Mt. Washington, and 2 at the airport.

Hotlines: Rape Action Hotline, ☎765-2731. 24hr. **Gay, Lesbian, Bisexual Center,**
☎422-0114. Operates M-F 6:30-9:30pm, Sa 3-6pm.

Post Office: 700 Grant St. (☎642-4472). Open M-F 7am-6pm, Sa 7am-2:30pm. **ZIP
code:** 15219. **Area code:** 412.

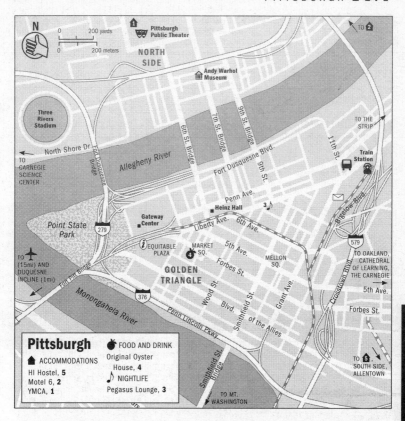

Pittsburgh

ACCOMMODATIONS
HI Hostel, **5**
Motel 6, **2**
YMCA, **1**

🍎 FOOD AND DRINK
Original Oyster
House, **4**
♪ NIGHTLIFE
Pegasus Lounge, **3**

ACCOMMODATIONS

Once a bank, the sparkling 🏠**Pittsburgh Hostel (HI-AYH),** 830 E. Warrington Ave., across the river and up a steep hill in Allentown 1 mi. south of downtown, delivers clean, grade-A hostel living. Amenities include spacious rooms, kitchen, A/C, free parking, a great 4th-floor common room view, and an elevator in a vault. Take bus #52, "Allentown." (☎431-1267. Check-in 8-10am and 5-10pm. Lock-out 10am-5pm. Laundry. Dorms $17, non-members $20. Semi-private singles $23/$26; doubles $41/$47; quads or family rooms $45-52. Linen $1, towels 50¢. Wheelchair accessible.) The **Allegheny YMCA,** 600 W. North Ave., has men's singles in the North Side. (☎321-8594. Laundry, gym, pool. Dorms $21, $64 per week; $5 key deposit.)

Several inexpensive motels can be found on the city's outskirts near the airport. **Motel 6,** 211 Beecham Dr., off I-79 at Exit 16/16B 10 mi. from downtown, supplies standard lodging with A/C and TVs. (☎922-9400. Singles $38; doubles $44; $3 per extra person. Reservations suggested for summer weekends.) **Pittsburgh North Campground,** 6610 Mars Rd., in Cranberry Township, has the area's closest camping, 20min. north of downtown; take I-79 to the Cranberry/Mars exit. (☎724-776-1150. Office open daily 8am-9pm. 110 campsites, showers, swimming. Tent sites for 2 $18, with hook-up $26; $3 per extra adult, $2 per extra child.)

BEES, DOGS, AND OTHER EDIBLE STUFF

Aside from the pizza joints and bars downtown, **Oakland** is the best place to look for a good inexpensive meal. Collegiate watering holes and cafes pack **Forbes Ave.** around the University of Pittsburgh; colorful eateries and shops line **Walnut St.** in Shadyside and **E. Carson St.** in South Side. The **Strip District** on Penn Ave. between 16th and 22nd St. (north of downtown along the Allegheny) bustles with Italian, Greek, and Asian cuisine; the Sa morning **farmers' market** sells an abundance of fresh produce and fish.

▨ **Cafe Zinho,** 238 Spahr St. (☎363-1500), in Oakland. An intimate, tastefully decorated cafe serving light, scrumptious selections. Try the ornately presented chicken salad sandwich with almonds, raisins, and tarragon orange mayonnaise in puff pastry ($8). Open Tu-Th 11:30am-3pm and 5:30pm-10pm, F-Sa until 11pm.

The Original Oyster House, 20 Market Sq. (☎566-7925). Pittsburgh's oldest and perhaps cheapest restaurant and bar. Serves seafood platters ($4-6) and fresh fish sandwiches ($3-5) in a smoky, marble and wrought-iron bar decorated with panoramic shots of Miss America pageants from ages past. Open M-Sa 9am-11pm.

Beehive Coffeehouse and Theater, 3807 Forbes Ave. (☎683-4483). Quirky coffeehouse brimming with cool wall paintings, self-described "fly" staff and clientele, and hot cappuccino ($1.50-2.75). A DJ (W-Th) and live bands (F-Sa) spice things up in the theater at night. Open M-F 10am-2am, Sa-Su 1pm-2am. Cover $5-15.

Union Grille, 413 S. Craig St. (☎681-8620), off Forbes Ave., in Oakland. Gains notoriety for its "honest American food" and cheap draughts ($1.75-3). Veggie sandwiches ($7), crabcakes ($6-14), and house wine ($3.25) please yuppies. Open M-Th 11:30am-10pm, F-Sa 11:30am-11pm, Su 11:30am-7pm.

👁 SIGHTS

The **Golden Triangle** is home to **Point State Park** and its famous 200 ft. fountain. A ride up the **Duquesne Incline,** in the South Side, gives a spectacular view of the city. *(1220 Grandview Ave. ☎381-1665. Open M-Sa 5:30am-12:45am, Su 7am-12:45am; round-trip $2.)* Founded in 1787, the **University of Pittsburgh** stands in the shadow of the 42-story **Cathedral of Learning,** at Bigelow Blvd. between Forbes and 5th Ave. in Oakland. The Cathedral, built in part due to the dimes of Depression-era Pittsburgh schoolchildren, features 25 "nationality classrooms" designed and decorated by artisans from the city's many ethnic traditions. *(☎624-6000. Cassette-guided tours M-F 9am-3pm, Sa 9:30am-3pm, Su 11am-3pm. $3, seniors $2, ages 8-18 50¢.)* **Carnegie-Mellon University** puts up scholars nearby on Forbes Ave. *(☎268-2000.)*

The **Andy Warhol Museum,** on the North Side, is the world's largest museum dedicated to a single artist, supporting seven floors of the Pittsburgh native's material, from pop portraits of Marilyn to screenings of films like *Eat* (39min. of a man eating) and a series of pieces entitled *Oxidation,* made from synthetic polymer paint and urine on canvas. *(117 Sandusky St. ☎237-8300. Open W-Th and Sa-Su 10am-5pm, F 10am-10pm. $7, seniors $6, students and children $4.)* A 20min. walk into the North Side, **The Mattress Factory** is actually a museum, created by light-worker James Turell and artist Yayoi Kausma, of cutting-edge visual and performance art. *(505 Jacksonia Way. ☎231-3169. Follow Sandusky St. to East Commons, then North Commons to Federal St. and then Jacksonia. Open Tu-Sa 10am-5pm, Su 1-5pm. $6, students and seniors $4.)*

Back when Pittsburgh was a bustling steel metropolis, Andrew Carnegie was its biggest robber baron—and its biggest benefactor. Carnegie's most spectacular gift, **The Carnegie,** across the street from the Cathedral of Learning, holds both an art museum and a natural history collection. *(4400 Forbes Ave. ☎622-3131, 622-3289 for tours. Take any bus to Oakland. Open Tu-Sa 10am-5pm, Su 1-5pm; M 10am-5pm in July-Aug. $6, students and ages 3-18 $4, seniors $5.)* Feel an earthquake, climb aboard a WWII submarine, or gaze at the coolest miniature railroad and village around at the **Carnegie Science Center.** *(1 Allegheny Ave., next to Three Rivers Stadium. ☎237-3400. Open Su-F 10am-6pm, Sa 10am-9pm. $10, seniors and ages 3-18 $8; with OmniMax or planetarium $14/$10.)*

Off I-376, east of town in Penn Hills, an eastern suburb of Pittsburgh, lies the first Hindu temple in the US. The **Sri Venkateswara (S.V.) Temple** *(☎373-3380)* is modeled after a temple in Andhra Pradesh, India, and has become a major pilgrimage site for American Hindus since its completion. Non-Hindus can walk through the Great Hall and observe prayer.

HOMESTEAD GRAYSBOX Past the shock-yellow Pirates pennants and computer-generated "Arrrr"-ing buccaneer lining the upper tiers of Three Rivers Stadium, a nondescript gray banner plainly states **"Homestead Grays."** A reminder of the days of the Negro Leagues, part of a segregationist past upon which America waxes both nostalgic and indignant, the pennant quietly reminds those in the know of a baseball team formed in 1910 from Homestead steelworkers. The Grays rose to become a league leader, winning every Negro National League pennant from 1931 to 1939 and several Negro World Series, including the league's last in 1948. Considered by many to be the greatest Negro League team, the Grays vanished into obscurity when the league split. Forbes Field, where they played, was doomed to destruction, and now Three Rivers, which mildly speaks of their legacy, is soon to follow.

▐▌ ENTERTAINMENT AND NIGHTLIFE

Most restaurants and shops carry the weekly *In Pittsburgh* or *City Paper*, great sources for free, up-to-date entertainment listings, nightclubs, and racy personals. The acclaimed **Pittsburgh Symphony Orchestra** performs Sept. through May at **Heinz Hall,** 600 Penn Ave. (☎392-4900), downtown. The **Pittsburgh Public Theater,** in Allegheny Sq. on the North Side, is world-renowned, but charges a pretty penny. (☎316-1600. Box office open daily Oct.-July 10am-showtime. Tickets $20-42; students and children under 27 $10 for shows Su-F.) At gritty **Three Rivers Stadium** on the North Side, the **Pirates** (☎321-2827) hit the hardball from Apr. through Sept., while the **Steelers** (☎323-1200) hit the gridiron from Sept. through Dec.

For nightlife, the Strip downtown is still relatively dense with revelers (relatively, that is, in a town that closes down at 5pm). The hip crowd fills **E. Carson St.** on the South Side, which overflows with regular guys and gals on weekend nights. **Metropol** and the more intimate **Rosebud,** 1600 Smallman St., in the Strip District, fill a spacious warehouse with two dance floors of steely partygoers .(☎261-4512. Metropol doors open 9pm, Rosebud doors open 6pm. Cover $5.) **Nick's Fat City,** 1601-1605 E. Carson St., South Side, features popular local rock 'n' roll bands and $2.75 draughts of Yuengling, a favorite PA brew. (☎481-6880. Open Tu-Sa 11am-2am. Cover varies.) **Jack's,** on E. Carson at S. 12th, South Side, repeatedly earns the moniker "Best Bar in the 'Burgh" by offering lifesaving specials like 25¢ hotdogs (M), 10¢ wings (W), and $2 chicken sandwich to a rowdy but friendly local crowd. (☎431-3644. Open M-Sa 7am-2am, Su 11am-2am. 21+.) The gay and lesbian community flocks to the **Pegasus Lounge,** 818 Liberty Ave., downtown, for house music and drag shows. (☎281-2131. Open Tu-Sa 9pm-2am.)

OHIOPYLE STATE PARK   ☎724

Lifted by steep hills and cut by cascading rivers, southwest Pennsylvania encompasses some lovely forests. Native Americans dubbed this region "Ohiopehhle" ("white frothy water") for the grand Youghiogheny River Gorge (*YOCK-a-GAY-nee*—or "The Yock" to locals), now the focal point of Pennsylvania's Ohiopyle State Park. The park's 19,000 acres offer hiking, fishing, hunting, whitewater rafting, and a variety of winter activities. The latest addition to the banks of the Yock, a graveled bike trail that winds 28 mi. north from the town of Confluence to Connellsville, was converted from a riverside railroad bed. Recently named one of the 19 best walks in the world, the trail is just one section of the "rails to trails" project that will eventually connect Pittsburgh and Washington, D.C.

Throngs come each year to raft Ohiopyle's 8 mi. long, class III rapids. Some of the best whitewater rafting in the East, the rapids take about 5hr. to conquer. Four outfitters front Rte. 381 in "downtown" Ohiopyle: **White Water Adventurers** (☎800-992-7238), **Wilderness Voyageurs** (☎800-272-4141), **Laurel Highlands River Tours** (☎800-472-3846), and **Mountain Streams** (☎800-723-8669). Trip prices on the Yock vary dramatically ($30-60 per person per day), depending on the season, day of the week, and difficulty. If you're an experienced river rat (or if you enjoy flipping boats), any of the above companies will rent you equipment. (Rafts about $12-15 per person; canoes $20; inflatable kayaks about $20-26.) In order to float anything, you need a **launch permit** from the park office. (M-F free, Sa-Su $2.50. Call at least 30 days in advance for Sa permits. Rental companies provide free permits.) To begin your trip, park at **Old Mitchell Parking Lot,** 7 mi. northwest of downtown, and purchase a $2.50 token. At the end of your trip, a shuttle will take you and your equipment back to your car. The Falls Market and Overnight Inn (see below) sells **fishing licenses** required in the park ($15 for 3 days; $30 per week; $35 per season, residents $17). Bike rental prices vary (generally $3-4 per hr.).

Inexpensive motels around Ohiopyle are scarce. The excellent **Ohiopyle State Park Hostel (HI-AYH),** on Ferncliffe Rd., sits next to a freight railroad line in the center of town off Rte. 381. (☎329-4476. Check-in 6-10pm. Check-out 7-9am. Curfew 11pm. 24 bunks, kitchen, laundry facilities. Dorms $10, non-members $13. Private rooms $18/ $24.) Down the street on Rte. 381, **Falls Market and Overnight Inn** rents nice rooms with shared baths. The downstairs store has groceries and a restaurant/snack bar. (☎329-4973. A/C, cable TV, VCR, laundry facilities. Store open daily 7am-9pm; in winter 7am-6:30pm. Triples $60; $10 additional person. Burgers $2, pancakes $3.) There are 226 **campsites** in Ohiopyle. (M-F $13, Sa-Su $16; PA residents $11/$14. Call at least 30 days in advance for weekend reservations in the summer.)

Ohiopyle borders on Rte. 381, 64 mi. southeast of Pittsburgh via Rte. 51 and U.S. 40. **Greyhound** serves Uniontown, 20 mi. to the west on U.S. 40, and travels to Pittsburgh (1¼hr., 2 per day, $12). The **Park Information Center,** P.O. Box 105, lies just off Rte. 381 on Dinnerbell Rd. (☎329-8591. Open daily 8am-4pm; Nov.-Apr. M-F 8am-4pm.) **Post Office:** Green St. (☎329-8605. Open M-F 7:30am-4:30pm, Sa 7:30-11:30am.) **ZIP code:** 15470. **Area code:** 724.

NEAR OHIOPYLE

Fallingwater, 8 mi. north of Ohiopyle on Rte. 381, is a masterpiece by the king of modern architecture, Frank Lloyd Wright. Designed in 1935 for Pittsburgh's wealthy Kaufmann family, "the most famous private residence ever built" blends into the surrounding terrain; huge boulders that predate the house are part of its architecture. The family wanted the house to be near the Bear Run Waterfall, but Wright daringly built it over the waterfall. As a result, the water's gentle roar can be heard in every room. A $12 million reinforcement project will be undertaken in the coming years before the house's steel girding bends beyond repair. This site can only be seen on a 1hr. tour; make reservations. (☎329-8501. Open Tu-Su 10am-4pm; Nov.-Dec. and Mar. Sa-Su only. Tours Tu-F $10, ages 6-18 $7; Sa-Su $15/$8. Children under 6 must be left in child care; $2 per hr.) The singular **Museum of Early American Farm Machines and Very Old Horse Saddles with a History** (☎438-5180), on U.S. 40 near Rte. 381 in Chalk Hill, exhibits rusted and zany Americana, as wascaly wabbits run amok amid a 12-ton cast-iron steam engine from 1905, a "cowboy's going courting saddle," and saddles from the Civil War.

DELAWARE

Tiny Delaware serves as a sanctuary from the sprawling cities of the Boston-New York-Washington megalopolis. The state's particular charm is well represented by the state bug, the ladybug, adopted in 1974 after an ardent campaign by elementary school children. Delaware was first to ratify the US Constitution on Dec. 7, 1787—hence the tag "First State." Since then its history has been dominated by the wealthy DuPont clan, whose gunpowder mills grew into a chemical giant. Tax-free shopping, scenic beach towns—and yes, convenient location—lure vacationers to here from all along the country's eastern shores.

> **NICE TO MEET YOU** Delaware, although rightfully esteemed by Americans as the first state to ratify the Constitution, is small—so small that when two Delawareans meet for the first time, they ask each other, "What exit are you from?"

⑦ PRACTICAL INFORMATION

Capital: Dover.

Visitor Info: 99 King's Hwy., Dover 19901 (☎ 739-4271 or 800-441-8846; www.state.de.us). Open M-F 8am-4:30pm. **Division of Fish and Wildlife,** 89 King's Hwy., Dover 19901 (☎ 800-523-3336).

Postal Abbreviation: DE. **Sales Tax:** 0%; 8% on accommodations.

DELAWARE SEASHORE

LEWES   ☎ 302

Founded in 1613 by the Zwaanendael colony from Hoorn, Holland, Lewes was Delaware's first town and for a brief stint of three years, a Dutch West India Company colony. Lewes hasn't changed much with the times. Featuring Victorian gingerbread houses, quiet streets, and a genuine lack of tourist culture, this ferry town has remained old-fashioned for ages. The town's main attraction—beautiful beaches—draw vacationers in and away from the chaos of nearby Rehoboth Beach.

⬛⑦ ORIENTATION AND PRACTICAL INFORMATION. From points north, take Rte. 1 S, which becomes the centrally-located Savannah Rd. From the west, travel east on Rte. 404, then take Rte. 9 E at Georgetown, continuing to Rte. 1. Greyhound/Trailways (☎ 800-231-2222) serves Lewes with **buses** to and from Washington, D.C. (3½hr., $32.75), Baltimore (3½hr., $28.75), and Philadelphia (4hr., $30.75). The buses stop in front of the Ace Hardware Store on Rte. 1. In Lewes and Rehoboth, the **Delaware Resort Transit** (☎ 800-553-3278) shuttle bus runs from the ferry terminal through Lewes to Rehoboth and Dewey Beach (every 30min.; operates daily late May to early Sept. 7am-3am; $1 per ride, seniors and disabled 40¢, day pass $2). **Seaport Taxis** (☎ 645-6800) will take you door to door anywhere in Lewes for a small fee. Note that the beach is not in town—a bridge separates the two, and it's a long walk to the beach without a car. Thankfully, the beach does offer abundant parking. The **Lewes Chamber of Commerce,** 20 King's Hwy., operates out of the Fisher-Martin House (ca. 1730) and offers useful Lewes info and a free walking tour. (☎ 645-8078. Open in summer M-F 10am-4pm, Sa 9am-3pm, Su 10am-2pm; off-season closed Sa-Su.) **Post Office:** 116 Front St. **ZIP code:** 19958. **Area code:** 302.

▚🖬 ACCOMMODATIONS AND FOOD. A charming, kid-friendly seven-room B&B with a lavish vegetarian breakfast, the **Savannah Inn,** 330 Savannah Rd., tops other Lewes accommodations in price and environmental spirit. Don't be fooled by the hints of peeling paint; this building is well-maintained and clean. (☎ 645-5592. Double rooms with shared bath $50, larger rooms sleep 3-4 and run $75-80. Oct.-May no breakfast and $10 off room rates.) **Captain's Quarters,** 406 Savannah Rd., a small motel on the beach side of the town drawbridge, offers comfy but less personal lodgings. (☎ 645-7924. Doubles $85, each additional person $5.) Sandy campsites are available in **Cape Henlopen State Park,** off Rte. 1. From the north, bypass Savannah Rd. and continue on Rte. 1 for ½ mi. before signs direct you to take a left, leading to the park. (☎ 645-2103. Campground open Apr.-Oct. 24hr. Park open year-round 8am-sunset. Sites $18. No RV hook-ups.)

The few restaurants in Lewes cluster primarily on 2nd St. **Rosa Negra,** 128 2nd St., offers filling Italian fare in a rather bare dining room. Be an anxious early bird, though, because the post-6pm menu is pricey. (☎ 645-1980. Open daily 4-11pm. Early bird special daily 4-6pm; pasta dish $7, seniors $6.) Locals jam to live music, including blues, rock, and karaoke at the wood-paneled **Rose and Crown Restaurant and Pub,** 108 2nd St. (☎ 645-2373. Open daily 11am-1am. Happy hour daily 4-6pm yields 75¢ discounts. Live music Tu-Sa.)

🖼 SIGHTS. While the towns on the Eastern Shore pride themselves on their independence from the tourism industry, Lewes is struggling to turn itself into a vacationer's historical playground. Unfortunately, Lewes has few notable historical sites—the real draw of the city is and always will be the beautiful **beach** (see below). The modest hub of Lewes lies along 2nd St. The town has gathered some historic buildings into the **Historical Society Complex,** located on Shipcarpenter St. near 2nd St. Amongst these preserved relics stands the town's oldest surviving home, the **Bunton House,** built in 1690. (☎645-7670. Open June-Labor Day Tu-F 11am-4pm, Sa 10am-12:30pm. Admission $5). Secluded among sand dunes and scrub pines 1 mi. east of Lewes on the Atlantic Ocean is the 4000-acre **Cape Henlopen State Park.** A family-oriented beach, youngsters frolic in the waves while their ever watchful parents soak up some rays in their lawn chairs. The park is home to a seabird nesting colony, sparkling white "walking dunes," a 2 mi. paved trail perfect for in-line skating, and an expansive, beautiful beach with a bathhouse. (Open daily 8am-sunset. $5 per car; bikes and walkers free.)

REHOBOTH BEACH   ☎302

The cotton candy, mini-golf, fast-food, beach volleyball, and discount t-shirt shops clustered on Rehoboth's boardwalk strip contrast sharply with the serenity of seaside Lewes. On the surface, Rehoboth appears to be little more than a commercial beach attraction, but if you venture inland past the hoopla of the beach, you'll find a well-heeled resort community with numerous Washington families and a burgeoning gay population.

■■ **ORIENTATION AND PRACTICAL INFORMATION.** Rehoboth is located about 6 mi. south of Lewes. To reach the town from Rte. 1, take Rte. 1B to Rehoboth Ave. and follow it to the water. The vibrant section of town is very concentrated within the beachside boardwalk, so walking is the preferred mode of transportation. **Greyhound/Trailways,** 251 Rehoboth Ave. (☎227-7223 or 800-231-2222), stops next to the Rehoboth Beach Chamber of Commerce. **Buses** go to and from Washington, D.C. (3½hr., 1 per day, $32.75), Baltimore (3½hr., 1 per day, $28.75), and Philadelphia (4hr., 2 per day, $30.75). The **Rehoboth Beach Chamber of Commerce,** 501 Rehoboth Ave., doles out Delaware info, free maps, and coupons (☎227-2233 or 800-441-1329. Open M-F 9am-5pm, Sa-Su 9am-noon.) **Post Office:** Rehoboth Ave. and 2nd St. **ZIP code:** 19971. **Area code:** 302.

■■ **ACCOMMODATIONS AND FOOD.** Inexpensive lodgings, mostly bed and breakfasts, abound in Rehoboth. **Mr. and Mrs. Downs of the Lord Baltimore,** 16 Baltimore Ave., half a block from the boardwalk, have clean, antiquated rooms with TVs, refrigerators, and A/C. Mr. and Mrs. Downs, the warm elderly couple at the helm of the motel, are very approachable sources of information. (☎227-2855. Singles and doubles $40-70; in winter $25-50; each additional person $5.) **The Abbey Inn,** 31 Maryland Ave., is just a street away from the noise of Rehoboth Ave. and always has a conversation waiting on the porch. (☎227-7023. Open late May to early Sept. 2-day minimum stay. Singles from $40; doubles from $50; 15% surcharge on weekends.) The wooded **Big Oaks Family Campground,** 1 mi. off Rte. 1 on Rd. 270, offers a rugged alternative to town lodging, with shaded sites, a bathhouse, and a pool. (☎645-6838. Sites $28.50, with hook-up $33.)

Rehoboth is known for its beach cuisine and its many bars. **Cafe Papillion,** 42 Rehoboth Ave., in the Penny Lane Mall, offers an authentic European twist to a very American town. French cooks speaking the international language of good food serve up fresh crepes ($2.50-5), croissants ($1.75-3), and stuffed baguette sandwiches for $5-7. (☎227-7568. Open daily May-Oct. 8am-11pm.) For filling breakfasts like mom used to make, saunter over to the **Royal Treat,** 4 Wilmington Ave., where a stack of pancakes and bacon is $5.25. The restaurant doubles as an ice-cream parlor in the afternoon and evening, catering to traditionalists with an old-fashioned ice cream soda ($3.50) and authentic Hershey's syrup on hot fudge sundaes ($3.50). (☎227-6277. Breakfast served 8-11:30am; ice cream 1-11:30pm.)

■■ **ENTERTAINMENT AND NIGHTLIFE.** The congestion on the sparkling **beach** thins to the north of the boardwalk. Early risers will find even the boardwalk beach deserted and may witness the daily southward commute of the dolphins. **The Blue**

Moon, 35 Baltimore Ave., rocks to the sounds of techno music for a predominantly gay crowd until 1am. (☎ 227-6515. Open daily 4pm-1am. Happy Hour M-F 4-6pm.) A new addition to the Rehoboth bar scene, the **Full Moon Saloon** uses the universal appeal of live classic rock 'n' roll to attract young and old. (Open M-Sa 10am-1am, Su 11am-1am. Happy Hour M-Th 5-8pm offers $1 drafts.) **The Frogg Pond,** 3 S. 1st St., welcomes young, old, gay, and straight to jam Tuesday through Sunday to live alternative music. The photo collage on the wall is a colorful chronicle of the patrons' exploits. (☎ 227-2254. Open M-F 10-1am, Sa-Su 9-1am. Occasional weekend cover $2.)

MARYLAND

Once upon a time, folks on Maryland's rural eastern shore captured crabs, raised tobacco, and ruled the state. Across the bay in Baltimore, workers loaded ships and ran factories. Then the federal government expanded, industry shrank, and Maryland had a new focal point: the Baltimore-Washington Pkwy. Suburbs grew, Baltimore revitalized, and the Old Line State acquired a new, liberal urbanity. As D.C.'s homogenized commuter suburbs continue to swell beyond the limits of Maryland's Montgomery and Prince Georges counties, Baltimore revels in its immensity, whereas Annapolis, the capital, remains a small town of sailors. The mountains of the state's western panhandle—geographic and cultural kin to West Virginia—are largely pristine to this day.

🛈 PRACTICAL INFORMATION

Capital: Annapolis.
Visitor Info: Office of Tourism, 217 E. Redwood St., Baltimore 21202 (☎ 800-543-1036; www.mdisfun.org). **Dept. of Natural Resources,** 580 Taylor Ave., Annapolis 21401 (☎ 410-260-8186; open M-F 8am-4:30pm).
Postal Abbreviation: MD. **Sales Tax:** 5%.

BALTIMORE   ☎ 410

The Native American name for Baltimore, *Patipasco*, means backwater, and nothing breeds crabs better than Baltimore's mucky waters. Crab cakes, Orioles games, the Inner Harbor, and the fabulous National Aquarium are all fine reasons to visit Baltimore. The true pulse of the city, however, lies beyond the glimmering Inner Harbor, in its overstuffed markets, coffee shops, and diverse cityfolk. Baltimore's Southern heritage is visible in its many neighborhoods. In Roland Park, for instance, every house has a front porch and everyone greets you in a friendly "Bawlmer" accent. Certain natives have gained notoriety for digging beneath this genial Southern complacency: John Waters' films capture the city's twisted side, while Edgar Allan Poe's writing evokes its gloominess.

▐ GETTING THERE AND GETTING AROUND

Baltimore is 35 mi. north of D.C. and about 150 mi. from the ocean. To get to Baltimore from D.C., take the **Capital Beltway (I-495)** to **I-95** at **Exit 27** or to the **Baltimore-Washington Parkway** at **Exit 22.** The two highways run roughly parallel. **Exit 53** for **Rte. 395** leads right into **Inner Harbor.** Without traffic, the trip takes less than an hour.

Airport: Baltimore-Washington International (BWI) (☎ 859-7111; www.bwiairport.com), on I-195 off the Baltimore-Washington Parkway (I-295), about 10 mi. south of the city center. Take MTA bus #17 to the Nursery Rd. light-rail station. Airport shuttles to hotels (☎ 859-0800; www.supershuttle.com) run daily every 30min. 5:45am-11:30pm ($11 to downtown Baltimore, $17 round-trip). For D.C., shuttles leave hourly 5:45am-11:30pm ($21-31). Amtrak trains from BWI run to Baltimore ($5) and D.C. ($12). MARC commuter trains are cheaper but slower, and only run M-F (Baltimore $3.25, D.C. $5).

Trains: Penn Station, 1500 N. Charles St. (☎800-872-7245), at Mt. Royal Ave. Easily accessible by bus #3 or 11 from Charles Station downtown. Amtrak trains run every 30min.-1hr. to: New York ($62-71); Washington, D.C. ($19), and Philadelphia ($35). On weekdays, 2 **MARC commuter lines** (☎800-325-7245 in MD) connect Baltimore to D.C.'s Union Station (☎859-7400 or 291-4268) via Penn Station (with stops at BWI Airport) or **Camden Station** (☎613-5342), at the corner of Howard and Camden St. near Oriole Park. Both are $5.75, round-trip $10.25. Open daily 5:30am-9:30pm, self-serve open 24hr. (credit card only).

Buses: Greyhound (☎800-231-2222) has 2 locations: downtown at 210 W. Fayette St. (☎752-7682), near N. Howard St.; and at 5625 O'Donnell St. (☎752-0908), 3 mi. east of downtown near I-95. Connections to New York ($24, round-trip $43); Washington, D.C. ($6, round-trip $10); and Philadelphia ($15, round-trip $24).

Public Transport: Mass Transit Administration (MTA), 300 W. Lexington St. (bus and Metro schedule info ☎539-5000 or 800-543-9809), near N. Howard St. Operator available M-F 6am-9pm. Bus, Metro, and light-rail service to most major sights in the city and outlying areas. Some buses run 24hr. Metro operates M-F 5am-midnight, Sa 6am-midnight. Light rail operates M-F 6am-11pm, Sa 8am-11pm, Su 11am-7pm. One way fare for all is $1.35, but may be higher depending on distance traveled. Bus #17 runs from the Nursery Rd. light-rail to BWI Airport.

Water Taxi: Main stop at Inner Harbor (☎563-3901 or 800-658-8947). Stops every 8-18min. (Nov.-Mar. every 40min.) at the harbor museums, Harborplace, Fells Point, Little Italy, and more. An easy way to travel to 40 of Baltimore's main sights. Service daily May-Aug. 9am-midnight, Apr. and Sept.-Oct. 9am-9pm, Nov.-Mar. 9am-6pm. 1 day unlimited rides $4.50, ages 10 and under $2. Run by **Harbor Boating, Inc.,** 1615 Thames St.

Taxis: Checker Cab, ☎685-1212. **Royal Cab,** ☎327-0330.

✳ 🛈 ORIENTATION AND PRACTICAL INFORMATION

The city is divided into quarters by **Baltimore St.** (east-west) and **Charles St.** (north-south). Directional prefixes indicate every other street's relation to these main streets. **Inner Harbor,** near the corner of Pratt and Charles St., is a scenic tourist trap and home to historic ships, a shopping mall, and an aquarium. The museum-laden **Mount Vernon** neighborhood—served by city buses #3, 9, and 11—occupies **N. Charles St.,** north of **Baltimore St.,** around Monument St. and **Centre Ave.** Ethnic **Little Italy** sits a few blocks east of the Inner Harbor, past the **Jones Falls Expressway.** Continuing past Little Italy, a short walk to the southeast brings you past Broadway to bar-happy **Fells Point.** Old-fashioned **Federal Hill** preserves Baltimore history, while the area east of **Camden Yards** has recently been re-urbanized.

The southern end of the **Jones Falls Expressway (I-83)** halves the city near the Inner Harbor, and the **Baltimore Beltway (I-695)** circles the city. I-95 cuts across the southwest corner of the city as a shortcut to the wide arc of the Beltway. During rush hour, these roads slow to a crawl. Baltimore, like any other major US city, lacks free parking. So either come fisting shiny quarters or expect to pay garages about $7 per day. Meters and garages away from the harbor are less expensive.

Visitor Information: Baltimore Area Visitors Center, 451 Light St. (☎837-7024). Open in summer M-Sa 9am-7pm, Su 10am-5pm; in winter daily 9am-5pm.

Traveler's Aid: ☎685-3569 (M-F 8:30am-3:30pm) or ☎685-5874, voice-mail only. Two desks at BWI Airport (☎859-7209; open M-F 9am-9pm, Su 1-9pm). Direct-line telephones at Penn Station and Greyhound terminal.

Help Lines: Suicide: ☎531-6677. **Sexual Assault and Domestic Violence:** ☎828-6390. Both open 24hr. **Gay and Lesbian:** ☎837-8888. Operators daily 7pm-midnight, recording all other times.

Post Office: 900 E. Fayette St. (☎347-4425). Open M-F 7:30am-9pm, Sa 7:30am-5pm. **ZIP code:** 21233. **Area code:** 410.

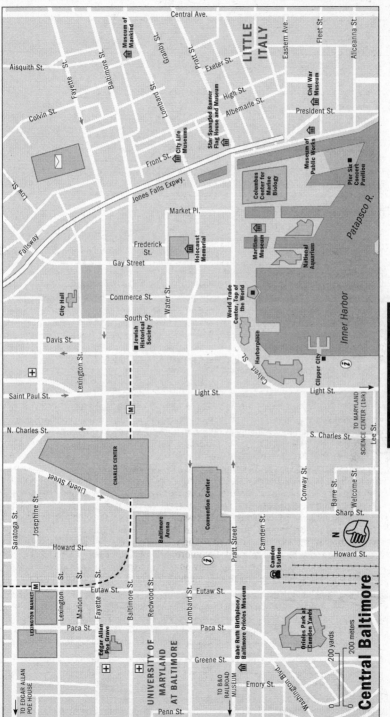

Central Baltimore

MID-ATLANTIC

Central Ave.

LITTLE ITALY

Aisquith St.

Fayette St.

Baltimore St.

Museum of Mankind

Granby St.

Pratt St.

Exeter St.

Eastern Ave.

Fleet St.

Aliceanna St.

Colvin St.

Lombard St.

High St.

Albemarle St.

Civil War Museum

President St.

Low St.

Front St.

Star Spangled Banner Flag House and Museum

City Life Museums

Jones Falls Expwy.

Museum of Public Works

Pier Six Concert Pavilion

Fallsway

Market Pl.

Columbus Center for Marine Biology

Patapsco R.

Frederick St.

Holocaust Memorial

Maritime Museum

Gay Street

National Aquarium

City Hall

Commerce St.

Water St.

South St.

World Trade Center, Top of the World

Inner Harbor

Davis St.

Lexington St.

Jewish Historical Society

Harborplace

Saint Paul St.

Light St.

Clipper City

Light St.

TO MARYLAND SCIENCE CENTER (10k)

Lee St.

N. Charles St.

S. Charles St.

Liberty Street

CHARLES CENTER

Convention Center

Conway St.

Barre St.

Welcome St.

Saratoga St.

Josephine St.

Howard St.

Baltimore Arena

Sharp St.

Camden St.

N

Howard St.

TO EDGAR ALLAN POE HOUSE

LEXINGTON MARKET

Lexington St.

Marion St.

Fayette St.

Eutaw St.

Baltimore St.

Redwood St.

Lombard St.

Eutaw St.

Pratt Street

Camden Station

Paca St.

Edgar Allan Poe Grave

Paca St.

Babe Ruth Birthplace/ Baltimore Orioles Museum

200 yards

200 meters

UNIVERSITY OF MARYLAND AT BALTIMORE

Greene St.

Oriole Park at Camden Yards

TO B&O RAILROAD MUSEUM

Emory St.

Washington Blvd.

Penn St.

ACCOMMODATIONS AND CAMPING

Expensive chain hotels dominate the Inner Harbor, and reputable inexpensive hotels elsewhere are hard to find. For a convenient way to reserve bed and breakfasts, call **Amanda's Bed and Breakfast Reservation Service,** 1428 Park Ave. (☎225-0001 or 800-899-7533. M-F 8:30am-5:30pm, Sa 8:30am-noon. Rates begin at $50 a night.)

Baltimore International Youth Hostel (HI-AYH), 17 W. Mulberry St. (☎576-8880), centrally located at Cathedral St. in the historic Mount Vernon neighborhood. Near bus and Amtrak terminals. Take MTA buses #3 or 11 along Charles St. **Note: The hostel is temporarily closed for renovations with plans to reopen in the summer of 2001. Prices quoted are from 1998. Call for new rates.** Elegantly shabby 19th-century brownstone harbors 35 beds in spacious dorm rooms. Full kitchen and laundry service. Lounge with marble fireplaces and a TV. Free baggage storage ($5 deposit) and linen ($10 deposit). Curfew 11pm, but house keys available with $10 deposit. 3-night max. stay (may be extended with manager's approval). Reservations recommended, especially in summer. $14, non-members $17. *Be careful at night.*

Duke's Motel, 7905 Pulaski Hwy. (☎686-0400), in Rosedale off the Beltway. The bulletproof glass in the front office is nothing to worry about—all the neighborhood motels have it, though the area is actually safer than most parts of downtown Baltimore. Clean and efficiently run. Simple, dark rooms have A/C and cable TV. $5 key deposit and ID required. King-sized beds optional. Singles from $47; doubles $48 and up. Rates increase in summer and weekends.

Capitol KOA, 768 Cecil Ave. (☎923-2771 or 800-562-0248, from Baltimore 987-7477), in Millersville, between D.C. and Baltimore. From D.C., take Rte. 50 E (John Hanson Hwy.) to Rte. 3 N (Robert Crain Hwy.). Bear right after 8 mi. onto Veterans Hwy.; after a short distance turn left under the highway onto Hog Farm Rd.; follow blue camping signs. Mostly RVs, some cabins, and a small wooded area for tents. Pool, volleyball courts, and bathroom/shower facilities centrally located. Open Mar. 25 to Nov. 1. Tent site for 2 $27; RV complete hook-up $35, water and electricity $32; 1-room cabin $46, 2 rooms $55. Each additional adult $5, child $3.

FOOD

🍴 **Mugavero's Confectionery,** 300 S. Exeter St. (☎539-9798). This menu-less deli has been a fixture for 54 years thanks to the unwavering service of the friendly proprietor. Patrons entrust their sandwich to his imagination or invent their own ($4). Cash only. Open daily 10am-9pm or 10pm.

🍴 **Amicci's,** 231 S. High St. (☎528-1096). Movie posters line the walls of Amicci's, paying homage to such Italian film classics as *The Godfather* and *La Vita è Bella.* Mediterranean zest is apparent on the menu as well; *ziti la rosa* (ziti in tomato pesto served with shrimp in marsala sauce; $13) is a standout. Loosen your belt to accommodate one of the 11 immense pasta dishes under $10. Open M-Th 11:30am-10pm, F-Sa 11:30am-11pm, Su 11:30am-9pm. Shorter off-season hrs.; call ahead.

🍴 **The Fudgery,** 301 Light St. (☎539-5260), on the first fl. in the Light St. Pavilion. Nirvana for chocolate-cravers. Vocal employees musically create and promote fudge while snagging some free samples. Products are pricey ($6 per ½ lb. slice) but worth the sacrifice for a delectable treat. Open M-Th 9am-10pm, F-Sa 9am-11:30pm, Su 9am-9pm.

Phillip's Restaurant, 301 Light St. (☎800-782-2722), on the 1st fl. of the Light St. Pavilion. Loyal fans flock to the Inner Harbor's seafood hot-spot for magnificent marine dishes. Indoor and outdoor seating. Sandwiches ($6-13) are just as delicious as the expensive entrees ($12 and up). Tykes under 5 years old eat for free. Or try **Phillip's Seafood Market** right next door for inexpensive takeout (crab cakes $7). Both open M-F 9am-10pm, Sa 9am-11pm, Su 9am-8pm.

SIGHTS

HARBORPLACE. Baltimore's gray harbor ends with a colorful bang in a five sq. block body of water bounded on three sides by an aquarium, shopping malls, a science museum, and a bevy of boardable ships. The nation's first pier-pavilion, the Harbor-place mall is Baltimore's most imitated building. Crowds flock to Harborplace's Pratt St. and Light St. Pavilions and to the Gallery across the street for a little wharf-side shopping and air-conditioned bliss. (☎ 332-4191. Open M-Sa 10am-9pm, Su 10am-6pm.)

NATIONAL AQUARIUM. The National Aquarium makes the Inner Harbor worth-while. Multi-level exhibits and tanks show off rare fish, big fish, red fish, and blue fish along with the biology and ecology of oceans, rivers, and rainforests. The Chil-dren's Cove (level 4) lets visitors handle inter-tidal marine animals. (Pier 3, 501 E. Pratt St. ☎ 576-3800. Entrance times July-Aug. daily 9am-8pm; Mar.-June and Sept.-Oct. Sa-Th 9am-5pm, F 9am-8pm; Nov.-Feb. Sa-Th 10am-5pm, F 10am-8pm. Aquarium remains open 2hr. after last entrance time. $14, seniors $10.50, children $7.50, under 3 free.)

MUSEUMS. Several ships bob by the aquarium; most belong to the **Baltimore Mari-time Museum,** at Piers 3 and 4. Visitors may board the USS Torsk submarine (which sank the last WWII Japanese combatant ships), the lightship Chesapeake, and the Coast Guard cutter Roger B. Taney. (☎ 396-3453.) At the Inner Harbor's far edge, the kid-oriented **Maryland Science Center** stuns audiences with its 5-story IMAX screen, 38-speaker sound system, and 50 ft. planetarium. (601 Light St. ☎ 685-5225. Open June-Aug. M-Th 9:30am-6pm, F-Su 10am-8pm; Sept.-May M-F 10am-5pm, Sa-Su 10am-6pm. $11; ages 13-17, seniors, and military $10; 4-12 $8.50; under 4 free.) **Fort McHenry National Monument,** at the foot of E. Fort Ave. off Rte. 2 (Hanover St.) and Lawrence Ave., commemorates the fort's victory against British forces in the War of 1812; the battle inspired Francis Scott Key's The Star-Spangled Banner. (☎ 962-4290. Take bus #1. Open daily June-Aug. 8am-8pm; Sept.-May 8am-5pm. $5, seniors and under 16 free.)

ART ATTRACTIONS. The **Walters Art Gallery** keeps one of the largest private art col-lections in the world, spanning five millennia. The museum's most esteemed pos-session is the Ancient Art collection, with sculptures and metalwork from Egypt, Greece, and Rome. (600 N. Charles St. at Centre St. ☎ 547-9000. Open Tu-F 10am-4pm, Sa-Su 11am-5pm. Tours W noon and Su 1:30pm. $5, students with ID and seniors $3, 6-17 $1, under 18 free Sa before noon.) The **Baltimore Museum of Art** exhibits a fine collection of Americana and modern art. The museum's two 20th-century **sculpture gardens** make wonderful picnic grounds. (10 Art Museum Dr. at N. Charles and 31st St. ☎ 396-7100. Open W-F 11am-5pm, Sa-Su 11am-6pm. $6, students and seniors $4, under 18 free; Th free.)

BALTIMORE ZOO. The Baltimore Zoo, off I-83 (Exit 7), offers a new Chimpanzee Forest exhibit, the spectacular Palm Tree Conservatory, a lake surrounded by lush greenery, and a simulated savanna with elephants and Siberian tigers. (☎ 396-7175. Open M-F 10am-4pm, Sa 10am-8pm, Su 10am-5:30pm; in winter closes daily 4pm. $9, seniors and ages 2-16 $5.50.)

🎵 ENTERTAINMENT

MUSIC, DANCE, AND THEATER. Vacationing in the city can be expensive, but for-tunately for the budget traveler, much of Baltimore's finest entertainment can be enjoyed free of charge. At **Harborplace,** performers are constantly entertaining tour-ists with magic acts, juggling, and clowning around during the day. At night, dance, dip, and dream to the sounds of anything from country to calypso to oldies at the Harborplace (occasional Th-Sa nights). The **Baltimore Museum of Art** offers free sum-mer jazz concerts in its sculpture garden. **Jazzline** (☎ 466-0600) lists jazz shows from Sept. to May; call for schedules and info. When the music isn't free in Baltimore, it's still just as good. Big-name musicians perform several times a week from May to October at **Pier 6 Concert Pavilion** (☎ 625-3100). Tickets ($15-30) are available at the pavilion or through Ticketmaster (☎ 625-1400 or 481-7328). The **Baltimore Symphony Orchestra** plays at Meyerhoff Symphony Hall, 1212 Cathedral St., from September to May and during their month-long Summerfest. (☎ 783-8000. Box office open M-F 10am-6pm, Sa-Su noon-5pm, and 1hr. before performances. Call for dates of Sum-merfest. Tickets $15-52.) The **Lyric Opera House,** down the street at 110 W. Mt. Royal Ave., near Maryland Ave., hosts the **Baltimore Opera Company** from late October to April. (☎ 727-6000. Box office open M-F 10am-5pm. Tickets $24-109.)

The **Arena Players,** a black theater group, perform comedies, drama, and dance at 801 McCullough St. at Martin Luther King, Jr. Blvd. (☎728-6500. Box office open M-F 9am-5pm. Tickets start at $15.) The **Showcase of Nations Ethnic Festivals** celebrate Baltimore's ethnic neighborhoods with a different culture featured each week (June-Sept.). The festivals take place all over the city; call the Baltimore Visitors Bureau (☎800-282-6632) for info.

SPECTATOR SPORTS. The beloved **Baltimore Orioles** play ball at **Camden Yards,** just a few blocks from the Inner Harbor at the corner of Russell and Camden St. Tickets for Orioles games range from $7 (standing room) to $35 (reserved boxes). Call ☎547-6234 to order tickets. The three-year-old **Ravens** represent Baltimore's 2nd chance at professional football. The Ravens, formerly the Cleveland Browns, play in **Raven Stadium,** adjacent to Camden Yards. To order individual game tickets, call ☎481-7328. Just outside of Baltimore, head off to the races at **Laurel** (☎792-7775; on Rte. 216 off I-95) and **Pimlico Race Tracks** (☎542-9400; on Rte. 129). The two tracks alternately hold thoroughbred horse races for much of the spring, summer, and fall. **The Preakness Stakes** (☎542-9400, ext. 4484 for tickets), leg two of the Triple Crown, is run annually at Pimlico on the 3rd Sa in May.

★ NIGHTLIFE

Baltimore law requires that bars close at 2am. Hearty partiers should plan to start their evenings early. After 2am, check out Fells Point to meet throngs of fellow revellers.

Cat's Eye Pub, 1730 Thames St. (☎276-9866), in Fells Point. An older crowd of regulars packs it in every weeknight for live blues, jazz, folk, or traditional Irish music (M-Th 9pm, F-Sa 4pm). Live blues Su 4-8pm. Occasional cover for national musical acts. Over 25 different drafts and 60 bottled beers. Open daily noon-2am. Happy Hour M-F 4-7pm.

Bohager's, 701 S. Eden St. (☎563-7220), in Fells Point. After undergoing extensive renovations, Bohager's has transformed into an enclosed tropical paradise for college students and locals. Under a 29,000 sq. ft. retractable dome, patrons rage to live island music until the wee hours of the morning. Tickets available at the club or through Ticket-Master (☎481-7328). Open M-F 11:30am-2am, Sa-Su 3pm-2am. Happy Hour Th-F 5-8pm.

Greene Turtle, 720 Broadway (☎342-4222). With foosball, pool (50¢), and an extensive CD jukebox, this relaxed bar is popular with the Baltimore college crowd, the Ravens, and anyone else interested in tanking up for next to nothing. Open daily 11:30am-2am. $2.50 drafts are a dollar cheaper during Happy Hour (M-F 4-7pm), which also offers half-price apps (M 7-close, Tu-F 4-7pm). Sandwiches $5-7.50. Sa-Su special yields ½lb. spicy steamed shrimp for $4.50.

Hippo, 1 W. Eager St. (☎547-0069), across the street from Central Station. Baltimore's largest gay bar provides pool tables, videos, and a packed dance floor in an industrial setting. First Su of every month is Ladies' Tea, one of the largest lesbian events this side of the Mississippi (6-10pm). Saloon open daily 4pm-2am; dance bar open Th-Sa 10pm-2am. Happy Hour 4-8pm daily. Men's Night Th. Cover Th-F $3, Sa $6.

ANNAPOLIS   ☎410

After its stint in 1783 as temporary capital of the US (hot on the heels of Philadelphia, New York, and Trenton, NJ), Annapolis relinquished the national limelight in favor of a more tranquil existence. Now, guests are treated to a surprisingly accurate taste of what coastal America once was: crowded, pastel row houses with gorgeous gardens, friendly strollers, and an endless array of boats. With its brick-paved sidewalks and narrow streets, the historic waterfront district retains its 18th-century appeal despite the presence of ritzy boutiques and pricey retail stores. Crew-cut "middies" (a nickname for Naval Academy students, or "midshipmen") mingle with longer-haired students from St. John's and couples on weekend getaways amid the highest concentration of historic homes in America.

🔁🔢 ORIENTATION AND PRACTICAL INFORMATION. The city extends south and east from two landmarks: **Church Circle** and **State Circle**. **School St.**, in a blatantly unconstitutional move, connects Church and State. **East St.** runs from the State House to the Naval Academy. **Main St.**, where food and entertainment congregate, starts at Church Circle and ends at the docks. Parking at the **Visitors Center** is the best bet for downtown. ($1 per hr.; M-F $8 maximum, Sa-Su $4 maximum.)

Greyhound stops at the local bus stop in the football field parking lot at Rowe Blvd. and Taylor St. and sends buses to Washington, D.C. (1hr., 1 per day, $10.50); Philadelphia (5-6hr., 2 per day, $42); and Baltimore (3hr., 1 per day, $10). **Mass Transit Administration** (☎539-5000 or 800-543-9809) has an express (#210) that runs to Baltimore M-F (1hr., $2.85) and a local (#14) that runs daily (1½hr., $1.35). Buses leave from St. John's and College Ave. and St. John's and Calvert St. **Annapolis Dept. of Public Transportation** operates a web of city buses connecting the historic district with the rest of town. (☎263-7964. Buses run M-Sa 5:30am-10pm, Su 8am-7pm. Base fare 75¢, over 60 or disabled 35¢.) **Annapolis Cab Co.,** ☎268-0022. **Checker Cab,** ☎268-3737. **Visitor Information: Annapolis and Anne Arundel County Conference & Visitors Bureau,** 26 West St., has free maps and brochures. (☎280-0445; www.visit-annapolis.org. Open daily 9am-5pm.) **Post Office:** 1 Church Circle (☎263-9292. Open M-F 8:30am-5pm.) **ZIP code:** 21401. **Area code:** 410.

🔪 ACCOMMODATIONS. The heart of Annapolis lacks cheap motels but has plenty of elegant and pricey bed and breakfasts. In general, these B&Bs prove a better choice than the hotels scattered about western Annapolis, which aren't actually cheaper and are far from central attractions. Rooms should be reserved in advance, especially for weekends and the busy summer months. **Bed and Breakfasts of Maryland** aids in arranging accommodations in Annapolis. (☎800-736-4667, ext. 15. Open M-F 9am-5pm, Sa 10am-3pm.) **Amanda's** offers a similar service. (☎225-0001. Open M-F 8:30am-5:30pm, Sa 8:30am-noon.) All lodgings listed are near the dock and within walking distance of major attractions.

Scotlaur Inn, 165 Main St., atop Chick and Ruth's Delly, has ten tiny guest rooms. This homey "bed & bagel," which is less fancy than the other B&Bs, is far more affordable. Huge complimentary breakfasts are available from **Chick & Ruth's** (see **Food,** below) and more than compensate for the rooms' lack of luxury. (☎268-5665. A/C, TVs, and private baths. Rooms range from $75-95.) **Gibson's Lodgings,** 110 Prince George St., 1 block from City Dock on Randall St., offers a patio and spacious common parlors among its three ivy covered buildings and 18 rooms. (☎268-5555. Continental breakfast and courtyard parking included. Single rooms start at $79; doubles at $109. Rollaway $20 extra. $10 discount in off season. One wheelchair accessible room available.) **Flag House Inn,** 26 Randall St., has a prime location next to the visitors entrance to the Naval Academy and, true to its name, six flags waving from the porch. (☎280-2721 or 800-437-4825. TV, A/C, and free off-street parking. King-sized beds and private baths in each of the 5 rooms. Breakfast included. Rooms begin at $95; 2-person suites $140; 4-person suites $220. Try to reserve 2-4 weeks in advance.)

🍴 FOOD. Most restaurants in the area cluster around **City Dock,** an area packed with people in summertime (especially Tu at 7:30pm when the spinnaker races finish at City Dock). The best place to find cheap eats is the Market House food court at the center of City Dock, where a hearty meal costs under $5. Numerous newspaper clippings adorn the walls, paying homage to an Annapolis institution of over 30 years, **Chick & Ruth's Delly,** 165 Main St., about a block from City Dock towards the State House. Dishes named for local and national politicians like the "Al Gore" Chicken Salad ($5). Omelettes ($3-7), corned beef sandwiches ($5), and malted milkshakes ($2.75) highlight an inexpensive menu. (☎269-6737. Open M-Tu 6:30am-4pm, W-Th, and Su 6:30am-10pm, F-Sa 6:30am-11pm. Delivery available.) The Middle Eastern **Moon Cafe,** 137 Prince George St., a block up East St. from the Naval Academy, attracts vegetarians, who flock here to sample creamy hummus ($4) and other "light fare" options. (☎280-1956. Poetry slams Tu 9:30pm; cover $3. Live music Th-Sa. Weekend brunch until 2pm.)

🔵 **SIGHTS.** The **US Naval Academy** is the institution that most typifies Annapolis. At the academy, harried, short-haired "plebes" (first-year students) in official, intentionally silly-looking sailor dress try desperately to remember and flawlessly recite the words of Navy fight songs while the rest of the undergraduates, "middies" (midshipmen), scream orders. By graduation rite, the outgoing 1st class leaps into the placid waters of the Severn River. The first stop should be the Armel-Leftwich Visitors Center, in the Halsey Field House. Tours include historic Bancroft Hall, the crypt, a dorm room, and the athletic facilities where the middies test their seafaring prowess on land. Visitors also view the original Tecumseh, a shiphead carving on the 3rd ship in the US Navy named after an Indian chief by joking midshipmen. The name stuck, and the icon is now one of the academy's mascots. *(52 King George St. ☎ 263-6933; www.nadn.navy.mil.; www.usna.com. Tours every 30min. M-Sa 9:30am-3:30pm, Su 12:15pm-3:30pm. $5.50, seniors $4.50, students $3.50.)*

Built from 1772 to 1779, the Corinthian-columned **State House,** in the center of State Circle, is the oldest working capitol building in the nation. It was the US Capitol building from 1783 to 1784, and the Treaty of Paris was signed inside on January 14, 1784. Visitors can explore the historical exhibits and silver collection, or watch the state legislature bicker in two exquisitely adorned marble halls from the 2nd W in January until mid-Apr. *(90 State Circle. ☎ 974-3400. Open daily 9am-5pm. Tours 11am and 3pm. Free.)*

Historic Hammond-Harwood House, an elegant 1774 building designed by Colonial architect William Buckland, retains period decor right down to the candlesticks. The house is most renowned for its impeccably preserved colonial doorway. *(19 Maryland Ave., at King George St. ☎ 263-4683. M-Sa 10am-4pm, Su noon-4pm. Tours on the hr.; last tour 1hr. before closing. $5, ages 6-18 $3, uniformed armed service personnel free. $10 joint tickets available for both the Hammond-Harwood and William Paca houses.)* The **William Paca House** is the first Georgian-style home built in Annapolis. The elegant house overlooks two acres of lush vegetation, and the garden hides shaded benches that gaze upon trellises, water lilies, and gazebos. *(186 Prince George St. ☎ 263-5553. M-Sa 10am-4pm, Su noon-4pm; Jan.-Feb. F-Sa 10am-4pm, Su noon-4pm. Tours given every hr. on the half-hour; arrive at least 1hr. before closing. House $5, garden $4, both $7. $10 joint tickets for Hammond-Harwood and William Paca houses.)*

It's difficult to escape the eats and greets at Annapolis' spirited **City Dock** which is easily accessed by following Main St. to its aquatic dead end. The city's main hub of activity, restaurants, and touristy shops line the waterfront, and Naval Academy ships (skippered by fresh-faced "plebes" in the summertime) ply the waters. The civilian yachtsmen congregate at bars to flex their alcohol tolerance and biceps simultaneously, earning the street its nickname, **"Ego Alley."** Smaller cruise boats leave on tours Apr.-Oct. *(☎ 268-7600. Boats depart M-F every hr. 11am-4pm, Sa-Su every hr. 11am-7pm. $6, under 12 $3.)*

📺🎭 **NIGHTLIFE AND ENTERTAINMENT.** Locals and tourists generally engage in one of two activities: wandering along City Dock or schmoozing 'n' boozing at upscale pubs. Bars and taverns line downtown Annapolis, drawing crowds every night. If you want more culture than drink can provide, Annapolis also has performance options. Theater-goers can check out **The Colonial Players, Inc.,** 108 East St., for innovative and often unknown works. (☎ 268-7373. Performances Th-Su at 8pm, additional Su show at 2:30pm. Tickets Th and Su $7, students and seniors $5, F-Sa $10.) During the summer, the **Annapolis Summer Garden Theater,** 143 Compromise St., offers musical "theater under the stars" in an open courtyard theater near the **City Dock.** (Tickets $10, students and seniors $8.)

McGarvey's, 8 Market Space, hosts mainly locals, who pack in among naval pilot-donated helmets in a candle-lit mezzanine level. (☎ 263-5700. Open M-Sa 11:30am-2am, Su 10am-2am. Happy hour M and W 10pm-2am. Th 6pm-2am the house beer is only $1.50.) After undergoing renovations and a change of ownership, **Armadillo's,** a sports bar at 132 Dock St., sports a homey brick interior and a cordial, talkative staff. (☎ 280-0028. Open daily 9am-1:30am. Happy hour M-F 4-7pm. Live music W-M 9:30pm. 21+ upstairs.) At **Ram's Head Tavern,** 33 West St., beer connoisseurs, midshipmen, and tourists enjoy 135 different beers, including international microbrews. (☎ 268-4545. Open M-Sa 11am-2am, Su 10am-2am. Happy hour M-F 4-7pm and midnight daily.)

ASSATEAGUE & CHINCOTEAGUE ISLANDS, VA ☎ 757

This is the place to see some really unique bands...of ponies, that is. Local legend has it that ponies first came to Assateague Island by swimming ashore from a sinking Spanish galleon—a story so captivating that it became the premise of the classic children's story, *Misty of Chincoteague*. A less romantic and more likely theory is that miserly colonial farmers put their horses out to graze on Assateague to avoid mainland taxes. Whatever their origins, the famous wild ponies now roam free across the unspoiled beaches and forests of the picturesque island.

▐▛ ORIENTATION AND PRACTICAL INFORMATION. The best way to get to Assateague Island is by car. From Rte. 50, take Rte. 611 south which leads directly to Assateague. If traveling from points south, use Rte. 113 north to Rte. 376 east in Berlin, Md. Follow Rte. 376 to access Rte. 611 and continue to the island. Although the two parks lie on opposite sides of the same island, a trip to Chincoteague requires park goers to inconveniently loop back through Maryland into Virginia via State Rd. 175 and onto the island at the opposite end, a 1½hr. trip. **Buses:** to reach the island by bus, take a **Greyhound** (☎800-752-4841) to Ocean City, via daily express or local routes from Greyhound stations in Baltimore ($25) or Washington, D.C. ($39-44). **Trailways** runs buses from **Salisbury, MD** ($8) and **Norfolk, VA** ($42), stopping on U.S. 13 at T's Corner store (☎824-5935), 11 mi. from Chincoteague. From Ocean City, take a **taxi** to the island (☎289-1313; about $30). There is no taxi service in the town. **Visitor Information: Chincoteague Chamber of Commerce,** P.O. Box 258, Chincoteague, VA 23336. The chamber is located at 6733 Maddox Blvd. (☎336-6161; www.chincoteaguechamber.com. Open in summer M-Sa 9am-4:30pm, Su 12:30-4:30pm; off-season M-Sa 9am-4:30pm.) **ZIP code:** 23336. **Area code:** 757.

▐▛ ACCOMMODATIONS AND FOOD. Due to Assateague's lack of civilization, visitors eat and sleep on **Chincoteague Island,** across an inlet from Assateague. Motels line the sides of **Maddox Boulevard** near the Assateague causeway. Midway down this motel mile, the **Mariner,** 6273 Maddox Blvd. offers comfortable rooms and features an outdoor pool and continental breakfast. (☎336-6565 or 800-221-7490. Four efficiency apartments are available for $125; doubles start at $58, in winter $47. Reserve in advance; the 10 economy rooms go fast.) Across from the Mariner lies a smaller version of the standard motel. The clean and quiet **Sea Hawk Motel,** 6250 Maddox Blvd., also offers an outdoor pool. (☎336-6527. Rooms $65-70, in winter $45-50; 1 double bed $38.) **Maddox Family Campground,** off to the right immediately before the causeway connecting Chincoteague and Assateague, has 550 sites, many with shade, and welcomes both RVs and tents. (☎336-3111. Pool and playground. Open Mar.-Dec. Sites $21.70, with hook-up $28.21.)

For fresh, absurdly cheap seafood takeout (no seats), head to **Melvin's Seafood,** situated in the family backyard of 3117 Ridge Rd., on the south side of the island (follow signs from Main St.). Don't be bashful, just drive right into their driveway where the owner family sells crab cakes for $8, a dozen steamed crabs for $12, and sandwiches for $3.50. (☎336-3003. Open daily 7am-7pm.) For sit-down seafood dining, locals swear by the all-you-can-eat steamed crabs ($18) and patriotic decor at **Wright's Seafood Restaurant,** on the mainland side of the Chincoteague inlet. From Rte. 175S, turn left on Atlantic Rd., go straight for 1½ mi., and turn left on Wright Rd. where you weave through cornfields for about one mi. before encountering the restaurant. (☎824-4012. Open daily 4-9pm. Entrees $10-23.) Chincoteague's most beloved dessert, nighttime snack, or breakfast treat is a Belgian waffle topped with ice cream and fruit ($5), found between the heart-stenciled walls of **Muller's Old Fashioned Ice Cream Parlor,** 4034 Main St. Single scoops are $1.50, extra scoops are $1. (☎336-5894. Open daily 11am-11pm when the family is in residence.)

▐▛ SIGHTS AND OUTDOORS. Maryland and Virginia share Assateague Island, which is divided into three distinct parts. The **Assateague State Park,** Rte. 611 in southeast Maryland, is a 2 mi. stretch of picnic areas, beaches, bathhouses, and campsites. Fishing without a license is permitted, but you must supply your own equipment. (☎410-641-2120 or 888-432-2267. Open daily Apr.-Oct. 8am-sunset.

Admission $2 per person, seniors free. Campsite registration open 9am-10pm. 2-night minimum on weekends. Sites $20, with hook-up $30.)

The **Assateague Island National Seashore** claims most of the long sandbar north and south of the park and has its own campground and beaches, most of which are inaccessible by car. The ranger station (☎641-3030) distributes $5 back-country camping permits from noon until 5pm; they go quickly, so arrive early. The **Barrier Island Visitors Center,** on Rte. 611, provides maps and info, an introduction to the park, and films on the park's natural treasures. (☎641-1441. Open daily 9am-5pm.) Secluded beachcombing to the north of the state park provides unguided, but adventurous, opportunities to unlock the park's natural treasures. Three meandering, ½ mi. nature trails give visitors a closer look at the island's flora and fauna: the **Forest Trail** offers the best viewing tower, but the **Marsh Trail** has fewer mosquitoes. If you feel safer within the confines of your own car, rental driving tours ($2) are available. Notorious gnats pester visitors all over the island, so bring plenty of repellent. (Campsites May-Oct. $14; Nov. to Apr. $10. No hook-ups.)

The **Chincoteague National Wildlife Refuge** stretches across the Virginia side of the island. Avid bird-watchers flock here to see rare species such as peregrine falcons, snowy egrets, and black-crowned night herons. The wild pony roundup, held the last consecutive W and Th in July, brings hordes of tourists to Assateague. During slack tide, local firemen herd the ponies together and swim them from Assateague to Chincoteague Island, where the fire department auctions off the foals the following day. The adults swim back to Assateague and reproduce, providing next year's crop. Can't make the round-up? Ponies can be seen almost every day along the refuge's trails, especially the Wildlife Loop Rd. (open 5am-10pm; for cars 3pm-sunset), which begins at the visitors center. If you are lucky enough to spot one of these awesome creatures, be careful to gawk from a safe distance—the ponies may appear harmless but are prone to violent outbursts. For more info, visit the **Chincoteague Refuge Visitor Contact Station.** (☎804-336-6122. Open daily 9am-4pm. $5 per car.) The **Piney Island Country Store,** 7085 Maddox Blvd. (☎336-6212), right outside the park entrance, rents bicycles for island rides.

OCEAN CITY   ☎410

Ocean City is a lot like a kiddie pool—it's shallow and plastic, but can be a lot of fun if you're the right age. This ten-mile strip of land packs endless bars, all-you-can-eat buffets, hotels, mini-golf courses, boardwalks, flashing lights, and sweaty tourists into a thin region between the Atlantic Ocean and the Assawoman Bay. Tourism is the town's only industry; in season the population swells from 5000 to 300,000, with a large migratory population of "June bugs," high school seniors that descend in swarms after graduation to celebrate. July and August cater more to families and singles looking for fun in the sun.

■ ▮ **ORIENTATION AND PRACTICAL INFORMATION.** Driving is the most sensible mode of transportation to reach the ocean resort. From the north, follow Rte. 1 which becomes Coastal Highway (Philadelphia Ave.). From the west, Rte. 50 leads directly to Ocean City. From points south, take Rte. 113 to Rte. 50 and follow that to town. Ocean City runs north-south, with numbered streets linking the ocean to the bay. Most hotels are in the lower numbered streets toward the ocean; most clubs and bars are uptown toward the bay. **Buses: Trailways,** at 2nd St. and Philadelphia Ave., buses to Baltimore (3½ hr., 7 per day, $25) and Washington, D.C. (4-6hr., $39-44). (☎289-9307. Open daily June-Aug. 7-8am and 10am-5pm, Sept.-May 10am-3pm.) **Public transportation:** in town, public buses run the length of the strip and are the best way to get around town 24 hours a day. (☎723-1607. $1 per day for unlimited rides.) **The Ocean City Visitors Center,** 4001 Coastal Hwy., at 40th St. in the Convention Center, gives out discount coupons. (☎800-626-2326. Open June-Aug. M-W 8:30am-5pm, Th-Sa 8:30am-8pm; Sept.-May daily 8:30am-5pm.) **Post Office:** 11805 Coastal Hwy. **Zip code:** 21842. **Area code:** 410.

⛶ ACCOMMODATIONS AND FOOD. The **Whispering Sands,** 15 45th St., rents out 11 spacious rooms with kitchen access. Lodging, available on a daily or a full-summer basis, draws a mostly European crowd in a location convenient to nightlife. Personable inn operator gladly provides visiting advice and conversation. (☎723-1874; Nov.-Apr. ☎202-362-3453 or 954-761-9008. Open May-Oct. A/C in all rooms but one. $20-25.) **Ocean City International Student Services,** 9 Somerset St., in the south end of town, provides a cheap summer boarding house for predominantly international college students. Private rooms and dorm rooms have access to kitchen, TV, living room, deck, hammock, and grill. (☎289-4542. Open Apr.-Oct. Cost averages $87 per week. Reservations necessary.) The **Cabana Motel,** 1900 Coastal Hwy. (Philadelphia Ave.), caters to families with small, comfortable rooms outfitted with A/C and TV. (☎289-9131. Open May-Oct. Singles and doubles $80-85; prices decrease in May and fall seasons.) The serene **Atlantic House Bed and Breakfast,** 501 N. Baltimore Ave., only a few bucks more, offers free breakfast and a wholesome change of pace from the Ocean City motel trend. (☎289-2333. A/C, cable TV, parking. Shared baths start at $50; private baths $125.) **Ocean City Travel Park,** 105 70th St., runs the only in-town campground (☎524-7601. Tents $25-38. RVs $25-53.)

Besides the beach, food is Ocean City's prime attraction. With freshly caught fish and a friendly atmosphere, **The Embers,** 24th St. and Coastal Hwy., flaunts the biggest seafood buffet and most potent fish stench in town. (☎289-3322 or 888-436-2377. Open daily July-Aug. 2-10pm; Sept.-June 3-9pm). When filling your belly matters more than aesthetics, **Fat Daddy's Sub Shop,** 216 S. Baltimore Ave., a grimy but economical dive around the corner from the hostel, offers satisfying deli sandwiches ($2-4.50) and subs ($4-6) on the beach until the early morning. (☎289-4040. Open daily 11am-4am. Free delivery.) Breakfast is the best meal of the day at the seaside **Brass Balls Saloon,** between 11th and 12th St. on the boardwalk. Enjoy oreo waffles ($4.75) or light, fluffy omelettes ($4.25-5.25) amid a mural of smiling celebrities. (☎289-0069. Open daily May-Oct. 8:30am-2am.)

⛶ ENTERTAINMENT AND NIGHTLIFE. Ocean City's star attraction is its beautiful **beach.** The wide stretch of surf and sand runs the entire 10 mi. length of town and can be accessed by taking a left onto any of the numerous side streets off of Philadelphia and Baltimore Ave. The breaking waves know no time constraints but beach-goers are technically limited to 6am-10pm. When the sun goes down, hard-earned tans glow under the glaring lights of Ocean City's bars and nightclubs. An amusement park for adults, the island oasis **Seacrets,** on 49th St., features 11 bars, including two floating bars on the bay. Barefoot barflies wander from bar to bar, sipping the signature frozen rum runner mixed with piña colada ($5.25) to the strains of three live bands nightly. A magnificent sunset view ushers in the early revelers. (☎524-4900. Open M-Sa 11am-2am, Su noon-2am. Cover $3-5.) The elder statesman of the bayside clubs, **Fager's Island,** 60th St. in the bay, attracts hordes across a plank walkway to its island location. No one seems to know the source of the classical music tradition but the 1812 Overture rings aloud daily with the sunset. Start the week with a festive bang at the M night deck party. (☎524-5500. Open daily 11am-2am. Happy hour Su-Th 4-7pm. Music plays nightly. Cover M $7.)

WASHINGTON, D.C. ☎202

Like many a young adult fresh out of college, the fledgling United States government quickly realized that independence meant little without a place to stay. Both Northern and Southern states wanted the capital on their turf. The final location—100 square miles pinched from Virginia and Maryland—was a compromise, an undeveloped swamp wedged between north and south. Congress commissioned French engineer Pierre L'Enfant to design the city.

Washington's wide avenues remained mostly empty, with a smattering of slave markets and boarding houses the only companions for the elegant government buildings. The city had hardly begun to expand when the British torched it in 1814; a post-war vote to give up and move the capital failed in Congress by just eight votes. Washington continued to disgust foreign diplomats—the district was a first stop for slave traders, whose shackled cargo awaited sales on the Mall and near the White House. The cessation of the slave trade after the Civil War transformed Washington from the Union's embarrassing appendage to its jugular vein.

The discrete cities of Federal Washington and local Washington coexist in the District. Federal Washington, the town of press conferences, power lunches, and presidential intrigue, is what most visitors come to see. The other part of Washington, the "second city," consists of a variety of communities, some prosperous, others overcome by poverty, drugs, and crime. These areas, sometimes within a few blocks of the seats of government, surprise many tourists with the troubling paradoxes of American democracy.

For everything about Washington D.C. you always wanted to know but were afraid to ask, check out the wildly revamped *Let's Go: Washington, D.C.*, available at fine bookstores.

✈ GETTING THERE AND AWAY

Airports: Ronald Reagan National Airport (☎703-417-8000). Metro: National Airport. It's best to fly here from within the US; National is on the Metro and closer to the city. Taxi $10-15 from downtown. The **Super Shuttle** (☎800-258-3826) runs between National and downtown M-F every 30min. **Dulles International Airport** (☎703-369-1600) is much farther from the city. Taxis cost $40 and up from downtown. The **Washington Flyer Dulles Express Bus** (☎888-927-4359) hits the West Falls Church Metro every 30min. 6-10am and 6-10:30pm, every 20min. from 10am-2pm, every 15min. from 2-6pm ($8). **Buses** to downtown (15th and K St. NW) take about 45min. and leave M-F every 30min. 5:20am-10:20pm; Sa-Su every hr. 5:20am-12:20pm, every 30min. 12:50-10:20pm ($16, family rate for groups of 3 or more $13 each).

Trains: Union Station, 50 Massachusetts Ave. NE (☎484-7540). **Amtrak** to: New York (3½hr., $67 reserved, $118 metroliner); Baltimore (40min., around $21); Philadelphia (2hr., $50); and Boston (8½hr., $68). Maryland's commuter train, **MARC** (☎410-859-7400, 24hr.), departs from Union to Baltimore ($5.75) and the suburbs.

⊑ GETTING AROUND

Public Transit: Metrorail and Metrobus (METRO), 600 5th St. NW (☎637-7000; M-F 6am-10:30pm), is relatively safe. Fare $1.10-3.25, depending on time and distance traveled. 1-day Metro pass $5. **Flash Pass** ($20) allows unlimited bus (and sometimes Metro) rides for 2 weeks. Trains run M-F 5:30am-midnight, Sa-Su 8am-midnight. For bus transfers, get a pass from machines on the platform *before* boarding the train. The **Metrobus** system serves Georgetown, downtown, and the suburbs. Fare $1.10.

Taxis: Yellow Cab, ☎544-1212.

Car Rental: Bargain Buggies Rent-a-Car, 3140 N. Washington Blvd. (☎703-841-0000), in Arlington, rents for $23 per day, $150 per week; 100 free mi. per day, 20¢. Must be 18 with major credit card or cash deposit of $250. Those under 21 need full insurance coverage of their own. Open M-F 8am-7pm, Sa 9am-3pm, Su 9am-noon.

Bike Rental: Big Wheel Bikes, 315 7th St. SE (☎543-1600). Metro: Eastern Market. Mountain bikes $5 per hr. (minimum 3hr.), $25 per business day. $32 per 24hr. Major credit card required for deposit. Open Tu-F 11am-7pm, Sa 10am-6pm, Su noon-5pm.

✦ ORIENTATION

Diamond-shaped D.C. stretches its tips in the four cardinal directions. The **Potomac River** forms the jagged southwest border, its waters flowing between the district and Arlington, VA. **North Capitol St., East Capitol St.,** and **South Capitol St.** slice up the city into four quadrants: NW, NE, SE, and SW. These four quadrants are named for where they stand vis-à-vis the Capitol. The **Mall,** stretching west of the Capitol,

Washington, D.C.

▲ ACCOMMODATIONS
Adams Inn & Int'l
Student Center, 1
Columbia Guest House, 2
Kalorama Guest House, 3
Washington International
Hostel (HI-AYH), 4

SEE COLOR INSERTS FOR MORE
WASHINGTON, D.C. MAPS

MID-ATLANTIC

makes a "West Capitol St." unnecessary. The suffixes of the quadrants distinguish otherwise identical addresses. For instance, you might find both an 800 G St. NW *and* an 800 G St. NE.

Washington's streets lie in a simple grid. Streets that run **east-to-west** are labeled **alphabetically** in relation to the north-south division, which runs through the Capitol. Since the street plan follows the Roman alphabet, in which "I" and "J" are the same letter, there is no J St. After W St., east-west streets take on **two-syllable names,** then **three-syllable names,** then the names of **trees and flowers.** The names run in alphabetical order, but sometimes repeat or skip a letter. Streets running **north-south** are **numbered** (1st St., 2nd St...) all the way out to 52nd St. NW and 63rd St. NE. Addresses on lettered streets indicate the number of the cross street. For instance, 1100 D St. SE is on the corner of D and 11th.

Major roads include **Pennsylvania Ave., Connecticut Ave., Wisconsin Ave., 16th St. NW, K St. NW, Massachusetts Ave., New York Ave.,** and **North Capitol St.** Washington, D.C. is ringed by the **Capital Beltway/I-495** (except where it's part of I-95); the Beltway is bisected by **U.S. 1,** and meets **I-395** from Virginia. The high-speed **Baltimore-Washington Pkwy.** connects Washington, D.C. to Baltimore. **I-595** trickles off the Capital Beltway east to Annapolis. **I-66** heads west into Virginia.

🚺 PRACTICAL INFORMATION

Visitor Info: Washington, D.C. Convention and Visitors Association (WCVA), 1212 New York Ave., #600 NW (☎789-7000; www.washington.org). Open M-F 9am-5pm. **D.C. Committee to Promote Washington,** 1212 New York Ave. NW, #200 (☎347-2873 or 800-422-8644). **Meridian International Center,** 1630 Crescent Pl. NW (☎667-6800). Metro: Dupont Circle. Brochures in a variety of languages. Office open M-F 9am-5pm.

Information lines: Dial-a-Museum (☎357-2020). **Dial-a-Park** (☎619-7275). **News** (☎334-9000). **Time** (☎844-1212). **Weather** (☎936-1212).

Hotlines: Rape Crisis Center, ☎333-7273. 24hr. **Gay and Lesbian Hotline,** ☎833-3234. Operates 7pm-11pm. **Traveler's Aid Society,** ☎546-3120. Offices at Union Station, National and Dulles Airports, and downtown at 512 C St. NE. Hours vary.

Hospitals and Clinics: Children's National Medical Center, 111 Michigan Ave. NW (☎884-5000). **Georgetown University Medical Center,** 3800 Reservoir Rd. NW (☎687-2000). **Whitman-Walker Clinic** (☎797-3500) provides AIDS and sexually transmitted disease counseling and a variety of other services. **Planned Parenthood,** 1108 16th St. NW (☎347-8500).

Internet Access: Atomic Grounds, 1555 Wilson Blvd., #105 (☎703-524-2157), in Arlington. Open M-F 6:30am-6:30pm, Sa-Su 8am-6:30pm. **The Cyberstop Cafe,** 1513 17th St. NW (☎234-2470), near P St. Open Su-Th 7:30am-midnight, F-Sa 7:30am-2am. **Myth.com Cybercafe,** 3241-3 M St. NW (☎625-6984). Open Su-Th 11am-1am.

Post Office: 900 Brentwood Rd. NE (☎636-1532). Indescribably inconvenient location. Open M-F 8am-8pm, Sa 8am-6pm, Su noon-6pm. **ZIP code:** 20066. **Area code:** 202.

🚹 ACCOMMODATIONS

Come nightfall, you're seeking sanctuary from the tourist dregs. But wherever should one squat in the District? Don't trip unwittingly into some chandeliered lobby. Trick these gold-digging taverns by shacking up with them on weekends or in summer months when discount rates crop up. Hostels also offer unbeatable rates and the chance to mingle with an international crowd. Don't forget that D.C. adds a 14.5% occupancy tax to your bill. Damn feds.

HOSTELS AND STUDENT CENTERS

Washington International Hostel (HI-AYH), 1009 11 St. NW 20001 (☎783-3262), 3 blocks north of the Metro Center stop. (11 St. exit). Located in the heart of D.C., just 5 blocks from the White House and a 20min. walk from the National Mall. Rooms with 4-

12 beds, shared baths. Common room, A/C, kitchen, game room, store, lockers, Internet access, laundry, luggage and bicycle storage. Reception 24hr. Check-in after noon. Check-out 11am. Use caution in this area at night. $22, non-members $25. Wheelchair accessible (give advance notice).

Washington International Student Center, 2451 18th St. NW (☎667-7681 or ☎800-567-4150). Metro: Woodley Park-Zoo and a 15min. walk. This hidden hostel barely squeezes itself into the fun-packed and lively Adams-Morgan area. 5 A/C bedrooms, with 3-4 bunkbeds per room, 2 kitchens, 3 shared bathrooms. No lockout. Breakfast included. Lockers. Common room. Bunks $16. Internet access $2 per 10min. Reserve at least a week in advance, especially in summer.

HOTELS

▨BullMoose, 101 5th St. NE (☎547-1050 or 800-261-2768) Metro: Capitol South. For fans of comfort, taste, and Teddy Roosevelt (pics of him dot the walls). BullMoose pampers its guests with continental breakfast, baked goods, and rustic elegance. 10 rooms, 4 with private bath. A/C, no smoking, kitchen, phones and data jacks. Reservations recommended. Twin beds approximately $89; doubles $129-149; queen beds $149-169.

Taft Bridge Inn, 2007 Wyoming Ave. (☎387-2007), at the intersection of 20th and Wyoming. Quiet hotel with beautiful antique-filled rooms in a stately Georgian building. Claw-legged bathtubs, fancy marble floors, canopy wood or big brass beds, window seats, and fireplaces. Modem hook-up, phones, voicemail, and A/C. Laundry facilities. Full breakfast included. Parking $8 per day. Wheelchair accessible. Singles $59-74, with private bath $110-125; off-season singles $99-114. Each additional person $15.

GUEST HOUSES

Kalorama Guest House at Woodley Park, 2700 Cathedral Ave. NW (☎328-0860), and at **Kalorama Park,** 1854 Mintwood Pl. NW (☎667-6369). Metro: Woodley Park-Zoo for both. Guest houses with Victorian charm. Clean, quiet rooms with A/C. Laundry. Continental breakfast. No children under 6. Limited parking by reservation. Reception M-F 8am-8pm, Sa-Su 9am-7pm. Singles with shared bath $45-65; doubles $50-70; with private baths $60-100/$65-105. Reservations with credit card required (or full payment with check at least 2 weeks in advance).

The Columbia Guest House, 2005 Columbia Rd. NW (☎265-4006), just off Connecticut Ave. Eccentric, patrician townhouse with dark wood paneling, polished hardwood floors, ornate fireplaces, and neatly furnished rooms (some with A/C and private bath). Most clientele are students or other budget travelers. Singles $29-33; doubles $36-59. $10 additional occupant. Students 10-15% discount.

Adams Inn, 1744 Lanier Pl. NW (☎800-578-6807). 3 elegant Victorian townhouses and a carriage house with garden. Cable TV, pay phones, and coin laundry facilities. Unique furnishings from 1913, the year the houses were erected. Friendly, helpful staff. Continental breakfast. Limited parking $7 per night. Reception M-Sa 8am-9pm, Su 1-9pm. Reservations require first night deposit. Singles $55, with private bath $70. Each additional person $10. ISIC 10% discount.

Tabard Inn, 1739 N St. NW (☎785-1277), between 17th and 18th St., just south of the Circle. 3 townhouses connected by a maze of passages, stairways, and lounges. Features large rooms beautifully decorated with ornate furniture. Offers a patio, bar, and lounges. Rooms have A/C and phone. Breakfast included. Reception 24hr. Singles $65-95, with private bath $99-155; doubles $90-110, with private bath $114-170. $15 per additional person.

◧ FOOD

How does one feast like a senator on an intern's slim budget? Savvy natives go grubbing at Happy Hours. Bars often leave out free appetizer platters to bait early evening clients (see **Nightlife**). As for budget eateries, **Adams-Morgan** and **Dupont Circle** are home to the creme de la creme of succulent ethnic delights.

ADAMS-MORGAN

▨ **Mixtec,** 1792 Columbia Rd. NW (☎332-1011), near 18th St. A familial, friendly staff serves some of the area's tastiest Mexican food to locals and travelers. *Tacos al carbon* (2 small beef-filled tortillas) $7, subs $4-6. Fruit drinks $1.75. Appetizers $3-6.50. Entrees $7-11; sangria $2.50 per glass. Open Su-Th 11am-10pm, F-Sa 11am-11pm.

Perry's, 1811 Columbia Rd. NW (☎234-6218), near 18th St. Nouvelle Japanese-American cuisine. Phyllo-wrapped salmon stuffed with crab on a bed of spicy beans, mango salsa, and asparagus ($17). Coveted rooftop patio with a view. Entrees $9-18; sushi 50¢-$5 per piece. Open M-Sa 5:30pm-1:30am, Su 5:30-11:30pm; kitchen closes daily 10:15pm, sushi closes daily 11:15pm; drag brunch Su 11am-2:30pm.

So's Your Mom, 1831 Columbia Rd. NW (☎462-3666). A sandwich shop with meats, cheeses, and breads as eye-popping as your mom. Portions as big as your mom and unexpected choices (sliced beef tongue $6). Take-out only. Sandwiches $3.25-6. Sweet pastries and your mom ($1.75). Open M-F 7am-8pm, Sa 8am-7pm, Su 8am-3pm.

ALEXANDRIA

Lite 'n' Fair, 1018 King St. (☎703-549-3717). Ki Choi, former chef of the ritzy Watergate Restaurant, runs this rough gem with carryout options. Exquisite seafood sandwiches and burgers $4-8, smoked salmon $4, calamari tempura $4, or seafood paella $9. Open M 11am-3pm, Tu-Th 11am-9pm, F-Sa 11am-10pm.

ARLINGTON

Cafe Dalat, 3143 Wilson Blvd. (☎703-276-0935). Metro: Clarendon. Premiere *pho* (Vietnamese noodle soup) $4. Specialties include *chao tom* (shrimp grilled on sugar cane with rice paper, vermicelli, cucumber, and peanut sauce; $10). Large vegetarian menu. All-you-can-eat lunch buffet M-F 11am-2pm $5. Dinner entrees $7-10. Open Su-Th 11am-9:30pm, F-Sa 11am-10:30pm.

BETHESDA

▨ **Tara Thai,** 4828 Bethesda Ave. (☎301-657-0488). Aqua-themed chitty-chitty-bang-bang-style dining. *Goong phuket* (grilled black tiger shrimp; lunch $8, dinner $13) and *pad thai* ($6/$8). Open M-Th 11:30am-3pm and 5-10pm, F 11:30am-3pm and 5-11pm, Sa noon-3:30pm and 5-11pm, and Su noon-3:30pm and 5-10pm.

CAPITOL HILL

▨ **Armands Chicago Pizzeria,** 226 Massachusetts Ave. NE (☎547-6600). Metro: Union Station. New York and Chicago style pizzas. Pizza ($6.50-15), pasta ($4-5.25), salads ($3.50-4.75), and subs ($3.75-4.75). Lunch buffet (11:30am-2:30pm, $6) with all-you-can-eat pizza. Open M-Sa 11:30am-11pm, Su 4pm-10pm.

Banana Cafe and Piano Bar, 500 8th St. SE (☎543-5906). Metro: Eastern Market. A crazy fiesta with fake banana trees and a garish yellow interior. Live Cuban music. Tex-Mex, Puerto Rican, and Cuban entrees ($7-16), tapas ($3.25-9), plantain soup ($4.50), shrimp fajitas ($15). Lunch entrees $6.25-9. Su brunch 11am-3pm ($13). Open M-Th 11:30am-10:30pm, F 11:30am-11pm, Sa noon-11pm, Su 11am-10pm.

CHINATOWN

Szechuan Gallery, 617 H St. NW (☎898-1180). Recognize this place? A scene from the movie *True Lies* was filmed here, and they've got autographed pictures to prove it. Locally renowned for its unusual dishes such as *congee*, a delicious Chinese gruel ($5). Lunch specials $5-8. Open Su-Th 11am-10pm, F-Sa 11am-11pm.

Burma Restaurant, upstairs at 740 6th St. NW (☎638-1280), between H and G St. Mild Burmese curries and a plethora of garnishes replace typical Chinese soy sauce. Fried golden prawns with sweet and sour chili sauce ($6). Squid, sauteed in garlic, ginger, and scallions ($8). Open M-F 11am-3pm and 6-10:30pm. Entrees $6-8.

DUPONT CIRCLE

▨ **Raku,** 1900 Q St. NW (☎265-7258, delivery 232-8646), off Connecticut Ave. Appropriately named after the Japanese word for "pleasure." Pan-Asian noodles ($9-13), salads

($5-11), sushi ($4-13), and "*tapas*" (dumplings, rolls, and skewers; $3-8). Open Su-Th 11:30am-10pm, F-Sa 11:30am-11pm.

▨ **Lauriol Plaza,** 1865 18th St. NW (☎387-0035), recently moved to the corner of 18th and T St. NW. Popular Latino eatery with a winding maze of dining rooms. F-Sa and holidays 11:30am-midnight. Appetizers like fried plantains and guacamole $2.50-7; entrees $6.50-16. Su brunch entrees $6-9 (11am-3pm). Open Su-Th 11:30am-11pm,

▨ **Mediterranean Blue,** 1910 18th St. NW (☎483-2583). Delectable Italian cuisine served in a dimly-lit dining room. Locals prefer the *penne estivi*, penne pasta tossed w/ fresh mozzarella, fresh basil, and sun-ripened tomatoes ($10). Also serves lamb, chicken, and shrimp kabobs ($9-16). Open daily 5pm-midnight, Su brunch 11am-3pm.

The Cyberstop Cafe, 1513 17th St. NW (☎234-2470), just north of P St. Upstairs lounge feels more like a living room than a cafe. Internet rates are $5 per 30min. and $8 per hr. Coffee $1-3, cookies $1. Open Su-Th 7:30am-midnight, F-Sa 7:30am-2am.

FARRAGUT

The Art Gallery Grille, 1712 I St. NW (☎298-6658). Metro: Farragut West. A combination of old-style Art Deco diner charm and healthy Middle Eastern eatery. Happy Hour 4-8pm. White Pizza (mozzarella, parmesan, and havarti cheese) $8, sandwiches $8.25-11. Open M-W 6:30am-11pm, Th-F 6am-2am.

GEORGETOWN

▨ **Cafe La Ruche,** 1039 31st St. NW (☎965-2684, takeout 965-2591), 2 blocks south of M St. Late at night, romantics buzz in to this beehive for French dessert and coffee. Soups $4, quiche $8, sandwiches $7-16, chocolate mousse $5, kiwi tart $5. Open M-Th 11:30am-11:30pm, F 11:30am-1am, Sa 10am-1am, Su 10am-10:30pm.

Bistro Med, 3288 M St. (☎333-0955), at the corner of M and 33rd St. Levantine cuisine from the eastern Mediterranean. Turkish style pizzas such as the *Lahmacun*, a favorite with ground beef ($11), as well as entrees ($11-17), including the *Merquez de Maroc-caire:* lamb sausage with eggplant and couscous ($11). Open daily 11:30am-10:30pm. Special late-night brunch served Th-Sa 11pm-5am.

Amma Vegetarian Kitchen, 3291 M St. NW (☎625-6025). South Indian cuisine, including dishes like *idli sambar* (steamed rice flour cakes served with a dazzling vegetable sauce, $3). Very affordable—the most expensive dish will set you back only $5. Open M-Th 11:30am-2:30pm and 5:30-9:30pm; F-Su 11:30am-3pm and 5:30-10pm.

OLD DOWNTOWN

▨ **Haad Thai,** 1100 New York Ave. NW (☎682-1111), entrance on 11th St. between H and I St. Serves popular *pad thai* (lunch $6.25, dinner $9) and *panang gai* (chicken sautéed with fresh basil leaves in curry peanut sauce; lunch $7.25, dinner $10) and vegetarian options. Open M-F 11:30am-2:30pm and 5-10:30pm, Sa noon-10:30pm, Su 5-10:30pm.

▨ **Harry's,** 436 11th St. (☎624-0053), on the corner of E and 11th. Metro: Metro Center. Spilling out onto the street during the summer, Harry's curries favor with its 8oz. burgers and fries ($6.25). Come to cool the night off and watch the Orioles game with a beer or daquiri ($3-5.25). Open Su-Th 11am-2am, F-Sa 11am-3am.

SHAW AND U DISTRICT

▨ **Polly's Cafe,** 1342 U St. NW (☎265-8385), near 14th St. Cozy dive serving grilled veggie sandwich ($5) and portabello mushroom steak ($9) as veggie faves. Sa-Su 10am-midnight. Live music W after 10pm. Hamburgers $5. Hearty Sunday brunch with drink pitchers ($5-9) and meat, potatoes, and eggs ($7-8). Open M-F 6pm-midnight.

FEELING CRABBY? Imported from nearby Maryland, **hard shell crabs** are an area favorite with a plethora of crab-houses in Maryland, Virginia, and in the District. These hard shell crabs are often cooked in a special **Old Bay Spice Seasoning,** the indigenous D.C. flavor. Many of these restaurants tantalize patrons with **all-you-can-eat** specials. Don't worry, they'll give you a bib, too!

MID-ATLANTIC

Wilson's, 700 V St. NW (☎462-3700 or 462-2992). Corner of V. St. and Georgia Ave. A sports diner with hot/cold sandwiches (hot sandwiches $5-6.50, cold sandwiches $3), salads ($1.60 tossed), or various dinner entrees (ribs $10, pork chops $8). Open M-Sa 7am-8pm, Su 8am-7pm.

UPPER NORTHWEST

🔲 **Jandara,** 2606 Connecticut Ave. NW (☎387-8876). Celestial blues and purples comple-ment an out-of-this-world dining with tasty Thai standards and specialty dishes like *gaeng ped yang* (roast duck simmered in a red curry sauce with pineapple, $8.95). Lunch entrees $5-10. Open Su-Th 11:30am-10:30pm, F-Sa 11:30am-11pm.

Mama Maria and Enzio's, 2313 Wisconsin Ave. NW (☎965-1337), near Calvert St. Southern Italian dishes such as *caprese* (tomato, fresh mozzarella with olive oil) or pro-sciutto and melon ($6.25-11.75), large shrimp in lemon sauce ($16), pastas ($9-13). Lunch entrees $7-11. Open lunch M-F 11:30am-3pm; dinner M-Sa 5-10:30pm.

Faccia Luna, 2400 Wisconsin Ave. NW (☎337-3132). A wood-fired oven cooks up thin, crisp-yet-tender crusts. Basic pie $6.50-12; toppings $1.25-2 each. Lunch special ($5-6) includes an entree and a drink. Open M-Th 11:30am-11pm, F-Sa 11:30am-midnight, Su 11am-midnight.

🏛 SIGHTS

Saw Washington Monument. Phallic. Appalling. A national catastrophe.
 —British writer Arnold Bennett

CAPITOL HILL

Capitol Hill is the heart of American government, Washington's principal tourist attraction, and one of democracy's most potent icons.

THE CAPITOL. The US Capitol may be an endless font of cynicism, but it still evokes the glory of the republican ideal. The **East Front** faces the Supreme Court. From the times of frontiersman Andrew Jackson (1829) to peanut-farmin' Jimmy Carter (1977), most presidents were inaugurated here. Recent presidential inaugu-rations have taken place on the mall-facing West Front. The East Front entrance brings you into the 180 ft. high **rotunda,** where soldiers slept during the Civil War. From the lower-level crypt, visitors can climb to the 2nd fl. for a view of the House or Senate visitors chambers. Americans may obtain a free gallery pass from the office of their representative or senator in the House or Senate office buildings near the Capitol. Foreigners may get one-day passes by presenting identification at the "appointments desks" in the crypt. *(☎225-6827. Metro: Capitol South. Open daily Mar.-Aug. 9am-8pm; Sept.-Feb. 9am-4:30pm. Tours Mar.-Aug. M-F 9am-7pm, Sa 9am-4pm; Sept.-Feb. M-Sa 9am-4pm. Free.)* The real business of Congress, however, is conducted in **com-mittee hearings.** Most are open to the public; check the *Washington Post's* "Today in Congress" box for times and locations. The free **Capitol subway** (a.k.a. the **"capitol choo-choo"**) shuttles between the basement of the Capitol and the House and Senate office buildings; a buzzer and flashing red light signals an imminent vote.

SUPREME COURT. In 1935, the justices of the Supreme Court decided it was time to take the nation's separation of powers literally and moved from their makeshift offices in the Capitol into a new Greek Revival courthouse across the street. Oral arguments are open to the public; show up before 8:30am to be seated, or walk through the standing gallery to hear 5min. of the argument. *(In session Oct.-June M-W 10am-noon and 1-3pm for 2 weeks every month. The courtroom itself is open when Justices are on vacation. 1 1st St. ☎479-3000. Court open M-F 9am-4:30pm. Free.)*

LIBRARY OF CONGRESS. The Library of Congress, between East Capitol and Inde-pendence Ave., is the world's largest library, with 113,026,742 objects stored on 532 mi. of shelves, including a copy of *Old King Cole* written on a grain of rice. The col-lection was torched by the British in 1814, and was restarted from Thomas Jeffer-son's personal collection. The collection is open to anyone of college age or older with a legitimate research purpose—exhibits of rare items and a tour of the facilities are available for tourists. *(1st St. SE. ☎ 707-5000.)* The **Jefferson Building's** green copper dome and gold-leafed flame seals a spectacular octagonal reading room. *(Great Hall open M-Sa 8:30am-5:30pm. Visitors Center and galleries open 10am-5:30am. Free.)*

UNION STATION. Trains converge at Union Station, 2 blocks north of the Capitol. Colonnades, archways, and domed ceilings allude to imperial Rome, if Rome was filled with stores and a food court. *(50 Massachusetts Ave. NE. ☎ 371-9441. Metro: Union Station. Retail shops open M-Sa 10am-9pm, Su 10am-6pm.)*

MONUMENTS

WASHINGTON MONUMENT. Currently undergoing a $9.4 million restoration project, this shrine to America's first president was once nicknamed the "the Beef Depot monument" after the cattle that grazed here during the Civil War. Construction was temporarily halted during the war and later resumed; the stone that was used came from a new quarry, which explains the different colors of the monument's stones. The **Reflecting Pool** mirrors Washington's obelisk. *(Metro: Smithsonian. Admission to the monument by timed ticket. Apr.-Aug. monument open daily 8am-midnight, ticket kiosk open from 7:30am until all tickets distributed; Sept.-Mar. monument open 9am-5pm, ticket kiosk from 8:30am. Free. No tickets needed after 8pm Apr.-Aug.)*

VIETNAM VETERANS MEMORIAL. Maya Ying Lin, who designed the Vietnam Veterans Memorial, south of Constitution Ave. at 22nd St. NW, received a "B" when she submitted her memorial concept for a grade as a Yale senior—but beat her professor in the public memorial design competition. In her words, the monument is "a rift in the earth—a long, polished black stone wall, emerging from and receding into the earth." The wall contains the names of the 58,132 Americans who died in Vietnam, indexed in books at both ends of the structure. *(☎ 634-1568. Metro: Foggy Bottom/GWU. 24hr.)*

LINCOLN MEMORIAL. The Lincoln Memorial, at the west end of the Mall, recalls the rectangular grandeur of Athens' Parthenon. From these steps, Martin Luther King, Jr. gave his "I Have a Dream" speech during the 1963 March on Washington. A seated Lincoln presides over the memorial, keeping watch over protesters, Nazi party vigils, and Fourth of July fireworks. Climbing the 19 ft. president is a federal offense; a camera will catch you if the rangers don't. *(☎ 426-6895. Metro: Smithsonian or Foggy Bottom/GWU. 24hr.)*

KOREAN WAR MEMORIAL. The 19 colossal polished steel statues of the Korean War Memorial trudge up a hill, rifles in hand, an eternal expression of weariness mixed with fear frozen upon their faces. The statue is accompanied by a black granite wall with over 2000 sandblasted photographic images from this war, in which 54,000 Americans lost their lives. The memorial is at the west end of the Mall, near Lincoln. *(☎ 632-1002. Metro: Smithsonian or Foggy Bottom/GWU.)*

FRANKLIN DELANO ROOSEVELT MEMORIAL. Occupying a long stretch of West Potomac Park (the peninsula between the Tidal Basin and the Potomac River) just a short walk from the Jefferson or Lincoln Memorials, the Franklin Delano Roosevelt Memorial is more of a stone garden than a monument. Whether to display the handicapped Roosevelt in his wheelchair was hotly debated when the memorial was being planned; in compromise, Roosevelt is seated, a position based on a famous picture taken at Yalta. The memorial is laid out in four "rooms" of red South Dakota granite, each of which represents a phase of FDR's presidency. *(☎ 376-6704. Metro: Smithsonian.)*

JEFFERSON MEMORIAL AND TIDAL BASIN. A 19 ft. bronze Thomas Jefferson stands enshrined in the domed rotunda of the Jefferson Memorial, designed to evoke Jefferson's home and own creation, Monticello. The memorial overlooks the Tidal Basin, where pedalboats ply a polluted pond in and out of the shrine's strange shadow. Quotes from the Declaration of Independence, the Virginia Statute of Religious Freedom, Notes on Virginia, and an 1815 letter adorn the walls. *(☎ 426-6821. Metro: L'Enfant Plaza.)*

SOUTH OF THE MALL

US HOLOCAUST MEMORIAL MUSEUM. A block off the mall lies the US Holocaust Memorial Museum, where excellent displays chronicle the rise of Nazism, the events leading up to the war in Europe, and the history of anti-Semitism. Films show troops entering concentration camps, shocked by the mass graves and emaciated prisoners they encounter. An eternal flame burns in "The Hall of Remembrance." *(100 Raul Wallenberg Pl. SW. ☎ 488-0400. Metro: Smithsonian. Open in summer daily 10am-8pm; in winter 10am-5:30pm. Free. Get in line early for tickets.)*

BUREAU OF ENGRAVING AND PRINTING. Also known as "the Mint," the Bureau offers tours of the presses that annually print over $20 billion worth of money. The love of money has made this the area's longest line; expect to grow old while you wait. *(☎ 847-2808. At 14th and C St. SW. Metro: Smithsonian. Open M-F 9am-2pm. Free.)*

WHITE HOUSE AND FOGGY BOTTOM

WHITE HOUSE. With its simple columns and expansive lawns, the White House seems a compromise between patrician lavishness and democratic simplicity. Thomas Jefferson proposed a contest for the design of the building, but he lost to amateur architect James Hoban when George Washington judged the competition. The President's staff works in the West Wing, while the First Lady's cohorts occupy the East Wing. Staff who cannot fit in the White House work in the nearby **Old Executive Office Building.** The President's official office is the **Oval Office,** site of many televised speeches, but the public tour is limited to public reception areas. *(1600 Pennsylvania Ave. NW. ☎ 456-7041. Open by tour only Tu-Sa 10am-noon. Free. Get tickets at the White House Visitors Center, 1450 Pennsylvania Ave. NW, at the corner of 15th and E St.)*

AROUND LAFAYETTE PARK. Historic homes surround Lafayette Park north of the White House. These homes include the Smithsonian-owned **Renwick Gallery** craft museum, which has some remarkable works, such as the 80s sculptures *Ghost Clock* and *Game Fish.* *(at 17th St. and Pennsylvania Ave. NW. ☎ 357-2700. Metro: Farragut West. Open daily 10am-5:30pm. Free.)* Once housed in the Renwick's mansion, the **Corcoran Gallery** now boasts larger quarters on 17th St. between E St. and New York Ave. NW. It displays American artists such as John Singer Sargent, Mary Cassatt, and Winslow Homer. *(☎ 639-1700. Open M, W, and F-Su 10am-5pm, Th 10am-9pm. Suggested donation $3, students and seniors $1, families $5.)* Nearby, the **Octagon,** a curious building designed by Capitol architect William Thornton, is reputedly filled with ghosts. Tour guides explain the history of the house. *(Open Tu-Su 10am-4pm. $5, students and seniors $3.)*

JFK CENTER FOR THE PERFORMING ARTS. A few blocks above Rock Creek Pkwy., the John F. Kennedy Center for the Performing Arts, off 25th St. and New Hampshire Ave. NW, rises like a marble sarcophagus. One could fit the Washington Monument in the gargantuan **Grand Foyer,** were it not for the 18 Swedish chandeliers, shaped like cubical grape clusters. *(☎ 467-4600. Metro: Foggy Bottom-GWU. Open daily 10am-midnight. Free tours every hr. on the hour. M-F 10am-5pm, Sa-Su 10am-1pm.)* Across the street is Tricky Dick's beloved **Watergate Complex.**

OLD DOWNTOWN

An architectural marvel houses the Smithsonian's **National Building Museum,** towering above F St. NW between 4th and 5th St. Montgomery Meigs' Italian-inspired edifice remains one of Washington's most beautiful. *(☎ 272-2448. Metro: Judiciary Sq. Open M-Sa 10am-4pm, Su noon-4pm; until 5pm in summer. Suggested donation $3, students and seniors $2.)*

At the **National Archives,** at 8th St. and Constitution Ave. NW, visitors line up to view the original Declaration of Independence, US Constitution, and Bill of Rights. *(☎ 501-5000; Metro: Archives-Navy Memorial. Open daily Apr.-Labor Day 10am-9pm; Labor Day-Mar. 10am-5:30pm. Free.)* The **Federal Bureau of Investigation** still hunts Communists, social activists, boogie-monsters, interstate felons, and Branch Davidians with undiminished vigor. Tour lines form on the **J. Edgar Hoover Building**'s outdoor plaza. *(☎ 324-3447. Open M-F 8:45am-4:15pm. Free.)*

John Wilkes Booth shot President Abraham Lincoln during a performance at **Ford's Theater,** 511 10th St. NW. National Park Rangers describe the events with animated gusto during a 20min. talk. *(☎ 426-6924. Metro: Metro Center. Open daily 9am-5pm. Free.)* The **Old Post Office,** at Pennsylvania Ave. and 12th St. NW, rebukes its contemporary neighbors with arched windows, conical turrets, and a clock tower, all sheathing a shopping mall. *(☎ 289-4224. Metro: Federal Triangle. Tower open mid-Apr. to mid-Sept. 8am-10:45pm; off season 10am-6pm. Shops open M-Sa 10am-8pm, Su noon-6pm.)*

The **National Museum of Women in the Arts** houses works by the likes of Mary Cassatt, Georgia O'Keeffe, and Frida Kahlo in a former Masonic Temple. *(1250 New York Ave. NW. ☎ 783-5000. Metro: Metro Center. Open M-Sa 10am-5pm, Su noon-5pm. Free.)*

GEORGETOWN

Georgetown's quiet, narrow, tree-lined streets are sprinkled with trendy boutiques and points of historic interest that make for an enjoyable walking tour. Retired from commercial use since the 1800s, the **Chesapeake & Ohio Canal** extends 185 mi. from Georgetown to Cumberland, MD. Today, the towpath where trusty mules pulled barges on the canal belongs to the National Park Service.

The **Dumbarton Oaks Mansion,** between R and S St., former home of John Calhoun, holds a beautiful collection of Byzantine and pre-Columbian art. The 1944 Dumbarton Oaks Conference helped write the United Nations charter. The spectacular pre-Columbian art gallery was designed by Phillip Johnson. The beautiful gardens are the best cheap date place in town. *(1703 32nd St. NW. ☎ 339-6401. Art gallery open Tu-Su 2-5pm. Suggested contribution $1. Gardens open daily Apr.-Oct. 2-6pm; Nov.-Mar. 2-5pm. $5, seniors and children $3.)*

In 1789, when Archbishop John Carroll learned where the new capital would be built, he rushed to found **Georgetown University,** at 37th and O St., the first Catholic institution of higher learning in the US.

DUPONT CIRCLE

Once one of Washington's swankier neighborhoods, Dupont Circle attracted embassies because of its stately townhouses and large tracts of land. Today, it is a haven for the international, artsy, and gay crowds; this mix of business, politics, and pleasure make it one of the more exciting parts of the city.

The **Art Gallery District,** bounded by Connecticut Ave., Florida Ave., and Q St., contains over two dozen galleries displaying everything from contemporary photographs to tribal crafts. *(General information ☎ 232-3610.)* Nearby, the **Phillips Collection,** at Q St. NW, was the 1st museum of modern art in the U.S. Everyone gapes at Auguste Renoir's masterpiece, *Luncheon of the Boating Party*, in the Renoir room. Works by Delacroix, Miró, and Turner line the Annex. *(1600 21st St. ☎ 387-2151. Open Tu-Sa 10am-5pm, Su noon-7pm. $7.50, students and seniors $4, under 12 free.)*

The stretch of Massachusetts Ave. between Dupont Circle and Observatory Circle is also called Embassy Row. Before the 30s, Washington socialites lined the avenue with extravagant edifices; status-conscious diplomats found the mansions perfect for their purposes, and embassies moved in by the dozen. Flags line the entrance to the **Islamic Center,** a brilliant white building within which stunning designs stretch to the tips of spired ceilings. No shorts allowed; women must cover their heads, arms, and legs. *(2551 Massachusetts Ave. NW. ☎ 332-8343. Open daily 10am-5pm; prayers held 5 times daily.)*

UPPER NORTHWEST

Washington National Zoological Park has been best known for its giant pandas, Hsing-Hsing and Ling-Ling, which Mao gave to Nixon. The zoo's orangutans are allowed to swing through the park via a series of 40 ft. high towers. The Valley Trail (marked with blue bird tracks) connects the bird and sealife exhibits, while the red Olmsted Walk (marked with elephant feet) links land-animal houses. *(3001 Connecticut Ave. ☎ 673-4800. Metro: Woodley Park-Zoo. Grounds open daily May 1 to Sept. 15 6am-8pm, Sept. 16 to Apr. 30 6am-6pm. Buildings open daily 10am-6pm, off-season 10am-4:30pm. Free.)*

MID-ATLANTIC

The **Washington National Cathedral,** at Massachusetts and Wisconsin Ave. NW, was built from 1907 to 1990. Rev. Martin Luther King, Jr. preached his last Su sermon from the pulpit. The elevator rises to the Pilgrim Observation Gallery, revealing D.C. from the highest vantage in the city. At the **Medieval Workshop,** children can carve stone, learn how a stained-glass window is created, or, for $2, mold a gargoyle out of clay. (☎ 537-6200 or 364-6616. Metro: Tenleytown, then take the #30, 32, 34, or 36 bus toward Georgetown; or walk up Cathedral Ave. from the equidistant Woodley Park-Zoo Metro. Cathedral open May-Aug. M-F 10am-9pm, Sa 10am-4:30pm, Su 12:30am-4:30pm; Sept.-Apr. M-Sa 10am-5pm, Su 12:30-4pm. Suggested donation $3 for tour, under 12 $1.)

🏛 MUSEUMS ON THE MALL

The **Smithsonian** is the catalogued attic of the United States, containing over 140 million objects. The Institute began as the brainchild of **James Smithson,** a British chemist who, though he never himself visited the US, left 105 bags of gold sovereigns—the bulk of his estate—to "found at Washington, under the name of the Smithsonian Institution, an establishment for the increase and diffusion of knowledge among men." The Smithsonian Museums on the Mall constitute the world's largest museum complex. The **Smithsonian Castle,** on the south side of the mall, has an introduction to and info on the Smithsonian buildings. (☎ 357-2700. Metro: Smithsonian or Federal Triangle. All Smithsonian museums are free, wheelchair accessible, and open daily 10am-5:30pm, with extended summer hours determined annually.)

National Air and Space Museum, on the south side of the Mall across from the National Gallery, is the world's most popular museum, with 7½ million visitors per year. Airplanes and space vehicles dangle from the ceilings; the Wright brothers' original biplane hangs in the entrance gallery. The space-age atrium holds a moon rock, worn smooth by tourists' fingertips. Walk through the Skylab space station, the Apollo XI command module, and a DC-7. IMAX movies on a 5-story screen thrill the endless throngs.

National Museum of American History, on the north side of the Mall, closest to the Washington Monument, houses several centuries' worth of machines, photographs, vehicles, harmonicas, and uncategorizable US detritus. When the Smithsonian inherits quirky artifacts of popular history, like Dorothy's slippers from *The Wizard of Oz*, they end up here. Hands-on exhibits are geared toward children.

Museum of Natural History, east toward the Capitol from American History, ruminates on the earth and its life in 3 big, crowded floors of exhibits. Objects on display in the spectacular golden-domed, neoclassical buildings include dinosaur skeletons, the largest African elephant ever captured, and an insect zoo with live creepy-crawlies. Visitors still line up to see the cursed Hope Diamond, mailed to the Smithsonian in 1958 for $145.29 (insured up to $1 million).

National Gallery of Art (☎ 737-4215), east of Natural History, is not technically a part of the Smithsonian, but a close cousin of the Institute due to its location on the mall. The **West Wing** houses its pre-1900 art in a domed marble temple in the Western Tradition, including works by El Greco, Raphael, Rembrandt, Vermeer, and Monet. Leonardo da Vinci's earliest surviving portrait, Ginevra de' Benci, the only one of his works in the US, hangs among a fine collection of Italian Renaissance Art. The **East Building** houses the museum's 20th-century collection, including works by Picasso, Matisse, Mondrian, Miró, Magritte, Pollock, Warhol, Lichtenstein, and Rothko. The building also holds the museum's temporary exhibits. The National Gallery recently unveiled an outdoor **Sculpture Garden.** Open M-Sa 10am-5pm, Su 11am-6pm.

Hirshhorn Museum and Sculpture Garden, on the south side of the mall west of Air and Space. The 4-story, slide-carousel-shaped brown building has outraged traditionalists since 1966. Each floor consists of 2 concentric circles: an outer ring of rooms with modern, postmodern, and post-postmodern paintings, and an inner corridor of sculptures. The museum claims a comprehensive set of 19th- and 20th-century Western sculpture.

National Museum of African Art and the **Arthur M. Sackler Gallery** hide together underground in the newest museum facility on the Mall, to the west of the Hirshhorn. The Museum of African Art displays artifacts from sub-Saharan Africa such as masks, textiles, ceremonial figures, and musical instruments. The Sackler Gallery showcases an extensive collection of art from China, South and Southeast Asia, and Persia. Exhibits include illuminated manuscripts, Chinese and Japanese painting, jade miniatures, and friezes from Egypt, Phoenicia, and Sumeria.

Freer Gallery of Art (☎ 357-4880), just west of the Hirshhorn, displays American and Asian art. The static American collection consists of the holdings of Charles L. Freer, the museum's benefactor, and focuses on works by James McNeill Whistler. The strong Asian collections include bronzes, manuscripts, and jade.

⚑ ENTERTAINMENT

MUSIC

The D.C. punk scene is, or at least was, one of the nation's finest. The biggest rock events take place at the sports arenas: **RFK Stadium** in the summer and the **USAir Arena** year-round. Tickets for many shows are available from **Protix** (☎ 410-481-6500, 703-218-6500, or 800-955-5566) or **TicketMaster** (☎ 432-7328). The **U District,** D.C.'s ear-blasting epicenter, has sent the D.C. punk and rock scene off the Richter scale for decades. *Be careful in the area at night.*

On summer Sa and Su, shows from jazz and R&B to the **National Symphony Orchestra** occupy the outdoor, 4200-seat **Carter Barron Amphitheater,** set into Rock Creek Park at 16th St. and Colorado Ave (☎ 426-6837, tickets vary from free to about $20).

THEATER AND DANCE

Arena Stage, 6th St. and Maine Ave. SW, is often called the best regional (non-New York) theater company in America. (☎ 488-4377. Metro: Waterfront. Box office open M-Sa 10am-8pm, Su noon-8pm. Tickets $25-45, lower for smaller stages, students 35% off, seniors 20% off; half-price rush usually available 1½hr. before show.) The **Kennedy Center** (☎ 416-8000), at 25th St. and New Hampshire Ave., offers scores of ballet, opera and dramatic productions, most of them expensive ($10-75); however, most productions offer half-price tickets the day of performance to students, seniors, military, and the disabled; call ☎ 467-4600 for details. The **Millennium Stage** presents free performances in the Grand Foyer of the Kennedy Center. The prestigious **Shakespeare Theater,** at the Lansburgh, 450 7th St. NW at Pennsylvania Ave., offers a Bard-heavy repertoire. Standing-room tickets are available 2hr. before curtain. (☎ 547-1122. TTY 638-3863. Metro: Archives-Navy Memorial. $10.) In the **14th St. theater district,** tiny repertory companies explore and experiment with enjoyable results (check *City Paper* for listings). **Woolly Mammoth,** 1401 Church St. NW (☎ 393-3939; Metro: Dupont Circle); **Studio Theater,** 1333 P St. NW (☎ 332-3300), at 14th St. (Metro: Dupont Circle); and **The Source Theater,** 1835 14th St. NW (☎ 462-1073; Metro: U St.-Cardozo), between S and T St., are all fine theaters in the neighborhood near Dupont Circle (tickets $25). *Use caution in this area at night.*

SPORTS

The 20,000-seat **MCI Center,** 601 F St. NW, in Chinatown, is D.C.'s premier sports arena (☎ 628-3200; Metro: Gallery Pl.-Chinatown). The **Washington Wizards,** the city's NBA team, continues its struggle against dismal play and a lame mascot (tickets $19-85). The **Washington Capitals** kick ice (Oct.-Apr.; tickets $20-75). Three-time Superbowl champions, the **Washington Redskins** draw crowds to **Fed-Ex Stadium,** Raljon Dr., in Raljon, MD, Sept.-Dec. (☎ 301-276-6050, $40-60). At **Robert F. Kennedy Stadium,** the **D.C. United** play soccer mid-Apr. to Oct. ($12-40; tickets ☎ 608-1119).

⚐ NIGHTLIFE

BARS AND CLUBS

Talk about leading a double life. When darkness falls, Washington swaps the flesh-toned nylons for the fishnet stockings. D.C. denizens who crawl through red tape by day paint the town red by night. If you accidentally find yourself taking Jell-O bodyshots off a beautiful stranger at an all-you-can-drink-fest, just don't say we didn't warn you.

Here's our advice on tripping the light fantastic: If you ache for a pint of amber ale, swing by the Irish pub-laden **Capitol Hill.** If you like girls (or boys) who wear Abercrombie & Fitch, hit up **Georgetown,** where youthful prepsters go to get happy. Gay and lesbian travelers traipse nightly through the glam **Dupont Circle,** while **Adams-Morgan** seethes with Eurotrash scuzziness. And to party *with* rock stars, head to none other than Shaw / U for the best live rock 'n' roll in all of Dixieland. To party *like* a rock star, find high times in the **Southeast** wasteland.

Dragonfly, 1215 Connecticut Ave. NW (☎331-1775). Beauty may be fleeting, but revel in the now than amidst the ultra-hot clientele of Dragonfly, *the* club in town to see and be seen. Ice-white interior, pod-like chairs, techno music, and video projections. Drinks are expensive but sushi is served all night for reasonable prices. DJs every night. Open M-Th 5:30pm-1am, F 5:30pm-2am, Sa 6pm-2am, Su 6pm-1am. No cover.

Zei, 1415 Zei Alley (☎842-2445), between 14th and 15th and H and I St. NW. Metro: McPherson Square. The streets of D.C. are a buzz about Club Zei's mix of hot hip-hop and hi-nrg house music. Mingle with D.C. college kids here. No sneakers or athletic gear, jeans ok. Open Th-Sa 10pm-3am. Cover $10. 18+.

State of the Union, 1357 U St. NW (☎588-8810), near 14th St. Partying and shaking some booty under the watchful eyes of Marx and Lenin might seem an unlikely combo (murals and busts of the Communist masterminds abound), but this cozy club's throbbing hip/hop, techno, and other jazzy genres keep the crowd dancing on a small dance floor. Happy Hour (daily until 8:30pm) means half-off beer and rails, with specialty twists on Russian faves—Starburst vodka, anyone? The back room has a movable wall for summer patio action. Open M-Th 5pm-2am, F-Sa 5pm-3am, Su 7pm-3am. Occasional $7 drink min. 21+.

Club Heaven and Club Hell, 2327 18th St. NW (☎667-4355), near Columbia Rd. The devoted reveler makes a pilgrimage to Club Heaven and Club Hell where everyone is a believer in Dionysian tenets. Hell is a hip, smoky bar greasily ornamented with pimpish gold tables and loud alterna-music. Heaven looks more like an old townhouse with scuffed wood, comfy couches, a small bar, and 3 TVs, but the dance floor throbs to pounding beats of techno that spill out onto the back patio. 80s dance party in Heaven is crammed (Th, cover $5). Mixed techno and progressive F-Sa. Heaven open Su, Tu-Th 9:30pm-2am; F-Sa 9:30pm-3am. Hell open Su-Th 7pm-2am; F-Sa 7pm-3am. Happy Hour in Hell M-Th until 10pm and F-Su until 8:30pm. Dancing at 10pm. No cover F-W. Domestic beer $3, imports $4-5.

Prive, 2424 18th St. NW (☎328-7194), between Belmont and Columbia Rd. The posh and crowded restaurant and bar, **Cities,** opens its stairwell to connoisseurs of pounding international music and the Euro-club scene F-Sa nights. The tragically hip lounge and dance in the Armani threads until the music dies (around 2:30am). The upstairs club offers a great view of the plebes below on 18th St. Opens at 9pm but doesn't really get lively until 11:30pm. International music F-Sa. Proper attire required. No cover. 21+.

Blue Room, 2123 18th St. (☎332-0800). A chic tapas restaurant by day, an alluring lounge and dance club at night. Trendy mid-twenties to early-thirties clientele gravitate to this stylish, blue world with polished chrome. Downtempo/deephouse/techno Th-Sa. The club starts jumping at around 11:30pm, closes at 3am. Proper attire required (no jeans, athletic gear, sneakers). Beer $4-9, cocktails $5-8.

Brickskeller, 1523 22nd St. NW (☎293-1885), between P and Q St. With a list of over 850 bottled brews, the Brickskeller claims to have the largest selection in the world. Basement bar "where everybody knows your name" embodies the typical neighborhood tavern atmosphere. "Beer-tails" are mixed drinks made with beer: a favorite is the classic Black Velvet (stout and champagne; $4.50). Monthly tastings hosted by brewers (call ahead for prices and schedule). Pub menu available. Open M-Th 11:30am-2am, F 11:30am-3am, Sa 6pm-3am, Su 6pm-2am.

GAY BARS AND CLUBS

The *Washington Blade* is the best source of gay news and club listings; published every Friday, it's available in virtually every storefront in Dupont Circle.

J.R.'s, 1519 17th St. NW (☎328-0090). Metro: Dupont Circle. D.C.'s busiest bar for good reason: beautiful bartenders, beautiful barhoppers, beautiful interior. Don't be intimidated by the seemingly snobby atmosphere; though, D.C. men can be *very* friendly. Packed every night with "guppies" (gay urban professionals). M Show-tune Sing-a-Long; W South Park. Open M-Th 11:30am-2am, F-Sa 11:30am-3am, Su noon-2am. Happy Hour (M-F 5-8pm) specials throughout the week including $7 all-you-can-drink (Th 5:30-8pm).

Badlands, 1415 22nd St. NW (☎296-0505), near P St. Metro: Dupont Circle. Ditch the inhibition, approach that hottie you've been eyeing, and invite him to bump and grind on Badlands' wild dance floor. The Annex upstairs hosts a mellower video bar with pool table, but most come for the drag queen karaoke F-Sa. Open Th-Sa 9pm-close (usually very late, whenever the crowd dies down). Cover F-Sa 9-10pm $4, after 10pm $8. Th no cover with a college ID. Tu, Th under 21 nights.

Hung Jury, 1819 H St. NW (☎785-8181). Metro: Farragut West. Lesbians from all over D.C., from older couples to young singles scoping the scene, spend their weekend nights bopping to Top 40. Open F-Sa 9pm-3:30am. Shooters $1. Cover $5.

Club Chaos, 1603 17th St. NW (☎232-4141), at Q St. Metro: Dupont Circle. Different nights cater to different crowds, though all nights are usually cool, crowded, and completely gender and orientation mixed. Open Tu-Th 4pm-1am, F-Sa 4pm-2am, Su 11am-1am. Happy Hour Tu-F 5-8pm. W lesbian night. Th Latin night. The best drag show in town Sa 10pm.

⑫ DAYTRIPS FROM D.C.

ARLINGTON, VA

The silence of the 612-acre **Arlington National Cemetery** honors those who sacrificed their lives in war. The Kennedy Gravesites hold the remains of President John F. Kennedy, his brother Robert F. Kennedy, and his wife Jacqueline Kennedy Onassis. The Eternal Flame flickers above JFK's simple memorial stone. The **Tomb of the Unknowns** honors all who died fighting for the US and is guarded by soldiers from the Army's Third Infantry. *(Changing of the guard every 30min.; Oct.-Mar. every hr. on the hr.)* Robert E. Lee's home, **Arlington House,** overlooks the cemetery; tours are self-guided. *(☎ 703-697-2131. Metro: Arlington Cemetery. Cemetery open daily Apr.-Sept. 8am-7pm; Oct.-May 8am-5pm. Free.)* Head down Custis Walk in front of Arlington House, exit the cemetery through Weitzel Gate, and walk for 20min. to get to the **Iwo Jima Memorial,** based on Joe Rosenthal's Pulitzer Prize-winning photo of Marines straining to raise the US flag on Mt. Suribachi.

The **Pentagon,** the world's largest office building, shows just how huge military bureaucracy can get. For security reasons, there are no bathroom breaks on the tour. *(☎695-1776. Metro: Pentagon. Tours every hour on the hour. M-F 9am-3pm. Free.)*

ALEXANDRIA, VA

Alexandria, VA traces its colonial origins over a century further back than Washington, D.C. Courtesy of a massive 80s restoration effort, **Old Town Alexandria** has cobblestone streets, brick sidewalks, tall ships, and quaint shops. *(Metro: King St.)* Sights cluster along **Washington** and **King St.** George Washington and Robert E. Lee prayed at **Christ Church,** a red brick Colonial building with a domed steeple. *(118 N. Washington St., at Cameron St. ☎703-549-1450.)* Both slept in **Robert E. Lee's Boyhood Home,** near Asaph St. *(607 Oronoco St. ☎703-548-8454.)* Thirty-seven different Lees inhabited the **Lee-Fendall House.** *(614 Oronoco St. ☎703-549-1789.)*

MID-ATLANTIC

MT. VERNON

George Washington had a fabulous estate called Mt. Vernon, easily accessible to Washingtonians in Fairfax County, VA. Visitors can see Washington's bedroom and tomb and the estate's fields, where slaves once grew corn, wheat, and tobacco. *(Take the Fairfax Connector 101 bus from Metro: Huntington or take I-395 S to George Washington Pkwy. S, which becomes Mt. Vernon Hwy. in Alexandria; use the Mt. Vernon exit. ☎ 703-780-2000. Open daily Apr.-Aug. 8am-5pm, grounds close at 5:30pm; Sept.-Oct. and Mar. 9am-5pm, grounds close at 5:30pm; Nov.-Feb. 9am-4pm, grounds close at 4:30pm. $8, seniors $7.50, ages 5-11 $4, under 5 free.)*

VIRGINIA

If Virginia is obsessed with its past, it has good reason: many of America's formative experiences—the English settlement of North America, the shameful legacy of the slave trade, the final establishment of American independence, and much of the Civil War—took place in Virginia. More recently, the state has begun to abandon its Old South lifestyle in search of a more cosmopolitan image. The western portion of the state, with montane forests and fascinating underground caverns, provides a welcome respite from nostalgia and relentless Southern heat.

ⓘ PRACTICAL INFORMATION

Capital: Richmond.
Visitor Info: Virginia Division of Tourism, 901 E. Byrd St., 19th fl., Richmond 23219 (☎804-786-4484 or 800-847-4882; www.virginia.org). Open daily 8am-5pm. **Dept. of Conservation and Recreation,** 203 Governor St., Richmond 23219 (☎804-786-1712). Open daily 8am-5pm.
Postal Abbreviation: VA. **Sales Tax:** 4.5%.

RICHMOND   ☎804

A little city fighting to live up to its capital status, Richmond is an assemblage of pastel facades, black historical roots, and lingering Confederate sentiments. The Civil War capital of the Confederacy, Richmond pays homage to secessionists like Jefferson Davis, Robert E. Lee, and Stonewall Jackson through statues, museums, and restored homes. At the same time, the city honors the rich African-American heritage of Jackson Ward, an area that once rivaled Harlem as a center of Black thought and culture.

▐ GETTING THERE AND GETTING AROUND

Trains: Amtrak, 7519 Staple Mills Rd. (☎264-9194 or 800-872-7245). Reservations required. To: Washington D.C. (2¼hr., 9 per day, $27); Williamsburg (1¼hr., 9 per day, $14); Virginia Beach (3hr., 1 per day, $23); New York City (7hr., 9 per day, $76); Baltimore (3½hr., 9 per day, $38); and Philadelphia (4¾hr., 9 per day, $55). Open 24hr. **Taxi** fare to downtown about $10.

Buses: Greyhound, 2910 N. Blvd. (☎254-5910 or 800-231-2222). 2 blocks from downtown. Take GRTC bus #24 north. To: Washington D.C. (18 per day, 2hr., $19.50); Charlottesville (6 per day, 1½-4hr., $19.50); Williamsburg (8 per day, 1hr., $9.50); Norfolk (9 per day, 3hr., $19.50); New York City (24 per day, 6½hr., $60); Baltimore (21 per day, 3½hr., $22.50); and Philadelphia (12 per day, 7hr., $39).

Public Transportation: Greater Richmond Transit Co., 101 S. Davis Ave. (☎358-4782). Maps available in the basement of City Hall, 900 E. Broad St., and in the Yellow Pages. Most buses leave from Broad St. downtown. Bus #24 goes south to Broad St. and downtown. Fare $1.25, transfers 15¢. Seniors 50¢ during off-peak hours. **Trolleys** provide dependable service to downtown, Shockoe Slip, and Shockoe Bottom daily 11am-11pm. Fare 25¢.

Taxi: Veterans Cab, ☎329-3333; **Yellow Cab,** ☎222-7300; **Colonial Cab,** ☎264-7960; and **Hansom,** ☎837-8524. Basic fare $1.50 first mi., 30¢ each additional mi.

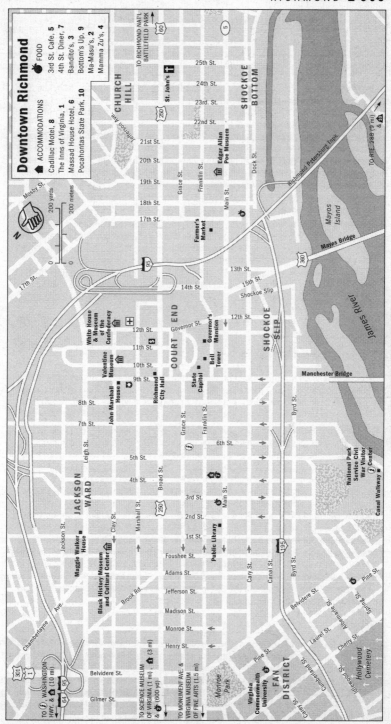

Downtown Richmond

▲ ACCOMMODATIONS

Cadillac Motel, **8**
The Inns of Virginia, **1**
Massad House Hotel, **6**
Pocahontas State Park, **10**

● FOOD

3rd St. Cafe, **5**
4th St. Diner, **7**
Bandito's, **3**
Bottom's Up, **9**
Ma-Masu's, **2**
Mamma Zu's, **4**

MID-ATLANTIC

✦ 🎙 ORIENTATION AND PRACTICAL INFORMATION

Broad Street is the city's central artery, and the streets that cross it are numbered from west to east. Most parallel streets to Broad St., including **Main St.** and **Cary St.**, run one-way. Both I-95, leading north to Washington, D.C., and I-295 encircle the urban section of the city. The **Court End** and **Church Hill** districts, on Richmond's eastern edges, comprise the city's historic center. Further southeast, **Shockoe Slip** and **Shockoe Bottom** overflow with after-dark partiers. **Jackson Ward,** in the heart of downtown (bounded by Belvedere, Leigh, Broad, and 5th St.) is currently undergoing renovations for an expanded City Center, which will revitalize the relatively rundown community. **The Fan,** named such because the neighborhood shape resembles the cooling device, is bounded by the Boulevard, I-95, the walk of statues along **Monument Ave.,** and **Virginia Commonwealth University.** The pleasant bistros and boutiques of **Carytown,** past the Fan on Cary St., and the tightly knit working community of **Oregon Hill** add texture to the cityscape.

Visitor Information: Richmond Visitors Center, 1710 Robin Hood Rd. (☎358-5511 or 358-5512), Exit 78 off I-95/64, in a converted train depot. Helpful 9min. video introduces the city's attractions. Walking tours and maps of downtown and the metro region. Offers same-day discounted accommodations. Open daily Memorial Day to Labor Day 9am-7pm; off-season 9am-5pm. **Smaller visitors centers,** located in the Bell Tower on the capitol grounds and at the airport, offer similar services without the shop.

Help Lines: Traveler's Aid: ☎643-0279 or 648-1767. Open M-F 9am-5pm. **Rape Crisis:** ☎643-0888. **Psychiatric Crisis Intervention:** ☎648-9224. Open 24hr. **AIDS/HIV:** ☎(800) 533-4148. Open M-F 8am-7pm. **Crisis Pregnancy Center:** ☎353-2320. Open 24hr. **Women's Health Clinic:** ☎800-254-4479. Open 24hr.

Post Office: 1801 Brook Rd. (☎775-6133). Open M-F 7am-6pm, Sa 10am-1pm. **ZIP code:** 23219. **Area code:** 804.

▌ ACCOMMODATIONS

Budget motels in Richmond cluster on **Williamsburg Rd.,** at the edge of town, and along **Midlothian Turnpike,** south of the James River; however, public transport to these areas is unreliable. As usual, the farther you stay from downtown, the less you pay. The visitors center can reserve accommodations, often at $20-35 discounts (see above).

Massad House Hotel, 11 N. 4th St. (☎648-2893). Surround yourself with antique furnishings, oil paintings, and a distinctly European atmosphere 5 blocks from downtown and the capitol. A/C and cable TV. Singles $56; doubles $62. Student and senior 10% off.

The Inns of Virginia, 5215 W. Broad St. (☎288-2800), 3 mi. from town; use bus #6. After being renamed two years ago, this motel with modest, but clean rooms and a lavish lobby seeks stability under new ownership. Provides A/C, cable TV, and an outdoor pool. Rooms $49-54; weekly rate $238.

Cadillac Motel, 11418 Washington Hwy. (☎798-4049), 10 mi. from town; no public transportation. Take I-95 to Exit 89. Not the Cadillac of motel rooms, but decent sleeping quarters with A/C and cable TV. Singles $45; doubles $55.

Pocahontas State Park, 10301 State Park Rd. (☎796-4255; for reservations, ☎225-3867 or 800-933-7275). From Richmond, take I-95 south to Rte. 288 and connect to Rte. 10. The park is 10 mi. south on Rte. 10 and Rte. 655 in Chesterfield. Showers, biking, boating, picnic areas, and the 2nd largest pool in Virginia. Rent a canoe or paddleboat ($4). Open year-round. Sites $18. No hook-ups.

◖ FOOD

The recipe for Richmond cuisine is simple: take one part Southern culture, one part hungry-but-short-on-cash college students, mix in a cultural blender, and you've got cheap, delicious food. The outdoor **Farmer's Market,** N. 17th and E. Main St., brings the freshest country crops into the city, brimming with farm fruits, veggies, and homemade delicacies. Surrounding the market in **Shockhoe Bottom,** pizza and deli food top the menu. The self-proclaimed "artsy" crowd of Virginia Commonwealth University convene in hip coffeehouses and restaurants.

▨ **Mamma Zu's,** 501 S. Pine St. (☎ 788-4205). Italian heaven blessed with the intoxicating aroma of garlic and spices. A staff of free-spirited 20-somethings serve up veggies from the restaurant's own garden. Exotic meats like rabbit liver $6.50 and healthy entrees $7-20. Open M-F 11am-2:30pm and 5:30-11pm, Sa 5:30-11pm.

▨ **Bottom's Up,** 1700 Dock St. (☎ 644-4400), at 17th and Cary St. Named "Richmond's Best Pizza" 4 years in a row. Choose-your-own-pizza adventure ($3-6 per slice). Drafts $1.50-3, bottles $2.50-3. Open M-W 11:30am-11pm, Th 11:30am-midnight, F 11:30am-2am, Sa noon-2am, Su noon-11pm.

Ma-Masu's, 2043 W. Broad St. (☎ 355-8063). Not to be confused with "Mamma Zu's." Ma-Masu, "Spiritual Mother" extraordinaire, inducts her guests to Liberian culture with a colorful mural. *Keli-willy* (fried plantains with spices and onions) and toywah Beans ($6), collard greens ($1.50), coconut juice ($1). Delivery available. Open M-F 11am-9pm.

3rd St. Diner (☎ 788-4750), at the corner of 3rd and Main St. Locals are served cheap eats by tattooed, pierced waitresses in combat boots. Breakfast special (2 eggs, biscuit or toast, and homefries, grits, or Virginia fried apples $2.25) and dinner sandwiches ($3-6) curb a late night greasy spoon craving. Open 24hr.

⬣ SIGHTS

AROUND ST. JOHN'S CHURCH. St. John's Church is the site of Patrick Henry's famed 1775 "Give me liberty or give me death" speech. Actors recreate the speech on summer Su at 2pm. *(2401 E Broad St. ☎ 648-5015. 25min. tours M-Sa 10am-3:30pm, Su 1-3:30pm. $3, seniors $2, ages 7-18 $1.)* Nearby is the **Edgar Allen Poe Museum.** Led by a moribund hostess, visitors try to unravel the mysterious death of the enigmatic and morbid author in Richmond's oldest standing house. Inspect a coffin fragment and a lock of hair to draw your own conclusions, then bristle with fear in the spooky garden. *(1914 E. Main St. ☎ 888-213-2763. Tu-Sa 10am-5pm, Su-M noon-5pm. $6, seniors and students $5).*

COURT END DISTRICT. Richmond's most important sites can be found in the **Court End** district. The **State Capitol,** at 9th and Grace St., is a Neoclassical masterpiece designed by Thomas Jefferson. The building was the seat of the Confederate government during the Civil War. Meet the real George Washington at the imposing Houdon statue, the only statue for which George actually posed. *(☎ 698-1788. Open daily 9am-5pm; Dec.-Mar. M-Sa 9am-5pm, Su noon-5pm.)*

CONFEDERATE SOUTH. The Civil War South is celebrated at the Museum of the Confederacy. To feel most welcome, wear hometown gray while wandering through the first floor's memorial to the "Great War of Northern Aggression." An extensive exhibit honoring war hero Robert E. Lee will run through 2001. The museum also runs 1hr. tours through the **White House of the Confederacy** next door, where a South-shall-rise-again feeling is almost palpable. *(1201 E. Clay St. ☎ 649-1861. Open M-Sa 10am-5pm, Su noon-5pm. $6, seniors $5, ages 7-18 $3, under 7 free. Tours M, W, and F-Sa 10:30am-4:30pm, Tu and Th 11:30am-4:30pm, Su 1:15-4:30pm. $7, seniors $6, students $4. Combination tickets available.)*

There are no cupids or candied hearts in **The Valentine Museum**—just the South's largest collection of costumes and textiles. Fantastic additions to the cultural elitism of the 18th century, ruffles and layers abound—and that's just the men's clothing. Admission price includes a **Wickham House** tour. In 2001, female chefs will display their abilities outside the kitchen in a "Women of Taste" exhibit. *(1015 E. Clay St. ☎ 649-0711. Open M-Sa 10am-5pm, Su noon-5pm. House tours on the hr. 10am-4pm. $5, students and seniors $4, ages 7-12 $3.)*

SHOCKOE SLIP. South of Court End, the Shockoe Slip district, running from Main, Canal, and Cary St. between 10th and 14th St., features fancy shops in restored and warehouses, but few bargains. The **Shockhoe Bottoms Arts Center** crams in 120 artist's cutting edge creations. *(2001 E. Grace St. ☎ 643-7959. Open Tu-Sa 10am-5pm, Su 1-5pm. Free)* Also in the Slip, the **Canalwalk,** linking the Kanaway Canal next to the James River, has gorgeous vistas, swaying trees, and stylish eateries.

MID-ATLANTIC

JACKSON WARD. Jackson Ward is the heart of African-American Richmond. The tiny **Black History Museum and Cultural Center of Virginia** showcases rotating exhibits on African-American history. Movie buffs, take note: February 2001 will see the opening of an exhibit commemorating 100 years of blacks in film. *(00 Clay St. ☎ 780-9093. Open Tu-Sa 11am-4pm. $4; seniors $3, under 12 $2. Wheelchair accessible.)*

THE FAN. In the Fan, **Monument Ave.**, a boulevard lined with trees, gracious old houses, and towering statues of Virginia heroes, is a Richmond memory lane. The statue of Robert E. Lee faces south toward his beloved Dixie; Stonewall Jackson faces north so that the general can perpetually scowl at the Yankees. The statue of African-American tennis hero Arthur Ashe, who died of AIDS, created a storm of controversy when built at the end of the avenue.

VIRGINIA MUSEUM OF FINE ARTS. On summer Th from 6:30-9:30pm, the Virginia Museum of Fine Arts—the South's largest art museum—draws sell-out crowds to its sculpture garden for **Jumpin'**, one of Richmond's most dynamic musical performance cycles. *(2800 Grove Ave. ☎ 367-0844. Open Tu-W and F-Su 11am-5pm, Th 11am-8pm in the North Wing Galleries. Suggested donation $4. Jumpin': ☎ 367-8148. Tickets $6 in advance, $7 at the door.)*

🎵🎭 ENTERTAINMENT AND NIGHTLIFE

One of Richmond's most entertaining and delightful diversions is the marvelous old **Byrd Theater**, 2908 W. Cary St. (☎ 353-9911). Movie buffs buy tickets from a tuxedoed agent and are treated on weekends to a pre-movie Wurlitzer organ concert. All shows are 99¢; on Sa the balcony opens for $1 extra. Free concerts abound downtown and at the **Nina Abody Festival Park**, near the bottom of 17th St. *Style Weekly*, a free magazine available at the visitors center, and its younger counterpart, *Punchline*, found in most hangouts, both list concert lineups. Cheer on the **Richmond Braves**, Richmond's AAA minor-league baseball team, on Boulevard St. for a fraction of major-league prices (☎ 359-4444; boxes $7, reserved seats $5, general $4). Student-driven nightlife enlivens **Shockoe Slip** and sprinkles itself throughout the **Fan.** After dark, **Shockoe Bottom** turns into a college-party central, with transient bars pumping bass-heavy music early into the morning.

Matt's Pub and Comedy Club, 109 S. 12th St. (☎ 643-5653), pours out a bit of Brit wit in wooden walls reminiscent of the old country. Stand-up comedy F 8 and 10:30pm, Sa 8 and 11pm; reservations recommended. Open F-Sa 11:30am-2am. Tex-Mex and pub cuisine $3-7; microbrews and drafts $2.75-$3.60; rails $3.25. Cover around $8.50.

Havana '59, 16 N. 17th St. (☎ 649-2822). Tipsy patrons sway with the palm trees while puffing on a Cuban at this salsa cabana. Cuban *flan* $4.25; cigars $9-20. Though you won't sunburn in this Havana, you might scorch your wallet eating dinner (entrees $12-20). Open M-Sa 4:30pm-2am, Su brunch 10:30am-3:30pm and 5:30pm-midnight.

Medley's, 1701 E. Main (☎ 648-2313). An older crowd drowns their sorrows with live blues and French-Cajun food. Open W-Sa 4pm-2am. Po' boy sandwiches $5.50-9; gumbo $4.50. Cover F-Sa $3-5.

Broadway Cafe, 1624 W. Broad St. (☎ 355-9931). Miss Scarlett, a fluffy white poodle, presides over this largely gay bar from her high stool. Open daily 2pm-2am. Drafts $1.60. Appetizers around $4.50, including the "wings of fire."

FREDERICKSBURG ☎ 540

Sometimes popularity really hurts. Smack dab between the Union capital at Washington, D.C., and the Confederate capital at Richmond, a foothold in Fredericksburg during the Civil War meant control of the road between the capitals and, thus, a distinct military advantage. As a result, Fredericksburg experienced merciless amounts of bloodshed as men battled for control of the city. Years before the battle of Fredericksburg shattered the silent landscape with gunshots, the colonial post was already established as an important tobacco port on the banks of the Rappahannock River. George Washington so loved his Fredericksburg childhood that he erected a retirement mansion for his mother among the tree-lined, cobblestone streets. After the Civil War dust cleared in 1865, Fredericksburg lay stained with carnage. The town has recovered, mixing gorgeous city plantations and somber battlefields with cafes and elegant boutiques.

■■ ORIENTATION AND PRACTICAL INFORMATION. Fredericksburg's position on I-95 directly between Washington and Richmond makes it an easily accessible and pleasant destination en route to either capital. Exit 130A off I-95 and onto Rte. 3 accesses the city, which is divided into two parts by **Lafayette Boulevard.** South of Lafayette lie personal residences, while the **Historic Downtown** crams museums, historical sites, and chic cafes into a network of one-ways that is easily traversed by foot. **William Street** (Rte. 3) runs northeast over the Rappahannock River into Falmouth. One-way **Caroline Street** is the main historic and commercial route.

Amtrak, 200 Lafayette Blvd. (☎872-7245 or 800-872-7245), near Caroline St., runs trains through twice daily as a stop on the long line from Maine to Florida. (No ticket office. Must call for reservations.) **Virginia Railway Express (VRE),** in the same building, makes several trips daily to Union Station in D.C. (☎703-684-1001 or 800-743-3873. Station open M-F 7am-7pm. Fare $6.70.) **Greyhound/Trailways,** 1400 Jefferson Davis Hwy. (☎373-2103) buses to Washington, D.C. (70 min., $9.50), Baltimore (65min., $22), and Richmond (1hr, $12.50). **Fredericksburg Regional Transit,** 1400 Jefferson Davis Hwy., offers extended bus service around the city with Caroline St. and Princess Anne St. as main thoroughfares. (☎372-1222. 25¢ per ride.) **Yellow Cab** (☎371-7075) and **Virginia Cab Service** (☎373-5111) provide taxis. **Fredericksburg Visitor Center,** 706 Caroline St. at the corner of Charlotte St., offers extensive free info on Historic Fredericksburg, including a walking tour, bike tours, maps, and a 14min. orientation video about the town. The center also assists in discount accommodation reservations and sells a "Pick Four" pass for admission to four sites ($13.75, ages 6-18 $5.50) and "Hospitality Pass" into seven of the major sites ($19.75, ages 6-18 $7). (☎373-1776 or ☎800-678-4748. Open daily 9am-7pm; in winter 9am-5pm. Free parking pass and *Fredericksburg, Spotsylvania & Stafford Visitor Guide*.) **Post Office:** Princess Anne St. between Charlotte St. and Lafayette Blvd (☎373-8860). **ZIP code:** 22401. **Area code:** 540.

▌ ACCOMMODATIONS AND CAMPING. Chain motels rule the areas around Fredericksburg's Exits 118, 126, 130, and 133 off I-95, while historic B&Bs scattered near the Rappahannock River cost more than a few pence, colonially speaking. Snag a copy of the *Traveler Discount Guide* in fast-food chains such as **Denny's** for discount coupons.

Econo Lodge, 7802 Plank Rd., Exit 130B off I-95 then left at 1st light, is where you'll forfeit colonial romance for the cheapest rates in Williamsburg. Desks, A/C, cable TV, and rosy interiors make for a comfortable stay. (☎786-8374. Free doughnuts, coffee, and juice. Singles $37; doubles $50. Off-season singles $35; doubles $48.) At **Fredericksburg Colonial Inn,** 1707 Princess Anne St., ascend the grand staircase to encounter walls decorated with Civil War nostalgia. TV, refrigerators, A/C, and antiques. (☎371-5666. Complimentary breakfast and papers. Singles and doubles $65; suites $90.) **Selby House,** 226 Princess Anne St., four blocks from the historic district, is a fragrant Victorian bed and breakfast operated by a certified Civil War battlefield tour guide. (☎373-7037. Private bathrooms, A/C, and a lounge with cable TV. Complimentary full breakfast served on fine china in the sunlight-washed dining room and patio. Singles $75; double with canopy bed $85.)

◨ FOOD. Nearly every fast food and restaurant chain known to man accompanies the motel mania off Exits 130A and 130B. Supermarkets thrive along the same strip, including **Ukrops,** 4250 Plank Rd. (☎785-2626). The locals head to **Caroline St.** for a barrage of healthy options and less congested dining.

Sammy T's, 801 Caroline St., a block from the visitors center, was formerly the Fredericksburg post office but now delivers a comprehensive menu capable of pleasing poultry-cravers (chicken parmesan $8.50) and animal-lovers (vegan sandwich $7).

Those of age can wash down their meal with a bottle from an impressive selection of imports. (☎371-2008. Open M-Sa 11am-10pm, Su 11am-9pm.) **Lee's Ice Cream,** 821 Caroline St., gives the most decadent dessert in Fredericksburg. Choose kahlua fudge or Arbuckle's, a finely grounded chocolate chip. (☎370-4390. Open M-Th 11am-10pm, F-Sa 11am-midnight, Su 10am-10pm. Single scoop $2, double $3, triple $3.25.) At **La Familia Castiglia's,** 324 William St., an effervescent staff of family greet customers with grins as wide as the broad menu. Indulge in the sumptuous veal marsala ($10) but not before a seafood start with *zuppa di cozze antipasti* (fresh mussels in wine sauce $6.50). (☎373-6650. Open M-Sa 11am-10pm, Su 11am-9pm.) While prescriptions are being filled in the back of **Goolrick's Pharmacy,** 901 Caroline St., patrons climb baby blue barstools to chow on cheap chicken salad ($2.50) in this time warp to the 50s. Thick milkshakes ($3) and freshly squeezed lemonade ($1) refresh on steamy summer days. (☎373-3411. Open M-F 8:30am-7pm, Sa 8:30am-6pm.)

🔯 **SIGHTS.** Mansions, medicine, and Monroe (James, not Marilyn) take center stage in Fredericksburg's **Historic District. Kenmore Plantation** was built in 1775 for Fielding Lewis and his wife, George Washington's sister, Betty. After being dazzled by the elegant dining room gawk at the garden so pristine it looks artificial. *(1201 Washington Ave. ☎373-4255. Open Mar.-Dec. M-Sa 10am-5pm, Su noon-4pm. $6, ages 6-17 $3. Grounds free.)* Since George was a bit busy founding a nation, he wanted his aging mother to be nearby the care of sister Betty. The result is the **Mary Washington House,** with tours packed with 18th-century trinkets. *(1200 Charles St. ☎373-1569. Open Mar.-Nov. daily 9am-5pm; Dec.-Feb.10am-4pm. $4, children $1.50.)* Learn why leeches purify the blood at the **Hugh Mercer Apothecary Shop,** which offers fascinating insights into old-fashioned, unhygienic medical technology. *(1020 Caroline St. ☎373-3362. Open daily Mar.-Nov. 9am-5pm; Dec.Feb. 10am-4pm. $4, ages 6-18 $1.50.)* **The James Monroe Museum,** originally Monroe's law office, is a repository of memorabilia. Parisian-purchased, Louis XVI-influenced furniture includes the desk where James drafted his famous doctrine. *(908 Charles St. ☎654-1043. Open daily Mar.-Oct. 9am-5pm; Nov.-Feb. 10am-4pm. $4, seniors $3.20, children $1.)*

🎭🎬 **ENTERTAINMENT AND NIGHTLIFE.** In the olden times, sundown meant bedtime. Well, not much has changed in Fredericksburg. Though flanked by **Mary Washington College** on the north, the town and its students usually quiet down when the tourists retire to their lodgings. The town does have a few postprandial pleasures. The **Colonial Theatre,** 907 Caroline St. (contact visitors center at ☎800-678-4748), showcases symphonic performances and the occasional play. At the **Klein Theater,** College Ave. and Thornton Ave., the **Fredericksburg Theatre Co.** performs in the summer. (☎654-1124. Performances W-Sa 8pm, Su 2pm. $13-15.)

Predominantly folk music attracts a local crowd among trendy, purple walls of **Orbits,** 406 Lafayette Blvd. Roaming rastafarians jam to a monthly reggae performance. You can open your mouth for an open-mic night M or for a $5.50 intercontinental alliance of pesto nachos. (☎371-2003. Open M-Th 11:30am-10pm, F-Sa 11:30am-2am, Su 11:30am-4pm. Drafts $3. Cover F-Sa $5.) **The Underground,** 106 George St., in the basement of George St. Grill, takes its name literally with its dark basement location and alternative rock players. While aged waitresses serve a relatively refined crowd upstairs, head-banging persists in the underground F-Sa and makes holding a brew ($2.75) difficult. (☎371-9500. Open F-Sa. Opening hrs. vary with shows; call ahead.)

NEAR FREDERICKSBURG: NATIONAL BATTLEFIELD PARKS

What today is a vast and serene green expanse witnessed bloody decimation between December 1862 and May 1864. Under the leadership of Confederate generals Robert E. Lee and "Stonewall" Jackson and Union Generals Ambrose E. Burnside, Joseph Hooker, and Ulysses S. Grant, four devastating Civil War battles were contested in the 20 mi. that surround the town. Today, a 76 mi. driving tour winds through the battlefields of **Fredericksburg, Chancellorsville,** the **Wilderness,** and **Spotsylvania,** paying homage to the many soldiers who risked their lives for the Confederate stripes.

Three walking tours—the **Sunken Road Walking Tour** following the entrenchment line at Fredericksburg, the **Chancellorsville History Trail,** and the **Spotsylvania History Trail**—encircle the battlefields and provide strategic viewpoints of all major sights of battle, including the Bloody Angle at Spotsylvania. A captivating and comprehensive journey into the Civil War, the battlefields inspire everyone to be a history buff for at least a day. *(Visitors center at 1013 Lafayette Blvd.* ☎*373-6122. Open daily 8:30am-6:30pm; in winter 9am-5pm. Six rotating tours offered by rangers highlight different features of the battlefield. $3, under 17 free.)*

WILLIAMSBURG ☎757

Economically floundering after colonial prosperity, Williamsburg was rescued in the late 20s by philanthropist John D. Rockefeller, Jr., who showered the troubled spots with money and restored a large chunk of the historic district, now known as **Colonial Williamsburg.** Nowadays a fife-and-drum corps marches down the streets, and costumed wheelwrights, bookbinders, and blacksmiths go about their tasks using 200-year-old methods on old gas station sites. Travelers who visit in late fall or early spring will avoid the crowds, heat, and humidity of summer. However, they will also miss the extensive array of special summer programs. December visitors will find an array of charming Colonial Christmas activities.

▐ GETTING THERE AND GETTING AROUND

Airport: Newport News/Williamsburg International Airport, 20min. away in Newport News with frequent connections to Dulles by United Express and USAir. Take Rte. 199 W to I-64 S.

Transportation Center, 408 N. Boundary St., behind the fire station. Houses offices for Amtrak, Greyhound, and taxi service.

Trains: Amtrak (☎229-8750 or ☎800-872-7245). To: New York (7½-8hr., 2 per day, $72); Washington, D.C. (3½hr., 2 per day, $33); Philadelphia (6hr., 2 per day, $56); Baltimore (5hr., 2 per day, $41); and Richmond (1hr., 2 per day, $14). Station open Tu-Th 7:30am-5pm, Su-M and F-Sa 7:30am-10:30pm.

Buses: Greyhound (☎229-1460 or ☎800-231-2222). To: Richmond (1hr., 8 per day, $10); Norfolk (1-2hr., 9 per day, $10); Washington, D.C. (3-4hr., 8 per day, $29); Baltimore (via D.C.; 6-7hr., 8 per day, $45); and Virginia Beach (2½hr., 4 per day, $14). Ticket office open M-F 8am-5pm, Sa 8am-2pm, Su 8am-noon.

Public Transportation: James City County Transit (JCCT) (☎220-1621). Bus service along Rte. 60, from Merchants Sq. in the historic district west to Williamsburg Pottery or east past Busch Gardens. Operates M-Sa 6:30am-5:15pm. Fare $1 plus 25¢ per zone-change. **Williamsburg Shuttle** (☎220-1621), provides service between Colonial Williamsburg and Busch Gardens every 30min. Operates May-Sept. daily 9am-9pm. $1 for an all day pass.

Taxi: Yellow Cab, ☎245-7777. 24hr. **Williamsburg Limousine Service,** ☎877-0279. To Busch Gardens or Carter's Grove $6-10 one-way. To Jamestown and Yorktown $20 round-trip. Call between 8:30am-midnight.

Bike Rental: Bikes Unlimited, 759 Scotland St. (☎229-4620), rents 21-speed bikes for $15 per day. $5 deposit required (includes lock). Open M-F 9am-7pm, Sa 9am-5pm, Su noon-5pm.

▟▐ ORIENTATION AND PRACTICAL INFORMATION

Williamsburg lies some 50 mi. southeast of Richmond between Jamestown (10 mi. away) and Yorktown (14 mi. away). **The Colonial Parkway,** which connects the three towns, has no commercial buildings and is a beautiful route between historic destinations. The general Colonial Williamsburg area is accessed by I-64 and the Colonial Parkway exit.

Visitor Information: Williamsburg Area Convention & Visitors Bureau, 201 Penniman Rd. (☎253-0192), ½ mi. northwest of the transportation center. Provides a free Visitor's Guide to Virginia's Historic Triangle. Open M-F 8:30am-5pm. **Colonial Williamsburg Visitors Center,** 102 Information Dr. (☎800-447-8679), 1 mi. northeast of the transport center. Tickets and transportation to Colonial Williamsburg. Maps and guides to historic district, including a guide for the disabled. Info on prices and discounts for Virginia sights. Open daily 8:30am-8pm; winter hrs. vary.

Post Office: 425 N. Boundary St. (☎229-4668). Open M-F 8am-5pm, Sa 10am-2pm. **ZIP codes:** 23185 (Williamsburg), 23690 (Yorktown), and 23081 (Jamestown). **Area code:** 757.

ACCOMMODATIONS AND CAMPING

The hotels operated by the **Colonial Williamsburg Foundation** are generally more expensive than other lodgings in the area. **Rte. 60 W** and **Rte. 31 S** are packed with budget motels, which grow cheaper the farther they are from the historic district. At the various B&Bs around William and Mary, guests pay more for gorgeous colonial decors. Guest houses don't serve breakfast, but still offer the bed, a reasonable price, abounding warmth, and "like-home" feelings.

■ **Lewis Guest House,** 809 Lafayette St. (☎229-6116), a 10min. walk from the historic district, rents three comfortable rooms, including an upstairs unit with private entrance, kitchen, partial A/C and shared bath. Rooms $25-35.

Carter Guest House, 903 Lafayette St. (☎229-1117). Two doors down from Lewis Guest House are 2 lovely, spacious rooms with 2 beds and a shared bath. Be forewarned: no bed till wed! The God-fearing Mrs. Carter—a woman of traditional Southern values—will not let unmarried men and women sleep in the same room. Singles $25; doubles $30.

Bryant Guest House, 702 College Terr. (☎229-3320). Offers rooms with private baths, TV and limited kitchen facilities in a stately, exquisitely landscaped brick home. Singles $35; doubles $45; 5-person suite $55.

Jamestown Beach Campsites, 2217 Jamestown Rd. (☎229-7609), immediately adjacent to the Jamestown Settlement. One of the largest campgrounds in the area. Frolic by the pool and waterslide or splash around in the more natural James River. Don't disturb the peace; quiet hours (11pm-8am) are strictly enforced. Sites $18, with water and electricity $23, full hook-up $25. Six-person maximum at each campsite.

FOOD

Instead of rowdy farmers and proper colonists, most of the authentic-looking "taverns" in Colonial Williamsburg are packed with sweaty tourists and are overpriced (lunch $5-10, dinner $18 and up). Jumping back into the 21st century for food proves the most price-savvy option.

■ **Chowning's Tavern** (☎220-7012), on Duke of Gloucester St. within the grounds of Colonial Williamsburg. Don your tri-cornered hat and let the wenches fulfill your every need. Odd dishes like "Bubble and Squeak" (cabbage and potatoes $5) and "Welsh Rarebit" (bread in beer sauce with ham, $7) will have you chowing like George Washington. After 9pm, the merriment continues as costumed waiters sing 18th-century ballads and challenge guests to card games ($3-7). Cover $3. Open daily 8am-midnight.

■ **Giuseppe's,** 5601 Richmond Rd. (☎565-1977), in Ewell Station shopping center on Rte. 60, about 2½ mi. from the historic district. Personable owner Joseph (that's Giuseppe in Italian) welcomes diners with a sterling sense of humor and an impressive wine list. 8 pasta dishes for under $6. Open M-Sa 11:30am-2pm and 5-9pm.

Green Leafe Cafe, 765 Scotland St. (☎220-3405). This classy restaurant draws William and Mary students with its hearty sandwiches ($5-6) like the pan-fried pumpernickel. Thirty brews on tap ($2.75-4), including savory Virginia micros. Su "Mug Night" brings half-price beer. Open daily 11am-2am.

The Cheese Shop, 424 Prince George St. (☎220-0298 or 800-468-4049). On weekdays, tourists overflow out the doors at this gourmet shop and deli. The local Virginia ham sandwich ($4) vies with the international Braunschweiger ($3.75). Outdoor seating only. Open M-Sa 10am-6pm, Su 11am-5pm.

BRIDGE O' LOVE A jaunt across the **Crim Dell Bridge** at William and Mary College means risky business. According to student lore, the fate of many a lovelife has been sealed in a single crossing (or shall we say in crossing singly?). Superstition dictates that those who tread the bridge's path alone will never marry. And if passion leads a couple to smooch with the bridge underfoot, destiny has eternally bound them together. Maybe this chance to say "I Do" has something to do with Playboy naming the bridge the "2nd most romantic spot on a college campus."

SIGHTS

Colonial Williamsburg will have you spending 1774 treasury notes and singing "my hat, it has three corners" while you dodge horse droppings all the way to the milliner's. The historic district itself doesn't require a ticket—walk around, march behind the fife-and-drum corps, and lock yourself in the stocks for free. Also open to the public is a colonial flea market where you can test your haggling skills or just peaceably buy a tri-cornered hat for $9. Most of the "colonial" shops and two of the historic buildings—the **Wren Building** and the **Bruton Parish Church**—are also open to the public. Monday's *Visitor's Companion* newsletter lists free events and evening programs. (☎ 800-447-8679. Most sights open 9:30am-5pm; for complete hrs., see the Visitor's Companion newsletter. Admission $27, ages 6-12 $16. 2-day pass $31/$18.)

The real fun of Colonial Williamsburg comes from interacting with its history. Trade shops afford wonderful opportunities to learn from skilled artisans such as the carpenter, and slightly less-skilled workmen like the brickmaster, who may invite you to take off your shoes and join him in stomping on wet clay. Colonial denizens are quick to play up their antiquated world view (admitted Floridians are likely to be greeted with startled cries of "Spanish territory!").

Spreading west from the corner of Richmond and Jamestown Rd., the **College of William and Mary** is the 2nd-oldest college in the US, having educated Presidents Jefferson, Monroe, and Tyler. The **Sir Christopher Wren Building,** was built two years after the college received its charter and restored with Rockefeller money. (Tours M-F 10am and 2:30pm.)

DAYTRIPS FROM WILLIAMSBURG

JAMESTOWN AND YORKTOWN. The **"Historic Triangle"** is a tri-cornered hat brimming with United States history. More authentic and less crowded than Colonial Williamsburg empire, Jamestown and Yorktown show visitors where it all *really* began. At the **Colonial National Park,** southwest of Williamsburg on Rte. 31, you'll see the remains of the first permanent English settlement in America (1607), as well as exhibits explaining colonial life. The **visitors center** offers a hokey film, a free 30min. "living history" walking tour, and a 45min. audio tape tour ($2) for the 5 mi. **Island Loop Route.** The **Old Church Tower,** built in 1639, is the only 17th-century structure still standing. Also featured is a statue of **Pocahontas.** In the remains of the settlement itself, archeologists uncover the original site of the triangular **Jamestown Fort.** (☎ 229-1733. Open daily 9am-5pm; off-season 9am-4:30pm. Visitors center closes 30min. after the park. Entrance fee $5.)

The nearby **Jamestown Settlement** is a commemorative museum with changing exhibits, a reconstruction of James Fort, a Native American village, and full-scale replicas of the three ships that brought the original settlers to Jamestown in 1607. The 20min. dramatic film details the settlement's history, including a discussion of settler relations with the indigenous Powhatan tribe. (☎ 229-1607. Open daily 9am-5pm. $10.25, ages 6-12 $5.)

The British defeat at **Yorktown** in 1781 signaled the end of the Revolutionary War. The Yorktown branch of **Colonial National Park** vividly re-creates the significant last battle with an engaging film and an electric map. The visitors center rents cassettes and players ($2) for driving the battlefield's 7 mi. automobile route. (☎ 757-898-3400.

MID-ATLANTIC

Center open daily 8:30am-5pm; last tape rented at 3:30pm. $4, under 17 free.) Brush up on your high school history as you listen to the rallying cries of revolutionary figures like Benjamin Franklin and Patrick Henry foretelling independence won at Yorktown. The **Yorktown Victory Center,** one block from Rte. 17 on Rte. 238, brims with Revolutionary War items and an intriguing "living history" exhibit: in an encampment in front, soldiers from the 1781 Continental Army take a break from combat. *(☎ 757-887-1776. Open daily 9am-5pm. $7.75, seniors $6.50, ages 6-12 $3.75).*

JAMES RIVER PLANTATIONS. Built near the water to ease the planters' commercial and social lives, these country houses buttressed the slave-holding Virginia aristocracy. Reconstructed **Carter's Grove Plantation,** 6 mi. east of Williamsburg on Rte. 60, maintains the colonial feel. Also redone were slave quarters and an archaeological dig. The **Winthrop Rockefeller Archaeological Museum,** built unobtrusively into a hillside, provides a fascinating case-study look at archaeology. *(☎ 757-229-1000, ext. 2973. Plantation open Tu-Su 9am-5pm; Nov.-Dec. 9am-4pm. Museum and slave quarters open Mar.-Dec. Tu-Su 9am-5pm. $18, ages 6-12 $11.)*

Berkeley Plantation, halfway between Richmond and Williamsburg on Rte. 5, claims to be the site of the invention of bourbon by British settlers. Beautiful, terraced box-wood gardens stretch from the original 1726 building to the James River. *(☎ 804-829-6018. Open daily 8am-5pm. $8.50, seniors $6.65, ages 13-16 $6.50, ages 6-12 $4. Grounds alone $5/$3.60/$2.50.)* To reach **Shirley Plantation,** follow Rte. 5 west from Williamsburg, or east from Richmond. Surviving war after war, this 1613 plantation has an exquisite Queen Anne-style mansion featuring a seemingly unsupported three-story staircase. *(☎ 800-232-1613. Open daily 9am-5pm. $8.50, ages 13-21 $5.50, ages 6-12 $4.50.)*

BEER AND ROLLERCOASTERS. At **Busch Gardens,** proceed with caution; an arduous journey fraught with dangerous dragons, monsters, and angry gods awaits the innocent tourist in "17th-Century Europe." For the 21+ crowd, indulge in a home-brewed Anheuser-Busch beer, but consume in moderation lest your stomach churn after a pulsating 70 mph scream on the **Apollo's Chariot** rollercoaster. *(☎ 253-3350. Open late June through Aug. Su-F 10am-10pm, Sa 10am-11pm; Sept.-Oct. M and F 10am-6pm, Sa-Su 10am-7pm; call for winter hrs. $37, seniors $34, ages 3-6 $26. Cheaper after 5pm.)*

A 3-day ticket ($55) is good for both Busch Gardens and **Water Country: USA,** 2 mi. away. Thirty-five water rides, slides, and attractions laced with a 1950s surfing theme keep barefooted waterbabies splashing with delight. *(Open late May to mid-June Sa-Su about 10am-6pm; mid-June to mid-Aug. daily about 10am-8pm; Sept. Sa-Su about 10am-7pm. Hrs. vary; call ahead. Admission $28, ages 3-6 $20.50; after 3pm $19 for all.)*

VIRGINIA BEACH ☎ 757

After decades as the capital of the cruising collegiate crowd, Virginia Beach is gradually shedding its playground image and maturing into a family-oriented vacation spot. The town has grown into Virginia's largest city. Along with its nearby neighbors, Norfolk, Newport News, and Hampton, the city is attempting to make the entire Hampton Roads region an attractive place to visit. For the time being, tipsy 20-somethings share the streets with parents and their baby carriages. Even the most dogged clean-up campaigns cannot conceal the omnipresence of fast-food joints, motels, and discount shops that characterize every beach town. But beyond all the slurpees and suntan oil, Virginia Beach's beautiful ocean sunrises, substantial dolphin population, and frequent military jet flyovers distinguish it from its East Coast counterparts.

▐ GETTING THERE AND GETTING AROUND

Trains: Amtrak (☎ 245-3589 or 800-872-7245). The nearest train station, in Newport News, runs 45min. bus service to and from the corner of 19th and Pacific St. When leaving, you must call to reserve your train ticket. To Newport News from: Washington, D.C. (6hr., $44); New York City (10hr., $73); Philadelphia (8½hr., $81); Baltimore (7hr., $58); Richmond (4hr., $19); and Williamsburg (2hr., $15).

Buses: Greyhound, 1017 Laskin Rd. (☎ 422-2998 or 800-231-2222). Connects with Maryland via the Bridge Tunnel. Station located ½ mi. from the oceanfront. From: Washington, D.C. (6½hr., $31); Richmond (3½hr., $24); and Williamsburg (2½hr., $15).

Public Transportation: Virginia Beach Transit/Trolley Information Center (☎ 640-6300), Atlantic Ave. and 24th St. Info on area transportation and tours, including trolleys, buses, and ferries. Trolleys transport riders to most major points in Virginia Beach. The Atlantic Avenue Trolley runs from Rudee Inlet to 42nd St. (May-Sept. daily noon-midnight; 50¢, seniors and disabled 25¢, day passes $1.50). Other trolleys run along the boardwalk, the North Seashore, and to Lynnhaven Mall. **Hampton Roads Regional Transit (HRT)** (☎ 222-6100), in the Silverleaf Commuter Center at Holland Rd. and Independence St., buses connect Virginia Beach with Norfolk, Portsmouth, and Newport News (fare $1.50, seniors and disabled 75¢, children under 38 in. free).

Bike Rental: RK's Surf Shop, 305 16th St. (☎ 428-7363). Rents bikes for $4 per hr. or $16 per day (in addition to aquatic entertainment).

Taxi: Yellow Cab, ☎ 460-0605.

✳❓ ORIENTATION AND PRACTICAL INFORMATION

In Virginia Beach, east-west streets are numbered and the north-south avenues, running parallel to the beach, have ocean names. Prepare to feel like a thimble on a Monopoly board: **Atlantic** and **Pacific Ave.** comprise the main drag. **Arctic, Baltic,** and **Mediterranean Ave.** are farther inland.

Tourist Office: Virginia Beach Visitors Center, 2100 Parks Ave. (☎ 437-4888 or 800-446-8038), at 22nd St. Info on budget accommodations and area sights. Helpful, knowledgeable docents. Open daily 9am-8pm; Labor Day to Memorial Day 9am-5pm.

Internet Access: WebCity Cybercafe, 1307 Atlantic Avenue, Suite 112, on the boardwalk. Minimum charge: $5 for 30 min.

Post Office: 2400 Atlantic Ave. (☎ 428-2821), at 24th St. and Atlantic Ave. Open M-F 8am-4:30pm. **ZIP code:** 23458. **Area code:** 757.

▐ ACCOMMODATIONS AND CAMPING

As could be expected with an ocean resort, a string of endless motels lines the waterfront in Virginia Beach. Oceanside, Atlantic and Pacific Aves. buzz with activity during the summer and boast the most desirable hotels. If you reserve in advance, rates are as low as $45 in winter and $65 on weekdays in summer. If you're traveling in a group, look for "efficiency" apartments, which are rented cheaply by the week. As with any beach town, the further from the shore, the lower the price of lodging.

Angie's Guest Cottage, Bed and Breakfast, and HI-AYH Hostel, 302 24th St. (☎ 428-4690). Filled with friendly staff, sparklingly clean rooms, and plenty of boogie boards in a prime area of town—only one block from the oceanfront. Barbara "Angie" Yates and her personable staff welcome predominantly young international and domestic guests with exceptional warmth, free trolley tokens, and great advice about the beach scene. Kitchen, lockers available. Linen $2. No lockout. No A/C. Open Apr.-Oct. Reservations helpful, but not required. Check-in 10am-9pm. Eight-guest capacity in each dorm room, HI-AYH members $14.50; off-season $14.50, HI-AYH members $11. Private hostel rooms with A/C $35.10, 2 people $26.90 per person, 3 people $23.40 per person; substantially less in off-season. Two-day minimum stay for private rooms.

Ocean Palms Motel, 2907 Arctic Ave. (☎ 428-8362), at 30th St. Two-person efficiencies with nondescript decor. Exchange a farther walk from beach locations for the chance to cook your own meal. Not likely to be mistaken for a five-star hotel, the brick building skimps on aesthetics, but, second only to Angie's hostel, offers the cheapest rates in the immediate resort area. TV, A/C, kitchen. $30-50 per night.

First Landings, 2500 Shore Dr. (☎ 412-2300, reservations 800-933-7275), about 8 mi. north of town on Rte. 60. Take the North Seashore Trolley. Located in the State Park bearing the same name, beachfront sites thrive on the natural beauty of Virginia's shore. Because of its desirable location amid sand dunes and cypress trees, the park is very popular; call 2-3 weeks ahead for reservations. The park features picnic areas, a private swimming area on a sprawling beach, a bathhouse and boat launching areas.

Coral Sand Motel, 2307 Pacific Ave. (☎425-0872), only two blocks from the ocean front, offers bland standard doubles with cable TV and A/C starting at $49 on week-days. Weekend prices around $109.

FOOD

Prepare for more $5 all-you-can-eat breakfast specials than you have ever previ-ously encountered. Alternatively, fish for a restaurant on **Atlantic Avenue** where each block is a virtual buffet of fried, fatty, sweet or creamy dining options.

■ **The Jewish Mother,** 3108 Pacific Ave. (☎422-5430). Let Mama fill your belly with deli where kids-at-heart can color on the walls with free crayons. Mama doesn't want no skin 'n' bones in her home, so feast on humongous sandwiches with a scoop of potato salad ($4-6.25), followed up by dessert ($3.50-4.50). The family restaurant transforms into a local barfly's delight after 11pm. Live music nightly with popular Blues Jam W. Happy Hour (daily 3-7pm) features $2 domestic drafts and $1.50 for a cooling mixed drink. Cover normally $3-5. Open M-F 8:30am-2am, Sa 8am-3am, Su 7am-2am.

■ **Giovanni's Pasta Pizza Palace,** 2006 Atlantic Ave. (☎425-1575). Young, outgoing wait-ers serve with gusto and speed in this affordable and plentiful pasta restaurant. The soft scrumptious rolls, inexpensive Italian pastas, pizzas, hot strombolis ($5-9), and a fabu-lous veggiboli ($6) satiate the appetite. Spinach ravioli ($7.25) is a delicious healthy option. Open daily noon-11pm.

Cuisine and Co., 3004 Pacific Ave. (☎428-6700). A local favorite, the pastel colored walls and plush furniture create a sophisticated departure from the glitter and noise of Atlantic Ave. Typical treats include veggie pita pizzas ($2), $6 per lb. stuffed baked potatoes, a chunky chicken salad ($5.25), and decadent cookies ($7.50 per lb.). Open M-Sa 9am-8pm, Su 9am-6pm.

Happy Crab's, 550 Laskin Rd. (☎437-9200). Get ready to fill your buckets with crab shells galore. Early-bird specials (daily 5-6:30pm) offer unbeatable 2-person size sea-food platters ($13) or huge 1-person servings big enough to split, like sumptuous ribs ($11). Lazybones, call ahead from the oceanfront and a free restaurant taxi will pick you up at the beach and bring you to the restaurant (after 5pm only). Open M-Th 11am-10pm, F-Su 11am-11pm.

SIGHTS

The **beach and boardwalk,** jam-packed with college revelers, bikini-clad sunbathers, and families, is the *raison d'être* at Virginia Beach. The **Old Coast Guard Station,** 24th St. and oceanfront, offers historic exhibits and a **Tower Cam** for voyeuristic peeks of sunbunnies. (☎422-1587. Open daily M-Sa 10am-5pm, Su noon-5pm. $3, seniors and military with ID $2.50, ages 6-18 $1, under 6 free.) The frequent roar of F-14 and Tom-cat jet engines will also remind you of the **Navy** base nearby. (☎433-3131 for info on visiting the base.) The **Virginia Marine Science Museum,** 717 General Booth Blvd., is home to over 50 species of fish, sharks and stingrays. (☎425-3474, excursion trips 437-2628. Open daily 9am-9pm, off-season 9am-5pm. $9, seniors $8, ages 4-11 $6.)

ENTERTAINMENT

On summer nights, the Virginia beach boardwalk becomes a haunt for lovers and teenagers, and **Atlantic Ave.,** a.k.a. "Beach Street, USA.," burgeons with minstrel shows and street performers. Rousing jazz and classic rock performances can be heard every other block. Larger outdoor venues at 7th, 17th, and 24th draw bigger names and bigger crowds. (☎440-6628 for more info. Schedules for the main events are posted along the street. Free.) Gay and lesbian bars can be found away from Virginia Beach in the chi chi Ghent neighborhood of nearby Norfolk.

Harpoon Larry's, 216 24th St. (☎422-6000), at Pacific Ave., 1 block from the HI-AYH hostel, serves tasty fish ($6) in an everyone-knows-your-name atmosphere. The amicable bartender and manager welcome 20- and 30-somethings to escape the sweat and raging hormones of "The Block." Specials include amazing seafood deals ($8-12) and rum runners (Tu, Th $2). Shout "Arriba!" W with 25¢ jalapeño poppers. Open daily noon-2am. Happy Hour M-F 7-9 pm.

Peabody's, 209 21st St. (☎422-6212). Boogie your body not your board at the biggest dance floor on the beach. A young, scantily-clad crowd bops to Top 40 hits, especially during "Hammertime" when drinks are only $1.50 (daily 7-9pm). All-you-can-eat crab legs and shrimp ($15). Peabody's scores big with the fresh-faced crowd on its theme nights: College Night on F (free admission with college ID) and Sa Summer Saturdaze (discount with tropical attire). Open Th-Sa 7pm-2am. Cover $5; pool $1.

Fat Daddy's, 1069 19th St. (☎491-1069), 1 mi. from the beach, recreates the French quarter of New Orleans with California wraps ($6-8) for a crowd dolled up in swanky duds. Don't be misled by the sloppy name. Opulence rules here at Fat Daddy's, decked as it is with fine wines and chandeliers. Festive deck party Th. Open Tu-Su 4pm-2am.

Abyss, 1065 19th St. (☎422-0486). While yuppies inhale martinis at Fat Daddy's, next door the Abyss fuels randy 18+ clubbers with pop and alternative dance music F-Sa, and W concerts. Open W and F-Sa 7pm-4am. Cover $3-6.

CHARLOTTESVILLE ☎804

Thomas Jefferson, composer of the Declaration of Independence and colonial Renaissance man, built his dream house, **Monticello,** high atop his "little mountain" just southeast of Charlottesville. Around his personal paradise, Jefferson endeavored to create the ideal community, primarily by transplanting fellow Presidents Monroe and Madison to the Charlottesville area for friendly visits. In an effort to breed further intellect (not to mention keep him busy in his old age), Jefferson humbly created the University of Virginia (UVA). Jefferson would be proud to know his time was not wasted—today the college sustains Charlottesville economically, geographically, and culturally.

▌ GETTING THERE AND GETTING AROUND

To reach Charlottesville by car, I-64 runs east-west and is the city's main feeder. From points north and south, Rte. 29 leads directly into Charlottesville where it becomes Emmet St.

Trains: Amtrak, 810 W. Main St. (☎296-4559 or 800-872-7245), 7 blocks from downtown. To: Washington, D.C. (3hr., 1 per day, $27); New York (7-8hr., 1 per day, $88); Baltimore (4hr., 1 per day, $44); and Philadelphia (5½hr., 1 per day, $67). Open daily 5:30am-9pm.

Buses: Greyhound/Trailways, 310 W. Main St. (☎295-5131), within 3 blocks of downtown. To: Richmond (1½-4hr., 6 per day, $18.50); Washington, D.C. (3hr., 5 per day, $18); Norfolk (4hr., 2 per day, $36); Baltimore (4-5hr., 4 per day, $50); and Philadelphia (7-11hr., 4 per day, $56.50). Open 7am-10pm daily.

Public Transportation: Charlottesville Transit Service (☎296-7433). Bus service within city limits. Maps available at both info centers, on the buses, the Chamber of Commerce, and the UVA student center in Newcomb Hall. Buses operate M-Sa 6:30am-6:30pm. Fare 75¢, seniors and disabled 33¢, under 6 free. The more frequent UVA buses technically require UVA student ID, but others report that a studious look usually suffices.

Taxi: Yellow Cab, ☎295-4131.

▌ ORIENTATION AND PRACTICAL INFORMATION

Charlottesville streets are numbered from east to west, using compass directions; 5th St. NW is 10 blocks from (and parallel to) 5th St. NE. There are two downtowns: one on the west side across from the university called **The Corner,** home to student-driven delis and hip coffee shops, and **Historic Downtown,** about a mile east and a couple notches higher on the price scale. The two are connected by **University Avenue,** running east-west, which starts as Ivy Rd. and becomes Main St. after a bridge terminates in The Corner district.

Visitor Information: Chamber of Commerce, 415 E. Market St. (☎295-3141), within walking distance of Amtrak, Greyhound, and downtown. Maps, guides, and info about special events available. Open M-F 9am-5pm. **Thomas Jefferson Visitors Center** (☎977-1783, ext. 121), off I-64 on Rte. 20. Arranges same-day discount lodgings; Monticello, Michie Tavern, and Ash Lawn-Highland combo tickets; and travel packages to sites associated with Jefferson. "The Pursuit of Liberty," a 30min. film about Jefferson's life, is shown on the hr. 10am-4pm ($2.50). Also features a free exhibit with 400 original Jeffersonian objects. Open daily Mar.-Oct. 9am-5:30pm; Nov.-Feb. 9am-5pm. **University of Virginia Information Center** (☎924-7969), at the Rotunda in the center of campus. Offers brochures, a university map, and tour information. Open daily 9am-4:45pm. The larger **University Center** (☎924-7166), Exit 120A off US 250W, is home to the campus police and hands out transport schedules, campus maps, entertainment guides, and hints on budget accommodations. Open 24hr.

Campus Police: ☎4-7166 on a UVA campus phone.

Hotlines: Region 10 Community Services: ☎972-1800. Open 24hr. **Mental Health:** ☎977-4673. Open 24hr. **Rape Crisis Center:** ☎977-7273. Open 24hr. **Lesbian and Gay:** ☎982-2773. Open Sept.-May M-W 7-10pm and Su 6-10pm. **Women's Health Clinic** (in Richmond): ☎800-254-4479. Open 24hr.

Post Office: 513 E. Main St. (☎963-2525). Open M-F 8:30am-5pm, Sa 10am-1pm. **ZIP code:** 22902. **Area code:** 804.

ACCOMMODATIONS

Emmet Street (U.S. 29) is home to generic hotels and motels ($40-60) that tend to fill up during summer weekends and big UVA events. The **Budget Inn,** 140 Emmet St., is the closest motel to the university, and offers big rooms with lots of sunlight and cable TV. (☎293-5141. Reception daily 8am-midnight. Singles $46; doubles $52. Each additional person $5.) **Charlottesville KOA Campground,** Rte. 708, 10 mi. outside Charlottesville has shaded campsites to keeps guests cool; the recreation hall, pool, and volleyball court entertain. Take U.S. 28 S to Rte 708 SE. (☎296-9881 or 800-562-1743. Open Mar.-Oct. Laundry facilities. Fishing and pets allowed. Sites $21, with water and electric $24, full hook-up $26.)

FOOD

Students and tourists dictate the menus in Charlottesville. Intellectual crowds dine at **The Corner** on University Ave. across from the university where good, cheap food overflows each plate. The chain motels on Emmet St. are complemented by fast food chains. For a glitzier culinary experience, a stroll down the cobblestone streets by the **Downtown Mall** unveils romantic, unique eateries, most of which offer outdoor dining in summer.

The Hardware Store, 316 E. Main St. (☎977-1518 or 800-426-6001), in the Downtown Mall. It requires a handyman's dexterity to go bottoms-up on the ½ meter and full meter beer tubes ($3-7). Eclectic grille food sends patrons to the head of the class with the cum laude sandwich (smoked salmon and ham on pumpernickel $8) and includes specialty potato *pierogies* ($4). Open M-Th 11am-9pm, F-Su 11am-10pm.

Southern Culture, 633 W. Main St. (☎979-1990). Delve deep into Cajun culture with the *pasta jambalaya* ($13) or the more affordable bayou burger ($6) served up by an amicable staff. Every Tu is Mardi Gras night. Open M-Th 5-10pm, F-Sa 5-10:30pm, Su 11am-2:30pm and 5-10:30pm.

Littlejohn's, 1427 University Ave. (☎977-0588). During lunch hours, this deli becomes as overstuffed with students and workers as its sandwiches. In the wee, wee hours of the morning, barflies trickle into Littlejohn's to kick back and relax with the easy rider (baked ham, mozzarella, and coleslaw $3.50). Many, many beers ($2). Open 24hr.

> **SMARTY PANTS** When Jefferson undertook the design of the **University of Virginia,** he envisioned an institution where knowledge flowed freely and without end. With this particular image in mind, he enclosed the lawn on three sides, with one side open to represent the limitless possibility of the human intellect. Ironically, the open side provided a spectacular view of his own home at Monticello, suggesting that the mind did indeed have a limit—and Thomas Jefferson had reached it.

👁 SIGHTS

Jefferson oversaw every stage of development of his beloved **Monticello,** a home that truly reflects the personality of its brilliant creator. The house is a quasi-Palladian jewel filled with fascinating innovations, such as a fireplace dumbwaiter to the wine cellar and a mechanical copier, all compiled or conceived by Jefferson. The grounds include orchards and flower gardens and afford magnificent views. *(1184 Monticello Loop. ☎984-9800. Open daily Mar.-Oct. 8am-5pm; Nov.-Feb. 9am-4:30pm. $11, ages 6-11 $6.)* Just west of Monticello on the Thomas Jefferson Pkwy. (Rte. 53) is the partially reconstructed **Michie Tavern,** which includes an operating grist mill and a general store. *(☎977-1234. Open daily 9am-5pm. $8, under 6 $7. Last tour 4:20pm.)* To reach **Ash Lawn-Highland,** the 535-acre plantation home of President James Monroe, continue east to the intersection with Rte. 795, 2½ mi. east of Monticello, and make a right. Although less distinctive than Monticello, Ash Lawn reveals more about family life in the early 19th century and hosts living history exhibitions including banjo music. Kids are mesmerized by the colorful peacocks in the backyard. *(☎293-9539. Open daily 9am-6pm; Nov.-Feb. 10am-5pm. Tour $7, seniors $6.50, ages 6-11 $4. AAA 10% discount. Wheelchair accessible.)*

Most activity on the grounds of the **University of Virginia** clusters around the **Lawn** and fraternity-lined **Rugby Road** *(☎924-3239).* Jefferson's Monticello is visible from the lawn, a terraced green carpet that is one of the prettiest spots in American academia. Professors live in the Lawn's pavilions; Jefferson designed each one in a different architectural style. Privileged Fourth Years (never called seniors) are chosen each year for the small Lawn singles. Room 13 is dedicated to ne'er-do-well **Edgar Allen Poe,** who was kicked out for gambling. The early-morning clanging of the bell that used to hang in the **Rotunda** provoked one incensed student to shoot at the building. *(☎924-3592. Open daily 9am-4:45pm. Tours 10am-4pm on the hr.)* The **Bayley Art Museum,** on Rugby Rd., features changing exhibits and a small permanent collection that includes a cast of Rodin's *The Kiss.* *(☎924-7969. Open Tu-Su 1-5pm.)*

🎵🎭 ENTERTAINMENT AND NIGHTLIFE

This preppy college town is full of jazz, rock, and pubs. A kiosk near the fountain in the center of the Downtown Mall has posters with club schedules; the free *Weekly C-ville* can tell you who's playing when. English-language opera and musical theater highlight the **Summer Festival of the Arts** in the Box Gardens behind Ash Lawn. *(☎293-4500. Open June-Aug. M-F 9am-5pm.)* Ash Lawn also hosts a "Music at Twilight" series on W evenings at 8pm ($10, students $6, seniors $9). There's daily skating at the **Charlottesville Ice Park,** 230 W. Main St., at the end of the Downtown Mall *(☎979-1423; call ahead for times and prices).*

Baja Bean, 1327 Main St. *(☎293-4507).* Cheap burritos, tamales and chimichangas go down smooth for under $8 at this Mexican bar and restaurant. Every 5th day of the month is the Cinco Celebration, a fiesta highlighted by $2 Corona and pinatas. Open daily 11am-2am. Happy Hour M-F 4-6pm for frozen fruit margaritas ($2.50).

The Max, 120 11th St. SW *(☎295-6299 or 295-8729).* Looking to kick up your heels? Tu features Top 40 DJ and dancing (cover $4), while Charlottesville turns to its southern roots with line dancing W (cover $4). F-Sa brings live country rock (cover $5). Drafts around $2. Open Th-Su 8pm-1:30am.

MID-ATLANTIC

TRAX, 122 11th St. SW (☎ 295-8729, 800-594-8499 for tickets and shows), next door to its rhyming neighbor Max, opens its doors as a concert venue Th-Sa for everything from heavy metal and rap to Christian rock. Tickets $5-20, depending on band.

Dürty Nelly's, 2200 Jefferson Park Ave. (☎295-1278). The slow southern twangs of older Bible-Belters declare the monstrous subs "the largest in the state" ($4.25-5.75). Over 50 beers: domestic drafts $1.50, $1.10 during Happy Hour (M-F 4-7pm). True to its downhome image, Tu nights and weekends feature live bluegrass and country music (cover $2-4). Deli open daily 11am-10pm; bar M-Sa 11am-2am, Su noon-midnight.

SHENANDOAH NATIONAL PARK ☎540

Shenandoah National Park was America's first great natural reclamation project. In 1926, Congress authorized Virginia to purchase a 280-acre tract of over-logged, over-hunted land. A 1936 decree from Franklin Roosevelt sought to improve the land, experimenting with trappers to foster new life upon the slowly rejuvenating soil. Today an enthralling national park spans 196,000 acres and contains 500 miles of trails and more plant species than all of Europe. On clear days, visitors can see miles of ridges and treetops. Such unspoiled views, however, are a rare commodity, as pollution has mixed with the natural dew in the area to create a murky mist cloaking the peaks. Shenandoah's amazing multicolored mountains—covered with foliage in the summer, streaked with brilliant reds, oranges, and yellows in the fall—offer relaxation and recreation throughout the year.

■🛈 **ORIENTATION AND PRACTICAL INFORMATION.** The park runs nearly 75 mi. along the famous 105 mi. **Skyline Drive,** which extends from Front Royal in the north to Rockfish Gap in the south before evolving into the Blue Ridge Parkway. Miles are measured north to south and denote the location of trails and stops. Three major highways divide the park into sections. The **North Section** runs from Rte. 340 to Rte. 211, the **Central Section** from Rte. 211 to Rte. 33, and the **South Section** from Rte. 33 to Rte. 250 and I-64. Entrance fee is $10 per vehicle, or $5 per hiker, biker, or bus passenger. Admission for disabled persons is free. Pass is valid for seven days and is necessary for re-admittance. Most facilities hibernate in the winter; call ahead. Skyline Dr. closes during and following bad weather.

The **Dickey Ridge Visitors Center,** at Mi. 4.6, and the **Byrd Visitors Center,** at Mi. 51, answer questions and maintain small exhibits about the park including a 12min. introductory slide show. (Dickey Ridge: ☎635-3566. Byrd: ☎999-3283. Both open daily Apr.-Oct. 8:30am-5pm, July 4 to Labor Day until 6pm. Dickey is open through Nov.) The stations and their knowledgeable rangers conduct informative presentations on local wildlife, short guided walks among the flora, and then wax romantic, outdoors-style, with lantern-lit evening discussions. Comprehensive and newly updated, the *Guide to Shenandoah National Park and Skyline Drive* ($7.50; worth every penny) is available at both visitors centers. For general park info call ☎999-3397 (daily 8am-4:30pm) or 999-3500 for a recorded message. Send mail to: **Superintendent,** Park Headquarters, Shenandoah National Park, Rte. 4, P.O. Box 348, Luray, VA 22835. In an emergency call ☎800-732-0911.

Greyhound sends buses once per day from Washington, D.C., to Waynesboro, near the park's southern entrance ($43); no bus or train serves Front Royal, near the park's northern entrance. **Area code:** 540.

▌ **ACCOMMODATIONS AND CAMPING. The Bear's Den (HI-AYH),** 18393 Blue Ridge Mountain Rd., 35 mi. north of Shenandoah on Rte. 601, in a miniature stone castle, can hold 20 mountain-weary travelers within its two standard dorm rooms; another room has one double bed and two bunk beds. Take Rte. 340 N to Rte. 7 E and follow it for 10 mi. to 601 N; travel ½ mi. on 601 and turn left at the gate. Aside from the more standard amenities, the hostel also offers simple, straightforward hiking trails geared towards inexperienced woodfolk. A convenience store spares budget-travelers a 9 mi. trek to the nearest supermarket. (☎554-8708. Reception 7:30-9:30am and 5-10pm. Front gate locked and quiet hrs. begin at 10pm; 24hr.

access to hikers' basement room. Check-out 9:30am. Beds $12, non-members $15; private room $30/$36. Camping $6/$7 per person with use of hostel facilities, $3 without.) The park also maintains three affordable "lodges," essentially motels with nature-friendly exteriors. **Skyland,** Mi. 42 on Skyline Dr., offers wood-furnished cabins and more upscale motel rooms. (☎999-2211. Cabins: Open Apr.-Oct. $53-100; $7 more in Oct. Motel rooms: Open Mar.-Nov. $116-155, Sa-Su $126-165.) **Big Meadows,** Mi. 51, has similar services, with a historic lodge and cabins. (☎999-2221. Cabins: Open late Apr. to Nov. $75-85. Lodge: $68-115, Sa-Su $73-121.) **Lewis Mountain,** Mi. 57, operates cabins with kitchens and less pricey tent cabins. (☎999-2255. Cabins: $62-67; $7 more in Oct. Tent cabins: $20-25.) Reservations are necessary at all three lodges, which can be accessed at ☎800-999-4714; call up to six months in advance. The park service (☎800-365-2267) also maintains four major campgrounds: **Mathews Arm** (Mi. 22), **Big Meadows** (Mi. 51), **Lewis Mountain** (Mi. 58), and **Loft Mountain** (Mi. 80). The latter three have stores, laundry, and showers, but no hook-ups. Heavily wooded and uncluttered by RVs, Mathews Arm and Lewis Mountain make for the happiest campers. Sites at Mathews Arm, Lewis Mountain, and Loft Mountain are $14, at Big Meadows $17. Reservations are possible only at Big Meadows.

⚑ CAMPING. Shenandoah houses more backpackers per mile than any other park. **Backcountry camping** is free, but you must obtain a permit at a park entrance, visitors center, ranger station, or the park headquarters. Camping without a permit or above 2800 ft. is illegal and unsafe. Trail maps and the PATC guide can be obtained at the visitors center. The PATC puts out 3 topographical maps ($5 each). The Appalachian Trail (A.T.) runs the length of the park. The **Potomac Appalachian Trail Club** (PATC) maintains six cabins in backcountry areas of the park. Campers who feel that they are sufficiently ready for a backpacking trip but not totally comfortable with staying in the woods on their own might consider staying at one of these rustic accommodations. You must reserve space in the cabins in advance by writing to the club at 118 Park St. SE, Vienna, VA 22180-4609 or calling ☎703-242-0693 or 703-242-0315 (M-Th 7-9pm, or Th-F noon-2pm). You may be under a roof but you'll still be in the wilderness, so bring lanterns and food; the primitive cabins contain only bunk beds, blankets, and stoves. (Su-Th $3 per person, F-Sa $14 per group. One group member must be 21+.) Though stamps from three different lodgings constitute eligibility, casual backpackers should avoid the shelters strewn at 7 mi. intervals along the park's segment of the A.T. Unwritten trail etiquette usually reserves the cabins for those hiking large stretches of the trail.

⚐ HIKING AND OUTDOORS. Many visitors choose to experience the park by taking a ride along Skyline Dr. and stopping occasionally to take short hikes, enjoy the views at scenic overlooks, or picnic. The drive is lined with seven picnic areas (located at Mi. 5, 24, 37, 51, 58, 63, and 80) with bathrooms, potable water, and scenic eating spots. The trusty *Guide to Shenandoah and Skyline Drive* includes an extensive hikes section with descriptions of every trail in the park. The trails off Skyline Dr. are heavily used and safe for cautious day-hikers with maps, appropriate footwear, and water. If you do not feel comfortable hiking on your own or want to try a longer hike, you might consider one of the free ranger-led tours arranged by the visitors center. The middle section of the park, from **Thorton Gap** (Mi. 30) to **South River** (Mi. 63), bursts with photo opportunities and moving views, although it tends to be crowded. The **Whiteoak Canyon Trail,** at Mi. 42.6, opens upon an impressive 86 ft. waterfall and is a strenuous 4½ mi. hike that rewards those who ascend the 1040 ft. and approximately 4 hrs. of trail with tremendous views of the ancient Limberlost hemlocks. The adjacent **Limberlost Trail** (5 mi. round-trip from Whiteoak Canyon; 1 mi. wheelchair-accessible loop from trailhead at Mi. 43) slithers into a hemlock forest. Weaving through orchards and remaining relatively level, Limberlost is recommended for beginners. Nearby, the popular **Old Rag Mountain Trail,** located 5 mi. from Mi. 45 (main trail starts outside park; from U.S. 211, turn right on Rte. 522, then right on Rte. 231 and watch for a sign), entices adventure-seekers to scramble up 3291 ft. to triumphant views of the valley below; the 8¾ mi. loop takes

6 to 8 hours. ($3 fee for Old Rag hikers 16 and older who have not paid Shenandoah admission). Farther south, at Mi. 50.7, hikers can feel the democratic pulse of the park by retracing Thomas Jefferson's footsteps along the 1½ mi. **Dark Hollow Falls Trail.** At Mi. 63, the 2½ mi. **South River Falls Trail** descends 850 ft. to a splendid viewing platform for the falls. Independent hikers can gain altitude on the self-guided **Stony Man Nature Trail,** at Mi. 41.7, which gradually climbs 1½ mi. to the park's 2nd-highest peak.

NEAR SHENANDOAH

LURAY CAVERNS. Mother Nature worked millions of years to sculpt the limestone bowels of the earth into delicate marvels of color and form. Chances are, it will seem like a million years as you wait in line to explore Luray Caverns' moist, 57° tunnels filled with mineral formations. A Mexican band entertains the droves of tourists as they wait in line to play some underground music of their own on the "Stalagpipe Organ." (☎540-743-6551. Exit 264 off I-81 to U.S. 211. Open daily June 15 to Labor Day 9am-7pm; Mar. 15 to June 14 and Labor Day to Oct. 31 9am-6pm; Nov. to Mar. 14 M-F 9am-4pm, Sa-Su 9am-5pm. $14, seniors $12, ages 7-13 $6; $1 AAA discount.)

ENDLESS CAVERNS. Escape the tourist congestion of Luray Caverns to discover the beauty of creation at Endless Caverns. The wildest of the caves was discovered in 1800 by two boys hunting a rabbit. Where the rabbit scurried remains a mystery to this day but chances are he had plenty of space to hop with 5½ mi. of passages documented and an unknown number still unexplored. Cave temperature is cool and the tour is relatively physical, so wear a jacket and sturdy shoes. (1800 Endless Caverns Rd. ☎540-896-2283. Follow signs from the intersection of U.S. 11 and U.S 211 in New Market. Open daily June 15 to Labor Day 9am-7pm; Labor Day to Nov. 14 and Mar. 15 to June 14 9am-5pm; Nov. 15 to Mar. 14 9am-4pm. $12, ages 3-12 $6; $1 AAA discount.)

SKYLINE CAVERNS. The smallest and the closest to D.C., Skyline Caverns tends an orchid-like garden of white rock spikes. Don't hold your breath in suspense of the next formation; one grows every 7000 years. Most notable are the anthodites (crystals), which can be found nowhere else in the world. (☎540-635-4545 or 800-296-4545. On U.S. 340, 1 mi. from the junction of Rte. 340 and Skyline Dr. Open daily June 5 to Labor Day 9am-6:30pm; Mar. 15 to June 4 and Labor Day to Nov. 14 9am-5pm; Nov. 15 to Mar. 14 9am-4pm. $12, senior, AAA, and military $10, ages 7-13 $6.)

OTHER SITES. The **Shenandoah Vineyards** hosts free tours and wine tastings daily. (3659 S. Ox Rd. off I-81. ☎540-984-8699. Open daily Mar.-Dec. 10am-6pm; Jan.-Feb. 9am-5pm. Free.) If a scenic paddle floats your boat, contact **Downriver Canoe Co.** in Bentonville, which offers canoe, kayak, raft, and tube trips and rentals. (☎540-635-5526 or 800-338-1963. From Skyline Dr. Mi. 20 follow U.S 211 W for 8 mi., then take U.S. 340 N 14 mi. to Bentonville; turn right onto Rte. 613 and go 1 mi.) Alternately, try **Front Royal Canoe** on U.S. 340 3 mi. south of Skyline Dr. (☎540-635-5440 or 800-270-8808.)

SCENIC DRIVE: BLUE RIDGE PARKWAY   ☎540

The beauty of unrestrained wilderness does not end at the southern gates of Shenandoah. Your jaw will continue to drop as you weave through the world's longest scenic drive, the 469 mi. Blue Ridge Pkwy. Continuous with Skyline Dr., the parkway winds through Virginia and North Carolina, connecting the Shenandoah (Virginia) and Great Smoky Mountains (Tennessee) National Parks, offering an endless barrage of stunning vistas along the way. Administered by the National Park Service, the parkway sprouts hiking trails, campsites, and picnic grounds with humbling mountain views. While still accessible in the winter, it lacks maintenance or park service between November and April. The steep, bending roads can be treacherous, so exercise caution, especially during inclement weather. Also be on the alert for darting deer, not an uncommon sight among the wild woods.

From Shenandoah National Park, the road extends south through Virginia's **George Washington National Forest** from Waynesboro to Roanoke. The forest's **visitors center** (☎291-1806), 12 mi. off the parkway at Mi. 70 at the intersection of Rte. 130

and Rte. 11 in Natural Bridge, distributes info on camping, canoeing, and mountain-lake swimming at Sherando Lake (4½ mi. off the parkway at Mi. 16; user fee $8).

Across from the forest's visitors center, a water-carved *Arch de Triomphe*, the **Natural Bridge,** towers 219 ft. above green-lined falls and an underground river. One of the seven natural wonders of the world, the Bridge still bears the initials carved into the side by vandalous George Washington. Not even this wondrous site, origi-nally known by Native Americans as "the Bridge of God," is safe from commercial invasion: a modest indoor miniature golf course entertains in the basement of the welcome center. The nightly "Drama of Creation" light and sound show chronicles the Bible's seven days of creation. (☎291-2121 or 800-533-1410. Bridge open daily 8am-8pm. Drama show Su-F 9pm, Sa 9 and 10pm. $8, seniors $7, ages 6-15 $4. Wheelchair accessible.)

Hiking trails vary in difficulty and duration, offering naturalists of all ages and abilities a chance to explore the peaks and valleys of Blue Ridge. **Humpback Rocks,** a greenstone formation (Mi. 5.8), is an easy hike to the namesake emerald mounds. The **Mountain Farm Trail** (Mi. 5.9) is another easy hike, about 20min., and leads to a reconstructed homestead. For a humbling hiking experience, 3-5 mi. trails start from **Peaks of Otter** (Mi. 84), where you can camp at the lowest point on the park-way among peaks as high as 4500 ft. The **Rock Castle Gorge Trail** (Mi. 167) takes about 3hr. to complete. For wheelchair accessibility, try the ¼ mi. **Linn Cove Viaduct Access Trail** (Mi. 304.4 in North Carolina). If you're hard-core and have the time to spare, venture onto the **Appalachian Trail,** which leads all the way to Georgia or Maine.

Although a hiker's paradise, the Blue Ridge Pkwy. features much more than wild-life trails. The **Otter Creek Restaurant** (Mi. 60) serves downhome southern fried chicken for $5.50 (open daily 8am-8pm). If you're overcome by the heat, seek aquatic refreshment in the **James River** (Mi. 63). The river is swimmable but can be dangerous; drownings have occurred in the past, so exercise extreme caution. **Mabry Mill** (Mi. 176.1) offers ham and biscuits ($4.35) in a mountain farmland. Between Mi. 292 and 295, the opulent manor at **Moses H. Cone Memorial Park** rents canoes on Price Lake, Mi. 291. (Open daily May 27 to Sept. 4 8:30am-6pm; May 6-21 and Sept. 9 to Oct. 29 Sa-Su 10am-6pm. $4 per hr., $3 per additional hr.) The Park Service hosts a variety of ranger-led activities; info is available at the **visitors centers** (see below).

There are nine **campgrounds** along the parkway, each with water (no showers) and restrooms, located at Mi. 60.9, 86, 120.5, 167.1, 239, 297, 316.3, 339.5, and 408.6 ($12; reservations not accepted). An inconspicuous iron gate hides the **Blue Ridge Country HI-AYH Hostel,** Mi. 214½, 7 mi. south on Rte. 89 from the town of Galax, housed in a recreated colonial building. (☎236-4962. Open Mar.-Dec. Lockout 9am-5pm. Curfew 11pm. 22 beds. Dorms $14-15, non-members $17-18.)

Galax hosts one mountain music concert per month and the famed **Fiddler's Con-vention** (☎236-8541) the 2nd weekend in Aug. The tiny hippie-redneck hamlet of Floyd, 40 mi. north, swells with its free weekly **jamboree** in the **Floyd County General Store** (☎745-4563) F at 7pm.

Where Skyline Dr. melts into Blue Ridge Pkwy., at the intersections of I-81 and I-64, more modern rooms crowd **Lexington,** a college town dripping with Confederate pride. Comfortable, 50s-style accommodations at **Overnight Guests,** 216 W. Washing-ton St., 8 mi. off the Blue Ridge Pkwy., directly across from Washington and Lee, are only $10 per night. Don't expect to be waited on hand and foot; the emphasis is on self-service. (☎463-2376. TV, no A/C. Call 9-11pm to reach the proprietor; other-wise, check the list of available rooms in the front hall and help yourself to an open room.) Hungry travelers grab pasta ($6) or overstuffed sandwiches like the "Old Gang" (turkey, ham, and bacon $4.25) in the garden at **Harb's Bistro,** 19 W. Washing-ton St. Mornings start with coffee and a huge muffin for $1.50. (☎464-1900. Open Tu-Sa 8am-3pm, Su 9am-3pm; in winter Tu-Th 8am-10pm, F-Sa 8am-11pm, Su 9am-3pm.) Before heading back to the parkway, check out the **Lee Chapel and Museum,** at the center of the Washington and Lee campus, which holds Confederate General (and college namesake) Robert E. Lee's sarcophagus and exhibits on his views on education. (☎463-8768. Open daily 8:30am-6pm. Free.) For further attractions and accommodations, contact the **Lexington Visitor Center,** 106 E. Washington St. (☎463-3777). Other cities and villages along the parkway also offer a range of accommodations, mostly motels (rates $35-55).

For general info on the parkway, call the park service in Roanoke, VA (☎857-2490) or write to **Blue Ridge Pkwy. Headquarters,** 400 BB&T Bldg., Asheville, NC 28801 (☎704-271-4779). Twelve **visitors centers** line the parkway at Mi. 5.8, 63.6, 85.9, 169, 217.5, 294, 304.5, 316.4, 364.5, and 382, located at entry points where highways intersect the Blue Ridge (most open daily 9am-5pm). **Area code:** 540.

WEST VIRGINIA

With 80% of the state cloaked in untamed forests, hope of commercial expansion and economic prosperity once seemed a distant dream for West Virginia. When the coal mines—formerly West Virginia's primary source of revenue—began to exhaust, the state appeared doomed, until government officials decided to capitalize on the area's evergreen expanses, tranquil trails, and raging rivers. Today, thousands of tourists forge paths into West Virginia's untamed, breathtaking landscape.

⚅ PRACTICAL INFORMATION

Capital: Charleston.
Visitor Info: Dept. of Tourism, 2101 Washington St. E., Bldg. #17, Charleston 25305; P.O. Box 50312 (☎800-225-5982; www.state.wv.uf/tourism). **US Forest Service Supervisor's Office,** 200 Sycamore St., Elkins 26241 (☎304-636-1800). Open M-F 8am-4:45pm.
Postal Abbreviation: WV. **Sales Tax:** 6%.

HARPERS FERRY   ☎304

Harpers Ferry earned its fame when abolitionist John Brown and his fighting friends raided the US Armory in 1859. Although Brown was captured and executed, the raid brought regional and moral divisions over slavery into the national spotlight. Brown's adamant belief in violence as the only means to overcome the persisting problem of slavery soon gained credence. It is widely believed that Brown's audacious attack on the Armory and slavery planted the seeds of the Civil War. Brown's raid would not be the last hostility Harpers Ferry would experience; the town was a major area of conflict and changed hands eight times during the Civil War. Today, Harpers Ferry attracts more mild-mannered guests, namely hikers, bikers, canoers, and rafters who enjoy the town's surrounding wilderness.

◪⚅ **ORIENTATION AND PRACTICAL INFORMATION.** Located on West Virginia's border with Maryland, Harpers Ferry is close enough to Washington for a convenient daytrip. **Trains: Amtrak,** on Potomac St., has one train per day to Washington, D.C. ($17); reservations are required, as no tickets are sold at the station. The same depot serves the **Maryland Rail Commuter (MARC)** (☎800-325-7245; open M-F 5:30am-8:15pm), a cheaper and more frequent service to D.C. (M-F 2 per day; $7.25). **Buses:** The closest **Greyhound** bus stations are 30min. away in Winchester, VA, to the southwest and Frederick, MD, to the northeast, but the most affordable option is the **Appalachian Trail Conference (ATC),** which runs buses to Charles Town for $2. **Bike Rental: Blue Ridge Outfitters** (☎304-535-6331), 2 mi. west of Harpers Ferry towards Charles Town, rents bikes for $20 per day. **Visitor Information:** ☎535-6223. Write to: Harpers Ferry National Historical Park, P.O. Box 65, Harpers Ferry, WV 25425. **Visitors center:** just inside the park entrance off Rte. 340 (☎535-6298; open daily 8am-5pm). Admission is $5 per car, $3 per hiker or bicyclist, and lasts for three consecutive days. A bus shuttles from the parking lot to town every 10min. **Post Office:** P.O. Box 9998, on the corner of Washington and Franklin St. (open M-F 8am-4pm, Sa 9am-noon). **ZIP code:** 25425. **Area code:** 304.

■ ACCOMMODATIONS. Ragged hikers find a warm welcome and a roof over their heads at the social and spacious **Harpers Ferry Hostel (HI-AYH)**, 19123 Sandy Hook Rd., at Keep Tryst Rd. off Rte. 340 in Knoxville, MD. This renovated auction house, replete with a backyard trail to pulsating Potomac overlooks, spreads guests into four rooms with 39 well-cushioned beds. (☎301-834-7654. Closed Nov. 15 to Mar. 15. Check-in 6-11pm. Laundry, limited parking. 3-night maximum stay. Beds $13, non-members $16. Camping $6/$9, includes use of hostel kitchen and bathrooms. "Primitive" campsites $3/$4.50. Credit card number required for phone reservation.) For private quarters, the **Hillside Motel**, 19105 Keep Tryst Rd., in Knoxville, MD, has 19 clean, adequate rooms. Location next to a restaurant and a liquor store may be particularly appealing to some. (☎301-834-8144. Singles $36; doubles $45; lower winter rates.) Camp along the **C&O Canal**, where free camping sites lie 5 mi. apart, or in one of the five Maryland state park campgrounds within 30 mi. of Harpers Ferry (for more information, call the ranger station ☎301-739-4200). **Greenbrier State Park**, on Rte. 40 E off Rte. 66, has camping and outdoor recreation revolving around a lake. (☎301-791-4767 or 888-432-2267. Open May-Oct. Sites $20, with hook-up $25.)

■ FOOD. Harpers Ferry has sparse offerings for hungry hikers. **Rte. 340** welcomes the fast food fanatic with various chain restaurants indicated by highway signs. Across the street from the Hillside Motel, at the **Cindy Dee Restaurant**, 19112 Keep Tryst Rd. at Rte. 340, Elvis is still very much alive. Enough chicken ($5) is fried to singlehandedly clog your arteries. The homemade apple dumpling ($2.50) is delectable. (☎301-695-8181. Open daily 7am-9pm.) The historic area, especially High St. and Potomac St., caters to lunchtime noshers but vacates for dinner. For nightlife and varied cuisine, the tiny **Shepherdstown**, 11 mi. north of Harpers Ferry, is practically a bustling culinary metropolis in these desolate parts. From the Ferry, take Rte. 340 S for 2 mi. to Rte. 230 N or pedal 13 mi. along the C&O towpath. Amid the colonial architecture of E. German St. can be found the center of town and the **Mecklinburg Inn**, 128 E. German St., where rock 'n' roll and $1.75 Rolling Rock provide alliterative entertainment on open-mic night every Tu from 9pm to midnight. (☎876-2126. Open M-Th 3pm-12:30am, F 3pm-1:30am, Sa 1pm-2am, Su 1pm-12:30am. Happy hour M-F 4:30-6:30pm. 21+ after 5pm.)

■ SIGHTS. Parking in town is nonexistent, so it's necessary to park at the visitors center and board the free bus to town or foot the 20min. walk. The bus stops at **Shenandoah St.**, where a barrage of replicated 19th-century shops will greet you. The shuttle ride through abandoned grounds where mills once stood creates the impression of being shipped to a desert island. Any fears of falling off the planet, however, will be assuaged upon encountering historical markers and actors attempting to recreate the Ferry's days as a Civil War hotbed. The **Harpers Ferry Industrial Museum**, on Shenandoah St., divulges methods used to harness the powers of the Sheanandoah and Potomac Rivers before the town was decimated by the Civil War. The unsung stories of the Ferry captivate visitors at **Black Voices from Harpers Ferry**, on the corner of High and Shenandoah St., where fettered slaves express their opinions of John Brown and his fiery raid. The plight of Harpers Ferry's slaves is tactfully elaborated through their words in the **Civil War Story**, next door on High St. Informative displays detail the importance of Harpers Ferry's strategic location to both the Union and Confederate armies. A ticket is required to enter some of the exhibits, but the park's *Lower Town Trail Guide* facilitates historical exploration. Park rangers provide free 45min. to 1hr. tours of the town (in summer daily 10:30am-4pm). In addition, the park offers occasional battlefield demonstrations, parades, and other re-enactments of Harpers Ferry's history (☎535-6298 for the schedule). The **John Brown Museum**, on Shenandoah St. just beyond High St., is the town's most captivating historical site. A 30min. video chronicles Brown's raid of the armory with a special focus on the moral and political implications of his actions. A daunting, steep staircase hewn into the hillside off High St. follows the **Appalachian Trail** to **Upper Harpers Ferry**, which has fewer sights

MID-ATLANTIC

but is graced with interesting tales. Allow 45min. to ascend past **Harper's House,** the restored home of town founder Robert Harper, and **St. Peter's Church,** where a pastor flew the Union Jack during the Civil War to protect the church.

▟ OUTDOORS. After digesting the historical significance of Harpers Ferry, many choose to immerse themselves in the town's flourishing outdoors. Go to the park's visitors center for trail maps galore. The **Maryland Heights Trail,** the town's most popular trail located across the railroad bridge in the Lower Town of Harpers Ferry, wanders for 4 mi. through Blue Ridge Mountains, including precipitous cliffs and glimpses of crumbling Civil War-era forts. More wooded, the 4 mi. **Loudon Heights Trail** starts in Lower Town off the Appalachian Trail. Both trails take a little over 3hr. to hike. History dominates the **Bolivar Heights Trail,** which starts at the northern end of Whitman Ave. Along the trail, exhibits and a three-gun battery now frame the Civil War battle line where Stonewall Jackson and his Confederate troops prevailed in battle. His horse didn't fail him; neither should your feet on the easy 1.1 mi. loop. The **Chesapeake & Ohio Canal** towpath, off the end of Shenandoah St. and over the railroad bridge, serves as a lasting reminder of the town's industrial roots. The **Appalachian Trail Conference,** 799 Washington St. at Washington and Jackson St., offers catalogs that feature deals on hiking books, trail info, and a maildrop for hikers. (☎ 535-6331. Open late May-Oct. M-F 9am-5pm, Sa-Su 9am-4pm; Nov. to mid-May M-F 9am-5pm. Membership $30, students and seniors $25.)

River & Trail Outfitters, 604 Valley Rd., 2 mi. out of Harpers Ferry off Rte. 340, in Knoxville, MD, rents canoes, kayaks, inner tubes, and rafts and organizes everything from scenic daytrips to wild overnights. For a more placid ride, Shenandoah River calm water floats run $15. (☎ 301-695-5177. Canoes $50 per day; raft trips $50 per person, children $40; tubing $30 per day.) **Blue Ridge Outfitters,** a few mi. west of Harpers Ferry on Rte. 340 N in Charles Town, arranges similar trips. In addition to rafting and canoe trips, water-adventurers can take a ride on the mutant half-raft-half-kayak "Ducky," or borrow an inner tube. (☎ 725-3444. Open daily 8am-6pm. Canoe or a seat on a half-day raft trip from $48, children $43; Ducky $40.50/$35.50.) Otherwise, at **Butt's Tubes, Inc.,** on Rte. 671 off Rte. 340, you can buy a tube for the day and sell it back before you go. (☎ 800-836-9911. Open M-F 10:30am-3pm, last pick-up at 5pm; Sa-Su 10am-4pm, last pick-up at 6pm. $5-20.) Horse activities in the area include a variety of recreational trips offered through **Elk Mountain Trails** (☎ 301-834-8882).

NEAR HARPERS FERRY: ANTIETAM NATIONAL BATTLEFIELD

Seventeen mi. north of the Ferry, blood soaked the soil at Antietam. On Sept. 17, 1862, in the single most devastating one-day battle of the Civil War, 22,728 Union and Confederate casualties were suffered as **Confederate General Robert E. Lee** failed to march north through the army of **Union General George B. McClellan.** Despite the severity of their losses, the Union garnered a modest victory as the objective of the war swung toward slavery—it was this Union triumph that prompted President Lincoln to decree the **Emancipation Proclamation,** freeing all slaves in the rebellious states as of Jan. 1, 1863. The **visitors center** orients visitors with a small room of soldiers' clothing and weaponry, an interactive Civil War explorer, free maps of an 8½ mi. driving tour, and rental tapes ($6) narrating the battle. Amicable and knowledgeable park rangers conduct 1hr. tours which begin in the observation room and spill outside onto the battlefield. Visits to bridges and trenches, formerly the site of

VICTORY CIGAR The battle of Antietam would have proved hopeless for the Union brigade if not for the carelessness of Lee's messenger. "Special Order 191" contained the precise whereabouts of Lee's troops at Harpers Ferry. Two copies of the order were made, but one was lost en route. A few days later, two Union soldiers from the 27th Indiana infantry spotted three wrapped cigars in a field. Thrilled that they had found stogies, they unwrapped the package to reveal Lee's plans, sending them straight to McClellan and victory.

ghastly bloodshed, illuminate the battle's history and send chills down the spine. (☎301-432-5124. *To get to Antietam from Harpers Ferry, take Rte. 340 W 2 mi. and take a right onto Rte. 230. Drive 9 mi. until you reach Shepherdstown, then turn right on Rte. 480, which becomes Rte. 34 E. Continue to Sharpsburg and follow signs. Visitors center open daily May-Sept. 8:30am-6pm; Oct.-Apr. 8:30am-5pm. 26min. film shown in visitors center 9am-5pm on the hr. Battlefield fee $2, family rate $4.*)

NEW RIVER GORGE ☎304

The New River Gorge is an electrifying testament to the raw beauty and power of nature. One of the oldest rivers in the world, the New River carves a narrow gouge through the Appalachian Mountains, creating precipitous valley walls which tower an average of 1000 ft. above the white waters. These steep slopes remained virtually untouched until 1873 when industrialists drained the region to uncover coal and timber galore. With the coal mines now defunct, the Gorge has come full circle, reverting into a natural spectacle burgeoning with wildlife.

⚑ PRACTICAL INFORMATION. Greyhound stops at 105 Third Ave. in Beckley (☎253-8333; open M-F 7-11am and 4-8:30pm, Sa-Su 7-9am and 4-8:30pm). **Amtrak** runs through the heart of the gorge, stopping on Rte. 41 N in Prince and Hinton. (☎253-6651. Trains Su, W, and F. Open Su, W, and F 10:30am-7pm, Th and Sa 7am-2:30pm.) Rentals are available at **Ridge Rider Mountain Bikes,** 103 Keller Ave., off U.S. 19 in Fayetteville. (☎574-2453 or 800-890-2453. Open daily 9am-5pm. $25 per half-day, $35 per full-day.) **Area code:** 304.

⚑ ACCOMMODATIONS. Budget motels can be found off I-77 in Beckley ($45-60), while smaller lodges and guest houses scatter through Fayetteville. Call ☎800-225-5982 for accommodations info. The aptly named **Whitewater Inn,** on the corner of Appalachian Dr. off U.S. 19, features small, but clean and homey rooms at affordable rates (☎574-2998; rooms $30-45). **Canyon Ranch** (☎574-3111 or 574-4111), off Gatewood Road next to Cunard Access for the river, offers two rooms with A/C and shared bath. Many of the raft companies operate private campgrounds, while four public campgrounds dot the general area. The most central public campground, **Babcock State Park,** on Rte. 41 south of U.S. 60, 15 mi. west of Rainelle, is the largest public campground in the gorge and has shaded, sometimes slanted sites. The park also rents 26 sites. (☎438-3004 or 800-225-5982. $11, with water and electricity $14.) On Ames Heights Rd., ½ mi. north of the New River Gorge Bridge, the private **Mountain State Campground** offers level and hilly tent sites with platforms (by request) and six-person primitive cabins. (☎574-0947. Open Apr.-Nov. Sites $7; cabins $65.)

⚑ ACTIVITIES. The **New River Gorge National River,** which runs north from Hinton to Fayetteville, falling over 750 ft. in 50 mi., is now protected, and the park service oversees the fishing, rock climbing, canoeing, mountain biking, and world-class rafting in the gorge. Whitewater rapids range from the family-friendly class I to the panic-inducing class V. A state info service (☎800-225-5982) connects you to some of the nearly 20 outfitters on the New River and the rowdier Gauley River, or pick up a brochure at the **Fayettesville County Chamber of Commerce,** 810 Oyler Ave. in Oak Hill. **USA Raft,** on Rte. 1 in Fayetteville, runs some of the cheapest express trips. (☎800-346-7238. New River: Su-F $48, Sa $58. Gauley River: $55/$65.)

Though the renowned rapids draw the most tourists, the park's numerous trails provide hikers with a sense of fulfillment and an appreciation for the river and the industry that once flourished here. The most rewarding trails are the 2 mi. **Kaymoor Trail** and the 3.4 mi. **Thurmond Minden Trail.** Kaymoor starts at the bridge on Fayette Station Rd. and runs past the abandoned coke ovens of Kaymoor, a coal-mining community that shut down in 1962. Thurmond Minden, left off Rte. 25 before Thurmond, has vistas of the New River and Thurmond. For a vertical challenge, climb the **Endless Wall** which runs southeast along the New River and is accessible from a trail off the parking lot at Canyon Rim Visitors Center. The park operates four **visitors centers: Canyon Rim,** off Rte. 19 near Fayetteville at the northern extreme of the park; **Grandview,** on Rte. 9 near Beckley; **Hinton,** on Rte. 20; and **Thurmond,** on Rte. 25 off I-19. Grandview attracts visitors in May when the rhododendrons are in bloom; otherwise, most stop at Canyon Rim, which has info on all park activities, including free and detailed hiking, biking, and climbing guides. (Canyon Rim: ☎574-2115. Grandview: ☎767-4756. Both open daily June-Aug. 9am-8pm; Sept.-May 9am-5pm. Hinton: ☎466-1597. Open daily June-Aug. 9am-5pm; Sept.-May Sa-Su 9am-5pm. Thurmond: ☎465-8550. Open daily June-Aug. 9am-5pm.)

🏛 **SIGHTS.** Where Rte. 19 crosses the river at the park's northern end, the man-made grandeur of the **New River Gorge Bridge,** the 2nd highest bridge in the US, over-looks the Canyon Rim cut of the gorge. The visitors center at this site offers a decent vista but, if you're feeling adventurous, descending innumerable stairs to the lower level lookout yields a spectacular view, not to mention a day's worth of exercise. Towering 876 ft. above New River, the bridge claims the world's largest single steel arch span. On **Bridge Day** (☎800-927-0263), the 3rd Sa of Oct., thousands of extreme sports enthusiasts leap off the bridge by bungee or parachute. For more stable flying, elderly "Five Dollar Frank" pilots $5 **scenic plane rides** at the Fay-etteville airstrip, 2 mi. south of town. Retired coal miners lead tours down a mine shaft at the **Beckley Exhibition Coal Mine,** 20 mi. south of Fayetteville at New River Park on Ewart Ave. in Beckley. Explore the mining industry as you ride behind a 30s engine through 150 ft. of underground passages. (☎256-1747. Open daily Apr.-Oct. 10am-5:30pm. $8, seniors $7, ages 4-12 $5, under 4 free.) **Horsebackriding** trips are another way to explore the gorge. (☎888-742-3982. Mar.-Oct. Rides start at $35.)

MONONGAHELA NATIONAL FOREST ☎304

Mammoth Monongahela National Forest sprawls across the Eastern portion of the state, sustaining wildlife, limestone caverns, weekend canoers, fly fisherman, spe-lunkers, and skiers. Over 500 campsites and 600 mi. of winding wilderness hiking trails lure adventurers to this outdoors haven.

🛈 **PRACTICAL INFORMATION.** Most public transportation in the forest area comes into White Sulphur Springs at the forest's southern tip. **Greyhound** has a flag stop at the Village Inn, 38 W. Main St. (One eastbound bus at 9am, and one west-bound bus per day at 4pm.) **Amtrak** stops at 315 W. Main St., across from the Green-brier resort. A flag stop in downtown Alderson can also be requested Su, W, or F. Trains run to Washington, D.C. ($53) and Charlottesville ($29). **Area code:** 304.

🏛 **SCENIC ROADS.** Surrounded by luscious green thicket, Monongahela's roads are indisputably scenic, though the beauty of **Rte. 39** from Marlinton down to Gos-hen, VA, past Virginia's swimmable Maury River, is unsurpassed. For more variety, turn off U.S. 219 onto Denmar Rd. and right on Locust Creek Rd. for a 10 mi. loop that passes fields of okapi and bison, a prison, an old country church, and finally a one-lane bridge adjacent to the 1888 covered bridge over Locust Creek. The **High-land Scenic Hwy.** (Rte. 150) runs near the Cranberry Visitors Center and stretches 43 mi. from Richwood to U.S. 219, 7 mi. north of Marlinton. Tempted as you may be to feast your eye on the forest's natural splendor, driving through the often fog-filled sinuous roads can be treacherous, so keep your eyes on the road.

🥾📷 **HIKING AND CAMPING.** Each of Monongahela's six districts have a camp-ground and a recreation area, with ranger stations off Rte. 39 east of Marlinton and in the towns of Bartow and Potomack (open M-F 8am-4:30pm). The forest **Supervi-sor's Office,** 200 Sycamore St., in Elkins, distributes a full list of sites and fees and provides info about fishing and hunting (☎636-1800; open M-F 8am-4:45pm). For area fishing, anglers can cast their lines for the abundant trout that flow through the Williams and Cranberry Rivers. Established sites are $5; sleeping in the backcoun-try is free. Indicate backcountry plans at the **Cranberry Mountain Nature Center,** near the Highland Scenic Hwy. at the junction of Rte. 150 and Rte. 39/55. (☎653-4826. Open daily Dec. and June-Aug. 9am-5pm; Sept.-Nov. and Jan.-May Sa-Su 10am-

4pm.) Aside from displaying an informative wildlife exhibit that includes hissing rattlesnakes, the nature center conducts weekend tours of the **Cranberry Glades** (Sa-Su 2pm, Memorial Day to Labor Day). Wrapping 6 mi. around the glades is the appealing **Cow Pasture Trail,** although spottings of mooing bovines named Bessie are unlikely. Two popular short hikes in the area are the panoramic **High Rocks** trail leading off of the Highland Scenic Hwy. and the awesome ¾ mi. **Falls of Hills Creek,** off Rte. 39/55 south of Cranberry Mountain Visitors Center. The first cascade is wheelchair accessible; steep steps take you to cascades two and three. *Remove valuables from vehicles as thieves are common in this area.* **Cranberry Campground** (☎ 296-9881), in the Gauley district 6 mi. west of U.S. 219 on Rte. 39/55, has hiking trails through cranberry bogs and $8 campsites.

Those with several days might choose to hike, bike, or cross-country ski a part of the **Greenbrier River Trail,** a 75 mi., 1% grade track from Cass to North Caldwell (trailhead on Rte. 38 off U.S. 60). Lined with numerous access points and campgrounds, the trail offers multiple vistas and arguably the highest concentration of butterflies in West Virginia. **Watoga State Park** (☎ 799-4087), in Marlinton, has maps.

OUTSIDE THE NATIONAL FOREST

Marlinton to the east and Elkins to the south lodge hikers, bikers, and tourists. In downtown Marlinton, the **Old Clark Inn,** 702 3rd Ave., offers a comfortable bed and hearty breakfast while the warm family proprietors provide a glimpse into mountaineer life. (☎ 799-6377 or 800-849-4184. Singles $35-45; doubles $50-60; $5 more in winter.) In Green Bank, year-round **cabins** can be rented; turn left off Rte. 92 N. (☎ 456-3470 or 456-4410; M-F $28-45, Sa-Su $38-55.) In eastern Monongahela, the **Middle Mountain Cabins,** on Forest Service Rd. 14 off Rte. 28, stock fireplaces, kitchens, drinking water, and field mice. (☎ 456-3335. Open May-Oct. one-week maximum stay. $30 per night; call well in advance.)

In the winter, the snow flurries, and skiers and snowboarders flock to test the slipperiness of the slopes in the **Canaan Valley** and the 54 trails at **Snowshoe** resort. (☎ 572-1000. Open daily Nov.-Apr. 8:30am-10pm. Lift tickets $38, students and seniors $30, Sa-Su $44; ski rental $26, children $18.) In summer, mountain biking is preferred. Cross-country skiers and mountain bikers can rent gear at **Elk River** (☎ 572-3771), off Rte. 219 in Slatyfork.

MID-ATLANTIC

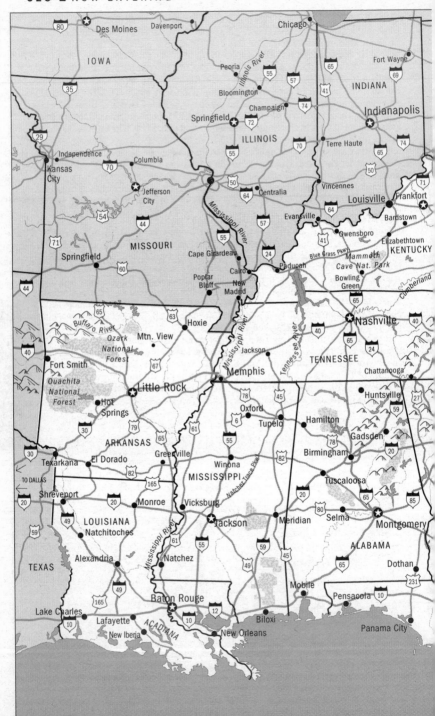

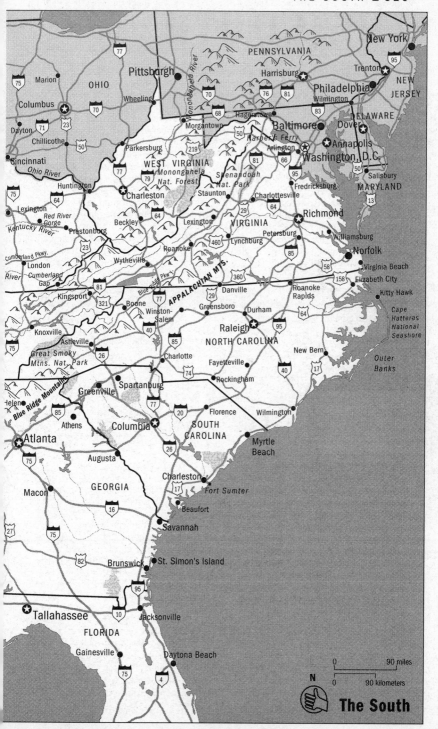

The South

THE SOUTH

The American consciousness has become much more homogeneous since the 1860s, when regional differences ignited the bloodiest conflict in the nation's history. Yet differences persist between North and South, as much in memory as in practice: what's known as "the Civil War" up North is here rather defiantly referred to as "The War Between the States." And outside the area's commercial capitals—Atlanta, Nashville, Charlotte, Orlando, and New Orleans—Southerners continue to live slower-paced and friendlier lives than their northern cousins.

Perhaps the greatest unifying characteristic of the South is its legacy of extreme racial division: slavery continues to place a nearly unbearable burden on Southern history, and the civil rights movement of the 50s and 60s remains too recent to be comfortably relegated to textbook study. At the same time, racial tensions and interactions have inspired many strands of American culture rooted in the South, from the novels of William Faulkner to nearly *all* American music: gospel, blues, jazz, country, R&B, and rock'n'roll. Although much of the South remains poor, the area maintains a rich cultural heritage; its architecture, cuisine, and language all borrow from Native American, English, African, French, and Spanish influences. Landscapes are equally varied—nature blessed the region with mountains, marshlands, sparkling beaches, and fertile soil.

HIGHLIGHTS OF THE SOUTH

FOOD. Some of the best Southern barbecue is at Dreamland in Mobile, AL (p. 396). New Orleans, LA (p. 403) has spicy and delicious Cajun cuisine. Southern "soul food" completes the spirit—Nita's Place, Savannah, GA (p. 387) will take you higher.

MUSIC. Make time for Tennessee—Nashville (p. 339) is the country music hotspot, but if you're a believer, you'll be heading to Graceland (p. 349).

CIVIL RIGHTS MEMORIALS. The Martin Luther King Center in Atlanta, GA (p. 376) and the Birmingham Civil Rights Institute, AL (p. 394) will move you to tears.

OLD SOUTH. Charm and Elegance. Nowhere is the antebellum way of life so well-kept as in stately Charleston, SC (p. 368) or Savannah, GA (p. 387).

KENTUCKY

Legendary for the duels, feuds, and stubborn spirit of its earlier inhabitants (such as the infamous Daniel Boone), but gentler than its past, Kentucky invites travelers to kick back, take a shot of local bourbon, grab a plate of burgoo (a spicy meat stew), and relax amid rolling hills and bluegrass. These days, Kentuckians' spirit erupts on the highways—they drive fast. Appropriately, Kentucky is home to the only American sports car, the Corvette. Of course, the most respected mode of transport is still the horse. Louisville ignores its vibrant cultural scene and active nightlife at Derby time, and Lexington devotes much of its most beautiful farmland to breeding champion racehorses. Farther east, the Daniel Boone National Forest preserves the virgin woods of the Kentucky Highlands, where trailblazers first discovered a route across the mountains to what was then the West.

⁊ PRACTICAL INFORMATION

Capital: Frankfort.
Visitor Info: Kentucky Dept. of Travel 500 Mero St., 22nd fl., Frankfort 40601 (☎502-564-4930 or 800-225-8747; www.kentuckytourism.com). **Kentucky State Parks,** 500 Mero St., 10th fl., Frankfort 40601 (☎800-255-7275; www.kystateparks.com).
Postal Abbreviation: KY. **Sales Tax:** 6%.

LOUISVILLE

☎502

Louisville (pronounced "Lua-Vul" by locals) is caught between two pasts. One past left a legacy of smokestacks, stockyards, and the occasional crumbling structure; the other entices with beautiful Victorian neighborhoods, ornate buildings, and the elegant, twin-spired Churchill Downs. Louisville's premier attraction, however, remains the Kentucky Derby; this extravagant event, the nation's most prestigious horse race, will pack the city with visitors on May 5, 2001.

⊞◪ ORIENTATION AND PRACTICAL INFORMATION. Interstates through the city include **I-65** (north-south expressway), **I-71,** and **I-64.** The easily accessible **Watterson Expwy.,** also called **I-264,** rings the city, while the **Gene Snyder Frwy. (I-265)** circles farther out. In central downtown, **Main St.** and **Broadway** run east-west, and **Preston Hwy.** and **19th St.** run north-south. The **West End,** beyond 20th St., is a rough area. The **Louisville International Airport** (☎376-4636) is 15min. south of downtown on I-65. A taxi downtown is $15, or take bus #2 into the city. **Greyhound,** 720 W. Muhammad Ali Blvd. (☎561-2805), at 7th St. runs to Indianapolis (1¼hr., 9 per day, $17.50), Cincinnati (2hr., 10 per day, $19.50), and Chicago (5hr., 7 per day, $38). Station open 24 hours. **Transit Authority River City's (TARC)** extensive bus system serves most of the metro area. (☎585-1234; daily 5am-11:30pm. Fare 75¢, $1 M-F 6:30-8:30am and 3:30-5:30pm.) Two free trolley routes service Main St. and 4th St. downtown from 8am to 5pm. **Taxis: Yellow Cab** (☎636-5511). **Highland Cycle,** 1737 Bardstown Rd. rents bikes. (☎458-7832. Open M-F 9am-5:30pm, Sa 9am-4:30pm. Bikes from $3.25 per hr., $12 per day.) **Visitor Info: Louisville Convention and Visitors Bureau,** 3rd and Market St. (☎584-2121; open M-F 8:30am-5pm, Sa 9am-4pm, Su 11am-4pm). **Hotlines: Rape Hotline** (☎581-7273) and **Crisis Center** (☎589-4313), both open 24 hours; **Gay/Lesbian Hotline** (☎454-7613; daily 6-10pm). **Post Office:** 1420 Gardner Ln. (☎454-1650; open M-F 7:30am-7pm, Sa 7:30am-3pm). **ZIP code:** 40213. **Area code:** 502.

⌐ HITCHIN' POSTS. Lodging in downtown Louisville is easy to find but pricey. Budget motels are on **I-65** near the airport or across the river in **Jeffersonville. Newburg,** 6 mi. south, is also a budget haven. To get Derby Week lodging, make reservations 6 to 12 months in advance and prepare to spend big; after Mar. 13, the visitors bureau will help you to secure a room for the event.

    Collier's Motor Court, 4812 Bardstown Rd., between I-264 and I-265, is 30min. from downtown by car; TARC buses serve this inconvenient area. Well-maintained, cheap rooms with A/C and free local calls. (☎499-1238. Singles $38.50; doubles $45.) **Super 8,** 927 S. 2nd St., has basic rooms; an airport shuttle can be secured by appointment. (☎584-8888. Singles $50; doubles $55; weekends $60/$65. Some wheelchair accessible rooms.) The local installation of the **KOA** regime, 900 Marriot Dr., has paved camping convenient to downtown. Follow I-65 N across the bridge and take Exit 1. (☎282-4474. Grocery, playground, free pool access, mini golf, and fishing lake. Sites for 2 $23, with hook-up $28; $4 per additional person, under 18 $2.50. Kabins for 2 $35. Rates drop mid-Nov. to mid-Mar.)

⌐ OATS AND HAY. Louisville's food is varied, but good budget fare can be hard to find in the heart of downtown. **Bardstown Rd.** is lined with cafes, budget eateries, and local and global cuisine, while **Frankfort Rd.** is rapidly becoming Bardstown-ized with restaurants and chi-chi cafes of its own. Downtown, **Theater Sq.,** at Broadway and 4th St., provides plenty of good lunch options. ◪**Twice Told,** 1604 Bardstown Rd. was the first coffeehouse in Louisville, and it's still funky after all these years. Poetry readings, comedy, punk, jazz, and blues entertain at the stage in the back, but get in earlier for a $5 homemade veggie burger. (☎456-0507. Open Su-Th 10am-midnight, F-Sa 10am-1am. Open stage every Tu. Shows M-Sa at 9pm. Some shows free; cover can go as high as $10.) The giant teapot in front of **Lynn's Paradise Cafe,** 984 Barret Ave., is a Louisville landmark where kid-friendly hammock-swings and animal sculptures complement adult-friendly prices. Breakfast ($4-9; served until 3pm) is the big meal here. (☎583-3447. Open Tu-Su 7am-10pm.) **Mark's Feed Store,** 1514 Bardstown Rd., serves award-winning barbecue in the company of metal pigs. (☎459-6275. Open Su-Th 11am-10pm, F-Sa 11am-11pm. Pork sandwich $3.50; free dessert M after 4pm.)

🔲 **NOT JUST A ONE-HORSE TOWN.** The **Highlands** strip runs along Baxter/Bard-stown and is bounded by Broadway and Trevilian Way on the south. This "anti-mall" of unfranchised cafes, pizza pubs, antique shops, and record stores is worth a look. *(Buses #17, 23, and 44.)* Nearby, the **American Printing House for the Blind** runs a small but fascinating museum on the development of Braille and other lesser-known systems for aiding the blind. *(1839 Frankfort Ave. ☎895-2405. Open M-F 9am-4:30pm; guided tours 10am and 2pm. Free.)* Farther south, near the University of Louisville, the impressive galleries of the **J.B. Speed Art Museum** house a large collection ranging from Dutch tapestries to contemporary art, as well as a stylish sculpture court. *(2035 S. 3rd St. ☎634-2700. Bus #2 or 4. Open Tu-W and F 10:30am-4pm, Th 10:30am-8pm, Sa 10:30am-5pm, Su noon-5pm. Free; parking $1.50 per hr.)*

The **Belle of Louisville**, an authentic paddle-wheel craft built in 1914, docks at 4th St. and River Rd. *(☎574-2355. 2hr. cruises depart from Riverfront Plaza early June to early Sept. daily 1pm. Sunset cruises Tu and Th 7pm. Dance cruise late July-Sept. Sa 8-11pm. $10, seniors $9, under 13 $6; dance cruise $12.50.)* The world's tallest baseball bat (120 ft.) leans against the **Hillerich and Bradsby Co. (Louisville Slugger Factory and Museum).** Inside awaits a nostalgic film and a tour showing how Sluggers are made. H&B will even give you a free miniature bat at tour's end. *(800 W. Main. ☎588-7228. Open M-Sa 9am-5pm. $5, over 60 $4.50, ages 6-12 $3.)*

Lovers of American kitsch will find a treat at the **Harland Sanders Museum** and **Kentucky Fried Chicken International Headquarters.** A room of artifacts and a short film honor the white-suited Colonel who brought us fried chicken with his secret recipe of 11 herbs and spices. *(1441 Gardiner Ln, off the Watterson Expwy. at Newburg Rd. ☎874-8300. Open M-F 8am-5pm. Free, as it should be.)*

🔲 **HORSIN' AROUND.** Each year, on the first Sa in May, Louisville stages the nation's most prestigious horse race, the **Kentucky Derby.** The drunken, week-long extravaganza leading up to the big day corrals over 500,000 visitors, but when the horses leave the gate, the stands are still for "the most exciting two minutes in sports;" after all, $15 million ride on each Derby Day. Even if you miss the Derby, be sure to visit **Churchill Downs.** You don't have to bet to admire the twin spires, the colonial columns, the gardens, and the sheer scale of the track. *(700 Central Ave., 3 mi. south of downtown. ☎636-4400. Take bus #4 "4th St." to Central Ave. Grounds open daily in racing season 10am-4pm. Races Apr. to late May W-Su from 1pm; June W-Su from 3pm; Nov. Tu-Su 1-5pm. Grandstand and clubhouse seats $2, 5th fl. reserved seats $4.50. Parking $3.)*

The **Kentucky Derby Festival** kicks off with the largest fireworks show in North America and continues for two weeks with balloon and steamboat races, concerts, and a parade. All of this is mere prelude to the climactic 80,000 mint juleps consumed at the **Run for the Roses,** the first Sa in May. A one- to ten-year waiting list stands between you and a ticket for the Derby, but never fear—on Derby morning, tickets are sold for standing-room-only spots in the infield ($35). Get in line early for good seats, lest the other 125,000 spectators get there first. Amazingly, no one is turned away. The **Kentucky Derby Museum,** at Churchill Downs, offers a short film on a 360° screen, footage of every Derby ever recorded (including Secretariat's record 1973 run), a simulated horse race for betting practice, tips on exactly what makes a horse a "sure thing," and seven tours of the Downs every day. *(☎637-7097. Open daily 9am-5pm; last tour at 3:45 pm. $6, seniors $5, ages 5-12 $2, under 5 free.)*

BILLIONS IN BULLION Security is so tight at Fort Knox, the holding station for American gold bullion reserves, 30 mi. south of Louisville, that all visitors can do is drive by. The best bet for those planning a heist is to examine the model used in the movie *Goldfinger,* which can be found at the nearby **Patton Museum.** The museum, north of Fort Knox off Dixie Hwy. (U.S. 31 W), holds exhibits on the history of armored warfare and more tanks than you can shake a stick at (were that, for some reason, your desire). *(☎624-3812. Open May-Sept. M-F 9am-4:30pm, Sa-Su 10am-6pm; otherwise, Sa-Su 10am-4:30pm. Free.)*

THE SOUTH

🎭🎵 **ENTERTAINMENT AND NIGHTLIFE.** The free weekly arts and entertainment newspaper, *Leo*, is available at most downtown restaurants or at the visitors center. What dreams may come when we have shuffled off this mortal coil at the **Kentucky Shakespeare Festival** at the zoo and in Central Park, which takes place over four weekends starting in late June. (☎583-8738. Performances 8pm. Free.) **The Louisville Palace,** 625 S. 4th Ave. (☎583-4555), is one of only 15 remaining "atmospheric theaters." Go to see both the lavish Spanish Baroque interior and the Broadway shows, comedy acts, and big-name music acts that play there.

Clubs cluster on Baxter Ave. near Broadway. **Phoenix Hill Tavern,** 644 Baxter Ave., features blues, rock, and reggae on four stages, including a deck and roof garden. (☎589-4957. Open W-Th and Sa 8pm-3:30am, F 5pm-3:30am. Cover W $2, Th-Sa $5.) **The Brewery,** 426 Baxter Ave. isn't a brewery, but hey, it's gigantic, with local bands and four volleyball courts. (☎583-3420. Open M-Sa 11am-4am, Su 5pm-4am. Cover for live music varies.) For gay nightlife, make **The Connection,** 120 Floyd St. This black-and-white-and-mirrored-all-over club features mostly gay male entertainment. (☎585-5752. Open Tu-Su 9pm-4am. Cover $2-5.)

NEAR LOUISVILLE

BARDSTOWN. Kentucky's second-oldest city, 17 mi. east on Rte. 245 from I-65 Exit 112, is proudly known as the "Bourbon Capital of the World." In 1791, Kentucky Baptist Reverend Elijah Craig left a fire unattended while heating oak boards to make a barrel for his aging whiskey. The boards were charred, but Rev. Craig carried on, and bourbon was born in that first charred wood barrel. Today, 90% of the nation's bourbon hails from Kentucky, and 60% of that is distilled in Nelson and Bullitt Counties. **Jim Beam's American Outpost,** 15 mi. west of Bardstown in Clermont off Rte. 245 features the "master distiller emeritus" himself, Jim Beam's grandson, Booker Noe, who narrates a film about bourbon. Tragically, Jim Beam's has no liquor license, but they do have free lemonade, coffee, and bourbon candies. (☎543-9877. Open M-Sa 9am-4:30pm, Su 1-4pm. Free.) Tours are offered at **Maker's Mark Distillery,** 19 mi. southeast of Bardstown on Rte. 52 E in Loretto; come any day but Su to buy a bottle of bourbon in the gift shop, and you can hand-dip it yourself in the red wax for which the label is famous. (☎865-2099. Tours M-Sa every hr. 10:30am-3:30pm, Su every hr. 1:30-3:30pm. Free.) The **Oscar Getz Museum of Whiskey History,** in Spalding Hall at 114 N. 5th St., contains exhibits on Kentucky's favorite beverage, and also on the state's other contribution to alcohol history—rabid prohibitionist Carry Nation. (☎348-2999. Open May-Oct. M-Sa 9am-5pm, Su 1-5pm; Nov.-Apr. Tu-Sa 10am-4pm, Su 1-4pm.) **Bardstown Visitors Center:** 107 E. Stephen Foster Ave. (☎348-4877 or 800-638-4877. Open M-F 8am-6pm, Sa 9am-6pm, Su 11am-3pm; Oct.-Mar. M-Sa 8am-5pm.)

MAMMOTH CAVE. Hundreds of enormous caves and narrow passageways cut through 🏞**Mammoth Cave National Park,** 80 mi. south of Louisville off I-65, then west on Rte. 70. Mammoth Cave comprises the world's longest network of cavern corridors—over 365 mi. in length. The first tours ran here in 1816. The first tour guides were slaves who worked the cave's salt-petre mining operation, shut down by the New Madrid earthquake in 1811. Nowadays tours are guided by park rangers. Devout spelunkers try the 6hr. "Wild Cave Tour" during the summer (16+; $35); less ambitious types generally take the 2hr., 2mi. historical walking tour ($8, seniors $4, ages 6-12 $5). Those in a rush can always opt for the unguided "Discovery Tour" ($3.50, seniors and ages 6-12 $2). Other tours accommodate disabled visitors (1½hr., $7). The caves are a chilly 54°F; the park also features numerous aboveground walking trails. (**Visitors center:** ☎758-2328 or 800-967-2283. Open daily 7:30am-7pm; off-season 8am-6pm.) Camping with toilets is available at the Headquarters campground, near the visitors center. (☎800-967-2283. Sites $13, showers in summer $2; reservations recommended.) For RV sites, check out Maple Springs Campground, across the river from the visitors center by ferry, or by a 35 mi. detour. (☎800-967-2283. $20; reservations required.) **Backcountry camping** permits can be obtained at the visitors center. **Greyhound** comes only as close as **Cave City,** just east of I-65 on Rte. 70. **Time Zone:** Central (1hr. behind Eastern).

THE SOUTH

WHISKEY BUSINESS All bourbon is whiskey, but not all whiskey is bourbon. So what makes bourbon so special? It's all in the making, codified by the US Government. For alcohol to be bourbon, it must fulfill these 6 requirements: 1. It must be aged in a new white oak barrel, flame-charred on the inside. (Scotch, alternatively, must be aged in used barrels.) 2. It must age at least 2 years in that barrel. 3. It must be at least 51% corn. 4. It cannot be distilled over 160 proof (80% alcohol). 5. It cannot go into the barrel over 125 proof. 6. It can have no additives or preservatives.

BOWLING GREEN. Home of the classic American sports car, auto enthusiasts inevitably pay their respects here. The extensive **National Corvette Museum,** 350 Corvette Dr. off I-65 Exit 28, displays 'Vettes from the original chrome-and-steel '53 to futuristic concept cars; the display rotates constantly. (☎800-538-3883. Open daily 8am-5pm. $8, ages 6-16 $4.50, seniors $5.) To see some action, visit the **General Motors Corvette Assembly Plant,** Exit 28 off I-65. With luck comes a chance to test-start one of the mint condition products. (☎745-8287. Tours M-F 9am and 1pm. Free.) **Time Zone:** Central (1hr. behind Eastern).

LEXINGTON   ☎859

In the early 1800s, Lexington was known as "the Athens of the West;" wealth from tobacco and hemp farms helped fund one of the most active cultural scenes west of the Appalachians and left a legacy of historic mansions near downtown. These days Lexington's most high-profile money comes from horse farming. Farms that have raised some of the most famous racehorses in the world ring the city in the scenic "bluegrass country" for which eastern Kentucky is famous. Within the Lexington city limits, the University of Kentucky (UK) keeps the banner of high culture flying.

▐ GETTING THERE AND GETTING AROUND

Airport: Blue Grass, 4000 Versailles Rd. (☎255-7218 or 800-845-3959), southwest of downtown. Ritzy downtown hotels run shuttles, but there is no public transportation. Taxi to downtown $20.

Buses: Greyhound, 477 New Circle Rd. NW (☎299-8804; open daily 7:30am-11pm); take LexTran bus #6 downtown. To: Louisville (2hr., 4 per day, $16.50); Cincinnati (1½hr., 4 per day, $22); and Knoxville (4hr., 5 per day, $45).

Public Transit: LexTran, 109 W. Louden Ave. (☎253-4636). Buses leave from the Transit Center, 220 E. Vine St., on a long block between Limestone and Rose St., generally 15min. before and after the hour. Serves the university and city outskirts. Most routes run 6am-midnight. Fare 80¢, ages 7-18 60¢, seniors 40¢. Transfers free. On racing days, LexTran runs a $1 shuttle to Keeneland.

Taxis: Lexington Yellow Cab, ☎231-8294.

✳🔢 ORIENTATION AND PRACTICAL INFORMATION

New Circle Rd. (Rte. 4/U.S. 60 bypass) loops the city, intersecting with many roads that connect the downtown district to the surrounding towns. **High, Vine,** and **Main St.** running east-west and **Limestone St.** and **Broadway** running north-south provide the best routes through downtown. Beware of the many curving one-way streets downtown and near UK.

Visitor Info: Lexington Convention and Visitors Bureau, 301 E. Vine St. (☎233-7299 or 800-845-3959; www.visitlex.com), at Rose St. Open in summer M-F 8:30am-5pm, Sa 10am-5pm, Su noon-5pm; off-season closed Su.

Hotlines: Crisis Intervention, ☎233-0444. **Rape Crisis,** ☎253-2511.

Hospitals: St. Joseph East Hospital, 150 N. Eagle Creek Dr. (☎268-4800). **Lexington Women's Diagnostic Center,** 1725 Harrodsburg Rd. (☎277-8485).

Internet access: Lexington Public Library, 140 E. Main St. (☎234-5573), at Limestone St. Lab open M-W noon-5pm, Th-F 9am-5pm, Sa noon-5pm, Su 1-5pm.

Post Office: 210 E. High St. (☎254-6156). Open M-F 8am-5pm, Sa 9am-noon. **ZIP code:** 40507. **Area code:** 859.

ACCOMMODATIONS

A concentration of horse-related wealth pushes up accommodation prices. The cheapest places are outside the city on New Circle Rd. or near I-75. **New Circle Rd. Dial Accommodations,** 301 E. Vine St., at the visitors center, can help you find a room. (☎233-1221 or 800-848-1224. Open M-F 8:30am-5pm, Sa 10am-5pm, Su noon-5pm; off-season reduced hrs.)

Catalina Motel, 208 W. New Circle Rd. (☎299-6281). Follow Broadway north of the city, and turn left onto New Circle Rd., or take bus #3. Large, clean rooms with A/C, cable TV, pool, and free local calls. Singles $33; doubles $40.

Microtel, 2240 Buena Vista Dr. (☎299-9600), off I-75 at the Winchester Rd. (Rte. 60) exit. Take bus #7. Pleasant motel rooms with window seats. A/C, cable; wheelchair-accessible rooms available. Singles $40 ($45 on weekends); doubles $50.

Congress Inn, 1700 N. Broadway (☎299-6226), just past New Circle Rd. Take bus #3. Clean, basic rooms with cable, pool, and free local calls. Singles $33.50; doubles $39.

Kentucky Horse Park Campground, 4089 Ironworks Pike (☎259-4257 or 800-370-6416), 10 mi. north of downtown off I-75 at Exit 120. Groomed camping plus laundry, showers, basketball courts, swimming pool, and a free shuttle to the KY Horse Park and Museum. Wide open tent sites. 260 RV sites nicely mix shade and lawn. 2-week maximum stay. Apr.-Oct. $13, with hook-up $18, seniors $15.50; Nov.-Mar. $11/$14/$12.

FOOD AND NIGHTLIFE

With a menu of fantastic international and veggie/vegan meals that change nightly, **Alfalfa Restaurant,** 557 S. Limestone St., offers complete dinners with salad and bread for under $12. Filling soups and salads price out at less than $4. (☎253-0014. Open M 11am-2pm, Tu-Th 11am-2pm and 5:30-9pm, F-Sa 10am-2pm and 5:30-10pm, Su 10am-2pm. Live jazz, folk, and other music W-Sa 8-10pm. No cover.) **Ramsey's** serves at five locations in the Lexington area, but the true experience can only be found at 496 E. High St. at Woodland. Real Southern grease abounds; even the veggies are cooked with pork parts. One meat and three vegetables for $8-10, sandwiches under $6. (☎259-2708. Open Su 10am-11pm, M-Tu 11am-11pm, W-F 11am-1am. Drinks two-for-one 4-7pm.) At the **Parkette Drive-In,** 1216 New Circle Rd. between Liberty and Winchester Rd., bargain food comes to you in a classic 1951 setting. A few booths inside give carless folks an equal opportunity to join in the nostalgia. (☎254-8723. Open M-Th 10am-10pm, F-Sa 10am-11pm.)

Lexington's nightlife surpasses expectations for a town its size, but lacks any real center. Generally, the area around Main St. west of Limestone St. and the eastern fringes of UK are most active. For current info, read the "Weekender" section of the F *Herald-Leader,* or pick up a free *Ace.* **The Bar,** 224 E. Main St., a popular disco cabaret/lounge complex, caters to gays and lesbians. (☎255-1551. Lounge open M-Sa 4pm-1am; club open Tu-Th 10pm-1am, F 10pm-2am, Sa 10pm-3:30am. Cover F $4, Sa $5.) **Lynagh's Pub and Club,** in University Plaza at Woodland and Euclid St., is more or less your typical neighborhood bar—the neighborhood just happens to include UK. Music plays next door to the pub. (Pub: ☎255-1292. Open M-Sa 11am-1am, Su noon-11pm. Club: ☎255-6614. Open Tu-Sa 4-9pm for pool and darts; music 10pm-1am. Cover from $3; up to $12 when national acts play.)

SIGHTS

CITY ATTRACTIONS. To escape the stifling swamp conditions farther south, antebellum plantation owners built beautiful summer retreats in milder Lexington. The most attractive of these stately houses preen only a few blocks northeast of the

THE SOUTH

town center, in the **Gratz Park** area near the old public library. Wrap-around porches, stone foundations, and rose-covered trellises distinguish these old estates from the neighborhood's newer homes. The **Hunt Morgan House** stands at the end of the park across from the old library at W. 2nd St. Built in 1814 by John Wesley Hunt, the first millionaire west of the Alleghenies, the house witnessed the birth of Thomas Hunt Morgan, who won a 1933 Nobel Prize for proving the existence of the gene. The house's most colorful inhabitant, however, was Confederate General John Hunt Morgan, the "Thunderbolt of the Confederacy." As legend has it, Hunt Morgan, while being pursued by Union troops, rode his horse up the front steps and into the house, leaned down to kiss his mother, and rode out the back door. *(201 N. Mill St. ☎ 233-3290 or 253-0362. Tours Tu-Sa 10am-4pm, Su 2-5pm at 15min. past the hr. $5, students $3. In the week before Halloween, Gratz Park "ghost tours" begin here in the evenings— brief tours of the area that focus on the neighborhood's many other-worldly inhabitants.)* Hollywood jewelry designer George W. Headley's exotic creations are displayed at the **Headley-Whitney Museum.** The three-car garage is blanketed with shells—you won't need an employee to tell you it's from the 70s. *(4435 Old Frankfort Pike. ☎ 255-6653. Open Tu-F 10am-5pm, Sa-Su noon-5pm. $4, students $2, seniors $3.)*

HORSE ATTRACTIONS. Lexington horse farms are pretty places to visit; the visitors bureau has a list of open farms. **Three Chimneys Farm** raised the 1977 Triple Crown winner Seattle Slew. *(On Old Frankfort Pike 4 mi. from I-64 and 8½ mi. from New Circle Rd. ☎ 873-7053. Tours daily 10am and 1pm, by appt. only. $5-10 tip customary.)* **Kentucky Horse Park** has extensive equine facilities, a museum tracing the history, science, and pageantry of these animals, and many live examples. The last weekend in Apr., the horse park hosts the annual Rolex tournament qualifier for the US equestrian team. *(4089 Ironworks Pike, Exit 120 off I-75. ☎ 233-4303. Open Apr.-Oct. daily 9am-5pm; Nov-Mar. W-Su 9am-5pm. $10, ages 7-12 $5; Nov.-Mar. $7.50/$4.50; live horse shows and horse-drawn vehicle tours included. 45min. horse ride and tour in addition to entrance fee $13; pony rides $4. Parking $2. Wheelchair accessible.)* Every Apr., the **Keeneland Race Track,** west on U.S. 60, holds the final prep race for the Kentucky Derby. The track kitchen may have the best breakfast deal in town: around $4 for a cafeteria-style full breakfast and the chance to chat with a jockey or horse owner. *(4201 Versailles Rd. ☎ 254-3412 or 800-456-3412. Races Oct. and Apr.; post time 1pm. $2.50. Workouts free and open to the public mid-Mar. to Nov. 6-10am. Breakfast daily 6-11am except the first 2 weeks in Feb.)*

▓ DAYTRIPS FROM LEXINGTON

WHITE HALL. At Exit 95 off I-75, the elegant Georgian-Italianate mansion **White Hall** was home to abolitionist (not the boxer) Cassius M. Clay, cousin of Senator Henry Clay. Cassius Clay was known not only for his views on abolition, but also for firing a cannon at tax collectors and for his book on the finer points of knife-fighting—a field in which he had good deal of personal expertise. *(☎ 623-9178. 45min. guided tours only. Open Apr.-Oct. daily 9am-5:30pm, last tour at 4:30pm; early Sept. to Oct. W-Su only. $4.50, under 13 $2.50, under 6 free.)*

BEREA. Further south, **Berea,** off Exits 76 and 77 from I-75, is a local crafts capital. High-priced and highly touristed crafts stores tend to dominate, but the town retains much of its charm nonetheless. At **Churchill Weavers,** 100 Churchill Dr., off U.S. 25, visitors can take a self-guided tour of the loomhouse and view one of the few remaining examples of the handloom industry. *(☎ 606-986-3127. Open M-F 9am-noon, 12:30-4pm.)* **Berea College,** located in the center of town, is known far and wide for its progressive past and present. The college, founded in 1855, educated women and African-Americans before the Civil War; students of the college now are given work to do in lieu of paying tuition. Many students help operate the handsome **Boone Tavern,** 100 Main St. *(☎ 606-986-9358 or 800-366-9358).* Information on these and other attractions is available at the **Tourist and Convention Commission,** 201 N. Broadway *(☎ 800-598-5263; open M-Sa 9am-5pm, Su 1-5pm).*

SCENIC DRIVE: KENTUCKY HEARTLAND

A drive along the Kentucky Heartland Drive is a drive through Kentucky history, with a bit of beautiful scenery thrown in for good measure. The scenic route actually begins on S. Broadway in Lexington. About 5 mi. south of New Circle Rd., the hustle, bustle, and endless strip malls fade away, replaced by verdant pastures and the miles of horse fences that run along U.S. 68.

This is classic Kentucky horse country. Thoroughbreds, some of which are more valuable than the cars that pass them, graze alongside the road. The most famous horse farm in the area is **Almahurst Farm,** 9 mi. south of Lexington, marked by a signpost by the side of the road. The farm was given to a certain James Knight in honor of his service in the Revolutionary War and has since raised a number of minor horse racing legends. Five mi. after Almahurst, U.S. 68 enters the **Kentucky River Gorge.** Limestone shelves overgrown with ivy lead up to what is undoubtedly the scenic high point of the trip: the Kentucky River itself.

Two historical attractions mark the further edge of the drive. The first of these, the **Shaker Village of Pleasant Hill,** is about 30 mi. from Lexington. The Shakers, a religious sect that spread to Kentucky in the early 19th century, marked themselves for impermanence by making celibacy an article of faith. This village was closed in 1910, but the buildings are preserved here as part of a "living history" production that involves tours, guided or otherwise, and craft demonstrations. **Riverboat excursions** are also run from here. (☎ 859-734-5411 or 800-734-5611. Open daily 9:30am-5:30pm. $10, students $5.50, ages 6-11 $3.50; with river trip $14/$7.50/$4.50. Oct.-Mar. reduced hrs. and prices. Wheelchair accessible.)

Eight mi. south of the Shakers is historic **Harrodsburg,** the oldest permanent English settlement west of the Alleghenies. Visitors can watch faux 18th-century craftspeople demonstrate their skills in the center of town at **Old Fort Harrod State Park,** Lexington and College St. The Park is a replica of the stockade built here in 1774. The Harrodsburg **visitors center,** 103 Main St. at U.S. 68, can supply visitors with information and a local tourbook. (☎ 734-2364 or 800-355-9192. Open M-F 9am-5pm; mid-June to Oct. also Sa 10am-3pm.)

DANIEL BOONE NATIONAL FOREST ☎ 606

The Daniel Boone National Forest cuts a vast green swath through Kentucky's Eastern Highlands. Encompassing 670,000 acres of mountains and valleys, the forest is layered with a gorgeous tangle of chestnut, oak, hemlock, and pine, as well as pristine lakes, waterfalls, and extraordinary natural bridges. This is bluegrass country, where seasoned backpackers and Lexington's day trippers still find the heart of old Appalachia deep in the forest—though, by some reports, you're less likely these days to stumble onto feuding Hatfields and McCoys than into some farmer's hidden field of marijuana, reputedly Kentucky's leading cash crop.

🖪 **PRACTICAL INFORMATION.** Six U.S. Forest Service Ranger Districts administer the National Forest. Ranger offices supply trail maps and specifics about the portions of the 254 mi. **Sheltowee Trace**—the forest's most significant trail—that pass through their districts. (Sheltowee was the name the Shawnee gave to Daniel Boone, meaning—enigmatically enough—"Big Turtle.") **Stanton Ranger District,** 705 W. College Ave., includes the **Red River Gorge and Natural Bridge** (☎ 663-2852; open M-F 8am-4:30pm). To the north, **Morehead Ranger District,** 2375 KY 801 S. (☎ 784-5628), 2mi. south of Rte. 60, includes **Cave Run Lake.** The **Morehead Tourism Commission,** 150 E. First St., Morehead 40351 (☎ 784-6221), has more info. To the south, **London Ranger District** (☎ 864-4163), on U.S. 25 S, covers Laurel River Lake, close to Cumberland Falls; Laurel River Lake's **visitors center** is at Exit 41 off I-75 (☎ 878-6900 or 800-348-0095; open M-Sa 9am-5pm, Su 10am-2pm). For forest-wide info, contact the **Forest Supervisor,** 1700 Bypass Rd., Winchester (☎ 745-3100). For information on campsites within the forest proper, check www.r8web.com/boone. **Greyhound** buses from Lexington to Morehead (1½hr., 1 per day, $14); London (1¾hr., 3 per day, $19); and Corbin (2hr., 5 per day, $21). **Area code:** 606.

THE SOUTH

STANTON RANGER DISTRICT. The Mountain Pkwy. runs through Stanton Ranger District, providing easy access to the District's two principle attractions: **Natural Bridge State Resort Park** and **Red River Gorge Geological Area.** South of the Parkway, **Natural Bridge,** off Rte. 11, is the area's absolute must-see site. A rather steep ¾ mi. trail leads to an expansive view at the top of the bridge's vast span; walk a little further for a spectacular view of the bridge itself. The **Red River Gorge Area,** on the other side of the Parkway, contains some of the most varied and ecologically rich terrain in this part of the country. A 32 mi. circuit (Rte. 77 E to Rte. 715) runs through the single-lane **Nada Tunnel,** an old railroad tunnel cut directly through the rock (scary as hell!), and past the restored **Gladie Historic Site Log House,** which also holds an information center (open 10am-6pm). Along the way, the drive takes in bison, curving mountain roads, forests, and picturesque wooden and metal bridges. If you don't mind driving down a 3 mi. gravel road, take a 1¼ mi. hike past the beautiful **Rock Bridge,** down Rock Bridge Rd. near the junction of Rte. 715 and Rte. 15. A few mi. north of Rock Bridge is **Sky Bridge** (off Rte. 715), which only requires a fairly-level ¼ mi. hike to reach the top. Standing high above the sheer drop-offs and green gorges on both sides is magical.

Both sites are best approached via the Slade exit off Mountain Pkwy., where a **red tourist caboose,** run by the **Natural Bridge/Powell County Chamber of Commerce,** hands out info. (☎663-9229. Open daily 10am-6pm; off-season 10am-5pm.) Budgetary concerns are best met by staying at the campgrounds at Natural Bridge. **Whittletown** has 40 well-shaded sites, and **Middle Fork** has 39 open sites. (Both campgrounds can be reached at the park's main line, ☎663-2214. Primitive sites $8.50, seniors $7.20; with hook-up $16 for 2 adults, seniors $13.60; $1 per additional adult, under 16 free. No reservations.) You can pitch a tent anywhere in the forest, as long as you stay more than 300 ft. from roads or marked trails and 200 ft. from any water source. **Li'l Abners** has large, clean rooms with a pool and free local calls, 2½ mi. from Red River Gorge on Rte. 11. (☎663-5384. Singles $49; doubles $55. July-Aug. reserve in advance.)

LONDON RANGER DISTRICT. There's boating, fishing, hiking, and just hanging out at the **Laurel River Lake. Camping** is available at two spacious and densely wooded Forest Service campgrounds on the lake, both off Rte. 193 and adjacent to marinas: **Grove** with 56 sites and **Holly Bay** with 90 sites. (☎877-444-6777. 10 primitive sites $7 for 1 person, $10 for 2; with hook-up $14/$24. Reservations recommended 10 days in advance.) Visitors to giant **Cumberland Falls**—"The Niagara of the South"—can camp at the state park that surrounds the falls. The campground, 18 mi. west of Corbin on Rte. 90, is signposted off Rte. 90. (☎528-4121. Open Apr.-Oct. 50 sites. Tents $8.50, seniors $7.20; RVs $14/$12.) Water mist during a full moon creates the fantastic moonbows for which the Cumberland Falls are famous. Onward, chicken soldiers: in nearby Corbin, deep-fried legions pay homage to the Colonel at the original **Kentucky Fried Chicken/Harland Sanders Cafe and Museum,** at the junction of Rte. 25 E and 25 W, in all its finger-lickin' glory (☎528-2163; open daily 10am-10pm). **Sheltowee Trace Outfitters,** on Rte. 90, 5 mi. east of the state park, arranges guided, 7hr. rafting trips down the Falls' class III rapids. (☎800-541-7238. Runs 9am-4:30pm with equipment, guide, and lunch. $48, ages 5-12 $38. Canoe rentals for trips on more placid sections of the river are $15 per person.)

CUMBERLAND GAP

Stretching from Maine to Georgia, the majestic Appalachian Mountain Range proved a formidable obstacle to the westward movement of early American settlers, but not to bison. By following these animals, Native Americans learned of the Cumberland Gap, a natural break in the mountains. Frontiersman Daniel Boone became famous when he blazed the Wilderness Trail through the Gap in 1775, thereby opening the West to colonization. The **Cumberland Gap National Historic Park,** best reached by U.S. 25 E from Kentucky or U.S. 58 from Virginia, sits on 20,000 acres shared by Kentucky, Virginia, and Tennessee. The Cumberland Gap **visitors center** (☎606-248-2817), on U.S. 25 E in Middleboro, KY, has a film and slide show on the Gap's history, as well as a small museum that narrates an abortive attempt in the 1880s to transform the area into a health resort. (Park and visitors center open daily 8am-6pm; off-season 8am-5pm.) The park's 160-site **campground,** on U.S. 58 in Virginia, has hot showers (sites $10, with electricity $15). **Backcountry camping** requires a free permit from the visitors center. A breathtaking view can be found at **Pinnacle Rock,** a 4 mi. drive or hike from the visitors center.

TENNESSEE

Sloping from the majestic Great Smoky Mountains to the verdant Mississippi lowlands, Tennessee makes and breaks stereotypes with the smooth ease of Jack Daniels. Those enchanted with the last state to secede from the Union (and the first to rejoin) often express their affection in the form of song—an ode to Davy Crockett deems this land the "greatest state in the land of the free," Dolly Parton finds her Heartsong in the mountains, and there ain't no place the Grateful Dead would rather be. Tennessee's economy is industry-based, with the world's largest Bible-producing business, but it is music that fuels the state's soul.

⚏ PRACTICAL INFORMATION

Capital: Nashville.
Visitor Info: Tennessee Dept. of Tourist Development, 320 6th Ave., Nashville (☎741-2159; www.state.tn.us/tourdev). Open M-F 8am-4:30pm. **Tennessee State Parks Information,** 401 Church St., Nashville (☎800-421-6683).
Postal Abbreviation: TN. **Sales Tax:** 6-8%.

NASHVILLE   ☎615

Long-forgotten Francis Nash is one of only four Revolutionary War heroes honored with US city names (Washington, Wayne, and Knox are the others), but his tenuous foothold in history pales in comparison to Nashville's notoriety as the banjo-pickin', foot stompin' capital of country music. Large, eclectic, and unapologetically heterogeneous, Tennessee's capital is not only the home of the Country Music Hall of Fame, but also "the Wall Street of the South." The city houses the Southern Baptists and still finds room for centers of fine arts and higher learning, such as Fisk University and Vanderbilt.

⌐ GETTING THERE AND GETTING AROUND

Airport: Metropolitan (☎275-1675), 8 mi. south of downtown. An airport **shuttle** (☎275-1180) operates out of major downtown hotels ($9, round-trip $15). Bus fare downtown $1.55 with a transfer. Taxi to downtown $20.
Buses: Greyhound, 200 8th Ave. S. (☎255-3556), at Broadway downtown. Borders on a rough neighborhood, but the station is bright. To: Memphis (4hr., 7 per day, $31); Chattanooga (2½hr., 5 per day, $16.50); Birmingham (3½hr., 6 per day, $28); and Knoxville (3½hr., 8 per day, $25). Station open 24hr.
Public Transit: Metropolitan Transit Authority (MTA) (☎862-5950). Buses operate on limited routes, usually once per hr. Times vary route to route, but none run before 5:30am or after 11:15pm M-F; less frequent service Sa-Su. Fare $1.45, transfers 10¢. MTA runs 4 **tourist trolleys.** Fare $1, all-day pass $3, seniors and under 13 $2.
Taxis: Nashville Cab, ☎242-7070. **Music City Taxi,** ☎262-0451.
Car Rental: Thrifty, 414 11th Ave. N. (☎248-8888), downtown. $33 per day, Sa-Su $27. Must be over 25 with a major credit card.

✦🛈 ORIENTATION AND PRACTICAL INFORMATION

Nashville's streets are fickle, often interrupted by curving parkways and one-ways. Names change constantly and without warning; **Broadway,** the main east-west thoroughfare, melts into **West End Ave.** just outside downtown at Vanderbilt and I-40. In downtown, numbered avenues run north-south, parallel to the Cumberland River. The curve of **James Robertson Pkwy.** encloses the north end, becoming **Main St.** on the other side of the river (later **Gallatin Pike**) and **McGavock St.** at the south end. *The area south of Broadway between 2nd and 7th Ave. and the region north of James Robertson Pkwy. are both unsafe at night.*

Visitor Info: Nashville Visitors Bureau, 501 Broadway (☎259-4747), in the Gaylord Entertainment Center (previously the Nashville Arena), I-65 at Exit 84, James Robertson Pkwy. Open daily 8:30am-7pm.

Internet access: Ben West Public Library, 225 Polk Ave. at Union St. (☎862-5800). Open M-F 9am-8pm, Sa 9am-5pm, Su 2-5pm.

Hotlines: Crisis Line, ☎244-7444. **Rape Hotline,** ☎256-8526. Both 24hr. **Gay and Lesbian Switchboard,** ☎297-0008. Operates nightly 6-9pm.

Hospitals: Metro General Hospital, 1818 Albion St. (☎341-4000). **The Women's Center,** 419 Welshwood Dr. (☎331-1200), across from Harding Mall.

Post Office: 901 Broadway (☎255-9453), next to Union Station. Open M-F 7:30am-6pm, Sa 9am-2pm. **ZIP code:** 37202. **Area code:** 615.

▞ ACCOMMODATIONS

Finding a room in Nashville isn't difficult, just expensive, especially in summer. Make reservations well in advance. Budget motels concentrate around **W. Trinity Ln.** and **Brick Church Pike,** off I-65. Dirt-cheap hotels inhabit the area around **Dickerson Rd.** and **Murfreesboro,** but the neighborhood is seedy at best. Closer to downtown (but still sketchy), several motels huddle on **Interstate Dr.** just over the Woodland St. Bridge. Rooms at **The Liberty Inn,** 2400 Brick Church Pike, come equipped with cable TV, A/C, and roomy showers—what more could you ask for? (☎228-2567. Singles and doubles $30-36. Wheelchair accessible.) **The Cumberland Inn,** 150 W. Trinity Ln. at Exit 87A off I-65 N, has cheerful rooms with A/C, laundry, and free continental breakfast. (☎226-1600 or 800-704-1028. Singles $30; doubles $43. Weekend singles $40.) Courtly splendor may be lacking at **Knights Inn,** 1360 Brick Church Pike, but all your needs will be met with A/C, HBO, and free coffee and doughnuts in the morning. (☎226-4500. Singles $28; doubles $33; weekends $33/$38.)

Two campgrounds lie near Opryland USA. By car, take Briley Pkwy. north to McGavock Pike Exit 12B and go north onto Music Valley Dr. **Nashville Holiday Travel Park,** 2572 Music Valley Dr., has a wooded area for tenting and densely packed RV sites. (☎889-4225. Sites for 2 $20, water and electricity $31.50; full hook-up $37.50; $4 per additional person over age 11.) The perks at **Opryland KOA,** 2626 Music Valley Dr., include a pool and live summer music. (☎889-0282. Sites $22, with hook-up $31. 1-room cabins with A/C and electricity $39, 2-room cabins $48.)

◖ FOOD

In Nashville, music influences even the local delicacies; **Goo-Goo Clusters** (peanuts, pecans, chocolate, caramel, and marshmallow), sold most places, bear the initials of the Grand Ole Opry. Nashville's other finger-lickin' traditions, barbecue or fried chicken followed by pecan pie, are no less sinful. Restaurants for collegiate tastes and budgets cram **21st Ave., West End Ave.,** and **Elliston Pl.,** near Vanderbilt.

▨ Loveless Cafe, 8400 Rte. 100 (☎646-9700 or 800-889-2432). A Nashville country cookin' tradition. Feast on nationally-renowned biscuits made from scratch with homemade preserves, country ham ($10), fried chicken ($11), and good ol' southern hospitality. Open M-F 8am-2pm and 5-9pm, Sa-Su 8am-9pm. Reservations recommended during peak times.

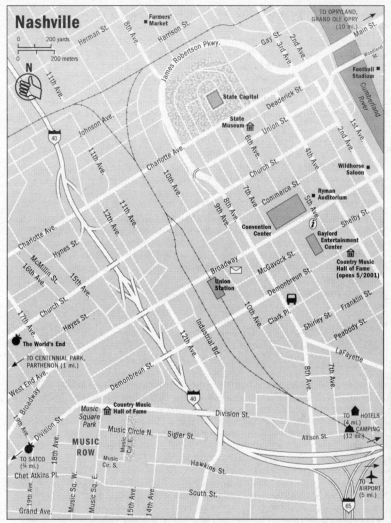

Nashville

0 ——— 200 yards
0 ——— 200 meters

N

TO OPRYLAND,
GRAND OLE OPRY
(10 mi.)

Farmers'
■ Market

Herman St.
8th Ave.
Harrison St.
Gay St.
2nd Ave.
3rd Ave.
Main St.
Woodland St.

James Robertson Pkwy.

11th Ave.

Football ■
Stadium

Cumberland River

Johnson Ave.

State Capitol

Deaderick St.

11th Ave.

Charlotte Ave.

State
Museum 🏛

Union St.

6th Ave.

1st Ave.

2nd Ave.

Church St.

Wildhorse ■
Saloon

12th Ave.

10th Ave.

7th Ave.

Commerce St.

4th Ave.

5th Ave.

■ Ryman
Auditorium

Charlotte Ave.

Hynes St.

8th Ave.

9th Ave.

Shelby St.

McMillin St.

16th Ave.

15th Ave.

Convention
Center

ℹ

Gaylord
Entertainment
Center

17th Ave.

Church St.

Broadway

McGavock St.

🏛 Country Music
Hall of Fame
(opens 5/2001)

Hayes St.

Union
Station

Demonbreun St.

🚌

● The World's End

12th Ave.

Industrial Blvd.

10th Ave.

Clark Pl.

Shirley St.

Franklin St.

TO CENTENNIAL PARK,
PARTHENON (1 mi.)

Peabody St.

West End Ave.

Broadway

Demonbreun St.

LaFayette

19th Ave.

Division St.

Music
Square
Park

🏛 Country Music
Hall of Fame

40

Division St.

8th Ave.

7th Ave.

TO ▲ HOTELS
(4 mi.)

MUSIC
ROW

Music Circle N.

Music
Cir. E.

Sigler St.

▲ CAMPING
(12 mi.)

Allison St.

TO SATCO
(¾ mi.)

18th Ave.

Music
Cir. S.

Hawkins St.

✈ TO
AIRPORT
(5 mi.)

Chet Atkins Pl.

19th Ave.

Music Sq. W.

Music Sq. E.

15th Ave.

14th Ave.

South St.

65

Grand Ave.

SATCO (San Antonio Taco Company), 416 21st Ave. S. (☎327-4322). Tex-Mex and beer abound at this student hangout. Fajitas $1.50, tacos $1; large combo platters $5. Single beers $2, bucket of 6 $10. Open Su-W 11am-midnight, Th-Sa 11am-1:30am.

The World's End, 1713 Church St. (☎329-3480). It's the end of the world as we know it, and I feel like a burger or a salad ($5-8), or maybe a beer ($2.50). Open Su and Tu-Th 4pm-12:30am, F-Sa 4pm-1:30am; happy hour nightly until 8pm.

👁 SIGHTS

COUNTRY MUSIC HALL OF FAME. Music Row, home of Nashville's signature industry, centers around Division and Demonbreun St. from 16th to 19th Ave. S., bounded to the south by Grand Ave. *(Take bus #3 to 17th Ave. and walk south.)* Once past the mobs outside the **Country Music Hall of Fame,** you can marvel at classic memorabilia, such as Elvis's "solid gold" Cadillac and 24-karat gold piano. The museum showcases everything from bluegrass to Cajun to Western swing: admission includes a tour of RCA's

THE SOUTH

historic Studio B, where stars like Dolly Parton, Chet Atkins, and The King recorded their early hits. *(4 Music Sq. E, at Division St. ☎256-1639. Open daily 9am-5pm. $10.75, ages 6-11 $5.75. Wheelchair accessible. In May of 2001, the museum will relocate to a glitzy new building at 5th and Demonbreun St., behind the Gaylord Entertainment Center.)*

PARTHENON. Nashville's pride and joy awaits in **Centennial Park,** a 15min. walk west along West End Ave. from Music Row. The "Athens of the South" boasts a full-scale replica of the **Parthenon.** Built as a temporary exhibit for the Tennessee Centennial in 1897, the Parthenon met with such success that it was rebuilt to last. In its first floor gallery, the building also houses the **Cowan Collection of American Paintings,** a refreshing but erratic selection of 19th- and early 20th-century American art. *(☎862-8431. Open Tu 10am-7:30pm, W–Sa 9am-4:30pm, Su 12:30-4:30pm; Apr.-Oct. closed Su. $3.50, seniors and ages 4-17 $2. Wheelchair accessible.)*

TENNESSEE STATE CAPITOL. A comely Greek Revival structure atop the hill on Charlotte Ave. next to downtown, the Capitol offers, among other things, tours of the tomb of former President James Knox Polk. *(☎741-1621. Tours hourly M-F 9-11am and 1-3pm, Sa-Su self-guided tours only. Free. Wheelchair accessible.)*

VAN VECHTEN GALLERY. Fisk University's Van Vechten Gallery consists of a portion of the private collection of Alfred Steiglitz and Georgia O'Keeffe; outstanding Steiglitz photographs hang among works by Picasso, Renoir, and American modernists. *(At Jackson St. and D.B. Todd Blvd. off Jefferson St. ☎329-8543. Open Tu-F 9am-5pm, Sa 1-4pm. Recommended donation $3.50. Wheelchair accessible.)*

CHEEKWOOD MUSEUM. If you tire of the downtown area, you can rest at the **Cheekwood Museum of Art and Tennessee Botanical Gardens.** The leisurely, well-kept gardens are a welcome change from Nashville glitz and complement the museum's 19th-century art perfectly. The museum also hosts high-caliber temporary exhibits on contemporary art. *(7 mi. southwest of town on Forrest Park Dr. between Hwy. 100 and Belle Meade Blvd. ☎356-8000. Bus #3 "West End/Belle Meade" from downtown to Belle Meade Blvd. and Page Rd. Open M-Sa 8:30am-4:30pm, Su 11am-4:30pm. $10, seniors $8, college students and ages 6-17 $5.)*

BELLE MEADE MANSION. Near Cheekwood Museum, the **Belle Meade Mansion,** dubbed "The Queen of Tennessee Plantations," offers a second respite. This lavish 1853 plantation was the site of the nation's first thoroughbred breeding farm and host to eight US presidents, including the 380 lb. Taft, who found himself stuck in the bathtub there. Prior to Taft's second visit, his hosts installed a rather amply-proportioned shower. *(5025 Harding Rd. ☎356-0501. Open M-Sa 9am-5pm, Su 11-5pm. 2 guided tours per hr.; last tour 4pm. $10, seniors $8.50, ages 6-12 $4. The bottom floor of the mansion is wheelchair accessible.)*

HERMITAGE. Andrew Jackson's beautiful manor, the **Hermitage,** sits atop 625 gloriously shaded acres 13 mi. from downtown Nashville. Admission includes a 15min. film, access to the house and grounds, and a visit to nearby Tulip Grove Mansion and Church. *(4580 Rachel's Ln., Exit 221A from I-40. ☎889-2941. Open daily 9am-5pm. $10, seniors $9, ages 6-12 $5, families $30. All of the grounds, except for the second floor of the mansion itself and the nature trail, are wheelchair accessible.)*

ENTERTAINMENT

The **Grand Ole Opry (GOO),** 2804 Opryland Dr., at Exit 11 off Briley Pkwy., the setting for America's longest-running radio show, has live music and a museum complete with a Randy Travis suit and Marty Robbin's race car. *(☎889-6611. Museum open M-Th 10am-5pm, F 10am-8pm, Sa 10am-10pm; free. Live music F 7:30pm, Sa 6:30 and 9:30pm; $20-22. The F *Tennessean* lists performers. Tours F-Sa 11am for $10. Call for reservations.)* The former home of the Opry, **Ryman Auditorium,** 116 Fifth Ave. N, also hosts live music most nights and offers tours in the day. *(☎889-3060. Open for tours 8:30am-4pm; adults $6, ages 4-11 $3. Showtimes and prices vary.)* The **Tennessee Performing Arts Center,** Deaderick and 6th Ave. N, hosts the Nashville Symphony, Opera, Ballet, and other highbrow entertainment *(☎782-4000; for tickets 255-2787).*

Listings for the area's music and events fill the free *Nashville Scene*, available at most area establishments. *Bone* has more music info, and *Q (Query)* contains gay and lesbian news and listings; both of these papers can be hard to locate.

Two new major-league franchises dominate the Nashville sports scene. The National Football League's **Tennessee Titans** play at **Adelphia Coliseum,** across the river from downtown at 460 Great Circle Rd. (☎565-4000. Tickets $12-52.) The **Nashville Predators,** a National Hockey League team whose inaugural season was 1998-99, play at the **Gaylord Entertainment Center,** 501 Broadway. (☎770-7825 for tickets, 770-2300 for info. $10-95.)

▉ NIGHTLIFE

Nightlife downtown centers around Broadway and 2nd Ave., where large tourist attractions like the Hard Rock Cafe and Planet Hollywood draw large crowds of tourists. Parking down here on a summer evening—especially when something is going on at the Gaylord Entertainment Center—can be either a huge hassle or a huge expense, depending on one's priorities. Near Vanderbilt, Elliston Pl. hops with a wide array of more college-oriented music venues.

  ◪ **Bluebird Cafe,** 4104 Hillsboro Rd. (☎383-1461), in Green Hills. This famous bird sings country, blues, and folk; Garth Brooks got his start here. Dinners of salads and sandwiches ($4-6.50) until 11pm. Open daily 5:30pm until the singing stops. Early show 7pm; cover begins around 9:30pm ($4-10). No cover Su.

  Wildhorse Saloon, 120 2nd Ave. N. (☎256-9453). Huge country dance hall and birthplace of TNN dance show. Bring your cowboy boots and hat for the two-step. Open daily 11am-2am. Dance lessons every hr. 4-9pm. Live music W-Sa. Cover $3-12 after 5pm.

  Exit/In, 2208 Elliston Pl. (☎321-4400), plays rock and alternative most nights to a funky crowd. Shows generally 8 or 9pm. Doors open one hr. before showtime. Tu is songwriters' night. Cover $5-15.

KNOXVILLE   ☎865

Knoxville was settled after the Revolutionary War and named for Washington's Secretary of War, Henry Knox. Once the capital of Tennessee, the city hosted the 1982 World's Fair (which attracted 10 million visitors) and continues to be home to the 26,000 students of the University of Tennessee (UT). Shaded by the stunning Smoky Mountains and hemmed by vast lakes created by the Tennessee Valley Authority, Knoxville offers friendly urbanity.

▊ PRACTICAL INFORMATION. Downtown stretches north from the **Tennessee River,** bordered by **Henley St.** and the **World's Fair Park** to the west. **Greyhound,** 100 Magnolia Ave. (☎522-5144), at Central St., buses to Nashville (3hr., 8 per day, $24); Chattanooga (2hr., 6 per day, $13.50); and Lexington (4hr., 5 per day, $40). **Public transit: KAT** buses run M-Sa from 6:15am-6:15pm or later, depending on the route; a few lines also run Su (☎637-3000; fare $1, transfers 20¢). Two **free trolley** lines run throughout the city: Blue goes downtown and eastward, while Orange heads downtown and westward to the park and UT (Orange line: 7am-6pm; Blue line: 6am-6:20pm). **Gateway Regional Visitors Center,** 900 Volunteer Landing, along the river on the southeast side of downtown, also hosts a small museum. (☎971-5550. Open M-Sa 9am-5pm, Su 1-5pm.) **Internet access:** Lawson McGhee Library, 500 W. Church St. (☎544-5750. Open M-Th 9am-8:30pm, F 9am-5:30pm, Sa-Su 1-5pm.) **Post Office:** 501 Main St. (☎521-8987; open M-F 7:30am-4:30pm). **ZIP code:** 37901. **Area code:** 865.

▐ ACCOMMODATIONS. Many not-quite-budget motels sit along **I-75** and **I-40,** just outside the city. If you're a woman, and they have space, the **YWCA,** 420 W. Clinch St., downtown at Walnut St., will take you. (☎523-6126. Call ahead M-F 9am-5pm. Small dorm-style rooms with shared bath $12.) **Microtel,** 309 N. Peters Rd., off I-75/40 at Exit 278, has admittedly small but spotless rooms. A/C, cable, local calls, and free admission to a nearby gym enlarge its appeal. (☎531-8041 or 800-579-1683; fax 529-1792. Wheelchair-accessible rooms available. Singles $40; doubles $45.

ANYONE FOR FUSION HANGMAN? Shrouded in secrecy and fenced in from outsides, the city of Oak Ridge was created in 1942 for the sole purpose of working on atomic bombs as part of the Manhattan Project. The city, 20 mi. from Knoxville on Rte. 62 or 162, was opened to the public in 1949 and hosts the **American Museum of Science and Energy.** The museum is "dedicated to person-alizing science and technology," and succeeds to a great extent with excellent interac-tive exhibits on the evolution of energy technology (including, yes, computerized games of "fusion hangman"). Some viewers, however, may find the relative lack of information on how science and technology were "personalized" to the citizens of Hiroshima and Nagasaki rather eerie. The museum also operates a bus tour, which runs through a graphite reactor to view the first nuclear reactor to operate at full capacity and the once top-secret Y-12 Plant, where the uranium used in the "Little Boy" bomb was produced. *(300 S. Tulane Ave. ☎576-3200. Open M-F 9am-5pm. The museum may begin charging admission in spring 2001. Tours M-F 12:30pm.)*

Rates are significantly higher on UT football weekends.) A charming replica of an Edinburgh split-level it is not, but the **Scottish Inns,** 301 Callahan Rd., at Exit 110 off I-75, keeps clean rooms equipped with A/C, free local calls, cable TV, and an out-door pool. (☎689-7777; fax 688-7749. Singles $29; doubles $32; on weekends $29/$34.) **Yogi Bear's Jellystone Park Campground,** 9514 Diggs Gap Rd., at Exit 117 off I-75, is located closer to the city than most other campgrounds. It features a pool, club-house, restaurant, and laundry, as well as cartoon cheer. (☎938-6600 or 800-238-9644. Sites with water and electricity $18; full hook-up $25.)

FOOD. The Strip (part of Cumberland Ave. along campus proper) is lined with student hangouts, bars, and restaurants. **Market Sq.,** a popular plaza to the east of World's Fair Park, presents restaurants, fountains, and shade, but mostly shuts down at night. The other center of chowing, browsing, and carousing, **Old City,** spreads north up Central and Jackson St. and stays active later than Market Sq. The ever-popular **Calhoun's on the River,** 400 Neyland Dr., claims to serve the "best ribs in America." (☎673-3355. Open M-Th 11am-10:30pm, F-Sa 11am-11pm, Su 11am-10pm. Meat on ribs $10-16; meat in a sandwich $7.) The **Crescent Moon Cafe,** 705 Market St. at Church St., tries hard to be relaxed (and offers significantly less meat). Excellent sandwiches with a side and fruit salad $6; hummus plate $7. (☎637-9700. Open M-F 7:30am-2:15pm. Dinner on some F by reservation only.)

SIGHTS. The must-see **Museum of Appalachia** is actually a village with houses, barns, a school, a spectacular Hall of Fame building complete with a dulcimer exhibit, livestock, and the cabin where Samuel Langhorne Clemens (Mark Twain) was conceived. Full of personal anecdotes and the tools and household items that make up the materials of the everyday, this museum does a magnificent job of con-veying a sense of Appalachian culture without turning its subject into spectacle. *(16 mi. north of Knoxville at I-75 Exit 122, in Norris. ☎494-7680 or 494-0514. Open daily dawn-dusk; live music Apr.-Dec. 9:30am-4:30pm. $7, ages 6-15 $4, families $17; senior and AAA discounts.)* For a taste of down-home Appalachia, visit the Farmers Market, 15 mi. from down-town on I-640, Exit 8. *(☎524-3276. Open M-Sa 9am-7pm, Su noon-6pm.)*

The self-guided **Cradle of Country Music Tour** runs through the eastern end of down-town; sights include the theater where Roy Acuff made his first public performance as well as the hotel where Hank Williams spent the last night of his life. Also on the tour is the site of the store from which *That's All Right, Mama,* performed by an unknown youngster named Presley, was played over loudspeakers to the public in Market Sq., attracting the attention of hundreds—including an RCA talent scout. Maps and information are available at the visitors center. Picnickers will appreciate **Krutch Park,** across the street from Market Sq., a tiny, perfectly manicured oasis of green in the midst of downtown. Larger expanses of greenery can be found at **Ijams Nature Cen-ter.** *(2915 Island Home Ave., 2 mi. east of downtown across Gay St. Bridge. ☎577-4717, Grounds open daily 8am-dusk. Museum open M-F 9am-4pm, Sa noon-4pm, Su 1-5pm. Free.)*

World's Fair Park makes for a fine stroll with a reflecting pool, grassy expanses, and a playground. The golden "sunsphere" is instantly recognizable from nearly anywhere in the city. The **Knoxville Museum of Art,** in the Park, houses changing exhibits of high caliber. *(1050 World's Fair Park Dr. ☎ 525-6101. Open Tu-Th and Sa 10am-5pm, F 10am-9pm, Su noon-5pm. $4, seniors and ages 12-17 $2. F free from 5-9pm.)* Downtown sits the **Blount Mansion,** the 1792 frame house of governor William Blount. *(200 W. Hill Ave. ☎ 525-2375. Open M-Sa 9:30am-5pm, Su 2-5pm; Nov.-Feb. Tu-F 9:30am-5pm. 1hr. tours leave on the hr.; last tour at 4pm. $5, seniors $4.50, ages 6-12 $2.50. AAA discount.)* Nearby, the **James White Fort** still preserves portions of the original stockade built in 1786 by Knoxville's first citizen and founder. *(205 E. Hill Ave. ☎ 525-6514. Tours run continuously until 3:30pm. Open M-Sa 9:30am-4:30pm. $5, children $2, seniors $4.25.)*

⌖🅜 ENTERTAINMENT AND NIGHTLIFE. UT sports some fantastic teams, particularly **football** and **women's basketball.** Call for tickets at ☎ 974-2491. In summer, the **Knoxville Smokies,** an AA baseball team, hit the field (☎ 637-9494; tickets $4-7). Knoxville will be in full bloom Apr. 6-22, 2001, for the **Dogwood Arts Festival** (☎ 637-4561), featuring food, folks, fun, and a lot of trees. Old City has the highest concentration of nightlife in the area. **The Underground,** 214 W. Jackson Ave., has been voted the town's best dance club six years in a row. (☎ 525-3675. Open M-W, F-Sa 10pm-3am. Cover $3-8.) The **Rainbow Club,** 133 S. Central St., is the more upscale gay club of the area. (☎ 522-6610. Open M, Tu, Th-Sa 5pm-3am; most crowded times are weekends after 10pm. F-Sa open after-hours 3-6am. Piano bar M, Th, and Su. Cover on weekends and on M.) The **Tennessee Theatre,** 604 S. Gay St., plays classic movies on weekends and occasionally hosts major bands (☎ 522-1174). For goings-on around town, pick up a free copy of *Metro Pulse.*

GREAT SMOKY MOUNTAINS NATIONAL PARK ☎ 865

The largest wilderness area in the eastern US, Great Smoky Mountains National Park encompasses 500,000 acres of gray-green Appalachian peaks bounded by misty North Carolina and Tennessee valleys. Black bears, wild hogs, groundhogs, wild turkeys, and a handful of red wolves inhabit the area, as well as more than 1500 species of flowering plants. Whispering conifer forests line the mountain ridges at elevations of over 6000 ft. Spring sets the mountains ablaze with wildflowers and azaleas; in June and July, rhododendrons burst into their full glory, and by mid-October, the mountains become a vibrant quilt of autumnal color. Unfortunately, the area has not remained untouched by human presence. Fifty years ago, a visitor at Newfound Gap could see, on average, 93 mi. Today, poorer air quality has cut visibility to only 15 mi.

🛈 PRACTICAL INFORMATION. Begin exploration at either visitors center: **Sugarlands** (☎ 436-1290), on Newfound Gap Rd. 2 mi. south of Gatlinburg, TN, next to the park's headquarters; or **Oconaluftee** (☎ 828-497-1900), 4 mi. north of Cherokee, NC (both open daily 8am-7pm; off-season hours vary). Rte. 441, known as the Newfound Gap Rd., is the only road that connects the Tennessee and North Carolina sides of the park. The *Smokies Guide* (25¢) details the park's tours, lectures, activities, and changing natural graces. **Info line:** ☎ 436-1200 (operates daily 8:30am-4:30pm). To get to and from Knoxville, contact **ETHRA** (☎ 428-1795; call 8am-3pm; $3-5; give 24hr. notice). **Area code:** 865.

🅕🅒 GRUB 'N' SLUMBER. Ten **campgrounds** lie scattered throughout the park, each with tent sites, limited trailer space, water, and bathrooms (no showers or hook-ups). **Smokemont, Elkmont,** and **Cades Cove** accept reservations from mid-May to late Oct. (sites $14-17, cancellation fee $10); the rest are first come, first served (sites $12-14). In summer, reserve spots near main roads at least eight weeks in advance (☎ 800-365-2267, park code GRE; 10am-10pm). **Backcountry camping** is by reservation only (☎ 436-1231; office open 8am-6pm). **Motels** lining Rte. 441 and Rte. 321 decrease in price with distance from the park. Small motels cluster in both Cherokee and Gatlinburg. In general, Cherokee motels are cheaper (from $35) and Gatlinburg motels are nicer (from $45); prices soar on weekends. In Cherokee, the **Gateway Inn,** 2418 Hwy. 441, south of town, supplies serviceable if somewhat shabby rooms for fantastic rates. (☎828-497-3777. TV, A/C, heat. Singles $25; doubles $29.) **Bell's Wa-Floy Retreat,** 3610 East Pkwy., is 10 mi. east of Gatlinburg on Rte. 321. This Christian retreat community includes a pool, tennis courts, and meditation area. (☎436-5575. Check-in before 10pm. $15 first night; thereafter, HI-YHA $10, non-members $12. Reservations required.)

Authentic Tennessee cookin' oozes from **Smokin' Joe's Bar-B-Que,** 8215 Rte. 73, Townsend. With succulent, slow-cooked meats and homemade side dishes like BBQ beans, Joe's smokes the competition. (☎448-3212. Usually open M-Th 11am-9pm, F-Sa 11am-10pm; Apr.-Oct. also Su 11am-8pm. Dinners with 2 sides, meat, and bread $7-10; sandwiches $2-4.)

SIGHTS AND ACTIVITIES. Over 900 mi. of hiking trails and 170 mi. of road meander through the park. Rangers at the visitors centers will help you devise a trip appropriate for your ability. Some of the most popular trails wind 5 mi. to **Rainbow Falls,** 4 mi. to **Chimney Tops,** and 2½ mi. to **Laurel Falls.** The 2 mi. walk along **Middle Prong Cascades,** accessible from the road to Cades Cove, includes views of several waterfalls. A 7 mi. drive from Newfound Gap Rd., followed by a steep (but paved) ½ mi. trail, runs to the top of **Clingmans Dome,** the highest peak in the Smokies. **Mingus Mill,** near the Oconaluftee visitors center, provides visitors with a glimpse at a working 19th-century mill, and the opportunity to purchase 19th-century quality flour. Less crowded but equally scenic areas not accessible from Rte. 441 include **Cosby** and **Cataloochee,** both on the eastern edge of the park. A **backcountry camping permit,** free from the visitors centers, is required to hike off marked trails. Wherever you go, bring water and don't feed the bears.

NEAR SMOKY MOUNTAINS: CHEROKEE RESERVATION

The **Cherokee Indian Reservation,** on the southeast border of the national park, features a number of museums, shops, attractions, and—most notably—a casino. Three historical attractions stand in marked contrast to miles and miles of rampant commercialism. From May to Oct., the reservation offers a tour of the **Ocunaluftee Indian Village,** a re-created mid-18th-century Native American village. (☎828-497-2315. Open May 15-Oct. 25 9am-5:30pm. $12, ages 6-13 $5.) Cherokee lifestyle, legends, and history are featured at the excellent **Museum of the Cherokee Indian** on Drama Rd. off Rte. 441. (☎828-497-3481. Open daily 9am-8pm; Sept. to mid-June 9am-5pm. $6, under 13 $4; 10% AAA and AARP discount.) **"Unto these Hills,"** an outdoor drama, retells the story of the Cherokees and the Trail of Tears. (☎828-497-2111. June-July M-Sa 8:45pm; Aug. M-Sa 8:30pm. $14-16, under 14 $6.) The **Cherokee Visitors Center** provides information; follow signs from Rte. 441 or Rte. 19 (☎800-438-1601; open M-F 8am-7pm, Sa 9am-7pm, Su 9am-6pm).

The **Nantahala Outdoor Center (NOC),** 13077 U.S. 19 W, 13 mi. southwest of Bryson City, NC, and just south of GSM Park, beckons with cheap beds, three restaurants, and the great outdoors. (☎704-488-2175 or 800-232-7238; call ahead. Showers, kitchen, laundry facilities. Bunks in simple cabins $13.) The NOC's **whitewater rafting expeditions** are pricey, but with some amount of rafting competency, you can rent your own raft for a trip down the Nantahala River. (Rafts Su-F $18, Sa $22. 1- or 2-person inflatable "duckies" Su-F $29/$44, Sa $32/$52. 60 lb. minimum. Group rates available. Higher prices weekends in July-Aug. Prices include transportation to site and all necessary equipment.) The 2144 mi. **Appalachian Trail** runs through here. **Mountain bike** rentals start at $30 (☎888-662-1662, ext. 600). The NOC staff can assist if you need help planning a daytrip.

SCENIC DRIVE: CADES COVE LOOP DRIVE

The Cades Cove loop road begins 24 mi. (40min. driving time) from Newfound Gap Rd., near the Sugarlands visitors center. May through Sept., from sunrise to 10am on M and W, the loop is closed to car traffic in order to accommodate bicylists. The main features of the one-way loop road are the stone and wooden buildings, some of which date as far back as the 1820s. Numerous private homes, three beautifully plain churches (one of which, the Methodist church, was built in 115 days for $115),

MOUNTAINS OF FUN A mythical American village created by Dolly Parton in the Tennessee hills, **Dollywood** dominates Pigeon Forge. The park celebrates the cultural legacy of the east Tennessee mountains and the country songmistress herself, famous for some mountainous topography of her own. In Dolly's world, craftspeople demonstrate their skills and sell their wares, 30 rides offer thrills and chills, and country favorites perform. While Dolly asserts that she wants to preserve the culture of the Tennessee mountains, she also seems to want you to pay to come again—Dollywood's motto is "Create Memories Worth Repeating." *(1020 Dollywood Ln. ☎865-428-9488. Open year-round; mid–June to mid-Aug. daily, most days 9am-9pm, but hours change constantly. $31, over 59 $26, ages 4-11 $22; enter after 3pm during summer and come in free the following day. Discount coupons available at tourist centers, restaurants, and motels.)*

a blacksmith shop, and a sawmill are accessible from the loop. Near the blacksmith shop and sawmill, at the far end of the loop, is the **Cades Cove Visitors Center** (open May-Aug. 9am-7pm; off-season hours vary). All of the historic buildings have been preserved to look more or less as they did when the federal government bought the land in 1927 and the 500 inhabitants of Cades Cove began to move elsewhere. Pamphlets providing extensive information on each building and on the cove in general are available at the information station at the start of the loop for $1.

Most visitors, however, also spend a good deal of time gawking at the **wildlife**— deer are nearly ubiquitous, and many also spot the occasional black bear. Wild European boars, turkeys, river otters, and that unfortunate animal known as both "groundhog" and "woodchuck" also inhabit the Cove, although they are more rarely seen by visitors. Drivers in a hurry beware: frequent animal sightings and the lines of cars they inevitably form as each family scurries for its cameras can make driving times astronomical. Unless you happen to be by one of the two roads that cut across the valley, there's no way of evading holdups. During summers, expect the 11 mi. of road to take anywhere between 1½ to 3hr.

Those wishing either to avoid bucolic traffic jams or to get that much closer to the historic experience can rent **horses** at the entrance to the loop across from the ranger station. (☎448-6286. Open Mar.-Nov. 9am-5pm. Horses $15 per hr. Hayrides $6-8, 5 per day. Buggy rides $7.) **Bikes** are also available at the same location. (☎448-9034. Open June-Aug. 9am-7pm, no rental after 4:30pm; May and Sept. 9am-5pm, no rental after 2:30pm. Opens at 7am on M and W. $3.25 per hr.)

CHATTANOOGA   ☎423

Anyone approaching Chattanooga by road will soon be made well aware of the city's star attraction; signs for Ruby Falls insistently surround the city in a 60 mi. radius. The city itself is, indeed, well-advertised and clearly commercial. Its downtown teems with tourists in peak season, and the prices and developments at its beautiful mountain attractions may leave some visitors longing for the National Park Service. Yet somehow Chattanooga, once famous only for its "choo-choo" connection, manages to cultivate a certain charm nonetheless.

◪ **PRACTICAL INFORMATION.** Chattanooga straddles the Tennessee/Georgia border at the junction of I-24, I-59, and I-75. **Greyhound,** 960 Airport Rd. (☎892-8814; station open 6:30am-9:30pm), buses to Atlanta (2hr., 8 per day, $14.50); Nashville (3½hr., 4 per day, $16.50); and Knoxville (2hr., 4 per day, $12.50). **Chattanooga Area Transportation Authority (CARTA)** runs buses 5am-11pm (☎629-1473; fare $1, transfers 20¢, children 50¢/10¢). **Visitors center:** 2 Broad St., next to the aquarium (☎756-8687 or 800-322-3344; open daily 8:30am-5:30pm). **Internet access: Public Library,** 1001 Broad St. at 10th St. (☎757-5310. Open M-Th 9am-9pm, F-Sa 9am-6pm; Sept.-May also Su 2-6pm.) **Post office:** 900 Georgia Ave. between Martin Luther King Blvd. and 10th St. (☎899-1198; open M-F 7:30am-5:30pm). **ZIP code:** 37402. **Area code:** 423.

THE SOUTH

⚑⚑⚑ ACCOMMODATIONS, FOOD, AND ENTERTAINMENT. Budget motels congregate on the highways coming into the city and on **Broad St.** at the base of Lookout Mountain. **Holiday Trav-I-Park,** 1623 Mack Smith Rd., in Rossville ½ mi. off I-75 at the East Ridge exit, enlivens sites for tents and RVs with a Civil War theme. (☎706-891-9766 or 800-693-2877. Laundry, pool. 2-person site $16.50, with water and electricity $20.50, full hook-up $22.50; cabins $35, $2 per additional person.) Two nearby lakes, **Chickamauga** and **Nickajack,** are surrounded by campgrounds. The ❚Pickle Barrel, 1012 Market St., downtown, moves beyond cucumbers to scrumptious sandwiches for $4-7 and a large selection of beers. When the weather's nice, the open-air deck upstairs is a must. (☎266-1103. Open daily 11am-3pm. 21+ after 9pm, except families.) For entertainment listings, check the free weekly *Outlook,* available at many restaurants and shops. The **Chattanooga Lookouts,** a minor league baseball farm team for the Reds, play at the new **BellSouth Park,** at 2nd and Chestnut St. (☎267-2208 or 800-852-7572. Tickets $4-8.)

⬢ SIGHTS. Downtown Chattanooga, a small area between 10th St. and the river, is full of attractions, shops, and restaurants. The biggest catch in town is the **Tennessee Aquarium,** on Ross's Landing, with the largest turtle collection in the world, as well as 7000 other animals. After the big tanks, check out the bigger IMAX screen. (☎800-322-3344. Open M-Th 10am-6pm, F-Su 10am-8pm; Oct.-Apr. daily 10am-6pm. $12, ages 3-12 $6.50; IMAX $7/$5; both $16/$10.) Somewhat lower-profile is the **International Towing and Recovery Hall of Fame and Museum,** also downtown. A big room full of gleaming tow trucks celebrates the unsung inventor of these vehicles, a Chattanooga native. (400 Broad St. ☎267-3132. Open M-F 10am-4:30pm, Sa-Su 11am-5pm. $3.50, seniors and ages 5-18 $2.50.) The **Chattanooga Regional History Museum** charts the city's involvement in the forced Cherokee removal in 1838 (the "Trail of Tears") and in the Civil War. (400 Chestnut St. ☎265-3247. Open M-F 10am-4:30pm, Sa-Su 11am-4:30pm. $4, seniors $3.50, children $3.)

A **riverwalk pathway** runs between downtown, near the aquarium, and the **Bluff View Art District.** Bluff View is a small district of upscale shops and cafes, anchored by the **Hunter Museum of Art.** The museum houses the South's most complete American art collection and an extensive Andy Warhol exhibit. (10 Bluff View. ☎267-0968. Open Tu-Sa 10am-4:30pm, Su 1-4:30pm. $5, students $3, seniors $4, ages 3-11 $2.50. Wheelchair accessible.) The riverfront is shut down for nine nights in mid-June for the **Riverbend Festival,** featuring four stages of live music. (☎265-4112. $20.)

The **Incline** takes passengers up a ridiculous 72.7° grade to **Lookout Mountain,** where six states can be seen on a clear day. (Incline: $9, ages 3-12 $4.50. Lookout Mountain: Take S. Broad or bus #15 or 31 and follow signs. Open daily Jun.-Aug. 8:30am-9:15pm; Sept.-May 9am-5:15pm; wheelchair accessible.) The highest peaks and the narrowest hikes are mixed with boulders, flowers, and tacky shops at **Rock City Gardens.** (☎706-820-2531. Open daily 8am-sunset; early Sept. to late May 8:30am-sunset. $11, ages 3-12 $6.) One thousand ft. inside the mountain, the ❚Ruby Falls cavern formations and a 145 ft. waterfall—complete with colored lights and sound effects—add a little Disney-style pizzazz to a day of sightseeing. (☎821-2544. Open daily in summer 8am-9pm; early Sept. to Oct. and Apr. to late May 8am-8pm; Nov.-Mar. 8am-6pm. 1hr. tour. $9.50, ages 6-12 $5.)

NEAR CHATTANOOGA: CHICKAMAUGA CREEK

The same railroads that immortalized Chattanooga in song gave the area great strategic importance in the Civil War. In the fall of 1863 some of the hardest fighting of the war took place here, near **Chickamauga Creek,** about three mi. over the Georgia border on U.S. 27. Chickamauga was the nation's first military park, initially intended as an opportunity for professional military study. As a result, the events of the battle are presented in nearly incomprehensible detail on countless plaques across the park. **Visitors center:** on U.S. 27. (☎706-866-9241. Open daily 8am-5:45pm, off-season 8am-4:45pm. 26min. video shown every hour; $3, seniors and children $1.50. Audio tour rentals until 3 hr. before closing; $3. The park is open until dusk.)

MEMPHIS ☎901

Memphis is a music mecca, especially for Elvis fans. The city has seen the creation of practically every important American music trend in the past century, including rock'n'roll and soul, but most visitors make the Memphis pilgrimage to see Graceland—the former home of the King and the tackiest mansion in the US. Beyond Graceland, Memphis offers a rich array of musical monuments, and popular blues clubs along Beale St. keep the city's greatest tradition alive. Traditional Southern accents like great barbecue, historic mansions, and manicured parks provide the perfect accompaniment to the more obvious musical treats.

▐ GETTING THERE AND GETTING AROUND

Airport: Memphis International, 2491 Winchester Rd. (☎922-8000), south of the southern loop of I-240. Taxi fare to the city around $20—negotiate in advance. Hotel express **shuttles** cost $10 (☎522-9229; service 6:30am-6:30pm). Public transport to and from the airport $1.10; service is sporadic and the trip can be confusing.

Trains: Amtrak, 545 S. Main St. (☎526-0052), at Calhoun on the southern edge of downtown. The surrounding area can be less than safe, but the Main St. Trolley line runs to the station. To: New Orleans (8½hr., 1 per day, $55); Chicago (10½hr., 1 per day, $93); and Jackson (4½hr., 1 per day, $39).

Buses: Greyhound, 203 Union Ave. (☎523-1184), at 4th St. downtown. *The area is unsafe at night.* To: Nashville (4hr., 10 per day, $28-31); Chattanooga (9hr., 4 per day, $37-41); and Jackson (4-5hr., 6 per day, $30-32). Open 24hr.

Public Transit: Memphis Area Transit Authority (MATA) (☎274-6282), corner of Union Ave. and Main St. Bus routes cover most suburbs but run infrequently. The major downtown stops are at the intersections of Front and Jefferson St., and 2nd St. and Madison Ave.; the major routes run on Front, 2nd, and 3rd St. Buses run M-F from 5:30am, Sa-Su from 6am and stop between 6pm and midnight, depending on the route. $1.10, transfers 10¢. Refurbished 19th-century **trolley cars** cruise Main St. (M-Th 6am-midnight, F 6am-1am, Sa 9:30am-1am, Su 10am-6pm) and roll along the Riverfront (M-Th 6:30am-midnight, F 6:30am-1am, Sa 9:30am-1am, Su 10am-6pm). 50¢; seniors 25¢, M-F 11am-1:30pm 25¢; children under 5 free. 1-day pass $2, 3-day $5.

Taxis: In taxi-deprived Memphis, expect a long wait. **City Wide,** ☎324-4202.

▚ ▌ ORIENTATION AND PRACTICAL INFORMATION

Downtown, named avenues run east-west and numbered ones run north-south. **Madison Ave.** divides north and south addresses. Two main thoroughfares, **Poplar** and **Union Ave.**, run east-west; **2nd** and **3rd St.** are the major north-south routes downtown. **I-240** and **I-55** encircle the city. **Bellevue** becomes **Elvis Presley Blvd.** and leads you south straight to Graceland. **Midtown,** a wonderful neighborhood, lies east of downtown. There's free, unmetered parking along the river.

Help Lines: Crisis Line, ☎274-7477, 24hr. **Gay/Lesbian Switchboard,** ☎324-4297. Operates daily 7:30-11pm. **HIV/AIDS Switchboard,** ☎278-2437.

Hospital: Baptist Memorial Hospital, 899 Madison Ave. (☎227-2727). **Memphis Area Medical Center for Women,** 29 S. Bellevue Blvd. (24hr. hotline ☎542-3809).

Visitor Info: Tennessee Welcome Center, 119 Riverside Dr. (☎543-5333), at Jefferson St. Open 24hr. The uniformed **blue suede brigade** roaming the city will happily give you directions or answer questions—just stay off of their blue suede shoes.

Internet access: Cossitt-Goodwin Public Library, 33 S. Front St. (☎526-1712), at Monroe. Open M-F 10am-5pm.

Post Office: 555 S. 3rd St. (☎521-2187). Open M-F 8:30am-5:30pm, Sa 10am-2pm. **ZIP code:** 38101. **Area code:** 901.

▎ SINCE M'BABY LEFT ME, I GOT A NEW PLACE T'DWELL

The fire-related demise of the Lowenstein-Long hostel in spring 2000 has made the once-difficult process of finding good budget accommodations in Memphis nearly impossible. A few downtown motels have prices in the budget range; otherwise, more distant lodgings are available near Graceland at **Elvis Presley Blvd.** and **Brooks Rd.** For the celebrations of Elvis's historic birth (Jan. 8) and death (Aug. 15), as well as for the Memphis in May festival, book six months to one year in advance.

Days Inn Riverbluff, 340 W. Illinois St. (☎948-9005), Exit 12C off I-55. Pleasant accommodation in a scenic (if somewhat run-down) location near downtown, next to the Mississippi. Cable, A/C, coffee, doughnuts, and newspaper. Rooms start at $33, but visitors center flyers can bring rates down to $33.

Airport Inn, 1441 E. Brooks Rd. (☎398-9211), Exit 5A from I-55, 10 mi. south of downtown. Large rooms near Graceland and the airport, but far from anything else. A/C, cable. Singles $36; doubles $47.

Red Roof Inn Memphis Medical Center, 210 S. Pauline St. (☎528-0650), at Union Ave., Exit 30 from I-240. Pricey, but convenient to downtown with sparkly clean rooms. Cable, A/C, free local calls, coffee, and newspaper. Singles $50; doubles $58; $10 more on weekends.

Memphis/Graceland KOA, 3691 Elvis Presley Blvd. (☎396-7125), right next door to Graceland with pool, laundry, and free shuttle to Beale St. No trees or privacy, but good location. Sites for 1-2 people $21, with hook-up $32. Kabins with A/C $36; $4 per extra person.

Memphis South Campground, 460 Byhalia Rd. (☎662-429-1818), Hernando, MS, 20 mi. south of Memphis, at Exit 280 off I-55. A relaxing, green spot with a pool and laundry. Office open daily 8-10am and 4:30-7:30pm. Tent sites $12, with water and electricity $15, full hook-up $17; $2 per additional person.

◖ MEALS FIT FOR THE KING

In Memphis, barbecue is as common as rhinestone-studded jumpsuits; the city even hosts the **World Championship Barbecue Cooking Contest** in May. But don't fret if gnawing on ribs isn't your thing—Memphis has plenty of other Southern restaurants with down-home favorites like fried chicken, catfish, chitterlings, and grits.

Rendezvous, 52 2nd St. (☎523-2746), around back on "Downtown Alley." A Memphis legend, serving large portions of ribs ($12-14) and cheaper sandwiches ($3-6), but be prepared to wait an hour. Open Tu-Th 4pm-11:30pm, F-Sa noon-midnight.

The Map Room, 2 S. Main St. (☎579-9924), where everything seems to move in delightfully slow motion. Business folk, travelers, and neo-hippies lounge on the sofas to read loaned books and sip "lateas" ($3.25). Sandwiches like pimento-and-cheese ($3.50) are a respite from Memphis's otherwise meaty options. Live music daily. Open 24hr.

The North End, 346 N. Main St. (☎526-0319 or 527-3663), at Jackson St. downtown, specializes in tamales, wild rice, stuffed potatoes, and creole dishes ($5-8). The orgasmic hot fudge pie is known as "sex on a plate" ($3.75). Very extensive beer list—domestics from $2.75, imports from $3.50. Open daily 10:30am-3am. Happy hour daily 4-7pm. Live music Tu-Sa 10pm; cover $2.

Java Cabana, 2170 Young Ave. (☎272-7210), in the Cooper-Young arts district in Midtown. Serves coffee drinks ($1-3), desserts ($2-3), and a limited selection of sandwiches ($4) to local alterna-types. Open Tu-Th 11am-10pm, F-Sa 11am-midnight, Su noon-10pm. Live music most nights at 8pm.

Huey's, 77 S. 2nd St. (☎527-2700), downtown. Voted best burgers ($3.80) in Memphis for 14 years straight. Open M-Th 11am-2am, F 11am-3am, Sa 11:30am-3am, Su noon-3am. Live music Su 4pm.

P and H Cafe, 1532 Madison Ave. (☎726-0906). The initials aptly stand for Poor and Hungry. The "beer joint of your dreams" serves grill food to students and locals. Although the patty melt with grilled onions ($3) might take away your moody blues, the friendly waitresses and the kitschy decor are the real draw. During Death Week in Aug., P and H hosts the infamous "Dead Elvis Ball." Open M-F 11am-3am, Sa 5pm-3am.

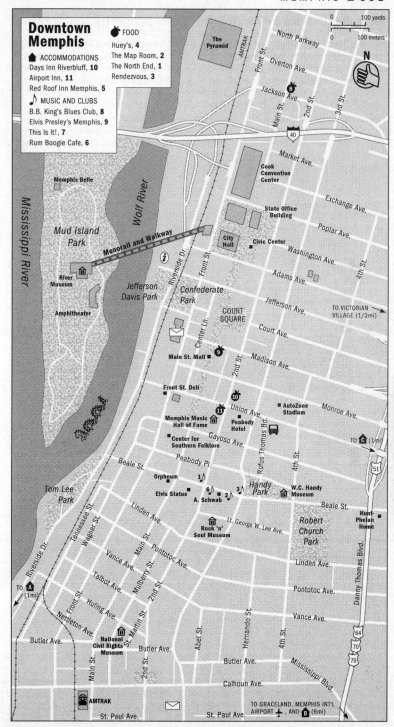

Downtown Memphis

🍎 FOOD

Huey's, **4**
The Map Room, **2**
The North End, **1**
Rendezvous, **3**

🏠 ACCOMMODATIONS

Days Inn Riverbluff, **10**
Airport Inn, **11**
Red Roof Inn Memphis, **5**

♪ MUSIC AND CLUBS

B.B. King's Blues Club, **8**
Elvis Presley's Memphis, **9**
This Is It!, **7**
Rum Boogie Cafe, **6**

THE SOUTH

0   100 yards
0   100 meters

N

The Pyramid

North Parkway

Overton Ave.

Jackson Ave.

AMTRAK

Front St.

Main St.

2nd St.

3rd St.

40

Market Ave.

Cook Convention Center

State Office Building

Exchange Ave.

Poplar Ave.

Memphis Belle

Wolf River

Mud Island Park

Monorail and Walkway

City Hall

Civic Center

Washington Ave.

4th St.

River Museum

Riverside Dr.

Front St.

Adams Ave.

Mississippi River

Jefferson Davis Park

Confederate Park

COURT SQUARE

Jefferson Ave.

TO VICTORIAN VILLAGE (1/2mi)

Amphitheater

Center Ln.

Court Ave.

Main St. Mall

9

2nd St.

Madison Ave.

Front St. Deli

11

10

Union Ave.

AutoZone Stadium

Monroe Ave.

Memphis Music Hall of Fame

Peabody Hotel

TO C (1mi)

Center for Southern Folklore

Gayoso Ave.

Rufus Thomas Bd.

4th St.

51

Beale St.

Peabody Pl.

Orpheum

1

Handy Park

W.C. Handy Museum

Elvis Statue

A. Schwab

6

2

3

Beale St.

Tom Lee Park

Linden Ave.

Lt. George W. Lee Ave.

Robert Church Park

Hunt-Phelan Home

Tennessee St.

Wagner St.

Main St.

Pontotoc Ave.

Rock 'n' Soul Museum

Linden Ave.

Vance Ave.

Mulberry St.

2nd St.

Pontotoc Ave.

Danny Thomas Blvd.

Talbot Ave.

TO A (1mi)

Riverside Dr.

Front St.

Huling Ave.

Nettleton Ave.

St. Martin St.

Butler Ave.

National Civil Rights Museum

Butler Ave.

Hernando St.

4th St.

Vance Ave.

64

70

Mississippi Blvd.

79

Main St.

2nd St.

Butler Ave.

Calhoun Ave.

AMTRAK

St. Paul Ave.

St. Paul Ave.

TO GRACELAND, MEMPHIS INT'L AIRPORT ✈ AND B (6mi)

■ MEMPHIS MUSIC AND MARVELS

GRACELAND. Bow down before **Graceland,** Elvis Presley's home and the paragon of Americana that every Memphis visitor must see. Unfortunately, any desire to learn about the man, share his dream, or feel his music requires the ability to transcend the mansion's crowd-control methods and audio-tape tour, to reach beyond the tacky commercialism and ignore the employees who seem to adhere to the saying "Taking Care of Business in a Flash." Still, you'll never forget the mirrored ceilings, carpeted walls, and yellow-and-orange decor of Elvis's 1974 renovations. By tour's end, even those who aren't die-hard Elvis fans may be genuinely moved. Be sure to gawk audibly at the **Trophy Building,** where hundreds of gold and platinum records line the wall. The King and his court are buried next door in the **Meditation Gardens,** where you can seek enlightenment while reciting a mantra to the tune of "You're So Square." *(3763 Elvis Presley Blvd. ☎ 332-3322 or 800-238-2000. Take I-55 S to Exit 5B or bus #13 "Lauderdale." Expect to wait 1-2hr. on summer weekends. Ticket office open M-Sa 9am-5pm, Su 10am-4pm; Nov.-Feb. mansion tour closed Tu. Attractions remain open 2hr. after ticket office closes. $12, students and seniors $10.80, ages 7-12 $5.)*

MORE ELVIS. If you love him tender, love him true—visit the peripheral Elvis attractions across the street from the mansion. The **Elvis Presley Automobile Museum** houses a score of pink and purple **Elvis-mobiles** in a huge hall, while an indoor drive-in movie theater shows clips from 31 Elvis movies. *($6, students and seniors $5.40, children $3.) Walk a Mile in My Shoes,* a free 20min. film with performance footage, screened every 30min., contrasts the early (slim) years with the later (fat) ones. **Elvis Airplanes** features the two Elvis planes: the *Lisa Marie* (named for Elvis's daughter) complete with blue suede bed and gold-plated seatbelt and the tiny *Hound Dog II* Jetstar. *($5, seniors $4.50, children $3.)* The **Sincerely Elvis** exhibit glimpses into Elvis's private side; see the books he read, the shirts he wore, the TVs he shot, and home movies with his wife Priscilla. *($4, seniors $3.60, children $2.50.)* The **Platinum Tour Package** discounts admission to the mansion and all attractions. *($22, students and seniors $19.80, ages 7-12 $11.)* All have wheelchair access except the airplanes and two rooms in the mansion tour.

Every year on the week of Aug. 15 (the date of Elvis's death), millions of the King's cortege get all shook up for **Elvis Week,** an extended celebration that includes a pilgrimage to his junior high school and a candlelight vigil. The days surrounding his birthday, Jan. 8, also see some Kingly activities.

ELVIS WHO? THE BLUES AND MORE. Long before Sam Phillips and Sun Studio produced Elvis, Jerry Lee Lewis, U2, and Bonnie Raitt, historic Beale St. saw the invention of the blues. Recently ousted from Beale St. by rampant commercialism, the **Center for Southern Folklore** celebrates local folk cultures with exhibitions, live music, and general exuberance. *(119 S. Main St. ☎ 525-3655. Open Su-W 11am-7pm, Th-Sa 11am-11pm. Live music, along with Southern food and a bar, generally M-W noon, Th-Sa 8pm, and Su at 5pm. Galleries free; shows around $5.)* The center can give you info on the **Music and Heritage Festival,** which fills Beale St. during Labor Day weekend. Gospel, country, blues, and jazz accompany dance troupes and craft booths. *(☎ 525-3655. Open 11am-11pm. Free.)* Of course, Memphis music history includes the soul hits of the Stax label and rockers like Big Star as well as the blues. The unmissable **Rock 'n' Soul Museum** examines the cultural movements surrounding that thing known as rock and the evolution of soul. Numerous artifacts are on display; best of all, the audio tour contains a hundred complete songs, from early blues classics to Isaac Hayes' theme from *Shaft. (145 Lt. George W. Lee Ave., one block south of Beale St. ☎ 543-0800. Open Su-Th 10am-6pm, F-Sa 10am-8pm. $6, seniors $5.50, ages 5-17 $4. Wheelchair accessible.)* The **Memphis Music Hall of Fame** fills in the history with a huge number of records, costumes, and photographs of local legends who recorded for Sun or Stax. *(97 S. 2nd St. ☎ 525-4007. Open Su-Th 10am-6pm, F-Sa 10am-8pm. $7.50, ages 7-14 $2.50. Wheelchair accessible. The Hall of Fame will relocate by Jan. 1, 2001.)* **Sun Studio** shows off the city's rock 'n' roll roots in the tiny recording studio where Elvis was discovered, Jerry Lee Lewis was consumed by great balls of fire, and Carl Perkins

AQUAMMODATIONS William Faulkner once said of Memphis that "the Delta meets in the lobby of the **Peabody Hotel.**" Every day at 11am and 5pm, the hotel rolls out the red carpet, and the ducks that live in their own luxury suites on the top floor ride down the elevator, with the help of a personal attendant, and waddle about the premises to John Phillip Sousa's *Stars and Stripes Forever* or *King Cotton March. (149 Union Ave, in downtown. ☎529-4000.)*

warned everyone to stay off of his blue suede shoes. Sun remains a one-room studio, so don't expect too much from the tour. *(706 Union Ave. ☎521-0664. 30min. tours every hr. on the ½hr. Open daily 10am-6pm. $8.50, under 13 free; some memorabilia is on display at the upstairs gift shop for free. Wheelchair accessible.)* Memphis is also the home of soul music legend **Al Green's Full Gospel Tabernacle,** where Su services display powerful music, dancing, speaking in tongues, and even exorcisms. *(787 Hale Rd. ☎396-9192. Services Su 11am-2:30pm; arriving late and leaving early is bad form.)*

MUD ISLAND. A quick monorail ride over the Mississippi, **Mud Island** has the **Mississippi River Museum,** the renowned World War II B-17 *Memphis Belle,* and a five-block scale model of the Mississippi River that you can splash in or stroll along. **Free tours** of the Riverwalk and Memphis Belle run several times daily. Summer Th from noon to 1pm on the island are free, featuring some live music. *(Monorail leaves from 125 Front St. ☎576-7241 or 800-507-6507. Open daily 10am-7pm; early Sept. to late May 9am-4pm. Park entrance fee $8, seniors and ages 5-17 $6. Parking $3. Wheelchair accessible.)*

MORE MUSEUMS. The ▧**National Civil Rights Museum** is housed at the site of Martin Luther King, Jr.'s assassination at the **Lorraine Motel** at Calhoun St. Historical documents, graphic photographs of lynching victims, and films chronicle key events of the Civil Rights Movement. *(450 Mulberry St. ☎521-9699. Open M and W-Sa 9am-6pm, Su 1-6pm. $6, students with ID and seniors $5, ages 4-17 $4; free M 3-6pm. Audio tours $2.50.)* The four seamlessly connected buildings of the **Brooks Museum of Art,** in the southwest corner of Overton Park east of downtown, showcase artwork as diverse as its architecture. *(1934 Poplar Ave. ☎722-3500. Open Tu-F 10am-4pm, first W of each month also 4-8pm, Sa 10am-5pm, Su 11:30am-5pm. $5, seniors $4, students $2; W free. Wheelchair accessible.)* South of downtown, the **National Ornamental Metal Museum,** the only such institution in the US, displays fine metalwork from contemporary artists as well as originally functional pieces. In the back is a working blacksmith shop and a sculpture garden with a view of the river. *(374 Metal Museum Dr., Exit 12C from I-55. ☎774-6380. Open Tu-Sa 10am-5pm, Su noon-5pm. $4, seniors $3, students $2.)*

The **Pink Palace Museum and Planetarium** is a fascinatingly strange conglomeration of exhibits ranging from a shrunken head (with recipe) to local history to a room-sized clockwork circus in miniature, as well as the obligatory IMAX theater. The museum also includes a replica of the world's first self-service grocery store, a Memphis Piggly-Wiggly; Clarence Saunders, the company's founder, built the pink Georgian structure as his home but had to relinquish it after losing his fortune on Wall Street. *(3050 Central Ave. ☎320-6320. Open M-Th 9am-4pm, F-Sa 9am-9pm, and Su noon-6pm. $7, seniors $5.50, ages 3-12 $4.50; IMAX film $6/$5.50/$4.50; planetarium show $3.50/$3/$3. Package deals available. Call for IMAX times. Wheelchair accessible.)*

HISTORIC MEMPHIS. Memphis is home to a few tastefully ornate houses, including the **Hunt-Phelan Home.** This antebellum Southern mansion, once visited by Jefferson Davis and soon after captured by Ulysses S. Grant, is worth visiting despite the Gracelandesque audio tour. *(533 Beale St. ☎344-3166 or 800-350-9009. Open M-Sa 10am-4pm, Su noon-4pm; early Sept. to late May Th-M 10am-4pm, Su noon-4pm. $10, students and seniors $9, ages 5-12 $6. Wheelchair accessible.)* **Victorian Village** is a cluster of 19th-century houses around the intersection of Orleans St. and Adams Ave., all in various stages of restoration. Two of these are open for visitation: **Mallory-Neeley House** and **Woodruff-Fontaine House.** *(Village open M-Sa 10am-4pm, Su 1-4pm, with the last tours leaving at 3:30pm. Mallory Neeley: 652 Adams Ave. ☎523-1484. Closed M and Jan.-Feb. Woodruff-Fontaine: 680 Adams Ave. ☎526-1469. Closed Tu. Each house $5, seniors $4, stu-*

dents *$3. Limited wheelchair access.)* **A. Schwab,** a small family-run department store (ca. 1876), still offers old-fashioned bargains. A "museum" of never-sold relics, including an array of voodoo potions, gathers dust on the mezzanine floor. Elvis bought some of his ensembles here. *(163 Beale St.* ☎ *523-9782. Open M-Th 9am-5pm, F-Sa 9am-7pm; off-season M-Sa 9am-5pm. Free tours upon request.)*

PARKS AND GARDENS. Memphis has almost as many parks as museums, each offering a slightly different natural setting. Brilliant wildflowers and a marvelous heinz of roses (57 varieties) bloom and grow forever at the **Memphis Botanical Garden.** *(750 Cherry Rd. in Audubon Park off Park Ave.* ☎ *685-1566. Open M-Sa 9am-6pm, Su 11am-6pm; Nov.-Feb. M-Sa 9am-4:30pm, Su 11am-4:30pm. $4, students and seniors $3, ages 6-17 $2.)* Across the street, the **Dixon Galleries and Garden** flaunts its manicured landscape and a collection of European art which includes works by Renoir, Degas, and Monet. *(4339 Park Ave.* ☎ *761-2409. Open Tu-Sa 10am-5pm, Su 1-5pm. $5, students $3, seniors $4, ages 4-11 $1. On M, only the gardens are open; admission is half-price. Seniors free on Tu.)* **Lichterman Nature Center** in East Memphis is a 65-acre wildscape with forests, wildlife, 3 mi. of trails, and a picnic area. *(5992 Quince Rd.; entrance at 1680 Lynnfield Rd.* ☎ *767-7322. Open Tu-Sa 9:30am-5pm, Su 1-5pm. $2; students, ages 3-18, and seniors $1.)*

♫ ARE YOU LONESOME TONIGHT?

BEALE ST. BLUES
The fourth line of W.C. Handy's 1917 "Beale St. Blues" claims that "You'll find that business never closes 'til somebody gets killed." Beale has changed a lot since Handy's day; today's visitors are more likely to encounter the Hard Rock Cafe and all the mega-commercialism that comes with it. But despite the commodification of Beale St., the strip between 2nd and 4th St. is still the place most visitors come for live music, and few clubs have set closing times. On F nights, a $10 wristband lets you wander in and out of any club on the strip. You can save a few bucks by buying a drink at one of the many outdoor stands as you meander from show to show. Hot blues joints wax and wane with the moon; ask the folks at the **Center for Southern Folklore** (see **Sights,** above), who are veritable archives of local info. The free *Memphis Flyer* and the "Playbook" section of the F morning *Memphis Commercial Appeal* can also tell you what's goin' down in town.

B.B. King's Blues Club, 143 Beale St. (☎524-5464 or 800-443-0972), where the club's namesake still makes appearances. Happily mixes young and old, tourist and native. Wash down entrees ($6-18) with a $3 beer. Open M-F noon, Sa-Su 11am. Cover $5-25; when B.B. himself plays, $35-100.

Elvis Presley's Memphis, 126 Beale St. (☎527-6900), Graceland-sponsored. Serves Elvis grub such as fried peanut butter and banana sandwiches ($5.75) and plain old beer ($3) to an older crowd. Open Su-Th 11am-1am, F-Sa 11am-2am. Shows begin 8:30-9:30pm. Su gospel brunch.

This is It!, 167 Beale St. (☎527-8200). A much smaller club than either of the big names, This is It! is about as close as it's going to get to the old Beale atmosphere. Open M-Tu 5pm-1am, W-Th 5pm-2am, F-Sa 5pm-4am, Su 7pm-1am. Shows generally at 8:30. Cover Th-Sa $5.

Rum Boogie Cafe, 182 Beale St. (☎528-0150). Friendly, relaxed atmosphere and honest homegrown blues with a touristy crowd. Check out the celebrity guitars on the wall and the original Stax records sign. Open daily 11am-2am. Music at 9pm. Cover $7.

NIGHTLIFE OFF BEALE ST.
For a more off-the-beaten-track club, try **Wild Bill's,** 1580 Vollintine Rd., which capitalizes on the juke joint/hole-in-the-wall tradition. (☎726-5473. Live music F-Sa; it's best to arrive after 11pm. Cover $3-5.) The hot gay spot, **J-Wag's Lounge,** 1268 Madison, served as the bar in *The People vs. Larry Flynt.* (☎725-1909. Open 24hr. DJ music F-Sa.) For a collegiate atmosphere, try the **Highland St.** strip near **Memphis State University,** with hopping bars like **Newby's,** 539 S. Highland St. (☎452-8408. Open daily 3pm-3am. Happy hour 4-7pm. Music F-Sa around 10:30pm. Cover $3-5.)

ENTERTAINMENT

The majestic **Orpheum Theater,** 203 S. Main St., shows classic movies in the summer at 7:15pm on F and 2pm on Su, along with an organ prelude and a cartoon. The grand old theater, with 15 ft. high chandeliers, has occasional live music and Broadway shows. (☎525-3000. Box office open M-F 9am-5pm and sometimes before shows. Movies $6, students and seniors $5, ages 4-17 $4. Music and shows $15-45.) **Memphis in May** (☎525-4611) celebrates through the month with concerts, art exhibits, food contests, and sporting events. The **Memphis Redbirds,** in Autozone Park downtown, are a brand-new AAA baseball team as of 1998. (☎721-6000. Tickets $5-12; discounts for seniors, military, and under 15.)

⌗ DAYTRIPS FROM MEMPHIS

SHILOH NATIONAL MILITARY PARK. On the morning of Apr. 6, 1862, Confederate troops, under the command of General A.S. Johnston, surprised General Grant's army of Tennessee, which was camped in the woods and fields around Shiloh. The next two days witnessed the largest artillery concentration seen in North America to that date; the horrible, bloody combat of Shiloh would soon become standard practice in the Civil War. The park's visitors center gives a pamphlet to the 9½ mi. automobile path and shows a 25min. video every half hour. From Memphis, take U.S. 64 E 100 mi. to U.S. 45 S and follow the signs. (☎901-689-5275. Park open during daylight hours; visitors center open daily 8am-5pm. $2, under 16 free, family $4.)

THE MISSISSIPPI DELTA. South of Memphis, U.S. 61 runs to Vicksburg through the swamps and flatlands of the Mississippi Delta region, where cotton was king and where the blues were born. **Clarksdale,** 70 mi. south of Memphis, houses the **Delta Blues Museum,** 1 Blues Alley, which displays mostly photographic exhibits on the history of the region with a definite hint of bitterness at the passing of an era. (☎662-627-6820. Open M-F 9am-5pm. Free.) Twenty mi. north on U.S. 49, across the river in Arkansas, lies **Helena.** The legendary King Biscuit Time radio show was first broadcast here in 1941, featuring live music from Sonny Boy Williamson. The first weekend of October, the town hosts the **King Biscuit Blues Festival,** the largest free blues festival in the South. The **Delta Cultural Center,** 141 Cherry St., displays exhibits on the rich land and poor people that figure so prominently in regional culture. (☎870-338-4350 or 800-358-0972. Open M-Sa 10am-5pm, Su 1-5pm. Free.)

NORTH CAROLINA

North Carolina can be split neatly into three regions: down-to-earth mountain culture in the west, mellow sophistication in the Research Triangle of the central piedmont, and beach culture in the east. Largely untouched by development, the natural beauty of the "Old North State" continues to be one of its greatest assets. Visitors in a hurry—definitely out of pace with most of the state—should stick to the scenery at the extremes of the state, in the Appalachian Mountains and the Outer Banks.

⌗ PRACTICAL INFORMATION

Capital: Raleigh.
Visitor Info: Dept. of Commerce, Travel and Tourism, 301 N. Wilmington St., Raleigh 27601-2825 (☎919-733-4171 or 800-847-4862; www.visitnc.com). **Dept. of Natural Resources and Community Development,** Division of Parks and Recreation, 1615 Mail Service Center, Raleigh 27699 (☎919-733-4181).
Postal Abbreviation: NC. **Sales Tax:** 6%.

THE RESEARCH TRIANGLE ☎919

Large universities and their students dominate "the Triangle," a regional identity born in the 50s with the creation of a spectacularly successful Research Triangle Park, where Nobel Prize-winning scientists toil for dozens of high-tech and biotech firms. **Raleigh**, the state capital and home to North Carolina State University (NC State), is a historic town that has recently renovated its tourist attractions. **Durham**, formerly a major tobacco producer, now supports multiple hospitals and medical research projects devoted to finding cancer cures. It's also purported to be one of the country's more gay-friendly cities. Chartered in 1789 as the nation's first state university, the University of North Carolina (UNC), is found just 20 mi. down the road in **Chapel Hill**. College culture predominates here—nearly every other store specializes in UNC t-shirts—and the music scene thrives.

┏ GETTING THERE AND GETTING AROUND

Airport: Raleigh-Durham International (☎840-2123), 15 mi. northwest of Raleigh on U.S. 70. A taxi to downtown Raleigh or Durham costs $20-30.

Trains: Amtrak, 320 W. Cabarrus St., Raleigh, 4 blocks west of the Civic Ctr. (☎833-7594). To Washington, DC (6hr., 2 per day, $66) and Richmond (3½hr., 2 per day, $31-42). Open 24hr.

Buses: Greyhound has a station in both Raleigh and Durham. **Raleigh:** 314 W. Jones St. (☎834-8275). To: Durham (40min., 9 per day, $5.50); Chapel Hill (80min., 4 per day, $8.50); and Charleston, SC (7½hr., 2 per day, $48). Open daily 7am-1am. **Durham:** 820 W. Morgan St., 1 block off Chapel Hill St. downtown, 2½ mi. northeast of Duke (☎687-4800). To Chapel Hill (25min., 4 per day, $6.50) and Washington, D.C. (6hr., 6 per day, $41). Open daily 7:30am-10pm. The **Chapel Hill** bus station was recently closed, but Triangle-area buses still pick up and drop off passengers in front of the old building at 311 W. Franklin St. Tickets must be bought at the next station on the route.

Public Transit: Capital Area Transit, Raleigh (☎828-7228). Buses run M-Sa. Fare 75¢; transfers free. **Durham Area Transit Authority (DATA),** Durham (☎683-3282). Most routes start downtown at Main and Morgan St. on the loop. Operates daily; hrs. vary by route; fewer on Su. Fare 75¢; seniors, under 18, and disabled 35¢; transfers free; children under 43 in. free. **Chapel Hill Transit,** Chapel Hill (☎968-2769). Buses run 6:30am-6:30pm. Office open M-F 6:30am-10pm. Fare 75¢. There is a free shuttle on the UNC campus.

Taxis: Associated Cab Co., ☎832-8807. **Cardinal Cab,** ☎828-3228.

▮ PRACTICAL INFORMATION

Visitor Info: Raleigh Visitors Center, 301 N. Blount St. (☎733-3456). Open M-F 8am-5pm, Sa 9am-5pm, Su 1-5pm. **Durham Convention Center and Visitors Bureau,** 101 E. Morgan St. (☎800-446-8604). Open M-F 8:30am-5pm. **Visitor Info Center and Chapel Hill Chamber of Commerce,** 104 S. Estes Dr. (☎967-7075). Open M-F 9am-5pm.

Hotline: Rape Crisis, ☎800-826-6200. 24hr.

Post Office: Raleigh: 311 New Bern Ave. (☎420-5333). Open M-F 8am-5pm, Sa 8am-noon. **ZIP code:** 27611. **Durham:** 323 E. Chapel Hill St. (☎683-1976). Open M-F 8:30am-5pm. **ZIP code:** 27701. **Chapel Hill:** 125 S. Estes St. (☎967-6297). Open M-F 8:30am-5:30pm, Sa 8:30am-noon. **ZIP code:** 27514.

Area code: 919.

▮ ACCOMMODATIONS

Durham's budget lodging can be found on Capital Blvd., about 2½ mi. northeast of town, a mile or so inside the 440 beltline. Probably the best bargain in the Triangle is the **Carolina-Duke Motor Inn,** 2517 Guess Rd, off I-85. Depending on your standards, the Inn may not precisely live up to its motto "luxury for less" but can certainly provide the weary traveler with a clean, budget-priced room. (☎286-0771 or 800-438-1158. Pool, laundry facilities, A/C, cable TV, free local calls, and shuttle to both the Duke and V.A. hospitals. Free continental breakfast. DATA access across the street. Singles $40; doubles $48; $3 per additional person. 10% discount for *Let's Go* users and AARP/AAA members. Wheelchair accessible.) In Raleigh, the best option is the **Regency Inn,** 300 N. Dawson St., at Lane St. (☎828-9081; fax 821-0654. A/C, cable TV, and coffee. Singles $44; doubles $48.) The **Capital Inn,** 1625 Capital Blvd., may show signs of wear but is quite a bargain nonetheless. (☎833-1901. Cable, A/C. Singles $36; doubles equipped with fridge and microwave $45.) Reasonably priced accommodations are slightly harder to come by in Chapel Hill; the **Red Roof Inn,** 5623 Chapel Hill Blvd. at the intersection of U.S. 15-501 and I-40, offers standard rooms. (☎489-9421; fax 489-8001. A/C, disabled access, free local calls, cable TV. Singles $47-51; doubles $54-59; $4 per additional person.) Area camping is best at **Falls Lake State Recreation Area,** about 12 mi. north of Raleigh, off State Hwy. 98. (☎676-1027. $12, with hook-up $17. Open year round; reservations taken with 7-14 days notice.)

◖ FOOD

Each of the area's major universities has spawned a region of affordable and interesting eateries nearby; Raleigh's **Hillsborough St.,** Durham's **9th St.,** and Chapel Hill's **Franklin St.** all cater to a college (and thus budget-oriented) crowd. The Franklin St. area offers the most variety. **█Skylight Exchange,** 405½ W. Rosemary St. (the entrance is in an alley off of Rosemary), a block over from Franklin, doubles as a cafe and used book/music store. The Exchange is home to a vast array of sandwiches ($4-7) and, most importantly, the legendary 50¢ cup of coffee. (☎933-5550. Open daily 11am-11pm; live music M-Sa 9pm.) The **█Rams Head Rathskeller,** 157A E. Franklin St., has been a local legend since 1948. Named for German meeting places located underneath courthouses where locals would drink beer and talk politics, the uniquely decorated interior of "the Rat" has seen more than 50 years of Tarheels come and go. (☎942-5158. Open M-Th 11am-10pm, F-Sa 11am-midnight, Su 4-10pm; summer hrs. vary. Meals $5-10.) In Raleigh, **Big Ed's,** 220 Wolfe St. in City Market, is far removed, both in location and in cuisine, from the college fare of Hillsborough St. Specializing in biscuits and country-cooked meats and vegetables, Big Ed's entices with homestyle fare at only slightly more than homestyle prices. (☎836-9909. Open M-F 7am-2pm, Sa 7am-noon. Very filling platters around $6.) In Durham, the slightly yuppified **Elmo's Diner,** on 9th St., serves breakfast all day for about $5. (☎416-3823. Open Su-Th 6:30am-10pm, F-Sa 6:30am-11pm.)

◉ SIGHTS

RALEIGH. Raleigh has grown rapidly in recent years—to the extent that it now needs a bypass to bypass its old bypass—but its downtown area still retains much of the character of an old North Carolina town, with added gleaming tourist attractions. Across from the capitol building are the **North Carolina Museum of History** and the **Museum of Natural Sciences** which features "Willo—the dinosaur with a heart," a rare dinosaur fossil with an iron concretion within the ribcage. *(5 E. Edenton St. Museum of History:* ☎ *715-0200. Open Tu-Sa 9am-5pm, Su noon-5pm. Free. Museum of Natural Sciences:* ☎ *733-7450. Open M-Sa 9am-5pm, Su 1-5pm. Free.)* The area around **Moore Square,** a few blocks southeast of the capitol, is a small district of youthful artsiness. Adjacent to the Square is **City Market,** a collection of shops, cafes, and bars.

CHAPEL HILL. Chapel Hill and neighboring Carrboro are virtually inseparable from the **University of North Carolina at Chapel Hill.** The university's **Smith Center** hosts sporting events and concerts. Until 1975, NASA astronauts trained at UNC's **Morehead Planetarium,** which now projects several different shows per year and also houses a small museum. *(☎962-1236. Open M-Sa 10am-5pm and 7-9:45pm, Su 12:30-5pm and 7-9:45pm. $4, students, seniors, and children $3. Exhibits free.)*

OFF TO A PIG PICKIN' Southerners are notoriously finicky about their barbecue, but eastern North Carolinians claim that theirs *is* authentic "Southern barbecue." To start, the terminology: to avoid ridicule or, worse yet, giving yourself away as a Yankee, remember that "barbecue" is a noun denoting a recognized food, *never* a verb. Say, rather, "We're goin' to cook a pig" or "We're havin' a pig pickin'." And keep in mind that purists insist only pig meat constitutes "barbecue," even if bovine-centric Texans get some slack. Most importantly, of course, the secret's in the sauce. The brown gooey stuff found in supermarkets is decidedly *not* real BBQ sauce, which should be much thinner and have a vinegar, not tomato, base. So sit back and enjoy your barbecue chipped, sliced, or, most festive of all, hot from a "pig pickin'." Southerners traditionally celebrate summertime weddings, reunions, and birthdays by gathering around a freshly cooked pig kept warm on an enormous grill. Parties line up buffet-style and have at it with forks, before heading off to the shade with a cool glass of sweet tea. And the livin' is easy...

DURHAM. The principle attractions of Durham center around the Duke family and their principle legacy, **Duke University,** which is split up into East and West campuses. The neo-gothic **Duke Chapel,** completed in the early 30s, is at the center of West Campus and contains over a million pieces of stained glass and numerous statues depicting both Christian and Southern figures. (☎684-2921. *Open daily Sept.- May 8am-10pm; June-Aug. 8am-8pm. Free; self-guided tour available.*) Nearby on Anderson St. sit the 55-acre **Sarah P. Duke Gardens,** which include both native plants and an Asiatic arboretum. (☎684-3698. *Open daily dawn-dusk. Free.*) The **Duke Homestead and Tobacco Museum,** on the other side of Durham, up Guess Rd., tells visitors about both the Duke family and the history of the tobacco industry. This quirky museum finds itself in a fascinatingly awkward position when discussing what it calls "the continuing debate" over the effects of tobacco on health. (*2828 Duke Homestead Rd.* ☎477-5498. *Open Apr.-Oct. M-Sa 9am-5pm, Su 1-5pm; Nov.-Mar. Tu-Sa 10am-4pm, Su 1-4pm. Free. Call for a schedule of Homestead tours.*) The 1988 movie *Bull Durham* was filmed in the **Durham Bulls'** ballpark. The AAA farm team for the Tampa Bay Devil Rays still plays here, minus Kevin Costner. (☎687-6500. *General admission $4.50-5.50.*)

♫ ENTERTAINMENT

Pick up a free copy of the *Spectator* and *Independent* weekly magazines, available at most restaurants, bookstores, and hotels, for listings of Triangle news and events. Chapel Hill offers the best nightlife, especially in terms of music. A number of live music clubs congregate near the western end of Franklin St., where it becomes Main St. in the neighboring town of Carrboro. **Cat's Cradle,** 300 E. Main St. in Carrboro, is the area's main venue, hosting a wide variety of local and national acts. Recent performers range from Kool Keith to L7. (☎967-9053. *Show times vary widely. Cover usually around $10; beer $1.50-3.*) Another nearby club focusing on indie and rock 'n' roll is **Local 506,** 506 W. Franklin St. (☎942-5506. *Cover around $5. 21+.*) **Gotham,** 306-H W. Franklin St., offers more of a dance club environment. (☎967-2852. *Open daily 10pm-2:30am. Cover around $5. 18+.*) Nightlife in Raleigh and Durham is harder to come by. **ComedySportz,** 204 Wolfe St. in Raleigh's City Market, turns standup into a sporting event: the home team, the Hillsborough Malamutes, takes on all comers. (☎829-0822. *F 8:30pm, Sa 7:30 and 9:45pm; $10. Sa matinee 1:20pm; $6.*)

CHARLOTTE   ☎704

The third-largest banking center in the nation and the largest city of the Carolinas, Charlotte seems unhaunted by any legacy of its past. The gleaming "uptown" region bustles with well-funded charm and vigor, attracting visitors with its top-notch science museum, ritzy clubs and bars, and successful sports teams. But beneath the veneer, patches of the past can still be found. Off Stonewall St., near the edges of Charlotte's city center, a set of concrete steps can be seen under the I-277 overpass.

They don't lead anywhere; before the predominantly black neighborhood of Brooklyn was bulldozed in the 60s, they would have been the front steps of a small house. Now they stand, in comparison to the polish of uptown Charlotte, as a somewhat eerie reminder of that which can be forgotten in the process of "urban renewal."

🛈 PRACTICAL INFORMATION. Amtrak, 1914 N. Tryon St. (☎376-4416) and **Greyhound,** 601 W. Trade St. (☎372-0456) stop in Charlotte. Both stations are open 24hr. **Charlotte Transit,** 901 N. Davidson St., operates local buses. (☎336-3366. Fare $1, $1.40 for outlying areas; free transfers.) Within the uptown area, **Center City Circuit** runs four free shuttle lines; call ☎332-2227 for more information. **Info Charlotte,** 330 S. Tryon St., offers 20 min. of free parking off 2nd St. (☎331-2700; open M-F 8:30am-5pm, Sa 10am-4pm, Su 1-4pm). **Rape Crisis line:** ☎375-9900. **Suicide Hotline:** ☎358-2800. **Gay/Lesbian Switchboard:** ☎535-6277. **Post Office:** 201 N. McDowell (☎333-5135; open M-F 7am-6pm, Sa 7am-1pm). **ZIP code:** 28204. **Area code:** 704.

🛏🍴 ACCOMMODATIONS AND FOOD. There are several clusters of budget motels in the Charlotte area: off I-85 at Sugar Creek Rd., Exit 41; off I-85 at Exit 33 near the airport; and off I-77 at Clanton St., Exit 7. The **Continental Inn,** 1100 W. Sugar Creek Rd., has clean, serviceable rooms. (☎597-8100. A/C, cable. Singles $40; doubles $45.) **Motel 6,** 3430 St Vardell Ln., Exit 7 on I-77, has similarly basic rooms. (☎527-0144 or 800-466-7356. Cable, A/C, laundry, pool, and free local calls. Singles $45, $6 per additional adult.)

Two areas outside of uptown offer attractive dining options. North Davidson ("NoDa"), around 36th St., is home to a small artistic community inhabiting a set of historic buildings. South from city center, the **Dilworth** neighborhood, along East and South Blvds., is lined with restaurants serving everything from ethnic cuisine to pizza and pub fare. Talley ho! veggie lovers, it's **Talley's Green Grocery and Cafe,** 1408-C East Blvd., an upscale grocery serving organic health food, $5 sandwiches, and hot soups for $3. (☎334-9200. Open M-Sa 7:30am-9pm, Su 10am-7pm.) The sign outside of **Bill Spoon's Barbecue,** 5524 South Blvd., reads "We cook the whole pig. It makes the difference." Many locals seem to agree. Serving east Carolina-style BBQ, this place can supply the hungry traveller with a pork sandwich for only $3.20, and the hush puppies and iced tea just don't stop. (☎525-8865. Open M-F 10:30am-3pm.) The **Charlotte Regional Farmers Market,** 1801 Yorkmont Rd., behind the Coliseum, hawks local produce, baked goods, and crafts year-round. (☎357-1269. Open Tu-Sa 8am-6pm, with additional Su hours 12:30-6pm May-Aug.)

🔟 SIGHTS. Most of Charlotte's museums are clustered around the intersection of Tryon St. and Trade St. at the very center of the city. The largest and most publicized of these museums is **The Discovery Place,** which draws crowds with its hands-on science museum, OmniMax theater, flight simulator, and planetarium. *(301 N. Tryon St. ☎372-6261 or 800-935-0553. Open M-Th 9am-6pm, F-Sa 9am-8pm, Su 1-6pm. One attraction $6.50, seniors and ages 6-12 $5.50, ages 3-5 $2.75; $3 per additional attraction.)* The **Museum of the New South** explores post-Reconstruction Charlotte and the Carolina Piedmont area. Currently closed for renovations, the museum should re-open in the fall of 2001. *(301 N. Tryon St. ☎333-1887.)* The excellently-curated **Mint Museum of Craft and Design** takes a rather narrow approach to its name, focusing on 20th century design. Admission also pays for the **Mint Museum of Art,** which displays American decorative and visual arts. *(Craft and Design: 220 N. Tryon St. Art: 2730 Randolph Rd. Information for both museums: ☎337-2000. Open Tu 10am-10pm, W-Sa 10am-5pm, Su noon-5pm. $6, students and seniors $4, under 13 free; free Tu after 5.)*

🎭🎵 ENTERTAINMENT AND NIGHTLIFE. Charlotte is a big sports town. Basketball's **Hornets** (men) and **Sting** (women) play in the **Coliseum** (☎357-4700), and the National Football League's **Panthers** play in Ericsson Stadium (☎358-3407). The Charlotte **Knights** play AAA minor league baseball at Knights Castle, off I-77 S at exit 88 in South Carolina (☎364-6637; tickets $5, seniors and children $3.50).

THE SOUTH

For nightlife, arts, and entertainment listings, grab a free *Creative Loafing* in one of Charlotte's shops or restaurants or check the E&T section in the F *Charlotte Observer*. The Elizabeth area along E. 7th St. and E. Independence Ave. parties with clubs like **Jack Straw**, 1936 E. 7th St. (☎347-8960. Th-Sa cover $5-8.) **The Baha**, 4369 S. Tryon St., is a "progressive dance complex" with nights like Disco Hump and College Quake. (☎525-3343. Open F-Sa until 4am. Women get in free Sa. 21+.)

CAROLINA MOUNTAINS

The sharp ridges and rolling slopes of the southern Appalachian range create some of the most spectacular scenery in the Southeast. Amid this beauty flourishes a mélange of diverse personalities, from scholars to ski bums to farmers to artists. The aptly named High Country includes the territory between Boone and Asheville, 100 mi. to the southwest, and fills the upper regions of the Blue Ridge Mountains. The central attraction of the mountains is the **Blue Ridge Parkway**, a national parkway that snakes through the mountains from northern Virginia to southern North Carolina. Views from many of the Parkway's scenic stops are simply staggering, particularly on rainy days when the peaks are wreathed in mist. Southwards is the Great Smoky Mountains National Park (see p. 345).

BOONE   ☎828

Named for frontiersman Daniel Boone, Boone is nestled among the breathtaking mountains of the High Country. Tourist attractions such as Mast General Store, Tweetsie Railroad, and ubiquitous antique shops lure young and old to eat family-style, flatten coins on railroad tracks, and, of course, shop. The small town lives on year-round, populated by summer tourists, winter skiers, locals, and the students of Appalachian State University (ASU).

▟ PRACTICAL INFORMATION. The **Boone AppalCart**, 274 Winkler's Creek Rd., provides local bus service with three main routes: Red links downtown Boone with ASU and motels and restaurants on Blowing Rock Rd.; Green serves Rte. 421; Blue runs within ASU. Red and Green routes run every hr., while Blue runs every 15min. (☎264-2278. Red: M-F 7:30am-11pm, Sa 8:30am-5pm. Green: M-F 7am-11pm, Sa 9am-5pm. Blue: M-F 7:30am-7pm. Fare 50¢; those wanting to make a transfer should notify the driver when they board.) **Ace Cab Co.** (☎265-3373) charges $1.50 base fare and $1.50 per additional mi. Runs 24 hours. **Rock and Roll Sports,** 280 E. King St., rents bikes for $30 a day. (☎264-0765. Open M-Sa 10am-6pm, Su noon-4pm. Helmets extra; car racks $5. Trail maps available.) **Boone Area Chamber of Commerce,** 208 Howard St. (☎264-2225 or 800-852-9506. Open M-F 9am-5pm.) **Visitor Info: North Carolina High Country Host Visitor Center,** 1700 Blowing Rock Rd. (☎264-1299 or 800-438-7500. Open M-Sa 9am-5pm, Su 10am-4pm.) Hikers should arm themselves with the invaluable, large-scale map *100 Favorite Trails* ($3.50), available at book stores. **Post Office:** 1544 Blowing Rock Rd. (☎264-3813; open M-F 9am-5pm, Sa 9am-noon.) **ZIP code:** 28607. **Area code:** 828.

▛▛ ACCOMMODATIONS AND FOOD. Catering primarily to vacationing families, the area fronts more than its share of expensive motels and B&Bs. Scratch the surface, though, and you'll find inexpensive rooms and campsites. Most budget hotels are concentrated along **Blowing Rock Rd. (Rte. 321)** or **Rte. 105.** The **Boone Trail Motel,** 275 E. King St./U.S. 421, south of downtown, has brightly painted rooms with quaint country baskets. (☎264-8839. Singles $30; doubles $40; F-Sa $40/$50. In winter, rooms are $25.)

Boone and the Blue Ridge Pkwy. offer developed and well-equipped campsites, as well as primitive camping options for those looking to rough it. Along the Pkwy. near Boone, spectacular tent and RV sites without hook-ups ($12) are available at the **Julian Price Campground,** Mi. 297 (☎963-5911); sites around Loop A are on a lake. Further down the Parkway towards Asheville are two other campsites run by the National Park Service: **Linville Falls,** Mi. 317, left onto Rte. 221 (☎765-7818; $12), and

Crabtree Meadows, Mi. 340 (☎675-5444; open May-Oct., hike-in sites only; $12). For hook-ups, try Rte. 194 N off 421. **Appalachian RV Park,** 3 mi. up the road, has laundry and TV. (☎264-7250. Full-hook-up $24; tent sites $18.50; 4-person cabins $33.)

Rte. 321 boasts countless fast-food options and family-style eateries. College students and professors alike hang out on **West King St.** (U.S. 441/221). **Our Daily Bread,** 627 West King St., offers sandwiches, salads, and super vegetarian specials for $3-6. (☎264-0173. Open M-F 8am-6pm, Sa 9am-5pm.) The **Dan'l Boone Inn,** at the Rte. 321/421 junction (King and Hardin Streets), satiates hearty appetites with all-you-can-eat country-style meals. (☎264-8657. Open for dinner M-F 11:30am-9pm, Sa-Su 11am-9pm; $12, ages 4-5 $4, ages 6-8 $5, ages 9-11 $6. Open for breakfast Sa-Su 8-11am; $7. No credit cards, but an ATM is on the premises.)

🔲📷 **SIGHTS AND ACTIVITIES. Horn in the West,** in an open-air amphitheater located near Boone off Rte. 105, dramatizes the part of the American Revolution fought in the southern Appalachians. (☎264-2120. Shows June-Aug. Tu-Su 8:30pm. $12, under 13 $6; group rates upon request; AAA and senior discount $1. Reservations recommended.) Near the theater, **Hickory Ridge Homestead** recreates 18th-century mountain life with restored cabins and demonstrations. (☎264-2120. Open daily June-Aug. 1-8:30pm; also open in late spring and early fall Sa 9am-4pm and Su 1pm-4am. Included in Horn admission price, or $2 alone.) Down the road, the **Daniel Boone Native Gardens** celebrate mountain foliage. (☎264-2120. Open May-Oct. daily 9am-6pm, until 8pm on show days. $2.) Also on the grounds is the **Watauga County Farmer's Market.** (☎264-2120. Open Sa and W 7am-1pm.) **An Appalachian Summer** is a July festival of high-caliber music, art, theater, and dance sponsored by ASU. (☎800-841-2787. $12-16 for individual shows.)

Downhill skiers enjoy the Southeast's largest concentration of alpine resorts (Nov.-Mar.): **Appalachian Ski Mountain,** off Rte. 221/321 (☎800-322-2373; lift tickets $23, Sa-Su $35); **Ski Beech,** 1007 Beech Mt. Pkwy., off Rte. 184 in Banner Elk (☎800-438-2093; lift tickets $28/$45); **Ski Hawksnest,** 2058 Skyland Dr., in the town of Seven Devils (☎888-429-5763; lift tickets $22/$39); and **Sugar Mountain,** in Banner Elk off Rte. 184 (☎898-4521; lift tickets $30/$47). It's best to call ahead to the resort for specific ski package prices. **Boone AppalCart** (see **Practical Information,** above) runs a free winter shuttle to Sugar Mountain and Ski Beech. Call ☎800-962-2322 for **daily ski reports.**

The 5 mi. road to **Grandfather Mountain,** off Rte. 221, near the intersection of Rte. 221 and the Parkway, provides an unparalleled view of the entire High Country area. (☎800-468-7325. Mountain open daily 8am-7pm, no entrance after 6pm; Dec.-Mar. 8am-5pm, weather permitting.) At the top, a private **park** features a 1 mi. high suspension bridge, a museum, and a small zoo ($10, ages 4-12 $5, under 4 free). Hiking or camping on Grandfather Mt. requires a **permit,** available at the park entrance or at the **Grandfather Mountain Country Store,** halfway between the mountain and Blowing Rock on Rte. 221. (☎295-6100. Store open M-Sa 7:30am-7:30pm, Su 1pm-7:30pm. Permit: Day use $5, camping $10.) Pick up a trail map at the entrance to learn which trails are available for overnight use. The mountain plays host to brawny men in kilts, second weekend in July, at the **Grandfather Mountain Highland Games & Gathering of Scottish Clans.** (☎828-733-1333. Shows $8-18.)

NEAR BOONE: BLOWING ROCK

Seven mi. south on Rte. 321, at the entrance to the Blue Ridge Pkwy., lies a town filled with craftmakers, folk artists, and the tourists who support them. **Blowing Rock,** the geographical oddity for which the town is named, overhangs Johns River Gorge; chuck something over the edge, and it will blow back. (☎828-295-7111. Open daily Apr.-Dec. 8:30am-7pm; Jan.-Feb. Sa-Su as weather permits. $4, ages 6-11 $1.)

In Blowing Rock, at the **Parkway Craft Center,** Mi. 294 Blue Ridge Pkwy., 2 mi. south of Blowing Rock Village in the Cone Manor House, members of the **Southern Highland Craft Guild** demonstrate their skills. (☎295-7938. Open mid-Mar. to Dec. daily 9am-6pm.) The craft center is on the grounds of the 3600-acre **Moses H. Cone Memorial Park;** for the less craftily inclined, the park's 25 mi. of trails are worth a stop in themselves. Check out *This Week's Activities* at the **National Park Service desk.** (☎295-3782. Open Apr.-Oct. daily 9am-5pm. Free.) Guided horseback rides from **Blowing Rock Stables** let you tour the park without hoofing it yourself. Exit the Blue Ridge Pkwy. at the Blowing Rock sign, turn left onto Rte. 221/Yonahlossee Rd. and follow the signs. (☎295-7847. Open Apr.-Oct. daily 9:30am-4pm. 1hr. $30, 1½ hr. $40, 2 hr. $50. Call at least 1 day in advance to reserve.)

Pricey food and lodging are as abundant as wildflowers in town, but the **Homestead Inn,** 153 Morris St., a half block off Main, lets you—and your wallet—rest easy. A gazebo, swing, and quilts transform this motel into a mountain lodge. Well, almost. (☎295-9559. Singles and doubles from $47 on weekdays, $65 on weekends; significantly lower in winter.) Blowing Rock is slightly north of Jimmy Buffet's beloved Caribbean, but there are **Cheeseburgers in Paradise** at Rte. 221 and Main St. This bar and grille has outdoor patios, great beef, and friendly waiters. (☎295-4858. Burgers $5, domestic beer $2.50. Open Su-Th 11am-9:30pm, F-Sa 11am-10:30pm.) **Blowing Rock Chamber of Commerce,** 132 Park Ave. (☎295-7851. Open M-Th 9am-5pm, F-Sa 9am-5:30pm.)

ASHEVILLE ☎828

Hazy blue mountains, deep valleys, and spectacular waterfalls all supply a splendid backdrop to this tiny town. Once a coveted layover for the nation's well-to-do, Asheville housed enough Carnegies, Vanderbilts, and Mellons to fill a 20s edition of *Who's Who on the Atlantic Seaboard.* Monuments such as the Biltmore Estate reflect the rich history of the town's gilded citizenry. The population these days tends more toward dreadlocks, batik, and vegetarianism, providing funky nightlife and festivals all year. In contrast to the laid-back locals, Asheville's sights are fanatically maintained and the downtown meticulously preserved, making for a pleasant respite from the Carolina wilderness.

🛈 PRACTICAL INFORMATION

Buses: Greyhound, 2 Tunnel Rd. (☎253-5353), 2 mi. east of downtown, near the Beaucatcher Tunnel. Asheville Transit bus #13 runs to and from downtown every hr.; last bus 6:30pm. To: Charlotte (3½hr., 6 per day, $25-27); Knoxville (2hr., 7 per day, $25-27); Atlanta (6½hr., 1 per day, $36-38); and Raleigh (8hr., 6 per day, $48.50-51.50). Open daily 8am-10pm.

Public Transit: Asheville Transit Authority, 360 W. Haywood St. (☎253-5691). Bus service within city limits. All routes converge on Pritchard Park downtown. Operates M-F (and some Sa) 6am-7:30pm, usually at 1hr. intervals. Fare 75¢, transfers 10¢. Discounts for seniors, disabled, and multi-fare tickets. Short trips within the downtown area (a quadrilateral defined by Hilliard St., Charlotte St., French Broad Ave. and I-240) are free.

Visitor Info: Chamber of Commerce, 151 Haywood St. (recorded info ☎800-257-1300; www.ashevillechamber.org), exit 4C off I-240, on the northwest end of downtown. Open M-F 8:30am-5:30pm, Sa-Su 9am-5pm.

Hotline: Rape Crisis, ☎255-7576.

Internet Access: Pack Memorial Library, 67 Haywood St. (☎255-5203), at Vanderbilt Pl. Open M-Th 10am-9pm, F-Sa 10am-6pm; Sept.-May also Su 2-6pm.

Post Office: 33 Coxe Ave. (☎271-6420), off Patton Ave. Open M-F 7:30am-5:30pm, Sa 9am-1pm. **ZIP code:** 28802. **Area code:** 828.

🛈 ACCOMMODATIONS

Motels cluster in three areas. The least expensive are on **Tunnel Rd.,** east of downtown, while slightly more expensive (and fewer) options can be found on **Merrimon Ave.,** just north of downtown. The ritziest of the budget circle hover around the Biltmore Estate on **Hendersonville Ave.,** south of downtown.

Peace House, 22 Ravenscroft Dr. (☎285-0230), off Church St. between Hilliard and Sawyer, is a funky new hostel in a brick house just south of downtown. With kitchen, deck, grill, laundry, common rooms, Internet access ($4 per hr.), and info on Asheville and the Smokies—give Peace a chance. Lockout 10:30am-4pm. Linen $1. Dorm rooms with 3-4 bunk beds at $18. Reservations recommended May-Oct.

Log Cabin Motor Court, 330 Weaverville Hwy. (☎645-6546). Take Rte. 240 to Rte. 19/23/70N to the New Bridge exit, then right, then left at the light; it's 1 mi. on the left. Though 10min. north of downtown, this motel provides quaint cabins with cable TV, laundry and pool access; some have fireplaces and kitchenettes, but none have A/C. Singles from $32; doubles from $46; quads from $73; quints from $78.

In Town Motor Lodge, 100 Tunnel Rd. (☎252-1811), has standard rooms for great prices; ask for one with a balcony. A/C, cable TV, and pool. Singles $32; doubles $36.

Powhatan (☎670-5627), on Wesley Branch Rd. 12 mi. southwest of Asheville off Rte. 191, the closest campsite in the Nantahala National Forest. Wooded sites on a 10-acre trout lake surrounded by hiking trails and a swimming lake. Open Apr.-Nov. Gates close 11pm. $14, no hook-ups.

Bear Creek RV Park and Campground, 81 S. Bear Creek Rd. (☎800-833-0798), features "luxury" camping with a pool, laundry facilities, groceries, and a game room. Take I-40 Exit 47, and look for the sign. Tent sites $20, with water and electricity $22; RV sites with hook-up $26-28.

FOOD AND ENTERTAINMENT

You'll find the greasy links of most fast-food chains on **Tunnel Rd.** and **Biltmore Ave.** The **Western North Carolina Farmers Market,** at the intersection of I-40 and Rte. 191, sells fresh produce and crafts. (☎253-1691. Open daily 8am-6pm.) At the **Laughing Seed Cafe,** 40 Wall St., behind Patton Ave, friendly servers vend veggie and vegan values. Su brunch draws a bustling crowd—and never disappoints. (☎252-3445. Salads $4 and sandwiches $4-8. Open M, W-Th 11:30am-9pm, F-Sa 11:30am-10pm, Su 10am-9pm.) **Beanstreets,** 3 Broadway St., brims with local sideburns and ill-fitting clothing. (☎255-8180. Open M-Tu 7:30am-6pm, W 7:30-10pm, Th-F 7:30am-midnight, Sa 7am-midnight, and Su 9am-4pm. Omelets and sandwiches $4.)

For a small town, Asheville really grooves. The downtown area, especially the southeast end around the intersection of Broadway and College St., offers music, munchies, and movies. Those in search of something a little more, well, European can find it at **Old Europe,** 18 Battery Park Ave., near Wall St., which doubles as a dessert shop and bar. Pastries are handmade by the Hungarian owners. (☎252-0001. Cookies $1, pastries $3; drinks $3-5.) **Tressa's,** 28 Broadway, hosts live jazz and blues most nights in a casual atmosphere. (☎254-7072. Open M-F 4pm-2am, Sa 7pm-2am. Cover $2-5.) Indie and artsy flicks play at the **Fine Arts Theater,** 36 Biltmore Ave. (☎232-1536; $6.50, matinees and seniors $5.) A popular bar, **Barley's Taproom,** 42 Biltmore Ave. (☎255-0504), hops with locals and $3 beers from 42 taps.

Summer shouldn't be anyone's season of discontent, not with free **Shakespeare in Montford Park.** (☎254-4540. June-Aug. F and Su 7:30pm at Hazel Robinson Ampitheater.) During the last weekend in July, put your feet on the street along with thousands of others at North Carolina's largest street fair, **Bele Chere Festival** (☎259-5800). Free weekly papers, *Mountain Express* and *Community Connections*, feature entertainment listings, as does *Take 5* in the F *Asheville Citizen-Times.*

SIGHTS

The ostentatious **Biltmore Estate** was built for George Vanderbilt in the 1890s under the supervision of architect Richard Morris Hunt and landscaper Frederick Law Olmstead (the man behind New York City's Central Park). Modeled on the chateaux of the Loire valley, the Biltmore is the largest private home in America. A tour can take all day; try to arrive early. Tours of the surrounding gardens and of the Biltmore winery (with generous wine tasting for those 21 and over) are included in the hefty admission price.

THE SOUTH

(1 North Pack Sq., 3 blocks north of I-40 Exit 50. ☎274-6333 or 800-543-2961. Open daily 9am-5pm. $32, ages 10-15 $24; Nov.-Dec. $2-3 more. Winery open M-Sa 11am-7pm, Su noon-7pm.) Free scenery blooms at the **Botanical Gardens** and the **North Carolina Arboretum.** *(Gardens: 151 Weaver Blvd., near Broadway. Take bus #2. ☎252-5190. Arboretum: Exit 2 on 191 S. ☎665-2492. Both open dawn-dusk. Gardens center open Mar.-Nov. daily 9:30-4pm.)*

Four museums will draw you into Pack Sq. at **Pack Pl.** The **Asheville Art Museum** displays 20th-century American paintings, while the **YMI Culture Center** focuses solely on African-American art. The kid-oriented **Health Adventure** lets you become one with your body, and the **Colburn Gem and Mineral Museum** showcases all that glitters. *(☎257-4500. All open Tu-Sa 10am-5pm; June-Oct. also Su 1-5pm. 1 museum $4, students, seniors, and ages 4-15 $3; all 4 museums $12/$9.)*

The interior of the **Thomas Wolfe Memorial,** between Woodfin and Walnut St., is closed due to fire, but tours around the exterior of the novelist's boyhood home are available. *(☎253-8304. Open Apr.-Oct. M-Sa 9am-5pm, Su 1-5pm; Nov.-Mar. Tu-Sa 10am-4pm, Su 1-4pm. Tours every hr. on the half-hr., with an multimedia program on the hr. $1, students 50¢.)* The scenic setting for *Last of the Mohicans* rises up almost ½ mi. in **Chimney Rock Park.** After driving to the base of the Chimney, take the 26-story elevator to the top, or walk up for a 75 mi. view. *(25 mi. southeast of Asheville on Rte. 74A. ☎625-9281 or 800-277-9611. Ticket office open daily 8:30am-5:30pm; in winter 8:30am-4:30pm. Park open 1½hr. after office closes. $11, ages 6-12 $5; in winter $7/$4.)*

NORTH CAROLINA COAST

Lined with "barrier islands" which shield inlanders from Atlantic squalls, the Carolina Coast has a history as stormy as the hurricanes that annually pummel its beaches. England's first attempt to colonize North America ended in 1590 with the peculiar disappearance of the Roanoke Island settlement. Later in its history, the coast earned a name as "The Graveyard of the Atlantic"—over 600 ships have foundered on the Outer Banks' southern shores. The same wind that sank ships lifted the world's first powered flight in 1903, thanks to some assistance from the Wright brothers, and now forms the basis of much of the area's recreational activity: hanggliding, paragliding, windsurfing, and good ol' kite-flying.

OUTER BANKS   ☎252

The Outer Banks descend from developed beach towns into heavenly wilderness. The three contiguous towns of Kitty Hawk, Kill Devil Hills, and Nags Head are located on the northern half of Bodie Island, which has come to seem like many other well-touristed beach areas on the East Coast. Crowds become less overpowering south on Rte. 12; Ocracoke Island, despite its growing popularity with visitors, still retains the feel of a small community.

▓ ORIENTATION

The Outer Banks are comprised of four narrow islands strung along half the length of the North Carolina coast. Three of them, Bodie, Hatteras, and Ocracoke, are connected by a single road—Rte. 12—that runs along the Atlantic. **Bodie Island,** the northernmost and joined to the mainland by U.S. 158, is most travelers' point of entry. For much of Bodie Island, Rte. 12 (known as the Beach Road) and U.S. 158 (called the Bypass) run parallel until the north edge of the **Cape Hatteras National Seashore.** After that, Rte. 12 continues south through the park to the great sandy elbow that is **Hatteras Island,** connected via bridge to Bodie. **Ocracoke Island,** the southernmost island, is linked by ferry to Hatteras Island and to towns on the mainland. Both Hatteras and Ocracoke are almost entirely park land. **Roanoke Island,** the only one of the four not on the Atlantic coast, lies between Bodie and the mainland on U.S. 64 and includes the town of **Manteo.** Directions to locations on Bodie Island are usually given in terms of distances in mi. from the Wright Memorial Bridge. There is **no public transit** on the Outer Banks. The flat terrain makes hiking and biking pleasant, but ferocious traffic calls for extra caution and extra travel time.

🛈 PRACTICAL INFORMATION

Ferries: Toll ferries run to Ocracoke (☎800-345-1665) from Cedar Island (☎800-856-0343; 2¼hr., 4-9 per day), east of New Bern on Rte. 12, off U.S. 70, and from Swan Quarter (☎800-773-1094; 2½hr., 6 per day), on the north side of Pamlico on U.S. 264. $1, $10 per car (reserve ahead), $2 per cyclist. **Free ferries** cross Hatteras Inlet between Hatteras and Ocracoke (40min., daily 5am-midnight). Call ☎800-293-3779 for all ferry times.

Taxis: Beach Cab, ☎441-2500, for Bodie Island and Manteo.

Bike Rental: Pony Island Motel (☎928-4411), on Ocracoke Island. $2 per hr., $10 per day. Open daily 8am-10pm.

Visitor Info: Dare County Tourist Bureau, 704 S. Hwy. 64 (☎473-2138 or 800-446-6262), in Manteo; info for all the islands. Open M-F 8:30am-6pm, Sa-Su noon-4pm by phone only. **Cape Hatteras National Seashore Information Centers: Whalebone Junction** (☎441-6644), Rte. 12 at the northern entrance to the park. Open May-Nov. 9am-5pm. **Bodie Island** (☎441-5711), Rte. 12 at Bodie Island Lighthouse, and **Ocracoke Island** (☎928-4531), next to the ferry terminal at the south end of the island, are both open daily June-Aug. 8:30am-6pm; Sept.-May 9am-5pm. **Hatteras Island** (☎995-4474), Rte. 12 at the Cape Hatteras Lighthouse. Open daily 9am-6pm.

Post Office: 3841 N. Croatan Hwy. Kitty Hawk (☎261-2211), Mi. 4 on the 158 Bypass. Open M-F 9am-4:30pm, Sa 10am-noon. **ZIP code:** 27949. **Area code:** 252.

🏠🍴 ACCOMMODATIONS AND FOOD

Most motels line **Rte. 12** on crowded Bodie Island. For more privacy, go further south; **Ocracoke** is the most secluded. On all three islands, rooming rates are highest from late May to early Sept. Reservations are needed 7 to 10 days ahead for weeknights and up to a month in advance for weekends. Long tent spikes (for the loose dirt), tents with fine screens (to keep out biting "no-see-ums"), and strong insect repellent are all recommended. Sleeping on the beach may result in fines.

BODIE ISLAND. Outer Banks International Hostel (HI-AYH), 1004 Kitty Hawk Rd. From Rte. 158, turn south onto The Woods Rd. and then right onto Kitty Hawk Rd. With 40 beds, two kitchens, A/C, heat, volleyball, and shuffleboard, this clean and friendly hostel is the best deal in the northern islands. (☎261-2294. Members $15, non-members $18; private rooms for one person $30/$35; for 2 $40/$50. Camping spots on the grounds $12, $6 per additional person; tent rental $6.) **Nettlewood Motel,** Mi. 7, Beach Rd., has bright cozy rooms with private beach access. (☎441-5039. TV, A/C, heat, refrigerators, pool. Doubles are equipped with a kitchenette. Singles $50; doubles $70; May 28-June 17 $40/$48; Sept. 25th-May 25th $33/$38.)

Caribbean-influenced seafood and grill items in a casual setting are the truth at **Tortuga's Lie,** Mi. 11 Beach Rd. Jamaican jerk chicken with beans and rice costs $6, to-die-for chocolate pecan pie $3. (☎441-7299. Open Su-Th 11:30am-midnight, F-Sa 11:30am-1am. W Sushi night. No reservations—expect to wait.) The **Flying Fish Cafe,** Mi. 10 Bypass 158, serves Mediterreanean food complemented by white stucco walls and maps of Italy. Early bird specials before 6pm have all entrees under $10. (☎441-6894. Open M-F 11:30am-4pm and 5-10pm, Sa-Su 5-10pm.)

THE SOUTH

> **"DAMNED IF THEY AIN'T FLEW!"** So exclaimed one eyewitness to humankind's first powered flight. On Dec. 17, 1903, two bicycle repairmen from Dayton, Ohio, launched the world's first true airplane in 27 mph headwinds from an obscure location on the North Carolina coast called Kill Devil Hills. Orville Wright, with his brother Wilbur watching anxiously from the ground, held on with his right hand and steered the 605 lb. Flyer with his left. 120 ft. and 12 sec. later, the Wright brothers had flown their craft into history—and then oblivion: the original Flyer was destroyed on the ground by a strong gust of wind.

MANTEO. Are you going to **Scarborough Inn,** romantically tucked away between the 7-11 and BP gas station on U.S. 64? Four-poster canopy beds, flowered linen, and wrap-around porches await. (☎473-3979. A/C, heat, fridges, microwaves, continental breakfast, and free bicycle use. Singles or doubles $60-65; off-season rates drop as low as $35-40.)

If romance and the 7-11 seem like an odd pairing, try bratwurst on the beach at **The Weeping Radish,** across the street from the Inn. The Radish, America's oldest restaurant/brewery, offers authentic German food and beer brewed according to the 1516 *Reinheitsgebot,* or Purity Law (0.5L $3.50). Complete with kitschy mini-theme park. (☎473-1157. Microbrewery tours daily 1 and 4pm. Open daily 11:30am-9pm; bar open until 10pm.)

HATTERAS AND OCRACOKE. ⬛**Ocracoke Island Wayfarer Hostel,** 125 Lighthouse Rd., can be your home away from home on Ocracoke Island—assuming, of course, that your home is comfortable, equipped with handmade bunk beds, and almost fanatically clean. Coming from the north, take a left off Rte. 12 at the Island Inn; the hostel will be on your left. (☎928-3411. Office hours 9-11am and 4-8pm. Free bike use, A/C, kitchen, 2 porches. Dorms $19; private room $39.) Beautiful juniper paneling at the **Sand Dollar Motel,** off Rte. 12 in Ocracoke, lends rooms a beach-cabin feel. Turn right at the Pirate's Chest gift shop, right again at the Back Porch restaurant, and left at the Edwards Motel. (☎928-5571. Open Apr. to late Nov. Refrigerators, A/C, heat, pool, and continental breakfast. Queen bed $65, 2 double beds $75; off-season rates vary.)

The **Cat Ridge Deli,** in Styron's Store at the corner of Lighthouse and Creek Rd. in Ocracoke, offers Asian-influenced wraps for around $6. (☎928-3354. Open M-Sa 11am-7pm, Su 11am-5pm.) On Hatteras Island, the **Orange Blossom Bakery Cafe,** just south of the lighthouse on Rte. 12, serves excellent sandwiches on freshly baked bread. (☎995-4109. Open M-Sa 7am-11am and 11:30am-1:30pm.)

CAPE HATTERAS NATIONAL SEASHORE. Three oceanside campgrounds off Rte. 12 in the Cape Hatteras National Seashore are open late April to early Oct.: **Oregon Inlet,** on the southern tip of Bodie Island, **Frisco,** near the elbow of Hatteras Island, and **Ocracoke,** in the middle of Ocracoke Island. **Cape Point** (in Buxton), is open late May to early Sept. All four have restrooms, water, and grills. Ocracoke is closest to the ocean, with its campsites clustered within a Frisbee throw of the water. Frisco is graced with dunes and hillocks. Cape Point is just dull. Ocracoke sites ($15) can be reserved from mid-May to mid-Sept. by calling ☎800-365-2267. All other sites ($15) are rented on a first come, first served basis. Listings of open sites at all four campgrounds are posted daily at Whalebone Junction. Contact **Cape Hatteras National Seashore** (☎473-2111) for park concerns.

👁 🔼 SIGHTS AND ACTIVITIES

The **Wright Brothers National Memorial,** Mi. 8 on U.S. 158, marks the spot where Orville and Wilbur Wright took to the skies. (☎441-7430. Open summer daily 9am-6pm; winter 9am-5pm. Presentations every hr. from 10am until 1hr. before closing. $2 per person, $4 per car.) **Kitty Hawk Aero Tours** offers 30min. airplane tours of the area. (☎441-4460. $29-39 per person.)

Flying of a different sort goes on at the nearby **Jockey's Ridge State Park,** Mi. 12 on U.S. 158, where hang-gliding lessons can be had from **Kitty Hawk Kites.** (☎441-4124 or 877-359-8447. 3hr. lesson, including 5 flights, $55-75. 85 lbs. minimum.) Those uninterested in hang-gliding can imagine themselves on a camel and walk up the tallest sand dune on the east coast, with a view of both the Atlantic and Albemarle Sound. (Park: ☎441-7132. Open daily 8am-9pm; off-season hrs. vary. Free.)

Roanoke Island offers several attractions. Coming on U.S. 64 from Bodie Island, the first of these is **Roanoke Festival Park** (follow signs from the highway). The park, staffed largely by persons in 16th-century garb, is centered around its interactive, kid-friendly museum and the sailing ship Elizabeth II, a representation of a 16th-century English merchant ship. (☎475-1500. Park open daily 9am-7pm; ship 10am-

THE SOUTH

6pm. Hours vary off-season. $8, students $5. In summer, performers from the North Carolina School for the Arts can be seen for free at the Park's outside pavilion.) The **Fort Raleigh National Historic Site,** off U.S. 64, offers several attractions. The **Lost Colony,** the longest-running outdoor drama in the US, has been performed here since 1937 and commemorates the first English colony in America, which mysteriously disappeared in 1590. (☎473-3414 or 800-488-5012. Shows June-Aug. M-Sa 8:30pm. $16, seniors $15, under 12 $8.) In the **Elizabethan Gardens,** antique statues and fountains punctuate a beautiful display of flowers, herbs, and trees. (☎473-3234. Open daily 9am-7pm; off-season hours vary. $5, seniors $4.50, ages 6-18 $1, under 6 free with adult.) The **North Carolina Aquarium** is 1 mi. west of U.S. 64 on Airport Rd., 3 mi. north of Manteo. Special exhibits change monthly; check out the huge brochure at the visitors center. (☎473-3493. Open daily 9am-7pm; off-season 9am-5pm. $4, seniors and military $3, ages 6-17 $2.) A pass for the aquarium, gardens, and Festival Park can be purchased at any of the three locations for $13 (adult) or $6 (under 12); add a Lost Colony ticket and pay $27/$14.

SCENIC DRIVE: CAPE HATTERAS NATIONAL SEASHORE

The **Cape Hatteras National Seashore,** for all of its 70 mi. length, is actually two shores: one that faces out to the Atlantic Ocean and the other that looks across the Pamlico Sound to North Carolina's mainland. The park's main appeal is this unique landscape, dotted with dunes, stunted trees and occasional stretches of marshland. Driving south from Hatteras to Ocracoke, the water stretches out to the horizon on either side; the park offers magnificent, largely empty beaches on both coasts.

Rte. 12 is the only means of ground transport in the park, running from the Whalebone Junction information station at the northern entrance of the park to the town of Ocracoke, except for a 40 min. stretch from Hatteras to Ocracoke which is covered by a free ferry. For its entire length, Rte. 12 is a paved two-lane road. Total transport time from Whalebone to Ocracoke is about 2½hr.

All of the major attractions of the park are accessible and clearly marked from Rte. 12. The chief of these are the Outer Banks' three **lighthouses** on Bodie, Hatteras, and Ocracoke islands. The tallest of these—and the tallest lighthouse in North America—is the spirally-striped Cape Hatteras lighthouse, built in 1870. The lighthouse is open for climbing (289 steps) 10am-4pm during the summer; for a schedule of the various daily programs run at the visitors centers located at each lighthouse, pick up a copy of the free paper *In The Park*. Another set of attractions along Rte. 12 serves to remind visitors that lighthouses have a value apart from the picturesque: various **shipwrecks** are visible from spots on the shore. Perhaps the most spectacular of these is the schooner *Laura A. Barnes*, which can be seen from Coquina Beach on Bodie Island.

The other attraction of the seashore is its rich wildlife, on display at the **Pea Island National Wildlife Refuge,** on the northern tip of Hatteras Island. Adjoining the **visitors center** is the marsh-country **Charles Kuralt Nature Trail,** which affords visitors a chance at glimpsing grackles, pelicans, and the Carolina salt marsh snake. (Visitors center usually open daily 9am-4pm in summer; weekends-only in the off-season. Beaches in the Refuge are open only in daylight and are often closed to preserve animal habitats.)

THE ROCK OF AGES IT ISN'T Lighthouses, built to ward ships from dangerous stretches of coasts, are generally taken as cultural symbols of safety and stability against the changing currents around them—as fixed points in a sea of change. They are also extremely large and very heavy. Given these two generalizations, it may come as a surprise that all 203 feet of the Cape Hatteras lighthouse were moved more then half a mile in the summer of 1999. The long-planned move, necessary to save the lighthouse from the ravages of erosion, was accomplished in only 23 days and took a position in the public eye unparalleled for an engineering project since the Apollo missions of the 60s. Having already weathered two hurricanes in its new position, the lighthouse seems stable as ever; of course, by current estimates they'll have to do it all over again in another 100 years.

THE SOUTH

SOUTH CAROLINA

South Carolina's pride in the Palmetto State may seem extreme. Inspired by the state flag, the palmetto tree logo dots hats, bottles and bumper stickers across the landscape. To some, pride lies in the unrivaled beaches of the Grand Strand; others revel in the stately elegance of Charleston. Columbia offers an impressive art and cultural experience without the smog and traffic which plague the New South metropoli of neighboring states. Tamed for tourists and merchandising, the Confederate legacy of the first state to secede from the Union is groomed as a cash cow. In recent years, South Carolina has been in the national news for its refusal to remove the controversial Confederate flag from the statehouse. In July 2000, state legislators approved moving the flag from the Statehouse dome to the lawn. However, the NAACP plans to boycott the state until it is removed entirely.

▣ PRACTICAL INFORMATION

Capital: Columbia.

Visitor Info: Dept. of Parks, Recreation, and Tourism, Edgar A. Brown Bldg., 1205 Pendleton St., #106, Columbia 29021 (☎803-734-1700; www.travelsc.com). **US Forest Service,** 4931 Broad River Rd., Columbia 29210 (☎803-561-4000).

Postal Abbreviation: SC. **Sales Tax:** 5%, 6% in Charleston.

CHARLESTON   ☎843

Built on rice and cotton, Charleston's antebellum plantation system yielded vast riches now seen in its numerous museums, historic homes, and ornate architecture. An accumulated cultural capital of 300 years flows like the long, distinctive drawl of the natives. Several of the south's most renowned plantations dot the city, while two venerable institutions, the College of Charleston and the Citadel, add a youthful eccentricity. With horse-drawn carriages, cobblestone streets, antebellum homes, beautiful beaches, and the best restaurants in the Southeast, it's no wonder that Charleston often heads the list of the nation's top destinations.

▮ GETTING THERE AND AROUND

Trains: Amtrak, 4565 Gaynor Ave. (☎744-8264), 8 mi. west of downtown. To: Richmond (6hr., 2 per day, $58-115); Savannah (1¾hr., 2 per day, $17-23); and Washington, D.C. (9½hr., 2 per day, $74-148). Open daily 6am-10pm.

Buses: Greyhound, 3610 Dorchester Rd. (☎747-5341), in N. Charleston. *Avoid this area at night.* To: Myrtle Beach (2½hr., 1 per day, $22), Savannah (2¾hr., 2 per day, $22-24) and Charlotte (4½hr., 2 per day, $38-40). Charleston Transit "Dorchester/Waylyn" bus goes to town from station area. Return on "Navy Yard: 5 Mile Dorchester Rd." bus.

Public Transit: CARTA, 36 John St. (☎724-7420). Fare 75¢, seniors and disabled 25¢, day pass $2, 3-day $5. CARTA's **Downtown Area Shuttle (DASH)** is made up of 5 trolley routes that circle downtown daily 8am-11pm. Visitors center has free schedules.

Bike Rental: The Bicycle Shoppe, 280 Meeting St. (☎722-8168), between George and Society St. $4 per hr., $15 per day. Open M-Th 9am-8pm, F-Su 9-7pm.

Taxis: Yellow Cab, ☎577-6565.

◤▮ ORIENTATION AND PRACTICAL INFORMATION

Old Charleston lies at the southernmost point of the mile-wide peninsula below **Calhoun St.** The major north-south routes through the city are **Meeting, King,** and **East Bay St.** The area north of the visitors center is mostly run-down and uninviting. **Savannah Hwy./U.S. 17** cuts across the peninsula going south to Savannah and north across two towering bridges to Mt. Pleasant and on to Myrtle Beach. There are plenty of metered parking spaces; there are also plenty of police officers giving tickets. Free unmetered parking is available on E. Bay St., near Calhoun.

Hotlines: **Crisis Line**, ☎ 744-4357 or 800-922-2283; general counseling. **People Against Rape**, ☎ 722-7273. Both operate 24hr.

Visitor Info: Charleston Visitors Center, 375 Meeting St. (☎ 853-8000 or 800-868-8118; www.charleston.com), across from Charleston Museum. Open daily 8:30am-5:30pm.

Post Office: 83 Broad St. (☎ 577-0690). Open M-F 9am-5pm, Sa 10am-noon. Also houses a cute little post museum. **ZIP code:** 29402. **Area code:** 843.

▌ ACCOMMODATIONS

Motel rooms in historic downtown Charleston are expensive. Cheap motels are a few miles out of the city, around Exits 209-11 on I-26 W in N. Charleston, or across the Ashley River on U.S. 17 S in Mt. Pleasant—not practical for those without cars.

Bed, No Breakfast, 16 Halsey St. (☎ 723-4450). The only budget option within walking distance of downtown. Two guest rooms available in this historical house. $45-70.

Masters Inn Economy, 6100 Rivers Ave. (☎ 744-3530 or 800-633-3434), at I-26 Exit 211B, 11 mi. from downtown. Spacious rooms with A/C and cable TV. Pool, free local calls, and laundry. Singles $35; doubles $43; Sa-Su $43/$49. There is also **Knight's Inn** (☎ 744-4900 or 800-845-1927) across the way with similar prices and another more expensive Master's Inn 3 mi. from downtown in Mt. Pleasant (☎ 884-2814).

Motel 6, 2058 Savannah Hwy. (☎ 556-5144), 4 mi. south of town. Clean and pleasant, but far from downtown and often full. Rooms $40, $3 per additional person.

Campground at James Island County Park (☎ 795-9884 or 800-743-7275). Take U.S. 17 S to Rte. 171 and follow the signs. Spacious but unwooded sites. The spectacular park is made up of 16 acres of lakes, bicycle and walking trails, and a small water park. Bike and boat rental. Tent sites $12; full hook-up $24.

▌ FOOD

Charleston has some of the best food in the country. While most restaurants cater to big-spending tourists, there are plenty of budget options to sample the southern cooking, barbecue, and fresh seafood that has made the low country famous.

Hyman's Seafood Company, 215 Meeting St. (☎ 723-6000). Since 1890, this casual restaurant has offered 15-25 different kinds of fresh fish daily ($7-12), served in any one of 8 styles. Expect long waits. Open daily 11am-11pm.

Southend Brewery, 161 E. Bay St. (☎ 853-4677). Outstanding ribs ($12), eclectic pizzas ($8-9), and burgers ($7-9) served in a 3-story brewhouse. Six home brewed beers. Food served Su-Th 11:30am-4pm and 5-10pm, F-Sa 11:30am-4pm and 5-11pm.

Jestine's Kitchen, 251 Meeting St. (☎ 722-7224). If your southern country grandma had a restaurant, this would be it. Excellent crispy fried chicken with 2 fresh veggies $8. Open Su and Tu-Th 11am-9pm, F-Sa 11am-10pm.

Andolini's Pizza, 82 Wentworth St. (☎ 722-7437), at King St. Hands down the best pizza in town 5 years running. Everything made from scratch. Large thin crust cheese pie $11. Calzones $5 and up. Open M-Th 11:30am-11pm, F-Sa 11:30-midnight, Su noon-10pm

Sticky Fingers, 235 Meeting St., (☎ 853-7427). Annually voted the best barbecue in town. Pulled pork sandwich $6. Ribs $11-15. Open daily 11am-11pm.

▌ SIGHTS

Charleston's ancient homes, historical monuments, churches, galleries, and gardens can be seen by foot, car, bus, boat, trolley, or horse-drawn carriage. The open-air **City Market,** downtown at Meeting St., has a deal on everything from porcelain sea lions to handwoven sweetgrass baskets. *(Open daily 9:30am-sunset.)*

PLANTATIONS AND GARDENS. The 300-year-old **Magnolia Plantation and Magnolia Gardens** is by far the most majestic of Charleston's plantations. Visitors can enjoy the Drayton family's absurd wealth by exploring their 50 acres of gorgeous gardens with 900 varieties of camelia and 250 varieties of azalea. Other attractions include a hedge maze, bike or canoe rental, and a swamp and bird sanctu-

THE SOUTH

ary. *(On Rte. 61 10 mi. out of town off U.S. 17. ☎ 571-1266. Open daily 8am-5:30pm. $10, teens $8, ages 6-12 $5. House $16/$14/$11; nature trail $15/$12/$8; swamp garden $5, ages 6-12 $3; canoes or bikes $3 per 3hr.)* A bit farther down the road is **Middleton Place,** a more manicured (and expensive) plantation with working stables, gardens, and house. *(On Rte. 61, 14 mi. northwest of downtown. ☎ 556-6020. Open Tu-Su 9am-5pm. $15, seniors $14, ages 6-12 $8, house museum $8.)* Even farther out, but well worth the trip, is **Cypress Gardens,** where you can paddle your own boat out onto the eerie swamps filled with gators. *(3030 Cypress Gardens Rd. ☎ 553-0515. Open daily Feb.-Dec. 9am-5pm.)*

CHARLESTON MUSEUM AND HISTORIC HOMES. The **Charleston Museum,** across the street from the visitors center, may be the nation's oldest museum, but it's clear time didn't bring quality. *(360 Meeting St. ☎ 722-2996. Open M-Sa 9am-5pm, Su 1pm-5pm. $7, children $4.)* Although a combo ticket is available for the museum and two historic homes located nearby (the 18th-century **Heyward-Washington House** and **Joseph Manigault House**), just pick one house and save your money. *(Heyward-Washington House: 87 Church St. ☎ 722-0354. Joseph Manigault House: 350 Meeting St. ☎ 723-2926. Both homes open M-Sa 10am-5pm, Su 1-5pm. Museum and 2 homes $18. One house $7, ages 3-12 $4.)* The **Nathaniel Russell House** and **Edmondston-Alston House** are similar, more unrefined 19th-century homes. *(Nathaniel Russell: 51 Meeting St. ☎ 723-1623. Open M-Sa 10am-5pm, Su 2-5pm. $7, under 6 free. Edmondston-Alston: 21 E. Battery. ☎ 722-7171. Open Su-M 1:30-4:30pm, Tu-Sa 10am-4:30pm. $8.)*

PATRIOT'S POINT AND FORT SUMTER. Climb aboard four Naval ships, including a submarine and the giant aircraft carrier *Yorktown*, in **Patriot's Point Naval and Maritime Museum,** the world's largest Naval museum. *(Across the Cooper River in Mt. Pleasant. ☎ 884-2727. Open daily Apr.-Sept. 9am-6pm; Oct.-Mar. 9am-5pm. $11, seniors $10, ages 6-11 $5.50.)* **Fort Sumter Tours** offers boat excursions to the National Historic Site from the City Marina off Lockwood Blvd. or Patriots Point. *(☎ 722-1691. 2¼hr.; 1-3 per day from each location; $9.50, ages 6-11 $4.75.)*

BEACHES. Over the James Island Bridge and U.S. 171, about 20 mi. southeast of Charleston, **Folly Beach** is popular with local students. **Isle of Palms** is more wide open and extends for miles down toward the less-crowded **Sullivan's Island.** To get there, cross the Cooper River Bridge, drive 10 mi. down Hwy 17 N. and turn right onto the Isle of Palms Connector. *(Folly Beach: ☎ 588-2426. Isle of Palms: ☎ 886-3862.)*

SOUTH CAROLINA AQUARIUM. This brand-new aquarium has quickly become Charleston's biggest attraction. Although a bit over-priced, exhibits showcasing aquatic life from the region's swamps, marshes, and oceans are well-executed and extremely interesting. *(At the end of Calhoun St. on the Cooper River, overlooking the harbor. ☎ 720-1990. Open daily July-Aug. 9am-7pm; Nov.-Feb. 10am-5pm; Mar.-June and Sept.-Oct. 9am-5pm. $14, ages 13-17 and seniors $12, ages 4-12 $7.)*

BULL ISLAND. To get away from human civilization, take a ferry to Bull Island, a 5000-acre island off the coast of Charleston. The boat is often greeted by dolphins swimming in some of the cleanest water on the planet, while the island is home to 278 different species of bird and 16 mi. of hiking trails. *(☎ 881-4582. 30min. ferries depart from Moore's Landing 5 mi. east of US 17 between Mt. Pleasant and Awendaw. Departs Mar.-Nov. Tu and F-Sa 9am and 12:30pm, Th 9am; returns Tu and Th-Sa noon and 4pm, Sa 3pm; Dec.-Feb. Sa 10am; returns 3pm. Round-trip $20, under 13 $10.)*

🎵 🎭 ENTERTAINMENT AND NIGHTLIFE

With nearby colleges and a constant tourist presence, Charleston's nightlife beats strong. Free copies of *Upwith* or *City Paper*, in stores and restaurants, list concerts and other events. Big name bands take center stage nightly at the **Music Farm,** 32 Ann St. (☎ 853-3276). **Club Tango,** 39 John St. (☎ 577-2822), and the adjacent **Cap'n Harry's Blue Marlin Bar** (☎ 577-2278) make the alley between John and Hutson St. the place to be when night falls. Club Tango is a more upscale dance club while Cap'n Harry's goes for a Key West theme with tropical drinks and reggae. For a more chill summertime setting, the outdoor patio at **Portside Cafe,** 462 King St., comes alive with nightly bands and an excellent blend of nouveau American and southern food. (☎ 722-0409. Open M-Th and Su 11:30am-10pm, F-Sa 11:30am-midnight.) Music, theater, dance, and opera fill the city late May and early June during **Spoleto Festival USA,** the nation's most comprehensive arts festival. (Tickets $10-75.)

DAYTRIP FROM CHARLESTON

BEAUFORT. Listen closely, and you will hear a musical language spoken in the coastal islands of southeastern South Carolina. During the slave trade, numerous African cultures merged with the European cultures of slave traders to produce **Gullah,** a unique blend of language, food, arts, and religion. After the Civil War, Gullah largely faded across the South, except in the geographically isolated South Carolina lowcountry. Bridges allow easy access to the area and exploration of this unique culture. St. Helena is considered the center of Gullah, largely due to the preservation efforts of the **Penn Center** (☎ 383-2432), about 1 mi. down Martin Luther King Jr. Dr. off U.S. 21, the first school for freed slaves in the south. King wrote his "I Have a Dream" speech on retreat at the center. The center preserves the area's unique culture and heritage in the **York W. Bailey Museum.** (☎ 838-2474. Open M-Sa 11am-4pm. $4, children $2.)

The best way to truly experience Gullah is on the **Gullah 'n' Geechie Tours,** led by community activist, historian, scholar, and all around expert Kitty Greene. More than a leisurely drive, Greene carefully conveys the Gullah culture by examining its language, religion, art, family, and food. Included is a trip to a "praise house," the 300-year-old religious center for local plantation slaves. (☎ 838-7516 or 838-3758. 2hr. tours leave from 847 Sea Island Parkway in St. Helena. M-F 9:45am, 1:45, and 4:30pm; Sa by arrangement. $17, children $12; reservations required.)

One of the Palmetto State's strangest sites is the **Kingdom of Oyotunji,** a Yoruba African village in Sheldon, 10 mi. north of Beaufort on Hwy. 17. The 30-year-old sanctuary for African priests is led by a self-proclaimed African king and his several wives. The heartfelt yet bizarre tour is worth every cent of its $5 charge; make an appointment beforehand to speak with the king. (☎ 846-2210. Open 10am-dusk.)

Stately Beaufort hosts the lively **Gullah Festival** every May and chows at the packed **Shrimp Festival** every Oct. Beaufort is 60 mi. from both Savannah and Charleston, on Rte. 21, 15 mi. south of I-95 Exit 33. From the **Greater Beaufort Visitors Center,** 1106 Carteret St., travel 5 mi. south on Rte. 210 to St. Helena. (☎ 986-5400. Open daily 9am-5:30pm.) **Greyhound,** 1307 Boundary Rd. (☎ 524-4646), runs to Savannah (1hr., 4 per day, $11.50-12.50). **Area code:** 843

COLUMBIA ☎ 803

Soon after the Revolutionary War, upstate resentment forced Charleston aristocrats to relocate the capital to the middle of the state, on Colonel Thomas Taylor's plantation along the Congaree River. As planned, Columbia quickly rose to prominence, only to be leveled by Sherman's marching torch. Yet Columbia has moved beyond its Civil War shadow with a thriving art community, historic neighborhoods, and an upscale entertainment district near the Congaree River. Town and gown prosper together, as the University of South Carolina (USC) adds its substantial cultural resources to the city.

> **A PIG PRIMER** Southerners have always found unique ways to prepare all parts of the pig. Chitlins, a tasty (but smelly) fall treat, are pig intestines cleaned, boiled, fried, and then seasoned. Hogmau is boiled and seasoned pig stomach. Throughout the South, pickled pig's feet soak in pool hall countertop jars. And those in a hurry can always grab a pig's ear sandwich.

THE SOUTH

▟▞ ORIENTATION AND PRACTICAL INFORMATION. The city is laid out in a square, with borders Huger St. (running north-south), Harden St. (north-south), Blossom St. (east-west), and Calhoun St. (east-west). **Assembly St.** is the main drag, running north-south through the heart of the city. **Gervais St.** is its east-west equivalent. The Congaree River marks the city's western edge.

Columbia Metropolitan Airport, 3000 Aviation Way (☎822-5000), is in West Columbia; a taxi to downtown costs about $15-17. **Amtrak,** 850 Pulaski St. (☎252-8246), sends one train per day to Miami (14hr., $62); Washington, D.C. (10hr., $65); and Savannah (2½hr., $23). The station is open daily 10am-5:30pm and 11pm-6:45am. **Greyhound,** 2015 Gervais St. (☎256-6465), at Harden, sends buses to Charlotte (1¾hr., 4 per day, $65); Atlanta (4-6hr., 8 per day, $46.50); and Charleston (2¼hr., 3 per day, $21.50). **South Carolina Electric and Gas (SCE&G)** runs public buses through Columbia from 5:30am to midnight. Most main routes depart from pick-up/transfer depots at Sumter St. and Laurel St. and at Assembly St. and Taylor St. (☎217-9019. Call for schedules. Fare 75¢, seniors and disabled 25¢, under 6 free. Free transfers.) **Taxis: Gamecock Cab,** ☎796-7700. **Hotlines: Crisis Intervention,** ☎790-4357, and **Rape Crisis,** ☎771-7273; both 24 hours. **Visitor info: Columbia Metropolitan Convention and Visitors Bureau,** 1012 Gervais St., has maps and info. (☎254-0479. Open M-F 9am-5pm, Sa 10am-4pm; winter hrs. vary.) For info on USC, try the **University of South Carolina Visitors Center,** 937 Assembly St. (☎777-0169 or 800-922-9755. Open M-F 8:30am-5pm, Sa 9:30am-2pm. Free visitor parking pass.) **Post office:** 1601 Assembly St. (☎733-4643; open M-F 7:30am-6pm). **ZIP code:** 29202. **Area code:** 803.

▛ ACCOMMODATIONS. Generally, the cheapest digs lie furthest from the city center; one exception is the **Masters Economy Inn,** 613 Knox Abbott Dr. Take Blossom St. across the Congaree River, where it becomes Knox Abbott Dr. The inn offers free local calls and morning coffee, a pool, and cable TV. (☎796-4300. Singles $37-41; doubles $39-45.) Inexpensive motels also line the three interstates (I-26, I-77 and I-20) that circle the city. Off I-26 near the airport at 1987 Airport Blvd., **Knights Inn** may not be a castle, but it has a great deal of amenities for a low price. All rooms have refrigerators, microwaves, cable TV, A/C, free local calls, and pool access. (☎794-0222. Singles and doubles Su-Th $35, F-Sa $39; 10% senior discount.) The **Sesquicentennial State Park** offers 1400 acres, a lake for swimming and fishing, a nature center, hiking and biking trails, and 87 wooded sites with electricity and water. Public transportation does not serve the park; take I-20 to the Two Notch Rd./U.S. 1, Exit 17, and head northeast for 3 mi. (☎788-2706. Gate open daily Apr.-Oct. 7am-9pm; Nov.-Mar. 8am-6pm. Campsites $15. Entrance $1.50 per person.)

☖ FOOD. It's little wonder that **Maurice's Piggie Park,** 800 Elmwood Ave. (☎256-4377) and 1600 Charleston Hwy. (☎796-0220) owns the world record for "Most BBQ sold in one day." Maurice's cash "pig" is his exquisite, mustard-based sauce that covers the Big Joe pork BBQ sandwich ($4). **Groucho's,** 611 Harden St., has received high marx from the collegiate crowd for 59 years, demonstrating the power of Groucho's own "45" sauce over deli-like $6 "dipper" sandwiches. (☎799-5708. Open M-Sa 11am-4pm, Su noon-4pm; June-Aug. M-Sa 11am-4pm.) Palmetto State farmers offer every kind of produce you could imagine within the confines of South Carolina at the **Columbia State Farmers Market,** 1001 Bluff Rd., across from the football stadium. (☎737-4664. Open M-Sa 6am-9pm, Su 1-9pm.) **Rosewood Market,** 2803 Rosewood Dr., specializes in healthy adaptations of sinful foods, including a $2.25 order of BBQ tofu and a bizarrely pleasing $3 currant tofu cheesecake. (☎765-1083. Deli open M-Sa 11:30am-2:30pm and 5-8pm.)

▣ SIGHTS. Over 2000 animals roam in recreated natural habitats at **Riverbanks Zoo and Garden,** which has been ranked as one of the top ten zoos in the country. In addition to an undersea fish and reptile kingdom, desert, and interactive southern farm, the bird pavilion is among their newest attractions. *(On I-126 at Greystone Blvd., northwest of downtown. ☎779-8717. Open M-F 9am-4pm, Sa-Su 9am-5pm; off-season daily 9am-4pm. $6.25, students $5, seniors $4.75, ages 3-12 $3.75.)*

THE SECRET OF LIFE Unknown to the rest of the world, mankind's secrets to wisdom and prosperity reside in **Elberton, GA** ("the granite capital of the world"), 150 mi. from Columbia. In 1980 a "group of Americans who seek the age of reason" sent a large check to a local mining firm with engraving instructions. On a hilltop 8 mi. out of town, several giant slabs of granite answer humanity's most burning questions. In English, Russian, Chinese, Hebrew, Swahili and Greek, the guidestones advise humanity to reproduce wisely, unite under a new living language, keep the population under 500 million, and resolve disputes in a world court. To prevent confusion, "Let these be guidestones" is announced in Babylonian Cuniform, Classical Greek, Sanskrit and Egyptian Hieroglyphics at the top of the tablets.

Bronze stars mark the impact of Sherman's cannonballs on the **Statehouse.** Lawmakers spent $70 million to restore Columbia's dominant structure to its turn-of-the-century glory. *(Between Sumter St., Assembly St., and Gervais St. ☎734-2430. Hourly tours July-Oct. M-F 9:30am-3:30pm, Sa 10:30am-3:30pm, Su 1:30-3:30pm; Nov.-June 12 tours per day. Free.)* Across Sumter St. from the Statehouse lies the verdant heart and original campus of USC, aptly named the **Horseshoe.** The **South Carolina Confederate Relic Room and Museum** houses an impressive and well-maintained collection of Civil War artifacts. *(920 Sumter St. ☎898-8095. Open M-F 8:30am-5pm; first and third Sa 10am-5pm. Free.)* At the head of the green, sitting at the intersection of Bull and Pendleton St., **McKissick Museum** explores the folklife of South Carolina and the southeast through music, science, art, and history. *(☎777-7251. Open M-F 9am-4pm, Sa-Su 1-5pm. Free.)*

Two 19th-century mansions, the **Robert Mills Historic House and Park** and the **Hampton-Preston Mansion,** compete in elegance as twin survivors of Sherman's Civil War rampage. Both have been lovingly restored with period fineries. *(1616 Blanding St., 3 blocks east of Sumter St. ☎252-1770. Hourly tours Tu-Sa 10:15am-3:15pm, Su 1:15-4:15pm. Tours $4, students $2.50, under 5 free. Buy tickets at Mills House Museum Shop.)*

🗹 **NIGHTLIFE.** Columbia's nightlife centers around the collegiate **Five Points District** (junction of Harden St. and Devine St.) and the blossoming, slightly more mature **Vista area** (Gervais St. before the Congaree River). Gamecocks (USC students) drink away at the **Knock Knock Club,** 634 Harden St. (☎799-1015; open M-F 5pm-5am, Sa-Su 7pm-2am), and **Jungle Jim's,** 724 Harden St. (☎256-1390; open M-F 5pm-6am, Sa-Su until 2am). In the Vista, the neon psychedelic decor of **Art Bar,** 1211 Park St., draws a diverse crowd (☎929-0198; open M-F 8pm-late, Sa-Su 8pm-2am). The weekly publication *Free Times* gives details on Columbia's club and nightlife scene. *In Unison* is a weekly paper listing gay-friendly nightspots.

MYRTLE BEACH AND THE GRAND STRAND

Each summer, millions of Harley-riding, RV-driving southerners make Myrtle Beach the second most popular summer tourist destination in the country. During spring break and in early June, Myrtle Beach is jam-packed with sunburned students, while the rest of the year, families, golfers, shoppers, and everyone else partakes in the fun tackiness of it all. The pace slows significantly on the rest of the 60 mi. Grand Strand. South of Myrtle Beach, Murrell's Inlet, a quaint port stocked with good seafood, and Pawley's Island are both dominated by private homes. Georgetown, once a critical Southern port city, showcases its history with white-pillared homes on 18th-century-style rice and indigo plantations.

⚡🛈 ORIENTATION AND PRACTICAL INFORMATION

Most attractions are on **Hwy. 17/Kings Hwy.,** which splits into a Business Route and Bypass, 4mi. south of Myrtle Beach. **Ocean Blvd.** runs right along the ocean and has a never-ending string of cheap motels. Avenue numbers repeat themselves after reaching 1st Ave. in the middle of town, so note whether the Ave. is "north" or "south." Also, take care not to confuse north **Myrtle Beach** with the town **North Myrtle Beach,** which has an almost identical street layout. **Rte. 501** runs west toward Conway, **I-95,** and, most importantly, the factory outlet stores. Unless otherwise stated, addresses on the Grand Strand are for Myrtle Beach.

Buses: Greyhound, 511 7th Ave. N (☎ 448-2471). To Charleston (2½hr., 1 per day, $22). Open M-F 7am-6:45pm, Sa-Su 10am-6:45pm.

Public Transit: Coastal Rapid Public Transit (CRPTA) (☎ 248-7277) provides minimal busing. Local fare $1. Runs M-Sa 7:30am-7:30pm.

Bike Rental: The Bike Shoppe, 711 Broadway (☎ 448-5335), at Main St. Cruisers $5 per half-day, $10 per day; mountain bikes $7/$15. Open M-F 8am-6pm, Sa 9am-5pm.

Visitor Info: Myrtle Beach Chamber of Commerce, 1200 N. Oak St. (☎ 626-7444 or 800-356-3015), parallel to Kings Hwy., at 12th N. Open M-F 8:30am-5pm, Sa-Su 9am-5pm.

Mini Golf: Everywhere.

Post Office: 505 N. Kings Hwy. (☎ 626-9533), at 5th. Open M-F 8:30am-5pm, Sa 9am-1pm. **ZIP code:** 29577. **Area code:** 843.

▌ ACCOMMODATIONS

There are hundreds of motels lining Ocean Blvd., and they're all pretty much the same. Cheaper options are across the street from the beach and thus have even numbered addresses. Cheap motels also line Hwy. 17. Prices plunge Oct. through Mar.—as low as $20-30 a night for one of the luxurious hotels right on the beach. If you'll be in town three to five days, call the free **Myrtle Beach Hospitality Reservation Service,** 1551 21st Ave. N., #20. (☎ 626-9970 or 800-626-7477. Open M-F 8:30am-5pm.)

Sea Banks Motor Inn, 2200 S. Ocean Blvd. (☎ 448-2434 or 800-523-0603), across the street from the ocean. Laundry, pool, beach access, large windows, and cable TV. Singles $45; doubles $68; mid-Sept. to mid-Mar. $20-26/$26-31.

Hurl Rock Motel, 2010 S. Ocean Blvd. (☎ 626-3531). The name may be foolish, but the big, clean rooms are stone-free. Pool and hot tub. Singles $45; doubles $55-58.

David's Landing, 2708 S. Ocean Blvd. (☎ 800-561-3504). Large, modern 2-room apartments perfect for families. $65-75; May 21 to June 10 and Aug. 11 to Sept. 2 $45-50.

Huntington Beach State Park Campground (☎ 237-4440), 3 mi. south of Murrell's Inlet on U.S. 17. A diverse environment with lagoons, salt marshes, and a beautiful beach. Gators come within yards of the campground. Office open daily 7am-9pm. 190 sites. Tent sites Apr.-Oct. $12; Nov.-Mar. $9.50. Full hook-up $26/$21. Day use $4.

Myrtle Beach State Park Campground (☎ 238-5325), 3 mi. south of town off U.S. 17. More crowded and less attractive than Huntington. 350 sites with a cool beach, fishing pier, a pool, and a nature trail. Water and electricity. Showers and bathrooms are nearby. Office open daily 8am-5pm. Sites $17.60. Cabins for 4-8 $39-67. Day use $2.

◖ ALL YOU CAN EAT

Over 1800 restaurants, serving anything you can imagine, can be found on the Grand Strand. Massive, family-style, all-you-can-eat joints await at every traffic light. Seafood is best on **Murrell's Inlet,** while **Hwy. 17** offers endless steakhouses, fast food joints, and buffets. **River City Cafe,** 404 21st Ave. N, serves free peanuts with its juicy burgers ($3-5), fries ($1.45), and beer ($1.50). The atmosphere is distinctively collegiate. (☎ 448-1990. Open daily 11am-10pm.) While most of the restaurants in Broadway by the Beach sacrifice food quality for elaborate decor, **Benito's,** in the northeast part of the complex, puts together fancy brick oven pizzas ($5-15) and excellent calzones ($6-7) and pasta dishes ($9-12). (☎ 444-0006. Open daily 11am-10:30pm.) Split your belly with one of the monstrous sandwiches at **Dagwood's Deli,** 400 11th. Ave. N. All sandwiches ($4-8) are made with fresh baked bread and pounds of juicy meat. (☎ 448-0100. Open M-Sa 11am-7pm.)

SIGHTS AND NIGHTLIFE

The cheapest and most amusing entertainment here is people-watching. Families, newlyweds, foreigners, and students flock to this incredibly popular area to lie out, eat out, and live out American beach culture. The boulevard and the length of the beach are both called "the strand." Cruising it at night is illegal—signs declare "You may not cross this point more than twice in two hours." You should never pay full price for any attraction in Myrtle Beach. Coupons are everywhere; pick up a copy of the *Sunny Day Guide, Myrtle Beach Guide,* or *Strand Magazine.*

The colossal **Broadway at the Beach,** Hwy. 17 Bypass and 21st Ave. N, is a sprawling complex impressive even by Orlando standards. In addition to the theaters, water park, mini-golf, rides, theme restaurants, and 100 shops, there is the new **Butterfly Pavilion** (☎839-4451), home to over 2000 butterflies in free flight and the absurdly over-priced **Ripley's Aquarium** (☎916-0888 or 800-734-8888; open daily 9am-11pm; $14, ages 5-11 $8, ages 2-4 $3). A better bet for animals is **Alligator Adventure,** Barefoot Landing, Hwy. 17 in North Myrtle Beach, home to over 800 gators. (☎361-0789. Open daily 9am-10pm. $12, seniors $10, ages 4-12 $8.)

When it comes to sports, nothing beats the fake thing. **Mini golf** holes outnumber permanent residents, with the most elaborate courses clustering on Kings Hwy. **NASCAR Speedpark,** U.S. 17 Bypass at 29th Ave. N, allows auto racing wannabees to race cars on eight different tracks, all with varying speed and difficulty. (☎626-8725. $25 unlimited rides, under 13 $11.)

The 9100-acre **Brookgreen Gardens,** Hwy. 17 opposite Huntington Beach State Park south of Murrell's Inlet, offers a respite from all the action. A large collection of American sculpture rests on over 9000 oak-shaded, relaxing acres. (☎235-6001. Open daily 9:30am-5pm. $8.50, ages 6-12 $4.)

For a night on the town, Broadway by the Beach's **Celebrity Square** makes the selection process easy. The Square houses *nine* nightclubs, all specializing in a different genre of the classic drinking and dancing combo. The soon-to-be-outdated **2001,** 920 Lake Arrowhead Rd. (☎449-9434), and now outdated **Club Millennium 2000,** 1012 S. Kings Hwy., continue to compete for the Spring Breakin' booty shakin' crowd, despite showing their age.

GEORGIA

Georgia presents two faces: the rural southern region contrasts starkly with the sprawling commercialism of the north. But the state somehow manages to balance its many different identities. The cosmopolitan capital city of Atlanta boasts of Coca-Cola and Ted Turner's CNN, both of which have networked the globe. Savannah fosters a different sort of life from the Atlanta metropolis by stubbornly preserving its distinctive antebellum atmosphere. And while collegiate Athens breeds "big" bands, Georgia's Gold Coast mellows in slow-paced sea-side existence. This state of countless contradictions was called home by two former presidents as well: Jimmy Carter's hometown of Plains and Franklin D. Roosevelt's summer home in Warm Springs both stand on red Georgia clay. No matter where you go in Georgia, however, one thing remains constant—the peachy Southern hospitality.

PRACTICAL INFORMATION

Capital: Atlanta.
Visitor Info: Dept. of Industry and Trade, Tourist Division, 285 Peachtree Center Ave., Atlanta 30303 (☎404-656-3590 or 800-847-4842; www.georgia.org), in the Marriot Marquis 2 Tower, 10th fl. Open M-F 8am-5pm. **Dept. of Natural Resources,** 205 Butler St. SE, #1352, Atlanta 30334 (☎404-656-3530 or 800-864-7275). **U.S. Forest Service,** 1800 NE Expressway, Atlanta 30329 (☎404-248-9142). Open W-Su 11am-7:30pm.
Postal Abbreviation: GA. **Sales Tax:** 4-7%, depending on county.

THE SOUTH

ATLANTA   ☎ 404

An increasingly popular destination for 20- and 30-somethings craving big city life but weary of more manic metropoli, Atlanta strives to be cosmopolitan with a smile. Although it has not yet caught up to the likes of Chicago, Los Angeles, or New York City, Atlanta continues to expand with corporate bigwigs, international sports events, and a wave of newcomers encouraging its growth. Northerners, Californians, the third-largest gay population in the U.S., and a host of ethnicities have diversified this unofficial capital of the South. A nationwide economic powerhouse, Atlanta holds offices for 400 of the Fortune 500 companies, including the headquarters of Coca-Cola, Delta Airlines, the United Parcel Service, and CNN. Nineteen colleges, including Georgia Tech, Morehouse College, Spelman College, and Emory University, call "Hotlanta" home. The city is just as blessed with subtle gems; getting lost on Atlanta's streets reveals a seemingly endless number of trendy restaurants and beautiful old houses.

✈ GETTING THERE AND AWAY

Atlanta sprawls across ten counties in the northwest quadrant of the state at the junctures of I-75, I-85, and I-20. **I-285** ("the perimeter") circumscribes the city.

Flights: Hartsfield International Airport (general info ☎ 222-6688, international services and flight info ☎ 530-2081; www.atlanta-airport.com), south of the city. MARTA (see Public Transit) is the easiest way to get downtown, with 15min. rides departing from the Airport Station every 8min. daily 5am-1am ($1.50). **Atlanta Airport Shuttle** (☎ 524-3400) runs vans from the airport to over 100 locations in the metropolis and outlying area (every 15min. daily 7am-11pm; shuttle downtown $12). Taxi to downtown $18.

Train: Amtrak, 1688 Peachtree St. NW (☎ 881-3062), 3 mi. north of downtown at I-85. Take bus #23 from "Arts Center" MARTA station. To New York (18½hr., 1 per day, $96-174) and New Orleans (11½hr., 1 per day, $44-80). Open daily 7am-9:30pm.

Buses: Greyhound, 232 Forsyth St. SW (☎ 584-1728), across from "Garnett" MARTA station. To: New York (18-23hr., 13 per day, $90); Washington, D.C. (15hr., 11 per day, $69); and Savannah (5hr., 5 per day, $43). Open 24hr.

▭ GETTING AROUND

Public Transit: Metropolitan Atlanta Rapid Transit Authority (MARTA) (☎ 848-4711; schedule info M-F 6am-11pm, Sa-Su 8am-10pm). Good combined rail and bus system. Rail operates M-F 5am-1am, Sa-Su and holidays 6am-12:30am in most areas. Bus hrs. vary. Fare $1.50, exact change needed, or buy a token at station machines; transfers free. Unlimited weekly pass $12. Pick up a system map at the **MARTA Ride Store,** Five Points Station downtown, or at the airport, Lindbergh, or Lenox stations. MARTA courtesy phones in each rail station. All trains, rail stations, and buses are lift-equipped.

Taxis: Atlanta Yellow Cab, ☎ 521-0200. **Checker Cab,** ☎ 351-1111.

Car Rental: Atlanta Rent-a-Car, 3185 Camp Creek Pkwy. (☎ 763-1110), just inside I-285 3 mi. east of the airport. 20 other locations in the area including 2800 Campelton Rd. (☎ 344-1060) and 3129 Piedmont Rd. (☎ 231-4898). $20 per day, 100 free mi. per day, 24¢ per additional mi. Must be 21 with major credit card.

✷ ORIENTATION

Getting around Atlanta is confusing—the city is more a conglomeration of several suburbs than a single metropolis. Maneuvering around the main thoroughfares, arranged much like the spokes of a wheel, challenges even the most experienced native. **Peachtree St.** (one of over 50 streets bearing the name in Atlanta), is a major north-south road. Two other significant roads, **Spring St.** and **Piedmont Ave.,** run parallel to Peachtree. On the eastern edge of the city, **Moreland Ave.** runs the length of the city, through Virginia Highland, Little Five Points (L5P), and E. Atlanta. Major east-west roads include **Ponce De Leon Ave.** and **North Ave.** In the heart of downtown, especially around the district known as Five Points, one-way streets run amok.

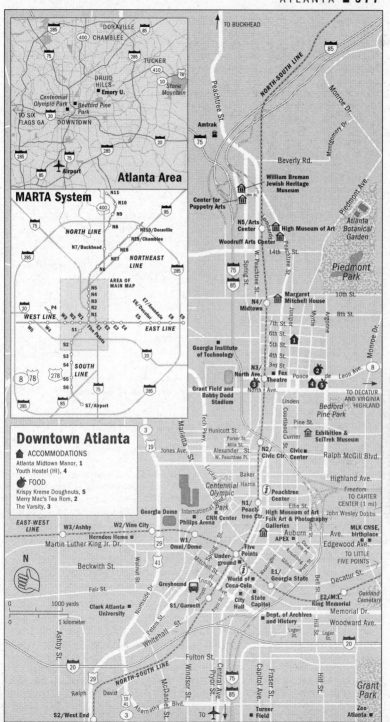

TO BUCKHEAD

Atlanta Area

DORAVILLE
CHAMBLEE
TUCKER
DRUID HILLS
Emory U.
Stone Mountain
Centennial Olympic Park
Bedford Pine Park
TO SIX FLAGS GA
DOWNTOWN
Airport

MARTA System

NORTH LINE
N11
N10
N9
N8
N7/Buckhead
N6
NORTHEAST LINE
N10/Doraville
N9/Chamblee
N8
N7
AREA OF MAIN MAP
N5
N4
N3
N2
N1
E6/Decatur
E7/Avondale
E5
WEST LINE
P4
W3 W2 W1
W6 W5 W4
S1
The Publix
E1 E2 E3 E4
EAST LINE
E8
E9
S2
SOUTH LINE
S3
S4
S5
S6
S7/Airport

Downtown Atlanta

🏠 ACCOMMODATIONS
Atlanta Midtown Manor, **1**
Youth Hostel (HI), **4**

🍗 FOOD
Krispy Kreme Doughnuts, **5**
Merry Mac's Tea Rom, **2**
The Varsity, **3**

Peachtree St.
Amtrak
William Breman Jewish Heritage Museum
Center for Puppetry Arts
N5/Arts Center
Woodruff Arts Center
High Museum of Art
Atlanta Botanical Garden
Beverly Rd.
Monroe Dr.
Montgomery Dr.
Piedmont Ave.
Piedmont Park
14th St.
N4/Midtown
Margaret Mitchell House
10th St.
8th St.
7th St.
6th St.
5th St.
4th St.
3rd St.
Georgia Institute of Technology
N3/North Ave.
Fox Theatre
Ponce de Leon Ave.
Grant Field and Bobby Dodd Stadium
North Ave.
Linden
Bedford Pine Park
TO DECATUR AND VIRGINIA HIGHLAND
Pine St.
Exhibition & SciTrek Museum
Hunicutt St.
Mills St.
Alexander St.
W. Peachtree Pl.
N2/Civic Ctr.
Civic Center
Ralph McGill Blvd.
Baker
Highland Ave.
Harris
Freedom
TO CARTER CENTER (1 mi)
Centennial Olympic Park
Peachtree Center
N1/Peachtree Ctr.
Ellis St.
High Museum of Art Folk Art & Photography Galleries
John Wesley Dobbs
MLK CNSE, birthplace
Georgia Dome
Philips Arena
CNN Center
Auburn Ave.
APEX
Edgewood Ave.
TO LITTLE FIVE POINTS
EAST-WEST LINE
W3/Ashby
W2/Vine City
Herndon Home
W1/Omni/Dome
Five Points
Underground
Decatur St.
Martin Luther King Jr. Dr.
Beckwith St.
World of Coca-Cola
E1/Georgia State
Greyhound
City Hall
State Capitol
E2/M.L. King Memorial
Oakland Cemetary
Memorial Dr.
Woodward Ave.
Fair St.
S1/Garnett
Clark Atlanta University
Dept. of Archives and History
Logan St.
Logan St.
N
1000 yards
1 kilometer
Fulton St.
Ashby St.
Whitehall St.
Peters St.
McDaniel St.
Windsor St.
Central Ave.
Pryor St.
Capitol Ave.
Fraser St.
Hill St.
Grant Park
NORTH-SOUTH LINE
Ralph
David
Abernathy Blvd.
S2/West End
TO
Turner Field
Zoo Atlanta

Anchoring downtown Atlanta, the **Peachtree Center** and **Five Points MARTA** stations deliver flocks of tourists to the Center and **Underground Atlanta,** respectively. From Five Points, head northeast to the **Midtown** area (from Ponce de Leon Ave. to 17th St.) to find Atlanta's art museums. Directly southwest of downtown is the **West End**—an African-American area and the city's oldest historic quarter. The **Little Five Points (L5P)** district, the local haven for eclecticism, artists, and youth subculture, lies only three subway stops east of Five Points, at the junction of Euclid and More-land Ave. **Virginia Highland,** a trendy neighborhood east of Midtown and Piedmont Park, attracts yuppies and college kids. And then there was **Buckhead,** a posher-than-thou area north on Peachtree and accessible on MARTA ("Buckhead").

■ PRACTICAL INFORMATION

Visitor Info: Atlanta Convention and Visitors Bureau, 233 Peachtree St. NE, (☎521-6600 or ☎800-285-2682; www.atlanta.com), Peachtree Center, Suite 100, downtown. Open M-F 8:30am-5pm. Automated **information service** (☎222-6688).

Bi-Gay-Lesbian Organizations: The Gay and Lesbian Center, 828 West Peachtree St., Suite 207 (☎876-5372; www.aglc.com), provides info, weekly events, and short-term counseling daily 6pm-11pm. Also check out the *Gay Yellow Pages* (☎351-6072).

Hotline: Rape Crisis Counseling, ☎616-4861. 24hr.

Post Office: 3900 Crown Rd. (☎765-7300). Open 24hr. **ZIP code:** 30321. **Area code:** 404 roughly inside the I-285 perimeter, 770 outside. Listings 404 unless noted. 10-digit dialing required.

■ ACCOMMODATIONS

Atlanta Hostel, 223 Ponce de Leon Ave. (☎870-0042), in Midtown. From MARTA: North Ave. station, exit onto Ponce de Leon, about 3½ blocks east on the corner of Myrtle St., or take bus #2 and ask the driver to stop. Attached to the Woodruff B&B, livened up by pooch "Fatty" and an amiable scarlet macaw. Clean, dorm-style rooms come with **Internet access,** coffee, and doughnuts. No sleeping bags allowed, but they distribute free blankets. Laundry facilities, pool table, arcade games, and renovated kitchen. Luggage storage $1. Linen $1. Free lockers. Dorms $18; private doubles $32.50.

Masters Inn Economy, 3092 Presidential Pkwy. (☎770-454-8373 or 800-633-3434; www.mastersinn.com), Chamblee Tucker Rd. Exit 94 off I-85 in Doraville. Renovated, large rooms with king-size beds, local calls, cable TV, and pool. Singles $39, F-Sa $41; doubles $44/$49.

Motel 6, 2820 Chamblee Tucker Rd. (☎770-458-6626), in Doraville, Exit 94 off I-85. Spacious and immaculate rooms. Offers free local calls, morning coffee, and A/C. Under 18 stay free with parents. Singles $40; doubles $46.

Atlanta Midtown Manor, 811 Piedmont Ave. NE (☎872-5846). 3 Victorian houses convenient to downtown. Nice rooms with floral shams, wooden 4-post beds, A/C, TV, and replica antique furnishings. Free coffee, doughnuts, and street parking. Shared bath, privacy costs extra. Laundry. Singles and doubles $49-89. Fills up in summer.

Stone Mountain Family Campground (☎770-498-5710), on U.S. 78 (see p. 382). Gorgeous sites; one-third are on the lake. Bike rentals, free laser show, nature trails, and **Internet access.** Maximum 2-week stay. Tent sites $20-26; full hook-up $30-35. Entrance fee $6 per car.

■ FOOD

From Vietnamese to Italian, baked to fried to fricaseed, Atlanta dining provides ample options, no matter what you're craving. "Soul food," designed to nurture the spiritual as well as the physical, is the heart of this town's palate. Some favorite dishes include fried chicken, ribs, okra, sweet-potato pie, and peach cobbler. Have a taste of the South and dip cornbread into "pot likker," water used to cook greens. For a sweet treat (60¢), you can't beat the Atlanta-based **Krispy Kreme**

Doughnuts, whose glazed delights are a Southern institution. The factory store, 295 Ponce de Leon Ave. NE (☎876-7307), is open 24 hours and continuously bakes their wares, visible through the back window. More healthy alternatives are available at the **Sweet Auburn Curb Market** in the Sweet Auburn District, 209 Edgewood Ave., a depot for soul food's raw materials. (☎659-1665. Open M-Sa 8am-6pm.)

BUFORD HIGHWAY

Little Szechuan, 5091-C Buford Hwy. (☎770-451-0192), at I-285, Exit 25. In the heart of the ethnically diverse Buford Hwy. area, lunch specials for $6 are served in heaping doses. Open M 11:30am-9:30pm, W-Sa 11:30am-9:30pm, Su noon-9:30pm.

Pho Hoa, 5150 Buford Hwy., Suite C-120. (☎770-455-8729), at I-285, Exit 25. Vietnamese noodle soup, *Pho*, provides a healthy one-dish alternative for any meal of the day. Whet your appetite with a taste of the *Cha Gio* ($2) and top it all off with a coffee drink, sinfully sweetened to suit your taste. Open daily 10am-10pm.

MIDTOWN

Tortillas, 774 Ponce de Leon Ave. (☎892-0193). The student crowd munches dirt-cheap and tasty Mexican food, with soft chicken tacos ($1.75) and a large variety of burritos (from $3). Try the upstairs patio for open-air eating. Open daily 11am-10pm.

The Varsity, 61 North Ave. NW at Spring St. (☎881-1706), at I-85. MARTA: North Ave. The world's largest drive-in and originator of the assembly-line school of food preparation. Best known for the greatest, greasiest onion rings in the South and the 2 mi. of hotdogs sold daily. Most menu items around $2. Open Su-Th 9am-11:30pm, F-Sa 9am-1:30am.

Mary Mac's Tea Room, 224 Ponce De Leon Ave. (☎876-1800), at Myrtle NE; take the "Georgia Tech" bus north. A "revival of Southern hospitality" with a 40s atmosphere and amazing cinnamon rolls ($3.75 per dozen after 5pm). Dinner (good enough for the Dalai Lama, along with a whole wall full of other celebs) with daily rotating entrees and sides is $6-9, or free to the expanding ranks of centenarians. Cash only. Open M-Sa 11am-9pm, Su 11am-3pm.

VIRGINIA HIGHLAND

Majestic Food Shop, 1031 Ponce de Leon Ave. (☎875-0276), at Cleburne. For the ravenous insomniac people watcher, there is no place better. The late, late night scene for Highland and L5P with doormen to prevent weekend nocturnal crowding. The Majestic offers "food that pleases" in the shape of burgers ($1.85), grits ($1.10), and the like. Open 24hr.

Everybody's, 1040 N. Highland Ave. (☎873-4545), has received high accolades for selling Atlanta's best pizza. Their inventive pizza salad, a colossal mound of greens and chicken on a pizza bed ($10.50) is more than enough for two. Open M-Th 11:30am-11pm, F-Sa 11:30am-1am, Su noon-11pm.

Manuel's Tavern, 602 N. Highland Ave. (☎525-3447), prime spot between L5P and the Highland. Longtime stomping ground for Atlanta's Democrats; Jimmy Carter is known to swing by for a burger ($5) and a beer. Open M-Sa 11am-2am, Su 12:30pm-midnight.

SURROUNDING AREA

Crescent Moon, 254 W. Ponce de Leon Ave. (☎377-5623), in Decatur. A heavenly breakfast spot. Indulge in phenomenal French toast ($1.75 per slice), or the Heap, an endless mound of potatoes, bacon, and cheese ($6). Whopping portions. Open M-F 7:30am-3pm, Sa-Su brunch 8am-2:30pm.

The Flying Biscuit, 1655 McLendon Ave. (☎687-8888). As expected, biscuits are the forte here. Chocolate lovers will appreciate the warm chocolate "biscuit" bread pudding ($4) with a cup of Ghirardelli hot cocoa ($2). Cafe, take-out, and cookbook available. Restaurant open daily 9am-9pm; bakery open M-F 7:30am-9pm, Sa-Su 8am-9pm.

Bridgetown Grill, 1156 Euclid Ave. (☎653-0110), in L5P. Reggae and salsa make for a hopping hole in the wall. Have a 20 oz. margarita ($6) with their famous seafood creole ($11) and a side of plantains ($2.30). Open S-Th 11am-11pm, F-Sa 11am-midnight.

SIGHTS

SWEET AUBURN DISTRICT

Atlanta's sights are scattered, but the effort it takes to find them pays off. The most powerful are the MLK sites along Auburn Ave. in Sweet Auburn. Reverend Martin Luther King, Jr.'s birthplace, church, and grave are all part of the 23-acre **⊠Martin Luther King, Jr. National Historic Site.** The **visitors center** houses poignant displays of photographs, videos, and quotations, oriented around King's life and the civil rights struggle. *(450 Auburn Ave.* ☎ *331-3920. MARTA: King Memorial.)* The **birthplace of MLK** offers frequent tours. *(501 Auburn Ave.* ☎ *331-5190.)* **Ebenezer Baptist Church** is the church where King was pastor from 1960 to 1968. *(407 Auburn Ave.* ☎ *688-7263.)* King's **grave** and reflecting pool are located at the **Martin Luther King, Jr. Center for Nonviolent Social Exchange.** The center also holds a collection of King's personal effects, an overview of his mentor, Gandhi, and an exhibit on Rosa Parks. *(449 Auburn Ave. NE.* ☎ *524-1956.)* Plaques lining Sweet Auburn point out the architecture and prominent past residents of this historically African-American neighborhood. *(All sites open daily 9am-5pm. Free.)*

DOWNTOWN AND AROUND

From Mar. through Nov., the **Atlanta Preservation Center** offers eight famous walking tours of popular areas. *(537 Peachtree St. NE.* ☎ *876-2041. $5, students and seniors $4.)*

GRANT PARK. In Grant Park, directly south of Oakland Cemetery and Cherokee Ave., is the 115-year-old **Cyclorama,** the world's largest painting in the round, which re-creates the 1864 Battle of Atlanta. *(*☎ *624-1071. Take bus #31 from Five Points. Open daily June-Sept. 9:30am-5:30pm; Oct.-May 9:30am-4:30pm. $5, students and seniors $4, ages 6-12 $3.)* Next door, **Zoo Atlanta** boasts komodo dragons, an artist-elephant, Allen the orangutan, a petting zoo, and their most recent addition, two giant pandas of Chengdu. *(800 Cherokee Ave. SE.* ☎ *624-5600 or 624-5856. Take bus #31 or 97 from Five Points. Open Apr.-Oct. M-F 9:30am-4:30pm, Sa-Su 9:30am-5:30pm; Nov.-Mar. daily 9:30am-4:30pm. $13, seniors $10, ages 3-11 $9.)*

WORLD OF COCA-COLA. Two blocks from the capitol, the World of Coca-Cola details "the real thing's" rise from humble beginnings in Atlanta to a position of world domination, from the classic print ads of the 20s, to the "Everyday of Your Life" video featuring Coke's international influence, to the sampling room, where more than 40 of the world's strangest soft drinks come direct to you, in a rainbow of flavors. *(55 Martin Luther King, Jr. Dr.* ☎ *676-5151. Open M-Sa 10am-9:30pm, Su noon-6pm. Summer hrs. may vary. $6, seniors $4, ages 6-12 $3.)* Adjacent to the WOC, redeveloped **Underground Atlanta** gets down with six subterranean blocks of urban marketplace and over 120 chain restaurants, shops, and night spots. Descend at the entrance beside the Five Points subway station. *(*☎ *523-2311. Shops open M-Sa 10am-9:30pm, Su noon-6pm. Bars and restaurants close later.)*

CNN. High-tech Atlanta reigns with multinational business powerhouses situated in the **Five Points District. Turner Broadcasting System** offers an overpriced, insider's peek with its **Cable News Network (CNN) Studio Tour,** at Techwood Dr. and Marietta St. Witness anchors broadcasting live while writers toil in the background. *(*☎ *827-2300. 45min. tours given every 15min. Open daily 9am-6pm. $8, seniors $6, ages 5-12 $5. Reservations optional.)* You're invited to join the punditocracy in the studio audience of *CNN Talk Back Live,* but they'll warn you not to pick your nose on camera. *(M-F 3pm. Take MARTA west to the Omni/Dome/GWCC Station at W1. Free.)*

THE REAL STORY ON THE REAL THING In

1886, chemist Dr. John Smyth Pemberton created a headache powder advertised to relieve even the greatest pangs. As old southern lore will tell it, a customer walked into Jacob's pharmacy shortly thereafter and asked the pharmacist to mix the powder with tonic water right there in the store, as his headache prevented him from waiting any longer to swallow the cure. This concoction, with its still secret formula, marked the birth of Coca-Cola and has not changed in over a century.

OLYMPICS. Despite the tragic bombing that occurred there during the Olympics, **Centennial Olympic Park,** adjacent to the Georgia World Congress Center, delights children of all ages with the **Fountain of Rings** (splashing and jumping encouraged). *(Four 20min shows daily: 12:30, 3:30, 6, and 9pm.)*

CARTER PRESIDENTIAL CENTER. The museum at the Carter Presidential Center, north of Little Five Points, documents Georgia peanut farmer Jimmy Carter's political career through exhibits and films. One of ten Presidential libraries, the **Jimmy Carter Library** at the center serves as an archival depository for preserving the historical materials from the 1977-81 Carter Administration. *(441 Freedom Pkwy. ☎ 331-0296. Take bus #16 to Cleburne Ave. Museum open M-Sa 9am-4:45pm, Su noon-4:45pm. $5, seniors $4, under 16 free.)*

WEST END

Dating from 1835, the West End is Atlanta's oldest neighborhood. Here can be found the **Wren's Nest,** home to author Joel Chandler Harris, who popularized the African folktale trickster Br'er Rabbit. Energetic storytellers continue to use the house to entertain young and old alike. *(1050 R.D. Abernathy Blvd. ☎ 753-7735. Take bus #71 from West End Station (S2). Open Tu-Sa 10am-3pm. $7, seniors and teens $5, ages 4-12 $4.)* The **Hammonds House** displays soulful works in Georgia's only collection dedicated entirely to African-American and Haitian art. *(503 Peeples St. SW. ☎ 752-8730. Take bus #71 from West End Station to Peeples St. and walk two blocks north. Open Tu-F 10am-6pm, Sa-Su 1-5pm. $2, students and seniors $1.)* The **Herndon Home,** a 1910 Beaux-Arts Classical mansion, was built by slave-born Alonzo F. Herndon. A prominent barber and founder of Atlanta Life Insurance Co., Herndon became Atlanta's wealthiest African American in the early 1900s. *(587 University Pl. NW. ☎ 581-9813. Take bus #3 from Five Points station to the corner of Martin Luther King, Jr. Dr. and Maple and walk one block north. Open Tu-Sa 10am-4pm. Free. Tours on the hr. 10am-3pm. $3.50.)*

MIDTOWN

PIEDMONT PARK. Piedmont Park sprawls around the 60-acre **Atlanta Botanical Garden** on Piedmont Ave., in the northwest corner of the park. Stroll through 15 acres of landscaped gardens, a 15-acre hardwood forest with trails, and an interactive children's garden focusing on health and wellness. *(☎ 876-5859. MARTA: Lindburgh Center, bus #31. Open Mar.-Sept. Tu-Su 9am-7pm; Oct.-Feb. Tu-Su 9am-6pm. $7, students and ages 6-12 $4, seniors $5.)* The Garden's **Dorothy Chapman Fuqua Conservatory** houses hundreds of species of endangered tropical plants. In 2001, a new **Fuqua Orchid House-Conservation Center** will open adjacent to the Conservatory. *(Take bus #36 from Arts Center Station or bus #31 from Five Points on Sundays. Opens at 10am.)* Near the park, **Scitrek (Science and Technology Museum of Atlanta),** with over 150 interactive exhibits for all ages, is one of the nation's top science centers. *(395 Piedmont Ave. NE. ☎ 522-5500. Take MARTA to Civic Center, walk two blocks east on Ralph McGill Blvd., and turn left on Piedmont. Open M-Sa 10am-5pm, Su noon-5pm. $7.50; students, seniors, military personnel, and ages 3-17 $6.)*

MARGARET MITCHELL. Newly opened in 1997 after two arson-related fires, the **Margaret Mitchell House and Museum** sit at 10th and Peachtree St., adjacent to the Midtown MARTA station. See the apartment in which Mitchell wrote *Gone With the Wind,* as well as her typewriter and autographed copies of the novel. The new museum includes the door to "Tara" and other paraphernalia from the *GWTW* movie set. *(990 Peachtree St. ☎ 249-7015. Open daily 9am-4pm. $10, students and seniors $8, ages 6-11 $7. 1hr. tours every 10min.; last one at 4pm.)*

WOODRUFF ARTS CENTER. Just to the west of Piedmont Park is the Woodruff Arts Center. It contains the **High Museum of Art,** Richard Meier's award-winning building of glass, steel, and white porcelain. The permanent collection contains one of Andy Warhol's Marilyn Monroe paintings. Recent visiting exhibits have brought renowned works of Picasso and Rockwell. *(WAC: 1280 Peachtree St. NE. ☎ 733-4200. Take MARTA to Arts Center and exit Lombardy Way. High Museum of Art: ☎ 733-4444. Open Tu-Th, Sa 10am-5pm, F 10am-9pm, Su noon-5pm. $6, students with ID and seniors $4, ages 6-17 $2; free Th 1-5pm.)* The **Folk Art & Photography Galleries,** one block south of Peachtree

Center Station, houses additional works as the High Museum's satellite facility. *(30 John Wesley Dobbs Ave. NE. ☎ 577-6940. Open M-F 10am-5pm. Free.)*

WILLIAM BREMAN JEWISH HERITAGE MUSEUM. The William Breman Jewish Heritage Museum, the largest Jewish museum in the southeast, features a moving Holocaust exhibit and a gallery tracing the history of the Atlanta Jewish community from 1845 to the present. *(1440 Spring St. NW. ☎ 873-1661. From Peachtree Center Station, walk three blocks north to 18th St. and Spring St. Open M-Th 10am-5pm, F 10am-3pm, Su 1-5pm. $5, students and seniors $3.)*

CENTER FOR PUPPETRY ARTS. Next to the Jewish Heritage Museum, across 18th St., the Center for Puppetry Arts has a museum featuring traditional Punch and Judy figures, some of Jim Henson's original Muppets, and daily puppet-making workshops. Stay for a puppet show to enjoy the latest revivals of classic tales. *(1404 Spring St. NW. ☎ 873-3391. Open M-Sa 9am-5pm. $5, students, seniors, and children $4. Shows $8/$7. Puppet workshop ages 5+: M-F 10 and 11:30am; Sa 11am and 1pm. $5.)*

BUCKHEAD

A drive through **Buckhead** (north of midtown and Piedmont Park, off Peachtree near W. Paces Ferry Rd.) uncovers Atlanta's Beverly Hills—the sprawling mansions of Coca-Cola CEOs and other specimens of high culture. This area is also a hub of local grub and grog, frequented often by Atlanta's 20-somethings (see **Entertainment,** below). One of the most exquisite residences in the Southeast, the Greek Revival **Governor's Mansion** has elaborate gardens and one of the finest collections of furniture from the Federal Period. *(391 W. Paces Ferry Rd. ☎ 261-1776. Take bus #40 "West Paces Ferry" from Lindbergh Station. Tours Tu-Th 10-11:30am. Free.)* In the same neighborhood, discover the **Atlanta History Center/Buckhead.** The **Atlanta History Museum** traces Atlanta's development from a rural area to an international cityscape. Its Civil War Gallery spotlights the stories of both Confederate and Federal soldiers. Also on the grounds are the **Swan House,** a lavish Anglo-Palladian Revival home built in 1928, and the **Tullie Smith Farm,** an 1845 Yeoman farmhouse. *(130 W. Paces Ferry Rd. NW. ☎ 814-4000. Open M-Sa 10am-5:30pm, Su noon-5:30pm. Ticket sales end at 4:30pm. $7, students and seniors $5, ages 6-17 $4.)*

EAST OF MIDTOWN

STONE MOUNTAIN PARK. A respite from the city is at Stone Mountain Park, where a fabulous Confederate Memorial is carved into the world's largest mass of granite. The "Mt. Rushmore of the South" features Jefferson Davis, Robert E. Lee, and Stonewall Jackson and rises 825 ft. The hike up the **Confederate Hall Trail** (1½ mi.) is rewarded with a spectacular view of Atlanta. The mount is surrounded by a 3200-acre "World of Family Fun" recreation area and historic park; check out the dazzling (and free) laser show on the side of the mountain every summer night at 9:30pm. *(16 mi. east of Atlanta on U.S. 78. ☎ 770-498-5690. Take bus #120 "Stone Mountain" from the Avondale subway stop. Park gates open daily 6am-midnight; attractions open 10am-8pm; off-season 10am-5pm. $6 per car; admission to other attractions $5.)*

FERNBANK MUSEUM OF NATURAL HISTORY. The Fernbank Museum of Natural History, off Ponce de Leon Ave., sports dinosaurs, an IMAX theater, discovery centers, and fossils embedded in the limestone floor tiles. *(767 Clifton Rd. NE. ☎ 370-0960. Take bus #2 from North Ave. or Avondale Station. Open M-Sa 10am-5pm, Su noon-5pm. Museum $9, students and seniors $8, ages 3-12 $7; IMAX film $7/$6/$5; both $14/$12/$10.)* The adjacent **Stanton Rose Garden,** on the corner of Ponce de Leon and Clifton Rd., contains over 1300 breeds that bloom from spring into Dec.

🎵 ENTERTAINMENT

For hassle-free fun, buy a MARTA pass (see **Practical Information,** p. 376) and pick up one of the city's free publications on music and events. *Creative Loafing, Music Atlanta,* the *Hudspeth Report,* or "Leisure" in the F edition of the *Atlanta Journal and Constitution* will give you the scuttlebutt. *Southern Voice* has complete listings on gay and lesbian news and nightclubs throughout Atlanta. Look for free summer concerts in Atlanta's parks.

The **Woodruff Arts Center** (see **Midtown**, p. 381) houses the Atlanta Symphony, the Alliance Theater Company, Atlanta College of Art, and the High Museum of Art. **Atlantix,** 65 Upper Alabama St., offers half-price rush tickets to dance, theater, music, and other attractions throughout the city. (☎770-772-5572. MARTA: Five Points. Walk-up service only, Tu 11am-3pm, W-Sa 11am-6pm, Su noon-3pm.) The recently completed **Philips Arena** hosts concerts, the **Atlanta Hawks** basketball team, and the **Atlanta Thrashers** hockey team. (100 Techwood Dr. ☎878-3000 or ☎800-326-4000.) The National League **Atlanta Braves** play at **Turner Field,** which features a Coke bottle over left field that erupts with fireworks after homeruns. (755 Hank Aaron Dr. ☎522-7630. MARTA: West End, bus #105. Call Ticketmaster at ☎800-326-4000. Tickets $5-15, $1 skyline seats available game day.) One-hour tours of Turner Field, including a glimpse from the $200,000 skyboxes, are offered. (☎614-2311. MARTA: Omni/Dome/World Congress Center. Open non-game days, M-Sa 9:30am-4pm, Su 1pm-4pm; game days M-Sa 9:30am-noon; off-season M-Sa 10am-2pm. $7, children $4, under 3 free.) See the **Atlanta Falcons** play football at the **Georgia Dome,** site of the 2000 Super Bowl and the world's largest cable-supported dome. Public tours are available. (MARTA: Omni/Dome/World Congress Center. Open W-F 10am-4pm. $2, seniors and ages 3-12 $1.)

Six Flags Over Georgia, at I-20 W, is one of the largest theme/amusement parks in the nation and features the new 54 mph rollercoaster "Georgia Scorcher." (7561 Six Flags Rd. SW. ☎770-948-9290. Take bus #201 "Six Flags" from Hamilton Homes. Open daily mid-May to Aug. 10am-10pm; times vary rest of year. $35, children and seniors $17; 2-day pass $40/$30.)

◪ NIGHTLIFE

Drink and dance hotspots center in **Little Five Points, Virginia Highland, Buckhead,** and oft-cheesy **Underground Atlanta. East Atlanta,** at the crossroads of Glenwood and Flat Shoals, is the up-and-coming part of town. A college-age crowd usually fills Little Five Points. Many bikers park their choppers outside **The Vortex,** 438 Moreland Ave., home of Atlanta's best burger, for a drink at their favorite watering hole. (☎688-1828. Open M-Sa 11am-2am, Su 11am-midnight.) Named after a medieval art forger, **Elmyr,** 1091 Euclid Ave., boasts 29 different tequilas ($4-8) and a waitstaff with sass. (☎588-0250. Open Su-Th noon-2am, F-Sa noon-3am.) For blues, feel your way to **Blind Willie's,** 828 N. Highland Ave. NE in Virginia Highland, a dim, bustling club with Cajun food and occasional big name acts. (☎873-2583. Open Su-Th 8pm-2am, F 8pm-3am, Sa 8pm-2:30am. Live music starts around 10pm. Cover $5-10.) Join the laid-back and often international crowd next door at **Limerick Junction Pub,** 822 N. Highland Ave., where contagious Irish music jigs nightly and open mic night happens every Tu at 9pm. (☎874-7147. Open M-W 5pm-1am, Th-Sa 5pm-2am, Su 5pm-midnight.) **Flatiron,** 520 Flat Shoals Ave., anchoring the expanding East Atlanta scene, bears the catchphrase, "If you love this country, you'll love this bar." (☎688-8864. Open Su-Th 11am-2am, F-Sa 11am-3pm.) In the heart of Buckhead's popular and young nightlife scene, cool off with a 96 oz. fishbowl at **Lu Lu's Bait Shack,** 3057 Peachtree Rd. (☎262-5220. Open Tu-F 5pm-4am, Sa 5pm-3am.) Towards downtown, the **Masquerade,** 695 North Ave. NE, occupies an original turn-of-the-century mill. The bar has three different levels: "heaven," with live music from touring bands; "purgatory," a more laid-back pub and pool house; and "hell," a dance club offering everything from techno to 1940s big band jazz. An outside space provides dancing with lights and celestial views. The 4000-seat amphitheater caters to metal and punk tastes. (☎577-8178; concert line ☎577-2007. Open W-Su 8pm-4am. Cover $3-8 and up. 18+.)

HELEN   ☎706

When your town's major industry dries up and tourism is stagnant, there is but one thing to do—redevelop and bill yourself as a Bavarian village. In the 60s, four Helen businesswomen transformed this once sleepy lumber town into Georgia's own Little Germany. Beer gardens and cobblestone streets line the overwhelmingly convincing downtown district; strict building codes ensure that even fast-food cabins fit the image. Burn off your weiner schnitzel exploring the nearby Chattahoochee River, Appalacian Trail, and Unicoi State Park. Willkommen, y'all!

7 PRACTICAL INFORMATION. Helen lies 85 mi. northeast of Atlanta, buttressing the mountains of the Chattahoochee National Forest. From I-85, take Exit 113 to Hwy. 365, then left onto Hwy. 384, right on Hwy. 75. Most everything Bavarian is accessible by foot from the **Alpine Helen/White County Convention and Visitors Bureau,** 726 Brucken Strasse (☎ 878-2181; open M-Sa 9am-5pm, Su noon-4pm). **Post Office:** S. Main St. (☎ 878-2422; open M-F 8:30am-5pm, Sa 8:30am-noon). **ZIP code:** 30545. **Area code:** 706.

ACCOMMODATIONS AND FOOD. All the major motel chains line Main St. The **Alpine Village Inn,** 1005 Edelweiss St., is a local alternative, sporting all the amenities in four garden-side "haus." (☎ 800-844-8466. Singles and doubles $49-69.) **Unicoi State Park,** 2 mi. up Hwy. 356, offers primitive campsites for $14, water and electricity for $19, and full hook-ups for $22. (☎ 800-573-9659. Park open 24hr.)

Fred's Famous Peanuts, 17 Clayton Rd. (☎ 878-3124), serves whooping pork rinds and goobers in all flavors. The owner's German mother supervises the schnitzel construction at **Alt Heidelburg,** in White Horse Sq. As they say, "Da wo man gut isst;" the schnitzel brot schmeckt sehr. (☎ 878-2986. Open daily 11:30am-9pm.)

⬚ SIGHTS. The owner of **Charlemagne's Kingdom** spent 20 years constructing a scale replica of Germany (what else?), including over 6000 handpainted models (8808 N. Main St. ☎ 878-2200. Open daily 11am-6pm. $5, ages 6-12 $2.50.) The magnificent twin waterfalls at **Anna Ruby Falls** roar with nature's power. (5 mi. down Hwy. 356 in the Chattahoochee National Forest. Open 9am-8pm; off-season 9am-6pm. $3 per car.) Various rafting packages at **Wildewood Outfitters** let you float way down yonder on the Chattahoochee. Their retail store meets the needs of forgetful backpackers and hikers. (7272 S. Main St. ☎ 865-4451 or 800-553-2715. Trip information 9am-2pm summer only. Store open M-Sa 10am-6pm, Su noon-6pm. Last trip leaves 2pm. From $16 per person, including transportation.) Tens of thousands flock to Helen for **Oktoberfest** in Oct. and Nov. (☎ 878-1619.)

ATHENS   ☎706

Athens is the peach state's version of the "Classic City." In 1795 a group of Georgia lawmakers chose Athens to host the first publicly-chartered college in the country, the University of Georgia (UGA). Since then, the school has expanded to over 30,000 students. UGA's enormous size, resources, and influence have forged an artsy downtown, a prolific music scene, extreme Georgia football fever, and varied nightclub offerings.

7 PRACTICAL INFORMATION. Situated 70 mi. northeast of Atlanta, Athens can be reached from I-85 via U.S. 316, which runs into U.S. 29. The **Athens-Clarke County Airport,** 1010 Ben Epps Dr. (☎ 613-3420), offers a **commuter shuttle** (☎ 800-354-7874) to various points in and around Atlanta ($30). **Greyhound,** 220 W. Broad St. (☎ 549-2255; station open M-F 7:30am-9:15pm, Sa-Su 7:30am-2:30pm and 7-9:15pm), buses to Atlanta (1¾-2hr, 3 per day, $16). The **Athens Transit System** runs buses on 30min. and 1hr. loops. Schedules and info are available at the welcome center and information center on Washington St. (☎ 613-3430. Buses run M-F 6:15am-7:15pm, Sa 7:30am-7pm. $1, seniors 50¢, ages 6-18 75¢.) The **University Transit System** runs several different routes through town and gown. (☎ 369-6220. Operates M-F 6:45am-12:40am. Free.) Two blocks north of the UGA campus is the **Athens Welcome Center,** 280 E. Dougherty St., in the Church-Waddel-Brumby House, the city's oldest Federal Period House (☎ 353-1820; open M-Sa 10am-6pm, Su noon-6pm). Help is available from **Public Health Information** (☎ 800-473-4357). **Post Office:** 575 Olympic Dr. (☎ 800-275-8777; open M-F 8:30am-6pm). **ZIP code:** 30601. **Area code:** 706.

■ ACCOMMODATIONS. Many of the city's affordable motels line **W. Broad St.,** also known as the Atlanta Hwy. (U.S. 78), a few mi. from downtown. Many hotels jack up their prices during football weekends in the fall. In the Five Points District, the **Downtowner Motor Inn,** 1198 S. Milledge Ave., has rooms in 70s colors near campus with A/C, continental breakfast, free local calls, cable TV, and pool access. (☎549-2626. Singles $42; doubles $50; $2 per additional person.) Closer to town, the **History Village Inn and Conference Center,** 295 E. Dougherty St., is across the street from the welcome center. (☎546-0410. A/C, cable TV, free local calls, pool and laundromat. Singles $40; doubles $45. 10% AAA, UGA, seniors discount. Wheelchair accessible.) A full-service campground with secluded sites, **Pine Lake RV Campground,** Rte. 186, 12 mi. outside of Athens off Rte. 441 in nearby Bishop, has full hook-ups and fishing lakes. (☎769-5486. Open daily 8am-dark. Tent sites $16.50, full hook-up $19.50. Wheelchair accessible.)

◨ FOOD. Low key and without frills, **Weaver D.'s,** 1016 E. Broad, lets his food do the talking. Spectacular BBQ and fried chicken (around $6) pack in native and visitor alike. The sign outside reads "Automatic For the People," owner Dexter Weaver's favorite expression; it inspired the title of REM's 1992 album. (☎353-7797. Open M-F 11am-6pm.) **The Grit,** 199 Prince Ave., is Athens at its crunchiest and coolest, serving up scrumptious, healthy meals, including a great weekend brunch. Popular dishes on the all-vegetarian menu include the Indian-flavored Dal Baby ($5.50) and the vegetable samosas. (☎543-6592. Open M-F 11am-10pm, Sa-Su brunch 10am-3pm and dinner 5-10pm. Entrees $3-6.) Athenians cheer the bakers behind **Big City Bread,** 393 N. Finley St., and their oven imported from France. Organic breads ($3-4 per loaf) and pastries proper for a Georgia peach (under $2.50) line the indoor/outdoor cafe. (☎543-1187. Open M-Sa 7am-6pm, Su 9am-3pm.) No Athenian culinary experience can lack an immense 50¢ scoop from **Hodgson's Pharmacy,** 1220 S. Milledge Ave., maybe the last place on earth where ice cream comes so cheap. (☎543-7386. Open M-Sa 9am-7pm, Su 2-7pm.)

◨◪ SIGHTS AND ENTERTAINMENT. For an in-depth look at Athens's old and new, take the 1½hr. **Classic City Tour.** This fascinating $10 driving tour tells the stories of the antebellum homes, the Civil War, and UGA. (☎353-1820 or 208-8687 for reservations. Tours leave from the welcome center daily at 2pm; walk-ins are welcome.) Athens is home to one of the state's grandest cultural institutions, the **Georgia Museum of Art,** 90 Carlton St., in the university's Performing and Visual Arts Complex. The museum houses a collection of over 8000 works and shows about 20 different exhibitions a year. (☎542-4662. Open Tu and Th-Sa 10am-5pm, W 10am-9pm, Su 1-5pm. Free.) At the **State Botanical Garden of Georgia,** 2450 S. Milledge Ave., folk cures for diabetes, epilepsy, and the flu grow in the international gardens. (☎542-1244. Open daily 8am-sunset. Visitors center open M-Sa 9am-4:30pm, Su 11:30am-4:30pm. Free.) Athens's grandest Greek Revival mansion, the **Taylor-Grady House,** 634 Prince Ave., once housed the newspaperman who coined the term "New South." (☎549-8688. Open M-F 10am-1pm and 2:30-5pm. $3.) Athenian legend recalls that Prof. W. H. Jackson deeded that the white oak standing at Dearing and S. Finley St. own itself and its shade. The original **"Tree that Owns Itself"** died in 1942 but was reborn from one of its own acorns.

The popular **Butts-Mehre Heritage Hall,** 1 Selig Circle, allows Dawgs fans to relive the greatest moments in UGA's infamous athletic program. (☎542-9094. Open M-F 8am-5pm, Sa-Su 2-5pm.) The **Morton Theater,** 195 W. Washington St., was the first theater in the US to be owned and run by African Americans. Ticket prices aren't what they were in 1910, but they're still low (☎613-3770; $5-15).

◪ NIGHTLIFE. If on an R.E.M. pilgrimage, check out the **40 Watt Club,** 285 W. Washington St., where the group started out and where many bands today attempt to follow their lead. (☎549-7871. Open daily 10pm-3am. Cover $5-12.) Appealing to a hatless, slightly more mature crowd, **The Globe,** 199 N. Lumpkin St., draws grad students in droves. The big brass bar offers over 100 types of beer. (☎353-4721.

THE SOUTH

Open M-Tu 4pm-1am, W-Sa 4pm-2am.) Bask in the warm Georgia sunshine at **Boar's Head,** 263 E. Washington St. (☎369-3040), the only downtown bar with a patio, and a grand one at that. Once an old Shell gas station, **Jittery Joe's,** 1210 S. Milledge Rd., is now a posh, 90s coffee sophisticate. Cozy and remote, Joe's provides a relaxed atmosphere for late night visitin'. (☎208-1979. Open Su 8:30am-midnight, M-Th 6:30am-midnight, F 6:30am-1am, Sa 8:30am-1am.) In the Five Points District, **Sons of Italy,** 1573 S. Lumpkin St., packs 'em in with a roadside ping-pong table and an outdoor bar with patio. (☎543-2516. Open M 3pm-2am, Tu-Sa 11am-2pm, Su 11am-midnight.) In mid-July, **Athfest** features hundreds of local bands playing in the downtown area (☎548-1973; $10 per day, both days $15). The free weekly *Flagpole*, found in local bars and restaurants, details upcoming shows and events.

ANDERSONVILLE NATIONAL HISTORIC SITE

The ☒**Andersonville National Historic Site,** Hwy. 49 in Andersonville, was home to the Civil War's deadliest prisoner-of-war camp. Located about an hour from Macon, this camp stands as a testament, like the battlefields of northern Virginia, to the brutality of the last two years of the American Civil War. Rampant disease, overcrowding, and slum conditions killed 13,000 of the 45,000 captured Union soldiers imprisoned there between 1864 and 1865. After the War, the Commandant of the Camp was the only Confederate officer to be hanged as a war criminal. On the site rests the **National Prisoner of War Museum,** a powerful collection of video personal testimonies and photographs, which cover captivity from the Revolutionary War to the Gulf War. Behind the Site and the Museum, the **Andersonville National Cemetery** continues to be a final resting place for veterans. (☎912-924-0343. Site and cemetery open 8am-5pm daily, museum open 8:30am-5pm. Free.)

OKEFENOKEE SWAMP   ☎912

Just inside the Georgia border, the Okefenokee Swamp has gained much attention for its wealth of biodiversity. The **Okefenokee National Wildlife Refuge,** established to preserve the swamp, includes 396,000 acres of one of the most well sustained freshwater areas in the US. While a bog covers a vast region, the refuge is comprised of many other habitats as well: lakes, cypress forests, islands, and open wet "prairies." With the sundry flora comes a motley crew of fauna, ranging from alligators to white ibis, red-cockaded woodpeckers to indigo snakes. Only a few of the refuge's trails can be traversed by foot, but a number of waterways permit bolder types to get a firsthand look at the swamp in a canoe.

The refuge is open daily 30min. before sunrise until 7:30pm. There is an entrance fee of $5 per vehicle. Three entrances guide visitors into the refuge, each offering their own unique opportunities for sighting wildlife. At the **East Entrance,** the main access located 11 mi. southwest of Folkston off Rte. 121/23, a brief stop at the **Richard S. Bolt Visitor Center** provides a wealth of trail maps and info on the indigenous species (☎496-7836; open daily 9am-5pm). The **West Entrance** is found at Stephen C. Foster State Park, 17 mi. east of Fargo off Hwy. Spur 177. The **Okefenokee Swamp Park** flanks the **North Entrance,** 8 mi. south of Waycross off U.S. 1. This private establishment makes the swamp available to landlubbers, safeguarding gators, otters, and snakes in a natural setting. The park also offers water tours and a museum on Walt Kelly and the comic strip (Pogo) he based on Okefenokee. (☎283-0583. Open daily 9am-5:30pm. $10, seniors and ages 5-11 $9. 1hr. boat tour $14, canoe tour $16.)

Right across from the East Entrance on Rte. 121/23, the **Okefenokee Pastimes Campground** sports nature trails, a wildlife habitat, and a gallery featuring regional artists. (☎496-4472. Primitive sites $12; $3 for 3rd person, $5 each additional person. RV with full hook-up $16; $3 per additional person.) **Stephen C. Foster State Park,** at the West Entrance, is the only campground located within the refuge. (☎637-5274. June-Feb. tents $13, RV with full hook-up $15; June-Feb. $16/$18.) Waycross, near the North entrance to the refuge, has a number of cheap motels along U.S. 1. Just 60 mi. east of the swamp, the historic port town of **Brunswick** often serves as headquarters for those who plan to make daytrips to either Okefenokee or the Golden Isles. The nearby **Hostel in the Forest,** off U.S. 82 (Mi. 11) provides a safe haven in, well, the forest. Dome-shaped huts and roosters lend this funky joint a tranquil ambience, but beware the dirt access road, not intended for the off-roading novice. (☎264-9738. Communal meals nightly at 8pm. Dorms $13, ages 7-12 $8. Linen $2, laundry $2.)

NEAR OKEFENOKEE SWAMP: CUMBERLAND ISLAND

About 50 mi. east of Okefenokee Swamp, the **Cumberland Island National Seashore** consists of 17½ mi. of salt marsh, live oak forest, and sand dunes laced with trails and a few decaying mansions. Phone reservations are necessary for entry into the parks. The effort is rewarded with seclusion; you can walk all day on these beaches without seeing a soul. (☎912-882-4335. Open M-F 10am-4pm.) The **ferry** leaves from St. Mary's, on the mainland at the terminus of Rte. 40 at the Florida border. (45min. In summer ferry runs to Cumberland Su-Tu twice daily, W-Sa thrice daily; returns once daily. In winter ferry runs to Cumberland twice daily, returns once daily. $10, seniors $8, under 13 $6.)

SAVANNAH   ☎912

In February 1733, General James Oglethorpe and a rag-tag band of 120 vagabonds founded the city of Savannah and the state of Georgia at Tamacraw Bluff on the Savannah River. General Sherman later spared the city during his famous rampage through the South. Some say he found it too pretty to burn, even presenting Savannah to President Lincoln as a Christmas gift. Today, the general's reaction is still believable to anyone who sees Savannah's antique stores and stately old trees, its Federalist and English Regency houses amid spring blossoms. More recently, the movie *Forrest Gump* has popularized a certain bench in Chippewa Sq., while John Berendt's best-seller *Midnight in the Garden of Good and Evil* continues to attract readers to this lovable town and its welcoming inhabitants.

ORIENTATION AND PRACTICAL INFORMATION

Savannah rests on the coast of Georgia at the mouth of the **Savannah River,** which runs north of the city along the border with South Carolina. The city stretches south from bluffs overlooking the river. The restored 2½ sq. mi. **downtown historic district,** bordered by East Broad, Martin Luther King, Jr. Blvd., Gwinnett St., and the river, is best explored on foot. *Do not stray south of Gwinnett St.; the historic district quickly deteriorates into an unsafe area.* **Tybee Island,** Savannah's beach, 18 mi. east on U.S. 80 and Rte. 26, makes a fine daytrip. Try to visit the city at the beginning of spring, when Savannah's streets are lined with flowers.

THE SOUTH

Trains: Amtrak, 2611 Seaboard Coastline Dr. (☎234-2611), 4 mi. outside the city. To Charleston (2hr., 2 per day, $23). Station open Sa-Th 4:30am-noon and 4:30pm-midnight; F 4:30am-midnight. Taxi to downtown $5.

Buses: Greyhound, 610 W. Oglethorpe Ave. (☎232-2135), at Fahm St. To: Jacksonville (2hr., 13 per day, $21); Charleston (3hr., 2 per day, $22-24); and Atlanta (6-8 hr., 5 per day, $41-43). Open 24hr.

Public Transit: Chatham Area Transit (CAT), 124 Bull St. (☎233-5767). Runs daily 7am-11pm. Fare 75¢, seniors 37¢; no transfers. Weekly pass $12. The CAT shuttle runs through the historic area daily M-Sa 7am-6pm, Su 9:40am-5pm. Free.

Taxis: Adam Cab, ☎927-7466.

Visitor Info: Savannah Visitors Center, 301 Martin Luther King, Jr. Blvd. (☎944-0455), at Liberty St., in a lavish former train station. Reservation service for local inns and hostels (☎877-728-2662). $5 parking pass allows unlimited use of all metered parking and city lots for 2 days. Open M-F 8:30am-5pm, Sa-Su 9am-5pm.

Hotlines: Rape Crisis Center, ☎233-7273. 24hr.

Post Office: 2 N. Fahm St. (☎235-4608), at Bay St. Open M-F 7am-6pm, Sa 9am-3pm. ZIP code: 31402. Area code: 912.

⌐ ACCOMMODATIONS

Downtown motels cluster near the historic area, visitors center, and Greyhound station. For those with cars, **Ogeechee Rd. (U.S. 17)** has several budget options.

Savannah International Youth Hostel (HI-AYH), 304 E. Hall St. (☎236-7744), in a restored Victorian mansion in the historic district 2 blocks east of Forsyth Park. Closed Dec. 1 to Feb. 28. Check-in 7:30-10am and 5-10pm; call Brian for late check-in. Lockout 10am-5pm. Flexible 3-night maximum stay. Dorm beds (6 per room) $18; hard-to-get private rooms $31. Linen $1. Bikes $10.

Thunderbird Inn, 611 W. Oglethorpe Ave. (☎232-2661), across from the Greyhound station. The least expensive rooms downtown. Modest exterior hides nice furnishings. A/C and cable TV. Su-Th singles $32, doubles $40; F-Sa $45/$50. 5% off with reservations and mention of *Let's Go.*

Motel 6, 4071 Rte. 17 (☎756-3543 or 800-466-8356), 20 mi. south of the historic downtown district; take Exit 87 off I-95. Clean and affordable rooms with cable TV and A/C. Singles Su-Th $34, F-Sa $35. $6 for second adult.

Skidaway Island State Park (☎598-2300 or 800-864-7275), 13 mi. southeast of downtown off Diamond Causeway. Inaccessible by public transportation. Follow Liberty St. east from downtown until it becomes Wheaton St.; turn right on Waters Ave. and follow it to the Diamond Causeway. Bathrooms, heated showers, electricity, and water. Swimming pool $2. Open daily 7am-10pm. Check-in before 10pm. Tent sites $16, RV $18.

Fort McAllister State Park (☎727-2339); take Exit 90 off I-95. Wooded sites with water and electricity, some with a water view. All located on island surrounded by marsh ("Savage Island"). Office open daily 8am-5pm; campground open 7am-10pm. Check-in before 10pm. Parking $2. Tent sites $13, RV $15.

⌐ FOOD

■ **Nita's Place,** 140 Abercorn St. (☎283-8233), gives reason enough to come to Savannah. Owner Juanita Dixon and family set the standard for soul food with tender fried chicken, all fresh veggies, and "spoon bread." The dessert-like squash casserole, a delight beyond description, will make you hug the chef. Open M-Tu 11:30am-3pm, W-Sa 11:30am-3pm and 4-8pm.

Wall's BBQ, 515 E. York Ln. (☎232-9754), in an alley between York and Oglethorpe. This tiny, nondescript house churns out fantastic ribs ($9.50), BBQ sandwiches ($4), and their specialty, baked deviled crabs ($3). Open W 11am-6pm, Th-Sa 11am-9pm.

Mrs. Wilkes Boarding House, 107 W. Jones St. (☎232-5997), a Southern institution. Friendly strangers sit around a large table eating luscious fried chicken, butter beans, and superb biscuits; don't leave before dessert! Breakfast ($5). All-you-can-eat lunch $10. *The wait in line is up to 2hr.* Get there at 11am. Open M-F 8-9am and 11am-3pm.

Clary's Cafe, 404 Abercorn St. (☎233-0402). A family spot since 1903 with a famous weekend brunch and friendly service. Malted waffle $4. Open M-F 7am-10pm, W 7am-5pm, Sa 8am-4pm and 5-10pm, Su 8am-10pm.

Olympia Cafe, 5 E. River St. (☎233-3131), on the river. Greek specialties and more, including veggie gyro ($6.55). Lunch or dinner $5-18. Open daily 11am-11pm.

⌐ SIGHTS

Most of Savannah's 21 squares contain some distinctive centerpiece. Elegant antebellum houses and drooping vine-wound trees often cluster around the squares, adding to the classic Southern aura. Bus, van, and horse carriage **tours** leave every 10-15min. from the visitors center ($13-15), but walking might be more fun.

Savannah's best-known historic houses are the **Davenport House,** on Columbia Sq., and the **Owens-Thomas House,** a block away on Oglethorpe Sq. The Davenport House, earmarked to be razed for a parking lot, was saved in 1955. Tours explore the 1st fl. every 30min.; the 3rd fl. is open to explore at your leisure. *(Davenport: 324 E. State St. ☎236-8097. Open daily 10am-4pm. Last tour 4pm. $6. Owens-Thomas: 124*

BETTER HOMES AND GARDENS A notorious and sophisticated antiques dealer, a scandalous and flamboyant drag queen, the prim and proper members of the Married Women's Card Club, and a melancholy soul with a vial of poison potent enough to kill every man, woman, and child in town: these are a few of the characters that have recently seized the attention of readers in 11 different countries. The colorful plot of *Midnight in the Garden of Good and Evil,* a *New York Times* best-seller, revolves around a highly publicized fatal shooting at Mercer House, a venerable and elegant old home on Monterey Sq. Was it murder or self-defense? Although the social elite about town have denounced "The Book's" exposure of their secrets in indignant whispered exchanges, tourism has skyrocketed by 46%, and it's hard to find a local who doesn't claim to be actually referred to in the book, however vaguely. **"The Book" Gift Shop,** 127 E. Gordon St. (☎233-3867), at Calhoun Sq., a fan club, Midnight tours, and a Hollywood adaptation all attest to the interest and revenue which "The Book" has generated.

Abercorn St. ☎233-9743. Open M noon-5pm, Tu-Sa 10am-5pm, Su 2-5pm. Last tour 4:30pm. $8, students $4, seniors $7, ages 6-12 $2.) The **Green Meldrim House,** on Madison Sq., is a Gothic Revival mansion that served as one of General Sherman's headquarters during the Civil War. *(1 W. Macon St. ☎233-3845. Open Tu and Th-F 10am-4pm, Sa 10am-1pm. Tours every 30min., last tour half-hr. before closing. $5.)*

Lovers of the cookies formerly known as Thin Mints and Tag-alongs make a pilgrimage to the **Juliette Gordon Low Birthplace,** near Wright Sq. The Girl Scouts' founder was born here on Halloween 1860, which might explain the Girl Scouts' door-to-door treat technique. The "cookie shrine" contains an interesting collection of Girl Scout memorabilia. *(142 Bull St. ☎233-4501. Open M-Tu and Th-Sa 10am-4pm, Su 12:30-4:30pm. $6, students, seniors, and children $5.)* The **Negro Heritage Trail Tour** visits African-American historic sights. *(502 E. Harris St. ☎234-8000. 2hr. tours daily from visitors center, 1 and 3pm. $15, ages 12 and under $12.)*

Savannah's four forts once protected the city's port from Spanish, British, and other invaders. The most interesting, **Fort Pulaski National Monument,** marks the Civil War battle where rifled cannons first pummeled walls, making Pulaski and similar forts obsolete. *(15 mi. east of Savannah on U.S. 80 E and Rte. 26. ☎786-5787. Open daily 8:30am-5:15pm; extended hrs. in summer; visitors center closes 5pm. $2, $4 maximum per car, under 17 free.)*

Special events in Savannah include the **Annual NOGS Tour of the Hidden Gardens of Historic Savannah,** when private walled gardens are opened to the public. *(☎238-0248; Apr. 27-28, 2001.)* Green is the theme of the **St. Patrick's Day Celebration on the River,** a five-day, beer-and-fun-filled party which packs the streets and warms celebrants up for the **Annual St. Patrick's Day Parade,** the 2nd largest in the US. *(Celebration: ☎234-0295. Parade: ☎233-4804, begins at 10:15am.)* A free paper, *Creative Loafing,* found in restaurants and stores, has the latest in news and entertainment.

 NIGHTLIFE

The waterfront area (River St.) offers endless oceanfront dining opportunities, street performers, and a friendly pub ambience. **Kevin Barry's Irish Pub,** 117 W. River St., stages live Irish folk music. *(☎233-9626. Open M-F 4pm-3am, Sa 11:30am-3am, Su 12:30pm-2am. Music W-Su after 8:30pm. Cover $2.)* For a drink that will keep you on your ear for days, check out **Wet Willies,** 101 E. River St., with its casual dining, young folks, and irresistible frozen daiquiris for $3.50-5.50. *(☎233-5650. Open M-Th 10:30am-1am, F-Sa 10:30am-2pm, Su 12:30pm-midnight.)* Local college students eat, drink, and shop at **City Market.** One hot spot is **Malone's Bar and Grill,** 27 Barnard St., with dancing, drinks, and daily live music. The lower floor opens up to a game room, while techno beats on the 3rd fl. *(☎234-3059. Open M-Sa 11am-3am, Su 11am-2am. Restaurant open until 1am. Happy hour 4-8pm.)* Hustlers will enjoy the ten Gandi pool tables and over 80 beers at **B&B Billiards,** 411 W. Congress St. *(☎233-7116. Open M-Sa 4pm-3am. Happy hour daily 4-8pm. Free pool Tu and Th.)*

The Lady Chablis, featured in *Midnight in the Garden of Good and Evil* (see box, p. 389), performs regularly at the popular gay/lesbian hotspot **Club One,** 1 Jefferson St., near City Market, at Bay St. (☎232-0200. Open M-Sa 5pm-3am, Su 5pm-2am. Cover $3-6.) All kinds of live music rocks W-Sa nights at **The Velvet Elvis,** 127 W. Congress St.; look for neon lights in the window. (☎236-0665. Open Tu-F 5pm-3am, Sa 6pm-3am. Cover $2-8.)

ALABAMA

The "Heart of Dixie" is often remembered for its controversial role in the civil rights movement of the 60s, when Governor George Wallace fought a vicious campaign opposing integration. Today, this once stalwart defender of segregation strives to broaden its image and reconcile its past. The legacy of that past comprises Alabama's most poignant attractions, as museums, statues, and sites pay homage to those it vilified 30 years ago. There is much more to this state than its history however; Southern cuisine, local festivities, and nationally acclaimed gardens mix to create the 'Bama of today.

■ PRACTICAL INFORMATION

Capital: Montgomery.

Visitor Info: Alabama Bureau of Tourism and Travel, 401 Adams Ave., Montgomery 36104 (☎334-242-4169 or 800-252-2262; www.touralabama.org.) Open M-F 8am-5pm. **Division of Parks,** 64 N. Union St., Montgomery 36104 (☎800-252-7275). Open daily 8am-5pm.

Postal Abbreviation: AL. **Sales Tax:** 4%, plus county tax.

MONTGOMERY   ☎334

Today Montgomery stands still and quiet, in sharp contrast to its tumultuous past as the first capital of the Confederacy and the birthplace of America's civil rights movement. Montgomery's role in the movement took off in 1955, when local authorities arrested Rosa Parks, a black seamstress, because she refused to give up her seat to a white man on a city bus. The success of an ensuing bus boycott, organized by local minister Dr. Martin Luther King, Jr., encouraged nationwide reform. Montgomery relies on its prominent past to overcome a nondescript today; civil rights movement battlegrounds are the main attractions, with some variety provided by Shakespearian drama, home cooking, and memories of Hank Williams.

■■ **ORIENTATION AND PRACTICAL INFORMATION.** Downtown follows a grid pattern: Madison Ave. and Washington Ave. are the major east-west routes; Union St. and Decatur St. run north-south. West of downtown, **I-65** runs north-south and intersects **I-85,** which forms Montgomery's southern border. **Greyhound,** 950 W. South Blvd. (☎286-0658; open 24hr.), at Exit 168 on I-65, runs to Mobile (3hr., 8 per day, $31); Atlanta (4hr., 6 per day, $33); and Tuskegee (45min., 6 per day, $9.50). **Amtrak,** 950 W. South Blvd., adjacent to the Greyhound station, offers limited bus service to the connecting city of Atlanta, but no actual trains; ask at Greyhound. **Downtown Area Runabout Transit (DART)** runs local buses 6am-6pm (fare $1.50, no transfers). **Taxis: Yellow Cab,** ☎262-5225. **Visitors Center:** 300 Water St., in Union Station (☎262-0013; open M-F 8:30am-5pm, Sa 9am-4pm, Su noon-4pm). **Hotlines: Council Against Rape,** ☎286-5987. **Help-A-Crisis,** ☎279-7837. Both 24 hours. **Post Office:** 135 Catoma St. (open M-F 7:30am-5:30pm, Sa 8am-noon). **ZIP code:** 36104. **Area code:** 334.

⌐ ACCOMMODATIONS. For those with a car, South Blvd., at I-65 Exit 168, overflows with inexpensive beds—beware the cheapest of the cheap, which are fairly seedy. Downtown is the comfortable and newly renovated ■**Town Plaza,** 743

Madison Ave., at N. Ripley St. near the visitors center. Rooms come with all the perks: A/C, TV, free local calls, and microfridges. (☎269-1561. Singles $24; doubles $30 for *Let's Go* toters.) Right next to I-65 on W. South Blvd., **The Inn South,** 4243 Inn South Ave., greets travelers with an unusually dramatic lobby for a budget motel. (☎288-7999 or 800-642-0890. Continental breakfast, free local calls, cable; microfridge upon request. Singles $29, Sa-Su $34; doubles $36; $2 per additional person. Wheelchair accessible.) The site of a 1763 French stronghold, **Fort Toulouse Jackson Park,** 12 mi. north of Montgomery on Rte. 6 off U.S. 231, has 39 rustic sites with water and electricity in beautiful woods. Other sites grace the Coosa River. (☎567-3002. Registration daily 8am-5pm. Tents $8, RVs $10; $2 senior discount. Make reservations at least 2 weeks in advance in spring and fall.)

FOOD. Martin's, 1796 Carter Hill at Mulberry, offers glorious fried chicken. (☎265-0757. Open M-F 11am-3pm and 4-7:45pm, Su 10:45am-1:45pm. Meat and 3 veggies $7.) With 20 vegetable options for burritos ($4.50-7.50), **El Reys,** 1031 East Fairview, provides a vegetarian option in a collegiate setting. (☎832-9688. Open M-Sa 11am-10pm, Su 4-10pm.) Munch down on some hot dogs at the oldest restaurant in town, **Chris's,** 138 Dexter Ave. An old haunt of Hank Williams (who allegedly got ejected more than once), Chris's makes hotdogs like nobody else. The special ($1.65) comes with mustard, onions, 'kraut and chili sauce. (☎265-6850. Open M-Sa 10am-7pm, F until 8pm.) Snag a bag of peaches for $2 at the **Montgomery State Farmers Market,** at Federal Dr. and Coliseum Blvd. (☎242-5350. Open daily 7am-5pm.)

SIGHTS. Maya Lin, the architect who designed the Vietnam Veterans Memorial in Washington, D.C. (p. 295), also designed Montgomery's newest sight, the **Civil Rights Memorial,** in front of the Southern Poverty Law Center. The outdoor monument, over which water continuously flows, pays tribute to 40 men, women, and children who died fighting for civil rights. *(400 Washington Ave. ☎264-0286. Open 24hr. Free. Wheelchair accessible.)* The legacy of African-American activism and faith survives one block away, at the 112-year-old **King Memorial Baptist Church.** This is where Dr. King first preached and the 1955 bus boycott was organized. The basement mural chronicles Dr. King's role in the nation's struggle for civil rights from Montgomery to Memphis. *(454 Dexter Ave. ☎263-3970. Tours M-Th 10am and 2pm, F 10am, Sa 10:30, 11:15am, noon and 12:45pm. Donations accepted.)*

The **Hank Williams Museum** honors country music's most beloved legend. His ballads filter among his outfits, memorabilia, and the '52 Cadillac he died in at age 29. *(118 Commerce. ☎262-3600. Open M-Sa 9am-6pm, Su 1-4pm. $5, under 12 $1.)* Country music fans make daily pilgrimages to the **Hank Williams Grave,** near downtown. *(1304 Upper Wetumpka Rd. in the Oakwood Cemetery Annex. Open M-F 10am-sunset.)*

THE SELMA TO MONTGOMERY MARCH In the Selma of 1964, only 1% of eligible blacks had the right to vote due to state-imposed restrictions. In 1965, to protest these conditions, civil rights activists organized an ill-fated march on the state capitol that was quashed by bayonet-carrying troops. Their spirits battered but not destroyed, the marchers tried again, this time encouraged by the likes of Dr. Martin Luther King, Jr., Joan Baez, Sammy Davis, Jr., Harry Belafonte, Lena Horne, and Mahalia Jackson. The second march, a 54 mi. trek from Selma to Montgomery, ended without conflict, prompting a weary Dr. King to declare the movement the "greatest march ever made on a state capitol in the South." King's analysis of the monumental significance of the event was not lost on President Lyndon B. Johnson, who noted with eloquence, "At times, history and fate meet at a single time in a single place to shape a turning point in man's unending search for freedom. So it was at Lexington and Concord. So it was a century ago at Appomattox. And so it was last week, in Selma, Alabama." A year later, Congress passed the Voting Rights Act, which prohibited states from using prerequisites to disqualify voters on the basis of color.

Old Alabama Town, two blocks off Madison and four blocks north of the King Memorial Baptist Church, reconstructs 19th-century Alabama with over 40 period buildings, including a pioneer homestead, an 1892 grocery, and an early African-American church. *(301 Columbus St.* ☎ *240-4500. Open M-F 9am-3pm.)*

A modest exterior hides the exquisitely decorated **State Capitol.** On the front steps, a bronze star commemorates the spot where Jefferson Davis took the oath of office as president of the Confederacy. *(Bainbridge St. and Dexter Ave.* ☎ *242-3935. Open M-F 9am-5pm, Sa 9am-4pm. Guided tours available. Free.)* The **First White House of the Confederacy** contains period furnishings and many of President Jefferson Davis's personal belongings. *(644 Washington Ave.* ☎ *242-1861. Open M-F 8am-4:30pm. Free.)*

The **F. Scott and Zelda Fitzgerald Museum** contains a few of her paintings and some of his original manuscripts, as well as their strangely monogrammed bath towels. *(919 Felder Ave., off Carter Hill Rd.* ☎ *264-4222. Open W-F 10am-2pm, Sa-Su 1-5pm. Free.)* The **Montgomery Museum of Fine Arts** houses a substantial collection of 19th- and 20th-century American paintings and graphics, as well as "Artworks," a hands-on gallery and art studio for kids. *(1 Museum Dr.* ☎ *244-5700. Open Tu-W and F-Sa 10am-5pm, Th 10am-9pm, Su noon-5pm. Free, donations appreciated.)*

⛫ ENTERTAINMENT. "Roses are red, violets are blue / Since you bought *Let's Go,* we love you." If you think that really sucked and want something a bit classier, head out to the **Alabama Shakespeare Festival,** the fifth largest in the world, staged at the **State Theater** on the grounds of the 250-acre private estate, **Wynton M. Blount Cultural Park;** take East Blvd. 15min. southeast of downtown onto Woodmere Blvd. The theater also hosts contemporary plays. (☎ 271-5353 or 800-841-4273. Box office open M-Sa 10am-6pm, Su noon-4pm, till 9pm on performance nights. Tickets $25-30; previews the week before opening $21.) For some blues and beers, try **1048,** 1048 E. Fairview Ave., near Woodley Ave. (☎ 834-1048. Open daily from 4pm.) The Th *Montgomery Advertiser* lists other entertainment options.

NEAR MONTGOMERY

TUSKEGEE. After Reconstruction, "emancipated" blacks in the South remained segregated and disenfranchised. **Booker T. Washington,** a former slave, believed that blacks could best improve their situation through hard work and learning a trade. The curriculum at the college Washington founded, Tuskegee Institute, revolved around such practical endeavors as agriculture and carpentry, with students constructing almost all of the campus buildings. Today, a more academically-oriented **Tuskegee University** fills 160 buildings on 1500 acres; the buildings of Washington's original institute comprise a national historical site (☎ 727-8349 for tours). Nearby is the **George Washington Carver Museum.** Artist, teacher, scientist, and head of the Agricultural Dept., Carver discovered many practical uses for the peanut, including axle grease and peanut butter. The **visitors center** for the University is inside the museum. (☎ 727-3200. Open daily 9am-5pm. Free.) Down the street on old Montgomery Rd. lies **The Oaks,** a restoration of Washington's home. Free tours depart from the museum on the hr. (daily 10am-4pm). To get to Tuskegee, take I-85 toward Atlanta and exit at Rte. 81 S. Turn right at the intersection of Rte. 81 and Old Montgomery Rd. onto Rte. 126. **Greyhound** (☎ 727-1290) runs from Montgomery (45min., 6 per day, $8-9). **Area code:** 334.

SELMA. Unfortunately for Selma, much of her fame originates in a history of defeat and dubious deeds. The small, historic Southern town was shaped by two momentous events that took place 100 years apart. As a stronghold for the Confederate armies (Selma's arsenal produced two-thirds of the South's ammunition during the last years of the war), her fall in 1865 marked a decisive victory for the North. A century later, Selma gained notoriety from the Voting Rights movement, specifically the clash between marchers and State troopers at Pettus Bridge that injured 65 people and sent 17 to the hospital (see **The Selma to Montgomery March** on p. 391). **The Old Depot Museum,** 4 Martin Luther King St., explores the history of Selma with artifacts of past and present, some dating back thousands of years to the area's original inhabitants. The Civil War is strongly represented with period relics, as is the civil rights movement. (☎874-2197. Open M-Sa 10am-4pm. $4, seniors $3, students $2.) The **National Voting Rights Museum & Institute,** 1012 Water Ave., houses memorabilia concerning the Voting Rights Act of 1965. (☎418-0800. Open Tu-F 9am-5pm, Sa 10am-3pm. $4, $2 students.) A companion sight to the museum is the **Brown Chapel AME Church and King Monument,** 410 Martin Luther King St., which served as the headquarters for many civil rights meetings.

Downtown Selma is bordered by **Jeff Davis Ave.** to the north and the **Alabama River** to the south. **U.S. 80,** which becomes **Broad St.,** runs straight through town. **Greyhound,** 434 Broad St. (☎874-4503; open daily 6:45am-10:45pm), runs to Montgomery (1hr, 6 per day, $13). **Visitors Center:** 2207 Broad St. (☎875-7485. Open daily 8am-8pm.) **Post Office:** 723 Alabama Ave. (☎874-4678. Open M-F 8am-4:40pm, Sa 8am-noon.) **Zip Code:** 36701. **Area code:** 334.

BIRMINGHAM ☎205

Birmingham, like its English namesake, sits atop soil rich in coal and iron ore—minerals responsible for its lightning-quick growth following the Civil War. "The Magic City" became the first industrial center of the South and the largest city of Alabama, a distinction it still carries. In the mid-20th century, however, the city was known to some as "Bombingham," and the Magic City became "The Tragic City" as it experienced some of the worst race-related violence of the period. To its credit, the city refuses to shy away from its controversial past: parks, museums, and memorials honor the heroes and martyrs of the Civil Rights Movement.

⊏ GETTING THERE AND GETTING AROUND

Trains: Amtrak, 1819 Morris Ave. (☎324-3033). To Atlanta (4hr., 1 per day, $27) and New Orleans (7hr., 1 per day, $33). Open 8:30am-5pm.

Buses: Greyhound, 618 19th St. N (251-3210). To: Montgomery (2hr., 5 per day, $20); Mobile (6-8hr., 6 per day, $41); and Atlanta (3hr., 10 per day, $22-24). 24hr.

Public Transit: Metropolitan Area Express (MAX) operates M-F 6am-6pm. Fare $1, transfers 25¢. **Downtown Area Runabout Transit (DART)** runs M-F 9am-4pm. Fare 50¢. For info on both, call ☎521-0101.

Taxi: Yellow Cab, ☎252-1131.

■■ ORIENTATION AND PRACTICAL INFORMATION

Downtown Birmingham is a regular grid, with numbered avenues running east-west and numbered streets running north-south. Richard Arrington, Jr. Blvd. is the one exception, running along what would have been called 21st St. The only complication is that downtown is in fact two grids, northside and southside, divided by railroad tracks—thus both avenues and streets are designated "N" or "S." **I-65, I-59,** and **Hwy. 31** form a U around downtown, leaving the southern side exposed.

Visitor Info: Greater Birmingham Convention and Visitors Center, 2200 9th Ave. N (☎458-8000 or 800-458-8085), 1st fl. Open M-F 8:30am-5pm.

Internet Access: 2100 Park Place (☎226-3600), at Richard Arrington, Jr. Blvd. Open M-Tu 9am-8pm, W-Sa 8am-6pm, Su 2-6pm.

Hotlines: Crisis Center, ☎323-7777. **Rape Response,** ☎323-7273. Both 24hr. **Gay info line:** ☎326-8600.

Post Office: 351 24th St. N (☎521-0302; open M-F 6am-11pm). **ZIP code:** 35203. **Area code:** 205.

■■ ACCOMMODATIONS AND FOOD

There are lots of cheap hotels and motels along the various interstates leading into Birmingham. A pleasant non-chain option in the city is **The Ranchouse Inn,** 2127 7th Ave. S, just north of Five Points. (☎322-0691. Singles $40; doubles $45. Wheelchair accessible.) Visitors may camp in Alabama's largest (10,000 acres) state park, **Oak**

Mountain State Park, 15 mi. south of Birmingham off I-65 in Pelham at Exit 246. Horseback rides, golf, hiking, and an 85-acre lake with beach and fishing are all available in the area. (☎ 620-2527 or 800-252-7275. Basic sites $10.50, water and electricity $14, full hook-up $16.50. Parking $1.)

With over 60 joints to choose from, barbecue reigns as the local specialty. **Five Points South,** an old streetcar suburb near the University at the intersection of 6th Ave. S and 20th St. S, is the best place to eat cheap and meet young people. **Jim 'N Nick's Barbecue,** 744 29th St. S, roasts chicken, pork, and beef BBQ sandwiches ($3) on a hickory wood fire in a brick pit out back. (☎ 323-7082. Open daily 10:30am-9pm, F closes at 10pm.) Birmingham's oldest seafood wholesaler doubles as the **Fish Market Restaurant,** 611 Richard Arrington, Jr. Blvd. S, a no-frills joint with cheap catch of the sea; fish entrees run $5-8. (☎ 322-3330. Open M-Th 10am-9pm, F-Sa 10am-10pm.) Closer to attractions downtown is **Hosie's Barbecue and Fish,** 321 14th St. N, a local landmark that serves greasy Southern classics like pig ear dinners ($6) and $1.35 sides like yams or collard greens. (☎ 326-3495. Open M 11am-8pm, Tu-Th 11am-10pm, F-Sa 11am-"till the customers stop walking.")

◉ SIGHTS

CIVIL RIGHTS SIGHTS. Birmingham's efforts to reconcile its turbulent past have culminated in the **Birmingham Civil Rights District,** centered around the intersection of 16th St. and 6th Ave. N., a six-block tribute to the fight for freedom and equality. The ◧**Birmingham Civil Rights Institute** traces the nation's civil rights struggle throughout the '50s and '60s, both through traditional displays and documentary footage. The institute also highlights contemporary human rights issues across the globe and serves as a public research facility. (*520 16th St. N, at 6th Ave. N.* ☎ *328-9696. Open Tu-Sa 10am-5pm, Su 1-5pm. $5, seniors $2, college students $1, 17 and under free. Th free.*) Across the street from the Institute is the **Sixteenth St. Baptist Church,** where four black girls died in a Sept. 1963 bombing by white segregationists. (*1530 6th Ave. N, at 16th St. N.* ☎ *251-9402. Open Tu-F 10am-4pm, Sa by appointment. $2 suggested donation.*) Protests spurred on by the deaths occurred in nearby **Kelly-Ingram Park,** at the corner of 6th Ave. and 16th St., where statues and sculptures commemorating the civil rights demonstrations now grace the green lawns.

HALLS OF FAME. In the same area as Kelly-Ingram Park is the **Alabama Jazz Hall of Fame,** which remembers the area's various stars, from Erskine Hawkins to Sun Ra and his Intergalactic Arkestra. (*1631 4th Ave. N, in the Carver Theatre.* ☎ *254-2731. Open Tu-Sa 10am-5pm, Su 1-5pm. Free.*) The **Alabama Sports Hall of Fame** honors the state's strangely rich tradition of great athletes, including Jesse Owens, Willie Mays, and Carl Lewis. (*Corner of Civic Center Blvd. and 22nd St. N.* ☎ *323-6665. Open M-Sa 9am-5pm, Su 1-5pm. $5, seniors $4, students $3.*)

OTHER ATTRACTIONS. Birmingham remembers its days as the "Pittsburgh of the South" at the gigantic **Sloss Furnaces National Historic Landmark.** Though the blast furnaces closed 20 years ago, they stand as the only preserved example of 20th-century iron-smelting in the world. Ballet, drama, and music concerts are held in a renovated furnace shed next to the stacks. (*Adjacent to the 1st Ave. N. viaduct off 32nd St. downtown.* ☎ *324-1911. Open Tu-Sa 10am-4pm, Su noon-4pm. Free tours Sa-Su 1, 2, and 3pm.*) Two blocks away is the **Birmingham Museum of Art,** the largest municipal art museum in the South, including over 17,000 works and a sculpture garden. (*2000 8th Ave. N.* ☎ *254-2565. Open Tu-Sa 10am-5pm, Su noon-5pm. $3.50 suggested donation.*)

OUTSIDE THE CITY. For a breather from an educational vacation, visit the 70-acre **Visionland** amusement complex. (*16 mi. southwest of Birmingham at I-20 and I-459.* ☎ *481-4750. Hrs. seasonal; in summer Su noon-9pm, M-Th 11am-9pm, F 11am-10pm, Sa 10am-10pm. $23, under 48 in. $18, seniors $15.*) Or revel in the marvelously sculpted grounds of the **Birmingham Botanical Gardens.** Spectacular floral displays, an elegant Japanese Garden (complete with teahouse), and an enormous greenhouse vegetate on 67 acres. (*2612 Lane Park Rd.* ☎ *879-1227. Garden Center open daily 8am-5pm. Gardens open daily dawn-dusk. Free.*)

🎵🎭 ENTERTAINMENT AND NIGHTLIFE

Historic Alabama Theater, 1817 3rd Ave. N, a gorgeous, renovated 1927 building, is booked 300 nights of the year with films and live performances. Their organ, the "Mighty Wurlitzer," entertains the audience pre-show. (☎252-2262. Order tickets through Ticketmaster ☎715-6000, or at the box office 1hr. prior to show. Showtimes generally 7pm; Su 2pm. Films $6, seniors and children under 12 $5.) In addition to the theater's **Infoline** (☎251-0418), the free *Birmingham Weekly* and the biweekly *black & white* list local entertainment events.

Those lucky enough to visit Birmingham Father's Day weekend can hear everything from country to gospel to big name rock groups at **City Stages.** The three-day festival, held in Linn Park, is the biggest thing to hit town all year and includes food, crafts, and children's activities. (☎251-1272. Daily pass $18, weekend pass $25.)

Nightlife centers around **Five Points South** (Southside). On spring and summer nights, many grab outdoor tables or loiter by the fountain until late. The hippest people jam year-round at **The Nick,** 2514 10th Ave. S. The poster-covered exterior says it clear and proud: "The Nick...rocks." (☎252-3831. Open M-F 3pm-late, Sa 8pm-6am. Happy hour M-F 3-9pm. Live music M-W. Cover $4-7; usually no cover M.) Live bands from reggae to alternative entertain a collegiate crowd at **The Hippodrum,** 2007 Highland Ave. (☎933-6565. Hrs vary, live music Tu-Sa.) Across the street, a better-dressed set lounges on the patio at **Dave's,** 1128 20th St. S. (☎933-4030. Open daily 3pm-4am, closes Sa 2am.)

🏃 DAYTRIPS FROM BIRMINGHAM

MOUNDVILLE. When white settlers first came across **Moundville,** 60 mi. southwest of Birmingham on I-59/20, they believed they had come across the city of some lost classical race. Archaeology would eventually place the two dozen flat-topped earthen mounds, the highest at 58 ft., as the work of the same Mississippian civilization that built **Cahokia** in Illinois (see p. 580). From 1000-1500 AD, the site was the ceremonial capital of a city of 10,000 people; the exact purposes of the mounds, and the causes of their builders' disappearance, are unknown. To reach the park from I-59/20, take Exit 71A to Rte. 69 south 13 mi. (☎371-2572. Park open daily 8am-8pm; visitors center open 9am-5pm. $4, students and ages under 16 $2.)

HUNTSVILLE. Eighty mi. north of Birmingham, Huntsville was the first English-speaking settlement in Alabama and the location of Alabama's constitutional convention in 1819. Far more momentous, however, was the 1950 decision to locate the nation's rocket program here, initially proposed by Wernher von Braun (better known to moviegoers as the basis of Stanley Kubrick's character Dr. Strangelove). The 363 ft. replica of a Saturn V rocket at the **US Space and Rocket Center** is easily recognizable for miles. This self-proclaimed "fun center of the universe" features various space-flight simulators, an IMAX theater, and also runs tours to the nearby Marshall Space Flight Center. (☎837-3400. Open daily 9am-6pm; off-season 9am-5pm. $15, ages 3-12 $11.)

Budget motels and chain restaurants cluster on **University Drive,** northwest of downtown. **Monte Sano State Park,** east of town off U.S. 431, has pleasant campsites in the midst of extensive recreational facilities. (☎534-6589. Primitive sites $9, water and electricity $14, full hook-up $15.) **RV sites** are also available adjacent to the Space and Rocket Center (☎830-4987; full hook-up $14). For food downtown, the friendly **Wild Rose Cafe,** 121 N. Side Square, is a traditional lunch counter serving quality meat-and-three (vegetables, that is) platters on styrofoam plates for $6. (☎539-3658. Open M-F 7:30-9:30am and 11am-2:30pm.)

Greyhound, 601 Monroe St. (☎534-1681; terminal hours 7:30am-11:30pm), runs buses to Nashville (2hr., 4 per day, $15.50); Birmingham (2¼hr., 3 per day, $16.50); and Memphis (7hr., 4 per day, $50). A **tourist shuttle,** mostly aimed at shoppers, runs hourly between downtown, points on University Dr., and the Space and Rocket Center. (M-F 6:40am-6:40pm, Sa 8:40am-7:10pm. $1, all-day pass $2.) **Huntsville Shut-**

THE SOUTH

tle also runs ten other routes, most running daily 6am-6pm. ($1, seniors and children under 7 50¢, transfers free.) Call ☎532-7433 for more info on both shuttles. **Taxis: Huntsville Cab Co.,** ☎539-8288. **Visitors center:** 700 Monroe St., in the Von Braun Center. (☎551-2230. Open M-Sa 9am-5pm, Su noon-5pm.) **Area code:** 256.

MOBILE   ☎334

Though Bob Dylan lamented being stuck here, Mobile (*mo-BEEL*) has had plenty of fans in its time—French, Spanish, English, Sovereign Alabama, Confederate, and American flags have each flown over the city since its 1702 founding. This historical diversity is revealed in local architecture: antebellum mansions, Italianate dwellings, Spanish and French forts, and Victorian homes line azalea-edged streets. Today, Mobile offers an untouristed version of New Orleans; the site of the first Mardi Gras, the city still holds a two-week long Fat Tuesday celebration, without the hordes that plague its Cajun counterpart.

⛰🛈 ORIENTATION AND PRACTICAL INFORMATION. The downtown district borders the Mobile River. **Dauphin St.** and **Government Blvd. (U.S. 90),** which becomes **Government St.** downtown, are the major east-west routes. **Royal St.** and **Broad St.** are major north-south byways. **Water St.** runs along the river in the downtown area, becoming the **I-10 causeway. Frontage Rd.,** along I-65, to the west of downtown, is the same as the **Beltline.**

   Amtrak, 11 Government St. (☎432-4052), runs the "Gulf Breeze" from Mobile to New York City via bus service to Birmingham or Atlanta. From Mobile, three trains per week roll to New Orleans (2½hr.; $32). **Greyhound,** 2545 Government Blvd at S. Conception downtown (☎478-6089; open 24hr.), runs buses to Montgomery (3hr., 7 per day, $29); New Orleans (2½hr., 8 per day, $23-25); and Birmingham (6hr., 5 per day, $37-41). **Mobile Transit Authority (MTA)** has major depots at Bienville Sq., Royal St. parking garage, and the Adams Mark Hotel. (☎344-5656. Runs M-F 6am-6pm; reduced service on Sa. Fare $1.25, seniors and disabled 60¢, transfers 10¢.) **Yellow Cab,** ☎476-7711. **Visitor Info: Fort Condé Info Center,** 150 S. Royal St., in a reconstructed French fort near Government St. (☎208-7304; open daily 8am-5pm). **Hotlines: Rape Crisis,** ☎473-7273. **Helpline,** ☎431-5111. Both 24 hours. **Post office:** 250 St. Joseph St. (☎694-5917; open M-F 7am-5pm, Sa 9am-noon). **ZIP code:** 36601. **Area code:** 334.

🛌 ACCOMMODATIONS. A slew of affordable hotels line I-65 on Beltline, from Exit 5 (Spring Hill Rd) to Exit 1 (Government Blvd). **Family Inn,** 980 S. Beltline Rd., I-65 at Airport Blvd., sports firm beds, free local calls, continental breakfast, cable, and a pool. (☎344-5500. Singles $28; doubles $40.) Downtown, the **Budget Inn,** 555 Government St., offers basic clean rooms with cable TV and A/C. (☎433-0590. Singles $35; doubles $40.) **I-10 Kampground,** 6430 Theodore Dawes Rd. E., lies 7½ mi. west on I-10, south off Exit 13. This is a great place, if you like RVs. (☎653-9816. Pool, playground, and laundry facilities. RV hook-up $20; $1 per additional person.)

🛈🍽 FOOD AND NIGHTLIFE. Mobile's Gulf location means fresh seafood (surf) and southern cookin' (turf). For surf, **⬛Wintzell's Oyster House,** 605 Dauphin St., a long-time local favorite, offers oysters 12 different ways. The 1hr. oyster eating record stands at 21½ dozen; beat it and the meal is on them. (☎432-4605. Open M-Sa 11am-10pm, Su noon-8pm. Lunch $6-8.) For turf, **⬛Dreamland,** 3314 Old Shell Rd. has ribs that will put you in a blissful food-coma, not to mention stain your shirt. (☎479-9898. Open M-Th 10am-10pm, F-Sa 10am-midnight, Su 11am-9pm. Half-slab $8.45, half-chicken $6.50.) To mix with the locals of Mobile, head to the well-worn and well-populated bar at **Hayley's,** 278 Dauphin St. (☎433-4970. Open daily 3pm-3am. Occasional live shows. Beer $2.25.) Eighteen pool tables, darts, and mega-subs ($3.50-5) make **Solomon's,** 5753 Old Shell Rd., the quintessential brew and cue college hangout. (☎344-0380. Open 24hr., though not all of 'em are so happening. Happy hour daily 11am-7pm.)

🔲 **SIGHTS.** Mobile's attractions lie scattered inland, around downtown, and near the bay. Three historic districts—Detonti Sq., Dauphin St., and Church St.—encompass the downtown area. The city's varied influences have led to an architecture unique to Mobile. In particular, the 27 buildings of the **Church St. East Historic District** showcase Federal, Greek Revival, Queen Anne, and Victorian architecture. **Bay City Tours** leads four different tours of Old Mobile and surrounding sights. (☎ 432-2229.)

Antebellum homes dominate the attractions of Old Mobile. In the **DeTonti Historical District,** north of downtown, brick townhouses with wrought-iron balconies surround the restored **Richards-DAR House Museum.** The museum's stained glass and Rococo chandeliers blend beautifully with its antebellum Italianate architecture and ornate iron lace. **Oakleigh Historical Complex,** two and a half blocks south of Government St., features a cantilevered staircase and enormous windows opening onto all the balconies upstairs. (*Richards-DAR: 256 North Joachim St. ☎ 208-7320. Open Tu-Sa 10am-4pm, Su 1-4pm. Tours $4, children $2; free tea and cookies. Oakleigh: 350 Oakleigh Pl. ☎ 432-1281. Open M-Sa 10am-4pm. Tours every 30min. $5, students $2, seniors $4.50, ages 6-18 $1.*)

For its lush rose and oriental gardens, its bayou boardwalk, and its 900-acre setting, *Southern Living* magazine has ranked **Bellingrath Gardens** one of the top three public gardens in the country. (*12401 Bellingrath Gardens Rd., Exit 15A off I-10. ☎ 973-2217. Open daily 8am-dusk. Gardens $8, ages 5-11 $5.*)

The **USS Alabama,** permanently moored 2½ mi. east of town at Battleship Park, fought in every major Pacific battle during WWII. Open portholes and passageways let land-lubbers explore the ship's deepest depths. (*☎ 433-2703. Open daily 8am-6pm. $8, ages 6-11 $4. Parking $2.*) **Spanish Plaza,** Hamilton and Government St., honors Mobile's sibling city (Málaga, Spain), while recalling Spain's early presence in Mobile. Amid sprouting fountains, Spanish flags flutter in the breeze.

February is a big month for Mobile. Locals await the blooming of the 27 mi. **Azalea Trail** and enjoy the parades, costumes, and "throws" of the oldest Fat Tuesday around at Mobile's **Mardi Gras.** (*Azalea Festival and Run: ☎ 334-473-7223. Mardi Gras: Feb. 14-27, 2001.*) The *Mobile Traveler* has an updated list of all Mobile attractions.

MISSISSIPPI

The "Deep South" bottoms out in Mississippi. The legacy of extravagant cotton plantations, dependence upon slavery, and subsequent racial strife and economic ruin are more visible here than in any other state. In the 1850s, Natchez and Vicksburg were two of the most prosperous cities in the nation; whites bathed in the riches that flowed from free slave labor. During the Civil War, the state was devastated by the siege of Vicksburg and the burning of Jackson. Hatred and injustice drowned Mississippi into the 60s as blacks protested against continuing segregation and whites reacted with campaigns of terror.

A number of remarkable triumphs have surfaced out of Mississippi's struggles. The state boasts an impressive literary and cultural heritage. Writers William Faulkner, Eudora Welty, Tennessee Williams, and Richard Wright called Mississippi home, as did blues musicians Bessie Smith, W.C. Handy, and B.B. King, who brought their riffs up the "Blues Highway" to Memphis, Chicago, and the world. Today, beautiful plantation homes are testament to the "good ol' days," while enduring rural poverty and low education levels are reminders of inequality.

🔲 PRACTICAL INFORMATION

Capital: Jackson.

Visitor Info: Division of Tourism, P.O. Box 1705, Ocean Springs 39566 (☎ 800-927-6378; www.decd.state.ms.us). **Dept. of Wildlife, Fisheries, and Parks,** P.O. Box 451, Jackson 39205 (☎ 800-546-4808).

Postal Abbreviation: MS. **Sales Tax:** 7%.

JACKSON

☎ 601

Jackson makes a concerted effort to overcome Mississippi's spotty past and lingering backwater image. One billboard even claims that Jackson is as "Rome was to Renaissance Europe." Impress your friends with the word "hyperbole;" Jackson simply ain't all that. Nonetheless, as the state's political, cultural, and commercial capital, Jackson strives to bring the world to its people. North Jackson's lush homes and plush country clubs epitomize wealthy Southern living, while shaded campsites, cool reservoirs, national forests, and Native American burial mounds invite exploration only minutes away.

⬛🔢 ORIENTATION AND PRACTICAL INFORMATION. West of I-55, downtown is bordered on the north by **Fortification St.**, on the south by **South St.**, and on the west by **Gallatin St.** North-south **State St.** bisects the city. **Jackson Municipal Airport** (☎932-2859) is east of downtown off I-20. Walk downtown via Capitol St. to **Amtrak**, 300 W. Capitol St. (☎355-6350; open daily 9:30am-7pm). Trains run to Memphis (4hr., 7 per week, $31) and New Orleans (4½hr., 7 per week, $17). **Greyhound**, 201 S. Jefferson (☎353-6342), sends buses to Montgomery (5hr., 7 per day, $48-51); Memphis (4hr., 8 per day, $26); and New Orleans (4½hr., 4 per day, $28). Station is open 24 hours; *avoid this area at night.* **Jackson Transit System (JATRAN)** provides limited public service. Bus schedules and maps posted at most bus stops downtown and available at JATRAN headquarters, 1025 Terry Rd. (☎948-3840. Headquarters open M-F 8am-4:30pm. Transit runs M-F 5am-7pm, Sa 5:30am-7pm. Fare $1, transfers free.) If JATRAN leaves you high and dry, flag down **City Cab** (☎355-8319). **Visitor Info: The Convention and Visitors Bureau,** 921 N. President St., downtown (☎960-1891; open M-F 8am-5pm). **Hotlines: Rape Hotline** (☎982-7273), 24 hours. **Post Office:** 401 E. South St. (open M-F 7am-6pm, Sa 8am-noon). **ZIP code:** 39205. **Area code:** 601.

🏚 ACCOMMODATIONS. If you have a car, head for the motels along **I-20** and **I-55**. Expect to pay $35 and up for decent accommodations in the area, unless you camp. **Sun 'n' Sand Motel,** 401 N. Lamar St., downtown, is a 60s time-warp—there's even a Polynesian suite. Lounge/restaurant in motel serves a $5 lunch buffet. (☎354-2501. Pool, cable TV. Singles $35-40; $5 per additional person.) **Parkside Inn,** 3720 I-55 N, at Exit 98B, has dark green furniture and wood-paneled walls to spruce up the clean, somewhat small rooms. (☎982-1122. Pool, cable TV, free local calls, and some rooms with whirlpools. Singles $29; doubles $39.) For camping, head to **Timberlake Campgrounds;** take I-55 N to Lakeland East (Exit 98B), turn left after 6 mi. onto Old Fannin Rd. and go 4 mi. (☎992-9100. Office open daily 8am-5pm. Gate closes 10pm. Pool, video games, tennis courts, playground. Tent sites $12, full hook-up $15; Oct.-Apr. $10/$13; seniors $1.)

📷📺 FOOD AND NIGHTLIFE. Franchised grease palaces can be found north to **County Line Rd.**, between I-55 and I-220, dubbed "restaurant alley" by natives. For the real Jackson scene, the **George St. Grocery**, 416 George St., is the place to be. Packed with state politicians by day and students by night, GSG's lunch deals ($5) ignite a sweet bang for your buck. (☎969-3573. Restaurant open M-Th 11am-9pm, F 11am-10pm, Sa 5-10pm. Live music Tu-Sa 9pm-1am.) **Keifer's**, 705 Poplar St., off State St., 1½ mi. north of downtown, serves gyros and other tasty pita wraps ($4.45-5.45) amid hanging greenery. (☎355-6825. Open Su-Th 11am-10pm, F-Sa 11am-11pm.) On Th, pick up *Clarion-Ledger* for a list of weekend events. **Hal & Mal's Restaurant and Brew Bar**, 200 S. Commerce St., stages live music in a converted warehouse. (☎948-0888. Restaurant open M 11am-3pm, Tu-Th 11am-10pm, F 11am-10:30pm. Bar open M-Th until 11pm, F-Sa until 1am. Cover up to $5 F-Sa.)

🔲 SIGHTS. The **Mississippi Museum of Art,** displays local art and a fabulous Americana collection. Adjacent to the MMA, the out-of-this-world **Russell C. Davis Planetarium** projects the splendors of the universe. *(201 E. Pascagoula, at Lamar St. MMA: ☎960-1515. Open M-Sa 10am-5pm, Tu until 8pm; Su noon-5pm. $5, children $2. Planetarium: ☎960-1550. Shows Tu-Sa 7:30pm, Sa-Su 2 and 4pm. $4, seniors and under 12 $2.50.)*

Built in 1833, the **Old State Capitol**, at the intersection of Capitol and State St., houses an excellent museum documenting Mississippi's turbulent history. (☎359-6920. Open M-F 8am-5pm, Sa 9:30am-4:30pm, Su 12:30-4:30pm. Free.) The state legislature currently convenes in the **New State Capitol**, completed in 1903. A huge restoration project preserved the *beaux arts* grandeur of the building. (400 High St., between West and President St. ☎359-3114. Open M-F 8am-5pm. 1hr. tours M-F 9, 10, 11am, 1:30, 2:30, and 3:30pm. Free.) A tour of the **Governor's Mansion** provides an enlightening introduction to Mississippi politics. (300 E. Capitol St. ☎359-3175. Tours Tu-F every 30min. 9:30-11am. Free.)

A recreated 20s farm village and a number of restored farm implements make up **Mississippi's Agriculture and Forestry Museum.** Also on site is the **National Agricultural Aviation Museum,** with vintage aircraft and tales of cornfield valor. (1150 Lakeland Dr., ½ mi. east of I-55 Exit 98B. ☎800-844-8687. Open M-Sa 9am-5pm, Su 1-5pm; closed Su early Sept. to late May. $4, seniors $3, ages 6-18 $2, under 6 50¢.)

VICKSBURG   ☎601

Vicksburg's verdant hills and prime Mississippi River location made it the focus of much strategic planning during the Civil War. President Abraham Lincoln called the town the "key," and maintained that the war "can never be brought to a close until that key is in our pocket." The Confederates' Gibraltar fell to Union forces on July 4, 1863, after resisting a 47-day bombardment. The loss hit the city hard—until the late 40s, Vicksburg refused to hold any 4th of July celebrations. Downtown, 19th-century mansions and Civil War monuments dominate the urban landscape. Lush parks lend Vicksburg a relaxed, pastoral feel, while brick-paved roads and festive casino riverwalks recreate a way of life that has long since passed.

⃞ PRACTICAL INFORMATION. A car is necessary in Vicksburg. The bus station, the info center, downtown, and the far end of the sprawling military park mark the city's extremes. **Greyhound** (☎638-8389; open daily 7am-8:30pm) pulls out at 1295 S. Frontage Rd. for Jackson (1hr., 6 per day, $11.50). The **Tourist Information Center,** on Clay St. across from the park (I-20 Exit 4, turn west), has a helpful map of sights. (☎636-9421 or 800-221-3536. Open daily 8am-5pm; in winter Sa-Su 8am-4pm.) **Post Office:** 3415 Pemberton Blvd., just off U.S. 61 S (open M-F 8am-5pm, Sa 8am-noon). **ZIP code:** 39180. **Area code:** 601.

⃞ ACCOMMODATIONS. Inexpensive lodging comes easy in Vicksburg. One of the best deals in town, the **Hillcrest Motel,** 40 Rte. 80 E, ¼ mi. east from I-20 Exit 4, offers well-worn yet well-kept and spacious rooms with pool access. (☎638-1491. Singles $26.50; doubles $32.) The **Beechwood Motel,** 4449 E. Clay St., a block in front of the Hillcrest, offers cable and standard rooms. (☎636-2271. Singles $27; doubles $35.) Most hotels cluster near the park; don't expect to stay downtown, unless you choose the **Relax Inn Downtown,** 1313 Walnut St. (☎631-0097. Rooms $30-40.) **Magnolia RV Park,** 211 Miller St., has 68 full RV hook-ups, a pool, game room, and playground. Head south on Washington (I-20 Exit 1A), and take a left on Rifle Range Rd. to Miller St. (☎631-0388. Office open daily 8:30am-8pm. Sites $18.) Closer to the military park and the highway is **Battlefield Kampground,** 4407 I-20 Frontage Rd., off Exit 4B, where the kampaign of the krazy "k" kontinues. (☎636-2025. Laundry, pool, and playground. Sites $10, with electricity and water $15, full hook-up $17.)

⃞⃞ FOOD AND NIGHTLIFE. While downtown, chow down at the **Burger Village,** 1220 Washington St., where a home-cooked southern meal costs under $5 and burgers are nothing but 100% all-American beef. (☎638-0202. Open M-Sa 9am-6pm.) **Walnut Hills,** 1214 Adams St., serves all-you-can-eat round table dinners (Su-F 11am-2pm) of catfish, hamburger steak, corn, green beans, etc. (☎638-4910. Open M-F 11am-9pm, Su 11am-2pm. 1 meat and 3 veggies $6.25, 2 meats and 6 veggies $8.)

The only-in-America **Red Carpet Washateria and Lanes,** 2904 Clay St., sports a bowling alley, pool room, and laundromat all in one. (☎631-0890. Laundry open daily 7am-9pm. Lanes open M-Th noon-11pm, F-Sa noon-1am, Su noon-10pm. $2.50 per game.) Despite the Red Carpet's many thrills, high-rollers might prefer spending their time at one of the four **casinos** that line the river.

■ **SIGHTS.** Vicksburg is a mecca for thousands of touring schoolchildren, Civil War buffs, and Confederate and Union army descendents. Memorials and markers of combat sites riddle the grassy 1700-acre ◪**Vicksburg National Military Park,** lending the grounds a sacred air. The park blockades the eastern and northern edges of the city, with its visitors center on Clay St., about ½ mi. west of I-20 Exit 4B, across from the city visitors center. Driving along the 16 mi. path, you have three options: guide yourself with a free map available at the entrance, buy an informative audio tour, or hire a person to help navigate the sights. (☎636-0583. Park center open daily 8am-5pm. Grounds open daily 7am-8pm; in winter 7am-sunset. $4 per car. Tape $4.50, CD $8. Live guide $20.) Within the park, the sunk and saved Union **USS Cairo Museum** contains countless artifacts salvaged in the early 60s from the old ironclad. The remains of ship are just next door. (☎636-2199. Open daily 9:30am-6pm; off-season 8am-5pm. Free with park fee.) The **Old Courthouse Museum** is one of the South's finest Civil War museums. During the siege of Vicksburg in 1863, Confederate troops used the cupola as a signal station and held Union prisoners in the courtroom. (1008 Cherry St. ☎636-0741. Open M-Sa 8:30am-5pm, Su 1:30-5pm; early Oct. to early Apr. closes 4:30pm daily. $3, seniors $2.50, under 18 $2.)

For an escape from Vicksburg's more serious war-related attractions, the **Attic Gallery** has a collection of Southern contemporary art and an eclectic display of glassware, pottery, books, and jewelry. (1101 Washington St. ☎638-9221. Open M-Sa 10am-5pm. Free.) Vicksburg's finest contribution to the historical home circuit, the **Martha Vick House,** was home to the daughter of the city's founder, Reverend Newitt Vick. (1300 Grove St. ☎638-7036. Open M-Sa 9am-5pm, Su 2pm-5pm. $5, under 12 free.)

NATCHEZ ☎601

In the late 18th century, Natchez distinguished itself as one of the wealthiest settlements on the Mississippi. Of the 13 millionaires in Mississippi at the time, 11 had their cotton plantations here. After the Civil War, the cotton-based economy crumbled, and the days of the mansion-building magnates passed. Many of the homes remain, however, affording visitors the opportunity to gaze at elegant dwellings from a vanquished era.

🖪 **PRACTICAL INFORMATION. Greyhound** makes connections to Vicksburg (1½hr., 1 per day, $16) and New Orleans (4½hr., 2 per day, $37) at the **Natchez Bus Station,** 103 Lower Woodville Rd. (☎445-5291. Open M-F 7:30am-5:30pm, Sa 9am-12:30pm and 3:30-5pm, Su 2-5pm.) The **Natchez Bicycling Center,** 334 Main St., rents bikes with basket, helmet, lock, and repair kit. (☎446-7794. Open Tu-F 10am-5:30pm, Sa 10am-3pm; other times by appointment. $15 per 4hr., $20 per day.) **Visitors center:** 640 S. Canal St., near the U.S. 84 Mississippi Bridge. (☎442-5849. Open daily 8:30am-6pm; early Nov.-Mar. 8am-5pm.) **Post Office:** 214 N. Canal St. (☎442-4361; open M-F 8:30am-5pm, Sa 10am-noon). **ZIP code:** 39120. **Area code:** 601.

🖩 **ACCOMMODATIONS AND FOOD.** The intersection of **U.S. 61** and **Highland Blvd.** supports lots of high-quality rooms. **Scottish Inns,** 40 Sgt. Prentiss Dr./U.S. 61, a coral-colored complex, has clean rooms equipped with microfridges and microwaves. (☎442-9141 or 800-251-1962. Singles $28; doubles $40.) Close to the Mississippi Bridge and visitors center is the **Natchez Inn,** 218 John Junkin Dr./U.S. 84, with spartan, tidy rooms, a pool, and cable TV. (☎442-0221. A/C, cable TV, and free local calls. Singles $30; doubles $40.) The secluded campground in **Natchez State Park** is less than 10 mi. north of Natchez on U.S. 61 in Stanton. (☎442-2658. Sites $7, with water and electricity $11, full hook-up $12.)

Lots of cafes and diners dish up budget eats in Natchez. **Cock of the Walk,** 200 N. Broadway, earns its title and stature with spicy catfish and complimentary jalapeño cornbread served in a bare wood dining room evocative of tough frontiersmen. (☎446-8920. Open daily 5pm until the manager's discretion, usually 9pm. Catfish fillet $10.) **The Pig Out Inn,** 116 S. Canal St., serves down-home, home-smoked, faster-than-fast-food BBQ with a spicy sauce on the side. (☎442-8050. Open M-Sa 11am-9pm. Sandwiches $3.75.) **Mammy's Cupboard,** 555 Hwy. 61, 4 mi. south of town, serves home-cookin' ($6-7.50) like chicken pot pie and desserts (about $2.50) in a country cottage beneath a huge statue of Mammy, the traditionally stereotyped southern black mother. (☎445-8957. Open Tu-Su 11am-2pm.)

⚅ SIGHTS. Natchez Pilgrimage Tours supervises tours of the restored manors left from Natchez's cotton days. A helpful staff has free tour schedules, maps, and pamphlets, plus a guidebook that details the histories of the 32 homes that Pilgrimage oversees. The central office sells tickets for individual house tours or tickets for a 35min. horse-drawn carriage tour and a 55min. air-conditioned bus tour. *(200 State St. at Canal St. ☎800-647-6742 or 446-6631. Open M-Sa 9am-5pm, Su 12:30-5pm. Guide book $5. House tours $6, children $3. Horse tour $9/$4. Bus tour $15/$7.50. Call ahead for seasonal schedules and prices.)* The largest octagonal house in America, **Longwood** astounds visitors with its imaginative floorplan; however, the six-story edifice remains unfinished. The builders, hired from the North, abandoned work at the beginning of the Civil War to fight for the Union, leaving only the basement completed (and furnished). **Stanton Hall,** on the other hand, arose under the direction of local Natchez architects and artisans. Completed in 1857, the mansion features French mirrors, Italian marble mantels, and exquisitely cut chandeliers. *(Longwood: 140 Lower Woodville Rd. ☎442-5193. Stanton Hall: 401 High St., off Union St. ☎442-6282. Both open daily 9am-5pm. Tours every 30min.)*

For centuries, the Natchez Indians flourished on this fertile land. The arrival of the French incited fighting in 1730, and French military successes brought an end to the thriving Natchez community. The **Grand Village of the Natchez Indians** pays homage to the tribe with a museum that documents their history and culture. *(400 Jefferson Davis Blvd., off U.S. 61 S. ☎446-6502. Open M-Sa 9am-5pm, Su 1:30-5pm. Free.)*

The 500 mi. **Natchez Trace Pkwy.** leads north from Natchez to Nashville, TN. Rambling through lush forests, swamps, and shady countryside, the road passes through historic landmarks and a beautiful national park.

OXFORD
☎662

Oxford gained great notoriety in the early 60s, when James Meredith attempted to be the first black student to enroll at the University of Mississippi (Ole Miss), just west of the city. This attempt, backed by a federal court, resulted in what many considered the largest constitutional crisis since the Civil War; Mississippi Governor Ross Burnett openly defied federal law, banning Meredith until the National Guard arrived. Above all else, however, Oxford is known as the "little postage stamp of native soil" that William Faulkner determined "was worth writing about." The result was what is widely regarded as the greatest American literature to date.

🛈 PRACTICAL INFORMATION. Oxford is 30 mi. east of I-55 on Rte. 6 (take Exit 243), 55 mi. south of Memphis and 140 mi. north of Jackson. **Oxford Tourism Info Center,** 111 Courthouse Sq., offers free audio walking tours. (☎800-758-9177. Open M-F 9am-5pm, Sa 10am-4pm, Su 1-4pm.) **Greyhound,** 2612B Jackson Ave. W (☎234-0094), runs once a day to Memphis (1½hr., $20) and Nashville (9hr., $59) and twice a day to Jackson (10hr., $49). **Internet access:** Public library, 401 Bramlett Blvd. at Jackson Ave. (☎234-5751; open M-Th 9:30am-8pm, F-Sa 9:30am-5:30pm, Su 2-5pm). **Post Office,** 401 McElroy Dr. (☎513-4685; open M-F 9am-5pm, Sa 9:30am-12:30pm). **ZIP code:** 38655. **Area code:** 662.

🛏 ACCOMMODATIONS. Spend a night in southern comfort at the **Oliver-Britt House Inn,** 512 Van Buren Ave., an unpretentious B&B. (☎234-8043. Breakfast on weekends. Singles and doubles $45-55, $10 surcharge F-Sa, $20 on football weekends.) **Ole Miss Motel,** 1517 E. University Ave., has basic rooms, but each has a heart on its door. (☎234-2424. Singles from $32; doubles from $42.) As a last resort, try the motels on the commercial strip of Jackson Ave., near Rte. 6 southwest of town. **Wall Doxy State Park,** 23 mi. north of town on Rte. 7, is a scenic spot with an expansive lake. (☎252-4231. Campsites with water and electricity $6, RV sites with dump stations $11. Cabins $43-49 per night, 3-night minimum stay. Entrance fee $2 per car, 50¢ per pedestrian or bicyclist.)

🖼🎭 FOOD AND ENTERTAINMENT. Food and such is best found at Courthouse Sq., at Jackson Ave. and Lamar Blvd. It's hip to be at **Square Books,** 160 Courthouse Sq., where a fine collection of southern works, coffee drinks ($2), and pastries ($3) may be enjoyed on a balcony overlooking the downtown area. (☎236-2262. Both open M-Th 9am-9pm, F-Sa 9am-10pm, Su 10am-6pm.) The **Bottletree Bakery,** 923 Van Buren Ave., serves Italian sodas and fresh pastries. (☎236-5000. Open Tu-F 7am-4pm, Sa 9am-4pm, Su 9am-2pm.) **Ajax Diner,** 118 Courthouse Sq., serves more substantial food: updated meat-and-two platters are $6, and traditional po' boy sandwiches are $5. (☎232-8880. Open M-Sa 11:30am-10pm.) At night, live music rolls from **Proud Larry's,** 211 S. Lamar, which keeps on burnin' all year. (☎236-0050. Music M-W and Su 10pm-midnight, F-Sa 10pm-1am. Cover $5-7.) For local listings, check the free weekly *Oxford Town.*

🎟 SIGHTS. Faulkner's home, **Rowan Oak,** lies just south of downtown on Old Taylor Rd. Faulkner bought the house in 1930 and named the property after the rowan tree, a symbol of peace and security. The rowan is not, in fact, a member of the oak family, a botanical tidbit which Oxford locals find most amusing. The house is interesting architecturally and has great value as a Faulkner pilgrimage: the plot outline of his 1954 novel *A Fable* is scribbled in pencil on the walls of the study. (☎234-3284. Open Tu-Sa 10am-noon and 2-4pm, Su 2-4pm. Grounds open sunrise to sunset. Free self-guided tours.)

Outside of Faulkner, Oxford's attractions are all affiliated with Ole Miss. The town's covered sidewalks and tall cedar trees help to make it a fitting home for the **Center for the Study of Southern Culture** in the old Barnard Observatory at Ole Miss, where visitors can pick up pamphlets or attend conferences, including the ever-popular **Faulkner Conference** in late July or early Aug. (☎915-5993. Center open M-F 8am-5pm. Free.) Blues buffs will revel in the memorabilia, sheet music, and over 40,000 records at the **Ole Miss Blues Archive,** Farley Hall room #340. (☎915-7753. Open M-F 9am-5pm. Free.) The **University Museums,** on University Ave., contain four main collections ranging from classical Greek pottery to 19th-century scientific instruments; easily the highlight, however, is the small collection of Southern folk and "outsider" art. (☎915-7073. Open Tu-Sa 10am-4:30pm, Su 1-4pm. Free.)

LOUISIANA

After exploring the Mississippi River valley in 1682, Frenchman René-Robert Cavalier proclaimed the land "Louisiane," in honor of Louis XIV. The name endured three centuries, though French ownership of the vast region did not. The territory was tossed between France, England, and Spain before Thomas Jefferson and the US snagged it in the Louisiana Purchase of 1803. Nine years later, a smaller, redefined Louisiana was admitted to the Union. Each successive government lured a new mix of settlers to the bayous: Spaniards from the Canary Islands, French Acadians from Nova Scotia, Americans from the East, and free blacks from the West Indies. Louisiana's multi-national history, Creole culture, and Napoleonic legal system are unlike anything found in the 49 other states.

🛈 PRACTICAL INFORMATION

Capital: Baton Rouge.

Visitor Info: Office of Tourism, P.O. Box 94291, Baton Rouge 70804-9291 (☎225-342-7317 or 800-261-9144; www.louisianatravel.com). Open M-F 8am-4:30pm. **Office of State Parks,** P.O. Box 44426, Baton Rouge 70804-4426 (☎225-342-8111 or 888-677-1400; www.crt.st.la.us). Open M-F 9am-5pm.

Postal Abbreviation: LA. **Sales Tax:** 8%.

NEW ORLEANS
☎ 504

Originally explored by the French, *La Nouvelle Orleans* was secretly ceded to the Spanish in 1762, though the citizens didn't find out until 1766. Spain returned the city to France just in time for the United States to grab it in the Louisiana Purchase of 1803. Centuries of cultural cross-pollination have resulted in a fabulous *mélange* of Spanish courtyards, Victorian verandas, Cajun jambalaya, Creole gumbo, and French *beignets*. New Orleans has its own style of cooking, its own distinct accent, and its own way of making music. In the beginning of the 20th century, its musicians even invented a completely new and different type of sound you might have heard of—*jazz*.

The city's nickname, the "Big Easy," reflects the carefree attitude characteristic of this fun-loving place. While New York may claim to be "the city that never sleeps," N'awlins holds the title for "the city that won't stop partying." Day or night, there's always something going on. The only thing that stifles this vivacity is the heavy, humid air that slows folks to a near standstill during the summer. But when the day's heat finally retreats into the night, the city begins to jump with drinking and dancing into the early morning. Come late February, there's no escaping the month-long celebration of Mardi Gras, the climax of the city's already festive mood.

THE SOUTH

ACCOMMODATIONS
India House, **3**
Jude Travel Park, **1**
Longpre House and St.
  Charles Guest House, **6**
Marquette House (HI), **5**
Mazant House, **4**
Sycamore Tree Travel Park, **2**
▬▬▬ St. Charles Streetcar
- - - - Ferry

SAFETY IN NEW ORLEANS. New Orleans plays down its high murder and crime rates. The tenement areas directly north of the French Quarter and directly northwest of Lee Circle pose particular threats to personal safety. At night, even quaint-looking side streets in the Quarter can be dangerous—stick to busy, well-lit roads and never walk alone after dark. Make some attempt to downplay the tourist image (e.g. don't wear a t-shirt that has the words "New Orleans" anywhere on it), and have a good idea of where you want to go. Many streets are poorly labeled, and one wrong turn can make a dangerous difference. *Avoid all parks, cemeteries, and housing projects at night.*

✈ GETTING THERE AND AWAY

Airport: Moisant International (☎464-0831), 15 mi. west of the city. Cab fare to the Quarter is set at $21 for 1-2 people; $8 per person for 3 or more. The **Louisiana Transit Authority,** 118 David Dr. (☎818-1077; open M-F 8am-4pm) runs buses from the airport downtown to Elk St., M-Sa 5:30am-5:40pm, every 15min. After 5:40pm, buses go to Tulane Ave. and Carollton Ave. (mid-city) until 11:30pm. Fare $1.50, exact change needed. Pick-up on the upper level, near the exit ramp.

Trains: Amtrak, 1001 Loyola Ave. (☎800-872-7245), in the Union Passenger Terminal, a 10min. walk to Canal St. via Elk. To: Houston (8hr., 3 per week, $49-87); Jackson (4hr., 7 per week, $17-34); and Atlanta (12hr., 7 per week, $45-80). Station open 24hr.; ticket office open Tu, Th, and Su 5:45am-11pm; M, W, and F-Sa 5:45am-8:30pm.

Buses: Greyhound, 1001 Loyola Ave. (☎524-7571 or 800-231-2222), in the Union Passenger Terminal. To Austin (11hr., 5 per day, $86.50) and Baton Rouge (2hr., 9 per day, $11.50). Open 24hr.

⊟ GETTING AROUND

Public Transit: Regional Transit Authority (RTA), 2817 Canal St. (☎248-3900; open M-F 8am-5pm). Most buses pass Canal St., at the edge of the French Quarter. Major buses and streetcars run 24hr. $1, seniors and disabled passengers 40¢; transfers 10¢. 1-day pass $4, 3-day pass $8; passes sold at major hotels in the Canal St. area. Office has bus schedules and transit info.

Taxis: Checker Yellow Cabs, ☎943-2411. **United Cabs,** ☎522-9771.

Bikes: French Quarter Bicycles, 522 Dumaine St. (☎529-3136), between Decatur and Chartres. Open M-F 11am-7pm, Sa-Su 10am-6pm. $4.50 per hr., $20 per 24hr., $84 per week (includes lock, helmet, and map). Credit card or $200 cash deposit required.

✤ ORIENTATION

Although it's fairly compact, New Orleans can be confusing. The city's main streets follow the curve of the **Mississippi River,** hence its nickname "the Crescent City." Directions from locals reflect watery influences—lakeside means north, referring to **Lake Ponchartrain,** and riverside means south. Uptown lies west, up river; downtown lies down river. The city is concentrated on the east bank of the Mississippi. However, **The East** (locally dubbed) refers only to the easternmost part of the city. Less populated regions of the city, like Algiers, are on **The West Bank,** across the river. Many streets run one-way or are separated with broad medians.

Tourists flock to the small **French Quarter (Vieux Carré),** bounded by the Mississippi River, **Canal St., Rampart St.,** and **Esplanade Ave.** Streets in the Quarter follow a grid pattern, making foot travel easy. The residential **Garden District** (uptown, bordered by **St. Charles Ave.** to the north and **Magazine St.** to the south) is distinguished by its elegant homes and well-cultivated gardens. The scenic **St. Charles Streetcar route** (fare $1), easily picked up at Canal St. and Carondelet St., passes through parts of the **Central Business District** ("CBD" or downtown), the Garden District via St. Charles Ave., and **S. Carollton Ave.**

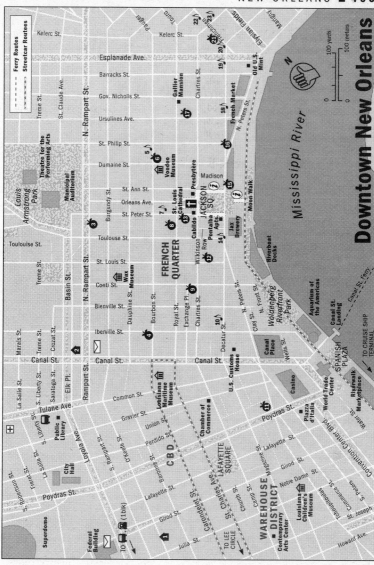

Downtown New Orleans

Mississippi River

THE SOUTH

Downtown
New Orleans

ACCOMMODATIONS
Depot House at Mme. Julia's, **1**
Hotel LaSalle, **2**

FOOD AND DRINKS
Café du Monde, **15**
Clover Grill, **6**
Laura's Candies, **9**
Mother's Restaurant, **11**
The Praline Connection, **21**
Gumbo Shop, **13**
Central Grocery, **16**
Acme Oyster House, **4**
Croissant d'Or, **17**
Mama Rosa's, **3**
Royal Blend, **8**
Johnny's Po' boys, **12**

MUSIC AND CLUBS
Café Brasil, **23**
Checkpoint Charlie's, **20**
Crescent City Brewhouse, **14**
El Matador, **19**
House of Blues, **10**
Lafitte's Blacksmith Shop, **5**
Snug Harbor, **22**
Pat O'Briens, **7**
Molly's at the Market, **18**

Parking in New Orleans is easier than driving in it. To park near the French Quarter, head for the residential area around **Marigny St.** and **Royal St.**, where many streets have no meters and no restrictions. *Avoid parking in this area at night; streets are dimly lit and deserted.* After sunset, it is best to take a cab.

🛈 PRACTICAL INFORMATION

Visitor Info: The **New Orleans Welcome Center,** 529 St. Ann St. (☎566-5031; www.neworleanscvb.com), by Jackson Sq. in the French Quarter. Open daily 9am-5pm.

Hotlines: Cope Line, ☎523-2673, for crises. **Rape Hotline,** ☎483-8888. Both 24hr.

Hospital: Charity Hospital, 1532 Tulane Ave. (☎568-2311). 24hr. emergency room.

Internet Access: New Orleans Public Library, 219 Loyola Ave., 1½ blocks from Canal St. (☎529-7323; open M-Th 11am-6pm, Sa 11am-5pm.

Post Office: 701 Loyola Ave. (☎800-275-8777), near the bus station. Open M-F 7am-11pm, Sa 7am-8pm, Su noon-5pm. **ZIP code:** 70113. **Area code:** 504.

🛏 ACCOMMODATIONS

Finding inexpensive, yet decent, rooms in the **French Quarter** can be as difficult as staying sober during Mardi Gras. Luckily, other parts of the city compensate for the absence of cheap lodging downtown. Several **hostels** pepper the area and cater to the young and almost penniless, as do B&Bs near the **Garden District.** Accommodations for Mardi Gras and the Jazz Festival get booked up to a year in advance. During peak times, proprietors will rent out any extra space—be sure you know what you're paying for. Rates tend to sink in June and early Dec., when accommodations become desperate for business; negotiation can pay off.

🏠 **India House,** 124 S. Lopez St. (☎821-1904), at Canal St. What this bohemian haunt lacks in tidiness it compensates for in character. Young backpackers come here to celebrate freedom and camaraderie. Kitchen, pool, and separate alligator pond out back. 1pm check-out designed for those with "morning grogginess." No lockout or curfew. Free linen. Key deposit $5. Dorms $14, up to $17 in summer and peak times.

🏠 **Marquette House New Orleans International Hostel (HI-AYH),** 2253 Carondelet St. (☎523-3014). The cleanest and classiest hosteling experience in New Orleans. Courtyards link several separate buildings with 176 beds, A/C, kitchens, and study rooms; wheelchair accessible. No lockout or curfew, no alcohol permitted. Exceptionally quiet. Linen $2.50. Key deposit $5. Dorms $16.75, non-members $19.75. Private rooms with queen-sized bed and pull-out sofa $52.50/$56. Weekly rates available.

St. Charles Guest House, 1748 Prytania St. (☎523-6556). In a serene neighborhood near the Garden District and St. Charles Streetcar. A big 3-building complex with 38 rooms, 8 with shared baths. Lovely pool and sunbathing deck. No-frills backpacker's singles $25-45. Rooms with 1 queen-sized bed or 2 twins $45-85. Breakfast included.

Depot House at Mme. Julia's, 748 O'Keefe Ave. (☎529-2952). Located ½ mi. from the Quarter and in the CBD, this B&B has plain—but comfortable—rooms for 1 or 2 people ($65-75). All have shared bathrooms. Breakfast included. Reservations required.

Longpre House, 1726 Prytania St. (☎581-4540), in a 145-year-old house 1 block off St. Charles, shows its age a bit. A 25min. walk from the Quarter. Dorm check-in 8am-10pm, 11am for private rooms. No curfew. Dorms $12, in peak times $16. Singles and doubles with shared bath $35, with private bath $40. Free coffee and linen.

Mazant House, 906 Mazant St. (☎944-2662). Tastefully furnished rooms, living room, well-equipped kitchen, and only 2 blocks from the Desire St. bus. Neighborhood could be better. Singles $25, with bath $39; doubles $35/$55; $5 per extra cot. Apartment accommodations and rates available for extended stays.

Hotel LaSalle, 1113 Canal St. (☎523-5831 or 800-521-9450), 3 blocks from Bourbon St., downtown. Convenient, not luxurious. Rooms are well maintained with TVs and phones. Lobby staffed 24hr. Singles $30, with bath $62; doubles $42/$75.

St. Bernard State Park (☎682-2101), 18 mi. southeast of New Orleans; take I-10 Exit 246A, turn left onto Rte. 46 for 7 mi., then right on Rte. 39 S for 1 mi. 51 sites with water and electricity. Office open daily 7am-8pm; winter 8am-7pm. Sites $12.

Jude Travel Park and Guest House, 7400 Chef Menteur Hwy./U.S. 90 (☎241-0632 or 800-523-2196), just east of the eastern junction of I-10 and U.S. 90. Bus #98 "Broad" drives past the front gate to #55 "Elysian Fields," which heads downtown. Showers, laundry, 24hr. security. 46 tent/RV sites $20 (all with water, sewage, and cable); rates rise at peak times.

Sycamore Tree Travel Park, 10910 Chef Menteur Hwy./U.S. 90 (☎244-6611), 3 mi. east of the eastern junction of I-10 and U.S. 90. Same RTA service as Jude Travel Park. Pool, showers, and laundry facilities. Tent sites $14, with full RV hook-up $17.

🍴 FOOD

If the eats in the Quarter prove too trendy, touristy, or tough on the budget, **Magazine St.'s** cafes, antique stores, and book fairs spill onto the sidewalk. Uptown, wander around **Tulane University** for late-night grub and collegiate character. The **French Market,** between Decatur and N. Peters St., on the east side of the French Quarter, sells pricey fresh vegetables.

FRENCH QUARTER

🏛 Cafe du Monde, 800 Decatur St. (☎525-4544), near the French Market. The consummate people-watching paradise since 1862 really only does 2 things–scrumptious *café au lait* ($1.25) and hot *beignets* ($1.25). Open 24hr. To take home some of that chicory coffee, cross the street to the Cafe du Monde Gift Shop, 813 Decatur St. (☎581-2914 or 800-772-2927; open daily 9:30am-6pm). 15 oz. of the grind $4.60.

Johnny's Po' boys, 511 St. Louis St. (☎524-8129). The po' boy is the right choice at this French Quarter institution, which offers 40 varieties of the famous sandwich ($3.75-6.50), with a combo plate available for the indecisive. Decent Creole fare (jambalaya $4.25, gumbo $6.25) is also on the menu. Open M-F 8am-4:30pm, Sa-Su 9am-4pm.

Gumbo Shop, 630 St. Peter St. (☎525-1486). Sit under a broad-leafed palm and savor a bowl of seafood okra or chicken andouille gumbo ($7); po' boys $5-8, entrees from $10. Expect a line. Recipes available. Open daily 11am-11pm.

Sabrina and Gabrielle's Secret Garden, 538 St. Philip St. (☎524-2041). A romantic rendezvous for the dinnertime crowd. A pleasant courtyard and gracious service add to the mood. Cajun and Creole specials come with soup and salad ($7-15). Open Su-Th 5:30-10pm, F-Sa 5:30-11pm.

Central Grocery, 923 Decatur St. (☎523-1620), between Dumaine and St. Philip St. Try an authentic *muffuletta* (deli meats, cheeses, and olive salad on Italian bread) at the place that invented them. A half ($4.50) serves 1; a whole ($8) is best split between 2. Open M-Sa 8am-5:30pm, Su 9am-5:30pm.

Acme Oyster House, 724 Iberville St. (☎522-5973). At the bar, patrons slurp fresh oysters shucked before their eyes (6 for $3.50, 12 for $6), or sit at the red checkered tables for a po' boy ($5-7). Open M-Sa 11am-10pm, Su noon-7pm.

Croissant d'Or, 617 Ursulines St. (☎524-4663). Fair-priced French pastries, sandwiches, and quiches. *Carré Mocca* $1.30, chocolate mousse $1.50. Open daily 7am-5pm.

Mama Rosa's, 616 N. Rampart (☎523-5546). Locals adore this Italian ristorante. Rosa's pizza was once rated among the 9 best in the country by *People Magazine*. 14 in. cheese pie $9. Open Su-Th 11am-10pm. F-Sa 11am-11pm.

Royal Blend, 621 Royal St. (☎523-2716). Quiet garden setting offers escape from hustle of Royal St. Over 20 hot and iced coffees available, as well as a mighty fine selection of teas–you can even brew your own. Light meals (croissant sandwiches, quiches) served daily; pastries $1-2. Open Su-Th 6:30am-8pm, F-Sa 7am-midnight.

Clover Grill, 900 Bourbon St. (☎598-1010). The Clover has been open 24hr. since 1950, serving greasy and delicious burgers ($4 and up) grilled under an American-made hubcap. The waiters behind the counter love to entertain and compliment patrons–for extra tips, of course.

SHO' NUFF, GOOD STUFF In addition to the international options which entice hungry visitors, New Orleans offers a long list of regional specialties which have evolved from the mixing of Acadian, Spanish, Italian, African, French, and Native American cuisines. **Jambalaya** (a Cajun jumble of rice, shrimp, oysters, sausage, and ham or chicken mixed with spices) and **gumbo** (chicken or seafood stew over rice) grace practically every menu in New Orleans. A Southern breakfast of grits, eggs, bacon, and buttermilk biscuits satisfies even the most ardent eaters. **Creole** cuisine (a mixture of Spanish, French, and Caribbean) is famous for red beans and rice, **po' boys** (French bread sandwiches filled with sliced meat or seafood and vegetables; "dressed" means with mayo, lettuce, tomatoes, pickles, etc.), and shrimp or crawfish *étouffé*. Get some of the best Creole pralines ($1.25) at **Laura's Candies,** 600 Conti St. (☎525-3880; open daily 9am-7pm).

OUTSIDE THE QUARTER

▨ **Camellia Grill,** 626 S. Carrollton Ave. (☎866-9573). Take the St. Charles Streetcar to the Tulane area. Classic, counter-service diner where cooks don't mind telling the whole restaurant about their marital problems. Big drippin' plates, crowds (especially weekend mornings), and excellent service. Chef's special omelette ($7), pecan pie ($2.80). Open M-Th 9am-1am, F 9am-3am, Sa 8am-3am, Su 8am-1am.

▨ **Franky and Johnny's,** 321 Arabella (☎899-9146), southwest of downtown towards Tulane off Tchoupitoulas St. Everybody at this joyous, noisy local hangout orders the succulent boiled crawfish (2 lbs. $5, seasonal), but the onion rings are good too ($3.25). Open daily 11am until late.

Taqueria Corona, 5932 Magazine St. (☎897-3974), between State and Nashville St. Some of the best Mexican food around. Loud but cozy atmosphere. Deliciously hot burritos $3-7. Open daily 11:30am-2pm and 5-9:30pm.

Tee Eva's, 4430 Magazine St. (☎899-8350). Creole woman sells bayou cooking out of her kitchen window. Peerless pies, creole pralines, and 9 oz. snow balls for 75¢. Crawfish pie only $3; sweet potato, pecan pie slices $2. Large 9 in. pies $10-17, by order only. Soul food lunches change daily ($3-5). Open daily 11am-7pm.

Joey K's Restaurant, 3001 Magazine St. (☎891-0997), at 7th St. Friendly neighborhood eatery, especially for the midday meal—lunch specials start at $6 and feature "Creole pot" cooking, stuffed eggplant, and fried seafood. Sandwiches $4.50-6 and beer $2. Open M-F 11am-10pm, Sa 8am-10pm.

Cafe Atchafalaya, 901 Louisiana Ave. (☎891-5271), at Laurel St. Take the #11 bus "Magazine St." This cozy cottage serves mouth-watering, traditional Southern cuisine. Simple dishes like red beans and rice with salad ($6.50) or delicacies like Shrimp Orleans ($13.50) are expensive but exquisite. Laid-back service. Lunch Tu-F 11:30am-2pm, Sa-Su 8:30am-2pm; dinner Tu-Th 5:30-9pm, F-Sa 5:30-9:30pm.

The Praline Connection, 542 Frenchman St. (☎943-3943). Finger-lickin' good soul food: fried chicken and seafood, stuffed crab, or *étouffées*. Entrees from $9. Open Su-Th 11am-10pm, F-Sa 11am-midnight.

Mother's Restaurant, 401 Poydras St. (☎523-9656), downtown at Tchoupitoulas St., 4 blocks southwest of Bourbon St. Serving up po' boys ($7-10) and some of the best jambalaya in town ($7.25) to locals for almost half a century. Delicious crawfish or shrimp *étouffé* omelette ($10). Open M-Sa 5am-10pm, Su 7am-10pm.

The Trolley Stop Cafe, 1923 St. Charles Ave. (☎523-0090). Breakfast served 24hr. and it's busy all the time, partly thanks to the police officers who convene here. Most meals under $5.50.

Bennachin Restaurant, 133 N. Carrollton Ave. (☎486-1313), off Canal St. Vegetarian, non-vegetarian, spicy, non-spicy—they'll make it the way you like it. Sway to African music as you peruse the selection of low-priced African dishes (specials around $5 before 4pm). Entrees $7-10. Open M-Th 11am-9pm, F 11am-10pm, Sa 5-10pm.

◉ SIGHTS

FRENCH QUARTER

Allow *at least* a full day in the Quarter. The oldest section of the city is famous for its ornate wrought-iron balconies; French, Spanish, and uniquely New Orleans architecture; and a raucous atmosphere. Known as the **Vieux Carré** (view-ca-RAY), or Old Sq., the historic district of New Orleans offers dusty used book and record stores, museums, and tourist traps. **Bourbon St.** is packed with touristy bars, strip clubs, and clowns. **Decatur St.** has more mellow coffee shops and bars.

ROYAL STREET. Once a streetcar named "Desire" rolled down Royal St., now one of the French Quarter's most aesthetically pleasing avenues. Two devastating fires, in 1788 and 1794, forced the neighborhood to rebuild during the era of Spanish domination in the city, and the renovations took on the flavor of Spanish colonial architecture. Most notable are the intricate iron-lace balconies, which are either hand-wrought or cast in molds. With balconies of wrought-iron oak leaves and acorns spanning three tiers, **LaBranche House,** at Royal and St. Peter St., may be the most photographed building in the French Quarter.

JACKSON SQUARE. During the day, most of the activity in the French Quarter centers around Jackson Sq., a park dedicated to General Andrew Jackson, victor of the Battle of New Orleans. The square swarms with artists, mimes, musicians, psychics, magicians, and con artists as **St. Louis Cathedral** presides over the hubbub; it is the oldest operational Catholic cathedral in the US. *(Tours every 15-20min. M-Sa 9am-4:50pm. Free.)* Behind the cathedral lies **St. Anthony's Garden,** named in memory of Father Antonio de Sedella, a priest who was locally renowned for his dedication to the poor. **Pirate's Alley** and **Père Antoine's Alley** border the garden. Legend has it that the former was the site of covert meetings between pirate Jean Lafitte and President Andrew Jackson, as they conspired to plan the Battle of New Orleans. Pirate's Alley is also home to **Faulkner House Books,** where the late American author wrote his first novel. Upholding the literary tradition, the bookshop is a treasure-trove of first-editions and quality hard-covers. *(624 Pirate's Alley. Open daily 10am-6pm.)*

FRENCH MARKET. The historic French Market takes up several city blocks just east of Jackson Sq., toward the water, along N. Peters St. *(☎522-2621. Shops open daily 9am-8pm.)* The market begins at the famous **Cafe du Monde** (see p. 407). Vendors sell everything from watermelons to earrings. For a map of the whole strip, stop at the **visitors center.** *(700 Decatur under Washington Artillery Park. ☎596-3424. Open daily 8:30am-5pm.)* Since 1791, visitors have been able to purchase fresh fruits, vegetables, herbs, and spices at the **Farmers Market,** which never closes. Scavengers should head for the **Flea Market,** where one gathers what another one spills. Tables are piled high with t-shirts, handmade furniture, and antique glasses; over it all, the scent of fish floats through the air. *(Open daily 8am-sunset.)*

TOURS OF THE QUARTER. The **Jean Lafitte National Historical Park and Preserve** conducts free 1½hr. walking tours through the Quarter which emphasize New Orleans' rich history. They also give daily presentations on regional topics at 3pm. *(419 Decatur St. ☎589-2636. In the back section of the French Market at Dumaine and St. Phillip St. Tours daily 10:30am. Office open daily 9am-5pm.)* It's always a great night to stroll the **Moon Walk,** a promenade stretching alongside the "Mighty" Mississippi. The walk offers a fantastic riverside view and chance for Michael Jackson jokes. *Don't go alone at night.*

OTHER ATTRACTIONS. At the southwest corner of the Quarter, by the World Trade Center, the **Aquarium of the Americas** houses an amazing collection of sea life and birds. Among the 500 species are black-footed penguins, endangered sea turtles, and extremely rare white alligators. *(1 Canal St. ☎565-3033. Open daily 9:30am-7pm. $13, seniors $10, ages 2-12 $6.50.)* The steamboat **Natchez** breezes down the Mississippi on 2hr. cruises, featuring live jazz and narration on riverside sights. A trip is normally an outrageous $15.75, so ask about two-for-one coupons at the visitors center. *(☎586-8777 or 800-233-2628. Departs 11:30am and 2:30pm from Jax Brewery.)*

OUTSIDE THE QUARTER

WATERFRONT. Take in the city from the revolving bar on the 33rd floor of the **World Trade Center** (see **Nightlife,** below). Looking southwest, the **Riverwalk,** a multi-million dollar conglomeration of overpriced shops overlooking the port, stretches along the Mississippi. *(Open M-Sa 10am-9pm, Su 11am-7pm.)* Take a chance on the newly opened **Harrah's New Orleans Casino,** at Canal and the river. Themed on the city from which it takes its name, experience an endless Mardi Gras as quarters plink into endless rows of slot machines. *(☎800-427-7247. Open 24hr.)* For an up-close view of the Mississippi River and a bit of African-American history, take the free **Canal St. Ferry** to Algiers Point. The Algiers of old housed many of New Orleans's African Americans and is a safe and beautiful neighborhood to explore by foot. At night, the ferry's outdoor observation deck affords a panoramic view of the city's sights. *(Departs daily 5:45am-midnight, every ½hr. from the end of Canal St. Cars $1 round-trip.)*

WAREHOUSE ARTS DISTRICT. Relatively new to the downtown area, the Warehouse Arts District, near the intersection of St. Charles and Julia St., contains several revitalized warehouse buildings that house contemporary art galleries. Exhibits range from Southern folk art to experimental sculpture. Individual galleries distribute maps of the area. In an old brick building with a modern glass and chrome facade, the **Contemporary Arts Center** mounts exhibits ranging from puzzling to positively cryptic. *(900 Camp St. ☎528-3805. Open Tu-Sa 11am-5pm, Su 11am-5pm. Exhibits $3, students and seniors $2, under 12 free; Th free.)* In the rear studio of the **New Orleans School of Glassworks and Printmaking Studio,** observe as students and instructors transform blobs of molten glass into vases and sculptures. *(727 Magazine St. ☎529-7277. Open M-F 11am-5pm; winter M-Sa 11am-5pm. Free.)* A few blocks farther down St. Charles St. stands a bronze Confederate General Robert E. Lee, in **Lee Circle.** The general continues to stare down the Yankees; he faces due North. *Lee Circle and the surrounding neighborhood should not be visited after dark.*

ST. CHARLES STREETCAR. Much of the Crescent City's fame derives from the **Vieux Carré,** but areas uptown have their fair share of beauty and action. The **St. Charles Streetcar** still runs west of the French Quarter, passing some of the city's finest buildings, including the 19th-century homes along **St. Charles Ave.** *Gone With the Wind*-o-philes will recognize the whitewashed bricks and elegant doorway of the house on the far right corner of Arabella St.—it's a replica of Tara. Frankly, my dear, it's not open to the public.

GARDEN DISTRICT. For more views of fancy living, get off the streetcar in the **Garden District,** an opulent neighborhood around Jackson and Louisiana Ave. French, Italian, Spanish, and American architectural legacies create an extraordinary combination of structures, colors, ironwork, and gardens. Some houses are raised above the ground for protection from the swamp on which New Orleans rests.

AUDUBON PARK. The St. Charles Streetcar eventually makes its way to **Audubon Park,** across from **Tulane University.** Designed by Frederick Law Olmsted, Audubon contains lagoons, statues, stables, and the award-winning **Audubon Zoo,** where white alligators swim in a re-created Louisiana swamp. *(☎861-2537. Streetcar stop #36; free museum shuttle between park entrance and zoo every 15min. Zoo open daily 9:30am-5pm; in summer Sa-Su until 6pm. $9, seniors $5, ages 2-12 $4.75.)*

BARATARIA PRESERVE. One of the most unique sights in the New Orleans area, the coastal wetlands along Lake Salvador make up a segment of the **Jean Lafitte National Historical Park** called the **Barataria Preserve.** There's a daily park-sponsored foot tour through the swamp; call for times. Countless commercial boat tours operate around the park; **Cypress Swamp Tours** will pick you up from your hotel for free. *(Preserve: 7400 Barataria Blvd./Rte. 45. ☎589-2330. Free. Cypress Swamp Tours: ☎581-4501, call for reservations. 2hr. tours at 9:30, 11:30am, 1:30, and 3:30pm. $20, $12 per child.)*

BEFORE YOU DIE, READ THIS: Being dead in New Orleans has always been a problem. Because the city lies 4 to 6 feet below sea level, a 6-foot hole in the earth fills up with 5 feet of water. At one time coffins literally floated in the graves, while cemetery workers pushed them down with long wooden poles. One early solution was to bore holes in the coffins, allowing them to sink. Unfortunately, the sight of a drowning coffin coupled with the awful gargling sound of its immersion proved too much for the squeamish families of the departed. Burial soon became passé, and stiffs were laid to rest in beautiful raised stone tombs. Miles and miles of creepy, cool marble tombs now fill the city's graveyards and ghost stories.

HISTORIC HOMES AND PLANTATIONS

Called the "Great Showplace of New Orleans," **Longue Vue House and Gardens** epitomizes the grand Southern estate with its lavish furnishings, opulent decor, and breathtaking sculpted gardens, dating back to the 30s. On the way, pause for a peek at the 85 ft. tall monument among the raised tombs in the **Metairie Cemetery.** (Longue Vue House: 7 Bamboo Rd., off Metairie Rd. ☎ 488-5488. Open M-Sa 10am-4:30pm, Su 1-5pm. $7, students $3, seniors $6, under 5 free. Gardens alone $3, students $1. Tours available in English, French, Spanish, Italian, and Japanese.) **River Rd.** curves along the Mississippi river across from downtown New Orleans, accessing several plantations preserved from the 19th century; copies of Great River Road Plantation Parade: A River of Riches, available at the New Orleans or Baton Rouge visitors centers, contain a good map and descriptions of the houses. Pick carefully, since a tour of all the privately-owned plantations is quite expensive. Those below are listed in order from New Orleans to Baton Rouge.

HERMANN-GRIMM HISTORIC HOUSE. Built in 1831, the house exemplifies French style, replete with a large central hall, guillotine windows, a fan-lit entrance, and the original parterre beds. On Thursdays, from Oct. to May, trained volunteers demonstrate period cooking in an 1830s Creole kitchen. (820 St. Louis St. ☎ 525-5661. Open M-Sa 10am-4pm. Tours every ½hr.; last tour 3:30pm. $6, ages 8-18 $5.)

GALLIER HOUSE MUSEUM. The elegantly restored residence of James Gallier, Jr., the city's most famous architect, resuscitates the taste and lifestyle of the wealthy in the 1860s. (1118-1132 Royal St. ☎ 525-5661. Open M-Sa 10am-4pm. Tours every 30min. to 1hr.; last tour 3:30pm. $6, students and seniors $5, ages 8-18 $4, under 8 free.)

SAN FRANCISCO PLANTATION HOUSE. Beautifully maintained from 1856, the San Francisco is an example of the Creole style, with a smurf blue, peach, and green exterior. (Rte. 44, 2 mi. northwest of Reserve, 42 mi. from New Orleans on the east bank of the Mississippi. Exit 206 off I-10. ☎ 535-2341. Tours daily Mar.-Oct. 10am-4:30pm; Nov.-Feb. 10am-4pm. $8, ages 12-17 $4, ages 6-11 $3.)

OAK ALLEY. The name, Oak Alley, refers to the magnificent driveway bordered by 28 evenly spaced oaks, all nearly 300 years old. The oaks correspond with 28 columns surrounding the Greek Revival house. The Greeks wouldn't have approved, though; the mansion is bright pink. (3645 Hwy. 18, between St. James and Vacherie St. ☎ 800-442-5539. Tours daily every 30 min. 9am-5:30pm. $10, ages 13-18 $6, ages 6-12 $4.)

HOUMAS HOUSE. This plantation served as the setting for the movie Hush, Hush, Sweet Charlotte, starring Bette Davis and Olivia DeHavilland. Huge, moss-draped oaks shade the spacious grounds and beautiful gardens. "Southern Belle" guides lead tours in authentic antebellum attire. (40136 Rte. 942, in Burnside just over halfway to Baton Rouge. ☎ 888-323-8314. Open daily 10am-5pm; Nov.-Jan. 10am-4pm. $8, ages 13-17 $6, ages 6-12 $3.)

NOTTOWAY. As the largest plantation home in the South, Nottoway is often called the "White Castle of Louisiana." A 64-room mansion with 22 columns, a large ballroom, and a 3-story stairway, it was David O. Selznick's first choice for filming Gone with the Wind, but the owners wouldn't allow it. (Rte. 405, between Bayou Goula and White Castle, 18 mi. south of Baton Rouge on the southern bank of the Mississippi. ☎ 832-2093. Open daily 9am-5pm. Admission and 1hr. tour $10, under 12 $4.)

🏛 MUSEUMS

National D-Day Museum, 945 Magazine St. (☎527-6012). Founded by renowned historian Stephen Ambrose and opened in June 2000, this excellent museum explores the economic, historical, and political nature of WWII. Open daily 9am-5pm. $7, seniors and students $6, ages 5-17 $5.

Louisiana State Museum, P.O. Box 2448 (☎800-568-6968), oversees 5 separate museums: the **Old US Mint,** 400 Esplanade; **Cabildo,** 701 Chartres St.; **Presbytère,** 751 Chartres St.; **1850 House,** 523 St. Ann St.; and **Mdme. John's Legacy,** 632 Dumaine St. All 5 contain artifacts, papers, and other changing exhibits on the history of Louisiana and New Orleans. The Old US Mint is particularly interesting, focusing not on currency or fresh breath, but on the history of jazz and the lives of greats like Louis "Satchmo" Armstrong. All open Tu-Su 9am-5pm. Old US Mint, Cabildo, Presbytere: $5, seniors and students $4. 1850 House, Mdme. John's Legacy: $3/$2. Under 12 free for all museums.

New Orleans Museum of Art (NOMA) (☎488-2631), in City Park. Take the Esplanade bus from Canal and Rampart St. This magnificent museum houses art from North and South America, a small collection of local decorative arts, opulent works by the jeweler Fabergé, and a strong collection of French paintings. Free tours available. Open Tu-Su 10am-5pm. $6, seniors and ages 3-17 $5.

Historic New Orleans Collection, 533 Royal St. (☎523-4662). Located in the aristocratic 18th-century Merieult House, this impressive cultural research center will teach you everything you wanted to know about Louisiana's history. The History Tour explores New Orleans past, while the Williams Residence Tour showcases the eclectic home furnishings of the collection's founders. Gallery open Tu-Sa 10am-4:30pm; free. Tours 10, 11am, 2, and 3pm; $4.

Musée Conti Wax Museum, 917 Conti St. (☎525-2605). Figures from 300 years of Louisiana lore. Perennial favorites include a voodoo display, a haunted dungeon, and a mock-up of Madame Lalaurie's torture attic. Open M-Sa 10am-5:30pm, Su noon-5:30pm. $6.25, under 17 $4.75, seniors $5.50.

Confederate Museum, 929 Camp St. (☎523-4522), in a brownstone building west of Lee Circle. The state's oldest museum, with a wide collection of Civil War records and artifacts. Open M-Sa 10am-4pm. $5, students and seniors $4, under 12 $2.

New Orleans Pharmacy Museum, 514 Chartres St. (☎565-8027), in the Quarter. This apothecary shop was built by America's first licensed pharmacist in 1823. On display are 19th-century "miracle drugs," voodoo powders, and the still-fertile botanical garden, where medicinal herbs are grown. Open Tu-Su 10am-5pm. $2, students and seniors $1, under 12 free. Admission includes 30min. tour.

Louisiana Children's Museum, 420 Julia St. (☎523-1357). This place invites kids to play and learn, as they star in their own news shows, run their own cafe, or shop in a re-created mini-mart. Kids under 16 must be accompanied by an adult. Open M-Sa 9:30am-4:30pm, Su noon-4:30pm; Sept.-May closed M. $5.

Louisiana Nature and Science Center, (☎246-5672) Joe Brown Memorial Park, off Read Blvd. Trail walks, exhibits, planetarium and laser shows, and 86 acres of natural wildlife preserve. From Basin St., take bus #64 "Lake Forrest Express" ($1.25) to reach this wonderful escape from the bedlam of the French Quarter. Open Tu-F 9am-5pm, Sa 10am-5pm, Su noon-5pm. $4.75, seniors $3.75, ages 4-13 $2.50.

🎭 ENTERTAINMENT

THEATER

Le Petit Théâtre du Vieux Carré, 616 St. Peters St., is one of the city's most beloved and historical theaters. The oldest continuously operating community theater in the US, the 1789 building replicates the early 18th-century abode of Joseph de Pontalba, Louisiana's last Spanish governor. Around five musicals and plays go up each year, as well as four fun productions in the "Children's Corner." (☎522-9958. Box office open Tu-Sa 10:30am-5:30pm, Su noon-4pm.)

MUSIC

Uptown tends to house authentic Cajun dance halls and popular university hangouts, while the Marigny is home to New Orleans's alternative/local music scene. Check out *Off Beat*, free in many local restaurants, or the F *Times-Picayune* to find out who's playing where.

Born at the turn of the century in **Armstrong Park,** traditional New Orleans jazz still wails nightly at the tiny, dim, historic **Preservation Hall,** 726 St. Peters St.; jazz is in its most fundamental element here. Those who don't come early can expect a lengthy wait in line, poor visibility, and sweaty standing-room only. (Daytime ☎ 522-2841, otherwise 523-8939. Eat and drink before you come. Doors open at 8pm; music begins at 8:30pm and ends at midnight. Cover $4.) Keep your ears open for **Cajun** and **zydeco** bands who use accordions, washboards, triangles, and drums to perform hot dance tunes (true locals two-step expertly) and saccharine waltzes. Anyone who thinks couple-dancing went out in the 50s should try a *fais do-do*, a lengthy, wonderfully energetic traditional dance. The locally based **Radiators** do it up real spicy-like in a rock-cajun-zydeco style.

FESTIVALS

New Orleans's **Mardi Gras** celebration is the biggest party of the year, a world-renowned, epic bout of lascivious debauchery that fills the three weeks leading up to Ash Wednesday. Parades, gala, balls, and general revelry take to the streets, as tourists pour in by the plane-full (flights into the city and hotel rooms fill up months in advance). In 2001, "Fat Tuesday," falls on Feb. 27; the biggest parades and the bulk of the partying will take place from Feb. 17 until Feb. 27.

The ever-expanding **New Orleans Jazz and Heritage Festival** attracts 7000 musicians from around the country to the city's fairgrounds. The likes of Aretha Franklin, Bob Dylan, Patti LaBelle, and Wynton Marsalis have graced this slightly "classier" fest, where music plays simultaneously on 12 stages in the midst of a huge Cajun and Creole food and crafts festival. The biggest names perform evening riverboat concerts. The festival grows more zoo-like and, unfortunately, more commercialized each year (☎ 522-4786; Apr. 26-May 6, 2001).

◪ NIGHTLIFE

Life in New Orleans is and always will be a party. On any night of the week, at any time of the year, the masses converge on **Bourbon St.** to drift in and out of bars and shop for romantic interludes. Though the street has become increasingly touristy of late, much of Bourbon's original charm remains. Several sleazy strip clubs and cross-dressing joints maintain the sense of sinful excitement that is the essence of the Quarter. College boys on balconies still throw beads to girls who flash their breasts, and drunken adults urinate on dark side streets. To escape the debauchery of Bourbon St., some flee to **Decatur St.,** between St. Ann and Barracks St.

While the Quarter offers countless bars and jazz, blues, and brass venues, be assured that there's more to New Orleans entertainment. When locals burn out on Bourbon, they head uptown, towards **Tulane University,** or to the **Marigny,** an up-and-coming district northeast of the Quarter. *Impact* and *Ambush* track the movements of New Orleans's large gay community; both are available at **Faubourg Marigny Books,** 600 Frenchmen St. (☎ 943-9875; open M-F 10am-8pm, Sa-Su 10am-6pm). Gay establishments cluster toward the northeast end of Bourbon St.; St. Ann St. is known to some as the **"Lavender Line."**

GIMME SOME SKIN French quarter shops sell beads for $1-5, but why buy them when you can *earn* them for free? Down on the 700th block of Bourbon St., and especially near the balconies above the Cat's Meow and Tricou House, lie the best bead bartering locations. Women who flash their breasts on the street earn beads. Only in New Orleans is exposing oneself so colorfully rewarded.

THE SOUTH

Bars in New Orleans stay open late, and few keep a strict schedule; in general, they open around 11am and close around 3am. Most blocks feature at least one establishment with cheap draft beer and Hurricanes (sweet juice-and-rum drinks). The party's fun, but the law is enforced, especially between 9pm and 1am. *All establishments are 21+ unless otherwise noted.*

BARS

FRENCH QUARTER

Pat O'Brien's, 718 St. Peters St. (☎525-4823). The busiest bar and one of the best in the French Quarter, bursting with happy (read: drunk) patrons. Listen to the piano in one room, mix with local students in another, or lounge near the fountain in the courtyard. Home of the original (and deliciously potent) Hurricane; purchase your first in a souvenir glass ($8). Open Su-Th 10am-4am, F-Sa 10am-5am.

Lafitte's Blacksmith Shop, 941 Bourbon St. (☎523-0066), at Phillip St. Appropriately, one of New Orleans's oldest standing structures is a bar. Built in the 1730s, the building is still lit by candlelight after sunset. Named for the scheming hero of the Battle of New Orleans, it offers shaded relief from the elements of the city and friendly company at night. Open noon until late; live piano 8pm until late.

Molly's at the Market, 1107 Decatur St. (☎525-5169). Molly's offers tasty and widely acclaimed frozen Irish coffee ($4), as well as a hang out space for eclectic locals. Vibrant late night retreat from the touristy frenzy of the quarter. Open daily 10am-6am.

Crescent City Brewhouse, 527 Decatur St. (☎522-0571). The only microbrewery in New Orleans, this classy brewpub sells its own 5 blends (12 oz. $3.50; 20 oz. pint $4.50). Glass walls and balcony make for good people-watching, a wonderful activity when set to live jazz (nightly 6-9pm). Open Su-Th 11am-10pm, F-Sa 11am-midnight.

O'Flaherty's Irish Channel Pub, 514 Toulouse St. (☎529-1317). An Irish Pub in New Orleans? Well, why not? O'Flaherty's bills itself as the meeting point of the disparate Celtic nations. Eavesdrop on Gaelic conversation while listening to Scottish bagpipes, watching Irish dances, and/or singing along to Irish tunes. Irish music daily at 8pm. Open daily noon-3am. Cover $2.

OUTSIDE THE QUARTER

Snug Harbor, 626 Frenchmen St. (☎949-0696), near Decatur St. Regulars include big names in modern jazz like Charmaine Neville, Astral Project, and Ellis Marsalis. The cover is steep ($8-15), but the music and its fans are authentic. Bar open daily 5pm-2am; restaurant open Su-Th 5-11pm, F-Sa 5pm-midnight. Shows nightly 9 and 11pm. All ages.

F&M Patio Bar, 4841 Tchoupitoulas St. (☎895-6784), near Napoleon. Mellow 20-somethings, students, doctors, lawyers, and ne'er-do-wells dance together on the pool tables in the heat of the night. Serves food after 6pm, mostly fajitas ($3.75) and burgers ($4.50) from a mega-grill on the patio. Open M-Th 1pm-4am, F 1pm-6am, Sa 3pm-6am, Su 8pm-4am.

Cafe Brasil, 2100 Chartres (☎949-0851), at Frenchmen St. Unassuming by day, Brasil is packed weekend nights by locals who come to see a wide variety of New Orleans talent. Open daily 7pm until late. Shows 8 and 11pm. Cover F-Sa after 11pm $6-10. All ages.

Checkpoint Charlie's, 501 Esplanade (☎947-0979), grunges it up like the best of Seattle. Do your laundry while listening to live music 7 nights a week. Julia Roberts sat on these machines in *The Pelican Brief.* Beer $2. Open 24hr. No cover.

Carrollton Station, 8140 Willow St. (☎865-9190), at Dublin St. A cozy neighborhood club with live R&B music and friendly folks. 12 beers on tap ($2-4). Open daily 3:30pm-2am. Music Th-Sa at 10pm.

Top of the Mart, World Trade Center, 2 Canal St. (☎522-9795). Ever had too many drinks and thought the world was spinning? Well, this time it's not your fault. The nation's largest revolving bar, this 500-seat cocktail lounge spins 33 stories above the ground. The sunset view is awe-inspiring. Open M-F 10am-midnight, Sa 11am-2am, Su 2pm-midnight. No cover, but a 1-drink minimum. ($2.50 and up). 18+.

DANCE CLUBS

FRENCH QUARTER

House of Blues, 225 Decatur St. (☎529-2583). A sprawling complex with a large (over 1000 capacity) music/dance hall, beefy bouncers, and a balcony and bar overlooking the action. Restaurant open Su-Th 11am-11pm, F-Sa 11am-midnight. Concerts nightly 9:15pm. Cover usually $5-10, but big names cost up to $30. 18+.

Bourbon Pub & Parade Disco, 801 Bourbon St. (☎529-2107). This gay dance bar has a "tea dance" on Su with $5 all-you-can-drink beer. Dance upstairs at the Paradise Disco nightly from 9pm (Tu-Su in summer); it lasts 'til you fall off. Open 24hr.

735 Nightclub and Bar, 735 Bourbon St. (☎581-6740). Great music and a hip mixed crowd keep this dance club energized well into the night. Techno plays downstairs, hip-hop and 80s on the 2nd floor. Open Tu-Su 10pm until late. Cover $3-10. 18+.

OUTSIDE THE QUARTER

Tipitina's, 501 Napoleon Ave. (☎891-8477, concert info 897-3943). The best local bands and some big national names, such as the Neville Brothers, John Goodman, and Harry Connick, Jr., play so close, you can almost touch them. Su evenings feature Cajun *fais-do-dos.* Cover $4-15, W free food and quarter draft with $5 cover; call ahead for times and prices.

The Red Room, 2040 St. Charles (☎528-9759). Latin beats and rhythm and blues mark this swanky throwback to the opulent, jazzy side of the 30s. One of the mellowest, classiest clubs. Dress up or look drab against the posh red decor. Open 7pm-2am, Sa until late. Music starts at 9pm. Cover $5-10. 18+.

Maple Leaf Bar, 8316 Oak St. (☎866-9359). The best local dance bar, offering zydeco, brass band, and Cajun music; everyone does the two-step. Large, pleasant, covered patio. Open daily 3pm. Poetry readings Su 3pm. Music and dancing start Su-Th 10pm, F-Sa 10:30pm. Cover $5.

Mid City Lanes, 4133 S. Carrollton Ave. (☎482-3133), at Tulane Ave. Uncut N'awlins. The "home of Rock 'n' Bowl" is bowling alley by day, dance club by night (you can bowl at night, too). Featuring good food and local zydeco, blues, and rock 'n' roll, this is where the locals party. Lanes $10 per hr. Open noon until late. Music Tu-Th 8:30pm, F-Sa 10pm; cover $5-7. The *Rock 'n' Bowlletin* has schedules (and a list of the regulars' birthdays). 18+.

El Matador, 504 Esplanade (☎569-8361). Tired of Bourbon Street? A good mix of patrons and a wide range of musical styles (jazz, hip-hop, techno, or rock, depending on the night) make this nightclub a good escape from the predictable drunken mayhem of more touristy locations. Live flamenco show on Sa night. Open M-Th 9pm until late, F-Su 4pm until late. Cover $2-4.

BATON ROUGE ☎225

Once the site of a tall cypress tree marking the boundary between rival Native American tribes, Baton Rouge ("red stick") has blossomed into Louisiana's capital and second largest city. State politics have shaped this town—it was once the home of the notorious governor, senator, and demagogue "Kingfish" Huey P. Long. The presence of Louisiana State University (LSU) adds an element of youth and rebellion. Nonetheless, Baton Rouge has a simple meat-and-potatoes flavor in contrast to the flamboyant sauciness of New Orleans.

◪ PRACTICAL INFORMATION. Close to downtown, **Greyhound,** 1253 Florida Blvd., at 13th St., sends buses to New Orleans (2hr., 8 per day, $11.50) and Lafayette (4hr., 12 per day, $12.50). *The area is unsafe at night.* (☎333-3811 or 800-231-2222; open 24hr.) **Visitor Info: State Capitol Visitors Center,** on the first fl. of the State Capitol. (☎342-7317; open daily 8am-4:30pm.) **Baton Rouge Convention and Visitors Bureau,** 730 North Blvd. (☎383-1825 or 800-527-6843; open M-F 8am-5pm.) **Post Office:** 750 Florida Blvd., off River Rd. (☎800-275-8777; open M-F 8:30am-5pm, Sa 9:30am-12:30pm.) **ZIP code:** 70821. **Area code:** 225.

ACCOMMODATIONS AND FOOD. Baton Rouge's cheapest accommodations are located on the outskirts of town. The **Corporate Inn,** 2365 College Dr., at Exit 158 off I-10, resembles the Emerald City—on the outside. (☎925-2451. Free local calls, HBO, and coffee and doughnuts in the morning. Singles $46; doubles $60.) The **KOA Campground,** 7628 Vincent Rd., 15 mi. east off I-12 at the Denham Springs exit, keeps well-maintained sites, clean facilities and a big pool. (☎664-7281 or 800-292-8245. Tent sites $20; full RV hook-up $26.50.)

Downtown, sandwich shops and cafes line 3rd St. Head to LSU at the intersection of Highland Rd. and Chimes St. for cheaper chow and an abundance of bars. **Louie's Cafe,** 209 W. State St., grills up fabulous omelettes $4.75-9.75. (☎346-8221. Open 24hr.) When you want a good sit-down meal, a good option is **The Chimes,** 3357 Highland Rd., a big restaurant and bar with more than 120 different beers. Louisiana alligator—farm-raised, marinated, and fried, served with Dijon mustard sauce—goes for $7. Do you dare? (☎383-1754. Open M-Sa 11am-2am, Su 11am-midnight.)

SIGHTS. In a move reminiscent of Ramses II, Huey Long ordered the construction of the unique **Louisiana State Capitol,** a magnificent, modern skyscraper, completed over a mere 14 months in 1931 and 1932. The **observation deck,** on the 27th floor, provides a view of the port. *(☎342-7317. Open daily 8am-4pm. Free.)* Of equal grandeur is the **Old State Capitol,** with a fantastic spiral staircase, domed stained glass, and many exhibits on the history of Louisiana, including the controversy over Long's assassination. *(100 North Blvd. ☎342-0500 or 800-488-2968. Open Tu-Sa 10am-4pm, Su noon-4pm. $4, seniors $3, students $2; $1 off with brochure from the new capitol.)* **Magnolia Mound Plantation,** 2161 Nicholson Dr., built in 1791, is a palatial French-Creole mansion spanning 16 acres. *(2161 Nicholson Dr. ☎343-4955. Open Tu-Sa 10am-4pm, Su 1-4pm. $5, seniors $4, students $2, ages 5-12 $1. Last tour 3:15pm.)* The **LSU Rural Life Museum** depicts the life of the less well-to-do Creoles through their authentically furnished shops, cabins, and storage houses. Adjacent to the museum are the lakes, winding paths, roses, and azaleas of the **Windrush Gardens.** *(4600 Essen Ln. ☎765-2437. Both open daily 8:30am-5pm. $5, seniors $4, ages 5-11 $3.)*

NATCHITOCHES ☎318

Pronounced *NAK-ah-tish*, the town is named after the original Native American inhabitants of the region. Founded in 1714 by the French to facilitate trade with the Spanish in Mexico, Natchitoches is the oldest permanent settlement in Louisiana, a point of pride for its residents. Back in the day, the strategic commercial and military location of Natchitoches along the banks of the Red River meant it should have become a major port city, much like New Orleans. However, fate (or a really big log jam) changed the course of Natchitoches's history, redirecting the Red River and leaving the town high and dry. Now called the Cane River National Heritage Area, only a 35-mile stretch of what used to be the Red River remains. Here, the influence of French, Spanish, African American, and Native American peoples is evident in the histories of the plantations lining its banks.

PRACTICAL INFORMATION. Downtown Natchitoches is organized in a grid-like fashion, with **Front St.** following the **Cane River** and numbered streets running parallel behind it. Most of the historic homes and plantations lie about 18 mi. south of downtown, near the river and off **Rte. 1 S. Greyhound,** 331 Cane River Shop Center (☎352-8341), buses to New Orleans (6½hr., 11 per day, $40) and Houston (8-10hr., 3 per day, $60). Station open M-F 8am-11am and noon-4pm. **Visitor Info: Natchitoches Convention and Visitors Bureau,** 781 Front St. (☎352-8072 or 800-259-1714; open M-F 9am-8pm, Sa 9am-5pm, Su 9am-3pm). **Post Office:** 240 Saint Denis St. (☎352-2161; open M-F 8am-4:30pm, Sa 9am-11pm). **ZIP code:** 71457. **Area code:** 318.

ACCOMMODATIONS. Don't say we didn't tell you: Natchitoches isn't a cheap town. As the "B&B Capital" of Louisiana, Natchitoches abounds with cozy rooms in historic homes. Unfortunately, most are far from budget-friendly. If the wallet's not a primary concern, ask at the **Natchitoches Convention and Visitors Bureau** for a listing of the area's top-notch B&Bs. During the Christmas Festival, room rates (even for motels!) can as much as triple, and reservations are booked months in advance.

With the recent opening of **I-49** through the area, a number of motels have sprouted-up west of town, where the interstate meets **Rte. 6.** One of the best deals is the **Microtel Inn,** 5335 Rte. 6 W. Brand-new rooms come well-furnished with A/C, cable, free local calls, microfridge, and microwave. There's also a pool and free continental breakfast. (☎214-0700 or 888-771-7171. Singles $45; doubles $53. 10% off for AAA and *Let's Go:USA* toters.) Campers have the advantage here. The 600,000-acre **Kisatchie National Forest** offers plenty of rustic, outdoor living in one of nature's untouched gems. All camping sites are primitive ($2-3 per night), but differ in "perks" (some have nearby swimming, others have hiking, etc.). Check-in first with the **Kisatchie Ranger District,** Rte. 6 W, ¼ mi. past the Microtel Inn, for maps, camping information, and park conditions. (☎352-2568. Open M-F 8am-4:30pm.)

🗒🍴 **FOOD AND NIGHTLIFE.** Famous for its meat pies, **Lasyone's,** 622 2nd St., is the place to go for hearty home cooking. You can have a meat pie by itself ($2.50) or get the full meal that comes with salad, a veggie, and mashed potatoes ($7). Lunch specials are $5.25. (☎352-3353. Open M-Sa 7am-7pm.) **Almost Home,** 5820 Rte. 1 N Bypass, lets you take what (and how much) you want from their buffet-line of traditional Southern fare. The price is set at one meat and three veggies for $6, except on F night when they have an all-you-can-eat seafood dinner for $10. (☎352-2431. Open M-Sa 6am-2:30pm, F night seafood dinner 5-9pm.)

Drink with a friendly, local crowd while listening to live music at **Pioneer Pub,** 812 Washington St., opposite the visitors center. (☎352-4884. Open Su-F 4:30pm-midnight, F-Sa 4:30pm-2am.) Being home to **Northwestern State University,** Natchitoches has its share of rowdy college bars. To find where the action is, flag down a young 20-something (there are about 8000 of them) and ask. The students tend to be a friendly group and will likely point you in the right direction.

📷🎭 **SIGHTS AND ENTERTAINMENT.** Much of Natchitoches's charm can be found near the Cane River, along **Front St.,** where coffee shops and antique parlors are the primary residents of historic buildings dating back to the mid-19th century. To see everything of significance that lies within city limits from the comfort of a large, green trolly, take a ride with the **Natchitoches Transit Company,** 100 Rue Beau Port. (☎356-8687. Call for departure times. 1½hr. tour $8, under 12 $5.)

Many of the popular tourist destinations are outside the city limits. For the next generation of handbags and belts, drive out to ⛳**Bayou Pierre Gator Park & Show,** 8 mi. north of Natchitoches off Rte. 1 N. Originally a conservation project for the scaly beasts, the park now entertains visitors with regular feeding shows and swamp-suspended walkways, allowing onlookers the chance to admire the toothy reptiles up-close and personal. (☎877-354-7001. Open daily Apr. 15 to Oct. 31 10am-6pm; call for hours during the winter months. $6, ages 3-12 $4.50.) A string of plantation homes follow the Cane River, south of downtown along Rte. 1. The **Melrose** plantation, 14 mi. south on Rte. 1 then left on Hwy. 493, is unique in origin; its female founder was an ex-slave herself. The tour covers the history of Melrose through the generations, walking visitors though five buildings on the site, including the old slave quarters. (☎379-0055. Open daily noon-4pm. $5, under 18 $3.) The **Kate Chopin House,** 20 mi. south off Rte. 1, is especially interesting for those curious about the roots of the feminist movement. Author of the controversial novel *The Awakening*, Kate Chopin broke with convention by doing such things as cigar-smoking and beer-drinking in a quiet Southern town. (☎379-2233. Open M-Sa 10am-5pm, Su 1-5pm. $5, under 18 $3.)

While Natchitoches may not see a *white* Christmas, she'll most definitely see a *light* Christmas. The town's residents spend months putting up some 300,000 Christmas bulbs, only to be greeted in-turn by 150,000 camera-toting tourists flocking like moths to the **City of Lights.** The peak of the month-long exhibition (Nov. 21 to Jan. 6, 2001) is the first weekend in Dec., when a carnival-like atmosphere fills the air during the **Festival of Lights.** If you miss the Dec. fun, don't fret; while they may not be as grand, there's a festival of some type going on nearly every weekend throughout the year. Call the **Natchitoches Convention and Visitors Bureau** for more info (see **Practical Information,** above).

ACADIANA

Throughout the early 18th century, the English government in Nova Scotia became increasingly jealous of the prosperity of French settlers *(Acadians)* and deeply offended by their refusal to kneel before the British Crown. During the war with France in 1755, the British rounded up the Acadians and deported them by the ship-load in what came to be called *le Grand Dérangement,* "the Great Upheaval." Of the 7000 Acadians who went to sea, one-third died of smallpox and hunger. Those who survived sought refuge along the Atlantic Coast, but were met suspicion and forced into indentured servitude. The Acadians soon realized that freedom waited in French Louisiana. The "Cajuns" (as they are known today) of St. Martin, Lafayette, New Iberia, and St. Mary parishes are descendants of these settlers.

Several factors have threatened Acadian culture since the relocation. In the 20s, Louisiana passed laws forcing Acadian schools to teach in English. Later, during the oil boom of the 70s and 80s, oil executives and developers envisioned the Acadian center of Lafayette (see below) as the Houston of Louisiana and threatened to flood the area with mass culture. The proud people of southern Louisiana have resisted homogenization. The state is officially bilingual, and a state agency preserves Acadian French in schools and in the media. "Cajun Country" spans the south of the state, from Houma in the east to the Texas border in the west.

LAFAYETTE   ☎337

The center of Acadiana, Lafayette is the perfect place to try boiled crawfish or dance the two-step to a fiddle and accordion. Though the city's French roots are often obscured by the chain motels that have accompanied its growth, there is no question that the Cajuns still own the surrounding countryside, where Cajun music and Creole zydeco heat up dance floors every night of the week and locals continue to answer their phones with a proud *bonjour.*

■■ **ORIENTATION AND PRACTICAL INFORMATION.** Lafayette stands at a crossroads. **I-10** leads east to New Orleans and west to Lake Charles; **U.S. 90** heads south to New Iberia and the Atchafalaya Basin; **U.S. 167** runs north into central Louisiana. Most of the city lies west of the **Evangeline Thruway (U.S. 49)** which runs north-south. Establishments are concentrated along Johnson St. (U.S. 167) and Ambassador Caffery Pkwy. **Amtrak,** 133 E. Grant St., sends three trains per week to New Orleans (4hr., $21); Houston (5½hr., $35); and San Antonio (10hr., $55). **Greyhound,** 315 Lee Ave., (☎235-1541), buses to New Orleans (3½hr., 10 per day, $17.50); Baton Rouge (1hr., 12 per day, $12.50); and New Iberia (30min., 2 per day, $7.50). Station open 24 hours. The **Lafayette Bus System,** 1515 E. University, is centered at Lee and Garfield St. (☎291-8570. Infrequent service M-Sa 6:30am-6:30pm. 45¢, ages 5-12 30¢, seniors and disabled 20¢.) **Taxi: Yellow/Checker Cab Inc.** (☎237-6196). **Hospital: University Medical Center,** 2390 W. Congress (☎261-6000; 24hr.). **Visitor Info: Lafayette Parish Convention and Visitors Commission,** 1400 NE Evangeline Thwy. (☎232-3808. Open M-F 8:30am-5pm, Sa-Su 9am-5pm.) **Post Office:** 1105 Moss St. (☎800-275-8777. Open M-F 8am-5:30pm, Sa 8am-12:30pm.) **ZIP code:** 70501. **Area code:** 337.

■■ **ACCOMMODATIONS AND FOOD.** Inexpensive hotels line the Evangeline Thwy. Simple rooms at **Super 8,** 2224 NE Evangeline Thruway, come with pool access and a highway view. (☎232-8826 or 800-800-8000. Singles $34; doubles $43.) **Travel Host Inn South,** 1314 N. Evangeline Thruway, also offers clean rooms with cable TV, pool, free breakfast, and a convenient location. (☎233-2090 or 800-677-1466. Singles $35; doubles $41.) One campground close to the center of Lafayette, **Acadiana Park Campground,** 1201 E. Alexander, off Louisiana Ave., has tennis courts and a soccer field. (☎291-8388. Office open Sa-Th 8am-5pm, F 8am-8pm. Full hookup $9.) The lakeside **KOA Lafayette,** 5 mi. west of town on I-10 at Exit 97, offers a store, mini-golf course, and two pools. (☎235-2739. Office open daily 7:30am-8:30pm. Tent sites $19, with water and electricity $24.50, full hook-up $26.)

Cajun restaurants with live music and dancing have popped up all over Lafayette. Unfortunately, some demand substantial funds. In central Lafayette, **Chris' Po' boys** offers seafood platters ($7-10) and—whadda ya' know—po' boys for under $6. (631 Jefferson St. ☎234-1696. Open M-Th 10:30am-8:30pm, F 10:30am-9pm, Sa 11am-9pm. Live blues and cajun F-Sa nights.) For the mild-mannered, the **Judice Inn**, 3134 Johnston St., provides tasty, no-nonsense hamburgers with a secret sauce for $2-3. (☎984-5614. Open M-Sa 10am-10pm.)

🎫 **SIGHTS.** Driving through south-central Louisiana means driving over America's largest swamp, the Atchafalaya *(a-chah-fa-LIE-a)* Basin. The **Atchafalaya Fwy.** (I-10 between Lafayette and Baton Rouge) crosses 32 mi. of swamp and cypress trees. To get down and dirty and maybe see some alligators, exit at Henderson (Exit 115), turn right, then immediately left for 5 mi. on Rte. 352. From there, follow signs to **McGee's Landing**, 1337 Henderson Rd., which sends four 1½hr. **boat tours** into the Basin each day. (☎228-2384 or 800-445-6681. Tours daily 8, 10am, 1, and 3pm. $12, seniors and under 12 $10, under 2 free.)

The **Acadian Cultural Center/Jean Lafitte National Park**, 501 Fisher Rd., features a 40min. documentary, *The Cajun Way: Echoes of Acadia*, as well as a terrific exhibit on the exodus and migration of these French settlers. (☎232-0789. Open daily 8am-5pm. Shows every hr. on the hr. 9am-4pm. Free.) Next door, the re-creation of an Acadian settlement at **Vermilionville**, 1600 Surrey St., has music, crafts, food, and dancing on the Bayou Vermilion banks. (☎233-4077 or 800-992-2968. Open daily 10am-5pm. Live music M-F 1:30-3:30pm, Sa-Su 2-5pm. Cajun cooking lessons daily 11:30am and 1:30pm. $8, seniors $6.50, ages 6-18 $5.) **Acadian Village**, 200 Greenleaf Rd., offers a look at the unpretentious homes of common 19th-century settlers (take U.S. 167 S to Ridge Rd., then left on Broussard, and follow the signs). While at the village, view Native American artifacts at the **Mississippi Valley Missionary Museum.** (☎981-2364 or 800-962-9133. Both open daily 10am-5pm. $6, seniors $5, children $2.50.) The 450-year-old **St. John's Cathedral Oak,** in the yard of **St. John's Cathedral,** 914 St. John St., shades the entire lawn with spidery limbs which spread 145 ft.; the weight of one limb is around 72 tons.

🎭 **ENTERTAINMENT.** Lafayette kicks off spring and fall weekends with **Downtown Alive!,** a series of free concerts featuring everything from New Wave to Cajun and zydeco. (☎291-5566. Apr.-June and Sept.-Nov. F 5:30pm; music 6-8:30pm.) The **Festival International de Louisiane** highlights southwest Louisiana in a francophone tribute. (☎232-8086. Apr. 24-29, 2001.) To find the best zydeco in town, pick up a copy of *The Times*, available free at restaurants and gas stations. For year-round entertainment, **Randol's,** 2320 Kaliste Saloom Rd., romps with live Cajun and zydeco music nightly and doubles as a restaurant. (☎981-7080. Open Su-Th 5-10pm, F-Sa 5-11pm.) On weekends, after the restaurants close, **Grant St. Dance Hall,** 113 Grant St., energizes with rajin' cajun tunes, fast-paced zydeco, and more mellow blues. (☎237-2255. Open F-Sa. Shows start at 10pm. Cover $5. All ages.)

NEW IBERIA AND ENVIRONS   ☎337

While Lafayette was being invaded by oil magnates eager to build a Louisiana oil-business center, New Iberia continued to maintain links to its bayou past. Several sights give visitors a good feel for the unique conditions of life in the area.

Most plantations in southern Louisiana grew sugarcane, not cotton. Many of these plantations are still private property, but **Shadows on the Teche,** 317 E. Main St. at the Rte. 14/Rte. 182 junction, welcomes the public with over 17,000 family documents and a first-hand look at antebellum life in the South. (☎369-6446. Open daily 9am-4:30pm. $6, ages 6-11 $3; AAA discount.) Time passes quickly at the **Rip Van Winkle Gardens,** 5505 Rip Van Winkle Rd., off Rte. 14. (☎365-3332. Open daily 9am-5pm. House and garden tour $9, seniors $8.50, students 14-18 $7, ages 5-13 $5.) **Avery Island,** 7 mi. away on Rte. 329 off Rte. 90 (50¢ toll to enter the island), sizzles with the world-famous **Tabasco Pepper Sauce Factory,** where the McIlhenny family has produced the famous condiment for nearly a century. Tours every 15min. include free recipes, samples, and tastings. (Factory open to visitors M-Th 9am-4pm; gift shop open M-Sa 9am-4pm. Free.) Bring sunglasses for the 1hr. **Airboat Tour** of the shallow swamps and bayous of Lake Fausse Pointe. (☎229-4457. Open Feb.-Oct. Tu-Su 8am-5pm. $15. Reservations required.)

Picturesque campsites on the banks of the Bayou Teche are available at **Belmont Campgrounds**, 1000 Belmont Rd., at the junction of Rte. 31 and 86. Within the well-kept grounds are nature trails and fishing areas in the stocked pond. (☎369-3252. Tent sites with showers and laundry $11, full RV hook-up $17.)

New Iberia lies 21 mi. southeast of Lafayette on U.S. 90. **Amtrak** stops at an unstaffed station, 402 W. Washington St., at Railroad St. Three trains per week set out for Lafayette (30min., $4) and New Orleans (3hr., $20). **Greyhound,** 1103 E. Main St. (☎364-8571), buses to New Orleans (4hr., 4 per day, $28) and Lafayette (40min., 2 per day, $7). Station open M-F 8am-5pm, Sa 8am-noon. The **Iberia Parish Convention and Visitors Bureau,** 2704 Rte. 14 (☎888-942-3742; open daily 9am-5pm), and the **Greater Iberia Chamber of Commerce,** 111 W. Main St. (☎364-1836; open M-F 8:30am-5pm), have maps. **Area code:** 337.

ARKANSAS

"The Natural State" lives up to its nickname, encompassing the Ozark and Ouachita mountains, the clear waters of Hot Springs, and miles of lush pine forests. The state's subcultures are just as varied as its geography. The bluesy Mississippi Delta region seeps into southeast Arkansas, while the northern mountains support a close-knit, no-pretenses community. All across Arkansas, however, one thing remains constant—travelers are easily accepted as part of the family (which happens to include former President Bill Clinton).

▮ PRACTICAL INFORMATION

Capital: Little Rock.
Visitor Info: Arkansas Dept. of Parks and Tourism, One Capitol Mall, Little Rock 72201 (☎501-682-1191 or 800-628-8725; www.arkansas.com). Open M-F 8am-5pm.
Postal Abbreviation: AR. **Sales Tax:** 6%.

LITTLE ROCK ☎501

In the early 19th century, a small rock just a few feet high served as an important landmark for boats pushing their way upstream. Sailors and merchants began settling around this stone outcrop, and, lo and behold, Little Rock was born. The capital became the focus of a nationwide civil rights controversy in 1957, when Governor Orval Faubus and local white segregationists violently resisted nine black students who entered Central High School under the shields of the National Guard. Fortunately, Little Rock has since become a more integrated community, one that strives to be a cosmopolitan centerpiece for the state.

▮ **PRACTICAL INFORMATION.** Little Rock is at the intersection of I-40 and I-30, 140 mi. west of Memphis. Downtown, numbered streets run east-west. Near the river, Markham St. is 1st St. and Capitol is 5th St. Markham St. will become Clinton St. sometime in the future, but street numbers will remain the same. **Greyhound,** 118 E. Washington St. (☎372-3007), is in North Little Rock; take bus #7 or 18. Runs to St. Louis (8½hr., 1 per day, $48); New Orleans (13½hr., 5 per day, $74); and Memphis (2½hr., 9 per day, $22). **Amtrak,** 1400 W. Markham St. (☎372-6841), runs from Union Station at Victory St.; take bus #1 or 8. Trains go most days to St. Louis (7hr., $58-72); Dallas (6½hr., $64-80); and Malvern ($9), near Hot Springs. (Station open Su and W-Th 6pm-1:30am, M 9:30am-7:30pm, Tu 3:30pm-1:30am, F-Sa 6am-4pm.) **Central Arkansas Transit (CAT)** operates a fairly extensive bus system. (Runs M-F 6am-11pm, with reduced service on weekends. Fare $1, seniors 50¢, transfers 10¢.) CAT also runs trolleys from the business district to River Market (M-F 11am-2pm; 25¢). **Little Rock Convention and Visitors Bureau,** 400 W. Markham St. (☎376-4781), in the Robinson Center at Broadway. **Internet access: Main Library,** 100 Rock St., near River Market. (☎918-3000. Open M, Tu, and Th 9am-8pm, W, F, and Sa 9am-6pm, Su 1-5pm). **Post Office:** 600 E. Capitol (☎375-5155; open M-F 7am-5:30pm). **ZIP code:** 72701. **Area code:** 501.

⌐ ACCOMMODATIONS. Budget motels are particularly dense on I-30 southwest of town and at the intersection of I-30 and I-40 in North Little Rock. **Master's Inn Economy,** 707 I-30, at 7th St. (Exit 140), is one of the few acceptable downtown motels, with spacious rooms, a pool, and complimentary breakfast. (☎372-4392 or 800-633-3434. Singles $35-42; doubles $47; $4 for each additional adult. Under 18 free with parent.) The **Cimarron Motel,** 10200 I-30 (Exit 130), has basic rooms. (☎565-1171. Key deposit $5. Singles $30; doubles $35.) If saving money is the only objective, the **Heritage House Inn,** 7500 S. University Ave. (☎565-2055), Exit 132 from I-30, has rooms from $20. Examine your room before you pay. **Maumell Park,** 9009 Pinnacle Valley Rd., on the Arkansas River, has 129 sites. From I-430, take Rte. 10 (Exit 9) west 3 mi., then turn right on the Pinnacle Valley Rd. for 3 mi. (☎868-9477. Sites with water and electricity $15. Boat launch $2; free for campers.)

☐☑ FOOD AND NIGHTLIFE. The downtown lunch crowd heads to the **River Market,** 400 E. Markham St., for something from a wide selection of food shops, coffee stands, and delis. (☎375-2552. Market open M-Sa 7am-6pm, but many shops are only open lunch hrs. Outdoor vegetable market Tu and Sa 7am-3pm.) **Vino's,** 923 W. 7th St. at Chester St., is Little Rock's original microbrewery with cheap Italian fare; slices are under $1, and calzones start at $5. (☎375-8466. Open M-W 11am-10pm, Th 11am-midnight, F 11am-1am, Su 11:30am-midnight, and Su 1-9pm. Live music Th-Sa. Cover $3-15.) **Juanita's,** 1300 S. Main St., is a local favorite, serving $6 Mexican lunches and $11 dinners. (☎372-1228. Open M-F 11am-2:30pm and 5:30-9pm, Sa 11am-9pm. Bar open M-F 11am-1am, Sa 11am-midnight. Live music most nights. Cover up to $10.)

☐ SIGHTS. Tourists can visit the **"little rock"** at Riverfront Park, a pleasant place for a walk along the Arkansas River. From underneath the railroad bridge at the north end of Louisiana St., look straight down; the rock is part of the embankment. The **State Capitol,** at the west end of Capitol St., may look familiar—it's a small-scale replica of the US Capitol in Washington D.C. Tape players at the police booth on the ground floor give a free 45min. audio tour. *(☎682-5080. Open M-F 9am-5pm, Sa-Su 10am-5pm.)* The **Arkansas Territorial Restoration** displays life in 19th-century Little Rock with tours of four restored buildings and a print shop built in 1824. A new visitors center will open in early 2001; until then, tours leave from a temporary structure at 3rd and Cumberland St. *(200 E. Third St. ☎324-9351. Open M-Sa 9am-5pm, Su 1-5pm; tours hourly until 4pm, except noon. $2, seniors $1, children 50¢.)* Little Rock's most important attraction lies to the south, at the corner of 14th St. and Park. **Central High School** is now a fully functional (and fully integrated) school and is closed to visitors. Across the street, however, a **visitors center** in a restored Mobil station contains an exhibit on the "Little Rock Nine." *(2125 W. 14th St. ☎374-1957. Open M-Sa 10am-4pm, Su 1-4pm. Free.)*

THE VINE THAT ATE THE SOUTH So some refer to the leafy kudzu plant, which seems to cover everything in the Deep South that stands still: trees, telephone poles, abandoned buildings, occasionally entire hillsides. Local legend has it that nervous Southern mothers often keep watch over their children on summer nights, for fear that the vine—capable of growing a foot daily—will choke their sleeping infants. Defined as a "weed" and a "pest plant" for its tendency to obliterate native vegetation, kudzu is nonetheless admired for its ability to enshroud ordinary landscape in surreal, biomorphic abstraction. Aesthetics aside, however: it's still best to close the window before turning out the light...

THE SOUTH

HOT SPRINGS   ☎ 501

Hot Springs has long had problems with tourism. In 1820, the citizens of the Arkansas territory asked the government to protect the area in order to prevent it from becoming as overly commercial as other spa resorts. Despite all efforts of the National Park Service, Hot Springs is currently home to such varied tourist traps as alligator farms, wax museums, and gift shops. Nevertheless, the town delivers the soothing relaxation it has advertised for nearly two centuries. Once you've bathed in these 143°F springs, you'll realize why everybody from Al Capone to the feds jumped into the bathhouse craze of the 20s. And, of course, yesterday's tourist economy is today's sightseeing; the historic bathhouses and hotels make Hot Springs worthwhile for its man-made scenery as well as its natural elixir.

⚡ PRACTICAL INFORMATION. Visitors center, 629 Central Ave., downtown off Spring St. (☎321-2277 or 800-543-2284; open daily 9am-5pm). **Post Office:** 100 Reserve St., at Central Ave. in the Federal Building (☎623-8217; open M-F 8am-4:30pm, Sa 9am-1pm). **ZIP code:** 71901. **Area code:** 501.

▚▞ ACCOMMODATIONS AND FOOD. In the days when the bathhouses were active, the local government gave a free bath to anyone who could prove financial need. You won't get quite the same treatment these days, but Hot Springs remains almost as budget-friendly in terms of lodging. Good deals can be found in the old-time motor inns north and south of town along **Rte. 7.** The **Tower Motel,** 755 Park Ave., offers clean rooms with wonderfully soft bedding. The friendly owners can give tips on good deals around town. Call ahead; if no one's staying, the motel shuts down. (☎624-9555. No phones in rooms. Singles $25; doubles $30.) The **Margarete Motel,** 217 Fountain St., is just a stone's throw away from the baths and offers an excellent deal on large rooms, many of which have full kitchens. (☎623-1192. Singles $30; doubles $45; slightly higher late Jan. to mid-Apr.) The **Best Motel,** 638 Ouachita Ave., has clean gingerbread-like cabins around a small pool. Some rooms have kitchens as well. (☎624-5736. Singles $25; doubles $40.) The closest campgrounds are at **Gulpha Gorge,** part of **Hot Springs National Park.** Follow Rte. 70 (Grand Ave.) 1 mi. east to Exit 70B, turn left, and drive ½ mi. north; it's on the left. (☎624-3383, ext. 640 for info and emergencies. Primitive sites $8.)

A number of restaurants line the strip near the bathhouses. **Granny's Kitchen,** 362 Central Ave., cooks up hearty country food. (☎624-6183. Open daily 7am-7pm. Plate lunches $5, dinners $6-10.) **Purity Barbecue,** 1000 Malvern Ave., offers sweet, smoky meat sandwiches ($2.50-4) and drippy vegetable sides ($1-4) in a loungy shack. (☎623-4006. Open 10:30am-8pm, later in summer.) The truly hungry can join the locals south of town at **King's,** 3310 Central Ave., which serves authentically Americanized Chinese food at low, low prices: all-you-can-eat dinner buffet $6, lunch buffet $5. (☎318-1888. Buffet daily 11am-2:30pm and 5-9pm.)

◼ SIGHTS. Still trickling through the earth after 4000 years, water gushes to the planet's crust in Hot Springs at a rate of 850,000 gallons per day. Visitors may fill bottles in the parking lot of the visitors center, or bathe in one of the many bathhouses; many cart the stuff away by the carload. As the only operating house on "Bathhouse Row," the **Buckstaff** retains the dignity and elegance of Hot Springs' heyday in the 20s. *(509 Central Ave. ☎623-2308. Open M-Sa 7-11:45am and 1:30-3pm; Nov.-Mar. Sa 7-11:45am. Bath $15, whirlpool $1.50 extra; massage $18.)* Around the corner, the **Hot Springs Health Spa** offers large common hot tubs and whirlpools. Yes, bathing suits are required. *(N. 500 Reserve, at Spring St. ☎321-9664. Open daily 9am-9pm. Bath $13; 30min. massage $17.50.)* The price for a hands-on, full treatment bath will be lowest in the hot springs at the **Downtowner,** but the quality is still comparable to the more expensive options elsewhere. *(135 Central Ave. ☎624-5521 or 800-251-1962. Open M-Tu and Th-F 7-11am and 1:30-3:15pm, W 7-11am, Sa 7-11am and 2-4:15pm. Bath $12.50, whirlpool $1.50 extra; massage $16.)*

The hydrophobic, or anyone else for that matter, can be bathed in information about the 20th-century leisure class at **Hot Springs National Park.** The park's **Fordyce**

THE SOUTH

Bathhouse Visitors Center shows a 17min. film on the history of the area and of the park, set aside as a national reserve by Andrew Jackson in 1832, long before the park system existed. The partially-restored bathhouse (those pesky stains from the "mercury rub" treatment for syphilis just don't come off), complete with obscure medical equipment, is also open for 2hr. self-guided tours. Ask at the front desk about guided tours. A number of trails run behind the bathhouses through the park, including the paved **Grand Promenade,** a 15min. walk, where visitors in the 20s paraded their high-falutin St. Louis fashions. *(Visitors center: 369 Central Ave. ☎624-3383, ext. 640. Open daily 9am-6pm. The front desk has a helpful chart for disabled and hearing-impaired visitors.)*

Hot Springs' natural beauty, like its schlocky tourist-oriented economy, is unmistakable. Folks can gaze at the green-peaked mountains while cruising Lake Hamilton on the **Belle of Hot Springs,** a 1½hr. narrated tour alongside Lake Ouachita and Lake Hamilton mansions. *(5200 Central Ave. ☎525-4438. Trips in summer daily 1, 3, and 7pm, Sa nights 6 and 8:30pm; call for exact times year-round. $10, seniors $8.50, ages 2-12 $5.)* A free shuttle runs from the city's visitors center to **Hot Springs Mountain Observatory Tower,** in the National Park, with a beautiful view of the surrounding mountains and lakes. On clear days, it's possible to see 140 mi. *(Turn off Central Ave. onto Fountain St. and follow the signs. ☎623-6035. Open daily Mar.-Oct. 9am-9pm; early Sept. to Oct. and Mar. to mid-May 9am-6pm; Nov.-Feb. 9am-5pm. $4, seniors $3.50, ages 5-11 $2.)*

SCENIC DRIVE: ARKANSAS 7

Arkansas isn't known as the "Natural State" for nothing; the Ouachita and Ozark mountain ranges in the northern part of the state offer some beautiful scenery. Arkansas Rte. 7, a scenic byway that travels through both ranges in its 160 mi. journey from Hot Springs north to Harrison, is perhaps the best way to see this part of the state, where the sky is certainly bluer and there's a whole lot of banjo music on the radio.

The road begins as Central Ave. in Hot Springs. Immediately after the small town of Jessieville, the road enters into the **Ouachita National Forest.** The helpful **ranger station** in Jessieville, on the west side of the road, can provide info; a short, wheelchair-accessible trail runs behind the station. (☎501-948-5313. Open M-F 8am-4:30pm; daily May-Sept.) The main trail of the park, the 192 mi. **Ouachita National Recreation Trail,** running from eastern Oklahoma to central Arkansas, intersects Rte. 7 just north of Jessieville. Fifteen mi. of densely wooded forest follow, much of it developed in the 30s by the Civilian Conservation Corps. This part of the drive is particularly popular in fall, when viewing the foliage here has become a bit of a local ritual.

About 40 mi. north of Hot Springs, Rte. 7 crosses the Fourche LaFave River, dammed in 1942 to form **Nimrod Lake.** After passing through the town of Ola, Rte. 7 intersects with Rte. 154 in the tiny crossroads town of Centerville. A right turn on Rte. 154 will take you on a practically unmissable detour east 16 mi. to **Petit Jean State Park** (☎501-727-5441; open daily 8am-8pm). Petit Jean offers a healthy portion of geological goodies—including a secluded waterfall and a natural bridge—as well as pleasant facilities and an extensive trail network.

Back on Rte. 7, the road crosses the dammed Arkansas River, 8 mi. north of Centerville. For a view of the dam and accompanying Lake Dardanelle, take a left just before the river at the sign for **Riverview Park** and drive about 1½ mi.; otherwise, continue north through Russelville, the largest town between Hot Springs and Harrison. Eighteen mi. north of Russellville, the highway enters the **Ozark National Forest** (☎501-968-2354), a land of forested mountains and one-room country churches. The only ranger station on Rte. 7 is north of much of the forest just outside of Jasper (open M-F 8am-4:30pm). About 8 mi. into the forest is **Booger Hollow Trading Post,** which for a town of "population 7—countin' one coon dog," sure does an impressive job of putting up billboards advertising its country wares.

Further north, the road comes out of the forest and runs through what's known as Arkansas' **"Grand Canyon."** The road descends from here, running 6 mi. to the town of Jasper and then entering the **Buffalo National River,** a national park that follows the sandstone and limestone bluffs of the river for almost all of its 150 mi. length. The **Pruitt Ranger Station,** at the entrance to the park, can give info on the numerous boating options, including the names of various rental agencies. (☎870-

446-5373. Open generally Mar.-Sept. M-F 9am-5pm.) Twelve mi. north, the road ends with more a whimper than a bang at the town of Harrison; from here, head 35 mi. north to Branson, MO (p. 586) or 60 mi. southeast to Mountain View (p. 424).

MOUNTAIN VIEW ☎ 870

Despite the commercialism that runs rampant in Mountain View—making the outskirts of town more like an interstate exit than a rural village—its core remains unpretentious, authentically Ozark, and unmistakably small (pop. 2439). Weekend nights, locals gather at Courthouse Square to make music; visitors and residents, young and old (mostly old), get an opportunity to listen in or dance.

⚠ PRACTICAL INFORMATION. Chamber of Commerce: on Washington and Howard St. (☎888-679-2859; open M-Sa 9am-5pm). **Post Office:** 802 Sylamore Ave. (☎269-3520; open M-F 8:30am-4:30pm). **ZIP code:** 72560. **Area code:** 870.

▓▓ ACCOMMODATIONS AND CAMPING. Mountain View offers many lodging options at moderate prices, but precious few at budget rates. This is particularly true on summer weekends, when rates are higher and motels are crowded—arriving without a reservation is tempting the fates. The **Mountain View Motel,** 407 E. Main St., has 18 orderly rooms with in-room coffee makers and cable TV. Each has a red chair outside for enjoying the evening air. (☎269-3209. Singles $33; doubles $39; $37/$45 on weekends.) A group of hexagonal cottages with padded rocking chairs make up the **Dry Creek Lodge,** on Spur 382 off Rte. 9, within the Ozark Folk Center. (☎269-3871 or 800-264-3655. Pool and restaurant. Rooms Su-W $52, Th-Sa $57; $5 each additional person. $12 less Nov.-Mar.) **Wildflower Bed & Breakfast,** on the northeast corner of the Courthouse Sq., rents nine attractive rooms with soft carpeting and antique furniture—but no TVs. (☎800-591-4879. Singles $56; doubles $64.)

Because Mountain View lies only 14 mi. south of the **Ozark National Forest,** the cheapest way to stay is free **camping.** Pitch a tent anywhere within the forest—it's free and legal as long as the campsite does not block any road, path, or thoroughfare. More camping info available at the **Sylamore Ranger District** of the National Forest, across the street from the post office. (☎757-2211 or 269-3228. Write P.O. Box 1279, Mountain View 72560.) Three safe, unattended campgrounds lie around the **Blanchard Springs Caverns,** off Rte. 14, 10-15min. west of the junction with Rte. 5 and 9: the **Blanchard Springs Recreation Area,** the **Gunner Pool Recreation Area,** and the **Barkshed Recreation Area.** All three border a clear creek ideal for swimming.

◻ FOOD. While visiting wonderful ▓**Tommy's Famous...a pizzeria,** about ½ mi. west of Courthouse Sq. off Rte. 66., sign Tom's copy of *Let's Go: USA* and swap stories with his son Clay. (☎269-3278. Open W-Th 3-9pm, F-Su 3-10pm. 12 in. pie $6.25, calzones start at $7.25, quality BBQ ribs $6.50.) Fried catfish is the local specialty of Mountain View, and **Jojo's Catfish Wharf,** 6 mi. north of town on Rte. 5, 1 mi. past the Rte. 5/9/14 junction, drops them into the pan fresh from the White River. Avoid the sandwiches and stick to the dinners, which vary in size from the $6 "Minnow" to the $11 "Hungry Fisherman." (☎585-2121. Open Su-Th 11am-8pm, F-Sa 11am-9pm.)

▓▐ SIGHTS AND ENTERTAINMENT. The **Ozark Folk Center,** 2 mi. north of Mountain View off Rte. 9 on Rte. 382, recreates a mountain village and showcases the cabin crafts, music, and lore of the Ozarks. Locals fiddle, pluck, and strum in the auditorium nightly, while dancers clog along. The center's seasonal events include the **Arkansas Folk Festival** (Apr. 20-22, 2001); the **Annual Dulcimer Jamboree** (Apr. 26-29, 2001); the **National Fiddle Championships** (Sept. 28-29, 2001); and the **Harvest Festival** (Oct. 13-27, 2001). (Center: ☎269-3851. Open daily mid-Apr. to Oct. 10am-5pm. Crafts area and 7:30pm musical performances each $8, ages 6-12 $5, family $19. 1-day combo $13.50/$7.25/$32.50.) Quintessential Ozark artist Jimmy Driftwood passed away, but his family continues his tradition of weekend music and revelry at the **Jimmy Driftwood Barn and Folk Museum,** also on Rte. 9. (☎269-8042. Shows F and Su around 7pm, doors open 6pm. Free.) The highlight of any visit to

Mountain View, however, is undoubtedly the impromptu music on F and Sa nights in **Courthouse Sq.** There are usually as many as six acts all at once; visitors can pick and choose from a wide range of styles, from the electrified twang of country-western to foot-stompin', banjo-pickin' family gospel acts. (Music generally begins around 6:30 or 7pm, before sundown, and sometimes runs as late as 10pm.)

To fish along the White River, non-residents can purchase a fishing license from **Wal-Mart,** 315 Sylamore Ave./Rt. 9 N. (☎269-4395. Open M-Sa 7am-9pm, Su 10am-6pm. 3-day license $11, 14-day $17; for trout, an additional $9 license is needed.) The folks at **Jack's Fishing Resort,** in the same building with Jojo's restaurant, rent a rod and reel for $5 per day and sell tackle and bait. (☎585-2211. Open daily 7am-7pm.) Visit the Sylamore Ranger District (see **Accommodations and Camping,** above) for info on hiking in the Ozark National Forest. The **OK Trading Post,** 3½ mi. west of the Rte. 5/9/14 junction on Rte. 14., has guided trail rides. (☎585-2217. Open daily 9am-dark. 1hr. rides $10, 2hr. $18.)

FLORIDA

Ponce de León landed in St. Augustine on the Florida coast in 1513, in search of the elusive Fountain of Youth. Although the multitudes who flock to Florida today aren't seeking fountains, many find their youth restored in the Sunshine State— whether they're dazzled by Disney World, or bronzed by the sun on the state's seductive beaches. Droves of senior citizens also migrate to Florida, where the sun-warmed air is just as good as Ponce de León's fabled magical elixir.

Anything attractive is bound to draw hordes of people, the nemesis of natural beauty. Florida's population boom has strained the state's resources; commercial strips and tremendous development have turned many pristine beaches into tourist traps. Still, it is possible to find a deserted spot on the peninsula on which to plop down with a paperback and get some sand in your toes.

HIGHLIGHTS OF FLORIDA

BEACHES. White sand, lots of sun, clear blue water. Pensacola (p. 464) and St. Petersburg (p. 459) win our thumbs-up for the best of the best.

DISNEY WORLD. Orlando's cash cow (p. 435)...what else is there to say?

EVERGLADES. The prime Florida haunt for fishermen, hikers, canoers, bikers, and wildlife watchers (p. 450). Check out the unique mangrove swamps.

KEY LIME PIE. This famous dessert hails from the Florida Keys (p. 452).

🛈 PRACTICAL INFORMATION

Capital: Tallahassee.
Visitor Info: Florida Division of Tourism, 126 W. Van Buren St., Tallahassee 32399 (☎888-735-2872; www.flausa.com). **Division of Recreation and Parks,** 3900 Commonwealth Blvd., #506, Tallahassee 32399 (☎850-488-6131).
Postal Abbreviation: FL. **Sales Tax:** 6%.

ST. AUGUSTINE   ☎904

Spanish adventurer Pedro Menéndez de Aviles founded St. Augustine in 1565, making it the first European colony in North America and the oldest continuous settlement in the United States. Thanks to preservation efforts, much of St. Augustine's Spanish flavor remains intact. This coastal city's pride lies in its provincial cobblestone streets and coquina rock walls rather than in its token Floridian beaches. And forget L.A.'s plastic surgeons. Eternal youth costs just $5.75 around here, the price of admission to the vaunted Fountain of Youth.

✦🛈 ORIENTATION AND PRACTICAL INFORMATION

St. Augustine has no public transportation; fortunately, most of the town lies within a pleasant walk from the hostel, motels, and bus station. Narrow streets, one-ways, and abundant parking meters can make driving unpleasant. The major east-west routes, **King St.** and **Cathedral Place,** run through the downtown and become the Bridge of Lions that leads to the beaches. **San Marco Ave.,** also known as **Avenia Menendez,** runs north-south. **Castillo Dr.,** the 3rd of the major east-west roads, grows out of San Marco Ave. at the visitors center. **Saint George St.,** a north-south pedestrian route, contains most of the shops and many sights in St. Augustine. **Greyhound,** 100 Malaga St. (☎829-6401; station open daily 7:30am-8pm), has service to Jacksonville (1hr., 6 per day, $10.50) and Daytona Beach (1¼hr., 5 per day, $13.50); if the station is closed, the driver accepts cash. **Taxi: Ancient City Taxi,** ☎824-8161. **Visitors Info Center:** 10 Castillo, at San Marco Ave. From the Greyhound station, walk north

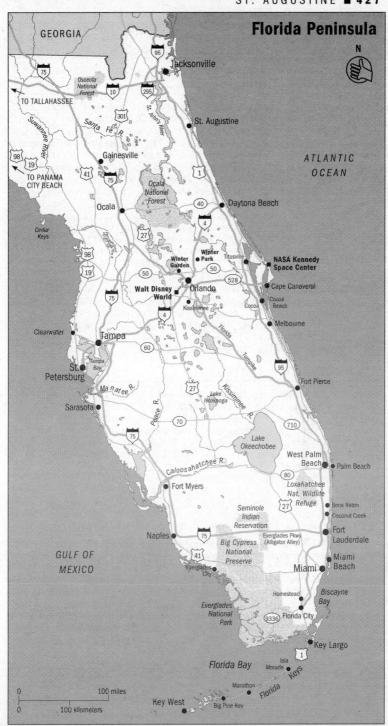

Florida Peninsula

N

GEORGIA

Jacksonville

Osceola National Forest

TO TALLAHASSEE

Santa Fe R.

Suwannee River

St. John's River

St. Augustine

Gainesville

TO PANAMA CITY BEACH

Cedar Keys

Ocala National Forest

Ocala

ATLANTIC OCEAN

Daytona Beach

Winter Garden

Winter Park

Titusville

NASA Kennedy Space Center

Walt Disney World

Orlando

Cape Canaveral

Kissimmee

Cocoa

Cocoa Beach

Florida

Clearwater

Tampa

Melbourne

St. Petersburg

Tampa Bay

Manatee R.

Sarasota

Peace R.

Lake Istokpoga

Kissimmee R.

Turnpike

Fort Pierce

Lake Okeechobee

West Palm Beach

Palm Beach

Caloosahatchee R.

Fort Myers

Loxahatchee Nat. Wildlife Refuge

Boca Raton

Coconut Creek

Seminole Indian Reservation

Naples

Big Cypress National Preserve

Everglades Pkwy (Alligator Alley)

Fort Lauderdale

GULF OF MEXICO

Everglades City

Miami

Miami Beach

Biscayne Bay

Homestead

Everglades National Park

Florida City

Florida Bay

Isla Morada

Key Largo

Key Keys

Marathon

Key West

Big Pine Key

Florida Keys

0   100 miles

0   100 kilometers

FLORIDA

on Ribeira, then right on Orange. (☎825-1000. Open daily late May to early Sept. 8am-7:30pm; Oct.-Apr. 8:30am-5:30pm.) **Post Office:** 99 King St., at Martin Luther King, Jr. Ave. (☎829-8716; open M-Tu and Th-F 8:30am-5pm, W 8:30am-5:30pm, Sa 9am-1pm). **ZIP code:** 32084. **Area code:** 904.

ACCOMMODATIONS

New owners and new amenities, including Internet access and free pancake breakfast, lie within walking distance of everything at the ▨**International Haus** youth hostel, 32 Treasury St. (☎808-1999. A/C, free lockers, and linen. Bikes $7 per day. Spacious dorms for 6 $15; private rooms $35.) Just over the Bridge of Lions, the **Seabreeze Motel,** 208 Anastasia Blvd. has clean rooms with refrigerators and access to a pool. (☎829-8122. A/C, cable TV, and free local calls. Kitchenette available. Singles $35, Sa-Su $42; doubles $40/$45.) The **American Inn,** 42 San Marco Ave., near the visitors center, rents small rooms in a location convenient to the restaurants and historic sights. (☎829-2292. TV, A/C, and pool. Singles $45, Sa-Su $55; doubles $55/$65.) The quaint and quiet **St. Francis Inn,** 279 Saint George St., a charming 16-room inn with a jungle of flowers, a tucked-away pool, and much of its original 18th-century interior, is an expensive treat. Juice and iced tea are served free all day, along with wine/beer social hour daily from 5:30-6:30pm. Guests receive free admission to the Oldest House museum. (☎824-6068 or 800-824-6062. Free full breakfast, use of bikes, parking. Cable TV, A/C. Rooms $79-159; F-Sa $99-219.)

Nearby, Salt Run and the Atlantic Ocean provide opportunities for great windsurfing, fishing, swimming, and hiking near the 139 campsites of the **Anastasia State Recreation Area,** on Rte. A1A, 4 mi. south of the historic district. From town, cross the Bridge of Lions and turn left just beyond the Alligator Farm. (☎461-2033. Office open daily 8am-sunset. Sites $16; electricity $2 extra. Entrance fee $3.25 for vehicles, $1 for pedestrians. Reservations recommended.)

FOOD AND NIGHTLIFE

The bustle of daytime tourists and abundance of budget eateries make lunch in St. Augustine's historic district a delight. Strolling down **Saint George St.** reveals the daily specials scrawled on blackboards outside each restaurant. **Anastasia Blvd.** also holds a wealth of budget options. An excellent healthy option is the **Manatee Cafe,** 179 San Marco Ave., just past the Fountain of Youth. They prepare cuisine with pure filtered water and certified organically grown produce. Tasty grilled hummus pita reuben ($5.25) gets originality points. (☎826-0210. Open daily 8am-4pm.) **Captain Jack's,** 410 Anastasia Blvd., will take you home tonight with fried shrimp for $9. (☎829-6846. Open M-F 11:30am-9pm, Sa-Su noon-9pm.) If, my dear, you do give a damn, go to **Scarlett O'Hara's,** 70 Hypolita St., at Cordova St., where monster burgers run $6 and live music entertains nightly. (☎824-6535. Open daily 11:30am-12:30am. Happy hour M-F 4-7pm. Occasional $2 cover.) **Peterson Bakery,** 113½ King St., has a carefully arranged and tasty array of fresh donuts, pastries, and other delights in the morning. (☎829-2964. Open M-F 6:30am-4:30pm, Sa 7am-4:30pm.)

St. Augustine supports an array of bars. *Today Tonight,* available at most grocery and convenience stores, has listings of current concerts and events. Local string musicians play on the two stages in the **Milltop,** 19½ Saint George St., a tiny bar situated above an old mill in the restored district. (☎829-2329. Open M-Sa 11am-1am, Su 11am-10pm. Music daily from 1pm until closing. Cover varies.) A favorite watering hole for the thirsty beach crowd is the **Oasis Deck and Restaurant,** 4000 Rte. A1A S./Beach Blvd., scheduling nightly entertainment with happy hours from 4-7pm. (☎471-3424 or 471-2451. Open daily 6:30am-1am.)

Cheap flicks and bargain eats await the weary traveler at **Pot Belly's,** 36 Granada St., across from the Lightner Museum (see **Sights,** below). This combination pub, deli, and cinema serves a vast array of junk food to tables in the theater. Remarkably cheap movie tickets run $3.75, and the ice cream drinks are divine. (☎829-3101. Shows start around 6:30 and 8:45pm.)

👁 SIGHTS

GATORS. Across the Bridge of Lions, the 🐊**St. Augustine Alligator Farm** allows visitors to get up close and personal with some of nature's finest reptilians. This century-old park features over 1500 alligators, specimens of all 22 crocodilian species from around the globe, and "Gomek Forever," the famous former resident of the farm now taxidermied in all his splendor. *(On Rte. A1A S. ☎824-3337. Open daily 9am-5pm; in summer 9am-6pm. Wildlife shows every hr. 10am-5pm. $12, ages 3-10 $8.)*

FOUNTAIN OF YOUTH. No trip to St. Augustine would be complete without a trek down beautiful Magnolia Drive to the **Fountain of Youth**, the infamous legend that sparked Ponce de Leon's voyage to the New World. To capture the historical significance of the sight, try to ignore the fact that the fountain now runs from a pipe. *(11 Magnolia Ave. ☎829-3168 or 800-356-8222. Go right on Williams St. from San Marco Ave. and continue until it dead ends into Magnolia Ave. Open daily 9am-5pm. $5.75, seniors $4.75, ages 6-12 $2.75.)*

SPANISH HERITAGE. Actors in period costumes describe the customs and crafts of the Spanish New World at the **Spanish Quarter,** a living museum that walks you through the daily activities of a military garrison community. *(29 Saint George St. ☎825-6830. Open Su-Th 9am-6pm, F-Sa 9am-7pm. $6.50, students and ages 6-18 $4, seniors, military, and AAA members 10%.)* Other 18th-century homes and shops fill the Restored Area. The oldest masonry fortress in the continental US, **Castillo de San Marcos National Monument** has 14 ft. thick walls built of coquina, the local shell-rock. Inside the fort (a four-pointed star complete with drawbridge and murky moat), you'll find a museum, a large courtyard surrounded by livery quarters for the garrison, a jail, a chapel, and the original cannon brought overseas by the Spanish. *(1 Castillo Dr., off San Marco Ave. ☎829-6506. Open daily 8:45am-4:45pm. $4, under 16 and seniors with Golden Age Passport free. Occasional tours; call ahead.)* Six blocks north of the info center, moss- and vine-covered **La Leche Shrine and Mission of Nombre de Dios** held the first US Catholic mass over 400 years ago. Above it, a 208 ft. steel cross commemorates the city's founding and the beginning of Christianity in the US. *(27 Ocean St., off San Marco Ave. ☎824-2809. Open M-F 8am-5:30pm, Sa-Su 9am-5pm. Mass M-F 8:30am, Sa 6pm, Su 8am. Donation suggested.)*

HISTORICAL SIGHTS. The historic district centers on Saint George St., beginning at the Gates of the City near the visitors center and running south past Cadiz St. and the Oldest Store. **Sightseeing Trains** hit all the major attractions. *(170 San Marco Ave. ☎829-6545 or 800-226-6545. Operates 8:30am-5pm. 20 stops. $12, ages 6-12 $5.)* The original **Ghostly Experience** walking tour will send chills up your spine as you saunter through the historical regions of St. Augustine and learn about the city's most celebrated spirits. *(Meets at Milltop water wheel nightly at 7:45pm. ☎461-1009 or 888-461-1009. $6, under 6 free. $1 discount at visitors center.)* Not surprisingly, the oldest continuous settlement in the US holds some of the nation's oldest stuff. The self-proclaimed **Oldest House** was occupied since its construction in the 1600s until 1918, when it became a museum. *(14 Saint Francis St. ☎824-2872. Open daily 9am-5pm. Last admission 4:30pm. $5, students $3, seniors $4.50, families $12.)* The **Oldest Store Museum** holds over 100,000 items from the 18th- and 19th-century, some of the store's original inventory. *(4 Artillery Ln. ☎829-9729. Open daily 10am-4pm. $5, ages 6-12 $1.50.)*

RESTORED HOTELS. For two decades, St. Augustine was the end of the line—the railroad line, that is. Swarms of wealthy northerners b-lined to railroad owner Henry Flagler's **Ponce de León Hotel**, at King and Cordova St. The hotel, decorated entirely by Louis Comfort Tiffany (son of the NY jeweler) and outfitted with electricity by Edison himself (the first hotel to feature this luxury), is now **Flagler College.** On summer days, free 25min. tours pass through some of the recently restored rooms; go, if only to see the exquisite stained glass windows. *(☎829-6481, ext. 383. Tours mid-May to mid-Aug. daily on the hr. 11am-4pm. $3, under 12 free.)* In 1947, Chicago publisher and art lover Otto Lightner converted the Alcazar Hotel, across the street, into the **Lightner Museum** to hold an impressive collection of cut, blown, and burnished glass, as well as old clothing and oddities like nun and monk beer steins. (☎824-2874. Open daily 9am-5pm. Last admission 4:30pm. $6, students and ages 12-18 $2.)

DAYTONA BEACH   ☎904

When locals first started autoracing on the hard-packed sands along the ocean in Daytona Beach, they were combining the two aspects of life that would come to define the entire town mentality: speed and sand. Daytona played an essential role in the founding of the National Association of Stock Car Auto Racing (NASCAR) in 1947, and race fans still congregate here to pay homage to the colossal Daytona International Speedway. But while the beach may no longer host racing, it has far from faded from the scene; every spring break season brings flocks of college students to roost in the 500-foot-wide sands and ample nightlife.

⌗ ORIENTATION. Daytona Beach lies 53 mi. northeast of Orlando and 90 mi. south of Jacksonville. I-95 parallels the ocean and the barrier island. Full of surf shops, motels and bars, **Atlantic Ave. (Rt. A1A)** is the main drag along the shore. **International Speedway Blvd. (U.S. 92)** runs east-west, from the ocean through the downtown area and past the racetrack. Daytona Beach is a collection of smaller towns that have expanded and converged but preserved their individual street-numbering systems. Many street numbers are not consecutive and navigation can be difficult. To avoid the gridlock on the beach, arrive early (8am) and leave early (3pm or so). You'll pay $5 to drive onto the beach (permitted 8am-7pm), and police strictly enforce the 10 mph speed limit. Free parking is plentiful during most of the year but sparse during peak seasons, especially Speedweeks, Bike Week, Biketoberfest, and the Pepsi 400 (see **Start your engines,** below), not to mention spring break (usually the 2nd half of Mar.).

⍈ PRACTICAL INFORMATION. Amtrak, 2491 Old New York Ave. in Deland (☎734-2322; open daily 8:30am-7pm), 24 mi. west on Rte. 92, tracks to Miami (7hr., 2 per day, $50). **Greyhound,** 138 S. Ridgewood Ave. (☎255-7076; station open daily 7am-10:30pm), behind the antique mall, 4 mi. west of the beach, goes to Orlando (80min., 7 per day, $9) and Jacksonville (2hr., 7 per day, $15). **Votran County Transit Co.,** 950 Big Tree Rd., on the mainland, operates local buses and a trolley that covers Rte. A1A between Granada Blvd. and Dunlawton Ave. (☎761-7700. Service M-Sa 6am-7:30pm with most running M-Sa 7am-7pm, Su 8am-5:30pm; trolley runs until midnight on Sa nights. $1, children 6-17 and seniors 50¢, transfers free. Free maps available at hotels.) **Taxi: Yellow Cab:** ☎255-5555. **Daytona Beach Area Convention and Visitors Bureau:** 126 E. Orange Ave., on City Island (☎255-0415 or 800-854-1234; open M-F 9am-5pm). **Rape Crisis and Sexual Abuse Line:** ☎254-4106. Operates 24 hours. **Post Office:** 220 N. Beach St. (open M-F 8am-5pm, Sa 9am-noon). **ZIP code:** 32115. **Area code:** 904.

⌂ ACCOMMODATIONS. Almost all of Daytona's accommodations front **Atlantic Ave./Rte. A1A,** either on the beach or across the street; those off the beach offer the best deals. Quieter hotels line **Ridgewood Ave.** During spring break and big race weekends, even the worst hotels are overpriced, and it's unwise to sleep on the well-patrolled shores. In summer and fall, prices plunge; most hotels offer special deals in June. The art deco **Streamline Hotel,** 140 S. Atlantic Ave. (A1A), one block north of E. International Speedway Blvd., stands out amid low level motels. Perks include A/C, cable TV, mini-fridges, free local calls, a recreation room, and proximity to the beach. (☎258-6937. Key deposit $5. Singles $19; doubles $24; during special events $150-200. Reservations not accepted.) The **Camellia Motel,** 1055 N. Atlantic Ave. (Rte. A1A), across the street from the beach, is an especially welcoming retreat, with cozy, bright rooms, free local calls, cable TV, and A/C. Owner speaks Slovak, German, Czech, Polish, English, and French. (☎252-9963. Singles $25; doubles $30; $10 per additional person. During spring break, singles $60; $10 per additional person. Rooms with kitchens cost $10 more. Reserve early.)

Tomoka State Park, 2099 N. Beach St., 8 mi. north of Daytona and 70min. from Disney World, has 100 sites under a tropical canopy near a salt marsh, along with salt-water fishing, nature trails, and a museum. Take bus #3 ("N. Ridgewood") to Domicilio and walk 2 mi. north. (☎676-4050. Open daily 8am-sunset. Sites $11, with electricity $13; Nov.-Apr. $16/$19; half-price FL resident and senior discount. $3.25 entrance fee. Canoe rentals $4 per hr.) **Nova Family Campground,** 1190 Herbert St., in Port Orange, is south of Daytona Beach and 3 mi. from the shore. From I-95, take Exit 85 to Dunlawton Ave. east. Make a left onto Clyde Morris Blvd. and a right on Herbert St., or take bus #7 or 15 from downtown or the beach. (☎767-0095. Reception daily 8am-7pm. Pool, laundry facilities, and shuffleboard. Sites $16, with electricity and water $18, full hook-up $22; higher during events.)

◻ **FOOD.** One of the most famous (and popular) seafood restaurants in the area is ◼**Aunt Catfish's,** just to the left of Port Orange Bridge (Dunlawton Ave.) as it connects to the mainland. Massive portions include delicious coconut fried shrimp ($8) and salad and hot bar. Their Boatsinker Pie ($4.50), a chocolate encrusted fudge dessert, has been lauded by *Bon Appetit.* (☎767-4768. Open M-Sa 11:30am-10pm, Su 9am-2pm.) "If it swims...we have it," boasts **B&B Fisheries,** 715 E. International Speedway Blvd. Take out your choice of fresh fish for lunch from $3.25. (☎252-6542. Open M-F 11am-8:30pm, Sa 4-8:30pm; takeout M-Sa 11:30am-8:30pm.) For cheap Chinese eats, hit the **Orient Palace Restaurant,** 2116 S. Atlantic Ave. (Rte. A1A), where chicken and broccoli is $7.25 (☎255-4183. Open daily 5-11pm; all-you-can-eat buffet 5-9:30pm. Happy hour with wicked scotch sours 4-6pm.)

🏎 **START YOUR ENGINES.** Experience the power of the true center of Daytona's world, the legendary **Daytona International Speedway.** Headquarters to NASCAR, the track annually hosts the Super Bowl of racing, the **Daytona 500.** *(Feb. 18, 2001; tickets $75-185.)* **SpeedWeek,** a 15-day series of races, qualifying, and build-up, precedes the Great American Race. *(Feb. 3-17, 2001.)* A "Disney for motorheads," **Daytona USA** thrills non-race fans as well with spectacular interactive exhibits and shows; learn to change all four tires in under 16sec. Inside, the **Daytona 500** IMAX film tears around the track at 180 mph. A 30min. tour of the facility provides an inside peak at the track. *(1801 W. International Speedway Blvd. ☎947-6800; call 253-7223 for NASCAR tickets. Open daily 9am-7pm. $12, seniors $10, ages 6-12 $6. Tours daily 9am-5pm on the hr. and half-hr. $6.)* NASCAR returns to Daytona in July for its mid-summer race under the lights, the **Pepsi 400.** *(July 7, 2001; tickets $45-115.)* **Bike Week** draws biker mamas for various motorcycle duels, and **Biketoberfest** brings them back for more. *(Bikeweek: Mar. 2-11, 2001. Biketoberfest: Oct. 18-21, 2001.)*

🌙 **NIGHTLIFE.** When spring break hits, concerts, hotel-sponsored parties, and other events cater to students questing for fun. News about these travels fastest by word of mouth, but the *Calendar of Events* and *SEE Daytona Beach,* available at the chamber of commerce, make good starting points. On more mellow nights, head to the boardwalk to play volleyball or shake your groove thing at the **Oceanfront Bandshell,** an open-air amphitheater constructed entirely of coquina rock. A fairly homogeneous collection of dance clubs tingle along Seabreeze Blvd. near the intersection with N. Atlantic Ave. At **St. Regis Bar and Restaurant,** 509 Seabreeze Blvd., live jazz flavors the veranda F and Sa 8-11pm. (☎252-8743. Open Tu-Sa 6-11pm. Happy hour with two-for-one drinks F 5-7pm.) Among the nightclubs, **Ocean Deck,** 127 S. Ocean Ave., where "everyday is like a weekend," stands apart with its beachfront location and live reggae music. (☎253-5224. Open daily 11am-3am; full menu until 2am. Music nightly 9:30pm-2:30am. 21+ from 9pm.)

ORLANDO ☎ 407

Every year, millions descend upon Orlando to visit Disney World, the most popular tourist attraction on earth. Comprised of the original Magic Kingdom, Epcot Center, Disney-MGM Studios, and the new Animal Kingdom and Downtown Disney area, Disney's sheer size and scope push it into a class by itself. Don't overlook the area's smaller perks though; the innovation of Universal Studios Escape and the natural talent of Sea World astounds. Choose and plan your time wisely—there are many ways to lighten your wallet in this land of illusions.

▐ GETTING THERE AND GETTING AROUND

Airport: Orlando International, 1 Airport Blvd. (☎ 825-2001); from the airport take Rte. 436 N, exit to Rte. 528 W (the Bee Line Expwy.), then head east on I-4 to the exits for downtown. City bus #42 or 51 make the trip for $1. **Mears Motor Shuttle,** 324 W. Gore St. (☎ 423-5566), has a booth at the airport for transportation to most hotels. No shuttle reservations are necessary from the airport (for return, call 1 day in advance).

Trains: Amtrak, 1400 Sligh Blvd. (☎ 843-7611), 3 blocks east of I-4. Take S. Orange Ave., head west on Columbia, then take a right on Sligh. To Jacksonville (3-4hr., 2 per day, $20-39). Station open daily 7:15am-7:45pm.

Buses: Greyhound, 555 N. John Young Pkwy. (☎ 292-3424). To Kissimmee (40min., 6 per day, $6.50-7.50) and Jacksonville (3-4½hr., 9 per day, $25-27). Open 24hr.

Public Transit: LYNX, 78 W. Central Blvd. (☎ 841-8240; open M-F 6:30am-8pm, Sa 7:30am-6pm, Su 8am-6pm). Buses operate daily 6am-9pm (times vary with route). Fare $1, ages 7-18 25¢ with ID, transfers 10¢. Downtown terminal between Central and Pine St., 1 block west of Orange Ave. and 1 block east of I-4. Schedules available at most shopping malls, banks, and at the downtown terminal. Serves the airport (bus #42 or 51 at side A, level 1) and Wet 'n' Wild (see p. 438).

Taxis: Yellow Cab, ☎ 422-4455.

◆❼ ORIENTATION AND PRACTICAL INFORMATION

Orlando lies at the center of hundreds of small lakes, toll highways, and amusement parks. Streets are divided north-south by **Rte. 17/92 (Orange Blossom Trail)** and east-west by **Colonial Dr.** The **Bee Line Expwy. (Rte. 528)** and the **East-West Expwy. (Rte. 408)** exact several tolls for their convenience. Supposedly an east-west expressway, **I-4** actually runs north-south through the center of town. **Disney World, Universal Studios** and **Sea World** await 15-20 mi. southwest of downtown on I-4 W; **Cypress Gardens** is 30 mi. south of Disney off **U.S. 27** near Winter Haven.

Visitor Info: Orlando Official Visitor Center, 8723 International Dr., Suite #101 (☎ 363-5872), several mi. southwest of downtown; take bus #8 and ask the driver to stop. Ask for the free "Magic Card" and receive discounts at various attractions, shops, restaurants, and hotels. Open daily 8am-7pm, tickets sold 8am-6pm.

Hotlines: Rape Hotline, ☎ 740-5408. **Crisis Hotline,** ☎ 843-4357. **Crisis Info,** ☎ 425-2624.

Post Office: 46 E. Robinson St. (☎ 843-5673). Open M-F 7am-5pm, Sa 9am-noon. **ZIP code:** 32801. **Area code:** 407.

▌ ACCOMMODATIONS

Orlando does not cater to the budget traveler. Prices for hotel rooms rise exponentially as you approach Disney World; plan to stay in a hostel or in downtown Orlando. **Bronson Memorial Hwy. (Rte. 192),** running through Kissimmee, provides a few choice motels at a reasonable price and distance from the theme parks. Visitors staying along this strip should bear in mind that **Greyhound runs to Kissimmee.** It is prudent to make reservations.

Orlando Theme Parks

♦ ACCOMMODATIONS
Disney's All-Star Resort, **1**
Hostelling International-
Orlando Resort (HI-AYH), **3**
KOA Camping, **4**
Sun Motel, **2**

FLORIDA

Hostelling International-Orlando Resort (HI-AYH), 4840 W. Irlo Bronson Memorial Hwy./ Rte. 192 (☎396-8282), in Kissimmee. Lakeside location 5 mi. from Disney World with swimming pool, fountains, and $3 summer BBQs on Tu and Th. Super-clean, motel-style rooms with bunk beds, A/C, pool, lake access, and transportation to Disney ($8). Lockers, linens, and towels free. Reception 24hr. Dorms $16, non-members $19; private rooms (with TV, A/C, phone) from $35 for 2 people. Ages 6-17 half-price, under 6 free.

Sun Motel, 5020 W. Irlo Bronson Memorial Hwy./Rte. 192 (☎396-6666 or 800-541-2674), in Kissimmee. Reasonable rates 4 mi. from Disney World. Pretty rooms with floral bedspreads, cable TV, fridge, phone, pool, and A/C. Sells discount tickets for theme parks. Key deposit $5. Singles $40; doubles $45; off-season $28/$30.

Disney's All-Star Resorts (☎934-7639), in Disney World. From I-4, take Exit 25B and follow the signs to Blizzard Beach—the resorts are just behind it. Pricey, but a great deal for groups. Large "theme" decorations from cowboy boots to surfboards adorn the courtyards. Pools, A/C, phone, fridge ($10 extra per day), and food court. Free parking and Disney transportation. Singles and doubles $74-104, depending on season; $10 additional adult (up to 4). No charge for children under 18 when with adults.

KOA, 4771 W. Irlo Bronson Memorial Hwy./Rte. 192 (☎396-2400 or 800-562-7791), in Kissimmee, 5 mi. east of I-4. Sites have lots of trees, a nice pool, tennis courts, and a store. Reception 24hr. Tent sites $22-28, with hook-up (for 2) $22-31; RVs $44. Kabins with A/C: 1-room $30-90, 2-room $40-100; $5 per additional adult (up to 5).

Turkey Lake Park, 3401 S. Hiawassee Rd. (☎299-5581), near Universal Studios. One of Orlando's 2 municipal campgrounds. Offers trails, a swimming pool, a petting farm, and fishing. Open daily 9:30am-7pm; in winter 9:30am-5pm. Tent sites with water and electricity $7, full hook-up $17. Cabins $28; $25 damage deposit. Key deposit $10.

Moss Park, 12901 Moss Park Rd. (☎273-2327), 10 mi. from the airport. 2nd municipal campgrounds. Garnished with Spanish moss, sites are lovely but far from civilization. Open daily 8am-7pm. Tent sites $15, with water and electricity $18; park entrance $1.

◖ FOOD

■ **Bakely's**, 345 W. Fairbanks Ave. (☎645-5767), in Winter Park. Take I-4 to Fairbanks Ave., Exit 45. The variety at this restaurant/bake shop is as large as the portions. Breakfast is served all day; the $5.50 burgers are Orlando's best. Save room for the 6-layer Boston cream cake ($3). Open Su-Th 7am-11pm, F-Sa 7am-midnight.

Champ's, 132 E. Central Blvd. (☎649-1230), in downtown across from the public library. Lilia and Chef George cook up specialty sandwiches and tasty pastries. Breakfast sandwiches ($1.50) and a hearty soup/salad lunch combo ($4). Open M-Sa 6am-6pm.

Francesco's Ristorante Italiano, 4920 W. Irlo Bronson Memorial Hwy./Rte. 192 (☎396-0889). Dine beneath Chianti bottles while Sinatra croons from a stereo. Large portions of pasta, steak, or seafood come complete with salad bar and homemade bread for $9-15. All-you-can-eat spaghetti $6. Open daily 4-11pm.

♫▥ ENTERTAINMENT AND NIGHTLIFE

N. Orange Ave., downtown, is the heart of Orlando nightlife. Relatively inexpensive bars line the city's main drag. **Tabu**, 46 N. Orange Ave., provides a safe haven for 20-somethings in search of a South Beach scene. (☎648-8363. Open Th-Sa 9pm-3am. 21+.) Voted one of America's best clubs by *Rolling Stone* and *Billboard*, **The Club at Firestone**, 578 N. Orange Ave., at Concord, features a raucous gay night (Sa) among a variety of theme nights. (☎872-0066. Open Su-Tu 10pm-3am, F-Sa 9pm-3am. Cover $5-12. Tu and F 21+, Sa-M 18+. Women 18+ allowed any night.) Improvisational comedy shows will keep you in stitches at the ■**SAK Theater**, 380 W. Amelia St., at Hughey Ave. Famous for good, clean fun, this house of humor launched Wayne Brady of "Whose Line is it Anyway?" (☎648-0001. Shows Tu 9pm; Th-F 8pm and 10pm; Sa 8pm, 10pm, and midnight. $3-12.) **Church Street Station**, 129 W. Church St., on the corner of Church and Garland St., is a slick, block-long entertainment, shopping, and restaurant complex. (☎422-2434. Open daily 11am-11pm; clubs and bars close later.) Inside, you can boogie down in the sci-fi-meets-wild-west wooden decor of **Phineas Phogg's Balloon Works.** (Open daily 8pm-2am, opens F at 5pm. Drink specials F 5-8:30pm help kick off the weekend. 21+.)

DISNEY WORLD   ☎ 407

Happiness can be bought at Disney World, where throngs of fun-seekers work assiduously to get their money's worth. "Amusement park" barely begins to describe the media empire, resort and hotel complex, four theme parks, three water parks, golf courses, sports venues, boardwalks, restaurants, and even night-clubs that constitute Disney World. Despite the flagrant over-commercialization and the competition rendered by nearby attractions, the central theme parks—the Magic Kingdom, Epcot Center, Disney/MGM Studios, and Animal Kingdom—and the entertainment complex Downtown Disney still rule after 25 years. If bigger is better, Disney World wins the prize for best park in the US by more than a mile.

⁊ PRACTICAL INFORMATION

Disney dominates **Lake Buena Vista,** 20 mi. west of Orlando via I-4. (☎ 824-4321. Call daily 8am-10pm.) The $46 one-day entrance fee (ages 3-9 $37) admits you to one of the four parks, allowing you to leave and return to the same park later in the day. A four- or five-day **Park-Hopper Pass** buys admission to all four parks for all days (4-day $176, ages 3-9 $142; 5-day $206/$167). The **Park Hopper Plus,** includes five days of admission to two other Disney attractions ($236/$192). A six-day package includes admission to three other Disney attractions ($266/$217). The Hopper passes allow for unlimited transportation between attractions on the Disney monorail, boats, buses, and trains. Multi-day passes need not be used on consecutive days, and never expire. Parking is $6 per day. Attractions that charge separate admissions include **River Country** ($16/$12.50); **Typhoon Lagoon** ($28/$22.50); **Pleasure Island** ($19, 18+ unless with adult); **Blizzard Beach** ($28/$22.50), and **Disney's Wide World of Sports Complex** ($9/$7). For descriptions, see **Other Disney Attractions** (p. 438).

Disney World opens its gates 365 days a year, but hours fluctuate with the season. Expect the parks to open at 9am and close between 7pm and 11pm, but call before-hand. The parks get busy during the summer when school is out, but the enor-mously crowded peak times are Christmas, Thanksgiving, and the month around Easter. More people visit between Christmas and New Year's than at any other time of year, but the parks are comatose in January, when almost no one is out of school. Disney has expanded the **FASTPASS** option from the Animal Kingdom into other parks. Show up for your assigned time to ride and bypass the line. Otherwise, expect a 45min. to 2hr. wait.

👁 THE PARKS

MAGIC KINGDOM

Seven lands comprise the Magic Kingdom: **Main St., USA; Tomorrowland; Fantasyland; Liberty Sq.; Frontierland; Adventureland;** and **Mickey's Toontown Fair.** More than any of the other Disney parks, this is geared for children.

MAIN ST., USA. Enter on Main St., USA, to capture the essence of early 20th-cen-tury America. The architects employed "forced perspective" here, building the ground floor of the shops nine-tenths of the normal size and making the 2nd and 3rd stories progressively smaller. Walt describes his vision in the "Walt Disney Movie" at the Hospitality House, to the right as you emerge from under the railroad station. Late in the afternoon, the "Magical Moments Parade" down Main St. showcases many of the Disney characters.

TOMORROWLAND. Tomorrowland received a neon-and-stainless-steel face-lift that skyrocketed it out of the space-race days of the 60s and into a futuristic inter-galactic nation. **Buzz Lightyear's Space Ranger Spin** is the newest attraction, a light-hearted save-the-planet quest made unique by "working" laser guns. The **ExtraTERRORestrial Alien Encounter** chills without spins or drops, creating suspense in pitch blackness—a claustrophobe's nightmare. **Space Mountain** still proves the high point of this section, if not the park. This is no secret; plan accordingly.

FANTASYLAND. The golden-spired Cinderella's Castle marks the gateway to the mildest of Mickey's regions, Fantasyland. Two classic rides, **Peter Pan's Flight** and **Snow White's Scary Adventures,** capture the original charm of the park and let children step into the Disney characters' shoes for a few minutes. Winnie, Piglet, Tigger, and friends bounce around happily in **The Many Adventures of Winnie the Pooh,** the latest addition to this land. You know the song, so see what it means at **It's a Small World,** a saccharine but endearing boat tour celebrating the children of the world. Killer A/C makes it a good bet for a hot day.

LIBERTY SQUARE AND FRONTIERLAND. Liberty Sq. and Frontierland devote their resources to a celebration of US history and Mark Twain. Escape from the concrete and crowds at **Tom Sawyer Island,** a wooded re-creation of outback life on the Mississippi, accessible only by raft. Adventurers should catch the classic, runaway **Big Thunder Mountain Railroad** roller coaster or the truly thrilling **Splash Mountain,** which takes you on a voyage with Br'er Rabbit—and four bear posteriors—and leaves you chilled inside and out. Spooky but charming, jovial ghouls bedeck the classic **Haunted Mansion.** Entertaining animatronics enliven the **Country Bear Jamboree.** A steamboat trip on the **Liberty Belle Riverboat** lets tired feet rest.

ADVENTURELAND. Adventureland romanticizes unexplored regions of the world in often trivial and tacky ways. The **Jungle Cruise** takes a tongue-in-cheek tour through tropical waterways populated by not-so-authentic-looking wildlife. **Pirates of the Caribbean** explores caves where animated swashbucklers spar, swig, sing and are chased by maidens. The **Swiss Family Robinson Treehouse** captures the family's clever tricks. Under new management, the birds of the **Enchanted Tiki Room** serenade their visitors with a tropical music revue.

EPCOT CENTER

In 1966, Walt dreamed up an "Experimental Prototype Community Of Tomorrow" (EPCOT), which would evolve constantly to incorporate new ideas from US technology—eventually becoming a self-sufficient, futuristic utopia. At present, Epcot splits into **Future World** and **World Showcase.**

FUTURE WORLD. The trademark 180 ft. high geosphere that forms the entrance to Future World houses the **Spaceship Earth** attraction, where visitors board a "time machine" for a tour through the evolution of communications and AT&T's latest ad campaign. A new veranda dominates the area behind the silver sphere. One of Epcot's biggest draws is **Test Track,** a 65 mph tear through a GM testing facility (fast). Uniquely creative, this is one of Disney's better rides, worth the 75min. wait (not fast). At the **Wonders of Life, Body Wars** takes visitors on a tour of the human body (with the help of a simulator). **Cranium Command** puts you at the helm of a 12-year-old boy as his animatronic "pilot" steers him around the pitfalls of daily life. **The Land** presents **The Circle of Life,** a live-action/animated film about the environment with characters from *The Lion King.* Fish, sharks, and manatees inhabit the re-created coral reef in **The Living Seas.** The immensely popular **Journey Into Imagination** pavilion screens *Honey, I Shrunk the Audience,* which boasts stellar 3D effects. The latest addition to this pedagogical world of fun is **Innoventions,** a double-pavilion attraction full of gadgets (IBM-sponsored, of course) and hands-on encounters with technology.

WORLD SHOWCASE. At the **World Showcase,** an architectural style or monument, as well as typical food and crafts, represent 11 countries from around the world. People in indigenous costumes perform dances, theatrical skits, and other "cultural" entertainment; each cast member is from the country he or she represents. To the east of Spaceship Earth, **Guest Relations** provides park info and can help arrange dinner reservations. Check the handy maps (available everywhere) for showtimes of the 25 various dance troupes, singers, and films throughout the World Showcase. The people with yellow-striped Disney-logoed shirts can answer questions throughout the park. The **360° film** made in China and the **200° film** made in France rate among the best of the attractions. In **The American Adventure,** Ben Franklin and Mark Twain dispense a patriotic interpretation of American history. Every night at 9pm, Epcot presents a magnificent mega-show called **IllumiNations,** with music from the represented nations accompanied by dancing fountains, laser lights, and fireworks.

The World Showcase pavilions specialize in regional cuisine. The all-you-can-eat meat, seafood, and salad buffet ($12) at **Restaurant Akershus** is the closest one gets to a Disney dining bargain. In other pavilions, sit-down meals will run $13-15 for lunch and upwards of $20 for dinner; it is wise to make reservations early in the morning at Guest Relations. The regional cafes (no reservations required) present cheaper options, but no real bargains.

DISNEY-MGM STUDIOS

Disney-MGM Studios (DMS) set out to create a "living movie set." Many familiar Disney characters stroll through the park, as do a host of characters dressed as directors, starlets, gossip columnists, and fans. Disney relative ABC-TV maintains a high profile and films programs. Stunt shows and mini-theatricals take place continually, although DMS also features some of the best thrill rides of all of the parks.

The **Aerosmith Rock n' Roller Coaster** blasted into the park in Aug. 1999 with a 2.8sec., 0-60 mph take off. "Sweet Emotion" blares during a stomach-numbing zip through L.A. en route to an Aerosmith performance. Next door, the **Twilight Zone Tower of Terror** climbs 13 stories in an old-time Hollywood hotel before the cable snaps; just when you think the ride is over, WHAM! it drops you again. All goes berserk in the well-crafted **Muppet Vision 3D,** a behind-the-scenes tour of top secret Muppets Labs. Beware the Swedish Chef. Of the two biggest attractions at this park, the underwhelming stuntshow **Indiana Jones Epic Stunt Spectacular** is no match for the other biggie, **Star Tours.** Based on the Star Wars movies, a novice droid pilot steers your tourist ship into enemy fire. Super-believable video and effects skim the craft across the feared Death Star. The real reason to cough up the money for this particular park, however, is the **Magic of Disney Animation,** a tour that introduces you to actual Disney animators, teaches you how they create Disney animated films, and offers a sneak peak at the sketches of upcoming Disney classics. The new and nocturnal **Fantasmic!,** the latest addition to the park's pyrotechnic shows, spotlights Mickey as the sorceror's apprentice, battling it out with antagonists from a variety of Disney films.

DISNEY'S ANIMAL KINGDOM

Amid the usual rides, shows and merchandise, bizarrely exotic creatures stare down bewildered tourists. Because it is brand-new—by Disney standards—park veterans and newcomers pack in during the day. Despite an earlier closing time than the other parks (7pm), the dinner crowd bails around 5pm, taking long lines with them. The rides are not among Mickey's greatest, but creative animal adventures and a classic 3-D show prove Disney still has the touch. Animal Kingdom is divided into five main regions: Camp Minnie-Mickey, Safari Village, Africa, Asia, and Dinoland USA. **Camp M-M** is a little kid's haven for singing and dancing to Disney favorites. In Africa, the bumpy ride through the **Kilimanjaro Safaris** offers up-close views of rhinos, giraffes, lions, and the occasional croc. The other Animal Kingdom biggie, **Countdown to Extinction** in Dinoland USA, is an overhyped, relatively slow thrill ride about time travel gone awry. The whole park is arranged around a single focal point, the **Tree of Life,** towering 14 stories tall, with over 325 animals carved into its roots, branches, and trunk. Beneath the tree, the show **It's Tough to be a Bug** combines 3-D tech with "audio animaltronics" for a creepily fun demo of insect talent. Also in Dinoland USA is the **Boneyard,** where kids can dig in a huge sandpit and uncover the remains of a woolly mammoth. Cool down in Asia on the **Kali River Rapids,** a soaking tour of the tropical rainforest. The **Discovery River Boats** of **Safari Village** are a relaxing break.

FLORIDA

OTHER DISNEY ATTRACTIONS

Besides the three main parks, Disney offers several other draws with different themes and separate admissions. The ▦**Richard Petty Driving Experience** at the **Walt Disney World Speedway** is undoubtedly the ride to top all rides. Blast around the track at over 145 mph in a custom-made NASCAR machine with a pro driver behind the wheel. Ain't no special effects here; this *is* the ultimate speed experience. (☎800-237-3889. Ride $94; must be 16. Free to watch the racing.) **Downtown Disney** is a larger than life, neon conglomeration of theme restaurants, nightlife, and shopping. **Pleasure Island** is a scantily-clad Disney with an attitude. Choose among the nightclubs—country, R&B, jazz, 70s and techno. ($19 to cross bridge. 18+ unless accompanied by parent.) **Blizzard Beach,** the most intense but least thematic of three water parks, was built on the harrowing premise of a melting mountain. Ride a ski lift to the peak of Mt. Gushmore and take the fastest water-slide in the world (Summit Plummet) down the 120 ft. descent. **Typhoon Lagoon,** a 50-acre water park, centers around one of the world's largest wave-making pools and the 7 ft. waves it creates. Besides eight water slides, the lagoon has a creek for inner-tube rides and a saltwater coral reef stocked with tropical fish and harmless sharks. Built to resemble a swimming hole, **River Country** offers water slides, rope swings, and plenty of room to swim. Water parks fill up early on hot days, so you might get turned away. **Disney's Wide World of Sports Complex** (☎939-1500) tests your skills in the **NFL Experience.**

LIFE BEYOND DISNEY   ☎407

🛈 PRACTICAL INFORMATION

The big non-Disney theme parks band together in competition with Mickey Mouse. "Flex Tickets," their mouse traps for Mickey, combine admission prices at a discount. A four-park ticket covers Sea World, both Universal Studios parks, and Wet 'n' Wild (a water park) and allows seven days of visiting with unlimited admissions and free transportation ($160, ages 3-9 $128). The five-park ticket (call Universal City Travel at ☎800-224-3838) adds Busch Gardens in Tampa (see p. 458) and lasts ten days ($197/$158).

👁 THE PARKS

SEA WORLD

One of the US's largest marine parks, **Sea World** makes a splash with marine-themed shows, rides and exhibits. Eels, barracudas, sharks, and other beasties lick their chops in **Terrors of the Deep,** the world's largest collection of dangerous sea creatures. In Shamu Stadium, the talented killer whale family remains Sea World's big draw. **The Shamu Adventure** thrills with plenty of amazing aquatic acrobatics executed smartly by a whole family of orcas and their trainers. Whale belly flops send waves of 52°F salt water into the cheering "soak zone"; try to wear a swimsuit. In the Atlantis Bayside Stadium, two teams of supremely gifted skiers, gymnasts and boaters square off in the **Intensity Games.** In recent years, SeaWorld has added roller coasters; the 1998 water coaster **Journey to Atlantis** gets rave reviews. Spring 2000 brought the much anticipated **Kraken,** a floorless ride billed as the highest, fastest, and longest coaster in Orlando. Upside down flips, turns and loops follow a 65 mph plunge into an underwater lagoon. The stunning **Anheuser-Busch Clydesdales** trot around for viewing (mesmerized tourists in tow). Adjacent to the park lies **Discovery Cove,** a new attraction where you can swim with dolphins and snorkel among tropical fish in a man-made lagoon. *(12 mi. southwest of Orlando off I-4 at Rte. 528. ☎351-3600. Take bus #8. Open daily 9am-7pm; extended hours in summer. $46, ages 3-9 $37. Parking $6. Sky Tower ride $3 extra. Most hotel brochure displays and hostels have coupons for $2-3 off regular admission. Discovery Cove admission by reservation only.)*

A HORSE OF A DIFFERENT COLOR Back in 1933 when Prohibition was repealed, the last thing August A. Busch, Sr. expected to receive in celebration of his resumed brewery business was a bunch of European war horses. His son, August Jr., introduced the first Budweiser Clydesdale hitch as a surprise gift to his father, and these magnificent steeds have now become a renowned symbol of Anheuser-Busch, the most popular beer company in America. As the most widely traveled horses in the world, the Bud Clydesdales must have white stockings on all four legs, a blaze of white on the face, and a black mane and tail or they don't make the team. Touring hitches are based all over the country, and you can get a first hand-look at these brawny beasts at the stables in Orlando's Sea World (p. 438) or Tampa's Busch Gardens (p. 458).

CYPRESS GARDENS

Cypress Gardens lies southwest of Orlando in Winter Haven. The botanical gardens feature over 8000 varieties of plants and flowers with winding walkways and electric boat rides for touring. Hoop-skirted Southern Belles patrol the grounds. Despite all the pretty flowers, the **water-ski shows** attract the biggest crowds and the loudest applause. (☎863-324-2111. Take I-4 southwest to Rte. 27 S, then Rte. 540 W. Open daily 9:30am-5pm; call ahead for exact hrs. Water-ski shows daily 11am and 4:30pm; times and frequency vary with crowd size. Park admission $32, ages 6-12 $15. Coupons can be found at most motels.)

UNIVERSAL STUDIOS ESCAPE

Opened in 1990, Universal Studios doubled its size in 1999 with the addition of another park and entertainment district within its grounds. With its three parks, **Universal Studios Florida, Islands of Adventure,** and **CityWalk,** Universal is no longer an afterthought to the "other park" down I-4; its attractions are also must-sees in Orlando. (I-4 Exit 29B or 30B. ☎363-8000. Open daily 9am, closing times vary. CityWalk open until 2am. Each park is $46, ages 3-9 $37; look for discount "upgrade" tickets to other park. CityWalk is ungated and free. Parking $7.)

UNIVERSAL STUDIOS FLORIDA. The original attraction is both amusement park and working film studio. Metal face villains appear so close you can kiss 'em at **Terminator 2: 3D,** an apocalyptic showdown with an evil cybertech regime. The original movie's director, actors, and effects wizards produced the 3D movie. Rides also take on movie themes: **Kongfrontation,** in which a 35 ft. King Kong roughhouses with your cable car, and the **E.T. Adventure** bike ride are hits with the kids. **Back to the Future...The Ride,** one of the staples of any Universal visit, utilizes seven-story OmniiMax surround screens and spectacular special effects. A photo with the cheery dino's stone statue at **A Day in the Park with Barney** makes the perfect dart board target. A classic attraction is **JAWS,** a pleasant tour of Amity gone awry when a bitter great-white gets the better of the town. Since the park also houses the largest film studio outside Hollywood, celebrity sightings are common. You may recognize a number of Universal's back-lot locations—Hollywood, Central Park, Beverly Hills, the Bates Motel from *Psycho*, and the streetfront from the *Cosby Show*. **Men In Black Alien Attack,** the latest (and most popular) ride here, puts a laser in your hand and lets you save the world from aliens.

■**ISLANDS OF ADVENTURE.** This park encompasses 110 acres of the most technologically sophisticated rides in the world and some of the weirdest eateries in Orlando. Five islands portray different themes, ranging from cartoons to the overhyped Jurassic Park. **The Amazing Adventures of Spider Man** is the crown jewel of Orlando theme parks; new technology and several patents sprung from its conception. A fast-moving car whizzes around a 3D video system as Spidey and you find the stolen Statue of Liberty. Riders go from 0-40 mph in 2sec., then shoot out of the **Incredible Hulk Coaster** with the same G-force as an Air Force F-16 fighter. In all the rides, waiting time is eased by ride narratives and creative distractions. The most

FLORIDA

entertaining island is the pastel-overload **Seuss Landing,** home of the **Green Eggs & Ham Cafe** (green eggs and ham-wich $5.60) and the **Moose Juice Goose Juice** stand. **The Cat in the Hat, Thing 1 and Thing 2** make the books come to life. Watch baby dinosaurs hatch in the **Discovery Center** nursery on Jurassic Park Island.

CITYWALK. Thirty free, ungated acres of shops, theme restaurants, and lively street entertainment make up Citywalk, Universal's answer to Downtown Disney. Overpriced restaurants range from the collectible-laden **NASCAR Cafe** to **Emeril's Restaurant** (yes, it's that guy from TV) and everything in between. The clubs are considerably laid-back and tourist heavy. What you save in covers (range $2-5 or $8 for all) will disappear over $4 beers and $6 drinks.

COCOA BEACH AND CAPE CANAVERAL   ☎ 321

Known primarily for rocket launches, space shuttle blast-offs, and NASA's enormous space center complex, the "Space Coast" also has uncrowded golden beaches, prime surfing, and vast wildlife preserves. Even during spring break, the place remains placid; most vacationers and sun-bathers here are Space Coast residents. Beware summer launch dates, when tourists pack the area and hotel prices follow NASA into the stratosphere.

■️🔢 ORIENTATION AND PRACTICAL INFORMATION. The Cocoa Beach area, 50 mi. east of Orlando, consists of mainland towns Cocoa and Rockledge, oceanfront towns Cocoa Beach and Cape Canaveral, and Merritt Island in between. Both **I-95** and **U.S. 1** run north-south on the mainland, while **Rte. A1A** (North Atlantic Ave.) is the beach's main drag, running through Cocoa Beach and Cape Canaveral. **Greyhound,** 302 Main St. (☎636-6531; station open daily 7am-5:30pm), in Cocoa, 8 mi. inland, runs to Orlando (1hr., 2 per day, $8.50-9.50); St. Augustine (3hr., 3 per day, $26-28); and Daytona (1¾hr., 4 per day, $13.50-14.50). **Space Coast Area Transit** (☎633-1878) runs North Beach and South Beach routes and makes stops at every town in Brevard County from 8am to 5pm (fare $1; students, seniors, and disabled 50¢; transfers free). **Taxi: Yellow Top Taxi** (☎636-7017), **Banana River Yellow Cab** (☎636-1234). **Blue Dolphin Shuttle** (☎433-0011) connects Cocoa Beach with Orlando International Airport ($25) and the Kennedy Space Center ($8 round-trip). Call in advance for availability. **Visitor Info: Cocoa Beach Chamber of Commerce,** 400 Fortenberry Rd. on Merritt Island (☎459-2200; open M-F 8:30am-5pm). **Space Coast Office of Tourism,** 8810 Astronaut Blvd. (A1A), #102 (☎800-936-2326; open M-F 8am-5pm). **Post Office:** 333 Crockett Blvd., Merritt Island (☎453-1366; open M-F 8:30am-5pm, Sa 9am-1pm). **ZIP code:** 32952. **Area code:** 321. Ten-digit dialing required.

📷🍴 ACCOMMODATIONS AND FOOD. Across from the beach, **Motel 6,** 3701 N. Atlantic Ave. (A1A) beats the rates of most accommodations in Cocoa Beach. (☎783-3103. A/C, TV, pool, laundry, shuffleboard. Singles Su-Th $42, F-Sa $46.) Behind the Greyhound station and the water tower is the **Dixie Motel,** 301 Forrest Ave., with clean rooms, floor-to-ceiling windows, A/C, cable TV, and a swimming pool. (☎632-1600. Laundry available. Singles $40; doubles $50; off-season $45/$55.) Pitch your tent at scenic **Jetty Park Campgrounds,** 400 E. Jetty Rd., at the northern tip of Cape Canaveral. (☎783-7111. 6 people per site. Jan.-Apr. rustic sites $18, with water and electricity $22, full hook-up $25; May-Dec. $16/$20/$23. Reserve 3 months in advance, especially before shuttle launches.)

Lines awaiting "famous" New York style pizza stream out the door of **Bizzarro,** #4 1st Ave. off AIA in Indiatlantic. (☎724-4799. Open M-Th 11am-9pm, F-Sa 11am-11pm, Su noon-9pm. Round or Sicilian slices $1.50; subs $4.) Nothing like soy milk and tofu on the beach; buy it at **Sunseed Food Co-op,** 6615 N. Atlantic Ave. (A1A), an impressive depot of all things organic, natural, and healthy. (☎784-0930. Open M-W 10am-7pm, Th-F 10am-8pm, Sa 10am-7pm, Su 11am-6pm.) The **Tea Room,** 6211 N. Atlantic Ave. (A1A), combines home-cookin' and a little TLC to rev your engine. Daily breakfast specials run around $3 while pastries range 50¢-$1.25. (☎783-5527. Open M-F 6:30am-2pm, Sa-Su 8am-2pm.)

▣ **BEAM ME UP, SCOTTY.** All of **NASA's** shuttle flights take off from the **Kennedy Space Center,** 18 mi. north of Cocoa Beach. **Kennedy Space Center Visitors Complex** provides a huge welcoming center for visitors, complete with a 3-D IMAX theater, the Rocket Garden, and several thoughtful exhibits and displays about the US space program. KSC offers two tours of their 220 sq. mi. grounds. The **Kennedy Space Center Tour** departs continuously from 9:30am to 5pm, hitting the three main tourist attractions: the LC 39 Observation Gantry, Apollo/Saturn V Center, and the International Space Station Center. The 2hr. **Then & Now Tour** highlights historic launch sites. The most impressive facility on the grounds is the **Apollo/Saturn V Center,** a $35 million, 100,000 sq. ft. interactive museum dedicated exclusively to the Apollo missions. A fully restored 363 ft. Saturn V rocket, one of only three in the world, runs the length of the daunting hanger. With NASA's ambitious launch schedule, you may have a chance to watch the space shuttles *Endeavor, Columbia, Atlantis,* or *Discovery* thunder off into the blue yonder above the Cape. For $15, KSC will transport you to a viewing area to watch the fiery ascension. *(☎452-2121; 449-4444 for launch info and schedules. On NASA Pkwy., accessible by car via Rte. 405; from Cocoa Beach, take Rte. A1A until it turns west onto Rte. 528, then follow Rte. 3 N to the Spaceport. Public transport: Blue Dolphin Shuttle (see Practical Information, above). Open daily in summer 9am-8:30pm; in winter 9am-5:30pm. Admission to Kennedy Space Center grounds, including all sights and tours, $24; ages 3-11 $15.)*

Surrounding the NASA complex, the **Merritt Island National Wildlife Refuge** stirs with sea turtles, alligators, wild hogs, otters, and over 300 bird species. *(☎861-0667. Open daily sunrise-sunset. Visitors center open M-F 8am-4:30pm, Sa 9am-5pm.)* Just north of Merritt Island, **Canaveral National Seashore,** the northeastern shore of the wildlife refuge, covers 67,000 acres of undeveloped beach and dunes. *(☎407-867-0677. Take Rte. 406 E off U.S. 1 in Titusville. Open daily 6am-8pm. $5 per car. Closed 3 days before and 1 day after NASA launches.)*

FORT LAUDERDALE ☎954

Fort Lauderdale's gleaming white sands stretch 23 miles down Florida's east coast, but it is the water that dominates the city's landscape. Often dubbed the "Venice of America," Fort Lauderdale supports an intricate intra-coastal waterway with over 165 miles of navigable waters. Numerous inlets cut streets in two; the town is home to 42,000 yachts and countless water sports. The number two activity in ritzy Fort Lauderdale is shopping, particularly along Los Olas Blvd.

▐ GETTING THERE AND GETTING AROUND

Airport: Fort Lauderdale/Hollywood International, 1400 Lee Wagoner Blvd. (call ☎359-1200 for recorded ramblings; 359-6100 for a human), 3½ mi. south of downtown on U.S. 1, or take I-595 E from I-95 to Exit 12B. Take bus #1 from downtown.

Trains: Amtrak, 200 SW 21st Terr. (☎587-6692), just west of I-95, ¼ mi. south of Broward Blvd. Take bus #22 from downtown. To Orlando (4¾hr., 2 per day, $29-56). Open daily 7:15am-9:15pm.

Buses: Greyhound, 515 NE 3rd St. (☎764-6551), 3 blocks north of Broward Blvd. downtown. *Be careful in the surrounding area, especially at night.* To: Orlando (5hr., 7 per day, $36-38); Daytona Beach (6½-7hr., 6 per day, $30-32); and Miami (1hr., 17 per day, $5). Open 24hr.

Public Transit: Broward County Transit (BCT) (☎357-8400; M-F 7am-10pm, Sa 7am-8pm, Su 8am-7pm). Most routes go to the terminal at the corner of 1st St. NW and 1st Ave. NW, downtown. Get a system map at any terminal. Operates daily 6am-11pm, every 30min. on most routes. $1; transfer 15¢; seniors, under 18, and disabled 50¢ (with ID). 7-day passes ($9), all-day passes ($3), and 10-ride passes ($8) available at beachfront hotels, libraries, and the central terminal. **TMAX** (☎761-3543) runs loops through downtown and on the beach strip between Sunrise Blvd. and Las Olas Blvd. Runs F and Sa 6pm-1am, every 30min. Free. **Tri-Rail** (☎728-8445 or 800-874-7245) connects West Palm Beach, Fort Lauderdale, and Miami. Trains run M-F 4am-10pm, Sa-

Su 7am-10pm. Schedules available at airport, motels, or Tri-Rail stops. $4-5.50, 50% discount for children, disabled, students and seniors with Tri-Rail ID.

Taxis: Yellow Cab, ☎ 777-7777. **Public Service Taxi,** ☎ 587-9090.

Car Rental: Alamo, 2601 S. Federal Hwy. (☎ 525-4713). Open 24hr. $39 per day, $225 per week with unlimited mi. Must be 21+ with a major credit card. $20 per day surcharge for those under 25.

Bike Rental: Mike's Cyclery, 5429 N. Federal Hwy. (☎ 493-5277). Open daily 10am-7pm. A variety of bicycles $20 per day, $50 per week. Some racing bikes cost slightly more. Credit card deposit required.

✴️🔢 ORIENTATION AND PRACTICAL INFORMATION

North-south **I-95** connects West Palm Beach, Fort Lauderdale, and Miami. **Rte. 84/I-75 (Alligator Alley)** slithers 100 mi. west from Fort Lauderdale across the Everglades to Naples and other small cities on Florida's Gulf Coast. Fort Lauderdale is bigger than it looks—and it looks huge. The city extends westward from its 23 mi. of beach to encompass nearly 450 sq. mi. Streets and boulevards are east-west and avenues are north-south. All are labeled NW, NE, SW, or SE according to quadrant. **Broward Blvd.** divides the city north-south, while **Andrews Ave.** cuts east-west. The unpleasant downtown centers around **Federal Hwy. (U.S. 1)** and **Las Olas Blvd.,** about 2 mi. west of the oceanfront. Between downtown and the waterfront, yachts fill the ritzy inlets of the **Intracoastal Waterway. The strip** (a.k.a. Rte. A1A, N. Atlantic Blvd., 17th St. Causeway, Ocean Blvd., and Seabreeze Blvd.) runs 4 mi. along the beach between **Oakland Park Blvd.** to the north and Las Olas Blvd. to the south.

Visitor Info: Greater Fort Lauderdale Convention and Visitors Bureau, 1850 Eller Dr., Ste. #303 (☎ 765-4466), in the Port Everglades. Particularly useful *Superior Small Lodgings,* a comprehensive and detailed list of low-priced accommodations. For published info, call ☎ 800-227-8669. Open M-F 8:30am-5pm. **Chamber of Commerce,** 512 NE 3rd Ave. (☎ 462-6000), 3 blocks off Federal Hwy. at 5th St. Open M-F 8am-5pm.

Internet Access: Floyd's Hostel/Crew House, see **Accommodations,** below.

Hotlines: First Call for Help, ☎ 467-6333. **Sexual Assault and Treatment Center,** ☎ 761-7273. Both 24hr.

Post Office: 1900 W. Oakland Park Blvd. (☎ 527-2028). Open M-F 7:30am-7pm, Sa 8:30am-2pm. **ZIP code:** 33310. **Area code:** 954.

🏠 ACCOMMODATIONS

Hotel prices increase exponentially as you approach prime beachfront and spring break. High season runs from mid-Feb. through early Apr. Investigate package deals at the slightly worse-for-wear hotels along the strip in Fort Lauderdale. Many hotels offer off-season deals for under $35. Small motels, many with tiny kitchenettes, crowd each other one or two blocks off the beach area; look along **Birch Rd.,** one block from Rte. A1A, and north along A1A. The **Greater Fort Lauderdale Lodging and Hospitality Association,** 1412 E. Broward Blvd., provides a free directory of area hotels (☎ 567-0766; open M-F 9am-5pm). The *Fort Lauderdale News* and the *Miami Herald* occasionally sport listings by local residents who rent rooms to tourists in spring. Sleeping on the well-patrolled beaches is illegal and virtually impossible between 9pm and sunrise.

Floyd's Hostel/Crew House, 445 SE 16th St. (☎ 462-0631; call ahead). A homey hostel catering to international travelers and boat crews. 42 beds, 5 kitchens, 5 living rooms with cable TV, and 8 bathrooms. Dorm rooms have 3-6 beds. Free daytime pick-up from anywhere in the Ft. Lauderdale area. Free pasta, cereal, local calls, linen, lockers, and laundry. Check-in by midnight or call for special arrangement. Passport or American driver's license required. Internet access $2.50 per 30min. About 2 mi. from beach and Las Olas district. The owners got engaged thanks to *Let's Go: USA 1995* (ask them for details). Beds $15.30, $14.55 with stay of 3 or more days; private rooms $35.

Estoril Paradise Inn, 2648 NE 32nd St. (☎563-3840 or 888-385-2322). Take bus #10 from downtown to Coral Ridge Shopping Center; walk 2 blocks east on Oakland Park Blvd. down to Bayview Dr. NE 32nd St. is one block north. Family-run for 30 years. A 10min. walk to the beach. Free pick-up from airport, bus, or train stations. Very clean rooms with A/C, cable TV, kitchenette, and free parking. Heated pool and grill. Rooms $29; mid-Dec. to Apr. Reservations accepted within 48hr. mid-Dec. to Apr.

Quiet Waters County Park, 401 S. Powerline Rd. (☎360-1315), off I-95's Exit 37B; take Hillsboro Blvd. west to Powerline Rd. From downtown, take bus #11 to Pompano Sq. Mall, then switch to bus #95. Fully equipped lake-side campsites (tent, grill, and free admission to beach) for up to 6 people ("don't feed the gators!"). Normal water sports and see-it-to-believe-it 8-person "boatless water skiing" at the end of a cable. No electricity or RVs. Office hours 8:30am-6pm. Check-in 2-6pm. Sites Su-Th $17, F-Sa and holidays $25; primitive sites $17. $25 refundable deposit. Wheelchair accessible.

☷☰ FOOD AND NIGHTLIFE

The clubs along the strip offer massive quantities of free grub during Happy Hour; wieners, chips, and hors d'oeuvres come on surfboard-sized platters or you can opt for the all-you-can-eat pizza and buffets. However, these bars have hefty cover charges (from $5) and drink minimums (from $3). The **Ocean Drive Cafe,** 401 Ft. Lauderdale Beach Blvd. (A1A), is one affordable option along the strip that provides both savory dishes and a great vantage point—people-watching breaks up a long day of sun and surf. Try the $7 homemade calzones or munch on a veggie burger for $6.50. (☎779-3351. Open daily 8:30am-midnight.) **La Spada's,** 4346 Seagrape Dr., off Commerical Blvd., has the best and biggest hoagies in southern Florida. The foot-long Italian sub ($7) is an absolute must, as most of Ft. Lauderdale, waiting in line with you, will agree. (☎776-7893. Open M-Sa 10am-8pm, Su 11am-8pm.) In aggressively marine decor, **Southport Raw Bar,** 1536 Cordova Rd., by the 17th St. Causeway behind the Southport Mall, serves spicy conch chowder ($2.95) and fried shrimp ($7), as well as a slew of clams, oysters, and other fruits of the sea. (☎525-2526. Open daily 11am-2am. Happy hour M-Th 3-6pm and 11pm-2am, F 3-6pm, Sa-Su 11pm-2am.) The traditional diner **Lester's,** 250 Rte. 84, furnishes each table with its own jukebox, mixing golden oldies with mouth-watering shakes and burgers. House specialties usually run $3-7. (☎525-5641. Open daily 24hr.)

Several popular nightspots line N. Atlantic Blvd. next to the beach. The **Elbo Room** sits on prime real estate at the corner of A1A and Las Olas Blvd; a camera on the second floor patio transmits the beach/strip scene to www.theelboroom.com. The booming sidewalk bar, chock full of scantily-clad beach beauties, is among the most visible and packed scenes on the strip. (☎463-4615. Open M-Th 11am-2am, F-Sa 11am-3am, Su noon-2am. Live music nightly.) In the popular Las Olas district, **O'Hara's Jazz Cafe,** 722 E. Las Olas Blvd., combines stacked sandwiches with nightly jazz and blues acts for a laid-back night out. Two-for-one daily drink specials will keep your whistle wet until 6pm. (☎524-1764. Open M-F 11:30am-2am, Sa 11:30am-3am, Su noon-2am. Live music nightly.)

LIVING THE JAI LIFE President Harry Truman and Eleanor Roosevelt were fans. Babe Ruth tried it, but failed. Anointed by Guiness as the **"fastest game in the world,"** Jai Alai generally still remains unknown to Americans outside the state of Florida. Players from the Basque region of France and Spain brought the game to the Sunshine State in the 20s, where it blossomed as a betting sport. Brave players whip the *pelota,* a rubber ball encased in layers of goat skin, from their *cesta,* a curved throwing/catching basket. Wild spins and speeds exceeding 180mph aim to keep the opponent from cleanly catching and releasing the pelota. **Dania Jai-Alai,** off U.S. 1 10min. south of Fort Lauderdale sports one of the largest *frontons* (courts) in the state. *(301 E. Dania Beach Blvd. ☎927-2841. Games Tu and Sa noon and 7:15pm, W-F 7:15pm, Su 1pm. General admission $1.50; reserved seats from $2.50.)*

FLORIDA

🔵 SIGHTS

Fort Lauderdale is a pleasant medium between the pretension of Miami Beach and the Redneck Riveria of panhandle beaches. Parts of "A1A: Beachfront Ave." demonstrate the class and sophistication of Vanilla Ice—signs for Jello might mean nude women. Yet Fort Lauderdale's well maintained palm-lined shore, emerald waters, and pink brick sidewalks make Miami Beach look shabby.

ON THE WATER. Fort Lauderdale Beach is at its most gorgeous along the beachfront between Las Olas Blvd. and Sunrise Blvd. **Los Olas Waterfront,** 2 W. 2nd St., the latest on-the-beach mall, boasts clubs, restaurants, bars, and over 20 movie screens to entertain until the ocean lures you back. Tour the city's waterways aboard the **Jungle Queen,** located at the Bahia Mar Yacht Center, on Rte. A1A three blocks south of Las Olas Blvd. The captain's commentary keeps you acquainted with the changing scenery as the 550-passenger riverboat cruises up the New River. *(801 Seabreeze Blvd. ☎462-5596. 3hr. tours daily 10am, 2, and 7pm. $11.50, ages 2-10 $7.75; 7pm tour $26/$13.75, dinner included.)* The **Water Taxi** offers a different way to get around town. The nautical mode of transit makes 20 stops along the Intracoastal Waterway and the New River. *(651 Seabreeze Blvd/Rte. A1A. ☎467-6677. Call 30min. before pick-up. Open daily 10am until they get tired. $14, under 12 $7 and free on Su when accompanied by an adult. All-day service $16.)* **Water Sports Unlimited,** on the beach, rents equipment for a variety of water sports, including wave runners. Parasailing trips are $65 (600 ft., 8min. duration), plus a little more if you want to get dipped. *(301 Seabreeze Blvd/Rte. A1A. ☎467-1316. Open daily 9am-6:30pm.)*

ON DRY LAND. Landlubbers can walk among three acres of tropical gardens, exotic birds, and thousands of live butterflies at 🦋**Butterfly World,** west of Florida's Turnpike, Exit #69, in Coconut Creek. *(3600 W. Sample Rd. ☎977-4400. Open M-Sa 9am-5pm, Su 1-5pm, gate closes 5pm. $13, ages 4-12 $8.)* Learn to fly-fish and reel in the virtual "big one" at the **International Game Fishing Association's Fishing Hall of Fame & Museum,** off I-95 at Griffin Rd., Exit 26. Adventures at the museum begin with an inspirational film, *Journeys,* in the big-screen theater. The galleries provide a detailed look at the art of fishing and hail history's most skillful anglers. *(300 Gulf Stream Way. ☎922-4212. Open daily 10am-6pm. $5, seniors $4.50, children $4. Wheelchair accessible.)* Amidst the commercial world of the beachfront area sits the secluded **Bonnet House,** a historic plantation, South Florida style. Forty-five spider monkeys roam the 35 subtropical acres. *(900 N. Birch Rd., off Sunrise Blvd. near the beach. ☎563-5393. Open W-F 10am-1:30pm, Sa-Su noon-2:30pm. Closed mid-Aug. thru mid-Sept. $9, students $7, seniors $8, children under 6 free.)*

MIAMI AND MIAMI BEACH   ☎305

Long a popular setting for TV shows and movies, Miami's Latin heart pulses to the beat of the largest Cuban population outside of Cuba—speaking Spanish is very useful. Many small cultural communities distinguish Miami's residential areas, from Little Havana (a well-established Cuban community) to Coconut Grove (an eclectic intellectual enclave turned stylized tourist mecca). Only seven miles away, across an arching causeway, Miami Beach's multiplying number of hotels triple the city's usual population. Throngs in thongs from the world over come to experience this "Hollywood of the East Coast" in all of its star-studded, bikinied gusto.

▐ GETTING THERE AND GETTING AROUND

Airport: Miami International (☎876-7000), at Le Jeune Rd. and NW 36th Ave., 7 mi. northwest of downtown. Bus #7 runs downtown; many other buses make downtown stops. From downtown, take bus "C" or "K" to South Miami Beach.

Trains: Amtrak, 8303 NW 37th Ave. (☎835-1223), near Northside station of Metrorail. Bus "L" goes directly to Lincoln Rd. Mall in South Miami Beach. To: Orlando (5hr., 2 per day, $33-64); New Orleans (24hr., 3 per week, $206-387); and Charleston (13-14hr., 2 per day, $64-149). Open daily 6:30am-10pm.

Miami

TO ORLANDO

TO FT. LAUDERDALE &
WEST PALM BEACH

Miami Gdns. Dr.

856

N.W. 37th Ave.

N.W. 27th Ave.

N.W. 47th Ave.

N.W. 57th Ave.

860

Florida Turnpike

441

95

Ocean Bd.

Palmetto Expwy.

826

N. Miami

826

1

OPA-LOCKA

817

N. Miami Beach Blvd.

NORTH
MIAMI
BEACH

Biscayne Blvd.

Oleta River State
Recreation Area

955

Opa-Locka
Airport

N.W. 138th St.

Tri-Rail

75

N.W. 135th St.

Gratigny Pkwy. (toll)

N.W. 42nd Ave.

Palm. Ave.

Red Rd.

N.W. 27th Ave.

924

N.W. 119th St.
(Gratigny Rd.)

N.E. 6th Ave.

N.E. 135th St.

NORTH MIAMI

915

922

Broad Cau seway (toll)

A1A

Collins Ave.

INDIAN
CREEK
VILLAGE

W. 49th St.

932

N.W. 103rd St.

Tri-Rail

HIALEAH

N.W. 95th St.

N.W. 7th Ave.

MIAMI SHORES

Biscayne Blvd.

Normandy Dr.
71st St.

Alton Rd.

A1A

W. 4th Ave.

Hialeah
Race
Track

Amtrak
Station

E. 25th St.

N.W. 79th St.

934

JFK Causeway

934

Metrorail

27

N.W. 37th Ave.

9

N.W. 79th St.

N.E. 2nd Ave.

Biscayne
Bay

MIAMI
BEACH

E. 9th St.

MLK Blvd.

N.W. 62nd St.

441

N.M. Miami Ave.
N.W. 1st Ave.

Hialeah Dr.

944

N.W. 54th St.

LIBERTY
CITY

MIAMI
SPRINGS

Airport
Expwy. (toll)

27

N.W. 36th St.

112

American
Police Hall
of Fame

1

Julia Tuttle Causeway

195

A1st St.

Collins Ave.

A1A

Miami River

N.W. 27th St.

Metrorail

N.W. 20th St.

Miami
International
Airport

836

Dolphin Expwy. (toll)

395

Venetian Causeway (toll)

Lincoln Rd.

Meridian Ave.

Collins Dr.

Ocean Dr.

WEST
MIAMI

N.W. 7th St.

Orange
Bowl

Government
Center

MacArthur Causeway

Port of Miami Bd.

5th St.

W. Flagler St.

LITTLE
HAVANA

968

Brickell

95

Port of
Miami

SEE SOUTH
BEACH MAP

Tamiami Trail

41

S.W. 8th St. (Calle 8)

933

95

DOWNTOWN
MIAMI

Fisher
Island

CORAL
GABLES

959

9

S.W. 24th St.

Vizcaya

Rickenbacker Causeway (toll)

Virginia
Key

972

S.W. 42nd Ave.
(Le Jeune Rd.)

Coral Way

Venetian
Pool

S.W. 57th Ave.

Metrorail

S. Dixie Hwy.

S. Bayshore Dr.

Vizcaya
Museum &
Gardens

Coconut
Grove

953

Coco-
Walk

COCONUT
GROVE

Miami
Seaquarium

Crandon
Park

ATLANTIC
OCEAN

Univ. of
Miami

1

SOUTH
MIAMI

Biscayne
Bay

Harbor Dr.

Crandon Park Bd.

TO FLORIDA KEYS,
THE EVERGLADES

KEY
BISCAYNE

Matheson
Hammock
Park

Red Rd.

Fairchild
Tropical
Garden

Cape Florida
State Park

N

0   2 miles

0   2 km

FLORIDA

Buses: Greyhound, Miami Station, 4111 NW 27th St. (☎871-1810). To: Atlanta (17-19hr., 13 per day, $85.50); Orlando (5-9hr., 10 per day, $36); and Fort Lauderdale (1hr., hourly, $5). Open 24hr.

Public Transit: Metro Dade Transportation (☎770-3131; info M-F 6am-10pm, Sa-Su 9am-5pm). The extensive Metrobus network converges downtown, where most long trips transfer. Lettered bus routes A, C, D, G, H, J, K, L, R, S, and T serve Miami Beach. After dark, some stops are patrolled (indicated with a sign). Buses run M-F 4:30am-2am. $1.25; transfers 25¢, to Metrorail 25¢. Call for weekend schedule. Exact change only. The **Metrorail** services downtown. $1.25, rail-to-bus transfers 50¢. The **Metromover** loop downtown is linked to the Metrorail stations. Runs daily 6am-midnight. Fare 25¢, seniors 10¢, free transfers from Metrorail. **Tri-Rail** (☎800-874-7245) connects Miami, Fort Lauderdale, and West Palm Beach. Trains run M-Sa 4am-8pm, Su 7am-8pm. M-F $6.75, Sa-Su $4; students, ages 5-12, and seniors 50% off. The **Electrowave** (☎843-9283) offers shuttles along Washington Ave. from S. Pointe to Dade Blvd. Runs M-W 8am-2am, Th-Sa 8am-4am, Su and holidays 10am-2am. 25¢; pick up a brochure or just hop on in South Beach.

Taxis: Metro, ☎888-8888. **Central Cab,** ☎532-5555.

Bike Rental: Miami Beach Bicycle Center, 601 5th St. (☎531-4161), at the corner of Washington Ave., Miami Beach. Open M-Sa 10am-7pm, Su 10am-5pm. $5 per hr., $20 per day, $70 per week. Must be 18+ with credit card or $200 cash deposit.

✈ ORIENTATION

Three highways criss-cross the Miami area. **I-95,** the most direct route north-south, merges into **U.S. 1 (Dixie Hwy.)** just south of downtown. U.S. 1 runs to the Everglades entrance at Florida City and then continues as the Overseas Hwy. to Key West. **Rte. 836,** a major east-west artery through town, connects I-95 to **Florida's Turnpike,** passing the airport in between. If you're headed to Florida City, taking Rte. 836 and the Turnpike will allow you to avoid the traffic on U.S. 1.

When looking for street addresses, pay careful attention to the systematic street layout; it's easy to confuse North Miami Beach, West Miami, Miami Beach, and Miami addresses. Streets in Miami run east-west, avenues north-south; both are numbered. Miami divides into NE, NW, SE, and SW quadrants; the dividing lines (downtown) are **Flagler St.** (east-west) and **Miami Ave.** (north-south). Some numbered streets and avenues also have names—e.g., Le Jeune Rd. is SW 42nd Ave., and SW 40th St. is Bird Rd. Get a map that lists both numbers and names.

Several causeways connect Miami to **Miami Beach.** The most useful is **MacArthur Causeway,** which becomes 5th St. in Miami Beach. Numbered streets run east-west across the island, increasing as you go north. In South Miami Beach, **Collins Ave. (A1A)** is the main north-south drag. Parallel to Collins is **Washington Ave.** and the beachfront riviera **Ocean Ave.** The commercial and entertainment district sits between 6th and 23rd St. To reach **Key Biscayne,** take the **Rickenbacker Causeway.**

The heart of **Little Havana** lies between SW 12th Ave. and SW 27th Ave.; take bus #8, 11, 17, or 37. The **Calle Ocho** (SW 8th St.) is central; one block north, the corresponding section of **W. Flagler St.** is a hub of Cuban business. **Coconut Grove,** south of Little Havana, centers around the shopping and entertainment district on **Grand Ave.** and **Virginia St. Coral Gables,** an upscale residential area, rests around the intersection of **Coral Way (SW 24th St.)** and **Le Jeune Rd.** A **car** can be an expensive liability in Miami. Posted signs indicate different parking zones; should you leave your car in a residential zone for even a few moments, you may return to find it towed. Never leave valuables visible in your car; automobile theft and break-ins are common.

ℹ PRACTICAL INFORMATION

Visitor Info: Miami Beach Visitors Center, 420 Lincoln Rd. (☎672-1270). Open M-F 9am-6pm, Sa-Su 10am-4pm. **Info booth,** 401 Biscayne Blvd. (☎539-2980), downtown outside of Bayside Marketplace. Open daily 10am-6:30pm. In South Beach, **The Art Deco**

Welcome Center, 1001 Ocean Dr. (☎531-3484) has tour info. Open M-F 11am-6pm, Sa 10am-10pm, Su 11am-10pm, extended hours in winter. **Coconut Grove Chamber of Commerce,** 2820 McFarlane Ave. (☎444-7270). Open M-F 9am-5pm. **Greater Miami Convention and Visitors Bureau,** 701 Brickell Ave. (☎539-3000 or 800-283-2707), 27th fl. of Barnett Bank Bldg. downtown. Open M-F 9am-5pm.

Internet Access: Kafka's Cafe, 1464 Washington Ave. (☎673-9669) in Miami Beach. 13 computers, $9 per hr. Open daily 9am-11pm. **Miami Beach International Travelers Hostel** (see **Accommodations,** below).

Hotlines: Crisis Line, ☎358-4357. **Rape Treatment Center and Hotline** (☎585-7273), at Jackson Memorial Hospital, 1611 NW 12th Ave. Both 24hr. **Gay Hotline,** ☎759-5210.

Post Office: 500 NW 2nd Ave. (☎639-4284), downtown. Open M-F 8am-5pm, Sa 9am-1:30pm. **ZIP code:** 33101. **Area code:** 305.

ACCOMMODATIONS

Cheap rooms abound in South Miami Beach's Art Deco hotels. Finding a "pullmanette" (in 40s lingo), a room with a refrigerator, stove, and sink, will save you money. In South Florida, many inexpensive hotels are likely to have 2-3 inch cockroaches ("palmetto bugs"). In general, high

South Beach

ACCOMMODATIONS
Banana Bungalow, 1

The Clay Hotel and International Hostel, 4
Sea Deck Hotel and Apartments, 3
Miami Beach International Travelers Hostel, 5
The Tropics Hotel/Hostel, 2

season for Miami Beach runs late Dec. through mid-Mar.; during the off season, when rooms are empty, hotel clerks are quick to bargain. The **Greater Miami and the Beaches Hotel Association,** 407 Lincoln Rd. #10G, can help you find a place to crash (☎531-3553; open M-F 9am-5pm), and the Miami Beach visitors center (see **Practical Information,** above) can finagle you the cheapest rates. **Camping** is not allowed in Miami Beach.

Banana Bungalow, 2360 Collins Ave. (☎538-1951), at 23rd St. along the northern edge of the Art Deco district. 180 bunk beds. Free coffee, tea, and toast. TV, pool, canal access, kitchen, free lockers, linen, bar, grill, and nightly movie at 8pm. Limited, free, guarded parking. Travel agent in lobby. Kayak/canoe rentals $10 per 2hr.; bikes $12 per day, $5 per hr. Shared rooms $15; hotel rooms $70-76. Reserve in advance.

The Tropics Hotel/Hostel, 1550 Collins Ave. (☎531-0361), across the street from the beach. From the airport, take bus "J" to 41st St., transfer to bus "C" to Lincoln Rd., and walk 1 block south on Collins Ave. Next to parking garage. Clean rooms with 4-6 beds, A/C, private baths, phone, pool access, and an outdoor kitchen. Free linen. Dorms $14. Private rooms have A/C, cable TV, and free local calls. Singles and doubles $50.

Miami Beach International Travelers Hostel (9th St. Hostel) (AAIH/Rucksackers), 236 9th St. (☎534-0268 or 800-978-6787), at Washington Ave. From the airport, take bus "J" to 41st and Indian Creek, then transfer to bus "C" or "K." Central location, but difficult parking. Lively international atmosphere near the beach. Laundry, common room with TV and movie library, and Internet access. 28 clean, comfortable rooms (maximum 4 people), all with A/C and bath. Dorms $15, $13 with any hosteling membership or student ID; private singles or doubles $55, off-season $32.

Sea Deck Hotel and Apartments, 1530 Collins Ave. (☎538-4361). Basic, cozy, and clean pullmanettes with floral bedspreads open onto a tropical courtyard. Limited parking available. Pullmanettes $49, other rooms $67, suites $78. *Let's Go* toters get 10% off.

The Clay Hotel and International Hostel (HI-AYH), 1438 Washington Ave. (☎534-2988 or 800-379-2529), in the heart of the Art Deco district; take bus "C" from downtown. Popular location for *Miami Vice*, also featured in *The Specialist*. Great archways in a Mediterranean-style building. International crowd. Kitchen, laundry facilities, A/C. Open 24hr. Dorm rooms of 4-8 beds come with phone and fridges; some also have TV. Key deposit $5. Lockers $1 per day. Dorms $15, non-members $16; private rooms $36-68.

⚫ FOOD

The rich ethnic diversity in Miami has brought notorious Latin cuisine to the city. Cuban specialties include *media noche* sandwiches (a sort of club sandwich on a soft roll, heated and compressed); bright red *mamey*-flavored ice cream and shakes; hearty *frijoles negros* (black beans); and *picadillo* (shredded beef and peas in tomato sauce, served with white rice). For sweets, seek out a *dulcería*, and punctuate your rambles with thimble-sized shots of strong, sweet *café cubano* (around 35¢). For other treats, try *platanos*, large starchy bananas served fried or caramelized, and *mojitos*, rum, lime and mint spritzers. Look for Florida stone crabs, in season from Oct. to May; seafood lovers will be easily caught by their sweet, meaty claws. Cheap restaurants are not common in Miami, but an array of bakeries can sustain you.

▨ **Macarena,** 1334 Washington Ave. (☎531-3440), in Miami Beach. Dance your way to wonderful food in an atmosphere that's equal parts intimate and festive. This place is a favorite of the Julio Iglesias family. *Paella* ($14, lunch $7) and the best rice pudding you'll encounter ($5.50) make for the perfect Spanish treat. Wine comes from their own vineyards. Flamenco dancing W and F; ladies night Th; live salsa on Sa. Open daily for lunch 12:30-3:30pm; dinner Su-Tu 7pm-1am, W-Th 7pm-1:30am; F-Sa 7pm-5am.

▨ **Wolfie's,** 2038 Collins Ave. (☎538-6626), at 21st St. in South Beach. "Famous the world over," this mega-deli is a throwback to old Miami Beach. One giant sandwich ($7-12) can be both lunch and dinner. Dessert selection is unreal: thick cheesecakes, dense black forest cakes, and gravity-defying pastries. Look for luminaries in the "celebrity room." Open 24hr.

The Versailles, 3555 SW 8th St./Calle Ocho (☎444-0240), in Miami. Palatial green and gilt dining room, seemingly packed with Little Havana's entire population. Versailles has served up good Cuban fare for 28 years. Breakfast $3.50-8, sandwiches $3.50-7, daily specials $3-8. Open M-Th 8am-2am, F-Su 8am-4am.

11th St. Diner, 1065 Washington Ave. (☎534-6373), at 11th St., in Miami Beach. Diner with the requisite soda fountain and ancient Coca-Cola clock. Breakfast all day ($3-7), sandwiches ($4-7), and grill items. Best shakes in Miami ($3.75). Open 24hr., making it a popular spot for beating the munchies after a long night of revelry.

King's Ice Cream, 1831 SW 8th St./Calle Ocho (☎643-1842), in Miami. Tropical fruit *helado* (ice cream) flavors include a regal coconut (served in its own shell), *mamey*, and mango (just $1 for a small cup). They also make tasty *churros* (fried dough, 12 for $1.50). Open M-Sa 10am-11pm, Su 1-11pm.

Flamingo Cafe, 1454 Washington Ave. (☎673-4302), near the Clay Hostel, in Miami Beach. Small diner with friendly service, all of which is in Spanish. Beef tacos and salad $2.75, *frijoles con queso* ($2.75). Lunch specials $5-7. Open M-Sa 7am-10pm.

📷 SIGHTS

South Miami Beach, between 6th and 23rd St., teems with hundreds of hotels and apartments whose sun-faded pastel facades conform to 20s ideals of a tropical paradise. An unusual mixture of people populates the area, including many retirees and first-generation Hispanic Americans. Models, tourists, and the occasional music superstar stroll down **Ocean Dr.,** the country's ultimate see-and-be-seen strip lined with many a bar or cafe for dodging the sun. **Walking tours** start at the **Oceanfront Auditorium.** *(1001 Ocean Dr. at 10th St. ☎672-2014. 1½hr. tours Th 6:30pm and Sa 10:30am; $10. 1¼hr. self-guided tours run daily 11am-4pm; $5.)* The **Holocaust Memorial,** across from the Miami Beach Visitors Center, commemorates the 6 million Jews who fell victim to Nazi terrorism in WWII. *(1933-45 Meridian Ave. ☎538-1663. Open daily 9am-9pm. Free.)* **The Wolfsonian** examines the art of design from 1885-1945 through over 70,000 objects. The permanent exhibit includes Russian political propaganda and London subway signs. *(1001 Washington Ave. ☎531-1001. Open M-Tu and F-Sa 11am-6pm, Th 11am-9pm, Su noon-5pm. $5, students and seniors $3.50. Free Th 6-9pm.)*

A stroll through the lazy streets of **Coconut Grove** uncovers an unlikely combination of haute boutiques and tacky tourist traps. On the bayfront between the Grove and downtown stands the **Vizcaya Museum and Gardens.** European antiques, tapestries, and art fill this 70-room Italianate mansion, surrounded by ten acres of lush gardens. *(3251 S. Miami Ave. ☎250-9133. Take bus #1 or the Metrorail to Vizcaya. Open daily 9:30am-5pm; last entry 4:30pm. $10, ages 6-12 $5.)* Blanketed with oversized ferns and leaves, the **Fairchild Tropical Garden** covers 83 acres and features 16 elaborate flower shows per year. *(10901 Old Cutler Rd. ☎667-1651. Open daily 9:30am-4:30pm. Tram tours hourly 10am-3pm, until 4pm on weekends. $8, under 12 free. Wheelchair accessible.)*

On the waterfront downtown, Miami's sleek **Bayside** shopping center hops nightly with talented street performers. *(Open M-Th 10am-10pm, F-Sa 10am-11pm, Su 11am-9pm.)* Near Bayside, the **American Police Hall of Fame and Museum** exhibits feature grisly execution equipment, the car from "Blade Runner," and "Old Sparky," Florida's infamous electric chair. *(3801 Biscayne Blvd. ☎573-0070. Open daily 10am-5:30pm. $6, seniors $4, and ages 6-12 $3; discounts at visitors center.)*

In **Coral Gables,** the family-friendly **Venetian Pool,** founded in 1923, once drew Hollywood stars like Esther Williams and Johnny Weissmuller. Waterfalls and Venetian-style architecture dress up this swimming hole. *(2701 DeSoto Blvd. ☎460-5356. Open summer M-F 11am-7:30pm, Sa-Su 10am-4:30pm; hrs. vary in winter and spring. $8, ages 12 and under $4; Nov.-Mar. $5/$2. Children under 36 months or 38 in. not admitted.)*

🎵📷 ENTERTAINMENT AND NIGHTLIFE

For the latest on Miami entertainment, the "Living Today," "Lively Arts," and F "Weekend" sections of the *Miami Herald* are logical places to start. Weekly *Oceandrive,* the *New Times, Street,* and the *Sun Post* list local happenings. *TWN* and *Miamigo* are the major gay papers. **Performing Arts and Community Education (PACE)** manages more than 400 concerts each year (jazz, rock, soul, dixieland, reggae, salsa, and bluegrass); most are free. **Carnaval Miami,** the nation's largest Hispanic festival, fills 23 blocks of Calle Ocho in early Mar. with salsa, music, and the world's longest conga line.

Nightlife in the Art Deco district of South Miami Beach starts late (usually after midnight) and continues until well after sunrise. Gawk at models and stars while eating dinner at one of Ocean Blvd.'s open cafes or bars, then head down to Washington Ave., between 6th and 7th St., for some serious fun. Many clubs charge covers only after midnight. Most clubs have dress codes, and everyone dresses to the nines. **Bash,** 655 Washington Ave., stands out among its neighbors; the large indoor dance floor grooves to house and progressive while the courtyard in back jams to worldbeat. *(☎538-2274. Open Th-Su 10pm-5am. Fashion shows on Th; Brazilian parties on F. Cover $10 Th, $20 Sa-Su; 21+.)* **The Tavern,** 3416 Main Hwy., is one of the most popular University of Miami watering holes. Enjoy a longneck for $1.75 on Tu or a Bud for $1.25 on Su. *(☎447-3884. Open M-F 3pm-3am, Sa-Su 1pm-3am. No cover; 21+.)* The beautiful and famous go to **Liquid,** 1439 Washington Ave., owned by Madonna chum Ingrid Casares and Madonna brother Michael Ciccione. (☎532-9154. Open 10pm-5am. Cover $20; 21+.) Arrive before midnight to dodge the cover and long lines at the **Groove Jet**, 323 23rd St. The front room of this massive hall plays trance, dance, and house; the back room churns out alternative rock. (☎532-2002. Open Th-Su 11pm-5am. Cover $10 after midnight; 21+.)

EVERGLADES ☎941

Encompassing the entire tip of Florida and spearing into Florida Bay, **Everglades National Park** spans 1.6 million acres of one of the world's most unique and fragile ecosystems. Vast prairies of sawgrass spike through broad expanses of shallow water, creating the famed "river of grass," while tangled mazes of mangrove swamps wind up the western coast. To the south, delicate coral reefs lie below the shimmering blue waters of the bay. A host of species found nowhere else in the world inhabits these lands and waters: American alligators, dolphins, sea turtles, and various birds and fishes, as well as the endangered Florida panther, Florida manatee, and American crocodile.

◪ PRACTICAL INFORMATION. Summer visitors can expect to get eaten alive by swarming mosquitoes. The best time to visit is winter or spring, when heat, humidity, storms, and bugs are at a minimum and wildlife congregate in shrinking pools of evaporating water. Whenever you go, be sure to bring mosquito repellent.

There are two primary roads into the park. Guarding the eastern section, the **Ernest Coe Visitors Center**, 40001 Rte. 9336, sits just inside the park (☎305-242-7700; open daily 8am-5pm). Take Rte. 9336 from U.S. 1 at Florida City; Everglades Park signs point the way. Rte. 9336 also cuts 40 mi. through the park past campgrounds, trailheads, and canoe waterways to the **Flamingo Visitors Center** (☎695-2945, open daily 9am-5pm; winter 7:30am-5pm) and the heavily developed Flamingo Outpost Resort. At the northern end of the park off U.S. 41 (Tamiami Trail), the **Shark Valley Visitors Center** provides access to a 15 mi. loop through sawgrass swamp that can be seen by foot, bike, or a 2hr. tram. (Open daily 8:30am-5pm.) **Shark Valley** is an ideal site for those who want a taste of the freshwater ecosystem, but can't commit to delving too far into the park. (☎305-221-8455. Open daily 8:30am-6pm. Tram tours in summer daily 9:30am, 11am, 1, and 3pm; Dec.-Apr. daily every hr. 9am-4pm; $10, seniors $9, under 12 $5.50. Reservations recommended. Wheelchair access available with reservations. Bike rental daily 8:30am-3pm; $4.25 per hr., includes helmets.) The **Gulf Coast Visitors Center**, 800 Copeland Ave. S, in Everglades City in the northwestern end of the park, provides access to the western coastline and the vast river network throughout the park (☎695-3311; open 8:30am-5pm in summer, extended hours in winter). **Emergency: Park headquarters** (☎305-247-7272). **Entrance fee for six days:** Ernest Coe: $10 per car, $5 bike- or walk-in; Shark Valley: $8 per car, $4 bike- or walk-in; Gulf Coast: free.

◪ ACCOMMODATIONS. Outside the eastern entrance to the park, **Florida City** offers some cheap options along U.S. 1. The only option for lodging inside the park, the **Flamingo Lodge**, 1 Flamingo Lodge Hwy., has large rooms with A/C, TV, private baths, pool, and a great bay view. Complimentary continental breakfast served each morning in the summer. (☎695-3101 or 800-600-3813. Singles and doubles $65; Nov.-Dec. and Apr. $79; Jan.-Mar. $95.) **Everglades International Hostel**, 20 SW 2nd Ave., is located off Palm Drive near the end of the Florida turnpike. You will soon find yourself at home at this 30s boarding house, adorned with a gazebo, gumbo limbo trees, a freshwater pool, tile mosaic floors, and 47 beds in the heart of Redlands Agricultural Community 10 mi. from the Everglades. (☎305-248-1122 or 800-372-3874. Canoes $20 per day; bikes $5 per day. Canoe tours available for $10. Linen $2. Dorms $12, $15 with A/C; private room $30, with A/C $40.) A few **campgrounds** line Rte. 9336; all have drinking water, grills, dump sites, and restrooms, but none have RV hookups. (☎800-365-2267. Reservations required Nov.-Apr. Sites free in summer; in winter $14.) **Backcountry camping** inside the park is accessible primarily by boat (see **Sights**, below). The required **permits** are available on a first come, first served basis at the Flamingo and Gulf Coast visitors centers ($10 for 1-6 people Dec.-Apr.; free May-Nov.). Applications must be made in person at earliest a day before starting.

Near the northwest entrance, motels, RV parks, and campgrounds scatter around Everglades City. The **Barron River Villa, Marina, and RV Park** offers 67 RV sites, 29 on the river, and precious motel rooms with TV and A/C. (☎695-3331 or 800-535-4961. RV sites: full hook-up $18, on the river $20; Oct.-Apr. $28/$34. Motel: rooms $41; Sept.-Dec. $49; Jan.-Apr. $57.) Most of **Collier-Seminole State Park,** 20200 Tamiami Trail E, is a wilderness preserve in a mangrove swamp, home to several of Florida's most endangered species. (☎394-3397. Park open 8am-sunset. Parking $3.25. 137 sites with water $16, off-season $8; electricity $2.)

◘ **FOOD.** If you're staying at the hostel, roll out of bed in the morning and cross the street for some eggs ($3.50) at **Rosita's,** 199 W. Palm Dr. Cheap but tasty Mexican entrees range $3.50-7.50 (☎246-3114; open daily 8:30am-9pm). Up Rte. 997 in Homestead, the **Main St. Cafe,** 128 N. Krome Ave., guarantees a good time when the community comes together for open mic nights. Try one of their gourmet smoothies for $2-4 or the all-you-can-eat soup & salad bar for $8. (☎245-7575. Open M-W 10am-5pm, Th-Sa 10am-midnight. Th teen open mic 8-11pm; F open mic 7pm-midnight; Sa folk country & acoustic rock 7pm-midnight.)

◉ **SIGHTS.** The park is positively swamped with fishing, hiking, canoeing, biking, and wilderness observation opportunities. *Forget swimming; alligators, sharks, and barracuda patrol the waters.* From Nov. through Apr., the park sponsors amphitheater programs, canoe trips, and ranger-guided Slough Slogs (swamp tours). Numerous trailheads lie off Rte. 9336; the ½ mi. **Mahogany Hammock Trail** passes the largest mahogany tree in the US, and the ¼ mi. **Pahayokee Overlook Trail** leads to a broad vista of grasslands and water. But if you really want to experience the Everglades, start paddling. The 99 mi. **Wilderness Waterway** winds its way from the northwest entrance to the Flamingo station in the far south. Adventurous camping spots along the journey include chickees (wooden platforms elevated above mangrove swamps), beaches, and groundsites. *(Free in summer; $10 in winter.)*

The **Everglades National Park Boat Tours** at the Gulf Coast Visitors Center rents canoes. *(☎695-2591 or 800-445-7724. $20 per day.)* The same company offers two boat tours into the park. Naturalists on the **Ten Thousand Island Cruise** lead the relaxing 1½hr. jaunt through the heart of the coastal "10,000 islands," and into the Gulf of Mexico, with the occasional manatee, bottle-nosed dolphin and bald eagle sighting. The **Mangrove Wilderness Cruise** guides passengers inland up Turner River for 2½hr., exploring the swampy mangrove forests of the southern Everglades. *(Tours daily, every ½hr. 9am-5pm; $16, ages 6-12 $8. Wheelchair accessible.)* Both cruises leave from the Gulf Coast visitors center. Shorter canoe trails wind from Rte. 9336; the **Hell's Bay Canoe Trail** threads through mangrove swamps past primitive campsites like Pearl Bay. Canoes are also available at the **Flamingo Marina.** *(☎695-3101 or 800-600-3813. $22 for 4hrs., $32 per day; $40 deposit.)*

No one ever saw little Ed Leedskalnin build his **Coral Castle** in Homestead, leading many to believe he possessed supernatural powers. Ed said he merely understood the secrets behind the ancient Egyptian pyramids, and applied them to carve his colossal coral stone palace. *(28655 South Dixie Hwy, Homestead. ☎305-248-6344. Open M-Th 9am-6pm, F-Su 9am-7pm. $7.75, seniors $6.50, ages 7-12 $5.)* View gators, crocs and snakes at the ◙**Everglades Alligator Farm,** 4 mi. south of Palm Dr. Thousands of gators, from little hatchlings clambering for sun to 18-footers clambering for...um...you, grace the premises. *(40351 SW 192 Ave. ☎305-247-2628 or 800-644-9711. Open daily 9am-6pm. $9, ages 4-10 $5. Airboat rides & wildlife shows $14.50/$8.)*

FLORIDA

MAIL CALL After a fire destroyed the local post office in 1953, Ochopee, FL, town leaders searched for a new location. Postmaster Sidney Brown quickly chose a small shack, originally an irrigation pipe shed for a tomato farm; ever since, the country's smallest post office has serviced a three-county area in a room barely big enough for two. Cram into the Ochopee mail room on U.S. 41 (Tamiami Trail) between the Gulf Coast and Shark Valley entrances to Everglades National Park.

FLORIDA KEYS

Intense popularity has transformed this long-time haven for pirates, smugglers, and treasure hunters into supreme beach vacationland. Whether smothered in tourists or outcasts, the Keys retain an "anything goes" mentality. When former Key West mayor Tony Tarracino arrived here decades ago, he did a quick inventory of bars and strip clubs, and concluded that he'd reached heaven (see p. 455). If this sounds more like hell, take a dive. Gardens of coral six miles off the coast grant relative solitude to scuba divers and snorkelers, as long as they don't mind millions of colorful fish, and form a 100-yard wide barrier reef between Key Largo and Key West. Don't believe the hype; sharks are scarce here.

🛈 PRACTICAL INFORMATION

The **Overseas Hwy. (U.S. 1)** bridges the divide between the Keys and the southern tip of Florida, stitching the islands together. **Mile markers** section the highway and replace street addresses. The first marker, Mi. 126 in Florida City, begins the long countdown to zero in Key West. **Greyhound** runs to the Keys from Miami ($32), stopping in Homestead, Key Largo, Marathon, Big Pine Key, and Key West. Most bus drivers can be convinced to stop at mile markers along the side of the road. Tiny Greyhound signs along the highway indicate bus stops (usually hotels), where you can buy tickets or call the Greyhound **info line** on the red phones provided. **Biking** along U.S. 1 is treacherous due to fast cars and narrow shoulders; instead of riding, bring your bike on the bus.

KEY LARGO   ☎ 305

Past the thick swamps and crocodile marshland of the Everglades, Key Largo opens the door to Caribbean-esque islands. With 120-foot visibility, the clear waters off Key Largo reveal shimmering coral reefs inhabited by darting, exotically colorful fish. Twenty feet down, an underwater statue of Jesus (meant to symbolize peace for mankind) blesses all those who explore the depths. Glass-bottom boats and fishing offer recreation without total submersion, though just plain swimming is a treat. Key Largo's exotic daytime adventures overcome the lack of nightlife; you will be so worn out, you won't care.

🛈 **PRACTICAL INFORMATION. Greyhound** (☎296-9072), Mi. 102 at the Howard Johnson, goes to Miami (3 per day, 1¾hr., $12.50-14.50) and Key West (4 per day, 3 hr., $26-29). Station open daily 8am-6pm. **Mom's Taxi:** ☎852-6000. **Key Largo Chamber of Commerce/Florida Keys Visitors Center:** 106000 U.S. 1, Mi. 106 (☎451-1414; open daily 9am-6pm). **The Key Largo Tourist and Reservation Center:** 103360 U.S. 1, Mi. 103 (☎453-0066; open M-Sa 9am-8pm, Su 10am-6pm). **Post Office:** 100100 U.S. 1, Mi. 100 (☎451-3155; open M-F 8am-4:30pm). **ZIP code:** 33037. **Area code:** 305.

🏠 **ACCOMMODATIONS. Ed and Ellen's Lodgings,** 103365 U.S. 1, Mi. 103.4, offers clean, spacious rooms with cable TV, A/C, and kitchenettes as well as help with diving or snorkeling reservations. (☎451-9949 or 888-333-5536. Doubles $49-79; off-season $39-49; $10 per additional person. Rates may vary on weekends, holidays, special events, and lobster season.) The waterside **Hungry Pelican,** Mi. 99½, boasts beautiful bougainvillea vines, tropical birds in the trees, and tidy, cozy rooms with double beds, fridges, and cable. Free use of paddle boats, canoes, and hammocks afford amazing sunset views. Complimentary continental breakfast is available every morning. (☎451-3576. Rooms $50-115; $10 per additional person.) Reservations are recommended for the popular **John Pennekamp State Park Campground** (see **Sights,** below); the 47 sites are clean, convenient, and well worth the effort required to obtain them. (☎451-1202. $24, with electricity $26.) Straight out of a Jimmy Buffet fantasy, **King's Kamp,** 103620 U.S. 1, Mi. 103½, offers easy water access and beautiful sites. (☎451-0010. Water, electricity. Tent sites $20, RV $30; $10 extra for boat.)

⌐⌐ **FOOD.** Follow your meal from the boat to the plate at **Calypso's,** 1 Seagate Blvd. on the marina across from Key Largo Fisheries. The coconut shrimp ($6) is a sweet, fried delight. (☎451-0600. Open M and W-Th noon-10pm, F-Sa noon-11pm.) The **Italian Fisherman,** Mi. 104, has fine food and a breathtaking view of Florida Bay. Some scenes from *Key Largo* were allegedly shot in this once-illegal casino. (☎451-4471. Open daily 11:30am-10pm. Lunch $5-10, dinner $7-17, $8 early bird special daily 4-6pm.) **Alabama Jack's,** 58000 Card Sound Rd., between Homestead and Key Largo, rocks the southern Florida wetlands with live country music Sa 2-5pm and Su 2-7pm. It is probably the southernmost place to enjoy "hoppin' john," a southern delight of black-eyed peas, rice and ham. (☎248-8741. Open M-F 11am-7pm, Sa-Su 11am-7:30pm.)

◙ **SIGHTS.** The nation's first underwater sanctuary, Key Largo's **John Pennekamp State Park,** Mi. 102½, 60 mi. from Miami, safeguards a 25 mi. stretch of the 120 sq. mi. coral reef that runs the length of the Florida Keys. (☎451-1202. Admission $4 per vehicle, $2 per vehicle with a single occupant, $1 walk- or bike-in; 50¢ per additional person on all fees.) The park's **visitors center,** about ¼ mi. past the entrance gate, provides maps of the reefs, info on boat and snorkeling tours, three aquariums, and films on the park. To see the reefs, visitors must take a boat or rent their own. (☎451-9570. Open daily 8am-5pm. 19 ft. motor boat $28 per hr. Deposit required. Call ☎451-6325 for reservations.) **Scuba trips** from the visitors center run at 9:30am and 1:30pm. (☎451-6322. $37 per person for a two-tank dive. Deposit required.) A **snorkeling tour** also allows you to partake of the underwater quiet. (☎451-1621. 2½hr. total, 1½hr. water time. Tours 9am, noon, and 3pm. $25, under 18 $20. Equipment $5. Deposit required.) For sailing, ask about the half-day sailing/snorkeling combo trip, just a bit more costly than snorkeling alone. (☎451-1621. 1½hr. water time. Tours 9am and 1:30pm. $32, under 18 $27. Deposit required.) **Glass Bottom Boat Tours,** leaving from the park shore at Mi. 102.5, provide a crystal clear view of the reefs without wetting your feet. (☎451-1621. 2½hr. Tours 9:15am, 12:15, and 3pm. $18, under 12 $10; discounts at the visitors center.)

KEY WEST   ☎305

Just 90 miles from Cuba, this is the end of the road. Key West boasts the southernmost point and perhaps the most laid-back attitude in the entire continental US. The island is cooler than mainland Florida in summer and far warmer in winter; the seeker of paradise in the States can do no better. Key West's tantalizing temperatures once drew writers Ernest Hemingway, Tennessee Williams, Elizabeth Bishop, and the chilly Robert Frost. Other colorful characters such as railroad magnate Henry Flagler and President Harry S. Truman appreciated the mystique of this island. Today, an easygoing diversity lures a new generation of artists, recluses, pirates, and eccentrics, along with a swinging gay population. Lacking stress, closing time, and indoor heat, the "Conch Republic" half-seriously jokes of its own independence. When it's full, it overflows; nightlife goes 24 hours as thousands of Parrotheads search for Margaritaville.

※⁊ **ORIENTATION AND PRACTICAL INFORMATION**

Key West lies at the end of U.S. 1, 155 mi. southwest of Miami (3-3½hr.). Divided into two sectors, the eastern part of the island, known as **New Town,** harbors tract houses, chain motels, shopping malls, and the airport. Beautiful old conch houses fill **Old Town,** west of White St. **Duval St.** is the main north-south thoroughfare in Old Town; **Truman Ave.**(U.S. 1) is a major east-west route.

Buses: Greyhound, 3535 S. Roosevelt Blvd. (☎296-9072), at the airport. To: Miami (4½hr., 3 per day, $32-36). Open daily 8am-6pm.

Public Transit: Key West Port and Transit Authority (☎292-8161), City Hall. Clockwise ("Old Town") and counterclockwise ("Mallory Sq. Rte.") routes. Service daily 7am-10:30pm, about every 1½hr. Fare 75¢, students and seniors 35¢.

Taxis: Keys Taxi, ☎296-6666.

Bikes/Mopeds: Keys Moped & Scooter, 523 Truman Ave. (☎294-0399). Open daily 9am-6pm. Bikes $4 per half-day, $30 per week. Mopeds $18 per 9am-5pm, $23 per 24hr.

Visitor Info: Key West Welcome Center, 3840 N. Roosevelt Blvd. (☎296-4444 or 800-284-4482), a private reservation service just north of the intersection of U.S. 1 and Roosevelt Blvd. Open M-Sa 9am-7:30pm, Su 9am-6pm. **Key West Chamber of Commerce,** 402 Wall St. (☎294-2587 or 800-527-8539), in old Mallory Sq. Open M-F 8:30am-6:30pm, Sa-Su 8:30am-6pm. **The Key West Business Guild Gay and Lesbian Information Center,** 728 Duval St. (☎294-4603). Open M-F 9am-5pm.

Hotlines: Help Line, ☎296-4357. 24hr.

Internet Access: Sippin', 424 Eaton St. (☎293-0555), off Duval. $10 per hr. Open daily 7am-10pm.

Post Office: 400 Whitehead St. (☎294-2557), 1 block west of Duval at Eaton. Open M-F 8:30am-5pm, Sa 9:30am-noon. **ZIP code:** 33040. **Area code:** 305.

▟ ACCOMMODATIONS

Key West is packed virtually year-round, particularly from Jan. through Mar., so reserve rooms far in advance. In **Old Key West,** the beautiful, 19th-century clapboard houses capture the charming flavor of the Keys. Some of the guest houses in the Old Town are for gay men exclusively. *Do not park overnight on the bridges—*this is illegal and dangerous.

Key West Hostel (HI-AYH), 718 South St. (☎296-5719), at Sea Shell Motel in Old Key West, 3 blocks east of Duval St. Rooms with 4-8 beds, shared bath. Reception 24hr. Common room with TV, Internet access. Free parking and linens. Key deposit $5. Lockers 25-75¢. Bike rentals $8 per 24hr. Reservations essential Dec-Mar. Call to check availability or for late arrival. Dorms $18.50, non-members $21.50.

Caribbean House, 226 Petronia St. (☎296-1600 or 800-543-4518), at Thomas St. in Bahama Village. Festive Caribbean-style rooms with A/C, cable TV, free local calls, and fridge. Comfy double beds. Free continental breakfast. Rooms from $49, in winter $69; cottages $69/$89. Reservations not accepted for cottages.

Wicker Guesthouse, 913 Duval St. (☎296-4275 or 800-880-4275). Excellent location on the main drag. Individually decorated rooms have pastel decor, private baths, A/C and cable TV; most have kitchenettes. Kitchen, pool access, and free parking. No telephones in rooms. Breakfast included. Rooms $85-98; late Dec. to May $125-135. Reservations suggested; ask for summer specials.

Eden House, 1015 Fleming St. (☎296-6868 or 800-533-5397), just 5 short blocks from downtown. Bright, clean, 20s Floridian Deco hotel with friendly staff. Cool rooms with private or shared bath, some with balconies. Pool, jacuzzi, hammock/swinging bench area and kitchens. Bike rentals $10 per day. Join other guests for free happy hour daily 4-5pm. Rooms with shared bath $105; off-season $80.

Boyd's Campground, 6401 Maloney Ave. (☎294-1465), at Mi. 5. Take a left off U.S. 1 onto Macdonald Ave., which becomes Maloney. 12 acres on the ocean. Full facilities, including showers. $34-57; in winter $39-68; $8 per additional person. Waterfront sites $6-14 extra. Water and electricity $10 extra, full hook-up $15 extra.

◑⊠ FOOD AND NIGHTLIFE

Expensive restaurants and B&Bs line festive **Duval St.** Side streets offer lower prices and fewer crowds. Hemingway once drank beer and refereed boxing at ▨**Blue Heaven,** 729 Thomas St., one block from the Caribbean House. Blue Heaven serves healthy breakfasts ($2-9), mostly vegetarian lunches ($2.50-10), and heavenly dinners ($9-19) that include plantains, corn bread, and fresh veggies—generally regarded as the best food in town. (☎296-8666. Open M-Sa 8am-3pm and 6-10:30pm, Su 8am-1pm and 6-10:30pm.) **Garden Cafe,** 310 Duval St., markets ½-lb. (cheese)burgers in an outdoor paradise for $5.75. Monster portabello and veggie burgers are $6.25. (☎294-2991. Open M-F 10am-1am, Sa-Su 10am-2am.) The best

Cuban food on the island can be found at **El Siboney,** 900 Catherine St., where $7 buys a lot of grub. (☎296-4184. Open M-Sa 11am-9:30pm.)

The free *Island News* and *Paradise, this week,* found in local restaurants and bars, list dining spots, music, and clubs; *Celebrate!* covers the gay and lesbian community. Nightlife in Key West revs up at 11pm and winds down very late. **Capt. Tony's Saloon,** 428 Greene St., the oldest bar in Key West and reputedly one of "Papa" Hemingway and Tennessee Williams' preferred watering holes, has been chugging away since the early 30s. Bras and business cards festoon the ceiling. Tony Tarracino, the 83-year-old owner, enters through a secret door on weekends (see box, below). (☎294-1838. Open M-Sa 10am-2am, Su noon-2am. Live entertainment daily and nightly.) An unabashed meat market under the stars, **Rick's,** 202 Duval St., boasts well-placed body shots and $7 all-you-can-drink nights W and Th. (☎296-4890. Open M-Sa 11am-4am, Su noon-4am. Happy hour daily 3-6pm features $1.75 longneck Bud.) For a real party, stop by **Sloppy Joe's,** 201 Duval St., undoubtedly Hemingway's favorite hangout. Grab a table and the *Sloppy Joe's News* to learn the latest on "Papa" look-alike contests, get entertainment and announcements, and read up on the bar's history. (☎294-5717. Open M-Sa 9am-4am, Su noon-4am.) Waste away again in **Margaritaville,** on Duval St., the Jimmy Buffet-inspired bar that specializes in, that's right, margaritas. The "cheeseburger in paradise" will tide you over for only $7. (☎296-3070. Open daily 11am-2am.) Most gay clubs line Duval St. south of Fleming Ave; **801 Bourbon,** 801 Duval St., is very popular. (☎294-4737. Open daily 11am-4am.) Key West nightlife reaches its annual exultant high during **Fantasy Fest** (☎296-1817; the third week of Oct.).

📀 SIGHTS

Seeing Key West by bike or moped is more convenient and comfortable than driving; the latest, safer transport craze is small electric cars. *(☎295-6686. $58 for a 2hr. minimum.)* The **Conch Tour Train,** a fascinating 1½hr. narrated ride through Old Town, leaves from Mallory Sq. at 3840 N. or from Roosevelt Blvd., next to the Quality Inn. *(☎294-5161. Runs daily 9am-4:30pm. $18, ages 4-12 $9.)* **Old Town Trolley** runs a similar tour 9am-5:30pm, but you can get on and off throughout the day at 14 stops. *(☎296-6688. Full tour 1½hr. $18, ages 4-12 $9.)* The **glass-bottomed boat** *Fireball* cruises to the reefs and back at noon, 2, and 6pm. *(☎296-6293. 2-2½hr. Tickets $20, at sunset $25, ages 5-12 $10/$12.50.)*

"Papa" wrote *For Whom the Bell Tolls* and *The Snows of Kilimanjaro* at the **Ernest Hemingway Home,** off Olivia St. Take a tour, or traipse through on your own among 50 descendants of Hemingway's cat, half of which have extra toes. *(907 Whitehead St. ☎294-1136. Open daily 9am-5pm. $8, ages 6-12 $5.)* The **Harry S. Truman Lit-**

"BRAINS DON'T MEAN SHIT" This brief profundity sums up the philosophy of Captain Tony Tarracino, gun runner, mercenary, casino owner, and one-time mayor of Key West. "All you need in this life is a tremendous sex drive and a great ego," proclaimed the Captain, who escaped to Key West over 40 years ago while evading the New Jersey bookies he cheated, having used a battered TV set to get racing results before they came over the wire. Tarracino arrived to find an island populated by bar-hoppers, petty criminals, and other deviants. In this setting, he thrived. Tony attempted to organize his local popularity into a political campaign, and after four unsuccessful bids, he was finally voted mayor in 1989, on the slogan, "Fighting for your future: what's left of it." Although he wasn't re-elected, Tarracino is certain that history will exonerate him. "I'll be remembered," he vows. With his own bar, countless t-shirts that bear his image, and even a feature film about his life, this is no idle assertion. But for now, Tony T. isn't going anywhere—he even mocks his own mortality. "I know every stripper in this town," he boasts. "When I'm dead, I've asked them all to come to my casket and stand over it. If I don't wake up then, put me in the ground."

FLORIDA

tle **White House Museum** sits in the restored vacation home of the President's get-away. *(111 Front St. ☎294-9911. Open daily 9am-5pm. $8, children $4. Admission includes tour.)* The **Audubon House** shelters fine antiques and a collection of original engravings by naturalist John James Audubon. *(205 Whitehead St. ☎294-2116. Open daily 9:30am-5pm. $8, students $5, seniors $7.50, ages 6-12 $3.50.)* Down Whitehead St., past Hemingway House, you'll come to the **southernmost point in the continental US** at the nearby **Southernmost Beach.** A small, conical monument and a few conch shell hawkers mark the spot, along with some hustlers who might offer to take your picture; they may not give your camera back until you pay them. **Mel Fisher's Maritime Heritage Society Museum** glitters with gold and quite a few busts of M.F., who uncovered the biggest sunken treasure ever. Feast your eyes on the $400 million booty of the shipwrecked *Atocha*, a 17th-century Spanish galleon. An illuminating film is included in the entrance fee. *(200 Greene St. ☎294-2633. Open daily 9:30am-5pm; last film 4:30pm. $6.50, ages 6-12 $2, students $4.)*

An old pier at **Monroe County Beach,** off Atlantic Ave., allows water access past the weed line, and the **Old US Naval Air Station** has deep-water swimming on **Truman Beach** ($1). Sunset lovers will enjoy the view from **Mallory Sq. Dock;** there, street entertainers (including Tomas the incredible living statue) and hawkers of tacky wares work the crowd, while boats showcase during the daily **Sunset Celebration.** The crowd cheers when the sun finally slips into the Gulf. Explore the old hanging tree and learn the story of Robert, the doll possessed by a spirit, on the **Ghost Tours.** *(☎294-9255. $18, children $10. Reservations required, call for hours.)*

GULF COAST

TAMPA   ☎813

Even with year-round warm weather and perfect beaches, Tampa has managed to avoid the plastic pink flamingos that plague its Atlantic Coast counterparts. One of the nation's fastest growing cities and largest ports, with booming financial, industrial, and artistic communities, its survival does not hinge on tourism. With the exception of Ybor City, its large Cuban neighborhood, few facets of Tampa deviate from the strictly functional. This pragmatism strips the city of the spunk endemic to Miami, but also makes Tampa a less commercial, more peaceful vacation spot.

▐ GETTING THERE AND GETTING AROUND

You can reach Tampa on I-75 from the north or I-4 from the east.

Airport: Tampa International (☎870-8700), 5 mi. west of downtown. HARTline bus #30 runs between the airport and downtown Tampa.

Amtrak: 601 Nebraska Ave. (☎221-7600), at the end of Zack St., 2 blocks north of Kennedy St. Ticket office open daily 5:30am-10:45pm. To: Miami (5hr., 1 per day, $32) and New Orleans (20hr., 3 per week, $78). 2 buses per day to Orlando if you are connecting there ($23).

Greyhound: 610 E. Polk St. (☎229-2174). To: Atlanta (11-14hr., 8 per day, $62.50), Orlando (1-3hr., 7 per day, $17.50), and Miami (7-10hr, 7 per day, $37). Open daily 5am-midnight.

Public Transit: Hillsborough Area Regional Transit (HARTline) (☎254-4278). $1.50, seniors and ages 5-17 55¢ (exact change only). The **Tampa Town Ferry** (☎223-1522) runs between the Florida Aquarium and Lowry Park Zoo.

✴▐ ORIENTATION AND PRACTICAL INFORMATION

Tampa wraps around Hillsborough Bay and sprawls north. **Nebraska Ave.** parallels I-275 as the main north-south route; **Kennedy Blvd., Columbus St.** and **Busch Blvd.** are main east-west arteries. With some exceptions, numbered streets run north-south and numbered avenues run east-west. **Ybor City**, Tampa's Latin Quarter and nocturnal playland, is bounded roughly by Nuccio Pkwy. on the north, 22nd St. on the south, Palm St. on the east, and 5th St. on the west. *Be careful not to stray outside these parameters, since the area can be dangerous.*

Visitor Info: Tampa/Hillsborough Convention and Visitors Association, 111 Madison St. (☎223-1111 or 800-826-8358), at Ashley Dr. Open M-Sa 9am-5pm.

Hotlines: Crisis Hotline, ☎234-1234. **Helpline**, ☎251-4000.

Post Office: 401 S Florida Ave. (☎800-725-2161). Open 8am-5pm. **ZIP code:** 33601. **Area code:** 813.

ACCOMMODATIONS

Gram's Place Bed & Breakfast, 3109 N. Ola Ave. (☎221-0596). From I-275, take Martin Luther King Blvd. west to Ola Ave., and then a left on Ola. Named for singer/songwriter Gram Parsons, this eclectic haven features a jacuzzi, lush courtyard, cable TV, BYOB outside bar, and continental breakfast. Recording studio available for guests in the basement. A smaller room is set aside as a hostel. B&B rooms $50-80; dorm $15-25; prices depend on availability.

Villager Lodge, 3110 W. Hillborough Ave. (☎876-8673), 5 mi from the airport at Exit 30 off I-275. 33 small rooms with A/C, cable, microfridge, and pool access. Singles $39-45; doubles $43-48; $5 per additional person.

Motel 6, 333 E. Fowler Ave. (☎932-4948), off I-275 Exit 34 near Busch Gardens. Big, newly renovated rooms 30 mi. from the beach on the northern outskirts of Tampa. Free local calls, cable, A/C, and pool. 1 adult $36-44; 2nd adult $4.

Super 8 Motel, 321 E. Fletcher Ave. (☎933-4545), 3 mi. from Busch Gardens in northwest Tampa; from I-275, take Exit 35 west. Clean rooms, some with fridge and stove. Pool and cable. Coffee and doughnuts each morning. Singles Sa-Su $39, M-F $37; doubles $46; king size suites $55; slightly more Jan.-Mar. Students with ID 10% discount.

Garden View Motel, 2500 E. Busch Blvd (☎933-3958), 4 blocks from Busch Gardens. A/C, cable, pool, and continental breakfast. Discount tickets to Busch Gardens sold at front desk. Singles $30-35; doubles $40-50. Students with ID 10% discount.

FOOD

Tampa is blessed with many unique, inexpensive restaurants. Heading that list is **Skipper's Smokehouse**, 910 Skipper Rd., off Nebraska Ave., a giant complex of thatched huts, wreckage, and wood planks in the northern outskirts of town. After downing a tender fried alligator tail sandwich ($5.50) and conch chowder ($2.50), walk to the adjacent "Skipper Dome" and groove to live zydeco, reggae or worldbeat tunes—a Tampa must-see. (☎971-0666. Restaurant and bar open Tu 11am-10pm, W-F 11am-11pm, Sa noon-11pm, Su 1-10pm. Happy hour Th-F 4-8pm. Cover varies.) The original hand-rubbed marinade behind **Kojak's House of Ribs**, 2808 Gandy Blvd., tenderly reminds you that you're still in the South. (☎837-3774. Open Tu-Th 11am-9:30pm, F-Sa 11am-10pm, Su 4pm-9pm. Ribs with two sides $8.50.) Tampa's gulf shore heritage is tasted at **Cafe Creole**, 1330 E. 9th Ave. a classy Ybor City establishment known for oysters and jambalaya. (☎247-6283. Open M-Th 11:30am-10pm, F 11:30am-11:30pm, Sa 5-11:30pm. Live jazz Th-Sa night. Happy hour M-F 4-7pm. Entrees $6-18.)

SIGHTS

Tampa blossomed only after the success of Ybor City, a planned community once known as the cigar capital of the world. Early 20th-century stogie manufacturer Vincent Martínez Ybor employed a wide array of immigrants, marking the area with a rich and varied ethnic heritage. The **Ybor City State Museum** details the rise and decline of the neighborhood's tobacco empire and the workers behind it. Photographs examine the art and culture of the hand-rolled cigar. *(1818 9th*

FLORIDA

Ave. ☎247-6323. Open daily 9am-5pm. Neighborhood walking tours Sa 10:30. $2, 6 and under free.) A 1½hr. **Ybor City Ghostwalk** relates haunting tales about the city's history. The tour leaves from **Joffrey's Coffee Co.** *(1616 E. 7th Ave. ☎242-9255. Th-Sa 7pm, Su 4pm. Adults $11 in advance, $12.50 on site; children $7.50. Advance reservations only.)* Buses #8, 3, and 46 run to Ybor City from downtown. The Tampa-Ybor Trolley runs during lunchtime between the two areas; schedules are available at the visitors center. *(Free.)*

The **Florida Aquarium** invites you to mash your face to the glass for a tête-á-tête with fish from Florida's various lagoons. Snakes, tarantulas and scorpions star in the wildly creepy "Frights of the Forest" exhibit. *(701 Channelside Dr. ☎273-4000. Open daily 9:30am-5pm. $13, seniors $12, ages 3-12 $8.)* At the **Henry B. Plant Museum,** in a wing of University of Tampa's Plant Hall, the exhibits include Victorian furniture and Wedgewood pottery but pale in comparison to the gaudy museum architecture, with lavish domes, minarets, and buttressed arches. *(401 W. Kennedy Blvd. ☎254-1891. Open Tu-Sa 10am-4pm, Su noon-4pm. $5, under 12 $2. Tours at 1:30pm.)* Downtown, the **Tampa Museum of Art** houses a noted collection of ancient Greek and Roman works as well as a series of changing, often family-oriented exhibits. *(600 N. Ashley Dr. ☎274-8130. Open Tu-W and F-Sa 10am-5pm, Th 10am-8pm, Su 1-5pm. Tours Th 5-8pm, Sa 10am-noon. Admission $5, seniors $4, ages 6-18 $3. Free Su and W 5-9pm.)*

It's never Miller time at **Busch Gardens,** Anheuser-Busch's addition to the world of Floridian theme parks. Eight mi. northeast of the city, Busch Gardens looms as Tampa's biggest tourist draw, but efficient shuttles minimize parking difficulties. The latest addition to the thrill-rides, Gwazi, flaunts a dueling set of roller coasters that approach 100 mph. You won't mind the workload of the "Budweiser Beer School" at the Anheuser Busch Hospitality House. Beermaster certificates and free samples follow a primer on the king of beers. *(Shows at 12:45, 1:45, 2:25, 3:45, and 4:45pm. Free.)* Over 2500 animals roam, fly, slither and swim through the African-themed zoo areas; the Edge of Africa safari experience remains among the park's most popular. *(Busch Gardens: E. 3000 Busch Blvd. ☎987-5082. Open daily 9:30am-7pm. $46, children age 3-9 $37. Parking $6.)* You can cool off at **Adventure Island,** a 13-acre water park about ½ mi. north of Busch Gardens. *(10001 Malcolm McKinley Dr. ☎987-5660. Open June 1 to Aug. 5 M-Th 9am-7pm, F-Su 9am-8pm. $25, ages 3-19 $23. Parking $4.)*

🎵 🎭 ENTERTAINMENT AND NIGHTLIFE

Brief yourself on city entertainment with the free *Tampa Weekend, Weekly Planet,* or *Stonewall,* found in local restaurants, bars, and streetcorners. On Jan. 26, 2001, the **Jose Gasparilla** (☎358-8070), a fully-rigged pirate ship loaded with hundreds of exuberant "pirates," will invade Tampa, kicking off a month of parades and festivals. The **Gasparilla Sidewalk Art Festival,** Mar. 3-4, 2001 (☎876-1747), awaits the congregation of talent from the world over. Thousands pack Ybor City every Oct. for **"Guavaween"** (☎621-7121), a Latin-style Halloween celebration.

With over 35 clubs and bars in a condensed area, **Ybor City** really does offer it all. Most nighttime hangouts are located on the well-lit 7th Ave.; use caution when walking down side streets. National blues, jazz, and reggae acts jam every weekend at the **Blues Ship Cafe,** 1910 E 7th Ave. (☎248-6097. Restaurant and bar open M-F 5pm-3am, Sa-Su 1pm-3am. Tu open mic, W open jam. $5 cover for bands. 18+.) Ybor offers a diverse range of clubs. **The Castle,** 2004 N 16th St. at 9th St., caters to the goth in you, but is open to all who enter the friendly sanctum. (☎247-7547. Open F-M 9:30pm-3am. F-Sa goth nights, Su gay night, M 80s night. Nipple night occasionally pokes up. Cover $4. 18+.) Spanning the pop spectrum, country line-dancing swings to everything from Alan Jackson to Puff Daddy at **Spurs,** 1915 7th Ave. (☎247-7787. Open Th-Sa 6pm-3am; free dance instructions 7-9pm.)

ST. PETERSBURG AND CLEARWATER ☎727

Twenty-two miles southwest of Tampa, across the bay, St. Petersburg caters to a
relaxed community of retirees and young singles. The town enjoys 28 miles of soft
white beaches, emerald-colored and bathtub-warm water, and about 361 days of
sunshine per year. The west coast of the narrow St. Petersburg-Clearwater stretch
encompasses one picturesque beach town after the next. While the scenery draws
the crowds, indoor activities will captivate as well—museum exhibits on Salvador
Dali and John F. Kennedy rival even the most superlative of sunsets.

⌷ GETTING THERE AND GETTING AROUND

Airport: St. Petersburg Clearwater International (☎535-7600) sits right across the bay
from Tampa, off Roosevelt St. **Airport Connection Limo** (☎572-1111) $19 per person.

Amtrak: (☎522-9475). Ticket office at Pinellas Sq. Mall, 7200 U.S. 19 N. Open 7am-
9pm. St. Pete has no train station, but Amtrak will connect you to Tampa from St. Pete
by bus ($10). Clearwater is inaccessible by train.

Buses: Greyhound, in St. Pete: 180 9th St. N. (☎898-1496). To: Panama City (9-10hr., 3
per day, $62-68); and Clearwater (30min., 7 per day, $8). Open daily 4:30am-11pm.
In Clearwater: 2811 Gulf-to-Bay Blvd. (☎796-7315). Open daily 6am-9pm.

Public Transit: Pinellas Suncoast Transit Authority (PSTA), ☎530-9911. Most routes
depart from Williams Park at 1st Ave. N. and 3rd St. N. Fare $1. Info kiosk at Williams
Park. To reach Tampa, take express bus #100X from the Gateway mall (fare $1.50). A
pink trolley (☎571-3440) loops through downtown (fare 50¢), and a green trolley runs
up and down the Pier (free). A 1-day unlimited bus pass is $2.50.

✴❷ ORIENTATION AND PRACTICAL INFORMATION

In St. Petersburg, **Central Ave.** parallels numbered avenues running east-west in the
downtown area. **34th St. (U.S. 19),** I-275, and 4th St. are major north-south fares.
The beaches line a strip of barrier islands on the far west side of town. Several
causeways, including the **Clearwater Memorial Causeway (I-60),** access the beaches
from St. Pete. Clearwater sits at the far north of the strip; **Gulf Blvd.** runs down the
long coastline, through Belleair Shores, Indian Rocks Beach, Indian Shores, Red-
ington Shores, Madeira Beach, Treasure Island, and St. Pete Beach. The stretch of
beach past the huge pink Don Cesar Hotel, in St. Pete Beach, and Pass-a-Grille
Beach have the best sand with less pedestrian and motor traffic.

Visitor Info: St. Petersburg Area Chamber of Commerce, 100 2nd Ave. N. (☎821-4715).
Open M-F 8am-5pm, Sa 9am-4pm, Su noon-3pm. **The Pier Information Center,** 800 2nd
Ave. NE (☎821-6164). Open M-Sa 10am-8pm, Su 11am-6pm.

Crisis Lines: Rape Crisis, ☎530-7233. **Helpline,** ☎344-5555. **Florida AIDS Hotline,** ☎800-
352-2437. All 24hr.

Post Office: 3135 1st Ave. N. (☎323-6516), at 31st St. Open M-F 8am-6pm, Sa 8am-
noon. **ZIP code:** 37370. **Area code:** 727.

⌷ ACCOMMODATIONS

St. Petersburg and Clearwater offer two hostels, as well as many cheap motels lining **4th St. N.** and **U.S. 19** in St. Pete. Some establishments advertise singles for as
little as $20, but these tend to be very worn down. To avoid the worst neighbor-
hoods, stay on the north end of 4th St. and the south end of U.S. 19. Several inexpensive motels cluster along the St. Pete beach.

St. Petersburg Youth Hostel, 326 1st Ave. N. (☎822-4141), downtown in the Bay Park
Arms Hotel. Bunk rooms ($15) for a maximum of 4 people with in-suite bathrooms.
Common room, TV, A/C; youth hostel card or student ID required. Also rents historic
hotel rooms ($39, weekly $125) with A/C and private bath, some with TV and fridge.

FLORIDA

Clearwater Beach International Hostel (HI-AYH), 606 Bay Esplanade Ave. (☎443-1211), off Mandalay Ave. at the Sands Motel in Clearwater Beach. Head to the superb white sand beach, just 2 blocks away, or take a free canoe to the nearby state park, where sports fields and equipment are free and bike rental is $5 per day. Common room, pool, and recreation center, with basketball and weight room. Office hours 9am-noon and 5-9pm. Linen $2. Dorms $12; non-members $13; private rooms $28-39.

Treasure Island Motel, 10315 Gulf Blvd. (☎367-3055), across the street from the beach. Big rooms with A/C, fridge, color TV, pull-out couch, and access to a beautiful pool. Catch dinner off a pier in back. Singles and doubles $45. Pirates welcome.

Grant Motel, 9046 4th St. N. (☎576-1369), 4 mi. north of town on U.S. 92. All rooms have A/C, fridge, and pronounced country-style decor, including straw hats and lacy curtains. Beautifully landscaped grounds. Pool. Singles and doubles $43. Weekly apartments $37-49 per day. Reservations strongly recommended.

Kentucky Motel, 4246 4th St. N. (☎526-7373). Large, clean rooms with friendly owners, located about 2 mi. north of downtown St. Petersburg. Cable TV, fridge, microwave, and free postcards. All rooms non-smoking. Singles $36; doubles $40; Jan.-Mar. $40/$45.

■ **Fort De Soto County Park,** 3500 Pinellas Bayway S. (☎582-2267), composed of 5 islands, has the best camping around. Also a wildlife sanctuary, the park makes a great oceanside picnic spot. Ranked among the best beaches in Florida. 233 palm-treed, private sites, many on the waterfront. No alcohol. $21, cash or traveler's checks only. 2-night minimum stay. Maximum 2 sites per individual per day. Front gate locked at 9pm. Curfew 10pm. Check-out 1pm. All sites have electricity, water, and a grill. Reservations must be made in person either at the park office, 501 1st Ave. N., #A116 on 5th St. entrance (☎582-7738; open 8am-4:30pm), or the Parks Dept. in Clearwater, 631 Chestnut St. (☎464-3347; open 8am-5pm).

◖ FOOD

Dockside Dave's, 13203 Gulf Blvd. S. in Madeira Beach, is one of the best-kept secrets on the islands. The ½ lb. grouper sandwich (market price, around $8) is simply sublime. (☎392-9399. Open M-Sa 11am-10pm, Su noon-10pm.) St. Petersburg's cheap, health-conscious restaurants cater to its retired population, and generally close by 8 or 9pm. City polls have repeatedly ranked **Tangelo's Bar and Grille,** 226 1st Ave. NE, as a top Cuban restaurant. Their imported sauce accents the $5.50 Oaxacan Mole Negro chicken breast sandwich. (☎894-1695. Open M-Sa 11am-7pm, Su seasonally.) Also in St. Pete is the **Fourth Street Shrimp Store,** 1006 4th St. N, purveyors of all things shrimp. Filling shrimp-taco salads cost $7. (☎822-0325. Open Su-Th 11am-9pm, F-Sa 11am-9:30pm.) Remember grease! Test the highly ranked burgers and "grouper cheeks" at **Frenchy's Cafe,** 41 Baymont St. The house specialty, boiled shrimp, comes dusted in their secret seasonings for $13. (☎446-3607. Open M-Th 11:30am-11pm, F-Sa 11:30am-midnight, Su noon-11pm.)

◣ NIGHTLIFE

Clearwater hotels, restaurants, and parks often host free concerts. Free copies of *Weekly Planet* or *Tampa Tonight/Pinellas Tonight* grace local restaurants and bars. With the combination of retirees in St. Pete and families on vacation in Clearwater, hot nocturnal spots can be hard to find. A smattering of establishments, however, hits the bullseye for those looking for a night on the town. **Beach Nutts,** 9600 W. Gulf Blvd., Treasure Island, has fresh grouper ($7.25) and decent burgers ($5), but go for the ambience; the restaurant/bar's newly expanded porch has a spectacular view of the beach, and bands play nightly. (☎367-7427. Open M-Sa 11am-2am, Su 1pm-2am.) Locals wind down with a beer and a game of pool at **Beach Bar,** 454 Mandalay Ave. If you're not in the mood for darts on the weekend, then walk around the corner to groove on their dance floor. (Bar open daily 10am-2am; dancing F-Sa 9pm-2am. No cover. 21+.) The younger crowd likes to make a dash for the mainland and party at **Liquid Blue,** 22 North Ft. Harrison St., Clearwater's premier nightspot for techno and weekly drink specials. (☎446-4000. Open Tu-Sa 9pm-2am. Cover varies; 18+.)

🔆 SIGHTS

Grab a copy of *See St. Pete* and *Beaches* or the *St. Petersburg Official Visitor's Guide* for the lowdown on area events, discounts, and useful maps. Beaches are the most worthwhile—but not the only—attraction for the coastline. The nicest beach may be **Pass-a-Grille Beach,** but its parking meters eat quarters; **Municipal Beach** at Treasure Island, accessible from Rte. 699 via Treasure Island Causeway, has free parking. **Clearwater Beach,** at the northern end of the Gulf Blvd. strand, is mainstream beach culture at its unspectacular height. For non-beach entertainment, the 🔆**Salvador Dalí Museum,** in Poynter Park on the Bayboro Harbor waterfront, makes you wonder what the talented Spaniard was smoking. The museum contains the world's most comprehensive collection of Dalí works and memorabilia—95 oil paintings, 1300 graphics, and many melting clocks. *(1000 3rd St. S. ☎823-3767. Open M-W 9:30am-5:30pm, Th 9:30am-8pm, F-Sa 9:30am-5:30pm, Su noon-5:30pm. $9, students $5, seniors $7, under 11 free.)* The **Florida International Museum** holds 🔆**John F. Kennedy: The Exhibition,** an exhaustive collection of over 500 artifacts. Personal effects from throughout JFK's life provide an intimate look at the President as both a political leader and an individual. *(100 2nd St. N. ☎822-3693. Open M-Sa 9am-6pm, Su noon-6pm. $14, seniors $13, students $8, ages 6-18 $6, under 6 free.)* The **Tampa Bay Holocaust Memorial Museum** covers pre-war Europe to the birth of Israel in the 4th largest museum of its kind in the country. A Nazi boxcar sitting in the center atrium once transported Jews to the camps. *(55 5th St. S. ☎820-0110. Open M-F 10am-5pm, Sa-Su noon-5pm; $6, students and seniors $5, ages 18 and under $2.)*

The **Sunsets at Pier 60 Festival** *(☎449-1036)* brings arts and entertainment to the Clearwater Beach daily from 2hr. before sundown until 2hr. after. The 🔆**sunsets** that happen every night are perhaps more spectacular; the sun crashes into the water of the Gulf. "Meet you at the 'Trop'" refers to the ballpark of **Tampa Bay Devil Rays,** 1 Tropicana Dr. *(☎825-3250. Apr.-Sept. Tickets $3-160.)*

GAINESVILLE   ☎352

Set equidistant from both coasts, Gainesville can't claim any beaches, but this Floridian version of a university town is a nice diversion from beach-and-theme-park monotony. The University of Florida (UF) lends the town a notably attractive population and an air of high culture equal parts bohemian, fraternity, and even Old South. From sophisticated professional theater to stuffed alligators to giant sinkholes to natural springs, Gainesville and its friendly residents insure a pleasant excursion for any visitor.

🔢 PRACTICAL INFORMATION.

Amtrak stops in Waldo, at an unstaffed station at U.S. 301 and State Rd. 24 *(☎468-1403)*. One train per day runs to Miami (9hr., $29-80) and Tampa (3½hr., $19-38); pay on board. **Greyhound,** 516 SW 4th Ave. *(☎376-5252; station open M-Sa 7am-11pm, Su and holidays 10am-10pm)* heads to Miami (14hr., 10 per day, $47-50), Tampa (3-5hr., 7 per day, $23-27), and Orlando (2½hr., 8 per day, $19). **Regional Transit System** runs trains and buses around the city. *(☎334-2602. $1; students, seniors, and handicapped 50¢; $2 buys a 1-day unlimited pass. M-F 6am-7pm, Sa-Su 7am-7pm.)* **Taxi: Gator Cab Co.,** ☎375-0313. **The Alachua County Visitors and Convention Bureau:** 30 E. University Ave., downtown *(☎374-5231; open M-F 8:30am-5pm)*. **Post Office:** 401 SE 1st Ave. *(☎371-7009; open M-Sa 8am-5:30pm, Sa 8am-noon)*. **ZIP code:** 32601. **Area code:** 352 or 904. Listings 352 unless noted.

🔥 ACCOMMODATIONS.

There are numerous inexpensive accommodations along 13th St., increasing as you near I-75. On football or Gatornationals race weekend, rates are at least double at any place you can squeeze into. The **Gainesville Lodge,** 413 W. University Rd., is a downtown steal, only a short stumble from the nightclubs. *(☎376-1224. TV, A/C, pool. Singles $36; doubles $40.)* The **Cape Cod Inn,** 3820 SW 13th St., has decor that will make New Englanders nostalgic. All rooms come with cable, pool, and continental breakfast. *(☎371-2500. Singles $44; doubles $47.)* Sleep amid bona-fide Floridian flora and fauna at **Paynes Prairie State Reserve** (see **Sights,** below), 10 mi. south on U.S. 441 (15 tent and 35 RV sites with water $11, $2 extra for electricity; bathroom facilities).

⌐ FOOD. Gainesville's diverse university population seems to have one taste they agree on: cheap, healthy food. At **Dish Yum,** 12 NW 13th St., gorge yourself with one of their signature sandwiches ($5.50), complete with freshly homemade ingredients. Don't be afraid to try their trademark concoction, "dishwater," a light blend of filtered water and fruit juices for 1.50. (☎336-3474. Open daily 11am-9pm.) In a cool atrium surrounded by flora, **Farah's,** 1120 W. University Ave., serves fine Mediterranean fare. Several types of wraps ($6) and rolled grape leaves with hummus ($8) are local favorites. (☎378-5179. Open M-Tu 11am-10pm, W-Sa 11am-11pm. Live jazz Sa 8pm.) **Leonardo's By the Slice,** 1245 W. University Ave., offers basic pastas ($4-6) and beautiful pizzas (slices $2-4), with a cafe that sells breakfasts and treats throughout the day. (☎375-2007. Open M-Th 9am-10pm, F 9am-11pm, Sa 10am-11pm, Su 11am-10pm.)

◙ SIGHTS. Teeming with gators, wild horses, and herds of buffalo, the 21,000 acres of **Paynes Prarie State Reserve** lie 10 mi. south on U.S. 441. A tower overlooks the many mi. of verdant, wet prairie landscape. Go it afoot either on your own or with an expert; in the winter, park rangers lead overnight expeditions through the basin. (☎466-3397 or 466-4100 for reservations. Open daily 8am-sunset. $3.25 per car.) The **University of Florida (UF)**—the cultural center of the area—houses its art at the **Samuel P. Harn Museum of Art.** The Harn, itself a breathtaking building, displays 5500 multicultural paintings, as well as at least 15 changing exhibitions a year. (SW 34th St. and Hull Rd. ☎392-9826. Open Tu-F 11am-5pm, Sa 10am-5pm, Su 1-5pm. Last admission time 4:45pm. Free.) A more bizarre collection can be found at the **Fred Bear Museum,** an endless parade of stuffed animals that met the famed archer's deadly aim. (4600 SW 41st Blvd. ☎376-2327. Open daily 10am-6pm. $5, seniors $4, ages 6-12 $3, families $12.) The nearby **Devil's Millhopper State Geological Site** is an enormous sinkhole named for its funnel-like shape and the discovery of fossilized bones and teeth at its bottom—legend claims bodies were once fed to the devil here. Your trip should be safer; to the tune of cascading water, a wooden walkway descends layer-by-layer through 20 million years of Florida's natural history. (4732 NW 53rd Ave. ☎955-2008. Open M-F 9am-5pm, Sa-Su 9am-sunset. Free.)

Poe Springs Park just over 3 mi. west of High Springs on County Rd., boasts sparkling natural springs and nature trails. (28800 NW 182nd Ave. ☎904-454-1992. Open 9am-dusk. $4.) Less ecologically sensitive is the **Gainesville Raceway,** home to the Gatornationals, a drag-racing extravaganza held every Mar. During the year the track hosts various gas-guzzling events. (11211 N. Country Rd. ☎377-0046.)

Gainesville has its share of the quirky. The **Retirement Home for Horses** in Alachua houses over 80 equine retirees. Admission is two carrots, but the horses request as many as you can smuggle in. (Mill Creek Farm, County Rd. 235-A. ☎904-462-1001. Open Sa only, 11am-3pm.) At the **Waldo Farmers and Flea Market,** on U.S. 301 1 mi. north of Waldo, over 400 vendors hawk "everything from blue jeans to green beans." (☎468-2255. Open Sa-Su 7:30am-4:30pm.) Down Museum Rd., in the middle of the UF campus, lies the **Bathouse.** Locals traditionally gather at sunset, turning their backs to the alligators in Lake Alice to watch the bats flock out of their abode.

♫▣ ENTERTAINMENT AND NIGHTLIFE. The annual **Alachua County Music Festival** showcases the local music scene; the likes of Tom Petty and Sister Hazel hail from Gainesville. The 3-day festival features 50 bands. (☎336-8360. 2nd week in Oct.) For live tunes year-round, head to the **Gainesville Community Plaza,** E. University Ave. and SE 1st St., where bands play every F night (☎334-5064; shows start at 8pm; free). The bi-weekly *Moon* and the UF's daily *Alligator* list local events and nightlife info. Look for them at Gainesville restaurants and street corners.

Clubs dot the intersection of W. University Ave. and 2nd Ave. downtown. **Orbit Lounge,** 238 W. University Ave., is the place in town for hip hop and techno, with three floors of dancing, a cigar lounge, and nightly drink specials. (☎335-9800. Open Th-Sa 10pm-2am. Cover $5. 18+.) Follow your ears to the wickedly hip **Soulhouse,** 15 SW 2nd Pl. and 1st St., off S. Main St. The house is a local secret known for its notorious Beanbag Room. (☎377-7685. Open M-Th 10pm-2am, F-Sa

FLORIDA

10am-3am. Cover $5.) **Lush,** 6 E. University Ave., covers everything from reggae to R&B to hip hop. Th-Sa guarantees drink specials and killer DJ's. Make sure to wash behind the ears—dress code required. (☎381-9044. Open M-Sa 10pm-2am. Cover varies.)

PANAMA CITY BEACH   ☎850

The people in PCB are quick to say that this isn't just a hot spring break destination (although it certainly is that), and they've got a point. But don't bother coming unless you're ready to have fun, Panama City Beach-style. Suntan lotion is the perfume of choice along these miles of snow-white beach and turquoise waters of the Gulf of Mexico. Heart of the "Redneck Riviera," PCB puts on no airs; leave those black suits and cell phones in Miami. Water parks, roller coasters, and surf shops complement the 27 miles of sandy shore.

⚆⚆ ORIENTATION AND PRACTICAL INFORMATION. After crossing Hathaway Bridge, **Front Beach Rd.** forks off from U.S. 98 and runs along the gulf. Also known as the "Miracle Strip," Front Beach Rd. is the place to see and be seen. To bypass the hubbub, take some of the smaller roads off U.S. 98.

Greyhound (917 Harrison Ave. ☎785-7861) makes a stop at the junction of U.S. 98 and U.S. 79 and continues on to Orlando (8-11hr., 3 per day, $62-65) and Atlanta (9hr., 3 per day, $48-51). **Bay Town Trolley,** 1021 Massalina Dr., shuttles along the beach, running 6am-6pm (☎769-0557; fare 50¢, students and seniors 25¢). **AAA Taxi:** ☎785-0533. **Yellow Cab:** ☎763-4691. **Panama City Beach Convention and Visitors Bureau:** 17001 Panama City Beach Pkwy., at corner of U.S. 98 and U.S. 79 (☎800-722-3224; open daily 8am-5pm). **Domestic Violence and Rape Crisis Hotline:** ☎763-0706. **Crisis and Mental Health Emergency Hotline:** ☎769-9481, ext. 405, both 24 hours. **Post Office:** 420 Churchwell Dr. (☎800-275-8777. Open M-F 8:30am-5pm, Sa 9am-12:30pm.) **ZIP code:** 32413. **Area code:** 850.

🏠 ACCOMMODATIONS. Depending on the Strip location and the time of year, rates range from can-do to outrageous. High season runs from the end of Apr. until early Sept.; rates drop in fall and winter. Call well in advance for summer reservations. Rates generally correspond to distance from the beach. One exception is **Sugar Beach Motel,** 16819 Front Beach Rd., with beach access, TV and in-room movies, A/C, pools, and hot-tub; kitchenettes available. (☎800-528-1273. www.sugarbeachmotel.com. Singles $59-75; doubles $80-115.) **La Brisa Inn,** 9424 Front Beach Rd., ½mi. from the beach, has clean, spacious rooms with two double beds, a pool, free cable, and coffee. (☎235-1122 or ☎800-523-4369; singles or doubles $45-79.) **Panama City Beach KOA,** 8800 Thomas Dr., two blocks south of U.S. 98 and directly across the street from the clubs, maintains 114 sites with showers, laundry, pool, cable TV, and storage. (☎234-5731 or 800-562-2483. Tent sites with water $20, full hook-up $26; cabins $40; in winter $13/$20/$23. Reservations recommended 6 months in advance.) Or camp on the beach at **St. Andrews State Recreation Area,** 4607 State Park Lane, 3 mi. east of PCB at the east end of Thomas Dr. Call ahead (up to 60 days) for reservations at this popular campground. All 176 sites are beneath the pines, on or close to the water. (☎233-5140. Sites $17, with electricity or waterside $19; in winter $10/$12.)

🍴📺 FOOD AND NIGHTLIFE. Buffets stuff the Strip and Thomas Dr. along the Grand Lagoon. "Early bird" specials, offered about 5pm, get you the same food at about half the price. **Scampy's,** 4933 Thomas Dr., offers seafare in a smaller, less harried atmosphere than the mega-troughs. (☎235-4209. Open daily 11am-3pm, 4-10pm; seafood salad $8, entrees $11-20.) Cool off at **Sharky's,** 15201 Front Beach Rd., with a hard lemonade ($3.25). More adventurous spirits will savor their signature appetizer, fried shark cubes, a.k.a. "shark bites." (☎235-2420. Open daily 11:30am-11:00pm. Live entertainment available on the beach deck most nights; cover $8.)

FLORIDA

Bars are a stumble away along the strip and Thomas Dr.; most have occasional live bands. The largest club in the US (capacity 8000) and MTV's former Spring Break headquarters, **Club LaVela**, 8813 Thomas Dr., offers eight clubs and 48 bar stations under one jamming roof. Live bands work the Rock pavilion every night, and national acts are no strangers. Wet t-shirt, bikini, and male hardbody contests fill the weekends and every night during Spring Break. (☎234-3866. Open daily 10am-4am. No cover during the day; cover varies at night. 18+.) Next door, **Spinnaker**, 8795 Thomas Dr., contains a restaurant (fresh seafood $8-20), a pool deck, and a playground for kids. This enormous wooden beach clubhouse has a happening daily happy hour (9-11pm) coupled with live bands throughout the week. (☎234-7882. Restaurant open daily 11am-10pm. Club open daily 10pm-4am; live entertainment 9pm. Cover $5-10. 18+.) The back patio bar at **Harpoon Harry's**, 12627 Front Beach Rd., overlooks the beach. Build a midnight sandcastle with their famous $6.50 margarita buckets. (☎234-6060. Open daily 11am-2am.)

🔊 **SIGHTS AND ENTERTAINMENT.** Over 1000 acres of gators, nature trails, and beaches make up the **St. Andrews State Recreation Area** (see **Accommodations**, above; open daily 8:30am-sunset; $4 per car). **Glass-bottom boat trips** take you on a dolphin-watching excursion and sail to Shell Island from Treasure Island Marina. (3605 Thomas Dr. ☎234-8944. 3hr. trips at 9am, 1, and 4:30pm. $17, seniors $16, under 12 $10; $3 coupon at visitors center.) Also in the Marina, the world's largest speed boat, the **Sea Screamer**, cruises the Grand Lagoon. (3601 Thomas Dr. ☎233-9107. Runs late May to early Sept. 11am, 1, 3pm, and sunset; in spring and fall 2 trips per day, 1pm and sunset. $12, ages 4-12 $8.) Sister to the Screamer is the **Sea Dragon**, an authentic pirate ship that fashions swashbucklers out of both young and old. (☎234-7400. 2hr. cruises in daytime, evening, and sunset. Call ahead for schedule of departure times. $16, seniors $13, ages 2-14 $11.) **Miracle Strip Amusement Park** is adjacent to **Shipwreck Island Water Park**, 2000 Front Beach Rd. The largest amusement complex in northeast Florida, these parks both have a number of thrill rides and shows for those who've had enough of the beach. (Amusement park: ☎234-5810. Open summer Su-F 6-11pm, Sa 1-11:30pm; spring and fall hours vary. $15, seniors $10. Water park: ☎234-0368. Open summer daily 10:30am-5:30pm; spring and fall hours vary. $20, seniors $10. Admission to both parks $28.) An assortment of dolphin shows, parasailing outfits, and amusement parks lines **Front Beach Rd.**

PENSACOLA   ☎ 850

Pensacola's military-infused population and reputation for conservatism have been a part of the city's make-up since before the Civil War, when three forts on the shores of Pensacola formed a triangular defense to guard the deep-water ports. Most visitors, however, will be drawn to the area for its sugar-white beaches and the secluded emerald waters along the Gulf Island National Seashore. For those seeking solace from sunburn, the naval aviation museum and historic district provide ample diversion.

📧 **PRACTICAL INFORMATION.** The city buttresses Pensacola Bay. **Palafox St.** and **I-110** are the main north-south byways; **Government St.** and **Main St.** run east-west. **Bayfront Pkwy.** runs along the edge of the bay and over the **Pensacola Bay Bridge.** On the other side, **Pensacola Beach Rd.** leads to Santa Rosa Island and Pensacola Beach. **Amtrak**, 980 E Heinburg St. (☎433-4966; open M, W, and F 12:30am-noon, Tu and Th 8:30am-4pm, Su 4:30-6:15pm) stops by on its east-west route between New Orleans (7hr., 3 per week, $38) and Orlando (13hr., 3 per week, $65). **Greyhound**, 505 W. Burgess Rd. (☎476-4800; open 24hr.) heads to Orlando (9hr., 7 per day, $69); Atlanta (9-14hr., 5 per day, $51); New Orleans (4-7hr., 2 per day, $29); and various locations in between. A **trolley** runs two lines through downtown, complete with tours; stops line Palafox St. (M-F 7am-6pm; 25¢). During the summer, two free Tiki Trolley shuttles run along the beach (F-Sa 10am-3am, Su 10am-10pm). **Taxi: Rainbow Taxi,** ☎437-1311. **Pensacola Convention and Visitors Bureau:** 1401 E. Gregory St., near the Pensacola Bay Bridge (☎800-874-1234; open daily 8am-5pm). **Post office:** 101 S. Palafox St. (open M-F 8am-5pm). **ZIP code:** 32501. **Area code:** 850.

ACCOMMODATIONS AND FOOD. Hotels along the beach cost at least $65. Better options lie inland, north of downtown on Pensacola Blvd., near I-10 (a 15min. drive to the beach). The **Civic Inn,** 200 N. Palafox St., is near the historic district, yet also budget friendly. The rooms are clean and well-furnished. (☎432-3441. A/C, pool, TV. Singles Su-Th $40, F-Sa $48; doubles $48/$58.) At the western edge of Santa Rosa Island, the ▓**Fort Pickens Campground** on the Gulf Islands National Seashore offers electric ($20) and non-electric ($15) sites within walking distance of the beach. (☎934-2622 for camping info, 800-365-2267 for reservations.)

Hopkin's House, 900 Spring St., serves their famous fried chicken and veggies on large, family style tables—$7.50 for all-you-can-eat. (☎438-3979. Open Tu-F 7-9:30am, 11:15am-2pm, and 5:15-7:30 pm, Sa-Su 7-9:30am and 11:15-2pm.) The owner of **King's BBQ,** 2120 N. Palafox St., built the drive-thru with his own hands and adds his personal touch to the colossal $5 pork, chicken, or beef sandwiches (open M-F 10:30am-6:30pm).

SIGHTS. Many visit Pensacola just to see the ▓**Naval Aviation Museum.** The excitement of more than 130 planes of past and present, dangling from the ceiling or parked within arm's reach, will have fly-boy wanna-bes soaring on natural highs. *(Inside the Naval Air Station, off I-10 Exit 2. ☎452-3604. Open daily 9am-5pm. Free.)* For fun that doesn't involve looking at winged killing machines, head across the 3 mi. Pensacola Bridge. From the visitors center at the **Naval Live Oaks Area** relaxing paths meander through a forest originally harvested for shipbuilding. *(1801 Gulf Breeze Pkwy. ☎934-2600. Open 8am-5:50pm.)* Pay $1 to cross the bridge to Santa Rosa Island for some of the best beaches around. Commanding the western part of the island—and past the string of condos marring nature's beauty—sits ▓**Fort Pickens,** where Apache leader Geronimo was once imprisoned. A $6 entrance fee to the park lets you explore the ruins, as well as sun-bathe and swim along the pristine seashore. *(Park open 7am-midnight.)*

FLORIDA

GREAT LAKES

During the Ice Age, massive sheets of ice flowed from the north, carving out huge basins. These glaciers eventually receded and melted, leaving expanses of rich topsoil, numerous basin pools, and five inland seas. Together, the Great Lakes comprise 15% of the earth's drinkable freshwater supply and an invaluable network of transport arteries for the surrounding region. Lake Superior is the world's largest freshwater lake, and its unpopulated, scenic coast hosts a significant wolf population. The sports lover's paradise of Lake Michigan boasts swimming, sailing, deepwater fishing, and sand dunes. Lake Erie has suffered from industrial pollution, but due to strict regulations, this shallow lake is gradually reclaiming its former beauty. The first Great Lake to be seen by Europeans, Lake Huron is still the least developed, though not in size or recreational potential. The runt of the bunch, Lake Ontario, still covers an area larger than New Jersey.

The Great Lakes region is not all unchartered beauty—Minneapolis and St. Paul have the panache of any coastal metropolis, while Chicago dazzles visitors with world-class music, architecture, and cuisine.

HIGHLIGHTS OF THE GREAT LAKES

FOOD. Wisconsin cheese, Chicago pizza (p. 504), pasties in MI's UP (p. 492), and Door County's fishboils (p. 525) are some of the regional specialties.

RECREATIONAL ACTIVITIES. Canoeing and kayaking are popular in the northern reaches of the Great Lakes; Grand Traverse Bay (p. 488) is an recreation hotspot.

SCENIC VISTAS. Reach the top of the Log Slide in MN (p. 493) or the Dune Climb in MI (p. 487), and you'll never want to come down.

SCENIC DRIVES. In MI, check out the Lake Michigan shore on U.S. 31 and M119 (p. 490); Brockway Mountain Dr. (p. 494); or the dirt roads of Pictured Rocks State Park (p. 493). In MN, drive Rte. 61 N from Duluth along the Lake Superior shore (p. 540).

OHIO

The glaciers that carved out the Great Lakes flattened the northern half of Ohio, creating the state's perfect farmland now patched with cornfields and soybean plants. The southern half, spared the bulldozing, rolls with endless wooded hills. The strikingly similar cities of Cincinnati, Cleveland, and Columbus, combined with unending farms and friendly small towns such as Oberlin, give Ohio its cheerfully acknowledged "Middle American" status.

▎ PRACTICAL INFORMATION

Capital: Columbus.

Visitor Info: State Office of Travel and Tourism, 77 S. High St., 29th Fl., Columbus 43215 (☎614-466-8844; www.ohiotravel.com). Open M-F 8am-5pm. **Ohio Tourism Line,** ☎800-282-5393. **Division of Parks and Recreation,** Fountain Sq., Columbus, 43224 (☎614-265-7000).

Postal Abbreviation: OH. **Sales Tax:** 5.75%.

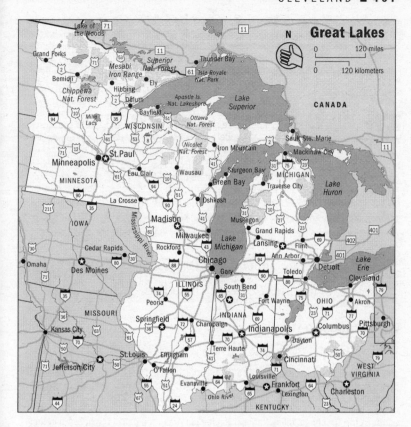

CLEVELAND ☎ 216

The city formerly known as the "Mistake on the Lake" has undertaken an extensive face-lift in recent years in an attempt to correct its beleaguered image. The arrival of the Rock and Roll Hall of Fame and three new sports stadiums have brightened the previously bleak visage of abandoned urbanity. Now, the downtown area is on the verge of flourishing, but Cleveland's outlying neighborhoods still face many challenges. Cleveland itself will remain a challenge for budget travelers until a new downtown hostel opens up—scheduled for completion in 2003.

⌐ GETTING THERE AND GETTING AROUND

Airport: Cleveland Hopkins International (☎265-6030), 10 mi. southwest of downtown in Brook Park. RTA line #66X "Red Line" to Terminal Tower $1.50. Taxi to downtown $20.

Trains: Amtrak, 200 Cleveland Memorial Shoreway NE (☎696-5115), across from Brown Stadium east of City Hall. To: New York City (12hr., 1 per day, $78-117); Chicago (7hr., 3 per day, $46-86); and Pittsburgh (3hr., 2 per day, $21-38). Open M-Th midnight-6:30pm, F-Su midnight-7:30am and 11am-6:30pm.

Buses: Greyhound, 1465 Chester Ave. (☎781-0520), at E. 14th St., 7 blocks from Terminal Tower. Near RTA bus lines. To: New York City (9-14hr., 12 per day, $78); Chicago (5¼-7½hr., 15 per day, $36); Pittsburgh (2½-4½hr., 11 per day, $19.50); and Cincinnati (4½-6½hr., 12 per day, $37). Most eastbound buses stopover in Pittsburgh.

Public Transit: Regional Transit Authority (RTA), 315 Euclid Ave. (☎621-9500, TDD 781-4271; open M-F 7am-6pm). Bus lines, connecting with Rapid Transit trains, travel from downtown to most of the metropolitan area. Service daily 5am-midnight; call for info on "owl" after-midnight service. Train fare $1.50. Bus fare $1.25, express $1.50, downtown loop 50¢, 1-day pass $4; ask the driver for free transfer tickets. The **Waterfront Line** accesses the Science Center, Rock and Roll Hall of Fame, and the Flats.

Taxis: Americab, ☎429-1111.

🔆🔢 ORIENTATION AND PRACTICAL INFORMATION

Terminal Tower in **Public Sq.** cleaves the city into east and west. Many street numbers correspond to the distance of the street from Terminal Tower; e.g., E. 18th St. is 18 blocks east of the Tower. To reach Public Sq. from **I-90** or **I-71,** follow the Ontario Ave./Broadway exit. From **I-77,** take the 9th St. exit to Euclid Ave., which runs into Public Sq. **The Flats,** along both banks of the Cuyahoga River, and **Coventry Rd.** in Cleveland Heights are the happenin' spots for food and nightlife.

Visitor Info: Cleveland Convention and Visitors Bureau, Tower City Center (☎621-4110 or 800-321-1001), first fl. of Terminal Tower at Public Sq. Open M-F 10am-4pm.

Internet access: Cleveland Public Library, 525 Superior Ave. 30min. limit. Open M-Sa 9am-6pm, Su 1-5pm; closed Su in summer.

Hotline: Rape Crisis Line, ☎619-6192 or 619-6194. 24hr.

Post Office: 2400 Orange Ave. (☎443-4494; after 5pm 443-4096). Open M-F 7am-8:30pm, Sa 8:30am-3:30pm. **ZIP code:** 44101. **Area code:** 216; 440 or 330 in suburbs. In text, 216 unless otherwise noted.

🏠 ACCOMMODATIONS

With hotel taxes (not included in the prices listed below) as high as 14.5%, budget lodging pickings are slim in Cleveland. So-called "budget" motels tend to run at least $60. **Cleveland Private Lodgings,** P.O. Box 18590, Cleveland 44118, will place you in a home around the city for as little as $35. (☎321-3213. Call M-F 9am-noon or 3-5pm. Allow 2-3 weeks for a letter of confirmation.) Travelers with cars might consider staying in the suburbs or near the airport, where prices tend to be lower, or heading south to the **Cuyahoga Valley National Recreation Area** (see p. 471), where hosteling and camping are inviting options. Off Exit 235 on I-71, 15 mi. southwest of the city, **Motel 6,** 7219 Engle Rd., has comfortable rooms with A/C and cable TV (☎440-234-0990. Singles $52, F-Sa $58; doubles $58/$64.) Closer to the airport, **Knights Inn,** 22115 Brookpark Rd., Exit 9 off I-480, provides standard motel rooms. Take the first two rights after the freeway. (☎440-734-4500. Singles $55; doubles $65. Must be 21+.)

🍴 FOOD

The delis downtown satiate most hot corned beef cravings, but Cleveland has more to offer elsewhere. A healthy dose of hipness infuses the shops near **Coventry Rd.** in Cleveland Heights. Italian cafes and restaurants cluster in Little Italy, around **Mayfield Rd.** Seafood and standard pub fare are abundant in **the Flats.** Over 100 vendors hawk produce, meat, and cheese at the **West Side Market,** 1995 W. 25th St., at Lorain Ave. (☎771-8885. Open M and W 7am-4pm, F-Sa 7am-6pm.)

Tommy's, 1824 Coventry Rd. in Cleveland Heights, up the hill from University Circle, whips up tantalizing veggie cuisine, like a falafel, veggie, and cheese pie for $5. Hedonists sock their guts with a Brownie Monster for $2.50. Take bus #9X east to Mayfield and Coventry Rd. (☎321-7757. Open M-Th 7:30am-10pm, F-Sa 7:30am-11pm, Su 9am-10pm.) **Mama Santa's,** 12305 Mayfield Rd., in Little Italy just east of University Circle, serves generous portions of Sicilian food in a no-frills setting. (☎231-9567. Open M-Th 11am-10:45pm, F-Sa 11am-11:45pm; closed most of Aug. Lasagna and cavatelli with meatballs both $7.) For good, cheap Chinese food downtown, the **China Sea Express,** 1507 Euclid Ave., offers $5.50 beef chop suey or $7 *moo sue* beef. (☎861-0188. Open M-Th 11am-9pm, F-Sa 11am-10pm.)

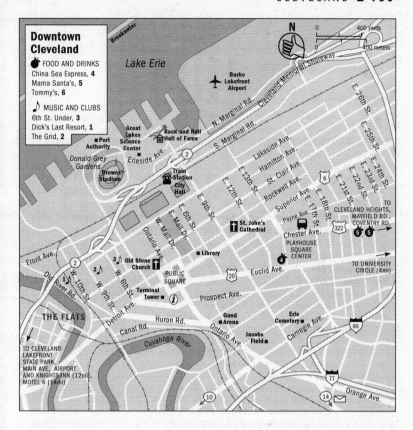

Downtown Cleveland

🍴 FOOD AND DRINKS
China Sea Express, **4**
Mama Santa's, **5**
Tommy's, **6**

♪ MUSIC AND CLUBS
6th St. Under, **3**
Dick's Last Resort, **1**
The Grid, **2**

👁 ⛰ SIGHTS AND ACTIVITIES

The aspirations of a new Cleveland show in the made-over downtown—a self-declared "Remake on the Lake." The **Rock and Roll Hall of Fame** is a dizzying exploration of the rock music world, where one can listen to hundreds of history-making tunes while reveling in the fashion sense of rock stars, from Jim Morrison's scout uniform to Elvis's sequined capes. *(1 Key Plaza. ☎ 781-7625. Open daily 10am-5:30pm, W until 9pm. $15, seniors and ages 9-11 $11.50. $5 W after 6pm.)* Next door, the **Great Lakes Science Center** holds gizmos, doodads, and interactive exhibits galore. *(601 Erieside Ave. ☎ 694-2000. Open Su-Tu and Th-F 9:30am-5:30pm, W and Sa 9:30am-9pm. $8, seniors $7, ages 3-17 $6; with IMAX $11/$10/$8. Parking for Hall of Fame and Science Center $7.)* **Cleveland Lakefront State Park,** is a 14 mi. park near downtown with three beaches and great swimming and picnic areas. *(☎ 881-8141. Accessible via Lake Ave., Cleveland Memorial Shoreway, or Lakeshore Blvd. Open daily 6am-11pm. Everett Beach closes at dusk.)*

Seventy-five cultural institutions cluster in **University Circle,** a micro-Smithsonian 4 mi. east of the city. The world-class **Cleveland Museum of Art** exhibits a survey of art from the Renaissance to the present, with exceptional collections of Impressionist and modern art. *(11150 East Blvd. ☎ 421-7340. Open Su 10am-5pm; Tu, Th, and Sa 10am-6pm; W and F 10am-9pm. Free.)* Nearby, the **Cleveland Museum of Natural History** displays the only existing skull of the fearsome dinosaur Pygmy Tyrant *(Nanatyrannus)* and one freaky-looking Ohio mastodon. *(1 Wade Oval Dr. ☎ 231-4600. Open M-Sa 10am-5pm, Su noon-5pm. $6.50; students,*

GREAT LAKES

seniors, and ages 7-18 $4.50.) The lovely, stream-laden **Cleveland Botanical Garden** provides a pacific respite from the urban decay that haunts much of the city. (11030 E. Blvd. ☎721-1600. Open until dusk.) The **Cleveland Orchestra,** one of the nation's best, performs at Severance Hall. (11001 Euclid Ave. ☎231-7300. Box office open M-F 9am-5pm. Tickets from $25.)

🎵 🎭 ENTERTAINMENT AND NIGHTLIFE

Baseball's **Cleveland Indians** (☎420-4200) hammer the hardball at **Jacobs Field,** 2401 Ontario St. Games have sold out for five straight years; the best bet is a 1hr. **stadium tour.** (☎241-8888 for tickets. May-Sept. every 30min. M-Sa 10am-2pm, June-Aug. Su noon-2:30pm when the team isn't in town. $6, seniors and under 15 $4.) The **Cleveland Cavaliers** (☎420-2000) pass the pill around **Gund Arena,** 1 Center Ct. (Nov.-Apr.), but not as well as the WNBA **Cleveland Rockers** (June-Aug.).

 Playhouse Square Center, 1519 Euclid Ave. (☎771-4444), a 10min. walk east of Terminal Tower, is the 2nd-largest performing arts center in the US. Inside, the **State Theater** hosts the **Cleveland Opera** (☎575-0900) and the renowned **Cleveland Ballet** (☎426-2500) from Oct. to June. The **Cleveland Cinemathique,** at the Institute of Art, screens off-beat and foreign films for $6 (☎421-7450).

 Most of Cleveland's nightlife is focused in **the Flats. Dick's Last Resort,** 1096 Old River Rd., jams to hits from the 50s, 70s, and 80s Th-Sa nights, while a swing band plays Su. (☎241-1234. Open M-Th 11am-1am, F-Sa 11am-2am, Su 10am-11pm. Comedy Sa night.) **6th St. Under,** 126 W. 6th St., hosts jazz and R&B jam sessions in one of the most chill downtown venues. (☎589-9313. Open Tu-F 5pm-2am, Sa 7pm-2am. No cover Tu-Th; F-Sa $6.) Hard-core rockers head for the **Grog Shop,** 1765 Coventry Rd. in Cleveland Heights, for local and national acts. (☎321-5588. Open M-Sa 7pm-2am, Su 2pm-2am.) Gays and lesbians frequent **The Grid,** 1281 W. 9th St., with a comfortable bar (decorated with male strippers W, F-Su nights) and a high-tech dance floor. (☎623-0113. Open M-Sa 5pm-2:30am, Su 4pm-2:30am.) For info on clubs and bands, pick up a copy of *Scene* or the *Free Times.* The *Gay People's Chronicle* and the bi-weekly *Out lines* are available at gay clubs, cafes, and bookstores.

🎫 DAYTRIPS FROM CLEVELAND

CEDAR POINT AMUSEMENT PARK. Recently declared "best amusement park in the world" by *Amusement Today,* Cedar Point Amusement Park, off U.S. 6, 65 mi. west of Cleveland in Sandusky, earns superlatives. The world's highest and fastest inverted roller coasters (riders are suspended from above), a "training coaster", and the brand-new **Millennium Force** (310 ft., 90 mph) offer a grand old adrenaline rush for all. Patriotic laser light shows take to the sky in summer at 10pm. (☎419-627-2350 or 800-237-8386. Open daily June-Aug. 10am-11pm; Sept. to early Oct. hrs. vary. $38, seniors $22, children under 4 or shorter than 48 in. $10. Parking $6.)

SEA AND INVENTURE. Sea World presents Shark Encounter, penguins, and wet, crowd-pleasing shows. (1100 Sea World Dr., 30 mi. south of Cleveland off Rte. 43 in Aurora. ☎330-995-2121. Open daily mid-June to late Aug. 10am-10pm; mid-May to mid-June 10am-7pm; late Aug. to late Oct. 10am-8pm. Sa-Su $35, ages 3-11 $20. Parking $6.) Innovative juices flow at **Inventure Place** and the **National Inventor's Hall of Fame,** 35 mi. south of Cleveland in Akron. (221 S. Broadway. ☎762-6565 or 800-968-4332. Open Tu-Sa 9am-5pm, Su noon-5pm; Sept.-Mar. W-Sa 9am-5pm, Su noon-5pm. $7.50, seniors, students, and children $6.)

FOOTBALL HALL OF FAME. The **Pro Football Hall of Fame** honors the pigskin greats. O.J. Simpson's jersey and helmet are displayed. (2121 George Halas Dr. NW, 60 mi. south of Cleveland in Canton. ☎330-456-8207. Take Exit 107A from I-77. Open daily 9am-8pm; early Sept. to late May 9am-5pm. $9, seniors $6, ages 6-14 $4.)

CUYAHOGA NATIONAL RECREATION AREA ☎330

Just 10 mi. south of Cleveland lies the northern edge of the surprisingly scenic **Cuyahoga Valley National Recreation Area (CVNRA),** established by Congress in the face of looming development in 1974. The **Cuyahoga River,** which once caught fire during the height of Cleveland's pollution woes a few decades ago, winds 22 miles through the dense forests and open farmland of the park, passing stables, aqueducts, and mills along the way.

◪ PRACTICAL INFORMATION. The Park Service operates three visitors centers, including the Depression-era **Happy Days Visitor Center,** on Rte. 303 off Rte. 8 in Peninsula. (☎650-4636. Open daily 8am-5pm; closed Jan.-Feb. and M-Tu in winter.) **Century Cycles,** 1621 Main St. in Peninsula, rents bikes for $5 per hr. (☎657-2209. Open M-Th 10am-8pm, F-Sa 10am-6pm, Su 10am-5pm.) **Post Office:** 1921 Bronson Ave. off Rte. 303 in Peninsula. (☎657-2500. Open M-F 8am-5pm, Sa 8am-noon.) **ZIP code:** 44264. **Area code:** 330.

▣◪ ACCOMMODATIONS AND FOOD. The genteel **Stanford House Hostel (HI-AYH),** 6093 Stanford Rd. in Boston, is the best accommodations option both in the park and in Cleveland. The clean, spacious hostel was built as a farmhouse in 1843 by George Stanford, one of the first settlers in the Western Reserve. Chill out with other hostelers on the old-fashioned front porch, or explore the gorgeous hiking and biking trails nearby. From Exit 12, turn right onto Boston Mills Rd., drive about 5 mi., then turn right on Stanford Rd. (☎467-8711. Call ahead. 7-night maximum stay. Check-in 5-10pm; check-out 9am. Curfew 11pm. 4-bed dorms and a smattering of family and private rooms. Dorms $14, under 18 $7. Linen $2. Laundry $1.75.) **Tamsin Park,** 5000 Akron-Cleveland Rd., 3 mi. south of Boston in Peninsula, offers the only **camping** around. (☎656-2859. Open May to Oct. 1. Sites $20, with hook-up $26.)

The village of Peninsula serves as the center of the park, and is home to most of its restaurants. **Fisher's Cafe and Pub,** 1607 Main St., serves delicious pancakes and $3-6 breakfast specials. (☎657-2651. Open M-Th 8am-10pm, F-Sa 8am-midnight, Su 8am-9pm.) **Tommy's Drive-In & Dairy Whip,** 1206 Aurora Rd. a few mi. east of the park in Macedonia, delivers the pleasing Tommyburger (with his own special sauce) and silky $2 milkshakes. (☎467-1004. Open in summer M-Sa 10:30am-10pm, Su 11:30am-10pm; in spring and fall closes at 9pm.)

▣◪ SIGHTS AND ACTIVITIES. The best way to see the soothing natural beauty of the park is by hiking or biking its elongated trails. The **Ohio & Erie Canal Towpath Trail** runs through shaded forests and past the numerous locks used by the canal during its heyday. **Hale Farm & Village,** 2686 Oak Hill Rd., 2 mi. south of Peninsula, recreates the rustic Ohio frontier life of the early 1800s. (☎666-3711. Open July-Aug. M-Sa 10am-5pm, Su 12-5pm; May-June and Sept.-Oct. closed M. $9.50, seniors $8.50, ages 3-12 $5.50.) **Beaver Marsh** was once an auto salvage yard until beavers built a dam and changed the environment into a flourishing swamp. To see the park by rail, **Cuyahoga Valley Scenic Railroad** runs several pleasing excursions along the banks of the river, from Peninsula, Independence, and Akron. (☎657-2000. Closed Jan. $11-20, seniors $10-18, children $7-12.) The park also has a few seasonal attractions. In the summer, the **Cleveland Orchestra** performs classical and pop evening concerts at the **Blossom Music Center,** 1145 W. Steels Corners Rd. in Cuyahoga Falls, a few mi. south of the park. (☎920-8040. Lawn seating $15-16.) In winter, **Boston Mills/Brandywine Ski Resorts** (☎467-2242) offer 16 lifts, snow tubing, and night skiing on both sides of the Cuyahoga.

COLUMBUS ☎614

Rapid growth, a huge suburban sprawl, and some gerrymandering have nudged Columbus's population beyond that of Cincinnati or Cleveland. The main drag, High St., heads north from the towering office complexes of downtown to the lively galleries in the Short North. It ends in the collegiate cool of Ohio State University (OSU), America's largest university with over 60,000 students. Columbus is America without glitz, smog, pretension, or fame—the clean, wholesome land of *Family Ties*. Bexley, a city suburb, was the model for the hit sitcom's setting.

GREAT LAKES

DAVE THOMAS, AMERICAN BEEFCAKE When R. David Thomas was a boy, he held the cartoon character Wimpy close to his heart. A mainstay on the Popeye show, Wimpy spent every episode incessantly gobbling hamburgers. In doing so, he cut an inspiring figure for the future fast-food entrepreneur. Born in 1932, Dave Thomas spent his early childhood in Atlantic City, dropping out of high school in 10th grade to chase his culinary dreams. In 1969, he opened the **first Wendy's restaurant,** in Columbus. From there, the freckled face and red pigtails of his daughter spread across the US like a midwest prairie fire. Today, Wendy's is an international fast-food chain, and Dave Thomas is a multimillionaire who enjoys eating in his own commercials. Thomas hasn't forgotten his humble beginnings and still loves to play the part of Wimpy, slipping out of board meetings to devour a quick burger...or 3.

■ **ORIENTATION AND PRACTICAL INFORMATION.** Columbus, a planned capital city, is laid out in an easy grid. High St., running north-south, and Broad St., running east-west, are the main thoroughfares, dividing the city into quadrants. **Greyhound,** 111 E. Town St. (☎221-2389), offers service from downtown to Cincinnati (2hr., 12 per day, $16); Cleveland (3hr., 14 per day, $17.50); and Chicago (7-10hr., 7 per day, $50.50). The **Central Ohio Transit Authority (COTA),** 177 S. High St., runs in-town transportation until 11pm or midnight depending on the route. (☎228-1776. Open M-F 8:30am-5:30pm. $1.10, express $1.50.) **Taxi: Yellow Cab,** ☎444-4444. **Greater Columbus Visitors Center,** 2nd fl. of City Center Mall, 111 S. 3rd St. (☎221-6623 or 800-345-4386). **Post office:** 850 Twin Rivers Dr. (☎469-4521. Open M-F 7am-8pm, Sa 8am-2pm.) .**ZIP code:** 43202. **Area code:** 614.

■ **ACCOMMODATIONS AND FOOD.** The **Heart of Ohio Hostel (HI-AYH),** 95 E. 12th Ave., 1 block from OSU, offers quality facilities (including a piano) and loans out bikes to guests. Stay free if you put on a 1hr. concert. (☎294-7157. Check-in 7:30-9:30am and 5-10pm. Lockout 9:30am-5pm. Dorms $14, nonmembers $17; 4 nights for $50.) **Motel 6,** 5910 Scarborough Dr., 20min. from downtown off I-70 at Exit 110A, has what you'd expect. (☎755-2250. Singles $37-45, $6 per extra adult.) Look for cheap motels on the outskirts of the city, where **I-70** and **I-71** meet **I-270.**

High St. features a variety of tasty budget restaurants. The **J&G Diner,** 733 N. High St., serves filling Belgian waffles ($4) and "hippie" or "rabbi" omelettes ($6) amidst evocative paintings of a green-clad Cinderella figure. (☎294-1850. Open M-F 10am-10pm, Sa-Su 9am-10pm.) **Bernie's Bagels and Deli,** 1896 N. High St., offers a variety of healthy $3-5 sandwiches. (☎291-3448. Open M-Sa 10am-2am, Su 5pm-2am.) **La Bamba,** 1980 N. High St., is the shiny, colorful home of the $5.65 burrito "Bigger Than Your Head." (☎294-5004. Open Tu-Sa 11am-3am, Su-M 11am-midnight.)

■ **SIGHTS. Ohio State University (OSU)** rests 2 mi. north of downtown. **The Wexner Center for the Arts** was Peter Eisenman's first public building. The four galleries display avant-garde art in all media, and the performance spaces host dance, music, and theater productions. (On N. High St. by 15th Ave. ☎292-3535. Exhibits open Tu-Sa 10am-6pm, Th until 9pm, Su noon-6pm. $3, students and seniors $2. Free Th 5-9pm. Wheelchair accessible.) The **Columbus Museum of Art** hosts Impressionist and European Modernist works. (480 E. Broad St. ☎221-6801. Open Tu-W and F-Su 10am-5:30pm, Th 10am-8:30pm. $4, students and seniors $2, under 5 free; Th free 5-8:30pm.) Fire, water, explosions, nylon mittens, uranium, and kids add up to some good ol' fun at the **Center of Science and Industry (COSI).** (333 W. Broad St. ☎288-2674. Open daily 10am-5pm. $12, students and seniors $7, ages 2-12 $6. Wheelchair accessible.) Several blocks east is the very first link in the **Wendy's** restaurant chain (see p. 472). Nearby, James Thurber's childhood home, the **Thurber House,** is decorated with drawings by the famous author and New Yorker cartoonist. (77 Jefferson Ave., off E. Broad 1 block west of I-71. ☎464-1032. Open daily noon-4pm. Free. Tours Su $2, students and seniors $1.50.)

South of Capitol Sq., the **German Village,** first settled in 1843, is now the largest privately funded historical restoration in the US, full of stately homes and beer halls. At **Schmidt's Sausage Haus,** traditional German oompah bands Schnickel-Fritz, Schnapps, and Squeezin' 'n' Wheezin' lead polkas at 7pm. Between dances, *liederhosen*-clad servers will bring you an $8.50 plate of homemade sausage. *(240 E. Kossuth St. ☎444-6808. Polkas W-Th at 7pm and F-Sa at 8pm in summer; no W rendition in winter. Open Su-M 11am-9pm, Tu-Th 11am-10pm, F-Sa 11am-11pm.)* You can grab free samples at **Schmidt's Fudge Haus,** one block west of the Sausage Haus. *(☎444-9217, call for hrs.)* The **German Village Society Meeting Haus** knows all. *(588 S. 3rd St. ☎221-8888. Open M-F 9am-4pm, Sa 10am-2pm.)* Ask about **Oktoberfest,** held in early Sept.

📋📺 ENTERTAINMENT AND NIGHTLIFE. Four free weekly papers available in shops and restaurants—*The Other Paper, Columbus Alive, The Guardian,* and *Moo*—list arts and entertainment options. The **Clippers,** minor league affiliate of the NY Yankees, swing away from Apr. to early Sept. (☎462-5250. Tickets $5-7.50.) A good place to start hopping is **Gallery V,** 694 N. High St., which exhibits contemporary paintings, sculptures, and works in less common media. (☎228-8955. Open Tu-W and F-Sa noon-6pm, Th noon-9pm; in winter Tu-Sa 11am-5pm.)

When you over-dose on art, Columbus has a sure cure: rock 'n' roll. Bar bands are a Columbus mainstay; it's hard to find a bar that doesn't have live music on the weekend. Bigger national acts stop at the **Newport,** 1722 N. High St. (☎228-3580. Tickets $5-40.) A famed chocolate martini and a lively, crowded atmosphere highlight the **Union Station Video Cafe,** 630 N. High St., which entertains a primarily gay crowd. (☎228-3740 or 228-3546. Open daily 11am-2:30am. Show tunes Su 6pm. Beers $2.50-3.50.) A few blocks south from that hip joint is the **Brewery District,** where barley and hops have replaced the coal and iron of the once industrial area.

NEAR COLUMBUS

A 1hr. drive south of Columbus, the area around **Chillicothe** (pronounce *CHILL-i-cozy* with a lisp) features several interesting attractions. The **Hopewell Culture National Historic Park** swells with 25 enigmatic Hopewell burial mounds spread over 13 acres, with an adjoining museum that theorizes about the mounds' configuration. Check with park officials for info on other nearby mounds. *(16062 Rte. 104. ☎740-774-1126. Museum open daily 8:30am-6pm; Sept.-May 8:30am-5pm. Grounds open dawn-dusk. $4 per car, $2 per pedestrian.)* From mid-June to early Sept., the Sugarloaf Mountain Amphitheater on the north end of Chillicothe off Rte. 23 presents **Tecumseh,** a drama re-enacting the life and death of the Shawnee leader. A behind-the-scenes tour will answer questions about how the stunt men dive headfirst off the 21 ft. cliff. *(Shows M-Sa 8pm. $13, F-Sa $15; under 10 $6 everyday. Hourly tour 2-5pm $3.50, children $2.)* **Scioto Trail State Park,** 10 mi. south of Chillicothe off U.S. 23, has walk-in camping across from Stuart Lake. (☎740-663-2125. Sites $9, with electricity $13.)

CINCINNATI   ☎513

Longfellow called it the "Queen City of the West." Founded by German pig salesmen, Cincinnati has also earned the less regal nickname of "Porkopolis." Located just across the Ohio River from Kentucky, Cincinnati has the feel—and sometimes the accent—of a Southern city, but its stellar ballet, world-class zoo, and one-of-a-kind chili draw travelers from all over.

▶ GETTING THERE AND GETTING AROUND

Airport: Greater Cincinnati International (☎606-767-3151), in Kentucky, 12 mi. south of Cincinnati and accessible by I-75, I-71, and I-74. **Jetport Express** shuttles to downtown (☎606-767-3702; $12, $16 round-trip), or call the **Transit Authority of Northern Kentucky (TANK)** (☎606-331-8265) for alternate shuttling info.

Trains: Amtrak, 1301 Western Ave. (☎651-3337), in Union Terminal. To Indianapolis (4hr., 1 per day, $18-34) and Chicago (8-9hr., 1 per day, $37-68). Open M-F 9:30am-5pm and Tu-Su 11pm-6:30am. *Avoid the area to the north, especially Liberty St.*

Buses: Greyhound, 1005 Gilbert Ave. (☎352-6012), past the intersection of E. Court and
Broadway. To: Louisville, KY (2hr., 11 per day, $19.50); Cleveland (4-6hr., 9 per day,
$37); and Columbus (2hr., 11 per day, $16). Open 24hr.

Public Transit: Cincinnati Metro and **TANK,** both in The Bus Stop, in the Mercantile Center,
115 E. 5th St. (☎621-9450; open M-F 8:30am-8pm). Most buses run out of Government Sq., at 5th and Main St., to outlying communities. In summer 50¢, in winter 65¢;
extra to suburbs. Office has schedules and info.

Taxi: Yellow Cab, ☎241-2100.

✴🔢 ORIENTATION AND PRACTICAL INFORMATION

The downtown business district is a simple grid centered around **Fountain Sq.,** at **5th**
and **Vine St.** Cross streets are numbered and designated E. or W. by their relation to
Vine St. The **University of Cincinnati** spreads out from Clifton, the area north of the
city. **Cinergy Field,** the **Serpentine Wall,** and the **Riverwalk,** all to the south, border the
river which marks the Ohio and Kentucky divide.

Visitor Info: Cincinnati Convention and Visitors Bureau, 300 W. 6th St. (☎621-2142 or
800-246-2987). Open M-F 9am-5pm. **Info Booth** in Fountain Sq. has limited offerings.
Open M-Sa 9am-5pm.

Hotlines: Rape Crisis Center, 216 E. 9th St. (☎872-9259), downtown. 24hr. **Gay/Lesbian
Community Switchboard,** ☎591-0222.

Post Office: 525 Vine St. (☎684-5667), on the Skywalk. Open M-F 8am-5pm, Sa 8am-1pm. **ZIP
code:** 45202. **Area codes:** 513; Kentucky suburbs 606. In text, 513 unless otherwise noted.

📷 ACCOMMODATIONS

Few cheap hotels can be found in downtown Cincinnati. About 30 mi. north of Cincinnati in Sharonville, budget motels cluster along **Chester Rd.;** 12 mi. south of the
city, inexpensive accommodations line **I-75** at Exit 184. Closer by, the motels at **Central Pkwy.** and **Hopple St.** offer solid, semi-cheap lodging. **Knights Inn-Cincinnati/
South,** 8048 Dream St., Florence, KY, just off I-75 at Exit 180, has renovated
rooms with an Arthurian flair and friendly service. (☎606-371-9711. Cable TV, A/
C, outdoor pool. Singles $36-40; doubles $40-45. 21+.) Ten min. from downtown
and the University of Cincinnati, **Budget Host Town Center Inn,** 3356 Central Pkwy.,
Exit 3 off I-75, is a smallish motel with a pool, and A/C and satellite TV in faded but
comfortable rooms. (☎283-4678 or 800-283-4678. Singles $45-60; doubles $50-65.)

⏲ GETTING FED AND GETTING BLOATED

Cincinatti's greatest culinary innovation is its chili. Unlike traditional beef or veggie
chili, Cincinnati chili consists of spaghetti noodles topped with meat, cheese,
chopped onions, and kidney beans...and a distinctive secret ingredient.

Skyline Chili, everywhere. Locations all over Cincinnati, including 643 Vine St. (☎241-
2020), at 7th St., dish up the best beans in town. The secret ingredient has been
debated for years; some say chocolate, but curry is more likely. 5-way large chili $5.55,
cheese coney (hot dog) $1.25. Open M-F 10:30am-7pm, Sa 11am-3pm.

Ulysses, 209 W. McMillan (☎241-3663), in Clifton. One-table vegetarian restaurant with
a distinctive hippie aura; draws ravenous veggies from all over town. Try the zesty and
refreshing fruit smoothies ($1.75), or the veggie chili ($2.75). Open in summer M-Sa
11am-8pm; in winter 11am-9pm.

Rookwood Pottery, 1077 Celestial St. (☎721-5456), on Mt. Adams. Patrons can sit in
giant, distinctive former kilns to enjoy some of the best burgers in town ($7-8) or whole-
some vegetable pesto ($10). Open Su-Th 11:30am-9:30pm, F-Sa 11:30am-11:30pm.

Graeter's, 41 E. 4th St. (☎381-0653), between Walnut and Vine St. downtown. One of
15 locations. Since 1870, Graeter's has been sending sweet-toothed locals into sen-
sory bliss with delectable ice cream blended with giant chocolate chips (single cone
$1.65). Sandwiches and baked goods also served. Open M-F 7am-6pm, Sa 7am-5pm.

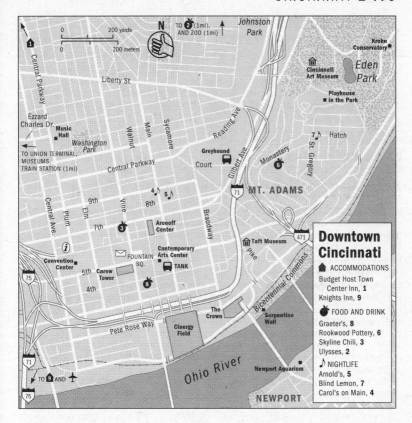

Map labels:

TO ② (1mi), AND ZOO (1mi)

Johnston Park

Krohn Conservatory ■

🏛 Cincinnati Art Museum

Eden Park

Playhouse ■ in the Park

Central Parkway

Liberty St

Ezzard Charles Dr.

■ Music Hall

Washington Park

Sycamore

Main

Walnut

Reading Ave

7 ♪ Hatch

St. Gregory

Monastery

TO UNION TERMINAL, MUSEUMS, TRAIN STATION (1mi)

Central Parkway

Greyhound 🚌 Court

Gilbert Ave

6

71 MT. ADAMS

9th

Vine

8th

4 ♪ 5 ♪

Elm

Plum

7th

3

Aronoff Center

Broadway

471

Central Ave.

ℹ

Convention Center ■

✉ FOUNTAIN SQ.

Contemporary Arts Center

■ TANK

🏛 Taft Museum

Pike

Bicentennial Commons

5th Carew Tower

4th

8

75

The Crown

Serpentine Wall

Cinergy Field

Pete Rose Way

71

TO ⑨ AND ✈

75

Ohio River

Newport Aquarium ■

NEWPORT

Downtown Cincinnati

🏠 ACCOMMODATIONS
Budget Host Town Center Inn, 1
Knights Inn, 9

🍎 FOOD AND DRINK
Graeter's, 8
Rookwood Pottery, 6
Skyline Chili, 3
Ulysses, 2

♪ NIGHTLIFE
Arnold's, 5
Blind Lemon, 7
Carol's on Main, 4

🔦 SIGHTS

Downtown Cincinnati orbits around the **Tyler Davidson Fountain,** a florid 19th-century masterpiece and an ideal people-watching spot. To the east, the expansive garden at **Procter and Gamble Plaza** is just one mark that the giant company has left on its home town. Around **Fountain Sq.** are business complexes and great shops, connected by a series of 2nd fl. skywalks; the observation deck at the top of **Carew Tower** provides the best view in the city.

Close to Fountain Sq., the **Contemporary Arts Center,** 2nd fl. of the Mercantile Center, has a strong national reputation. (*115 E. 5th St. ☎ 721-0390. Open M-Sa 10am-6pm, Su noon-5pm. $3.50, students and seniors $2. Free M. Wheelchair accessible.*) Also downtown is the **Taft Museum,** at the east end of 4th St., which houses a nice collection of painted enamels and pieces by Rembrandt and Whistler. (*316 Pike St. ☎ 241-0343. Open M-Sa 10am-5pm, Su 1-5pm. $4, students and seniors $2, under 18 free. Free W and Su.*)

Eden Park, northeast of downtown and Mt. Adams, provides a nearby respite from the city with rolling hills, a pond, and cultural centers. (*Take bus #49 to Eden Park Dr. Open daily 6am-10pm.*) The collections at the **Cincinnati Art Museum,** inside the park, span 5000 years, from Near Eastern artifacts to Andy Warhol's rendition of Cincinnati's infamous baseball great Pete Rose. (*☎ 721-5204. Open Tu-Sa 10am-5pm, Su noon-6pm. $5, students and seniors $4, under 18 free, Sa by donation.*) The nearby **Krohn Conservatory** is one of the largest public greenhouses in the world, boasting a lush rainforest simulation. (*☎ 421-5707. Open M-Tu and Th-Su 10am-5pm, W 10am-6pm. Free; donations accepted. Wheelchair accessible.*)

THE PARAMOUNT KING BEAST For an utimate amusement park experience, head to **Paramount's Kings Island** in Mason, 24 mi. north of Cincinnati off I-71 at Exit 24. In addition to a "faux" Eiffel Tower and an expanded waterpark, this fun center cages **The Beast,** the world's longest wooden rollercoaster, which spreads its tentacles over 35 acres and 2 ZIP codes. (☎573-5800 or 800-288-0808. Open late May to late Aug. Su-F 9am-10pm, Sa 9am-11pm. $40, seniors and ages 3-6 $20. Parking $6. Wheelchair accessible.)

♫ ENTERTAINMENT

The free newspapers *City Beat*, *Everybody's News*, and *Downtowner* list the happenings around town. The cliff-hanging community of **Mt. Adams** supports a thriving arts and entertainment district. Perched on its own wooded hill in Eden Park, the **Playhouse in the Park,** 962 Mt. Adams Circle, performs theater-in-the-round. (☎421-3888. Performances mid-Sept. to June Tu-Su. Tickets $26-40; senior rush 2hr. before show, student rush 15min. before show, both $13.50.)

The **Music Hall,** 1243 Elm St. (☎721-8222), hosts the **Cincinnati Symphony Orchestra** and the **Cincinnati Pops Orchestra** (☎381-3300) Sept. through May (tickets $12-60). The orchestra's summer seasons (June-July) take place at **Riverbend,** near Coney Island (tickets $16-32). The **Cincinnati Opera** performs in the Music Hall as well (☎241-2742; tickets $12-85). For updates, call **Dial the Arts** (☎621-4744). The **Cincinnati Ballet Company** (☎621-5219) is at the **Aronoff Center for the Arts,** 650 Walnut, which also houses a Broadway series. (☎241-7469. Ballet performances Oct.-May. Tickets $12-47, matinee $8-20. Musical tickets $15-45. Wheelchair accessible.)

Escape the high-brow lot and beat the summer heat in the world's largest recirculating pool at the **Coney Island Amusement Center,** 6201 Kellogg Ave., off I-275 at the Kellogg Ave. exit. (☎232-8230. Pool open daily 10am-8pm; rides M-F noon-9pm, Sa-Su 11am-9pm. Pool $11, ages 4-11 $9, seniors $8; rides $7; both $16/$14/$13.) Cincinnati's sports fanatics watch baseball's **Reds** (☎421-7337; tickets $5-21) and football's **Bengals** (☎621-3550; tickets $35-50) at **Cinergy Field,** 201 E. Pete Rose Way.

◆ NIGHTLIFE

Overlooking downtown from the east, **Mt. Adams** has spawned some funky bars and late-night coffee shops. Antiques adorn the walls of **Blind Lemon,** 939 Hatch St., at St. Gregory St., while live blues and acoustic rock fill its courtyard. (☎241-3885. Open M-Th 5pm-2:30am, F 4pm-2:30am, Sa-Su 3pm-2:30am. Music M-Sa 9:30pm, Su 7pm. No cover. Domestic draft $2.) For a drink straight out of the 19th century, try Cincinnati's oldest tavern, **Arnold's,** 210 E. 8th St., between Main and Sycamore. This wood-paneled mainstay provides good, uncomplicated beer ($3) as well as pasta and sandwiches ($4-10). After 9pm, Arnold's does ragtime, bluegrass, and swing. (☎421-6234. Open M-F 11am-1am, Sa 4pm-1am.) **Carol's On Main,** 825 Main St., inserts funk and style into downtown Cincinnati. Drawing theater groups and yuppies galore, this restaurant/bar is known for great food (Cock-a-Noodle-Do Salad $8) and late hours. (☎651-2667. Bar open Su 4pm-1:30am, M-Tu 11:30am-1:30am, W-F 11:30am-2:30am, Sa 4pm-2:30am.)

MICHIGAN

Orbiting the earth in a space shuttle, Michiganers would have no trouble identifying their state; with its 3000 miles of coastline along four of the irregularly outlined Great Lakes, Michigan easily lays claim to the title of "Most Readily Apparant State When Viewed from Space." Michigan's industrially developed Lower Peninsula paws the Great Lakes like a huge mitten, while its pristine and oft-ignored Upper Peninsula hangs above, quietly nursing moose, vacation homes, and a famed population of wolves. The state once famous for its booming automotive industry is now starting to make waves as a natural getaway, blending a coastal character with thousands of fresh water lakes at an inland location.

⁊ PRACTICAL INFORMATION

Capital: Lansing.
Visitor Info: Michigan Travel Bureau, 333 S. Capitol, Ste. F, Lansing 48909 (☎888-784-7328 or 800-543-2937; www.travel-michigan.state.mi.us). **Dept. of Parks and Recreation,** Information Services Center, P.O. Box 30257, Lansing 48909 (☎517-373-1270). Entry to all state parks requires a motor vehicle permit; $4 per day, $20 annually. Call ☎800-447-2757 for reservations at any state park campground.
Postal Abbreviation: MI. **Sales Tax:** 6%.

DETROIT ☎313

Decades of hardship recently prompted an author to proclaim Detroit "America's first Third-World city." Violent race riots in the 60s caused a massive flight to the suburbs; the population has more than halved since 1967, turning neighborhoods into ghost towns. The decline of the auto industry in the late 70s added unemployment to the city's ills, beleaguring an already depressed area. Today, the five gleaming towers of the riverside Renaissance Center symbolize the hope of a city-wide renewal. Aggressive tourist media focus attention on Detroit's attractions: Michigan's largest and most comprehensive museums, a fascinating ethnic history, and the still-visible (though soot-blackened and slightly crumbling) evidence of the city's former architectural grandeur.

⌐ GETTING THERE AND GETTING AROUND

Airport: Detroit Metropolitan (☎942-3550 or 800-351-5466), 2 mi. west of downtown off I-94 at Merriman Rd. in Romulus. **Commuter Express** (☎941-3252 or 800-488-7433) runs shuttles downtown daily 7am-midnight every hr. on the hr. (45min., $15), stopping at major hotels. Reservations necessary. A taxi to downtown costs $30.
Trains: Amtrak, 11 W. Baltimore (☎873-3442), at Woodward. To: Chicago (6hr., 3 per day, $19-50) and New York (16hr., 1 per day, $72-135). Open daily 5:45am-11:30pm. For Canadian destinations, go through **VIA Rail,** 298 Walker Rd., Windsor, ON (☎519-256-5511 or 800-561-3949). To Toronto (4hr., 5-7 per day, CDN$71).
Buses: Greyhound, 1001 Howard St. (☎961-8011). *At night, the area is unsafe.* To: Chicago (5½hr., 8 per day, $24); Cleveland (4hr., 9 per day, $20); and Ann Arbor (1hr., 5 per day, $7). Station open 24hr.; ticket office open daily 6am-12:30am.
Public Transit: Detroit Dept. of Transportation (DOT), 1301 E. Warren St. (☎933-1300). Policed public transport system serves downtown, with limited service to the suburbs. Many buses stop service at midnight. Fare $1.25, transfers 25¢. **DOT Attractions Shuttle** (☎259-8726) delivers camera-toting tourists to the metro area's most popular sights 10am-5:45pm. All-day ticket $5. **People Mover,** 150 Michigan Ave. (☎962-7245 or 800-541-7245). Ultramodern elevated tramway circles the Central Business District

on a 2.7 mi. loop; worth a ride just for the view. Runs M-Th 7am-11pm, F 7am-midnight, Sa 9am-midnight, Su noon-8pm. Fare 50¢. **Southeastern Michigan Area Regional Transit (SMART),** ☎962-5515 or 223-2100. Bus service to the suburbs. Fare $1.50, transfers 25¢. Get free maps of the system at the office on the first fl. of First National Bank at 600 Woodward Ave. Buses run 4am-midnight, depending on route.

Taxis: Checker Cab, ☎963-7000.

✳ 🔢 ORIENTATION AND PRACTICAL INFORMATION

Detroit lies on the Detroit River, which connects Lakes Erie and St. Clair. Across the river to the south, the town of **Windsor, ON,** can be reached by tunnel just west of the Renaissance Center (toll $2.25), or by the Ambassador Bridge. Detroit is a tough town, but you probably won't encounter trouble during the day, especially within the People Mover loop. Driving is the best way to negotiate this sprawling city where good and bad neighborhoods alternate at whim; public transportation is often inefficient and less safe.

Detroit's streets form a grid. **The Mile Roads** run east-west as major arteries. **Eight Mile Rd.** is the city's northern boundary and the beginning of the suburbs. **Woodward Ave.** heads northwest from downtown, dividing city and suburbs into "east side" and "west side." **Gratiot Ave.** flares out northeast from downtown, while **Grand River Ave.** shoots west. **I-94** and **I-75** pass through downtown. For a particularly helpful map, check the pull-out in the invaluable *Detroit Metro Visitor's Guide.*

Visitor Info: Convention and Visitors Bureau, 211 W. Fort St. (☎202-1813 or 800-338-7648). Open M-F 8:30am-5pm. **Windsor Travel Info,** 110 Park St. (☎519-973-1338).

Hotlines: 24hr. Crisis Hotline, ☎224-7000. **Sexual Abuse Helpline,** ☎876-4180. 24hr.

Bi-Gay-Lesbian Organizations: Triangle Foundation of Detroit, ☎537-3323. **Between the Lines,** ☎248-615-7003. **Affirmations,** 195 W. 9 Mile Rd. 48220 (☎248-398-7105), in Ferndale, has a large library, info on gay nightlife, and copies of *Pride Source Guide,* a comprehensive gay guide to MI.

Post Office: 1401 W. Fort St. (☎226-8304. Open 24hr.) **ZIP code:** 48233. **Area codes:** 313, 810, and 248 (north); or 734 (southwest). In text, 313 unless otherwise noted.

▐ ACCOMMODATIONS

Detroit's suburbs harbor loads of chain motels. Ones near the airport in **Romulus** tend to be overpriced, and others along **E. Jefferson,** near downtown, can be skanky. For a mix of convenience and affordability, look along **Telegraph Rd.** off I-94, west of the city. If the exchange rate is favorable, good deals can be found in **Windsor** just across the border. The *Detroit Metro Visitor's Guide* lists accommodations by area and includes price ranges. Devoted campers should resign themselves to a 45min. commute.

🏚 **Country Grandma's Home Hostel (HI-AYH),** 22330 Bell Rd. (☎734-753-4901), in New Boston, 6 mi. south of I-94 off I-275, between Detroit and Ann Arbor. Though it's inaccessible by public transportation, the comfort and hospitality make it worth the trip. 6 beds, a kitchen, and free parking. Dorms $11, non-members $14. Call for required reservations and directions. Wheelchair accessible.

Shorecrest Motor Inn, 1316 E. Jefferson Ave. (☎568-3000 or 800-992-9616), as close to downtown as the budget traveler can get. Clean, comfortable singles $59; doubles $79. Key deposit $5. Reservations recommended. Wheelchair accessible.

University of Windsor, 401 Sunset Ave. (☎519-973-7074), in Windsor, just over the Ambassador Bridge, rents rooms from early May to late Aug. Free use of university facilities. Singles CDN$31, CDN$18.50 for students with college ID; doubles CDN$46. Wheelchair accessible.

Motel 6, 32700 Barrington St. (☎248-583-0500), 15 mi. north of downtown off I-75 in Madison Heights, just off 12 Mile Rd. Enormous, well-kept, cookie-cutter rooms with free local calls and HBO. Singles $43; doubles $49. Reservations recommended.

Downtown Detroit

TO CRANBROOK
MUSEUM OF
SCIENCE (15mi),
DETROIT ZOO (5mi)

Woodward Ave.

TO MOTEL 6(15mi),
PONTIAC LAKE
RECREATION AREA (35mi)

TO MOTOWN
HISTORICAL
MUSEUM
(1mi)

Palmer St.

TO DETROIT
METROPOLITAN AIRPORT
& HENRY FORD MUSEUM

Ferry St.

Historical
Museum

Children's
Museum

International
Institute

Kirby St.

Frederick St.

Public
Library

Frederick Douglass Ave.

Institute
of Art

Farnsworth St.

Wayne State
University

Putnam St.

CULTURAL
CENTER

Science
Center

Museum
of African
American
History

Warren Ave.

Warren Ave.

Hancock St.

Forest St.

Forest St.

Forest St.

Lysander St.

Garfield St.

Prentis St.

Calumet St.

2nd St.

Cass St.

John R. St.

Canfield St.

St. Antoine

Willis St.

Willis St.

Willis St.

Superior St.

Alexandrine St.

Alexandrine St.

Brush St.

Alexandrine St.

Selden St.

Leland St.

Avery St.

Commonwealth St.

3rd St.

Illinois St.

Scripps
Park

St. Joseph St.

Grand River Ave.

Lincoln St.

Orchestra Hall ■

John R. St.

Rivard St.

Martin L. King Jr. St.

Davenport St.

Mack St.

Pierce St.

Sycamore St.

Myrtle St.

Stimson St.

Elliot St.

Beaubien St.

Erskine St.

Erskine St.

Ash St.

4th St.

Erskine St.

Watson St.

Brush St.

Watson St.

Elm St.

Butternut St.

Charlotte St.

Edmund St.

Wilkins St.

Temple St.

Brooklyn St.

Brewster St.

Brewster St.

Perry St.

Cass
Park

Alfred St.

Alfred St.

St. Antoine

Alfred St.

Spruce St.

Sproat St.

Divison St.

Divison St.

Pine St.

Ledyard St.

Sibley St.

Adelaide St.

Eastern
Market ■

Kaline St.

Henry St.

Plum St.

Montcalm St.

Brooklyn St.

Plume St.

Fox Theater ■

Columbia St.

CORKTOWN

Elizabeth St.

State Theatre ■

Elizabeth St.

Adams St.

TO MEXICAN
TOWN

Grand Circus
Park

Gratiot Ave.

Trumbull St.

Bagley St.

Madison St.

Mullet St.

Bagley St.

Broadway

Clinton St.

Michigan Ave.

6th St.

Labrosse St.

Cass St.

DPM

Rivard St.

Porter St.

Abbott St.

Macomb St.

GREEK-
TOWN

Joliet Pl.

Savage
Memorial
Park

Abbott St.

3rd St.

2nd St.

1st St.

State St.

Woodward Ave.

Library St.

Monroe St.

Lafayette St.

Howard St.

Brooklyn St.

5th St.

Lafayette St.

Beaubien St.

St. Antoine St.

Navarre Pl.

TO AMBASSADOR
BRIDGE (3mi)

Griswold St.

Shelby St.

Washington Blvd.

People Mover ⓘ

Congress St.

Fort St.

Larned St.

People Mover

DPM

Jefferson St.
Woodbridge St.

TO DETROIT

Detroit-
Windsor
Tunnel (Toll)

Dieppe
Park

Riverside Dr.

Joe Louis
Arena

Casino
Windsor

Cobo
Center

HART
PLAZA

Renaissance
Center

RIVERTOWN

Atwater St.

TO CHENE PARK →

Ouellette Ave.

University St.

ⓘ

City
Hall

Detroit River

Detroit-
Windsor
Tunnel
(Toll)

MICHIGAN (USA)
ONTARIO (CANADA)

TO WINDSOR (400m)

0   500 yards
0   500 meters

N

GREAT LAKES

Pontiac Lake Recreation Area, 7800 Gale Rd. (☎248-666-1020), in Waterford 45min. northwest of downtown; take I-75 to M59 W, a right on Will Lake northbound and left onto Gale Rd. Huge wooded sites in rolling hills, just 4 mi. from the lake. 176 sites with electricity $11. Vehicle permit $4.

FOOD

Although many downtown restaurants have migrated to the suburbs, there are still some in-town budget dining options. In **Greektown,** at the Greektown People Mover stop, Greek restaurants and excellent bakeries line one block of Monroe St. near Beaubien St. To snag a *pierogi,* cruise Joseph Campau Ave. in **Hamtramck** (*Ham-TRAM-eck*), a Polish neighborhood northeast of Detroit. No budget traveler should miss the **Eastern Market,** at Gratiot Ave. and Russell St., an 11-acre produce-and-goodie festival with everything imaginable. (☎833-1560. Open Sa 5am-5pm.)

Lafayette Coney Island, 118 W. Lafayette, (☎964-8198). Detroit's most famous culinary establishment, Lafayette doles out its $1.79 coney dogs to Detroiters of all walks of life. Join the crowd and bring some antacids. Open M-Th 8am-3:30am, F-Sa 8am-4:30am or 5am, Su 9am-3:30am.

Cyprus Taverna, 579 Monroe St., (☎961-1550). A local favorite for Greek cuisine. In the heart of Greektown, it features tasteful decor and a charmingly subdued atmosphere. Entrees $9-13. Open Su-Th 11am-2am, F-Sa 11am-4am.

Ivanhoe Cafe, 5249 Joseph Campau at Frederick St., (☎925-5335). Lunch spot for authentic $6 kielbasa dishes. Open daily 11:30am-3pm, must be seated by 2:30pm.

Soup Kitchen Saloon, 1585 Franklin St., (☎259-1374). Where once there was a speakeasy and brothel, now there's some of Detroit's best live blues, plus fresh seafood, steaks, and cajun eats. BBQ catfish and seafood creole $12. Open Tu-F 11am-midnight, Sa-Su 5pm-midnight. Music Tu-Sa; cover $5-7.

SIGHTS

ODDITIES. Detroit's art isn't confined to museums. Artist and activist Tyree Guyton created the block-long **Heidelburg Project,** an ever-changing amalgamation of polka dots and found objects. (*Turn west on Heidelburg St. from Mt. Elliott, which is between I-94 and E. Jefferson, and follow the dots.*) For wandering bibliophiles, **John K. King Used and Rare Books** holds over a million books on four floors, making browsing an overwhelming but rewarding enterprise. (*901 W. Lafayette.* ☎961-0622. *Right off the Lodge Freeway. Open M-Sa 9:30am-5:30pm.*)

DETROIT ZOOLOGICAL PARK. If the gowns of the Supremes aren't wild enough for you, try the well-funded **Detroit Zoological Park,** just off the Woodward exit of 696 in Royal Oak. North America's first National Amphibian Conservation Center is currently under construction, but until then stroll the grounds and the the relatively new Wildlife Interpretive Gallery. (☎248-398-0900. *Open daily Apr.-Oct. 10am-5pm, Nov.-Mar 10am-4pm. Open until 6pm on Su from mid-May to Labor Day and until 8pm on W from late June to late Aug. $7.50, ages 2-18 and seniors $5.50, under 2 free. Parking $3.*)

CRANBROOK. Fifteen mi. north of Detroit in posh Bloomfield Hills, **Cranbrook's** scholarly campus holds public gardens, several museums, and an art academy. Far and away the best of the lot is the **Cranbrook Institute of Science,** with rotating exhibits emphasizing educational fun. (*1221 N. Woodward Ave.* ☎248-645-3209 *or 877-462-7262. Open Sa-Th 10am-5pm, F 10am-10pm. $7, children, seniors, and students, $4.*)

BELLE ISLE. The largest urban island park in the US and one of the best escapes from Detroit's hectic pace, **Belle Isle** maintains a **conservatory, nature center, aquarium, maritime museum,** and small **zoo** for animal lovers with short attention spans. (☎852-4078. *3 mi. from downtown via the MacArthur Bridge. Belle Isle accessible daily 6am-10pm; all attractions open 10am-5pm. $2 each, ages 2-12 $1; zoo $3, ages 2-12 $2, under 2 free.*)

MUSEUMS

Detroit Institute of Arts, 5200 Woodward Ave. (☎833-7900). One of the nation's finest art museums, features Van Gogh's "Self-Portrait" and Diego Rivera's massive mural "Detroit Industry"—one masterpiece that will never go on loan. Open W-F 11am-4pm, Sa-Su 11am-5pm, first F of each month 11am-9pm. Suggested donation $4, children and students $1.

Henry Ford Museum & Greenfield Village, 20900 Oakwood Blvd. (☎982-6100, 271-1620 for 24hr. info). Off I-94 in nearby Dearborn; take SMART bus #200 or 250. More than just a tribute to planes, trams, and automobiles (though there's plenty of that), the museum exhibits deliver a comprehensive running commentary on 20th-century America. The premises boast the limousine in which President Kennedy was assassinated and a copy of the Lunar Rover. Over 80 historic edifices from around the country have been moved to **Greenfield Village,** next to the museum; visit the workshop of the Wright Brothers or the factory where Thomas Edison researched. Museum and village open daily 9am-5pm. Museum or village $12.50, seniors $11.50, ages 5-12 $7.50. Combination ticket valid 2 consecutive days. $23/$22/$13.

Automotive Hall of Fame, 21400 Oakwood Blvd. (☎240-4000). Glorifies the innovators of the car industry with an interactive tour through the industry's history. Open daily 10am-5pm; Nov.-May Tu-Su 10am-5pm. $6, seniors $5.50, ages 5-12 $3.

Spirit of Ford, 1151 Village Rd. (☎317-7478). Thrills visitors with its racing exhibits, notably a jolting simulator ride around a racetrack and a realistic Pit Stop Challenge. Open daily 9am-6pm. $6, seniors $5, ages 5-12 $4, under 5 free.

Museum of African-American History, 315 E. Warren Rd. (☎494-5808). Exhibits include harrowing accounts of the history of slavery and displays of present day African-American culture. Open W-Su 9:30am-5pm. Suggested donation $3, under 13 $2.

Motown Historical Museum, 2648 W. Grand Blvd. (☎875-2264). East of Rosa Parks Blvd. about 1 mi. west of the Lodge Freeway/Rte. 10; take the "Dexter Avenue" bus. Downstairs, the Jackson 5, Marvin Gaye, Smokey Robinson, and Diana Ross recorded in the primitive Studio A. Open Su-M noon-5pm, Tu-Sa 10am-5pm. $6, under 12 $3.

ENTERTAINMENT AND NIGHTLIFE

Newly renovated and restored, Detroit's theater district, around Woodward and Columbia, is witnessing a cultural revival. The **Fox Theater,** 2211 Woodward Ave., near Grand Circus Park, features high-profile drama, comedy, and musicals, as well as the nation's largest movie theater hall (seats 5000) for occasional epic films. (☎596-3200. Box office open M-F 10am-6pm. Tickets $25-100; movies under $10.) The **State Theater,** 2115 Woodward Ave., brings in a variety of popular concerts (☎961-5450; 810-932-3643 for event info) and is also home to **Ignition,** a giant party that enlists DJs from a local radio station to play alternative dance music. (Sa 10pm-2am. Cover starts at $5.) **Orchestra Hall,** 3711 Woodward Ave., at Parsons St., houses the Detroit Symphony Orchestra. (☎962-1000, box office 576-5111. Open M-F 9am-5pm. Half-price rush tickets 1½hr. prior to show for seniors and students with ID.) For some of Detroit's best jazz, check out the **Harmony Park** area near Orchestra Hall. The weekly *Metro Times* contains complete entertainment listings.

For info on the trendiest nightspots, pick up a free copy of *Orbit* in record stores and restaurants. *Between the Lines*, also free, has entertainment info for gays, lesbians, and bisexuals. Alternative fans looking for a little live music should check out **St. Andrew's Hall,** 431 E. Congress, which hosts local and national alternative acts. (☎961-6358. Shows F-Su. Advance tickets sold through Ticketmaster; $7-10.) **Shelter,** the dance club downstairs, draws young, hip crowds on non-concert nights. Young party animals take advantage of Ontario's lower drinking age (19) at bars and clubs along **Ouellette Ave.** in Windsor. Those with too much cash rid themselves of the burden with three floors of gambling at the shiny **Windsor Casino,** 377 Riverside Dr. (☎519-258-7878, 800-991-8888 for reservations or 800-991-7777 for info. Open 24hr. 19+.)

FESTIVALS

Detroit's numerous festivals draw millions of visitors. Hip jazz fans jet to Hart Plaza during Labor Day weekend for the four-day **Montreux-Detroit Jazz Festival** (☎963-7622). With more than 70 acts on three stages and mountains of international food at the World Food Court, it's the largest free jazz festival on the continent. The nation's oldest state fair, the **Michigan State Fair** (☎369-8250), at Eight Mile Rd. and Woodward Ave., gathers together bake-offs, art, and livestock birth exhibits during the two weeks before Labor Day. A two-week extravaganza in late June, the international **Freedom Festival** (☎923-8259), held jointly with Windsor, Ontario, celebrates the friendship between the US and Canada by igniting North America's largest fireworks display over the Detroit River. **Detroit's African World Festival** (☎877-8073) brings over a million people to Hart Plaza on the 3rd weekend in Aug. for an open-air market and free reggae, jazz, blues, and gospel concerts.

ANN ARBOR ☎734

For a small town tucked between some major industrial hubs, Ann Arbor hasn't done too badly. Named after Ann Rumsey and Ann Allen, wives of two of the area's early pioneers (who supposedly enjoyed sitting under grape arbors), the city has managed to prosper without losing its relaxed charm. In 1837, the gargantuan and well-respected University of Michigan moved to town, giving rise to a hip collage of leftists, granolas, yuppies, and middle Americans.

▊ GETTING THERE AND GETTING AROUND

Trains: Amtrak, 325 Depot St. (☎994-4906). To: Chicago (5hr., 3 per day, $22) and Detroit (1hr., 3 per day, $8-16). Tickets sold daily 6:45am-11:30pm.

Buses: Greyhound, 116 W. Huron St. (☎662-5511). To: Detroit (1-1½hr., 4 per day, $8); Chicago (6hr., 5 per day, $26); and Grand Rapids (2-4hr., 3 per day, $19). Open M-Sa 8am-6:30pm, Su 8am-9am and noon-6:30pm.

Public Transit: Ann Arbor Transportation Authority (AATA), Blake Transit Center, 331 S. 4th Ave. (☎996-0400 or 973-6500). Service in Ann Arbor and a few neighboring towns. Buses run M-F 6:45am-10:45pm, Sa-Su 8am-6:15pm. Fare 75¢, students and seniors 35¢. Station open M-F 7:30am-9pm, Sa noon-5:30pm. **AATA's Nightride,** ☎663-3888. Safe door-to-door transportation M-F 11pm-6am, Sa-Su 7pm-6am. Call to book a trip; the wait is 5-45min. Fare $2 per person. **Commuter Transportation Company,** ☎941-9391 or 800-488-7433. Frequent shuttle service between Ann Arbor and Detroit Metro Airport. Vans depart Ann Arbor 5am-7pm and return 7am-midnight. $24, round-trip $48. Door-to-door service for up to 4 $65-75. Reserve up to 48hr. in advance.

✴ ▊ ORIENTATION AND PRACTICAL INFORMATION

Ann Arbor's streets lie in a grid, but watch out for the *slant* of Packard St. and Detroit St. **Main St.** divides the town east-west, and **Huron St.** cuts it north-south. The central campus of the **University of Michigan,** where restaurants and bars live, lies four blocks east of Main St. and south of E. Huron (a 5min. walk from downtown). Although street meter parking is plentiful, authorities ticket ruthlessly. One-way streets and unexpected dead ends also make driving near the campus stressful.

Visitor Info: Ann Arbor Convention and Visitors Bureau, 120 W. Huron St. (☎995-7281 or 800-888-9487), at Ashley. Open M-F 8:30am-5pm.

Hotlines: Sexual Assault Crisis Line, ☎483-7273. **U. Michigan Sexual Assault Line,** ☎936-3333. **S.O.S. Crisis Line,** ☎485-3222. All 24hr. **U. Michigan Gay/Lesbian Referrals,** ☎763-4186. Operates M-F 9am-5pm.

Post Office: 2075 W. Stadium Blvd. (☎665-1100. Open M-F 7:30am-5pm.) **ZIP code:** 48103. **Area code:** 734.

ACCOMMODATIONS

Due to the many business travelers and college sports fans who flock to the town, expensive hotels, motels, and B&Bs dominate the lodging scene in Ann Arbor. Reservations are always advisable, especially during the school year. Reasonable rates exist at discount chains farther out of town or in **Ypsilanti** (*Ip-si-LAN-tee*), 5 mi. southeast along I-94. Just south of I-94 on the outskirts of Ann Arbor, good ol' **Motel 6**, 3764 S. State St., rents well-kept, reliable rooms. (☎665-9900. Singles $46-50; doubles $52-56.) The **Hotel Embassy**, 200 E. Huron, at 4th Ave., a short walk from the main campus downtown, offers tidy rooms in the middle of the action. (☎662-7100. Singles $40; doubles $45; key deposit $3.) For the wilderness-oriented, seven campgrounds lie within a 20 mi. radius of Ann Arbor. Both the **Pinckney Recreation Area**, 8555 Silver Hill (☎426-4913), in Pinckney, and the **Waterloo Recreation Area**, 16345 McClure Rd. (☎475-8307), in Chelsea, have rustic ($6) and modern ($14) sites and require a $4 vehicle permit.

 FOOD

Where there are students, there are cheap eats. Here the cheapest cram the sidewalks of **State St.** and **S. University St.**, while the more upscale line **Main St.** Next to the Kerrytown shops, growers haul their crops to the popular **farmers market**, 315 Detroit St. (☎761-1078. Open May-Dec. W and Sa 7am-3pm; Jan.-Apr. Sa 8am-3pm.) When it comes to deli fare, the renowned **Zingerman's Deli**, 422 Detroit St., doesn't mess around. Even *goyim* crowds line up for huge, excellent sandwiches for $6-12. (☎663-3354. Open daily 7am-10pm.) In the birthplace of Domino's, the readers of *Ann Arbor News* voted **Cottage Inn Pizza**, 512 E. William St., at Thompson St., purveyor of "best pizza." (☎663-3379. Open M-Th 11am-midnight, F-Sa 11am-1am, Su noon-midnight. Pizza $7-18.) Plants tremble at the mention of **Seva** (*say "VAH!"*), 314 E. Liberty, Ann Arbor's long-established veggie haven. It's comforting, earthy decor complements a meatless menu that covers Mexican, stir-fry, and all points in-between. (☎662-1111. Open M-Th 10:30am-9pm, F 10:30am-10pm, Sa 9am-10pm, Su 10am-9pm. Entrees $7-10.) The best (and cheapest) **Krazy Jim's Blimpy Burger**, 551 S. Division, near campus, is a favorite of kollege kids for their great, self-proclaimed $1.50 "cheaper than food" burgers. (☎663-4590. Open daily 11am-10pm.)

SIGHTS AND ENTERTAINMENT

Most of Ann Arbor's attractions stem from its identity as home to a major university. The U of M offers a handful of free museums near the main campus; while all are intriguing, only a couple merit a special trip. A limited but impressive collection of artwork from around the world fills the **University of Michigan Arts Museum (UMAM)**, 525 S. State St., at the corner of S. University St. (☎764-0395. Open Tu-W, F-Sa 10am-5pm, Th 10am-9pm, Su noon-5pm. Free.) The **University of Michigan Exhibit Museum of Natural History**, 1109 Geddes Ave., at Washtenaw, displays an assortment of dinosaur skeletons and other exhibits on zoology, astronomy, and geology. The planetarium offers indoor star-gazing on weekends. (☎764-0478. Open M-Sa 9am-5pm, Su noon-5pm. Museum free; planetarium $3, seniors and kids $2.)

Outside the university, the **Ann Arbor Hands-On Museum**, 219 E. Huron St., offers a tactile wonderland of exhibits designed to be felt, turned, touched, pushed, and plucked by children of all ages. (☎995-5437. Open Tu-F 10am-5:30pm, Sa 10am-5pm, Su 1-5pm. $4; seniors, students, and ages 3-17 $2.50.) Numerous local artists display their creations at the **artisan market**, 315 Detroit St., which shares the farmers market grounds (open May-Dec. Su 11am-4pm). It's nigh-impossible to get tickets for a **Wolverine football** game at UM's 115,000 capacity stadium, but fans can give it a shot by calling the athletics office at ☎764-0247.

As tens of thousands of students depart for the summer, locals indulge in a little celebration. In late July, thousands pack the city to view the work of nearly 600 artists at the **Ann Arbor Summer Art Fair** (☎995-7281). The **Ann Arbor Summer Festival** (☎647-2278) draws crowds from mid-June through early July for a collection of comedy, dance, and theater productions, as well as musical performances including jazz, country, and classical. The festival includes nightly outdoor movies at **Top of the Park,** on top of the Fletcher St. parking structure, next to the Health Services Building. The **County Events Hotline** (☎930-6300) has more info. Classical music lovers should contact the **University Musical Society,** in the Burton Memorial Clock Tower at N. University and Thouper, which sponsors 60 professional concerts per season at various area venues. (☎764-2538 or 800-221-1229. Open M-F 10am-5pm, Sa 10am-1pm. Tickets $10-55.)

 NIGHTLIFE

The monthlies *Current, Agenda, Weekender Entertainment,* and the weekly *Metrotimes,* all free and available in restaurants, music stores, and elsewhere, print up-to-date nightlife and entertainment listings. For gay and lesbian info pick up a copy of *OutPost* or *Between the Lines.* The **Blind Pig,** 208 S. First St., is the hottest spot in town for live music, with rock 'n' roll, reggae, blues, and swing. (☎996-8555. Open M-Sa until 2am. Cover $3-18; 19+. Happy hour bands each F 6-9pm with no cover.) Showcasing big names F and Sa, the **Bird of Paradise,** 207 S. Ashley, sings with live jazz every night at 9:30pm. (☎662-8310. Cover usually $3 during the week; F-Sa $5-20 depending on band. Free jam sessions on Su nights.) **The Nectarine,** 516 E. Liberty, is the place for young hipsters to shake their groove thing to DJ-controlled dance music. (☎994-5436. Open Tu-Sa until 2am; Tu is gay night.) **Conor O'Neill's,** 318 S. Main St., is a hearty Celtic-flavored hangout for ale-loving locals and students. (☎665-2968. Open daily 11am-2am.) On weekends, locals hang out at **Del Rio,** 122 W. Washington St., at Ashley, for cheap burgers and Mexican food, good vegetarian options, and free jazz Su evenings. (☎761-2530. Open M-Sa noon-2am, Su 5:30pm-2am with jazz until 9pm.) Sports fans unable to snag a ticket to the big game should head to **Touchdown Cafe Grill & Bar,** 1220 S. University on campus, to guzzle beer, play pool, and indulge their inner quarterback with enormous TVs. (☎665-7777. Open daily 11am-2am.)

GRAND RAPIDS   ☎616

From its humble beginning as one among many fur trading posts, Grand Rapids worked hard to distinguish itself from its neighbors. While many towns opted for tourist chic with quaint, old-fashioned looks, Grand Rapids plowed ahead to become a city of concrete and tall buildings. While attractive to businesses, Grand Rapids offers precious little in the way of entertainment for the traveler. Most use it as a transportation hub to reach the rest of western Michigan.

🛈 **PRACTICAL INFORMATION.** Most of Grand Rapids' streets are neatly gridded. The town is quartered by the north-south Division St. and the east-west Fulton St. **Greyhound,** 190 Wealthy St. (☎456-1709; station open daily 6:45am-10pm), connects to: Detroit (3½hr., 4 per day, $19-23); Chicago (4½hr., 3 per day, $27-29); and Ann Arbor (3hr., 1 per day, $18-21). **Amtrak,** 507 Wealthy St., at Market, has service to the south and west, including Chicago (4hr., 1 per day, $32-46, round-trip $58). The station, which does not sell tickets, only opens when trains pass through. **Grand Rapids Transit Authority (GRATA),** 333 Wealthy St. SW, sends buses throughout the city and suburbs. (☎776-1100. Runs M-F 6am-6pm, Sa 9am-9pm. Fare $1.25, seniors 60¢; 10-ride pass $7, students and seniors $6.) **Veterans Taxi:** ☎459-4646. The **Grand Rapids-Kent County Convention and Visitors Bureau,** 134 Monroe Center (☎459-8287 or 800-678-9859; open M-F 9am-7pm) and the **West Michigan Tourist Association,** 1253 Front Ave. NW (☎456-8557 or 800-442-2084; open M-Th 8:30am-5pm, F 8:30am-6pm, Sa 9am-1pm) furnish general area info. **24hr. Suicide, Drug, Alcohol, and Crisis Line,** ☎336-3535. **Post Office:** 225 Michigan St. N.W. (☎532-2109; open M-F 8am-5:30pm, Sa 9am-12:30pm). **ZIP code:** 49503. **Area code:** 616.

■■■ ACCOMMODATIONS, FOOD, AND NIGHTLIFE. Most of the cheaper motels and restaurants cluster south of the city along Division and 28th St. **The Knights Inn,** 35 28th St. SW, offers 102 large rooms, with an indoor pool and hot tub (☎452-5141 or 800-843-5644; singles $38, doubles $50). Men are in luck at the **YMCA,** 33 Library St. NE, downtown (☎222-9626; $26, $15 per additional night; no reservations). Just 12 mi. northeast of downtown, **Grand Rogue Campgrounds,** 6400 W. River Dr., sports wooded, riverside sites. Take Rte. 131 north to Comstock Park Exit 91, then head left on W. River Dr. for 4 mi. (☎361-1053; $18.50, with hook-up $23).

Throngs of locals pack the **Beltline Bar and Café,** 16 28th St. SE, for Grand Rapids' most popular Mexican food. Wet burritos, the house specialty, start at $5. (☎245-0494. Open M-Tu 7am-midnight, W-Sa 7am-1am, Su noon-10:30pm.) The ■**Four Friends Coffeehouse,** 136 Monroe Center, has excellent coffee concoctions (from $2), fresh muffins ($1.25), and delicious sandwiches (from $3) in a bright, trendy atmosphere. (☎456-5356. Open M-Th 7am-10pm, F 7am-midnight, Sa 9:30am-midnight; Sept.-May open until 11pm. Live music on F and Sa during the school year.) The **Grand Rapids Brewing Company,** 3689 28th St. SE, makes tasty $6 burgers, steaks, and $3 hand-crafted beers. (☎285-5970. Open M-Th 11am-10pm, F-Sa 11am-11pm, Su noon-10pm; bar open M-Th 11am-midnight, F-Sa 11am-1am, Su 11am-11pm.)

Detailed listings on events and nightlife in Grand Rapids can be found in *On the Town* or *In the City,* both available in most shops, restaurants, and kiosks. The artsy Eastown District houses the bulk of the local music scene, but dance clubs overshadow other forms of city nightlife. The wild **Diversions,** 10 Fountain NW, is *the* place to showcase your funkiest dance moves. (☎451-3800. Open daily from 8pm, dance floor opens at 10pm. Karaoke W, Sa at 10pm. Cover Th-Sa $3; 18+.)

■ SIGHTS. The attractive **Public Museum of Grand Rapids,** showcases marvels such as one of the world's largest whale skeletons (76 ft.), a 50-animal carousel, and a planetarium. *(Open M-Sa 9am-5pm, Su noon-5pm. $5, seniors $4, ages 3-17 $2. Planetarium $1.50.)* The largest year-round conservatory in Michigan, the **Frederik Meijer Gardens** keeps over 100 sculptures among numerous tropical plants on its 70 acres. A $12.8 million addition and a three-story replica of a Da Vinci horse sculpture were purchased in celebration of the millenium. *(3411 Bradford St. at Beltline. ☎957-1580. Open M-W and F-Sa 9am-5pm, Th 9am-9pm, Su noon-5pm; Sept.-May M-Sa 9am-5pm, Su noon-5pm. $5, seniors $4, ages 5-13 $2.)* Architecture enthusiasts shouldn't miss the **Meyer May House,** an authentic Frank Lloyd Wright-designed masterpiece. *(450 Madison Ave. SE at Logan St. ☎246-4821. Open Tu, Th 10am-2pm and most Su 1pm-5pm. Free.)*

LAKE MICHIGAN SHORE

The freighters that once powered the rise of Chicago still steam along the coast of Lake Michigan, but have long since been supplanted by pleasure boats. With dunes of sugary sand, superb fishing, abundant fruit harvests, and deep winter snows, the eastern shore of Lake Michigan is a midwestern vacationer's dreamland. The coastline stretches 350 miles north from the Indiana border to the Mackinaw Bridge; its southern end is a scant 2 hours from downtown Chicago.

■■ ORIENTATION AND PRACTICAL INFORMATION

Many of the region's attractions are to be found in the small coastal towns that cluster around Grand Traverse Bay in the north. **Traverse City,** at the southern tip of the bay, is famous as the "cherry capital of the world," and fishing is best in the Au Sable and Manistee Rivers. However, the rich Mackinac Island Fudge, sold in numerous specialty shops on and around the Island, seems to have the biggest hold on tourists ("fudgies" to locals; see **Mackinac Island,** p. 489). The main north-south route along the coast is U.S. 31. Numerous detours, marked by green "Lake Michigan Circle Tour" signs, twist closer to the shoreline, providing an excellent way to explore the coast. Coastal accommodations can be exorbitantly expensive; for cheaper lodging, head inland. Based in Grand Rapids, the **West Michigan Tourist Association,** 1253 Front Ave. NW hands out literature on the area. (☎ 456-8557 or 800-442-2084. Open M-Th 8:30am-5pm, F 8:30am-6pm, Sa 9am-1pm.) The Lake Michigan Shore's **area codes** are 616 and 231.

SOUTHERN MICHIGAN SHORE

HOLLAND   ☎ 616

Thirty mi. southwest of Grand Rapids off I-196, Holland was founded in 1847 by Dutch religious dissenters and remained mostly Dutch well into the 20th century. The town cashes in on its heritage with a bevy of tacky Dutch-inspired attractions; still, it's worth visiting around May when the tulips bloom. The small but high-quality **Holland Museum,** 31 W. 10th St., displays ceramics, furniture from the home country, and exhibits on town history. (☎ 392-9084. Open M and W-Sa 10am-5pm, Su 2-5pm. $3, students and seniors $2.) The harvest at the jubilantly arrayed **Veldheer Tulip Gardens,** 12755 Quincy St., at U.S. 31, would be the envy of the Amsterdam market. (☎ 399-1900. Open M-F 8am-6pm, Sa-Su 9am-5pm. $2.50, ages 3-13 $1.50. In tulip time $5/$3.) Next door, the **DeKlomp Wooden Shoe and Delftware Factory** caters to tourists who want to take home a wooden or porcelain souvenir. (☎ 399-1900. Open M-F 8am-6pm. Free.) A nearby "authentic" **Dutch Village,** 12350 James St., at U.S. 31, is worth a look, although its oversized wooden shoe and windmill attractions can resemble a mini-golf course *sans* holes. (☎ 396-1475. Open daily late Apr. to mid-Oct. 9am-5pm. $6.50, ages 3-11 $4.50.) DeZwaan, the nation's only operating Dutch windmill, turns on **Windmill Island,** at the corner of Lincoln and 7th St. downtown. (☎ 355-1030. Open daily May-Oct. with variable hours; call for info. $5.50, ages 5-12 $2.50, under 5 free.)

The **Blue Mill Inn,** 409 U.S. 31, at 16th St., rents decent singles from $52 and doubles from $64 (☎ 392-7073 or 888-258-3140; off-season rates lower). **Holland State Park,** 2215 Ottawa Beach Rd., 8 mi. west of Holland, has 306 sparsely wooded sites nestled between Lake Macatawa and Lake Michigan. (☎ 399-9390 or 800-447-2757. Sites $15; $4 vehicle permit.) **Greyhound,** 171 Lincoln Ave. (☎ 396-8664), runs through Holland to Detroit (4hr., 2 per day, $25-27); Chicago (4hr., 3 per day, $24-26); and Grand Rapids (35min., 3 per day, $7). **Amtrak,** in the same building, runs a daily train to Chicago (3hr., $31). Reserve train tickets in advance; there are no Amtrak representatives at the station. (Station open M-F 7-11am and 12:30-4:30pm.) **Holland Convention and Visitors Bureau:** 76 E. 8th St. downtown (☎ 394-0000 or 800-506-1299; open M-F 8am-5pm, May-Oct. also Sa 10:30am-3pm).

GRAND HAVEN   ☎ 616

Thirty-five mi. west of Grand Rapids off I-96, Grand Haven is one of the best beach communities in the area. The town offers a relaxed, resort-like atmosphere and lots of sand—so pure that auto manufacturers use it to make cores and molds for engine parts. The small downtown area attracts visitors to its pleasant "boardwalk" along the lake. In the heart of downtown, **Washington St.** is lined with shops, restaurants, and laidback people. The spectacular **Musical Fountain,** at the end of Washington St., pulses with water and light to the beat of different music each night at dusk. (☎ 842-4910 or 842-2550. Operates Memorial Day to Labor Day around 9:30pm.)

An upscale northwoods hostel, the ▨**Khardomah Lodge,** 1365 Lake Ave., has charmingly decorated rooms and enormous common areas. Its Americana character, warm service, and location less than 200 yd. from the beach, make it one of the best budget lodgings on all of Michigan's lakeshore. (☎ 842-2990. Kitchen, shared bath. Doubles $58, $10 per additional person. Reservations strongly recommended.) Campers who don't mind sand between their toes will love picturesque **Grand Haven State Park,** 1001 Harbor Dr. (☎ 800-447-2757. Open early Apr.-Oct. $15 plus $4 permit for site and electrical hook-up.) **Grand Haven Area Visitors Bureau:** 1 S. Harbor Dr., at Washington St. (☎ 842-4499 or 800-303-4096. Open M 9:30am-5pm, Tu-F 8:30am-5pm, Sa 10am-2pm in summer.)

CENTRAL MICHIGAN SHORE

MANISTEE   ☎ 231

Manistee's claim to be a "Victorian Port City" is overshadowed by the impressive trio of natural beauties that surround it. Lake Michigan tempts boaters, swimmers, and beachgoers, while fishing buffs are drawn to Manistee Lake. Manistee National Forest blankets the outer reaches of the city, giving it a pleasantly sheltered feel.

There are several relatively inexpensive motel options in and near Manistee. The friendly **Riverside Motel,** 520 Water St., has dock space for boats and large waterfront rooms. (☎723-3554. Singles $69-99 in summer, $29-69 in winter; doubles $69-109/$35-79.) Fourteen mi. north in Onekama, the **Traveller's Motel,** 5606 Eight Mile Rd., a half block from Rte. 22, rents enormous rooms with kitchenettes. (☎889-4342. Singles $45; doubles $60; with kitchenettes for up to 6 people $80; in winter $32/$42/$55.) The **National Forest** supplies copious camping at 11 campgrounds in the area ($5 per person; no reservations). Those who enjoy roughing it are free to camp anywhere in the forest.

More info on hiking and canoeing is available from the **Manistee Ranger Station,** 1658 Manistee Hwy., 2 mi. north of Manistee on U.S. 31. (☎723-2211. Open M-F 8am-5pm, Sa-Su 8:30am-5pm.) Thirty mi. to the south, the **Lake Michigan Car Ferry** shuttles people and cars between Ludington and Manitowoc, WI, granting easy access Wisconsin's major cities and attractions. (☎800-841-4243. 4hr., 2 per day late June to Aug., in spring and fall 1 per day; $38, seniors $35, ages 5-15 $17, for cars an additional $46. Reservations recommended.) The **Manistee County Chamber of Commerce,** 50 Filer St. in Briny Bldg., Suite 224, stocks pamphlets on local attractions (☎723-2575 or 800-288-2286. Open M-F 8am-5:30pm.)

SLEEPING BEAR DUNES   ☎ 231

The Sleeping Bear Dunes lie along the western shores of the Leelanau Peninsula, 20 mi. west of Traverse City on Rte. 72. According to Chippewa legend, the mammoth sand dune represents a sleeping mother bear, waiting for her drowned cubs—the Manitou Islands—to finish a swim across the lake after fleeing a forest fire. Each cub has a distinctive personality—South Manitou is small and more civilized, while rugged North Manitou is vast and untamed. The sleepy town of **Empire** serves as the gateway to the **Sleeping Bear Dunes National Lakeshore,** which includes both the Manitou Islands and 25 mi. of lakeshore on the mainland. Near the historic Fishtown shops, **Manitou Island Transit,** in Leland, makes daily trips to South Manitou and ventures five times per week in July and Aug. to North Manitou. (☎256-9061. Check-in 9:15am. Call ahead for schedule in May-June and Sept.-Nov. Round-trip $22, under 13 $13.) **Camping** is available on both islands with the purchase of a **permit** ($5; plus required park entrance fee $7 for 7 days; buy at the visitors center); the Manitou Islands do not allow cars.

Willing climbers can be king of the sandhill at **Dune Climb,** 5 mi. north of Empire on Rte. 109. From there, a strenuous 2½ mi. hike over sandy hills leads to Lake Michigan in all its refreshing glory. If you'd rather let your car do the climbing, drive to an overlook along the 7 mi. **Pierce Stocking Scenic Drive,** off Rte. 109 just north of Empire, where a 450 ft. sand cliff descends to the cool water below (open daily mid-May to mid-Oct. 9am-10pm). For maps and info on the numerous cross-country skiing, hiking, and mountain biking trails in the lakeshore area, stop by the helpful **National Parks Service Visitors Center,** 9922 Front St., in Empire (☎326-5134; open daily in summer 9am-6pm; mid-Sept. to mid June 9am-4pm).

Sleeping Bear Dunes has four **campgrounds: DH Day** (☎334-4634), in Glen Arbor, with 83 primitive sites ($10); **Platte River** (☎325-5881 or 800-365-2267), off the southern shore, with 179 sites and showers ($14, with electricity $19); and two cheaper **backcountry campsites** accessible by 1½ mi. trails (no reservations; $5 permit required, available at visitors center or at either developed campground). The Platte River (at the southern end of the lakeshore) and the Crystal River (at the northern end) are ideal for canoeing or for lazy floating. **Crystal River Outfitters,** 6249

Western Ave. (Rte. 22), near Glen Arbor, offers 1-4hr. kayak excursions. (☎334-7490. $12.50-20 per person.) **Riverside Canoes,** 5042 Scenic Hwy. (Rte. 22), at Platte River Bridge, lets less adventurous types play with water toys. (☎325-5622. Inner tubes $4-6 for 1hr., $11-13 for 2hr.; canoes $25-29; kayaks $16.)

TRAVERSE CITY   ☎231

Named after the "Grand Traverse" that French fur traders once made between the Leelanau and Old Mission Peninsulas, Traverse City offers the summer vacationer a slew of sandy beaches and more than a bowl full of cherries (half of the nation's cherries are produced in the surrounding area).

🛈 PRACTICAL INFORMATION. Indian Trails and **Greyhound,** 3233 Cass Rd. (☎946-5180), tie Traverse City to Detroit (7½hr., 3 per day, $38) and to the Upper Peninsula via St. Ignace (2½hr., 2 per day, $17). The **Bay Area Transportation Authority** has a demand-response service; you call them and they'll pick you up. (☎941-2324. Available M-Sa 6:30am-2am, Su 8am-12am. Fare $2, daily pass $4.) **Traverse City Convention and Visitors Bureau:** 101 West Grandview Pkwy./U.S. 31 N. (☎947-1120 or 800-872-8377. Open M-Sa 9am-6pm, Su 11am-3pm; in winter M-F 9am-5pm, Sa 9am-3pm.) **Post Office:** 202 S. Union St. (☎946-9616; open M-F 9am-4pm). **ZIP code:** 49684.

🛏 ACCOMMODATIONS. East Front St. (U.S. 31) is lined with motels, but it is nearly impossible to find a room for under $50 in the popular summer months. **Northwestern Michigan College,** 1701 E. Front St., West Hall, has some of the cheapest beds in the city. (☎922-1409. Open early June to Aug. Singles $30; doubles $40; suite with bathroom $55. Reserve several weeks in advance.) The **Shoestring Resort,** at the intersection of Garfield and River Rd., 12 mi. south of town, offers exceptionally pleasant cabins with one to three bedrooms, kitchens, cable TV, and A/C at reasonable rates. (☎946-7935. Cottages start at $35 per night; in winter $10 lower; weekly rates available. Reserve several weeks in advance.) For those who prefer to commune with nature, or at least 300 other campers, **Traverse City State Park,** 1132 U.S. 31 N, 2 mi. east of town, has 344 wooded sites across the street from the beach. (☎922-5270 or 800-447-2757. Sites with hook-up $15; $4 vehicle permit fee.)

🍽 FOOD AND NIGHTLIFE. Front St. downtown offers a range of appealing food options. **Poppycock's,** 128 E. Front St. doles out $7-8 homemade linguini lunches and $5-7 gourmet sandwiches (vegetarian and otherwise) in a stylish setting. (☎941-7632. Open in summer M-Th 11am-10pm, F-Sa 11am-10:30pm, Su noon-9pm; in winter M-Th 11am-9pm, F-Sa 11am-10pm.) The **North Peak Brewing Company,** 400 W. Front St., dishes out local specialties like a Sesame Walleye Sandwich ($7), along with more standard pub fare and house brew North Peak Pale Ale. (☎941-7325. Open daily from 11am.) The **U & I Lounge,** Front St. downtown, is the hottest bar in town, thanks in part to the intimate atmosphere and tasty local beer. (☎946-8932. Open M-Sa 11am-2am, kitchen until 1:35am, Su noon-2am, kitchen until 1:15am.) For more entertainment info, pick up the weekly *Traverse City Record-Eagle Summer Magazine* or *Northern Express* at corner kiosks around the city.

🎿 ACTIVITIES. In the summer, swimming, boating, and scuba diving interests focus on Grand Traverse Bay; free beaches and public access sites speckle the shore. The area's scenic waterfront also makes for excellent biking. The **TART** bike trail runs 8 mi. along E. and W. Grand Traverse Bay, while the 30 mi. loop around Old Mission Peninsula, just north of the city, provides great views of the Bay on both sides. **Ralston Cycles,** 750 E. 8th St., rents bikes. (☎941-7161. Open M-Th 9am-6pm, F 9am-7pm, Sa 9am-5pm, Su 11am-4pm. $15 per day, $25 all weekend.)

Most other attractions in the Traverse City area focus on its fruit. The annual **National Cherry Festival,** held the first full week in July, is a rousing tribute to the fruit's annual harvest with concerts, parties and lots of cherry pie. (☎947-4230.)) In early to mid-July, five orchards near Traverse City let visitors pick their own cherries, including **Amon Orchards,** 10 mi. north on U.S. 31. (☎938-9160. Open daily 9am-

6pm. $1.25 per lb.; eat while you pick for free.) More sophisticated fruit connois-
seurs might indulge their tastebuds at one of the area's many well-respected wineries. **Château Grand Traverse,** 12239 Center Rd., 8 mi. north of Traverse City on M37, offers free tours and tastings amid acres of gorgeous vineyards. (☎223-7355 or 800-283-0247. Open M-Sa 10am-7pm, Su noon-6pm; Nov.-Apr. M-Sa 10am-5pm, Su noon-5pm. In summer, tours on the hr. noon-4pm.)

NORTHERN MICHIGAN SHORE

STRAITS OF MACKINAC   ☎231

Only fur'ners say *"mackinACK;"* in the Land of the Great Turtle (as early Native Americans called it), Mackinac is pronounced *"mackinAW."* Colonial **Fort Michilimackinac** still guards the straits between Lake Michigan and Lake Huron, but tourists, not troops, flock to **Mackinaw City.** Along with Fort Michilimackinac, **Fort Mackinac** (on Mackinac Island, see below) and **Historic Mill Creek** (3½ mi. south of Mackinaw City on Rte. 23) form a trio of State Historic Parks in the area. (☎436-5563. All open daily mid-June to early Sept. 9am-6pm; early Sept. to Oct. and mid-May to mid-June 10am-5pm. Each park $7.25, ages 6-12 $4.25, families $20.) The **Mackinac Bridge** ("Mighty Mac"), connecting Mackinaw City to St. Ignace in the Upper Peninsula, is the world's longest suspension bridge. A local tradition not to be missed is the annual **Labor Day Bridge Walk,** where Michigan's governor leads thousands of pilgrims across the bridge from Mackinaw City to St. Ignace.

The best lodging deals in the area lie across the Mackinac Bridge and away from the lakeshore on the I-75 Business Loop in St. Ignace. Five minutes from the docks, the **Cedars Motel,** 2040 I-75 Business Loop, rents cushy rooms. (☎905-643-9578. Open early May to Oct 1. Singles $32-41; doubles $40-65.) Back near Mackinaw City, campers can crash at the enormous **Mackinac Mill Creek Campground,** 3 mi. south of town on Rte. 23. Most of its 600 sites lie near the lake. (☎436-5584. Sites $12.50, full hook-up $15; cabins $35, 2nd night $30, 3rd $25.) Sites at the **Wilderness State Park,** 11 mi. west of the city on Wilderness Park Dr., have showers and electricity. (☎436-5381. $15; 4- to 8-person cabins $40; 20-person bunkhouse $55.)

For transportation outside the city, **Indian Trails** (☎517-725-5105 or 800-292-3831) has a flag stop at the Big Boy restaurant on Nicolet Ave. One bus runs north and one south daily; buy tickets at the next station. The **Michigan Dept. of Transportation Welcome and Travel Information Center,** on Nicolet St. off I-75 at Exit 338, has loads of helpful info on lodging, food and area attractions. (☎436-5566. Open Sa-Th 9am-7pm, F 9am-8pm; Sept. to mid-June daily 9am-5pm. Free reservation service.)

MACKINAC ISLAND   ☎231

Posh Mackinac Island, an 18min. ferry ride from the mainland, has long been considered Mackinaw City's classier cousin. The prohibition of cars on the heavily touristed island, and the resulting proliferation of horse-drawn carriages, have given it a snobbish air and a decidedly equine aroma. Nevertheless, travelers flock to the island for its coastal, old-world charm.

The main draws include **Fort Mackinac,** magnificent Victorian homes, and countless roamable beaches. (Fort ☎906-847-3328. Open daily 9:30am-6:30pm, closed in winter. $7.50, ages 6-12 $4.50, under 6 free.) Connoisseurs will immediately recognize the island as the birthplace of Mackinac Fudge, sold in shops all over the island and along the entire Michigan coastline (1 lb. box $7). **Horse-drawn carriages** cart guests on tours all over the island, showcasing architectural wonders such as the ritzy Grand Hotel. (Carriage tours ☎906-847-3325. Open daily 8:30am-5pm; $14, ages 4-11 $7.) Saddle horses ($25 per hr.) are also available at various stables around the isle. Perhaps the best way to see the island and escape the tourist mayhem is by bicycle. Rentals line Main St. by the ferry docks ($4 per hr.). Encompassing 80% of the island, **Mackinac Island State Park** features a circular 8.2 mi. shoreline road for biking and hiking.

GREAT LAKES

Transportation to the island via ferry is quick and pleasant, providing terrific views of the Mackinac Bridge. Three ferry lines leave Mackinaw City and St. Ignace with overlapping schedules, though service from St. Ignace is less frequent. The catamarans operated by **Arnold Transit Co.** (☎847-3351 or 800-542-8528) are a fun way to jet to the island. During the summer, a ferry leaves Mackinaw City every 30min. from 8am-11pm (round-trip $14.50, under 16 $5.50, bike passage $5.50). Prices on the island are exorbitantly high; the mainland is the place to stay. For food, **Mighty Mac** cooks it good and cheap, with huge ¼ lb. burgers under $4 (☎847-6384; open daily 8am-8pm). The invaluable *Mackinac Island Locator Map* ($1) and the *Discover Mackinac Island* book ($2) can be found at the **Mackinac Island Chamber of Commerce,** on Main St. (☎906-847-3783 or 800-454-5257. Open daily 8am-7pm; Oct.-May 9am-5pm.)

SCENIC DRIVE: NORTHERN MICHIGAN SHORE DRIVE

Vibrant cherry trees, tranquil lake shores, and intimate resort villages dot the Northern Michigan Shore. Once a trade route used by Native Americans and French fur traders, the path along the coast now offers a glimpse into the diversity of Michigan's lands.

U.S. 31 winds its way 65 mi. north from Traverse City to Petoskey, where tortuous M119 takes over and completes the 31 mi. journey to Cross Village. It takes about 3hr. to do justice to the drive, stopping along the way to admire both the natural and manmade wonders that line the route. Although the roads are generally well maintained, drivers should exercise special caution in the spectacular 27 mi. stretch of M119 between Cross Village and Harbor Springs, known as the **Tunnel of Trees.** This patch of road is extremely narrow and twists through many sharp curves, necessitating slow speeds and care in passing. Luckily, the slow pace is rewarded with more time to absorb the natural beauty of the area.

Just 12 mi. outside of bustling Traverse City, lush cherry orchards line the road around the sleepy town of **Acme.** Twenty mi. north of Acme, then west on Barnes Park Road, the village of **Torch Lake** harbors pristine, isolated beaches on **Grand Traverse Bay** at **Barnes County Park.** More cherry trees line the route north of **Atwood,** one of the most prolific areas of the cherry harvest.

Rolling hills and increasingly elaborate homes mark the entrance into **Charlevoix** (*SHAR-le-voy*), a resort village that inhabits the narrow strip of land between Lake Michigan and Lake Charlevoix. The yacht-filled, high-brow town now attracts more tourists than it did earlier in the century, when one-time resident Ernest Hemingway used the area as the setting for many of his Nick Adams stories. The **Charlevoix Area Chamber of Commerce,** 408 Bridge St., dishes the dirt on area attractions such as golfing, boating, and shopping. (☎547-4045 or 800-367-8557. Open in summer M-Sa 9am-7pm; in winter M-F 9am-5pm and Sa 10am-4pm.) Lodging rarely comes cheap in this coastal resort town, but the **Colonial Motel,** 6822 U.S. 31 S, is better than the rest with free coffee, A/C, and cable TV. (☎547-6637. Open May-Oct. Singles $38-60; doubles $48-70. Lower rates off season.) Campers who don't mind doing without showers and electricity can bask in 90 sites on the shores of Lake Michigan at **Fisherman's Island State Park,** on Bells Bay Rd., 5 mi. south of Charlevoix on U.S. 31. (☎547-6641 or 800-447-2757. Rustic sites $6; $4 vehicle permit fee.) Charlevoix also serves as the gateway to **Beaver Island,** the Great Lakes region's most remote inhabited island. Hiking, boating, biking, and swimming abound on the island's 53 sq. mi., just a 2¼hr. ferry trip from shore. (**Ferries** depart from 102 Bridge St. 1-3 times per day. Round-trip $31, ages 5-12 $15.50; bikes $12. Call ☎547-2311 or 888-446-4095 for more info.) **Beaver Island Chamber of Commerce:** ☎448-2505.

PETOSKEY   ☎231

Eighteen mi. north of Charlevoix on the mainland, the slightly larger resort town of Petoskey is best known for its Petoskey Stones, fossilized coral from an ancient sea that remains strewn about the area's beaches. Another vacation haunt of Hemingway, the town honors him with a feature at the **Little Traverse History Museum,** on the waterfront downtown at 1 Waterfront Park. (☎347-2620. Open Memorial Day-Labor

Day M-Sa 10am-4pm; May and Sept.-Oct. Tu-Sa 10am-4pm. $3.) Nearby, the **Sunset Park Scenic Overlook** is an unbeatable place to watch the sun sink below the horizon.

The cheapest rooms in town are at homely **North Central Michigan College,** 1515 Howard St., which rents single dorm rooms within a suite. (☎348-6611 or 348-6612 for reservations. Singles $30; doubles $40; 4-person suite $70. Linen provided. Reservations recommended; cash or check only.) The **Petoskey Motel,** at the corner of U.S. 31 and U.S. 131, rents well-kept, spacious rooms with A/C and cable. (☎347-8177. Singles $39-49.) Petoskey's **Gaslight District,** just off U.S. 31 downtown, features local crafts and foods in period shops. In the heart of the district, the nautical-themed **Roast and Toast Cafe,** 309 E. Lake St., serves pasta and chicken dishes for $7-10. (☎347-7767. Open daily in summer 7am-9:30pm; in winter 7am-8pm.) The **City Park Grill** sells sandwiches ($5-7) and contemporary cuisine ($7-12) in an elegant 1910 setting dear to Hemingway. (☎347-0101. Open M-Th 11:30am-10pm, bar open later; live entertainment W-Sa 10pm. $2-3 cover.)

Although it lies 20 mi. east of Petoskey in a remote woodland just outside Indian River, the **Cross in the Woods,** 7078 M68, (☎238-8973) is worth straying from the charted path to see. Here, a 31 ft. bronze Jesus cleaved onto a 55 ft. tall wooden cross—the world's tallest—forms an anguished yet oddly imposing monument to the national obsession with size.

UPPER PENINSULA

A multi-million-acre forestland bordered by three of the world's largest lakes, Michigan's Upper Peninsula (U.P.) is among the most scenic, unspoiled stretches of land in the Great Lakes region. In 1837, though, Michigan only grudgingly accepted this "wasteland to the north" in the unpopular deal that gave the territory statehood. From the start, Michigan exploited most of the land, laying waste to huge tracts of forest destined for the fireplaces of Chicago. In the past century, however, the now-protected forests have returned to their original grandeur, and the U.P.'s spectacular waterfalls and miles of coastline have won the hearts of nature lovers.

Only 24,000 people live in the U.P.'s largest town, **Marquette.** The region is a paradise for fishing, camping, hiking, snowmobiling, and escaping hectic urban life. Hikers here enjoy numerous treks, including Michigan's section of **North Country Trail,** a national scenic trail extending from New York to North Dakota. The **North Country Trail Association,** 49 Monroe Center NW, Suite 200B, Grand Rapids 49503 (☎616-454-5506) provides details on the path. A vibrant spectrum of foliage makes autumn a beautiful time to hike; in the winter, skiers and snowmobilers replace hikers as layers of snow blanket the trails. After the ice thaws, dozens of pristine rivers beckon canoers. Those who heed the call of the water should contact the **Michigan Association of Paddlesport Providers,** P.O. Box 270, Wellston, MI 49689 (☎616-862-3227).

Outside the major tourist towns, motel rooms in the U.P. generally start at around $24. The peninsula has 200 **campgrounds,** including those at both national forests (call ☎800-447-2757 for reservations). Sleep with your dogs or bring extra blankets—temperatures in these parts drop to 50°F, even in July. For regional cuisine, indulge in the Friday night **fish-fry:** all-you-can-eat whitefish, perch, or walleye buffets served in almost every restaurant in every town. The local ethnic specialty is a **pasty** (*PASS-tee*), a meat pie imported by Cornish miners in the 19th century.

▣ PRACTICAL INFORMATION

Helpful **welcome centers** guard the U.P. at its six main entry points: **Ironwood,** 801 W. Cloverland Dr. (☎932-3330; open daily June-Aug. 8am-6pm, in winter daily 8am-4pm); **Iron Mountain,** 618 S. Stephenson Ave. (☎774-4201; open daily June-Aug. 7am-5pm, in winter 8am-4pm); **Menominee,** 1343 10th Ave. (☎863-6496; open daily Memorial Day to Labor Day 8am-5pm, in winter 8am-4pm); **Marquette,** 2201 U.S. 41 S (☎249-9066; open daily 9am-6pm); **Sault Ste. Marie,** 943 Portage Ave. W. (☎632-8242; open daily June-Sept. 8am-6pm, Oct.-May 9am-5pm); and **St. Ignace,** on I-75 N just

GREAT LAKES

> # DEER SEASON
> Lasting only 2 weeks in late November, "Deer Season" might seem relatively innocuous to the unwary traveler, yet in this part of the country, Deer Season is fraught with cultural significance. Many schools in the Upper Peninsula and the northern Lower Peninsula close on Opening Day (the first day of Deer Season) because of the sheer number of student absences. The song "The Second Week of Deer Camp" is played incessantly on the radio. Hunter's orange, an eye-catching fabric hue designed to prevent accidental shootings, becomes *de rigeur* in every bar and tavern. The same old jokes are bandied around with equal enthusiasm each year: "What's the difference between beer nuts and deer nuts? Beer nuts are $2.50; deer nuts are under a buck." Groan if you want, but he has a gun....

north of the Mackinac Bridge (☎643-6979; open daily June-Aug. 8am-6pm, Sept.-May 9am-5pm). The invaluable *Upper Peninsula Travel Planner* is published by the **Upper Peninsula Travel and Recreation Association** (☎800-562-7134; info line staffed M-F 8am-4:30pm). For additional help planning a trip into the wilderness, write to or call the **U.S. Forestry Service** at the **Hiawatha National Forest,** 2727 N. Lincoln Rd., Escanaba 49829 (☎786-4062). **Area code:** 906.

SAULT STE. MARIE AND THE EASTERN U.P. ☎906

The shipping industry rules in gritty Sault ("Soo") Ste. Marie, where "the locks" are the primary attraction for both tourists and prospective residents. Back in the day, St. Mary's River dropped 21 vertical ft. over 1 mi. in this area, rendering the river impassable by boat. In 1855, entrepreneurs built the first lock here, opening up industrial opportunities that led the region to relative economic prosperity. Now the busiest in the world, the city's four locks float over 12,000 ships annually, gradually lowering them through successive, emptying chambers. A 2hr. **Soo Locks Boat Tour,** which leaves from both 1157 and 515 E. Portage Ave., grants a close-up look at the locks operation. (☎632-6301 or 800-432-6301 for departure times. Open mid-May to mid-Oct. $15, ages 13-18 $12, ages 4-12 $6.50.) For landlubbers, the **Locks Park Historic Walkway** parallels the water for 1 mi. and offers a slightly different perspective.

On the waterfront, at the end of Johnston St., lies the **Museum Ship Valley Camp,** a 1917 steam-powered freighter housing the Great Lakes's largest maritime museum and the **Marine Hall of Fame.** (☎632-3658. Open daily July-Aug. 9am-9pm; mid-May to June and Sept. to mid-Oct. 10am-6pm. $6.50, children $3.50.) A different, wilder side of the Soo rewards intrepid travelers who cross the 2 mi. long **International Bridge** into Ontario (toll $1.50). Although the Canadian Sault Ste. Marie is more urban and larger than its American cousin, it has more immediate access to wilderness. The **Agawa Canyon Train Tour** is an all-day excursion into a picturesque North that gives new meaning to the words "sparsely populated." (☎800-242-9287. Departs from the Station Mall, 129 Bay St. Operates early June to late Oct. In summer, CDN$54, seniors CDN$46, ages 5-18 CDN$17, under 5 CDN$12. In fall when the trees are in full color, CDN$66/CDN$66/CDN$40/CDN$15.)

The Ontario side of the city is also home to the area's best lodging deal. **The Algonquin Hotel (HI-C),** 864 Queen St. E., features intimate private rooms in a fun, welcoming atmosphere just 1 mi. from the bridge. (☎705-253-2311. Singles CDN$21.25, nonmembers $28; doubles CDN$33.60/$39. Cash or travelers checks only.) Otherwise, affordable accommodations line the I-75 Business Spur on the American side. For those who insist on staying within walking distance of the locks, the **Mid City Motel,** 304 E. Portage, is a relaxed establishment in the shadow of the campy Tower of History. (☎632-6832. Singles $36-44; doubles $45-54.) Just down the road, get stuffed with a Paul Bunyan burger ($6) and other classic American entrees at **The Antlers,** 804 E. Portage St. (☎632-3571). Animal lovers beware—the walls of the wildly popular restaurant have eyes (and heads and bodies).

West of the city, the uncrowded eastern branch of the **Hiawatha National Forest** and the appealing town of **Paradise** are other attractions in the eastern U.P. At **Tahquamenon Falls State Park** (☎492-3415), 15min. east of Paradise, amateur voyageurs can rent a canoe ($6 per half-day) or **rowboat** ($1.50 per person) at the Lower Falls, or gawk at the spectacular 50 ft. Upper Falls (no barrel riders here). North of Tahquamenon, over **300 shipwrecks** protected in an Underwater Preserve lie off Whitefish Point, affording divers an unbeatable opportunity to search for sunken treasure.

MIDDLE OF THE PENINSULA   ☎906

The western branch of the **Hiawatha National Forest** dominates the middle of the Peninsula, offering limitless wilderness activities and many rustic **campsites** ($7-11; pit toilets, no showers; first come, first served). **Rapid River** is home to the southern office of the west branch on Hwy. 2. In the north, **Munising,** on Hwy. 28, accesses the forest and the not-to-be-missed **Pictured Rocks National Lakeshore,** where water saturated with copper, manganese, and iron oxide paints the cliffs with multicolored bands. **Pictured Rocks Boat Cruise** (☎387-2379), at the city dock in Munising, gives the best view (tours approximately 3hr.; $24, ages 6-12 $7, under 6 free), but various car- or foot-accessible overlooks within the park offer spectacular glimpses of their own. The Forest and Lakeshore share a **visitors center** at the intersection of Rte. 28 and Hwy. 58 in Munising. (☎387-3700. Open daily mid-May to mid-Oct. 8am-6pm; mid-Oct to mid-May M-Sa 9am-4:30pm.) From Munising, M58—a bumpy, partially unpaved gem of a road—weaves along the lakeshore past numerous trailheads and campsites; spare tires are often necessary for extensive travel in the Hiawatha Forest. For a paved, but less scenic alternative from Munising to Grand Marais, go east on M28, then north on Rte. 77.

Within the park, ▓**Miner's Castle Overlook,** 12 mi. east of Munising off M58, allows trekkers to walk up to the edge of the cliffs, providing an unbeatable image of multicolored rocks and deep blue water as far as the eye can see. Twenty mi. east of Miner's Castle off M58, visitors can stroll, birdwatch, or collect smooth stones along the shore at **Twelve Mile Beach** (self-registered campsites $10; pump water only). From atop the sandy **Log Slide,** 5 mi. west of Grand Marais on M58, the adventurous can survey the magnitude of Lake Superior; in the winter months, "polar bears" (read: fat guys with balls of steel) take the plunge in the ice water. As an alternative to the developed campsites at Twelve Mile Beach, **backcountry camping permits** for 1-6 people ($15) are available from the Munising or **Grand Sable Visitors Center,** 2 mi. west of Grand Marais on Hwy. 58. (☎494-2660. Open mid-May to early Oct. daily 10am-7pm.) For those who prefer to avoid camping altogether, **Poplar Bluff Cabins,** Star Rte. Box 3118, have lakeview rooms with kitchens. Head 12 mi. east of Munising on Rte. 28, then 6 mi. south from Shingleton on M94 to get there. (☎452-6271. Cottages $40-50 per night, from $200 per week. Free use of boats on lake.)

KEWEENAW PENINSULA   ☎906

In 1840, Dr. Douglas Houghton's mineralogical survey of the Keweenaw (*KEE-wa-naw*) Peninsula, a curved finger of land on the U.P.'s northwest corner, incited a copper mining rush which sent the area booming. When mining petered out around 1969, the land was left barren and exploited. Today, reforestation and government support have helped Copper Country find new life as a tourist destination. Every year, 250 in. of snow fall on the towering pines, smooth-stone beaches, and low mountains of the Keweenaw. Visitors ski, snowshoe, and snowmobile in winter and enjoy the gorgeous green coasts in the summer.

The rugged **Porcupine Mountain Wilderness State Park** (☎885-5275 or 800-447-2757), affectionately known as "The Porkies," hugs Lake Superior at the base of the peninsula. Eight mi. inside the park on M107, **Lake of the Clouds** etches out a path between rugged cliffs and mountains, giving way to a spectacular overlook view of the Big Carp River valley below. The park also sports campsites ($9-14 sites with toilets and showers, electricity at Union; rustic sites $6), rustic cabins (sleeps 2-8; $32; reservations required), and paths into the **Old Growth Forest,** the largest tract of uncut forest between the Rockies and the Adirondacks. The **visitors center,** near the junction of M107 and South Boundary Rd. inside the park, provides required **permits** good for all Michigan state parks. (Open in summer daily 10am-6pm.)

The twin towns of **Houghton** and **Hancock** link the Porkies to the rest of the Keweenaw. Eight mi. north of Hancock on M203, **Mclain State Park** is home to some of the best camping in Copper Country. The campground rests along a 2 mi. beach and harbors an impressive lighthouse. (☎482-0278. Sites with electricity $14; $4 state parks vehicle permit required.) From the state park, U.S. 41 winds north through the Keweenaw. By far the most scenic path to the tip of the peninsula, the breathtaking **Brockway Mountain Dr.** (6 mi.), between Eagle Harbor and Copper Harbor, is a must for those who want to reach the summit. Rising 1337 ft. above sea level, its peak provides some of the best panoramic views on the entire U.P. (Accessible from M26 off U.S. 41.)

The northernmost town in Michigan, **Copper Harbor** functions as a gateway to **Isle Royale National Park** (see below). **Brockway Inn,** three blocks west of the junction between M26 and U.S.41 in Copper Harbor, pleases patrons with cable TV, free coffee, and some rooms with a private whirlpool. (☎482-0278. Singles $35-45; doubles from $53.) **The Pines,** on U.S. 41 in Copper Harbor, serves huge cinnamon rolls ($1.50) to locals and visitors alike. (☎289-4222. Restaurant open M-Sa 6:30am-3pm, Su 8am-3pm; adjacent bar open noon-2am.) Across the street, the **Keweenaw Adventure Company** (☎289-4303)—look for the bikes out front—can make anyone's wilderness dreams come true with kayaking outings (2½hr. intro paddle $26), bike rentals (half-day $25, full-day $35), and more.

ISLE ROYALE NATIONAL PARK

Around the turn of the century, moose swam from the Canadian coast to this pristine 45 miles long, 10 miles wide island. With no natural predators, the animals overran the land. Today, wild animals, including a pack of wolves, are the island's only permanent inhabitants. After the island was designated a national park in 1940, the fisherfolk who once lived here left. For backcountry seclusion, this is the place—no cars, phones, or medical services pamper visitors. Come prepared.

◪ **PRACTICAL INFORMATION.** Despite the fact that it's closer to the Ontario and Minnesota mainlands, Isle Royale is part of Michigan. The park **headquarters** is in **Houghton** at 800 E. Lakeshore Dr., in the Upper Peninsula. (☎906-482-0984. Open M-Sa 8am-4:30pm.) The headquarters operates a 6hr. ferry to the island. (Tu and F 9am, returns W and Sa 9am. Round-trip $94, under 12 $48, kayaks $40.) **Isle Royale Ferry Service,** at the dock in Copper Harbor, makes 4½hr. trips. (☎906-289-4437. Round-trip $80, under 12 $40.) Both ferries land at Rock Harbor. To access other parts of the island, take any of several shuttles from Rock Harbor, or leave from **Grand Portage, MN;** the **Grand Portage-Isle Royale Transportation Line** (☎715-392-2100 or 888-746-2305), sends a boat to Rock Harbor via Windigo, which stops at trailheads around the island (7½hr.; round-trip $108, under 12 $60). In summer, additional trips go just to Windigo (3hr.; round-trip $66, under 12 $33; same day round-trip $39). On the island, the park's **ranger stations** include **Windigo** on the west tip, **Rock Harbor** on the east tip, and **Malone Bay,** between Windigo and Rock Harbor.

◪◪ **CAMPING AND ACCOMMODATIONS.** Scattered about the island lie many **campgrounds** for which free permits, available at any ranger station, are required. Some sites have three-sided, screened-in shelters. They go quickly on a first come, first served basis, so bringing your own tent is a good idea. Visitors will need warm clothes and insect repellent; nights are always frigid (about 40°F in June) and biting bugs peak in June and July. Intestinal bacteria, tapeworms, and giardia lurk in the waters of Isle Royale; use a 0.4-micron filter, or boil water for at least 2min. Purified water is available at Rock Harbor and Windigo. Very few places on the island permit fires, so bring a small campstove as well. The **Rock Harbor Lodge** controls most of the island's commercial activity. The store carries a decent selection of overpriced food and camping staples. The lodge and associated cabins are the only indoor lodging on the island—remember, you're here to camp. (☎906-337-4993. Singles $143, doubles $229.)

ACTIVITIES. Streams, lakes, and 170 mi. of trails traverse the park. The **Greenstone Ridge Trail,** the main artery of the trail system, follows the backbone of the island from Rock Harbor Lodge, passing through several spectacular vistas. Serious backpackers conquer the **Minong Ridge Trail,** which runs parallel to the Greenstone Trail to the north for 30 mi. from McCargoe Cove to Windigo; the remains of early Native American copper mines line the trail. Shorter hikes near Rock Harbor include **Scoville Point,** a 4.2 mi. loop out onto a small peninsula, and **Suzy's Cave,** a 3.8 mi. loop to an inland sea arch. The park office has info on cruises, evening programs, and ranger-led interpretive walks. **Canoeing** and **kayaking** allow access to otherwise inaccessible parts of the island; both Rock Harbor and Windigo have **boat** and **canoe rental** outfitters. (Motors $12.50 per half-day, $21 per day. Boats and canoes $11 per half-day, $18.75 per day.) After registering at the park office, **scuba divers** can explore shipwrecks in the treacherous reefs off the northeast and west ends of the island. Divers need to bring filled tanks; no compressors are available.

INDIANA

The cornfields of southern Indiana's Appalachian foothills give way to expansive plains in the industrialized north, where Gary's smokestacks spew black clouds over the waters of Lake Michigan and urban travel hubs string along the interstates. Despite its lofty official motto—"The Crossroads of America"—Indiana is a modest, slow-paced state, where farms roll on and on, big cities are a rarity, and countless Hoosier school boys grow up dreaming of becoming the next Larry Bird.

▣ PRACTICAL INFORMATION

Capital: Indianapolis.

Visitor Info: Indiana Division of Tourism, 1 N. Capitol, #700, Indianapolis 46204 (☎800-289-6646; www.state.in.us/tourism). **Division of State Parks,** 402 W. Washington #W-298, Indianapolis 46204 (☎317-232-4125).

Postal Abbreviation: IN. **Sales Tax:** 5%.

INDIANAPOLIS   ☎317

Surrounded by flat farmland, Indianapolis feels like an average American city. Folks shop and work all day among downtown's skyscrapers and drive home to sprawling suburbs in the evening. Life ambles here—until May, when 350,000 spectators and crew members overrun the city, and the road warriors of the Indianapolis 500 speed into the spotlight.

▣ GETTING THERE AND GETTING AROUND

Airport: Indianapolis International (☎487-7243), 7 mi. southwest of downtown off I-465, Exit 11B. Take bus #8 "West Washington" or a cab ($17).

Amtrak: 350 S. Illinois St. (☎263-0550), behind Union Station. Trains travel east-west only. To Chicago (5hr., 1 per day, $17-32) and Cincinnati (3hr., 1 per day, $18-34). Open daily 6:30am-10pm.

Buses: Greyhound, 350 S. Illinois St. (☎267-3076). To: Chicago (4hr., 12 per day, $29); Cincinnati (3-7hr., 4 per day, $17.50); and Bloomington (1hr., 1 per day, $14.50). Open 24hr.

Public Transit: Indy Go, 139 E. Ohio St. (☎635-3344). Office open M-F 8am-6pm, Sa 9am-4pm. $1, children under 6 free. Patchy coverage of outlying areas; get a map.

Taxis: Barrington Cab, ☎786-7994.

✦❷ QUALIFYING FOR THE BIG RACE

The city is laid out in concentric circles, with a dense central cluster of skyscrapers and low-lying outskirts. The very center of Indianapolis is just south of **Monument Circle**, at the intersection of **Washington St. (U.S. 40)** and **Meridian St.** Washington St. divides the city north-south; Meridian St. divides it east-west. **I-465** circles the city and provides access to downtown. **I-70** cuts through the city east-west. Plentiful 2hr. metered parking can be found along the edges of the downtown area.

   Visitor Info: Indianapolis City Center, 201 S. Capitol Ave. (☎237-5200 or 800-233-4639), in the Pan Am Plaza across from the RCA Dome, has a helpful model of the city. Open M-F 10am-5:30pm, Sa 10am-5pm, Su noon-5pm.
   Hotlines: Rape Crisis Line, ☎800-221-6311. **Gay/Lesbian Info Line,** ☎923-8550.
   Post Office: 125 W. South St. (☎464-6376), across from Amtrak. Open M-W and F 7am-5:30pm, Th 7am-6pm. **ZIP code:** 46206. **Area code:** 317. **Time zone:** Central.

❙ PARK IT!

Budget motels line the I-465 beltway, 5 mi. from downtown. Make reservations a year in advance for the Indy 500, which inflates rates throughout May.

   Fall Creek YMCA, 860 W. 10th St. (☎634-2478), just north of downtown. Small, dorm-style rooms; access to a pool, gym, and laundry facilities. Free parking. 87 rooms for men, 10 for women. Singles $25, with bath $30; $77/$87 per week. Key deposit $5.
   Motel 6, 6330 Debonair Lane, just off Crawfordsville Rd., at Exit 16A off I-465, near the Speedway. Clean, pleasant rooms with A/C and cable TV at reasonable prices. Singles Su-Th $37, F-Sa $40; doubles $43/$46.
   Dollar Inn, 6331 Crawfordsville Rd. (☎248-8500), off I-465 at Exit 16A. Not the lap of luxury, but a very good deal. About 10min. from downtown. Decent rooms with HBO. Singles $26; doubles $31. F-Sa singles and doubles $31. Key deposit $2. Check-out 11am (strictly enforced). Must be 21+.
   Indiana State Fairgrounds Campgrounds, 1202 E. 38th St. (☎927-7520). Bus #4 or 39 from downtown. To get close to nature, go elsewhere. 170 sod-and-gravel sites, mostly packed by RVs. Sites $10.50, full hook-up $12.60. Busy during the state fair.

◐ HIGH-OCTANE FUEL

Ethnic food stands, produce markets, and knick-knack vendors fill the spacious **City Market,** 222 E. Market St., in a renovated 19th-century building. As if America didn't have enough malls, Indianapolis's newly constructed **Circle Centre,** 49 West Maryland St. (☎681-8000), hosts a slew of restaurants and a food court.

   Bazbeaux Pizza, 334 Massachusetts Ave. (☎636-7662), and 832 E. Westfields Blvd. (☎255-5711). Indianapolis's favorite pizza. The Tchoupitoulas pizza is a Cajun master-piece ($12, serves 2). Construct your own culinary wonder ($5.75) from a choice of 53 toppings ($1.40 each). Open M-Th 11am-10pm, F-Sa 11am-11pm, Su 4:30-10pm.
   The Abbey, 771 Massachusetts Ave. (☎269-8426), with other locations at 5905 E. 86th St. and 74 W. New York St. Sit in overstuffed velvet chairs while you sip cappucino ($2.25) or sample the wide selection of salads and sandwiches ($5-7). Open Su 11am-midnight, M-Th 8am-midnight, F 8am-1am, Sa 11am-1am.

◉ SUNDAY DRIVE

The newly restored canal at **White River State Park,** near downtown, entices locals to stroll, bike, or nap on the banks. *(Take bus #8.)* Pedal boats are available for rent at **Central Canal Rental.** *(☎634-1824.)* The **visitors center** is located within the park in the old pumphouse. *(801 W. Washington St. ☎233-2434 or 800-665-9056. Open M-F 8:30am-7pm, Sa 10am-7pm, Su noon-7pm.)* Near the park entrance, the **Eiteljorg Museum of American Indians' and Western Art** features an impressive collection of art from the Old

West—both white and Native American. *(500 W. Washington St. ☎636-9378. Open Tu-Sa 10am-5pm, Su noon-5pm; in summer also M 10am-5pm. Tours daily at 1pm. $5, seniors $4, students with ID and children $2.)* It may be 38 blocks from downtown, but the **Indianapolis Museum of Art** is well worth a visit. The museum's beautiful 152 acres offer nature trails, art pavilions, the Eli Lilly Botanical Garden, a greenhouse, and a theater. *(1200 W. 38th St. ☎923-1331. Open Tu-W and F-Sa 10am-5pm, Th 10am-8:30pm, Su noon-5pm. Free. Special exhibits $5.)*

Brass chandeliers and a majestic stained-glass dome grace the marbled interior of the **State House.** *(Between Capitol and Senate St. near W. Washington St. ☎233-5293. Open daily 8am-5pm, main floor only Sa-Su. 4 guided 1hr. tours per day M-F. Self-guided tour brochures are available inside.)* The Indy area is also home to a few quality options for animal lovers. The seemingly cageless **Indianapolis Zoo** holds one of the world's largest enclosed whale and dolphin pavilions. *(1200 W. Washington St. ☎630-2101. Open daily 9am-5pm; Sept.-May 9am-4pm. $9.75, seniors $7, ages 3-12 $6. Parking $3.)* Wolves and bison roam under researchers' supervision at **Wolf Park** on Jefferson St. in Battle Ground. The wolves, who howl constantly, are let out into the moonlight some nights. *(1hr. north of Indianapolis off I-65. ☎765-567-2265. Open May-Nov. Tu-Su 1-5pm; open later for wolf howls, F-Sa 7:30pm; Tu-Sa and Howl night $4, ages 6-13 $3; Su $5/$3.)*

🎵🎹 IN THE FAST LANE

The **Walker Theatre,** 617 Indiana Ave., named in honor of African-American beautician Madame Walker, America's first self-made woman millionaire, is now home of the bi-weekly **Jazz on the Avenue** series. Take a 15min. walk northwest of downtown. (☎236-2087. F 6-10pm; $5.)

By day a boring Clark Kent, the **Broad Ripple** area, 6 mi. north of downtown at College Ave. and 62nd St., transforms after dark into a nightlife super-mecca. The party fills the clubs and bars and spills out onto the sidewalks off Broad Ripple Ave. until about 1am on weekdays and 3am on weekends. The **Monkey's Tale,** 925 E. Westfield Blvd. (☎253-2883), is a good place to meet other happening folks and play a tune on the jukebox. The attached **Jazz Cooker** heats up when the Dick Liswell Trio begins jamming (Th-Sa at 10pm). **Average Joe's Sports Pub,** 814 Broad Ripple Ave., is a standard bar offering five pool tables and $2.50 beers. (☎253-5844. Open M-F 5pm-3am, Sa 6pm-3am, Su 6pm-midnight.) If you need some laughs, head to the **Crackers Comedy Club,** 6281 N. College Ave., at Broad Ripple Ave. (☎255-4211. Shows Tu-Sa, M amateur night.) After the clubs close, make a run for tacos ($2.50) and burritos ($4.50) at **Paco's Cantina,** 737 Broad Ripple Ave. (☎251-6200. Open 24hr.)

🏁 DAYS OF THUNDER

When the **Indianapolis Motor Speedway** lies dormant, buses take tourists around the 2½ mi. track. *(4790 W. 16th St., off I-465 at the Speedway exit. ☎481-8500. Take bus #25. Track tours daily 8am-4pm. $3, ages 6-15 $1.)* The adjacent **Speedway Museum** houses Indy's Hall of Fame. *(☎484-6747. Open daily 9am-5pm. $3, ages 6-15 $1.)* The country's passion for fast cars reaches fever pitch during the **500 Festival**—a month of parades, a mini-marathon, and hoopla leading up to race day. *(☎636-4556.)* The festivities begin with time trials in mid-May and culminate with the bang of the **Indianapolis 500** starter's gun the Su before Memorial Day. Tickets for the race go on sale the day after the previous year's race and usually sell out within a week. NASCAR's **Brickyard 400** sends stock cars zooming down the speedway in early Aug. *(☎800-822-4639 for ticket order forms for any event.)*

BLOOMINGTON ☎812

Bloomington's rolling hills may have made the area inadequate for farming, but they create an exquisite backdrop for its most prominent institution, Indiana University. At its core Bloomington is a campus town, offering up numerous cafes, nightlife hotspots, and great college basketball.

GREAT LAKES

🛈 PRACTICAL INFORMATION. Bloomington lies south of Indianapolis on Rte. 37; **N. Walnut** and **College St.** are the main north-south thoroughfares. **Greyhound,** 219 W. 6th St. (☎332-1522; station open M-F 9am-5pm, Sa-Su noon-4pm), connects Bloomington to Chicago (5hr., 1 per day, $50.50) and Indianapolis (1hr., 1 per day, $14.50). **Bloomington Transit** sends buses on seven routes. Service is infrequent; call ☎332-5688 for info. (75¢, seniors and ages 5-17 35¢.) **Yellow Cab** (☎336-4100) charges by zone. The **visitors center,** 2855 N. Walnut St., offers free local calls. (☎334-8900 or 800-800-0037. Open M-F 8:30am-5pm, Sa 9am-4pm, Su 10am-3pm; Nov.-Apr. M-F 8:30am-5pm, Sa 10am-3pm; 24hr. brochure area.) **Post office:** 206 E. 4th St., two blocks east of Walnut St. (☎334-4030. Open M and F 8am-6pm, Tu-Th 8am-5:30pm, Sa 8am-1pm.) **ZIP code:** 47404. **Area code:** 812. **Time zone:** Central.

🛈 ACCOMMODATIONS. Budget hotels cluster around the intersection of N. Walnut St. and Rte. 46. **College Motor Inn,** 509 N. College Ave., is close to the university and offers plush rooms with basic cable and comfortable furniture. (☎336-6881. Singles from $45; doubles from $50.) **Motel 6,** 1800 N. Walnut St., provides big, clean rooms, free HBO, and an outdoor pool. (☎332-0820. Singles $36 Su-Th, $40 F-Sa; doubles $42/$46.) **Paynetown State Park,** 10 mi. southeast of downtown on Rte. 446, has open field campsites in a well-endowed park on Lake Monroe with access to a boat ramp and hiking trails. Boat rentals are available. (☎837-9490. Primitive sites $5, with shower $7, with electricity $11. Vehicle registration $5, in-state $2.)

🛈 FOOD. Downtown Sq. boxes in a wealth of veggie-heavy restaurants, bookstores, and cute clothing shops in a two-block radius, most on Kirkwood Ave. near College Ave. and Walnut St. **🛈Snow Lion,** 113 S. Grant St., just off Kirkwood Ave., is owned by the Dalai Lama's nephew and is one of only a few Tibetan restaurants in the country. *Momo*'s Dinner ($7) and Tibetan Butter Tea ($1.50) make for a splendid meal. (☎336-0835. Open daily 11am-10pm.) **The Laughing Planet Café,** 322 E. Kirkwood Ave., serves up organic delights such as the superb $4 burritos. (☎323-2233. Open daily 11am-9pm.) Join hordes of Hoosiers at **Jimmy John's,** 430 E. Kirkwood Ave., home of the self-pronounced "World's Greatest Sandwiches." (☎332-9265. Open M-W 10:30am-2am, Th-Sa 10:30am-4am, Su 10:30am-1am.)

🛈 NIGHTLIFE. Bloomington's nightlife scene is about what you would expect from a college town in Middle America: beer and rock. **The Crazy Horse,** 214 W. Kirkwood Ave. drafts an alcohol army of 80 beers. (☎336-8877. Open M-W 11am-1am, Th-Sa 11am-2am, Su noon-midnight.) Everyone who's anyone (at IU, that is) shimmies over to **Nick's,** 423 E. Kirkwood Ave., to play drinking games. (☎332-4040. Beers $2-3.) **Bluebird,** 216 N. Walnut St., showcases local musical talent for a small cover charge (☎336-2473. Open M-Sa 9pm-3am.) The doors at **Rhino's,** 325½ S. Walnut St. (☎333-3430), are open to those under 21 for dancing and performances. **Bullwinkle's,** 201 S. College Ave., caters to a gay crowd with drag shows (M and W) and dance music. (☎334-3232. Open M and W-Sa 7pm-3am.)

🛈 SIGHTS. The **Tibetan Cultural Center** offers meditation and info on Tibetan culture. *(3655 Snoddy Rd. ☎334-7046. Grounds open Sa-Su noon-4pm. Center open Su noon-3pm.)* IU's architecturally striking **Art Museum,** on the University campus, maintains an excellent collection of Oriental and African artworks. *(E. 7th St. ☎855-5445. Open Tu-Sa 10am-5pm, Su noon-5pm. Free.)* Nearby, the **Mathers Museum of World Cultures** features somewhat interesting archaeology exhibits, idiophones and chordophones, and an authentic Mongonlian tent. *(416 N. Indiana St., near E. 8th St. ☎855-6873. Open Tu-F 9am-4:30pm, Sa-Su 1-4:30pm.)* **Oliver Winery** not only has beautiful grounds, but also offers free (and generous) tastings of all of its 15 wines, including the local favorite, blackberry wine. *(8024 N. State Rd. 37. ☎876-5800 or 800-258-2783. Open M-Sa 10am-6pm, Su noon-6pm.)*

ILLINOIS

The "Land of Lincoln" is one of compromise between sharply contrasting lifestyles, from the bustling urban center of Chicago to the vast farm country of most of the rest of the state. First known for its arable soil, the growth of big industry diversified the state and made its extremes more disparate. Always a gateway between east and west, present-day Illinois encompasses patches of coastal sophistication amid acres and acres of Midwest prairies. They may vote in the same elections and pay the same sales tax, but a farmer in Galena and a banker on Lake Shore Drive have little else in common. Visitors benefit from this diversity, finding a little bit of everything American in the mix of terrains and attitudes.

⚡ PRACTICAL INFORMATION

Capital: Springfield.
Visitor Info: Illinois Office of Tourism (☎800-226-6632; www.enjoyillinois.com). **Springfield Office of Tourism,** 109 N. Seventh St., Springfield 62701 (☎800-545-7300).
Postal Abbreviation: IL. **Sales Tax:** 6.25-8.75%, depending on the city.

CHICAGO   ☎312

Situated snugly along the banks of Lake Michigan—the only topological boundary to its development—Chicago is the Midwest version of urban sprawl. A burgeoning commercial center by the mid-1800s, the town drew millions of immigrants and freed slaves who encountered more tribulation than economic triumph. Machine politics soon flourished, blurring any line between organized government and organized crime. Chicago proudly weaves this checkered past into its brighter present. The diverse "Windy City"—so named for its politicians' hot air, not for its cold, fierce gusts—sings a sweeter song than it used to. From a collection of renowned museums to a varied and vibrant musical and entertainment scene, visitors to the city are never at a loss for something to do.

✈ GETTING THERE AND AWAY

Airports: O'Hare International (☎773-686-2200), off I-90. 1,000,000 planes take off and land here every minute. Well, maybe not that many, but it's a really big number. Depending on traffic, a trip between downtown and O'Hare can take up to 2hr. The blue line **Rapid Train** runs between the Airport El station and downtown (40min.-1hr., $1.50). **Midway Airport** (☎773-767-0500), on the western edge of the South Side, often offers less expensive (though less frequent) flights. To get downtown, take the El orange line from the Midway stop. **Airport Express** (☎454-7799 or 800-654-7871) connects the airports to downtown hotels from O'Hare (45min.-1hr., every 5-10min. 6am-11:30pm, $17) and Midway (30-45min., every 10-15min. 6am-10:30pm, $12).

Trains: Amtrak, Union Station, 225 S. Canal (☎558-1075), at Adams St. just west of the Loop, is Amtrak's nationwide hub. The bus is the easiest way to get there; buses #1, 60, 125, 151, and 156 all stop at the station. Otherwise, take the El to State and Adams, then walk 7 blocks west on Adams. To: Milwaukee (1½hr., 5 per day, $20); Detroit (8hr., 3 per day, $37-42); and New York (19hr., 2 per day, $82-151). Station open 6:15am-10pm; tickets sold daily 6am-9pm. Lockers $1 per day.

Buses: Greyhound, 630 W. Harrison St. (☎408-5980), at Jefferson and Desplaines Ave. Take the El to Linton or buses #60, 125, 156, or 157 to the terminal. *The* hub of the central US and home-base for several smaller companies covering the Midwest. To: Detroit (6-7hr., 6 per day, $24-27); Milwaukee (2hr., 13 per day, $13); St. Louis (5-7hr., 9 per day, $28-31); and Indianapolis (3½-4½hr., 9 per day, $28-31). Station and ticket office open 24hr.

Chicago is a big city with big city problems. It is a good idea to stay within the boundaries made apparent by tourist maps. Aside from small pockets such as Hyde Park and the U. of Chicago, areas south of the loop and west of the "little ethnic" enclaves are mostly industrial or residential and pose a safety threat to the unwary tourist. **Cabrini Green** (bounded by W. Armitage Ave. on the north, W. Chicago Ave. on the south., Sedgwick on the east, and Halsted on the west), an infamously dangerous public housing development, sits within tourist map borders—other unsafe neighborhoods are usually outside them.

⊟ GETTING AROUND

Public Transportation: The **Chicago Transit Authority (CTA),** 350 N. Wells (☎836-7000 or 888-968-7282), 7th fl., runs efficient trains, subways, and buses. The **elevated rapid transit train system,** called the **El,** encircles the Loop. Some downtown routes run underground but are still referred to as the El. The El operates 24hr., but late-night service is infrequent and unsafe in many areas. Also, some buses do not run all night; call the CTA for schedules and routes. Extremely helpful CTA maps are available at many stations and the Water Tower Information Center. Don't step blindly onto a train; many are "express" and different routes may run along the same track. Train and bus fare is $1.50; add 25¢ for express routes. Get a transfer (30¢) from bus drivers or when you enter the El stop, which allows for up to 2 more rides on different routes during the following 2hr. Buy or add value to **transit cards** (from $3 for 2 rides; $13.50 for 10 rides or $16.50 for 10 rides and transfers) at all CTA stations and some supermarkets and museums. CTA also offers a variety of consecutive-day passes for tourists, available at airports and Amtrak stations: 1-day $5, 2-day $9, 3-day $12, and 5-day $18. On Sa from mid-June through mid-Oct., a **Loop Tour Train** departs on a free 40min. elevated tour of the downtown area at 12:15, 12:55, 1:35, and 2:15pm (tickets must be picked up at the Chicago Office of Tourism; see **Practical Information** below).

Taxis: Yellow Cab, ☎829-4222. **Flash Cab,** ☎773-561-1444.

Car Rental: Dollar Rent-a-Car (☎800-800-4000), at O'Hare and Midway. $26 per day, $170 per week; under 25 surcharge $15 per day.

METRA, 547 W. Jackson (☎836-7000), distributes free maps and schedules for its extensive commuter rail network, with 11 rail lines and 4 downtown stations (open M-F 8am-5pm; fare $2-6.60, depending on distance).

PACE (☎836-7000) operates the suburban bus system. Numerous free or cheap shuttle services run throughout the loop, with brochures and schedules available just about everywhere.

⊞ ORIENTATION

Chicago has overtaken the entire northeastern corner of Illinois, running north-south along 29 mi. of the southwest Lake Michigan shorefront. The city sits at the center of a web of interstates, rail lines, and airplane routes; most cross-country traffic swings through the city. A good map is essential for navigating Chicago; pick up a free one at the tourist office or any CTA station.

Although flat and sprawling, the grids mostly make sense, and navigation is pretty straightforward, by car or ubiquitous public transportation. At the city's center is the **Loop,** Chicago's downtown business district and hub of the public transportation system. The block numbering system begins from the intersection of State and Madison, increasing by about 800 per mi. The Loop is bounded by the Chicago River to the north and west, Lake Michigan to the east, and Roosevelt Rd. to the south. Directions in *Let's Go* are generally from downtown. South of the Loop, numbered east-west streets increase towards the south. Many ethnic neighborhoods lie in this area (see **Neighborhoods,** below), but farther out, the struggling South Side should be mostly avoided. Most of the city's favored destinations for food and nightlife jam the first few mi. north of the Loop. **Lake Shore Dr.,** a scenic pseudo-freeway hugging Lake Michigan (beware the 45 mph speed limit), provides express north-south connections.

To avoid driving (and parking) in the city, daytrippers can leave their cars in one of the suburban park-and-ride lots ($1.75); call CTA (see below) for info. Parking downtown costs around $8-15 per day.

North Ave.
Second City
TO ❶ (1mi)

Chicago Historical Society

TO ❸ AND LINCOLN PARK (1mi) ❹ (5mi)

❷ Burton Pl.

International Museum of Surgical Science

W. Schiller St.

La Salle St.

N. Lake Shore Dr.

Goethe St.

Downtown Chicago

▲ ACCOMMODATIONS	● FOOD
Arlington House (HI-AYH, AAIH), 1	The Berghoff, 16
Cass Hotel, 10	Billy Goat's Tavern, 11
Chicago Int'l Hostel, 4	Frontera Grill, 8
Days Inn Gold Coast, 3	Gold Coast Dogs, 9
Eleanor Residence, 2	Lou Malnati's, 7
Hotel Wacker, 5	Lou Mitchell's, 15
International House, 18	The Original Gino's East, 6
Hostelling International (HY-AYH), 17	Pizzeria Due, 13
Motel 6, 14	Pizzeria Uno, 12

N

0   300 yards
0   300 meters

Division St.

Elm St.

Cedar St.

Oak St.

Bellevue Pl.

Oak St. Beach

Larabee St.

Washington Square

Locust St.
Hudson Ave.
Sedgwick St.
Orleans St.
Franklin St.
Wells St.

Delaware Pl.

Walton St.

John Hancock Bldg. and Observatory

Outer Harbor

Bush St.

Old Water Tower

Pearson St.
Chicago Ave.
Superior St.

Huron St.
Erie St.
Ontario St.
Ohio St.

La Salle St.
Clark St.
Dearborn St.
State St.
Wabash Ave.
Michigan Ave.

Museum of Contemporary Art

Olive Park

❺
❻

❶❸

❶❹

70

Ohio St.

Navy Pier

Grand Ave.
Illinois St.
W. Hubbard St.

Fairbanks Ct.

❼ ❽

❶❷

❾ ❿ ❶❶

E. North Water St.

Merchandise Mart

Kinzie St.

Chicago River

N. Kingsbury St.
Chicago River

Wacker Dr.

S. Water St.

Field Rd.

Lake St.

Franklin St.

Wacker Dr.

State of Illinois Center

Chicago Theater

E. Lake St.

Lake Michigan

Canal St.
Clinton St.

Randolph St.

City Hall

Daley Plaza

Wabash Ave.

E. Randolph Dr.

ℹ **Visitors Center**

Northwestern Station

Washington St.

Madison St.

Carson Pirie Scott Shop

Grant Park

Monroe Harbor

Monroe St.

Sears Tower and Observ.

Union Station

E. Monroe Dr.

Art Institute of Chicago

Goodman Theatre

Petrillo Music Shell

❶❻

Adams St.

Board of Trade

Jackson Blvd.

E. Jackson Dr.

❶❺

Chicago Board of Options Exchange

290

Van Buren St.

Chicago Public Library

Buckingham Fountain

Chicago Harbor

❶❼

Congress Dr.

Congress Parkway

Harrison St.

Columbia College

TO MAIN BUS STATION, GREEKTOWN (2mi)

E. Balbo Ave.

Spertus Museum of Judaica

E. Balbo Dr.

W. Polk St.

E. 8th St.

9th St.

S. Wells St.

E. 11th St.

John G. Shedd Aquarium

Roosevelt Rd.

Field Museum Of Natural History

Solidarity Dr.

Adler Planetarium

Canal St.
Clinton St.

E. 13th St.

Clark St.
State St.
Wabash St.
Michigan Ave.
Indiana Ave.
Columbus Dr.

W. 14th St.   E. 14th St.

S. Lake Shore Dr.

Soldier Field

Burnham Park Harbor

South Branch
Chicago River

TO ❶❽ AND MUSEUM OF SCIENCE & INDUSTRY

41

GREAT LAKES

NEIGHBORHOODS

The diverse array of enclaves that compose the Windy City justifies its title as a "city of neighborhoods." North of the Loop, LaSalle Dr. loosely defines the west edge of the posh **Near North** area, whose activity is largely centered along the **Magnificent Mile** of Michigan Ave. between the Chicago River and Oak St. The trendy restaurant- and nightlife-packed **River North** district lines N. Clark St., just north of the Loop and west of Michigan Ave. The primarily residential **Gold Coast** shimmers on N. Lakeshore Dr. between Oak St. and North Ave. Northwest of the Gold Coast, the **Bucktown/Wicker Park** area, at the intersection of North, Damen and Milwaukee Aves., is the place to be for artsy, cutting-edge cafes and night-life. **Lincoln Park,** a hotbed of hip activity, revolves around the junction of N. Clark St., Lincoln Ave., and Halsted St. To the north Lincoln Park melts into **Lakeview,** near the 3000s of N. Clark St. and N. Halsted St., a gay-friendly area teeming with food and nightlife, and then becomes **Wrigleyville** in the 4000s. **Andersonville,** 5 mi. farther down N. Clark St. north of Foster Ave., is the historic center of the **Swedish** community, though immigrants from **Asia** and the **Middle East** have recently settled here.

The near south and west sides are filled with other vibrant ethnic districts. The center of the **Chinese** community lies 2 mi. south of the Loop, at Cermak Rd. and Wentworth Ave. The **German** community has scattered, but the beer halls, restaurants, and shops in the 3000s and 4000s of N. Lincoln Ave. remain. The former residents of **Greektown** have also moved, but S. Halsted St., just west of the Loop, houses authentic Greek restaurants. The area is bustling and safe until the restaurants close, at which point tourists clear out. Nearby **Little Italy** fell prey to the **University of Illinois at Chicago (UIC),** but a shadow of what once existed remains along W. Taylor St., west of the UIC campus. **Jewish** and **Indian** enclaves center on Devon Ave., from Western Ave. to the Chicago River. The **Pilsen** neighborhood, southwest of the loop, around 18th St., offers a slice of **Mexico.** The search for **Polish** cuisine leads hungry travelers near Bucktown to N. Milwaukee Ave. between blocks 2800 and 3100. Chicago's Polish population is the largest of any city outside Warsaw.

☑ PRACTICAL INFORMATION

Visitor Info: Chicago Office of Tourism, 78 E. Washington St. (☎744-2400 or 800-226-6632). Open M-F 10am-6pm, Sa 10am-5pm, Su noon-5pm. In the same building is the **Chicago Cultural Center Welcome Center,** 77 E. Randolph St., at Michigan Ave. Open M-F 10am-6pm, Sa 10am-5pm, Su noon-5pm. **Chicago Visitor Information Center,** 163 E. Pearson St. (☎744-2400), at Michigan Ave, in the Water Tower Pumping Station. Open M-F 9:30am-7pm, Sa 10am-7pm, Su 11am-6pm. On the lake, **Navy Pier Info Center,** 600 E. Grand (☎595-7437). Open Su-Th 10am-10pm, F-Sa 10am-noon. The **International Visitors Center,** 520 N. Michigan Ave. (☎645-1836), aids foreign visitors with their itineraries. (Call for assistance.)

Hotlines: Crisis Line, ☎800-866-9600. **Rape Crisis Line,** ☎847-872-7799. Both 24hr.

Bi-Gay-Lesbian Concerns: Gay and Lesbian Hotline/Anti-Violence Project, ☎871-2273. **Gay and Lesbian Hotline,** ☎773-929-4357. Both 24hr. For current info on events and nightlife, pick up a copy of the *Windy City Times* or *Gay Chicago* at Lakeview's **Unabridged Books,** 3251 N. Broadway (☎773-883-9119).

Medical Services: Northwestern Memorial Hospital, 251 E. Huron St. near Michigan Ave. (☎908-2000); emergency division at 250 E. Erie St. nearby (☎926-5188). Open 24hr. Farther out, **Cook County Hospital,** 1835 W. Harrison (☎633-6000). Take the Congress A train to the Medical Center Stop. Open 24hr.

Internet Access: Free at the **Chicago Public Library.** Main branch at 400 S. State St., at Congress. Open M 9am-7pm, Tu and Th 11am-7pm, W, F, and Sa 9am-5pm, Su 1-5pm.

Post Office: 433 W. Harrison St. (☎654-3895), at the Chicago River. Free parking. Open 24hr. **ZIP code:** 60607. **Area code:** 312 (downtown) or 773 (elsewhere in Chicago); 708, 630, or 847 (outside the city limits). In text, 312 unless otherwise noted.

ACCOMMODATIONS

A cheap, convenient bed can be found at one of Chicago's many hostels; the moderately priced motels on **Lincoln Ave.** in Lincoln Park are accessible by car. Motel chains off the interstates, about 1hr. from downtown, are inconvenient and expensive (from $35), but are an option for late-night arrivals. **Chicago Bed and Breakfast,** P.O. Box 14088, Chicago 60614 (☎773-248-0005 or 800-375-7084), runs a referral service. Few B&Bs have parking, but the majority are near public transit. (2-night minimum stay. Singles from $75; doubles from $85. Reservations required.) Chicago has a 15% tax on most accommodation rates.

HOSTELS

Hostelling International–Chicago (HI-AYH), 24 E. Congress Pkwy. (☎360-0300), off Wabash St. in the Loop. Take the El Orange Line to State & Van Buren, walk 1 block east to Wabash St., turn right, walk 1 block to Congress. This brand-new, immense hostel is packed with amenities that make it the best budget option in Chicago. Its location offers easy access to the major museums during the day, but *be careful on the deserted streets of the Loop at night.* Student center, performance center, library, kitchen, laundry. Dorms $19-20, non-members $22-23. Reservations recommended.

Arlington House, 616 W. Arlington Pl. (☎773-929-5380 or 800-467-8355), off Clark St. just north of Fullerton in the Lincoln Park area. The social atmosphere and brilliant location ensure a lively stay in this enormous Lincoln Park hostel. All rooms are tidy and breezy, and the dorm rooms let you get to know your neighbors. Safe, central neighborhood near food and nightlife. Kitchen, TV room, laundry facilities. Dorms $19.50; private doubles with shared bath $41, with private bath $51. Reservations recommended.

Eleanor Residence, 1550 N. Dearborn Pkwy. (☎664-8245). *Women only, must be over 18.* A location near Lake Michigan, Lincoln Park, and the Gold Coast is the ideal setting for a majestic common room and lobby, as well as spotless rooms. Singles $55, breakfast and dinner included. Reserve at least 1 day in advance; 1-night deposit required.

Chicago International Hostel, 6318 N. Winthrop St. (☎773-262-1011). Take the Howard St. northbound train to Loyola Station; walk 3 blocks south on Sheridan Rd. to Winthrop, and a ½-block south. Simple, sunny rooms with 4-6 beds, near Loyola University. A fairly safe location during the day close to the lake, beaches, and many fast food joints; *don't wander around alone at night.* Linens provided. Free parking. Kitchen and laundry access. Lockout 10am-4pm. Check-in 7-10am and 4pm-midnight. Curfew Su-Th midnight, F-Sa 2am. Dorms $13, double with bath $35-40. Lockers $1. Key deposit $5.

HOTELS AND GUEST HOUSES

Cass Hotel, 640 N. Wabash Ave. (☎787-4030 or 800-227-7850), just north of the Loop. Take El to State or Grand St. Its reasonable rates and convenient location near the Magnificent Mile make this newly renovated hotel a favorite find of the budget-conscious. The in-house bar is ideal for bonding, and the $2 breakfast downstairs at the coffee shop is a great deal. Parking available. Laundry room. Singles from $64. Key deposit $5. Reservations recommended. Wheelchair accessible.

International House, 1414 E. 59th St. (☎773-753-2270), Hyde Park, off Lake Shore Dr. *Students only.* Take the Illinois Central Railroad from the Michigan Ave. station (20min.) or METRA South Shore Line to 59th St. and walk a half-block west. On the grounds of the University of Chicago; *don't wander off campus at night.* Expansive common areas filled with student activity augment neat, spacious singles with shared bath. Rooms $38. Kitchen and laundry; tennis courts, game room, weight room, cafeteria. Linen provided. Reservations with credit card required.

Hotel Wacker, 111 W. Huron St. (☎787-1386), at N. Clark St. Insert your own joke. A green sign on the corner makes this place easy to find. Small, well-appointed rooms are overshadowed by reasonable prices and convenient Near North location. TV, A/C, phone. Check-in 24hr. Singles $40; doubles $50; $250 per week. Key and linen deposit $5. Wheelchair accessible.

GREAT LAKES

ⓘ FOOD

Chicago's culinary delights are among its main attractions. One of the best guides to city dining is the monthly *Chicago* magazine, which includes an extensive restaurant section, cross-indexed by price, cuisine, and quality. It can usually be found at tourist offices, as well as newsstands everywhere.

PIZZA

Chicago's deep-dish pizza is known 'round the world, either standard-style, with the cheese on top, or stuffed, with "toppings" in the middle.

🍕 **Lou Malnati's,** 439 N. Wells St. (☎828-9800), at Hubbard downtown. The name may not be as famous as Uno's, but the pizza is just as fantastic. A Chicago mainstay for 30 years, Lou's is a local sports memorabilia-themed chain with bubbling deep-dish masterpieces. Pizzas $6-20. Open M-Th 11am-11pm, F-Sa 11am-midnight, Su noon-10pm.

Pizzeria Uno, 29 E. Ohio St. (☎321-1000), and younger sister **Due,** 619 N. Wabash Ave. (☎943-2400). It may look like any other Uno's, but this is where the delicious legacy of deep-dish began. Pizza, pasta, or bust. Lines are long, and pizza takes 45min. to prepare. Same short menu at Due (right up the street), with a terrace and more room than Uno's. Pizzas $6-19. Uno open M-F 11:30am-1am, Sa 11:30am-2am, Su 11:30am-11:30pm. Due open Su-Th 11am-1:30am, F-Sa 11am-2am.

The Original Gino's East, 633 N. Wells St. (☎943-1124), at Ontario downtown. Bring a marker to claim history on the heavily decorated walls of this legendary deep-dish joint. Pizza $9-22. Open daily 11am-11pm.

'ROUND THE LOOP

Many of Chicago's best restaurants, from ragin' Cajun to tried-and-true German, inhabit the streets of the Loop.

🍴 **Lou Mitchell's,** 565 W. Jackson Blvd. (☎939-3111), 2 blocks west of the Sears Tower. Undoubtedly the city's best breakfast place, this retro diner has been stuffing faithful customers for 75 years. Visitors should plan to leave the diet elsewhere and indulge in a sinfully good omelette ($6-8) and the "world's finest cup of coffee" ($1.30). Lines are long but move fast, and female customers get a free box of Milk Duds while they wait. Open M-Sa 5:30am-3pm, Su 7am-3pm.

Heaven on Seven, 111 N. Wabash Ave. (☎263-6443), 7th fl. of the Garland Bldg. This is heaven Cajun-style, from the mardi gras and voodoo decor to endless hot sauce and spicy cuisine. The line is long, but hell, the gumbo is great ($4; entrees $9-11). Open M-F 8:30am-5pm, Sa 10am-3pm.

Billy Goat's Tavern, 430 N. Michigan (☎222-1525), underground on lower Michigan Ave. Descend through what looks like a subway entrance in front of the Tribune building. The gruff service in this bar/diner was the inspiration for the legendary *Saturday Night Live* "Cheezborger, cheezborger—no Coke, Pepsi" skit. Cheezborgers $2.50. "Butt in anytime" M-F 7am-2am, Sa 10am-3am, Su 11am-2am.

Gold Coast Dogs, 418 N. State St. (☎527-1222), at Hubbard St. Hot dogs are sacred in Chicago, but only when they're done Second City-style with a veritable salad of relish, onions, pickles, tomatoes, etc. on top. Locals think Gold Coast's are among the best. Hot dogs from $2. Open M-F 7am-10pm, Sa-Su 11am-8pm.

The Berghoff, 17 W. Adams St. (☎427-3170). Take the El to Adams. This dim, cavernous German restaurant filled with lunching traders has been a Chicago institution for over 100 years. Bratwurst $6, stein of Berghoff's own beer $3. Open M-Th 11am-9pm, F 11am-9:30pm, Sa 11am-10pm.

RIVER NORTH

River North houses some of the trendiest eateries in town, as well as Chicago's pizza institutions (see **Pizza,** above).

🍴 **Frontera Grill,** 455 N. Clark St. (☎661-1434), between Illinois and Hubbard. Take El Red Line to Grand/State. A delightful departure from chain tacos and burritos, Frontera delivers what many claim is the best authentic Mexican cuisine in the country. Entrees (from $9) change often but are always superb. The usual 2hr. wait is bearable if you snag a bar seat and order appetizers (from $4). Open Tu-Th 11:30am-2:30pm and 5:30-10pm, F 11:30am-2:30pm and 5-11pm, Sa 10:30am-2:30pm and 5-11pm. Reservations only accepted for parties of 5 or more.

Garrett Popcorn Shop, 670 N. Michigan Ave. (☎944-2630), near Ontario. The line of locals that snakes out the door points the way to delectable, warm-from-the-popper caramel popcorn ($3.50 per lb.) Open daily 10:30am-9pm.

SOUL FOOD SOUTH OF THE LOOP

The area of the Loop between Jackson and Roosevelt St. is the South Loop, home to good, cheap American-style soul food like ribs, fried chicken, and greens. More of the same peppers the South Side, but travelers should be very careful south of the Loop, especially after dark.

▨**Army & Lou's,** 422 E. 75th (☎773-483-6550), on the South Side. Locals from all over the city come here for a surprisingly upscale setting and some of the best southern fare north of the Mason-Dixon line. Fried chicken with 2 sides $8.75, mixed greens with ham $8. Open M and W-Su 9am-10pm.

Dixie Kitchen & Bait Shop, 5225 S. Harper St. (☎773-363-4943), tucked back in a parking lot at 52nd in Hyde Park. Fried green tomatoes ($3.75) and oyster po' boy sandwiches ($8) are among Dixie's southern highlights. Fried catfish $10. Blackened Voodoo beer $2. Open M-Th and Su 11am-10pm, F-Sa 11am-11pm.

The Smokedaddy, 1804 W. Division St. (☎773-772-6656), west of the Loop in Wicker Park. Fantastic ribs ($8), vegetarian BBQ sandwiches ($5.45) and pulled pork sandwiches ($5) merit the "WOW" proclamation of the neon sign out front. Open M-Sa until 2am, Su until 1am; opening hrs. vary. Live blues some nights.

CHINATOWN

Chinatown is lined with restaurants. Take the Red Line to Cermak/Chinatown to get here, *but don't go too far south of Cermak St. after dark.*

Hong Min, 221 W. Cermak Rd. (☎842-5026). Spartan decor, Epicurean dining. Daily dim sum and fresh oysters are local favorites. Sweet-and-sour fish $8. Open Su-Th 10am-2am, F-Sa 10am-3am. Dim sum M-F 10am-3pm, Sa-Su 10am-4pm.

Three Happiness, 209 W. Cermak Rd. (☎842-1964). The smaller of 2 locations, this site receives constant local acclaim. Chicken entrees around $7. Open daily 9am-2am.

LITTLE ITALY

What is left of Little Italy can be reached by taking the El to UIC, then walking west on Taylor St. or taking bus #37 down Taylor St. As is the case with all west and south side areas, tourists should clear out when the restaurants close.

▨**Mario's Italian Lemonade,** 1074 W. Taylor St., across from Al's. A classic neighborhood stand that churns out sensational Italian ices ($1-4.75) in flavors from cantaloupe to cherry. Open daily mid-May to mid-Sept. 10am-midnight.

Al's Italian Beef, 1079 W. Taylor St. (☎226-4017), at Aberdeen near Little Italy; also at 169 W. Ontario in the Near North. Churns out top-notch Italian beef with lots of spices. Italian beef sandwich $3.75. Great fries $1.50. Open daily 9am-1am.

GREEKTOWN

▨**The Parthenon,** 314 S. Halsted St. (☎726-2407). The golden ratio ain't in the architecture, but the staff converses in Greek, the murals transport you to the Mediterranean, and the food wins top awards. The delicious Greek Feast family-style dinner ($15) includes everything from the original *saganaki* (flaming goat cheese, invented here) to *baklava.* Open daily 11am-1am.

Rodity's, 222 S. Halsted St. (☎454-0800), between Adams St. and Jackson Blvd. With slightly cheaper fare than the other Greektown options (daily specials under $9), Rodity's prepares more than generous portions of *spanakopita* (spinach pie; $4) and other delectable Greek treats. Open Su-Th 11am-midnight, F-Sa 11am-1am.

LINCOLN PARK

Penny's Noodle Shop, 950 W. Diversey Ave. (☎773-281-8448), at Sheffield. One of the best budget options in town, the unassuming Penny's delivers outstanding, generous Asian noodle dishes (all under $6) to scores of locals who pack the place at all hours. No reservations; sit at the counter or prepare to wait. BYOB. Open daily 10am-10pm.

Cafe Ba-Ba-Reeba!, 2024 N. Halsted St. (☎935-5000), just north of Armitage. Well-marked by the colorful, glowing facade, the sprawling Ba-Ba-Reeba pleases with unbeatable *tapas* ($3-8) and hearty Spanish *paellas* ($10-15 per person; there will be plenty to take home). The outdoor terrace provides some of the best people-watching in town. Glass of *sangria* $3.50. Reservations recommended. Open M-Th noon-10pm, F-Sa noon-midnight, Su noon-10pm. Su brunch *tapas* noon-3pm.

The Bourgeois Pig, 738 Fullerton Ave. (☎773-883-5282). Take the El brown line to Fullerton. Low-key, soothing coffee shop with faux marble tables, board games, veggie specials and desserts to boot. Cappuccino $1.75, scones $1.50. Parking can be difficult. Open M-Th 6:30am-11pm, F 6:30am-midnight, Sa 8am-midnight, Su 9am-11pm.

Potbelly Sandwich Works, 2264 N. Lincoln Ave. (☎773-528-1405), between Belden and Webster. Potbellied locals might have had one too many Italian sandwiches from this laid-back deli, appropriately decorated with a potbelly stove and a player piano. Huge, delicious subs $3.50-5.50. Open daily 11am-11pm. Call for additional locations.

ANDERSONVILLE

Kopi, A Traveller's Cafe, 5317 N. Clark St. (☎773-989-5674), near Foster St. in Andersonville. A 10min. walk from the Berwyn El, 4 blocks west on Berwyn. As visitors quickly learn, *kopi* is Indonesian for (really good) "coffee." Espresso $1.50. Music M and Th nights. Open M-Th 8am-11pm, F 8am-midnight, Sa 9am-midnight, Su 10am-11pm.

Ann Sather, 929 W. Belmont Ave. (☎773-348-2378). Take El Red Line to Belmont. This authentic Swedish diner draws a huge breakfast crowd with their wildly popular, gooey cinnamon rolls ($4). Although there hasn't yet been a formal study, locals report that they're addictive. Open Su-Th 7am-10pm, F-Sa 7am-11pm. Call for other locations.

BUCKTOWN/WICKER PARK

Busy Bee, 1546 N. Damen Ave. (☎773-772-4433), at Milwaukee Ave. in Bucktown. Take El to Milwaukee Ave. In a city known for its Polish roots, this is where locals get their pierogis and boiled beef. Entrees $3-9. Open daily 10am-10pm.

Kitsch'n on Roscoe, 2005 W. Roscoe St. (☎773-248-7372), at Damen Ave. in nearby Roscoe Village. Kitsch abounds at this breakfast and lunch spot, which serves a surprisingly good "Let-Go-My-Belgian-Pecan-Waffle" and "Jonny's Lunch Box" (soup, sandwich, fruit, and a snack cake served in a lunch box) on campy theme tables. (Star Trek, anyone?) Meals $3-7. Open Tu-Th and Su 9am-3pm, F-Sa 9am-3pm and 6-10pm.

◉ SIGHTS

Chicago's sights range from well-publicized museums to undiscovered back streets, from beaches and parks to towering skyscrapers. The tourist brochures, bus tours, and downtown area reveal only a fraction of Chicago. As a famous art historian once said, "no one will learn the city of Chicago without using their feet."

THE LOOP

When Mrs. O'Leary's cow kicked over a lantern and started the **Great Fire of 1871,** Chicago's downtown flamed into a pile of ashes. The city rebuilt with a vengeance, turning the functional into the fabulous and creating one of the most concentrated clusters of architectural treasures in the world. The downtown area, hemmed in by the Chicago River and Lake Michigan, grew upward rather than outward.

TOURS. Visitors can explore this street museum via **walking tours,** organized by the **Chicago Architectural Foundation.** The 2hr. tours, one of early skyscrapers and one of modern architecture, start at the foundation's gift shop. Highlights include Louis

Sullivan's arch, the Chicago window, and Mies van der Rohe's revolutionary sky-scrapers. *(224 S. Michigan Ave. ☎ 922-8687. $12 for 1 tour, $18 for both.)*

CHICAGO BOARD OF TRADE. Those who prefer to explore the Loop on their own can observe the frantic trade of Midwestern farm goods at the world's oldest and largest commodity exchange, the Chicago Board of Trade. For tours, contact the **visitors office.** *(141 W. Jackson Blvd., on the 5th fl. ☎ 435-3590. Open M-F 8am-2pm. Tours M-F 9:15am, every 30min. 10am-12:30pm. Free.)*

SEARS TOWER. A few blocks west on Jackson, the 1454 ft. **Sears Tower** is undoubt-edly Chicago's most immediately recognizable architectural landmark. Built in 1973 and named for American retail giant Sears-Roebuck, its former tenant, the Tower is the 2nd-tallest building in the world (first, in the minds of staunch Chicagoans). On a clear day, visitors to the 103rd floor Skydeck can see three bordering states, as well as the city's 2nd-tallest structure, the towering white Amoco Building. *(233 S. Wacker Dr., enter on Jackson. ☎ 875-9696. Open daily 9am-11pm; Oct.-Feb. 9am-10pm. $8.50, seniors $6.50, children $5.50, families $20. Lines are long, usually at least 1hr.)*

THE PLAZA. The **First National Bank Building and Plaza** sits about two blocks north-east at the corner of Clark and Monroe St. One of the world's largest bank build-ings, it leads gazes skyward with its diamond-shaped, diagonal slope. Back on the ground, Marc Chagall's vivid mosaic, *The Four Seasons*, lines the block and sets off a public space often used for concerts and lunchtime entertainment. The mural is a fabulous sight at night, when it is lit by various colored bulbs. Two blocks north at the corner of Clark and Washington St., the Methodist **Chicago Temple**, the world's tallest church, sends its babelesque steeples heavenward.

STATE STREET. State and Madison St., the most famous intersection of "State St. that great street," forms the focal point of the Chicago street grid as well as another architectural haven. Here, Louis Sullivan's adored **Carson Pirie Scott** store is adorned with exquisite ironwork and the famous extra-large Chicago window. Sul-livan's other masterpiece, the **Auditorium Building,** sits several blocks south at the corner of Congress St. and Michigan Ave. Intricate design and flawless acoustics highlight this Chicago landmark.

OTHER ARCHITECTURAL WONDERS. Burnham and Root's **Monadnock Building,** 53 W. Jackson, deserves a glance for its serene, alternating bays of purple and brown rock. Just to the southeast, the **Sony Fine Arts Theatre** screens current artistic and foreign films in the grandeur of the **Fine Arts Building.** *(418 S. Michigan Ave. ☎ 939-2119. Open M-Th. $8.25; students $6; seniors, children, or matinee $5.)* In 1988, the city held a contest to design a building in honor of the late mayor. The result is the $144 million **Harold Washington Library Center,** a researcher's dream and a postmodern architec-tural delight. *(400 S. State St. ☎ 747-4300. Open M 9am-7pm, Tu and Th 11am-7pm, W and F-Sa 9am-5pm, Su 1-5pm. Tours M-Sa noon and 2pm, Su 2pm.)* Two blocks away near Washington and Dearborn, the **State of Illinois Building** is a postmodern town square designed by Helmut Jahn in 1985; the elevator to the top gives a thrilling (and free) view of its sloping atrium, circular floors, and hundreds of employees.

SCULPTURE. In addition to its architectural masterpieces, Chicago is decorated with one of the country's premier collections of outdoor sculpture. Large, abstract designs punctuate many downtown corners, making a walking tour of Loop out-door sculpture a terrific way to spend an afternoon. The Chicago Cultural Center sells the *Loop Sculpture Guide* for $4 (see **Practical Information,** above). "The Pic-asso" at the foot of the **Daley Center Plaza,** at Washington and Dearborn St., is the most famous and an unofficial symbol of Chicago, although no one is quite sure if it represents a bird, dog, or woman. *(☎ 443-3054 for more info.)* Directly across Washing-ton St. rests surrealist Joan Miró's *Chicago*, the artist's voluptuous gift to the city. *(69 W. Washington.)* Three blocks south on Dearborn at Jackson, Alexander Calder's *Flamingo*, a stark red structure that is half-statue, half-mobile, stands in front of the Federal Center Plaza. Calder's other Chicago masterpiece, *The Universe*, swirls in the lobby of the Sears Tower.

NEAR NORTH

TRIBUNE TOWER. The city's ritziest district lies north of the Loop along the lake, just past the Michigan Ave. Bridge. An international design competition in the 1920s resulted in the Tribune Tower, a Gothic skyscraper just north of the bridge which overlooks this stretch. Chicago's largest newspaper, *The Chicago Tribune*, is produced here. *(435 N. Michigan Ave.)*

THE MART. Over 8 mi. of corridors fill the nearby Merchandise Mart; the entrance is on N. Wells or Kinzie, north of the river. One of the largest commercial buildings in the world (25 stories high and 2 blocks long), it even has its own zip code. The first two floors house a mediocre public mall; the remainder contains private showrooms where design professionals converge to choose home and office furnishings. **Tours at the Mart** guides visitors through the building. *(Bus #114. 1½hr. tours M-F at noon. $12; seniors and students over 15 $10.)*

NAVY PIER. Big, bright, and always festive, touristy Navy Pier, east of Grant Park on Lake Michigan, captures the carnival spirit 365 days a year. No small jetty, the mile-long pier has it all: a concert pavilion, dining options, nightspots, sight-seeing boats, a spectacular ferris wheel, a crystal garden with palm trees, and an Omnimax theater. Now *that's* America. From here, explorers can rent **bicycles** to navigate the Windy City's streets. *(600 E. Grand Ave. Take El Red Line to Grand/State and transfer to a free pier trolley bus. Bike rental open daily June-Sept. 8am-11pm; May 8am-8pm; Apr. and Oct. 10am-7pm. $9 per hr., $36 per day.)*

MAGMILE. Chicago's showy Magnificent Mile, a row of glitzy shops along N. Michigan Ave. between the Chicago River and Oak St., can magnificently drain the wallet. Several of these retail stores, including **Banana Republic** and **Crate & Barrel,** were designed by some of the country's foremost architects and merit a look. The relatively plain **Chicago Water Tower** and **Pumping Station** stick out among the ritzy stores at the corner of Michigan and Pearson Ave. Built in 1867, these two structures were the only in the area to survive the Great Chicago Fire. The pumping station houses the multimedia show *Here's Chicago* and a comprehensive tourist center (see **Practical Information,** above). Across Pearson St., expensive, trendy stores pack **Water Tower Place,** the first urban shopping mall in the US. One block north of the Water Tower shops, the **John Hancock Building** (Chicago's 3rd tallest) rockets toward the sky in black steel and glass.

OLD TOWN. The bells of the pre-fire **St. Michael's Church** ring 1 mi. north of the MagMile in **Old Town,** a neighborhood where eclectic galleries, shops, and nightspots crowd gentrified streets. Architecture buffs will enjoy a stroll through the W. Menomonee and W. Eugenie St. area. In early June, the **Old Town Art Fair** attracts artists and craftsmen from across the country. *(Take bus #151 to Lincoln Park and walk south down Clark or Wells St.)*

NORTH SIDE

LINCOLN PARK. Urban renewal has made **Lincoln Park,** a neighborhood just west of the park that bears the same name, a popular choice for wealthy residents. Bounded by Armitage to the south and Diversey Ave. to the north, lakeside Lincoln Park offers splendid harbors and parks. Cafes, bookstores, and nightlife pack its tree-lined streets; some of Chicago's liveliest clubs and restaurants lie in the area around N. Clark St., Lincoln Ave., and N. Halsted St.

LAKEVIEW. North of Diversey Ave. on N. Clark St., the streets of Lincoln Park become increasingly diverse as they melt into the community of Lakeview around the 3000s block. In this self-proclaimed "gay capital of Chicago," supermarket shopping plazas alternate with tiny markets and vintage clothing stores, while apartment towers and hotels spring up between aging two-story houses. Polish diners share blocks with Korean restaurants in this ethnic potpourri, and Mongolian eateries face Mexican bars.

WRIGLEYVILLE. Around the 4000s block of N. Clark, Lakeview shifts into **Wrigleyville.** Although they finally lost their battle against night baseball in 1988, Wrigleyville residents remain fiercely loyal to the **Chicago Cubs.** Tiny, ivy-covered **Wrigley Field,** 1060 W. Addison, just east of the junction of Graceland and N. Clark, is the North Side's most famous institution. A pilgrimage here is a must for the serious or curious baseball fan, and for *Blues Brothers* nuts who want to visit the famous pair's falsified address. Along Clark St. in both Lakeview and Wrigleyville—one of the city's busiest nightlife districts—restaurants, sports bars, and music clubs abound. Window shopping here beckons in the funk, junk, and 70s revival stores. For an alternative form of nightlife, go bowling, one of the most cherished midwest pastimes, at **Southport Lanes & Billiards.** The 75 year-old Southport is one of the only remaining alleys anywhere to use pin-boys to set the lanes. *(3325 N. Southport Ave. near N. Clark St. ☎ 773-472-1601. Open 24hr. Game prices vary; tips appreciated.)* An even more raucous bowling experience awaits at the **Diversey Rock-n-Bowl,** in Lakeview, where "athletes" guzzle beers and bowl to deafening rock music. *(2211 W. Diversey. ☎ 773-227-5800. Open 24hr.)*

NEAR WEST SIDE

The Near West Side, bounded by the Chicago River to the east and Ogden Ave. to the west, assembles a veritable cornucopia of vibrant ethnic enclaves. **Greektown** and **Little Italy** draw culinary acclaim from all over the city (see **Food,** above).

HULL HOUSE. The primary inedible attraction on the Near West Side lies a few blocks north on Halsted, where activist Jane Addams devoted her life to historic Hull House. This settlement house bears witness to Chicago's role in turn-of-the-century reform. Although the house no longer offers social services, it's been painstakingly restored as a museum. *(800 S. Halsted St. ☎ 413-5353. Take El Blue Line to Halsted/U of I or bus #8 "Halsted." Open M-F 10am-4pm, Su noon-5pm. Free.)*

SOUTH OF THE LOOP

HYDE PARK AND THE UNIVERSITY OF CHICAGO. Seven mi. south of the Loop along the lake, the scenic campus of the **University of Chicago** dominates the **Hyde Park** neighborhood. A former retreat for the city's artists and musicians, the park's community underwent urban renewal in the 50s and is now an island of intellectualism in a sea of degenerating neighborhoods. University police patrol the area bounded by 51st St. to the north, Lakeshore Dr. to the east, 61st St. to the south, and Cottage Grove to the west, but don't test these boundaries, even during the day. Lakeside Burnham Park, east of campus, is fairly safe during the day but not at night. The impressive **Oriental Institute, Museum of Science and Industry** (see **Museums,** p. 510), and **DuSable Museum of African-American History** are all in, or border on, Hyde Park. *(From the Loop, take bus #6 "Jefferson Express" or the METRA Electric Line from the Randolph St. Station south to 59th St.)*

ROBIE HOUSE. On campus, Frank Lloyd Wright's famous ▓**Robie House** blends into the surrounding trees. A seminal example of Wright's Prairie style, which sought to integrate house with environment, its low horizontal lines now hold university offices. *(5757 S. Woodlawn, at the corner of 58th St. ☎ 708-848-1976. Tours M-F 11am-3pm, Sa-Su 11am-3:30pm. $8, over 64 and ages 7-18 $6.)*

PULLMAN. In 1885, George Pullman, inventor of the sleeping car, attempted to create a model working environment so that his Palace Car Company employees would be "healthier, happier, and more productive." The result of this quest was the town of **Pullman,** 14 mi. southeast of downtown. It was considered the nation's ideal community until 1894, when a stubborn Pullman evicted fired workers from their homes. The community soon after held a monumental strike, and Pullman's vision was shattered. In the center of town, **Hotel Florence** houses a museum and gift shop. *(11111 S. Forrestville Ave. ☎ 773-785-8181. I-94W to 111th St. Illinois Central Gulf Railroad to 111th St. and Pullman or METRA Rock Island Line to 111th St.)* The **Historic Pullman Foundation Visitors Center** leads guided tours. *(11141 S. Cottage Grove Ave. ☎ 773-785-3111. Tours leave the first Su of each month May-Oct. at 12:30 and 1pm. $5, students and seniors $4.)*

GREAT LAKES

WEST OF THE LOOP

OAK PARK. A must-see destination for any visitor to Chicago, the magnificent town of Oak Park sprouts off of Harlem St., 10 mi. west of downtown on I-290. *(I-290 W to Harlem St.)* Frank Lloyd Wright endowed the community with 25 of his spectacular homes and buildings, all of which dot the Oak Park Historic District. Here, his one-time home and workplace, the ⬛**Frank Lloyd Wright House and Studio,** offers an unbeatable look at his interior and exterior stylings and is an ideal starting point for walking tours of the district. *(951 Chicago Ave. Open daily 10am-5pm. 45min. tours of the house M-F 11am, 1, and 3pm, Sa-Su every 15min. 11am-4pm. 1hr. self-guided tours of Wright's other Oak Park homes can be taken with a map and audio cassette available daily 10am-3pm. Guided tours Sa-Su 10:30am, noon, and 2pm. Tours $8, seniors and under 18 $6; combination interior/exterior tour tickets $14/$10.)* The **visitors center** also offers maps, guidebooks, and tours. *(158 Forest Ave. ☎ 708-848-1500 or 888-625-7275. El Green Line to Harlem.)*

🏛 MUSEUMS

Chicago's major museums admit visitors free at least one day per week. The first five listings, the Big Five, provide a diverse array of exhibits, while a handful of smaller collections target specific interests. Lake Shore Drive has been diverted around Grant Park, linking the Field Museum, Adler, and Shedd; the compound, known as Museum Campus, offers a free shuttle between museums. Visitors who plan on seeing all five, plus the Sears Tower Observation Deck, can also save money by purchasing a half-price CityPass, which grants admission to the sights as well as discount coupons for food and shopping ($30.50, seniors $25, ages 3-11 $22.75; available at each included attraction).

- ⬛ **The Art Institute of Chicago,** 111 S. Michigan Ave. (☎443-3600), at Adams St. in Grant Park; take the El Green, Brown, Purple, or Orange Lines to Adams. The city's premier art museum, with 4 millennia of art from Asia, Africa, Europe, and beyond. The Institute's Impressionist and Post-Impressionist collections have won international acclaim. Highlight tour daily 2pm, includes Wood's *American Gothic* and Seurat's *A Sunday Afternoon on the Island of La Grande Jatte*, among others. Free jazz in the courtyard in summer Tu after 4:30pm. Open M and W-F 10:30am-4:30pm, Tu 10:30am-8pm, Sa-Su 10am-5pm. $8, students, seniors, and children $5, under 5 free; free on Tu.

- ⬛ **Museum of Science and Industry,** 5700 S. Lake Shore Dr. (☎773-684-1414), at 57th St. in Hyde Park; take bus #6 "Jeffrey Express" or METRA South Shore line to 57th St. Housed in the only building left from the 1893 World's Columbian Exposition, the expansive and impressive Museum includes the *Apollo 8* command module, a full-sized replica of a coal mine, a cantilevered 727 airplane, and Omnimax shows. Call for schedule. Open daily M-F 9:30am-4pm, Sa-Su and holidays 9:30am-5:30pm. $7, seniors $6, ages 3-11 $3.50, under 3 free; with Omnimax $13/$11/$8.50; free on Th (except Omnimax). Parking $7 per day.

- ⬛ **Field Museum of Natural History,** 1400 S. Lake Shore Dr. (☎922-9410), at Roosevelt Rd. in Grant Park; take bus #146 from State St. Sue, the largest T-rex skeleton ever found, is newly assembled and alone worth the trip to Chicago. Excellent geological, anthropological, botanical, and zoological exhibits lie in the shadow of her 40 ft. bad-ass self. Other highlights include Egyptian mummies, Native American halls, and a dirt exhibit. Open daily 8am-5pm, Labor Day to Memorial Day 9am-5pm. $8, students, seniors, and ages 3-11 $4, under 3 free; free on W. Parking $7 per day.

- **The Adler Planetarium,** 1300 S. Lake Shore Dr. (☎922-7827), on Museum Campus in Grant Park. Lets amateur astronomers discover their weight on Mars, read the news from space, and examine astronomy tools. Open June-Aug. Sa-W 9am-6pm, Th-F 9am-9pm; Sept.-May M-F 9am-5pm, Sa-Su 9am-6pm. $5, seniors and ages 4-17 $4; free on Tu and Th evenings. Some exhibits $5 extra. Skyshow daily on the hr. $5.

- **Shedd Aquarium,** 1200 S. Lake Shore Dr. (☎939-2438), in Grant Park. The world's largest indoor aquarium has over 6600 species of fish in 206 tanks, along with a fascinating new Amazon Rising exhibit. The Oceanarium features beluga whales, dolphins, seals, and other marine mammals in a giant pool that appears to flow into Lake Michigan. Open daily 9am-6pm, Th until 10pm (Oceanarium until 8pm); Labor Day to Memorial Day M-F 9am-5pm, Sa-Su 9am-6pm. Feedings M-F 11am, 2, and 3pm. Combined admission to Oceanarium and Aquarium $15, seniors and ages 3-11 $11; Aquarium free on M, Oceanarium $6, seniors and ages 5-17 $5. Tour of Oceanarium $3.

The Museum of Contemporary Art, 220 E. Chicago Ave. (☎280-2660), 1 block east of Michigan Ave.; take #66 (Chicago Ave.) bus. The MCA showcases outstanding permanent and temporary collections of modern art. Warhol, Javer, and Nauman highlight a vibrant list of artists. Open Tu 10am-8pm, W-Su 10am-5pm. $8, students and seniors $5, under 12 free; free on Tu.

Chicago Historical Society, 1601 N. Clark St. (☎642-4600), at North Ave. in Lincoln Park. A research center for scholars with an excellent interactive museum open to the public. Permanent exhibit on America in the age of Lincoln, plus changing exhibits. Open M-Sa 9:30am-4:30pm, Su noon-5pm. $5, students and seniors $3, ages 6-12 $1; free on M.

Museum of Holography, 1134 W. Washington Blvd (☎226-1007), just west of the Loop. This unconventional museum explores the seemingly inexplicable world of holograms, those funny little 3D pictures on credit cards. The hologram pictures of famous people are fantastic. Open W-Su 12:30-5pm. $2.50.

Spertus Institute of Jewish Studies, 618 S. Michigan Ave. (☎322-1747), near Harrison downtown. Take El Red Line to Harrison. A fabulous collection of synagogue relics rests on the first fl., as does the diminutive but moving Holocaust Memorial. Open Su-W 10am-5pm, Th 10am-8pm, F 10am-3pm. Artifact center open Su-Th 1-4:30pm. $5, students, seniors, and children $3; free on F.

Terra Museum of American Art, 664 N. Michigan Ave. (☎664-3939), at Erie St. One of few galleries to exclusively showcase American art from colonial times to the present, focusing on 19th-century Impressionism. Open Tu 10am-8pm, W-Sa 10am-6pm, Su noon-5pm. $7, seniors $3.50, students and teachers with ID and under 12 free; free on Tu and first Su of month. Free tours Tu-F noon and 6pm, Sa-Su noon and 2pm.

International Museum of Surgical Science, 1524 N. Lake Shore Dr. (☎642-6502), at North Ave. A sculpture of a surgeon holding his wounded patient marks the entrance to this unique museum, a harrowing journey through the history of surgery that's better than it sounds. Highlights, if they can be so called, include a fascinating collection of gallstones and bladderstones. Open Tu-Sa 10am-4pm. $5, seniors and students $3.

⚃ OUTDOORS

A string of lakefront parks fringe the area between Chicago proper and Lake Michigan. On sunny afternoons, a cavalcade of sunbathers, dog walkers, in-line skaters, and skateboarders storm the shore. The two major parks, close to downtown, are **Lincoln** and **Grant**. Lincoln extends across 5 mi. of lakefront on the north side, and rolls in the style of a 19th-century English park: winding paths, natural groves of trees, and asymmetrical open spaces. The **Lincoln Park Zoo,** the nation's oldest, is an excellent spot for a stroll among the gorillas and tigers. *(Open daily 10am-5pm, and summer Sa-Su until 7pm. Free.)* Next door, the **Lincoln Park Conservatory** encloses fauna from varied eco-systems in its glass palace. *(☎742-7736. Open daily 9am-5pm. Free.)*

Grant Park, covering 14 lakefront blocks east of Michigan Ave., follows the 19th-century French park style: symmetrical and ordered, with corners, a fountain in the center, and wide promenades. The Grant Park Concert Society hosts free summer concerts here in the **Petrillo Music Shell.** *(520 S. Michigan Ave. ☎742-4763.)* Colored lights illuminate **Buckingham Fountain** from 9-11pm. On the north side, Lake Michigan lures swimmers and sun-bathers to **Lincoln Park Beach** and **Oak St. Beach.** Be aware that the rock ledges are restricted areas, and swimming from them is illegal. Although the beaches are patrolled 9am to 9:30pm, they can be unsafe after dark. The **Chicago Parks District** (☎747-2200) has further info.

🎵 ENTERTAINMENT

The weeklies *Chicago Reader* and *New City*, available in many bars, record stores, and restaurants, list the latest events. The *Reader* reviews all major shows, with times and ticket prices. *Chicago* magazine has exhaustive club, music, dance, and opera listings, along with theater reviews. *The Chicago Tribune* includes an entertainment section each F. *Gay Chicago* provides info on social activities and other news for the area's gay community.

THEATER

One of the foremost theater centers of North America, Chicago's more than 150 theaters show everything from blockbuster musicals to off-color parodies. Downtown theaters cluster just north of the Loop and around Michigan Ave. and Madison Ave. Smaller, community-based theaters are scattered throughout the city. Most tickets are expensive. Half-price tickets are sold on the day of performance at **Hot Tix Booths,** 108 N. State St., or at the 6th level of 700 N. Michigan Ave. Purchases must be made in person. Lines form 15-20min. before the booth opens. (☎977-1755. Open M-F 10am-7pm, Sa 10am-6pm, Su noon-5pm.) **Ticketmaster** supplies tickets for many theaters; ask about senior, student, and child discounts at all Chicago shows (☎559-1212). The "Off-Loop" theaters on the North Side specialize in original production, with tickets usually under $18.

Steppenwolf Theater, 1650 N. Halsted St. (☎335-1888), where Gary Sinise and the eerie John Malkovich got their start and still stop by. Tickets Su-Th $34, F-Sa $39; half-price Tu-F after 5pm, Sa-Su after noon. Office open Su-M 11am-5pm, Tu-F 11am-8pm, Sa 11am-9pm.

Goodman Theatre, 200 S. Columbus Dr. (☎443-3800), presents consistently solid original works. Tickets around $18-40; half-price after 6pm, or after noon for matinee. Box office open 10am-5pm; 10am-8pm show nights, usually Sa-Su.

Shubert Theater, 22 W. Monroe St. (☎902-1500), presents big-name Broadway touring productions. Ticket $15-70. Box office open M-Sa 10am-6pm.

Annoyance Theatre, 3747 N. Clark St. (☎773-929-6200), in Wrigleyville. Original works that play off pop culture, such as *Co-ed Prison Sluts.* 7 different shows per week. Often participatory comedy. Tickets ($5-10) sold just before showtime, usually 8 or 9pm.

Bailiwick Repertory, 1225 W. Belmont Ave. (☎773-327-5252), in the Theatre building. A mainstage and experimental studio space. Tickets from $10. Box office open W noon-6pm, Th-Su noon until showtime.

Live Bait Theatre, 3914 N. Clark St. (☎773-871-1212). Shows with titles like *Food, Fun, & Dead Relatives* and *Mass Murder II.* Launched a multi-play *Tribute to Jackie* (Onassis, that is). Tickets $20, Th $10. Box office open M-F noon-5pm.

COMEDY

Chicago boasts a plethora of comedy clubs. The most famous, **Second City,** 1616 N. Wells St. (☎337-3992), at North Ave. in Old Town, spoofs Chicago life and politics. Second City graduated Bill Murray and late greats John Candy, John Belushi, and Gilda Radner, among others. Most nights, a free improv session follows the show. **Second City e.t.c.** offers yet more comedy next door at 1608 N. Wells. (☎642-8189. Shows for both M-Th 8:30pm, F-Sa 8 and 11pm, Su 8pm. Box office hrs. daily 10:30am-10pm. Tickets $15. Reservations recommended; during the week you can often get in if you show up 1hr. early.) Watch improv actors compete to bust your gut at **Comedy Sportz,** 2851 N. Halsted (☎773-549-8080; shows F-Sa 8 and 10:30pm).

DANCE, CLASSICAL MUSIC, AND OPERA

Ballet, comedy, live theater, and musicals are performed at **Auditorium Theater,** 50 E. Congress Pkwy. (☎922-2110; box office open M-F 8:30am-5pm.) From Oct.-May, the **Chicago Symphony Orchestra,** conducted by Daniel Barenboim, resonates at **Symphony Center,** 220 S. Michigan Ave. (☎294-3000). **Ballet Chicago** pirouettes in theaters throughout Chicago (☎251-8838; tickets $12-45). The acclaimed **Lyric Opera of Chi-cago** performs from Sept.-Mar. at the **Civic Opera House,** 20 N. Wacker Dr. (☎332-2244). While other places may suck your wallet dry, the **Grant Park Music Festival** affords a taste of the classical for free; from mid-June through late Aug., the acclaimed Grant Park Symphony Orchestra plays a few free evening concerts per week at the Grant Park Petrillo Music Shell (usually W-Su; schedule varies; call ☎819-0614 for details).

SEASONAL EVENTS

The city celebrates summer on a grand scale. The **Taste of Chicago** festival cooks for eight days through July 4th. Seventy restaurants set up booths with endless samples in Grant Park, while crowds chomp to the blast of big name bands (free entry, food tickets 50¢ each). The Taste's fireworks are the city's biggest and most popular, though they are held on July 3rd. The first week in June, the **Blues Festival** celebrates the city's soulful, gritty music; the **Chicago Gospel Festival** hums and hollers in mid-June; and Nashville moves north for the **Country Music Festival** at the end of June. The **¡Viva Chicago!** Latin music festival steams up in late Aug., while the **Chicago Jazz Festival** scats Labor Day weekend. All festivals center at the Grant Park Petrillo Music Shell. The Mayor's Office **Special Events Hotline** (☎744-3370 or 800-487-2446) has more info on all six free events. On summer Sa, Navy Pier has a free fireworks show (☎595-7437 for times).

The regionally famous **Ravinia Festival** (☎847-266-5100), in the northern suburb of Highland Park, runs from late June to early Sept. The Chicago Symphony Orchestra, ballet troupes, folk and jazz musicians, and comedians perform throughout the festival's 14-week season. (Shows M-Sa 8pm, Su 7pm. Lawn seats $8; other tickets $15-35. On certain nights, the Orchestra allows students free lawn admission with student ID. Call ahead. Round-trip on the METRA costs about $7; the festival runs charter buses for $12. The bus ride takes 1½hr.)

SPORTS

The National League's **Cubs** step up to bat at **Wrigley Field,** 1060 W. Addison St., at N. Clark St. in Wrigleyville, one of the few ballparks in America to retain the early grace and intimate feel of the game; it's definitely worth a visit (☎831-2827; tickets $10-22). The **White Sox,** Chicago's American League team, swing on the South Side at the new **Comiskey Park,** 333 W. 35th St. (☎674-1000; tickets $12-24). Da **Bears** of the NFL kick off at **Soldier Field Stadium,** at McFetridge Dr. and S. Lakeshore Dr. (☎708-615-2327). Da **Bulls** have won many an NBA championship at the **United Center,** 1901 W. Madison just west of the Loop, known fondly as "the house that Michael Jordan built" (☎943-5800; tickets $30-450). Hockey's **Blackhawks** skate in his shadow there (☎455-4500; tickets $25-100). **Sports Information** (☎976-4242) has up-to-the-minute info on local sports events. For tickets to all games, call **Ticketmaster** (Bulls and Blackhawks ☎559-1212, White Sox ☎831-1769, Cubs ☎831-2827).

🎵 NIGHTLIFE

"Sweet home Chicago" takes pride in the innumerable blues performers who have played here. Jazz, folk, reggae, and punk clubs throb all over the **North Side.** The **Bucktown/Wicker Park** area, west of Halsted St. in Northwest Chicago, stays open late with bucking bars and dance clubs. Aspiring pick-up artists swing over to **Rush** and **Division St.,** an intersection that has replaced the stockyards as one of the biggest meat markets in the world. Full of bars, cafes, and bistros, **Lincoln Park** is frequented by singles and young couples, both gay and straight. The vibrant center of gay culture is between 3000 and 4500 **N. Halsted St.;** many of the more festive and colorful clubs and bars line this area. For more upscale raging, raving, and discoing, there are plenty of clubs near **River North,** in Riverwest, and on Fulton St.

▓ **Funky Buddha Lounge,** 728 W. Grand Ave. (☎666-1695. El Blue Line: Chicago), West Town just west of River North. Extremely trendy, eclectic dance club and lounge where hip-hop and funk harmonize with outrageous leopard, velvet, and Buddha decor. Open Tu-F and Su 9pm-2am, Sa 9pm-3am. Cover $10-20.

▓ **Biology Bar,** 1520 N. Fremont St. (☎266-1234), in West Town. This ultra-hip, Latin-flavored dance club is much more fun and less educational than its name implies. A fur-covered bar and ultrasuede chairs provide a cushy rest after the pulsating salsa beats on the dance floor. Open M 11pm-4am, F 9:30pm-4am, Sa 10pm-5am. Cover $5-15.

B.L.U.E.S., 2519 N. Halsted St. (☎773-528-1012). El to Fullerton, then take the eastbound bus "Fullerton." Crowded and intimate, with unbeatable music. Success here led to the larger **B.L.U.E.S. etc.,** 1124 W. Belmont Ave. (☎773-525-8989). El to Belmont, then 3 blocks west on Belmont. The place for huge names: Albert King, Bo Diddley, Dr. John, and Wolfman Washington have played here. Live music every night 9pm-1:30am. Cover for both places M-Th $6-8, F-Sa $8-10. 21+.

Buddy Guy's Legends, 754 S. Wabash Ave. (☎427-0333), southern downtown. Buddy officially plays in Jan., but he is known to stop by when not on tour. The rest of the time, major and rising blues stars take over and enchant crowds in the soul-filled space. Blues M-Th 5pm-2am, F 4pm-2am, Sa 5pm-3am, Su 6pm-2am. Cover Su-W $6, Th $7, F-Sa $10-15. 21+.

Metro, 3730 N. Clark St. (☎773-549-0203), in Wrigleyville. Outstanding live alternative and pop music venue, ranging from local bands to Soul Asylum and the hometown favorite Smashing Pumpkins. Tu new band showcase. Cover $5-12; much more for big bands. 18+; occasionally all ages are welcome. Downstairs, the 21+ **Smart Bar** (☎773-549-4140) has pool tables and a dance floor that spins punk, techno, hip-hop or house. Opening times vary (around 10pm); closes around 4am on weekends. Cover $5-9. Metro concertgoers pay no cover.

Wild Hare & Singing Armadillo Frog Sanctuary, 3530 N. Clark St. (☎773-327-4273., between Addison and Roscoe St. El: Addison), in Wrigleyville. Live Roots Reggae acts sing Jah's praises in front of an intimate dance floor filled with both dreadlocked hipsters and yuppies. Arrive before 9:30pm to avoid cover. Open Su-F until 2am, Sa until 3am. Cover $5-8, M-Tu free; W ladies free.

Crobar Night Club, 1543 N. Kingsbury St. (☎413-7000. El Red Line: North & Clybourn), Near North. Cavernous, candle-strewn dance club where a young, leather-clad crowd slithers to house beats in cages and on the floor. Open W, F, and Su 10pm-4am, Sa 10pm-5am. GLEE gay night Su. Cover $5-20.

Circus, 901 W. Weed St. (☎266-1200), near North Ave. in the Near North. A blue, rotating sign marks the entrance into this three-ring (well, three-room) nightclub where ahead-of-the-trends attendees share the dance floor with fire-breathing, trapeze-swinging circus sideshows. Rock/hip-hop. Open Tu-F, Su 8pm-2am, Sa 8pm-3am. Cover $10.

Checkerboard Lounge, 423 E. 43rd St. (☎773-624-3240), at King Dr. Drive or take a cab. The true Blues bar experience, the Checkerboard is the most authentic, intimate joint in town. The down-and-out neighborhood infuses the music with its spirit; be careful. Open M-F 1pm-2am. Cover $5-7.

Berlin, 954 W. Belmont Ave. (☎773-327-7711. El Red or Brown line: Belmont), in Lakeview. Anything and everything goes at Berlin, a mainstay of Chicago's gay nightlife scene. Crowds pulsate to house/dance music amid drag contests, disco nights, and other theme parties. W ladies night. Open M-F until 4am, Sa until 5am. Cover F-Sa after midnight $5. 21+.

⚑ DAYTRIPS FROM CHICAGO

LAKE SHORE DRIVE. The full length of Lake Shore Dr. is an absolutely gorgeous drive on a sunny day. Starting from the Hyde Park area in the south, the road offers sparkling views of Lake Michigan all the way past the city and one of the best views of the downtown skyline. At its end, Lake Shore becomes Sheridan Rd., which twists and turns its way through the picturesque northern suburbs. Just north of Chicago is **Evanston,** a lively, affluent college town (home to Northwestern University) with an array of parks and nightclubs. Ten min. farther north is upscale **Wilmette,** home to the ornate and striking ▧**Baha'i House of Worship,** at Sheridan Rd. The intricate archtectual wonder is topped by a stunning nine-sided dome. *(100 Linden Ave. ☎847-853-2300. Open daily 10am-10pm; Oct.-May 10am-5pm. Services M-Sa 12:15pm, Su 1:15pm.)*

THE DUNES. The ▧**Indiana Dunes State Park** and **National Lakeshore** lie 45min. east of Chicago on I-90. The State Park's gorgeous dune beaches on Lake Michigan are packed on summer weekends, when Chicagoans flee the frantic pace of the city for swimming and sunning. Options for the more adventuresome include hikes through dunes, woods, and marshes. Info about the State Park is available at the **visitors center.** *(1600 N. 25 East in Chesterton. ☎219-926-1952.)* National Lakeshore details come from their visitors center. *(1100 N. Mineral Springs Rd. in Porter. ☎219-926-7561.)*

SPRINGFIELD ☎217

Springfield, "the town that Lincoln loved," owes much to its most distinguished former resident. A hotbed of political activity during the increasingly fractured antebellum years, the small town hosted the heated Lincoln-Douglass debates of 1858, attracting the attention of the entire nation. Although Springfield has since declined from national prominence into obscurity, the town welcomes tourists to learn everything about Honest Abe.

◪ PRACTICAL INFORMATION. Amtrak, 3rd and Washington St. (☎753-2013; station open daily 6am-9:30pm), near downtown, runs trains to Chicago (3½hr., 3 per day, $21-44) and St. Louis (2hr., 3 per day, $19-31). **Greyhound,** 2351 S. Dirksen Pkwy. (☎800-231-2222; depot open M-F 9am-8pm, Sa 9am-noon and 2-4pm), on the eastern edge of town, rolls to Chicago (6 per day, 5hr., $38); Indianapolis (7hr., 2 per day, $47.50); St. Louis (2hr., 4 per day, $24); and Bloomington (1hr., 1 per day, $54.50). **Springfield Mass Transit District:** 928 S. 9th St. Pick up maps at transit headquarters, most banks, or the Illinois State Museum. (☎522-5531. Buses operate M-Sa 6am-6pm. Fare 75¢, seniors 35¢, transfers free.) The **downtown trolley** system is designed to take tourists to eight designated places of historic interest. (☎528-4100. Trolleys run 9am-4pm; hop-on/off all fare $10, seniors $9, kids 5-12 $5; circuit fare $5.) **Taxi: Lincoln Yellow Cab,** ☎523-4545. **Springfield Convention and Visitors Bureau:** 109 N. 7th St. (☎789-2360 or 800-545-7300; open M-F 8am-5pm). **Internet access: Lincoln Library,** 326 S. 7th St. (☎753-4900; open M-Th 9am-9pm, F 9am-6pm, Sa 9am-5pm; Sept.-May also Su noon-5pm). **Post Office:** 411 E. Monroe, at Wheeler St. (☎788-7470; open M-F 7:30am-5pm). **ZIP code:** 62701. **Area code:** 217.

▛▟ ACCOMMODATIONS AND FOOD. Bus service to the cheap lodgings off I-55 and U.S. 36 on Dirksen Pkwy. is limited. Downtown hotels may be booked solid on weekdays when the legislature is in session, but ask the visitors office about weekend packages. Rooms should be reserved early for holiday weekends and the **State Fair** in mid-Aug. Take bus #3 "Bergen Park" to Milton and Elm St. and walk a few blocks east to the **Dirksen Inn Motel/Shamrock Motel,** 900 N. Dirksen Pkwy., for clean, pleasant rooms with refrigerators. (☎523-5302. Reception 8am-10pm. Rooms $30.) **Mister Lincoln's Campground,** 3045 Stanton Ave. (☎529-8206; take bus #10), off Stevenson Dr., has free showers. (Reception daily 8am-8pm; in winter until 6pm. Sites $14, with hook-up $19; cabins with A/C $25.)

Interesting cuisine is sparse in Springfield. Still, you can get some kicks down on historic Rte. 66 at the **Cozy Drive-In,** 2935 S. 6th St., a three-generation family diner devoted to memorabilia of the old road and great greasy food. (☎525-1992. Open M-Sa 8am-8pm. Cozy Dog $1.35.) Downtown, pink-and-orange **Cafe Brio,** 6th and Monroe (☎544-0574), stirs up typical soup and sandwich fare with a Mexican, Mediterranean, and Caribbean flair. The cafe has a full bar and is open daily for lunch ($5-8), dinner ($5-17), and weekend brunch.

SIGHTS. Springfield makes money by zealously re-creating Lincoln's life. Walking from sight to sight allows you to retrace the steps of the monumental man himself. Happily, many Lincoln sights are free. *(Info line ☎800-545-7300.)* The **Lincoln Home Visitors Center** screens a 19min. film on "Mr. Lincoln's Springfield" and doles out free tickets to see the **Lincoln Home.** The only house Abe ever owned and the main Springfield draw, it sits at 8th and Jackson St. in a restored 19th-century neighborhood replete with hoops-playing girls and rickety boardwalks. *(426 S. 7th St. ☎492-4241. Open daily 8am-6pm. 10min. tours every 5-10min. from the front of the house. Arrive early to avoid the crowds.)* The magnificent limestone **Old State Capitol,** where Lincoln delivered his stirring and prophetic "House Divided" speech in 1858, also witnessed the epic Lincoln-Douglass debates which catapulted Lincoln to national prominence the same year. *(☎785-7961. Open daily Mar.-Oct. 9am-5pm, Nov.-Feb 9am-4pm. Last tour 1hr. before closing. Donation suggested.)* Lincoln, his wife Mary Todd, and three of their sons rest at the massive **Lincoln Tomb,** at Oak Ridge Cemetery. *(1500 Monument Ave. ☎782-2717. Open daily Mar.-Oct. 9am-5pm, Nov.-Feb. 9am-4pm.)*

Those unwilling to endure all of Lincolnland should walk to the **Dana-Thomas House,** six blocks south of the Old State Capitol. Built in 1902, the stunning and well-preserved home was one of Frank Lloyd Wright's early experiments in Prairie Style and still features Frank's original fixtures. *(301 E. Lawrence Ave. ☎782-6776. Open W-Su 9am-4pm. 1hr. tours every 15-20min. Suggested donation $3.)* Rte. 66, that fabled American highway of yesteryear, is remembered in Springfield by **Shea's,** 2075 Peoria Rd., a truck shop with masses of memorabilia, including gas pumps, signs, and license plates. *(☎522-0475. Open Tu-F 7am-4pm, Sa 7am-noon.)*

WISCONSIN

Oceans of milk and beer flood the Great Lakes' most wholesome party state. French fur trappers first explored this area in search of lucrative furry creatures. Later, miners burrowed homes in the hills during the 1820s lead rush (earning them the nickname "badgers"), and hearty Norsemen set to clearing vast woodlands. By the time the forests fell and the mines were exhausted, German immigrant farmers had set dairy cows to graze and planted rolling fields of barley for beer amid the state's 15,000 lakes. Visitors to "America's Dairyland" pass cheese-filled country stores to delight in the ocean-like vistas of Door County and the ethnic fêtes (and less refined beer bashes) of Madison and Milwaukee.

⛶ PRACTICAL INFORMATION

Capital: Madison.
Visitor Info: Division of Tourism, 123 W. Washington St., P.O. Box 7606, Madison 53707 (☎608-266-2161, out of state 800-432-8747; www.tourism.state.wi.us).
Postal Abbreviation: WI. **Sales Tax:** 5.5%.

MILWAUKEE ☎414

Home to beer and countless festivals, Milwaukee is a city given to celebration. Ethnic communities take turns throwing rollicking city-wide parties each summer weekend, giving the city its reputation for *gemütlichkeit* (hospitality). Milwaukee's famous beer industry fuels the revelry, supplying more than 1500 bars and taverns with as much of the good stuff as anyone could ever need—or take. Aside from merrymaking, the city boasts top-notch museums, German-inspired architecture, and a long expanse of scenic lakeshore.

▐ GETTING THERE AND GETTING AROUND

Airport: General Mitchell International Airport, 5300 S. Howell Ave. (☎747-5300). Take bus #80 from 6th St. downtown (30min.). **Limousine Service,** ☎769-9100 or 800-236-5450. 24hr. pick-up and drop-off from most downtown hotels. $10, round-trip $18. Reservations required.

Trains: Amtrak, 433 W. St. Paul Ave. (☎271-0840), at 5th St. downtown. In a fairly safe area, but less so at night. To: Chicago (1½hr., 6 per day, $21) and St. Paul (6½hr., 1 per day, $75). Open daily 5:30am-9pm.

Buses: Greyhound, 606 N. 7th St. (☎272-2156), off W. Michigan St., 3 blocks from the train station. To: Chicago (2-3hr., 18 per day, $12) and Minneapolis (6½-9hr., 6 per day, $47). Station open 24hr.; office open daily 6:30am-11:30pm. **Wisconsin Coach** (☎262-544-6503 or 262-542-8861), in the same terminal, covers southeast Wisconsin. **Badger Bus,** 635 N. 7th St. (☎276-7490 or 608-255-1511), across the street, burrows to Madison (1½hr., 6 per day, $10). Open daily 6:30am-10pm. *Be cautious at night.*

Public Transit: Milwaukee County Transit System, 1942 N. 17th St. (☎344-6711). Efficient metro area service. Most lines run 5am-12:30am. Fare $1.35, seniors and children 65¢; weekly pass $10.50/$6.50. Free maps at the library or at Grand Ave. Mall info center. Call for schedules. **Milwaukee Loop** (☎344-6711) runs around historic downtown. $1 pass good all day. Operates June-Sept. Th 5pm-1am, F-Sa 10am-1am.

Taxis: Veteran, ☎291-8080. **Yellow Taxi,** ☎271-6630.

✴▌ ORIENTATION AND PRACTICAL INFORMATION

Most of Milwaukee's action is centered on the east side of downtown, which lies between **Lake Michigan** and 10th St. Address numbers increase north and south from **Wisconsin Ave.,** the center of east-west travel. Most north-south streets are numbered, increasing from Lake Michigan toward the west. The **interstate system** forms a loop around Milwaukee: **I-43 S** runs to Beloit, **I-43 N** runs to Green Bay, **I-94 E** is a straight shot to Chicago, **I-94 W** goes to Madison and then Minneapolis/St. Paul, **I-794** cuts through the heart of downtown Milwaukee, and **I-894** is the downtown bypass and connects with the airport.

Visitor Info: Greater Milwaukee Convention and Visitors Bureau, 510 W. Kilbourne St. (☎273-7222 or 800-554-1448), downtown. Open M-F 8am-5pm; in summer also Sa 9am-2pm.

Hotlines: Crisis Intervention, ☎257-7222. **Rape Crisis Line,** ☎542-3828. Both 24hr. **Gay People's Union Hotline,** ☎562-7010. Operates daily 7-10pm.

Post Office: 345 W. St. Paul Ave. (☎270-2004), south along 4th Ave. from downtown, by the Amtrak station. Open M-F 7:30am-8pm. **ZIP code:** 53202. **Area code:** 414.

▌ ACCOMMODATIONS

Downtown lodging options tend to be expensive; travelers with cars should head out to the city's two hostels. **Bed and Breakfast of Milwaukee** (☎277-8066) finds rooms in picturesque B&Bs around the area (from $55).

University of Wisconsin at Milwaukee (UWM), Sandburg Hall, 3400 N. Maryland Ave. (☎229-4065 or 299-6123). Take bus #30 north to Hartford St. Convenient to nightlife and east-side restaurants, the UWM sports spotless, unadorned dorm suites, divided into single and double bedrooms. Laundry facilities, cafeteria, free local calls. Open June to mid-Aug. Singles with shared bath $27; doubles $35; 4 bed suite $60, 5 beds $71. Parking $6.50 for 24hr. 2-day advance reservations required.

Wellspring Hostel (HI-AYH), 4382 Hickory Rd. (☎675-6755), in Newburg. Take I-43 N to Rte. 33 W to Newburg and exit on Main St.; Hickory Rd. intersects Newburg's Main St. just northwest of the Milwaukee River. The idyllic setting, far from downtown on a riverside vegetable farm, is worth the 45min. drive for those looking to get back to nature. Well-kept with 25 beds, kitchen, and nature trails. Office open daily 8am-8pm. Dorms $15, non-members $18. Private room with bath $40. Linen $3. Reservations required.

Red Barn Hostel (HI-AYH), 6750 W. Loomis Rd. (☎529-3299), in Greendale 13 mi. south-west of downtown via I-894; take the Loomis exit. Dim rooms with stone walls comprise the bottom floor of this enormous, 85-year-old red barn. 20 dorm-style bunk beds, full kitchen, lockers, shared bathrooms. Check-in 5-10pm. Open May-Oct. Dorms $11, non-members $14. Linen $1.50. Reservations recommended.

Motel 6, 5037 S. Howell Ave. (☎482-4414), near the airport off I-894, in a remodeled building 15min. from downtown. Any airport shuttle will take you within walking dis-tance of this dependable chain motel, which houses airy rooms with A/C, cable, and a pool. Singles $44; doubles $48; Sa-Su $46/$48.

🍴 FOOD

Milwaukee is best known for its food and beer. German influences run especially strong, as bier-guzzling locals take pride in the best *schnitzel* and *wurst* this side of the Atlantic. On a distinctly less exotic note, Milwaukeeans take advantage of nearby Lake Michigan with a local favorite called the **Friday night fish fry.** For those who prefer to skip straight to the sweet stuff, extra-creamy ice cream, known as **fro-zen custard,** is the dairy state's special treat.

German restaurants are scattered along nearly every street in the city, particu-larly downtown where most have high-brow prices and continental attitude to match their 100 or so years of experience. Polish and Serbian influences dominate the **South Side,** and good Mexican food prevails in **Walker's Point,** at National and 5th St. **East Side** eateries are cosmopolitan and quirky, with a mix of ethnic flavors. Downtown, the Riverwalk project has revitalized the **Water St. entertainment district,** which boasts hot new restaurants for a range of palates. On the north end of the Riverwalk, **Old World Third St.** is home to the city's best brew-pubs.

Leon's, 3131 S. 27th St. (☎383-1784). A cross between *Grease* and *Starlight Express,* Leon's scoops some of the best frozen custard in town (2 scoops $1.25). Hot dogs $1. Open Su-Th 11am-midnight, F 11am-12:30am, Sa 11am-1am.

Casablanca, 730 W. Mitchell St. (☎383-2363), on the South Side. Herbivores feast on falafel and tabouli at the unbeatable all-you-can-eat lunch buffet ($5) in this serene Middle Eastern storefront. Carnivores get their fix with delectable shish kababs ($5-7). Entrees $5-10. Lunch buffet Tu-F 11am-2pm. Open Tu-Sa 11am-9pm, Su noon-6pm.

Mader's German Restaurant, 1037 N. Old World Third St. (☎271-3377), downtown. In a town known for its German cuisine, Mader's is a local favorite. The *schnitzels* and *schaumtorte* are worth the steep prices. The stern decor, suits of armor along the halls, and gorgeous wooden bar will make you think you're eating them in Bavaria. Entrees from $12. Open M 11:30am-9pm, Tu-Th 11:30am-10pm, F-Sa 11:30am-11pm, Su 10:30am-9pm. Reservations recommended.

King and I, 823 N. 2nd St. (☎276-4181). The lunch buffet ($6.50) is a favorite at this elegant Thai place. Entrees $9-11. Open M-F 11:30am-9pm, Sa 5-10pm, Su 4-9pm.

👁 SIGHTS

BREWERIES. Although many of Milwaukee's breweries have left, the city's name still evokes images of a cold one. No visit to the city would be complete without a look at the yeast in action. The ◼**Miller Brewery,** a corporate giant that produces 43 million barrels of beer annually, leads a free 1hr. tour followed by a trip to the bier-garten for three generous samples. *(4251 W. State St. ☎931-2337. 2 tours per hr. M-Sa 10am-3:30pm; 3 per hr. during busy days; call for winter schedule. Under 18 must be accompa-nied by adult. ID required.)* The **Lakefront Brewery,** off Pleasant St., produces five popu-lar year-round beers and several seasonal specials, including pumpkin beer and cherry lager. *(1872 N. Commerce St. ☎372-8800. Tours F 3:30pm, Sa 1:30, 2:30, and 3:30pm, Su 1pm. $3 for plastic cup, $5 for tour with souvenir mug.)* One of the state's most renowned microbreweries, **Sprecher Brewing,** 5 mi. north of the city on I-43 then east on Port Washington St., doles out four beer samples following a 1hr. tour. *(701 W.*

GREAT LAKES

Glendale. ☎ 964-2739. Tours M-F 4pm, Sa every 30min. 1-3pm. $2, under 12 free. Reservations required.) At most breweries, tour prices are discounted for non-drinkers.

MUSEUMS. Several excellent museums dot the shores of Milwaukee. One of the nation's first and finest natural history spots, the ▧**Milwaukee Public Museum,** at N. 8th St., attracts visitors with dinosaur bones, a replicated Costa Rican rainforest, a Native American exhibit, and a re-created European village. *(800 W. Wells St. ☎ 278-2700 or 278-2702 for recorded info. Open daily 9am-5pm. $6.50, seniors $5, ages 4-17 $4. Parking available.)* The newly expanded, spectacular **Milwaukee Art Museum,** on the lakefront downtown, is worth a visit just for its innovative architecture: moveable, sail-like wings jut out from the building and control its light and temperature, sheltering Haitian folk art, 19th-century German art, and American works from folk to Warhol. *(750 N. Lincoln Memorial Dr. ☎ 224-3200. Open Tu-W and F-Sa 10am-5pm, Th noon-9pm, Su noon-5pm. $5.50, students and seniors $3.50, under 12 free.)* The **Charles Allis Art Museum** houses a fine collection of East Asian and Classical artifacts in a surprisingly intimate mansion. *(1801 N. Prospect Ave. at E. Royal Pl., 1 block north of Brady. ☎ 278-8295. Take bus #30 or 31. Open W-Su 1-5pm. $3, students and seniors $2, children free.)*

PARKS. Better known as "The Domes," the **Mitchell Park Horticultural Conservatory,** at 27th St., recreates a desert and a rainforest and mounts seasonal floral displays in a series of seven-story conical glass domes. *(524 S. Layton Ave. ☎ 649-9800. Open daily 9am-5pm. Take bus #10 west to 27th St., then #27 south to Layton. $4, students 6-17 and seniors $2.50, under 6 free.)* The **Boerner Botanical Gardens,** in Whitnall Park between Grange and Rawsen St. in suburban Hales Corners, boast billions of beautiful blossoms as well as open-air concerts on Th nights. *(5879 S. 92nd St. ☎ 425-1130. Open mid-Apr. to Oct. daily 8am-7pm. Parking $3.50.)* County parks line much of Milwaukee's waterfront, providing free recreational areas and trails.

OTHER SIGHTS. A road warrior's nirvana, locally-headquartered **Harley-Davidson** gives 1hr. tours of its engine and transmission plant that will enthrall the aficionado. *(11700 W. Capitol Dr. ☎ 342-4680. Tours M-F 9:30, 11am, and 1pm. Call ahead—the plant sometimes shuts down in summer. Reservations required for groups larger than 6.)* For a brush with Olympic glory, amateur ice skaters should head to daily open skates at the **Pettit National Ice Center,** next to the state fairgrounds. Home to the US Speedskating team, the Pettit encloses several hockey and figure-skating rinks within a vast 400m speed oval. *(500 S. 84th St. at I-94. ☎ 266-0100. Call for open skating schedules. $5, seniors and children $4. Skate rental $2.)*

🎵 ENTERTAINMENT

The modern **Marcus Center for the Performing Arts,** 929 N. Water St., across the river from Père Marquette Park, is the area's major arts venue and plays host to the **Milwaukee Symphony Orchestra,** the **Milwaukee Ballet,** and the **Florentine Opera Company.** (☎ 273-7206 or 800-472-4458. Symphony tickets $17-52, ballet $13-62, opera $15-80. Ballet and symphony offer half-price student and senior rush tickets.) During the summer months, the center's Peck Pavilion hosts **Rainbow Summer,** a series of free lunchtime concerts—jazz, bluegrass, you name it. (☎ 273-7206. Concerts M-F noon-1:15pm.) **The Milwaukee Repertory Theater,** 108 East Wells St., stages innovative shows alongside the classics from Sept. through May. (☎ 224-1761. Tickets $8-30; half-price student and senior rush tickets available 30min. before shows.)

The **Milwaukee Brewers** baseball team steps up to bat at the brand-new, convertible **Miller Park,** at the interchange of I-94 and Rte. 41 (☎ 933-9000 or 800-933-7890), while the **Milwaukee Bucks** hoop it up at the **Bradley Center,** 1001 N. 4th St., downtown (☎ 227-0500).

🌸 FESTIVALS

Summertime livens up Milwaukee's cultural scene with countless free festivals and live music events. On any given night, a free concert is happening somewhere; call the **visitors bureau** (☎ 273-7222) to find out where. On summer Th, **Jazz in the Park**

(☎271-1416) jams for free in **Cathedral Square Park,** at N. Jackson St. between Wells and Kilbourn St. In Père Marquette Park, by the river between State and Kilbourn St., **River Flicks** (☎270-3560) screens free movies at dusk Th in Aug.

Locals line the streets far in advance for ☒**The Great Circus Parade** (☎356-8341), held in mid-July, a re-creation of turn-of-the-century processions with trained animals, daredevils, costumed performers, and 65 original wagons. **Summerfest,** the largest and most lavish of Milwaukee's festivals, spans 11 days in late June and early July; daily life halts as a potpourri of big-name musical acts, culinary specialities, and an arts and crafts bazaar take over. (☎273-3378 or 800-273-3378. Tickets M-Th $9, F-Su $10.) In early Aug., the **Wisconsin State Fair** rolls into the fairgrounds toting 12 stages, exhibits, contests, rides, fireworks, and a pie-baking contest. (☎266-7000 or 800-884-3247. $6, seniors $5, under 11 free.) Ethnic festivals abound during festival season. The most popular are: **Polish Fest** (☎529-2140) and **Asian Moon** (☎821-9829), both in mid-June; **Festa Italiana** (☎223-2193), in mid-July; **Bastille Days** (☎271-7400), near Bastille Day (July 14); **German Fest** (☎464-9444), in late July; **Irish Fest** (☎476-3378), in mid-Aug.; **Mexican Fiesta** (☎383-7066), in late Aug.; **Indian Summer Fest** (☎774-7119), in early Sept.; and **Arabian Fest** (☎342-4909), in mid-Sept. (Most festivals $7, under 12 free; some free plus price of food.) Pick up a copy of the free weekly *Downtown Edition* for the scoop on festivals and other events.

 NIGHTLIFE

Milwaukee never lacks something to do after sundown. The downtown business district gets a bit seedy at night, but the area along **Water St.** between Juneau and Highland Ave. offers hip, lively bars and clubs. Nightspots that draw a college crowd cluster around the intersection of **North Ave.** and **North Farwell St.,** near the UW Campus. One of the hottest places to be in Milwaukee after hours is bar- and coffeehouse-lined **Brady St.,** which runs east-west between Farwell and the river. **South 2nd St.** is a hothouse for eclectic, ultra-trendy nightclubs, including dance clubs, sports bars, lounges, and the town's best gay bars.

☒ **Safehouse,** 779 N. Front St. (☎271-2007), across from the Pabst Theater downtown. A brass plate labeled "International Exports, Ltd." welcomes guests to this bizarre world of spy hideouts, James Bond music, *mata hari* outposts, and drinks with names like Rahab the Harlot. A briefing with "Moneypenny" in the foyer is just the beginning of the intrigue. Draft beer $2.75; 24 oz. specialty drinks $5.75. Open M-Th 11:30am-1:30am, F-Sa 11:30am-2am, Su 4pm-midnight. Cover $1-3.

Hi-Hat, 1701 Brady St. (☎225-9330), 3 blocks west of Farwell Ave. M-W swing and jazz and other assorted live acts play on the loge in this trendy jazz joint, while Milwaukee's hep night-hawks roost in the cavernous depths below. The Su brunch is a local favorite. Beer $2-6. Open daily 4pm-2am, Su 10am-3pm for brunch. No attitude, no dress code, no cover.

Rochambo, 1317 Brady St. (☎241-0095), across the street from Hi-Hat. A coffee/teahouse hip almost to a fault. Crowds of the trying-not-to-be-trendy thronging the outdoor seating may intimidate at first, but the friendly staff, vintage music, sociable atmosphere and incredible tea selection make it one of Brady St.'s best spots. $1.50 for a mug of Oolong. Open M-F 7am-midnight, Sa 8am-midnight, Su 9am-midnight.

Von Trier, 2235 N. Farwell Ave. (☎272-1775), near Brady St. *Deutsch* down to the last detail, Von Trier is a packed biergarten with fantastic outdoor seating. The intricate wood carvings, big oak bar, and walls lined with steins create a laid-back atmosphere for enjoying some serious beer. A house special is German beer topped with German gin ($5). Beer from $2. Open Su-Th 4pm-2am, F-Sa 4pm-2:30am.

Lacage, 801 S. 2nd Ave. (☎383-8330). The largest pub in town attracts a mostly 20- and 30-something gay clientele, but crowds are often mixed due to the welcoming atmosphere. DJ's spin to keep 2 large floors grooving. F and Sa the bar splits: dancing on one side and drag shows on the other. B-Y-O-Wig. Cover W-Th $3, F-Sa $6. Open Su-Th 9pm-2am, F-Sa until 2:30.

MADISON
☎ 608

Building cities on isthmi is like shaking someone's left hand; it's generally avoided and, when attempted, usually comes off quite awkwardly. Madison's awkward development owes much to Judge James Doty, who in 1836 cajoled lawmakers into moving the capital to this narrow strip of land sandwiched between lakes Menona and Mendota. The resulting proximity of the Capitol to the University now gives Madison its peculiar flavor, blending the youth culture of activity and activism with the solemn, devout atmosphere of government and the Midwest.

✷ ORIENTATION

Madison's main attractions are centered around the Capitol and the University of Wisconsin-Madison. **State St.,** which connects the two, is the city's hub for eclectic food, shops, and nightlife; it is a pedestrian-only street. The northeast and southwest ends of the isthmus house malls, chain restaurants, and chain motels and are joined by **Washington Ave./US 151,** the city's main thoroughfare. **I-90** and **I-94** are joined through the city, but separate on either side of it. I-94 E goes to Milwaukee, then Chicago; I-94 W goes to Minneapolis/St. Paul; I-90 E goes directly to Chicago through Rockford, IL; I-90 W goes to Albert Lea, MN.

⑦ PRACTICAL INFORMATION

Greyhound, 2 S. Bedford St. (☎257-3050), has buses to Chicago (3-5hr., 8 per day, $18-20) and Minneapolis (6hr., 5 per day, $38-40). **Badger Bus** (☎255-6771) departs from the same depot to Milwaukee (1½hr., 6 per day, $12). The station is open daily from 5:30am-11pm. **Madison Metro Transit System,** 1101 E. Washington Ave. (☎266-4466), travels through downtown, UW campus, and surrounding areas ($1.50; free M-Sa 10am-3pm in the Capitol-UW campus area). The **Greater Madison Convention and Visitors Bureau,** is at 615 E. Washington Ave. (☎255-2537 or 800-373-6376; open M-F 8am-4:30pm). **Post Office:** 3902 Milwaukee St., at Hwy. 51 (☎246-1249; open M 7:30am-7pm, Tu-F 7:30am-6pm, Sa 8:30am-2pm). **ZIP code:** 53714. **Area code:** 608.

▛ ACCOMMODATIONS

Among the motels stretching along Washington Ave. (U.S. 151), near the intersection with I-90, rates start at $40 per weeknight and rise dramatically on weekends. From the Capitol, Bus A shuttles the 5 mi. between the Washington Ave. motels and downtown. Prices steepen downtown, starting around $60.

Hostelling International–Madison (HI-AYH), 141 S. Butler St. near State St. (☎441-0144 or 282-9031). Take bus to Capitol Sq., turn right on King St., then left on S. Butler St. This brand-new, ideally located hostel is a good bet for social, nightlife-loving travelers. Vibrant, homey setting and spotless rooms. Open year-round. Office hours 8-11am and 5-9pm. 24 beds; 34 beds June-Aug. Kitchen, laundry, internet access. Dorms $15, non-members $18; private rooms $33/$36; discounts for bikers, families, and groups of 5 or more.

Memorial Union, 800 Langdon St., on the UW campus (☎265-3000). Large, elegant rooms with excellent lake and city views, cable TV, A/C, and free parking. They only have 8, so call ahead. Rooms from $60. The no-frills **college cafeterias** here dole out the quickest, cheapest food in town. Meals from $3.

Select Inn, 4845 Hayes Rd., near the junction of I-94 and U.S. 151 (☎249-1815). Large rooms with cable TV, A/C, and a whirlpool. Singles $42; doubles from $50; Sa-Su $46/$54. Continental breakfast included.

Motel 6, 1754 Thierer Rd., behind Denny's (☎241-8101). A solid choice with A/C and cable TV. Singles from $39; doubles from $44.

Lake Kegonsa State Park, 2405 Door Creek Rd., 20min. south on I-90 in Stoughton (☎873-9695). Pleasant sites in a wooded area near the beach. Showers, flush toilets. Sites $9, WI residents $7; more on weekends. Parking permits $7/$5 per day.

◖ FOOD

Good, unique restaurants pepper Madison; clusters of them spice up the university and Capitol areas. **State St.** hosts a variety of cheap restaurants, including chains and Madison originals.

Himal Chuli, 318 State St. (☎251-9225). This State St. storefront stirs up excellent Nepalese favorites, such as *tarkari, dal,* and *bhat.* In English, that's great veggie meals and lentil soup ($3). Vegetarian entrees $5.25-7.50, meat entrees $8-10. Open M-W 11am-9pm, Th-Sa 11am-9:30pm, Su noon-8:30pm.

Nitty Gritty, 223 N. Frances St. (☎251-2521), near State St. A popular college hangout, this laid-back grill celebrates a gazillion birthdays each day with balloons and free beer (for the birthday person only). Just don't wear your birthday suit. Entrees $2-7. Open M-Sa 11am-midnight, Su 5-10pm.

Noodles and Co., 232 State St. (☎257-6393), at Johnson St. A truly global array of cheap, wonderful noodle dishes is just about all there is in this corner shop, where Japanese pan-fried noodles and Pad Thai share counter space with Stroganoff and Wisconsin-style Macaroni and Cheese. Entrees $3-7. Open M-Sa 11am-9pm, Su noon-8pm.

◉ ♫ SIGHTS AND ENTERTAINMENT

DOWNTOWN. With its double nature as a seat of government and home to a thriving college scene, there's lots to see on the isthmus. The imposing, Roman Renaissance-style **State Capitol,** in Capitol Sq. at the center of downtown, boasts beautiful ceiling frescoes and the only granite dome in the US. (☎266-0382. Open daily 6am-8pm. Free tours from the ground fl. info desk M-Sa on the hr. 9-11am and 1-3pm, Su 1-3pm.) Every Sa morning from late Apr. to early Nov., visitors swarm the Capitol grounds for the **farmers market,** which has grown into a premiere attractions. Leading out from the Capitol, Madison's pedestrian-only **State St.** exudes a lively college atmosphere, sporting many funky clothing stores, art galleries, and record shops. The **Madison Civic Center,** 211 State St., frequently stages arts and entertainment performances in the Oscar Mayer Theatre, and hosts the **Madison Symphony Orchestra.** (☎266-9055. Office open M-F 11am-5:30pm, Sa 11am-2pm. Season runs late Aug. to May. Tickets from $20.) The **Madison Repertory Theatre,** 122 State St., #201, performs classic and contemporary musicals and dramas. (☎256-0029. Showtimes vary; tickets $6.50-22.) At the southwest end of State St. is the **University of Wisconsin–Madison (UW),** where students and locals pass their days and nights hanging out at Memorial Union's gorgeous, lakeside **Union Terrace.** In summer, the terrace is home to free weekend concerts on the lake shore. Although the concerts move indoors in winter, the volume remains the same.

UNIVERSITY OF WISCONSIN. UW itself has a few noteworthy museums. One of the state's most acclaimed art museums, the **Elvehjem Museum of Art** (*EL-vee-hem*), 800 University Ave., boasts an astounding collection of Ancient Greek coins and vases, several galleries of American and European painting, and decorative arts dating from BC 2300. (☎263-2246. Open Tu-F 9am-5pm, Sa-Su 11am-5pm. Free.) UW produces its own Babcock brand of ice cream at the **Babcock Dairy Plant,** 1605 Linden Dr. near Charter St. and Observatory Dr. An observation deck allows visitors to watch their favorite flavor being made before they buy some at the store. (☎262-3047. Store open M-F 9:30am-5:30pm, Sa 10am-1:30pm.) Also part of UW, the outdoor **Olbrich Botanical Gardens** and indoor **Bolz Conservatory,** 3330 Atwood Ave., house a plethora of plant life. The Gardens showcase a variety of floral settings, from butterfly-attracting plants to an English herb garden; free-flying birds, waterfalls, and tropical plants grace the inside of the conservatory dome. (☎246-4550. Gardens open daily 8am-8pm; Sept.-May M-Sa 10am-4pm, Su 1am-5pm. Free. Conservatory open M-Sa 10am-4pm, Su 10am-5pm. $1, under 5 free; free W and Sa 10am-noon.) Botanists and Bedouins alike will enjoy the **University Arboretum,** 1207 Seminole Hwy. (☎263-7888), off I-94. A 6 mi. walking loop encircles the Arboretum's 1200 acres. For more info visit the **UW Visitors Center,** at the corner of Observatory Dr. and N. Park St., on the west side of the Memorial Union.

OUTDOORS. For more personal contact with nature, Madison's many parks and lakeshores offer endless recreational activities. There are 13 gorgeous public **beaches** for swimming or strolling along the two lakes (call ☎266-4711 for info). Back on dry land, **bicycling** is possibly the best way to explore the isthmus and surrounding park lands. **Budget Bicycle Center,** 1202 Regent St. (☎251-8413), loans out all types of two-wheel transportation. ($15 per day.) Hikers, picnickers, and other explorers should head to a city park; the **Parks Department,** 215 Martin Luther King Jr. Blvd., in the Madison Municipal Building, can help with specific park info. (☎266-4711. Open daily 4:30am-10pm. Admission to Madison parks is free.)

OUTSIDE MADISON. Some of Madison's most unique sights are far from the isthmus. 45min. west of Madison off U.S. 14, ◨**House on the Rock,** 5754 Rte. 23, in Spring Green, is an unparalleled multilevel house built into a chimney of rock. The 40-acre complex of gardens and fantastic architecture includes the world's largest carousel—of its 269 animals, not one is a horse. (☎935-3639. Open daily 9am-8pm; mid-Mar. to late May and Sept.-Oct. 9am-7pm. $15, ages 7-12 $9, ages 4-6 $4.) Nine mi. north of the House on the Rock, Frank Lloyd Wright's famed **Taliesin** home and school, on Rte. 23 in Spring Green, sprawls across acres of prairie land. The **visitors center,** Rte. 23 at Hwy. C, runs tours of the architect's buildings and living quarters. (☎588-7900. Open daily May-Oct. 9am-5pm. Prices vary according to tour; call for rates and schedules.)

◪ NIGHTLIFE

Fueled by the 40,000-plus students who pack the reputed party school, Madison's nightlife scene is active and eclectic. Clubs and bars are scattered throughout the isthmus, particularly along **State St.** and **U.S. 151.**

Essen Haus, 514 E. Wilson St. (☎255-4674), off US 151. This lively German bar and grill plays host to live polka bands, semi-rowdy crowds, and 2-gallon hats. Incredible beer selection (from $1.50). Open Tu-Sa 4pm-1am, Su 3pm-1am.

Cardinal, 418 E. Wilson St. (☎251-0080), near Essen Haus. Salsa Cubana and other themed dance nights bring some spice to the Madison nightlife scene. Renowned for its quirky, mixed crowds, Cardinal is the liveliest dance club in the city. Hrs. vary; call first. Usually open Su-Th until 2am, F-Sa until 2:30am. Cover from $4.

Crystal's Corner Bar, 1302 Williamson St. (☎256-2953). A slightly older crowd downs draught beers ($1.50-4) and grooves to live bands (usually blues). Hrs. and cover vary.

BARABOO'S BIZARRE The Greatest Show on Earth is in Baraboo, Wisconsin—permanently. Twenty mi. northwest of Madison along the Baraboo River, a swath of bank has been set aside by the State Historical Society to honor the one-time winter home of the world-famous **Ringling Brothers** circus. The **Circus World Museum,** in Baraboo, packs a full line-up of events from big-top performances to street parades. *(426 Water St. ☎356-0800. Open daily in summer from 9am to 6pm, mid-May through early Sept. 9am-9pm. Various shows at 11am, 1:15pm, 3pm. $14, seniors $13, under 12 $7.)* If seeing some plumed horse parade through town leaves you unfulfilled, Baraboo has more to offer. The **fantastical sculpture garden of Dr. Evermore** lies just south of Baraboo on Rte. 12. Here iron relics from an industrial age are given new life by the good doctor's welding torch. Thousands of critters, from plier-beaked, trumpet-necked birds, to spring-tailed robot legions clutter the two-acre plot. The centerpiece is a massive and fanciful palace/rocketship structure which has been recognized by *Guiness* as the largest junk sculpture in the world.

GREAT LAKES

NEAR MADISON: EFFIGY MOUNDS

Mysterious and striking, the Effigy Mounds are earthy windows into North American prehistory. Built by Native Americans as early as BC 1000, the enigmatic effigies are low-lying mounds of piled earth formed into distinguishable geometric and animal shapes. Though they once covered much of the Midwest, farmers' plows have ensured that only a scattering of them remain, mostly in western Wisconsin and eastern Iowa. One of the largest concentrations of intact mounds composes the **Effigy Mounds National Monument,** 151 Hwy. 76, 100 mi. west of Madison in Harpers Ferry, Iowa. Offering striking views of the Mississippi from high, rocky bluffs, the trails winding through the park explore the lives of these indigenous people and the meaning the mounds had for them. *(☎319-873-3491. Take Rte. 18 W from Madison. Visitors center open daily 8am-5pm.)* **Wyalusing State Park,** just across the Mississippi in Wisconsin, offers campsites overlooking the stunning confluence of the Wisconsin River and the Mighty Miss, as well as its own assortment of mounds and trails. *(☎608-996-2261. Campsites $8.)*

DOOR COUNTY   ☎920

Jutting out like a 🖑thumb from the Wisconsin mainland between Green Bay and Lake Michigan, the Door peninsula exudes a coastal spirit unlike any other in the nation's heartland. With 250 miles of rocky coastline, Lake Michigan's ocean-like tides, miles of bike paths, acres of apple and cherry orchards, and stunning scenery, Door County is the Midwest's vacationland. Despite its undeniable popularity as a tourist destination, the Door has managed to carefully avoid the fast-paced, neon-lit commercialism that plagues so many resort communities. Its 12 villages swing open on a summer-oriented schedule, so visitors are advised to make reservations for just about everything if they plan to be on the peninsula during a weekend in either July or August. Temperatures can dip to 40°F at night, even in July.

■⚡ **ORIENTATION AND PRACTICAL INFORMATION.** Door County begins north of **Sturgeon Bay,** where Rte. 42 and Rte. 57 converge and then split again. Rte. 57 runs up the eastern coast of the peninsula; Rte. 42 runs up the western. The peninsula's west coast, which borders the Green Bay, tends to be warmer, artsy-er, and more expensive. The colder, calmer, and less expensive east coast, contains the bulk of the peninsula's park area. From south to north along Hwy. 42, **Egg Harbor, Fish Creek, Ephraim, Sister Bay,** and **Ellison Bay** are the largest towns. Public transportation comes only as close as **Green Bay,** 50 mi. southwest of Sturgeon Bay, where **Greyhound** has a station at 800 Cedar St. *(☎432-4883.* Open M-F 6:30am-5pm, Sa-Su 6:30am-6:50am, 10am-noon and 3:30-5:10pm.) To: Milwaukee (3 per day, $24). Reserve tickets at least a day in advance. **Door County Chamber of Commerce:** 6443 Green Bay Rd., on Rte. 42/57 entering Sturgeon Bay. *(☎743-4456 or 800-527-3529.* Open M-F 8:30am-5pm, Sa-Su 10am-4pm; mid-Oct. to mid-May M-F 8:30am-4pm.) Visitors centers are also in each of the villages. **Post Office:** 359 Louisiana, at 4th St. in Sturgeon Bay. *(☎743-2681.* Open M-F 8:30am-5pm, Sa 9:30am-noon.) **ZIP code:** 54235. **Area code:** 920.

⚑ **ACCOMMODATIONS AND CAMPING.** Unique, country-style lodgings crowd Rte. 42 and Rte. 57 (from $60 in summer); reservations for July and Aug. should be made far in advance. The **Century Farm Motel,** 10068 Rte. 57, 3 mi. south of Sister Bay on Rte. 57, rents intimate, carefully maintained two-room cottages hand-built by the owner's grandfather in the 20s. *(☎854-4069.* Open mid-May to mid-Oct. A/C, TV, private bath, fridge. $45-60.) A bevy of gnome statues, 1000 Barbies, 600 animated store window mannequins, and 35 cars grace the premises of the **Chal-A Motel,** 3910 Rte. 42/57, 3 mi. north of the bridge in Sturgeon Bay, which also houses guests in large, homey rooms. *(☎743-6788.* July-Aug. singles $49, doubles $54; Nov. to mid-May $29/$34; mid-May to June $34/$39.) Relaxed but convenient, the **Lull-Abi Motel,** 7928 Egg Harbor Rd. (Rte. 42) in Egg Harbor, entices visitors with spacious rooms, a patio, an indoor whirlpool, and free coffee. *(☎868-3135.* Open May to mid-Oct. Doubles $50-84, depending on season. Suites with wet bar and refrigerator $62-95.)

Four out of the area's five **state parks** (all but **Whitefish Dunes**) offer outstanding camping ($10, WI residents $8; F-Sa $12/$10). All state parks require a motor vehicle permit ($7/$5 per day; $25/$18 per year; $3 per hr.). **Peninsula State Park,** just past Fish Creek village on Rte. 42, contains 20 mi. of shoreline and 17 mi. of trails alongside the largest of the state park campgrounds. (☎868-3258. 469 sites with showers and toilets. Make reservations *well* in advance or come in person to put your name on the waiting list for one of 70 walk-in sites.) The relatively uncrowded **Potawatomi State Park,** 3740 Park Dr., sits just outside Sturgeon Bay off Rte. 42/57, south of the bridge. (☎746-2890. 125 campsites, 19 open to walk-ins.) **Newport State Park** is a shaded wildlife preserve at the tip of the peninsula, 7 mi. from Ellison Bay off Rte. 42. Vehicles are permitted, but sites are accessible by hiking only. (☎854-2500. 16 sites, 3 open to walk-ins.) The untamed **Rock Island State Park,** offers 40 remote sites on Washington Island, which take some planning to reach. (☎847-2235. Open mid-Apr. to mid-Nov.)

◘ **FOOD AND DRINK.** Many people come to Door County just for **fishboils,** a Scandinavian tradition dating back to 19th-century lumberjacks in which cooks toss potatoes, onions, spices, and fresh whitefish into an enormous kettle over a wood fire. To remove the fish oil from the top of the water, the boilmaster judges the proper time to throw kerosene into the fire, producing a massive fireball; the cauldron boils over, signaling chow time—it's much better than it sounds. Most fishboils conclude with a big slice of cherry pie, made from locally famous Door peninsula cherries. Door County's original, best-known fishboils bubble up at **The Viking Grill,** in Ellison Bay. (☎854-2998. Mid-May to Oct. every 30min. 4:30-8pm. $12, under 12 $9; regular dining 6am-10pm.)

Fishboils aren't all there is in Door, however. **White Gull Inn,** 4225 Main St. in Fish Creek, is the peninsula's breakfast spot of choice, serving delicious cherry-stuffed french toast ($5.40) and outstanding coffee cake ($3) in an elegant country inn. (☎868-3517. Open daily 7:30am-9pm. Lunch from $4.50, dinner from $15.50. Reservations required for dinner.) **Al Johnson's Swedish Restaurant,** in the middle of Sister Bay on Rte. 42, has excellent entrees from $9, a waitstaff in traditional Swedish dress, and goats on the thick sod roof. Be prepared for long waits in summer. (☎854-2626. Open daily 6am-9pm; in winter M-Sa 6am-8pm, Su 7am-8pm.) At the ▓**Bayside Tavern,** on Rte. 42 in Fish Creek, Bob cooks up his world-famous chili ($4). At night, it's a lively bar with local music on M (cover $2), Tu pint nights, and Th open-mic keeping friendly locals and exuberant vacationers in good spirits. (☎868-3441. Open Su-Th 11am-2am, F-Sa 11am-2:30am.)

Guests can hurl dollars to the ceiling at **Husby's Food & Spirits,** on Rte. 42 entering Sister Bay from the south. The well-chosen beer selection includes $2.50 imports, while the menu ranges from Mexican to fish fry. (☎854-2624. Open Su-Th 11am-2am, F-Sa 11am-2:30am.) Just across the street, local favorite **Sister Bay Bowl and Supper Club** rolls out generous portions of chicken, fish, and sandwiches along with a six-lane bowling alley. (☎854-2841. Open daily June-mid-Oct. noon-10pm; call for off-season hours. Entrees from $5, bowling from $3.)

EAST SIDE. Biking is the best way to take in the largely untouched lighthouses, rocks, and white sand beaches of the Door's rugged eastern coastline; village tourist offices have free bike maps. **Whitefish Dunes State Park,** off Rte. 57 on the peninsula's east side, glimmers with Wisconsin's most extensive sand dunes, hiking/biking/skiing trails, and a well-kept wildlife preserve. (Open daily 8am-8pm; $7 vehicle permit required.) Just north of the Dunes on Cave Point Rd. off Rte. 57, **Cave Point County Park** stirs the soul with its rocky coastline and some of the most stunning views on the peninsula. (Open daily 6am-9pm. Free.)

Five mi. north of Cave Point in the sleepy town of **Jacksonport, Lakeside Town Park** offers a wide, sandy expanse of beach backed by a shady, picnic-perfect park and playground. (Open daily 6am-9pm. Free.) Another natural highlight of the East Side lies 3 mi. to the north in laidback **Baileys Harbor.** Here, waves and wind have carved miles of sand ridges that swirl along the coastline. Trails at the **Ridges Sanctuary,** north of Baileys Harbor off Hwy. Q, enable exploration of over 30 of the ridges, an amazing orchid collection, great birdwatching, and a unique boreal forest at **Toft's Point.** (☎839-2802. Nature center open daily 9am-4pm. $2.) Adjoining the sanctuary on Ridges Rd. is **Baileys Harbor Ridges Beach,** a usually uncrowded stretch of sand ideal for secluded swimming. Just past the ridges off Hwy. Q, **Cana Island Lighthouse** juts out from the Lake, beckoning visitors to cross the narrow sandpath (at low tide) or wade through the frigid waters (at high tide) to reach its oft-photographed shores. (Reached from Cana Island Rd. off Hwy. Q. No phone. No facilities. Free.)

WEST SIDE. The more populated West Side offers alternating stretches of developed villages and unmitigated nature. At the base of the peninsula, Sturgeon Bay houses the intriguing **Door County Maritime Museum,** 120 N. Madison St. downtown. The museum offers the best insight into the area's ship-building, water-charting history with antique boats and interactive, pilot-your-own exhibits. (☎743-5958. Open daily May-Oct. 9am-6pm, Nov.-Apr. 10am-5pm. $3.) The nearby **Door County Historical Museum,** 4th Ave. and Michigan St., explains such important traditions as the fishboil, cherry orchards, and commercial fishing. (☎743-5809. Open daily May-Oct. 10am-5pm. Free, donations appreciated.)

The award-winning **Door Peninsula Winery,** 5806 Rte. 42 in Sturgeon Bay, invites vine- (or orchard-) lovers to partake of 30 different fruit wines. (☎743-7431 or 800-551-5049. 15-20min. tours and tastings daily in summer 9am-6pm; off-season 9am-5pm.) At **Peninsula State Park,** in Fish Creek, visitors rent boats and ride mopeds and bicycles along 20 mi. of shoreline road. Sunbathing at Nicolet Beach is a more relaxed way to get close to nature. At the top of **Eagle Tower,** 1 mi. and 110 steps up from the beach, a clear day allows a glimpse of Michigan's shores across the waters of Green Bay. (Open daily 6am-11pm. Vehicle permit required $3 per hr.) Directly across from the Fish Creek entrance, **Nor Door Sport and Cyclery,** 4007 Hwy. 42., rents out various kinds of bikes and winter sport equipment. (☎868-2275. From $3 per hr./$10hr. per day. Cross-country skis $9 per day.) The park also hosts the musical troupe **American Folklore Theatre,** home to the Door County hit *Lumberjacks in Love.* (☎869-2329. $10.) Just north of the Peninsula State Park, on Rte. 42 between Fish Creek and Ephraim, is the fabulously retro ◼Skyway Drive-In, showcasing current releases at unbeatable prices. (☎854-9938. Current release double-feature $5. Call for schedules.)

The shipping town of **Green Bay,** 50 mi. south of Sturgeon Bay at the foot of the Door peninsula, is best known as home to the Green Bay Packers. Unless you know a Packer, you won't find a ticket, but the appropriately green and yellow Lambeau Field is worth a look. (☎496-5719. Tickets $32-39.) The unique **Packer Hall of Fame,** 855 Lombardi Ave., across from the stadium, has a cathedral-like feel, for thousands come here to worship at the altars of their gridiron heroes. The Hall also offers stadium tours. (☎499-4281. Open daily June-Aug. 10am-6pm; Sept.-May 10am-5pm. Tours June-Sept. only; 1½hr. $8, under 15 $5.50.)

APOSTLE ISLANDS   ☎ 715

The National Lakeshore protects 21 of the breathtaking islands off the coast of Wisconsin, as well as a 12 mi. stretch of mainland shore. Glaciers created these land masses that once supported loads of shipping activity during the Voyageur fur trade. Lighthouses still dot six of the islands and recall their industrially prosperous past. Today, summer tourists enjoy kayaking, hiking, spelunking, and camping among the unspoiled sandstone bluffs.

◼ **PRACTICAL INFORMATION.** All Apostle Islands excursions begin in the sleepy mainland town of **Bayfield** (pop. 686), in northwest Wisconsin on the Lake Superior coast. The **Bay Area Rural Transit (BART),** 300 Industrial Park Rd., 21 mi. south on Rte. 13 in Ashland, offers a shuttle to Bayfield (☎682-9664; 4 per day, M-F 7am-5pm; $1.80, students $1.50, seniors $1.35). **Bayfield Chamber of Commerce,** 42 S. Broad St. (☎779-3335 or 800-447-4094; open M-Sa 9am-5pm, Su 10am-2pm). **National**

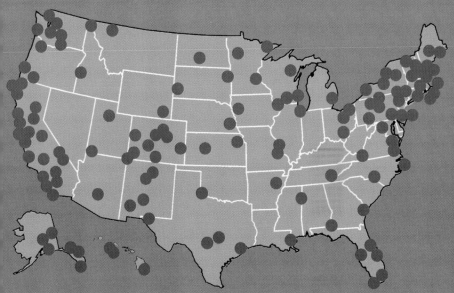

MAKING RESERVATIONS HAS NEVER BEEN SO EASY!

choose HOSTELLING INTERNATIONAL

Call **800 • 909 • 4776** and at the prompt dial the two digit access code listed below

California
74 Klamath
05 Los Angeles/Santa Monica
25 Los Angeles/Fullerton
26 Los Angeles/South Bay
63 Midpines/Yosemite
64 Montara
73 Pescadero
61 Point Reyes Nat'l Seashore
40 Sacramento
42 San Clemente
43 San Diego/Downtown
44 San Diego/Point Loma
03 San Francisco/ Fisherman's Wharf
02 San Francisco/Downtown
45 Santa Cruz
62 Sausalito
82 Tecopa (Death Valley)

Colorado
67 Denver
69 Durango
75 Glenwood Springs

Connecticut
21 Hartford

District of Columbia
04 Washington, DC

Florida
16 Clearwater Beach
86 Florida City/Everglades
55 Key West

06 Miami Beach
33 Orlando

Illinois
10 Chicago

Louisiana
09 New Orleans

Massachusetts
07 Boston
14 Cape Cod/Eastham
15 Cape Cod/Truro
78 Littleton
27 Martha's Vineyard
29 Nantucket

Missouri
70 St. Louis

New Hampshire
51 White Mountains

New York
60 Buffalo
01 New York City
31 Niagara Falls
59 Syracuse

North Carolina
54 Kitty Hawk

Ohio
11 Akron/Cleveland
18 Columbus
52 Malabar Farm/Lucas

Oregon
39 Portland
76 Portland/City Center

46 Seaside

Pennsylvania
17 Collegeville
22 La Anna
30 Newtown
79 Ohiopyle State Park
35 Philadelphia/ Chamounix Mansion
36 Pine Grove Furnace State Park
66 Pittsburgh

South Dakota
77 Deadwood

Texas
89 Austin
88 Galveston
41 San Antonio

Utah
71 Salt Lake City

Vermont
68 White River Junction

Virginia
81 Galax
50 Virginia Beach

Washington
08 Seattle
37 Port Townsend
49 Vashon Island/Seattle

Wisconsin
24 Laona
80 Madison

HOSTELLING INTERNATIONAL

MAKE YOUR RESERVATIONS TODAY!
800 • 909 • 4776 www.hiayh.org **One number. 135 locations**

POW WOW. Throughout the Midwest, and scattered around the rest of the country, are hundreds of small nations, commonly known as Indian Reservations. Countless stereotypes exist regarding reservation conditions—many Americans think of them now as hotbeds for casinos and gambling. But instead of pouring money into a tribal casino, tourists can support an alternative—go to a party—and learn something in the meantime. Most reservations have two Pow Wows annually, making for a wonderful mix of celebration and reverence—for participants and guests alike. In the words of one young dancer, "A Pow Wow is a family." The festival, often a 4-day weekend affair for $5-10, normally comes with free camping. Food from vendors' trucks is ridiculously cheap and satisfying (2 pancakes, 2 eggs, hashbrowns, juice and coffee for $3), and crafts, kitsch, and cultural items are also sold cheaply too. To learn more on the **Menominee** reservation, in Keshena, call ☎ 715-799-3341. For info on schedules at other locations, stop by the tribal offices, call the above number, or pick up a local reservation newspaper or the international publication, *Indian Country Today*.

Lakeshore Headquarters Visitors Center, 410 Washington Ave., distributes hiking info and **camping permits** (☎779-3397; open daily 8am-6pm, in winter M-F 8am-4:30pm; $15 permit for 2 weeks, must be 14 consecutive days). **Weather:** ☎682-8822. Bayfield's **post office:** 22 S. Broad St. (☎779-5636; open M-F 9am-4:30pm, Sa 9am-11am). **ZIP code:** 54814. **Area code:** 715.

▶ ACCOMMODATIONS. In summer months, the budget pickings are slim in Bayfield. Would-be lodgers without reservations may be out of luck on July and Aug. weekends; it's wise to call far in advance to reserve a room. The best deal in town is **The Seagull Bay Motel,** off Rte. 13 at S. 7th St., offering spacious, enticing rooms with cable TV and a lake view. (☎779-5558. From $50; mid-Oct. to mid-May $35.) Just south on Rte. 13, **Lakeside Lodging** has rooms with a private entrance and bath, patio, and continental breakfast. (☎779-5545. Open mid-May to mid-Oct. In summer, reservations highly recommended one month in advance. Rooms $60.) **Dalrymple Park,** ¼ mi. north of town on Rte. 13, has 30 campsites in a majestic setting under tall pines on the lake. (Sites $12. No showers; self-regulated; no reservations.) **Apostle Islands Area Campground,** ½ mi. south of Bayfield on County Rd. J off Rte. 13, has a few sites overlooking the islands. (☎779-5524. Sites $12, with hook-up $16, with hook-up and cable $19, with view $22; cabins for 3 without A/C or private bathroom $35. Reservations recommended 1 month in advance in July-Aug.) The chamber of commerce has info on **guest houses** (from $35).

◘ FOOD. With a look that is more Key West than Midwest, **Maggie's,** 257 Manypenny Ave., serves satisfying burgers ($6) and daily specials amid a flamingo-filled decor (☎779-5641; open Su-Th 11am-10pm, F-Sa 11am-11pm). The **Gourmet Garage,** just south of Bayfield on Rte. 13, has local flavor and any kind of pie (☎779-5365; open daily 9am-6pm). **Greunke's Restaurant,** 17 Rittenhouse Ave. at 1st St., specializes in huge breakfasts by day ($4-6) and famous fishboils by night (☎779-5480; open M-Sa 6am-10pm, F-Su 7am-9:30pm; fishboils Th-Su 6-8pm, $12, children $6). **Egg Toss Cafe,** 41 Manypenny Ave., serves a variety of breakfasts and sandwiches in a casual, patio setting (☎779-5181; open daily from 6am). Outfit your stomach at the **Wild By Nature Market,** 100 Rittenhouse Ave., with bulk trail food or $4 wraps (☎779-5075; open in summer M-Sa 8am-6pm, Su 8am-4pm).

◙♫ SIGHTS AND ACTIVITIES. Though often overshadowed by Bayfield and Madeline Island (see below), the other 21 islands have their own subtle charms. The sandstone quarries of Basswood and Hermit Islands and the abandoned logging and fishing camps on some of the other islands serve as silent reminders of a more vigorous era. The restored **lighthouses** on Sand, Raspberry, Long, Michigan, Outer, and Devil's Islands offer spectacular views of the surrounding country. **Sea caves,** carved out by thousands of years of winds and water, pocket the shores of several islands; a few on Devil's Island are large enough to explore by boat. The **Apostle Islands Cruise Service** runs narrated 3hr. cruises for a less exorbitant fee than most companies. From late June to early Sept., the cruise service runs an inter-island shuttle that delivers campers and lighthouse lovers to their destinations. (☎779-3925 or 800-323-7619. Tours depart the Bayfield City Dock mid-May to mid-Oct. daily 10am. $22.50, children $11.) The best beach on the mainland is **Bay View Beach,** just south of Bayfield along Rte. 13, near Sioux Flats, reached by a poorly marked path to the left about 8 mi. out of town. **Swimming** in chilly Lake Superior can be quite uncomfortable. **Trek and Trail,** at Rittenhouse and Broad St., rents bikes and kayaks. (☎800-354-8735. Bikes $5 per hr., $20 per day; 4hr. kayak rental $38, all equipment included. Renters must complete $50 safety course.)

Bayfield is the proud home of some awfully good apples. In early Oct., up to 40,000 gather for the **Apple Festival.** The **Bayfield Apple Company,** on County J near the intersection of Betzold Rd., has fresh-picked ones and excellent jam (☎779-5700 or ☎800-363-4526; open May-Jan. daily 9am-6pm).

MADELINE ISLAND   ☎715

Several hundred years ago, the Chippewa tribe came to Madeline Island from the Atlantic in search of the megis shell, a light in the sky purported to bring prosperity and health. The island maintains its allure, as thousands of summer visitors seek this relaxing retreat's clean, sandy beaches. At day's end, a jaunt to Sunset Bay on the island's north side reveals why the bay got its name.

The **Madeline Island Motel,** on Col. Woods Ave. across from the ferry landing, has clean rooms named for local personalities, as well as private patios. (☎747-3000. Mid-June to Labor Day doubles $80; Sept. M-Th $70, Sa-Su $80; Oct.-May $70.) Rooms in the area fill during the summer; call ahead for reservations. Madeline Island has two campgrounds. **Big Bay Town Park,** 6½ mi. from La Pointe off Big Bay Rd., sits next to tranquil Big Bay Lagoon. (☎747-6913. Sites $9, with electricity $13. No reservations accepted.) Across the lagoon, **Big Bay State Park** rents 55 primitive sites. (☎747-6425; Bayfield office 779-4020; for reservations 888-475-3386. Sites $10-12. Daily vehicle permit $7, WI residents $5. Reservations $4.) **Grampa Tony's,** next to the Chamber of Commerce, offers good, no-frills dining. (☎747-3911. Sandwiches $4-5, salads $3-6, ice cream from $1.50. Open Su-Th 7am-9pm, F-Sa 7am-10pm.)

With roughly five streets, Madeline Island is easy to navigate. **Visitors Info: Madeline Island Chamber of Commerce,** on Middle Rd. (☎747-2801 or 888-475-3386; open M-Sa 8am-4pm). **Madeline Island Ferry Line** shuttles between Bayfield and La Pointe on Madeline Island. (☎747-2051 or 747-6801. 20min. ride; in summer, daily every 30min. 9:30am-6pm, every hr. 6:30-9:30am and 6-11pm. $3.50, ages 6-11 $2; bikes $1.75; cars $7.75—driver not included. Mar.-June and Sept.-Dec. ferries run less frequently and prices drop.) In winter, the state highway department builds a road across the ice. During transition periods, the ferry service runs **windsleds** between the island and the mainland. "Moped Dave" rents the technical marvels at **Motion to Go,** 102 Lake View Pl., about one block from the ferry. (☎747-6585. $12 per hr., $50 per day. Mountain bikes $6/$22. Open daily 10am-8pm; mid-May to mid-June and Sept.-Oct. 10am-6pm.) La Pointe's **post office** is just off the dock on Madeline Island (☎747-3712; open M-F 9am-4:20pm, Sa 9:30am-12:50pm). **ZIP code:** 54850.

MINNESOTA

In the 19th century, floods of German and Scandinavian settlers forced the native Sioux and Ojibwe tribes from the rich lands now known as Minnesota. Minnesota's white pioneers transformed the southern half of the state into a stronghold of commercial activity; however, the north remains largely untouched, an expanse of wilderness quilted with over 14,000 lakes. Attempts at preserving this rugged wilderness have helped raise awareness about Minnesota's natural resources and the culture of the Ojibwe, the state's Native American antecedents.

⚑ PRACTICAL INFORMATION

Capital: St. Paul.

Visitor Info: Minnesota Office of Tourism, 500 Metro Sq., 121 7th Pl. E., St. Paul 55101-2112
(☎651-296-5029 or 800-657-3700; www.exploreminnesota.com). Open M-F 8am-5pm.

Postal Abbreviation: MN. **Sales Tax:** 6.5%.

MINNEAPOLIS AND ST. PAUL ☎612

Native son Garrison Keillor wrote that the "difference between St. Paul and Minneapolis is the difference between pumpernickel and Wonder bread." Keillor's quote
plays on St. Paul's characterization as an old Irish Catholic, conservative town and
Minneapolis's reputation as a young, fast-paced metropolis of the future. Minneapolis's theaters and clubs rival those of New York, while both the traditional capitol
and the cathedral rest atop St. Paul. In both cities, consumer culture (e.g. the Mall
of America), the youth bohemianpunk world (e.g. the myriad upstart coffeehouses), corporate America (e.g. the downtown and the skyway systems), and an
international community (e.g. Swahili is taught in public schools) thrive.

⌷ GETTING THERE AND GETTING AROUND

Downtown Minneapolis lies about 10 mi. west of downtown St. Paul via **I-94. I-35**
splits in the Twin Cities, with **I-35 W** serving Minneapolis and **I-35 E** serving St.
Paul. **I-494** runs to the airport and the Mall of America, while **I-394** heads to downtown Minneapolis from the western suburbs.

Airport: Twin Cities International, 15min. south of the cities on Hwy. 5 (☎726-5555), off
I-494 in Bloomington. Take bus #7 to Washington Ave. in Minneapolis or bus #54 to
St. Paul. **Airport Express** (☎827-7777) shuttles to either downtown and to some hotels
roughly every 30min. 6am-midnight. To: Minneapolis ($13) and St. Paul ($10).

Trains: Amtrak, 730 Transfer Rd. (☎651-644-1127 or 800-872-7245), on the east bank
off University Ave. SE, between the Twin Cities. City bus #7 runs from the station to St.
Paul, and #16 connects to both downtowns. To: Chicago (8hr., 1 per day, $42-92) and
Milwaukee (6hr., 1 per day, $41-89). Open daily 6:30am-11:45pm.

Buses: Greyhound, in Minneapolis, 29 9th St. (☎371-3325), at 1st Ave. N. downtown. In
St. Paul, 166 W. University Ave. (☎651-222-0509), 2 blocks west of the capitol. To
Chicago (8½-10hr., 7 per day, $60) and Milwaukee (7-8hr., 6 per day, $45); both
routes depart from Minneapolis and St. Paul stations. Minneapolis station open 24hr.
St. Paul station open M-F 6:30am-1am, Sa-Su 6:30am-10pm.

Public Transit: Metropolitan Transit Commission, 560 6th Ave. N. (☎373-3333), serves
both cities M-F 6:30am-11pm, Sa 7am-11pm, Su 9am-9pm; some buses operate
4:30am-12:45am, others shut down earlier. $1; seniors and ages 6-12 50¢ discount;
disabled 50¢. Peak fare (M-F 6-9am and 3:30-6:30pm) $1.50. Express 50¢ more. Bus
#16 connects the 2 downtowns 24hr. (50min.); bus #94 (b, c, or d) takes 30min.

Taxis: Yellow Taxi, ☎824-4444 in Minneapolis; ☎651-222-4433 in St. Paul.

✴⚑ ORIENTATION AND PRACTICAL INFORMATION

Curves and one-way streets tangle both of the downtown areas; even the numbered
grids in the cities are skewed, making north-south and east-west designations
tricky without a map. Skyways keep pedestrian commuters and shoppers warm
within both downtown areas.

Visitor Info: Minneapolis Convention and Visitors Association, 40 S. 7th St. (☎335-5827),
near Hennepin Ave. in the City Center skyway. Open M-F 10am-7pm, Sa 10am-6pm, Su
noon-6pm. **St. Paul Convention and Visitors Bureau,** 175 W. Kellogg, suite 502 (☎800-
627-6101), in the RiverCentre. Open M-F 8:30am-5pm. **The Connection** has 24hr. state
park info (☎922-9000).

Hotlines: Crisis Line, ☎340-5400. **Rape/Sexual Assault Line,** ☎825-4357. Both 24hr. **Gay-Lesbian Helpline,** ☎822-8661 or 800-800-0907; M-F noon-midnight, Sa 4pm-midnight. **Gay-Lesbian Information Line,** ☎822-0127; M-F 2-10pm, Sa 4-10pm.

Post Office: In Minneapolis, 100 S. 1st St. (☎349-4957), at Marquette Ave. on the river. Open M-F 7am-11pm, Sa 9am-1pm. **ZIP code:** 55401. In St. Paul, 180 E. Kellogg Blvd. (☎651-293-3268). Open M-F 8am-6pm, Sa 8:30am-1pm. **ZIP code:** 55101. **Area codes:** Minneapolis 612, St. Paul and eastern suburbs 651, southwestern suburbs 952, northwestern suburbs 763. In text, 612 unless otherwise noted.

◤ ACCOMMODATIONS

The Twin Cities are filled with unpretentious, inexpensive accommodations. The visitors bureaus have lists of **B&Bs** (but no price info), while the **University of Minnesota Housing Office** (☎624-2994) keeps a list of local rooms ($15-60) which rent on a daily or weekly basis. The section of I-494 at Rte. 77, near the Mall of America, is lined with budget chain motels from $40. The nearest private campgrounds are about 15 mi. outside the city; the closest state park camping is in the **Hennepin Park** system, 25 mi. out. Call **The Connection** (see **Practical Information,** above) for info.

City of Lakes International House, 2400 Stevens Ave. S (☎871-3210), Minneapolis, just south of downtown next to the Institute of Arts. Take bus #10, 17, or 18 from Nicollet Mall to 24th St. and walk 2 blocks east to Stevens. From airport, take bus #7 downtown and then buses above. A good bet for social travelers, this hostel fosters an international spirit with common areas, well-kept dorms, and a young, diverse clientele. Kitchen, TV, lockers, on-site parking. Bike rentals ($3 per night). Free local calls. Check-in daily 9am-noon, 6:30pm-midnight. Checkout 11am. Beds $17, students $16; 2 singles $34/$32. Linen $2, towel $1. Key deposit $5. Reservations recommended.

Evelo's Bed and Breakfast, 2301 Bryant Ave. (☎374-9656), South Minneapolis. Convenient location just off Hennepin Ave., a 15min. walk from uptown; take bus #17 from downtown to Bryant Ave. Hospitable owners rent out 3 lovingly cared for rooms in a house with elegant Victorian artifacts. Singles $55; doubles $65. Reservations and deposit required.

Kaz's Home Hostel (☎822-8286), in South Minneapolis. Bright shag carpet, a ton of family photos, a dog, and friendly hosts make this house better than home. Kitchen, laundry facilities. Towels $1. No children allowed. Checkout 9am. Lockout 9am-5pm. Curfew 11pm. 2 beds in a large 2nd fl. room $10. Call for reservations and directions.

Hotel Amsterdam, 830 Hennepin Ave. (☎288-0459), between 8th and 9th St. in downtown Minneapolis. Quiet considering its location above the wildly popular **Saloon** nightclub, this warm, gay- and lesbian-owned hotel offers visitors comfortable rooms and easy access to downtown action and attractions. Singles from $33; doubles from $38. Reservations recommended.

◖ FOOD

The Twin Cities' cosmopolitan, cultured vibe is reflected in their culinary choices. Posh, big city restaurants share the streets with intimate cafes. **Uptown** Minneapolis, around the intersection of Lake St. and Hennepin Ave., packs plenty of funky restaurants and bars with reasonable prices. In downtown Minneapolis, the **Warehouse District,** on 1st Ave. N between 8th St. and Washington Ave., and **Nicollet Mall,** a pedestrian stretch of Nicollet Ave., attract hordes of locals and tourists with trendy shops and lively cafes. In St. Paul, **Grand Ave.,** between Lexington and Dale, is lined with laid-back restaurants and bars. In downtown St. Paul, **Lowertown,** along Sibley St. near 6th St., is the newest nighttime hotspot. Near the UM campus between the downtowns, **Dinkytown,** on the east bank of the river, and the **Seven Corners** area of the **West Bank,** on Cedar Ave. across the river, cater to student appetites with unique, low-end eateries. To get to either one, follow the signs off of I-94 for East Bank or West Bank. In the Twin Cities, many forego restaurants for the plentiful **cafes** (see p. 535). For do-it-yourselfers, the **St. Paul Farmers Market,** on Wall St., between E. 4th and 5th St. downtown, sells fresh produce and baked goods. (☎227-6856. Open late Apr. to mid-Nov. Sa 6am-1pm.)

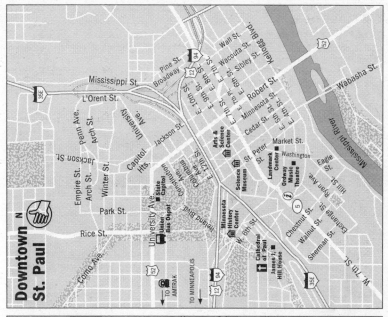

Downtown St. Paul

N

St. Anthony Falls

35E
Mississippi St.
L'Orent St.
Penn Ave.
Arch Ave.
University Ave.
Jackson St.
Pine St.
Broadway
Wall St.
Wacouta St.
Sibley St.
Kellogg Blvd.
Robert St.
Minnesota St.
Cedar St.
E. 4th St.
E. 5th St.
Wabasha St.
52
12
94
E. 10th St.
E. 9th St.
E. 8th St.
E. 7th St.
E. 6th St.
Jackson St.
Capitol Hts.
Empire St.
Arch St.
Winter St.
Park St.
Rice St.
Como Ave.
Constitution Ave.
12th St.
State Capitol
Union Bus Depot
Ireland Blvd.
Minnesota History Center
W. 8th St.
Arts & Science Center
Science Museum
St. Peter St.
Landmark Center
Market St.
Washington
Ordway Music Theatre
Eagle St.
Hill St.
Ryan Ave.
Exchange St.
Chestnut St.
Walnut St.
Sherman St.
W. 7th St.
Mississippi River
52
5
i
Cathedral of Paul
James J. Hill House
TO AMTRAK
TO MINNEAPOLIS
52
12
94
35E

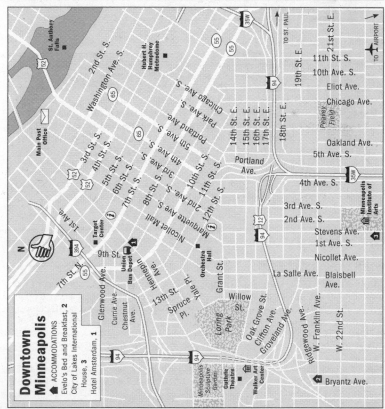

Downtown Minneapolis

N

ACCOMMODATIONS
Evelo's Bed and Breakfast, 2
City of Lakes International House, 3
Hotel Amsterdam, 1

GREAT LAKES

MINNEAPOLIS

▨ **Chino Latino,** at the corner of Hennepin Ave. and Lake St. (☎824-7878), Uptown. An amazing array of gold sequins dangles above the outside entrance, but beware: "no iron gut, no service" at this Latin-Asian fusion that stirs up spicy food "from the hot zone." Opened in Jan. 2000, the trendiest restaurant in town packs in the (young, hipper-than-thou) crowds with its satay bar ($7-9), drinks bar, pupu platter ($28; serves an army), tostadas ($7.50), and Bali Fertility Feast (don't ask.) Open M-F 4:30pm-1am, Sa-Su 11am-1am. Reservations strongly recommended.

Bryant Lake Bowl, 810 W. Lake St. (☎825-3737), at Bryant St. near Uptown. Built in the 30s, this funky bowling alley-cum-bar-cum-cabaret is also—surprise—a really good, inexpensive restaurant. The "BLB Scramble" (a breakfast dish of eggs and vegetables), ravioli, soups, and sandwiches ensure that the stylish patrons throw strikes with pleasantly full stomachs. Entrees from $4. Open daily 7am-1am.

Pasqual's Salsaria, 2528 Hennepin Ave. S. (☎374-1415), between 25th and 26th St., Uptown. Adorned with geckos and strings of chili pepper lights, this cafe serves unbelievably delicious and huge burritos (from $3), enchilada dinners ($5), and fresh salsas and sides. Open M-Sa 11am-10pm, Su 9am-9pm.

Al's Breakfast, 413 14th Ave. SE (☎331-9991), between 4th and 5th Sts. in Dinkytown. The walls may be bare, but that only adds to the coolness of this tiny 50 year-old diner that serves the best breakfast in town. Blueberry and blackberry pancakes ($4) and huge omelettes draw crowds and have sustained many a U of M student through 4 years of dorm food. Open M-Sa 6am-1pm, Su 9am-1pm.

Mud Pie, 2549 Lyndale Ave. S. (☎872-9435), at 26th St., Uptown. Vegans and vegetarians will be in heaven, choosing from a great selection of meat-free dishes with Mexican and Middle Eastern accents. Famous veggie burger $7. Open in summer M-Th 11am-10pm, F 11am-11:30pm, Sa 10am-11:30pm, Su 10am-9:30pm.

ST. PAUL

▨ **Cafe Latte,** 850 Grand Ave. (☎651-224-5687), at Victoria St. More gourmet than its prices and cafeteria-style setup would suggest. Meals are consistently wonderful; desserts are to die for. Chicken-salsa chili ($5) and turtle cake ($4) fill the 2 floors with chic, hungry locals. Open M-Th 9am-11pm, F-Sa 9am-midnight, Su 9am-10pm.

Mickey's Diner, 36 W. 7th St. (☎651-698-0259), at St. Peter St. A real 30s diner on the National Register of Historic Places, Mickey's food manages to outshine its bright history and chrome-and-vinyl decor. Steak and eggs from $5; pancakes $2.50. Open 24hr.

Table of Contents and **Hungry Mind Bookstore,** 1648 Grand Ave. (☎651-699-6595), near Snelling Ave. In this excellent gourmet cafe/unique college bookstore combo, the wafer-crust pizza ($6) is a delicious alternative to pricier dinners ($12-25). Open M-Th 11:30am-10pm, F-Sa 9am-10:30pm, Su 10am-7pm. Another location at 1310 Hennepin Ave. (☎339-1133), Minneapolis. Open M-Th 11:30am-9pm, F-Sa 11:30am-10pm, Su 10am-2pm and 5-9pm.

◉ SIGHTS

MINNEAPOLIS

LAKES AND RIVERS. In the land of 10,000 lakes, Minneapolis boasts many of its own. **Lake Calhoun,** on the west end of Lake St. Uptown, is the largest of the bunch and a recreational paradise. Scores of in-line skaters and runners loop the lake on all but the coldest days. Ringed by stately mansions, serene **Lake of the Isles** is an excellent place to commune with Canadian geese. Just southeast of Lake Calhoun on Sheridan St., **Lake Harriet** brings out the locals with tiny paddleboats and a bandshell with nightly free concerts in summer. The city maintains 28 mi. of lakeside trails around the three lakes for strolling and biking. **Calhoun Cycle Center,** three blocks east of Lake Calhoun, rents out bikes for exploring the paths. (*1622 W. Lake St. ☎827-8231. Open daily 9am-9pm. $8 per hr.,*

$18 per half-day, $26 per day. Must have credit card and driver's license.) At the northeast corner of Lake Calhoun, the **Minneapolis Park and Recreation Board** handles canoe and rowboat rentals. *(☎ 370-4964. Open daily 10am-8pm. Canoes $6 per hr., rowboats $12 for 4hr.)*

You can get a good look at the Mighty Mississippi from several points in town. Off Portland Ave. downtown, **Stone Arch Bridge** offers pedestrians and bikers a scenic view of **St. Anthony Falls;** several mi. downstream, **Minnehaha Park** *(near the airport; take bus #7 from Hennepin Ave. downtown)* allows a gander at the much more impressive **Minnehaha Falls,** immortalized in Longfellow's *Song of Hiawatha. (Off Minnehaha Ave., south of Godfrey Pkwy.)* The **visitors center** at the **Upper St. Anthony Lock and Dam,** at Portland Ave. and West River Pkwy., provides a sweeping view and a helpful explanation of the locks that allow big boats access to the city. *(☎ 651-332-5336. Observation tower open daily mid-Mar. to mid-Dec. 9am-10pm).*

MUSEUMS. The lakes are only the beginning of Minneapolis's appeal—locals and visitors have plenty to do during the (at least) six months of frigid winter. The **Minneapolis Institute of Arts,** south of downtown, has an exceptionally varied and well-chosen collection, including Rembrandt's *Lucretia* and the world-famous *Doryphoros,* Polykleitos's perfectly proportioned man. *(2400 3rd Ave. S. ☎ 870-3131. Take bus #9. Open Tu-W and F-Sa 10am-5pm, Th 10am-9pm, Su noon-5pm. Free.)* A few blocks southwest of downtown, the world-renowned **◪Walker Art Center** counts daring exhibits by Lichtenstein, Rothko, and Warhol among its amazing galleries of contemporary art. *(725 Vineland Pl. at Lyndale Ave. ☎ 375-7622. Open Tu-W and F-Sa 10am-5pm, Th 10am-8pm, Su 11am-5pm. $4; students, seniors, and ages 12-18 $3; free Th and 1st Sa of the month.)* Next to the Walker lies the **Minneapolis Sculpture Garden,** the largest urban sculpture garden in the US. The tongue-in-cheek, postcard-friendly **Spoonbridge and Cherry** is the highlight of the worthwhile gardens; the adjacent **Cowles Conservatory** houses an array of plants and a Gehry fish sculpture. *(Gardens open daily 6am-midnight; conservatory open Tu-Sa 8am-8pm. Free.)* Frank Gehry also holds the honor of having designed the Cities' most unique and controversial structure: the **Weisman Art Museum,** on the East Bank of the UM campus. The indescribable metallic pseudo-building does not overshadow the galleries' inspired collection of modern art, including works by O'Keeffe, Hartley, and Lichtenstein. *(333 E. River Rd. ☎ 625-9494. Open Tu, W, F 10am-5pm, Th 10am-8pm, Sa-Su 11am-5pm. Free.)* The **Museum of Questionable Medical Devices,** north of the river near St. Anthony Falls, has a sure cure for absolutely anything. The Solorama Bedboard (meant to cure brain tumors) and a fully operational phrenological device are among the highlights of the collection. *(201 Main St. SE. ☎ 379-4046. Open Tu-Th 5-9pm, F noon-9pm, Sa 11am-9pm, Su noon-5pm. Donation requested, toenails preferred.)*

ST. PAUL

ARCHITECTURE. St. Paul's history and architecture are among its greatest assets. Nowhere is this more evident than along **Summit Ave.,** the nation's longest continuous stretch of Victorian houses. Built on the tracks of an old railroad, the avenue includes a former home of novelist **F. Scott Fitzgerald** *(599 Summit Ave.)* and the Minnesota **Governor's Mansion,** now home of the state's most famous ex-wrestler, Governor Jesse "The Body" Ventura. *(☎ 651-297-8177. 1006 Summit Ave. Tours May-Oct. Tu 2-3:15pm. Reservations required. Free.)* Also on Summit, the magnificently intricate home of railroad magnate **James J. Hill** offers 1¼hr. tours every 30min. *(☎ 651-297-2555. 240 Summit Ave. Open W-Sa 10am-3:30pm. $5, seniors $4, ages 6-15 $3. Reservations preferred.)* Golden horses top the ornate **state capitol,** on Aurora Ave. at Cedar St., the world's largest unsupported marble dome. *(☎ 651-296-3962. Open M-F 9am-5pm, Sa 10am-4pm, Su 1-4pm. Tours on the hr. M-F 9am-4pm, Sa 10am-3pm, Su 1-3pm. Free.)* Overlooking the capitol at the end of Summit Ave. stands the **Cathedral of St. Paul,** a scaled-down version of St. Peter's in Rome. *(239 Selby Ave. ☎ 651-228-1766. Mass M-F 7:30am and 5:15pm, no evening mass W or F; Sa mass 8am and 7pm; call for Su mass schedule. Tours M, W, F 1pm; free.)*

HISTORICAL SIGHTS. Along the river, the innovative, exciting ☒**Minnesota History Center** houses ten interactive, hands-on exhibit galleries on Minnesota history. *(345 Kellogg Blvd. W. ☎ 651-296-1430. Open M-W and F-Sa 10am-5pm, Th 10am-9pm, Su noon-5pm. Free.)* Downtown's historic **Landmark Center** is a grandly restored 1894 Federal Court building replete with towers and turrets, along with a collection of pianos, a concert hall, and four restored courtrooms. *(75 W. 5th St. ☎ 651-292-3225. Open M-W, Th until 8pm, F-Sa, Su 1-5pm. Free tours Th 11am, Su 1pm.)* Out front, **Rice Park** is an ideal place for a stroll or a picnic.

AMUSEMENTS. Out in suburban Apple Valley, the **Minnesota Zoo** harbors local and exotic animals in their natural habitats. The snow monkeys and the Northern Trails are must-sees. *(13000 Zoo Blvd. Take Rte. 77 S to zoo exit and follow signs. ☎ 952-431-9200 or 952-432-9000. Open Memorial Day to Labor Day M-Sa 9am-6pm, Su 9am-8pm; daily Labor Day to Oct. 1 9am-6pm; daily Oct. 2 to Memorial Day 9am-4pm. $8, seniors $5, ages 3-12 $4, under 3 free.)* In Shakopee, even the most daring thrill-seekers can get their jollies at **Valleyfair,** a better-than-usual amusement park with five coasters and the brand new Power Tower, which drops over ten stories in free fall. *(1 Valleyfair Dr. Take Hwy. 169 south to Rte 101 W. ☎ 952-445-7600. Open daily Memorial Day to Labor Day; hrs. vary so call first. Usually 10am-10pm. $25; seniors and kids under 3 $9.)*

🎵 ENTERTAINMENT

Second only to New York in number of theaters per capita, the Twin Cities are always full of drama (and comedy, music, etc.) Most parks feature free evening concerts in the summer. The thriving alternative, pop, and classical music scenes fill out the wide range of cultural options. For general info on the local music scene and other events, read the free *City Pages* or *Skyway News.*

THEATER. The renowned repertory ☒**Guthrie Theater,** 725 Vineland Pl., Minneapolis, adjacent to the Walker Art Center just off Hennepin Ave., draws lots of praise for its mix of daring and classical productions. *(☎ 377-2224. Season Apr.-Nov., also shows in Dec. Box office open M-F 9am-8pm, Sa 10am-8pm, Su 11am-7pm. Tickets $18-40, students and seniors $5 discount. Rush tickets 10min. before show $12, line starts 1-1½hr. before show.)* Touring Broadway shows that land in Minneapolis take the stage at either the **Historic State Theatre,** 805 Hennepin Ave. downtown, or the **Orpheum Theatre,** across the street at 910 Hennepin Ave. N. (For tickets to both, call Ticketmaster at ☎ 989-5151.) For family-oriented productions, the **Children's Theater Company,** at 3rd Ave. and 24th St., next to the Minneapolis Institute of Arts, comes through with first-rate plays. *(☎ 874-0400. Season Sept.-June. Box office open M-Sa 9am-5pm; summer hrs. vary slightly. Tickets $18-27; students, seniors, and children $12-21. Rush tickets 15min. before show $8.)* The ingenious **Theatre de la Jeune Lune,** 105 1st St. N., stages critically acclaimed, off-the-beaten path productions in an old warehouse. *(☎ 332-3968, box office 333-6200. Open M-F 10am-6pm. Tickets $15-25.)* **Brave New Workshop,** 2605 Hennepin Ave. in Uptown, stages satirical sketch comedy shows, based on current events, in an intimate club; there are great improv sessions Sa at midnight. *(☎ 332-6620. Box office open June-July M 5-9pm, F-Sa 4-9:30pm, Th and Su 4pm-midnight. In summer M shows $5, Sa-Su $8-12; Aug.-May W-F and Su 4-9pm, Sa 4pm-12:15am. Tickets $12-18.)*

SHOP 'TIL YOU DROP About 10min. south of downtown, the **Mall of America,** Bloomington, corrals an indoor roller coaster, ferris wheel, mini-golf course, and 2 mi. of stores. Welcome to the largest mall in America, the consummation of an American love affair with all that is obscenely gargantuan. With hundreds of specialty stores, a movie megaplex, amusement park, and aquarium, plus all your old favorites and a large and better-than-average food court, the Mall is a good idea for a day of mind-numbing entertainment or a good old-fashioned shopping spree. *(60 E. Broadway. ☎ 883-8800. From St. Paul, take I-35 E. south to I-494 W. to the 24th Ave. exit. Open M-F 10am-9:30pm, Sa 9:30am-9:30pm, Su 11am-7pm.)*

GREAT LAKES

MUSIC. The Twin Cities' vibrant music scene offers everything from opera and polka to hip-hop and alternative. **Sommerfest,** a month-long celebration of Viennese music put on by the **Minnesota Orchestra,** is the best of the cities' classical offerings during July and Aug.; **Orchestra Hall,** 1111 Nicollet Mall, downtown Minneapolis, hosts the event. (☎800-292-4141. Box office open M-Sa 10am-6pm. Tickets $15-50; rush tickets for students 30min. before show $10.) Nearby **Peavey Plaza,** on Nicollet Mall, holds free nightly concerts and occasional film screenings. The **St. Paul Chamber Orchestra,** the **Schubert Club,** and the **Minnesota Opera Company** all perform at St. Paul's glass-and-brick **Ordway Music Theater,** 345 Washington St., which also hosts touring Broadway productions. (☎651-224-4222. Box office open M-F 9am-5pm, Sa 10am-5pm, Su 11am-5pm. Tickets $20-55.) The artist once again known as **Prince** brought his seductive and energetic pop lyrics from local rave to worldwide fame—all in high-heeled boots. Today, his state-of-the-art **Paisley Park** studio complex, outside the city in Chanhassen, draws bands from all over.

FESTIVALS. Countless festivals celebrate the coming of summer and liven up the dreary cold days. In Jan., the fun ten-day **St. Paul Winter Carnival,** near the state capitol, cures cabin fever with ice sculptures, ice-fishing, parades, and skating contests. In June, the 12-day **Fringe Festival** for the performing arts (tickets $4-5) stages edgy plays around town. On the 4th of July, St. Paul celebrates **Taste of Minnesota** with fireworks, concerts, and regional and ethnic cuisine from hordes of local vendors. On its coattails rides the nine-day **Minneapolis Aquatennial,** with concerts, parades, and art exhibits glorifying the much talked about lakes. The first weekend in Aug., the excellent **Uptown Art Fair** takes over the junction of Hennepin and Lake, drawing hundreds of thousands of people. In the two weeks prior to Labor Day, just about everyone in town heads to the **Minnesota State Fair,** at Snelling and Como St. in St. Paul (☎651-642-2200), the nation's largest. With lots of pigs and agricultural delights, cheese curds and walleye-on-a-stick, the fair provides a sampling of the area's flavor. ($5, seniors and ages 5-12 $4, under 5 free.)

SPORTS. The puffy **Hubert H. Humphrey Metrodome,** 900 S. 5th St. (☎332-0386), in downtown Minneapolis, houses baseball's **Minnesota Twins** and football's **Minnesota Vikings.** Basketball's **Timberwolves** howl at the **Target Center,** 600 1st Ave. (☎673-0900), between 6th and 7th St. in downtown Minneapolis. The brand-new NHL team, the **Wild,** takes to the ice at St. Paul's **RiverCentre** this winter (☎651-333-7825). The soccer craze hits the Midwest with the **Thunder,** at the **National Sports Center** in suburban Blaine. (☎785-3668).

◄ CAFES

More so than anywhere else outside of Seattle, cafes are an integral part of the Twin Cities' nightlife. Particularly in Uptown Minneapolis, quirky, one-of-a-kind coffeehouses caffeinate the masses and draw crowds as large as any bar. Come hungry, since most complement their java with some of the cheapest food in town.

Pandora's Cup and Gallery, 2516 Hennepin Ave., at 25th St., Uptown. One of the newest coffee spots in town, Pandora's is also the most lively, with hordes of 20-somethings packing the shop's 2 stories inside and out. The tragically hip sip their espresso ($1.25-2) and munch on PB&J "sammiches" ($1.40) and free ginger snaps on one of the patios or in the red-hued, overstuffed couch-filled interior. Coffee drinks $1.25-4. Sandwiches $1.50-5.25. Open daily 7am-1am.

Plan B Coffeehouse, 2727 Hennepin Ave. (☎872-1419), between 27th and 28th St. Plan B is first-rate. The desk toward the back may be littered with boring dictionaries, but the animated conversation, intriguing artwork, and mismatched furniture tell a different story. Engaging staff and a chill atmosphere jive with drinks like the "tripper's revenge" ($3.75), an iced concoction made with chocolate, honey, many, many shots of espresso, and "some other stuff." Open Su-Th 7am-midnight, F-Sa 7am-1am.

Uncommon Grounds, 2809 Hennepin Ave. S. (☎872-4811), at 28th St., Uptown. This coffeeshop in a small, Victorian house lives up to its name, with exceptionally cushy velour booths, dim lighting, and relaxing music in its smoke-free interior. The crowd of students and with-it GenXers belies the genteel setting. Espresso $1.30, Turtle Mocha $3.20, Zoom $1.65. Open M-Th 7am-midnight, F-Sa 7am-1am, Su 8am-midnight.

Muddy Waters, 2401 Lyndale Ave. S. (☎870-9508), at 24th St., Uptown. The linoleum tables and vinyl chairs of this self-proclaimed "caffeine canteen" recall a smoky 50s diner, but the varied music, funky mosaic, outstanding coffee, and pierced staff keep it firmly planted on the cutting edge. Mochas, hot cows ($1.25-2.25), cereal and milk, and spaghetti-o's (with half a bagel $4) are just the beginning of the eclectic menu. Open Su-Th 7am-1am, F-Sa 8am-1am.

⎙ NIGHTLIFE

Minneapolis's vibrant youth culture feeds the Twin Cities' nightlife. The post-punk scene thrives in the Land of 10,000 Aches: **Soul Asylum** and **Hüsker Dü,** as well as the best bar band in the world, **The Replacements,** rocked here before they went big (or bad). A cross-section of the diverse nightlife options can be found in the downtown **Warehouse District** on Hennepin Ave., in **Dinkytown** by the U of M, and across the river on the **West Bank** (bounded on the west by I-35 W. and to the south by I-94), especially on **Cedar Ave.** The Twin Cities card hard, even for cigarettes, so carry your ID with you. The top floor of the **Mall of America** (see **Shop 'til You Drop,** p. 534) invites bar-hopping after the screaming kids have gone to bed.

▨ **Loring Bar and Cafe,** 1624 Harmon Pl. (☎332-1617), off Hennepin Ave. near I-94. Velvet-draped and bohemia-soaked, the Loring oozes character and attitude from its indoor, light-strung trees to its artsy waitstaff. Live music, a theatrical feel, and a see-and-be-seen outdoor patio keep the stylish patrons satisfied. Beer starts at $3; wine $4.50; entrees $9. Cover (for live music) $1-5. Open Su-F 11am-1am, Sa 5pm-1am.

The Quest, 117 4th St. N. (☎359-0915), between 1st Ave. N. and 2nd Ave. N. in the Warehouse District. Once owned by Prince, this poppin' dance club pays homage to his purple highness with purple windows and lots of funk. Live salsa on M and house music draw in a young, cosmopolitan crowd. Cover $5-10. Hrs. vary; call ahead.

Ground Zero, 15 4th St. NE (☎378-5115), off Hennepin Ave. just north of the river, has something for every mover and shaker with a different theme each night. Live music on M and W, Bondage A Go-Go on Th. Open M, W, and Su until 1am; Tu and Th until 2am; F-Sa until 3am.

First Avenue and 7th St. Entry, 701 1st Ave. N. (☎332-1775), downtown Minneapolis, rocks with the area's best live music several nights a week. Prince's frequent hangout during the *Purple Rain* era, First Ave. is still where cutting-edge 20-somethings go to dance and be seen. Music varies from grunge to hip hop and everything in between. Cover $1-6, for concerts $7-18. Open M-Sa 8pm-3am, Su 7pm-3am.

Nye's Bar, 112 E. Hennepin Ave. (☎379-2021), across the river from downtown Minneapolis, pumps live polka (Th-Sa) and a piano band every night for a younger, hipper crowd than you'd expect. Open daily 11am-1am.

Fine Line Music Cafe, 318 1st Ave. N (☎338-8100), in the Warehouse District. Even musicians love to sit in the audience at the Fine Line, where a range of local and national folk, blues, rock, and jazz acts induce toe-tapping from the accessible stage. Cover varies by concert. Sunday gospel brunch from 11am. Nightly shows at 9pm.

The Gay 90s (☎333-7755), on Hennepin Ave. at 4th St., claims the 7th highest liquor consumption rate of all clubs in the nation. This superplex hosts thousands of mostly gay and lesbian partymongers in its many bars and showrooms, though the straight crowd is sizeable. Open M 9am-1am, Tu 8am-2am, W-Sa 8am-3am, Su 10am-1am.

DULUTH   ☎218

If cities were sold at auctions, Duluth would fetch a high price: the people are nice, the parks are clean, the streets are safe, and the location is amazing. Bidders on a vacation to Duluth can expect to eat well, find relatively inexpensive lodging, and watch some serious shipping action. As the largest freshwater port in the world, Duluth harbors ships from over 60 different countries. The recently restored area of Canal Park, along Lake St., has tempted microbreweries, restaurants, theaters, and museums to occupy the old factories and depots down on the wharf, turning a once-overlooked tourist destination into a spunky hotspot of northern activity.

⊟ GETTING THERE AND GETTING AROUND. Greyhound, 2122 W. Superior (☎722-5591), stops 2 mi. west of downtown; take bus #9 "Piedmont" from downtown. Buses run to Milwaukee (11hr., 3 per day, $70) and St. Paul (3hr., 3 per day, $21). Buy tickets daily 6:45am-5:30pm. The **Duluth Transit Authority,** 2402 W. Michigan St. (☎722-7283), sends buses throughout the city (peak fare M-F 7-9am and 2:30-6pm $1, off-peak 50¢). The **Port Town Trolley** (☎722-7283) moves tourists around the city's districts (runs late May to early Sept. daily 11am-7pm; fare 50¢).

⚐ PRACTICAL INFORMATION. Visitor Information: Convention and Visitors Bureau, 100 Lake Place Dr. at Endion Station in Canal Park (☎722-4011; open M-F 8:30am-5pm); the **Summer Visitors Center** at Vista dock on Harbor Dr. (☎722-6024; open mid-May to mid-Oct. daily 8:30am-7:30pm; hrs. variable); and **The Depot,** 506 W. Michigan St. (☎727-8025; open Sa-Th 9:30am-6pm, F 9:30am-8pm; mid-Oct. to Apr. M-Sa 10am-5pm, Su 1-5pm). **24hr. Crisis Line:** ☎726-1931. **Post Office:** 2800 W. Michigan St. (☎723-2590; open M-F 8am-5pm, Sa 9am-1pm). **ZIP code:** 55806. **Area code:** 218.

⚑ ACCOMMODATIONS. Motel rates rise and rooms fill during the warm months. The postcard-worthy **College of St. Scholastica,** 1200 Kenwood Ave., exit 258 off I-35 N., rents out quiet dorm rooms with free local calls, kitchen access, and laundry facilities. (☎723-6000 or 800-447-5444; ask for the housing director. Singles $21; doubles $40. Reservations recommended. Open early June to mid-Aug.) Reasonably priced motels line London Rd.; the **Chalet Motel,** 2 mi. west of downtown at 1801 London Rd., offers decent rooms seemingly out of a fairy tale. (☎728-4238 or 800-235-2957. Apr.-Sept. Sa-Su singles $46, doubles $55; M-F $39/$49. Lower in winter.) A few mi. south of town, the warm **Duluth Motel,** 4415 Grand Ave., houses visitors in affordable well-kept rooms (☎628-1008; from $50 in summer; $25 in winter).

With a decidedly less urban feel, the rocky **Jay Cooke State Park,** southwest of Duluth on I-35 exit 242, draws in families and travelers with hiking, snowmobiling, cross-country skiing, and 83 campsites among the tall trees of the St. Louis River valley. (☎384-4610 or 800-246-2267 for reservations. Open daily 9am-9pm, park gates open until 10pm. Sites with showers $12, plus electricity $14.50. Vehicle permit $4. Reservations recommended; $6.50 reservation fee.)

⚃⚄ FOOD AND NIGHTLIFE. Upscale **Fitger's Brewery Complex,** 600 E. Superior St., and the **Canal Park** region, south from downtown along Lake Ave., feature plenty of pleasant eateries. The **Brewhouse,** in Fitger's Brewery Complex, has beer and pub food. (☎726-1392. Live entertainment Tu and Th-Sa; cover $1-2. Open daily 11am-1am. Grill closes 10pm. Big Boat Oatmeal Stout $3.50.) The **DeWitt-Seitz Marketplace,** in the middle of Canal Park Dr., has slightly pricier restaurants. **Blue Note Cafe,** 357 Canal Park Dr., creates delicious sandwiches ($5-7) and desserts ($3.25) in a coffeehouse setting. (☎727-6549. Open M-Th 9am-10pm, F-Sa 9am-11pm, Su 9am-8pm.) Located in an old pipe-fitting factory in Canal Park, **Grandma's Sports Garden** is the mother of all Duluthian nightlife, with dining, a bar, and a huge dance floor. (☎722-4724. Restaurant open daily Memorial Day to Labor Day 11am-10pm; Labor Day to Memorial Day 11:30am-10pm. Club open daily 11:30am-1am; dancing W-Sa nights.) At the large, social **Backstage,** 1612 Tower Ave., across the river in Superior, WI, house and dance DJs spin the tables for a young, suburban crowd (☎715-392-3737; open daily until 2am; mixed drinks $2 and up).

⚅⚆ SIGHTS. Duluth's proximity to majestic Lake Superior is its biggest draw; many visitors head right down to **Canal Park** and watch the big ships go by at the ◪**Aerial Lift Bridge.** Accompanied by deafening horn blasts, the unique Aerial Lift Bridge climbs 138 ft. in 55sec. to allow vessels to pass; late afternoon is prime viewing time. Ships get loaded at the **Ore Docks Observation Platform,** at 35th Ave. W. and Superior St. downtown. The **Boatwatcher's Hotline** has up-to-the-minute info on ship movements (☎722-6489). Within Canal Park, the **Lake Superior Maritime Visitors Center** prepares extensive displays on commercial shipping in Lake Superior. (☎727-2497. Open daily 10am-9pm.) Canal Park also serves as the beginning and end of the **Duluth Lakewalk,** a worthwhile 3 mi. promenade which connects Fitger's Brewery, Canal Park, and the near north shore.

A 39-room neo-Jacobean mansion built on iron-shipping wealth, **Glensheen,** 3300 London Rd., lies on the eastern outskirts of town and provides visitors with a glimpse of Duluth's most prosperous period. (☎724-8863 or 888-454-4536. Open late May to early Sept. 9:30am-4pm; off-season hrs. vary. $8.75, seniors and ages 12-15

$7, ages 6-11 $4; reservations recommended.) Waterfront tours aboard the steamer **William A. Irvin** reveal more of Duluth's shipping past. (☎722-7876 May-Oct.; 722-5573 year-round. Open daily May 10am-4pm; Memorial Day to Labor Day Su-Th 9am-6pm, F-Sa 9am-8pm; Labor Day to mid-Oct. Su-Th 10am-4pm, F-Sa 10am-6pm. $6.50, students and seniors $5.50, ages 3-12 $4.) Across the Aerial Lift Bridge, **Park Point** has excellent swimming areas (for those who don't mind 55°F water in June), parks, and sandy beaches. The scenic **Willard Munger State Trail** links West Duluth to Jay Cooke State Park, providing 14 mi. of paved path perfect for bikes and in-line skates—**Willard Munger Inn,** 7408 Grand Ave., rents both. (☎624-4814 or 800-982-2453. Bikes $10 per half-day, $13 per day; in-line skates $10/$14.)

History buffs should seek out the outstanding **Karpeles Manuscript Library Museum,** which houses original drafts of the Bill of Rights, Handel's Messiah, and the Emancipation Proclamation. (☎728-0630. Open daily June-Aug. noon-4pm; Sept.-May Tu-Su noon-4pm. Free.) **The Depot,** 506 W. Michigan St., a former railroad station, appeals to locals and families as well as travelers with its four performing arts groups and several museums. (☎727-8025. Open daily May to mid.-Oct. 10am-5pm; mid-Oct. to Apr. M-Sa 10am-5pm, Su 1-5pm. $6 includes all museums and a trolley ride, families $18, ages 3-11 $4.) Featuring exhibitions on animal life in Lake Superior, the brand-new **Great Lakes Aquarium,** 353 Harbor Dr., is the world's only all-freshwater aquarium. (☎525-2265. Open late May to Sept. M-Th 10am-9pm, F-Su 10am-6pm; call for off-season hours. $11; seniors $9; children 4-7 $6; under 4 free.)

CHIPPEWA NATIONAL FOREST ☎218

Gleaming white stands of birch lace the Norway pine forests of the **Chippewa National Forest,** home to the highest density of breeding bald eagles—America's national symbol—in the continental US. The national forest shares territory with the **Leech Lake Indian Reservation,** home to 4560 Ojibwe tribespeople. The Ojibwe, mistakenly called Chippewa, migrated from the Atlantic coast in the 1700s, displacing the Sioux. In the mid-1800s, the US government seized most of their land and established reservations like Leech Lake.

🛈 PRACTICAL INFORMATION. For the northbound traveler, **Walker,** a small town in the southwest corner of the park and reservation, is an ideal gateway. **Leech Lake Area Chamber of Commerce** is on Rte. 371 downtown (☎547-1313 or 800-833-1118; open May-Sept. M-F 9am-5pm, Sa 9am-3pm, call ahead for winter hrs.). The **Forest Office** (☎547-1044; superintendent 335-8600), just east of town on Rte. 371, has the dirt on outdoor activities (open M-F 8am-4:30pm). **Greyhound** runs from Minneapolis to Walker (5½hr., 1 per day, $35), stopping at Hardee's (☎547-9585), with a ticket office at Ben Franklin's, downtown. A southbound bus leaves daily at 8:30am, a northbound at 4:30pm; buy tickets at the next station. **Post office:** 602 Michigan Ave. (☎547-1123; open M-F 9am-4pm). **ZIP code:** 56484. **Area code:** 218.

WHERE IT ALL BEGINS Near Chippewa, step across the Mighty Mississippi at its source at the **Beginning of the Mississippi,** in **Lake Itasca State Park,** 30 mi. west of Chippewa National Forest on Rte. 200. More like the vacation home you wish you owned than a cheap place to spend the night, the ■ **Mississippi Headwaters Hostel (HI-AYH)** within the park attracts locals as well as travelers with its friendly service and authentic log cabin decor. All of its cushy rooms offer spectacular views of the surrounding woods and the hostel stays open in the winter to facilitate access to the park's excellent cross-country skiing. (☎266-3415. Laundry, kitchen, multiple bathrooms. 2-night minimum stay some weekends. Check-in Su-Th 5-10pm, F-Sa 5-11pm. Check-out M-F 10am, Sa-Su noon. Dorms $15, non-members $18. Linen $2-4. $4 per day vehicle permit required for entrance to park. Private rooms available.) The **park office,** through the north entrance and down County Rd. 122, has camping info. (☎266-2100. Office open M-F 8am-4:30pm, Sa-Su 8am-4pm; mid-Oct. to Apr. M-F 8am-4:30pm. Ranger on call after hrs.) In the park, **Itasca Sports Rental** offers mountain bikes ($3.50 per hr., $20 per day), canoes ($34/$20), and pontoons ($25 for 2hr.) for those who wish to become one with the meandering river. (☎266-2150. Open daily May-Oct. 7am-9pm; must be 18+ with driver's license.)

ACCOMMODATIONS AND CAMPING. Cheap, plentiful, and available in varying degrees of modernity, **camping** is the way to stay in the forest. The Forest Office (see above) has info on campsites; over 400 of them are free. Billboards for private campgrounds string the edges of Rte. 71 along the western border of the forest. For those who prefer more permanent forms of shelter, modern lakeside cabins at **Stony Point Resort,** 8724 Stoney Point Camp Trail NW, 7 mi. east of town off Rte. 200 then 4 mi. north on Onigum Rd., sleep up to 12 people (☎547-1665 or 800-338-9303; open May-Sept.; from $96 for 4-person cabin with A/C). The **National Forest Campground** next door provides a budget-friendly alternative (☎800-280-2267; $18; $8 reservation fee; sites are self-regulated).

IRON RANGE   ☎218

It was the cry of *"Goald!"* that brought a flood of miners to join loggers and trappers already in the area, but it was the staying power of iron that kept them here. The Iron Range—120 mi. of wilderness and small towns along Minnesota Rte. 169—produces over 50% of the country's steel. Although taconite mining techniques have usurped the profitablility of their underground mines, Iron Rangers continue to celebrate their heritage proudly with exhibitions of past industrial glory.

HIBBING. The answer, my friend, is blowing in **Hibbing,** hometown of Robert Zimmerman (a.k.a. **Bob Dylan**). Then again, maybe it's not—a stay long over a day will illustrate why the legendary songwriter refused for years to acknowledge where his oats were sown. Nonetheless, the **Hibbing Tourist Center,** 1202 E. Howard St., off Rte. 169, mixes up the medicine on the area. (☎262-4166. Open June-Aug. M-F 9am-5pm; Sept.-May M-F 9am-4pm.) Spectacular swirled-red cliffs and water-filled valleys comprise the **Hull Rust Mahoning Mine,** 3 mi. north of Howard St. on 3rd Ave. E., the world's largest open pit-mine. If you're sleepy and there is no place you're going to, **Adams House,** one block south of Howard St. at 201 E. 23rd St., an outstanding Tudor-style mansion masquerading as a B&B, can put you up in a beautifully renovated double room. (☎263-9742 or 888-891-9742. Shared bath $45-$50; private bath $50-$60. Full breakfast included; reservations recommended.)

CHISOLM. Ten mi. east of Hibbing on Rte. 169, the town of **Chisolm** cultivates its iron-laden history at the **Ironworld Discovery Center,** W Hwy. 169 at Rte. 73. Half amusement park and half museum, Ironworld leads interested teams of pseudo-miners on a trolley ride through historical equipment and above an obsolete open-pit mine. (☎254-3321 or 800-372-6437. Open mid-June to mid-Sept. daily 9:30am-5pm; genealogy research center open year-round M-F 8am-4:30pm. $8, senior citizens $7, students under 18 $6, under 7 free.) On the way out, the 85 ft. tall **Iron Ore Miner Statue** is a can't-miss tribute to the workers of the Iron Range's glory days.

SOUDAN. For those who feel the need to dig deeper, the town of Soudan, 50 mi. northeast of Chisolm on Rte. 169, features an unforgettable journey ½ mi. underground in a high-speed elevator, or "cage," at the ▓Soudan Underground Mine State Park, off Rte. 1. This, the "Cadillac of underground mines," offers fascinating tours given by retired miners and their families. Visitors go by train almost a mi. into the underground maze to glimpse the dark, difficult lives of ore workers in the Iron Range. Bring sturdy shoes and a jacket—it's always a chilly 50°F underground. (☎753-2245. Park open late May through Labor Day daily 9am-6pm; tours given 10am-4pm on the ½hr. $6, ages 5-12 $4, under 5 free; $4 state park vehicle permit required.) Next door, the McKinley Park Campground rents semi-private campsites overlooking Lake Vermilion. (☎753-5921. Sites $12, with hook-up $14. Canoe and paddleboat rentals $4 per hr., $16 per day.)

ELY. The charming town of **Ely** serves as a launching pad into both the **Boundary Waters Canoe Area Wilderness (BWCAW)** (see **Boundary Waters,** p. 541) and the Iron Range, and so supports its share of wilderness outfitters and attractions. The **International Wolf Center,** just north of downtown at 1396 Rte. 169, houses three timber wolves, packs BWCAW permits, and has informative displays on *Canis lupus.* (☎365-4695. Open daily May-June and Sept.-Oct. 9:30am-6pm; July-Aug. 9:30am-7pm; Nov.-May Sa-Su only, 10am-5pm. $5.50, seniors $4, ages 6-12 $2.75. Call for wolf presentation times.) Next door, the **Dorothy Molter Museum** honors the "Root Beer Lady of Knife Lake" by inviting visitors into her kitschy, memorabilia-filled cabins which remain much as she left them. The last year-round resident of the BWCAW, Ms. Molter brewed 11-12,000 bottles of root beer each year and stubbornly refused to vacate the

GREAT LAKES

540 ■ MINNESOTA

declared wilderness until her death in 1986. (☎365-4451. Open Memorial Day to Labor Day daily 10am-6pm. $3, children $1.50; root beer $1.) **Stony Ridge Resort**, 60 W. Lakeview Pl., has a tidy loft full of comfortable bunks for $12 per night, including linen and showers, plus some RV campsites and cabins. (☎365-6757. RV sites $15 with water and electricity. 1-bedroom cabins from $65 for weeknights. Canoe rental $10 per day.)

VOYAGEURS ☎218

Voyageurs National Park sits on Minnesota's boundary with Ontario, accessible almost solely by boat. Named for the French Canadian fur traders who once traversed this area, the park invites today's voyagers to leave the auto-dominated world and push off into the longest inland lake waterway on the continent. Preservation efforts have kept the area much as it was in the late 18th century, and wolves, bear, deer, and moose roam freely. Sadly, undeveloped can mean unregulated; water should be boiled for at least 2min. before consumption, and some fish in these waters contain mercury. Ticks bearing Lyme disease have been found as well; visitors should take precautions (see **Preventing Disease,** p. 46).

7 PRACTICAL INFORMATION. The park can be accessed through (from southeast to northwest) **Crane Lake, Ash River, Kabetogama Lake,** or **Rainy Lake** (all east of Rte. 53), or through **International Falls,** at the northern tip of Rte. 53 just below Ft. Frances, ON. There are many visitors centers. **Crane Lake Visitor and Tourism Bureau,** 7238 Handberg Rd. (☎993-2481 or 800-362-7405; open M-F 9am-5pm); **International Falls Chamber of Commerce,** 301 2nd Ave. (☎800-325-5766; open M-F 8am-5pm); and, within the park, three more: **Rainy Lake,** at the end of Rte. 11, 12 mi. east of International Falls (☎286-5258; open May-Sept. daily 9am-5pm; Oct.-Apr. W-Su 9am-4:30pm); **Ash River,** 8 mi. east of Rte. 53 on Rte. 129, then 3 mi. north (☎374-3221; open early May to early Sept. daily 10am-4pm); and **Kabetogama Lake,** 1 mi. north of Rte. 122, follow the signs (☎875-2111; open mid-May to Sept. daily 9am-5pm).

⌐ ACCOMMODATIONS. Many of the numerous campsites in the park are accessible only by water. Several car-accessible sites lie outside Voyageurs in the state forest, including **Wooden Frog** about 4 mi. from Kabetogama Lake Visitors Center on Rte. 122 (☎757-3489; primitive sites $9, showers available at lodge $3), and **Ash River,** 3 mi. from the visitors center on Rte. 129 (☎757-3489; primitive sites $9). The **Ash Trail Lodge,** 10 mi. east of Rte. 53 on Rte. 129, is a good option for the wilderness-challenged, offering roomy cabins, a restaurant/bar, and lots of socializing in a wooded environment. (☎374-3131 or 800-777-4513. Singles and doubles $55.)

International Falls, the inspiration for Rocky and Bullwinkle's hometown of Frostbite Falls, offers other lodging options and a few attractions outside Voyageurs. Rte. 53 is loaded with motels. **The Tee Pee Motel,** 1501 2nd Ave. at Rte. 53, features homey rooms with cable, fridge, and seldom-needed A/C (☎283-8494 or 800-850-1518; singles $39, doubles $60). Near downtown, the **Voyageur Motel,** 1210 3rd Ave., embraces the region's wilderness feel with a rustic, lodge-like atmosphere and vast bedrooms (☎283-9424; rooms from $39 in summer). **International Voyageurs RV Campground,** 5min. south of town on Rte. 53, provides decent camping with showers, and laundry (☎283-4679; tent sites $11 for 2 people, RV sites $18 for 2 people; $2 each additional person; showers $5.)

SCENIC DRIVE: NORTH SHORE DRIVE

Vast and mysterious, Lake Superior shapes the landscape of Northeastern Minnesota with its jagged, glacier-carved edges and seemingly limitless surface. Scenic overlooks on the lake's North Shore allow harrowing views down steep cliffs toward the fickle waters below. Inland, the **Sawtooth Mountains** hover over the lake with stunning rock formations and tall, sweeping birch trees.

The true Lake Superior North Shore extends 646 mi. from Duluth, MN to Sault Ste. Marie, ON; but **Rte. 61,** winding 150 mi. along the coast from Duluth to Grand Portage, gives travelers an abbreviated version of the spectacular journey. Most of the small, touristy fishing towns along the shore maintain visitors centers. The **R.J. Houle Visitor Information Center** (☎834-4005 or 800-554-2116), 21 mi. from Duluth up Rte. 61 in scenic **Two Harbors,** has lodging guides and info for each town along the MN stretch of the North Shore. (Open Su-Th 10am-4pm, F-Sa 9am-7pm; mid-Oct. to May W-Sa 9am-1pm.) Rte. 61 is often glutted with boat-towing pick-up trucks and family-filled campers on summer weekends. Accommodations flanking the roadside fill up fast in summer; make reservations early. Remember to bring warm clothes; temperatures can drop into the low 40s (°F) on summer nights.

Striking views of the jagged cliffs that descend to the massive lake are Rte. 61's greatest appeal. State parks scattered along the route not only afford more in-depth looks at the shore but, in many cases, stunning attractions of their own. Twenty mi. northeast of the visitors center, **Gooseberry Falls** crashes down to the lake with five rugged waterfalls and scenic overlooks. The adventuresome can climb on the middle or lower falls for a head-on view. (☎834-3855. Visitors center open daily 8:30am-6pm; park open daily 8am-10pm. $4 vehicle permit fee.) **Camping** near the cataract is an appealing lodging option (primitive sites with shower $12; vehicle permit $4).

Eight mi. down the road, the **Split Rock Lighthouse** takes visitors back to the lake's industrial heyday and elevates them to a birds-eye view atop a 130 ft. cliff. (☎226-6372. Open daily late May, June, Sept. and early Oct. 9am-6pm; July through Labor Day 9am-7pm. Call for winter hrs. $3-6.) Rte. 61 becomes more convoluted as it enters the **Lake Superior National Forest** and passes over countless winding rivers toward **Tofte**, where the 1,526 ft. **Carlton Peak** dominates the landscape. The pine-paneled **Cobblestone Cabins,** off Rte. 61 2 mi. north of Tofte, offer the road-weary a place to stay and access to a cobblestone beach, canoes, a woodburning sauna, and kitchenettes (☎663-7957; open May-Oct.; cabins for 1-12 $40-85).

GRAND MARAIS

Near the north end of the 150 mi. scenic drive, this fishing resort town and former artists' colony is both a popular tourist destination and a good place to sleep and eat. **Nelson's Traveler's Rest,** on Rte. 61, ½ mi. west of town, provides fully equipped cabins with a lake view (☎387-1464 or 800-249-1285; from $43; open mid-May to mid-Oct.; call in advance). **Grand Marais Recreation Area RV Park–Campground,** off Rte. 61 in Grand Marais, has new wooded and mostly private primitive campsites along the lake. (☎387-1712 or 800-998-0959. Office open 6am-10pm. Primitive sites $15, with water and electricity $18; use of municipal pool $1.)

Cheap and popular with locals and fishermen, **South of the Border Cafe,** 4 W. Rte. 61, in Grand Marais, specializes in huge breakfasts (served all day) and satisfying diner food. The bluefin herring sandwich (fried, of course) will run you $2.75; breakfast less than $4. (☎387-1505. Open daily 5am-2pm.) Sweet-tooths should try **World's Best Doughnuts,** at the intersection of Wisconsin and Broadway, whose pastries live up to their bold moniker. (☎387-1345. Open late May to mid-Oct. M-Sa 7:30am until sold out, usually around 5pm, Su 7am-2pm. Doughnut 40¢.) The **Grand Marais Chamber of Commerce:** N. Broadway off Rte. 61. (☎387-2524 or 888-922-5000. Open mid-May to Oct. M-Sa 9am-5pm. Call for winter hrs.)

BOUNDARY WATERS. Grand Marais also serves as a gateway to the **Boundary Waters Canoe Area Wilderness (BWCAW),** a designated wilderness comprising 1.2 million acres of lakes, streams, and forests in which no human-made intrusions—phones, roads, electricity, private dwellings—are allowed. The BWCAW is even finicky about when, where, and how many people it will allow to enter; phoning ahead is essential (day permits free, camping permits $10 per person per trip). One mi. south of Grand Marais, the **Gunflint Ranger Station** distributes permits. (☎877-550-6777. Open May-Sept. daily 6am-8pm; Oct.-Apr. M-F 8am-4:30pm.) Running northwest from town, the 60 mi. paved **Gunflint Trail** (County Rd. 12) is the only developed road offering access to the wilderness from Rte. 61; resorts and outfitters gather alongside this lone strip of civilization. **Bear Track Outfitters,** 2011 W. Rte. 61, across from the Gunflint Ranger Station, rents boats and sells camping necessities. (☎387-1162. 1-day canoe rental $20, includes all accessories. 1-day kayak rental $30.)

A good option for those who would rather not camp in the Wilderness, the well-kept, seldom-full cabins of **"Spirit of the Land" Island Hostel (HI-AYH)** are located on an island in Seagull Lake, near the end of the Gunflint Trail. The Christian-oriented **Wilderness Canoe Base** leads canoe trips and summer island camps for various groups and administers at the hostel. Call from Grand Marais to arrange a boat pick-up. (☎388-2241 or 800-454-2922. Full kitchen, outhouses. Beds $14, non-members $18, F-Sa $18/$20. Sleeping bag $5, sleepsack $3. Meals $4-6. Hot showers free. Saunas $3. Canoe rental $10 per half day, $18 per day. Snowshoe rentals in winter. Closed Nov.-Dec.)

GREAT LAKES

GREAT PLAINS

In 1803, the Louisiana Purchase doubled America's size, adding French territory west of the Mississippi at the bargain price of 4¢ per acre. Over time, the plains spawned legends of pioneers and cowboys and of Native Americans struggling to defend their homelands. The arrival of railroad transportation and liberal land policy spurred an economic boom, until a drought during the Great Depression transformed the region into a dust bowl. Modern agricultural techniques have since reclaimed the soil, and the heartland of the United States thrives on the trade of farm commodities. The Great Plains is a vast land of prairies and farms, where open sky stretches from horizon to horizon, broken only by long, thin lines of trees. Grasses and grains paint the land green and gold, and the plains' breadbasket feeds much of the world. Yet, in spite of man, the land rules here, and the most staggering sights in the region are the work of nature, from the Badlands to the Black Hills to the mighty Missouri and Mississippi Rivers.

HIGHLIGHTS OF THE GREAT PLAINS

NATIONAL PARKS AND MONUMENTS. Discover the uncrowded gems of Theodore Roosevelt National Park, SD (p. 547), and the Badlands, SD (p. 550), or join the crowds in the Black Hills around Mt. Rushmore (p. 554).

HISTORICAL SITES. sNational Monument, NE (p. 571) and Chimney Rock, NE (p. 571) will fascinate anyone interested in the pioneers.

NORTH DAKOTA

An early visitor to the site of present-day Fargo declared, "It's a beautiful land, but I doubt that human beings will ever live here." Posterity begs to differ. The stark, haunting lands that so intimidated early settlers eventually found willing tenants, and the territory became a state along with South Dakota on Nov. 2, 1889. The inaugural event was not without confusion—Benjamin Harrison concealed the names when he signed the two bills, so both Dakotas claim to be the 39th state.

North Dakota has remained largely isolated geographically. In the western half of the state, the colorful buttes of the Badlands rise in desolate beauty, while in the eastern half mind-numbing flatness rules; the 110 miles of Rte. 46 from U.S. 81 to Rte. 30 is the longest stretch of highway in the US without a single curve. Perhaps North Dakota is overshadowed as a destination by South Dakota's high-gear tourist industry, but those smart enough to head to North Dakota find stark, untainted beauty minus the crowds.

▊ PRACTICAL INFORMATION

Capital: Bismarck.

Visitor Info: Tourism Dept., 604 East Blvd., Bismarck 58505 (☎ 701-328-2525 or 800-435-5663; www.ndtourism.com). **Parks and Recreation Dept.,** 1835 Bismarck Expwy., Bismarck 58504.

Postal Abbreviation: ND. **Sales Tax:** 5-7%, depending on city.

Great Plains

FARGO ☎ 701

Although it is North Dakota's largest city, Fargo existed in anonymity until the 1996 Oscar-winning film *Fargo* brought it name-recognition. However, very little of the movie was filmed in the town, and its parodied accents are more northern Minnesota than North Dakota. Fargo and its sister city, Moorhead, MN, are home to 20,000 students who pack lectures at North Dakota State University, Moorhead State, and Concordia College and add a touch of energy to a withering downtown.

⅔ PRACTICAL INFORMATION. Fargo and Moorhead flank the Red River on the east and west, respectively. The two cities are connected by a messy network of streets, with numbered streets running north-south and increasing from the river outward and numbered avenues running east-west. Main Ave. is the central east-west thoroughfare and intersects I-29. **Hector International Airport** is at 2801 32nd Ave. N.W. (☎241-8168), off 19th Ave. N. in northern Fargo. **Amtrak** can be found at 420 4th St. N. (☎232-2197). **Greyhound** is at 402 Northern Pacific (N.P.) Ave. (☎293-1222. Open daily 6:30am-6:20pm and 9:30pm-1:20am.) **Metro Area Transit,** 502 North Pacific Ave., runs buses across the city (☎232-7500; operates M-Sa). **Taxi:** Doyle's Yellow Checker Cab (☎235-5535). **Internet access** is available at the Fargo Public Library, 102 N. 3rd St. (☎241-1492. Open M-Th 9am-9pm, F 11am-6pm, Sa 9am-6pm; winter also Su 1-6pm.) Sort out your visit at the **Fargo-Moorhead Convention and Visitors Bureau,** 2001 44th St. SW, off 45th St. Follow the blue signs from I-29 Exit 63B. (☎282-3653 or 800-235-7654. Open May-Aug. M-Sa 8am-7pm, Su 9am-6pm; Sept.-Apr. M-F 8am-5pm, Sa 10am-4pm.) **Crisis Line:** ☎235-7335; 24hr. **Post Office:** 657 2nd Ave. N. (Open M-F 7:30am-5:30pm, Sa 8am-2pm.) **ZIP code:** 58103. **Area code:** 701.

⌂ ACCOMMODATIONS. In summer, Moorhead State University rents tidy rooms with linen and phones in **Ballard Hall,** just north of 9th Ave. S and 14th St. S in Moorhead. (☎218-236-2231. Check-in 24hr. $12 per person.) Cheap chain motels abound at I-29 and 13th Ave.; take Exit 64 off I-29. **The Sunset Motel,** 731 W. Main, in West Fargo, about 3 mi. west off I-29 Exit 65, offers clean rooms, free local calls, continental breakfast, and an indoor pool with a snazzy two-story waterslide. (☎800-252-2207. Call early on weekends. Singles $25-28; doubles $43-48; kitchenettes $5 extra.) Follow signs from I-94 Exit 351 to **Lindenwood Park,** at 17th Ave. and 5th St. S. The campground offers sites close to the peaceful Red River. The park also has extensive trails ideal for mountain biking. (☎232-3987. Sites $8, with hook-up $15.)

◨▨▱ FOOD, NIGHTLIFE, AND ENTERTAINMENT. Erbert & Gerbert's, 63 Broadway, puts together great club sandwiches and subs on freshly baked bread. Vegetarians will be delighted with the "Jacob Bluefinger" ($3.40), though there are plenty of meat options as well. (☎235-3445. Open F-Sa 10:30am-2am, Su-Th 10:30am-11pm.) **Cafe Aladdin,** 530 6th Ave. N, is popular for its scrumptious Greek and Middle Eastern food ($4-7.50) and sweet, flaky baklava for $1.50. (☎298-0880. Open M 10:30am-8pm, Tu-Sa 10am-8pm.) The **I Beam,** at Center Ave. and 11th St. in Moorhead, is an alternative bar with a great dance floor. (☎233-7700. Open M-Sa 7pm-1am. Tu men's night. Th ladies' night. Cover F-Sa after 10pm $2.) NDSU students tend to go to the bars along Broadway near Northern Pacific Ave. If it's culture, not beer you're craving, head to the **Fargo Theater,** 314 Broadway. The recently restored 30s theater now shows art films (☎239-8385; tickets $6.50).

◧ SIGHTS. The **Heritage Hjemkomst Center,** 202 1st Ave. N. in Moorhead, pays tribute to the two cities' Norwegian heritage. Inside looms the Hjemkomst (pronounced "*yem-komst*"), a 76 ft. Viking ship replica built by Moorhead native Robert Asp that actually sailed the 6100 mi. from Duluth, MN, to Bergen, Norway, in 1982. Outside, a 72 ft. stave church replica, built by Moorhead native Guy Paulson, impresses visitors with its raw beauty. (☎218-299-5511. Open M-W and F-Sa 9am-5pm, Th 9am-9pm, Su noon-5pm. $3.50, students and seniors $3, ages 4-17 $1.50.) The **Scandinavian Hjemkomst Festival** is a big draw, complete with cultural exhibits, music and dance shows, and local food (☎800-235-7654; June 20-24, 2001). From June to Aug., **Trollwood Park Weekends** (☎241-8160) feature similar enticements.

I-94, ROAD OF CONCRETE WONDERS
Two gargantuan concrete monuments separated by 131 mi. of interstate symbolize the past and present of North Dakota and the entire Great Plains. Looming against the horizon in Jamestown, ND, at Exit 258, is the world's largest buffalo—a towering, 60 ton, 24 ft., monument to the animals that once roamed the plains. Near the statue, a herd of real buffalo regards their concrete brother apathetically from behind a protective fence. With luck, you'll see White Cloud, a rare albino buffalo sacred to many Native American tribes. Adjacent to the monument is the **National Buffalo Museum,** documenting the evolution and adulation of the buffalo. (☎800-222-4766. Open daily 9am-8pm. $3, students $1, families $7.) 131 mi. west in Salem, at Exit 127, Salem Sue, the world's largest Holstein Cow (38 ft. tall and 50 ft. long), keeps an eye on the interstate and the seas of cows that munch on the grasses of the plains. ($1 suggested donation.)

BISMARCK
☎701

Bismarck is hardly a rough, urban capital. The city is impeccably clean, the people are open and friendly, and the scenery is spectacular. Even with only about 55,000 residents, it still has the look and feel of a large town. The city was founded on land that defies the misconception that all prairies are flat. The terrain is an array of color, texture, and shapes. Seas of yellow wildflowers, grids of green farmland, and fields of golden wheat blend with surprising harmony. The city of Bismarck itself offers a number of notably trendy eating establishments and vibrant nightspots. As far as North Dakotan cities go, Bismarck is the most interesting and comfortable place to spend a few days relaxing, enjoying the scenery, and learning about pioneer culture and heritage.

⑦ PRACTICAL INFORMATION. Bismarck is on I-94, about half-way between Fargo and Theodore Roosevelt National Park. The Missouri River separates Bismarck from Mandan, its neighboring city to the West. In Bismarck, Washington and 9th St. are the main north-south thoroughfares and are intersected by Main Ave., Divide Ave., and Interstate Ave., all running east-west. The **Bismark Municipal Airport** (☎222-6502) is located on Airport Rd., 2 mi. southeast of the city. Buses to neighboring cities depart from the **Greyhound** station, 3750 E. Rosser Ave. (☎223-6576. Open daily 9am-1pm and 5:30-9pm; Tu and Sa also open 1:30-5:30am.) For a taxi, try **Taxi 9000** (☎223-9000). **Internet access** is free at the **Bismarck Public Library,** 515 N. 5th St. (Open M-F 9am-9pm, Sa 9am-5pm, Su 1-5pm, summer F 9am-6pm. 1hr. time slots.) **Visitors Center:** 1600 Burnt Boat Rd., Exit 157 off I-94. (☎222-4308. Open daily 7am-7pm.) **Post Office:** 220 E. Rosser Ave. (☎221-6550. Open M-F 7:45am-5:30pm, Sa 10am-noon.) **ZIP code:** 58501. **Area Code:** 701.

⌐ ACCOMMODATIONS. Budget motels abound at I-94 Exit 159. The **Bismarck Motor Hotel,** 2301 E. Main Ave., offers clean rooms with a microwave and a fridge. (☎223-2474. Singles $29; doubles $33.) The best value around is the **Select Inn,** 1505 Interchange Ave, I-94 at Exit 159. The rooms are clean and spacious, with laundry access and continental breakfast. (☎223-8060 or 800-641-1000. Singles $36, $41 for 2 people; doubles $43. AAA discount.) Camping is a relaxing experience in the beautiful **Fort Abraham Lincoln State Park** (see **Sights,** below), 7 mi. south on Hwy. 1806 in Mandan. Tent sites line the banks of the Missouri River and feature an amazing view of the surrounding prairie. (☎663-9571. $7, with electricity $12; vehicle fee $4.)

⍓ FOOD. Bismarck offers a surprising array of posh restaurants, each with a unique dining room atmosphere. Aliens have landed in Bismarck, ND, for certainly **▓Space Aliens Grill and Bar,** 1304 E. Century Ave., is no earthly dining experience. Human visitors are offered an array of typical human foods—with an alien twist, of course. The BBQ ribs won first prize in the National BBQ Cookoff in Memphis, TN (perhaps due to scientific advancements gained through pig abductions?) (☎223-6220. Open Su-Th 11am-11pm, F-Sa 11am-1am.) With an enormous menu of pasta, chicken, seafood, and sandwiches ($5.50-10), the **Walrus,** 1136 N. 3rd. St. in Arrow-head Plaza, is understandably a popular local favorite. The $9.50 Italian Sausage Pizziola is a house specialty. (☎ 250-0020. Open M-Sa 10:30am-1am.) Housed in the old train depot, **Fiesta Villa** (☎ 222-8075), 411 E. Main Ave. at the corner of 4th and Main, serves quesadillas, tacos, enchiladas and other Mexican fare, complimented by their homemade sauces ($6-9). Enjoy your selection inside the historic building or soak up the atmosphere on the open-air patio.

🔟 **SIGHTS.** The unique **North Dakota State Capitol,** 600 E. Boulevard Ave, was built between 1932-34, with a budget of only $2 million. To stretch the money to the max, the usual dome-style capitol design was replaced by a more efficient 19-story office-style building. Inside, visitors view paramount examples of Art-Deco architecture in beautiful Memorial Hall. The observation deck on the 19th floor is a great place to see the prairie and the Capitol's 130 acres of well-manicured grounds. (☎ 328-2000. Open M-F 7am-6pm. Informative 45min. tours leave hourly M-F 8am-4pm; Memorial Day to Labor Day additional tours Sa 9am-4pm, Su 1-4pm. Free.) Right next door to the Capitol is the **North Dakota Heritage Center,** 612 E. Boulevard Ave., an excellent historical museum dedicated to illustrating the development of North Dakota life and society from prehistoric times to the present. (☎ 328-2666. Open M-F 8am-5pm, Sa 9am-5pm, Su 11am-5pm. Free.) On Hwy. 1806 in Mandan, **Fort Abraham Lincoln State Park** proves that there are irregularities on the prairie; odd shaped hills engulf the road. The state park houses "On-a-Slant" Mandan Indian village and replicas of the cavalry post and Victorian-style home of Lt. Col. George Armstrong Custer. Those wishing to "visit the General" can follow a host dressed in period-garb through the Custer home. (☎ 663-3069 or 663-9571. Buildings open daily 9am-7pm; park 9am-9:30pm. $4, high school students $2; additional $4 vehicle fee.)

🔟🎵 **NIGHTLIFE AND ENTERTAINMENT.** Locals agree that the coolest place to be in Bismarck these days is **Borrowed Buck's Roadhouse,** 118 S. 3rd St. Decorated like an old service station, Buck's has a full dance floor and a live DJ every night. Rock music is the focus, but W are "Dance Ranch," featuring good country music. Live bands take the stage at Bucks once or twice a month; the performances are well-advertised around the city. (☎ 224-1545. Open M-F 4pm-1am, Sa noon-1am. 21+.) If only one night a week of country isn't enough for you, there's always **Lonesome Dove,** 3929 Memorial Hwy. on the border of Mandan, the *real* country joint in Bismarck. Lonesome Dove has a large dance floor and live, toe-tappin' country music six nights a week. (☎ 663-2793. Open daily noon-1am.) The **Bismarck Symphony** (☎ 258-8345) plays in the magnificent Belle Mehus Auditorium, 201 N. 6th St. The symphony celebrates holidays in style—8000 people turn up for their 4th of July concert on the Capitol steps. A variety of musical programs run throughout the year, and chamber music can be heard every Su afternoon.

SCENIC DRIVE: SASKAWEA TRAIL

Drivers along Hwy. 200 in North Dakota witness an extraordinary transformation, as smooth green prairie hills abruptly give way to red and white jutting buttes and canyons. The change in terrain occurs without warning and can be startling. Aside from the scenery, the Saskawea Trail offers travelers interested in Lewis and Clark or Native American history ample opportunity to learn and explore the countryside.

The Saskawea Trail begins in **Washburn,** north of Bismarck on Rte. 83. At the junction of Rte. 83 and Rte. 200A lies the **Lewis and Clark Interpretive Center.** The museum presents an overview of the wilderness journey, and visitors can don buffalo robes and schlep around with a cradle board like the one Saskawea wore. (☎ 701-462-8535. Open Memorial to Labor Day 9am-7pm; rest of year 9am-5pm.) Just down the street at **Fort Mandan,** modern-day trailblazers can enter a replica of the expedition's rugged riverside lodgings. (☎ 701-462-8535. Open daily 8:30am-sunset.)

Back on Rte. 200A, rustic, secluded camping can be found at the **Cross Ranch State Park Campground.** Follow the paved road at the sign on 200A for about 14 mi. (☎ 702-794-3731. $4 vehicle charge. Tent sites $5, RVs with no electricity $7.) About

10 mi. west of Washburn, a scenic overlook is marked with a small sign. On the left-hand side lie the Arroda Lakes, blue and sparkling against the green land. On the right, vibrant-colored fields meet the Missouri River. Down the road, plaques and sign posts mark the former site of **Fort Clark;** over time, forceful prairie winds eradicated any evidence of its existence on the plains. About 8 mi. west of Fort Clark you can follow signs for the **Knife River Indian Villages National Historic Site.** There is a 15min. video detailing the life of Plains Indians and a ½ mi. wheelchair accessible trail to the Knife River. (☎ 701-745-3309. Open 7:30am-6pm; Labor Day to Memorial Day 8am-4:30pm. Earth lodge tours 10am, 1, 3pm. Free.)

After the Knife River Indian Villages, there's not much standing in the way of **Theodore Roosevelt National Park.** For the next 40 mi. or so, the road is fairly straight. Just before the junction with Rte. 85, however, the landscape begins to change dramatically. At first, only a few solitary buttes break the tranquility of the hills. Then—before you know it—they are everywhere; the earth becomes a stark red and white and dotted with jagged formations. The southern entrance to Theodore Roosevelt National Park lies in the tiny frontier town of **Medora,** about 16 mi. south on Rte. 85 and another 15 mi. west on I-94. Signs on Rte. 85 N also point the way to the northern entrance to the park.

THEODORE ROOSEVELT NATIONAL PARK ☎ 701

After both his mother and wife died on the same day, pre-White House Theodore Roosevelt moved to his ranch in the Badlands for a dose of spiritual renewal. He was so influenced by the red- and brown-hued lunar formations, horseback riding, big-game hunting, and cattle ranching in this unforgiving land that he later claimed, "I never would have been President if it weren't for my experiences in North Dakota." Inspired by his wilderness days, Roosevelt created numerous national parks, monuments, and bird refuges. Theodore Roosevelt National Park was created in 1947 as a monument to his conservationist policies. Visitors can garner the inspiration he did, among quiet canyons, secluded glens, and dramatic rocky outcroppings which have earned the park the nickname "rough-rider country." The park teems with wildlife; prairie dog towns, bison, and deer are all common.

◪ PRACTICAL INFORMATION. The park is split into southern and northern units and bisected by the border separating Mountain and Central Time Zones. The entrance to the more-developed southern unit is just north of I-94 in **Medora,** a frontier town revamped into a tourist mecca. **Greyhound** serves Medora from the Sully Inn (see below), with buses to Bismarck (3½hr., 3 per day, $23-25) and Billings (6hr., 2 per day, $45-48). There is no ticket office in Medora; board the bus and buy your ticket during the Dickinson layover. The park entrance fee ($5 per person or $10 maximum per vehicle, under 17 free) covers admission to both units of the park for seven days. The **South Unit's Visitors Center,** in Medora, maintains a mini-museum displaying T.R.'s guns, spurs, and old letters, as well as a beautiful 13min. film about the Badlands. (☎623-4466. Open daily 8am-8pm; Sept. to mid-June 8am-4:30pm.) The **North Unit's Visitors Center** has an interesting exhibit on the nature and wildlife in the park and offers a shorter film. (☎842-2333. Open daily 9am-5:30pm Central Time.) In an **emergency** in the north unit, call the **ranger** (☎842-2333; available 9am-5:30pm Central Time; after hours call ☎842-4266) or the **sheriff** at ☎842-3654. The **South Unit's Emergency** number is ☎623-4765. For more info, write to **Theodore Roosevelt National Park,** P.O. Box 7, Medora 58645, or call the visitors centers. **Provisions/pharmacy:** Medora lacks a real pharmacy and grocery store. However, both the **Ferris Store,** 251 Main St. (☎623-4447; open daily 8am-8pm) and **Medora Liquor Convenience,** Pacific Ave. (☎623-4479; open daily 7am-10pm), sell basic pharmaceutical goods. The Ferris Store also sells a variety of basic food and cooking items. There is a 24-hour **Walmart** in Dickinson (30 mi. east on I-90). **Bike Rental: Dakota Cyclery,** 275 3rd Ave. (☎623-4830. Open daily 9am-6pm. $6 per hr., $10 per 2hr., $15 per 4hr., $25 per day.) *Off*-road biking is not allowed in either unit of Theodore Roosevelt National Park. The Cyclery also leads bike tours of the plains and badlands at 10am and 2pm daily. **South Unit Time Zone:** Mountain (2hr. behind Eastern).

North Unit Time Zone: Central (1hr. behind Eastern). Medora's **post office:** 355 3rd Ave. (Open M-Sa 8am-7pm; window service M-F 8am-4:30pm, Sa 8:15am-9:45am.) **ZIP code:** 58645. **Area code:** 701.

▛▟ **ACCOMMODATIONS AND FOOD.** Free backcountry camping permits are available at the visitors centers. **Cottonwood Campgrounds** lies just inside the south entrance. In the north, **Juniper Campground,** 5 mi. west of the north unit entrance, is in a beautiful valley. The campground is a popular buffalo nightspot all year, so be aware. (Both campgrounds have toilets and running water; sites $10).

It's not easy to find inexpensive, non-camping lodging in Medora. The **Sully Inn,** 428 Broadway, offers clean rooms at the lowest rates in town, free local calls, and 10% off in its bookstore. (☎623-4455. Singles $35-45, in winter $20-35; doubles $40-50; under 13 free.) Teddy Roosevelt was known to bunk down at the **Rough Riders Hotel,** 3rd St. and 3rd Ave. The hotel's room rates are far from budget, but the restaurant serves reasonable breakfasts and lunches (huge omelettes, salads, and sandwiches) in an upscale atmosphere for $5-7. (☎623-4444, ext. 497. Open daily 7am-8:30pm. In winter, B&B only.) The **Cowboy Cafe** on 4th St., rustles up less expensive meals ($2-10), including their famous pies, buffalo burgers, and the tasty popcorn chicken salad. (☎623-4343. Open daily May-Nov. 6am-8pm.)

▣ **SIGHTS AND ACTIVITIES. Painted Canyon Overlook,** 7 mi. east of Medora off I-94, has its own **visitors center** with picnic tables and a breathtaking view of the Badlands. The occasional buffalo roams through the parking lot. The **Painted Canyon Trail** is a worthwhile 1 mi. loop that undulates gently through shady wooded areas and scorching buttes. (☎575-4020. Open daily 8am-6pm; mid-Apr. to late May and early Sept. to mid-Nov. 8:30am-4:30pm. Free.) The **south unit** is busier and more crowded than the north unit, consisting of a 36 mi. **scenic automobile loop** from which all sights and trails are accessible. **Peaceful Valley Ranch,** 7 mi. into the park, offers a variety of horseback riding excursions, 1½hr. or longer. (☎623-4568. Rides leave daily 8:30am-2pm, evening ride 6pm. $16.) The **Ridgeline Trail** is a short, self-guided hiking trail about ½ mi. long. Signs along the way instruct about the ecology and geology of the terrain. The ¾ mi. **Coal Vein Trail** traces a seam of lignite coal that ignited and burned from 1951 to 1977. The searing heat of the blaze served as a natural kiln, baking the adjacent clay and sand. **Buck Hill** is accessible by car, but a short climb up a steep paved path earns you a 180° view of the badlands landscape. Constant winds continue to morph the soft sands of **Wind Canyon.** A short, dirt path leads you along the bluffs for a close look at the canyon walls and the river below. The third-largest **petrified forest** in the US lies a day's hike into the park; if you prefer to drive, ask the ranger for specific directions and expect to walk about ¾ mi. Learn more about Teddy Roosevelt through a tour of his **Maltese Cabin,** circa 1883. Tours leave periodically from the **Southern Unit Visitors Center** in the summer.

The less-visited **north unit** of the park is 75 mi. from the south unit on U.S. 85. Equally as scenic as the south unit, it is infinitely more conducive to hiking and exploring. Most of the land is wilderness, resulting in virtually unlimited **backcountry hiking** possibilities. The seclusion provides ample opportunity for wildlife contact, but be careful not to surprise the buffalo; one ranger advises singing while hiking so they can hear you coming. For those eager to escape the crowds but reluctant to leave the car, the north unit does award a look at the badlands on its **14 mi. scenic drive.** It connects the entrance and visitors center to **Oxbow Overlook,** and is as unsullied as possible considering it's a car trail—there are no turnouts and signs to mar the setting. Everyone can enjoy the **Little Mo Trail.** Weaving through woodlands and badlands, three-fourths of the 1 mi. trail is wheelchair accessible. The **Buckhorn Trail** is a long but relatively easy 11 mi. walk that includes a visit to a prairie dog town. The **Caprock Coulee Trail** (1½ mi round-trip) connects with the Buckhorn Trail and journeys on fairly level ground through prairie and dry water gulches. Seasoned hikers and adventurers will thrive on the challenging **Achenbach Trail.** The 16 mi. sojourn features numerous vertical drops and uphill climbs as it winds around the Little Missouri River.

■ **ENTERTAINMENT.** The popular **Medora Musical** is a comical singing, dancing, and theater experience that attracts hoards of people nightly. The show, held in the open-air Burning Hills Amphitheater west of town, incorporates the magnificent natural landscape into the performance. The Medora Musical also stages various outside talent acts, ranging from magicians to comedians to Argentinian Gauchos. Shows nightly at 8:30pm from early June to early Sept. ($17-19, ages 6-18 $10-11). Before the show, clog your arteries at the **Pitchfork Fondue.** The "chef" puts ten steaks on a pitchfork and dips them into a vat of boiling oil for 5 min. ($18, age 17 and under $10, includes buffet. Reservations required.) Tickets for both are available at 335 4th St. at the **Harold Schafer Heritage Center** (☎623-4444).

SOUTH DAKOTA

From the forested granite crags of the Black Hills to the glacial lakes of the northeast, the Coyote State has more to offer than casual passers-by might expect. In fact, with only ten people per square mile, South Dakota has the highest ratio of sights-to-people in all of the Great Plains. Colossal man-made attractions like Mt. Rushmore and the Crazy Horse Memorial and stunning natural spectacles like the Black Hills and the Badlands make tourism the state's largest industry.

■ PRACTICAL INFORMATION

Capital: Pierre.
Visitor Info: Department of Tourism, 711 E. Wells Ave., Pierre 57501 (☎605-773-3301 or 800-952-3625; www.travelsd.com). Open M-F 8am-5pm. **U.S. Forest Service,** 330 Mt. Rushmore Rd., Custer 57730 (☎605-673-4853). Open M-F 7:30am-4:30pm. **Game, Fish, and Parks Dept.,** 523 E. Capitol Ave., Foss Bldg., Pierre 57501 (☎605-773-3391), has info on state parks and campgrounds. Open M-F 8am-noon and 1-5pm. Call ☎800-710-2267 for a campground reservation or 800-732-5682 for a packet of info.
Postal Abbreviation: SD. **Sales Tax:** 6%.

SIOUX FALLS   ☎605

South Dakota's eastern gateway, Sioux Falls is the typical "nice guy": quiet, friendly, clean-cut, and a little boring—a better stopping point than a destination in itself. The city's namesake rapids are at Falls Park, north of downtown on Falls Park Dr. The Sioux River Greenway Recreation Trail circles the city from Falls Park in the northeast to the Elmwood golf course in the northwest.

■ **PRACTICAL INFORMATION. Main St.** divides the city east-west, **Minnesota Ave.** north-south. **10th** and **12th St.** intersect them; 10th connects with **I-229** in the east and 12th connects with **I-29** in the west. **Jack Rabbit Buses,** 301 N. Dakota Ave. (☎336-0885; open daily 7:30am-5pm) hop to Minneapolis (6hr., 2 per day, $43-46), Omaha (4hr., 2 per day, $30-32), and Rapid City (9hr., 1 per day, $114). **Sioux Falls Transit** buses run during the day for $1 with free transfers (☎367-7183; operates M-Sa). **Taxi: Yellow Cab,** ☎336-1616. **Visitors Center:** in Falls Park, follow signs to Falls Park from Main St. (☎367-7430. Open daily Apr. 15 to Sept. 30 9am-9pm, Oct. 1 to Apr. 14 Sa-Su 9am-5pm.) Aside from the plethora of info available, the visitors center offers a free climb up its observation tower for a glimpse at the surrounding countryside. **Post Office:** 320 S. Second Ave. (☎357-5000. Open M-F 7:30am-5:30pm, Sa 8am-1pm.) **ZIP code:** 57104. **Area code:** 605.

> **YOU ARE NOW ONLY THREE PAGES FROM WALL DRUG.**

╠╬ ACCOMMODATIONS AND FOOD. Budget motels flank 41st St. at Exit 77 off I-29. The **Select Inn,** 3500 Gateway Blvd., is a particularly good value. (☎361-1864. Free continental breakfast. Singles $33; doubles $38, with twin beds $45.) There are a number of state parks nearby; **Split Rock City Park,** 20 mi. northeast in Garretson has the cheapest camping. From I-90 E, take Rte. 11 N. (Corson) and drive 10 mi. to Garretson; turn right at the sign for Devil's Gulch, and it will be on your left before the tracks. (Pit toilets and drinking water. Sites $4-6.) At the **Sioux Falls Brewing Co.,** 431 N. Phillips, the only remotely trendy restaurant in Sioux Falls, you can grab a slice of buffalo pie (cheesecake with stout beer and dark chocolate) with your burger or salad. (☎332-4847. Open M-Th 11:30am-midnight, F-Sa 11:30am-1:30am.)

▨ SIGHTS. At **Buffalo Ridge,** 5 mi. west of Sioux Falls on I-90, Exit 390, you can visit a ghost town with over 50 exhibits portraying life in the old West. A herd of over 50 buffalo is also known to make appearances near the town. (☎528-3931. Open early Apr.-Oct. sunrise to sunset. $4, children 5-12 $3.) At **Jesse James Pontoon Rides,** 505 3rd St. in Garretson (see **Split Rock Park** below), adventurers can enjoy a 45min. nature tour down Split Rock River to the cave where the infamous outlaw Jesse James hid. (☎594-2225. Open M-Sa 9am-5:30pm, Su 1-5:30pm. $6, children under 12 $4. Reservations required.) The **Corn Palace,** 604 N. Main St., in Mitchell, 70 mi. west of Sioux Falls on I-90, poses as a regal testament to granular architecture. Dating back to 1892, the structure is redecorated yearly to demonstrate the richness of South Dakota's soil. (☎800-257-2676. Open in summer daily 8am-9pm; daily May and Sept. 8am-5pm, Oct.-Apr. M-F 8am-5pm. Free.) On a warm summer night, head to the visitors center (see below) for the **Wells Fargo Falls Park Light and Sound Show.** The spectacle enhances the natural beauty of Sioux Falls, the city's namesake, with a little help from technology. (Nightly Memorial Day to Labor Day, starting a half hr. after sunset. Free.) **Great Bear Ski Valley,** 5901 E. Rice St., close to downtown, has skiing, snowboarding, and snowshoeing. (Call ☎367-4309 after Dec. 1 for lift ticket and rental prices.)

THE BADLANDS   ☎605

When architect Frank Lloyd Wright first saw the Badlands it appeared to him as "an endless supernatural world more spiritual than earth but created out of it." Earlier explorers, when faced with the mountainous rock formations that suddenly appear out of the prarie, were less enthusiastic; "Hell with the fires out," General Alfred Sully called these arid and treacherous formations at first encounter. The French (perhaps erroneously) translated the Sioux name for the area, *mako sica,* as *les mauvaises terres:* "bad lands." Some 60 million years ago, when much of the Great Plains was under water, tectonic shifts thrust up the Rockies and the Black Hills. Mountain streams deposited silt from these nascent highlands into the area now known as the Badlands, capturing and fossilizing in layer after multicolored layer the remains of wildlife that once wandered these flood plains. Erosion has carved spires and steep sills into the earth, and it is still at work today. According to geologists, the Badlands lose about 6 in. every year; at this rate it will disappear in 500,000 years—so hurry up before it is too late. Late spring and fall in the Badlands offer pleasant weather that can be a relief from the extreme temperatures of midsummer and winter, but no matter how bad it gets, it is always well worth a visit.

▨ PRACTICAL INFORMATION. Badlands National Park smolders about 50 mi. east of Rapid City on I-90. **Jack Rabbit Buses,** 333 6th St. (☎348-3300), leaves from Rapid City for Wall at 11:30am daily ($24). Driving tours can start at either end of Rte. 240, which winds through wilderness in a 32 mi. detour off I-90 (Exit 110 or 131). The **Ben Reifel Visitors Center** (☎433-5361; open daily Sept.-Jun. 7am-8pm; Aug.-May hrs. vary), 5 mi. inside the park's northeastern entrance, is larger and more convenient than **White River Visitors Center** (☎455-2878; open June-Aug. 10am-4pm, hrs. may vary), 55 mi. to the southwest off Rte. 27 in the park's less-visited southern section. Both visitors centers have potable water. The **entrance fee,** collected at the park entrance, is $10 per car, $5 per person (a free copy of *The Prairie Preamble* with trail map included). At the **National Grasslands Visitors Center (Buffalo Gap),** 708 Main St., down the street from Wall Drug in Wall, there are several films and an exhibit on the complex ecosystem that comprises much of the surrounding area (☎279-2125; open daily 7am-8pm, off-season 8am-4:30pm). **Area code:** 605.

░░ ACCOMMODATIONS AND FOOD. The closest decent motel to the Badlands, the **Badlands Inn** sits just outside the park, south of the Ben Riefel Visitors Center in Interior. (☎433-5401 or 800-341-8000. Singles $32-40, with 2 people $34-50; doubles $39-55.) The **Hillcrest Motel,** 412 Fourth Ave in Wall, doesn't look like much from the outside, but the rooms are clean and spacious, and it's the best value around. (☎279-2415 or 800-888-1326. Open mid-May to mid-Sept. Free continental breakfast. Singles $40, with 2 people $45; doubles $55-65.) Next to the Ben Reifel Visitors Center inside the park, **Cedar Pass Lodge** rents cabins with A/C and showers. (☎433-5460. Open mid-Apr. to mid-Oct. 1 person $43, $4 per additional person.; fills up early, call ahead.)

Two campgrounds lie within the park. **Cedar Pass Campground,** just south of the Ben Reifel Visitors Center, has sites with water and restrooms ($10). It's best to get there early, since it sometimes fills up by late afternoon in summer. At **Sage Creek Campground,** 13 mi. from the Pinnacles entrance south of Wall (take Sage Creek Rim Rd. off Rte. 240), you can sleep in an open field; there are restrooms, but no water and no fires allowed—but hey, it's free. **Backcountry camping** (½ mi. from the road and out of sight) allows a more intimate introduction to this austere landscape, but water must be packed in. For more info, contact one of the rangers. Wherever you sleep, don't cozy up to the bison; nervous mothers can become just a tad protective.

At the lodge's mid-priced **restaurant** (the only one in the park), brave diners try the $3.45 buffalo burger (open daily May 15 to late Oct. 7am-8:30pm; hrs. may vary). When your stomach demands more loving fare, head to the ▧**Cuny Table Cafe,** 8 mi. west of the White River Visitor Center on Rte. 2, only a short detour to or from Wounded Knee. It's worth the drive to get the area's best Indian Tacos ($4.50)— home-cooked fry bread piled with veggies, beans, and beef raised in the backyard.

▨ SIGHTS AND ACTIVITIES. The 244,000-acre park protects large tracts of prairie and stark rock formations. The Ben Reifel Visitors Center has a video on the Badlands, as well as a wealth of info on nearby parks, camping, and activities. Park rangers offer free talks and excursions into the park daily during the summer; check the handy *Prairie Preamble* for the schedule.

For stunning vistas, a drive along Rte. 240/Loop Rd. is an excellent way to see the park. The road makes its way through rainbow colored bluffs and around hairpin turns, all the while affording views of many distinct types of Badlands terrain.

Trail guides from the visitors centers facilitate **hiking** through the Badlands. Hiking is permitted throughout the entire park, although climbing on the formations is discouraged. For backcountry hikers, it's a good idea to bring a compass, a map, and lots of water. Planning your route with a park ranger is also wise. Despite the burning heat in summer, long pants are advisable to protect from poison ivy, stinging and biting insects, and the park's one venomous snake—the prairie rattlesnake. Five hiking trails begin off Loop Rd. near the Ben Reifel Visitor Center. The **Door Trail** is wheelchair accessible for the first 100m. The rest of the trail winds through buttes and crevices for spectacular views of the surrounding countryside. A self-guiding brochure is available for 50¢ at the start of the trail. The **Window Trail** is an almost ridiculously short wheelchair accessible ramp that redeems itself with the view at the finish. **The Cliff Shelf Nature Trail** also sells self-guiding brochures (50¢). Half of the trail is wooded and unpaved. Wooden steps connect this less-traveled, tranquil half to the trodden wooden plank path. Not for the weak at heart, the **Notch Trail** demands sure footing and a willingness to climb a shaky ladder at a 45° angle. The trail blazes around narrow ledges before making its way to the grand finale: an unbelievable view of the Cliff Shelf and White River Valley. The short but steep **Saddle Pass Trail**, for more experienced hikers, climbs to the top of the Badlands Wall before connecting with the longer and more level **Castle and Medicine Root Trails.** The gravel **Sage Creek Rim Rd.,** west of Rte. 240, has fewer people and more animals; highlights are **Roberts Prairie Dog Town** and the park's herds of bison and antelope. Across the river from the Sage Creek campground lies another prairie dog town and some popular bison territory. Fresh buffalo chips reveal recent activity. It is easy to lose your bearings in this territory; rangers and maps will help.

RAPID CITY ☎ 605

Rapid City's location makes it a convenient base from which to explore the Black Hills and the Badlands. In summer, the area welcomes 3 million tourists, over 60 times the city's permanent population. If you have a car, pick up a map of the Rapid City Circle Tour at the Civic Center or at any motel; the route leads you to numerous free attractions and includes a jaunt up Skyline Drive for a bird's-eye view of the city and the seven concrete dinosaurs of Dinosaur Park.

■◪ ORIENTATION AND PRACTICAL INFORMATION. Driving in Rapid City is easy; roads are laid out in a sensible grid pattern; **St. Joseph St.** and **Main St.** are the main east-west thoroughfares, and Mt. Rushmore/Rte. 16 is the main north-south route. Many north-south roads are numbered, and numbers go up as you move from east to west. East streets are denoted as such (St. Joseph St. becomes East St. Joseph, etc.). Call ☎ 394-2255 to check on **road conditions** in extreme weather. **Jack Rabbit Lines** scurries east from the Milo Barber Transportation Center, 333 6th St. (☎ 348-3300), downtown, with one bus daily to Pierre (4hr., $65), Sioux Falls (10hr., $114), and Omaha (12hr., $134). **Powder River Lines,** also in the center, runs once per day to Billings (8hr., $57) and Cheyenne (8hr., $65). Station open M-F 8am-5pm, Sa-Su 10am-noon and 2-5pm. **Grayline Tours** lead regional tours based out of Rapid City (see the **Black Hills Region,** p. 553). Take flight from **Rapid City Regional Airport** (☎ 393-9924), off Rte. 44 8½ mi. east of the city. **Rapid Ride** runs **buses** M-F 6:35am-6:05pm. (☎ 394-6631. $1, seniors 50¢. pick up schedule at terminal in the Milo Barber Transportation center.) **Rapid Taxi:** ☎ 348-8080. **Bike Rental: Two Wheeler Dealer,** 100 E. Blvd. N., rents bikes with helmets. (☎ 343-0524. Open M-F 9am-8pm, Sa 9am-5pm, Su noon-4pm. Rentals $16.75 for 5hr. or $27 per day.) **Car Rental: Casey's Car Rentals,** 1318 5th St., has the cheapest rental rates in town. (☎ 800-733-9735. Open M-Sa 9am-5:30pm, Su 11am-2pm. Summer $29.50 per day; off-season $19.50; 150 mi. per day free. $500 credit card or check deposit required. Ages 18-25 extra $5 per day.) **Rapid City Chamber of Commerce and Visitors Information Center:** 444 Mt. Rushmore Rd. N., in the Civic Center (☎ 343-1744; open M-F 8am-5pm). **Rapidcare Health Center:** 408 Knollwood (☎ 341-6600; open M-F 7am-7pm, Sa 9am-4pm, Su 11am-4pm). **Rape and Assault Victims Helpline:** ☎ 341-2046. 24hr. **Black Hills Gay and Lesbian Resource Line:** ☎ 394-8080. M-Sa 6-10pm. **Internet Access:** First come, first served for up to 90min. at Rapid City Public Library, 610 Quincy St. (☎ 394-4171. Open M-Th 9am-9pm, F-Sa 9am-5:30pm; Labor Day to Memorial Day also Su 1-5pm.) **Post Office:** 500 East Blvd., several blocks east of downtown. (☎ 394-8600. Window service M-F 8am-5:30pm, Sa 8:30am-12:30pm.) **ZIP code:** 57701. **Area code:** 605.

HAVE YOU DUG WALL DRUG? There is almost no way to visit the Badlands without being importuned by advertisements from **Wall Drug,** 510 Main St., a towering monument to the success of saturation advertising. (☎ 279-2175. Open daily 6am-10pm; mid-Sept. to Apr. 6:30am-6pm.) After seeing billboards for Wall Drug from as far as Greenland and Amsterdam, Holland, travelers feel obligated to make a stop in Wall to see what all the ruckus is about—much as they must have done 60 years ago, when Wall first enticed parched travelers with free water. The "drug store" itself is now a conglomeration of shops containing Old West memorabilia, kitschy souvenirs, Western books, and numerous photo opportunities with statues of oversized animals; you can even pray for a safe trip at their traveler's chapel. Wall itself is hardly worth a visit. All in all, the town is just another brick in the...oh, never mind.

⌐ ACCOMMODATIONS. Rapid City accommodations are more expensive during the summer. Make reservations; motels often fill weeks in advance, especially during the first two weeks in Aug., when nearby Sturgis hosts its annual motorcycle rally. Winter travelers are in luck because of an abundance of off-season bargains (roughly Labor Day to Memorial Day). **Robert's Roost Hostel,** 627 South St., has the best rates, a great location just a few blocks from downtown, and a social atmosphere. Robert's offers one private room and two single-sex, dorm-style rooms, with kitchen, laundry, and a breezeway with a view of the city. (☎341-3434 or 348-7799. Includes linen and breakfast. Call ahead. No key, door kept unlocked. Dorms $16 per person; private room $25 for one person, $36 for 2, $40 for 3 or more.) **Kings X Lodge,** 525 E. Omaha St., has clean rooms, cable, and free local calls. (☎342-2236. Singles $33; doubles $37-39; less in off-season.) **Big Sky Motel** is located just south of town on a service road off Mt. Rushmore St. (large billboards guide the way). Many rooms have great views, but can be chilly. (☎348-3200 or 800-318-3208. June-Sept. singles $40, doubles $56; less off-season.) **Camping** is available at **Badlands National Park** (p. 550), **Black Hills National Forest** (p. 553), and **Custer State Park** (p. 556).

⌐▨ FOOD AND NIGHTLIFE. Sixth St. Bakery and Delicatessen, 516 6th St., next to the $2 cinema, sells various day-olds for 50¢. The goofy staff makes good sandwiches for $4-5. (☎342-6660. Open M-Sa 6:30am-7pm, Su 10am-2pm; in winter daily 6:30am-5pm.) The cosmopolitan **Once Upon a Vine,** 513 6th St., feels like an art museum cafe. The chef puts together delectable sandwiches ($4.50-5.75) for gourmet tastebuds. The curried chicken salad on hazelnut bread ($4.75) is superb, and you can savor wine, beer, or tea with your meal. (☎343-7802. Open M-Sa 11am-2pm, 5-9pm; F-Sa until 10pm.) The popular **Sirloin and Buffet,** 306 Omaha St., puts out a huge all-you-can-eat buffet, including steak, chicken, and vegetables. Pies, brownies, and sundaes complete the meal—if you've left room. (☎341-6967. Open M-Th 11am-2pm, 5-9pm; F-Sa 11am-2pm, and 4:30-9pm; Su 11am-8pm. Su brunch $7.25; M-F lunch $6, kids $4, dinner $7.69, kids $4. Sa and Su lunch and dinner $8.)

Nightlife lines **Main St.** between 6th and Mt. Rushmore St. For a beer as black as the Hills, toss back a Smokejumper Stout ($3) at the **Firehouse Brewing Co.,** 610 Main St., *the* bar in Rapid City. Located in a restored 1915 firehouse, the company brews five beers in-house and serves sandwiches, burgers, salads ($6-10, a bit pricier at dinner). (☎348-1915. Open M-Th 11am-midnight, F-Sa 11am-2am, Su 4-10pm.) After dinner at the firehouse, head upstairs to **Fat Boys Saloon** for pool, foosball, music, and, well, more beer. (☎348-1915. Open M-Sa 7pm-2am.)

BLACK HILLS REGION ☎605

The Black Hills, named for the dark hue that distance lends the green pines covering the hills, have long been considered sacred by the Sioux. The Treaty of 1868 gave the Black Hills and the rest of South Dakota west of the Missouri River to the tribe. But when gold was discovered in the 1870s, the US government snatched back the land. The dueling monuments of Mt. Rushmore (a national memorial, see p. 554) and Crazy Horse (an independent project, see p. 555) strikingly illustrate the clash of the two cultures that reside among these hills. Today, white residents dominate the area, which contains a trove of natural treasures, including Custer State Park, Wind Cave National Park, and Jewel Cave National Monument.

BLACK HILLS NATIONAL FOREST ☎605

Most the land in the Black Hills is part of the Black Hills National Forest and exercises the "multiple use" principle—mining, logging, ranching, and recreation all take place in close proximity. Don't-miss attractions like reptile farms and Flintstone campgrounds lurk around every bend of the sinuous roads. The forest itself provides opportunities for backcountry hiking and camping, as do park-run campgrounds and private tent sites. In the hills, the **visitors center,** on I-385 at Pactola Lake, has details on backcountry camping and great $6 maps (☎343-8755; open daily May 15 to Oct. 1 8:30am-6pm). **Backcountry camping** in the national forest is free. Camp 1 mi. away from any campground or visitors center and at least 200 ft. off the side of the road (leave your car in a parking lot or pull off); open fires are prohibited, but controlled fires in provided grates are allowed. Good campgrounds include **Pactola,** on the Pactola Reservoir just south of the junction of Rte. 44 and U.S. 385; **Sheridan Lake,** 5 mi. northeast of Hill City on U.S. 385 (north entrance for group sites, south entrance for individuals); and **Roubaix Lake,** 14 mi. south of Lead on U.S. 385 (sites for all three $14). All National Forest campgrounds are quiet and wooded, offering fishing, swimming, and pit toilets, but no hook-ups. (☎877-444-6777. Reservations recommended during peak times.) The national forest extends into Wyoming with a **ranger station** in Sundance (☎307-283-1361; open M-F 7:30am-5pm). The Wyoming side of the forest permits campfires, allows horses, and draws fewer visitors. **Hostelling International Black Hills at the Penny Motel (HI-AYH)** (see **Deadwood,** p. 558) is the cheapest indoor accommodation in the Black Hills area.

I-90 skirts the northern border of the Black Hills from Spearfish in the west to Rapid City in the east; **U.S. 385** twists from Hot Springs in the south to Deadwood in the north. The road system that interconnects through the hills covers beautiful territory, but the roads are difficult to navigate without a good map; pick one up for free almost anywhere in the area. Don't expect to get anywhere fast—these convoluted routes will hold you to half the speed of the interstate.

The off-season in the Black Hills offers stellar skiing and snowmobiling (see **Lead,** p. 557), but many attractions are closed or have limited hours, and most resorts and campgrounds close for the winter. Unless you are astride a flashy piece of chrome and steel, steer clear of the Hills in early Aug., when over 12,000 motorcyclists converge on the area for the **Sturgis Rally** (☎605-347-2556; Aug. 6-12, 2001).

Of the **Grayline tours,** P.O. Box 1106, Rapid City, 57709, tour #1 is the most complete. Make reservations or call 1hr. before departure for pick-up from motels in Rapid City. (☎342-4461. Runs daily mid-May to mid-Oct., 9hr., $34 includes admission prices.) The **Black Hills Visitor Information Center,** Exit 61 off I-90, in Rapid City, has info. (☎355-3700. Open daily 8am-8pm, off-season 8am-5pm; hrs. subject to change.) **Area code:** 605.

MOUNT RUSHMORE   ☎ 605

After all the tourist traps that dot the region, **Mt. Rushmore National Memorial** is refreshingly impressive. South Dakota historian Doane Robinson originally conceived of this "shrine of democracy" in 1923 as a memorial for local Western heroes like Lewis and Clark and Kit Carson; sculptor Gutzon Borglum chose four presidents. Borglum initially encountered opposition from those who felt the work of God could not be improved, but the tenacious sculptor defended the project's size, insisting that "there is not a monument in this country as big as a snuff box." Throughout the Depression work progressed slowly; a great setback occurred when the nearly completed face of Thomas Jefferson had to be blasted off Washington's right side and moved to his left due to insufficient granite. In 1941, the 60 ft. heads of George Washington, Thomas Jefferson, Theodore Roosevelt, and Abraham Lincoln were finished. The 465 ft. tall bodies were never completed, as work ceased when US funds were diverted to WWII, but the millions of visitors who come here every year don't seem to mind the disembodiment.

From Rapid City, take U.S. 16 and 16A to Keystone and Rte. 244 up to the mountain. Remote parking is free, but the lot fills early. There is an $8 per car "annual parking permit" for the lot adjacent to the entrance. The **info center** (☎574-3198) details the monument's history and has ranger tours. A state-of-the-art **visitors center** (☎574-3165) chronicles the history of the monument, the lives of the featured presidents, and shows a film explaining how the carving was accomplished. About 90% of the sculpting was done with dynamite. (Both info center and visitors center open daily June-Aug. 8am-10pm; off-season hrs. generally 8am-5pm.)

From the visitors center, along the **Presidential Trail,** it is 4 mi. and over 100 steps down on a planked wooden path to **Borglum's Studio.** Here visitors can stare at Borglum's full-bodied plaster model of the carving as well as tools and designs for Mt.

Rushmore (open daily May-Sept. 9am-6pm). During the summer, the **Mt. Rushmore Memorial Amphitheater** hosts a monument-lighting program. A patriotic speech and film commence at 9pm, and light floods the monument 9:30-10:30pm. Trail lights are extinguished at 11pm.

The rather commercialized **Mt. Rushmore KOA Palmer Gulch Lodge** lies 5 mi. west of Mt. Rushmore on Rte. 244. With campsites for two ($24, with water and electricity $31) or kabins ($41-47) come showers, stoves, pool, laundry, and free shuttle service to Mt. Rushmore. (☎574-2525 or 800-562-8503. Open May-Oct. Make reservations early, up to 2 months in advance for cabins and special requests.) **Horsethief Campground** lies 4 mi. west of Mt. Rushmore on Rte. 244. More rustic and cheaper than Palmer Gulch, the former President George Bush fished here in 1993; rumor has it that the lake was overstocked with fish to guarantee his success. (☎877-444-6777. Water and flush toilets in the woods. Lakeside sites $18. Sites set back from the lake $16. Reservations recommended on weekends and during peak times.)

CRAZY HORSE MEMORIAL ☎605

If you thought Mt. Rushmore was big, think again. The Crazy Horse Memorial is a wonder of the world in progress; an entire mountain is metamorphosing into a 563 ft. high memorial sculpture of the great Lakota war leader Crazy Horse. When completed, it will be the largest sculpture in the world. A famed warrior, Crazy Horse was revered by many tribes for refusing to sign treaties or live on a government reservation. In 1877, Crazy Horse was treacherously stabbed in the back by a white soldier who was bearing a flag of truce.

The project was initiated by Lakota Chief Henry Standing Bear as a rebuttal to nearby Mt. Rushmore. The memorial also stands as a haunting reminder of the seizure of the Black Hills in the year before Crazy Horse was assassinated; it wasn't the first or last time gold fever glossed over the niceties of US diplomatic decorum. The project began in 1947 and, to no one's surprise, didn't receive any initial government funding. The sculptor, Korczak Ziolkowski, went solo for years, later refusing $10 million in federal funding. Today, his ten children carry on the work. Crazy Horse's completed face was unveiled in June 1998 (all four of the Rushmore heads could fit inside it), and part of his arm is now visible; eventually, his entire torso and head will be carved into the mountain. The memorial, 17 mi. southwest of Mt. Rushmore on U.S. 16/385, includes the Indian Museum of North America, the Sculptor's Studio-Home, and the Native American Educational and Cultural Center where native crafts are displayed and sold. The orientation center shows a moving 17min. video. (☎673-4681; www.crazyhorse.org. Open daily 7am-dark; Oct.-Apr. 8am until dark. Monument lit nightly for 1hr. $8, $19 per carload, $14 with a senior, under 6 free. $2 AAA discount per car. Free coffee at the restaurant.)

WIND CAVE AND JEWEL CAVE ☎605

In the cavern-riddled Black Hills, the subterranean scenery often rivals the aboveground sites. Local entrepreneurs will attempt to lure you into the holes in their backyards, but the government owns the area's prime underground real estate: **Wind Cave National Park** (☎745-4600), adjacent to Custer State Park on U.S. 385, and **Jewel Cave National Monument** (☎673-2288), 13 mi. west of Custer on Rte. 16. There is no public transportation to the caves. Bring a sweater on all tours—Wind Cave remains a constant 53°F, Jewel Cave 49°F. **Area code:** 605.

WIND CAVE. Wind Cave was discovered in 1881 by Tom Bingham, who heard the sound of air rushing out of the cave's only natural entrance. In fact, the wind was so strong it knocked his hat off. Air forcefully gusts in and out of the cave due to outside pressure changes. When Tom returned to show his friends the cave, his hat got sucked in. Today, the amazing air pressure leads scientists to believe that only 5% of the cave's passages have been discovered. Currently, 91 mi. have been explored, and geologists have even found a lake over 200 ft. long within the depths of the cave. Wind Cave is known for its "boxwork," a honeycomb-like lattice of calcite covering its walls. There are five tours; all have more than 150 stairs. The **Garden of**

Eden Tour is the least strenuous. (1hr., 7 per day June-Aug. 8:40am-5:30pm. Call for off-season times. $6, seniors and ages 6-15 $3.) The **Natural Entrance Tour** and the **Fairgrounds Tour** are both moderately strenuous and one or the other leaves about every 30min. (1¼hr. and 1½hr. respectively, June-Aug. 9am-6:30pm. Call for off-season times. $8, seniors and ages 6-16 $4.) Light your own way on the more rigorous **Candlelight Tour**. (Limited to 10 people. 2 hr; 2 per day at 10:30am and 1:30pm, Jun.-Aug.; $9, seniors and kids $4.50. Kids under age 8 not admitted. "Non-slip" soles on shoes required.) The rather difficult **Caving Tour,** an intro to basic caving, is limited to ten people ages 16 and over who can fit through a 10 in. high passageway. (Parental consent required for under 18. 4hr. tour at 1pm. $20, seniors $10. Reservations required.) In the afternoon, all tours fill about 1hr. ahead of time, so buy tickets early (☎ 800-967-2283). **Wind Cave National Park Visitors Center,** RR1, P.O. Box 190, Hot Springs 57747, can provide more info. (☎ 745-4600. Open daily June to mid-Aug. 8am-7:30pm; winter hrs. vary. Tours for the disabled can be arranged.) The **Elk Mountain Campground** rarely fills up during the summer, though it is an excellent site in the woods with potable water and restrooms (sites $10).

JEWEL CAVE. In striking contrast to nearby Wind Cave's boxwork, the walls of this sprawling underground labyrinth (the 2nd longest cave in the US) are covered with a layer of calcite crystal. The ½ mi. **Scenic Tour** includes 723 stairs and a peek at a 27 ft. cave formation that bears a striking resemblance to a strip of bacon. (Leaves roughly every 20min. 8:30am-6pm; in winter call ahead. $8, ages 6-16 $4.) The **Historic Tour** is more interesting. (Every hr. 9am-5pm; in winter call ahead; $8, ages 6-16 $4.) Reservations, pants, a long-sleeve shirt, knee-pads, sturdy boots, and a willingness to get down and dirty are required for the 4hr. **Spelunking Tour,** limited to five people ages 16 and up. (Runs daily June-Aug. 12:30pm. $20; you must be able to fit through an opening only 8½ in. by 2 ft.) The **visitors center** has more info. (☎ 673-2288. Open daily 8am-7:30pm; mid-Oct. to mid-May 8am-4:30pm.) Behind the visitors center, Jewel Cave offers visitors two alluring hiking tails. The **Roof Trail** is only ¼ mi. long, but provides a memorable introduction to the Black Hills' beauty. The bucolic 3½ mi. **Canyons Trail** winds in and around small canyons, through fields, and up forested hills before returning to the visitors center.

NEAR WIND CAVE: HOT SPRINGS

The well-heeled once flocked from the four corners to bathe in the mineral waters of picturesque Hot Springs, located on scenic **U.S. 385.** Still quiet and less crowded than the rest of the Black Hills, the town's charming pink sandstone buildings and budget lodgings make it a nice stop on a tour of the southern Hills.

The Sioux and Cheyenne once fought over possession of the 87°F spring here; in 1890, a public pool was erected at the site. The waterslide at **Evan's Plunge,** on U.S. 385, empties into the world's largest naturally heated pool. The water in the pool is naturally replaced by fresh water 16 times daily, but it still smells like any other crowded public pool. (☎ 745-5165. June-Aug. M-F 5:30am-10pm, Sa-Su 8am-10pm; winter hrs. vary. $8, ages 3-12 $6. Wheelchair accessible.) **Kidney Spring,** just to the right of the waterfall near U.S. 385 and Minnekahta Ave., is rumored to have healing powers. At the **Mammoth Site** on the U.S. 18 bypass, three woolly mammoths and 48 Columbian mammoths fell into a sinkhole and fossilized near Hot Springs about 26,000 years ago. (☎ 745-6017. Open daily 8am-8pm. Last tour 7:15pm. Winter hrs. vary. 30min. tour $5, seniors $4.75, ages 6-12 $3.25.)

CUSTER STATE PARK   ☎ 605

Peter Norbeck, governor of South Dakota in the late 1910s, loved to hike among the thin, towering rock formations that haunt the area south of Sylvan Lake and Mt. Rushmore. In order to preserve the land, he created Custer State Park. The spectacular **Needles Hwy. (Rte. 87)** within the park follows his favorite hiking route (see below). Norbeck designed this road to be especially narrow and winding so that newcomers could experience the pleasures of discovery. Custer's biggest attraction is its herd of **1500 bison,** which can best be seen near dawn or dusk wandering near Wildlife Loop Rd. If you are "lucky," they, along with some friendly burros, will come right up to your car. Don't get out; they are dangerous.

The **entrance fee** is $4 per person, $10 per carload for a seven-day pass from May to Oct. (Nov.-Apr. $2 per person, $5 per car). The **Peter Norbeck Visitors Center**, on U.S. 16A, ½ mi. west of the State Game Lodge, serves as the park's info center. (☎255-4464. Open daily Memorial Day to Labor Day 8am-8pm; early Sept. to Oct. and May 9am-5pm.) Seven **campgrounds** in the park charge $12-16 and have showers and restrooms, but no hook-ups. Primitive camping ($2 per night) is available in the **French Creek Natural Area;** the visitors center can give you more info. Two hundred of the park's 350 sites are reserveable. The entire park fills by early afternoon in the summer. (call ☎800-710-2267 daily Jun.-Sept. 7am-7pm, early Sept. to late May 7am-5pm. $5 non-resident users fee.) The **Elk Mountain Campground** in nearby Wind Cave National Park is an excellent alternative and rarely fills up (see **Wind Cave**, p. 555). Motels in the surrounding area include the clean and friendly **Chalet Motel** on 16A just west of the Stockade Lake entrance to the park. (☎673-2393 or 800-649-9088. Call ahead. Rooms start at $42.) Food and concessions are available at all four park lodges, but the local general stores in Custer, Hermosa, or Keystone generally charge less. **The Bank House**, 548 Mt. Rushmore Rd., serves classic sandwiches ($3-4), and great pie ($3). (☎605-673-5698. Open Oct.-May M-Sa 6am-9pm.)

At 7242 ft., **Harney Peak** is the highest point east of the Rockies and west of the Pyrenees. At the top are a few mountain goats and a great view of the Black Hills. Bring water and food, wear good shoes, and leave as early in the morning as possible. There are more than 30 other trails in the park. You can hike, fish, paddle boats, or canoe at popular **Sylvan Lake,** on Needles Hwy. (Sylvan Lake Resort ☎574-2561; kayak rental $4 per person per 30min.) Horse rides are available at **Blue Bell Lodge,** on Rte. 87 about 8 mi. from the south entrance (☎255-4531, stable 255-4571; 1hr. for $18, under 12 $15). Mountain bikes can be rented at the **Legion Lake Resort,** on U.S. 16A 6 mi. west of the visitors center. (☎255-4521. $8.50 per hour, $36 per day.) All lakes and streams permit fishing with a daily license ($12; 3-day nonresident license $30). Fishing licenses and rental equipment are available at the area lodges. Summer trout fishing is the best. The strong granite of the Needles makes for great rock climbing. For more info contact **Granite Sports/Sylvan Rocks** at the corner of Elm and Main St. in Hill City. (☎574-2121 or 574-2425. Open daily 8:30am-8:30pm; off-season hrs. vary.) **Area code:** 605.

LEAD   ☎605

Lead (rhymes with *bead*, not *bed*) is actually named for the ore veins that marked the path to gold in the mines of this town. The **Open Cut** invites indignation or silent awe; it's a giant hole in the earth created by the **Homestake Mining Company,** 160 W. Main St. Mining ceased here in Sept., 1998, but the giant void remains indefinitely. The company still mines thousands of ft. beneath Lead, and offers interesting surface tours. (☎584-3110. Visitors center open M-F 8am-7pm, Sa-Su 10am-5pm; Sept.-May M-F 8am-5pm. 1hr. hard-hat tours leave every 45min. until 4:30pm. $5.25, students $4.25, seniors $4.75.) The **Ponderosa Mountain Lodge,** on U.S. 14A just outside of Lead heading toward Deadwood, offers a variety of cabins nestled among the pines and stocked with TVs and fridges but no phones. (☎584-3321. From $50-65 depending on season and size.) **Hanna Campground** offers 13 lovely sites about 9 mi. from town off U.S. 85; turn onto the dirt road just south of the junction with 14A at Cheyenne Crossing (pit toilets and water; sites $10). Interesting sandwich combinations ($4.75-9) are the main fare at the **Stampmill Saloon,** 305 W. Main St. (open Su-Th 11am-9pm, F-Sa 11am-10pm).

Wintertime in the Black Hills provides fine skiing and snowboarding opportunities. **Terry Peak Ski Area** and **Deer Mountain** are both west of Lead off U.S. 85. (Terry: ☎584-2165 or 342-7609. Lift ticket $32, under 13 $25, over 69 and under 5 free. Ski rental $18, junior ski rental $12, snowboard rental $25. Deer: ☎800-410-3337 or 584-3230. Lift ticket weekends and holidays $24, children $19. Weekdays $20/$16. Ski rental $15, snowboard rental $22.50.) **Lead Chamber of Commerce,** 640 W. Main St. (☎584-1100. Open M-F 9am-3pm.) **Post Office:** 329 W. Main St. (☎584-2110. Open M-F 8:15am-4:15pm, Sa 10am-noon.) **ZIP code:** 57754. **Area code:** 605.

DEADWOOD   ☎ 605

Continue along Main St. from Lead for 3 mi., and you'll find yourself in Deadwood. Gunslingers **Wild Bill Hickock** and **Calamity Jane** sauntered into this town during the height of the Gold Rush. Bill stayed just long enough—two months—to spend eternity here. They lie side-by-side in the **Mt. Moriah Cemetery,** just south of downtown. (Admission $1, ages 5-12 50¢—is nothing sacred?) If you have a car, take Cemetery St. off of Rte. 85 and follow the signs. Hiking up the hill on foot is quite a challenge, but **Alkali Ike Tours** will take you on their 1hr. narrated bus tour. Tickets are sold at the booth on Main St., just outside Saloon #10. (☎578-3147. Tours July-Aug. at 10am, noon, 2, 4, and 6pm. $6, ages 7-13 $3, under 7 free.) The forever immortalized **Saloon #10,** 657 Main St., is where Hickock was shot holding black aces and eights, the infamous "dead man's hand." Every summer the shooting is re-enacted on location. (☎578-3346. 4 times daily at 1, 3, 5, and 7pm.) At 7:45pm Tu-Su outside of Saloon #10, assassin Jack McCall is apprehended by authorities, and those willing to pay $8 can follow the angry mob to a comical reenactment of **McCall's trial** in the **Old Town Hall,** 12 Lee St. (☎578-3583 for ticket reservations. Pick up reserved tickets at the Old Town Hall, or purchase them at Saloon #10.) If you miss the Hickock saga or just can't get enough of hullabaloo, there are **random shootouts** along Main St. at 2, 4, and 6pm. Listen for gunshots and the sound of Calamity Jane's whip.

If Lead is where the gold is found, then Deadwood is where the gold is lost. It's a challenge to avoid **gambling** entertainment in Deadwood—casinos line **Main St.,** and even the most innocent-looking establishments may hide slot machines within. At the **Buffalo Saloon,** 658 Main St. (☎578-1300), you can gamble 24hr. a day, seven days a week, and there's live music outside the Stockade. For the fun of gambling without the high stakes, many casinos offer nickel slot machines. **Free parking** is available in the Sherman St. parking lot on Rte. 85 heading towards Lead. If you lose most of your money at the gambling tables, you can probably still afford to stay at ▨**Hostelling International Black Hills at the Penny Motel (HI-AYH),** 818 Upper Main St. Look for the Penny Motel sign. A great kitchen, comfortable beds, and super clean rooms await. (☎877-565-8140 or 578-1842. Dorms $12, non-members $15. One private room $24. Motel singles $49; doubles $56.) The **Whistler Gulch Campground,** off U.S. 85, has a pool, laundry facilities, and showers (☎578-2042 or 800-704-7139. Tent sites $17, full hook-up $27.) Food in Deadwood varies as casinos try new hooks—the best deals are advertised on the windows.

The **Deadwood History and Information Center,** 3 Siever St. (☎800-999-1876), is open in summer daily 8am-8pm. **Bike Rentals: Penny Motel.** (See above. $7 per hr., $30 per day. Deposit required.) **Internet access: Biff Malibu's,** 670 Main St. Biff's is the just about the only place in Deadwood *without* slot machines. (☎578-1919. Open daily 5pm until the music ends. $3 per 30min.) **Area code:** 605.

SPEARFISH   ☎ 605

Located on the northwest edge of the Black Hills, Spearfish makes a pleasant, short stop to or from the Black Hills. Nearby, the spectacular **Spearfish Canyon Scenic Byway** (U.S. 14A) winds through 18 miles of forest along Spearfish Creek. Amazing views of the Black Hills, waterfalls, and picnic spots await around every corner of the byway. The site where *Dances with Wolves* was filmed is marked by a small sign and lies 2¾ miles west of U.S. 14A on Rte. 222.

▨ **PRACTICAL INFORMATION.** The **Spearfish Ranger Station,** 2014 N. Main St., has free maps and hiking advice. (☎642-4622. Open M-F 8am-5pm, Sa 8am-4:30pm; in winter M-F 8am-4:30pm; foyer with maps and info open 24hr.) The **Chamber of Commerce:** 106 W. Kansas St., at the corner of Main St. (☎642-2626 or 800-626-8013. Open M-F 8am-7pm, Sa 9am-3pm, Su noon-7pm; Sept.-May M-F 8am-5pm.) **Internet Access: Public Library,** 625 N. 5th St. Sign up for ½hr. time slots. (☎642-1330. Open M-Th 10am-8pm, F 10am-5pm, Sa 9am-5pm.) **Post Office:** 120 Yankee St., north of downtown off North Ave. (☎642-2521. Open M-F 8:30am-4:30pm, Sa 9:30am-noon.) **ZIP code:** 57783. **Area code:** 605.

◨ⵕ FOOD AND ACCOMMODATIONS. The **Canyon Gateway Hotel,** south of town on U.S. 14A, offers cozy rooms in a pleasant setting. (☎ 642-3402 or 800-281-3402. No phones. Singles $40; doubles $43.) The weary traveler can ring in at **Bell's Motor Lodge,** on Main St. at the east edge of town. (☎ 642-3812. Open May-Sept. Free local calls, TV, pool. Singles $36; doubles $48.) Three and four mi. west of U.S. 14A on Rte. 222 are two spectacular campgrounds: **Rod and Gun Campground** (sites $10) and **Timon Campground** (sites $10). Both have pit toilets and potable water. Right in town, at the southern end of Canyon St. two blocks west of Main St., the **Spearfish City Campground** caters to those who want full hook-ups. (☎ 642-1340. Full hook-up $21. Tent site $12 for 1 person, $1 each additional person. Showers 25¢. Reservations needed Sa-Su.) The buffet at the **Pizza Ranch,** 715 Main St., has pizza, pasta, and salad. (☎ 642-4422. Open Su-Th 11am-10pm, F-Sa 11am-11pm. Lunch buffet M-F 11:30am-1:30pm $4.59. Dinner buffet M-F 6-8pm $5.59. M is student discount night.) For authentic English pub fare like chicken and mushroom pie and fish and chips, trot on over to the **Knight's Cellar** on E. Hudson St. There's live music by local artists on W, F, and Sa. (☎ 642-4292. Open daily 4-11pm.)

◧ SIGHTS. There are no trout native to the Black Hills, but you can feed tens of thousands of hatchery-raised fish at the unique **D.C. Booth Historic Fish Hatchery.** View the Booth home, stroll through the manicured gardens, or check out the old railroad "fish car." From Main St., go two blocks west to Canyon and turn south. (☎ 642-7730. Grounds open daily from dawn to dusk. Buildings open May-Sept. M-F 9am-6pm.) Dick Termes paints rotating spheres and calls his work, cleverly enough, Termespheres; more than 30 examples are on display at the **Termesphere Gallery.** From downtown, go south on Main St. and follow it as it becomes Colorado Blvd. Turn right on Christensen Dr. and go about 1½ mi. (☎ 642-4805. Open M-Sa 9am-5pm or just show up; if they're there, they'll let you look.) The **Passion Play Amphitheater** attracts large audiences with the **Passion Play,** which recounts the last week of Jesus's life. The outdoor performance features 23 professional actors, Spearfish townspeople as extras, and live animals like camels and donkeys. (☎ 800-457-0160. Performances every Su, Tu, and Th from the beginning of June to late Aug. Reserved tickets $12-18, unreserved seats $10, under 13 half-price. Tickets are sold only at the amphitheater.)

IOWA

Named for the Ioway Native Americans who farmed by the state's many river banks, Iowa contains one fourth of all US Grade A farmland. Farming truly is the way of life in Iowa, a land where men are measured by the size of their John Deere tractor, not the by kind of car they drive. Besides being fertile, the land is subtly beautiful. Gentle hills roll throughout the state; particularly striking are the Loess Hills in the west. Created by wind-blown quartz silt, these hills are a geological rarity found only in Iowa and China. The Mississippi River Valley in Eastern Iowa is also gorgeous, offering amazing views of the "Big Muddy" from limestone bluffs. Iowa preserves its European heritage in the small towns that maintain their German, Dutch, and Swedish traditions.

◪ PRACTICAL INFORMATION

Capital: Des Moines.

Visitor Info: Iowa Dept. of Economic Development, 200 E. Grand Ave., Des Moines 50309 (☎ 800-345-4692 or 888-472-6035; www.traveliowa.com).

Postal Abbreviation: IA. **Sales Tax:** 5%.

DES MOINES ☎515

Travelers accustomed to large cities may ask, "Did we miss it?" upon entering the Des Moines (*Duh-moyn*) metropolitan area. Still, the downtown area is worth a look—nearly all buildings are linked by the Skywalk, a series of passages above the street. The Skywalk contains offices, hotels, malls, and restaurants, so there's almost no reason to leave. If you do, Des Moines is perhaps better visited for its unique ambiance and cultural events rather than its museums. You can see art anywhere, but how often can you say you've been to the World Pork Expo, where they crown a Pork Queen and host the world's largest barbecue? (June 7-9, 2001 at the Iowa State Fair Grounds.)

▌ GETTING THERE AND GETTING AROUND

Des Moines idles at the junction of I-35 and I-80.

Airport: Des Moines International, Fleur Dr. at Army Post Rd. (☎256-5195), 5 mi. southwest of downtown; take bus #8 "Havens" M-F. Taxi to downtown $7-9.

Buses: Greyhound, 1107 Keosauqua Way (☎243-5283) at 12th St., just northwest of downtown; take bus #4 "Urbandale." To: Iowa City (2hr., 7 per day, $22); Omaha (2hr., 8 per day, $22); and St. Louis (10hr., 5 per day, $64). Station open 24hr.

Public Transportation: Metropolitan Transit Authority (MTA), 1100 MTA Lane (☎283-8100), south of the 9th St. viaduct. Open M-F 8am-5pm. Buses run M-F approximately 6am-10:45pm, Sa 6:45am-5:50pm. Fare $1, seniors (except M-F 3-6pm) and disabled persons 50¢; transfers 10¢. Routes converge at 6th and Walnut St. Maps at the MTA office or any Dahl's or Hy-Vee.

Taxis: Yellow Cab, ☎243-1111.

Car Rental: Enterprise, 5601 Fleur Dr. just outside the airport (☎285-2525), with speedy airport pick-up. $35 with 150 free mi. per day; 25¢ per additional mi. They also offer weekend specials. Must be 21+ with major credit card. No surcharge for under 25. Open M-F 8am-10pm, Sa 9am-3pm, Su 11am-4pm.

✳▌ ORIENTATION AND PRACTICAL INFORMATION

Numbered streets run north-south, named streets east-west. Addresses are zero downtown at the **Des Moines River** and increase as you move east or west; **Grand Ave.** divides addresses north-south. Other east-west thoroughfares are **Locust St.,** and moving north, **University Ave.** (home to Drake University), **Hickman Rd.,** and **Euclid/Douglas Ave.** Note: Des Moines and West Des Moines are different places, and the numbered streets within each are not the same.

Visitor Info: Greater Des Moines Convention and Visitors Bureau, 2 Ruan Ctr., suite 222 (☎286-4960 or 800-451-2625), at 6th and Locust in the Skywalk. Open M-F 8:30am-5pm. Downstairs is the **Chamber of Commerce** (☎286-4950). Open M 9:30am-5pm, Tu-Th 8am-5pm, F 8am-4pm.

Internet Access: Des Moines Public Library, 100 Locust (☎283-4152), and all other branches. Free 1hr. per day. It's best to sign up one day in advance. Open M-W 10am-9pm, Th-F 10am-6pm, Sa 10am-5pm. Su hours vary, call for current schedule.

Post Office: 1165 2nd Ave., downtown just north of I-235. Open M-F 7:30am-5:30pm. **ZIP code:** 50318. **Area code:** 515.

▌ ACCOMMODATIONS

Finding cheap accommodations in Des Moines is usually no problem, though you should make reservations at least one month in advance for visits during the State Fair in Aug. and during the high school sports tournament season in Mar. Beware of the 7% hotel tax. Several campgrounds can be found west of the city off I-80 and cheap motels are sprinkled along I-80 and Merle Hay Rd., 5 mi. northwest of downtown. Take bus #4 "Urbandale" or #6 "West 9th" from downtown.

■ **The Carter House Inn,** 640 20th St. (☎288-7850), at Woodland St. in historic Sherman Hill. The Nelson family has converted this old Victorian home into a beautifully furnished and immaculately clean B&B. A large homecooked breakfast is served on fine china, by candlelight, to classical music. $65-75. Student discounts around 15% can be arranged if extra rooms are available. Call ahead.

Motel 6, 4817 Fleur Dr. (☎287-6364), at the airport, 5min. south of downtown. Newly renovated rooms with free local calls. Singles Su-Th $40, F-Sa $47; doubles Su-Th $46/$53. Two wheelchair-accessible rooms.

Iowa State Fairgrounds Campgrounds, E. 30th St. (☎262-3111 or 800-545-3247; fax 262-6906), at Grand Ave. Take bus #1 "Fairgrounds" to the Grand Ave. gate and follow East Grand Ave. straight east through the park. No fires. Sites with water and electricity $12; full hook-up $15. Fee collected in the morning. Rates go up at fair time in Aug.; make reservations well in advance. Check-in until 10pm. Open mid-Apr. to mid-Oct.

◓ FOOD

Good eating places tend to congregate on **Court Ave.** downtown, or in antique-filled **Historic Valley Jct.** in West Des Moines, on 5th St. south of Grand Ave. The supermarkets **Dahl's** and **Hy-Vee** are sprinkled throughout the city and have cafeterias that serve hot food for cheap. At Dahl's, breakfast is under $2, lunch under $4, dinner under $5. Hy-Vee is just a little more expensive, but they have an all-you-can-eat salad bar ($5). A breakfast buffet ($5) is served at some of the bigger locations on weekends. The popular **Farmer's Market** (☎243-6625) sells loads of fresh fruit and vegetables, baked goods, and ethnic food on Sa mornings (7am-noon mid-May to Nov.) and much of Court Ave. and 4th St. are blocked off for the extravaganza.

■ **Bauder Pharmacy and Fountain,** 3802 Ingersoll (☎255-1124), conveniently located at the corner of 38th and Ingersoll. This old fashioned soda fountain attracts an eclectic local following. Nuns and bikers both agree, "Man, that's good ice cream!" ($1.15 per scoop). Bauder's also sells simple sandwiches for $2-3. Open M-F 8:30am-7pm, Sa 9am-5pm, Su 10am-3pm.

Stella's Blue Sky Diner, 400 Locust St. (☎246-1953), at the Skywalk level in the Capital Sq. Mall. At this 50s-style diner, you can slide into a vinyl booth and enjoy classic diner food with a touch of pizzazz. Spruce up your fries with Stella's jalapeno and cheese "neutron" sauce ($2). A thick malt is the perfect way to end the meal. Open M-F 6:30am-6pm, Sa 8am-6pm. Also at 3281 100th St. in Urbandale (☎278-0550). Open M-Th 10:45am-10pm, F-Sa 10:45am-11pm, Su 10:45am-9pm.

Billy Joe's Pitcher Show, 1701 25th (☎224-1709), off University Ave. in West Des Moines. This combo smoke-filled restaurant and movie theater is a popular date spot for people of all ages. Waitresses serve beer (pitchers $5.75) and assorted grub ($4-10) while you watch the second-run flick on the big screen ($3.50). $2.50 matinees; $1.50 on M, $1.50 on Su with student ID. 4 shows per day, 12:30-9:30pm; experience the *Rocky Horror Picture Show* at midnight on F. Call for exact times.

◓ SIGHTS

LIVING HISTORY FARMS. Ten mi. northwest of downtown in Urbandale, Living History Farms is a 600-acre open-air museum with four working farms and a frontier town, each depicting a different time period from 1700 to the present. Dressed in period garb, the staff milks cows, feeds chickens, sows crops, and interacts with curious visitors. *(2600 NW 111th St. at Hickman Rd. ☎ 278-5286. Open daily May to mid-Oct. 9am-5pm. Last tour 3pm. $8, seniors $7, ages 4-12 $5.)*

STATE CAPITOL. If cities were judged by their capitol buildings alone, Des Moines would be New York. Despite ongoing renovations (until 2002), the copper-and-gold-domed **state capitol** is still breathtaking. From its lofty hilltop position on E. 9th St. across the river and up Locust Ave., the site provides a spectacular view of the Des Moines skyline. Take #1 "Fairgrounds," #4 "E. 14th," or #7 "Walker." *(☎281-5591. Open M-F 8am-5pm, Sa-Su 8am-4pm. Free tours M-Sa 9:30am-2:30pm; call for exact times.)*

BOTANICAL CENTER. The geodesic greenhouse dome of the Botanical Center, just north of I-235 and the capitol, encompasses a desert, rainforest, bonsai exhibit, and various species of birds, fish, and turtles. (909 E. River Dr. ☎ 323-8900. Open M-Th 10am-6pm, F 10am-9pm, Sa-Su 10am-5pm. $1.50, students 50¢, seniors 75¢.)

GRAND AVENUE ATTRACTIONS. Most cultural sights cluster west of downtown on Grand Ave. The intimate **Des Moines Art Center** is composed of three architecturally different buildings. The museum exhibits an interesting collection of African art, gigantic sculptures, and a smattering of paintings by favorites like Picasso, Monet, and Andy Warhol. Take bus #1 "West Des Moines." (4700 Grand Ave. ☎ 277-4405. Open T-W, F-Sa 11am-4pm, Th 11am-9pm, Su noon-4pm. Free.) Behind the Art Center, through the immaculately groomed **Rose Garden,** is **Greenwood Pond,** a rather scummy lagoon. Nonetheless, its creative structures and bridges made of wood and steel make it a worthy place for an afternoon picnic or winter skate. Across from Greenwood Pond, the **Science Center of Iowa** has great exhibits for kids, dazzling laser shows set to popular music, and planetarium spectacles. (4500 Grand Ave. ☎ 274-6868. Open M-Sa 10am-5pm, Su noon-5pm; $5.50, seniors and ages 3-12 $3.50.)

🎵🎭 ENTERTAINMENT AND NIGHTLIFE

The **Civic Center,** 221 Walnut St. (☎ 243-1120), sponsors theater and concerts; call for info. On Th, a copy of the Des Moines *Register* provides "The Datebook," a helpful listing of concerts, sporting events, and movies. *Cityview*, a free local weekly, lists free events and is available at most supermarkets. The **Iowa State Fair,** one of the nation's largest, captivates Des Moines for ten days in mid-Aug. with prize cows, crafts, cakes, and corn (Runs Aug. 9-19, 2001. $7 per day, children over 5 $4; $2 less if purchased in advance). Tickets for **Iowa Cubs** baseball games are a steal. Chicago's farm team plays at **Sec. Taylor Stadium,** 350 SW 1st St. Call for game dates and times. (☎ 243-6111. General admission $5, children $3; reserved grandstand $7, children $5.) From late Apr. to late July, Des Moines flips over for **Seniom Sed;** it attracts the after-work crowd for a city-wide block party held F 6-9pm at Nollen Plaza downtown. (☎ 282-2022. $5, with 3-beverage tickets included.) **Jazz in July** (☎ 280-3222) presents free concerts at locations throughout the city every day of the month; pick up a schedule at area restaurants, concert sites, or the visitors bureau. **Music Under the Stars** (☎ 237-1386) presents free concerts on the steps of the Iowa State Capitol. Performances occur every Su evening at 7:30pm through the end of July.

Court Ave., in the southeast corner of downtown, is a yuppified warehouse district packed with almost-trendy restaurants and bars. At **Papa's Planet,** 208 3rd St., 20- and 30-somethings move to 80s and 90s dance music on two dance floors and listen to classic rock cover bands on the patio outside. (☎ 284-0901. Open Th-Sa 7pm-2am. Live music F-Sa. 25¢ beers on Th with $5 cover; F-Sa cover $3-5 includes drink specials. 21+.) **Java Joe's,** 214 4th St., a mellow coffeehouse with Internet access ($1 for 9½ minutes), sells exotic coffee blends and beer ($2.50-3). Vegetarians will be delighted with the creative array of sandwiches. (☎ 288-5282. Open M-Th 7:30am-11pm, F-Sa 7:30am-1am, Su 9am-11pm.)

🗺 DAYTRIPS FROM DES MOINES

PELLA. Forty-one mi. east of Des Moines on Rte. 163, Pella blooms in May with its annual **Tulip Time** festival, featuring Dutch dancing, a parade, concerts, and *glöckenspiel* performances (☎ 746-3882; May 10-12, 2001). In **Indianola,** 12 mi. south on U.S. 69, the **National Balloon Museum,** 1601 N. Jefferson, holds the annual **National Balloon Classic** in late July for hot-air balloons. (☎ 961-3714. Museum open M-F 9am-4pm, Sa 10am-4pm, Su 1-4pm. Free. Call to arrange a tour; $1, children 50¢.)

WINTERSET. Twenty mi. south of Des Moines is the town of **Winterset,** where John Wayne, the toughest of American film cowboys, was christened Marion Robert Morrison (now there's a name that'll make you tough) in 1907. Wayne's birthplace

> **"CHRIST, WE'RE IN LOVE..."** Winterset happens to be
> the setting for Robert Kincaid and Francesca Johnson's transcendent 4-day love affair
> in the best-selling *Bridges of Madison County*. Robert Waller's romantic novel of adul-
> tery between an Iowa farm wife and an itinerant *National Geographic* photographer
> was decried by the literary establishment, but it sold millions of copies across the
> world. Lines such as, "We have both lost ourselves and created something else, some-
> thing that exists only as an interlacing of the two of us. Christ, we're in love," left critics
> aghast and readers enthralled. The book was made into a film starring Clint Eastwood
> and Meryl Streep, and the movie site is now open for tours. (Open daily May-Oct.
> 10am-6pm. $5, seniors $4, children $3, car tour $4.) Take U.S. 35 S from Des
> Moines, exit at Cummings/Norwalk, and turn right. Follow the signs reading
> "Francesca's House." The bridges themselves are free and located 10-12 mi. beyond.

is just outside of downtown at 216 S. 2nd St. The house has been converted into a
museum, the **John Wayne Birthplace,** with two rooms of memorabilia and two rooms
authentically furnished in the style of the Duke's parents' era. (☎462-1044. Open
daily 10am-4:30pm; $2.50, seniors $2.25, children $1.)

IOWA CITY   ☎319

Iowa City is a classic college town and an oasis of liberalism in a conservative state.
In essence, Iowa city *is* the University of Iowa; the campus fills the city with a
plethora of student bars, frozen yogurt stands, and street musicians. Every other
autumn weekend, hordes of Iowans make a pilgrimage to the city to cheer on the
university's football team, the Hawkeyes. Iowa City's streets are busy with people,
but its carefully tempered vibrancy—this is Iowa, after all—promises a spell of welcome relief from the compulsive fury of big city life.

PRACTICAL INFORMATION. Iowa City is on I-80, 112 mi. east of Des
Moines. North-south **Madison** and **Gilbert St.** and east-west **Market** and **Burlington
St.** bind the downtown. **Greyhound** and **Burlington Trailways** are both located at 404
E. College St. (☎337-2127. Station open M-F 6:30am-8pm, Sa-Su 10am-8pm.)
Buses head out for Des Moines (2-4hr., 9 per day, $22); Chicago (5-6½hr., 7 per
day, $38); and St. Louis (10hr., 1 per day, $62). The free **Cambus** runs daily all over
campus and downtown. (☎335-8633. M-F 5am-midnight, Sa-Su noon-midnight;
summer Sa-Su noon-6pm.) **Iowa City Transit** runs downtown. (☎356-5151. M-F
6:30am-10:30pm and Sa 6:30am-7pm. Fare 75¢, seniors with pass 35¢.) The **convention and visitors bureau,** 408 1st Ave., sits across the river in Coralville off U.S.
6. (☎337-6592 or 800-283-6592. Open M-F 8am-5pm, Sa-Su 10am-4pm.) More area
info is available at the University of Iowa's **Campus Information Center,** in the **Iowa
Memorial Union** at Madison and Jefferson St. (☎335-3055. Open M-F 8am-8pm, Sa
10am-8pm, Su noon-4pm; reduced hrs. in summer and interims.) **Internet access**
is available at the Iowa City Public Library, 123 S. Linn St., free with photo ID as
deposit. (☎356-5200. Open M-Th 10am-9pm, F-Sa 10am-6pm, Su 1-5pm.) **Post
Office:** 400 S. Clinton St. (☎354-1560. Open M-F 8:30am-5pm, Sa 9:30am-1pm.) **ZIP
code:** 52240. **Area code:** 319.

ACCOMMODATIONS AND FOOD. Cheap motels line U.S. 6 in **Coralville,** 2
mi. west of downtown, and **1st Ave.** at Exit 242 off I-80. The cheapest of the bunch is
the **Big Ten Inn,** 707 1st Ave. off U.S. 6. (☎351-6131. Singles $36; doubles $46.) Up the
street at **Motel 6,** 810 1st Ave., rooms are newer and cleaner, and there's a pool.
(☎354-0030 or 800-466-8356. Singles $40; doubles $46.) Six blocks from downtown
is **Haverkamp's Linn Street Homestay,** 619 N. Linn St., an unbeatable value. This bed
and breakfast contains only three rooms, so call ahead. (☎337-4636. Rooms $35/
$45/$50.) **Kent Park Campgrounds,** 9 mi. west on U.S. 6, manages 86 secluded first
come, first served sites pleasantly huddled near a lake. (☎645-2315. Check-in by
10:30pm. $6, with electricity $10.)

Downtown boasts cheerful, moderately-priced restaurants and bars. At the open-air **Pedestrian Mall,** on College and Dubuque St., the melodies of street musicians drift through the eateries and shops and vendors sell food until 3am if demand is strong. **The Airliner,** 22 Clinton St., is Iowa City's oldest restaurant, popular with both faculty and students. (☎338-5463. Kitchen open daily 11am-10pm; bar open until 2am. Pizza slices $2.25, Su $1.25; entrees $5-9.) The super cheap but tasty **Panchero's,** 108 Washington St. (☎338-6311), whips up several types of decent-sized quesadillas ($3.45), tacos ($3.45), and burritos ($4.50) in homemade tortillas. **Masala,** 9 S. Dubuque St. (☎338-6199), Iowa city's award winning vegetarian Indian restaurant, presents a lunch buffet ($6.25) and offers mango and pistachio ice cream for dessert ($2). Student discounts are given. At downtown's Swan Parking Ramp, folks find the **Iowa City Farmers Market,** Gilbert and Washington St. (☎356-5110. Open May-Oct. W 5:30-7:30pm, Sa 7:30-11:30am.)

🖼 **SIGHTS.** The **Old Capitol** building between Clinton and Madison St. is the focus of the **Pentacrest,** a formation of five university buildings. The gorgeous Capitol was restored with much attention to detail. (☎335-0548. Open M-Sa 10am-3pm, Su noon-4pm.) More quirky is the **Museum of Natural History** in the Pentacrest building at Jefferson and Clinton St. Its dioramas on the Native Americans of Iowa are well-presented, and the stuffed birds of prey and the giant sloth (the size of a small car!) shouldn't be missed. (☎335-0482. Open M-Sa 9:30am-4:30pm, Su 12:30-4:30pm. Free. Wheelchair accessible.) In West Branch, 15min. northeast of the city (Exit 254 on I-80; follow signs) lies the 31st President's birthplace, now known as the **Herbert Hoover National Historic Site.** The vintage American town chronicles this fascinating man's life with his birthplace cottage, the presidential library/museum, and a ½ mi. trail through restored prairie that leads to his gravesite. (☎643-2541. Open daily 9am-5pm; $2, seniors $1, under 16 free. Wheelchair accessible.)

🎵 **NIGHTLIFE.** Nightspots are plentiful downtown. **Deadwood,** 6 S. Dubuque St. (☎351-9417), is often lauded as the city's best bar. For live music running the gamut of musical tastes visit **Gabe's,** 330 E. Washington St. (☎354-4788. Cover $5-10.) Local jazz, folk, and blues musicians play Th-Sa at 9:30pm in **The Sanctuary,** 405 S. Gilbert St., a cozy, wood-paneled restaurant and bar with 120 beers. (☎351-5692. Open M-Sa 4pm-2am, Su 4pm-2am. Closes earlier in summer. Cover $1-4.) **The Union Bar,** 121 E. College St., brags that it's the "biggest damn bar in college football's 'Big Ten.'" (☎339-7713. Open Tu-Sa 8pm-2am. Cover varies.) From May-Aug. in the Pedestrian Plaza downtown, the **Friday Night Concert Series** (☎354-0863; 5-9pm) features everything from jazz to salsa to blues..

SCENIC DRIVE: GREAT RIVER ROAD

With its winding roads, steep bluffs, and breathtaking views of the Mississippi River, the Great River Road defies all stereotypes of Iowa's terrain. This is perhaps Iowa's most beautiful country, and for those who've never seen the great Mississippi in all her majesty, the Great River Road grants an excellent introduction. Graced with lush vegetation, interesting nature sights, tiny historic towns, and lots of roadkill, this roadtrip offers something for everyone. The trip is 62 mi. and best experienced spring through fall.

FIELD OF DREAMS Movie buffs and baseball fanatics alike may want to go the distance to the **Field of Dreams** in Dyersville, where the movie *Field of Dreams* was shot. (☎800-443-8981. Open Apr.-Nov. Free.) In the film, mysterious voices direct a farmer (played by Kevin Costner) to build a baseball field amidst Iowa's acres of corn. In doing so, the farmer is able to exorcise his demons. The folks there will provide you with bats, balls, and gloves at no cost so you can try to hit one into the stands, er, stalks. Dyersville is about 25 mi. west of Dubuque in northeast Iowa. Take Rte. 20 west from Dubuque to Rte. 136 N; go right after the railroad tracks for 3 mi.

The Great River roadtrip begins in **Dubuque,** Iowa's oldest city, on Rte. 52 N. Dubuque is a rather unattractive industrial city, but is quickly left behind. In the small town of **Sageville,** turn onto Country Road C9Y heading north. On C9Y the going gets a bit tough. Gas stations are few and far between, portions of the road are unpaved, and you're likely to be the only car on the road. But the relative isolation affords the perfect opportunity to leisurely enjoy the corn stalks, groomed fields, and silos that line the road. In **Millville,** pick up Rte. 52 north again to the town of **Guttenberg.** This historic river town is the home to **Lock and Dam No. 10,** and the path to the river from Rte. 52 is marked by signs. Hungry travelers can find gourmet sandwiches ($3.75-5) at the sassy **Guttenberg Bakery and Cafe,** 422 S. River Park Dr. but "If you are grouchy, irritable, or just plain mean, there will be a $10 charge just for putting up with you." ($3.5. ☎ 319-252-2225. Open Tu-Sa 6am-2pm, Su 7am-1pm.) The park that stretches along the river is the perfect place to picnic.

Follow green Great River Rd. signs to navigate your way out of Guttenberg onto Rte. X56. Where X56 becomes Rte. 340 lies **Pike's Peak Park,** offering campgrounds, hiking trails, and mountain biking. (☎ 319-873-2341. Sites $9, with electricity $12.) To finish the drive, pick up Rte. 340 north and pass through **McGregor.** The quiet town features a small-town commercial strip, reminiscent of the time before malls destroyed the quintessential American downtown. The journey officially ends in Marquette, but 3 mi. away on Rte. 18, **Effigy Mounds National Monument** fascinates visitors with 191 mysterious mounds of earth (see p. 524).

SPIRIT LAKE AND OKOBOJI   ☎ 712

Not to be outdone by its neighbors, Iowa, too, has its Great Lakes: Spirit Lake, West Okoboji Lake, and East Okoboji Lake, all popular vacation destinations. West Okoboji Lake ranks with Switzerland's Lake Geneva and Canada's Lake Louise as one of the world's three blue-water lakes.

◪ PRACTICAL INFORMATION. A handful of towns are scattered around the lakes, and several highways criss-cross the area. U.S. 71 runs between West and East Okoboji Lakes, through Okoboji and Arnold's Park. Rte. 86 skirts the side of West Okoboji Lake, and Rte. 276 lines the western half of Spirit Lake. The **Iowa Great Lakes Chamber of Commerce,** at the **Iowa Welcome Center** just through the gate to the amusement park, overflows with info about the area. (☎ 322-2107 or 800-839-9987. Open M-F 9am-5pm, Sa 10am-2pm.) **Area code:** 712.

▓ ACCOMMODATIONS AND FOOD. Budget accommodations in the immediate lake area are as scarce as snowballs in hell—especially in summer, when prices rise. To stay indoors for cheap, head 15 mi. south on U.S. 71 to Spencer. **The Northland Inn,** at the convergence of Rte. 9 and Rte. 86 just north of West Okoboji Lake, offers wood-paneled rooms and a continental breakfast. (☎ 336-1450. May-Sept., 1 bed for 1-2 people $55, 2 beds for up to 4 people $65; Oct.-Apr. 1 bed $30, 2 beds $40.) Pitch your tent year-round at tranquil **Marble Beach Campground** in the state park on the shores of Spirit Lake. (☎ 336-4437, in winter ☎ 337-3211. Sites $9, full hook-up $12.) Other camping options include **Emerson Bay** ($9, $13 with electricity) and **Gull's Point** ($9/$12) both off Rte. 86 on West Okoboji Lake. The **Koffee Kup Kafe,** off U.S. 71 in Arnold's Park, is a kozy place with kountry kooking. Try the delicious pancakes ($1-3), or order a sandwich ($3.25-5.25). Breakfast is served all day. (☎ 332-7657. Open daily 6am-2pm.) **Tweeter's,** also off U.S. 71 in Okoboji, is a local lunch favorite that grills burgers ($5), tosses salads, and melts sandwiches. (☎ 332-9421. Open 11am-midnight, in winter 11am-11pm. Bar open 10pm-2am.)

☎ SIGHTS. One block west of the amusement park (see below) is **Abbie Gardner Historic Log Cabin.** (☎ 332-7248. Open Memorial Day to Sept. 30 M-F noon-4pm, Sa-Su 9am-4pm. Free, but donation suggested.) The museum presents an unbiased 13min. video explaining the unfurling of the dispute between encroaching settlers and members of the Sioux that led to the Spirit Lake Massacre in March 1857. It's hard to miss the **amusement park** in Arnold's Park, off Rte. 71, with a roller coaster, kiddie rides, and ice cream shops. (☎332-2183 or 800-599-6995. Hrs. vary. $14 with rides, children 3-4 ft. tall $10, under 3 ft. free; $5 without rides.) The park's **Roof Garden** plays open air concerts (call for info). You can hike, in-line skate, or bike **The Spine**, a 14½ mi. trail that runs through the area; bike rental ($10 per day) is available at **Allan's Hardware,** on Rte. 71 (☎332-7131).

NEBRASKA

Travelers rush through Nebraska toward the West, but those who stop for a breather are rewarded. The Nebraskan prairie—the little that hasn't been turned into farmland—is astoundingly beautiful in its stark nothingness; early pioneers once called this land the "Great American Desert," mistakenly believing that if trees did not grow here, neither would crops. Visitors to the state are constantly reminded of the state's pioneer heritage and the continuing importance of agriculture and farming. Although Nebraska lacks a cosmopolitan air—even in Omaha and Lincoln—its midwestern flavor is unmistakably unique and worth experiencing.

◪ PRACTICAL INFORMATION

Capital: Lincoln.
Visitor Info: Nebraska Tourism Office, P.O. Box 94666, Lincoln 68509 (☎402-471-3796 or 800-228-4307; www.visitnebraska.org). Open M-F 8am-5pm. **Nebraska Game and Parks Commission,** 2200 N. 33rd St., Lincoln 68503 (☎402-471-0641). Open M-F 8am-5pm.
State Soft Drink: Kool-Aid. **Postal Abbreviation:** NE. **Sales Tax:** 5-6.5%, depending on city.

OMAHA   ☎402

Frankly, Omaha makes a lousy first impression. The outskirts of the sprawling city are lined with unattractive buildings, warehouses, and highway overpasses. But once within the heart of the city, Omaha exudes charm and a surprisingly comfortable ambiance. The Old Market in downtown Omaha lures visitors with its quiet sidestreet cafes, trendy restaurants, and relatively stimulating nightlife. In addition to its downtown, Omaha also prides itself on a number of popular tourist attractions, including a world-class zoo.

▐ GETTING THERE AND GETTING AROUND

Trains: Amtrak, 1003 S. 9th St. (☎342-1501), at Pacific St. To Chicago (9¾hr., 1 per day, $100) and Denver (8hr., 1 per day, $100). Open nightly 10:30pm-7:30am, Sa-Su also from 7:30am-4pm.
Buses: Greyhound, 1601 Jackson (☎341-1906). To: Des Moines (2-2½hrs, 3 per day, $22); Cheyenne (9½hrs., 2 per day, $72); and Lincoln (1hr., 4 per day, $11.50). Open 24hr.
Public Transportation: Metro Area Transit (MAT), 2222 Cumming St. (☎341-0800). Open M-F 8am-4:30pm. Schedules available at Park Fair Mall, at 16th and Douglas St. near the Greyhound station, and the library,14th and Farnam St. Fare 90¢, transfers 5¢.
Taxis: Happy Cab (☎339-0110).

◪ ORIENTATION AND PRACTICAL INFORMATION

Omaha rests on the west bank of the Missouri River, brushing up against Iowa's border. While it wears a facade of geometric order, Omaha is actually an imprecise grid of numbered streets (running north-south) and named streets (east-west). **Dodge St.** (Rte. 6) divides the city west. **I-80** runs across the southern half of town and intersects with **I-480/Rte. 75** (the Kennedy Expwy.), which leads to nearby Bellevue. **I-29,** just over the river in Iowa, will take you north to Sioux City or south to Kansas City. *At night, avoid N. 24th St.*

Visitor Info: Visitors Center/Game and Parks Commission, 1212 Bob Gibson Blvd. (☎595-3990), get off I-80 at 13th St. Open daily 9am-5pm. **Greater Omaha Convention and Visitors Bureau,** 6800 Mercy Rd., suite 202 (☎800-332-1819), at the Ak-Sar-Ben complex off S. 72 St. north of I-80. Open M-F 8am-4:30pm. **Events Hotline,** ☎444-6800.

Hotlines: Rape Crisis, ☎345-7273. 24hr. **First Call for Help** for information and referrals, ☎444-6666, M-F 8am-5pm.

Hospital: Methodist Hospital, 8303 Dodge St. (☎354-4434), 84th and Dodge. **Women's Services,** 201 South 46th St., one block south of Dodge St. (☎554-0110).

Internet Access: Omaha Public Library, 215 S. 15th St. (☎444-4800), between Douglas and Farnham. Open M-Th 9am-9pm, F-Sa 9am-5:30pm, Su 1-5pm. Free.

Post Office: 1124 Pacific St. Open M-F 7:30am-6pm, Sa 7:30am-noon. **ZIP code:** 68108. **Area code:** 402.

ACCOMMODATIONS

Budget motels in Omaha proper are not particularly budget-friendly. For better deals, head for the city outskirts or across the river into Council Bluffs, Iowa.

YMCA, 430 S. 20th St. (☎341-1600). Clean, single rooms with phones (no long-distance). $5 per day for use of on-site facilities. 4th fl., men only (common bathroom) $11. Other rooms (with individual bathrooms) $12.23. Free parking.

Satellite Motel, 6006 L St. (☎733-7373), just south of I-80 Exit 450 (60th St.). A round 2-story building with lots of personality. Clean, wedge-shaped rooms equipped with fridge, microwave, coffee-maker, and TV. In winter singles $36-40, doubles $46-48; in summer $38-40/$46-48.

Haworth Park Campground (☎291-3379 or 293-3098), in Bellevue on Payne St. at the end of Mission St. Take the exit for Rte. 370 E. off Rte. 75, turn right onto Galvin St., left onto Mission St., and right onto Payne St. just before the toll bridge. Tent sites are far enough away from the RV area to tone down the trailer-park feel although the setting of the campgrounds isn't particularly beautiful. Sites $5, with hook-up $10. Showers, toilets, shelters. Open daily 6am-10pm; stragglers can enter after hrs. Check-out 3pm.

FOOD FOR THOUGHT

It's no fun being a chicken, cow, or vegetarian in Omaha, with a fried chicken joint on every block and a steakhouse in every district. Once a warehouse area, the brick streets of the **Old Market,** on Jackson, Howard, and Harney St. between 10th and 13th, now feature popular shops, restaurants, and bars. The **farmers market,** 11th and Jackson St. (☎345-5401), is held on Sa 8am-12:30pm from mid-May to mid-Oct. and on W 5:30-8pm from mid July to mid-Aug.

McFoster's Natural Kind Cafe, 302 S. 38th St. (☎345-7477), at Farnam St. Housed in a unique, castle-like building, McFoster's sells healthy dishes ($4-13), including free-range chicken, vegan eggplant parmesan, and artichoke specialties. Open M-Th 11am-10pm, F-Sa 11am-11pm, Su 10am-3pm. 1st fl. wheelchair accessible.

The Diner, 409 S. 12 St. at Harney (☎341-9870), is as straight-forward as its name suggests. It's not one of those chains that tries to recreate the 50s; it really is lost in the 50s. Good homemade food at really good prices. (Everything on the menu under $6, most breakfast $2-4, lunch $3-5.) Open M-Sa 6am-4pm.

Délice European Cafe, 1206 Howard St. (☎342-2276), in the Old Market., sells scrumptious pastries and deli fare ($2-6) in a light, spacious setting. They also serve wine and beer to help make your meal appropriately European. Ask about availability of day-old baked goods. Open M-Th 7:30am-10pm, F-Sa 7:30am-11pm, Su 7:30am-7pm.

Upstream Brewing, 514 S. 11th St. (☎344-0200), at Jackson St. Creative entrees ($9-18) can be enjoyed inside, out on the patio, or on the roof-top deck. Pizza and burgers $6-8. Features 8 home brewed beers. Seasonal brews, such as raspberry beer, are particularly good. Bar open M-Sa until 1am, Su until midnight.

SIGHTS

ART. Within a monumental Art Deco artifice, Omaha's **Joslyn Art Museum** displays a decent collection of 19th- and 20th-century European and American art. The exterior is pink Georgian marble; the interior dazzles with 30 different types of stone. From mid-July to mid-Aug., the museum hosts free "Jazz on the Green" concerts each Th 7:30-9pm. *(2200 Dodge St. ☎342-3300. Open Tu-Sa 10am-4pm, Su noon-4pm. $5, seniors and college students $3, ages 5-17 $2.50, free Sa 10am-noon.)*

ZOO. One of the largest indoor jungles in the nation, complete with monkeys, low-flying bats, and exotic birds, has made the **Henry Doorly Zoo** the #1 tourist attraction between Chicago and Denver. *(3701 S. 10th St. ☎733-8401. Exit at 13th St. off I-80, at Bert Murphy Blvd. Open M-Sa 9:30am-5pm, Su 9:30am-6pm; early Sept. to late May daily 9:30am-5pm. $7.75, seniors $6.25, children $4.)*

SAC. See the gargantuan remnants of US air power of the last half-century in an equally enormous **Strategic Air Command Museum.** The museum displays various military aircraft, including a B-52 bomber, as well as many different exhibits on military history. Particularly interesting is the model 50s bomb shelter and its provisions. *(☎800-358-5029. Adjacent to Mahoney Park, off route I-80 between Omaha and Lincoln. Open daily 9am-5pm. $6, seniors and military $5, children $3.)*

SAFARI. Just down the road is the **Simmons Wildlife Safari Park.** Just like Jurassic Park, except instead of dinosaurs, drive your all-terrain vehicle (or beat-up Chevette) 4½ mi. through a nature preserve with bison, pronghorns, and other beasts roaming inside. *(☎944-9453. Open Apr.-Oct. 9:30am-5pm. $4, seniors $3.50, children $2. Guided tram runs every hr. on the hr.)*

ENTERTAINMENT AND NIGHTLIFE

At I-80 and 13th St. (across the street from the zoo) is **Johnny Rosenblatt Stadium,** where you can watch the minor league **Omaha Golden Spikes** battle opponents from Apr. to early Sept. (☎734-2550. General admission $4. Box seat $6-8. $1 off all tickets for high school students and seniors. Wheelchair accessible.) The stadium also hosts the College Baseball World Series in June. In late June and early July, **Shakespeare on the Green** stages free performances in Elmwood Park, on 60th and Dodge St. (☎280-2391. Th-Su 8:30pm.)

Punk and progressive folk have found a niche at the several area universities; check the window of the **Antiquarian Bookstore,** 1215 Harney, in the Old Market, for the scoop on shows. Several good bars await nearby. **The Dubliner,** 1205 Harney, below street level, stages live traditional Irish music on F and Sa evenings (☎342-5887; cover $2-3). The **13th Street Coffee Company,** 519 13th St., sells interesting coffee concoctions. The Mexican latte—chocolate, orange, cinnamon, steamed milk, a double shot, and whipped cream—is particularly rich and tasty. Live music plays F at 9pm, with no cover. (☎345-2883. Open M-Th 6:30am-10pm, F 6:30am-midnight, Sa 8am-11pm, Su 9am-10pm.)

One of the most popular gay bars in the state, **The Max,** 1417 Jackson (a brown building with no sign outside), caters to men and women with 5 bars, a disco dance floor, DJ, fountains, patio, and a leather bar. (☎346-4110. Open daily 4pm-1am. Happy hour 4-7pm. Cover F-Sa $3.) For country tunes and line dancing, dig out your cowboy boots and head to **Guitars and Cadillacs,** 10865 W. Dodge Rd. On F and Sa the club hosts after-hours dancing (1-3am) for those 18 and over. (☎333-5500. Open Tu-W 7pm-1am, Th 8pm-1am, F 6pm-3am, Sa 7pm-3am, and Su 6pm-1am.)

LINCOLN   ☎402

Lincoln's impressively clean streets are ordered alphabetically; it's a hint—don't expect "named street" sophistication in this very down-to-earth city. The University of Nebraska campus lies in the heart of the city, and the students and football team, the Cornhuskers, are a significant town presence. The Sabbath happens to arrive a day early in Lincoln: on game days, businesses shut down and locals gnash their teeth in communal woe after every loss. Aside from football, Lincoln is also known for its breathtaking capitol, the "Tower on the Plains," which houses the only unicameral (one-house) state legislature in the US and pays homage to the state's vital tradition of agriculture.

▐ GETTING THERE AND GETTING AROUND

Airport: Lincoln Airport (☎474-2770), 5 mi. northwest of downtown on Cornhusker Hwy., or take Exit 399 off I-80. Taxi to downtown $14.

Trains: Amtrak, 201 N. 7th St. (☎476-1295). Once daily to: Omaha (1hr., $8-15); Denver (7½hr., $65-115); and Chicago (11hr., $67-120). Prices vary with availability. Some seasonal specials. Open M-W 7:30am-4pm and daily 11:30pm-7am.

Buses: Greyhound, 940 P St. (☎474-1071), close to downtown and city campus. To: Omaha (1 hr., 4 per day, $11.50); Chicago (11-14hr., 5 per day, $46); Kansas City (6½-8½hr., 2 per day, $48.50); and Denver (33hr., 1 per day, $118). Open M-F 6:30am-6:00pm, Sa 9:30am-6:00pm. On Su, meet the bus at departure time.

Public Transportation: Star Trans, 710 J St. (☎476-1234). Schedules are available on the bus, at many downtown locations, and at the office. Buses run M-Sa 6am-6pm. Fare 85¢, seniors 40¢, ages 5-11 50¢.

Taxis: Yellow Cabs, ☎477-4111.

Car Rental: U-Save Auto Rental, 101 W. O St., (☎477-5236). $12 per day with 100 free mi.; 10¢ per additional mi. Must be 21+. $100 deposit. Open daily 7:30am-5:30pm.

▐ ORIENTATION AND PRACTICAL INFORMATION

Lincoln is easily navigated. Numbered streets increase as you go east; lettered streets progress through the alphabet as you go north. **O St.** is the main east-west drag. It becomes Cornhusker Hwy. (U.S. 6) if you head west of the city and Hwy. 34 if you're heading east. **R St.** runs along the south side of the **University of Nebraska-Lincoln (UNL)** city campus.

Visitor Info: Visitors Center, 201 N. 7th St. in the Haymarket district (☎434-5348 or 800-423-8212). Open M-F 9am-8pm, Sa 8am-5pm, Su noon-5pm; in winter M-F 9am-6pm, Sa 10am-4pm, Su noon-4pm. **Lincoln Convention and Visitors Bureau,** P.O. Box 83737, Lincoln, 68501 (☎434-5335; www.lincoln.org/cvb).

Hotlines: Personal Crisis Line, ☎475-5171. **University of Nebraska Gay/Lesbian/Bisexual/ Transgender Resource Center,** ☎472-5644 (inactive in summer).

Quadratic Formula: $(-b \pm \sqrt{b^2-4ac})/2a$.

Internet Access: Lincoln Public Library, 136 S. 14th St. at N St. (☎444-8500). Open M-Th 9am-9pm, F-Sa 9am-6pm, Su 1:30pm-5:30pm. 45min. sessions. Free.

Post Office: 700 R St. Open M-F 7:30am-6pm, Sa 9am-1pm. **ZIP code:** 68501. **Area code:** 402.

▐ ACCOMMODATIONS

There are few inexpensive motels downtown; most lie east of the city center around the 5600 block of Cornhusker Hwy. (U.S. 6). The **Cornerstone Hostel (HI-AYH),** 640 N. 16th St., at U St. just south of Vine St., is conveniently located in a church basement in the university's downtown campus and rarely fills up. There's not much of an atmosphere, but for the price and location, it can't be beat. (☎476-0355 or 476-0926. Two single-sex rooms; 5 beds for women, 3 for men. Full kitchen and laundry facilities. Curfew 11pm. Dorms $10, non-members $13. Free parking and linen.) The **Great Plains Budget Host Inn,** 2732 O St., has large rooms with fridges. Take bus #9 "O St. Shuttle." (☎476-3253 or 800-288-8499. Free parking and kitchenettes available. Singles $42; doubles $46-50.) The **Nebraska State Fair Park Campground,** 2400 N. 14th St. at Cornhusker, is conveniently located but next to a highway and train tracks; take bus #7 "Belmont."

(☎473-4287. Open Mar.-Oct. Sites for 2 $14, with electricity $16, full hook-up $18; $1 per additional person. Fills up early in Aug., but no reservations accepted.) To get to the more pleasant **Camp-A-Way**, 1st and Superior St., take Exit 401 or 401a from I-80, then Exit 1 on I-180/Rte. 34. Lots of trees, but a bit out of the way, and also next to a highway. (☎476-2282. Reservations recommended during fair time in Aug. Showers, laundry, pool, and convenience store. Sites $14, water and electricity $18.50, full hook-up $22.)

FOOD AND NIGHTLIFE

Historic Haymarket, 7th to 9th and O to R St., is a renovated warehouse district near the train tracks, with cafes, bars, several restaurants, and a **farmers market.** (☎435-7496. Open mid-May to mid-Oct. Sa 8am-noon.) All downtown buses connect at 11th and O St., two blocks east of Historic Haymarket. Every renovated warehouse district has its yuppie brewery; **Lazlo's Brewery and Grill,** 710 P St., is the oldest one in Nebraska, founded in 1991. The oatmeal stout is excellent, and you can fill up with salads, sandwiches, and meat entrees for $5-15. (☎434-5636. Open M-Sa 11am-1am, Su 11am-10pm. Wheelchair accessible.) Right next door, **Ja Brisco,** 700 P St., serves pizzas, pasta, and deli sandwiches ($6-10) that are sure to please. (☎434-5644. Open daily 11am-10:30pm. Wheelchair accessible.) **Valentino's,** 232 N. 13th St., a regional chain with roots in Lincoln, offers pasta ($5-7) and six different all-you-can-eat buffets. (☎475-1501. Open Su-Th 11am-10pm, F-Sa 11am-11pm. $6, after 4pm $8. F and Sa 9:30-11pm pizza $3, $1 draughts and $3 pitchers.)

Nightspots abound in Lincoln, particularly those of the sports-bar variety. For the biggest names in Lincoln's live music scene, try the suitably dark and smoky **Zoo Bar,** 136 N. 14th St. Cover varies, as does the music, but the emphasis is on blues. (☎435-8754. Open M-Sa 3pm-1am, and some Su if there's a show. 21+.) **Q,** 226 S. 9th St. between M and N, is a great gay/lesbian bar with a large dance floor. (☎475-2269. Open Tu-Su 8pm-1am. 19+ on Tu.) For the best of the college sports bar genre, head to **Iguana's** at 1426 O St. (☎476-8850. Open M-Th and Sat 6pm-1am and F 3pm-1am. Happy hour 3-7pm on F with free appetizers.)

SIGHTS

The "Tower on the Plains," the 400 ft. **Nebraska State Capitol Building** at 14th and K St., an unofficial architectural wonder of the world, wows with its streamlined exterior and detailed interior, highlighted by a beautiful mosaic floor. (☎471-0448. Open M-F 8am-5pm, Sa 10am-5pm, Su 1-5pm. Free, enthusiastically led 30min. tours are given every 30min. M-F in summer, every hr. Sa-Su.) The **Museum of Nebraska History** on Centennial Mall, a renamed portion of 15th St., has a phenomenal collection of headdresses, moccasins, jewelry, and other beautiful artifacts in its exhibit on the Plains Indians. (☎471-4754. Open M-F 9am-4:30pm, Sa 9am-5pm, Su 1:30-5pm. Free.) The **University of Nebraska State Museum,** 14th and U St., in Morrill Hall, boasts an amazing fossil collection that includes the largest mounted mammoth in any American museum. (☎472-6302. Open M-Sa 9:30am-4:30pm, Su 1:30-4:30pm. Requested donation $2.) In the same building, the **Mueller Planetarium** lights up the ceiling with several shows daily and laser shows several days a week. (☎472-2641. Closed on home game days. Planetarium $4; students, seniors, and under 13 $3. Laser shows $5, with college ID $4, under 12 $3.)

In addition to livestock, crafts, and fitter family contests, the **Nebraska State Fair** offers car races, tractor pulls, and plenty of rides to please all comers. It lasts 11 days in late Aug. and early Sept. (☎473-4109. $5.)

Pioneers Park, ¼ mi. south off W. Van Dorn on Coddington St. (watch for the signs along Van Dorn), is great for a real prairie picnic. The Pioneer Park Nature Center harbors bison and elk within its sanctuary and is also the starting point for 5 mi. of trails. (3201 S. Coddington Ave. ☎441-7895. Open M-Sa 8:30am-8:30pm, Su noon-8:30pm; Sept.-May M-Sa 8:30am-5pm, Su noon-5pm. Free. Wheelchair accessible.)

CARHENGE OR BUST Everything looks the same as you drive through the low plains and small bluffs of western Nebraska, until, suddenly, a preternatural power sweeps the horizon and the ultimate shrine to bizarre on-the-road Americana springs into view—Carhenge. Consisting of 36 old cars painted gray, this oddly engaging sculpture has the same orientation and dimensions as Stonehenge in England. When asked why he built it, the artisan Reinders replied, "plane, loqui deprehendi," or, "clearly, I spoke to be understood." This wonder of the cornhuskers can be found right off 385, 2 mi. north of Alliance, NE, which is 60 mi. northwest of Scotts Bluff. (☎800-738-0648. Open daily 24hrs.)

SCOTTS BLUFF   ☎308

Known to the Plains Indians as "Ma-a-pa-te" ("hill that is hard to go around"), the imposing clay and sandstone highlands of **Scotts Bluff National Monument** were landmarks for people traveling the Mormon and Oregon Trails in the 1840s. For some time the bluff was too dangerous to cross, but in the 1850s a single-file wagon trail was opened just south of the bluff through narrow **Mitchell's Pass,** where traffic wore deep marks in the sandstone. Evidence of the early pioneers can still be seen today on the ½ mi. stretch of the original **Oregon Trail** preserved at the pass; tourists can gaze out at the distant horizons to the east and west as pioneers once did. The **visitors center,** at the entrance on Rte. 92, will tell you of the mysterious death of Hiram Scott, the fur trader who gave the Bluffs their name. Don't miss the 12min. slide show. (☎436-4340. Open daily 8am-8pm; in winter 8am-5pm. $5 per carload, $2 per motorcycle.) To get to the top of the bluffs, hike challenging **Saddle Rock Trail** (1½ mi. each way) or motor up **Summit Dr.** At the top, you'll find two short **nature trails.** Guides are available at the trailheads for 25¢. The **North Overlook** is a ½ mi. paved walk for a view of the North Platte River Valley. The **South Overlook** is 0.2 mi. and provides a spectacular view of Scotts Bluff. Take U.S. 26 to Rte. 71 to Rte. 92; the monument is on Rte. 92 about 2 mi. west of **Gering** (*not* in the town of Scottsbluff). A 1.2 mi. bike trail links Gering with the base of the bluffs. In mid-July, the four-day **Oregon Trail Days Festival** packs the towns near Scotts Bluff with festive folk. Twenty mi. east on Rte. 92, just south of Bayard, the 500 ft. spire of **Chimney Rock,** visible from more than 30 mi. away, marks another landmark which once inspired travelers of the Oregon Trail. A gravel road leads from Rte. 92 to within ½ mi. of the rock. There you can find the first graveyard of settlers on the Oregon Trail. Unfortunately, there is no path up to the base of the rock due to the rough terrain and rattlesnakes. The Nebraska State Historical Society operates a **visitors center.** (☎586-2581. Open daily 9am-6pm; in winter 9am-5pm. $2, under 18 free.) **Area code:** 308. **Time Zone:** Mountain.

KANSAS

Kansas has served as a major stop-over for various travelers since the 1820s: families on the Oregon and Santa Fe Trails drove their wagons west in search of new homes, while cowboys on the Chisholm Trail drove their longhorns north in search of railroads and good times. The influx of people resulted in fierce battles over land, as white settlers forced Native Americans to move into the arid regions farther west. Grueling feuds over Kansas's slavery status before the Civil War gave rise to the term "Bleeding Kansas." The wound has healed, and Kansas now presents a serene blend of kitschy tourist attractions and miles of farmland. Highway signs subtly remind that "every Kansas farmer feeds 75 people—and *you.*"

🄝 PRACTICAL INFORMATION

Capital: Topeka.

Visitor Info: Division of Travel and Tourism: 700 S.W. Harrison, #1300, Topeka 66603-3712 (☎800-452-6727 or 785-296-2009; www.state.ks.us). Open M-F 7am-10pm, Sa-Su 7:30am-10pm. **Kansas Wildlife and Parks,** 900 S.W. Jackson, 5th fl., Topeka 66612-1233 (☎785-296-2281). Open M-F 8am-5pm.

Postal Abbreviation: KS. **Sales Tax:** 4.9%, plus some city taxes.

WICHITA   ☎316

In 1541, Coronado came to the site of present-day Wichita in search of the mythical, gold-laden city of Quivira. Upon arriving, he was so disappointed that he had his guide strangled for misleading him. Miraculously, Wichita grew to become the largest city in Kansas, and is now a key city for airplane manufacturing: Lear, Boeing, Beech, and Cessna all have factories in town. Much of the downtown is painfully suburban in its tree-lined stillness. As the Old Town area gets revamped, however, yuppies party further and further into the Kansas night.

🄝 **PRACTICAL INFORMATION.** Wichita lies on I-35, 170 mi. north of Oklahoma City and about 200 mi. southwest of Kansas City. A small and quiet downtown makes for easy walking or parking. **Broadway** is the major north-south artery. **Douglas Ave.** divides the numbered east-west streets to the north from the named east-west streets to the south. **Kellogg Ave. (U.S. 54)** is the main commercial strip east and west of town; through downtown it serves as an expressway. The closest **Amtrak** station, 414 N. Main St. (☎283-7533; station open Su-Tu and Sa midnight-8am, W-F midnight-4pm), 25 mi. north of Wichita in the town of Newton, sends one very early train northeast to Kansas City (5hr., $46) and another west to Dodge City (2½hr., $46).

GEOGRAPHIC CENTER OF THE US. Have you ever wanted to be the center of the action? Go 2 mi. northwest of Lebanon, KS. Sit by the stone monument and feel special—you are the center of the United States.

Greyhound, 312 S. Broadway, 2 blocks east of Main St. and 1½ blocks southwest of the transit station (☎265-7711; open daily 2:30am-6:30pm), services Kansas City (3-5hr., 3 per day, $30-35); Oklahoma City (4hr., 3 per day, $30-32); and Denver (13hr., 2 per day, $59-75). **Wichita Transit,** 214 S. Topeka Blvd., runs 18 bus routes in town. (☎265-7221. Station open M-F 8am-5pm. Buses run M-F 5:30am-6:30pm, Sa 6:30am-5:30pm. Fare $1, seniors 50¢, ages 6-17 75¢; transfers 25¢.) **Convention and visitors bureau:** 100 S. Main St., on the corner of Douglas Ave. (☎265-2800 or 800-288-9424; open M-F 8am-5pm). **Internet access: Public library,** 223 S. Main St. (☎261-8500; open M-Th 10am-9pm, F-Sa 10am-5:30pm, Su 1-5pm). **Post Office:** 330 W. 2nd St., at Waco (☎262-6245; open M-F 7am-5:30pm, Sa 9am-1pm). **ZIP code:** 67202. **Area code:** 316.

🄜 **ACCOMMODATIONS.** Wichita offers a bounty of cheap hotels. South Broadway has plenty of mom-'n'-pop places, *but be wary of the neighborhood.* The chains line **E. and W. Kellogg Ave.** 5 to 8 mi. from downtown. Only ten blocks from downtown, the **Mark 8 Inn,** 1130 N. Broadway, has small, comfortable rooms that come with free local calls, cable TV, A/C, fridge, and laundry facilities. (☎265-4679 or 888-830-7268. Singles $30; doubles $33; no checks). The **English Village Inn,** 6727 E. Kellogg, though American, urban, and a motel, keeps large rooms with aging furnishings in tidy repair for very reasonable rates. (☎683-5613 or 800-365-8455. Cable and HBO in the rooms, popcorn in the lobby. Singles from $30; doubles from $36.) **USI Campgrounds,** 2920 E. 33rd St., right off Hillside Rd., is the most convenient of Wichita's hitchin' posts, with laundry, showers, playground, and storm shelter, in case there's a twister a-comin'. (☎838-0435. Sites $17, partial hook-up $19, full hook-up $20.50; weekly rates available.)

◌ FOOD. Beef: it's what's for dinner in Wichita. Everything old is new in the **Old Town** area, a few blocks east of downtown on Washington and Mosley St., between 1st St. and Douglas Ave., where revitalized warehouses now house breweries and restaurants. The area isn't a bad choice for a weekday lunch, when a few of the local pizzerias offer $5 buffets. Neon lights are on **N. Broadway** around 10th St., with all kinds of fairly authentic Asian food, mostly Vietnamese. If you eat only one slab here, make it one from **Doc's Steakhouse**, 1515 N. Broadway, where the most expensive entree—a 17 oz. T-bone with salad, potato, and bread—is only $9.75. Take bus #13 "N. Broadway." (☎264-4735. Open M-Th 11:30am-9:30pm, F 11:30am-10pm, Sa 4-10pm.) The large paper umbrellas hanging from the ceiling at **Pho 99**, 1015 N. Broadway, may be questionable, but the food certainly isn't. Good *pho* and vermicelli dishes are $4-6; only in Kansas would Vietnamese noodles be accompanied by strips of rib-eye steak. (☎267-8188. Open daily 10am-8:30pm.)

▣ SIGHTS. The **Four Museums-on-the-River** are located within a few blocks of each other; take the trolley or bus #12 "Riverside." Walk through the rough and tumble cattle days of the 1870s in the **Old Cowtown**, lined with many original buildings. (1871 Sim Park Dr. ☎264-6398 or 264-0671. Open M-Sa 10am-5pm, Su noon-5pm; Nov.-Mar. Sa-Su only. $7, seniors $6.50, ages 5-11 $3.50, under 5 free; seniors 2-for-1 Tu and W. Call for special events info.) The **Mid-America All-Indian Center and Museum** displays Native American artifacts. The late Blackbear Bosin's awe-inspiring sculpture, *Keeper of the Plains*, stands guard over the grounds. The center holds the **Mid-America All-Indian Intertribal Pow Wow** during the last weekend in July with traditional dancing, foods, arts, and crafts. (650 N. Seneca. ☎262-5221. Open M-Sa 10am-5pm, Su 1-5pm; Jan.-Mar. closed M. $2, ages 6-12 $1.) The **Wichita Art Museum** has an excellent collection of American art, particularly from the 20th century. (619 Stackman Dr. ☎268-4921. Open Tu-Sa 10am-5pm, Su noon-5pm. Free.)

More art hides on the **Wichita State University**, at N. Fairmont and 17th St., accessible by the "East 17th" bus, including over 50 sculptures and the **Corbin Education Center**, designed by Frank Lloyd Wright. Free sculpture maps are available at the **Edwin A. Ulrich Museum of Art** office, in the McKnight Arts Center, also on campus. A gigantic glass mosaic mural by Joan Miró forms one wall of the building. (☎978-3644. Open daily noon-5pm. Free.) North of campus, the **Bright Spot for Health** features a 40 ft. pyramid, used for reflection and receptions, with the world's largest FDA food pyramid painted on its side. (3100 N. Hillside. ☎682-3100. Tours M-F 1:30pm; $4.)

Most of Wichita's museums and historic points of attraction are part of the **Wichita Western Heritage Tour,** which focuses on the city's contributions to culture. Visiting all the sites earns a free **belt buckle** at the last stop, **Sheplers,** the world's largest Western store. (6501 W. Kellogg. ☎946-3600. M-Sa 10am-9pm, Su noon-6pm.) All the hard sightseeing work may result in overheating, in which case there's the **Museum of the American Fan Collectors,** which touts itself as having the "most comprehensive collection of air moving devices in the world," including devices from as early as 1876. The museum is one room in the lobby of the Vornado fan plant and rather informal, but certainly wins the Wichita-area prize for sheer oddity. (415 E. 13th St., 30min. east in Andover. ☎733-0035. From I-35, take 21st St. west from Exit 57, turn left on Andover St., and left again on 13th St. Open M-F 8:30-5pm. Free.)

WHAT'S THAT SMELL? In its heyday in the 1870s, Dodge City ("the wickedest little city in America") was a haven for gunfighters, prostitutes, and other lawless types; at one time, the main drag had a saloon for every 50 citizens. Disputes were settled man to man, with a duel. The slower draw ended up in Boot Hill Cemetery, so named for the boot-clad corpses buried there. Legendary lawmen Wyatt Earp and Bat Masterson earned their fame cleaning up the streets of Dodge City. Today, the town's most noticeable residents, about 50,000 cows, reside on the feedlots on the east part of town. Hold your nose and whoop it up during the **Dodge City Days** (☎316-227-3119), the last weekend in July through the first weekend in Aug., complete with rodeo, carnival, and lots of steak. You'll know when you're getting close.

MISSOURI

Pro-slavery Missouri applied for statehood in 1818, but due to Congress's fear of upsetting the balance of free and slave states, was forced to wait until Maine entered the Union as a free state in 1821. Missouri's Civil War status as a border state was a harbinger of its future ambiguity; close to the center of the country, Missouri still defies regional stereotyping. Its large cities are defined by wide avenues, long and lazy rivers, numerous parks, humid summers, and blues and jazz wailing into the night. In the countryside, Bible factory outlets stand amid firework stands and barbecue pits. Missouri's patchwork geography further complicates character-ization. In the north, near Iowa, amber waves of grain undulate. Along the Missis-sippi, towering bluffs inscribed with Native American pictographs evoke western canyonlands, while Hannibal's spelunkers enjoy some of the world's largest lime-stone caves, made famous by Mark Twain's Tom Sawyer.

🛈 PRACTICAL INFORMATION

Capital: Jefferson City.

Visitor Info: Missouri Division of Tourism, P.O. Box 1055, Jefferson City 65102 (☎573-751-4133 or 800-877-1234; www.missouritourism.org). Open M-F 8am-5pm; 800 number operates 24hr. **Dept. of Natural Resources,** Division of State Parks, P.O. Box 176, Jefferson City 65102 (☎573-751-2479 or 800-334-6946). Open M-F 8am-5pm.

Postal Abbreviation: MO. **Sales Tax:** Varies, averaging 6.75%.

ST. LOUIS   ☎314

Located directly south of the junction of the Mississippi, Missouri, and Illinois riv-ers, St. Louis gained prominence in the 18th and 19th centuries as the US expanded west. Musically, St. Louis has also played an important role in American history: the city contributed both to the development of the blues and witnessed Scott Joplin's invention of ragtime in the early 20th century. St. Louis remains a prototypical American metropolis and one of the country's largest inland trading ports. Gener-ally considered the best baseball town in America, it is also home to innovative musicians, infamous ghettoes, and Eero Saarinen's magnificent Gateway Arch, a silvery landmark of westward expansion.

▐ GETTING THERE AND GETTING AROUND

Airport: Lambert-St. Louis International (☎426-8000), 12 mi. northwest of the city on I-70. Hub for **TWA.** MetroLink and Bi-state bus #66 "Maplewood-Airport" provide easy access to downtown ($3). Taxis to downtown are less economical ($18). A few west-bound Greyhound buses stop at the airport.

Trains: Amtrak, 550 S. 16th St., 2 blocks south of Kiel Center. To: Chicago (6hr., 3 per day, $27-57) and Kansas City (5½hr., 2 per day, $48-96). Office open daily 6am-1am.

Buses: Greyhound, 1450 N. 13th St. (☎231-4485), at Cass Ave. Bi-state bus #30 "Cass" takes less than 10min. from downtown. *Be cautious at night.* To: Chicago (6½hr., 6 per day, $31) and Kansas City (5hr., 5 per day, $31).

Public Transportation: Bi-State (☎231-2345). Extensive daily service; infrequent off-peak hrs. Info and schedules available at the **Metroride Service Center** in the St. Louis Cen-ter (☎982-1485; open M-F 6am-8pm, Sa-Su 8am-5pm). **MetroLink,** the light-rail sys-tem, runs from 5th St. and Missouri Ave. in East St. Louis to Lambert Airport M-Sa 5am-midnight and Su 6am-11pm. Travel for free in the "Ride Free Zone" (from Laclede's Landing to Union Station) M-F 11:30am-1pm. Fare for Bi-State or MetroLink $1.25, transfers 10¢; seniors and ages 5-12 50¢/5¢. 1-day pass $4, available at MetroLink stations. **Shuttle Bug,** a small bus painted like a ladybug, cruises around Forest Park and the Central West End. (M-F 6:45am-6pm, Sa-Su 10am-6pm. $1.25.) The **Shuttle**

Bee buzzes around Forest Park, Clayton, Brentwood, and the Galleria. (M-F 6am-11:30pm, Sa 7:30am-10:30pm, Su 9:30am-6:30pm. $1.25.)

Taxis: Yellow Cab, ☎ 361-2345.

ORIENTATION AND PRACTICAL INFORMATION

U.S. 40/I-64 runs east-west through the entire metropolitan area. Downtown, **Market St.** divides the city running north-south. Numbered streets parallel the Mississippi river, increasing to the west. The historic **Soulard** district borders the river south of downtown. **Forest Park** and **University City,** home to **Washington University** and old, stately homes, lie west of downtown; the Italian neighborhood called **The Hill** is south of these. St. Louis is a driving town: parking comes easy, wide streets allow for lots of meters, and private lots are cheap ($2-8 per day).

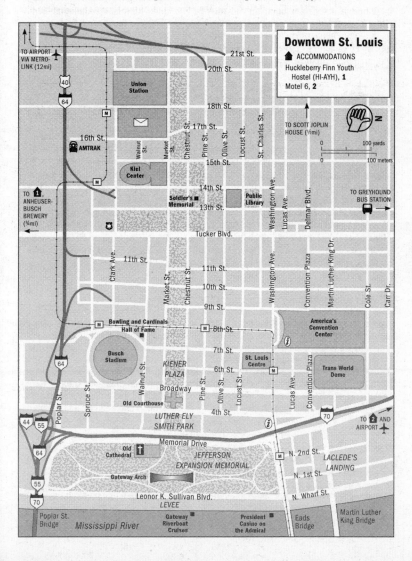

Downtown St. Louis

ACCOMMODATIONS
Huckleberry Finn Youth Hostel (HI-AYH), **1**
Motel 6, **2**

Visitor Info: St. Louis Visitors Center, 308 Washington Ave. (☎241-1764). Open daily 9:30am-4:30pm. The *Official St. Louis Visitors Guide* and the monthly magazine *Where: St. Louis,* both free, contain much info and decent maps.

Hotlines: Rape Hotline, ☎531-2003. **Suicide Hotline,** ☎647-4357. **Kids Under 21 Crisis,** ☎644-5886. All 24hr. **Gay and Lesbian Hotline,** ☎367-0084. Open M-Sa 6-10pm.

Hospitals: Barnes-Jewish Hospital, 216 S. Kingshighway Blvd. (☎747-3000). **Metro South Women's Health Center,** 2415 N. Kingshighway Blvd. (☎361-1606).

Post Office: 1720 Market St. (☎800-275-8777). Open M-F 6:30am-2:30pm, Sa 6:30am-1pm. **ZIP code:** 63103. **Area code:** 314 (in St. Louis), 636 (in St. Charles), 618 (in IL); in text, 314 unless noted.

▚ ACCOMMODATIONS

Most budget lodging is far from downtown. For chain motels, try **Lindbergh Blvd. (Rte. 67)** near the airport, or the area north of the I-70/I-270 junction in **Bridgeton,** 5 mi. beyond the airport. **Watson Rd.** near Chippewa is littered with cheap motels; take bus #11 "Chippewa-Sunset Hills" or #20 "Cherokee."

▧ **Huckleberry Finn Youth Hostel (HI-AYH),** 1908 S. 12th St. at Tucker Blvd. (☎241-0076), 2 blocks north of Russell Blvd. in a sketchy neighborhood of the Soulard District. Take bus #73 "Carondelet." A very accommodating hostel with TV, lockers, full kitchen, free parking, and friendly staff. Reception daily 8-10am and 6-10pm. Check-out 9:30am. Linen $3. Key deposit $5. Dorm-style rooms with 5-9 beds $15, non-members $18. Ask about work opportunities, like whitewashing the fence.

Motel 6, 4576 Woodson Rd. (☎427-1313), near the airport. From downtown, Metrolink to the airport or take bus #4 "Natural Bridge." Most motels match the price, but few can touch the cleanliness. A/C, cable, pool. Singles $46-50; doubles $52-56.

Royal Budget Inn, 6061 Collinsville Rd. (☎618-874-4451), 20min. east of the city off Exit 6 of I-55/I-70 in Fairmont City, IL. Clean, one-bed purple-lit rooms with an aqua-green Taj Mahal flavor. Rooms Su-Th $35, F-Sa $38.

Rainbow Motel, 5280 Collinsville Rd. (☎618-875-2800), in Fairmont City. Basic rooms with A/C and cable TV get the job done. Singles $34; doubles $38.

Horseshoe Lake State Park, 3321 Rte. 111 (☎618-931-0270), north off I-70 in Granite City, IL, about 3 mi. from Cahokia Mounds. Sites are on an island (connected by a causeway) in a relatively secluded area. No electricity or water. Sites $7.

◖ FOOD

In St. Louis, the difference of a few blocks can mean vastly different cuisine. The area surrounding **Union Station,** at 18th and Market St. downtown, is being revamped with hip restaurants and bars. The **Central West End** offers coffeehouses and outdoor cafes; a slew of impressive restaurants await just north of Lindell Blvd. along **Euclid Ave.** (MetroLink to "Central West End" and walk north, or catch the Shuttle Bug.) St. Louis's historic Italian neighborhood, **The Hill,** southwest of downtown and just northwest of Tower Grove Park, produces plenty of inexpensive pasta; take bus #99 "Lafayette." Cheap Thai, Philippine, and Vietnamese restaurants spice the **South Grand** area, at Grand Blvd. just south of Tower Grove Park; board bus #70 "Grand." The intellectual set hangs out on **University City Loop,** on Delmar Blvd. between Skinker Blvd. and Big Bend Blvd.

▧ **Blueberry Hill,** 6504 Delmar Blvd. (☎727-0880), on the Loop. Eclectic rock 'n' roll restaurant with 9 different rooms including the "Duck Room" and the "Elvis Room," record covers, Howdy Doody toys, a *Simpsons* collection, and giant baseball cards. The jukebox plays 2000 songs, and live bands play F-Sa and some weeknights (cover $4-15). Performers have included Chuck Berry, Sarah McLachlan, and Bonnie Raitt. Burgers are big and juicy ($4.50). Open M-Sa 11am-1am, Su 11am-midnight. 21+ after 8pm.

▧ **Ted Drewe's Frozen Custard,** 4224 S. Grand Blvd. (☎352-7376); or 6726 Chippewa (☎481-2652), on Rte. 66. *The* place for the summertime St. Louis experience since

1929. Standing in line for the "chocolate-chip banana concrete shake" is rewarding; the blended toppings are thick enough to hang in an overturned cup ($1.50-3.50). Open daily 11am-midnight in summer; until 11pm the rest of the year; closed Jan.

Pho Grand, 3191 S. Grand Blvd. (☎664-7435), in the South Grand area. Good Vietnamese food, with vegetarian and thinly-cut beef options. Their specialty is *pho* (noodle soup; $4); entrees are $4-6. Open Su-M and W-Th 11am-10pm, F-Sa 11am-11pm.

Mangio Italiano, 3145 S. Grand Blvd. (☎664-8585). Offers fresh pasta made on site ($5-9), jazz on weekend nights, a handpainted mural wall, and mismatched tables. Serves food M-F noon-10pm and Sa-Su 12:30-10:30pm; bar open until 1:30am.

Kaldi's Coffeehouse and Roasting Company, 700 De Mun Ave. (☎727-9955), in Clayton. Home-roasted java and the food is fresh. Intellectuals swarm for panini ($5) and whole-wheat pizza ($3) in this intimate, veggie-friendly establishment. Open daily 7am-11pm.

 SIGHTS

DOWNTOWN. The nation's tallest monument at 630 ft., the 🏛**Gateway Arch** towers gracefully over all of St. Louis and southern Illinois. The ground-level view is impressive, but the 4min. ride to the top in elevator modules straight out of a sci-fi film is more fun. Waits are shorter after dinner or in the morning but are uniformly long on Sa. Beneath the arch, the underground **Museum of Westward Expansion** adds to the appeal of the grassy park complex known comprehensively as the **Jefferson Expansion Memorial.** The museum celebrates the Louisiana Purchase and its exploration. *(☎982-1410. Museum and arch open daily 8am-10pm; in winter 9am-6pm. Tickets for 1 attraction $6, ages 13-16 $4, ages 3-12 $2.50; 2 attractions $10/$8/$5; 3 attractions $14/ $12/$7.50. Limited Wheelchair accessible.)* Scope out the city from the water with **Gateway Riverboat Cruises;** tours leave from the docks in front of the arch. *(☎621-4040 or 800-878-7411. 1hr. tours 11am-3:30pm. $9, ages 3-12 $4.)*

Beneath the arch, St. Louis's oldest church, **Old Cathedral,** holds masses daily. *(209 Walnut St. ☎231-3250.)* Within walking distance is the magnificently ornate **Old Courthouse,** across the highway from the arch. In 1847, Dred Scott sued for freedom from slavery here. *(11 N. 4th St. ☎425-6156. Open daily 8am-4:30pm. Tours usually on the hr. in summer, less frequently in winter. Free. Limited wheelchair access.)*

It's a strike either way at the **International Bowling Museum and Hall of Fame** and the **St. Louis Cardinals Hall of Fame Museum,** across from Busch Stadium. The amusing bowling museum features little-known facts about bowling (only here can you learn how monopolistic German dwarfs played Su night games with gold and silver pins), while the baseball museum exhibits memorabilia from the glory days of St. Louis hardball. *(111 Stadium Plaza. ☎231-6340. Open in summer M-Sa 9am-5pm, Su noon-5pm; Oct-Mar. daily 11am-4pm; game days until 6:30pm. $6, ages 5-12 $4. Includes 4 frames in the lanes downstairs. Wheelchair accessible.)* Historic **Union Station,** 1 mi. west of downtown, houses a shopping mall, food court, and entertainment center in a magnificent structure that was once the nation's largest and busiest railroad terminal. *(18th and Market St. ☎421-6655. MetroLink to Union Station.)* "The Entertainer" lives on at the **Scott Joplin House,** just west of downtown at Geyer Rd., where the ragtime legend lived and composed from 1901 to 1903. The detailed 1hr. tour delves into Joplin's long-lasting influence on American music and his tortured love life and includes a few live performances of ragtime classics. *(2658 Delmar. ☎340-5790. Open in summer M-Sa 10am-5pm, Su noon-6pm. $2, ages 6-12 $1.25. Wheelchair accessible.)*

SOUTH AND SOUTHWEST OF DOWNTOWN. Soulard is bounded by I-55 and Seventh St.; walk south on Broadway or 7th St. from downtown, or take bus #73 "Carondelet." In the early 70s, the city proclaimed this area a historic district, because it once housed German and East European immigrants, many of whom worked in the breweries. The district surrounds the **Soulard Farmers Market,** at Lafayette and 7th St. Despite its age (220 years), Soulard *still* has fresh produce. *(730 Carroll St. ☎622-4180. Open W-F 8am-5:30pm, Sa 6am-5:30pm; hrs. vary among merchants.)* The end of 12th St. features the largest brewery in the world, the **Anheuser-Busch Brewery,** 12th and

Lynch St. The 1½hr. tour is markedly less thrilling than sampling the beer at the end. *(1127 Pestalozzi St. ☎577-2626. Take bus #40 "Broadway" south from downtown. Tours M-Sa 9am-5pm; Sept.-May M-Sa 9am-4pm. Get free tickets at the office. Wheelchair accessible.)* The internationally acclaimed 79-acre **Missouri Botanical Garden** thrives north of Tower Grove Park on grounds left by entrepreneur Henry Shaw. Among the flora from all over the globe, the Japanese Garden is guaranteed to soothe the weary budget traveler—but watch out for the thousands of freaky-looking orange fish. *(4344 Shaw Blvd. ☎800-642-8842. From downtown, take I-44 west by car or ride MetroLink to "Central West End" and hop on bus #13 "Union-Missouri Botanical Gardens" to the main entrance. Open daily 9am-8pm; early Sept. to late May 9am-5pm. $5, seniors $3, under 12 free. Guided tours daily at 1pm. Wheelchair accessible.)* **Grant's Farm,** the former home of President Ulysses S. Grant, is now a bustling wildlife preserve. The tram-ride tour traverses an environment where over 1000 animals roam and interact freely, as evidenced by the zebrass (donkey-zebra), and concludes with free beer in the historic Baurnhof area. *(10501 Gravois Rd. ☎843-1700. Take I-55 west to Reavis Barracks Rd. and turn left onto Gravois. Open May-Aug. Tu-Sa 9am-4pm, Su 10am-5pm., hrs. in Apr. and Sept.-Oct. vary; call for hrs. Free. Parking $4.)*

WEST OF DOWNTOWN. Forest Park, the country's largest urban park, contains three museums, a zoo, a planetarium, a 12,000-seat amphitheater, and a grand canal, as well as countless picnic areas, pathways, and flying golf balls. Take MetroLink to Forest Park and catch the Shuttle Bug. All Forest Park sites are wheelchair accessible. Marlin Perkins, the late host of TV's *Wild Kingdom*, turned the **St. Louis Zoo** into a world-class institution, replete with frisbee-playing sea lions. *(☎781-0900. Open late May-early Sept. W-M 9am-5pm, Tu 9am-dusk; Sept.-May daily 9am-5pm. Free.)* Atop **Art Hill,** just to the southwest, a statue of France's Louis IX, the city's namesake, beckons with his raised sword in front of the **St. Louis Art Museum,** which contains masterpieces of Asian, Renaissance, and Impressionist art. *(☎721-0072. Open Tu 1:30-8:30pm, W-Su 10am-5pm. Main museum free; special exhibits usually $7, students and seniors $6, ages 6-12 $5, free Tu.)*

From Forest Park, head east a few blocks to gawk at the lavish residential sections of the **Central West End,** where every house is a turn-of-the-century version of a French château or Tudor mansion. The vast **Cathedral of St. Louis** is a strange combination of Romanesque, Byzantine, Gothic, and Baroque styles, with gold-flecked mosaics depicting 19th-century church history in Missouri. *(4431 Lindell Blvd. ☎533-2824 or 533-0544 to schedule tours. MetroLink stop "Central West End", or bus #93 "Lindell" from downtown. Open daily 6am-7pm, off-season 6am-5pm. Guided tours M-F 10am-3pm, Su after the noon Mass. Wheelchair accessible.)*

The **St. Louis Car Museum** houses over 150 legendary cars that have cruised the highways and byways of America, from the Model T to the '57 Chevy to the VW Bus. *(1575 Woodson Rd. at I-170. ☎993-1330. Open M-Sa 9am-5pm, Su 11am-5pm. $3.75, under 12 $2.75.)* Less exalted autos are crushed under the 66 in. wheels of **Bigfoot,** the "Original Monster Truck." The first Bigfoot and its descendants live near the airport and I-270. *(6311 N. Lindbergh. ☎731-2822. Open M-F 9am-6pm, Sa 9am-3pm. Free.)*

The Loop, just northwest of the Central West End, has more than just shops full of ethnic items and cafes full of intellectuals—the sidewalk, for instance. All along the loop runs the **St. Louis Walk of Fame,** with stars and biographies celebrating famous St. Louisians like Kathleen Turner, Kevin Kline, Tennessee Williams, Bob Costas, and John Goodman. *(6504 Delmar. ☎727-7827.)*

🎵 ENTERTAINMENT

Founded in 1880, the **St. Louis Symphony Orchestra** is one of the country's finest. **Powell Hall,** 718 N. Grand Blvd., holds the 101-member orchestra in acoustic and visual splendor. Take bus #91 "Delmar" or #94 "Washington Ave." to Grand Blvd. The symphony has a "summer series" in June at the Music School and in July at Queenie Park. *(☎534-1700. Performances Sept. 17 to May 14 Th-Sa 8pm, Su matinee 3pm.*

Box office open M-Sa 9am-5pm and before performances. Tickets from $10; rush tickets often available for half-price on day of show.)

St. Louis offers theater-goers many choices. The outdoor **Municipal Opera**, the "Muny," performs tour productions of hit musicals on summer nights in Forest Park. Back rows provide 1456 free seats on a first come, first served basis. The gates open at 7:30pm for 8:15pm shows. (☎361-1900. Box office open daily June to mid-Aug. 9am-9pm. Tickets $7-48.) Productions are also regularly staged by the **St. Louis Black Repertory**, 634 N. Grand Blvd. (☎534-3807), and the **Repertory Theatre of St. Louis,** 130 Edgar Rd. (☎968-4925). The **Fox Theatre,** 537 N. Grand, was originally a 30s movie palace, but now hosts Broadway shows, classic films, and Las Vegas, country, and rock stars. (☎534-1111. Box office open M-Sa 10am-6pm, Su noon-4pm. Tours Tu, Th, Sa at 10:30am. $5, under 12 $2.50. Call for reservations.) **Metrotix** (☎534-1111) has tickets to most theatrical events.

A recent St. Louis ordinance permits gambling on the river. The **President Casino on the Admiral** floats below the Arch on the Missouri side. (☎622-3000 or 800-772-3647. Open Su-Th 8am-4am, F-Sa 24hr. $2.) On the Illinois side, the **Casino Queen** claims "the loosest slots in town." (☎618-874-5000 or 800-777-0777. Open daily 9am-5am.) Parking for both is free; both are wheelchair accessible.

Six Flags St. Louis, 30min. southwest of St. Louis on I-44 at Exit 261, reigns supreme in the kingdom of amusement parks. Last year brought the addition of the vaunted "Boss" wooden roller-coaster, which features a 570° helix. (☎636-938-4800. Hrs. vary by season. $39, seniors and under 48 in. $19.50.) The **St. Louis Cardinals** play ball at **Busch Stadium** Apr. through early Oct. (☎421-3060; tickets $8-16). The 2000 Super Bowl champion **Rams,** formerly of L.A., have brought the ol' pigskin back to St. Louis in shining fashion at the **Trans World Dome** (☎425-8830; tickets $32). The **Blues** hockey team slices ice at the **Kiel Center** at 14th St. and Clark Ave. (☎843-1700 or 622-2500; tickets from $15).

▼ NIGHTLIFE

Music rules the night in St. Louis. The *Riverfront Times* (free at many bars and clubs) and the *Get Out* section of the *Post-Dispatch* list weekly entertainment. The *St. Louis Magazine*, published annually, lists seasonal events, as does the comprehensive calendar distributed at the tourist office. The bohemian **Loop** parties hearty at the coffeehouses and bars of Delmar Blvd. **Brandt's Market & Cafe,** 6525 Delmar Blvd., does it all with wine, beer, espresso, and a varied menu. (☎727-3663. Open daily 11am-midnight; live jazz W-Su.)

For beer, outdoor tables, and live music, often without a cover charge, St. Louis offers **Laclede's Landing,** a collection of restaurants, bars, and dance clubs housed in 19th-century industrial buildings north of the Arch on the riverfront. Most bars offer mainstream rock and draw clean-cut, touristy crowds. In the summer, bars take turns sponsoring "block parties," with food, drink, music, and dancing in the streets. (☎241-5875. Generally open 9pm-3am, with some places open for lunch and dinner. 21+.) **Mississippi Nights,** 914 N. 1st St., hosts big local and national bands. (☎421-3853. Box office open M-F 11am-6pm.) **Train Wreck,** 720 N. 1st St., features alternative cover bands in its nightclub F-Sa nights. (☎436-1006. Open Su-Th 11am-10pm, F-Sa 11am-3am. Cover $3.)

Also downtown, **Union Station** and its environs have spawned some off-beat nightlife. **Hot Locust Cantina,** 2005 Locust St., is home to hip-hop *and* rockabilly performances. (☎231-3666. Lunch M-F 10am-2pm, dinner Tu-Th 5-10pm and F-Sa 5-11pm. Music weekend nights. Entrees $6-9. Cover $3-4.) The less touristy and quite gay-friendly **Soulard** district has been known to ripple with the blues. The **1860 Hard Shell Cafe & Bar,** 1860 S. 9th St., hosts some gritty blues and rock performances. (☎231-1860. Open M-F 9am-1:30am, Sa-Su 10am-12:30am. Music nightly and Sa-Su afternoons. Cover $3 after 9pm F-Sa.) **Clementine's,** 2001 Menard, contains a crowded restaurant and St. Louis's oldest gay bar, established in 1978. (☎664-7869. Open M-F 10am-1:30am, Sa 8am-1:30am, Su 11am-midnight.)

◪ DAYTRIPS FROM ST. LOUIS

CAHOKIA MOUNDS STATE HISTORIC SITE. Fifteen minutes from the city in Collinsville, IL (8 mi. east of downtown on I-55/70 to Rte. 111), over 65 earthen mounds rising from the flat land mark the site of Cahokia, a complex Native American settlement inhabited from 700 to 1500 AD and now a World Heritage Site. In constructing these mammoth building foundations, workers had to carry over 15 million loads of dirt on their backs. The largest mound, **Monk's Mound,** took 300 years to complete; today it offers a faraway view of the smog-filled St. Louis skyline. The Cahokians, once a community of 20,000, faced the same problems of pollution, overcrowding, and resource depletion that we do today—which might help explain their mysterious disappearance. Celebrate equinoxes and solstices at dawn on the Su closest to the big day at **Woodhenge,** a solar calendar built by the Cahokians. The **Interpretive Center** offers booklets or a narrated audio tape to guide the curious. (☎618-346-5160. Site open daily 8am-dusk; free. Center open daily 9am-5pm; suggested donation $2, booklet $1. Wheelchair accessible.)

HANNIBAL. Hannibal hugs the Mississippi River 100 mi. west of Springfield, IL, and 100 mi. northwest of St. Louis. Founded in 1819, the town remained a sleepy village until Samuel Clemens (a.k.a. Mark Twain) distinguished his boyhood home by making it the setting of *The Adventures of Tom Sawyer*. Tourists flock to Hannibal to imagine Tom, Huck, and Becky romping around the quaint streets and nearby caves. Despite all its tourist traps, Hannibal retains its considerable small-town hospitality and charm.

The **Mark Twain Boyhood Home and Museum,** 208 Hill St. (☎221-9010), marks the downtown historic district with restored rooms and an assortment of memorabilia from the witty wordsmith's life. Across the street sit the **Pilaster House** and **Clemens Law Office,** where a young Twain awoke one night to find a murdered man lying on the floor next to him. Further down Main St., the new **Mark Twain Museum** includes a collection of Norman Rockwell's "Tom and Hucks." (Open June-Aug. daily 8am-6pm; off-season hrs. vary dramatically. All sites included $6.) The **Mark Twain Riverboat,** at Center St. Landing, steams down the Mississippi for a 1hr. sight-seeing cruise that is part history, part folklore, and part advertisement for the land attractions. (☎221-3222. Late May to early Sept. 3 per day; May and Sept.-Oct. 1 per day. $8.50, ages 3-12 $5.50; dinner cruises 6:30pm $26/$16.) Both Injun Joe's ghost and rare bats haunt the **Mark Twain Cave,** 1 mi. south of Hannibal on Rte. 79, the complex series of caverns Twain explored as a boy. (☎221-1656. Open daily 8am-8pm; Apr.-May and Sept.-Oct. 9am-6pm; Nov.-Mar. 9am-4pm. 1hr. tour $12, ages 5-12 $6.) Nearby **Cameron Cave** provides a slightly longer and far spookier lantern tour ($14, ages 5-12 $7). Every 4th of July weekend, 100,000 fans converge on Hannibal for the fence-painting, frog-jumping fun of the **Tom Sawyer Days** festival (☎221-2477).

Chain motels, some of which differ in name but share the same owner, swarm about Hannibal, particularly on **Mark Twain Ave.** (Rte. 36) and on U.S. 61 near the Rte. 36 junction. Numerous **B&Bs** are located downtown. The cheapest singles are $60—times have changed from Twain's Hannibal, when "there was not enough money in the first place to furnish a conversation!" Shiningly well-maintained, the **Howard Johnson Lodge,** 3603 McMasters Ave., at the U.S. 36/U.S. 61 junction, provides quality rooms with A/C, cable TV, and a pool. (☎221-7950. Singles $35-60; doubles $40-79; prices highest in summer.) The **Mark Twain Cave Campgrounds,** adjacent to the cave 1 mi. south of Hannibal on Rte. 79, are cheery and family-oriented, but not too secluded. (☎221-1656. Sites $14, full hook-up $18.) As befits a state bordering the Deep South, Hannibal is home to a few tasty barbecue establishments. ◙**Bubba's,** 101 Church St. on the waterfront, pit-smokes painstakingly prepared BBQ pork and beef sandwiches ($5.50) that come with home-style vegetable sides such as cole slaw and jambalaya. (☎221-5552. Open daily 11am-9pm.) **Ole Planters,** 316 N. Main St., serves tasty $4.75 BBQ beef sandwiches and $2.50 German chocolate pie. (☎221-4410. Open M-W and F-Sa 11am-3pm and 4:30-8pm, Th and Su 11am-

3pm. Closed Jan.-Feb. and on Su in winter.) The **Twainland Cheesecake Company,** 101 N. Main St., concocts sandwiches ($5) and over 99 flavors of cheesecake. (☎221-3355. Open M-Sa 9am-3pm.)

From **Trailways Bus Lines,** at the junction of MM and 61 (☎221-0033), in front of Abel's Quik Shop, buses blaze to Cedar Rapids (1 per day, $54.50) and St. Louis (1 per day, $22). The **Hannibal Convention and Visitors Bureau,** 505 N. 3rd St., offers free local calls (☎221-2477; open M-F 8am-6pm, Sa 9am-6pm, Su 9:30am-4:30pm). **Post Office:** 801 Broadway (☎221-0957; open M-F 8:30am-5pm, Sa 8:30am-noon). **ZIP code:** 63401. **Area code:** 573.

KANSAS CITY ☎816

With over 200 public fountains and more miles of boulevard than Paris, Kansas City looks and acts more European than one might expect from the "Barbecue Capital of the World." KC has a strong tradition of booze and good music; when Prohibition stifled most of the country's fun in the 20s, Mayor Pendergast let the good times continue to roll, and Count Basie and Duke Ellington both flourished. The Kansas City of today maintains its big bad blues-and-jazz rep in a metropolis spanning two states: the highly suburbanized and mostly bland half in Kansas (KCKS) and the quicker-paced commercial and touristed half in Missouri (KCMO).

▊ GETTING THERE AND GETTING AROUND

Airport: Kansas City International (☎243-5237), 18 mi. northwest of KC off I-29 (take bus #29). **KCI Shuttle** (☎243-5000 or 800-243-6383) departs over 100 times daily, servicing downtown, Westport, Crown Center, and Plaza of KCMO and Overland Park, Mission, and Lenexa of KCKS (one-way $13, round-trip $21). Taxi to downtown $23-26.

Trains: Amtrak, 2200 Main St. (☎421-3622), at Pershing Rd., next to old Union Station (take bus #27). To: St. Louis (5½hr., 3 per day, $28) and Chicago (8hr., 2 per day, $72). Open 24hr.

Buses: Greyhound, 1101 N. Troost (☎221-2835). Take bus #25. *The terminal is in an unsafe area.* To: St. Louis (5hr., 5 per day, $29) and Chicago (10-15hr., 6 per day, $43). Open daily 5:30am-11pm.

Public Transit: Kansas City Area Transportation Authority (Metro), 1200 E. 18th St. (☎221-0660), near Troost. Excellent downtown coverage. 90¢, $1 for KCKS, $1.10 for Independence; discounts for seniors, Medicare cardholders, and under 18. Free transfers. Buses run 5am-6pm (outer routes) or 5am-midnight (downtown routes). Two **Downtowner Shuttle** routes run between the business district, Union Station, Crown Center, and City Market every 10min. M-F 6:30am-6pm. Fare 25¢.

Taxis: Yellow Cab, ☎471-5000.

✴▐ ORIENTATION AND PRACTICAL INFORMATION

The KC metropolitan area sprawls almost interminably, making travel difficult without a car. Most sights worth visiting lie south of downtown on the Missouri side. All listings are for KCMO, unless otherwise indicated. Although parking around town is not easy, there are many lots that charge $4 or less per day. **I-70** cuts east-west through the city, and **I-435** circles the two-state metro area. KCMO is laid out on an extensive grid with numbered streets running east-west from the Missouri River well out into suburbs, and named streets running north-south. **Main St.** divides the city east-west.

Visitor Info: Convention and Visitors Bureau of Greater Kansas City, 1100 Main St. (☎221-5242 or 800-767-7700), 25th fl. of the City Center Sq. Bldg. Open M-F 8:30am-5pm. Two more conveniently-located info centers are at 4709 Central, in the Plaza (open M-Sa 10am-6pm, Su noon-5pm), and in Union Station (open M-F 10am-5pm). **Missouri Tourist Information Center,** 4010 Blue Ridge Cut-Off (☎889-3330 or 800-877-1234 for a travel package); follow signs from the exit from I-70. Open daily Mar.-Nov. 8am-5pm, Dec.-Feb. M-Sa 8am-5pm.

Hotlines: Crisis Line, ☎531-0233. **Gay and Lesbian Hotline,** ☎931-4470. **Suicide Prevention,** ☎395-3091. **Troubled Youth Line,** ☎741-1477. All 24hr.

Hospitals: Truman Medical Center, 2301 Holmes St. (☎556-3000). **Women's Clinic of Johnson County,** 5701 W. 119th St. (☎491-4020).

Internet Access: Kansas City Public Library, 311 E. 12th St. (☎221-2685). Open M-Th 9am-9pm, F-Sa 9am-5pm, Su 1-5pm

Post Office: 315 W. Pershing Rd. (☎374-9180), at Broadway (take bus #40 or 51). Open M-F 8am-6:30pm, Sa 8am-2:30pm. **ZIP code:** 64108. **Area code:** 816 in Missouri, 913 in Kansas; in text 816 unless noted.

◤ ACCOMMODATIONS

The least expensive lodgings are near the interstate highways, especially I-70, and towards Independence. Downtown, most hotels are either expensive, uninhabitable, or unsafe—sometimes all three. For help finding a bed in an inn or a home closer to downtown (from $50), call **Bed and Breakfast Kansas City** (☎913-888-3636).

Serendipity Bed and Breakfast, 116 S. Pleasant St. (☎833-4719 or 800-203-4299), 20min. from downtown KC in Independence. A Victorian mansion with all the trimmings and an ample breakfast. Historic tours and train pick-ups are available in a 1926 Studebaker, weather and time permitting. Singles $30-80; doubles $45-100.

American Inn, a chain that dominates the KC budget motel market, has locations at 4141 S. Noland (☎373-8300 or 800-905-6343); Woods Chapel Rd. (☎228-1080) off I-70 at Exit 18; 1211 Armour Rd. (☎471-3451) in North Kansas City off I-35 at Exit 6B; and 7949 Splitlog Rd. (☎913-299-2999) in KCKS off I-70 at Exit 414. Despite the gaudy neon facades, the rooms inside are large, cheap, and good-looking, with A/C, free local calls, cable, and outdoor pools. Rates are subject to a rather annoying game: the motels have a cheap set of rooms (singles from $30, doubles from $45) that are reserved for walk-ins only and usually disappear by evening. When these are gone, singles from $50. Prices (except walk-in rate) drop with reservations and distance from KC.

Interstate Inn (☎229-6311), off I-70 at Exit 18. A great deal if you get one of a small set of walk-in, non-reserveable singles and doubles are $30; other singles start at $50.

YMCA, 900 N. 8th St. (☎913-371-4400) in KCKS. Varying rooms for men with access to the Y's gym and pool. Take bus #1 or 4. Key deposit $7. $25 per night, $81 per week.

Lake Jacomo (☎229-8980), 22 mi. southeast. Take I-470 south to Colbern, then head east on Colbern for 2 mi. Forested campsites, lots of water activities, and a nifty dam across the street. Sites $10, with electricity $14, plus water $16, full hook-up $20.

◖ BBQ AND OTHER GRUB

Kansas City rustles up a herd of barbecue restaurants that serve unusually tangy ribs. The **Westport** area, at Westport Rd. and Broadway just south of 40th St., has eclectic menus, cafes, and coffeehouses. Ethnic fare clusters along **39th St.** just east of State Line. For fresh produce, visit **City Market,** at 5th and Walnut St. along the river. (☎842-1271. Open Su-F 9am-4pm, Sa 6am-4pm.)

▨ Arthur Bryant's, 1727 Brooklyn St. (☎231-1123). Take the Brooklyn exit off I-70 (bus #110 from downtown). A KC tradition, this restaurant is invariably on the short list for best barbecue in the country. "Sandwiches"—little wimpy triangles of bread drowning in a mass of perfectly-cooked meat—are $6.55. Vegetarians can choose from beef, pork, chicken, and turkey. Open M-Th 10am-9:30pm, F-Sa 10am-10pm, Su 11am-8:30pm.

Corner Restaurant, 4059 Broadway (☎931-6630), in the heart of Westport. The best breakfast in all of KC ($4-5), and it is served through lunch. Plate-sized buttermilk or cornmeal pancakes $2.50, homestyle lunch and dinner specials $4-7. Open M-F 7am-3pm, 5-9pm, Sa-Su 7am-2pm.

Strouds, 1015 E. 85th St. (☎333-2132), at Troost, 2 mi. north of the Holmes exit off I-435. Enormous dinners ($7-22) in a weathered wooden hut crammed between the train tracks and an overpass. Early birds get prompt service. Open M-Th 4-9:30pm, F 11am-10:30pm, Sa 2-10:30pm, Su 11am-9:30pm.

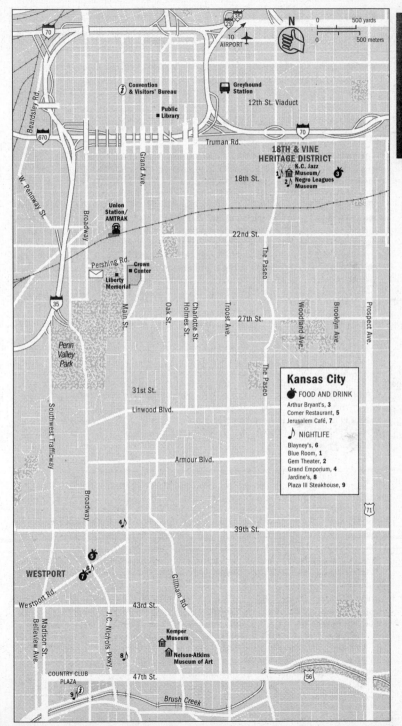

0   500 yards
0   500 meters

TO AIRPORT

Convention & Visitors' Bureau

Greyhound Station

12th St. Viaduct

Public Library

Truman Rd.

70

670

Grand Ave.

18th & VINE HERITAGE DISTRICT

K.C. Jazz Museum/ Negro Leagues Museum

18th St.

Union Station/ AMTRAK

22nd St.

The Paseo

Pershing Rd.

Crown Center

Liberty Memorial

W. Pennway St.

Broadway

35

Oak St.

Charlotte St.

Holmes St.

Troost Ave.

27th St.

Woodland Ave.

Brooklyn Ave.

Prospect Ave.

Penn Valley Park

31st St.

Southwest Trafficway

Linwood Blvd.

The Paseo

Kansas City

🍎 FOOD AND DRINK

Arthur Bryant's, 3
Corner Restaurant, 5
Jerusalem Café, 7

♪ NIGHTLIFE

Blayney's, 6
Blue Room, 1
Gem Theater, 2
Grand Emporium, 4
Jardine's, 8
Plaza III Steakhouse, 9

Armour Blvd.

71

39th St.

Broadway

WESTPORT

Westport Rd.

Madison St.

Belleview Ave.

J.C. Nichols Pkwy.

Gillham Rd.

43rd St.

Kemper Museum

Nelson-Atkins Museum of Art

COUNTRY CLUB PLAZA

47th St.

56

Brush Creek

d'Bronx, 3904 Bell St. (☎531-0550), on the 39th St. restaurant row. A New York deli transplanted to middle America. 35 kinds of subs (half-sub $4-5, whole $6-10) and huge brownies ($1.50). Open M-Th 10:30am-10:30pm, F-Sa 10:30am-midnight.

Jerusalem Cafe, 431 Westport Rd. (☎756-2770). Vegetarians of all faiths claim it as a holy land. Vats of hummus, baba ghanoush, and tabouli garnered praise for this restaurant as the best Middle Eastern food in KC. Sandwiches with rice and salad $4-5, entrees $8-10. Open M-Sa 11am-10pm, Su noon-8pm.

▣ SIGHTS

AFRICAN-AMERICAN SIGHTS. Jazz once flourished in what has been recently designated as the **18th and Vine Historic District.** (☎474-8463.) The **Kansas City Jazz Museum** brings back the era with classy displays, music listening stations, neon dance hall signs, and everything from Ella Fitzgerald's eyeglasses to Louis Armstrong's lip salve. In the same building swings the **Negro Leagues Baseball Museum,** where the era of segregation of the American pastime is recalled with photographs, interactive exhibits, and bittersweet nostalgia. (1616 E. 18th St. Jazz museum: ☎474-8463. Baseball museum: ☎221-1920. Both museums open Tu-Sa 9am-6pm, Su noon-6pm. One museum $6, under 12 $2.50; both museums $8/$4.) The nearby **Black Archives of Mid-America** holds a large collection of paintings and sculpture by African-American artists but focuses on artifacts of local black history. (2033 Vine St. ☎483-1300. Take bus #8 "Indiana." Open M-F 9am-4:30pm, tours start 10am. $2, under 17 50¢.)

ART COLLECTIONS. A taste of KC's masterpieces is available at the **Nelson-Atkins Museum of Art,** at 45th, three blocks northeast of Country Club Plaza. The museum contains one of the best East Asian art collections in the world and a sculpture park with 13 Henry Moores. (4525 Oak St. ☎561-4000. Take bus #47, 55, 56, or 57. Open Tu-Th 10am-4pm, F 10am-9pm, Sa 10am-5pm, Su 1-5pm. Jazz F 5:30-8:30pm. $5, students $2, ages 6-18 $1; free Sa. Free tours Tu-Sa until 2pm, Su until 3pm.) Two blocks northwest, through the **Art Institute** campus, the entrance to the **Kemper Museum of Contemporary Art and Design** is marked by an enormous glass spider. Modern sculptures and works by Georgia O'Keeffe and Robert Mapplethorpe are scattered throughout this young museum. (4420 Warwick Blvd. ☎561-3737. Open Tu-Th 10am-4pm, F 10am-9pm, Sa 10am-5pm, Su 11am-5pm. Free.)

THE PLAZA. A few blocks to the west at 47th and Southwest Trafficway, **Country Club Plaza,** known as "the Plaza," is the oldest and perhaps most picturesque shopping center in the US. Modeled after buildings in Seville, Spain, the Plaza boasts fountains, sculptures, hand-painted tiles, and reliefs of grinning gargoyles. During summer, the Plaza hosts free concerts Th 5-8pm and Sa-Su 2-5pm. It is lit at night from Thanksgiving to New Year's; catch a glimpse from the **riverwalk** along Bush Creek. (☎753-0100. Buses #39, 40, 47, 51, 56, 57, and 155.) A few blocks south of the Plaza is the **Toy and Miniature Museum,** containing a vast collection of mostly 19th-century toys that are more historical than kid-oriented. (5235 Oak St. ☎333-2055. Open W-Sa 10am-4pm, Su 1-4pm; closed the first two weeks after Labor Day. $4, seniors and students $3.50, ages 3-12 $2.)

CROWN CENTER. **Crown Center** sits 2 mi. north of the Plaza at Pershing. The center, headquarters of Hallmark Cards, houses a maze of restaurants and shops, plus the children's **Coterie Theatre** and the **Ice Terrace,** KC's only public outdoor ice-skating rink. On the 3rd level of the center, say "I care!" and see how cards and accessories are made at the **Hallmark Visitors Center.** (Center: 2450 Grand Ave. ☎274-8444. Take bus #40, 56, or 57 or any trolley from downtown. Coterie: ☎474-6785. $8, children $6. Ice Terrace: ☎274-8412. Rink open Nov.-Dec. Su-Th 10am-9pm, F-Sa 10am-11pm; Jan.-Mar. daily 10am-9pm. $5, under 13 $4. Rentals $1.50. Visitors center: ☎274-3613 or 274-5672 for a recording. Open M-F 9am-5pm, Sa 9:30am-4:30pm. Free.)

🎵 ENTERTAINMENT

The **Missouri Repertory Theatre,** 50th and Oak St., stages American classics. (☎235-2700. Season Sept.-May. Tickets $20-34, students and seniors $3 off. Box office open M-F 10am-5pm; call for in-season weekend hrs.) **Quality Hill Playhouse,** 303 W. 10th St., produces off-Broadway plays and revues year-round (☎235-2700; tickets $17-19, seniors and students $2 off). Late June to mid-July, the **Heart of America Shakespeare Festival** (☎531-7728) in Southmoreland Park, 47th and Oak St., puts on free shows nearly every night at 8pm. For more entertainment news, *Pitch Weekly* is helpful, as is the guide at the visitors center.

Sports fans will be pierced to the heart by **Arrowhead Stadium,** at I-70 and Blue Ridge Cutoff, home to football's **Chiefs** (☎920-9400 or 800-676-5488; tickets from $30) and soccer's **Wizards** (☎472-4625; tickets $10-15). Next door, a water-fountained wonder, **Kauffman Stadium** (☎921-8000 or 800-676-9257), houses the **Royals** baseball team (tickets $7-17, M and Th most seats half-price). A stadium express bus runs from downtown and Country Club Plaza on game days.

🌃 NIGHTLIFE

In the 20s, Kansas City played hot spot to the nation's best jazz. Pianist **Count Basie** and his "Kansas City Sound" reigned at the River City bars; 20 years later, saxophonist **Charlie "Bird" Parker** spread his wings and soared. The **Crown Center** celebrates annually with the **Kansas City International Jazz Festival,** on the last weekend in June (☎888-337-8111; tickets from $12). The restored **Gem Theater**, 1615 E. 18th St., stages blues and jazz like in the old days (☎842-1414; box office open M-F 10am-4pm). Across the street, the **Blue Room**, 1600 E. 18th St. (☎474-2929), cooks M, Th, F, and Sa nights with some of the smoothest acts in town—after all, they have to live up to the legends next door at the museum. The **Grand Emporium**, 3832 Main St., twice voted the best blues night club in the US, has live jazz F-Sa; M and W-Th feature bands of all types. (☎531-1504. Open daily noon-3am. Cover $5-15.)

A few blocks west, noisy nightspots pack the restored **Westport** area, near Broadway and Westport Rd. There's pool, a new deck, and intense rhythm and blues at **Blayney's,** 415 Westport Rd. (☎561-3747. Open Tu-Sa until 3am. Acts usually begin around 9pm. Cover $2-5.) **Kiki's Bon-Ton Maison,** 1515 Westport Rd., features KC's best in-house soul band (Sa 10:30pm) and whips up Cajun food with bayou flavor—jambalaya and crawfish is $10-13; sandwiches are $6-7. (☎931-9417. Open M-Th 11am-10pm, F 11am-11pm, Sa 11am-1:30am, Su 11:30am-8pm. Live music W and Sa.) Kiki's also hosts the annual **Crawfish Fiesta** around the first weekend in June. **Gilhouly's,** 1721 39th St., at Bell St., has over 125 bottled imports, a large selection of Irish and Scottish beers on tap, and several pool tables. (☎561-2899. Open M-Sa 11am-1:30am.) **Cabaret,** 5024 Main St., is a popular gay bar and dance club. (☎753-6504. Open Tu-Su 6pm-2:30am. Cover $3-5.)

🏞 DAYTRIP FROM KANSAS CITY

INDEPENDENCE. The buck stops at Independence, the hometown of former President Harry Truman and a 15min. drive east of KC on I-70; it is also accessible by bus #24 "Independence." The **Harry S. Truman Library and Museum,** at U.S. 24 and Delaware St., has a replica of the Oval Office and exhibits about the man, the times, and the presidency. (☎833-1225 or 800-833-1225. Open M-W and F-Sa 9am-5pm, Th 9am-9pm, Su noon-5pm. $5, seniors $4.50, ages 6-18 $3.) When Washington, D.C. overheated, the Trumans would retreat to the 14-room **Harry S. Truman Home,** 219 N. Delaware St., known as the Summer White House. Get tickets to tour the Victorian mansion at the **Truman Home Ticket and Info Center,** 223 Main St. (☎254-2720. Open daily 9am-4:45pm. Home closed M from Sept.-May. $2, under 16 free.)

Independence's history goes back farther than just Truman. Thousands of pioneers ventured west along the California, Oregon, and Santa Fe trails, which all began here. Go west at the **National Frontier Trails Center,** 318 W. Pacific, and imagine 2000 mi. in a covered wagon—are we there yet? (☎325-7575. Open M-Sa 9am-4:30pm, Su 12:30-4:30pm. $3.50, ages 6-17 $2.) The gothic **Vaile Mansion,** 1500 N. Liberty St., built in 1881, has 112 windows and 2 ft. thick walls. (☎325-7430. Open Apr.-Oct. and Dec. M-Sa 10am-4pm, Su 1-4pm. $3, seniors $2.50, ages 6-16 $1.)

Inspired by the chambered nautilus, the computer-designed world headquarters of the **Reorganized Church of Jesus Christ of Latter Day Saints,** 1001 W. Walnut St., at River and Walnut St. is a bizarre and beautiful seashell that spirals up nearly 200 ft. (☎833-1000. Tours M-Sa 9-11:30am and 1-5pm, Su 1-5pm. Organ recitals Su 3pm; daily in summer. Free.) Nearby, in the City Hall building, the **Dept. of Tourism,** 111 E. Maple, has the skinny on Independence (☎325-7113; open M-F 8am-5pm).

BRANSON ☎417

The Presley family had no idea what the impact would be when they opened a tiny music theater on **West Hwy. 76.** Over 7 million tourists, seemingly all retirees, clog Branson's strip each year (Rte. 76, a.k.a. Country Music Blvd.) to visit the "live country music capital of the Universe." Billboards, motels, and giant showplaces beckon the masses that visit Branson each year to embrace this collage of all things plastic or franchised, with a dash of country music and variety entertainment sprinkled on the surface (of course, Branson is *all* surface). Theaters of all types line the Blvd.; big-name acts, such as Loretta Lynn and Billy Ray Cyrus, play the **Grand Palace,** 2700 W. Rte. 76. (☎336-1220 or 800-884-4536. Shows Apr.-Dec. $27-45, children $12-45.) Other acts, like the **Platters** ($22, 16 and under free) and the **Osmond Family** ($22/$5), love Branson too much to ever leave; they play in their established venues all season long. For full listings, pick up one of the many guides available, more or less, at every store within a 30 mi. radius of town.

Motels along Rte. 76 generally start around $30, but prices often increase during the busy season from July to Sept. Less tacky, inexpensive motels line Rte. 265, 4 mi. west of the strip or Gretna Rd. at the west end of the strip. **Budget Inn,** 315 N. Gretna Rd., has slightly dim but spacious rooms with A/C, free local calls, cable, and pool access very close to the action. (☎334-0292. Rooms from $24.50.) **Indian Point,** at the end of Indian Point Rd., south of Hwy. 76, has lakeside sites with swimming and a boat launch (☎338-2121 or 888-444-6777. Reception Su-Th 9am-7pm, F-Sa 8am-8pm. Sites $12, with electricity $16.)

The off-season runs from Jan. to Mar.; many attractions close. **Visitors info: Branson Chamber of Commerce,** on Rte. 248 just west of the Rte. 248/65 junction (☎334-4136; open M-F 8am-6pm, Sa 8am-5pm, Su 10am-4pm). **Greyhound's** nearest location is 20 mi. south in Harrison, but there is a **flag stop** in town at Bob Evans, on the corner of Hwy. 76 and Hwy. 65. **Area code:** 417.

OKLAHOMA

From 1838 to 1839, President Andrew Jackson forced the relocation of "The Five Civilized Tribes" from the southeastern states to the designated Oklahoma Indian Territory in a tragic march which came to be known as "The Trail of Tears" (see p. 589). After rebuilding their tribes in Oklahoma, the Indians were again dislocated in 1889 by whites rushing to stake claims. Their unseemly past behind them, the people of Oklahoma now treat each other with "old-fashioned" respect and courtesy. Moreover, the depression-era "dustbowl" wasteland depicted in *The Grapes of Wrath* is now blanketed by the green crops of Oklahoma's rolling red hills, hemmed in by calming lakes and rivers. All this leaves Oklahoma a surprisingly scenic and friendly place to visit, putting the "OK" back in Oklahoma.

🚺 PRACTICAL INFORMATION

Capital: Oklahoma City.

Visitor Info: Oklahoma Tourism and Recreation Dept., 15 N. Robinson, Rm. 801, Oklahoma City 73152 (☎521-2406 or 800-652-6552; www.travelok.com), in the Concord Bldg. at Sheridan St. Open M-F 8am-5pm.

Postal Abbreviation: OK. **Sales Tax:** 6-8%. **Tolls:** Damn annoying. Oklahoma is fond of toll-booths, so keep a wad of bills handy when driving around.

TULSA ☎918

Though Tulsa is not Oklahoma's political capital, it is in many ways the center of the state. First settled by Creek Native Americans arriving on the Trail of Tears, Tulsa's location on the banks of the Arkansas River made it a logical trading out-post. The town's Art Deco skyscrapers, French villas, Georgian mansions, and dis-tinctively large Native American population reflect its varied heritage. Rough-riding motorcyclists and slick oilmen have recently joined the city's cultural mélange, seeking the good life on the Great Plains.

🔛🚺 ORIENTATION AND PRACTICAL INFORMATION. Tulsa sections off neatly into one sq. mi. quadrants. Downtown surrounds the intersection of **Main St.** (north-south) and **Admiral Blvd.** (east-west). Numbered streets lie in ascending order north or south from Admiral. Named streets run north-south in alphabetical order; those named after western cities are west of Main St., while eastern cities lie to the east. **Tulsa International Airport** (☎838-5000; call M-F 8am-5pm) is just northeast of downtown and accessible by I-244 or U.S. 169. **Greyhound,** 317 S. Detroit Ave. (☎584-4428), departs for Oklahoma City (2hr., 8 per day, $18); St. Louis (7-10hr., 6 per day, $76); Kansas City (7hr., 3 per day, $39); and Dallas (7hr., 4 per day, $47). Station open 24 hours. **Metropolitan Tulsa Transit Authority,** 510 S. Rockford, runs local buses. Maps and schedules are at the main office or on buses. (☎582-2100. Open M-F 8am-5pm. Buses operate M-Sa 6am-7pm. Fare 75¢, transfers 5¢, seniors and disabled 35¢, ages 5-18 60¢, under 5 free.) **Taxis: Yellow Cab,** ☎582-6161. **Hospitals: Hillcrest Medical Center,** 1120 S. Utica Ave. (☎579-1000), and **Center for Women's Health,** 1822 E. 15th St. (☎749-4444). **Metropolitan Tulsa Chamber of Commerce:** 616 S. Boston Ave. (☎585-1201 or 800-558-3311; open M-F 8am-5pm). **Post office:** 333 W. 4th St. (open M-F 7:30am-5pm). **ZIP code:** 74101. **Area code:** 918.

📍 ACCOMMODATIONS. Decent budget accommodations are scarce downtown. Try the budget motels around the junction of **I-44** and **I-244** (Exit 222 from I-44); take bus #17 "Southwest Blvd." **Georgetown Plaza Motel,** 8502 E. 27th St., off I-44 at 31st and Memorial St., offers clean, if frayed, rooms with free local calls and cable TV. (☎622-6616. Singles $28; with microfridge $31; doubles $28/$34.) The **Gateway Motor Hotel,** 5600 W. Skelley, at Exit 222 C, has functional rooms decorated in pea-green and timber fashion. (☎446-6611. Singles $29; doubles $34.) The 250-site **Mingo RV Park,** 801 N. Mingo Rd., at the northeast corner of the I-244 and Mingo Rd. intersection, provides laundry and showers in a semi-urban setting. (☎832-8824 or 800-932-8824. Reception daily 8:30am-8pm. Sites $9, full hook-up $19.) **Heyburn Park,** 28165 W. Heyburn Park Rd., 20 mi. southwest of the city in Kellyville, sits off I-44 or Rte. 66. Turn right for 4 mi. on Rte. 33 and watch for the Shepards Pt. sign. Shady sites line the shores of Heyburn Lake, far removed from the hubbub of town. (☎247-6601 or 887-444-6777. Sites $10, with water and electricity $14.)

🍽🎭 NIGHTLIFE. Most downtown restaurants cater to lunching business people, closing on weekends and at 2pm on weekdays. **Nelson's Buffeteria,** 514 S. Boston Ave., is an old-fashioned diner that has served their blue plate special (two scram-bled eggs, hash browns, biscuit and gravy $2.50) and famous chicken-fried steak ($6) since 1929. (☎584-9969. Open M-F 6am-2pm.) For extended hours, S. Peoria Ave. has more to offer. **The Brook,** 3401 S. Peoria, in a converted movie theater, has classic art-deco appeal. A traditional menu of chicken, burgers, and salads ($5-7) is complemented by an extensive list of $5.25 signature martinis. (☎748-9977. Open M-Sa 11am-2am, Su 11am-11pm.)

Read the free *Urban Tulsa*, at local restaurants, and *The Spot* in the F *Tulsa World* for up-to-date specs on arts and entertainment. Good bars line the 3000s along S. Peoria Ave., an area known as **Brookside**, and 15th St. east of Peoria. Let the party-animal inside reveal itself at **ID Bar**, 3340 S. Peoria Ave. With a posh interior and quality DJs, this newly-opened dance club has a decidedly un-Oklahoma feel. (☎743-0600. Open W-Su 9pm-2am. Live music W. Cover F-Sa $5-7. 21+.) 18th and Boston Ave. raises a ruckus at night, catering to the young adult crowd. College kids flock to the blues-happy **Steamroller**, 1738 Boston Ave., commonly billed as "the snob-free, dork-free, band-and-brewski place to be." (☎583-9520. Open M-Th 11am-10pm, F 11am-2am, Sa 5pm-2am. Local bands F-Sa 10pm. Cover $3-10.)

▣▯ **SIGHTS AND ENTERTAINMENT.** The **Philbrook Museum of Art**, 2727 S. Rockford Rd., presents tastefully selected works of Native American and international art in a renovated Italian Renaissance villa, complete with a grassy sculpture garden. Take bus #5 "Peoria." (☎749-7941 or 800-324-7941. Open Tu-W and F-Sa 10am-5pm, Th 10am-8pm, Su 11am-5pm. $5.40, students and seniors $3.25, under 13 free.) Perched atop an Osage foothill 2 mi. northwest of downtown, the **Thomas Gilcrease Museum**, 1400 Gilcrease Museum Rd., houses the world's largest collection of Western American art, as well as 250,000 Native American artifacts. Take the Gilcrease exit off Rte. 412 or bus #47. (☎596-2700. Open M-Sa 9am-5pm, Su 11am-5pm; Mid-Sept. to mid-May closed M. $3 donation requested.)

The ultra-modern, gold-mirrored architecture of **Oral Roberts University**, 7777 S. Lewis Ave., rises out of an Oklahoma plain about 6 mi. south of downtown between Lewis and Harvard Ave.; take bus #12. In 1964, Oral had a dream in which God commanded him to "Build Me A University," and Tulsa's most-frequented tourist attraction was born. The **visitors center**, located in the spiky Prayer Tower, offers free 35min. tours. (☎495-6807. Open Jun.-Aug. M-Sa 9am-5pm, Su 1-5pm; Sept.-May 10am-5pm, Su 1-5pm. Tours begin every 15min.)

Tulsa thrives during events like the **International Mayfest** (☎582-6435; May 17-20, 2001). The **Intertribal Pow-Wow**, at the Tulsa Fairgrounds Pavilion (Expo Sq.), attracts Native Americans and thousands of on-lookers for a three-day festival of food, arts and crafts, and nightly dance contests. (☎744-1113. Usually in Aug., call for exact dates. $4, seniors $1, under 5 free.)

NEAR TULSA: TAHLEQUAH

Buried deep in the lush hills of northeast Oklahoma, 66 mi. east of Tulsa on Rte. 51, the sleepy hamlet of Tahlequah historically marks the end of the Cherokee tribe's forced movement west. In the center of town, on Cherokee Sq., stands the capitol building of the **Cherokee Nation**, 101 S. Muskogee Ave., easy to find since Hwy. 51, 82, and 62 all intersect and run together on Muskogee. Built in 1870, the building, together with other tribal government buildings such as the Supreme Court building and the Cherokee National Prison (one and two blocks south of Cherokee Sq. respectively), formed the highest authority in Oklahoma until statehood in 1907. Across from the northeast corner of Cherokee Sq., the **visitors center**, 123 E. Delaware St. (☎456-3742), offers free maps of the major sites downtown.

The **Cherokee Heritage Center**, 4 mi. south of town on Hwy. 82, left on Willis Rd., then right at the sign, includes both **Ancient Village**, a recreation of a 16th-century Cherokee settlement with ongoing demonstrations of skills such as flint knapping and basket weaving, and the well-executed **Cherokee National Museum**. (☎456-6007 or 888-999-6007. Village and Museum open Feb.-Apr. M-Sa 10am-5pm; daily May-Oct. 10am-5pm; Nov.-Dec. M-Sa 10am-5pm, Su 1-5pm. Last tour 4:15pm. $7.50, under 13 $3.50.) **Area code:** 918.

TRAIL OF TEARS President Jackson ignored a Supreme Court ruling when he forced 13,000 Cherokee Indians to march from North Carolina, Tennessee, Georgia, and Alabama to the Indian Territories. Between 1838 and 1839, many walked the trail at gunpoint, and by the end thousands had died of hunger and disease. The Trail of Tears National Historic Trail, established in Dec. 1987, commemorates this journey by designating the remaining parts of the Trail of Tears as National Historic Sites. Auto routes (Rte. 10 and 62) follow the northern land trail as closely as possible. For more info, contact Trail of Tears National Historic Trail, Southwest Region, National Park Service, P.O. Box 728, Santa Fe, NM 87504 (☎505-988-6888).

OKLAHOMA CITY   ☎405

At noon on Apr. 22, 1889, a gunshot sent settlers scrambling into the Oklahoma Territory—the "landrush" was afoot. By sundown, Oklahoma City, set strategically along the Santa Fe Railroad, was home to over 10,000 homesteaders. These settlers have since multiplied, maintaining the thriving stockyards and horseshows that often vanished with the civilizing of the Old West. In recent years, Oklahoma City has had more than its share of tragedy; the city remains an unobstrusive and tranquil place, in spite of the traumatic 1995 bombing of the Alfred R. Murrah federal office building and the devastating 1999 tornado which left whole sections of the city in ruin.

🖥🛈 ORIENTATION AND PRACTICAL INFORMATION. Oklahoma City is constructed on a nearly perfect grid. Almost all of the city's attractions are outside the city center, but the Metro Transit bus reaches many of them. Cheap and plentiful parking makes driving the best way to go. **Will Rogers World Airport** (☎680-3200), is on I-44 southwest of downtown, Exit 116 B. To get to the **Greyhound** station, 427 W. Sheridan Ave. (☎235-6425), at Walker St., take city bus #4, 5, 6, 8, or 10. *Be careful at night.* Buses run to Tulsa (2hr., 7 per day, $18); Dallas (5hr., 4 per day, $40); and Kansas City (10hr., 6 per day, $69). Station open 24 hours. **Amtrak**, 100 S. E.K. Gaylord Blvd., rumbles to Ft. Worth (4½ hr., 1 per day, $25-49). The station is open 24 hours, but unattended. **Oklahoma Metro Transit** has bus service M-Sa 6am-6pm; all routes radiate from the station at 200 N. Shartel St. The office at Union Station, 300 S.W. 7th, distributes free schedules. (☎235-7433. Open M-F 8am-5pm. Fare $1, seniors and ages 6-17 50¢.) **Yellow Cab,** ☎232-6161. The **Oklahoma City Convention and Visitors Bureau**, 189 W. Sheridan at Robinson St., has city-specific info (☎297-8910; open M-F 8:30am-5pm). **Post Office:** 320 S.W. 5th St. (open M-F 6am-10pm, Sa 8am-5pm). **ZIP code:** 73125. **Area code:** 405.

🏠 ACCOMMODATIONS. Cheap lodging in OKC lies along the interstate highways, particularly on I-35 north of the I-44 junction; the I-40 cluster east of town was depleted by the tornado. The most inexpensive options are chains, like **Motel 6**, 6166 Tinker Diagonal, across from the Sixpence, off I-40 Exit 156B. Rooms have cable, free local calls, and access to a pool. (☎737-6676. Singles $32; doubles $38.) **The Royal Inn**, 2800 S. I-35, south of the junction with I-40, treats you to free local calls, HBO, and adequate rooms. (☎672-0899. Singles $27; doubles $34.) Behind a strip mall are the 172 sites of **RCA,** 12115 Northeast Expwy./I-35 N. Take southbound Frontage Rd. off Exit 137; it's ¼ mi. to the red-and-white "RV" sign. (☎478-0278. Open daily 8am-8pm; in winter 8am-6pm. Pool, laundry, and showers. Sites $12, full hook-up $17.) In contrast, **Lake Thunderbird State Park** offers campsites near a beautiful lake fit for swimming or fishing. Take I-40 east to Choctaw Rd. (Exit 166), then south 10 mi. until the road ends and make a left for another mi. (☎360-3572. Office open M-F 8am-5pm; there's a campsite host for late or weekend arrivals. Showers available. Sites $7, full hook-up $13-19; huts $40.)

◨☑ **FOOD AND NIGHTLIFE.** Oklahoma City contains the largest feeder cattle market in the US, and beef tops most menus. Most places downtown close early in the afternoon after they've served business lunchers. After-hours restaurants lie immediately east of town on Sheridan Ave. (in the Bricktown district) and north of downtown, along Classen Blvd. and Western Ave. Everyone's fighting for the rights to the late Leo's recipes at **Leo's Original BBQ,** 3631 N. Kelley St., a classic, hickory smoking outfit in the northwest reaches of town. (☎424-5367. Open M 11am-2pm, Tu-Sa 11am-7pm.) The **Classen Grill,** 5124 Classen St., serves breakfast and middle American meals. (☎842-0428. Open M-Th 7am-9pm, F-Sa 7am-10pm, Su 8am-2pm.) The *Oklahoma Gazette* has listings of local eateries and nightlife. Unfortunately, nightlife here is almost as rare as the elusive jackalope. The Bricktown district has restaurants with live music. The **Bricktown Brewery,** 1 N. Oklahoma St., at Sheridan Ave., brews beer on the premises. (☎232-2739. Open Su-M 11am-10pm, Tu-Th 11am-midnight, F-Sa 11am-1:30am. Live music Tu and F-Sa 9pm. Cover $5 for bands. Upstairs 21+.) There are a number of solid dance clubs in the converted warehouses of the gay district, near **39th St.** and **Penn Ave.**

◨◪ **SIGHTS AND ENTERTAINMENT.** Monday morning is the time to visit the **Oklahoma City Stockyards,** 2500 Exchange Ave. (☎235-8675), the busiest in the world. Take bus #12 from the terminal to Agnew and Exchange Ave. Cattle auctions (M-Tu) begin at 8am and may last into the night. Visitors enter free of charge via a catwalk soaring over cow pens and cattle herds, leading from the parking lot northeast of the auction house. The auction is as Old West as it gets; only those with a wide-brim cowboy hat, blue jeans, boots, and faded dress shirt fit in.

Plant lovers should make a bee-line for **Myriad Gardens,** 301 W. Reno Ave., downtown at Robinson Ave., where a 70 ft. diameter glass cylinder, called the Crystal Bridge, perches above a large pond. The gardens include both a desert and a rainforest. (☎297-3995. Open M-Sa 9am-6pm, Su noon-6pm. $4, seniors and students $3, ages 4-12 $2. Outdoor gardens open daily 7am-11pm. Free.) The **National Cowboy Hall of Fame,** 1700 N. E. 63rd St., features an extensive collection of Western art. (☎478-2250. Open daily June-Aug. 8:30am-6pm, Sept.-May 9am-5pm. $8.50, seniors $7, ages 6-12 $4, under 6 free.) The **Oklahoma City National Memorial,** at 5th and Harvey downtown, is a powerful tribute to the victims of the 1995 bombing of the Murrah Federal Bldg. The **Red Earth Festival** is the country's largest celebration of Native America; the Myriad Convention Center hosts art fairs and intense dance competitions. (☎427-5228. June 8-10, 2001. $7.)

TEXAS

Covering an area as wide as the span of Wisconsin and Montana and as long as the stretch from North Carolina to Key West, Texas has more the brawn of a country than a state. The fervently proud, independent citizens of the "Lone Star State" seem to prefer it that way. After revolting against the Spanish in 1821 and splitting from Mexico in 1836, the Republic of Texas stood alone until 1845, when it entered the Union as the 28th state. The state's unofficial motto proclaims that "everything is bigger in Texas;" this truth is evident in prolific wide-brimmed hats, styled and sculpted ladies' coifs, boat-sized American autos, giant ranch spreads, countless steel skyscrapers, and towering urban cowboys who seem ready and willing to conquer the frontier and fight for independence all over again.

HIGHLIGHTS OF TEXAS

FOOD. Drippin' barbecue and colossal steaks reign supreme in this state where beef is king and vegetables are for the cows. Some of the best beef awaits in Austin (p. 598) and Amarillo (p. 617).

SAN ANTONIO . Remember the Alamo! A city rich with Spanish heritage. (p. 615).

RODEOS/COWBOYS. The ol' West lives on in Fort Worth (p. 608) and at the Mesquite Rodeo in Dallas (p. 607), with some of the finest rope-riders in the land.

✱ PRACTICAL INFORMATION

Capital: Austin.

Visitor Info: Texas Travel Information Centers (800-452-9292; www.tourtexas.com), near state lines on all major highways into Texas. Call 8am-6pm (centers open daily 8am-5pm) for a free guidebook. **Texas Division of Tourism,** P.O. Box 12728, Austin 78711 (800-888-8839). **Texas Parks and Wildlife Dept.,** Austin Headquarters Complex, 4200 Smith School Rd., Austin 78744 (512-389-8950 or 800-792-1112).

Postal Abbreviation: TX. **Sales Tax:** 6-8.25%.

SAN ANTONIO ☎210

The skyline may be dominated by aging office buildings, but no Texan city seems more determined to preserve its rich heritage than the romantic San Antone. Founded in 1691 by Spanish missionaries, the city is home to the famed Alamo, historic Missions, and La Villita, once a village for San Antonio's original settlers and now a workshop for local artisans. Many attractions, including the magnificent (though slightly artificial) Riverwalk, make San Antonio a popular vacation destination; hotel occupancy rates and prices rise on weekends, unlike most other cities of comparable size. Though both Native Americans and Germans have at one time claimed San Antonio as their own, Spanish speakers (55% of the population) outnumber any other group; the city's food, architecture, and language reflect this influence.

▰ GETTING THERE AND GETTING AROUND

Flights: San Antonio International Airport, 9800 Airport Blvd. (☎207-3411), north of town. Accessible by I-410 and U.S. 281. Bus #2 ("Airport") connects the airport to downtown at Market and Alamo. Taxi to downtown $14-15.

Trains: Amtrak, 350 Hoefgen St. (☎223-3226), facing the northern side of the Alamodome. To: Houston (5hr., 3 per week, $30); Dallas (9hr., daily, $28); and Los Angeles (27hr., 4 per week, $135). Open daily 10am-4pm.

Buses: Greyhound, 500 N. Saint Mary's St. (☎270-5824). To: Houston (4hr., 9 per day, $21) and Dallas (5-6hr., 15 per day, $34). Open 24hr.

Public Transit: VIA Metropolitan Transit, 800 W. Myrtle (☎362-2020; open M-Sa 7am-7pm, Su 8am-5pm). Buses operate daily 4:30am-11:30pm, but many routes stop at 6pm. Infrequent service to outlying areas. Fare 75¢. One-day "day tripper" passes $2, available at 112 Soledad St.

Taxis: Yellow Cab, ☎226-4242.

Car Rental: American Auto Rental, 3249 SW Military Dr. (☎922-9464). $20.80 per day with 100 free mi. Must be 21 with credit card or cash deposit. Customer pick-up service available for $12. Open M-F 8am-6pm, Sa 9am-3pm, Su noon-5pm.

✱ PRACTICAL INFORMATION

Visitor Info: 317 Alamo Plaza (☎270-8748), downtown across from the Alamo. Open daily 8:30am-6pm. Free maps and brochures.

Hotlines: Rape Crisis, ☎349-7273. 24hr. **Supportive Services for the Elderly and Disabled,** ☎226-9212. Referrals and transport.

Hospital: Metropolitan Methodist Hospital, 1310 McCullough Ave. (☎208-2200). 24hr.

Post Office: 615 E. Houston (☎800-275-8777), 1 block from the Alamo. Open M-F 8:30am-5:30pm. **ZIP code:** 78205. **Area code:** 210.

▮ ACCOMMODATIONS

For cheap motels, try **Roosevelt Ave.,** a southern extension of Saint Mary's St., and **Fredericksburg Rd.** Inexpensive motels also line **Broadway** between downtown and Brackenridge Park. Drivers should follow **I-35 N** to find cheaper and often safer lodging within a 15 mi. radius of town.

Downtown San Antonio

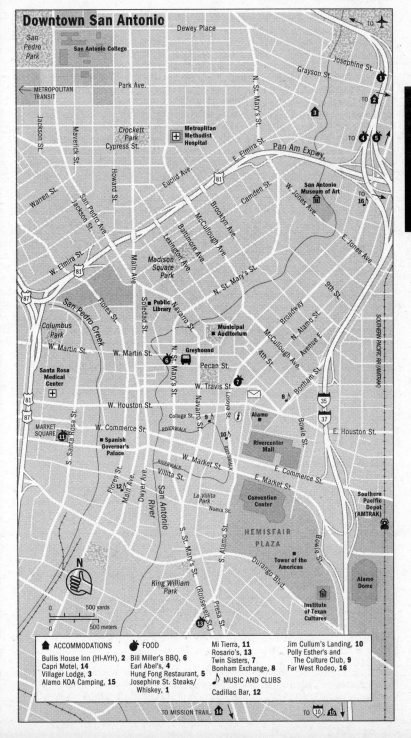

Dewey Place

San Pedro Park

San Antonio College

Park Ave.

METROPOLITAN TRANSIT

Crockett Park
Cypress St.

Metroplitan Methodist Hospital

Josephine St.

Grayson St.

Pan Am Expwy.

San Antonio Museum of Art

E. Jones Ave.

Jackson St.
Maverick St.
Warren St.
Jackson St.
San Pedro Ave.
Howard St.
Main Ave.
N. St. Mary's St.
Euclid Ave.
Brooklyn Ave.
McCullough Ave.
Baltimore Ave.
Lexington Ave.
Camden St.
W. Jones Ave.

Madison Square Park

N. St. Mary's St.

9th St.
Broadway
McCullough Ave.
N. Alamo St.
Avenue E
Bonham St.

W. Elmira St.

Flores St.
San Pedro Creek

Columbus Park

Public Library

Soledad St.
Navarro St.

Municipal Auditorium

W. Martin St.
W. Martin St.

Greyhound

Pecan St.

4th St.

Santa Rosa Medical Center

N. St. Mary's St.

W. Travis St.

Losoya St.

Alamo

SOUTHERN PACIFIC RR (AMTRAK)

MARKET SQUARE

Spanish Governor's Palace

W. Houston St.

W. Commerce St.

College St.

RIVERWALK

Navarro St.

Bowie St.

E. Houston St.

E. Commerce St.

S. Santa Rosa St.

Flores St.
Main Ave.
Dewey Ave.
San Antonio River

RIVERWALK

Villita St.

W. Market St.

La Villita Park

Nueva St.

Rivercenter Mall

Convention Center

E. Market St.

Southern Pacific Depot (AMTRAK)

S. St. Mary's St. (Roosevelt St.)

King William Park

S. Alamo St.

HEMISFAIR PLAZA

Tower of the Americas

Durango Blvd.

Bowie St.

Institute of Texan Cultures

Alamo Dome

N

0   500 yards
0   500 meters

Presa St.

TO MISSION TRAIL, 14

TO 10 15

TEXAS

🏠 ACCOMMODATIONS

Bullis House Inn (HI-AYH), **2**
Capri Motel, **14**
Villager Lodge, **3**
Alamo KOA Camping, **15**

🍴 FOOD

Bill Miller's BBQ, **6**
Earl Abel's, **4**
Hung Fong Restaurant, **5**
Josephine St. Steaks/ Whiskey, **1**

Mi Tierra, **11**
Rosario's, **13**
Twin Sisters, **7**
Bonham Exchange, **8**

🎵 MUSIC AND CLUBS

Cadillac Bar, **12**

Jim Cullum's Landing, **10**
Polly Esther's and The Culture Club, **9**
Far West Rodeo, **16**

Bullis House Inn San Antonio International Hostel (HI-AYH), 621 Pierce St. (☎223-9426), 2 mi. north of downtown on Broadway, right on Grayson. From the bus station, walk to Navarro St. and take bus #11 or 15 to Grayson and New Braunfels; walk 2 blocks west. A spacious, ranch-style hostel in a quiet neighborhood. Pool, kitchen, Internet access. Fills quickly in summer. Reception daily 8am-10pm. No curfew. Linen $2. Breakfast $4.50. $16.75, non-members $19.75.

Villager Lodge, 1126 E. Elmira (☎222-9463 or 800-584-0800), about 3 blocks east of St. Mary's; 1 mi. north of downtown; take bus #8. The caring management provides the cleanest rooms at this price. Cable TV, 5 free local calls, A/C, and Microfridges in some rooms. Outdoor pool. Small singles for $27, large singles or doubles $34.

Capri Motel, 1718 Roosevelt Ave. (☎533-2583), about 2 mi. south of downtown near the missions. Fairly clean rooms at reasonable prices. Singles $35; doubles $40.

Alamo KOA, 602 Gembler Rd. (☎224-9296 or 800-833-7785), 6 mi. from downtown; take bus #24 ("Industrial Park") from the corner of Houston and Alamo downtown. From I-10 E, take Exit 580/W.W. White Rd., drive 2 blocks north, then take a left onto Gembler Rd. Beautiful, well-kept grounds with lots of shade. Each site has a grill and patio. Showers, laundry facilities, pool, and free movies. Reception daily 7:30am-9:30pm. Tent sites $20, full RV hook-up $22.75; $3 per additional person.

◖ FOOD

Expensive cafes and restaurants line the **Riverwalk**—breakfast alone can clean you out if you don't settle for a muffin and coffee. North of town, Asian restaurants open onto **Broadway** across from Brackenridge. On weekends, hundreds of carnival food booths crowd the walkways of **Market Sq.** Come late in the day when prices drop and vendors are willing to haggle. (☎207-8600. Open daily 10am-8pm; Sept.-May 10am-6pm.) **Pig Stand** diners offer cheap but decent grub all over this part of Texas; the branches at 801 S. Presa, off S. Alamo, and 1508 Broadway (both near downtown) stay open 24 hours. The omnipresent **Bill Miller's BBQ,** one location at 501 N. Saint Mary's St., at Pecan St., dishes out serious BBQ (☎212-4343; open M-F 10am-6pm).

Mi Tierra, 218 Produce Row (☎225-1262), in Market Sq. Perpetually smiling mariachi musicians serenade patrons who also smile after filling up on chicken enchiladas slathered in chocolate-based mole sauce ($8.25). Lunch specials $6. Grab desert on the run from their bakery. Open 24hr.

Rosario's, 910 S. Alamo St. (☎223-1806), at S. Saint Mary's St., is widely acknowledged by locals to be the best eatery in town. Scrumptious chicken quesadillas for $6 uphold the reputation. Live music F-Sa nights. Open M 10:45am-3pm, Tu-Th 10:45am-10pm, F-Sa 11am-12:30am.

Josephine St. Steaks/Whiskey, 400 Josephine St. (☎224-6169), at McAllister. Josephine's specializes in thick Texan steaks, but offers an assortment of big, tasty dishes in a relaxed cafe atmosphere. Entrees $5-12, lunch specials $5-7. Open M-Th 11am-10pm, F-Sa 11am-11pm.

Twin Sisters, 124 Broadway (☎354-1559). This cafe and bakery is located downtown and makes the best vegetarian eats around. Try the caesar with eggless tofu salad ($8) or the tofu quesadillas ($6). Open M-F 7:30am-3pm.

Earl Abel's, 4220 Broadway (☎822-3358). A professional organist for silent movies, Mr. Abel found himself out of work once the "talkies" hit the silver screen. Consequently, he opened a restaurant in 1933 and not much has changed since (even some of the patrons, by the looks of them). Abel's family still runs the operation. Fried chicken, Old Earl's speciality, for $5-7. Bacon, eggs, hash browns, and toast served with a friendly smile $4.75. Dinner $5-10. Breakfast served all day. Open daily 6:30am-1am.

◉ SIGHTS

Much of historic San Antonio lies in the present-day downtown and surrounding areas. The city may seem diffuse, but almost every major site or park is within a few miles of downtown and is accessible by public transportation.

THE MISSIONS

THE ALAMO. "Be silent, friend, here heroes died to blaze a trail for other men." **The Alamo,** which has always been set apart from the other missions, is not maintained by the National Historical Park but by the Daughters of the Republic of Texas—oh, brother! If the core of Texas pride were stored in a strongbox, it would be deposited here. Disobeying orders to retreat with their cannons, the 189 defenders of the Alamo, outnumbered 20 to one, held off the Mexican army for 12 days. Then, on the morning of the 13th day, the Mexicans commenced the infamous *deguello* (throat-cutting). The only survivors of the Alamo defenders were women, children, and slaves. Forty-six days later, General Sam Houston's small army defeated the Mexicans at San Jacinto amid cries of "Remember the Alamo!" *(☎ 225-1391. At the center of Alamo Plaza near Houston and Alamo St. Open M-Sa 9am-5:30pm, Su 10am-6:30pm. Free.)*

THE OTHER MISSIONS. The five missions along the river once formed the soul of San Antonio; the city preserves their remains in the San Antonio Missions National Historical Park. To reach the missions, follow the brown and white "Mission Trail" signs beginning on S. Saint Mary's St. downtown. **Mission San José,** a.k.a. the "Queen of the Missions," has remnants of its own irrigation system, a gorgeous sculpted rose window, and numerous restored buildings. As the largest of San Antonio's missions, it best conveys the self-sufficiency of these institutions. **Mission Concepción** is the oldest unrestored stone church in North America. Traces of the once-colorful frescoes are still visible. **Mission San Juan Capistrano** and **Mission San Francisco de la Espada,** smaller and simpler than the others, evoke the isolation of such outposts. Between them lies the Espada Aqueduct, the only remaining waterway built by the Spanish. *(☎ 534-8833 for info on all missions. Bus #42 stops within walking distance of Mission Concepción and right in front of Mission San José. Park headquarters is located at Mission San José. San José: 6701 San José Dr. off Roosevelt Ave. ☎ 932-1001. 4 Catholic services held each Su 7:45, 9, 10:30am, and a noon "Mariachi Mass." Concepción: 807 Mission Rd., 4 mi. south of the Alamo off E. Mitchell St. ☎ 534-1540. San Juan: 9101 Graf St. ☎ 534-0749. San Francisco: 10040 Espada Rd. ☎ 627-2021. All missions open daily 9am-5pm. Free.)*

SECULAR SAN ANTONE

DISTRICTS. Southwest of the Alamo, black signs indicate access points to the 2½ mi. **Paseo del Río (Riverwalk),** a series of well-patrolled shaded stone pathways which follow a winding canal built by the Works Progress Administration in the 30s. Lined with picturesque gardens, shops, and cafes, and connecting most of the major downtown sights, the Riverwalk is the hub of San Antonio's nightlife. A few blocks south, the recreated artisans' village, **La Villita,** 418 Villita, houses restaurants, craft shops, and art studios. *(☎ 207-8610. Shops open daily 10am-6pm, restaurant hrs. vary.)* On weekends, **Market Sq.,** between San Saba and Santa Rosa St., features the upbeat tunes of Tejano bands, the omnipresent buzzing of frozen margarita machines, and jangling wind chimes. *(☎ 207-8600. Open daily 10am-8pm; Sept.-May 10am-6pm.)*

HEMISFAIR PLAZA. The site of the 1968 World's Fair, **HemisFair Plaza,** on S. Alamo, draws tourists with nearby restaurants, museums, and historic houses. The observation deck of the **Tower of the Americas** rises 750 ft. above the dusty plains; the view is best at night. *(600 HemisFair Park. ☎ 207-8617. Open Su-Th 9am-10pm, F-Sa 9am-11pm; $3, seniors $2, ages 4-11 $1.)*

OTHER ATTRACTIONS. The adobe-walled **Spanish Governor's Palace,** completed in 1749, revives Spanish Colonial-style architecture with restored rooms and an enclosed garden. *(105 Plaza de Armas. ☎ 224-0601. Directly behind City Hall, between Commerce and Dolorosa St. at Laredo. Open M-Sa 9am-5pm, Su 10am-5pm; $1, ages 7-14 50¢.)* Home to the **San Antonio Spurs,** the **Alamodome,** at Hoefgen St., resembles a Mississippi riverboat. *(100 Montana. ☎ 207-3600. Take bus #24 or 26. Tours Tu-Sa 11am and 1pm, except during scheduled events. $4, seniors and ages 4-12 $2.)* The **San Antonio Museum of Art,** just north of the city center, showcases an extensive collection of Latin American folk art, as well as Texan furniture and pre-Colombian, Native American, and Mexican folk art. *(200 W. Jones Ave. ☎ 978-8100. Open Tu 10am-9pm, W-Sa 10am-5pm, and Su noon-5pm. $5, college students with ID and seniors $4, ages 4-11 $1.75; free Tu 3-9pm. Free parking.)*

OUTSIDE CITY CENTER

BRECKENRIDGE PARK. The truly adventurous will break beyond the confines of the Alamo and Riverwalk and make their way to the city's fringes. **Brackenridge Park,** 5 mi. north of the Alamo, is an escape from the urban congestion. The 343-acre show ground includes playgrounds, stables, a miniature train, and an aerial tramway that glides to a sunken Japanese garden. Directly across the street, the **San Antonio Zoo,** one of the country's largest, houses over 3500 animals from 800 species in reproductions of their natural settings, including an extensive African mammal exhibit. *(Park: 3910 N. Saint Mary's St. ☎ 736-9534. Take bus #7 or 8. Open M-F 10am-5:15pm, Sa-Su 10am-6pm. Tramway: $2.25, ages 1-11 $1.75. Zoo: 3903 N. Saint Mary's St. ☎ 734-7184. Open daily summer 9am-6pm; winter 9am-5pm. $7, seniors and ages 3-11 $5.)*

A LITTLE SOMETHING DIFFERENT. The phallic, 140-million-year-old rock formations of **Natural Bridge Caverns** change continuously; they are different every millennia. *(26495 Natural Bridge Caverns Rd. ☎ 651-6101. Take I-35 N to Exit 175 and follow the signs. Open daily 9am-6pm; off-season 9am-4pm. $9, ages 4-12 $6. 1¼hr. tours every 30min.)*

If you're itching for the trigger, **A Place to Shoot** is—well, just that. This 22-acre shooting facility offers five types of shotgun ranges: skeet, trap, crazy quail, dove tower, and country doubles. *(13250 Pleasanton Rd. ☎ 628-1888. Exit 46 off I-410 S. Open M-F 10am-7pm, Sa-Su 9am-7pm; $7 per person; $5 per 25 clays. 50¢ earplug rental.)* If you're in the mood to see some cowboy paraphernalia, **Pioneer Hall** contains a splendid collection of artifacts, old guns, documents, and portraits of the rangers, trail drivers, and pioneers who helped settle Texas. *(3805 Broadway. ☎ 822-9011. Open May-Aug. M-Sa 10am-5pm, Su 10am-4pm; Sept.-Apr. M-Sa 11am-4pm, Su 12pm-4pm; $2, seniors $1.50, ages 6-12 50¢.)*

🎵🎭 ENTERTAINMENT AND NIGHTLIFE

From Apr. 20-29, 2001, **Fiesta San Antonio** (☎ 227-5191) will usher in spring with concerts, parades, and plenty of Tex-Mex celebrations to commemorate the victory at San Jacinto and to pay homage to the heroes of the Alamo. For excitement after dark any time, any season, stroll down the Riverwalk. *The Friday Express* or weekly *Current* (available at the tourist office) will guide you to concerts and entertainment.

For authentic **Tejano music,** a Mexican and country amalgam, head to **Cadillac Bar,** 212 S. Flores, where every weeknight a different band whips the huge crowd (anywhere from 500-1000 people) into a cheering and dancing frenzy. (☎ 223-5533. Open M-Sa 11am-2am. 21+.) Right around the corner from the Alamo, the **Bonham Exchange,** 411 Bonham, San Antonio's biggest gay dance club, plays high-energy music with some house and techno on the side. A younger, more mixed crowd files in on Wednesdays for college night. (☎ 271-3811. Open M-Th 4pm-2am, F 4pm-3am, Sa 8pm-3am. Cover for 21+ $3-5, for 18-20 up to $10.) Some of the best traditional jazz anywhere taps at **Jim Cullum's Landing,** 123 Losoya, in the Hyatt downtown. The legendary Cullum plays with his jazz band M-Sa 8:30pm-1am. Tidy dress is recommended at this sophisticated venue. The improv jazz quintet Small World performs on Su nights. (☎ 223-7266. Open M-Th 4:30pm-12:30am, F 4:30pm-1:30am, Sa noon-1:30am, Su noon-midnight. Cover Sa $6.50. All ages.) Also along the Riverwalk, **Polly Esther's** and **The Culture Club,** 212 College St., pump up the crowd with 70s disco on the 2nd floor and 80s retro on the 3rd floor. (Open Su-W 8pm-2am, Th 8pm-3am, F-Sa 8pm-4am. Cover $3-7. 21+.) **Far West Rodeo,** 3030 NE Loop 410, plays two types of music—country *and* western. With an indoor rodeo on F and Sa nights, a mechanical bull and two dance floors, you'd better bring your 10-gallon hat to enjoy the fun. (☎ 646-9378. Open W-Th 7pm-2am, F-Sa 8pm-2am. Cover $3-6. 18+.)

SCENIC DRIVE: TEXAS HILL COUNTRY DRIVE

Parts of the **Texas Hill Country** are about as cliché as they come. Rolling expanses of scraggly brush interrupted by jagged hills dominate the landscape, while rusty pickup trucks driven by big men in big hats dominate the roads. Longhorns (or for city-

TEXAS

HOW MANY WORDS CAN YOU MAKE FROM "SCHLITTERBAHN?"

The entire local economy of New Braunfels depends upon the innertube. Almost 2 million visitors per year come to this town, hoping to spend a day floating along the waters of the spring-fed **Comal River**. **Rockin' "R" River Rides** will send you off with a life jacket and a trusty tube and pick you up downstream 2½hr. later. *(193 S. Liberty. ☎830-620-6262. Open May-Sept. daily 9am-7pm. Tube rentals $9, $7 for bottomless floats. Car keys, proper ID, or $25 deposit required during rental.)* If the Comal don't float your boat, head for the chlorinated waters of **Schlitterbahn**, a 65-acre extravaganza of a waterpark with 17 water slides, nine tube chutes, and five giant hot tubs. The park has recently built the planet's only uphill watercoaster, the Master Blaster. To find both attractions, take I-35 N to Exit 189, turn left, and follow the signs for Schlitterbahn. *(400 N. Liberty. ☎830-625-2351. Open May-Sept. Call for hrs., generally around 10am-8pm. Full-day passes $27.50, ages 3-11 $22.75.)*

folk, "moo-moos" with weapons) graze roadside as vehicles hurtle past at 70 mph. Yet the Texas Hill Country is more than ranches and cattle: the limestone-rich soil is well suited for wine-making and peach-growing. German influence dating back to 1846 with the founding of **Fredericksburg** is prominent, visible in the *biergartens* and billboards along the way. Finally, a series of well-maintained parks offers campers and day visitors alike the chance to experience the wilds of nature firsthand.

The drive, with occasional stops along the way, takes about two days and links San Antonio and Austin. While it is not the most direct route between these two cities, the trip is worthwhile for its unique diversions and beautiful scenery. From San Antonio, take I-35 to New Braunfels. After high-priced visits to the **Schlitterbahn** and/or **Natural Bridge Caverns** (see p. 596), you might be eager for less touristy attractions. Take Rte. 46 west for 6.5 mi., then turn left on Herbelin Rd. Here you'll find **Dry Comal Creek Vineyards**, which offers free tastings and tours of the small vineyard. (☎830-885-4121. Open W-Su noon-5pm.) Yes, Texas makes wine. While vineyards are a new addition to the region (many are less than ten years old), the wine they produce is surprisingly drinkable—and improving, as locals are quick to point out. Twenty-five mi. past Dry Comal Creek along Rte. 46 west brings you to **Guadalupe River State Park,** where you can swim in the cliff-lined river or camp for the night in nearby tent sites. (☎830-438-2656. Open M-F 9am-8pm, Sa 9am-midnight. Day entrance $4 per person, children under 12 free. Tent sites $15 for water and electricity, $12 for water only.)

Further down Rte. 46 is **Boerne** (pronounced BUR-nee), an antique lover's paradise; a string of converted barns and old farmhouses sell a wide array of odds n' ends. After 12 mi. of twists and turns through a series of low hills along the way to **Bandera,** Rte. 46 intersects with Rte. 16; take Rte. 16 north. Bandera's central street passes through a row of ramshackle buildings that could easily serve as facades for an old cowboy movie. Consistent with the image, Bandera is home to the **Frontier Times Museum,** 506 13th St., which has an eclectic assortment of objects dating back to the settlin' days of Texas. (☎830-796-3864. Open M-Sa 10am-4:30pm, Su 1pm-4:30pm. $2, students 25¢.) Continuing down 15 mi. of zig-zag roads through dramatic countryside, Rte. 16 north then brings you to the town of **Medina,** the "apple capital of Texas." Stop off at **Love Creek Orchards** (☎800-449-0882), on the north side of town, to buy some fresh cider for the trip (½ gallon $4) or sample their assortment of apple pies—after all, nothing's more American than fresh apple pie.

Leaving Medina on Rte. 16 north, the next 35 mi. winds through some of the most breathtaking country around. Be especially cautious driving this leg of the trip; hairpin turns and steep inclines can catch even the most alert off-guard. Safety aside, the real reason to proceed slowly is to enjoy the surrounding scenery. This is the Texas of childhood imagination, where less than a hundred years ago "cowboys and Indians" rode horseback, chasing each other through rugged canyons and shallow streams.

On the way through **Kerrville,** be sure to stop by the **Cowboy Artists of America Museum,** 1550 Bandera Hwy. Action-packed scenes and sculptures of the Wild West introduce visitors to the medium of cowboy art, depicting a scene of Texan life before "horseless carriages" and "moving pictures." (Open M-Sa 9am-5pm, Su 1pm-5pm. $5, ages 6-18 $1, seniors $3.50.)

Twenty-two mi. along Rte. 16 from Kerrville sits historic **Fredericksburg,** a German-rooted town of beer and sausage. For history buffs, Fredericksburg's **Admiral Nimitz Historic Center,** 340 E. Main St., contains an excellent exhibit on World War II in the Pacific. (☎830-997-4379. Open daily 10am-5pm. $5, students $3.)

An 18 mi. detour north of Fredericksburg on Rte. 965 brings you to **Enchanted Rock State Natural Park.** Enchanted Rock has the double allure of being a natural wonder in its own right (a tree-less, 440 ft. dome of pink granite) as well as a place to pitch one's tent. It also offers hiking and rock-climbing for the technically proficient. (☎800-792-1112. Open daily 8am-5pm. Entrance fee $5, under 12 free. Regular tent sites $9, primitive $7. Reservations strongly recommended.)

Back in Fredericksburg, take U.S. 290 E heading towards **Johnson City,** the birthplace of 36th President Lyndon Baines Johnson. Ten mi. later you'll find **Becker Vineyards,** on Jenschke Ln., which offers free tours of the vineyard and winery as well as tastings (☎830-644-2681; open daily 10am-5pm). Thirst quenched, follow U.S. 290 to Johnson City. Nine mi. east is **Pedernales Falls State Park,** off FM 2766. Waterfalls, extensive hiking trails, tent sites, and swimming/tubing areas make it a favorite getaway from Austin, which lies 60 mi. east on U.S. 290. (☎800-792-1112. Open daily 9am-6pm; entrance fee $2 per person, under 12 free. Water and electric sites $16, primitive sites $7.)

AUSTIN ☎512

If the "Lone Star State" still inspires images of rough 'n' tumble cattle ranchers riding horses across the plains, Austin does its best to put the stereotype to rest. In recent years, big money and big industry have become increasingly prominent, with Fortune 500 companies and Internet start-ups seeking to redefine the city's essence. Add to the mix Austin's history of musical innovation (she's ambitiously nicknamed the "Live Music Capital of the World"), plus the 50,000 college students that attend the University of Texas, and you've got a truly vibrant city. What makes Austin worthy of a visit is her nightlife; only after sunset does the city truly come alive with enough variety and diversity to please any type of traveler.

▐ GETTING THERE AND GETTING AROUND

Airport: Austin Bergstrom International, 3600 Presidential Blvd. (☎530-2242). Heading south from the city on I-35, go east on Ben White Blvd. (Hwy. 71) 8 mi. from downtown. Take bus #100. Taxi to downtown $12-14.

Trains: Amtrak, 250 N. Lamar Blvd. (☎476-5684 or 800-872-7245); take bus #38. To: Dallas (6hr., daily, $29); San Antonio (3hr., daily, $12); and El Paso (19hr., 4 per week, $98). Office open daily 8am-10pm.

Buses: Greyhound, 916 E. Koenig, several mi. north of downtown off I-35. Easily accessible by public transportation. Bus #15 and 7 stop across the street and run downtown. To: San Antonio (2hr., 13 per day, $13.50); Houston (3½hr., 7 per day, $17); and Dallas (3hr., 11 per day, $25). Schedules and prices vary. Station open 24hr.

Public Transit: Capitol Metro, 106 E. 8th St. (☎474-1200 or 800-474-1201; call M-F 6am-10pm, Sa 6am-8pm, Su 7am-6pm). Fare 50¢; students 25¢; seniors, children, and disabled free. Office has maps and schedules (open M-F 7:30am-5:30pm). The **'Dillo Bus Service** (☎474-1200) runs on Congress and Lavaca St. M-F every 10-15min. during rush hrs.; varies during off-peak times. Park for free in the lot at Bouldin and Barton Springs.

Taxis: American Yellow Checker Cab, ☎472-1111.

Bike Rental: If you come upon a **completely yellow bicycle,** hop on it for free—compliments of the city. Just make sure to leave it in a conspicuous spot for the next person to use.

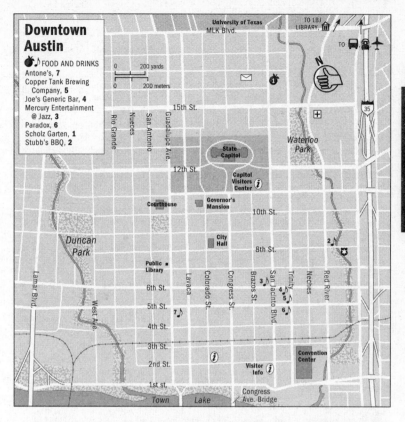

Downtown Austin

🍴♪ FOOD AND DRINKS
Antone's, 7
Copper Tank Brewing Company, 5
Joe's Generic Bar, 4
Mercury Entertainment @ Jazz, 3
Paradox, 6
Scholz Garten, 1
Stubb's BBQ, 2

Most buses have bicycle racks. **Waterloo Cycles,** 2815 Fruth St. (☎472-9253), offers rentals $15 per day, $20 on weekends. Fee includes helmet. Lock rental $5. Delivery available. Open M-W and F-Sa 10am-7pm; Th 10am-8pm; Su noon-5pm.

ORIENTATION AND PRACTICAL INFORMATION

The majority of Austin lies between **Hwy. 1** and **I-35,** both running north-south and parallel to one another. UT students inhabit central **Guadalupe St. ("The Drag"),** where plentiful music stores and cheap restaurants thrive on their business. The state capitol governs the area a few blocks to the southeast. South of the capitol dome, **Congress Ave.** features upscale eateries and classy shops. The many bars and clubs of **6th St.** hop and clop at night. Much nightlife has moved to the growing **Warehouse Area,** around 4th St., west of Congress. Away from the urban gridiron, **Town Lake** offers a verdant haven for the town's joggers, rowers, and cyclists.

Visitor Info: Austin Convention and Visitor's Bureau/ Visitor's Information Center, 201 E. 2nd St. (☎478-0098 or 800-926-2282). Open M-F 8:30am-5pm, Sa-Su 9am-5pm.

Hospital: St. David's Medical Center, 919 E. 32nd St. (☎476-7111). Off I-35, close to downtown. Open 24hr.

Hotlines: Crisis Intervention Hotline, ☎472-4357. **Austin Rape Crisis Center Hotline,** ☎440-7273. Both 24hr. **Outyouth Gay/Lesbian Helpline,** ☎800-969-6884, www.outy-outh.org. W, F, Su 5:30-9:30pm.

Post Office: 510 Guadalupe (☎800-275-8777) at 6th St. Open M-F 7am-6:30pm, Sa 8am-3pm. **ZIP code:** 78701. **Area code:** 512.

ACCOMMODATIONS

If you insist on your Motel 6, cheap accommodations lie along **I-35,** running north and south of Austin. However, this funkified city is a great place to find cheap options with character. In town, **co-ops,** run by college houses at UT, peddle rooms and meals to hostelers. The co-ops work on a first come, first served basis. Patrons have access to all their facilities, including fully stocked kitchens. Unfortunately, most UT houses are only open from May through Aug. Call ☎ 476-5678 for information about several co-ops. If you're interested in camping, however, a 10-20 min. drive separates Austin and the nearest campgrounds.

■ **Hostelling International-Austin (HI-AYH),** 2200 S. Lakeshore Blvd. (☎ 800-725-2331 or 444-2294), about 3 mi. from downtown. From the Greyhound station, take bus #7 "Duval" to Burton and walk 3 blocks north. From I-35, exit at Riverside, head east, and turn left at Lakeshore Blvd. Beautifully situated hostel with a 24hr. common room overlooking Town Lake. Kitchen, with a convenient cubby for each guest. 40 dorm-style beds, single-sex rooms. No curfew. Alcohol prohibited. Linen provided; no sleeping bags allowed. Rents bikes and kayak. Reception open daily 8-11am and 5-10pm. $14, nonmembers $17.

Taos Hall, 2612 Guadalupe (☎ 476-5678), at 27th St. The UT co-op where you are most likely to get a private room. For stays of a week or more, they'll draft you into the chores corps. Open June-Aug. Three meals and a bed $20.

21st St. Co-op, 707 W. 21st St. (☎ 476-5678). Take bus #39 on Airport St. to Koenig and Burnet, transfer to the #3 S, and ride to Nueces St.; walk 2 blocks west. Treehouse style building arrangement and hanging plants recall Robinson Crusoe's island home; its residents call it the "Ewok Village." A bit grungy, but only from all the good fun. Suites with A/C, and common room on each floor. $15 per person for 3 meals (when school is in session) and kitchen access. Fills up rapidly in summer.

The Goodall Wooten, 2112 Guadalupe (☎ 472-1343). The "Woo's" comfortable but somewhat sterile rooms are essentially UT dorms, but come with private baths, small fridges, and access to a big-screen TV lounge, laundry, basketball courts, and a computer lab. Reception M-Sa 9am-5pm and 8pm-midnight, Su 1-5pm and 8pm-midnight. Call ahead. Singles $25; doubles $30. Linen $5.

McKinney Falls State Park, 5808 McKinney Falls Pkwy. (☎ 243-1643, reservations 389-8900), southeast of the city. Turn right on Burleson off Rte. 71 E and go right on McKinney Falls Pkwy. Caters to both RV and tent campers. Swimming permitted in the stream; 7 mi. of trails to hike or bike. Primitive sites (accessible only by foot) $9; sites with water and electricity $12. Daily park usage fee $2, under 13 free.

Austin Lonestar RV Resort (☎ 444-6322 or 800-284-0206), 6 mi. south of the city along I-35 off Exit 227 on the northbound service road. Offers a pool, clean bathrooms, a game room, laundry facilities, a grocery store, and a playground. RV and tent sites with water and electricity $32-36; 3rd night free if on a weekday. Cabins for 4 $37; for 6 $46. 10% off with AAA.

FOOD

Scores of fast-food joints line the west side of the UT campus on **Guadalupe St.** Around **6th St.,** south of the capitol, the battle for happy hour business rages with unique intensity; patrons can often enjoy drink specials and free hors d'oeuvres. Although a bit removed from downtown, **Barton Springs Rd.** offers a diverse selection of inexpensive restaurants, including Mexican and Texas-style barbecue joints. The **Warehouse District** offers more expensive seafood and Italian eateries.

■ **Ruby's BBQ,** 512 W. 29th St. (☎ 477-1651). Ruby's barbecue is good enough to be served on silver platters, but that just wouldn't seem right in this cow-skulls-and-butcher-paper establishment. The owners only order meat from farm-raised, grass-fed cows, with "none of that steroid crap." A monster of a brisket sandwich goes for $4.25. Two black bean tacos $4. Open daily 11am-midnight.

Guero's, 1412 S. Congress (☎707-8232), across the river from downtown. This wholesome Mexican taco bar and restaurant is very popular with locals, as well it should be. Polish off 2 tacos for $3 or have a full meal with rice and beans for $7. Combination plates $8.50-12.50. Open M-F 11am-11pm, Sa-Su 8am-11pm.

Trudy's Texas Star, 409 W. 30th St. (☎477-2935), and 8800 Burnet Rd. (☎454-1474). Fine Tex-Mex dinner entrees ($5.25-8) and a fantastic array of margaritas. Famous for *migas*, a corn tortilla soufflé ($5.25). Pleasant outdoor porch bar. Open M-Th 7am-midnight, F-Sa 7am-2am, Su 8am-midnight; bar always open until 2am.

Threadgill's, 301 W. Riverside Dr. (☎472-9304). Another location at 6416 N. Lamar Blvd. (☎451-5440). A legend in Austin since 1933, serving up terrific Southern soul food and $8 fried chicken among creaky wooden floors, slow-moving ceiling fans, and antique beer signs. Surprisingly large variety of vegetarian and non-dairy options. Open M-Sa 11am-10pm, Su 11am-9pm.

Scholz Garten, 1607 San Jacinto Blvd. (☎474-1958), near the capitol. UT students and state politicians alike gather at this Austin landmark, recognized by the legislature for "epitomizing the finest traditions of the German heritage of our state." Popular chicken-fried steak dinners ($7) and sausage 'n' bratwurst po' boys ($5). The "Wurst" um-pah band in Austin plays W 8-10pm. Open M-W 11am-10pm and Th-Sa 11am-11pm.

Casa De Luz, 1701 Toomey Rd. (☎476-2535). Those familiar with Macrobiotic cooking (essentially vegetarian) will enjoy the lovingly prepared meals served in a tranquil, communal setting. Lovers of the furry, fishy or feathered might find themselves asking "Where's the beef?" All meals are $9, except brunch, $11. Open M-F 11:30am-2pm and 6-8pm; Sa-Su 11:30am-2pm for brunch.

⊙ SIGHTS

Not to be outdone, Texans built their **state capitol** 7 ft. higher than the national one. *(At Congress Ave. and 11th St. ☎463-0063. Open M-F 7am-10pm, Sa-Su 9am-8pm. 45min. tours every 15min. Free.)* The **Capitol Visitors Center** is located in the southeast corner of the capitol grounds. *(112 E. 11th St. ☎305-8400. Open daily 10am-5pm.)* There is a free 2hr. garage at 12th and San Jacinto St.; in the nearby trees resides the **Governor's Mansion.** *(1010 Colorado St. ☎463-5516. Free tours M-F every 20min. 10-11:40am.)* From Mar. to Nov., the **Austin Convention Bureau** sponsors free walking tours of the area. *(☎454-1545. Tours Th-F 9am, Sa-Su 9, 11am, 2pm. Tour starts at the capitol steps.)*

The **University of Texas at Austin (UT)** is both the wealthiest public university in the country, with an annual budget of almost a billion dollars, and America's largest, with over 50,000 students. UT forms the backbone of city cultural life. Bus #20 heads to the **Lyndon B. Johnson Library and Museum.** The first floor focuses on Texas-native LBJ and the history of the American presidency; the 8th floor features a model of the Oval Office. *(2313 Red River St. ☎916-5137. Open daily 9am-5pm. Free.)*

The **Austin Museum of Art,** housed in a Mediterranean-style villa, blends art, architecture, and nature. On rolling grounds overlooking Lake Austin, the museum displays 20th-century artwork. *(3809 W. 35th St. at Laguna Gloria. ☎458-8191. Open Tu-W and F-Sa 10am-5pm, Th 10am-8pm, Su noon-5pm. Admission $2, under 12 free; Th free. Group tours Aug.-June by appt.)* The museum hosts **Fiesta Laguna Gloria,** a mid-May arts and crafts festival with evening concerts and plays *(☎458-6073).* The museum also has a branch downtown, which rotates their exhibitions every few months *(823 Congress St. ☎495-9224).*

WHERE HAVE ALL THE HIPPIES GONE?

About 15 mi. northeast of downtown Austin lies **Hippie Hollow,** Texas's only public nude swimming and sunbathing haven. Here, free spirits go au naturel in the waters of the lovely Lake Travis. Take Mopac (Loop 1) north to the exit for F.M. 2222. Follow 2222 west and turn left at the I-620 intersection; Comanche Rd. will be on your right. (7000 Comanche Trail. ☎473-9437. 18+ only. Open daily 8am-9pm, no entry after 8:30pm. $5 per car, pedestrians $2.)

Just before dusk, head underneath the south side of the **Congress Ave. Bridge,** near the Austin American-Statesman parking lot, and watch for the massive swarm of **Mexican free-tail bats** that emerge from their roosts to feed on the night's mosquitoes. When the bridge was reconstructed in 1980, the engineers unintentionally created crevices which formed ideal homes for the migrating bat colony. The city began exterminating the night-flying creatures until **Bat Conservation International** moved to Austin to educate people about the bats' harmless behavior and the benefits of their presence—the bats eat up to 3000 lbs. of insects each night. Today, the bats are among the biggest tourist attractions in Austin. The colony, seen from mid-Mar. to Nov., peaks in July, when a fresh crop of pups increases the population to around 1½ million. For **flight times,** call the bat hotline. *(☎416-5700 ext. 3636.)*

Mt. Bonnell Park, 3800 Mt. Bonnell Rd., off W. 35th St., offers a sweeping view of Lake Austin and Westlake Hills from the highest point in the city. On hot afternoons, Austinites come in droves to riverside **Zilker Park,** just south of the Colorado River. *(2201 Barton Springs Rd. ☎477-7273. Take bus #30. Open daily 5am-10pm. Free.)* Flanked by walnut and pecan trees, **Barton Springs Pool,** a spring-fed swimming hole in the park, stretches 1000 ft. long and 200 ft. wide. The pool's temperature hovers around 68°F. *(☎476-9044. Pool open F-W 5am-10pm, Th 5-9am and 7-10pm. Admission M-F $2.50, Sa-Su $2.75; ages 12-17 $1, under 12 50¢; late Mar. to early Oct. free.)* The **Barton Springs Greenbelt** offers challenging trails for hikers and bikers.

🎵🎭 ENTERTAINMENT AND NIGHTLIFE

Beverly Sheffield Zilker Hillside Theater, across from the Barton Springs pool, hosts free outdoor bands, ballets, plays, musicals, and symphony concerts every weekend May to Oct. (☎397-1463 for events schedule). From Mar. 9-18, 2001, the **South by Southwest Music, Media, and Film Festival** will draw entertainment industry's giants and thousands of eager fans (☎467-7979). Austin's smaller events calendar is a mixed bag, like the **Spamarama** on Apr. 1, 2001. Spam fans from all walks of life pay homage to...this, er, product...with food, sports, and live music at the **Spam Jam.**

Austin has replaced Seattle as the nation's underground music hotspring, so keep an eye out for rising indie stars, as well as old blues, folk, country, and rock favorites. On weekends, nighttime swingers seek out dancin' on **6th St.,** an area bespeckled with warehouse nightclubs and fancy bars. More mellow cigar-smoking night owls gather at the **4th St. Warehouse District.** The weekly *Austin Chronicle* and *XLent* provide details on current music performances, shows, and movies. The *Gay Yellow Pages* is free at stands along the Drag.

■ **Antone's,** 213 W. 5th St. (☎474-5314). Antone's has attracted the likes of B.B. King and Muddy Waters. This blues paradise was also the starting point for Stevie Ray Vaughn. All ages. Shows at 10pm. Cover $5-25. Open daily 9pm-2am.

■ **Mercury Entertainment @ Jazz,** 214 E. 6th (☎478-6372). Representing the new side of Austin that has moved away from the usual country music and classic rock, the Mercury caters to sophisticated 20-somethings looking for the latest in jazz, funk and hip-hop. Cover $9 and up for ages 18-20, $6 and up for 21+. Open daily 9:30pm-2am.

Stubb's BBQ, 801 Red River (☎480-8341). The 21+ club downstairs has nightly acts, but the big draw of Stubb's is the occasional big names that appear in the 2000 capacity amphitheater out back. Swing by earlier for some scrumptious, inexpensive grub like beef brisket and 2 side dishes for $7. All ages welcome for amphitheater shows. Cover $3-25. Shows at 10:30pm. Open Tu-W, Su 11am-10pm, Th-Sa 11am-1am.

Hole in the Wall, 2538 Guadalupe St. (☎472-5599), at 26th St. Its self-effacing name disguises this renowned music spot, which features college alternative bands and an occasional country-western group. Music nightly. 21+. Cover $3-5; no cover Su-M. Open M-F 11am-2am, Sa-Su noon-2am.

Cactus Cafe, at 24th and Guadalupe St., in the Texas Union (☎475-6515). Features adventurous acoustic music every night. Specializing in folk-rock and Austin's own "New Country" sound, the Cactus gave Lyle Lovett his start. All ages welcome. Music starts 9pm. Cover $2-15. Open M-F 8pm-1am, Sa 8pm-2am.

Joe's Generic Bar, 315 E. 6th St. (☎480-0171). Find your way here for some raunchy Texas-style blues washed down with cheap beer. 21+. No cover. Open daily 7:30pm until the wayward crawl home at 2am, when the bar closes.

Paradox, 311 E. 5th St. at Trinity (☎469-7615). In a city hurting for dance clubs, this warehouse-style dance club with retro-80s and Top 40 music draws 20-somethings by the pack. Cover $5-10. Open Th-Su 9pm-4am.

Copper Tank Brewing Company, 504 Trinity St. (☎478-8444). Probably the city's best microbrewery. On W, a pint of any of the freshly brewed beers costs just $1—normally $3.75. 21+. Open daily 11am-2am.

DALLAS   ☎214

Dallas began as a trading outpost at a fort across the Trinity River in 1841. Rapidly boosted by the oil industry, Dallas is now the nation's largest inland city. Nevertheless, it has yet to be recognized as the cosmopolitan center it aspires to be—visitors are more interested in the image of oil and cowboys fostered by the television show *Dallas*. In truth, golf courses and swimming pools far outnumber genuine ropers or oilers here, and Dallasites prefer to point out plush cultural venues such as Myserson Symphony Hall and the Museum of Art. The city's overwhelming prosperity means slim-pickings for slim wallets, so be prepared to shell out big bucks for decent accommodations and attractions.

▐ GETTING THERE AND GETTING AROUND

Airport: Dallas-Ft. Worth International (☎972-574-8888), 17 mi. northwest of downtown; take bus #202 ($2). For door-to-gate service, take the **Super Shuttle,** 729 E. Dallas Rd. (☎800-258-3826). First passenger $16, $6 per additional passenger. 24hr. service. Taxi to downtown $30.

Trains: Amtrak, 400 S. Houston St. (☎653-1101), in Union Station. To: Los Angeles (42hr., 4 per week, $138); Austin (6½hr., daily, $22); and Little Rock (7½hr., daily, $53). Open daily 9am-6:30pm.

Buses: Greyhound, 205 S. Lamar St. (☎655-7727), 3 blocks east of Union Station. To: New Orleans (13hr., 11 per day, $78); Houston (4hr., 11 per day, $34); and Austin (4hr., 15 per day, $28). Open 24hr.

Public Transit: Dallas Area Rapid Transit (DART), 1401 Pacific Ave. (☎979-1111; open M-F 5am-10pm, Sa-Su 8am-6pm). Buses radiate from 2 downtown transfer centers, East and West, and serve most suburbs. Runs daily 5:30am-9:30pm, to suburbs 5:30am-8pm. Fare $1, $2 to suburban park-and-ride stops; transfers free. Maps at Elm and Ervay St. office (open M-F 7am-6pm). **DART Light Rail** runs north-south through downtown (5:30am-12:30am; fare $1).

Taxis: Yellow Cab Co., ☎426-6262 or 800-749-9422.

▟ ▐ ORIENTATION AND PRACTICAL INFORMATION

Most of Dallas lies within the **I-635** loop, which is bisected east-west by **I-30** and north-south by **I-35 E (Stemmons Frwy.)** and **U.S. 75 (Central Expwy.).** Nicer suburbs stretch along the northern reaches of Central Expwy. and the **Dallas North Toll Rd.** Many of downtown Dallas's shops and restaurants lie underground in a maze of tunnels accessible from any major office building.

Visitor Info: Dallas Convention and Visitors Bureau, administrative office at 1201 Elm S., Renaissance Tower, 20th fl. (☎571-1000). Open M-F 7:30am-5:30pm. Operates a 24hr. hotline (☎571-1301) and an **info center** in the Old Red Courthouse, 100 S. Houston St. at the intersection with Main St. Open M-F 8am-5pm, Sa-Su 9am-5pm.

Hotlines: Suicide and Crisis Center, ☎828-1000. **Contact Counseling,** ☎972-233-2233, for general counseling. Both 24hr.

Post Office: 400 N. Ervay St. (☎800-275-8777), near Bryan St. downtown. Open M-F 8am-6pm. **ZIP code:** 75201; for General Delivery, 75221. **Area codes:** 214, 817, and 972. In text, 214 unless otherwise noted.

TEXAS

TEXAS

ACCOMMODATIONS

Cheap lodging in Dallas is difficult to come by; big events such as the Cotton Bowl (Jan. 1) and the State Fair in Oct. exacerbate the problem. Look 15-20min. along three major roads for inexpensive motels: north of downtown on **U.S. 75,** north along **I-35,** and east on **I-30. Bed and Breakfast Texas Style,** 4224 W. Red Bird Ln., will place you in a home, usually near town, with friendly residents anxious to make y'all as comfortable as possible. It's an especially good deal for two people. Call a few days ahead. (☎972-298-8586. Open M-F 8:30am-4:30pm. Singles from $55; doubles from $65.) The **Super 7 Motel Mesquite,** 3629 U.S. 80 E, lies 10min. out of downtown; after bearing right onto U.S. 80 from I-30, exit at Town East Blvd. Perks include TV, free local calls, and a small pool. (☎613-9989. Singles $30.50; doubles $35.) Downtown, the **Paramount Hotel,** 302 S. Houston St., near Dealey Plaza and the West End, stands 2½ blocks from the Light Rail and CBD West transfer center. (☎761-9090. Singles $69; doubles $79.)

Near Lake Joe Pool, southwest of the city, **Cedar Hill State Park** provides 355 tent sites. Take I-35 E to Rte. 67, turn right onto FM 1382, and the park is on the left. The area fills up early for summer, so call at least two weeks in advance. There is a swimming area, marina, jet-ski rental, and three walking trails in the park. (☎972-291-3900, ☎512-389-8900 for reservations. Office open M-F 10am-5pm, Sa-Su 10am-10pm; 24hr. gate access with reservations. Sites $15, primitive $7. Additional $5 daily fee for each adult.) RV campers should take I-35 E north of the city to Exit 444, then go left under the highway about a mile to **Sandy Lake RV Park,** 1915 Sandy Lake Rd. RV sites are $20-22, depending on the vehicle size. (☎972-242-6808. Office open M-F 8am-8pm, Sa 8am-7pm, Su 1-6pm.)

FOOD

Dallas prides itself on just about everything, and food is no exception. The city supports more restaurants per capita than any other in the US, and Dallasites love to talk about their favorite eateries. For the lowdown on dining options, pick up the "Friday Guide" of the *Dallas Morning News.*

EatZi's, 3403 Oaklawn Ave. (☎526-1515), at Lemmon Ave., 1 mi. east of Oaklawn exit from 35E, north of downtown, #51 or 2 buses from downtown. A paradise for the frugal gourmet, this grocery, cafe, kitchen, and bakery forms an 8000 sq. ft. venue of glorious food. Sounds of Vivaldi and Verdi surround heapings of focaccia ($3), sandwiches ($4-7) and a multitude of delights. Open daily 7am-10pm.

Sonny Bryan's Smokehouse, 302 N. Market St. (☎744-1610), in the West End. A landmark of Dallas BBQ with a funky, run-down atmosphere where school desks replace tables. Try a beef sandwich ($4) or combine 3 smokehouse delicacies ($11). Vegetarian options available. Open M-Th 11am-10pm, F-Sa 11am-11pm, Su noon-9pm.

Flying Burro, 2831 Greenville Ave. (☎827-2112). The patio strewn with chili-pepper-shaped Christmas lights and cheesy overhangings may look a bit artificial, but this fine establishment serves New Mexico-style dishes that would make Santa Fe proud. Hits include stacked enchiladas ($7.25-9). Lunch specials from $5.25-7. Restaurant open Tu-Th and Su 11am-11pm, F-Sa 11am-12:30am. Bar open until 2am.

Baker's Ribs, 2724 Commerce (☎748-5433), east of downtown in Deep Ellum. If good BBQ and meat is what you're craving, Baker's is the answer. A hearty meal between walls covered in banjos, washpans, cowboy pictures and other Texan glory. Sandwiches ($3.25), combination plates ($7-8.50). Open M-Th 11am-7pm, F-Su 11am-9pm.

SIGHTS

Oil-flushed Dallas is packed with showy displays of 20th-century architecture and sculpture. Encircled by the skyscrapers of modern engineering that is present-day downtown, historic Dallas can easily be seen on a walking tour. Dallas is more

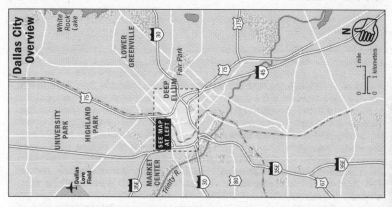

Dallas City Overview

White Rock Lake

LOWER GREENVILLE

Fair Park

DEEP ELLUM

SEE MAP AT LEFT

UNIVERSITY PARK

HIGHLAND PARK

MARKET CENTER

Dallas Love Field

Trinity R.

Industrial Blvd.

N

0   1 mile
0   1 kilometers

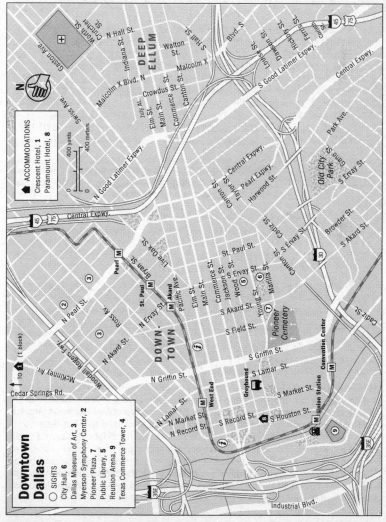

Downtown Dallas

○ SIGHTS
City Hall, **6**
Dallas Museum of Art, **3**
Myerson Symphony Center, **2**
Pioneer Plaza, **7**
Public Library, **5**
Reunion Arena, **9**
Texas Commerce Tower, **4**

▲ ACCOMMODATIONS
Crescent Hotel, **1**
Paramount Hotel, **8**

N

0   400 yards
0   400 meters

Worth St.
Crutcher St.
N Hall St.
Gaston Ave.
Swiss Ave.
Malcolm X Blvd. N
July Al.
Elm St.
Main St.
Crowdus St.
Commerce St.
Canton St.
Walton St.
Indiana St.
Malcolm X
S Hall St.
DEEP ELLUM

N Good Latimer Expwy.
S Good Latimer Expwy.
Central Expwy.

Blvd. S
Louise St.
Dawson St.
Hickory St.

45 75

Central Expwy.
45 75

Pearl
Bryan St.
Live Oak St.
St. Paul
Akard
Pacific Ave.
N Pearl St.
Ross Av.
N Akard St.
N Ervay St.

Canton St.
Taylor St.
Central Expwy.
Pearl Expwy.
Harwood St.

Park Ave.
Old City Park
Bass St.
S Ervay St.
Browder St.
S Akard St.

Commerce St.
St. Paul St.
Elm St.
Main St.
Jackson St.
Wood St.
Young St.
S Ervay St.
Cadiz St.
Marilla St.
Commerce St.
Cadiz St.

Pioneer Cemetery

30

DOWN TOWN

S Akard St.
S Field St.
S Griffin St.

McKinney Av.
Woodall Rogers Fwy.
Cedar Springs Rd.
TO 1 (1 block)

N Griffin St.
N Lamar St.
N Market St.
N Record St.

West End
Greyhound
S Lamar St.
S Market St.
S Record St.
S Houston St.

Convention Center
Union Station

Cadiz St.

35E
45 75
35E

Industrial Blvd.

notorious for its recent history, however; JFK's assassination during a campaign parade in 1963 is permanently preserved in various museums and landmarks.

JFK SIGHTS. On the corner of Houston Ave. and Elm St., the 6th floor of the unassuming **Texas School Book Depository** still gives people the chills as they look out the window through which Lee Harvey Oswald allegedly fired the shot that killed President John F. Kennedy on Nov. 22, 1963. Now this floor is a fascinating museum devoted to the Kennedy legacy, tracing the dramatic and macabre moments of the assassination through various media. (☎ 747-6660. Open daily 9am-6pm. Self-guided tours $6, seniors and students $4. Audio cassette rental $3.) To the south of the depository, Elm St. runs through **Dealy Plaza,** a national landmark beside the infamous grassy knoll where Kennedy's convertible passed as the shots were fired. Philip Johnson's **Memorial** to Kennedy looms nearby at Market and Main. Allegedly just across the street at 110 Market St. is the **Conspiracy Museum.** This bizarre and engaging shrine to elaborate CIA plots and mafia intrigue chronicles the assassinations of JFK, RFK, and Lincoln. (☎ 741-3040. Open daily 10am-6pm. Free walking tour of Dealy Plaza with entry, Sa-Su at noon and 3pm. $7, students and seniors $6, children $3.)

ART AND ARCHITECTURE. The Dallas Museum of Art's architecture is as graceful and beautiful as its collections of Egyptian, African, Early American, Impressionist, modern, and decorative art. (1717 N. Harwood St. ☎ 922-1200. Open Tu-W and F 11am-5pm, Th 11am-9pm, Sa-Su 11am-5pm. Free; special exhibits $5-8.) Directly across Harwood St., the **Trammel Crow Center** has a sculpture garden featuring Rodins and Bourdelles as well as a museum of Asian art. (☎ 979-6430. Open Tu, W, F 11am-6pm, Th 11am-9pm, Sa 10am-6pm, Su 11am-5pm. Free.) The ubiquitous **I.M. Pei** designed many downtown Dallas buildings. The spectacular Fountain Place at the Wells Fargo Building is on Ross St. just past Field St. The Morton H. Meyerson Symphony Center, 2301 Flora St., a few blocks east, and the imposing Dallas City Hall, 100 Marilla St. off of Young St., were also designed by Pei.

ATTRACTIONS. At the **Dallas World Aquarium,** admission is steep, but the multi-level rainforest exhibit with caged bats, swimming penguins, sleepy crocodiles, and birds zooming by your head make this aquarium worthwhile. The museum anchors northeast of the West End, a block north of Ross Ave. (1801 N. Griffin St. ☎ 720-2224. Open daily 10am-5pm. $11.85, seniors and children $6.50.) On the east shore of White Rock Lake, resplendent flowers and trees fill the 66-acre **Dallas Arboretum.** The lake also provides a haven for walkers, bikers, and in-line skaters. (Arboretum: 8617 Garland Rd. ☎ 327-8263. Take bus #19 from downtown. Open M-F 10am-6pm, Sa-Su 8am-6pm; Nov.-Feb. daily 10am-5pm. $6, seniors $5, ages 6-12 $3. Parking $3.)

FAIR PARK. Home to the state fair since 1886, **Fair Park** earned national landmark status for its Art Deco architecture. During the fair, **Big Tex**—a 52 ft. smiling cowboy float—towers over the land; only a huge ferris wheel, the **Texas Star,** looms taller. The 277-acre park also hosts the **Cotton Bowl** (Jan. 1). The park holds the **Science Place,** where toddlers can indulge in hands-on exhibits and everyone can enjoy the planetarium and IMAX theater. (Fair Park: ☎ 421-9600. Southeast of downtown on I-30, on #12 Dixon bus from CBD East. Science Place: ☎ 428-5555. Open Su-Th 9:30am-5:30pm, F-Sa 9:30am-9pm. Museum $6, seniors and ages 3-12 $3. Movies $6, children $5.)

HISTORIC DALLAS. Thirty-five late 19th-century buildings from around Dallas (including a dentist's office, a bank, and a farmstead which still raises animals) have been restored and moved to **Old City Park,** the city's oldest and most popular recreation and lunch spot. (☎ 421-5141. Nine blocks south of City Hall on Ervay St. at Gano. Open daily 9am-6pm. Exhibit buildings open Tu-Sa 10am-4pm, Su noon-4pm. $6, seniors $4, children $3.) The **West End Historic District and Marketplace,** full of broad sidewalks, shops, and restaurants, lies north of Union Station. (Most stores open M-Th 11am-10pm, F-Sa 11am-10pm, Su noon-6pm.) Dallas's **mansions** are in the **Swiss Avenue Historic District** and the streets of the **Highland Park** area, between Preston Rd. and Hillcrest Ave. south of Mockingbird Ln.

🎵 ENTERTAINMENT

The Met, a free weekly released W in restaurants and bookstores, has unrivaled entertainment coverage. For the scoop on Dallas' **gay scene,** pick up copies of the *Dallas Voice* and *Texas Triangle* in **Oak Lawn** shops and restaurants.

Prospero works his magic at the **Shakespeare in the Park** festival, at Samuel-Grand Park just northeast of Fair Park. During June and July, two free plays run 6 nights a week. (☎ 559-2778. Tu-Su 8:15pm; $4 donation is optional.) At Fair Park, the **Music Hall** showcases **Dallas Summer Musicals.** (☎ 421-0662 or 373-8000 for tickets; 696-4253 for half-price tickets on performance days. Shows run June-Oct. $9-70.) The **Dallas Symphony Orchestra** plays in the Morton H. Meyerson Symphony Center, at Pearl and Flora St. in the arts district (☎ 692-0203; Sept.-May; tickets $12-87).

If you come to Dallas looking for cowboys, the **Mesquite Rodeo,** 1818 Rodeo Dr., is the place to find them. Take I-30 east to I-635 S to Exit 4 and stay on the service road. Nationally televised, the rodeo is one of the most competitive in the country. (☎ 972-285-8777 or 800-833-9339. Shows Apr. to early Oct. F-Sa 7:30pm. Gates open at 6pm. $10, seniors $7, children 3-12 $4. Dinner $9.50, children $6.50.)

Six Flags Over Texas, 15 mi. from downtown off I-30 in Arlington, between Dallas and Fort Worth, boasts 38 rides, including the speedy, looping new roller coasters "Batman: the Ride" and "Mr. Freeze." (☎ 817-640-8900. Open June to early Aug. daily from 10am; late Aug.-Dec. and Mar.-May Sa-Su from 10am. Closing times vary. $40, over 55 or under 4 ft. $20.) Across the highway lies the mammoth 47-acre waterpark, **Hurricane Harbor.** Shoot down superspeed water flumes or experience simulated seasickness in the one million gallon wave pool. (☎ 817-265-3356. Open late May to early Aug. daily 10:30am-8pm. $27, seniors and under 4 ft. $13.50.) Find coupons for both parks on soda cans.

In Dallas, the moral order is God, country, and the **Cowboys.** Football devotees flock to **Cowboys Stadium** at the junction of Loop 12 and Rte. 183, west of Dallas in Irving. (☎ 972-785-5000. Sept.-Jan. Ticket office open M-F 9am-4pm. Tickets from $36.) **The Ballpark in Arlington,** 1000 Ballpark Way, plays host to the **Texas Rangers.** (☎ 817-273-5100. Apr.-Sept. Ticket office open M-F 9am-6pm, Sa 10am-4pm, Su noon-4pm. Tickets $4-30.) Experience the mystique of the game with a tour of the locker room, dugout, and the press box on the **ballpark tour.** (☎ 817-273-5098. Hours vary with the Ranger's schedule. $5, seniors and students $4, under 13 $3.)

🌙 NIGHTLIFE

For nightlife, head to **Deep Ellum,** east of downtown. In the 20s, the area was a blues haven for legends Blind Lemon Jefferson, Lightnin' Hopkins, and Robert Johnson; in the 80s, Bohemians revitalized the area. **Trees,** 2709 Elm St., rated the best live music venue in the city by the *Dallas Morning News*, occupies a converted warehouse with a loft full of pool tables. Bands tend to be alternative rock groups. (☎ 748-5009. Open W-Sa 9pm-2am. Cover $2-10. 17+.) A diverse clientele populates **Club Dada,** 2720 Elm St., the former haunt of Edie Brickell and the New Bohemians, which recently added an outdoor patio and live local acts. (☎ 744-3232. Open F 5pm-2am, Sa 9pm-2am, Su 8pm-2am. Cover Th-Sa $3-5. 21+.)

The touristy **West End** jams seven clubs into **Dallas Alley,** 2019 N. Lamar St., all under one cover charge (☎ 880-7420; $3-6). Guests sample Top 40, techno, country-western, karaoke, dueling pianos, and slot machines. **Lower Greenville Ave.** provides a refreshing change from the downtown mania. **Poor David's Pub,** 1924 Greenville Ave., stages live music ranging from Irish folk tunes to reggae. Music is the main, and only, event: if there's no group booked, Poor David's doesn't open. (☎ 821-9891. Open M-Sa 8pm-2am. Tickets available after 6pm at the door; cash only. Cover $1-20.) More popular nightspots also line Yale Blvd., near Southern Methodist University's fraternity row. **Green Elephant,** 5612 Yale Blvd., full of pseudo-60s psychedelica, is the bar of choice. (☎ 750-6625. Open M-Sa 11am-2am, Su 6pm-2am.) Many gay clubs rock north of downtown in **Oak Lawn.** Among the more notable is **Roundup,** 3912 Cedar Springs Rd., at

Throckmorton, a huge, cover-free country-western bar which packs a mixed gay and straight crowd of up to 1600 on weekends. "Best Gay Bar" in Dallas according to the *Dallas Observer*. (☎522-9611. Open Th-Su 8pm-2am; free dance lessons Th 8:30pm. Daytime bar opens M-F 3pm, Sa-Su noon.)

FORT WORTH   ☎817

If Dallas is the last Eastern city, Fort Worth is undoubtedly the first Western one. Dallas's slightly less refined brother lies less than 40min. west on I-30, providing a worthwhile daytrip and some raw Texan entertainment. Fort Worth is divided into three cultural districts, each marked by red brick streets: the **Stockyards Historic District, Sundance Square,** and the **Museum District.**

The Stockyards Historic District, which lies along East Exchange Ave., 10min. north of downtown on Main St., attracts the felt hat and leather boot crowd like nowhere else in the metroplex. A walk along Exchange Ave., the main drag, provides a window into the Wild West, offering a slew of saloons, restaurants, shows, and gambling parlors. The **White Elephant Saloon,** 106 Exchange Ave., with its live country music, brass footrails, and prodigious collection of cowboy hats, is a longtime favorite. (☎624-1887. Open Su-Th noon-midnight, F-Sa noon-2am.)

Down Exchange Ave., the **Cowtown Coliseum** (☎625-1025 or 888-269-8696) hosts two weekly events: **rodeos** are held here F-Sa at 8pm ($8, seniors $7, children $5), and **Pawnee Bill's Wild West Show** features sharp-shooting, trick-roping, and a bullwhip act every Sa-Su at 2:30 and 4:30pm ($7, ages 3-12 $4). **Billy Bob's Texas,** 2520 Rodeo Plaza, ropes in the Stockyards crowds for some honky-tonk night clubbing with big names in country music. With 100,000 sq. ft. of floor space, including a bull ring, a BBQ restaurant, pool tables, slot machines, and 42 bar stations, the place bills itself as the world's largest honky-tonk. On one night alone, during a Hank Williams, Jr. concert, Billy Bob's sold 16,000 bottles of beer. (☎624-7117. Open M-Sa 11am-2am, Su noon-2am. Professional bull-riding F-Sa 9 and 10pm. Free dance lessons Th 7pm. Afternoon cover $1, Su-Th after 6pm $3; F-Sa evenings $6.50-11, depending on performers. 18+ with ID or under 18 with parent.)

The **Chisholm Trail Round-Up,** a three-day jamboree in the Stockyards during either the second or third week of June, preserves the heritage of the cowhands who led cattle drives to Kansas 150 years ago. (☎624-4741. Calls taken M-Th 9am-6pm, F 9am-6pm, Sa 9am-7pm, Su 11am-6pm.) The **Armadillo Races** are a Round-Up must-see; children and visitors are allowed to participate in ground-beating attempts to make the critters move. For more on the stockyards, grab a copy of the *Stockyards Gazette* at the **visitors center,** 130 E. Exchange Ave.

Downtown, **Sundance Sq.,** a pedestrian-friendly area, offers quality shops, museums, and eats. In the square, the **Sid Richardson Collection,** 309 Main St., displays an impressive stash of 56 paintings by the Western artists Remington and Russell. (☎332-6554. Open Tu-W 10am-5pm, Th-F 10am-8pm, Sa 11am-8pm, Su 1-5pm. Free.) Be sure to visit the little boys/girls room before going to the **Water Gardens** at Commerce and 5th St., where the wet stuff cascades down a series of man-made terraces as onlookers relax in the shade and picnic. (Open daily 7am-11:30pm. Free.) For an escape from the Texas weather, strap on some blades at the ice skating rink inside the **Fort Worth Outlet Square,** 100 Throckmorton St. (☎415-4800. Open M-Sa 10am-5:30pm and 7-9:30pm, Su noon-5:30pm and 7-9:30pm. $5; skate rental $2.)

A few min. west of downtown down 7th St., the **Museum District** offers an array of intimate collections and exhibitions. The **Kimbell Museum,** 3333 Camp Bowie Blvd., arguably the best museum in the Southwest, exhibits some of the world's most sophisticated art. (☎332-8451. Open Tu-Th and Sa 10am-5pm, F noon-8pm, Su noon-5pm. Free.) **Ft. Worth Visitor's Bureau:** ☎336-8791. **Area code:** 817.

HOUSTON ☎713

Born in 1836, when Augustus and John Allen came slicing through the weeds of the Buffalo Bayou, Houston now spreads its borders as a huge mega-metropolis, with monster trucks on superhighways, awe-inspiring glass-and-steel skyscrapers, enormous oil plants, and the largest strip malls in the country. As if all this was not enough, the Houston-based NASA space center reaches toward the stars. Unfortunately, Houston is a difficult place to navigate. Several interstates and highways tangle together at its downtown, and the city counters its growth by swallowing surrounding suburbs, leading to a sloppy and diffuse layout. But while the city grapples with its burgeoning borders, it continues to offer the cultural benefits of a large city in distinctive Texan style.

▌ GETTING THERE AND GETTING AROUND

Flights: Houston Intercontinental Airport (☎281-230-3100), 25 mi. north of downtown. Get to city center via **Express Shuttle** (☎523-8888); buses daily every 30min. to 1hr., depending on the destination hotel in the downtown area. (Runs 7am-11:30pm, $17-21, under 12 free.) A second and smaller airport, **Hobby Airport,** 7800 Airport Blvd. (☎640-3000), lies south of city center and specializes in regional travel.

Trains: Amtrak, 902 Washington Ave. (☎224-1577), *in a rough neighborhood.* During the day, catch a bus west on Washington Ave. (away from downtown) to Houston Ave.; at night, call a cab. To San Antonio (5hr., 3 per week, $30-55) and New Orleans (9hr., 3 per week, $48-55). Open Su and M 7am-9pm, Tu-Sa 7am-midnight.

Buses: Greyhound, 2121 Main St. (☎759-6565). *At night call a cab—this is an unsafe area.* To: Dallas (4-5hr., 10 per day, $32); San Antonio (3½hr., 11 per day, $20); and Santa Fe (24hr., 5 per day, $119). Open 24hr.

Public Transit: Metropolitan Transit Authority (METRO Bus System) (☎635-4000). Offers reliable service anywhere between NASA (15mi. southeast of town) and Katy (25 mi. west of town). Operates M-F 6am-9pm, Sa-Su 8am-8pm; less frequently on weekends. The METRO operates a free trolley throughout downtown. Free maps available at the **Houston Public Library,** 500 McKinney (☎236-1313), at Bagby St. (open M-F 9am-9pm, Sa 9am-6pm, Su 2-6pm), or at a Metro Rides store. Fare $1, seniors 40¢, ages 5-11 25¢; day pass $2.

Taxis: United Cab, ☎699-0000.

✳❼ ORIENTATION AND PRACTICAL INFORMATION

Though the flat Texan terrain supports several mini-downtowns, true downtown Houston, a squarish grid of interlocking one-way streets, borders the **Buffalo Bayou** at the intersection of I-10 and I-45. **The Loop (I-610)** encircles the city center with a radius of 6 mi. Anything inside the Loop is easily accessible by car or bus. The shopping district of **Westheimer Blvd.** grows ritzier to the west. Nearby, restaurants and shops line **Kirby Dr.** and **Richmond Ave.;** the upper portion of Kirby Dr. winds past spectacular mansions. *Be careful in the south and east areas of Houston, as they may be unsafe.* The downside to Houston's booming economy is the ongoing roadwork that affects visitors and natives alike—be on the look-out for detours.

Visitors Info: Greater Houston Convention and Visitors Bureau, in City Hall (☎227-3100 or 800-365-7575, at the corner of McKinney and Bagby St.). Open daily 9am-4pm.

Hotlines: Crisis Center, ☎228-1505. **Rape Crisis,** ☎528-7273. **Women's Center,** ☎528-2121. All 24hr. **Gay and Lesbian Switchboard of Houston** (☎529-3211 or www.gay-switchboardhouston.org) has entertainment info. Operates M-F 7-10pm.

Hospital: Columbia Bellaire Medical Center, 5314 Dashwood (☎512-1200), has a 24hr. emergency room. **Columbia Woman's Hospital of Texas,** 7600 Fannin (☎790-1234).

Internet Access: see **Houston Public Library** (above in Public Transit).

Post Office: 701 San Jacinto St. (☎800-275-8777). Open M-F 8am-5pm. **ZIP code:** 77002. **Area codes:** 713 and 281 (in text 713, unless indicated).

ACCOMMODATIONS

A few cheap motels dot the **Katy Freeway (I-10W).** Budget accommodations along **S. Main St.** are more convenient, but not all are safe. Prices start at $30 for a single room. (Bus #8 goes down S. Main.)

Perry House, Houston International Hostel (HI-AYH), 5302 Crawford St. (☎523-1009), at Oakdale St. In the museum district near Hermann Park. From the Greyhound station, take bus #8 or 15 south to Southmore St.; walk 6 blocks east to Crawford St. and 1 block south to Oakdale St. Helpful management provides 30 beds in 6 spacious rooms. Well-equipped kitchen, email access ($3 per hr.), choose-your-own chore. Room lock-out 10am-5pm, common area open all day; sleepsacks required. Free use of bicycles with a $20 deposit. Dorms $15.

YMCA, 1600 Louisiana Ave. (☎659-8501), between Pease and Leeland St. Downtown location features cubicle-like rooms, all singles, with daily maid service, TV, and telephones for incoming calls; some have private baths. Key deposit $10; towel deposit $2.50. Newly renovated. Singles $25-30. **Another branch,** 7903 South Loop (☎643-2804), is farther out (off the Broadway exit from I-610 near I-45) but less expensive. Take bus #50 to Broadway. Key deposit $10. Singles $22.

White House Motel, 9300 S. Main (☎666-2261). Close to I-610. Large, decently maintained rooms at solid prices. There's also an "Olympic Pool," but don't think Sydney is willing to share the spotlight. Singles $35; doubles $40.

Red Carpet Inn, 6868 Hornwood Dr. (☎981-8686 or 800-251-1962). Near the Bellaire exit off U.S. 59 S/SW Fwy. Plain but well-kept rooms. Free coffee and continental breakfast. Singles $35; doubles $42.

Most campgrounds in the Houston area lie a considerable distance from the city center. **KOA Houston North,** 1620 Peachleaf, has sites with pool and shower access. From I-45 N, go east on Aldine-Bender Rd., then turn right on Aldine-Westfield Rd., and then right again on Peachleaf. (☎281-442-3700 or 800-562-2132. Tent sites for 2 $18, RV hook-up $24; $2 per additional adult. 1 room cabins $28, 2 rooms $40.)

FOOD

Houston's port has witnessed the arrival of many immigrants (today the city's Indochinese population is the second largest in the nation), and its restaurants reflect this diversity. Houston's cuisine features Mexican, Greek, Cajun, Asian, and Southern soul food. Look for reasonably priced restaurants along the chain-laden streets of **Westheimer** and **Richmond Ave.,** especially where they intersect with **Fountainview.** Houston has two **Chinatowns:** a district south of the George R. Brown Convention Center and a newer area on **Bellaire Blvd.** called **DiHo.** Many small Mexican restaurants line the strip malls outside of the downtown region and are usually a good value for an empty stomach.

Goode Company BBQ, 5109 Kirby Dr. (☎522-2530), near Bissonnet St. This might be the best (and most popular) BBQ in Texas. Goode Company's mesquite-smoked brisket, ribs, and sausage links (all smothered in homemade sauce) will make your mouth water. Sandwiches $3.50 and up; dinner, featuring one meat and two veggie dishes, $7-10. Open daily 11am-10pm.

Bibas/One's A Meal, 607 W. Gray St. (☎523-0425), at Stanford St. This family-owned institution serves everything from chili 'n' eggs ($5.75) to a gyro with fries ($6). Their Greek pizza (6 in., $5.75) is hard to beat, and #8 on the breakfast menu is colossal (egg, bacon, sausage or ham, grits or hash browns, toast or biscuits, and juice for $5.25). Open 24hr.

Kim Son, 300 Milam St. (☎222-2790), a short wok from all major downtown sights. Lunch specials are reasonable (sesame chicken $5.95) and dinners start at $7.50. Open M-F 11am-9pm.

Ragin' Cajun, 4302 Richmond Ave. (☎623-6321). A local favorite that specializes in (you guessed it) fish, cajun style. Indoor picnic tables and a casual atmosphere. Po-boys $5.70-8.50, gumbo $4. Open M-Th 11am-10pm, F-Sa 11am-11:30pm.

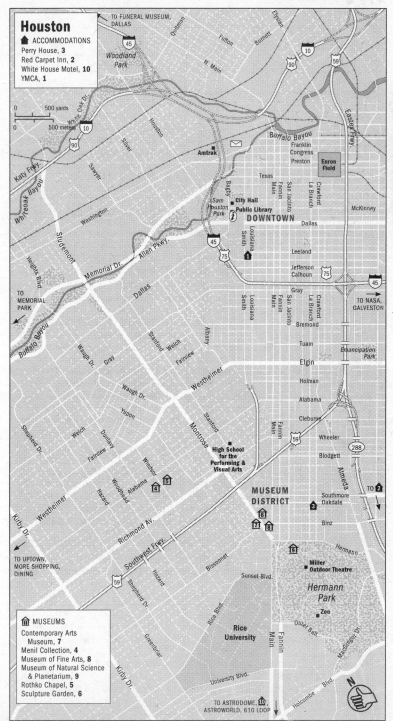

Houston

ACCOMMODATIONS
Perry House, **3**
Red Carpet Inn, **2**
White House Motel, **10**
YMCA, **1**

MUSEUMS
Contemporary Arts
  Museum, **7**
Menil Collection, **4**
Museum of Fine Arts, **8**
Museum of Natural Science
  & Planetarium, **9**
Rothko Chapel, **5**
Sculpture Garden, **6**

TEXAS

TO FUNERAL MUSEUM,
DALLAS

Woodland Park

Quitman
Fulton
Burnett
Elysian

N. Main

Buffalo Bayou

Franklin
Congress
Preston

Enron Field

Easter Frwy.

Amtrak

Texas

Crawford
La Branch

McKinney

Katy Frwy.

Whiteoak Bayou

White Oak Dr.
Silver
Houston
Sawyer

City Hall
Public Library

Sam Houston Park

San Jacinto
Fannin
Main

Dallas

DOWNTOWN

Louisiana
Smith

Leeland

Jefferson
Calhoun

TO MEMORIAL PARK

Heights Blvd.
Studemont

Washington

Memorial Dr.

Allen Pkwy.

Dallas

Buffalo Bayou

Gray

Louisiana
Smith

San Jacinto
Fannin
Main

Crawford
La Branch

Bremond

TO NASA,
GALVESTON

Waugh Dr.
Gray

Stanford
Welch

Fairview

Albany

Westheimer

Tuam

Emancipation Park

Elgin

Shepherd Dr.
Welch
Dunlavy
Fairview

Yupon

Waugh Dr.

Montrose

Stanford

Holman

Alabama

Cleburne

Fannin
Main

Wheeler

High School
for the
Performing &
Visual Arts

Windsor
Woodhead
Alabama
Hazard

MUSEUM DISTRICT

Southmore
Oakdale

Binz

Almeda

TO

Kirby Dr.

Westheimer

Richmond Av.

Southwest Frwy.

Hermann

Bissonnet

Sunset Blvd.

Hermann Park

Miller
Outdoor Theatre

TO UPTOWN,
MORE SHOPPING,
DINING

Shepherd Dr.
Hazard

Rice Blvd.

Rice
University

Zoo

Outer Bell

Greenbriar

Kirby Dr.

University Blvd.

Fannin
Main

MacGregor Dr.

Holcombe

Blvd.

TO ASTRODOME,
ASTROWORLD, 610 LOOP

N

0   500 yards
0   500 meters

SIGHTS

JOHNSON SPACE CENTER. The city's most popular attraction, ▓**Space Center Houston,** is technically not even in Houston, but 20 mi. from downtown in Clear Lake, TX. The active Mission Control Center still serves as HQ for modern-day Major Toms. When astronauts ask, "Do you read me, Houston?" these folks answer. Admission includes three separate hour-long tours of the mission control center, the underwater weightless training pool, and other astronaut training facilities. Among the attractions are out-of-this-world harnesses that will have you bouncing around like a real spaceman. The complex also houses models of Gemini, Apollo, and Mercury craft, as well as galleries and hands-on exhibits. *(1601 NASA Rd. 1. ☎ 281-244-2100 or 800-972-0369. Take I-45 south to NASA Rd. exit, then head east 3 mi. or take bus #246. Open June-Aug. daily 9am-7pm; Sept.-May M-F 10am-5pm, Sa-Su 10am-7pm. $14, seniors $13, ages 4-11 $10. Parking $3.)*

BAYOU BEND. The 17th- to 19th-century American decorative art at **Bayou Bend Collection and Gardens** in **Memorial Park** is an antique-lover's dream. The collection, housed in the mansion of millionaire Ima Hogg (we *swear*), daughter of former Gov. Jim "Boss" Hogg, includes John Singleton Copley portraits and a silver sugar bowl by Paul Revere. *(1 Westcott St. ☎ 639-7750. Collection open Tu-F 10am-2:45pm, Sa-Su 1-5pm. $10, seniors and students $8.50, ages 10-18 $5, under 10 not admitted. Gardens open Tu-Sa 10am-5pm, Su 1-5pm. $3, under 10 free. 1½hr. garden tours by reservation.)*

HERMANN PARK. Museums, gardens, paddle boats, and golfing are all part of **Hermann Park,** 388 acres of beautifully landscaped grounds by Rice University and the Texas Medical Center. Near the northern entrance of the park, the **Houston Museum of Natural Science** offers a butterfly center, some formidable looking dinosaurs (all dead), a splendid display of gems and minerals, a planetarium, an IMAX theatre, and a hands-on gallery geared towards grabby little children. At the southern end of the park, crowds flock to see more animated attractions—such as gorillas, hippos, and reptiles—in the **Houston Zoological Gardens.** The park grounds also encompass the Miller Outdoor Theater (see **Entertainment,** below), sports facilities, a kiddie train, and a Japanese garden. *(Museum of Natural Science: 1 Hermann Circle Dr. ☎ 639-4629. Exhibits open daily 9am-6pm. Museum $4, seniors and under 12 $3; IMAX $6/$4; planetarium $4/$3; butterfly center $4/$3. Zoo: 1513 N. MacGregor. ☎ 284-8300. Open daily 10am-6pm. $2.50, seniors $2, ages 3-12 50¢.)*

ART ATTRACTIONS. The Museum of Fine Arts hosts Impressionist and post-Impressionist Art, as well as fine works from Asia, Africa, and the American West. The museum's **Sculpture Garden** includes pieces by artists such as Matisse and Rodin. Across the street, the **Contemporary Arts Museum** displays changing exhibits. *(Museum of Fine Arts: 1001 Bissonet. ☎ 639-7300. Open Tu-W and Sa 9am-7pm, Th-F 9am-9pm, Su 12:15-6pm. $5, students and seniors $2.50; free Th. Garden: 5101 Montrose St. Open daily 9am-10pm. Free. Contemporary Arts Museum: 5216 Montrose St. ☎ 284-8250. Open Tu-W and F-Sa 10am-5pm, Th 10am-9pm, Su noon-5pm. Suggested donation $3.)*

The Menil Foundation exhibits an array of artwork in four buildings grouped within a block of each other. The **de Menil Collection** includes an eclectic assortment of Surrealist paintings and sculptures, Byzantine and medieval artifacts, and European, American, and African art. *(1515 Sul Ross. ☎ 525-9400. Open W-Su 11am-7pm;*

WE'RE DYING TO GET IN If you've got a car and a funeral fascination, head to the **American Funeral Service Museum.** The museum aims to "take the fear out of funerals." It contains exhibits on funerals of notable political figures, embalming artifacts, over two dozen funeral vehicles, and (of course) coffins of all shapes and sizes—from glass to iron, from chicken-like to airplane-shaped. *(415 Barren Springs Dr. ☎ 281-876-3063 or 800-238-8861. From I-45, exit at Airtex, go west to Ella Blvd., turn right, and proceed to Barren Springs. Open M-F 10am-4pm, Sa-Su noon-4pm. $5, seniors and under 12 $3. Tours by appt. only.)*

chapel closes at 6pm. Free.) A block away, the **Rothko Chapel** houses 14 of the artist's paintings in a sanctuary. Fans of modern art will delight in Rothko's ultra-simplicity; others will wonder where the paintings are. *(3900 Yupon. ☎524-9839. Open daily 10am-6pm. Free.)*

JUST FOR FUN. In downtown, earthly pleasures can be found underground. Hundreds of shops and restaurants line the 18 mi. **Houston Tunnel System,** which connects all the major buildings in downtown Houston, extending from the Civic Center to the Tenneco Building and the Hyatt Regency. Duck into the air-conditioned passageways via any major building or hotel. *(Most entries closed Sa-Su.)*

Many a Bacchanalian fest must have preceded the construction of the **Beer Can House,** 222 Malone, off Washington Ave. Adorned with 50,000 beer cans, strings of beer-can tops, and a beer-can fence, the house was built by the late John Mikovisch, an upholsterer from the Southern Pacific Railroad. At 5¢ a can, the tin abode has a market price of $2500 for the decorations alone.

SAN JACINTO. The **San Jacinto Battleground State Historical Park** is the most important monument to Lone Star independence. The 18min. battle brought Texas its freedom from Mexico and gave the city its namesake in the person of Sam Houston. A ride to the top of the 50-story **San Jacinto Monument** yields a 570 ft. tall view of the area. The **museum** inside the monument celebrates Texas history. *(Monument: ☎281-479-2421. 21 mi. east on Rte. 225 and 3 mi. north on Rte. 134. Open daily 9am-6pm. Elevator to top $3, seniors $2.50, under 12 $2. Museum: ☎281-479-2431. Open daily 9am-6pm. Free. Slide show daily 10am-5pm. $3.50/$3/$2.50. Combo tickets with elevator ride $6/$5/$2.)*

🎵🎭 ENTERTAINMENT AND NIGHTLIFE

From Apr. to Oct., symphony, opera, and ballet companies and various professional theaters stage free performances at the **Miller Outdoor Theater** in Hermann Park (☎284-8352). The annual **Shakespeare Festival** struts and frets upon the stage from late July to early Aug. The downtown **Alley Theater,** 615 Texas Ave., puts on Broadway-caliber productions at moderate prices. (☎228-8421. Tickets $32-44; Su-Th $12 student rush tickets 1hr. before the show.) **Jones Hall,** 615 Louisiana Blvd. (☎227-3974), stages Houston's high-brow entertainment. The **Houston Symphony Orchestra** performs here Sept. through May (☎227-2787; tickets $20-70). Between Oct. and May, the **Houston Grand Opera** produces six operas in the nearby **Wortham Center,** 500 Texas Ave. (☎546-0200. Tickets $25-186; 50% student discount available at noon on the day of some shows and $20-70 off tickets bought 1hr before start time.)

In Apr. 2000, baseball's **Astros** moved into **Enron Field,** a new, state of the art stadium located at the intersections of Texas, Crawford, and Congress St. near Union Station downtown (☎295-8000; outfield deck seats $5). Houston's basketball team, the **Rockets,** hoop it up at the **Compaq Center,** 10 Greenwald Plaza (☎843-3995).

For downtown entertainment, **Bayou Place,** 500 Texas Ave., holds a multi-screen movie complex, a pool hall, and a Hard Rock Cafe. Additionally, there's a growing number of upscale bars, restaurants and clubs surrounding nearby **Market Sq.** Most of Houston's nightlife, however, happens west of downtown around Richmond and Westheimer Ave. Several gay clubs cluster on lower Westheimer, while enormous, warehouse-style dancehalls line the upper reaches of Richmond. A variety of bars and music venues fill the streets in between. Located in the mother of all strip malls, **City Streets,** 5078 Richmond Ave., is a multi-venue complex with six different clubs offering everything from country and live R&B to disco and a pool hall. (☎840-8555. Open W-F 5pm-2am, Sa 7:30pm-2am. $2-5 cover good for all six clubs.) All sorts come to converse in the distinctly English atmosphere of **The Ale House,** 2425 W. Alabama, at Kirby St. The bi-level bar and beer garden offers over 130 brands of beer ($3-5). Upstairs, you'll find old-time rock 'n' roll or the blues on F-Sa nights. (☎521-2333. Open M-Sa 11am-2am, Su noon-2am.) Good natured drinkers gather on the patio of **Sam's Boat/Sam's Place,** 5720 Richmond Ave., to drink, chat, and hear live music. (☎781-2628. Open daily 11am-2am; food served until 2am. Live music Tu 5pm-2am, F 8pm-2am, Sa 6pm-2am. Cover up to $3.)

GALVESTON ISLAND   ☎409

In the 19th century, Galveston was the "Queen of the Gulf," Texas's most prominent port and wealthiest city. The glamour came to an abrupt end on Sept. 8, 1900, when a devastating hurricane ripped through the city, claiming 6000 lives. The Galveston hurricane still ranks as one of the worst natural disasters in US history. Today, the narrow, sandy island of Galveston (pop. 65,000), 50 mi. southeast of Houston on I-45, meets beach resort quotas for t-shirt shops and ice cream stands but redeems itself with beautiful vintage homes and antique shops.

🔃 PRACTICAL INFORMATION. Galveston's streets follow a grid; lettered avenues run east-west, while numbered streets run north-south. **Seawall Blvd.** follows the southern coastline. Most routes have two names; Ave. J and Broadway, for example, are the same street. Greyhound-affiliate **Kerrville Bus Co.,** 714 25th St. (☎765-7731; station open M-F 8am-7pm, Sa 8am-3:15pm), travels to Houston (1½hr., 4 per day, $13). **Galveston Island Convention and Visitors Bureau,** 2428 Seawall Blvd. (☎763-4311 or 888-425-4753; open daily summer 8:30am-6pm, winter 8:30am-5pm), is conveniently located on the beach. **Heritage Visitors Center,** 2328 Broadway in the Ashton Villa (☎762-3933; open 10am-5pm) has information dealing mostly with the area's historical sites. **Post Office:** 601 25th St. (☎763-1527; open M-F 8am-5pm, Sa 6am-5pm). **ZIP code:** 77550. **Area code:** 409.

🍴🏨 ACCOMMODATIONS AND FOOD. The price of lodging in Galveston fluctuates by season, rising to exorbitant heights ($50 and way up) during the summer, holidays, and weekends. Especially during the summer, consider making Galveston a daytrip from Houston. Otherwise, visitors can find reasonable rates for RVs and tents at any of several parks on the island. The closest to downtown, the **Bayou Shores RV Resort,** 6310 Heards Ln., off 61st St., is located on a peaceful waterfront with laundry facilities and bug-free restrooms and showers. (☎744-2837. Sites for 2 with full hook-up $18, waterfront sites $22; $3 per additional person. Tents welcome.) **Galveston Island State Park,** on 13½ Mile Rd., 6 mi. southwest of Galveston on FM3005 (a continuation of Seawall Blvd.), rents tent sites. (☎737-1222. Restrooms, showers, and barbecue pits available. $12, plus $3 entrance fee per person.)

The oldest restaurant on the island, **The Original Mexican Cafe,** 1401 Market, cooks up great Tex-Mex meals with homemade flour tortillas, and daily lunch specials for $4.50-6.50. (☎762-6001. Open M-Th 11am-9:30pm, F 11am-10pm, Sa-Su 8am-10pm.) **Benno's,** 1206 Seawall Rd., serves tasty cajun seafood with an ocean view. Po'boys and lunch specials $5, seafood dinners $8.25-11.50. (☎762-4621. Open Su-Th 11am-10pm, F-Sa 11am-11pm.) Indulge your sweet tooth at **LaKing's Confectionery,** 2323 Strand St., a large, wonderfully old-fashioned ice cream and candy parlor. (☎762-6100. Open Su-Th 10am-9pm, F 10am-10pm, Sa 10am-11pm.)

📷🏖 SIGHTS AND ACTIVITIES. Galveston recently spent more than $6 million to clean up and restore its shoreline. The money was well spent—finding a pleasant beach is as easy as picking a spot once you're there. The only beach in Galveston which permits alcoholic beverages is **Apffel Park,** on the far eastern edge of the island (known as East Beach). **#3 Beach Pocket Park** (numbers 1 and 2 destroyed by the ocean) lies on the west end of the island, east of Pirates Beach, with bathrooms, showers, playgrounds, and a concession stand. (Car entry for beaches generally $5. Open daily 9am-9pm; some open later.)

Strand St., near the northern coastline, between 20th and 25th St., is a national landmark, with over 50 Victorian buildings. The district, restored with authentic gas lights and brick-paved walkways, provides a pastiche of cafes, restaurants, gift shops, and clothing stores. The **Galveston Island Trolley** shuttles between the seawall beach area and Strand St. Pick up the trolley at either visitors center. (Runs daily 6:30am-7pm; 60¢ per 30min.)

You'll find fabulous and pricey attractions at **Moody Gardens;** turn onto 81st from Seawall. The area, though filled with touristy gift shops and restaurants, makes room for three glass pyramids. One pyramid houses over 30 interactive space exhibits and three IMAX ride-film theaters (rides every 15min.), a second contains a tropical rainforest and 2000 exotic species of flora and fauna, while the third features an aquarium. An additional IMAX theater adjoins the visitors center. (☎683-4200 or 800-582-4673. Open summer daily 10am-9pm; winter Su-Th 10am-6pm, F and Sa 10am-9pm. Attractions $7.50 each, ride/films $7.50, aquarium $11, seniors and children $1 off; discounts for multiple exhibits.)

CORPUS CHRISTI   ☎361

Corpus Christi's economy depends almost entirely on its shoreside location; while local refineries are fed by the crude oil found offshore in the Gulf, year-round warm beaches bring the tourists in droves. As a result, there is no typical "off-season." Motels and beaches are packed by vacationers in the summer season, only to be replaced in the cooler months by "winter Texans," many of them elderly mobile home owners fleeing the chill of the northern states. Corpus Christi is defined equally by its pricey knick-knacks, cheap gas, natural stretches of sand, and the encroaching waste that floats in from the Gulf.

GETTING THERE AND GETTING AROUND. Greyhound, 702 N. Chaparral (☎882-2516; open daily 8am-2:30am), travels to Dallas (9-10hr., 7 per day, $39); Houston (5hr., 9 per day, $21); and Austin (5-7½hr., 4 per day, $25). **Regional Transit Authority (The "B")** (☎289-2600) buses within Corpus Christi; pick up maps and schedules at the visitors bureau or at **The B headquarters,** 1806 S. Alameda (☎883-2287; open M-F 8am-5pm). City Hall, Port Ayers, Six Points, and the Staples St. stations serve as central transfer points. (Runs M-Sa 5:30am-9:30pm, Su 11am-6:30pm. Fare 50¢; students, seniors, and children 25¢; disabled 10¢; Sa 25¢, transfers free.) The **Harbor Ferry** follows the shoreline and stops at the aquarium (10:30am-6:30pm daily, $1 each way). On the north side of Harbor Bridge, the free **Beach Shuttle** also travels to the beach, the Aquarium, and other nearby attractions (runs May-Sept. 10:30am-6:30pm). **Yellow Cab** (☎884-3211) charges $1.50 for the first mi., $1.50 per additional mi.

PRACTICAL INFORMATION. Corpus Christi's tourist district follows **Shoreline Dr.,** which borders the Gulf Coast, 1 mi. east of the downtown business district. **Convention and Visitors Bureau,** 1823 Chaparral, 6 blocks north of I-37 and 1 block from the water (☎561-2000 or 800-678-6232; open M-F 8:30am-5pm, Sa 9am-3pm). **Medical Care: Spohn Hospital Shoreline,** 600 Elizabeth St. (☎881-3000). **Hotlines: Hope Line** (☎855-4673) and **Battered Women and Rape Victims Shelter** (☎881-8888); both 24 hours. **Post Office:** 809 Nueces Bay Blvd. (☎800-275-8777; open M-F 7:30am-5:30pm, Sa 8am-1pm). **ZIP code:** 78469. **Area code:** 361.

ACCOMMODATIONS. Cheap accommodations are scarce downtown, and posh hotels and motels take up much of the shoreline. However, hostelers need not fear. **The Purple Parrot,** 2900 N. Shoreline Dr. (☎883-7100 or 800-883-8507), next to the USS Lexington, boasts bay-view decks, a courtyard with constant music, beach volleyball courts, and its own bar and restaurant. Consider The Purple Parrot a small resort to which hostelers are given privileged access. (Open daily 8-11am, 5-10pm. Key and linen deposit $10. Single-sex 6-person dorms $19; private rooms $39 for 2, $10 per additional person, ages 6-11 $5.) The best motel bargains lie several mi. south on Leopard St. (take bus #27) or I-37 (take #27 Express). The **Super 8** is at 910 Corn Products Rd. (☎289-1216; singles $33; doubles $38). Campers should head for the **Mustang State Park** or the **Padre Island National Seashore** (see below). Nueces River **City Park** (☎241-1464), off I-37 N from Exit 16 and approximately 18 mi. from downtown Corpus, has free tent sites, but only pit toilets and no showers.

FOOD AND NIGHTLIFE. The mixed population and seaside locale of Corpus Christi have resulted in a wide range of cuisines. Non-chain restaurants can be found on the "south side" of the city, around Staples St. and S. Padre Island Dr. **BJ's,**

6335 S. Padre Island Dr., serves cheese-laden, crispy-crusted pizzas (8 in. $4.50) while patrons shoot pool and drink 300 varieties of beer. (☎992-6671. Open M-Sa 11am-10:30pm, Su noon-9:30pm.) Next to the USS Lexington, **Pier 99,** 2822 N. Shoreline Dr., specializes in fried fresh fishies, such as $7 shrimp or oyster baskets. (☎887-0764. Open daily 11am-10pm.)

The city shuts down early, but several clubs manage to survive on Chaparral. **Tom, Dick, and Harry's,** 301 N. Chaparral St., provides three clubs under one cover. **Tom Foolery's** is a spacious bar with rock music and plenty of video screens, complemented by the adjacent **Dead Eye Dick's Saloon** and **Harry's Piano Bar.** (☎887-0029. Open W-Sa 11am-2am. Cover $3-5.) **Planet Luna,** 309 N. Chaparral St., is a dance oriented venue with a funky interior and late closing hours on the weekend. (☎884-4229. Open W-Th 9pm-2am, F-Sa 9pm-4am. $5-10 cover. 18+.)

🔲 **SIGHTS.** Corpus Christi's most significant sight is the shoreline, bordered by miles of rocky seawall and wide sidewalks with graduated steps down to the water. Overpriced seaside restaurants, sail and shrimp boats, and aggressive, hungry seagulls overrun the piers. To find beaches that allow swimming (some lie along Ocean Dr. and north of Harbor Bridge), just follow the signs, or call **Nueces County Parks** (☎949-7023) for directions. On the north side of Harbor Bridge, the **Texas State Aquarium** showcases creatures from the Gulf of Mexico. (*2710 N. Shoreline Blvd.* ☎881-1200 or 800-477-4853. Open M-Sa 9am-6pm, Su 10am-6pm; early Sept. to late May closes at 5pm. $8.75, seniors and ages 12-17 $6.75, ages 4-11 $5.*)

Just offshore floats the aircraft carrier **USS Lexington,** a World War II relic now open to the public. In her day, the "Blue Ghost" set more records than any carrier in the history of naval aviation. Be sure to check out the crews' quarters—you won't complain about small hostel rooms ever again. (☎888-4873 or 800-523-9539. Open daily 9am-6pm; early Sept. to late May 9am-5pm. $9, seniors $7, ages 4-12 $4.)

PADRE ISLAND   ☎361

With over 80 mi. of painstakingly preserved beaches, dunes, and wildlife refuge land, the **Padre Island National Seashore (PINS)** is a priceless, though debris-flawed gem, sandwiched between the condos of North Padre Island and the spring break hordes of South Padre Island. The seashore provides excellent opportunities for **windsurfing, swimming,** or **surf fishing.** For up-to-date info on prices and activities within PINS, call ☎800-766-2322. Garbage from nearby ships frequently litters the sands, but a lucky few may spot one of the endangered Kemp's Ridley sea turtles which PINS nutures. A weekly pass into PINS costs $10 for cars, $5 for hikers and bikers. Windsurfing or launching a boat from the Bird Basin will dock you an extra $5. Many beachcombers avoid these hefty fees by going to the free **North Beach.**

Five mi. south of the entrance station, **Malaquite Beach** makes your day on the sand as easy as possible with restrooms and rental picnic tables. In summer, the rental station is set up on the beachfront (inner tubes $2 per hr., chairs $1 per hr., body boards $2.50 per hr.). The **Malaquite Visitors Center,** has free maps and exhibits about the island (☎949-8068; open daily summer 8:30am-6pm; winter 8:30am-4:30pm). Motorists enter the PINS via the JFK Causeway, from the Flour Bluff area of Corpus Christi. PINS is difficult to reach via Corpus Christi's public bus system.

Visitors with four-wheel-drive and a taste for solitude should make the 60 mi. trek to the **Mansfield Cut,** the most remote and untraveled area of the seashore; loose sands prevent most vehicles from venturing far onto the beach. If you decide to go, tell the folks at the **Malaquite Ranger Station** (☎949-8173), 3½ mi. south of the park entrance; they handle emergency assistance and like to know who's out there. No wheels? Hike the **Grasslands Nature Trail,** a ¾ mi. loop through sand dunes and grasslands. Guide pamphlets are available at the trailhead.

The **PINS Campground,** less than 1 mi. north of the visitors center, consists of an asphalt area for RVs, restrooms, and cold-rinse showers—no soap is permitted on PINS (sites $8). Outside of this area—excluding the 5 mi. pedestrian-only beach—wherever vehicles can go, camping is free. For camping with amenities, the **Padre Balli County Park,** on Park Rd. 22, 3½ mi. from the JFK Causeway, near the national seashore, provides running water, electricity, laundry, and hot showers for campers. (☎949-8121. Sites with water and hook-up $15, "primitive" tent sites $6. 3-day maximum reservation, 14-day maximum stay.) **Area code:** 361.

WESTERN TEXAS

On the far side of the Río Pecos lies a region whose stereotypical Texan character verges on self-parody. This is the stomping ground of Pecos Bill—the mythical cowpoke who was raised by coyotes and lassoed a tornado. The land was colonized in the days of the Republic of Texas, during an era when the "law west of the Pecos" meant a rough mix of vigilante violence and frontier gunslinger machismo. The border city of El Paso and its Chihuahuan neighbor, Ciudad Juárez, beckon way, *wayyyy* out west—700 mi. from the Louisiana border—while Big Bend National Park dips down into the desert, cradled by a curve in the Río Grande.

AMARILLO   ☎806

Named for the yellow clay of a nearby lake (*amarillo* is "yellow" in Spanish), Amarillo opened for business as a railroad construction camp in 1887 and, within a decade, became the nation's largest cattle-shipping market. For years, the economy depended largely on the meat industry, but the discovery of oil gave Amarillo a kick in the 20s. More recently, the city has been boosted by a surge in tourism. Amarillo is the prime overnight stop for motorists en route from Dallas, Houston, or Oklahoma City to Sante Fe, Denver, and points west. It's a one-day city—there isn't much to do on the Texas plains—but a grand, shiny truck stop it is.

7 PRACTICAL INFORMATION. Amarillo sprawls at the intersection of I-27, I-40, and U.S. 287/87; you'll need a car to explore. Rte. 335 (the Loop) encircles the city. Amarillo Blvd. (historic Rte. 66) runs east-west, parallel to I-40. **Greyhound,** 700 S. Tyler (☎374-5371; station open 24hr.), buses to Dallas (7-8hr., 5 per day, $52) and Santa Fe (6-10hr., 4 per day, $56). **Amarillo City Transit,** 801 S.E. 23rd, operates eight bus routes departing from 5th and Pierce St. (☎378-3094. Buses run every 30min. M-Sa 6am-6pm. Maps at office. Fare 75¢.) The **Texas Travel Info Center,** 9400 I-40E, at Exit 76, dispenses state info (☎335-1441; open daily 8am-5pm). **Amarillo Convention and Visitors Bureau:** 1000 S. Polk at 10th St. (☎374-1497 or 800-692-1338; open M-F 8am-5pm). **Internet access:** Central Library, 413 E. 4th St. at Buchanan (☎378-3054; open M-Th 9am-9pm, F-Sa 9am-6pm, Su 2-6pm). **Post Office:** 505 E. 9th Ave., in Downtown Station at Buchanan St. (open M-F 7:30am-5pm). **ZIP code:** 79105. **Area code:** 806.

▮▊ ACCOMMODATIONS AND FOOD. There are cheap motels on the outskirts of town on I-40; prices rise near the downtown area. **Camelot Inn,** 2508 I-40 E, at Exit 72A, is a pink, castle-like motel with palatial rooms, a princely staff, shiny wood furniture, cable, and free morning grog—ranks among the best of the I-40 offerings. (☎373-3600. Singles $24-26; doubles $35-40; varies seasonally. 21+.) Kampers commune with nature at the **KOA Kampground,** 1100 Folsom Rd., 6 mi. east of downtown; take I-40 to Exit 75, head north to Rte. 60, then east 1 mi. (☎335-1792. Reception daily 7:30am-10pm; early Sept. to late May 8am-8pm. Pool, laundry, basketball court, free coffee, and shady sites. Sites $19, full hook-up $24.)

Dine amid plants, fountains, and Mexican murals at **Abuelo's,** 3501 45th St. The *cena mexicana* ($10) is best suited for two. (☎354-8294. Open Su-Th 11am-10pm, F-Sa 11am-11pm.) **OHMS,** 619 S. Taylor St., downtown, serves an assortment of ready-made dishes such as fettuccine and enchiladas with salad and bread. (Open M-F 11:30am-1:30pm, F-Sa 6:30-9pm.)

▣▙ SIGHTS AND ENTERTAINMENT. The outstanding **Panhandle-Plains Historical Museum,** 2401 4th Ave., in nearby Canyon (I-27 S to Rte. 87), has fossils, an old drilling rig, local history and geology exhibits, and a fine collection of Southwestern art. (☎651-2244. Open M-Sa 9am-5pm, Su 1-6pm; in summer daily until 6pm. $4,

> **BIG TEXAN WOMEN** The 72 oz. steak on display at the big, leathery, tourist-trap of a beef joint, the **Inn of the Big Texan**, at Lakeside Exit 75 from I-40, makes you feel full before even taking a bite. Anyone who eats the steak in 1hr. gets it free; the defeated pay $54. Over 25,000 have tried to consume the beast; the names, weights (before), and home cities of some of the 5000+ success stories are listed under the glass-top bar. A third of the women have been victorious, compared to only a fifth of the men. (☎372-6000 or 800-657-7177. Open daily 10:30am-10:30pm.)

seniors $3, ages 4-12 $1.) The **Amarillo Zoo,** off the 24th St. exit from U.S. 287, in Thompson Park, has 20 acres of open prairie laden with bison, roadrunners, and other Texas fauna. (☎381-7911. Open Tu-Su 9:30am-5:30pm. Free.) At **Cadillac Ranch,** Stanley Marsh III has planted ten gleaming Cadillacs at the same angle as Cheops pyramids. Get off I-40 at the Hope Rd. exit, 9 mi. west of Amarillo, cross to the south side of I-40, and drive ½ mi. down the highway access road to the west.

PALO DURO CANYON STATE PARK   ☎806

Known as the "Grand Canyon of Texas," Palo Duro covers 16,000 acres of jaw-dropping beauty. The canyon—1000 ft. from rim to rugged floor—exposes red, yellow, and brown cliffs. The park is 23 mi. south of Amarillo. Take I-27 to Exit 106 and head east on Rte. 217; from the south, get off I-27 at Exit 103. (Park open daily 7am-10pm; in winter 8am-10pm. $3, under 12 free.) The park **headquarters,** just inside the park, has maps of hiking trails and info on park activities (☎488-2227; open daily 7am-10pm, in winter 8am-5pm). A ½ mi. past the HQ, the **visitors center** displays exhibits on the canyon's history (open M-Sa 9am-5pm, Su 1-5pm). **Area code:** 806.

The beautiful 16 mi. **scenic drive** through the park, beginning at the HQ, provides many photo opportunities. The **Chuckwagon Restaurant,** 1½ mi. along the drive, has a restaurant (sandwiches $3) and a small selection of groceries. (☎488-2152. Open daily 8:30am-9pm.) To experience the canyon from the saddle, **Old West Stables,** ¼ mi further, rents horses with a saddle and riding hat. (☎488-2180. Open 8:30am-dusk. $15 per hr., wagon rides $8. Reservations recommended.)

Rangers allow backcountry hiking, but the majority of visitors stick to the marked trails. Most hikers (even children) can manage the 5 mi. **Lighthouse Trail,** but only experienced hikers should consider the rugged 9 mi. **Running Trail.** Temperatures in the canyon frequently climb to 100°F; bring at least two quarts of water. **Backcountry camping** is allowed in designated areas. (☎512-389-8900 for reservations. Primitive sites $9, with water $10, hook-up $12; cabins $65.)

The official play of the State of Texas, the musical ▧**Texas,** performed in Pioneer Amphitheater, is a must-see attraction in Palo Duro. The song and dance extravaganza covers the state's early days against the backdrop of the park's famous canyon scenery. (☎655-2181. In summer M-Sa 8:30pm. $8-21, children under 12 $4-21.)

GUADALUPE MOUNTAINS   ☎915

The Guadalupe Mountains rise out of the vast Texas desert to unexpected heights. Mescalero Apaches hunted and camped on these lands, until they were driven out by the US army. Before being forced out, Apache chief Geronimo claimed that the greatest gold mines in the world were hidden in the peaks. Happy prospectin'—the legendary mines remain undiscovered. Few settlers bought the prophecy; by the late 1800s, only a few ranchers and guano miners inhabited the rugged region. Today, **Guadalupe Mountains National Park** encompasses 86,000 acres of desert, caves, canyons, and highlands. Drivers can glimpse the park's most dramatic sights from U.S. 62/180: **El Capitán,** a 2000 ft. limestone cliff, and **Guadalupe Peak,** the highest point in Texas (8749 ft.). The mountains promise over 80 mi. of challenging desert hikes to those willing to explore the area. Entrance to the park is free. **Carlsbad, NM** (see p. 778), 55 mi. northeast, makes a good base town, with many cheap motels, campgrounds, and restaurants.

The major trails begin at the Pine Springs Campground, near the headquarters (see below). Imposing Guadalupe Peak can be scaled in a difficult but rewarding full-day hike (8½ mi.). Another full-day trail leads from the campground to The **Basin,** a high-country forest of Douglas fir and Ponderosa pine. A shorter trek (2-3hr.) traces the canyon floor of **Devil's Hall**—tread softly, and you may see deer along the trail. The 2½ mi., 1½hr. **Spring Trail** leads from the **Frijole Ranch,** about 1 mi. north of the visitors center, to a mountain spring. An easy 2-3hr. trail leading to the historic **Pratt Cabin** in the McKittrick Canyon (a major attraction in itself) begins at the **McKittrick Visitors Center,** several mi. northeast of the main visitors center off U.S. 62/180. Some trails are marked more clearly than others so take a map. Another full-day hike leads from the campground to The **Bowl** (9 mi.), a high-country forest of Douglas fir and Ponderosa Pines.

The park's lack of development is attractive to backpackers, but it creates some inconveniences. *Gas and food are not available in the park.* The park's two simple campgrounds, **Pine Springs** (☎828-3251), just past park headquarters, and **Dog Canyon** (☎828-3251, ranger station 505-981-2418), south of the New Mexico border at the north end of the park, have water and restrooms but no hook-ups or showers (sites $8; reservations for groups only). Dog Canyon is accessible only via Rte. 137 from Carlsbad, NM (72 mi.), or by a full-day hike from the **Visitors Center and Park Headquarters,** off U.S. 62/180. (☎828-3251. Open daily June-Aug. 8am-6pm; Sept.-May 8am-4:30pm. After hrs., info is posted on the bulletin board outside.) Free **backcountry camping** permits are at the visitors center.

Guadalupe Park lies 110 mi. east of El Paso. For additional info, contact the visitors center or write to **Guadalupe Mountains National Park,** HC 60, Box 400, Salt Flat 79847. **TNM&O Coaches** (☎505-887-1108) runs along U.S. 62/180 between Carlsbad, NM, and El Paso, making a flag stop in the Guadalupe Mountains National Park at the Headquarters Visitors Center (from Carlsbad 2½hr., $26). **Area code:** 915.

EL PASO ☎915

The largest of the US border towns, El Paso boomed in the 17th century as a stop-over on an important east-west wagon route that followed the Rio Grande through "the pass" (*el paso*) between the Rocky Mountains and the Sierra Madre. Today, modern El Paso is a stopover for travelers crossing between the US and Mexico, and the town's mixture of Mexican and American gives those crossing into Mexico a taste of what awaits them. After dark, activity leaves the center of town, migrating either toward the University of Texas at El Paso (UTEP) or south of the border to raucous Ciudad Juárez.

🛈 **PRACTICAL INFORMATION.** San Jacinto Plaza, at the corner of Main and Oregon, is the heart of El Paso. **I-10** runs east-west and **U.S. 54** north-south to the city. El Paso is divided into east and west by **Santa Fe Ave.** and into north and south by **San Antonio Ave.** *Tourists should be wary of the streets between San Antonio and the border late at night.* Sun Metro bus #33 runs 50min. to downtown from the airport, northeast of the city center. **Greyhound,** 200 W. San Antonio (☎532-2365; open 24hr.), across from the Civic Center, has daily service to Dallas (12hr., 7 per day, $60) and Los Angeles (16hr., 6 per day, $45). **Public Transportation:** Sun Metro departs from San Jacinto Plaza. (☎533-3333. Fare $1, students 50¢.) **Visitors Center:** 1 Civic Center Plaza, at Santa Fe and San Francisco. (☎544-0062. Open daily 8am-5pm.) **Post Office:** 219 E. Mills, between Mesa and Stanton. (☎532-2652. Open M-F 9am-5pm, Sa 8am-noon.) **ZIP code:** 79901. **Area code:** 915.

🏠🍴 **ACCOMMODATIONS AND FOOD.** El Paso offers safer, more appealing places to stay than Ciudad Juárez. Several good budget hotels can be found in the town center near Main St. and San Jacinto Square. The best place in town is the ▨**El Paso International Hostel,** 311 E. Franklin, between Stanton and Kansas in the Gardner Hotel. From the airport, take bus #33 to San Jacinto Park, walk two blocks north to Franklin, turn right, and head east one and a half blocks. The hostel takes great pride in meeting the needs of backpackers. (☎532-3661. Dorms $17.50, with

US university ID, ISIC, or ISTC $14.) **Budget Lodge Motel,** 1301 N. Mesa, is at California, six blocks from UTEP. A small cafe serves breakfast and lunch. (☎533-6821. A/C, cable TV. Singles $30; doubles $34.)

El Paso's cheap restaurants cluster around Stanton and Texas. **La Malinche,** 301 Texas, near San Jacinto Square, has authentic Mexican food in substantial portions. *Menudo* (a local speciality) is served Sa and Su. (☎544-8785. Open M-Sa 7:30-4pm. Breakfasts $2.75, chili specials $3.50-5.75.) **Manolo's Cafe,** 122 S. Mesa, between Overland and San Antonio, has *menudo* ($2), burritos ($1), and generous *comida corrida* ($4). Bullfighting and boxing photographs give it character. (☎532-7661. Open M-Sa 7am-6pm, Su 7:30-4pm.)

SIGHTS AND NIGHTLIFE. Most visitors are either stopping on the long drive through the desert or heading south to Ciudad Juárez. For a whirlwind tour, hop aboard the **Border Jumper Trolleys,** departing from the tourist office. Historic **San Jacinto Plaza** swarms with daily activity and affords an opportunity to rest on a shaded bench. To take in a view of the Rio Grande Valley, head northwest of downtown along Stanton and make a right turn on Rim Road (which becomes Scenic Dr.) to reach **Murchison Park,** at the base of the ridge. The Park offers a commanding vista of El Paso, Ciudad Juárez, and the Sierra Madre mountains.

Most nightlife seekers follow the younger drinking age across the border to Ciudad Juárez. If you decide to stick to the US side, **The Tap,** 408 E. San Antonio, remains El Paso's nightlife staple, serving authentic Mexican food (burritos $1.75-3.75) and drinks (Coronas $2) under its neon lights. (Open M-Sa 7am-2am, Sa 12pm-2am.) For something racier, **Club 101,** 500 San Francisco, is El Paso's oldest club. The club manages to keep up with the times with its two dance floors and changing party scene. (Open F-Sa until 2am. 21+.) **OP,** 301 S. Ochoa, is El Paso's premier gay club. (☎533-6055. Open Th and Su 9pm-2am, F-Sa 9pm-4am.)

BIG BEND   ☎915

Roadrunners, coyotes, wild pigs, mountain lions, and 450 species of birds make their home in Big Bend National Park, an 800,000-acre tract (about the size of Rhode Island) that is cradled by a helluva meander of the Río Grande. Spectacular canyons, vast stretches of the Chihuahuan Desert, and the Chisos Mountains occupy this literally and figuratively "far-out" spot. If you're in search of solitude, avoid the high season (Feb.-Apr.). During the summer, the predominantly desert park is excruciatingly hot, but you might have it all to yourself.

PRACTICAL INFORMATION. Big Bend is very geographically isolated, accessible only by car, via Rte. 118 or U.S. 385, both of which meet I-10. There are no gas stations or services of any kind on these roads; *fill your tank before leaving I-10.* **Park headquarters** is at **Panther Jct.,** about 26 mi. inside the park. (☎477-2251. Open daily 8am-6pm; vehicle pass $10 per week, pedestrians and bikers $5. National parks passes accepted.) For info, write the **Superintendent,** Big Bend National Park, P.O. Box 129, 79834. **Ranger stations** are located at Panther Jct., Río Grande Village, Persimmon Gap, and Chisos Basin. (Panther open daily 8am-6pm; Chisos open daily 8am-4:30pm; others closed May-Nov.) **Amtrak** stops in **Alpine,** 70 mi. north of the park (4hr.; El Paso to Alpine, $43-64). From there, rent a car from **Air Flight Auto Rental,** 414 E. Holland St., next to the Sonic. (☎837-3463. From $35 per day, 10¢ per mi. Must be 18+. $100 deposit required. Call for reservations.) **Groceries** and **gas** are available in Panther Jct., Río Grande Village, and Chisos Basin; Castalon has groceries, no gas. The Río Grande Village Store has **public showers** (75¢). **Emergency:** ☎477-2251 until 5pm; afterwards, call 911. **Area code:** 915.

ACCOMMODATIONS AND FOOD. The expensive **Chisos Mountains Lodge,** 10 mi. from park headquarters, offers the only motel-style shelter within the park. (☎477-2291. Singles $64; doubles $72. $10 per additional person.) They also rent lodges equipped with showers and baths but no A/C (singles $61; doubles $70; $10 per additional person), and stone cottages with three double beds and bath (3

TEXAS

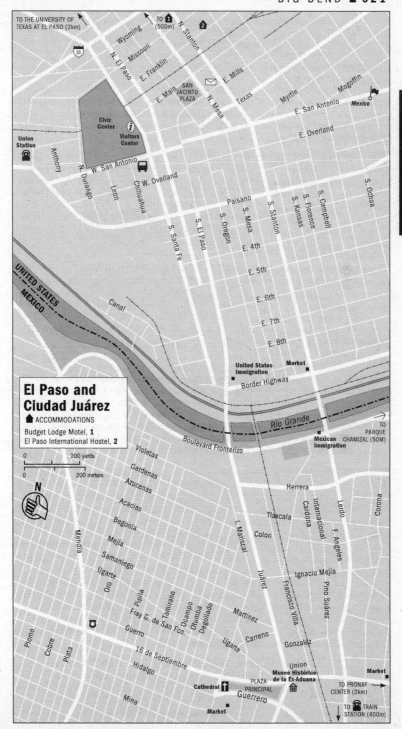

TO THE UNIVERSITY OF TEXAS AT EL PASO (2km)

TO 1 (500m)

TO 2

Wyoming

Missouri

N. Stanton

E. Franklin

E. Mills

E. Main

N. El Paso

SAN JACINTO PLAZA

N. Mesa

Texas

Myrtle

E. San Antonio

Magoffin

Mexico

Civic Center

Visitors Center

E. Overland

Union Station

Anthony

N. Durango

Leon

W. San Antonio

Chihuahua

W. Overland

Paisano

S. Oregon

S. El Paso

S. Mesa

S. Stanton

S. Florence

S. Kansas

S. Campbell

S. Ochoa

S. Santa Fe

E. 4th

E. 5th

E. 6th

E. 7th

E. 8th

UNITED STATES

MEXICO

Canal

United States Immigration

Market

Border Highway

Río Grande

TO PARQUE CHAMIZAL (50M)

Boulevard Fronterizo

Mexican Immigration

El Paso and Ciudad Juárez

🏠 ACCOMMODATIONS

Budget Lodge Motel, **1**
El Paso International Hostel, **2**

0   200 yards
0   200 meters

N

Violetas

Gardenas

Azucenas

Acacias

Begonia

Mejía

Samaniego

Ugarte

Oro

Mendía

Tepía

Tamirano

Ocampo

Otumba

Desolado

Fray G. de San Fco.

Guerro

16 de Septiembre

Hidalgo

Plomo

Cobre

Plata

Mina

Herrera

Tlaxcala

Colon

L. Mariscal

Cardona

Internacional

F. Angeles

Leido

Corona

Ignacio Mejía

Pino Suárez

Juárez

Francisco Villa

Martinez

Carreno

Ugarte

Gonzalez

Union

Museo Histórico de la Ex-Aduana

PLAZA PRINCIPAL

Cathedral

Guerrero

Market

Market

TO PRONAF CENTER (2km)

TO TRAIN STATION (400m)

people $81; $10 per additional person). Reservations are a must for high season; the lodge is often booked a year in advance. The restaurant and coffee shop at the lodge serve basic diner food (open daily 7am-8pm).

Designated campsites within the park are first come, first served. **Chisos Basin** and **Río Grande Village** offer sites with flush toilets ($8; cash only); the sites at **Castalon** have pit toilets. In summer, the sites in Chisos Basin are cool. During high season the campgrounds fill early. The **RV park** at Río Grande Village has 25 full-hookup sites ($14.50 for up to two people; $1 per additional person). For free overnight backcountry camping obtain a free **backcountry permit** at the park headquarters.

Cheap motels lurk off U.S. 170 near the dusty towns of **Terlingua** and **Lajitas,** 21 and 28 mi. respectively from park headquarters. Terlingua, named for the three languages spoken in the town in the late 1800s (English, Spanish, and a Native American dialect), lies on Rte. 170 just past Study Butte, about 35 mi. from park headquarters, but only 7 mi. from the park's western entrance; Lajitas is 7 mi. farther down the road. The **Chisos Mining Co. Motel,** on Rte. 170 1 mi. west of the junction of 170 and 118, provides clean rooms with an offbeat atmosphere. (☎371-2430. A/C. Singles $42; doubles $46.) Farther up Rte. 170 in **Terlingua Ghost Town,** the **Starlight Theater Bar and Grill** has large portions of cheap Tex-Mex ($3-9) and free live music on weekends. (☎371-2326. Food served daily 6-10pm; bar open Su-F 5pm-midnight, Sa 5pm-1am. No credit cards.)

◪ **OUTDOORS.** Big Bend encompasses several hundred mi. of hiking trails, ranging from 30min. nature walks to backpacking trips several days long. *When hiking in the desert, always carry at least a gallon of water per person per day.* The 43 mi. **scenic drive** to Santa Elena Canyon is handy for those short on time. Many of the park's roads can **flood** during the rainy summer.

Park rangers at the visitors centers are happy to suggest hikes and sights; the *Hiker's Guide to Big Bend* pamphlet ($2), available at Panther Jct., is a good investment. The **Lost Mine Trail,** a 3hr. hike up a peak in the Chisos, leads to an amazing summit-top view of the desert and the Sierra de Carmen in Mexico. A shorter walk (1¾ mi.) ambles through the **Santa Elena Canyon** along the Río Grande—the canyon walls rise as high as 1000 ft. over the banks of the river.

Rafting is big fun on the Río Grande. Free permits and info are at all visitors center. Several companies offer **river trips** down the 133 mi. of the Río Grande in the park. **Far-Flung Adventures,** next door to the Starlight Theater Bar and Grill in Terlingua, organizes one- to seven-day trips. (☎800-359-4138. 1-day trip to Santa Elena around $110 per person if water flows permit; 1-day trip to Colorado Canyon $84.)

ROCKY
MOUNTAINS

Created by immense tectonic forces some 65 million years ago, the Rockies mark a vast wrinkle in the North American continent. Sculpted by wind, water, and glaciers over eons, their weathered peaks extend 3000 miles from northern Alberta to New Mexico and soar to altitudes exceeding two vertical miles. Cars overheat and humans gulp thin alpine air as they ascend into grizzly bear country. Dominated by rock and ice, the highest peaks of the Rockies are accessible only to veteran mountain climbers and wildlife adapted for survival in scant air and deep snow.

Although the whole of the Rocky Mountain area supports less than 5% of the US population, every year millions flock to its spectacular national parks, forests, and ski resorts, while hikers follow the Continental Divide along the spine of the Rockies. Nestled in valleys or appearing out of nowhere on the surrounding plains, the region's mountain villages and cowboy towns welcome travelers year-round.

HIGHLIGHTS OF THE ROCKY MOUNTAINS

HIKING. Memorable trails include the Gunnison Rte. in the Black Canyon, CO (p. 691); the hike to Monument Canyon at the Colorado National Monument (p. 687); and just about anything in the Grand Tetons (p. 654).

SKIING. The Rockies are filled with hotspots, but try Sawtooth, ID (p. 628); Vail, CO (p. 683); or Whitefish, MT (p. 642).

SCENIC DRIVES. Going-to-the-Sun Rd. in Glacier National Park (p. 638) is truly unforgettable, as is phenomenally high San Juan Skyway in southern Colorado (p. 695). The North Fork (p. 653) offers an alternative, more rewarding passage into Yellowstone; the full-day Centennial Scenic Drive (p. 659) explores the rugged Wyoming wilderness.

ALPINE TOWNS. Aspen, CO (p. 684), and Stanley, ID (p. 628): two of the loveliest.

IDAHO

When Lewis and Clark first laid eyes on Idaho in 1805, they observed pristine, snow-capped mountains, clear lakes, frothing rivers, and thick stands of conifers—little has changed since: Idaho offers miles of untouched National Forest and wilderness areas ripe for adventure. The wilderness adventurer's opportunities are maximized by the diversity of the land; the Rocky Mountains divide Idaho into three distinct regions. To the southeast, world-famous potatoes thrive in volcanically rich valleys. To the north, pine forests envelop frigid lakes and reclusive souls. In the center, ski slopes, hiking trails, and hot springs attract nature lovers.

🗺 PRACTICAL INFORMATION

Capital: Boise.

Visitor Info: Idaho Information Line, ☎800-847-4843; www.visitid.org. **Parks and Recreation Dept.,** 5657 Warm Springs Ave., Boise 83712 (☎334-4199). **Skier Info,** ☎800-243-2754. **Idaho Outfitters and Guide Association,** 711 N. 5th St.; P.O. Box 95, Boise 83701 (☎342-1438; www.ioga.org).

Hotlines: Mental Health Emergency, ☎334-0808 or 800-600-6474. **Women's Crisis Line,** ☎343-7025. **Rape Crisis Line,** ☎345-7273.

Postal Abbreviation: ID. **Sales Tax:** 5%. **Area code:** 208.

BOISE

☎ 208

Surprisingly cosmopolitan Boise (pronounced *BOY-see*, not *BOY-zee*) is a verdant residential oasis with a happening downtown. Idaho's capital city offers a small-town feel, a warm population, numerous grassy parks, and airy shopping plazas. Most of the city's sights are within the ten square blocks between the capitol and the Boise River, easily manageable on foot.

⚡ PRACTICAL INFORMATION

The pedestrian-friendly Grove is a brick walkway parallel to and between Main St. and Front St. **Greyhound,** 1212 W. Bannock (☎343-3681), a few blocks west of downtown, runs to Salt Lake City (8hr., 4 per day, $37-40); Portland (11hr., 3 per day, $33-36); and Seattle (14hr., 3 per day, $36-38). **Boise Urban Stages** runs several routes throughout the city. (☎336-1010. Maps available at visitors center. Buses operate M-Sa 6:15am-6:45pm. Fare 75¢, seniors 35¢, ages 6-18 50¢; all fares 35¢ on Sa.) **McU's Sports,** 822 W. Jefferson St. (☎342-7734), rents a good selection of gear and offers tips on hiking. The ski shop is located at 2314 Bogus Basin Rd. (☎336-2300. In-line skates $5 for 1hr., $15 for 8hr. Mountain bikes $15 per half-day, $25 per day. Ski equipment $15 per day, kids $12.) **Visitors center:** 850 W. Front St., at Boise Center on the Grove (☎344-5338; open M-F 10am-4pm, Sa 10am-2pm). **Internet access: Boise Public Library,** 715 S. Capitol Blvd. (☎384-4114; open M 10am-6pm, Tu-Th 10am-9pm, F 10am-6pm, Sa 10am-5pm). **Post Office:** 770 S. 13th St. (open M-F 7:30am-5:30pm, Sa 10am-2pm). **ZIP code:** 83702. **Area code:** 208.

▛ ACCOMMODATIONS

The recently opened **Hostel Boise,** 17322 Can-Ada Rd., is located 15-20min. from downtown Boise in the town of Nampa. This country-style home has mountain views, evening campfires, and Internet access. To get to the hostel, take Exit 38 from I-84 and follow Can-Ada Rd. north from the interstate; the hostel is about 2 mi. up the road. (☎467-6858. Dorm-style beds $12-15.) **University Inn,** 2360 University Dr., bordering on Boise State University has free local calls, cable TV, and HBO, as well as a pool and jacuzzi and shuttle service to the airport. (☎345-7170 or 800-345-7170. Singles $45; doubles $50.) The **Cabana Inn,** 1600 Main St., is at the other end of downtown. (☎343-6000. Rooms from $30-55.) Reasonable motels cluster around Exit 53 of I-84, near the airport.

The **Boise National Forest Office/Bureau of Land Management,** 1387 S. Vinnell Way, provides info about campgrounds in Boise, most of which are RV-oriented. (☎373-4007. Open M-F 7:45am-8pm.) **Fiesta Park,** 11101 Fairview Ave., offers tent sites for $22. Amenities include a pool, restroom with running water, and a pay phone. (☎375-8207. Reception daily Oct.-Mar. 8am-5pm; Apr. 8am-6pm; May 8am-7pm; June-Sept. 8am-9pm. RV sites with partial hook-up $23, full hook-up $24.) The **Americana Kampground,** 3600 Americana Terrace Blvd., next to the river, colludes in the stale overuse of "K" in place of "C" but has riverside views. (☎344-5733. $17 includes full hook-up for a night, $92 for a week; $2 each additional person. $3 showers.) The closest non-RV camping is at **Bogus Basin,** about a 45min. drive out of Boise (open M-F 7:30am-4:30pm).

◑▨ FOOD AND NIGHTLIFE

Boise offers other dining options besides Idaho's famous potatoes. The downtown area, centered around **8th and Main St.,** is bustling with lunchtime delis, coffee shops, ethnic cuisine, and several stylish bistros. After work lets out in summer, young professionals relax with food and drink on numerous restaurants' patios. For amazingly fresh and creative vegetarian food, try **Kulture Klatsch,** 409 S. 8th. This hip and multi-cultural eatery has an extensive veggie menu, including numerous vegan options, and hosts live music with no cover five nights a week. (☎345-0452. Open M

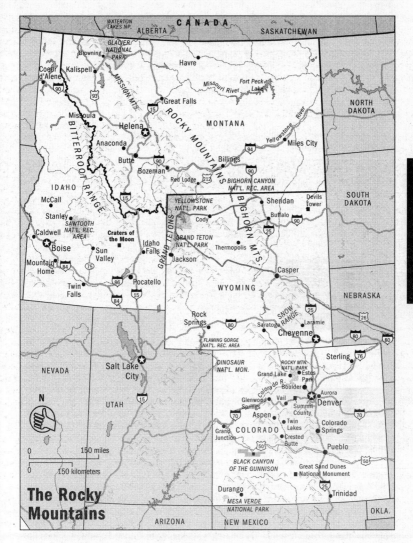

The Rocky Mountains

7am-3pm, T-Th 7am-10pm, F 7am-11pm, Sa 8am-11pm, Su 8am-3pm. Breakfasts $3-8, lunch specials $5, dinners $7-9.) **Moon's Kitchen,** 815 W. Bannock St., an institution among politicians from the nearby capitol, has been serving classic American food since 1955. (☎385-0472. Open M-F 7am-3pm, Sa 8am-3pm. Breakfast specials $4-7, famous shakes $3.) For a traditional 50s diner, complete with working Wurlitzers, try the family-oriented **Galaxy Diner,** 500 S. Capitol Blvd. Burgers start at $4, shakes are $3. (☎343-6191. Su-Th 7am-10pm, F-Sa 7am-midnight.)

Musicians perform on Main St. from 5-9pm, while vendors from nearby restaurants hawk food and beer. Cheap beer and live music draw the locals to **Blues Bouquet,** 1010 Main St., downtown Boise's only western saloon. (☎345-6605. Open M-F 1pm-2:30am, Sa-Su 8pm-2am. 21+.) The youthful and trendy gather at **The Balcony,** upstairs at Capitol Terrace, one block from the Grove Center on Grove St., to dance, play pool, and socialize (open 2pm-2am; 21+).

BOISE'S BASQUE BACKGROUND

In 1848, the California Gold Rush brought a flood of immigrants to the US. Among them were the Basques, who moved from a small corner of Spain to the goldfields of the Sierras. The Basques, whose native language is supposedly unrelated to any in the world, had a particularly difficult time learning English. Unable to find jobs, the American Basques spread out into the Western rangelands and mountains to become sheep herders. Although historians have recently found links between the mysterious language and Caucasian, the ancient language spoken in the Caucasus region, no conclusive evidence of a tie has been found, and Basque remains without linguistic relatives. Today, southern Idaho is home to the largest concentrated Basque population outside of Europe. Basque culture is preserved at the **Basque Museum and Cultural Center** at the corner of Grove and Capital in downtown Boise. This fascinating museum includes a gallery with changing exhibits, Basque art, and a replica of a Basque herder's house. (☎343-2671. Open Tu-F 10am-4pm, Sa 11am-3pm. $1, 12 and under free.) Next door to the museum, sample Basque cuisine at **Bar Gernika,** 202 S. Capitol Blvd., a pub and eatery named for the capital of the Basque homeland. In the summer, enjoy the hearty meals outside on the patio. Authentic Basque dishes include Solomo sandwiches (marinated pork tenderloin $6-8) and Dorothy's famous beef tongue ($11-12), served only on Sa, from 10am until it's gone. (☎344-2175. Open M 11am-11pm, Tu-Th 11am-midnight, F 11am-1am, Sa 11:30am-1am.)

👁 SIGHTS

The logical starting point for exploring Boise is the beautiful **Julia Davis Park.** Free parking is available around the museums, just off of Capitol Blvd. The **Boise Tour Train** whisks you around 75 city sights in 1¼hr. Tours begin and end in the parking lot of Julia Davis Park. (☎342-4796. Tours June to early Sept. M-Sa 5 per day 10am-3pm, Su 4 per day noon-3:45pm; in fall, W-F 1 per day at 1:30pm, Sa 4 per day 10:30am-3pm, Su 3 per day noon-3pm. $6.50, seniors $6, ages 13-17 $5, ages 4-12 $3.50.) To learn about Idaho and the Old West at your own pace, stroll through the **Historical Museum,** in Julia Davis Park, which showcases a replica 19th-century bar complete with a display of a two-headed calf. Other notable exhibits include Native American artifacts and a timeline of Ernest Hemingway's life. (☎334-2120. Open M-Sa 9am-5pm, Su and holidays 1-5pm. Free; donations encouraged.) Also in the park, the **Boise Art Museum** displays an impressive selection of contemporary international and local works while offering educational programs, lectures, and tours. (670 Julia Davis Dr. ☎345-8330. Open all year M-F 10am-5pm, Sa-Su noon-5pm. $4, students and seniors $2, ages 6-12 $1; free the 1st Th of every month.) Raptors perch and dive at the **World Center for Birds of Prey.** (566 W. Flying Hawk Ln. ☎362-3716. From I-85, take the Overland exit. Go south on S Cole until you reach the center. Open daily 9am-5pm; off-season 10am-4pm. $4, seniors $3, children $2, under 4 free.) For more back-to-nature fun, try the 22 mi. **Boise River Greenbelt,** a pleasant path ideal for a leisurely walk or picnic along the Boise River. In the summer, visitors can go tubing in the river at Berber Park. The ever-growing **Boise Shakespeare Festival** hits town from June to Sept. (☎336-9221.) Every year in late June, Boise hosts a **River Festival,** featuring hot-air balloon rallies, a carnival, live music, fireworks, and sporting events. (☎338-8887.) Upcoming events are showcased in *The Boise Weekly*, available Th.

KETCHUM AND SUN VALLEY   ☎208

In 1935, Union Pacific heir Averill Harriman sent Austrian Count Felix Schaffgotsch to scour the US for a site to develop a ski resort area rivaling Europe's best. The Count dismissed Aspen, reasoning that its air was too thin for East Coasters, and selected the small mining and sheep-herding town of Ketchum in Idaho's Wood River Valley. Celebrities and other privileged people have been flocking to the area ever since. While Ketchum's permanent population is only 5300, traffic extends for miles in each direction during peak months. Ketchum features numerous shops and expensive eateries, but the real attraction lies in the hills outside of town.

⁊ PRACTICAL INFORMATION

The best time to visit is during the rare "slack" period (late Oct. to late Nov. and May to early June). **Sun Valley Express** runs one bus daily to the Boise airport. (☎877-622-8267. Leaves Ketchum 7:15am, return bus from the Boise airport leaves at 2pm. $50. Reservations recommended.) **KART,** Ketchum's **bus service,** tours the city and its surrounding areas. (☎726-7576. Runs daily 7:20am-midnight maps available at Chamber of Commerce. No fare.) **Sawtooth National Recreation Area (SNRA) Headquarters,** 6 mi. north of Ketchum off Rte. 75, stocks detailed info on the recreation area, hot springs, and area forests and trails, including National Recreation Area maps for $4 and Margaret Fuller's excellent trail guides for $15. (☎727-5013, 727-5000, or 800-280-2267. Open daily 8am-5pm.) **Chamber of Commerce/Visitors Center:** 4th and Main St. in Ketchum. (☎726-3423 or 800-634-3347. Open daily in peak season 9am-7pm, hrs. vary during spring and fall.) **Post office:** 301 1st Ave. (☎726-5161; open M-F 8am-5:30pm, Sa 11am-2pm). **ZIP code:** 83340. **Area code:** 208.

⁊⌂ ACCOMMODATIONS AND FOOD

From early June to mid-Oct., camping is the best option for cheap sleep in the Sun Valley area. Check with the **Ketchum Ranger District,** on Sun Valley Rd., just outside of Ketchum on the way to Sun Valley. (☎622-5371. Open M-F 8am-4:30pm, Sa-Su 8am-5:30pm.) **Boundary Campground,** 3 mi. northeast of town on Trail Creek Rd. past the Sun Valley resort, is the closest to town and has ten wooded sites near a creek. (Restrooms, water. Sites $10.) Further up the road, free, scattered sites are available along Trail Creek Rd. although they have no restrooms or water. Up Rte. 75 into the SNRA lie several scenic camping spots; the cheapest ($8) are **Murdock** (11 sites) and **Caribou** (7 sites). They are, respectively, 2 and 3 mi. up a dirt road called North Fork Rd., which begins as a paved road to the right of the visitors center. At $11, **North Fork** (29 sites) and **Wood River** (30 sites) are 8 mi. north of Ketchum, along Rte. 75. For North Fork, take the first campground road north of SNRA headquarters. Wood River is 2 mi. beyond SNRA headquarters. **Easley Campground and Pool,** about 8 mi. on the way to Stanley from SNRA headquarters, is adjacent to a tiny hot spring ($11). For those looking for indoor accommodations, the towns of Hailey and Bellevue, approximately 15 mi. south of Ketchum, have more affordable lodging. The **High Country Motel,** 765 S. Main in Bellevue, with spacious, wood-paneled rooms, is the best deal around. (☎788-2050 or 800-692-2050. Rooms $45-55.)

Ketchum's small confines bulge with over 80 restaurants, catering to the gourmet tastes of resort visitors. Ketchum's cheapest eats can be found at **The Hot Dog Adventure Company,** 210 N. Main St. A vast array of hot dogs ($2-4), including veggie dogs, are served with fries and shakes. (☎726-0117. Open M-Sa noon-6pm and 10:30pm-2:30am.) The soups and chowders ($3-6) at the **Burger Grill,** corner of 4th and Main, are filling and inexpensive. (Open M-Sa 11am-8pm. Burgers $5-7.) **The Starrwood Bakery,** 591 4th St., has fresh baked goods and a solid lunch deal: $5.50 buys a deli sandwich with soup and a side salad. (☎726-2253. Open M-F 6:30am-5pm, Sa 7am-5pm, Su 7am-4pm; hrs. shorter in winter.) Chase back some stiff drinks for just $1 on Su and Tu at Hemingway's old haunt, **Whiskey Jacques,** 251 Main St. (☎726-5297, take-out 726-3200. Open daily 4pm-2am. Live music 9:30pm-2am most nights.)

⚟ OUTDOORS

See and be seen on the **Wood River and Sun Valley trail system.** Over 20 mi. of paved trails follow Hwy. 75 south of town, beginning in Bellevue and continuing through Ketchum and Sun Valley, and pass by ski slopes and historic sites. Available at the visitors center, *Wood River Trails,* has more info.

ROCKY MOUNTAINS

SKIING. Visible from miles around, **Bald Mountain,** affectionately called Baldy, is a beacon for serious skiers. Two plazas serve Baldy River Run on the north side of town and Warm Springs on the south side. The gentle slopes of **Dollar Mountain,** accessible from the Sun Valley Rd., are perfect for beginners. Both ski areas are run by Sun Valley Resort. (☎800-786-8259, ski conditions 800-635-4150. Full-day lift ticket $59, under 12 $32.)

MOUNTAIN BIKING. The Sawtooth area is nationally renowned for its stunning mountain bike trails, which run through the gorgeous canyons and mountain passes of the SNRA. Beware; trails might be snowbound or flooded well into July. Take a high-speed quad to the top of Bald Mountain and ride down on a mountain bike during summer months. (☎800-726-8259. Open daily in summer 9am-3:45pm. $15 per ride, $20 per day.) Inquire about trail conditions at **Formula Sports,** on the corner of 5th and Main at 460 N. Main St. (☎726-3194. Bikes from $12 per 4hr., $18 per day; tandems $20/$30.) **The Elephant's Perch,** 280 East Ave., at East Ave. and Sun Valley Rd., has a complete stock of outdoor gear. (☎726-3497. Open M-Sa 9am-6pm, Su 10am-6pm. Bikes $12 per 4hr., $20 per day, backpack $15 per day, sleeping bag $25 per day, tents $20 per day, ski pages $12-30 per day.) Before hitting the forest, pick up info on mountain biking and trail suggestions at the Chamber of Commerce or the SNRA Headquarters north of town.

HOT SPRINGS. After a hard day of biking or hiking, Ketchum locals soak in their favorite geothermal hot spring. The hot springs, hidden in the hills and canyons of Ketchum, are not the secret they once were. Springtime melt and rain can put the springs underwater, rendering them inaccessible. They are normally safe only in July and Aug. The Chamber of Commerce has suggestions on which pools are safe and accessible. Two of the more accessible, non-commercial springs are **Warfield Hot Springs,** on Warm Springs Creek, 11 mi. west of Ketchum on Warm Springs Rd., and **Russian John Hot Springs** (called a "sheep dip" by locals for its lukewarm temperature), 8 mi. north of the SNRA headquarters on Rte. 75, just west of the highway. A safer alternative to chancing these uncontrolled pools can be found at **Easley Hot Springs,** 12 mi. north of Ketchum on Hwy. 75. (☎726-7522. Open Tu-Sa 11am-7pm, Su 11am-5pm. $4, children $3, seniors $2.50.) For the best info on **fishing,** including equipment rentals, stop by **Silver Creek Outfitters,** 500 N. Main St. (☎726-5282. Open M-Sa 9am-6pm, Su 9am-5pm, longer hrs. in peak season. Fly rods $15 per day.)

SAWTOOTH ☎208

Home to the Sawtooth and White Cloud Mountains in the north and the Smokey and Boulder Ranges in the south, the Sawtooth National Recreation Area (SNRA) sprawls over 756,000 acres of untouched land and is surrounded by four national forests, encompassing the headwaters of five of Idaho's rivers. A great (but slow) 60 miles drive heads north to Stanley on Rte. 75. Pause at the Galena Overlook, 31 miles north of Ketchum and ¼ mile downhill from the 8701-foot Galena Pass.

THE SUN VALLEY ALSO RISES Ernest Hemingway's love affair with both rugged outdoor sports and wealthy celebrities fits Ketchum's dualistic spirit. After spending many of his vacations hunting and fishing in the Sawtooth Range, the author built a cabin in Sun Valley where he died from a self-inflicted gunshot wound on July 2, 1961. While Hemingway's house is off-limits, there are a number of sites in town that commemorate the author. His grave is located in the Ketchum Cemetery, just north of town on Hwy. 75. The **Ketchum-Sun Valley Heritage and Ski Museum,** at the corner of 1st St. and Washington Ave., displays exhibits on Hemingway's life. (☎726-8118. Open daily 1-4pm.) A bust of Hemingway is tucked away in a shady spot along the river at the **Hemingway Memorial,** about 1 mi. outside of Sun Valley on the way to Boundary Campground (see above). Each year on Hemingway's birthday, July 21, the community library hosts a lecture. (☎726-3493.)

7 PRACTICAL INFORMATION. The tiny (pop. 69), frontier-style town of **Stanley,** located 60 mi. north of Ketchum at the intersection of Rte. 21 and 75, serves as a northern base for exploring Sawtooth. The small business district is located one block to the south of Rte. 21, along Ace of Diamonds St. The **Stanley Ranger Station** offers maps, SNRA passes, and sage advice. The station is located 3 mi. south of Stanley on Rte. 75 (☎ 774-3000; open M-Sa 8am-4:30pm; off-season M-F 8am-5pm). At the entrance to Redfish Lake (5 mi. south of Stanley and 55 mi. north of Ketchum on Rte. 75), the **info booth** dispenses a wide range of info about hiking, camping, and outdoor sports. (☎ 774-3536. Sporadic hrs.; the booth is usually staffed during sunny, busy weekends.) Stanley's **post office:** Ace of Diamonds St. (☎ 774-2230. Open M-F 1-5pm; in winter M-F 8-11am and noon-5pm.) In the Chamber of Commerce building, the **Stanley Library** offers public **Internet access** (☎ 774-2470. Open M noon-6pm, Th noon-4pm, Sa noon-4pm.) **ZIP code:** 83278. **Area code:** 208.

⌐ ACCOMMODATIONS. The SNRA boasts 33 campgrounds scattered throughout the park, making the maps and advice available at rangers stations and the SNRA headquarters invaluable. **Alturas Lake,** 21 mi. south of Stanley on Rte. 75 (the turn-off is marked about 10 mi. north of Galena Pass) has three campgrounds with fishing, swimming, and scenery. (55 sites. Vault toilets and water. Sites $11-13.) The area around **Redfish Lake,** 5 mi. south of Stanley off Rte. 75, is a scenic but sometimes overcrowded spot. The eight campgrounds in the area are located conveniently close to Stanley and many trailheads into the SNRA. (Sites $11-13.)

East on Rte. 75, past the town of Stanley, numerous sites are available alongside the wild and scenic **Salmon River.** (Water available; no hook-up. First come, first served sites $11, $5.50 with Golden Age and Golden Access, free with Golden Eagle.) One of the best is **Mormon Bend,** 5 mi. east of Stanley on Rte. 75, with 15 sites convenient to whitewater. Other scenic and inviting spots are **Casino Creek,** 8 mi. east of Stanley on Rte. 75, and the **Salmon River Campground,** 9 mi. east of Stanley on Rte. 75. In most areas, a trailhead pass is required for parking. These are available at the Stanley Ranger Station (see **Practical Information,** above).

For a real bed, Stanley provides more scenic and more reasonable lodging than Ketchum. On Ace of Diamonds St. in downtown, the charming and historic **Sawtooth Hotel** is the best deal on indoor lodging for miles. (☎ 774-9947. Open May-Sept. Singles $35, with private bath $50; doubles $40/$60.) Stop downstairs for breakfast at the **Sawtooth Cafe** and pick up a picnic for hiking. (Open 6am-3pm. Breakfasts $3-5; picnics $6.75-8.75.) At **Danner's Log Cabin Motel,** on Rte. 21, town ex-mayor and Stanley history buff Bunny Danner rents historic cabins built by goldminers in 1939. The office, built in 1906, was the first building in town and served originally as the ranger station. (☎ 774-3539. Cabins $50-80; $35-80 in spring and fall.)

◻ FOOD. Dining options are rather limited in Stanley. Stock up on eats for the trail at the **Mountain Village Grocery Store.** (☎ 774-3500. Open daily 7am-9pm, 6am-10pm in the summer months.) The **Mountain Village Resort Restaurant and Saloon,** on Rte. 21 near the intersection with Rte. 75, offers sandwiches ($5-6) and breakfast entrees for $2.50-7. (☎ 774-3317. Open daily 7am-10pm.) The local watering hole is the **Rod and Gun Club Bar,** at the end of Ace of Diamonds St. in Stanley. This authentic western bar has pool tables, Internet access ($5 per ½hr.) and live music on weekends. (☎ 774-9920. Open daily from 4pm. Last call 2am. 21+.)

◪ OUTDOORS. The rugged backcountry of the SNRA is perfect for hiking, boating, fishing, and mountain biking. Pick up a free map of the area and inquire about trail conditions at SNRA headquarters before hitting the trail or the lake, particularly in early summer, when trails may be flooded out. Much of the backcountry stays buried deep in the snow well into summer. The SNRA is home to black bears; ranger stations have information about necessary precautions.

Redfish Lake is the source of many trails; some popular, leisurely hikes include those to **Fishhook Creek** (excellent for children), **Bench Lakes,** and the **Hell Roaring trail.** The long, gentle loop around **Yellow Belly, Toxaway,** and **Petit Lakes** is a moderate overnight suitable for novices. Two mi. northwest of Stanley on Rte. 21, the 3 mi. Iron Creek Rd.

leads to the trailhead of the **Sawtooth Lake Hike.** This 5½ mi. trail, steep but well-worn, is not too taxing if you stop to rest. Bionic hikers can try the steep, 4 mi. hike to **Casino Lakes,** which begins at the Broadway Creek trailhead southeast of Stanley.

The Sawtooths have miles of mountain biking, but check a map first; riding is allowed in the National Forest areas, but prohibited in the Sawtooth Wilderness. **Riverwear,** on Rte. 21 in Stanley, rents bikes from $17 per day. (☎774-3592; open daily 7am-10pm.) Beginners will enjoy riding the dirt road that accesses the North Fork campgrounds from the visitors center. This gorgeous passage parallels the North Fork of the Wood River for 5 mi. before branching off into other narrower and steeper trails, suitable for more advanced riders. These trails can be combined into loops; consult the trail map or the ranger station. **Boulder Creek Rd.,** 5 mi. from SNRA headquarters, leads to pristine Boulder Lake and an old mining camp. The steep, 10 mi. roadtrip ride is suitable for skilled riders. Check with the ranger station in Stanley or the SNRA Headquarters to find out if trails are flooded out.

Topographical maps ($4) and various trail books ($3-20), including Margaret Fuller's invaluable books ($14-18), are available at **McCoy's Tackle and Gift Shop,** on Ace of Diamonds St. McCoy's also sells a full range of outdoor equipment. (☎774-3377. Open daily Memorial Day to June 21st 8am-7pm, June 22 to Labor Day 7:30am-9pm, Sept. 9am-6pm.) **Sawtooth Rentals,** ¼ mi. north of the Rte. 21/75 junction, specializes in water vehicle rentals. (☎774-3409 or 800-243-3185. Kayaks $30 per day, doubles $40; rafts $15 per person per day; mountain bikes $25 per day.) For pontoon boat tours of the lake, head for **Redfish Lake Lodge Marina.** (☎774-3536. Open daily in summer 9am-10pm. 1½hr. tours $6.50, children $4.50; schedule varies. Paddleboats $5 per 30min. Canoes $5 per hr., $15 per half-day, $25 per day. Outboards $10 per hr., $33.50 for half-day, $60 per day.)

The most inexpensive way to enjoy the SNRA waters is to visit the **hot springs** just east of Stanley. **Sunbeam Hot Springs,** 10 mi. east of Lower Stanley on Rte. 75, is the best of the batch. Be sure to bring a bucket or cooler to the stone bathhouse; you'll need to add about 20 gallons of cold Salmon River water before you can get into these hot pools (120-130°F). High water can wash out the hot springs temporarily. Check with locals for info about other hot springs.

CRATERS OF THE MOON   ☎208

The unearthly landscape at Craters of the Moon National Monument seems more like the aftermath of a disaster movie than a vacation spot. The twisted lava formations were formed by a moving "hot spot" underneath the earth's surface that today causes the geological phenomenon found in Yellowstone National Park. Located 70 mi. southeast of Sun Valley at the junction of Rte. 20 and 26/93, this strange attraction is worth at least a quick detour (admission $4 per car, $2 per individual).

The monument's single campground, located just past the entrance station, scatters 52 sites with views of the lava formations. (Water but no hook-up; $10.) Wood fires are prohibited, but charcoal fires are permitted. Camping in unmarked sites in the dry lava beds of the park itself is permitted with a free backcountry permit, available from the **visitors center** (☎527-3257; open daily 8am-4:30pm). **Echo Crater,** accessible by a 4 mi. hike from the Tree Molds parking lot, is the most frequented and comfortable of these sites.

The visitors center offers videos, displays, and printed guides on the geological past of the area. A 7 mi. drive winds through much of the monument, accessing most major sights. There are several short trails that lead to stranger sites; the visitors center has guides. Don't forget sturdy shoes, water, sunscreen, and hats; the rocks are black and there are no trees for miles. For more information, write the **Superintendent**, Craters of the Moon National Monument, Box 29, Arco, ID 83213.

The town of **Arco,** 20 mi. east of the Craters of the Moon on Rte. 20, which claims to be the "first city in the world lit by atomic power," has the nearest services for travelers. The **Arco Deli Sandwich Shop,** on Rte. 20/26/93, corner of Grand Ave. and Idaho St., serves fresh ingredients to an appreciative local crowd. (☎527-3757. Open M-Sa 8am-8pm. Foot-long sandwiches $6.) The **Chamber of Commerce** (☎527-8977, P.O. Box 46, Arco, ID 83213), in the town hall on Grand Ave., has info.

MONTANA

When you've seen the sunset splash vibrant colors over a canopy of clouds, or the full spread of brilliant stars unfold at midnight, you'll know why they call Montana Big Sky country. With 25 million acres of national forest and public lands, the state's population of pronghorn antelope seems to outnumber the people, while grizzly bears, mountain lions, and extreme weather serve as reminders of human vulnerability. Out of this unfettered country has emerged a culture of wilderness; authors such as Norman MacLean, A.B. Guthrie, James Welch and Ivan Doig all infuse the spirit of the land into their work, while the Unabomber and fringe militia groups have sought refuge here. Copious fishing lakes, 500 species of wildlife (not including millions of insect species), beautiful rivers, mountains, glaciers, and thousands of ski trails make Montana an American paradise.

◪ PRACTICAL INFORMATION

Capital: Helena.

Visitor Info: Travel Montana, P.O. Box 7549, Missoula 59807 (☎406-444-2654 or 800-847-4868; www.travel.state.mt.us). **National Forest Information,** Northern Region, Federal Bldg., 200 E. Broadway, Box 7669, Missoula 59807 (☎406-329-3511).

Gay/Lesbian info: PRIDE!, P.O. Box 775, Helena 59624 (☎406-442-9322; www.gaymontana.com).

Postal Abbreviation: MT. **Sales Tax:** 0%.

BILLINGS ☎406

Located at the junction of I-90 and I-94 and served by major airlines, Billings is more of a stopover, or point of entry, than a destination. The **Billings Logan International Airport,** 1901 Terminal Circle (☎238-3420) can be found right at the end of N. 27th St. Both **Greyhound** and **Rimrock Trailways** operate from 2502 1st Ave. N. (☎245-5116; open 24hr.); buses run to Bozeman (3hr., 5 per day, $26); Missoula (7-9hr., 5 per day, $50); and Bismarck (9hr., 4 per day, $59). For car rentals, head to **Thrifty,** 2600 6th Ave. N. In summer, rentals start at just $40 per day with 150 free mi. and $239 per week with 1050 free mi. (Open daily 5:30am-11:30pm. 25¢ each additional mi. $10 per day surcharge for ages 21-24.) **Billings Metropolitan Transit** runs buses M-F approximately 6:45am-6:00pm, Sa 8:45am-5:45pm. Maps are available at many stores, banks, and at the library. (☎657-8218. 75¢, seniors 25¢). **Visitors center:** 815 S. 27th St. (☎252-4016 or 800-735-2635. Open May 31-Sept. 6 M-Sa 8:30am-6pm; off-season M-F 8:30am-5pm.) **Post Office:** 841 S. 26th St. (☎657-5700; open M-F 8am-6pm, Sa 10am-2pm). **ZIP code:** 59101. **Area code:** 406.

Billings's lodgings are spread throughout the city. The **Cherry Tree Inn,** 823 N. Broadway, has immaculate, spacious, Colonial-themed rooms at chopped-down prices. Take Exit 450 off I-90; go north on 27th St. then turn left onto 9th Ave. (☎252-5603 or 800-237-5882. A/C, phones, cable TV. Singles $37; doubles $42.) Convenient to the Interstate, **Motel 6,** 5400 Midland Road, offers clean rooms at reasonable rates. (☎252-0093. A/C, phones, pool, cable TV. Singles $41; doubles $46.)

Downtown, **Jake's,** 2701 1st Ave. N., has hearty soups ($3-4), burgers ($5.50), and a selection of microbrews and less trendy liquids, but eat at the bar—the restaurant is a pricey steak place. (☎259-9375. Bar open M-Th 11:30am-1am, F 11:30am-2am, Sa 4:30pm-2am. Restaurant open M-Th 11:30am-2pm and 5:30-10pm, F-Sa 11:30am-2pm and 5:30-10:30pm.) Also downtown, **Cafe Jones,** 2712 2nd Ave. N., is a coffeehouse/juice bar that also serves salads ($4-5) and sandwiches for around $5. (☎259-7676. Open M-F 7am-4pm, Sa 8am-4pm.) **Khanthaly's Eggrolls,** 1301 Grand Ave., serves tasty Laotian fast food, like fried rice noodles and spring rolls, at prices more likely to be found in Laos than the US. From downtown, go west on 6th Ave. N, and bear right at the fork and onto Grand Ave. (☎259-7252. Open M-Sa 11am-9pm.)

LITTLE BIG HORN

Little Big Horn National Monument, 60 mi. southeast of Billings off I-90 on the Crow Reservation, marks the site of one of the most dramatic episodes in the conflict between Native Americans and the US Government. Here, on June 25, 1876, Sioux and Cheyenne warriors, led by Sioux chiefs Sitting Bull and Crazy Horse, retaliated for years of genocide by annihilating five companies of the US Seventh Cavalry under the command of Lt. Colonel George Armstrong Custer. White stone graves mark where the US soldiers fell. The exact Native American casualties are not known, since their families and fellow warriors removed the bodies from the battle-field almost immediately. The renaming of the monument, formerly known as the Custer Battlefield Monument, signifies the US Government's admission that Custer's brutal acts against Native Americans merit no glorification. Congress also prescribed that a memorial be built in honor of the Native Americans killed at the battle. This memorial, which the Cheyenne have been working towards since 1925, is still being built; the completion date is unknown.

Rangers give great explanatory talks in the summer, every 30min., daily 9am-6pm. Visitors can also ride through the monument guided by an audio tour that narrates the battle movements ($13; open daily 8am-8pm). A 1hr. **bus tour** leaves the visitors center (9, 10:30am, noon, 2, and 3:30pm. $10; seniors $8, under 12 $5). The **visitors center** has a small movie theater, an electronic map of the battlefield, and a weapons display. (☎638-2621, ext. 124. Monument open daily late May to early Sept. 8am-9pm; visitors center open 8am-7:30pm. In fall monument and visitors center open 8am-6pm; in winter 8am-4:30pm. Entrance $6 per car, $3 per person.)

HELENA ☎406

Exploring historic Helena is a painless way to get acquainted with the miners, corrupt politicians, and prostitutes that define much of Montana's past. When gold was discovered at Last Chance Gulch, shanty-towns, opium-dens and brothels quickly followed, and many of these structures have been preserved and lovingly restored. The town that began as a seedy mining camp has become a culturally-savvy capital city, complete with a symphony, theaters, and a boisterous walking mall. The added bonus of close proximity to national forests, the Continental Divide, and the reservoirs along the Missouri River make Helena an accommodating host. Don't pronounce it He-*leen*-a or He-*lane*-a; the early miners thought these pronunciations were too citified and opted for Hell-*uh*-na.

⁊ PRACTICAL INFORMATION. I-15, U.S. 12 and U.S. 287 intersect Helena. **Rimrock Trailways,** at the High Country Travel Plaza Truck stop, 3122 Hwy. 12 E. (☎442-5860), buses to Missoula ($18; departs 6:45pm), Bozeman ($14.50; departs 8:15am, 6:45pm), and Billings ($34; departs 8:15am 6:45pm), with Greyhound connections in Missoula and Bozeman. **Helena Area Chamber of Commerce,** 225 Cruse Ave, has visitor information. (☎442-4120. Open M-F 8am-5pm.) **Post Office:** 2300 N. Harris (☎443-3304). **ZIP Code:** 59601. **Area Code:** 406.

⌂⊡ ACCOMMODATIONS AND FOOD. Budget accommodations aren't that easy to find in Helena. **Budget Inn Express,** 524 N. Last Chance Gulch, has an attractive downtown location and large, tidy rooms. (☎442-0600 or 800-862-1334. Laundry, cable, kitchenettes. Singles $38; doubles $43.) The **Helena Campground and RV Park,** 5820 N. Montana Ave, north of Helena, just west of I-15, has grassy, shaded tent sites. (☎458-4714. Laundry, showers. Sites $20, full hook-up $23.) Just to the southeast of Helena, a number of free-$10 public campgrounds line Canyon Ferry Reservoir. The free Fish Hawk campground, on West Shore Drive is reserved for tents and has toilets but no drinking water. Take either Canyone Ferry Rd. or Rte. 284 from U.S. 12. The **BLM/BOR Canyon Ferry Office** (☎475-3319), at 7661 Canyon Ferry Rd., has more info.

Rub elbows with state legislators and officials at the **Windbag Saloon and Grill,** 19 S. Last Chance Gulch, in the walking mall, and enjoy Montana-sized burgers for $5-7. (☎443-9669. Open M-Sa 11am-2:20pm and 5pm-9:30pm.) The **Staggering Ox,** 400

Euclid, in the Lundy Center, claims that their clubfoot sandwich ($4-6) is the "World's Best Sandwich." It's certainly is one of the most innovative. (☎443-1729. Open M-Th 9am-8pm, F-Su 9am-9pm.)

🔆 **SIGHTS.** A logical starting point for exploration of Helena is the museum of the **Montana Historical Society,** 225 N. Roberts St., which preserves Montanan history from Native American times through the pioneer days and into the 20th century. (☎444-2694. Open Memorial Day to Labor Day M-F 8am-6pm, Sa-Su 9am-5pm. Open in winter M-F 8am-5pm, Sa 9am-5pm. Free.) Nearby, the **State Capitol** building, 6th Ave. and Montana Ave., has several pieces of notable artwork, including C.M. Russell's "Lewis and Clark Meeting the Flathead Indians at Ross' Hole" and a statue of Jeannette Rankin. (Self-guided tours daily 8am-6pm; in summer guided tours on the hr., M-Sa 10am-4pm, Su 11am-3pm. Free.) The gold vanished from **Last Chance Gulch** long ago; today this walking mall, which begins at the intersection of Last Chance Gulch and 6th Ave., offers restaurants, shops, and public artwork commemorating the past. In **Reeders Alley,** 100 S. Park Ave., the redbrick boarding houses built for miners have been restored and now contain galleries and restaurants. Housed in the old jail, the **Myrna Loy Center,** N. Ewing St. (☎443-0287), is a multi-purpose theater, presenting foreign film, dance, music and performance art.

Take in all of Helena and the surrounding area from the top of **Mt. Helena** (elevation 5460 ft.); the trail begins from the Adams St. Trailhead, just west of Reeders Alley. You can see the Missouri River just as Lewis and Clark did in 1805 by taking the boat ride to the **Gates of the Mountains,** 18 mi. north of Helena, just off I-15. The boat also stops near the place of the Mann Gulch fire, made famous by Norman MacLean's book, *Young Men and Fire.* (☎458-5241. Tours June M-F 11am, 2pm, Sa-Su 10am, noon, 2pm, 4pm; July-Aug. M-F 11am, 1pm, 3pm, Sa-Su every hr. 10am-4pm; Sept. M-F 11am, 2pm, Sa-Su 11am, 1pm, 3pm. $8.50, ages 4-17 $5.50.)

BOZEMAN ☎406

Surrounded by the Gallatin National Forest, close to world-class skiing, and renowned for its nearby fly-fishing streams, Bozeman has lately become a magnet for outdoor enthusiasts. To Montanans, however, Bozeman is better known as "that boisterous college town." While rodeo, cowboy hats, and pick-up trucks are still popular among quite a few students, a recently diversified student body reflects the growing cultural vibrancy of this thriving community.

🛈 **PRACTICAL INFORMATION.** Greyhound and **RimRock Stages,** 625 N. 7th Ave. (☎587-3110), both serve Bozeman. To: Butte (1½hr., 4 per day, $14-15); Billings (3-4hr., 5 per day, $21-25); Helena (2hr., 3 per day, $16-26); and Missoula (5hr., 5 per day, $24-32). Open M-F 7:30am-noon, 1-5:30pm, 8-11pm; Sa-Su 7:30am-noon, 3:30-5:30pm, 8:30-10pm. **Budget Rent-a-Car,** at the airport, rents for $45-60 per day. (☎388-4091. Open daily 7am-11pm, or until last flight. 100 free mi., 25¢ per additional mi. Ages 21-24 $15 per day surcharge; credit card required.) **Bozeman Area Chamber of Commerce:** at 19th Ave. and Baxter Ln. (☎586-5421 or 800-228-4224. Open M 9am-5pm, Tu-F 8am-5pm.) **Internet access: Library,** 220 E. Lamme St. (☎582-2400. Open M-Th 10am-8pm, F-Sa 10am-5pm, Su 1-5pm, closed Su in summer. Free.) **Post Office:** 32 E. Babcock St. (open M-F 9am-5pm). **ZIP code:** 59715. **Area code:** 406.

SHAKESPEARE IN THE PARK No, New York's famed production didn't make a wrong turn at W. 86th St. and Central Park West to end up in Montana. Rather, this is **Montana Shakespeare in the Park,** a roving band of thespians who make the rounds of the Big Sky state from the 4th of July to Labor Day. In the words of one young Montanan, "In the summer, if I'm not camping, I'm watching this." (☎406-994-3901 or www.montana.edu/wwwmtsip for schedule.)

ⅢⅢⅢ ACCOMMODATIONS, FOOD, AND NIGHTLIFE. A number of budget motels line Main St. and 7th Ave. north of Main. The **Bozeman International Backpackers Hostel,** 405 W. Olive St., situated on a quiet street near the university, has a relaxed and welcoming atmosphere. The first floor is a comfortable living and eating area, while the upstairs has rooms with bunkbeds. There are only 15 beds; call ahead if you can. Owners advise where to eat, drink, and hike; they also rent bikes. (☎586-4659. $14, children $6; 1 double $32. Bikes half-day $6, full-day $10.) The **Alpine Lodge,** 1017 E. Main St., has reasonable prices and spacious rooms (☎586-0356 or 888-922-5746. Summer $35.) The **Bear Canyon Campground** has great views, if you can see around the RVs. The park is 4 mi. east of Bozeman, south of I-90 at Exit 313. (☎587-1575 or 800-438-1575. Laundry, showers, and pool. $15 for 2, with water and electricity $16-18; full hook-up $20; $2 per additional person.) Several **national forest campgrounds** line U.S. 191, on the way to Big Sky, south of town ($8-10).

Thrifty eateries aimed at the college crowd line W. College near the University. Now a popular Montanan chain, the original **Pickle Barrel** resides at 809 W. College. Enormous sandwiches with fresh ingredients and free pickles have drawn MSU students for years. A hefty half-sandwich is $4-5.30. (☎587-2411. Open daily 10:30am-10pm; in winter 11am-10:30pm.) At **tombo's,** 815 W. College St., giant bowls of hearty rice and noodles are available for both veggies and carnivores. (☎585-0234. Open M-Sa 11am-9pm, Su 4-9pm, closed Su in summer. Bowls $3.75-6.) **Brandi's,** 717 N. 7th, at the Cat's Paw Casino, greases up great breakfast at ridiculously low prices: two eggs, hash browns, coffee, and toast goes for $2 (☎587-3848. Open daily 8am-9:30pm. Breakfast all day.)

The **Zebra Cocktail Lounge,** in the basement at the corner of Rouse Ave. and Main St., has a huge selection of beer and a supercool atmosphere that draws college folk and outdoorsy types. (☎585-8851. Open daily 8pm-2am. Music every other night.) Sample some of Montana's best beer at the **Spanish Peaks Brewery,** 120 N. 19th Ave. (☎585-2296. Alehouse open daily 11am-2am.) Get the scoop on music and other nightlife from *The BoZone* and *Tributary,* both published weekly.

ⅢⅢ SIGHTS AND OUTDOORS. Get up close and personal with dinosaurs and other artifacts of Rocky Mountain history at the **Museum of the Rockies,** 600 West Kagy Blvd., near the university. Dr. Jack Horner (the basis for the main character in *Jurassic Park*) and other paleontologists make this their base for excavating prehistoric remains throughout the West. The exhibit on Native American culture is also noteworthy. (☎994-2251. Open daily in summer 8am-8pm, in winter M-Sa 9am-5pm, Su 12:30-5pm. $7, ages 5-18 $4, under 5 free.)

Surrounded by three renowned trout-fishing rivers—Yellowstone, Madison, and Gardiner—the small town of **Livingston,** about 20 mi. east of Bozeman off I-90, is an angler's heaven. This is gorgeous country; *A River Runs Through It* was shot in Bozeman and Livingston. Livingston's Main St. features a strip of circa-1900 buildings, housing bars (with gambling), restaurants, fishing outfitters, and only a few modern businesses. **Dan Bailey's,** 209 West Park St., provides licenses (2-day $15, season $50), and rents fishing gear and wear. (☎222-1673 or 800-356-4052. Open M-Sa 7am-7pm, Su 8am-5pm; in winter M-Sa 8am-6pm. Float tubes $15, rod and reel $10, waders and boots $10.)

Bozeman provides its share of downhill thrills. The world-class ski area, **Big Sky,** 45 mi. south of town on U.S. 191, has runs as long as 6 mi. and short lift lines. The Lone Peak trams reach an altitude of 11,166 ft. and offer extreme skiing options. (☎800-548-4486. Full-day ticket $52, ages 11-17 and college students with I.D. $40, under 10 free. Rentals: skis $24-39, kids skis $18, snowboard $33. Season mid-Nov. to mid-Apr.) More intimate and less expensive than Big Sky, **Bridger Bowl Ski Area,** 15795 Bridger Canyon Rd., 16 mi. northeast of town, has trails for a variety of abilities. (☎586-2389 or 800-223-9609. Season mid-Dec. to early April. Full-day ticket $31, over 72 free, children $13. Rentals: skis $15-20, junior skis $10, snowboard $25.) In summer, scenic **lift rides** soar up Big Sky (June-Sept. Th-M 10:30am-4:30pm; $12, under 10 free). Equestrian types gallop at nearby **Dalton's Big Sky Stables,** on the spur road off U.S. 191 about 2 mi. before Big Sky's entrance. (☎995-2972. Open June-Sept. $25 per hr.; 1 day's notice required). **Yellowstone Raft Co.** shoots the rapids 7 mi. north of the Big Sky area on U.S. 191 (☎995-4613. Half-day $37.)

RED LODGE ☎406

Upscale but inviting, Red Lodge sits amid beautiful mountains. With so much going on in this small town, however, you may never get to the hills. Shops, galleries and restaurants make Broadway, the main street, a good place to spend a few hours; most stores are open 8am to 6pm.

🗗 PRACTICAL INFORMATION. The closest bus stop is in Billings, but the **Red Lodge Shuttle** offers affordable transportation between Billings and Red Lodge (☎446-2257 or 888-446-2191). The friendly folks at the **visitors center,** 601 N. Broadway, on the north side of town, can help you find ways to occupy your days and nights. (☎446-1718. Open daily in summer 8am-7pm; in winter M-F 9am-5pm.) **Hospital:** Beartooth Hospital and Health Clinic, 600 W. 21st St. (☎446-2345). **Post Office:** 119 S. Hauser (☎446-2629; open M-F 8am-4:30pm, Sa 9am-1pm). **ZIP code:** 59068. **Area code:** 406.

🖪🖫 ACCOMMODATIONS AND FOOD. Most accommodations in Red Lodge are a tad pricey. **The Eagles Nest,** 702 S. Broadway, has affordable rates and a location both adjacent to Rock Creek and close to downtown. (☎446-2312. Phone, cable TV. Singles $36; doubles $41; ski-house for 8 with kitchen $107.) Four mi. north of Red Lodge on Highway 212, the **Red Lodge KOA** has treed sites on Rock Creek. (☎446-2364. Open late May to mid-Sept. Tent sites $18, full hook-up $26, kabins $39.) A number of free and inexpensive campsites can be found south of Red Lodge on Hwy. 212, along Rock Creek.

Satisfy your cravings for meat at **The Smokehouse,** 202½ S. Broadway. (☎446-2566. Open daily 11am-3:30pm. Sausages $3.75, burgers $3.75-5.) **Genesis Health Foods and Deli,** 123 S. Broadway, creates salads and sandwiches that are veggie friendly. (☎446-3204. Open M-F 8am-6pm, Sa 9am-5pm. Sandwiches $3-5, salads $4-6.) Sample microbrews ($3.75) and creative wraps ($5-$6) at the **Red Lodge Alehouse,** 11 N. Broadway (☎446-1426). Wallpapered with personalized license plates and irreverent bumper stickers, the raucous 🗎**Snow Creek Saloon** is one of the best bars around. (☎446-2542. Open daily 2pm-2am. Live music on weekends.)

🖾🎿 SIGHTS AND ACTIVITIES. Red Lodge Mountain offers 69 runs and is snowboard friendly. (☎446-2610. Open early Nov. to mid-Apr. $34, ages 13-18 $28, 12 and under $12. Rentals $15, snowboards $25.) A variety of cross-country skiing options are also available. The **Red Lodge Nordic Center** (☎446-9191), located 2 mi. west of Red Lodge on Hwy. 78, has groomed trails. The roads along Rock Creek south of town are good for beginners. Mountain bikers converge at Red Lodge each year in late July for the **Fat Tire Frenzy,** an off-road and slalom competition. The **Meeteetse Trail,** off Hwy. 212 south of Red Lodge, and the **Silver Run Trails** near the West Fork of Rock Creek are popular mountain biking spots.

A number of other festivals and special events attract visitors to Red Lodge in both winter and fall. Hosted jointly by the town and the ski area, the **Winter Carnival,** held the first weekend in March, makes good use of abundant snow with ice sculptures, sledding, and music. The 4th of July **Home of Champions Rodeo** celebrates a local infatuation with the cowboy sport. Red Lodge's first settlers were miners who came from all over Europe, and today Red Lodge pays tribute to this multicultural heritage with the week-long **Festival of Nations** held each Aug. Every summer weekend F-Su, beginning at 7pm, **Bearcreek Downs,** 7 mi. east of Red Lodge on Hwy. 308, features pig races that draw visitors from all over the world. The races are sponsored by the Bearcreek Saloon where you can get a healthy portion of beef, but no pork. (☎446-3482. Open F-Sa 2pm-2am. Burgers $5.) A more refined style of entertainment can be found at the **Round Barn Restaurant and Theater,** just south of Red Lodge on Hwy. 212. (☎446-1197. Plays performed most summer weekends.)

ROCKY MOUNTAINS

MISSOULA ☎406

A liberal haven amidst a largely conservative state, Missoula attracts new residents
every day with its revitalized downtown and bountiful outdoors opportunities: the
mountains and valleys that surround town make for cold winters but offer beautiful
scenery. For some Missoulians, the 60s were slow to fade, and today a new generation of counter-culture youth has spawned chic bars and coffeehouses.

▯ PRACTICAL INFORMATION

You can fly into and out of **Missoula International Airport,** 5225 Hwy. 10 W (☎728-
4381); follow Broadway (which turns into Rte. 10/200) west out of town 6 mi. **Greyhound:** 1660 W. Broadway (☎549-2339); to Bozeman (6hr., 4 per day, $24-30) and
Spokane (4hr., 5 per day, $31-33). From the same terminal, **RimRock Stages** serves
Whitefish via St. Ignatius and Kalispell (3½hr., 1 per day, $21) and Helena (2½hr., 1
per day, $18). Catch a ride on the reliable **Mountain Line City Buses** from the Transfer
Center, located behind the County Courthouse at the corner of Ryman and Pine St.,
or a curbside around town. (☎721-3333. Buses operate M-F 6:45am-6:15pm, Sa
9:45am-5:15pm. Fare 85¢.) **Taxis: Yellow Cab** (☎543-6644). **Ugly Duckling Car Rental,**
3010 S. Reserve, has beautiful prices. (☎542-8459. $25 per day with 150 free mi., 25¢
each additional mi. Reservations essential. 21+.) **Missoula Chamber of Commerce:** 825
E. Front St. at Van Buren. (☎543-6623. Open in summer M-F 8am-7pm, Sa 8am-6pm;
early Sept. to late May M-F 8am-5pm.) **Internet Access: Cyber Shock,** 821 S. Higgins.
(☎721-6251. Open Su-Th 7am-2am, F-Sa 24hr.; $3 per hr.) **Post Office:** 1100 W. Kent,
between Brooks and South St. (☎329-2200. Open M-F 8am-6pm, Sa 9am-1pm.) **ZIP
code:** 59801. **Area code:** 406.

▯ ACCOMMODATIONS

Unfortunately, the town's only hostel closed down last year. Cheap lodgings still
exist and cluster along **Broadway.** Some rooms at the **Sleepy Inn Motel,** 1427 W.
Broadway near the bus depot, have zany shag rugs. (☎549-6484. Singles $34; dou-
bles $42.) To reach the **Aspen Motel,** 3720 Rte. 200 E in East Missoula, get off I-90 at
exit 107 and travel ½ mi. east. (Clean rooms, cable, A/C. Singles $35; 1-bed doubles
$42; 2-beds $51). Rooms at the **City Center Motel,** 338 E. Broadway, have funky
murals, cable, fridges, and microwaves. (☎543-3193. Singles $42; doubles $45.) A
world unto itself, the **Missoula/El-Mar KOA Kampground,** 3450 Tina Ave., just south of
Broadway off Reserve St. is one of the best KOAs around. Offers shaded tent sites
apart from RVs. (☎549-0881 or 800-562-5366. 2 people $18, water and electricity $24,
full hook-ups $26, kabins $35-40; $3 per additional person.)

▯▯ FOOD AND NIGHTLIFE

Missoula, the culinary capital of Montana, boasts a number of innovative, delicious,
and thrifty eating establishments. Head downtown, north of the Clark Fork River
along Higgins Ave., to find out which new lunch place or coffeehouse is this
month's hot spot. The **Farmers Market** and the **Peoples Market** showcase edible and
inedible wares at N. Higgins (open in summer Sa 9am-noon and Tu 5:30-7pm). **Torrey's** is just like Mom's; as long as your mom served huge portions of all natural
health food. All meals are an absurd $3. (☎721-2510. Open M-F 11:30am-3pm and M-
Th 4:30-8:30pm.) You can gorge yourself on great vegetarian Indian food at **Tipu's,**
115½ S. 4th St., in the alley just west of the corner of S 4th and Higgins St. (look for
the neon sign), during their lunch buffet for just $6, served from 11:30am-5pm.
(☎452-0622. Open daily 11:30am-9:30pm. Full meal $4-7). Hungry UM students
crowd **Food for Thought,** 540 Daly, for breakfast and lunch. The A+ sandwich is
above average at $5.25. (☎721-6033. Open daily 7am-4pm, breakfast served until
11am weekdays, 2pm weekends. Omelettes $5-$6, huge bowl of vegan chili with roll
$3.) **Loco's Burritos** first location is at 311 N. Higgins, the other is the "Burrito Bus"

that cruises town looking for hungry shoppers and pub crawlers. The burritos, enchiladas, and tacos are made from fresh ingredients, and every item on the menu is under $5. (☎549-6742. Store open M-F 11am-7pm, Sa 11am-5pm.)

College students swarm the downtown bar area around Front St. and Higgins Ave. during the school year; bars have a more relaxed atmosphere in summer. A rowdy, youngish crowd gathers at **The Rhinoceros** or "Rhino's," 158 Ryman Ave., to partake of the 51 beers on tap. (☎721-6061. Open daily 11am-2am.) Live music and an affable waitstaff make **Sean Kelly's,** 131 W. Pine St., the place to be on weekends. (☎542-1471. Open daily 11am-2pm.) **The Kettle House Brewing Co.,** 602 Myrtle, one block west of Higgins between 4th and 5th, has its priorities straight; they don't serve food, only delectable beer straight from their brewery. (Open M-Th 3-9pm, F-Sa noon-9pm; no beer served after 8pm. 2 free samples, then $2.50 for pints.)

👁🗾 SIGHTS AND OUTDOOR ACTIVITIES

BICYCLING. Nearby parks, recreation areas, and surrounding wilderness areas make Missoula an outdoor enthusiast's dream. Bicycle-friendly Missoula is located along both the Trans-America and the Great Parks bicycle routes; all major streets have designated bike lanes. **Open Road Bicycles and Nordic Equipment,** 517 W. Orange St., has bike rentals. (☎549-2453. Open M-F 9am-6pm, Sa 10am-5pm, Su 11am-3pm. $3.50 per hr., $17.50 per day.) The national **Adventure Cycling,** 150 E. Pine St., is the place to go for info about the Trans-America and Great Parks routes. (☎721-1776 or 800-755-2543. Open M-F 8am-5pm.) **Missoulians on Bicycle** is a local organization that hosts rides and events for cyclists; write to P.O. Box 8903 for more information.

SKIING. Alpine and Nordic skiing occupy the thoughts of Missoulians during winter; the folks at Open Road (see above) can take care of your cross-country needs (X-C ski package $12 per day). **Pattee Canyon Recreation Area** has groomed trails that are conveniently close to town; take Pattee Canyon Drive from SW Higgins 3½ mi. east. Family-oriented **Marshall Mountain** is a great place to learn how to downhill ski. (☎258-6000. Full-day $19, seniors and under 19 $15; rentals: skis $12, snowboard $16; night skiing and free shuttles from downtown.) More experienced skiers should check out the extreme **Montana Snowbowl** (☎549-9777; full-day $25).

WET FUN. Floating on rafts and tubes is a favorite activity for locals on weekends. The Blackfoot River, along Rte. 200 east of Bonner, makes a good afternoon float. The **Montana State Regional Parks and Wildlife Office,** 3201 Spurgin Rd., sells float maps for $4. (☎542-5500. Open M-F 8am-5pm.) Rent tubes ($3 per day with $20 deposit) or rafts ($30-60; credit card required) from the **Army and Navy Economy Store,** 322 N. Higgins. (☎721-1315. Open M-F 9am-7:30pm, Sa 9am-5:30pm, Su 10am-5:30pm.) **Pangaea Expeditions** runs rafting trips, and leaves from Bernice's Bakery at 190 S. 3rd St. W. (☎721-7719. 2hr. $25, half-day $40-45, full-day $55.)

HIKING. Hiking opportunities abound in the Missoula area. Rub elbows with UM football players on the steep hike to the "M" (for the U of M, not Missoula) on Mount Jumbo. After taking in the view from the "M" (1½ mi. round-trip), you can continue up the trail for even more spectacular views of the surrounding mountains. The Chamber of Commerce has info on area day hikes. **The Rattlesnake Wilderness National Recreation Area,** named after the shape of the river (there are no rattlers for mi.), is 11 mi. northeast of town off the Van Buren St. exit from I-90, and makes for a great day of hiking. Other popular areas include Pattee Canyon (see **Skiing,** above) and **Blue Mountain,** which is located south of town. Maps ($6) and more info on the area, including longer hikes in the Bitterroot and Bob Marshall areas, are available from the **US Forest Service Information Office,** 200 E. Broadway; the entrance is at 200 Pine St. (☎329-3511. Open M-F 7:30am-4pm.) For equipment rentals, stop by **Trailhead,** 110 E. Pine St., at Higgins St. (☎543-6966. Open M-F 9:30am-8pm, Sa 9am-6pm, Su 11am-6pm. Tents $9-18; backpacks $9-15; sleeping bags $5-9.)

NUTS TO YOU The folks at the Rock Creek Lodge (☎825-4868), east of Missoula, promise you'll "have a ball" at the annual **Testicle Festival** (www.testyfesty.com; Sept. 20-24, 2001). In the past, as many as 12,000 ballsy souls have gathered to sample delicious **rocky mountain oysters** (a.k.a. bull's testicles) and join in wild revelry. Feasting isn't the only activity here; the wary can take part in the bullshit pitch or hairy chest contest instead! Even if you're not around for the festival, **Kathy's Kitchen** at the lodge serves the scrumptious "tender-groin" (open Apr.-Oct. daily 9am-8pm). You may not be able to look a bull in the eyes again, but to show your sack, take I-90 22 mi. east of Missoula to Exit 126 in Clinton (coincidence?).

OTHER ATTRACTIONS. Missoula's hottest sight, the **Smokejumper Center,** 7 mi. west of town on Broadway (Rte. 10, just past the airport), depicts the life of courageous aerial firefighters who parachute into flaming, remote forests. (☎329-4934. Open daily 8:30am-5pm. Tours May-Sept. on the hr. 10-11am and 2-4pm. Free.)

The handcrafted **Carousel,** in Caras Park, offers a wholesome spin. (☎549-8382. Open daily June-Aug. 11am-7pm; Sept.-May 11am-5:30pm. $1, seniors and under 19 50¢.) **Out to Lunch,** in Caras Park, a Missoula tradition, offers free performances in the summer, every W 11:30am-1:30pm. The **Western Montana Fair and Rodeo,** held in early August, has live music, a carnival, fireworks, and exhibits (call ☎721-3247 for more information). The *Independent* and *Lively Times* offer the low-down on the Missoula music scene (available at newsstands and cafes), while the *Entertainer*, in the F *Missoulian*, has movie and event schedules.

FROM MISSOULA TO GLACIER

The ⌧**Miracle of America Museum,** on U.S. 93 at the southern end of **Polson,** houses one of the country's greatest collections of Americana, unswervingly dedicated to the belief that the good ol'-fashioned American way of life is miraculous. A general store, saddlery shop, barber shop, soda fountain, and gas station sit among the classic memorabilia. (☎883-6804. Open daily June-Sept. 8am-8pm; Oct.-May M-Sa 8am-5pm, Su 2-6pm. $3, ages 3-12 $1.)

The **National Bison Range** was established in 1908. Before they were hunted to near-extinction, 50 million of these animals roamed the plains; the Range is home to 300-500 of the imposing creatures in addition to deer, antelope, elk, bighorn sheep and mountain goats. The two-hour Red Sleep Mountain self-guided tour offers spectacular views of the Flathead Valley and the best chance for wildlife viewing. To access the range, travel 40 mi. north of Missoula off U.S. 93, then 5 mi. west on Rte. 200, and 5 mi. north on Rte. 212. (☎644-2211. Range open daily mid-May to mid-Oct. 7am-dusk. Visitors center open daily 8am-4:30pm; off-season hrs. vary. Scenic drive $4.) Fresh fruits stands line **Flathead Lake,** renowned for its cherries as well as trout and whitefish fishing opportunities, along U.S. 93 between Polson and Kalispell.

St. Ignatius Campground and Hostel, off U.S. 93 in **St. Ignatius** (look for the camping sign), offers lodging in its "earthship," an eco-friendly structure built into a hillside and made from recycled tires and aluminum cans. The new owner has info and gear available to explore the backcountry. Stay at the hostel and ski Marshall Mountain near Missoula all for $35 a day. (☎745-3959. Showers, laundry, kitchen. $12; tent sites for 1 $10, for 2 $12.) **RimRock Stages** (☎745-3501) makes a stop ½ mi. away in St. Ignatius, at the Malt Shop on Blaine St.

WATERTON-GLACIER PEACE PARK

Waterton-Glacier transcends international boundaries to encompass one of the most strikingly beautiful portions of the Rockies. A geographical metaphor for the peace between the US and Canada, the park provides sanctuary for many endangered bears, bighorn sheep, moose, mountain goats, and grey wolves. Perched high in the Northern Rockies, Glacier is sometimes called the "Crown of the Continent" and the high alpine lakes and glaciers seem like the jewels.

Technically one park, Waterton-Glacier is actually two distinct areas: the small **Waterton Lakes National Park** in Alberta, and the enormous **Glacier National Park** in Montana. Each park charges its own admission fee, and you must go through customs to pass from one to the other. Several **border crossings** are nearby: **Piegan/Carway** at U.S. 89 (open daily 7am-11pm); **Roosville** on U.S. 93 (open 24hr.); and **Chief Mountain** at Rte. 17 (open daily mid-May to early June and mid-Sept. to early Oct. 9am-6pm; early June to mid-Sept. 7am-10pm). The fastest way to Waterton is to head north from the east side of Glacier. Go through Chief Mountain if it's open.

Since snow melting is an unpredictable process, the parks are usually in full operation only from late May to early Sept.; it is worth your while to check conditions in advance. The *Waterton Glacier Guide*, provided at any park entrance, has dates and times of trail, campground, and border crossing openings. To find out which park areas, hotels, and campsites will be open when you visit, contact the Superintendent, Waterton Lakes National Park, Waterton Park, AB T0K 2M0 (☎403-859-5133), or the Superintendent, Glacier National Park, West Glacier 59936 (☎406-888-7800). Mace, bear spray, and firewood are not allowed into Canada.

GLACIER NATIONAL PARK   ☎406

⚡ ORIENTATION. There are few roads in Glacier, and the locals like it that way. Glacier's main thoroughfare is the **Going-to-the-Sun Rd.** which connects the two primary points of entry, West Glacier and St. Mary. **U.S. 2** skirts the southern border of the park and is the fastest route from Browning and East Glacier to West Glacier. Check out the "Goat Lick" near Walton where mountain goats traverse steep cliffs to lap up the natural salt deposits here. While most of Glacier is primitive backcountry, a number of villages provide amenities for those seeking a more civilized experience, including Many Glacier, St. Mary, and East Glacier in the east and West Glacier, Apgar, and Polebridge in the west.

🔢 PRACTICAL INFORMATION. Admission is $10 per week per car and $5 for pedestrians and cyclists. Yearly passes are available for $20. The accessible and knowledgeable rangers at each of the three visitors centers can give you the inside scoop on campsites, day hikes, weather, flora, and fauna. **St. Mary** guards the east entrance of the park. (☎732-7750. Open daily mid-May to mid-June 8am to 5pm; mid to late-June 8am to 6pm; late June to early Sept. 8am to 9pm; early Sept. to mid-Oct. 8am-5pm.) **Apgar** aids at the west entrance. (☎888-7939. Open daily late May-late June 8am-4:30pm; late June-early Sept. 8am-8pm; early Sept. to late Oct. 8am to 4:30 pm.) A third visitors center graces **Logan Pass** on Going-to-the-Sun Rd. (Open daily early June to late June 9am-4:30 pm; late June to early Sept. 9am-7pm; early Sept. to late Sept. 10am-4:30pm; early Oct. to mid-Oct. 10am-4pm.) The **ranger station** at Many Glacier can answer questions. (Open daily late May to late June 8am-4:30 pm; late June to early Sept. 8am-6pm; early Sept. to mid-Sept. 8am-4:30pm.) The **Backcountry Permit Center,** located on the main street in Apgar, is an invaluable resource for those seeking to explore Glacier's less-traveled areas (open daily May to early Oct.). Backcountry permits are also available at other visitors centers.

Amtrak (☎226-4452) traces a dramatic route along the southern edge of the park. The station in West Glacier is open mid-May to Sept.; the train stops at an unstaffed station in the winter. Trains chug daily to East Glacier (1½hr., $17), Whitefish (30 min., $5), Seattle (14½ hr., $120), and Spokane (6hr., $50-60); Amtrak also runs from East Glacier to Chicago (31hr., $250) and Minneapolis (21½hr., $172-207). **RimRock Stages** (☎800-255-7655), the only bus line that nears the park, stops in Kalispell at the Kalispell Bus Terminal, 3974 U.S. 2., and goes to Missoula ($18) or Billings ($58). As in most of the Rockies, a car is the most convenient mode of transport, particularly within the park. **Rent-A-Wreck,** 2622 U.S. 2 E, in Kalispell, rents cars. (☎755-4555. $37.50 per day. 100 free mi., 21¢ each additional mi. 21+; under 25 $5 per day surcharge.) The famous red jammer buses are currently out of service as they undergo repairs, but **Sun Tours** offers interpretive tours of the park, leaving from East Glacier and St. Mary. (☎800-786-9220 or 226-9220. $45 for all day tour.)

Shuttles for hikers ($6-18) roam the length of Going-to-the-Sun Rd.; schedules are at visitors centers (☎888-9187). **Kalispell Regional Medical Center:** 310 Sunnyview Ln. (☎752-5111), north of Kalispell off Rte. 93. **Post Office:** In West Glacier. (☎888-5591. Open M-F 8:30am-12:30pm and 1:30-4:45pm.) **ZIP code:** 59936. **Area code:** 406.

▌ ACCOMMODATIONS. Staying indoors within Glacier is expensive, but several affordable options lie just outside the park boundaries. On the west side of the park, the electricity-less town of **Polebridge** provides access to Glacier's remote and pristine northwest corner. From Apgar, take Camas Rd. north, and take a right onto the poorly-marked gravel Outside North Fork Road, just past a bridge over the North Fork of the Flathead River. From Columbia Falls, take Rte. 486 north. Don't take Inner N Fork Rd.; its potholes are legendary. Follow the signs through town to the **North Fork Hostel,** 80 Beaver Drive, where the wooden walls and kerosene lamps are reminiscent of a deep woods hunting retreat. The price includes showers, but no flush toilets. During the winter, old-fashioned wood stoves warm frozen fingers and toes after skiing or snowshoeing. Call ahead for a $25 pick-up from the West Glacier Amtrak station. (☎888-5241. Check-in 10pm, check-out noon. Lock-out 9am-5pm. Light chores. Use of canoes, mountain bikes, snowshoes, and nordic ski equipment included. Dorms $13, $10 after 2 nights; cabins $26; log homes $50-52. Showers $4. Linen $2. Reservations recommended, especially during winter.) In the east, inexpensive lodging is just across the park border in **East Glacier,** on U.S. 2, 30 mi. south of the St. Mary entrance and about 5 mi. south of the Two Medicine entrance. At **Brownies Grocery (HI-AYH),** 1020 Rte. 49, come downstairs from the comfortable hostel for thick huckleberry shakes ($4) and $5 sandwiches made especially for your backpack. (☎226-4426. Open May-Sept., weather permitting. Check in by 9pm, call ahead for late arrivals. Check out 9am. Light chores. Dorms $12, non-members $15; private singles $17/$20; doubles $25/$28; triples $25/$28; family room for 4-6 $35. Tent sites $10. Extra bed $5. Key deposit $5. Reservations recommended.) The **Backpacker's Inn Hostel,** 29 Dawson Ave., just south of the East Glacier Amtrak station and behind Serrono's Mexican Restaurant, has 22 clean beds in co-ed rooms and hot showers for only $10 per night. (☎226-9392. Open May-Sept. Bring a sleeping bag or rent one for $1.) The one budget motel, the **Swiftcurrent Motor Inn** in Many Glacier Valley, has cabins for $41. (☎732-5531. Open early June to early Sept. No toilets. 2 bedrooms $51.) The distant offices of **Glacier Park, Inc.,** handle reservations for all in-park lodging. (☎602-207-6000. Write 925 Dial Corporate Center, Phoenix, AZ 85077-0928.)

⌂ FOOD. To hungry backpackers, the homemade pastries ($1-3) at the **Polebridge Mercantile Store** (☎888-5105) are as splendid as the surrounding peaks. The **Northern Lights Saloon** next door serves fabulous $5 cheeseburgers, and $3 cold pints (open daily June-Sept. 4-9pm for food, until midnight for drinks).

Sample homemade Montana delicacies at the **Whistle Stop Cafe** in East Glacier next to Brownie's Grocery; this is where huckleberries go to die (☎226-9292; huckleberry french toast $5.50). In St. Mary on Hwy. 89, just north of the park entrance, the **Park Cafe** provides sustenance to those who dare to traverse the Going-to-the-Sun Rd. The "Hungry Hiker" (2 eggs with hashbrowns and toast, $3.50) and the vegetarian Caribbean Burrito ($4.75) are local favorites. (☎732-4482. Open May-Sept. M-F 7:30am -9pm; Sa-Su 7:30am-10pm.)

▟ HIKING AND BIKING. *There are bears and mountain lions out there. Familiarize yourself with the precautions necessary to avoid an encounter. Ask the rangers about wildlife activity in the area in which you plan to hike.* Most of Glacier's spectacular scenery lies off the main roads and is accessible only by foot. An extensive trail system has something for everyone, from short, easy day hikes to hard-core backcountry expeditions. Stop by one of the visitors centers for maps with day hikes. The most popular day-hike in the park wanders through old-growth forest to emerge at the breathtaking **Avalanche Lake.** (4 mi. round-trip; 500 ft. elevation gain; approximately 3hr.) The short and wheelchair accessible **Trail of the**

Cedars begins at the same trailhead, north of Lake McDonald on the Going-to-the-Sun Rd. (¼ mi. loop on level boardwork; approximately 20 mi.) The hike to **Numa Ridge Lookout** begins from the Bowman Lake campground, near Polebridge, and ends with sweeping vistas of Glacier's rugged northeast corner. (12 mi. round-trip; 2930 ft. elevation gain; approximately 9hr.) To get up close and personal with a glacier, try the **Grinnell Glacier trail** (trailhead at the Many Glacier Picnic Area; 11 mi.; 1600 ft. elevation gain; approximately 7hr.). On a clear day, from Scenic Point, you can see the Sweetgrass Hills, nearly 100 miles away (trailhead ¼ mi. east of the Two Medicine Ranger Station; 6¼ mi. round-trip; 2350 ft. elevation gain, approximately 5hr.) The **Hidden Lake Nature Trail** begins at the Logan Pass Visitor Center and offers a chance to stretch your legs while traversing the Going-to-the-Sun Rd. (3 mi. round-trip; 460 ft. elevation gain; approximately 2hr.)

Visitors planning overnight backpacking trips must obtain the necessary **backcountry permits.** With the exception of the Nyack/Coal Creek camping zone, all backcountry camping must be done at designated campsites that are equipped with pit toilets, tent sites, food preparation areas, and food hanging devices. During the summer season (June 1-Sept. 30), the fee for overnight camping is $4 per person per night for age 17 and over; $2 for ages 9-19; there are no fees for winter permits. Advance reservations are after Apr. 15 each year for a $20 fee and must be made more than 24 hours in advance. Reservations can be made in person at the Apgar Permit Center and other park offices, over the web at www.nps.gov/glac/home.htm, or write to Backcountry Reservation Office, Glacier National Park, West Glacier, MT 59936. The free *Backcountry Camping Guide* is available at the visitors centers and permit stations. The helpful staff at the Backcountry Permit Center in Apgar (see **Practical Information**) are good resources for trip planning. The North Fork and the Belly River areas are particularly isolated areas, while the trails around Many Glacier, Two Medicine, and Logan Pass are more crowded.

Opportunities for bicycling are limited and confined to roadways and designated bike paths; cycling on trails is strictly prohibited. Although Going-to-the-Sun Rd. is a popular **bike route,** only experienced cyclists with appropriate gear and legs of titanium should attempt this grueling ride. The sometimes nonexistent shoulder of the road can create a hazardous situation. From June 15 through Labor Day, bike traffic is prohibited 11am-4pm from the Apgar campground to Sprague Creek, and east-bound (uphill) from Logan Creek to Logan Pass. The Inner Fork Rd. (which runs from Kintla Lake to Fish Creek on the west side of the park) and the old logging roads in the Flathead National Forest are good for **mountain biking.** Ask at a visitors center for more details. **Equestrian** explorers should check to make sure trails are open; fines for riding on closed trails are steep. **Trail rides** from Mule Shoe Outfitters ($35 for 2hr.) are available at Many Glacier (☎732-4203), Apgar (☎888-5010), and Lake McDonald (☎888-5121).

⚑ BOATING AND FISHING. Boat tours explore all of Glacier's large lakes. Tours leave from **Lake McDonald** (☎888-5727; 1hr., 4-5 per day, $8.50, ages 4-12 $4.25); **Two Medicine** (☎226-4467; 45min., 5 per day, $8); **Rising Sun** at St. Mary Lake (☎732-4430; 1½hr., 5 per day, $10, children $5); and **Many Glacier** (☎732-4480; 1¼hr., 5-6 per day, $9.50). The tours from Two Medicine, Rising Sun, and Many Glacier provide access to Glacier's backcountry, and there are sunset cruises from Rising Sun and Lake McDonald. **Glacier Raft Co.,** in West Glacier, hawks trips down the middle fork of the Flathead River. (☎888-5454 or 800-235-6781; half-day $38, under 13 $29; full-day trip $71 with lunch, under 13 $46.)

Rent **rowboats** ($8 per hr.) at Lake McDonald, Many Glacier, Two Medicine, and Apgar; **canoes** ($8 per hr.) at Many Glacier, Two Medicine, and Apgar; **kayaks** at Apgar ($8 per hr.) and Many Glacier; and **outboards** ($15 per hr.) at Lake McDonald, Two Medicine, and Apgar. No permit is needed to **fish** in the park, and limits are generally high, though some areas are restricted and certain species may be catch-and-release. It's all explained in *Fishing Regulations,* available at visitors centers. Lake Ellen Wilson, Gunsight Lake, and Lake Elizabeth are good places to sink a line. Outside the park, on Blackfoot Indian land, you *do* need a special permit, and everywhere else in Montana you need a state permit.

SCENIC DRIVE: GOING-TO-THE-SUN ROAD

The high country of Glacier National Park is a paradise of purple mountains, cascading waterfalls, alpine wildflowers, and permanent snowpack. This land, mostly inhabited by snow and mountain goats, was made accessible to everyone when the Going-to-the-Sun Road was opened in 1932. Today, most visitors to Glacier see only the scenery visible from this road. Going-to-the-Sun is not for the faint of heart. Hairpin turns, narrow shoulders, thousand-foot drop-offs, and nonexistent guardrails make for some serious white-knuckling for drivers. Stories of campers in the valley seeing headlights sailing through the night as cars go over the edge are part of the park's folklore. Sun Tours will do the driving for you if you like (see **Practical Information** for details). Going-to-the-Sun runs 50 mi. through the mountains from St. Mary to Apgar. Driving time is usually a bit over two hours, depending on weather and traffic conditions. Due to late-melting snow and early winters, high portions of the road are usually only open from late May or early June to late Oct. The tall wooden poles on the edges of the road are used by the snowplows to prevent them from careening off the cliffs when they plow in the spring. Vehicles over 21 ft. in length or 8 ft. in width are prohibited.

Travelers can begin from either Apgar or St. Mary. Some prefer starting at St. Mary, as the road hugs the inside of the mountains for the majority of the drive. Beginning from St. Mary, the drive passes through the wind-swept plains of the Rocky Mountain front as it follows the blue-green of **St. Mary Lake.** A turnout at **Wild Goose Island** offers a stunning view of the lake, a tiny island, and looming peaks that have graced many a postcard. Going-to-the-Sun Mountain and Mount Siyeh appear to the right as the road continues to ascend to **Logan Pass.** The road crosses the Continental Divide here at an elevation of 6646 ft. Be sure to visit the **Logan Pass Visitor Center** for information on wildlife; mountain goats are also frequent visitors to the parking lot here. The road follows the **Garden Wall** as it begins to descend below the treeline. From **Bird Women Falls Overlook,** cascading streams on distant mountains are visible. Be sure to slow down for the **Weeping Wall** where water runs down the cliffs next to the road and sprays the windshields of unexpecting drivers. At **The Loop,** a giant hairpin turn, the road goes back into trees and begins to follow McDonald Creek until it reaches **Lake McDonald.**

NEAR GLACIER

WHITEFISH. Whitefish's proximity to skiing, Glacier National Park, Flathead Lake and other outdoor attractions has largely contributed to its recent boom. Fortunately, the sprawling shops and malls that are spreading throughout the Flathead Valley haven't detracted from Whitefish's vibrant downtown where bars crowd with ski bums in winter and cyclists in summer.

The Big Mountain, southwest of the park in Whitefish, has 78 superb ski trails in the winter. (☎800-858-5439. Full-day $40, students and seniors $30, ages 7-18 $27; night skiing $12. Rentals $18, seniors and kids $12, snowboards $25.) Mountain bikers take over the trails in the summer. (Bikes $15 for 4hr. Lift ticket $18 per day or $13 per ride. Family packages available.) Other activities include horseback riding, gondola rides, and folf (frisbee golf).

The **Tally Lake District** of the Flathead National Forest has great (but hard-core) mountain bike riding. **Glacier Cyclery,** 336 2nd St., sells maps ($6) and rents bikes. (☎862-6446; half-day $20, full-day $25-40).

After a long day, many crash at one of Whitefish's two hostels. **The Bunkhouse Traveler's Inn and Hostel,** 217 Railway St., has a summertime sundeck and offers winter ski pick-up. (☎862-3377. Closes in spring and fall, call ahead to see if they're open. Kitchen and laundry facilities. Dorms $13; private rooms $30.) The **Non-Hostile Hostel,** 300 E. 2nd St., is one helluva friendly place. This apartment building-esque hostel has Internet access ($1.50 for email, $5 per ½hr.), a pool table, and the **Wrap and Roll Cafe** (wrap sandwiches from $4) downstairs (☎862-7383; rooms $13).

Truby's, at 115 Central Ave., offers a lunch special that consists of half a gourmet pizza, a salad, and a soda for $5.25. (☎862-4979; lunch served M-Sa 11am-3pm).

Whitefish is the area's nightlife hotspot; the **Dire Wolf Pub,** 845 Wisconsin Ave., on the way to Big Mountain, is a popular après-ski stop and has live music during the ski season (☎862-4500; open daily 11am-2am). The **Great Northern Saloon,** 27 Central St., rocks on the patio in summer and offers a variety of cures for the tired skier or snowboarder (☎862-2816; open daily 11am-2am). Both bars serve burgers and sandwiches ($5-6). **Black Star Brewery,** 2 Central Ave., has free samples of good beer (☎863-1000; open M-Sa noon-6pm; in winter M-Sa 3-7pm).

   RimRock buses (☎800-255-7655) stop at the Conoco station across E. 2nd St. and run to Missoula (1 per day, $21). Whitefish can be reached by **Amtrak. Post office:** 424 Baker St. (☎862-2151. Open M-F 8:30am-5:30pm, Sa 10am-2pm.) **ZIP code:** 59937.

BROWNING. The center of the Blackfoot Indian Reservation, Browning, 12 mi. east of East Glacier, provides a glimpse into the past and present of Native American life. The **Museum of the Plains Indian,** at the junction of U.S. 2 and U.S. 89, displays traditional Native American clothing, artifacts, and crafts. (☎338-2230. Open daily June-Sept. 9am-4:45pm; Oct.-May M-F 10am-4:30pm. $4, ages 6-12 $1; groups of 10 or more $1 per person; Oct.-May free.) During **North American Indian Days** (from the 2nd Th through the 2nd Su of July), Native Americans from the surrounding Blackfoot reservation and elsewhere gather for a celebration that includes tribal dancing, rodeo, and a fantastic parade (☎338-7406).

WATERTON LAKES NATIONAL PARK, AB ☎403

Only a fraction of the size of its Montana neighbor, Waterton Lakes National Park offers spectacular scenery and activities without the crowds that plague Glacier during July and August. The town of Waterton is a genuine alpine town, complete with a Swiss-style chalet. Traffic jams are common on account of the town's four-legged denizens, the bighorn sheep and mule deer that also call Waterton home. Admission is CDN$4 per day, CDN$8 per group of two to ten people. The park is free in the winter, but a credit card is required from 10pm to 8am.

🔁 **PRACTICAL INFORMATION.** The only road from Waterton's park entrance leads 8½km south to **Waterton Park.** En route, stop at the **Waterton Visitors Center,** 8km inside the park on Rte. 5 for a schedule of events and hikes. (☎859-5133. Open daily mid-June to Aug. 8am-8pm; mid-May to mid-June 8am-6pm; Sept.-Oct. hrs. vary.) In the off-season, pick up info at **Park Administration,** 215 Mt. View Rd. (☎859-2224; open M-F 8am-4pm). Greenbacks (US dollars) can be exchanged for Loonies (Canadian dollars) at the **Tamarac Village Sq.** on Mt. View Rd. (Open daily July-Aug. at least 9am-6pm; May-June and Sept.-Oct. usually 9am-5pm.) **Pat's Mohawk and Cycle Rental,** Mt. View Rd., Waterton, rents bikes. (☎859-2266. Mountain bikes CDN$6 per hr., CDN$30 per day.) **Ambulance:** ☎859-2636. **Post office:** in Waterton on Fountain Ave. at Windflower Ave. (open M, W, and F 8:30am-4:30pm, Tu and Th 8:30am-4pm). **Postal code:** T0K 2M0. **Area code:** 403.

👥 **ACCOMMODATIONS AND FOOD.** At the entrance to the park, the enormous(ly pricey) **Prince of Wales Hotel** serves traditional afternoon tea from June to Sept. (☎859-2231. Daily 2-4:30pm. CDN$25.) Check out the spectacular view from the lobby—complete with kilted bellhops—even if you can't afford high tea.

   The park's three campgrounds are much more affordable. **Belly River,** on Chief Mountain Hwy. outside the park entrance, has scenic and uncrowded primitive sites for CDN$10. **Crandell,** on Red Rock Canyon Rd., is situated in a forest area with sites for CDN$13. Camp with 200 of your best RV pals at **Townsite** in Waterton Park, which has showers and a lakeside vista, but no privacy. The walk-in sites are satisfactory and generally the last to fill (sites CDN$17, walk-in sites CDN$15, full hook-up CDN$23). **Backcountry camping** is CDN$6 per person per night and requires a permit from the visitors center (call ☎859-5133 for a CDN$10 permit, up to 90 days in advance). The backcountry campsites are rarely full, and several, including beautiful **Crandell Lake,** are less than a 1hr. hike from the trailhead.

Travelers preferring to stay indoors should reserve one of the 21 comfy beds, with real mattresses, at the **Waterton International Hostel (HI),** in the Lodge at Waterton Lakes. One of the cushiest hostels around, amenities include a 10% discount at the health club and pool next door, laundry, and kitchen. (☎ 859-2151 ext. 2016, 888-985-6343 for toll-free reservations; member CDN$20, non-member CDN$24, family room CDN$27/31 per person, ages 6-17 CDN$10/12.) The **Country Bakery and Lunch Counter,** 303 Windflower Ave., cooks up CDN$2.75 meat pies and CDN$3.50 Belgian waffles. (☎ 859-2181. Open daily May-Sept. 7am-7pm.)

⚑ HIKES AND ACTIVITIES. Waterton Lakes includes 191 mi. of trails of varying difficulty. In addition to exploring the mountain lakes and snow-capped peaks of Waterton Lakes, many of these trails link up with the network of trails in Glacier National Park. **Waterton-Glacier International Peace Park Hike,** a free guided hike, takes off every Saturday morning at 10am (July-Sept.) from the Bertha Trailhead, just south of the Waterton townsite, and crosses the border into the US. After 8.5 mi. of moderately easy hiking led by interpreters from both the US and Canada, participants can take a boat back from the Goat Haunt Ranger Station. The **Carthew-Alderson Trail** starts from Cameron Lake and leads through 18km of incredible views to end up at the town (11¾ mi one-way, 1440 ft. elevation gain, approximately 7½ hr.) A shorter day-hike follows the shore of Cameron Lake. (2¼ mi., no elevation gain, approximately 1hr.) The **Hiker Shuttle** runs from Tamarack Village in town to Cameron Lake and other trailheads. (☎ 859-2378. CDN$4.50. Reservations strongly recommended.) The popular **Crypt Lake Trail** leads past waterfalls in a narrow canyon, through a 20m natural tunnel, and after 6km arrives at icy, green Crypt Lake, which straddles the international border. (10½ mi. round-trip, 2100 ft. elevation gain, approximately 7hr.) To get to the trailhead, you must take the **water taxi** run by **Waterton Shoreline Cruises** in Waterton Park (☎ 859-2362). The boat leaves four times a day (CDN$12, ages 4-12 CDN$6). The marina also runs a 2hr. boat tour of Upper Waterton Lake (open mid-May to mid-Sept.; CDN$21, ages 13-17 CDN$12, ages 4-12 CDN$8). Gear is available for purchase at **Waterton Sports** in the Tamarack Village Sq. (☎ 859-2378; open 9am-6pm). Horses are allowed on many trails. **Alpine Stables,** 1km north of the townsite, conducts trail rides. (☎ 859-2462. Open May-Sept. 1hr. ride CDN$17, 4hr. CDN$55.)

Fishing in Waterton requires a **license** (CDN$6 per week, CDN$13 per season), available from the park offices, campgrounds, warden stations, and service stations in the area. Lake trout cruise the depths of **Cameron** and **Waterton Lakes,** while northern pike prowl the weedy channels of **Maskinonge Lake.** Most of the backcountry lakes and creeks support rainbow and brook trout. Try the creek that spills from Cameron Lake, about 200m to the east of the parking lot, or hike 1½km to Crandell Lake for plentiful fish. Rent **rowboats, paddleboats,** or **canoes** at Cameron Lake (2 people $17 first hr., $14 per additional hr.; 4 people CDN$20/$17). On summer evenings at 8:30pm, take in a free **interpretive program** at the **Cameron Theater** in town or at the Crandell campsite. There are programs daily in summer at 8:30pm; the visitors center has a schedule.

WYOMING

The ninth-largest state in the Union, Wyoming is also the least populated. This is a place where livestock outnumber citizens, and men wear cowboy hats and boots for real. Yet this rugged land was more than just a frontier during westward expansion. It was the first state to grant women the right to vote without later repealing it, and the first to have a national monument (Devils Tower, p. 663) and a national park (Yellowstone, p. 645) within its borders. Wyoming has everything you'd want to see in a state in the Rockies: a Frontier Days festival, spectacular mountain ranges, breathtaking panoramas, and, of course, cattle and beer.

⓱ PRACTICAL INFORMATION

Capital: Cheyenne.
Visitor Info: Wyoming Business Council Tourism Office, I-25 and College Dr., Cheyenne 82002 (☎307-777-7777 or 800-225-5996; www.wyomingtourism.org). Info center open daily 8am-5pm. **Dept. of Commerce, State Parks and Historic Sites Division,** 122 W. 25th St., Herschler Bldg., 1st fl., Cheyenne 82002 (☎307-777-6323). Open M-F 8am-5pm. **Game and Fish Dept.,** 5400 Bishop Blvd., Cheyenne 82006 (☎307-777-4600). Open M-F 8am-5pm.
Postal Abbreviation: WY. **Sales Tax:** 5%.

YELLOWSTONE ☎307

Geysers, mountains, wildlife, and water draw millions of tourists to **Yellowstone National Park** every year. Geologists believe that the unique forces at work in Yellowstone result from a "hot spot" underneath the earth's crust. Three immense volcanic explosions have occurred as a result of this hot spot, one 2 million years ago, one 1.3 million years ago, and one 600,000 years ago, leading geologists to believe that the Yellowstone caldera is on a 600,000 year cycle. You do the math. While this "hot spot" may mean certain death for humanity at some point, it also makes Yellowstone a place of tangible geological power, where the landscape can change in minutes, not eons.

Today, Yellowstone's roads are clogged with RVs and tourists gawking at geysers and wildlife. The Greater Yellowstone ecosystem, consisting of Yellowstone National Park and the surrounding National Forest lands, has diverse and abundant animals, including grizzlies, bison, elk, moose, and bighorn sheep. With the reintroduction of wolves in 1995, all of the animals that lived in this area before the arrival of Europeans are still present, with the exception of the black-footed ferret.

⌗ GETTING THERE AND GETTING AROUND

The bulk of Yellowstone National Park lies in the northwest corner of Wyoming, with slivers in Montana and Idaho. **West Yellowstone, MT,** and **Gardiner, MT,** are the most developed and expensive entrance points to the park. For a rustic beginning, **Cooke City, MT,** the northeast entrance, leads to U.S. 212, a gorgeous stretch of road known as **Beartooth Hwy.** (open only in summer). From the east, enter through **Cody** (see p. 660) via Rte. 14/16/20. Southern entry to the park is through **Grand Teton National Park** (see p. 654). **Entrance fee** is $20 for cars, $10 for pedestrians, $15 for motorcycles; pass good for one week at Yellowstone and Grand Teton.

Buses: Greyhound: West Yellowstone Office Services, 132 Electric St., West Yellowstone. To: Bozeman (2hr., 1 per day, $15); Salt Lake City (9hr., 1 per day, $48); and Boise (17hr., 1 per day, $90). **Powder River Transportation** departs from Cody (see p. 660).

Car Rental: Big Sky Car Rental, 429 Yellowstone Ave. (☎646-9564 or 800-426-7669), West Yellowstone, MT. $45 per day, 10% discount for 7 days or more, unlimited mi. Must be 21 with a credit card. Open daily May to mid-Oct. 8am-5pm.

Bike Rental: Yellowstone Bicycle and Video, 132 Madison Ave. (☎646-7815), West Yellowstone, MT. Mountain bikes with helmet and water $3.50 per hr., $12.50 per half-day, $19.50 per day. Open May-Oct. daily 8:30am-8:30pm; Nov.-Apr. 11am-7pm.

Horse Rides: AmFac (☎344-7311; call at least a day ahead), from Mammoth Hot Springs, Roosevelt Lodge, and Canyon Village. Late May to early Sept. $20 per hr., 2hr. From early June to early Sept., **stagecoach rides** ($6.50, ages 2-11 $5.25) are available at Roosevelt Lodge.

Tours: With time and transportation, you can do better on your own, but **AmFac Parks and Resorts** (☎344-7311) offers the cheapest tours. 8½-9hr. bus tours of part of the park leave daily from Old Faithful Inn, Grant Village, Lake Yellowstone Hotel, Fishing Bridge RV Park, Canyon Lodge and Bridge campground. ($24-30, ages 12-16 $15-16.) Full-day tours around the park's figure-eight road system also available, leaving from Gardiner, MT, and Mammoth Hot Springs ($34-35, ages 12-16 $18). **Grayline Tours** runs from West Yellowstone through both loops. Free pick-up from area motels and camp-grounds (☎406-646-9374 or 800-523-3102. $40.) Alternatively, **Buffalo Bus Lines,** 429 Yellowstone Ave. (☎406-646-9564 or 800-426-7669) in West Yellowstone tours Upper Loop every day, and Lower Loop on M, W, and F ($35, children $25).

ORIENTATION

Yellowstone is huge; both Rhode Island and Delaware could fit within its bound-aries. Yellowstone's roads circulate millions of visitors in a rough figure-eight con-figuration, with side roads branching off to park entrances and some of the lesser-known sites. The natural wonders which make the park famous (e.g. Old Faithful) dot the Upper and Lower Loops. Construction and renovation of roads are planned for the next 80 years; call ahead or consult *Yellowstone Today*, available at the entrance, to find out which sections will be closed during your visit…and your life-time. Even without construction you won't be getting anywhere fast. The speed limit is 45mph and much of the time you'll be going slower because of the steep grades, tight curves, and traffic jams caused by wildlife sightings.

> Yellowstone can be a dangerous place. While roadside wildlife may look tame, these large beasts are unpredictable and easily startled, particularly mothers with babies. Stay at least 25 yards from any animal and at least 100 yards away from bears. Both black bears and grizzly bears inhabit Yellowstone; all necessary precautions should be taken. Before hiking, consult with rangers to find out about the latest sightings. If you should encounter a bear, let a ranger know for the safety of the bear and other visitors. Many visitors regard bison as simply overgrown cows, but these enormous creatures can travel at speeds of up to 30mph. Visitors have been gored. While the pools of sulfuric, boiling water may look like a tempting place for a hot dip, don't venture off the marked trails, because "scalding water can ruin your trip." The fires of 1988 left thousands of "widow-makers;" dead trees that can fall over at anytime, especially during high winds. Exercise caution when near Yellowstone's other large beasts, cars and RV's; wildlife, pedestrians, distracted drivers, and bumpy, narrow roads are a recipe for an accident.

PRACTICAL INFORMATION

The park's high season extends from about mid-June to mid-Sept. If you visit during this period, expect large crowds, clogged roads, and motels and campsites filled to capacity. Much of the park shuts down from Nov. to mid-Apr., then opens gradually as the snow melts.

Visitor Info: Most regions in this vast park have their own central station. All centers offer general information and backcountry permits, but each has distinct hiking and camping regulations and regional exhibits. **Albright Visitors Center** (☎344-2263) at Mammoth Hot Springs: history of Yellowstone Park and the beginnings of the National Park Idea; **Grant Village** (☎242-2650): wilderness and the 1988 fire; **Fishing Bridge** (☎242-2450): wild-life and Yellowstone Lake; **Canyon** (☎242-2550): bison; **Old Faithful** (☎545-2750): gey-sers; **Norris** (☎344-2812): geothermic features of the park. All stations are usually open late May to early Sept. daily 8am-7pm; Albright and Old Faithful are open through the winter. **Info centers: Madison** (open 8am-7pm), and at **West Thumb** (open 8am-5pm), on the southern edge of the Lake. **West Yellowstone Chamber of Commerce,** 30 Yellow-stone Ave. (☎406-646-7701 or 406-646-9488 for lodging info), West Yellowstone, MT, 2 blocks west of the park entrance. Open late May to early Sept. daily 8am-8pm; early Sept. to late May M-F 8am-5pm.

General Park Information, including campground info: ☎344-7381, TDD 344-2386.

Radio Information: Tune in to 1610AM for park info.

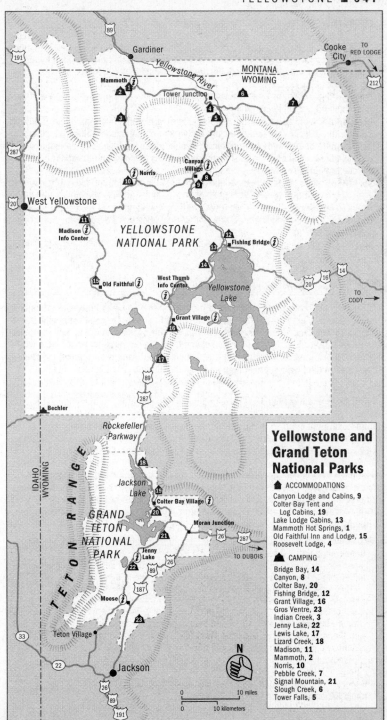

ROCKY MOUNTAINS

Yellowstone and Grand Teton National Parks

▲ ACCOMMODATIONS

Canyon Lodge and Cabins, 9
Colter Bay Tent and
  Log Cabins, 19
Lake Lodge Cabins, 13
Mammoth Hot Springs, 1
Old Faithful Inn and Lodge, 15
Roosevelt Lodge, 4

▲ CAMPING

Bridge Bay, 14
Canyon, 8
Colter Bay, 20
Fishing Bridge, 12
Grant Village, 16
Gros Ventre, 23
Indian Creek, 3
Jenny Lake, 22
Lewis Lake, 17
Lizard Creek, 18
Madison, 11
Mammoth, 2
Norris, 10
Pebble Creek, 7
Signal Mountain, 21
Slough Creek, 6
Tower Falls, 5

N

0   10 miles
0   10 kilometers

Medical Services: Lake Clinic, Pharmacy, and **Hospital** (☎242-7241), across the road from the Lake Yellowstone Hotel. Clinic open late May to mid-Sept. daily 8:30am-8:30pm. Emergency room open May-Sept. 24hr. **Old Faithful Clinic** (☎545-7325), near the Old Faithful Inn. Open early May to mid-Oct. daily 8:30am-5pm; May and mid-Sept. to mid-Oct. closed Th-F. **Mammoth Hot Springs Clinic** (☎344-7965), open year-round M-F 8:30am-1pm and 2-5pm. The **Clinic at West Yellowstone,** 236 Yellowstone Ave. (☎406-646-7668), in West Yellowstone, open late May to early Sept. M-Sa 8:30am-5:30pm; off season hours vary.

Disabled Services: All entrances, visitors centers, and ranger stations offer the *Visitor Guide to Accessible Features.* Fishing Bridge RV Park, Madison, Bridge Bay, Canyon, and Grant campgrounds have accessible sites and restrooms, while Lewis Lake and Slough Creek each have a site. Write the **Accessibility Coordinator,** P.O. Box 168, Yellowstone National Park, WY, 82190, for more info, or call ☎344-2386 (TDD only).

Post Office: There are 5 post offices in the park at **Lake, Old Faithful, Canyon, Grant,** and **Mammoth Hot Springs** (☎344-7764). All 3 open M-F 8:30am-5pm. Specify which station at Yellowstone National Park when addressing mail. **ZIP code:** 82190. In **West Yellowstone, MT:** 209 Grizzly Ave. (☎406-646-7704). Open M-F 8:30am-5pm, Sa 8-10am. **ZIP code:** 59758.

Area codes: 307 (in the park), 406 (in West Yellowstone, Cooke City, and Gardiner, MT). In text, 307 unless otherwise noted.

ACCOMMODATIONS AND FOOD

Camping is far cheaper, but affordable indoor lodging can be found with advanced preparation. Lodging within the park can be hard to come by on short notice but is often a better deal than the motels found on the park's outskirts. During peak months, motel rooms that are $35 in April or Oct. can go for as much as $100, while in-park lodging remains relatively inexpensive. Without reservations, rooms—much less budget ones—are scarce and motels fill early in the afternoon.

IN THE PARK

AmFac Parks and Resorts (☎344-7311) controls all accommodations within the park with an iron fist, using a secret code for cabins: "Roughrider" means no bath, no facilities; "Budget" offers a sink; "Economy" guarantees a toilet and sink; "Pioneer" offers a shower, toilet, and sink; "Frontier" is bigger, more plush; and "Western" is the biggest and most plush. Facilities are located close to the more rustic cabins. All cabins or rooms should be reserved well in advance of the June to Sept. tourist season. Be choosy buying food in the park, as many, but not all, of the restaurants, snack bars, and cafeterias are quite expensive. If possible, stick to the **general stores** at each lodging location; they sell provisions. The stores at Fishing Bridge, Lake, Grant Village, and Canyon sell lunch-counter style food (open daily 7:30am-10pm, though times may vary by around 30min.).

Roosevelt Lodge, in the north of the park, 19 mi north of Canyon. A favorite of Teddy Roosevelt, who seems to have frequented every motel and saloon west of the Mississippi. Provides some of the cheapest and most scenic indoor accommodations around, and is located in a relatively isolated section of the park. Roughrider cabins with wood-burning stoves $43. More spacious Economy with toilet $57. Frontier cabins with full bath $83.

Mammoth Hot Springs, 18 mi. west of Roosevelt area, near the north entrance, is a less scenic area than some, but makes a good base for early-morning wildlife sighting excursions. Lattice-sided Budget cabins $50. Frontier cabins (some with porches) from $83. Hotel Room without bath $60.

Old Faithful Inn and Lodge, 30 mi. southwest of the west Yellowstone entrance, is a sea awash with ice cream-toting tourists and RVs, but is conveniently located. Pleasant Budget cabins $35. Pioneer cabins $43. Frontier cabins $62. Well-appointed hotel rooms from $64 without bath, with private bath $91.

Lake Lodge Cabins, a stone's throw from Yellowstone Lake 4 mi. south of Fishing Bridge, is a cluster of cabins dating from the 20s and 50s, with interior decorating from the 70s. Pioneer cabins $49. Larger Western cabins $106. Next door, **Lake Yellowstone Hotel and Cabins** has yellow Frontier cabins with no lake view for $83.

Canyon Lodge and Cabins, in the middle of the figure-eight of the park loop 15 mi north of Fishing Bridge. Less authentic and more expensive than Roosevelt Lodge's cabins, but slightly closer to the popular Old Faithful area. Pioneer cabins $54. Frontier cabins $78. Western cabins $106.

WEST YELLOWSTONE, MT

Guarding the west entrance of the park, West Yellowstone capitalizes on the hordes of tourists who pass through en route to the park. The closest of the border towns to popular park attractions, West Yellowstone has scads of budget motels, with more reasonable prices than Gardiner.

Grab an inexpensive breakfast or lunch at the **Running Bear Pancake House** at the corner of Madison and Hayden (☎406-646-7703; open daily 7am-2pm) or stockpile provisions at the **Food Round-Up Grocery Store,** 107 Dunraven St. (☎406-646-7501; open in summer daily 7am-10pm; in winter 7am-9pm).

West Yellowstone International Hostel (AAIH/Rucksackers), 139 Yellowstone Ave. (☎406-646-7745 or 800-838-7745), at the **Madison Hotel** is the best bet for indoor budget accommodations near the park. A friendly manager presides over this old but clean, wood-adorned hostel. Open late May to mid-Oct. Dorms $20; private singles and doubles $40.

Lazy G Motel, 123 Hayden St. (☎406-646-7586), has an affable staff and big rooms with queen beds, refrigerators, and TVs. Singles $43; doubles $53, with kitchenette $53-63.

Ho Hum Motel, 126 Canyon (☎406-646-7746) is a straight-forward motel that offers clean rooms with 1 queen bed for $40 and 2 queen beds for $50.

GARDINER, MT

Located about 1½hr. northeast of West Yellowstone, Gardiner is the park's original entrance. It's smaller and less touristy than West Yellowstone, but also more expensive and less scenic. Pick a bundle of cheap food at **Food Farm,** on U.S. 89 across from the Super 8 (☎406-848-7524; open M-Sa 7am-9pm, Su 8am-8pm). A few blocks west on U.S. 89, **Helen's Corral Drive-In** rounds up killer ½ lb. burgers (open in summer daily 11am-11pm, burgers $3.75-6.75).

The Town Cafe and Motel (☎406-848-7322), on Park St. across from the park's northern entrance. These wood-paneled, carpeted rooms are one of the best deals in town. TVs but no phones. Singles $45; doubles $55; Oct.-May $35/$45.

Jim Bridger Court Modern Cabins (☎406-848-7371), on U.S. 89, has clean, no frills cabins with TVs but no phones. 1 queen bed $50, 2 queen beds $65.

Hillcrest Cottages (☎406-848-7353 or 800-970-7353), on U.S. 89 across from the Exxon, rents out homey cabins with kitchenettes. Open May to early Sept. Singles $60; doubles $70; $6 per additional adult, $2 per additional child under 18.

COOKE CITY, MT

Cooke City is located at the northeast corner of the park. The Nez Percé slipped right by the US cavalry here, Lewis and Clark deemed the area impassable, and even today few people visit this rugged little town. Most things are cheaper here than in the other entrance towns, particularly gas (up to 10¢ cheaper per gallon). Far away from the attractions that draw the majority of tourists, Cooke City makes a good base for exploring the more remote parts of Yellowstone.

The **Grizzly Pad Grill and Cabins,** Rte. 212 on the eastern side of town offers the Grizzly Pad Special—an incredible milkshake, fries, and a large cheeseburger for only $5.50. (☎406-838-2161. Open in summer daily 7am-9pm, off season hours vary, but generally 7am-4pm; closed mid-Oct. to late Dec. and mid-Apr. to late May.)

ROCKY MOUNTAINS

Yellowstone Yurt Hostel (☎406-838-2349), at the corner of W. Broadway and Montana St. (turn north onto Republic St. from U.S. 212). Rustic but cheap lodging in a round tent with a skylight, wood stove, and six bunks. The hostel is oriented toward backcountry skiers in the winter, and may be a bit stuffy in summer. $14 buys a bunk, a hot shower, and access to an outdoor kitchen. Bring a sleeping bag. Check-in is before 9pm; call ahead for late arrivals.

Antler's Lodge (☎406-838-2432). Ernest Hemingway spent a few nights editing *For Whom the Bell Tolls* here. Rustic cabins in a renovated US cavalry outpost. Singles $45; doubles $55.

▓ CAMPGROUNDS

Getting a campsite in Yellowstone can be a pain in the buttocks. If you've already arrived in Yellowstone, call **Park Headquarters** (☎344-7381) for info on campgrounds—they may be able to tell you which campgrounds are full. Five of the 12 developed campgrounds allow advance reservations. **AmFac,** P.O. Box 165, Yellowstone National Park 82190 (☎344-7311), controls **Canyon, Grant Village, Madison, Bridge Bay** (all $16), and **Fishing Bridge RV** ($27; RVs only). For advance reservations call ☎344-7311. For same day reservations call ☎344-7901, or, if you're in West Yellowstone, go to **Northern Bear Trading Company,** between the IMAX theater and the Grizzly Discovery Center (☎406-646-7345). Generally, Fishing Bridge is the first to fill up each day, followed by Madison, Canyon, Grant Village, and Bridge Bay. Reservations are accepted up to two years in advance, and on crowded days (generally weekends and holidays) all spots may be reserved beforehand. On quieter days it is possible to reserve a site if you call before 9am. Sometimes you can reserve Grant Village and Bridge Bay as late as 7pm, but the earlier the better. **Madison's** 280 campsites are close to good flyfishing, while the sites at **Canyon** are enveloped in pine trees. **Grant Village** and **Bridge Bay** are both conveniently near beautiful Yellowstone Lake, but **Grant Village** is much more scenic.

Seven campgrounds offer rustic first come, first served sites with potable water. In summer, most of these fill by 10am and finding a site can be frustrating since info on full campgrounds is hard to come by. Check-out time is 10am; most sites empty out from the previous evening between 8 and 10am and this window is your best chance to claim popular spots. All of these campgrounds are nice, but two of the most beautiful areas are **Slough Creek Campground** (29 sites, 10 mi. northeast of Tower Junction; open late May to Oct.; $10) and **Pebble Creek Campground** (32 sites; no RVs; open mid-June to early Sept.; $10). Both are located in the northeast between Tower and the Northeast Entrance—generally the least congested area—and offer relatively uncrowded spots and good fishing. You can also try **Lewis Lake,** south of the Lake halfway between West Thumb and the South Entrance, with 85 pine treed-sites ($10), or **Tower Falls,** between the Northeast entrance and Mammoth Hot Springs, with 32 sites high on a hill ($10). **Norris** (116 sites; open late May-late Sept.; $12); **Indian Creek,** between the Norris Geyser Basin and Mammoth Hot Springs (75 sites; open mid-June to mid-Sept.; $10); and **Mammoth** (85 sites; open year-round; $12) are a bit less scenic, but are still great places to camp. Campgrounds at Grant Village, Fishing Bridge, and Canyon all have coin laundries ($1.25 wash, $1 dry) and pay showers ($3). The lodges at Mammoth and Old Faithful have showers for $3 (towels and shampoo included) but no laundry facilities.

If all sites are full, $8 campgrounds lurk outside the park in the National Forests. Options line U.S. 14/16/20, 287, 191, 89, and Rte. 212 (near Cooke City). Often nearly empty, they are worth camping in, even if there are spots open at Yellowstone. Help can be found at the visitors center in West Yellowstone.

Over 95% (almost 2 million acres) of the park is backcountry. To venture overnight into the wilds of Yellowstone, you need a free **backcountry permit** from a ranger station (near all major visitors centers). There is almost always space available in the backcountry, though the more popular areas fill up in high season. You can reserve a permit in person no more than 48hr. in advance. To reserve a permit ahead of time you must pay $15 and fill out a **trip planning worksheet,** which you can get by writing to the **Backcountry Office,** P.O. Box 168, Yellowstone National Park 82190, or by calling ☎344-2160 or 344-2163. Follow backcountry regulations regarding sanitation, pets, firearms, and firewood. In many backcountry areas campfires are not permitted, and in particularly dry years none may be permitted at all; plan on bringing a stove and related cooking gear. Consult a ranger before embarking on a trail; they can offer tips on how to avoid bears, ice, and other natural hindrances. Areas and trails may be closed due to bears and other factors. The **Backcountry Trip Planner,** available at visitors centers or by writing to the above address, is an invaluable resource, containing information on trails, campsites, and necessary safety precautions.

👁 SIGHTS AND ACTIVITIES

For mountains of cash, **AmFac** (☎344-7311) sells tours, horseback rides, and chuckwagon dinners until the cows come home. Given enough time, however, eyes and feet will do a better job than AmFac's tours, and you won't have to sell your firstborn. The main attractions feature informative self-guiding tour pamphlets with maps (25¢, except for Old Faithful, 50¢) and are accessible from the road by walkways, usually extending ¼ to 1½ mi. through various natural phenomena.

What sets Yellowstone apart from the myriad of other National Parks and Forests in the Rockies are its **geothermal features**—the park protects the largest geothermic area in the world. Beware: *the crust around some of these features is paper thin and underneath may lie boiling, acidic water. Stay on the marked paths, or, in the backcountry, give wide berth lest scalding water ruin your trip.* The bulk of these geothermal wonders can be found on the western side of the park between Mammoth Hot Springs in the North and Old Faithful in the South. The most dramatic of this bizarre bunch are the **geysers.** Incredibly hot molten rock, close to the surface of the earth in the geothermic areas superheats water until it boils and bubbles and eventually builds up enough pressure to burst through the cracks with steamy force. The extremely volatile nature of this area means that attractions may change, appear, or disappear due to forces beyond human control.

While bison-jams and bear-gridlock may make wildlife seem more of a nuisance than an attraction, wildlife viewing in Yellowstone affords a unique opportunity to see a number of native species co-existing in their natural environment. The best times for viewing are early morning and just before dark, as most animals nap in the shade during the hot midday. The road between Tower-Roosevelt and the northeast entrance, in the Lamar Valley, is a good place to go looking for wolves and grizzlies (among other species). Ranger may have some pointers on where the creatures are.

OLD FAITHFUL AREA. Yellowstone's trademark attraction, Old Faithful is the most predictable of the large geysers and has consistently pleased audiences since its 1870 discovery. Eruptions typically occur every 30min. to 1½hr. and are usually 106 ft. to 184 ft. in height. Predictions for the next eruption, usually accurate to within 10 min., are posted at the Old Faithful Visitors Center. Old Faithful lies in the **Upper Geyser Basin,** 16 mi. south of the Madison area and 20 mi. west of Grant Village. Numerous other geysers and hot springs are in this area and trails connect them all. The walk to beautiful **Morning Glory Pool** is an easy 1½ mi. from Old Faithful, and is a nice diversion while waiting for the geyser to erupt.

FIREHOLE RIVER. Between Old Faithful and Madison, along the Firehole River, lie the **Midway Geyser Basin** and the **Lower Geyser Basin.** Almost everything you'll see along the side of the road is interesting, even if only for a brief stop. The **Excelsior Geyser Crater,** a large, steaming lake carved out of the earth by a powerful geyser blast, and its partner the **Grand Prismatic Spring,** the largest hot spring in the park, are both located about 5 mi. north of Old Faithful and are worth a look. Eight mi. north of Old Faithful (or 8 mi. south of Madison, depending on your world-view) you'll find the **Fountain Paint Pot,** a bubbling pool of hot milky mud. Along this area's trails lie examples of all four types of geothermal activity (geysers, mudpots, hot springs, and fumaroles—muddy steam vents) which bubble, steam, and spray together in cacophonous harmony. The temptation is strong to wash off the grime of camping in all of this hot water, but swimming in the hot springs is prohibited. You can **swim** in the Firehole River, three-fourths of the way up Firehole Canyon Dr. (just south of Madison Jct.), though be prepared for a chill; the name of the river is quite deceiving. Call park info (☎ 344-7381) to make sure the river is open.

NORRIS GEYSER BASIN. Farther north, 14 mi. past Madison, 21 mi. south of Mammoth and 15 mi. south of the Indian Creek Campground, is the colorful **Norris Geyser Basin,** one of the most active areas in the park. **Echinus,** whose dramatic blasts from a clear basin of water consistently please, is predictable about half the time and eruptions occur once an hour. The geyser has erratic fits the other half of the time, exploding once every one to four hours. Its neighbor, **Steamboat,** is the tallest geyser in the world, topping 400 ft. and erupting for up to 20min. but it is entirely unpredictable. After more than nine years of inactivity, Steamboat surprised a group of people illegally camped in the parking lot on May 2, 2000.

MAMMOTH HOT SPRINGS. Shifting water sources, malleable limestone deposits, and temperature-sensitive, multicolored bacterial growth create the most rapidly changing natural structure in the park, the hot spring terraces that resemble huge wedding cakes at **Mammoth Hot Springs,** 21 mi. to the north of the Norris Basin and 29 mi. west of Tower. Ask a local ranger where the most active springs are on the day of your visit. Also ask about area trails, which feature some of the park's best wildlife viewing. **Horse rides** are available through AmFac (see **Practical Information,** p. 645) just south of the Hot Springs, and **swimming** is allowed in the **Boiling River,** whose name-giver was a big liar, 2½ mi. north. Call the info line (☎ 344-7381) to make sure that this area is open.

CANYON. The east side's featured attraction, the **Grand Canyon of the Yellowstone,** wears rusty red-orange colors created by hot water acting on the volcanic rock. For a close-up view of the mighty **Lower Falls,** hike down the short but steep **Uncle Tom's Trail** (over 300 steps). **Artist Point** on the southern rim and **Inspiration Point** on the northern rim offer broader canyon vistas and both are accessible from the road between Canyon and Fishing Bridge. All along the canyon's 19 mi. rim, keep an eye out for bighorn sheep. At dawn or dusk, the bear-viewing area (at the intersection of Northern Rim and Tower roads) should have you dusting off your binoculars. **Horse rides** are available at Canyon, as well as in the Tower-Roosevelt area 19 mi. north (see **Practical Information,** p. 645).

YELLOWSTONE LAKE AREA. Situated in the southeast corner of the park, **Yellowstone Lake** is the largest high-altitude lake in North America and home to a recovery program for the cutthroat trout. While the surface of the lake may appear calm, geologists have found that the bottom of the lake contains evidence of underwater geothermal features. **AmFac** offers lake cruises that leave from the marina at Bridge Bay. (☎ 344-7311. Open daily early June to mid-Sept. 5-7 per day. $8.75, ages 2-11 $4.75.) The **West Thumb** area, named after the vaguely hand-like shape of the lake, is home to geysers and hot springs that spill into the lake, with an average rate of 3100 gallons per day. This barely affects the chilly temperature of the lake. Early visitors to the park cooked their freshly-caught trout in the boiling water of the **Fishing Cone,** but this is forbidden today. Due to efforts to help the endangered cutthroat population, fishing off the **Fishing Bridge** has also been outlawed. You may smell the sulphurous odors of the **Mud Volcano** area from miles away, but these unique features are worth the assault on your nose. Located 6 mi. north of Fishing Bridge and 10 mi. south of Canyon Junction, these strange geothermal features have descriptive names such as **Dragon's Mouth, Sour Lake,** and **Black Dragon's Cauldron.**

Fishing and **boating** are both allowed within the park, provided you follow a number of regulations. Permits are required for fishing; areas may be closed due to feeding patterns of bears, and some species are catch-and-release only (permits age 16 and older $10 for 10-day pass; $20 for season; available at rangers stations, visitors centers, and general stores). In addition to the lake, popular fishing spots include

FEDERAL WOLF PACKS In Jan. 1995, after years of public debate, the federal government began to reintroduce gray wolves into the greater Yellowstone ecosystem. Before the program, the last known wolves in Yellowstone were killed in 1929 as part of a federally funded bounty hunt to eradicate the predators. Local and state response to the federal initiative has been mixed. Many ranchers have denounced the reappearance of wolves, fearing they will kill livestock. Others hail the program as the first step in a return to a healthy ecosystem. Montana's State Senate and House of Representatives responded with a caustic joint resolution that made their position clear: "Now, therefore, be it resolved that if the United States government is successful in its efforts to reintroduce wolves into the Yellowstone Park ecosystem, the U.S. Congress be urged to take the steps necessary to ensure that wolves are also reintroduced into every other ecosystem and region of the United States, including Central Park in New York City, the Presidio in San Francisco, and Washington, D.C."

the Madison and Firehole rivers. To go boating or even floating on the lake, you'll need a **boating permit** (motorized vessels $10 for 10-day pass; motor-free boats $5 for 10-day pass), available at many ranger stations, backcountry offices (check *Yellowstone Today*), Bridge Bay marina, a few park entrances, and the Lewis Lake campground. **AmFac** (☎344-7311) rents row boats ($6.50 per hr.), outboards ($30 per hr.), and dockslips ($10-16 per night) at Bridge Bay Marina. Parts of Yellowstone Lake and some other lakes are limited to non-motorized boating; inquire at the Lake Village or Grant Village ranger stations for more advice.

OFF THE (EXTREMELY WELL) BEATEN PATH. Most visitors to Yellowstone never get out of their cars and miss out on the over 1200 mi. of trails in the park. Options for exploring Yellowstone's more pristine areas range from short dayhikes to extended backcountry trips. When planning a hike, pick up a topographical trail map ($8-9) at any visitors center and ask a ranger to describe forks in the trail. Allow extra time (at least 1hr.) in case you lose the trail as they are occasionally poorly marked. The fires of 1988 scarred on over a third of the park; hikers should consult rangers and maps on which areas are burned. Burned areas have less tree cover; hikers should equip themselves with hats, extra water, and sunscreen.

In addition to the self-guiding trails at major attractions, many worthwhile sights are only a few miles on other trails. In the Old Faithful area, the short flat hike to a spectacular cascade, **Fairy Falls,** offers a unique perspective on the geysers of the Midway Geyser basin. The trail begins in the parking lot marked Fairy Falls just south of Midway Geyser basin and is 5¼ mi. round-trip. The petrified trees at Specimen Ridge are accessible only by foot; the trail begins in the Yellowstone River Picnic Area and is a challenging hike, suitable for those comfortable with backcountry navigation. The trail to the top of **Mt. Washburn** is enhanced by an enclosed observation area and offers sweeping views of the park. This trail begins at Chittenden Rd. or Dunraven Pass parking areas and totals about 6 mi. round-trip. The free *Backcountry Trip Planner* and rangers can help plan more extended trips. Always consult with a ranger before heading off into the backcountry.

SCENIC DRIVE: NORTH FORK DRIVE

Linking Yellowstone National Park with Cody, WY, the **Buffalo Bill Cody** scenic byway, also known as U.S. 14/16/20, bridges the majestic peaks of the Absaroka mountains (pronounced *ab-SOR-ka*) with the sagebrush lands of the Wyoming plains. This 52 mi. drive winds through the canyon created by the North Fork of the Shoshone River and is spectacular as a departure from or entrance to Yellowstone. The high granite walls and sedimentary formations of the **Shoshone Canyon** are noticeable from the road, as is the smell of sulfur from the DeMaris springs located in the Shoshone River. Once the world's tallest dam, the **Buffalo Bill Dam Visitors**

Center and Reservoir celebrates the human desire to control the flow of water to fit human needs. (Visitors center: ☎527-6076. Open daily May-Sept. 8am-8pm.) Continuing west past the dam, **strange rock formations** created millions of years ago by lava flow from volcanic eruptions in the Absarokas dot the dusty hillsides. These rocks have odd names, such as Chimney Rock, the Slipper, the Old Woman and the Cabin, and Laughing Pig. Sagebrush and small juniper trees gradually lead into the thick pine cover of the **Shoshone National Forest,** the nation's first national forest. This area is known as the **Wapiti Valley** and is home to over 18 dude ranches. Wapiti is an Indian word for elk, and travelers should keep an eye out for wildlife of all kinds, including grizzlies. The **East Entrance** to Yellowstone National Park guards the west end of this road and is closed in winter.

GRAND TETON ☎307

When John Colter explored Wyoming's wilderness in the early 1800s, he found himself before a spectacular mountain range. The range's crowning glories were (and are) three craggy peaks—South Teton, Grand Teton and Mt. Teewinot—each over 12,000 feet. While many western peaks have miles of foothills gradually gaining elevation, these mountains rise straight up out of an idyllic valley. Later, solitary French mountain men attempted to make the rugged landscape more trapper-friendly, and so dubbed the mountains "Les Trois Tetons," French for "the three tits." When they found that the triple nipples had many smaller companions, they named the range "Les Grands Tetons." Now, the snowy heights of Grand Teton National Park delight hikers with miles of strenuous trails and steep rock faces.

ORIENTATION AND PRACTICAL INFORMATION

Hwy. 89 runs the length of the park, connecting Yellowstone to Jackson, and offers great views of the Tetons. A side road allows lake access and a closer look at the peaks between Jackson Lake Junction and Moose Junction. There are two entrance stations to the park, at Moose and at Moran Junction. It is possible to drive a stretch of Hwy. 89 without entering the park, thereby getting the view but not paying the fee. The park **entrance fee** is $20 per car, $10 per pedestrian or bicycle, and $15 per motorcycle. The pass is good for seven days in both the Tetons and Yellowstone.

Public Transit: Grand Teton Lodge Co. (☎733-2811) runs in summer from Colter Bay to Jackson Lake Lodge ($3 each way). Shuttles also run to the Jackson Hole airport (5 per day, $20) and Jackson (3 per day, $15).

Visitor Info: Moose Visitors Center (☎739-3399), Teton Park Rd., at the southern tip of the park, ½ mi. west of Moose Jct. Open early June to early Sept. 8am-7pm; early Sept. to mid-May 8am-5pm. **Jenny Lake Visitors Center** (☎739-3392), next to the Jenny Lake Campground. Open daily early June to early Sept. 8am-7pm, early Sept. to early Oct. 8am-5pm. **Colter Bay Visitors Center** (☎739-3594), on Jackson Lake in the northern part of the park. Open daily early June to early Sept. 8am-8pm; early May to mid-May and early Sept. to early Oct. 8am-5pm; late May to early June 8am-7pm. Visitors centers and campgrounds have free copies of the **Teewinot** newspaper which has info on special programs, hiking, camping and news. For general info, info on ranger-led activities, and a visitor's packet, contact **Park Headquarters** (☎739-3600) or write the **Superintendent,** Grand Teton National Park, P.O. Drawer 170, Moose WY 83012.

Info lines: Weather, ☎739-3611. **Wyoming Hwy. Info Center,** ☎733-1731. **Wyoming Dept. of Transportation,** ☎888-996-7623. **Road Report,** ☎336-6600 or 888-432-7623. **Backcountry Permits and River Info,** ☎739-3309.

Emergency: Sheriff's office, ☎733-2331. **Park dispatch,** ☎739-3300.

Medical Services: Grand Teton Medical Clinic, Jackson Lake Lodge (☎543-2514, after hrs. 733-8002). Open daily late May to mid-Oct. 10am-6pm. **St. John's Hospital,** 625 E. Broadway (☎733-3636), in Jackson.

Post Office: In Moose (☎733-3336), across from the Park HQ. Open M-F 9am-1pm and 1:30-5pm, Sa 11am-12:30pm. **ZIP code:** 83102. **Area code:** 307.

▓ CAMPGROUNDS AND BACKCOUNTRY CAMPING

To stay in the Tetons without emptying your savings account, find a tent and pitch it; call ☎739-3603 for camping info. The park service maintains five campgrounds, all first come, first served. Campsites are generally open mid-May to late Sept. or early Oct. (vehicle sites $12, bicycle campsites $3). Maximum length of stay is 14 days at all sites except Jenny Lake (7 day maximum stay). All have restrooms, cold water, fire rings, dump stations, and picnic tables. RVs are welcome in all but the Jenny Lake area, but only Colter Bay (sites $31) and Flagg Ranch sites have hook-ups. Large groups can go to Colter Bay and Gros Ventre; all others allow a maximum of six people and one vehicle per site. The 49 quiet, woodsy sites at **Jenny Lake** are among the most beautifully developed in the US. Mt. Teewinot towers 6000 ft. above tents pitched at the edge of the lake. These sites usually fill before 8am; get there early. **Lizard Creek,** closer to Yellowstone than the Tetons, has 60 spacious, secluded sites along the northern shore of Jackson Lake. The campsites fill up by about 2pm. While not exactly a wilderness experience, the 350 crowded sites at **Colter Bay** offer the most amenities, including $3.50 showers, a grocery store, a laundromat, and two restaurants. At **Signal Mountain,** 10 mi. south of Colter Bay, the 86 sites are a bit roomier and more secluded than at Colter Bay and are usually full by 10am. **Gros Ventre** is the biggest campground (360 sites, 5 group sites), located along the edge of the Gros Ventre River at the southern border of the park, convenient to Jackson. However, the Tetons are hidden by Blacktail Butte. The campsite rarely fills and is the best bet for late arrivals. (☎739-3516; Jan.-May 739-3473.)

To **backcountry camp** between Jan. 1 and May 15 in a mountain canyon or on the shores of a lake, make a reservation by submitting an itinerary and $15 to the **permit office.** (☎739-3309 or 739-3397; fax 739-3438. Or write Grand Teton National Park, Moose HQ, Attn.: Permits, P.O. Drawer 170, Moose WY 83012.) After May 15, three-fourths of all backcountry spots are available first come, first served; get a free permit up to 24hr. before setting out at the Moose, Colter Bay (permit office open daily 8am-6pm), or Jenny Lake visitors centers. The staff can also help plan routes and find campsites. Wood fires are not permitted above 7000 ft. in the backcountry and generally not at lower elevations; be sure to check with rangers before singing 'round the campfire. Snow often remains at high-elevation campsites into July, and the weather can become severe (deadly to those unprepared for it) any time of the year. Taking severe weather gear is advised.

▓ ACCOMMODATIONS AND FOOD

The Grand Teton Lodge Co. runs all indoor accommodations in the park. (Reservations ☎543-2811 or 800-628-9988; or write **Reservations Manager,** Grand Teton Lodge Co., P.O. Box 240, Moran 83013. Deposits often required.) Most lodges are pricey, but there are two options for affordable, rustic cabins at Colter Bay, open late May to early Oct. **Colter Bay Tent Cabins** are the cheapest, but potentially the coldest. The cabins are charming but primitive log and canvas shelters with dusty floors, wood-burning stoves, tables, and bunks. Sleeping bags, cots, and blankets are available for rent. (☎543-2828. Office open early June to early Sept. 24hr. Tent cabins $31 for 2; $3 per additional person. Restrooms and $3.50 showers nearby.) **Colter Bay Log Cabins** maintains 208 quaint log cabins near Jackson Lake. The cabins with shared baths are probably the best deal in the entire Jackson Hole area; book early. The friendly staff dispenses sage advice about local hikes and excursions. (☎543-2828. Open late May to late Sept. 2-person cabins with semi-private bath from $32, with private bath $66-94; 2-room cabins with bath $97-120.)

The best way to eat in the Tetons is to bring your own food. Non-perishables are available at **Dornan's General Store** in Moose (☎733-2415; open daily 8am-7pm). Jackson has **Albertson's** supermarket, 105 Buffalo Way, at the intersection of W. Broadway and Hwy. 22 (☎733-5950; open daily 6am-midnight). The **Chuck Wagon Restaurant,** in Colter Bay, serves breakfast (buffet $7), lunch, and dinner, and will cook your catch of the day for $10. (☎543-1077. Open M-F 7:30-10am, 11:30am-2pm, 5:30-9pm.) The connected **Cafe Court** has affordable cafeteria-style food. (Open daily 6:30am-10pm; breakfast served until 11am. Sandwiches and salads $3-7.)

👁 🏔 SIGHTS AND ACTIVITIES

While Yellowstone wows visitors with geysers and mudpots, the Grand Tetons boast some of the most scenic mountains in the US, if not the world. The youngest range in North America (2-3 million years old), the Tetons stand 13,771 ft. high, almost without foothills, providing vistas more weathered peaks lack. The steep rock faces draw scores of climbers, but less-experienced hikers can still experience the beauty of the Teton's backcountry. A number of self-guiding trails allow even novices to get off the beaten path for a few hours.

HIKING. All visitors centers provide pamphlets about the day hikes and sell many guides and maps ($3-10). Ranger also lead informative hikes; check the *Teewinot* or at visitors centers for more info. Before hitting the trail or planning extended hikes, be sure to check in at the ranger station, as trails at higher elevations may still be snow-covered. Prime hiking season does not begin until well into July during years with heavy snow.

The **Cascade Canyon Trail** begins on the far side of tranquil Jenny Lake and follows Cascade Creek through some spectacular terrain. The **Hidden Falls Waterfall** is located ½ mi. up and views of Teewinot, Mt. Owen, and Grand Teton are visible to the south. Hikers with more stamina can continue upwards towards **Inspiration Point** (another ¾ mi.), but only the lonely can trek 6¾ mi. further to **Lake Solitude**, which stands at 9035 ft. Expanded trail guides for Cascade Canyon are available for a small fee at visitors centers. The trail can be reached by following part of the 6.6 mi trail around Jenny Lake or by taking one of the shuttles offered by **Teton Boating**. (☎733-2703. *Boats leave from Jenny Lake visitors center every 20min. beginning at 8am; last boat returns from other side at 6pm. One-way $4, ages 7-12 $3; round-trip $5/$3.50.*)

The 3¼ mi. trail to **Taggert Lake** is another self-guided hike. This moderate trail winds through a broad spectrum of plant life, including a recently burned area, and emerges for spectacular views of the mountains at the lake. The trail begins in the Taggert Lake parking area, 3 mi. north of Moose.

The 4½ mi. walk from Colter Bay to **Hermitage Point** offers a unique perspective on Jackson Lake and is a prime spot for wildlife spotting. Leave the crowds behind and hike the **Amphitheater Lake Trail,** beginning just south of Jenny Lake at the Lupine Meadows parking lot, which takes you 4¾ breathtaking mi. to one of the park's glacial lakes. (Lupines, the purple, clumpy flowers visible all along the roads throughout the park, bloom June-July.) **Static Peak Divide,** a steep 15½ mi. loop trail up 4020 ft. from the Death Canyon trailhead (4½ mi. south of Moose Visitors Center), offers some of the best vistas in the park. The Death Canyon area is prime for longer two- to three-day hikes. Two areas offer short, flat walks that explore the history of the area. The ½ mi. loop at **Menor's Ferry** leads to a historic cabin and ferry, dating back to frontier times. In the same parking area, the **Chapel of the Transfiguration** is a tiny church with an enormous view and a pair of charming stained glass windows. The **Cunningham Cabin Trail** relives the history of cattle ranching in the valley. The trail begins 6 mi. south of Moran; the walk is ¾ mi. to the cabin.

CLIMBING. Two climbing guide companies offer more extreme backcountry adventures, including four-day packages that let beginners work their way up to the famed Grand Teton. **Jackson Hole Mountain Guides and Climbing School,** 165 N. Glenwood St. in Jackson, offers a one-day beginner course for $80; prices escalate rapidly from there. (☎733-4979 or 800-239-7642. *Reservations necessary.*) **Exum Mountain Guides** has similar classes and rates. (☎733-2297. *Reservations necessary.*)

BOATING, FISHING, AND BIKING. Boating is permitted on a number of lakes; Jackson, Jenny, and Phelps Lakes allow motorboats; hand-powered crafts are allowed on most lakes. Permits for boating can be obtained at the Moose or Colter Bay visitors centers. (*Motorized boats $10 for 7 days, $20 annual; non-motorized $5/$10.*)

Grand Tetons Lodge Company rents boats at Colter Bay and Jenny Lake and offers scenic cruises of Jackson Lake, leaving from Colter Bay. (☎543-3100. Cruises $14, ages 3-11 $7. Canoes $9 per hr.; motor boats $18 per hr.) **Fishing** is permitted within the park with a Wyoming license, available at Moose Village Store, Signal Mountain Lodge, Colter Bay Marina, and Flagg Ranch Village. ($6 per day for non-residents.) A number of companies offer float trips on the Snake River within the park, including the **Grand Teton Lodge Company.** (☎543-3100. $38, ages 6-11 $19.) **Mountain biking** is a popular activity on roads in the park, but is strictly forbidden on hiking trails.

Outdoor equipment rentals can be found both in Jackson and at Moose Village. **Adventure Sports,** a division of Dornan's in Moose, rents bikes and provides advice on where to bike. (☎733-3307. Open daily 9am-6pm; spring and fall hrs. vary. Mountain bikes from $7 per hr. for a basic model. Credit card or deposit required.) **Snake River Angler,** next to Dornan's, rents spinning rods for $10 per day. (☎733-3699. Open daily 9am-7pm, off-season 9am-6pm.) Next door, **Moosely Seconds** rents climbing equipment. (Open daily 8am-9pm; climbing shoes $6-10, crampons $10, ice axes $6, trekking poles $4.)

WINTER ACTIVITIES. In the **winter,** all hiking trails and the unploughed sections of Teton Park Rd. are open to **cross-country skiers.** Pick up winter info at Moose or Colter Bay visitors centers. Naturalists lead free **snowshoe hikes** from the Moose Visitors Center. (☎739-3399. Jan.-Mar. Th-Tu at 1pm. Snowshoes distributed free.) **Snowmobiling** along the park's well-powdered trails and up into Yellowstone is a noisy but popular winter activity; pick up a free permit at Moose Visitors Center (Moose is *the* visitors center in the winter) and grab a map and guide at the Jackson Chamber of Commerce. For about $100 per day, you can rent snowmobiles at **Signal Mt. Lodge, Flagg Ranch Village,** or in **Jackson.** A well-developed snowmobile trail runs from Moran to Flagg Ranch, and numerous other snowmobiling opportunities exist in the valley. The Colter Bay and Moose parking lots are available for parking in the winter. All **campgrounds** close in winter, but **backcountry snow camping** (only for those who know what they're doing) is allowed with a permit bought from the Moose Visitors Center. Before making plans, consider that temperatures regularly drop below -20°F. Be sure to carry extreme weather clothing and check with a ranger station for current weather conditions and avalanche danger; many early trappers froze to death in the 10 ft. drifts.

JACKSON   ☎307

Jackson Hole describes the valley bounded by the Teton and Gros Ventre ranges. Nearby Jackson is a ski village gone ballistic—its downtown streets are lined with Gap and Banana Republic shops, chic restaurants, faux-Western bars, and wooden-plank sidewalks. Home to 5000 permanent residents, a dynamic mix of money and energy, international tourists and locals, people-watchers and nature lovers, Jackson is a truly cosmopolitan place. Although a sliver of the area's beauty can be seen from town, striking out into the nearby Tetons or onto the Snake River—whether by foot, boat, horse, or llama—yields a richer experience.

🏔📑 ORIENTATION AND PRACTICAL INFORMATION. The center of downtown Jackson is at the intersection of Broadway St. and Cache St. and is marked by the **Town Sq. Park.** The majority of shops and restaurants are within a four-block radius of this intersection. South of town, W. Broadway becomes U.S. 191/89/26 at the intersection with Hwy. 22. To get to **Teton Village;** take Hwy. 22 to Hwy. 390, also called Teton Village Rd., just before the town of Wilson. A bumpy, winding and sometimes gravel road connects Teton Village with Moose and the park. North of town, Cache St. becomes Hwy. 89, leading to Grand Teton National Park.

Public Transportation: Jackson START runs buses 6:15am-10pm. (☎733-4521. 50¢ in town, $1 on village road, $2 to Teton Village; over 60 half-price, under 9 free.) **Jackson Hole Express** (☎733-1719 or 800-652-9510) runs to the Salt Lake City airport (5½hr., $45) and the Idaho Falls airport (2hr., $20). Reservations are required. **Leisure Sports,** 1075 Hwy. 89, has the best deals on camping and backpacking rentals. (☎733-3040. Hrs. vary by season. Tents $7.50-25, sleeping bags $5-8, backpacks $3.50-7.50.) **Jackson Hole and Greater Yellowstone Information Center,** 532 N. Cache St. is a crucial stop for visitor info. (Open daily early June to early Sept. 8am-7pm; in winter M-F 8am-5pm, Sa-Su 10am-2pm.) For guided trips to nearby parks, **Grayline Tours** offers 8hr. tours of Grand Teton ($50 including boat ride; leaves Jackson at 8:30am on M, W, Sa and returns at 4pm), and an 11hr. tour of Yellowstone National Park's lower loop ($60; leaves Jackson at 7:30am on Tu, Th, Su, and returns at 6:30pm). (☎733-4325 or 800-443-6133. Office takes calls daily 7am-7pm. Tour picks up at hotels. Call for reservations.) **Post Office:** at Powderhorn and Maple Way. (☎733-3650. Open M-F 7:30am-5:30pm, Sa 10am-2pm.) **ZIP code:** 83002. **Area code:** 307.

⌐ ACCOMMODATIONS. Jackson draws hordes of visitors year-round, making rooms expensive and hard to get without reservations. ◪**The Hostel X (HI-AYH),** 12 mi. northwest of Jackson in Teton Village, lets skiers and others stay close to the slopes without mortgaging their home. More ski lodge than hostel, each room has a private bath and maid service. Other amenities include a lounge with TVs and games and a ski-waxing room. The hostel is also a close stumble from the Mangy Moose (see **Nightlife,** below) next door. (☎733-3415. 4 beds in dorm rooms; 20 rooms with king-size beds. $45 for 1-2 people, non-members $55; $60 for 3-4. In winter, $47 for 1-2; $60 for 3-4; no member discount.) A cheaper option is **The Bunkhouse,** 215 N. Cache St., in the basement of the Anvil Motel. (☎733-3668. Showers, coin laundry, and ski storage. Beds $22.) Rooms are costly during peak months, but **The Pioneer,** 325 N. Cache St., is a bargain during the spring. It offers lovely rooms with microwaves, refrigerators, free local calls, and hand-crafted quilts. (☎733-3673 or 800-550-0330. Singles peak at $90 in the summer; early Apr. to mid-May $50.)

For those willing to rough it, the primitive campgrounds in Grand Teton National Park and the **Bridger-Teton National Forest** are the cheapest accommodations around. **Gros Ventre** campground (see p. 655) is only a 10min. drive from Jackson. There are 45 developed campgrounds in the Bridger-Teton National Forest, including a number on U.S. 26 west of Jackson. The publication **The Bridge,** available at the visitors center in Jackson, has more info, as do the National Forest offices. (Some have water, no showers. Free-$15.) Dispersed camping is free within the national forest; campers must stay at least 200 ft. from water and 100 ft. from roads or trails. Consult with a ranger before attempting this as some areas may be restricted.

◻ FOOD. Jackson has dozens of restaurants, but few are suited for the budget traveler. Get your buns into **The Bunnery,** 130 N. Cache St., and pick up some of their special O.S.M. bread (made of oats, sunflower, and millet). (☎733-5474. Open daily 7am-10pm. Sandwiches $5-8.) For a homeopathic remedy, or just a healthy bite to eat, try the **Harvest Bakery and Cafe,** 130 W. Broadway, a New Age jack-of-all-trades. Stop in for breakfasts priced under $4.25, soup and salad ($4), fresh pastries ($2), and $3-4 smoothies. (☎733-5418. Cafe open 7am-3pm. Bakery open daily 7am-8pm; in winter 8am-6pm.) At **Bubba's,** 515 W. Broadway, generous portions of ribs and sides (full rack $8.75) stick to your ribs. (☎733-2288. Open daily 7am-10pm.) Locals and tourists alike frequent **LeJay's 24 Hour Sportsmen Cafe,** at the corner of Glenwood and Pearl, for authentic Western grub after the bars close. (☎733-3110. Open 24hr. Burgers and sandwiches with fries $4-6; breakfast special $3.25-8.) **Bagel Jax** and **Jamba Juice,** 145 and 135 N. Glenwood, combine creative sandwiches and nutritious smoothies for a healthy and filling meal. (☎733-9148 or 734-1084. Open daily 6:30am-6:00pm. Sandwiches $3-4; breakfast scramblers $2-3, smoothies $2-4.)

◪ OUTDOORS. Jackson puts on a good show, but the feature presentation here is the quality of outdoor adventure. World-class skiing, climbing, and whitewater all lie within minutes of Jackson, and the plethora of guiding companies can make anyone feel extreme. **Whitewater rafting** on the legendary Snake River is a popular activity. **Lone Eagle** runs 8 mi., 3hr. trips for a bargain price of $26. (☎800-321-3800 or 733-1090. Must find own transportation to meeting point at Hoback Junction. $31 includes lunch at Bubba's Barbecue. Reservations recommended.) **Mad River,** 1255 S. Hwy. 89, 2 mi. south of Town Sq., offers similar trips with the promise that their small boats mean big action. (☎733-6203 or 800-458-7238. $40.) During winter months, skiing enthusiasts flock to Jackson to experience pure Wyoming powder. **Jackson Hole Mountain Resort,** 12 mi. north of Jackson in Teton Village, has some of the best runs in the US, including the jaw-droppingly steep Corbet's Couloir. (☎733-2292. Open Dec. 4 to April 2. Lift tickets $51, seniors and under 14 $26.) Even after the snow melts, the **aerial tram** whisks tourists to the top of Rendezvous Mountain (elevation 10,450 ft.) for a panoramic view of the valley. (☎739-2753. Open daily May 26 to June 23 9am-5pm; June 24 to Sept. 4 9am-7pm; Sept. 5 to Sept. 24 9am-5pm. $12, seniors $13; ages 6-17 $5.) Located in the town of Jackson, **Snow King** offers less expensive and more relaxed skiing. (☎733-5200. Lift tickets full-day $30, half-day $20, night $14; juniors and seniors $20/$12/$9. $8 per hr.) Snow King also has summer rides to the summit for views of the Tetons. ($8, seniors $6, under 12 $6. Ride down $1.) Jackson Hole is a prime locale for **cross-country skiing;** the knowledgeable folks at **Skinny Skis,** 65 W Delorney in downtown Jackson, can point you in the right direction. (☎733-6094. Rentals with skis, boots, and poles full-day $12, half-day $8.)

🔊🍽 **ENTERTAINMENT AND NIGHTLIFE.** When the sun goes down on a long day of skiing, hiking, or rafting, Jackson has bars, concerts, and festivals to suit all tastes. Catch cowboy fever at the **JH Rodeo,** held at the fairgrounds, two blocks west of the Snow King ski area. (☎733-2805. Late May to early Sept. W and Sa 8pm. $9, reserved tickets $11, families $28, ages 4-12 $7.) Over Memorial Day weekend, the town bursts its britches as tourists, locals, and nearby Native American tribes pour in for the dances and parades of **Old West Days.** World-class orchestras roll into Teton Village each summer for the **Grand Teton Music Festival.** (☎733-1128. Festival orchestra concerts F-Sa 8pm; $27, students $13.50. Spotlight concerts Th 8pm; $20/$10. Chamber music concerts Tu-W 8pm; $15/$7.50. Open rehearsal F 9:30am; $5/$2.50.) The **Jackson Hole Fall Arts Festival** (☎733-3216; mid-Sept.) showcases artists, musicians, and dancers in a week-long celebration.

Ski bums and bunnies complete their ski experience at **The Mangy Moose,** in Teton Village at the base of Jackson Hole Ski Resort, a quintessential après-ski bar. Things are a bit more sedate during the rest of the year, but in winter, this is the place to be. The eclectic but sporadic entertainment line-up has featured everything from Blues Traveler to Dr. Timothy Leary. (☎733-4913. Dinner daily 5:30-10pm; bar open nightly 11pm-2am. Cover $3-15.) Live music and good beer make the **Stagecoach Bar,** 7 mi. west of Jackson on Rte. 22 in Wilson, a popular nightspot, particularly on Disco Night (Th). (☎733-4407. Open daily 11am-2am. Live bands Sa and Su.) Local microbrews can be found at the **Snake River Brewery,** 265 S. Millward St., Wyoming's first brew-pub. One particularly powerful beer is the "Zonkers Stout," otherwise known as penzoil (pints $3, pitchers $10). (☎739-2337. Open daily noon-1am; food is served until 11pm.)

SCENIC DRIVE: CENTENNIAL SCENIC DRIVE

Passing through some of the most beautiful country on earth, this all-day drive is like a vacation unto itself. For 162 mi., the Centennial Scenic Byway passes by the high peaks, roaring whitewater rivers, and broad wind-swept plains of western Wyoming. The drive is open all year but may occasionally close due to snow.

Begin your drive in the small frontier town of **Dubois,** home of the **National Bighorn Sheep Interpretive Center,** 907 W. Ramshorn (☎455-3429; open Th-M 9am-5pm). As you leave town on Rte. 26, the crumbly breccia of the volcanic Absaroka mountains will become visible to the north. The high towering mountain is **Ramshorn Peak** at 11,920 ft. The road follows the **Wind River,** a favorite swimming spot for moose, especially early in the morning. Aspen groves are found along the river and the road. A "grove" of these delicate trees is actually just one tree with many different branches rising up from a root system that can go for miles. The road gently rises through a conifer forest and reaches **Togwotee Pass,** elevation 9544 ft.

As the road begins to descend, the famed skyline of the Teton mountain range becomes visible. The highest peak is the Grand Teton; stop at the Teton Range Overlook for a peak-finder. After entering **Grand Teton National Park** (see p. 654), the road winds through the flat plain of the Buffalo Fork River, a strikingly beautiful

ROCKY MOUNTAINS

contrast to the high peaks and mountain forests. This floodplain is the beginning of the wide and long valley known as Jackson Hole; early trappers referred to any high mountain valley as a Hole.

In the park, the road begins to follow the legendary Snake River, a mecca for whitewater enthusiasts. As you near **Jackson** (see p. 657), the National Elk Refuge, the winter home of some 10,000 elk, becomes visible to the east. The town of Jackson was once home to mountain men, explorers, and trappers, but today caters more to tourists. To escape Jackson, take U.S. 189/191 south. As the peaks of the Tetons grow small in your rear-view mirror, the Wind River Range appears on the horizon. The road enters the Green River Valley, which offers great views of the Winds. From here the highest peak in Wyoming is visible: **Gannet Peak,** elevation 13,804 ft. The drive ends in the tiny, rustic town of **Pinedale.**

CODY   ☎ 307

William F. "Buffalo Bill" Cody was more than a Pony Express rider, scout, and sportsman. He also started "Buffalo Bill's Wild West Show," an extravaganza that catapulted the image of the cowboy into the world's imagination. Cody's show traveled all over the US and Europe, attracting the attention of royalty and statesmen.

☎ PRACTICAL INFORMATION. Cody lies at the junction of Rte. 120, 14A, and 14/16/20. The town's main street is **Sheridan Ave.,** which turns into **Yellowstone Ave.** west of town. **Powder River Transportation** (☎800-442-3682) runs buses to Denver (17-19½hr., 2 per day, $79); Cheyenne (10-13hr., 2 per day, $63); and Billings (3hr., 1 per day, $27) from Daylight Donuts, 1452 Sheridan Ave. **Powder River Tours** offers guided daytrips through Yellowstone National Park and departs from several locations in town (☎527-6316; $60, 16 and under $30, seniors $54; reservations recommended). The **Chamber of Commerce Visitors Center** is at 836 Sheridan Ave. (☎587-2297. Open M-Sa 8am-6pm, Su 10am-3pm; off-season M-F 8am-5pm.) **Post Office:** 1301 Stampede Ave., from downtown take 13th St. north for about 1 mi. (☎527-7161. Open M-F 8am-5:30pm, Sa 9am-noon.) **ZIP code:** 82414. **Area code:** 307.

☎ ACCOMMODATIONS AND FOOD. Rates go up in the summertime, but a strip of reasonable motels lines **W. Yellowstone Ave.** The **Pawnee Hotel,** 1032 12th St., is just a block from downtown and has 18 unique rooms. (☎587-2239. Unique rooms $22-38.) **Buffalo Bill State Park** offers two **campgrounds** on the Buffalo Bill Reservoir with incredible views. The North Shore Bay campground (☎527-6274) is the better of the two, 9 mi. west of town on U.S. 14/16/20. The **North Fork Campground,** about 14 mi. west of town on U.S. 14/16/20, is a little less nice, but is still much more picturesque than those in town (☎527-6057; sites at both $9). The **Gateway Motel and Campground,** 203 Yellowstone Ave., has campsites with views of the surrounding hills. (☎587-2561. Open May-Sept. Showers and laundry. Campsites $12 for 2, $2 for each additional person, with water and electricity $16, full hook-up $18.)

Peter's Cafe and Bakery, at 12th St. and Sheridan Ave., fries up cheap breakfasts (three buttermilk pancakes $3) and stacks a meaty mountain-man sub and a meatless Calamity Jane Sub, for $3 apiece. (☎527-5040. Open daily 7am-8pm.) The **Irma Hotel and Restaurant,** 1192 Sheridan Ave., originally owned by Buffalo Bill and named after his daughter, has affordable lunch eats (buffet $7) and dinner if you choose carefully. The original cherrywood bar was sent as a gift from Queen Victoria. (☎587-4221. Open daily Apr.-Sept. 6am-10pm; Oct.-Mar. 6am-8pm.)

☎ SIGHTS. To this day, as numerous billboards proclaim, Cody *is* Rodeo and a visit to this cowboy town is your best chance to catch the sport. The Cody Nite Rodeo performs every night from June through Aug. at 8:30pm. (☎587-5155. Tickets $10-12, ages 7-12 $4-6.) Each year over the 4th of July weekend, the **Cody Stampede Professional Rodeo Cowboy Association Rodeo,** voted by the cowboys themselves as the best "large outdoor rodeo" in the world, rough-rides into town (☎587-5155; tickets $15; reserve ahead).

The **Buffalo Bill Historical Center,** 720 Sheridan Ave., known affectionately as the "Smithsonian of the West," contains four museums under one roof. **The Buffalo Bill Museum** documents the life of you-know-who; the **Whitney Gallery of Western Art** shows off Western paintings, including some Remingtons; the **Plains Indian Museum** contains several exhibits about its namesake group; and the **Cody Firearms Museum** holds the world's largest collection of American firearms. (☎587-4771. Open daily June-Sept. 7am-8pm, Oct. 8am-5pm; Nov.-Mar. Th-M 10am-5pm, Apr. 10am-5pm, May 8am-8pm. $10, students $6, seniors $6.50, ages 6-17 $4. Tickets good for 2 consecutive days.) **Rafting** trips on the Shoshone provide more energetic diversions. To make arrangements, call **Wyoming River Trips,** 1701 Sheridan Ave., at Rte. 120 and 14. (☎587-6661 or 800-586-6661. Open May-Sept. Easy 2hr. trip $18, half-day trip $45.)

BUFFALO AND SHERIDAN ☎307

Away from the beaten path of tourists heading to Yellowstone, these two small towns offer up some authentic western flavor. Real ranchers and cowboys walk the historic streets of Buffalo and Sheridan. Located at the magic place where prairies rise up into mountains, Buffalo and Sheridan make perfect base-camps for travelers venturing into the wilds of the Bighorns.

BUFFALO

Situated at the crossroads of I-90 and I-25, Buffalo lies appreciably close to the **scenic byway U.S. 16.** Before heading for the mountains, however, absorb some Old West character in the elegant rooms of the **Occidental Hotel,** 10 N. Main St., which opened its doors as the town hall in 1880 and, as the story goes, was won by the Smith Family in a 1917 poker game. The hotel was the setting for Owen Wister's western novel, *The Virginian.* (☎684-0451. Open in summer M-Sa 10am-5pm. $2.)

In Buffalo, budget motels line **Main St. (Rte. 87)** and **Fort St.** The friendly management at the **Mountain View Motel and Campground,** 585 Fort St., keeps appealing pine cabins with TV, A/C, and heating. (☎684-2881. Showers and laundry. Cabins $46; $35 in winter; up to six people in big cabin with kitchenette $78/$50; campsites $12, full hook-up for 2 $18.) A few doors down, the **Z-Bar Motel** has TVs with HBO, refrigerators, and A/C. (☎684-5535 or 800-341-8000. Singles $43; doubles $47; Nov.-Apr. $34/37; kitchen $6 extra. Reservations recommended.)

Tom's Main Street Diner, 41 N. Main St., is a great little eatery downtown. Lunch specials ($4-5.75, including beverage) and bread pudding with whipped cream ($2.25) are best. (☎684-7444. Open M and W-Sa 5:30am-2pm, Su 8am-1pm.) **Dash Inn,** 620 E. Hart St., offers great chicken, ribs, and Texas Toast for $6-9. (☎684-7930. Open Tu-Su 11am-9:30pm; in winter M-Sa 11am-8pm.)

There is no bus service to Buffalo; **Greyhound** (☎674-6188) goes to nearby Sheridan and Gillette. **Alabam's,** 421 Fort St., sells topographical maps ($4); hunting, fishing, and camping supplies; and **fishing licenses** (1-day $6). (☎684-7452. Open daily roughly 7am-6pm.) The **Buffalo Chamber of Commerce Visitors Center,** 55 N. Main St. has info. (☎684-5544 or 800-227-5122. Open June-Aug. M-F 8am-6pm, Sa-Su 10am-4pm; Sept.-May M-F 8am-5pm.) The **US Forest Service Offices,** 1425 Fort St., sells a map of the area for $4. (☎684-1100. Open M-F 8am-4:30pm.) **Post Office:** 193 S. Main St. (☎684-7063. Open M-F 8am-5pm, Sa 10am-noon.) **ZIP code:** 82834. **Area code:** 307.

SHERIDAN

Larger than its counterpart to the south, Sheridan still manages to capture a true Wyoming feeling with a historic downtown where professionals and cowboys rub elbows. About 10 mi. south of **scenic byway U.S. 14/14A,** a winding route marked by steep drops (cars with trailers, RVs, and buses are not recommended on 14A), spectacular mountain views and never-ending prairie are visible. **King's Saddlery and Cowboy Museum,** 184 N. Main St. in the building behind their main store, ropes 'em in with over 550 remarkably crafted, award-winning saddles on display. Watch as ropes and saddles are made in their warehouse. Each saddle takes four to six weeks to complete and can cost $1800-6000. (☎672-2702, 672-2755, or 800-443-8919.

Open M-Sa 8am-5pm. Free.) The **Trail End State Historic Site**, 400 Clarendon Ave., showcases the impressive mansion and gardens of rags-to-riches cattle baron and former governor John B. Kendrick. (☎674-4589. Open daily mid-May to Aug. 9am-6pm, Oct.-Dec. 1 and Apr. 1 to mid-May W-Su noon-4pm. $2 for non-residents, $1 for residents, under 18 free.)

Sheridan Inn, at 5th and Broadway, saw scores of colorful characters in its day; Buffalo Bill Cody used the porch as an audition room for cowpokes aspiring to his *Wild West Show*. (☎674-5440. Self-guided tours free. Guided tour $3, seniors $2, under 12 free; call ahead.) Locals flock to town several days a week for **polo** games (☎751-3802 for schedule and information; June to mid-Sept.). There are motels aplenty along Main St. and Coffeen Ave. The **Aspen Inn**, 1744 N. Main St., offers the best deal. (☎672-9064. Singles $31; doubles $38.) Kamping can be found at the **Sheridan KOA** with the typical KOA amenities: laundry, showers, water, pool, restaurant, video arcade, etc. Go south at Exit 20 off I-90, turn right at the Port of Entry, take an immediate right on Rte. 338 and go about ¾ mi. (☎674-8766. $15 for 2, water and electricity $19, full hook-up $22; Kabins $28. $2.50 for each additional person.) Camping is more rustic at **Connor Battlefield Campground**, which offers pit toilets, water, a river for fishing, and $4 sites. (In Ranchester, 14 mi. north of Sheridan; take Rte. 14 west at Exit 9 off I-90, turn left on to Gillette St. and follow the signs to the battlefield/campground.)

Round up some veggies at **Sanford's Grub Pub and Brewery**, 1 E. Alger Ave. This friendly eatery offers respite from the traditional steak-and-burgers Wyoming cuisine with nearly 40 sandwiches ($5.75-6.50), from the "Fat Albert" to the "Fonz-A-Relli," and 20 different salads ($2.50-6.25). (☎674-1722. Open daily 11am-10pm.) A real cowboy joint, The **Mint Bar**, 151 Main St., has pleased customers since 1907. (☎674-9696. Open M-Sa 8am-2am.)

Powder River buses leave twice daily for Billings (2hr., $27) and Cheyenne (8hr., $51) from the Texaco station at the Evergreen Inn, 580 E. 5th St. (☎674-6188. Terminal open daily 3am-11:30pm.) The **visitors center** (☎672-2485 or 800-453-3650) sits just off I-90 at Exit 23. The Sheridan **Ranger Station** is on the south end of town at 1969 S. Sheridan Ave, off Coffeen St. (☎672-0751; open M-F 8am-4:30pm). **Post Office:** 101 E. Laucks St. (☎672-0713. Open M-F 7:30am-5:30pm, Sa 8am-noon.) **ZIP code:** 82801. **Area code:** 307.

BIGHORN MOUNTAINS   ☎307

The **Bighorn National Forest** may be one of the best kept secrets in the Rocky Mountains; it is relatively uncrowded and offers great hiking and wildlife viewing. The Bighorns erupt from the hilly pasture land of northern Wyoming, a dramatic backdrop to grazing cattle, sprawling ranch houses, and valleys full of wildflowers. Visitors can hike through the woods or follow **scenic highways U.S. 14/14A** in the north and **U.S. 16** in the south to waterfalls, layers of prehistoric rock, and views above the clouds. The **Medicine Wheel** on U.S. 14A is a mysterious 80 ft. wide stone formation at 10,000 ft. dating from around AD 1300; prepare for a 3 mi. round-trip hike from where the dirt road off the highway ends. This site is sacred to 89 Native American tribes and several people pray there each day. **Cloud Peak Wilderness** offers sheer solitude. Registration at major trailheads is required to enter the Cloud Peak area. The most convenient access to the wilderness area is from the trailheads off U.S. 16, around 20 mi. west of Buffalo. From the **Hunter Corrals Trailhead**, move to beautiful **Seven Brothers Lake**, 3 mi. off U.S. 16 on Rd. 19 (13 mi. west of Buffalo on U.S. 16), an ideal base for day-hikes into the high peaks beyond. You can also enter the wilderness area on U.S. 14/14A to the north. To get to the top of 13,175 ft. Cloud Peak, most hikers enter at **West Tensleep Trailhead**, accessible from the town of **Tensleep** on the western slope, 55 mi. west of Buffalo on U.S. 16. Tensleep was so named because it took the Sioux ten sleeps to travel from there to their main winter camps. Check with a forest office to find out about more out-of-the-way treks, and always check on local conditions with a ranger before any hike. A listing of all the Bighorn's attractions along with other helpful information and a map of the area can be found in *Bighorn Bits and Pieces*, available at all of the visitors centers.

Ranger stations can be found in Buffalo (see p. 661), Lovell at 604 E. Main St. (☎548-6541; open M-F 8am-4:30pm), and Sheridan (see p. 661), as well as within the park. The Burgess Junction Visitors Center, off U.S. 14 about halfway into the area, houses loads of great info and a theater with several films on the surroundings (open daily mid-May to mid-Sept. 9am-5pm). The Bighorn Canyon Visitor's Center on Rte. 14A in Lovell shows movies on the Medicine Wheel and can help out if the Lovell station is closed. (☎548-2251. Open daily in-season 8am-6pm; off-season 8:30am-5pm.) Campgrounds fill the forest. Doyle Campground, near a fish-rich creek, has 19 sites ($6) and toilets, but no water. (Drive 26 mi. west of Buffalo on U.S. 16 and south 6 mi. on Hazelton Rd./County Rd. 3—it's a rough ride.) There is no fee to camp at the uncrowded Elgin Park Trailhead, 16 mi. west of Buffalo off U.S. 16, which promises good fishing along with parking and toilets. Off U.S. 14 (roughly 27 mi. in from I-90 in the east), the Sibley Lake Campground is one of several nice campgrounds in the northern half of the park ($10, with electricity $13; wheelchair access). If Sibley is crowded, Tie Flume and Dead Swede (both $9) are great campgrounds off Rte. 14 about 10 mi. south of the Burgess Jct. Visitors Center. Many other campgrounds line Rte. 14 and 16 and the map in *Bighorn Bits and Pieces* will guide the way. For reservations within the park, call ☎877-444-6777. Campgrounds rarely fill up in the Bighorns, but if they do, or if you're looking to get away from civilization altogether, free dispersed camping is permitted at least 100 yd. from the road. For more information call ☎672-0751. Area code: 307.

DEVILS TOWER ☎307

A Native American legend tells of seven sisters who were playing with their little brother when the boy turned into a bear and began to chase them. Terrified, the girls ran to a tree stump and prayed for help. The stump grew high into the sky and the girls became the stars of the Big Dipper. Others tell of a core of fiery magma that shot up without breaking the surface 60 million years ago, and of centuries of wind, rain, and snow that eroded the surrounding sandstone, leaving a stunning spire. Still others, not of this world, have used the stone obelisk as a landing strip *(Close Encounters of the Third Kind)*. The massive column that figures so prominently in the myths of Native Americans, geologists, and space aliens is the centerpiece of Devils Tower National Monument in northeastern Wyoming ($8 per car, $3 per person on bike, foot, or motorcycle; free map on entry.)

Devils Tower is considered one of the best technical rock climbing sites in North America, and scaling the monument's 1280 ft. is a feat indeed. Native Americans, on the other hand, consider the tower a sacred site and would rather rock climbing were banned. A semi-compromise reached in 1995 calls for a voluntary refrain from climbing in the month of June—the most sacred time because of the solstice. The park has reached a level of 85% compliance with this policy.

Read about the rock and register to climb at the visitors center, 3 mi. from the entrance. (☎467-5283, ext. 20. Open daily late-May to Sept. 8am-8pm; Mar.-Apr. and Oct.-Nov. usually 9am-4:45pm.) Cool climbing demos are given outside the visitors center (May, July and Aug.; call for times). For more horizontally-oriented climbers, there are several hiking trails; the most popular, the paved 1.3 mi. Tower Trail, loops the monument and provides great views. The Red Beds Trail, a 3 mi. loop, takes hikers up and around the bright red banks of the Belle Fourche River. Hikers can opt for a longer hike by connecting with the shorter Valley View Trail (0.6 mi.) for a flat walk through the prairie dog town and the South Side Trail (0.6 mi.), which climbs back to the bluffs of the Red Beds Trail. Ask a ranger to identify leafy spurge and poison ivy; they irritate the eyes and skin. The park maintains a campground near the red banks of the Belle Fourche River. (Open roughly Apr.-Oct.; call to be sure. Water, bathrooms, grills, picnic tables, and lots of noise-making prairie dogs; no showers. Sites $12.) The best camping deal around is at the Devils Tower View Store Campground on Rte. 24, a few miles before the monument. Though there's not much shade, there's a great view of the monument and an inexpensive restaurant next door. (Open May-Sept. Water and nice port-o-potties. Donation requested.) To reach the monument from I-90, take U.S. 14, 25 mi. north to Rte. 24. Area code: 307.

ROCKY MOUNTAINS

CASPER ☎ 307

From 1841 to 1866, some 350,000 pioneers passed through Casper on famed routes like the Oregon Trail. This proliferation of travelers earned Casper the moniker "Crossroads of the West," and Casper continues this tradition today, hosting some of the hordes of tourists en route to Yellowstone, the Black Hills, and elsewhere. Stalwartly midwestern in atmosphere, Casper has managed to escape the hokey Western commercialism that overruns much of the area.

🛈 PRACTICAL INFORMATION. Powder River Transportation Services (☎266-1904, 265-2353 or 800-433-2093), at I-25 and Center St. in the Parkway Plaza Hotel, sends buses to Cheyenne (4hr., 2 per day, $31) and Denver (7hr., 2 per day, $47). Office open M-F 6am-8pm, Sa 6-11am and 3:30-4:30pm, Su 6-7:30am and 3:30-4:30pm. **Casper Area Convention and Visitors Bureau:** 500 N. Center St. (☎234-5311 or 800-852-1889; open daily M-F 8am-5pm). **Post office:** 411 N. Forest Dr. (☎266-4000; open M-F 8:30am-5pm, Sa 9am-noon). **ZIP code:** 82609. **Area code:** 307.

🍴 ACCOMMODATIONS AND FOOD. Convenient to the interstate, the **Showboat National 9 Inn,** 100 W. F St., has spacious rooms and free continental breakfast. (☎235-2711 or 800-524-9999. Singles $34; doubles $41.) **Fort Casper Campground,** 4205 Ft. Caspar Rd., is a friendly community of RVers, but tent sites are available. (☎234-3260. Free showers and laundry. Sites for 2 people $12, $60 per week; full hook-up $17. 10% AAA discount.)

Locals swear by **Granny's Eastside Diner,** 1705 E. 2nd St., for breakfasts ($3-5), burgers ($5), and shakes ($3). Dinner specials are a good bargain; fried chicken dinners range from $3-6. (☎234-4204. Open M-F 6:30am-9pm, Sa-Su 6:30am-10pm.) Get the local scoop with your coffee at the **Blue Heron,** 201 E. 2nd St., in the Atrium Plaza. (☎265-3774. Open M-F 8am-6pm, Sa 9am-4pm.) **Alpenglow Natural Foods,** 109 E. 2nd St., is a combination health food store and deli that serves organic smoothies, soups, and sandwiches. (☎234-4196. Open M-W 9am-6pm, Th-Sa 9am-8pm. Soup and sandwich $5.)

📷 SIGHTS. Relive the pioneer experience at **Fort Caspar,** where pioneers crossed the North Platte River and cavalrymen prepared for wars with Native Americans. The fort sponsors re-enactments in June, July, and Dec. (☎235-8462. Open M-Sa 8am-7pm, Su noon-7pm. Free.) The **Nicolayson Art Museum,** 400 E. Collins Dr., called the "Nic," exhibits Wyoming and world artwork and houses a children's art discovery center. (☎235-5247. Open Tu-W, F-Sa 10am-5pm, Th 10am-8pm, Su noon-4pm.) The real fun, however, is on the 3rd floor in the kid-orientated **Science Adventure Center.** (Open Tu-F noon-5pm, Sa 1-5pm. Admission to both museums $3, ages 2-12 $2.) The **Central Wyoming Fair and Rodeo,** 1700 Fairgrounds Rd. (☎235-5775), gets excited about livestock in mid-July.

CHEYENNE ☎ 307

Originally the name of the Native American tribe that inhabited the region, "Cheyenne" was considered a prime candidate for the name of the Wyoming Territory. The moniker was struck down by vigilant Senator Sherman, who pointed out that the pronunciation of Cheyenne closely resembled that of the French word *chienne*, meaning, er, "bitch." Once one of the fastest growing frontier towns, Cheyenne has tried to maintain its Old Western image through simulated gunfights and rodeos, but most of its charm is found in the historical downtown area.

🛈 PRACTICAL INFORMATION. Greyhound, 222 Deming (☎634-7744), off I-80, makes daily trips to Salt Lake City (9hr., 4 per day, $74); Chicago (19hr., 4 per day, $128); Laramie (1hr., 4 per day, $14); Rock Springs (5hr., 4 per day, $55); and Denver (3-5hr., 5 per day, $19-26). Station open 24hrs. **Powder River Transportation** (☎634-7744), in the Greyhound terminal, honors Greyhound passes and buses daily to Rapid City (10hr., 1 per day, $65); Casper (4hr., 2 per day, $36); and Billings (11½hr., 2 per day, $70). For local jaunts, flag down one of the shuttle buses provided by the

Cheyenne Transit Program (☎637-6253; buses run M-F 6:30am-6:30pm; fare $1). **Cheyenne Area Convention and Visitors Bureau:** 309 W. Lincolnway (☎778-3133 or 800-426-5009), just west of Capitol Ave. **Domestic Violence and Sexual Assault Line:** ☎637-7233. 24hr. **Internet Access: Laramie County Public Library,** 2800 Central Ave. (☎634-3561. Open M-Th 10am-9pm, F-Sa 10am-6pm; Sept. 15 to May 15 also Su 1pm-5pm. First come, first served 30min. slots available.) **Post office:** 4800 Converse Ave. (☎800-275-8777. Open M-F 7:30am-5:30pm, Sa 7am-1pm.) **ZIP code:** 82009. **Area code:** 307.

▛ ACCOMMODATIONS. It's easy to land a cheap room here among the plains and pioneers, unless your visit coincides with **Frontier Days,** the last full week of July (see **Festivals and Sights,** below). Beware of doubling rates and disappearing rooms in the days approaching this week. Many budget motels line Lincolnway (U.S. 30/16th St.). **Plains Hotel,** 1600 Central Ave., across from the I-180 on-ramp, one block away from the center of downtown, offers cavernous, retro hotel rooms with marble sinks and free cable. (☎638-3311. Singles $35; doubles $43. Additional $5 for the 3rd person in a single or a 5th in a double.) Holster your peacemaker before walking into the **Frontier Motel,** 1400 W. Lincolnway (☎634-7961), and grab a latté ($2) or an Italian soda ($2) at the front desk. The motel offers singles with a living room, large bathroom, free cable, and A/C. Call for prices. The **Guest Ranch Motel,** 1100 W. Lincolnway, rents large rooms with cable TV and free local calls. (☎634-2137. Singles $30; doubles $40; winter $25/$35.) Camp at **Curt Gowdy State Park,** 1319 Hynds Lodge Rd., 24 mi. west of Cheyenne on Rte. 210/Happy Jack Rd. This year-round park is centered around two lakes with excellent fishing, horseback riding (bring your own horse), and archery. (☎632-7946. $4 per night plus $5 entrance fee.)

▛ FOOD. Cheyenne has only a smattering of non-fast food restaurants that provide reasonably-priced cuisine. For a dirt-cheap breakfast or lunch, head to the **Dirtwood Cafe,** on the corner of 18th and Warren St. The cafe has a ma-and-pop atmosphere and the food to match. The menu features $1.25 cinnamon rolls, $4 burgers, and $2 slices of pie. (☎634-5304. Open M-F 7am-4pm.) Popular **Sanford's Grub and Pub,** 115 E. 17th St., is packed with every type of kitschy decor imaginable. In the giant menu (giant in both content and size) you'll find burgers, sandwiches, and salads for $6-7. Sanford's has 55 beers on tap, 108 bottled beers, and 132 different liquors. While you're waiting for your food, check out the game room downstairs. (☎634-3381. Open M-Sa 11am-12am, Su 11am-10pm.) **Lexie's Cafe,** 216 E. 17th St., has cheerful, cottage-style decor featuring wicker chairs and flowers. You'll find filling breakfast combos for $4-7, towering stacks of pancakes for $3, and burgers for $5. (☎638-8712. Open Tu-Th 7:30am-8pm, F-Sa 7:30am-9pm, Su 10:30am-2:30pm.) Relax with a light sandwich ($3-6) at **The Java Joint,** 1711 Carey Ave., or simply enjoy a latté. (☎638-7332. Open M-F 7am-4:30pm, Sa 8:30am-volume.)

▛▛▛ FESTIVALS, SIGHTS, AND NIGHTLIFE. During the last week in July, make every effort to attend the one-of-a-kind **Cheyenne Frontier Days,** nine days of non-stop Western hoopla. The town doubles in size as anyone who's anyone in the West comes to see the world's largest outdoor rodeo competition ($10-20) and partake of the free pancake breakfasts, parades, big-name country music concerts, and square dancing. (☎778-7222 or 800-227-6336. July 20-29, 2001.) During June and July, a "gunfight is always possible," and the entertaining **Cheyenne Gunslingers** (☎778-3133), at W. 16th and Carey, shoot each other M to F at 6pm (Sa high noon); their soda saloon sits at 218 W. 17th St. The **Wyoming State Capitol Building** (☎777-7220), at the base of Capitol Ave. on 24th St., features beautiful stained glass windows and a gorgeous rotunda under the gold-leaf dome. Pick up an informative brochure to find your way around (open M-F 8am-4:30pm). The **Old West Museum,** 4501 N. Carey Ave., in Frontier Park, houses a collection of Western memorabilia, including clothing and a surrey with its original fringe. Don't miss the rodeo video with hair-raising footage of cowboys riding (and falling off) bucking broncos. (☎778-7290. Open M-F 9am-5pm, Sa-Su 10am-5pm. $4, under 12 free.)

NAW, THAT LOOKS LIKE A... Instead of lame alphabet games or car bingo to pass the time, try a variation on the Native American vision quest. The odd formations of the Vedauwoo Rocks loom off in the distance from I-80 Exit 329 between Cheyenne and Laramie. The strange rocks look something like piles of gigantic pebbles, deliberately placed to form all kinds of shapes. Sort of like cloud watching, it's fun to try to identify different forms in the rock. The Vedauwoo rocks, pronounced *VEE-dah-voo*, take their name from the Arapaho word meaning "earthborn," and young men on vision quests placed great spiritual significance on what they saw in the formations. Today, the Vedauwoo Recreation Area offers over 100 wooded picnic sites, a campground, and hiking and mountain biking trails. ($3 per vehicle daily fee. Water and toilets, but no hook-ups. Sites $10.) The Summit Rest Area on I-80 just west of the Vedauwoo hands out info on the rocks and also displays the impressive Lincoln Monument, visible from the highway, on its grounds.

When you want to shoot stick in a haze of smoke, look for a pink elephant above **D.T.'s Liquor and Lounge,** 2121 E. Lincolnway. A patio bar and sun room offer an alternative to the dark interior. (☎632-3458. Open M-Sa 7am-2am, Su 10am-10pm.)

WEST OF CHEYENNE

THE SNOWY RANGE. Local residents call the forested granite mountains to the east of the Platte Valley the Snowy Mountain Range because snow falls nearly year-round on the higher peaks. Even when the snow melts, quartz outcroppings reflect the sun, creating an illusion of a snowy peak. Enjoy 25 downhill trails, cross-country trails, and a snowboard halfpipe at **Snowy Range Ski and Recreation Area**. Take Exit 311 off I-80 to Hwy. 130 west. (☎800-462-7669. Open mid-Dec. to Easter. Lift ticket $29, children 6-12 $15.) The Snowy Range is part of the **Medicine Bow National Forest,** spread over much of southeastern Wyoming. Cross-country skiing is popular in the winter months; campsites and hiking trails usually don't open until mid-July.

From late May to Nov., the **Snowy Range Scenic Byway (Rte. 130)** is cleared of snow, and cars can drive 27 mi. through seas of pine trees and around treeless mountains and picture-perfect crystal lakes to elevations nearing two vertical mi. Along the Byway, the **Libby Flats Observation Point** features a very short wildflower nature walk and an awe-inspiring view of the surrounding land. The challenging 4½ mi. **Medicine Bow Trail** starts at **Lewis Lake** and climbs to **Medicine Bow Peak** (12,013 ft.), the highest point in the forest. Nearby **Silver Lake** offers 17 first come, first served quiet, wooded camp sites close to the lake ($10). Two hiking trails depart from Silver Lake. A little west of the Centennial entrance, **Nash Fork** is another serene and untrammeled campground, with 27 well-shaded sites ($10). All 16 of the park's developed campgrounds are open only in summer and have toilets and water, but no hook-ups or showers. Reservations for some campgrounds are available (☎800-280-2267; $8.65 reservation fee). A drive up **Kennaday Peak** (10,810 ft.), at the end of Forest Rd. 215 off Rte. 130, leads to an impressive view.

Mountain biking is generally not allowed on the high country trails because of the frail alpine plants and the rocky terrain. However, you can bike or four-wheel drive on trails in the high country or on trails below about 10,000 ft. The 7 mi. **Corner Mountain Loop,** just west of Centennial Visitors Center (see below), is an exhilarating roller coaster ride through forest and small meadows. The visitors centers hand out maps of mountain biking trails. During the winter, mountain biking and hiking trails are used for cross-country skiing.

Visitors Centers: Brush Creek Visitors Center at the west entrance. The visitors center is also home to an outrageous number of hummingbirds that love to show themselves to curious visitors. In fact, there are so many hummingbirds that the ranger station feeds them more than 48 lb. of sugar every summer. (☎326-5562. Open daily mid-May to Oct. 8am-5pm.) **Centennial Visitors Center,** 1 mi. west of Centennial, at the east entrance. (☎742-6023. Open late May to early Sept. Tu-Su 9am-4pm; in winter Sa-Su only). **Cross Country Ski Rental: Cross Country Connection,** 222 S. 2nd St., Laramie. (☎721-2851. Open M-Sa 10am-6pm; Su noon-4pm. $10 per day, no deposit required.) **Downhill Ski/Snowboard Rental: The Fine Edge,** 1660E. N. 4th St. (☎745-4400. Call for hrs. Full-day $16, children $12. Snowboards $22/$17. Boots $9. $300 credit card or check deposit required for snowboards only.) **Area code:** 307.

SARATOGA. On the west side of the Snowy Range along Rte. 130, Saratoga, like its New York sister, is known for its **hot mineral springs.** Running between 104° and 120°F, these springs will warm you up and won't leave you reeking of sulfur. The free, 24hr. soaking wonders are located at the end of E. Walnut St., behind the public pool. A few feet away from the hot springs, the **North Platte River** offers excellent fishing. Fishing permits ($6) are available from the **Country Store** (☎326-5638) on Rte. 130. **Medicine Bow Drifters,** at 1st and Bridge St. also sells fishing permits; the knowledgeable owner can offer advice and completely outfit fishermen of any level. (☎326-8002. Open Apr.-May and Sept.-Oct. 6am-6pm, June-Aug. 6am-9pm. $40 per day for complete outfit.) The **Hotel Wolf,** 101 E. Bridge St., a renovated Victorian inn, is a howlin' good deal. (☎326-5525. Singles from $37; doubles from $43.) The local favorite **Wolf Hotel Restaurant** serves expensive dinners but reasonably priced sandwiches and salads ($5.50-7) for lunch. (☎326-5525. Open M-Th 11:30am-2pm and 6-9:30pm, Su 5-9pm). For a more casual dining atmosphere, drop in on **Mom's Kitchen,** on the corner of First and Hickory. The "big daddy burger" will fill you up, and pot roast, meatloaf, and other comfort foods are only $6. (☎326-5136. Open Tu-Su 7am-8pm.) Next door to the Wolf, **Lollypops,** 107 E. Bridge St., sells ice cream (single cone $1.85), latté ($2.75), and gourmet lollipops ($2). (☎326-5020. Open daily 7am-10pm.) Across from the Wolf, the **Lazy River Cantina** tempts hungry pedestrians with wafting aromas and a good selection of Mexican dishes. (☎326-8472. Open M-Th 11am-9:30pm, F 11am-10pm, Su 7am-9:30pm. Lunch $5-8; dinner specialties $8.) **Area code:** 307.

LARAMIE   ☎307

Laramie, home of the University of Wyoming (UW), the state's only four-year college, is a comfortable stop-over for those traveling across Wyoming. Laramie is a mix of collegiate coffee-shop chic and cowboy grit. Drifters can get a dose of youthful pluck in town and then relax in nearby **Medicine Bow National Forest** or **Curt Gowdy State Park.** From Cheyenne, take **Happy Jack Rd. (Rte. 210)** for a cow-filled scenic tour or I-80 for expedience and a glimpse of the **Vedauwoo Rocks** (see box, p. 666).

🔃 PRACTICAL INFORMATION. Chamber of Commerce: 800 S. 3rd. St., Exit 313 off I-80. (☎745-7339; open M-F 8am-5pm). **Laramie Events Hotline:** ☎721-7345. **Post Office:** 152 N. 5th St. (Open M-F 8am-5:15pm, Sa 9am-1pm.) **Bike Rental: Rocky Mountain Sports Outlet,** 217 E. Grand Ave. (☎742-3220. Open M-F noon-6pm, Sa 10am-5:30pm. $15 per day. Deposit the value of the bike required.) **Internet Access: Albany County Public Library,** 310 S. 8th St. (☎721-2580. Open M-Th 10am-8pm, F-Sa 1pm-5pm. First come, first served 1hr. time slots.) **ZIP code:** 82070. **Area code:** 307.

▚▙ ACCOMODATIONS AND FOOD. The rooms are large and comfortable at the sprawling **Motel 8,** 501 Boswell, down the street from the Caboose on the outskirts of town. (☎745-4856. Singles $45-50; doubles $51-56; cheaper in winter.) **Ranger Motel,** 453 N. 3rd St., patrols downtown, within walking distance of many attractions. (☎742-6677. HBO, fridge, microwave. Singles $37; doubles $46.) Lined with hotels and fast food, 3rd St. leads south into the heart of town, crossing Ivinson and Grand St., both of which burst with student hangouts. **Jeffrey's Restaurant,** 123 Ivinson St. at 2nd. St., doles out homemade bread and hot sandwiches for $5-9. (☎742-7046. Open M-Sa 11am-9pm.) The air in **The Home Bakery,** 304 S. 2nd St., smells of fresh loaves and cookies. Baked goods start at 45¢. (☎742-2721. Open M-Sa 5:30am-5:30pm; deli closes 2pm.) Check out the local scene at the tragically hip **Coal Creek Coffeehouse,** 110 Grand Ave. Coffee is the speciality, but they also pan some gourmet "light fare" for $4-6. (☎745-7737. Open during school year M-F 7am-11pm, Sa-Su 7:30am-11pm; in summer M-F 6am-10pm, Sa-Su 6:30am-10pm.)

▣▧▨ **SIGHTS, FESTIVALS, AND NIGHTLIFE.** Laramie does its darndest to bring its rough and rugged 19th-century history back to life at the **Wyoming Old West Park,** 975 Snowy Range Rd., a reconstructed frontier town where for $5, you can have a friend or family member arrested by the town marshal. (☎800-845-2287. Open daily early June to late Aug. 10am-5pm. $5, ages 6-12 $4, under 6 free.) The adjacent **Wyoming Territorial Prison** (tours every hr.) is a well-presented look at all aspects of prison life in the Old West. The **National US Marshals Museum** presents the history of the US marshals and their dealings with Native Americans and Western outlaws. (☎800-845-2287. Open daily early May to early Oct. 9am-6pm. $6, children $4, under 6 free; includes museum and prison. AAA discount.) At night, splurge to attend the renowned **Summer Dinner Theatre,** right next to the Frontier Town. Prices run about $30, $20 for children, but include the show, non-alcoholic drinks, dinner, and dessert. (☎800-845-2287. Shows W-Sa evenings; dinner at 6pm. Reservations required.) In early July, don't miss the chance to attend a rodeo at Laramie's **Jubilee Days** festival. (☎745-7339. Adult rodeo tickets start at $9.) Both students and Harleys steer their way into the **Buckhorn Bar,** 114 Ivinson St., a neighborhood hangout featuring busy pool tables and live music Sa and Su nights. (☎742-3554. Open M-Sa 8am-2am, Su 10am-midnight.) UW students can honestly tell mom they spent the weekend in the **Library,** 1622 Grand Ave. Pull up a table in their stacks for a salad ($4-7), a steak ($11-14), or a daily special ($5-6). Next door, the library's more lived-in bar has $2 beers on tap. (☎742-3900. Restaurant open Su-W 11am-9pm, Th-Sa 11am-10pm. Bar open M-Sa 11am-2am, Su 11am-midnight.)

COLORADO

In the high, thin air of Colorado, golf balls fly farther, eggs take longer to cook, and visitors tend to lose their breath just getting out of bed. Oxygen deprivation lures athletes looking to loosen their lungs for a competitive edge, but most hikers, skiers, and climbers worship Colorado for its peaks and mountain enclaves. Denver— the country's highest capital—serves as the hub for the entire Rocky Mountain region, providing a resting place for cross-country travelers and a "culture fix" for those heading to the mountains. Colorado's extraordinary heights are matched by its equally spectacular depths. Over millions of years, the Gunnison and Colorado Rivers have etched the natural wonders of the Black Canyon and the Colorado National Monument. Early settlers mined Colorado for its silver and gold, and the US military burrowed enormous intelligence installations into the mountains around Colorado Springs, but most visitors dig their feet into the state's soil simply to get down and dirty with Mother Nature.

⚡ PRACTICAL INFORMATION

Capital: Denver.

Visitor Info: Colorado Travel and Tourism Authority, CTTA, 1625 Broadway suite 1700, Denver, 80202 (☎303-892-3885). For a packet of info, call ☎800-265-6723 or visit www.colorado.com. **US Forest Service,** Rocky Mountain Region, 740 Sims St., Golden, 80401 or P.O. Box 25127, Lakewood 80225 (☎303-275-5350). Open M-F 7:30am-4:30pm. **Ski Country USA,** 1560 Broadway, #2000, Denver 80202 provides info on all Colorado ski resorts (☎303-837-0793; ski report 825-7669; open M-F 8am-5:30pm). **National Park Service,** 12795 W. Alameda Pkwy., P.O. Box 25287, Denver 80225 (☎303-969-2000). For reservations for Rocky Mountain National Park or any national park, call ☎800-365-2267. **Colorado State Parks,** 1313 Sherman St., #618, Denver 80203 (☎303-866-3437). Open for calls M-F 7am-4:45pm. For reservations for any Colorado state park, call ☎470-1144 or 800-678-2267. There is a $7 reservation fee.

Postal Abbreviation: CO. **Sales Tax:** 7.4%.

DENVER ☎303

In 1858, the discovery of gold in the Rocky Mountains brought a rush of eager miners to northern Colorado. After an excruciating trek through the plains, the desperados set up camp for a breather and a stiff shot of whiskey before heading west into "them thar hills." Today, Denver is still a good place to take a breather, despite the high altitude. While everyone knows Denver as the "Mile High City," the city boasts many other claims to fame: it is a bonafide melting pot of cultures and peoples, and, interestingly, America's fittest city. Denver has the fewest number of overweight residents, which is surprising considering the range and quality of its restaurants. Perhaps Denver's best characteristic is its vibrant, lived-in feel. City residents seem always to be out and about, enjoying the atmosphere; live bands, free concerts, and radio station promotions are pervasive and offer ample opportunity to enjoy Denver's combination of urban sophistication and more traditional Western grit.

✈ GETTING THERE AND AWAY

Airport: Denver International (DIA) (☎342-2000), 23 mi. northeast of downtown off I-70. Shuttles run from the airport to downtown and ski resorts in the area. The **RTD Sky Ride** (☎800-366-7433 or 299-6000; RTD office hours M-F 6am-10pm, Sa-Su 8am-8pm) costs $6 (disabled and seniors 65+ $3) to DIA from downtown; buses run hourly from the Market St. Station downtown from 5am-10:30pm. From the main terminal, **Supershuttle** (☎370-1300 or 800-525-3177, airport desk 342-5452) shuttles to downtown hotels (1hr., $17). A **taxi** to downtown costs about $45. The Supershuttle also heads north to Boulder. (☎444-0808. 1hr.+, $18 from hotels and University of CO at Boulder campus, $22 from homes and businesses.)

Trains: Amtrak, Union Station, 1701 Wynkoop St. (☎534-2812 for arrivals/departures, 825-2583 for ticket office), at 17th St. To: Salt Lake City (14½hr., 1 per day); St. Louis (26½hr., 1 per day); and Chicago (18½hr., 1 per day). Ticket office open daily 5:30am-9pm. **Río Grande Ski Train,** 555 17th St. (☎296-4754), leaves from Amtrak Union Station and chugs 2¼hr. through the Rockies, stopping in Winter Park within walking distance of the lifts; free ground transport to town provided; lift discounts included. (Dec.-Apr. same-day round-trip $40, reservations required. Runs Sa-Su only; F added after early Feb., special runs from, but not including, Dec. 25 to Jan. 1. Mid-Jun. to mid-Aug. trains run to the mountains on Sa. Round-trip $40.)

Buses: Greyhound, 1055 19th St. (☎293-6555). To: Santa Fe (7½-9hr., 4 per day, $60.50); Salt Lake City (10-13hr., 3 per day, $43.50); Colorado Springs (1½hr., 10 per day, $16.50); and Chicago (20-22hr., 7 per day, $76). Ticket office open daily 6am-midnight.

⌐ GETTING AROUND

Public Transportation: Regional Transportation District (RTD), 1600 Blake St. (☎299-6000 or 800-366-7433). Serves Denver, as well as Longmont, Evergreen, Golden, and suburbs. Route hrs. vary; many shut down by 9pm. M-F 6-9am and 4-6pm $1.25; other hrs. 75¢, disabled and seniors 25¢. Exact change required. Major terminals are at Market and 17th St. and at Colfax and Broadway. The free 16th St. **Mall Shuttle** covers 14 blocks downtown and runs daily 5:45am-1am. **Light Rail** services the perimeter of the city and suburbs, from I-25 and Broadway north to 30th and Downing.

Taxis: Yellow Cab, ☎777-7777. **Zone Cab,** ☎444-8888.

Car Rental: Enterprise, 7720 Calawaba Ct., Denver, at DIA (☎800-720-7222). Compact cars start at $55 per day with an extra $15 charge per day for drivers 21-25. Security deposit of $250 on a major credit card required. Open daily 7am-10pm.

ROCKY MOUNTAINS

✳ 🔢 ORIENTATION AND PRACTICAL INFORMATION

Running north-south, **Broadway** slices Denver in half. East of Broadway, **Colorado Blvd.** is also a major north-south thoroughfare. **Colfax Ave.**, running east-west, is the main north-south dividing line. Both named and numbered streets run diagonally in the downtown area. In the rest of the city, numbered avenues run east-west and count upwards as you head north. Named streets run north-south. Many of the avenues on the eastern side of the city become numbered *streets* downtown. The **16th St. Mall** is the hub of Denver's downtown and could easily be called the social, dining, and entertainment center of the city. *Avoid the west end of Colfax Ave., Federal Blvd., S. Santa Fe Blvd, the east side of town beyond the capitol (the Capitol Hill area), and the west side of the* **Barrio** *(25th-34th St.) at night.*

Visitor Info: Denver Visitors Bureau, 1668 Larimer St. (☎892-1112 or 892-1505), just north of the 16th St. Mall. Open M-F 8am-5pm, Sa 9am-1pm.

Hotlines: Rape Emergency, ☎322-7273.

Bi-Gay-Lesbian Organizations: Gay and Lesbian and Bi-Sexual Community Services Center of Colorado, ☎733-7743. Open M-F 10am-6pm.

Internet Access: Public Library, 10 W. 14th Ave. Open M-W 10am-9pm, Th-Sa 10am-5:30pm, Su 1-5pm.

Post Office: 951 20th St. (☎800-275-8777). Open M-F 7am-6pm, Sa 9am-1pm. General delivery open M-F 8:30am-4pm. **ZIP code:** 80202. **Area code:** 303. Ten digit dialing required.

🏠 ACCOMMODATIONS

Hostel of the Rocky Mountains (HI-AYH), 1530 Downing St. (☎861-7777). Right off E. Colfax Ave., the hostel is 10 blocks from the Capitol, next to 2 major bus routes and a trolley stop. Cheerful dorms and private rooms, make this hostel Denver's best value. The hostel features TVs with built-in VCR in every room, laundry facilities, library, kitchens, a small gym, and email access. Pick-up from the Greyhound depot or Union Station. Bike rental ($2); tours of Denver area ($5-25). Reception 7am-noon, 5-10pm. Dorms $14; private rooms $30-45. Linen $2, key deposit $5. Reservations recommended.

Hostel of the Rocky Mountains B&Bs. The friendly staff at the hostel also operate two well-priced B&Bs right next door. Classier and decidedly quieter than the hostel, the rooms here are clean and spacious with shared baths. Guests can enjoy free breakfast next door at the hostel or use the kitchen facilities to fend for themselves. Prices run $32, $36, and $40, depending on the room. Call the hostel for reservations.

YMCA, 25 E. 16th Ave. (☎861-8300), at Lincoln St. Divided into sections for men, women, and families. Laundry and TV rooms. Singles without bath (men only) $32, with shared bath $36, with private bath from $41; doubles (women only) $58-$60. Weekly rates available. Key deposit $12 and ID. Reserve in advance. Must be 18+

Motel 6, 12020 E. 39th Ave, (☎371-1980), take the Peoria St. exit off I-70. Tidy rooms, cable TV, free local calls, and an outdoor pool make Motel 6 a good bet. Singles M-F $40, Sa-Su $46; doubles $46/$54.

Rodeaway Inn, 12033 E. 38th Ave (☎371-0740), just down the street from Motel 6. Rooms have A/C, free local calls, HBO, coffee makers, and free morning paper delivery. An indoor pool sweetens the deal. Clean, spacious singles $40; doubles $45.

Two state parks lie in the Denver metro area. **Cherry Creek State Park,** 4201 S. Parker Rd., Aurora, is located in a rather sterile urban area but is conveniently located. A few stands of pine trees make an attempt at providing shade. The park often fills up, so arrive early. Take I-25 to Exit 200, then head north on I-225 for about 3 mi. and take the Parker Rd. exit. (Open Apr.-Oct. Sites $10, with electricity $14; daily entrance fee $5.) The beautiful, but much less convenient **Golden Gate Canyon State Park** offers 106 rustic sites. Take I-70 west to 6th Ave., go west about 20 mi. towards Central City, and then go north about 19 mi. on Rte. 119. (Tent sites $10, with electricity $14; backcountry shelters $6; daily entrance fee $4.) Contact the **State Parks Office** for info. (Reservations ☎470-1144 or 800-678-2267. Open M-F 8am-5pm. $7.)

Denver

⌂ ACCOMMODATIONS
Hostel of the Rocky Mtns.
(HI-AYH) & B&Bs, **10**
Motel 6, **9**
Rodeaway Inn, **8**
YMCA, **6**

🍴 FOOD
Corner Bakery, **5**
Lemon Sisters Market, **2**
The Market, **3**
Mercury Cafe, **4**
Pearl Street Grill, **7**
Swing Thai, **11**
Wynkoop Brewery, **1**

TO I-70, COORS FIELD, RED ROCKS, AIRPORT

TO ROCKY MOUNTAIN ARSENAL (4.1m)

TO COORS FIELD

TO MILE HIGH STADIUM (1.25mi)

TO I-70, (8 mi.) RED ROCKS (15 mi.)

TO I-70 (2 mi.)

TO (3¾ mi.)

TO ELLSWORTH AVE. (1.1mi)

Court Pl.

24th St.

23rd St./Park Ave.

22nd St.

21st St.

Tremont Pl.

Glenarm Pl.

Welton St.

California St.

Stout St.

Champa St.

Curtis St.

Arapahoe St.

Lawrence St.

Larimer St.

Market St.

Blake St.

Wazee St.

Wynkoop St.

Wewatta St.

Delgany St.

Little Raven St.

Ehrich Cir.

Speer Blvd.

Cherry Creek

Auraria Pkwy.

19th St.

18th St.

17th St.

16th St.

15th St.

14th St.

13th St.

12th St.

11th St.

9th St.

8th St.

7th St.

5th St.

La Veta Way

Curtis Ave.

Colfax Ave.

14th Ave.

Rio Ct.

Shoshone St.

Osage St.

Mariposa St.

Lipan St.

Kalamath St.

Delaware St.

Speer Blvd.

Downing St.

Corona St.

Ogden St.

Emerson St.

Clarkson St.

Washington St.

E. 18th Ave.

E. 17th Ave.

E. 16th Ave.

E. Colfax Ave.

Pennsylvania St.

E. 20th Ave.

E. 19th St.

Pearl St.

Logan St.

Grant St.

Sherman St.

Lincoln St.

Broadway

Cleveland Pl.

Court Pl.

Tremont Pl.

Glenarm Pl.

Welton St.

California St.

Stout St.

Champa St.

Curtis St.

Skyline Park

E. 14th Ave.

Colfax Ave.

Cheyenne Pl.

Speer Blvd.

Union Station

Wynkoop Brewery

RTD Market St. Bus Terminal

Market

WRITER SQ.

LARIMER SQ.

Federal Bldg.

Museum of Western Art

Brown Palace

RTD Civic Center Station

State Capitol

Colorado History Museum

Library

Civic Center Park

Greek Amphitheater

Denver Art Museum

Byers/Evans House

Denver History Museum

US Mint

Firefighter's Museum

Colorado Convention Center

Denver Performing Arts Complex

Denver Community College

UNIVERSITY OF COLORADO-DENVER AURARIA

Library & Media Center

St. Elizabeth's

Student Union

Pepsi Center

Six Flags Elitch Gardens

8   9

2

3

4

5

6

7

1

N

0   300 yards
0   300 meters

FOOD

Downtown Denver is great for cheap Mexican and Southwestern food. Dining al fresco and people-watching are available along the **16th St. Mall.** Southwest of the mall on Larimer St., **Larimer Sq.** has several more gourmet eateries. Along with sports bars, trendy restaurants cluster around **LoDo,** the neighborhood extending from Wynkoop St. to Larimer Sq. between Speer Blvd. and 20th St. Outside of downtown, **Colorado Blvd.** and **6th Ave.** also have their share of posh restaurants. **E. Colfax Ave.** offers a number of reasonably priced ethnic restaurants ranging from Greek to Ethiopian cuisine. Colorado's distance from the ocean may make you wonder about **"Rocky Mountain oysters."** These salty-sweet delicacies (bison testicles) are sold at the **Denver Buffalo Company,** 1109 Lincoln Ave. (☎832-0880).

Mercury Cafe, 22nd and California (☎294-9241 or 294-9258 to "speak to a human"). Decorated with a new age flair, the Merc specializes in home-baked wheat bread and a slew of reasonably-priced soups, salads, enchiladas, and vegetarian specials. Live bands provide music in the dining room and upstairs dance area: Tu jazz and indie hop, W open stage and tango, Su and Th big band swing, F Argentine tango. Low cover and free dancing lessons. All ages admitted unless otherwise specified. Open for meals Tu-F 5:30-11pm, Sa-Su 9am-3pm and 5:30-11pm; dancing until 2am F-Sa and 1am on Tu-Th and Su.

Pearl Street Grill, 1477 S. Pearl St. (☎778-6475), in the trendy and laid-back Washington Park area. Serves gourmet food, but an evening there won't break the bank. On the dinner menu, the "PSG Favorites" range from $6.50-11 (the majority cost $8). Enjoy your food and the night on the elegant outdoor patio. Open daily 11am-2am (brunch served 11am-3pm).

Corner Bakery, 500 16th St. (☎572-0170), is a trendy establishment that's taken the term "bakery" to a higher level of sophistication. Chicken pesto sandwiches and a variety of soups, salads, gourmet pizzas, homemade breads, and goodies are served cafeteria style with a classy spin. Sit inside, or tempt pedestrians along the Mall with your delicious food. Open M-Th 7am-8pm, F 7am-10pm, Sa 8am-10pm, Su 9am-5pm.

Swing Thai, 845 Colorado Blvd (☎777-1777), is an understandably popular restaurant. With a wide assortment of high-quality food at cheap prices, Swing Thai stands out. Those sick of pizza and burgers can indulge on Thai specialties like the *hot* Jungle Curry ($6.50) or Pineapple Fried Rice ($5.50). A number of wok specials with gigantic portions are available for a mere $6.50. Open daily 11am-10pm.

Lemon Sisters Market, 1530 Blake St. (☎825-4133), downtown, is a hidden treasure. The tasty breakfast burritos cost just $2.50. Deli Sandwiches made fresh to order are $5. Hearty soups and a variety of specials ($3-5) are available daily. Sesame noodles, tabouli, and hummus satisfy those with more exotic cravings. Open M-F 8am-9pm, Sa-Su 10am-6pm.

The Market, 1445 Larimer Sq. (☎534-5140), downtown, is popular with a young, artsy crowd, as well as suits. A variety of busy specialty counters serve cappuccino for $2.20, sandwiches for $5.50, and exotic salads for $5-9 per lb. Grab your goods to go, or have a seat. Open M-Th 6:30am-11pm, F 6:30am-midnight, Sa-Su 7:30am-midnight.

Wynkoop Brewery, 1634 18th St. (☎297-2700), at Wynkoop across from Union Station in LoDo. Colorado's first brewpub serves beer (20 oz. $2.50), homemade root beer, lunch, and dinner (burgers from $6). Pool tables upstairs and an independent **comedy club** downstairs (☎297-2111). Happy hour M-F 3-6pm, $2 pints. Brewery open daily M-Sa 11am-2am, Su 11am-midnight. Food service M-Th until 11pm, F-Sa until midnight, Su until 10pm. Free brewery tours Sa 1-5pm.

SIGHTS

CULTURAL CONNECTION TROLLEY. One of the best tour deals around, the trolley visits over 20 of the city's main attractions. The fare is good all day on any local bus or light rail. The easiest place to begin a tour is along the 16th St. Mall, near the Mall Ride stops, but the tour can be joined at many local attractions; look for the green-and-red sign. (☎299-6000. Runs daily early May to early Sept. 9:30am-6pm. Buses come every 30min.; buy your ticket from the driver. $3.)

DENVER STATE CAPITOL. Many of the best sights in Denver center around down-town, which makes touring on foot easy. The **Capitol Building** is a sensible place to start your visit to the Mile High City—the 15th step (marked by a small plaque) leading to the building's entrance sits exactly 5280 ft. (1 mi.) above sea level. Guided tours show off the many riches of Colorado that were employed in the building's construction. Ambitious visitors can climb 93 stairs to the dome observatory for an interesting look at the Capitol's architecture as well as a view of the city and the surrounding mountains. (☎866-2604. 40min. tours run every 30min. M-F 7am-5:30pm and Sa 9:30am-2:30pm. Visitors are welcome to climb the stairs to the dome until M-F 3:30pm and Sa-Su 2:15pm.)

DENVER ART MUSEUM. Just a few blocks west of the Capitol stands the Denver Art Museum, a unique seven-story "vertical" museum. The DAM houses a world-class collection of Native American art and pre-Colombian artifacts. Guided tours of the European and American Art Galleries run every Sa and Su at 2:30pm. You could spend hours in this museum and still not see it all, but it's worth a brave attempt. (100 W. 14th Ave. Pkwy. ☎640-4433. Open Tu and Th-Sa 10am-5pm, W 10am-9pm, Su noon-5pm. Tours: Jul. and Aug. Tu-Sa 11am and 1:30pm, Su 1:30pm; after Aug. 31, daily at 1:30pm, Sa also at 11:30am. $4.50; students, seniors, and children $2.50; under 5 free.)

US MINT. A mere two blocks west of the Art Museum is a remnant of Colorado's silver mining days, the US Mint. The Mint issues the majority of coins in the US; just look for the small "D" embossed beneath the date to see if your pocket change was made in Denver. The lines are often horrendously long, so arrive early or call ahead. (320 W. Colfax Ave. ☎405-4761. Open M-F 8am-3pm. In summer free 20min. tours every 15-20min. Call for reservation Oct.-Apr.)

SIX FLAGS. Next door, make a splash of your own at the Island Kingdom water park at Six Flags Elitch Gardens, at Elitch Circle and Speer Blvd., across the free-way from Mile High Stadium. The Boomerang, Mind Eraser, Sidewinder, and Tower of Doom keep thrill seekers content. (☎595-4386. Open June-Aug. daily 10am-10pm, spring and early fall Sa-Su call to confirm. $33, seniors $20, under 4 ft. tall $16.50. Look for money-saving coupons in the Elitch Gardens brochures. AAA discounts available.)

DENVER MUSEUM OF NATURE AND SCIENCE. This gigantic museum hosts a variety of interesting exhibits under its roof. You won't want to miss the Hall of Life or the Prehistoric Journey room. A super-cool **IMAX** theater with a six-story screen shows three different movies on a daily basis. (2001 Colorado Blvd. ☎370-6357. Open daily Labor Day to Memorial Day 9am-5pm; summer W-M 9am-5pm, Tu 9am-7pm. Museum entrance $7; seniors, students, and children 3-12 $4.50. Combination tickets to IMAX and museum $11/$7. Call for IMAX shows and times.)

COORS BREWERY. Located in nearby Golden, this is the world's largest one-site brewery. The Brewery also holds the honor of having one of the nicest wellness centers in the corporate world—not too long ago, the workout center was deemed a necessary company addition. All 42,000 workers are allowed two free beers after every shift, and waistlines were noticeably growing. Interesting 40min. walking tours take you through the entire Coors brewing process from start to finish. Those parched and exhausted at the end of the tour can indulge themselves by sampling up to three different Coors products. (☎303-277-2337. Take I-70 to 6th Ave. (Rte. 6 West) in Golden. Follow signs for Brewery Tours. A shuttle bus runs from the parking lot to the brewery, but not before a very short historical tour of Golden. Tours run M-Sa 10am-4pm. Bring ID if you plan on sampling the alcohol. Otherwise, there are free Pepsi products for the taking.)

RED ROCKS AMPHITHEATER AND PARK. The mammoth park, 12 mi. southwest of Denver on I-70 at the Morrison exit, is carved into red sandstone. As the sun sets over the city, performers such as R.E.M., U2, and the Denver Symphony Orchestra compete with the view behind them. The actual Red Rocks park contains more than 600 acres and features numerous hiking trails. For concert tickets, call Ticket-master (☎830-8497).

ROCKY MOUNTAINS

PUBLIC PARKS. Denver has more public parks per sq. mi. than any other city, providing prime space for bicycling, walking, or lolling about. **Cheesman Park,** 8th Ave. and Humboldt Sts., offers picnic areas and a view of the snow-capped peaks of the Rockies. **Confluence Park,** at Cherry Creek and the South Platte River, lures bikers and hikers with paved paths along the river. Every Th in July, **Confluence Concerts** (☎637-2645) hosts live music for a broad range of musical tastes along the banks of the South Platte. **City Park** (☎331-4113) houses a museum, zoo, running path, and golf course. **Colorado State Parks** has the low-down on nearby state parks. (☎866-3437. Open M-F 8am-5pm.) A local favorite is **Roxborough State Park,** where visitors can hike and ski among red rock formations. (Take U.S. 85 S, turn right on Titan Rd., and follow it 3½ mi. to the park. Open year-round. Day use only.) Forty mi. west of Denver, the road to the summit of **Mt. Evans** (14,260 ft.) is the highest paved road in North America. (☎303-567-2901. Take I-70 W to Rte. 103 in Idaho Springs. Open late May to early Sept.)

ROCKY MOUNTAIN ARSENAL. Incredibly, the best spot for bald eagles in Denver is also the town's most radioactive plot. The Rocky Mountain Arsenal, a former nuclear waste site, is a wildlife refuge. (☎289-0232. The bald eagle viewing area open Oct.-Mar. 8:30am-dusk; refuge open Sa 12:30-8pm, in winter 8am-3pm. Call ahead.)

🌸🎵 FESTIVALS AND ENTERTAINMENT

Every Jan., Denver hosts the nation's largest livestock show and one of the biggest rodeos, the **National Western Stock Show,** 4655 Humbolt St. Here, cowboys compete for prize money while over 10,000 head of cattle compete for "Best of Breed." **Cinco de Mayo** (☎534-8342, ext. 122)—yes, on the 5th of May—attracts 250,000 visitors per year in celebration of Mexico's victory over the French in 1862. The **Capitol Hill People's Fair** (☎830-1651), the first full week of June, is a large outdoor celebration with food vendors and local bands at **Civic Center Park,** near the capitol. The **Renaissance Festival** brings guests back in time with jousting, music, and plenty of free spirits in medieval garb. (☎688-6010. Every Sa-Su early June to late July.) **The Festival of Mountain and Plain: A Taste of Colorado** (☎892-7004) packs Civic Center Park Labor Day weekend for one last summer shebang. Booths with food and crafts, free entertainment, and carnival rides are all part of the fun.

Life in Denver is never boring for sports fans. Denver's baseball team, the **Colorado Rockies,** plays at **Coors Field,** at 20th and Blake St. (☎800-388-7625. Tickets $4-35; some $4 Rockpile tickets available day of game.) In the fall, the 1998 Super Bowl champion **Denver Broncos** put on the blitz at **Mile High Stadium,** 19th and Eliot St. (☎433-7466); soccer mania takes over the joint during the spring and summer as the **Colorado Rapids** shoot (☎299-1570). The NBA **Nuggets,** and the NHL squad, the **Colorado Avalanche,** play in the brand-spanking-new **Pepsi Center,** 901 Auraria Pkwy. (☎405-1100 for info on the Nuggets and the Avalanche.)

📺 NIGHTLIFE

Downtown Denver in and around the 16th St. Mall is an attraction in itself. With ample shopping, dining, and people-watching opportunities, there's something for everyone. Many restaurants host radio stations and live bands on a regular basis, and concerts are never lacking in the Civic Center Park area. Denver's local restaurants and bars cater to a college-age and slightly older singles crowd. A copy of *Westword* gives the lowdown on LoDo. For a great evening, visit the ■**Mercury Cafe** (see Food). The "Hill of the Grasshopper," El Chapultepec, at 20th and Market St., is an honest-to-goodness bebopping jazz bar that has survived since Denver's Beat era of the 50s. (☎295-9126. Open daily 11am-2am. No cover. 1-drink min. per set.) Hungry after all that jazz? Check out "the Pec's" **burrito joint** next door. A remodeled chapel, **The Church,** 1160 Lincoln, offers four full bars (try a Fat Tire on tap), a cigar lounge, and a weekend sushi bar—that is, if Joe lets you off the dance floor. On weekends, the congregation swells with two floors of dancing. (☎832-3528. Doors open Tu-Su 8-9pm until 1-2am.) The **Bluebird Theater,** 3317 E. Colfax (☎322-2308), hosts local and the occasional national act. The theater runs a free movie once a month. The movies span a variety of categories, but due to the drinking opportunity that accompanies the films, only 21+ are allowed. **Charlie's**, 900 E. Colfax Ave., at Emerson, is a popular gay bar with country Western dancing. (☎839-8890. Open daily 10am-4am.)

MOUNTAIN RESORTS NEAR DENVER   ☎970

WINTER PARK
Nestled among delicious-smelling mountain pines in the upper Fraser River valley, The popular **Winter Park Resort** is the closest ski and summer resort to Denver, only 67 miles away.

🚩 **PRACTICAL INFORMATION.** To reach Winter Park from Denver, take I-70 W to U.S. 40. The Chamber of Commerce (see below) also serves as the **Greyhound** depot. **Home James Transportation Services** (☎970-726-5060 or 800-451-4844) runs door-to-door shuttles to and from Fraser or the Winter Park and Denver airport. (Office hours daily 8am-6pm. Reservations required. $37.) The same phone number reaches **Mad Adventures** river rafting (half-day $38.50; full-day $58.50). From Dec. to Apr., the **Río Grande Ski Train** (☎303-296-4754) leaves Denver's Union Station for Winter Park. **Winter Park-Fraser Valley Chamber of Commerce:** 78841 Hwy. 40 (☎726-4118, 303-422-0666 or 800-903-7275; open daily 8am-5pm). **Area code:** 970.

🍴 **ACCOMMODATIONS AND FOOD.** The **Viking Lodge,** on Rte. 40 in Winter Park, offers tiny rooms with phones and color TVs. Stays include access to the hot tub and sauna and a 10% discount on rentals at the adjacent store, and winter shuttle service to the lifts. (☎726-8885 or 800-421-4013. Reception 8am-9pm. Singles $35-65; doubles $35-70; varies with season.) Perhaps the best family lodging deal in the Fraser Valley is the **Snow Mountain Ranch YMCA,** 12 mi. past the town of Winter Park (take I-70 west to U.S. 40 west). The ranch features a host of recreational activities, including nordic skiing. (☎887-2152, ext. 4110. Quad with private bath $64. Campsites range from $17-21 per night.) Deliciously healthy breakfasts and lunches (each $5-8) are served on the patio at **Carver's Bakery Cafe,** at the end of the Cooper Creek Mall off U.S. 40. Try the massive cinnamon rolls ($2.75) or the Almond Joy Latte ($4). (☎726-8202. Open daily 7am-2pm, until 3pm during peak season.) The local favorite for breakfast, brunch, and lunch is **The Last Waltz,** at Kings Crossing Center off Hwy. 40. Hearty breakfasts like chocolate chip pancakes ($5) or black Bean Huevos ($6) will tide you over until lunch, when you can return for a Chicken Mango Tango sandwich ($7) or "la comida" Mexican dishes ranging from $6.25-8.25. (☎726-4877. Open daily 7am-2pm.)

🎿 **ACTIVITIES. Winter Park Mary Jane Ski Area** (☎726-5514 or 800-453-2525) packs bowls all winter long with a 3060 ft. vertical drop and 1467 acres of glade skiing on 2886 total acres. **Slopeside Gear and Sport,** right at the base of Winter Park Resort, rents skis starting at $18 per day, snowboards from $25 per day. For snow conditions and summertime fun info, call ☎303-572-7669 or 800-729-5813. The **Alpine Slide** twists and turns 26 times; at 3030 ft., it is Colorado's longest. (Open daily June to early Sept. 10am-6pm; mid- to late Sept. Sa-Su only 10am-5pm. $8, seniors and children $7. Under 6 and over 70 free.) In the summer, mountain biking and hiking trails climb the mountains of the Continental Divide. The **Zephyr Express** chairlift blows to the summit of Winter Park Mountain, allowing mountain bikers to reach the peak, then ride down on 50 mi. of single track trails. (Open daily mid-June to early Sept. 10am-5pm, mid- to late Sept. Sa-Su only. Full-day chair pass costs $19. Mountain bike rentals from $9 per hr., $32 per day. A 2hr. clinic will teach you how to ride or hone your skills for $15.) Winter Park is on the vanguard of summer mountain fun, with mountain scooters, a maze, and a zip-line. (Full park pass for all summer activities $40 weekdays, $45 weekends.) The **High Country Stampede Rodeo** bucks every Sa at 7:30pm in July and Aug. at the John Work Arena, west of Fraser on County Rd. 73. (☎726-4118 or 800-903-7275. $10, children $6, seniors $8.)

ROCKY MOUNTAINS

SUMMIT COUNTY

Skiers, hikers, and mountain bikers can tap into a sportsman's paradise in the US's highest county, about 70 mi. west of Denver on I-70. The ski resorts of **Breckenridge** (☎453-5000 or 800-846-9240), **Copper Mountain** (☎968-2882 or 800-458-8386), and **Keystone** (☎496-2316 for operator, 800-255-3715 for info, or 888-222-9298 for reservations) are alternatives to the more expensive resorts of Aspen and Vail. **Arapahoe Basin** usually has skiing until early July, depending on snow conditions; it is the highest skiable terrain in North America (☎888-272-7246, 468-0718).

The **Alpen Hütte,** 471 Rainbow Dr., in Silverthorne, has welcoming hosts, a familial atmosphere, clean rooms with beautiful mountain views, and year-round outdoor activities, including fly-fishing on the Blue River behind the hostel. Greyhound (from Denver) and Summit Stage stop outside the door. (☎468-6336. Reception daily 7am-11am and 4pm-midnight. Laundry. Free ski storage. Parking. Midnight curfew. Dorms $17; in winter $27. Linen and towels $1.50. Lockers $5 deposit. Reserve for winter 1-2 months in advance.) Several Forest Service campgrounds lie nearby in the **White River National Forest.** The **Dillon Ranger District Office,** 680 Blue River Pkwy. (☎468-5400; 877-444-6777 for campground reservations), can supply more info (open M-F 8am-5pm and until Labor Day, also Sa-Su 9am-4pm). **Summit Stage** buses (free) connect these resorts with the towns of **Frisco, Dillon,** and **Silverthorne.** Call ☎668-0999 for schedule information. **Summit County Chamber of Commerce:** 11 Summit Blvd., in Frisco. (☎668-2051. Open daily 9am-5pm.) **Silverthorne-Dillon Info Center:** in the Summit Place Mall off Rte. 6 in Dillon, ¼ mi. south of I-70 on Rte. 6. (☎262-0817. Open daily 9am-5pm.) **Area Code:** 970.

BRECKENRIDGE

Fashionable Breckenridge lies west of Silverthorne on I-70, 9 mi. south of Frisco. Despite the many expensive restaurants and stores, you can still find reasonably priced, smoke-free accommodations at the **Fireside Inn (HI-AYH),** 114 N. French St., two blocks east of Main St. on the corner of Wellington. The indoor hot tub is great for *après-ski.* (☎453-6456. Closed in May. Office hours daily 7am-10pm. Dorms $20, private rooms $50-75; in height of winter prices rise as high as $31/$95-145.) Start your day at the **Paintbrush Cafe,** 311 S. Main St., in the Main St. Mall, where the breakfast and lunch menu items are under $7. (☎453-7656. Open Tu-F 8am-3pm, Sa-Su 8am-3pm. Winter hrs. may vary.) **Rasta Pasta,** 411 S. Main St., is a small but jammin' with the sound of twirling forks. The Rasta Pasta namesake dish, (flamin' jerk chicken, penne pasta, and a garlic tomato sauce) will make you wail with delight. Dishes range from $6-13. (☎453-7467. Open daily 11:30am-9pm.) **Riverside Info Center:** on the corner of Washington and Main St. (☎453-5579; open daily 9am-5pm). **Ski Conditions and Weather:** ☎800-789-7609. **Area code:** 970.

BOULDER
☎303

Combining yuppie tastes with collegiate earthiness, Boulder lends itself to the pursuit of higher knowledge and better karma. It is home to both the central branch of the University of Colorado (CU) and the only accredited Buddhist university in the US, Naropa University. Only here can you take summer courses in Mystical Writing, Yoga, and Buddhist Meditation or attend poetry and healing workshops at the Jack Kerouac School of Disembodied Poetics. Boulder is, in a word, transcendent; enjoy it while you can—the real world lurks just outside the city borders.

▐ GETTING THERE AND GETTING AROUND

Buses: Greyhound, at 30th and Diagonal Hwy. (☎443-1574). To: Denver (1hr., 2 per day, $6); Glenwood Springs (6-7hr., 2 per day, $35-37); and Vail (5-5½hr., 2 per day, $28-30). Open 24hrs.

Public Transportation: HOP, 4880 Pearl St. (☎447-8282). Shuttles connect the Pearl St. Mall, the Hill, CU, and the Crossroads Mall in a 2-way loop. Runs M-F 7am-7pm, with stops every 10min., and Sa 9am-7pm every 15min. 75¢, seniors 25¢. During term

BOULDER ■ 677

time, shuttles also run Th-Sa 10pm-3am every 20min. **SKIP** (☎299-6000) runs up and down Broadway and makes a loop through the west Table Mesa area. Pick up a map at the station or the visitors center (see below). **RTD** (☎299-6000 or 800-366-7433), at 14th and Walnut St. in the center of town, runs M-F 6am-8pm, Sa-Su 8am-8pm. 75¢, seniors free; higher during peak hrs. Also runs to: Denver Airport ($8, seniors and under 12 $4); Denver ($3); and Coors Field (round-trip $4). Buses operate 5:30-10pm.

Taxis: Boulder Yellow Cab, ☎442-2277.

Car Rental: Budget Rent-a-Car, 1345 28th St. (☎800-527-7000), in the Harvest Hotel. Must be 21+ with major credit card. Ages 21-25 $20 per day surcharge. Economy size $19-45 per day. Unlimited mi. Open M-F 7:30am-5:30pm, Sa-Su 8am-1pm.

Bike Rental: University Bicycles, 839 Pearl St. (☎444-4196), downtown. Rents mountain bikes with helmet and lock $15 per 4hr., $20 per 4-8hr., $25 overnight; kids' bikes $12/$15/$20. Open M-F 10am-7pm, Sa 9am-6pm, Su 10am-5pm.

✴🎤 ORIENTATION AND PRACTICAL INFORMATION

Boulder is a small, manageable city, accessible by Rte. 36. The most developed area lies between **Broadway (Rte. 93)** and **28th St. (Rte. 36),** two busy streets running north-south through the city. **Baseline Rd.,** connecting the Flatirons with the eastern plains, and **Canyon Blvd. (Rte. 7),** following the Boulder Canyon into the mountains, both border the **University of Colorado (CU)** campus. The area around the school is known as **the Hill.** The pedestrian-only **Pearl St. Mall,** between 9th and 15th St., is the hip center of town with plenty of cafes, restaurants, and posh shops. On 28th St. you'll find all of your practical stores. Most east-west roads are named, while north-south streets are numbered; Broadway is a conspicuous exception.

Visitor Info: Boulder Chamber of Commerce/Visitors Service, 2440 Pearl St. (☎442-1044), at Folsom about 10 blocks from downtown. Take RTD bus #200; also accessible by HOP. Open M-Th 8:30am-5pm, F 8:30am-4pm. **University of Colorado Information** (☎492-6161), 2nd fl. of University Memorial Center (UMC) student union. Free local calls. Open M-Th 7am-11pm, F-Sa 7am-midnight, Su 11am-11pm; term-time open M-Th 7am-midnight, F-Sa 7am-1am, Su 11am-midnight. **CU Ride Board:** UMC first fl.

Hotlines: Rape Crisis, ☎443-7300. **Crisis Line,** ☎447-1665 for counseling. Both 24hr.

Internet Access: Kiosks are scattered throughout the **UMC** (see **Visitor Info**).

Post Office: 1905 15th St., at Walnut St. Open M-F 7:30am-5:30pm, Sa 10am-2pm. **ZIP code:** 80302. **Area code:** 303. Ten digit dialing required.

🛏 ACCOMMODATIONS

After spending all your money on tofu and yogurt at the Pearl St. Mall, you may find yourself strapped for cash and without a room; Boulder doesn't offer many budget accommodations. In the summer, at least you can rely on the hostel.

Boulder International Hostel, 1107 12th St. (☎442-0522), at College Ave., 2 blocks up College Hill; 15min. south of the RTD station. From Denver, take the A or B bus as close to College Ave. as possible. The vibrance of youth is well manifested here; optimism abounds. Good facilities. The front door is locked after midnight, but guests are given a code to enter after hrs. Dorm lockout 10am-5pm. $15 gets you shared hall bathrooms, a large kitchen, laundry, and TV; linen $4. Shower and towels free. Key deposit $10. Private singles $35 per night, $150 per week; doubles $40/$180.

Lazy L Motel, 1000 28th St. (☎442-7525), on the Frontage Rd., has smallish rooms, but they're clean and as cheap as you'll find in Boulder. Conveniently located near busy Rte. 36. Singles $81; doubles $91. In winter $63/$73.

Chautauqua Association (☎442-3282), off Baseline Rd. at the foot of the Flatirons. Turn at the Chautauqua Park sign and take Kinnikinic to Morning Glory Dr., where the office is located, or take RTD bus #203. Office hours M-F 8:30am-7pm, additional summer hrs. Sa-Su 9am-3pm. In summer, lodge rooms ($57, one bedroom suites $73) and private cottages with kitchens (4-night minimum stay; 2 bedrooms $90-98; 3 bedrooms $120-126) are available in a gorgeous setting. Reserve months in advance.

ROCKY MOUNTAINS

The Boulder Mountain Lodge, 91 Four Mile Canyon Dr. (☎444-0882), 3 mi. west on Canyon Rd. (which becomes Rte. 119). 15 sites in a grove of pines next to a creek. Pay phone, 2 hot tubs, seasonal pool, and free showers. Check-out 10am; no reservations for camping. Cramped 3-person sites $14; $5 per additional person; $84 per week. Motel rooms for 1 or 2 people in summer $68; in winter from $53.

Camping info for **Arapahoe/Roosevelt National Forest** is available from the **Boulder Ranger District,** 2140 Yarmouth Ave at the corner of Hwy. 36. (☎444-6600; open M-F 8am-4:30pm). **Kelly Dahl** (46 sites) lies among pine trees and picnic tables 3 mi. south of Nederland on Rte. 119. **Rainbow Lakes** (18 sites, first come, first served; no water) is 6½ mi. northwest of Nederland: turn at the Mountain Research Station (CR 119) and follow the road for 5 mi. (open late May-mid-Sept.). The two gems of the forest are **Peaceful Valley** (18 sites) and **Camp Dick** (46 sites). Both lie north on Rte. 72 and offer cross-country skiing in the winter. (☎800-280-2267; Rainbow Lakes: 970-444-6600. All sites are $12, $6 per additional car, except Rainbow Lakes, $6/$3. Reservations recommended, especially on weekends.)

◖ FOOD AND HANGOUTS

The streets on the **Hill** surrounding CU and along the **Pearl St. Mall** burst with good eateries, natural foods markets, and colorful bars. Boulder may have more options for vegetarians than carnivores.

The Sink, 1165 13th St. (☎444-7465), on the Hill. This Boulder classic still awaits the return of its former janitor, Robert Redford, who quit his job and headed to California in the late 50s. Surprisingly upscale new cuisine and great pizzas are served amid wild graffiti, low ceilings, and pipes. Burgers $6-7. Open M-Sa 11am-2am, Su noon-2am; food served until 10pm.

Foolish Craig's, 1611 Pearl St. (☎247-9383). Craig foolishly gave the French crepe an American twist ($5-7.50); take for example the "Homer" crepe —"Doh!" However, the Breast 'o Pesto chicken crepe is anything but foolish. For those who pine for Paris or simply enjoy Nutella, try the classic chocolate Nutella crepe for dessert. Open M-F 8am-9pm, Sa-Su 8am-10pm. Occasional live music on weekends.

Alfalfa's, 2651 Broadway (☎442-0909). A delightful supermarket that specializes in organic food. A good place to buy provisions. The kitchen also sells a huge selection of prepared goods at cheap prices. Pasta salads galore start at just $4 per lb., and fresh wraps range $4.50-5. There's an extensive salad bar with a number of creative components ($4.60 per lb.), and, of course, an oh-so-trendy juice bar. Open daily 7am-10pm.

Daddy Bruce's Barbecue (☎449-8890), corner of 20th and Arapahoe, is the place to be with a hankerin' for meat. You'll know it by the heavenly aroma of beef brisket ($8) and BBQ chicken ($8) floating from this pantry-sized restaurant. Open daily 11am-3pm.

▧ **TEALIGHTFUL TREATS** Plopped down next to the Boulder Museum of Contemporary Art is an honest-to-goodness **Dushanbe teahouse,** 1770 13th St., built by artists from Tajikstan (part of the former Soviet Union), in Boulder's sister city, Dushanbe. The structure was then piece-mailed to Boulder, where it was assembled in 1998. The building is owned by the city and leased to restaurateur Lenny Martinelli, who lays out a scrumptious spread. It's more than worth the price of a cup of tea ($2-4) to sit on a *topchan* in this artistic wonderworld and contemplate life in ancient Persia. Lunch starts at $5.50 and dinner at $7. Don't forget to say *hush omaded* (thank you) to the people of Dushanbe when you go. (☎442-4993. Open M-F 8am-9pm, Sa-Su 8am-10pm.)

👁 SIGHTS

The tiny **Boulder Museum of Contemporary Art,** 1750 13th St., focuses on regional art. (☎443-2122. Open W-F noon-8pm, Su noon-5pm; in winter Tu-Sa 11am-5pm, Su noon-5pm. $4, seniors and students $3. Kids free.) The intimate **Leanin' Tree Museum,** 6055 Longbow Dr., presents 200 paintings and 80 bronze sculptures that focus on Western themes. The Lloyd Mitchell paintings are good for a chuckle. (☎530-1442. Open M-F 8am-4:30pm, Sa-Su 10am-4pm. Free.) **The Celestial Seasonings Tea Company,** 4600 Sleepytime Dr., just min. from the Leanin' Tree Museum, lures tourists with tea samples and free tours through the factory. Don't bother doing your hair—all visitors into the factory must wear a fashionable hairnet. Putting vanity aside, the hairnet is worth a trip into the infamous "Peppermint Room." All leave Celestial Seasonings with clear sinuses and a new found appreciation for tea. (☎581-1202. Tea shop open M-F 9am-6pm, Sa 9am-5pm, Su 11am-5pm. Tours M-Sa at 10, 11am, noon, 1, 2, and 3pm. Su on the hr. from 11am-3pm.) Writers give readings in the Beat/Buddhist tradition at the small **Naropa University,** 2130 Arapahoe Ave., while others participate in meditation workshops. (☎444-0202; call for current office hrs.) The **Rockies Brewing Company,** 2880 Wilderness Pl., off Velmont, offers tours and free beer. (☎444-8448. Pub open M-F 11am-10pm, Sa 11am-8pm; in winter M-F 11am-8pm. 25min. tours M-Sa 2pm.)

Due to its proximity to the mountains, Boulder's location supports many outdoor activities. **Boulder Creek,** at the foot of the mountains, is prime hiking and biking territory, as is **Scott Carpenter Park. Chautauqua Park** has a number of trails varying in length and difficulty that climb up and around the **Flatirons. The Enchanted Mesa/McClintock Trail** is a self-guided nature trail that is partially wheelchair accessible. Before heading out, prepare yourself on how to deal with potentially lurking mountain lions, and grab a trailmap at the entrance of Chautauqua Park.

🎵🎭 ENTERTAINMENT AND NIGHTLIFE

A perennially outrageous street scene rocks the Mall and the Hill; the university's kiosks have the low-down on downtown happenings. The **University Memorial Center,** 1609 Euclid (16th St. becomes Euclid on campus), hosts many events (☎492-6161). On the 3rd fl., its Cultural Events Board (☎492-3221) has the latest word on all CU-sponsored activities. Late June through early Aug., the **Colorado Shakespeare Festival** suffers the slings and arrows of outrageous fortune. (☎492-0554. Tickets $16-40; previews $10-20; $2 student and senior discount.) The **Colorado Music Festival** plays in July and Aug. (☎449-2413. Tickets $12-35; seniors and students $12 or $2 off higher-priced tickets.) The local indie music scene is on display at the popular **Fox Theater and Cafe,** 1135 13th St. (☎447-0095). From Apr.-Oct., Boulder shuts down 13th St., between Canyon and Arapahoe, for a good ol' **farmer's market** (open W 10am-2pm, Sa 8am-2pm).

Boulder literally overflows with nightlife hotspots, each with its own unique spin. For bluegrass and funk, head to **Mountain Sun,** 2535 Pearl St. (☎546-0886. Open M-Sa 11:30am-1am, Su noon-midnight. Su nights feature acoustic performances from 10pm-1am.) The **Bookend Cafe,** 1115 Pearl St., attached to the famous **Boulder Bookstore,** is an established local favorite where people go to see and be seen. Snarf down a chocolate caramel bar, muffin, cookie, or piece of pie while you're watching from the best vantage point, the outdoor patio. (☎440-6699. Open M-Th 6:45am-10pm, F 6:45am-11pm, Sa 8am-11pm, Su 8am-10pm.) For house and trance, head over to **Soma,** 1915 Broadway. If the music doesn't get to you, the red lighted interior and dizzyingly large dance floor will make your world spin 'round. (☎402-1690. Open daily 8pm-2am.)

ROCKY MOUNTAIN NATIONAL PARK ☎970

Of all the US national parks, Rocky Mountain National Park is closest to heaven. A third of the park lies above treeline and Longs Peak pierces the sky at 14,255 feet. Here among the clouds, bitterly cold winds whip through a craggy landscape carpeted with dwarf wildflowers, arctic shrubs, granite boulders, and crystalline lakes.

The city of Estes Park, located immediately east of the park, hosts the vast majority of would-be mountaineers and alpinists, who crowd the shopping areas and boulevards in the summer. To the west of the park, the town of Grand Lake, located on the edges of two glacial lakes, is a more tranquil base from which to explore the park's less traversed but equally stunning western side. Trail Ridge Rd./U.S. 34 runs 48 miles through the park from Grand Lake to Estes Park.

✳❓ ORIENTATION AND PRACTICAL INFORMATION

You can reach the national park from Boulder via U.S. 36 or scenic Rte. 7, or from the northeast up the Big Thompson Canyon via U.S. 34 (but beware flash floods).

Visitor Info: Park Headquarters and Visitors Center (☎586-1206), 2½ mi. west of Estes Park on Rte. 36, at the Beaver Meadows entrance to the park. Open daily mid-June to late Aug. 8am-9pm; Labor Day to mid-June 8am-5pm. Winter evening programs on park-related topics are offered Sa 7pm; in summer daily at 7:30pm; a park introduction film is shown every 30min. 8:30am-4pm. **Kawuneeche Visitors Center** (☎627-3471), just outside the park's western entrance and 1¼ mi. north of Grand Lake, offers similar info. Open daily mid-May to late Aug. 8am-6pm; Sept. 8am-5pm; Oct. to mid-May 8am-4:30pm. Evening programs Sa 7pm (during winter, on the 2nd Sa of the month). The high-altitude **Alpine Visitors Center,** at the crest of Trail Ridge Rd., has a great view of the tundra. Open daily mid-June to late Aug. 9am-5pm; late May to mid-June and late Aug. to mid-Oct. 10am-4:30pm. **Lily Lake Visitors Center,** 6 mi. south of Park Headquarters on Rte. 7, opens only in summer (daily 9am-4:30pm). Park **entrance fee** is $10 per vehicle, $5 per cyclist or pedestrian; the pass is valid for 7 days.

Park Weather and Road Conditions: ☎586-1333.

Internet Access: Estes Park Public Library, 335 E Elkhorn (☎586-8116). Open summer M-F 9am-9pm, F-Sa 9am-5pm, Su 1-5pm; in winter M-Th 10am-9pm, F-Sa 10am-5pm, Su 1-5pm.

Hospital: Estes Park Medical Center, ☎586-2317.

Park Emergency: ☎586-1399.

Post Office: Grand Lake, 520 Center Dr. Open M-F 8:30am-5pm. **ZIP code:** 80447. **Estes Park,** 215 W. Riverside Dr. Open M-F 8:30am-5:30pm, Sa 10am-2pm. **ZIP code:** 80517. **Area code:** 970.

▟ ACCOMMODATIONS

ESTES PARK

Although Estes Park has an abundance of expensive lodges and motels, there are a few good deals on indoor beds near the national park, especially in winter when temperatures drop and tourists leave.

The Colorado Mountain School, 351 Moraine Ave. (☎586-5758). Tidy, dorm-style accommodations are open to travelers unless already booked by mountain-climbing students. Wood bunks with comfortable mattresses, linen, and showers. 17 beds. $20 per person, $18 in winter. Reservations recommended 1 week in advance.

Estes Park Center YMCA, 2515 Tunnel Rd. (☎586-3341, ext. 1010), follow Rte. 36 to Rte. 66; 2 mi. from the park entrance. Extensive facilities on the 860-acre complex include mini-golf and a pool, as well as daily hikes for guests and horseback rides ($20 per hr.). A 4-person cabin with kitchen and bath from $60; 5-person cabins $113; 7-person cabins $153. A 1-day guest membership is required to stay ($3, families $5). Call ahead; reservations for summer accepted starting May 1st.

GRAND LAKE

Though inaccessible without a car in the winter, this town is the "snowmobile capital of Colorado" and offers spectacular cross-country routes.

 Shadowcliff Hostel (HI-AYH), 405 Summerland Park Rd. (☎627-9220); from the western entrance, veer left to Grand Lake, then take the left fork ¼ mi. into town on W. Portal Rd. In downtown Grand Lake, take a left at Garfield, and turn right onto W. Portal. Hand-built pine lodge perched on a cliff overlooking Shadow Mountain Lake and the Rockies. Hiking trails, kitchen, showers and a wood burning stove. Open late May to Oct. Dorms $10, non-members $12, bedding rental $1. Private singles $27, doubles $33; $5 per additional person. Cabins sleeping 6-8 $66-77 per day; 6-day minimum stay. Make cabin reservations as far as a year in advance.

Sunset Motel, 505 Grand Ave. (☎627-3318). With a yellow front and baby blue trim, you can't miss the Sunset Motel. Friendly owners, cozy rooms, and the only heated indoor pool in Grand Lake equals a warm stay. Singles $50-60; doubles $70-100; 10% discount with *Let's Go: USA.*

Bluebird Motel, 30 River Dr. (☎627-9314), on Rte. 34 west of Grand Lake. Variety is the key word here. Some rooms have couches, many have fridges, others have complete kitchenettes. The clean and cheerful Bluebird Motel overlooks Shadow Mountain Lake and the snow-capped Continental Divide. Singles $30-50; doubles $40-55.

▌ CAMPING

You can camp a total of seven days anywhere within the park, at which point you must look for other accommodations. All national park sites are $16 (winter sites are $10). A **backcountry** camping permit ($15) is required in the summer. On the eastern slope, permits are available inside the park from the **Backcountry Permits and Trip Planning Building,** a 2min. walk from the park headquarters. (☎586-1242. Open daily in summer 7am-7pm, in winter 8am-4:30pm.) The friendly staff will ensure you're prepared. In the west, see the folks at the **Kawuneeche Visitors Center.**

GRAND LAKE

The cheapest camping in the National Park is in the surrounding national forests. **Stillwater Campground,** west of Grand Lake on the shores of the hot boating spot Lake Granby, has 123 tranquil sites. ($15-18, with electricity $20.) **Green Ridge Campground,** located on the south end of Shadow Mountain Lake (81 sites; $12), is also a good bet. Both campgrounds have toilets, water, and boat ramps, and are open late May to early Sept. Make reservations for a $9 fee (☎800-260-2267) or arrive early for a first come, first served spot. **Timber Creek,** 10 mi. north of Grand Lake, is the only national park campground on the western side of the park. Open year-round, it is comprised of 100 woodsy sites. There is no water at Timber Creek in the winter.

EAST SIDE OF THE PARK

Moraine Park, 3 mi. west of Beaver Meadows Park Headquarters on Bear Lake Rd., is open all year and has 247 sites with open, sunny spots. **Glacier Basin** (9 mi. from Estes, south of Moraine Park) is open in summer only and offers 150 secluded sites and a spectacular view of the mountains. Both Moraine Park and Glacier Basin *require* reservations in summer (☎800-365-2267). **Aspenglen,** 5 mi. west of Estes Park near the Fall River entrance, has 54 sites early May through Sept. **Longs Peak Campground** has tent sites only on a first come, first served basis and is a prime location to begin climbing Longs Peak. There is a three-night maximum stay within this campground and no water in winter.

◖ FOOD

ESTES PARK

The Notchtop Pub (☎586-0272), in the upper Stanley Village Shopping Plaza, east of downtown off Rte. 34. Locals and bohemians flock to the Notchtop for homemade everything, including breads, pastries, and pies baked fresh every morning. A mean lunch of soups ($3), salads ($4-6), and sandwiches (starting at $5). Open daily 8am-9pm; bakery open Su-Th 7am-10pm, F-Sa 7am-11pm.

Mama Rose's, 338 E. Elkhorn Ave. (☎586-3330), on the riverwalk in Barlow Plaza. Heaping portions of Italian food. Mama's special gives carbo-depleted mountain hoppers all-you-can-eat soup, salad, garlic bread, pasta, and spumoni for $11. All-you-can-eat breakfast special $6. Open daily 4-9pm.

GRAND LAKE

Marie's Grand Lake Cafe, 928 Grand Ave. (☎627-9475), located on the lake. A watering hole for locals. Huge breakfast of 2 eggs, steak, pancakes, and hashbrowns for $5. Open daily 6am-10pm, in winter W-Su 6am-8pm.

Pancho and Lefty's, 1120 Grand Ave. (☎627-8773). The price is right, as are the portions; their deliciously spicy tamales ($5.75) or crunchy *chimichangas* ($6.75) are cases in point. Open daily 11am-9pm; in winter W-M 6am-8pm.

▲ EXPLORING ROCKY MOUNTAIN NATIONAL PARK

TRAIL RIDGE ROAD. The star of the park is **Trail Ridge Rd.** (U.S. 34), a 48 mi. stretch that rises 12,183 ft. above sea level into frigid tundra. This main drag through the park is the highest continuously paved road in the world. Best done in the morning before the crowds, the round-trip drive takes roughly 3hr. by car; beware of slow-moving tour buses and people who stop without warning to ogle at wildlife. The road is closed Oct. to May for weather reasons and is passable only in the afternoon well into the summer. Many sights within the park are accessible from Trail Ridge Rd. Heading west, you'll come to the **Forest Canyon Overlook,** which offers an impressive look at the vast tree-carpeted landscape. The interesting 30min. **Tundra Communities Trail** provides a most likely once-in-a-lifetime-look at the fragile tundral environment. Signposts along the paved trail instruct on the geology and wildlife pertinent to the tundra. The **Lava Cliffs** attract large crowds, but are worth the hassle. The **Alpine Visitors Center** lies just beyond the Lava Cliffs to the west and is probably the most difficult place along Trail Ridge Rd. to find parking.

After the Alpine Visitors Center, the traffic and crowds become noticeably thinner. Enjoy the western half of the park; it has all the eastern half has to offer, without the frustration of dealing with humans. Numerous trailheads lie in the western half, as does the Continental Divide, which has an accompanying hiking trail. Trail Ridge Rd. ends in **Grand Lake,** a small but refreshing town with ample outdoor opportunities of its own. An overnight trek into the scenic and remote **North** or **East Inlets** leaves camera-toting crowds behind. An 11 mi. trail ascends 2240 ft. through pristine wilderness to **Lake Nanita** (leave from North Inlet). From East Inlet, a 7 mi. course leads to **Lake Verna,** where plump trout make for excellent fishing. Grand and Shadow Mountain Lakes are great spots for water activities, and numerous hiking trails start in the town.

OLD FALL RIVER ROAD. A wilder alternative to Trail Ridge Rd. is **Old Fall River Rd.** Entering Rocky Mountain National Park from the east side on Rte. 34 will take you by **Sheep Lakes,** a popular crossing for Bighorn Sheep. After Sheep Lakes, veer right toward the **Alluvial Fan** and Old Fall River Rd. The road is paved only at first; drivers will notice the destruction caused by flooding in 1982 along the way. After **Endovalley** picnic area, Old Fall River Rd. becomes one-way only, unpaved, and uphill. For 9 mi. the road twists around the mountain, working its way above timberline. From Old Fall River Rd., you can access the **Mt. Chapin** trailhead. Because most of the trail lies above timberline, start this one early. Climb Mt. Chapin or hike around it to the saddle, a great place to picnic. From here, the adventurous can continue on to **Mt. Chiquita** and **Ypsilon Mountain.** The hike to Mt. Chapin takes just a morning, but the other mountains require most of the day. Watch for afternoon thunderstorms and plan accordingly—the tundra offers little protection. Back on the road, the view of the mountaintops is spectacular. The finale is worth the drive, unless you're afraid of heights. The road empties out behind the Alpine visitors center.

BEAR LAKE ROAD. Bear Lake Rd. lies south of Trail Ridge Rd. and leads to the most popular hiking trails within the park. **Moraine Park Museum,** en route to the campsites, has exhibits on the park's geology and ecosystem, as well as some comfy rocking chairs with a view of the mountains. (Open in summer 9am-5pm.) **Hollowell Park** is usually an uncrowded area with picnic tables and an unfrequented but beautiful trail. The path crosses an open meadow and then empties out into a serene field of aspens. The Hollowell trail also provides a look at the significant beaver activity along **Mill Creek.** Hollowell park may not take you through the tundra, but at least the size of the crowds on the trail doesn't scare away the wildlife.

The park's premier hiking is the **Bear Lake Trailhead.** In the summer, the parking lot fills up by 9am, but if you're slow to rise, a shuttle bus runs from points along the road to the trailhead where you can begin the ½ mi. hike around Bear Lake. Trails also go up to **Nymph** (½ mi. one way), **Dream** (1.1 mi.), and **Emerald Lakes** (1¾ mi.), three glacial pools which offer inspiring glimpses of the higher rock tops. The last leg of the trail up to Emerald lake is steep and rocky at points, although finding a place to sit and enjoy the view among the cluster of people at the end of the trail is the hardest part. To leave the excessive crowds behind, choose the trail that forks to the left towards **Lake Haiyaha** (2¼ mi.)—the trail offers superb views of the mountains. A scramble over the rocks at the end of the trail earns you a peek at hidden Lake Haiyaha—it's more beautiful than the other three lakes anyway.

VAIL ☎970

The largest one-mountain ski resort in all of North America, Vail also holds the ruby-encrusted crown of 2nd most-visited ski resort in the US (Breckinridge Mountain, p. 676, holds the diamond-encrusted one). The trendy town has its fair share of ritzy hotels, swank saloons, and sexy boutiques, while the mountain wows skiers with its prime snow conditions, a vertical drop of 3330 feet, 174 ski runs, and 31 lifts. Discovered by Lord Gore in 1854, Vail and its surrounding valley were invaded by miners during the Rockies gold rush in the 1870s. According to local lore, the Ute Indians adored the area's rich supply of game, but they became so upset with the white man that they set fire to the forest, creating the resort's open terrain.

⚅ PRACTICAL INFORMATION. **Vail Village** and **Lionshead Village** form the entity known as Vail. They are pedestrian only, so visitors must park in garages off **Frontage Rd.** Parking is free during the summer. A free bus links the two villages; the stops are marked by signs. Vail's two **visitors centers** are at either end of the village; the larger one is at the **Vail Transportation Center** on S. Frontage Rd. (☎479-1394 or 800-525-3875. Open M-F 9am-6pm, Sa-Su 9:30am-5:30pm. Hrs. subject to change.) The other is in Lionshead Village, also on S. Frontage Rd. (☎479-1385. Open daily 9am-7pm; in winter 8am-5pm.) **Greyhound** (☎476-5137; ticket office open daily 8am-6:30pm) buses eager skiers out of its depot, in the Transportation Bldg. next to the main visitors center, to Glenwood Springs (1½hr., 4 per day, $16); Denver (2hr., 5 per day, $18-19); and Grand Junction (3½hr., 4 per day, $15.50-16.50). **Avon/Beaver Creek Transit** (☎748-4120 for schedule info; office hrs. daily 8am-noon and 1-5pm) runs bus routes between Vail and its surrounding areas, including Eagle and Edwards (each $2). Free bus service covers the area around Vail Village, Lionshead, and East and West Vail. **Weather conditions:** ☎476-5677. **Internet Access: Vail Public Library,** 292 W. Meadow Dr. Three terminals are available for email in 20min. first come, first served slots. (☎479-2184. Open M-Th 10am-8pm, F 10am-6pm, Sa-Su 11am-6pm.) **Post office:** 1300 N. Frontage Rd. W. (☎476-5217. Open M-F 8:30am-5:30pm, Sa 8:30am-noon.) **ZIP code:** 81657. **Area code:** 970.

⌐ ACCOMMODATIONS. The phrase "cheap lodging" is not part of Vail's vocabulary. Rooms in the resort town rarely dip below $175 per night in winter, and summer lodging is often equally pricey. **The Prairie Moon,** 738 Grand Ave., offers some of the cheapest lodging outside the expensive resort area. Located in Eagle, about 30 mi. west of Vail, The Prairie Moon has large, clean rooms with fridges and micro-

ROCKY MOUNTAINS

waves. (☎328-6680. Singles and doubles from $35; triples $45.) A bus shuttles visitors daily between Eagle and Vail (see **Anon/Beaver Creek Transit** above). Closer summer lodgings await at the **Roost Lodge,** 1783 N. Frontage Rd., in West Vail. Average-sized, but nicely decorated and impressively clean rooms come with cable and phones, as well as continental breakfast and access to a jacuzzi, sauna, and pool. (☎476-5451 or 800-873-3065. Singles $55-62; in winter $134-150.) The **Holy Cross Ranger District,** right off I-70 at Exit 171 (follow signs), provides info on the six campgrounds near Vail. (☎827-5715. Open M-F 8am-5pm, Sa-Su 8am-4:30pm. Closed weekends after Labor Day.) With 25 sites, **Gore Creek** is the closest and most popular campground. It's well-situated right outside East Vail, among birch trees, wild flowers, and mountains, and it is within hiking distance of the free Vail bus. ($12; sites have water and 10-day limit.)

◖◗ FOOD. Garfinkel's, a hidden hangout accessible by foot in Vail's Lionshead Village (directly across from the gondola) offers nightly specials that include $5 burgers, $3 margaritas, and $7 steak fajitas Enjoy your meal on a porch that practically merges with the ski slope. (☎476-3789. Restaurant open daily 11am-10pm; bar open until 2am. DJs and the occasional live band supply Garfinkel's with tunes; Su nights are disco night.) **DJ's Classic Diner,** in nearby Concert Hall Plaza, whips up old-fashioned specialty omelettes from $5, as well as $4-6 crepes and $4.50 blintzes. (☎476-2336. Open daily 7am-1am, in winter 24hr.)

▣▥ SIGHTS AND ACTIVITIES. The **Colorado Ski Museum,** in the Transportation Bldg. in Vail Village, offers a glimpse into Vail's past and houses the **Ski Hall of Fame.** (☎476-1876. Open Tu-Su 10am-5pm. $1, under 12 free.) Before slaloming, the unequipped visit **Ski Base,** 675 W. Lionshead Circle. (☎476-5799. Open daily in winter 9am-7pm. Skis, poles, and boots start from $13 per day; snowboard and boots from $19 per day.) It becomes **Wheel Base Bike Shop** in summer. (Open M-Sa 9am-6pm, Su 9am-5pm. Path bikes $14 per 8 hrs; mountain bikes $20 per 8 hrs.)

Vail caters to sun worshippers in the summer, when the ski runs become **hiking and biking trails.** The **Eagle Bahn Gondola** at Lionshead and the **Vista Bahn chairlift,** part of the **Vail Resort** in Vail village, whisk hikers, bikers, and sightseers to the top of the mountains for breathtaking views. (☎476-9090, office hours 8:30am-4:30pm. Eagle Bahn is open in summer Th-Sa 10am-9pm, Su-W 10am-4pm; after Labor Day, F-Su only. Vista Bahn open daily late May-early Sept. 10am-4pm. An all-day summer pass on the Vista Bahn and Eagle Bahn includes hauling fees and costs $15, ages 65-69 $10, 70 and over free.) Rental **bikes** are available atop Vail Mountain. (☎476-9090. $15 per hr., $35 per day.) During the summer months, enjoy the **Eagle Bahn Gondola Twilight Ride** from 6-8pm. (Th and Sa $8, children 5-12 $6, F free.) The **Gore Creek Fly Fisherman,** 183-7 Gore Creek Dr., reels in the daily catch of river info. (☎476-3296 or 800-369-3044. Open daily 8am-10pm; May 15 to June and Sept. to Oct. 15 Su-Th 8am-8pm. Rod rentals $15 per day, $25 with boots and waders.)

The **Gerald R. Ford Amphitheater** presents a number of outdoor concerts, dance festivals, and theater productions on its grounds. (☎476-2918. Open Tu-Sa 2pm-6pm. Prices free-$85, depending on production and seat location.) The **Vilar Center for the Arts** (☎845-8497 or 888-920-2787), at Beaver Creek, also hosts world renowned musicians, actors, and dancers.

ASPEN ☎970

Aspen was founded as a silver mining camp, but the silver ran out quickly and by 1940 the town was almost gone. Wealthy visionaries took one look at the location of the floundering village and transformed it into a winter playground. Today, Aspen's skiing, scenery, and festivals are matched only by the prices in the exclusive boutiques downtown. To catch Aspen on the semi-cheap, stay in Glenwood Springs (40 miles north on Rte. 82; see p. 686) and make a daytrip here or camp amid aspen groves in the nearby national forest.

■ **PRACTICAL INFORMATION. Visitors centers:** 320 Hyman Ave., in the opera house (open M-Sa 9am-6pm, Su 10am-5pm); and 425 Rio Grand Pl. (☎925-1940 or 800-262-7736; open M-Sa 10am-4pm). The **Aspen Ranger District,** 806 W. Hallam, provides info on hikes and camping within 15 mi. of Aspen. (☎925-3445; weather info 920-1664. Open M-F 8am-5pm, in summer also Sa 8am-4:30pm. Topographic maps $4.) **Roads and Weather:** ☎945-2221. **Area code:** 970.

ACCOMMODATIONS. If you stay in Aspen, you'll have to bite the bullet and reach deep into your pockets. The last sound deal in town, **St. Moritz Lodge,** 344 W. Hyman Ave., charms ski bums with a pool, sauna, and hot tub. (☎925-3220 or 800-817-2069. Dorm beds $26-55 depending on season. Hotel accommodations from $59.) Unless 6 ft. of snow covers the ground, **camping** is available in one of the many National Forest campgrounds that lie within 5 mi. of Aspen. Reservable and first come, first served sites scatter just west of town on Maroon Rd. (accessible from 5pm-8:30am) and southeast on Rte. 82. (☎800-280-2267. Open June to mid-Sept. 5-day maximum stay throughout the district. Sites fill before noon. $7-12 per night.) Free **backcountry camping permits** are available at the Ranger District and sporting goods stores (see below). When you pick up your permit, consider paying $1 for insurance which will cover the cost in case you need "extraction" and rescue.

FOOD. Main Street Bakery, 201 E. Main St., serves gourmet soups ($4.25), homemade granola with fruit ($5.50), and vegetarian sandwiches ($6.50). The patio is a prime people-watching spot. (☎925-6446. Open daily 7am-9:30pm.) **In and Out House,** 233 E. Main St., is just that: a revolving door of fresh, innovative lunches for $3-7. (☎925-6647. Open M-F 8am-5pm, Sa-Su 9am-4pm.) **The Big Wrap,** 530 E. Durant Ave., rolls up creatively named veggie and Mexican wraps for $5-6.25 and mixes smoothies for $4. (☎544-1700. Open daily 10am-6pm; in winter 10am-6pm.) American favorites, such as burgers ($6-8) and grilled cheese ($5), take center stage at **Boogies Diner,** 534 Cooper. Obey the house rules: "schnoodling in booths only." (☎925-6610. Open M-F 11am-10pm; off-season M-F 11am-9pm.)

SKIING AND FESTIVALS. Skiing is the main attraction in Aspen. The hills surrounding town contain four ski areas: **Aspen Mountain, Aspen Highlands, Buttermilk Mountain,** and **Snowmass Ski Area.** Interchangeable lift tickets mean that the areas operate as one extended resort; for the best deal, buy multi-day passes in advance by calling ahead. (☎925-1220 or 800-525-6200. Day passes vary by season, expect $60+, ages 13-27 $45, ages 7-12 $37, 65-69 $55, over 70 and under 7 free.) Each of the mountains has a different character and difficulty. Beginners are welcomed to Buttermilk's gentle slopes for lessons and snowplowing. Aspen Highlands has the most diverse offering of trails and is being prepared for expansion. Aspen Mountain caters to expert skiers; there are no easy trails on this hill. The granddaddy of the Aspen ski areas, Snowmass boasts 20 lifts and countless runs. All but the most timid of beginners will find something to occupy them here. Half-pipes and a terrain course also make this a favorite of snowboarders.

The **Glenwood Springs Hostel** offers a $39 full-day lift ticket for the Aspen ski resorts (see p. 686). In summer, the **Silver Queen Gondola** heads to the top of the mountains. (☎925-1220 or 800-525-6200. Open daily late May to early Sept. 10am-4pm. $19 per day, $29 per week.) At **Snowmass Mountain,** you can take a chairlift to the top and ride your mountain bike down (in summer daily 9:30am-3pm; free). The mountains of **Maroon Bells** and the well-known 1¾ mi. hike to **Cascade Lake** are not to be missed, but Maroon Creek Rd. is closed to traffic from 8:30am to 5pm daily. To avoid paying $5 for a long, slow bus ride, which departs every 30min. from **Rubey Park,** plan an early morning or a sunset hike. In Aspen proper, the **Ute Trail** leaves Ute Ave. and climbs to a rock ledge, following a windy and hairy course. The peak is a spectacular spot to watch the sunset (climbing time 30min.). The gentler **Hunter Trail** wanders through town and is a favorite place to jog or bike.

Aspen's most famous event, the **Aspen Music Festival,** features jazz, opera, and classical music from late June through Aug. A variety of shows are held every night in many venues around town. (☎925-9042; 925-3254 for a schedule. Free shuttle bus for listeners. Many concerts are free.) **Aspen Theatre in the Park** presents a variety of shows each night from July through late Aug. (☎920-5770. Tickets $25-30.)

GLENWOOD SPRINGS   ☎970

Glenwood Springs, located along I-70, 40 miles north of Aspen on Rte. 82, allows budget travelers to stay near Aspen's famed slopes and keep their souls out of pawn. However, this small town has attractions of its own, notably the hot springs.

🛂 PRACTICAL INFORMATION. Amtrak, 413 7th St. (☎945-9563; open daily 9:30am-4:30pm) runs to Denver (6¾hr., $42-64) and Salt Lake City (8¼hr., $48-87). **Greyhound,** at the W. Glenwood Mall, (☎945-8501; open M-F 8am-4:30pm), buses to Denver (3½hr., 5 per day, from $28) and Grand Junction (2hr., 5 per day, $12). The **Roaring Fork Transit Agency (RFTA),** at Durant and Mill St. in Aspen (☎925-8484; open M-F 6am-7:30pm, Sa-Su 8:30am-6:30pm) screams to Aspen (1½hr.; $6, children $5). The **White River National Forest Headquarters,** 9th and Grand Ave., has info on the outdoors (☎945-2521; open M-F 8am-5pm). **Glenwood Springs Chamber Resort Association:** 1102 Grand Ave. (☎945-6589. Open June-Aug. M-F 9am-6pm, Sa-Su 10am-3pm; Aug.-June M-F 8:30am-5pm. Printed info available 24hr.) **Post Office:** 113 9th St. (☎945-5611. Open M-F 8am-6pm, Sa 9am-1pm.) **ZIP code:** 81601. **Area code:** 970.

🖼🖼 ACCOMMODATIONS AND FOOD. Within walking distance of the springs and downtown, you'll find the **Glenwood Springs Hostel (HI-AYH),** 1021 Grand Ave., which consists of a spacious Victorian house and a newer building next door. This hostel offers a wide variety of trips and tours in the area, including discounts on skiing at Aspen. Other amenities include a meditation room, a darkroom, and the owner's amazing vinyl collection. (☎945-8545 or 800-946-7835. Lockout 10am-4pm. Free pick-up from train and bus stations. Kitchen use and some food included. Linen $1. Dorms $12, 4 nights $39; private singles $19; private doubles $26.) Relatively cheap (compared to Aspen) motels can be found in Glenwood Springs. The most affordable motel is the **Frontier Lodge,** 2834 Glen Ave. (☎970-945-5496 or 888-606-0602. Singles $35; doubles $45.)

The **Daily Bread Cafe and Bakery,** 729 Grand Ave., draws in the locals for fresh, wholesome breakfasts and lunches. For a veggie-friendly breakfast, there are many innovative omelettes for under $7. (☎945-6253. Open M-F 7am-2pm, Sa 8am-2pm, Su 8am-noon.) For hearty eats or a late-night snack, try the **Village Inn,** 102 W. 6th St. (☎945-9275. Open Su-Th 6am-11pm, F-Sa 6am-midnight.) **Doc Holliday's Saloon,** 724 Grand Ave., is the place for burgers ($6-8) and beers. (☎945-9050. Open daily 10am-2am, food served 11am-11pm.)

🏃 ACTIVITIES. Glenwood Hot Springs Lodge and Pool, 401 N. River Rd., in a huge resort complex, contains the world's largest outdoor hot springs pool, a waterslide, and spas with different water temperatures. (☎945-6571 or 800-537-7946. Open daily 7:30am-10pm. Day pass $7.50, after 9pm $5; ages 3-12 $5.25/$4.50.) Pamper yourself at **Yampah Spa and Vapor Caves,** 709 E. 6th St. Sweat the stress of travel out in these 125°F natural steam caves and then relax in the Solarium. (☎945-0667. Open daily 9am-9pm. $8.75, hostelers $4.75 with hostel pass/receipt.)

While most skiers are heading to Aspen's fab four, relaxed family-style skiing is available at the uncrowded **Sunlight,** 10901 County Rd. 117, 10 mi. west of town. (☎945-7491 or 800-445-7931. $30 per day, ages 6-13 $20; hosteler discount.) Take a tour of the 8th wonder of the world, as the **Fairy Caves** were dubbed in 1896. A new company called **Glenwood Caverns,** 508 Pine St., behind the Colorado Hotel, has just opened them to the public. (☎945-4228. Open Apr. 15 to Nov. 1. 2hr. tours depart every hour 9am-6pm. M-F $10, Sa-Su $12; children $5/$6.)

Call the USA

"feel free to call"

1-800-COLLECT

When in Ireland
Dial: 1-800-COLLECT (265 5328)

When in N. Ireland, UK & Europe
Dial: 00-800-COLLECT USA (265 5328 872)

Member of
Dublin Tourism

Australia	0011	800 265 5328 872
Finland	990	800 265 5328 872
Hong Kong	001	800 265 5328 872
Israel	014	800 265 5328 872
Japan	0061	800 265 5328 872
New Zealand	0011	800 265 5328 872

GRAND JUNCTION ☎970

Grand Junction gets its name from its seat at the junction of the Colorado and Gunnison Rivers and the conjunction-junction of the Río Grande and Denver Railroads.
Today, the name aptly describes Grand Junction's role as a transportation hub for
the masses heading to southern Utah and the Colorado Rockies. Most travelers will
want to get out of Grand Junction quickly, but if you're stuck there for a while,
inquire at the Visitors Bureau (see below) about tasting tours of local wineries.

⚐ PRACTICAL INFORMATION. Amtrak, 339 S. 1st St. (☎241-2733; station open
daily 10am-6pm), shoots twice daily to Denver ($43-79) and Salt Lake City ($39-71).
The **Greyhound** station, at 5th and Ute St. (☎242-6012; ticket window open 24hr.),
has service to Denver (5½hr., 7per day, $33); Durango (5hr., 1 per day, $37); Salt
Lake City (6-11hr., 1 per day, $47-50); and Los Angeles (16hr., 2 per day, $95-100).
The **Grand Junction Visitor Bureau,** 740 Horizon Dr., Exit 31 off I-70, behind the Taco
Bell. (☎244-1480. Open daily May to mid-Oct. 8:30am-8pm; late Oct. to Apr. 8:30am-
5pm.) **Domestic violence line:** ☎241-6704. **Internet access** is available via **Cyber Cafe,** at
8th and North Ave. (☎244-3400). **Post Office:** 241 N. 4th St. (☎244-3401. Open M-F
8am-5:15pm, Sa 9am-12:30pm.) **ZIP code:** 81501. **Area code:** 970.

⚐⚐ ACCOMMODATIONS AND FOOD. The lovely, historic **Melrose Hotel (HI-
AYH),** 337 Colorado Ave., between 3rd and 4th St., assists travelers in navigating the
nearby natural wonders. In winter, owner Marcus can direct you to Powderhorn for
the best local skiing. In addition to dorm rooms, 22 meticulously decorated private
rooms are available. (☎242-9636 or 800-430-4555. Reception 8-10am and 4-9pm; call
if arrival time will not coincide. Dorms $15; singles $24, with bath $34; doubles $27/
$39.) **Columbine Motel,** 2824 North Ave., offers rooms with TVs and fridges. (☎241-
2908. Singles $42; doubles $52.) More camping is available at **Island Acres State Park,**
10 mi. east on the banks of the Colorado River, off I-70 Exit 47. (☎464-0548. 6 tent
sites $9, 34 partial hook-ups $12, 40 full hook-ups $15; $4 per day entrance fee.)
    Rockslide Restaurant and Brew Pub, 401 S. Main St., joins the avalanche of micro-
breweries blanketing the nation. The Big Bear Stout comes in an $8.50 grotler (half
gallon). Salmon and chips are $8; half-price appetizers during happy hour M-F 4-
6pm. (☎245-2111. Open daily 10am-midnight.) Mouth-watering breakfasts are the
specialty at **The Crystal Cafe,** 314 Main St. (☎242-8843. Open M-F 7am-1:45pm, Sa
8:30am-1:25pm. Bakery open until 3pm.) Grand Junction lies at the intersection of
U.S. 50 and U.S. 6 between Denver and Salt Lake City; its pit stop location draws
touring bands who refuse to drive 500 mi. between gigs. **Chameleon Club,** 234 Main
St. (☎245-3636), grooves to live music nightly until 2am. Su night is Service Industry
Night; anybody in "public service" gets happy hour prices all night.

COLORADO NATIONAL MONUMENT ☎970

Four mi. west of Grand Junction off Monument Rd., the Colorado National
Monument is a 32 sq. mi. sculpture of steep cliff faces, canyon walls, and obelisk-
like spires wrought by the forces of gravity, wind, and water. The **Rim Rock Drive**
runs along the edge of red canyons, providing views of awe-inspiring rock monoliths, the Grand Mesa, and the city of Grand Junction. **Window Rock Trail** (¼ mi.)
and **Otto's Trail** (½ mi.) are easy walks to points from which you can gaze at the
eerie, skeletal rock formations. The 6 mi. **Monument Canyon Trail** inspires visions
of grandeur, as it wanders amid the giant rocks. Check in at the monument **headquarters and visitors center,** near the western entrance. (☎858-3617. Open daily
June-Sept. 8am-6pm; off-season 9am-5pm. Entrance fee $4 per vehicle, $2 per
cyclist or hiker.) **Saddlehorn Campground,** near the visitors center, provides over
50 partially shaded sites. (First come, first served. Restrooms, water. Sites $10.)
The **Bureau of Land Management,** 2815 H Rd. (☎244-3000; open M-F 7:30am-
4:30pm), with its office across from the airport, maintains 12 sites at **Mud
Springs,** near **Glade Park** ($5). Primitive camping is permitted on all adjoining
BLM land (free).

ROCKY MOUNTAINS

DREAMS DO COME TRUE There is a good chance that the Colorado National Monument would not exist if it weren't for the efforts and antics of one man: John Otto. Otto moved to the canyon on the outskirts of Grand Junction in 1906 and was immediately entranced. He spent years living alone in the canyon, building trails so individuals could enjoy the place he loved and badgering government officials to declare the canyon a national monument. Sometimes his letters were more threats than requests. Perhaps his most interesting escapade came when President Taft was making a train stop in Grand Junction: Otto knew that Taft was a huge fan of peaches, so he lured the president to what is now the monument with a promise of delicious fruit. His tactics worked. In 1911, the monument was created, and Otto was named caretaker.

COLORADO SPRINGS   ☎ 719

Early Colorado gold seekers were shocked to find bizarre rock formations among the peaks; they named the region Garden of the Gods, in part because of the Ute legend that the rocks were petrified bodies of enemies hurled down by the gods above. The US Olympic Team, housed in Colorado Springs, continues the quest for gold, while jets from the US Air Force Academy barrel-roll overhead.

🔆🛈 ORIENTATION AND PRACTICAL INFORMATION

Colorado Springs is laid out in a grid of broad thoroughfares. **Nevada Ave.**, the main north-south strip, just east of I-25, is known for its bars and restaurants. **Cascade Ave.** is the east-west axis, while **Pikes Peak Ave.** divides the city north and south. The numbered streets west of Nevada ascend as you move west. **I-25** from Denver plows through downtown. East of Nevada Ave. remains largely residential.

Buses: Greyhound, 120 S. Weber St. (☎635-1505). To: Denver (1½-2hr., 7 per day, $12); Pueblo (1hr., 5 per day, $8); and Albuquerque (8hr., 4 per day, $58). Tickets sold daily 5:15am-10pm.

Public Transit: City Bus Service, 127 E. Kiowa (☎385-7433), at Ridefinders Transport Ctr., at Kiowa and Nevada. Serves Widefield, Manitou Springs, Ft. Carson, Garden of the Gods, and Peterson AFB (#1). Hourly service M-F 6am-6pm; 6-10am, 11am and 2-6pm every 30min.; irregular evening service until 10pm; Sa hourly service 6am-10pm, except #1 bus every 30min. $1, seniors and children ages 5-11 50¢, under 6 free; to Ft. Carson, Widefield, Fountain, Manitou Springs 25¢ extra; exact change required.

Taxis: Yellow Cab, ☎634-5000.

Tours: Pikes Peak Tours, 3704 Colorado Ave. (☎633-1181 or 800-345-8197), offers trips to the U.S. Air Force Academy and Garden of the Gods (4hr., $20, under 13 $12.50) and Pikes Peak (4hr., $30/$20), as well as a 10mi. whitewater rafting trip on the Arkansas River (7hr., includes lunch; $65/$45). Office open daily 8am-5pm.

Visitor Info: Visitors Bureau, 104 S. Cascade, #104, entrance on Colorado Ave. (☎635-7506 or 800-888-4748). Open daily 8:30am-5pm.

Post Office: 201 E. Pikes Peak Ave., at Nevada Ave. Open M-F 7:30am-5:30pm, Sa 8am-1pm. **ZIP code:** 80903. **Area code:** 719.

▌ ACCOMMODATIONS

The motels along **Nevada Ave.** are fairly shabby; opting for nearby campgrounds and spots along **W. Pikes Peak Ave.** and **W. Colorado Ave.** is a good idea.

Apache Court Motel, 3401 W. Pikes Peak Ave., off of 34th and Colorado (☎471-9440). Take bus #1 west down Colorado Ave. to 34th St. Motel sign is visible from the bus stop. Pink adobe rooms with A/C, TV, refrigerator, and a common hot tub. Summer singles M-F $45, Sa-Su $50. In winter and on some summer weekdays, $40/$55.

Amarillo Motel, 2801 W. Colorado Ave., at 34th and Colorado (☎635-8539 or 800-216-8539). Take bus #1 down Colorado Ave. toward the mountains to 28th St. The hotel sign is visible from the bus stop. Simple rooms, stayin' alive with 70s decor, have clean kitchens and TV. In summer singles $40; doubles $45; in winter $35/$40. Laundry.

Tree Haven Cottages, 3620 W. Colorado Ave. (☎578-1968). Tiny rooms fully-equipped with cable, fridge, microwaves, and a pool. Singles $43; off-season $30.

About 30min. from Colorado Springs, several **Pikes Peak National Forest** campgrounds lie in the mountains flanking Pikes Peak (generally open May-Sept.), but no local transportation serves this area. Campgrounds clutter Rte. 67, 5-10 mi. north of **Woodland Park,** 18 mi. northwest of the Springs on U.S. 24. For example, try **Colorado, Painted Rocks,** or **South Meadows** near Manitou Park. Others border U.S. 24 near the town of Lake George, 50 mi. west of the Springs (sites $9-12). You can camp on national forest property for free if you are at least 500 ft. from a road or stream. The **Pikes Peak Ranger District Office,** 601 S. Weber, has maps of the area (☎636-1602. Open M-F 8am-5pm. $4-6.) Farther afield, visitors may camp in the **Eleven Mile State Recreation Area,** off a spur road from U.S. 24 near Lake George, on a reservoir (☎748-3401; 800-678-2267 for reservations. Reservation 7am-4:45pm. Pay showers and laundry. Sites $7-9, with electricity $12; vehicle fee $4.)

🌙🍴 FOOD AND NIGHTLIFE

Students and the young-at-heart perch among outdoor tables in front of the cafes and restaurants lining **Tejon Ave.,** a few blocks east of downtown. **Old Colorado** city is home to a number of fine eateries, as well as a **farmer's market** on summer Sa between Colorado Ave. and Pikes Peak, on 24th St. **Poor Richard's Restaurant,** 324½ N. Tejon Ave., is a local coffeehouse hangout, serving pizza (cheese slices $2.50; cheese pies $11), sandwiches, and $3-6 salads (☎632-7721. Open daily 11am-10pm. Live bluegrass W, Celtic Th.) **La Baguette,** 2714 W. Colorado Ave., bakes bread and melts fondues better than you might expect in a place so far from Paris. Cheese fondue with apple slices is $6.50. (☎577-4818. Open M-Sa 7am-6pm, Su 8am-5pm.) **Jose Muldoon's,** 222 N. Tejon St., a short walk from Colorado College, allows students to put down their books and enjoy live music, canned dance tunes, or the occasional dunk tank. It is also home to the "world's largest margarita." (☎636-2311. Food served M-Th 11am-10pm, F-Sa 11am-11pm, Su 9:30am-3pm.)

👁 SIGHTS

GARDEN OF THE GODS. Between Rte. 24 (also Colorado Ave.) and 30th St. in northwest Colorado Springs, the redrock towers and spires of the "Garden," as locals call it, rise strikingly against a mountainous backdrop. *(Open daily 5am-11pm; Nov.-Apr. 5am-9pm.)* **Climbers** are regularly lured by the large red faces, while a number of exciting **mountain biking** trails cross the Garden as well. The park's hiking trails give great views of the rock formations and each can be done in 1 day. A map is available from the park's **visitors center.** *(1805 N. 30th at Gateway Rd. ☎634-6666. Open daily June-Aug. 8am-8pm; in winter 9am-5pm. Walking tours depart in summer at 10, 11am, 2 and 3pm, in winter 10am and 2pm.)*

PIKES PEAK. From any part of the town, one can't help noticing the 14,110 ft. summit of Pikes Peak on the horizon. The willing can climb the peak via the strenuous but well-maintained 26½ mi. round-trip **Barr Trail;** the trailhead is in Manitou Springs by the "Manitou Incline" sign off Ruxton Ave. Make sure you are in marathon shape and check the weather and with rangers before departing. But don't despair if you don't reach the top—explorer Zebulon Pike never reached it, either. There is a fee to drive up the gorgeous 19 mi. **Pikes Peak Hwy.,** a well-maintained dirt road. *(☎684-9383. Hwy. open daily June-Aug. 7am-7pm; daily Sept. 7am-5pm, Oct.-May 9am-3pm, weather permitting. $35 per car or $10 per person.)* Five mi. west in Manitou Springs, visitors can reserve a seat on the **Pikes Peak Cog Railway,** which takes visitors to the top every

80min. From the summit, Kansas, the Sangre de Cristo Mountains, and the Continental Divide unfold before you. This lofty view inspired Kathy Lee Bates to write "America the Beautiful." *(515 Ruxton Ave. ☎685-5401. May to early Oct. daily 8am-5:20pm; call for times in May and Aug.-Oct. Round-trip $22, children $11; reservations required.)*

CAVE OF THE WINDS. For adventurous hiking through subterranean passages, head for the contorted caverns of the **Cave of the Winds.** A laser light show dances on the canyon walls nightly at 9pm during the summer. *(On Rte. 24, 6 mi. west of Exit 141 off I-25. ☎685-5444. Guided tours daily every 15min. 9am-9pm; Sept. to late May 10am-5pm. $12, ages 6-15 $6. Light show adults $6, children $3.)* Just above Manitou Springs on Rte. 24 lies the **Cliff Dwellings Museum,** which contains replicas of ancient Anasazi pueblos dating from AD 1100-1300. *(☎800-354-9971, 685-5242, or 685-5394. Open daily June-Aug. 9am-8:30pm; Sept.-May 9am-6:30pm. $7, seniors $6, ages 7-11 $5, under 7 free.)* The **Seven Falls,** west on Cheyenne Blvd., are lit up at night. *(☎632-0765. $6.50 before 5pm, $7 after 5pm, ages 6-15 $4, seniors $5.50.)* As you drive to town, the **Starr-Kempf Residence** boasts a yard full of fantastic chrome-colored sculptures created by the couple who lives inside. *(2057 Evans Ave.)*

GOING FOR THE GOLD AND AIMING HIGH. Olympic hopefuls train with some of the world's most high-tech sports equipment at the **US Olympic Complex,** at I-25 Exit 156A; take bus #1 east to Farragut. Every 30min. to 1hr., the complex offers free 1hr. tours that include a tear-jerking film of struggle and glory. *(750 E. Boulder St. ☎578-4644 or 578-4618. Open M-Sa 9am-5pm, Su 10am-5pm.)* Earlier searches for gold are recorded at the **Pioneers' Museum,** downtown, which recounts the settling of Colorado Springs. *(215 S. Tejon St. ☎578-6650. Take Exit 156a off I-25. Open Tu-Sa 10am-5pm, in summer only Su 1-5pm. Free.)*

The **United States Air Force Academy,** 12 mi. north of town off I-25, hosts over 1 million visitors annually. The cadets' chapel was constructed of aluminum, steel, and other materials used in building airplanes. M through F during the school year, cadets gather at noon near the chapel for the cadet lunch formation (i.e., to eat). *(☎333-4515, office hours 7:30am-4:30pm. Open M-Sa 9am-5pm, Su 1-5pm.)* The **Barry Goldwater Visitors Center** has info. *(☎472-0102, tours 333-2025. Open mid-May to early Sept. daily 8am-6pm; early Sept. to mid-May 8am-5pm.)*

GREAT SAND DUNES ☎719

When Colorado's mountains all begin to look the same, head to the **Great Sand Dunes National Monument** at the northwest edge of the San Luis Valley. A sea of 700 ft. sand dunes, representing eons of wind-blown accumulation, laps silently at the base of the **Sangre de Cristo Range,** 37 mi. northeast of Alamosa and 127 mi. west of Pueblo on U.S. 160. The progress of the dunes through passes in the range is checked by the shallow **Medano Creek;** visitors can wade across the creek when it flows (Apr. to mid-July). While there aren't any trails through the dunes, visitors can dive right in. Hiking to the top takes about 1½hr. and is extremely difficult,

GROUND ZERO While most Cold War era bomb shelters are buried under 5-10 ft. of dirt, the **North American Air Defense Command Headquarters (NORAD)** was constructed 1800 ft. below Cheyenne Mt. Contrary to popular myth and legend, Cheyenne Mt. is the eyes and ears of an intricate intelligence network, as opposed to a center for nuclear action. However, the center does look like something out of a James Bond movie; a 3 mi. tunnel leads to buildings on massive springs which house computers and detectors scanning the heavens for incoming inter-continental ballistic missiles. The center was designed to be operational even after a direct nuclear attack. Call in advance to make reservations for an information session. *(M at 2pm, F at 10:30am. ☎474-2238 or 474-2239.)* The **Peterson Air Force Base,** east of Academy Blvd., houses the **Edward J. Peterson Air and Space Museum,** which showcases exhibits on the history of the base, as well as on space and satellite operations. *(☎556-4915. Museum open Tu-Sa 8:30am-4:30pm, closed on national holidays. Free.)*

since your feet sink a good 6 in. with each step. Take at least a quart of water per person, and beware the summer's intense heat—the sand can reach 140°F (60°C). Those with high-clearance four-wheel-drive can motor over the **Medano Pass Primitive Rd.** At the southern boundary of the monument, the **Oasis** complex offers four-wheel-drive tours that huff over Medano Pass Primitive Rd. to the dunes' nether regions. (☎378-2222. 2hr. tours daily 10am and 2pm. $14, ages 5-11 $8.)

Schedules of daily ranger-led hikes and talks can be found at the **visitors center,** ½ mi. past the entrance gate. The newsletter *Sand Dune Breezes* suggests drives and hikes. For more info, contact the **Superintendent,** Great Sand Dunes National Monument, Mosca, CO 81146. (☎378-2312. Open daily 8:30am-4:30pm; Sept.-May 8am-6pm. $3 per person, under 17 free. National Parks passes accepted.)

Pinyon Flats, the monument's primitive campground, is open year-round and includes drinking water. Bring mosquito repellent in June. (☎378-2312. Arrive by early afternoon. Sites $10. No reservations.) Get free **backcountry camping** permits for the dunes from the visitors center. If the park's sites are full, **Oasis** (see above) will fulfill your needs with showers and two-person sites ($12, with hook-up $18.50; $2.50 per additional person), cabins ($33 for 2 people) or teepees ($27.50 for 2 people). **San Luis State Park,** 8 mi. away in Mosca, has showers and 51 electrical sites. (☎378-2020, 800-678-2267 for camping reservations. Closed in winter. Sites $12; $4 vehicle entrance fee.) For info on nearby National Forest Campgrounds, contact the **Río Grande National Forest Service Office,** 11571 County Rd. T5, La Jara, CO 81140. (☎274-5193. Open M-F 8am-4:30pm. All sites $10.) **Area code:** 719.

SAN JUAN MOUNTAINS

Ask Coloradans about their favorite mountain retreats, and they'll most likely name a peak, lake, stream, or town in the San Juan Range of southwestern Colorado. Four **national forests**—the **Uncompahgre** (*un-cum-PAH-gray*), the **Gunnison,** the **San Juan,** and the **Río Grande**—encircle this sprawling range. **Durango** is an ideal base camp for forays into these mountains. Northeast of Durango, the **Weminuche Wilderness** tempts the hardy backpacker with a vast expanse of rugged terrain where wide, sweeping vistas stretch for miles. Get $4 maps and hiking info from **Pine Needle Mountaineering,** 835 Main Ave., Durango 81301. (☎970-247-8726. Open in summer M-Sa 9am-9pm, Su 10am-5pm; off-season M-Sa 9am-6pm, Su 10am-5pm.)

The San Juan area is easily accessible on U.S. 50, which is traveled by hundreds of thousands of tourists each summer. **Greyhound** serves the area, but very poorly; traveling by car is the best option in this region. On a happier note, the San Juans are loaded with HI-AYH hostels and campgrounds, making them one of the more economical places to visit in Colorado.

BLACK CANYON ☎970

Native American parents used to tell their children that the light-colored strands of rock streaking through the walls of the Black Canyon were the hair of a blond woman—and that if they got too close to the edge they would get tangled in it and fall. The edge of **Black Canyon of the Gunnison National Monument** is a staggering place, literally—watch for those trembling knees. The Gunnison River slowly gouged out the 53 miles long canyon, crafting a steep 2500-foot gorge dominated by inky shadows (hence black). The Empire State Building, if placed at the bottom of the river, would reach barely halfway up the canyon walls.

🗾 **PRACTICAL INFORMATION.** The Black Canyon lies 10 mi. east of the town of Montrose in western Colorado. The **South Rim** is easily accessible via a 5 mi. drive off U.S. 50 ($7 per car, $4 walk-in or motorcycle); the wilder **North Rim** can only be reached by detouring around the canyon and taking a gravel road from Crawford off Rte. 92. **Greyhound** shuttles once a day ($12) between Montrose at 132 N. 1st St. (☎249-6673) and the **Gunnison County Airport,** 711 Rio Grande (☎641-0060), and will drop you off on U.S. 50, 6 mi. from the canyon. Western Express **taxi** (☎249-8880) is located near the airport. For $39, **Gisdho Shuttles** (☎800-430-4555) conducts tours of the Black Canyon and the Grand Mesa from Grand Junction. The trip includes transportation, entrance fees, and tours off the beaten path. (10-11hr. Trips May-Oct. W and Sa.) The Canyon has two **visitors centers:** one on the South Rim (☎249-1914, ext. 23. Open daily in summer 8am-6pm; in winter 8am-4pm), and another on the North Rim. **Area code:** 970.

◪◪ ACCOMMODATIONS AND FOOD. The **South Rim** has a **campground** with 102 small, busy sites amid sagebrush ($8). Pit toilets, charcoal grills, water, and paved wheelchair-accessible sites are available. On the **North Rim,** another campsite offers more space. It rarely fills, but is popular with climbers (water and toilets; $8).

Many inexpensive motels line Main St./U.S. 50 in downtown **Montrose.** The **Traveler's B&B Inn,** 502 S. 1st St., parallel to Main St., offers cozy rooms. (☎249-3472. Singles $32; with private bath $34-36, doubles $42.) The **Log Cabin Motel,** 1034 E. Main St., at the end of town nearest the Monument, has small but comfortable rooms. (☎249-7610. Singles $30; doubles $38; family room with kitchen $58.) For tasty sandwiches ($4.50) and delightful omelettes ($5.50), head for the **Daily Bread Bakery and Cafe,** 346 Main St. (☎249-8444. Open in summer M-Sa 6am-3pm.)

◪ SIGHTS. The 8 mi. scenic drive along the South Rim boasts the spectacular **Chasm View,** where you can peer 2300 ft. down a sheer vertical drop—the highest cliff in Colorado—at the Gunnison River and the "painted" wall. Don't throw stones; you might kill an exhausted hiker in the canyon below. There are no well-established trails to the bottom, but you can scramble down the **Gunnison Rte.,** which drops 2000 ft. over the course of 1 mi. A free **wilderness permit** (from the South Rim visitors center) is required for all inner canyon routes. Bring at least 3L of water per person, and be prepared to use your hands to climb back up. In the canyon, camp and enjoy the beauty; unimproved sites (no water) are available on a beach along the river. Pack in water or use a purification system. The rock walls of the Black Canyon are a **rock climbing** paradise. Register at the South Rim visitors center to climb some of the tallest rock faces in the Rocky Mountains. Less strenuous hikes follow the canyon rim, providing dizzying views.

CRESTED BUTTE   ☎970

Crested Butte, 27 miles north of Gunnison on Rte. 135, was once a mining town. The coal was exhausted in the 50s, and a few years later, the steep powder fields on the Butte began attracting skiers. The historic downtown district is a throwback to those mining days, thanks to strict zoning rules prohibiting homogenizing chains.

◪ PRACTICAL INFORMATION. Crested Butte Chamber of Commerce: 601 Elk (☎349-6438 or 800-545-4505; open daily 9am-5pm). A free **shuttle** to the mountain departs from the chamber. (☎349-7318. Every 40 min. 7:20am-10:20am and 8pm-midnight, every 20min. 10:20am-8pm.) **Post Office:** 217 Elk Ave. (☎349-5568; open M-F 7:30am-4:30pm, Sa 10am-1pm). **ZIP code:** 81224. **Area code:** 970.

◪ ACCOMMODATIONS. Finding budget accommodations in the winter is about as easy as striking a vein of gold, but there are a few possibilities. **Crested Butte International Hostel,** 615 Teocalli Ave., offers a cheap place for skiers and bikers to crash. This beautifully built and situated hostel provides guests with meal plans, kitchen, TV room with fireplace, and laundry. (☎349-0588 or 888-389-0588. Reception 7:30am-10pm, lockout 10am-2pm. Dorms $20, stays of 2 or more nights $18; in winter $30/$27; private room $50, with private bath $60; $3 discount for HI members. $4-6 dinners in peak seasons. Shower for non-guests $5. Packages available, such as the Mar. deal of 5 nights accommodation, 4 days skiing for $300 per person.) **Forest Queen,** 129 Elk Ave., rents out comfortable doubles at reasonable prices. (☎349-5336. Doubles $59, off-season $49; with private bath $69/$59; $10 per additional person.) **Gunnison National Forest Office,** 216 N. Colorado, 30 mi. south in Gunnison, and the Chamber of Commerce (see above), have info on many **campgrounds.** (☎641-0471. Open M-F 7:30am-5pm.) Camp for $8 in achingly beautiful surroundings at the

Gothic Campsite, 3 mi. past the town of Gothic on Gothic Rd. (no water, composting toilets), or park in one of the turnouts and find your own tent site, as long as you're at least 150 ft. away from roads and streams (open June-Nov.).

◻ **FOOD. Brick Oven Pizza,** 3rd and Elk St., replenishes calories lost skiing and biking with authentic NY and Chicago pizza; tasty slices loaded with toppings are $2, and large pizzas start at $10.50. (☎349-5044. Open daily 11am-9pm.) **The Bakery Cafe,** 401 Elk Ave., is a popular lunch spot, with $4-6.50 sandwiches and awe-inspiring pastries for 50¢-$1.50. (☎349-7280. Open daily 7am-6pm; in winter 9am-6pm. Wheelchair accessible.) **The Eldo,** upstairs from Red Lady Realty on Elk St., packs a small bar and a large patio for cheap food and cheaper beer. (☎349-6125. Open daily 3pm-2am. $1.50 pints and 50¢ off drinks during the daily 4-8pm happy hour.)

▣ **OUTDOORS.** Three mi. north of town, **Crested Butte Mt. Resort** takes skiers to "the extreme limits" and offers over 800 acres of bowl skiing. Many of the other 85 runs are less spine-tingling, but the thin air and panoramic views may leave you feeling extreme anyway. During parts of Nov. and Apr., lift tickets are free. (☎800-544-8448. Open Nov.-Apr. Prices vary by season, expect around $50 for day passes.)

Come summertime, Crested Butte becomes the mountain biking capital of Colorado. During the last week of June, the town hosts the **Fat Tire Bike Festival,** four days of mountain biking, racing, and fraternizing. In 1976, a group of cyclists rode from Crested Butte to Aspen, starting the oldest mountain biking event in the world. Every Sept., enduring and experienced bikers repeat the trek over the 12,705 ft. pass to Aspen and back during the **Pearl Pass Tour.** Biking trail maps are available from bike shops and **The Alpineer,** near the visitors center (☎349-5210; open daily 9am-6pm). Trails begin at the base of Mt. Crested Butte and extend into the exquisite Gothic area. **Trail 401** is a demanding and famous 24 mi. round-trip loop with an excellent view. The Gothic area is also accessible with a car; follow Rte. 135 past Mt. Crested Butte and keep driving. When bumpy Gothic Rd. begins to get the best of you, park the car and explore the tiny town of **Gothic,** home to a grand outdoor biology laboratory. Excellent intermediate bike trails depart Brush Creek Road in Crested Butte.

TELLURIDE ☎970

Site of the first bank Butch Cassidy ever robbed (the San Miguel), Telluride has a history right out of a 30s film. Prize fighter Jack Dempsey used to wash dishes in the Athenian Senate, a popular saloon/brothel that frequently required Dempsey to double as a bouncer when he was between plates. William Jennings Bryan delivered his "Cross of Gold" speech in Telluride from the front balcony of the Sheridan Hotel. Locals believe that their city's name derives from a contraction of "to hell you ride," a likely warning given to travelers to the once hell-bent city. Things have quieted down a bit in the last few years; outlaw celebrities have been replaced with film celebrities, and six-shooter guns with cinnamon buns. Skiers, hikers, and vacationers come to Telluride to pump gold and silver *into* the mountains, while the town is gaining popularity and may be the Aspen of the future. Still, a small-town feeling prevails—rocking chairs sit outside brightly painted, wood-shingled houses, and dogs lounge on storefront porches.

▣ **PRACTICAL INFORMATION.** Telluride is only accessible by car, via U.S. 550 or Rte. 145. **Public Transportation:** Galloping Geese. (☎728-5700. Runs 8am-6pm. Free.) **Between town and Mountain Village:** Gondola. (☎728-8888. Runs 7am-11pm. Free.) The **visitors center** is upstairs from **Rose's Grocery Store,** 666 W. Colorado Ave., near the entrance to town. (☎728-6265 or 800-525-2717. Open daily in summer 9am-7pm; ski season 8am-6pm.) **Telluride Medical Center:** ☎728-3848. **Taxi:** Telluride Express (☎728-6000 or 888-212-8294). **Road Conditions:** ☎249-9363. **Free Box:** A Telluride tradition—people drop-off stuff they no longer want and take stuff that they do. On Pine across from Post Office. **Post Office:** 101 E. Colorado Ave. (☎728-3900. Open M-F 9am-5pm, Sa 10am-noon.) **ZIP code:** 81435. **Area code:** 970.

ROCKY MOUNTAINS

◤ ACCOMODATIONS. If you're visiting Telluride during a festival, bring a sleeping bag; the cost of a bed is outrageous. The **Oak Street Inn,** 134 N. Oak St., offers cozy rooms. (☎728-3383. Singles $42, with private bath $66; doubles $58/$66. Rates $20 higher during festivals. Showers $3 for non-guests.) Camping is available at the east end of Telluride in a town-operated facility with 46 sites, water, restrooms, and showers. (☎728-2173. Sites $10-12. 1-week maximum stay.) **Sunshine,** 8 mi. southwest on Rte. 145 toward Cortez, is a developed campground. (14 sites. Sites $8. 7-day maximum stay. Closed until summer 2001.) For info on National Forest Campgrounds, call the **Forest Service.** (☎327-4261. Open M-F 8am-noon and 1-5pm.) Several free primitive sites huddle nearby. During festival times, you can crash anywhere; hot showers ($2) are available at the high school.

◪▣ FOOD AND NIGHTLIFE. Baked in Telluride, 127 S. Fir St., has enough rich coffee, delicious pastries, pizza, sandwiches, and 60¢ bagels to get you through a festival weekend even if you *are* baked in Telluride. The apple fritters ($2) are rightly famous, and their pizza ($2.25 a slice) might be your only route to a dirt-cheap meal in town. (☎728-4775. Open daily 5:30am-10pm.) **Steaming Bean Coffee,** 221 W. Colorado Ave., offers coffee ($1 if you bring your own mug), as well as smoothies ($3-4) and **Internet access.** (☎728-0793. Open M-F 7am-9pm, Sa-Su 7:30am-9pm. Access $6.50 per hr., price includes any drink on the menu.) The hip-hop-blaring and celebrity-snaring **La Cocina de Luz,** 123 E. Colorado Ave., attracts those roughing it to be chic and those roughing it just to eat. (☎728-9355. Open M-Sa 9am-9pm. Taco dinners $7-9, burrito dinners $7-9.) Eighteen different subs ($5) and interesting sandwich creations called "jaffles" ($3) are the main attractions at **Deli Downstairs,** 217 W. Colorado Ave. (☎728-4004. Open daily 10am-midnight.)

The taps at **Floradora,** 103 W. Colorado Ave., flow with home-brewed beer. (☎728-3888. Open daily 11am-2am. Pints $3.50.) **The House, a Tavern,** 131 N. Fir St., is where college-students-gone-ski-bums hang out. (☎728-6207. Open daily 11am-2am. Happy hour 5-7pm, $1 off margaritas and 21 oz. drafts. Drafts $2-5.) The cool, conversational **Last Dollar Saloon,** 100 E. Colorado, near Pine, will take it with a smile. (☎728-4800. Open daily 11:30am-2am. Beer $2.75-3.75). Jiving with Telluride's hip and swank, **Fly Me to the Moon,** 132 E. Colorado Ave. (☎728-6666), shines with some of the area's best musical talent.

▨▨ FESTIVALS AND ACTIVITIES. Given that only 1500 people live in Telluride, the sheer number of summer arts festivals in the town seems staggering. For general festival info, contact the visitors center. Gala events occur just about every weekend in summer and fall; the most renowned is the **Bluegrass Festival.** (☎800-624-2422. 3rd weekend in June. Tickets $35-40 per night, 4-day pass $120.) The **Telluride International Film Festival** premiers some of the hippest independent flicks; *The Crying Game* and *The Piano* were both unveiled here. (☎603-643-1255. 1st weekend in Sept.) Telluride also hosts the **Talking Gourds** poetry fest and a **Jazz Celebration.** (☎728-7009. Poetry: 2nd weekend in July. Jazz: 1st weekend in Aug.) For some festivals, volunteering to usher or perform other tasks can be exchanged for free admission.

Biking, hiking, and backpacking opportunities are endless; ghost towns and lakes are tucked behind almost every mountain crag. The tourist office has a list of suggestions for hikes in the area. The most popular trek (about 2hr.) is up the jeep road to **Bridal Veil Falls,** the waterfall visible from almost anywhere in Telluride. The trailhead is at the end of Rte. 145. Continuing another 2½ mi. from the top of the falls will lead you to Silver Lake, a steep but very rewarding and serene climb. For more Rocky Mountain highs, ride the **free gondola** to the top of the mountain. A number of hiking and mountain biking trails run from the St. Sophia station. With a skateboard ramp, numerous playing fields, a basketball court, and a swimming pool, the **Town Park,** at the east end of town, is a popular lazy Su destination.

In winter, even self-proclaimed atheists can be spied praying before hitting the "Spiral Stairs" and the "Plunge," two of the Rockies' most gut-wrenching ski runs. For more info, contact the **Telluride Ski Resort.** (*P.O. Box 11155, Telluride 81435.* ☎728-3856.) A free year-round gondola connects the mountain village with the rest of the town and runs from 7am-11pm. **Paragon Ski and Sport** rents bikes in summer and skis in winter. Longer rentals are cheaper. *(213 W. Colorado Ave. ☎ 728-4525. Open daily 9am-8pm; in ski season 8:30am-9pm. Bikes $26 per day; skis and boots $20 per day.)*

SCENIC DRIVE: SAN JUAN SKYWAY

Place your traytables in their upright and locked positions as you embark on the heavenly San Juan Skyway. Winding its way through the San Juan and Uncompahgre National Forests, Old Western mountain towns, and ancient Native American ruins, the 236 mi. scenic byway visits nearly all of southwestern Colorado's splendors. With breathtaking views of the southwest corner of Colorado and reaching altitudes up to 11,000 ft., the San Juan Skyway is widely considered America's most beautiful drive. Travelers in this area inevitably drive at least parts of it as they head to places like Telluride, Durango and Mesa Verde. Many sections of the skyway skirt along steep drop-offs and involve twisty mountain driving. Call the San Juan (☎970-247-4874) or Uncompahgre (☎970-874-6600) National Forests to check on road conditions or to inquire about driving the skyway.

The San Juan Skyway is a loop road, piggie-backing on Rte. 550, Rte. 62, Rte. 146, and Rte. 160. The voyage can be started from anywhere along the loop, at towns such as Durango, Silverton, Telluride, or Cortez. Beginning in Durango, the skyway heads north along Rte. 550 N (a.k.a. the Million Dollar Highway) climbing into the San Juan Mountains. Paralleling the Animas River, the road passes **Purgatory Ski Area** (see p. 696) as it ascends. At Mi. 64 on Rte. 550, the road peaks at Molas Point, a whopping 10,899 ft. above sea level. **Molas Lake** (☎970-749-9254 or 800-846-2172) offers visitors an oasis with tent and RV sites ($12), cabins, canoe rentals ($5 per hr.), horseback riding ($20 per hr.), and picnic tables. Descending to a mere 9000 ft., the skyway arrives in the easy-going Silverton. A mining town until the early 90's, **Silverton** (see p. 696) is a subdued mountain village that boasts some of Colorado's best ice climbing. The visitors center is to the left as you enter town on Rte. 550 (☎970-387-5654; open M-Sa 9am-6pm, Su 9am-5pm). With dirt roads and a 14,000 ft. peak surrounding it, Silverton seems straight from an old Western movie. Hiking, mountain biking, and local skiing at Kendal Mountain ($6 lift tickets) await those who can still catch their breath.

From Silverton, the San Juan Skyway climbs higher until it reaches 11,018 ft. at Mi. 80 on Rte. 550. Known as **Red Mountain Pass,** this scenic point has some hiking and more than a few Kodak-moments. Continuing north, the drive from Silverton to Ouray showcases stellar 14,000 ft. mountain peaks and **defunct mines.** In 1991, the Reclamation Act shut down most of the mines, leaving only remnants of the past. The skyway next arrives in **Ouray,** a yoddler's delight. With fabulous mountain views and hedonistic hot springs, this heavily Swiss-influenced town is a relaxing stop for the weary. Beyond Ouray, the skyway returns to Earth. Traversing mesas, Rte. 550 junctions with Rte. 62 in Ridgeway. Rte. 62 assumes the reigns of the skyway and leads travelers to Placerville, where the skyway connects with Rte. 145.

Telluride (see p. 693) next awaits travelers along Rte. 145. Past the Mountain Village, the dubiously-named **Lizard's Pass** offers a tranquil 6 mi. hike reaching over 12,000 ft. From the pass, the skyway glides down along the Taylor Mesa through the quiet towns of Rico, Stoner, and Dolores. Rte. 145 connects with Rte. 160 just east of Cortez and west of **Mesa Verde National Park** (see p. 698). Moving east along Rte. 160, the skyway cuts through **Mancos** (see p. 697) and finally returns to Durango.

DURANGO   ☎970

Durango has two sides: the side Will Rogers described as "out of the way and glad of it," and the side where, as many in the town proclaim, "every night is a Saturday night." After a day of stereotypical Colorado "extreme" fun, some people tend to take it easy. Conversely, some take it easy during the day (after an evening of stereotypical Western evenin' fun, of which there is plenty). It's either on-the-go or on-the-porch action in Durango, keeping the yin and the yang of the town in a nice balance. Predominantly yang-seeking tourists come here to see Mesa Verde (see p. 698), raft down the Animas River, hike the San Juan Mountains, or ski at Purgatory.

ROCKY MOUNTAINS

◼ PRACTICAL INFORMATION. Durango is at the intersection of U.S. 160 and U.S. 550. Streets run perpendicular to avenues, but everyone calls Main Ave. "Main St." On southern Main Ave., the town becomes less touristy. **Greyhound,** 275 E. 8th Ave. (☎259-2755; open M-F 7:30am-noon and 3:30-5pm, Sa 7:30am-noon, Su and holidays 7:30-10am), runs once per day to Grand Junction (5½hr., $35-37); Denver (11½hr., $56-60); and Albuquerque (5hr., $42-45). The **Durango Lift** provides trolley service up and down Main Ave. every 30min. (☎259-5438. Runs daily 6am-10pm. 50¢.) The **Durango Area Chamber Resort Association,** 111 S. Camino del Rio, on the southeast side of town at Santa Rita Park along Rte. 160, offers info on sights and hiking. (☎247-0312 or 800-525-8855. Open M-Sa 8am-6pm, Su 10am-4pm.) **Internet access** is free at the **Durango Public Library,** 1188 E. 2nd Ave. (☎385-2970. Open M-W 9am-9pm, Th-Su 9am-5:30pm.) Taxi: Durango Transportation, ☎259-4818. **Road Conditions:** ☎247-3355. **Weather Info:** ☎247-0930. **Post Office:** 222 W. 8th St. (☎247-3434. Open M-F 8am-5:30pm, Sa 9am-1pm.) **ZIP code:** 81301. **Area code:** 970.

◼◻ ACCOMMODATIONS AND FOOD. The **Durango Youth Hostel (HI-AYH),** 543 E. 2nd Ave., one block from downtown, maintains clean, simple bunks in a large converted house. Located near the heart of downtown, this hostel jives with the younger and less touristy side of Durango. While the men's dorm room is barrack-styled, the women enjoy more comfortable accommodations. Ask the manager about local cafes, hangouts, and activities. (☎247-9905. Check-in 7-10am and 5-10pm. Check-out 7-10am. Key deposit $5. Dorms $13, non-members $15.) The **Country View Lodge,** 6 mi. west of Durango on Rte. 160, fixes travelers up with an array of lodging options in a quiet rural surrounding. Clean and carpeted hostel dorm rooms are $13 and include linen. (☎247-5701. Office hours 7am-10:30pm. Motel room $46; in winter $26.) For the cheapest motels in town, look to northern Main Ave. The lowest price for a summer double hovers around $45, and these rooms are away from the downtown action. The big rooms at **Budget Inn,** 3077 Main Ave., aren't cheap—but include access to a pool and hot tub. (☎247-5222 or 800-257-5222. Singles $50; doubles $72; in winter $25/$44.) Durango's nearest campground is **Cottonwood Camper Park,** on U.S. 160, ½ mi. west of town. (☎247-1977. 2-person tent sites $17; $2 per additional person; full hook-up $22.)

Silverton, 47 mi. north on U.S. 550, has less expensive lodging options. The **Silverton Hostel,** 1025 Blair St., offers snowbirds cheap lodging year-round. Dorm rooms are simple and clean. (☎387-0115 or 888-276-0088. Office open 8am-10pm. Dorms $12, in winter $10; private rooms $30/$25. Reservations recommended in July.) The **Avon Hotel,** 144 E. 10th St., offers high Victorian decor and comfort for peasant wages. (☎387-5140. Open June-July. Rooms $30.) Locals head to **Rocky Mountain Funnel Cakes,** 1249 Green St., for cheap eats. (☎387-5450. Open daily 9:30am-8:30pm. Burritos $2-4; sandwiches $4.)

Back in Durango, locals eat breakfast at **Carver's Bakery and Brewpub,** 1022 Main Ave., which has delicious bread, breakfast specials ($2-6), the usual pizza and burgers ($5-6), and $8 pitchers of home-brewed beer. (☎259-2545. Open M-Sa 6:30am-10pm, Su 6:30am-1pm.) "Dill-icious" pickles and subs abound at **Johnny McGuire's Deli,** 552 Main Ave., where choosing between the more than 25 sandwiches ($5) will leave you in a pickle. (☎259-8816. Open daily 7am-9pm.) Every year, **Olde Tymer's,** 1000 Main Ave., wins an award for Durango's best burger ($7, $4 on M nights). Vegetarians dig the $4-9 salad options (☎259-2990; open daily 11am-10pm). To catch some of the best area bands or hang with Durango hipsters, head to the **San Juan Room,** 601 E. 2nd Ave. (☎382-9880).

◼ ACTIVITIES. Unlike most Colorado towns that thrive on tourism, Durango's busiest season is summer, though winter is no stranger to strangers. **Purgatory Resort,** 27 mi. north on U.S. 550, hosts skiers of all levels. When the heat is on, travelers can trade in their skis for a sled and test out the **alpine slide** or take a free **scenic chairlift ride.** The ski slope also offers **mountain biking** in the summer. (☎259-9671 or 800-982-5850. Open daily 9:30am-4:45pm; in winter 8:30am-5pm. Slide: 1 ride $8, 3 rides $22. Bike uplifts $5; $12 per day. Lift tickets $43, ages 6-12 $23.)

The entire Durango area is engulfed by the **San Juan National Forest;** the headquarters is located in Durango. Call for info on hiking and camping in the forest, especially if you're planning a trip into the massive **Weminuche Wilderness,** northeast of Durango. *(Headquarters:* ☎ *247-4874. Open M-F 8am-5pm.)*

The largest outfitter in the area is **Mild to Wild Rafting.** Anything from family trips on placid class II rapids to intense class V battles are offered. *(701 Main Ave.* ☎ *247-4789 or 800-567-6745. Open daily 8am-10pm. Half-day mild $38; full-day mild $65; full-day intense $105. Reservations recommended.)* Bikes are available at **Hassle Free Sports,** but you must have a driver's license and major credit card. *(2615 Main St.* ☎ *259-3874 or 800-835-3800. Open M-Sa 8:30am-6pm, Su 10am-5pm; in winter M-Sa 7:30am-7pm. Half-day $16; full-day $25. Ski rental packages from $12-25 per day.)* **Horseback riding** opportunities abound in the San Juan. **Rimrock Outfitters** offers an array of trips. *(*☎ *533-7588. 1hr. $20, half-day $60, full-day $90.)*

Although it's definitely more of a tourist attraction than a means of transportation, the **Durango and Silverton Narrow Gauge Train** runs along the Animas River Valley to the glistening old town of **Silverton.** Old-fashioned, 100% coal-fed locomotives wheeze through the San Juans, making a 2hr. stop in Silverton before returning to Durango. In the summer, be prepared for heat and dust. It is often more comfortable and cheaper to drive the route yourself (see p. 695). The train also drops off and picks up **backpackers** at various scenic points; call for more info on this service. *(479 Main St.* ☎ *247-2733. Office open daily 6am-9pm; May and mid-Aug. to Oct. 7am-7pm; Nov.-Apr. 8am-5pm. Morning and afternoon trains, 7hr. $53, ages 5-11 $27.)*

🎬 **ENTERTAINMENT.** Less-interactive activity moseys into town every summer with the **Durango Pro Rodeo Series,** at the LaPlata County Fairgrounds at 25th and Main Ave. Saddling up on Tu and W nights, the action starts at 7:30pm with a barbecue at 6pm. (☎ 247-1666. $13, children under 12 $5.) One of the best **Victorian-style melodramas** in the US—full of high-flying vocals and tap dancing—takes place at the Strater Hotel and Theater at 7th St. and Main Ave. (☎ 247-3400. Early June to late Sept. M-Sa. Doors open at 7:30pm, curtain at 8pm. Tickets $15.) In June and July, the annual **Shakespeare Festival** occurs. (☎ 247-7657. $12, students $8, under 12 $5.)

NEAR DURANGO: PAGOSA SPRINGS

The Ute people—the first to discover the waters of Pagosa—believed that the springs were a gift of the Great Spirit; it's not hard to see why. Pagosa Springs, some of the hottest and largest in the world, bubble from the San Juan Mountains 62 mi. east of Durango on Rte. 160. Follow the sulfur smell to **The Spring Inn,** 165 Hot Springs Blvd., where 15 different outdoor pools ranging from 98° to 114°F are available. (☎ 264-4168 or 800-225-0934. Open 24hr. $10 per person.) **Chimney Rock Archeological Area,** 17 mi. west of Pagosa Springs on U.S. 160 and Rte. 151 S, contains the ruins of a high-mesa Ancestral Puebloan village. (☎ 883-5359. Open daily mid-May to late Sept. 9am-4pm. 2½hr. tours leave at 9:30, 10:30am, 1, and 2pm. $5, ages 5-11 $3.) Skiing is available at **Wolf Creek,** 20 mi. east of Pagosa, which claims to have the most snow in Colorado. (Lift tickets $37, under 13 and over 64 $24; rates often change.) For nearby fishing, hiking, and camping, contact the San Juan National Forest (see Durango **Activities,** p. 697). The **Pagosa Springs Chamber of Commerce,** intersection of San Juan St. and Hot Springs Blvd. (☎ 264-2360. Open M-F 8am-5pm, Sa-Su 10am-2pm; in winter daily 9am-5pm.) Occasional mudslides, stampedes, and a **local bus** (50¢) provide public transportation in Pagosa.

The **Sky View Motel,** 1 mi. west of downtown on Rte. 160, has rooms with cable TV; some have kitchenettes. (☎ 264-5803. Singles $40; doubles $45.) **Pinewood Inn,** 157 Pagosa St., four blocks from downtown, rents cozy wood-paneled rooms with TVs and phones. (☎ 800-655-7463 or 264-5715. Singles $35-44; doubles $40-55.) **Los Amigos,** a small Mexican grill 3 mi. west of downtown on Rte. 160, befriends budget travelers with $2 tacos. (☎ 731-2188. Open M-Sa 10:30am-9pm.) The award-winning green chili stew ($4) at the **Rolling Pin Bakery Cafe,** 214 Pagosa St., deserves attention with its unique combo of spices, chili, and chicken. Big breakfast flapjacks are $4 and sandwiches are $5-6. (☎ 264-2255. Open M-Sa 7am-2pm.) **Area code:** 970.

FOUR CORNERS **New Mexico, Arizona, Utah,** and **Colorado** meet at an unnaturally neat intersection about 40 mi. northwest of **Shiprock, NM,** on the Navajo Reservation. **Four Corners** epitomizes American ideas about land; these state borders were drawn along scientifically determined lines of longitude and latitude, disregarding natural boundaries. There's little to see; nonetheless, a large number of people veer off the highway to marvel at the geographic anomaly. At the very least, getting down on all fours to put a limb in each state is a good story for a cocktail party. *(Open daily in summer 7am-8pm; in winter 8am-5pm. $2.)*

MESA VERDE ☎ 970

Mesa Verde (Green Table) rises from the deserts of southwestern Colorado, its flat top noticeably friendlier to vegetation than the dry lands below. The spectacular land is not, however, the main attraction—some of the most elaborate Pueblo dwellings in existence, as otherworldly and awesome as any of the rock formations that grace the Southwest, draw the largest crowds. Fourteen hundred years ago, Native American tribes began to cultivate the area now known as Mesa Verde National Park. These people—today called the Ancestral Puebloan, and formerly the Anasazi, or "ancient ones"—constructed a series of expansive cliff dwellings beneath the overhanging sandstone shelves surrounding the mesa. Then, around AD 1275, 700 years after their ancestors had arrived, the Pueblo people abruptly and mysteriously vanished from the historical record, leaving behind their eerie and starkly beautiful dwellings. Mesa Verde is not for the snap-a-shot-and-go tourist; the best views require a bit of a physical effort to reach and are too extraordinary to let the camera do all the marveling anyway.

⛏ PRACTICAL INFORMATION. The park's main entrance is off U.S. 160, 36 mi. from **Durango** and 7 mi. from **Mancos.** The **entrance fee** is $10 for vehicles, $5 for pedestrians and bikers. The visitors center is closed during the winter; head to the museum (see above) or the **Colorado Welcome Center/Cortez Chamber of Commerce,** 928 E. Main, in Cortez. (☎565-4048 or 565-3414. Open daily 8am-6pm; in winter 8am-5pm.) Sights here are up to 40 mi. apart; a car is essential. **Area code:** 970.

🍴 ACCOMMODATIONS AND FOOD. The **Far View Lodge,** across from the visitors center, offers two half-day bus tours that depart from the Lodge at 9am and 1pm en route to the **Spruce Tree House.** The Lodge also offers a full-day tour which departs at 9:30am. Arrive at least 30min. before the tour. (☎529-4421. Half-day tours $31-33, under 12 $21-23; full-day $48/$38.)

Lodging in the park is pricey. Mesa Verde's only motel-style lodging, the rooms at **Far View Lodge** (☎592-4421), are expensive (from $96). Six mi. west of the park entrance, in Mancos, the **Old Mancos Inn,** 200 W. Grand Ave., lavishes guests with antique-laden private rooms for near-hostel prices. Outgoing owners and a nap-friendly porch add to the homey feeling of the Inn. (☎533-9019. Shared bath $25-30, private bath $45.) The **Ute Mountain Motel,** 531 S. Broadway (☎565-8507; singles $20-35, doubles $28-46), or the well-lit rooms of **Tomahawk Lodge,** 728 S. Broadway (☎565-8521 or 800-643-7705; singles $35-49, doubles $43-69; in winter $31-35), both in Cortez, are other options. The **Durango Hostel** (see Durango **Accommodations,** p. 696) also has cheap beds. Mesa Verde's **Morfield Campground** is located 4 mi. inside the park and almost never fills up. (☎564-1675. 452 beautiful, secluded sites $16, full hook-up $23. Showers $1 per 5min.)

📷 SIGHTS. A good starting point, the **Far View Visitors Center** is a long 15 mi. drive from the entrance gate along Rte. 160. A comprehensive visitor guide and tour tickets are available here, as well as friendly park rangers (☎529-4465; open daily in summer 8am-5pm). At the visitors center, the park divides into **Chapin Mesa,** featuring the largest number of cliff dwellings, and the smaller and quieter **Wetherill Mesa.** The **Chapin Mesa Museum,** on the first loop on the Chapin branch (before the dwellings), can give you an overview of the Ancestral Puebloan lifestyle and is a good place to start before exploring the mesa. (☎529-4465. Open daily 8am-6:30pm; Oct.-May 8am-5pm.) From their respective overlooks on Chapin Mesa, rangers lead three tours of the cliff dwellings; all last about 1hr. and depart every 30min. Tickets ($1.75) can be purchased at the visitors center in summer and at the museum in winter. Tours of the spectacular **Cliff Palace** run from 9am-6pm and explore the largest cliff dwelling in North America with over 200 preserved rooms. The impressive **Balcony House** (open in summer only), is a 40-room dwelling 600 ft. above the floor of the Soda Canyon; tours run from 9am-5:30pm. Finally, tours of the Wetherill Mesa's **Long House,** composed of 150 rooms and 21 kivas, are offered 10am-5pm. For all three locations, tours in the early morning tend to be less crowded and more pleasing than those in the afternoon. Make sure you are up to the rigor of the tours; the Balcony House tour is especially strenuous, requiring visitors to crawl through a tunnel at one point. Bring water on both tours, as none is available on the trail. An easier approach to seeing the Chapin Mesa is the self-guided **Mesa Top Loop Road,** passing a chronological progression of the ruins from AD 600 to the classic 13th-century dwellings (open 8am-sunset).

ROCKY MOUNTAINS

THE SOUTHWEST

The Ancestral Puebloans (formerly Anasazi) of the 10th and 11th centuries were the first to discover that the arid lands of the Southwest could support an advanced agrarian civilization. Years later, in 1803, the United States laid claim to parts of the Southwest with the Louisiana Purchase. The idealistic hope for a western "empire of liberty," where Americans could live the virtuous farm life, both motivated further expansion and helped create the region's individualist mythology.

Today, the steel blue of the Superstition peaks, the rainbow expanse of the Painted Desert, the deep gorges of the Grand Canyon, the murky depths of Carlsbad Caverns, and the red stone arches and twisted spires of southern Utah and northern Arizona lure visitors and keep Kodak in business. The vastness of the Southwestern desert and its peculiar colors—of red rock, sandstone, scrub brush, and pale sky—invite contemplation; farther north, Utah's mountains offer equally breathtaking vistas. Although the Southwest is best known for dramatic landscape, its kaleidoscopic mix of cultures is just as intriguing. True to eccentric and spirit of the land, aging conservative Midwesterners, hippies hold out from the 60s, cowboys and cowboys-at-heart, New Age spiritualists, Native Americans, Mexicans and Mexican Americans, outdoor enthusiasts, government scientists, droves of tourists, and suburban families have all rambled their way here, the real American desert.

HIGHLIGHTS OF THE SOUTHWEST

MEXICAN FOOD. You can't get away from it, and in the tasty eateries of New Mexico's Albuquerque (p. 766) and Santa Fe (p. 760), you may not want to.

NATIONAL PARKS. Utah's "Fab Five" (p. 717) and Arizona's Grand Canyon (p. 727) reveal a stunning landscape of bizarre rock formations and brilliant colors.

SKIING. In a region famous for its blistering sun, the Wasatch Mountains (p. 711) near Salt Lake City, UT receive some of the nation's choicest powder in winter.

LAS VEGAS, NV. Attractions include casinos, casinos, and casinos (p. 702).

NEVADA

Nevada once walked the straight and narrow. Explored by Spanish missionaries and settled by Mormons, the Nevada Territory's scorched expanses seemed a perfect place for ascetics to strive for moral uplift. However, with the discovery of gold in 1850 and silver in 1859, the state was won over permanently to the worship of filthy lucre. When the precious metals ran out, gambling and marriage-licensing became big industries. The final moral cataclysms came when the state legalized prostitution on a county by county basis and spawned lounge idol Wayne Newton. But there *is* another side to Nevada. Lake Mead National Recreation Area, only 25 mi. from Las Vegas, is an oasis in stunning desert surroundings, and the forested slopes of Lake Tahoe provide serene resorts for an escape from the cities.

ⓘ PRACTICAL INFORMATION

Capital: Carson City.

Visitor Info: Nevada Commission on Tourism, Capitol Complex, Carson City 89701 (☎800-638-2328; line staffed 24hr.). **Nevada Division of State Parks,** 1300 S. Curry St., Carson City 89703-5202 (☎702-687-4384). Open M-F 8am-5pm.

Postal Abbreviation: NV. **Sales Tax:** 6.75-7%; 8% room tax in some counties.

The Southwest

Lincoln

81

80

North Platte

NEBRASKA

83

Platte River

Cheyenne

WYOMING

Laramie

30

ROCKY MOUNTAINS

80

Salt Lake City

Provo

Great Salt Lake

15

UTAH

IDAHO

Ely

93

6

NEVADA

50

Carson City

Reno

Lake Tahoe

395

OREGON

95

Redding

Eureka

5

101

San Francisco

Sacramento

SIERRA NEVADA MTNS.

COAST RANGE

Fresno

Yosemite Nat'l Park

Kings Canyon Nat'l Park

CALIFORNIA

Death Valley National Monument

395

San Luis Obispo

101

Los Angeles

5

San Diego

PACIFIC OCEAN

Barstow

15

Joshua Tree National Monument

40

Las Vegas

Lake Mead National Recreation Area

Zion National Park

Bryce Canyon National Park

Capitol Reef National Park

Green River

Moab

191

Arches National Park

Canyonlands National Park

70

Dinosaur National Monument

Grand Junction

COLORADO

Denver

Rocky Mountain National Park

76

Pueblo

25

666

Colorado

Lake Powell

89

Grand Canyon National Park

Flagstaff

Petrified Forest Nat'l Park

ARIZONA

Phoenix

Tuscon

Saguaro National Monument

Organ Pipe National Monument

8

Yuma

10

Canyon de Chelly National Monument

Gallup

Gila Cliff Dwellings National Monument

666

Chaco Culture National Monument

Santa Fe

40

Albuquerque

64

Taos

Tucumcari

285

Roswell

Truth or Consequences

NEW MEXICO

White Sands Nat'l Monument

El Paso

10

Rio Grande

Carlsbad Caverns National Park

Guadalupe Mtns National Park

10

Odessa

20

TEXAS

Lubbock

27

Amarillo

54

Wichita Falls

Red River

83

Abilene

83

Oklahoma City

40

OKLAHOMA

Dodge City

KANSAS

Arkansas River

Wichita

83

50

70

N

0   160 miles

0   160 kilometers

LAS VEGAS

☎ 702

Las Vegas, a city of 880,000, draws three times that many tourists every month. Most come to witness the spirit of capitalism (minus the Protestant ethic) and to partake in what might be the most direct economic alienation known to man—funneling earnings into a well-oiled, privately owned profit machine. The lights and glitter of the Strip comprise a Disney-esque league of mock-ups, from ancient Egypt to New York, each leading to a similar gauntlet of gaming rooms—thresholds of fun without substance, triumph without responsibility, loss without meaning.

█ GETTING THERE AND GETTING AROUND

Driving to Vegas from L.A. is a straight 300 mi. shot on I-15 (5hr.). From Arizona, take I-40 W to Kingman and then U.S. 93/95 N.

Airport: McCarran International (☎261-5743), at the southeastern end of the Strip. Main terminal on Paradise Rd. Vans to the Strip and downtown $3-5; taxi $10-12.

Buses: Greyhound, 200 S. Main St. (☎384-8009 or 800-231-2222), at Carson Ave. downtown. To: L.A. (5-7hr., 22 per day, $35-37) and San Francisco (13-16hr., 6 per day, $59-62). Tickets sold daily 4:30am-1am.

Public Transportation: Citizens Area Transit (CAT) (☎228-7433). Bus #301 serves downtown and the Strip 24hr. Buses #108 and 109 serve the airport. All buses wheelchair accessible. Most operate every 10-15min. (less frequently off the Strip). Buses run daily 5:30am-1:30am (24hr. on the Strip). Fares for routes on the Strip $2, for residential routes $1.25, seniors and ages 6-17 75¢. **Las Vegas Strip Trolleys** (☎382-1404), are not strip joints. They cruise the Strip every 15min. daily 9:30am-2am (fare $1.50 in exact change).

Taxis: Yellow, Checker, Star, ☎873-2000. Initial charge $2.20, each additional mi. $1.50. For pick-up, call 30min. before you need a cab. 24hr.

Car Rental: Sav-Mor Rent-A-Car, 5101 Rent-A-Car Rd. (☎736-1234 or 800-634-6779). Rentals from $35 per day, $149 per week. 150 mi. per day included, each additional mi. 20¢. Must be 21+; under 25 surcharge $8 per day. Open daily 5:30am-1am.

✹ ▨ ORIENTATION AND PRACTICAL INFORMATION

Las Vegas has two major casino areas: **downtown,** around Fremont and 2nd St., is a pedestrian promenade, and the **Strip** is a collection of mammoth casinos on both sides of **Las Vegas Blvd.** Parallel to the Strip is **Paradise Blvd.,** also strewn with casinos. Many areas of Las Vegas are unsafe. Always stay on brightly lit pathways and do not wander too far from the major casinos and hotels. The neighborhoods just north and west of downtown can be especially dangerous.

Despite all its debauchery, Las Vegas has a **curfew.** Cruisers under 18 are not allowed unaccompanied in public places from midnight to 5am, those under 14 from 10pm to 5am. On weekends, no one under 18 is allowed unaccompanied on the Strip or in other designated areas 9pm-5am.

Visitor Info: Las Vegas Convention and Visitor Authority, 3150 Paradise Rd. (☎892-0711; fax 226-9011), 4 blocks from the Strip in the big pink convention center by the Hilton. Up-to-date info on headliners, conventions, shows, hotel bargains, and buffets. Open daily 8am-5pm.

Tours: Gambler's special bus tours leave L.A., San Francisco, and San Diego for Las Vegas early in the morning and return at night or the next day. Ask at tourist offices in the departure cities or call casinos for info. **Gray Line,** 4020 E. Lone Mountain Rd. (☎384-1234 or 800-634-6579). City Tours (7½hr., 1 per day, $35). Bus tours from Las Vegas to **Hoover Dam/Lake Mead** (3 per day, $30 includes Dam admission) and the **Grand Canyon's South Rim** (full-day $149). Discounts with coupons in tourist publications and for ages 2-9. Reserve in advance.

Las Vegas: The $trip

ACCOMMODATIONS
Circus Circus, 3
Goldstrike, 6
Las Vegas Int'l Hostel (AAIH/Rucksackers), 1
Palace Station, 2
Silverton, 7
Somerset House Motel, 4
Whiskey Pete's, 5

SOUTHWEST

Marriage: Marriage License Bureau, 200 S. 3rd St. (☎455-4415). Must be 18+ or obtain parental consent. Licenses $35; cash only. No waiting period or blood test required. Open Su-Th 8am-midnight, F-Sa 24hr.

Bi-Gay-Lesbian Organization: Gay and Lesbian Community Center, 912 E. Sahara Ave. (☎733-9800). Open M-F 9am-7pm.

24-Hour Crisis Lines: Gamblers Anonymous, ☎385-7732. **Rape Crisis Center Hotline,** ☎366-1640. **Suicide Prevention,** ☎731-2990.

Post Office: 301 E. Stewart Ave., downtown. Open M-F 8:30am-5pm. General Delivery pick-up M-F 9am-2pm. **ZIP Code:** 89101. **Area code:** 702.

ACCOMMODATIONS AND CAMPGROUNDS

Even though Vegas has over 100,000 rooms, most hotels fill up on weekend nights. If you get stuck, call the **Room Reservations Hotline** (☎800-332-5333). Room rates at most hotels in Vegas fluctuate all the time, and many hotels have different rate ranges for weeknights and weekend nights. A room that costs $30 during a promotion can cost hundreds during conventions (two major ones are in Jan. and Nov.).

Strip hotels are at the center of the action and within walking distance of each other, but their inexpensive rooms sell out quickly. Many have reasonable rates Su through Th, but prices can triple on the weekends. There is a cluster of inexpensive motels north of the Strip (1200-1400 S. Las Vegas Blvd.).

▨ **Whiskey Pete's,** Primm Valley, NV (☎800-248-8453), 45 mi. south of Vegas on I-15, just before the California border. Cheap as fool's gold and home to the wildest roller-coaster in Nevada ($6). Su-Th $19, F-Sa $60; prices vary with availability.

Las Vegas International Hostel (AAIH/Rucksackers), 1208 S. Las Vegas Blvd. (☎385-9955). Extremely helpful staff is an excellent source for advice about budget Vegas. Shared bathrooms. Reception 7am-11pm. Check-out 10am. 6-person dorms Apr.-Nov. $14 with IHA membership. Singles $26-28. Key deposit $5. Rates lower Dec.-Mar.

Somerset House Motel, 294 Convention Center Dr. (☎735-4411 or 888-336-4280; fax 369-2388). A straightforward, no-frills establishment within short walking distance of the major Strip casinos. Many rooms feature kitchens. Singles Su-Th $35, F-Sa $44; doubles $44/$55; additional person $5. Rates lower for seniors.

Palace Station, 2411 W. Sahara Ave. (☎367-2411 or 800-634-3101). Free shuttle to airport and Las Vegas Blvd. The largest slot win in history—$25,000,000—was won here. Rooms Su-Th $29-49, F-Sa $59-69; additional person $10.

Circus Circus, 2880 S. Las Vegas Blvd. (☎734-0410 or 800-444-2472). Check out the awesome Adventuredome Theme Park and the super-wacky clown shop. Su-Th $29-79, F-Sa $69-119, holidays $69-159; rollaway bed $12. Fills 2-3 months in advance for Su-Th, 3-4 months for F-Sa.

Lake Mead National Recreation Area (☎293-8906), 25 mi. south of town on Rte. 93/95. Numerous campsites available throughout. Check with rangers at fee station. Sites $10, with hook-up $14-18.

Valley of Fire State Park (☎397-2088), 60 mi. south of Vegas. A spectacular campground near the ancient petroglyph site of Atlatl Rock. No electricity. Sites $10, RV hook-ups $16-18.

Circusland RV Park, 500 Circus Circus Dr. (☎734-0410), a part of the Circus Circus hotel on the strip. Pool, jacuzzi, convenience store, showers, and laundry. Hook-ups Su-Th $17.50, F-Sa $20.

◐ FOOD

Almost every hotel-casino in Vegas courts tourists with cheap buffets, but expect bland, greasy food and long lines at peak hours. Beyond the buffets, Vegas has some of the best restaurants in the world, though there's little for the frugal. Wander the Strip and ask around at the major casinos for the cheap little places.

▨ **Carnival World Buffet at the Rio,** 3700 W. Flamingo Rd. (☎364-9192). Hands down the greatest buffet in Vegas. Enjoy truly delicious food from any of the 11 stations, each reflecting a different theme. Breakfast 7-11am $8.50, lunch 11am-3pm $9.50, dinner 4-11pm $11.50.

The Plaza Diner, 1 Main St. (☎386-2110), near the entrance to Jackie Gaughan's Plaza Hotel/Casino. Cheap prime rib dinner $4 (noon-midnight). $1 beers. Open 24hr.

Rincon Criollo, 1145 S. Las Vegas Blvd. (☎388-1906), across from Las Vegas International Hostel. Dine on filling Cuban food beneath a wall-sized photograph of palm trees. Daily special including rice and black beans $6.50. Hot sandwiches $3.50-4.50. Open Tu-Su 11am-10pm.

Battista's Hole in the Wall, 4041 Audrie Ave. (☎732-1424), right behind the Flamingo. Adorning the walls are 28 years' worth of celebrity photos and novelties from area brothels, as well as the head of "Moosolini," the fascist moose. Though pricey at $18, dinner (includes house wine) is worth it. Open M-Th 4:30-10:30pm, F-Su 4:30-11pm.

Luxor's Pharaoh's Pheast, 3900 S. Las Vegas Blvd. (☎262-4000), at the Luxor Hotel. A delicious pheast phit for a pharaoh. Breakfast 6-11:30am $7.50; lunch 11:30am-4pm $8; dinner 4-11pm $11.50.

◪ CA$INO-HOPPING AND NIGHTLIFE

Once the quintessentially Vegas themes of cheap buffets, booze, and entertainment were enough; now casinos spend millions of dollars to fool guests into thinking they are somewhere else. Spittin' images of Venice, New York, Rio, Paris (complete with Eiffel Tower), Cairo (complete with the Pyramids), and Monte Carlo already thrive on the Strip.

Remember: *gambling is illegal for those under 21.* If you are of age, look for casino "funbooks" which allow gamblers to buy $50 in chips for only $15. *Never bring more money than you're prepared to lose cheerfully,* and remember, in the long run, you will almost definitely lose cash. Keep your wallet in your front pocket, and beware of prowling thieves trying to nab winnings from jubilants.

Casinos, nightclubs, and some wedding chapels are open 24hr. There are far more casinos and far more attractions within them than can be listed here; use the following as a compendium of the best, but explore the Strip for yourself. Check with the visitors center for more casino listings.

At **Circus Circus,** 2880 S. Las Vegas Blvd. (☎734-0410), parents run to card tables and slot machines downstairs while their children spend their quarters upstairs on the souped-up carnival midway and in the titanic video game arcade. The majestic confines of the **Mirage,** 3400 S. Las Vegas Blvd. (☎791-7111), banish all illusions from the halls of entertainment. Among its attractions are a dolphin habitat, illusionists Siegfried and Roy's white tigers, and an equally flaming volcano that erupts in fountains and jets of fire. A huge bronze lion guards the **MGM Grand,** 3799 S. Las Vegas Blvd., and a couple of live felines can be seen inside at the lion habitat. In addition to more than 5000 rooms, MGM also contains the Grand Adventures Amusement Park. (Amusement park ☎891-7979. Hrs. vary seasonally.) At **Caesar's Palace,** 3570 S. Las Vegas Blvd. (☎731-7110), busts abound: some are plaster, while others are barely concealed by the low-cut costumes that the cocktail waitresses have to wear; neither are real. At **New York, New York,** 3790 S. Las Vegas Blvd. (☎740-6969), towers mimic the Manhattan skyline, re-creating the glory of the Big Apple at this tacky casino. You can roll through the mean streets of New York aboard the muscular Manhattan Express Rollercoaster, a fast and acrobatic thrill.

Nightlife in Vegas gets rolling around midnight and keeps going until everyone drops or runs out of money. **C2K** at the **Venetian,** 2800 S. Las Vegas Blvd. is the newest resort-casino's palatial showroom transformed nightly into a mind-shattering über-club. You don't simply dance, but swim in a virtual ocean of synchronized, cyber-driven lights. (☎933-4255. Open W-Su 11pm-until whenever.) **Ra,** 3900 S. Las Vegas Blvd., is a superhot Egyptian-themed night club at the **Luxor.** Pretty people only, please. (☎262-4000. Open W-Sa 10pm-6am.)

🖪 DAYTRIPS FROM LAS VEGAS

HOOVER DAM. Built to subdue the flood-prone Colorado River, Hoover Dam took 5000 men five years of seven-day weeks to construct. When their sweat finally dried, over 6.6 million tons of concrete had been crafted into a 726 ft. colossus that now shelters precious agricultural land, pumps big voltage to Vegas and L.A., and furnishes the frazzled jet-skier with azure waters to churn. Ultimately, 96 men died during construction. The excellent tours and interpretive center explore the dam's history, though in a varnished and self-congratulatory way. This is a prize artifact from America's "think-big" era of ambitious landscaping and culturally transforming public works projects. The visitors center leads tours to the generators at the structure's bottom. (☎294-3510 or 294-3523. Open daily 8:30am-5:45pm.)

LAKE MEAD. Dubbed "the jewel of the desert" by its residents, **Lake Mead** and its environs offer more than the social planning and deficit spending that created it. Backcountry hiking and camping is permitted in most areas and hunting in some, but the lake is really sustained by the multitude of Californians driving white pick-up trucks with jet-skis in tow. For those who come unprepared, boats and other watercraft can be rented at the various concessionaires along the shores. **Boulder Beach** is accessible by Lakeshore Dr., off U.S. 93. (☎800-752-9669. Jet-skis $50 per hr., $270 per day; fishing boats $55 for 4hr., $100 per day.)

Alongside the ubiquitous Park Service campsites ($10), concessionaires usually operate RV parks, marinas, restaurants, and occasionally motels. More remote concessionaires include **Echo Bay Resort** (☎702-394-4000 or 800-752-9669; RV hook-up $18), which offers motel rooms from $80 for singles and $90 for doubles (lower in winter). Its restaurant, **Tale of the Whale,** is decorated in nautical motifs, features a stunning view of Lake Mead, and cooks up $5 burgers. The resort rents jet-skis ($50 per hr., $270 per day) and fishing boats ($12/$60).

RENO   ☎775

If a Hollywood exec ever got the great idea to cross *Showgirls* with *The Golden Girls*, the result would be Reno. Hoping to strike it rich at the card tables, busloads of the nation's elderly flock to its hedonistic splendor. A punchy kaleidoscope of casinos, 24 hour bars, seedy motels, mountain vistas, strip clubs full of aspiring dancers, and neon-lit pawnshops makes Reno a strange and memorable place.

🛈 PRACTICAL INFORMATION. Amtrak, at 135 E. Commercial Row, speeds to San Francisco (1 bus/train combo per day, $35-85). **Greyhound,** 155 Stevenson St., a half-block from W. 2nd St., rolls to San Francisco (18 per day, $30-32); Salt Lake City (4 per day, $45-48); L.A. (12 per day, $52); and Sacramento (12 per day, $20). **Reno Citifare** (☎348-7433), at 4th and Center St., serves the Reno-Sparks area. Most of its buses operate daily 5am-7pm, though city center buses operate 24 hours. Buses stop every two blocks. (Fare $1.25, seniors and disabled 60¢, ages 6-18 90¢.) **Reno-Sparks Convention and Visitors Center,** 300 N. Center St., sits on the first floor of the National Bowling Stadium. (☎800-367-7366. Open M-Sa 7am-8pm, Su 9am-7:30pm.) **Post Office,** 50 S. Virginia St. at Mill St., two blocks south of city center (open M-F 8:30am-5pm, Sa 10am-2pm). **ZIP code:** 89501. **Area code:** 775.

⌂ ACCOMMODATIONS. While weekend prices at casinos are usually on the high side, gamblers' specials, weekday rates, and winter discounts provide some great, cheap rooms. Prices fluctuate, so call ahead. **Fitzgerald's,** 225 N. Virginia St. (☎786-3663), **Atlantis,** 3800 S. Virginia St. (☎825-4700), **Circus Circus,** 500 N. Sierra St. (☎329-0711), and **Sundowner,** 450 N. Arlington Ave. (☎786-7050), have been known to offer some good deals to go along with their central locations and massive facilities. Be advised: Heterosexual prostitution is legal in most of Nevada (though not in Reno itself), and a few cheap motels may be lacking a particularly wholesome feel. Members of the same sex sharing a hotel room may be required to book a room with two beds. Southwestern downtown has the cheapest lodging.

To escape the constant jingle of slot machines in Reno, campers can make the drive to the woodland campsites of **Davis Creek Park,** 17 mi. south on U.S. 395, then a ½ mi. west; follow signs. (☎849-0684. Open year-round. Sites $11, each additional car $5; pets $1. Free picnic area open daily 8am-9pm.) Wrap yourself in a blanket of pines and sage at the base of **Mount Rose** and camp at one of the 63 sites with full service, including showers and a small pond stocked with fish, but no hook-ups. Sites available on a first come, first camp basis. (Sites with 1 vehicle $10, pets $1.) The nearby 14 mi. Offer Creek Trail leads to Rock and Price Lakes and interlocks with the Tahoe Rim Trail. Camping and fishing on the trail are free but require permits (available at grocery and sporting goods stores). You can also camp along the shore at **Pyramid Lake** (see p. 707). To stay closer to Reno, park and plug in your RV overnight at the **Reno Hilton,** 2500 E. 2nd St. (☎789-2129. Full hook-up $21.) Call ahead; people reserve up to a year in advance.

🍴 FOOD. Eating in Reno is cheap. To entice gamblers and to prevent them from wandering out in search of food, casinos offer a wide range of all-you-can-eat buffets and 99¢ breakfasts. However, buffet fare can be greasy, overcooked, and tasteless, and rumors of food poisoning abound. Reno's other inexpensive eateries offer better quality food. The large Basque population, who immigrated from the Pyrenees to herd sheep in Nevada, has brought a spicy and hearty cuisine locals enthusiastically recommend. **The Blue Heron,** 1091 S. Virginia St. (☎786-4110), nine blocks from downtown, is a rare bird in Reno, appealing to a younger crowd. The **Santa Fe Restaurant,** 235 Lake St., has just reopened but already has a clientele that swears by its tangy Basque cuisine. (☎323-1891. Open daily 11am-2pm and 6-9pm. Lunch $7-9. 7-course dinner $14.)

🎭 ENTERTAINMENT. Reno is one big amusement park. Many casinos offer free gaming lessons; minimum bets vary between establishments. Drinks are either free or incredibly cheap if you're gambling, but be wary of a casino's generous gift of risk-inducing, inhibition-dropping alcohol. Don't forget that gambling is illegal if you're under 21; if you hit the jackpot at age 20, it'll be the casino's lucky day and not yours. Almost all casinos offer live nighttime entertainment, but the shows are generally not worth the steep admission prices. **Harrah's,** 219 N. Center St. (☎786-3232), is the self-consciously "hip" complex where **Planet Hollywood** capitalizes on movie lust, magically transforming Hollywood knick-knacks into precious relics. Harrah's also features a rockumentary featuring all sorts of past dance crazes entitled **Dancin' in the Street.** At **Circus Circus,** 500 N. Sierra (☎329-0711), a small circus above the casino performs "big top" shows every 30min.

NEAR RENO: PYRAMID LAKE
Thirty mi. north of Reno on Rte. 445, on the Paiute Indian Reservation, lies emerald green Pyramid Lake, one of the most heart-achingly beautiful bodies of water in the US. The pristine tides of Pyramid Lake are set against the backdrop of a barren desert, making it a soothing and otherworldly respite from neon Reno. **Camping** is allowed anywhere on the lake shore, but only designated areas have toilet facilities. A $5 permit is required for use of the park, and the area is carefully patrolled by the Paiute tribe. Permits are available at the **Ranger Station,** 3 mi. left from Rte. 445 at Sutcliffe (☎476-1155; open daily 8am-7pm). **Boat rental** (☎476-1156) is available daily at the marina near the Ranger Station; call for reservations. **Area code:** 775.

UTAH

Beginning in 1848, persecuted members of the Church of Jesus Christ of Latter-Day Saints (colloquially called Mormons) settled on the land that is now Utah, intending to establish and govern their own theocratic state. President James Buchanan struggled to quash the Mormons' efforts in 1858, as many others had tried before. The Mormons eventually gave up their dreams of theocracy, and statehood was finally granted on Jan. 4, 1896. Today the state's population is 70% Mormon—a religious presence that creates a haven for family values. Utah's citizens dwell primarily in the 100-mile corridor along I-15 stretching from Ogden to Provo. Outside this area, Utah's natural beauty dominates, intoxicating visitors in a way that Utah's watered-down 3.2% beer never can. Immediately east of Salt Lake City, the Wasatch range beckons skiers in the winter and bikers in the summer. Southern Utah is part of a region like no other place on Earth; red canyons, river gorges, and crenellated cliffs attest to the creative powers of wind and water.

🛈 PRACTICAL INFORMATION

Capital: Salt Lake City.

Visitor Info: Utah Travel Council, 300 N. State St., Salt Lake City 84114 (☎801-538-1030 or 800-200-1160; www.utah.com), across from the capitol building. Distributes the *Utah Vacation Planner* lists of motels, national parks, and campgrounds, as well as statewide biking, rafting, and skiing brochures. **Utah Parks and Recreation,** 1594 W. North Temple, Salt Lake City 84116 (☎801-538-7220). Open M-F 8am-5pm.

Controlled Substances: Mormons dispense with "strong drinks" (coffee and tea), nicotine, alcohol, and, of course, illegal drugs. While you won't have any trouble getting a pack of cigarettes, a cup of coffee or, a coke, alcohol is another matter. State liquor stores are sprinkled sparsely about the state and have inconvenient hours. Grocery and convenience stores can only sell beer. While most upscale restaurants serve wine, licensing laws can split a room, and drinkers may have to move a few feet down a bar to get a mixed drink. Diners wanting a drinks list must request one, law requires that waiters not offer drink menus. Also, establishments that sell hard alcohol are required to be "members only"; tourists can either find a "sponsor"—i.e., an entering patron—or get a short-term membership. If the rigmarole gets to be too much, try a smoothie.

Postal Abbreviation: UT. **Sales Tax:** 5.75-7.75%.

SALT LAKE CITY   ☎ 801

Tired from five exhausting months of travel, Brigham Young looked out across the desolate valley of the Great Salt Lake and said, "this is the place." Young knew that his band of Mormon pioneers had finally reached a haven where they could practice their religion freely, away from the persecution they had faced in the East. Today, Salt Lake City is still dominated by Mormon influence. The Church of Jesus Christ of Latter-Day Saints (LDS) owns the tallest office building downtown and welcomes visitors to Temple Sq., a city block that includes the Mormon Temple and cool, shady gardens. Despite its commitment to preserving tradition, Salt Lake is rapidly attracting high-tech firms, as well as outdoor enthusiasts drawn by world-class ski resorts, rock climbing, and mountain trails. The city has already landed perhaps the biggest prize of all, the 2002 Winter Olympics, which has the city looking temporarily war-torn from construction.

▐ GETTING THERE AND GETTING AROUND

Airport: Salt Lake City International, 776 N. Terminal Dr. (☎575-2400), 6 mi. west of Temple Sq. UTA bus #50 runs between the terminal and downtown for $1-2, but don't count on it after 10pm. Taxi to Temple Sq. costs about $11.

Trains: Amtrak, in Rio Grande Station, 340 S. 600 W. (☎531-0188), *in an unsafe area.* To San Francisco (19hr., 1 per day, $77-115) and Denver (15hr., 1 per day, $75-112). Station open M-F 10pm-1:30pm, Sa-Su 10pm-6am

Buses: Greyhound, 160 W. South Temple St. (☎355-9579), near Temple Sq. To: Las Vegas (8hr., 2 per day, $40); Los Angeles (16-17hr., 2 per day, $77); and Denver (10-18hr., 5 per day, $40). Open daily 4am-11pm, ticket window open 6:30am-7:30pm.

Public Transit: Utah Transit Authority (UTA), 3600 S. 700 W. (☎287-4636). Frequent service to University of Utah campus; buses to Ogden (#70/72 express), suburbs, airport, mountain canyons, and the #11 express runs to Provo (fare $2). Buses every 20min.-1hr. M-Sa 6am-11pm. Fare $1-2, senior discounts, under 5 free. Maps available at libraries and the visitors bureau. UTA also runs the **Sites Trolley,** which visits all the major sites for $2.

Taxis: Ute Cab, ☎359-7788. **Yellow Cab,** ☎521-2100.

Bike Rental: Wasatch Touring, on the corner of 700 E. and 100 S. St. (☎359-9361). 24-speed mountain bikes with helmets $25 per day. Open M-Sa 9am-7pm.

▐▌▐ ORIENTATION AND PRACTICAL INFORMATION

Salt Lake City's grid system may seem confusing at first but makes navigation easy once you get the hang of it. Brigham Young designated **Temple Sq.** as the heart of downtown. Street names increase in increments of 100 and indicate how many blocks east, west, north, or south they lie from Temple Sq.; the "0" points are **Main St.** (north-south) and **South Temple St.** (east-west). State St., W. Temple, and N. Temple are 100 level streets. Occasionally, streets are referred to as 13th S. or 17th N. which are the same as 1300 S or 1700 N. Local address listings often include two numerical cross streets, acting as a type of coordinate system (no maps needed!). A building on 13th S St. (1300 S) might be listed as 825 E. 1300 S, meaning the cross street is 800 E (8th E). Smaller streets and those that do not fit the grid pattern sometimes have non-numeric names.

Salt Lake City

ACCOMMODATIONS
Scenic View Motel, **4**
Ute Hostel, **6**
Skyline Inn, **5**
Avenue's Hostel, **1**

Visitor Info: Salt Lake Valley Convention and Visitors Bureau, 90 S. West Temple St. (☎534-4902). Located in Salt Palace Convention Center, 1 block south of Temple Sq. Open in summer M-F 8am-6pm, Sa-Su 9am-5pm; early Sept. to late May M-F 8am-5pm, Sa-Su 9am-5pm.

Hotlines: Rape Crisis, ☎467-7273. **Suicide Prevention,** ☎483-5444. Both 24hr.

Medical Services: University hospital emergency, ☎581-2291.

Post Office: 230 W. 200 S. St., 1 block south and 1 block west of visitors bureau. Open M-F 8am-5pm, Sa 9am-2pm. **ZIP code:** 84101. **Area code:** 801.

ACCOMMODATIONS

Affordable chain motels cluster at the southern end of downtown, around 200 W. and 600 S.

The Avenue's Hostel (HI-AYH), 107 F St. (☎359-3855), 15min. walk from Temple Sq. toward the foothills. Relaxed atmosphere in a residential area. Guests make frequent use of TV lounge, library, and video collection. Reception 7:30am-10:30pm. Free pick-up from Amtrak and Greyhound stations. Winter ski bus to nearby resorts $2-4. Blankets and linen free. Dorm rooms $14; doubles $33-34.

Ute Hostel (AAIH/Rucksackers), 21 E. Kelsey Ave. (☎595-1645), near the intersection of 1300 S and Main St. Young international crowd. Check-in 24hr. Free pick-ups can be arranged from airport, Amtrak, Greyhound, or the visitors center. Free tea and coffee, parking, linen, and safe. Dorm rooms $15; comfortable doubles $35.

Skyline Inn, 2475 E. 1700 S (☎582-5350), near the university. Friendly service and very clean singles $57.

Scenic Motel, 1345 S. Foothill Drive, (☎582-1527). Charming rooms in a safe residential area. Singles $38; doubles $45.

The mountains rising to the east of Salt Lake City offer comfortable summer camping with warm days and cool nights. Rocky **Little Cottonwood Canyon,** on Rte. 210 east of the city, features two of the closest campgrounds for summer camping: **Albion Basin** (26 sites) and **Tanners Flat** (39 sites; both $10). Two more campgrounds lie just north of the city on I-15: **Sunset** (17 sites; $6) and **Bountiful Peak** (22 sites; $8). On weekends, get there early to ensure a space. The **Salt Lake Ranger District** fields calls for more info (☎943-1794).

Camp out in the middle of the Great Salt Lake on **Antelope Island,** (access via 7¼ mi. Davis County Causeway from the mainland). The 13 sites are popular; call early for reservations. (Headquarters ☎550-6155, visitors center 721-9569. $2, $7 entrance fee for motorized vehicles.) If you need a hook-up, **Camp VIP,** 1400 W. North Temple St., has 450 RV sites and 17 tent sites. (☎328-0224. Sites $19, full hook-up $26.)

☼ MORAL FIBER

Good, cheap restaurants are sprinkled around the city and its suburbs. The area near the University of Utah has the best selection of trendy and inexpensive restaurants. If you're in a hurry downtown, **ZCMI Mall** and **Crossroads Mall,** both located across from Temple Sq., have standard food courts.

W.H. Brumby's, 224 S. 1300 E. (☎581-0888). Mouth-watering breakfasts, lunches, and desserts. Students and locals swarm for Su brunch. Breakfast and lunch $5-7. Open Tu-F 8am-9pm, Sa-Su 8am-9pm.

The Pie, 1320 E. 200 S. (☎582-0193), next to the University of Utah. This graffiti-buried college hangout serves up large pizzas (starting at $7) late into the night. Open M-Th 11am-1am, F-Sa 11am-3am, Su noon-midnight.

Park Cafe, 604 E. 1300 S. (☎487-1670), at the south end of Liberty Park. Homestyle food in a classy little joint with a patio and a view of a park. Lunches $6-7, light dinners $8. Open M-F 7am-3pm and 5-9pm, Sa 7am-3pm and 5-10pm, Su 7am-3pm.

Squatter's Salt Lake Brewing Company, 147 W. Broadway (☎363-2739). Microbrewery ($3 pints) with reasonably priced American cuisine and a variety of sandwiches ($7-8), pizzas, and salads ($4). Open M-Sa 11:30am-1am, Su 11:30am-midnight.

☉ SIGHTS

MORMON SIGHTS. The majority of Salt Lake City's sights are sacred to the Church of Jesus Christ of Latter-Day Saints and are all free. The seat of the highest Mormon authority and the central temple, **Temple Sq.** is the symbolic center of the Mormon religion. The square has two **visitors centers,** North and South. Visitors can wander around the flowery ten-acre square, but the sacred temple is off-limits to non-Mormons. A 45min. tour leaves from the flagpole every 10min., showing off the highlights of Temple Sq. *Legacy,* a film detailing the Mormon trek to Salt Lake City, is screened at the **Joseph Smith Memorial Building.** *(☎240-2609; 240-4383 for film show times. Open daily 8am-10pm, in winter 9am-9pm. Tours daily 8:30am-8:30pm. Free.)*

Temple Sq. is also home to the **Mormon Tabernacle** and its famed choir. Weekly rehearsals and performances are free and open to the public. *(Organ recitals M-Sa noon-12:30pm, Su 2-2:30pm, in summer also M-Sa 2-2:30pm. Choir rehearsals Th 8-9:30pm; Choir broadcasts Su 9:30am, must be seated by 9:15am.)* During summer months, there are frequent free concerts at **Assembly Hall** next door. *(☎800-537-9703 for schedules.)*

The **Church of Jesus Christ of Latter Day Saints Office Building** is the tallest skyscraper in town. The elevator to the 26th floor grants a view of the Great Salt Lake in the west and the Wasatch Range in the east. *(50 E. N. Temple St. ☎240-3789. Observation deck open M-F 9am-5pm.)* The LDS church's collection of genealogical materials is available and free. The **Family Search Center,** 15 E. S Temple St., in the Joseph Smith Memorial Building, has computers and staff to aid in your search. The actual collection is housed in the **Family History Library.** *(35 N. W. Temple. ☎537-9703. Center: Open M-Sa 9am-9pm. Library: Open M 7:30am-6pm, Tu-Sa 7:30am-10pm.)*

CAPITOL HILL. At the northernmost end of State St., Utah's **capitol building** features beautiful grounds, including a garden that changes daily. *(☎538-3000. Open M-F 8am-5pm. Tours M-F 9am-4pm.)* Also on Capitol Hill, the **Hansen Planetarium,** has free exhibits and laser shows set to music. *(15 S. State St. ☎538-2104. Open M-Th 9am-9pm, F-Sa 9am-midnight, Su noon-6pm. Laser show $7.50, star and science show $4.50.)*

MUSEUMS. At the **Children's Museum,** pilot a 727 jet or implant a Jarvik artificial heart in a life-sized "patient." *(840 N. 300 W. St. ☎328-3383. Take bus #70. Open M-Th and Sa 10am-6pm, F 10am-8pm. 2 and under $3, F after 5pm $2.)* A permanent collection of world art wows enthusiasts at the **Utah Museum of Fine Arts,** on the University of Utah campus. *(☎581-7332. Open M-F 9am-5pm, Sa-Su 2-5pm. Free.)* The **Salt Lake Art Center,** displays an impressive array of contemporary art, as well as the less abstract Kidspace, where modern art appreciation is hands-on. *(20 S. W. Temple St. ☎328-4201. Open Tu-Th and Sa 10am-5pm, F 10am-9pm, Su 1-5pm; Kidspace open W-F and Su 1-4pm, Sa 10am-4pm. Suggested donation $2.)*

THE GREAT SALT LAKE. The Great Salt Lake, administered by Great Salt Lake State Marina, is a remnant of primordial Lake Bonneville and is so salty that only blue-green algae and brine shrimp can survive in it. The salt content varies from 5-27%, providing unusual buoyancy. No one has ever drowned in the Great Salt Lake—a fact attributable to the Lake's chemical make-up, which also makes the water reek. *(☎250-1822.)* **Antelope Island State Park,** in the middle of the lake, has beaches, hiking trails, picnic spots, and buffalo. *(☎595-4030. It is nearly impossible to get to the Lake without a car; bus #37 "Magna" will take you within 4 mi., but no closer. To get to the south shore of the lake, take I-80 17 mi. west of Salt Lake City to Exit 104. To get to the island, take Exit 335 from I-15 and follow signs to the causeway. Open daily 7am-10pm; in winter dawn to dusk. $7 per vehicle, $3 per bicycle.)*

⚠ SKIING

Skiing is a major attraction in Salt Lake City. Many claim that the Wasatch Mountains are home to the greatest snow on earth, and seven ski areas within an hour of Salt Lake offer the opportunity to put this hypothesis to the test. The neighboring town of Park City is a quintessential ski town, complete with expensive restaurants, luxury hotels, and few options for budget-minded travelers. Staying in Salt Lake is a more affordable option.

Alta (☎359-1078), 27 mi. southeast of Salt Lake City in Little Cottonwood Canyon. The cheapest lift tickets around, but the skiing is still magnificent. Alta's powdery slopes are strictly for skiing, so leave the snowboard behind. Open Nov.-Apr. Day pass $35; half-day $27.

Brighton (☎532-4731), south of Salt Lake in Big Cottonwood Canyon. A favorite for families, with its friendly terrain. More experienced skiers may be looking for more challenging runs, but Brighton is a great place to start. Open Nov.-Apr. Day pass $35; day and night $39; twilight $33; half-day $28; night pass $20.

The Canyons (☎435-649-5400), in Park City. Has recently undergone renovations, adding new lifts, mountains, half-pipes, and other facilities. With 125 trails, 13 lifts, and 6 half-pipes, the Canyon's terrain wows skiing enthusiasts but may be intimidating to beginners. Open Nov.-May. Day pass $52, ages 6-12 and seniors $25, under 6 free.

Deer Valley (☎435-649-1000), in Park City. Host of the slalom, moguls, and aerial events in the 2002 Winter Olympics and a genuine world-class ski area. While Deer Valley doesn't cater to the snowboarding crowd, skiers will be mesmerized by the bowl skiing. Open Dec.-Apr. Day pass $60; under age 13 $32, seniors $42; half-day $42.

Park City (☎435-649-8111). Facilities earned it the job of hosting the Olympic snowboarding events in 2002; the skiing's not bad either. The 750 acres of open bowl skiing might make you feel a bit extreme. Open Nov.-Apr. Day passes vary by season, expect $60+ in high season, seniors ages 65-69 $30, seniors 70+ free; half-day $42.

Snowbird (☎933-2222 or 800-453-3000), in Little Cottonwood Canyon south of Salt Lake. May frighten those who don't like steeps, but the adventurous types will relish in the back bowl feeling here. A 125-passenger aerial tram ascends to an 11,000 ft. peak for spectacular views and extreme-style skiing. Open Nov.-May. Day pass with tram access $52, chairs only $42.

Solitude (☎543-1400), in Big Cottonwood Canyon south of Salt Lake. Budget prices and luxury slopes. The uncrowded runs are accessible for skiers and snowboarders of all abilities. Open Nov.-Apr. Day pass $39, seniors 60-69 $32, 70+ free; half-day $33; multi-day $37.

🎵🎭 ENTERTAINMENT AND NIGHTLIFE

Concerts abound in the sweltering summer months. At 7:30pm every Tu and F, the **Temple Sq. Concert Series** conducts a free outdoor concert in Brigham Young Historic Park, with music ranging from string quartet to unplugged guitar (☎240-2534; call for a schedule of concerts). The **Utah Symphony Orchestra** performs in **Abravanel Hall,** 123 W. South Temple St. (☎533-6683. Office open M-F 10am-6pm. Call 1 week in advance. Tickets Sept. to early May $15-40.) On W evenings in summer, the Gallivan Center, at the corner of State St. and 200 S St., hosts **Alive After Five,** a laid-back celebration of live music, beer, and food.

Women's basketball's **Utah Starzz** (season June-Aug.; tickets $5-40) and the 1998 NBA Western Conference Champion **Utah Jazz** (season Oct.-Apr.; tickets $10-83) take the court at the **Delta Center,** 301 W. South Temple St. (☎355-3865).

Free copies of *The Event, Mountain Times, City Weekly,* or *Utah After Dark* are available from bars, clubs, and restaurants and list events. While most of Salt Lake's nightlife spots are private clubs for members, temporary memberships for around $5 are often available. The **Dead Goat Saloon,** 165 S. W. Temple St., showcases local acts in a relaxed atmosphere that includes pool, darts, and a grill. (☎328-4628. Open M-Sa 6pm-2am, Su 6pm-around midnight.) **The Zephyr,** 301 S. Temple St., thumps live music nightly and attracts national acts. (☎355-2582. Hrs. vary. Get a member to sponsor you.) Dance the night away at **Club DV8,** 115 S. W. Temple St., to a variety of dance music. (☎539-8400. Open F-Sa 9pm-2am. Half-price drafts 9-10pm.) Classic movies are accompanied by microbrews at **Brewvies,** 667 S. 200 W (☎355-5500), a movie theater and brewpub combination.

🗺 DAYTRIP FROM SALT LAKE CITY

TIMPANOGOS CAVE. Legend has it that a set of mountain lion tracks first led Martin Hansen to the mouth of the cave that today bears his name. While Utah's Wasatch Mountains brim with natural wonders, the cave system of American Fork Canyon, collectively called Timpanogos Cave, is a true gem for speleologists (cave nuts) and tourists alike. Though early gem pirates stole and shipped boxcar loads of stalactites and other mineral wonders back east to sell to universities and museums, enough remain to bedazzle guests for the 1hr. walk through the caves. Today the cave is open only to visitors via tours led by rangers.

Timpanogos Cave National Monument is solely accessible via Rte. 92 (20 mi. south of Salt Lake City off I-15, Exit 287). The **visitors center** dispenses tour tickets and info on the caves. Summer tours tend to sell out by early afternoon; reservations may be made by phone two weeks in advance, or at the visitors center up to the day before the tour. Bring water and warm layers: the rigorous hike to the cave is a climb, but the temperature drops dramatically once inside. (☎756-5238. Open daily mid-May to mid-Oct. 7am-5:30pm. 3hr. hikes depart daily 7am-4:30pm every 15min. $6, ages 6-15 $5, seniors with Golden Age Passport and under 5 $3.)

The national monument is dwarfed by the surrounding **Uinta National Forest,** which blankets the mountains of the Wasatch Range. The **Alpine Scenic Drive (Rte. 92)** leaves the visitors center and heads southwest, providing excellent views of Mt. Timpanogos and other snow-capped peaks. The loopy 20 mi. drive is laden with switchbacks and takes close to 1hr. in one direction. This road will take you past many trailheads; for detailed trail descriptions of area hikes such as the 9 mi. (one-way) trek up Mt. Timpanogos, inquire at the **Pleasant Grove Ranger District,** 390 N. 100 E. Pleasant Grove (☎785-3563).

Camping in the national monument is strictly forbidden. The Pleasant Grove Ranger District (see above) has info on the four **campgrounds** in the area (☎800-280-2267 for reservations; sites $11-13) and **backcountry camping** throughout the forest, which requires no permit or fee as long as you respect minimum-impact guidelines. Once inside the monument, services are extremely limited. Rte. 89 in nearby **Orem** and **Pleasant Grove** has gas stations, supermarkets and fast food joints.

DINOSAUR NATIONAL MONUMENT AND VERNAL ☎ 435

Dinosaur National Monument was created in 1915, seven years after paleontologist Earl Douglass happened upon an array of fossilized dinosaur bones here. The rugged landscape that today includes the beautiful Green and Yampa rivers was once home to legions of dinosaurs that left their remains for tourists to ogle. The monument's main attraction is the dinosaur quarry, but adventurous types may find more distractions in the less explored parts of the area. The town of Vernal, west of Dinosaur on U.S. 40, is a popular base for exploring the monument, Flaming Gorge, and the Uinta Mountains.

⌕ PRACTICAL INFORMATION. Greyhound, 15 S. Vernal Ave. (☎789-0404), at Frontier Travel near the corner Main St. in Vernal, makes daily runs east and west along U.S. 40 (2 each way), stopping in Dinosaur, CO, en route from Denver and Salt Lake City. Jensen is a flag stop, as is monument headquarters, 2 mi. west of Dinosaur, CO. The park collects an **entrance fee** of $10 per car, and $5 per cyclist, pedestrian, or tour-bus passenger. The monument's more interesting and varied **west side** lies along Rte. 149 off U.S. 40 just outside of Jensen and 30 mi. east of Vernal. The rugged **east side** of the park is accessible only from a road off U.S. 40, outside Dinosaur, CO. The **Dinosaur Quarry Visitors Center,** near the fee collection booth, is accessible only by a free shuttle bus running every 15min. or an uphill ½ mi. walk in the summer; in the winter you can drive up to the center. (☎789-2115. Open daily 8am-6pm; in winter 8am-4:30pm.) The **Dinosaur National Monument Headquarters** is on the other side of the park at the intersection of U.S. 40 and the park road in Dinosaur, CO. (☎970-374-3000. Open daily May-Sept. 8am-4:30pm; Sept.-May M-F 8am-4:30pm.) No services are available in the park; fill up in Dinosaur, Jensen, or Vernal. The **Ashley National Forest Service Office,** 355 N. Vernal Ave., in Vernal, has info about hiking, biking, and camping in the surrounding forests. (☎789-1181. Open M-F 8am-4:30pm.) Vernal's **Post Office** is on the corner of 67 N and 800 W. (☎789-2393. Open M-F 9am-5pm, Sa 10am-1pm.) **ZIP code:** 84078. **Area code:** 435.

⌕ ACCOMMODATIONS AND FOOD. For the lowdown on campgrounds, contact the park visitors center or the National Forest Headquarters in Vernal. **Green River Campground** consists of 88 shaded sites along the Green River. (Open late spring to early fall. Flush toilets, water, RVs, wheelchair accessible sites. Sites $12.) There are also several free **primitive campsites** in and around the park. Thirteen mi.

THE WILD BUNCH Of all the stalwart pioneers and daring outlaws of the Old West, perhaps Butch Cassidy is most deeply etched in the era's legends. The "Robin Hood of the West" rose to notoriety as a cunning train and bank robber. He later joined forces with the Sundance Kid to form the Wild Bunch, a group of thieving renegades who worked out of Brown's Park and wreaked havoc on Utah, Colorado, and Wyoming. Vernal's Outlaw Trail Theater brings the Cassidy lore back to life in its outdoor musical *Cassidy: The Mostly True Story of Butch Cassidy and the Wild Bunch.* This lively production fires from the hip, consciously blurring the distinction between the myth and the man. The show runs from late June through early Aug.; call ☎789-6932 or 800-477-5558 for tickets and info.

east of Harper's Corner, off a four-wheel drive road (impassable when wet) on the park's east side, **Echo Park Campground** provides the perfect location for a crystal-line evening under the stars (vault toilets and water; 8 sites $6). Free **backcountry camping** permits are available from the headquarters or from Quarry Center. For hook-ups and other amenities head outside the park, to **Campground Dina RV Park,** 930 N. Vernal Ave., about 1 mi. north of Main St. on U.S. 191 in Vernal. (☎789-2148 or 800-245-2148. Heated pool, showers, laundry, convenience store. Grassy sites $6.50 per person, ages 7-17 $2; full hook-up $20.)

For those less inclined to rough it, Vernal is civilization's beacon. The comfortable **Sage Motel,** 54 W. Main St., has big, clean rooms, A/C, cable TV, and free local calls. (☎789-1442 or 800-760-1442. Singles $39; doubles $42; 2 beds $47; $5 per additional person.) The **Lazy K Motel,** on U.S. 40, has clean, minimalist rooms, on the outskirts of town toward the monument. (☎789-3277. Singles $25; doubles $30.)

Finding a budget meal isn't difficult in Vernal. The **Seven Eleven Cafe,** 77 E. Main St., in Vernal, packs in locals and tourists for monster breakfasts ($5) and fresh java. (☎789-1170. Open M-Sa 6am-10pm.) Mouthwatering homemade salsa is the special at **LaLa's Fiesta,** 550 E. Main St. Lunch and dinner specialties begin with the *chile relleno* ($5 for 2), and all meals are under $9. (☎789-2966. Open M-Sa 11am-9pm; if busy, open later and on Su.)

SIGHTS AND ACTIVITIES. Some 350 million tons of dinosaur remains have been carted away from this Jurassic cemetery, but over 1600 fossils remain exposed in the **Quarry Visitors Center** (see **Practical Information,** above.)

Scenic drives and hikes are the best way to appreciate the unique beauty and history of the area. Stop by the visitors center in Vernal to pick up free guides to auto tours in the area. These kitschy pamphlets direct motorists to historical sights and beautiful vistas. **Harper's Corner,** at the confluence of the Green and Yampa Rivers, has one of the best views around. To get to the corner, take the Harper's Corner road from the monument headquarters. At the end of the road, an easy 2 mi. round-trip hike leads to the view.

River trips are a popular summer diversion along the Green and Yampa Rivers. **Dan Hatch River Expeditions,** in Vernal, floats through the monument and the nearby Flaming Gorge. Trips meet at 221 N. 400 E. (☎789-4316 or 800-342-8243. 1-day trip $65, age 6-12 $56; seniors 10% off.)

FLAMING GORGE   ☎435

Seen at sunset, the contrast between the red canyon lands and the aquamarine water of the Green River makes the landscape glow, hence the moniker "Flaming Gorge." Apparently not everyone was satisfied with this natural beauty; legislation was passed in 1963 to dam the Green River. The resulting body of water is now home to the **Flaming Gorge National Recreation Area.** Boating and fishing enthusiasts descend into the gorge every summer to take advantage of this altered landscape.

PRACTICAL INFORMATION. From Wyoming, travel on U.S. 191 S to the Gorge through the high desert. A recreation pass is $2 and can be obtained at the **Flaming Gorge Visitors Center,** on U.S. 191 atop the Flaming Gorge Dam. The visitors center also offers free tours of the dam. (☎885-3135. Open daily 8am-6pm; off-season 9am-5pm.) A few mi. off U.S. 191 and 3 mi. off Rte. 44 to Manila, the **Red Canyon Visitors Center** hangs 1360 ft. above Red Canyon. (☎889-3713. Open daily 10am-5pm; closed in winter.) **Post Office:** 4 South Blvd., in Dutch John. (☎885-3351. Open M-F 7:30am-3:30pm, Sa 9:30am-12:30pm.) **ZIP code:** 84023. **Area code:** 435.

ACCOMMODATIONS. Camping in the area is scenic and accessible. With over 30 camps spread around the lake, the visitors centers can offer sound advice on what is best for the season. A number of sites can be reserved by calling ☎888-444-6777 at least five days in advance. Prices for camping range from free to $14 depending on available services. The 18 secluded sites at **Dripping Springs** are some of the most coveted, due to prime fishing location (reservable; sites $12). **Red Canyon** offers a feeling of high-country camping with nearby views of the red-walled gorge (sites $12).

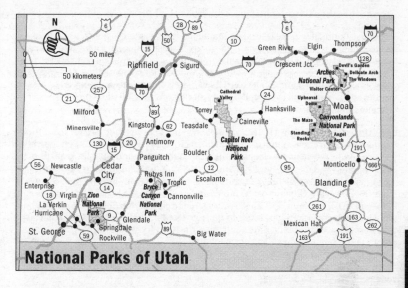

National Parks of Utah

While camping is cheapest, indoor lodging can be found at **Red Canyon Lodge** west on Rte. 44, 2 mi. before the visitors center. While this lodge offers location, views, and activities more in line with a luxury resort, budget cabins are available. (☎889-3759. Private lake, restaurants. Single cabins for 2 $35, for 4 $45, with private bath $50/$60; $6 per additional adult; $2 per child under 12; rollaway beds $6 per night.)

🔥 **OUTDOORS.** The Green River Gorge below the dam teems with trout, making for top-notch **fishing,** and the Green River offers some of the best fly fishing in the country. To fish, obtain a **permit,** available at Flaming Gorge Lodge, Dutch John Recreation Services, and most stores in Manila. For more info, call the **Utah Division of Wildlife Resources,** 1594 W. North Temple, in Salt Lake City. (☎800-538-4700. Open M-F 7:30am-6pm.) Several establishments rent the requisite gear for recreation. **Cedar Springs Marina,** 3 mi. before the dam, rents boats. (☎889-3795. Open daily 8am-6pm. Pontoon boats for 8 people from $90 for 3hr., from $160 per day. Ski boats for 6 $110 for 3hr., $190 per day; skis $15 per day.) Nearby, friendly **Flaming Gorge Lodge** rents fishing rods (☎889-3773; $10 per day). At **Lucerne Valley Marina,** 7 mi. east of Manila off Rte. 43, you can procure a small, 14 ft. fishing boat for $75, plus a $50 deposit per day. (☎784-3483. Open daily around 7am-9pm.)

The **Sheep Creek Geologic Loop,** an 11 mi. scenic drive off Hwy. 530 just south of Manila, takes you past strata and wildlife. For a hideout from tourists, the valley of **Brown's Park,** 23 mi. east of Flaming Gorge, is accessible via narrow, sometimes paved roads winding through three states. Nineteenth-century outlaws **Butch Cassidy, the Sundance Kid,** and their **Wild Bunch** found the valley's isolation and its proximity to three state lines ideal for evading the law (see **The Wild Bunch** p. 713).

Most visitors prefer to enjoy the area from the comfort of boats, leaving **hiking** and **biking** trails deserted. The most scenic trail follows the colorful gorge for 5 mi. There are four trailheads to the **Canyon Rim** trail, including one at the visitors center. Most trails are open to mountain biking, but no biking is allowed in the adjacent High Uintas Wilderness. The **Dowd Mountain** trail begins from Rte. 44 between Manila and the Red Canyon Visitors Center and offers panoramic views of the area. The 10 mi. round-trip trek is mostly moderate, but is can be rough toward the finish. Maps and more info are available at both visitors centers.

MOAB
☎**435**

Moab first flourished in the 50s, when uranium miners rushed to the area and transformed the town from a quiet hamlet into a gritty desert outpost. Today, the mountain bike has replaced the Geiger counter, as tourists rush into the town eager to bike the red slickrock, raft whitewater rapids, or explore surrounding Arches and Canyonlands National Parks. The town itself has changed to accommodate the new visitors and athletes; microbreweries and t-shirt shops now fill the rooms of the old uranium building on Main St.

⁊ PRACTICAL INFORMATION. Moab sits 50 mi. southeast of I-70 on U.S. 191, 5 mi. south of Arches. **Amtrak** comes only as close as Green River, 52 mi. northwest of town. **Greyhound's** closest stop is in Crescent Junction, 32 mi. north of Moab at the junction of Hwy. 191 and I-70. Some hotels and hostels will pick guests up from these distant points for a small fee. **Bighorn Express** makes trips from the Salt Lake City airport to Moab. (☎587-3061 or 888-655-7433. Open M-F 9am-5pm, Sa 10am-2pm. $49. Reservations required.) **Coyote Shuttle** (☎259-8656) will also take you where you want to go (rates and hrs. vary). The **Moab Information Center,** 3 Center St., doles out info on the city and nearby parks and monuments. (Open daily July-Aug. 8am-9pm; Sept.-Oct. and Apr.-May 8am-7pm; May-June 8am-8pm; Nov. 9am-7pm; Dec.-Mar. 9am-5pm.) **Post Office:** 50 E. 100 N. St. (☎259-7427; open M-F 8:30am-4:30pm, Sa 8:30am-noon). **ZIP code:** 84532. **Area code:** 435.

⁊ ACCOMMODATIONS. Chain motels clutter Main St., but Moab fills up fast in the summer, especially on weekends; call ahead. Off-season rates can drop as much as 50%, and during that time the weather is more conducive to hiking. John Wayne and you too! can sleep at **Apache Motel,** 166 S. 400 E. Wash off the red dust in their swimming pool. (☎259-5755. Rooms $31-75; AAA discount.) The owners of the **Lazy Lizard International Hostel (AAIH/Rucksackers),** 1213 S. U.S. 191 (look for the "A1 Self Storage" sign 1 mi. south of Moab on U.S. 191), go out of their way to be helpful—they'll pick you up (usually for $10-15) and arrange trips through local companies. The kitchen, VCR, laundry, and hot tub are at your disposal. (☎259-6057. Dorms $8. Private rooms for 1 or 2 from $20. Cabins from $25. Tent sites $6. No curfew.) A miner's hat, fishing nets, and a Victrola accent the quirky and luxurious theme rooms of **Hotel Off Center,** 96 E. Center St., a block off Main St. (☎259-4244. Open Mar.-Nov. Shared bath. Dorms $12; singles $40; doubles $50.) **The Prospector Lodge,** 186 N. 1st W. St., a block west of Main St., offers comfy rooms with TV. (☎259-5145. Singles $34; doubles $41, with a queen-size bed $48. $6 per additional person.)

Arches National Park (see p. 717) has the area's best campground. In town, the **Canyonlands Campground,** 555 S. Main St., next to the Shell Station, provides well-shaded sites and a pool. (☎259-6848 or 800-522-6848. Sites for two $15, with water and electricity $18, full hook-up $20; $3 per additional adult or teen.) **Slickrock Campground,** 1301½ Hwy. 191, beckons the budget traveler with the slogan, "funpigs stay at Slickrock." Yes, "funpig"—a person who relaxes and has fun. (☎259-7660 or 800-448-8873. Pool, 3 hot tubs, showers, and laundry. Tent sites $17, with water and electricity $21, full hook-up $23. Cabins with A/C $30 plus $5 per extra person.)

⁊ FOOD. I say, what about **Breakfast at Tiffany's,** 90 E. Center? The filling meals are accompanied by snazzy decor. (☎259-2553. Open daily 7am-3pm. Lunch 11:30am-3pm.) Seating on the patio or inside among simulated redrocks heightens the pleasure of fresh lunch wraps like the Ragin' Cajun ($7) at **Honest Ozzie's Cafe,** 60 N. 100 W. Veggie and vegan menu items complement a wide variety of fresh, quick meals. (☎259-8442. Open W-M 8am-3pm.) The retro booths might take you back to the 50s at **The Moab Diner and Ice Cream Shoppe,** 189 S. Main St. Veggie specials and excellent french fries are big draws. (☎259-4006. Open Su-Th 6am-10pm, F-Sa 6am-10:30pm. Sandwiches and burgers $5-6.) **Moab Community Coop,** 111 N. 100

W, a block off Main St., can fill your saddlebags with organic and health foods for your journey. (☎259-5712. Open M-F 9am-6pm, Sa 9-10:30am, and 1-6pm.) After a hot day in the desert, cool off at the **Peach Tree Juice Cafe,** 20 Main St. (☎259-6333), with a $2.25 smoothie. The **Moab Brewery,** 686 S. Main St., serves delicious food (full meals all under $10) and their own ales. (☎259-6333. Open Su-Th 11:30am-10pm, F-Sa 11:30am-11pm.) A search for live music will lead to **The Rio Colorado Restaurant and Bar,** 200 S. 100 W St., off Main St. (☎259-6666. Restaurant open F-Sa 3-8:30pm, Su-Th 3-10pm. Bar open M-Sa until 2am, Su until midnight.)

🔲🅰 **SIGHTS AND ACTIVITIES. Mountain biking** and **rafting,** along with nearby national parks, are the big draws in Moab. The **Slickrock** trail is a 10 mi. loop which rolls up and down the slickrock outside of Moab. The trail has no big vertical gain, but it's technically difficult, and temperatures often reach 100°F. **Rim Cyclery,** 94 W. 1st St., rents bikes and distributes info about the slickrock trails. (☎259-5333. Open daily 9am-6pm. $31-35 per day includes helmet.)

Countless raft companies are based in Moab. **OARS/North American River Expeditions,** 543 N. Main, offers great deals and the best guides on the rivers. (☎259-5865 or 800-342-5938. Half-day $36, ages 5-17 $27; includes snacks and a natural history lesson.) **Western River Expeditions** offers good deals as well. (☎259-7019 or 800-453-7450. Half-day $34, children $27; full-day $47/$34; includes lunch.) Various Moab outfitters also arrange horseback, motorboat, canoe, jeep, and helicopter rides. **Pack Creek Ranch** offers horseback rides into the La Sal Mountains. (☎259-5505. 1½hr. $20 per person.)

Albert Christensen spent 12 years creating the bizarre **Hole 'n the Rock,** 15 mi. south of Moab on U.S. 191, a 14-room house carved out of a sandstone cliff. His wife Gladys kept the dream alive after his death in 1957 and opened the house to the public. Christensen's nearby rendering of Franklin D. Roosevelt is somethin', really somethin'. (☎668-2250. Open daily mid-Apr. to mid. Oct. 9am-6pm; late Oct. to early Apr. 9am-5pm. $2.75, children $1.75; includes informative tour.) Utah's only winery, **Arches Vineyards,** 420 Kane Creek, is located in the Moab area. (☎259-5397. Tasting room open M-Sa noon-8pm. Free.)

FINDING THE FAB FIVE

The five **National Parks** that cover this majestic area can be reached by several roads. From Moab, take U.S. 191 N 5 mi. to **Arches** (see below). Continue 60 mi. north on U.S. 191 to Rte. 313 S to the Islands in the Sky area of **Canyonlands** (see p. 719). Or, take U.S. 191 south from Moab to Rte. 211 W to reach the Needles area of Canyonlands (87 mi.). To reach **Capitol Reef** (see p. 720), continue driving north on U.S. 191 and then west on I-70; leave I-70 at Exit 147, and follow Rte. 24 S to Hanksville and then west to the park (81 mi. from I-70). Rte. 24 W runs to Torrey, where scenic Rte. 12 branches south and west through the Dixie National Forest to **Bryce Canyon** (see p. 721). For **Zion** (see p. 723), continue on Rte. 12 W to U.S. 89 S through Mt. Carmel Jct., and pick up Rte. 9 W.

The two national forests in Southern Utah are divided into districts, some of which lie near the national parks and serve as excellent places to stay on a cross-country jaunt. **Manti-La Sal National Forest** has two sections near Arches and the Needles area of Canyonlands. **Dixie National Forest** stretches from Capitol Reef through Bryce all the way to the western side of Zion.

ARCHES   ☎435

"This is the most beautiful place on earth," novelist Edward Abbey wrote of Arches National Park. Thousands of sandstone arches, spires, pinnacles, and fins tower above the desert in overwhelming grandeur. Some arches are so perfect in form that early explorers believed they were constructed by a lost civilization. Deep red sandstone, green pinyon trees and juniper bushes, ominous grey thunderclouds, and a strikingly blue sky combine to etch an unforgettable palette of color that is best explored on foot.

⁊ PRACTICAL INFORMATION. The park entrance is on U.S. 191, 5 mi. north of Moab. Although no public transportation serves the park, shuttle bus companies travel to both the national park and Moab from surrounding towns and cities (see Moab **Practical Information,** p. 716). While most visitors come in the summer, 100°F temperatures make hiking difficult; bring at least one gallon of water per person per day. The weather is best in the spring and fall when temperate days and nights combine to make a comfortable stay. In the winter, white snow provides a brilliant contrast to the red arches. The **visitors center,** to the right of the entrance station, distributes free park service maps. (☎259-8161. Open daily mid-Apr. to Sept. 7:30am-6pm, in winter 8am-4:30pm.) An **entrance pass** covers admission for a week ($10 per carload, $5 per pedestrian or biker). Write the **Superintendent,** Arches National Park, P.O. Box 907, Moab 84532. For more details on accommodations, food, and activities, see **Moab,** p. 716. **Area code:** 435.

⌐ CAMPGROUNDS. The park's only campground, **Devil's Garden,** has 52 excellent campsites nestled amid pinyon pines and giant red sandstone formations. The campsite is within walking distance of the Devil's Garden and Broken Arch trailheads; however, it is a long 18 mi. from the visitors center. Because Devil's Garden doesn't take reservations, sites go quickly. In spring and fall, visitors show up early; a line forms at the visitors center at 7:30am. (No wood-gathering. Running water mid-Mar. to Oct.; 1-week max. stay. Sites $10, in winter $5.)

If the heat becomes unbearable at Arches, the aspen forests of the **Manti-La Sal National Forest** offer respite. Take Rte. 128 along the Colorado River and turn right at Castle Valley; or go south 21 mi. from Moab on U.S. 191 7 mi. and turn off to the left. These beautiful sites sit 4000 ft. above the national park and are usually several degrees cooler. All sites cost $8, except the free sites at **Oowah Lake.** Oowah, 3 mi. down a dirt road, is a rainbow trout haven. Fishing permits are available at most stores in Moab and at the Forest Service office ($5 per day).

◉⚑ SIGHTS AND ACTIVITIES. While the striking red slickrock around Arches may seem like attraction enough, the real points of interest here lie off the paved road. Load up on water and sunscreen and seek out on foot some of the arches that make this place famous. There are thousands of natural arches in the park, and each one is pinpointed on the free map and guide that is passed out at the fee collection booth. For more detailed maps and info on hiking, especially desert precautions, stop at the visitors center. Hiking in the park is unparalleled, especially in the cool days of spring and fall. Stay on trails; the land may look barren but the soil actually contains cryptobiotic life forms that are easily destroyed by footsteps. The most popular hike in the parks leads to the oft-photographed **Delicate Arch.** The trail leaves from the Wolfe Ranch parking area and climbs 480 ft. The 3 mi. hike takes about 2½hr.; bring lots of water (at least 1 quart per person.) To view the spectacular Delicate Arch without the 3 mi. hike, take the **Delicate Arch Viewpoint** trail which begins, appropriately, in the Delicate Arch Viewpoint parking area. This 300 ft. trail takes around 15min. and is wheelchair accessible. The 7¼ mi loop through **Devils Garden** requires some scrambling over rocks, but hearty travelers will be rewarded by the eight arches visible from this trail. The trek usually takes 3-5hrs. and is not recommended in wet or snowy conditions. A much easier trail traverses the **Windows** area. Three arches (North and South Windows and Turret Arch) are visible along this 1 mi. loop. Visitors occasionally come across petroglyphs left on the stone walls by the Ancestral Puebloans and Ute who wandered here centuries ago.

Arches aren't the only natural wonders of the area. One of the more popular trails, the moderately strenuous 2 mi. **Fiery Furnace Trail,** leads down into the canyon bottoms, providing new perspective on the imposing cliffs and monoliths above. Only experienced hikers should attempt this trail. Rangers lead groups from the visitors center into the labyrinth twice daily in summer. ($6, children $3. Tours tend to fill up 2 days before; reservations can be made 7 days in advance in person.)

CANYONLANDS ☎ 435

Those who make the trek to Canyonlands National Park are rewarded with a pleasant surprise: the absence of people. The sandstone spires, roughly cut canyons, and vibrantly colored rock layers of this awe-inspiring landscape are often passed-up by those on a time budget. There are none of the amenities of Western culture in the park, and those who come commit themselves to a real outdoor experience.

ORIENTATION AND PRACTICAL INFORMATION. The Green and Colorado Rivers divide the park into three sections. The **Needles** region contains spires, arches, canyons, and Native American ruins, but is not as rough as the Maze area. To get to the Needles, take Rte. 211 W from U.S. 191, about 40mi. south of Moab. (☎259-4711. Open daily 8am-5pm.) Farther north, **Island in the Sky,** a towering mesa which sits within the "Y" formed by the two rivers, affords fantastic views of the surrounding canyons and mountains; take Rte. 313 W from U.S. 191 about 10 mi. north of Moab. (☎259-4712. Open daily 8am-5pm.) The most remote district of the park, the rugged **Maze** area, is a veritable hurly-burly of twisted canyons made for *über*-pioneers with four-wheel-drive vehicles only. (☎259-2652. Open daily 8am-4:30pm.) Once you've entered a section of the park, getting to a different section involves retracing your steps and reentering the park, a tedious trip that can last from several hours to a full day.

Monticello's **Multiagency Visitors Center,** 117 S. Main. St., sells area maps. (☎587-3235 or 800-574-4386. Open M-F 8am-5pm, Sa-Su 10am-5pm.) **Entrance fees:** $10 per car, $5 per hiker or cyclist. Write to **Canyonlands National Park,** 2282 S. West Resource Blvd., Moab 84532 (☎259-7164). **Moab** makes an excellent base town for exploring the park (see p. 716). *There are no gas, water, or food services in the park.* Just outside the boundary in the Needles district, however, the **Needles Outpost** houses a limited and expensive grocery store and gas pump (☎979-4007; open daily 8:30am-6pm). Hauling in groceries, water, and first-aid supplies from Moab or Monticello makes the most sense for travelers on a budget. **Area code:** 435.

CAMPGROUNDS AND HIKING. Before **backcountry camping** or **hiking,** outdoors-types must register at the proper visitors center for one of a limited number of permits. ($10 for backpack and overnight permit. Backcountry voyages not recommended in summer.) Four-wheel drivers should also register at the visitors center ($25 permit). Each region has its own official **campground.** In the Needles district, **Squaw Flat's** 26 sites occupy a sandy plain surrounded by giant sandstone towers, 40 mi. west of U.S. 191 on Rte. 211. In June, insects swarm. Fuel is not abundant and water is not available Oct.-Mar. (sites $8; Oct.-Mar. free). **Willow Flat Campground,** in the Island in the Sky district, sits high atop the mesa on Rte. 313, 41 mi. west off U.S. 191 (12 sites $5 in summer, free in off-season; pit toilets). You must bring your own water. Willow Flat and Squaw Flat both provide picnic tables and grills. The backcountry campground at the **Maze Overlook** offers no amenities. All campgrounds operate on a first come, first served basis.

Each visitors center has a brochure of possible hikes and advice on length and difficulty. With summer temperatures regularly climbing over 100°F, at least 1 gallon of water per person per day is a must. Hiking options from the Needles area are probably the best developed. Island in the Sky offers spectacular views; a short trail makes a quick diversion. In the Maze district, a 6hr., 6 mi. guided hike into Horseshoe Canyon leaves the Horseshoe Canyon Trailhead at 9am on Sa and Su. If hiking in desert heat doesn't appeal to you, you can rent Jeeps or mountain bikes in Moab.

For some great overlooks at elevations above 8000 ft., the **Monticello District** of the **Manti-La Sal National Forest,** south of Needles, delivers. The campsites in Canyonlands may be sweltering, but the air is almost always cooler in the forest here. This section of the forest has two campgrounds on **Blue Mountain: Buckboard,** 6½ mi. west of U.S. 191 (16 sites, 10 with full hook-up), and **Dalton Springs,** 5 mi. west of U.S. 191 (18 sites, 16 with full hook-up). Both campgrounds operate from late May to Sept. and charge $8.50 per site. From Moab, head south on U.S. 191 to Monticello and then west on Rte. 1 S. More info on the Monticello District awaits at the **Multi-Agency Visitors Center** (see **Practical Information,** above).

> **ABBEY'S ROAD** For many, the essays and novels of Edward Abbey most eloquently capture the harsh beauty of the American West. Born in Pennsylvania, he fell in love with the region upon his first visit and devoted the rest of his life to fiercely defending it from the United States' westward march of "progress." He spent three seasons as a park ranger at Arches National Park, delighting in the solitude of the desert. Abbey penned a celebrated series of essays on life in the desert based on his years spent wandering around Moab and Canyonlands. He captured their enigmatic beauty in his passionate and often acerbic manner—Abbey's passages vividly evoke the unforgiving, sun-parched landscape he loved. *The Monkey Wrench Gang,* Abbey's novel about an amusingly radical foursome rebelling against the pillaging of the wilderness, became the inspiration for Earth First!, an activist environmental group. As Abbey once wrote, "For us the wilderness and human emptiness of this land is not a source of fear but the greatest of its attractions."

Farther away, **Dead Horse Point State Park** perches on the rim of the Colorado Gorge. (Visitors center open daily 8am-5pm. Entrance fee $5.) The park, south of Arches and 14 mi. south of U.S. 191, accessible from Rte. 313, offers camping, with water, hook-ups, and covered picnic tables (21 sites, half are available on a first come, first served basis; $11). Write the **Park Superintendent,** Dead Horse Point State Park, P.O. Box 609, Moab 84532 (☎259-2614 or 800-322-3770; open daily 6am-10pm).

CAPITOL REEF   ☎435

A geologist's fantasy and Capitol Reef National Park's feature attraction, the Waterpocket Fold bisects the park, presenting visitors with 65 million years of stratified natural history. This 100-mile furrow in the earth's crust, with its rocky scales and spines, winds through Capitol Reef like a giant medieval serpent. The sheer cliffs that border the Fold were originally called a "reef," not for their oceanic origins, but because they posed a barrier to travel.

⌗ PRACTICAL INFORMATION. The middle link in the Fab Five chain, east of Zion and Bryce Canyon and west of Arches and Canyonlands, Capitol Reef is unreachable by major bus lines. The closest Greyhound stop is in Green River. For a fee, **Wild Hare Expeditions** (see **Sights and Activities,** below) will provide a shuttle service between Richfield and the park. **Entrance** to the park is free except for the scenic drive that costs $4 per vehicle. The **visitors center,** on Rte. 24, supplies travelers with waterproof topographical maps ($8), regular maps ($4), free brochures on trails, and info on daily activities such as ranger-led jaunts. (☎425-3791. Open daily 8am-6pm; Sept.-May 8am-4:30pm.) The free park newspaper, *The Cliffline,* lists a schedule of park activities. *When hiking, keep in mind that summer temperatures average 95°F and beware of flash-floods after rain.* Contact the **Superintendent,** Capitol Reef National Park, HC 70 Box 15, Torrey 84775 (☎425-3791). **Post Office:** 222 E. Main St. (☎425-3488; open M-F 8am-1pm, Sa 7:30-11am). **ZIP code:** 84775. **Area code:** 435.

⌂⌂ ACCOMMODATIONS AND FOOD. The park's campgrounds provide sites on a first come, first served basis. The main campground, **Fruita,** 1¼ mi. south off Rte. 24, presides over 71 sites (1 reserved for the disabled), with drinking water and toilets ($10). Sites are nestled among orchards; visitors can eat the fruit. **Cedar Mesa Campground,** in the park's south end, and **Cathedral Valley,** in the north, have only five sites each; neither has water or a paved road—but hey, they're free. To get to Cedar Mesa, take Rte. 24 past the visitors center to Notom-Bullfrog Rd. and head about 25 mi. south. Cathedral Valley is accessible only by four-wheel-drive or on foot. Both of these sites and unmarked backcountry campsites require a free **backcountry permit,** easily obtained at the visitors center. Outside the park, off scenic Rte. 12 between Boulder and Capitol Reef, a stretch of **Dixie National Forest** shelters three lovely campgrounds. All perch at elevations over 8000 ft. and have drinking water and pit toilets. (Open May-Sept. First come, first served sites $7.) The **Oak Creek Campground** has eight sites, and the **Pleasant Creek Campground** has 18 sites. **Single Tree Campground** offers 26 sites and two family sites, one of which can be reserved ahead of time (☎800-283-2267). Visitors can ask the **Teasdale Ranger District Office** (☎425-3702) for more info.

Torrey, 11 mi. west of the visitors center on Rte. 24, has the nearest indoor lodging. The cheapest bed in town can be found at the friendly **Sandcreek Hostel,** 520 Hwy. 24. A single dorm room houses comfy beds, a TV/VCR, and a microwave. (☎425-3577. Dorms $10; linens $2; tent sites $10; RV hook-up $15-18; showers $3.) The **Trading Post,** 75 W. Main St., offers small cabins that sleep up to four people and share a common bath (☎425-3716; $30). The **Boulder View Inn,** 385 W. Main St., provides comfortable rooms with private baths (☎425-3800; from $30).

Capitol Reef Inn and Cafe, 360 W. Main St., features local rainbow trout (smoked or grilled) and a dining room that looks out on the russet hills. The grilled trout sandwich ($6.75) served on a bagel with cream cheese is not to be missed. (☎425-3271. Open Apr.-Oct. daily 7am-11pm.) Greasier offerings awaits at **Brink's Burgers,** 163 E. Main St. (☎425-3710. Open daily 11am-9pm.)

SIGHTS AND ACTIVITIES. The Reef's haunting landforms can be explored from the seat of your car on the 25 mi. scenic drive, a 1½hr. (round-trip) jaunt next to the cliffs along paved and improved dirt roads. Along Rte. 24, you can ponder the bathroom-sized **Fruita Schoolhouse** built by Mormon settlers, 1000-year-old **petroglyphs** etched on the stone walls, and **Panorama Point. Chimney Rock** and the **Castle** are two of the more striking and abstruse of sandstone formations along the route. For many of the park's most spectacular vistas visitors must temporarily abandon their air-conditioned comfort. **Wild Hare Expeditions,** 2600 E. Hwy. 24, in the Best Western Capitol Reef Resort, embarks on a variety of backpacking and hiking tours. (☎425-3999 or 888-304-4273. $40-50 per half-day, children $35; full-day $60-75/$50. Scenic drives and four-wheel-drive tours are also available.)

SOUTHWEST

For a change of scenery, the bucolic **orchards** which lie within the park in the Fruita region might suffice. Guests can eat as much fruit as they like while in the orchards, but cold, hard cash is necessary to take some home.

BRYCE CANYON ☎435

If Nature enjoys painting with a big brush in the Southwest, she discarded her usual course tools for finer instruments when creating **Bryce Canyon National Park;** the canyon brims with slender, fantastically-shaped rock spires called hoodoos. What it lacks in Grand Canyon-esque magnitude, Bryce makes up for in intricate beauty. Early in the morning or late in the evening the sun's rays bring the hoodoos to life, transforming them into color-changing stone chameleons. The first sight of the canyon can be breathtaking: as Ebenezer Bryze, a Mormon carpenter with a gift for understatement, put it, the canyon is "one hell of a place to lose a cow."

PRACTICAL INFORMATION. Approaching from the west, Bryce Canyon lies 1½hr. east of Cedar City; take Rte. 14 to U.S. 89. From the east, take I-70 to U.S. 89, turn east on Rte. 12 at Bryce Jct. (7 mi. south of Panguitch), and drive 14 mi. to the Rte. 63 junction; head south 4 mi. to the park entrance. There is no public transportation to Bryce Canyon. The park's **entrance fee** is $20 per car, $10 per pedestrian.

Visitors center: Just inside the park. (☎834-5322. Open Jun.-Aug. 8am-8pm; Apr.-May and Sept.-Oct. 8am-6pm; Nov.-Mar. 8am-4:30pm.) Or, write: Bryce Canyon National Park, P.O Box 170001, Bryce Canyon, UT 84717. **Shuttle Bus**: New this year, a three-line bus system has been implemented to cut down on traffic. The buses run during daylight hours and stop at a number of trailheads and points of interest. Contact the visitor center for details. **Post office:** in Bryce Lodge (☎834-5361; open M-F 8am-noon and 1-5pm, Sa 8am-noon). **ZIP code:** 84717. **Area code:** 435.

CAMPGROUNDS AND FOOD. **North** and **Sunset Campgrounds,** both within 3 mi. of the visitors center, offer toilets, picnic tables, potable water, and 210 sites on a first come, first served basis (sites $10). **Backcountry camping permits** are free from the ranger at the visitors center. Two campgrounds lie just west of Bryce on scenic Rte. 12, in Dixie National Forest. The **King Creek Campground,** 11 mi. from Bryce on a dirt road off Rte. 12 (look for signs to Tropic Reservoir), features lakeside sites surrounded by pine trees. Group sites are available with reservations. ($8. ☎800-280-2267.) At an elevation of 7400 ft., the **Red Canyon Campground** has 36 sites on a first come, first served basis amid the glory of the red rocks ($10). **Ruby's Inn** rents teepees starting at $22 (☎834-5301).

There are no indoor budget accommodations in the park itself, though groups might wind up making out well. Only a few min. from the park entrance, the **Bryce Canyon Resort,** at the junction of Rte. 12 and Rte. 63, offers pricey and conventional deluxe doubles. (☎834-5351. Pool and restaurant on site. $85, $39 in the winter.) Although expensive for single travelers, **Bryce Lodge** is a decent deal for a group. (☎834-5361. Open Apr.-Oct. Motel-style doubles $88; western-style cabins $98; $5 per each additional person.) **Canyonlands International Youth Hostel** hosts travelers 60 mi. south of Bryce in **Kanab** while the **Dixie Hostel** is 105 mi. away in **Hurricane** (see p. 724 for both). Forty mi. from Bryce on U.S. 89 at Mi. 22, the **Paria Canyon Adventure Ranch,** has great outdoor facilities, including horseback riding, a climbing wall, and shuttle service to trailheads in the Paria Canyon wilderness area, in addition to budget lodging and camping. (☎689-0398. Dorms $12; teepees $10; camping sites $5.)

The **grocery store** at Ruby's Inn, just outside the park entrance, has a wide selection of provisions for reasonable prices (open daily 7am-10pm). If you're stuck in the park without any food, the **general store** at Sunrise Point has basic fast food and showers in back. (☎834-5361, ext. 167. Open daily 8am-8pm; closed in winter. Showers $2 for 10min.)

🔘🏔 **SIGHTS AND OUTDOORS.** Bryce's 18 mi. **main road** winds past spectacular look-outs such as **Sunrise Point, Sunset Point, Inspiration Point,** and **Rainbow Point,** but a range of hiking trails makes it a crime not to leave your car. A few warnings: the air is thin; if you start to feel giddy or short of breath, take a rest. Also, very sturdy shoes or hiking boots are a must for hiking into the canyon. One oft-missed viewpoint is **Fairlyland Point,** at the north end of the park, 1 mi. off the main road, with some the best sights in the canyons. The **Rim Trail** parallels the Amphitheater and offers views over 100 mi. The section between Sunrise Point and Sunset Point is wheelchair accessible and is a good way to peer onto the sea of hoodoos. The 3 mi. loop of the **Navajo** and **Queen's Garden** trails leads into the canyon and includes some natural bridges. More challenging options include **Peek-A-Boo Loop,** winding in and out through hoodoos for 4 mi., and the **Trail to the Hat Shop,** an extremely steep 4 mi. descent. (And if climbing down was tough...) **Canyon Trail Rides** arranges guided horseback rides (☎679-8665. $27-40 per person.)

NEAR BRYCE

Utah's scenic **Hwy. 12,** running from the Red Canyons near Bryce to the layered domes of Capital Reef National Park, is a worthwhile drive. Twisting its way through rugged and varied landscapes, Hwy. 12 originates 7 mi. south of Panguitch at a junction with Rte. 89 and traverses 120 mi. until it reaches Rte. 24, 9 mi. east of Capital Reef. The road offers spectacular mountain-top views of a wide diversity of landscapes, as well as hiking and backcountry driving options. It is also the best way to see the newly-christened 1.2 million-acre Grand Staircase Escalante National Monument.

BOX-DEATH HOLLOW OUTSTANDING NATURAL AREA. Daring hikers flirt with death in the network of sandstone canyons that comprises the ominously named park, just north of **Escalante** along Hwy. 12 in Dixie National Forest. The full trail through the canyons, starting at the **Hell's Backbone** trailhead north of town, requires four to five days to complete (30 mi. one-way). For the first 11 mi., there's no water at all; then the trail requires hikers to swim across a series of deep pools. A free backcountry permit (required), directions, and weather reports await at the **Escalante Interagency Office,** 755 W. Main St., on Rte. 12 just west of town (☎826-

5499; open daily 7:30am-5:30pm; off-season M-F 8am-4:30pm). A shorter, almost as stunning day hike starts in the **Upper Escalante Canyon** and heads through some of the Death Hollow area. The **Calf Creek** campground, 15 mi. east of Escalante on Rte. 12, has a cascading waterfall, drinking water, and toilets (sites $8).

GRAND STAIRCASE ESCALANTE NATIONAL MONUMENT. Designated by President Bill Clinton in 1996, this region is the newest national monument. In terms of geologic age, though, the Grand Staircase is the granddad of the region—the "steps," a series of cliffs and plateaus, reveal hundreds of millions of years of sedimentary rock formation. The relatively few visitors come less for the staircase than for the hiking opportunities among tucked-away rock fields, extraordinary formations, and wildlife. The best hiking can be found in the Escalante Canyons, along **Hole-in-the-Rock Rd.**, which connects with Hwy. 12 just east of the town of Escalante. Most of these trails are overnighters and meander in Glen Canyon National Recreation Area—it is not unusual to stumble onto a natural bridge or petroglyph. The best way to enter the park from the south is by turning onto Cottonwood Canyon from U.S. 89 N. in Utah, between Mi. 17 and 18. From the north, use Hwy. 12. The roads are unpaved and bumpy, so be sure the weather is okay. The **Bureau of Land Management** has more information (☎ 826-5499).

ZION ☎ 435

Russet sandstone mountains loom over the puny cars and hikers that flock to **Zion National Park** in search of the promised land, or at least the land promised to be beautiful by enthusiastic travel guides. Some 13 million years ago, the ocean flowed over the cliffs and canyons of Zion. When the sea subsided, it left behind only the raging Virgin River, whose watery fingers sculpt the smooth white rock hills. In the northwest corner of the park, the walls of Kolob Terrace tower thousands of ft. above the river. Elsewhere, branching canyons and rock formations show off erosion's unique artistry. In the 1860s, Mormon settlers came to the area and enthusiastically proclaimed that they had found Zion, the promised land. Brigham Young disagreed, however, and declared that the place was awfully nice, but "not Zion." The name "not Zion" stuck for years until a new wave of entranced explorers dropped the "not," giving the park its present name.

◪ PRACTICAL INFORMATION. The main entrance to Zion is in **Springdale,** on Rte. 9, which borders the park to the south along the Virgin River. Approaching Zion from the west, take Rte. 9 from I-15 at Hurricane. In the east, pick up Rte. 9 from U.S. 89 at Mt. Carmel Jct. **Greyhound** is in St. George (☎ 673-2933; 43 mi. southwest of the park on I-15), departing from a McDonald's, 1235 S. Bluff St., at St. George Blvd. Buses run to Salt Lake City (6hr., 3 per day, $38); Los Angeles (9 hr., 5 per day, $57); Denver (8 hr., 3 per day, $89); and Las Vegas (2hr., 5 per day, $27). The main newly remodeled **Zion Canyon Visitors Center** has an introductory slide program and an interesting museum (☎ 772-3256; open daily 8am-7pm; off-season 8am-6pm). **Kolob Canyons Visitors Center** lies in the northwest corner of the park, off I-15 at Exit 40 and issues backcountry permits (☎ 586-9548; open daily 7am-7pm; off-season 9am-4pm). The park's **entrance fee** is $20 per car, $10 per pedestrian. **Emergency:** ☎ 772-3322. Zion's **post office** is located inside the Zion Canyon Lodge. **ZIP code:** 84767. **Area code:** 435.

▮ CAMPGROUNDS AND ACCOMMODATIONS. More than 300 sites are available on a first come, first served basis in the **South** and **Watchman Campgrounds,** both near the park's south entrance ($14; water, toilets, and sanitary disposal station). Campgrounds fill quickly in summer. Six free but primitive sites at **Lava Point** are accessible from a hiking trail, or from the gravel road which turns off Rte. 9 in Virgin (toilets but no water; open June-Nov.). A permit ($5) from the visitors center is required for **backcountry camping.** Camping along the rim is *not* allowed, but a free map from the visitors center shows other spots you may (and may not) pitch a tent.

Mukuntuweep Campground, ¼ mi. outside the east entrance, doesn't have just altitude on its side. Not only is it 1000 ft. higher and about 10°F cooler than the sites inside the park, but it also offers a laundromat, showers, restaurant, and gas station. (☎648-2154. Office open 24hr. 70 tent sites $15, 30 full hook-ups $20, cabins and teepees $25.) **Zion Canyon Campground,** 479 Zion Park Blvd., in Springdale just south of the park, soothes the weary, hungry, and filthy with a convenience store, restaurant, grocery store, showers, and coin-op laundry. (☎772-3237. Sites for 2 $16, full hook-up $20; $3.50 per additional adult, $2 per additional child under 15. Cabins for $40. Office open daily 8am-9pm. Store open daily 8am-9pm; off-season 8am-5pm.)

The **Zion Canyon Lodge,** along the park's main road, offers premium rooms at premium prices, along with a restaurant. (☎303-297-2757 for reservations. Singles and doubles $91; cabin singles and doubles $101; $7 per additional person.) Cheap motels are available in nearly any of the towns near Zion, including **Springdale** and **Rockville,** 2-5 mi. south of the park; **Mt. Carmel Junction,** 20 mi. east; **Kanab,** 40 mi. east; or **Cedar City,** 70 mi. north of the park on Rte. 15.

The closest hostel is the ⊠**Dixie Hostel (HI-AYH),** 73 S. Main St., 20 mi. west in Hurricane. Fresh-smelling, pink-hued, and without a speck of dust, the hostel is a comfortable stay and only 2hr. from Las Vegas. (☎635-8202 or 635-9000. Linen, laundry, kitchen, continental breakfast, and 20% discount at hot springs nearby. Dorm beds $15; private doubles $35.) In the other direction, the **Canyonlands International Youth Hostel,** 143 E. 100 S., Kanab, lies 20 mi. south. Though the place is a bit too primitive and earthy for some, the hostel's location, 1hr. north of the Grand Canyon's North Rim and roughly equidistant from Zion, Bryce, and Lake Powell, makes it a good base for exploring northern Arizona and southern Utah. (☎644-5554. Linen, laundry, TV, kitchen, continental breakfast, and Internet. Dorms $10.) Fifty mi. away, the **Paria Canyon Adventure Ranch,** also has budget accommodations (see p. 722).

🔲 **SIGHTS AND ACTIVITIES.** Zion seems to have been made for hiking; unlike in the forboding canyons that surround it, most of the trails won't have you praying for a stray mule to show up. However, a number of trails spiral around cliffs with narrow trails and long drop-offs. Hiking boots are recommended on trails like Angel's Landing of Hidden Canyons. The trails are serviced by a prompt shuttle bus system that delivers bright-eyed hikers to and from trailheads (runs 6:30am-11:15pm). Shuttle maps are available at the visitors center.

The **Riverside Walk,** paved and wheelchair accessible with assistance, begins at the Temple of Sinawava and stretches 1 mi. from the north end of Zion Canyon Dr., Running alongside the Virgin River and some beautiful wildflower displays, Riverside is Zion's most popular and easiest trail. The **Emerald Pools trail,** which starts opposite the Zion Lodge, is 1.2 mi. round-trip for the lower section which leads to a waterfall. The trail has wheelchair access along its lower loop, but the middle and upper loops are steep and narrow. Swimming is not allowed in any of the pools. Another easier trail leads to **Weeping Rock** (½ mi. round-trip), a dripping spring surrounded by hanging gardens, at the Weeping Rock parking lot toward the north of the park. The challenging **Angel's Landing** (5 mi. round-trip) trail begins in the Grotto picnic area, and rises 1488 ft. above the canyon; the last terrifying ½ mi. climbs a narrow ridge with guide chains blasted into the rock. A shorter, but equally harrowing trail is **Hidden Canyon** (2 mi. round-trip) which rewards hikers with impressive valley views. The difficult trail to **Observation Point** (8 mi. round-trip) leads through **Echo Canyon,** a spectacular kaleidoscope of sandstone, where steep switchbacks explore the unusually gouged canyon. Overnight hikers can spend days on the 27 mi. **West Rim Trail.** One of the best ways to take in Zion's splendor is to ride the shuttle bus loop. Called the **Zion Canyon Scenic Loop,** this 90min. narrated ride gives great views of the rocks from below. Another motorized way to take in the scenery is the 10 mi. **Zion-Mt. Carmel Highway,** which connects the east and south entrances. Spiralling around the Canyon, the highway gives excellent views of the valley, as well as fun trip through an 80 yr.-old mountain tunnel.

When visiting the **Kolob Canyons,** check out **Zion Canyon.** The 7 mi. dead-end road on the canyon floor rambles past the giant **Sentinel, Mountain of the Sun,** and the overwhelming symbol of Zion, the **Great White Throne.** A shuttle from the Lodge runs this route every hour on the hour. (During summer daily 9am-5pm. $3.) Horseback tours by **Canyon Trail Rides** also leave from the Lodge (☎772-3810; $15-40).

Despite being overshadowed by the boastful Moab, the Zion valley has a loyal **mountain biking** following and trails to compete with the big-boy to the north. **Gooseberry Mesa,** about 15 mi. from Springdale, has some great single tracks, as well as trails for novice riders. **Bike Zion,** 1458 Zion Park Blvd., can hook you up with some wheels and trail advice. (☎772-3929. Open daily 8am-8pm. $7-15 per hr., $17-35 per half-day, $23-45 per day.)

NEAR ZION: CEDAR BREAKS

Heading east on Rte. 14 from Cedar City, the flowered slopes of the **Cedar Breaks National Monument** descend 2000 ft. into chiseled depths. The rim of this giant amphitheater stands a lofty 10,350 ft. (entrance $4 per car, $2 per pedestrian). A 30-site campground (sites $9) and the visitors center (☎586-0787; open in summer daily 8am-6pm, closed Oct. to Apr.) await at Point Supreme. For more info, contact the Superintendent, Cedar Breaks National Monument, 82 N. 100 E., Cedar City 84720 (☎586-9451).

There are many hikes in the neighboring Dixie National Forest. The trail to **Cascade Falls** (1 mi. round-trip) is located on a dirt road just off Rte. 14 at Mi. 25 and gives excellent views of the valley and a babbling fall. **Navajo Lake,** just 2 mi. down the dirt road, is a popular fishing venue.

NATURAL BRIDGES, ROUTE 95, AND HOVENWEEP

NATURAL BRIDGES NATIONAL MONUMENT. The Paiutes who inhabited this region nearly 3000 years ago called it *Ma-Vah-Talk-Tump*, or "under the horse's belly." Although Utah's first national monument now carries the more prosaic moniker of "Natural Bridges," the three rock formations are no less impressive. To appreciate the size of the monuments fully—the highest is more than 200 feet—leave the overlooks and hike down to the bridges. Once you do, it's easy to understand why the Hopi named the largest one "Sipapu," or "place of emergence"—they believed it to be the entry way through which their ancestors came into this world. The park's paved **Bridge View Drive** is about 9 mi. and passes the overlooks and trailheads to each of the three major bridges. It's also possible to hike various loop trails connecting the bridges—trails range from 5.6 to 8.6 mi.

The **visitors center,** several mi. past the monument's entrance, offers a slide show and exhibits. (☎692-1234. Open daily Mar.-Oct. 8am-6pm; Nov.-Feb. 9:30am-5pm. Park entrance $6 per vehicle, $3 per hiker or bicyclist, good for 7 days; National Parks Passes accepted.) Sleep under the stars at the **campground** near the visitors center. Thirteen shaded sites set amid pinyon pines accommodate up to nine people each and include grills and picnic tables. (Campground usually fills up by 2pm. First come, first served. Sites $10.) **Water** is available at the visitors center. For more info, write the Superintendent, Natural Bridges, HC 60 Box 1, Lake Powell 84533. If the park campground is full, primitive overflow camping is available off a gravel road originating at the intersection of Rte. 95 and Rte. 261, 6 mi. from the visitors center. The free sites are flat and shaded but have no facilities.

To reach Natural Bridges from northern Utah, follow U.S. 191 S. from Moab to its junction with **Rte. 95.** From Colorado, U.S. 66 heads west to U.S. 191 S (junction in Monticello). From the south, Rte. 261 from Mexican Hat climbs a mesa in a heart-wrenching and axle-grinding series of 5mph gravel switchbacks, providing a spectacular view of Monument Valley across the Arizona border.

ROUTE 95. A true Rocky Mountain high, Rte. 95 connects Natural Bridges to I-191, 4 mi. south of Blanding. Showcasing the variety of landscape that the Four Corners area has to offer, Rte. 95 is a wonder unto itself, as it parallels the ascent of the

Rockies mountains along a 29 mi. canyon-cradled pedestal. The route gives stellar views of the receding arid landscape as it morphs to the jagged Rockies. It is more spectacular heading east, especially during sunset, as the mountains grow on the horizon. Rte. 95 is a tranquil road that receives little traffic and has no visible signs of civilization; bring water, provisions, and a camera.

HOVENWEEP NATIONAL MONUMENT. Hovenweep, from the Ute meaning "deserted valley," was aptly named—it's still in one of the emptiest regions in the US. The few who make the trip to the area, in the Utah section of the four corners, are treated to national park solitude (not always an oxymoron) and six groups of Pueblo ruins dating back more than 1000 years, a few hundred years older than the Navajo Monument ruins. The best preserved and most impressive ruins, **Square Tower Ruins,** lie footsteps away from the visitors center (see below). The **Square Tower Loop Trail** (2 mi. round-trip) loops around a small canyon, accessing **Hovenweep Castle** and the **Twin Towers.** A shorter trail, the ½ mi. **Tower Point Loop,** accesses the ruins of a tower perched on a canyon. The outlying ruins—**Cujon Ruins** and **Huckberry Canyon** in Utah and **Cutthroat Castle** and **Goodman Point Ruins** in Colorado—are isolated and difficult to reach.

Desolate but beautiful roads usher you to Hovenweep. In Utah or Arizona, follow U.S. 191 to its junction with Rte. 262 E (14 mi. south of Blanding, 11 mi. north of Bluff). After about 30 mi., watch for signs to the monument. From Cortez, CO, go south on U.S. 666/U.S. 160 to County Rd. G (the airport road); follow the Hovenweep signs for 45 mi. It's wise to check road conditions at the **visitors center,** accessible from both the Utah and Colorado sides. (☎970-562-4282. Open daily 8am-6pm, offseason 8am-5pm, except when the ranger is out on patrol. $3 per person, $6 per car, National Parks Passes accepted.) There is no gasoline, telephone, or food at the monument. The Hovenweep **campground** has recently reopened and is located close to the visitors center. Water and toilets are available, though campers must carry out all of their trash. ($10.) For more info, contact the Superintendent, Hovenweep National Monument, McElmo Rte., Cortez, CO 81321 (☎970-562-4282).

⚃ NEARBY CIVILIZATION. Three small towns provide lodging and services for travelers to the monuments and the valley. In the agricultural town of **Blanding** (45 mi. from Hovenweep, 60mi. from Natural Bridges), the **Prospector Motor Lodge,** 591 U.S. 191 S., has spacious rooms, some with kitchenettes. (☎678-3231. Singles $41-50; doubles $45-55; off-season $27/$39; prices somewhat negotiable.) The cheaper **Blanding Sunset Inn,** 88 W. Center St., has basic, phoneless rooms. (☎678-3323. Singles $25; doubles $35.) The **Old Tymer,** 733 S. Main St., is great for down-home food all the tyme; breakfast $2-6, sandwiches $4-6. (☎678-2122. Open M-Sa 6:30am-9pm, Su 7am-8pm.)

Nestled among the sandstone canyons, the tiny town of **Bluff** (40 mi. from Hovenweep, 65 mi. from Natural Bridges) welcomes the budget traveler. The gigantic, austere sandstone sculptures of the **Valley of the Gods,** which provided the backdrop for some of the road scenes in *Thelma and Louise,* are worth the detour. A tough but incredible 17 mi. drive departs from U.S. 163, 15 mi. south of Bluff on the right side of the road, and runs right through the valley. Inexpensive and comfortable lodges and motels line U.S. 191, including The **Recapture Lodge.** (☎672-2281. Singles $40; doubles $46.) Tasty Navajo sheepherder sandwiches (roast beef on Indian fry bread, $5.25) hit the tables at the **Turquoise Restaurant,** opposite the lodge on U.S. 191 S. (☎672-2279. Open M 7am-9:30pm, Tu-Su 7:30am-9:30pm.)

Mexican Hat sits along the San Juan River on the border of the Navajo nation. The town is 20 mi. south of Bluff on U.S. 163 and 20 mi. north of Arizona. Rest your head at the newly renovated **Canyonlands Motel,** on U.S. 163. (☎683-2230. Singles $30; doubles $45.) The **restaurant** at Burch's Indian Trading Co., on U.S. 163, serves Mexican and Southwestern food on picnic tables, including tasty $6 mutton stew and $4.75 burgers. (☎683-2221. Open daily 12-4pm, 6-9pm.)

ARIZONA

Populated primarily by Native Americans until the end of the 19th century, Arizona has been hit in the past hundred years by waves of settlers—from the speculators and miners of the late 1800s, to the soldiers who trained here during World War II and returned after the war, to the more recent immigrants from Mexico. Traces of lost Native American civilization remain at Canyon de Chelly, Navajo National Monument, and Wupatki and Walnut Canyons, while deserted ghost towns scattered throughout the state illustrate the death of the mining lifestyle—but both civilizations persevere. The descendents of area tribes now occupy reservations on one-half of the state's land, making up one-seventh of the US' Native American population, while urban Phoenix sprawls wider and wider. Arizona is a state always in flux, yet perhaps the majesty of the land is the one constant. No man-made structures can overshadow Arizona's natural masterpieces—the Grand Canyon, Monument Valley, and the gorgeous landscapes viewed from the state's highways.

⚡ PRACTICAL INFORMATION

Capital: Phoenix.
Visitor Info: Arizona Tourism, 2703 N. 3rd St. Suite 4015, Phoenix 85004 (☎602-230-7733 or 888-520-3434; www.arizonaguide.com). Open M-F 8am-5pm. **Arizona State Parks,** 1300 W. Washington St., Phoenix 85007 (☎602-542-4174 or 800-285-3703). Open M-F 8am-5pm.
Postal Abbreviation: AZ. **Sales Tax:** variable 5%.
Time Zone: Mountain Standard Time. *With the exception of the Navajo reservation, Arizona does not observe Daylight Saving Time.*

GRAND CANYON

Despite the prevalence of its image on everything from postcards to screensavers, nothing can prepare you for the first sight of the Grand Canyon. After the initial humbling shock of emerging on the canyon's rim, stay awhile and let its sheer enormity and majesty sink in; stories of grungy hermits descending into the canyon and emerging weeks or months later demonstrate the inexplicable draw of this rock sensation. One of the seven natural wonders of the world (277 mi. long, 10 mi. wide, and over 1 mi. deep), the canyon descends to the Colorado River past looming walls of multi-colored limestone, sandstone, and shale. Hike down into the gorge to experience the immensity and beauty of this natural phenomenon, or just watch the colors and shadows change from one of the many rim viewpoints.

Grand Canyon National Park (www.thecanyon.com/nps) is divided into three areas: the **South Rim,** which includes Grand Canyon Village; the **North Rim;** and the canyon gorge itself. The Canyon itself extends from Lake Mead, NV, to Lee's Ferry, AZ. West of the park's boundaries, the Canyon cuts through two Native American Reservations: the Hualapai and Havasupai. Within the park, the slightly lower, more accessible South Rim draws ten times as many visitors as the higher, more heavily forested North Rim. The South Rim is open all year, while the North Rim welcomes travelers only from mid-May to mid-Oct. (mid-Oct. to early Dec. for day use), depending on the weather. The 13 mi. trail that traverses the canyon floor furnishes sturdy hikers with a minimum two-day adventure, while the 214 mi. perimeter road is a good 5hr. drive for those who would rather explore from above. If you observe all safety precautions, use common sense, and drink lots of water, you are sure to have an unforgettable experience.

SOUTHWEST

SOUTH RIM   ☎ 520

During the summer, everything on two legs or four wheels converges on this side of the Grand Canyon. If you plan to visit during the mobfest, make reservations for lodging, campsites, or mules well in advance—and prepare to battle the crowds. That said, it's much better than Disney World. A friendly Park Service staff, well-run facilities, and beautiful scenery help ease crowd anxiety. Fewer tourists brave the canyon's winter weather; many hotels and facilities close during the off-season.

⌐ GETTING THERE AND GETTING AROUND

There are two park entrances: the main **south entrance** is about 6 mi. from the visitor center while the eastern **Desert View** entrance is 27 mi. away. Both are accessed from Rte. 64 (coming north for the south entrance, west for Desert View). From Las Vegas, the fastest route to the South Rim is U.S. 93 S to I-40 E, and then Rte. 64 N. From Flagstaff, head north on U.S. 180 to Rte. 64.

Buses: Nava-Hopi Bus Lines (☎ 877-467-3329) leaves the Flagstaff Amtrak station for the Grand Canyon daily at 7:45am and 2:30pm, returning from Maswik Lodge at 10am and 4:30pm (about 2hr.). $20, under 15 $13; round-trip $34/$20, including entrance fee. Times vary by season, so call ahead.

Public Transit: Free shuttle buses ride the West Rim Loop (daily 1 hr. before sunrise-1 hr. after sunset) and the Village Loop (daily 1 hr. before sunrise-10:30pm) every 10-30min. A free **hiker's shuttle** runs every 30min. between Grand Canyon Village and the South Kaibab Trailhead, on the East Rim near Yaki Point.

Taxis: Call ☎ 638-2822. Open 24hr.

Auto Repairs: Grand Canyon Garage (☎ 638-2631), east of the visitors center on the main road, near Maswik Lodge. Open daily 8am–5pm. 24hr. emergency service.

◄ ■ ？ ORIENTATION AND PRACTICAL INFORMATION

Posted maps and signs in the park make orienting easy. Lodges and services concentrate in **Grand Canyon Village,** at the end of Park Entrance Rd. The east half of the Village contains the visitors center and the general store, while most of the lodges and the challenging **Bright Angel Trail** lies in the west section. The shorter but more difficult **South Kaibab Trail** is off East Rim Dr., east of the village. Free shuttle buses to eight rim overlooks run along **West Rim Dr.** (closed to private vehicles during the summer). Avoid walking on the drive; the rim trails are safer and more scenic.

The **entrance pass** is $20 per car and $10 for travelers using other modes of transportation—even bus passengers must pay (National Parks Pass, Golden Age, and Golden Access passports accepted). The pass lasts for one week. For most services in the Park, call the **main switchboard** number at ☎ 638-2631.

Visitor Info: The **visitors center** (☎ 638-7888) is 6 mi. north of the south entrance station. Open daily 8am-7pm; off-season 8am-5pm. Hikers should get the *Backcountry Trip Planner;* the regular old *Trip Planner* is for regular old mortals (both free). Free and informative, *The Guide* is also available here. Write **Trip Planner,** Grand Canyon National Park, P.O. Box 129, Grand Canyon, 86023 or call ☎ 638-2631. The **transportation info desks** in **Bright Angel Lodge** and **Maswik Lodge** (☎ 638-2631 for both) handle reservations for mule rides, bus tours, plane tours, Phantom Ranch, taxis, and more. Both open daily 6am-8pm.

Equipment Rental: General Store (☎ 638-2262), in Grand Canyon Village near Yavapai Lodge and the visitors center. Comfy hiking boots, socks included ($8 first day, $5 per additional day); sleeping bags ($7-9/$5); tents ($15-18/$9); and other camping gear. Hefty deposits required on all items. Open daily 8am-8pm.

Luggage Storage: In Bright Angel Lodge. Open 6:30am-9pm. $1 per day.

Weather and Road Conditions: ☎ 638-7888.

Medical Services: Grand Canyon Clinic (☎ 638-2551), several mi. south of the visitors center on Center Rd. Open M-F 8am-8pm, Sa 9am-1pm. 24hr. emergency aid.

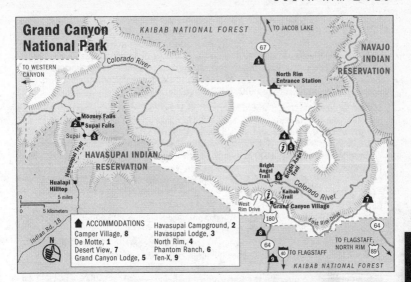

Grand Canyon National Park map with legend:

ACCOMMODATIONS
Camper Village, **8**
De Motte, **1**
Desert View, **7**
Grand Canyon Lodge, **5**
Havasupai Campground, **2**
Havasupai Lodge, **3**
North Rim, **4**
Phantom Ranch, **6**
Ten-X, **9**

Post Office: (☎638-2512), across the street from the visitors center, next door to the General Store. Open M-F 9am-4:30pm, Sa 11am-3pm. **ZIP code:** 86023. **Area code:** 520.

ACCOMMODATIONS

Compared to the 6 million years it took the Colorado River to carve the Grand Canyon, the year it will take you to get indoor lodging near the South Rim is nothing. Summer rooms should be reserved *11 months in advance.* That said, there are cancellations every day; if you arrive unprepared, check for vacancies, or call the Grand Canyon operator at ☎638-2631 and ask to be connected with the proper lodge. Reservations for **Bright Angel Lodge, Maswik Lodge, Trailer Village,** and **Phantom Ranch** can be made through **Grand Canyon National Park Lodges,** P.O. Box 699, Grand Canyon 86023 (☎303-297-2757 or 530-638-2631). Most accommodations on the South Rim are very pricey.

Bright Angel Lodge (☎638-2631), Grand Canyon Village. The cheapest indoor lodging on the rim. Very convenient to Bright Angel Trail and shuttle buses. "Rustic" lodge singles and doubles with shared bath $44-50; with private bath $60. "Historic" cabins available for 1 or 2 people $73; $7 per additional person in rooms and cabins.

Maswik Lodge (☎638-2631), Grand Canyon Village. Small, clean cabins (singles or doubles) with showers but no heat $63; motel rooms $73-118; $7-9 per additional person.

Phantom Ranch (☎638-2631), on the canyon floor, a day's hike down the Kaibab Trail. Dorm beds $23; rarely available cabins for 1 or 2 people $68; $11 per additional person. Don't show up without reservations. Reservations taken up to 23 months in advance. Meals must be reserved in advance. Breakfast $15; box lunch $8; stew dinner $18, steak dinner $29. If you're dying to sleep on the canyon floor but don't have a reservation, show up at the Bright Angel transportation desk at 6am, and they may be able to arrange something.

CAMPGROUNDS

The campsites listed here usually fill up early in the day. In the **Kaibab National Forest,** along the south border of the park, you can pull off a dirt road and camp for free. No camping is allowed within ¼ mi. of U.S. 64. Sleeping in cars is *not* permitted within the park, but it is allowed in the Kaibab Forest. For more info, contact the **Tusayan Ranger District,** Kaibab National Forest, P.O. Box 3088, Grand Canyon 86023 (☎638-2443). Overnight hiking or camping within the park outside of designated campgrounds requires a **backcountry use permit** ($20 application fee plus $4 per person per night), available at the **backcountry office,** ¼ mi. south of the visitors center (☎ 638-7875; open daily 8am-noon and 1-5pm). Permit requests are accepted by mail, fax, or in person up to four months in advance. Responses take a minimum of three weeks, unless done in person. Guests with reservations at Phantom Ranch (see above) do not need permits. Reservations for some campgrounds can be made through **BIOSPHERICS** (☎ 800-365-2267).

Mather Campground (call BIOSPHERICS, ☎ 800-365-2267), Grand Canyon Village, 1 mi. south of the visitors center. 320 shady, relatively isolated sites with no hook-ups. Check at the office, even if the sign says the campground is full. 7-day maximum stay. For Mar.-Nov., reserve up to 3 months in advance; Dec.-Feb. sites go on a first come, first served basis. Sept.-May $12; June-Aug. $15.

Ten-X Campground (☎ 638-2443), in the Kaibab National Forest, 10 mi. south of Grand Canyon Village off Rte. 64. Open May-Sept. Shady sites surrounded by pine trees. Toilets, water, no hook-ups, no showers. First come, first served sites $10.

Desert View Campground (☎ 638-7888), 26 mi. east of Grand Canyon Village. Open mid-May to Oct. 50 sites with phone and rest room access, but no hook-ups. Sites $10. No reservations; usually full by early afternoon.

Camper Village (☎ 638-2887), 7 mi. south of the visitors center in Tusayan. RV and tent sites $15-23 for 2 people; $2 per additional adult. First come, first served tent sites; reservations required for RVs.

Indian Gardens, 4½ mi. from the Bright Angel trailhead and 3100 ft. below the rim. 15 free sites, toilets, and water. Reservations and backcountry permit required.

Trailer Village (☎ 638-2631), next to Mather Campground. Office open daily 8am-noon and 1-5pm. Designed with the RV in mind. Showers and laundry nearby. 84 sites for 2 with hook-up $20; $1.75 per additional person. Reserve 6-9 months in advance.

Havasupai Campground, see **Near South Rim,** below.

🍴 FOOD

Fast food has yet to sink its greasy talons into the South Rim (the closest McDonald's is 7 mi. south in Tusayan), but you *can* find meals at fast-food prices. **General Store,** near the visitors center, has a deli counter and a wide selection of groceries, as well as a camping supplies department. (☎ 638-2262. Open daily 8am-8pm; deli open 8am-7pm. Sandwiches $2-4.) The well-stocked **Canyon Cafe,** across from the General Store, offers a wider variety of food than the nearby deli (open daily 6am-10pm; hamburgers $3, pizza $3-4, dinners $5-7). **Maswik Cafeteria,** in Maswik Lodge, serves a variety of inexpensive grill-made options in a wood-paneled cafeteria atmosphere (open daily 6am-10pm; hot entrees $5-7, sandwiches $2-4). **Bright Angel Dining Room,** in Bright Angel Lodge, serves hot sandwiches for $6-8. (☎ 638-2631. Open daily 6:30am-10pm.) The **soda fountain** at Bright Angel Lodge chills 16 flavors of ice cream for hot folks (open daily 8am-8pm; 1 scoop $2).

🏔 OUTDOORS

Hikes into and around the Grand Canyon can be broken down into two categories: day hikes and overnight hikes. Confusing an overnight hike for a day hike can lead to disaster and a permanent residency in the canyon. Hiking to the Colorado River is reserved for overnight trips; plan to make it at least a two-day excursion. All overnight trips require permits obtained through the Backcountry Office. In determining what is an appropriate day hike, remember that the Canyon does not have any loop hikes. Be prepared to retrace every single footstep uphill on the way back. For longer day-hikes, it is strongly recommended to begin before 7am. Consult a ranger before heading out. Park Service rangers also present a variety of free, informative **talks** and **guided hikes;** times and details are listed in *The Guide.*

Beyond hiking, there are others ways to conquer the canyon. **Mule trips** from the South Rim are expensive and booked up to one year in advance, although cancella-

From your first glimpse of the canyon, you may feel a compelling desire to see it from the inside, an enterprise that is harder than it looks. Even the young at heart and body should remember that an easy downhill hike can become a nightmarish 50° incline on the return journey. Also keep in mind that the lower you go, the hotter it gets; when it's 85°F on the rim, it's around 100°F at Indian Gardens, and around 110°F at Phantom Ranch. Heat exhaustion, the greatest threat to any hiker, is marked by a monstrous headache and red, sweatless skin. *For a day hike, you must take at least a gallon of water per person; drink at least a liter per hour hiking upwards under the hot sun.* Hiking boots or sneakers with excellent tread are also necessary—the trails are steep, and every year several careless hikers take what locals morbidly call "the 12 second tour." A list of hiking safety tips can be found in *The Guide*. It is advisable to speak with a ranger or drop by the visitors center before embarking on a hike: they may have important information about the trail. Parents should think twice about bringing children more than 1 mi. down any trail—kids remember well and may exact revenge when they get older.

tions do occur (call ☎303-297-2757 for reservations; day trip $106, overnight $280). Mule trips from the North Rim are cheaper and more readily available (☎638-9875). **Whitewater rafting** trips through the canyon last from three days to two weeks; advance reservations are required. Call the transport info desk for a list of trips.

The **Rim, Bright Angel, South Kaibab,** and **River** trails are the only South Rim trails regularly maintained and patrolled by the park service. There are a number of other trails and paths into and around the Canyon, such as **South Bass, Grandview,** and **Tonto.** These trails are only for the experienced hiker and may contain steep chutes and technical terrain. Consult a Park Ranger and *The Guide* before heading out.

Rim Trail. With only a mild elevation change (about 200 ft.) and the constant security of the nearby shuttle, the Rim Trail is excellent for hikers seeking a tame way to see the Canyon. The trail follows the shuttle bus routes along Hermit Rd. past the Visitors Center toward Yavapai Point. From start to finish, the Rim Trail covers almost 10 mi. of paved and unpaved path, with 8 view points along Hermit Rd. and 3 east of it. Hopi Point is a great place to watch the sun set with its panoramic canyon views (*The Guide* and the visitors center list times for sunsets and sunrises). Bring plenty of water before you head out, as little is available along the trail.

Bright Angel Trail. Bright Angel is outfitted for the average hiker. Depending on distance, the trail can be either a day or overnight hike. Rest houses are strategically stationed 1½ mi. and 3 mi. from the rim, each with water available between May and Sept. Indian Gardens, 4½ mi. down, offers tired hikers restrooms, picnic tables, and blessed shade. From the rim to the river, the trail drops 4420 ft. Although spread over 7.7 mi, this drop is far too big for a day-hike. Overnighters can camp (with permit) at Indian Gardens or the Bright Angel Campground, while day-hikers are advised to go no further than Plateau Pt. (12.2 mi round trip) or Indian Gardens (9.2 mi).

South Kaibab Trail. Those seeking a more challenging hike down might consider the S. Kaibab Trail. Beginning at Yaki Pt., Kaibab is trickier, steeper, and lacks shade or water, but it rewards the intrepid with a better view of the canyon. Day hikes to Cedar Ridge (3 mi.) and Skeleton Pt. (6 mi.) are reasonable for experienced, well-conditioned hikers, due to the trail's steep grade. For overnight hikes, Kaibab meets up with Bright Angel at the Colorado River. It is 1.7 mi. shorter than the Bright Angel to this point. Guests staying at the Phantom Ranch use either the Bright Angel or S. Kaibab to reach the ranch. Many hikers believe that the best route is the South Kaibab Trail (4-5hr., depending on conditions) and back up the Bright Angel (7-8hr.) the following day.

River Trail. Connecting the Bright Angel to the S. Kaibab, the River Trail follows the Colorado and offers close-up views of the creator of the Canyon. Two bridges cross the river along the trail, and there is only a little elevation change. This trail (1.7 mi) is only available to overnight hikers due to its distance from the rim.

SOUTHWEST

NORTH RIM   ☎ 520

If you're coming from Utah or Nevada, or want to avoid the crowds at the South Rim, the park's North Rim is a bit wilder, a bit cooler, and much more serene—all with a view *almost* as groovy as that from the South Rim. Unfortunately, because the North Rim is less frequented, it's hard to reach by public transportation, and by car, it's a long drive. From October 15 until December 1, the North Rim is open for day use only; from December 1 until May 15, it is closed entirely.

✴☌ ORIENTATION AND PRACTICAL INFORMATION

To reach the North Rim from the South Rim, take Rte. 64 E to U.S. 89 N, which runs into Alt. 89; from Alt. 89, follow Rte. 67 S to the edge. Altogether, the beautiful drive is over 200 mi. From Utah, take Alt. 89 S from Fredonia. From Page, take U.S. 89 S to Alt. 89 to Rte. 67 S. Snow closes Rte. 67 from mid-Oct. through mid-May; park visitor facilities (including the lodge) close for the winter. The **entrance fee** covers both rims for 7 days ($20 per car; $10 per person on foot, bike, bus, or pilgrimage).

Public Transit: Transcanyon, P.O. Box 348, Grand Canyon 86023 (☎638-2820). Buses to South Rim depart 7am (4½hr.); return buses depart 1:30pm. $60, round-trip $100. Reservations required. A **hikers' shuttle** runs from the Lodge to the North Kaibab trailhead at 5:30am and 7:45am. Tickets ($5) must be purchased in advance at the Lodge. Both run late May to Oct.

Visitor Info: North Rim Visitors Center (☎638-7864), in the lobby of Grand Canyon Lodge (see below). Open daily 8am-6pm. **Kaibab Plateau Visitors Center** (☎643-7298), located at Jacob Lake, next to Inn. Open 8am-5:30pm.

Weather Info: ☎638-7888. Updated at 7am daily.

Camping Supplies: General store abuts North Rim Campground. Open daily 7am-9pm.

Post Office: in Grand Canyon Lodge (☎638-2611), like everything else. Open M-F 8am-11am, 11:30am-4pm, Sa 8am-2pm. **ZIP code:** 86052. **Area code:** 520.

▟◖ ACCOMMODATIONS AND FOOD

Camping within the confines of the Grand Canyon National Park is limited to designated campgrounds. **BIOSPHERICS** (☎800-365-2267) handles reservations; otherwise, mark your territory by 10am. If you can't get in-park lodgings, head for the **Kaibab National Forest,** which runs from north of Jacob Lake to the park entrance. You can camp for free, as long as you're ¼ mi. from the road or official campgrounds. Less expensive accommodations may be found in **Kanab, UT,** 80 mi. north (p. 724), where motel rooms tend to hover around $40.

Grand Canyon Lodge (☎303-297-2757 for reservations, 638-2611 for front desk), on the edge of the rim. The only indoor rim lodging in the park. Reception 24hr. Reserve several months in advance. Open mid-May to Oct. Pioneer cabins shelter 4 people for $91. Singles or doubles in frontier cabins $78; Western cabins and motel rooms $84-94.

Jacob Lake Inn (☎643-7232), 45 mi. north of the North Rim entrance at Jacob Lake. Reception daily 6am-9pm. Cabins for 2 $69-75; for 3 $82-84; for 4 $86-88. Pricier motel units available for $10-15 more.

Kaibab Camper Village (☎643-7804), 1 mi. south of Jacob Lake Inn. Open May to mid-Oct. 50 tent sites $12; 60 sites with hook-ups for 2 $22; $2 per extra person.

North Rim Campground (call BIOSPHERICS, ☎800-365-2267), on Rte. 67 near the rim, the only campground in the park. You can't see into the canyon from the pine-covered sites, but you know it's there. Food store nearby, laundry, recreation room, and showers. No hook-ups. Open mid-May to mid-Oct. 7-day maximum stay. 83 sites $15.

DeMotte Park Campground, 16 mi. north of the park entrance in Kaibab National Forest. First come, first served. 23 woodsy sites $10 per vehicle per night.

Feeding options on the North Rim are placed strategically at the **Grand Canyon Lodge.** The restaurant serves breakfast for $4-8, lunch for $6-8, and dinner for $13 and up (☎638-2612 ext. 160. Open daily 6:30-10am, 11:30am-2:30pm, and 5-9:30pm; reservations required for dinner.) A sandwich at the **Cafe on the Rim** costs $4-6 (open daily 6:30am-9pm). There is also a **Saloon** in the lodge that has baked goods in the morning (open daily 5am-9am and 11am-10pm). North Rim-ers are better off eating in Kanab or stopping at the **Jacob Lake Inn** for $5-6 sandwiches and great $2 milkshakes. (☎643-7232. Open daily 6am-9pm.)

🅰 OUTDOORS

Hiking in the leafy North Rim seems like a trip to the mountains. This mountain, however, is upside-down—the hike back up comes after the legs are already a little weary from hiking down. All precautions for hiking at the South Rim are even more important at the North Rim, where the elevations are higher and the air is thinner. In-depth information on trails can be found in the North Rim's version of *The Guide*. Park Rangers also run nature walks, lectures, and evening programs at the North Rim Campground and Grand Canyon Lodge. Check the info desk or campground bulletin boards for schedules. One-hour ($15) or half-day **mule trips** ($40) through **Canyon Trail Rides** circle the rim or descend into the canyon from the lodge. (☎435-679-8665. Open daily 7am-7pm. No credit cards.) To tour the Canyon wet, pick up a Grand Canyon River Trip Operators brochure and select from among the 20 companies offering trips.

Overnight hikers must get permits from the **Backcountry Office** in the ranger station (open daily 8am-noon and 1-5pm), or write to the **Backcountry Office**, P.O. Box 129, Grand Canyon, AZ 86023; it may take a few days to get a permit in person.

Bright Angel Point Trail (½ mi.) begins near the visitors center and winds around behind the Lodge, ending with a seraphic view of the Canyon. Nature pamphlets are available along this easier trail. **North Kaibab Trail,** meaning "upside-down mountain," is the only maintained trail that leads into the Canyon. The Coconino Overlook (1½ mi. round-trip), Supai Tunnel (4 mi.), and Roaring Springs (9½ mi.) are day-hike destinations along the trail. Hiking beyond Roaring Springs should be left for overnight trips. A **shuttle** runs to the trailhead from Grand Canyon Lodge (daily at 5:30 and 7:45am; $5; reservations required). **Ken Patrick Trail** (10 mi.) is a forested walk along the rim that runs from Point Imperial to the N. Kaibab parking lot.

In addition, **Point Imperial,** an 11 mi. drive from the lodge, overlooks **Marble Canyon** and the **Painted Desert. Cape Royal** lies 23 mi. from the lodge; en route, you'll pass the enchanting **Vista Encantadora.** Short trails include the **Cape Final Trail** (4 mi.), which heads from a parking lot a few mi. before Cape Royal to Cape Final, and the **Transept Trail** (3 mi.), which follows the rim from the lodge to the campground.

NEAR GRAND CANYON: HAVASUPAI RESERVATION   ☎ 520

To the west of the hustle and bustle of the South Rim lies the tranquility of the Havasupai Reservation. Meaning "people of the blue-green water," the Havasupai are operate beyond the jurisdiction of the National Park Service, and maintain the only village on the Canyon floor. **Supai,** their village, can only be reached by an 8 mi. hike and lies just south of the Canyon's most beautiful waterfalls. A sequence of four waterfalls carries the Caribbean-like water of the Havasu Creek to its mothership, the Colorado. With lagoons forming at the base of each falls, these areas invite reflection and comparisons to the Garden of Eden.

📧 **GETTING THERE.** Supai and the campground can only be reached by a trail that originates on the rim at the Hualapai Hilltop. No roads lead to Supai, although mules can be hired to carry bags or people (contact the **Havasupai Tourist Enterprise** at ☎448-2141 for rates and details). The hike down to Supai and then onto the campground is not to be underestimated. The well-marked trail is a grueling, sun-exposed 8 mi. to the Supai village and then an additional 2 mi. to the campground. Bring at least a gallon of water per hiker. It is also best to start hiking at dawn whether entering or leaving the Canyon. Hiking in during the mid-day is dangerous. *Do not hike down without a reservation.* You may have to hike right back out.

⚡ PRACTICAL INFORMATION. Reservations for the campground, lodge, and mules can be made by calling the **Havasupai Tourist Enterprise** at ☎448-2141. Credit cards are accepted and a deposit is required. The trailhead is located at Hualapai Hilltop. Take I-40 E from Flagstaff or Williams until Rte. 66 at Seligman (40 mi. from Williams). Continue on Rte. 66 for 30 mi. until it meets with Indian Rd. 18, which ends at the Hilltop (60 mi.). Visitors must first check-in at the Tourist Office in Supai before heading onto the campground. In the village, there's a post office, general store, and cafe. Prices are high, because everything must be brought in by mule or helicopter. Bringing your own food to the campground is advised. All trash must be packed-out. No gas or water is available past Rte. 66; stock up beforehand.

⚡⚡ ACCOMMODATIONS AND OUTDOORS. The Havasupai graciously share their natural paradise with the outside world. The tribe operates the two accommodations: the **⚡Havasupai Campground** and the **Havasupai Lodge** both on the Canyon floor. The friendly campground, 2 mi. beyond Supai, lies between the **Havasu** and **Mooney Falls.** Many campers consider the camp sites to be heaven-on-earth, because they border the blue-green water of the Havasupai Creek and are near to the swimmer-friendly lagoons. The Tribe charges a one-time entry of $15 per visitor and $12 per night at the campground. Facilities are sparse: non-flush toilets and no showers. A spring provides fresh water. For those willing to brave the rough conditions, nature rewards them with glorious natural surroundings. The **Lodge,** in Supai, offers basic, roofed accommodation between $75-95 for up to six people (in addition to the entrance fee).

The trail from Supai to the campground extends to **Mooney Falls** (1 mi. from campground), **Beaver Falls** (4 mi.), and the **Colorado** (7 mi.). The hike down to Mooney Falls is stomach-turningly steep. Extreme caution should be exercised and well-treaded shoes are a must. Handrails are provided. Swimming and general frolicking are available at the lush lagoons that collect at the bottom of the falls.

FLAGSTAFF   ☎520

Born on the 4th of July, Flagstaff began as a reststop along the transcontinental railroad; its mountain springs provided precious aqueous refreshment along the long haul to the Pacific. The past hundred years have echoed with the innumerable "timber!" cries of the logging industry, seen a scientist in search of canal-digging Martians, witnessed an emerging milieu of diverse cultures and ideologies, and felt the unrelenting onslaught of backpackers and fannypackers alike. One thing hasn't changed, though: Flagstaff is still a major rest-stop on the way to Southwestern must-sees. Trains plow through town 72 times a day, while travelers pass through on their way to the Grand Canyon, Sedona, and the Petrified Forest, which are all within day-trip distance. The fabled, and perhaps over-hyped, Rte. 66 cuts through downtown, parallel to the still-buzzing railroad. The energetic citizens welcome travelers to their rock formations by day and their breweries by night; many wandered into town with camera in hand and ended up settling down. Retired cowboys, earthy Volvo owners, New Agers, and serious rockclimbers comprise much of the remaining population.

⬛ GETTING THERE AND GETTING AROUND

Flagstaff sits 138 mi. north of Phoenix (take I-17), 26 mi. north of Sedona (take U.S. 89A), and 81 mi. south of the Grand Canyon's south rim (take U.S. 180).

Trains: Amtrak, 1 E. Rte. 66 (☎774-8679). To Los Angeles (12hr., 1 per day, $58-105) and Albuquerque (7hr., 1 per day, $54-99). Station open daily 4:15am-10:45pm; ticket office closed 12:30-3:15pm.

Buses: Greyhound, 399 S. Malpais Ln. (☎774-4573), across from NAU campus, 3 blocks southwest of the train station on U.S. 89A. Turn off 89A by Dairy Queen. To: Phoenix, including airport (3hr., 4 per day, $21); Albuquerque (6½hr., 4 per day, $39); Los Angeles (10-12hr., 9 per day, $47.50); and Las Vegas (6-7hr., 3 per day via Kingman, casino special round-trip $50.50). Terminal open 24hr. **Grayline/Nava-Hopi,** 114 W. Rte. 66 (774-5003 or 877-467-3329). Shuttle buses to the Grand Canyon (2hr., 2 per day, $20 including admission fee) and Phoenix (3hr., 3 per day, $24).

Public Transit: Pine Country Transit, (☎779-6624). Routes cover most of town. Buses run once per hr.; route map and schedule available at visitors center in Amtrak station. One-way 75¢; seniors and disabled 35¢; children 60¢; book of 20 passes $13.

Taxis: Friendly Cab, ☎214-9000. 24hr.

Car Rental: Budget Rent-A-Car (☎779-5235), at the Flagstaff Airport. Cars with unlimited mileage. Must be 21 with major credit card. Under 25 surcharge $20 per day. Open daily 7am-8pm. *Let's Go* toters get 10% off.

✴❔ ORIENTATION AND PRACTICAL INFORMATION

Downtown surrounds the intersection of **Beaver St.** and **Rte. 66** (formerly Santa Fe Ave.). Both bus stations, two hostels, the tourist office, and a number of inexpensive restaurants lie within ½ mi. of this spot. Other commercial establishments line **S. San Francisco St.**, two blocks east of Beaver. As a mountain town, Flagstaff stays fairly temperate and receives frequent afternoon thundershowers.

Equipment Rental: Peace Surplus, 14 W. Rte. 66 (☎779-4521), 1 block from Grand Canyon Hostel. Daily tent rental ($5-8; $100-200 deposit), packs ($6; $300 deposit), plus a good stock of cheap outdoor gear. 3-day minimum rental on all equipment. Credit card or cash deposit required. Open M-F 8am-9pm, Sa 8am-8pm, Su 8am-6pm.

Visitor Info: Flagstaff Visitors Center, 1 E. Rte. 66 (☎774-9541 or 800-842-7293), in the Amtrak station. Open M-Sa 7am-6pm, Su 7am-5pm.

24-Hour Pharmacy/Grocery: Fry's Food and Drug Store (☎774-2719), 1 mi. north of San Francisco St. on Rte. 66. Open 24hr.

Internet Access: NAU's **Cline Library** (☎523-2171). Open M-Th 7:30am-10pm, F 7:30am-6pm, Sa 9am-6pm, Su noon-10pm. **Flagstaff Public Library**, 300 W. Aspen Ave. (☎774-4000). Open M-Th 10am-9pm, F 10am-7pm, Sa 10am-6pm, Su 11am-6pm.

Post Office: 2400 N. Postal Blvd. (☎714-9302), for general delivery. Open M-F 9am-5pm, Sa 9am-1pm. **ZIP code:** 86004. There's one closer to downtown at 104 N. Agassiz St., 86001, open the same hr. **Area code:** 520.

▚ ACCOMMODATIONS

When swarms of summer tourists descend on Flagstaff, accommodations prices shoot up. Thankfully, the town is blessed with excellent hostels. Historic **Rte. 66** is home to many cheap motels. *The Flagstaff Accommodations Guide*, available at the visitors center, lists all area hotels, motels, hostels, and bed and breakfasts. If you're here to see the Grand Canyon (who isn't?), check the noticeboard in your hotel or hostel; some travelers leave their still-valid passes behind.

▨ **Grand Canyon International Hostel,** 19 S. San Francisco St. (☎779-9421 or 888-442-2696; www.grandcanyonhostel.com), near the train station. Sunny, clean, and classy. Despite its large size (60 beds), the hostel is blessed with friendly guests and a staff to match. Free tea and coffee, breakfast, parking, and linen. Access to kitchen, TV room with cable, Internet ($2), and laundry facilities. Free pick-up from Greyhound station. Tours to the Grand Canyon ($38-40). Reception 7am-midnight. 4-bed dorms $16; private rooms $32-35.

Motel Du Beau, 19 W. Phoenix St. (☎774-6731 or 800-398-7112), also just behind the train station. The Du Beau lives up to its ritzy name with freshly reconstructed dorm rooms (4-8 beds) and private bathrooms (also refurbished). The lively, well-equipped common room is a highlight. Reception 7am-midnight. Under the same ownership as the Grand Canyon Hostel, the Du Beau offers all the same services (free linen, tours, etc.) in house and charges all the same prices.

The Weatherford Hotel, 23 N. Leroux St. (☎779-1919), on the other side of the tracks 1 block west of San Francisco St. The oldest hotel in Flagstaff, dating back to 1897, the Weatherford has spacious rooms with amazing balconies and bay windows. Equipped with elegant furnishing, the Weatherford is ideally located in the middle of downtown Flagstaff. Hotel singles with shared bathroom $38-49; with private baths $50-60. Reservations recommended.

Hotel Monte Vista, 100 N. San Francisco St. (☎779-6971 or 800-545-3068), downtown. Feels like a classy hotel, with charmingly quirky decor and a bar (with pool tables, video games, and off-track betting) downstairs. The place is phasing out hostel accommodations, but some dorm beds are still available. 4-bed dorms by gender with private baths $12; private rooms named after movie stars who slept there start at $40.

KOA Campground, 5803 N. U.S. 89 (☎526-9926), a few mi. northeast of town. Local buses stop near this beautiful campground. Showers, restrooms, cheap bike rentals, and kitchen during summer. Tent sites for 2 $20, cabins $34; $4 per additional person.

Camping in the surrounding **Coconino National Forest** is a pleasant and inexpensive alternative, but you'll need a car to reach the designated camping areas. Forest maps ($6) are available at the Flagstaff Visitors Center. The **Peaks Ranger Station** (☎526-0866), northeast of Flagstaff at the intersection of Rte. 89A and Railhead Dr., provides descriptions of all the campgrounds, as well as helpful advice on camping and hiking. **Lakeview,** 11½ mi. southeast of Flagstaff on Forest Hwy. 3 (U.S. 89A), is open from early May through late Oct. and has 30 sites. (Sites $10 per night per vehicle.) **Bonito Campground,** 14 mi. northeast on 89A, has 42 sites. (Open from mid-Apr. to early Sept. $12 per vehicle per night.) Lakeview and Bonito both feature running water and flush toilets. Camping is free anywhere in the national forest outside the designated campsites, unless marked. For info on campgrounds and backcountry camping, call the **Coconino Forest Service** (☎527-3600; open M-F 7:30am-4:30pm).

🍴🎵 FOOD, NIGHTLIFE, AND ENTERTAINMENT

All the arch-wielding, deep-fat frying chains are readily available outside of downtown, but near the heart of Flagstaff, the creative and off-beat rules. **Macy's,** 14 S. Beaver St., behind Motel Du Beau, is a cheery student hangout serving only vegetarian food (excellent vegan selection, too) in an earthy atmosphere. (☎774-2243. Open M-W 6am-8pm, Th-Sa 6am-9pm, Su 6am-6pm. Food served until 1hr. before closing.) Behind demure lace curtains, **Kathy's Cafe,** 7 N. San Francisco St., prepares delicious and inexpensive breakfasts accompanied by biscuits and fresh fruit ($4-6). Lunch sandwiches include $5 veggie options. (☎774-1951. Open M-F 6:30am-3pm, Sa-Su 7am-3:30pm. No credit cards accepted.) Never buy magic beans, except at **The Black Bean,** 12 E. Rte. 66, a great place for on-the-go burritos ($3-5). (☎779-9905. Open M-Th 11am-9pm, F-Sa 11am-10pm.) **Alpine Pizza,** at 7 N. Leroux, skillfully blends the time-honored American traditions of pizza-eating and beer-drinking. Slices are large (Alpine-sized) and $2, while beer is comparably inexpensive. A local hang-out, Alpine has a pool table and wood-carved booths. (☎774-4109. Open Su-Th 11am-11pm, F-Sa 11am-midnight.)

At night, head for the pool tables of **Mad Italian,** 101 S. San Francisco St. (☎779-1820. Open daily noon-1am. Happy hour daily 4-7pm.) **Charly's,** 23 N. Leroux St., plays live jazz and blues in one of the classiest buildings in town. (☎779-1919. Open daily 11am-10pm. Bar open daily 11am-1am.) If country/western is your thang, the **Museum Club,** 3404 E. Rte. 66, a.k.a. the **Zoo,** will rock your world. This place is the real deal—it was built during the Great Depression as a premiere roadhouse to liven spirits. Cowboy gusto is re-enacted daily with liquid spirits and first-class country. (☎526-9434. Open daily 11am-3am. Cover $3-5.)

In early June, the annual **Flagstaff Rodeo** (☎800-638-4253) comes to town with competitions, barn dances, a carnival, and a cocktail waitress race. For the month of July, the **Festival of the Arts** attracts chamber concerts, orchestras, and individual performers. The town's birthday, also known as the **4th of July,** is a knee-slapping good time with festivals and fireworks. At the (cow) tail-end of the summer (Labor Day), the **Coconino Country Fair** digs its heals into Flagstaff. For indoor entertainment, the **Flagstaff Symphony** plays from Oct. to May (☎774-5107; tickets $12-25, under 18 half-price). **Theatrikos,** 11 W. Cherry Ave. (☎774-1662), a local theater group, stages plays year-round in their own playhouse.

CITY IN A BUBBLE The planned city of **Arcosanti,** off I-17 at Exit 262, is designed to embody Italian architect Paolo Soleri's concept of an "arcology," or "architecture and ecology working together as one integral process." When complete, the city will be entirely self-sufficient, supplying its own food, power, and all other resources. Arcosanti has been under construction since 1970 but is expected to be finished rather later than the original goal of 2000—so far, only one building is up. The pace of the construction might have something to do with the restrictions on who is allowed to participate; rather than hiring workers, all the labor is done by students and others who take part in the community's "workshops." (☎632-7135. Tours daily every hr. 10am-4pm; $5 donation requested. Visitors center open daily 9am-5pm.)

SIGHTS

In 1894, Percival Lowell chose Flagstaff as the site for an astronomical observatory, and then spent the rest of his life here, devoting himself to the study of heavenly bodies and culling data to support his theory that life exists on Mars. The **Lowell Observatory** (west of downtown off Rte. 66), where he discovered the planet Pluto, doubles as a general tribute to his genius and a high-powered research center sporting five super-duper telescopes. In the day, admission includes tours of the telescopes, as well as a museum with hands-on astronomy exhibits. If you have stars in your eyes, come back at night for an excellent program about the night's sky and the constellations. (M-Sa 7:30pm; in summer, 8:30pm.) Nightly presentations include gazing through the 100-year-old Clark telescope and an informative talk by one of the perky guides. (1400 W. Mars Hill Rd. ☎774-2096; www.lowell.edu. Open daily 9am-5pm. $3.50, ages 5-17 $1.50.)

The more down-to-earth **Museum of Northern Arizona,** off U.S. 180 a few mi. north of town, houses impressive collections of Native American, Hispanic, and Western art. There's also an intimidating dinosaur skeleton. (☎774-5213. Open daily 9am-5pm. $5, students $3, seniors $4, ages 7-17 $2.)

OUTDOORS

With the northern **San Francisco Peaks** and the surrounding **Coconino National Forest,** Flagstaff offers numerous options for the rugged outdoorsperson or those simply interested in walking off last night's fun. Nature's playground provides skiing, hiking, biking, and general awe-struckedness. Due to the 7000 ft. plus altitudes, bring plenty of water, regardless of the season or activity. In late spring and summer, National and State Park Rangers may close trails if the potential for fire gets too high. The mountains occupy national forest land, so backcountry camping is free.

SKIING. The Arizona Snow Bowl, open from mid-Dec. to Apr., operates four chairlifts and maintains 32 trails. The majestic Humphrey's Peak, standing a whopping 12,670 ft., is the backdrop for the Snowbowl, as well as the Hopi's sacred home of the Kachina spirits. With an average snowfall of 260 in. and 2300 ft. of vertical drop, the Snow Bowl rivals the big-boy ski resorts of the Rockies. (☎779-1951. Open daily 8am-5pm. Lift tickets $37.) To reach the Snow Bowl, take U.S. 180 about 7 mi. north to the Fairfield Snow Bowl turn-off. Cross-country skiing is available at the Flagstaff Nordic Center (☎779-1951), 8 mi. north of Snow Bowl Rd. on Hwy. 180.

HIKES. In the summer, these peaks attract different species: hikers and bikers. The Coconino National Forest has many trails for hikers of all abilities. Consult the **Peaks Ranger Station,** 5075 N. 89A (☎526-0866), for trail descriptions and possible closures. For the more energetic hiker, the **Elden Lookout Trail** is ideal for jaw-dropping mountain-top views. Only 3 mi. in length (one-way), the trail climbs 2,300 ft.; it is demanding, but worth the view. The trail begins at the Peaks Ranger station. The **Inner Basin Trail** leads hikers and bikers into the ancient volcano that formed the San Francisco Peaks. Wildflowers and the remains of lava flows decorate this 3 mi. (one-way) trail. Inner Basin is located 15 mi. north of Flagstaff; contact the Ranger Station for directions.

DEEP IMPACT Perhaps the recent American obsession with all things extraterrestrial explains the popularity of **Meteor Crater,** 35 mi. east of Flagstaff off I-40, because not much else could. Originally thought to be a volcanic cone, the crater is now believed to be the impact site of a giant nickel-iron meteorite that fell to earth 50,000 years ago. Visitors are not allowed to hike down into the crater, which measures 4100 ft. across, but must fight the hordes for an unspectacular view over the guard-railed edge. Conspicuously missing in action is the meteor itself; scientists believe that most of it was vaporized at the moment of impact, since it was traveling at an impressive 10 mi. per second. The site was used to train Apollo astronauts in the 60s, and a museum in the building near the admissions booth patriotically celebrates the US space program (free with crater admission). (☎520-289-5898. Open daily 6am-6pm; off-season 8am-5pm. $10, seniors $9, ages 6-17 $5.)

CHAIRLIFT. Reluctant hikers and those who love mountain views will find the vista at the top of the **Snow Bowl's Skyride** stunning. When the air is clear, the North Rim of the Grand Canyon, the Painted Desert, and countless square miles of Arizona and Utah can be seen from the peak. (30min. Runs daily late May to early Sept. 10am-4pm; early Sept. to mid-Oct. F-Su 10am-4pm. $9, seniors $6.50, ages 6-12 $5.)

MOUNTAIN BIKING. Flagstaff also offers excellent mountain biking. The **Dry Lake Hills** and the **Elden Moutains** are two great areas, both north of Flagstaff, to tear it up on two wheels. **Schultz Creek Rd.,** off Hwy. 180, is a more low-key, less-demanding trail, while **Brookbanks** and **Little Bears** are recommended only for the experienced. Seek out the experts at **Single Track,** 575 Riordan Rd. (☎773-1862), for trail advice and general bike info. They also offer repairs for all of (mountain biking) life's little accidents. Bike rentals are available at **Absolute Bikes,** 18 N. San Francisco St. (☎779-5969), starting at $25 per day.

◪ DAYTRIPS FROM FLAGSTAFF

WALNUT CANYON NATIONAL MONUMENT. The ruins of more than 300 rooms in 13th-century Sinagua dwellings make up Walnut Canyon National Monument, constructed within a 400 ft. deep canyon. A glassed-in observation deck in the **visitors center** overlooks the whole canyon. The steep, self-guided **Island Trail** snakes down from the visitors center past 25 cliff dwellings. Markers along the 1 mi. trail describe aspects of Sinagua life and identify plants used for food, dyes, medicine, and hunting. The ¾ mi. **Rim Trail** offers some great views of the canyon and passes the rim-top inhabitances. Every Sa morning, rangers lead 2 mi. hikes into Walnut Canyon to the original Ranger Cabin and more remote cliff dwellings. Hiking boots and long pants are required for these challenging 2½hr. hikes. Walnut Canyon lies 10 mi. east of Flagstaff off I-40 at Exit 204. (☎520-526-3367. Open daily 8am-6pm; off season 9am-5pm. $3, under 16 free. Call ahead, hrs. change frequently.)

SUNSET CRATER VOLCANO NATIONAL MONUMENT. The crater encompassed by Sunset Crater Volcano National Monument, 12 mi. north of Flagstaff on U.S. 89, appeared in AD 1065. Over the next 200 years, a 1000 ft. high cinder cone took shape as a result of periodic eruptions. The self-guided **Lava Flow Nature Trail** wanders 1 mi. through the surreal landscape surrounding the cone, 1½ mi. east of the visitors center, where gnarled trees lie uprooted amid the rocky black terrain. Lava tube tours have been permanently discontinued due to falling lava, and hiking up Sunset Crater itself is not permitted. The **visitors center** supplies additional info. (☎520-526-0502. Open daily 8am-6pm; off season 8am-5pm. $3 per person, under 16 free; includes admission to Wupatki.) The **Bonito Campground,** in the Coconino National Forest at the entrance to Sunset Crater, provides tent sites (see p. 736).

WUPATKI NATIONAL MONUMENT. Wupatki possesses some of the Southwest's most scenic Pueblo ruins, situated 18 mi. northeast of Sunset Crater, along a stunning road with views of the Painted Desert. The Sinagua moved here in the 11th century, after the Sunset Crater eruption forced them to evacuate the land to the south. In less than 200 years, however, droughts, disease, and over-farming led the Sinagua to abandon these stone houses perched on the sides of *arroyos* in view of the San Francisco Peaks. Five deserted pueblos face the 14 mi. road from U.S. 89 to the visitors center. Another road to the ruins begins on U.S. 89, 30 mi. north of Flagstaff. The largest and most accessible, **Wupatki Ruin,** located on a ½ mi. round-trip loop trail from the visitors center, rises three stories. The spectacular **Doney Mountain trail** rises ½ mi. from the picnic area to the summit. Get info and trail guide brochures at the **visitors center.** (☎520-679-2365. Open daily 8am-5pm. Monument open daily 8am-5pm.) Backcountry hiking is not permitted.

SEDONA   ☎520

Being that Sedona is a UFO sighting hotspot, one wonders if the Martians are simply mistaking its deep red-rock towers for home. The scores of tourists who descend upon the town year-round (Sedona rivals the Grand Canyon for tourist mass) certainly aren't; they come for sights that would make Newton question gravity's effectiveness. Dramatic copper-toned behemoths dotted with pines tower over Sedona, rising from the earth with such flair and crowd appeal that they feel like a perfectly manufactured tourist attraction. Some folks in town will tell you that they were man-made, perhaps by the Egyptians—Sedona is also the New Age capital of the US. The downtown is overrun with overpriced boutiques and cafes, but the rocks are simply spectacular.

🛈 **PRACTICAL INFORMATION.** Sedona lies 120 mi. north of Phoenix (take I-17 north to Rte. 179 W) and 30 mi. south of Flagstaff (take I-17 S to Rte. 179 W or use U.S. 89A SW). The **Sedona-Phoenix Shuttle** (☎282-2066) runs six trips daily ($35). The **Sedona Chamber of Commerce,** at Forest Rd. and U.S. 89A. (☎282-7722), provides information on accommodations including camping and local attractions (open M-Sa 8:30am-5pm, Su 9am-3pm). **Area code:** 520. **Zip code:** 86336.

⌂ ACCOMMODATIONS. Lodging in town is a bit pricey, but a few deals can be had; however, it's not a bad idea to make Sedona a daytrip from Flagstaff or Cottonwood. **Hostel Sedona,** 5 Soldiers Wash Dr., off Brewer Rd., which connects with U.S. 89A uptown at the Burger King, provides basic, camp-like accommodations at a great location. (☎282-2772. Kitchen and common room. Chores required. Dorm beds $15; private room $30.) **White House Inn,** 2986 W. U.S. 89A (☎282-6680), is the second cheapest option, with singles and doubles, some with kitchenettes, at $46-58. A popular alternative to commercial lodging is renting a room in a private residence. Check the local papers or bulletin boards at a New Age shop for opportunities. In addition, cheaper options can be found in Cottonwood, 15 mi. away, where a number of budget motels line U.S. 89. The **Willow Tree Inn,** 1089 Hwy. 260 (☎634-3678), offers comfortable single rooms for $38-48.

There are a number of **campgrounds** within **Coconino National Forest,** along Oak Creek Canyon on U.S. 89A. (☎527-3600. Sites $12 per vehicle.) The largest, **Cave Springs,** 20 mi. north of town, administers 78 sites (call ☎800-283-2267 for reservations). For more info on Coconino Forest, including hiking maps, visit the **ranger station,** 250 Brewer Rd.; turn off U.S. 89A at Burger King. (☎282-4119. Open M-Sa 7:30am-4:30pm; in winter M-F 7:30am-4:30pm.) Free **backcountry camping** is allowed in the forest anywhere outside of Oak Creek and more than 1 mi. from any official campground or trailhead.

🍴 FOOD . Like many things in Sedona, restaurants can be expensive. However, there are a few good deals to be had. The **Coffee Pot Restaurant,** 2050 W. U.S. 89A, a local favorite, dishes up 101 varieties of omelettes ($4-7) and three varieties of tacos for $4. (☎282-6626. Open daily 6am-9pm.) Freshly made ice cream and bakery treats draw in the masses at **Black Cow Cafe,** 229 N. U.S. 89A, a great spot to cool off. Baked goods ($1-3) and sandwiches ($4-6) are for breakfast and lunch. (☎203-9868. Open daily 7am-9pm.) The **Red Planet Diner,** 1665 W. 89A, beams patrons in with a flying saucer and extraterrestrial charm. Martian milkshakes ($3) and Universal noodle bowls ($6) are "out-of-this-world" (☎282-6070; open daily 11am-11pm). For more down-to-earth fare, **Thai Spices,** 2986 W. U.S. 89A, offers authentic Thai cuisine. Good vegetarian options include Almond Curry Vegetables and Tempeh Garlic Vegetables (both for $8; ☎282-0599; open M-Sa 5-9pm).

⚄ OUTDOORS. The incredible formations at **Red Rock State Park** (☎282-6907) invite strolling or just contemplation. Located 15 mi. southwest of Sedona, the Park entrance can be found along the Red Rock Loop Road off U.S. 89A. Rangers lead daily nature hikes into the nearby rock formations and are happy to give trail recommendations. **Eagle's Nest Loop** (2½ mi.) is a good trail for gazing at amazing panoramic views. For the do-it-yourselfer, trail maps are available at the visitors center. (Center open daily 9am-5pm. Park open daily 8am-6pm; Oct.-Mar. 8am-5pm. $5 per car, $1 per pedestrian or cyclist.) The **Chapel of the Holy Cross,** on Chapel Rd., lies just outside a 1000 ft. rock wall in the middle of red sandstone. (☎282-4069. Open daily 9am-5pm.) The view from the parking lot is a religious experience itself.

Considered a rival to Moab, UT, by those in the mountain-biking know, Sedona has some of the best tracks in the world. The **Solider's Pass Secret Trails,** just north of town, are a playground for intense bikers. Tamer trails can be found along the **Bell Rock Pathway,** which lies south of town. Bike rentals (starting at $25 per day) and good trail information can be found at **Mountain Bike Heaven,** 1695 W. U.S. 89A. They also lead occasional free bike trips (call for dates and times) and do repairs for any devilish spill. (☎282-1312. Open M-F 9am-6pm, Sa-Su 9am-5pm.)

Wading like water-buffaloes in Sedona's natural water holes is another recreational favorite. At **Slide Rock State Park,** 10 mi. north of Sedona on U.S. 89A, rocks form a natural waterslide into the cold waters of Oak Creek. In the summer, locals come in droves to swim and picnic. (☎282-3034. Open daily 8am-7pm; closes earlier in off-season. $5 per car, $1 per pedestrian or cyclist.) Another popular spot is **Grasshopper Point,** a recreation site in the **Coconino National Forest,** 2½ mi. north of Sedona on 89A. (☎527-3600. Open daily 8am-7pm; closes earlier in off season. $5 per car, $1 per pedestrian or cyclist.)

Scenic driving is nearly as plentiful as the red rocks. The Chamber of Commerce is very helpful in suggesting routes. The Red Rock Loop provides views of mind-blowing rock formations and a little dirt road adventure. Dry Creek and Airport Rd. are also good drives. For those hoping to see Sedona's wild off-road side, jeep tours are available from a number of companies. Generally, trips range from $35 to $75 and 2-4hr. in length. **Sedona Adventures,** 276 N. U.S. 89A (☎282-3500 or 800-888-9494), offers some of the less expensive trips in the area.

NEAR SEDONA

Montezuma Castle National Monument, 10 mi. south of Sedona on I-17, is a 20-room cliff dwelling built by the Sinagua tribe in the 12th century. Unfortunately, you can't get very close to the ruins, but the view from the paved path below is excellent and wheelchair accessible. (☎567-3322. Open daily 8am-7pm, off-season 8am-5pm. $2, under 16 free.) A beautiful lake formed by the collapse of an underground cavern, **Montezuma Well,** off I-17 11 mi. north of the castle, once served as a source of water for the Sinagua who lived here. (Open daily 8am-7pm. Free.) Take U.S. 89A to Rte. 279 and continue through Cottonwood to reach **Tuzigoot National Monument,** 20mi. southwest of Sedona, a dramatic Sinaguan ruin overlooking the Verde Valley and a copper smelting waste area. (☎634-5564. Open daily 8am-7pm; in winter 8am-5pm. $2, under 17 free.) For different type of ruin, check out the **Cliff Castle Casino** (☎800-381-7568) in Camp Verde, 10 mi. south of Sedona off I-17. From poker to bowling to a kid's playland, Cliff can win over even the most discerning gambler.

IS THE FORCE WITH YOU? Could a powerful force be lurking near the Sedona airport or parks? Psychic **Page Bryant** thought so in 1980, when he divined several vortexes, or areas of great psychic and spiritual energy, around town. People who enter the vortexes have claimed to have experienced episodes of extreme psychic and emotional alertness, and sometimes **spiritual healing** in the long term. Vortexes have become a sensation among the New Age crowd since Bryant's discovery, and much conjecturing and scientific study has been done. **Extra-terrestrial meddling,** spiritual presences, high magnetism from the Sedona's metal-rich rocks, and **parallel universe cross-over** have all been cited as causes. Perhaps you can unlock their mystery: the main vortexes are at the airport, Bell Rock, Cathedral Rock, and Boyton Canyon.

JEROME   ☎ 520

Precariously perched on the side of Mingus Mountain, Jerome once attracted miners, speculators, saloon owners, and madams who came to the city following the copper boom of the late 1800s. By 1920, the town ranked as Arizona's third-largest city. The 1929 stock market crash threw Jerome's economy into an irrecoverable downward spiral. By mid-century Jerome was a ghost town. Recently, bikers, hippies, ex-cowboys, and artists have arrived, drawn by the charm and spectacular scenery of the town. Jerome's current incarnation is, in one respect, drastically different from its start—tourist mining has replaced copper mining as the main industry. Yet the lively, quirky flavor of this awkward town continues to thrive. Just driving down Main St. you get a feel for why Jerome is special: it is steeper than a horse's brow. The **Jerome State Historic Park,** ½ mi. off U.S. 89A just as you enter town, provides a worthwhile panoramic view of the town and a small museum. (☎634-5381. Open daily 8am-5pm. $2.50, ages 7-13 $1.)

Budget travelers should make Jerome a daytrip from Flagstaff or Phoenix, as lodging tends to be expensive. Staying over in Cottonwood, 15 mi. from both Jerome and Sedona, is a good alternative. The **Willow Tree Inn** (☎634-3678), off I-17 in Cottonwood, offers comfortable single rooms for $38-48. In addition, a number of budget motels are situated along U.S. 89 in Cottonwood. In town, **The Inn at Jerome,** 309 Main St., is one of the lower-priced joints. (☎634-5094 or 800-634-5094. Rooms $55-85 including breakfast.) The oldest restaurant in Arizona, **The English Kitchen,** 119 Jerome Ave., has a large array of salads and sandwiches for $5-6. (☎634-2132. Open Tu-Su 8am-3:30pm.) At night, float over to **The Spirit Room,** at Main St. and Jerome Ave., for live music and mayhem. (☎634-8809. Open daily 11am-1am; live music Sa from 9pm, Su 2-6pm.) **Paul and Jerry's Saloon,** 206 Main St., has been helping people get sloppy for three generations. (☎634-2603. Open daily noon-1am.)

U.S. 89A slinks its way to Jerome 30 mi. southwest of Sedona; the drive between them is simply gorgeous. The **Chamber of Commerce,** 310 Hull St., is staffed somewhat sporadically by volunteers; the recorded message lists food and lodging info. (☎634-2900. Usually open daily 10am-4pm.) **Area code:** 520.

NAVAJO RESERVATION   ☎ 520

In the 1830s, federal policymakers planned to create a permanent Native American country in the West. By mid-century, however, those plans had been washed away by the tide of American expansion. Indian reservations evolved out of the US government's subsequent *ad hoc* attempts to prevent fighting between Native Americans and whites while facilitating white settlement. Initially, the reservation system imposed a kind of wardship on the Native Americans, which lasted for over a century, until a series of Supreme Court decisions, beginning in the 60s, reasserted the tribes' legal standing as semi-sovereign nations. Today, the **Navajo Nation,** or the "rez," is the largest reservation in America and covers more than 27,000 sq. mi. of northeastern Arizona, southeastern Utah, and northwestern New Mexico. With over 210,000 Navajo, or Diné (*dih-NEH,* "the People") as they call themselves, the reservation is home to one-tenth of the US Native American population. Within the Navajo boundaries, the smaller **Hopi Reservation** is home to around 10,000 Hopi ("Peaceable People").

For visitors to the reservation, cultural sensitivity takes on a new importance; despite the many state and interstate roads that traverse the reservation, the land is legally and culturally distinct. Superficially, much of the Navajo Nation and other reservations resemble the rest of the US. In reality, deep rifts exist between Native American and "Anglo culture"—the term used to refer to the non-reservation US society. The Reservation has its own police force and laws. Possession and consumption of alcohol are prohibited on the reservation. General photography is allowed, unless otherwise stated, but photographing the Navajo people requires their permission (a gratuity is usually expected). Tourist photography is not permitted among the Hopi. As always, the best remedy for cultural friction is usually simple respect.

Lively reservation politics are written up in the local *Navajo-Hopi Observer* and *Navajo Times* as well as in regional sections of Denver, Albuquerque, and Phoenix newspapers. For a taste of the Navajo language and Native American ritual songs, tune your **radio** to 660AM, "The Voice of the Navajo." Remember to advance your watch 1hr. during the summer; the Navajo Nation runs on **Mountain Daylight Time,** while the rest of Arizona, including the Hopi reservation, remains on **Mountain Standard Time.** The **area code** for the entire reservation is 520.

Monument Valley, Canyon de Chelly, Navajo National Monument, Rainbow Bridge, Antelope Canyon, and the roads and trails that access these sights all lie on Navajo land. Driving or hiking off-road without a guide is considered trespassing. Those planning to hike through Navajo territory should head to the visitors center in Window Rock (see below) for a backcountry permit, or mail a request along with a money order or certified check to P.O. Box 9000, Window Rock, AZ 86515 ($5 per person). Fill up your gas tank before exploring the reservation; gas stations are few and far between. The "border towns" of Gallup, NM (see p. 772), Flagstaff, AZ (see p. 734), and Page, AZ (see p. 746) are good gateways to the reservations, with car rental agencies, inexpensive accommodations, and frequent Greyhound service on I-40. The only budget accommodation in the Navajo territory is the **Grey Hills Inn** (see p. 743) located in Tuba City. Budget travelers can also camp at the national monuments or Navajo campgrounds, or stay in a border town.

WINDOW ROCK

Unlike many historical presentations of Native Americans, **Window Rock** is a celebration of modern tribal life. The capital of the Navajo Nation and the epicenter of Reservation life, Window Rock is the seat of tribal government and home to most of the Reservation's infrastructure. For travelers, Window Rock, named after its unique geological formation, is a good starting place.

The limited lodging in town is expensive, but Navajo sights make Window Rock a good stopover en route to or from Gallup. A terrific view of the eponymous rock itself can be had from **Window Rock Tribal Park,** off Rte. 12 just past the government offices. The **Navajo Tribal Museum,** on Rte. 264 ½ mi. east of Rte. 12, has four rooms of Navajo and Navajo-related artwork and photography. (☎871-7941. Open M-Sa 8am-5pm. Free.) For those who want to observe the tribal government in action, in the Navajo language, the **Navajo Council Tribal Chambers** offers free tours of the governing body's meeting rooms. (☎871-6417. Open M-F 8am-noon and 1-5pm.) The animals in the **Navajo Nation Zoo and Botanical Park,** across from the Tribal Museum, might look familiar, although you may not have seen them in a zoo before. Recent tribal debates have centered on whether the zoo should remain open, since many of the animals featured are considered sacred. Check that the zoo is open before visiting. (☎871-6573. Open daily 8am-5pm. Free.) The oldest trading post in the US and a national historic site, the **Hubbell Trading Post,** 30 mi. west of Window Rock on Rte. 264 in the town of Ganado, has functioned as a store since 1876. It still sells Navajo arts and crafts, and now also houses a museum. The work put into the rugs justifies their steep prices, though it makes the post a museum stop and not a store for most. (☎755-3475. Open daily 8am-6pm, in winter 8am-5pm. Free.)

The **Navajoland Tourism Dept.,** P.O. Box 1840, Window Rock 86515, in downtown Window Rock in the same building as the tribal museum (see above), offers the free pamphlet *Discover Navajoland*, which has a list of accommodations and jeep and horseback tours. The **tourist office** also sells a detailed map ($3) entitled *The Visitors' Guide to the Navajo Nation* (☎871-6436; open M-Sa 8am-5pm).

CANYON DE CHELLY NATIONAL MONUMENT

The red hue of the cliffs of Canyon de Chelly (pronounced *"Canyon de Shay"*) and the adjoining canyons in the national monument have enchanted settlers for over four millennia, giving the area a history far greater than anywhere else in the four-corners region. However, like much of the region, the canyon's history has been colored by repeated conflicts between Native Americans and whites. In 1805, in what is now called **Massacre Cave,** 115 Native American women and children were shot by Spanish men. Later in the 1860s, the famed Kit Carson starved the Navajo out of the canyon.

To the Navajo, it is the nature of *Tsegi* (*say-he*), the spirit of their home, that brings new life to this region. The fertile **Beautiful Valley** is testament to the vitality of the land. So central is this region to the local Native American culture that the Navajo Nation was purposely created with Canyon de Chelly at its center. Although **Canyon de Chelly National Monument** lies on Navajo Nation land, it is administered by the National Park Service. Visitors are only allowed to enter the canyon via the **White House Ruin trail.** A 3 mi. round-trip hike, the trail descends into the belly of the Canyon, from a South Rim overlook. Winding its way down 600 ft., the trail passes a Navajo farm and traditional hogan and cliff dwelling ruins.

To explore beyond the White House Ruin trail, a **private guide** must be hired. Reservations can be made through the visitors center, but are not required. (3hr., $15 per hr. You provide the four-wheel-drive vehicle; free permit from visitors center.) Horseback tours can be arranged at **Justin's Horse Rental,** on South Rim Dr., at the canyon's mouth. (☎674-5678. Open daily 9am-sundown. Horses $10 per hr.; mandatory guide $15 per hr.) You can also take one of the paved **Rim Drives** (North Rim 15 mi. one-way to last overlook, South Rim 16 mi. one-way) skirting the edge of the 300-700 ft. cliffs; the South Rim is more dramatic. Get booklets (50¢) on the White House Ruin and Rim Drives at the visitors center. On the North Rim Drive, the large dwellings in **Mummy Cave Ruin** are impressive. Nearby is the somber Massacre Cave. **Spider Rock Overlook,** 16 mi. from the visitors center, on the South Rim Drive, is a narrow sandstone monolith towering hundreds of feet above the canyon floor. Native American lore says the whitish rock at the top contains the bleached bones of victims of the *kachina* spirit, or Spider Woman, who has a taste for disobedient children.

The most common route to the park is from **Chambers,** 75 mi. south, at the intersection of I-40 and U.S. 191; you can also come from the north via U.S. 191. Entrance to the monument is free. The **visitors center** sits 2 mi. east of Chinle on Navajo Rte. 7. (☎674-5500. Open daily 8am-6pm; Oct.-Apr. 8am-5pm.) One of the larger towns on the reservation, **Chinle,** adjacent to U.S. 191, has restaurants and gas stations. There is no public transportation to the park. In an **emergency,** contact the park ranger (☎674-5523, after hrs. 674-5524) or the Navajo Police (☎674-2111).

Camp for free in the park's **Cottonwood Campground,** 1½ mi. from the visitors center. This giant campground, located in a pretty cottonwood grove, can get noisy with the din of the stray dogs who wander about the area at night. Sites are first come, first served. (☎674-5500. Restrooms, picnic tables, water except in winter, and dump station. 5-day maximum stay.) The least expensive lodging on the Rez is in Tuba City. Less than 1 mi. east on Rte. 160 off the Rte. 264 and Rte. 160 intersection, the **Grey Hills Inn** has hostel beds and motel rooms all with shared bathrooms. (☎283-6271. Dorms $16; private room $23; motel rooms $42.) **Farmington, NM,** and **Cortez, CO,** are the closest major cities with multiple cheap lodging options.

SOUTHWEST

MONUMENT VALLEY

The red sandstone towers of Monument Valley are one of the southwest's most otherworldly sights. Paradoxically, they're also one of the most familiar, since countless Westerns have used the butte-laden plain as their backdrop. Some years before John Wayne, Ancestral Puebloans managed to sustain small communities here, despite the hot, arid climate. The park's looping 17 mi. **Valley Drive** winds around 11 of the most spectacular formations, including the famous pair of **Mittens** and the slender **Totem Pole.** However, the gaping ditches, large rocks, and mudholes on this road can be jarring to both you and your car—drive at your own risk and observe the 15mph speed limit. The drive takes at least 1½hr. Other, less-touristed parts of the valley can be reached only by four-wheel-drive vehicle, horse, or foot. *Leaving the main road without a guide is not permitted.* The visitors center parking lot is crowded with booths run by small companies selling jeep, horseback, and hiking tours. (1½hr. jeep tour about $15 per person, 1½hr. horseback tour $30, 4hr. hiking tour $45; prices higher for a single person.) In winter, snow laces the rocky towers, and most tourists flee. Call the visitors center for snow and road conditions.

Accommodations in the area are hard to come by. **Mitten View Campground,** ¼ mi. southwest of the visitors center, offers 99 sites, showers, and restrooms, but no hook-ups. (Sites $10; in winter $5. Register at the visitors center. No reservations.) The **Navajo National Monument** (see below) has more camping. Cheap motels are in **Mexican Hat, UT** (see p. 726); **Bluff, UT** (see p. 726); and **Page, AZ** (see p. 746).

The park entrance lies on U.S. 163 just across the Utah border, 24 mi. north of the Navajo town **Kayenta,** which is at the intersection of U.S. 163 and U.S. 160. The **visitors center** has info. (☎435-727-3353. Park and visitors center open daily 7am-7pm; Oct.-Apr. 8am-5pm. The drive closes at 6:30pm; begin by 4:30pm to complete it. Admission $3, under 7 free.)

NAVAJO NATIONAL MONUMENT

Until the late 1200s, a small population of the ancestors of the modern Hopi inhabited the region, though hard times left the villages vacant by 1300. From U.S. 160, 20 mi. west of Kayenta, Rte. 564 travels 9 mi. north to the park entrance. Today, the site contains three cliff dwellings. **Inscription House** has been closed to visitors indefinitely (since the 60s) due to its fragile condition; the other two admit a very limited number of visitors. The stunning **Keet Seel** (open late May to early Sept.) can be reached only via a challenging 16 mi. round-trip hike. Hikers can stay overnight in a free campground nearby (no facilities or drinking water). Reservations for permits to visit Keet Seel must be made up to two months in advance through the **visitors center;** total reservations are limited to 20 people per day. (☎520-672-2366. Open daily 8am-5pm.) Ranger-led tours to **Betatakin,** a 135-room complex, are limited to 25 people. (Open May to late Sept. 1 per day at 8:15am; first come, first served the morning of the tour. A strenuous 5 mi., 5-6hr. hike.) If you're not up for the trek to the ruins, the paved, 1 mi. round-trip **Sandal Trail** lets you gaze down on Betatakin from the top of the canyon. The **Aspen Forest Overlook Trail,** another 1 mi. hike, overlooks canyons and aspens, but no ruins. Write to **Navajo National Monument,** HC 71 Box 3, Tonalea 86044 for more info. The free **campground,** next to the visitors center, has 30 sites. An additional overflow campground nearby has no running water. (First come, first served. 7-day maximum stay. No hook-ups.)

HOPI RESERVATION

In the southwestern corner of the Navajo Nation, the Hopi Reservation clusters around three mesas connected by Rte. 264, First Mesa, Second Mesa, and Third Mesa. On Second Mesa, the **Hopi Cultural Center,** 63 mi. north of Winslow, AZ, and 5 mi. west of the intersection of Rte. 264 and 87, contains the reservation's only museum, which displays Hopi baskets, jewelry, pottery, and info about the tribe's history. (☎734-2401. Open M-F 8am-5pm, Sa-Su 9am-3pm; $3, under age 14 $1.)

Visitors are welcome to attend some of the Hopi **village dances.** Announced only a few days in advance, these religious ceremonies usually occur on weekends and last from sunrise to sundown. The dances are highly formal occasions; do not wear shorts, tank tops, or other casual wear. Photographs, recordings, and sketches are strictly forbidden. Often several villages will hold dances on the same day, giving tourists the opportunity to go village-hopping. The **Harvest Dance,** occurring in mid-Sept. at the Second Mesa Village, is a spectacular ceremony bringing together tribes from all over the US; and there is no admission charge for observing. For all dances inquire at the cultural center, the Flagstaff Chamber of Commerce, or the **Hopi Cultural Preservation Office,** P.O. Box 123, Kykotsmovi 86039 (☎734-2244), for the dates and sites.

PETRIFIED FOREST AND PAINTED DESERT   ☎520

Spreading over 60,000 acres, the Petrified Forest National Park looks like an imploded box of crayons dotted with fallen trees turned to stone. Some 225 million years ago, when Arizona's desert was a floodplain, volcanic ash covered the logs, slowing their decay. When silica-rich water seeped through the wood, the silica crystallized into quartz, producing rainbow hues. One of the most unique attractions in the Southwest, the park also contains a scenic chunk of the Painted Desert, named for the stunning colors that stripe its rock formations.

▪ ORIENTATION. Roughly speaking, the park can be divided into two parts: the northern Painted Desert and the southern Petrified Forest. An entrance station and visitors center welcomes guests at each end and a 28 mi. road connects the two sections. With lookout points and trails strategically located along the road, driving from one end of the park to the other is a good way to digest all of this natural splendor.

▶▌ PRACTICAL INFORMATION AND ACCOMMODATIONS. Enter the park either from the north or the south. (Open daily 7am-7pm; in winter 8am-5pm. Entrance fee $10 per vehicle, $5 per pedestrian.) To enter the southern section of the park, exit I-40 at Holbrook and take U.S. 180 W to the **Rainbow Forest Museum.** The museum provides a look at petrified logs up close and serves as a **visitors center.** (☎524-6822. Open daily 8am-7pm; off-season 8am-5pm. Free.) There are no established campgrounds in the park, but **free backcountry camping** is allowed in several areas with a permit. To enter the Painted Desert section of the park, take I-40 to Exit 311 (107 mi. east of Flagstaff). The **Painted Desert Visitors Center** is less than 5 mi. from the exit. (☎524-6228. Open daily 7am-7pm; off-season 8am-5pm.) There is no public transportation to either part of the park. **Nava-Hopi Bus Lines, Gray Line Tours,** and **Blue Goose Backpacker Tours** offer services from **Flagstaff** (see p. 734). Budget accommodations abound in **Holbrook** (27 mi. west of the park). The rooms at **Royal Thrifty Inn,** 310 W. Hopi Dr., could use some paint, but you can't beat the price. (☎524-6490. Singles $20; doubles $27.) **Gallup, NM** (see p. 772), and **Flagstaff, AZ** (see p. 734), also offer cheap lodging.

▣ SIGHTS. The Petrified Forest is the largest concentration of petrified wood in the world. Located near the southern visitors center, the **Long Logs, Agate House,** and **Giant Logs Trails** are all peppered with fragments of the petrified wood. All three trails are less than 1 mi. and involve little elevation change. Farther north, the more strenuous **Blue Mesa** trail (1 mi.) leads hikers into the belly of the badlands, an area brimming with brilliant blue clay hills. Past the Blue Mesa turn-off is the **Puerco Pueblo,** a 500-year old dwelling, and **Newspaper Rock,** covered with Native American petroglyphs. The **Painted Desert** section lies at the park's north end; here, a number of overlooks allow for unimpeded gazing. No established trails traverse the Painted Desert, but backcountry hiking is allowed (permit required for overnights). Beware that shoes will be eternally coated in red sand. Picking up fragments of the wood is illegal and traditionally unlucky; if the district attorney doesn't get you, then the demons will. Those who *must* have a piece should buy one at any of the myriad stores along I-40.

LAKE POWELL AND PAGE   ☎ 520

"Dammit!" said President Dwight Eisenhower in 1953, pressing a large red button on his desk. Many hundreds of miles away, a massive explosion shook the earth. Thus began a tremendous effort to provide water and energy to the desert: ten years and ten million tons of concrete later, **Glen Canyon Dam,** the second-largest dam in the country, was completed. With no particular place to go, the Colorado River flooded **Glen Canyon,** which spanned northern Arizona and southern Utah, to form the 186-mile-long **Lake Powell.** Ironically named after John Wesley Powell, a one-armed Civil War veteran who led and chronicled the first expedition down the then-raging but now-sedated Colorado, the lake offers 1960 miles of shoreline. Water sports and fishing are the most popular activities on the lake, but hiking opportunities also abound. Spectacular **Antelope Canyon** sits outside the resort town of **Page** near the southwest tip of Lake Powell at the U.S. 89/Rte. 98 junction.

❼ PRACTICAL INFORMATION. Visitor Information: The **Carl Hayden Visitor Center** (2 mi. north of Page on U.S. 89N, ☎ 608-6404) offers a wealth of Lake Powell and Glen Canyon Dam information. The **Page Chamber of Commerce,** 644 N. Navajo Dr. (☎ 645-2741), in the Dam Plaza is open daily 8am-8pm; in winter M-F 9am-5pm. **Internet Access: Mailboxes Etc.** at Page Plaza. $3 per 15min. (Open M-F 9am-6pm, Sa 10am-4pm.) **Post Office:** 44 6th Ave., ☎ 645-2571. Open M-F 8:30am-5pm, Sa 1-4pm. **ZIP Code:** 86040. **Area code:** 520.

▌ ACCOMMODATIONS. Despite the influx of pricey chain hotels to Page, many low-cost quality accommodations remain. A cluster of budget accommodations resides on 8th Ave. (between S. Navajo and Elm), which has been deemed the small motel district. Motels in this area are manned by personable, friendly staff. **Uncle Bill's Place,** 117 8th Ave. (☎ 645-1224), is perfect for those looking for a peaceful, intellectually-stimulating stay. Elegantly decorated singles and doubles ($36) have shared bathrooms and include kitchens and living rooms. **K.C.'s Motel,** 126 8th Ave. (☎ 645-2947), is across the street from Bill's. K.C.'s offers spacious former-apartment suites for room prices. With cable TV, private bathrooms, and kitchens, the doubles are a steal at $39-49 ($29 in the winter). **Bashful Bob's Motel,** 750 S. Navajo Dr., isn't embarrassed about its huge rooms with kitchens, sitting areas, cable TV, and Internet access. (☎ 645-3919. Singles and doubles $35, around $29 in the winter.) About 30 mi. from Page, half-way to Kanab, UT, the **Paria Canyon Adventure Ranch,** offers hostel beds, teepees, camping, and outdoor activities (see p. 722). **Wahweap Campground,** 100 Lake Shore Dr., is adjacent to the exorbitant Wahweap Lodge, (☎ 645-1059). 146 sites offered on a first come, first served basis. $15 for tent sites, $25 for full hook-up sites at campground and neighboring **Wahweap RV Park.**

▢ FOOD. Cactus & Tropicals Garden and Cafe, 809 N. Navajo Dr., owned by a former town mayor, is your best bet for healthy, high quality food in town. Adorned with a beautiful outdoor garden and indoor boutique, the atmosphere and food are a nice change from the usually grease-fortified Page offerings. (☎ 645-6666. Open M-Sa 8am-3pm. Sandwiches $5.) The **Sandwich Place,** in the Page Plaza, also whips up 'fast food fit for grown-ups' and killer onion rings. (Open M-Sa 11am-8pm. Sandwiches $4-5.) Make **Dos Amigos,** 608D Elm St. in the Page Plaza, your new pals by feasting on their delicious Mexican fare. The a la carte menu is friendly to budget travelers with tacos starting at $2. (☎ 645-3036. Open daily 11am-10pm.) For breakfast fare, the **Glen Canyon Steakhouse,** 201 N. Lake Powell Blvd., serves an all-you-can-eat morning buffet for $6.

▣▟ SIGHTS AND ACTIVITIES. Neighboring the Glen Canyon Dam, the **Carl Hayden Visitors Center,** 3 mi. north of Page on U.S. 89 N, offers free tours of the dam (☎ 608-6404; open daily May-Sept. 8am-7pm; off-season 8am-5pm). Tours, lasting one hour, are offered every half hour (8:30am-4:30am) and are the only way to see the insides of the dam. History buffs will dig the **John Wesley Powell Museum,** 6 N.

Lake Powell Blvd., where friendly staff extend the legacy of the one-armed local hero. (☎645-9496. Visitor information is also available at the museum. $1.)

Lake Powell's man-made shores are rocky rather than sandy, with skimpy beaches that vanish when the water rises. Completely unnatural, smurf-blue, "97% pure," 80°-in-the-summer waters more than make up for the rocky shore. Recreation opportunities abound at **Wahweep Marina,** where you can swim, rent a boat or take a boat tour. (☎645-2433. 6-person skiff $70; off-season $42; tours $11-99.) **Free swimming** is available at "The Chains," a group of quiet coves surrounded by rocky shoreline, found off a dirt road just before the dam on Rte. 89. Many companies lead **boat tours** to the famous **Rainbow Bridge National Monument,** the world's largest natural bridge. The bridge, which is sacred to the Navajo, takes its name from the Navajo word *nonnoshoshi,* "rainbow turned to stone." It can be reached by a strenuous two-day hike or a half-day boat tour. **ARAMARK Leisure Services** conducts boat tours (☎800-528-6154. Full-day $99, under 12 $73; half-day $55-75. Call ahead for reservations.) Hiking permits must be obtained in advance from the Navajo Nation, since the trails cross Navajo land. Write to **Navajo Nation,** P.O. Box 308, Window Rock, AZ 86515. If you want to see the Canyon downstream of the dam, try a relaxing **Colorado River Float Trip** (☎800-528-6154; half-day $53, full-day, $75)

No less spectacular for its great accessibility, the kaleidoscopic **Antelope Canyon** is one of the only slot canyons in the US. The entrance is on U.S. 98 several mi. south of Page, by the Navajo Power Plant. The trail through the **upper canyon,** while moderately strenuous, is wider and easier to negotiate than the one through the **lower canyon,** which requires many tight squeezes so is less touristed. Sunlight illuminating the canyon's twisting sandstone walls is nothing short of incredible. The canyon lies on Navajo land, so a **guide** is required (1½hr.; $13 per person).

A short, beautiful hike leads to **Horseshoe Bend Overlook,** which provides a view of the Colorado River as it curves around a huge rock formation. Evening hikes reveal spectacular sunsets. The trail leads from a parking lot down a dirt road off U.S. 89, just south of Mi. 545—the tourist office can provide directions.

PHOENIX ☎602

The name Phoenix was chosen for a small farming community in the Sonoran desert by Anglo settlers who believed that their oasis had risen from the ashes of ancient Native American settlements, like the legendary phoenix of Greek mythology. The 20th century has seen this unlikely metropolis live up to its name; the expansion of water resources, the proliferation of railroad transportation, and the introduction of air-conditioning have fueled Phoenix's ascent to its standing among America's leading cities. Shiny high-rises now crowd the business district, while a vast web of six-lane highways and strip malls surrounds the downtown. Phoenix's rise has not been without turmoil, though: its greatest asset, the sun, is also its greatest nemesis. The scorching heat and arid landscape may put a damper on expansion, as the wet stuff is now in short supply. For the traveler, the Phoenix sun can also be either friend or foe. During the balmy winter months, tourists, golfers, and business conventioneers flock to the resort-perfect temperatures and increasingly posh accommodations. In the summer, the city crawls into its air-conditioned shell as temperatures climb to an average of 100°F and lodging prices plummet.

▊ GETTING THERE AND GETTING AROUND

Phoenix operates a major international airport that is, of all Southwestern cities, probably the easiest and cheapest to fly into. Southwest Airlines offers some of the cheapest flights. Amtrak and Greyhound have frequent service to the downtown area. Many car rental agencies line the streets near the airport.

Airport: Sky Harbor International (☎273-3300), just southeast of downtown. Take the Valley Metro Red Line bus ($1.25) into the city (5:45am-10pm).

Trains: Amtrak, 401 W. Harrison (☎253-0121); follow 4th Ave. south 2 blocks past Jefferson St. *Be careful at night.* To: Los Angeles via Tuscon (12hr., 4 per week, $94); and San Antonio via Tuscon (20hr., 3 per week, $116). Open Sa-M 1:15-9:45am and 5:15pm-12:45am, Tu-W 1:15-9:45am, Th-F 5:15pm-12:45am.

Buses: Greyhound, 2115 E. Buckeye Rd. (☎389-4200). To: El Paso (8hr.,13 per day, $35); Los Angeles (7hr., 12 per day, $37); Tucson (2hr., 13 per day, $13); and San Diego (8hr., 6 per day, $43). Open 24hr.

Public Transit: Valley Metro, ☎253-5000. Most lines run to and from the Central Bus Station, at Central and Van Buren St. Routes tend to operate M-F 5am-8pm with reduced service on Sa. Fare $1.25; disabled, seniors, and children 60¢. All-day pass $3.60, 10-ride pass $12. Bus passes and system maps at the Terminal.

Taxis: Ace Taxi, ☎254-1999. 24hr.

Car Rental: ABC Rent-a-Car, 2532 E. Jefferon St. (☎681-9000). Cars from $40-50 per day with unlimited mi. on older models. Cash deposit and under 25 accepted with surcharge. Open daily 8am-8pm.

✴🛈 ORIENTATION AND PRACTICAL INFORMATION

The intersection of **Central Ave.** and **Washington St.** marks the heart of downtown. Central Ave. runs north-south. One of Phoenix's peculiarities is that numbered avenues and streets both run north-south; avenues are numbered sequentially west from Central, while streets are numbered east. Some avenues and streets dead-end abruptly. A few of the largest north-south thoroughfares are **7th St., 16th St., 7th Ave.,** and **19th Ave.** Washington St. divides streets north-south. You'll need a car or a bus pass to see much of Phoenix; this city sprawls forever.

Visitor Info: Phoenix and Valley of the Sun Convention and Visitors Center (☎254-6500, recorded info and events calendar ☎252-5588). Downtown location: 2nd and Adams St. Open M-F 8am-5pm. Biltmore Fashion Park location: 24th St. and East Camelback. Open daily 8am-5pm. Good camping and outdoors advice available at the **Bureau of Land Management** Office, 222 N. Central.

Hotlines: Crisis Hotline, ☎254-4357. 24hr. **Gay Hotline,** ☎234-2752. Daily 10am-10pm.

Internet Access: At the beautiful copper-and-glass **Burton Barr Central Library,** 1221 N. Central Ave. (☎262-4636). Open M-Th 9am-9pm, F-Sa 9am-6pm, Su 1-5pm. Sign-up required, but computers usually available.

Post Office: 522 N. Central Ave., downtown. Open M-F 8:30am-5pm. General delivery: 1441 E. Buckeye Rd. Open M-F 7:30am-5pm. **ZIP code:** 85026. **Area code:** 602.

🛈 ACCOMMODATIONS

Budget travelers should consider visiting Phoenix during July and Aug. when motels knock their prices down by as much as 70%. In the winter, when temperatures and vacancies drop, prices go up; make reservations if possible. The reservationless should cruise the rows of motels on **Van Buren St.** east of downtown, toward the airport. The strips are full of 50s-era ranch-style motels, some touting adult movies as their main attraction, as well as the requisite modern chains. Parts of these areas can be unsafe; *guests should examine a motel thoroughly before checking in.* Safer, but more distant, the area around **Bell Rd.,** north of the city, is also loaded with motels. **Mi Casa Su Casa/Old Pueblo Homestays Bed and Breakfast,** P.O. Box 950, Tempe 85280 (☎800-456-0682), arranges stays in B&Bs throughout Arizona, New Mexico, southern Utah, southern Nevada, and southern California. (Open M-F 9am-5pm, Sa 9am-noon. Singles $40-70; doubles from $60. Make winter reservations a month in advance.)

Metcalf House (HI-AYH), 1026 N. 9th St. (☎254-9803), a few blocks northeast of downtown. From the Central Bus Station, take bus #10 down 7th St. to Roosevelt St., walk 2 blocks east to 9th St., and turn left—the hostel is ½ block north in a shady and quiet residential area. Last bus leaves at 7:15pm. The owner, who gushes helpful advice about the area, fosters a lively community in this uniquely decorated converted house. Evening gab-sessions common on the front porch. Dorm-style rooms with wooden bunks adjoin a kitchen and common room. Check-in 7-10am and 5-10pm. Chores required. $12, non-members $15.

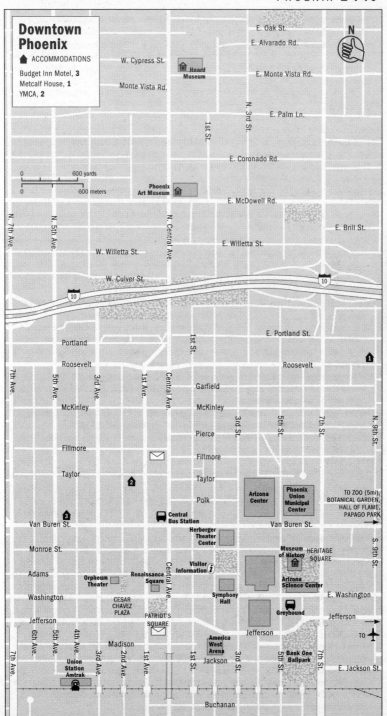

Downtown Phoenix

🏠 ACCOMMODATIONS

Budget Inn Motel, **3**
Metcalf House, **1**
YMCA, **2**

N

0 ——— 600 yards
0 ——— 600 meters

E. Oak St.
E. Alvarado Rd.
W. Cypress St.
Heard Museum
E. Monte Vista Rd.
Monte Vista Rd.
N. 3rd St.
1st St.
E. Palm Ln.
E. Coronado Rd.
Phoenix Art Museum
E. McDowell Rd.
N. 7th Ave.
N. 5th Ave.
N. Central Ave.
E. Brill St.
E. Willetta St.
W. Willetta St.
W. Culver St.
10
10
Portland
E. Portland St.
Roosevelt
Roosevelt
1st St.
7th Ave.
5th Ave.
3rd Ave.
1st Ave.
Central Ave.
Garfield
McKinley
McKinley
Pierce
3rd St.
5th St.
7th St.
N. 9th St.
Fillmore
Fillmore
Taylor
Taylor
Polk
Arizona Center
Phoenix Union Municipal Center
TO ZOO (5mi), BOTANICAL GARDEN, HALL OF FLAME, PAPAGO PARK
Central Bus Station
Van Buren St.
Van Buren St.
Monroe St.
Herberger Theater Center
Museum of History
HERITAGE SQUARE
S. 9th St.
Adams
Visitor Information ⓘ
Arizona Science Center
Washington
Orpheum Theater
Renaissance Square
Symphony Hall
E. Washington
Jefferson
CESAR CHAVEZ PLAZA
PATRIOT'S SQUARE
Greyhound
Jefferson
TO ✈
6th Ave.
5th Ave.
4th Ave.
3rd Ave.
2nd Ave.
1st Ave.
Madison
1st St.
America West Arena
Jackson
3rd St.
Bank One Ballpark
5th St.
7th St.
E. Jackson St.
7th Ave.
Union Station Amtrak
Jefferson
Buchanan

SOUTHWEST

Budget Inn Motel, 424 W. Van Buren St. (☎257-8331), near the junction of 4th Ave. and Van Buren. Downtown location with newly remodeled rooms. Singles $40; doubles $42.

Phoenix Destiny RV Resorts (☎623-853-0537), 11 mi. west of Phoenix on Citrus Rd. Take I-10 to Exit 124; head ¾ mi. south to Van Buren St., then 1 mi. west to Citrus Rd. An RV paradise with shuffleboard and a fitness center. 284 sites, pool, and jacuzzi. RV sites with hook-up $28. Tent sites $21.

FOOD

Aside from food courts in malls, it's difficult to find several restaurants together amid Phoenix's expanse. Downtowners feed mainly at small coffeehouses, most of which close on weekends. Heavily touristed places tend to be pricey, but hidden jewels can be found. **McDowell** or **Camelback Rd.** offer a (small) variety of Asian restaurants. The **Arizona Center,** an open-air shopping gallery at 3rd St. and Van Buren, boasts food venues, fountains, and palm trees. Pricey sports bar and grilles hover around the America West Arena and Bank One Ballpark. Tempe (along Mill Ave.) brims with college-friendly restaurants and moderately priced menus. The *New Times* gives extensive restaurant recommendations (☎271-4000).

La Tolteca, 1205 E. Van Buren St. (☎253-1511). A local favorite, this unassuming cafeteria-style restaurant/Mexican grocery serves up uncommercialized Mexican fare in huge portions. Familiar dishes with refreshing authenticity are offered alongside specialities like cocido soup ($5) and refreshing horchata ($1-2), a sweet milk and rice drink. Big burritos $3-4, dinner plates $5-6. Open daily 6:30am-9pm.

Gourmet House of Hong Kong, 1438 E. McDowell Rd. (☎253-4859). For those who think that quality Chinese food vanishes between the Mississippi and the West Coast, this decor-free, little fortune of a cookie will impress. 40 varieties of soup, innumerable noodle dishes, and rare Hong Kong specialities (such as chicken feet) are unceremoniously dished up. Entrees $5-7. Lunch specials $3-5. Open Su-Th 11am-9:30pm, F-Sa 11am-10:30pm.

Los Dos Molinos, 8646 S. Central Ave. (☎243-9113). Live music at lunch and dinner, a huge menu, and lemonade in jelly jars. Enchiladas $3, burritos $4-7. Open Tu-F 11am-3pm and 5-9pm, Sa 11am-9pm.

5 & Diner, 5220 N. 16th St. (☎264-5220). 24hr. service and all the sock-hop music that one can stand. Vinyl booths, smiley service, and the menu are as good a history lesson as a museum. Burgers $4, sandwiches $5-7. Outdoor seating with view of scenic N. 16th St. available.

SIGHTS

DOWNTOWN. Downtown Phoenix offers a few museums and mounting evidence of America's growing consumer culture. The price of most downtown attractions hovers around $7; fortunately, the majority are worth it. The **Heard Museum** is renowned for its presentation of ancient Native American art, and also features exhibits focusing on contemporary Native Americans. There are many interactive and traveling exhibits and some for kids. The museum occasionally sponsors lectures and Native American dances. *(2301 N. Central Ave., 4 blocks north of McDowell Rd. ☎252-8840; recorded info ☎252-8848. Open daily 9:30am-5pm. Free tours at noon, 1:30, and 3pm. $7, seniors $6, ages 4-12 $3.)* Three blocks south, the **Phoenix Art Museum** exhibits art of the American West, including paintings from the Taos and Santa Fe art colonies. There's also impressive collections of abstracts, 19th-century European, and American works. *(1625 N. Central Ave. at McDowell Rd. ☎257-1222. Open Tu-Su 10am-5pm, Th 10am-9pm; closed M. $7, students and seniors $5, ages 6-18 $2. Free on Th.)* The **Arizona Science Center** offers interactive science exhibits along with an IMAX theater and a planetarium. *(600 E. Washington St. ☎716-2000. Open daily 10am-5pm. $8, seniors and ages 4-12 $6. IMAX or planetarium ticket $3 extra.)* Neighboring the Science Center is the **Phoenix Museum of History,** a small tribute to the historical maturation of this "new American city." *(105 N. 5th St. ☎253-2734. Open M-Sa 10am-5pm, Su noon-5pm. $5, seniors and students $3.50, children under 12 $2.50.)*

PAPAGO PARK AND FATHER EAST. The **Desert Botanical Garden,** in Papago Park, 5 mi. east of downtown, grows a colorful collection of cacti and other desert plants. *(1201 N. Galvin Pkwy. ☎941-1217, recorded info ☎481-8134. Open daily May-Sept. 7am-8pm; Oct.-Apr. 8am-8pm. $7, seniors $6, ages 5-12 $1.)* Take bus #3 east to **Papago Park,** on the eastern outskirts of the city. The park with wildlife-rich expanses has spectacular views of the desert along its hiking, biking, and driving trails. If you spot an orangutan strolling around the cacti, it's either a mirage or you're in the **Phoenix Zoo,** located within the park and boasting a formidable collection of South American, African, and Southwestern critters. *(455 N. Galvin Pkwy. ☎273-1341. Open daily mid-Sept. to Apr. 9am-5pm; mid-May to mid-Sept. 7:30am-4pm. $8.50, seniors $7.50, ages 3-5 $1.50.)* Don't pull any fire alarms at the **Hall of Flame Museum of Firefighting,** also in Papago Park, featuring antique fire engines and other fire-fighting equipment. *(6101 E. Van Buren St. ☎275-3473. Open M-Sa 9am-5pm, Su noon-4pm. $5, ages 6-17 $3, ages 3-5 $1.50.)* Still farther east of the city, past Tempe in Mesa, flows the **Salt River,** one of the last remaining desert rivers in the US. Salt River Recreation arranges tubing trips, even for ice-chests. *(☎984-3305. Open daily May-Sept. 9am-4pm. Tube rental $9.)*

FRANK LLOYD WRIGHT ATTRACTIONS. In nearby Scottsdale, **Taliesin West** served as the architectural studio and residence of Frank Lloyd Wright in his later years. *(Corner of Frank Lloyd Wright Blvd. and Cactus St. ☎860-8810 or 860-2700. Open daily June-Sept. 9am-4pm. 1hr. and 1½hr. guided tours required. $10-14, students and seniors $8-12, children $3-8.)* The beautifully designed studio seems to blend naturally into the surrounding desert. Wright also designed the **Arizona Biltmore** hotel. *(24th St. and Missouri. ☎955-6600.)* One of the last buildings designed by Wright, the **Gammage Memorial Auditorium,** wears the pink-and-beige earth tones of the surrounding environment. *(Mill Ave. and Apache Blvd. on the Arizona State University campus in Tempe. ☎965-3434. Take bus #60, or #22 on weekends. 20min. tours daily in winter.)*

🎭🎵 NIGHTLIFE AND ENTERTAINMENT

The free *New Times Weekly,* available on local magazine racks, lists club schedules for Phoenix's after-hours scene. The *Cultural Calendar of Events* covers area entertainment in three-month intervals. **Char's Has the Blues,** 4631 N. 7th Ave., houses dozens of wanna-be John Lee Hookers, so the music is pretty good. *(☎230-0205. Doors open 7pm. Cover F-Sa $6.)* **Phoenix Live,** 455 N. 3rd St., at the Arizona Center, quakes the complex, with three bars and a restaurant. *(☎252-2112. $5 weekend cover buys access to it all.)* For a more mellow evening, **The Willow House,** 149 W. McDowell Rd., a self-proclaimed "artist's cove," combines the best aspects of chic coffee house, New York deli, and quirky musicians' hangout in a colorful little house with a small theater beside it. *(☎252-0272. Open M-Th 7am-midnight, F 7am-1am, Sa 8am-1am, Su 8am-midnight. Live music Th-Sa starting at 8pm.)*

The Western Front, found in bars and clubs, covers gay and lesbian nightlife. **Ain't Nobody's Biz,** 3031 E. Indian School Rd., #7, is a large lesbian bar with Th beer busts. *(☎224-9977. Open M-F 4pm-1am, Sa-Sun 2pm-1am. $2 pitchers 9pm-midnight.)* **Roscoe's,** 4531 N. 7th St., a gay sports pub, has pool and dart tournaments. *(☎285-0833. Open M-Sa 3pm-1am, Su 11am-1am. Happy hour M-Sa 3-7pm.)*

Phoenix also offers many options for the sports lover. NBA basketball action rises with the **Phoenix Suns** *(☎379-7867),* at the **America West Arena,** while the **Arizona Cardinals** *(☎379-0101)* provide American football excitement. In the summer, the women's basketball team **Phoenix Mercury** takes it to the hoop at the America West Arena. The newest addition to the Phoenix sports family are the **Arizona Diamondbacks** *(☎514-8400),* the Major League baseball team that arrived on the scene in 1998. Their home, the new **Bank One Ballpark,** neighbors the America West arena and is an architectural wonder, complete with a retractable roof, an outfield swimming pool, and "beer gardens." Baseball fever, fueled by low ticket prices and the exciting stadium, is sweeping Phoenix. *(☎462-6799. Tickets start at $4. Tours of the stadium are offered throughout the year and proceeds benefit local charities.)*

SCENIC DRIVE: APACHE TRAIL

Steep, gray, and haunting, the **Superstition Mountains** derive their name from Pima Native American legends. Although the Native Americans were kicked out by the Anglo gold prospectors who settled the region, the curse stayed. In the 1840s, a Mexican explorer found gold in these hills, but was killed before he could reveal the location of the mine. More famous is the case of Jacob Waltz, known as "Dutchman" despite having come from Germany. During the 1880s, he brought out about $250,000 worth of high-quality gold ore from somewhere in the mountains. Upon his death in 1891, he left only a few clues to the whereabouts of the mine. Strangely, many who have come looking for it have died violent deaths—one prospector burned to death in his own campfire, while another was found decapitated in an arroyo. Needless to say, the mine has never been found.

Rte. 88, a.k.a. **Apache Trail,** winds from **Apache Junction,** a small mining town 40 mi. east of Phoenix, through the mountains. Although the road is only about 50 mi. long, it's only partially paved; trips require at least 3-4hr. behind the wheel. The carless can leave the driving to **Apache Trail Tours,** which offers on- and off-road Jeep tours. (☎480-982-7661. 2-4hr. tours. $60 per person. Reserve at least a day in advance.) For more info, head to the **Apache Junction Chamber of Commerce,** 112 E. 2nd Ave. (☎480-982-3141. Open M-F 8am-5pm.)

The scenery is the Trail's greatest attraction; the dramatic views of the arid landscape make it one of the most beautiful driving routes in the nation. The deep blue waters of the man-made **Lake Canyon, Lake Apache,** and **Lake Roosevelt** contrast sharply with the red and beige-hued rock formations surrounding them. **Goldfield Ghost Town Mine Tours,** 5 mi. north of the U.S. 60 junction on Rte. 88, offers tours of the nearby mines and gold-panning in a resurrected ghost town. (☎480-983-0333. Open daily 10am-5pm. Mine tours $5, ages 6-12 $3; gold-panning $4.) "Where the hell am I?" said Jacob Waltz when he came upon **Lost Dutchman State Park,** 1 mi. farther north on Rte. 88. At the base of the Superstitions, the park offers nature trails, picnic sites, and campsites with showers but no hook-ups. (☎480-982-4485. Entrance $5 per vehicle; first come, first served sites $10.) Grab a saddle for a barstool at **Tortilla Flat,** another refurbished ghost town 18 mi. farther on Rte. 88. The town keeps its spirits up and tourists nourished with a restaurant, ice cream shop, and saloon. (☎480-984-1776. Restaurant open M-F 9am-6pm, Sa-Su 8am-7pm.) **Tonto National Monument,** 5 mi. east of Lake Roosevelt on Rte. 88, preserves 800-year-old masonry and pueblo ruins built by Ancestral Puebloans. (Open daily 8am-4pm. $4 per car.) **Tonto National Forest** offers nearby camping (☎602-225-5200; sites $4-11). The trail ends at the **Theodore Roosevelt Dam** (completed in 1911), the last dam constructed by hand in the US. For those who complete the Trail, Rte. 60 is a scenic trip back to Phoenix; the increased moisture and decreased temperatures of the higher elevations give rise to lush greenery (by southern Arizona standards).

TUCSON   ☎ 520

A little bit country, a little bit rock 'n' roll, Tucson is a city that carries its own tune. Emerging from the shadow of its neighbor to the north, Phoenix, Tucson blends a spunky university, an artsy downtown, urbane foothills, and cacti-ed surroundings seamlessly. Mexican property until the Gaddsen Purchase, the city retains many of its south-of-the-border influences. And with arguably better tourist attractions than any other Southwestern city, Tucson offers the conveniences of a metropolis without the nasty aftertaste.

▐ GETTING THERE AND GETTING AROUND

Airport: Tucson International (☎573-8000), on Valencia Rd., south of downtown. Bus #25 runs every hr. to the Laos Transit Center; from there, bus #16 goes downtown. **Arizona Stagecoach** (☎889-1000) goes downtown for around $13. Runs 24hr. Reservations recommended.

SOUTHWEST

Downtown Tucson

⚓ ACCOMMODATIONS
Hotel Congress and Hostel, **10**
La Siesta Hotel, **14**
Roadrunner Hostel, **9**

🍴 FOOD
El Charro Cafe, **13**
India Oven, **2**
Little Café Poca Cosa, **11**
Maya Quetzal, **6**
Time Market, **1**

♪ NIGHTLIFE
3rd Stone, **4**
Bar Toma, **12**
Gotham, **15**
IBT's, **5**
New West, **16**
O'Malley's, **3**
The Rock, **8**

● SERVICES
Fairwheels Bicycles, **7**

Park Ave.
Tyndall Ave.
Euclid Ave.
1st Ave.
2nd Ave.
3rd Ave.
4th Ave.
5th Ave.
6th Ave.
7th Ave.
Stone Ave.
9th Ave.
2nd St.
3rd St.
4th St.
5th St.
6th St.
7th St.
8th St.
9th St.
10th St.
Broadway Blvd.

Catalina Park

Stevens Ave.
Toole Ave.
Amtrak
Greyhound
Congress St.
Jackson St.
Ochoa St.
Church Ave.
Stone Ave.
Pennington St.
Armory Park
12th St.
Granada Ave.

Court Ave.
Council St.
Washington St.
Meyer Ave.
Franklin St.
Alameda St.
El Presidio Park
Tucson Museum of Art

TO SAGUARO NATIONAL PARK (12 mi), ARIZONA-SONORA DESERT MUSEUM (15 mi), (1.2 mi)
Granada Ave.

TO **16**, **15** (10 mi)

200 yards / 200 meters

N

Trains: Amtrak, 400 E. Toole Ave. (☎623-4442), at 5th Ave., 1 block north of the Greyhound station. To: Los Angeles (9hr., 3 per week, $38-104). Open Sa-M 6:15am-1:45pm and 4:15-11:30pm, Tu-W 6:15am-1:45pm, Th-F 4:15-11:30pm.

Buses: Greyhound, 2 S. 4th Ave. (☎882-4386), between Congress St. and Broadway. To: Phoenix (2hr., 16 per day, $14); Los Angeles (9-10hr., 4 per day, $38); Albuquerque (12-14hr., 5 per day, $77); and El Paso (6hr., 12 per day, $35). Open 24hr.

Taxis: Yellow Cab, ☎624-6611. 24hr.

Public Transit: Sun-Tran (☎792-9222). Buses run from the Ronstadt terminal downtown at Congress and 6th St. Service roughly M-F 5:30am-10pm, Sa-Su 8am-7pm; times vary by route. Fare 85¢, under 19 60¢, seniors and disabled 35¢. Day pass $2.

Car Rental: AAA Tucson Auto Rental, 3150 E. Grant Rd. (☎320-1495). Rates start at $17 per day. Under 21 surcharge $10 per day. Credit card deposit preferred, cash deposit accepted for local rentals. Open M-F 8am-6pm, Sa 8am-4pm.

Bike Rental: Fairwheels Bicycles, 1110 E. 6th St. (☎884-9018), at Freemont. $20 first day, $10 per additional day. Credit card deposit. Open M-F 9am-6pm, Sa 9am-5:30pm, Su noon-4pm.

▚▐ ORIENTATION AND PRACTICAL INFORMATION

Just east of I-10, Tucson's downtown area surrounds the intersection of **Broadway Blvd.** (which runs west) and **Stone Ave.,** two blocks from the train and bus terminals. The **University of Arizona** lies 1 mi. northeast of downtown at the intersection of **Park** and **Speedway Blvd.** "Avenues" run north-south, "streets" east-west; because some of each are numbered, intersections such as "6th and 6th" are possible. Speedway, Broadway, and **Grant Ave.** are the quickest east-west routes through town. To go north-south, follow **Oracle Rd.** through the heart of the city, **Campbell Ave.** east of downtown, or **Swan Rd.** farther east. The hip, young crowd swings on **4th Ave.** and on **Congress St.,** both with small shops, quirky restaurants, and a slew of bars.

Visitor Info: Tucson Convention and Visitors Bureau, 130 S. Scott Ave. (☎624-1817 or 800-638-8350), near Broadway. Open M-F 8am-5pm, Sa-Su 9am-4pm.

Bi-Gay-Lesbian Organization: Gay, Lesbian, and Bisexual Community Center, 300 E. 6th St. (☎624-1779). Open M-Sa 11am-7pm.

Hotline: Rape Crisis, ☎624-7273. **Suicide Prevention,** ☎323-9373. Both 24hr.

Internet Access: Free access at the **University of Arizona main library,** 1510 E. University Blvd. Open M-Th 7:30am-1am, F 7:30am-9pm, Sa 10am-9pm, Su 11am-1am.

Post Office: General delivery: 1501 S. Cherry Bell (☎388-5129). Open M-F 8:30am-8pm, Sa 9am-1pm. **ZIP code:** 85726. **Area code:** 520.

▐ ACCOMMODATIONS

There's a direct correlation between the temperature in Tuscon and the warmth of its lodging industry toward budget travelers: expect the best deals in summer. Rain-cooled evenings and summer bargains are strong consolation for the mid-day scorch. A home away from home, the ▓**Roadrunner Hostel,** 346 E. 12th St., wows guests with unparalleled amenities such as a giant 52 in. TV, a formidable movie collection, free high-speed Internet access, purified water, free soup, and A/C. Located in a pleasant house a few blocks from downtown, the hostel also is exceptionally clean and friendly. (☎628-4709. Free linen, towels, lockers, and laundry soap. Kitchen and laundry. Dorms $14, non-members $16; private doubles $30/$35.) The swank old **Hotel Congress and Hostel,** 311 E. Congress, conveniently located across from the bus and train stations, offers superb lodging to night-owl hostelers. Club Congress, downstairs, booms until 1am on weekends, making it rough on early birds. Private rooms come with bath, phone, vintage radio, and ceiling fans. The cafe downstairs serves great salads and omelettes. (☎622-8848. Dorms $15 per person. Singles $29; doubles $32-42; 10% discount for students and artists.) Located between the university and downtown, the **University Inn,** 950 N. Stone Ave., has clean rooms with A/C, cable TV, telephones, and pool access. (☎791-7503 or 800-233-8466. Singles from $32; doubles $37.)

Mt. Lemmon Recreation Area, in the **Coronado National Forest,** offers beautiful camp sites. Campgrounds lie away from Tucson via the **Catalina Hwy. Rose Canyon,** 33 mi. northeast of Tucson, at 7000 ft., are wooded and cool, and have a small lake. Sites ($15) at higher elevations fill quickly on summer weekends. The **National Forest Service,** 300 W. Congress Ave., has more info (☎670-4552; open M-F 8am-4:30pm).

🍴 FOOD

Good, cheap Mexican restaurants are everywhere. **Little Cafe Poca Cosa,** 20 S. Scott Ave., the less expensive *niño* of the Cafe Poca Cosa on Broadway, prides itself on fresh ingredients and an ever-changing menu—patrons often walk in and say "give me something good." (Open M-F 7:30am-2:30pm. Lunch specials $5.75. Cash only.) On chic 4th Ave., **La Indita,** 622 N. 4th Ave, delights customers with traditional Mexican cuisine served on tasty tortillas. (☎792-0523. Open M-Th 11am-9pm, F 11am-6pm, Sa 6-9pm, Su 9am-9pm.) When you've had it with Mexican food, **India Oven,** 2727 N. Campbell Ave., between Grant and Glenn, offers relief. The garlic *naan* ($2.35) is exquisite. (☎326-8635. Open daily 11am-10pm. Vegetarian dishes $6-7; tandoori meats and curries $6-9.) The $1.75 pizza slices at **Time Market,** 444 E. University Blvd., are enhanced by gourmet toppings like piñon nuts, shrimp, and smoked gouda (open daily 7:30am-10pm). A hole-in-the-wall, **Maya Quetzal,** 429 N. 4th Ave., serves authentic Guatemalan food at rock-bottom prices. The veggie or meat *empanadas* ($4) and the $3 veggie *taquitos* are good choices. (☎622-8207. Open M-Th 11:30am-11:30pm, F 11:30am-9:30pm, Sa noon-9:30pm.)

👁 SIGHTS

UNIVERSITY OF ARIZONA. Lined with cafes, restaurants, galleries, and vintage clothing shops, **4th Ave.** is an alternative magnet and a great place to take a stroll. Between Speedway and Broadway Blvd., the street becomes a historic shopping district with increasingly touristy shops. Lovely for its varied and elaborately irrigated vegetation, the **University of Arizona's** mall sits where E. 3rd St. should be, just east of 4th Ave. The **Center for Creative Photography,** on campus, houses various exhibits, including the archives of Ansel Adams and Richard Avedon. (☎621-7968. Open M-F 9am-5pm, Sa-Su noon-5pm. Free.) The **Flandrau Science Center,** on Cherry Ave. at the campus mall, dazzles with a public observatory, a laser light show, and interactive exhibits. (☎621-7827. Open M-Sa 9am-5pm, Su noon-5pm, W-Sa also 7-9pm. $3, under 14 $2. Shows $5/$4, seniors and students $4.50.)

TUSCON MUSEUM OF ART. This major attraction presents impressive traveling exhibits in all media, in addition to its permanent collection of varied American art. (140 N. Main Ave. ☎624-2333. Open Tu-Sa 10am-4pm, Su noon-4pm. $2, students and seniors $1, children free; free Su.)

DOWN SPEEDWAY. A museum, zoo, and nature preserve rolled into one, the **Arizona-Sonora Desert Museum** is an enchanting spectacle. The living museum recreates a range of desert habitats and features over 300 kinds of animals. A proper visit requires at least 2hr., preferably during the cool morning hours before the animals take their afternoon siestas. (2021 N. Kinney Rd. ☎883-2702. Follow Speedway Blvd. west of the city as it becomes Gates Pass Rd., then Kinney Rd. Open Mar.-Sept. Su-F 7:30am-6pm, Sa 7:30am-10pm; Oct.-Feb. daily 8:30am-5pm. $9, Nov.-Apr. $10; ages 6-12 $1.75.) West of Tucson via Speedway Blvd., the **International Wildlife Museum** is wild but lifeless—the creatures were stuffed long ago. (4800 W. Gates Pass Rd. ☎617-1439. Open M-F 9am-5pm, Sa-Su 9am-6pm, last entrance at 4:15pm. $7, seniors $5.50, ages 6-12 $2.50.)

SAGUARO NATIONAL PARK. North of the desert museum, the western half (Tucson Mountain District) of Saguaro National Park has limited hiking trails and an auto loop. The paved nature walk near the **visitors center** passes some of the best specimens of Saguaro cactus in the Tucson area. (☎733-5158. Park open 24hr, autoloop 7am-sunset. Visitors center: open daily 8:30am-5pm.) The towering cacti take decades to reach maturity, and don't start sprouting their trademark raised arms until around age 75. **Gates Pass,** on the way to the Tucson Mountain District and the Desert Museum, is an excellent spot for watching the rising and setting sun. **Saguaro National Park East,** a.k.a. Rincon Mountain District, lies east of the city on Old Spanish Trail; take I-10 E to Exit 279 and follow Vail Rd. to Old Spanish Trail. (☎733-5153. Visitors center open daily 8:30am-5pm. $4 per vehicle, $2 per pedestrian.) Within the park, 128 mi. of trails and an 8 mi. scenic drive lead through the cactus forest. Before noon, the visitors center has free permits for **backcountry camping.**

CAVES. Caves are all the rage in Tuscon. The recently opened **Kartchner Caverns State Park,** located 8 mi. off I-10 at Exit 302, is enormously popular, filled with magnificent rock formations and home to over 1000 bats. Taking a tour is the only way to enter the cave. (☎586-4100. Open daily 7:30am-6pm. 1hr. tours run every 30min. 8:30am-4:30pm. Entrance fee $10 per vehicle, tour $14, ages 7-13 $6. Reservations strongly recommended.) Located near Saguaro National Park East, **Colossal Cave** is one of the only dormant (no water or new stala(ct/gm)ites) caves in the US. (☎647-7275. Open mid-Mar. to mid-Sept. M-Sa 8am-6pm, Su 8am-7pm; mid-Sept. to mid-Mar. M-Sa 9am-5pm, Su 9am-6pm. $7, ages 6-12 $4.)

PIMA AIR AND SPACE MUSEUM. This impressive museum follows aviation history from the days of the Wright brothers to its modern military incarnations. Exhibits on female and African-American aviators are particularly interesting. (☎574-0462. Open M-F 7am-3pm, Sa-Su 7am-5pm; off-season daily 9am-5pm. $7.50, seniors $6.50.) Tours of the **Davis-Monthan Air Force Base** are offered at the museum. (5 tours per day M-F. $5, ages 6-12 $3.)

♫ 🎭 ENTERTAINMENT AND NIGHTLIFE

The free *Tucson Weekly* is the local authority on nightlife, while the weekend sections of the *Star* or the *Citizen* also provide good coverage. Throughout the year, the city of the sun presents **Music Under the Stars,** a series of sunset concerts performed by the **Tucson Symphony Orchestra** (☎792-9155). **Downtown Saturday Nights,** on the first and 3rd Sa of each month, Congress St. is blockaded for a celebration of the arts with outdoor singers, crafts, and galleries. Every Th, the **Thursday Night Art Walk** lets you mosey through downtown galleries and studios. The **Tucson Arts District** has more info (☎624-9977).

UA students rock and roll on **Speedway Blvd.,** while other folks do the two-step in country music clubs on **N. Oracle. Club Congress,** 311 E. Congress St., has DJs during the week and live bands on weekends. The friendly hotel staff and a cast of regulars make it an especially good time. M is 80s night with 80¢ drinks. (☎622-8848. Open daily 9pm-1am. Cover $4) **Rhino Pub,** 1112 E. 6th St. (☎903-9039), caters to a college crowd. For a quiet drink, **Bar Toma,** 311 N. Cart Ave., offers a wide selection of tequilas. (☎622-5465. Open Su-Th 5-9pm, F-Sa 5-10pm.) **El Parador,** 2744 E. Broadway Blvd. (☎881-2808), attracts all ages with Latin music and Salsa dancing. Young locals hang out on **4th Ave.** at night; most bars have live music and low cover charges. **O'Malley's,** 247 N. 4th Ave., is a good spot with decent bar food, pool tables, and pinball. (☎623-8600. Open daily 11am-1am. Cover Th-Sa varies.) Despite its name, **New West,** 4385 W. Ina Rd., is an authentic Old West saloon playing continuous country-western music on the largest dance floor in Arizona (6000 sq. ft.). The newly-renovated club offers $2 beers and occasional two-stepping lessons. (☎744-7744. Open Tu-Th 8pm-2am, Th-Sa 7pm-2am. Cover $4, 7-11pm $2.) On the same grounds, **Gotham** throbs to a heavy urban beat. (Open Tu 7pm-2am, Th 9pm-2am, F-Sa 7pm-2am. Cover $4, ages 18-20 $6, Tu and Th 7-11pm $2.) **IBT's,** on 4th Ave. at 6th St., leads the gay scene. (☎882-3053. Open daily 9am-1am.)

DAYTRIPS FROM TUCSON

BIOSPHERE 2. Ninety-one ft. high, with an area of more than three acres, Biosphere 2 is sealed off from Earth—"Biosphere 1"—by 500 tons of stainless steel. In 1991, eight research scientists locked themselves inside this giant greenhouse to cultivate their own food and knit their own socks as they monitored the behavior of five man-made ecosystems: savanna, rainforest, marsh, ocean, and desert. After 2 years, they began having oxygen problems and difficulty with food production. No one lives in Biosphere 2 now, but it's still used as a research facility. The Biosphere is 30min. north of Tucson; take I-10 west to the "Miracle Mile" exit, follow the miracles to Oracle Rd., then travel north until it becomes Rte. 77 N. From Phoenix, take I-10 to Exit 185, follow Rte. 387 to Rte. 79 (Florence Hwy.), and proceed to Oracle Junction and Rte. 77. Guided 2hr. tours. include two short films, a walk through the laboratory's research and development models for the Biosphere 2 ecosystems, and a stroll around Biosphere 2 itself, including the crew's living quarters. Walking around unchaperoned is also permitted. *(Tours daily 9am-4:30pm; grounds open 8:30am-5:30pm; last admission at 5pm. $13, seniors and students $11.50, ages 13-17 $9, ages 6-12 $6.)* **Area code:** 520.

SABINO CANYON. North of Tucson, the cliffs and desert pools of **Sabino Canyon** provide an ideal backdrop for picnics and day hikes. Locals beat the Tucson heat by frolicking in the water holes during the summer. No cars are permitted in the canyon, but a **tram** makes trips through it. *(☎ 749-2861. Runs every hr. 9am-4pm, Dec.-June every 30min. $6, ages 3-12 $2.)* Biking within the park is only permitted before 9am, after 5pm, and never on W or Sa. The National Forest's **visitors center** lies at the canyon's entrance. *(☎ 749-8700. Open M-F 8am-4:30pm, Sa-Su 8:30am-4:30pm.)* Sabino is located northeast of downtown; take Speedway Blvd. to Swan Rd. to Sunrise Dr. The entrance is at the cross of Sunrise Dr. and Sabino Canyon Rd. **Area code:** 520.

SCENIC DRIVE: MT. LEMMON DRIVE

Climbing to 9157 ft. above sea level, the Mt. Lemmon Drive is a virtual transnational trip from the deserts of Mexico to the conifer forests of Canada. Along the ascent, drivers are witness to a breathtaking metamorphosis of terrain. *Road construction will plague the Mt. Lemmon Drive until Sept. 2001. Road closures and delays are frequent. Call ☎ 520-751-9405 for current info.*

The 50 mi. round-trip drive begins northwest of downtown Tucson along the **Catalina Hwy.,** off Tanque Verde Rd. Venturing into the **Coronado National Forest,** the road passes rolling hills of Sonoran desert scrub, Saguaro cacti, and mesquite trees. Past the Molino Canyon Vista point, a NFS entrance station collects fees. There is no charge to drive, but if you plan on hiking any of the numerous trails or picnic grounds that line the road, a $5 day-use permit must be purchased. Beyond the entrance station, the road continues to climb on its way through five different life zones. Desert lowland gives way to semi-desert grassland and oak forests which change into mixed pine and oak woodlands at about 6000 ft. **Windy Point,** true to its name, provides views of Tucson, the **Patagonia Mountains,** and on clear days, the **Sierra de San Antonio** of Mexico. Located just before Mi. 20, the **Palisades Visitor Center** offers restrooms, brochures, and ranger advice. From there, the vegetation continues to morph into a ponderosa pine forest, as the road climbs to over 8000 ft. The final life zone is the mixed conifer forest with temperatures that are on average 20°F cooler than Tucson. At Mi. 25, the drive meets the access road for the **Mt. Lemmon Ski Valley** (☎ 520-576-1321). The climax of the drive is the small village of Summerhaven, whose surroundings look more like the Rockies than southern Arizona.

TOMBSTONE ☎ 520

Founded in the wake of the gold and silver rush of the 1870s, Tombstone—home to more than 3000 prostitutes and 100 saloons—was once the largest city between St. Louis and San Francisco. But water gradually seeped into the mines that were the city's lifeline. When the equipment installed to pump it out failed in 1909, the mines were inundated and they remain flooded to this day. In recent years, "the town too tough to die" has lived up to its title. Tourism now keeps the old blood pumping.

⚠ PRACTICAL INFORMATION. To get to Tombstone, head to the Benson exit off I-10, then go south on Rte. 80. The nearest **Greyhound** station is in **Benson,** 6080 W. 4th St. (☎586-3141), at the Benson Flower Shop. **Amtrak** is across the street. **Douglas Shuttle** (☎364-9442) has $15 service from Tucson to Tombstone, $5 from Tombstone to Bisbee. **Visitor Info: Tombstone Visitors Center.** (☎457-3929. Open M-Tu and Th-F 9am-4pm, W and Sa-Su 10am-4pm.) **Area code:** 520.

⚠ ACCOMMODATIONS AND FOOD. The **Larian Motel,** on the corner of Fremont and 5th, is clean, nicely furnished, and within easy walking distance of all sights. (☎457-2272. Singles $39-42; doubles $45-55.) The rooms at the **Tombstone Motel,** across the street, are basic and woody, but clean. (☎457-3478 or 888-455-3478. Singles $39-42; doubles $55.)

Blake's Char-Broiled Burgers and BBQ Ranch, 511B Allen St., slaps the cow on the bun for as little as $4.25 (☎457-3646; open daily 11am-4pm). **Don Teodoro's,** 15 N. 4th St., serves Mexican plates accompanied by live guitar music for under $6. (☎457-3647. Open Su-Th 11am-9pm, F-Sa 11am-10pm. Live music W-M 6-9pm.) For a bit of moonshine and country music, smell your way to **Big Nose Kate's Saloon,** on Allen St., named for "the girl who loved Doc Holliday and everyone else too." Bartenders serve drinks like "Sex in the Desert." (☎457-3107. Open daily 10am-midnight.)

⚠ SIGHTS. By inviting visitors to view the barnyard where Wyatt Earp and his brothers kicked some serious butt, Tombstone has turned the **shootout at the O.K. Corral,** on Allen St. next to City Park, into a year-round tourist industry. (☎457-3456. Open daily 9am-5pm. $2.50.) The **Boothill Gunslingers,** the **Wild Bunch,** and the **Vigilantes/Vigilettes** perform re-enactments of famous gunfights (2nd and 4th Su of the month at 1pm; $2.50, ages 6-12 $1.50). The **Hanging Chairman** can treat a friend or relative to a **public mock hanging** by one of these groups (☎457-3434). The voice of Vincent Price narrates the town's history next door to the O.K. Corral in the **Tombstone Historama,** while a plastic mountain revolves onstage and a dramatization of the gunfight is shown on a movie screen. (☎457-3456. Shows daily on the hr. 9am-4pm. $2.50.) Site of the longest poker game in western history (8 years, 5 months, and 3 days), the **Bird Cage Theater,** at 6th and Allen, was named for the compartments suspended from the ceiling that once housed prostitutes. (☎457-3421. Open daily 9am-6pm.) John Slaughter battled outlaws at the **Tombstone Courthouse,** at 3rd and Toughnut St. The courthouse is now a museum housing extremely diverse exhibits related to the town's history. (☎457-3311. Open daily 8am-5pm. $2.50, ages 7-13 $1.) The **tombstones** of Tombstone, largely the result of all that gunplay, stand on Rte. 80 just north of town (open daily 7:30am-6pm; free). For something completely different, the **Rose Tree Museum,** at 4th and Toughnut St., shelters the largest rose tree in the world. (☎457-3326. Open daily 9am-5pm. $2, under 14 free.)

BISBEE   ☎520

One hundred mi. southeast of Tucson and 20 mi. south of Tombstone, mellow Bisbee, a former mining town, is known throughout the Southwest as a chic but laid-back artists' colony. Visitors revel in the town's proximity to Mexico, picture-perfect weather, and excellent, relatively inexpensive accommodations. The few sights in town are mine-related, but Bisbee is a terrific place to stroll, window-shop, and drink coffee in a cute cafe. **Queen Mines,** on the Rte. 80 interchange entering Old Bisbee, ceased mining in 1943 but continues to give educational 1¼hr. tours. (☎432-2071. Tours at 9, 10:30am, noon, 2, and 3:30pm. $10, ages 7-15 $3.50, ages 3-6 $2.) The Smithsonian-affiliated **Mining and Historical Museum,** 5 Copper Queen, highlights the discovery of Bisbee's copper surplus and the lives of the fortune-seekers who extracted this resource. (☎432-7071. Open daily 10am-4pm. $4, seniors $3.50, under 16 free.)

Located in the heart of downtown, the **Red Metal Miner's Hostel,** 59B Subway St., offers guests comfortable rooms, amenities, and peace of mind—proceeds from the hostel help fund local children's programs. (☎432-6671. Kitchen privileges, free

Internet access, cable TV and bike rentals. Dorms $16; private rooms $40.) At the intersection of Douglas Rd. and Rte. 80, 1½ mi. from downtown, the **Shady Dell** (☎432-3567), squares guests away in restored vintage trailers, each decorated in a different motif. Trailers range from the 1954 Crown ($35) to the luxurious Royal Mansion ($70). About a 10min. walk from downtown, the **Jonquil Inn,** 317 Tomb-stone Canyon, offers clean and smoke-free rooms. (☎432-7371. Singles $40-45; dou-bles $50-60; in winter about $10 higher.) A number of cheap eateries line the main drags of downtown. **El Zarape Cafe,** 46 Main St., cooks up tasty Mexican entrees for under $6 and sandwiches starting at $2. (☎432-5031. Open M, W, and F 8am-6:45pm; Tu, Th, and Sa 8am-2:45pm.) **Chamber of Commerce:** 31 Subway St. (☎432-5421. Open M-F 9am-5pm, Sa-Su 10am-4pm.)

NEAR BISBEE: CHIRICAHUA NATIONAL MONUMENT

Over 25 million years ago Chiricahua was a thick heap of volcanic ash extruded from the nearby Turkey Creek Cauldera. Fortunately, since then the never-to-be-underestimated powers of erosion have sculpted the hardened rock into spectacular rock formations with forboding mountains in the back-ground. A cross between Zion and Bryce Canyon, Chiricahua was aptly called the "Land of the Standing-Up Rocks" by Apaches and the "Wonderland of Rocks" by pioneers. And while Chiricahua nearly equals the natural splendor of Bryce and Zion, it happily falls short of their popularity, indulging in peace and tranquility.

Chiricahua is located 40 mi. off I-10; take Rte. 186 from Willcox. The monument is 70 mi. from Bisbee; take Rte. 80 E to Rte. 191 N to 181 N. The **visitors center** is located just beyond the entrance station. (☎824-3560, ext. 104. Open daily 8am-5:30pm. Entrance fee $6 per vehicle.) The park offers many day hikes, but overnight backcountry camping is not permitted. Handy hiking maps are 25¢. The **Bonita Creek Campground** within the park offers 24 sites with toilets and running water, but no showers (sites $8).

NEW MEXICO

Sometimes overshadowed by its more flamboyant neighbors, New Mexico is nevertheless a dreamscape of varied terrains and peoples. Going back to the days when Spaniards arrived with delusions of golden riches, this expansive land of high deserts, mountain vistas, and roadrunners has always been a place where people come to fulfill their fantasies. Today, most explorers arrive in search of natural beauty, adobe architecture, and cultural treasures rather than gold. It makes sense that New Mexico is a haven for hikers, backpackers, cyclists, mountain-climbers, and skiers. Six national forests within the state pro-vide miles and miles of beautiful and challenging opportunities for lovers of the outdoors, while the Sandía, Mogollon, and Sangre de Cristo mountains fulfill mountain-climbers' upward thrust. And with the mixings of Spanish, Mexican, Native American, and Anglo cultures, New Mexico is as culturally diverse as it is geographically diverse.

◪ PRACTICAL INFORMATION

Capital: Santa Fe.

Visitor Info: New Mexico Dept. of Tourism, 491 Old Santa Fe Trail, Santa Fe 87501 (☎800-545-2040; www.newmexico.org). Open M-F 8am-5pm. **Park and Recreation Division,** 2040 S. Pacheco, Santa Fe 87505 (☎505-827-7173). Open M-F 8am-5pm. **US Forest Service,** 517 Gold Ave. SW, Albuquerque 87102 (☎505-842-3292). Open M-F 8am-4:30pm.

Postal Abbreviation: NM. **Sales Tax:** 6.25%.

SANTA FE ☎505

The 2nd oldest city in the US, Sante Fe glistens with modern sophistication and New World luxuries. Meaning "Holy Faith," the city, with its adobe facades and twisting street alleys, is sometimes referred to as Albuquerque's theme park. With internationally-renowned museums and a vibrant artistic community, however, Sante Fe ain't Disney World. Lying at the convergence of the Santa Fe Trail, an old trading route running from Independence, MO, and El Camino Réal ("Royal Road"), which originates in Mexico City, Santa Fe has always been a place of commerce and cultural interaction. Today is no different, though the people are more diverse and the prices are steeper. Santa Fe's popularity has recently bloomed like a desert flower, giving rise to gated communities, ritzy restaurants and jacked-up prices.

▆ GETTING THERE AND GETTING AROUND

Buses: Greyhound, 858 St. Michael's Dr. (☎471-0008). To: Taos (1½hr., 2 per day, $17); Albuquerque (1½hr., 4 per day, $11.55); and Denver (8-10hr., 4 per day, $59). Open M-F 7am-5:30pm and 7:30-9:45pm, Sa-Su 7-9am, 12:30-1:30pm, 3:30-5pm, and 7:30-9:30pm.

Trains: Amtrak's nearest station is in Lamy (☎466-4511), 18 mi. away on Country Rd. 41. Call ☎982-8829 to shuttle to Santa Fe ($14). Open daily 9am-5pm.

Public Transit: Santa Fe Trails (☎955-2001) runs 6 downtown bus routes (M-F 6am-10pm). Bus #10 leaves every 30min. from the downtown Sheridan Transit Center, 1 block from the plaza between Marcy St. and Palace Ave., and heads to the museums on Camino Lejo. 50¢, ages 6-12 25¢; day pass $1. **Sandia Shuttle Express** (☎474-5696) runs to the Albuquerque airport (10 per day, $20) from downtown hotels. Reserve 2 days in advance. Open M-F 7am-6pm, Sa-Su 7am-5pm.

Car Rental: Enterprise Rent-a-Car, 2641 Cerrillos Rd. (☎473-3600). $37 per day, $169 per week. Must be 21 with major credit card. Open M-F 8am-6pm.

Taxis: Capital City Taxi, ☎438-0000. 24hr.

✴ ⚡ ORIENTATION AND PRACTICAL INFORMATION

Except for the museums southeast of the city center, most upscale restaurants and sights in Santa Fe cluster within a few blocks of the **downtown plaza** and inside the loop formed by the **Paseo de Peralta.** Narrow streets make driving troublesome; park your car and pound the pavement. You'll find **parking lots** behind Santa Fe Village, near Sena Plaza, and one block east of the Federal Courthouse near the plaza, while metered spaces (2hr. maximum) line the streets just south of the plaza. Parking is also available along the streets near the galleries on Canyon Rd.

Visitor Info: Santa Fe Welcome Center, 491 Old Santa Fe Trail (☎875-7400 or 800-545-2040). Open daily 8am-7pm; off-season 8am-5pm. **Santa Fe Convention and Visitors Bureau,** 201 W. Marcy St. (☎800-777-2489). Open M-F 8am-5pm. **Info booth,** in the First National Bank, Lincoln and Palace St. Open mid-May to mid-Oct. 9:30am-4:30pm.

Hotline: Rape Abuse, ☎800-721-7273 or 986-9111. Operates 8am-5pm, on-call 24hr.

Internet Access: Santa Fe Public Library (☎984-6780), at the corner of Lincoln St. and Washington Ave. Open M-Th 10am-9pm, F-Sa 10am-6pm, Su 1pm-5pm.

Post Office: 120 S. Federal Pl. (☎988-6351), next to the courthouse. Open M-F 7:30am-5:45pm, Sa 7:30am-1pm. **ZIP code:** 87501. **Area code:** 505.

▙ ACCOMMODATIONS

Hotels in Santa Fe tend towards the expensive side. As early as May, they become swamped with requests for **Indian Market** (3rd week of Aug.) and **Fiesta de Santa Fe** (2nd weekend of Sept.). Make reservations early or plan to sleep

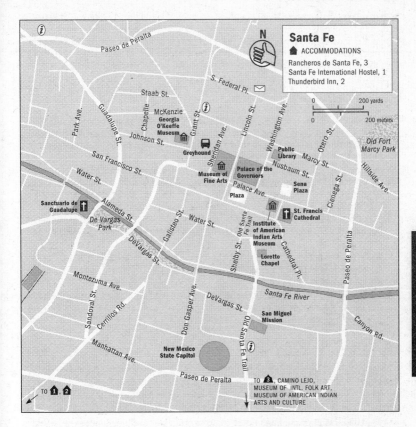

Santa Fe
🏠 ACCOMMODATIONS
Rancheros de Santa Fe, 3
Santa Fe International Hostel, 1
Thunderbird Inn, 2

SOUTHWEST

standing up. At other times, the **Cerrillos Rd.** area has the best prices, but travelers should use caution and evaluate the motel (read: see the room) before checking in. At many of the less expensive motels, bargaining is possible for stays of more than one night.

A car is necessary to camp around Santa Fe. In addition to Rancheros de Santa Fe (see below), there are several campsites run by the **Santa Fe National Forest** (☎438-7840) in the scenic Sangre de Cristo Mountains along Rte. 475. The **Black Canyon Campground**, 7 mi. northeast of Santa Fe, has 43 sites ($8.50). Reserve by calling ☎877-444-6777. Four mi. further, primitive camping (no water) is free at one of **Big Tesuque's** seven sites. (Both open May-Oct. Call the National Forest for info.)

Santa Fe International Hostel and Pension (AAIH), 1412 Cerrillos Rd. (☎988-1153), 1 mi. from the bus station and 2 mi. from the plaza. Busy, but big enough to accommodate the masses. Kitchen, library, and large dorm rooms. Internet access $2 per day. Dorms $14, non-members $15. Linen free. B&B singles $25; doubles $35; with private bath $33/$43; no discount for members. No credit cards. Office open daily 7am-11pm. Chores required.

Thunderbird Inn, 1821 Cerrillos Rd. (☎983-4397). Slightly farther from town than the hostel, but an excellent value (for Santa Fe, anyway). Large, very clean singles $44; doubles $49; some with fridge and microwave; winter rates $10-15 lower.

Rancheros de Santa Fe, 736 Old Las Vegas Hwy. (☎466-3482). Take I-25 N to Exit 290. Big, friendly campground with pool. Sites $18, full hook-up $25; cabins $34.

FOOD

Spicy Mexican food served on blue corn tortillas is a Santa Fe staple. Bistros near the plaza dish up savory chiles to tourists, businessmen, and local artists, but most run $20 an entree. Cheaper alternatives lie south of the plaza on Cerillos and on Guadalupe St. Wandering down side streets uncovers smaller Mexican restaurants where the locals eat; grill carts in the plaza can sell you fragrant fajitas ($3) and fresh lemonade ($1).

Tia Sophia's, 210 W. San Francisco St. (☎983-9880). It looks and feels like a diner (the servers are quick and curt), but the food is exceptional. The most popular item is the Atrisco plate ($6)—chile stew, cheese enchilada, beans, *posole*, and a *sopapilla*. Arrive before noon for the fastest service. Open M-Sa 7am-2pm.

The Shed, 113½ E. Palace Ave. (☎982-9030), up the street from the plaza, feels like an open garden, even in the enclosed section. Vegetarian quesadilla ($6) and amazing chicken enchilada verde ($9). Lunch daily 11am-2:30pm; dinner M-Sa 5:30-9pm.

Upper Crust Pizza, 329 Old Sante Fe Trail (☎982-0000). With a lackadaisical porch and live music Th-M, "crustomers" are treated to the best pizza in Sante Fe in a fantastic setting. Pizzas start at $6; sandwiches $5. Open Su-Th 11am-10pm, F-Sa 11am-11pm.

Carlo's Gospel Cafe, 125 Lincoln St. #117 (☎983-1841). A popular spot with locals, Carlo's is pure temptation with divinely delicious sandwiches ($5 and up) and biblically-rich pies. Open M-Sa 11am-3pm.

Zia Diner, 326 S. Guadalupe St. (☎988-7008). A classy diner, Zia's has all the traditional fixin's (burgers $6) plus some snazzy dinners from $10. Leave room for their award-winning desserts. Open daily 11am-10pm.

OLD STYLE SIGHTS

The grassy **Plaza de Santa Fe** is a good starting point for exploring the museums, sanctuaries, and galleries of the city. Since 1609, the plaza has been the site of religious ceremonies, military gatherings, markets, cockfights, and public punishments—now it holds ritzy shops and relaxing tourists.

MNM MUSEUMS. Sante Fe is home to six world-class and imaginative museums. Four are run by **The Museum of New Mexico.** They all hold the same hours and charge the same admission. A worthwhile four-day pass ($10) includes admission to all four museums; it can be purchased at any of them. (☎827-6463. Open Tu-Su 10am-5pm; single visit $5, under 17 free. The two downtown museums—Fine Arts and Palace of the Governors—are both free on F 5-8pm. All four MNM museums offer free tours; hrs. vary based on day and museum; call ahead for details.)

Inhabiting a large adobe building on the northwest corner of the plaza the **Museum of Fine Arts** dazzles visitors with the works of major Southwestern artists, like Georgia O'Keeffe and Gustave Baumann, as well as very adventurous contemporary exhibits of often controversial American art. (107 W. Palace Ave. ☎476-5072.) The **Palace of the Governors,** on the north side of the plaza, is the oldest public building in the US and was the seat of seven successive governments after its construction in 1610. The *haciendas* palace is now a museum with exhibits on Native American, Southwestern, and New Mexican history. The craft and jewelry displays in front have cheaper and better quality wares than you'll find in other stores around town. (107 W. Palace Ave. ☎476-5100.) Two more inventive museums lie 2 mi. south of downtown. The fascinating **Museum of International Folk Art,** houses the jumbled Girard Collection, which includes over 100,000 handmade dolls, doll houses, and other toys from around the world. Other galleries hold changing ethnographic exhibits. (706 Camino Lejo. ☎827-6350.) Next door, the **Museum of American Indian Arts and Culture** displays Native American photos and artifacts with high-tech savvy. (710 Camino Lejo. ☎827-6344.)

OTHER PLAZA MUSEUMS. While the two other Sante Fe museums have no affiliation with the Museum of New Mexico, they are, however just as worthwhile. The popular **Georgia O'Keeffe Museum** attracts the masses with O'Keeffe's famous flower paintings and her more abstract works. Spanning her entire life, the museum's collection demonstrates the artist's versatility. *(217 Johnson St.,* ☎*995-0785. Open Th-Tu 10am-5pm, W noon-8pm. $5, under 17 free; F 5-8pm free. Audio tour $5.)* The **Institute of American Indian Arts Museum,** downtown, houses an extensive collection of contemporary Indian art. *(108 Cathedral Place.* ☎*988-6281. Open M-Sa 9am-5pm, Su noon-5pm. $4, students and seniors $2, under 16 free.)*

CHURCHES. Santa Fe's Catholic roots are evident in the Romanesque **St. Francis Cathedral,** built in 1884 under the direction of the pope to bring Catholicism to the "ungodly" westerners. The cathedral's architecture is especially striking against the New Mexican desert. *(213 Cathedral Pl.* ☎*982-5619.)* The neo-gothic **Loretto Chapel** is famous for its "miraculous" spiral staircase. *(207 Old Santa Fe Trail.* ☎*982-0092. Open M-Sa 9am-6pm, Su 10:30pm-5pm; $2.50, seniors and children $2.)* About five blocks southeast of the plaza lies the **San Miguel Mission,** at DeVargas St. and the Old Santa Fe Trail. Built in 1710, the mission is the oldest functioning church in the US. The original altar was built by Native Americans. *(*☎*983-3974. Open M-Sa 9am–5pm, Su 1:30-4pm; Nov.-Apr. M-Sa 10am-3:45pm, Su 1:30-4:30pm. $1.)*

GALLERIES. Along **Canyon Rd.** Santa Fe's most successful artists live and sell their work. Head away from the Plaza on San Francisco Dr., take a left on Alameda St., a right on Paseo de Peralta, and a left on Canyon Rd. Extending for about 1 mi., the road is lined on both sides by galleries displaying all types of art, as well a number of indoor/outdoor cafes. Most galleries are open from around 10am until 5pm. At the **Hahn Ross Gallery,** the art is hip, enjoyable, and occasionally affordable. *(409 Canyon Rd.* ☎*984-8434. Open daily 10am-5pm.)* **Off the Wall** vends truly offbeat jewelry, pottery, clocks, and sculpture. *(616 Canyon Rd.* ☎*983-8337. Open daily 10am-5pm.)*

🎵🎭 ENTERTAINMENT AND NIGHTLIFE

YEEHAW! Native American ceremonies, fairs, arts, and crafts shows complement Santa Fe's active theater scene and the roster of world-famous musicians who frequently play in the city's clubs. Everybody's famous at the **Cowgirl Hall of Fame,** 319 Guadalupe St., where live music hoe-downs happen every night. (Open M-Sa 10:30am-2am, Su 8:30am-2am. Happy hour M-F 3pm-6pm with $3.50 Cowgirl Margaritas.) **El Farol,** 808 Canyon Rd., features up-and-coming rock, salsa, and R&B musicians. (☎983-9912. Shows nightly 9:30pm. Cover W-Sa varies depending on band). The **Catamount Bar and Grill,** 125 E. Water St., has live bands and dancing F and Sa nights. Cool down with a 16 oz. margarita for $6. (☎988-7222. Open M-Sa 11am-2am, Su noon-midnight. Sandwiches $7.)

A BIT OF CLASS. Strange verse and distinguished acting invade the city each summer when **Shakespeare in Sante Fe** raises its curtain. Running from late June to late Aug., the festival consists of two plays in an open-air theater on the St. John's College campus. Reserved seating tickets range from $10-28; lawn seating is free, although a $5 donation is requested. (Tickets available at show or call ☎982-2910. Shows run F-Su.) The **Santa Fe Opera,** on Opera Dr. 7 mi. north of Santa Fe on Rte. 84/285, performs outdoors against a gorgeous mountain backdrop. Nights are cool; bring a blanket. The season runs July through Aug. The box office is at the opera house. (☎877-999-7499. July W and F-Sa at 9pm; Aug. M-Sa at 8:30pm. Tickets $15-200, rush standing-room tickets $8-15; 50% student discount on same-day reserved seats. Call the day of the show for specific prices and availability.) The **Santa Fe Chamber Music Festival** celebrates the works of great Baroque, Classical, Romantic, and 20th-century composers in the St. Francis Auditorium of the Museum of Fine Arts. (☎983-2075. Mid-July to mid-Aug. Tickets $25-40, students $10.)

FESTIVALS. Santa Fe is also home to two of the US's largest festivals. In Aug., the nation's largest and most impressive **Indian Market** floods the plaza. The **Southwestern Association on Indian Affairs** has more info (☎983-5220). Don Diego De Vargas's peaceful reconquest of New Mexico in 1692 marked the end of the 12-year Pueblo Rebellion, now celebrated in the three-day **Fiesta de Santa Fe** (☎988-7575). Held in early Sept., festivities include street dancing, processions, and political satires. The *New Mexican* publishes a guide and a schedule of the fiesta's events.

SKIING. Only 16 mi. northeast of downtown, **Ski Sante Fe** heats up the winters. Located in the towering Sangre De Cristo Mountains on Rte. 475, the ski area is home to 600 acres of terrain and over 200 in. of snowfall. (☎800-776-7669. Lift tickets $40, children and seniors $28; rental packages start at $15.)

⬛ DAYTRIPS FROM SANTA FE

LOS ALAMOS. Known only as the mysterious P.O. Box 1663 during the heyday of the Manhattan Project, Los Alamos is no longer the nation's biggest secret. With the infamous distinction of being the birthplace of the Atomic Bomb, Los Alamos now attracts visitors with its natural beauty and outdoor activities. Overlooking the Rio Grande Valley, Los Alamos hovers above the Pueblo and Bayo Canyons on thin finger-like mesas, 35 mi. to the northeast of Sante Fe. In town, the **Bradbury Science Museum,** corner of 15th St. and Central, explains the history of the Los Alamos National Laboratory and its endeavors with excellent videos and hands-on exhibits. (☎647-4444. Open Tu-Sa 9am-5pm, Su-M 1-5pm. Free.) Outdoors, the town brims with great activities. The **Sante Fe National Forest** provides countless trails for hiking and biking in and along the town's many canyons. The **Valle Grande,** an expansive and lush volcanic caldera, is a wonder to see. It's 15 mi. to the east on Rte. 4 along the scenic Jemez Mountain Trail. **Los Alamos visitors center** is at 109 Central Park Square. (☎662-8105. Open M-Sa 9am-4pm, Su 10am-3pm.)

BANDELIER NATIONAL MONUMENT. Bandelier, 40 mi. northwest of Santa Fe (take U.S. 285 to 502 W, then follow the signs), features some amazing pueblos and cliff dwellings, as well as 50 sq. mi. of dramatic mesas, ancient ruins (remains of stone houses and *kivas,* underground ceremonial chambers), and spectacular views of surrounding canyons. The most accessible, **Frijoles Canyon,** is the site of the **visitors center.** (☎672-3861, ext. 517; 672-0343 24hr. recorded info. Open daily in summer 8am-6pm; off-season hrs. vary between 8am-4:30pm and 9am-5:30pm; call ahead to verify.) From the visitors center, a self-guided 1hr. tour leads through nearby pueblo **cliff dwellings** and an additional ½ mi. hike continues to the **Alcove House,** which offer an incredible view. The 5 mi. **Falls Trail** hike descends 700 ft. into the mouth of the canyon, past two waterfalls, to the Río Grande. A strenuous two-day, 20 mi. hike leads from the visitors center to **Painted Cave,** decorated with over 50 Ancestral Puebloan pictographs. Free permits are required for backcountry hiking and camping; topographical maps ($10) are sold at the visitors center. The 95-site **Juniper Campground,** ¼ mi. off Rte. 4 at the entrance to the monument, is the only campground (sites $10, with Golden Age passport $5). The park entrance fee is $10 per vehicle, $5 per pedestrian; National Parks passes are accepted.

PECOS NATIONAL HISTORICAL PARK. Located in the hill country 25 mi. southeast of Santa Fe on I-25 and Rte. 63, Pecos features ruins of a pueblo and a Spanish mission church. The small park includes an easy 1 mi. hike through various archaeological sites. Especially noteworthy are the renovated *kivas,* built after the Rebellion of 1680. Off-limits at other ruins, the *kivas* at Pecos are open to the public. (Open daily 8am-5pm. Entrance $2 per person, $4 per car. National Parks passports accepted.) The **visitors center** (☎757-6032) has a small museum and a 10min. film shown on the hour. The park is not accessible by public transportation. Backcountry camping is permitted in the **Santa Fe National Forest,** 6 mi. north on Rte. 63 (see Santa Fe **Accommodations**).

TAOS
☎505

Those who now inhabit Taos are but the latest in a diverse series of settlers lured by the fertility and stark beauty of the Taos Valley region. First came the Native American tribes, whose pueblos still speckle the valley. In the 17th century, Spanish missionaries arrived, in hopes of converting the Native Americans to Christianity while farming alongside them. The 20th century saw artists captivated and inspired by Taos's mountainous beauty, including Georgia O'Keeffe and R.C. Gorman. Aspiring artists still flock here, but recent trends indicate that the next generation of immigrants may be a mixed bag of thrill-seekers and spiritualists who come to take advantage either of Taos's natural surroundings or its thriving New Age culture. Increasingly, hikers and skiers infest the nearby mountains, rafters brave the nearby Río Grande, and New Agers drawn by the desert vibe set up house.

🛈 **PRACTICAL INFORMATION.** In town, **Rte. 68** becomes Paseo del Pueblo Sur. Drivers should park on Camino de la Placita, a block west of the plaza, or at the meters scattered on side streets. **Greyhound,** 114 Alexander St. (☎758-1144; open daily 9-10am, 2-3pm, and 6-7pm), sends two buses per day to Albuquerque (3hr., $22); Santa Fe (1½hr., $17); and Denver (7hr., $50). The **Chile Line** runs vans from Ranchos de Taos, south of town, up to the pueblo and back (☎751-4459; runs M-Sa 7am-10pm; Sept.-May M-Sa 7am-7pm, Su 9am-6pm; 50¢). **Faust's Transportation** (☎758-3410) taxis daily 7am-9pm. **Chamber of Commerce:** 1139 Paseo del Pueblo Sur, south of town at the junction of Rte. 68 and Paseo del Cañon, (☎758-3873 or 800-732-8267; open daily 9am-5pm). **Post Office:** 318 Paseo Del Pueblo Norte, ¼ mi. north of the plaza (☎758-2081; open M-F 8:30am-5pm). **ZIP code:** 87571. **Area code:** 505.

🛏 **ACCOMMODATIONS.** The **Abominable Snowmansion Hostel (HI-AYH)**, in the village of Arroyo Seco, is a snowbird's delight with spacious dorm rooms and a pool table adorning the common room. A hostel by summer, ski lodge by winter, the Snowmansion is located 9 mi. north of the town and 9 mi. west of the ski valley. Teepees and camping are available in the warmer months. (☎776-8298. Reception daily 8-11am and 5-10pm; in winter 8-11am and 4-10pm. Summer dorms $14, nonmembers $16; private doubles $36/$40; teepees $14/$16. Winter dorms $20. Reserve ahead for winter and spring break.) Closer to town, the **Sun God Lodge,** 919 Paseo del Pueblo Sur, has sizeable and clean rooms with Southwestern-style wooden furniture. (☎758-3162. Singles $45-65; doubles $65-75.) **Taos Valley RV Park,** 120 Estes Rd., just off Paseo del Pueblo Sur has tent sites and full hook-ups. (☎758-4469 or 800-999-7571. Sites $16-18 for 2 people; full hook-ups $25-27 for 2.)

Camping around Taos is easy with a car. Up in the mountains on wooded Rte. 64, 20 mi. east of Taos, the **Kit Carson National Forest** operates three campgrounds. **Las Petacas** is free but has no drinking water; **La Sombra** and **Capulin,** down the same road, charge $6. Four free campgrounds also line Rte. 150 north of town. **Backcountry camping** doesn't require a permit. For maps of area campgrounds contact the **forest service office,** 208 Cruz Alta Rd. (☎758-6200; open M-F 8am-4:30pm).

🍴 **FOOD.** Restaurants cluster around Taos Plaza and Bent St. Cheaper options can be found north of town along Paseo Del Pueblo. **Michael's Kitchen,** 304 Paseo del Pueblo Norte, is popular with locals, offering some good $2-7 breakfast specials. (☎758-4178. Open daily 7am-8:30pm.) **Taos Pizza Outback,** north of town on Rte. 64, serves the town's best pizza in slices large enough to warrant their price ($2.75 and up). (☎758-3112. Open daily 11am-10pm.) The **Bent Street Deli and Cafe,** 133A Bent St., straightens out patrons with creative sandwiches ($4-8) and soups ($2.50). (☎758-5787. Open daily 8am-9pm.)

🔆 **SIGHTS.** Taos comes in 2nd only to Santa Fe as a center for Southwestern art. Galleries, ranging from high-quality operations to glorified curio shops, can be found in **Taos Plaza** and on **Kit Carson Rd.** A well-chosen selection of early Taos paintings hangs at the **Harwood Foundation Museum,** 238 Ledoux St., off Camino de la Placita. *(☎758-9826. Open Tu-Sa 10am-5pm, Su noon-5pm; $5, under 12 free.)* The **Taos**

Arts Festival celebrates local art from mid-Sept. to early Oct. In the tiny village of Ranchos de Taos, 4 mi. south of Taos Plaza, the **Mission of San Francisco de Asis** displays a "miraculous" painting that changes into a shadowy figure of Christ when the lights go out. A video documents the miracle in the parish office, to your left as you're facing the church. (☎758-2754. *Video shown every 30min. daily 9am-4pm. $2.*) Four mi. north of Taos off Rte. 522, exhibits of Native American art including Pueblo jewelry, black-on-black pottery, and Navajo rugs grace the **Millicent Rogers Museum,** 1504 Museum Rd. (☎758-2462. *Open daily 10am-5pm, Nov.-Mar Tu-Su 10am-5pm. $6, students and seniors $5, ages 6-16 $1.*)

Taos Pueblo, 3 mi. northwest of the plaza, remarkable for its five-story houses, is one of the last inhabited pueblos; many buildings are off-limits to visitors. The pueblo has capitalized on its popularity—visitors must pay up. (☎758-1028. *Open daily 8am-5pm; in winter 9am-4pm. $10 per person, under 12 free. Camera permit $10, video camera permit $20.*) Feast days are celebrated with tribal dances; **San Gerónimo's Feast Days** (Sept. 29-30) also feature a fair and races. The **Taos Pueblo Annual Powwow** (2nd weekend of July) is the highlight of the summer. The tribal office can supply you with schedules of dances and other info. Best known for its sparkling pottery molded from mica and clay, **Picuris Pueblo,** 25 mi. south of Taos on Rte. 75 near Peñasco, is smaller, less touristed, and somewhat more accessible. (☎587-2519. *Open daily 8am-5pm.*) A free guide to Northern New Mexican Indian pueblos is available at the Taos visitors center.

▲ ACTIVITIES. Skiers flock to the Taos area when the snow falls. Hailed as one of the best ski resorts in the country, **Taos Ski Valley,** about 15 mi. northeast of town on Rte. 150, offers powder conditions in bowl sections and short but steep downhill runs that rival Colorado's. With 72 trails and 12 lifts, Ski Valley boasts over 2500 ft. of vertical drop and over 300 in. of annual snowfall. (☎776-2291, lodging info 800-992-7669, ski conditions 776-2916. Lift tickets $41-45; equipment rental from $19 per day.) Reserve a room well in advance if you plan to come during the winter holiday season. There are also two smaller, more family-oriented ski areas near Taos: **Angel Fire** (☎377-6401 or 800-633-7463; lift tickets $39) and **Red River** (☎800-494-9117; lift tickets $39). Money-saving multi-day passes are available for use at all three resorts (from $36 a day). In summer, the nearly deserted ski valley area becomes a hiker's paradise (most trails begin off Rte. 150). Due to the town's prime location near the Río Grande, **river rafting** is very popular in Taos. **Far-Flung Adventures,** next door to the Río Grande Gorge Hostel (see **Accommodations,** above), offers half-day ($40) to three-day ($375) river trips. Reservations up to six weeks in advance are required for longer trips; call for details. (☎758-9072. Open daily 8am-5pm; closed in winter.) **Cottam's Ski and Outdoor,** 207A S. Pueblo del Sur rents mountain bikes. (☎758-2822. Open daily 9am-6pm. $8 per hr., $20 per day.)

Taos hums with New Age services: vibrasound relaxation, drum therapy, harmony massage, and cranial therapy, just for starters. **Taos Drums,** 5 mi. south of the plaza on Rte. 68, features the world's largest collection of Native American drums. (☎800-424-3786. Open M-Sa 9am-6pm, Su 11am-6pm.)

ALBUQUERQUE ☎505

With the infamous Rte. 66 and Sante Fe railroad cutting through the heart of downtown, Albuquerque is a city that many travelers whizz through without a second thought. This place is definitely, however, worth a rest on the way from here to there. A mellow university, the dramatic Sandia Mountains, and hospitable residents all surprise travelers who take the time to explore New Mexico's largest city. Downtown bustles with urban sophistication, while Old Town is a trip back to the 19th century, and the university district jives with youthful exuberance.

GETTING THERE AND GETTING AROUND

Airport: Albuquerque International, 2200 Sunport Blvd. SE (☎842-4366), south of downtown. Take bus #50 from 5th St. and Central Ave, or pick it up along Yale Blvd. **Airport Express** (☎765-1234) shuttles to the city ($11, two people $16.50). Their booth is open 9:30am-12:30am. A taxi downtown costs under $10, to Old Town $15.

Trains: Amtrak, 214 1st St. SW (☎842-9650). 1 train per day to Los Angeles (16hr., $61-109); Kansas City (17hr., $106-189); Santa Fe (1hr. to Lamy, $14-26; 20min. shuttle to Santa Fe, $14); and Flagstaff (5hr., $56-99). Reservations required. Open daily 10am-6pm.

Buses: Greyhound (☎243-4435) and **TNM&O Coaches** (☎242-4998) run from 300 2nd St. SW, 3 blocks south of Central Ave. Buses go to Santa Fe (1½hr., 4 per day, $11.15); Flagstaff (6hr., 4 per day, $39-41); Denver (10hr., 5 per day, $61); Phoenix (10hr., 4 per day, $41); and Los Angeles (18hr., 5 per day, $65-69).

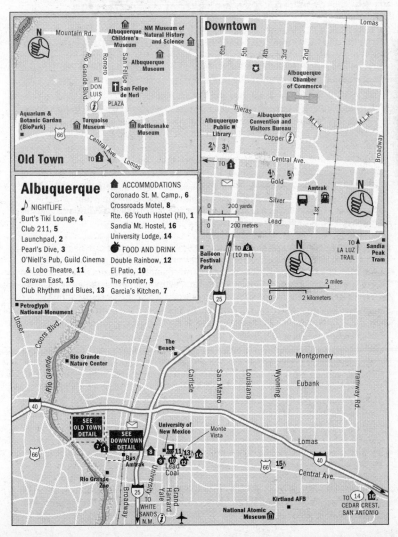

SOUTHWEST

Public Transit: Sun-Tran Transit, 601 Yale Blvd. SE (☎843-9200; open M-F 8am-5pm). Most buses run M-Sa 6am-10pm. Pick up maps at visitors centers, the transit office, or the main library. 75¢, seniors and ages 5-18 25¢. Request free transfers from driver.

Taxis: Albuquerque Cab, ☎883-4888. 24hr.

Car Rental: Rent-a-Wreck, 500 Yale Blvd. SE (☎232-7552 or 800-247-9556). Cars from $20 per day with 150 free mi.; 20¢ per additional mi.; $120 per week. Insurance $11 per day, $70 per week. Must be 21+ with credit card or $250-500 cash deposit; under 25 surcharge $3 per day. Open M-F 8am-5:30pm, Sa 8am-4pm, Su 11am-2pm. Reservations recommended.

Bike Rental: Old Town Bicycles, 2209 Central Ave. NW (☎247-4926), several blocks from Old Town Plaza. Rents hybrid bikes for city use ($5 per hr., $16 overnight, $60 per week) and mountain bikes ($7/$20/$60). Open M-F 10am-6pm, Sa 10am-5pm. Credit card required for deposit. Reservations recommended on weekends.

✴🛈 ORIENTATION AND PRACTICAL INFORMATION

The city divides into four quadrants: NE, NW, SE, SW. **Central Ave.** divides the north and south, and **I-25** is a rough division between east and west. The all-adobe campus of the **University of New Mexico (UNM)** spreads along Central Ave. from University Ave. to Carlisle St. **Old Town Plaza** lies between San Felipe, North Plaza, South Plaza, and Romero, off Central Ave.

Visitor Info: Albuquerque Convention and Visitors Bureau, 20 First Plaza, galleria level (☎800-284-2282). Open M-F 8am-5pm. Recorded info 24hr. **Old Town Visitors Center** (☎243-3215), at Plaza Don Luís on Romero NW across from the church. Open daily 9am-5pm; Nov.-Mar. 9:30am-4:30pm. Airport **info booth** open daily 8:30am-8:30pm.

Hotlines: Rape Crisis Center, 1025 Hermosa SE (☎266-7711). Center open M-F 8am-noon and 1-5pm. **Gay and Lesbian Information Line,** ☎891-3647. Both 24hr.

Internet Access: UNM Zimmerman Library, at the heart of campus. Open fall and spring semesters M-Th 8am-midnight, F 8am-9pm, Sa 9am-6pm, Su 10am-midnight; in summer M-Th 8am-9pm, F 8am-5pm, Sa 10am-5pm, Su 10am-9pm.

Post Office: 1135 Broadway NE, at Mountain (☎346-8044). Open M-F 7:30am-6pm. **ZIP code:** 87101. **Area code:** 505.

▌ ACCOMMODATIONS

Cheap motels line **Central Ave.,** even near downtown. Evaluate the motel carefully before paying; a bit more money might mean a bit more safety. During the Oct. **balloon festival** (see **Sights,** below), rooms are scarce; call ahead for reservations.

Route 66 Youth Hostel, 1012 Central Ave. SW (☎247-1813), at 10th St. Get your kicks at this lively and friendly hostel. Well located between downtown and Old Town, Route 66 pleases guests with a well-stocked kitchen and enthusiastic staff. Dorm and private rooms are simple but clean. Reception daily 7-10:30am and 4-11pm. Check-out 10:30am. Chores required. Bunks $13 with any hostel card. Private singles with a shared bath are a bargain at $18, while spacious doubles with private bath are $28. Linen $1. Key deposit $5.

Sandía Mountain Hostel, 12234 Hwy. 14 N (☎281-4117), in nearby Cedar Crest. With top-to-bottom wood paneling, this hostel feels like a giant mug of hot chocolate. Comfortable living room with fireplace, kitchen, and a family of resident donkeys. Sandía hiking and mountain biking trails are nearby. Beds in clean and spacious dorms $12; private rooms $30. Linen $1. Wheelchair accessible.

University Lodge, 3711 Central Ave. NE (☎266-7663). About a 15min. walk from campus, in the historic and cool Nob Hill district. Unusually cozy rooms. In summer singles $33, doubles $40; in winter $30/$30.

Crossroads Motel, 1001 Central Ave NE (☎242-2757). Large, bright rooms, some with fridge, all with A/C, cable, and phone. Singles $26; doubles $34.

Coronado State Monument Campground (☎ 867-5589), about 15 mi. north of Albuquerque. Take I-25 to Exit 242 and follow the signs. A unique camping experience near the haunting Sandía Mountains. Adobe shelters on the sites offer a respite from the heat. Toilets, showers, and drinking water available. Sites $8, with hook-up $14. Office open daily 8am-5pm; see host to check-in after hrs.

FOOD

A diverse ethnic community, a lot of hungry interstate travelers, and one big load of green chiles render Albuquerque surprisingly tasty. The area around **UNM** is the best bet for inexpensive eateries. A bit farther east, the hip neighborhood of **Nob Hill** offers more offbeat options.

El Patio, 142 Harvard St. SE (☎ 268-4245). Behind blue-wooden fencing, a softly strumming guitarist beckons passers-by to sit, relax, and down a few enchiladas. Mexican plates $5-8, including lots of veggie options. Open M-Th 11am-9pm, F-Sa 11am-9:30pm, Su noon-9pm.

Double Rainbow, 3416 Central Ave. SE (☎ 255-6633). This magazine-stocked establishment is known for its desserts ($4). Generous, hearty lunches and dinners ($4-8), including soup ($3). Open Su-Th 6am-midnight, F-Sa 6am-1am.

Garcia's Kitchen, 1736 Central Ave. SW (☎ 842-0273). This restaurant is authentic. From burritos ($3 and up) to *gringo* breakfasts favorites ($2-5), Garcia's offers a large menu and long hours. Open daily 6am-10pm.

The Frontier, 2400 Central Ave. SE (☎ 266-0550). If it's 3am and an insatiable appetite for some sort of ground beef product has you pressing hard on the accelerator, you'll wind up here. College kids, a friendly staff, lively-to-the-wee-hours atmosphere, and good eats. Remarkable green chile stew $2; burgers $2-3; sweet rolls $1. Open 24hr.

SIGHTS

OLD TOWN. When the railroad cut through Albuquerque in the 19th-century, it missed Old Town by almost 2 mi. and thus sentenced the plaza to 90 years of being overlooked. As downtown grew around the railroad, Old Town remained untouched until the 50s, when the city realized that it had a tourist magnet right under its nose. Just north of Central Ave. and east of Rio Grande Blvd, the adobe-styled plaza looks today, for the most part, as it did over 100 years ago, except for the ubiquitous restaurants, gift shops, and jewelry vendors. Old Town is an architectural marvel and a stroll through it is worthwhile. Free insightful **walking tours of Old Town,** lasting 1hr. are offered Tu-Su at 11am; meet at the Museum of Albuquerque. On the north side of the plaza, the **San Felipe de Neri** Church, dating back to 1793, has stood the test of time. *(Open daily 9am-5pm; Su mass in English 7am and 10:15am, in Spanish 8:30am.)* A posse of museums and attractions surrounds the plaza. To the north, the **Albuquerque Museum** showcases New Mexican art and history. *(2000 Mountain Rd. NW. ☎ 242-4600. Open Tu-Su 9am-5pm. Free. Wheelchair accessible.)* Across the street from the museum, Spike and Alberta, two statuesque dinosaurs, greet tourists outside the kid-friendly **New Mexico Museum of Natural History and Science;** inside the museum, interactive exhibits present the geological and evolutionary history of New Mexico. *(1801 Mountain Rd. NW. ☎ 841-2800. Open daily 9am-5pm. $5, seniors $4, children $2; combination Dynamax theater ticket $9/$6/$3. Wheelchair accessible.)* A modern addition, the unusual **Rattlesnake Museum,** south of the plaza, houses the world's most extensive display of rattlesnakes. *(202 San Felipe NW. ☎ 242-6569. Open daily 10am-6pm; $3, students $2, children $1.)*

UNIVERSITY MUSEUMS. The University of New Mexico has a number of small but thought-provoking museums. The **University Art Museum** and the **Maxwell Museum of Anthropology** are two of the more popular ones. All the UNM museums are located on-campus, along Central Ave, from University Ave, to Carlisle Ave., and are free of charge. *(Art Museum: ☎ 277-4001. Open Tu-F 9am-4pm, Su 1pm-4pm. Anthropology: ☎ 277-5963. Open Tu-F 9am-4pm, Sa 10am-4pm.)*

OTHER ATTRACTIONS. On Central Ave just east of Rio Grande Blvd. lies two-thirds of the Albuquerque **BioPark:** the aquarium and botanic garden. *(2601 Central Ave SW. ☎ 764-6200. Both open daily Tu-Su 9am-5pm; in winter 9am-6pm. Admission to both $4.50, seniors and children $2.50. Both wheelchair accessible.)* The zoo is south of Central on 10th St. *(903 10th St. SW. Same hrs. $4.50/$2.50.)* The **National Atomic Museum,** on Kirtland Air Force Base, tells the story of Little Boy and Fat Man, the atomic bombs dropped on Hiroshima and Nagasaki. *Ten Seconds that Shook the World,* a documentary on the making of the atomic bomb, shows on the hour. The Air Force base is a few mi. southeast of downtown, east of I-25. Ask at the visitor control gate on Wyoming Blvd. for a museum visitors pass; you'll need *several* forms of ID. *(20358 Wyoming Blvd. ☎ 284-3243. Museum open daily 9am-5pm. $3, children $2.)*

▲ OUTDOORS

SKIING, BIKING, AND SUNSETS. Serving as the spectacular backdrop to the city, Albuquerque's mountains captivate outdoor enthusiasts. The **Sandía Mountains,** on Albuquerque's east side in the Cíbola National Forest, were named by the Spanish for the pink color they turn at sunset (*sandía* means watermelon). In the snowy months, skiers flock to the mountains; hikers and bikers lay siege the rest of the year. Located 30min. north of Albuquerque on I-25, **Sandía Peak** welcomes skiers from mid-Dec. to mid-Mar. With 30 trails and four chairlifts, the mountain offers solid intermediate skiing. *(☎242-9052.)* However, the lack of snow during the last two winters shortened the season; call ahead for snow reports. *(☎857-8977.)* From mid-May to mid-Sept., the mountain becomes a **mountain biking** haven. A chairlift accesses miles of trails for both bikers and hikers. *(Open Th-Su. $5; round-trip $7.)* The mountain is also home to the **Sandía Peak Aerial Tramway,** the world's longest aerial tramway. Ascending the west face of the Sandia Peak, the tram overlooks Albuquerque, the Río Grande Valley, and western New Mexico; the ascent is especially striking at sunset. *(Recorded info ☎856-7235. To reach the tram, take Tramway Rd. from I-25 (Exit 234) or Tramway Blvd. from I-40 (Exit 167). Tramway open daily 9am-10pm; in winter 9am-8pm, weather permitting. 30min. trip, times vary. $14, children $10.)*

DRIVING AND HIKING. Winding through lovely forests of piñon and ponderosa pines, oaks, and spruce, a 19 mi. **driving loop** climbs to the Sandía's summit, **Sandía Crest,** elevation 10,678 ft. *(To reach the road, take I-40 E through Tijeras Canyon, turn north onto Rte. 14, and turn west onto Rte. 536 at San Antonio. $3 per vehicle permit fee.)* A ranger station *(☎248-0190)* greets visitors at the top as does views of Albuquerque and the **Cíbola National Forest.** A dazzling 1½ mi. **ridge hike** connects the Crest with the top of the tram. In addition, the road is lined with hiking trails. For those wanting to tackle the mountain by foot, the **La Luz** trail runs to the top of the tram. The strenuous 8 mi. hike takes 3 to 5hr.; call first to make sure the trail isn't blocked by snow, which can happen even in early summer. To reach the La Luz, follow the signs from Tramway Blvd. to the trailhead, about 1 mi. from the road to the tramway. Rangers lead guided hikes through the Cíbola National Forest; you'll need reservations for the challenging winter snowshoe hikes. In the summer, some hiking and biking trails are open to the public only during specific hours. *(☎242-9052 for reservations or details. Usually staffed Th-Su 10am-4pm.)*

> **STUFF.** Housed within walls made of glass bottles, the **Tinkertown Museum** is unlike anything you've ever seen before. From a collection of wedding cake garnishes to Otto the one-man-band to a sailboat that has sailed around the world to the pants of the tallest man that ever lived, this place is full of, well, do-dads...whatchamacallits...you know...um, *stuff.* For full enjoyment, bring lots of quarters. Located 20min. from Albuquerque, Tinkertown sits along the Turquoise Trail on Rte. 536. Take Exit 175 N off I-40. *(Open daily Apr.-Nov. 9am-6pm. $3, seniors $2.50, children $1.)*

SOUTHWEST

NATIVE AMERICAN ATTRACTIONS. Located at the edge of suburbia on Albuquerque's west side, **Petroglyph National Monument** features more than 20,000 images etched into lava rocks between 1300 and 1680 by Pueblo Indians and Spanish settlers. Short paved trails access small sections of the park's **Boca Negra Canyon,** but most of the area can be explored only by backcountry hiking—ask rangers for suggested routes. (☎899-0205. Take I-40 to Unser Ave. (Exit 154), and follow the signs to the park. Alternatively, take bus #9 from 6th and Silver to Coors Blvd., a few blocks away. Park open M-F 8am-5pm. $1, Sa-Su $2; National Parks passports accepted.) **The Pueblo of Acoma,** about 60 mi. west of Albuquerque, is one of the most spectacular Native American pueblo dwellings in the area. (Take I-40 to Exit 102 and Hwy. 30 to Acomita. From there, take Hwy. 32 south about 11 mi. to the visitors center. Tours given Apr.-Oct. 8am-7pm, Nov.-Mar. 8am-4:30pm; last tour leaves 1hr. before closing. Hrs. change often; call ahead. $6, seniors $5, children $4.)

🎵🎭 ENTERTAINMENT AND NIGHTLIFE

Compared to the sometimes stale nightlife options that the Southwest offers, Albuquerque is an oasis. Hopping with quirky bars, jamming nightclubs, art film houses, and a sizeable university, Albuquerque feels truly alive. Check flyers posted around the university area for live music shows, or pick up a copy of *Alibi,* the free local weekly. Over the first week of Oct., hundreds of aeronauts take flight in beautifully colored hot-air balloons during the **balloon festival.** Even the most grounded of landlubbers will enjoy the week's barbecues and musical events.

Nightlife can be found downtown and near the university. In the heart of downtown, **Launchpad,** 618 Central Ave. SW, draws a young, colorful crowd, lured by local alternative bands and occasional big acts. (☎764-8887. Open Su-F 4pm-2am, Sa 7pm-2am. Cover varies with band.) **Pearl's Dive,** 509 Central Ave., attracts those who appreciate their blues and jazz. (☎244-9405. Open M-Tu 11am-midnight, W-F 11am-2am, Sa 4pm-2am.) **Burt's Tiki Lounge,** 313 Gold Ave. SW, is a surfin' themed bar. (☎243-2878. Doors open M-F 5pm, Sa 8pm.) For those who know that a grinder isn't just a sandwich, **Club 211,** 211 Gold Ave. SW, busts a move W-Sa nights. (☎766-9601. Doors open W-Th 10pm, F-Sa 9pm.)

Farther east down Central Ave., the university's influence is prevalent as Lobo banners and student deals emerge from every corner. **O'Niell's Pub,** 3211 Central Ave. NE, is an Irish tavern with class, music, and stouts. (☎256-0564. Open M-Sa 11:30am-2am, Su 11:30am-midnight.) **Club Rhythm and Blues,** corner of Central and Carlisle Ave., has African music on M, Latin on W, and blues and jazz the others. (☎256-0849. Open M-Sa 9pm-1:15am. Tu and Th no cover, M and W $5, F and Sa $7.) At **Caravan East,** 7605 Central Ave. NE, "there is always a dancin' partner" and live country music. (☎265-7877. Open daily 4:30pm-2am. Cover F-Sa $3.)

Two independent film houses grace Central Ave, attracting the artsy. The **Lobo Theatre,** 3013 Central Ave. NE (☎265-4769), hosts film festivals and daily showings. The less-glitzy but more off-beat **Guild Cinema,** 3405 Central Ave. NE (☎255-1848), runs two shows M-Th (4:30 and 7pm) and three F-Su (2:15, 4:30, and 7pm).

🚗 DAYTRIP FROM ALBUQUERQUE

MADRID. The scenic and historic **Turquoise Trail** extends along Rte. 14 between Albuquerque and Sante Fe. Miners once harvested copious amounts of turquoise, gold, silver, and coal from the surrounding area, but the towns suffered greatly during the Depression. Established in 1892 as a coal mining town, Madrid (*MA-drid*), 40 mi. from Albuquerque along Rte. 14, was a ghost town until the 70s, when artists began to resettle the area. Now the town cranks out funky and off-beat art instead of minerals, claiming artists, refugees from the 60s hippie revolution, and craftmakers as some of its 300 residents. Over 30 galleries showcase the local art ranging from estrogen-laced dresses to Native American-styled jewelry. The locally-revered **Mine Shaft Tavern,** 2840 Rte. 14, busts out "the best burgers west of the Mississippi" ($5-8) along with other traditionals. (☎473-0743. Open M-Th 11am-4pm, bar until 10pm; F-Su 11am-8pm, bar until closing. Live music Su 1-6pm.) **Java**

Junction, smack in the middle of town, offers lattés ($2.60), mochas ($3.10), and the cheapest grub around (tamales $1.50), as well as a selection of wacky coffee-themed t-shirts (open 7:30am-6pm). **Area code:** 505.

GALLUP   ☎ 505

Gallup, located at the intersection of **I-40** and **U.S. 666,** falls into the unfortunate class of Western cities that seem to have been built too quickly, filling their cultural void with an empty supermarket-and-styrofoam-cups modernity. However, Gallup's proximity to the **Petrified Forest National Park** (see p. 745), the **Navajo Reservation** (see p. 741), **Chaco Culture National Park** (see below), and **El Morro National Monument** (see below) somewhat redeems it for travelers. Gallup is also a good base for exploring the four-corners area.

Old Rte. 66, which runs parallel to I-40 through downtown, is lined with cheap motels. **The Colonial Motel,** 1007 W. Coal Ave., a bit west of downtown, rents large rooms with cable TV. (☎863-6821. Singles $21; doubles $25.) Near the center of downtown, the **Arrowhead Inn,** 1115 E. Rte. 66, might be an even better deal, with large and pleasant rooms, phones, cable TV, and sometimes microfridges. (☎863-5111. Doubles $20; quads $27.) You can pitch a tent in the shadow of red sandstone cliffs at **Red Rock State Park Campground,** which offers 141 sites and a convenience store. From I-40, take Exit 33 and follow the signs. (☎863-1329. Sites $10, RV hook-ups $14.) In addition to the usual fast-food suspects, a number of diners and cafes line both sides of I-40. **Ranch Kitchen,** 3001 W. Rte. 66, serves up tasty country cooking and real-deal barbecue in a wood-beamed dining room. (☎722-2537. Open daily 7am-10pm. 3 pancakes $4; barbecue chicken $11.)

Greyhound, 255 E. Rte. 66 (☎863-3761), runs to Flagstaff (4hr., 4 per day, $38) and Albuquerque (2½hr., 4 per day, $22). **Visitors center:** 701 Montoya Blvd., just off Rte. 66. (☎863-4909. Open daily 8am-5pm.) **Post Office:** 950 W. Aztec. (☎722-5265. Open M-F 8:30am-5pm, Sa 10am-1:30pm.) **ZIP code:** 87301. **Area code:** 505.

NEAR GALLUP

CHACO CULTURE NATIONAL HISTORICAL PARK. Sun-scorched **Chaco Canyon** (*CHAH-co*) served as the first great settlement of the Ancestral Puebloans. The ruins here, which date from the 9th century, are among the best-preserved in the Southwest. Evidence of inhabitance thousands of years older than even the most ancient Ancestral Pueblo dwellings also enrich the landscape, though the societies that flourished during the turn of the first millennium are what make the site awesome. The Chaco societies demonstrated superior scientific knowledge and designed their building in accordance to solar patterns. One such structure, **Pueblo Bonito,** is the canyon's largest pueblo; it was once four stories high and housed more than 600 rooms. Nearby **Chetro Ketl** houses one of the Southwest's largest *kivas,* a prayer room used in religious rituals. The largest pueblos are accessible from the main road, but **backcountry hiking trails** lead to many other ruins; snag a free **backcountry permit** from the visitors center before heading off.

The park lies 92 mi. northeast of Gallup. From the north, take Rte. 44/550 to County Rd. 7900 (3 mi. east of **Nageezi**); from the south, take Rte. 9 from Crownpoint to the turn-off for the park. At the turn of the century, it took a government archaeologist almost a year to get here from Washington, DC—not much has changed. From the highways, a 20 mi. dirt road leads to the park; this part alone may take 1hr. *There is no gas in the park, and gas stations en route are few and far between.* In addition, call the park in advance (☎988-6727) to inquire about the conditions of the roads, which may close due to bad weather.

The **visitors center,** at the east end of the park, has an excellent museum that exhibits Ancestral Puebloan art and architecture and includes an enlightening film. Star-gazing like the Chacos is offered at the center's observatory, open to visitors four nights a week (call ahead for available nights). Stock up on water here. (☎786-7014. Open daily 8am-6pm; in winter 8am-5pm. $8 per vehicle.) No food is available at the park. **Camping,** located a little more than a mile from the visitors center, costs $10 per site; register at the campground. Arrive by 11am; there are only 48 sites.

Most visitors to the **Circle A Ranch Hostel,** 5 mi. east of Cuba, come for no other reason than to stay at the ranch, but the hostel is also a convenient base for the park. Be forewarned: with 360 acres of forest, lakes, and canyons, and all the quiet and rustic appeal of a turn-of-the-century ranch, it may be hard to leave. Heading north on Hwy. 44/550, just north of Cuba, turn right onto Los Pinos Co. Rd., where an upside-down triangle advertises a camp, and follow the signs to the hostel for 5 mi. (☎289-3350. Open May-Oct. Kitchen, large living room, indoor and solar showers. Dorms $13; doubles $24-44.) **Area code:** 505.

EL MALPAIS NATIONAL MONUMENT. Home to a spectacle of converging lava flows and sandstone landscape, El Malpais contradicts its meaning of "the badlands." A young'n, this 11-year-old national monument features some of the Southwest's most diverse environments, from 114,000 acres of lava flow to sandstone bluffs to natural arches to ponderosa forests.

Due to its youth, much of El Malpais remains serene and at times inaccessible. Off I-40 at Exit 85, the **Northwest New Mexico Visitors Center** sits at the northern part of the monument and is the best place to begin the venture. (☎876-2783. Open daily 9am-6pm; Oct.-Apr. 8am-5pm.) Rte. 53 runs along the western side of the monument, while Rte. 117 borders the eastern side. Both roads are the means to accessing the trailheads and are themselves excellent ways to see the diverse landscape. In addition, Rte. 42 runs into the monument's belly; however, because it is unmaintained, a high-clearance vehicle is recommended. Off Rte. 42, two of the lava tube caves can be found at the **Big Tubes Area,** while the other one is at **Junction Cave.** Rte. 117 dazzles visitors with views of the mere 3000-year-old lava flows and offers access to **La Ventana Natural Arch.**

In addition to the Northwest New Mexico Visitors Center, El Malpais maintains two other venues for info. The Park Service's **El Malpais Information Center** (☎783-4774) is located 23 mi. south of I-40 on Rte. 53, while the **Bureau of Land Management's Ranger Station** is off I-40 at Exit 89 on Rte. 117. (Both open daily 8:30am-4:30pm.) There are no campgrounds at El Malpais; however, **backcountry camping** is free. Obtaining a permit at one of the visitors centers is requested but not mandatory. For more info, contact any of the visitors centers or write National Park Service, P.O. Box 939, Grants NM 87020. **Area code:** 505.

EL MORRO NATIONAL MONUMENT. While traveling through what is now New Mexico, Native Americans, Spanish *conquistadores*, and Anglo pioneers left their inscriptions on a giant boulder. **Inscription Rock** is now part of El Morro National Monument, just west of the Continental Divide on Rte. 53, 13 mi. southeast of the Navajo town of Ramah. A ½ mi. loop trail winds past the boulder and neighboring spring. A longer trail continues on past two pueblos. The **visitors center** includes a small museum and warnings against emulating the graffiti of old. A small tranquil campground has running water and primitive toilets ($5 per site; no reservations). Trails close 1hr. before visitors center. (☎783-4226. Open daily 8am-7pm; off-season 9am-5pm. $4 per vehicle, $2 per pedestrian.) **Area code:** 505.

TRUTH OR CONSEQUENCES   ☎505

In 1950, the popular radio game show "Truth or Consequences" celebrated its 10th anniversary by renaming a small town, formerly Hot Springs, NM, in its honor. As its maiden name suggests, T or C was a tourist attraction prior to the publicity stunt. The mineral baths infuse the town with fountain-of-youth effects and a funky down-home spirit. Maybe it's something in the water.

∎ PRACTICAL INFORMATION. T or C sits approximately 150 mi. south of Albuquerque on I-25. **Greyhound,** in cooperation with TNM&O coaches (☎894-3649), runs two buses daily from Albuquerque (3hr., $31.50). The **tourist office,** 201 S. Foch St., has info, shminfo. (☎800-831-9487. Open M-F 9am-5pm, Sa 9am-1pm.) **Post Office:** 300 Main St., in the middle of town (open M-F 9am-3pm), or 1507 N. Date St. (open 8:30am-5pm). **ZIP code:** 87901. **Area code:** 505.

ⅠＩ ACCOMMODATIONS. On the banks of the Río Grande, the laid-back ▨River-bend Hot Springs Hostel (HI-AYH), 100 Austin St., offers relief to weary travelers; prices include use of the mineral baths and the tranquil lapping of the Río Grande. With a meditation cove and canoe-trips down the river, Riverbend is an excellent spot to take it easy and certainly worth a stop—many travelers plan to stay a night and spend a week. (☎894-6183. Kitchen and laundry. Teepees or dorms $13, non-members $15; private rooms $30-45.) More traditional accommodations can be found at the **Charles Motel,** 601 Broadway, which also has mineral baths on the premises. The adobe rooms are large and most have kitchens. (☎894-7154. Singles $35; doubles $39.) **Campsites** at the nearby **Elephant Butte Lake State Park** have access to restrooms and cold showers. (Primitive sites $8; developed sites $10; with electricity $14.)

☐ FOOD. Nearly all of T or C's restaurants are as easy on the wallet as the baths are on the body. The popular **La Cocina,** 280 N. Date St., pleases with huge portions of Mexican and New Mexican food, including free chips and salsa. (☎894-6499. Open daily 10:30am-10pm. Burritos around $3, combination plates $6.) **Bar-B-Que on Broadway,** 308 Broadway (☎894-7047), has excellent breakfast specials (starting at $3) and hardy lunch entrees ($5-6). Find a decent selection of **groceries** at **Bullock's,** at the corner of Broadway and Post (open M-Sa 7:30am-8pm, Su 8am-7pm). That **Dam Site,** located next to the dam on the lake, hosts live music on its relaxing patio every Sa in the summer. (☎894-2073. Opens daily at 11am. Drafts $2.75.)

▣ SIGHTS AND ACTIVITIES. T or C's **mineral baths** are the town's main attraction; locals claim that it heals everything from blisters to sunburn. The only outdoor tubs are located at the **Riverbend Hostel,** where four co-ed tubs (bath suits must be worn) adorn the Río Grande. Public access to the baths is $6 per hr., complementary for hostel guests (baths run daily 7am-10am, and 7pm-10pm). The private indoor baths at the **Charles Motel's spa** cost $4 for guests and $5 per hr. for non-guests (open Su-Th). The spa also offers a variety of other New Age-y services, from reflexology to ear candling. The town's other claim to fame is dazzlingly blue **Elephant Butte Lake.** New Mexico's largest lake, Elephant Butte abounds with boating, water sports, and swimming. A few miles northeast of town, the lake is a popular weekend destination. (Entrance fee $4 per vehicle.)

Approximately 55 mi. north of T or C on I-25, the **Bosque del Apache Wildlife Refuge** is a favorite spot of migrating birds in winter, including cranes, eagles, and snow geese. (☎835-1828. Park open until 1hr. after sunset. Entrance fee $3.) In the summer you can see a surprising number of deer, coyote, porcupines, roadrunners, and snakes from the 15 mi. driving loop. The park also offers some short **hiking trails.** (Maps at visitors center. Open M-F 7:30am-4pm, Sa-Su 8am-4:30pm.)

GILA CLIFF DWELLINGS   ☎505

The mysterious **Gila Cliff Dwellings National Monument** preserves over 40 stone and timber rooms carved into the cliff's natural caves by the Mogollon tribe during the late 1200s. About a dozen families lived here for about 20 years, farming on the mesa top and along the river. During the early 1300s, however, the Mogollon abandoned their homes for reasons unknown, leaving the dwellings as their only trace. (Dwellings open daily 8am-6pm, off-season 9am-4pm. **Entrance fee** $3, under 12 free. National Parks passes accepted.) The **visitors center,** at the end of Rte. 15, shows an informative film and sells various maps of the **Gila National Forest** (☎536-9461; open daily 8am-5pm; off-season 8am-4:30pm). The picturesque 1 mi. round-trip **hike** to the dwellings begins past the Upper Scorpion campground. A trail guide (50¢) can be purchased at the trail head or visitors center. With flush toilets and running water, the **Upper Scorpion campground** operates on a first come, first served basis.

The **Gila National Forest** encompasses hundreds of mi. of hiking trails, as well as **free backcountry camping,** including some designated campsites. The forest includes more wilderness than any other Southwestern national forest. Rugged, mountainous terrain makes it ideal for extended and intense backpacking trips. Many trails start at the two corrals on the road to the cliff dwellings; rangers have hiking suggestions. To reach the monument, take Rte. 15 from Silver City, a slow and gorgeous drive that winds through the heavily-forested mountains to the canyon of the Gila River (44 mi.). In winter, call ahead for road conditions before attempting the drive. If you're coming from Truth or Consequences, take Rte. 152 in San Lorenzo to Rte. 35, then head north on Rte. 15. This route is less steep, just as beautiful, and takes about the same amount of time.

The nearest accommodation to the cliff dwellings is the comfy **Grey Feathers Lodge**, 20 mi. south at the intersection of Rte. 15 and Rte. 35. Attracting as many as 4000 hummingbirds over certain summer weekends, the lodge is an excellent place to relax and bird watch. (☎536-3206. Singles $40; doubles $45.) The adjoining **cafe** outfits travelers with sandwiches ($3-7) and tasty ice cream ($1 per scoop).

NEAR GILA: SILVER CITY

More beds and food await 44 mi. south of the Cliff Dwellings in **Silver City**, a good base for a trip to the monument, 60 mi. west of Truth or Consequences on Rte. 152. Life circulates around the historic downtown area where art galleries and small eateries please visitors. Downtown is bracketed by College Ave to the north and Broadway to the south; Rte. 90 (a.k.a. Hudson St.) runs along the eastern side. **Bullard St**. is the main drag, where most of the eateries and gift stores are located; galleries tend to be found on the side streets.

Fortunately two budget, but comfortable, accommodations are located in the downtown vicinity. The squeaky-clean **Carter House (HI-AYH)**, 101 N. Cooper St., has a kitchen, large common area, laundry facilities, and a huge wrap-around porch; a B&B occupies the upstairs. To find Carter House, follow the signs to the historic district, or take Broadway up the hill and turn left on Cooper—Carter is to the left of the courthouse. (☎388-5485. Check-in 8-10am and 4-9pm. $13, non-members $16; double $25/$31. B&B singles $62-72; doubles $70-80.) A half block from Bullard St., The **Palace Hotel**, 106 W. Broadway, has beautiful antique rooms. (☎388-1811. Doubles $32.50-55. Reservations recommended.)

The best food in Silver City can also be found downtown. True to its name, **The Corner Cafe**, 200 N. Bullard St., a local favorite, has an all-you-can-eat salad and soup buffet for $5. Sandwiches like the New Mexican Downtowner ($4.50) and especially delicious pancakes ($2.75) are crowd-pleasers. (☎388-2056. Open M-Sa 7am-4pm, Su 8am-2pm.) The eponymous owner of **Vicki's Downtown Deli**, 108 W. Yankie St., makes authentic Reuben, with chips and salsa, for $5.25. (☎388-5430; open M-F 11am-8:30pm, Sa 11:30am-4pm).

The **Gila Hike and Bike Shop**, 103 E. College St., rents mountain bikes to explore Gila and the surrounding foothills. (☎388-3222. Open M-F 9am-5:30pm, Sa 9am-5pm, Su 10am-4pm. Rentals 1st day $20, each additional day $10.) **Silver Stage Lines** (☎388-2586 or 800-522-0162) has bus service twice daily to Silver City from the El Paso airport (round-trip $50, home pick-up $2 extra). **Las Cruces Shuttle Service** (☎800-288-1784) offers daily trips between Silver City and Deming (3 per day, $20); Las Cruces (3 per day, $30); and El Paso (3 per day, $35). Both pick up passengers from The Corner Cafe, 200 N. Bullard St. **Visitors Center:** 201 N. Hudson St. (☎538-3785 or 800-548-9373. Open M-Sa 9am-5pm, in summer also Su noon-4pm.) **Internet access:** Public Library, 515 W. College Ave. (☎538-3672. Open M 9am-8pm, T-W 9am-6pm, Th 9am-8pm, F 9am-5pm, Sa 9am-1pm.) **Post office:** 500 N. Hudson St. (☎538-2831. Open M-F 8:30am-5pm, Sa 10am-noon). **ZIP code:** 88061. **Area code:** 505.

WHITE SANDS NATIONAL MONUMENT   ☎505

The giant sandbox of White Sands evokes nostalgia for playground days. Situated in the Tularosa Basin between the Sacramento and San Andres mountains, the world's largest gypsum dunes formed as rainwater dissolved gypsum in a nearby mountain, collecting in the basin's Lake Lucero. As desert heat evaporated the lake, the gypsum crystals were left behind and now form the blindingly white sand dunes. These drifts of fine sand create an arctic tundra look, but don't be fooled: the midday sun assaults the shadeless with a light and heat that can be unbearable.

Trekking or rolling through the dunes provides hours of mindless fun or mindful soul-searching; the sand is particularly awe-inspiring at sunset.

◪ PRACTICAL INFORMATION. White Sands lies on Rte. 70, 15 mi. southwest of Alamogordo and 52 mi. northeast of Las Cruces. Rte. 70 is prone to closures due to missile testing at the nearby military base. Delays can run up to an hour; call ☎479-9199 to check the status of Rte. 70 closures. You'll find the **White Sands Visitors Center,** P.O. Box 1086, Holloman AFB 88330, as you enter the park from Rte. 70. (☎479-6124. Open daily 8am-7pm; mid-Aug. to late May 8am-5pm.) **Area code:** 505.

▟ ACCOMMODATIONS. To use the park's **backcountry campsites,** register at the park entrance ($3 per adult plus entrance fee). More free backcountry camping can be found at **Lincoln National Forest** (☎682-2551), 13 mi. to the east. **Aguirre Springs** (☎525-4300), 30 mi. to the west on Rte. 70, doesn't charge for camping, but you must pay $3 to enter. For info, contact the **Forest Supervisor,** Lincoln National Forest, 1101 New York Ave., Alamogordo 88310. **Oliver Lee Memorial State Park,** 10 mi. south of Alamogordo on U.S. 54, then 5 mi. east on Dog Canyon Rd., has a campground at the canyon mouth on the west face of the Sacramento Mountains. (☎437-8284. Sites $10-14, with hook-up $17. Visitors center open daily 9am-4pm. Park entrance fee $3 per vehicle.)

A destination unto itself, the relaxing ◪**High Desert Hostel Ranch** revels in its quiet, rural way of life. Located in the hamlet of Oscuro about 1hr. north of the park, this working adobe ranch comes complete with chickens, cows, orchard, and organic vegetable garden. Oscuro is a flag stop on the Greyhound route from El Paso to Albuquerque ($24 one-way from either city); call ahead, and the owner will pick you up from the bus stop. Driving, the hostel is about 1 mi. down a dirt road from U.S. 54 at Mi. 108—follow the signs. (☎648-4007. Free laundry. Dorm beds $14; private doubles $27; triples $32.) Closer to White Sands, the town of **Alamogordo** has a large motel selection, most of which line White Sands Blvd. The bright pink **Western Motel,** 1101 S. White Sands Blvd., has pleasant rooms with cable TV and A/C. (☎437-2922. Singles $30; doubles $35.)

◪ SIGHTS AND ACTIVITIES. Hiking possibilities include the **Big Dune Trail,** a 1 mi. nature trail adorned with plaques describing the unique fauna and flora of the dunes, and the difficult **Alkali Flat Trail,** a backcountry hike to a dry lake bed where gypsum sand is formed (4.5 mi., 3-4hr.; ask at the visitors center for a topographical map before starting out). Bring plenty of water, even for short hikes. The paved **Dunes Drive** leads 8 mi. into the heart of the dunes. (Open 7am-9pm; off-season 7am-sunset. $3 per adult. Wheelchair accessible.) Summer evening events include ranger-led sunset strolls (7pm) and lectures (8:30pm). Ask about special programs for full moon nights, when the park is open until midnight. The basin is also home to a missile test range—duck if you hear a sharp whistle—and the **Trinity Site,** 65 mi. north of White Sands, where the world's first atomic bomb was detonated in July 1945 (open to visitors on the first weekends of Apr. and Oct.).

The **Space Center,** 2 mi. northeast of U.S. 54, brings the great beyond down to earth with a museum, an OmniMax, and a planetarium. (☎437-2840 or 877-333-6589. Open daily 9am-5pm. Museum $2.50, seniors $2.25, ages 6-17 $2; OmniMax film $5.50/$5/$4.50; Planetarium $3.50/$2.25/$2.) The **White Sands Missile Range** runs a small museum and outdoor exhibit of missiles. Located 30 mi. west off the national park on Rte. 70, the exhibit is free. (Open M-F 8am-4:30pm. Several forms of ID are required to enter the military base.)

ROSWELL   ☎505

With giant inflatable martians advertising used cars, streetlights with painted-on pointy eyes, and flying saucers adorning fast food signs, one thing is certain: aliens *have* invaded Roswell. Located 76 miles north of Carlsbad, Roswell is a celebration of extra-terrestrial life and all the mania that accompanies it. The fascination began in July 1947, when an alien spacecraft reportedly plummeted to the earth near the

SOUTHWEST

dusty town. The official Army press release reported that the military had recovered pieces of some form of "flying saucer," but a retraction arrived the next day—the mysterious wreckage, the brass claimed, was actually a harmless weather balloon. Everyone admits that something crashed in the desert northwest of Roswell on that fateful night some 50 years ago. Was the initial Army admission just a poor choice of words by some PR hack or a crack in an elaborate cover-up?

■■ ORIENTATION AND PRACTICAL INFORMATION. Aside from a few things, Roswell is a fairly normal town. The intersection of 2nd St. (Rte. 70/380) and Main St. (Rte. 285) is the sun that the Roswell solar system orbits. To reach Roswell from Albuquerque, head 89 mi. south on I-25 to San Antonio, then 153 mi. east on U.S. 380. The cheery and helpful **visitors center** is at 426 N. Main St. (☎624-0889. Open M-F 8:30am-5:30pm, Sa-Su 10am-3pm.) **Greyhound,** 1100 N. Virginia Ave. (☎622-2510), in conjunction with TNM&O runs buses to Albuquerque (4hr., 2 per day Tu-Sa, 1 on M, $31.50) and El Paso (4½hr., 3 per day, $38). The **Pecos Trails Transit,** 515 N. Main St., runs buses all over town. (☎624-6777. M-F 6am-10:30pm, Sa 7:10am-10pm, Su 10:30am-7pm. 75¢, students 50¢, seniors 35¢.) The main **Post office:** 415 N. Pennsylvania Ave. (☎623-7231. Open M-F 7:30am-5:30pm, Sa 8am-noon.) **ZIP code:** 88202. **Area code:** 505.

■■ ACCOMMODATIONS AND FOOD. Main St. and 2nd St. are lined with budget motels. Many chain motels have settled on Main St. north of downtown and tend to be pricier than those on 2nd St. The **Budget Inn,** 2200 W. 2nd St., has newly remodeled rooms with telephones and microwaves. (☎623-3811 or 800-806-7030. Singles $27-37; doubles $31-45.) On Main St., the best deal can be found at the woody **Zuni Motel,** 1201 N. Main. All rooms have fridges and some suites are available. (☎622-1930. Singles $22; doubles $28.) The nearest **camping** can be found at **Bottomless Lakes State Park.** To reach the park, drive 15 mi. east on Rte. 380, then 5 mi. south on Rte. 409. (☎624-6058. Sites $10, full hook-up $18.)

Although fast food restaurants are as prevalent in Roswell as allusions to alien life, they are concentrated along N. Main St. and 2nd St. Side streets are home to less commercial budget eateries. **Martin's Capitol Cafe,** 110 W. 4th St. delights earthling or otherwise with tasty Mexican dishes at down-to-earth prices. The gigantic burritos (starting at $3.50) with red or green salsa are out of...um, good. Another inexpensive option is **Teresa's Restaurant,** 505 N. Main St. where breakfast and lunch specials range from $3-5. (☎623-9691. Open Tu-Su 7am-2pm.)

■■ SIGHTS AND ENTERTAINMENT. Believer or skeptic, most visitors will find the alien side of Roswell entertaining, if not enlightening. During the first week of July, the UFO Festival commemorates the anniversary of the alleged encounter, drawing thousands for live music, an alien costume contest, and a 5km "Alien Chase" race. With a plastic flying saucer above its diminutive storefront, the popular **International UFO Museum and Research Center,** 114 N. Main St., has invented some novel ways to cash in on the alienophile hysteria. Some remain skeptical of its scholarly credentials, but the museum's backers say the reading rooms and archives are academically legitimate. (☎625-9495. Open daily 10am-5pm; in summer 9am-5pm. Free. Audio tour $1.) No pilgrimage would be complete without a trip to the sun-scorched crash site itself, the 24 sq. mi. **Hobb Corn Ranch,** 20 mi. north of Roswell on U.S. 285. A sign near the entrance greets the faithful: this "universal sacred site" is dedicated "to the beings who met their destinies near Roswell, New Mexico, July 1947." For $25 (under 14 free), the owners will escort the curious 8 mi. to the low butte where the saucer allegedly met its destiny amid dust devils and parched cacti (by appointment only; call ☎622-0628 10am-5pm).

If you can tear yourself away from all the alien mania, Roswell's tamer side features a worthy stop. The **Roswell Music and Art Center,** 100 W. 11th St., houses a superb art museum that showcases innovative and daring artwork alongside traditional Southwestern fare. The center also has a **Planetarium** which runs $3 shows Th-Sa nights in the summer and one week per month in the winter. (☎624-6744. Open M-Sa 9am-5pm, Su 1pm-5pm. Free.)

SOUTHWEST

CARLSBAD CAVERNS

☎**505**

Imagine the surprise of the first European wanderers in southeastern New Mexico when 250,000 bats appeared at dusk, seemingly out of nowhere. It was the turn of the century when this swarm led to the discovery of the Carlsbad Caverns. By 1923, colonies of tourists clung to the walls of this desolate attraction. Carlsbad Caverns National Park marks one of the world's largest and oldest cave systems; even the most jaded spelunker will be struck by its unusual geological formations.

⁊ PRACTICAL INFORMATION. The closest town is **White's City,** a tiny tourist trap on U.S. 62/180, 20 mi. southeast of Carlsbad, 6 mi. from the park visitors center. Flash floods occasionally close the roads, so call ahead to the visitors center. **El Paso, Texas** (see p. 619), is the nearest major city, 150 mi. to the west past **Guadalupe Mountains National Park** (see p. 618). **Greyhound,** in cooperation with **TNM&O Coaches** (☎887-1108), runs two buses per day to White's City from El Paso ($25) and Carlsbad (35min., $4). **Visitor Info: Carlsbad Caverns Visitors Center.** (☎785-2232. Open daily 8am-7pm; late Aug. to May 8am-5:30pm.) White's City's **post office:** 23 Carlsbad Caverns Hwy., next to the Best Western gift shop. (☎785-2220. Open M-F 8am-noon and 12:30-4:30pm, Sa 8am-noon.) **ZIP code:** 88268. **Area code:** 505.

⁊ ACCOMMODATIONS. Drive 20 mi. north to **Carlsbad** to find a plethora of cheap motels. **Carlsbad Inn,** 2019 S. Canal St., has clean rooms, many with a microwave and fridge. (☎887-1171. Singles $33; doubles $38.) Even less expensive motels line S. Canal St. (U.S. 285), but it's always a good idea to see the room before you pay. The **White's City Resort RV Park,** outside the park entrance, has water, showers, and a pool. (☎785-2291 or 800-228-3767. Tent sites or full hook-up $20. Register in the Best Western lobby.) **Backcountry camping** is free; get a permit at the visitors center. For more camping, see **Guadalupe Mountains National Park, TX,** p. 618.

⧉ SIGHTS. The belly of the cave can be explored by embarking on any of three tours. Plaques guide you along the self-guided **Big Room Tour** and **Natural Entrance Tour.** The Big Room tour is relatively easy and popular, making use of the elevator on both the descent and ascent. The steep Natural Entrance tour is less trafficked as it winds its way down from the surface to the Big Room area. The elevator is used for the ascent. *(Open 8:30am-5pm; mid-Aug.-May. 1½hr., depending on how often you stop to gawk in amazement. $6, ages 6-15 and Golden Age Passport holders $3, under 6 free. Partially wheelchair accessible.)* The 3rd option is the ranger-guided **King's Palace Tour,** which passes through four of the cave's lowest rooms and some of the most awesome anomalies. *(1½hr. tours on the hr. 9-11am and 1-3pm. Advance reservations required. $8, Golden Age Passport holders and ages 6-15 $4.)* Plan your visit for late afternoon to catch the magnificent **bat flight.** The ritual, during which hungry bats storm out of the cave at a rate of 6000 per min., is preceded by a ranger talk. *(Daily May-Oct. just before sunset.)* **Backcountry hiking** is permitted in the park (not in the caves), but a permit, a map, and massive quantities of water are required.

Tours of the undeveloped **Slaughter Canyon Cave** offer a more rugged caving experience. A reliable car is required to get there, however. There's no public transportation, and the parking lot is 23 mi. down a dirt road off U.S. 62/180, several mi. south of the main entrance to the park. The cave entrance is a steep, strenuous ½ mi. from the lot. Ranger-led tours (bring a flashlight) traverse difficult and slippery terrain; there are no paved trails or handrails. Call to reserve at least two days ahead. *(☎785-2232. Two 2hr. tours; early Sept. to late May Sa-Su only. $15, Golden Age Passport holders and ages 6-15 $7.50.)* Other tours of remote areas of the caves are offered, the more adventurous of which require crawling and climbing through tight passages. *(☎800-967-2283. Tours 1-4hr. $7-20. Call at least a month in advance for reservations.)*

Just north of Carlsbad, **Living Desert State Park** preserves and protects the various flora and fauna native to New Mexico. The 1¼ mi. **self-guided walking tour** passes a variety of exhibits, including an aviary, bears, porcupines, and a reptile house. *(Open daily 8am-7pm; off-season 9am-4pm. $4, ages 7-12 $2. Wheelchair accessible.)*

CALIFORNIA

For centuries, settlers have come to California in search of the elusive and the unattainable. Spanish conquistadors saw in it a utopian paradise and '49ers plumbed its depths for the gloriously imagined Mother Lode. Today, adventurers flock to its mountains and deserts, and stampedes of families overrun its national parks, seeking peace among forests, granite cliffs, and lava beds. Dreamy-eyed, disenfranchised flower children converge on San Francisco's Haight Street, while technology wizards inundate booming Silicon Valley. And aspiring actors still seek stardom on Hollywood's silver screen.

Glaring movie spotlights, clanging San Francisco trolleys, and *barrio* bustle all belong to California. Vanilla-scented Jeffrey pines, alpine lakes, and ghostly, shimmering desert landscapes all belong to California. The breezy tolerance of the San Francisco Bay Area, the plastic style of L.A., and the military-fueled Republicanism of San Diego all belong to California. It is the West of the West, the testing ground of the superlative, the drawing board for the American dream. There's so much going on you'd need a whole book (like *Let's Go: California 2001*) to describe it.

HIGHLIGHTS OF CALIFORNIA

LOS ANGELES. Follow your star to the place where media legends carouse, Ice Age fossils calcify, and boardwalk freaks commune (p. 779).

SAN FRANCISCO. Here, bluesmen resonate, iconoclasts castigate and students demonstrate, and old hippies recreate (p. 825).

SCENIC DRIVES. Along the coast, Rte. 1 and U.S. 101 breeze past earthy beach towns and along soaring cliffs, passing Santa Barbara (p. 816), Hearst Castle (p. 820), and Redwood National Park (p. 859).

NATIONAL PARKS. Hike among the granite peaks of Yosemite (p. 868), or climb a boulder and see the sunset at Joshua Tree (p. 813).

🛈 PRACTICAL INFORMATION

Capital: Sacramento.
Visitor Info: California Office of Tourism, 801 K St. #1600, Sacramento 95814 (☎800-862-2543; www.gocalif.ca.gov).
Postal Abbreviation: CA. **Sales Tax:** 7-8%, depending on county.

LOS ANGELES ☎213

Myth and anti-myth stand comfortably juxtaposed in Los Angeles. Some see in its sweeping beaches and dazzling sun a demi-paradise, a land of opportunity where the most opulent dreams can be realized. Others point to its congestion, smog, and crime, and declare Los Angeles a sham—a converted wasteland where TV-numbed masses go to wither in the sun. Regardless, L.A. is a wholly American phenomenon, one that developed at the same time as America's international ascendancy. It is this autonomy that makes L.A. feel like a city without a past, a city where nothing seems more than 30 years old. Many come to this historical vacuum to make or remake themselves. And what better place? Without the tiresome duty of kowtowing to the gods of an established high culture, Angelenos are free to indulge not in what they must, but in what they choose. The resulting atmosphere is delicious with potential. It's a hell of a show.

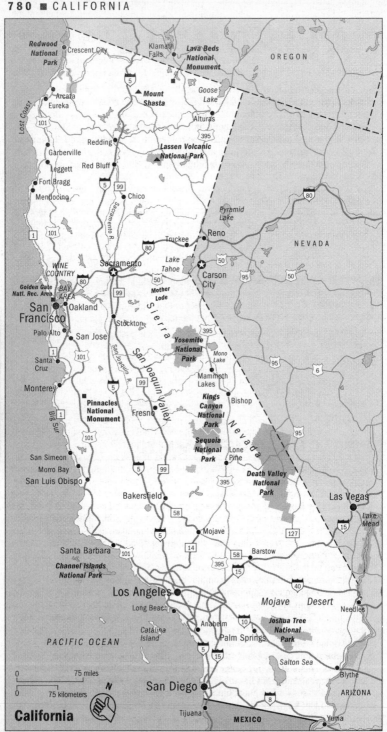

California

0   75 miles
0   75 kilometers

N

PACIFIC OCEAN

OREGON
NEVADA
ARIZONA
MEXICO

✈ GETTING THERE AND GETTING AWAY

Six main arteries pump into Greater L.A. Three of them run north from the city: the **Santa Ana Freeway (I-5)**, the **Ventura Freeway (U.S. 101)**, and the **Pacific Coast Highway (Rte. 1).** Santa Ana Fwy. also runs south, and **I-10** and **I-15** run east.

   Airport: Los Angeles International (LAX) (☎310-646-5252), in Westchester, 15 mi. southwest of downtown. Metro buses, car rental companies, cabs, and airport shuttles offer rides from here to requested destinations. Cab fare to downtown is $24-33.

   Buses: Greyhound-Trailways Information Center, 1716 E. 7th St., at Alameda, downtown. Call for fares, schedules, and local ticket info.

   Trains: Union Station, 800 N. Alameda St. (☎683-6729), serves Amtrak trains.

▛ GETTING AROUND

Nowhere is the god *Automobile* revered more than in L.A., often making the city a transportation hell. The freeway is perhaps the most enduring of L.A.'s images. When uncongested, these well-marked, 10- and 12-lane concrete roadways offer speed and convenience. But the most frustrating aspect of driving is the sheer unpredictability of L.A. traffic. It goes without saying that rush hours, both morning and evening, are always a mess and well worth avoiding. Since construction is performed at random hours, there can be problems at any time. A little reminder: no matter how crowded the freeway is, it's almost always quicker and safer than taking city streets. For freeway info, call **CalTrans** (☎897-3693). *Do not hitchhike!* In Los Angeles, it's not just dangerous, it is suicidal.

 Public transportation can be confusing, slow, and even useless in L.A. Because sights are so spread out and buses are such a headache, those looking to sightsee should get behind the wheel of a car. If this is not possible, try to base yourself in Hollywood or downtown, where many sights are clustered. While driving isn't much fun in L.A., it's usually the better way to get around.

   Public Transit: The **Metropolitan Transit Authority (MTA)** does work—sort of. Some older buses may still be labeled RTD (Rapid Transit District), the MTA's former name. Bus service is dismal in the outer reaches of the city and 2hr. journeys are not unusual. Write for "sector maps," MTA, P.O. Box 194, Los Angeles 90053, or stop by a **customer service center.** There are **three centers** downtown: Gateway Transit Center, Union Station (open M-F 6am-6:30pm); Arco Plaza, 505 S. Flower St., Level C (open M-F 7:30am-3:30pm); and 5301 Wilshire Blvd. (open daily 9am-5pm). MTA's basic fare is $1.35, seniors and disabled 45¢; transfers 25¢/10¢. Exact change is required. The **DASH shuttle** (☎808-2273) serves Chinatown, Union Station, Gateway Transit Center, and Olvera Street. DASH also operates shuttles in Hollywood (along Sunset Blvd.), Pacific Palisades, Venice, Watts, Fairfax, Midtown, Crenshaw, Van Nuys/Studio City, Warner Center, and Southeast L.A. Downtown DASH operates approximately M-F 6:30am-6:30pm, Sa 10am-5pm. Pacific Palisades shuttles do not run on Sa. Venice DASH operates June-Aug. Sa-Su every 10min. 11am-6pm. Fare 25¢. Parking $2.50. With over 1000 stops in Santa Monica, L.A., and Culver City, **Santa Monica Municipal Bus Lines** (☎310-451-5444), the "Big Blue Bus" (BBBus), is faster and cheaper than the MTA. Fare 50¢ and transfer tickets for MTA buses 25¢; transfers to other BBBuses free.

   Taxi: Checker Cab, ☎482-3456. **Independent,** ☎385-8294.

   Car Rental: Avon, 7080 Santa Monica Blvd. (☎323-850-0826), at La Brea Blvd. Open M-F 6am-7pm, Sa-Su 7am-5pm. Economy cars $29 per day with 150 mi. free, $175 per week with 750 mi. free. CDW $9 per day. No under-25 surcharge. **Avis,** 11901 Santa Monica Blvd. (☎310-914-7700), between Barrington Ave. and Bundy St. Open M-F 7:30am-5pm, Sa 8am-5pm, Su 9am-4pm. Economy cars $34 per day or $180 per week with unlimited mileage. CDW $9 per day. Under-25 surcharge $10 per day.

CALIFORNIA

⚡ ORIENTATION

A mere 419 mi. south of San Francisco and 127 mi. north of San Diego, the City of Angels spreads its wings across the flatland basin between the coast of Southern California and the inland San Gabriel Mountains. Greater L.A. is like a club to which the surrounding 'burbs try to belong, a vast conceptual conglomerate of over 80 cities. Before you even think about navigating L.A.'s 6500 mi. of streets and 40,000 intersections, get yourself a good **map**. Locals swear by the *Thomas Guide: Los Angeles County Street Guide and Directory* ($16 for L.A. county, $26 for L.A. and Orange County).

A legitimate **downtown** Los Angeles does exist, but it won't help orient you to the rest of the city. The predominately Latino section of L.A. known as **East L.A.** begins east of downtown's Western Ave. South of downtown are the **University of Southern California (USC), Exposition Park,** and the predominantly African-American districts of **Inglewood, Watts,** and **Compton.** The area south of downtown, known as **South Central,** suffered the brunt of the fires and looting that erupted in 1992. South Central and East L.A. are considered crime-ridden and offer little to attract tourists.

Northwest of downtown is **Hollywood.** Running from downtown to the ocean, Sunset Blvd. (east-west) presents a cross-section of virtually everything L.A. has to offer: beach communities, lavish wealth, famous nightclubs, and sleazy motels. Hollywood Blvd. (east-west) runs just beneath the star-studded Hollywood Hills.

West of Hollywood, the **Westside** encompasses West Hollywood, Westwood, Century City, Culver City, Bel Air, Brentwood, and (for our purposes) the independent city of **Beverly Hills.** The affluent Westside also is home to the University of California at Los Angeles (UCLA) and some trendy, off-beat Melrose Ave. hangouts. The area west of downtown is known as the **Wilshire District** after its main boulevard.

The Valley spreads north of the Hollywood Hills and the Santa Monica Mountains. For most people, *the* valley, is, like, the **San Fernando Valley,** where more than a million people live in the suburbs, in a basin bounded to the north and west by the Santa Susanna Mountains and the Simi Freeway (Rte. 118), to the south by the Ventura Freeway (Rte. 134), and to the east by the Golden State Freeway (I-5). The Valley also contains the suburb of **Burbank** and the city of **Pasadena.**

Eighty mi. of beach line L.A.'s **Coastal Region. Zuma** is northernmost, followed by **Malibu,** which lies 15 mi. up the coast from **Santa Monica.** Just a bit farther south is the funky beach community of **Venice.** The beach towns south of Santa Monica, comprising an area called the **South Bay,** are **Marina del Rey, Manhattan, Hermosa,** and **Redondo Beach.** South across the hob nobby **Palos Verdes Peninsula** is **Long Beach.** Farthest south are the **Orange County** beach cities. Confused yet? Everyone is. Get a good map.

🗒 PRACTICAL INFORMATION

Visitor Info: Los Angeles Convention and Visitor Bureau, 685 S. Figueroa St. (☎ 689-8822), between Wilshire Blvd. and 7th St. in the Financial District. Staff speaks French, German, Spanish, Japanese, Tagalog, and Klingon. Open M-F 8am-5pm, Sa 8:30am-5pm, Sa 8:30am-5pm.

Hotlines: Rape Crisis, ☎ 310-392-8381. 24hr.

Post Office: 71301 S. Central Ave. Open M-F 7am-7pm, Sa 7am-3pm. **ZIP Code:** 90001.

AREA CODES **213** covers downtown L.A., Huntington Park, Vernon, and Montebello. **213** and **323** cover Hollywood. **310** and **424** cover Malibu, Pacific Coast Highway, Westside, parts of West Hollywood, Santa Monica, southern and eastern L.A. County, and Catalina Island. **626** covers the San Gabriel Valley and Pasadena. **818** covers Burbank, Glendale, San Fernando Valley, Van Nuys, and La Cañada. **909** covers the eastern border of L.A. County. In text, **213** unless noted.

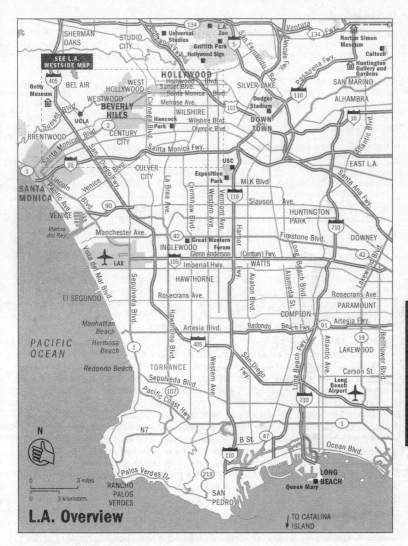

L.A. Overview

ACCOMMODATIONS

Cheap accommodations in Los Angeles are often unsafe. It can be difficult to gauge quality from the exterior, so ask to see a room before you plunk down any cash. Be suspicious of rates below $35; they're probably not the kind of hotels in which most travelers would feel secure. In choosing where to stay, the first consideration should be car accessibility. If you don't have wheels, you would be wise to decide which element of L.A. appeals to you the most. Those visiting for the beaches would do well to choose lodgings in Venice or Santa Monica. Avid sightseers will probably be better off in Hollywood or the more expensive (but cleaner and nicer) Westside. Downtown has numerous public transportation connections but is unsafe after dark. *Listed prices do not include L.A.'s 14% hotel tax.*

HOLLYWOOD

Although Tinseltown has tarnished in recent years, its location, sights, and nightlife keep the tourists coming. Exercise caution if scouting out one of the many budget hotels on **Hollywood** or **Sunset Blvd.;** *especially east of the main strips, the area can be dangerous, particularly at night.* Nevertheless, the hostels here are generally excellent and a much better value than anything else in L.A. If the ones listed below are full, try **Orange Drive Manor,** 1764 N. Orange Dr. (☎323-850-0350); **Student Inn International Hostel,** 7038½ Hollywood Blvd. (☎323-469-6781 or 800-557-7038), on the Walk of Fame, which offers a 25% *Let's Go* discount; or a second **Hollywood International Hostel,** 6820 Hollywood Blvd. (☎323-463-0797 or 800-750-6561).

Banana Bungalow Hollywood, 2775 W. Cahuenga Blvd. (☎323-851-1129 or 800-446-7835), just north of the Hollywood Bowl. Free shuttles from airport ($12 per person to airport) and to area beaches and attractions. Hollywood Hills locale affords a relentlessly wacky and frisky summer-camp atmosphere. Free nightly movies, pool, hoops, weight room, Internet access ($1 per 10min.), and "snack shack." Continental breakfast, linen, and parking included. Meals $5. Car rental available. Check-in 24hr. Check-out 10:30am. Stay 7 nights and the 8th night is free. *Passport and international airline ticket or college ID required.* Co-ed dorms (6-10 beds) with bathroom and TV $18-20; private doubles $55.

USA Hostels Hollywood, 6772 Hawthorn Ave. (☎323-462-3777 or 800-524-6783), off Highland Ave. between Hollywood and Sunset Blvd. Free pick-up from airport, bus, and train stations. Daily tours to local attractions. Kitchen, patio, bike rental, party room with bar, billiards, Internet access ($1 per 10min.), and TV. BBQs and comedy nights twice per week. Linen, lockers, parking, and breakfast of unlimited waffles and pancakes included. *Passport or proof of travel required.* Meals $4-5. Co-ed dorms (6-8 beds) with private bath June-Aug. $17, Sept.-May $16; private rooms $40. Weekly rates $109/$254.

Re-Tan Hotel, 1732 N. Whitley Ave. (☎323-462-9275), off Hollywood Blvd. Re-Tan's rooms receive loving care. Sinks in rooms; sparklingly clean shared baths. Laundry and linens available. No parking. Reception 7am-noon. Check-out noon. Singles $16; doubles $18, with private bath $25. Weekly rates singles/doubles $95, with bath $125. No credit cards; $25 deposit required.

Hollywood International Hostel, 1057 Vine St. (☎323-462-6351 or 800-750-1233), at Santa Monica Blvd. Free pick-up from airport, bus, and train stations. Large rooms and a lounge with leather couches, cable TV, and a PacMan video game. Kitchen, gym, Internet access, nightly movies, billiards room with cable TV. Rooftop deck has a bar and grill, as well as a killer view of the Hollywood sign. Breakfast and parking included. All rooms have private bath and lockers. Reception 24hr. *International passport or college ID required.* Dorms June-Aug. $15, Sept.-May $13; doubles $37/$32. Weekly rates $90/$84; doubles $245/$210.

SANTA MONICA, VENICE, MARINA DEL REY

Venice Beach hostels beckon to all the young budget travelers, especially foreign students, who are lured by the area's blend of indulgent beach culture and lively nightlife. Most of the cheap accommodations that pepper the coast cater to raucous party kids, but there are some quiet gems in the mix.

▨ **Los Angeles/Santa Monica (HI-AYH),** 1436 2nd St., Santa Monica (☎310-393-9913), 2 blocks from the beach and across from the 3rd St. Promenade. Take MTA #33 from Union Station to 2nd St. and Broadway, BBBus #3 from LAX to 4th St. and Broadway, or BBBus #10 from Union Station. Rooms are small but clean. Quiet hours 10pm-8am. Lobby manned 24hr. Colossal kitchen, 2 nightly movies, library, central courtyard, laundry, and biweekly barbecues ($5). 4-week maximum stay. Dorms (4-10 beds) $19-21, non-members $22-24; private doubles $58/$61. In summer, reserve 2 weeks in advance.

Cadillac Hotel, 8 Dudley Ave., Venice (☎310-399-8876), directly off the Ocean Front Walk, overlooking the beach. International crowd and helpful staff. Tour desk, sauna,

TO GRIFFITH PARK

Hollyhock House ■ Barnsdall Park

Franklin Ave.

Hollywood Fwy.

Vermont Ave.

Normandie Ave.

Western Ave.

Van Ness Ave.

Sunset Blvd.

Vine St.

Cahuenga Blvd.

Highland

HOLLYWOOD

Paramount Studios ■

3rd St.

6th St.

TO DOWNTOWN

Olympic Blvd.

Pico Blvd.

N

1 mile
1 kilometer
0
0

Crenshaw Blvd.

Jefferson Blvd.

Franklin Ave.

Hollywood Blvd.

Fountain Ave.

Sierra Bonita Ave.

Fairfax Ave.

Crescent Heights Blvd.

Santa Monica Blvd.

WEST HOLLYWOOD

Melrose Ave.

La Brea Blvd.

Gardner St.

Pan Pacific Park

CBS Studios

Farmer's Market

Hancock

La Brea Park
Tar Pits ■

L.A. County
Museum of Art

Miracle Mile

Wilshire Country Club

WILSHIRE DISTRICT

San Vicente Blvd.

Fairfax Ave.

Venice Blvd.

Washington Blvd.

10

Sweetzer Ave.

Kings Rd.

Le Parc ■

Beverly Center ■

La Cienega Blvd.

Robertson Blvd.

Crescent Hts. Blvd.

Beverly Blvd.

Sunset Strip

Santa Monica Blvd.

Doheny Dr.

Hillcrest Rd.

3rd St.

Burton Way

Wilshire Blvd.

Olympic Blvd.

Pico Blvd.

Museum of Tolerance ■

Beverwil Dr.

WEST LOS ANGELES

Santa Monica Fwy.

Greystone Mansion and Park ■

Doheny Rd.

Hillcrest Rd.

Elm Dr.

BEVERLY HILLS

Crescent Dr.

Canon Dr.

Beverly Dr.

Rodeo Dr.

Golden Triangle

CENTURY CITY

Moreno Dr.

Park E

Century Plaza Towers ■

Ave. of the Stars

Century Park W.

Fox Studios

Rancho Park

405

Sta. Monica Mtns. Nat'l Recreation Area

Lake Franklin

Coldwater Canyon Drive

Sunset Blvd.

Beverly Hills Hotel ■

Benedict Canyon

Tower Rd.

Los Angeles Country Club

Roxbury Dr.

Mapleton Dr.

Beverly Glen Blvd.

Beverly Glen Blvd.

Hilgard Ave.

Little S. Mona Blvd.

Westwood Memorial Cemetery

Westwood Blvd.

Veteran Ave.

Sepulveda Blvd.

Santa Monica Fwy.

10

Bel Air Rd.

Stone Canyon Rd.

BEL AIR

Sunset Blvd.

WESTWOOD

UCLA

Gayley Ave.

Landfair Ave.

Le Conte Dr.

UCLA Hammer Museum ■

San Diego Fwy.

Wilshire Blvd.

Santa Monica Blvd.

Federal Ave.

Barrington Ave.

Veteran Ave.

BRENTWOOD

405

J. Paul Getty Museum and Getty Center ■

Bristol Ave.

San Vicente Blvd.

Bundy Dr.

Montana Ave.

Wilshire Blvd.

Santa Monica Blvd.

Olympic Blvd.

Olympic Blvd.

2

TO SANTA MONICA AND VENICE

CALIFORNIA

L.A. Westside

▲ ACCOMMODATIONS

Beverly Inn, **5**
Bevonshire Lodge Motel, **6**
Claremont Motel, **1**
Hotel del Flores, **4**
The Little Inn, **2**
Stars Inn, **3**

101

2

rooftop sundeck, and well-equipped gym. Lounge has cable TV, pool table, Internet access. Lockers and luggage storage. Parking included with private rooms. 4-bunk dorms with private bath $25; impressive for the area, private suites start at $80. Airport shuttle $7. No reservations for bunks; call before coming or show up at 1pm and hope.

Venice Beach Hotel, 25 Windward Ave., Venice (☎310-399-7649; fax 399-1930), 1 block from the boardwalk. From the L.A. airport, take BBBus #3, transfer to #2, get off at the Venice Beach post office, and walk 1 block toward shore. Airport shuttle $7. Pristine rooms, some with ocean views. Lively BYOB bar area has colorful tables. Free cocktail at check-in; free tea and coffee throughout your stay. Excellent security. No kitchen or laundry. Free use of tennis rackets, table tennis, and boogie boards ($20 deposit). Linen included. Reception 24hr. *International or American passport required.* Dorms (3-6 beds) $15, with private bath $17; doubles (some with private bath and TV) $35-49; slightly cramped but manageable triples $55.

Share-Tel Apartments, 20 Brooks Ave., Venice (☎310-392-0325), half a block from the beach. Fun-loving hostel has a lounge with TV and games. Dorm rooms are spacious and clean, with private baths, kitchenettes, and fridges. Breakfast (daily) and dinner (M-F) included. Lockers $1. Linen and key deposit $20. Reception 8am-11pm. *International passport or proof of travel required.* 4-8 bed dorms $17; weekly July-Aug. $125, Sept.-June $110; private rooms $22-25. No reservations. No credit cards.

BEVERLY HILLS, WESTWOOD, WILSHIRE

The relatively safe Westside has excellent public transportation to the beaches. The area's affluence, however, means less bang for your buck, and there are no hostels. Those planning to stay at least one month in summer or six months during the school year can contact the **UCLA Off-Campus Housing Office,** 350 Deneve Dr. (☎310-825-4491; cho.ucla.edu).

Claremont Hotel, 1044 Tiverton Ave., Westwood Village (☎310-208-5957 or 800-266-5957), near UCLA. Clean rooms with antique dressers, ceiling fans, private baths, and phones. Microwave and free coffee offered in the lobby. Check-in 24hr. Check-out noon. Reservations recommended, especially in June graduation season. Singles $43; doubles $49; triples $55. Bi-weekly rates available.

The Little Inn, 10604 Santa Monica Blvd., West L.A. (☎310-475-4422). On Little Santa Monica Blvd., the smaller road paralleling the divided boulevard to the south. Budget-travel nirvana. The rooms are clean and color-coordinated. A/C, cable TV, and fridges. Parking included. *Let's Go* toters get special rates Sept.-July (excluding major holiday periods). One bed (up to 2 people) $55; two beds $65. Kitchens extra.

Bevonshire Lodge Motel, 7575 Beverly Blvd. (☎323-936-6154), near Farmer's Market. Pool in the central courtyard. Spacious rooms have sparkling bathrooms (to make the shower scenes fun). A/C, cable TV, and in-room phones. Parking included. Singles $44.50; doubles $48.50; rooms with kitchen $56.50. 10% ISIC discount.

DOWNTOWN

Downtown L.A. is not the best place to look for accommodations. Although busy and fairly safe by day, the area empties and becomes dangerous after 6pm and Sa-Su. Cheaper weekly rates are sometimes available. Remember to travel in packs, especially between Broadway and Main St.

Milner Hotel, 813 S. Flower St. (☎627-6981 or 800-827-0411). Free pick-up from airport, bus, and train stations. Central location, pub and grill in lobby. Small, well-furnished rooms have A/C and cable TV. Breakfast included. Singles $60; doubles $70.

Hotel Stillwell, 838 S. Grand Ave. (☎627-1151). The historic building was recently restored and refurbished with modern conveniences. A/C and cable TV. Parking area next door ($3.50 per day). Singles $50, weekly $250; doubles $59/$325.

◘ FOOD

Eating in Los Angeles, the city of the health-conscious, is more than just *eating*. Thin figures and fat wallets are a powerful combination. Of course, there are also restaurants where the main objective is to be seen, and the food is secondary, as well as those where the food itself seems too beautiful to be eaten—it was here, after all, that 80s nouvelle cuisine reached its height.

Fortunately for the budget traveler, Los Angeles elevates fast-food and chain restaurants to heights virtually unknown in the rest of the country. For the optimal burger-and-fries experience, try **In 'n' Out Burger,** a chain as beloved as the '57 Chevy. **Johnny Rocket's** revives the never really lost era of the American diner. Their milkshakes are the food of the gods. The current hot 'n' spicy craze is lard-free, cholesterol-free "healthy Mexican"—☒**Baja Fresh** leads the pack. The ubiquitous smoothie allows the health-conscious to indulge in a sweet blend of fruit, juice, frozen yogurt, and energy-boosting additives like wheat grass. **Jamba Juice** makes the biggest and the best, with shots of fresh-blended grass for die-hard fiberphiles.

The range of culinary options in L.A. is directly proportional to the city's ethnic diversity. Certain food types are concentrated in specific areas. Jewish and Eastern European food is most prevalent in Fairfax; Mexican in East L.A.; Japanese, Chinese, Vietnamese, and Thai around Little Tokyo, Chinatown, and Monterey Park; and seafood along the coast. Vietnamese, Italian, Indian, and Ethiopian restaurants are scattered throughout the city.

HOLLYWOOD

Hollywood offers the best budget dining in L.A. **Melrose** is full of chic cafes, many with outdoor patios.

☒ **Roscoe's House of Chicken and Waffles,** 1514 Gower St. (☎323-466-7453). Roscoe makes the best waffles of any dive anywhere. Try "1 succulent chicken breast and 1 delicious waffle" ($5.60). The down-home feel has been known to attract celebrities. Be prepared to wait on weekends. Open Su-Th 8:30am-midnight, F-Sa 9am-4am.

☒ **Duke's Coffee Shop,** 8909 Sunset Blvd., West Hollywood (☎310-652-3100), at San Vicente Blvd. The legendary Duke's is the best place in L.A. to see hung-over rockers. Try the "Spinach Special" (with mushrooms, onions, ground beef, scrambled eggs, cheese and spices) for $8.25. Entrees $5-8. Attendant parking in rear $1. Open M-F 7:30am-8:45pm, Sa-Su 8am-3:45pm.

Pink's Famous Chili Dogs, 709 N. La Brea Ave. (☎323-931-4223), at Melrose. More of an institution than a hot dog stand, Pink's has been serving up chili-slathered doggies on its outdoor patio since 1939. Mouthwatering chili dogs $2.20 and chili fries $1.85. Rumor has it that Orson Welles scarfed down 15 of Pink's chili dogs in one sitting. Open Su-Th 9:30am-2am, F-Sa 9:30am-3am. No credit cards.

Swingers Hollywood Diner, 8020 Beverly Blvd. (☎323-653-5858), at Laurel Ave. in the rump of the Beverly Laurel Hotel. Where the hippest L.A. club kids (and *Swingers* Mikey and Trent) come to eat healthy food and 5 flavors of "smart drinks" that organically stimulate the brain ($5.50-6.50). This place is *so* money! Open daily 6am-4am.

SANTA MONICA

Elevated patios along the 3rd St. Promenade and Ocean Ave. herald Santa Monica's upscale eating scene—and it is a scene. Most menus offer plentiful organic and vegetarian choices.

☒ **Fritto Misto,** 601 Colorado Ave. (☎310-458-2829), at 6th St. This authentic Italian cafe has a distinct Santa Monica twist in its long list of vegetarian entrees ($9-13). The biggest deal is the mix 'n' match pastas, which are served quickly and in healthy portions ($6-7). Worth the wait. BYOB for a $1.50 per person surcharge. Lunch specials until 5:30pm ($6-8). Open M-F 11:30am-10pm, Sa-Su 11:30am-11pm.

Big Dean's "Muscle-In" Cafe, 1615 Ocean Front Walk (☎310-393-2666). Home of the management-proclaimed "Best Cheeseburger on the West Coast" ($4), this bar and grill

---

TOURING THE BURGER KINGDOM Los Angeles has spurred many tasteless trends, but few realize that it's also the birthplace of perhaps the world's furthest sweeping trend, one guaranteed to leave a curious taste in your mouth: good ol' American fast food. Unlikely as it sounds, this obsessively health-conscious city spawned some of the nation's greasiest, most cholesterol-packed grub. An international synonym for fast food, **McDonald's** was founded by Angeleno brothers Richard and Maurice McDonald in 1937 (serving, incidentally, hot dogs only). The oldest standing golden arches still glare proudly at 10807 Lakewood Blvd. in Downey, which has walk-up rather than drive-thru service. (The brothers granted Ray Kroc exclusive U.S. franchising rights, and in 1955 he opened the first outlet of what has become the McDonald's Corporation in Des Plaines, Illinois.) Home to the original double-decker hamburger, the oldest **Bob's Big Boy,** 4211 Riverside Dr. (☎818-843-9334), in Burbank, still looks as sleek and streamlined as the day it opened in 1949. Check out the honest-to-goodness car-hop service (Sa-Su 5-10pm). **Carl's Jr.** started off as a downtown hot dog stand at Florence and Central Ave. in 1941, and the **Denny's** and **Winchell's** chains also got their start in the Los Angeles basin.

---

is just a few steps from the Santa Monica Pier. Paul Newman muscled in here for *Twilight.* Bratwurst $2 (with kraut $2.50), veggie burgers $6. Happy Hour with beers for $2 (M-F 4-8pm). Open daily 10am-dark.

El Cholo, 1025 Wilshire Blvd. (☎310-899-1106), at 11th. Huge portions of Mexican food. Cheese enchilada, beans, rice, and choice of a taco, chile relleno, or tamale $8. *L.A. Magazine* named the "L.A. Lemonade" the city's best margarita. Make reservations; it's always crowded. Open M-Th 11am-10pm, F-Sa 11am-11pm, Su 11am-9pm.

VENICE

Venetian cuisine runs the gamut from greasy to ultra-healthy, as befits its beachy-hippie crowd. The boardwalk offers cheap grub in fast food fashion.

■ **Van Go's Ear 24 Hour Restaurant and Gallery,** 796 Main St. (☎310-314-0022). Quintessential Venice, with a psychedelic mural of the cafe's namesake wearing an earring. Entrees named for 3rd-rate celebs, such as the Kato Kaelin "guest house" Salad ($5). "Tightwad menu" has 8 breakfast combos under $2 (served M-F 6-11am). Open 24hr.

■ **Rose Cafe and Market,** 220 Rose Ave. (☎310-399-0711; fax 396-2660), at Main St. Rose wall murals and industrial architecture might make you think this is a museum— complete with gift shop. But the colorful cuisine is the main display. Deli specials, sandwiches ($5), and salads ($5-8). Open M-F 7am-7pm, Sa 8am-7pm, Su 8am-5pm.

On The Waterfront Cafe, 205 Ocean Front Walk (☎310-392-0322). Lovely bar/cafe, with a pool table and boardwalk seating. Erdinger Weißbier and Bitburger on tap. Salads, bratwurst sandwiches, and pasta. Mussels ($12, serves 2). Beer half-price during Sunset Hour (M-F 6-8pm). Open M-F 11am-midnight, Sa-Su 9am-midnight.

WILSHIRE DISTRICT AND HANCOCK PARK

The Wilshire District's eateries are sadly out of step with its world-class museums. Inexpensive (and often kosher) restaurants dot **Fairfax** and **Pico Blvd.**

Nyala Ethiopian Cuisine, 1076 S. Fairfax Ave. (☎323-936-5918), south of Olympic Blvd. The Fairfax area is known for its kosher delis, but it's also the backbone of L.A.'s Ethiopian community. Large plates of crepe (*injera*) with your choice of spicy stews (lunch $7.50, dinner $10.50). Vegetarian lunch buffet (M-F 11:30am-3pm) a steal at $5. Live music F-Sa 11pm-2am. Open M-F 11:30am-11pm, Sa-Su 11:30am-2am.

The Apple Pan, 10801 W. Pico Blvd. (☎310-475-3585), 1 block east of Westwood Blvd. across from the Westside Pavilion. Suburban legend has it that *Beverly Hills 90210*'s Peach Pit was modeled after The Apple Pan. Paper-plated burgers $3-6; pies $2.40. Open Tu-Su 11am-midnight. No credit cards.

BEVERLY HILLS

There is budget dining in glamorous Beverly Hills; it just takes a little looking. A tip: do not eat on Rodeo Dr., stay south of Wilshire Blvd.

■ **The Breakfast Club,** 9671 Wilshire Blvd. (☎ 323-271-8903), 2 blocks west of Rodeo Dr. Beverly Hills's own designer diner. Brightly colored vinyl booths, framed vintage movie posters, and Coca-Cola clocks. Omelettes $5-7, burgers $7. Open M-Sa 7am-3pm, Su 8am-3pm.

Finney's in the Alley, 8840 Olympic Blvd. (☎ 310-888-8787). Heading east on Olympic Blvd. from Rodeo Dr., turn right on Clark, and immediately right into the alley; look for a yellow awning. Started by the publisher of the *Beverly Hills Courier* to feed his staff, Finney's opened to the public 3 years ago and has since become a back-alley sensation. Most delectable Philly steak sandwich $5. Open M-Sa 11am-6pm.

Nate n' Al Delicatessen, 414 N. Beverly Dr. (☎ 310-274-0101). Serves up hand-pressed potato pancakes, blintzes ($9), and reuben sandwiches ($10). The tables are fake wood, there's a bottle of Hebrews National Deli Mustard on every table, and the waitresses wear pink pin-striped deli dresses and tennis shoes. Open daily 7am-9pm.

WESTWOOD AND UCLA

With UCLA nearby, cheap food and beer can be found in abundance. If you're down to your last few bucks, head to **Subbie's Roll-Inn,** 972 Gayley Ave., for $2 subs (open daily 10am-3am), or **Jose Bernstein's,** 935 Broxton Ave., which has burritos for $4 (open Su-Th 11am-1am, F-Sa 10am-2:30am).

■ **Gypsy Cafe,** 940 Broxton Ave. (☎ 310-824-2119). The food is more Italian than French (penne cacciatore $7.25), and the mood is more Turkish than Italian (hookahs for rent, $10 per hr.). Elegant dining (tile floors, chandeliers, dark wood paneling). Stand-up comedy Tu and F nights. Open Su-Th 8am-midnight, F-Sa 8am-1am.

Arrosto Coffee, 923 Broxton Ave. (310-824-2277). Arrosto attracts students in droves at lunch, dinner, and after-party hours. 12 in. sub ($2.45), gyros platter ($3). Open M-Th 6am-1am, F 6am-3am, Sa 8am-3am, Su 8am-1am.

Mongols B-B-Q, 1064 Gayley Ave. (☎ 310-824-3377). A feast for the rapacious carnivore. For $6, put as much raw meat, veggies, and noodles of your choice as you can possibly balance in your bowl. Then watch the BBQ chefs as they dance around their circular, glass-enclosed grill to toss around the contents of your bowl. Includes rice vegetable soup and sesame buns. Open M-F 11:30am-10pm, Sa noon-11pm, Su 3-10pm.

Diddie Riese Cookies, 926 Broxton Ave. (☎ 310-208-0448). You'll be singin' "doo-wa-diddie" as you walk away from this hotspot for fresh cookies ($3 per dozen). 10 delicious flavors to choose from. Open M-Th 7am-midnight, F 7am-1am, Su noon-midnight.

DOWNTOWN

Financial District eateries vie for the business-person's coveted lunchtime dollar. Their secret weapon is the lunch special, but you shouldn't hang out here that late anyway—it's a rough neighborhood.

■ **Philippe, The Original,** 1001 N. Alameda St. (☎ 628-3781), 2 blocks north of Union Station. "Carvers" (counter waitresses dressed in vintage server garb) prep the best French Dip sandwiches around (Philippe's invented 'em!); varieties include beef, ham, turkey, or lamb ($3-4). Top it off with a glass of lemonade (50¢) or a cup of coffee (10¢), and you've got a colossal lunch at this L.A. institution. Open daily 6am-11pm.

The Pantry, 877 S. Figueroa St. (☎ 972-9279). Since 1924, it hasn't closed once—not for the earthquakes, not for the riots (when it served as a National Guard outpost), and not even when a taxicab drove through the front wall. There aren't even locks on the doors. Known for large portions, free cole slaw, and fresh sourdough bread. Giant breakfast specials ($6). Lunch sandwiches $3-5. Open forever. Cash only.

SAN FERNANDO VALLEY

Ventura Blvd. is lined with restaurants. Eating lunch near the studios in **Studio City** is your best stargazing opportunity. The unwritten law: Stare all you like, *but don't ask for autographs.*

CALIFORNIA

▨ **Miceli's,** 3655 W. Cahuenga Blvd., Burbank (☎323-851-3444), across from Universal Studios. Would-be actors serenade dinner guests. Don't worry about losing your appetite during the Broadway, cabaret, and opera numbers—waiters have passed vocal auditions. Pasta, pizza, or lasagna $9-12. If you're looking for a romantic splurge, ask about the Valentine's table. Open Su-Th 11:30am-11pm, F 11:30am-midnight, Sa 4pm-midnight.

   Poquito Más, 3701 W. Cahuenga Blvd., Burbank (☎818-760-8226), opposite Universal Studios. This is as close to healthy as Mexican food gets: no lard, no MSG, no canned anything. Fabulous *carnita* plate only $2. Shrimp tacos ($4 for 2). Open Su-Th 11am-midnight, F-Sa 10am-1am. Cash only.

▣ SIGHTS

HOLLYWOOD

Hollywood is no longer the upscale home of movie stars and production studios. In fact, all the major studios, save Paramount, have moved to the roomier San Fernando Valley. Left behind are historic theaters and museums, a crowd of souvenir shops, famous boulevards, and an American fixation. Aside from the endless string of movie premieres, the only star-studded part of Hollywood is the sidewalk, though it is tread upon by prostitutes and panhandlers, and lined by tattoo parlors and porn shops.

HOLLYWOOD SIGN. The 50 ft. high, slightly erratic letters on Mt. Cahuenga north of Hollywood form a universally recognized symbol of the city. The original 1923 sign, which read HOLLYWOODLAND, was an advertisement for a new subdivision in the Hollywood Hills. You can't go frolic on the sign like Robert Downey, Jr. did in *Chaplin*—there is a $500 fine if you're caught (which is likely). *(You can snap a great picture by driving north on Vine, turning right on Franklin, left on Beachwood, and left on Belden into the Beachwood Supermarket parking lot. To get a close-up of the sign, continue up Beachwood, turn left on Ledgewood, and drive all the way up to Mulholland Hwy.)*

MANN'S CHINESE THEATER. This theater is a garish rendition of a Chinese temple and the hottest spot for a Hollywood movie premiere. Pay homage to impressions made by movie stars in the cement, including Whoopi Goldberg's dreadlocks, Jimmy Durante's nose, and George Burns's cigar. *(6925 Hollywood Blvd., between Highland and La Brea Ave. ☎323-461-3331.)*

WALK OF FAME. Things get a little seedier all along Hollywood and Vine St., where the sidewalk is embedded with over 2000 bronze-inlaid stars, inscribed with the names of the famous, the infamous, and the downright obscure. The stars have no particular order so don't try to find a method to the madness. To catch a glimpse of today's (or yesterday's) stars in person, call the Chamber of Commerce for info on star-unveiling ceremonies. *(☎323-469-8311.)*

HOLLYWOOD BOWL AND MUSEUM. Nestled in the hills, this famous outdoor performance space is the perfect spot to have a picnic lunch and listen to the L.A. Philharmonic strike it up at rehearsals on M, Tu, Th, and F. The Bowl also hosts a summer jazz concert series. The museum-within-a-bowl has several exhibits, as well as listening stations where you can swoon to Stravinsky, Aaron Copland, and the Beatles, all of whom played the Bowl in the same week during the 60s. *(2301 N. Highland Ave. ☎323-850-2058; concert line 323-850-2000. Open Tu-Sa 10am-4:30pm. Free.)*

HOLLYWOOD MUSEUMS. The **Hollywood Heritage Museum** provides a glimpse into early Hollywood filmmaking. Antique cameras, costumes worn by Douglas Fairbanks and Rudolph Valentino, props, and vintage film clips fill the museum. *(2100 N. Highland Ave., across from the Hollywood Bowl. ☎323-874-2276. Open Sa-Su 11am-3:45pm; call ahead. $2, ages 3-12 $1, under 3 free. Ample free parking, except during Bowl events.)* The **Hollywood Entertainment Museum** is a treasure chest of authentic set designs, costumes, and props, and a lesson in the how-to's of the business. Entrance to the original sets from *Star Trek* and *Cheers* deserves the ooh-ing and aah-ing it usually receives. The *Cheers* bar is functional and open for drinks on Th nights and for Monday Night Football. *(7021 Hollywood Blvd. ☎323-465-7900. Museum open daily July-Aug. 11am-6pm; Sept.-June Th-Tu 10am-6pm. Decent tours every 30min. $7.50, students and seniors $4.50, ages 5-12 $4, under 5 free. Parking $2. Cheers cover $5; proceeds go to educational programs.)*

OTHER SIGHTS. The alternately fascinating and horrifying **Hollywood Wax Museum** contains 200 figures, from Austin Powers to Jesus. *(6767 Hollywood Blvd. ☎323-462-8860. Open Su-Th 10am-midnight, F-Sa 10am-1am. $10, seniors $8.50, ages 6-12 $7, under 6 free.)* **Frederick's of Hollywood** gives a free peep at celebrity-worn corsets and bosom-boosting bras in its lingerie museum. *(6608 Hollywood Blvd. ☎323-957-5953. Open M-F 10am-9pm, Sa 10am-7pm, Su 11am-6pm. Free.)* The **Capital Records Tower,** a monument to the recording industry, was designed to look like a stack of records, with fins sticking out at each floor (the "records") and a needle on top, which blinks H-O-L-L-Y-W-O-O-D in Morse code. *(1750 Vine St., just north of Hollywood Blvd.)* The ornate **El Capitán Theatre** hosted the 1941 Hollywood premiere of *Citizen Kane.* Current Disney movies play here with interactive post-show activities. *(6838 Hollywood Blvd. ☎467-9545 or 800-347-6396. Tickets $12, ages 3-11 and over 60 $10.)* If you still haven't had enough glitz from years gone by, visit the creepy cemetery at **Hollywood Memorial Park,** decaying between Vine St. and Western. Here rest deceased stars Rudolph Valentino, Jayne Mansfield (hubba-hubba), Douglas Fairbanks Sr., and Cecil B. DeMille. *(6000 Santa Monica Blvd. Open M-F 8am-5pm. Mausoleums close at 4:30pm.)*

SANTA MONICA

Santa Monica is known more for its shoreside scene than its shore. Filled with gawkers and hawkers, the area on and around the carnival pier is the hub of local tourist activity. The fun fair spills over into the pedestrian-only **Third Street Promenade,** where street performers and a farmers' market (W and Sa mornings) make for cinematic "crowd" scenes. People with clipboards often sign people up for **free movie passes.** Farther inland, along Main St. and beyond, a smattering of galleries, design shops, and museums reveal the city's love affair with art and design.

THE PIER AND PACIFIC PARK. The heart of the Santa Monica Beach is the famed **Santa Monica Pier,** home of the carnivalesque family funspot **Pacific Park.** The centerpiece of the pier is the unrideable 1922 carousel. Look for free TV show tickets near the north entrance. *(Off PCH on the way to Venice Beach from Santa Monica Beach. Open daily 10am-11pm; ticket window closes at 10:30pm. Tickets $1.25, most rides 2-3 tickets. Parking off PCH $5 per day.)*

BERGAMOT STATION ARTS CENTER. This converted warehouse is moving contemporary L.A. area artists to higher ground. The Gallery of Functional Art sells inspired art object creations such as toasters-turned wall lamps and the more affordable fork-chops (a cosmic merging of forks and chopsticks, $4). The **Santa Monica Museum of Art,** in building G-1, exhibits the work of emerging artists. "Friday Evening Salons" are free informal public forums with artists who are currently having their work exhibited. *(2525 Michigan Ave. Near the intersection of Olympic and Cloverfield Blvd. ☎310-586-6467; fax 586-6487. Santa Monica Museum usually open Tu-Su 11am-6pm, but call ahead. Colleagues Gallery open M noon-2pm and Th 10:30am-2pm. Suggested donation to SMMoA $3, students and seniors $2; galleries free.)*

VENICE

Venice is a carnivalesque beach town with rad politics and mad diversity. Its guitar-toting, Bukowski-quoting, wild-eyed, tie-dyed residents sculpt masterpieces in sand and compose them in graffiti, all before heading to the beach to slam a volleyball around. A stroll in in-line skating, bikini-flaunting, tattooed Venice is like an acid trip for the timid. *(To get to Venice from downtown L.A., take MTA #33 or 333; take 436 during rush hour. From downtown Santa Monica, take Santa Monica Blue Bus #1 or 2. Avoid hourly meter-feedings by parking in the $5-per-day lot at Pacific and Venice.)*

CALIFORNIA

OCEAN FRONT WALK. Venice's main beachfront drag, is a seaside circus of fringe culture. Bodybuilders of both sexes pump iron in skimpy spandex outfits at **Muscle Beach.** *(1800 Ocean Front Walk.)* Fire-juggling cyclists, joggers, sand sculptors, groovy elders (such as the "skateboard grandma"), and bards in Birkenstocks make up the balance of this playground population. Vendors of jewelry, henna body art, and snacks overwhelm the boardwalk.

OTHER SIGHTS. Venice's anything-goes attitude attracts some of L.A.'s most innovative artists (and not just the guy who makes sand sculptures of Jesus). The **Chiat Day offices** were designed by Frank Gehry, Claes Oldenburg, and Coosje Van Brueggen to look like a pair of enormous binoculars. *(340 Main St.)* Venice's **street murals** are another free show. Don't miss the homage to Botticelli's *Birth of Venus* on the beach pavilion at the end of Windward Ave.—a woman of ostensibly divine beauty sporting short shorts, a band-aid top, and roller skates boogies out of her seashell.

MALIBU

Malibu's public beaches are cleaner and less crowded than any others in L.A. County, and as a whole offer better surfing. Surf's up at **Surfrider Beach,** a section of Malibu Laguna State Beach located north of the pier at 23000 PCH. You can walk onto the beach via the **Zonker Harris** access way (named after the beach-obsessed *Doonesbury* character), at 22700 PCH. **Malibu Ocean Sports,** across from the pier, rents surfboards, kayaks, boogie boards, and wetsuits, and offers surfing lessons. *(22935 PCH. ☎ 310-456-6302. Open daily 9am-7pm. Surfboards $10 per hr., $25 per day. Kayaks: single $15 per hr., $35 per day; double $20/50. Boogie boards $12 per day. Wetsuits $10 per day. Surfing lessons $100 for 2hr. lesson and full-day gear.)*

Corral State Beach, a remote windsurfing, swimming, and scuba-diving haven, lies on the 26000 block of PCH, followed by **Point Dume State Beach,** which is larger and generally uncrowded, and has better currents for scuba diving. Along the 30000 block of PCH lies **Zuma,** L.A. County's northernmost, largest, and most user-friendly county-owned sandbox. Restrooms, lifeguards, and food stands guarantee that Zuma regularly draws a diverse crowd. Sections 6-8 are popular with local kids, sections 9-11 are less populated. Swimmers should only dive near manned lifeguard stations; because of the devastating **riptide,** rescue counts are high. The free street parking is highly coveted, so expect to park in the beach lot. *($6, off-peak $2.)* Just south of Zuma, before Point Dume, is a clothing-optional strip nicknamed Pirate's Cove. There are fewer footprints at **Westward Beach,** just southeast of Zuma, where cliffs shelter the beach from the highway.

WILSHIRE AND HANCOCK PARK

LOS ANGELES COUNTY MUSEUM OF ART (LACMA). At the west end of Hancock Park, LACMA rebuts those who say that L.A.'s only culture is in its yogurt. Opened in 1965, the LACMA is the largest museum in the West, with six major buildings clustered around the **Times-Mirror Central Court.** The **Steve Martin Gallery,** in the Anderson Bldg., houses the famed benefactor's collection of Dada and Surrealist works, including Rene Magritte's *Treachery of Images.* (This explains how Steve was allowed to in-line skate through LACMA in *L.A. Story.*) The museum sponsors free jazz, chamber music, film classics and documentaries, and free daily tours. *(5905 Wilshire Blvd. General info ☎ 323-857-6000, Docent Council 323-857-6108. Open M-Tu and Th noon-8pm, F noon-9pm, Sa-Su 11am-8pm. $7, students and seniors $5, under 18 $1; free 2nd Tu of each month. Free jazz F 5:30-8:30pm, chamber music Su 6-7pm. Film tickets $7, seniors $5. Parking $5, after 6pm free. Wheelchair accessible.)*

OTHER SIGHTS. Across the street from LACMA, the **Petersen Automotive Museum** showcases L.A.'s most recognizable symbol—the automobile. With 300,000 sq. ft., PAM is the world's largest car museum and the nation's 2nd-largest history museum (the Smithsonian is the largest). Bo and Luke's General Lee and Herbie the Love Bug are here. *(6060 Wilshire Blvd., at Fairfax. ☎ 323-930-2277. Open Tu-Su 10am-6pm; Discovery Center closes at 5pm. $7, students and seniors $5, ages 5-12 $3, under 5 free. Full-*

day parking convenient to LACMA $4.) Nearby, archaeologists excavate trapped prehistoric critters at the **La Brea tarpits.** *(5801 Wilshire Blvd., at Curson Ave. Wilshire Blvd. buses stop in front of the museum. ☎323-934-7243 or 857-6311. Open daily July-Sept. 9:30am-5pm; Oct.-June Tu-Su 9:30am-5pm. Tours of grounds 1pm, museum tours Tu-Su 2:15pm. $6, students and seniors $3.50, ages 5-12 $2; 1st Tu of each month free. Parking $5.)*

WEST HOLLYWOOD

Melrose Ave. running from the southern part of West Hollywood to Hollywood, is lined with chi-chi restaurants, art galleries, and shops catering to all levels of the counter-culture spectrum. The choicest stretch is between La Brea and Fairfax Ave. North of Beverly Center is the **Pacific Design Center,** a sea-green glass complex, nicknamed the **Blue Whale** and constructed in the shape of a wave. It hosts an awesome **Gay Pride Weekend Celebration** in late June. *(8687 Melrose Ave., at San Vicente Blvd. ☎310-657-0800.)*

BEVERLY HILLS

Ready to gawk? Conspicuous displays of wealth sometimes border on the vulgar in this storied center of extravagance and privilege. On the palm-lined 700-900 blocks of **Beverly Dr.,** each and every manicured estate begs for attention. The heart of the city is in the **Golden Triangle,** a wedge formed by Beverly Dr., Wilshire Blvd., and Santa Monica Blvd., centering on **Rodeo Dr.,** known for its flashy boutiques. Farther north, the **Beverly Hills Hotel,** 9641 Sunset Blvd. (☎310-276-2251), is a pink, palm-treed collection of poolside cottages. Marilyn Monroe reportedly had affairs with both JFK and RFK in bungalows here. You can get a room for a mere $275.

A conspicuous way to tour the city is in the trolley car replica operated by the **Beverly Hills Chamber of Commerce.** *(☎310-271-8126. June-Sept. Tu-Sa 1-5pm every hr. $5.)* If you prefer a cooler approach, go solo with a star map ($8), sold along Sunset Blvd. but not within Beverly Hills.

Just south of Beverly Hills is the sobering **Museum of Tolerance.** This hands-on, high-tech museum has interactive exhibits on the Holocaust, the Croatian genocide, the L.A. riots, and the US civil rights movement. Visit the Point of View Diner, a recreation of a 50s diner that serves a menu of controversial topics on video jukeboxes. *(9786 W. Pico Blvd., at Roxbury St. ☎310-553-8043. Open M-Th 10am-4pm, F 10am-1pm, and Su 11am-5pm. Closing times are for the time of the last entry into the museum. $8.50, students $5.50, seniors $6.50, ages 3-11 $3.50. Free parking. Wheelchair accessible.)*

WESTWOOD AND UCLA

To reach the campus by car, take the San Diego Fwy. (I-405) north to the Wilshire Blvd./Westwood exit, heading east into Westwood. Take Westwood Blvd. north off Wilshire, heading straight through the center of the village and directly into the campus. By bus, take MTA route #2 along Sunset Blvd., #21 along Wilshire Blvd., #320 from Santa Monica, or #561 from the San Fernando Valley, or Santa Monica Blue Bus #1, 2, 3, 8, or 12. Parking passes ($5) from campus information stands are a must—traffic cops like to ticket unsuspecting visitors here.

Get a feel for mass academia UC-style at the **University of California at Los Angeles (UCLA),** which sprawls in the foothills of the Santa Monica Mountains. A prototypical Californian university, UCLA sports an abundance of grassy spaces, bike and walking paths, dazzling sunshine, and pristine buildings in a hodge-podge of architectural styles.

The **Murphy Sculpture Garden,** which contains over 70 pieces scattered through 5 acres, lies directly in front of the Art Center. The collection includes works by Rodin, Matisse, and Miró. Opposite the sculpture garden is **MacGowen Hall,** which contains the **Tower of Masks.** UCLA has loads of events, exhibitions, and performances year-round; call the **UCLA Arts Line** *(☎310-825-2278)* for tickets, a calendar, and directions.

The **Armand Hammer Museum of Art and Cultural Center** houses a small collection of Western art from the 16th century to the present day. A "Who's Who" of European painters, Hammer's collection includes works by Rembrandt, Chagall, and

Cézanne, but its real gem is Van Gogh's *Hospital at Saint Rémy*. *(10899 Wilshire Blvd.* ☎ *310-443-7000. Open Tu-W and F-Sa 11am-7pm, Th 11am-9pm, Su 11am-5pm. $4.50, students and seniors $3, under 17 free with adult; Th free. Free tours of permanent collection Su 2pm, of traveling exhibits Th 6pm, Sa-Su 1pm. 3hr. parking $2.75.)*

BEL AIR, BRENTWOOD, PACIFIC PALISADES

Most of today's stars live in these affluent communities. Next to UCLA is the well-guarded community of **Bel Air,** where **Ronald Reagan** has retired. His estate is at 668 St. Cloud, adjacent to the *Beverly Hillbillies* mansion (750 Bel Air Rd.) and a few blocks up from the former home of **Sonny and Cher** (364 St. Cloud). **Elizabeth Taylor** is literally around the corner (700 Nimes).

Farther west on Sunset Blvd. is **Brentwood,** home to many young actors and, until recently, **O.J. Simpson.** O.J.'s estate (360 Rockingham) was repossessed and auctioned off for a mere $2.63 million. On Aug. 4, 1962, **Marilyn Monroe** was found dead at her home (12305 Fifth Helena Dr.). The celeb-city of Brentwood also includes the homes of Michelle Pfeiffer, Harrison Ford, Meryl Streep, and Rob Reiner.

The considerably more secluded **Pacific Palisades** is the place to live these days. Many streets are entirely closed to anyone but residents and their guests, but if you keep your eyes wide shut, you might catch a glimpse of **Tom Cruise** and **Nicole Kidman** outside 1525 Sorrento, or **Steven Spielberg** at 1515 Amalfi. **Arnold Schwarzenegger** and **Maria Shriver** practice family fitness at 14209 Sunset Blvd., **Tom Hanks** lives at 321 S. Anita Ave., and **Michael Keaton** resides at 826 Napoli Dr. Billy Crystal, Chevy Chase, and John Travolta also own homes in the area.

In the Santa Monica Mountains above Bel Air is the **J. Paul Getty Museum and Getty Center.** The center unites L.A.'s beloved Getty museums with its institutes on one site, designed by renowned architect Richard Meier. The museum itself is housed in five pavilions overlooking the three-acre Robert Irwin-designed Central Garden, a living work of art that changes with the seasons. The museum includes the permanent Getty collection, which includes Van Gogh's *Irises*, James Ensor's *Christ's Entry into Brussels in 1889*, Impressionist paintings, Renaissance drawings, and one of the nation's best Rembrandt collections. "Friday Nights at the Getty" feature plays, films, and readings. *(1200 Getty Center Dr.* ☎ *310-440-7330. Take the San Diego Fwy./I-405 to Getty Center Dr. BBB #14 and MTA #561 stop at the museum's front entrance on Sepulveda Blvd. Open Tu-W 11am-7pm, Th-F 11am-9pm, Sa-Su 10am-6pm. Free. Parking $5; requires advance reservations.)*

DOWNTOWN

The **Los Angeles Conservancy** offers Sa tours of downtown's historic spots. *(*☎*213-623-2489. Tours $5. Reserve one week in advance.)* Those who prefer to travel solo can walk each of the respective sections but should take **DASH Shuttles** for travel between. *(References below are for M-F travel. Sa-Su the Discovery Direct "DD" route covers almost all of the sights below.)* If driving, park in a secure lot, rather than on the streets. Parking is costly; arriving before 8am enables visitors to catch early-bird specials; the guarded lots around 9th and Figueroa charge $3-4 per day. **The L.A. Visitors Center** is at 685 S. Figueroa St. *(Open M-F 8am-5pm, Sa 8:30am-5pm.)*

HISTORIC NORTH. The historic birthplace of L.A. lies in the northern section of downtown, bordered by Spring and Arcadia St. Where the city center once stood, **El Pueblo de Los Angeles Historical Monument** preserves a number of historically important buildings from the Spanish and Mexican eras. *(125 Paseo St. DASH B.* ☎ *213-628-1274. Open daily 9am-9pm. Free.)*

Olvera St., one of L.A.'s original roads, resembles a small Mexican street market. The street is the site of the Cinco de Mayo and Día de los Muertes celebrations of L.A.'s Chicano population (see **Seasonal Events,** p. 801). Across Alameda St. from El Pueblo is the grand old **Union Station,** famous for its appearances in many Hollywood productions; and **Chinatown** lies north of this area, roughly bordered by Yale, Spring, Ord, and Bernard St. Pick up walking tour maps at the **Chinatown Heritage and Visitors Center.** *(DASH B.)*

CIVIC CENTRAL. The **Civic Center** is best seen from the outside. *(Bounded by Rte. 101, Grand Ave., 1st, and San Pedro St. DASH B and D.)* One of the best-known buildings in the Southland, **City Hall** "has starred in more movies than most actors." *(200 N. Spring St.)* L.A.'s royalty try to get their hands on Hollywood's golden boy, the short but popular Oscar, at the **Dorothy Chandler Pavilion.** The pavilion will be the site of the annual Academy Awards for one last year before the event moves to the new Kodak center planned in Hollywood.

Upscale **Little Tokyo** lies southeast of the Civic Center, on 2nd and San Pedro St. on the eastern edge of downtown. *(DASH A.)* The **Japanese-American National Museum,** housed in a refurbished Buddhist temple, is a community-oriented museum featuring interactive computers with access to WWII relocation camp records.

NEAR DOWNTOWN

EXPOSITION PARK

Southwest of downtown, off Rte. 110, bounded by Exposition Blvd., Vermont Ave., Figueroa, and Santa Barbara St. From downtown, take DASH shuttle F or MTA #81 or 442. From Hollywood, take MTA #204 or 354 down Vermont Ave. From Santa Monica, take MTA #20, 22, 320, or 322 on Wilshire Blvd.; transfer to #204 at Vermont Ave. Parking: at Figueroa St. and Exposition Blvd. ($5).

Once an upscale suburb of downtown, the area began to decline around the turn of the century, plummeting in the 20s. In spite of revitalization efforts for the 1932 and 1984 Olympic Games, the area is still pretty rough; its museums are safe but *visitors should exercise caution outside the park, especially at night.*

The park is dominated by several major museums, including the **California Science Center (CSC),** which is dedicated to the phenomena of California—from earthquakes to smog. The expansive, formal **rose garden** in front of the CSC is the last remnant of the blessed days when all of Exposition Park was an exposition of horticulture. More than 19,000 specimens of 200 varieties of roses surround walking paths, green lawns, gazebos, fountains, and a lily pond. *(700 State Dr. ☎323-724-3623. Open daily 10am-5pm. Free. Rose garden: Open daily Mar. 16-Dec. 31 8:30am-5:30pm.)*

OTHER SIGHTS

GRIFFITH PARK AND GLENDALE. Griffith Park stretches for 4107 acres from the hills above North Hollywood to the intersection of the Ventura (Rte. 134) and Golden State Fwy. (I-5). Several of the mountain roads through the park (especially the **Vista Del Valle Dr.**) offer panoramic views of downtown L.A., Hollywood, and the Westside. Unfortunately, heavy rains have made them unsafe for cars, but foot traffic is allowed on most. The 5 mi. hike to the top of **Mt. Hollywood,** the highest peak in the park, is quite popular. For info, stop by the **Visitors Center and Ranger Headquarters.** *(4730 Crystal Spring Dr. ☎323-913-7390. Park open daily 5am-10pm.)*

OBSERVATORY AND PLANETARIUM. The white stucco and copper domes of the Art Deco Observatory and Planetarium are visible from around the park. You might remember the planetarium from the dénouement of the James Dean film *Rebel Without A Cause.* The planetarium presents popular **Lazerium** light shows. A telescope with a 12 in. lens is open to the public every clear night until 9:45pm. *(Drive to the top of Mt. Hollywood on Vermont Ave. or Hillhurst St. from Los Feliz Blvd., or take MTA #180 or 181 from Hollywood Blvd. ☎323-664-1181, recording 664-1191. Free parking, use Vermont St. entrance to Griffith Park. Planetarium: shows M-F at 1:30, 3, and 7:30pm, Sa-Su 1:30, 3, 4:30, and 7:30pm; in winter Tu-F 3 and 7:30pm, Sa-Su 1:30, 3, 4:30, and 7:30pm. $4, seniors $3, ages 5-12 $2, under 5 free but only admitted to 1:30pm show. Observatory: ☎323-663-8171. Open in summer daily 12:30-10pm; in winter Tu-F 2-10pm, Sa-Su 12:30-10pm. Lazerium: ☎818-901-9405. Shows Su-M 6 and 8:45pm, Tu-Sa 6, 8:45, and 9:45pm. $7-8, ages 5-12 $6-7; under 5 not admitted.))*

CALIFORNIA

FOREST LAWN CEMETERY. A rather twisted sense of celebrity sightseeing may lead some travelers to Glendale, where they can gaze upon stars who won't run away when chased for a picture. Among the illustrious dead are Clark Gable, George Burns, Sammy Davis, Jr., and Errol Flynn. Forest Lawn allegedly inspired the "Whispering Glades Cemetery" (of Evelyn Waugh's renowned satirical novel *The Loved One*), where death and showbiz combine to transform sorrow and spirituality into something more marketable and cliché. *(1712 Glendale Ave. ☎800-204-3131. From downtown, take MTA #90 or 91 and get off just after the bus leaves San Fernando Rd. to turn onto Glendale Ave. By car from I-5 or the Glendale Fwy., take Los Feliz Blvd. south to Glendale Ave./Rte. 2. Grounds open daily Mar.-Oct. 8am-6pm, Nov.-Feb. 8am-5pm; mausoleum open 9am-4:30pm.)*

SAN FERNANDO VALLEY

Movie studios have replaced the Valley Girl as the Valley's defining feature. As the Ventura Fwy. (Rte. 134) passes Burbank, you can see what are today the Valley's trademarks: the **NBC peacock,** the **Warner Bros. water tower,** and the carefully designed **Disney dwarves.** Urban legend says that the water pipes are orchestrated such that the seven dwarves appear to urinate on daddy Disney when it rains. For those who find watching TV on TV slightly cliché, most of the studios have **free TV show tapings** (see **Entertainment,** p. 797).

UNIVERSAL STUDIOS AND CITY WALK. This movie-themed amusement park is the most popular spot in today's expatriate Tinseltown. Universal is best loved by those with a healthy knowledge of America's blockbuster movie tradition. Expect long, long waits (and lots of heat) in the summer. *(☎818-622-3801. Take MTA bus #420 bus west from downtown or east from the Valley. Open daily July-Aug. 8am-10pm, Sept.-June 9am-7pm. Last tram leaves at 6:15pm, 4:15pm in the off-season. Tours in Spanish daily. $41, seniors $36, ages 3-11 $31. Parking $7.)* If, somehow, you have a few dollars left after Universal Studios, head to the adjacent **Universal City Walk** for food, shopping, and entertainment. *(City Walk parking $7. Full refund if you buy two movie tickets before 6pm, $2 refund after 6pm.)* The jewel in City Walk's technicolor crown is **B.B. King's Blues Club,** where the thrill is far from gone. *(☎818-622-5464. Open Su-Th 4pm-midnight, F-Sa 4pm-2am; M-Th dinner served 4-11pm, Sa-Su lunch 2-6pm and dinner 6-11pm. Su Gospel Brunch noon-2pm $30, children $15. Cover $5-14, $3 for dinner guests. Must be 21 after 10pm.)*

MAGIC MOUNTAIN. At the opposite end of the Valley, 40min. north of L.A. in Valencia, is Six Flags Magic Mountain. Not for novices, Magic Mountain has the hairiest roller coasters in Southern California, if not the world. Next door, Six Flag's waterpark **Hurricane Harbor** features the world's tallest enclosed speed slide. *(At the I-5 Magic Mountain Pkwy. exit. Magic Mountain: recorded info ☎661-255-4111; operator ☎661-255-413. Open Memorial Day weekend to Aug. Su-Th 10am-10pm, F-Sa 10am-midnight; Sept. to Memorial Day Sa-Su 10am-6pm. $41, seniors $21, under 48 in. tall $10, under 2 free. Parking $6. Hurricane Harbor: open M-Th 10am-7pm, F-Su 10am-8pm. $20, seniors and under 48 in. tall $13, under 2 free. Combo admission to both parks $50.)*

PASADENA AND AROUND

With its world-class museums, graceful architecture, lively shopping district, and idyllic weather, Pasadena is a welcome change from its noisy downtown neighbor. **Old Town** Pasadena sequesters intriguing historic sights and an up-and-coming entertainment scene. The **Pasadena Fwy.** (Rte. 110) is one of the nation's oldest. The city provides **free shuttles** approximately every 12min. that loop between Old Town and the downtown area around Lake Ave. *(☎626-744-4055. Shuttles run downtown M-Th 11am-7pm, F 11am-10pm, Sa-Su noon-8pm; uptown M-F 7am-6pm, Sa-Su noon-5pm.)*

NORTON SIMON MUSEUM OF ART. The recently revamped museum features a world-class collection, chronicling Western art from Italian Gothic to 20th-century abstract, with paintings by Raphael, Botticelli, Monet, Picasso, and others. The Impressionist and Post-Impressionist hall is particularly impressive, and the collection of Southeast Asian sculpture is one of the world's best. *(411 W. Colorado*

Blvd., at Orange Grove Blvd. ☎626-449-6840. Take MTA bus #180 or 181 west on Colorado Blvd. between Lake and N. Orange St. or #180 south on Lake between Washington and Colorado St. Open W-Th and Sa-Su noon-6pm, F noon-9pm. $6, seniors $3, students with ID and children under 12 free. Wheelchair accessible.)

HUNTINGTON LIBRARY, ART GALLERY, AND BOTANICAL GARDENS. This massive institute in San Marino has stunning botanical gardens, which are home to 150 acres of plants (but no picnicking or sunbathing—both are forbidden). The library houses rare books and manuscripts, including a Guttenberg Bible, Benjamin Franklin's handwritten autobiography, a 1410 manuscript of Chaucer's *Canterbury Tales*, and a number of Shakespeare's first folios. The art gallery is known for its 18th- and 19th-century British paintings. American art is on view in the Virginia Steele Scott Gallery. The Annabella Huntington Memorial Collection features Renaissance paintings and 18th-century French decorative art. Tea is served in the Rose Garden daily. *(1151 Oxford Rd., between Huntington Dr. and California Blvd. in San Marino, south of Pasadena, about 2 mi. south of the Allen Ave. exit from I-210. ☎626-405-2100. From downtown L.A., take MTA bus #79 out of Union Station to San Marino Ave. and walk ½ mi.; 45min. trip. Open Memorial Day to Labor Day Tu-Su 10:30am-4:30pm; in winter Tu-F noon-4:30pm, Sa-Su 10:30am-4:30pm. $8.50, students $6, seniors $8, under 12 free; first Th of each month free.)*

🎵 ENTERTAINMENT

A visit to the world's entertainment capital isn't complete without some exposure to the actual business of making a movie or TV show. Fortunately, most production companies oblige. **Paramount** (☎323-956-5000), **NBC** (☎818-840-3537), and **Warner Bros.** (☎818-954-1744) offer 2hr. guided walking tours, but as they are made for tourists, they tend to be crowded and overpriced.

TELEVISION

The best way to get a feel for the industry is to land yourself some tickets to a TV taping. All tickets are free, but most studios tend to overbook, so holding a ticket does not always guarantee that you'll get into the taping. Show up early and you might see your favorite stars up close in the backlot of an operating studio.

NBC, 3000 W. Alameda Ave., at W. Olive Ave. in Burbank, is your best spur-of-the-moment bet. Show up at the ticket office on a weekday at 8am for passes to Jay Leno's **Tonight Show,** filmed at 5pm the same evening (2 tickets per person, must be 16+). Studio tours run on the hour. (M-F 9am-3pm; additional tours July-Aug. Sa 10am-2pm. $7, ages 5-12 $3.75.) Many of NBC's "Must-See TV" shows are taped at **Paramount Pictures,** 5555 Melrose Ave. (☎323-956-1777), in Hollywood. Sitcoms like *Dharma and Greg, Sister, Sister,* and *Frasier,* are taped September

---

SO, YOU WANNA BE IN PICTURES? Honey!

Baby! Sweetheart! You don't have to be beautiful and proportionally perfect to grace celluloid—just look at Tom Arnold or Lily Tomlin. The quickest way to get noticed is to land yourself a job as an extra—no experience necessary. One day's work will land $40-130 in your pocket and two meals in your tummy. Step 1 is to stop calling yourself an extra—you're an "atmosphere actor" (it's better for both your ego and your resumé). Step 2 is to contact a reputable casting service. **Cenex Central Casting,** 220 Flower St., Burbank 91506 (☎818-562-2755), is the biggest, and a good place to start. You must be at least 18 and a US citizen or Green Card holder. Step 3 is to show up on time; you'll need the clout of DeNiro before you can waltz in after call. Don't forget to bring $20 in cash to cover the "photo fee." Step 4 is to dress the part: don't wear red or white, which bleed on film and render you unusable. Finally, after you collect 3 **Screen Actors Guild (SAG)** vouchers (☎213-937-3441), you'll be eligible to pay the $1234 to join showbiz society. See you in the movies!

through May—call the studio five working days in advance to secure tickets. NBC's most popular sitcoms, like *Friends* and *Will and Grace*, are filmed before a private audience, so unless you are a friend of a Friend, you're out of luck. As it is one of the few major studios still in Hollywood, Paramount's tours are very popular. (Every hr. M-F 9am-2pm. $15.)

A **CBS box office,** 7800 Beverly Blvd., next to the farmer's market in West Hollywood, hands out free tickets to Bob Barker's seminal game-show masterpiece *The Price is Right* (taped M-Th) up to one week in advance. (☎323-575-2458. Open non-taping days M-Th 9am-5pm, taping days M-Th 7:30am-5pm.) Audience members must be over 18. You can request up to 10 tickets on a specific date by sending a self-addressed, stamped envelope to *The Price is Right* Tickets, 7800 Beverly Blvd., L.A. 90036, about four weeks in advance.

If all else fails, **Hollywood Group Services,** 1422 Barry Ave. #8, L.A. 90025 (☎310-914-3400), and **Audiences Unlimited, Inc.,** 100 Universal City Plaza, Universal City, CA 91608 (☎818-506-0067), offer guaranteed seating, but charge $10 to no-shows. To find out what shows are available during your visit, send a self-addressed, stamped envelope to either of the services. Hollywood Group Services will fax a list of all available shows within 24 hours of a call-in request.

CINEMA

Countless theaters show films the way they were meant to be seen: in a big space, on a big screen, with top-quality sound. It would be a cinematic crime not to take advantage of the incredible experience that is movie-going in L.A. **Loews Cineplex Cinemas** (☎818-508-0588), atop the hill at Universal City Walk; **Pacific Cinerama Dome,** 6360 Sunset Blvd. (☎323-466-3401), near Vine; and **Mann's Chinese Theater,** 6925 Hollywood Blvd. (☎323-464-8111), are some of the best movie houses.

To see an **on-location movie shoot,** stop by in person at the Entertainment Industry Development Company's L.A. Film Office, 7083 Hollywood Blvd., Suite 500, for a "shoot sheet" ($10), which lists current filming locations. Be aware that film crews may not share your enthusiasm for audience participation. (☎323-957-1000. Open M-F 8:30am-6pm.) The same information is free at www.eidc.com.

MUSIC AND THEATER

L.A.'s music venues range from small clubs to massive amphitheaters. The **Wiltern Theater** (☎213-380-5005) shows alterna-rock/folk acts. The **Hollywood Palladium** (☎323-962-7600) is of comparable size, with 3500 seats. Mid-size acts head for the **Universal Amphitheater** (☎818-777-3931) and the **Greek Theater** (☎323-665-1927). Huge indoor sports arenas, such as the **Great Western Forum** (☎310-673-1300) and the new **Staples Center** (☎213-742-7100), double as concert halls for big acts. Few dare to play at the 100,000-seat **Los Angeles Memorial Coliseum and Sports Arena**—only U2, Depeche Mode, and the mighty Guns n' Roses have filled the stands in recent years. Call Ticketmaster (☎323-365-3500) to purchase tickets for any of these venues. During the week, you can catch the L.A. Philharmonic or visiting performers as they rehearse at the ⬛**Hollywood Bowl,** 2301 N. Highland Ave. (☎323-850-2000).

The live theater scene isn't quite the spectacle it is in New York. On the other hand, 115 "equity waiver theaters" (under 100 seats) offer a dizzying choice for theater-goers, who can also take in small productions in museums, art galleries, universities, parks, and even garages. For the digs on what's hot, browse the listings in the *L.A. Weekly.*

SPORTS

Exposition Park and the often dangerous city of **Inglewood,** southwest of the park, are home to many sports teams. The **USC Trojans** football team plays at the **Los Angeles Memorial Coliseum,** 3939 S. Figueroa St. (tickets ☎740-4672), at Martin Luther King Blvd., which seats over 100,000 spectators. It is the only stadium in the world to have the honor of hosting the Olympic Games twice. Basketball's doormat, the

Los Angeles Clippers (☎ 213-742-7500), and the dazzling, star-studded 2000 NBA Champion Los Angeles Lakers (☎ 310-426-6031) play at the new Staples Center, 1111 S. Figueroa St. (☎ 742-7100; box office 742-7300), along with the Los Angeles Kings hockey team (☎ 888-546-4752). The city's women's basketball team, the Los Angeles Sparks (☎ 310-330-3939), plays at the Great Western Forum, at the corner of Manchester and Prairie in Inglewood (☎ 310-673-1300). Tickets are in high demand (Lakers season runs Nov.-June; Sparks June-Aug.). Kings tickets start at $19, Lakers at $21, and Sparks at $8. For tickets, call Ticketmaster (☎ 480-3232).

Elysian Park, about 3 mi. northeast of downtown, curves around the northern portion of Chavez Ravine, home of Dodger Stadium and the popular Los Angeles Dodgers baseball team. Tickets ($6-17) are a hot commodity during the April to October season, especially if the Dodgers are playing well (but they rarely seem to live up to their potential). Call ☎ 323-224-1448 for info and advance tickets.

◪ NIGHTLIFE

L.A. clubs range from tiny danceterias and ephemeral warehouse raves to exclusive lounges catering to showbiz elite. The hub of L.A. nightlife is the Sunset Strip along Sunset Blvd. in West Hollywood.

LATE-NIGHT RESTAURANTS

With the unreliability of clubs and the short shelf-life of cafes, late-night restaurants have become reliable hangouts. The 24hr. Jerry's Famous Deli has numerous locations, including 8701 Beverly Blvd., West Hollywood (☎ 310-289-1811); 10923 Weyburn Ave., Westwood (☎ 310-208-3354); and 12655 Ventura Blvd., Studio City (☎ 818-980-4245).

◪ Canter's, 419 N. Fairfax Ave., Fairfax (☎ 651-2030). An L.A. institution. Grapefruit-sized matzoh ball in chicken broth ($3.40). Giant sandwiches $6-8. Visit the Kibbitz Room nightly for live rock, blues, jazz, and cabaret-pop (from 9pm). Cheap beer ($2.50) served until 2am. Open 24hr.

◪ Fred 62, 1850 N. Vermont Ave., Los Feliz (☎ 323-667-0062). "Eat now, dine later." Headrests and toasters at every booth. Hip, edgy East L.A. crowd's jukebox selections rock the house. The waffles ($4.62) are divine. All prices end in .62. Open 24hr.

The Rainbow Grill, 9015 Sunset Blvd., West Hollywood (☎ 310-278-4232), next to the Roxy. Goth girl waitresses, rock n' roll types, and an insane rainbow of guests play their parts here. Marilyn Monroe met Joe DiMaggio on a blind date here. Brooklyn-quality pizza $6; calamari $7; and grandma's revitalizing chicken soup $2.50 per cup, $4 per bowl. Open M-F 11am-2am, Sa-Su 5pm-2am.

Barney's Beanery, 8447 Santa Monica Blvd., Hollywood (☎ 323-654-2287). Cracked rainbow vinyl booths and tacky low-hanging Coors lamps. Over 600 items on the menu, 250 bottled beers, and 200 on tap. Avoid (or target) the loud, riotous karaoke nights Su, M, and W 9:30pm-1am. Happy Hour M-F 4-7pm ($2.50 well, $2 draft, $3 appetizer). Valet parking $1.50. Open daily 10am-2am.

COFFEEHOUSES

In a city where no one eats very much for fear of rounding out that bony figure, espresso, coffee, and air are vital dining options.

◪ Un Urban Coffeehouse, 3301 Pico Blvd., Santa Monica (☎ 310-315-0056). Three separate rooms of campy voodoo candles, Mexican wrestling masks, musty books, and leopard-print couches. Iced mocha blends $3.25, Italian sodas $2. Open mic comedy Th 7pm, open mic songwriters F 7pm, music showcase Sa 7pm, spoken word Su 8pm. Open M-W 6am-6pm, Th-F 6am-1am, Sa 8am-1am, Su 8am-10pm.

Highland Grounds, 742 N. Highland Ave., Hollywood (☎ 323-466-1507). Nightly live shows (8pm) range from folk singers, to performance artists, to empowerment speakers. Outdoor patio with blazing fire. Full menu. Beer and wine. After 8pm, cover $2 and 1-drink min. Open M 9am-6pm, Tu-Sa 9am-midnight, Su 10am-3:30pm and 7-10pm.

Wednesday's House, 2409 Main St., Santa Monica (☎310-452-4486). A popular site for movie shoots. Grab some threads from clothing racks beside the coffee. Nutty trip mocha (with peanut butter, chocolate, and almond) $3.25. Internet access ($1 for 10min.). Open M-F 8am-2am, Sa 11am-2am, Su 11am-2pm. No credit cards.

BARS

While the 1996 film *Swingers* may not have transformed every bar into The 3 of Clubs, it has had a sadly homogenizing effect on L.A.'s hipsters. Grab your retro-70s polyester shirts, sunglasses, goatees, and throwback Cadillac convertibles, 'cause if you can't beat them, you have to swing with them, daddy-o.

■ **Beauty Bar,** 1638 Cahuenga Blvd., Hollywood (☎323-464-7676). A combination bar and beauty parlor. Manicures, "up 'dos," and henna tattoos are offered select nights of the week with a specialty drink ($10). Drinks like "Shampoo" or "Platinum Blonde" are $5-7. Smoking with hair-setting seats. DJ nightly at 10pm. Open Su-M 9pm-2am, Tu-W 8pm-2am, Th-F 6pm-2am, Sa 8pm-2am.

■ **Miyagi's,** 8225 Sunset Blvd. (☎323-656-0100), Sunset Strip. With 3 levels, 5 sushi bars, and 7 liquor bars, this Japanese-themed restaurant, bar, and lounge is the latest Strip hotspot. "*Sake* bomb, *sake* bomb, *sake* bomb" $4. Open daily 5:30pm-2am.

■ **The 3 of Clubs,** 1123 N. Vine St., Hollywood (☎323-462-6441). In a small strip mall beneath a "Bargain Clown Mart" sign, this simple, classy, spacious, hardwood bar is famous for appearing in 1996's *Swingers*. DJ W, live bands Th. Open daily 7pm-2am.

The Room, 1626 Cahuenga St., Hollywood (☎462-7196). A speakeasy that empties into an alley, the very popular Room almost trumps The 3 of Clubs. No advertising, no sign on the door. Open daily 8pm-2am.

Daddy's, 1610 N. Vine St., Hollywood (☎323-463-7777), between Hollywood and Sunset Blvd. A large New York-style lounge with low-to-the-ground booths, candle lighting, and the cheapest jukebox in town. Sip $5 drinks and $4 beers to the mellow stylings of Al Green. Open daily 9am-2am.

CLUBS

L.A. is famous, even infamous, for its club scene. With the highest number of bands per capita in the world, most clubs book top-notch acts night after night. These clubs can be the hottest thing in L.A. one month and extinct the next, so check the *L.A. Weekly* (free everywhere) before venturing out.

■ **The Derby,** 4500 Los Feliz Blvd., Hollywood (☎323-663-8979). This joint is jumpin' with the kings of swing. Ladies, grab your snoods, because many dress the 1940s part. Choice Italian fare from Louise's Trattoria next door. Full bar. The best of big band music nightly. Free dance lessons nightly at 8pm: Lindy Hop M, salsa Tu, swing W-Su. Happy Hour daily 5-7pm; 2nd Happy Hour Su-Th midnight-closing ($1.50 off drinks). Open daily 5pm-2am. Cover $7-10.

■ **Largo,** 432 N. Fairfax Ave., West Hollywood (☎323-852-1073). Elegant and intimate sit-down (or, if you get there late, lean-back) club. New talent and original rock, pop, and folk sounds. Open M-Sa 9pm-2am. Cover $2-12.

Luna Park, 665 N. Robertson Blvd., West Hollywood (☎310-652-0611). Hosts many record/CD release parties and an eclectic, ultra-hip crowd. Live funk, jazz, and rock nightly; Th club DJ. Supper club, full bar, outdoor patio, trancy dance floor. "New Music Mondays" land L.A.'s best improvisational talent. Open daily until 2am. Cover $3-10, big-name acts $20.

Key Club, 9039 Sunset Blvd., Sunset Strip (☎310-274-5800). A colossal, crowded multimedia experience complete with black lights, neon, and a frenetic dance floor. Live acts and DJ productions, depending on the night. Tequila library on the first floor. Open daily 8pm-2am. Cover M-Th $10, F-Sa $22.

COMEDY CLUBS

L.A.'s comedy clubs are the best in the world, unless you happen to chance upon an amateur night, which is generally a painful experience.

■ **The Improvisation,** 8162 Melrose Ave., West Hollywood (☎651-2583). L.A.'s best talent, including Robin Williams and Jerry Seinfeld, have shown their faces here. Shows Su-Th 8pm, F-Sa 8:30 and 10:30pm. Bar open daily until 1:30am. 2-drink min. Reservations recommended. Cover $8-11. 18+, or 16+ with parent.

■ **Groundling Theater,** 7307 Melrose Ave., Hollywood (☎323-934-9700). The best improv and comedy "forum" in town. The Groundling's alums include Pee Wee Herman and many *Saturday Night Live* regulars such as Julia Sweeney, Will Farrell, Cheri Oteri, and Chris Kattan. Shows W-Th 8pm, F-Sa 8 and 10pm, Su 7:30pm. Cover $10-18.50.

GAY AND LESBIAN NIGHTLIFE

Many ostensibly straight clubs have gay nights. Check the *L.A. Weekly* for more listings or the free weekly magazine *fab!* Gay and lesbian nightlife centers around **Santa Monica Blvd.** in West Hollywood.

Micky's, 8857 Santa Monica Blvd., West Hollywood (☎310-657-1176). Large, popular spot filled with delectable men. Music is mostly Top 40 dance. Serves lunch daily noon-4pm and hot go-go boys Tu-F and Su. "Cocktails with the stars" (many of them porno stars) Th 6-8pm. Open daily noon-2am. Happy Hour daily 4-7pm. Cover $3-20.

Rage, 8911 Santa Monica Blvd., West Hollywood (☎310-652-7055). This institution rages on with nightly DJs, drag nights, and disco 'til you drop. Mostly gay men; some lesbians during the day. Full lunch and dinner menu served 2-10pm. Open Su-Th 2pm-2am, F 2pm-3:30am, Sa 2pm-3am. Happy Hour (half-price drinks) M-F 2-8pm. Th 18+.

El Rey, 5515 Wilshire Blvd., Miracle Mile (☎323-936-4790). This palatial art deco establishment is a venue for an assortment of clubs, ranging from 70s flash to trashy drag shows. F is gal's bar, Hotbox. Many Sa gay nights. Call for schedule. Open F-Su, 9pm-2am. Cover $10. 18+.

✿ SEASONAL EVENTS

New Year's Day is always a perfect day in Southern California, or so the **Tournament of Roses Parade and Rose Bowl** (☎626-449-7673), Pasadena, would have it. Some of the wildest New Year's Eve parties happen along **Colorado Blvd.,** the parade route. **Cinco de Mayo** (☎625-5045) explodes May 5, especially downtown at Olvera St. Huge celebrations mark the day the Mexicans drop-kicked France out of Mexico. In mid-May, **UCLA Mardi Gras** (☎310-825-8001), at the athletic field, is billed as the world's largest collegiate activity (a terrifying thought). During **Gay Pride Weekend,** Pacific Design Center, 8687 Melrose Ave., West Hollywood, L.A.'s lesbian and gay communities celebrate in full effect with art, politics, dances, and a big parade. (☎860-0701. Last or second-to-last weekend in June. Tickets $12). ■**Día de los Muertos** is a rousing Mexican cultural celebration for the spirits of dead ancestors revisiting the world of the living. (Nov. 1, along Olvera St., downtown.)

◪ SOUTH BAY BEACHES

South Bay life is beach life. **Hermosa Beach** wins both bathing suit and congeniality competitions. Its slammin' volleyball scene, gnarly waves, and killer boardwalk make this the überbeach. The mellower **Manhattan Beach** exudes a yuppified charm, while **Redondo Beach** is by far the most commercially suburban. Ritzy **Rancho Palos Verdes** is a coast of a different breed. From early morning to late evening, these beaches are overrun by swarms of eager skaters, bladers, volleyball players, surfers, and sunbathers. At night, the crowds move off the beach and toward Manhattan and Hermosa Ave. for an affordable nightlife scene. South Bay harbors two of L.A.'s finest hostels; the one in Hermosa Beach has an awesome social scene, while the one in San Pedro may make you want to take up *tai chi.* ■**Los Angeles South Bay (HI-AYH),** 3601 S. Gaffey St., Bldg. #613, in Angels Gate Park (entrance by 36th) in San Pedro, pleases with a kitchen, laundry, TV room, volleyball courts, and free parking. (☎831-8109. Reception 7am-noon and 1pm-midnight; in winter 7am-11am and 4pm-midnight. $13; twins $15; private rooms $38. Non-members add $3. Linen

$2. 7-night maximum stay.) **Los Angeles Surf City Hostel,** 26 Pier Ave., half a block from the beach in Hermosa Beach, is a good-natured spot to rest with free linen, body-boards, and breakfast. Take the #439 bus from Union Station to 11th and Hermosa, walk 2 blocks north, and make a left on Pier. They will pick you up from the airport for free and drop you off for $5. (☎798-2323. Discount car rentals, laundry, kitchen, and TV lounge, but no parking. 4-6 bunk dorms $17; Dec.-Apr. $15; private rooms $45. Key deposit $10. Reservations recommended. Passport or proof of out-of-state residence required.)

ORANGE COUNTY   ☎714

Directly south of L.A. County is Orange County, or "O.C." It is a microcosm of Southern California: dazzling stretches of sandy shoreline, bronzed beach bums, endless strip malls, frustrating traffic snarls, and the stronghold of the late Walt Disney's ever-expanding cultural empire. One of only two staunchly Republican counties in California, Orange County has won fame for its economy (as big as Arizona's, and one of the world's 30 largest). Disneyland is the premier inland attraction, an island of dancing, singing critters with plastic smiles in the midst of the suburban sprawl. O.C.'s amazing beaches run the gamut from the budget and party-friendly Huntington Beach to the opulent Newport Beach.

🛈 PRACTICAL INFORMATION

John Wayne Orange County Airport, on Campus Dr., 20min. from Anaheim, is newer, cleaner, and easier to get around than LAX. (☎949-252-5006. Domestic flights only.) **Amtrak** runs to Fullerton, 120 E. Santa Fe Ave. (☎992-0530); Anaheim, 2150 E. Katella Blvd. (☎714-385-1448); Santa Ana, 1000 E. Santa Ana Blvd. (☎547-8389); Irvine, 15215 Barranca Parkway (☎949-753-9713); San Juan Capistrano, Santa Fe Depot, 26701 Verdugo St. (☎949-240-2972); and San Clemente, 1850 Avenida Estacion. **Greyhound** has three stations in the area: Anaheim, 100 W. Winston St., three blocks south of Disneyland (☎999-1256; open daily 6:30am-9pm); Santa Ana, 1000 E. Santa Ana Blvd. (☎542-2215; open daily 6am-8:30pm), and San Clemente, Dad's Liquor & Deli, 2421 S. El Camino Real (☎949-366-2646; open daily 7am-8:30pm). **Orange County Transportation Authority (OCTA),** 550 S. Main St., Garden Grove, provides thorough service useful for getting from Santa Ana and Fullerton Amtrak stations to Disneyland and for coastal beach-hopping. (☎636-7433. Fare $1, day pass $2.50.) **MTA** (☎800-266-6883 or 213-626-4455) runs buses daily from L.A. to Disneyland and Knott's Berry Farm. The **Anaheim Area Visitors and Convention Bureau,** 800 W. Katella Ave., is in the Anaheim Convention Center (☎999-8999. Open M-F 8:30am-5pm.) Anaheim's **post office:** 701 N. Loara (☎520-2601). **ZIP code:** 92803.

> **ORANGE COUNTY AREA CODES. 714** in Anaheim, Fullerton, Fountain Valley, Santa Ana, Orange, Garden Grove; **949** in Newport, Laguna, Irvine, Mission Viejo, San Juan Capistrano, and surrounding areas; **310** in Seal Beach. In text, **714** unless noted.

🛈 ACCOMMODATIONS

The Magic Kingdom is the sun around which the Anaheim solar system revolves, so budget motels and garden-variety "clean comfortable rooms" flank it on all sides. Keep watch for family and group rates posted on marquees and seek out establishments offering the three-for-two passport (3 days of Disney for the price of 2). O.C.'s beach communities have a few excellent hostels.

ANAHEIM

Fullerton (HI-AYH), 1700 N. Harbor Blvd., Fullerton (☎738-3721 or 800-909-4776), 15min. north of Disneyland. Shuttle from L.A. airport $17. OCTA bus #43 runs along

Harbor Blvd. to Disneyland. In the woods and away from the thematic craziness of nearby Anaheim. Kitchen, Internet access, relaxing living room, communal bathrooms. Free laundry. Linen $1. 5-night maximum stay. Check-in 8-11am and 4-11pm. Dorms $14, non-members $17; less in off-season. Reservations encouraged.

Magic Inn & Suites, 1030 W. Katella Ave., Anaheim (☎772-7242 or 800-422-1556). The rugs can't show you a whole new world, but it *is* just opposite Disneyland. Pools, A/C, TVs, fridges, and microwaves. Continental breakfast included. Laundry. 2 full-sized beds $69, 1 queen bed $59. Reservations recommended.

Econolodge, 1126 W. Katella Ave., Anaheim (☎533-4505), at the southwest corner of Disneyland. Clean rooms with HBO, phones, and A/C. Small pool, many kids. View of Disney's nightly fireworks. Queen bed $69; 2 beds $79. In winter $49/$59. Reservations recommended.

ORANGE COUNTY BEACH COMMUNITIES

🏠 **Huntington Beach Colonial Inn Youth Hostel,** 421 8th St., Huntington Beach (☎536-9206), 4 blocks inland at Pecan Ave. Take OCTA #29 (which also goes to Knott's) or #50. Quiet hours after 11pm. Large kitchen, reading/TV room, coin-op laundry, Internet access, deck, and surfboard shed. Linen and breakfast included. Check-in 7am-11pm. Reserve 2 days in advance for summer weekends. *International passport required; American college IDs accepted on space available basis.* Dorms $15; dorm doubles $17. Key deposit $20.

HI San Clemente Beach (HI-AYH), 233 Ave. Granada, San Clemente (☎949-492-2848), 2 blocks west of El Camino and within walking distance of the shore. This airy surfer's haven is so laid-back it's almost comatose. 20-bed male dorm, 14-bed female dorm, and private room with 3 beds ($2 surcharge per person). Reception 8-10:30am and 5-11pm. Quiet hours 11pm-7am. 14-day maximum stay. Open May-Oct. Dorms $12, non-members $15.

🍴 FOOD

Inexpensive ethnic restaurants tucked into Anaheim's strip malls allow escape from fast food. Many specialize in take-out or will deliver chow to your motel room. **Rutabegorz,** 211 N. Pomona Blvd., Fullerton, has a name derived from the unloved rutabaga and a style acquired from the worship thereof. Crepes, curries, quesadillas, and club sandwiches are all fresh and veggie-licious. (☎738-9339. Open M-Th 11am-10pm, F-Sa 11am-11pm, Su 4-9pm.)

👁 SIGHTS

DISNEYLAND

Main **entrance** *on Harbor Blvd. and a smaller one on Katella Ave. May be approached by car via I-5 to Katella Ave. From L.A., MTA bus #460 travels from 4th and Flower St. (about 1hr.) to the Disneyland Hotel (service to the hotel begins at 4:53am, service back to L.A. until 1:20am). Free shuttles link the hotel to Disneyland's portals, as does the Disneyland monorail. The park is served by Airport Service, OCTA, Long Beach Transit, and Gray Line (see* **Practical Information,** *p. 802).* **Parking** *in the morning is painless, but leaving in the evening is not.* ☎781-4565; www.disneyland.com. **Open** *approximately Su-Th 10am-9pm, F-Sa 8am-midnight (hours vary; call for info.)* **Admission:** *unlimited use passport ($41, seniors $39, ages 3-12 $31, under 3 free) allows repeated single-day entrance into the park, as does the parking pass ($7 per day). 2- and 3-day passes available. Lockers west of the ticket booths outside the main entrance and at the lost and found facility on Main Street, USA.*

Disneyland calls itself the "Happiest Place on Earth," and there is an oh-so-smiley part of every pop culture pilgrim that agrees. Weekday and off-season visitors will undoubtedly be the happiest, but the enterprising can take advantage of the new FastPass system or wait for parades to distract the children, leaving shorter lines. *Disneyland Today!* lists parade and show times, as well as breaking news from Frontierland.

K(NOT)T DISNEYLAND

Buena Park offers a cavalcade of non-Disney diversions, some of which are better than others. The first theme park in America, **Knott's Berry Farm,** is at La Palma Ave. in Buena Park just 5 mi. northeast of Disneyland. *(8039 Beach Blvd. at La Palma Ave., 5 mi. northeast of Disneyland. Recorded info* ☎ *714-220-5220. From downtown L.A., take MTA bus #460 from 4th and Flower St.; 1¼hr. If driving from L.A., take the I-5 S to Beach Blvd; turn right at the end of the exit ramp and proceed south 2 mi. Park hours vary, but are approximately Su-Th 9am-10pm, F-Sa 9am-midnight. $38, seniors $28, ages 3-11 $28, under 3 free; after 4pm all ages $17. Summer discounts. Parking $7.)* The major league **Anaheim Angels** play baseball from early Apr.-Sept. *(☎940-2000 or 800-626-4357. General tickets $6-22.)* Happy, happy hockey takes place at the **Arrowhead Pond,** home to the NHL's **Mighty Ducks.** *(2695 E. Katella Ave, one block east of Rte. 57.* ☎ *704-2500.)*

Farther inland is the highly uncritical, privately funded monument to Tricky Dick, the **Richard Nixon Library and Birthplace.** Skeptics can investigate the Watergate Room. Museum curators portray Nixon as a victim of circumstance, plotting enemies, and his own immutable honor. *(18001 Yorba Linda Blvd.* ☎ *993-5075. Open M-Sa 10am-5pm, Su 11am-5pm. $6, seniors $4, ages 8-11 $2, under 8 free.)*

ORANGE COUNTY BEACH COMMUNITIES

O.C.'s various beach communities have cleaner sand and better surf than their L.A. county counterparts. **Huntington Beach** is a legendary epicenter of the surfing craze, which transformed California coast life in the early 1900s. It's still a fun hotspot for wave-shredders, with a pristine pier for ogling. **Newport Beach** is the Beverly Hills of beach towns, though the beach itself displays few signs of ostentatious wealth; it is crowded with young, rowdy hedonists cloaked in neon. The sands of the beach run south to **Balboa Peninsula,** which can be reached by Rte. 1. At the end of the peninsula, **the "dirty old" Wedge,** pounded by waves, is a bodysurfing mecca.

Laguna Beach, 4 mi. south of Newport, is between canyons. Back in the day, Laguna was a bohemian artists' colony, but no properly starving artists can afford to live here now. The surviving galleries and art supply stores nevertheless add a unique twist to the standard SoCal beach culture that thrives on Laguna's sands. **Main Beach** and the shops nearby along Ocean Ave. are the prime parading areas, though there are other, less crowded spots as well. One accessible beach is **Westry Beach,** which spreads out south of Laguna just below **Aliso Beach Park.**

More tourists than swallows return every year to **Mission San Juan Capistrano,** 30min. south of Anaheim on I-5. Take Ortega Hwy. to Camino Capistrano. The most beautiful of California's missions, it's still used by the Catholic Church. *(☎949-248-2048. Open daily 8:30am-5pm. $6, seniors $4, ages 3-12 $4.)*

BIG BEAR ☎909

Hibernating in the San Bernardino Mountains, Big Bear Lake draws hordes with fluffy winter skiing and stellar summer hiking, biking, and boating. Interestingly, the consistent winds (no doubt the sighs of relaxing Angelenos) make for some of the best sailing in the state.

The **hiking** here is both free and priceless. Maps, trail descriptions, and the *Visitor's Guide to the San Bernardino National Forest* are available at the **Big Bear Discovery Center,** on Rte. 38. (☎866-3437. Open daily Apr.-Sept. 8am-6pm; Oct.-Mar. 8am-4:30pm.) The **Woodland Trail** or the more challenging **Pineknot Trail** offer views of the lake; high altitudes here make slow climbing necessary.

Mountain biking is a popular activity in Big Bear when the snow melts. Grab a pulpy *Ride and Trail Guide* at the Discovery Center and at **Snow Summit,** which runs lifts in summer so adrenaline monsters can grind serious downhill terrain. (☎866-4621. 1 mi. west of Big Bear Lake. $9 per ride, day pass $19; ages 7-12 $4, $9. Helmet required.) Those without wheels of their own can rent them from **Big Bear Bikes,** 41810 Big Bear Blvd. (☎866-2224. Open daily 10am-5pm.) Many summer activities take place on the water. **Fishing licenses** are available at area sporting goods stores ($10 per day, season $28), and the **Big Bear Fishing Association** (☎866-

6260) cheerfully dispenses info. **Holloway's Marina,** 398 Edgemor Rd., on the South Shore, rents **boats.** (☎ 800-448-5335. Full-day $46-130.)

When conditions are favorable, ski areas run out of lift tickets quickly. Tickets for the resorts listed below may be purchased over the phone through **Ticketmaster** (☎ 740-2000). The **Big Bear Hotline** (☎ 866-7000 or 800-424-4232) has info on lodging, local events, and ski and road conditions. **Big Bear Resort,** 1½ mi. southeast of downtown Big Bear Lake, has 12 lifts covering 195 acres of terrain, including huge vertical drops, plus many more acres of undeveloped land for adventurous skiers. (☎ 585-2519. Lift tickets $32, holidays $45. Skis $23, snowboards $28. New skier/snowboarder packages include group lesson, lift ticket, and equipment rental.)

Big Bear has few budget accommodations, especially in the winter. The best option for daytrippers is probably to stay in Redlands or San Bernardino, although the drive down Rte. 18 can be difficult at night. **Big Bear Boulevard,** the main drag on the lake's south shore, is lined with lodging possibilities, but groups can find the best deals by sharing a cabin. **Mountain Lodging Unlimited** arranges lodging and lift packages. (☎ 800-487-3168. From about $100 per couple. Open in ski season 7am-midnight; off season 9am-midnight.) **Hillcrest Lodge,** 40241 Big Bear Blvd., is a favorite for honeymooners. Pine paneling and skylights give these cozy rooms a ritzy feel at a budget price. (☎ 866-7330, reservations 800-843-4449. Jacuzzi, cable, and free local calls. Small rooms $35-49, 4-person units with kitchen $64-89, deluxe doubles with hearth and kitchen $57-79; in winter $44-69/$74-125/$74-125.) **Pineknot,** south of Big Bear on Summit Blvd., has 52 isolated sites with flush toilets and water. At the base of Snow Summit, this spot is popular with mountain bikers. (☎ 877-444-6777 for reservations. Sites $15. Wheelchair accessible.) Groceries can be procured at **Stater Bros.,** 42171 Big Bear Blvd. (☎ 866-5211. Open daily 7am-11pm.)

To reach Big Bear Lake, take the San Bernardino Fwy. (I-10) to the junction of Rte. 30 and 330. Follow Rte. 330, also known as Mountain Rd., to Rte. 18, a *very* long and winding uphill road. About halfway up the mountain, Rte. 18 becomes Big Bear Blvd., the main route encircling the lake. Driving time from L.A. is about 2½hr., barring serious weekend traffic or road closures. **Mountain Area Regional Transit Authority (MARTA)** runs one bus per day from the Greyhound station in San Bernardino to Big Bear. (☎ 584-1111. $5, seniors and disabled $3.75.) Buses also run the length of Big Bear Blvd. (end-to-end trip 1hr.; $1, students 75¢, seniors and disabled 50¢). MARTA also operates **Dial-A-Ride** ($2, students $1.75, seniors and disabled $1).

SAN DIEGO ☎ 619

San Diegans are fond of referring to their garden-like town as "America's Finest City." This claim is difficult to dispute—San Diego has all the virtues of other California cities without their frequently cited drawbacks. No smog fills this city's air, and no sewage spoils its silver seashores. Its zoo is the nation's best, and its city center contains a greater concentration of museums than any spot in America save Washington, D.C. The city was founded when the seafaring Spanish prolonged an onshore foray in 1769 and began the first permanent settlement on the US's West Coast, but it didn't become a city proper until the 40s, when it became the headquarters of the US Pacific Fleet following the Pearl Harbor attack.

▐ GETTING THERE AND AROUND

San Diego rests in the extreme southwest corner of California, 127 mi. south of L.A. and 15 mi. north of Mexico. **I-5** runs south from L.A. and skirts the eastern edge of downtown; **I-15** runs northeast to Nevada; and **I-8** runs east-west along downtown's northern boundary, connecting the desert with Ocean Beach. The major downtown thoroughfare, **Broadway,** also runs east-west.

San Diego has an extensive system of fairly easy **bike routes.** The flat, paved route along Mission and Pacific Beaches toward La Jolla affords ocean views and soothing sea breezes. But bikers beware: pedestrian traffic along the beaches rivals the automobile blockades on the boulevards.

Airport: San Diego International (Lindbergh Field), at the northwest edge of downtown. Call the Travelers Aid Society (☎231-7361) for info. Open daily 8am-11pm. Bus #2 goes downtown ($1.75), as do cabs ($8).

Trains: Amtrak, 1050 Kettner Blvd. (☎239-9021 or 800-872-7245), just north of Broadway. To: L.A. (11 per day; $28, off-season $23). Station has info on bus, trolley, car, and boat transportation. Ticket office open daily 5:15am-10:20pm.

Buses: Greyhound, 120 W. Broadway (☎239-8082 or 800-231-2222), at 1st St. To: L.A. (30 per day 5am-11:35pm; $15, round-trip $25). Ticket office open 24hr.

Public Transit: San Diego Metropolitan Transit System (MTS). 24hr. info line (☎685-4900), has info on buses, trains, and trolleys. The **Transit Store,** at 1st Ave. and Broadway, has bus, trolley, and ferry tickets and timetables (open M-F 8:30am-5:30pm, Sa-Su noon-4pm). The **Day Tripper** allows unlimited rides on buses, ferries, and trolleys for 1 day ($5), 2 days ($8), 3 days ($10), or 4 days ($12). The pass can be purchased at the Transit Store or at trolley stations.

Car Rental: Academy Car, Jet Ski, and Boat Rental, 2270 Hotel Circle N. (☎294-2227 or 888-920-2227), in the Hanalei Mission Valley Hotel. Cars from $19 per day, $139-198 per week; 150 mi. free per day, 700 mi. per week. Ages 18-21 pay $8 per day surcharge, ages 21-25 pay $4. Insurance to take the car into Mexico $6-12. Credit card required. Waverunners and boats also for rent. Open daily 8am-6pm.

Bike Info: Buses equipped with bike carriers make it possible to cart bikes almost anywhere in the city (call ☎233-3004 to find out which routes have carriers). Bikes are also allowed on the San Diego Trolley with a $4 permit (available at **Transit Store,** see above). For more bike info, contact the **City Bicycle Coordinator** (☎533-3110), or **Cal-Trans,** 4040 Taylor St., San Diego 92110 (☎231-2453), in Old Town. Biking maps and pamphlets are available. Rent bikes from **Action Sports,** 4000 Coronado Bay Rd. (☎424-4466), at the Marina Dock of the Loews Coronado Bay Resort. Beach cruiser bikes $7 per hr., $20 per 4hr.; mountain bikes $9/$25; full-suspension bikes $10/$30. Open M-F 9am-6pm, Sa-Su 8:30am-6:30pm.

✳❓ ORIENTATION AND PRACTICAL INFORMATION

In northeast downtown sits **Balboa Park,** home to many museums and to the justly heralded San Diego Zoo. The cosmopolitan **Hillcrest** and **University Heights** districts, both centers of the gay community, border the park to the northeast. South of downtown, between 4th and 6th St., is the **Gaslamp District,** full of nightclubs, chic restaurants, and coffeehouses. **Downtown** is situated between San Diego's two major bays: **San Diego Bay,** formed by **Coronado Island,** lies just to the south, while **Mission Bay,** formed by the **Mission Beach** spit, lies to the northwest. Up the coast from Mission Beach are **Ocean Beach, Pacific Beach,** and wealthy **La Jolla.**

Visitor Info: International Visitor Information Center, 11 Horton Plaza (☎236-1212), downtown at 1st Ave. and F St. Multilingual staff. 3hr. parking validation for lots with entrances on G St. and 4th Ave. Open June-Aug. M-Sa 8:30am-5pm, Su 11am-5pm; Sept.-May M-Sa 8:30am-5pm. **Old Town and State Park Info,** 4002 Wallace Ave. (☎220-5422), in Old Town Sq. Take the Taylor St. exit off I-8 or bus #5. Free walking tours leave daily at 11am and 2pm. Open daily 10am-5pm.

Post Offices: 2535 Midway Dr. Take bus #6, 9, or 35. Open M 7am-5pm, Tu-F 8am-5pm, Sa 8am-4pm. **ZIP Code:** 92186. **Area code:** 619 for most of the city; 858 in the north. In text, 619 unless noted.

▌ ACCOMMODATIONS

San Diego offers a variety of accommodations, but rates predictably rise on weekends and during the summer season. Reservations are recommended. There is a popular cluster known as **Hotel Circle** (2-3 mi. east of **I-5** along **I-8**), where summer prices at the cheaper places begin at $55 for a single and $62 for a double during the week ($70/$80 on weekends). Those with cars and tents can camp on the beaches outside of the city. Reservations are available through ReserveAmerica. (☎800-444-7275. Open daily 8am-5pm.)

Downtown San Diego

⌂ ACCOMMODATIONS

J Street Inn, **3**
San Diego Metropolitan, **2**
USA Hostels San Diego, **1**

■ **San Diego Metropolitan (HI-AYH),** 521 Market St. (☎525-1531 or 800-909-4776, ext. 43), at 5th Ave., in the heart of the Gaslamp. Quiet, impeccable hostel near San Diego's most popular attractions and clubs. Lockers (bring a lock) and laundry. Reception 7am-midnight. Groups welcome. Dorms (4-6 beds) $17, non-members $20; doubles $40/$46.

■ **USA Hostels San Diego,** 726 5th Ave. (☎232-3100 or 800-438-8622), between G and F St. in the Gaslamp. This Euro-style fun house hosts keg parties every Sa and organizes Tijuana tours ($10). Breakfast included. Free linen and lockers. Coin-op laundry. Free shuttle to nearby sights. *International passport required.* Clean and spacious dorms $15-18; twin $35-40.

■ **Ocean Beach International (OBI),** 4961 Newport Ave. (☎223-7873 or 800-339-7263), **Ocean Beach.** Free transport to and from airport, train, and bus terminals. The OBI features cable TV and kitchen near the beach. Breakfast included. Beach gear rental. Laundry. Free BBQ and keg parties Tu and F night; free pasta Tu in winter. 29-day maximum stay. *Proof of international travel required.* Dorms (4-6 beds) $15-18; doubles (some with bath) $34-40.

Banana Bungalow, 707 Reed Ave. (☎273-3060 or 800-546-7835), just off Mission Blvd. in Mission Beach. Free pick-up from airport and Greyhound terminal (call ahead), or take bus #34 to Mission Blvd. and Reed Ave. This beachfront party central rocks with cheap keg parties and beach bonfires. Internet access $1 per 10min. Breakfast included. Free linen. Bikes, skates, surfboards for rent. Checkout 11am. 2-week maximum stay. Call in advance. *Must have an international passport.* Dorms (4-12 beds) $20. Single room with private bath June-Aug. $55, Sept.-May $45.

J Street Inn, 222 J St. (☎696-6922; fax 696-1295), near the convention center and ritzy waterfront, downtown. All 221 fabulous studio rooms have cable TV, microwave, fridge, and bath. Gym and reading room. Enclosed parking $5 per day, $20 per week. Singles and doubles $50-70; each additional person $20. Weekly $179-249.

South Carlsbad Beach State Park (☎760-438-3143), off Pacific Coast Hwy. (Rte. 21) near Leucadia, in north San Diego County. Half of the 222 sites accommodate RVs. Beautiful beaches with good surfing conditions. Showers and laundry. Mar.-Nov. ocean view $22, inland $17; Dec.-Feb. $19/$14. Hook-ups $6 more. Extra vehicle $4. Dogs $1 each.

San Elijo Beach State Park (☎760-753-5091), off Pacific Coast Hwy. (Rte. 21) south of Cardiff-by-the-Sea. 171 sites (23 with full RV hook-ups) on seaside cliffs. Fresh breezes and glorious sunsets. Laundry and showers. Same prices as South Carlsbad Beach State Park, above. Wheelchair accessible.

◖ FOOD

Good restaurants cluster downtown along **C St., Broadway,** and in the **Gaslamp.** The best food near Balboa Park and the Zoo is north and west in nearby **Hillcrest** and **University Heights. Old Town** is absolutely *the* place to eat Mexican cuisine.

▨ **Casa de Bandini,** 2754 Calhoun St. (☎297-8211). An Old Town institution and repeatedly voted best Mexican restaurant in San Diego. Set in a Spanish-style architectural landmark (built in 1829), Bandini dishes out superb food and boisterous Mariachi music. The colossal combo plates ($8) and heavyweight margaritas ($4-7) are the stuff of legend. Open M-Th 11am-9:30pm, F-Sa 11am-10pm, Su 10am-9:30pm.

▨ **The Vegetarian Zone,** 2949 5th Ave. (☎298-7302), at Quince St., near Balboa Park. The motto here is that "the human body doesn't require any form of meat to operate wonderfully." Open M-Th 11:30am-3pm and 5:30-9pm, F 11:30am-3pm and 5:30-10pm, Sa 9:30am-3pm and 5:30-10pm, Su 8:30am-3pm and 5:30-9pm.

Kono's Surf Club, 704 Garnet Ave. (☎483-1669), across from the Crystal Pier in Pacific Beach. A surfer's shrine. Breakfast all day ($3-4). The Egg Burrito #3 includes bacon, cheese, potatoes, and pica sauce, all for $3.25. Open M-F 7am-3pm, Sa-Su 7am-4pm.

El Indio Mexican Restaurant, 409 F St. (☎299-0385), downtown. Good food at good prices. Combo plates $4-6, burritos $3-4. Open M-Th 11am-8pm, F-Sa 11am-2am.

Karl Strauss' Old Columbia Brewery and Grill, 1157 Columbia St. (☎234-2739), downtown. A favorite for power lunches. BBQ ribs and pasta $8-12, lighter fare $6-8. Open M-Th 11:30am-midnight, F-Sa 11:30am-1am, Su 11:30am-10pm.

Rancho El Nopal, in the Bazaar (☎295-0584), in Old Town. Sumptuous and bubbling concoctions of beans, rice, and cheese. Entrees $6-9. Open daily 10am-9pm.

◖ SIGHTS

DOWNTOWN

San Diego's downtown attractions are concentrated in the corridor that includes its business, Gaslamp, and waterfront districts—all testaments to San Diego's continuing renaissance. **San Diego Museum of Contemporary Art** is a steel-and-glass structure that encases 20th-century works of art from the museum's permanent collection and visiting works on a rotational basis. *(1001 Kettner Blvd. ☎234-1001 or 454-3541. Open Tu-Sa 10am-5pm, Su noon-5pm. $2.)* The **Gaslamp Quarter** houses antique shops, Victorian buildings, and trendy restaurants. Formerly the city's Red Light District and home to the original Pappy's, Inc. adult bookstore, the area's new bars and bistros have grown popular with upscale revelers. By day, the area's charm lies in its history. The **Gaslamp Quarter Foundation** offers guided walking tours. *(William Heath Davis House, 410 Island Ave. ☎233-4692. Museum open M-F 10am-2pm, Sa 10am-4pm, Su noon-4pm. $5; students, seniors, and ages 12-18 $3; under 12 free.)* The **Horton Grand Hotel,** like most old buildings in San Diego, is supposedly haunted. Believers may catch a glimpse of Wyatt Earp or even Babe Ruth. *(311 Island Ave. ☎544-1886. Tours W at 3pm.*

Free.) The **San Diego Maritime Museum** displays showcase San Diego's rich maritime history. *(1306 N. Harbor Dr. ☎234-9153. Open daily June-Aug. 9am-9pm, Sept.-May 9am-8pm. $6; seniors, military, and ages 13-17 $5; ages 6-12 $3; under 6 free.)*

THE SAN DIEGO ZOO AND BALBOA PARK

SAN DIEGO ZOO. With over 100 acres of exquisite fenceless habitats, this zoo well deserves its reputation as one of the finest in the world. Its unique "bioclimatic" exhibits group animals and plants together by habitat. The zoo currently showcases several **pandas** and invests over a million dollars a year on panda habitat preservation in China. Young *Homo sapiens* can watch the hatching and feeding of other species' toddlers in the **children's petting zoo.** The **Skyfari Aerial Tramway** rises 170 ft. above the park and lasts about 2min. If the tramway appeals to you, purchase your tickets in advance when you buy your zoo admission. *(☎234-3153. Late June to early Sept. 7:30am-10pm; off-season 9am-dusk. $18, ages 3-11 $8, military in uniform free. Combined Zoo, Wild Animal Park, and Seaworld admission $79, ages 3-11 $56. Skyfari Aerial Tramway $1.50 one-way.)*

BALBOA PARK AND THE EL PRADO MUSEUMS. Although they may not be Smithsonian-quality, the museums in Balboa Park form the highest concentration of museums in the US outside of Washington, D.C. It would take several days to see all of them. Most of the museums reside within the resplendent Spanish colonial-style buildings that line **El Prado Street,** which runs west-to-east through the Park's central **Plaza de Panama.** The **Balboa Park Visitors Center** is in the House of Hospitality on El Prado St. at the Plaza de Panama and sells park maps ($1) and the Passport to Balboa Park ($25), which allows admission into 12 of the park's museums. Passports are also available at participating museums. *(☎239-0512. Open daily 9am-5pm.)* Formerly a state building, the sizeable **Museum of Man** anchors the west end of the park. The museum traces human evolution with exhibits on primates and early man. *(☎239-2001. Open daily 10am-4:30pm. $6, seniors $5, ages 6-17 $3, military in uniform free.)* At the east end of Balboa Park, the **Natural History Museum** displays stuffed mammals and birds. Live insects and arthropods enhance the exhibition of standard fossils. A re-created mine displays gems. *(☎232-3821. Open daily 9:30am-5pm; in off-season 9:30am-4:30pm. Admission varies depending on traveling exhibits, call for exact prices.)* The **Aerospace Museum** displays 24 full-scale replicas and 44 original planes, as well as aviation history exhibits in the drum-shaped Ford Pavilion. *(2001 Pan American Plaza. ☎234-8291. Open daily 10am-5:30pm; in off-season 10am-5pm. $8, seniors $6, ages 6-17 $3, under 6 and military in uniform free; free 4th Tu of each month.)*

OLD TOWN

In 1769, Father Junípero Serra, supported by a brigade of Spanish infantry, established the first of 21 missions that eventually would line the California coast. Now known as Old Town, the remnants of this early settlement are one of San Diego's tourist mainstays. The **Mission Basilica San Diego de Alcalá** is still an active parish church and contains a chapel, gardens, a small museum, and a reconstruction of Serra's living quarters. *(☎281-8449. Mass held daily at 7am and 5:30pm; visitors welcome.)* The most popular of the area's attractions, the **Old Town State Park** contain museums, shops, and restaurants. **Seely Stable** gives visitor info and free tours of the stable's agricultural exhibits. *(☎220-5422. Open 10am-9pm. Tours hourly 11am-2pm.)* Take a tour of the **Whaley House,** which displays an authentic Lincoln life mask and the piano used in *Gone With the Wind*. The house stands on the site of San Diego's first gallows, which might explain why it is one of two **official haunted houses** recognized by the State of California. *(2482 San Diego Ave. ☎298-2482. Open daily 10am-4:30pm. $4, seniors $3, ages 6-12 $2.)* Across the street is **Heritage Park,** a group of seven 150-year-old Victorian buildings (6 houses and a temple) collected from around the city. Four are open to the public. The **Serra Museum** houses exhibits documenting the settlement; outside is a really, really huge flagpole marking the former location of **Fort Stockton.** *(In Presido Park. ☎279-3258. Open Tu-Sa 10am-4:30pm, Su noon-4:30pm. $3, under 12 free.)*

CORONADO ISLAND

Lovely Coronado Island is in fact a peninsula. A slender 7 mi. strip of sand known as the "Silver Strand" tethers it to the mainland. Famous for its elegant colonial Hotel Del Coronado, the island is perfect for strolling and browsing. Water babies frolic in the frothy waves that break all along the southern shore, and outdoor enthusiasts jog and bike along paved trails. Coronado has a huge military presence, and the entire northern chunk comprises the **North Island Naval Air Station,** the birthplace of American naval aviation. Among the island's many naval enterprises is the training area of the infamous SEAL (sea, air, and land) commando teams. Coronado would undoubtedly win "Island Least Likely to Be Invaded," if there were such a contest. The super-helpful **Coronado Visitors Bureau** provides info on every aspect of the island. *(1047 B Ave., just off Orange Ave. near the Hotel Del Coronado. ☎ 437-8788 or 800-622-8300. Open M-F 9am-5pm, Sa 10am-5pm, Su 11am-4pm.)*

SEA WORLD

Take Disneyland, subtract the rides, add a whole lot of fish, and you've got Sea World. Sea World aspires to be both fun and educational. Though critics have long condemned the practice of training highly intelligent marine mammals to perform unnatural circus acts, most visitors find the playful goofballs irresistible. The A-list star here is the behemoth killer whale **Shamu,** whose signature move is a cannonball splash that soaks anyone in the first 20 rows (the original Shamu died long ago, but each of his ten successors has proudly borne the moniker). If it's your mind and not your water-filled pockets that needs emptying, head for the **Baywatch at Sea World** ski show, where high-speed hilarity and prominent bodices are a way of life. The performance's plot is just as gripping as the TV show's, and part of the event is narrated by international heartthrob **David Hasselhoff.** The park's newest attraction is **Shipwreck Rapids,** Sea World's first-ever adventure ride. Those who feel they need a little cooling down should head to the **Anheuser-Busch Hospitality Tent,** which will give each guest (21 and over) up to two free cups of beer. *(☎ 226-3901. Open M-Th 9am-11:30pm, F-Su 9am-11pm. Hours shorter in off-season. $40, ages 3-11 $30. Two-day pass $44/$34. Parking $7, $9 for RVs.)*

◪ NIGHTLIFE

Nightlife in San Diego is not centered around a particular strip, but scattered in several distinct pockets of action. Upscale locals and trendy tourists flock to the **Gaslamp Quarter,** where numerous restaurants and bars feature live music. The **Hillcrest** area, next to Balboa Park, draws a young, largely gay crowd. Away from downtown, the **beach areas** (especially Garnett Ave. in Pacific Beach) are loaded with clubs, bars, inexpensive eateries, and college-age revelers. The city's definitive source of entertainment info is the free *San Diego Reader*.

Lesbian and gay clubs cluster in **University Heights** and **Hillcrest. Gaymart,** 550 University Ave., a clothing and video emporium, has info on the gay scene. (☎ 543-1221. Open daily 10am-10pm.) **The Flame,** 3780 Park Blvd., in Hillcrest, is a popular lesbian dance club. (☎ 295-4163. Open Sa-Th 5pm-2am, F 4pm-2am.) **Bourbon Street,** 4612 Park Blvd., in University Heights, is a piano bar with a gay following. (☎ 291-0173. Open daily 11am-1:30am.) **The Brass Rail,** 3796 5th Ave., in Hillcrest, feature dancing and drag on weekends. (☎ 298-2233. Open daily 5pm-2am.)

▨ **Croce's Top Hat Bar and Grille** and **Croce's Jazz Bar,** 802 5th Ave. (☎ 233-4355), at F St. in the Gaslamp. Ingrid Croce, widow of singer Jim Croce, created this rock/blues bar and classy jazz bar side-by-side on the first fl. of the historic Keating building. Open daily 7:30am-3pm and 5pm-midnight; bar open until 2am. Live music nightly. Cover $5-10, includes 2 live shows.

Pacific Beach Bar and Grill and **Club Tremors,** 860 Garnet Ave. (☎ 858-272-1242 and 277-7228, respectively), Pacific Beach. Live DJ packs the 2-level dance floor with a young and slinky crowd. The Bar and Grill has cheap, delicious food. Club open Th-Sa 9pm-1:30am. Bar open 11am-1:30am, kitchen closes at midnight. Cover $5.

Cafe Lu Lu, 419 F. St. (☎858-238-0114), Gaslamp. Vegetarian coffeehouse was designed by local artists. See and be seen as you eat for under $7, surreptitiously sipping a raspberry-mocha espresso ($3.75). Standing room only after midnight. Open Su-Th 9am-2am, F-Sa 9am-3am.

Dick's Last Resort, 345 4th Ave. (☎858-231-9100), Gaslamp. Buckets of Southern grub attract a wildly hedonistic bunch. Dick's stocks beers from around the globe, from Africa to Trinidad, on top of native brews like the Dixieland Blackened Voodoo Lager. No cover for the nightly rock or blues, but you'd better be buyin'. Lunch burgers under $4; dinner entrees $10-18. Open daily 11am-1:30am.

NORTH OF SAN DIEGO

LA JOLLA. Pronounced "*la-HOY-a*," this affluent locality houses few budget accommodations or eateries, but its fabulous beaches are largely open to the public. The **La Jolla Cove** is popular with scuba divers, snorkelers, and brilliantly colored Garibaldi goldfish (the state saltwater fish). Surfers are especially fond of the waves at **Tourmaline Beach** and **Windansea Beach,** which can be too strong for novices. **La Jolla Shores,** next to Scripps/UCSD, has clean and gentle swells ideal for bodysurfers, boogie boarders, swimmers, and families. **Black's Beach** is not officially a nude beach, but let's just say there are plenty of wieners and buns at *this* lunchcart. To reach La Jolla, turn from I-5 and take a left at the Ardath exit or take buses #30 or 34 from downtown. **Area code:** 858.

ESCONDIDO. The **San Diego Wild Animal Park** is an essential part of any trip to San Diego. Visitors gawk at the beasties from the open-air **Wgasa Bush Line Railway,** a 55min. monorail safari through four simulated habitat areas. Patrons also watch butterflies and birds flutter as they walk through the Hidden Jungle greenhouses. The park has shops, restaurants, and animal shows, but for adventure, try the 1 mi. Heart of Africa hike, the open-air Photo Caravan, or the Roar and Snore overnight camping safari, available May to Sept. (☎738-5049 or 800-934-2267, Photo Caravan 738-5049, Roar and Snore 800-934-2267. Open daily at 9am; closing times vary. $22, ages 3-11 $15. Parking $5.) **Area code:** 760.

TIJUANA ☎66

In the shadow of swollen, sulphur-spewing factories lies the most notorious specimen of a peculiar border subculture: Tijuana, Mexico. By day, swarms of tourists cross the US border to haggle with street vendors, pour gallons of tequila down their throats, and get their pictures taken with donkeys painted as zebras. By night, Revolución, the city's wide main drag, becomes a big, bad party with *mariachi* bands and exploding bottle rockets doing little to drown out the thumping dance beats blaring from the packed nightclubs. Rife with flashy sleaze and border intrigue, it's hard to say whether it's the city's strange charm, its cheap booze, or its sprawling, unapologetic hedonism that attracts tourists to Tijuana like flies.

■🛈 **ORIENTATION AND PRACTICAL INFORMATION.** From San Diego, grab a trolly at Kettner and Broadway downtown (25 min., US$20); then catch the southbound **Mexicoach** or walk across the pedestrian footbridge which continues as a walkway over the Río Tijuana and ends at the corner of Calle 1a and Revolución (10min.). The area surrounding Revolución is known as the **Zona Centro.** East-west *calles,* which are both named and numbered, cross Revolución; perpendicular to the *calles, avenidas* run north-south. Tijuana has two bus stations, the conveniently located **downtown station,** at Calle 1a and Madero, and the more remote **Central Camionera** (☎21 29 82). **Greyhound** (☎88 19 79) picks up passengers downtown before leaving for **Los Angeles** (3hr., every hr. 5am-midnight, US$24), and connecting to other North American cities. The **Tourist Office,** Revolución 711, at Calle 1. has friendly, English-speaking staff who dole out maps and advice. (☎88 05 55. Open M-Sa 8am-5pm, Su 10am-5pm.) The **Customs Office** lies at the border on the Mexican side, after crossing the San Ysidro bridge. (☎83 13 90. Open 24hr.) Numerous countries have **consulates: Canada,** German Gedovius 10411-101, in the Zona Río. (☎84 04 61 or 800-706-2900; open M-F 9am-1pm); the **UK,** Salinas 1500, in Col. Aviación, La Mesa. (☎81 73 23 or 86 53 20; open M-F 9am-3pm); and the **US,** Tapachula Sur 96, in Col. Hipódromo, adjacent to the racetrack southeast of town (☎81 74 00 or 619-692-2154; open M-F 8am-4:30pm). **Red Cross:** Gamboa at Silvestre, across from Price Club (☎21 77 87, emergency 066). **Post office:** Negrete at Calle 11 (☎84 79 50; open M-F 8am-5pm). **Postal Code:** 22000. **Area code:** 66.

▐▛▐▘ ACCOMMODATIONS AND FOOD. There's no shortage of budget hotels in Tijuana, especially on Calle 1, between Revolución and Mutualismo. Rooms tend to be roachy—ask to see them before paying. *Exercise caution when walking in this area at night.* The strangely decorated **Hotel Perla de Occidente,** Mutualismo 758, between Calles 1 and 2, four blocks from the bedlam of Revolución, has large, soft beds, roomy bathrooms, and fans on request. (☎85 13 58. Singles 120 pesos; doubles 150 pesos.) **Hotel El Jaliscense,** Calle 1 7925, sits between Niños Héroes and Martínez. Small rooms have resilient beds, baths, fans, and phones. If you want to sleep soundly, ask for a room that doesn't face Calle 1. (☎85 34 91. Singles 140 pesos; doubles 160 pesos.) For some great food try **El Pipirín Antojitos,** Constitución 878, between Calles 2 and 3. (☎88 16 02. Open daily 8:30am-9pm. Chicken burritos with rice and beans 28 pesos.) **Los Panchos Taco Shop,** Revolución at Calle 3, serves steak tacos ($1) and bean and cheese burritos ($2). (☎85 72 77. Open Su-Th 8am-midnight, F-Sa 8am-4am; off season Su-Th 8am-midnight, F-Sa 8am-2am.)

▣ SIGHTS AND SPORTS. Photo-ops abound on Revolución, where zebra-striped donkeys and gaudily costumed cowboys vie for your attention. The multi-tiered dance clubs and curio shops that share the street are often the only sights that Tijuana tourists care to see. Dedicated in 1924 to the memory of Vicente Guerrero, the beautiful and shady **Parque Teniente Guerrero,** on Calle 3a and 5 de Mayo, is a favorite gathering place for local families and an oasis from the noisy circus of Revolución. The **Catedral de Nuestra Señora de Guadalupe** was originally built in 1902 as a modest adobe chapel; modern expansions and reinforcement have made it into a huge stone cathedral checkered in adobe orange and gray and crowned with a giant image of the Virgin of Guadalupe. The cathedral's daily mass attracts a diverse congregation of devout locals and curious passersby. The grandiose baroque **Frontón Palacio,** on Revolución at Calle 7a, hosts daily competitions of **jai alai.** (☎85 16 12. Games take place M-Sa at 8pm. Free.) If you're in town on the right Su, you can watch the graceful and savage battle of man versus bull in one of Tijuana's two bullrings. **El Toreo de Tijuana,** southeast of town just off of Agua Caliente, hosts the first round of fights (alternate Su, May-July). To get to El Toreo, catch a bus on Calle 2a west of Revolución.

▣ NIGHTLIFE. For nightlife, head to **Eclipse,** Revolución at Calle 6a—a three-tiered party palace with some of the cheapest booze in town: two beers and a shot of tequila for $3. (Open M-W 11am-9:30pm, Th-Su 9am-6am.) **People's,** Revolución and Calle 2a, has fluorescent constellations and silver-painted sports equipment on its purple arches. Revelers guzzle 10 beers for $18. (☎85 45 72. Open M-W 10am-2am, Th-Su 10am-5am.) **Iguanas-Ranas,** Revolución at Calle 3, serves beers ($2.50) in a yellow school bus dangling above Revolución and is packed on weekends with US and Mexican 20-somethings. (☎85 14 22. Open M-Th 10am-2am, F-Su 10am-5am.) Clubs catering to gays and lesbians cluster in the southern part of the *centro* around Calle 6a and 7a or down the hill to the north of Calle 1a.

THE CALIFORNIA DESERT

Mystics and misanthropes have long been fascinated by the austere scenery and the vast open spaces of the California desert. In winter the desert is a pleasantly warm refuge; in spring, a technicolor floral landscape; in summer, a blistering wasteland; and in fall, more of the same. The desert's beauty lies in its emptiness as well as in its elusive treasures: diverse flora and fauna, staggering topographical variation, and scattered relics of the American frontier.

PALM SPRINGS   ☎ 760

From its first known inhabitants, the Cahuilla Indians, to today's geriatric fun-lovers, the restorative oasis of Palm Springs has drawn many to its sandy bosom. With warm temperatures, celebrity residents, and more pink than a *Miami Vice* episode, this desert city provides a sunny break from everyday life.

Mt. San Jacinto State Park, Palm Springs's primary landmark, offers outdoor recreation opportunities for visitors of all fitness levels. If Mt. San Jacinto's 10,804 ft. escarpment seems too strenuous, try the **Palm Springs Aerial Tramway,** on Aerial Tramway Rd. off North Palm Canyon Dr. The observation deck has great views of the Coachella Valley. (☎325-1391. Trams run every 30min., M-F 10am-8pm, Sa-Su 8am-8pm. Round-trip fare $19, seniors $17, ages 5-12 $12.50.) The **Desert Hot Springs Spa,** 10805 Palm Dr., features six naturally heated mineral pools of different temperatures, as well as saunas, massage professionals, and bodywraps. Take Indian Canyon Dr. to Pierson Blvd., turn right, then turn left onto Palm Dr. (☎329-6495. Simmer daily 8am-10pm. M and W $5; Tu $3; Th men $3, women $5; F men $5, women $3; Sa-Su $6. After 3pm $3. Holidays $7.) **Oasis Water Park,** off I-10 South on Gene Autry Trail between Ramon and E. Palm Canyon Dr., has a wave pool, inner tube river, and 13 waterslides. (☎325-7873 or 327-0499. Open daily mid-Mar. to mid-Sept. 11am-6pm, mid-Sept. to Oct. Sa-Su 11am-5pm. $20, children under 5 ft. $13, seniors $11, under 3 ft. free. Parking $4.)

Like most famous resort communities, Palm Springs caters mainly to those seeking a tax shelter, not a night's shelter—the cheapest way to stay here is to find a nearby state park or national forest campground. If you've gotta stay in town, there is a particular concentration of inexpensive motels at the bend in Palm Canyon Dr. where East Palm Canyon Dr. becomes South Palm Canyon Dr. **Motel 6** has the cheapest rates, especially during winter. Locations include 660 S. Palm Canyon Dr. (☎327-4200), south of city center; 595 E. Palm Canyon Dr. (☎325-6129); and 63950 20th Ave. (☎251-1425), near the I-10 off-ramp. Each has A/C rooms and pool access. (Singles $35; doubles $41; in winter $6-12 more.)

Palm Springs offers a kaleidoscope of sumptuous food, from the classic greasy spoon to ultra-trendy fusions of cuisines. However, high prices limit the scope of viable options. **Thai Smile,** 651 N. Palm Canyon Dr., is an authentic and inexpensive foray into Thai cuisine. Don't miss the $6 lunch specials (☎320-5503; open daily 11:30am-10pm). **Las Casuelas—The Original,** 368 N. Palm Canyon Dr., was the first establishment in this restaurant chain. Authentic Mexican dishes (from $6) and dingy lighting give it that slightly outlaw south-of-the-border feel. (☎325-3213. Open daily 10am-10pm.)

Palm Springs Regional Airport, 3400 S. Tahquitz-Canyon Rd. (☎323-8161), offers mainly in-state service. **Greyhound,** 311 N. Indian Canyon Dr. (325-2053), buses to Los Angeles (9 per day; $19, round-trip $35). The local **Sun Bus** (343-3451) connects Coachella Valley cities. (Operates daily 5am-10pm. Fare 75¢, transfers 25¢.) **Visitor Info: Chamber of Commerce,** 190 W. Amado Rd. (☎325-1577; open M-F 8:30am-4:30pm). **Post office:** 333 E. Amado Rd. **ZIP code:** 92262, General Delivery 92263.

JOSHUA TREE NATIONAL PARK   ☎ 760

When the Mormon pioneers crossed this desert in the 19th century, they named the enigmatic desert tree they encountered after the Biblical prophet Joshua. Perhaps it was the heat, but the tree's crooked limbs seemed to them an uncanny image of the Hebrew general, who with arms upraised, beckoned them to the promised land. Stacks of wind-sculpted boulders, Joshua trees, five oases, and a spectrum of high and low desert ecologies create a vast mosaic of landscape and vegetation. In recent years, climbers, campers, and daytrippers from Southern California have added to the mosaic. History buffs will appreciate the vestiges of human occupation—ancient rock petroglyphs, dams built in the 19th century to catch the meager rainfall for livestock, and gold mine ruins dot the landscape.

CALIFORNIA

⚡ PRACTICAL INFORMATION. About 160 mi. east of L.A., Joshua Tree National Park covers 558,000 acres northeast of Palm Springs. The park is ringed by three highways: **I-10** to the south, **Rte. 62 (Twentynine Palms Hwy.)** to the west and north, and **Rte. 177** to the east. The northern entrances to the park are off Rte. 62 at the towns of **Joshua Tree** and **Twentynine Palms.** The south entrance is at **Cottonwood Spring,** off I-10 at **Rte. 195,** south of Palm Springs near the town of Indio. The park entrance fee is $5 per person or $10 per car, valid for seven days. **Headquarters and Oasis Visitors Center:** 74485 National Park Dr., Twentynine Palms, ¼ mi. off Rte. 62. (☎367-5500. Open daily 8am-5pm. Water available.) **Post office:** 73839 Gorgonio Dr., Twentynine Palms (open M-F 8:30am-5pm). **ZIP Code:** 92277. **Area code:** 760.

⚡⚡ ACCOMMODATIONS AND CAMPING. Most campgrounds in the park operate on a first come, first served basis. Reservations can be made for group sites only at Cottonwood, Sheep Pass, Indian Cove, and Black Rock Canyon through **DESTINET** (☎800-436-7275). **Backcountry** camping is also an option. Ask at a ranger station for details. All campsites have tables, fireplaces, and pit toilets, and are **free** unless otherwise noted. Those who plan any sort of extended stay should pack supplies, water, and cooking utensils. Campground stays are limited to 30 days in the summer and to 14 days Oct. through May. **Hidden Valley,** in the center of the park, off Quail Springs Rd., has secluded alcoves shaded by enormous boulders. Its proximity to Wonderland of Rock and the Barker Dam Trail make this a rock climber's heaven. **Jumbo Rocks,** located near Skull Rock Trail on the eastern edge of Queen Valley, is the highest, and therefore the coolest, campground in the park. Front spots have the best shade. **Indian Cove,** on the north edge of the Wonderland of Rocks, has dramatic waterfalls and rock climbing nearby. **Black Rock Canyon,** at the end of Joshua Ln. off Rte. 62 near Yucca Valley, has wooded sites near flush toilets and running water (sites $10; reservations accepted). Those who cannot stomach the thought of desert campgrounds can find indoor accommodations in **Twentynine Palms.** The **29 Palms Inn,** 73950 Inn Dr., facing the Mara Oasis, offers the indoors. (☎367-3505. Doubles June-Sept. Su-Th $50-80, F-Sa $65-105; Oct.-May $10-20 extra. Cottages for 4-8 people and air-stream trailers also available for rent. Reservations required Feb.-Apr.)

◙ SIGHTS. Over 80% of the park is designated wilderness area, safeguarded against development, and lacking paved roads, toilets, and campfires. Joshua Tree offers truly remote territory for backcountry hiking and camping. There's no water in the wilderness except when a flash flood comes roaring down a wash (beware your choice of campsite). The park's most temperate weather is from Oct. to Dec. and Mar. to Apr.; temperatures in other months span uncomfortable extremes.

A self-paced **driving tour** is an easy way to explore the park and linger to a later hour. All park roads are well-marked, and "Exhibit Ahead" signs point the way to unique floral and geological formations. One sight that should not be missed is **Key's View,** 6 mi. off the park road just west of Ryan campground. It's a great spot for watching the sunrise. The **Cholla Cactus Garden,** a grove of spiny succulents resembling 3D asterisks, lies in the Pinto Basin just off the road. Four-wheel-drive vehicles can use dirt roads, such as **Geology Tour Road,** climbing through fascinating rock formations to the Li'l San Bernardino Mountains.

Hiking through the park's trails is perhaps the best way to experience Joshua Tree. Only on foot can visitors tread through sand, scramble over boulders, and walk among the park's hardy namesakes. Although the **Barker Dam Trail,** next to Hidden Valley, is often packed with tourists, its painted petroglyphs and eerie tranquility make it a worthwhile hike. Bring plenty of water for the strenuous, unshaded climb to the summit of **Ryan Mountain,** where the boulder formations bear an unsettling resemblance to herculean beasts of burden slouching toward a distant destination. The visitors center has info on the park's many other hikes, which range from the 15min. stroll to the **Oasis of Mara** to a three-day trek along the **California Riding and Hiking Trail** (35 mi.). Joshua Tree teems with flora and fauna that you're unlikely to see anywhere else in the world. Larger plants like Joshua trees, cholla,

Here's your ticket to freedom, baby!

*Airline Tickets | Hotel Rooms | Rental Cars
New Cars | Long Distance*

Wherever you want to go, priceline.com can get you there for less. Our customers regularly save up to 40% or more off the lowest published airfares. But we're more than just airline tickets. At priceline.com, you can Name Your Own Price℠ and save big on brand-name hotels nationwide. Get great rates on all your long distance calls — without changing your long distance carrier. Even get the car of your dreams, at the price *you* want to pay. If you haven't tried priceline.com, you're missing out on the best way to save. **Visit us online today at www.priceline.com.**

and the spidery ocotillo have adapted to the severe climate in fascinating ways, and the **wildflowers** that dot the desert terrain each spring attract thousands of visitors.

Energetic visitors are often drawn to Joshua Tree for its **rock climbing;** the world-renowned boulders at **Wonderland of Rocks** and **Hidden Valley** are especially challenging and attract thousands of climbers each year. The visitors center provides info on established rope routes and on wilderness areas where the placement of new bolts is restricted. **Joshua Tree Climbing School,** Box 29, Joshua Tree (☎800-890-4745), provides instruction and equipment rental.

DEATH VALLEY   ☎760

Satan owns a lot of real estate in Death Valley National Park. Not only does he grow crops (at the Devil's Cornfield) and hit the links (at the Devil's Golf Course), but the park is also home to Hell's Gate itself. Not surprisingly, the area's astonishing topographical and climactic extremes can support just about anyone's idea of the Inferno. Winter temps dip well below freezing, and summer readings rival even the hottest Hades. The 2nd-highest temperature ever recorded on Earth (134°F in the shade) was measured at the valley's Furnace Creek Ranch on July 10, 1913. Few venture to the valley floor during the summer, and it is foolish to do so; the average high in July is 116°F. Ground temperatures hover near an egg-frying 200°F. A visit in winter lets visitors enjoy the splendor in comfort.

▣ GETTING THERE AND GETTING AROUND. There is no regularly scheduled public transportation into Death Valley. **Guaranteed Tours,** with a depot at the World Trade Center on Desert Inn Rd. between Swensen and Maryland Pkwy. in Las Vegas, runs bus tours from Las Vegas to Death Valley. (☎702-369-1000. Open for reservations daily 6am-10:45pm. 9½hr. Tours depart Tu, Th, and Sa 8am. $120, includes continental breakfast and lunch.) The best way to get around Death Valley is by car. Of the nine **park entrances,** most visitors choose Rte. 190 from the east. The road is well-maintained, the pass is less steep, and you arrive more quickly at the visitors center. But the visitor with a trusty vehicle will be able to see more of the park by entering from the southeast (Rte. 178 west from Rte. 127 at Shoshone) or the north (direct to Scotty's Castle via NV Rte. 267 from U.S. 95). Unskilled mountain drivers should not attempt to enter via Titus Canyon or Emigrant Canyon Drive roads; neither has guard rails to prevent your car from sliding over **precipitous cliffs.** If you **hitchhike,** you walk through the Valley of the Shadow of Death. Don't.

⬛ PRACTICAL INFORMATION. Visitor Info: Furnace Creek Visitors Center, on Rte. 190 in the east-central section of the valley (☎786-3244; open daily 8am-6pm); or write the **Superintendent,** Death Valley National Park, Death Valley 92328. **Ranger stations** are located at **Grapevine** (☎786-2313), at the junction of Rte. 190 and 267 near Scotty's Castle; **Stovepipe Wells** (☎786-2342), on Rte. 190; and **Shoshone** (☎832-4308), outside the southeast border of the valley at the junction of Rte. 178 and 127. The weather report, weekly naturalist programs, and park info are posted at each station. (All open daily 8am-5pm.) The $5 per vehicle **entrance fee** is collected at the visitors center in the middle of the park. **Get gas** outside Death Valley at Olancha, Shoshone, or Beatty, NV. **Radiator water** (*not* for drinking) is available at critical points on Rte. 178 and 190 and NV Rte. 374, but not on unpaved roads. Those who *do* drive along the backcountry trails should carry chains, extra tires, gas, oil, radiator and drinking water, and spare parts. **Post Office:** Furnace Creek Ranch (☎786-2223). **ZIP code:** 92328. **Area code:** 760.

▮ ACCOMMODATIONS. In Death Valley, enclosed beds and fine meals within a budget traveler's reach are as elusive as the desert bighorn sheep. During the winter months, camping out with a stock of groceries is a good way to save both money and driving time. **Furnace Creek Ranch Complex** is deluged with tour-bus refugees who challenge the adjacent 18-hole golf course and relax in the 85°F spring-fed swimming pool. (☎786-2345 or 800-236-7916. Cabins with A/C and 2 beds $94, motel-style rooms $124-149.) **Stovepipe Wells Village** is right in Death Valley. (☎786-2387. $58 per night for 1-2 people; each additional person $11; RV sites $15.) The National Park Service maintains nine **campgrounds,** but only Texas Springs and Furnace Creek accept reservations. Call ahead to check availability and be prepared to battle for a space if you come during peak periods. Water availability is not reliable and supplies can be unsafe at times; always pack your own. Roadside camping is not permitted, but **backcountry camping** is free and legal, provided you check in at the visitors center and pitch tents at least 1 mi. from main roads, 5 mi. from any established campsite, and ¼ mi. from any water source.

🗺 **SIGHTS.** Death Valley has hiking to bemuse the gentlest wanderer and challenge the hardiest adventurer. Backpackers and day-hikers should inform the visitors center of their trip and take along the appropriate topographical maps. The National Park Service recommends that valley-floor hikers plan a route along roads where assistance is readily available and outfit a party of at least two people.

Artist's Drive, 10 mi. south of the visitors center on Rte. 178, is a one-way loop that twists its way through rock formations of colors akin to those found in Crayola sets. About 5 mi. south is **Devil's Golf Course,** a plane of sharp salt pinnacles made of the precipitate from the evaporation of Lake Manly, the 90 mi. long lake that once filled the lower valley. **Badwater** lies 3 mi. south of Devil's Golf Course, on I-90, a briny pool four times saltier than the ocean. The surrounding salt flat dips to the lowest point in the Western Hemisphere—282 ft. below sea level.

Immortalized by Antonioni's film of the same name, **Zabriskie Point** is a marvelous place from which to view Death Valley's corrugated badlands. Perhaps the most spectacular sight in the park is the vista at **Dante's View,** reached by a 13 mi. paved road from Rte. 190. Just as the poet stood with Virgil looking down on the damned, so the modern observer gazes upon the vast inferno that is Death Valley.

THE CENTRAL COAST

The 400-mile stretch of coastline between Los Angeles and San Francisco embodies all that is purely Californian: surf crashing onto secluded beaches, dramatic cliffs and mountains, self-actualizing New Age adherents, and always a hint of the off-beat. This is the solitary magnificence that inspired Robinson Jeffers's paeans, John Steinbeck's novels, and Jack Kerouac's musings. Among the smog-free skies, sweeping shorelines, dense forests, and plunging cliffs, there is a point where inland farmland communities and old seafaring towns join, beckoning citified residents to journey out to the quiet drama of the coast. The landmarks along the way—Hearst Castle, the Monterey Bay Aquarium, Carmel, the historic missions—are well worth visiting, but the real point of the Central Coast is the journey itself.

SANTA BARBARA   ☎805

Santa Barbara epitomizes worry-free living and abandonment of responsibility—all memory seems to melt away in the endless sun. The town is an enclave of wealth and privilege, true to its soap opera image, but in a significantly less aggressive way than its Southern Californian counterparts. Spanish Revival architecture decorates the residential hills that rise gently over a lively pedestrian district.

▐ GETTING THERE AND GETTING AROUND

Santa Barbara is 96 mi. northwest of Los Angeles and 27 mi. past Ventura on the **Ventura Freeway** (U.S. 101). Built along an east-west traverse of shoreline, the street grid is slightly skewed. The beach lies at the south end of the city, and **State St.,** the main drag, runs northwest from the waterfront. All streets are designated east and west from State St. The major east-west arteries are U.S. 101 and **Cabrillo Blvd.**

Airport: Santa Barbara Municipal Airport (☎683-4011), in Goleta. Offers state and limited national service.

Trains: Amtrak, 209 State St. (☎963-1015). *Be careful around the station after dark.* To: L.A. ($16-21) and San Francisco ($46-73). Reserve in advance. Open daily 6:30am-9pm. Tickets sold until 8pm.

Buses: Greyhound, 34 W. Carrillo St. (☎962-2477), at Chapala St. To: L.A. ($13) and San Francisco ($30). Open M-Sa 5:30am-8pm and 11pm-midnight, Su 7am-8pm and 11pm-midnight. **Green Tortoise** (☎415-956-7500 or 800-227-4766), picks up from Banana Bungalow Hostel. To: L.A. ($15) and San Francisco ($35).

Santa Barbara Metropolitan Transit District (MTD), 1020 Chapala St. (☎683-3702), at Cabrillo Blvd. behind the Greyhound station. Bus schedules available at this transit center (open M-F 6am-7pm, Sa 8am-6pm, Su 9am-6pm). All buses wheelchair accessible. Fare $1, seniors and disabled 50¢, under 5 free; transfers free. The MTD runs a **downtown-waterfront shuttle** along State St. and Cabrillo Blvd. every 10min. Su-Th 10:15am-6pm, F-Sa 10:15am-8pm. Stops designated by circular blue signs. Fare 25¢.

Taxis: Yellow Cab Company, ☎965-5111.

Bike Rental: Cycles-4-Rent, 101 State St. (☎966-3804), 1 block from the beach. Rent a 1-speed beach cruiser for $5 per hr., $21 per day; 21-speed $7/$28.

✴🔢 ORIENTATION AND PRACTICAL INFORMATION

Driving in Santa Barbara can be bewildering; dead-ends and one-way streets abound. Many downtown lots and streets offer 90min. of free **parking,** including two subterranean lots at Pasco Nuevo, accessible from the 700 block of Chapala St. Parking is free on Su. Most streets are equipped with **bike lanes.** The **Cabrillo Bikeway** runs east-west along the beach from the Bird Refuge to the City College campus.

Visitor Information: Tourist Office, 1 Garden St. (☎965-3021), at Cabrillo Blvd. near the beach. Open July-Aug. M-Sa 9am-6pm, Su 10am-6pm; Sept.-Nov. and Feb.-June M-Sa 9am-5pm, Su 10am-5pm; Dec.-Jan. M-Sa 9am-4pm, Su 10am-4pm. Outdoor computer kiosk open 24hr.

Post Office: 836 Anacapa St., 1 block east of State St. Open M-F 8am-6pm, Sa 9am-5pm. **ZIP Code:** 93102. **Area code:** 805.

▌ACCOMMODATIONS

A 10-minute drive north or south on U.S. 101 rewards with cheaper lodgings than those found in Santa Barbara proper. All Santa Barbara accommodations are more expensive on the weekends. State campsites can be reserved through ReserveAmerica (☎800-444-7275). **Carpinteria Beach State Park,** 12 mi. southeast of Santa Barbara along U.S. 101, has 261 developed tent sites with hot showers. (☎684-2811. Sites $17, with hook-up $22-28; weekends $18/$23-29; off-season $15/$20-26.) There are two other state beaches within 30 mi. of Santa Barbara, but neither are served by buses. North of Santa Barbara off U.S. 101, **El Capitán** (☎968-1033) has 140 well-kept sites, some with views of the Channel Islands. **Refugio** has 84 crowded, wheel-chair-accessible sites just steps from the beach. (☎968-1033. Sites at both $17, weekends $18; off-season $15; seniors $2 discount.) North of Santa Barbara are more than 100 sites in the **Los Padres National Forest** (☎968-6640).

▨ **Hotel State Street,** 121 State St. (☎966-6586; fax 962-8459), on the main strip 1 block from the beach. Welcoming, comfortable, and run by a self-proclaimed clean freak. Pristine common bathrooms. Private rooms have sinks and cable TV; a few have skylights. Continental breakfast included. Free parking. One double bed $40; 2 single beds $45; 2 queen beds $55; $15-25 higher July-Aug. Reservations recommended.

Traveler's Motel, 3222 State St. (☎687-6009; fax 687-0419). Take bus #6 or 11 from downtown. Although it's a bit far from the action, this motel is clean and spacious. Cable TV, A/C, direct-dial phones, and fridges. Singles June-Sept. $50-60, Oct.-May $35; rooms with kitchenettes $55, Oct.-May $40; each additional person (up to 4) $5.

Banana Bungalow Santa Barbara, 210 E. Ortega St. (☎963-0154), just off State St., in a busy area. Party-oriented hostel with lived-in feel and tropical motif. Young, international crowd. Kitchen, TV room, pool table, video games. Equipment rentals. Laundry, coin lockers. Free parking. No reservations; show up around 11am. Doors lock at 2:30am. *Passport or student ID required.* Co-ed and women-only dorms $17-22; thatched-roof bunks $19.

FOOD

State and Milpas St. both have many places to eat; State St. is hipper, while Milpas St. is cheaper. Ice cream lovers flock to award-winning **McConnel's,** 201 W. Mission St. (☎569-2323. Open daily 10am-midnight.) There's an open-air **farmer's market** packed with bargains on the 400 block of State St. (Tu 4-7:30pm), and another on Santa Barbara St. at Cota St. (Sa 8:30am-12:30pm). **Tri-County Produce,** 335 S. Milpas St., sells fresh produce and prepared foods. (☎965-4558. Open M-Sa 9am-7:30pm, Su 9am-6pm.)

Palazzio, 1026 State St. (☎564-1985). They say "people don't usually leave here hungry," and you certainly shouldn't buck the trend. The depiction of the Sistine Chapel on the ceiling is nearly as impressive as the enormous pasta dishes and the amazing garlic rolls. Lunch daily 11:30am-3pm, dinner Su-Th 5:30pm-11pm, F-Sa 5:30pm-midnight.

Pacific Crepes, 705 Anacapa St. (☎882-1123). Comfortable, classy French cafe is filled with the delicious smells of a full menu of crepe creations. The make-your-own plate starts with an empty crepe for just $3, which you can have filled for as little as $4. Sandwiches $6-7. Open T-Sa 8:30am-9pm, Su 8:30am-4pm.

La Super-Rica Taqueria, 622 N. Milpas St. (☎963-4940), has received rave reviews, both from culinary experts and the long lines of customers that extend out its door. Outstanding and inexpensive. Open Su-Th 11am-9:30pm, F-Sa 11am-10pm.

Napoleon, 808 State St. (☎899-1183), at De Laguerra St. This patisserie and boulangerie bakes incredible desserts (lemon tart $3.50) and serves sandwiches (Croque Monsieur $5.75). Open Su-Th 8am-10:30pm, Sa 8am-11:30pm.

SIGHTS

Santa Barbara is best explored in three sections—the beach and coast, swingin' State St., and the mountains. *Santa Barbara's Red Tile Tour,* a map and walking tour guide, is free at the visitors center. Recently revamped, the coastal drive Cabrillo Blvd. serves as the first leg of the city's **scenic drive.** Follow the green signs as they lead you in a loop into the mountains and around the city.

SANTA BARBARA ZOO. The delightfully leafy habitat has low fences and such an open feel that the animals seem kept in captivity only through sheer lethargy. Attractions include a miniaturized African plain, or *veldt,* where giraffes stroll lazily, silhouetted against the Pacific. A miniature train provides a park tour. *(500 Niños Dr., off Cabrillo Blvd. from U.S. 101. ☎962-5339. Take bus #14 or the downtown-waterfront shuttle. Open daily 10am-5pm. $7, seniors and ages 2-12 $5, under 2 free. Train $1.50, children $1.)*

BEACHES AND ACTIVITIES. Santa Barbara beaches are unmistakably breathtaking. **East** and **Leadbetter Beaches** flank the wharf on either side. **Beach Rentals** will rent beachgoers a retro surrey: a covered carriage, Flintstone-esque **bicycle.** You and up to eight friends can cruise along the beach paths in this stylish buggy. Beach Rentals also rents in-line skates. *(22 State St. ☎966-6733 or 966-2282. Open daily 8am-8pm. Surreys $12-32 per hr., depending on number of riders. Skates, including safety gear, 1hr. $6; 2hr. $9; 6hr. $18.)* For the best **sunset** view in the area, have a drink at the bar at the Four Seasons Biltmore Hotel. This five-star lodging is just a li'l bit steep for the budget traveler, but the view of the Pacific is priceless. *(1260 Channel Dr. ☎969-2261. Montecito.)*

STATE STREET. Santa Barbara's monument to city planning, State St. runs a straight tree-lined 2 mi. in the center of the city. Shops, restaurants, and cultural and historical landmarks are slathered in Spanish tile. The **Santa Barbara Museum of Art** owns an impressive collection of classical Greek, Asian, and European works spanning 3000 years, most donated by wealthy local residents. *(1130 State St. ☎ 963-4364. Open Tu-Th and Sa 11am-5pm, F 11am-9pm, Su noon-5pm. Tours Tu-Su noon and 2pm. $5, students and ages 6-16 $2, seniors $3. Free on Th and 1st Su of each month.)*

MISSION SANTA BARBARA. At the so-called "Queen of Missions" there are towers containing splayed Moorish windows on either side of a Greco-Roman facade, and a Moorish fountain bubbles in front. The museum contains period rooms and a sampling of items from the mission archives. *(At the end of Las Olivas St. ☎ 682-4149. Take bus #22. Open daily 9am-5pm. $4, under 12 free. Self-guided museum tour starts at the gift shop. Mass M-F 7:30am, Sa 4pm, Su 7:30am-noon.)*

SANTA BARBARA BOTANICAL GARDEN. Though it is quite a distance from town by car, these gardens offer enjoyable hikes through 65 acres of native Californian trees, wildflowers, and cacti. *(1212 Mission Canyon Rd. ☎ 682-4726. Open Mar.-Oct. M-F 9am-5pm, Sa-Su 9am-6pm; Nov.-Feb. M-F 9am-4pm, Sa-Su 9am-5pm. Tours M-W and F at 2pm, Th and Sa-Su at 10:30am and 2pm. $5; students, seniors, and ages 13-19 $3; ages 5-12 $1.)*

HIKING TRAILS. The trailhead for **Seven Falls Trail** is at the junction of Tunnel and Spyglass Rd. From the end of Las Canoas Rd. off Mission Canyon Rd., you can pick up the 3½ mi. **Rattlesnake Canyon Trail,** has many waterfalls, pools, and secluded spots. The 7¼ mi. trek from the **Cold Springs Trail** to **Montecito Peak** is considerably more strenuous. *(From U.S. 101 South, take a left at the Hot Springs Rd. Exit, and another left on Mountain Dr. to the creek crossing.)*

 NIGHTLIFE

Every night of the week, the clubs on **State Street** are packed. This town is full of locals and tourists who love to eat, drink, and be mirthful. Consult the *Independent* to see who's playing on a given night. Bars on State St. charge $4 for beer fairly uniformly, so search for a special.

The Hourglass, 213 W. Cota Street (☎ 963-1436), in a residential part of town. Rent a private hot tub here by the hour. Pick a sensuous indoor bath or watch the stars from a private outdoor tub. Locals report that "this is what we do in Santa Barbara." No alcohol allowed. Towels $1. 2 people $25 per hr.; each additional person $7. $2 students discount; children free with parent. Open Th-Su 5pm-midnight.

Q's Sushi A-Go-Go, 409 State St. (☎ 966-9177). Leopard skin decor, a tri-level bar, and a State St. balcony. Stomach some sushi ($3.50-8.50) in front of your date and you'll score! M Brazilian night, W karaoke. Open daily 4pm-2am. Cover F-Sa after 9pm $5.

Madhouse, 434 State St. (☎ 962-5516). Decadent dive for the jet set. Sounds of Sinatra, mambo, and Afro-Cuban music mix retro and funk. Live music, drink specials W-Th night. DJ Th-Sa. Pool table. Open W-Sa 5pm-2am, Su-Tu 7pm-2am. 21+.

SAN LUIS OBISPO ☎ 805

With its sprawling green hills and its proximity to the rocky coast, San Luis Obispo (SLO) is a town where things don't move fast. Ranchers and oil-refinery employees make up a significant percentage of the population, but Cal Poly State University students add a young, energetic component.

🛈 PRACTICAL INFORMATION. Greyhound, 150 South St. (☎ 543-2121), ½ mi. from downtown, is open daily 7:30am-9:30pm. **Visitor Info: Chamber of Commerce,** 1039 Chorro St. (☎ 781-2777. Open M-W 8am-5pm, Th-F 8am-8pm, Sa 10am-8pm.) **State Parks Office,** 3220 S. Higuera St. #311 (☎ 549-3312; open M-F 8am-5pm). **Post Office:** 893 Marsh St. (☎ 543-3062. Open M-F 8:30am-5:30pm, Sa 9am-5pm.) **ZIP Code:** 93405. **Area code:** 805.

▐ ACCOMMODATIONS. Rates in San Luis Obispo tend to "depend"—on the weather, the season, the number of travelers that day, or even on the position of the waxing and waning moon. **San Luis Obispo (HI-AYH),** 1617 Santa Rosa St., has a tight-knit atmosphere. (☎544-4678. Reception 7:30-10:30am and 4:30-10pm. Lockout 10am-4:30pm. Linen $1, towels 50¢. Parking available. No credit cards. Dorms $16.50; private rooms $38.50; $2 more for non-members.) The **Sunbeam Hotel,** 1656 Monterey St., looks like an apartment complex; rooms are as sunny as the staff. (☎543-8141. Cable TV, A/C, fridges, phones, coffeemakers. Singles $33-36; doubles $38-45.) **Morro Bay State Park,** 12 mi. west of SLO on Rte. 1., has a popular camp-ground between the ocean and forest with 135 developed sites, 30 with hook-ups. ($17, in winter $14; hook-up $24/$20. Reserve year-round.) All state park sites can be reserved through ReserveAmerica (☎800-444-7275).

▐▌ FOOD AND NIGHTLIFE. Monterey St. and its cross streets are lined with restaurants and cafes. The area just south of the mission along the creek is popular with lunchtime crowds. **▐Big Sky Cafe,** 1121 Broad St., was voted "Best Restaurant in SLO" by the local magazine poll for delivering hearty, vegetarian-friendly food. (☎545-5401. Open M-Sa 7am-10pm, Su 8am-8pm.) **Tio Alberto's,** 1131 Broad St., has the best burritos between L.A. and San Francisco. (☎546-9646. Open Su-Th 9am-11pm, F-Sa 9am-3am. Burritos $3.50-5.50, combo plates $5.) One half of SLO's pop-ulation is under the age of 24, so the town can't help but party. It gets particularly wild after the Th evening **farmer's market** along Higuera St. between Nipomo and Osos St., which is more of a raging block party than a produce market. Weekdays slow down a bit while the students rescue their grades. The free weekly *New Times* lists goings-on.

▐ SIGHTS. San Luis Obispo grew around the **Mission San Luis Obispo de Tolosa,** and the city continues to engage in celebrations and general lunchtime socializing around its front steps. (☎543-6850. Open daily early Apr. to late Oct. 9am-5pm; late Oct. to early Apr. 9am-4pm. $2 donation requested.) The mission faces Mission Plaza, where Father Serra held the area's first mass. The visitors center may try to deny its exist-ence, but **Bubble Gum Alley,** 735 Higuera St., is a crazy, squishy fact. If you'd like to add your own wad of gum to the alley, head down to the 7-11 on the corner of Broad and Marsh for a pack of Wrigley's.

South of San Luis Obispo, **Pismo Beach** is popular and congested; the lines for the public restrooms are practically social events. This raging spring break party spot is accessible by **Central Coast Area Transit** (☎541-2228) as well as **Greyhound.** Rent all kinds of beach equipment at **Beach Cycle Rentals,** 150 Hinds Ave., next to the pier. (☎773-5518. Open daily 9am-dusk.) **Shell Beach,** 1½ mi. from Pismo Beach, is the launching point for many a kayak. Gray whales, seals, otters, dolphins, and the occasional orca frequent **Montana de Oro State Park** (☎528-0513), 30min. west of SLO on Los Osos Valley Rd. The 8000 acres and 7 mi. of shoreline remain relatively secluded. North of San Luis Obispo, **Morro Bay** has dramatic coastlines, formed by volcanic activity.

NEAR SAN LUIS OBISPO: HEARST CASTLE

On Rte. 1, 3 mi. north of San Simeon and 9 mi. north of Cambria. Info ☎927-2020, reserva-tions through 800-444-4445, international reservations 916-638-5883; wheelchair accessi-ble reservations 805-927-2020. Tours: 4 daytime tours; 1¾hr.; $10, ages 6-12 $5, under 6 free. Evening tours feature costumed docents acting out the Castle's legendary Hollywood his-tory; 2hr.; $20, ages 6-12 $10. Each of the tours involves 150-370 stairs.

Driving along this stretch of Rte. 1, the last thing you would expect to see is a castle that would put Disney to shame. Newspaper tycoon William Randolph Hearst built this palatial abode and invited wealthy elite to visit the most extravagant edifice this side of the Taj Mahal. Casually referred to by its founder as "the ranch," Hearst Castle is a decadent conglomeration of castle, cottages, pools, gardens, and Medi-terranean *esprit* perched high above the Pacific. It stands as a testament to Hearst's unfathomable wealth and Julia Morgan's architectural genius. **Tour One** covers the photogenic Neptune Pool, the opulent Casa del Sol guest house, fragrant gardens, and the main rooms of the house; this is the best bet for first-time visitors. **Tours Two, Three,** and **Four** are recommended for those already familiar with Tour One. Call weeks in advance; tours sell out.

BIG SUR   ☎831

Host to expensive campsites and even more expensive restaurants, Big Sur holds big appeal for big crowds eager to experience the power of the redwoods, the crash of the surf, and the rhythm of the river. There are no signs to announce that you are in Big Sur, but you'll know you're there because it's the first time you'll see signs of civilization for miles in either direction. The drive from Carmel to Big Sur on **Rte. 1** is breathtaking and everyone knows it; try going early in the morning.

Big Sur's state parks and **Los Padres National Forest** beckon outdoor enthusiasts of all types. Their **hiking** trails penetrate redwood forests and cross low chaparral, offering even grander views of Big Sur than those available from Rte. 1. The northern end of Los Padres National Forest, accessible from Pfeiffer Big Sur, has been designated the **Ventana Wilderness** and contains the popular **Pine Ridge Trail,** which runs 12 mi. through primitive sites and the Sikes hot springs. The Forest Service ranger station supplies maps and permits for the wilderness area.

Within **Pfeiffer Big Sur State Park** are eight trails of varying lengths (75¢ map available at park entrance). The **Valley View Trail** is a short, steep trail offering a view of the valley below. **Buzzard's Roost Trail** is a rugged 2hr. hike up tortuous switchbacks, but at its peak are rewarding panoramic views of the Santa Lucia Mountains, the Big Sur Valley, and the Pacific Ocean.

Big Sur's most jealously guarded treasure is splendid, USFS-operated **Pfeiffer Beach,** 1 mi. south of Pfeiffer Burns State Park and roughly 10½ mi. north of Julia Pfeiffer Burns State Park. Turn off Rte. 1 at the stop sign and the "Narrow Road Not Suitable For Trailers" sign, just past the bridge by Loma Vista. Follow the road 2 mi. to the parking area, where a path leads to the beach. An offshore rock formation protects sea caves and seagulls from the pounding ocean waves. Frequent winds can make sunbathing uncomfortable, and even if there were lifeguards, riptides make swimming and other water sports dangerous. (Parking fee $5; annual pass $15; walk-in, bike-in, and Golden Age passport holders free.)

Camping in Big Sur is heavenly, but site prices and availability reflect high demand. Camping is free in the Ventana Wilderness, a backpack-only area at the northern end of Los Padres National Forest (permits at Big Sur Station). Roadtrippers may also spend cramped nights in their cars within the cradle of deep turnouts, since the Highway Patrol encourages sleepy drivers to take 2-3hr. breaks when tackling the dark and curvy road. **Ventana Big Sur,** on Rte. 1, 30 mi. south of Carmel, has 75 shady sites in a gorgeous redwood canyon with picnic tables, fire rings, and water faucets. (☎667-2688. Up to 2 people $25, leashed dogs $5. Day use $10. Reservations accepted at least 2 weeks in advance.)

MONTEREY   ☎831

Although Father Serra targeted the area for a mission in 1770, it was the growing whaling industry that kept Monterey alive until 1880, when sardine fishing and packaging stepped in to take its place. In the next half century, the wharfside flourished like the fisherman's world immortalized by John Steinbeck in the 40s. Monterey has since become a sedate and tourist-oriented community. The remnants of the past and the spectacle of the present result in a restrained beauty well worth the journey.

7 **PRACTICAL INFORMATION. Monterey-Salinas Transit (MST),** 1 Ryan Ranch Rd., runs buses (☎899-2555, call M-F 7:45am-5:15pm, Sa 10am-2:30pm). The free *Rider's Guide* has schedules and route info (available on buses, at motels, and at the visitors center). **Monterey Peninsula Visitor and Convention Bureau:** 380 Alvarado St. (☎649-1770; open M-F 8:30am-5pm). **Post Office:** 565 Hartnell St. (☎372-5803; open M-F 8:45am-5:10pm). **ZIP Code:** 93940. **Area code:** 831.

█▐ ACCOMMODATIONS AND FOOD. Reasonably priced hotels line **Lighthouse Ave.** in Pacific Grove (bus #2 and some #1 buses) and the 2000 block of **Fremont St.** in Monterey (bus #9 or 10). Others cluster along **Munras Ave.** between downtown and Rte. 1. The cheapest hotels in the area, however, are in the less-appealing towns of Seaside and Marina, just north of Monterey. Call the **Monterey Parks** line (☎755-4895 or 888-588-2267) for camping info and **PARKNET** (☎800-444-7275) for reservations. **Del Monte Beach Inn**, 1110 Del Monte Blvd., is near downtown and across from the beach, is a Victorian-style inn with a TV room. (☎649-4410. Check-in 2-6pm. Rooms with shared bath Su-Th $55-66, F-Sa from $77. Reservations recommended.) Set to open in October 2000, the **Monterey Hostel (HI-AYH)**, 778 Hawthorne St., is four blocks from Cannery Row. From Lighthouse Ave., turn left onto Irving Ave. The hostel parking lot will be on your left. From the Transit Center, take bus #1. (☎649-0375. Dorms $17. Reservations essential June-Sept.)

The sardines have left, but Monterey Bay teems with squid, crab, red snapper, and salmon. Seafood is bountiful, but expensive—try an early-bird special (usually 4-6:30pm). **Fisherman's Wharf** has smoked salmon sandwiches ($6) and free chowder samples. Don't despair if you loathe seafood—this is also the land of artichokes and strawberries. The Monterey **farmer's market,** which takes over Alvarado St., has free fruit, cheese, and seafood samples (☎655-2607; Tu 4-8pm, 4-7pm in winter). The **Old Monterey Cafe**, 489 Alvarado St., has hot, hefty portions favored by locals. (☎646-1021. Open daily 7am-2:30pm. Lunch specials from $5.50.) **Thai Bistro II**, 159 Central Ave., Pacific Grove, has good service and a patio ringed with flowers. Lunch combos ($6) come with delicious soup. (☎372-8700. Open daily 11:30am-3pm and 5-9:30pm.)

█ SIGHTS. The extraordinary ▓**Monterey Bay Aquarium** provides visitors with a window (literally) into the most curious creatures of the Pacific. Gaze through the **world's largest window** at an enormous marine habitat containing green sea turtles, giant ocean sunfish, large sharks, and impressive yellow- and blue-fin tuna. Don't miss the oozingly graceful and mesmerizing jellyfish. Arrive with a surfeit of patience; the lines for tickets, admission, viewing, and food are as unbelievable as the exhibits themselves. Pick up tickets the day before and save 20-40min. *(886 Cannery Row. ☎648-4888. Open daily June to early Sept. and major holiday periods 9:30am-6pm; early Sept. to late May 10am-6pm. $16; students, seniors, and ages 13-17 $13; disabled and ages 3-12 $8.)*

Lying along the waterfront south of the aquarium, **Cannery Row** was once a depressed street of languishing sardine-packing plants. The ¾ mi. row has been converted into glitzy mini-malls, bars, and a pint-sized carnival complex. For a series of interpretive looks at Steinbeck's *Cannery Row*, take a peek at the **Great Cannery Row Mural;** local artists have covered 400 ft. of construction-site barrier on the 700 block with depictions of Monterey in the 30s. The lavish **Wine and Produce Visitors Center**, 700 Cannery Row, offers tastes of the county's burgeoning wine industry, with well-priced bottles, fresh produce, and free winery maps. *(☎888-646-5446. Open daily 11am-6pm. 3 tastings $2. 21+.)*

Several companies on Fisherman's Wharf offer critter-spotting boat trips around Monterey Bay. The best time to go is during gray whale migration season, Nov. through Mar., but the trips are hit-or-miss at any time of year. **Chris's Fishing Trips** has 2-3hr. daily tours at 11am and 2pm. *(☎375-5951. $25, under 16 $20.)* Sea kayaking on top of kelp forests and among prancing otters can be a heady experience. **Monterey Bay Kayaks** provides rentals, instruction, and tours. *(693 Del Monte Ave. ☎373-5357 or 800-649-5357. Call for lesson and tour information. Open daily 9am-6pm. $25 per person, includes gear and wetsuit.)*

In nearby Carmel, the extraordinary 550-acre state-run ▓**Point Lobos Reserve** is a wildlife sanctuary popular with skindivers and day-hikers. Otters, sea lions, seals, brown pelicans, and gulls are visible from paths along the cliffs (bring binoculars). Point Lobos has tide pools and marvelous vantage points for watching the whale migration, which peaks in winter but continues throughout spring. *(On Rte. 1, 2 mi. south of Carmel. ☎624-4909. Park on Rte. 1 before the tollbooth and walk or bike in for free.)*

Accessible by MST bus #22. Open daily Apr.-Oct. 9am-7pm, Nov.-Mar. 9am-4:30pm. $4 per car, seniors $3. Day-use free for campers registered with one of the state parks. Map included with car entry fee; extra copy $1. Free daily tours; call for times. Divers must call 624-8413 or email ptlobos@mbay.net for diving reservations. Dive fee $7.)

SANTA CRUZ   ☎831

One of the few places where the 60s catch-phrase "do your own thing" still applies, Santa Cruz simultaneously embraces macho surfers, aging hippies, free-thinking students, and a large lesbian, gay, and bisexual community. Along the beach and boardwalk, tourism runs rampant and surf culture reigns supreme. Nearby Pacific Ave. teems with independent bookstores, cool bars, and trendy cafes, which provide a safe, clean hangout for local teens and tourists alike. On the inland side of Mission St., the University of California at Santa Cruz (UCSC) sprawls luxuriously across miles of rolling forests and grasslands, filled with prime biking routes and wild students.

▌ GETTING THERE AND AROUND

Buses: Greyhound, 425 Front St. (☎423-1800, 423-1801, or 800-231-2222). To: L.A. (8 per day, $37); San Francisco (4 per day, $12); and San Jose (M-Th 4 per day, $5). Open daily 9-11:30am and 1:30-9pm and during late bus arrivals and departures.

Public Transportation: Santa Cruz Metropolitan Transit District or **SCMTD,** 920 Pacific Ave. (☎425-8600 for info M-F 6am-7pm, TDD 425-8993; www.scmtd.com), at the Metro Center in the middle of the Pacific Garden Mall. The free *Headways* has route info. Fare $1, seniors and disabled 40¢, under 46 in. free; day pass $3/$1.10/free. Buses run daily 6am-11pm.

Taxis: Yellow Cab, ☎423-1234.

Bike Rental: The Bicycle Rental Center, 131 Center St. (☎426-8687). Rents 21-speed mountain/road hybrids, tandems, and children's bikes. Bikes $7 for first hr., $2 each additional 30min.; $25 per day; $5 overnight. Helmets and locks provided. Open daily in summer 10am-6pm; off-season 10am-5pm.

▌ PRACTICAL INFORMATION

Santa Cruz is on the northern tip of Monterey Bay, 65 mi. south of San Francisco on Rte. 1. Passing through westside Santa Cruz, Rte. 1 becomes **Mission Street.** The **University of California at Santa Cruz (UCSC)** blankets the hills inland from Mission St. Southeast of Mission St. lie the waterfront and the downtown. Down by the ocean, **Beach Street** runs roughly east-west.

Visitor Info: Santa Cruz County Conference and Visitor Council, 701 Front St. (☎425-1234 or 800-833-3494). Publishes the free *Santa Cruz County Traveler's Guide* with restaurant info. Open M-Sa 9am-5pm, Su 10am-4pm. **California Parks and Recreation Dept.,** 600 Ocean St. (☎429-2850), across from the Holiday Inn. Info on camping and beaches (☎800-444-7275 for reservations). Open M-F 8am-5pm.

Post Office: 850 Front St. (☎426-5200). Open M-F 8:30am-5pm, Sa 9am-4pm. **ZIP Code:** 95060. **Area code:** 831.

▌ ACCOMMODATIONS

Santa Cruz is packed solid during the summer, especially on weekends; rates skyrocket, availability plummets, and price fluctuation can be outrageous. Reservations are recommended. Sleeping on the beach is strictly forbidden and fined. Reservations for all state campgrounds can be made through ReserveAmerica (☎800-444-7275) and should be made early. **New Brighton State Beach** and **Big Basin Redwoods State Park,** the most scenic spots, are both accessible by public transportation. (Campground fees June-Sept. Su-Th $17, F-Sa $18; Oct.-May $16.)

Carmelita Cottage Santa Cruz Hostel (HI-AYH), 321 Main St. (☎423-8304). 4 blocks from the Greyhound stop, 2 blocks from the beach. Sporadic summer barbecues ($4) to fuel up for days at the beach. Two kitchens, common room. Chore required. Linen $1. Strict curfew 11pm. July-Aug. 3-night maximum stay and HI members preferred. Call for reservations. Reception 8-10am and 5-10pm. Lockout 10am-5pm. Dorms $15, non-members $18, ages 12-17 $13, ages 4-11 $9, under 4 free.

Harbor Inn, 645 7th Ave. (☎479-9371), near the harbor and a few blocks north of Eaton St. A beautiful 19-room hotel well off the main drag. Queen-sized beds, microwaves, and fridges. Check-in 2-7pm, check-out 11am; call to arrange late check-in. Rooms Su-Th $75, F-Sa $95; off-season $65/$75. Reservations recommended.

🍴 FOOD

Santa Cruz offers an astounding number of budget eateries in various locations. Fresh local produce sells at the **farmer's market** at Lincoln and Cedar St. in downtown (W 2:30-6:30pm).

🏆 **Zoccoli's,** 1534 Pacific Ave. (☎423-1711), across from the post office. Without a doubt the best pre-picnic stop in town, this phenomenal deli churns out "special sandwiches" ($4-5). Daily pasta specials (about $5) come with salad, garlic bread, cheese, and a cookie. Only the freshest ingredients. Open M-Sa 10am-6pm, Su 11am-5pm.

Zachary's, 819 Pacific Ave. (☎427-0646). With excellent potatoes, freshly baked bread, and enormous omelettes, laid-back and earthy Zachary's will fill you with reasons to laze about the beach for the rest of the day. Basic breakfast (2 eggs, oatmeal-molasses toast, and hash browns) for under $5. Beware of the crowds that congregate here on weekends. Open Tu-Su 7am-2:30pm.

Saturn Cafe, 145 Laurel St. at Pacific Ave. (☎429-8505). Excellent vegetarian meals (most under $6). Table decorations include the "body manipulations" theme and the "ruined picnic" with plastic ants. The Alien sandwich (tofu, hummus, avocado, and cheese; $6.75) is delicious. Open 24hr.

Taquería Vallarta I, 608 Soquel Ave. (☎457-8226). Outstanding Mexican manna. Vegetarian plate $4; mind-blowing *agua fresca* $1.20. Open M-F 10am-midnight.

📷 SIGHTS

SANTA CRUZ BEACH BOARDWALK. Santa Cruz has a great beach, but the water is frigid. Without wetsuits for warmth, many casual beachgoers catch their thrills on the Boardwalk, a three-block-long strip of over 25 amusement park rides, guess-your-weight booths, shooting galleries, and caramel apple vendors. The boardwalk is a gloriously tacky throwback to 50s-era beach culture, providing a loud and lively diversion. Highly recommended is the Giant Dipper, a 1924 wooden roller coaster ($3), where Dirty Harry met his enemy in 1983's *Sudden Impact* (Harry finally impaled him on the merry-go-round's unicorn). While the Boardwalk is relatively safe, be cautious of the surrounding community at night. *(Boardwalk open daily Memorial Day to Labor Day, plus many off-season weekends and holidays. Rides $1.50-3; all-day pass $22. Mini golf $4, with all-day pass to Boardwalk $3.)*

SANTA CRUZ WHARF. Jutting off Beach St. is the longest car-accessible pier on the West Coast. Seafood restaurants and souvenir shops will try to distract you from the expansive views of the coast. Munch on candy from local favorite Marini's while you feed fish to the sea lions hanging out on rafters beneath the pier. *(Marini's: ☎423-7258. Parking $1 per hr., under 30min. free. Disabled patrons free.)*

🏖 BEACHES AND ACTIVITIES

The **Santa Cruz Beach** (officially named Cowell Beach) is broad, reasonably clean, and packed with volleyball players. **Beach access** points line Rte. 1; railroad tracks, farmlands, and dune vegetation make several of these access points somewhat difficult, but correspondingly less crowded.

To try your hand at riding the waves, contact the **Richard Schmidt Surf School,** or ask around for him at the beach. (☎423-0928. 1hr. private lesson $65, 2hr. group lesson $70. Lessons include equipment.) To learn more about the activity, stop by the well-known and ever-popular **Steamer's Lane**—the deep water off the point near the Lighthouse along West Cliff Dr.

Around the point at the end of W. Cliff Dr. is **Natural Bridges State Park.** While all but one of its natural bridges have collapsed, the park nevertheless offers a pristine beach, awe-inspiring tidepools, and tours during Monarch butterfly season from Oct. to Mar. In Nov. and Dec. thousands of the stunning *lepidoptera* swarm along the beach. (☎423-4609. Open daily 8am-dusk. Parking $6, seniors $5.)

Parasailing and other pricey pastimes are popular on the wharf. **Kayak Connection,** 413 Lake Ave., has ocean-going kayaks at reasonable rates. Rentals include paddle, life jacket, and a skirt or wetsuit. (☎479-1121. Open M-F 10am-6pm, Sa-Su 8:30am-6pm. Rentals: open-deck single $27 per day, closed-deck single $30. 4½hr. lessons $40.)

◼ NIGHTLIFE

There are comprehensive weekly events listings in the free local publications *Good Times* and *Metro Santa Cruz*, and also in the *Spotlight* section of the F *Sentinel*. The Boardwalk bandstand offers free summertime F night concerts, usually by oldies bands, around 6:30 and 8:30pm.

▨ Caffe Pergolesi, 418A Cedar St. (☎426-1775). Look for the "Dr. Miller's" sign. Chill coffeehouse/bar for reading, writing, or socializing. Cheerful color scheme and intimate tables give "Perg's" a supremely friendly atmosphere. $2.50 pints daily 7-9pm; large coffee for the price of a small M-F 1-3pm. 4 varieties of hot chocolate! Open M-Th 6:30am-11:30pm, F-Sa 7:30am-midnight, Su 7:30am-11:30pm.

Kuumbwa Jazz Center, 320-322 Cedar St. (☎427-2227). Great jazz and innovative off-night programs. The big names play here on M; locals have their turn on F. Tickets ($10-20) sold through **Logos Books and Music,** 1117 Pacific Ave. (☎427-5100; open daily 10am-10pm), as well as **BASS outlets** (☎998-2277). Most shows around 8pm. All ages welcome.

Blue Lagoon, 923 Pacific Ave. (☎423-7117). Mega-popular gay-straight club has won all awards from "best bartender" to "best place you can't take your parents" from the local press. Happy Hour with $2.50 drinks daily 6-9pm. Su Bloody Marys $3. Open daily 4pm-2am. Cover Su and Tu $1, M and W $3, Th-Sa $4.

The Catalyst, 1011 Pacific Ave. (☎423-1338). The town's primary music/dance venue draws national, college, and local bands. Shows W-Sa. Open M-Sa 9am-2am, Su 9am-5pm. Food served daily 9am-3pm; 9am-11pm on show days. Cover and age restrictions vary widely with show; adjacent bar area strictly 21+.

SAN FRANCISCO ☎415

By California standards, San Francisco is steeped in history, but it's a history of oddballs and eccentrics that resonates more loudly in street culture than in museums and galleries. Deeply rooted in America's great westward expansion, San Francisco has always attracted artists, dreamers, and outsiders. Most famous are the hippies and flower children of the late 60s, who turned on one generation and freaked out another in Haight-Ashbury's "Summer of Love." Before them were the Beats—angry young writers who captured the rhythms of bebop jazz in their poetry and lives. The lineage of free spirits and troublemakers runs back to the smugglers and pirates of the Barbary Coast and to the '49ers who flocked here during the mad boom of the California Gold Rush.

And the tradition continues. Anti-establishment politics have almost become establishment here. The gay community emerged in the 70s as one of the city's most visible and powerful groups. At the same time, immigrants have made San

Francisco one of the most racially diverse cities in the US. Not to be outdone, many young computer workers have ditched the bland suburbs of Silicon Valley for the cooler breezes of San Francisco, with Internet start-up companies infiltrating the forgotten spaces of lower-rent neighborhoods. Like so many chameleons, San Francisco is ever-changing with the times, but some things remain constant: the Bay is foggy, the hills are steep, and the tourists are the only ones wearing shorts.

✈ GETTING THERE AND AWAY

Driving from L.A. takes 6hr. on I-5, 8hr. on U.S. 101, or 9½hr. via Rte. 1. U.S. 101 compromises between vistas and velocity, but the stunning coastal scenery along Rte. 1 makes getting there fun. From inland California, **I-5** approaches the city from the north and south via **I-580** and **I-80,** which runs across the **Bay Bridge** (westbound toll $2). From the north, U.S. 101 and Rte. 1 come over the **Golden Gate Bridge** (southbound toll $3).

Airport: San Francisco International (☎650-761-0800), 15 mi. south of downtown via U.S. 101. Ground transportation information (☎800-736-2008). **San Mateo County Transit (SamTrans)** (☎800-660-4287) runs 2 buses to downtown. Express bus #7F allows one carry-on bag per person (35min., 5:30am-12:50am, $3, seniors at off-peak times $1.25, under 17 $1.25). Bus #7B stops frequently and allows all luggage (1hr., 5am-12:30am, $2/50¢/75¢).

Trains: Amtrak, 425 Mission St. (☎800-872-7245), in the Transbay Terminal, between Fremont and 1st St. downtown. To: Los Angeles ($42). Free shuttles to the 3 Amtrak stations near the city. Office open daily 6:45am-10:45pm. **CalTrain** (☎800-660-4287) leaves from the CalTrain Depot at 4th and King St. in SoMa to Palo Alto ($4, seniors and under 12 $2), San Jose ($5.25/$2.50), and Santa Cruz.

Buses: Golden Gate Transit (Marin County, ☎923-2000), **AC Transit** (East Bay, ☎510-891-4777), and **SamTrans** (San Mateo County) all stop at the **Transbay Terminal,** 425 Mission St. (☎495-1575), between Fremont and 1st St. downtown. **Greyhound** runs buses from the terminal to Los Angeles ($36) and Portland, OR ($51).

⌁ GETTING AROUND

San Francisco Municipal Railway (MUNI) (☎673-6864). System of buses, cable cars, subways, and streetcars. Fare $1, seniors and ages 5-17 35¢. Cheapest and most efficient way to get around the city. **MUNI passports** are valid on all MUNI vehicles (1-day $6, 3-day $10, 7-day $15). Weekly Pass ($9) is for a single work week and requires an additional $1 to ride the cable cars. The Monthly FastPass ($35) includes in-town BART trips and cable cars. Free transfers (valid for 1½hr.). Coverage decreases considerably after dark. Wheelchair access varies among routes; all below-ground subway stations, but not all above-ground sites, are accessible. Runs daily 6am-12:30am.

Cable cars: Noisy, slow, and usually crammed full, but charming relics. To avoid mobs, ride in the early morning. The **Powell-Mason (PM)** line, which runs to the wharf, is the most popular. The **California (C)** line, from the Financial District up through Nob Hill, is usually the least crowded, but the **Powell-Hyde (PH)** line, with the steepest hills and the sharpest turns, may be the most fun. All lines run daily 6am-12:45am. Fare $2, seniors and disabled $1 before 7am and after 9pm. No transfers.

Bay Area Rapid Transit (BART) (☎989-2278). BART operates carpeted trains along 4 lines connecting San Francisco with the East Bay, including **Oakland, Berkeley, Concord,** and **Fremont.** All stations provide maps and schedules. There are 8 BART stops in San Francisco proper, but BART is not a local transportation system. Runs M-F 4am-midnight, Sa 6am-midnight, Su 8am-midnight. Fare $1.10-6. Wheelchair accessible.

Car Rental: City, 1748 Folsom St. (☎861-1312), between Duboce St. and 14th St. Must be 21; under 25 surcharge $8 per day. From $28 per day, $160 per week. Unlimited mi. for a small fee. Sa-Su specials. Advance booking specials. Open M-F 7:30am-6pm, Sa 9am-4pm, Su 10am-4pm.

Taxis: Yellow, ☎626-2345. **De Soto,** ☎970-1399. **National,** ☎648-4444.

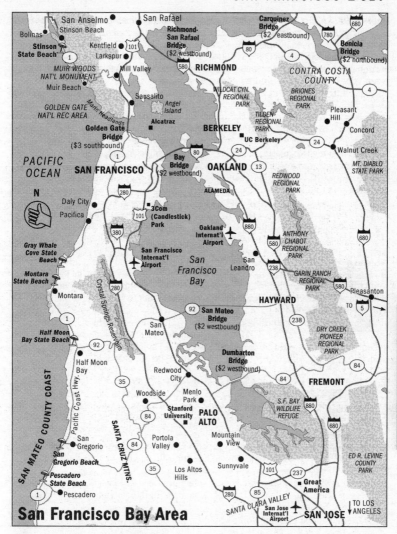

San Francisco Bay Area

✈ ORIENTATION

San Francisco is 403 mi. north of Los Angeles and 390 mi. south of the Oregon border. The city lies at the northern tip of the peninsula separating the San Francisco Bay from the Pacific Ocean. San Francisco radiates outward from its docks, which lie on the northeast edge of the 30 mi. peninsula, just inside the lip of the Bay. Many of the city's most visitor-friendly attractions are found within a wedge formed by **Van Ness Ave.**, which runs north-south; the **Embarcadero** along the coast; and **Market St.**, which runs northeast-southwest and interrupts the regular grid of streets.

At the top of this wedge lies touristy **Fisherman's Wharf.** From here, ferries service **Alcatraz Island. Columbus Ave.** extends southeast from the docks to **North Beach**, a district shared by Italian-Americans, artists, and professional-types. **Telegraph Hill**, which is topped by Coit Tower, emerges as the focal point of North Beach amid a mass of terrific eateries. To the west of Columbus Ave. are residential **Russian Hill** and **Nob Hill.** South of North Beach, the largest **Chinatown** in North America covers 24 sq. blocks between Broadway in the north, Bush St. in the south, and Kearny St. in the east. On the other side of the Bush St. gateway of Chinatown lies the heavily developed **Financial District,** where skyscrapers fill the blocks above the northeast portion of Market St. To the west, the core downtown area centered on **Union Sq.** gives way to the well-pounded **Tenderloin,** where, despite attempts at urban renewal, drugs, crime, and homelessness prevail. The area is roughly bounded by Larkin St. to the west, Taylor St. to the east, and Post St. to the north, and bleeds down Market St. for a few blocks. In the **Civic Center,** which occupies the acute angle formed by Market St. and Van Ness Ave. at the southern point of the wedge, cultural heavyweights like the Opera House crown a collection of municipal buildings. Just to the west, artists inhabit the newly-hip **Hayes Valley.**

South of the wedge, directly below Market St., lies the **South of Market Area (SoMa).** Here, the best of San Francisco's nightclubs are scattered among warehouses. SoMa extends inland from the Bay to 10th St., at which point the largely Latino and very trendy **Mission District** begins and spreads south to quiet **Bernal Heights.** The **Castro,** center of the gay community, abuts the Mission District on its west side, roughly along Church St. From the landmark **Castro Theater** on the corner of Castro and Market St., the neighborhood stretches to the less flamboyant **Noe Valley** in the south and the undeveloped oasis of **Twin Peaks** in the southeast.

Some interesting strips are sprinkled among the residential neighborhoods west of Van Ness Ave. The posh stucco of the **Marina** and Victorians of **Pacific Heights** run south to funkier **Fillmore St.,** which leads to the few *udon*-filled blocks of **Japantown.** Vast **Golden Gate Park** and its neighboring **Sunset District** to the south dominate the western half of the peninsula. At the park's eastern end sits the former hippie haven of **Haight-Ashbury** to the southeast. The park is bounded by Lincoln St. and the Sunset District to the south, and by Fulton St. and the residential **Richmond District** to the north, stretching out to **Ocean Beach** along the Pacific. **Lincoln Park** and the **Presidio,** at the northwestern corner, culminate in the **Golden Gate Bridge.**

⌕ PRACTICAL INFORMATION

Visitor Info: Visitor Information Center (☎391-2000; 24hr. info recording 391-2001, in Spanish 391-2122), in Hallidie Plaza at Powell St. beneath street level at the BART exit. MUNI passports and maps for sale. Open M-F 9am-5pm, Sa-Su 9am-3pm.

Hotlines: Rape Crisis Center, ☎647-7273. **Helplink,** ☎772-4357. **Drug Crisis Line,** ☎362-3400. **Suicide Prevention,** ☎781-0500. **Crisis Line for the Handicapped,** ☎800-426-4263.

Internet Access: Free at all public libraries. **Main Branch,** 100 Larkin St. (☎552-4400), between Grove and Fulton St. Open M 10am-6pm, Tu-Th 9am-8pm, F 11am-5pm, Sa 9am-5pm, Su noon-5pm.

Post Office: Federal Building Station, 450 Golden Gate Ave. (☎800-275-8777) at Larkin St. Open M-F 8:30am-5pm. **ZIP Code** 94142. **Area code:** 415.

⌂ ACCOMMODATIONS

Beware that some of the cheapest budget hotels may be located in areas requiring extra caution at night. Reservations are recommended at hotels.

HOSTELS

▨ **San Francisco International Guest House,** 2976 23rd St. (☎641-1411), in the blue house at the corner of Harrison in the Mission. TV area, 2 kitchens (smoking and non-smoking), and guest phones. Neighborhood parking. Dorms $14; private double $28. 5-night minimum stay, 3-month maximum. Passport with international stamps required.

AYH Hostel at Union Square (San Francisco Downtown; HI-AYH), 312 Mason St. (☎788-5604), between Geary and O'Farrell St., 1 block from Union Sq. TV, Internet access ($1 for 10min.), walking tours, and a seminar on nightlife. Kitchens have no

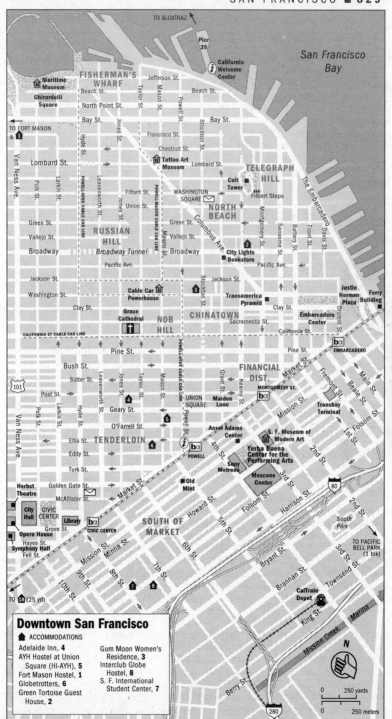

TO ALCATRAZ

Pier 39

California Welcome Center

San Francisco Bay

FISHERMAN'S WHARF

Jefferson St.

Maritime Museum

Ghirardelli Square

Beach St.

North Point St.

Bay St.

TO FORT MASON &

Francisco St.

Chestnut St.

Lombard St.

Tattoo Art Museum

TELEGRAPH HILL

Van Ness Ave.

Polk St.

Larkin St.

Hyde St.

Leavenworth St.

Jones St.

Filbert St.

Union St.

Green St.

Vallejo St.

Broadway

RUSSIAN HILL

Broadway Tunnel

Pacific Ave.

Jackson St.

Washington St.

Clay St.

WASHINGTON SQUARE

Colt Tower

Filbert Steps

NORTH BEACH

Columbus Ave.

Green St.

Vallejo St.

Broadway

City Lights Bookstore

Pacific Ave.

Montgomery St.

Sansome St.

Battery St.

Front St.

Davis St.

The Embarcadero

Justin Herman Plaza

Ferry Building

Cable Car Powerhouse

Grace Cathedral

NOB HILL

CHINATOWN

Stockton St.

Jackson St.

Transamerica Pyramid

Clay St.

Sacramento St.

California St.

Embarcadero Center

CALIFORNIA ST CABLE CAR LINE

Pine St.

Pine St.

EMBARCADERO

101

Bush St.

Sutter St.

Post St.

Van Ness Ave.

Polk St.

Larkin St.

Hyde St.

Leavenworth St.

Jones St.

Taylor St.

Mason St.

Geary St.

O'Farrell St.

Ellis St.

Eddy St.

Turk St.

TENDERLOIN

UNION SQUARE

Maiden Lane

Grant St.

Kearny St.

FINANCIAL DIST.

MONTGOMERY ST.

Mission St.

Market St.

Fremont St.

Beale St.

Main St.

1st St.

Transbay Terminal

Folsom St.

Ansel Adams Center

S. F. Museum of Modern Art

Yerba Buena Center for the Performing Arts

Sony Metreon

Moscone Center

3rd St.

2nd St.

POWELL

4th St.

Herbst Theatre

City Hall

CIVIC CENTER

Library

Golden Gate St.

McAllister St.

Grove St.

Opera House

Hayes St.

Symphony Hall

Fell St.

CIVIC CENTER

Old Mint

SOUTH OF MARKET

Market St.

Mission St.

Minna St.

Howard St.

Folsom St.

Harrison St.

80

South Park

2nd St.

TO PACIFIC BELL PARK (1 blk)

TO 18 (25 yd)

9th St.

10th St.

8th St.

7th St.

6th St.

5th St.

Bryant St.

Brannan St.

3rd St.

Townsend St.

CalTrain Depot

King St.

Marina

Mission Creek

N

South Park

280

Berry St.

0   250 yards

0   250 meters

Downtown San Francisco

🏠 ACCOMMODATIONS

Adelaide Inn, 4
AYH Hostel at Union Square (HI-AYH), 5
Fort Mason Hostel, 1
Globetrotters, 6
Green Tortoise Guest House, 2

Gum Moon Women's Residence, 3
Interclub Globe Hostel, 8
S. F. International Student Center, 7

CALIFORNIA

stoves. Quiet hours (midnight-7am) not always respected by Mason St. traffic. Reception 24hr. Dorms July-Oct. $24, Nov.-Feb. $19, Mar.-June $20; non-members $3 more; under 13 half-price with parent. Key deposit $5. Reserve by phone with credit card, or show up around 8am. Wheelchair accessible.

San Francisco International Student Center, 1188 Folsom St. (☎255-8800), at 8th in SoMa. Hall bathrooms. Chummy international crowd. Hostelers pay no cover at Cat Club downstairs—bring dancing shoes or earplugs. Free coffee and tea. Reception 10am-9pm. Check-out 11am. Dorms $17, off-season $14. No credit cards. Foreign passport or out-of-state ID required.

Fort Mason Hostel (HI-AYH), Bldg. #240 (☎771-7277), in Fort Mason in the Marina. Entrance at Bay and Franklin St., 1 block west of Van Ness Ave., or on McDowell on the water side. Take MUNI bus #42 or from SFO #7B or 7F. Beautiful surroundings. No smoking or alcohol. Movies, walking tours, kitchen, bike storage, laundry. Parking included. Minor chores. A small number of beds for walk-ins each morning at 7am. Reception 24hr. Check-in 7-11:30am and 12:30pm-1am. Check-out 11am. Limited access 11:30am-2:30pm. Lights out midnight. Dorms $20.

Easy Goin' Travel and California Dreamin' Guesthouse, 3145-47 Mission St. (☎552-8452; fax 552-8459), near César Chavez St., in the Mission. Super-friendly staff. TV, kitchen, lounge, laundry, Internet access, bike rental, and travel services. Check-in noon. Check-out 11am. $20 security and key deposit. Dorm beds $16; private rooms $35. Reservations recommended. 2-night minimum stay.

Globetrotters, 225 Ellis St. (☎346-5786), between Mason and Taylor St. near Union Sq. Common room has couches and TV. Large and fully-equipped kitchen. Laundry. Check-in 8am-midnight. Check-out 11am. Dorms $15, weekly $90; doubles $30.

Green Tortoise Guest House, 494 Broadway (☎834-1000), at Kearny St. in North Beach. Take MUNI bus #9X or 15 to Columbus Ave. and Broadway. From the Transbay Terminal, take MUNI bus #12 or 42 to Kearny St. and Pacific Ave. Common room with huge TV, couches, pool table. Sauna, free Internet access, kitchens, laundry, lockers (bring a lock). Continental breakfast included. Reception 24hr. Check-in noon. Check-out 11am. Dorms $19-22; private doubles $48. No credit cards

Interclub Globe Hostel, 10 Hallam Pl. (☎431-0540), off Folsom St. between 7th and 8th St. in SoMa. From Transbay Terminal take MUNI bus #12 to 7th and Howard St. Smoky crowded common room has pool table, TV, microwave, and fridge. Linen included. Dorms $21; 3 nights $48. Lower off-season rates. Passport with international stamps required. No credit cards.

GUESTHOUSES

▓ **The Red Victorian Bed, Breakfast, and Art,** 1665 Haight St. (☎864-1978), in the Upper Haight. Rooms are individually decorated to honor peace, sunshine, or butterflies. Even the hall baths have their own motifs and names. Free tea and coffee. Breakfast included. F-Sa 2-night minimum stay. Reception 9am-9pm. Check-in 3-6pm or by appt. Check-out 11am. Most doubles $86-126; discount on stays of 3 days or more. Reserve well in advance.

▓ **Adelaide Inn,** 5 Isadora Duncan (☎441-2261), off Taylor St. between Geary and Post St., 2 blocks west of Union Sq. Warm hosts and lovely furnishings. Steep stairs. All rooms have large windows, TV, and sink. Kitchen. Shared bathrooms. Continental breakfast included. Reception Tu-F 9am-1pm and 5-9pm, M and Sa-Su flexible. Singles $42-50; doubles $52-58.

▓ **Inn On Castro,** 321 Castro St. (☎861-0321), at Market St., in the Castro. Trendy 70s, tongue-in-cheek luxury in each of the Inn's 8 rooms belie the brightly refurbished Victorian exterior. Breakfast included. Gay-owned and operated, but "straight-friendly." Singles $95-160; doubles $110-180. Parking $15 per day.

▓ **Gum Moon Women's Residence,** 940 Washington St. (☎421-8827), between Stockton and Powell St., in Chinatown. Bright, spacious rooms with shared bath in a large, clean house run by a very friendly staff. Piano, TV, and VCR, kitchen, laundry. Very secure. Reception 9am-midnight. Curfew midnight. Reservations no more than 1 week in advance. Women over 18 only. Singles $27; doubles $22. Weekly $110/$90.

◌ FOOD

FISHERMAN'S WHARF

The archetypal Wharf meal is a loaf of sourdough bread ($2-4) from **Boudin Bakery**, 156 Jefferson St. (☎928-1849), and clam chowder ($4-5) from a seafood stand.

Rico's, 943 Columbus Ave. (☎928-5404), between Taylor and Lombard St., at the top of North Beach. Well worth the 10min. walk, Rico's enormous burritos ($3-5) and bottled Mexican beers ($2.75) are a fraction of the price of Wharfside snacks. Open daily 10am-10pm. No credit cards.

NORTH BEACH

▨ **Italian French Bakery,** 1501 Grant Ave. (☎421-3797), at Union St. *Bastoni,* maca- roons, and zucchini muffins—all at the best prices around. Although you'd never guess it from the innocent facade, the basement was used as the set of the murder scene in *Basic Instinct.* Open Su-Th 7am-6pm, F-Sa 6am-7pm. Cash only.

Sodini's Green Valley Restaurant, 510 Green St. (☎291-0499), at Grant Ave. One of the area's oldest restaurants, established in 1906. The *Ravioli alla Casa* rocks the house ($9.25). Restaurant open M-Th 5-10pm, F-Su 5-11pm; bar open daily 5pm-1am.

Mario's Bohemian Cigar Store Cafe, 566 Columbus Ave. (☎362-0536), near Union St. A hip cafe right at the corner of Washington Sq. Park. Hot sandwiches on slabs of *focac- cia* $6.25-7; half-sandwich $3. Open M-Sa 10am-midnight, Su 10am-11pm. Cash only.

NOB HILL AND RUSSIAN HILL

The Golden Turtle, 2211 Van Ness Ave. (☎441-4419), at Vallejo St., in **Russian Hill.** Fabulous Vietnamese restaurant serves sensational entrees ($10-12) like the Red Sea Diamond ($11). Open Tu-Su 5-11pm. Reservations recommended on weekends.

Bob's Broiler Restaurant, 1601 Polk St. (☎474-6161), at Sacramento St., in **Nob Hill.** Comforting diner fare like pancakes ($4.50) and BLTs ($4.25). Open daily 7am-10pm.

CHINATOWN

▨ **Brandy Ho's,** 217 Columbus Ave. (☎788-7527), at Pacific St. This food is spicy. Let the chef suggest dishes. Three Delicacies (toss fried scallops and shrimp) $11. Lunch spe- cials $5-6 (11:30am-3pm). Open Su-Th 11:30am-11pm, F-Sa 11:30am-midnight.

▨ **Chef Jia,** 925 Kearny St. (☎398-1626), at Pacific St. Cheap, fabulous food in a small, informal space. Lunch specials $4.50 (11:30am-4pm). Entrees $4-7. Open M-Th 11:30am-10pm, F 11:30am-10:30pm, Sa 5-10:30pm, Su noon-10pm.

UNION SQUARE AND THE TENDERLOIN

▨ **Cafe Bean,** 800 Sutter St. (☎923-9539). Steaming eggs and toast ($3.50) and brie- and-olive sandwich ($6.25). Open M-Sa 6am-9pm, Su 6am-5pm.

Shalimar, 532 Jones St. (☎928-0333), at Geary St. and 417 O'Farrell St., (☎447- 4041), between Jones and Taylor St. Authentic Indian and Pakistani food made to order in clay firepots. Open daily noon-3pm and 5:30-11:30pm.

CIVIC CENTER AND HAYES VALLEY

Millennium, 246 McAllister St. (☎487-9800), at Larkin St. Organic ingredients and a vegan menu don't limit Millennium; dining here is elegant and romantic. The creamy Plantain Torte appetizer ($7.75) or the Szechuan Eggplant Crepe entree ($15.25) are subtly flavored and filling. Reservations recommended. Open daily 5-9:30pm

Momi Tobys Revolution Cafe and Art Bar, 528 Laguna St. (☎626-1508), between Hayes and Fell St. Local artists break free from their iron cages and unite under the common cause of coffee. Open M-F 7:30am-10pm, Sa-Su 8am-10pm.

SOUTH OF MARKET AREA (SOMA)

▨ **Hamburger Mary's,** 699 12th St. (☎626-1985), at Folsom St. Excellent burgers ($6.50- 10). Spicy home fries, and a handful of veggie options. Open Tu-Th 11:30am-10:30pm, F 11:30am-midnight, Sa 10am-midnight, Su 10am-10:30pm. Bar open F-Sa until 2am. Breakfast served all day; brunch served Sa-Su until 4pm.

Lisa's on Folsom, 299 9th St. (☎551-1688), at Folsom St. Super-goddess Lisa, harnessing the ancient decorative powers of *feng shui*, brings fresh noodles, homemade potstickers, and potent drinks to SoMa. Lunch served M-F 11am-3pm; dinner served M-Sa 5pm-midnight. Happy Hour M-F 5-7pm; after hours F-Sa until 4am.

THE MISSION DISTRICT

☒ **Taquería El Farolito,** 2279 Mission St. (☎824-7877), at 24th St. The spot for cheap and authentic Mexican *comida*. Chow down as Latin beats blast through this fast food joint. After any kind of evening activity in the Mission, El Farolito is a late-night must. Tacos $1.75. Open Su-Th 9am-2am, F-Sa 9am-4am.

☒ **Ti Couz,** 3108 16th St. (☎252-7373), at Valencia St. Savory ($2.50-6.50) and sweet ($2.50-5.25) crepes, plus dozens of tempting additions and toppings. Long waits on weekends. Open M-W 11am-11pm, Th-F 11am-2am, Sa 10am-2am, Su 10am-11pm.

Herbivore, 983 Valencia St. (☎826-5657), at 21st St. All vegan, all the time. Immaculate eatery hangs fresh-off-the-vine produce as decor. Grilled *seitan* $6.50. Lasagna with tofu ricotta $8. Open Su-Th 11am-10pm, F-Sa 11am-11pm.

CASTRO

☒ **Welcome Home,** 464 Castro St. (☎626-3600), across from the Castro Theater. If grandma were a drag queen, this would be her kitchen: the antique ovens and pride flags, fried chicken, and milkshakes bring an all-American and decidedly queer comfort to the Castro. Dinners $7-9. Open daily 7:30am-10:30pm.

Orphan Andy's, 3991A 17th St. (☎864-9795), at Castro and Market St. Red vinyl booths and a vintage jukebox. Burgers $6.50, huge milkshakes $4.45. Open 24hr. Cash only.

Hot 'n' Hunky, 4039 18th St. (☎621-6365), at Hartford St. near Castro St. Hunker down with a Macho Man Burger or I Wanna Hold Your Ham (both $4.40). Open Su-Th 11am-midnight, F-Sa 11am-1am. No credit cards.

MARINA AND PACIFIC HEIGHTS

Soku's Teriyaki and Sushi, 2280 Chestnut St. (☎563-0162), at Scott St. Great service and a $4 lunch box special (2-item combo plus miso soup and rice; served 11:30am-3pm). Open M-Sa 11:30am-10pm.

Pizza Orgasmica, 3157 Fillmore St. (☎931-5300), at Greenwich St. "We never fake it," says the sign out front. With pizzas named "menage a trois" and "doggi style," it's hard not to get excited. Open Su-W 11am-midnight, Th 11am-2am, F-Sa 11am-2:30. No credit cards.

JAPANTOWN

Mifune, 1737 Post St. (☎922-0337), in the Kintetsu Bldg., upper level. Excellent and much-loved noodle restaurant. Sit with 6 or *Seven Samurai* and slurp some soups with choice of *udon* (heavy flour noodles) or *soba* (slender buckwheat noodles) for $4-7. Walk, don't *Ran* for the *Sake* $2.25-4.25. Open Su-F 11am-9:30pm, Sa 11am-10pm.

Isobune, 1737 Post St. (☎563-1030), in the Kintetsu Bldg., upper level. A flotilla of tiny wooden sushi boats sails in a moat around an immense counter. Your bill is based on the price-coded plates you stack up (2 pieces $1.20-3). Open daily 11:30am-10pm.

HAIGHT-ASHBURY

Locals linger over omelettes, home fries, and Marlboros until late afternoon. There are several **grocery stores** along and near Haight St.

☒ **Sweet Heat,** 1725 Haight St. (☎387-8845). Filling tacos $3-4 each; quesadillas $3.75-8 (for fancy Dungeness crab). Open Su-Th 11am-10pm, F-Sa 11am-11pm. Happy Hour 4-7pm with $2 draft beers and sangria and $3 margaritas.

☒ **Citrus Club,** 1790 Haight St. (☎387-6366). Dishes cross borders to bring you the best of many Asian cuisines. Prices range from $3.50 for spring rolls to $7.50 for the Spicy Curry Tiger Shrimp. Open Su and Tu-Th 11:30am-10pm, F-Sa 11:30am-11pm.

All You Knead, 1466 Haight St. (☎552-4550). The 8-page menu of this spacious diner includes a large selection of pizzas, sandwiches, burgers, entrees, and huge breakfasts. Many vegetarian and vegan options. Breakfast and lunch served all day; dinner 4pm-closing. Open M and W-Su 8am-10:50pm, Tu 8am-6pm.

RICHMOND

Lee Hou Restaurant, 332 Clement St. (☎668-8070), at 5th Ave. Some of the best dim sum New Chinatown has to offer. 13 pieces of dim sum $8. Lunch $4-10. Open M-Th and Su 9am-1am, F-Sa 9am-2am.

Taiwan Restaurant, 445 Clement St. (☎387-1789), at 6th Ave. Super-yummy, super-cheap spot dishing up Northern Chinese cuisine. Lunch $3.50; dinner $5-8. Open M-Th 11am-10pm, F 11am-midnight, Sa 10am-midnight, Su 10am-10pm.

👁 SIGHTS

FISHERMAN'S WHARF

Piers 39 through 45 provide access to San Francisco's most famous and visited attractions. Easily visible from boats and the waterfront is **Alcatraz Island.**

ALCATRAZ. Named in 1775 for small cormorants (*alcatraceo*) which nest on the island, this former federal prison looms over San Francisco Bay, 1½ mi. from Fisherman's Wharf. In the 30s, the federal government used it to imprison those who had wrought too much havoc in other prisons, including infamous criminals like Al Capone, "Machine Gun" Kelly, and Robert "The Birdman" Stroud. Of the 23 men who attempted to escape, 18 were recaptured or killed, and five are "presumed drowned," although their bodies have never been found. In 1964, Attorney General Robert Kennedy closed the prison, and the island remained empty until 1969-71, when 80 Native Americans occupied it as a symbolic gesture, claiming "the Rock" as theirs under terms of a broken 19th-century treaty. Alcatraz is now part of the **Golden Gate National Recreation Area.** The **Blue and Gold Fleet** runs boats to Alcatraz from **Pier 41.** Once on Alcatraz, wander alone or take the audiotape-guided tour, full of clanging chains and the ghosts of prisoners past. (☎773-1188 for info, tickets 705-5555. Call in advance, daily 7am-8pm. Blue and Gold Fleet boats at Pier 41 depart every 30min. in summer 9:15am-4:15pm; in winter 9:45am-2:45pm. Arrive 20min. before departure. $8.75, seniors $7, ages 5-11 $5.50. Audio tours add $3.50, ages 5-11 $2.50. Other boating companies run shorter tours up to and around—but not onto—the island for about $10 per person.)

GHIRARDELLI SQUARE. Pronounced "*GEAR-ah-DEH-lee*," Ghirardelli Sq. is the most famous shopping mall in the area around Fisherman's Wharf, known for producing some of the world's best chocolate. Today, the remains of the machinery from Ghirardelli's original factory display the chocolate-making process in the rear of the **Ghirardelli Chocolate Manufactory,** an old-fashioned ice-cream parlor. The nearby soda fountain serves up loads of its world-famous hot fudge sauce on huge sundaes ($6). If your sweet tooth outpaces your financial resources, file through the Ghirardelli store for a free sample. (900 North Point St. Square: ☎775-5500. Store: ☎771-4903. Open Su-Th 9am-11pm, F-Sa 9am-midnight.)

OTHER SIGHTS. Pier 39 juts toward Alcatraz on pilings several hundred yards into the harbor. Toward the end of the pier is **Center Stage,** where mimes, jugglers, and magicians play the crowds. A number of the marina docks have been claimed by **sea lions** that pile onto the wharf to gawk at human tourists on sunny days. (Pier ☎981-7437. Shops open daily 10am-9pm.) **Pier 45** and the **Hyde St. Pier** serve as docks to old submarines and boats which can be toured. **The Cannery** is a mini-plaza on the wharf, with garden seating, a few cafes, and the popular Belle Roux Voodoo Lounge, a Cajun restaurant, bar, and host of Cobb's Comedy Club. (On Jefferson St., between Hyde and Leavenworth St. Belle Roux ☎771-5225; comedy club ☎938-4320.)

CALIFORNIA

NORTH BEACH

WASHINGTON SQUARE. Sunny North Beach is well worth visiting in the daytime as well as during its neon-lit evenings. Bordered by Union, Filbert, Stockton, and Powell St. is Washington Sq., a pretty lawn edged by trees and watched over by a statue of not Washington, but Benjamin Franklin. The wedding site of Marilyn Monroe and Joe DiMaggio, the park fills every morning with men and women practicing tai chi. Across Filbert, to the north of the square, the **Church of St. Peter and St. Paul** beckons tired sightseers to take refuge in its dark, wooden nave. (☎ 421-0809. *Mass in Italian, English, and Cantonese.*) Lillie Hitchcock Coit, rescued from a fire as a girl, donated the **Volunteer Firemen Memorial,** in the middle of the square.

TELEGRAPH HILL. Telegraph Hill is its own neighborhood, and a nice one at that, but North Beach provides the best up-close views. Lillie Coit also put up money to build **Coit Tower,** which stands a few blocks to the east of the memorial. The tower commands a spectacular view of the city and the bay from Telegraph Hill, the steep mount from which a semaphore signalled the arrival of ships in Gold Rush days. To get to the tower, take MUNI bus #39, or trundle up the **Filbert Steps** that rise from the Embarcadero to its eastern base. The walk is short, allows excellent views, and passes attractive Art Deco buildings. (☎ 362-0808. *Open daily 10am-7pm; Oct.-May 9am-4pm. Elevator fare $3.50, over 64 $2.50, ages 6-12 $1.50.*)

CITY LIGHTS BOOKSTORE. Drawn to the area by low rents and cheap bars, the Beat writers came to national attention when Lawrence Ferlinghetti's City Lights Bookstore published Allen Ginsberg's *Howl.* Banned in 1956, a judge found the poem "not obscene" after an extended trial, but the resulting publicity vaulted the Beats into literary infamy and turned North Beach into a must-see. Rambling and well-stocked, City Lights has expanded since its Beat days, but remains committed to publishing young poets and other writers under its own imprint. (*201 Columbus Ave.* ☎ 362-8093. *Open daily 10am-midnight.*)

NOB HILL AND RUSSIAN HILL

LOMBARD ST. The famous curves of Lombard St.—installed in the 20s so that horse-drawn carriages could negotiate the extremely steep hill—are one-of-a-kind. From the top of Lombard St., pedestrians and passengers alike enjoy the view of city and harbor. The view north along Hyde St. isn't too shabby either. (*Between Hyde and Leavenworth St. at the top of Russian Hill.*)

GRACE CATHEDRAL AND HUNTINGTON PARK. Grace Cathedral, the most immense Gothic edifice west of the Mississippi, crowns Nob Hill. The castings for its portals are such exact imitations of Lorenzo Ghiberti's on the Baptistery in Florence that they were used to restore the originals. Inside, modern murals mix San Franciscan and national historical events with scenes from saints' lives. (*1100 California St.* ☎ 749-6300. *Open Su-F 7am-6pm; Sa 8am-6pm; Su services at 7:30, 8:30, 11am, and 3:30pm. Suggested donation $3.*) The quaint spot of turf and trees in front of Grace Cathedral is Huntington Park, literally the playground of the rich. (*On Taylor St. between California and Sacramento St.*)

OTHER SIGHTS. After the journey up Nob Hill, you will understand what inspired the development of the vehicles celebrated at the **Cable Car Powerhouse and Museum,** still the working center of the cable-car system. Displays teach about the picturesque cars, some of which date back to 1873. (*1201 Mason St.* ☎ 474-1887. *Open daily Apr.-Oct. 10am-6pm; Nov.-Mar. 10am-5pm. Free.*) Once the site of the enormous mansions of the four mining and railroad magnates who "settled" Nob (Charles Crocker, Mark Hopkins, Leland Stanford, and Collis Huntington), the hilltop is now home to upscale hotels and bars. Kitsch connoisseurs must check out the **Tonga Room.** In a city blessed with several faux-Polynesian tiki bars, King Tonga has to be seen to be believed. (*In the Fairmont Hotel.*)

CHINATOWN

GRANT AVE. The oldest street in San Francisco, Grant Ave. is a sea of Chinese banners, signs, and architecture. During the day, Grant Ave. and nearby streets fill up with a slow-moving tourist horde stopping every block to buy health balls and chirping boxes and trying to ignore the Chinese porn mags in some shop windows. Most of the picturesque pagodas punctuating the blocks were designed around 1900 or more recently. At Bush and Grant St. stands the ornate, dragon-crested **Gateway to Chinatown,** given as a gift by the Taiwanese in 1969. "Everything in the world is in just proportion," say the Chinese characters above the gate.

ROSS ALLEY. Once lined with brothels and opium dens, Ross Alley, running from Jackson to Washington St. between Grant and Stockton St., still has the cramped look of old Chinatown. It has stood in for Asia in such films as *Big Trouble in Little China*, *Karate Kid II*, and *Indiana Jones and the Temple of Doom*. Watch fortune cookies being shaped by hand in the **Golden Gate Cookie Company.** *(56 Ross Alley. ☎ 781-3956. Bag of cookies $2; with "funny" or "sexy" fortunes $4.)*

ARCHITECTURE. Noteworthy Chinatown buildings include **Buddha's Universal Church,** 720 Washington St., at Kearny St., and **Old St. Mary's,** 660 California St., at Grant St., built from Chinese granite in 1854, and San Francisco's only cathedral for decades. **Portsmouth Square,** at Kearny and Washington St., made history in 1848 when Sam Brennan stood there to announce his discovery of gold at Sutter's Mill. Today, hangings are no longer for the public, and the square is filled with young children and Chinese men playing board games. A stone bridge leads from the square over construction refuse to the **Chinese Culture Center,** in the Holiday Inn, which houses exhibits of Chinese-American art and sponsors two walking tours of Chinatown. The **Heritage Walk** surveys the history of Chinatown, while the **Culinary Walk** teaches the preparation of Chinese food. *(750 Kearny St. ☎ 986-1822. Gallery open Tu-Su 9am-5:30pm. Heritage Walk Sa and Su 2pm, $15, under 18 $6. Culinary Walk M-F 10:30am by arrangement only. $30, under 12 $15; includes dim sum at Four Seas on Grant St. Walks require reservations.)*

FINANCIAL DISTRICT

TRANSAMERICA PYRAMID. The leading lady of the area is the **Transamerica Pyramid.** New Age sources claim the pyramid is directly centered on the telluric currents of the Golden Dragon ley line between Easter Island and Stonehenge. An architect's joke co-opted by one of the country's leading architectural firms, the building earned disdain from purists and reverence from city planners after the fact. Without a business suit and some chutzpah, one must make do with the virtual viewscapes in the lobby. A pillar of the establishment, the address was once a site of revolutionary disgruntlement, and Sun Yat-Sen scripted a dynastic overthrow in one of its apartments. *(600 Montgomery St., between Clay and Washington St.)*

OTHER BUILDINGS. **Justin Herman Plaza** and its formidable **Vallaincourt Fountain,** at the foot of Market St., invite total visitor immersion. Bands and rallyists often rent out the area during lunch. One free concert, performed by U2 in the fall of 1987, resulted in the arrest of lead singer and madcap non-conformist Bono for spray-painting "Stop the Traffic—Rock and Roll" on the fountain. The 660 ft. waterfront **Ferry Building,** at the foot of Market St., has lost a bit of grandeur over the years, as other buildings along the Embarcadero stole the spotlight.

UNION SQUARE AND THE TENDERLOIN

While Union Sq. is filled with boutiques, stores, and retail, the blocks west have cultural offerings as well, in the form of theaters and galleries. When the Barbary Coast (now the Financial District) was down and dirty, Union Sq.'s Morton Alley was dirtier. Around 1900, murders on the alley averaged one per week, and prostitutes waved to their favorite customers from 2nd-story windows.

MAIDEN LN. After the 1906 earthquake and fires destroyed most of the flop-houses, merchants moved in and renamed the area Maiden Ln. in hopes of changing the street's image. It worked. Today, the pedestrian street is as virtu-ous as they come. The lane's main architectural attraction is the windowless face of the **Frank Lloyd Wright Building,** the city's only Wright-designed building, which now houses the **Folk Art International Gallery.** *(140 Maiden Ln. ☎392-9999. Open M-Sa 10am-6pm.)*

MARTIN LAWRENCE GALLERY. The Martin Lawrence Gallery is a modest corner space that displays works by pop artists like Andy Warhol and Keith Haring, as well as some studies by Pablo Picasso and Marc Chagall. Haring once distributed his work for free to New York commuters in the form of graffiti; it now commands upwards of $13,000 in print form. *(366 Geary St. ☎956-0345. Open M-Th 9am-8pm, F-Sa 9am-9pm, Su 10am-6pm.)*

OTHER SIGHTS. Just south-west of Union Square the aptly-named Tenderloin hosts not only more traditional ladies (and men) of the night, but also San Fran-cisco specials: transvestite, transsexual, and transgendered streetwalkers. Witness the scene more safely by day and check out the surprisingly vibrant cultural offer-ings. The **509 Cultural Center/Luggage Store** presents performing arts events and exhibitions. *(1007 Market St., near 6th St. ☎255-5971.)* The small **Institute of Interna-tional San Francisco Art** hosts occasional student shows in its lobby. *(1172 Market St. ☎865-0198.)*

CIVIC CENTER AND HAYES VALLEY

CIVIC CENTER. Home to the opera, the symphony, and most of San Francisco's major theater, the Civic Center district is grandest at night, when beautifully lit flags and fountains flank bumper-to-bumper limousine traffic. The **Louise M. Davies Symphony Hall** glitters at Grove St. The seating in this glass-and-brass $33 million hall was designed to give most audience members a close-up view of per-formers. Visually, the building is a smashing success, and the San Francisco Symphony is equally highly rated. *(201 Van Ness Ave. ☎552-8000; symphony tickets 864-6000. Open M-F 10am-6pm, Sa noon-6pm.)* The recently renovated **War Memorial Opera House** hosts the well-regarded San Francisco Opera Company and the San Francisco Ballet. *(301 Van Ness Ave., between Grove and McAllister St. ☎865-2000.)* The **Veteran's Building,** where Herbst Theater hosts solo singers, string quartets, ensembles, and lecturers also houses the **Performance Art Library and Museum.** *(On Van Ness Ave. between Grove and McAllister St., 4th fl. Herbst Theater: ☎392-4400. PALM: ☎255-4800; Open Tu and Th-Sa 11am-5pm, W 11am-7pm. Free Tours of Symphony Hall, War Memorial Opera House, and Herbst Theater: ☎552-8338. Tours depart from Symphony Hall every hr. M 10am-2pm. $5, students and seniors $3.)*

THE BONAPARTE OF THE BAY By nature California is a populist constituency, putting more questions to voter referendum than any other state—but San Franciscans have made at least one notable exception. From 1853 to 1880, locals recognized the self-proclaimed rule of **Joshua Norton the First, Emperor of the United States and Defender of Mexico.** Norton assumed the grandiose title after tough luck in rice speculation wiped out all his money—and perhaps his sanity. He donned an ostrich feather hat and faux-military attire and roamed San Francisco's streets with his dogs, Bummer and Lazarus. When he wasn't busy sending suggestions to Abraham Lincoln, Queen Victoria, and the Czar of Russia, Norton's decrees for San Francisco included starting the tradition of a Christmas tree in Union Sq. and building a bridge across the Bay. Locals didn't mind his eccentricities; good-natured merchants accepted the money he printed, and the Central Pacific Railroad allowed him to travel for free. The city even footed the bill for his new clothes. When he died, 20,000 people came to wave him on to the next world.

HAYES VALLEY. Hayes Valley is the latest San Francisco neighborhood to come into its own. Artists of all types, from architects to fashion and interior designers, have begun to open studios around Hayes St. One precursor to the current boom, the **Women Artists Gallery** began in the 1880s as the Young Ladies Sketch Club. It exhibits women's photographs, paintings, and prints. *(370 Hayes St. ☎ 552-7392. Open Tu-W and F-Sa 11am-6pm, Th 11am-8pm. Free.)*

SOUTH OF MARKET AREA (SOMA)

The area's main draw is its fantastic collection of modern and contemporary art museums (see p. 841).

THE MISSION DISTRICT

MISSION DOLORES. Extant for over two centuries and in the old heart of San Francisco, **Misión de los Dolores** is thought to be the city's oldest building (built in 1776 by Father Junipero Serra). Bougainvillea, poppies, and birds-of-paradise bloom in its cemetery, which was featured in Alfred Hitchcock's 1958 film *Vertigo.* *(At 16th and Dolores St. ☎ 621-8203. Open daily May-Oct. 9am-4:30pm; Nov.-Apr. 9am-4pm. $2, ages 5-12 $1. Masses: In English M-F 7:30 and 9am; Sa 7:30, 9am, 5pm; Su 8 and 10am. In Spanish Su noon.)*

MISSION MURALS. A walk east or north along Mission St. from the 24th St. BART stop leads to the great ▨Mission murals. Continuing the long muraling tradition brought to fame by Diego Rivera and José Orozco, the Mission murals have been a proud mark of Chicano artists, schoolchildren, and community members since the 80s. Standouts include: the more political murals of Balmy Alley, off 24th St. between Harrison and Folsom St.; a three-building tribute to guitar god Carlos Santana at 22nd St. and Van Ness Ave.; the face of St. Peter's Church at 24th and Florida St.; and the urban living center on 19th St. between Valencia and Guerrero St. The library leads free weekly tours of the Mission murals in summer, meeting at Precita and Harrison St., behind Flynn Elementary School on Saturdays at 11am. *(Library tours ☎ 557-4266; free.)*

OTHER SIGHTS. La Galeria de la Raza celebrates local Chicano and Latino artists with exhibitions and parties. Attached to the gallery is **Studio 24,** a space where Chicano and Latino artists sell artwork, crafts, and jewelry. *(2857 24th St., between Bryant and Florida St. ☎ 826-8009. Open Tu-Su noon-6pm. Free.)*

CASTRO AND NEARBY

THE CASTRO. Rainbow flags raised high, out and proud lesbians, gays, bisexuals, and transgendered folk find comfort and fun on the streets of the Castro. The concept, as well as the reality, of an all-queer neighborhood draws gay tourists and their friends from around the world, carrying the already absolutely fabulous Castro scene over the top. The people out and about are the main attraction on the picture-perfect streets, and the shops are an added novelty. **Cruisin' the Castro** is a guided tour of the area. Trevor Hailey, a resident since 1972, is consistently recognized as one of San Francisco's top tour leaders. Her 4hr. walking tours cover Castro life and history. *(☎ 550-8110. Tours Tu-Sa 10am. $40; brunch included. Call ahead.)*

Shoppers, like queens (both the royal and the drag types), do *not* climb hills; thus, the steeply sloped areas to the south and west of Castro Village tend to be residential. The vibrantly painted old **Victorians** here are worth wandering for—Collingwood and Noe St. both have their share. For architecture without the walk, look for the faux-baroque **Castro Theatre,** 429 Castro St.—not that you could miss it.

VIEWS. West of the Castro, the peninsula swells with several large hills. From **Twin Peaks,** between Portola Dr., Clarendon Ave., and Market St., are some of the more spectacular views of the city. On rare fogless nights, the views are particularly sublime. At the hulking three-masted radio tower, known by some as the Great Satan, a pair of red warning lights blink ominously beneath a Mephisthophelean crown. Significantly south of the peaks is **Mount Davidson,** the highest spot in San Francisco at 938 ft. The 103 ft. concrete cross is the resilient replacement of two earlier versions destroyed by fire. *(Off Portola Dr. Accessible by MUNI bus #36.)*

MARINA AND PACIFIC HEIGHTS

PALACE OF FINE ARTS. The main attractions in this area are almost all along the waterfront; the neighborhoods themselves are residential with bouts of commerce. The Palace of Fine Arts, an imposing domed structure with curving colonnades, has been reconstructed from remnants of the 1915 Panama Pacific Exposition which commemorated the opening of the Panama Canal and signaled San Francisco's recovery from the 1906 earthquake. The grounds, complete with swans, make one of the best picnic spots in the city, and the nighttime illumination is glorious. *(On Baker St., between Jefferson and Bay St. near the Exploratorium. Open 24hr. Free.)*

FORT MASON. Fort Mason is the site of a popular hostel and headquarters for the **Golden Gate National Recreation Area.** *(At Laguna and Marine St. east of Marina Green, west of Fisherman's Wharf's Municipal Pier.)* Sam Shepard served as the playwright-in-residence at the **Magic Theater** from 1975 to 1985. Today, the theater stages both world and American premieres. *(Bldg. D, 3rd fl. ☎ 441-8822.)* Fort Mason also holds several excellent **museums** (see p. 842).

OTHER SIGHTS. Near Union and Sacramento St., **Pacific Heights** boasts the greatest number of **Victorian buildings** in the city. The **Octagon House** was built in 1861 with the belief that the odd architecture would bring good luck to its inhabitants. Its survival of San Francisco's many earthquakes and fires is proof of fortune's favor, so far. *(2645 Gough St., at Union St. ☎ 441-7512. Open Feb.-Dec. 2nd Su and 2nd and 4th Th of each month noon-3pm.)* Along the water, joggers and walkers crowd **Marina Green.** Play pick-up soccer on weekends, or just plain pick-up—the wide sidewalk's uninterrupted sight lines make cruising optimal.

JAPANTOWN

PEACE PAGODA AND SOKOJI BUDDHIST TEMPLE. Stores hawk the latest Pokemon paraphernalia and karaoke bars warble J-pop along Post St. around the Japan Center. The five-tiered Peace Pagoda, a gift to the community from the Japanese government, is in a featureless paved lot. A brighter example of Japanese architecture is the Sokoji Buddhist Temple, where some meditation services are open to the public. *(1691 Laguna St., at Sutter St. ☎ 346-7540. Public Zazen meditation services Su 8:30am, W and F 6:30pm—arrive 15min. early.)*

HEAVEN. Weary travelers may want to invest in a massage at **Fuji Shiatsu.** *(1721 Buchanan Mall, between Post and Sutter St. ☎ 346-4484. By appointment only; morning $33 per hr., afternoon $36.)* Or you can steam at **Kabuki Hot Springs.** *(1750 Geary St. ☎ 922-6000. Men-only M-Tu, Th, and Sa 10am-10pm; women-only Su, W, and F 10am-10pm. Sauna, steam room, and baths M-F before 5pm $12, evenings and Sa-Su $16. Other services by appointment.)*

GOLDEN GATE PARK

The park should not be rushed through. Intriguing museums (see p. 842) and cultural events pick up where the lush flora and fauna finally leave off, and athletic opportunities abound. In addition to cycling and skating paths, the park also has a municipal golf course, an equestrian center, sports fields, tennis courts, and a stadium. On Sundays, traffic is banned from park roads, and bicycles and in-line skates come out in full force. A **visitors center** for Golden Gate Park is located in the remodeled Beach Chalet on the Western edge of the park on the Great Hwy., south of Fulton St. *(☎ 751-2766. Open daily 9am-6pm.)* **Surrey Bikes and Blades in Golden Gate Park** rents equipment. *(50 Stow Lake Dr. ☎ 668-6699. Open daily 10am-dusk. Bikes from $6 per hr., $21 per day; skates $7 per hr.)*

GARDENS. Despite its sandy past, the soil of Golden Gate Park is rich enough to support a wealth of flowers. The **Garden of Fragrance** is designed especially for the visually impaired; all labels are in Braille and the plants are chosen specifically for their textures and scents. Near the Music Concourse off South Dr., the **Shakespeare Garden** contains almost every flower and plant ever mentioned by the Bard. Plaques with the relevant quotations are hung on the back wall, and there's a map to help you find your favorite hyacinths and rue. *(Open daily in summer dawn-dusk; in winter Tu-Su. Free.)* **Rhododendron Dell,** between the Academy of Sciences and John F. Kennedy Dr., honors John McLaren with a splendid profusion of his favorite flower. The **Japanese Cherry Orchard,** at Lincoln Way and South Dr., blooms intoxicatingly the first week in Apr. Created for the 1894 Mid-Winter Exposition, the elegant **Japanese Tea Garden** is a serene collection of dark wooden buildings, small pools, graceful footbridges, carefully pruned trees, and lush plants. In 1953, small donations made by Japanese schoolchildren funded a 9000 lb. Lantern of Peace to be given as a token of friendship to the new generations of the US. Sip tea and munch cookies for $2.50 and watch the giant carp circle the central pond. *(☎ 752-4227. Open daily 8:30am-6pm. $3.50, seniors and ages 6-12 $1.25. Free daily 8:30-9am and 5:30-6pm.)*

OTHER SIGHTS. Across JFK Dr. from the Conservatory, just south of **Lily Pond,** among the fragile, flowering dogwoods and giant redwoods of **De Laveaga Dell,** rests the **National AIDS Memorial Grove.** The grove is a site for remembrance and renewal, at once somber and rejuvenating. *(☎ 750-8340. Tours Th 9:30am-12:30pm starting at the Main Portal of the Grove, near the corner of Middle Dr. East and Bowling Green Dr.)*

In the extreme northwest of the park, the **Dutch Windmill** has done its last good turn. Once the muscle behind the park's irrigation system, the outdated but renovated old powerhouse (114 ft. from sail to sail) is now the purely ornamental centerpiece of the cheery **Queen Wilhelmina Tulip Garden.** Rounding out the days of yore is the **carousel** (c. 1912), accompanied by a $50,000 Gebruder band organ. *(Open daily June-Sept. 10am-5pm; Oct-May Tu-W and F-Su 9am-4pm. $1, ages 6-12 25¢.)*

Brimming **Spreckels Lake,** on John F. Kennedy Dr., is populated by crowds of turtles who pile onto a turtle-shaped rock to sun themselves—it's turtles all the way down. A dozen **bison** loll about a spacious paddock just west of Spreckels.

HAIGHT-ASHBURY

All around Haight and Ashbury St., vestiges of the 60s exist in harmony with chain stores and boutiques. Music and clothing top the list of legal merchandise. Inexpensive bars and ethnic restaurants, action-packed street life, anarchist literature, and shops selling pipes for…um, tobacco…also contribute to groovy browsing possibilities. While the **Upper Haight** tends to attract a younger tourist crowd, the **Lower Haight** is the stomping ground for longtime locals, though visitors are always welcome. Can't you just feel the love?

FAMOUS HOMES. The former homes of several counterculture legends survive beautifully. Starting at the corner of Haight and Ashbury St., walk up Ashbury St. to #710, just south of Waller St., to check out the house occupied by the **Grateful Dead** when they were still the Warlocks. Look across the street for the **Hell's Angels'** house. If you walk back to Haight St., go right three blocks, and make a left on Lyon St., you can check out **Janis Joplin's** old abode, 122 Lyon St., between Page and Oak St. Cross the Panhandle, and continue three blocks to Fulton St., turn right, and wander seven blocks toward the park to see where the Manson "family" planned murder and mayhem at the **Charles Manson** mansion, 2400 Fulton St., at Willard St.

WALKING TOURS. The **Flower Power Walking Tour** explains the Haight's history and visits the sights. *(☎ 221-8442. 2½hr., Tu and Sa 9:30am. $15.)* The **San Francisco Public Library** offers a free walking tour focused on the area's pre-hippie incarnation as a Victorian-era resort. *(☎ 557-4266. Tours leave Su at 11am from the Park Branch Library at 1833 Page St., near Cole St.)*

OTHER SIGHTS. Several parks dot the Haight. You may see police lurking in the bushes—the parks are rumored to be great places to buy pot. **Buena Vista Park,** which runs along Haight St. between Central and Baker St. and continues south, resembles a dense jungle. An unofficial crash pad and community center for San Francisco skaters, Buena Vista is supposedly safer than **Alamo Square,** which lies northeast of the Haight at Hayes and Steiner St. Across Alamo Square's gentle grassy slope, a string of brightly colored Victorian homes known as the **Painted Ladies**—subjects of a thousand postcards—glow against the backdrop of the metropolitan skyline.

CALIFORNIA

LINCOLN PARK AND OCEAN BEACH

CLIFF HOUSE. The precarious **Cliff House,** built in 1909, is the 3rd of that name to occupy this spot—the previous two burned down. *(At the end of Pt. Lobos Ave./Geary Blvd. in the southwest corner of Lincoln Park.)* Along with overpriced restaurants, the Cliff House hosts a **Camera Obscura,** the **Golden Gate National Recreation Area Visitors Center,** and the **Musée Mecanique,** an arcade devoted to games of yesteryear—not Donkey Kong and Space Invaders, but wooden and cast-iron creations dating back to the 1890s. The ingenious and addictive games are accompanied by fortune tellers, love testers, "naughty" kinescopes, and player pianos. Presiding over them all is "Laughing Sal," a roaring mechanical clown. *(Camera Obscura:* ☎ *750-0415. Open daily 11am-sunset. $1. Visitors Center:* ☎ *556-8642. Open daily 10am-5pm. Musée Mecanique:* ☎ *386-1170. Open daily in summer 10am-8pm; in winter M-F 11am-7pm, Sa-Su 10am-8pm. Free, but most games are 25¢.)*

LINCOLN PARK. The beaches and park at the western edge of Richmond offer more views and wanderings than works of art. The grounds around Lincoln Park, which include the **Land's End Path,** offer a romantic view of the Golden Gate Bridge. Swimming is allowed at **China Beach** at the end of Seacliff Ave. on the eastern edge of Lincoln Park. The water is cold, but the views are stunning. Adolph Sutro's 1896 **bathhouse** lies in ruins on the cliffs. Cooled by ocean water, the baths were capable of squashing in 25,000 occupants at a time, but after an enthusiastic opening surge, they very rarely did. Be careful when exploring the ruins and nearby cliffs. *(East of Cliff House. Paths lead there from Point Lobos Ave.)*

OCEAN BEACH. Ocean Beach, the largest and most popular of San Francisco's beaches, begins south of Point Lobos and extends down the northwestern edge of the city's coastline. The strong undertow along the point is very dangerous, but die-hard surfers brave the treacherous currents and the ice-cold water anyway.

THE PRESIDIO AND THE GOLDEN GATE BRIDGE

PRESIDIO. The Presidio, a sprawling preserve that extends from the Marina in the east to the wealthy Sea Cliff area in the west, was occupied by the US Army for nearly a century between the Mexican War and World War II. Now administered by the National Park Service, the Presidio is ideal for biking, jogging, and hiking. The preserve supports the southern end of San Francisco's world-famous Golden Gate Bridge. *(MUNI bus #28, 29, 42, or 76 or Golden Gate Transit buses into the Presidio.)*

GOLDEN GATE BRIDGE. Synonymous with the city itself, the majestic Golden Gate Bridge spans the mouth of San Francisco Bay, a rust-colored symbol of the West's boundless confidence. Countless photos can't pack the punch of a personal encounter with the suspended colossus itself. The bridge's overall length is 8981 ft.; the main span is 4200 ft. long and the stolid towers are 746 ft. high. Although disaster-proofed against seismic threat, the bridge still claims victims—it is the most popular site for suicides in the world, and it lacks a traffic divider. Across the bridge, Vista Point offers incredible views of city and bridge on rare fogless days.

OTHER SIGHTS. At the northern tip of the Presidio (and the peninsula), under the tower of the Golden Gate Bridge, **Fort Point** keeps watch over the entrance to San Francisco Bay. Film buffs may recognize the spot where Kim Novak dove into the Bay in Alfred Hitchcock's *Vertigo* (1958). Fort Point's museum is dedicated to past military occupants, but the thrilling view of sea-savaged surfers below is more interesting. *(Museum open daily 10am-5pm. Grounds open dawn-dusk. Guided tours.)* **Baker Beach,** in Golden Gate National Recreation Area, offers a picturesque but chilly place to tan and swim. Wind shelter makes the north half of the beach one of the city's most popular nude beaches.

🏛 MUSEUMS

FISHERMAN'S WHARF

Maritime Museum (☎556-3002), at Beach and Polk St. across from Ghirardelli. The free museum has large, fairly clean bathrooms as well as a quiet deck with a water view. Open daily 10am-5pm. Free.

NORTH BEACH

North Beach Museum, 1435 Stockton St. (☎391-6210), at Columbus Ave. inside Bay View Bank, depicts the North Beach of yesteryear in a series of vintage photographs. Most of the photographs long predate the Beats, but a handwritten manuscript of Ferlinghetti's *The Old Italians Dying* is on display. Open M-Th 9am-5pm, F 9am-6pm.

Tattoo Art Museum, 841 Columbus Ave. (☎775-4491), displays a fantastic collection of tattoo memorabilia, including hundreds of designs and exhibits on different tattoo techniques (the largest collection of its kind). $50 will buy a quick rose on the hip; larger tattoos are $100 per hr. Open M-Th noon-9pm, F-Su noon-10pm.

SOMA

San Francisco Museum of Modern Art (SFMOMA), 151 3rd St. (☎357-4000), between Mission and Howard St. Fascinating from an architectural perspective, as well as for the art it contains, this black-and-gray, marble-trimmed museum consists of 5 spacious floors of art, with an emphasis on design. Its contemporary European and American collections also impress—SFMOMA has the largest selection of 20th-century art this side of New York. Open M-Tu and F-Su 11am-6pm, Th 11am-9pm. $9, students $5, over 61 $6, under 12 free; Th 6-9pm half-price; 1st Tu of each month free. 4 free tours daily.

Yerba Buena Center for the Arts, 701 Mission St. (☎978-2787). The center runs an excellent gallery space and vibrant programs, emphasizing performance, film, viewer involvement, and local multicultural work. It is surrounded by the **Yerba Buena Rooftop Gardens,** a huge expanse of concrete, fountains, and very intentional-looking foliage next to the huge Sony Metreon. Open Tu-Su 11am-6pm, Th-F 11am-8pm. $5, seniors and students $3; 1st Th of each month free 5-8pm.

ZEUM, 221 4th St., at Howard St. (☎777-2800). Within the Yerba Buena gardens but a sight unto itself, this recently opened "art and technology center" is aimed at children and teenagers. The best draw may be the reopened **carousel,** first installed in Seattle in 1907. Open W-F noon-6pm, Sa-Su 11am-5pm; in winter Sa-Su 11am-5pm. $7, students and seniors $6, ages 5-18 $5, under 5 free. Carousel: Open Su-Th 10am-6pm, F-Sa 10am-8pm. $2 for 2 rides.

Friends of Photography Ansel Adams Center, 555 Mission St. (☎495-7000), between 3rd and 4th St. Although the center only exhibits a small number of the master's photographs, rotating shows by other photographers make up one of the largest and best collections of art photography in the country. Open daily 11am-5pm. Open until 8pm first Th each month. $5, students $3, seniors and ages 13-17 $2, under 13 free.

Cartoon Art Museum, 814 Mission St., 2nd fl. (☎227-8666). Showcases the history of comic strip art from *The Yellow Kid* to *Calvin and Hobbes.* Changing exhibits on cartoon masters and research archives for funny scholars. Open W-F 11am-5pm, Sa 10am-5pm, Su 1-5pm. $5, students and seniors $3, ages 6-12 $2, under 6 free; first W each month is pay-what-you-wish.

MARINA

Exploratorium, 3601 Lyon St. (☎563-7337). *Scientific American* called this "the best science museum in the world," and it is indeed a mad scientist's dream. Displays include interactive tornadoes, computer planet-managing, and giant bubble-makers poised to take over the universe. Open Memorial Day to Labor Day M-Tu and Th-Su 10am-6pm, W 10am-9pm; Labor Day to Memorial Day Tu and Th-Su 10am-5pm, W 10am-9pm. $9, students and seniors $7, disabled and ages 6-17 $5, ages 3-5 $2.50, under 3 free. Free first W of each month. **Tactile Dome** (☎561-0362), inside the Exploratorium, is a pitch-dark maze of tunnels, slides, nooks, and crannies designed to help refine your sense of touch. Claustrophobes beware. Open during museum hours. Reservations required. $12 includes museum admission.

FORT MASON

Mexican Museum, Bldg. D, first fl. (☎202-9700). Presents exhibits by historic and contemporary Chicano and Latino artists. Open W-F noon-5pm, Sa-Su 11am-5pm. $4, students and seniors $3. Free first W of month 11am-7pm.

African-American Historical and Cultural Society Museum, Bldg. C #165 (☎441-0640). Focuses on contemporary African arts and crafts. Open W-Su noon-5pm. $2, seniors and children $1.

Craft and Folk Art Museum, Bldg. A (☎775-0990). Stocks a lot more than apple dolls and driftwood sculpture. Open Tu-F and Su 11am-5pm, Sa 10am-5pm. $3, students and seniors $1, under 12 free, families $5. Free Sa 10am-noon.

GOLDEN GATE PARK

▨ **California Academy of Sciences,** on the east side of the park at 9th Ave. (☎750-7145) Houses several smaller museums devoted to different fields of science. The **Steinhart Aquarium,** holds over 600 aquatic species. Shark feedings M-W and F-Su 10:30am, 12:30, 2:30, and 4:30pm. The **Morrison Planetarium** recreates the heavens above with impressive sky shows. Shows M-F 2pm, with additional summer showings. $2.50; students, seniors, and ages 6-17 $1.25. The **Laserium** offers evening laser shows. ☎750-7138. $7, students and seniors $6, ages 6-12 $4. The rest of the Academy is considered the **Natural History Museum,** with an Earthquake Theater and a Far Side of Science gallery paying tribute to Gary Larson. Moo. Open daily Memorial Day to Labor Day 9am-6pm; Labor Day to Memorial Day 10am-5pm. $8.50; students, seniors, and ages 12-17 $5.50; ages 4-11 $2. Open until 8:45pm first W each month; free.

M. H. de Young Memorial Museum, on the east side of the park at 9th Ave. (☎863-3330), offers excellent snapshots of American art. It has expanded its collection of art from Africa and Oceania to complement the Asian wing. Open Tu-Su 9:30am-5pm. $11, ages 12-17 $10. Open until 8:45pm 1st W of each month, $6. Audio tours $4.

LINCOLN PARK

California Palace of the Legion of Honor (☎863-3330), in the middle of Lincoln Park. A copy of Rodin's *Thinker* beckons visitors into the grand courtyard. A thorough catalogue of great masters, from medieval to Matisse, hangs inside. Other draws include a pneumatically operated 4500-pipe organ, played in weekly recitals (Sa-Su 4pm) and a gilded ceiling from a 15th-century *palacio* in Toledo, Spain. Open Tu-Su 9:30am-5pm. $8, seniors $6, under 17 $5, under 12 free.

♬ ENTERTAINMENT

MUSIC

S.F. Weekly and the *Guardian* are the place to start looking for the latest live music listings. Hard core audiophiles might snag a copy of *BAM*. Many of the bars and a few of the clubs listed above feature live bands at various times. *The List* lists rock gigs all over Northern California.

▨ **Cafe du Nord,** 2170 Market St. (☎861-5016), between Church and Sanchez St. in the **Castro.** Excellent live music nightly—pop and groove to garage-trash rock. Vintage jazz, blues, and R&B. Open daily 4pm-2am. Happy Hour 5-7pm. Cover $5.

▨ **Bottom of the Hill,** 1233 17th St. (☎621-4455, ticket info 510-601-8932), between Missouri and Texas St. in Potrero Hill. Intimate rock club with tiny stage is the last, best place to see up-and-comers before they move to bigger venues. Open M-Th and Su 3pm-2am, Sa 8pm-2am. Cover $3-7.

▨ **The Fillmore,** 1805 Geary Blvd. (☎346-6000), at Fillmore St. south of Japantown. Bands that would pack stadiums in other cities are often eager to play at the legendary Fillmore. All ages. Tickets $15-25. Wheelchair accessible.

▨ **Boom Boom Room,** 1061 Fillmore St. (☎673-8000), at Geary St. near Japantown. Don't miss this bad-ass blues joint, often featuring big-name acts. Open daily 2pm-2am. Cover Tu $1, $20 for more well-known musicians.

Louise M. Davies Symphony Hall, 201 Van Ness Ave. (☎552-8000), near the Civic Center, houses the **San Francisco Symphony.** The cheapest seats are on the center terrace, directly above the orchestra—the acoustics are slightly off, but they afford an excellent (and rare) face-on view of the conductor (and the rest of the audience).

San Francisco Opera, 301 Van Ness Ave. (☎864-3330), in the **War Memorial Opera House,** near the Civic Center. Open M-Sa 10am-6pm. Tickets start at $30; box office is at 199 Grove St. Discounted standing-room-only tickets on sale at the Opera House 2hr. before performances.

THEATER

Theater Artaud, 450 Florida St. (☎437-2700, box office 621-7797), at Mariposa St. in the Mission. Shows some of the best and most diverse contemporary theater and dance in the Bay Area. Box office open Tu-Sa 1-6pm and 1hr. before each show. Ticket prices vary. Students and seniors get a $2 discount. Volunteer to usher and see the show for free.

Geary Theater, 415 Geary St. (☎749-2228), at Mason St. in Union Square. Home to the renowned **American Conservatory Theater.** Tickets $14-55. Box office open Tu-Sa noon-8pm, Su-M noon-6pm. Student, teacher, and senior discounts with ID. Wheelchair accessible.

Theatre Rhinoceros, 2926 16th St. (☎861-5079; open for reservations Tu and Sa 1-6pm), at Van Ness Ave. in the Mission. The oldest queer theater in the world. Box office open 1hr. before show.

The Orpheum, 1192 Market St. (☎551-2000), at Hyde St. near the Civic Center. This famous San Francisco landmark hosts the big Broadway shows.

FESTIVALS

Some of San Francisco's more popular festivals: the **Asian American International Film Showcase,** AMC Kabuki 8 Theater, Japantown (☎863-0814; mid-Mar.); the **Cherry Blossom Festival,** Japantown (☎563-2313; Apr.); the **San Francisco International Film Festival,** the oldest film festival in America (☎929-5000; Apr.-May); the **San Francisco International Gay and Lesbian Film Festival,** Roxie Cinema (16th St. at Valencia) and Castro Theater (Castro St. at Market; ☎703-8663; June); **Pride Day,** the High Holy Day of the queer calendar (☎864-3733; June 25); the **San Francisco Blues Festival,** Fort Mason, the oldest blues festival in America (☎826-6837; 3rd weekend in Sept.); the **Folsom Street Fair,** on Folsom St., leather and chains (☎861-3247; last Su in Sept.); **Halloween,** the Castro (Oct. 31); **Día de los Muertos (Day of the Dead),** the Mission (☎821-1155; Nov. 1); and **Chinese New Year Celebration and Parade,** Chinatown (☎982-3000; in Feb.).

◪ NIGHTLIFE

Nightlife in San Francisco is as varied as the city's personal ads. Everyone from the "shy first-timer" to the "bearded strap daddy" to the "pre-op transsexual top" can find places to go on a Sa (or Tu) night. The spots listed below are divided into coffeehouses, bars, clubs, and music venues, but these lines get pretty blurred in San Francisco after dark. There are 10,000 night spots in the city, and you're sure to find something that fits you like a warm leather glove. Ahem. Check out the nightlife listings in *S.F. Weekly,* the *Guardian,* and *Metropolitan.*

DJs are artists here, and **clubbing** is practically a second job for many young San Franciscans. *S.F. Weekly* and *Bay Guardian* have listings and reviews, and record stores are littered with flyers. **Housewares,** 1322 Haight St. (☎252-1440), is a **rave** clothing store and a source of flyers for parties and events. They maintain a rave hotline (☎281-0125). Up the street, **F-8,** 1816 Haight St. (☎221-4142), provides flyers and a telephone hotline (☎541-5019), but is more geared toward trance and techno. There is an online rave bulletin at www.hyperreal.org/raves/sf. The **Be-At Line** (☎626-4087), established by the son of Mayor Willie Brown, is a rundown of the night's most happening happenings. It's the first and only resource for many avid club-goers. *Unless otherwise noted, all clubs are 21+.*

BARS

Specs, 12 Saroyan Pl. (☎421-4112), in a little alley off Columbus Ave. between Broadway and Pacific Ave. in North Beach. Memorabilia packs every inch of the walls, floor, and ceiling. Start your scavenger hunt by finding a gold toilet plunger, a walrus penisbone, a human skull, and a bottle of Anchor Steam. Open daily 5pm-2am.

The Red Room, 827 Sutter St. (☎346-7666), at Jones St. in Union Square. The virtual heart of the local bar scene, this blood-red lounge pumps away every night. Intimate early, packed after 11pm. Don't try to be cute—just wear black. Open daily 5pm-2am.

An Bodhran, 668 Haight St. (☎431-4724), at Pierce St. in the Lower Haight. Bar staff pulls some of the city's best pints of Guinness. Open M-F and Su 4pm-2am, Sa 6pm-2am. Happy Hour daily 4-7pm.

Zeitgeist Bar, 199 Valencia St. (☎255-7505), at Duboce St. in the Mission. Biker boys, biker babes, and beer. Pool tables and a huge patio out back. A haven for puffers in the smoke-free California bar scene. 50¢ off pints and $1 off pitchers M-F 9am-8pm. Open daily 9am-2am.

Beauty Bar, 2299 Mission St. (☎285-0324), at 19th St. in the Mission. Surrounds you with vintage hair dryers and lots of pink. Manicures W-F 6-10pm mostly by appointment (manicure and martini $10). Makeovers Su 7-10pm. Drinks like Dippity-do (Malibu and Midori) $5. Open M-F 5pm-2am, Sa-Su 7pm-2am. Happy Hour daily 5-8pm.

Attic, 3336 24th St. (☎643-3376), between Bartlett and Mission St. in the Mission. Barely lit, womblike booths in back once you squeeze past the bar. Romantic and hip. Jazz music plays in the background. Open daily 5pm-2am. Happy Hour daily 5-7:30pm.

CLUBS

■ **Ten 15 Folsom,** 1015 Folsom St. (☎431-1200) at 6th St. in SoMa. Schizophrenic dance cavern where disco, deep house, and acid jazz are all popular. Strict dress code and inflated cover on weekends. Hours vary, but parties usually start at 10pm. Cover F-Sa $10, Su-Th $5.

■ **Nickie's Barbecue,** 460 Haight St. (☎621-6508), at Fillmore St. in the Lower Haight. One of the chillest, friendliest small clubs in the whole city, with a low cover and even less attitude. Live DJ every night with themes ranging from world music to hip-hop to funk. Great dancing, diverse crowd. Open daily 9pm-2am. Cover M-F $3, Sa-Su $5.

■ **The Top,** 424 Haight St. (☎864-7386), at Fillmore St. in the Lower Haight. The finest House DJs in San Francisco. Open daily 6pm-2am. Cover M-F $3, Sa-Su $5.

Liquid, 2925 16th St. (☎431-8889), at Van Ness Ave. between SoMa and the Mission. Nightly mix usually includes trip-hop or jungle beats. Young crowd. Don't look for a sign advertising the club—head for the awning with the 2925. Open daily 7pm-2am.

El Rio, 3158 Mission St. (☎282-3325), at Precita St. in the Mission. Unbelievably cool patio with a stage, dance space, outdoor bar, and tables. Salsa Su, belly dancing Th, funk and soul M, women only Sa. El Rio has some of the most diverse clientele in the city. Open Su-Tu 3pm-midnight, W-Sa 3pm-2am. Cover free-$8.

GAY AND LESBIAN NIGHTLIFE

Politics aside, nightlife alone is enough to make San Francisco a queer mecca. From the buff gym boys in nipple-tight Ts to tattooed dykes grinding to NIN, there's something for everybody. The boys hang in the **Castro** (around the intersection of Castro and Market St.), while the grrrls prefrrr the **Mission** (on and off Valencia St.); both genders frolic along **Polk St.** (several blocks north of Geary Blvd.), and in **SoMa.** Polk St. can be seedy and SoMa barren, so keep a watchful eye for trouble. Most of the clubs and bars listed above are gay-friendly any night of the week. *The Sentinel* offers information on gay community events. The free *Odyssey* and *Oblivion* are excellent guides.

■ **The Cafe,** 2367 Market St. (☎861-3846), in the Castro. The dance floor, balcony, and patio crowds rotate in a constant game of see-and-be-seen. Repeat *Guardian* awards for best gay bar. Open M-F 2pm-2am, Sa-Su 12:30pm-2am.

The Lexington Club, 3464 19th St. (☎863-2052), at Lexington St. in the Mission. Only bar in San Francisco that is all lesbian, all the time. Jukebox plays all the tuff muff favorites (k.d. lang, Sleater-Kinney, Liz Phair). Open daily 3pm-2am. Happy Hour M-F 4-7pm.

The EndUp, 401 6th St. (☎357-0827), at Harrison St. in SoMa. Theme nights run from mostly straight KitKat Th to Fag F to Girl Spot Sa. Sa morning GSpot goes until 4pm. Open W-F 10pm-4am. Sa night 9pm-4am; infamous Su Tea Dance (26 years strong) 5:30am-2am the next day. Cover $5-10.

Esta Noche, 3079 16th St. (☎861-5757), at Valencia St. in the Mission. The city's premier gay Latino bar hosts regular drag shows, both on stage and off. Gringos are asked to refrain from dancing salsa without instruction. Open Su-Th 1pm-2am, F-Sa 1pm-3am.

The Stud, 399 9th St. (☎252-7883), at Harrison St. in SoMa. Go Tu for the wild and wacky drag and transgendered parties known as "Trannyshack," Th for Reform School boy-cruising party, F for Doll House dykes. Crowd is mostly gay male. Open 5pm-2am; Sa until 4am; Su until 3am. Cover around $5.

Twin Peaks, 401 Castro St. (☎864-9470), at Market St. in the Castro. The wide-open picture windows were radical for a gay bar when Twin Peaks opened over 20 years ago. It's the granddaddy of the Castro, with a mellow crowd. Open daily noon-2am.

THE BAY AREA

BERKELEY   ☎510

Famous for being an activist center and a haven for iconoclasts, Berkeley lives up to its reputation. Although its political outrage peaked in the 60s and 70s, when students attended more protests than classes, UC Berkeley continues to rebel against the establishment, even if no longer as "Berserkeley." The vitality of the population infuses the streets, which are strewn with hip cafes and top-notch bookstores. Telegraph Ave. remains Berkeley's commercial and social heart, home to street-corner soothsayers, hirsute hippies, and itinerant street musicians who never left.

CALIFORNIA

▐ GETTING THERE AND GETTING AROUND

Berkeley lies across the bay northeast of San Francisco, just north of Oakland. Reach the city by BART from downtown San Francisco or by car (I-80 or Rte. 24). Crossing the bay by BART ($2.70) is quick and easy; driving in the city is difficult and frustrating. The choice is yours.

Bay Area Rapid Transit (BART) (☎465-2278), has 2 Berkeley stops. The Downtown Berkeley station, 2160 Shattuck Ave., at Center St., is close to the western edge of campus, while the North Berkeley station, at Delaware and Sacramento St., lies 4 blocks north of University Ave. (to downtown SF 20-30min., $2.65).

Alameda County (AC) Transit (☎817-1717). Buses #15, 43, and 51 run from the Berkeley BART station to downtown Oakland on Martin Luther King, Jr. Way, Telegraph Ave., and Broadway, respectively. ($1; seniors, disabled, ages 5-12 65¢; under 5 free; 1hr. transfers 25¢.)

▐ PRACTICAL INFORMATION

Berkeley Convention and Visitor Bureau, 2015 Center St. (☎549-7040 or 800-847-4823), at Milvia St. Helpful street, park, and area maps. Usually open M-F 9am-5pm.

Internet Access: UC Computer, 2569 Telegraph Ave. (☎649-6089). $3 for 15min., $5 for 30min., $7 per hr. Open M-Sa 10am-6pm.

Post Office: 2000 Allston Way (☎649-3100), at Milvia St. Open M-F 8:30am-6pm, Sa 10am-2pm. **ZIP code:** 94704. **Area code:** 510.

ACCOMMODATIONS

There are surprisingly few cheap accommodations in Berkeley. **The Oakland Bed and Breakfast Network** (☎547-6380) coordinates 20 East Bay B&Bs with a range of rates. A popular option is to stay in San Francisco and make daytrips to Berkeley.

UC Berkeley Summer Visitor Housing (☎642-5925; www.housing.berkeley.edu). Visitors housed in **Stern Hall**, 2700 Hearst Ave., at Highland St. Shared baths, free Internet access, local phone calls, games, and TV room. Parking ($3 per day), laundry (wash 75¢), meals, and photocopying. Open June to mid-Aug. Singles $44; doubles $57.

Capri Motel, 1512 University Ave. (☎845-7090), at Sacramento St. Clean, tasteful rooms with cable TV, A/C, and microfridge. Singles $55-70, doubles $70-100; in winter $45-50/$55-70.

YMCA, 2001 Allston Way (☎848-6800), at Milvia St. Adequate but worn rooms in co-ed hotel portion of this YMCA. Shared bath. Use of pool and fitness facilities included. In-room phones for incoming calls; pay phones in hall. 4-night maximum stay; special applications available for longer stays. Reception daily 8am-9:30pm. Singles $38; doubles $50; triples $65. *Must be 18+ with ID.*

FOOD

The north end of **Telegraph Ave.** caters to student appetites and wallets with a high concentration of pizza joints and trendy cafes. If you've maxed out on caffeine and have a car, head out to **Solano Ave.** in Albany to the north for Asian cuisine or cruise down to **San Pablo Ave.** in the west for American fare. If you want to make your own meals, the best grocery shopping in the bay awaits at **Berkeley Bowl**, 2777 Shattuck Ave., at Stuart St., a former bowling alley filled with fresh produce, seafood, and bread. (☎843-6929. Open M-Sa 9:30am-8pm, Su 10am-6pm.)

Cafe Intermezzo, 2442 Telegraph Ave. (☎849-4592), at Haste St. This veggie-lover's paradise serves heaping salads, huge sandwiches on freshly baked bread, and tasty soups. Salad and sandwich combo $4. Sandwiches $4; salads $3-6. Open M-F 10:30am-9pm; coffee from 8:30am.

Ann's Soup Kitchen, 2498 Telegraph Ave. (☎548-8885), at Dwight St. Towering portions compensate for sometimes crowded dining. 2 eggs with toast or homefries $3. Open M and W-F 8am-6pm, Tu 8am-3pm, Sa-Su 8am-5pm.

Long Life Vegi House, 2129 University Ave. (☎845-6072), between Shattuck Ave. and Walnut St. Vast menu vegetable and "vegetarian meat" Chinese options. Huge portions; most entrees $5-7. Open M-Th and Su 11:30am-9:30pm, F-Sa 11:30am-10pm.

Oscar's, 1890 Shattuck Ave. (☎849-2164), at Hearst St. Unassuming hamburger shack justly lauded by locals. Cheeseburger $3. Open Su-Th 10am-midnight, F-Sa 10am-2am.

Vik's Chaat Corner, 726 Allston Way (☎644-4412). Take a left off University Ave. onto 6th St., then turn right onto Allston. *Chaat* is the term for greasy, spicy Indian roadside snacks, and Vik's is the deep-fried, chili-filled, customer-packed mother of all Bay Area *chaat* houses. Make a light meal of giant samosas or basketball-sized *puri*, both with side sauces ($3 per dish). Open Tu-Su 11am-6pm.

Kabna, 1106 University Ave (☎845-3355), at San Pablo Ave. A Pakistani hole-in-the-wall that locals adore. If you like South Asian food, it's well worth the walk from campus. Vegetarian dishes $5; lamb curry $6. Open daily 11am-3:30pm and 5-9:30pm.

SIGHTS

UC BERKELEY. In 1868, the private College of California and the public Agricultural, Mining, and Mechanical Arts College became one as the **University of California.** Berkeley was the first of the nine University of California campuses, so by seniority it has sole rights to the nickname "Cal." Pass through **Sather Gate** into **Sproul Plaza,** both sites of celebrated student sit-ins and bloody confrontations with police, to enter the 160-acre Berkeley campus. The Plaza, suspended between Berkeley's idyllic campus and raucous Telegraph Ave., is now a perfect place for people-watching. Maps of campus are posted everywhere; the **UC Berkeley Visitors Center,** also sells campus maps and offers campus tours which leave from the center M-F at 10am. *(101 University Hall, 2200 University Ave. ☎ 642-5215. Open M-F 8:30am-4:30pm. Tours Sa 10am and Su 1pm.)* Tours leave from **Sather Tower,** the tallest building on campus. You can ride to its observation level for a great view. *(Open M-F 8:30am-4:30pm. $1.)*

The **Lawrence Hall of Science,** on Centennial Dr., atop the eucalyptus-covered hills east of the main campus, is one of the finest science museums in the Bay Area. Take bus #8 or 65 from the Berkeley BART station (and keep your transfer for $1 off admission) or a university shuttle (☎ 642-5132); otherwise it's a long, steep walk. *(☎ 642-5132. Open daily 10am-5pm. $6; seniors, students, and ages 7-18 $4; ages 3-6 $2.)*

You haven't really visited Berkeley until you've been on **Telegraph Ave.** which runs south from Sproul Plaza all the way to downtown Oakland. The action is near the university, where Telegraph Ave. is lined with a motley assortment of cafes, bookstores, and used clothing and record stores. Businesses come and go by the whims of the marketplace, but the scene, a rowdy jumble of 1960s and 1990s counterculture, abides.

TILDEN REGIONAL PARK. When you're ready to get out of town, Berkeley is happy to oblige. Tilden Regional Park, in the pine- and eucalyptus-forested hills east of the city, is the anchor of the extensive East Bay park system. *(☎ 635-0135. By car or bicycle, take Spruce St. to Grizzly Peak Blvd., then to Canon Ave. AC Transit buses #7 and 8 run from the Berkeley BART station to the park entrance at Grizzly Peak Blvd. and Golf Course Dr. Open daily dawn-dusk.)* Hiking, biking, running, and riding trails crisscross the park and provide impressive views of the Bay Area. The **ridgeline trail** is an especially spectacular bike ride. Within the park, a 19th-century carousel delights juvenile thrill-seekers. The small, sandy beach of **Lake Anza** is a popular swimming spot during the summer, often overrun with squealing kids. *(☎ 848-3385. Open 11am-6pm. $3, seniors and children $1.50.)*

ENTERTAINMENT AND NIGHTLIFE

The university offers a number of quality entertainment options. Hang out with procrastinating students in or around the **Student Union** (☎ 643-0693). **The Underground** contains a ticket office, an arcade, bowling alleys, foosball tables, and pool tables, all run from a central blue desk. (☎ 642-3825. Open M-F noon-8pm, Sa 10am-6pm.) **Caffe Strada,** 2300 College Ave., at Bancroft, is a glittering jewel of the caffeine-fueled-intellectual scene. (☎ 843-5282. Open daily 6:30am-midnight.) **Spats,** 1974 Shattuck Ave., between University and Berkeley, lures locals and students with the warmth of the staff, the original drinks (Danko Bar Screamer $5.75), and the quirky surroundings. (☎ 841-7225. Open M-F 11:30am-2am, Sa 4pm-2am.) **924 Gilman,** 924 Gilman St., at 8th, is a legendary all-ages club and a staple of California punk. (☎ 524-8180; 24hr. info 525-9926. Cover $5 with $2 membership card, good for 1 year and sold at the door.)

OAKLAND   ☎ 510

Long-suffering Oakland sings the blues. In the 30s and 40s, Oakland's black majority gave birth to the sound that came to be known as the West Coast blues. Sometimes the city's sound has been more overtly political. In the 60s, North and West Oakland were the proving ground for violent revolutionary movements like the Black Panthers. Today, Oakland's City Center and Jack London Square smell like urban renewal, with crisp office buildings and clean streets.

ORIENTATION AND PRACTICAL INFORMATION. Drivers can take **I-80** from San Francisco across the Bay Bridge to **I-580** and connect with Oakland **I-980 S,** which has downtown exits at 12th St. and 19th St. **Bay Area Rapid Transit (BART)** (☎ 465-2278) provides another option, running from downtown San Francisco to Oakland's stations at **Lake Merritt** (Dublin/Pleasanton or Fremont trains), **12th St.** (Richmond or Pittsburg/Bay Point trains), or **19th St.** (Richmond or Pittsburg/Bay

Point trains). **Port of Oakland Information Booth** (☎272-4864), on Broadway in Jack London Sq., under the Barnes and Noble bookstore. **Area code:** 510.

▐▝▙ ACCOMMODATIONS AND FOOD. Cheap and safe accommodations are nearly non-existent in Oakland. Food options include ◙**Lois the Pie Queen,** 851 60th St., North Oakland, at Adeline St. Down-home breakfasts ($3-6) and diner standards (burgers, root beer floats) are popular, but pastry made Lois the Queen. (☎658-5616. Open M-F 8am-2pm, Sa 7am-3pm, Su 7am-4pm.) **The Red Tractor Cafe,** 5634 College Ave., 1 block from Rockridge BART station, serves wholesome heartland food. (☎595-3500. Open M-F 11:30am-9pm, Sa-Su 9am-9pm. Dishes $5-9.)

▐▞▟ ENTERTAINMENT AND SIGHTS. The best reason to visit is to catch some live music: whether they're playing the West Coast blues, Oaktown hip-hop, or progressive jazz, Oakland's music venues are unsurpassed. **Koncepts Cultural Gallery** is not a venue but an organization that hosts some of the most groundbreaking progressive jazz sessions (☎763-0682. Cover $5-25.) ◙**Eli's Mile High Club,** 3629 Martin Luther King Jr. Way, is the home of the West Coast blues. (☎655-6661. Soul food kitchen opens at 7pm; music starts by 10pm. Cover $5-10.) Not the most famous, just the best, jazz and blues musicians take the stage at **The Fifth Amendment,** 3255 Lakeshore Ave., at Lake Park. (☎832-3242. Shows start at 9pm. No cover.) **Yoshi's,** 510 Embarcadero, at Jack London Sq., is not cutting-edge, but it's still an upscale Oakland institution, bringing together world-class sushi and jazz. (☎238-9200. Shows M-Sa 8 and 10pm, Su 2 and 8pm. Box office open daily 10am-11pm. $5-30.)

Outside of Oakland's music scene, the most impressive sight is probably the **Oakland Museum of California,** 1000 Oak St. at 10th, on the southwest side of the lake near the Lake Merritt BART station. A complex of three museums devoted to California's history, art, and ecology, the Museum's highlights include photography by Edward Weston and Dorothea Lange, quick-snap panoramic photos of San Francisco by Eadweard Muybridge, and multicultural modern works. (☎238-2200. Open W-Sa 10am-5pm, Su noon-5pm; 1st F of each month open until 9pm. $6, students and seniors $4; 2nd Su of each month free.) The **Ebony Museum of Art,** 208-209 Jack London Village, combines African and African-American art and artifacts with images from two centuries of pop culture. (☎763-0745. Open Tu-Sa 11am-6pm, Su noon-5pm. Free.)

SAN JOSE   ☎408

In 1851, San Jose was deemed too small to be California's capital, and Sacramento assumed the honors. Today, San Jose is the civic heart of the Silicon Valley and the fastest-growing city in California. The FBI named it the 3rd-safest city in the country, and taking a trip to San Jose is like taking a trip through a mental image of 50s suburbia.

▐▞▟ ORIENTATION AND PRACTICAL INFORMATION. San Jose lies at the southern end of San Francisco Bay, about 50 mi. from San Francisco (via U.S. 101 or I-280) and 40 mi. from Oakland (via I-880). San Jose is centered around the convention-hosting malls and plazas near the intersection of east-west **San Carlos St.** and north-south **Market St. San Jose International Airport** is at 1661 Airport Blvd. (☎277-4759). **Amtrak,** 65 Cahill St. (☎287-7462), runs to San Francisco (2hr., 1 per day, $9) and Los Angeles (10½hr., 1 per day, $77). **CalTrain,** 65 Cahill St., at W. San Fernando, runs to San Francisco (1½hr.; ☎291-5651 or 800-660-4287; every hr. M-F 5am-10pm, Sa 6:30am-10pm, Su 7:30am-10pm) with stops at peninsula cities. **Greyhound,** 70 S. Almaden, at Santa Clara, buses to San Francisco (1hr., $6.50) and Los Angeles (7hr., $37). **Bay Area Rapid Transit (BART)** (☎510-441-2278) goes to San Francisco (1¼hr., $4.05). **Visitor Information and Business Center:** in the San Jose McEnerny Convention Center at San Carlos and Market St. Free maps. (☎977-0900, events line 295-2265. Open M-F 8am-5:30pm, Sa-Su 11am-5pm.) **Post Office:** 105 N. 1st St. Open M-F 9am-5:30pm. **ZIP code:** 95113. **Area code:** 408.

⚑⚑⚑ ACCOMMODATIONS, FOOD, AND NIGHTLIFE. San Jose is surrounded by county parks with campgrounds. The idyllic hamlet of **Saratoga,** 14 mi. southwest of San Jose on Rte. 85, has a number of campsites (open Apr. to mid-Oct.; tent sites $8; RVs $25) and mi. of horse and hiking trails in wooded **Sanborn-Skyline County Park** (☎867-9959, reservations 358-3751), on Sanborn Rd. From Rte. 17 S, take Rte. 9 to Big Basin Way. Along the way sits **Saratoga Springs,** a private campground with 32 sites, hot showers, and a general store. (☎867-9999. $25 for 2 people, $30 for RV.) **Sanborn Park Hostel (HI-AYH),** 15808 Sanborn Rd., in Sanborn-Skyline Park, 13 mi. west of San Jose, has dorms. (☎741-0166. $10, US non-members $12, foreign non-members $13; under 18 $5.) **San Jose State University,** 375 S. 9th St., at San Salvador, opens to visitors June to early Aug. (☎924-6192. Single $20, double $30.)

House of Siam, 55 S. Market St., serves excellent $7-10 meat and meatless dishes. (☎279-5668. Open M-F 11am-3pm and 5-10pm, Sa-Su 11:30am-10pm). **La Guadalajara,** 45 Post St., has been serving delicious Mexican food and pastries since 1955. (☎298-7768. Open daily 7:30am-8pm. Jumbo burritos $3.25.) **White Lotus,** 80 N. Market St., between Santa Clara and St. John, is one of the few vegetarian restaurants in the area. (☎977-0540. Open M-Th 11am-2:30pm and 5:30-9pm, F-Sa 11am-9:30pm, Su noon-9pm.) A wacky jukebox suits the fly clientele of **The Flying Pig Pub,** 78 S. 1st St. This mega-chill bistro serves drinks from its full bar, as well as food. (☎298-6710. Open M 3pm-2am, Tu-F 11am-2am, Sa 4pm-2am.)

▣ SIGHTS. The **Tech Museum of Innovation,** in downtown San Jose, is the closest thing to a Silicon Valley tourist attraction. Underwritten by area high-tech firms, "the Tech" features hands-on exhibits on robotics, DNA engineering, and space exploration. *(201 S. Market St. ☎294-8324. Open daily 10am-5pm. $9, students, seniors, and ages 3-12 $7.)* Science-based toys also grace the **Children's Discovery Museum.** *(180 Woz Way. ☎298-5437. Open Tu-Sa 10am-5pm, Su noon-5pm. $6, seniors $5).* The **Rosicrucian Egyptian Museum** rises out of the suburbs like the work of a mad pharaoh. *(1342 Naglee Ave., at Park Ave. ☎947-3635. Open Tu-Su 10am-5pm. $7, students and seniors $5, ages 6-15 $3.50. Under 15 must be accompanied by an adult.)*

PALO ALTO   ☎650

Well-manicured Palo Alto looks a lot like "Collegeland" in a Disney-esque theme park. Jane and Leland Stanford founded the secular, co-educational **Stanford University** in 1885, to honor a son who died of typhoid on a family trip to Italy. The Stanfords loved Spanish architecture and collaborated with Frederick Law Olmsted, designer of New York City's Central Park, to create a red-tiled campus of uncompromising beauty. Berkeley students sometimes refer to Stanford as "the World's Largest Taco Bell."

⚏⚐ ORIENTATION AND PRACTICAL INFORMATION. Palo Alto is 35 mi. southeast of San Francisco, near the southern shore of the bay. From the north, take **U.S. 101** to the University Ave. exit, or take the Embarcadero Rd. exit directly to the Stanford campus. Alternatively, motorists from San Francisco can split off onto the **Junípero Serra Hwy. (I-280)** for a slightly longer but more scenic route. Palo Alto-bound trains also leave from San Francisco's **CalTrain** station, at 4th and King. (Run M-F 5am-midnight, Sa 7am-midnight, Su 8am-10pm. Fare $3.25; seniors, disabled and children $1.75; off-peak hrs. $2.50.) The **Palo Alto Transit Center** on University Ave., serves local and regional buses and trains. (☎323-6105. Open daily 5am-12:30am.) There is a train-only depot on California Ave., 1¼ mi. south of the Transit Center. (☎326-3392. Open daily 5:30am-12:30am.) The Transit Center connects to points south via **San Mateo County buses** and to the Stanford campus by the free **Marguerite University Shuttle. Alto Chamber of Commerce:** 325A Forest Ave. (☎324-3121. Open M-F 9am-noon and 1-5pm.) **Stanford University Information Booth:** across from Hoover Tower in Memorial Auditorium. Free student-led tours depart daily 11am and 3:15pm; times vary on holidays and during exam periods. (☎723-2053 or 723-2560. Open daily 8am-5pm.) **Area code:** 650.

╓╥ ACCOMMODATIONS AND FOOD. Hidden Villa Ranch Hostel (HI-AYH), 26870 Moody Rd., is about 10 mi. southwest of Palo Alto in Los Altos Hills. (☎949-8648. Reception 7:30-9:30am and 4:30-9pm. Open Sept.-May. 35 beds; dorms $10.) About half of Stanford's social life happens at **The Coffee House,** in Tresidder Union, the Stanford student center, in the heart of campus. (☎723-3592. Open term-time M-F 10am-11pm, Sa-Su 10am-midnight; in summer daily 10am-7pm.) The **Mango Cafe,** 435 Hamilton Ave., one block east of University Ave., boasts reggae music, fan-backed wicker chairs, and Caribbean cuisine. (☎325-3229. Open M-Th 6-9:30pm, F 11:30am-2pm and 6-10pm, Sa 6-10pm.)

╓╥ SIGHTS AND ENTERTAINMENT. The oldest part of campus is the colonnaded **Main Quadrangle,** the site of most undergraduate classes. Chipper student tour guides will point to other quirky Stanford tidbits on twice-daily tours. **Memorial Church** (☎723-1762), in the Main Quad, is a non-denominational gold shrine with stained glass windows and glittering mosaic walls like those of an Eastern Orthodox church. East of the Main Quad, the observation deck in **Hoover Tower** has views of campus, the East Bay, and San Francisco. (☎723-2053 or 723-2560. Open daily 10am-5pm. $2, seniors and under 13 $1.) The **Iris and B. Gerald Cantor Center for Visual Arts,** on Museum Way off Palm St. between the Main Quad and El Camino Real, displays its collection for free. (☎723-4177. Open W and F-Su 11am-5pm, Th 11am-8pm.)

SAN MATEO COAST ☎650

The rocky bluffs of the San Mateo County Coast quickly obscure the hectic urban pace of the city to the north. Most of the energy here is generated by the coastal winds and waves. The Pacific Coast Hwy. (Rte. 1) maneuvers its way through a rocky shoreline, colorful beach vistas, and generations-old ranches. Although it's possible to drive quickly down the coast from San Francisco to Santa Cruz, haste is waste—especially if you drive off a cliff.

Half Moon Bay is an old coastal community 29 mi. south of San Francisco. Recent commercialization has not infringed much on this small, easy-going beach town. The fishing and farming hamlet of **San Gregorio** rests 10 mi. south of Half Moon Bay. **San Gregorio Beach** is a delightful destination; you can walk to its southern end to find little caves in the shore rocks. (Open daily 8am-dusk; day use $4, seniors $3.)

The **Pigeon Point Lighthouse Hostel (HI-AYH),** is on Rte. 1, 6 mi. south of Pescadero and 20 mi. south of Half Moon Bay. (☎879-0633. Dorms $12, non-members $15; private rooms $22/$25. Call ahead.) **Point Montara Lighthouse Hostel (HI-AYH)** is on Lighthouse Point, 25 mi. south of San Francisco and 4 mi. north of Half Moon Bay. (☎728-7177. Dorms $12, non-members $15; private rooms $22/$25.) **The Flying Fish Grill,** at the corner of Main St. and Rte. 92, serves inexpensive, airborne seafood straight from the coast. (☎712-1125. Open in summer Tu-Su 11:30am-8:30pm; off-season until 7:30pm.) *The* social spot for locals is ▨**San Gregorio General Store,** 7615 Stage Rd., 1 mi. east of Rte. 1 on Rte. 84, 8 mi. south of Half Moon Bay. This quirky store has served San Gregorio since 1889 with an eclectic selection of hardware, cold drinks, groceries, gourmet coffee, cast iron pots, books, candles, and more. (☎726-0565. Open M-Th 9am-6pm, F-Su 9am-7pm.) **Area code:** 650.

MARIN COUNTY ☎415

Marin is physically beautiful, politically liberal, and stinking rich. If the new Beetle were sold nowhere but Marin (*muh-RIN*), Volkswagen would still reap a profit. The yuppie reincarnation of the quintessential hippie car strikes just the right chord of upscale chic and counterculture nostalgia to have taken this county by storm.

▛ GETTING THERE AND GETTING AROUND

The Marin peninsula lies at the northern end of the Bay and is connected to the city by **U.S. 101** via the **Golden Gate Bridge.** U.S. 101 extends north and inland to Santa

Rosa and Sonoma County, while **Rte. 1** winds north along the coast. The **Richmond-San Rafael Bridge** connects Marin to the East Bay via **Interstate 580.**

Buses: Golden Gate Transit (☎455-2000). M-F buses #20 and 50 serve Marin City and Sausalito from San Francisco's Transbay Terminal; Sa-Su buses #10 and 25 will take you there ($2.35, seniors and disabled $1.15, under 18 $1.75, under 6 free). Buses #20, 50 and 80 go to San Rafael. ($2.95, seniors and disabled $1.45, under 18 $2.25, under 6 free).

Ferries: Golden Gate Ferry (☎455-2000) runs from San Francisco to the Sausalito terminal at the end of Market St. ($5, seniors and disabled $2.50, under 18 $3.75, under 6 free), and the Larkspur terminal (M-F $2.95, seniors and disabled $1.45, under 18 $2.25, under 6 free; Sa-Su $5, seniors and disabled $2.50, under 18 $3.75). No bike fees. **Blue and Gold Ferry** (☎773-1188, tickets 705-5555) runs ferries from Pier 41 at Fisherman's Wharf to Sausalito and Tiburon ($6, under 5 free; bikes $1)

PRACTICAL INFORMATION

Visitor Information: Marin County Visitors Bureau, 1013 Larkspur Landing Circle (☎499-5000). Open M-F 9am-noon and 1-5pm. **Sausalito Visitors Center,** 780 Bridgeway Ave. (☎332-0505). Open Tu-Su 11:30am-4pm.

Park Visitor Information: Marin Headlands Visitors Center, Bldg. 948, Fort Barry, (☎331-1540), at Bunker and Field Rd. One of the best information centers in the Golden Gate National Recreation Area. Open daily 9:30am-4:30pm. **Point Reyes National Seashore Headquarters** (☎663-1092), on Bear Valley Rd., ½ mi. west of Olema. Open M-F 9am-5pm, Sa-Su 8am-5pm.

Post Office: 150 Harbor Dr., at Bridgeway Ave., in **Sausalito.** Open M-Th 8:30am-5pm, F 8:30am-5:30pm. **ZIP code:** 94965. 40 Bellam Blvd., at Francisco St. in **San Rafael.** Open M-F 8:30am-5pm, Sa 10am-1pm. **ZIP code:** 94901. **Area code:** 415.

ACCOMMODATIONS

Point Reyes Hostel (☎663-8811 or 800-909-4776, ext. 61), in the Pt. Reyes National Seashore. Exit west from Rte. 1 at Olema onto Bear Valley Rd. Take the 2nd possible left at Limantour Rd. (no sign indicates the turn) and drive 6 mi. into the park. Turn left at the 1st crossroad. 2 cabins occupy a site near Limantour Beach, wildlife areas, and hiking trails. Kitchen, barbecue, and cozy common room. Chores expected. Reception open 7:30-9:30am and 4:30-9:30pm. Check-in 4:30-9:30pm. Check-out and chores finished by 10am. Linen $1; towels $1. Dorms $13-15. Reservations recommended.

Marin Headlands Hostel, Bldg. 941 in old Fort Barry (☎331-2777 or 800-909-4776, ext. 62), up the hill from the visitors center and next to the Headlands Center for the Arts. Spacious and immaculate, with 109 beds, game room, kitchens, and common rooms. Linen $1, towels 50¢. Laundry $1.50. Key deposit $10. Check-in 7:30-10am and 3:30-11:30pm. Check-out 8:45am. Lockout 10am-3:30pm. Dorms $13-15, under 17 (with parent) $6.50; private doubles $39. Reservations with credit card.

The Marin Headlands (☎331-1540), offers 3 small walk-in (100 yd. to 3 mi.) campgrounds with a total of 11 primitive campsites for individual backpackers and small groups, as well as sights for large groups. In the backpack camps, picnic tables and chemical toilets are available. Bring your own water and camp stove. 3-day maximum stay. Showers and kitchen ($2 each) at Headlands Hostel. Free outdoor cold showers at Rodeo Beach. Reserve up to 90 days in advance. Groups sites $20.

FOOD

Marinites take their fruit juices, tofu, and nonfat double-shot cappuccinos very seriously; restaurateurs know this, and raise both the alfalfa sprouts and the prices. A number of cafes and pizzerias along **4th St.** in San Rafael, and **Miller Ave.** on the way into Mill Valley, provide welcome exceptions; others are listed below.

Sartaj Indian Cafe, 43 Caledonia St. (☎332-7103), 1 block from Bridgeway. Generous portions of excellent Indian food. Low prices (curries $8; samosas $1.75; sandwiches $3.75). Open daily 6:30am-9:30pm.

Mama's Royal Cafe, 387 Miller Ave. (☎388-3261). Unusual but wonderful dishes (Enchilada El Syd $7). Decorated with lawn ornaments and psychedelic murals. Entrees $7-11.50. Open M-F 7:30am-2:30pm, Sa-Su 8:30am-3pm.

Olema Liquor and Deli, 10003 Shoreline Hwy. (☎663-8615), at Sir Francis Drake Blvd. in Olema. Olema's budget option. Sandwiches ($3-5), liquor, rolling tobacco, fishing tackle, and Häagen-Dazs ice cream. Open Su-Th 8am-9pm, F-Sa 8am-10pm.

SIGHTS

Marin's proximity to San Francisco makes it a popular daytrip destination. Virtually everything worth seeing or doing in Marin is outdoors. An efficient visitor can hop from park to park and enjoy several short hikes along the coast and through the redwood forests in the same day, topping it off with a pleasant dinner in one of the small cities. Those without cars, however, may find it easier to use one of the two well-situated hostels as a base for explorations.

SAUSALITO

Originally a fishing center full of bars and bordellos, the city at Marin's extreme southeastern tip has long since traded its sea-dog days for retail boutiques and overpriced seafood restaurants. **Bridgeway** is the city's main thoroughfare, and practically the only one shown on Sausalito visitors center maps. A block away from the harbor and Bridgeway's smug shops, **Caledonia St.** offers more charming restaurants and a few more affordable stores. Perhaps the best thing to see in Sausalito is the view of San Francisco. For the best views of the city, take the ferry (see **Ferries,** p. 851) or bike across the Golden Gate Bridge. Half a mile north of the town center is the **Bay Model,** 2100 Bridgeway, a massive working model of San Francisco Bay. Built in the 50s to test proposals to dam the bay and other diabolical plans, the water-filled model re-creates tides and currents in great detail. (☎332-3871. Open Tu-F 9am-4pm, Sa 10am-6pm; off-season Tu-F 9am-4pm. Free.)

MARIN HEADLANDS

Fog-shrouded hills just to the west of the Golden Gate Bridge constitute the Marin Headlands. Its windswept ridges, precipitous cliffs, and hidden sandy beaches offer superb hiking and biking within minutes of downtown San Francisco. For instant gratification, choose one of the coastal trails, which offer easy access to dark sand beaches and dramatic cliffs of basalt greenstone. One of the best short hikes is to the lighthouse at **Point Bonita,** a prime spot for seeing sunbathing California sea lions in summer and migrating gray whales in the cooler months. The **Marine Mammal Center,** at Rodeo Beach, is dedicated to saving injured, sick, or orphaned marine mammals. (☎289-7325. Open daily 10am-4pm. Donation requested.) Also at Rodeo Beach, the **Golden Gate Raptor Observatory** studies the annual migration of thousand of hawks across the Marin Headlands each fall. (☎331-0730. Ideal hawk viewing Sept.-Oct. 10am-3pm.)

MT. TAMALPAIS, MUIR WOODS, AND POINT REYES

Between the upscale towns of East Marin and the rocky bluffs of West Marin rests beautiful **Mt. Tamalpais State Park** (*tam-ull-PIE-us*). The park has miles of hilly, challenging trails on and around 2571 ft. Mt. Tamalpais, the highest peak in the county and the original "mountain" in "mountain bike." At the center of the state park is **Muir Woods National Monument,** a 560-acre stand of primeval coastal redwoods, located about 5 mi. west of U.S. 101 along Rte. 1. Spared from logging by the steep sides of Redwood Canyon, these centuries-old redwoods are massive and enshrouded in silence. (Monument open daily 8am-sunset; visitors center 9am-6pm.)

Rte. 1 reaches the Pacific at Muir Beach and from there twists its way up the rugged coast. It's all beautiful, especially when driving south, on the sheer-drop-to-the-ocean side of the highway. Sheltered **Muir Beach** is scenic and popular with families. (Open daily dawn-9pm.) The crowds thin out significantly after a 5min. climb on the shore rocks to the left. Six mi. to the north, **Stinson Beach** attracts a younger, rowdier crowd of good-looking surfer dudes and dudettes, though cold and windy conditions often keep them landlocked. (Open daily dawn-dusk.)

A near-island surrounded by nearly 100 mi. of isolated coastline, the **Point Reyes National Seashore** is a wilderness of pine forests, chaparral ridges, and grassy flatlands. Rte. 1 provides direct access to the park from the north or south; Sir Francis Drake Blvd. comes west from U.S. 101 at San Rafael. After a day or ten exploring the seashore, the little town of **Point Reyes Station**, 2 mi. north of Olema on Rte. 1, makes a welcoming dinner destination. Point Reyes is a cow town, built on dairy farming, and its main streets look appropriately Western.

WINE COUNTRY

NAPA VALLEY   ☎707

While not the oldest, the Napa Valley is certainly the best-known of America's wine-growing regions. The gentle hills, fertile soil, ample moisture, and year-round sunshine are ideal for viticulture. During the 70s, Napa's rapidly improving offerings won the attention of those in the know, and word-of-mouth cemented the California bottle as a respectable choice. In 1976, a bottle of red from Napa's Stag's Leap Vineyard beat a bottle of Château Lafitte-Rothschild in a blind taste test in Paris, and American wine was suddenly *très* cool. Today, local vineyards continue to reap awards, and the everyday tasting carnival dominates life in the valley's small towns.

▐ GETTING THERE AND GETTING AROUND

Rte. 29 (St. Helena Hwy.) runs through the Napa Valley from **Napa** through **Yountville** and **St. Helena** to **Calistoga.** Slow with visitors stopping at each winery, the relatively short distance takes a surprisingly long, if scenic, time. The **Silverado Trail,** parallel to Rte. 29, is a less crowded route, but watch out for cyclists. Napa is 14 mi. east of Sonoma on **Rte. 12.** From the city, take U.S. 101 over the Golden Gate, then Rte. 37 E to Rte. 121 N, which will cross Rte. 12 N (to Sonoma) and Rte. 29 (to Napa). The nearest **Greyhound** station is in Vallejo, but one bus per day passes through the valley, stopping in Napa (6:15pm, Napa State Hospital, 2100 Napa-Vallejo Hwy.), Yountville, St. Helena, and Calistoga. **Public Transportation: Napa City Bus,** or **Valley Intercity Neighborhood Express (VINE),** 1151 Pearl St., covers the Vallejo (fare $1.50, students $1.10, disabled 75¢) and Calistoga ($2/$1.45/$1); transfers are free. (☎800-696-6443 or 255-7631, TDD 226-9722. Buses run M-F 6:30am-6pm, Sa 7:30am-5:30pm.) **Car Rental: Budget,** 407 Soscol Ave., Napa. (☎224-7846. From $35 per day; under 26 surcharge $20. Unlimited mi. Must be 21+ with credit card).

✴▐ ORIENTATION AND PRACTICAL INFORMATION

On Sa mornings and Su afternoons the roads are packed with cars traveling from San Francisco. Although harvest, in early Sept., is the most exciting time to visit, winter weekdays provide space for personal attention. **Winery tours** are offered by **Napa Valley Wine Shuttle,** 3031 California Blvd. (☎800-258-8226; day pass $30, children free), and **Napa Valley Holidays** (☎255-1050; 3hr., $30). **Visitor Info: Napa Visitors Center,** 1310 Town Center. (☎226-7459. Open daily 9am-5pm, phones closed Sa-Su.) **St. Helena Chamber of Commerce,** 1010A Main St. (☎963-4456. Open M-F 10am-4:30pm.) **Calistoga Chamber of Commerce,** 1458 Lincoln Ave. (☎942-6333. Open M-F 9am-5pm, Sa 10am-4:30pm, Su 11am-4pm.) **Post office:** 1351 2nd St., Napa. (☎255-1268. Open M-F 8:30am-5pm.) **ZIP code:** 94559. **Area code:** 707.

▐▚ ACCOMMODATIONS AND CAMPGROUNDS

Rooms in Napa are scarce and go fast despite high prices. Camping is a good alternative, although the heat can be intense in summer.

Calistoga Ranch Club, 580 Lommel Rd. (☎800-847-6272), 4 mi. off the Silverado Trail, south of Calistoga. Campground caters to families. Hiking trails lace 167 wooded acres, which include a fishing lake, volleyball, and pool. Sites $20, with full hook-up $27; 4-person cabins with shared bath $49; 5-person trailers with kitchen $89.

Discovery Inn, 500 Silverado Trail (☎253-0892), near Soscol Ave., in Napa. Rooms have kitchenettes, cable TV, and personality. Check-in noon-6pm. M-Th $70, F-Su $100.

Bothe-Napa Valley State Park, 3801 Rte. 29 (☎942-4575, reservations 800-444-7275), north of St. Helena. 50 sites near Ritchey Creek Canyon often full. 1 site fully wheelchair accessible. No hook-ups. Pool $3, under 18 $2. Rustic, but hot showers. Check-in 2pm. Park open 8am-dusk. Su-Th $15, F-Sa $20; seniors $14; vehicles $5.

▐ FOOD

Eating in Wine Country ain't cheap, but the food is usually worth it. Picnics are an inexpensive and romantic option—supplies can be bought at the numerous delis or Safeway stores in the area. Most wineries have shaded picnic grounds, often with excellent views. The **Napa farmer's market,** at Pearl and West St., offers a sampling of the valley's *other* produce. (☎252-7142. Open daily 7:30am-noon.)

Curb Side Cafe, 1245 1st St. (☎253-2307), at Randolph St., in Napa. Sublime sandwiches $6-7. This diner-like cafe's heavy breakfasts include the pancake special: 2 buttermilk pancakes, 2 eggs, and ham or sausage $7. Open daily 9am-4pm.

Calistoga Natural Foods and Juice Bar, 1426 Lincoln St. (☎942-5822), in Calistoga. One of few natural foods stores in the area. Organic juice and sandwich bar with vegetarian specialties like the Garlic Goddess ($5). Open M-Sa 9am-6pm, Su 10am-5pm.

Ana's Cantina, 1205 Main St. (☎963-4921) at Spring St., in St. Helena. A glimmer of nightlife in a quiet town. Nightly music or karaoke, great Mexican food 11am-9pm, and pool tables. Combo platters $7. Open daily 10am-2am. 21+.

WINERIES

There are more than 250 wineries in Napa County, nearly two-thirds of which line Rte. 29 and the Silverado Trail in the Napa Valley. Wine Country's heavyweights call this valley home; vineyards include national names such as Inglenook, Fetzer, and Mondavi. Few wineries in Napa have free tastings, so choose your samples carefully. The smaller name vineyards are in general friendlier. Visitors must be 21 or older to taste or purchase alcohol (yes, they do card).

◪ V. Sattui, 1111 White Lane (☎963-7774 or 800-799-2337), at Rte. 29 in Calistoga. One of the best kept secrets of Napa Valley, it is one of the handful of wineries in the nation that only sells at its winery. The family-owned operation has an exceptionally friendly and helpful staff that will treat you right whether you're 21 or 71. Picnic area. Free tastings. Open daily Mar.-Oct. 9am-6pm; Nov.-Feb. 9am-5pm.

Domaine Chandon, 1 California Dr. (☎944-2280), in Yountville. Owned by Moët Chandon (the makers of Dom Perignon), this winery produces 5 million bottles of sparkling wine annually. Tours (every hr. 11am-5pm) and tastings ($8 for 3 wines, $12 for all 5). Open May-Oct. M-Tu 10am-6pm, W-Su 10am-8pm; Nov.-Apr. W-Su 10am-6pm.

Robert Mondavi Winery, 7801 Rte. 29 (☎963-9611 or 800-666-3284), 8 mi. north of Napa in Oakville. This triangular winery offers some of the best tours in the valley, covering subjects from tasting to soil conditions. Call for tour times. Wine by the glass from $3. Open daily 9am-5pm.

Hakusan Sake Gardens, 1 Executive Way (☎258-6160 or 800-425-8726), in Napa. Take Hwy. 12 off Rte. 29, turn left on N. Kelly, then left onto Executive Way. Japanese gardens offer a welcome change of pace. Try the *sake,* a strong Japanese wine with a fruity taste. Open daily 10am-5pm.

TASTING 101 While European wines are often known by their region of origin, California wines are generally known by the type of grape from which they are made. California **white** wines include Chardonnay, Riesling, and Sauvignon Blanc; **reds** are Pinot Noir, Merlot, Cabernet Sauvignon, and Zinfandel, which is indigenous to California. **Blush** or **rosé** wines issue from red grapes that have had their skins removed during fermentation–to leave just a kiss of pink. **Dessert** wines, such as Muscat, are made with grapes that have acquired the "noble rot" *(botrytis)* at the end of picking season, giving them an extra-sweet flavor.

When tasting, be sure to follow proper procedures. Always start with a white, moving from **dry** to **sweet.** Proceed through the reds, which go from **lighter** to more **full-bodied,** depending on tannin content. You should cleanse your palate between wines with a biscuit, some *fromage,* or fruit. Tasting proceeds thus: stare, sniff, swirl, swallow (first three steps are optional). You'll probably encounter tasters who slurp their wine and make concerned faces, as though they're trying to cram the stuff up their noses with the back of their tongues. These are serious tasters, and are aerating the wine in their mouths to better bring out the flavor. Key words to help you seem more astute during tasting sessions are: dry, sweet, buttery, light, crisp, fruity, balanced, rounded, subtle, rich, woody, and complex. Feel free to banter these terms about.

SIGHTS AND OUTDOOR ACTIVITIES

Napa's gentle terrain makes for an excellent bike tour. The 26 mi. **Silverado Trail** has a wider bike path than Rte. 29. **Yountville** and **Saint Helena,** which lie between the busy city of **Napa** and the soothing spas of **Calistoga,** are very similar, ritzy towns that both host several small restaurants and trendy shops. **⬛St. Helena Cyclery** rents bikes. *(1156 Main St. ☎963-7736. Open M-Sa 9:30am-5:30pm, Su 10am-5pm. $7 per hr., $25 per day with maps, helmet, lock, and picnic bag.)*

The annual **Napa Valley Wine Festival** takes place in Nov. Every weekend in Feb. and Mar. the **Mustard Festival** puts together a different musical or theatrical presentation. The **Napa Valley Fairgrounds** hosts a weekend fair in August, with wine tasting, music, juggling, rides, and a rodeo. *(☎942-5111.)* In summer, there are free afternoon concerts at **Music-in-the-Park,** downtown at the riverfront.

CALISTOGA. Calistoga is also known as the "Hot Springs of the West." After a hard day of wine-tasting, the rich and relaxed converge on Calistoga to luxuriate in mud baths, massages, and mineral showers. Prices are as high as the water temperatures, hitting $80 in many spas. Massage your wallet by sticking to **Nance's Hot Springs.** *(☎942-6211. 30min. massage $25.)* **Golden Haven,** which specializes in private couple baths, is known to be one of the less pretentious. *(☎942-6793. 30min. massage 30min. $45; 30min. facial 30min. $45; also has hot springs.)* Cooler water is at **Lake Berryessa,** 20 mi. north of Napa off Hwy. 128, where swimming, sailing, and sunbathing are popular along its 169 mi. of shoreline. *(☎966-2111.)*

OLD FAITHFUL GEYSER OF CALIFORNIA. This steamy wonder should not be confused with its more famous namesake in Wyoming, although it performs similarly—it's one of only three Old Faithful geysers in the world. The geyser regularly jets boiling water 60 ft. into the air about every 40min. *(On Tubbs Ln. off Hwy. 128., 2 mi. outside Calistoga. ☎942-6463. Open daily 9am-6pm; in winter 9am-5pm. $6, seniors $5, disabled free, ages 6-12 $2.)*

MARINE WORLD AFRICA/USA. This 160-acre Vallejo attraction is an enormous zoo-oceanarium-theme park. It has animal shows and special attractions like the Lorikeet Aviary, the Butterfly Walk, and the Shark Experience, which provides patron-fish interaction. *(Off Rte. 37, 10 mi. south of Napa. ☎643-6722. Vallejo is accessible from San Francisco by BART ☎510-465-2278 and the Blue and Gold fleet ☎415-705-5444. Open daily Mar.-Aug. 10am-10pm; Sept.-Oct. F-Su 10am-6pm. $34, seniors $25, ages 4-12 or under 48 in. $17. Parking $6. Wheelchair accessible.)*

ST. HELENA. The hike up Mt. St. Helena is a moderate 3hr. climb culminating in dizzying views of the valley. There is no ranger station or facilities; bring water. *(Open daily 8am-dusk.)* **Robert Louis Stevenson State Park** has a plaque where the Scottish writer, sick and penniless, spent a rejuvenating honeymoon in 1880. *(On Rte. 29, 4 mi. north of St. Helena. ☎942-4575.)* The **Silverado Museum** is a labor of love created by a devoted collector of Stevenson memorabilia. Manuscript notes from *Dr. Jekyll and Mr. Hyde* are on display. *(1490 Library Ln., off Adams St. ☎963-3757. Open Tu-Su noon-4pm. Free.)*

SONOMA VALLEY ☎707

The sprawling Sonoma Valley is a quieter alternative to Napa. Wineries are approachable via winding side roads rather than down a freeway strip, making for a more intimate and adventurous feel. Less straggling than Napa's strip of small towns, the valley showcases a beautiful, expansive eight-acre plaza in the town of Sonoma. Petaluma, which is west of the Sonoma Valley, has a better variety of budget lodgings than the expensive wine country.

▐ GETTING THERE AND GETTING AROUND

From San Francisco, take **U.S. 101** over the Golden Gate Bridge, then follow Rte. 37 E to Hwy. 121 N, which crosses Hwy. 12 N to Sonoma. Alternatively, follow U.S. 101 N to Petaluma, then cross over to Sonoma by Hwy. 116. Allow one to 1½hr. from San Francisco. **Hwy. 12** traverses the length of Sonoma Valley, from **Sonoma** to **Kenwood** in the north. The center of downtown Sonoma is **Sonoma Plaza**, which contains City Hall and the Visitors Center. **Broadway** dead-ends in front of City Hall at Napa St. The numbered streets run north-south. **Petaluma** lies to the west and is connected to Sonoma by **Rte. 116,** which becomes **Lakeville St.** in Petaluma.

Public Transportation: Sonoma County Transit (☎576-7433 or 800-345-7433) serves the entire county, from Petaluma to Cloverdale and the Russian River. **Golden Gate Transit** (☎541-2000 from Sonoma County, 415-923-2000 from SF, TDD 257-4554) runs buses frequently between SF and Santa Rosa. **Volunteer Wheels** (☎800-992-1006) offers door-to-door service for the disabled. Open daily 8am-5pm.

Bike Rental: Sonoma Valley Cyclery, 20093 Broadway (☎935-3377), in Sonoma. Bikes $6 per hr., $25 per day. Open M-Sa 10am-6pm, Su 10am-4pm. **Bicycle Factory,** 110 Kentucky St. (☎763-7515), in downtown Petaluma. Mountain bikes $8 per hr., $22 per day. Helmet included. Major ID or credit card required as deposit. Open M-F 10am-6:30pm, Sa 9am-5pm, Su 10am-4pm.

Taxis: A-1 Taxi of Petaluma, ☎763-3393.

▌ PRACTICAL INFORMATION

Visitor Information: Sonoma Valley Visitors Bureau, 453 E. 1st St. (☎996-1090), in Sonoma Plaza. Maps $2. Open daily June-Oct. 9am-7pm; Nov.-May 9am-5pm. **Petaluma Visitors Program,** 799 Baywood Dr. (☎769-0429), at Lakeville St. Open May-Oct. M-F 9am-5:30pm, Sa-Su 10am-6pm; shorter hours off-season.

Crisis Lines: Sonoma Valley Crisis Line, ☎938-9357. Open 24hr. **Crisis Line for the Handicapped,** ☎800-426-4263.

Hospital: Petaluma Valley, 400 N. McDowell Blvd. (☎781-1111).

Post Office: Sonoma: 617 Broadway, at Patten St. Open M-F 8:30am-5pm. **Petaluma:** 120 4th St. Open M-F 8:30am-5:30pm, Sa 10am-2pm. **ZIP code:** 95476 in Sonoma; 94952 in Petaluma. **Area code:** 707.

▐▐ ACCOMMODATIONS AND CAMPGROUNDS

Pickings are pretty slim for lodging; rooms are scarce even on weekdays and generally start at $75. Cheaper motels cluster along **U.S. 101** in Santa Rosa and Petaluma.

Motel 6, 1368 N. McDowell Blvd. (☎765-0333), off U.S. 101, in Petaluma. Spacious and tastefully decorated. Cable TV. Well-maintained pool open 9am-9pm. Reservations recommended weekends. M-Th and Su singles $45, doubles $51. F-Sa $48/$54. Each additional adult $3. Under 17 free with family.

Sugarloaf Ridge State Park, 2605 Adobe Canyon Rd. (☎833-5712), off Hwy. 12, north of Kenwood. 50 sites around a meadow. Flush toilets and running water, but no showers. M-Th and Su sites $15, for seniors $13; F-Sa $16, $14. Reserve through ReserveAmerica (☎800-444-7275; www.reserveamerica.com).

◖ FOOD

Fresh produce is seasonally available directly from area farms or at roadside stands and farmer's markets. *Farm Trails* maps are free at the Sonoma Valley Visitors Bureau. The **Sonoma Market,** 520 W. Napa St., in the Sonoma Valley Center, is an old-fashioned grocery store with deli sandwiches ($4-6) and *very* fresh produce. (☎996-0563. Open daily 7am-9pm.)

▨ **Quinley's,** 310 D St. (☎778-6000), in Petaluma. This hugely popular burger counter first opened its doors in 1952, and that old-time rock 'n' roll plays on. Outdoor bar and picnic tables. Burgers $4-5; 4-scoop shake or malt $3. Open M-Th 11am-9pm, F-Sa 11am-10pm, Su 11am-6pm.

Sonoma Cheese Factory, 2 Spain St. (☎996-1931 or 800-535-2855), in Sonoma. Forget the *vino* for now—take a toothpick and enjoy the free cheese samples. You can even watch the cheese-making process in the back room. Sandwiches $4.50-5.50. Open daily 8:30am-5:30pm.

WINERIES

Sonoma Valley's wineries, near Sonoma and Kenwood, are less touristy but just as elegant as Napa's. Most of the tastings in the Sonoma Valley are complimentary. Near Sonoma, white signs will help guide you through backroads. Bring a map along on the ride, as the signs will often desert you when they're most needed.

Buena Vista, 18000 Old Winery Rd. (☎800-926-1266), off E. Napa St. in Sonoma. The oldest winery in the valley. Famous old stone buildings are preserved just as Mr. Haraszthy built them in 1857, when he founded the California wine industry. Theatrical performances July-Sept. Historical presentations in summer at 2pm. Self-guided tours. Free tastings daily 10:30am-5pm.

Glen Ellen Winery, 14301 Arnold Dr. (☎939-6277), in Jack London Village, 1 mi. from Glen Ellen. Nearby cafes have *très cher* food to enjoy at picnic tables outside. Adjacent olive press with oil tasting. Open daily 10am-5pm. The winery expects to relocate soon, and to reopen by spring 2001; call 939-6200 for the new location.

Kenwood, 9592 Sonoma Hwy. (☎833-5891), in Kenwood. One of the few wineries in the region that uses organic grapes, Kenwood prides itself on its attention to the environment. Free tastings, with recipe samples Sa-Su noon-4pm. Tours daily at 11:30am and 2:30pm. Open M-F 10am-4:30pm.

Ravenswood, 18701 Gehricke Rd. (☎938-1960), in Sonoma. Edgar Allen Poe himself would have approved of their red Zinfandels, which are often described as "gothic." Fabulous wines produced by a surprisingly light-hearted group who believe "wine should also be fun." Summer weekend BBQs ($7-10). Free tastings. Tours by appointment. Open daily 10am-4:30pm.

◉ ▨ SIGHTS AND SEASONAL EVENTS

SONOMA STATE HISTORIC PARK. Within the park, an adobe church stands on the site of the **Mission San Francisco-Solano,** the northernmost and last of the 21 Franciscan missions. Built in 1826 by Padre Jose Altimira, the mission houses a remnant of the original California Republic flag, the rest of which was burned in the

1906 fires. *(E. Spain and 1st St., in the northeast corner of town. ☎ 938-9560. Open daily 10am-5pm. $1, children under 16 free.)*

JACK LONDON STATE PARK. Jack London, author of *The Call of the Wild*, bought 1400 acres here, determined to create his dream home. When London died before the house could be built, he was buried under a boulder intended for the construction of his house. The nearby **House of Happy Walls,** built by his widow, is now a two-story museum devoted to the writer. The park's scenic ½ mi. **Beauty Ranch Trail** passes the lake, winery ruins, and quaint cottages. *(Take Hwy. 12, 4 mi. north from Sonoma to Arnold Ln. and follow signs. ☎ 938-5216. Park open daily 9:30am-7pm, in winter 9:30am-5pm. Museum open daily 10am-5pm.)* **Sonoma Cattle and Napa Valley Trail Rides** also amble through the forests. *(☎ 996-8566. 2hr. ride $45.)*

SEASONAL EVENTS. Sonoma Plaza hosts festivals and fairs nearly every summer weekend. **Kenwood** heats up **July 4,** when runners gather for the Kenwood Footrace, a tough 7½ mi. course through hills and vineyards. A chili cook-off and the **World Pillow Fighting Championships** pass the rest of the day.

NORTHERN CALIFORNIA

MENDOCINO   ☎ 707

Perched on bluffs overlooking the ocean, isolated Mendocino is a highly stylized coastal community of art galleries, craft shops, bakeries, and B&Bs. The town's weathered wood shingles, sloping roofs, and clustered homes seem out of place on the West Coast.

▉⁷ ORIENTATION AND PRACTICAL INFORMATION. Mendocino sits on **Rte. 1,** right on the Pacific Coast, 30 mi. west of U.S. 101 and 12 mi. south of Fort Bragg. Although driving is the best way to reach Mendocino, once there the tiny town is best explored on foot (plentiful street parking available). Given Mendocino's 40 to 70°F weather, travelers should prepare for the chill of coastal fog.

The nearest **bus station** is 2hr. away in Ukiah. Greyhound runs two buses per day to Ft. Bragg. **Mendocino Stage** (☎ 964-0167) runs buses between Ft. Bragg and Ukiah (2 per day, $10). **Mendocino Transit Authority,** 241 Plant Rd. makes one round-trip daily between Santa Rosa, Ukiah, Willits, Fort Bragg, and Mendocino. (☎ 800-696-4682. $16.) **Fort Bragg Door-to-Door Taxis** has an on-call passenger van service. (☎ 964-8294. Operates daily 10am-2am.)

For **visitor info,** contact the **Ford House,** 735 Main St. (☎ 937-5397. Open in summer daily 11am-4pm.) For **Parks General Information,** call ☎ 937-5804, or visit **Russian Gulch Park,** on the west side of Rte. 1 (open daily 5am-10pm). **Catcha Canoe and Bicycles, Too!,** at Rte. 1 and Comptche Rd., rents somewhat pricey but top quality bikes, canoes, and kayaks. (☎ 937-0273. Open daily 9am-5:30pm.) **Lost Coast Kayaking** gives fantastic guided tours. (☎ 937-2434. 2hr.; $45 per person. Call to reserve 24hr. in advance.) **Post office,** 10500 Ford St., two blocks west of Main St. (☎ 937-5282; open M-F 7:30am-4:30pm). **ZIP code:** 95460. **Area code:** 707.

▉▉ ACCOMMODATIONS AND CAMPING. It's impossible to find a hotel room in Mendocino for under $60. Fortunately, hundreds of campsites are nearby; interested travelers should call **ReserveAmerica** (☎ 800-444-7275) to make reservations. Otherwise, look to Ukiah or Fort Bragg for budget motels. **Jug Handle Creek Farm,** 5 mi. north of Mendocino off Rte. 1 before the Caspar exit, is a beautiful 120-year-old house sitting on 40 acres of gardens, campsites, and small rustic cabins. Guests have access to the beach and trails in Jug Handle State Park (see **Sights,** p. 859). (☎ 964-4630. 30 beds. No linen. One hour of chores or $5 required per night. Dorms $18, students $12, children $4; sites $8. Cabins $25 per person. Reserve in advance.) **MacKerricher State Park campground,** 3½ mi. north of Ft. Bragg, has excellent views of tidepool life, passing seals, sea lions, and migratory whales, as well as 9 mi. of beaches and a murky lake for trout fishing. (☎937-5804. Showers, bathrooms, and water. Sites $16; day-use free. Reservations recommended.)

☐ FOOD. All of Mendocino's breads are freshly baked, all vegetables locally grown, all wheat unmilled, all coffee cappuccino, and almost everything expensive. Most restaurants close at 9pm. Picnicking on the Mendocino Headlands is the cheapest option and should be preceded by a trip to **Mendosa's Market,** 10501 Lansing St., the closest thing in Mendocino to a real supermarket. It's pricey (of course), but most items are fresh and delicious. (☎937-5879. Open daily 8am-9pm.) **Tote Fête,** 10450 Lansing St., has delicious tote-out food, and the crowds know it. An asiago, pesto, and artichoke heart sandwich ($4.25) hits the spot. (☎937-3383. Open M-Sa 10:30am-7pm, Su 10:30am-4pm; bakery open daily 7:30am-4pm.)

◙ SIGHTS. Mendocino's greatest attribute lies 900 ft. to the west, where the earth comes to a halt and falls off into the Pacific, forming the impressive fog-shrouded coastline of the **◙Mendocino Headlands.** Beneath wildflower-laden meadows, fingers of eroded rock claw through the pounding ocean surf and seals frolic in secluded alcoves.

In **Fort Bragg,** the **Skunk Train,** at Rte. 1 and Laurel St., offers a jolly, child-friendly diversion through deserted logging towns and a recuperating forest. (☎964-6371 or 800-777-5865. Trips depart at 9am and 2pm, off-season 9:30am and 1:30pm.) A steam engine, diesel locomotive, and vintage motorcar take turns running between Fort Bragg and Willits via Northspur, with whole- and half-day trips available. Schedule changes make it necessary to call ahead for reservations.

AVENUE OF THE GIANTS ☎707

About 6 mi. north of **Garberville** off U.S. 101, the **Avenue of the Giants** winds its way through 31 mi. of the largest living creatures this side of sea level. Scattered throughout the area are several commercialized attractions such as the **World Famous Tree House, Confusion Hill,** and the **Drive-Thru Tree.** Travelers looking for a more authentic taste of the redwood forests may want to bypass these hokey attractions in favor of more rugged and natural tours. There are a number of great hiking trails in the area, marked on free brochures available at the **Humboldt Redwoods State Park Visitors Center,** just south of Weott on the Avenue (☎946-2263; open daily 9am-5pm; Nov.-Mar. Th-Su 10am-3pm.) The **Canoe Creek Loop Trail,** across the street from the visitors center, is an easy start. Uncrowded trails snake through the park's northern section around **Rockefeller Forest,** which contains the largest grove of old-growth redwoods (200 years and growing) in the world. The **Dyerville Giant,** in the redwood graveyard at Founder's Grove about midway through the Avenue, deserves a respectful visit. The ½ mi. loop trail includes the **Founder's Tree** and the **Fallen Giant,** whose massive trunk stretches 60 human body-lengths long and whose three-story rootball looks like a mythical ensnarlment of evil. The **Standish Hickey Recreation Area,** north of Leggett on U.S. 101, offers fishing, camping, swimming, and hiking. (☎925-6482. Parking $5.)

With its sizable artist population, Garberville's art festivals are a big draw. **Jazz on the Lake** and the **Summer Arts Fair** begin in late June, followed by **Shakespeare at Benbow Lake** in late July. Early Aug. brings **Reggae on the River,** a three-day music fest on the banks of the Eel River. **Visitor Info: Chamber of Commerce,** 773 Redway (☎800-923-2613), in Garberville. **Area code:** 707.

REDWOOD NATIONAL PARK ☎707

With ferns that grow to the height of humans and redwood trees the size of skyscrapers, Redwood National Park, as John Steinbeck said, "will leave a mark or create a vision that stays with you always." The redwoods in the park are the last remaining stretch of the old-growth forest which once blanketed two million acres of Northern California and Oregon. Wildlife runs rampant here, with black bears and mountain lions in the backwoods and Roosevelt elk grazing in the meadows.

CALIFORNIA

🛈 PRACTICAL INFORMATION

Redwood National Park is only one of four redwood parks between Klamath and Orick, the others being **Jedediah Smith State Park, Del Norte Coast Redwoods State Park,** and **Prairie Creek Redwoods State Park.** The name "Redwood National Park" is an umbrella term for all four parks.

Buses: Greyhound, 500 E. Harding St., Crescent City (☎ 464-2807). To San Francisco (2 per day, $55-61) and Portland, OR (2 per day, $55-61). Open M-F 7-10am and 5-7:30pm, Sa 7-9am and 7-7:30pm. No credit cards.

Visitor Info: Redwood Info Center (☎ 464-6101, ext. 5265), on U.S. 101, 1 mi. south of Orick. Shows free films on redwoods, gray whales, and black bears. Free maps. Info on trails and campsites from enthusiastic and helpful rangers. Open daily 9am-5pm.

Post Office: Crescent City, 751 2nd St. (☎ 464-2151). Open M-F 8:30am-5pm, Sa noon-2pm. **ZIP Code:** 95531. **Orick,** 121147 U.S. 101 (☎ 488-3611). Open M-F 8:30am-noon and 1-5pm. **ZIP Code:** 95555. **Klamath,** 141 Klamath Blvd. (☎ 482-2381). Open M-F 8am-4:30pm. **ZIP Code:** 95548. **Area code:** 707.

🛏🍴 ACCOMMODATIONS AND FOOD

A pleasant pad is the **Redwood Youth Hostel (HI-AYH),** 14480 U.S. 101, 7 mi. north of Klamath at Wilson Creek Rd. Overlooking the crashing Pacific surf and housed in the historic DeMartin House, this 30-bed hostel suggests Shaker simplicity. Chores and rules keep the house immaculate. (☎ 482-8265. Check-in 4:30-9:30pm. Check-out 9:30am. Dorms $13. Linen $1.) **Nickel Creek campground,** at the end of Enderts Beach Rd. outside Crescent City, has ocean access and toilets, but no showers or water. State Park campsites (☎ 464-9533) are all fully developed and easily accessible. Call **ReserveAmerica** (☎ 800-444-7275) for reservations, which are necessary in summer (sites $16). **Green Valley Motel,** on U.S. 101 in Orick, has clean, basic rooms, and a deli. (☎ 488-2341. Phones and TV. Singles $35; doubles $45.)

There are more picnic table sites than restaurants in the area, so the best option for food is probably **Orick Market,** which has reasonably priced groceries (☎ 488-3225; open M-Sa 8am-7pm, Su 9am-7pm). In Crescent City, head to the 24-hour **Safeway** in the shopping center on U.S. 101 (M St.) between 2nd and 5th. Hungry visitors can grab breakfast or lunch at the **Wild Rocket Juice Bar & Cafe,** 309 U.S. 101 in Crescent City. The fresh vegetables in the Rocket's scrumptious wraps ($5) and salads ($4-5) are all from locally based Reese Hydro Farms. Delightful fruit smoothies ($3-5) will soothe your weariness. (☎ 464-2543. Open M-F 6am-6pm, Sa 9am-3pm. Drive-thru available.) **Glen's Bakery and Restaurant,** 3rd and G St., serves basic diner fare such as huge pancakes ($3), sandwiches ($4-5), and burgers ($3-4), for visitors and regulars alike. (☎ 464-2914. Open Tu-Sa 5am-6:30pm).

👁🎿 SIGHTS AND ACTIVITIES

In the parks, you may gather berries, but all other plants and animals are protected—even feathers dropped by birds of prey are off-limits. The National Parks Sevice and the California Department of Parks and Recreation conduct many ranger-led activities for all ages in summer; call the **Redwood Information Center** (☎ 464-6101) for more info.

ORICK AREA. The Orick Area covers the southernmost section of Redwood National and State Parks. Its **visitors center** lies on U.S. 101 1 mi. south of Orick and a ½ mi. south of the Shoreline Deli (the Greyhound bus stop). A popular sight is the **Tall Trees Grove,** accessible by car to those with free permits available at the visitors center when the road is open. Allow at least 3-4hr. for the trip.

PRAIRIE CREEK AREA. The Prairie Creek Area, equipped with a **ranger station, visitors center,** and **state park campgrounds,** is perfect for hikers, who can explore 75 mi. of trails in the park's 14,000 acres. Be sure to pick up a trail map ($1) at the ranger station before heading out; the loops of criss-crossing trails may be confusing without one. Starting at the Prairie Creek visitors center, the **James Irvine Trail** (4½ mi. one-way) winds through a prehistoric garden of towering old-growth redwoods of humbling height. Snaking past small waterfalls that trickle down 50 ft. fern-covered walls, the trail ends at **Fern Canyon** on **Gold Bluffs Beach,** whose sands stretch for miles upon elk-scattered miles.

KLAMATH AREA. The Klamath Area to the north consists of a thin stretch of park land connecting Prairie Creek with Del Norte State Park. The town itself consists of a few stores stretched over 4 mi., so the main attraction here is the ruggedly spectacular coastline. The **Klamath Overlook,** where Requa Rd. meets the Coastal Trail, is an excellent **whale-watching** site with a fantastic view.

CRESCENT CITY AREA. An outstanding location from which to explore the parks, Crescent City calls itself the city "where the redwoods meet the sea." The **Battery Point Lighthouse** houses a museum open only during low tide. The curious should consult guides about the resident ghost. The lighthouse is on a causeway jutting out of Front St. Turn left onto A St. at the top of Front St. (☎ 464-3089. Open Apr.-Sept. W-Su 10am-4pm, tide permitting. $2, children 50¢.) From June through Aug., the National Park offers **tidepool walks,** which leave from the Enderts Beach parking lot. (☎ 464-6101 for schedules. Turn-off 4 mi. south of Crescent City.)

HIOUCHI AREA. This inland region, known for its rugged beauty, sits in the northern part of the park region along U.S. 199 and contains some excellent hiking trails, most of which are in **Jedediah Smith Redwoods State Park.** The wheelchair-accessible **Stout Grove Trail** is a ½ mi. loop through lush redwoods. The trailhead is near the eastern end of Howland Hill Rd.; the paved section is just past the trail.

GOLD COUNTRY

In 1848, California was a rural backwater of only 15,000 people. The same year, sawmill operator James Marshall wrote in his diary: "This day some kind of mettle…found in the tailrace…looks like goald." In the next four years, some 90,000 '49ers from around the world headed for California and the 120 miles of gold-rich seams called the **Mother Lode.** Despite the hype, few of the prospectors struck it rich. Miners, sustained by dreams of instant wealth, worked long and hard, yet most could barely squeeze sustenance out of their fiercely guarded claims.

Although gold remains in them thar hills, today the towns of Gold Country make their money mining the tourist traffic. Gussied up as **"Gold Rush Towns,"** they solicit tourists traveling along the appropriately numbered **Rte. 49,** which runs through the foothills along rivers, cliffs, and pastures, connecting dozens of small Gold Country settlements. Traffic from the coast connects with Rte. 49 via I-80 through Sacramento, which today serves as a supply post for tourists. If you tire of Gold Country lore, you're not alone. Vineyard touring, river rafting, and spelunking are popular as well. Most of Gold Country is about two hours from Sacramento, three hours from San Francisco.

SACRAMENTO   ☎916

Sacramento is a good place from which to explore the hills of Gold Country or head onward to the Sierra Nevada or Cascade mountain ranges. ▨**Sacramento Hostel (HI-AYH),** 900 H St., at 9th St., in a restored Victorian mansion (c. 1885), has a huge modern kitchen, 3 large living rooms, and a library. (☎ 443-1691. Chore required. Check-in 7-10am and 5-10pm. Check-out 9:30am. Doors lock at 11pm. Dorms $15, nonmembers $18. Wheelchair accessible.) At **Sacramento Econo Lodge,** 711 16th St., between G and H St., most rooms have refrigerators and free HBO, CNN, and ESPN. (☎ 443-6631 or 800-553-2266. Room with queen bed $55; with 2 doubles or king bed $65.) ▨**The Fox and Goose,** 1001 R St., at 10th St. is a funky English pub and restaurant. (☎ 443-8825. Food served M-Th 7am-midnight, F 7am-2am, Sa 8am-2am, Su 8am-1pm. Open mic nights, live bands, and wizards performing live magic. Wheelchair accessible.)

> **PANNIN' FER GOALD** Panning for gold is easy and fun. Find one of many public stretches of river and a 12- or 18-inch gold pan, which can be easily acquired at local stores. Dig in old mine tailings, at turns in the river, around tree roots, and at the upstream ends of gravel bars, places where heavy gold may settle. Swirl water, sand, and gravel in a tilted gold pan, slowly washing materials over the edge. Be patient, and keep at it until you are down to black sand, and—hopefully—gold. Gold has a unique color. It's shinier than brassy-looking pyrite (Fool's Gold), and it doesn't break down upon touch, like mica, a similarly glittery substance.

CALAVERAS COUNTY   ☎ 209

Unsuspecting Calaveras County turned out to be literally sitting on a gold mine—the richest, southern part of the "Mother Lode"—when the big rush hit. Over 550,000 pounds of gold were extracted from the county's earth. A journalist from Missouri named Samuel Clemens, a hapless miner but a gifted spinner of yarns later known as **Mark Twain,** allegedly based "The Celebrated Jumping Frog of Calaveras County" on a tale he heard in Angels Camp Tavern. Life in this area has since imitated (or capitalized on) art; Calaveras has held **annual frog-jumping contests** since 1928. Thousands of people gather on the 3rd weekend of May for the festivities.

A drive along the scenic **Rte. 49** is a great way to glimpse Calaveras County. **San Andreas,** at the juncture of Rte. 26 and 49, is the county hub and most densely populated area, but it isn't very big. The **Calaveras County Information Center,** in downtown Angels Camp, is a great resource for info on and history of sights in the area. (☎ 800-225-3764. Open M-F 9am-4pm, Sa 11am-4pm, Su 11am-3pm.)

The real attractions of Calaveras County are the natural wonders. About 20 mi. east of Angels Camp on Rte. 4 lies **Calaveras Big Trees State Park.** Here the *Sequoiadendron giganteum* (Giant Sequoia) reigns with might: the *giganteum* is the largest living thing on land. The 1 mi. **North Grove Trail** is wheelchair accessible, gently graded, and heavily trafficked. The less-traveled, more challenging 4 mi. **South Grove Trail** better captures the forest's beauty and timelessness. The park also offers swimming in **Beaver Creek** and camping. Summertime visitors should prepare for gnats and mosquitoes. Be aware that the snow comes early (sometimes in Sept.) and leaves late (mid-Apr.) at Big Trees. (☎ 795-2334, 800-365-2267 for site reservations. Open 24hr. Day use $2, seniors $1. Sites $16.)

Calaveras County boasts gargantuan natural wonders below ground as well as above. **Moaning Cavern** is a vast vertical cave so large that the Statue of Liberty could live there comfortably. From Angels Camp, follow Rte. 4 east for 4 mi., turn right onto Parrot's Ferry Rd., and follow signs. Descend the 236 steps or rappel 180 feet down into the cave. (☎ 736-2708. Open daily 9am-6pm; in winter M-F 10am-5pm, Sa-Su and holidays 9am-5pm. Stairs $8.75, ages 3-13 $4.50; rappelling first time $39.50, each additional time $20.) **Mercer Caverns,** 9 mi. north of Angels Camp, off Rte. 4 on Sheep Rd. in Murphys, offers 1hr. walking tours of 10 internal rooms. Although smaller and less dramatic than Moaning Cavern, the caves are nearly a million years old. (☎ 728-2101. Open M-Th 9am-6pm, F-Sa 9am-8pm. Tours every 20min. $8, ages 5-11 $4, under 5 free.) **California Caverns,** at Cave City, served as a naturally air-conditioned bar and dance floor during the Gold Rush when a shot of whiskey could be purchased for a pinch of gold dust. The caverns sobered up on Su for church services when one stalagmite served as an altar. Walking tours and "wild cavern expedition trips" explore cramped tunnels, waist-high mud, and underground lakes. (☎ 736-2708. Tours $9, ages 3-13 $4.75. Expeditions 2-3hr.; over 16 $99; less-strenuous for ages 9-16 $65.25.)

Calaveras County has been a producer of fine wines for nearly 150 years. Vineyards stretch along Rte. 49, and wineries abound near Plymouth. The **Stevenot Winery,** 2 mi. north of Murphy's Main St. on Sheep Ranch Rd., is the county's largest. (☎ 728-3436. Free tastings M-F 8am-noon and 1-5pm.) **Kautz Ironstone Vineyards,** on Six Mile Rd. 1½ mi. south of Murphy's Main St., stores wine in caverns hewn from rock. (☎ 728-1251. Tours daily 11am-5pm. Tasting room open M-F 10am-6pm.)

COLOMA   ☎530

The 1848 Gold Rush began in Coloma at John Sutter's water-powered lumber mill, operated by James Marshall. Today, the town tries its darnedest to hype this claim to fame. Accommodations are sparse, so visitors will probably want to stay in Placerville. The town basically revolves around the **James Marshall Gold Discovery State Historic Park.** Near the site where Marshall struck gold is a replica of the original mill. (☎622-1116. Open daily 8am-dusk. Day-use fee $2 per car, seniors $1; walk-ins $1, under 16 free.) Picnic grounds across the street surround the **Gold Discovery Museum,** 310 Back St., which presents the events of the Gold Rush through dioramas and film. (☎622-3470. Open daily 8am-5pm; in winter 10am-4pm.) The real reason to come to Coloma, however, may be for the nearby natural attractions. The American River's class III currents, among the most accessible rapids in the West, attract thousands of rafters and kayakers every weekend. Contact **Ahwahnee** (☎800-359-9790), **Motherlode River Trips** (☎800-427-2387), **Oars Inc.** (☎800-346-6277), or **Whitewater Connection** (☎800-336-7238).

THE CASCADES   ☎916

The Cascade Mountains interrupt an expanse of farmland to the northeast of Gold Country. In these ranges, recent volcanic activity has left behind a surreal landscape of lava beds, mountains, lakes, waterfalls, caves, and recovering forest areas. The calm serenity and haunting beauty of these mountains draw visitors in a way that the Central Valley and Gold Country cannot.

   Lassen Volcanic National Park is accessible by **Rte. 36** to the south and **Rte. 44** to the north. Both roads are about 50 mi. from **Rte. 5.** In 1914, the earth radiated destruction as tremors, streams of lava, black dust, and a series of huge eruptions ravaged the land, climaxing in 1915 when Mt. Lassen belched a 7 mi. high cloud of smoke and ashes. The destructive power of this eruption is still evident in the strange, unearthly pools of boiling water and the stretches of barren moonscape. Winter is long and snowy here. **Lassen Volcanic National Park Headquarters** are located in Mineral. (☎595-4444. Open daily in summer 8am-4:30pm; off-season closed Sa-Su.)

   Every summer, thousands of New Age believers, yuppie vacationers, and crunchy hikers come to **Mt. Shasta** to carouse, climb, commune, and contemplate its rugged snow-capped top. **Shasta-Trinity National Forest Service,** 204 W. Alma St. (☎926-4511 or 926-4596), charges info-crystals. The **Alpenrose Cottage Hostel,** 204 Hinckley St., sends rose scents and sounds of windchimes up to the majestic mountain. (☎926-6724. $15, children $7.50; reservations recommended. Showers $3.)

THE SIERRA NEVADA

The Sierra Nevada is a high, steep, and physically stunning mountain range. Thrust skyward 400 million years ago by gigantic plate collisions and shaped by erosion, glaciers, and volcanoes, this enormous hunk of granite stretches 450 miles north from the Mojave Desert to Lake Almanor near Lassen Volcanic National Park. The glistening clarity of Lake Tahoe, the heart-stopping sheerness of Yosemite's rock walls, the craggy alpine scenery of Kings Canyon and Sequoia National Parks, and the abrupt drop of the Eastern Sierra into Owens Valley are sights to behold. Temperatures in the Sierra Nevada are as diverse as the terrain. Even in the summer, overnight lows can dip into the 20s. Normally, only U.S. 50 and I-80 are kept open during the snow season. Exact dates vary from year to year, so check with a ranger station for local road conditions, especially from October to June.

LAKE TAHOE   ☎530

In February of 1844, fearless explorer John C. Fremont led his expedition over the Sierra—a fool's errand, as anyone in the Donner Party could have told you between bites of human flesh. Luckily for him, the sight of the beautiful alpine lake was enough to boost the morale of his 36 starved and weary companions. The lake went through several identities, from Bigler to Lake of Beer, before the state of California officially named it Tahoe in 1945. Since settlers rolled into California in the late 18th century, Lake Tahoe has been a playground for the wealthy and an outdoor adventurist's dream in any season, with miles of biking, hiking, and skiing trails, long stretches of beach, and hair-raising whitewater.

▐ GETTING THERE AND GETTING AROUND

In the northern Sierra on the California-Nevada border, Lake Tahoe is a 4hr. drive from San Francisco. The two main trans-Sierra highways, **I-80** and **U.S. 50 (Lake Tahoe Boulevard)**, run east-west through Tahoe, skimming the northern and southern shores of the lake, respectively. Lake Tahoe is 118 mi. northeast of Sacramento and 35 mi. southwest of Reno on I-80. From the Carson City and Owens Valley area, **U.S. 395** runs north along Tahoe's eastern shores.

Buses: Greyhound (☎530-543-1050), in the Thunderbird Motel on Laurel Ave. 1 block north of U.S. 50 in South Lake Tahoe. To San Francisco (3 per day, $27) and Sacramento (3 per day, $20). No lockers. Station open daily 8am-7pm.

Trains: Amtrak runs a bus from its San Joaquin and Capitol train routes to Pre-Madonna Casino, off I-5 at Pre-Madonna exit, and Whiskey Pete's Casino in Stateline, NV. These trips are long and costly. To: San Francisco (11hr., $80).

Public Transit: Tahoe Casino Express provides shuttle service between the Reno airport and South Shore Tahoe casinos (☎800-446-6128; runs daily 6:15am-12:30am; $17, round-trip $30, up to 2 children under 12 free). **Tahoe Area Regional Transport (TART)** (☎550-1212) connects the western and northern shores from Incline Village to Tahoe City to Tahoma (Meeks Bay in summer). Stops daily every hour 6:30am-6pm. Buses also run out to Truckee and Squaw Valley 5 times per day. Fare $1.25, exact change required; day pass $3. **South Tahoe Area Ground Express (STAGE)** (☎542-6077) operates buses around South Tahoe and hourly to the beach and connects Stateline and Emerald Bay Rd. $1.25; day pass $2; 10-ride pass $10. Most casinos operate free shuttle service along U.S. 50 to California ski resorts and motels. A summer bus program connects STAGE and TART at Meeks Bay for the entire lake area 6am-midnight.

▟▐ ORIENTATION AND PRACTICAL INFORMATION

The lake is roughly divided into two main regions: North Shore and South Shore. The North Shore includes King's Beach, Tahoe City, and Incline Village, while the South Shore includes Emerald Bay and South Lake Tahoe City. Rte. 28 and 89 form a 75 mi. ring of asphalt around the lake; the complete loop takes nearly 3hr.

Visitor Info: ☎573-2674 (available daily Memorial Day to Oct. 1.) **South Lake Tahoe Chamber of Commerce,** 3066 Lake Tahoe Blvd. (☎541-5255). Open M-Sa 8:30am-5pm. **Lake Tahoe/Douglas Chamber of Commerce,** 195 U.S. 50, Stateline, NV (☎775-588-4591). Open M-F 9am-6pm, Sa-Su 9am-5pm. **Tahoe North Visitor and Convention Bureau and Visitor Info,** 245 N. Lake Blvd. (☎583-3494). Helpful staff makes lodging reservations. Open M-F 9am-5pm, Sa-Su 9am-4pm.

Internet Access: South Lake Tahoe Library, 1000 Rufus Allen Blvd. (☎573-3185). Open Tu-W 10am-8pm, Th-Sa 10am-5pm. **Kings Beach Library,** 301 Secline Ave., 1 block north of N. Lake Blvd. in Kings Beach. Open Tu 1-5pm, W 2-6pm, Th 10am-2pm, F 1-5pm, Sa 11am-3pm. Internet access free.

Medical Services: Barton Memorial Hospital (☎541-3420), at 4th St. and South Ave., in S. Lake Tahoe. **Stateline Medical Center,** 176 U.S. 50, Stateline, NV (☎702-588-3561), at Kahle St. Open daily 8am-8pm. **Tahoe Forest Hospital** (☎587-6011), at Donner Pass Rd. and Pine Ave., Truckee.

Post Office: Tahoe City, 950 N. Lake Blvd. #12 (☎800-275-8777), in the Lighthouse Shopping Center. Open M-F 8:30am-5pm. **ZIP Code: 96145. South Lake Tahoe,** 1046 Tahoe Blvd. (☎544-2208). Open M-F 8:30am-5pm, Sa noon-2pm. **ZIP Code: 96151. Area code:** 530 in Lake Tahoe, 775 in Nevada. In text, 530 unless noted.

ACCOMMODATIONS

The strip off U.S. 50 on the California side of the border supports the bulk of Tahoe's motels. Particularly glitzy and cheap in South Lake Tahoe, motels also line the quieter area along Park Ave. and Pioneer Trail. The North Shore offers more woodsy accommodations along Rte. 28, but rates are especially high in Tahoe City, where lodgings are booked solid and well in advance for weekends and holidays at sky-high prices. Fall and spring are the most economical times of the year to visit.

Tamarack Lodge, 2311 N. Lake Tahoe Blvd. (☎583-3350 or 888-824-6323), 3 mi. north of Tahoe City, across from Star Harbor. Clean, quiet motel in the woods. Newly refurbished exterior, outdoor BBQ and fireplace, phones, cable TV, and friendly management. Rooms with queen beds $39-54.

Cedar Glen Lodge, 6589 N. Lake Blvd., Tahoe Vista (☎546-4281 or 800-500-8246). Family-operated motel with a private beach, pool, and indoor and outdoor hottub and sauna. Grounds include BBQ pits, playground, hammock, lots of flowers, and spectacular rabbit hutch. Morning newspaper and continental breakfast included. Cottages with kitchens also available. Singles from $60.

Hostel at Squaw Valley, 1900 Squaw Valley Rd. (☎581-3246). A 100-bed hostel in Squaw Valley. Roll out of bed and stroll to the ski lifts. Common area but no kitchen. Often closed for school groups on weekends. Open mid-Nov. to mid-Apr. Dorms $24.

Doug's Mellow Mountain Retreat, 3787 Forest St., S. Lake Tahoe (☎544-8065). 1 mi. west of the state line, turn left onto Wildwood Rd., and after 3 blocks take a left on Forest. St. Doug's hostel is the 6th house on the left. Modern kitchen, BBQ, fireplace, Internet access. Very friendly international atmosphere. Bedding and laundry included. Dorms $15 per person, private rooms available; discounts for stays of a week or longer.

Budget Inn, 3496 Lake Tahoe Blvd., S. Lake Tahoe (☎544-2834 or 888-615-1424). Standard rooms with HBO and pool access. Continental breakfast included. Singles Su-Th $32, F-Sa $59; doubles $39/$69.

Bayview (☎544-5994) has 10 first come, first camp sites right on Emerald Bay with pit toilets but no water. 7-night maximum stay. Sites $5.

D.L. Bliss State Park (☎525-7277), on Rte. 89 a few miles north of Emerald Bay. Camp by the beach near emerald waters and granite boulders or in secluded forest sites. Popular day-use beach, but entrance restricted by the number of parking spaces. 168 sites. 14-night maximum stay. Open June to Labor Day but open for day-use May-Oct. Sites $16, beach-side $20. Day parking free.

FOOD

In the south, the casinos on the Nevada side offer perpetually low-priced buffets, but there are restaurants along the lakeshore with reasonable prices, similarly large portions, and much better food. Groceries are cheaper on the California side.

Lakehouse: Pizza-Spirits-Fun, 120 Grove St., Tahoe City (☎583-2222). On the water with a sunny lakefront deck. Standard breakfast specials $3-7, California salad $7, sandwiches, and reasonably priced pizzas. Open M-Th 7am-10pm, F-Sa 7am-11pm. No checks but major credit cards accepted. Free delivery in area after 5pm.

Syd's Bagelry and Natural Foods, 550 N. Lake Tahoe Blvd., Tahoe City (☎583-2666). A bagel shop with a million-dollar view. "Hummus Among Us" (fat bagel sandwich with hummus, cucumber, mushrooms, tomato, carrots, onion, and sprouts) $4.50; garden burgers $4.25. Syd's prides itself on its espresso drinks. Open daily 6am-8pm. No credit cards.

Red Hut Waffles, 2749 Lake Tahoe Blvd. (☎541-9024). Homestyle cooking. Waffle piled with fruit and whipped cream ($5.50), 4-egg monster omelettes ($5.75-7), fresh fruit bowl ($4), and bottomless coffee ($1.25). Open daily 6am-2pm. No credit cards.

Sprouts Natural Foods Cafe, 3123 Harrison Ave. (☎541-6969), at the intersection of Hwy. 50 and Alameda Ave. in S. Lake Tahoe. With all-natural food and portions fit for a wrestler, this place keeps everyone satisfied. Try the pasta dinner ($6.50), the tuna burrito ($5), or the tasty smoothies ($2.50-3.25). Open daily 8am-10pm.

CALIFORNIA

🏔 OUTDOOR RECREATION

BEACHES. Lake Tahoe supports many beaches perfect for a day of sunning and people-watching. Parking generally costs $3-5. Bargain hunters leave cars in turnouts on the main road and walk to the beaches. **Sand Harbor Beach,** south of Incline Village, has gorgeous granite boulders and clear waters that attract swimmers, sunners, and scuba divers in droves. The parking lot ($6) is usually full by 11:30am. One mi. away at Memorial Point, lakeside paved parking is free. **Hidden Beach,** also south of Incline Village, and **Kings Beach,** just across the California border on Rte. 28, comes complete with the latest rage (waveboards) and an alternative-rock feel. Kings Beach has volleyball nets, a basketball court, and a playground. **Pope Beach,** at the southernmost point of the lake off Rte. 89, is a wide, pine-shaded expanse of shoreline, which becomes less trafficked on its east side. **Nevada Beach,** 8 mi. north of South Lake Tahoe, is close to the casinos off U.S. 50, offering a quiet place to reflect on gambling losses while gazing upon the mountains. **Zephyr Cove Beach,** about 15 mi. north of South Lake Tahoe, is a favorite spot for the younger college crowd. **Meeks Bay,** 10 mi. south of Tahoe City, is family-oriented and social: picnic tables, volleyball, motorboat and kayak rental, and a petite store. In the summer the Tahoe City and South Tahoe Buses connect here. Five mi. south of Meeks Bay, the **D.L. Bliss State Park** has a large beach on a small bay (Rubicon). The Rubicon Trail leads to the peaceful Vikingsholm mansion. Parking here ($3) is very limited, so think about parking on the road and walking in.

OTHER WATER ACTIVITIES. River rafting can be a refreshing way to appreciate the Tahoe scenery, but depending on the water levels of the American and Truckee Rivers, rafting can range from a thrilling whitewater challenge to a boring bake in the sun. If water levels are high, check out raft rental places along the Truckee River and at Tahoe City. For more info, call **Mountain Air Sports Truckee River Rafting** (☎ 583-7238 or 888-584-7238; open daily 8:30am-3:30pm), in Tahoe City, across from Lucky's at Fanny Bridge, or **Tahoe Truckee River Raft Co.** (☎ 583-0123; open daily 8:30am-3:30pm). If paddling in the north, ask around about (privately owned) **natural hot springs** on the way to the spectacular Crystal Bay. Local lore maintains that the bay's frigid temperatures (average 39°F) prevent the decomposition that would ordinarily make corpses float to the surface. Spoooky. **Fishing** information and regulations can be found at visitors centers, and licenses are available at local sporting good stores. Because of its depth (1600 ft. in places) and strange formation, Tahoe is a notoriously difficult lake to fish; bring a good book and be prepared to walk away empty-handed.

BIKING. Lake Tahoe is a biking paradise. The excellent paved trails, logging roads, and dirt paths have not gone unnoticed; be prepared for company if you pedal around the area. The U.S. Forest Service and bike rental stores can provide advice, publications like *Bike West* magazine, maps, and info about trails. No cycling is allowed in the Desolation Wilderness, or on the Pacific Crest or Tahoe Rim Trails. **Olympic Bike Shop,** 60 N. Lake Tahoe Blvd., Tahoe City, has an expert staff equipped with multitudes of maps and trail options. (☎ 581-2500. Open daily 9am-6pm. Mountain bikes $5 per hr., $15 for 4hr., $21 per day.)

Known more for its ski trails, the North Shore is equipped with both flat lakeside jaunts and steeper woodsy rides. The **Tahoe Rim Trail,** from Kings Beach to Tahoe City, offers intermediate-level hilly biking. The trail can be accessed from Tahoe City or Brockway Summit (see below for more info). **Squaw Valley,** northwest of the lake on Rte. 89, opens its slope to hikers and mountain bikers during the summer. The cable car transports bikers and their wheels 2000 vertical ft. (1 ride $19, full-day pass $26). You find your own way down—the slopes are steep, but fairly easy. The South Shore boasts a variety of scenic trails for all abilities. **Fallen Leaf Lake,** just west of South Lake Tahoe, is a dazzling destination by bike or by car, but watch out for the swerving tourists in boat- and trailer-towing vehicles, especially on the narrow mountain roads. The steep mountain peaks that surround the lake are breathtaking when viewed from beside Fallen Leaf's icy blue waters. Bikers looking for a challenge can try the 7 mi. ring around the lake, but beware—it's more difficult than it looks. **U.S. 50, Rte. 89,** and **Rte. 28** are all bicycle-friendly, but the drivers aren't, especially in heavy traffic areas like South Lake Tahoe. Angora Ridge (4 mi.), accessible from Rte. 89, meanders past Fallen Leaf Lake to the Angora Lakes for a moderate challenge. For serious mountain bikers, **Mr. Toad's Wild Ride** (3 mi.), reaches from U.S. 50 or Rte. 89 and is a difficult, winding trail that climbs to 9000 ft. The **Flume Trail** has magnificent views of the lake 1500 ft. below. This advanced 23 mi. loop begins at Spooner Lake campground with the Marlette Lake Trail, a 5 mi. sandy road. Several paved paths offer undemanding touring adventures around the lake. The **Pope-Baldwin Bike Path** (3½ mi.) runs parallel to Rte. 89, while the **South Lake Tahoe Bike Path** runs from El Dorado Beach over the Upper Truckee River. The lake views and smooth, easy ride make these trails quite popular. Parking is available at the Truckee River trailhead (Rte. 89, south of Tahoe City), Kaspian campground (Skyland), and General Creek campground at Sugar Pine Point State Park (south of Homewood). The **West Shore Bike Path,** a paved 10 mi. stretch from Tahoe City to Sugar Pine Point, is a flat, scenic way to tour the lake.

HIKING. The visitors center and ranger stations provide detailed info and maps for all types of hikes. Backcountry users must obtain a wilderness permit from the US Forest Service for any hike into the Desolation Wilderness. The almost completed **Tahoe Rim Trail** encircles the lake, following the ridge tops of the Lake Tahoe Basin. Hiking is moderate to difficult. On the western shore, the trail is part of the Pacific Crest Trail. Current trailheads are at Spooner Summit on U.S. 50, off Rte. 89 on Fairway Dr. in Tahoe City, Brockway on Rte. 267, and Mt. Rose on Rte. 431. (Mt. Rose is a 1¼ mi. wheelchair-accessible loop.)

ROCK CLIMBING. The **Alpenglow Sport Shop,** 415 N. Lake Blvd., Tahoe City, provides free rock and ice climbing literature and rents climbing shoes. (☎583-6917. Open M-F 10am-6pm, Sa-Su 9am-6pm.) **The Sports Exchange,** 10095 W. River St., houses Gym Works, a challenging indoor climbing gym with over 2500 sq. ft. of bouldering and climbing space. (☎582-4510. Open daily 10am-6pm. $7 per day, indoor shoe rental $3 per day.) **Headwall Climbing Wall** at Squaw Valley, offers several challenging routes in the Cable Car Building. (☎583-7673. Open daily 10am-5pm. $12 per day, indoor shoe rental $4 per day.)

DOWNHILL SKIING. With its world-class alpine slopes, knee-deep powder, and notorious California sun, Tahoe is a skier's paradise. There are approximately 20 ski resorts in the Tahoe area. The visitors center provides info, maps, publications like *Ski Tahoe* (free), and coupons. For daily ski info updates, use the website www.tahoesbest.com/skitahoe. All the major resorts offer lessons and rent equipment. Look for multi-day packages that offer significant discounts over single-day rates. Lifts at most resorts operate daily 9am to 4pm; arrive early for the best skiing and shortest lines. Prices do not include ski rental, which generally costs $15 to $20 for a full day. Skiers on a tight budget should consider night skiing or half-day passes. Numerous smaller ski resorts offer cheaper tickets and shorter lines. **Squaw Valley,** off Rte. 89 just north of Alpine Meadows, was the site of the 1960 Olympic Winter Games, and with good reason—the groomed bowls and tree runs make for some of the West's best skiing. The 32 ski lifts access high-elevation runs for all levels. (☎583-6955 or 800-545-4350. Day pass $52, half-day $35, seniors and under 13 $26, over 75 free.) **Alpine Meadows,** on Rte. 89, lies 6 mi. northwest of Tahoe City. An excellent, accessible family vacation spot with more than 2000 skiable acres. (☎583-4232 or 800-441-4423. Full-day $50, ages 7-12 $10, ages 65-69 $28, over 70 or under 6 $6. Basic ski rental $26, ages 7-12 $17, under 6 $11.) **Heavenly,** on Ski Run Blvd. off U.S. 50, is the largest and most popular resort in the area, with over 4800 skiable acres, 27 lifts, and 82 trails. Reaching over 10,000 ft., it is Tahoe's highest ski resort. (☎800-243-2826. Full-day lift ticket $46, seniors and under 13 $20; half-day $30/$15.) **Mount Rose,** 11 mi. from Incline Village on Rte. 431, is a local favorite because of its long season, short lines, intermediate focus, and less expensive lift tickets. (☎800-754-7673. Full-day lift ticket $42, half-day $34; ages 13-19 $35/ $30; seniors M-F half-price, ages 6-12 $10, over 70 and under 5 free.)

CROSS-COUNTRY SKIING AND SNOWSHOEING. One of the best ways to enjoy the solitude of Tahoe's pristine snow-covered forests is to cross-country ski at a resort. Alternatively, rent skis at an independent outlet and venture onto the thick braid of trails around the lake. **Porters** (☎587-1500), at the Lucky-Longs Center, in Truckee, and 501 N. Lake Blvd., Tahoe City (☎583-2314), rents skis for $9-12 (both open daily 8am-6pm).

Royal Gorge (☎426-3871), on Old Hwy. 40 below Donner Summit, is the nation's largest cross-country ski resort, with 80 trails covering 170 mi. of beginner and expert terrain. **Spooner Lake,** at the junction of U.S. 50 and Rte. 28, offers 21 trails and incredible views. (☎749-5349. Adult trail fee $15, children $3; mid-week special $11.) **Hope Valley** (☎694-2266) has 11 free trails of varying difficulty; take Rte. 89 South from South Lake Tahoe and turn left on Rte. 88.

Snowshoeing is easier than cross-country skiing and allows you to traverse more varied terrain. Follow hiking or cross-country trails, or trudge off into the woods (make sure to bring a map). Equipment rentals are available at many sporting goods stores for about $15 per day. Check local ranger stations for ranger-guided winter snowshoe hikes.

YOSEMITE NATIONAL PARK ☎209

In 1868, a Scotsman named John Muir arrived by boat in San Francisco and asked for directions to "any place that is wild." Anxious to run this crazy youngster out of town, Bay Area folk directed him to the heralded lands of Yosemite. The wonders that Muir beheld there sated his wanderlust and spawned a lifetime of conservationism. His efforts won Yosemite its national park status by 1880 and Sequoia and Kings Canyon the same reward by 1890. The swarms of tourists from around the world who flock to Yosemite today are a measure of just how far removed we feel from nature. Despite the summer swarm, Yosemite remains a paradise for outdoor enthusiasts; most visitors congregate in only 6% of the park (Yosemite Valley), leaving expanses of beautiful backcountry in relative peace and quiet.

▌ GETTING THERE AND GETTING AROUND

BY BUS OR TRAIN. Yosemite runs public **buses** that connect the park with Merced and Mariposa. **Yosemite VIA** runs buses from the Merced bus station at 16th and N streets to Yosemite. (☎384-1315 or 800-842-5463. 7, 8:55, 10:15am, and 4:15pm. $20, round-trip $38.) VIA also runs **Yosemite Gray Line (YGL),** which meets trains arriving in Merced from San Francisco and takes passengers to Yosemite. Tickets can be purchased from the driver. (☎384-1315. Operates M-F 8am-5pm.) YGL also runs buses to and from Fresno/Yosemite International Airport, Fresno hotels, and Yosemite Valley ($20). A new service called **YARTS** (☎209-372-4487 or 877-989-2787) provides two daily trips to Yosemite from Merced. Call ahead to ask about fares and schedules, which vary widely. Amtrak runs a **bus** from Merced to Yosemite (4 per day, $10). Amtrak **trains** run to Merced from San Francisco (4 per day, $22-29) and L.A. (5 per day, $28-51). The trains connect with the waiting YGL bus.

The best bargain in Yosemite is the **free shuttle bus system.** Comfortable but often crowded, the buses have knowledgeable drivers and wide viewing windows. (Daily every 10min. 7am-6pm, every 20min. 6pm-10pm.) **Hikers' buses** run daily to Glacier Point (spring-fall) and to Tuolumne Meadows/Lee Vining. (☎372-1240. Late June to Labor Day; $20.50 round-trip.)

BY CAR. Although the inner valley is often congested with traffic, the best way to achieve a rapid overview of Yosemite is by car. Gas-guzzlers should keep in mind that there are no gas stations in the valley; be prepared to get ripped off in a gateway town. Within the park, there are gas stations with high prices at Tuolumne Meadows and Wawona. A more relaxing (and environmentally friendly) option is to park at one of

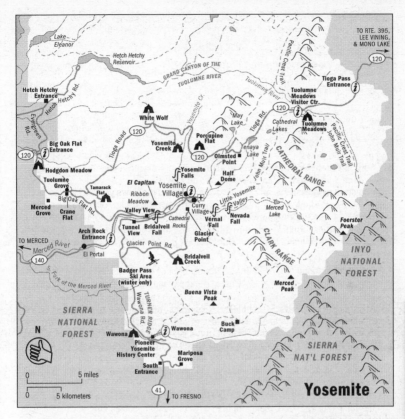

Yosemite

the lodging areas and ride the free shuttle to see the valley sights, using your car only to explore sights outside of the valley. Drivers intending to visit the high country in spring and fall should have snow tires (sometimes required even in summer).

✳ ❷ ORIENTATION AND PRACTICAL INFORMATION

General Park Information (☎372-0200). Info on weather, accommodations, and activities. Call the general line before calling a specific info station. All visitors centers have free maps and copies of *Yosemite Guide*. **All hours listed are valid late May-Sept. unless otherwise noted.**

Yosemite Valley Visitors Center (☎372-0200), in Yosemite Village. Sign language interpreter in summer. Open daily mid-June to Labor Day 8am-7pm; Labor Day to mid-June 9am-5pm.

Wilderness Center (☎372-0308), in Yosemite Village. P.O. Box 545, Yosemite National Park 95389. Backcountry and map info (☎379-2648). Wilderness permit reservations (☎372-0740) up to 24 weeks in advance ($5 per person per reservation, M-F 9am-4pm), or first come, first served (free). Helpful staff cannot plan your trips, but provides a wealth of info for those who do their homework. Open daily 7:30am-7pm.

Bike Rental: Yosemite Lodge (☎372-1208) and **Curry Village** (☎372-8319) for $5.25 per hr., $20 per day. Wheelchairs also available at both shops for $5 per hr., $20 per day. Both open daily 8:30am-6:45pm, weather permitting.

Equipment Rental: Yosemite Mountaineering School (☎372-8344 or 372-8436), on Rte. 120 at Tuolumne Meadows. Sleeping bags $10 per day, backpacks $8 per day; 3rd day half-price. Climbing shoes rented to YMS students only. Driver's license or credit card required for deposit. Rock climbing classes offered daily. Open daily 8:30am-5pm.

Laundromat: Laundry facilities open at **Housekeeping Camp.** Wash $1.25, 10min. dry 25¢. Open daily 8am-8pm. In winter, laundry facilities available at **Camp 6,** across the street from the Village Store. Open daily 7am-10pm.

Weather and Road Conditions: ☎372-0200. 24hr.

Internet Access: Yosemite Bug Hostel (☎966-6666), on Rte. 140, 30 mi. west of Yosemite in Midpines (see p. 870). Internet access $1 for 10min.

Post Office: Yosemite Village, next to the visitors center. Open M-F 8:30am-5pm, Sa 10am-noon. Lobby open 24hr. **Curry Village,** near the registration office. Open Memorial Day-Labor Day M-F 11:30am-3pm. **Yosemite Lodge,** open M-F 9am-1pm, 2-4:30pm. **Wawona,** open M-F 9am-5pm, Sa 9am-noon. **Tuolumne Meadows,** open M-F 9am-12:30pm and 1:30-4:30pm, Sa 9am-noon. **ZIP Code:** 95389. **Area code:** 209.

ACCOMMODATIONS

INSIDE THE PARK

Advance reservations are necessary and can be (and almost always are) made up to one year in advance by calling ☎252-4848. Rates fluctuate, but tend to be higher on weekends and during the summer (those given below are for summer weekends). Check-in hovers around 11am. *All park lodgings provide access to dining and laundry facilities, showers, and supplies.*

Housekeeping Camp (☎372-8338) ¼ mi. west of Curry Village. Canvas-capped concrete "camping shelters" accommodate up to 4 people and include 2 bunk beds, a double bed, a picnic table, a firepit with grill, lights, and electrical outlets. Cottages $48.

Curry Village (☎252-4848), southeast of Yosemite Village. Pool, nightly shows at the amphitheater, snack stands, cafeteria, and an ice rink Nov.-Feb. Ranger programs nearly every night feature stories about the history of Yosemite. Back-to-back cabins $62, with bath $82; canvas-sided cabins on raised wooden floors $44.

Tuolumne Meadows Lodge (☎372-8413), on Tioga Pass Rd., in the northeastern corner of park. Canvas-sided cabins, wood stoves, no electricity. Maid service $4. Doubles $48; additional adult $9, child $4.

White Wolf Lodge (☎372-8416), on Tioga Pass Rd. in the western area of the park. Open late June to early Sept. Cabins with bath $73; tent cabin doubles $48; each additional adult $8, child $4.

Yosemite Lodge (☎372-1274), west of Yosemite Village and directly across from Yosemite Falls. Tiny cabins are as close to motel accommodations as the valley gets. Singles and doubles $100, with bath $125.

OUTSIDE THE PARK

Yosemite Bug Hostel (☎966-6666), on Rte. 140 in Midpines, 25 mi. west of Yosemite. Look carefully for sign. Up in the woods, a low-budget resort spot. International backpacking crowd lounges in hammocks. Discounts on public transportation (45min., $5.50) to park. Internet access $1 for 10min. Wheelchair accessible. Dorms $15; tent sites $17; private rooms with shared bath $40-50.

Oakhurst Lodge, 40302 Rte. 41, Oakhurst (☎683-4417 or 800-655-6343). Clean, simple motel rooms with shag carpeting, pool, large grassy back lawn. Continental breakfast included in an adjoining coffeeshop. 1 queen bed $70 ($55 with various local coupons); 2 queen beds $80-95.

CAMPGROUNDS

Yosemite is camping country; most of the valley's campgrounds are choked with tents, trailers, and RVs. Reservations can be made up to five months in advance (☎800-436-7275, TDD 888-530-9796, outside the U.S. 301-722-1257; www.reservations.nps.gov; phones and web site available daily 7am-7pm, or mail NPRS, P.O. Box 1600, Cumberland, MD 21502). Backcountry camping is prohibited in the valley but is encouraged outside it.

IN YOSEMITE VALLEY

Sunnyside, at the western end of the valley past Yosemite Lodge. The only first come, first camp site in the valley. Be prepared to meet new friends; every site is filled with 6 people. Water, flush toilets, and tables. 35 sites fill up early. $3 per person.

Lower Pines, in the busy eastern end of Yosemite Valley. Commercial, crowded, and plagued by the noises of cars driving by. Next to **North Pines** campsite (81 sites; open Apr.-Sept.) and the enormous **Upper Pines** campsite (238 sites). Pets allowed. Water, toilets, tables, and showers. Open Mar.-Sept. Sites $15.

BEYOND YOSEMITE VALLEY

Outside of the valley, campsite quality vastly improves. All of the parks' campgrounds have at least 50 sites, and all have RV sites except for Tamarack Flat, Yosemite Creek, and Porcupine Flat. *All sites have firepits and nearby parking.*

Hodgdon Meadow, on Rte. 120 near Big Oak Flat Entrance, 25 mi. from valley. Warm enough for winter camping. 105 thickly wooded sites provide some seclusion even when the campground is full. Water, toilets, and tables. May-Sept. sites $15; Oct.-Apr. first come, first camp $10.

Tuolumne Meadows, on Rte. 120, 55 mi. east of the Valley. 157 sites require advance reservations, 157 saved for same-day reservations. Drive into the sprawling campground or escape the RVs by ambling to the 25 sites saved for hikers without cars. Ranger programs every night and nearby trailheads. Water, toilets, and tables. Open July-Sept. Drive-in sites $15; backpacker sites $3 per person.

FOOD

Restaurants in the park are nothing special. A slim supply of pricey groceries can be found at the **Yosemite Lodge** or the **Village Store** (both open daily June-Sept. 8am-10pm; Oct.-May 8am-9pm), or at **Wawona** (open daily 8am-8pm). Consider buying all of your cooking supplies, marshmallows, and batteries in Merced, Fresno, or Oakhurst en route to the park. These gateway towns are also home to many affordable restaurants.

THE OUTDOORS

THE VALLEY

BY CAR. Although the view is better if you get out of the car, you can see a large portion of Yosemite from the bucket seat. The **Yosemite Road Guide** ($4 at every visitors center) is keyed to roadside markers and outlines a superb tour of the park—it's almost like having a ranger tied to the hood. Spectacular panoramas are omnipresent during the drive east along **Tioga Pass Road (Rte. 120).** This stretch of road is the highest highway strip in the country; as it winds down from Tioga Pass through the park's eastern exit, it plunges nearly 1 mi. to reach the lunar landscape of Mono Lake. The drive west from the pass brings you past **Tuolumne Meadows** with its open spaces and rippling creeks, to shimmering Tenaya Lake and its countless scenic views of granite slopes and canyons. No less incredible are the views afforded by the southern approach to Yosemite, **Rte. 41.** Most recognizable is the Wawona Tunnel turnout (also known as **Inspiration Point**), which most visitors will immediately recognize as the subject of many Ansel Adams photographs.

El Capitan, a gigantic granite monolith (7569 ft.), looms over awestruck crowds. If you stop and look closely (with binoculars if possible), you will see what appear to be specks of dust moving on the mountain face—they are actually world-class climbers inching toward fame. At night their flashlights shine from impromptu hammocks hung from the granite. Nearby, **Three Brothers** (three adjacent granite peaks) and misty **Bridalveil Falls** pose for hundreds of snapshots every day. A drive into the heart of the valley leads to **Yosemite Falls** (the highest in North America at 2425 ft.), **Sentinel Rock,** and mighty **Half Dome.**

CALIFORNIA

Glacier Point, off Glacier Point Rd., opens up a different perspective on the valley. This gripping overlook, 3214 ft. above the valley floor, can stun even the most wilderness-weary traveler. Half Dome rests majestically across the valley, while Nevada Falls looks deceptively peaceful from such a distance.

DAY HIKING IN THE VALLEY. To have the full Yosemite experience, visitors must travel the outer trails on foot. A wealth of opportunities reward anyone willing to lace up a pair of boots, even if only for a daytrip. Day-use trails are usually as busy as the New York Stock Exchange, and are sometimes as packed as a Pearl Jam concert. Hiking just after sunrise is the best, and sometimes the only, way to beat the crowds. But even then, trails like Half Dome are already busy. A colorful trail map with difficulty ratings and average hiking times is available at the visitors center (50¢). The **Mirror Lake Loop** is a level 3 mi. walk. **Bridalveil Falls,** another Ansel Adams favorite, is an easy ¼ mi. stroll from the nearby shuttle bus stop, and its cool spray is as close to a shower as many Yosemite campers ever get. This trail, as well as **Lower Yosemite Falls Trail,** is wheelchair accessible. The Lower Yosemite Falls Trail is a favorite of all ages and starts just opposite the Yosemite Lodge. **Upper Yosemite Falls Trail,** a back-breaking 3½ mi. trek to the windy summit, rewards the intrepid hiker with an overview of the 2425 ft. drop. Those with energy to spare can trudge on to **Yosemite Point,** where views of the valley below rival those from more-heralded Glacier Point. The trail begins with an extremely steep, unshaded ascent. Leaving the marked trail is not a wise idea—a sign warns, "If you go over the waterfall, you will die."

From the Happy Isles trailhead, the **John Muir Trail** leads 211 mi. to Mt. Whitney, but most visitors prefer to take the slightly less strenuous 1½ mi. **Mist Trail** past **Vernal Falls** to the top of **Nevada Falls.** This is perhaps the most popular day-use trail in the park, and with good reason—views of the falls from the trails are outstanding, and the indefatigable drizzle that issues from the nearby water-assaulted rocks is more than welcome during the hot summer months. From Nevada Falls, the trail continues to the base of **Half Dome,** Yosemite's most recognizable monument and strong testament to the power of glaciation.

CLIMBING AND RAFTING. The world's best **climbers** come to Yosemite to test themselves at angles past vertical. If you've got the courage (and the cash), you can join the stellar Yosemite rock climbers by taking a lesson with the **Yosemite Mountaineering School** (see p. 869). Basic rock climbing classes (mid-Apr. to Oct.) teach simple skills on the ground such as bouldering, rappelling, and ascending an 80 ft. high cliff. Reservations are useful and require advance payment, although drop-ins are accepted if space allows. (☎372-8344. Open daily 8:30am-5pm.)

Rafting is permitted on the Merced River (10am-4pm) when deemed safe (when the water is warm and high enough), but no motorized crafts are allowed. For organized rafting trips, **All Outdoors,** 1250 Pine St. #103, Walnut Creek 94596 (☎925-932-8993 or 800-247-2387) leads trips on the north fork of Stanislaus River (leave from Calaveras Big Trees State Park), the Merced River (Mt. View Store, Midpines), the Kaweah River (Kaweah General Store), and Goodwin Canyon (Stanislaus River Park, Sonora).

ORGANIZED ACTIVITIES. Open-air tram tours (☎372-1240) leave from Curry Village, the Ahwahnee Hotel, Yosemite Lodge, and the Village Store. Tickets are available at lodging facilities and the Village Store tour desk. The basic, 2hr. **Valley Floor Tour** points out Half Dome, El Capitan, Bridalveil Falls, and Happy Isles (departs every 30min; $17.50, seniors $15.75, ages 5-12 $9.50). The 4hr. **Glacier Point Tour** climbs 3200 ft. to the point for a view of the valley 7300 ft. below (June-Oct.; $20.50, ages 5-12 $11). The 2hr. **Moonlight Tour,** on nights with a full (or nearly full) moon, offers unique nighttime views of the valley (2hr.; $17.50).

Park rangers lead a variety of informative hikes and other activities for visitors of all ages. Daily **junior ranger** (ages 8-10) and **senior ranger** (ages 11-12) activities allow children to hike, raft, and investigate aquatic and terrestrial life. (Free. Reservations required at least a day in advance through the **Yosemite Valley Visitors Center,** see p. 869.) Rangers also guide a number of free walks. **Discover Yosemite Family Pro-**

grams address a variety of historical and geological topics (3hr., daily 9am; most wheelchair accessible). Rangers also lead strenuous, 4-8hr. **Destination Hikes** into the high country from Tuolumne Meadows. **Sunrise photo walks** leave most mornings from the Yosemite Lodge tour desk (free).

THE BACKCOUNTRY

Most folks never leave the valley, but a wilder, more isolated Yosemite awaits those who do. Topographical maps and hiking guides are especially helpful in navigating Yosemite's nether regions.

WINTERTIME IN YOSEMITE. Cross-country skiing is free, and several well-marked trails cut into the backcountry of the valley's South Rim at Badger Pass and Crane Flat. Both areas have markers on the trees so trails can be followed even under several feet of snow; this same snow transforms many summer hiking trails into increasingly popular **snowshoe trails.** Rangers host several snowshoe walks, but the serene winter forests are perhaps best explored *sans* guidance. Snowshoes and skis can be rented from the **Yosemite Mountaineering School** (see p. 869).

The state's oldest ski resort, **Badger Pass Ski Area,** on Glacier Point Rd. south of Yosemite Valley, is the only downhill ski area in the park. The resort's powder may not rival the soft stuff of Tahoe, but its family-fun atmosphere fosters learning and restraint (but no snowboards). Free shuttles connect Badger Pass with Yosemite Valley. (☎372-8430. Lifts open 9am-4:30pm. Group ski lessons $22 for 2hr., private lessons from $44. Rental packages $18 per day, under 12 $13. 1-day lift tickets M-F $22, Sa-Su $28; under 12 daily $13; some specials for those over 60 or exactly 40. Some weekday discounts available through Yosemite Lodge.)

NEAR YOSEMITE: STANISLAUS NATIONAL FOREST

This highly preserved land circles Yosemite and connects the forests along the northern Sierra. Well-maintained roads and campsites, craggy peaks, dozens of topaz lakes, wildflower meadows, and forests of Ponderosa pines make up the 900,000 acres of the Stanislaus National Forest. Peregrine falcons, bald eagles, mountain lions, and bears sometimes surprise the lucky or tasty traveler. Besides great fishing, campsites, and hiking trails, Stanislaus offers solitude—something its better-known neighbor, Yosemite, doesn't have. **Park headquarters** are at 19777 Greenly Rd., Sonora. (☎532-3671. Open M-F 8am-5pm, until 4:30pm in winter.) Camping permits are required for Carson-Iceberg, Mokelumne, and Emigrant Wilderness; permits are also needed to build fires in wilderness areas. Only Pinecrest accepts reservations.

MONO LAKE ☎760

As fresh water from streams and springs drains into this "inland sea," it evaporates, leaving behind a mineral-rich, 13 mi.-wide expanse Mark Twain once called "the Dead Sea of the West." The lake derives its lunar appearance from towers of calcium carbonate (similar to giant drip sandcastles) called tufa, which form when calcium-rich springs well up in the carbonate-filled salt water. At 1 million years old, the lake is the oldest enclosed body of water in the Western Hemisphere.

The Mono Lake Committee offers **canoe tours** of the lake that include a crash course in conservation and Mono's natural history. (☎647-6595. Tours $17, ages 4-12 $7. Reservations required.) The unique terrain of this geological playground makes it a great place for hikers of all levels. Easy trails include the quarter-mile **Old Marina Area Trail,** east of U.S. 395 1 mi. north of Lee Vining, the **Lee Vining Creek Nature Trail,** which begins behind the Mono Basin Visitors Center, and the **Panum Crater Trail,** 5 mi. south on U.S. 395.

The **El Mono Motel,** on Main and 3rd St., offers a slice of modern California: faux Spanish name, white stucco exterior, espresso bar, and alternative rock in the lobby. Clean and bright rooms have cable TV but no phone. (☎647-6310. Open Apr.-Oct. Singles $49-65.) None of the area's campgrounds take reservations, but sites are ubiquitous, so a pre-noon arrival time will almost always guarantee a spot. Most sites are clustered west of Lee Vining along Rte. 120. Try **Inyo National Forest Camp-**

grounds, which are close to town. **Lundy** and **Lee Vining Canyons** are the best locations for travelers headed for Mono Lake. (No water. Open May-Oct. Sites $7.) **Ellery Lake,** on Tioga Pass Rd. at Rte. 120 across from Tioga Pass Resort, has 12 first come, first camp sites near a brook. (Running water, chemical toilets. Sites $11.)

In 1984, Congress set aside 57,000 acres of land surrounding Mono Lake and named it the **Mono Basin National Forest Scenic Area** (☎ 873-2408). For a $3 fee (Golden Eagle, Golden Age, and Golden Access passes accepted), investigate the **South Tufa Grove,** which harbors and awe-inspiring hoard of calcium carbonate formations. Take U.S. 395 S to Rte. 120, then go 4 mi. east and take the Mono Lake South Tufa turn-off 1 mi. south to Tufa Grove.

The town of Lee Vining provides stunning access to Yosemite as well as the best access to Mono Lake and the ghost town of Bodie. Lee Vining is 70 mi. north of Bishop on U.S. 395 and 10 mi. west of the Tioga Pass entrance to Yosemite. **Mono Lake Committee and Lee Vining Chamber of Commerce** (☎ 647-6595) offers lodging, dining, and local services at Main and 3rd St., in the orange-and-blue building. **Mono Basin National Forest Scenic Area Visitors Center,** Inyo National Forest, off U.S. 395 a half-mile north of Lee Vining, is housed in a new structure that resembles a modern-day cathedral or *Architectural Digest* centerfold. (☎ 873-2408. Open M-F 9am-5:30pm.) **Post Office:** 4th St., Lee Vining, in the big brown building. (☎ 647-6371. Open M-F 9am-2pm and 3-5pm.) **ZIP Code:** 93541. **Area code:** 760.

MAMMOTH LAKES   ☎ 760

Home to one of the most popular ski resorts in the US, the town of Mammoth Lakes has transformed itself into a giant year-round playground. Mammoth Mountain metamorphosizes from ski park in winter to bike park in summer, with fishing, rock climbing, and hiking to boot. Even the McDonald's looks like a ski lodge. The weekend nightlife is lively and entirely full of athletes who come to this alpine paradise to get vertical and have mammoth fun. Mammoth Lakes is on U.S. 395 160 mi. south of Reno and 40 mi. southeast of the eastern entrance to Yosemite. Rte. 203 runs through the town as Main St. and then veers off to the right as Minaret Summit Rd. In the winter, the roads from L.A. are jammed with weekend skiers making the 6hr. journey up to the slopes.

As with most ski resorts, lodging is much more expensive in the winter, but prices tend to be cheaper on weekdays. Condo rentals are a comfortable choice for groups of three or more, and start at $65 per night. **Mammoth Reservation Bureau** (☎ 800-462-5571) can make rental arrangements. For lone travelers, dorm-style motels are the cheapest option. Make reservations far in advance. There are nearly 20 Inyo Forest public campgrounds (sites $12-14) in the area, at Mammoth Lakes, Mammoth Village, Convict Lake, Red's Meadow, and June Lake. All sites have piped water, and most are near fishing and hiking. Interested parties should contact the **Mammoth Ranger District** (☎ 924-5500) for info. Reservations can be made for all sites, as well as at nearby Sherwin Creek (☎ 800-280-2267; reservation fee $8.65).

One of the best views in town is from the **Davison St. Guest House,** 19 Davison Rd. (☎ 924-2188. Dorms $16, singles $32; in winter $18/$55.) **The Stove,** 644 Old Mammoth Rd., 4 blocks from Main St., serves big breakfasts. There's down-home cooking for dinner—the bacon avocado burger is heaven on a bun ($7). Vegetarian options are also available. (☎ 934-2821. Open daily 6:30am-9pm.)

Devil's Postpile National Monument was formed when lava flows oozed through Mammoth Pass thousands of years ago, forming 40-60 ft. basalt posts. A pleasant 3 mi. walk from the center of Devil's Postpile Monument is Rainbow Falls, where the middle fork of the San Joaquin River drops 101 ft. into a glistening green pool. From U.S. 395, the trailhead is a 15 mi. drive past Minaret Summit on Rte. 203. A quick ½ mi. hike from the Twin Lakes turn-off culminates in spectacular views from **Panorama Dome.** Lake Mamie has a picturesque picnic area and many short hikes lead out to Lake George, where exposed granite sheets attract climbers. These trailheads and scenic spots are accessible from the **MAS shuttle.**

Mammoth Mountain High Adventure gets people high. (Through adventure. And mountains.) The stately climbing wall stands like a modern-day shrine to extreme sports, beckoning both the inexperienced and the professional. (☎924-5683. Open daily 10am-6pm. $13 per hr., $22 per day; discount for groups of 3 or more.) The **Mammoth Mountain Gondola** reaches a view miles above the rest. (☎934-2571. Open daily 8am-4pm. Round-trip $16, children $8; day pass $25 for gondola and trail use.) Exit the gondola at the top for a mountain biking extravaganza over the twisted trails of **Mammoth Mountain Bike Park,** where the ride starts at 11,053 ft. and heads straight down rocky ski trails. (☎934-0706. Helmets required. Open 9am-6pm.)

With 150 downhill runs, over 28 lifts, and miles of nordic skiing trails, Mammoth is one of the country's premier winter resorts. The season extends from mid-Nov. to June; in a good year, downhill skiing can last through July. Mammoth Mountain lift tickets can be purchased at the Main Lodge on Minaret Rd. (☎934-2571. Open daily 7:30am-3pm.) A free **shuttle bus (MAS)** transports skiers between lifts, town, and the **Main Lodge**. The U.S. Forest Service provides information and tips on the area's cross-country trails. For info, contact the **Inyo National Forest Visitors Center and Chamber of Commerce** (☎924-5500 or 934-0210), east off U.S. 395 north of town. **Post Office:** 3330 Main St. (open M-F 8:30am-5pm). **ZIP code:** 93546. **Area code:** 760.

CALIFORNIA

THE PACIFIC NORTHWEST

Until the encroachment of European settlement, Native American tribes like the Palouse and Spokane were on the move nine months of every year, hunting buffalo herds across the flat, dry region east of the Cascades. Coast dwellers like the Salish formed stable, stationary communities ruled by a hereditary chief and sustained by abundant resources. President Thomas Jefferson commissioned Meriwether Lewis and William Clark to explore the Pacific Northwest in 1803. Accompanied by Sacajawea, a Shoshone translator, the expedition traveled about 4000 miles each way from St. Louis to the mouth of the Columbia River and back.

In the 1840s, Senator Stephen Douglas argued, sensibly, that the Cascade Range would make the perfect natural border between two new states. Sense has little to do with politics, of course, and the Columbia River, running perpendicular to the Cascades, became the border between Washington and Oregon. Yet even today, the range and not the river is the region's most important geographic and cultural divide: west of the rain-trapping Cascades lie the microchip, mocha, and music meccas of Portland and Seattle; to the east sprawl farmland and an arid plateau.

For comprehensive coverage of the Northwest, refer to *Let's Go: Alaska and the Pacific Northwest*.

HIGHLIGHTS OF THE PACIFIC NORTHWEST

SEATTLE. The off-beat neighborhoods, fine museums, ample green space, and pioneering cafes of this thriving city are not to be missed (p. 877).

NATIONAL PARKS. Oregon's Crater Lake National Park (p. 915) puts the region's volcanic past on display. In Washington, Olympic National Park (p. 894) has mossy grandeur and deserted beaches; life beautifully blankets the dormant Mt. Rainier (p. 898).

SCENIC DRIVES. Rte. 20 (p. 901) winds through the emerald North Cascades, while U.S. 101 takes visitors on a spin through the Oregon Coast (p. 910).

WASHINGTON

On Washington's western shores, wet Pacific storms feed one of the world's only temperate rainforests in Olympic National Park, and low clouds linger over Seattle, hiding the Emerald City. Visitors to Puget Sound enjoy both island isolation in the San Juan islands and cosmopolitan entertainment in the concert halls and art galleries of the mainland. Over the Cascades, the state's eastern half spreads out into fertile farmlands and grassy deserts, while fruit bowls runneth over around Yakima, Spokane, and Pullman.

◪ PRACTICAL INFORMATION

Capital: Olympia.

Visitor Info: Washington State Tourism, Dept. of Community, Trade and Economic Development, P.O. Box 42500, Olympia, WA 98504 (☎800-544-1800; www.tourism.wa.gov). **Washington State Parks and Recreation Commission,** P.O. Box 42650, Olympia, WA 98504 (☎360-902-8500, info 800-233-0321; www.parks.wa.gov).

Postal Abbreviation: WA. **Sales Tax:** 7-9.1%, depending on county.

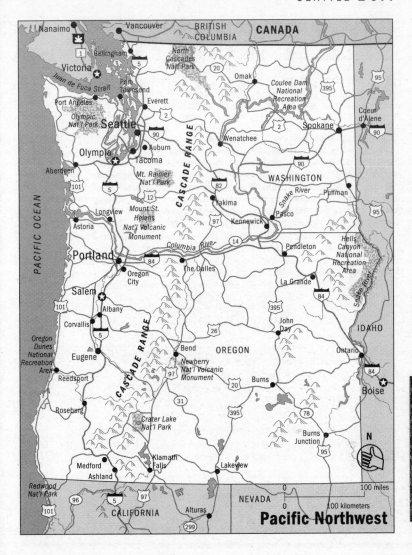

Pacific Northwest

SEATTLE   ☎ 206

Seattle's mix of mountain views, clean streets, espresso stands, and rainy weather proved to be the magic formula of the 90s, attracting transplants from across the US. Even today, newcomers arrive in droves, armed with college degrees and California license plates, hoping for computer industry jobs and a different lifestyle. Seattle duly blesses them with a magnificent setting and a thriving artistic community. The city is one of the youngest and most vibrant in the nation, and a nearly epidemic fascination with coffee has also made it one of the most caffeinated. Every hilltop in Seattle offers an impressive view of Mt. Olympus, Mt. Baker, and Mt. Rainier. The city is shrouded in cloud cover 200 days a year, but when the skies clear, Seattleites rejoice that "the mountain is out" and head for the country.

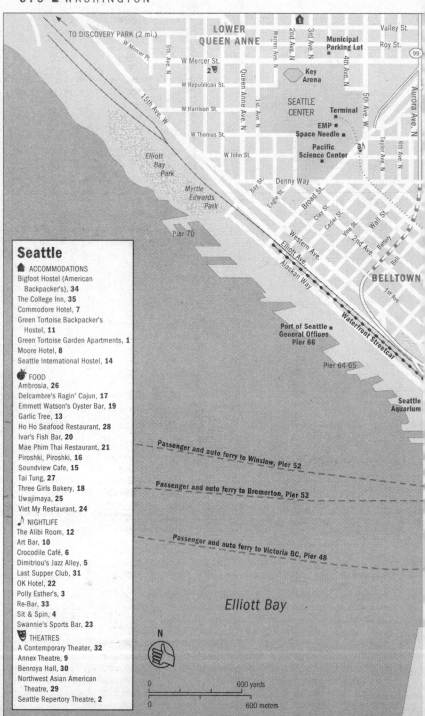

Seattle

ACCOMMODATIONS
Bigfoot Hostel (American
    Backpacker's), **34**
The College Inn, **35**
Commodore Hotel, **7**
Green Tortoise Backpacker's
    Hostel, **11**
Green Tortoise Garden Apartments, **1**
Moore Hotel, **8**
Seattle International Hostel, **14**

FOOD
Ambrosia, **26**
Delcambre's Ragin' Cajun, **17**
Emmett Watson's Oyster Bar, **19**
Garlic Tree, **13**
Ho Ho Seafood Restaurant, **28**
Ivar's Fish Bar, **20**
Mae Phim Thai Restaurant, **21**
Piroshki, Piroshki, **16**
Soundview Cafe, **15**
Tai Tung, **27**
Three Girls Bakery, **18**
Uwajimaya, **25**
Viet My Restaurant, **24**

NIGHTLIFE
The Alibi Room, **12**
Art Bar, **10**
Crocodile Café, **6**
Dimitriou's Jazz Alley, **5**
Last Supper Club, **31**
OK Hotel, **22**
Polly Esther's, **3**
Re-Bar, **33**
Sit & Spin, **4**
Swannie's Sports Bar, **23**

THEATRES
A Contemporary Theater, **32**
Annex Theatre, **9**
Benroya Hall, **30**
Northwest Asian American
    Theatre, **29**
Seattle Repertory Theatre, **2**

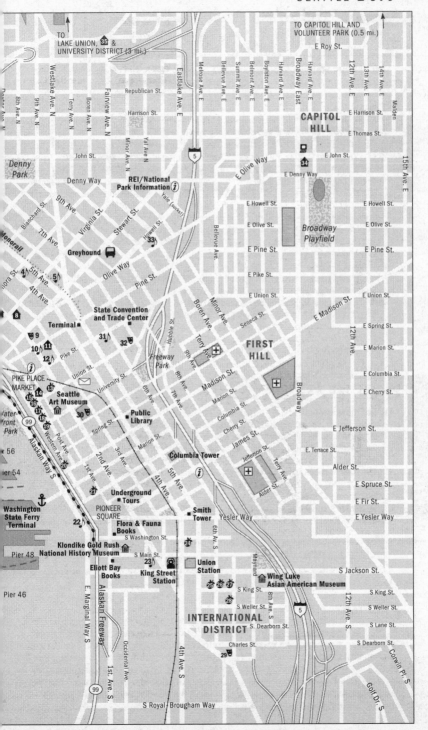

✈ GETTING THERE AND AWAY

Seattle is easily accessible by car via **I-5,** which runs north-south through the city, east of downtown, and by **I-90** from the east, which ends at I-5.

Airport: Seattle-Tacoma International (Sea-Tac) (☎431-4444), on Federal Way, 15 mi. south of Seattle. Bus #194 departs the underground tunnel at University St. & 3rd Ave.

Trains: Amtrak (☎382-4125), King St. Station, at 3rd and Jackson St., 1 block east of Pioneer Square next to Kingdome. To: Portland, OR (4 per day, $21-34), Spokane (1 per day, $42-74), San Francisco, CA (1 per day, $110-157), and Vancouver, BC (1 per day, $24-33). Ticket office and station open daily 6:15am-8pm.

Buses: Greyhound (☎628-5526), at 8th Ave. and Stewart St. To: Spokane (6 per day, $31); Vancouver, BC (16 per day, $21.50); and Portland, OR (14 per day, $20). Ticket office open daily 6:30am-2:30am. **Quick Shuttle** (☎604-940-4428 or 800-665-2122) makes 8 cross-border trips daily from the Travelodge hotel at 8th and Bell St. in Seattle and the Sea-Tac airport to the Vancouver, BC, airport and the Sandman Inn on Granville St. in downtown Vancouver (4-4½hr., $29 from downtown, $35 from Sea-Tac). **Green Tortoise Bus Service** (☎800-867-8647) departs 9th Ave. and Stewart St. Cushioned seats fold into beds at night on this bus-turned-lounge that stops en route for barbecues, swimming holes, and saunas at their own private retreat. To: Portland, OR (4½hr., $15); Eugene, OR (7½hr., $30); Berkeley, CA (24hr., $69); San Francisco, CA (25hr., $69); and Los Angeles, CA (overnight in San Francisco, 2 days, Th only; $89).

Ferries: Washington State Ferries (☎464-6400 or 800-843-3779), Colman Dock, Pier 52, downtown. Service from downtown to Vashon Island (25min.). No Su service; passengers only. To reach the **Fauntleroy ferry terminal** in West Seattle, drive south on I-5 and take Exit 163A down Fauntleroy Way. From Fauntleroy to Vashon Island (15min.). All eastbound ferries crossing the Sound have the same price: June to mid-Oct. $3.70, car and driver $8.25 each way; off-season $6.50. Westbound foot traffic travels for free. **Victoria Clipper** (☎448-5000 or 800-668-1167) takes passengers from Seattle to Victoria only. Departs from Pier 48 (3hr.; 2-4 per day; one-way $60-69, seniors $54-63, under 12 half-price).

▐ GETTING AROUND

Public Transportation: Metro Transit, 801 2nd Ave. (☎553-3000 or 800-542-7876; TTY 689-1739), in the Exchange Building downtown. The bus tunnel under Pine St. and 3rd Ave. is the heart of the downtown bus system. Open M-F 9am-5pm. Fares are based on a 2-zone system. **Zone 1** includes everything within the city limits ($1.25, off-peak $1). **Zone 2** includes everything else ($1.75/$1.25). Ages 5-18 always 75¢. **Peak hours** in both zones M-F 6-9am and 3-6pm. Exact fare required. Weekend day passes $2. Ride free daily 6am-7pm in the downtown "ride free" area, bordered by S. Jackson on the south, 6th and I-5 on the east, Blanchard on the north, and the waterfront on the west. Free transfers can be used on any bus, including a return trip on the same bus within 2hr. **Mono Rail** runs from Space Needle to Westlake Center, on the 3rd fl. Every 15min. 9am-11pm; $1.25, seniors 50¢, ages 5-12 75¢.

Ride Board: First fl. of **Husky Union Building (HUB),** behind Suzallo Library on University of Washington main campus. Matches cars and riders, within geographical reason. Also check the board at **Seattle HI** (p. 881) and the **Green Tortoise Hostel** (p. 881).

Taxi: Farwest Taxi, ☎622-1717. **Metro Cab,** ☎901-0707.

✦ ORIENTATION

Seattle is a long, skinny city, stretched north to south on an isthmus between **Puget Sound** to the west and **Lake Washington** to the east, linked by locks and canals (for more on cities and isthmi, see **Madison,** p. 521). From I-5, downtown (including Pioneer Sq., Pike Place Market, and the waterfront) can be accessed by taking any of the exits from James St. to Stewart St. The less crowded **Rte. 99,** also called Aurora Ave. or the Aurora Hwy., runs parallel to I-5 and skirts the western side of downtown, with great views from the Alaskan Way Viaduct.

Downtown, **avenues** run northwest to southeast, and **streets** run southwest to northeast. Outside downtown, avenues run north-south and streets east-west. The city is split into **quadrants:** 1000 1st Ave. NW is a long walk from 1000 1st Ave. SE. **Parking** is cheap, plentiful, and well lit at the **Seattle Center,** near the Space Needle. Park there and take the monorail to the convenient **Westlake Center** downtown. The **City of Seattle Bicycle Program** (☎684-7583) furnishes bicycle maps.

⚡ PRACTICAL INFORMATION

Visitor Information: Seattle-King County Visitors Bureau (☎461-5840), at 8th and Pike St., on the first fl. of the convention center. Helpful staff doles out maps, brochures, newspapers, and Metro and ferry schedules. Open June-Oct. M-F 8:30am-5pm, Sa-Su 10am-4pm; Nov.-May M-F 8:30am-5pm, Sa 10am-4pm.

Outdoor Information: Seattle Parks and Recreation Department, 100 Dexter St. (☎684-4075). Open M-F 8am-5pm. **National Park Service,** 222 Yale Ave. (☎470-4060), in REI (see **Equipment Rental,** below). Open Tu-F 10:30am-7pm, Sa 9am-7pm, Su 11am-6pm; winter hrs. may be shortened.

Equipment Rental: REI, 222 Yale Ave. (☎223-1944 or 888-873-1938), near Capitol Hill. The mothership of camping supply stores. Open M-F 10am-9pm, Sa 9am-7pm, Su 11am-6pm. **The Bicycle Center,** 4529 Sand Point Way (☎523-8300), near the Children's Hospital. Rents mountain and hybrid bikes ($3 per hr., $15 per day; 2hr. minimum). Open M-F 10am-8pm, Sa 10am-6pm, Su 10am-5pm.

Internet Access: Every 3rd cafe in Seattle charges about $6 per hr., as does **Capitol Hill Net,** 219 Broadway Ave E #23 (☎860-6858), upstairs in Alley Mall. But here *Let's Go* toters and all hostelers get 15min. free. Open daily 10am-midnight.

Hotlines: Crisis Line, ☎461-3222. **Rape Crisis,** ☎800-825-7273. **Harborview Medical,** ☎521-1800. All 24hr.

Gay and Lesbian Services: 1820 E. Pine (☎323-0220 or 800-527-7683). Open M-F 3-9pm. **Lesbian Resource Center,** 2214 S. Jackson St. (☎264-4409), at 23rd St. Support groups, drop-ins, library, workshops. Open Tu-F noon-7pm, Su noon-5pm. **AIDS Information,** 400 Yesler Way, 3rd. fl. (☎205-7837). Open M-F 9am-5pm.

Medical Services: International District Emergency Center (☎623-3321). Multilingual staff. 24hr. **Aradia Women's Health Center,** 1300 Spring St. (☎323-9388). Open M-F 10am-4pm. **Health South Medical Center,** 1151 Denny Way (☎682-7418). Walk-in. **Providence Medical Center,** 500 17th Ave. (☎320-2111), for urgent care. 24hr.

Post Office: at Union St. and 3rd Ave. downtown. Open M-F 8am-5:30pm. General delivery window open M-F 10am-noon, 1-3pm. **ZIP Code:** 98101. **Area Code:** 206.

▗ ACCOMMODATIONS

Seattle's hostel scene is alive, friendly, and clean. **Pacific Lodging Association** arranges B&B singles in the $55-65 range. (☎784-0539. Open M-F 9am-5pm.) Those tired of urban high-rises can head for the **Vashon Island Hostel** (see p. 889).

■ **Green Tortoise Backpacker's Hostel,** 1525 2nd Ave. (☎340-1222; fax 623-3207), between Pike and Pine St. on the #174 or 194 bus route. A young party hostel downtown; lots of people, lots of activities. Free beer common on Tu and F; pub-crawls F. Laundry, kitchen. Internet access $1 per 5min. $20 cash key deposit required. Linens $1 with $9 deposit. Free continental breakfast 6-9:30am. Free dinner on M night. Reception 24hr. 150 beds in 48 rooms $18, $17 with cash, $1 off with HI or ISIC. 10 private rooms $50, winter $45.

Seattle International Hostel (HI), 84 Union St. (☎622-5443 or 888-622-5443), at Western Ave., right by the waterfront. Walk west/northwest from the airport bus stops in downtown, then head down the stairs under the "Pike Pub & Brewery." Overlooks the water. TV lounge off common room. Coin laundry. Ride board. Internet $6 per hr. 7-night maximum stay in summer. Reception 24hr. 199 beds, 6-10 per room $17, non-members $20. Private rooms for 2-3 $41/$47. Reservations recommended.

Moore Hotel, 1926 2nd Ave. (☎448-4851 or 800-421-5508), at Virginia, 1 block east from Pike Place Market, next to historic Moore Theater. Open lobby, cavernous halls, and attentive service makes the Moore more reminiscent of the 20s. Singles $35, with bath $57; doubles (1 bed) $39/$60. Big room with 2 beds and bath $67. Large suites, some with kitchen, $80-120. HI discount 15%.

Green Tortoise Garden Apartments, 715 2nd Ave. N (☎340-1222; fax 623-3207), on the south slope of Queen Anne Hill, 3 blocks east from the Space Needle and Seattle Center. Long-term accommodations with backyard, kitchen, garden, laundry, free tea/coffee. Beds $260 per month and $80 per additional week (one-month minimum stay), with 4 people per room. $90 deposit.

Bigfoot Hostel (American Backpacker's), 126 Broadway Ave. E (☎720-2965 or 800-600-2965). From Broadway, follow Olive Way east, taking the first right. Free pick-up from bus, train or downtown. Free kitchen, linens, laundry, pool table, Internet, parking, and breakfast. Beer on F. Reception 7am-2am. Curfew weekdays 2am, weekends 4am. 48 beds: $17, $15 winter, $1 off with ISIC. $10 key deposit.

The College Inn, 4000 University Way NE (☎633-4441), at N.E. 40th St. Quiet place near UW campus and its youthful environs. Rooms are tiny, but turn-of-the-century bureaus and brass fixtures are s'durned *charming*. Free continental breakfast. Singles from $49; doubles from $65. Credit card required.

☕ FOOD

Although Seattleites appear to subsist solely on espresso and steamed milk, they do occasionally eat. When they do, they seek out healthy cuisine, especially seafood. The **University District** supports inexpensive and international cuisine. The **Chinatown/International District** offers tons of rice, pounds of fresh fish, and enough veggies to keep your mother happy, all at ridiculously low prices. Capitol Hill, the U District, and Fremont close main thoroughfares on summer Sa for **farmers' markets.**

■ **Bimbo's Bitchin' Burrito Kitchen,** 506 E. Pine (☎329-9978). The name explains it, and the decorations (fake palm trees and dancing monkeys) prove it. An experience. Spicy Bimbo's burrito $4. Open M-Th noon-11pm, F-Sa noon-2am, Su 2-10pm.

Piroshki, Piroshki, 1908 Pike Pl. (☎441-6068). The Russian Piroshki is a croissant-like dough baked around sausages, mushrooms, cheeses, salmon, or apples, doused in cinnamon. Open daily 8:30am-6pm.

Delcambre's Ragin' Cajun, 1523 1st Ave. (☎624-2598), near Pike Place. A tremendous portion of spicy red beans with *andouille* (a flavorful sausage) was enjoyed here by former President Clinton in 1995. Lunch $6-8. Dinner almost twice that. Open M-Sa 11am-3pm and Th-Sa 5:30-8:30pm.

Ivar's Fish Bar, Pier 54 (☎624-6852), north of the square, is named for late Seattle shipping magnate Ivar Haglund. Enjoy the definitive Seattle clam chowder ($2). Four-piece fish and chips $5.69. Open daily 11am-2am.

Tai Tung, 655 S King St. (☎622-7372). Select authentic Chinese and Mandarin cuisine from one of the largest menus around. Grab a bite at the bar where menus are plastered on the wall. Entrees $5-12. Open Su-Th 10am-11:30pm, F-Sa 10am-1:30am.

Ho Ho Seafood Restaurant, 653 S. Weller St. (☎382-9671). Generous portions of tank-fresh seafood. Great place for large parties to share food on round, spinning tables. Lunch $5-7; dinner $7-12. Open Su-Th 11am-1am, F-Sa 11am-3am.

Flowers, 4247 University Way NE (☎633-1903). This 20s landmark was once a flower shop. The mirrored ceiling tastefully reflects an all-you-can-eat vegetarian buffet ($7). Great drink specials: W $1 tequila shots, Th $2 Well sours, Sa $2 margaritas. Open M-Sa 11am-2am; kitchen closes at 10pm, but late night snacks go on.

☕ CAFES

Bauhaus, 305 E. Pine St. (☎625-1600). The Reading Goddess looks from above the towering bookshelves, protects patrons, and oversees service of drip coffee ($1) or Kool-Aid ($1). Open M-F 6am-1am, Sa-Su 8am-1am.

CONVOLUTED CONVENTIONS OF A CAFFEINE-CRAZED CULTURE

Visiting Seattle without drinking the coffee would be like traveling to France without tasting the wine. Espresso stands line streets and infiltrate office buildings, and "Let's go for coffee sometime" is a clichéd local pick-up line. It all started in the early 70s, when the fledgling Starbucks started roasting its coffee on the spot in Pike Place Market. Soon, Stewart Brothers Coffee, now Seattle's Best Coffee, presented Starbucks with a rival, and the race was on both for the best cup o' joe and for global hegemony. Today, hundreds of bean-brands compete for the local market, and Seattle coffeeholics often claim undying allegiance to one or another. Learning a few basic terms for ordering espresso drinks can only endear you to locals and enrich your cultural experience: **Espresso:** The foundation of all espresso drinks—a small amount of coffee brewed by forcing steam through finely ground, dark-roasted coffee. **Cappuccino:** Espresso topped by the foam from steamed milk. Order "wet" for more liquid milk and big bubbles, or "dry" for stiff foam. **Frappuccino:** Cold blended coffee drink, with milk shake consistency. **Latte:** Espresso with steamed milk and a little foam. More liquid than a cappuccino. **Americano:** Espresso with hot water—an alternative to classic drip coffee. **Short:** 8 oz. **Tall:** 12 oz. **Grande** (or Large): 16 oz. **Single:** One shot of espresso. **Double:** Two singles. Add shots (usually about 60¢) until you feel you've reached your caffeine saturation point. Triples are common. **Skinnies:** skim (nonfat) milk drinks. **Drip Coffee:** normal coffee.

Espresso Roma, 4201 University Way NE (☎632-6001). Pleasant patio, when sun abides, and quasi-former warehouse interior result in spacious tables with an open-air feel. Mocha $1.65. Internet access $6 per hr. Open daily 7am-11pm.

🔎 SIGHTS

It takes only two frenetic days to get a decent look at most of Seattle's major sights, since most are within walking distance of one another or are within the Metro's "ride free" zone (see **Getting Around,** p. 880). Any one of the ferries that leave from the waterfront affords a great glimpse of the city's skyline.

DOWNTOWN. The new **Seattle Art Museum** lives in a grandiose building with an entire floor dedicated to the art of Pacific Northwest Native Americans, plus an extensive collection of modern and contemporary regional works. Admission is good for the fabulous **Seattle Asian Art Museum** (see p. 885) as well. *(100 University Way, near 1st Ave. ☎654-3100 or 654-3255, TDD 654-3137. Open Tu-W and F-Su 10am-5pm, Th 10am-9pm. Free tours 12:30, 1, and 2pm; sometimes Th 6:15pm. $7, students and seniors $5, under 12 free; first Th of the month free.)* **Seattle Art Museum Gallery** displays work by local artists. *(Open M-F 11am-5pm, Sa-Su 11am-4pm.)* Beside the Westlake monorail stop, **Westlake Park's** Art Deco brick patterns and surprisingly dry **Wall of Water** provide nice scenery in which to kick back and listen to steel drums on Pike St.

THE WATERFRONT. The **Pike Place Hillclimb** descends from the south end of Pike Place Market past chic shops and ethnic restaurants to Alaskan Way and the waterfront. *(Elevator available.)* The star attraction of the super-popular ◪**Seattle Aquarium** is an underwater dome, home to harbor seals, fur seals, otters, and others. Touch tanks and costumes delight kids. The world's only aquarium salmon ladder is part of a $1 million salmon exhibit; 11:30am feedings are a sight. *(Pier 59, near Union St. ☎386-4330, TTD 386-4322. Tours 10:30am and 3:30pm. Open daily 9:30am-8pm; in winter 10am-6pm. $8.50, seniors $7.50, ages 6-18 $5.75, ages 3-5 $3.75.)* Next door, the **Omnidome** makes you feel like you're *in* the movie. The sound system may scare small children and scar delicate psyches. *(☎622-1868. Films daily 10am-10pm. $7, seniors $6.50, ages 6-18 $6. Aquarium/Omnidome ticket $14, seniors and ages 13-18 $13, ages 6-13 $10.25, ages 3-5 $3.75.)* You can explore the waterfront by foot or be **streetcar.** The 20s-era cars were brought in from Melbourne after Seattle sold its originals to San

Francisco as "cable cars." Streetcars are wheelchair accessible and run from the Metro opposite the King St. Station in Pioneer Square north to Pier 70 and Myrtle Edwards Park. *(Every 20-30min. M-F 7am-11pm, Sa 8am-11pm, Su 9am-11pm; in winter until 6pm. $1, during peak hours $1.25; children 75¢. Weekend or holiday day pass $2. Under 12 with a paying passenger free Su. Metro passes accepted.)*

SEATTLE CENTER. The 1962 World's Fair demanded a Seattle Center to herald the city of the future. It is home to everything from carnival rides to ballet, but Seattle-ites generally leave the center to tourists and suburbanites, except for during concerts and festivals. The center is bordered by Denny Way, W. Mercer St., 1st Ave., and 5th Ave. The **Space Needle** is a useful landmark for the disoriented. It houses an observation tower and a high-end 360° rotating restaurant. *(☎443-2111. $11, seniors $9, ages 5-12 $5.)* Undoubtedly the biggest and best attraction at the Seattle Center is the new, futuristic, abstract, and technologically brilliant **Experience Music Project (EMP).** The museum is the brainchild of Seattle billionaire Paul Allen, who originally wanted to create a shrine to worship his music idol Jimmy Hendrix. Splash together the technological sophistication and foresight of Microsoft, dozens of ethnomusicologists and multimedia specialists, the world-renowned architect Frank Gehry, and enough money to make the national debt seem small (OK, OK...it was only $350 million), and you have *the* rock and roll museum of the future. *(325 5th St. at Seattle Center. ☎367-5483 or 877-367-5483; TDD 770-2771. From I-5 Exit 167, follow signs to Seattle Center. Bus #15, 4, 3. Open daily 9am-11pm; in winter Su-Th 10am-6pm, F-Sa 10am-11pm. $20, seniors and students 13-17 $16, children $15.)*

PIONEER SQUARE AND ENVIRONS. From the waterfront or downtown, it's just a few blocks south to historic **Pioneer Square,** centered around Yesler Way and 2nd Ave., home of the first Seattleites. The 19th-century buildings, now housing shops and pubs, retain historical intrigue and great crowds of tourists. Originally, downtown was 12 ft. lower than it is. Logs dragged to the local mill's front door earned **Skid Row** its epithet, and the smell of the oil used to lubricate the slide was so noxious that self-respecting Seattleites left the neighborhood. The **Underground Tour** raucously guides visitors through the subterranean city of old. Tours depart from Doc Maynard's Pub. *(610 1st. Ave. ☎682-4646 or 888-608-6337. 90min. tours daily and roughly hourly 9am-7pm. $8, seniors and students ages 13-17 $7, children $4; AAA, ISIC or military $6. Reservations recommended. Cash only.)* **Klondike Gold Rush National Historic Park** depicts Seattle's role in the Klondike gold rush. *(117 S. Main St. ☎553-7220. Open daily 9am-5pm. Tours of Pioneer Square daily at 10am; gold panning demonstration 1 and 3pm. Free.)*

THE INTERNATIONAL DISTRICT. Seattle's **International District** is three blocks east of Pioneer Square, up Jackson on King St. The tiny **Wing Luke Memorial Museum** has a thorough description of Asian-American community life, a permanent exhibit on Asian nationalities in Seattle, and work by local Asian artists. *(407 7th Ave. S ☎623-5124. Open Tu-F 11am-4:30pm, Sa-Su noon-4pm. $2.50, seniors and students $1.50, ages 5-12 75¢. Th free.)* Landmarks of the district include the abstract **Tsutakawa sculpture** at the corner of S. Jackson and Maynard St. and the gigantic dragon mural and pagoda in **Hing Hay Park** at S. King and Maynard St. The **community gardens** at Main and Maynard St. provide a well-tended retreat with free parking spaces nearby.

CAPITOL HILL. Capitol district's leftist and gay communities set the tone for its nightspots, while the neighborhood supports collectives, radical bookstores, and

The Gap. **Broadway** is a center for both alternative lifestyles and mainstream commercialism. **Volunteer Park** was named for the veterans of the Spanish-American War. Though it is unsafe (and closed) at night, it is a popular afternoon destination. The **outdoor stage** often hosts free performances on summer Su. Scale the **water tower** at the 14th Ave. entrance for a stunning 360° panorama of the city and the Olympic Range. The **glass conservatory** houses dazzling orchids. *(Between 11th and 17th Ave. at E Ward St., north of Broadway. Open daily 10am-4pm; summer 10am-7pm. Free.)* The world-renowned ▨**Seattle Asian Art Museum** displays Ming vases and ancient kimonos. *(☎ 654-3100. Open Tu-Su 10am-5pm, Th 10am-9pm. $3, under 12 free; free with SAM ticket, same day.)* North of Volunteer Park on 15th St. is **Lake View Cemetery. Bruce** and **Brandon Lee,** and many founders of Seattle, are buried here. One of the most famous martial artists of the century, Bruce Lee moved to Seattle in his youth; his son Brandon was known for his own formidable skills. Near the top of the cemetery, a row of small evergreen trees are lined behind a bench in their memory.

The ▨**University of Washington Arboretum** nurtures over 4000 species, trees, shrubs, and flowers, and maintains superb walking and running trails. Tours depart the **Graham Visitor Center,** at the southern end of the arboretum on Lake Washington Blvd. *(☎ 543-8800. 10 blocks east of Volunteer Park. Bus #11 from downtown. Open daily sunrise to sunset. Free tours Sa and Su at 1pm.)* Across the street, the tranquil 3½-acre **Japanese Tea Garden** is a retreat of sculpted gardens, fruit trees, a reflecting pool, and a traditional tea house. *(☎ 684-4725. Open daily Mar.-Nov. 10am-dusk. $2.50, seniors, disabled, students, and ages 6-18 $1.50, under 6 free.)*

THE UNIVERSITY DISTRICT. With over 33,000 students, the **University of Washington** comprises the state's cultural and educational center. The U District swarms with students year-round, and Seattleites of all ages take advantage of the area's bohemian bookstores, shops, taverns, and restaurants. The **visitors center** offers campus maps, a self-guided tour book, and information about the university. *(4014 University Way NE at N.E. Campus Way. ☎ 543-9198. Buses #71-73 from downtown, or #7, 9, 43, or 48 from Capitol Hill. Open M-F 8am-5pm. Guided tours leave from center at 10:30am.)* The **Thomas Burke Museum of Natural History and Culture** exhibits a superb collection on Pacific Rim cultures, as well as kid-friendly exhibits. *(45th St. NE and 17th Ave. NE. ☎ 543-5590. In the northwest corner of the campus. Open F-W 10am-5pm, Th 10am-8pm. $5.50, seniors $4, students $2.50, under 5 free.)* Across the street, the astronomy department's old stone **observatory** is open to the public on clear nights. *(☎ 543-0126.)* The red concrete basin in the center of campus is a hub of student radicalism and skateboarding known as **Red Square.** The ▨**Henry Art Gallery,** opposite the visitor center, displays superb modern art in a stark white setting. *(At the western edge of the University campus, at the intersection of 41st NE and 15th NE Ave. ☎ 543-2280. Open Tu-Su 11am-5pm, Th 11am-8pm. $5, seniors $3.50, students free; free Th after 5pm.)*

FREMONT. Fremont, under Rte. 99, is home to residents who pride themselves on their love of art and antiques and the liberal atmosphere of their self-declared "center of the world." Twice in the past ten years Fremont has applied to secede from the US. The **immense troll** who sits beneath the Aurora Bridge on 35th St. grasps a Volkswagen Bug and bears a confounded expression on his cement face. Some say kicking the bug's tire brings good luck; others say it hurts. A flamin' **Vladimir Lenin** resides at the corner of N 36th and N Fremont Pl.

BALLARD. Next door to the U District, the primarily Scandinavian neighborhood of **Ballard** offers a taste of Europe, with a wide variety of eateries and shops lining Market St. The **Nordic Heritage Museum** presents exhibits on the Nordic immigration and influence in the US. *(3014 N.W. 67th St. ☎ 789-5707. Bus #17 from downtown, and bus #44 from the U District, transferring to #17 at 24th and Market. Open Tu-Sa 10am-4pm, Su noon-4pm. $4, seniors and students $3, ages 6-18 $2.)*

WATERWAYS AND PARKS

The waterways that link Lake Washington and Puget Sound are a haven for summer boaters. By **Lake Union,** situated between Capitol Hill and the University District, the **Center for Wooden Boats** maintains a moored flotilla of new and restored small craft for rent. *(1010 Valley St.* ☎*382-2628. Open daily noon-6pm. Rowboats weekends $30, weekdays $19; sailboats $38/$24.)* **Gasworks Park,** a celebrated kite-flying spot at the north end of Lake Union, hosts a furious ◨**4th of July Fireworks show.** *(Take bus #26 from downtown to N 35th St. and Wallingford Ave. N.)* **Gasworks Kite Shop** is one block north of the park. *(3333 Wallingford N.* ☎*633-4780. Open M-F 10am-6pm, Sa 10am-5pm, Su 11am-5pm.)* **Urban Surf,** opposite the park entrance, rents surfboards and in-line skates. *(2100 N Northlake Way.* ☎*545-9463. Boards $15 per day. Skates $5 per hr., $16 per day.)*

Directly north of Lake Union, athletes run, ride, and roll around **Green Lake.** The lake is also given high marks by windsurfers. *(Take bus #16 from downtown.)* Nearby, the habitats at the **Woodland Park Zoo** are highly realistic. *(5500 Phinney Ave.* ☎*684-4800. I-5 N to 50th St. exit or N. 50th St. Bus #5 from downtown. Open May to mid-Sept. 9:30am-6pm; mid-March to April and mid-Sept. to mid-Oct. until 5pm; winter until 4pm. $8.50, students and seniors $7.75, ages 6-17 $6, ages 3-5 $3.75, disabled $5.50.)* Farther west, crowds gather at the **Hiram M. Chittenden Locks,** on N.W. 54th St., to watch a circus of nitwit skippers crossing between Lake Washington and Puget Sound. Salmon jockey up the passage themselves at the **fish ladder.** The **visitors center** for both sights leads free tours. *(N.W. 54th St. Visitors center:* ☎*783-7059. Bus #42 from U District or #17 from downtown. Open daily June-Sept. 10am-6pm. Tours Sa-Su 1 and 3pm, M-F 11am.)*

Across the canals and west of the locks lie the 534 bucolic acres of **Discovery Park,** at 36th Ave. W and W. Government Way, on a lonely point west of the Magnolia District and south of Golden Gardens Park. Eroding bluffs, while dangerous for hikers, provide a haven for birds forced over Puget Sound by bad weather. The park supports much of the flora and fauna of the Pacific Northwest. *(Park:* ☎*386-4236. Open daily 6am-11pm. Visitors center: 3801 W Government Way. Bus#24. Open daily 8:30am-5pm.)* The **Indian Cultural Center** at the park's north end, operated by the **United Indians of All Tribes Foundation,** houses a gallery of modern Native American art. *(*☎*285-4425. Open M-Sa 10am-5pm, Su noon-5pm. Free.)*

Seward Park lies at the south end of a string of beaches and forest preserves on the west shore of Lake Washington; take bus #39. The area offers sweeping views of the lake and Mercer Island and a popular bike loop half-way around the lake.

◩ OUTDOORS

Ever since the Klondike gold rush, Seattle has been in the business of equipping wilderness expeditions. Cyclists should gear up for the 19 mi., 1600-competitor **Seattle to Portland Race** in mid-July. Call the **bike hotline** for more info (☎522-2453). On five **Bicycle Sundays** from May-Sept., Lake Washington Blvd. is open exclusively to cyclists from 10am to 6pm. Call the **Citywide Sports Office** for info (☎684-7092). Many whitewater rafting outfitters are based in the Seattle area, and **Washington State Outfitters and Guides Association** provides advice and info; although their office is closed in summer, they do return phone calls (☎877-275-4964). The **Northwest Outdoor Center,** 2100 Westlake Ave., on Lake Union, gives instructional programs in whitewater and sea kayaking and leads three-day kayaking excursions through the San Juan Islands. (☎281-9694. Open M-F 10am-8pm, Sa-Su 9am-6pm. Kayak rentals $10-15 per hr. Weekdays 3rd and 4th hrs. are free. Make reservations.) Skiing near Seattle is every bit as good as the mountains make it look. Get lift ticket rates and conditions for **Alpental, Ski-Acres,** and **Snoqualmie** by calling ☎232-8182. **Crystal Mountain** (☎663-2265) is the region's newest resort.

♫ ENTERTAINMENT

Seattle has one of the world's most notorious underground music scenes and the 3rd largest theater community in the US. The city supports performance in all sorts of venues, from bars to bakeries. Risers seem to grow from the asphalt in spring, when street fairs and outdoor theater please parkgoers. During summer lunch hours, the free **Out to Lunch** series brings everything from reggae to folk dancing to the parks, squares, and office buildings of downtown Seattle (☎623-0340). The **Seattle Public Library** screens free films as part of the program and hosts daily poetry readings and children's book-reading competitions (☎386-4636). The **Seattle Opera** performs at the Opera House in the Seattle Center from Aug.-May. (☎389-7676; Ticketmaster 292-2787. From $31; half-price rush tickets on the day of the performance for seniors and students.) The **Seattle Symphony Orchestra,** performs in the new Benaroya Hall, 200 University St. at 3rd Ave., from Sept. to June (☎212-4700, tickets 215-4747. Ticket office open M-F 10am-6pm, Sa 1-6pm. Tickets $25-39, seniors half-price, students $10; rush tickets from $6.50.) The **Pacific Northwest Ballet** peforms at the Opera House from Sept.-June. (☎441-9491. From $15; half-price rush tickets available to students and seniors 30min. before showtime.) The **University of Washington** offers the World Series of dance, theater and chamber music. Contact the Meany Hall box office, 400 University Way. (☎543-4880. Open Sept.-June M-F 10:30am-6pm, summer 10:30am-4:30pm. Tickets $25-40. Half-price student rush tickets available 1hr. before show.)

THEATER. Theater rush tickets are often available at nearly half-price on the day of the show (cash only) from **Ticket/Ticket** (☎324-2744). Comedies in the small ⓦ**Empty Space Theatre,** 3509 Fremont Ave. N, one and a half blocks north of the Fremont Bridge, draw the entire city. (☎547-7500. Season Oct. to early July. Box office open Tu-Su from noon. Tickets $14-24; previews and under 25 $10; half-price rush tickets 10min. before curtain.) The **Seattle Repertory Theater,** 155 W. Mercer St., performs at the wonderful Bagley Wright Theater in Seattle Center. (☎443-2222. Box office open M-F 10am-6pm. Tickets $15-45, seniors $29, under 25 $10.) A **Contemporary Theater (ACT),** 700 Union St., puts up modern and off-beat premieres in the summer. (☎292-7670. Box office open M-F 9am-5pm. Tickets $20-45. Under 25 $10.) **Northwest Asian American Theater,** 409 7th Ave. S., in the International District, stages pieces by and about Asian Americans. (☎340-1445. Tickets $6-12.)

MOVIES. Most of the cinemas that screen non-Hollywood films are on Capitol Hill and in the University District. Large, first-run theaters are everywhere, including the mammoth 16-screen **Loews Cineplex Meridian** (☎223-9600) at 7th Ave. and Pike. **Seven Gables,** a local company, has recently bought up the Egyptian, the Metro, the Neptune, and about 25 other theatres. $28 buys admission to any five films at any of their theaters. Call ☎443-4567 for local movie times and locations. On summer Sa, **outdoor cinema** in Fremont begins at dusk at 670 N 34th St., in the U-Park lot by the bridge. (☎767-2593. $5. Music starts at 8pm.) **TCI Outdoor Cinema** shows everything from classics to cartoons for free at the Gasworks Park (☎720-1058; live music 7pm-dusk). **The Egyptian,** 801 E. Pine St., at Harvard Ave. on Capitol Hill, is a handsome Art Deco theater showing artsy flicks. It hosts the **Seattle International Film Festival** in the last week of May and first week of June. (☎323-4978. Festival tickets available at a discount. $7.50, matinees $4.25.) **The Harvard exit,** 807 E. Roy St., on Capitol Hill, shows quality classic and foreign films. The theater is haunted by a ghost and an enormous antique projector. (☎323-8986. $7.50, matinees $4.25.)

SPORTS. Seattle baseball fans cheered when the **Mariners** moved out of the Kingdome; in 1995, sections of the roof fell into the stands. The half-billion dollar, retractable-roofed, hangar-like **Safeco Field,** at First Ave. S and Royal Brougham Way S., is now home to the Ms. (☎622-4487. Tickets from $10.) Seattle's football team, the **Seahawks,** are stuck playing in UW's Husky Stadium until construction on their own stadium is finished. (Tickets ☎628-0888. From $10.) On the other side of town, the sleek **Key Arena** in the Seattle Center is packed to the brim when Seattle's pro basketball team, the **Supersonics,** plays (☎281-5800). For college sports fans, the **University of Washington Huskies** football team has dominated the PAC-10 for years and doesn't plan to let up. Call the Athletic Ticket Office (☎543-2200) for Huskies schedules and prices.

FAIRS AND FESTIVALS. The first Th evening of each month, the arts community sponsors **First Thursday,** a free gallery walk. Street fairs enliven the University District in mid- to late May; at Pike Place Market over Memorial Day weekend; and in Fremont in mid-June, with the **Fremont Fair and Solstice Parade's** music, frivolity, and craft booths. The International District holds an annual two-day bash in mid-July, with East Asian and Pacific food. Call **Chinatown Discovery** for info (☎236-0657 or 583-0460). **Northwest Folklife Festival,** on Memorial Day weekend, is one of Seattle's most notable events, held at the Seattle Center. Dozens of booths, artists, musicians, and dancers congregate to celebrate the area's heritage. (☎684-7300. $5 suggested donation.) The free **Wooden Boat Show** (☎382-2628), on Lake Union, draws a 4th of July weekend crowd. The year-end blow-out is the **Quick and Daring Boatbuilding Contest,** when hopefuls go overboard with a limited kit of tools and materials. The **Seattle Seafair** (☎728-0123), from mid-July to early Aug., is the biggest festival of them all. Neighborhoods contribute with street fairs, parades, music, and a seafood orgy. Big-name rock bands, buskers, and a young crowd flock to **Bumbershoot,** over Labor Day weekend. This massive, four-day arts festival in the Seattle Center caps off the summer. (☎281-7788. 4 days $44; 2 days $28; 1 day $16. Tickets cheaper if you buy them in advance.)

◤ NIGHTLIFE

Seattle has moved beyond beer to a new nightlife frontier: the cafe-bar. The popularity of espresso bars in Seattle might lead one to conclude that caffeine is more intoxicating than alcohol. Seattle establishments posing as diners by day bring on a band, break out the disco ball, and pour microbrews by night. **Pioneer Square** area bars participate in a joint cover ($8, Su-Th $5) to encourage band sampling: **Fenix Cafe and Fenix Underground** (☎467-1111) and **Central Tavern** (☎622-0209) rock constantly, while **Larry's** (☎624-7665) and **New Orleans** (☎622-2563) feature jazz and blues nightly. Many locals tell tourists that Pioneer Sq. is the spot for good beer, music, and crowds—these Seattleites are lying to you like curs. They probably take their beer bucks downtown to **Capitol Hill,** or up Rte. 99 to **Fremont,** where the atmosphere is more laid-back.

■ **Sit and Spin,** 2219 4th St. (cafe/laundromat ☎441-9484; band info 441-9474). Board games keep patrons busy while they wait for their clothes to dry or for alternative bands to stop playing in the back room. The cafe sells everything from local microbrews on tap to bistro food to boxes of laundry detergent. Open Su-Th 9am-midnight, F-Sa 9am-2am. Kitchen opens daily at 11am. F-Sa night cover $6-8.

■ **ARO.space,** 925 E. Pike (☎860-7322), entrance on 10th Ave. What every club should be like, and will be...in the year 2100. No one laughs when they say they're involved in a revolution in art. Drum & bass Th, R&B/pop Su, electronic W and F-Sa. Vegetarian fare $5-7.50. Restaurant open daily 5pm-1am, club 10pm-2am.

Last Supper Club, 124 S. Washington St. (☎748-9975), at Occidental. Two dance floors, playing acid jazz and 70s disco F, funky house, drum & bass and trance Sa. Su nights salsa at 9:30pm. Open W-Su 4pm-2am. Cover F-Sa $10; W, Th, and Su $5.

Art Bar, 1516 2nd Ave. (☎622-4344), opposite the Green Tortoise Hostel. Gallery/bar. Grooving local bands on M. DJs Tu-Su. Tu funk, Th Dancehall Reggae, F jungle, Sa hip-hop. Pints $2.50 from 4-9pm. Open M-F 11am-2am, Sa-Su 4pm-2am. Cover $5-6.

Crocodile Cafe, 2200 2nd Ave. (☎448-2114), at Blanchard in Belltown. Cooks from scratch by day, and plays host to local and national bands by night. House W. Some shows need tix in advance. Open Tu-Sa 8am-2am, Su 9am-3pm for brunch. Cover $5-20. 21+ after 9pm.

The Alibi Room, 85 Pike St. (☎623-3180), across from the Market Cinema in the Post Alley in Pike Place. Self-proclaimed indie filmmaker hangout. Live jazz trio Tu, DJ downstairs W and Th. DJ dance party upstairs F and Sa. Open daily 11am-2am. No cover.

Red Door Alehouse, 3401 Fremont Ave. N (☎547-7521), at N 34th St., across from the Inner-Urban Statue. Throbbing with university students who attest to the good local ale selection and a mile-long beer menu. Try the Pyramid Wheaton or Widmer Hefeweizen with a slice of lemon. Open daily 11:30am-2am. Kitchen closes at 11pm.

Re-Bar, 1114 Howell (☎233-9873). A mixed gay and straight bar. 70s disco Th, Hard house F, Funk/soul/hip-hop Sa, House Su. Ladies night on Sa means lesbian-friendly. Open Th-Sa 10pm-2am. Cover $5-6.

Vogue, 1516 11th Ave. (☎324-5778) off Pike St. Anything goes during this angsty club's Theme nights: house M, live music Tu, Goth W, drag Th, Industrial F, 80s/90s New Wave Sa, Fetish Su. Open 9pm-2am. Cover $2-5.

Neighbours, 1509 Broadway (☎324-5358), in Capitol Hill. A very gay dance club with techno slickness. Open Su-W 9pm-2am, Th 9pm-3am, F-Sa 9pm-4am. Cover Su-Th $1; F-Sa $5.

■ DAYTRIP FROM SEATTLE

VASHON ISLAND. Only a 25min. ferry ride from Seattle, Vashon Island has remained inexplicably invisible to most Seattleites. With its forested hills and expansive sea views, this artists' colony feels like the San Juan Islands without the tourists or an economy to cater to them, though budget travelers will feel well cared for in the island's hostel. Most of the island is covered in Douglas fir, rolling cherry orchards, wildflowers, and strawberry fields, and, on Vashon, all roads lead to rocky beaches. **Vashon Island Bicycles,** 7232 Vashon Hwy., rents bikes (☎463-6225; $10 per hr., $25 per day). **Point Robinson Park** is a gorgeous spot for a picnic, and **free tours** (☎217-6123) of the 1885 **Coast Guard lighthouse** are available. **Vashon Island Kayak Co.,** at Burton Acres Boat Launch, runs guided tours and rents sea kayaks. (☎463-9527. Open F-Su 10am-5pm. Call for weekday rentals. Singles $14 per hr., $35 per half-day, $50 per day; doubles $20/$50/$65. Tours from $48.) More than 500 acres of woods in the middle of the island are laced with moderate **hiking trails.** The Vashon Park District has info (☎463-9602; open daily 9am-5pm). Many of Vashon's residents are artists. **Blue Heron Arts Center,** 19704 Vashon Hwy., coordinates free gallery openings on the first F of each month 7-9:30pm. (☎463-5131. Open Tu-F 11am-5pm, Sa noon-5pm.)

The **Vashon Island AYH Ranch Hostel (HI-AYH),** at 12119 S.W. Cove Rd., west of Vashon Hwy., is sometimes called the "Seattle B." Resembling an old Western town, the hostel offers bunks, open-air teepees and covered wagons. (☎463-2592. Open May-Oct. Free pancake breakfast, free firewood. $11; bicyclists $10; non-members $14. Sleeping bag $2.) The hostel runs **The Lavender Duck B&B** down the road ($55).

Vashon Island stretches between Seattle and Tacoma on its east side and between Southworth and Gig Harbor on its west side. **Washington State Ferries** (☎464-6400 or 800-843-3779) runs ferries to Vashon Island from Seattle (see p. 880). The local **Thriftway** (9740 S.W. Bank Rd.) provides maps, as does the Vashon-Maury **Chamber of Commerce,** 17633 S.W. Vashon Hwy. (☎463-6217). **Area code:** 206.

OLYMPIA   ☎360

While the Evergreen State College campus lies a few miles from the city center, its liberal, highly-pierced student body spills into the state capital to mingle with preppy politicos. Some locals, nostalgic for the era when "Oly" was a smaller city with a thriving fishing industry, scorn upstart youth and their raucous ways. Judging by the nightlife, they have plenty to scorn.

■ PRACTICAL INFORMATION. Olympia is at the junction of I-5 and U.S. 101. **Amtrak,** 6600 Yelm Hwy. (☎923-4602), runs to Seattle (1¾hr., 4 per day, $8.50-16) and Portland, OR (2½hr., 4 per day, $11.50-22). Station open daily 8-11:30am, 12:45-

3:30pm, and 4:30-8:15pm. **Greyhound,** 107 E 7th Ave. (☎357-5541), at Capitol Way, goes to Seattle (1¾hr., 6-7 per day, $9.50); Portland, OR (2¾hr., 6-7 per day, $20); and Sea-Tac ($5 one way, $8 round-trip). **Intercity Transit (IT)** provides service almost anywhere in Thurston County, even with bicycles. (☎786-1881 or 800-287-6348. Fare 60¢; day passes $1.25.) The free **Capitol Shuttle** runs from the Capitol Campus to downtown or to the east side and west side (every 15min., 6:45am-5:45pm). For the standard fare, **Custom** buses pick up where normal fixed routes stop (☎943-7777. Runs M-Sa after 7pm.) **Washington State Capitol Visitors Center** is on Capitol Way at 14th Ave., next to the State Capitol; follow the signs on I-5. (☎586-3460. Open M-F 8am-5pm.) **The Olympic National Forest Headquarters,** 1835 Black Lake Blvd. SW, provides info on land in and outside the park. (☎956-2400. Open M-F 8am-4:30pm.) **Post Office:** 900 Jefferson SE. (☎357-2289. Open M-F 7:30am-12:25pm and 1-6pm, Sa 9am-12:25pm and 1-4pm.) **ZIP code:** 98501. **Area code:** 360.

▐▛▟ ACCOMMODATIONS AND FOOD. Motels in Olympia cater to policy-makers ($60-80), but chains in nearby Tumwater are fine. ▓**Grays Harbor Hostel,** 6 Ginny Ln., 25 mi. west of Olympia just off Rte. 8 in Elma, is a home away from home and the perfect place to start a trip down the coast. (☎482-3119. Hot tub, 3-hole golf course, and a shed for bike repairs. Dorms $13.50; private rooms $27. Bikers can camp on the lawn for $8.) **Millersylvania State Park,** 12245 Tilly Rd. S., is 10 mi. south of Olympia. Take Exit 99 off I-5 S or Exit 95 off I-5 N, then take Rte. 121 N, and follow signs to 6 mi. of trails and Deep Lake. (☎753-1519 or 800-452-5687. 10-day maximum stay. 164 sites $12; hook-ups $17; walk-ins $6. Showers 25¢ per 6min. Wheelchair accessible.) Diners, veggie eateries, and Asian quickstops line bohemian 4th Ave. east of Columbia. The **Olympia Farmer's Market,** 700 N Capital Way, proffers produce and fantastic, cheap fare. (☎352-9096. Open Apr.-Oct. Th-Su 10am-3pm, Nov.-Dec. Sa-Su 10am-3pm.) **The Spar Cafe & Bar,** 114 E. 4th Ave., is an ancient logger haunt that moonlights as a sweet-smelling pipe and cigar shop. (☎357-6444. Restaurant open M-Th 6am-10pm, F-Sa 6am-11pm, Su 6am-9pm. Bar open Su-Th 11am-midnight, F-Sa 11am-2am. Sandwiches and burgers $7.)

▣ SIGHTS. Olympia's crowning glory is the **State Capitol Campus,** a complex of state government buildings, fabulous fountains, manicured gardens, and veterans' monuments. (☎586-3460. Tours depart from just inside the front steps daily on the hr. 10am-3pm. Building open M-F 8am-5:30pm, Sa-Su 10am-4pm.) The mansionesque **State Capitol Museum,** 211 W. 21st Ave., houses historical and political exhibits. (☎753-2580. Open Tu-F 10am-4pm, Sa-Su noon-4pm. $2, seniors $1.75, children $1.) Several different free tours of campus buildings leave hourly on weekdays; call ☎586-8677 for info and options for the disabled. The **4th Ave. Bridge** is a perfect place to spot **spawning salmon,** as the leaping lox-to-be cross the lake from late Aug. through Oct. The high walls of the **Yashiro Japanese Garden,** at Plum and Union next to City Hall, contain Olympia's secret garden. (☎753-8380. Open daily 10am-dusk to picnickers and ponderers.) **Wolf Haven International,** 3111 Offut Lake Rd., 10 mi. south of Olympia, shelters 19 wolves and two coyotes reclaimed from zoos or illegal owners. Take Exit 99 off I-5, turn east, and follow the brown signs. (☎264-4695 or 800-448-9653. Open May-Sept. W-M 10am-4pm; Oct.-Apr. 10am-4pm. 45min. tours on the hour. $6, ages 5-12 $4.) At the campfire **Howl-In,** humans and canines tell stories. (Late May-Sept. F-Sa 6:30-9:30pm. $6, children $4.)

◪ NIGHTLIFE. Olympia's ferocious nightlife seems to have outgrown its daylife. *The Rocket* and the daily *Olympian* list live music. At **Eastside Club and Tavern,** 410 E 4th St., old men play pool, college students slam micro pints, and local bands play often. (☎357-9985. Open M-F noon-2am, Sa-Su 3pm-2am.) The **4th Ave. Alehouse & Eatery,** 210 E 4th St., serves "slabs" of pizza ($2.25), 26 micropints ($3), and live tunes, from blues to reggae. (☎956-3215. Restaruant open M-F 11:30am-8pm, F-Sa noon-8pm. Music Th-Sa 9pm.) DJs spin tunes nightly at gay-friendly **Thekla,** 155 E 5th Ave., under the neon arrow off N. Washington St. between 4th Ave. and Capitol. (☎352-1855. Open Tu-Su 5pm-2am. Cover up to $5; 21+.)

BELLINGHAM
☎360

Right between Seattle and Vancouver, Bellingham is the southern terminus of the Alaska Marine Hwy.; most over-nighters are contemplating or completing an overseas journey to or from Alaska. Commercial fishing, coal mining, and a paper mill support the economy, and the Lummi, Nooksack, and Semiahmoo of the region maintain strong ties to their fishing legacy.

⑦ PRACTICAL INFORMATION. Bellingham lies along I-5, 90 mi. north of Seattle and 57 mi. south of Vancouver, and is the only major city between the two. The train and bus terminals are both at 401 Harris Ave; take Exit 250 off I-5, then Rte. 11 W. **Amtrak** (☎734-8851) sends one train per day to Seattle (2½hr., $23) and Vancouver, BC (1½hr., $15). **Greyhound** (☎733-5252) runs to Seattle (2hr., 8 per day, $13) and Vancouver (2hr., 6 per day, $13). The **Alaska Marine Highway Ferry,** 355 Harris Ave. (☎676-8445 or 800-642-0066), runs 2 boats per week to Ketchikan, AK ($164) from July to Aug. All **Whatcom County Transit** routes begin at the Railroad Ave. Mall terminal, between Holly and Magnolia St. (☎676-7433. Buses run every 15-60min. M-F 5:50am-6:30pm; reduced service M-F 7:30-11pm and Sa-Su 9am-6pm. 50¢, under 6 and over 90 free. No free transfers.) The **Great Adventure on Water** (☎733-5888), near the Bell Cruise Terminal, rents kayaks. **Fairhaven Bikes,** 1103 11th St., rents bikes and in-line skates. To reach the **Visitor Information Center,** 904 Potter St., take Exit 253 from I-5 (☎671-3990; open daily 8:30am-5:30pm). **Post Office:** 315 Prospect (☎676-8303; open M-F 8am-5:30pm, Sa 9:30am-3pm). **ZIP code:** 98225. **Area code:** 360.

⟦⟧ ACCOMMODATIONS AND FOOD. Fairhaven Rose Garden Hostel (HI), 107 Chuckanut Dr., next to Fairhaven Park, is about ¾ mi. from the ferry terminal. The hostel is clean and tiny, with sleeping quarters, bathrooms, and showers all in the basement. Take I-5 Exit 250, and go west on Fairhaven Pkwy. to 12th St.; bear left onto Chuckanut Dr. From downtown Bellingham, take bus #1A or 1B. (☎671-1750. Open Feb.-Nov. Reception 5-10pm. Beds $13. Linen $2. Call ahead, especially on W or Th night, when Alaska-bound travelers fill the hostel. Reservations mandatory July-Aug.) **Larrabee State Park,** on Chuckanut Dr., 7 mi. south of town, has sites tucked in among the trees on Samish Bay. Check out the nearby tide pools or hike to alpine lakes. (☎676-2093 or 800-452-5687. Open daily 6:30am-dusk. Sites $11, with hook-up $16.) **⬛Casa Que Pasa,** 1415 Railroad Ave., serves humongous fresh burritos from $2.75. (☎738-8226. Open daily 11am-11pm.)

⬛ SIGHTS. The **Whatcom Museum of History and Art,** 121 Prospect St. (☎676-6981), displays Darius Kinsey's photographs of 1900s-era logging scenes. In the 2nd weekend of June, the **Deming Logging Show** displays the skills. The showgrounds are 12 mi. east on Mt. Baker Hwy. (Rte. 542), off Cedarville Rd. to the left. (☎592-3051. $5, ages 3-12 $3.) The **Bellingham Festival of Music** is in the first two weeks of Aug. (☎676-5997; $18-23).

SAN JUAN ISLANDS
☎360

The San Juan Islands are home to great horned owls, puffins, sea otters, sea lions, and more deer, raccoons, and rabbits than they can support. Pods of orcas (killer whales) patrol the waters, and pods of tourists circle the islands in all manner of watercraft. Over 1½ million visitors come ashore each year, usually in July and Aug. To avoid the rush but still enjoy good weather, visit in late spring or early fall.

⑦ PRACTICAL INFORMATION

Washington State Ferries (☎206-464-6400 or 800-843-3779) serves Lopez (50min.), Shaw (1¼hr.), Orcas (1½hr.), and San Juan Island (2hr.), from Anacortes; check the schedule at visitors centers in Puget Sound. Foot passengers travel free. To save on car fares, travel directly to the westernmost island on your itinerary, then return:

eastbound traffic travels for free. In summer, arrive at least 1hr. prior to departure. ($5.30, vehicle $17-22.75, bike $3; cash only.) To reach Anacortes, take I-5 N from Seattle to Mt. Vernon, then Rte. 20 west to town and follow signs. The **Bellingham Airporter** (☎800-235-5247) shuttles between Sea-Tac and Anacortes (M-F 10 per day, Sa-Su 7 per day; $31, round-trip $56). Short hops and good roads make the islands excellent for **biking.**

SAN JUAN ISLAND

The biggest and most popular of the islands, San Juan Island is the easiest island to explore, since the ferry docks right in town, roads are fairly flat, and a shuttle bus runs throughout the island. Seattle weekenders flood the island throughout the summer, bringing fleets of traffic. A drive around the 35 mi. perimeter of the island takes about 2hr., and the route is good for a day's cycle. The **West Side Rd.** traverses gorgeous scenery and provides the best chance for sighting **orcas** offshore. Mullis Rd. merges with Cattle Point Rd. and goes straight into **American Camp,** on the south side of the island. The camp dates from the Pig War of 1859, and a visitors center explains the history of that curious conflict. In the summer, every Sa from 12:30 to 3:30pm, volunteers in period costume reenact daily Pig-War era life. (☎378-2902. Visitors center open 8:30am-5pm. Camp open daily June-Aug. dawn-11pm; Sept.-May Th-Su. Guided walks Sa 11:30am.) **British Camp,** the second half of the **San Juan National Historical Park,** lies on West Valley Rd., on the sheltered **Garrison Bay.** (Buildings open Memorial Day to Labor Day daily 8am-5pm.) **Limekiln Point State Park,** along West Side Rd., is renowned as the best **whale-watching** spot in the area. Killer whales frequent this stretch of coastline and perform occasional acrobatics. The annual **San Juan Island Jazz Festival** swings in late July (☎378-5509).

 San Juan County Park, 380 Westside Rd., 10 mi. west of Friday Harbor on Smallpox and Andrews Bays, offers the chance to catch views of whales and a great sunset. (☎378-2992. Park open daily 7am-10pm. Office open daily 9am-7pm. Water and flush toilets, no showers or RV hook-ups. Vehicle sites $18; walk-ins $5. Reservations highly recommended.) At **⛰Katrina's,** 135 2nd St., the daily menu invariably includes organic salads, fresh bread, and gigantic cookies. (☎378-7290. Open M-F 11:30am-4pm, Sa 10am-1pm.)

 San Juan Transit (☎378-8887 or 800-887-8387) circles the island every 35-55min. and will stop on request (point to point $4; day pass $10; 2-day pass $19, also good on Orcas Island). If you plan to see San Juan Island only, it may be cheaper to leave your car in Anacortes and use the shuttles. **Island Bicycles,** 380 Argyle St., up Spring St., rents for $5 per hr., $25 per day (☎378-4941; open daily 9am-6pm). The **Chamber of Commerce** (☎378-5240 or 888-468-3701) is a booth on East St. up from Cannery Landing. The **San Juan National Historic Park Information Center** is at 1st and Spring St. (☎378-2240. Open M-F 8:30am-4:30pm; in winter until 4pm.)

ORCAS ISLAND

A small population of retirees, artists, and farmers dwell on Orcas Island in understated homes, surrounded by green shrubs and the red bark of madrona trees. The trail to **Obstruction Pass Beach** is the best way to clamber down to the rocky shores. **Moran State Park** is unquestionably Orcas' star outdoor attraction, with over 30 mi. of hiking trails ranging from a 1hr. jaunt around **Mountain Lake** to a day-long trek up the south face of **Mt. Constitution** (2047 ft.), the highest peak on the islands. The summit of Constitution looks out over the Olympic and Cascade Ranges, Vancouver Island, and Mt. Rainier. Part-way down is **Cascade Falls,** spectacular in the spring and early summer. The **Orcas Tortas** makes a slow drive on a green bus from Eastsound to the peak (☎376-4156; $8). **Shearwater Adventures** runs a fascinating **sea kayak tour** of north Puget Sound and is a great resource for experienced paddlers. (☎376-4699. 3hr. tour with 30min. of dry land training. $43.) **Crescent Beach Kayak,** on the highway 1 mi. east of Eastsound, rents. (☎376-2464. Open daily 9am-5pm. $10 per hr.; $25 per half-day.)

 Doe Bay Village Resort, Star Rte. 86, Olga, off Horseshoe Hwy. on Pt. Lawrence Rd., 5 mi. out of Moran State Park, includes kitchen facilities, a health food store and cafe, a treehouse, guided kayak trips, and a steam sauna and mineral bath. (☎376-2291. Reception 8am-10pm. Baths $4 per day, non-guests $7; bathing suits optional; coed. Beds $16 for members; campsites $12-22. Yurts $49. Reservations recommended.) To reach **Moran State Park,** Star Rte. 22 in Eastsound, follow Horseshoe Hwy. (☎376-2326 or 800-452-5687. About 12 sites and restrooms are open year-round. Standard sites $12; hiker/biker $6. Rowboats and paddleboats $12-13 for 1hr., $35-45 for full day. Reservations strongly recommended May to Labor Day.) ▨**Chimayo,** in the Our House Bldg. on North Beach Rd., has a Southwestern theme and comfy booths. (☎376-6394. Open M-Sa 11am-7pm. Funky burritos $3-5.)

The ferry lands on the southwest tip of Orcas, and the main town of **Eastsound** is 9 mi. northeast. **Olga** and **Doe Bay** are an additional 8 and 11 mi. down the eastern side of the horseshoe. **San Juan Transit** (☎376-8887) runs about every 1½hr. to most parts of the island (ferry to Eastsound $4). **Wildlife Cycle,** at A St. and North Beach Rd. in Eastsound, rents 21-speeds. (☎376-4708. Open M-Sa 10am-5:30pm, Su 11am-3pm. $6 per hr., $25 per day.)

LOPEZ ISLAND

Smaller than either Orcas or San Juan, "Slow-pez" lacks some of the tourist facilities of larger islands. The small **Shark Reef** and **Agate Beach County Parks,** on the southwest end of the island, have tranquil and well-maintained hiking trails, and Agate's beaches are calm and deserted. Roads on the island are ideal for biking. **Lopez Village** is 4½ mi. from the ferry dock off Fisherman Bay Rd. To rent a bike or kayak, head to **Lopez Bicycle Works,** south of the village. (☎468-2847. Open daily July-Aug. 9am-9pm. Apr.-Jun. and Sept.-Oct. 10am-5pm. Bikes $5 per hr., $25 per day; kayaks from $10-15 per hr.) **Spencer Spit State Park,** on the northeast corner of the island 3½ mi. from the ferry terminal, has primitive sites on the beach and the hill. (☎468-2251 or 800-452-5687. Open Feb.-Oct. daily until 10pm. Toilets. Sites $12; hiker/biker $6. Reservations recommended; fee $6.) Ferry transport means price inflation, so it may be wise to bring a lunch. Or munch on fresh pastries, bread, and pizza at **Holly B's.** (☎468-2133. Open M and W-Sa 7am-5pm, Su 7am-4pm.)

OLYMPIC PENINSULA

Due west of Seattle and its busy Puget Sound neighbors, the Olympic Peninsula is a remarkably different world. To the west, the Pacific Ocean stretches to a distant horizon; to the north, the Strait of Juan de Fuca separates the Olympic Peninsula from Vancouver Island; and to the east, Hood Canal and the Kitsap Peninsula isolate this sparsely inhabited wilderness from the sprawl of Seattle. While getting around the peninsula is easiest by car, the determined traveler with ample time can make the trip by bus.

PORT TOWNSEND ☎360

Unlike the salmon industry, Port Townsend's Victorian splendor has survived the progression of time and weather. Countless cafes, galleries, and bookstores line somewhat drippy streets, cheering the urbanites who move here to escape the rat race. The **Ann Starret Mansion,** 744 Clay St., has nationally renowned Victorian architecture, frescoed ceilings, and a free-hanging, three-tiered spiral staircase. (☎385-3205 or 800-321-0644. Tours daily noon-3pm; $2.)

Two hostels crouch in old military haunts, offering bright, clean rooms: **Olympic Hostel (HI-AYH),** in Fort Worden State Park, 1½ mi. from town, and **Fort Flagler Hostel (HI-AYH),** in Fort Flagler State Park on gorgeous Marrowstone Island, 20 mi. from Port Townsend. To get to Fort Flagler, go south on Rte. 19, which connects to Rte. 116 E and leads directly into the park; miles of pastoral bike routes wind over Marrowstone. (Olympic: ☎385-0655. Check-in 5-10pm, check out 9:30am. Private rooms with kitchens. Dorms $14, non-members $17; hiker/biker $2 off. Fort Flagler: ☎385-1288. Check-in 5-10pm, check-out 9:30am; lockout 10am-5pm. Book ahead. Dorms $13, non-members $16; private room add $6; hiker/biker $2 off.) You can camp on the beach at **Fort Flagler State Park** (☎385-1259; 116 sites; tents $12, RVs $17, hiker/biker $7; book ahead) or **Fort Worden State Park** (☎385-4730; seaside sites $17).

Port Townsend sits at the terminus of Rte. 20 on the northeastern corner of the Olympic Peninsula. Over land, it can be reached by U.S. 101 on the peninsula, or from the Kitsap Peninsula across the Hood Canal Bridge. **Washington State Ferries** (☎206-464-6400 or 800-808-7977) runs from Seattle to **Winslow** on Bainbridge Island, where a **Kitsap County Transit** bus runs to Poulsbo. From Poulsbo, **Jefferson County Transit** (☎385-4777) runs to Port Townsend. A **free shuttle** goes into downtown from the Park 'N' Ride lot. (Most buses do not run on Su. 60¢, seniors, disabled travelers, and ages 6-18 30¢; 30¢ extra fare per zone. Day passes $1.50.) **Chamber of Commerce:** 2437 E. Sims Way, 10 blocks southwest of town on Rte. 20. (☎385-3628 or 888-365-2722. Open M-F 9am-5pm, Sa 10am-4pm, Su 11am-4pm.) **P.T. Cyclery,** 100 Tyler St., rents mountain bikes. (☎385-6470. Open M-Sa 9am. $7 per hr., $25 per day.) **Kayak P.T.,** 435 Water St., rents kayaks. (☎385-6240. Singles $25 per 4hr., doubles $40 per 4hr.) **Post Office:** 1322 Washington St. (☎385-1600; open M-F 9am-5pm). **ZIP code:** 98368.

OLYMPIC NATIONAL PARK ☎360

With glacier-encrusted peaks, dripping river valley rainforests, and jagged shores along the Pacific Coast, the landscape of ONP is wonderfully diverse. A little effort and planning may yield an afternoon shell-hunting on an isolated beach, a day salmon fishing on the Hoh River, or a week glacier-gazing from the tree-line.

⁊ PRACTICAL INFORMATION

Only a few hours from Seattle, Portland, and Victoria, the wilderness of Olympic National Park is most easily and safely reached by car. U.S. 101 encircles the park in the shape of an upside-down U, with Port Angeles at the top. The park's vista-filled **eastern rim** runs up to Port Angeles, from which the much-visited **northern rim** extends westward. The tiny town of **Neah Bay** and stunning **Cape Flattery** perch at the northwest tip of the peninsula; farther south on U.S. 101, the slightly less tiny town of **Forks** is a gateway to the park's rainforested **western rim.** Separate from the rest of the park, much of the peninsula's Pacific coastline comprises a gorgeous **coastal zone.** July, Aug., and Sept. are best for visiting Olympic National Park, since much of the backcountry remains snowed-in until late June, and only summers are relatively rain-free.

Olympic National Park Visitors Center, 3002 Mt. Angeles Rd., is off Race St. in Port Angeles. ONP's main info center fields questions about the entire park, including camping, backcountry hiking, and fishing. (☎452-0330, TDD 452-0306. Open in summer approximately Su-F 8:30am-6:30pm, Sa 8:30am-8pm; in winter daily 9am-4pm.) Staff at the **Olympic National Park Wilderness Information Center** (☎452-0300), just behind the visitors center, helps design trips within the park. The **entrance fee,** good for seven days' access to the park, is $10 per car and $5 per hiker or biker, charged during the day at ranger stations and developed entrances such as Hoh, Heart o' the Hills, Sol Duc, Staircase, and Elwha. **Backcountry** users must pay $2 extra per night to ranger offices. $3 passes are required to park in Olympic National Forest.

⌓ ACCOMMODATIONS

The closest budget accommodations are at the **Rainforest Hostel,** 169312 U.S. 101, 20 mi. south of Forks. Follow the signs from U.S. 101 or come by bus from North Shore Brannon's Grocery in Quinault (1 per day; 9am, 1, and 4:35pm; 50¢). Two family rooms, a men's dorm (5 double bunks in summer), and rooms for couples require deposits. (☎374-2270. Dorms $12. Curfew 11pm. Wakeup 8am. Morning chore required of hostelers.)

Olympic National Park maintains six free campgrounds in the Hood Canal Ranger District, and others within its boundaries (sites $8-12); three can be reserved (☎800-280-2267): **Seal Rock, Falls View,** and **Klahowga.** A **backcountry permit** is always required. Quota limits apply to popular spots, including **Lake Constance** and **Flapjack Lakes** in the east; **Grand Valley, Badger Valley,** and **Sol Duc** in the north; **Hoh** in the west; and the coastal **Ozette Loop.** Most drive-up camping is first come, first served. Olympic National Forest requires a **trailhead pass** to park at sites located off a main trail. The Washington Department of Natural Resources allows **free backcountry camping** at least 100 yards off any state road on DNR land, mostly near the western shore along the Hoh and Clearwater Rivers. From July to Sept., most spaces are taken by 2pm. Popular sites such as those at Hoh River fill by noon.

👁 🏔 SIGHTS AND OUTDOORS

EASTERN RIM. What ONP's western regions have in ocean and rainforest, the eastern rim matches with canals and grandiose views. Canyon walls rise treacherously, their jagged edges leading to mountaintops that offer glimpses of the entire peninsula and Puget Sound. Steep trails lead up **Mt. Ellinor,** 5 mi. past Staircase on Rte. 119. Once on the mountain, hikers can choose the 3 mi. path or an equally steep but shorter journey to the summit; look for signs to the Upper Trailhead along Forest Road #2419-04. Adventure-seekers who hit the mountain before late July should bring snow clothes to "mach" (as in Mach 1, the speed to which sliders accelerate) down a ¼ mi. **snow chute.**

A 3¼ mi. hike ascends to **Lena Lake,** 14 mi. north of Hoodsport off U.S. 101; follow Forest Service Rd. 25 off U.S. 101 for 8 mi. to the trailhead. The Park Service charges a $3 trailhead pass. The **West Forks Dosewallip Trail,** a 10½ mi. trek to **Mt. Anderson Glacier,** is the shortest route to any glacier in the park. The road to **Mt. Walker Viewpoint,** 5 mi. south of Quilcene on U.S. 101, is steep, has sheer drop-offs, and should not be attempted in foul weather or a temperamental car. Yet another view of Hood Canal, Puget Sound, Mt. Rainier, and Seattle awaits intrepid travelers on top. Inquire about base camps and trails at **Hood Canal Ranger Station,** southeast of reserve lands on U.S. 101 in Hoodsport. (☎877-5254. Open daily 8am-4:30pm; in winter M-F 8am-4:30pm.)

NORTHERN RIM. The most developed section of Olympic National Park lies along its northern rim, near Port Angeles, where glaciers, rainforests, and sunsets over the Pacific are all only a drive away. Farthest east off U.S. 101 lies **Deer Park,** where trails tend to be uncrowded. Past Deer Park, the **Royal Basin Trail** meanders 6¼ mi. to the **Royal Basin Waterfall.** The road up **Hurricane Ridge** is an easy but curvy drive. Before July, walking on the ridge usually involves a bit of snow-stepping. Clear days give splendid views of Mt. Olympus and Vancouver Island, set against a foreground of snow and indigo lupine. From here, the uphill **High Ridge Trail** is a short walk from Sunset Point. On weekends from late Dec. to late Mar., the Park Service organizes free guided **snowshoe walks** atop the ridge.

Farther west on U.S. 101, 13 mi. of paved road penetrates to the popular **Sol Duc Hot Springs Resort,** where retirees de-wrinkle in the springs and eat in the lodge. (☎327-3583. Open daily late May-Sept. 9am-9pm; spring and fall Th noon-6pm, F-Su 9am-6pm. $7.50, seniors $6.50; suit or towel rental $3. Pools wheelchair accessible.) The **Sol Duc trailhead** is a starting point for those heading on up; crowds thin dramatically above **Sol Duc Falls.** The **Eagle Ranger Station** has info and permits. (☎327-3534. Open late June-Sept. Su-Th 8am-4:30pm, F-Sa 8am-8:30pm.)

NEAH BAY AND CAPE FLATTERY. At the westernmost point on the Juan de Fuca Strait and north of the park's western rim lies **Neah Bay,** the only town in the **Makah Reservation,** renowned as the "Pompeii of the Pacific," a remarkably-preserved 500-year-old village buried in a landslide at Cape Alava. You can reach Neah Bay and Cape Flattery by a 1hr. detour from U.S. 101. From Port Angeles, Rte. 112 leads west to Neah Bay; Rte. 113 runs north from Sappho to Rte. 112. The **Makah Cultural and Research Center,** in Neah Bay on Hwy. 112, just inside the reservation, beautifully presents artifacts from the archaeological site. (☎645-2711. Open daily

June-Aug. 10am-5pm; Sept.-May M-F 10am-5pm. $4, seniors and students $3. Free tours W-Su 11am.) The Makah Nation, whose recorded history goes back 2000 years, still lives, fishes, and produces artwork on this land. During **Makah Days,** on the last weekend of Aug., Native Americans from around the region come for canoe races, dances, and bone games (a form of gambling). Visitors are welcome; call the center for details. **Clallam Transit System** runs bus #14 from Oak St. in Port Angeles to Sappho, then #16 to Neah Bay. (☎452-4511. $1, seniors 50¢, ages 6-19 85¢.)

Cape Flattery is the most northwesterly point in the contiguous US and is drop-dead gorgeous. Get directions at the Makah Center or just take the road through town until it turns to dirt, past the "Marine Viewing Area" sign 4 mi. to a parking area where a trailhead leads toward the cape. To the south, the reservation's **beaches** are solitary and peaceful; respectful visitors are welcome.

WESTERN RIM. In the temperate rainforests of ONP's western rim, ferns, mosses, and gigantic old growth trees blanket the earth in a sea of green. The drive along the **Hoh River Valley,** actively logged land, is alternately overgrown and barren. **Hoh Rainforest Visitors Center** sits a good 45min. drive from U.S. 101 on the park's western rim. (☎374-6925. Open mid-June to Labor Day daily 9am-6:30pm; Labor Day to mid-June 9am-4:30pm.) From there, take the quick ¾ mi. **Hall of Mosses Trail** for a whirlwind tour of the rainforest. The slightly longer **Spruce Nature Trail** leads 1¼ mi. through lush forest and along the banks of the Hoh River, with a smattering of educational panels explaining bizarre natural quirks. The **Hoh Rainforest Trail** is the most heavily traveled path in the area, beginning at the visitors center and paralleling the Hoh River for 18 mi. to **Blue Glacier** on the shoulder of Mt. Olympus.

Several other trailheads from U.S. 101 offer less crowded opportunities for exploration of the rainforest, amid surrounding ridges and mountains. The **Queets River Trail** hugs its namesake east for 14 mi. from the free **Queets Campground;** the road is unpaved and unsuitable for RVs or large trailers. High river waters early in the summer can thwart a trek; hiking is best in Aug., but there's still a risk that water will cut off trail access. A shorter 3 mi. loop passes a broad range of rainforest, lowland river ecosystems, and the park's largest Douglas fir.

From the **Quinault Ranger Station,** 353 S. Shore Rd. (☎288-2525; open daily 8am-4:30pm; in winter M-F 9am-4:30pm), try the 4 mi. **Quinault Lake Loop** or the ½ mi. **Maple Glade Trail.** Snow-seekers flock to **Three Lakes Point,** an exquisite summit covered with powder until July. **Quinault Lake** lures anglers, rowers, and canoers. The **Lake Quinault Lodge,** next to the ranger station, rents canoes and rowboats (☎288-2900 or 800-562-6672; $10 per hr.). Jim Carlson offers **horseback rides** around the lake and through the forest in summer (☎288-2293; $40 per 2hr.).

COASTAL ZONE. Pristine coastline traces the park's slim far western region for 57 mi., separated from the rest of ONP by U.S. 101 and non-park timber land. Eerie fields of driftwood, sculptured arches, and dripping caves frame flamboyant sunsets, while the waves are punctuated by rugged sea stacks—chunks of coast stranded at sea after erosion swept away the surrounding land. Between the Quinault and Hoh Reservations, U.S. 101 hugs the coast for 15 mi., with parking lots just a short walk from the sand. North of where the highway meets the coast, **Beach #4** has abundant tidepools, plastered with sea stars; **Beach #6,** 3 mi. north at Mi. 160, is a favorite whale-watching spot. Near Mi. 165, sea otters and eagles hang out amid tide pools and sea stacks at **Ruby Beach. Beach camping** is only permitted north of the Hoh Reservation between **Oil City** and **Third Beach,** and north of the Quileute Reservation between **Hole-in-the-Wall** and **Shi-Shi Beach.** Day hikers and backpackers adore the 9 mi. loop that begins at **Ozette Lake.** The trail is a triangle with two 3 mi. legs leading along boardwalks through the rainforest. One heads toward sea stacks at **Cape Alava,** the other to a sublime beach at **Sand Point.** A 3 mi. hike down the coast links the two legs, passing ancient petroglyphs. More info is available at the **Ozette Ranger Station** (☎963-2725; open intermittently). Overnighters must make **permit reservations** (☎452-0300) in advance; spaces fill quickly in summer.

CASCADE RANGE

Intercepting the moist Pacific air, the spectacular Cascades divide Washington into the lush, wet green of the west and the low, dry plains of the east. The Cascades are most accessible in July, Aug., and Sept. Many high mountain passes are snowed in during the rest of the year. Mounts Baker, Vernon, Glacier, Rainier, Adams, and St. Helens are accessible by four major roads. The **North Cascades Hwy. (Rte. 20)** is the most breathtaking and provides access to North Cascades National Park. Scenic **U.S. 2** leaves Everett for Stevens Pass and descends along the Wenatchee River. Rte. 20 and U.S. 2 can be traveled in sequence as the Cascade Loop. **U.S. 12** approaches Mt. Rainier through White Pass and passes north of Mt. St. Helens. I-90 sends four lanes from Seattle past the ski resorts of Snoqualmie Pass. Rainstorms and evening traffic can slow hitching; locals warn against thumbing Rte. 20.

MOUNT ST. HELENS ☎360

In a single cataclysmic blast on May 18, 1980, the summit of Mt. St. Helens erupted, transforming what had been a perfect cone into a crater 1 mile wide and 2 miles long. The force of the ash-filled blast robbed the mountain of 1300 feet and razed entire forests, strewing trees like charred matchsticks. Ash from the crater rocketed 17 mile upward, blackening the sky for days. The explosion was 27,000 times the force of the atomic bomb dropped on Hiroshima. **Mt. St. Helens National Volcanic Monument** encompasses most of the blast zone, the rebounding ecosystem immediately affected by the explosion. The volcano still threatens to erupt, but is well-monitored, and there's a good chance it won't blow while you're there.

🛈 PRACTICAL INFORMATION. Vigorous winter rains often decimate access roads; check at a ranger station for road closures before heading out. From the **west,** take Exit 49 off I-5 and use Rte. 504, otherwise known as the **Spirit Lake Memorial Hwy.** For most, this is the quickest and easiest daytrip to the mountain, and the main visitors centers line the way to the volcano. **Rte. 503** parallels the **south** side of the volcano until it connects with **Forest Service Rd. 90.** Though views from this side don't highlight recent destruction, green glens and remnants of age-old explosions make this the best side for hiking and camping. From the **north,** the towns of **Mossyrock, Morton,** and **Randle** line **U.S. 12** and offer the closest major services to the monument. From U.S. 12, both **Forest Service Rd. 25** and **Forest Service Rd. 26** head south to **Forest Service Rd. 99,** a 16 mi. dead-end road that travels into the most devastated parts of the monument past a handful of lookouts.

The monument charges an **entrance fee** at almost every visitors center, viewpoint, and cave. (One day, all access $6, ages 4-15 $2. Individual monument fees cost $3; ages 4-15 $1.) It is possible to stop at the viewpoints after 6pm without paying (though you risk a ticket), or to drive through the park without stopping at the main centers. **Mt. St. Helens Visitors Center,** across from Seaquest State Park on Rte. 504, is most visitors' first stop, with displays and interactive exhibits. (☎274-2100 or 274-2103. Open daily 9am-5pm.) **Coldwater Ridge Visitors Center** is 38 mi. farther on Rte. 504. This sprawling glass-and-copper building has a superb view of the collapsed cavity, with an emphasis on the area's recolonization by living things. (☎274-2131. Open daily 9am-6pm.) **Johnston Ridge Observatory,** at the end of Rte. 504, overlooking the crater, focuses on geological exhibits and offers the best roadside view of the steaming dome and crater. (☎274-2140. Open daily May-Sept. 10am-6pm.)

Woods Creek Information Station, 6 mi. south of Randle on Rd. 25 from U.S. 12, is a drive-through info center. (Open daily June-Aug. daily 9am-4pm.) **Pine Creek Information Station,** 17 mi. east of Cougar on Rd. 90, shows an interpretive film of the eruption. (☎238-5225. Open mid-May to Sept. daily 9am-6pm.) **Apes Headquarters,** at Ape Cave on Rd. 8303, on the south side of the volcano, answers all lava tube questions. (Open daily June-Sept. 9:30am-5:30pm.) **Monument Headquarters,** 42218 N.E. Yale Bridge Rd., 3 mi. north of Amboy on Rte. 503, is in charge of **crater-climbing permits.** (☎247-3900 or 247-3903. Open M-F 7:30am-5pm.) From May 15 to Oct. 31, the

Forest Service allows 100 people per day to hike to the crater rim (applications accepted from Feb. 1; $15). Procrastinators should head for **Jack's Restaurant and Country Store,** 13411 Louis River Rd., on Rte. 503, 5 mi. west of Cougar (I-5 Exit 21), where a lottery is held at 6pm each day to distribute the next day's 50 unreserved permits. (☎231-4276. Open daily 5:30am-9pm.)

CAMPING. Although the monument itself contains no campgrounds, a number are scattered throughout the surrounding national forest. Free dispersed camping is allowed within the monument, but finding a site is a matter of luck. **Iron Creek Campground** is just south of the Woods Creek Information Station on Rd. 25, near its junction with Rd. 76. This is the closest campsite to Mt. St. Helens, with good hiking and striking views of the crater and the blast zone. (☎800-280-2267. Water available 8-10am and 6-8pm. Sites $13-15.) Spacious **Swift Campground** is on Rd. 90, just west of the Pine Creek Info Station. (☎503-813-6666. Sites $15.) **Beaver Bay** is west of Swift Campground on the Yale Lake. (Toilets and showers. Sites $15.)

OUTDOORS. Along each approach, short interpretive trails loop into the landscape. The 1hr. drive from the Mt. St. Helens Visitors Center to Johnston Ridge offers spectacular views of the crater and of the resurgence of life. Another 10 mi. east, the hike along **Johnston Ridge** approaches incredibly close to the crater where geologist David Johnston died studying the eruption. On the way west along Rd. 99, **Bear Meadow** provides the first interpretive stop, an excellent view of Mt. St. Helens, and the last restrooms before Rd. 99 ends at **Windy Ridge.** The monument begins just west of Bear Meadow, where Rd. 26 and 99 meet. Rangers lead ½ mi. walks around emerald **Meta Lake;** meet at Miner's Car at the junction of Rd. 26 and 99 (late June-Sept. daily 12:45 and 3pm). Farther west on Rd. 99, **Independence Pass Trail #227** is a difficult 3½ mi. hike, with overlooks of Spirit Lake and superb views of the crater and dome. For a serious hike, continue along this trail to its intersection with the spectacular **Norway Pass Trail,** which runs 6 mi. directly through the blast zone and ends on Rd. 26. Farther west, the 2 mi. **Harmony Trail #224** provides access to Spirit Lake. From spectacular **Windy Ridge** at the end of Rd. 99, a steep ash hill grants a magnificent view of the crater from 3½ mi. away. The **Truman Trail** leaves from Windy Ridge and meanders 7 mi. through the **Pumice Plain,** where hot pyroclastic flows sterilized the landscape. From the Pine Creek Information Station, 25 mi. south of the junction of Rd. 25 and 99, take Rd. 90 12 mi. west and then continue 3 mi. north on Rd. 83 to **Ape Cave,** a broken 2½ mi. lava tube formed by an ancient eruption. When exploring, wear a jacket and sturdy shoes, and take at least two **flashlights** or **lanterns.** Rangers lead ten free 30min. guided cave explorations per day. Rd. 83 continues 9 mi. farther north, ending near **Lava Canyon Trail #184** and three hikes past the **Muddy River Waterfall.**

MOUNT RAINIER NATIONAL PARK ☎360

At 14,411 ft., Mt. Rainier presides regally over the Cascade Range. The Klickitat native people called it Tahoma, "Mountain of God," but Rainier is simply "the Mountain" to most Washington residents. Perpetually snow-capped, this dormant volcano draws thousands of visitors from all around the globe. Clouds mask the mountain 200 days per year, frustrating visitors who come solely to see its distinctive summit. Over 305 miles of trails weave among old growth forests and alpine meadows, rivers, and bubbling hot springs, for the non-alpinists among us.

PRACTICAL INFORMATION. To reach Mt. Rainier from the **west,** take I-5 to Tacoma, then go east on Rte. 512, south on Rte. 7, and east on Rte. 706. This road meanders through the town of **Ashford** and into the park by the **Nisqually entrance,** which leads to the visitors centers of **Paradise** and **Longmire.** Snow usually closes all other park roads from Nov. to May. **Stevens Canyon Rd.** connects the southeast corner of the national park with Paradise, Longmire, and the Nisqually entrance, unfolding superb vistas of Rainier and the Tatoosh Range.

Gray Line Bus Service, 4500 S. Marginal Way, Seattle, runs from Seattle to Mt. Rainier. Buses leave from the Convention Center at 8th and Pike in Seattle at 8am and return at 6pm, allowing about 3½hr. at the mountain. (☎206-624-5208 or 800-426-7532. Runs daily May to mid-Sept. 1-day round-trip $50, under 12 $25.) **Rainier Shuttle** (☎569-2331), runs daily between Sea-Tac Airport, Ashford (2hr., 2 per day, $40), and Paradise (3hr., 1 per day, $45). The best place to plan a backcountry trip is at the **Longmire Wilderness Center** (☎569-4453; open Su-Th 7:30am-6:30pm, F-Sa 7am-7pm), east of the Nisqually entrance; or the **White River Ranger Station** (☎663-2273; open Su-Th 8am-4:30pm, F-Sa 7am-7pm), off Rte. 410 on the park's east side. Both distribute **backcountry permits.** The **entrance fee** is $10 per car, $5 per hiker; permits are good for seven days, and gates are open 24 hours. **Rainier Mountaineering, Inc. (RMI),** in Paradise, rents climbing gear and expert guides lead summit climbs and programs. (☎569-2227. Open daily May-Oct. 9am-5pm. Winter office at 535 Dock St. #209, in Tacoma; ☎253-627-6242). **Post Office:** In the **National Park Inn,** Longmire (open M-F 8:30am-noon and 1-5pm), and in the **Paradise Inn,** Paradise (open M-F 9am-noon and 12:30-5pm, and Sa 8:30am-noon). **ZIP code:** Longmire 98397; Paradise 98398. **Area code:** 360.

⚑🗒 ACCOMMODATIONS AND FOOD. Hotel Packwood, 102 Main St., in Packwood, is a charming reminder of the Old West with crisp, clean rooms and antique furniture. (☎494-5431. Shared or private bath; singles $20-38; double bunks $25-35.) **Whittaker's Bunkhouse,** 6 mi. west of the Nisqually entrance, offers spiffy rooms with firm mattresses and sparkling clean showers, as well as a homey espresso bar, but no kitchen. Bring your own sleeping bag. (☎569-2439. Bunks $25; private rooms $65-90. Reservations strongly recommended.)

Camping in the park is first come, first served from mid-June to late Sept. (Sites $10-14. Reservations for off-season ☎800-365-2267.) National park campgrounds all have facilities for the handicapped, but no hook-ups or showers (coin-op showers are available at Jackson Memorial Visitors Center, in Paradise). **Sunshine Point** (18 sites), near the Nisqually entrance, and **Cougar Rock** (200 sites), 2¼ mi. north of Longmire, are in the southwest. The serene high canopy of **Ohanapecosh** (205 sites) is 11 mi. north of Packwood on Rte. 123, in the southeast. **White River** (112 sites) is 5 mi. west of White River on the way to Sunrise, in the northeast. **Backcountry camping** in the park requires a **permit,** free from ranger stations and visitor centers in person 24 hours beforehand, or by reservation up to two months in advance. (☎569-4453. $20 per group. Quotas limit group size.) Hikers with valid permits can use any of the free, well-established trailside camps scattered in the park. Most camps have toilet facilities and a nearby water source, and some have shelters for groups of up to 12. **Glacier climbers** and **mountain climbers** intending to scale above 10,000 ft. must register in person at ranger stations to be granted permits. Camping in **national forests** outside the park is free. Avoid eroded lakesides and riverbanks; flash floods are frequent. **Campfires** are prohibited except during the rainy season.

Blanton's Market, 13040 U.S. 12, in Packwood, is the closest decent supermarket to the park and has an **ATM** in front. (☎494-6101. Open daily 6am-10pm.) **Ma & Pa Rucker's** on U.S. 12 in Packwood, is a pizza parlor/grill/mini-mart/icecream store/cafe. (☎494-2651. Open M-Th 9am-9pm, F-Su 9am-10pm. Pizza $8-12.)

◩▨ SIGHTS AND OUTDOORS. Ranger-led **interpretive hikes** delve into everything from area history to local wildflowers. Each visitor center conducts hikes on its own schedule and most of the campgrounds have evening talks and campfire programs. Mt. Adams and Mt. St. Helens aren't visible from the road, but can be seen from mountain trails like **Paradise** (1½ mi.), **Pinnacle Peak** (2½ mi.), **Eagle Peak** (7 mi.), and **Van Trump Park** (5½ mi.). A segment of the **Pacific Crest Trail,** which runs from Mexico to the Canadian border, dodges in and out of the park's southeast corner. The **Wonderland Trail** winds 93 mi. up, down, and around the mountain. Hikers must get permits for the arduous but stunning trek and must complete the hike in 10 to 14 days. Call the Longmire Wilderness Center (see **Practical Information,** above) for details on both hikes. A trip to the **summit** of Mt. Rainier requires substantial preparation and expense. The ascent involves a vertical rise of more than 9000 ft. over a distance of 9 or more mi., usually taking two days and an overnight stay at **Camp Muir** on the south side (10,000 ft.) or **Camp Schurman** on the east side (9500 ft.). **Permits** for summit climbs cost $15 per person. Although in opposite corners of the park, the **Ohanapecosh** and **Carbon Rivers** are in the same ranger district. One of the oldest stands of trees in Washington, the **Grove of Patriarchs,** grows near the Ohanapecosh visitors center. An easy 1½ mi. walk leads to these 500- to 1000-year-old Douglas firs, cedars, and hemlocks. The **Summerland** and **Indian Bar Trails** are excellent for serious backpacking—this is where rangers go on their days off. **Carbon River Valley,** in the northwest corner of the park, is one of the only inland rainforests in the US and has access to the **Wonderland Trail** (see above). Winter storms keep the road beyond the Carbon River entrance in constant disrepair.

NORTH CASCADES (ROUTE 20)

A favorite stomping ground for grizzlies, deer, mountain goats, black bears, and Jack Kerouac *(The Dharma Bums)*, the North Cascades are one of the most rugged expanses of land in the continental US. The dramatic peaks stretch north from Stevens Pass on U.S. 2 to the Canadian border, with the centerpiece of **North Cascades National Park** straddling the crest of the Cascades. Rte. 20 (open Apr.-Nov., weather permitting), a road designed for unadulterated driving pleasure, is the area's primary means of access and awards jaw-dropping views at every curve.

SEDRO WOOLLEY TO MARBLEMOUNT. The **Sedro Woolley Visitor Information Center** (☎360-855-0974; open daily 9am-4pm), in the train caboose at Rte. 20 and Ferry St., explains the **Sedro Woolley Loggerodeo** (☎855-1129), held over 4th of July weekend. Sedro Woolley houses the **North Cascades National Park and Mt. Baker-Snoqualmie National Forest Headquarters,** 2105 Rte. 20 (☎360-856-5700; open Sa-Th 8am-4:30pm, F 8am-6pm). Inquire here about camping in the forest and trail park passes and permits required. Call ☎206-526-6677 for snow avalanche info.

Rte. 9 leads north from Sedro Woolley, providing indirect access to **Mt. Baker** through the forks at the Nooksack River and Rte. 542. The turn-off for **Baker Lake Hwy.** is 23 mi. east of Sedro Wooley at Mi. 82, which dead-ends 25 mi. later at Baker Lake and free **hot springs.** Along this road, the crowded **Kulshan Campground** has drinking water and flush toilets ($7), and **Horseshoe Cove** ($12) and **Panorama Point** ($7) are wheelchair accessible (reservations ☎800-280-2267).

Farther east on Rte. 20, near the relatively small **Rockport State Park** (☎853-8461; sites $10, hook-ups $15), Sauk Mountain Rd. (Forest Service Rd. 1030) makes a stomach-scrambling climb up **Sauk Mountain.** Trailers, RVs, and the faint of heart should not attempt it. The **Sauk Mountain Trail** near the top winds 3½ mi. to stunning views and campsites near Sauk Lake.

Three miles east of Marblemount, bunnies romp outside the **Eatery,** 5675 Rte. 20. Dine under the American flag which 88-year-old Tootsie's grandmother made in 1890 when Washington celebrated its first 4th of July as a state. (Open daily 8am-8pm.) The **Marblemount Wilderness Information Center,** 728 Ranger Station Rd., Marblemount 98267, 1 mi. north of Marblemount on a well-marked road from the west end of town, is the place to go for a **backcountry permit** and to plan longer hiking excursions. (☎360-873-4500, ext. 39. Open in summer Su-Th 7am-6pm, F-Sa 7am-8pm; call for winter hrs.)

ROSS LAKE. Newhalem is the first town on Rte. 20 after it crosses into the **Ross Lake Recreation Area,** a buffer zone between the highway and the national park. At the tourist-friendly **North Cascades Visitors Center and Ranger Station,** off Rte. 20, a mystical and atonal slide show is shown. (☎206-386-4495. Open daily 8:30am-6pm; in winter Sa-Su 9am-4:30pm.) Among the easiest hikes is the **Thunder Creek Trail,** which extends through old-growth cedar and fir forests, beginning from the Colonial Creek Campground (see below) at Rte. 20 Mi. 130. The 3¼ mi. **4th of July Pass Trail** begins approximately 2 mi. into the Thunder Creek Trail and climbs 3500 ft. toward eye-poppin' views. The park's **Goodell Creek Campground,** just south of Newhalem, has 22 sites for tents and trailers, with drinking water, pit toilets, and a launch site for whitewater rafting on the Skagit River (sites $7; water turned off after Oct., when sites are free). **Colonial Creek Campground,** 10 mi. to the east, is a fully developed, wheelchair-accessible campground with flush toilets, a dump station, and occasional campfire programs (164 sites, no hook-ups; $10).

SCENIC DRIVE: ROSS LAKE TO TWISP

This is the most beautiful segment of Rte. 20. Leaving the basin of Ross Lake, the road begins to climb, exposing the jagged, snowy peaks of the North Cascades. Thirty mi. of astounding views east, the **Pacific Crest Trail** crosses Rte. 20 at **Rainy Pass** on one of the most scenic and difficult legs of its 2500 mi. Canada-to-Mexico route. Near Rainy Pass, groomed scenic trails can be hiked in sneakers, provided the snow has melted (about mid-July). Just off Rte. 20, an overlook at **Washington Pass** (Mi. 162) rewards a ½ mi. walk on a wheelchair-accessible paved trail with an astonishing view of the red rocks in **Copper Basin.** The popular 2½ mi. walk to **Blue Lake** begins just east of Washington Pass. An easier 2 mi. hike to **Cutthroat Lake** departs from an access road 4½ mi. east of Washington Pass. From the lake, the trail continues 4 mi. farther and almost 2000 ft. higher to **Cutthroat Pass,** treating hikers to a stellar view of towering peaks. The hair-raising 23 mi. road to **Hart's Pass** begins at **Mazama,** on Rd. 1163, 10 mi. east of Washington Pass. Awesome views await steel-nerved drivers, from both the pass and from **Slate Peak,** the site of a lookout station 3 mi. past the pass. The road prohibits trailers and closes for snow.

Farther east is **Winthrop,** a town desperately and somewhat successfully trying to market its frontier history. **Winthrop Information Station,** 202 Riverside, is at the junction with Rte. 20. (☎509-996-2125. Open daily early May to mid-Oct. 10am-5pm.) Winthrop's summer is bounded by rodeos on Memorial and Labor Day weekends. Late July brings the top-notch **Winthrop Rhythm and Blues Festival,** where big name blues bands flock to belt their tunes, endorse radio stations, and play cowboy. Tickets for the three-day event cost $35. (☎509-997-2541. $40 in advance; $48 at the door.) The **Methow Valley Visitors Center,** Bldg. 49, Rte. 20, hands out info on area camping, hiking, and cross-country skiing. (☎509-996-4000. Open daily 9am-5pm; call for winter hrs.) For more in-depth skiing and hiking trail info, call the **Methow Valley Sports Association** (☎509-996-3287), which maintains 100 mi. of trails. Between Winthrop and Twisp on East Country Rd. #9129, the **North Cascades Smokejumper Base** is a center for airborne forest-firefighters. (☎509-997-2031. Open in summer and early fall daily 8am-6pm; tours 10am-5pm.)

Nine mi. south of Winthrop on Rte. 20, the peaceful village of **Twisp** offers lower prices and far fewer tourists than its neighbor. The **Twisp Ranger Station,** 502 Glover St., employs a crunchy and helpful staff fortified with essential trail and campground guides. (☎509-997-2131. Open M-F 7:45am-4:30pm.) At **The Sportsman Motel,** 1010 E. Rte. 20, a barracks-like facade masks tastefully decorated rooms with kitchens. (☎509-997-2911. Singles $35; doubles $40.) The **Sisters Cafe,** 104 N. Glover St., serves California-style wraps. (☎509-997-1323. Open M-F 8am-5pm, Sa 9am-2pm.) **Campgrounds** and **trails** await 15-25 mi. up Twisp River Rd. off Rte. 20. Most of the campsites are primitive and have a $5 fee. **Riverbend RV Park,** 19961 Rte. 20, is only 2 mi. west of Twisp. (☎509-997-3500 or 800-686-4498. Office open 9am-9pm. Sites $14, hook-ups $19; $2 per additional person after 2 people.) From Twisp, Rte. 20 continues east to **Okanogan** and Rte. 153 runs south to **Lake Chelan.**

EASTERN WASHINGTON

SPOKANE ☎509

A city built on silver mining, grown fat and prosperous after decades as a central rail link for regional agriculture, Spokane has regressed to become a gateway rather than a destination. Copious middle-Americana, fused with bottom-of-the-barrel prices, makes Spokane a convenient, inexpensive stopover.

PACIFIC NORTHWEST

⚐ PRACTICAL INFORMATION. Spokane lies 280 mi. east of Seattle on I-90. **Spokane International Airport** (☎624-3218) is off I-90, 8 mi. southwest of town. **Amtrak,** W. 221 1st St. (☎624-5144), at Bernard St., sends one train per day to Seattle (7hr.) and Portland, OR (8hr.) for $34-74. **Greyhound** (☎624-5251), in the same building, runs to Seattle (6hr., 5 per day, $26) and Portland, OR (8-10hr., 4 per day, $36). **Spokane Transit Authority** serves all of Spokane, including Eastern Washington University in Cheney. (☎328-7433. Runs until 12:20am downtown. 75¢, under 5 free.) **Spokane Area Convention and Visitors Bureau,** 201 W. Main St., is at Exit 281 off I-90. (☎747-3230 or 800-248-3230. Open May-Sept. M-F 8:30am-5pm, Sa 8am-4pm, Su 9am-2pm; Oct.-Apr. M-F 8:30am-5pm). **Internet access: Library,** W. 906 Main St. (☎444-5333. Open M-Tu noon-8pm, W-F 10am-6pm.) **Post Office:** W. 904 Riverside Ave., at Lincoln (☎800-275-8777; open M-F 6am-5pm). **ZIP code:** 99210. **Area code:** 509.

⛺ ACCOMMODATIONS AND FOOD. Boulevard Inn, 2905 W. Sunset Blvd, 2 mi. west of town on Rte. 2., rents rooms so clean you could eat off the floor. (☎747-1060. Singles $33; doubles $39.) **Riverside State Park** is 6 mi. northwest of downtown on Rifle Club Rd., off Rte. 291 (Nine Mile Rd.); take Division St. north and turn left on Francis, then follow signs. Sites lie in a sparse Ponderosa forest next to the river. (☎800-452-5687 or 800-233-0321. Showers. Sites $12; hiker/cyclist sites $6. Wheelchair accessible.) **The Spokane Marketplace,** 1100 N Ruby St., northwest of town at DeSmet St., sells fresh fruit, vegetables, baked goods, and crafts. (☎456-0100. Open Apr. Sa 9am-4pm; May W and Sa 9am-4pm; June-Dec. W and Sa 9am-4pm, F 11am-6pm.) At **Dick's,** E. 10 3rd Ave., at Division St., patrons eat in their cars and pay prices out of the 50s. (☎747-2481. Open M-Th 8am-midnight, F-Sa 8am-1am, Su 9am-midnight; mid-June to Aug. M-Th 8am-1am, F-Sa 8am-2am and Su 9am-2am. Burgers 59¢; shakes 89¢.)

🔦 SIGHTS. Riverfront Park, N. 507 Howard St. (☎456-4386), just north of downtown, is Spokane's civic center and greatest asset. Developed for the 1974 World's Fair, the park's 100 acres are divided down the middle by the roaring rapids that culminate in **Spokane Falls.** In the park, the **IMAX Theater** houses your basic five-story movie screen. (☎625-6686. Shows June-Sept. on the hr.; call for winter schedule. Open daily 11am-8pm. $7, under 12 $5, seniors $6.) A 1-day pass ($15) covers all these and more, including the exquisitely hand-carved **Looff Carousel.** (Open daily June-Sept. 11am-8pm, F-Sa 11am-10pm. $1.75 per whirl, under 12 $1.) The park hosts **ice-skating** in the winter. South of downtown off Stevens St., at **Manito Park,** 4 W. 21st Ave., carp blow bubbles in the **Nishinomiya Japanese Garden** and roses bloom in June at **Rosehill.** (☎625-6622. Open daily 8am-8pm. Free.)

OREGON

Over a century ago, families liquidated their possessions and sank their life savings into covered wagons, corn meal, and oxen, high-tailing it to Oregon in search of prosperity and a new way of life. Today, Oregon remains as popular a destination as ever for backpackers, cyclists, anglers, beachcrawlers, and families. The caves and cliffs of Oregon's coastline are a siren call to tourists, and inland attractions include Crater Lake National Park and Ashland's Shakespeare Festival. Portland is casual and idiosyncratic—its name was determined by a coin toss—while the collegetown of Eugene embraces hippies and Deadheads. For everything from microbrews to snow-capped peaks, Oregon is worth crossing the Continental Divide.

⚐ PRACTICAL INFORMATION

Capital: Salem.

Visitor Info: Oregon Tourism Commission, 775 Summer St. NE, Salem, OR 97310 (☎800-547-7842; www.traveloregon.com). **Oregon State Parks and Recreation Dept.,** P.O. Box 500, Portland, OR 97207-0500 (☎800-551-6949; www.prd.state.or.us).

Postal Abbreviation: OR. **Sales Tax:** 0%.

PORTLAND

☎ 503

With over 200 parks, the pristine Willamette River, and snow-capped Mt. Hood in the background, Portland is an oasis of natural beauty. Portlanders have also nursed a love of art, music, and books. Culture is constantly cultivated in the endless theaters, galleries, and bookshops around town. As the microbrewery capital of America, Portland is a flowing font of the nation's finest beer. During the rainy season, locals flood neighborhood pubs and coffeehouses for shelter and conversation. But on rare sunny days, a battalion of hikers, bikers, and runners take advantage of their sylvan surroundings.

◪ GETTING THERE AND AWAY

Portland lies in the northwest corner of Oregon, where the Willamette River flows into the Columbia River. **I-5** connects Portland with San Francisco and Seattle, while **I-84** follows the route of the Oregon Trail through the Columbia River Gorge, heading along the Oregon-Washington border toward Boise, ID. West of Portland, **U.S. 30** follows the Columbia downstream to Astoria, but **U.S. 26** is the fastest path to the coast. **I-405** runs just west of downtown to link I-5 with U.S. 30 and 26.

Airport: Portland International Airport (☎ 460-4234 or 877-739-4636). For a cheap ride from downtown, take bus #12 (Sandy Blvd.) outside baggage claim (45min.; 6 per hr. am, 2 per hr. pm; $1.15). **Gray Line** provides **airport shuttles** that stop at most major hotels in Portland (☎ 285-9845; every 45min. from 5:15am-midnight; $15).

Trains: 800 N.W. 6th Ave. (☎ 273-4866), at Hoyt St., in Union Station. To Seattle, WA (4hr., 4 per day, $34) and Eugene (2½hr., 2 per day, $27). Open daily 7:45am-9pm.

Buses: Greyhound, 550 N.W. 6th Ave. (☎ 243-2310), next to Union Station. To: Seattle (3-4½hr.; 15 per day; $20); Eugene (2½-4hr.; 9 per day; $12); and Spokane, WA (8hr.; 5 per day; $36). Lockers $5 per day. Open daily 5am-12:30am. **Green Tortoise** (☎ 956-7537 or 800-867-8647) picks up at Union Station. One per day to Seattle (4hr.; $15) and San Francisco (22hr.; $159). Confirm 2 days in advance.

▐ GETTING AROUND

Public Transportation: Tri-Met, 701 S.W. 6th Ave. (☎ 238-7433), in Pioneer Courthouse Sq. Open M-F 7:30am-5pm. Buses generally run 5am-midnight with reduced hrs. on weekends. Fare $1.15-1.45, ages 7-18 85¢, seniors or disabled 55¢, free in the downtown **Fareless Square.** All-day pass $3.60; 10 fares for $10. All buses and bus stops are marked with one of 7 symbols and have bike racks ($5 permit available at area bike stores). **MAX** (☎ 228-7246), based at the Customer Service Center, is Tri-Met's efficient light-rail train running between downtown, Hillsboro in the west, and Gresham in the east. Transfers from buses can be used to ride MAX. Runs M-F 4:30am-1:30am.

Taxis: Radio Cab, ☎ 227-1212. **Broadway Cab,** ☎ 227-1234.

Car Rental: Crown Rent-A-Car, 1315 N.E. Sandy Blvd. (☎ 224-8110 or 800-722-7813), across from the huge 7-Up bottle. Open M-F 8am-5pm. Transport from airport. From $25-40 per day, $140-160 per week. Must be 21 with credit card.

◪▐ ORIENTATION AND PRACTICAL INFORMATION

Portland is divided into five districts by which all street signs are labeled: **N, NE, NW, SE,** and **SW. Burnside St.** divides the city into north and south, while east and west are separated by the **Willamette River.** SW Portland is known as **downtown** but also includes the southern end of Old Town and a slice of the wealthier **West Hills. Old Town,** in NW Portland, encompasses most of the city's historic sector. Some areas in the NW and SW around W. Burnside are best not walked alone at night, although on weekends district clubs and live music draw crowds. West of Old Town and Chinatown, **Pearl District** is known for art galleries and antique stores. Farther west, N.W. 21st and N.W. 23rd St. are known as **Nob Hill,** a hot spot for boutique shopping and dining. **Southeast** Portland contains parks, factories, local businesses, and residential areas of all income brackets; a rich array of cafes, stores, theaters, and restaurants also lines **Hawthorne Blvd. Williams Ave.** frames "the North." **North** and **Northeast** Portland are chiefly residential, punctuated by a few small and quiet parks and the site of the **University of Portland.**

> **Visitor Info: Portland Oregon Visitors Association (POVA),** 25 S.W. Salmon St. (☎222-2223 or 877-678-5263), at S.W. 1st Ave. in the Two World Trade Center complex. From I-5, follow signs for City Center. Free *Portland Book* has maps and info on local attractions. Open June-Aug. M-Sa 9am-5pm, Su 10am-4pm; Sept.-May closed Su.
>
> **Internet Access: Library,** 801 S.W. 10th Ave. (☎248-5123), between Yamhill and Taylor, has free 1hr. access. Open M-Th 9am-9pm, F-Sa 9am-6pm, Su 1-5pm.
>
> **Women's Crisis Line:** ☎235-5333. 24hr.
>
> **Post Office:** 715 N.W. Hoyt St. Open M-F 7am-6:30pm, Sa 8:30am-5pm. **ZIP code:** 97208. **Area code:** 503.

ACCOMMODATIONS

Although downtown is studded with Marriott-esque hotels and the smaller motels are steadily raising prices, Portland still welcomes the budget traveler. Prices tend to drop away from the City Center, and inexpensive motels can be found on S.E. Powell Blvd. and the southern end of S.W. 4th Ave. Portland accommodations fill up, especially during the Rose Festival, so early reservations are wise.

> ▨ **Portland International Hostel (HI),** 3031 S.E. Hawthorne Blvd. (☎236-3380), at 31st Ave. From the airport, take bus #12 to 5th. Ave, then walk to the corner of 5th and Washington to take #14. Th open mic attracts local and hostel talent. BBQ every Th. Porch, laundry. Internet access $1 per 20min. Discount ski passes to Mt. Hood and guided tours to the Columbia River Gorge, Mt. Hood, and Mt. St. Helens ($38.50). Fills early in summer. Reception daily 9am-10pm. 34 beds. Dorms $18, non-members $21.
>
> ▨ **McMenamins Edgefield,** 2126 S.W. Halsey St. (☎669-8610 or 800-669-8610; fax 492-7750), in Troutdale, a 20min. drive east of Portland or a 50min. MAX ride. By car, take I-84 east to Exit 16 and turn left at the first stoplight onto S.W. Halsey St. Continue down Halsey, turn right just after Edgefield's vineyards. Or take MAX east to the Gateway Station, then Tri-Met bus #24 (Halsey) east to the main entrance. The beautiful 33-acre former farm does bed and breakfast European style. Movie theater, winery, brewery, 18-hole golf course, three restaurants, and the Little Red Shed, the smallest free-standing bar in North America. Free summer outdoor concerts Th. Reception 24hr. Two single-sex dorms with 12 beds. $20 includes lockers, towels, and bedding.
>
> **Northwest Portland International Hostel (HI),** 1818 N.W. Glisan St. (☎241-2783), at 18th Ave. From S.W. 6th and Salmon or the Greyhound Station, take bus #17 to corner of 19th Ave. Between trendy Nob Hill and Pearl District. New hostel has deck, kitchen, laundry, and Su sundaes ($1). Reception 8am-11pm. 34 dorm beds (co-ed available). Dorms $17, non-members $21.
>
> **Ainsworth State Park** (Oregon Park Info Center ☎695-2301 or 800-551-6949, M-F 8am-5pm). 37 mi. east of Portland, Exit 35 off I-84 on U.S. 30, in Columbia Gorge. Wooded and lovely, but highway noise prevails. Showers, toilets, hiking. Open Apr.-Oct. Tent sites $13, full hook-up $18. Non-camper showers $2.
>
> **Champoeg State Park,** 8239 N.E. Champoeg Rd. (☎678-1251 or 800-452-5687). Take I-5 south 27 mi. to Exit 278, then follow the signs west for 6 mi. Play along miles of paved bikeway or hike by the Willamette River. Water, electricity. Little privacy. Yurts $27, RV sites $19, tent sites $15, $4 per person, $3 per vehicle.

FOOD

Portland has more restaurants per capita than any other American city, and dining is seldom dull. Downtown tends to be expensive, but restaurants and quirky cafes in the NW and SE quadrants offer great food at reasonable prices.

Downtown Portland

PACIFIC NORTHWEST

ACCOMMODATIONS
Downtown Value Inn, 19
McMenamins Edgefield, 31
Northwest Portland International
 Hostel (HI), 6
Portland International Hostel (HI), 30

FOOD
Accuardi's Old Town Pizza, 13
Dog's Dig, 14
Escape From New York Pizza, 4
Garbonzo's, 1
Komblatt's, 3
Little Wing Cafe, 7
Montage, 29
Muu-Muu's Big World Diner, 5
Nicholas Restaurant, 28
The Roxy, 26
Santa Fe Taqueria, 2
Western Culinary Institute:
 Chef's Corner Deli, 22
 Chef's Diner, 22
 Restaurant, 23

THEATERS
Artist's Repertory Theater, 25
Oregon Ballet Theater, 21
Portland Center Stage, 20
Portland Civic Auditorium, 18
Portland Opera, 24

NIGHTLIFE
Berbati's Pan, 16
Boxxes, 27
Brig, 27
Crystal Ballroom, 10
Embers, 11
Jimmy Mak's, 9
The Laurel Thirst Public House, 8
Lotus Card Room and Cafe, 17
Ohm, 15
Panorama, 27
Satyricon, 12

🖾 **Western Culinary Institute** (☎294-9770) has several opportunities for scrumptious dining. **Chef's Diner,** 1231 S.W. Jefferson, lets cheerful students serve, taste, and discuss sandwiches, the breakfast special ($2), or the occasional all-you-can-eat buffet ($5). Open Tu-F 7am-noon. **Chef's Corner Deli,** 1239 S.W. Jefferson, is good for a quick meal on-the-go. Open Tu-Th 8am-5:30pm, F 8am-6pm. Elegant **Restaurant,** 1316 S.W. 13th Ave., serves a classy 5-course lunch ($8) rivaled by its superb 6-course dinner (Tu-W and F, $12-18) and the tastebud-tingling international buffet (Th, $17). Reservations recommended. Open Tu-F 11:30am-1pm and 6-8pm.

🖾 **Montage,** 301 S.E. Morrison St. (☎234-1324). Take bus #15 to the end of the Morrison Bridge and walk under it. Louisiana-style cooking. Munch gator ($10) or oyster shooters ($2) while pondering a mural of *The Last Supper*. Open M-Th 11am-2pm and 6pm-2am, F 11am-2pm and 6pm-4am, Sa 6pm-4am, Su 6pm-2am.

🖾 **Coffee Time,** 712 N.W. 21st Ave. (☎497-1090). Sip a cup of chai ($2-3) amid ancient wonders in the main room or over Jenga in a 3-sided niche. The intelligentsia mingle on the couches; bohemians chill to music in the tapestried parlor. Lattés $2-3. Open 24hr.

Accuardi's Old Town Pizza, 226 N.W. Davis St. (☎222-9999), at 2nd Ave. A typical whorehouse-turned-saloon-style pizzeria. Small cheese $5.25, large $10. Open Su-Th 11:30am-11pm, F-Sa 11:30am-midnight.

Hawthorne Street Cafe, 3354 S.E. Hawthorne Blvd. (☎232-4982). Bus #14. Some come just for the marionberry coffee cake ($3). Enticing sandwiches $6-7. Breakfast all day. 15% discount for Hawthorne HI guests. Open daily 7:30am-3pm.

Saigon Kitchen, 835 N.E. Broadway (☎281-3669). Best Vietnamese and Thai restaurant in town. The *chả giò* rolls, deep-fried and served with fresh herbs and sauce ($7), are a perennial favorite. Most entrees $7-9. Open M-Sa 11am-10pm, Su noon-10pm.

Cup and Saucer, 3566 S.E. Hawthorne Blvd. (☎236-6001). Ask Chef Kerby to scramble you up an Ultimate Omelette ($6) any time of day. Decor is questionable; service is not. Ani DiFranco has been spotted here more than once. Open daily 7am-9pm.

👁 SIGHTS

PIONEER COURTHOUSE AND OLD TOWN. The fully-functioning **Pioneer Courthouse,** a downtown landmark at 5th Ave. and Morrison St., is the centerpiece of **Pioneer Courthouse Sq.,** which opened in 1983 and has since become "Portland's Living Room." During the summer, the **High Noon Tunes** draw thousands of music lovers. *(701 S.W. 6th Ave. ☎223-1613. W noon-1pm.)* The section of downtown just south of the Burnside Bridge and along the river comprises **Old Town.** Intended as a place where "horses, men and dogs" might drink, **Skidmore Fountain,** at S.W. 1st Ave. and S.W. Ankeny St., marks the end of **Waterfront Park,** a 20-block swath of grass and flowers along the Willamette River. The 185 jets of **Salmon St. Springs** spout down the street from the visitors center (see **Practical Information,** above).

ARTWORK. Catch the best of Portland's dizzying arts scene on the first Th of each month, when the Portland Art Museum and Southwest and Northwest galleries stay open until 9pm. For details contact the **Regional Arts and Culture Council** or grab the *Art Gallery Guide* at the visitors center. *(620 S.W. Main St. #420. ☎823-5111.)* On the west side of the South Park Blocks sits the venerable **Portland Art Museum (PAM),** at Jefferson St. PAM holds over 32,000 works of Western, Native American, Asian, and African art spanning the past 3500 years. *(1219 S.W. Park. ☎226-2811. Open Tu-Sa 10am-5pm, Su noon-5pm, and until 8pm on the first Th of the month. $7.50, seniors and students $6, under 19 $4; special exhibitions may be more.)*

PARKS AND GARDENS. Portland has more park acreage than any other American city, thanks in good measure to **Forest Park,** the 5000-acre tract of wilderness in Northwest Portland. Washington Park (see below), provides easy access by car or foot to this sprawling sea of green, where a web of trails leads through lush forests, scenic overviews, and idyllic picnic areas. At the **Crystal Springs Rhododendron Garden,** over 2500 rhododendrons surround a lake and border an 18-hole public golf course. *(S.E. 28th Ave., at Woodstock. Take bus #63. Open daily Mar. to Labor Day dawn-dusk;*

Oct.-Feb. 8am-7pm. $3, under 12 free.) Less than 2 mi. west of downtown, in the middle of the posh neighborhoods of **West Hills,** is mammoth **Washington Park.** Its **Rose Garden** is the pride of Portland. In summer months, a sea of blooms arrests the eye, showing visitors exactly why Portland is the City of Roses. *(400 S.W. Kingston. ☎ 823-3636.)* Across from the Rose Garden are the scenic **Japanese Gardens,** reputed to be the most authentic this side of the Pacific. *(611 S.W. Kingston Ave. ☎ 223-1321. Open daily Apr.-Sept. 10am-7pm; Oct.-Mar. 10am-4pm. Tours daily at 10:45am and 2:30pm. $6, seniors $4, students $3.50, under 6 free.)* The **Hoyt Arboretum,** at the crest of the hill above the other gardens, features 200 acres of trees and trails. *(4000 S.W. Fairview Blvd. ☎ 228-8733 or 823-3655. Visitors center open M-F 9am-4pm, Sa-Su 10am-5pm.)*

MUSEUMS. Across the park from the Portland Art Museum, the **Oregon Historical Society Museum and Library** stores photographs, artifacts, and records of Oregon's past two centuries. *(1200 S.W. Park Ave. ☎ 222-1741. Open Tu-W and F-Sa 10am-5pm, Th 10am-8pm, Su noon-5pm. $6, students $3, ages 6-12 $1.50. Seniors free on Th.)* The **Oregon Museum of Science and Industry (OMSI)** keeps visitors mesmerized with science exhibits, including an earthquake simulator chamber and an Omnimax theater. *(1945 S.E. Water Ave., at S.E. Clay St. ☎ 797-4000 or 797-4569. Open daily Labor Day to Memorial Day 9:30am-7pm, Th until 8pm; in winter 9:30am-5:30pm, Th until 8pm. $6.50, ages 4-13 and seniors $4.50.)* While at OMSI, visit the **USS Blueback,** the Navy's last diesel submarine; she never failed a mission. *(☎ 797-4624. Open daily 10am-5pm. 40min. tour $3.)*

UNIQUE ATTRACTIONS. At the first and only **24-Hour Church of Elvis,** you can listen to synthetic oracles, witness satirical miracles, and experience a tour in the Art-o-Mobile. Visits to the gift store grant exit from the land of eternal grace. *(720 S.W. Ankeny St. ☎ 226-3671. Usually open M-Th 2-4pm, F-Sa noon-5pm and 8pm-midnight, Su noon-5pm, but call ahead.)* Downtown on the edge of the Northwest district is the gargantuan **Powell's City of Books,** a cavernous establishment with almost a million new and used volumes, more than any other bookstore in the US. *(1005 W. Burnside St. ☎ 228-4651 or 800-878-7323. Open daily 9am-11pm.)*

OTHER SIGHTS. The Grotto, a 62-acre Catholic sanctuary, houses magnificent religious sculptures and gardens just minutes from downtown. *(On Sandy Blvd./U.S. 30, at N.E. 85th. ☎ 254-7371. Open daily May-Oct. 9am-6pm, Nov.-Jan. 9am-4pm, Feb.-Apr. 9am-6:30pm.)* The **Oregon Zoo** is renowned for its scrupulous re-creation of natural habitats and its successful elephant breeding. *(4001 S.W. Canyon Rd. ☎ 226-1561. Take #63 "zoo bus" or the MAX light-rail to Washington Park stop. Open daily 9am-6pm. $6.50, seniors $5, ages 3-11 $4; 2nd Tu of each month is free after 1pm.)*

🎵 🌸 ENTERTAINMENT AND FESTIVALS

Portland's major daily newspaper, the **Oregonian,** lists upcoming events in its F edition. **Oregon Symphony Orchestra,** 923 S.W. Washington St. plays classics from Sept. to June. *(☎ 228-1353 or 800-228-7343. Box office open M-Sa 9am-5pm; off-season M-F 9am-5pm. $15-60. "Symphony Sunday" afternoon concerts $10-15. "Monday Madness" offers $5 student tickets one week before showtime.)* **Sack Lunch Concerts,** 1422 S.W. 11th Ave. *(☎ 222-2031),* at Clay St. and the Old Church, presents free concerts, usually classical or jazz, every W at noon.

Portland Center Stage, in the Newmark Theater at S.W. Broadway and S.W. Main, stages a five-play series of classics and modern adaptations. *(☎ 248-6309. Late Sept.-Apr. Su and Tu-Th $11-31, F-Sa $12-39; under 26 $10. Half-price tickets may be available 1hr. before curtain.)* The **Bagdad Theater and Pub,** 3702 S.E. Hawthorne Blvd. *(☎ 669-8754),* and the **Mission Theater and Pub,** 1624 N.W. Glisan *(☎ 223-4031),* put out 2nd-run films and an excellent beer menu ($2-3; 21+). Sports fans can watch basketball's **Portland Trailblazers** at the **Rose Garden,** 1 Center Ct. *(☎ 321-3211).*

Northwest Film Center, 1219 S.W. Park Ave., hosts the **Portland International Film Festival** in the last two weeks of Feb., with 100 films from 30 nations. *(☎ 221-1156. Box office opens 30min. before each show. $6, seniors $5.)* Portland's premier summer event is the **Rose Festival** *(☎ 227-2681)* during the first three weeks of June. The city decks itself in finery, coming alive with waterfront concerts, art festivals, celebrity entertainment, auto racing, parades, an air show, Navy ships, and the largest children's parade in the world. Not too long afterward, the outrageously good three-day **Waterfront Blues Festival** draws some of the world's finest blues artists. (☎282-0555 or 973-3378; July 4-8, 2001. Suggested donation is $3 and two cans of food to benefit the Oregon Food Bank.) The **Oregon Brewers Festival,** on the last full weekend in July, is the continent's largest gathering of independent brewers and models for one incredible party at Waterfront Park. (☎778-5917. $3 mug and $1 per taste. Those under 21 must be accompanied by a parent.)

◪ NIGHTLIFE

Once an uncouth and rowdy frontier town, always an uncouth and rowdy frontier town. Portland's nightclubs cater to everyone from the clove-smoking college aesthete to the nipple-pierced neo-goth aesthete.

Biddy McGraw's, 3518 S.E. Hawthorne Blvd. (☎233-1178). Bus #14. Fast and friendly bartenders. Live Celtic and Gaelic tunes Th-Su. Raucous dancing to reggae Su, funk M, and jazz Tu. 22 kegs of Guinness consumed weekly; do your part for $3.75 per imperial pint. Microbrews $3. Open daily 2pm-2:30am.

Crystal Ballroom, 1332 W Burnside Blvd. (☎225-0047), near I-405. Look past the grand ballroom's immense paintings, gaudy chandeliers, and arching balcony, and jump onto the newest in stage technology: the infamous "floating dance floor." Portland's longest bar. Microbrewery on site. Open daily 11:30am-2:30am.

Panorama, Brig, and **Boxxes,** 341 S.W. 10th St. (☎221-7262), form a network of clubs along Stark St. between 10th and 11th. A thriving mixed crowd. The beats reach back in the Brig with 70s and 80s classics F. The 23-screen video/karaoke bar is where matchmaking magic happens. Open F-Sa 9pm-4am, Su-Th noon-2:30am. Cover $2-5.

Ohm, 31 N.W. 1st Ave. (☎223-9919), at Couch under the Burnside Bridge. Specializing in unclassifiable beats you're unlikely to hear anywhere else. Open M-F 8pm-2:30am, Sa 11am-4am, Su 11am-2:30am. After-hours for some shows and special events stretch past 6am. Kitchen service until 2am. Cover $5-20.

Satyricon, 125 N.W. 6th Ave. (☎243-2380), on the bus mall. Live alternative and punk since the days when grunge rock was the new kid on the block. Open daily 10pm-2:30am. Nightly cover $4-10, bigger draws $10-15. 21+.

Embers, 110 N.W. Broadway (☎222-3082), at Couch St. Follow rainbows to the dance floor, or watch fish swim in the bar counter. Retro and house music. Alternative crowd enjoys nightly drag show at 10pm. Open daily 11am-2:30am. Happy hour until 7pm.

MOUNT HOOD   ☎503

The magnificent, snow-capped peak juts above its cohorts at 11,235 feet, evidence of its much more recent volcanic activity. The seismic activity and high ground temperatures (closely monitored by the authorities) don't stop thousands of outdoor enthusiasts from enjoying the mountain year-round: in winter, snowboarders and skiers attack the slopes, while summer brings climbers, bikers, and hikers.

◪ PRACTICAL INFORMATION. Mt. Hood stands near the junction of U.S. 26 and Rte. 35, 1½hr. east of Portland and 1hr. south of the Hood River. The **Mt. Hood Information Center,** 65000 E U.S. 26, 16 mi. west of the junction of U.S. 26 and Hwy. 35 and 30 mi. east of Gresham, has topographic maps and info on both area ranger districts. (☎622-7674 or 888-622-4822. Open daily June-Oct. 8am-6pm; Nov.-May 8am-4:30pm.) **Hood River District Ranger Station,** 6780 Rte. 35, has more specialized info. (☎541-352-6002. Open daily Memorial Day to Labor Day M-F 8am-4:30pm; closed Sa-Su in winter.) The other station is **Zigzag District Ranger Station,** 7020 E. U.S. 26. (☎622-3191. Open M-F 8am-4:30pm.) **Area code:** 503.

◪ CAMPING. Government Camp, 50 mi. east of Portland, has food, accommodations, and gear rental. Camping spots in the **Mt. Hood National Forest** cluster near the junction of U.S. 26 and Rte. 35. **Trillium Lake Campground,** 2 mi. east of the Timberline turn-off on U.S. 26, has trails around the crystal-clear lake and paved sites with water and toilets. Pine trees offer some privacy. (Sites $14; premium lakeside sites $16.) Just 1 mi. west of Trillium Lake, down a dirt road off U.S. 26, **Still Creek Campgrounds** has a quieter, woodsier feel, unpaved sites, and a babbling brook. (Sites $13.) Well worth the trip out, **Lost Lake Campground** has lakeside sites with water, showers, and toilets. Turn east off Hwy. 35 onto Woodworth Dr. (2 streets north of Hood River Ranger Station), right onto the Dee Hwy., then left onto Lost Lake Rd. (Forest Service Rd. 13). A 3 mi. hike around the lake provides stunning views of Mt. Hood and of old growth forest. (☎541-386-6366. 121 sites. Tent sites $15; RV sites without electricity $18; cabins from $45-100.) **Reservations** for all of these campgrounds except Alpine and Lost Lake can be made at ☎877-444-6777.

◪ SKIING. Three Mt. Hood ski areas are convenient to Portland. All offer **night skiing** and **snowboard parks. Timberline,** off U.S. 26 at Government Camp, is a largely beginner and intermediate area, with the longest ski season in Oregon. (☎622-0717, snow report 222-2211. Open daily in winter 9am-4pm, in spring and fall 8:30am-2:30pm, in summer 7am-1:30pm. Lift tickets $34. Night skiing Jan.-Feb. W-F 4-9pm, Sa-Su 4-10pm. Rentals: ski package $21, ages 7-12 $13; snowboard and boots $33/$23. Cash deposit or credit card required.) Smaller **Mt. Hood Ski Bowl,** 87000 E. U.S. 26, in Government Camp, 2 mi. west of Hwy. 35, has the best night skiing and a snowboard park, though the season is limited. (☎222-2695. Season mid-Nov. to May. Open M-Tu 3:30-10pm, W-Th 9am-10pm, F 9am-11pm, Sa 8:30am-11pm, Su 8:30am-10pm. Lift tickets $16 per day, ages 7-12 $13. $16 per night, $22-28 for both. Ski rental $18/$13. Snowboards $26.) **Mt. Hood Meadows,** 9 mi. east of Government Camp on Hwy. 35, is the largest and nicest resort in the area, offering a wide range of terrain and the most high-speed lifts. At a medium elevation (7300 ft.), it often stays open through May. Mt. Hood Meadows offers $20 lift tickets through participating hotels. (☎337-2222, snow report 227-7669 or 541-386-7547. Open daily mid-Nov. to May 9am-4pm. Lift tickets $41, ages 7-12 $21. Night skiing Dec.-Mar. W-Su 4-10pm; $17. Ski rental package $20, ages 7-12 $15; snowboard $28/$21. Beginner package with lift ticket, lesson, and rental $45.)

◪ SUMMER ACTIVITIES. The most popular day hike is **Mirror Lake,** a 6 mi. loop that starts 1 mi. west of Government Camp (open June-Oct.). **ART of Adventure** offers mountain climbing training trips through Portland Parks and Recreation from late May to early Aug. (☎823-5132. 2-day trip is 1-day snow class, 1-day climb, with lodging and meals in Government Camp. $205; equipment rental not included.) In summer, Mount Hood Ski Bowl opens its **Action Park,** which features Indy Kart racing, "extreme" frisbee golf, bungee jumping, and an alpine slide. (☎222-2695. Open M-F 11am-6pm, Sa-Su 10am-6pm.)

COLUMBIA RIVER GORGE ☎509

The magnificent Columbia River Gorge stretches 75 stunning miles east from Portland and plunges into canyons more than 1000 feet deep. Heading inland along the Gorge, heavily forested peaks give way to broad, bronze cliffs and golden hills. Mt. Hood and Mt. Adams loom nearby, and breathtaking waterfalls plunge over steep cliffs into the river.

◪ PRACTICAL INFORMATION. To follow the gorge, which divides Oregon and Washington, take I-84 E to Exit 22. Continue east uphill on the **Columbia River Scenic Hwy. (U.S. 30),** which follows the crest of the gorge past unforgettable views. The largest town in the gorge is **Hood River,** at the junction of I-84 and Rte. 35. **Vista House,** hanging on the edge of an outcropping, is a visitors center in **Crown Point State Park,** 4 mi. east of Exit 22 off I-84 E. (☎503-695-2230. Open daily mid-Apr. to mid-Oct. 8:30am-6pm.) **Amtrak** runs trains from Portland to the foot of Walnut St. in Bingen, WA (2hr., $8-17). Station open M-Sa 8:30am-7pm and some Su afternoons. **Greyhound** runs from 600 E. Marina Way (☎386-1212) to Portland (1¼hr., 4 per day,

$11.50). **Hood River County Chamber of Commerce,** 405 Portway Ave., is just off City Center Exit 63. (☎386-2000 or 800-366-3530. Open Apr.-Oct. M-F 9am-5pm, Sa-Su 10am-5pm; Nov.-Mar. M-F 9am-5pm.) **Columbia Gorge National Scenic Area Headquarters,** 902 Wasco St., in Wyeth, offers info on hiking and a friendly earful of local lore (☎386-2333; open M-F 7:30am-5pm). **Post Office:** 408 Cascade Ave., in Hood River (open M-F 8:30am-5pm). **ZIP code:** 97031. **Area codes:** In WA 509, in OR 541. In text, 509 unless noted.

⌕ ACCOMMODATIONS. The **Bingen School Inn Hostel,** a converted schoolhouse, is just across the Hood River Toll Bridge (75¢), three and a half blocks from the Amtrak stop in Bingen, WA. (☎493-3363. Dorms $14; private rooms $35. Sailboards $30 per day.) **Beacon Rock State Park,** across the Bridge of the Gods (Exit 44) and 7 mi. west on Washington's Rte. 14, has secluded sites (☎427-8265; $12). The **Port of Cascade Locks Marine,** ½ mi. east off the bridge on the Oregon side, has a lawn on the river which doubles as a campground. (☎272-3380. Closed summers. $10.)

◪ WINDSURFING. The river widens out and the wind picks up at the town of Hood River, providing some of the world's best **windsurfing.** Though it was once "as fast as a waterfall turned on its side" and so full of fish that Lewis and Clark quipped that they could walk across without getting wet, the Columbia's waters now run slower and emptier due to damming upstream. The water near **Spring Creek Fish Hatchery** on the Washington side is the place to watch the best windsurfers in the business. Another hub is the **Event Site,** off Exit 63 behind the visitors center. All-day parking costs $3, although it's free if you just sit and watch. **Big Winds,** 207 Front St., at the east end of Oak St., has cheap beginner rentals. (☎386-6086. $8 per hr.; $15 per half-day; $25 per day.)

▨ OUTDOORS. **Discover Bicycles,** 1020 Wasco St., rents mountain bikes, suggests routes, and sells all manner of trail maps. (☎386-4820. Open M-Sa 9am-7pm, Su 9am-5pm. Bikes $6 per hr., $30 per day.) The 11 mi. round-trip **Hospital Hill Trail** provides views of Mt. Hood, the gorge, Hood River, and surrounding villages. To reach the unmarked trail, follow signs to the hospital, fork left to Rhine Village, and walk behind the power transformers through the livestock fence. At **Latourell Falls,** 2½ mi. east of Crown Point, a jaunt down a paved path leads right to the base of the falls; 5 mi. farther east, **Wahkeena Falls** is visible from the road and hosts both a short, steep scramble over loose rock and a ¼ mi. trip up a paved walk. Just ½ mi. farther on U.S. 30 is **Multnomah Falls,** which attracts 2 million visitors annually; I-84 Exit 31 leads to an island in the middle of the freeway from which visitors can only see the upper falls. The steep **Wyeth Trail,** near the hamlet of Wyeth (Exit 51), leads 4½ mi. to a wilderness boundary and 7¼ mi. to the road to Hood River and the incredible 13 mi. **Eagle Creek Trail** (Exit 44). Chiseled into cliffs high above Eagle Creek, this trail passes four waterfalls before joining the Pacific Crest Trail.

OREGON COAST

From Astoria in the north to Brookings down south, U.S. 101 hugs the shore along the Oregon Coast, linking a string of resorts and fishing villages that cluster around the mouths of rivers feeding into the Pacific. Breathtaking ocean views spread between these towns, while state parks and national forests allow direct access to the big surf. Seals, sea lions, and waterfowl lounge on rocks just offshore, watching the human world whiz by on wheels.

ASTORIA   ☎503

Astoria's long-standing dependence on maritime industries has only recently begun to yield to the tourist industry. With its Victorian homes, bustling waterfront, rolling hills, and persistent fog, tiny Astoria reminds many tourists of San Francisco; every so often, the clouds around Astoria Column lift to reveal a stupendous view of the town cradled between Saddle Mountain to the south and the Columbia River estuary to the north. The **Fort Clatsop National Memorial,** 5 mi. southwest of town, reconstructs Lewis and Clark's winter headquarters from detailed descriptions in their journals. Astoria was their last stop in 1805. Take U.S. 101 south from Astoria to Alt. U.S. 101, and follow the signs 3 mi. to the park. (☎861-2471. Open mid-June to Labor Day 8am-6pm; off-season 8am-5pm. $2, under 17 free, families $4 per car.) At the **Shallon Winery,** 1598 Duane St., owner Paul van der Velt provides tours and tastings of his vintages, including chocolate flavor. (☎325-5978. Open almost every afternoon; 21+ to drink.)

Grandview B&B, 1574 Grand Ave., offers intimate, luxurious rooms and a delicious breakfast spread. (☎325-0000, reservations 325-5555. From $45, with private bath from $71; 2nd night $36 off-season.) **Fort Stevens State Park,** over Youngs Bay Bridge on U.S. 101 S, 10 mi. west of Astoria, is the largest state park in the US, with rugged, empty beaches and bike trails. (☎861-1671, reservations 800-452-5687. Hot showers. Facilities for the disabled. $18, full hook-up $21; hiker/biker $4.25 per person; yurts $29. Reservations $6.) Seventeen mi. further south, and worth it, **Seaside International Hostel (HI-AYH),** 930 N. Holladay Dr., in Seaside, is a pastoral wonderland. (☎738-7911. Office open 8am-11pm. Kayaks and canoes $7-8 per hr. 34 large bunks $15, non-members $18; 4-person private rooms with bath and cable TV $38/$58. Call well ahead.)

Pierce Pacific Stages (☎692-4437) picks up travelers at Video City, 95 W. Marine Dr., and runs to Portland (3hr., $22). **Astoria/Warrenton Area Chamber of Commerce:** 111 W. Marine Dr. (☎325-6311. Open June-Sept. M-F 8am-6pm, Sa-Su 9am-6pm; Oct.-May M-F 8am-5pm, Sa-Su 11am-4pm.) **Post Office:** 748 Commercial St., at 8th St. (open M-F 8:30am-5pm). **ZIP code:** 97103. **Area code:** 503.

CANNON BEACH ☎503

Cannon Beach presents a somewhat more refined version of Astoria's commercialism, but the beach is the real draw. **Ecola State Park** attracts picnickers and hikers (☎436-2844; $3). **Ecola Point** offers a view of hulking **Haystack Rock,** which is spotted with (and splattered by) gulls, puffins, barnacles, anemones, and the occasional sea lion. Ecola Point also affords views of the Bay's centerpiece, the **Tillamook Lighthouse,** which clings to a rock like a phallic barnacle. A huge **Sand Castle Competition** transforms Cannon Beach into a fantastic menagerie on the 2nd Sa of June.

Pleasant motels line Hemlock St.; none costs under $40 in summer, but family units can make a good deal. In winter, most motels offer two-nights-for-one deals. **The Sandtrap Inn,** 539 S. Hemlock St. offers picturesque, cozy rooms with fireplaces, cable TV, and kitchens. (☎436-0247 or 800-400-4106. Singles from $60; off-season $50; 2-night minimum stay summer Sa-Su.) **Seaside International Hostel (HI-AYH)** is only 7 mi. north (see **Astoria,** above), and the stunning **Oswald West State Park** is 10 mi. south. The park provides wheelbarrows for transporting gear from the parking lot to the 36 sites which teem with surfers; arrive early. (Sites mid-May to Oct. $14; Oct.-Apr. $10.)

Sunset Transit System (☎800-776-6406) runs buses to Astoria ($2.25). **Cannon Beach Shuttle** traverses the downtown area daily 9am-6pm (75¢). **Mike's Bike Shop,** 248 N. Spruce St., rents mountain bikes. (☎436-1266 or 800-492-1266. Open daily 9am-6pm. $6-8 per hr., $20-30 per day.) **Cannon Beach Chamber of Commerce:** 207 N. Spruce St. (☎436-2623; open M-Sa 10am-6pm, Su 11am-4pm). **Post Office:** 155 N. Hemlock St. (☎436-2822; open M-F 9am-5pm). **ZIP code:** 97110. **Area code:** 503.

THE THREE CAPES LOOP

Between Tillamook and Lincoln City, the **Three Capes Loop,** a 35 mi. circle to the west of the straying U.S. 101, connects a trio of spectacular promontories. **Cape Meares State Park** and **Lighthouse,** at the tip of the promontory jutting out from Tillamook, protect one of the few remaining old-growth forests on the Oregon Coast. Another 12 mi. southwest of Cape Meares, **Cape Lookout State Park** (☎842-4981) offers picnic tables and access to the beach for drive-by dawdlers as well as some fine camping. A spectacular view of **Haystack Rock** awaits at the end of the 2½ mi. **Cape Trail. Cape Kiwanda State Park,** the southernmost promontory on the loop, reserves its magnificent shore for day use (open 8am-dusk). Home to one of the most sublime beaches on the Oregon coast, the sheltered cape draws all sorts. Massive rock outcroppings in a small bay mark the launching pad of the flat-bottomed **dory fleet,** one of the few fishing fleets in the world that launches beachside, directly from sand to surf. **Pacific City,** a hidden gem that most travelers on U.S. 101 never even see, is home to another **Haystack Rock,** just as impressive as its Cannon Beach sibling to the north.

NEWPORT   ☎541

After the miles of malls along U.S. 101, Newport's renovated waterfront area of pleasantly kitschy restaurants and shops are a delight. Newport's claim to fame lies in its world-class fish tank, also known as the **Oregon Coast Aquarium,** 2820 Ferry Slip Rd. SE, at the south end of the bridge. The six-acre complex features pulsating jellyfish, attention-seeking sea otters, and giant African bullfrogs. (☎867-3474. Open May-June 9am-6pm; July-Sept. 9am-8pm; winter 10am-5pm. $9.25, seniors $8.25, ages 4-13 $4.75. Wheelchair accessible.) The ▓**Mark O. Hatfield Marine Science Center,** at the south end of the bridge on Marine Science Dr., is the hub of Oregon State University's coastal research and an overshadowed, superior facility. Intricate exhibits explain marine science. (☎867-0100. Open daily 10am-5pm; in winter Th-M 10am-4pm. Admission by donation.)

   City Center Motel, 538 Coast Hwy. SW (☎265-7381 or 800-627-9099), opposite the visitors center is smack in the middle of town. It has spacious, oddly empty rooms with sparkling bathrooms, cable, phones, and ice. (In summer, singles start at $35; doubles $58.) **Beverly Beach State Park,** 198 123rd St. NE, 7 mi. north of town, is a year-round campground set amid gorgeous, rugged terrain. (☎265-9278 or 800-452-5687. Sites $14-17, with electricity $16-20, full hook-up $18-21; yurts $28; hiker/biker $4.25. Non-camper showers $2.) **April's,** 749 3rd St. NW, down by Nye Beach, is the undisputed pinnacle of local dining. The serene ocean view and devastatingly good food are worth every penny. (☎265-6855. Open Tu-Su for dinner from 5pm. Dinners $11-19. Call ahead.)

   Greyhound, 956 10th St. SW (☎265-2253), at Bailey St. runs buses to Portland (4hr., 2 per day, $18); Seattle (9hr., 2 per day, $44); and San Francisco (17-21hr., 3-4 per day, $72-76). **Chamber of Commerce,** 555 Coast Hwy. SW (☎265-8801; open M-F 8:30am-5pm; in summer also Sa-Su 10am-4pm). **Post office:** 310 2nd St. SW (open M-F 8:30am-5pm, Sa 10am-1pm). **ZIP code:** 97365. **Area code:** 541.

OREGON DUNES   ☎541

Millennia of wind and water action have formed the Oregon Dunes National Recreation Area, a 50-mile expanse between Florence and Coos Bay. Endless mounds of sand rise 500 feet above the water, shifting so quickly that the entire face of a dune can disappear and reform in the course of a day. The dunes' shifting grip on the coastline is broken at Reedsport, where the Umpqua and Smith Rivers empty into Winchester Bay, near a town of the same name. **Dunes Odyssey, Inc.,** on Hwy. 101 in Winchester Bay, was the first ATV rental business on the Oregon Coast. Rent a Honda Odyssey or a Polaris Quad and explore over 10,000 acres of dunes. (☎271-3863. Open daily 8am-dusk; call for winter hours. Both $35 for the first hr., $30 for each additional hr. Odyssey: $50 deposit. Polaris Quad: $100 deposit.) Even those with little time can at least stop at the **Oregon Dunes Overlook,** off U.S. 101, about halfway between Reedsport and Florence. Wooden ramps lead to a peek at untrammeled dunes and the ocean. (Overlook staffed daily Memorial Day to Labor Day 10am-3pm. Guided hikes are available. $1 parking fee.)

   The **Harbor View Motel,** 540 Beach Blvd., off U.S. 101 in Winchester Bay, is so close to the marina there are boats in the parking lot. Aging rooms to charm an antique hound are comfortable and clean. (☎271-3352. Singles $34; doubles $39.) Motels with singles from $40 abound on U.S. 101, though they often fill in summer. The national recreation area is administered by **Siuslaw National Forest.** Dispersed camping is allowed on public lands, 200 ft. from any road or trail. The campgrounds with dune buggy access—**Spinreel, Driftwood II, Horsfall,** and **Horsfall Beach**—are generally loud and rowdy in the summer. All have flush toilets, drinking water, and are open year-round (☎800-280-2267 for reservations; $10-13). **Carter Lake Campground,** 12 mi. north of Reedsport on U.S. 101, is as quiet as it gets. (Open May-Sept. No ATVs. Nice bathrooms, no showers. $13.)

Greyhound, 265 Rainbow Plaza (☎271-1025), in old town Reedsport, runs to Portland (6hr., 2 per day, $26) and San Francisco, CA (15hr., 2 per day, $67). The station is open daily 11am to 3pm and 2:30am until the last bus comes in. **Oregon Dunes National Recreation Area Information Center,** 855 U.S. 101 (☎271-3611), at Rte. 38 in Reedsport, south of the Umpqua River Bridge, happily answers questions on fees, regulations, hiking, and camping throughout the area. **Reedsport/Winchester Bay Chamber of Commerce** (☎271-3495 or 800-247-2155) is at the same location and has dune buggy rental info and motel listings. (Both open daily June-Oct. 8am-4:30pm; Nov.-May M-F 8am-4:30pm, Sa 10am-4pm.) **Post Office:** 301 Fir Ave., off Rte. 38 (open M-F 8:30am-5pm). **ZIP code:** 97467. **Area code:** 541.

INLAND OREGON

EUGENE ☎541

Known as "Track Capital, USA", the home of the University of Oregon takes due credit for its role in the running revolution of the 80s. Producing legends such as Steve Prefontaine, the U of O distance running program inspired all of Oregon to "hit the trails." Fitness enthusiasts flock to this running capital of the universe which is also the original hometown of Nike, Inc. (now based in Beaverton). With U of O students riding mountain bikes and hippies eating organic food, Eugene has also earned itself a liberal reputation. Many of the cities businesses are owned by active radicals, and environmental issues motivate its people. Outdoor types raft on the Willamette River and hike in nearby Willamette National Forest.

▐ GETTING THERE AND GETTING AROUND

Eugene is 111 mi. south of Portland on I-5.

Trains: Amtrak, 433 Willamette St. (☎687-1383), at 4th Ave. To: Seattle, WA (6-8hr., 2 per day, $29-56); Portland (2½-3hr., 2 per day, $14-27); Berkeley, CA (14hr., 1 per day, $55-111). Open daily 5:30-7pm.

Buses: Greyhound, 987 Pearl St. (☎344-6265), at 10th Ave. Open daily 6:15am-9:35pm. To: Seattle, WA (6-9hr., 9 per day, $30-32); San Francisco, CA (12-15hr., 6 per day, $47-50); Portland (2-4hr., 10 per day, $12.50-13.50). **Green Tortoise** (☎800-867-8647) stops at the U of O library, 14th and Kincaid St. To San Francisco, CA (21hr., two per week, $49), and Seattle, WA (7hr., two per week, $30) via Portland (4½hr., $15). Some routes require reservations. Office open daily 8am-8pm.

Public Transportation: Lane Transit District (LTD) (☎687-5555). Map and timetables at the LTD Service Center at 11th Ave. and Willamette St. Runs M-F 6am-11:40pm, Sa 7:30am-11:40pm, Su 8:30am-8:30pm. $1, seniors and 18 and under 50¢. Wheelchair accessible.

Taxis: Yellow Cab, ☎746-1234.

▟ 🛈 ORIENTATION AND PRACTICAL INFORMATION

The **University of Oregon** campus lies in the southeast corner of Eugene, bordered on the north by **Franklin Blvd.,** which runs from the city center to I-5. **First Ave.** runs alongside the winding Willamette River; numbered **streets** go north-south. **Hwy. 99** is split in town—**6th Ave.** runs north and **7th Ave.** goes south. **Willamette Ave.** intersects the river, dividing the city into east and west. It is interrupted by the **pedestrian mall,** between 6th and 7th Ave. on Broadway downtown. Eugene's main student drag, **13th Ave.**, heads east to the University of Oregon.

Visitor Info: 115 W 8th Ave. #190 (☎484-5307 or 800-547-5445), but the door is on Olive St. Courtesy phone. Sells an indexed map for $4. Open May-Aug. M-F 8:30am-5pm, Sa-Su 10am-4pm; Sept.-Apr. M-Sa 8:30am-5pm. **University of Oregon Switchboard,** in the Rainier Building at 1244 Walnut St. (☎346-3111). Referral for almost anything, from rides to housing. Open M-F 7am-6pm.

Post Office: 520 Willamette St., at 5th Ave. Open M-F 8:30am-5:30pm, Sa 10am-2pm. **ZIP code:** 97401. **Area code:** 541.

ACCOMMODATIONS AND FOOD

The cheapest motels are on E. Broadway and W. 7th Ave. and tend toward seediness. Make reservations early; motels are packed on big football weekends. **Hummingbird Eugene International Hostel (HI-AYH),** 2352 Willamette St., a graceful neighborhood home, is a wonderful escape from the city. Take bus #24 or 25 and get off at 24th Ave. and Willamette, or park in back on Portland St. (☎349-0589. Check-in 5-10pm. Lockout 11am-5pm. Cash or traveler's check only. Dorms $14, non-members $17.50; private rooms from $37.) **Downtown Motel,** 361 W. 7th Ave., is in a prime location, with clean rooms under a green Spanish roof. (☎345-8739 or 800-648-4366. Cable, A/C, refrigerators, free coffee, and doughnuts in the morning. Singles $35; doubles $40.) Tenters have been known to camp by the river, especially in the wild and woolly northeastern side near Springfield. Farther east on Rte. 58 and 126, the immense **Willamette National Forest** is packed with campsites ($3-16). A swamp gives the tree bark and ferns an eerie phosphorescence in the beautiful, mysterious **Black Canyon Campground,** 28 mi. east of Eugene on Hwy. 58 (☎877-444-6777. $10.)

Eugene's downtown area specializes in gourmet food; the university hangout zone at 13th Ave. and Kincaid has more grab-and-go options, and natural food stores encircle the city. The creative menu and organic ingredients at ▧**Keystone Cafe,** 395 W. 5th St., give diners a true taste of Eugene. (☎342-2075. Open daily 7am-5pm. Plate-sized pancakes $3.) **Chez Ray's North Beach,** 44 W 10th Ave., has tie-dyed bar stools and floating heads of the Grateful Dead. Brunch and breakfast is served all day for $6 to 8, and Chez Ray's world famous salmon burger is only $6.50. (☎344-1530. Open Su-F 9am-11pm, Sa 9am-1am. Live entertainment every night.)

SIGHTS AND EVENTS

Take time to pay homage to the ivy-covered halls that set the scene for *National Lampoon's Animal House* at Eugene's centerpiece, the **University of Oregon.** The visitor parking and info booth is just left of the main entrance on Franklin Blvd. A few blocks away, the **Museum of Natural History,** 1680 E. 15th Ave., at Agate, shows a collection of relics from indigenous cultures worldwide, including a 7000-year-old pair of shoes. A primitive "swoosh" logo is still visible. (☎346-3024. Open W-Su noon-5pm. Suggested donation $2.) Northwest of the city, just after the I-5 overpass, the **Owen Memorial Rose Garden** is perfect for a picnic, accompanied by the sweet strains of rumbling traffic. *The surrounding neighborhood of Whittaker can be unsafe at night.*

The weekly **Saturday Market,** at 8th Ave. and Oak St., offers produce, crafts, clothing, jewelry, artwork, flowers, food, and music. (☎686-8885. Apr.-Nov. Sa 10am-5pm.) From June 22 to July 8, 2001, during the **Oregon Bach Festival,** Baroque authority Helmut Rilling leads some of the country's finest musicians in performances of Bach's concerti and cantatas, as well as selections from Verdi and Dvôrak. (☎346-5666 or 800-457-1486. Concert and lecture series $12; main events $10-42; senior and student discounts for selected events.) The vast **Oregon Country Fair** actually takes place in **Veneta,** 13 mi. west of town on Rte. 126, but its festive quakes can be felt in Eugene. July 13-15, 2001, 50,000 people will drop everything to enjoy ten stages' worth of shows, 300 booths of art, clothing, crafts, herbal remedies, furniture, food, and free hugs. Advance tickets are available through **Fastixx** (☎800-992-8499) or at the **Hult Center.** (☎343-4298. Advance tickets F and Su $10, Sa $15. No tickets sold on site.)

OUTDOORS

Adventure Supply, 2101B W. 10th St. runs guided trips on the Willamette River and rents gear. (☎343-6883. Open M 10am-2pm, W-Sa 10am-6pm, Su noon-6pm. 4hr. rafting trip $45, 4-person minimum. Kayaks $25 per day; canoes $25 per day. Credit card required.) The visitors center has a full list of outfitters. To fill a free hour, canoe or kayak the **Millrace Canal,** which parallels the Willamette for 3 mi. The large and popular Cougar Lake features the Terwilliger Hot Springs, known by all as **Cougar Hot Springs.** To get there, go 4 mi. east of Blue River on Rte. 126, turn right onto Aufderheide Dr. (Forest Service Rd. 19), and follow the road 7¼ mi. as it winds on the right side of Cougar Reservoir. ($3 day fee per person.)

East from Eugene, Rte. 126 runs adjacent to the beautiful McKenzie River, and on a clear day, the mighty snowcapped Three Sisters of the Cascades are visible. Just east of the town of McKenzie Bridge, the road splits into a scenic byway loop; Rte. 242 climbs east to the vast lava fields of McKenzie Pass, while Rte. 126 turns north over Santiam Pass and meets back with Rte. 242 in Sisters. Often blocked by snow until the end of June, Rte. 242 is an exquisite drive, tunneling its narrow, winding way between Mt. Washington and the Three Sisters Wilderness before rising to the high plateau of McKenzie Pass, where lava outcroppings served as a training site for astronauts preparing for lunar landings.

The 26 mi. **McKenzie River Trail** parallels Rte. 126 through mossy forests and leads to some of Oregon's most spectacular waterfalls, Koosah Falls and Sahalie Falls. They flank Clear Lake, a volcanic crater now filled with crystal clear waters. The trail starts about 1½ mi. west of the ranger station and ends up north at Old Santiam Rd. near the Fish Lake Old Growth Grove. The trail is now open to mountain bikers.

◪ NIGHTLIFE

According to some, Eugene nightlife is the best in Oregon. Not surprisingly, the string of establishments by the university along 13th St. are often dominated by fraternity-style beer bashes. **Sam Bond's Garage,** 407 Blair Blvd., is a supremely laid-back gem of a cafe and pub in a soulful neighborhood. Live entertainment goes on every night, plus an ever-changing selection of local microbrews ($3 per pint). Take bus #50 or 52 or a cab at night. (☎431-6603. Open daily 3pm-1am.) Downstairs at **Jo Federigo's Jazz Club and Restaurant,** 259 E. 5th Ave., across the street from the 5th St. Market., the jazz club swings with music every night, and the whole place rattles when the train goes by. (☎343-8488. Open M-F 11:30am-2pm and 5-10 pm, Sa-Su 5-10pm. Jazz club open daily 2:30pm-1am. Shows usually at 9:30pm. Blues night W. Happy hour 2:30-6:30pm. No cover, but $5 drink minimum.) **John Henry's,** 136 E. 11th Ave., in the heart of downtown, is a cavernous warehouse-style venue that plays host to a diversity of musical acts. (☎342-3358. Open M-Sa 4pm-1am. Call for schedule. Microbrew pints $3. Cover $3-7.)

CRATER LAKE AND KLAMATH FALLS ☎541

Crater Lake, the namesake of Oregon's only national park, was regarded as sacred by Native American shamans who forbade their people to look upon it. The fantastic depth of the lake (1932 ft.), combined with the clarity of its waters, creates its intensely blue effect. About 7700 years ago, Mt. Mazama created this serene scene in a massive eruption that buried thousands of square miles of the western US under a thick layer of ash. The cataclysmic eruption left a deep caldera that gradually filled with centuries of rain. Klamath *(kuh-LAH-math)* Falls, one of the closest towns, houses most of the services, motels, and restaurants listed below.

7 PRACTICAL INFORMATION. The park is accessible from **Rte. 62** and the **south access** road that leads up to the caldera's rim, but the park is not completely open until after the snow has melted; call the Steel Center for road conditions (see below). To reach the park from Portland, take I-5 to Eugene, then Rte. 58 E to U.S. 97 S. During the summer, you can take Rte. 138 W from U.S. 97 and approach the lake from the park's **north entrance,** but this route is one of the last to be cleared. The **Amtrak** Spring St. depot (☎884-2822; open 6:45-10:15am and 9-10:30pm) is in Klamath Falls, on the east end of Main St.; turn right onto Spring St. and immediately left onto Oak St. One train per day runs to Portland ($35-58). **Greyhound,** 1200 Klamath Ave. (☎882-4616; open M-F 6am-2:30pm and midnight-12:45am, Sa 6-9am and midnight-12:45am), rolls one per day to Bend (3hr., $20); Eugene (10hr., $39-41); and Redding, CA (4hr., $27-29). **Visitor Info: Klamath County Dept. of Tourism,** 507 Main St. (☎884-0666 or 800-445-6728; open M-Sa 9am-5pm). **Post Office:** 317 S. 7th St. (open M-F 7:30am-5:30pm, Sa 9am-noon). **ZIP code:** 97604.

The **William G. Steel Center,** 1 mi. from the south entrance of the park, issues free **backcountry camping** permits (☎594-2211, ext. 402; open daily 9am-5pm). **Crater Lake National Park Visitors Center:** on the lake shore at Rim Village (☎594-2211, ext. 415; open daily June-Sept. 8:30am-6pm). The **park entrance fee** is $10 for cars, $5 for hikers and cyclists.

𝕲 ACCOMMODATIONS AND FOOD. Klamath Falls has several affordable hotels; it's an easy base for forays to Crater Lake. **Fort Klamath Lodge Motel and RV Park,** 52851 Rte. 62, is 15 mi. from the southern entrance in Fort Klamath. Cozy, quiet, countrified motel rooms have knotted pine walls. (☎381-2234. Open May-Oct. Fan, heater, TV, no phones. Singles $42; doubles $58.) **Lost Creek Campground** is in the park, 3 mi. off Rim Dr. in the southeast corner. Sites are set amid thin, young pines. (☎594-2255. Usually open mid-July to mid-Oct., but call the visitors center to confirm. Drinking water, flush toilets, sinks. Tents only. Sites $10. No reservations.) **Waldo's Mongolian Grill and Tavern,** 610 Main St., will grill your choice of veggies, meats, and sauces. (☎884-6863. Open M-Th 11am-11:30pm, F-Sa 11am-1am. 81 beers, 15 microbrews. All-you-can-eat $10.)

𝕶 OUTDOORS. From the visitors center at the rim to the **Sinnott Memorial Overlook** is an easy 100 yd. walk to the park's most panoramic and accessible view. **Rim Dr.,** which does not open entirely until mid-July, is a 33 mi. loop around the rim of the caldera, high above the lake. Trails to **Garfield Peak** (one-way 1¾ mi.), which starts at the lodge, and **Watchman Peak** (one-way ¾ mi.), on the west side of the lake, are the most spectacular. The sweaty, 2½ mi. hike up **Mt. Scott,** the park's highest peak (shy of 9000 ft.), begins from near the lake's eastern edge. The steep **Cleetwood Trail,** 1 mi. of switchbacks on the lake's north edge, is the only route down to the water. It is also the home of **Wizard Island,** a cinder cone rising 760 ft. above the lake, and **Phantom Ship Rock,** a spooky rock formation. Picnics, fishing, and swimming are allowed, but surface temperatures reach a maximum of only 50°F. Park rangers lead free walking tours daily in the summer and periodically in the winter (on snowshoes). The **Red Cone trailhead,** on the north access road, makes a 12 mi. loop of the **Crater Springs, Oasis Butte,** and **Boundary Springs Trails.**

ASHLAND   ☎541

Set near the California border, Ashland mixes hippies and history to create an unlikely but perfect stage for the world-famous **Oregon Shakespeare Festival,** P.O. Box 158, Ashland 97520 (☎482-4331). From mid-Feb. to Oct., drama devotees can choose among 11 Shakespearean and newer works performed in Ashland's three elegant theaters: the outdoor **Elizabethan Stage,** the **Angus Bowmer Theater,** and the intimate **Black Swan.** Ticket purchases are recommended six months in advance; mail-order and phone ticket sales begin in Jan. ($22-39 in spring and fall, $29-52 in summer; $5 fee per order for phone, fax, or mail orders.) At 9:30am, the **box office,** 15 S. Pioneer St., releases any unsold tickets for the day's performances and sells 20 standing room tickets for sold-out shows on the Elizabethan Stage ($11). Half-price rush tickets are sometimes available 1hr. before performances that are not already sold out. Some half-price student-senior matinees are offered in the spring and in Oct., and all three theaters hold full-performance previews in the spring and summer. **Backstage tours** provide a wonderful glimpse of the festival from behind the curtain (Tu-Su 10am; $9-12, ages 6-17 $4.50-9, under 6 not admitted).

In winter, Ashland is a budget paradise of vacancy and low rates; in summer, hotel and B&B rates double, and the hostel bulges. Only rogues and peasant slaves arrive without reservations. ◪**Ashland Hostel,** 150 N. Main St., is well-kept and cheery, with an air of elegance. (☎482-9217. Laundry and kitchen. Check-in 5-11pm. Lockout 10am-5pm. Curfew midnight. Dorms $16; private rooms $45.) The incredible selection of food on N. and E. Main St. has earned the plaza a culinary reputation independent of the festival. ◪**Geppetto's,** 345 E. Main St., is *the* spot for a late-night bite. The staff is congenial, the walls covered in baskets, and dinners start at $11. (☎482-1138. Open daily 8am-midnight. Wheelchair accessible.)

Ashland is located in the foothills of the Siskiyou and Cascade Ranges, 285 mi. south of Portland and 15 mi. north of the California border, near the junction of **I-5** and **Rte. 66. Greyhound** (☎482-8803) runs from the **BP station,** 2073 Rte. 99 N, at the north end of town, and sends three per day to Portland (7hr., 3 per day, $42.50-47); Sacramento, CA (7hr., 3 per day, $43-47); and San Francisco, CA (11hr., 3 per day, $48-52). **Chamber of Commerce:** 110 E. Main St. (☎482-3486). **Ashland District Ranger Station,** 645 Washington St., off Rte. 66 by Exit 14 on I-5, provides info on hiking, biking, and the Pacific Crest Trail (☎482-3333; open M-F 8am-4:30pm). **Post Office:** 120 N. 1st St., at Lithia Way (open M-F 9am-5pm). **ZIP code:** 97520. **Area code:** 541.

BEND   ☎541

At the foot of the Cascades's east slope, Bend is at the epicenter of an impressive array of outdoor opportunities, wooing waves of skiers and nature-lovers. Oregon's biggest little city in the east is rapidly losing its small-town feel to a stream of California, Portland, and Seattle refugees in search of the perfect blend of urban excitement, pristine wilderness, and sun-filled days.

🛈 PRACTICAL INFORMATION. Bend is 160 mi. southeast of Portland either on U.S. 26 E through Warm Springs Indian Reservation to U.S. 97 S or south on I-5 to Salem, then east on Rte. 22 E to Rte. 20 E through Sisters; 144 mi. north of Klamath Falls on U.S. 97; and 100 mi. southeast of Mt. Hood via U.S. 26 E and Rte. 97 S. **U.S. 97 (3rd St.)** bisects the town. Downtown lies to the west along the **Deschutes River; Wall** and **Bond St.** are the two main arteries. **Greyhound,** 63076 US 97N (☎382-2151; open M-F 8-1:30pm and 2:30-5pm, Sa-Su 8:30am-3pm), runs to Portland (5 hr., 1 per day, $22-24) and Eugene (2½hr., 1 per day, $21). **Taxi: Owl Taxi,** ☎382-3311. **Bend Chamber and Visitors Bureau,** 63085 U.S. 97 N, stocks free maps, free coffee, and Internet access (☎382-3221; open M-Sa 9am-5pm, Su 11am-3pm). **Deschutes National Forest Headquarters,** 1645 U.S. 20 E, has forest and wilderness info (☎383-5800; open M-F 7:45am-4:30pm). **Post Office:** 2300 N.E. 4th St., at Webster (open M-F 8:30am-5:30pm, Sa 10am-1pm). **ZIP code:** 97701. **Area code:** 541.

🛏🍴 ACCOMMODATIONS AND FOOD. Most of the cheapest motels line **3rd St.** just outside of town, and rates are surprisingly low. To reach **Bend Cascade Hostel,** 19 S.W. Century Dr., take Greenwood west from 3rd St. until the name changes to Newport. After ½ mi., take a left on 14th St.; the clean, fairly safe, and tidy hostel is ½ mi. up on the right side, just past the Circle K. (☎389-3813 or 800-299-3813. Foosball, laundry, kitchen, linen. $15; students, seniors, cyclists, and HI members $14; under 18 with parents half-price.) **Deschutes National Forest** maintains a huge number of lakeside campgrounds along the **Cascade Lakes Hwy.,** west of town; all have toilets. Sites with potable water cost $8-12 per night; those without water are free. Camping anywhere in the national forest area is free.

Devore's Good Food Store and Wine Shop, 1124 Newport NW peddles all things organic (☎389-6588; open M-Sa 8am-7pm, Su 11am-6pm). **Deschutes Brewery and**

Public House, 1044 N.W. Bond St., has homemade sausage and smoked salmon, but they're overshadowed by the specials ($5-7) and $3.25 imperial pints. (☎382-9242. Open M-Th 11am-11:30pm, F-Sa 11am-12:30am, Su 11am-10pm.)

🔲🏔 SIGHTS AND OUTDOORS. South of Bend by 3½ mi., the **High Desert Museum,** 59800 S. Hwy. 97, is one of the premier natural and cultural history museums in the Pacific Northwest. Visitors walk through stunning life-size dioramas of life in the Old West, while the indoor desertarium houses bats, burrowing owls, and collared lizards. A brand-new Native American Wing features a walk-through exhibit on post-reservation Indian life. (☎382-4754. Open daily 9am-5pm. $7.75, seniors and ages 13-18 $6.75, ages 5-12 $3.75.)

The **Three Sisters Wilderness Area,** north and west of the Cascade Lakes Highway, is one of Oregon's largest and most popular wilderness areas. A parking permit is required at most trailheads: pick one up at any of the ranger stations or at the visitor center ($5). Mountain biking is not allowed in the wilderness area itself, but Benders have plenty of other places to spin their wheels. Try **Deschutes River Trail** (one-way 10½ mi.) for a fairly flat, basic, forested trail ending at **Deschutes River.** To reach the trailhead, go 7½ mi. west of Bend on Century Dr. (Cascade Lakes Hwy.) until Forest Service Rd. 41, then turn left and follow the signs to Lava Island Falls. For a difficult, technical ride, hit the **Waldo Lake Loop,** a grueling 22 mi. trail around the lake. To get there, take Cascade Lakes Hwy. to Forest Service Rd. 4290. A slick new guide to mountain bike trails around Bend is available for $7 at the Bend/Ft. Rock District Ranger Station and at most bike shops in the area, but some of the hottest trails aren't on the maps; talk to locals.

HELLS CANYON AND WALLOWA MOUNTAINS   ☎541

The northeast corner of Oregon is the state's most rugged, remote, and arresting country, with jagged granite peaks, glacier-gouged valleys, and azure lakes. East of La Grande, the Wallowa Mountains (*wa-LAH-wah*) rise abruptly, looming over the plains from elevations of more than 9000 feet. Thirty miles east, North America's deepest gorge, Hells Canyon, plunges to the Snake River. Dusty slopes and scorching heat lend credence to the canyon's name. It may take a four-wheel-drive vehicle to get off the beaten path, but those with the initiative and the horsepower will find stunning vistas and heavenly solitude in the backcountry.

🔃 PRACTICAL INFORMATION. Hells Canyon National Recreation Area and the Eagle Cap Wilderness lie on either side of the Wallowa Valley, which can be reached from Baker City, La Grande, and Clarkston, WA. Three main towns offer services within the area: **Enterprise, Joseph,** and **Halfway.** The **Wallowa Valley Stage Line** (☎569-2284) makes one round-trip M-Sa from Joseph to La Grande. Pick-up at the Chevron on Rte. 82 in Joseph, the Amoco on Rte. 82 in Enterprise, and the Greyhound terminal in La Grande. One-way from La Grande to: Enterprise ($10); Joseph ($11); and Wallowa Lake ($15). **Wallowa County Chamber of Commerce** is at S.W. 1st St. and W. Greenwood Ave. in Enterprise, in the mall (☎426-4622 or 800-585-4121; open M-F 9am-5pm). **Hells Canyon Chamber of Commerce:** (☎742-4222), in the office of Halfway Motels. **Outdoor Information: Wallowa Mountains Visitor Center,** 88401 Rte. 82, on the west side of Enterprise. $4 map a necessity for navigating area roads. (☎426-5546. Open Memorial Day to Labor Day M-Sa 8am-5pm; off-season M-F 8am-5pm.)

🏠 ACCOMMODATIONS. **Indian Lodge Motel,** 201 S. Main St., on Rte. 82 in Joseph, has elegant rooms with dark wood furniture and plush blue carpet. (☎432-2651 or 888-286-5484. A/C, cable, coffee-makers, fridges. Singles $37; doubles $49. Winter $31.50/$40.) Campgrounds here are plentiful, inexpensive, and sublime. Pick up the *Campground Information* pamphlet at the Wallowa Mountains Visitors Center for a complete listing of sites in the area. Due to 1996 budget cutbacks, most campgrounds are not fully serviced, and are therefore **free**—check at the visitors center to see whether a campground has potable water. Inexplicably, the massive **Wallowa**

Lake State Park campground books solid up to a year in advance. Try your luck there if in the market for full-service camping. (☎432-4185 or 800-452-5687. Toilets, drinking water, and showers. Sites $16.50, full hook-ups $21.)

⚠ HIKING AND DRIVING. Hiking is the best way to comprehend the vast emptiness of Hells Canyon, and to really get into the canyon requires a trip of at least a few days. There are over 1000 mi. of trails, only a fraction of which are regularly maintained. Bring snakebite kits, good boots, and lots of water. The dramatic 56 mi. **Snake River Trail** runs beside the river for the length of the canyon. At times, the trail is cut into the side of the rock with just enough clearance for a horse's head. Come prepared for any hazard, though outfitters and rangers patrol the river by boat at least once a day. This trail can be followed from **Dug Bar** in the north clear down to the Hells Canyon Dam or accessed by treacherously steep trails along the way. From north to south, **Hat Point, Freezeout,** and **P.O. Saddle** are possible access points. To reach Dug Bar, take Forest Rd. 4260, a steep, slippery route recommended only for 4-wheel drive or high-clearance vehicles, for 27 mi. northeast from Imnaha; check conditions before heading out. The only way to get close to the canyon without taking at least a full day is to drive the **Hells Canyon National Scenic Loop Drive,** which begins and ends in Baker City, following Rte. 86, Forest Rd. 39 and 350, Rte. 82, and finally I-84. Even this paved route takes 6hr. to two days to drive; closures are routine. The most eye-popping views are from the 90 ft. fire lookout at **Hat Point Overlook;** go 24 mi. up the steep gravel Forest Rd. 4240 from Imnaha, then turn off onto Rd. 315 and follow the signs.

Without a catchy, federally approved name like "Hells Canyon," the Wallowas often take 2nd place to the canyon in the minds of tourists, though they possess a scenic beauty equally magnificent. The canyons echo with the deafening rush of rapids, and the jagged peaks are covered with wildflowers in spring. Over 600 mi. of **hiking trails** cross the **Eagle Cap Wilderness** and are usually free of snow from mid-July to Oct. Deep glacial valleys and high granite passes make hiking this wilderness tough going: it often takes more than a day to get into the most beautiful and remote areas. Still, several high alpine lakes are accessible to dayhikers. The 5 mi. hike to **Chimney Lake** from the Bowman trailhead on the Lostine River Rd. (Forest Rd. 8210) traverses fields of granite boulders sprinkled with a few small meadows. A little farther on lie the serene **Laverty, Hobo,** and **Wood Lakes,** where the path is less beaten. The **Two Pan trailhead** at the end of the Lostine River Rd. is the start of a forested 6 mi. hike to popular **Minam Lake,** which makes a good starting point for those heading to other backcountry spots like **Blue Lake,** 1 mi. above Minam. From the **Wallowa Lake trailhead,** behind the little powerhouse at the end of Rte. 82, a 6 mi. hike leads up the East Fork of the Wallowa River to Aneroid Lake. From there, hikes to Pete's Point and Aneroid Mountain offer great views.

WESTERN CANADA

> **!** **A NOTE TO OUR READERS.** Canada is **not** a part of the United States. All prices listed in this chapter are in Canadian dollars unless otherwise noted.

HIGHLIGHTS OF WESTERN CANADA

THE YUKON. Flightseeing in Kluane National Park (p. 934) and gold-panning in boomtown Dawson City (p. 931) are both unusual and memorable.

SCENIC DRIVES. The glorious Dempster Hwy. (p. 935) leads way up to Inuvik, NWT.

NATIONAL PARKS. Banff (p. 936) and Jasper (p. 939) in Alberta reign as two of the region's most beautiful. Pacific Rim National Park, BC contains the West Coast Trail (p. 930) with its isolated beaches and old growth rainforest.

BRITISH COLUMBIA

British Columbia (BC) is Canada's westernmost province, with over 890,000 square kilometers bordering four US states (Washington, Idaho, Montana, and Alaska) and three Canadian entities (Alberta, the Yukon Territory, and the Northwest Territories). It's natural beauty and vibrant cities attract so many visitors that tourism has become its 2nd-largest industry after logging.

🛈 PRACTICAL INFORMATION

Capital: Victoria.

Visitor Info: Tourism British Columbia, 1117 Wharf St., Victoria, BC V8W 2Z2 (☎250-387-1642 or 800-663-6000; www.travel.bc.ca). **British Columbia Parks Headquarters** P.O. Box 9398, Stn. Prov. Govt., Victoria, BC V8W 9M9 (☎250-387-5002; www.elp.gov.bc.ca/bcparks).

Drinking Age: 19. **Postal Abbreviation:** BC. **Sales Tax:** 7%.

VANCOUVER   ☎604

Like any self-respecting city on the west coast of North America, Vancouver boasts a thriving multicultural populace; the Cantonese influence is so strong so that it is often referred to by its nickname, "Hongcouver." The completion of the cross-Canada railroad at the turn of the century was made possible in large part by the work of tens of thousands of Chinese immigrants, many of whom settled at the western terminus, founding Vancouver's extensive Chinatown. Recent cultural developments include a tendency for young Canadians from all points east to migrate, seemingly instinctively, to this western city. And while diversity may be the norm for big cities, Vancouver couples it with the stunning surroundings of the Pacific Ocean and the forested Coast Mountain range.

▣ GETTING THERE AND GETTING AROUND

Airport: Vancouver International Airport (☎276-6101), on Sea Island, 23km south of the city center. A visitors center (☎303-3601) is on level 2. Open daily 8am-midnight. To reach downtown, take bus #100 "New Westminster Station" to the intersection of Granville and 70th Ave. Transfer there to bus #20 "Fraser." An **Airport Express** (☎946-8866) bus leaves from level 2 for downtown hotels and the bus station. 4 per hr. 6:30am-10:30pm; $10, seniors $8, ages 5-12 $5.

British Columbia and the Yukon Territory

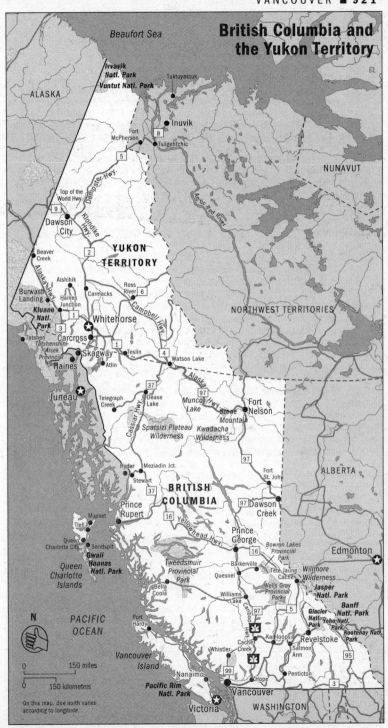

Beaufort Sea

ALASKA

Ivvavik Natl. Park
Vuntut Natl. Park

Tuktoyaktuk

8 Inuvik

Fort McPherson

Tsiigehtchic

5

Dempster Hwy.

NUNAVUT

9 Top of the World Hwy.

Dawson City

Klondike Hwy.

2

YUKON TERRITORY

Beaver Creek

Aishihik

Ross River 6

Arctic Red River

NORTHWEST TERRITORIES

Burwash Landing

Carmacks

Alaska Hwy.

Haines Junction

Kluane Natl. Park

1 Whitehorse

Campbell Hwy.

3

Carcross

Tatshenshini-Alsek Provincial Park

1 Skagway

Teslin

4

Watson Lake

Tatshen

Haines

Atlin

Alaska Hwy.

Juneau

37

Telegraph Creek

Dease Lake

97

Muncol Lake

Stone Mountain

Fort Nelson

Cassiar Hwy.

Spatsizi Plateau Wilderness

Kwadacha Wilderness

97

ALBERTA

Hyder

Meziadin Jct.

Stewart

Fort St. John

37

BRITISH COLUMBIA

97

Dawson Creek

Prince Rupert

16 Yellowhead Hwy.

Masset

Tlell

Prince George

16

Bowron Lakes Provincial Park

Edmonton

Queen Charlotte City

Sandspit

Gwaii Haanas Natl. Park

Tweedsmuir Provincial Park

Barkerville

Tete Jaune Cache

Willmore Wilderness

Quesnel

Wells Gray Provincial Park

Jasper Natl. Park

Queen Charlotte Islands

Bella Coola

Williams Lake

5

Glacier Natl. Park

Banff Natl. Park

Yoho Natl. Park

PACIFIC OCEAN

N

Port Hardy

97

Cariboo Hwy.

Kamloops

Revelstoke

Kootenay Natl. Park

95

Whistler

Cache Creek

Salmon Arm

0   150 miles

0   150 kilometers

Vancouver Island

Nanaimo

99

Penticton

3

Hope

Vancouver

Pacific Rim Natl. Park

Victoria

WASHINGTON

On this map, due north varies according to longitude.

WESTERN CANADA

Ferries: BC Ferries (☎888-223-3779). To the Gulf Islands, Sechelt, and Vancouver Island ($7.50-9, ages 5-11 $4.25, car $30-32, bike $2.50; fares cheapest mid-week). Ferries to Victoria, Nanaimo, and the Gulf Islands leave from the **Tsawwassen Terminal,** 25km south of the city center (take Hwy. 99 to Hwy. 17). To reach downtown from Tsawwassen by bus, take #640 "Scott Rd. Station" or #404 "Airport" to the Ladner Exchange, then transfer to bus #601. Ferries to Nanaimo and Sechelt depart the **Horseshoe Bay Terminal** at the end of the Trans-Canada Hwy. in West Vancouver. Take "Blue Bus" #250 or 257 on Georgia St. from downtown.

Downtown Vancouver

🔺 ACCOMMODATIONS
Backpackers Hostel, **11**
Cambie Hostel, **9**
Global Village
  Backpackers, **4**
Kingston Hotel, **7**
Vancouver Hostel
  Downtown, **1**

🎵 NIGHTLIFE
The Cambie, **12**
Odyssey, **3**
Purple Onion, **15**
Sonar, **14**
Wett Bar, **21**

🍎 FOOD
Deserts Falafel, **2**
La Luna Cafe, **13**
Lingo Cyberbistro, **10**
Subeez Café, **6**

⬤ OTHER
Dr. Sun Yat-Sen Classical
  Chinese Garden, **17**
GM Place, **18**
Library, **8**
Orpheum Theatre, **5**
Science World, **19**
World's Skinniest
  Building, **16**

Trains: VIA Rail, 1150 Station St. (☎800-561-8630, in US 800-561-9181). 3 trains per week to eastern Canada via Jasper, AB (17hr., $187.25). Open M, W, Th, and Sa 9:30am-6pm; Tu, F, and Su 9am-7pm. **BC Rail,** 1311 W. 1st St. (☎984-5246), in North Vancouver at the foot of Pemberton St. Take the BC Rail Special bus on Georgia St. (June-Sept.) or the SeaBus to North Vancouver, then bus #239 west. Daily train to Whistler (2½hr., $33). Tu and F trains depart at 7pm for Williams Lake (10hr., $133); Prince George (14hr., $196); and other points north. Open daily 8am-8pm.

Buses: Greyhound, 1150 Station St., in the VIA Rail station (☎482-8747; open daily 5:30am-12:30am). To Calgary, AB (15hr., 4 per day, $117). Pacific Coach Lines, 1150 Station St. (☎662-8074) to Victoria (3½hr., $26.50 includes ferry). Quick Shuttle (☎940-4428 or 800-665-2122) makes 8 trips per day from downtown via the airport to Seattle, WA (3-3½hr., $42) and the Sea-Tac airport (3½-4hr. $50). **Greyhound USA** (☎402-330-8552) goes to Seattle (3-4½hr.; US$20).

Public Transit: Coast Mountain Buslink (☎521-0400) covers most of the city and suburbs, with direct transport or easy connections to airport and ferry terminals. **Central zone** encompasses most of the city ($1.75 per 1½hr.). During peak hours (M-F before 6:30pm), it costs $2.50 to travel between 2 zones and $3.25 to travel through 3 zones. During off-peak hours all zones are $1.75. Ask for a **free transfer** (good for 1½hr.) when you board buses. **Day passes** ($7) are sold at 7-11, Safeway, and HI-C hostels. Seniors and ages 5-13 $1.25 for 1 zone or off-peak travel, $1.75 for two zones, $2.25 for 3 zones, and $5 for day passes. **SeaBus** and **SkyTrain** included in the normal BusFare. The SkyTrain is a light rapid transit system, running from Vancouver to Burnaby. The SeaBus shuttles passengers across the waters of Burrard Inlet from the foot of Granville St. downtown (SkyTrain: Waterfront) to **Lonsdale Quay** at the foot of Lonsdale Ave. in North Van.

Car Rental: Resort Rent-a-Car, 3231 No. 3 Rd., in Richmond (☎232-3060; free pick-up in Vancouver). From $34 per day, $164 per week; unlimited km. Must be 21. Open M-F 7am-9pm and Sa-Su 7am-7pm.

✦🛈 ORIENTATION AND PRACTICAL INFORMATION

Vancouver lies in the southwestern corner of mainland British Columbia. South of the city flows the **Fraser River,** and to the west lies the **Georgia Strait,** separating the mainland from Vancouver Island. **Downtown** juts north into the Burrard Inlet from the core of the city, and **Stanley Park** goes further north. The **Lions Gate** suspension bridge over Burrard Inlet links Stanley Park with North and West Vancouver **(West Van),** known collectively as the **North Shore;** the bridges over False Creek south of downtown link it with **Kitsilano ("Kits")** and the rest of the city. West of Burrard St. is the **West Side** or **West End. Gastown** and **Chinatown** are east of downtown. The **University of British Columbia (UBC)** lies on the west end of Kits on Point Grey, while the **airport** is on Sea Island in the Fraser River delta. The **Trans-Canada Hwy. (Hwy. 1)** enters town from the east and **Hwy. 99** runs north-south through the city.

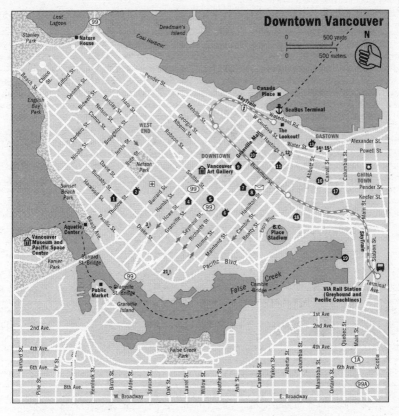

Visitor Information: 200 Burrard St. (☎683-2000). Open daily 8am-6pm.

Internet Access: Library, 350 W Georgia St. (☎331-3600). Free email terminals or pay $5 per hr. Open M-Th 10am-8pm and F-Sa 10am-5pm. Free email at 20 other branches; check white pages.

Gay and Lesbian Info: Gay and Lesbian Centre, 1170 Bute St., counseling and info. *Xtra West* is the city's gay and lesbian biweekly. Vancouver **Prideline** (☎684-6869), staffed daily 7am-10pm. Open M-F 3:30-9:30pm, Sa 6:30-9:30pm.

Special Concerns Info: Women's Resource Center, 1144 Robson St. (☎482-8585), near downtown. Open July-Aug. M-Th 10am-2pm; Sept.-June M-F 10am-4pm. **Crisis Center,** ☎872-3311. 24hr.

Hospital: Vancouver Hospital, 855 W 12th Ave. (☎875-4111). **UBC Hospital,** 221 Westbrook Mall (☎822-7121), on the UBC campus.

Post Office: 349 W Georgia St. (☎662-5725). Open M-F 8am-5:30pm. **Postal code:** V6B 3P7. **Area code:** 604.

ACCOMMODATIONS

Greater Vancouver B&Bs are a viable option for couples or small groups (singles from $45, doubles from $55). The visitors center and agencies like **Town and Country Bed and Breakfast** (☎731-5942) and **Best Canadian** (☎738-7207) list options. HI hostels are a good bet for clean rooms and quiet nights; others can be rowdy or seedy.

Vancouver Hostel Downtown (HI), 1114 Burnaby St. (☎684-4565 or 888-203-4302), in the West End. Ultra-modern and ultra-clean 225-bed facility between downtown, the beach, and Stanley Park. 4-bunk rooms, game room, kitchen, rooftop patio, free linen, tours of the city. Free shuttle to Jericho Beach Hostel. Internet access $6 per hr. Pub crawls almost every night. Travel agency in the basement. Open 24hr. Dorms $20, non-members $24; private doubles $55/$64. Reservations crucial in summer.

Vancouver Hostel Jericho Beach (HI), 1515 Discovery St. (☎224-3208 or 888-203-4303), in Jericho Beach Park. Follow 4th Ave. west past Alma, bear right at the fork, or take bus #4 from Granville St. downtown. Institutional but clean. Peaceful location with great view across English Bay. 285 beds in 14-person dorm rooms. Family rooms. Kitchens, TV, laundry, cafe, free linen. Bike $20 per day. Organizes tours and trips to Vancouver bars. Free shuttle to Vancouver Hostel Downtown (see above). Stay-and-ski package with Grouse Mountain for $37 includes bed, lift ticket, free shuttle to slopes. Dorms $17.50; non-members $21.50. Reservations imperative in summer.

The Globetrotter's Inn, 170 W. Esplanade (☎988-2082), in North Van. Near the Lonsdale Quay Market and SeaBus terminal on the water for easy access to downtown. Kitchen, pool table, free laundry. Reception 8am-8pm. Dorms $18; singles $25; doubles $30. Weekly rates from $100. Reservations recommended.

Kingston Hotel, 757 Richards St. (☎684-9024; fax 684-9917), between Robson and Georgia St. A B&B/hotel hybrid. Feel like a monarch in small, quiet, cushioned-and-carpeted rooms. Pay parking available. Coin laundry and sauna. Singles $45-65; doubles $55-105. Cheaper rates for shared bath. Breakfast included.

Cambie Hostel, 515 Seymour St. (☎684-7757). The quieter of two downtown Cambie hostels. Pub crawls (W), movie nights (Su-M), soccer games (Sa), free tours of Granville Island Brewery (Tu at noon, 2pm, and 4pm) and pancake breakfast (Sa). Internet access. Open 24hr. Dorms $25, $20 with student or HI card; $40 private room.

Global Village Backpackers, 1018 Granville St. (☎682-8226 or 888-844-7875), on corner of Nelson, next to Dakota Hotel. Shuttle from bus/train station; call for details. Airporter Bus stops at Granville St. New hostel offers fresh fun karma. Internet, pool. Linen included. Key, linen deposit. Dorms $24; doubles $59; doubles with bath $66. $3 discount for those with HI, ISIC, or other hosteling membership.

Backpackers Hostel, 347 W. Pender St. (☎688-0112), downtown. Cheap rates make this hostel popular with the true budget traveler. Beds packed tightly into rooms. TV and video-game room, rooftop smoking affords room to stretch out. Internet access $6 per hr. Sa free beer. Dorms $10; singles $25; doubles $30.

Capilano RV Park, 295 Tomahawk Ave. (☎987-4722), at foot of Lions Gate Bridge in North Van; closest RV park to downtown. Turn south off Marine Dr. onto Lower Capilano Rd., take first right on Welch, right on Tomahawk. Showers, pool, laundry. Reception open daily 8am-11pm. 2-person sites $25; extra person $3.50; hook-ups $30-35.

FOOD

The diversity and excellence of Vancouver's international cuisine makes the rest of BC seem provincial. Vancouver's **Chinatown** is second in size to only San Francisco's. The **Punjabi Village** along Main and Fraser, around 49th St., serves cheap, authentic Indian food. The entire world, from Vietnamese noodle shops to Italian cafes to succulent yet cheap sushi, seems represented along **Commercial Drive,** east of Chinatown. Produce peddled along "The Drive" puts supermarkets to shame.

Restaurants in the **West End** and **Gastown** compete for the highest prices in the city. The former caters to consumers taking a break from shopping and executives on expense accounts, while the latter lures tourists fresh off the cruise ships. Many cheap and grubby establishments along Davie and Denman St. stay open around the clock. Dollar-a-slice, all-night pizza places pepper downtown.

The Naam, 2724 W. 4th Ave. (☎738-7151), at MacDonald St. Bus #4 or 7 from Granville Mall. The most diverse vegetarian menu around with great prices. Crying Tiger Thai stir fry $8; tofulati ice cream $3.50. Live music nightly 7-10pm. Birthday discounts equal to the nearest decade of your new age (e.g. 22 years old, 20% off!). Open 24hr.

■ **Benny's Bagels,** 2505 W. Broadway (☎731-9730). Every college student's dream. Serves the requisite beer (W bucket $10.25), bagels (75¢, $2.25 with cream cheese), and hot sandwiches (from $5). Open Su-W 7am-1am and Th-Sa 24 hr.

■ **Deserts Falafel,** 1183 Davie St. (☎684-4760). Delicious falafel sandwiches ($3.75) and heaping hummus plates ($3.50). Free delivery. Open daily 11am-midnight.

WaaZuBee Cafe, 1622 Commercial Dr. (☎253-5299), at E. 1st St. Sleek, metallic decoration, ambient music, and artwork temper the brilliantly prepared food. Veggie Spinach and Ricotta Agnoilotti pasta $12, Thai prawns $8, veggie burger $7. Open M-F 11:30am-1am, Sa 11am-1am and Su 11am-midnight.

La Luna Cafe, 117 Water St. (☎687-5862), in Gastown. Loyal patrons swear by the coffee, roasted on premises. Cheap, satisfying sandwiches ($3.75-4.50), homemade soups ($3). Open M-F 7:30am-5pm and Sa 10am-6pm.

Thai Away Home, 1918 Commercial Dr. (☎253-8424). Small, colorful cafe serves tasty Thai at a good price. Delicious *pad thai* ($7) and 5 colors of curry ($5). Open M-Sa 11:30am-9:30pm and Su noon-9:30pm.

Hon's Wun-Tun House, 268 Keefer St. (☎688-0871). Two kitchens (one vegetarian); phenomenal service. Cash only. Open daily 8:30am-10pm.

SIGHTS

WORLD'S FAIR GROUNDS AND DOWNTOWN

EXPO '86. On the city's centennial, the World Exposition brought attention, prestige, and roller-coasters to Vancouver. The big-screen star of Expo '86 was the **Omnimax Theatre,** part of **Science World.** In addition to the 27m spherical screen, Science World also features hands-on exhibits and fact-crammed shows for kids. *(1455 Quebec St., at the Main St. stop of the Skytrain. ☎268-6363. Open daily July-Aug. 10am-6pm; call for winter hours. $11.75; students, seniors, and children $7.75. Omnimax shows Su-F 10am-5pm and Sa 10am-9pm. $10. Combined ticket $14.75/$10.50.)*

CANADA PLACE. The Canada Pavilion, or **Canada Place,** was built to resemble giant sails; the cavernous roof dominates the harbor. The shops and restaurants inside are outrageously expensive, but the promenades around the complex make for terrific gawking at luxury liners and their camera-toting cargo. **Lookout!** offers fantastic 360° views of the city! Tickets are expensive! But they're good for the whole day! Come back for a more sedate nighttime skyline! *(555 W. Hastings St. ☎689-0421. SkyTrain from the main Expo site or walk across the street from the visitors center on Burrard St. Open daily 8:30am-10:30pm; in winter 10am-9pm. $9, students $6, seniors $8. 50% off with HI membership or receipt from Vancouver International Hostel.)*

VANCOUVER ART GALLERY. An entire floor of the gallery is devoted to the surreal paintings of British Columbian Emily Carr. *(750 Hornby St. in Robson Square. ☎662-4700. Open W-M 10am-5:30pm and Th 10am-9pm; in winter Tu-Su 10am-5:30pm. $10; students $6; under 12 free. Th 5-9pm pay-what-you-can. Two-for-one HI discount.)*

CHINATOWN

Southeast of Gastown. Bus #22 north on Burrard St. leads to Pender and Carrall St., in the heart of Chinatown. ☎689-7133. Open daily 9:30am-7pm; in winter 10:30am-4:30pm. Tours every hr. 10am-6pm. $7.50, students $5, seniors $6, children free, families $18.

The neighborhood bustles with restaurants, shops, bakeries, and **the world's skinniest building.** In 1912, the city expropriated all but a 1.8m strip of Chang Toy's property in order to expand the street; he built on the land anyhow. *(8 W. Pender St.)* The serene **Dr. Sun Yat-Sen Classical Chinese Garden** maintains imported Chinese plantings, carvings, and rock formations in the first full-size authentic garden of its kind outside China. *(578 Carrall St.)* Don't miss the **night market** along Pender and Keefer St., the first in North America. *(F-Su 6:30-11pm.)*

UNIVERSITY OF BRITISH COLUMBIA (UBC)

*6393 N.W. Marine Dr. Bus #4 or 10 from Granville St. Museum (☎822-3825 or 822-5087). Open M and W-Su 10am-5pm in Tu 10am-9pm; Sept.-May closed M. $7, students $4, seniors $5, under 6 free Tu after 5pm free. **Nitobe Garden** (☎822-6038). Open daily Mar.-Oct. 10am-6pm; Nov.-Feb. M-F 10am-2:30pm. **Botanical Garden,** 6804 S.W. Marine Dr. (☎822-9666). $2.50, students $1.75. **Gallery** (☎822-2759). $3, students free. **Concerts** (☎822-3113). Call ☎822-8687 to arrange a walking tour May-Aug.*

The high point of a visit to UBC is the breathtaking ▧**Museum of Anthropology.** The high-ceilinged glass and concrete building houses totems and other massive carvings, highlighted by Bill Reid's depiction of Raven discovering the first human beings in a giant clam shell. Across the street caretakers tend to **Nitobe Memorial Garden,** the finest classical Shinto garden outside of Japan. The **Botanical Gardens** are a collegiate Eden encompassing eight gardens, including the largest collection of rhododendrons in North America. It also boasts a **Fine Arts Gallery** and free daytime and evening concerts. Just east of campus in **Pacific Spirit Regional Park,** woods stretch from inland hills to the beaches of Spanish Banks. With 50km of gravel and dirt trails through dense forest, the park is ideal for jogging and mountain biking. Grab free maps at the **Park Centre** on 16th Ave., near Blanca.

STANLEY PARK

Established in 1889 at the tip of the downtown peninsula, the 1000-acre **Stanley Park** is a testament to the foresight of Vancouver's urban planners. An easy escape from the nearby West End and downtown, the thickly wooded park is laced with cycling and hiking trails, and surrounded by an 11km **seawall** promenade popular with cyclists, runners, and in-line skaters.

VANCOUVER AQUARIUM. The aquarium, on the park's eastern side not far from the entrance, features exotic aquatic animals; BC, Amazonian, and other ecosystems are skillfully replicated. Dolphin and beluga whales demonstrate their advanced training and intelligence by drenching gleeful visitors in educational shows. Outside the aquarium, an **orca fountain** by sculptor Bill Reid glistens black. *(☎659-3474. Open daily July-Aug. 9:30am-7:30pm; Sept.-June 10am-5:30pm. Shows throughout the day 10:30am-5:30pm. $13, students and seniors $11, under 12 $9.)*

FALSE CREEK AND GRANVILLE ISLAND

GRANVILLE ISLAND MARKET. Granville Island Market, southwest of downtown under the Granville Street Bridge, intersperses trendy shops, art galleries, restaurants, and countless produce stands. *(☎666-5784. From downtown, bus #50 "False Creek" or #51 "Granville Island" from Granville St. Open daily 9am-6pm; in winter closed M.)*

MARITIME MUSEUM. The ferry shares the Maritime Museum dock with historic vessels. The wood-and-glass A-frame museum on shore houses **RCMP. St. Roch,** a schooner that patrolled the Northwest Passage in the 40s; in 1950, she was the first to circumnavigate North America.

VANCOUVER MUSEUM. The circular building displays artifacts from local native cultures and more recent relics of Vancouver history. In the same building, the **Pacific Space Centre** runs a motion-simulator ride, planetarium, and exhibit gallery, as well as laser-light rock shows. *(1100 Chestnut St. ☎736-4431. Bus #22 south on Burrard St. from downtown. Open daily 10am-5pm; in winter closed M. $8, under 18 $5.50. Pacific Space Centre $12.50, students and seniors $9.50; laser-light show $8.)*

▧ PARKS AND BEACHES

Vancouver is blessed with remarkably clean beaches. Follow the western side of the Stanley Park seawall south to **Sunset Beach Park,** a strip of grass and beach extending all the way along **English Bay** to the Burrard Bridge.

Kitsilano Beach, across Arbutus St. from Vanier Park, is another local favorite for tanning and beach volleyball. For fewer crowds, more young 'uns, and free showers, visit **Jericho Beach.** North Marine Dr. runs along the beach, and a cycling path at the side of the road leads to the westernmost end of the UBC campus. West of Jericho Beach is the quieter **Spanish Banks;** at low tide the ocean retreats almost 1km, allowing for long walks on the flats.

Most of Vancouver's 31km of beaches are patrolled daily by lifeguards from late May to Labour Day between 11:30am and 9pm. Frolic in true West Coast spirit during summer weekend **volleyball tournaments,** offering all levels of competition. Scare up a team at the hostel, then call ☎291-2007 to find out where to play.

"Co-ed Naked Beach Volleyball" would make a fine t-shirt slogan, but you wouldn't wear it at **Wreck Beach.** Take entry trail #6 down the hill from S.W. Marine Dr. opposite the UBC campus. A steep wooden staircase leads to a totally secluded, self-contained sunshine community of nude sunbathers and guitar-playing UBC students. There are no lifeguards, but naked entrepreneurs peddle vegetarian-friendly foods, beer, and other awareness-altering goods for premium prices. Call **Wreck Beach Preservation Society** (☎273-6950) for more info.

🎵📺 ENTERTAINMENT AND NIGHTLIFE

The **Vancouver Symphony Orchestra** (☎684-9100) plays Sept. to May in the refurbished **Orpheum Theatre** (☎665-3050), at the corner of Smithe and Seymour. The new **Ford Center for the Performing Arts** (☎602-0616) plays Broadway musicals. The **Vancouver Playhouse** (☎873-3311), on Dunsmuir and Georgia St., and the **Arts Club Theatre** (☎687-5315), on Granville Island, stages low-key shows, often including local work. **Theatre Under the Stars** (☎687-0174), in Stanley Park's Malkin Bowl, puts on outdoor musicals. The annual **Fringe Theater Festival** features 600 performances in venues in Granville Island and Yaletown. (☎257-0350. Runs Sept. Tickets under $11.)

- 🎵 **Purple Onion,** 15 Water St. (☎602-9442), in Gastown. Sucks in the crowd with an eclectic music selection and inviting lounge chairs. The lounge features live blues, R&B, jazz, and funk acts. DJs spin acid jazz, disco, soul, funk, Latin, swing, and reggae in the back room. Open M-Th 8pm-2am, F-Sa 7pm-2am, and Su 7pm-midnight. Cover $3-8.
- 🎵 **Sonar,** 66 Water St. (☎683-6695), in Gastown. A new arrival on the club scene, this former live rock venue is now a popular 2-level beat factory. House Th and Sa, hip-hop W, and break-beat F. Pints $3.50-4.75. Open M-Sa 8pm-2am, and Su 8pm-midnight.
- **The King's Head,** 1618 Yew St. (☎738-6966), at 1st St., in Kitsilano. Cheap drinks, cheap food, relaxing atmosphere, and a great location near the beach. Bands play acoustic sets on a tiny stage. Daily drink specials. $3 pints. Gullet-filling Beggar's Breakfast ($4). Open M-F 7am-1:30am, Sa 7:30am-2am, and Su 7:30am-midnight.
- **Wett Bar,** 1320 Richards St. (☎662-7707), downtown. Candlelit dining booths, a weekend dress code, and one of the most advanced stereo and light systems in Vancouver. Drum 'n' bass M, hip-hop F, top 40 Sa. Open M and W-Sa 9pm-2am, and Tu 9pm-1am.
- **The Cambie,** 300 Cambie St. (☎684-6466), in Gastown. Young crowds from all over the cultural spectrum, picnic tables made from bowling lanes, loud music, sports TVs, and beer as cheap as it gets. Pitcher of Molson $8.25. Open daily 9am-1:30am.
- **Odyssey,** 1251 Howe St. (☎689-5256). F-Sa cranks out beats to a mainly gay crowd. Male go-go dancers F; Drag Night Su and W. Open daily 9pm-2am. Cover $2-4.

🏔 DAYTRIP FROM VANCOUVER

WHISTLER. Only 125km north of Vancouver on the dangerously twisty Hwy. 99, Whistler and Blackcomb mountains provides some of North America's best skiing and snowboarding and are popular mountain destinations in summer, too. The **"Village"** is overproduced and overpriced, but no amount of Disneyfication can take away from the striking beauty of the mountains or the challenge of the terrain. Whistler is currently bidding to host the 2010 Winter Olympics.

Seven thousand acres of terrain, 33 lifts, and 2km of vertical drop make recently merged **Whistler/Blackcomb** the largest ski resort in North America. Parking and lift access for this behemoth is available at six points, with Whistler Creekside offering the shortest lines and easiest access to those coming from Vancouver. A lift ticket is good for both mountains. (☎932-3434 or 800-766-0449. $58; $38 from June 12 to Aug. 7. Multi-day discounts available.) Cheap tickets are often available at Super-Valu's and 7-11's in Vancouver and Squamish. While skiing is God in Whistler and lasts on the glaciers until August, the **Whistler Gondola** whisks sightseers to the top of the mountain year-round for $22 ($25 with bike), providing access in summer to the resort's extensive mountain bike park.

The gorgeous lakeside **Whistler Hostel (HI-C)**, 5678 Alta Lake Rd., lies 5km south of Whistler Village on Hwy. 99. BC Rail stops at the hostel on request. (☎932-5492. $18.50; non-members $22.75.) Rooms at the **Shoestring Lodge,** 7124 Nancy Greene Dr., 1km north of the village, offer cable, private baths, and a shared kitchen. (☎932-3338. Bunk $16-30; doubles $90-140. Peak prices, mandatory reservations, and free shuttle transport to the slopes Dec.-Apr.)

Greyhound (☎932-5031) runs to Vancouver from the Village Bus Loop (2½hr., 6 per day, $20). **BC Rail's** 2½-hr. Cariboo Prospector (☎984-5246) departs North Vancouver for Whistler Creek at 7am and returns at 6:20pm daily ($33). **Activity and information center:** in the heart of the Village. (☎932-2394. Open daily 9am-5pm.) **Post office:** in the Village Marketplace. (☎932-5012. Open M-F 8:30am-5:30pm and Sa 8:30am-12:30pm.) **Postal Code:** V0N 1B0. **Area code:** 604.

VANCOUVER ISLAND

VICTORIA ☎250

Clean, polite, and tourist-friendly, today's Victoria is a homier alternative to cosmo-politan Vancouver. Although many tourist operations would have you believe that Victoria fell off Great Britain in a neat little chunk, its High Tea tradition began in the 50s to draw American tourists. Double-decker buses motor past native art galleries, new-age bookstores, and countless English pubs.

🛈 **PRACTICAL INFORMATION.** Victoria surrounds the **Inner Harbour;** the main north-south thoroughfares downtown are **Government Street** and **Douglas Street.** To the north, Douglas St. becomes Hwy. 1, which runs north to Nanaimo. **Blanshard Street,** one block to the east, becomes Hwy. 17.

The **E&N Railway** (☎383-4324 or 800-561-8630), near the Inner Harbour at the Johnson St. Bridge, runs daily to Nanaimo (2½hr., $19, students with ISIC $11). **Laid-law,** 700 Douglas St. (☎385-4411 or 800-318-0818), at Belleville St., and its affiliates, **Pacific** and **Island Coach Lines,** run buses to Nanaimo (2½hr., 6 per day, $17.50); Vancouver (3½hr., 8-14 per day, $27); and Port Hardy (9hr., 1-2 per day, $84). **BC Ferries** (☎656-5571 or 888-223-3779; operator 7am-10pm 386-3431) depart Swartz Bay to Vancouver's Tsawwassen ferry terminal (1½hr.; 8-16 per day; $9, bikes $2.50, car and driver $39-41), and to the Gulf Islands. **Washington State Ferries** (☎381-1551 or 656-1831; in the US ☎206-464-6400 or 800-843-3779) depart from Sidney to Anacortes, WA (1-2 per day; US$9, car with driver US$41). Free stopovers allowed in the San Juan Islands. **Victoria Clipper** (☎382-8100 or 800-888-2535) passenger ferries travel to Seattle (2-3hr.; 4 per day May-Sept., 1 per day Oct.-Apr.; US$79-91). **Black Ball Transport** (☎386-2202) runs to Port Angeles, WA (1½hr.; 2-4 per day; US$6.75, car and driver US$28.50). **Public Bus #70** ($2.50) runs between downtown and the Swartz Bay and Sidney ferry terminals. **Victoria Taxi,** ☎383-7111, runs 24 hours. **Tourism Victoria:** 812 Wharf St., at Government St. (☎953-2033. Open daily 8:30am-7:30pm; in winter 9am-5pm.) **Post Office:** 621 Discovery St. (☎963-1350. Open M-F 8am-6pm.) **Postal code:** V8W 1L0. **Area code:** 250.

🛏 **ACCOMMODATIONS.** The colorful new 🏠**Ocean Island Backpackers Inn,** 791 Pandora St., downtown, boasts a better lounge than most clubs, tastier food than most restaurants (see **Food,** below), and accommodations comparable to most hotels. Undoubtedly one of the finest urban hostels in Canada. (☎385-1788 or 888-888-4180. 140 beds in small rooms; free linen and towels, laundry, email. Dorms

$19.50, $16.25 for students and HI members; doubles $40. Parking $4.) To reach the **Selkirk Guest House,** 934 Selkirk Ave., in West Victoria, take bus #14 along Craigflower to Tillicum; Selkirk is one block north with co-ed and all-female dorms with flowery sheets, free canoes, and a hot tub on the water. (☎389-1213. Kitchen, free linen and towels, laundry. Dorms $18; private rooms $50-70. Breakfast $5.) **Goldstream Provincial Park,** 2930 Trans-Canada Hwy., 20km northwest of Victoria, offers a forested riverside area with great hiking trails and swimming. (☎391-2300 or 800-689-9025. Flush toilets and firewood. $18.50.) The sites at **Thetis Lake Campground,** 1938 Trans-Canada Hwy., 10km north of the city center, are not large, but some are peaceful and removed. (☎478-3845. Showers 25¢ per 5min. Flush toilets, laundry. $16, full hook-up $20.)

🍴📷 FOOD AND NIGHTLIFE. A diversity of food can be found in Victoria, if you know where to go; ask locals, or wander the downtown core. **Chinatown** extends from Fisgard and Government St. to the northwest. In **Fernwood Village,** three blocks north of Johnson St., accessible by bus #10, creative restaurants are scattered among craft shops. **◪John's Place,** 723 Pandora St., is a hopping joint serving wholesome Canadian fare with international twists. (☎389-0711. Open M-Th 7am-10pm, F-Sa 7am-11pm, and Su 8am-10pm. Entrees $5-11.) A trip to Victoria is improper without a spot of tea; the tea with sandwiches and pastries ($7) or Su high tea ($10) at the **James Bay Tea Room & Restaurant,** 332 Menzies St., behind the Parliament Buildings, is a lower-key and significantly less expensive version of the famous High Tea at the Empress Hotel. (☎382-8282. Open M-Sa 7am-8pm, Su 8am-8pm.)

The free weekly *Monday Magazine*, out on Wednesday and available downtown, lists who's playing music where. **Steamers Public House,** 570 Yates St., attracts a young, happy crowd dancing to different music every night. (☎381-4340. Open M-Sa 11:30am-2am, Su 11:30am-midnight. Open stage M, jazz night Tu. Cover $3-5 at night.) **Big Bad John's** is the bar that invites you to leave a piece of yourself behind; everything from bras to bills line the walls. (☎383-7137. Open M-Sa noon-2am and Su noon-midnight.)

📷⛰ SIGHTS AND OUTDOORS. The fantastically thorough **◪Royal British Columbia Museum** presents excellent exhibits on the biological, geological, and cultural history of the province, from protozoans to the present. A new IMAX theater shows films that are larger than life. *(675 Belleville St. ☎387-3014. Open daily 9am-5pm. $8; students, youths, and seniors $5; under 5 free. IMAX $9.50; seniors $8; youth $6.50; child $3.50.)* The public **Art Gallery of Greater Victoria** culls magnificent exhibits from its collection of 14,000 pieces covering contemporary Canada, traditional and contemporary Asia, North America, and Europe. *(1040 Moss St. ☎384-4101. Open Tu 10am-10pm, W-Sa 10am-5pm, and Su 1pm-5pm. $5; students and seniors $3; free M.)* Across the street from the museum stands the imposing **Parliament Buildings,** home of the provincial government. *(501 Belleville St. ☎387-3046. Open M-F 8:30am-5pm; Sa-Su for tours only. Free tours leave from main steps in summer daily 9am-4:30pm, 3 times per hr.)* Just north of Fort St. on Wharf St. is Bastion Sq., home to the **Maritime Museum,** which houses ship models, nautical instruments, and a torpedo. *(28 Bastion Sq. ☎385-4222. Open daily 9:30am-4:30pm. $5; students $3; seniors $4; ages 6-11 $2. Tickets good for 3 days.)*

The elaborate **Butchart Gardens** sprawl across a valley. Immaculate landscaping includes a rose garden, Japanese and Italian gardens, fountains, and wheelchair-accessible paths. *(21km north of Victoria off Hwy. 17. Take bus #75 Central Saanich from downtown at Douglas and Pandora. ☎652-5256 or 652-4422. Open daily July-Aug. 9am-10:30pm. Fireworks Sa around dusk. $16.50; ages 13-17 $8.25; ages 5-12 $2; under 5 free.)*

Mountain bikers can tackle the **Galloping Goose,** a 60km trail beginning downtown and continuing to the west coast of the Island through towns, rainforests, and canyons. **Ocean River Sports** offers kayak rentals, tours, and lessons. *(☎381-4233 or 800-909-4233. Open M-Th and Sa 9:30am-5:30pm, F 9:30am-8:30pm, and Su 11am-5pm. Full day single kayak $42, double $50; canoe $42.)* Many whale-watching outfits give discounts for hostel guests. **Ocean Explorations** runs 3hr. tours from Apr. to Oct. *(532 Broughton St. ☎383-6722. $69, hostelers and children $50, less in early season. Free pick-up at hostels.)*

PACIFIC RIM NATIONAL PARK ☎ 250

Pacific Rim National Park, a thin strip of land on the island's remote western coast, is separately accessible at all three of its disparate regions and features beautiful remote hiking, popular sandy surfing beaches, and quirky small towns. The south end of the park—the head of the West Coast Trail at Port Renfrew—lies at the end of Hwy. 14, west of Victoria. **West Coast Trail Express** runs one bus per day from Victoria to Port Renfrew. (☎477-8700; 2¼hr.; $32. Reservations are required.) The fantastic **West Coast Trail,** covering the southern third of the park between Port Renfrew and Bamfield, traces the shoreline for 75km of forests and waterfalls and scales ladders and rocky slopes; recommended hiking time is about one week ($20 reservation fee, $70 trail use fee, $25 ferry crossing fee). The **Trail Information Centre** in Port Renfrew (☎647-5434), is at the first right off Parkinson Rd. (Hwy. 14) once in "town." The trail is open May to Sept.; reservations should be made three months in advance at **Parks Canada,** Box 280, Ucluelet V0R 3A0 (☎800-663-6000).

The park's middle section—Bamfield and the Broken Group Islands in Barkley Sound—is far more difficult to reach. Hwy. 18 connects to Hwy. 1 at Duncan about 60km north of Victoria. West Coast Trail Express buses (see above) run daily from Nanaimo (3hr., $50) and Victoria (4½hr., $50). **Alberni Marine Transportation** floats Apr. to Sept. from Port Alberni. (☎723-8313 or 800-663-7192; 4½hr.; $20.)

To reach Long Beach, at the park's northern reaches, take the spectacular drive across Vancouver Island on Hwy. 4 to the **Pacific Rim Hwy.** This stretch connects the towns of sleepy but expensive Ucluelet and crunchy and friendly Tofino. Hwy. 4 branches west of Hwy. 1 about 35km north of Nanaimo, leads 50km through Port Alberni, and continues 92km to the Pacific coast. **Chinook Charters** (☎725-3431) sends buses to the towns from Victoria (7hr., $47.50). Alberni Marine Transportation (see above) runs from Port Alberni to Ucluelet (5hr., $23). **Parks Canada Visitor Information** is 3km north of the Port Alberni junction on the Pacific Rim Hwy. (☎726-4212. Open mid-June to mid-Sept. daily 9:30am-5pm.) ▨**Whalers on the Point Guesthouse (HI),** on Main St. in Tofino, is a newly-constructed deluxe hostel offering 60 beds (4 to a room), a free sauna, billiards, Sega, linen, and harborside views. (☎725-3443. Check-in 7am-noon and 5pm-11pm. $22, non-members $24; private rooms available.) Camping is extremely popular in summer. The golf course on the way to Tofino often has showerless gravel sites ($15) when no one else does.

Hiking is the highlight of a trip to the west side of the Island. **The Rainforest Centre,** 451 Main St., in Tofino, has assembled an excellent trail guide for Clayoquot Sound, Tofino, Ucluelet, the Pacific Rim, and Kennedy Lake (available by donation). The trails grow even more beautiful in the frequent rain and fog. (☎725-2560. Park passes available in parking lots. $8 per day; season passes $45.)

PRINCE RUPERT ☎ 250

At the western end of Hwy. 16, Prince Rupert is an emerging transportation hub— a springboard for ferry travel to Alaska, the spectacular Queen Charlotte Islands, and northern Vancouver Island.

▐ **GETTING THERE AND AWAY. Prince Rupert Airport** is on Digby Island, with a ferry and bus connection to downtown (45min., $11). **VIA Rail** (☎627-7304 or 800-561-8630, outside BC 800-561-3949), toward the water on Bill Murray Way, runs to Prince George (12hr., 3 per week, $169); **BC Rail** (☎604-984-5500 or 800-339-8752, outside BC 800-663-8238) continues the next morning from Prince George to Vancouver (14hr., $194). **Greyhound,** 822 3rd Ave. (☎624-5090), near 8th St., runs to Prince George (10hr., 2 per day, $88) and Vancouver (24hr., 2 per day, $175). **Alaska Marine Highway** ferries (☎627-1744 or 800-642-0066), at the end of Hwy. 16 (Park Ave.), run north from Prince Rupert along the Alaskan Panhandle to Ketchikan (6hr., US$38) and Juneau (1-2 days, US$104). Next door, **BC Ferries** (☎624-9627 or 888-223-3779) runs to the Queen Charlotte Islands (6-7hr.; 6 per week; $24, car $90) and Port Hardy on the northern tip of Vancouver Island (15hr.; every other day; $104/$214). **Seashore Charter Services** (☎624-5645) runs a shuttle from the mall on

2nd Ave. to the ferry terminal by request ($3). **Prince Rupert Bus Service** (☎624-3343) runs downtown (Su-Th 7am-6pm; F until 10pm; $1); about every 30min., bus #52 runs from 2nd Ave. and 3rd St. to within a 5min. walk of the ferry terminal.

◧◪ ORIENTATION AND PRACTICAL INFORMATION. The only major road into town is the Yellowhead Highway (Hwy. 16), leading to the ferry docks; it is known as **McBride St.** within city limits, **2nd Ave.** at the north end of downtown, and **Park Ave.** at the south end. From the docks, downtown is a 30min. walk. The **Info Centre,** at 1st Ave. and McBride St., is in a cedar building modeled after a Tsimshian bighouse. (☎624-5637 or 800-667-1994. Open May 15 to Labor Day M-Sa 9am-8pm and Su 9am-5pm; off-season M-Sa 10am-5pm.) **Internet access: Public Library,** 101 6th Ave. W. (☎627-1345. Open M and W 1-9pm, Tu and Th 10am-9pm, F-Su 1-5pm; closed Su July-Aug. $2 per hr.) **Post office:** in the mall at 2nd Ave. and 5th St. (☎624-2353. Open M-F 9:30am-5:30pm.) **Postal code:** V8J 3P3. **Area code:** 250.

▛▟ ACCOMMODATIONS AND FOOD. Nearly all of Prince Rupert's hotels are within the six-block area defined by 1st Ave., 3rd Ave., 6th St., and 9th St. **▨Andree's Bed and Breakfast,** 315 Fourth Ave. E, in a spacious 1922 Victorian-style residence, overlooks the harbor and city. (☎624-3666. Singles $55; doubles $65; twins $70; $10 per extra person. Includes breakfast.) **Park Ave. Campground,** 1750 Park Ave., is less than 2km east of the ferry terminal via Hwy. 16. Some of the well-maintained sites in this RV metropolis are forested; others have a view of the bay. (☎624-5861 or 800-667-1994. Laundry facilities. $10.50; hook-up $18.50. Showers for non-guests $3.50.) **▨Cow Bay Cafe,** 201 Cow Bay Rd., offers an ever-changing menu, including lunch delights like Santa Fe corn pie ($7) and shrimp quesadillas ($9), and an extensive wine list. (☎627-1212. Open Tu noon-2:30pm and W-Sa noon-2:30pm and 6-9pm.)

▨▟ SIGHTS AND OUTDOORS. The **Museum of Northern British Columbia,** in the same building as the info centre, documents the history of logging, fishing, and Haida culture. (☎624-3207. Open late May to mid Sept. M-Sa 9am-8pm and Su 9am-5pm; mid-Sept. to late May M-Sa 9am-5pm.) Prince Rupert's harbor has the highest concentration of archaeological sites in North America; **archaeological boat tours** leave from the info center daily. (2½hr. tours depart daily mid-June to early Sept. $22, children $13, under 5 free.) Tiny **Service Park,** off Fulton St., offers panoramic views of downtown and the harbor beyond. A trail winding up the side of **Mt. Oldfield,** east of town, yields an even wider vista. The trailhead is at **Oliver Lake Park,** about 6km from downtown on Hwy. 16 (contact the info center about guided nature walks May-Oct.; $5). The best time to visit Prince Rupert may be during **Seafest,** a four-day event held in mid-June.

DAWSON CREEK   ☎250

Mile 0 of the Alaska Highway (a.k.a. the Alcan) is Dawson Creek, BC (not to be confused with Dawson City, YT, or *Dawson's Creek*, WB), first settled in 1890 as just another pip-squeak frontier village of a few hundred souls. Its later status as a railroad terminus made it a natural place to begin building the 2600km Alcan.

◧◪ ORIENTATION AND PRACTICAL INFORMATION. From Prince George, drive 402km north to Dawson Creek on the John Hart section of Hwy. 97. **Greyhound,** 1201 Alaska Ave. (☎782-3131; open M-F 6am-5:30pm and 8-8:30pm; Sa 6-10:30am, 3-5:30pm, and 8-8:30pm; Su 7-10:30am, 3-4:30pm, and 8-8:30pm), runs to Whitehorse, YT (20hr., 3 per week, $165); Prince George (6½hr., 2 per day, $50); and Edmonton (8hr., 2 per day, $70). For road reports, stop at the **visitors center,** 900 Alaska Ave. (☎782-9595. Open daily May 15 to Labor Day 8am-7pm; in winter Tu-Sa 9am-5pm). **Internet access: Public Library,** at 10th St. and McKellar Ave. (☎782-4661. Open Tu-Th 10am-9pm, F 10am-5:30pm, and Sa 1:30-5:30pm. Free.) **Post office:** 104th Ave. and 10th St. (☎782-9429. Open M-F 8:30am-5pm.) **Postal code:** V1G 4E6. **Area code:** 250.

█.█ ACCOMMODATIONS AND FOOD. For a bargain price, great location, and an off-beat aura, head straight for the historic **Alaska Hotel,** above the Alaska Cafe & Pub on 10th St., one and a half blocks from the visitors center. (☎ 782-7998. Shared bath; no TV or phone. Singles $35; doubles $40; in winter $5 less.) The newer **Voyageur Motor Inn,** 801 111th Ave., facing 8th Ave., offers phones and cable in a sterile environment. (☎ 782-1020. Singles $40; doubles $45.) **Mile 0 Campground,** 1km west of Alaska Hwy. Mile 0 and adjacent to the Pioneer Village, is a RV city with free showers and coin laundry. (☎ 782-2590. Sites $10, hook-ups $15.)

For excellent $5 burgers., head to the **Alaska Cafe & Pub,** "55 paces south of the Mile 0 Post" on 10th St. (☎ 782-7040. Open Su-Th 10am-10pm and F-Sa 11am-11pm; pub open noon-3am.) Pick up a loaf for the road at the **Organic Farms Bakery,** 1425 97th Ave. From the visitors center, go west along Alaska Ave. and take a right at 15th St. Breads (from $1.70) are baked with local grain. (☎ 782-6533. Open Tu-F 9:30am-6pm, Sa 9am-4pm.)

▣ SIGHTS AND EVENTS. Travelers cruising through Dawson Creek can't miss the **Mile 0 Cairn** and **Mile 0 Post,** both commemorating the birth of the Alcan, within a stone's throw of the visitors center. This town boomed during construction, literally. On February 13, 1943, 60 cases of exploding dynamite leveled the entire business district save the COOP building, now Bing's Furniture, opposite the Mile 0 post. In early Aug., the town plays host to the **Fall Fair & Stampede** (☎ 782-8911) with a carnival, fireworks, chuckwagon races, and a professional rodeo.

ALASKA APPROACHES

THE ALASKA HIGHWAY. Built during World War II, the Alcan traverses an astonishing 2378km route between Dawson Creek, BC, and Fairbanks, AK. In recent years, the US Army has been replaced by an annual army of over 250,000 tourists, many of them RV-borne. In general, there's a trade-off between the excitement you'll find on the Alcan and the speed with which you'll reach Alaska. Countless opportunities lurk off the highway for hiking, fishing, and viewing wildlife. A 1hr. video shown at the Dawson Creek visitors center provides a praiseworthy introduction to the road and region. The free *Driving the Alaska Highway* includes a listing of emergency medical services and phone numbers throughout Alaska, the Yukon, and British Columbia, plus tips on preparation and driving; get it at visitors centers. **Road conditions:** ☎ 867-667-8215.

CASSIAR HIGHWAY (HWY. 37). A growing number of travelers prefer the Cassiar Hwy. to the Alaska Hwy., which has become an RV institution. The highway slices through charred forests and snow-capped peaks on its way from Hwy. 16 in BC to the Alcan (Hwy. 97) in the Yukon. Three evenly spaced provincial parks right off the highway offer good camping, and the Cassiar's services, while sparse, are numerous enough to keep cars and drivers running. Hitchhiking is less popular here than on the Alaska Hwy. Advantages include a shorter distance, consistently interesting scenery, and fewer crowds. On the other hand, the Cassiar is remote, less well maintained, and large sections are very slippery when wet and harder on tires than the better-paved Alcan. This causes little concern for the large, commercial trucks that roar up and down the route, but keeps the infrequent service stops busy with overambitious drivers in need of tire repair.

THE YUKON TERRITORY

The Yukon Territory is among the most remote and sparsely inhabited regions of North America, averaging one person per 15 square kilometers. While summers usually bring comfortably warm temperatures and more than 20 hours of daylight, travelers should still be prepared for difficult weather. The territory remains a bountiful, beautiful, and largely unspoiled region, yet many travelers mimic gold-crazed prospectors and zoom through without appreciating its uncrowded allure.

▓ PRACTICAL INFORMATION

Capital: Whitehorse.

Visitor Info: Tourism Yukon, P.O. Box 2703, Whitehorse, YT Y1A 2C6 (☎867-667-5340; www.touryukon.com).

Police: ☎867-667-5555. For *emergencies* outside Whitehorse, ☎911 may not work.

Drinking Age: 19. **Postal Abbreviation:** YT. **Sales Tax:** 7% national sales tax (GST).

WHITEHORSE   ☎867

Named for the once-perilous Whitehorse Rapids, whose crashing whitecaps were said to resemble the flowing manes of white mares, Whitehorse is a modern crossroads in an ageless frontier. With over 23,000 residents, Whitehorse prides itself on being Canada's largest city north of 60° latitude. The mountains, rivers, and lakes in all directions are a powerful reminder that "south of 60" is far, far away.

▐ GETTING THERE AND GETTING AROUND. The **airport** is off the Alaska Hwy., just southwest of downtown. **Greyhound,** 2191 2nd Ave. (☎667-2223; open M-F 7:30am-6pm, Sa 9am-1:30pm, and Su 4-8am and 5-6pm), on the northeast edge of town, runs once per day to Vancouver, BC (41hr., $300); Edmonton, AB (30hr., $232); and Dawson Creek, BC (18hr., $165). Service is reduced from Sept. to late June. **Alaska Direct** (☎668-4833 or 800-770-6652) runs to Anchorage (15hr., 3 per week, US$165); Fairbanks (12hr., 3 per week, US$140); and Skagway (3hr., 1 per day, US$50); in winter, buses run once per week to above destinations. The local buses of **Whitehorse Transit** arrive and depart downtown next to Canadian Tire on Ogilvie St. (☎668-7433. Runs M-Th 6:15am-7:30pm, F 6:15am-10:30pm, and Sa 8am-7pm. $1.50, seniors and disabled 75¢.)

▐▐ ORIENTATION AND PRACTICAL INFORMATION. Whitehorse lies 1500km north of Dawson Creek, BC, along the Alaska Hwy. and 535km south of Dawson City, YT. **Visitors center:** 100 Hanson St., in the Tourism and Business Centre at 2nd Ave. (☎667-3084. Open daily mid-May to mid-Sept. 8am-8pm; in winter M-F 9am-5pm.) The **Yukon Conservation Society,** 302 Hawkins St., offers maps and great ideas for area hikes. (☎668-5678. Open M-F 10am-2pm.) The **Kanoe People,** at Strickland and 1st Ave., rent outdoor gear. (☎668-4899. Open daily 9am-6pm. Mountain bikes $25 per day, canoes $45 per day, kayaks $35-45 per day. Credit card or deposit required.) **Internet access: Public Library,** 2071 2nd Ave. (☎667-5239. Open M-F 10am-9pm, Sa 10am-6pm and Su 1-9pm. Free.) **Post Office:** 211 Main St. (☎667-2485. Open M-F 9am-6pm, Sa 11am-4pm.) **General Delivery** is at 3rd Ave. and Wood St., in the Yukon News Bldg. (Open M-F 8am-6pm.) **General delivery postal code:** last names A-L, Y1A 3S7; M-Z, Y1A 3S8. **Area code:** 867.

▐▐ ACCOMMODATIONS AND FOOD. Interchangeable motels in town cost around $65. The **Roadhouse Inn,** 2163 2nd Ave., near the Greyhound depot, has shared rooms and hall showers with a bathtub. (☎667-2594. Reception 7am-2:30am. Free local calls. $20; private rooms with cable and private bathroom $50; $10 per additional person. Key deposit $10.) **Robert Service Campground,** 1km from town on South Access Rd. along the Yukon River, is a convenient stop for tenting types, with no RV sites. (☎668-3721. Open late May to early Sept. Gates open 7am-midnight. Food trailer, firewood, playground, drinking water, toilets, coin showers. 68 sites. $12.) The 62km drive to the **Takhini Hot Springs,** the Yukon's only hot springs, offers tenting plus thermal relief. Follow the Alaska Hwy. northwest from downtown, turn right onto the North Klondike Hwy., and then left to the end of Takhini Hot Springs Rd. (☎633-2706. Restaurant, showers, and laundry. $11; $3-5 entry charge.)

   ▓**Klondike Rib and Salmon Barbecue,** 2116 2nd Ave., serves charred fresh salmon or halibut with homemade bread for lunch. (☎667-7554. Open mid-May to Sept. M-F 11:30am-2pm and 4pm-10pm, Sa-Su 5-10pm. Lunch $8.) ▓**The Talisman Cafe,** 2112 2nd Ave., is elegantly decorated with local art and has the best vegetarian menu in town. (☎667-2736. Open daily 9am-9pm.)

🎦🖼 SIGHTS AND OUTDOORS. Visitors hungry for local history can feed their heads at the **MacBride Museum,** at 1st Ave. and Wood St. The sod-roofed cabin in the courtyard was built by Sam Mcgee whose demise was famously related in verse by Robert Service. (☎667-2709. Open daily June-Aug. 10am-6pm; call for winter hrs. $4, students and seniors over 60 $3.50.) The new **Yukon Beringia Interpretive Centre,** on the Alcan, 2km west of the junction with the S. Access Rd., pays homage to the forgotten continent that joined Siberia, Alaska, and the Yukon. (☎667-8855. Open daily mid-May to Sept. 8am-8pm; in winter Su 1-5pm. $6, seniors $5, children $4.)

Grey Mountain, partly accessible by gravel road, is a somewhat rigorous day hike. Take Lewes Blvd. across the bridge by the **S.S. Klondike,** then take a left on Alsek Ave. Turn left again at the "Grey Mt. Cemetery" sign and follow the gravel road to its end. Joggers, bikers, and cross-country skiers love the **Miles Canyon trail network** that parallels the Yukon River. To get there, take Lewes Blvd. to Nisutlin Dr. and turn right; just before the fish ladder turn left onto the gravel Chadbum Lake Rd. and continue for 4km to the parking area. The **Conservation Society** leads nature walks. (Office open July-Aug. M-F 10am-2pm.) **Up North Boat and Canoe Rentals,** 86 Wickstrom Rd., lets you paddle 25km to Takhini River. (☎667-7905. 4hr. $30 including transportation. 8-day trip on the Teslin $200. Kayaks and canoes $25-30 per day.) The tiny islands around **Sanfu Lake,** 1½hr. south of town on Atlin Rd., are ideal for kayaking.

KLUANE NATIONAL PARK   ☎867

Together with adjacent Wrangell-St. Elias National Park in Alaska and Tatshenshini/Alsek Provincial Park in BC, Kluane (*kloo-AH-nee*) is part of one of the world's largest wilderness areas. It contains Canada's highest peak, Mt. Logan (5959m), as well as the world's most massive non-polar ice fields. The ice-blanketed mountains of Kluane's interior are a haven for experienced expeditioners, but render two-thirds of the park inaccessible to humbler hikers. Fortunately, the northeast part of the park (bordering the Alaska Hwy.) offers splendid, easily accessible backpacking, canoeing, rafting, biking, fishing, and dayhiking.

🎊 PRACTICAL INFORMATION. Haines Junction, at the eastern park boundary, 158km west of Whitehorse, serves as park gateway and headquarters. **Alaska Direct** (☎668-4833 or 800-770-6652) runs from Haines Jct. three times per week in the summer to Anchorage (13hr., US$125), Fairbanks (11hr, US$100), and Whitehorse (2hr, US$20). **Kluane National Park Visitor Reception Centre,** on Logan St. (Km 1635 on the Alcan), provides wilderness permits ($5 per night, $50 per season), fishing permits ($5 per day, $35 per season), maps ($11), and trail and weather info. (☎634-7207. Open daily May-Sept. 9am-7pm; in winter M-F 10am-noon and 1-5pm.) **Sheep Mountain Info Centre,** 72km north of town at Alaska Hwy. Km 1707, registers hikers headed into the park. **24hr. road service: Triple S Garage** (☎634-2915), 1km north of Haines Jct. **Emergency:** ☎634-5555. **Ambulance/Clinic:** ☎634-4444. **Post office:** in Madley's Store on Haines Rd. (☎634-3802. Open M-F 10am-noon and 1-5pm.) **Postal code:** Y0B 1L0. **Area code:** 867.

🖼🖼 ACCOMMODATIONS AND FOOD. Camping by a gorgeous lakeside beats staying at a clean-but-forgettable highway motel or RV park any day. The idyllic **Kathleen Lake Campground,** off Haines Rd. 27km south of Haines Junction, is close to hiking and fishing. (Open mid-May to mid-Sept. Toilets, fire pits, and firewood. Sites $10. Wheelchair accessible.) Popular **Pine Lake,** 7km east of town, features a sandy beach. (Water, firewood, pit toilets. $8 with Yukon camping permit only.) The **Dezadeash Lake Campground,** about 50km south of Haines Junction on Haines Rd., offers the same deal and similarly sweet lakefront property. **Laughing Moose B&B,** 120 Alsek Crescent, four blocks from the junction, offers a sparkling-clean kitchen, spacious common room with TV and VCR, and a view of the Auriol Mountains. (☎634-2335. Singles $60; doubles $70; shared bath.) The **Stardust Motel,** 1km north of town on the Alcan, has spacious rooms with TVs and tubs, but no phones.

(☎634-2591. Singles $49; doubles $59; shared bath.) **Village Bakery and Deli,** on Logan St. across from the visitors center, serves up substantial soups with bread ($3.50) and mushroom quiche ($2.50). Watch out for (or join in) live music and salmon BBQs ($13) on M. (☎634-2867. Open daily May-Sept. 7:30am-9pm.)

⚑ OUTDOORS. A $1 pamphlet lists about 25 trails and routes ranging from 500m to 96km. Routes, as opposed to trails, are not maintained, do not have marked paths, are more physically demanding, and require backcountry navigation skills. Overnight visitors must register at one of the visitors centers ($5 per night, ages 5-16 $2.50), and use bear-resistant food canisters, which the park rents for $5 per night. The **Dezadeash River Loop** trailhead is downtown at the day-use area across from Madley's on Haines Rd. This flat, forested 5km trail will disappoint those craving vert, but it makes for a nice stroll. The more challenging 15km **Auriol Loop** has a primitive campground halfway along. The trail begins 7km south of Haines Junction on Haines Rd. and cuts through boreal forest, leading to a subalpine bench (elevation gain 400m) just in front of the Auriol Range. This is a popular overnight trip, though 4-6hr. is adequate time without heavy packs. The 5km (one-way) **King's Throne Route** is a very challenging but rewarding day hike with a 1220m elevation gain and a panoramic view. It begins at the **Kathleen Lake** day-use area at the campground (see **Accommodations,** above).

Excellent hiking awaits near **Sheep Mountain** in the park's northern section. An easy 500m jaunt up to **Soldier's Summit** starts 1km north of the Sheep Mountain Info Centre and leads to the site where the original highway was officially opened in 1942. The **Sheep Creek** trail, down a short gravel access road just north of the visitors center, is a satisfying dayhike up Sheep Mountain, and one of the better bets to see Dall sheep in summer (5km one-way; 430m elevation gain; 3-6hr. round-trip). Only experienced backpackers should attempt the trek along the **Slims River** to the magnificent **Kaskawulsh Glacier.** Two rough routes along the either bank of the river are available and require three to five days to complete. One stretches 23km with an elevation gain of 910m; the other is 30km and has an elevation gain of 1340m.

The **Alsek River Valley Trail,** starting from Alcan Km 1645 and following a bumpy old mining road 14km to Sugden Creek, makes for good mountain biking. **Paddle-Wheel Adventures,** down the road from the Village Bakery in Haines Junction, arranges flightseeing over the glaciers and full-day rafting trips on the Class III and IV rapids of the **Blanchard** and **Tatshenshini Rivers.** (☎634-2683. $90 per person for a 30min. flight over the Kaskawulsh. Rafting $100 per person, including lunch.)

SCENIC DRIVE: THE DEMPSTER HIGHWAY

The Dempster Hwy. (Hwy. 5) begins 41km east of Dawson City at the **Klondike River Lodge** on the Klondike Hwy. (Hwy. 2) and winds a spectacular 741km to Inuvik, becoming Hwy. 8 upon crossing into the Northwest Territories. Like no other highway in North America, the Dempster confronts its drivers with real wilderness devoid of logging scars or ads. The Dempster is reasonably navigable and well-maintained, but services are limited, weather is erratic, and its dirt-and-gravel stretches can give cars a thorough beating. Although the drive can be made in 13hr., it deserves at least two days each way to be fully and safely appreciated. Rainstorms can create impassable washouts, closing down parts of the highway or disrupting ferry service—and leaving travelers stranded in Inuvik—for as long as two weeks. **Northwest Territories Tourism** (☎800-661-0788) and **Road and Ferry Report** (☎867-777-2678 or 800-661-0752) provide up-to-date road info. The **Northwest Territories Visitor Centre,** in Dawson City, has a free Dempster brochure. (☎867-993-6167. Open daily late May to early Sept. 9am-8pm.) There are **government campgrounds** at Tombstone (Km 72), Engineer Creek (Km 194), Nitainlii (Km 541), and Chuk (Km 731). Hook-ups are only available at Nitainlii and Chuk. The **Interpretive Centre** at Tombstone loans out a kilometer-by-kilometer travelogue of the Dempster's natural history and wildlife. The drive out to Tombstone makes a pleasant overnight for those not willing to charge forth to the NWT.

ALBERTA

With its gaping prairie, oil-fired economy, and conservative politics, Alberta is the Texas of Canada. Petro-dollars have given birth to gleaming, modern cities on the plains, while the natural landscape swings from the mighty Canadian Rockies down to beautifully desolate badlands.

🔢 PRACTICAL INFORMATION

Capital: Edmonton.
Visitor Info: Travel Alberta, Commerce Pl., 10155 102 St., 3rd fl., Edmonton, AB T5J 4G8 (☎780-427-4321 or 800-661-8888; www.discoveralberta.com). **Parks Canada,** 220 4th Ave. SE, #552, Calgary, AB T2G 4X3 (☎403-292-4401 or 800-748-7275). **Alberta Environmental,** 9820 106 St., 2nd Fl., Edmonton, AB T5K 2J6 (☎780-427-7009; www.gov.ab.ca/env/parks.html).
Drinking Age: 18. **Postal Abbreviation:** AB. **Sales Tax:** 0%.

THE ROCKIES

Every year, some 5 million visitors make it within sight of the Rockies' majestic peaks and stunning glacial lakes. Thankfully, much of this traffic is confined to highwayside gawkers, and only a tiny fraction of these visitors make it far into the forest. Of the big two national parks—Banff and Jasper—Jasper feels a little further removed from the crowds and offers great wildlife viewing from the road. Without a car, guided bus rides may be the easiest way to see some of the park's main attractions. **Brewster Tours** buses from Banff to Jasper. (☎762-6767. 9½hr.; $89.) **Bigfoot Tours** take two days to make the trip. (☎888-244-6673 or 604-278-8224. $89.)

BANFF NATIONAL PARK   ☎403

Banff is Canada's best-loved and best-known natural park, with 6641 square kilometers of peaks, forests, glaciers, and alpine valleys. Even streets littered with gift shops, clothing shops, and chocolatiers cannot mar Banff's beauty. Transient 20-somethings arrive with mountain bikes, climbing gear, skis, and snowboards, but a trusty pair of hiking boots remains the park's most popular outdoor equipment.

📑 PRACTICAL INFORMATION. The park hugs Alberta's border with British Columbia, 129km west of Calgary. Civilization in the park centers around the towns of **Banff** and **Lake Louise,** 58km apart on Hwy. 1. All of the following info applies to Banff Townsite, unless otherwise specified. **Greyhound,** 106 Railway Ave. (800-661-8747; depot open daily 7:30am-9pm), runs 4 buses per day to Lake Louise (1hr., $12); Calgary (2hr., $21); and Vancouver, BC (13hr., $100). **Brewster Transportation,** 100 Gopher St. (☎762-6767), runs buses to Jasper (5hr., $51); Lake Louise (1hr., $11); and Calgary (2hr., $36).

Banff Visitor Centre, 224 Banff Ave., includes **Banff/Lake Louise Tourism Bureau** and **Canadian Parks Service.** (Tourism Bureau: ☎762-8421. Parks Service: ☎762-1550. Open daily June-Sept. 8am-8pm; Oct.-May 9am-5pm.) The **Lake Louise Visitor Centre,** at Samson Mall in Lake Louise, shares a building with a museum. (☎522-3833. Open daily July-Aug. 8am-8pm; June and Sept. 8am-6pm; Oct.-May 9am-5pm.) **Emergency: Banff Police,** ☎762-2226. **Lake Louise Police,** ☎522-3811. **Banff Warden Office,** ☎762-4506. **Lake Louise Warden Office,** ☎522-1200. **Post Office:** 204 Buffalo St. (☎762-2586. Open M-F 9am-5:30pm.) **Postal code:** T0L 0C0. **Area code:** 403.

🗿 ACCOMMODATIONS AND FOOD. HI runs a **shuttle service** connecting all the Rocky Mountain hostels and Calgary ($8-90). Wait-list beds become available at 6pm, and the larger hostels save some stand-by beds for shuttle arrivals. **◼Lake Louise International Hostel (HI),** 500m west of the info center in Lake Louise Townsite, on Village Rd., is more like a hotel than a hostel, with a reference library, common

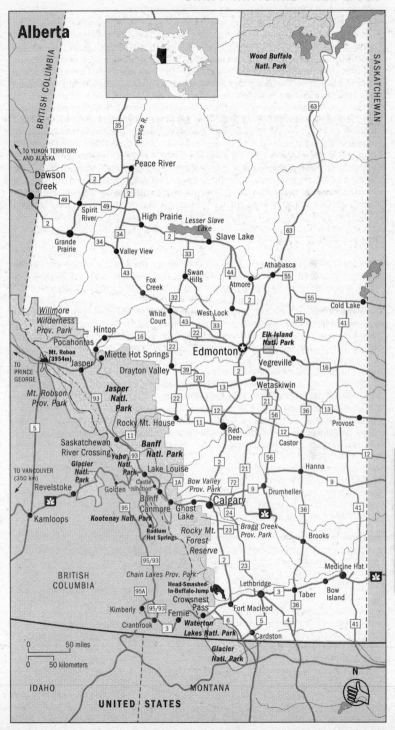

Alberta

BRITISH COLUMBIA

SASKATCHEWAN

Wood Buffalo
Natl. Park

Peace R.

35

63

TO YUKON TERRITORY
AND ALASKA

Peace River

Dawson
Creek

49

2

Spirit
River

49

2

High Prairie

Lesser Slave
Lake

Slave Lake

63

34

34

2

Grande
Prairie

Valley View

33

Athabasca

55

43

Fox
Creek

Swan
Hills

44

Atmore

55

Cold Lake

Willmore
Wilderness
Prov. Park

32

White
Court

West Lock

2

36

41

Hinton

16

43

33

22

Pocahontas

22

Elk Island
Natl. Park

Mt. Robon
(3954m)

Jasper

Miette Hot Springs

Edmonton

Vegreville

16

TO
PRINCE
GEORGE

Drayton Valley

39

Mt. Robson
Prov. Park

93

20

2

Wetaskiwin

22

13

21

36

13

5

Jasper
Natl.
Park

Rocky Mt. House

12

56

Provost

11

Red
Deer

12

Saskatchewan
River Crossing

11

Banff
Natl. Park

93

2

21

56

Castor

12

Hanna

TO VANCOUVER
(350 km)

Glacier
Natl.
Park

Yoho
Natl.
Park

93

Lake Louise

1A

Bow Valley
Prov. Park

72

9

9

Drumheller

Revelstoke

Castle
Junction

Golden

Banff

Calgary

36

41

95

Canmore

Ghost
Lake

24

Kamloops

Kootenay Natl. Park

Radium
Hot Springs

Rocky Mt.
Forest
Reserve

Bragg Creek
Prov. Park

Brooks

2

23

Medicine Hat

95/93

Chain Lakes Prov. Park

Head-Smashed-
In-Buffalo-Jump

Lethbridge

BRITISH
COLUMBIA

95A

Crowsnest
Pass

3

Taber

Bow
Island

36

Kimberly

95/93

Fernie

6

Fort Macleod

5

4

41

Cranbrook

3

Waterton
Lakes Natl. Park

Cardston

0   50 miles

0   50 kilometers

Glacier
Natl. Park

N

IDAHO

MONTANA

UNITED STATES

WESTERN CANADA

rooms with open, beamed ceilings, a stone fireplace, two full kitchens, a sauna, ski/ bike workshops, and a cafe. (☎522-2200. Dorms $21, non-members $25. Private rooms available for $6 more per person. Wheelchair accessible.) **Banff International Hostel (HI)** is 3km from Banff Townsite, on Tunnel Mountain Rd.; take the Happy Bus from downtown ($1). This big hostel has the look and feel of a ski lodge, with three lounge areas, two large fireplaces, a game room with pool table, a kitchen, cafe, laundry facilities, and hot showers. (☎762-4122. Reception 24hr. Linen $1. Dorms $20, non-members $24. Private rooms $12 more. Wheelchair accessible.) ▩**Castle Mountain Hostel (HI),** on Hwy. 1A, 1.5km east of the junction of Hwy. 1 and Hwy. 93, between Banff and Lake Louise, is a quieter alternative, with running water, hot showers, and electricity, general store, library, and fireplace. (Linen $1. Dorms $13, non-members $17). Three other rustic hostels—**Hilda Creek, Rampart Creek** and **Mosquito Creek**—can be booked by calling Banff International Hostel. At any of Banff's nine park campgrounds, sites are first come, first served ($10-24). On Hwy. 1A between Banff Townsite and Lake Louise, **Johnston Canyon** and **Castle Mountain** are close to relatively uncrowded hiking. Only Village 2 of **Tunnel Mountain Village,** 4km from Banff Townsite, on Tunnel Mountain Rd., remains open in winter.

The Banff and Lake Louise Hostels serve affordable meals ($3-8), but **Laggan's Deli** (☎522-2017), in Samson Mall in Lake Louise, is the best thing going. Thick sandwich on whole wheat cost $4; a fresh-baked loaf for later runs $3. **Aardvark's,** 304A Caribou St., does big business after the bars close. The place is skinny on seating but serves thick slices of pizza. (☎762-5500. Open daily 11am-4am. 10% HI discount on large pizzas. Slices $2.85; small pizza $6-9, large $13-21.)

▨ OUTDOORS. Near Banff Townsite, **Fenland Trail** winds 2km (1hr.) through an area shared by beaver, muskrat, and waterfowl (closed for elk calving in late spring and early summer). Follow Mt. Norquay Rd. out of town and look for signs across the tracks on the road's left side. The summit of **Tunnel Mountain** provides a dramatic view of the **Bow Valley** and **Mt. Rundle.** Follow Wolf St. east from Banff Ave., and turn right on St. Julien Rd. to reach the head of the steep 2.3km (2hr.) trail. At 2949m (9675 ft.), **Mt. Rundle** offers a more demanding fair-weather-only dayhike (7-8 hr., 5.5km one-way, 1600m/5248 ft. elev. gain). **Johnston Canyon,** about 25km out of Banff toward Lake Louise, along the Bow Valley Pkwy. (Hwy. 1A), is a popular half-day hike which runs past waterfalls to seven blue-green cold-water springs known as the **Inkpots.**

The park might not exist if not for the **Cave and Basin Hot Springs,** southwest of town on Cave Ave., once rumored to have miraculous healing properties. The **Cave and Basin National Historic Site,** a refurbished resort built circa 1914, is now a museum. (☎762-1566. Open daily in summer 9am-6pm; in winter 9:30am-5pm. Tours at 11am. $2.50, seniors $2, children $1.50.) For a dip in the hot water, follow the rotten-egg smell to the 40°C (104°F) **Upper Hot Springs,** up the hill on Mountain Ave. (☎762-1515. Open daily 9am-11pm; winter 10am-10pm. $7, seniors and children $6. Swimsuits $1.50, towels $1, lockers 50¢.)

The highest community in Canada at 1530m (5018 ft.), Lake Louise and its surrounding glaciers have often passed for Swiss scenery in movies. Once at the lake, the hardest task is escaping fellow gawkers at the posh **Château Lake Louise.** Several hiking trails begin at the water; the 3.6km **Lake Agnes Trail** and the 5.5km **Plain of Six Glaciers Trail** both end at teahouses.

Fishing is legal in most of the park's bodies of water during specific seasons, but live bait and lead weights are not. **Permits** are available at the info center. (7-days; $6.) Winter activities in the park range from world-class ice climbing to ice fishing. Those 1600km of hiking trails make for exceptional **cross-country skiing,** and three allied resorts offer a range of **skiing and snowboarding** opportunities from early Nov. to mid-May. **Sunshine Mountain** has the largest snowfall (☎762-6500, snow report 760-7669; lift tickets $53); **Mt. Norquay** is smaller, closer to town and less busy (☎762-4421; $39); while **Lake Louise** is the 2nd-biggest ski area in Canada and has the most expert terrain (☎522-3555, snow report 762-4766; $53). Shuttles to all three resorts leave from most big hotels in the townsites, and most hostels have **ticket and transportation discounts** available for guests.

SCENIC DRIVE: ICEFIELDS PARKWAY

The 230km Icefields Pwy. is one of the most beautiful routes in North America, heading north from Lake Louise in Banff National Park to Jasper Townsite in Jasper National Park. Free maps of the parkway are available at info centers in Jasper and Banff, or at the **Icefield Centre**, at the boundary between the two parks, 132km north of Lake Louise and 103km south of Jasper Townsite. (☎780-852-6288. Open May to mid-Oct. daily 9am-5pm.) Although the center is closed in winter, the parkway is only closed for plowing after heavy snowfalls. An extensive campground and hostel network along the parkway makes longer trips along the length of Jasper and Banff convenient and affordable. **Cycling** the highway is also a popular option; bikes can be rented in Banff or Jasper for a one-way trip.

However you travel the parkway, set aside time for hikes and magnificent vistas. At **Bow Summit**, 40km north of Lake Louise, the parkway's highest point (2135m), a 10min. walk leads to a view of fluorescent aqua **Peyto Lake,** especially vivid toward the end of June. The Icefield Centre (see above) lies in the shadow of the tongue of the **Athabasca Glacier,** a great white whale of an ice flow that flows from the 325 sq. km **Columbia Icefield,** the largest accumulation of ice and snow south of the Arctic Circle (yes, excepting Antarctica, smart-ass). **Columbia Icefield Snocoach Tours** carries visitors right onto the glacier in bizarre monster buses for an 80min. trip. (☎877-423-7433. Apr.-Oct. daily 9am-5pm. $26, ages 6-15 $10.)

JASPER NATIONAL PARK   ☎780

Northward expansion of the Canadian railway system led to the exploration of the Canadian Rockies and the creation of Jasper National Park in 1907. The largest of the four National Parks in the region, Jasper encompasses herculean peaks and plummeting valleys that dwarf the battalion of motorhomes and charter buses parading through the region. In the face of this annual bloat, Jasper Townsite's permanent residents struggle to keep their sheltered home looking and feeling like a genuine small town. In the winter, the crowds melt away, a blanket of snow descends, and a ski resort welcomes visitors to a slower, more relaxed town.

◪ PRACTICAL INFORMATION. All of the addresses below are in **Jasper Townsite,** near the center of the park. **VIA Rail** (☎800-561-8630) sends 3 trains per week from the station on Connaught Dr. to Vancouver, BC (16½hr., $156) and Edmonton (5hr., $91). **Greyhound** (☎852-3926), in the train station, runs to Edmonton (4½hr., 4 per day, $50) and Vancouver, BC (11½hr., 2per day, $99). **Brewster Transportation Tours** (☎852-3332), in the station, runs daily to Calgary (7½hr., $71) via Banff (5½hr., $51). The **Park Information Centre,** 500 Connaught Dr., has trail maps. (☎852-6176. Open daily mid-June to early Sept. 8am-7pm; early Sept. to late Oct. and late Dec. to mid-June 9am-5pm.) **Emergency:** ☎852-4421. **Post Office:** 502 Patricia St. (☎852-3041. Open M-F 9am-5pm.) **Postal code:** T0E 1E0. **Area code:** 780.

Rocky Mountain Unlimited serves as a central reservation service for many local outdoor businesses. They provide prices and recommendations for rafting, fishing, horseback riding, and wildlife safaris. (☎852-4056. Open daily 9am-9pm; in winter 8am-6pm.) **Currie's,** in The Sports Shop, 406 Patricia St., rents fishing equipment and gives tips on good spots. (☎852-5650. Rod, reel, and line $10. 1-day boat or canoe rental $30, after 2pm $20, after 6pm $15. Pick-up and drop-off service available.) **Fishing permits** are available at fishing shops and the Parks Canada info center ($6 per week, $13 per year).

ꞃ ACCOMMODATIONS. HI runs a shuttle service connecting all the Rocky Mountain hostels and Calgary (1-way $7-65). The modern **Jasper International Hostel (HI),** 3km up Whistlers Rd. from Hwy. 93, 4km south of the townsite, also known as **Whistlers Hostel,** anchors the chain of HI hostels stretching from Jasper to Calgary. Jasper International attracts gregarious backpackers and cyclists, but a "leave-your-hiking-boots-outside" rule keeps the hardwood floors and dorm rooms clean. (☎852-3215 or 877-852-0781. Dorms $16, non-members $21. Curfew 2am.) **Maligne**

Canyon Hostel (HI), 11km east of town on Hwy. 16, has small cabins on the bank of the Maligne River. (Closed W Oct.-Apr. $11, non-members $16.) **Mt. Edith Cavell Hostel (HI),** 12km up Edith Cavell Rd., off Hwy. 93, offers small but cozy quarters heated by wood-burning stoves. In winter, the road is closed, but you can pick up keys at Jasper International Hostel and ski uphill from the highway. (Propane light, pump water, solar shower, firepit. $11, non-members $16; in winter $10/$15.)

Most of Jasper's campgrounds have primitive sites with few facilities ($13-22). They are first come, first served, so get there early. Call the park info center (☎852-6176) for details. None of the surrounding campgrounds are open in winter. A 781-site behemoth, **Whistlers,** on Whistlers Rd., 3km south of the townsite, off Hwy. 93, is closest to the townsite. (Open early May to mid-Oct. $17, full hook-ups $24.) The highlight of the Icefields Pkwy. campgrounds is **Columbia Icefield,** 109km south of the townsite, which lies close enough to the Athabasca Glacier to intercept an icy breeze and even a rare summer night's snowfall.

▲ OUTDOORS. The info center in town distributes *Day Hikes in Jasper National Park.* Snow-capped **Mt. Edith Cavell** is a rewarding half-day hike. The trailhead is 30km south of the townsite; take Hwy. 93 to 93A to the end of the bumpy, twisty 15km Mt. Edith Cavell Rd. (open June-Oct.). To scale a peak in a day, climb the Sulpher **Skyline Trail,** a challenging 4 to 6hr. hike with views of the limestone Miette Range and Ashlar Ridge (9.6km round-trip, 700m elevation gain). The trail leaves all too conveniently from the **Miette Hot Springs,** 42km north of the townsite on Hwy. 16 and 15km along Miette Hot Springs Rd., blending chlorinated and filtered heat therapy with panoramic views. (Open daily May 19 to June 21 and Sept. 5 to Oct. 9 10:30am-9pm; June 22 to Sept. 4 8:30am-10:30pm. $5.50; swimsuit $1.50.)

The spectacular if over-touristed **Maligne Canyon** is 11km east of the townsite on Maligne Lake Rd. From the trailhead, a 4km path follows the Maligne River as it plunges through the narrow limestone gorge, across footbridges, and eventually into Medicine Lake. Brilliant turquoise **Maligne Lake,** the longest (22km) and deepest (97km) lake in the park, sprawls at the end of Maligne Lake Rd. The **Opal Hills Trail** (8.2km loop) winds through subalpine meadows and ascends 460m to views of the lake. **Maligne Tours,** 626 Connaught Dr., rents kayaks and leads fishing canoeing, rabbiting, horseback riding, hiking, and whitewater rafting tours (☎852-3370. Kayaks half-day $30, full-day $60.)

The **Jasper Tramway,** 4km up Whistlers Rd., climbs 1200m up Whistlers Mt., leading to a panoramic view of the park and, on a clear day, very far beyond. (☎852-3093. Open daily Apr.-Aug. 8:30am-10pm; Sept.-Oct. 9:30am-4:30pm. $15, under 14 $8.50, under 5 free.) The demanding 9km **Whistlers Trail** covers the same ground, beginning behind Jasper International's volleyball court.

CALGARY   ☎403

Mounties founded Calgary in the 1870s to control the flow of illegal whiskey, but another liquid—oil—made this city great. Petroleum fuels Calgary's economy; the city holds the most corporate headquarters in Canada outside of Toronto. Calgary's dot on the map grew larger when it hosted the 1988 Winter Olympics; it is now Canada's 2nd-fastest-growing city. The world-class Calgary Stampede, the "Greatest Outdoor Show on Earth," garbs the city in cowboy duds every July.

▣▨ ORIENTATION AND PRACTICAL INFORMATION. Calgary is divided into quadrants: NE, NW, SE, and SW. **Centre St.** is the east-west divider; the **Bow River** splits the north and south sections. **Avenues** run east-west, **streets** run north-south, and numbers count up from the divides. **Calgary International Airport** is about 17km northeast of the city center. **Greyhound,** 877 Greyhound Way SW (☎265-9111 or 800-661-8747), runs to Edmonton (3½hr., 13 per day, $40); Banff (2hr., 4 per day, $20); and Drumheller (1½hr., 3 per day, $22). **Brewster Tours** (☎221-8242) runs from the airport or downtown to Banff (2½hr., 3 per day, $36) and Jasper (8hr., 1 per day, $71) and offers a 15% HI discount. **Calgary Transit,** 240 7th Ave. SW, runs **C-Trains,**

which are free in the downtown zone. (☎262-1000. Runs M-F 6am-11pm, Sa-Su 6am-9:30pm. Bus fare and C-Trains outside downtown $1.60, ages 6-14 $1; day pass $5/$3; 10 tickets $14.50/$9.) The **Visitor Service Centre,** 131 9th Ave. SW, is under the Calgary Tower. (☎750-2397. Open daily 8am-5pm.) **Post Office:** 207 9th Ave. SW. (☎974-2078. Open M-F 8am-5:45pm.) **Postal code:** T2P 2G8. **Area code:** 403.

▞▚ ACCOMMODATIONS, FOOD, AND NIGHTLIFE. The ▨**Calgary International Hostel (HI),** 520 7th Ave. SE, is several blocks east of downtown. Go east along 7th Ave. from the 3rd St. SE C-Train station; the hostel is on the left just past 4th St. SE. (☎269-8239. Open 24hr. Kitchen, game room, laundry, email, and barbecue facilities. $16, non-members $20. Linen $1. Wheelchair accessible.) **University of Calgary,** in the NW quadrant, has rooms booked through **Kananaskis Hall,** 3330 24th Ave., a 12min. walk from the University C-Train stop. (☎220-3203. Open 24hr. Rooms available May-Aug. only. Shared rooms $20; singles $32, with student ID $23; doubles $39/$32. Suites with private bathrooms about $35.)

The cheapest, most satisfying food is located in Calgary's tiny Chinatown, the two square blocks at the north end of Centre St. S and 1st St. SE. Five dollars buys a feast in Vietnamese noodle-houses and Hong-Kong style cafes, many of which don't close until 3 or 4am. At ▨**Thi-Thi Submarine,** 209 1st St. SE, $2.50 will buy a 10 in. "super-sub" with three kinds of pork, chicken, cilantro, carrots, cucumbers, and special sauce, served hot on a fresh baguette. The veggie sub is a ludicrous $1.50. (☎265-5452. Open daily 10am-7pm.) **Take Ten Cafe,** 304 10th St. NE, attracts clientele not for panache, but for good food. All burgers under $5.75. (☎270-7010. Open Tu-Sa 9am-6pm, Su 9am-3pm.)

▨**The Nightgallery,** 1209B 1st St. SW, attracts scenesters with one large dance floor, one bar, and one oversized disco ball. The club breaks out the best House in town at "Sunday School" and on Th. Reggae-Dub draws a slightly older crowd M. (☎269-5924. Open daily 7:30pm-3am. Cover $5, $1.50 highballs before 11pm.) **The Ship and Anchor,** 534 17th Ave. SW, is the meeting place for the city's young and beautiful scurvy dogs. (☎245-3333. Open daily 11:30am-2:30am.)

▣ SIGHTS. Over a decade later, Calgary still clings to its two weeks of Olympic stardom at the **Canada Olympic Park,** 10min. west of downtown on Hwy. 1, site of the four looming ski jumps and the quick bobsled and luge tracks. *(☎247-5452. Open daily 8am-9pm.)* The **Olympic Hall of Fame** honors Olympic achievements with displays, films, and bobsled and ski-jumping simulators. In summer, the park opens its hills to mountain bikers. Take the lift up the hill, then cruise down—no work necessary. *(☎247-5452. Open daily 9am-9pm. $3.75, seniors and students $3, under 6 free. Mountain biking open daily May-Sept. 10am-9pm. $7 ticket includes chair lift and entrance to ski jump buildings. Guided tour $10. Hill pass $6 for cyclists. Bike rental $6 per hr., $24 per day.)*

The **Glenbow Museum** brings rocks and minerals, Buddhist and Hindu art, and native Canadian history under one roof. *(130 9th Ave. SE. ☎268-4100. Open Su-W 9am-5pm, Th-F 9am-9pm. $8, seniors and students $6, under 6 free. 10% HI discount. $2 for everyone Su 9am-noon.)* Footbridges stretch from either side of the Bow River to **Prince's Island Park,** a natural refuge blocks from the city center. Calgary's other island park, **St. George's Island,** is accessible by the river walkway to the east, and houses the **Calgary Zoo.** *(Parking is off Memorial Dr. on the north side of the river. ☎232-9300. Open daily 9am-8pm; winter 9am-4pm. Grounds open daily 9am-9pm; Oct.-Apr. 9am-5:30pm. $10, children $5, seniors half-price Tu and Th; winter $8, seniors and children $4. 25% AAA and 10% HI discounts.)* On July 6-15, 2001, 1 million cowboys and tourists will converge on **Stampede Park,** just southeast of downtown, bordering the east side of Macleod Trail between 14th and 25th Ave. SE. For ten days, the grounds are packed for world-class steer wrestling, saddle bronc, bareback- and bull-riding, pig racing, wild-cow-milking, and chuckwagon races. *(☎269-9822 or 800-661-1767. Take C-Train to the Stampede. Gate admission $9; seniors and ages 7-12 $4. Rodeo and evening cost $19-50; if not sold out, rush tickets are $9, at the grandstand 1½hr. before showtime.)*

ALBERTA BADLANDS

In the late Cretaceous period, these were the fertile shores of an inland sea, conditions that have created one of the richest dinosaur fossil sites in the world. Once the sea dried up, wind, water, and ice cut twisting canyons down into the sandstone and shale bedrock, creating the desolate splendor of the Alberta Badlands. The **Royal Tyrrell Museum of Paleontology** lies on the North Dinosaur Trail (Secondary Hwy. 838), 6km northwest of Drumheller. The museum is the world's largest display of dinosaur specimens. (☎ 403-823-7707 or 888-440-4240. Open daily Victoria Day to Labour Day 9am-9pm; Labour Day to Victoria Day Tu-Su 10am-5pm. $7.50, seniors $5.50, ages 7-17 $3, under 7 free; winter half-price Tu.) The museum's immensely popular 12-person **Day Digs** include instruction in paleontology and excavation techniques, and a chance to dig in a dinosaur quarry. The fee includes lunch and transportation, but all finds go to the museum. (Daily July-Aug. 8:30am, returning at 4:30pm. $85, ages 10-15 $55. Reservations required.) **Greyhound** runs from Calgary to Drumheller (1½hr., 2 per day, $21).

ALASKA

Alaska's beauty and intrigue are born of extremes: North America's highest mountains and broadest flatlands, windswept tundra and lush rainforests, and 15 incredible national parks cover an area roughly equal to that of England and Ireland combined (586,412 square miles, over one-fifth of the land mass of the US). The US bought Alaska for about 2¢ per acre in 1867, from a Russia deep in debt after losing the Crimean War. Critics mocked "Seward's Folly," named after the Secretary of State who negotiated the deal, but just 15 years after the purchase, huge deposits of gold were unearthed in the Panhandle's Gastineau Channel. Prospectors quickly struck gold in rivers such as the Yukon, Charley, Fortymile, and Klondike. The Trans-Alaska Pipeline, running 800 miles through the heart of the Alaskan wilderness, has had a revolutionary effect on the state's political, social, and economic landscape since its construction in 1977. In August of 1998, the federal government gave the go-ahead for drilling in about one-fifth of the National Petroleum Reserve's 23 million acres. Environmentalists argue that drilling will disrupt the pristine wilderness, while oil companies want the entire area to be opened.

For more comprehensive coverage of Alaska and its arctic allures, see *Let's Go: Alaska & the Pacific Northwest, Including Western Canada 2001*.

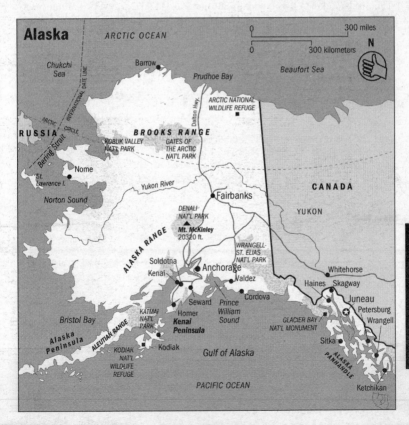

HIGHLIGHTS OF ALASKA

NATURAL WONDERS. Denali National Park (p. 948) is the state's crown jewel. Wrangell-St. Elias National Park (p. 947) houses massive glaciers, while Glacier Bay National Park (p. 955) basks in a symphony of sea and ice.

WILDLIFE. Cruises out of Seward into Kenai Fjords National Park (p. 947) are stuffed with opportunities to view sea critters.

RECREATION. Southeast Alaska's grandest features include kayaking in Misty Fiords National Monument (p. 953), climbing Deer Mountain in Ketchikan (p. 952), and hiking the West Glacier Trail in Juneau (p. 955).

■ PRACTICAL INFORMATION

Capital: Juneau.
Visitor Info: Alaska Division of Tourism, P.O. Box 110801, Juneau 99811 (☎907-465-2010; www.dced.state.ak.us/tourism). **Alaska Department of Fish & Game, Division of Wildlife Conservation,** P.O. Box 25526 Juneau, AK 99802 (☎907-465-4190; www.state.ak.us/local/akpages/FISH.GAME/wildlife/wildmain.htm).
Postal Abbreviation: AK. **Sales Tax:** 0%.

■ GETTING THERE AND AWAY

The **Alaska Railroad Corporation (ARRC)** (☎800-544-0552), covers 470 mi. from Seward to Fairbanks, with stops in Anchorage and Whittier. The **Alaska Marine Hwy.,** Homer Ferry Terminal, 4667 Spit Rd. Suite #1, Homer 99603 (☎800-642-0066), remains the most practical and enjoyable way to explore much of the Panhandle, Prince William Sound, and the Kenai Peninsula. The **AlaskaPass,** P.O. Box 351, Vashon, WA 98070 (☎800-248-7598 or 206-463-6550), offers unlimited access to Alaska's railroad, ferry, and bus systems (15 days $700, 30 days $950; 12 non-consecutive days over a 21-day period $730). Most of the state's major **highways** are known by their name as often as their number (e.g., George Parks Hwy. is the same as Rte. 3 which is the same as The Parks). Driving to and through Alaska is not for the faint of car. Highways reward drivers with stunning views and access to true wilderness, but they barely scratch the surface of the massive state. See p. 932 for the two major highway approaches into the state from points south. For Alaska's most remote destinations, **air travel** is an expensive necessity. Intrastate airlines and charter services, many of them based at the busy Anchorage airport, transport passengers and cargo to virtually every village in Alaska.

CLIMATE
Weather varies from the coast inland. Anchorage temperatures range from 8°F in winter to 65°F in summer. In Alaska's interior, the temperature ranges from around 70°F in summer to -30°F and lower in winter. Progressing farther north, summer days and winter nights become longer. North of the Arctic Circle, the sun does not set at all on the nights around the summer solstice in late June, nor does it rise on the days around the winter solstice in December.

ANCHORAGE ☎907

Alaska's primary metropolis, Anchorage is home to 254,000 people—two-fifths of the state's population. As far north as Helsinki and almost as far west as Honolulu, the city achieved its large size (2000 square miles) by hosting three major economic projects: the Alaska Railroad, WWII military developments, and the Trans-Alaska Pipeline. Anchorage serves as a good place to get oriented and stock up on supplies before journeying to the breathtaking wilderness just outside.

⟦ GETTING THERE AND GETTING AROUND

Most Alaskan airstrips can be reached from **Anchorage International Airport** (☎266-2437) either directly or through a connection in Fairbanks. **Alaska Railroad,** 411 W. 1st Ave., runs to Denali (8hr., $120); Fairbanks (12hr., $160); and Seward (4hr., in summer only, $50). Flagstops are anywhere along route; wave the bus down with a white cloth. (☎265-2494 or 800-544-0552. Ticket window open M-F 5:30am-5pm, Sa-Su 5:30am-1pm.) **Grayline Alaska** (☎800-544-2206) sends buses daily to Seward (4hr., $40) and Valdez (10hr., $70); three times per week to Skagway ($209, overnight). **Parks Hwy. Express** (☎479-3065 or 888-600-6001) runs buses daily May through Sept. to Denali ($35) and Fairbanks ($55). **Alaska Marine Hwy.,** 605 W. 4th Ave., sells ferry tickets. (☎800-642-0066. Open daily 7:30am-4:30pm; in winter M-F.) **People Mover Bus,** in the Transit Center on 6th Ave. between G and H St., sends local buses all over the Anchorage area. (☎343-6543. Office open M-F 8am-5pm. Runs M-F 6am-10pm; restricted schedule Sa-Su. Fare $1, ages 5-18 50¢, over 65 25¢; tokens 90¢; day passes $2.50.) **Airport Car Rental,** 502 W. Northern Lights Blvd., charges $45 per day, with unlimited mileage. (☎277-7662. Open M-F 8am-8pm, Sa-Su 9am-6pm. Must be 21+; under 25 surcharge $5 per day; cash or credit card deposit required.) **Taxi: Yellow Cab,** ☎272-2422.

⟦ ORIENTATION AND PRACTICAL INFORMATION

Downtown Anchorage is laid out in a grid: numbered avenues run east-west, with addresses designated east or west from **C St.** North-south streets are lettered alphabetically to the west and named alphabetically to the east of **A St.** The rest of Anchorage spreads out along major highways. The **Log Cabin Visitor Information Center,** on W. 4th Ave. at F St., sells a $3.50 bike guide. (☎274-3531, events 276-3200. Open daily June-Aug. 7:30am-7pm; May and Sept. 8am-6pm; Oct.-Apr. 9am-4pm.) The **Alaska Public Lands Information Center,** Old Federal Building, 605 W. 4th Ave., between F and G St., combines the Park, Forest, State Parks, and Fish and Wildlife Services under one roof. (☎271-2737 or 271-2744. Open daily 9am-5:30pm.) **Internet access: Oscar's Roast and Smoke,** 508 W. 6th Ave. (☎868-3028. Open M-F 10am-9pm, Sa-Su noon until the crowd leaves. $2 per 15min.) **Post Office:** W. 4th Ave. and C St., on the lower level in the yellow mall. (Open M-F 10am-5:30pm.) **ZIP code:** 99510. **Area code:** 907.

⟦ ACCOMMODATIONS

Alaska Private Lodgings (☎258-1717; call M-Sa 9am-6pm) or the **Anchorage reservation service** (☎272-5909) arrange out-of-town B&Bs (from $70). Two of the best campgrounds in **Chugach State Park** (☎354-5014) are **Eagle River** ($15; 12½ mi. from town) and **Eklutna** ($10; 36½ mi. from town) along Glenn Hwy. Both fill up early, especially on weekends. Public-use cabins can also be found in Chugach. (☎800-280-2267. $25 per night; $8.25 reservation fee.)
⟦**Anchorage Guesthouse,** 2001 Hillcrest Dr., gets full marks for its outstanding service and homey atmosphere. Take bus #3, 4, 6, 36, or 60 from downtown, get off at West High School, and walk ¼ mi. up Hillcrest. From the airport, take bus #6 to the intersection of Spenard and Hillcrest and walk towards the school. (☎ 274-0408, same number for faxes. Bikes $2 per hr. Continental breakfast included. Free local calls. Internet $2.50 per 15min. No alcohol. 1-week maximum stay. Bunks $24; private room $64. $5 key deposit.) ⟦**Spenard Hostel,** 2845 W. 42nd Place, is a comfortable, clean, and welcoming alternative. Take bus #7 from downtown to Gweenie's Restaurant. Turn down Spenard to Turnagain Blvd.; go north and 42nd Place is the first left from Turnagain. (☎248-5036. 3 kitchens, free local calls, bike rental $5, Internet access $5, laundry, lockers, Denali Shuttle drop-off/pick-up. Quiet hours. Chore requested. 6-night maximum stay. Dorms or tent sites $15.)

LET'S MUSH Charlie Darwin would have liked these odds: snow, wind, and frigid cold, separating the women from the girls. The celebrated **Iditarod** dog sled race begins in Anchorage on the first weekend in March. Dogs and their drivers ("mushers") traverse a 1150 mi. trail over two mountain ranges, along the mighty Yukon River, and over the frozen Norton Sound to Nome. The Iditarod Trail began as a dog sled supply route from Seward on the southern coast to interior mining towns. The race commemorates the 1925 rescue of Nome, when drivers ferried 300,000 units of life-saving diptheria serum from Nenana, near Fairbanks, to Nome. Today, up to 70 contestants speed each year from Anchorage to Nome, competing for a $450,000 purse but surprisingly willing to help fellow mushers in distress. The fastest time was recorded by Doug Swingley—9 days, 2hr. You can visit the **Iditarod Headquarters** at Mi. 2.2 Knik Rd. in Wasilla. Contact ☎376-5155 or www.iditarod.com for more info.

FOOD AND NIGHTLIFE

◼**Moose's Tooth,** 3300 Old Seward, serves pizza and brews as hearty as the climbers who tackle the nearby peak. Take bus #2 or 36. (☎258-2537. Open M-Th 11am-midnight, F-Sa noon-1am, Su noon-midnight. Local bands Th; open mic M 9-11pm.) **Sweet Basil Cafe,** 335 E St., is run by the black labrador retriever/CEO Buba, who keeps the owner-chefs turning out tasty treats. (☎274-0070. Open M-F 7:30am-4pm, Sa 9am-4pm.) **Snow City Cafe,** 1034 W 4th St., at L St., is bedecked with art and blessed by live music F-Sa. Their other claim to fame is the best breakfasts in town. (☎272-2489. Open M-Tu 7am-4pm, W-Su 7am-4pm and 5-9pm; winter M-Th 7am-4pm, F 7am-4pm and 5-9pm, Sa-Su 8am-4pm and 5-9pm. Salads and big sandwiches $4-10.)

The brew-pub revolution has hit Anchorage, and microbrews gush from taps like oil through the pipeline. Catch a flick with brew in hand at the **Bears Tooth,** 1230 W 27th St. (Pints $3.75. $2 cover for movie.) At **Bernie's Bungalow Lounge,** 626 D St., relax in one of many wingback chairs or couches as you sip your lemon drop martini ($5), puff on a cigar, and play a round of croquet in a hotspot frequented by the young and retro. (☎276-8808. Open daily noon-2am; in winter 3pm-2am.) **Chilkoot Charlie's,** 2435 Spenard Rd., at Fireweek, has cavernous dance floors and rock music. "Koots" is the place to dance into the night; take bus #7. (Open Su-Th 10:30am-2:15am, F-Sa 11am-2:45am. $1 drink specials until 10pm. Escalating cover from 8pm $2-5.)

SIGHTS AND OUTDOORS

Near town off Northern Lights Blvd., **Earthquake Park** recalls the 1964 Good Friday quake, the strongest ever recorded in North America, registering 9.2 on the Richter scale. At the ◼**Anchorage Museum of History and Art,** 121 W. 7th Ave., at A St., permanent Native Alaskan artifacts and art mingle with national and international works. (☎343-4326. Open daily Su-Th 9am-9pm, F-Sa 9am-6pm; Sept.-May Tu-Sa 9am-6pm, Su 1-5pm. Tours daily at 10, 11am, 1, and 2pm. $6.50, seniors $6, under 18 free.) At the **Alaska Zoo,** Mi. 2 on O'Malley Rd., Binky the polar bear mauled an Australian tourist in 1994 and became a local hero. (☎346-3242. Open daily 9am-6pm. $7, seniors $6, ages 12-18 $5, 3-11 $3.)

The 13 mi. **Tony Knowles Coastal Trail** is arguably one of the best urban bike paths in the country; in the winter, it's groomed for cross-country skiing. The serene **Chugach State Park,** cornering the city to the north, east, and south, has 25 established dayhiking trails. A 15min. drive from the city center, **Flattop Mountain** (4500 ft.) is the most frequently climbed mountain in Alaska, providing an excellent view of the inlet, the Aleutian Chain, and on the rare clear day, Denali. Parking at the trailhead costs $5, or take bus #92 to Hillside Rd. and Upper Huffman Rd. From there, the trailhead is a ¾ mi. walk along Upper Huffman Rd., then right on Toilsome Hill Dr. for 2 mi.; it's a 2 mi. hike to the summit. Less frequented hikes branch from the **Powerline Trail,** which begins at the same parking lot as the Flattop Trail. The **Eklutna Lakeside Biking Trail** extends 13 mi. one-way from the Eklutna Campground, off Mi. 26 of the Glenn Hwy. (Rte. 1). A relatively flat dirt road, the trail follows the blue-green Eklutna Lake for 7 mi. before entering a steep river canyon, ending at the base of the Eklutna River. **Nancy Lake State Recreation Area,** just west of the Parks Hwy. (Rte. 3) at Mi. 67.3, and just south of Willow, contains the **Lynx Lake Canoe Loop,** which takes two days and weaves through 8 mi. of lakes and portages, with designated campsites along the way. The loop begins at Mi. 4½ of the Nancy Lake Parkway, at the Tanaina Lake Canoe Trailhead. For canoe rental or shuttle service in the Nancy Lake Area, call **Tippecanoe.** (☎495-6688. Canoes $25 per day, $70 per week. Shuttle free for backpackers.)

SEWARD AND KENAI FJORDS ☎907

Seward serves as a gateway to the waterways and yawning ice fields of **Kenai Fjords National Park. Exit Glacier,** the only road-accessible glacier in the park, lies 9 mi. west on a spur from Mi. 3.7 of the Seward Hwy. (Rte. 9). A **shuttle** runs here four times daily from downtown Seward; parking for the day is $5. (☎224-5770. Round-trip $20.) Beyond this glacier, boat cruises are the easiest and most popular way to see the park. **Kenai Fjords Tours** are informative and amusing. (☎224-8068 or 800-478-8068. Tours last 6-9½hr. $109-139, children $54-60.) **Major Marine Tours** brings along a ranger to explain wildlife and glacier facts. (☎224-8030 or 800-764-7300. $99; with salmon, halibut, and shellfish dinner $109.) **Wildlife Quest** is the only outfit with speedy catamarans. (☎888-305-2515. 5½hr. $99, children $49.) **Sunny Cove Sea Kayaking** offers a joint trip with Kenai Fjords Tours, including the wildlife cruise, a salmon bake, kayaking instruction, and a 2½hr. wilderness paddle. (☎345-5339. 8hr. $139-159.)

◪**Kate's Roadhouse,** 5½ mi. outside town on the Seward Hwy., has huge continental breakfasts with home-baking and a quietly sleeping pig in the sitting room. (☎224-5888. Free shuttle service, laundry, bedding, and towels. Shared baths. Clean dorms $17; private rooms $59; 4 private cabins with electricity, cable TV, and heat $29-49.) **Ballaine House Lodging,** 437 3rd Ave. at Madison St., two blocks from downtown, is bright, clean, and well-furnished, with pleasant rooms and a scrumptious breakfast. (☎224-2362. Singles $55; doubles $84; lower rates without breakfast. Free laundry with notice.) Camping is available at the **Municipal Waterfront Campground,** along Ballaine Rd. between Railway Ave. and D St. (Open May 15 to Sept. 2-week maximum stay. Sites $6; RV sites $10, hook-ups $15.)

Seward is 127 mi. south of Anchorage on the scenic **Seward Hwy. (Rte. 9).** Most services and outdoor outfits cluster in the small boat harbor on Resurrection Bay. Across from the visitors center at the **Alaska Railroad** depot, trains leave for Anchorage at 6:45am in summer. (☎800-544-0552. 4½hr. $50, ages 2-11 $25.) **Seward Bus Lines,** 1914 Seward Hwy. (☎224-3608), runs to Anchorage (9am, $35; airport service $5). The **Alaska Marine Hwy.** (☎224-5485 or 800-642-0066) docks at 4th Ave. and Railway St., running three per month in summer to Valdez (11hr., $58) and Homer (25hr., $96). The **Seward Chamber of Commerce** is at Mi. 2 on the Seward Hwy. (☎224-8051. Open M-F 8am-5pm, Sa 9am-6pm, Su 9am-4pm.) **Kenai Fjords National Park Visitors Center** is at the small-boat harbor. (☎224-3175, info 224-2132. Open daily 8am-7pm; in winter M-F 8am-5pm.) **Post Office:** at 5th Ave. and Madison St. (☎224-3001; open M-F 9:30am-4:30pm, Sa 10am-2pm). **ZIP code:** 99664. **Area code:** 907.

WRANGELL-ST. ELIAS NATIONAL PARK ☎907

Wrangell-St. Elias National Park is the largest national park in the US (13¼ million acres). Beyond towering peaks and extensive glaciers, Wrangell teems with wildlife. With only two rough roads that penetrate its interior, and almost no established trails, the park's inaccessibility keeps many tourists away. **Ranger stations** lurk exclusively outside the park boundaries in Copper Center, south of Glennallen (☎822-7261; open daily 8am-6pm); Yakutat in the east (☎784-3295; open daily 8am-5pm); Chitina in the west (☎823-2205; open daily 10am-6pm); and Slana on the park's northern boundary (☎822-5238; open daily 8am-5pm). They have the lowdown on all the must-knows and go-sees of the park and sell invaluable topographical maps (entire park $9; quadrants $4). **Backcountry Connection** (☎822-5292 or 800-478-5292) runs buses daily from Glennallen (4hr., $65) and Chitina (3hr., $50) to McCarthy. **Charter flights** from McCarthy or Nabesna start at around $60 per person.

One of the park's access routes is the scenic **Nabesna Rd.**, extending a harsh 46 mi. from the Richardson Hwy. (Rte. 4) into the park's northern portion. The turn-off for the road is at Slana, 65 mi. southwest of Tok on the Tok Cutoff. Nabesna, at the end of the 42 mi. road, is little more than a mining ghost town, home to the **End-of-the-Road Bed & Breakfast.** (☎822-5312. Bunks $20; singles $50; doubles $65.)

The more harrowing **McCarthy Rd.** plunges 60 mi. into the park from Chitina (*CHIT-nuh*) to the western edge of the Kennicott River, where travelers must cross a footbridge and walk ½ mi. into the town of McCarthy. Free parking is available another ½ mi. back before the river. Deep in the heart of the park, McCarthy and its sister town Kennicott are quiet today, but abandoned log-hewn buildings and forgotten roads bear witness to a boom town past. **Wrangell Mountain Air** flies to McCarthy twice daily from Chitina and farther afield by arrangement. (☎554-4411 or 800-478-1160. Round-trip $140.) A **shuttle** runs the 5 mi. road between the towns from 9am to 7:30pm (round-trip $10). McCarthy's cheapest beds, six-person cabins, and a cozy common room await a ¼ mi. before the river at the **Kennicott River Lodge and Hostel.** (☎554-4441, winter 479-6822. Rooms $25; cabins $85.) Camping is free at the lot ½ mi. back along the road toward Chitina (pit toilets, no water). If you want to dine out, try **Tailor-Made Pizza and Morning Moonshine,** as it's the only non-lodge restaurant in town that serves dinner. (☎554-1155. Open daily 8am-8pm. Calzones $9.)

This is the place for flightseeing in Alaska. Even a short flight to 16,390 ft. Mt. Blackburn and the surrounding glaciers offers soul-stunning views. **Wrangell Mountain Air** makes a 35min. tour of the amazing icefalls of the Kennicott and Root Glaciers (☎554-4411 or 800-478-1160; $50). The best bargain is the 70min. trip up the narrow Chitistone Canyon to view the thundering Chitistone Falls and on to a slew of glaciers and peaks ($95 per person; minimum 2 people). **Copper Oar** runs a day-long whitewater rafting trip down the Class III Kennicott River with a flightseeing jaunt back from Chitina (☎554-4453 or 800-523-4453; $225). **St. Elias Alpine Guides** (☎554-4445 in McCarthy, 888-933-5427 in Anchorage) lead a variety of guided hikes and explorations. The park maintains no trails around McCarthy; consult with a ranger station before setting out. Ranger stations need a written itinerary for independent overnight trips.

DENALI NATIONAL PARK AND PRESERVE ☎907

Nine thousand square miles of snow-capped peaks, braided streams, and glacier-carved valleys, interrupted only by a lone gravel road, Denali National Park and Preserve is not a place made for humans; nevertheless, more than a million visitors invite themselves here year after year. And why not? Such untamed, beautiful wilderness is hard to find. Visitors to the park are guests of grizzly bears, moose, caribou, wolves, Dall sheep, and wildflowers. Denali's 20,320 ft. centerpiece, called Mt. McKinley by the US Geological Survey but known to locals as Denali or "the Mountain," is the world's tallest mountain from base to peak. (Mt. Everest reaches a higher elevation but is not taller.) Mid- to late August is the best time to visit—fall colors peak, berries ripen, mosquito season is virtually over, and September snows have not yet arrived.

⊟ GETTING THERE AND AROUND. The **George Parks Hwy. (Rte. 3)** makes for smooth and easy traveling to the park entrance north from Anchorage or south from Fairbanks. Leading east away from the park, the gravel **Denali Hwy. (Rte. 8)** starts 27 mi. south of the park entrance at Cantwell and proceeds to Paxson (closed in winter). The **Alaska Railroad** makes regular stops at Denali Station, 1½ mi. from the park entrance (☎683-2233 or 800-544-0552; open daily 10am-5pm), and runs out to Fairbanks (4½hr.; $48, bikes $10) and Anchorage (8hr.; $120/$20); reserve ahead. **Parks Hwy. Express** (☎888-600-6001) runs to the park from Anchorage (5hr., $42) and Fairbanks (3½hr., $27).

Only the first 14 mi. of the park road are accessible by private vehicle; the remaining 75 mi. of dirt road can be reached only by shuttle bus, camper bus, or bicycle. **Shuttle buses** leave from the visitors center daily 5am to 6pm, pause at the almost inevitable sighting of any major mammal ("MOOOOOSE!"), and turn back at various points along the park road, such as Toklat, Mi. 53 ($12.50); Eielson, Mi. 66 ($21); Wonder Lake, Mi. 85 ($27); and Kantishna, Mi. 89 ($31). (Most buses are wheelchair accessible.) **Camper buses** ($15.50) transport only those visitors with campground permits and backcountry permits and move faster than the shuttle buses. Unlike private vehicles, bikes *are* permitted on all park roads.

🅱 **PRACTICAL INFORMATION.** All travelers must stop at the **Denali Visitors Center,** ½ mi. from the Parks Hwy. (Rte. 3), for orientation. Park rangers collect the **entrance fee** ($5 per person, good for 1 week). Most park privileges are first come, first served; conduct all business at the visitors center as early in the day as possible. (☎683-2294. Open daily late Apr. to Memorial Day 10am-4pm, Memorial Day to Labor Day 7am-8pm, Memorial Day to late Sept. 10am-4pm. Lockers 50¢.) **Denali Outdoor Center,** at Mi. 238.9, just north of the park entrance, rents bikes. (☎683-1925. Half-day $25; full-day $40; 5 or more days $35 per day.) **Healy Clinic** is 13 mi. north of the park entrance. (☎683-2211. Open M-F 9am-5pm; Oct.-Apr. M-F 10am-3pm.) **Post Office:** next to Denali Hotel, 1 mi. from the visitors center. (☎683-2291. Open May-Sept. M-F 8:30am-5pm, Sa 10am-1pm; Oct.-Apr. M-Sa 10am-1pm.) **ZIP code:** 99755. **Area code:** 907.

🅵🅵 **ACCOMMODATIONS AND FOOD.** To reach the **Denali Hostel,** go 9½ mi. north of the park entrance, turn left onto Otto Lake Rd., and continue straight 1¼ mi. past the golf course. It's the 2nd house on the right, with a beautiful setting (oh, the sunsets!), international clientele, helpful owners, clean rooms, full kitchen, TV room, showers, and coin-operated laundry. (☎683-1295. Open May-Sept. Check-in 5:30-10pm. Shuttle to the park and Alaska Railroad. Dorms $25. Linen $3. Reservations recommended.) Campers must obtain a permit from the visitors center and may stay for up to 14 nights in the park's seven campgrounds, which line the park road. (☎272-7275 or 800-622-7275 for advance reservations. First come, first served sites are distributed rapidly at the visitors center.) **Riley Creek** is the only campground open year-round and has the only dump station. Most campgrounds are wheelchair accessible.

Once you board that park bus, there is no food available anywhere. At **Black Bear Coffee House,** 1 mi. north of the park entrance, the coffee is hot and strong, the muffins are fresh, and the staff is all smiles. (☎683-1656. Open daily May-Sept. 7am-10pm. Veggie sandwich with hot cup of soup $7.) **Denali Smoke Shack,** north of the park entrance at Mi. 238½, serves real Alaskan barbecue and a large vegetarian menu. (☎683-7665. Open daily 8am-10:30am and noon-1am.)

THIS BOX IS PLANE BORING Alaska has the highest per capita ownership of small planes, the greatest number of pilots, the greatest number of float planes, and in Anchorage, one of the nation's busiest airports. Throughout much of the interior, small planes aren't simply the best way to get there—they're the only way. Some of the state's most colorful lore is steeped in aviation—like the story of Alaska's 3rd governor, who broke both ankles crash-landing his small plane to avoid endangering the children playing on the airstrip. Tales of unusual landings are as common as tales of unusual cargo: Bush pilots have been known to transport canoes, beer, furniture, and even moose to the farthest reaches of the state.

ALASKA

▲ **OUTDOORS.** The best way to experience Denali is to get off the bus and explore the land. Beyond Mi. 14, the point which only shuttle and camper buses can cross, there are no trails. You can begin dayhiking from anywhere along the park road by riding the shuttle bus to a suitable starting point and asking the driver to let you off. It's rare to wait more than 30min. to flag a ride back. **Primrose Ridge,** beginning at Mi. 16 on the right side of the road, is bespangled with wildflowers and has spectacular views of the Alaska Range and its carpeted emerald valley below. A walk north from Mi. 14 along the **Savage River** provides a colorful, scenic stroll through this valley. The more challenging **Mt. Healy Overlook Trail** starts from the hotel parking lot and climbs to an impressive view at 3400 ft. (5 mi. round-trip; 1700 ft. elevation gain; 3-4hr.) **Discovery hikes** are guided 3-5hr. hikes, departing on special buses from the visitors center. Topics vary; a ranger might lead you on a cross-country scramble or a moose trail excursion. The hikes are free but require reservations and a bus ticket. More sedate 45min. **tundra walks** leave from Eielson Visitors Center daily at 1:30pm. More guided talks and walks are posted at the visitors center.

There are no trails in the backcountry. While dayhiking is unlimited and requires no permit, only 2-12 backpackers can camp at one time in each of the park's 43 units. Overnight stays in the backcountry require a **free permit,** available no earlier or later than one day in advance at the backcountry desk in the visitors center. The quota board there reports which units are still available. Type-A hikers line up outside as early as 6:30am to grab permits for popular units. Talk to rangers and research your choices with the handy *Backcountry Description Guides* and *The Backcountry Companion,* available at the visitors center bookstore. The visitors center sells essential topographic maps ($4). All but two zones in Denali require that food be carried in **bear resistant food containers (BRFC),** available for free at the backcountry desk. These are bulky things; be sure to leave space in your backpack. With the park's cool, often drizzly weather and its many rivers, streams, and pools, your feet will get wet. **Hypothermia** can set in quickly and quietly; talk with rangers about prevention and warning signs.

FAIRBANKS   ☎907

Fairbanks stands unchallenged as North American civilization's northernmost hub—witness such landmarks as the "World's Northernmost Woolworth's," "World's Northernmost Denny's," and "World's Northernmost Southern Barbecue." From here, adventuresome travelers can drive, fly, or float to the Arctic Circle and into the tundra. Most do not make the long and arduous trip to Fairbanks merely to stay put, although the town is fostering reasons to stay.

🛈 **PRACTICAL INFORMATION.** Most tourist destinations lie within the square formed by **Airport Way, College Rd., Cushman Blvd.,** and **University Way.** The city center lies north of the intersection of Cushman and Airport Way. Fairbanks is a bicycle-friendly city, with wide shoulders, multi-use paths, and sidewalks. The **airport** is 5 mi. from downtown on Airport Way. **Alaska Railroad,** 280 N. Cushman St. (☎456-4155; open M-F 7am-3pm, Sa-Su 7-11am), runs one train per day to Anchorage ($160) via Denali ($48); service is reduced during the winter. **Parks Hwy. Express** (☎479-3065 or 888-600-6001) runs daily to Denali (one per day, $27); Anchorage (one per day, $55); Glennallen (3 per week, $45); and Valdez (3 per week, $62). **Municipal Commuter Area Service (MACS),** at 5th and Cushman St., runs through downtown and its surroundings. (☎459-1011. Fare $1.50; students, seniors, and disabled 75¢; under 5 free. Day pass $3.) **Fairbanks Taxi,** ☎452-3535. **Visitor Info:** 550 1st Ave., at Cushman. (☎456-5774 or 800-327-5774. Open daily 8am-8pm; in winter M-F 8am-5pm.) **Alaska Public Lands Info Center (APLIC):** 250 Cushman St. #1A, at 3rd. St. in the basement of the Federal building. (☎456-0527. Open daily 9am-6pm; in winter Tu-Sa 10am-6pm.) **Post Office:** 315 Barnette St. (☎452-3203; open M-F 9am-6pm, Sa 10am-2pm). **ZIP code:** 99707. **Area code:** 907.

ACCOMMODATIONS AND FOOD. Grandma Shirley's Hostel, 510 Dunbar St., is the Fairbanks überhostel. From the Steese Expwy., turn right onto the Trainor Gate Rd., then left at E. St., and right on Dunbar St. (☎451-9816. Spectacular kitchen, showers, TV room, big backyard, and free bike use. Dorms $16.25.) **Billie's Backpackers Hostel,** 2895 Mack Rd., is a somewhat cluttered but welcoming place to meet many international travelers. Take Westwood Way one block off College to Mack Rd. (☎479-2034. Shower and kitchen in each room. Beds $20. Breakfast $7. Tent sites $10 per person.) **Chena River State Campground,** off Airport Way on University Ave., is landscaped, clean, and on a quiet stretch of the Chena River. (56 sites. $15. In summer, 5-night maximum stay per vehicle.)

An artery-blocking good time fills Airport Way and College Rd. **Sam's Club,** 48 College Rd., is good for stocking up on groceries. (☎451-4800. Open M-Sa 9am-8pm, Su 10am-7pm.) **Bun on the Run,** located in a trailer in the parking lot between Beaver Sports and the Marlin on College Rd., across from the Campus Corner Mall, whips up the best pastries in Alaska. (Open M-F 7am-5pm, Sa 7am-4pm.) **Gambardella's Pasta Bella,** 706 2nd Ave., turns out the "Mother of all Lasagnas" for $15 in true Italian ambiance. (Open daily M-Sa 11am-10pm.) Grab a cuppa joe in the log cabin coffeehouse **Into the Woods,** 3560 College Rd. (Open Tu 6pm-midnight, W-Su noon-midnight.)

SIGHTS AND OUTDOORS. The **University of Alaska Museum,** a 10min. walk up Yukon Dr. from the Wood Center, features a thorough look at the Aleut/Japanese evacuation during WWII, indigenous crafts, and Blue Babe, a 36,000 year-old steppe bison recovered from the permafrost. (☎474-7505. Open daily June-Aug. 9am-7pm; May and Sept. 9am-5pm; Oct.-Apr. M-F 9am-5pm and Sa-Su noon-5pm. $5, seniors $4.50, ages 7-17 $3.) Stand upwind of the **Large Animal Research Station,** which offers a rare chance to see baby musk oxen and other arctic animals up close. Take Farmer's Loop to Ballaine Rd. and turn left on Van Kovich; the farm is 1 mi. up on the right. (☎474-7207. Tours June-Aug. Tu, Th, Sa at 11am and 1:30pm; Sept. Sa 1:30pm. $5, students $2, seniors $4.)

Moose Mountain, 20min. northeast of town, has over 20 downhill skiing trails. (☎479-8362. Lift tickets $25; college students, seniors, military, and ages 13-17 $20; ages 7-12 $15; over 70 or under 6 free. $5 off after 1pm or if the temperature is below 0°F.) Maps for multi-use trails are available at the Wood Center, in the UAF Activities Office. Cross-country skiing trails stripe the UAF campus. The **Chena River State Recreation Area** has a variety of multi-use trails. Maps are available at the Public Lands Information Center.

NIGHTLIFE AND ENTERTAINMENT. **Howling Dog Saloon,** 11½ mi. north on the Steese Hwy. (Rte. 6) toward Fox, at the intersection of the Old and New Steese Hwys., is, as the manager says "rough, tough, and good-lookin." Volleyball, pool, and horseshoe games go on until 4am or so. (☎457-8780. Open May-Oct. Su-Th 4pm-2am, F-Sa 4pm-4am. Live music W-Sa.) In mid-July, Fairbanks citizens don old-time duds and whoop it up for **Golden Days,** a celebration of Felix Pedro's 1902 discovery that sparked the Fairbanks gold rush. Although its relation to the actual gold rush days is questionable, the **rubber duckie race** is one of the biggest events. The Fairbanks Goldpanners play their annual **Midnight Sun Baseball Game** on the solstice itself (June 21, 2001). The game begins as the sun dips at 10:30pm, features a short pause near midnight for the celebration of the midnight sun, and ends at about 2am, in full daylight. For a true sports spectacular, see the **World Eskimo-Indian Olympics,** in mid to late July. Native Alaskans from all over the state compete for three days in traditional tests of strength and survival. Witness the ear pull, for which sinew is wrapped around the ears of contestants, who then tug to see who can endure the most pain. *Ears have been pulled off in this event.* (☎452-6646. Daily pass $6, season pass $20.)

SOUTHEAST ALASKA

Southeast Alaska sometimes goes by "the Panhandle" or "the southeast." It spans 500 miles from the basins of Misty Fiords National Monument to Skagway at the foot of the Chilkoot Trail. The waterways weaving through the Panhandle, collectively known as the Inside Passage, make up an enormous saltwater soup spiced with islands, inlets, fjords, and the ferries that flit among them. The absence of roads in the steep coastal mountains has helped Panhandle towns maintain their small size and hospitable personalities. The **Alaska Marine Hwy.** system (see p. 944) provides the cheapest, most exciting way to explore the Inside Passage.

KETCHIKAN   ☎907

Ketchikan is the first stop in Alaska for cruise ships and would-be cannery workers. An average of nearly 12½ feet of rainfall a year can not deter visitors' delight in the fabulous proximity to Tongass National Forest (one-third of which lies in the Ketchikan area) and the Misty Fiords National Monument. A revamped "historical district" is dressed for the tourists who support the newest growth industry, but parts of Ketchikan remain economically depressed. The adjustment to a tourism-based economy has not been easy for many residents, who would prefer to turn back the clock to when fishing and logging were the only shows in town.

◪ PRACTICAL INFORMATION

Ketchikan rests on **Revillagigedo Island** (*ruh-VIL-ya-GIG-a-doe*). Upon reaching Ketchikan from Canada, roll back your watch an hour to get in step with Alaska Time. The town caters to the elite, and its attractions are extremely spread out, making bike rental a wise option. A small **ferry** runs from the airport, across from Ketchikan on Gravina Island, to just north of the state ferry dock (every 30min.; $2.50). **Alaska Airlines** (☎800-225-2141) makes daily flights to Juneau. **Alaska Marine Hwy.** (☎225-6181 or 800-642-0066) sends wheelchair-accessible boats from the far end of town on N. Tongass Hwy. to Wrangell ($24), Juneau ($74), and Sitka ($54). The main bus route runs a loop between the airport parking lot near the ferry terminal at one end, and Dock and Main St. downtown at the other. (Runs every 30min. M-F 5:15am-9:45pm; 1 per hr. Sa 6:45am-8:45pm, Su 8:45am-3:45pm. $1, students, seniors, and children 75¢.) **Taxi: Sourdough Cab,** ☎225-5544. **Ketchikan Visitors Bureau:** 131 Front St., at the cruise ship docks downtown. (☎225-6166 or 800-770-3300. Open daily 8am-5pm.) **Southeast Alaska Visitors Center (SEAVC),** 50 Main St., provides trip-planning service, plus info on public lands around Ketchikan, including Tongass and Misty Fiords. (☎228-6220. Open daily Apr.-Sept. 8am-5pm; Oct.-Mar. Tu-Sa 8:30am-4:30pm.) **Post Office:** by the ferry terminal (☎225-9601; open M-F 8:30am-5pm). **ZIP code:** 99901. **Area code:** 907.

▮◖ ACCOMMODATIONS AND FOOD

The **Ketchikan Reservation Service** provides info on B&Bs. (☎800-987-5337; fax 247-5337. Singles from $65.) Because of boardwalk stairs, these accommodations aren't wheelchair accessible. The **Ketchikan Youth Hostel (HI-AYH)** is at Main and Grant St. in the First Methodist Church. The social scene is skimpy since the doors close at 11pm sharp. Bring a sleeping bag for the foam mats. (☎225-3319. Open June-Aug. Common area, showers, kitchen, and free tea, coffee, and popcorn every night. 4-night maximum stay when full. Lockout 9am-6pm. Lights out 11pm-7am. Call ahead if arriving on a late ferry. $10, non-members $13. Make reservations.) **Eagle View Bed & Breakfast and Backpacker Bunks,** 2303 5th Ave., is reached via Jefferson Ave. uphill from Tongass, turn right on 5th Ave.; it's a big brown house at the end of the street. Not as cheap as the hostel, but the B&B has free use of a kitchen, TV, sauna, BBQ, and hammocks. (☎225-5461. Laundry $2.50 per load.

Campgrounds usually have stay limits of a week or two and are really out of the way. **Signal Creek** sits on Ward Lake Rd. Drive north on Tongass Ave. and turn right at the sign for Ward Lake, approximately 5 mi. from the ferry terminal. (Open May-Sept. Water, pit toilets. 14-night maximum stay. $10.) Anyone can camp for up to 30 days in **Tongass National Forest,** but may not return for six months after that time. Any clearing is free.

The freshest seafood swims in **Ketchikan Creek;** in summer, anglers frequently hook king salmon from the docks by Stedman St. **Ocean View Restaurante,** 3159 N. Tongass Ave., serves up enchiladas ($9) and pizza ($7.50) with equal gusto. The fried ice cream is a winner for desert. (☎ 225-7566. Open daily 11am-11pm.) **Burger Queen,** 518 Water St., is a block past the tunnel. The regal veggie burgers, chicken troika sandwiches, and guacamole cheddar burgers ($2-8) please the pickiest. (☎ 225-6060. Open M-Sa 11am-8pm; in winter until 4pm.)

👁️🏔️ SIGHTS AND OUTDOORS

Ketchikan's primary cultural attraction is the **Saxman Totem Park,** the largest totem park in Alaska, 2½ mi. southwest of town on Tongass Hwy. ($10 by cab, or a short ride on the Hwy. bike path.) The **Totem Heritage Center,** up Park St. on the hill above downtown, houses 33 well-preserved totem poles from Tlingit, Haida, and Tsimshian villages. It is the largest collection of authentic, pre-commercial totem poles in the US, but only a few are on display. (☎ 225-5900. Open daily May-Sept. 8am-5pm, Oct.-Apr. Tu-F 1-5pm. $4, under 13 free.) A $10 combination ticket also provides admission to the **Deer Mountain Fish Hatchery and Raptor Center,** across the creek. (☎ 225-6761. Open daily May-Sept. 8am-4:30pm.)

From Ketchikan, a trail up 3001 ft. **Deer Mountain** makes a good dayhike. Walk up the hill past the city park on Fair St.; the marked trailhead branches off to the left just behind the dump. The ascent is steep but manageable, and on a rare clear day the walk yields sparkling views of the sea and surrounding islands. While most hikers stop at the 2½ mi. point, the trail continues above the treeline to the summit along an 8 mi. route that passes Blue Lake and leads over John Mountain to Little Silvis Lake and the Beaver Falls Fish Hatchery. This portion of the trail is poorly marked, and snow and ice are common on the peaks even in the summer; only experienced and well-prepared hikers should attempt it. An A-frame cabin between Deer Mountain and John Mountain can be reserved through the Forest Service desk at SEAVC (see p. 952). The trail emerges 12 mi. south of Ketchikan at the Beaver Falls power station parking lot. For swimming, a sandy beach, and picnic tables, head to **Ward Lake** at the Signal Creek Campground. A 1¼ mi. trail circles the grassy pond. Bikers can explore surrounding logging roads.

NEAR KETCHIKAN: MISTY FIORDS

The jagged peaks, plunging valleys, and dripping vegetation of **Misty Fiords National Monument,** 20 mi. east of Ketchikan, make biologists dream and outdoors enthusiasts drool. Only accessible by kayak, boat, or float plane, the 2.3-million-acre park offers superlative camping, kayaking, hiking, and wildlife-viewing. **Camping** is permitted throughout the park, and the Forest Service maintains four first come, first served shelters (free) and 14 cabins ($25). Contact the **Misty Fiords Ranger Station,** 3031 Tongass Ave., Ketchikan (☎ 225-2148), and ask ahead at the SEAVC (see p. 952). Kayaking neophytes might contact **Alaska Cruises,** 220 Front St.; they'll drop off at the head of Rudyard Bay. (☎ 225-6044. $200 per person.) **Area code:** 907.

JUNEAU
☎ 907

Alaska's state capital has an air of modernity and progressiveness usually not found in the rural fishing villages of Southeast Alaska. Accessible only by water and air, Juneau is the 2nd-busiest cruise ship port in the US, after Miami. Hordes of travelers come to Juneau for the Mendenhall Glacier, numerous hiking trails, and close access to Glacier Bay. Be prepared to share the beauty.

🛈 PRACTICAL INFORMATION

Franklin St. is the main drag downtown. **Glacier Hwy.** connects downtown, the airport, the residential area of the Mendenhall Valley, and the ferry terminal. The ferry and airport are both annoyingly far from the glacier and downtown. **Juneau International Airport,** 9 mi. north of Juneau on Glacier Hwy., is served by **Alaska Airlines** (☎789-0600 or 800-426-0333). **Capital Transit** runs buses from downtown to the airport and Mendenhall Glacier, with hourly express service downtown. The closest stop to the ferry is across from DeHart's General Store. (☎789-6901. Office open M-F 8:10am-5:10pm. Runs M-Sa 7am-10:30pm, Su 9am-5:30pm. Fare $1.25; exact change required.) **MGT Ferry Express** (☎789-5460) meets all ferries and runs to downtown hotels or to the airport ($5). **Alaska Marine Hwy.,** 1591 Glacier Ave. (☎465-3941 or 800-642-0066), docks at the Auke Bay terminal, 14 mi. from the city on the Glacier Hwy., and runs to Ketchikan ($74); Sitka ($26); and Bellingham, WA ($226). **Taku Cab** (☎586-2121) runs to the glacier ($15), the ferry ($20), and the airport ($15). **Davis Log Cabin Visitor Center,** 134 3rd St., at Seward St., is a great source of pamphlets and maps. (☎586-6304 or 888-581-2201. Open M-F 8:30am-5pm, Sa-Su 9am-5pm; Oct.-May M-F 9am-5pm.) **Forest Service Info Center,** 101 Egan Dr., at Willoughby in Centennial Hall, provides info on hiking and fishing in the area and reservations for Forest Service cabins in Tongass National Forest. (☎586-8751. Open M-F 8am-5pm.) **Internet access: Library,** at Admiral Way and S. Franklin St. **Post Office:** 709 W. 9th St. (☎586-7987; open M-F 9am-5:30pm). **ZIP code:** 99801. **Area code:** 907.

🛏🍴 ACCOMMODATIONS AND FOOD

The **Alaska B&B Association** can help find a room downtown (from $65). On a steep hill, lovely **Juneau International Hostel (HI-AYH)**, 614 Harris St., at 6th St., enforces strict rules in a prime location. (☎586-9559. Lockout 9am-5pm and 11pm curfew. 48 beds. Wash $1.25, dry 75¢. 3-night maximum stay if they're full. $7, non-members $10. $10 deposit mailed in advance secures a phone reservation.) **Alaskan Hotel,** 167 Franklin St., downtown, has been meticulously restored to its original 1913 decor. (☎586-1000 or 800-327-9347. Kitchenettes and TVs. Laundry for guests. Rooms $60-89; rates lower in winter.) **Mendenhall Lake Campground** is about 6 mi. from the ferry terminal on Montana Creek Rd.; take Glacier Hwy. north 10 mi. to Mendenhall Loop Rd., continue 3½ mi., and take the right fork. Bus drivers will stop within 2 mi. of camp. The 60 sites have stunning views of the glacier and convenient trails to go even closer. (Open June 15 to Sept. Reception 7am-10:30pm. Firepits, water, flush toilets, showers, firewood. 14-night maximum stay. Sites $10-20. No reservations.)

  Silverbow Bagels, 120 2nd. St., is the oldest operating bakery in Alaska, and the years of experience shine through in the quality of their food. (☎526-9566. Open M-F 7am-4:30pm, Sa 8am-3:30pm, Su 9am-2:30pm. Movies Tu, Th, and Sa night. Back Room restaurant open for dinner.) **Armadillo Tex-Mex Cafe,** 431 S. Franklin St., shelters locals in the heart of the cruise ship district with fast, saucy service and hot, spicy food. (☎586-1880. Open M-Sa 11am-10pm, Su 4-10pm. 2 enchiladas $6.)

👁🏔 SIGHTS AND OUTDOORS

The excellent **Alaska State Museum,** 395 Whittier St., leads through the history and culture of Alaska's four major native groups: Tlingit, Athabascan, Aleut, and Inuit. (☎465-2901. Open mid-May to mid-Sept. M-F 9am-6pm, Sa-Su 10am-6pm; mid-Sept. to mid-May Tu-Sa 10am-4pm. $5, under 19 free.) The hexagonal and onion-domed 1894 **St. Nicholas Russian Orthodox Church,** on 5th St. between N. Franklin and Gold St., holds rows of icons and a glorious altar. Services, held Sa at 6pm and Su at 10am, are conducted in English, Old Slavonic, and Tlingit. (Open daily in summer 9am-5pm. $1 donation requested.)

The **West Glacier Trail** begins off Montana Creek Rd., by the Mendenhall Lake Campground. The 5-6hr. walk yields stunning views of **Mendenhall Glacier** from the first step to the final outlook. The 3½ mi. trail parallels the glacier through western hemlock forest and up a rocky cairn-marked scramble to the summit of 4226 ft. **Mt. McGinnis.** At the end of Basin Rd., the easy **Perseverance Trail** leads to the ruins of the Silverbowl Basin Mine and booming waterfalls. The **Granite Creek Trail** branches off the Perseverance Trail and follows its namesake to a beautiful basin, 3¾ mi. from the trailhead. The summit of Mt. Juneau lies 3 mi. farther along the ridge and, again, offers terrific views. The shorter, steeper **Mt. Juneau Trail,** which departs from Perseverance Trail about 1 mi. from the trailhead, opens up to similar vistas. Many trails are well-maintained and excellent for mountain biking. Biking off-road is sometimes prohibited.

Tracy Arm, a mini-fjord near Juneau, is known as "the poor man's Glacier Bay," offering much of the same spectacular beauty and wildlife as the national park at well under half the cost. **Auk Nu Tours,** 76 Egan Dr., is the biggest tour company. (☎800-820-2628. 8hr. $110. Lunch included.) **Juneau Outdoor Center** (☎586-8220), on Douglas Island, and **Alaska Paddle Sports,** 800 6th St. (☎463-5678), provide rental kayaks, pick-ups and drop-offs in Glacier Bay and elsewhere, and **guided kayak tours** in about the same price range as the tour boats. In winter, the **Eaglecrest Ski Area,** on Douglas Island, offers decent alpine skiing. (☎586-5284. $25 per day, ages 12-17 $17, under 12 $12; ski rental $20, children $14.) The Eaglecrest **ski bus** departs from the Baranov Hotel at 8:30am and returns from the slopes at 5pm on winter weekends and holidays. (Round-trip $6.)

GLACIER BAY NATIONAL PARK   ☎907

Glacier Bay was once referred to by explorer Jean François de Galaup de la Perouse as "perhaps the most extraordinary place in the world." Crystal monoliths, broken off from glaciers, float peacefully in fjords, while humpback whales maneuver the maze of the icy blue depths. Glacier Bay National Park encloses nine tidewater glaciers, as well as the **Fairweather Mountains,** the highest coastal range in the world. Charter flights, tours, and cruise ships all probe Glacier Bay, providing close encounters with glaciers, rookeries, whales, and seals. The bay itself is divided into two inlets: the westward **Tarr Inlet** advances as far as the Grand Pacific and Margerie Glaciers, while the eastward **Muir Inlet** ends at the Muir and Riggs Glaciers.

Glacier Bay provides a rare opportunity to see geological and ecological processes radically compressed. A mere two centuries ago, the **Grand Pacific Glacier** covered the entire region under a sheet of ancient ice. Severe earthquakes separated the glacier from its terminal moraine (the silt and debris that insulates advancing ice from the relatively warm surrounding seawater), and the glacier retreated 45 mi. in 150 years—light speed in glacial time. As a result, the uncovered ground is virgin territory, colonized by pioneering vegetation.

Getting to Bartlett Cove, the principal access point to the bay, is relatively easy: a plane or ferry takes visitors to Gustavus, and from there a taxi or shuttle (about $12) goes to **Glacier Bay Lodge** (☎697-2225 or 800-451-5952) and the visitors center, both steps from the cove. The few ways to see the glaciers are expensive. Sightseers take one of a range of packages on a sightseeing cruise boat; backcountry travelers are dropped off by the same ship for their trips. Visitors should contact **Glacier Bay National Park's Superintendant** at P.O. Box 140, Gustavus 99826 (☎697-2230), for assistance in planning a backcountry trip. Glacier Bay is becoming *the* destination for extended kayak trips in the region. The only food available at Bartlett Cove is at the dining room in the lodge, which is rather expensive, so trippers bring provisions with them.

Wilderness camping and hiking are permitted throughout the park, though there are no trails except the two near the lodge, and hiking is very difficult in most of the park because of thick alder brush. Backcountry hiking and kayaking are possible in the Dry Bay area (the northwest corner of the park), as is rafting down the Alsek River. For info on these activities contact the **Yakutat District Office of the National Park Service,** P.O. Box 137, Yakutat, AK 99689 (☎784-3295).

ALASKA

APPENDIX

DISTANCES (MI.) AND TRAVEL TIMES (BY BUS)

	Atlanta	Boston	Chicago	Dallas	D.C.	Denver	L.A.	Miami	N. Orl.	NYC	Phila-delphia	Phoenix	St. Louis	San Fran.	Seattle	Toronto	Vancouver	Montreal
Atlanta		1108	717	783	632	1406	2366	653	474	886	778	1863	560	2492	2699	959	2825	1240
Boston	22hr.		996	1794	442	1990	3017	1533	1542	194	333	2697	1190	3111	3105	555	3242	326
Chicago	14hr.	20hr.		937	715	1023	2047	1237	928	807	767	1791	302	2145	2108	537	2245	537
Dallas	15hr.	35hr.	18hr.		1326	794	1450	1322	507	1576	1459	906	629	1740	2112	1457	2255	1763
D.C.	12hr.	8hr.	14hr.	24hr.		1700	2689	1043	1085	225	139	2350	845	2840	2788	526	3292	665
Denver	27hr.	38hr.	20hr.	15hr.	29hr.		1026	2046	1341	1785	1759	790	860	1267	1313	1508	1458	1864
L.A.	45hr.	57hr.	39hr.	28hr.	55hr.	20hr.		2780	2005	2787	2723	371	1837	384	1141	2404	1285	2888
Miami	13hr.	30hr.	24hr.	26hr.	20hr.	39hr.	53hr.		856	1346	1214	2368	1197	3086	3368	1564	3505	1676
New O.	9hr.	31hr.	18hr.	10hr.	21hr.	26hr.	38hr.	17hr.		1332	1247	1535	677	2331	2639	1320	2561	1654
NYC	18hr.	4hr.	16hr.	31hr.	5hr.	35hr.	53hr.	26hr.	27hr.		104	2592	999	2923	2912	496	3085	386
Phila.	18hr.	6hr.	16hr.	19hr.	3hr.	33hr.	50hr.	23hr.	23hr.	2hr.		2511	904	2883	2872	503	3009	465
Phoenix	40hr.	49hr.	39hr.	19hr.	43hr.	17hr.	8hr.	47hr.	30hr.	45hr.	44hr.		1503	753	1510	2069	1654	2638
St. Louis	11hr.	23hr.	6hr.	13hr.	15hr.	17hr.	35hr.	23hr.	13hr.	19hr.	16hr.	32hr.		2113	2139	810	2276	1128
San Fran.	47hr.	60hr.	41hr.	47hr.	60hr.	33hr.	7hr.	59hr.	43hr.	56hr.	54hr.	15hr.	45hr.		807	2630	951	2985
Seattle	52hr.	59hr.	40hr.	40hr.	54hr.	25hr.	22hr.	65hr.	50hr.	55hr.	54hr.	28hr.	36hr.	16hr.		2623	146	2964
Toronto	21hr.	11hr.	10hr.	26hr.	11hr.	26hr.	48hr.	29hr.	13hr.	11hr.	13hr.	48hr.	14hr.	49hr.	48hr.		4563	655
Vancvr.	54hr.	61hr.	42hr.	43hr.	60hr.	27hr.	24hr.	67hr.	54hr.	57hr.	56hr.	30hr.	38hr.	18hr.	2hr.	53hr.		4861
Montreal	23hr.	6hr.	17hr.	28hr.	12hr.	39hr.	53hr.	32hr.	31hr.	7hr.	9hr.	53hr.	23hr.	56hr.	55hr.	7hr.	55hr.	

ABOUT LET'S GO

FORTY-ONE YEARS OF WISDOM

As a new millennium arrives, *Let's Go: Europe*, now in its 41st edition and translated into seven languages, reigns as the world's bestselling international travel guide. For over four decades, travelers criss-crossing the Continent have relied on *Let's Go* for inside information on the hippest backstreet cafes, the most pristine secluded beaches, and the best routes from border to border. In the last 20 years, our rugged researchers have stretched the frontiers of backpacking and expanded our coverage into Asia, Africa, Australia, and the Americas. This year, we've introduced a new city guide series with books on San Francisco and our hometown, Boston. Now, our seven city guides feature sharp photos, more maps, and an overall more user-friendly design. We've also returned to our roots with the inaugural edition of *Let's Go: Western Europe*.

It all started in 1960 when a handful of well-traveled students at Harvard University handed out a 20-page mimeographed pamphlet offering a collection of their tips on budget travel to passengers on student charter flights to Europe. The following year, in response to the instant popularity of the first volume, students traveling to Europe researched the first full-fledged edition of *Let's Go: Europe*, a pocket-sized book featuring honest, practical advice, witty writing, and a decidedly youthful slant on the world. Throughout the 60s and 70s, our guides reflected the times. In 1969 we taught travelers how to get from Paris to Prague on "no dollars a day" by singing in the street. In the 80s and 90s, we looked beyond Europe and North America and set off to all corners of the earth. Meanwhile, we focused in on the world's most exciting urban areas to produce in-depth, fold-out map guides. Our new guides bring the total number of titles to 51, each infused with the spirit of adventure and voice of opinion that travelers around the world have come to count on. But some things never change: our guides are still researched, written, and produced entirely by students who know first-hand how to see the world on the cheap.

HOW WE DO IT

Each guide is completely revised and thoroughly updated every year by a well-traveled set of nearly 300 students. Every spring, we recruit over 200 researchers and 90 editors to overhaul every book. After several months of training, researcher-writers hit the road for seven weeks of exploration, from Anchorage to Adelaide, Estonia to El Salvador, Iceland to Indonesia. Hired for their rare combination of budget travel sense, writing ability, stamina, and courage, these adventurous travelers know that train strikes, stolen luggage, food poisoning, and marriage proposals are all part of a day's work. Back at our offices, editors work from spring to fall, massaging copy written on Himalayan bus rides into witty, informative prose. A student staff of typesetters, cartographers, publicists, and managers keeps our lively team together. In September, the collected efforts of the summer are delivered to our printer, who turns them into books in record time, so that you have the most up-to-date information available for your vacation. Even as you read this, work on next year's editions is well underway.

WHY WE DO IT

We don't think of budget travel as the last recourse of the destitute; we believe that it's the only way to travel. Living cheaply and simply brings you closer to the people and places you've been saving up to visit. Our books will ease your anxieties and answer your questions about the basics—so you can get off the beaten track and explore. Once you learn the ropes, we encourage you to put *Let's Go* down now and then to strike out on your own. You know as well as we that the best discoveries are often those you make yourself. When you find something worth sharing, please drop us a line. We're Let's Go Publications, 67 Mount Auburn St., Cambridge, MA 02138, USA (email: feedback@letsgo.com). For more info, visit our website, www.letsgo.com.

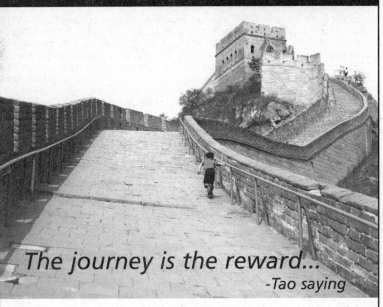
APPENDIX

INDEX

INDEX

A

Acadia National Park, ME
 93
Acadiana, LA 418
accommodations 49
Adirondacks, NY 245
adventure trips 57
airlines 67
Alabama 390–397
 Birmingham 393
 Mobile 396
 Montgomery 390
Alaska 943–955
 Anchorage 944
 Denali National Park and
  Preserve 948
 Fairbanks 950
 Glacier Bay National
  Park 955
 Juneau 953
 Ketchikan 952
 Seward and Kenai Fjords
  947
 Wrangell-St. Elias
  National Park 947
Alaska Highway 932
Albany, NY 237
Alberta 936–942
 Alberta Badlands 942
 Banff National Park 936
 Calgary 940
 Jasper National Park 939
Alberta Badlands, AB 942
Albuquerque, NM 766
alcohol 44
Alexandria, VA 301
alternatives to tourism 84
Amarillo, TX 617
Amherst College, see
 Amherst, MA
Amherst, MA 142

Amtrak 73
Anaheim, CA, see Orange
 County, CA
Anchorage, AK 944
Andersonville National
 Historic Site, GA 386
Ann Arbor, MI 482
Annapolis, MD 282
Antietam, WV 324
Apostle Islands, WI 526
Appalachian State
 University, see Boone, NC
Appalachian Trail 94, 98,
 142, 319, 321, 323, 346
Arches National Park, UT
 717
architecture 25
Arizona 727–759
 Bisbee 758
 Flagstaff 734
 Grand Canyon 727
 Havasupai 733
 Jerome 741
 Lake Powell and Page
  746
 Navajo Reservation 741
 Petrified Forest and
  Painted Desert 745
 Phoenix 747
 Sedona 739
 Tombstone 757
 Tucson 752
Arkansas 420–425
 Hot Springs 422
 Little Rock 420
 Mountain View 424
Arlington National
 Cemetery, VA 301
art 23
Asheville, NC 362
Ashland, OR 916
Aspen, CO 684

Assateague Island, VA 285
Astoria, OR 910
Athens, GA 384
Atlanta, GA 376
Atlantic City, NJ 250
ATMs 40
Austin, TX 598
auto transport companies
 79
automobile clubs 77
Avenue of the Giants, CA
 859

B

Badlands, SD 550
Baltimore, MD 277
Bandelier National
 Monument, NM 764
Banff National Park, AB
 936
Bardstown, KY 333
bargaining 41
Baseball Hall of Fame, NY
 239
Basketball Hall of Fame,
 MA 143
Baton Rouge, LA 415
Beaufort, SC 371
bed and breakfasts 53
Bellingham, WA 891
Bend, OR 917
Berea, KY 336
Berkeley, CA 845
Berkshires, MA 139
Beverly Hills, CA 793
bicycles 79
Big Bear, CA 804

Big Bend, TX 620
Big Sur, CA 821
Bighorn Mountains, WY 662
Billings, MT 631
Biosphere 2, AZ 757
Birmingham, AL 393
Bisbee, AZ 758
bisexual travelers 81
Bismarck, ND 545
Black Canyon, CO 691
Black Hills National Forests, SD 553
Black Hills Region, SD 553–558
Block Island, RI 147
Bloomington, IN 497
Blowing Rock, NC 361
Blue Ridge Parkway, VA 320
Boise, ID 624
Boone, NC 360
Boston, MA 111
Boulder, CO 676
Bowling Green, KY 334
Box-Death Hollow Outstanding Natural Area, UT 722
Bozeman, MT 633
Branson, MO 586
Brattleboro, VT 109
Breckenridge, CO 676
British Columbia 920–932
    Dawson Creek 931
    Pacific Rim National Park 930
    Prince Rupert 930
    Vancouver 920
    Victoria 928
Bronx, NY 223
Brooklyn, NY 221
Brown University, see Providence, RI
Browning, MT 643
Bryce Canyon, UT 721
budgets 41
Buffalo, NY 241
Buffalo, WY 661
Burlington, VT 103
buses 75

C

Cahokia Mounds, IL 580
Calaveras County, CA 862

Calgary, AB 940
California 779–875
    Avenue of the Giants 859
    Berkeley 845
    Big Bear 804
    Big Sur 821
    Calaveras County 862
    Cascades 863
    Coloma 863
    Death Valley 815
    Joshua Tree National Park 813
    Lake Tahoe 863
    Los Angeles 779
    Mammoth Lakes 874
    Marin County 850
    Mendocino 858
    Mono Lake 873
    Monterey 821
    Napa Valley 853
    Oakland 847
    Orange County 802
    Palm Springs 813
    Palo Alto 849
    Redwood National Park 859
    Sacramento 861
    San Diego 805
    San Francisco 825
    San Jose 848
    San Luis Obispo 819
    San Mateo Coast 850
    Santa Barbara 816
    Santa Cruz 823
    Sonoma Valley 856
    Tijuana 811
    Yosemite National Park 868
California Desert 812
Cambridge, MA 125
Camden, ME 94
campers 57
camping 55
camping and the outdoors National Forest info 55
Canada
    Eastern Canada 152–195
    Western Canada 920–942
Cannon Beach, OR 911
Canyon de Chelly, AZ 743
Canyonlands National Park, UT 719
Cape Canaveral, FL 440
Cape Cod, MA 130
Cape May, NJ 253
Capitol Reef National Park, UT 720
Carlsbad Caverns, NM 778
cars 76

    maintenance 77
    rental 78
Cascade Range, WA 897
Cascades, CA 863
cash cards 40
Casper, WY 664
Cassiar Highway 932
Catskill Forest Preserve 236
Catskills, NY 236
Cave of the Winds, CO 690
Cedar Breaks National Monument, UT 725
Chaco Culture National Historic Park, NM 772
Champlain Valley, VT 105
Chapel Hill, NC, see Research Triangle, NC
Charlemont, MA 140
Charleston, SC 368
Charlotte, NC 358
Charlottesville, VA 315
Chattanooga, TN 347
Cherokee Reservation, TN 346
Cheyenne, WY 664
Chicago, IL 499
Chickamauga Creek, TN 348
children 83
Chillicothe, OH 473
Chincoteague Island, VA 285
Chippewa National Forest, MN 538
Chiricahua National Monument, AZ 759
Chisolm, MN 539
Cincinnati, OH 473
civil rights 13
    sights 380, 391, 392, 394
Civil War 10
    sights 117, 135, 268, 305, 308, 323, 324, 348, 355, 373, 382, 386, 389, 392, 400, 412
Clearwater, FL 459
Cleveland, OH 467
climate 32
Cocoa Beach, FL 440
Cody, WY 660
College of William and Mary, see Williamsburg, VA
Coloma, CA 863
Colorado 668–699
    Aspen 684
    Black Canyon 691
    Boulder 676
    Colorado National

Monument 687
Colorado Springs 688
Crested Butte 692
Denver 669
Durango 695
Glenwood Springs 686
Grand Junction 687
Great Sand Dunes 690
Mesa Verde 698
Rocky Mountain National
 Park 680
Telluride 693
Vail 683
Colorado National
 Monument, CO 687
Colorado Springs, CO 688
Columbia River Gorge, OR
 909
Columbia University, see
 New York City, NY
Columbia, SC 371
Columbus, OH 471
Concord, MA 128
Coney Island, NY 222
Connecticut 148–151
 Hartford 148
 Mystic and the
  Connecticut Coast 151
 New Haven 149
consulates 32
Conway, NH 101
Cooperstown, NY 238
Cornell University, see
 Ithaca, NY
Corpus Christi, TX 615
Crater Lake, OR 915
Craters of the Moon, ID 630
Crazy Horse Memorial, SD
 555
credit cards 40
Crested Butte, CO 692
Cumberland Gap, KY 338
Cumberland Island, GA 387
currency 37
current events 15
Custer State Park, SD 556
customs 36
Cuyahoga National
 Recreation Area, OH 471

D

Dalhousie University, see
 Halifax, NS
Dallas, TX 603

Daniel Boone National
 Forest, KY 337
Dawson Creek, BC 931
Daytona Beach, FL 430
Deadwood, SD 558
Death Valley, CA 815
Delaware 274–277
 Lewes 275
 Rehoboth Beach 276
Denali National Park and
 Preserve, AK 948
Denver, CO 669
Des Moines, IA 560
Detroit, MI 477
Devils Tower, WY 663
dietary concerns 83
Dinosaur National
 Monument, UT 713
disabled travelers 82
Disney World, FL 435
Disneyland, CA 803
Dodge City, KS 573
Dollywood, TN 347
Door County, WI 524
dorms 53
driving permits 76
drugs 44
Duke University, see
 Durham, NC
Duluth, MN 536
Durango, CO 695
Durham, NC, see Research
 Triangle, NC

E

Eastham, MA 133
Effigy Mounds, IA 524
El Malpais National
 Monument, NM 773
El Morro National
 Monument, NM 773
El Paso, TX 619
election 2000 15
embassies 32
emergency 42
Endless Caverns, VA 320
entrance requirements 34
environmentally responsible
 tourism 59
Epcot Center, FL 436
Escondido, CA 811
Eugene, OR 913

Everglades, FL 450
exchange rates 37

F

Fairbanks, AK 950
Fargo, ND 544
Festivals 31
 Albuquerque, NM 771
 Ann Arbor, MI 484
 Apostle Islands, WI 528
 Ashland, OR 916
 Aspen, CO 685
 Baltimore, MD 282
 Beaufort, SC 371
 Bellingham, WA 891
 Boise, ID 626
 Boston, MA 119, 120
 Boulder, CO 679
 Burlington, VT 105
 Calaveras County, CA 862
 Calgary, AB 941
 Casper, WY 664
 Charlottesville, VA 317
 Chattanooga, TN 348
 Cheyenne, WY 665
 Chicago, IL 508, 513
 Dallas, TX 606
 Daytona Beach, FL 431
 Denver, CO 674
 Des Moines, IA 562
 Detroit, MI 482
 Durango, CO 697
 Eugene, OR 914
 Fairbanks, AK 951
 Fargo, ND 544
 Flagstaff, AZ 736
 Halifax, NS 157
 Helena, AR 355
 Houston, TX 613
 Indianapolis, IN 497
 Jackson, WY 659
 Kansas City, MO 585
 Key West, FL 455
 Lafayette, LA 419
 Laramie, WY 668
 Lenox, MA 141
 Lincoln, NE 570
 Los Angeles, CA 801
 Louisville, KY 332, 333
 Memphis, TN 350, 355
 Milwaukee, WI 519
 Minneapolis and St. Paul,
  MN 535
 Missoula, MT 638
 Montana 633
 Montgomery, AL 392

Montréal, PQ 171, 173
Mountain View, AR 424
Natchitoches, LA 417
New Haven, CT 150
New York City, NY 228
Newport, RI 147
Oklahoma City, OK 590
Omaha, NE 568
Ottawa, ON 195
Pella, IA 562
Portland, ME 90
Portland, OR 907
Red Lodge, MT 635
San Antonio, TX 596
San Francisco, CA 843
San Juan Island, WA 892
Santa Fe, NM 764
Savannah, GA 389
Seattle, WA 888
Sonoma Valley, CA 858
Stockbridge, MA 142
Stratford, ON 190
Tampa, FL 458
Telluride, CO 694
Toronto, ON 188
Traverse City, MI 488
Tulsa, OK 588
Vancouver, BC 927
film 20
Finger Lakes, NY 240
Fire Island, NY 235
Flagstaff, AZ 734
Flaming Gorge, UT 714
Florida 426–465
Cocoa Beach and Cape
Canaveral 440
Daytona Beach 430
Everglades 450
Fort Lauderdale 441
Gainesville 461
Key Largo 452
Key West 453
Miami 444
Orlando 432
Panama City 463
Pensacola 464
St. Augustine 426
St. Petersburg and
Clearwater 459
Tampa 456
Florida Keys, FL 452–456
food 27
Football Hall of Fame, OH
470
Forests, see National
Forests
Fort Knox, KY 332
Fort Lauderdale, FL 441
Fort Worth, TX 608

Franconia Notch, NH 99
Fredericksburg, VA 306
Freeport, ME 94
Fundy National Park, NB 159

G

Gainesville, FL 461
Gallup, NM 772
Galveston Island, TX 614
gambling
Arizona 740
Louisiana 410
Michigan 481
Mississippi 399
Missouri 579
Nevada 704, 707
New Jersey 252
South Dakota 558
Tennessee 346
gay pride celebrations
Los Angeles, CA 793
San Francisco, CA 843
Toronto, ON 188
gay travelers 81
Georgetown University, see
Washington, D.C.
Georgia 375–390
Andersonville National
Historic Site 386
Athens 384
Atlanta 376
Helen 383
Okefenokee Swamp 386
Savannah 387
Gettysburg, PA 268
Gila Cliff Dwellings, NM 774
Glacier Bay National Park,
AK 955
Glacier National Park, MT
639
Glenwood Springs, CO 686
Golden Access Passport 55
Golden Age Passport 55
government 16
Grand Canyon, AZ 727
Grand Haven, MI 486
Grand Junction, CO 687
Grand Marais, MN 541
Grand Rapids, MI 484
Grand Staircase Escalante
National Monument, UT
723
Grand Strand, SC 373
Grand Teton National Park,

WY 654
Grayboxes
"Christ, we're in love..."
563
A horse of a different color
439
A pig primer 371
Abbey's Road 720
All lit up 218
All you need is a dream
688
Aquammodations 353
Baraboo's Bizarre 523
Before you die, read this
411
Better homes and gardens
389
Big Texan women 618
Boise's Basque
background 626
Boom. 157
Brains don't mean shit 455
Bridge o' love 311
Carhenge or bust 571
Cheap seats 229
City in a bubble 737
Convoluted conventions of
a caffeine-crazed culture
883
Damned if they ain't flew!
365
Dave Thomas, American
beefcake 472
Deep impact 738
Deer season 492
Federal wolf packs 653
Feeling crabby? 293
Field of Dreams 564
Fornicating falcons 119
Four corners 698
Geographic center of the
US 572
Gimme some skin 413
Ground zero 690
Have you dug wall drug?
552
Hershey's candyland 269
Hip-Hop (R)evolution 223
Homestead Graysbox 273
How many words can you
make from
"Schlitterbahn?" 597
I-94, road of concrete
wonders 545
Is the force with you? 741
Let's mush 946
Living the jai life 443
Mail call 451
Mountains of fun 347
Naw, that looks like a...
666

Nice to meet you 274
Nuts to you 638
Off to a pig pickin' 358
Pannin' fer goald 862
Pie in your eye 267
Pop quiz, hotshot 884
Pow wow 527
Shakespeare in the park 633
Shop 'til you drop 534
Smarty pants 317
Smoked meat on rye 169
So, you wanna be in pictures? 797
Stuff 770
Tasting 101 855
Tealightful treats 678
The Appalachian Trail 94
The Paramount King Beast 476
The real story on the real thing 380
The rock of ages it isn't 367
The secret of life 373
The Selma to Montgomery march 391
The Sun Valley Also Rises 628
The wild bunch 713
This box is plane boring 949
Touring the burger kingdom 788
Trail of Tears 589
Victory cigar 324
We're dying to get in 612
What's that smell? 573
Where have all the hippies gone? 601
Whiskey business 334
Your chariot awaits... 189
Great Depression 11
Great Sand Dunes, CO 690
Great Smoky Mountains National Park, TN 345
Greyhound 75
Greyhound Canada 76
Guadalupe Mountains,TX 618

H

Haines Falls, NY 237
Halifax, NS 155
Hannibal, MO 580
Harlem, NY 220

Harpers Ferry, WV 322
Harrodsburg, KY 337
Hartford, CT 148
Harvard University, see Cambridge, MA
Havasupai Reservation, AZ 733
health 44
  environmental hazards 45
  precautions 45
  preventing disease 46
Hearst Castle, CA 820
Helen, GA 383
Helena, MT 632
Hells Canyon, OR 918
Hemingway, Ernest 453, 455, 490, 626, 627, 628, 650
Hershey, PA 269
Hibbing, MN 539
Historic Sites, see National Historic Sites
history
  Canada 28
  US 7
hitchhiking 80
holidays 31
Holland, MI 486
Hollywood, CA 790
home exchanges and rentals 53
Hoover Dam, NV 705
Hopewell Culture National Historic Park, OH 473
Hopi Reservation, AZ 744
Hostels 51
  Albuquerque, NM 768
  Anchorage, AK 945
  Ashland, OR 917
  Astoria, OR 911
  Austin, TX 600
  Baltimore, MD 280
  Banff National Park, AB 936
  Bellingham, WA 891
  Bend, OR 917
  Bisbee, AZ 758
  Blue Ridge Parkway, VA 321
  Boise, ID 624
  Boston, MA 112
  Boulder, CO 677
  Bozeman, MT 634
  Brattleboro, VT 109
  Breckenridge, CO 676
  Bryce Canyon, UT 722
  Buffalo, NY 242
  Burlington, VT 104
  Calgary, AB 941

Canyon de Chelly, NM 743
Capitol Reef, UT 721
Cascades, CA 863
Chaco Canyon, NM 773
Charlottetown, PEI 161
Chicago, IL 503
Chippewa National Forest, MN 538
Clearwater, FL 460
Columbia River Gorge, OR 910
Columbus, OH 472
Concord, MA 129
Conway, NH 101
Corpus Christi, TX 615
Crested Butte, CO 692
Cuyahoga National Recreation Area, OH 471
Deadwood, SD 558
Denali National Park and Preserve, AK 949
Denver, CO 670
Detroit, MI 478
Durango, CO 696
Eastham, MA 133
El Paso, TX 619
Eugene, OR 914
Everglades, FL 450
Fairbanks, AK 951
Fort Lauderdale, FL 442
Fundy National Park, NB 159
Gettysburg, PA 268
Glacier National Park, MT 640
Glenwood Springs, CO 686
Grand Junction, CO 687
Grand Marais, MN 541
Halifax, NS 156
Harpers Ferry, WV 323
Hartford, CT 148
Houston, TX 610
Jackson, WY 658
Jasper National Park, AB 939
Juneau, AK 954
Ketchikan, AK 952
Key West, FL 454
Lake Placid, NY 247
Lake Tahoe, CA 865
Las Vegas, NV 704
Lincoln, NE 569
Los Angeles, CA 784
Madison, WI 521
Marin County, CA 851
Martha's Vineyard, MA 137
Miami, FL 447
Milwaukee, WI 517
Minneapolis and St. Paul, MI 530
Moab, UT 716

Monterey, CA 822
Montréal, PQ 167
Mt. Desert Island, ME 92
Mt. Rainier National Park, WA 899
Nantucket, MA 138
New Orleans, LA 406
New York City, NY 203
Niagara Falls, NY and ON 243
North Conway, NH 101
Ocean City, MD 287
Ohiopyle State Park, PA 274
Olympia, WA 890
Olympic National Park, WA 894
Orange County, CA 802
Orcas Island, WA 892
Orlando, FL 434
Ottawa, ON 192
Outer Banks, NC 365
Pacific Rim National Park, BC 930
Palo Alto, CA 850
Philadelphia, PA 258
Phoenix, AZ 748
Pine Hill, NY 237
Pittsburgh, PA 271
Plymouth, MA 130
Port Townsend, WA 893
Portland, OR 904
Provincetown, MA 134
Québec City, PQ 175
Rapid City, IA 553
Redwood National Park, CA 860
Rocky Mountain National Park, CO 681
Sacramento, CA 861
Saint John, NB 158
Salt Lake City, UT 709
San Antonio, TX 594
San Diego, CA 807
San Francisco, CA 828
San Jose, CA 849
San Mateo Coast, CA 850
Santa Barbara, CA 818
Santa Cruz, CA 824
Santa Fe, NM 761
Sault Ste. Marie, ON 492
Savannah, GA 388
Searsport, ME 95
Seattle, WA 881
Seward, AK 947
Shenandoah National Park, VA 318
Silver City, NM 775
South Bay, CA 801
St. Augustine, FL 428
St. Ignatius, MT 638

St. Louis, MO 576
Stowe, VT 107
Summit County, CO 676
Taos, NM 765
Thousand Island Seaway, NY 249
Toronto, ON 184
Truro, MA 134
Truth or Consequences, NM 774
Tucson, AZ 754
Vancouver, BC 923
Vashon Island, WA 889
Victoria, BC 928
Virginia Beach, VA 313
Washington, D.C. 290
Waterton Lakes National Park, AB 644
Whistler, BC 928
White Mountains, NH 98
White River Junction, VT 109
White Sands, NM 776
Whitefish, MT 642
Wrangell-St. Elias National Park, AK 948
Yellowstone National Park, WY 649
Yosemite National Park, CA 870
Zion National Park, UT 724
Hot Springs, AR 422
hotels 49
Houston, TX 609
Hovenweep National Monument, UT 726
Hunter Mt., NY 237
Huntsville, AL 395
Hyannis, MA 132

I

Idaho 623–630
  Boise 624
  Craters of the Moon 630
  Ketchum and Sun Valley 626
  Sawtooth 628
identification 36
Iditarod Trail 946
Illinois 499–516
  Chicago 499
  Springfield 515
immunizations 45
Independence, MO 585
Indian, see Native American

Indiana 495–498
  Bloomington 497
  Indianapolis 495
Indianapolis, IN 495
insurance 47
International Student Identity Card (ISIC) 36
interstates 78
Iowa 559–565
  Des Moines 560
  Iowa City 563
  Spirit Lake and Okoboji 565
Iowa City, IA 563
Iron Range, MN 539
Isle Royale National Park, MI 494
Ithaca, NY 240

J

Jackson, MS 398
Jackson, WY 657
Jamestown, VA 311
Jasper National Park, AB 939
Jerome, AZ 741
Jewel Cave, SD 556
Joshua Tree National Park, CA 813
journalism 26
Juneau, AK 953

K

Kansas 571–573
  Dodge City 573
  Wichita 572
Kansas City, MO 581
Kenai Fjords National Park, AK 947
Kennebunk, ME 90
Kennebunkport, ME 90
Kentucky 330–339
  Cumberland Gap 338
  Daniel Boone National Forest 337
  Lexington 334
  Louisville 331
Ketchikan, AK 952
Ketchum, ID 626
Keweenaw Peninsula, MI 493

Key Largo, FL 452
Key West, FL 453
Klamath Falls, OR 915
Kluane National Park, YT 934
Knoxville, TN 343
Kouchibouguac National Park, NB 160

L

La Jolla, CA 811
Labor Day 31
Lafayette, LA 418
Lahave, NS 154
Lake Champlain, VT 105
Lake Mead, NV 705
Lake Michigan Shore, MI 485
Lake Placid, NY 247
Lake Powell, AZ 746
Lake Tahoe, CA 863
Lakeshores, see National Lakeshores
Lancaster County, PA 266
Laramie, WY 667
Las Vegas, NV 702
Lead, SD 557
Lebanon, KS 572
Lenox, MA 141
lesbian travelers 81
Lewes, DE 275
Lexington, KY 334
Lincoln, NE 568
literature 16
Little Big Horn, MT 632
Little Rock, AR 420
Long Island, NY 234
Lopez Island, WA 893
Los Alamos, NM 764
Los Angeles, CA 779
Louisiana 402–420
  Baton Rouge 415
  Lafayette 418
  Natchitoches 416
  New Iberia 419
  New Orleans 403
Louisiana State University, see Baton Rouge, LA
Louisville, KY 331
Lunenberg, NS 154
Luray Caverns, VA 320

M

Mackinac, MI 489
Madeline Island, WI 528
Madison, WI 521
Mahone Bay, NS 154
mail 61
Maine 86–95
  Acadia 93
  Camden 94
  Freeport 94
  Mt. Desert Island 91
  Portland 88
  Searsport 95
Malibu, CA 792
Mammoth Cave National Park, KY 333
Mammoth Lakes, CA 874
Manistee, MI 487
Marin County, CA 850
Martha's Vineyard, MA 136
Mary Washington College, see Fredericksburg, VA
Maryland 277–287
  Annapolis 282
  Assateague and Chincoteague Islands, VA 285
  Baltimore 277
  Ocean City 286
Massachusetts 110–143
  Berkshires 139
  Boston 111
  Cambridge 125
  Cape Cod 130
  Lexington and Concord 128
  Martha's Vineyard 136
  Nantucket 138
  Pioneer Valley 142
  Plymouth 129
  Provincetown 134
  Salem 128
Massachusetts Institute of Technology (MIT), see Cambridge, MA
McGill University, see Montréal, PQ
media 25
Memorial Day 31
Memorials
  Civil Rights Memorial, AL 391
  Crazy Horse Memorial, SD 555
  Fort Clatsop National Memorial, OR 911
  Franklin Delano Roosevelt

Memorial, D.C. 295
Hemingway Memorial, ID 628
Holocaust Memorial, FL 449
Holocaust Memorial, MA 118
Jefferson Memorial, D.C. 295
Korean War Memorial, D.C. 295
Lincoln Memorial, D.C. 295
Mt. Rushmore National Memorial, SD 554
National War Memorial, ON 194
Oklahoma City National Memorial, OK 590
Robert Gould Shaw and 54th Regiment Memorial, MA 117
Vietnam Veterans Memorial, D.C. 295
Witch Trials Memorial, MA 128
Wright Brothers National Memorial, NC 366
Memphis, TN 349
Mendocino, CA 858
Mesa Verde National Park, CO 698
Miami, FL 444
Michigan 477–494
  Ann Arbor 482
  Detroit 477
  Grand Rapids 484
  Isle Royale National Park 494
  Lake Michigan Shore 485
  Upper Peninsula 491
Middlebury College, see Middlebury, VT
Middlebury, VT 106
mileage chart 956
Milwaukee, WI 516
Minneapolis and St. Paul, MN 529
Minnesota 528–541
  Chippewa National Forest 538
  Duluth 536
  Grand Marais 541
  Iron Range 539
  Minneapolis and St. Paul 529
  Voyageurs National Park 540
minority travelers 83

Mississippi 397–402
  Jackson 398
  Natchez 400
  Oxford 401
  Vicksburg 399
Mississippi Delta 355
Missoula, MT 636
Missouri 574–586
  Branson 586
  Kansas City 581
  St. Louis 574
Misty Fiords, AK 953
Moab, UT 716
Mobile, AL 396
Mohawk Trail, MA 140
money 37
money wiring 40
Mono Lake, CA 873
Monongahela National
  Forest, WV 326
Montana 631–644
  Billings 631
  Bozeman 633
  Glacier National Park 639
  Helena 632
  Little Big Horn 632
  Missoula 636
  Red Lodge 635
Monterey, CA 821
Montezuma Castle National
  Monument, AZ 740
Montgomery, AL 390
Montréal, PQ 163
Monument Valley, AZ 744
Monuments, see National
  Monuments
motorcycles 79
Moundville, AL 395
Mount Hood, OR 908
Mount Rainier National Park,
  WA 898
Mount St. Helens, WA 897
Mountain View, AR 424
Mt. Desert Island, ME 91
Mt. Greylock, MA 140
Mt. McKinley, AK 948
Mt. Rushmore, SD 554
Mt. Tremper, NY 236
Mt. Vernon, VA 302
Mt. Washington, NH 99
music 19
Myrtle Beach, SC 373
Mystic, CT 151

N

Nantucket, MA 138
Napa Valley, CA 853
Nashville, TN 339
Natchez, MS 400
Natchitoches, LA 416
National Forest info 55
National Forests
  Bighorn, WY 662
  Black Hills, SD 553
  Chippewa, MN 538
  Daniel Boone, KY 337
  Monongahela, WV 326
  Stanislaus, CA 873
  White Mountains, NH 97
National Historic Sites
  Andersonville, GA 386
  Cave and Basin, AB 938
  Chaco Canyon, NM 772
  Cumberland Gap, KY 338
  Fort Raleigh, NC 367
  Fort Sumter, SC 370
  Gettysburg National
    Cemetery, PA 268
  Halifax Citadel National
    Historic Park, NS 156
  Herbert Hoover, IA 564
  Hopewell Culture National
    Historic Park, OH 473
  Independence National
    Historical Park, PA 260
  Klondike Gold Rush
    National Historic Park,
    WA 884
  Knife River Indian Villages,
    ND 547
  Longfellow House, MA 127
  Minuteman National
    Historic Park, MA 129
  Pecos National Historical
    Park, NM 764
  Salem Maritime, MA 128
  San Antonio Missions
    National Historical Park,
    TX 595
  San Juan National Historic
    Park, WA 892
  Shiloh, TN 355
  Trail of Tears National
    Historic Trail 589
  Valley Forge National
    Historic Park, PA 265
  Vicksburg, MI 400
National Lakeshores
  Apostle Islands, WI 526
  Indiana Dunes, IL 515
  Pictured Rocks, MI 493
  Sleeping Bear Dunes, MI

National Monuments
  Bandelier, NM 764
  Black Canyon of the
    Gunnison, CO 691
  Canyon de Chelly, AZ 743
  Castillo de San Marcos, FL
    429
  Cedar Breaks, UT 725
  Chiricahua, AZ 759
  Colorado, CO 687
  Craters of the Moon, ID
    630
  Devil's Postpile, CA 874
  Devils Tower, WY 663
  Dinosaur, UT 713
  Effigy Mounds, IA 524
  El Malpais, NM 773
  El Morro, NM 773
  Fort McHenry, MD 281
  Fort Pulaski, SC 389
  Gila Cliff Dwellings, NM
    774
  Grand Staircase
    Escalante, UT 723
  Great Sand Dunes, CO 690
  Hovenweep, UT 726
  Jewel Cave, SD 556
  Little Big Horn, MT 632
  Misty Fiords, AK 953
  Montezuma Castle, AZ 740
  Mt. St. Helens National
    Volcanic Monument, WA
    897
  Muir Woods, CA 852
  Natural Bridges, UT 725
  Navajo, AZ 744
  Petroglyph, NM 771
  Rainbow Bridge, AZ 747
  Scotts Bluff, NE 571
  Sunset Crater Volcano, AZ
    738
  Timpanogos Cave, UT 712
  Tonto, AZ 752
  Tuzigoot, AZ 740
  Walnut Canyon, AZ 738
  White Sands, NM 775
  Wupatki, AZ 739
National Park info
  Golden Access Passport
    55
  Golden Age Passport 55
  in Canada 57
National Parks
  Acadia, ME 93
  Arches, UT 717
  Badlands, SD 550
  Banff, AB 936
  Big Bend, TX 620
  Bryce Canyon, UT 721
  Canyonlands, UT 719

Carlsbad Caverns, NM 778
Crater Lake, OR 915
Death Valley, CA 815
Denali, AK 948
Everglades, FL 450
Fundy, NB 159
Glacier Bay, AK 955
Glacier, MT 639
Grand Canyon, AZ 727
Grand Teton, WY 654
Great Smoky Mountains,
  TN 345
Guadalupe Mountains, TX
  618
Isle Royale, MI 494
Jasper, AB 939
Joshua Tree, CA 813
Kenai Fjords, AK 947
Kluane, YT 934
Kouchibouguac, NB 160
Mammoth Cave, KY 333
Mesa Verde, CO 698
Mount Rainier, WA 898
North Cascades, WA 900
Olympic, WA 894
Pacific Rim, BC 930
Petrified Forest, AZ 745
Prince Edward Island, PEI
  161
Redwood, CA 859
Rocky Mountain, CO 680
Saguaro, AZ 755
Shenandoah, VA 318
Theodore Roosevelt, ND
  547
Voyageurs, MN 540
Waterton Lakes, AB 643
Wind Cave, SD 555
Wrangell-St. Elias, AK 947
Yellowstone, WY 645
Yosemite, CA 868
Zion, UT 723
National Recreation Areas
Cuyahoga, OH 471
Flaming Gorge, UT 714
Golden Gate, CA 833
Hells Canyon, OR 918
Lake Mead, NV 705
Oregon Dunes, OR 912
Rattlesnake Wilderness,
  MT 637
Sawtooth, ID 628
National Seashores
Assateague Island, MD
  286
Canaveral, FL 441
Cape Cod, MA 132
Cape Hatteras, NC 366
Cumberland Island, GA
  387
Fire Island, NY 235

Gulf Island, FL 464
Padre Island, TX 616
Point Reyes, CA 853
National Wildlife Refuges
Chincoteague, MD 286
Great Meadows, MA 129
Merritt Island, FL 441
Missisquoi, VT 105
Okefenokee, GA 386
Pea Island, NC 367
Rachel Carson, ME 90
Native American
Blackfoot Indian
  Reservation, MT 643
Cherokee Nation, OK 588
Cherokee Reservation, TN
  346
Havasupai Reservation
  733
Hopi Reservation, AZ 744
Navajo Reservation, AZ
  741
Natural Bridges National
  Monument, UT 725
Navajo National Monument,
  AZ 744
Navajo Reservation, AZ 741
Nebraska 566–571
Lincoln 568
Omaha 566
Scotts Bluff 571
Nevada 700–707
Las Vegas 702
Reno 706
New Brunswick 157–160
Fundy National Park 159
Saint John 158
New Hampshire 95–99
Franconia Notch 99
North Conway and Conway
  101
Pinkham Notch 99
Portsmouth 95
Ski resorts 96
White Mountains 97
New Haven, CT 149
New Iberia, LA 419
New Jersey 250–??
Atlantic City 250
Cape May 253
New Mexico 759–778
Albuquerque 766
Carlsbad Caverns 778
Gallup 772
Gila Cliff Dwellings 774
Santa Fe 760
Silver City 775
Taos 765
Truth or Consequences 773

White Sands 775
New Orleans, LA 403
New River Gorge, WV 325
New York 196–250
Adirondacks 245
Albany 237
Buffalo 241
Catskills 236
Cooperstown 238
Ithaca and the Finger
  Lakes 240
Lake Placid 247
New York City 198
Niagara Falls 243
Thousand Island Seaway
  248
New York City, NY 198
New York University, see
  New York City, NY
Newport, OR 912
Newport, RI 145
Niagara Falls, NY 243
North Adams, MA 140
North Carolina 355–367
Asheville 362
Boone 360
Charlotte 358
Outer Banks 364
Research Triangle 356
North Carolina State
  University, see Raleigh, NC
North Cascades, WA 900
North Conway, NH 101
North Dakota 542–549
Bismarck 545
Fargo 544
Theodore Roosevelt
  National Park 547
Northhampton, MA 142
Northwestern State
  University, see
  Natchitoches, LA
Nova Scotia 152–157
Atlantic Coast 152
Halifax 155

O

Oakland, CA 847
Ocean City, MD 286
Ogunquit, ME 90
Ohio 466–476
Cincinnati 473
Cleveland 467
Columbus 471

Cuyahoga National
Recreation Area 471
Ohio State University, see
Columbus, OH
Ohiopyle State Park, PA 273
Okefenokee Swamp, GA 386
Oklahoma 586–590
Oklahoma City 589
Tulsa 587
Oklahoma City, OK 589
Okoboji, IA 565
Old Orchard Beach, ME 90
Olympia, WA 889
Olympic National Park, WA
894
Olympic Peninsula, WA 893
Omaha, NE 566
Onation's Niagara
Escarpment, ON 190
Ontario 179–195
Ottawa 190
Toronto 181
Oral Roberts University, see
Tulsa, OK
Orange County, CA 802
Orcas Island, WA 892
Oregon 902–919
Ashland 916
Bend 917
Columbia River Gorge 909
Crater Lake and Klamath
Falls 915
Eugene 913
Hells Canyon and Wallowa
Mountains 918
Mount Hood 908
Oregon Coast 910
Portland 903
Oregon Dunes, OR 912
Orlando, FL 432
Ottawa, ON 190
outdoors 55
Outer Banks, NC 364
Ovens Natural Park, NS 154
Oxford, MS 401

P

Pacific Rim National Park,
BC 930
packing 47
Padre Island, TX 616
Page, AZ 746
Pagosa Springs, CO 697

Painted Desert, AZ 745
Palm Springs, CA 813
Palo Alto, CA 849
Palo Duro Canyon State
Park, TX 618
Panama City, FL 463
Parks, see National Parks
passports 34
Pearl Harbor, HI 12
Pecos National Historic
Park, NM 764
Pella, IA 562
Pennsylvania 254–274
Gettysburg 268
Lancaster County 266
Ohiopyle State Park 273
Philadelphia 255
Pittsburgh 270
Pensacola, FL 464
Petoskey, MI 490
Petrified Forest, AZ 745
Philadephia, PA 255
Phoenicia, NY 237
Phoenix, AZ 747
Pine Hill, NY 237
Pinkham Notch, NH 99
Pioneer Valley, MA 142
Pittsburgh, PA 270
Pittsfield, MA 141
planes 65
Plymouth, MA 129
Port Townsend, WA 893
Portland, ME 88
Portland, OR 903
Portsmouth, NH 95
Prince Edward Island 160–
162
Prince Edward Island
National Park, PEI 161
Prince Rupert, BC 930
Prohibition 11
Providence, RI 143
Provincetown, MA 134
Pullman, IL 509
Pyramid Lake, NV 707

Q

Québec 162–??
Montréal 163
Québec City 173
Québec City. PQ 173
Queens, NY 222

R

Raleigh, NC, see Research
Triangle, NC
Rapid City, SD 552
Recreation Areas, see
National Recreation Areas
Red Lodge, MT 635
Redwood National Park, CA
859
Rehoboth Beach, DE 276
Reno, NV 706
Research Triangle, NC 356
Rhode Island 143–147
Newport 145
Providence 143
Rhode Island School of
Design, see Providence, RI
Richmond, VA 302
Roanoke Island, NC 366
Rocky Mountain National
Park, CO 680
RVs 57

S

Sabino Canyon, AZ 757
Sacramento, CA 861
safety 42
Saint John, NB 158
Salem, MA 128
Salt Lake City, UT 708
San Antonio, TX 592
San Diego, CA 805
San Fernando Valley, CA 796
San Francisco, CA 825
San Jose, CA 848
San Juan Island, WA 892
San Juan Islands, WA 891
San Luis Obispo, CA 819
San Mateo Coast, CA 850
Sandwich, MA 132
Santa Barbara, CA 816
Santa Cruz, CA 823
Santa Fe, NM 760
Santa Monica, CA 791
Sault Ste. Marie, MI 492
Savannah, GA 387
Sawtooth, ID 628
Scenic Drives
Apache Trail, AZ 752
Arkansas 7, AK 423
Blue Ridge Parkway, VA

320
Cades Cove Loop Drive, TN 346
Cape Hatteras National Seashore, NC 367
Centennial Scenic Drive, WY 659
Dempster Highway, YT 935
Going-to-the-Sun Road, MT 642
Great River, IA 564
Icefields Parkway, AB 939
Kentucky Heartland, KY 337
Mt. Lemmon Drive, AZ 757
North Fork Drive, WY 653
North Shore Drive, MN 540
Northern Michigan Shore Drive, MI 490
Ross Lake to Twisp, WA 901
Saskawea, ND 546
Texas Hill Country Drive, TX 596
Scotts Bluff, NE 571
Searsport, ME 95
Seashores, see National Seashores
Seattle, WA 877
security 42
Sedona, AZ 739
Selma, AL 392
senior citizens 81
Seward, AK 947
sexually transmitted diseases 46
Shelburne Falls, MA 140
Shenandoah National Park, VA 318
Sheridan, WY 661
Shiloh National Military Park, TN 355
Sierra Nevada, CA 863
Silver City, NM 775
Sioux Falls, SD 549
skiing
   Alaska 946, 951, 955
   Alberta 938
   Arizona 737
   British Columbia 927
   California 805, 867, 873, 874
   Colorado 675, 684, 685, 686, 693, 696
   Idaho 627
   Montana 634, 637, 642
   New Hampshire 96
   New Mexico 764, 766
   New York 237, 248
   North Carolina 361
   Ohio 471
   Oregon 909
   South Dakota 550, 557
   Utah 711
   Vermont 102
   Virginia 327
   Washington 886
   Wyoming 657, 666
Skyline Caverns, VA 320
slavery 9
Sleeping Bear Dunes, MI 487
Snowy Mountain Range, WY 666
solo travelers 81
Sonoma Valley, CA 856
Soudan, MN 539
South Carolina 368–375
   Charleston 368
   Columbia 371
   Myrtle Beach and the Grand Strand 373
South Dakota 549–558
   Badlands 550
   Crazy Horse Memorial 555
   Custer State Park 556
   Deadwood 558
   Lead 557
   Mt. Rushmore 554
   Rapid City 552
   Sioux Falls 549
   Spearfish 558
   Wind Cave and Jewel Cave 555
Spearfish, SD 558
Spirit Lake, IA 565
Spokane, WA 901
sports 26
Springfield, IL 515
Springfield, MA 143
St. Augustine, FL 426
St. Louis, MO 574
St. Mary's University, see Halifax, NS
St. Paul, MN 529
St. Petersburg, FL 459
Stanford University, see Palo Alto, CA
Stanislaus National Forest, CA 873
Staten Island, NY 224
Stockbridge, MA 141
Stowe, VT 107
Stratford, ON 190
studying abroad 84
Summit County, CO 676
Sun Valley, ID 626
Sunset Crater Volcano National Monument, AZ 738

T

Tahlequah, OK 588
Tampa, FL 456
Taos, NM 765
taxes 42
telephones 63
television 25
Telluride, CO 693
Tennessee 339–355
   Chattanooga 347
   Great Smoky Mountains 345
   Knoxville 343
   Memphis 349
   Nashville 339
Testicle Festival, MT 638
Texas 591–622
   Amarillo 617
   Austin 598
   Big Bend 620
   Corpus Christi 615
   Dallas 603
   El Paso 619
   Galveston Island 614
   Guadalupe Mountains 618
   Houston 609
   Padre Island 616
   Palo Duro Canyon State Park 618
   San Antonio 592
Theodore Roosevelt National Park, ND 547
Thousand Island Seaway, NY 248
Three Capes Loop, OR 911
Tijuana, Mexico 811
Timpanogos Cave, UT 712
tipping 41
Tombstone, AZ 757
Toronto, ON 181
trains 73
transportation 65
travel agencies, budget and student 65
traveler's checks 39
traveling alone 81
Traverse City, MI 488
Truro, MA 134
Truth or Consequences, NM 773

INDEX

Tucson, AZ 752
Tulane University, see New Orleans, LA
Tulsa, OK 587
Tuskegee University, see Tuskegee, AL
Tuskegee, AL 392
Tuzigoot National Monument, AZ 740
Twain, Mark 149, 344, 580, 862, 873

U

University of Alaska, see Fairbanks, AK
University of Arizona, see Phoenix, AZ
University of British Columbia, see Vancouver, BC
University of California, see Berkeley, CA
University of California-Los Angeles, see Los Angeles, CA
University of Colorado, see Boulder, CO
University of Illinois at Chicago, see Chicago, IL
University of Kentucky, see Lexington, KY
University of Massachusetts-Amherst, see Amherst, MA
University of Michigan, see Ann Arbor, MI
University of New Brunswick at Saint John, see Saint John, NB
University of New Mexico, see Albuquerque, NM
University of North Carolina, see Chapel Hill, NC
University of Oregon, see Eugene, OR
University of South Carolina, see Columbia, SC
University of Texas at Austin, see Austin, TX
University of Texas at El Paso, see El Paso, TX
University of Toronto, see Toronto, ON
University of Vermont, see Burlington, VT

University of Virginia, see Charlottesville, VA
University of Washington, see Seattle, WA
University of Wisconsin-Madison, see Madison, WI
University of Wyoming, see Laramie, WY
Upper Peninsula, MI 491
US Naval Academy, see Annapolis, MD
Utah 707–726
Arches 717
Bryce Canyon 721
Canyonlands 719
Capitol Reef 720
Dinosaur National Monument and Vernal 713
Flaming Gorge 714
Hovenweep National Monument 726
Moab 716
Natural Bridges 725
Salt Lake City 708
Zion 723

V

Vail, CO 683
Valley Forge, PA 265
Vancouver Island, BC 928
Vancouver, BC 920
Vashon Island, WA 889
Venice, CA 791
Vermont 102–110
Brattleboro 109
Burlington 103
Middlebury 106
Ski resorts 102
Stowe 107
Vernal, UT 713
Via Rail 75
Vicksburg National Military Park 400
Vicksburg, MS 399
Victoria, BC 928
Virginia 302–322
Charlottesville 315
Fredericksburg 306
Richmond 302
Shenandoah National Park 318
Virginia Beach 312
Williamsburg 309

Virginia Beach, VA 312
visas 35
Voyageurs National Park, MN 540

W

Walden Pond, MA 129
Wall Drug, SD 552
Wall Street, NY 213
Wallowa Mountains, OR 918
Walnut Canyon National Monument, AZ 738
Washington 876–902
Bellingham 891
Mount Rainier National Park 898
Mount St. Helens 897
North Cascades 900
Olympia 889
Olympic National Park 894
Port Townsend 893
San Juan Islands 891
Seattle 877
Spokane 901
Washington, D.C. 287–302
Waterton Lakes National Park, AB 643
Wellfleet, MA 133
West Virginia 322–327
Harpers Ferry 322
Monongahela National Forest 326
New River Gorge 325
Whistler, BC 927
White Hall, KY 336
White Mountains, NH 97
White River Junction, VT 109
White Sands, NM 775
Whitefish, MT 642
Whitehorse, YT 933
Wichita State University, see Wichita, KS
Wichita, KS 572
wilderness safety 57
Wildlife Refuges, see National Wildlife Refuges
Williams College, see Williamstown, MA
Williamsburg, VA 309
Williamstown, MA 141
Wind Cave, SD 555
Window Rock, AZ 742
Wine Country, CA 853

Winter Park, CO 675
Winterset, IA 562
Wisconsin 516–528
  Apostle Islands 526
  Door County 524
  Madison 521
  Milwaukee 516
women travelers 80
Woodstock, NY 236
working abroad 84
Wrangell-St. Elias National
  Park, AK 947
Wupatki National
  Monument, AZ 739
Wyoming 644–668
  Bighorn Mountains 662
  Buffalo and Sheridan 661
  Casper 664
  Cheyenne 664
  Cody 660
  Devils Tower 663
  Grand Teton 654
  Jackson 657
  Laramie 667
  Yellowstone 645

Y

Yale University, see New
  Haven, CT
Yarmouth, NS 154
Yellowstone National Park,
  WY 645
YMCAs 53
Yorkstown, VA 311
Yosemite National Park, CA
  868
Yukon Territory 932–935
  Kluane National Park 934
  Whitehorse 933
YWCAs 53

Z

Zion National Park, UT 723

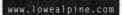

If I had my life to live over again,

I would relax. I would limber up. I would take more chances.

I would take more trips.

I would climb more mountains, swim more rivers, and watch more sunsets.

I would go places and do things and travel lighter than I have.

I would ride more merry-go-rounds.

Excerpt from Nadine Stair, 85 years old / photo> John Norris

technical packs & apparel

Find Yourself. Somewhere Else.

Don't just land there, do something. Away.com is the Internet's preferred address for those who like their travel with a little something extra. Our team of travel enthusiasts and experts can help you design your ultimate adventure, nature or cultural escape. Make Away.com your destination for extraordinary travel. Then find yourself. Somewhere else.

away.com
1.877.769.2929

Will you have enough stories to tell your grandchildren?

Yahoo! Travel

Do You YAHOO!?

L.A. Westside

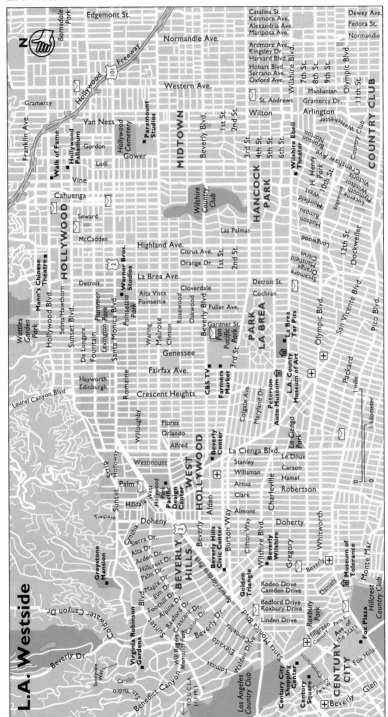

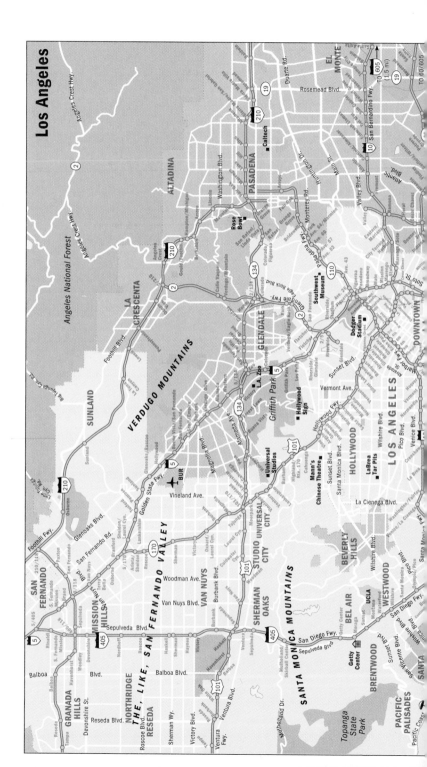

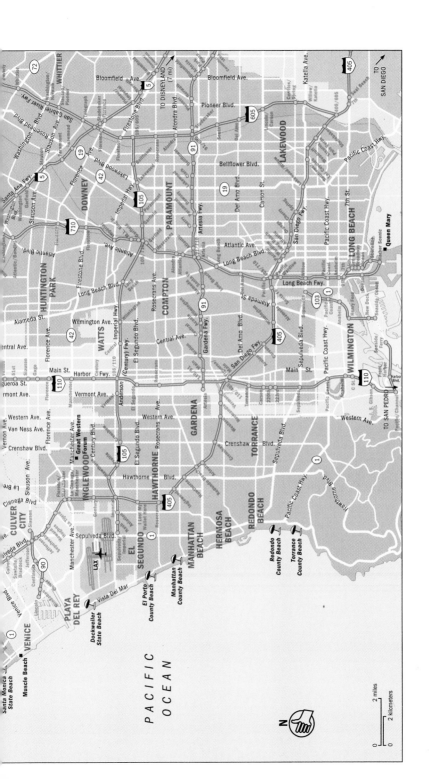

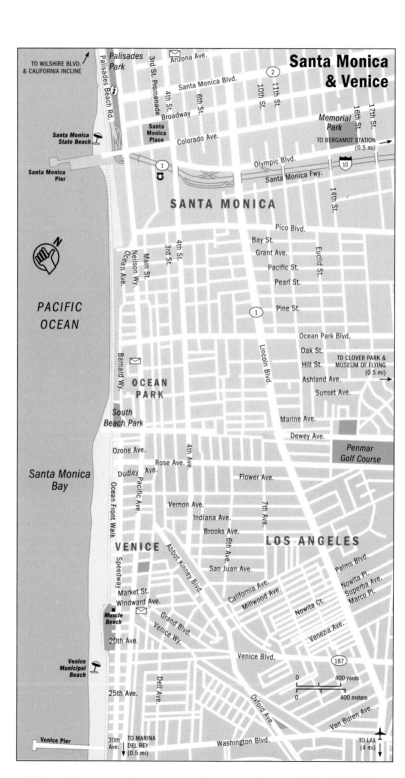

Santa Monica & Venice

TO WILSHIRE BLVD.
& CALIFORNIA INCLINE

Palisades Park

Arizona Ave.

Santa Monica Blvd.

3rd St. Promenade

Palisades Beach Rd.

4th St.

6th St.

Broadway

10th St.

11th St.

Memorial Park

16th St.

17th St.

Santa Monica State Beach

Santa Monica Place

Colorado Ave.

TO BERGAMOT STATION (0.5 mi)

Santa Monica Pier

Olympic Blvd.

Santa Monica Fwy.

14th St.

SANTA MONICA

Pico Blvd.

Bay St.

Grant Ave.

Pacific St.

Euclid St.

4th St.

3rd St.

Main St.

Neilson Wy.

Ocean Ave.

Pearl St.

Pine St.

Ocean Park Blvd.

Oak St.

Hill St.

Ashland Ave.

TO CLOVER PARK & MUSEUM OF FLYING (0.5 mi)

Sunset Ave.

Lincoln Blvd.

PACIFIC OCEAN

Barnard Wy.

OCEAN PARK

South Beach Park

Marine Ave.

Dewey Ave.

Penmar Golf Course

Ozone Ave.

4th Ave.

Rose Ave.

Dudley Ave.

Pacific Ave.

Flower Ave.

Santa Monica Bay

Ocean Front Walk

Vernon Ave.

Indiana Ave.

7th Ave.

Brooks Ave.

6th Ave.

LOS ANGELES

VENICE

Abbot Kinney Blvd.

San Juan Ave.

Speedway

California Ave.

Millwood Ave.

Palms Blvd.

Nowita Pl.

Superba Ave.

Market St.

Nowita Ct.

Marco Pl.

Windward Ave.

Muscle Beach

Grand Blvd.

Venice Wy.

Venezia Ave.

20th Ave.

Venice Municipal Beach

Venice Blvd.

187

Dell Ave.

25th Ave.

0   400 yards
0   400 meters

30th Ave.

Oxford Ave.

Van Buren Ave.

Venice Pier

TO MARINA DEL REY (0.5 mi)

Washington Blvd.

TO LAX (4 mi)

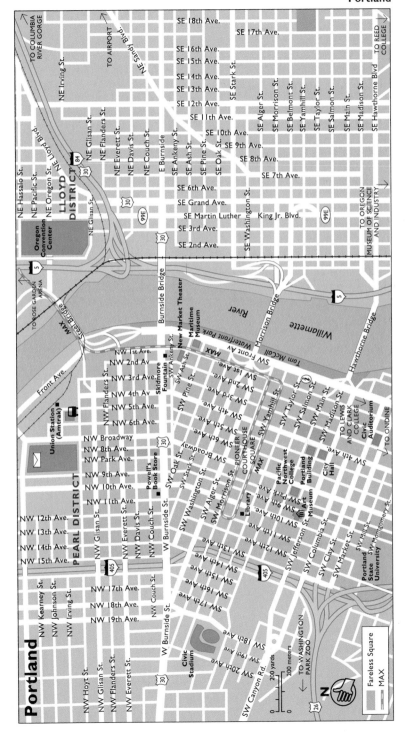

Portland

SE 18th Ave.
SE 17th Ave.
SE 16th Ave.
SE 15th Ave.
SE 14th Ave.
SE 13th Ave.
SE 12th Ave.
SE 11th Ave.
SE 10th Ave.
SE 9th Ave.
SE 8th Ave.
SE 7th Ave.
SE 6th Ave.
SE Grand Ave.
SE Martin Luther   King Jr. Blvd.
SE 3rd Ave.
SE 2nd Ave.

SE Stark St.
SE Alger St.
SE Morrison St.
SE Belmont St.
SE Yamhill St.
SE Taylor St.
SE Salmon St.
SE Main St.
SE Madison St.
SE Hawthorne Blvd

SE Ankeny St.
SE Ash St.
SE Pine St.
SE Oak St.
E Burnside
SE Couch St.
SE Washington St.

NE Irving St.
NE Glisan St.
NE Flanders St.
NE Everett St.
NE Davis St.
NE Couch St.
NE Hassalo St.
NE Pacific St.
NE Oregon St.
NE Lloyd Blvd.
NE Glisan St.
NE Glisan St.

NE Sandy Blvd.

TO COLUMBIA
RIVER GORGE
TO AIRPORT
TO REED
COLLEGE
TO OREGON
MUSEUM OF SCIENCE
AND INDUSTRY

LLOYD
DISTRICT

Oregon
Convention
Center

84
30
30
99E
30
99E
5
5

Burnside Bridge
Morrison Bridge
Hawthorne Bridge

River
Willamette

New Market Theater
Maritime Museum
Tom McCall
Waterfront Park

ROSE GARDEN
ARENA

Steel Bridge
MAX

Front Ave.

Union Station
(Amtrak)

NW 1st Ave.
NW 2nd Av
NW 3rd Ave.
NW 4th Av
NW 5th Ave.
NW 6th Ave.
NW Broadway
NW 8th Ave.
NW Park Ave.
NW 9th Ave.
NW 10th Ave.
NW 11th Ave.
NW 12th Ave.
NW 13th Ave.
NW 14th Ave.
NW 15th Ave.

PEARL DISTRICT

Powell's
Book Store

Skidmore
Fountain

SW Ash St.
SW Pine St.
SW Oak St.
SW Stark St.
SW Washington St.
SW Alger St.
SW Morrison St.

SW Ankeny St.
SW Front Av
SW 1st Ave.
SW 2nd Ave.
SW 3rd Ave.
SW 4th Ave.
SW 5th Ave.
SW 6th Ave.
SW Broadway
SW Park Ave.
SW 9th Ave.
SW 10th Ave.
SW 11th Ave.
SW 12th Ave.
SW 13th Ave.
SW 14th Ave.
SW 15th Ave.
SW 16th Ave
SW 17th Ave
SW 18th Ave
SW 19th Ave
SW 20th Ave

MAX

SW Yamhill St.
SW Taylor St.
SW Salmon St.
SW Main St.
SW Madison St.
SW Jefferson St.
SW Columbia St.
SW Clay St.
SW Market St.
SW Mill St.
SW Montgomery St.

PIONEER
COURTHOUSE
SQUARE

MAX

Pacific
Northwest
College

Portland
Building

Art
Museum

Library

City
Hall

Civic
Auditorium

Portland
State
University

TO LEWIS
AND CLARK
COLLEGE

TO ONDINE

NW Hoyt St.
NW Glisan St.
NW Flanders St.
NW Everett St.
NW 17th Ave.
NW 18th Ave.
NW 19th Ave.
NW Glisan St.
NW Everett St.
NW Davis St.
NW Couch St.
NW Couch St.
W Burnside St.
W Burnside St.

NW Kearney St.
NW Johnson St.
NW Irving St.

405
405

30
30

SW Canyon Rd.

Civic
Stadium

TO WASHINGTON
PARK ZOO

26

N

0   200 yards
0   200 meters

Fareless Square
MAX

Seattle

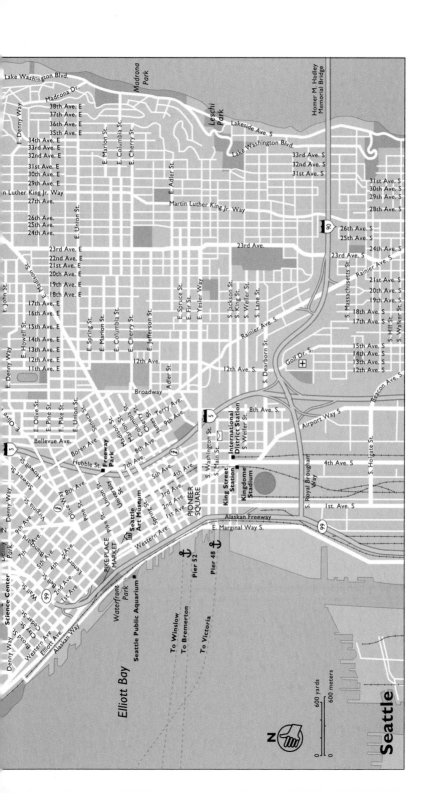

Seattle

Vancouver

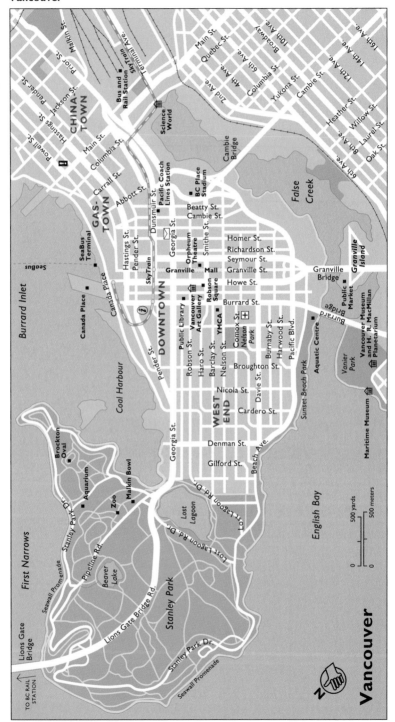

Vancouver

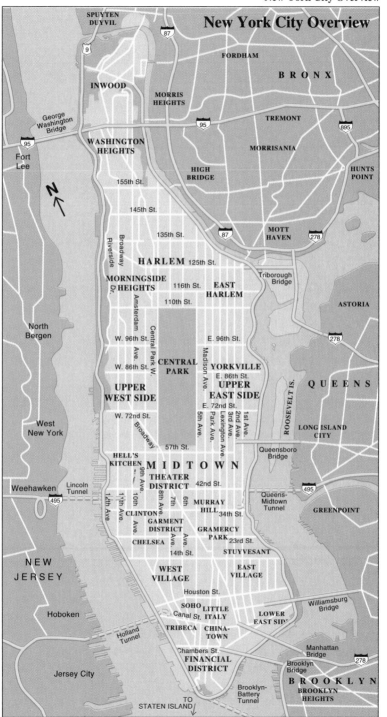

New York City Overview

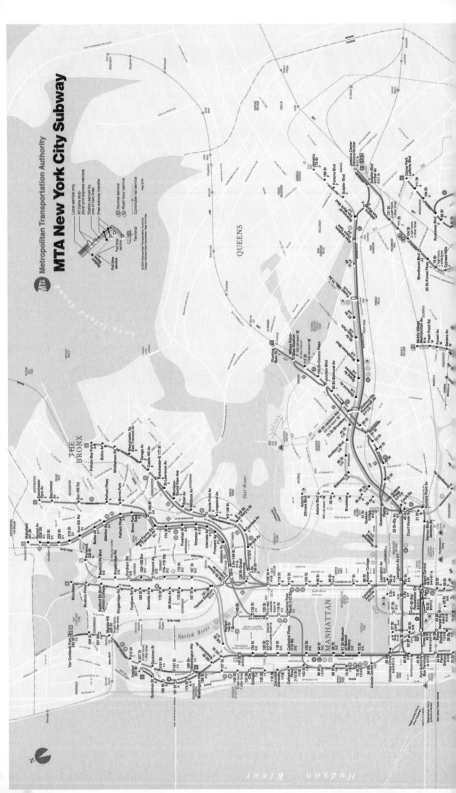

MTA New York City Subway

Metropolitan Transportation Authority

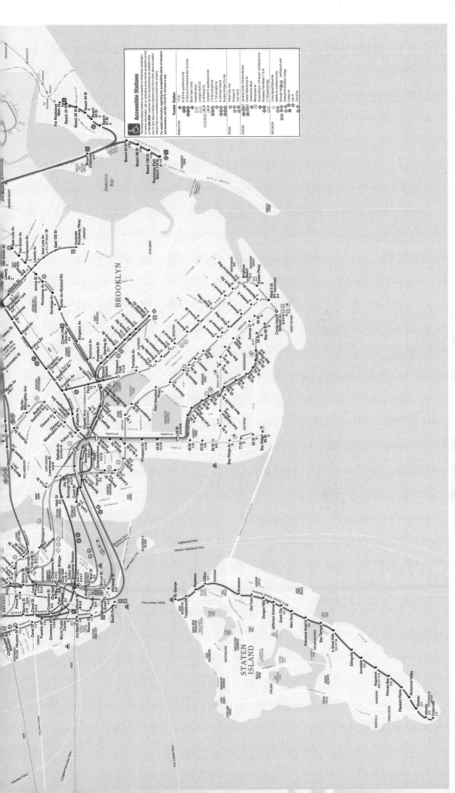

Downtown Manhattan

Downtown Manhattan

New Museum of
Contemporary Art, 31
New School of Social
Research, 46
New York Stock
Exchange, 14
New York University, 37
Puck Building, 32
St. John's Episcopal
Methodist Church, 19
St. Luke's Chapel, 35
St. Mark's in the Bowery
Church, 40
St. Paul's Chapel, 20
South Street Seaport
Museum, 18
Staten Island Ferry
Terminal, 7
Statue of Liberty and Ellis
Island Ferry Terminal, 3
Strand Bookstore, 42
Tower Records, 36
Trinity Church, 12
Umberto's Clam House, 30
U.S. Customs House, 11
Woolworth Building, 23
World Financial Center, 22
World Trade Center, 21

Downtown

Alternative Museum, 28
Anthology Film
Archives, 33
Buddhist Temple, 27
Castle Clinton, 1
Cherry Lane Theatre, 34
Chinatown Fair, 26
Church of the
Ascension, 44
Church of Our Lady of the
Rosary, 8
City Hall, 24
Clocktower Gallery, 25
Cooper Union, 39
Downtown Heliport, 9
East Coast Memorial, 2
Federal Hall, 15
Federal Reserve Bank, 16
Forbes Magazine
Galleries, 47
Forbidden Planet, 43
Fraunces Tavern, 10
Fulton Fish Market, 17
Grace Church, 41
Jefferson Market
Library, 45
Joseph Papp Public
Theater, 38
Morgan Guaranty Trust
Company, 13
Museum of Holography, 29

Midtown Manhattan

East River

Queensboro Bridge

Queens-Midtown Tunnel

FDR Dr.

TURTLE BAY

United Nations

First Ave.

Second Ave.

Third Ave.

Lexington Ave.

Park Ave.

Madison Ave.

Fifth Ave.

Grand Central Terminal

New York Public Library

MURRAY HILL

Empire State Building

Bryant Park

Broadway

HERALD SQUARE

GARMENT DISTRICT

TIMES SQUARE

Seventh Ave.

Eighth Ave.

Ninth Ave.

Port Authority Bus Terminal

General Post Office

Dyer Ave.

Tenth Ave.

Eleventh Ave.

Twelfth Ave.

HELL'S KITCHEN

Lincoln Tunnel

Grand Army Plaza

Park South

Central

Carnegie Hall

Museum of Modern Art

Rockefeller Center

COLUMBUS CIRCLE

New York Convention & Visitors Bureau

Chicorp Center

A,B,C,D, 1,2,3,9

N,R

B,Q

4,5,6

B,Q

N,R

C,E

1,2,3,9

N,R

A,C,E

B,D,F,Q

1,2,3, N,R,9

B,D,F, Q,7

4,5,6,S

E,F

E,F

6

6

7

B,D,E

B,D,F,Q

A,C,E

E. 60th St. · E. 59th St. · E. 58th St. · E. 57th St. · E. 56th St. · E. 55th St. · E. 54th St. · E. 53rd St. · E. 52nd St. · E. 51st St. · E. 50th St. · E. 49th St. · E. 48th St. · E. 47th St. · E. 46th St. · E. 45th St. · E. 44th St. · E. 43rd St. · E. 42nd St. · E. 41st St. · E. 40th St. · E. 39th St. · E. 38th St. · E. 37th St. · E. 36th St. · E. 35th St. · E. 34th St. · E. 33rd St. · E. 32nd St.

W. 60th St. · W. 59th St. · W. 58th St. · W. 57th St. · W. 56th St. · W. 55th St. · W. 54th St. · W. 53rd St. · W. 52nd St. · W. 51st St. · W. 50th St. · W. 49th St. · W. 48th St. · W. 47th St. · W. 46th St. · W. 45th St. · W. 44th St. · W. 43rd St. · W. 42nd St. · W. 41st St. · W. 39th St. · W. 38th St. · W. 37th St. · W. 36th St. · W. 35th St. · W. 34th St. · W. 33rd St.

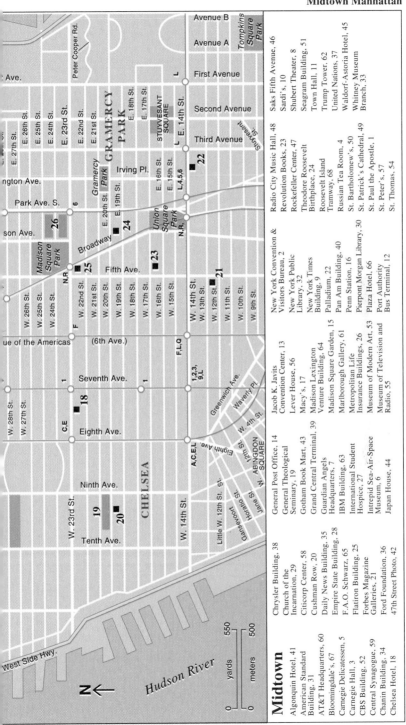

Saks Fifth Avenue, 46
Sardi's, 10
Shubert Theater, 8
Seagram Building, 51
Town Hall, 11
Trump Tower, 62
United Nations, 37
Waldorf-Astoria Hotel, 45
Whitney Museum Branch, 33

Radio City Music Hall, 48
Revolution Books, 23
Rockefeller Center, 47
Theodore Roosevelt Birthplace, 24
Roosevelt Island Tramway, 68
Russian Tea Room, 4
St. Bartholomew's, 50
St. Patrick's Cathedral, 49
St. Paul the Apostle, 1
St. Peter's, 57
St. Thomas, 54

New York Convention & Visitors Bureau, 2
New York Public Library, 32
New York Times Building, 9
Palladium, 22
Pan Am Building, 40
Penn Station, 16
Pierpont Morgan Library, 30
Plaza Hotel, 66
Port Authority Bus Terminal, 12

Jacob K. Javits Convention Center, 13
Lever House, 56
Macy's, 17
Madison Lexington Venture Building, 64
Madison Square Garden, 15
Marlborough Gallery, 61
Metropolitan Life Insurance Buildings, 26
Museum of Modern Art, 53
Museum of Television and Radio, 55

General Post Office, 14
General Theological Seminary, 19
Gotham Book Mart, 43
Grand Central Terminal, 39
Guardian Angels Headquarters, 7
IBM Building, 63
International Student Hospice, 27
Intrepid Sea-Air-Space Museum, 6
Japan House, 44

Midtown

Algonquin Hotel, 41
American Standard Building, 31
AT&T Headquarters, 60
Bloomingdale's, 67
Carnegie Delicatessen, 5
Carnegie Hall, 3
CBS Building, 52
Central Synagogue, 59
Chanin Building, 34
Chelsea Hotel, 18

Chrysler Building, 38
Church of the Incarnation, 29
Citicorp Center, 58
Cushman Row, 20
Daily News Building, 35
Empire State Building, 28
F.A.O. Schwarz, 65
Flatiron Building, 25
Forbes Magazine Galleries, 21
Ford Foundation, 36
47th Street Photo, 42

Uptown

American Museum of Natural History, 53
The Ansonia, 55
The Arsenal, 25
Asia Society, 14
Belvedere Castle, 36
Bethesda Fountain, 33
Blockhouse No. 1, 42
Bloomingdale's, 22
Bridle Path, 30
Cathedral of St. John the Divine, 47
Central Park Zoo, 24
Chess and Checkers House, 28
Children's Museum of Manhattan, 51
Children's Zoo, 26
China House, 19

Cleopatra's Needle, 38
Columbia University, 46
Conservatory Garden, 2
Cooper-Hewitt Museum, 7
The Dairy, 27
Dakota Apartments, 56
Delacorte Theater, 37
El Museo del Barrio, 1
Fordham University, 60
Frick Museum, 13
Gracie Mansion, 10
Grant's Tomb, 45
Great Lawn, 39
Guggenheim Museum, 9
Hayden Planetarium (at the American Museum of Natural History), 53
Hector Memorial, 50
Hotel des Artistes, 57

Hunter College, 16
International Center of Photography, 5
Jewish Museum, 6
The Juilliard School (at Lincoln Center), 59
Lincoln Center, 59
Loeb Boathouse, 34
Masjid Malcolm Shabazz , 43
Metropolitan Museum of Art, 11
Mt. Sinai Hospital, 4
Museum of American Folk Art, 58
Museum of American Illustration, 21
Museum of the City of New York, 3
National Academy of Design, 8
New York Convention & Visitors Bureau, 61

New York Historical Society, 54
New York Hospital, 15
Plaza Hotel, 23
Police Station (Central Park), 40
Rockefeller University, 20
7th Regiment Armory, 17
Shakespeare Garden, 35
Soldiers and Sailors Monument, 49
Strawberry Fields, 32
Studio Museum in Harlem, 44
Symphony Space, 48
Tavern on the Green, 31
Temple Emanu-El, 18
Tennis Courts, 41
Whitney Museum of American Art, 12
Wollman Rink, 29
Zabar's, 52